COMPACT SCHOOL & OFFICE EDITION

# WEBSTER'S NEW WORLD DICTIONARY

THE WORLD PUBLISHING COMPANY
Cleveland and New York

Library of Congress Catalog Card Number: 76-130439
ISBN-0-529-04676-8

PRINTED IN THE UNITED STATES OF AMERICA

# KEY TO PRONUNCIATION

| *Symbol* | *Key Words* | *Symbol* | *Key Words* | *Symbol* | *Key Words* |
|---|---|---|---|---|---|
| a | fat | u | up | n | not, ton |
| ā | ape | ū | use | p | put, tap |
| â | bare | ũr | fur | r | red, dear |
| ä | car | | | s | sell, pass |
| | | ə | a *in* ago | t | top, hat |
| e | ten | | e *in* agent | v | vat, have |
| ē | even | | i *in* sanity | w | will, always |
| ê | here | | o *in* comply | y | yet, yard |
| ẽr | over | | u *in* focus | z | zebra, haze |
| i | is | | | | |
| ī | bite | b | bed, dub | ch | chin, arch |
| | | d | did, had | kh | loch |
| o | lot | f | fall, off | ŋ | ring, drink |
| ō | go | g | get, dog | sh | she, dash |
| ô | horn | h | he, ahead | th | thin, truth |
| o͞o | tool | j | joy, jump | *th* | then, father |
| oo | book | k | kill, bake | zh | azure, beige |
| oi | oil | l | let, ball | ʼ | (see explanatory note below) |
| ou | out | m | met, trim | | |

A few explanatory notes on the more involved of these symbols follow.

**a** This symbol represents essentially the sound of *a* in *far* but may also represent the *a* intermediate between (a) and (ä) occasionally heard in New England for *bath.*

**â** This symbol is used, always followed and hence colored, by *r*, to represent the range of sounds (ā, e, a) heard variously in such words as *care* and *prayer.*

**ê** Like (â), this symbol followed, and hence colored, by *r*, represents a range of sounds (i through ē) heard variously in such words as *here* and *dear.*

**i** This symbol, representing essentially the vowel in *hit*, has also been used to indicate the neutralization of vowel in the unstressed syllables of such words as *garbage* (gär′bij) and *goodness* (good′nis). In some persons' pronunciation of such words, total neutralization is heard; hence, (gär′bəj) and (good′nəs) can be assumed as possible variants.

**ô** This symbol, representing essentially the vowel in *fork*, has also been used to represent the sound midway between (ä) and (ô) heard in an Eastern variant of *fob.*

**ə** This symbol, called the schwa, is borrowed from the International Phonetic Alphabet, and has been used to represent the reduced, weakened, and dulled vowel of neutral coloration heard in the unstressed syllables of *ago, agent, sanity, comply,* and *focus.* See also note on i above.

**ũr ẽr** These two symbols represent respectively the stressed and unstressed r-colored vowels heard successively in the two syllables of *murder* (mũr′dẽr). Where these symbols are given, Southern and Eastern speakers will, as a matter of course, pronounce them by "dropping their *r*'s."

**ŋ** This symbol, also borrowed from the International Phonetic Alphabet, represents the nasal sound of the *-ng* of *sing* and of the *n* before *k* and *g* in *drink* (driŋk) and *finger* (fiŋ′gẽr).

**kh** This symbol represents the sound made by arranging the speech organs as for (k) but allowing the breath to escape in a continuous stream, as in pronouncing (h).

**ʼ** The apostrophe before an *l, m,* or *n* indicates that this consonant has formed a syllable with no appreciable vowel sound, as in *apple* (ap′'l) or *season* (sē′z'n). In some persons' speech such syllabic consonants are often replaced with syllables having neutralized vowels, as (sē′zən). The apostrophe is also used after final *l* and *r* in some French words, to indicate that they are voiceless after an unvoiced consonant, as in *double-entendre* (do͞o′bl'-än′tän′dr'). In such cases the final *l* and *r* often tend to be lost entirely.

# ABBREVIATIONS USED IN THIS DICTIONARY

**abbrev.**, abbreviation
**acc.**, accusative
**act.**, active
**A.D.**, anno Domini
**adj.**, adjective
**adv.**, adverb
**Afr.**, African
**alt.**, altered, alternative
**Am.**, American
**Ar.**, Arabic
**Aram.**, Aramaic
**art.**, article
**AS.**, Anglo-Saxon
**B.C.**, before Christ
**Brit.**, British
**c.**, circa (about); century
**Canad.**, Canadian
**Celt.**, Celtic
**cf.**, *confer* (compare)
**chem.**, chemistry
**Chin.**, Chinese
**Colloq.**, colloquial
**comp.**, compound
**compar.**, comparative
**conj.**, conjunction
**contr.**, contraction
**D.**, Dutch
**Dan.**, Danish
**deriv.**, derivative
**Dial.**, dialect; dialectal
**dim.**, diminutive
**E**, eastern
**E.**, East
**eccl.**, ecclesiastical
**e.g.**, for example
**Eng.**, English
**esp.**, especially
**etc.**, et cetera (and others)
**etym.**, etymology
**fem.**, feminine
**ff.**, following
**fig.**, figurative(ly)
**Finn.**, Finnish
**Fl.**, Flemish
**Fr.**, French
**ft.**, feet
**fut.**, future
**G.**, German
**Gael.**, Gaelic
**genit.**, genitive
**Gmc.**, Germanic
**Gr.**, Greek
**Heb.**, Hebrew
**Hind.**, Hindu
**Hung.**, Hungarian
**hyp.**, hypothetical
**Ice.**, Icelandic
**i.e.**, *id est* (that is)
**in.**, inches
**Ind.**, Indian
**indic.**, indicative
**inf.**, infinitive
**infl.**, influenced
**intens.**, intensive
**interj.**, interjection
**Ir.**, Irish
**It.**, Italian
**Japan.**, Japanese
**L.**, Latin
**LG.**, Low German
**LGr.**, Late Greek
**lit.**, literally
**LL.**, Late Latin
**M**, Middle; Medieval
**masc.**, masculine
**math.**, mathematics
**MD.**, Middle Dutch
**ME.**, Middle English
**Med.**, Medieval
**Mex.**, Mexican
**mi.**, mile; miles
**ML.**, Medieval Latin
**Mod.**, **mod.**, modern
**myth.**, mythology
**N**, northern
**N.**, North
**n.**, noun
**naut.**, nautical
**NE**, northeastern
**n.fem.**, noun feminine
**nom.**, nominative
**Norm.**, Norman
**Norw.**, Norwegian
**n.pl.** noun plural
**NW**, northwestern
**O**, Old
**Obs.**, **obs.**, obsolete
**occas.**, occasional(ly)
**OFr.**, Old French
**OHG.**, Old High German
**ON.**, Old Norse
**orig.**, original(ly)
**p.**, page
**pass.**, passive
**perf.**, perfect
**pers.**, person; personal
**philos.**, philosophy
**phr.**, phrase
**pl.**, plural
**Pol.**, Polish
**pop.**, population
**Port.**, Portuguese
**poss.**, possessive
**pp.**, pages; past participle
**ppr.**, present participle
**Pr.**, Provençal
**prec.**, preceding
**prep.**, preposition
**pres.**, present
**prob.**, probable; probably
**pron.**, pronoun
**pronun.**, pronunciation
**psych.**, psychology
**pt.**, past tense
**R.C.**, Roman Catholic
**refl.**, reflexive
**Rom.**, Roman
**Russ.**, Russian
**S**, southern
**S.**, South
**Sans.**, Sanskrit
**Scand.**, Scandinavian
**Scot.**, Scottish
**SE**, southeastern
**sing.**, singular
**Slav.**, Slavic; Slavonic
**Sp.**, Spanish
**sp.**, spelling; spelled
**specif.**, specifically
**sq.**, square
**subj.**, subjunctive
**superl.**, superlative
**SW**, southwestern
**Swed.**, Swedish
**t.**, tense
**TV**, television
**ult.**, ultimate(ly)
**unc.**, uncertain
**U.S.**, United States
**v.**, verb
**var.**, variant
**v.aux.**, verb auxiliary
**v.i.**, verb intransitive
**v.t.**, verb transitive
**W**, western
**W.**, West
**Yid.**, Yiddish
**‡** foreign word or phrase
**<** derived from; from
**?** perhaps; uncertain
**+** plus
**&** and

# A

**A, a** (ā), *n.* [*pl.* A's, a's, As, as], the first letter of the English alphabet.

**A,** *n.* 1. in *chem.*, argon. 2. in *music*, the sixth tone in the scale of C major.

**a** (ə; *stressed*, ā), *adj.*, *indefinite article* [< *an*], 1. one; one sort of. 2. each; any one. 3. per: as, once *a* day. *A* is used before words beginning with a consonant sound (*a* child, *a* union, *a* history). Cf. **an.**

**a-,** a prefix meaning: 1. [< AS.], *a*) *in, into, on, at, to*, as in *aboard*. *b*) *in the act* or *state of*, as in *asleep*. *c*) *up, out*, as in *arise*. *d*) *off, of*, as in *akin*. 2. [< Gr.], *not*, as in *agnostic*.

**a.,** 1. about. 2. acre(s). 3. answer.

**aard·vark** (ärd′värk′), *n.* [D., earth pig], a burrowing African mammal that eats ants.

**Aar·on** (âr′ən), *n.* in the *Bible*, the first high priest of the Hebrews.

**ab-,** [L.], a prefix meaning *away, from, off, down*, as in *abdicate*.

**A.B.,** Bachelor of Arts.

**a·back** (ə-bak′), *adv. & adj.* [Archaic], backward. —**taken aback,** surprised; startled.

**ab·a·cus** (ab′ə-kəs), *n.* [*pl.* -CUSES, -CI (-sī′)], [< Gr. *abax*], 1. a frame with sliding beads for doing arithmetic. 2. in *architecture*, a slab forming the top of the capital.

**a·baft** (ə-baft′), *prep.* [AS. *on-be-æftan*], in *naut. usage*, behind. *adv.* aft.

**ab·a·lo·ne** (ab′ə-lō′ni), *n.* [Sp.], a sea mollusk with a spiral shell.

**a·ban·don** (ə-ban′dən), *v.t.* [< OFr. *mettre a bandon*, to put under (another's) ban], 1. to give up completely. 2. to desert. *n.* unrestrained activity. —**a·ban′don·ment,** *n.*

**a·ban′doned,** *adj.* 1. deserted. 2. given up to wickedness; shameless. 3. unrestrained.

**a·base** (ə-bās′), *v.t.* [ABASED, ABASING], [< LL. *abassare*, to lower], to humble; humiliate. —**a·base′ment,** *n.*

**a·bash** (ə-bash′), *v.t.* [< L. *ex* + *bah* (interj.)], to make self-conscious and embarrassed. —**a·bashed′,** *adj.* —**a·bash′ment,** *n.*

**a·bate** (ə-bāt′), *v.t. & v.i.* [ABATED, ABATING], [< OFr. *abattre*, to beat down], 1. to make or become less. 2. in *law*, to end; quash. —**a·bat′a·ble,** *adj.* —**a·bate′ment,** *n.*

**ab·at·toir** (ab′ə-twär′), *n.* [Fr.; see ABATE], a slaughterhouse.

**ab·ba·cy** (ab′ə-si), *n.* [*pl.* -CIES], an abbot's position, jurisdiction, or term of office.

**ab·bé** (ä′bā′), *n.* [Fr.; see ABBOT], in France, a priest's title.

**ab·bess** (ab′is), *n.* [see ABBOT], a woman who is head of a nunnery.

**ab·bey** (ab′i), *n.* [*pl.* -BEYS], 1. a monastery or nunnery. 2. a church of an abbey.

**ab·bot** (ab′ət), *n.* [< Aram. *abba*, father], a man who is head of a monastery.

**abbrev.,** 1. abbreviated. 2. abbreviation.

**ab·bre·vi·ate** (ə-brē′vi-āt′), *v.t.* [-ATED, -ATING], [< L. *ad-*, to + *brevis*, short], to make shorter; esp., to shorten (a word) by omitting letters. —**ab·bre′vi·a′tor,** *n.*

**ab·bre′vi·a′tion** (-ā′shən), *n.* 1. a shortening. 2. a shortened form of a word or phrase, as *Mr.* for *Mister*.

**A B C** (ā′ bē′ sē′), *n.* [*pl.* A B C's], 1. *usually pl.* the alphabet. 2. the basic elements (*of* a subject); rudiments.

**ab·di·cate** (ab′də-kāt′), *v.t. & v.i.* [-CATED, -CATING], [< L. *ab-*, off + *dicare*, to proclaim], to give up formally (a throne, etc.); surrender (a power). —**ab′di·ca′tion,** *n.*

**ab·do·men** (ab′də-mən, ab-dō′-), *n.* [L.], the part of the body between the diaphragm and the pelvis, containing the intestines, etc.; belly. —**ab·dom′i·nal** (-dom′ə-n'l), *adj.*

**ab·duct** (ab-dukt′), *v.t.* [< L. *ab-*, away + *ducere*, to lead], to kidnap. —**ab·duc′tion,** *n.* —**ab·duc′tor,** *n.*

**a·beam** (ə-bēm′), *adv.* at right angles to a ship's length or keel.

**a·bed** (ə-bed′), *adv.* in bed.

**A·bel** (ā′b'l), *n.* in the *Bible*, the second son of Adam and Eve, killed by Cain, his brother.

**ab·er·ra·tion** (ab′ẽr-ā′shən), *n.* [< L. *ab-*, from + *errare*, wander], 1. deviation from what is right, true, normal, etc. 2. mental derangement.

**a·bet** (ə-bet′), *v.t.* [ABETTED, ABETTING], [< OFr. *a-*, to + *beter*, to bait], to urge on or help, esp. in crime. —**a·bet′ment, a·bet′tal,** *n.* —**a·bet′tor, a·bet′ter,** *n.*

**a·bey·ance** (ə-bā′əns), *n.* [< LL. *badare*, to gape], temporary suspension, as of an activity or ruling.

**ab·hor** (əb-hôr′), *v.t.* [-HORRED, -HORRING], [< L. *ab-*, from + *horrere*, to shudder], to shrink from in disgust, hatred, etc; detest. —**ab·hor′rence,** *n.*

**ab·hor·rent** (əb-hôr′ənt), *adj.* causing disgust, hate, etc. —**ab·hor′rent·ly,** *adv.*

**a·bide** (ə-bīd′), *v.i.* [ABODE or ABIDED, ABIDING], [AS. *abidan*], 1. to remain. 2. [Archaic], to reside. *v.t.* 1. to await. 2. to endure. —**abide by,** 1. to live up to (a promise, etc.). 2. to submit to and carry out.

**a·bid′ing,** *adj.* enduring. —**a·bid′ing·ly,** *adv.*

**a·bil·i·ty** (ə-bil′ə-ti), *n.* [*pl.* -TIES], 1. a being able; power to do. 2. talent; skill.

**ab·ject** (ab-jekt′, ab′jekt), *adj.* [< L. *ab-*, from + *jacere*, to throw], 1. miserable; wretched. 2. degraded. —**ab·jec′tion,** *n.*

**ab·jure** (əb-joor′), *v.t.* [-JURED, -JURING], [< L. *ab-*, away + *jurare*, to swear], to give up (rights, allegiance, etc.) on oath; renounce. —**ab·ju·ra·tion** (ab′joo-rā′shən), *n.*

**ab·la·tive** (ab′lə-tiv), *n.* [< L. *ablatus*, carried away], in Latin, etc., the case expressing removal, direction from, cause, etc.

**a·blaze** (ə-blāz′), *adv.* on fire. *adj.* 1. flaming. 2. greatly excited.

**a·ble** (ā′b'l), *adj.* [ABLER, ABLEST], [< L. *habere*, have], 1. having power, skill, etc. (*to* do something). 2. talented. —**a′bly,** *adv.*

**-able** [< L.], a suffix meaning: 1. *able to*, as in *durable*. 2. *capable of being*, as in *drinkable*. 3. *worthy of being*, as in *laudable*. 4. *having qualities of*, as in *comfortable*. 5. *tending to*, as in *perishable*.

**a′ble-bod′ied,** *adj.* strong and healthy.

**ab·lu·tion** (ab-lōō′shən), *n.* [< L. *ab-*, off + *luere*, wash], a washing of the body, esp. as a religious ceremony. —**ab·lu′tion·ar′y,** *adj.*

**-ably,** a suffix of adverbs corresponding to adjectives ending in *-able*.

**ab·ne·gate** (ab′ni-gāt′), *v.t.* [-GATED, -GATING], [< L. *ab-*, from + *negare*, deny], to deny and refuse; renounce. —**ab′ne·ga′tion,** *n.*

**ab·nor·mal** (ab-nôr′məl), *adj.* not normal, average, or typical. —**ab·nor′mal·ly,** *adv.*

**ab·nor·mal·i·ty** (ab′nôr-mal′ə-ti), *n.* 1. an abnormal condition. 2. [*pl.* -TIES], an abnormal thing.

**a·board** (ə-bôrd′), *adv. & prep.* 1. on or in (a train, car, etc.). 2. alongside.

**a·bode** (ə-bōd′), pt. and pp. of **abide.** *n.* a home; residence.
**a·bol·ish** (ə-bol′ish), *v.t.* [< L. *abolere,* destroy], to do away with; put an end to.
**ab·o·li·tion** (ab′ə-lish′ən), *n.* 1. complete destruction; annulment. 2. [also A-], the abolishing of slavery in the U.S. **—ab′o·li′tion·ar·y,** *adj.* **—ab′o·li′tion·ist,** *n.*
**A-bomb** (ā′bom′), *n.* an atomic bomb.
**a·bom·i·na·ble** (ə-bom′ə-nə-b'l), *adj.* 1. vile. 2. very bad. **—a·bom′i·na·bly,** *adv.*
**a·bom·i·nate** (ə-bom′ə-nāt′), *v.t.* [-NATED, -NATING], [< L. *abominari,* regard as an ill omen], 1. to hate; loathe. 2. to dislike. **—a·bom′i·na′tion,** *n.*
**ab·o·rig·i·nal** (ab′ə-rij′ə-n'l), *adj.* 1. existing (in a region) from the beginning; first. 2. of aborigines. *n.* an aborigine.
**ab′o·rig′i·nes′** (-ə-nēz′), *n.pl.* [*sing.* -NE (-nē′)], [L. < *ab-,* from + *origine,* the beginning], the first known inhabitants of a region.
**a·bort** (ə-bôrt′), *v.i.* [< L. *aboriri,* miscarry], to have a miscarriage. *v.t.* to check before fully developed.
**a·bor′tion,** *n.* premature expulsion of a fetus so that it does not live; miscarriage. **—a·bor′tion·ist,** *n.*
**a·bor′tive,** *adj.* 1. born too soon. 2. unsuccessful; fruitless. 3. causing abortion.
**a·bound** (ə-bound′), *v.i.* [< L. *ab-* + *undare,* to rise in waves], to be plentiful (often with *in* or *with*). **—a·bound′ing,** *adj.*
**a·bout** (ə-bout′), *adv.* [< AS. *onbutan,* around], 1. all around. 2. near. 3. in an opposite direction. 4. nearly: as, *about* ready. *adj.* astir: as, he is up and *about* now. *prep.* 1. on all sides of. 2. near to. 3. with. 4. intending; on the point of. 5. concerning.
**a·bout-face** (ə-bout′fās′), *n.* a reversal of position or opinion.
**a·bove** (ə-buv′), *adv.* [AS. *abufan*], 1. in a higher place; up. 2. earlier (in a book, etc.). 3. higher in rank, etc. *prep.* 1. over; on top of. 2. better or more than: as, *above* average. *adj.* mentioned earlier.
**a·bove′board′,** *adv. & adj.* in plain view; without dishonesty.
**ab·ra·ca·dab·ra** (ab′rə-kə-dab′rə), *n.* [L.], 1. a word supposed to have magic powers, used in incantations, on amulets, etc. 2. a magic spell or formula. 3. gibberish.
**ab·rade** (ə-brād′), *v.t.* [-RADED, -RADING], [< L. *ab-,* away + *radere,* scrape], to rub off; wear away by scraping. **—ab·rad′er,** *n.*
**A·bra·ham** (ā′brə-ham′), *n.* in the *Bible,* the first patriarch of the Hebrews.
**ab·ra·sion** (ə-brā′zhən), *n.* 1. an abrading. 2. an abraded spot.
**ab·ra′sive** (-siv), *adj.* causing abrasion. *n.* a substance used for grinding, polishing, etc., as sandpaper.
**a·breast** (ə-brest′), *adv. & adj.* side by side. **—abreast of,** in line with.
**a·bridge** (ə-brij′), *v.t.* [ABRIDGED, ABRIDGING], [< L. *ad-,* to + *brevis,* short], 1. to shorten, lessen, or curtail. 2. to shorten by using fewer words but keeping the substance. **—a·bridg′ment, a·bridge′ment,** *n.*
**a·broad** (ə-brôd′), *adv.* 1. far and wide. 2. current: as, rumors are *abroad.* 3. outdoors. 4. to or in foreign lands.
**ab·ro·gate** (ab′rə-gāt′), *v.t.* [-GATED, -GATING], [< L. *ab-,* away + *rogare,* propose], to abolish; repeal; annul. **—ab′ro·ga′tion,** *n.*
**a·brupt** (ə-brupt′), *adj.* [< L. *ab-,* off + *rumpere,* break], 1. sudden; unexpected. 2. brusque. 3. very steep. 4. disconnected, as some writing. **—a·brupt′ly,** *adv.*
**Ab·sa·lom** (ab′sə-ləm), *n.* in the *Bible,* David's favorite son, who rebelled against him.
**ab·scess** (ab′ses), *n.* [< L. *ab(s)-,* from + *cedere,* go], an inflamed area in body tissues, containing pus. *v.i.* to form an abscess.
**ab·scond** (ab-skond′), *v.i.* [< L. *ab(s)-,* from + *condere,* to hide], to leave hastily and secretly to escape the law. **—ab·scond′er,** *n.*
**ab·sence** (ab′s'ns), *n.* 1. a being absent. 2. the time of this. 3. a lack.
**ab·sent** (ab′s'nt), *adj.* [< L. *ab-,* away + *esse,* be], 1. not present; away. 2. not existing; lacking. 3. not attentive. *v.t.* (ab-sent′), to keep (oneself) away.
**ab·sen·tee** (ab′s'n-tē′), *n.* one who is absent, as from work. *adj.* by one who is absent. **—ab′sen·tee′ism,** *n.*
**ab′sent-mind′ed,** *adj.* 1. not attentive; preoccupied. 2. habitually forgetful. **—ab′sent·mind′ed·ly,** *adv.*
**ab·sinthe, ab·sinth** (ab′sinth), *n.* [Fr. < Gr. *apsinthion*], a green alcoholic liquor with the flavor of wormwood and anise.
**ab·so·lute** (ab′sə-lōōt′), *adj.* [see ABSOLVE], 1. perfect. 2. complete; whole. 3. not mixed; pure. 4. unrestricted: as, *absolute* rule. 5. certain; positive. 6. real: as, *absolute* truth. *n.* something that is absolute. **—the Absolute,** in *philos.,* that which is thought of as existing completely in and by itself. **—ab′so·lute′ly,** *adv.* **—ab′so·lute′ness,** *n.*
**absolute zero,** the hypothetical point at which matter would have neither molecular motion nor heat: theoretically equal to −273.18°C. or −459.72°F.
**ab′so·lu′tion** (-lōō′shən), *n.* 1. a freeing (from guilt); forgiveness. 2. remission (*of* sin or its penalty).
**ab·so·lut·ism** (ab′sə-lōōt′iz'm), *n.* government in which the ruler has unlimited powers; despotism. **—ab′so·lut′ist,** *n. & adj.*
**ab·solve** (ab-solv′), *v.t.* [-SOLVED, -SOLVING], [< L. *ab-,* from + *solvere,* to loose], 1. to free from guilt, a duty, etc. 2. to give religious absolution to. **—ab·solv′a·ble,** *adj.*
**ab·sorb** (əb-sôrb′), *v.t.* [< L. *ab-,* from + *sorbere,* drink in], 1. to suck up; take in. 2. to engulf wholly. 3. to interest greatly. **—ab·sorbed′,** *adj.* **—ab·sorb′ing,** *adj.*
**ab·sorb′ent,** *adj.* capable of absorbing moisture, etc. *n.* a thing that absorbs. **—ab·sorb′en·cy,** *n.*
**ab·sorp·tion** (əb-sôrp′shən), *n.* 1. an absorbing. 2. great interest. 3. the passing of nutrient material into the blood or lymph. **—ab·sorp′tive,** *adj.*
**ab·stain** (əb-stān′), *v.i.* [< L. *ab(s)-,* from + *tenere,* hold], to voluntarily do without; refrain. **—ab·sten′tion** (-sten′shən), *n.*
**ab·ste·mi·ous** (ab-stē′mi-əs), *adj.* [< L. *ab(s)-,* from + *temetum,* strong drink], eating and drinking sparingly.
**ab·sti·nence** (ab′stə-nəns), *n.* an abstaining from some or all food, liquor, etc. **—ab′sti·nent,** *adj.* **—ab′sti·nent·ly,** *adv.*
**ab·stract** (ab-strakt′, ab′strakt), *adj.* [< L. *ab(s)-,* from + *trahere,* to draw], 1. thought of apart from material objects. 2. expressing a quality so thought of. 3. theoretical. *n.* (ab′strakt), a summary. *v.t.* 1. (ab-strakt′), to take away. 2. (ab′strakt), to summarize. **—in the abstract,** in theory as apart from practice. **—ab′stract·ly,** *adv.*
**ab·stract′ed,** *adj.* withdrawn in mind; preoccupied. **—ab·stract′ed·ly,** *adv.*
**ab·strac′tion,** *n.* 1. an abstracting. 2. an abstract idea. 3. an unrealistic notion. 4. mental withdrawal. **—ab·strac′tion·ism,** *n.*
**ab·struse** (ab-strōōs′), *adj.* [< L. *ab(s)-,* away + *trudere,* to thrust], hard to understand.
**ab·surd** (əb-sũrd′), *adj.* [< L. *absurdus,* not to be heard of], unreasonable, hence ridiculous. **—ab·surd′ly,** *adv.* **—ab·surd′ness,** *n.*
**ab·surd′i·ty,** *n.* 1. a being absurd. 2. [*pl.* -TIES], an absurd idea or thing.
**a·bun·dance** (ə-bun′dəns), *n.* [see ABOUND], great plenty; more than enough. **—a·bun′dant,** *adj.* **—a·bun′dant·ly,** *adv.*
**a·buse** (ə-būz′), *v.t.* [ABUSED, ABUSING], [<

L. *ab-*, away + *uti*, to use], 1. to use wrongly. 2. to mistreat. 3. to insult; revile. ***n.*** (ə-būs'), 1. wrong use. 2. mistreatment. 3. a corrupt practice. 4. insulting language. **—a·bu'sive** (-bū'siv), ***adj.*** **—a·bu'sive·ly, *adv.***

**a·but** (ə-but'), ***v.i.*** [ABUTTED, ABUTTING], [< OFr. *a-*, to + *bout*, end], to border (*on*).

**a·but'ment, *n.*** 1. an abutting. 2. a part supporting an arch, strut, etc.

**a·bys·mal** (ə-biz'm'l), ***adj.*** of or like an abyss; not measurable. **—a·bys'mal·ly, *adv.***

**a·byss** (ə-bis'), ***n.*** [< Gr. *a-*, without + *byssos*, bottom], 1. a bottomless gulf. 2. anything too deep for measurement: as, an *abyss* of shame. 3. hell. **—a·byss'al, *adj.***

**-ac,** [Gr.], a suffix meaning: 1. *relating to*, as in *cardiac*. 2. *affected by*, as in *maniac*.

**Ac,** in *chem.*, actinium.

**A.C., a.c.,** alternating current.

**a·ca·cia** (ə-kā'shə), ***n.*** [< Gr. *akakia*, thorny tree], 1. a tree or shrub with yellow or white flower clusters. 2. the locust tree.

**ac·a·dem·ic** (ak'ə-dem'ik), ***adj.*** 1. of schools or colleges. 2. having to do with liberal arts rather than technical education. 3. formal; pedantic. Also **ac'a·dem'i·cal.**

**a·cad·e·mi·cian** (ə-kad'ə-mish'ən), ***n.*** a member of an academy (sense 3).

**a·cad·e·my** (ə-kad'ə-mi), ***n.*** [*pl.* -MIES], [< Gr. *akadēmeia*, place where Plato taught], 1. a private secondary school. 2. a school for special instruction. 3. an association of scholars, writers, etc. for advancing an art or science.

**a·can·thus** (ə-kan'thəs), ***n.*** [*pl.* -THUSES, -THI (-thī)], [< Gr. *akantha*, thorn], 1. a prickly plant with large leaves. 2. in *architecture*, a representation of these leaves.

**‡a cap·pel·la** (ä' kä-pel'lä), [It., in chapel style], unaccompanied: said of choral singing.

**ac·cede** (ak-sēd'), ***v.i.*** [-CEDED, -CEDING], [< L. *ad-*, to + *cedere*, to yield], 1. to enter upon the duties (of an office). 2. to assent; agree (*to*). **—ac·ced'ence, *n.***

**ac·cel·er·an·do** (ak-sel'ẽr-an'dō), ***adv. & adj.*** [It.], in *music*, with gradually quickening tempo: abbrev. **accel.**

**ac·cel·er·ate** (ak-sel'ẽr-āt'), ***v.t.*** [-ATED, -ATING], [< L. *ad-*, to + *celerare*, hasten], 1. to increase the speed of. 2. to cause to happen sooner. ***v.i.*** to go faster. **—ac·cel'er·a'tion, *n.***

**ac·cel'er·a'tor, *n.*** a person or thing, as the foot throttle of an automobile, that accelerates something.

**ac·cent** (ak'sent), ***n.*** [< L. *ad-*, to + *canere*, sing], 1. emphasis given a syllable or word in speaking. 2. a mark showing such emphasis or indicating pronunciation. 3. a distinguishing manner of pronouncing: as, an Irish *accent*. 4. in *music & verse*, rhythmic stress. ***v.t.*** (*also* ak-sent'), 1. to emphasize; stress. 2. to mark with an accent.

**ac·cen·tu·ate** (ak-sen'chōō-āt'), ***v.t.*** [-ATED, -ATING], accent; stress.**—ac·cen'tu·a'tion, *n.***

**ac·cept** (ək-sept'), ***v.t.*** [< L. *ad-*, to + *capere*, take], 1. to receive willingly. 2. to approve. 3. to agree to. 4. to believe in. 5. to agree to pay. **—ac·cept'er, ac·cep'tor, *n.***

**ac·cept'a·ble, *adj.*** satisfactory. **—ac·cept'a·bil'i·ty, *n.* —ac·cept'a·bly, *adv.***

**ac·cept'ance, *n.*** 1. an accepting. 2. approval. 3. belief in. 4. a promise to pay.

**ac·cept·ed** (ək-sep'tid), ***adj.*** generally regarded as true, proper, etc.; conventional.

**ac·cess** (ak'ses), ***n.*** [see ACCEDE], 1. approach or means of approach. 2. the right to enter, use, etc.

**ac·ces'si·ble, *adj.*** 1. easy to approach or enter. 2. obtainable. 3. open to the influence of (with *to*). **—ac·ces'si·bil'i·ty, *n.***

**ac·ces·sion** (ak-sesh'ən), ***n.*** 1. an attaining (the throne, power, etc.). 2. assent. 3. *a*) increase by addition. *b*) an addition.

**ac·ces·so·ry** (ak-ses'ə-ri), ***adj.*** [see ACCEDE], 1. additional; extra. 2. helping in an unlawful act. ***n.*** [*pl.* -RIES], 1. something extra or complementary. 2. one who, though absent, helps another to break the law.

**ac·ci·dent** (ak'sə-dənt), ***n.*** [< L. *ad-*, to + *cadere*, to fall], 1. an unexpected happening. 2. an unfortunate occurrence. 3. chance.

**ac'ci·den'tal** (-den't'l), ***adj.*** occurring by chance; fortuitous. **—ac'ci·den'tal·ly, *adv.***

**ac·claim** (ə-klām'), ***v.t.*** [< L. *ad-*, to + *clamare*, to cry out], to greet or announce with loud approval; hail. ***n.*** loud approval.

**ac·cla·ma·tion** (ak'lə-mā'shən), ***n.*** 1. an acclaiming or being acclaimed. 2. loud applause. 3. an approving vote by voice.

**ac·cli·mate** (ə-klī'mit, ak'li-māt'), ***v.t. & v.i.*** [-MATED, -MATING], [see AD- & CLIMATE], to accustom or become accustomed to a new climate or environment: also **ac·cli'ma·tize'** (-mə-tīz') [-TIZED, -TIZING]. **—ac'cli·ma'tion, *n.***

**ac·cliv·i·ty** (ə-kliv'ə-ti), ***n.*** [*pl.* -TIES], [< L. *ad-*, to + *clivus*, hill], an upward slope.

**ac·co·lade** (ak'ə-lād'), ***n.*** [Fr. < It. *accollare*, to embrace], a praising mention; award.

**ac·com·mo·date** (ə-kom'ə-dāt'), ***v.t.*** [-DATED, -DATING], [< L. *ad-*, to + *com-*, with + *modus*, a measure], 1. to adjust; adapt. 2. to supply (*with* something). 3. to do a favor for. 4. to have space for; lodge.

**ac·com'mo·dat'ing, *adj.*** obliging.

**ac·com'mo·da'tion, *n.*** 1. adjustment. 2. willingness to do favors. 3. a help; convenience. 4. *pl.* *a*) lodgings. *b*) traveling space, as in a train.

**ac·com·pa·ni·ment** (ə-kump'ni-mənt), ***n.*** 1. anything that accompanies something else. 2. an instrumental part supporting a solo voice, etc.

**ac·com'pa·nist, *n.*** one who plays an accompaniment.

**ac·com·pa·ny** (ə-kum'pə-ni), ***v.t.*** [-NIED, -NYING], [see AD- & COMPANION], 1. to add to; supplement. 2. to go with; attend. 3. to play an accompaniment for or to.

**ac·com·plice** (ə-kom'plis), ***n.*** [< *a* (the article) + L. *complex;* see COMPLEX], one who helps another break a law; partner in crime.

**ac·com·plish** (ə-kom'plish), ***v.t.*** [< L. *ad*, to + *complere*, fill up], to succeed in doing.

**ac·com'plished, *adj.*** 1. done; completed. 2. skilled; expert.

**ac·com'plish·ment, *n.*** 1. completion. 2. work completed. 3. social art or skill.

**ac·cord** (ə-kôrd'), ***v.t.*** [< L. *ad*, to + *cor*, heart], 1. to make agree. 2. to grant. ***v.i.*** to agree; harmonize. ***n.*** mutual agreement; harmony. **—of one's own accord,** voluntarily.

**ac·cord'ance, *n.*** agreement; conformity. **—ac·cord'ant, *adj.***

**ac·cord'ing, *adj.*** in harmony. ***adv.*** accordingly. **—according to,** 1. consistent with. 2. as stated by.

**ac·cord'ing·ly, *adv.*** 1. in accord with what has preceded. 2. therefore.

**ac·cor·di·on** (ə-kôr'di-ən), ***n.*** [< It.; see ACCORD], a keyed musical instrument with a bellows, which is pressed to force air through reeds. **—ac·cor'di·on·ist, *n.***

**ac·cost** (ə-kôst'), ***v.t.*** [< L. *ad-*, to + *costa*, side], to approach and speak to.

**ac·count** (ə-kount'), ***v.t.*** [< L. *computare;* see COMPUTE], to judge to be. ***v.i.*** 1. to give a financial reckoning. 2. to give reasons (*for*). ***n.*** 1. a counting. 2. *often pl.* a record of business transactions. 3. worth; importance. 4. an explanation. 5. a report. **—on account,** as partial payment. **—on account of,** because of.**—on no account,** under no circumstances. **—take into account,** to consider.

**ac·count'a·ble, *adj.*** 1. liable; responsible. 2. explainable. **—ac·count'a·bil'i·ty, *n.***

**ac·count·ant** (ə-koun′t'nt), *n.* one whose work is accounting. **—ac·count′an·cy,** *n.*
**ac·count′ing,** *n.* the setting up and auditing of commercial accounts.
**ac·cou·ter** (ə-ko͞o′tẽr), *v.t.* [? < L. *consuere*, to sew], to outfit; equip: also **ac·cou′tre** [-TRED, -TRING].
**ac·cou′ter·ments** (-mənts), *n.pl.* 1. clothes. 2. a soldier's equipment.
**ac·cred·it** (ə-kred′it), *v.t.* 1. to authorize; certify. 2. to believe in. 3. to attribute. 4. to give (someone) credit for (with *with*).
**ac·cre·tion** (ə-krē′shən), *n.* [< L. *ad-*, to + *crescere*, to grow], 1. growth in size by addition. 2. accumulated or added matter. 3. a growing together of parts.
**ac·crue** (ə-kro͞o′), *v.i.* [-CRUED, -CRUING], [see ACCRETION], to come as a natural growth or increase, as interest on money. **—ac·cru′al, ac·crue′ment,** *n.*
**ac·cu·mu·late** (ə-kūm′yoo-lāt′), *v.t. & v.i.* [-LATED, -LATING], [< L. *ad-*, to + *cumulare*, to heap], to pile up; collect. **—ac·cu′mu·la′tive,** *adj.* **—ac·cu′mu·la′tor,** *n.*
**ac·cu′mu·la′tion,** *n.* 1. an accumulating. 2. collected material; heap.
**ac·cu·ra·cy** (ak′yoo-rə-si), *n.* the state of being accurate; precision.
**ac·cu·rate** (ak′yoo-rit), *adj.* [< L. *ad-*, to + *cura*, care], 1. careful and exact. 2. free from errors. **—ac′cu·rate·ly,** *adv.*
**ac·curs·ed** (ə-kũr′sid, -kũrst′), *adj.* 1. under a curse. 2. damnable. Also **ac·curst′.**
**ac·cu·sa·tion** (ak′yoo-zā′shən), *n.* 1. an accusing. 2. what one is accused of.
**ac·cu·sa·tive** (ə-kū′zə-tiv), *adj.* [see ACCUSE], in *linguistics*, designating or in the case **(accusative case)** expressing the goal of an action or motion. *n.* 1. the accusative case. 2. a word in this case.
**ac·cuse** (ə-kūz′), *v.t.* [-CUSED, -CUSING], [< L. *ad-*, to + *causa*, a cause], 1. to blame. 2. to bring charges against (*of* doing wrong).
**ac·cused′,** *n. sing. & pl.* in *law*, the person or persons accused of a crime (with *the*).
**ac·cus·tom** (ə-kus′təm), *v.t.* to make familiar by custom, habit, or use.
**ac·cus′tomed,** *adj.* 1. usual; customary. 2. wont or used (*to*).
**ace** (ās), *n.* [< L. *as*, unit], 1. a playing card, etc. with one spot. 2. a point, as in tennis, won by a single stroke. 3. an expert, esp. in combat flying. *adj.* [Colloq.], first-rate.
**ace in the hole,** [Slang], any advantage held in reserve.
**ac·er·bate** (as′ẽr-bāt′), *v.t.* [-BATED, -BATING], [< L. *acerbare*], 1. to make sour or bitter. 2. to irritate; exasperate.
**a·cer·bi·ty** (ə-sũr′bə-ti), *n.* [*pl.* -TIES], [< L. *acerbus*, sharp], 1. a sour, astringent quality. 2. sharpness of temper, etc.
**ac·et·an·i·lide** (as′ə-tan′'l-īd′, -id), *n.* [< *acetic* + *aniline*], a drug used to lessen pain and fever: also **ac′et·an′i·lid** (-id).
**ac·e·tate** (as′e-tāt′), *n.* a salt or ester of acetic acid.
**a·ce·tic** (ə-sē′tik), *adj.* [< L. *acetum*, vinegar], of the sharp, sour liquid **(acetic acid)** found in vinegar.
**ac·e·tone** (as′ə-tōn′), *n.* [< *acetic*], a colorless liquid used as a solvent.
**a·cet·y·lene** (ə-set′'l-ēn′), *n.* [< *acetic* + *-yl* + *-ene*], a gas used for lighting, and, with oxygen in a blowtorch, for welding, etc.
**ache** (āk), *v.i.* [ACHED (ākt), ACHING], [AS. *acan*], 1. to have or give dull, steady pain. 2. [Colloq.], to yearn. *n.* a dull, steady pain.
**a·chene** (ā-kēn′), *n.* [< Gr. *a-*, not + *chainein*, to gape], any small, dry, one-seeded fruit which ripens without bursting.
**a·chieve** (ə-chēv′), *v.t.* [ACHIEVED, ACHIEVING], [< L. *ad-*, to + *caput*, head], 1. to do successfully. 2. to get by effort. *v.i.* to effect a desired result. **—a·chiev′a·ble,** *adj.*
**a·chieve′ment,** *n.* 1. an achieving. 2. a thing achieved, as by skill, work, etc.; feat.
**A·chil·les** (ə-kil′ēz), *n.* Greek hero killed in the Trojan War.
**Achilles' heel,** (one's) vulnerable spot.
**ach·ro·mat·ic** (ak′rə-mat′ik), *adj.* [< Gr. *a-*, without + *chrōma*, color], refracting white light without breaking it up into its component colors.
**ac·id** (as′id), *adj.* [< L. *acidus*, sour], 1. sour; sharp; tart. 2. of an acid. *n.* 1. a sour substance. 2. [Slang], LSD. 3. in *chem.*, any compound that reacts with a base to form a salt. **—a·cid·i·ty** (ə-sid′ə-ti) [*pl.* -TIES], *n.*
**a·cid′i·fy′** (-ə-fī′), *v.t. & v.i.* [-FIED, -FYING], 1. to make or become sour or acid. 2. to change into an acid. **—a·cid′i·fi·ca′tion,** *n.*
**ac·i·do·sis** (as′i-dō′sis), *n.* a condition in which the alkali reserve of the body is lower than normal.
**acid test,** a crucial, final test.
**a·cid·u·late** (ə-sij′oo-lāt′), *v.t.* [-LATED, -LATING], to make somewhat acid or sour.
**a·cid·u·lous** (ə-sij′oo-ləs), *adj.* somewhat acid or sour. **—a·cid′u·lous·ly,** *adv.*
**-acious,** [< L.], a suffix meaning *inclined to, full of*, as in *tenacious*.
**-acity,** a suffix used to form nouns corresponding to adjectives ending in *-acious*.
**ack-ack** (ak′ak′), *n.* [Slang], 1. an antiaircraft gun. 2. its fire.
**ac·knowl·edge** (ək-nol′ij), *v.t.* [-EDGED, -EDGING], [cf. KNOWLEDGE], 1. to admit as true. 2. to recognize the authority or claims of. 3. to respond to a greeting, etc. 4. to state that one has received (a letter, etc.). 5. to express thanks for. **—ac·knowl′edg·ment, ac·knowl′edge·ment,** *n.*
**ac·me** (ak′mi), *n.* [< Gr. *akmē*, a point, top], the highest point.
**ac·ne** (ak′ni), *n.* [? < Gr.; see ACME], a skin disease causing pimples on the face, etc.
**ac·o·lyte** (ak′ə-līt′), *n.* [< Gr. *akolouthos*, follower], 1. an altar boy. 2. an attendant.
**ac·o·nite** (ak′ə-nīt′), *n.* [< Gr.], 1. a poisonous plant with hoodlike flowers. 2. a sedative drug made from its roots.
**a·corn** (ā′kôrn), *n.* [< AS. *æcern*, nut], the nut of the oak tree.
**acorn squash,** a kind of squash shaped like an acorn.
**a·cous·tic** (ə-ko͞os′tik), *adj.* [< Gr. *akouein*, to hear], having to do with hearing or acoustics: also **a·cous′ti·cal.**
**a·cous′tics** (-tiks), *n.pl.* 1. the qualities of a room, etc. that have to do with how clearly sounds can be heard in it. 2. [construed as sing.], the science of heard sound.
**ac·quaint** (ə-kwānt′), *v.t.* [< L. *ad*, to + *cognoscere*, know], 1. to familiarize (oneself *with*). 2. to inform.
**ac·quaint′ance,** *n.* 1. knowledge got from personal experience. 2. a person whom one knows slightly. **—ac·quaint′ance·ship,** *n.*
**ac·quaint′ed,** *adj.* having an acquaintance with a person or thing.
**ac·qui·esce** (ak′wi-es′), *v.i.* [-ESCED, -ESCING], [< L. *ad-*, to + *quiescere*, to be at rest], to consent without protest (with *in*). **—ac′qui·es′cence,** *n.* **—ac′qui·es′cent,** *adj.*
**ac·quire** (ə-kwīr′), *v.t.* [-QUIRED, -QUIRING], [< L. *ad-*, to + *quaerere*, to seek], 1. to gain by one's own efforts. 2. to get as one's own. **—ac·quire′ment,** *n.*
**ac·qui·si·tion** (ak′wə-zish′ən), *n.* 1. an acquiring. 2. something acquired.
**ac·quis·i·tive** (ə-kwiz′ə-tiv), *adj.* eager to acquire (money, etc.); grasping.
**ac·quit** (ə-kwit′), *v.t.* [-QUITTED, -QUITTING], [< L. *ad*, to + *quietare*, to quiet], 1. to pay (a debt). 2. to declare (a person) not guilty (*of* something). 3. to conduct (oneself); behave. **—ac·quit′tal,** *n.*

**ac·quit'tance,** *n.* 1. a settlement of, or release from, debt, etc. 2. a record of this.

**a·cre** (ā'kēr), *n.* [AS. *æcer*, field], 1. a measure of land, 43,560 sq. ft. 2. *pl.* lands.

**a·cre·age** (ā'kēr-ij), *n.* acres collectively.

**ac·rid** (ak'rid), *adj.* [< L. *acer*, sharp], 1. sharp or bitter to the taste or smell. 2. sharp in speech, etc.

**ac·ri·mo·ny** (ak'rə-mō'ni), *n.* [*pl.* -NIES], [< L. *acer*, sharp], bitterness or harshness of manner or speech. —**ac'ri·mo'ni·ous,** *adj.*

**ac·ro·bat** (ak'rə-bat'), *n.* [< Gr. *akrobatos*, walking on tiptoe], a performer on the trapeze, tightrope, etc. —**ac'ro·bat'ic,** *adj.*

**ac'ro·bat'ics** (-iks), *n.pl.* 1. an acrobat's tricks. 2. agile feats: as, mental *acrobatics.*

**ac·ro·nym** (ak'rə-nim), *n.* [< Gr. *akros*, at the end; + homo*nym*], a word formed from the first (or first few) letters of several words, as *radar.*

**a·crop·o·lis** (ə-krop'ə-lis), *n.* [< Gr. *akros*, at the top + *polis*, city], the fortified hill of an ancient Greek city; esp., [A-], that of Athens, on which the Parthenon was built.

**a·cross** (ə-krôs'), *adv.* 1. crosswise. 2. from one side to the other. *prep.* 1. from one side to the other of. 2. on the other side of. 3. into contact with.

**a·cros·tic** (ə-krôs'tik), *n.* [< Gr. *akros*, at the end + *stichos*, verse], a verse, etc. in which certain letters in each line, as the first or last, spell out a word, motto, etc.

**act** (akt), *n.* [< L. *agere*, to do], 1. a thing done. 2. a doing. 3. a law. 4. a main division of a drama or opera. 5. a short performance, as on a vaudeville program. *v.t.* 1. to play the part of. 2. to perform in (a play). *v.i.* 1. to perform on the stage. 2. to behave. 3. to function. 4. to have an effect (*on*). 5. to appear to be: as, to *act* angry. —**act as,** to perform the functions of. —**act up,** [Colloq.], to misbehave.

**ACTH,** [< *a*drenocortico*t*ropic *h*ormone], a pituitary hormone used in the treatment of arthritis, etc.

**act·ing** (ak'tiŋ), *adj.* 1. functioning. 2. temporarily doing the duties of another. *n.* the art of an actor.

**ac·tin·ic** (ak-tin'ik), *adj.* designating or of violet or ultraviolet rays that produce chemical changes. —**ac·tin'i·cal·ly,** *adv.*

**ac·tin·i·um** (ak-tin'i-əm), *n.* [< Gr. *aktis*, ray], a radioactive chemical element found in pitchblende: symbol, Ac.

**ac·tion** (ak'shən), *n.* 1. the doing of something. 2. a thing done. 3. *pl.* behavior. 4. an effect, as of a drug. 5. the way of working, as of a machine. 6. the moving parts, as of a gun. 7. the sequence of events, as in a story. 8. a lawsuit. 9. military combat.

**ac·ti·vate** (ak'tə-vāt'), *v.t.* [-VATED, -VATING], 1. to make active. 2. to organize (a military unit, etc.). 3. to make radioactive. 4. to aerate (sewage) in order to purify it. —**ac'ti·va'tion,** *n.* —**ac'ti·va'tor,** *n.*

**ac·tive** (ak'tiv), *adj.* 1. acting; working. 2. causing motion or change. 3. lively; agile. 4. requiring action: as, *active* sports. 5. in *grammar*, indicating the voice of a verb whose subject performs the action. *n.* in *grammar*, the active voice. —**ac'tive·ly,** *adv.* —**ac'tive·ness,** *n.*

**ac·tiv·i·ty** (ak-tiv'ə-ti), *n.* [*pl.* -TIES], 1. a being active. 2. liveliness. 3. a specific action.

**ac·tor** (ak'tēr), *n.* 1. one who does a thing. 2. one who acts in plays, motion pictures, etc. —**ac'tress,** *n.fem.*

**ac·tu·al** (ak'choo-əl), *adj.* [< L. *agere*, to do], 1. existing in reality; real. 2. existing at the present moment. —**ac'tu·al·ness,** *n.*

**ac'tu·al'i·ty** (-al'ə-ti), *n.* 1. reality. 2. [*pl.* -TIES], an actual thing; fact.

**ac'tu·al·ize'** (-əl-īz'), *v.t.* [-IZED, -IZING], to make actual or real.

**ac'tu·al·ly,** *adv.* really.

**ac·tu·ar·y** (ak'choo-er'i), *n.* [*pl.* -IES], [L. *actuarius*, clerk], one who figures insurance risks, premiums, etc. —**ac'tu·ar'i·al,** *adj.*

**ac·tu·ate** (ak'choo-āt'), *v.t.* [-ATED, -ATING], 1. to put into action. 2. to impel to action. —**ac'tu·a'tion,** *n.* —**ac'tu·a'tor,** *n.*

**a·cu·men** (ə-kū'mən), *n.* [L. < *acuere*, sharpen], keenness of mind; sharp insight.

**a·cute** (ə-kūt'), *adj.* [< L. *acuere*, sharpen], 1. sharp-pointed. 2. keen of mind. 3. sensitive: as, *acute* hearing. 4. severe, as pain. 5. severe but not chronic: as, an *acute* disease. 6. shrill; high in pitch. 7. less than 90°: said of angles. —**a·cute'ness,** *n.*

**acute accent,** a mark (') showing the quality of a vowel, stress, etc.

**-acy,** [ult. < Gr.], a suffix meaning *quality, condition*, etc., as in *celibacy.*

**ad** (ad), *n.* [Colloq.], an advertisement.

**ad-,** [L.], a prefix meaning *motion toward, addition to, nearness to:* also **a-, ac-, af-, ag-, an-,** etc. before certain consonants.

**A.D.,** *Anno Domini*, [L., in the year of the Lord], of the Christian era: used with dates.

**ad·age** (ad'ij), *n.* [< L. *ad-*, to + *aio*, I say], an old saying; proverb.

**a·da·gio** (ə-dä'jō), *adv.* [It. *ad agio*, at ease], in *music*, slowly. *adj.* slow. *n.* [*pl.* -GIOS], 1. a slow movement in music. 2. a slow ballet dance.

**Ad·am** (ad'əm), *n.* in the *Bible*, the first man.

**ad·a·mant** (ad'ə-mant', -mənt), *n.* [< Gr. *a-*, not + *daman*, subdue], a very hard stone or substance. *adj.* 1. too hard to be broken. 2. unyielding; firm.

**Adam's apple,** the projection of cartilage in the front of a man's throat.

**a·dapt** (ə-dapt'), *v.t.* [< L. *ad-*, to + *aptare*, to fit], 1. to make suitable, esp. by changing. 2. to make (oneself) conform to new circumstances. —**a·dapt'er, a·dap'tor,** *n.*

**a·dapt'a·ble,** *adj.* 1. that can be adapted. 2. that adapts easily to new circumstances. —**a·dapt'a·bil'i·ty,** *n.*

**ad·ap·ta·tion** (ad'əp-tā'shən), *n.* 1. an adapting. 2. a thing or change resulting from adapting. Also **a·dap'tion.**

**a·dap·tive** (ə-dap'tiv), *adj.* 1. showing adaptation. 2. able to adapt. —**a·dap'tive·ness,** *n.*

**add** (ad), *v.t.* [< L. *ad-*, to + *dare*, give], 1. to join (*to*) so as to increase. 2. to state further. 3. to combine (numbers) into a sum. *v.i.* 1. to cause an increase (*to*). 2. to find a sum. —**add up to,** to mean; signify.

**ad·dend** (ad'end, ə-dend'), *n.* [< *addendum*], a number or quantity to be added to another.

**ad·den·dum** (ə-den'dəm), *n.* [*pl.* -DA (-də)], [L.], a thing added, as an appendix to a book.

**ad·der** (ad'ēr), *n.* [AS. *nædre*], 1. a poisonous snake of Europe; viper. 2. any of several harmless snakes of N. America.

**ad·dict** (ə-dikt'; *for n.*, ad'ikt), *v.t.* [< L. *addicere*, give assent], to give (oneself) up habitually (*to*). *n.* one addicted to a habit, as to taking drugs. —**ad·dict'ed,** *adj.* —**ad·dict'ed·ness, ad·dic'tion,** *n.*

**ad·di·tion** (ə-dish'ən), *n.* 1. an adding of numbers to get a sum. 2. a joining of a thing to another thing. 3. a part added. —**ad·di'tion·al,** *adj.* —**ad·di'tion·al·ly,** *adv.*

**ad·di·tive** (ad'ə-tiv), *n.* something added. *adj.* 1. of addition. 2. to be added.

**ad·dle** (ad''l), *adj.* [< AS. *adela*, mire], 1. rotten: said of an egg. 2. muddled; confused. *v.t. & v.i.* [-DLED, -DLING], 1. to make or become rotten. 2. to make or become confused.

**ad·dress** (ə-dres'; *for n. 2 & 3, also* ad'res), *v.t.* [< LL. *directiare*, to direct], 1. to direct (words *to*). 2. to speak or write to. 3. to write the destination on (a letter, etc.).

4. to apply (oneself *to*). *n.* 1. a spoken or written speech. 2. the place where one lives or receives his mail. 3. the destination indicated on an envelope, etc. 4. skill; tact.
**ad·dress·ee** (ad'res-ē'), *n.* the person to whom mail, etc. is addressed.
**ad·duce** (ə-dōōs', -dūs'), *v.t.* [-DUCED, -DUCING], [< L. *ad-*, to + *ducere*, to lead], to give as a reason or proof; cite.
**-ade,** [ult. < L.], a suffix meaning: 1. *the act of*, as in *blockade*. 2. *participant in an action*, as in *brigade*. 3. *drink made from*, as in *limeade*.
**ad·e·noid** (ad''n-oid'), *adj.* 1. glandular. 2. of or like lymphoid tissue. Also **ad'e·noi'dal.**
**ad·e·noids** (ad''n-oidz'), *n.pl.* [< Gr. *adēn*, gland; + *-oid*], lymphoid growths in the throat behind the nose.
**a·dept** (ə-dept'), *adj.* [< L. *ad-*, to + *apisci*, pursue], highly skilled; expert. *n.* (ad'ept, ə-dept'), an expert. **—a·dept'ly,** *adv.*
**ad·e·quate** (ad'ə-kwit), *adj.* [< L. *ad-*, to + *aequare*, make equal], equal to a requirement; sufficient or suitable. **—ad'e·qua·cy, ad'e·quate·ness,** *n.* **—ad'e·quate·ly,** *adv.*
**ad·here** (əd-hêr'), *v.i.* [-HERED, -HERING], [< L. *ad-*, to + *haerere*, to stick], 1. to stick fast; become attached. 2. to give allegiance or support (*to*). **—ad·her'ence,** *n.*
**ad·her'ent,** *adj.* sticking fast; attached. *n.* a supporter or follower (*of* a cause, etc.).
**ad·he·sion** (əd-hē'zhən), *n.* 1. a sticking or being stuck together. 2. devoted attachment. 3. in *physics*, the force that holds together the unlike molecules of substances.
**ad·he'sive** (-siv), *adj.* 1. sticking. 2. gummed; sticky. *n.* an adhesive substance. **—ad·he'sive·ness,** *n.*
**adhesive tape,** tape sticky on one side, used in bandaging, etc.
**a·dieu** (ə-dū', -dōō'; *Fr.* ä'dyö'), *interj.* & *n.* [*pl.* ADIEUS; Fr. ADIEUX (-dyö')], [Fr.], good-by.
**ad in·fi·ni·tum** (ad in'fə-nī'təm), [L.], endlessly; without limit.
**ad in·te·rim** (ad in'tə-rim), [L.], 1. in the meantime. 2. temporary.
‡**a·dios** (ä-dyôs'), *interj.* & *n.* [Sp.], good-by.
**ad·i·pose** (ad'ə-pōs'), *adj.* [< L. *adeps*, fat], of animal fat; fatty. *n.* animal fat. **—ad'i·pos'i·ty** (-pos'ə-ti), *n.*
**adj.,** adjective.
**ad·ja·cent** (ə-jā's'nt), *adj.* [< L. *ad-*, to + *jacere*, to lie], near or close (*to*); adjoining. **—ad·ja'cen·cy, ad·ja'cence,** *n.*
**ad·jec·tive** (aj'ik-tiv), *n.* [< L. *adjicere*, add to], a word used to limit or qualify a noun or other substantive: *good* and *every* are *adjectives*. **—ad'jec·ti'val** (-tī'v'l), *adj.*
**ad·join** (ə-join'), *v.t.* [< L. *ad-*, to + *jungere*, join], to be next to. *v.i.* to be in contact or proximity. **—ad·join'ing,** *adj.*
**ad·journ** (ə-jūrn'), *v.t.* & *v.i.* [< L. *ad*, to + *diurnus*, of a day], to suspend business of (a legislature, etc.) for a time. **—ad·journ'ment,** *n.*
**ad·judge** (ə-juj'), *v.t.* [-JUDGED, -JUDGING], [< L. *ad-*, to + *judicare*, to judge], 1. to decide by law. 2. to order or sentence by law.
**ad·ju·di·cate** (ə-jōō'di-kāt'), *v.t.* [-CATED, -CATING], in *law*, to hear and decide (a case); adjudge. *v.i.* to act as judge (*in* or *on*).
**ad·junct** (aj'uŋkt), *n.* [see ADJOIN], a secondary or nonessential addition.
**ad·jure** (ə-joor'), *v.t.* [-JURED, -JURING], [< L. *ad-*, to + *jurare*, swear], 1. to charge solemnly on oath. 2. to ask earnestly. **—ad'ju·ra'tion,** *n.*
**ad·just** (ə-just'), *v.t.* [< L. *ad*, to + *juxta*, near], 1. to alter so as to make fit. 2. to regulate, as a watch. 3. to settle rightly. 4. to decide the amount to be paid in settling (an insurance claim). *v.i.* to adapt oneself. **—ad·just'a·ble,** *adj.* **—ad·just'ment,** *n.*
**ad·ju·tant** (aj'ə-tənt), *n.* [< L. *adjuvare*, to help], 1. an assistant. 2. an army staff officer who helps the commanding officer. 3. a large stork of India and Africa.
**Adjutant General,** the U.S. Army general in charge of all records.
**ad-lib** (ad'lib'), *v.t.* & *v.i.* [-LIBBED, -LIBBING], [< L. *ad libitum*, at pleasure], [Colloq.], to improvise; extemporize.
**ad·min·is·ter** (əd-min'ə-stēr), *v.t.* [< L. *ad-*, to + *ministrare*, serve], 1. to manage; direct. 2. to give out, as punishment. 3. to apply (medicine, etc.). 4. to tender (an oath, etc.). Also **ad·min'is·trate'** [-TRATED, -TRATING]. *v.i.* to furnish help (*to*).
**ad·min'is·tra'tion** (-strā'shən), *n.* 1. management. 2. [often A-], the executive officials of a government, etc. and their policy. 3. their term of office. 4. the administering (*of* punishment, medicine, etc.). **—ad·min'is·tra'tive,** *adj.*
**ad·min'is·tra'tor** (-tēr), *n.* 1. one who administers. 2. in *law*, one appointed to settle an estate.
**ad·mi·ra·ble** (ad'mə-rə-b'l), *adj.* 1. deserving admiration. 2. excellent.
**ad·mir·al** (ad'mə-rəl), *n.* [< Ar. *amir al*, ruler of], 1. the commanding officer of a fleet. 2. a naval officer of the highest rank.
**ad'mi·ral·ty** (-ti), *n.* [*pl.* -TIES], [often A-], a governmental department in charge of naval affairs.
**ad·mi·ra·tion** (ad'mə-rā'shən), *n.* 1. an admiring. 2. high esteem.
**ad·mire** (əd-mīr'), *v.t.* [-MIRED, -MIRING], [< L. *ad-*, at + *mirari*, wonder], 1. to regard with wonder and delight. 2. to have high regard for. **—ad·mir'er,** *n.*
**ad·mis·si·ble** (əd-mis'ə-b'l), *adj.* that can be accepted or admitted.
**ad·mis·sion** (əd-mish'ən), *n.* 1. an admitting or being admitted. 2. an entrance fee. 3. a conceding, confessing, etc. 4. a thing conceded, confessed, etc.
**ad·mit** (əd-mit'), *v.t.* [-MITTED, -MITTING], [< L. *ad-*, to + *mittere*, send], 1. to permit or entitle to enter or use. 2. to allow; leave room for. 3. to concede or confess. *v.i.* to allow (with *of*). **—ad·mit'tance,** *n.*
**ad·mit'ted·ly,** *adv.* by admission or general agreement.
**ad·mix·ture** (ad-miks'chēr), *n.* [< L. *ad-*, to + *miscere*, mix], 1. a mixture. 2. a thing added in mixing.
**ad·mon·ish** (əd-mon'ish), *v.t.* [< L. *ad-*, to + *monere*, warn], 1. to warn; caution. 2. to reprove mildly. 3. to advise. **—ad·mo·ni·tion** (ad'mə-nish'ən), *n.*
**ad·mon'i·to'ry** (-ə-tôr'i), *adj.* warning.
‡**ad nau·se·am** (ad nô'shi-am'), [L.], to the point of disgust.
**a·do** (ə-dōō'), *n.* fuss; trouble.
**a·do·be** (ə-dō'bi), *n.* [Sp.], 1. unburnt, sun-dried brick. 2. clay for making this brick. 3. a building of adobe.
**ad·o·les·cence** (ad''l-es''ns), *n.* the time of life between puberty and adulthood; youth.
**ad'o·les'cent,** *adj.* [< L. *ad-*, to + *alescere*, grow up], 1. growing up. 2. of or in adolescence. *n.* a person during adolescence.
**A·do·nis** (ə-dō'nis, -don'is), *n.* 1. in *Gr. myth.*, a young man loved by Aphrodite. 2. any very handsome young man.
**a·dopt** (ə-dopt'), *v.t.* [< L. *ad-*, to + *optare*, choose], 1. to take legally into one's own family and raise as one's own child. 2. to take as one's own. 3. to choose or accept. **—a·dopt'a·ble,** *adj.* **—a·dop'tion,** *n.*
**a·dop·tive** (ə-dop'tiv), *adj.* 1. adopted. 2. adopting. **—a·dop'tive·ly,** *adv.*
**a·dor·a·ble** (ə-dôr'ə-b'l), *adj.* 1. worthy of adoration or love. 2. [Colloq.], delightful.
**ad·o·ra·tion** (ad'ə-rā'shən), *n.* 1. a worshiping or paying homage. 2. great love.

**a·dore** (ə-dôr′), ***v.t.*** [-DORED, -DORING], [< L. *ad-*, to + *orare*, speak], 1. to worship as divine. 2. to love greatly. 3. [Colloq.], to like very much. —**a·dor′ing,** ***adj.***

**a·dorn** (ə-dôrn′), ***v.t.*** [< L. *ad-*, to + *ornare*, deck out], 1. to serve as an ornament to. 2. to put decoration on. —**a·dorn′ment,** ***n.***

**ad·re·nal** (ad-rē′n'l), ***adj.*** [*ad-* + *renal*], 1. near the kidneys. 2. of two ductless glands (**adrenal glands**) on top of the kidneys in mammals. ***n.*** an adrenal gland.

**ad·ren·al·in** (ad-ren′'l-in), ***n.*** a drug used to raise blood pressure, stop bleeding, etc.: a trademark (**Adrenalin**).

**a·drift** (ə-drift′), ***adv. & adj.*** floating without mooring or direction; untied.

**a·droit** (ə-droit′), ***adj.*** [Fr., *à*, to + *droit*, right], skillful and clever. —**a·droit′ly,** ***adv.***

**ad·u·late** (aj′ə-lāt′) ***v.t.*** [-LATED, -LATING], [< L. *adulari*, fawn upon], to flatter servilely. —**ad′u·la′tion,** ***n.***

**a·dult** (ə-dult′, ad′ult), ***adj.*** [see ADOLESCENT], grown up; mature. ***n.*** a mature person, animal, or plant. —**a·dult′hood,** ***n.***

**a·dul·ter·ate** (ə-dul′tēr-āt′), ***v.t.*** [-ATED, -ATING], [< L. *ad-*, to + *alter*, other], to make inferior, impure, etc. by adding a poor or improper substance. —**a·dul′ter·a′tion,** ***n.***

**a·dul·ter·y** (ə-dul′tēr-i), ***n.*** [*pl.* -IES], [see ADULTERATE], sexual intercourse between a married person and another not the spouse. —**a·dul′ter·er,** ***n.*** —**a·dul′ter·ess,** ***n.fem.***

**ad·um·brate** (ad-um′brāt, ad′əm-brāt′), ***v.t.*** [-BRATED, -BRATING], [< L. *ad-*, to + *umbra*, shade]. 1. to outline vaguely. 2. to overshadow. —**ad′um·bra′tion,** ***n.***

**adv.,** 1. adverb. 2. advertisement.

**ad·vance** (əd-vans′, -väns′), ***v.t.*** [-VANCED, -VANCING], [< L. *ab-*, from + *ante*, before], 1. to bring forward. 2. to suggest. 3. to promote. 4. to raise the rate of. 5. to lend. ***v.i.*** 1. to go forward. 2. to improve; progress. 3. to rise in rank, price, etc. ***n.*** 1. a moving forward. 2. an improvement. 3. rise in value. 4. *pl.* approaches to get favor. 5. a payment before due. ***adj.*** 1. in front: as, *advance* guard. 2. beforehand. —**in advance,** 1. in front. 2. ahead of time. —**ad·vance′ment,** ***n.***

**ad·vanced′,** ***adj.*** 1. in advance; in front. 2. old. 3. ahead of the times.

**ad·van·tage** (əd-van′tij), ***n.*** [< L. *ab ante*, from before], 1. superiority. 2. a favorable circumstance, event, etc. 3. gain; benefit. —**take advantage of,** 1. to use for one's own benefit. 2. to impose upon. —**to advantage,** to good effect. —**ad·van·ta·geous** (ad′vən-tā′jəs), ***adj.***

**Ad·vent** (ad′vent), ***n.*** [< L. *ad-*, to + *venire*, come], 1. the period including the four Sundays before Christmas. 2. [a-], a coming.

**ad·ven·ti·tious** (ad′ven-tish′əs), ***adj.*** [see ADVENT], not inherent; accidental.

**ad·ven·ture** (əd-ven′chēr), ***n.*** [see ADVENT], 1. an exciting and dangerous undertaking. 2. an unusual, stirring, often romantic experience. ***v.t. & v.i.*** [-TURED, -TURING], to risk; venture. —**ad·ven′tur·ous, ad·ven′ture·some,** ***adj.*** —**ad·ven′tur·ous·ly,** ***adv.***

**ad·ven′tur·er,** ***n.*** 1. one who has or likes to have adventures. 2. a soldier of fortune. 3. one who tries to advance socially by dubious schemes. —**ad·ven′tur·ess,** ***n.fem.***

**ad·verb** (ad′vērb), ***n.*** [< L. *ad-*, to + *verbum*, word], a word used to modify a verb, adjective, or another adverb, by expressing time, place, manner, degree, etc. —**ad·ver′bi·al·ly,** ***adv.***

**ad·ver·sar·y** (ad′vēr-ser′i), ***n.*** [*pl.* -IES], [see ADVERT], an opponent; foe.

**ad·verse** (əd-vũrs′), ***adj.*** [see ADVERT], 1. hostile; opposed. 2. unfavorable; harmful.

**ad·ver·si·ty** (əd-vũr′sə-ti), ***n.*** [*pl.* -TIES], 1. misfortune; wretched or troubled state. 2. an instance of misfortune; calamity.

**ad·vert** (əd-vũrt′) ***v.i.*** [< L. *ad-*, to + *vertere*, to turn], to call attention; refer (*to*).

**ad·ver·tise, ad·ver·tize** (ad′vēr-tīz′), ***v.t.*** [-TISED, -TISING; -TIZED, -TIZING], [see ADVERT], to describe or praise publicly, usually to promote sales. ***v.i.*** 1. to call public attention to things for sale. 2. to ask (*for*) by public notice. —**ad′ver·tis′er, ad′ver·tiz′er,** ***n.*** —**ad′ver·tis′ing, ad′ver·tiz′ing,** ***n.***

**ad·ver·tise·ment, ad·ver·tize·ment** (ad′vēr-tīz′mənt, əd-vũr′tiz-), ***n.*** a public notice, usually paid for, as of things for sale.

**ad·vice** (əd-vīs′), ***n.*** [< L. *ad-*, at + *videre*, to look], 1. opinion given as to what to do; counsel. 2. *usually pl.* information or report.

**ad·vis·a·ble** (əd-vīz′ə-b'l), ***adj.*** to be recommended; prudent. —**ad·vis′a·bil′i·ty,** ***n.***

**ad·vise** (əd-vīz′), ***v.t.*** [-VISED, -VISING], 1. to give advice to; counsel. 2. to offer as advice. 3. to inform. ***v.i.*** to consult (*with*). —**ad·vi′ser, ad·vis′or,** ***n.***

**ad·vised′,** ***adj.*** thought out; planned: now chiefly in *well-advised, ill-advised.*

**ad·vis′ed·ly** (-id-li), ***adv.*** with due consideration; deliberately.

**ad·vise′ment,** ***n.*** careful consideration. —**take under advisement,** to consider carefully.

**ad·vi·so·ry** (əd-vī′zə-ri), ***adj.*** 1. advising or empowered to advise. 2. relating to advice.

**ad·vo·cate** (ad′və-kit, -kāt′), ***n.*** [< L. *ad-*, to + *vocare*, to call], one who pleads another's cause or in support of something. ***v.t.*** (-kāt′), [-CATED, -CATING], to speak or write in support of. —**ad′vo·ca·cy** (-kə-si), ***n.*** —**ad′vo·ca′tor,** ***n.***

**advt.,** [*pl.* ADVTS.], advertisement.

**adz, adze** (adz), ***n.*** [AS. *adesa*], an axlike tool for dressing wood, etc.

**ae·gis** (ē′jis), ***n.*** [< Gr. *aigis*, goatskin], 1. protection. 2. sponsorship.

**Ae·ne·as** (i-nē′əs, ē-), ***n.*** in *Gr. & Rom. legend*, a Trojan warrior whose adventures are told in an epic poem by Virgil.

**ae·on** (ē′ən, ē′on), ***n.*** [Gr. *aiōn*, an age], an extremely long, indefinite period of time.

**a·er·ate** (ā′ēr-āt′, âr′-), ***v.t.*** [-ATED, -ATING], [< *aero-* + *-ate*], 1. to expose to air. 2. to charge (liquid) with gas, as in making soda water. —**a·er·a′tion,** ***n.*** —**aer′a·tor,** ***n.***

**aer·i·al** (âr′i-əl, ā-ēr′i-), ***adj.*** [< L. *aer*, air; + *-al*], 1. of or like air. 2. not substantial; unreal. 3. of aircraft or flying. ***n.*** a radio or television antenna.

**aer′i·al·ist** (-ist), ***n.*** an acrobat who performs on a trapeze, high wire, etc.

**aer·ie, aer·y** (âr′i, ēr′i), ***n.*** [prob. < L. *ager*, field], the high nest of an eagle, hawk, etc.

**aero-, aëro-,** [< Gr. *aēr*], a combining form meaning: 1. *air, of the air.* 2. *of aircraft.* 3. *of gases.*

**aer·o·dy·nam·ics** (âr′ō-dī-nam′iks, ā′ēr-ō-), ***n.pl.*** [construed as sing.], the branch of physics dealing with the forces exerted by air or other gases in motion.

**aer·o·naut** (âr′ə-nôt′, ā′ēr-ə-), ***n.*** [< Gr. *aēr*, air + *nautēs*, sailor], the pilot of a balloon or dirigible.

**aer′o·nau′tics** (-nô′tiks), ***n.pl.*** [construed as sing.], the science of making and flying aircraft; aviation. —**aer′o·nau′tic,** ***adj.***

**aer′o·plane′** (-plān′), ***n.*** an airplane.

**aer′o·sol′** (-sōl′, -sol′), ***n.*** [*aero-* + *sol*ution], a suspension of insoluble particles in a gas.

**aer·o·space** (âr′ə-spās′), ***n.*** the earth's atmosphere and the space outside it. ***adj.*** of aerospace, or of spacecraft or missiles designed for flight in aerospace.

**aes·thete** (es′thēt), ***n.*** [Gr. *aisthētēs*, one who perceives], 1. a person highly sensitive to art and beauty. 2. one who exaggerates the value of artistic sensitivity.

**aes·thet·ic** (es-thet′ik), *adj.* 1. of aesthetics. 2. of beauty. 3. sensitive to art and beauty.
**aes·thet′ics** (-iks), *n.pl.* [construed as sing.], the study or philosophy of beauty.
**a·far** (ə-fär′), *adv.* at, to, or from a distance.
**af·fa·ble** (af′ə-b'l), *adj.* [< L. *ad-*, to + *fari*, speak], pleasant and polite. —**af′fa·bil′i·ty,** *n.* —**af′fa·bly,** *adv.*
**af·fair** (ə-fâr′), *n.* [< L. *ad*, to + *facere*, do], 1. a thing to do. 2. *pl.* matters of business. 3. any matter, event, etc. 4. an amorous episode.
**af·fect** (ə-fekt′), *v.t.* [< L. *ad-*, to + *facere*, do], 1. to have an effect on; influence. 2. to move or stir the emotions of.
**af·fect′,** *v.t.* [< L. *affectare*, strive after], 1. to like to have, use, wear, etc. 2. to make a pretense of being, feeling, etc.
**af·fec·ta·tion** (af′ek-tā′shən), *n.* 1. a pretending to like, have, etc. 2. artificial behavior.
**af·fect′ed,** *adj.* 1. assumed for effect; artificial. 2. behaving in an artificial way.
**af·fect′ed,** *adj.* 1. diseased. 2. influenced. 3. emotionally moved.
**af·fect′ing,** *adj.* emotionally moving.
**af·fec·tion** (ə-fek′shən), *n.* 1. *often pl.* fond or tender feeling. 2. a disease.
**af·fec′tion·ate** (-it), *adj.* tender and loving.
**af·fer·ent** (af′ẽr-ənt), *adj.* [< L. *ad-*, to + *ferre*, to bear], bringing inward to a central part, as nerves: cf. **efferent**.
**af·fi·ance** (ə-fī′əns), *n.* [< L. *ad*, to + *fidare*, to trust], betrothal. *v.t.* [-ANCED, -ANCING], to betroth.
**af·fi·da·vit** (af′ə-dā′vit), *n.* [ML., he has made oath], a written statement made on oath, as before a notary public.
**af·fil·i·ate** (ə-fil′i-āt′), *v.t.* [-ATED, -ATING], [< L. *affiliare*, adopt as a son], 1. to take in as a member. 2. to associate (oneself). *v.i.* to join. *n.* (-it), an affiliated person, club, etc.; member. —**af·fil′i·a′tion,** *n.*
**af·fin·i·ty** (ə-fin′ə-ti), *n.* [*pl.* -TIES], [< L. *affinis*, adjacent], 1. relationship by marriage. 2. close relationship. 3. a likeness implying common origin. 4. a spontaneous attraction to a person or thing.
**af·firm** (ə-fũrm′), *v.t.* [< L. *ad-*, to + *firmare*, make firm], 1. to declare positively; assert. 2. to confirm; ratify. *v.i.* in *law*, to declare solemnly, but not under oath.
**af·fir·ma·tion** (af′ẽr-mā′shən), *n.* 1. an affirming or confirming. 2. a positive declaration. 3. in *law*, a solemn declaration.
**af·firm·a·tive** (ə-fũr′mə-tiv), *adj.* affirming; answering "yes." *n.* 1. an expression of assent or agreement. 2. the side upholding the proposition in a debate.
**af·fix** (ə-fiks′), *v.t.* [-FIXED or -FIXT, -FIXING], [< L. *ad-*, to + *figere*, fasten], 1. to fasten; attach. 2. to add at the end. *n.* (af′iks), 1. a thing affixed. 2. a prefix or suffix.
**af·fla·tus** (ə-flā′təs), *n.* [< L. *ad-*, to + *flare*, blow], inspiration, as of an artist.
**af·flict** (ə-flikt′), *v.t.* [< L. *ad-*, to + *fligere*, strike], to cause pain or suffering to; distress greatly. —**af·flict′er,** *n*
**af·flic·tion** (ə-flik′shən), *n.* 1. pain; suffering. 2. any cause of suffering.
**af·flu·ence** (af′lo͞o-əns), *n.* [< L. *ad-*, to + *fluere*, flow], 1. great plenty; abundance. 2. riches; wealth; opulence.
**af′flu·ent,** *adj.* 1. plentiful. 2. wealthy. *n.* a stream flowing into a river; tributary.
**af·ford** (ə-fôrd′), *v.t.* [AS. *geforthian*, advance], 1. to spare (money, time, etc.) without much inconvenience. 2. to give; yield: as, to *afford* pleasure.
**af·fray** (ə-frā′), *n.* [< OFr. *esfrai*, an attack], a noisy brawl; public fight or riot.
**af·front** (ə-frunt′), *v.t.* [< L. *ad-*, to + *frons*, forehead], 1. to insult openly. 2. to confront defiantly. *n.* an open insult.
**af·ghan** (af′gən, -gan), *n.* [< *Afghanistan*], a crocheted or knitted blanket or shawl.
**a·field** (ə-fēld′), *adv.* 1. in or to the field. 2. away (from home); astray.
**a·fire** (ə-fīr′), *adv.* & *adj.* on fire.
**a·flame** (ə-flām′), *adv.* & *adj.* in flames.
**AFL-CIO,** American Federation of Labor and Congress of Industrial Organizations, merged in 1955.
**a·float** (ə-flōt′), *adj.* 1. floating. 2. at sea. 3. flooded, as a ship's deck.
**a·flut·ter** (ə-flut′ẽr), *adv.* & *adj.* in a flutter.
**a·foot** (ə-foot′), *adv.* & *adj.* 1. on foot. 2. in motion; astir.
**a·fore** (ə-fôr′), *adv.*, *prep.*, *conj.* [Archaic or Dial. except in nautical use], before.
**a·fore′said′** (-sed′), *adj.* spoken of before.
**a·foul** (ə-foul′), *adv.* & *adj.* in a collision or tangle. —**run** (or **fall**) **afoul of,** to get into trouble with.
**Afr.,** 1. Africa. 2. African.
**a·fraid** (ə-frād′), *adj.* [< obs. *affray*, to frighten], feeling fear; frightened (*of*, *that*, or *to*): often merely indicating regret.
**a·fresh** (ə-fresh′), *adv.* again; anew.
**Af·ri·can** (af′ri-kən), *adj.* of Africa, its peoples, etc. *n.* a native of Africa.
**aft** (aft, äft), *adj.* & *adv.* [< AS. *afta*, behind], at, near, or toward the stern (within the ship).
**af·ter** (af′tẽr, äf′-), *adv.* [see AFT]. 1. behind. 2. later. *prep.* 1. behind. 2. in search of. 3. later than. 4. as a result of. 5. in spite of: as, *after* all I've said, he's still going. 6. lower in rank or order than. 7. in imitation of. 8. for: as, named *after* Lincoln. 9. concerning: as, she asked *after* you. *conj.* following the time when. *adj.* 1. next; later. 2. more aft.
**af′ter·birth′,** *n.* the placenta and fetal membranes expelled after childbirth.
**af′ter·ef·fect′,** *n.* an effect coming later, or as a secondary result.
**af′ter·glow′,** *n.* the glow remaining after a light has gone, as in the sky after sunset.
**af′ter·math′** (-math′), *n.* [*after* + < AS. *mæth*, cutting of grass], a result or consequence, usually an unpleasant one.
**af′ter·most′,** *adj.* hindmost; last.
**af′ter·noon′,** *n.* the time from noon to evening. *adj.* in the afternoon.
**af′ter·thought′,** *n.* 1. later reflection or explanation. 2. a thought coming too late to be apt.
**af′ter·ward** (-wẽrd), *adv.* later; subsequently: also **af′ter·wards.**
**Ag,** *argentum*, [L.], in *chem.*, silver.
**a·gain** (ə-gen′, -gān′), *adv.* [< AS. *on-*, up to + *gegn*, direct], 1. back into a former condition. 2. once more. 3. besides. 4. on the other hand. —**again and again,** repeatedly.
**a·gainst** (ə-genst′, -gānst′), *prep.* [see AGAIN], 1. in opposition to. 2. toward so as to strike: as, throw it *against* the wall. 3. next to; adjoining. 4. in preparation for.
**a·gape** (ə-gāp′), *adv.* & *adj.* [*a-*, on + *gape*], 1. with the mouth wide open. 2. wide open.
**ag·ate** (ag′it), *n.* [< Gr. *Achatēs*, Sicilian river], 1. a hard semiprecious stone with clouded coloring. 2. a playing marble made of or like this.
**a·ga·ve** (ə-gā′vi), *n.* [< proper name in Gr. myth], a desert plant of the amaryllis family, esp. the American century plant.
**age** (āj), *n.* [< L. *aetas*], 1. the length of time that a person or thing has existed. 2. a lifetime. 3. the time when one is qualified for full legal rights: as, to come of *age*. 4. a stage of life. 5. old age. 6. a historical or geological period. 7. *often pl.* [Colloq.], a long time. *v.i.* [AGED, AGING or AGEING], to grow old. *v.t.* to make old.
**-age,** [< LL. *-aticum*], a suffix meaning *act* or *state of*, *amount of*, *cost of*, *place of* or *for*,

*collection of*, as in *passage*, *postage*, *orphanage*, *acreage*.
**a·ged** (ā'jid), *adj.* 1. old. 2. (ājd), of the age of. —**the aged** (ā'jid), old people.
**age'less,** *adj.* 1. not aging. 2. eternal.
**a·gen·cy** (ā'jən-si), *n.* [*pl.* -CIES], [see AGENT], 1. action; power. 2. means. 3. *a*) a firm, etc. empowered to act for another. *b*) its business, office, etc.
**a·gen·da** (ə-jen'də), *n.pl.* [*sing.* -DUM (-dəm)], [< L. *agere*, do], [also construed as sing.], a list of things to be dealt with (at a meeting, etc.).
**a·gent** (ā'jənt), *n.* [< Gr. *agein*, to drive], 1. an active force or substance producing an effect. 2. a person, firm, etc. empowered to act for another.
**age-old** (āj'ōld'), *adj.* ages old; ancient.
**ag·glom·er·ate** (ə-glom'ẽr-āt'), *v.t. & v.i.* [-ATED, -ATING], [< L. *ad-*, to + *glomerare*, form into a ball], to gather into a mass or ball. *adj.* (-it), gathered into a mass or ball. *n.* (-it), a jumbled heap, cluster, etc. —**ag·glom'er·a'tion,** *n.*
**ag·glu·ti·nate** (ə-glōō't'n-it), *adj.* [< L. *ad-*, to + *gluten*, glue], stuck together. *v.t. & v.i.* (-āt'), [-NATED, -NATING], to stick together, as with glue. —**ag·glu'ti·na'tion,** *n.*
**ag·gran·dize** (ag'rən-dīz', ə-gran'dīz), *v.t.* [-DIZED, -DIZING], [< L. *ad*, to + *grandis*, great], to increase in power, position, riches, etc. —**ag·gran'dize·ment** (-diz-mənt), *n.*
**ag·gra·vate** (ag'rə-vāt'), *v.t.* [-VATED, -VATING], [< L. *ad-*, to + *gravis*, heavy], 1. to make worse. 2. [Colloq.], to exasperate. —**ag'gra·vat'ing,** *adj.* —**ag'gra·va'tion,** *n.*
**ag·gre·gate** (ag'ri-git), *adj.* [< L. *ad-*, to + *grex*, a herd], total. *n.* a total or whole; mass of distinct things gathered together. *v.t.* (-gāt'), [-GATED, -GATING], 1. to amount to; total. 2. to gather into a mass. —**ag'gre·ga'tion,** *n.*
**ag·gres·sion** (ə-gresh'ən), *n.* [< L. *aggredi*, to attack], 1. an unprovoked attack or invasion. 2. a being aggressive. —**ag·gres'sor,** *n.*
**ag·gres·sive** (ə-gres'iv), *adj.* 1. boldly hostile; quarrelsome. 2. bold and active; enterprising. —**ag·gres'sive·ly,** *adv.*
**ag·grieve** (ə-grēv'), *v.t.* [-GRIEVED, -GRIEVING], [see AGGRAVATE], to cause grief or injury to; offend; slight; wrong.
**a·ghast** (ə-gast', -gäst'), *adj.* [< AS. *a* + *gast*, demon], terrified; horrified; dismayed.
**ag·ile** (aj'əl, -īl), *adj.* [< L. *agere*, do], quick and easy of movement; nimble; deft. —**ag'ile·ly,** *adv.* —**a·gil·i·ty** (ə-jil'ə-ti), *n.*
**ag·i·tate** (aj'ə-tāt'), *v.t.* [-TATED, -TATING], [< L. *agere*, do], 1. to stir up; shake up. 2. to excite; fluster. *v.i.* to stir people up so as to produce changes. —**ag'i·tat'ed,** *adj.* —**ag'i·ta'tion,** *n.* —**ag'i·ta'tor,** *n.*
**a·glow** (ə-glō'), *adv. & adj.* in a glow (of color or emotion).
**ag·nos·tic** (ag-nos'tik), *n.* [< Gr. *a-*, not + base of *gignōskein*, know], one who thinks it is impossible to know whether God exists. *adj.* of an agnostic. —**ag·nos'ti·cal·ly,** *adv.* —**ag·nos'ti·cism** (-tə-siz'm), *n.*
**a·go** (ə-gō'), *adj.* [< AS. *agan*, pass away], gone by; past: used following the noun, as, years *ago*. *adv.* in the past: as, long *ago*.
**a·gog** (ə-gog'), *adv. & adj.* [Fr. *en gogues*, in mirth], with eagerness or excitement.
**ag·o·nize** (ag'ə-nīz'), *v.i.* [-NIZED, -NIZING], 1. to struggle. 2. to be in agony. *v.t.* to torture. —**ag'o·niz'ing,** *adj.*
**ag·o·ny** (ag'ə-ni), *n.* [*pl.* -NIES], [< Gr. *agōn*, a contest], 1. great mental or physical pain. 2. death pangs.
**a·gou·ti, a·gou·ty** (ə-gōō'ti), *n.* [*pl.* -TIS, -TIES], [< S. Am. Ind.], a rodent related to the guinea pig, found in Latin America.
**a·grar·i·an** (ə-grâr'i-ən), *adj.* [< L. *ager*, field], 1. of land or the ownership of land. 2. of agriculture. *n.* one who favors more equitable division of land.
**a·gree** (ə-grē'), *v.i.* [AGREED, AGREEING], [< L. *ad*, to + *gratus*, pleasing], 1. to consent (*to*). 2. to be in harmony. 3. to be of the same opinion (*with*). 4. to arrive at an understanding (*about* prices, etc.). *v.t.* to acknowledge; grant.
**a·gree'a·ble,** *adj.* 1. pleasing; charming. 2. willing to consent. 3. conformable. —**a·gree'a·bil'i·ty,** *n.* —**a·gree'a·bly,** *adv.*
**a·gree'ment,** *n.* 1. an agreeing. 2. an understanding between people, countries, etc. 3. a contract.
**ag·ri·cul·ture** (ag'ri-kul'chẽr), *n.* [< L. *ager*, field + *cultura*, cultivation], the work of producing crops and raising livestock; farming. —**ag'ri·cul'tur·al,** *adj.* —**ag'ri·cul'tur·ist, ag'ri·cul'tur·al·ist,** *n.*
**a·gron·o·my** (ə-gron'ə-mi), *n.* [< Gr. *agros*, field + *nemein*, manage], the management of farm land. —**a·gron'o·mist,** *n.*
**a·ground** (ə-ground'), *adv. & adj.* on or onto the ground, a reef, etc., as a boat.
**a·gue** (ā'gū), *n.* [< ML. (*febris*), *acuta*, violent (fever)], 1. a fever, usually malarial, marked by chills. 2. a fit of shivering.
**ah** (ä, ô), *interj.* an exclamation of pain, delight, surprise, etc.
**a·ha** (ä-hä'), *interj.* an exclamation of satisfaction, triumph, etc.
**a·head** (ə-hed'), *adv. & adj.* 1. in or to the front. 2. forward; onward. 3. in advance. —**be ahead,** [Colloq.], to be winning or profiting. —**get ahead of,** to outdo.
**a·hoy** (ə-hoi'), *interj.* in *naut. usage*, a call used in hailing a person or a vessel.
**a·i** (ä'i), *n.* [*pl.* AIS (-iz)], [Tupi < the animal's cry], a S. American sloth with three toes.
**aid** (ād), *v.t. & v.i.* [< L. *ad-*, to + *juvare*, to help], to help; assist. *n.* 1. help; assistance. 2. a helper; assistant. 3. an aide.
**aide** (ād), *n.* [Fr.], a military officer who is assistant to a superior.
**aide-de-camp, aid-de-camp** (ād'də-kamp'), *n.* [*pl.* AIDES-, AIDS-], [Fr., lit., camp assistant], a general's aide.
**ai·grette, ai·gret** (ā'gret, ā-gret'), *n.* 1. an egret. 2. an egret's plumes, used for a woman's headdress, etc.
**ail** (āl), *v.t.* [AS. *eglan*, to trouble], to cause pain or trouble to. *v.i.* to be ill.
**ai·le·ron** (ā'lə-ron'), *n.* [Fr. < *aile*, wing], a hinged section of an airplane wing, for banking.
**ail'ing,** *adj.* sickly; ill.
**ail'ment** (-mənt), *n.* a mild illness.
**aim** (ām), *v.i. & v.t.* [< L. *ad-*, to + *aestimare*, to estimate], 1. to point (a weapon, blow, etc.) so as to hit. 2. to direct (one's efforts). 3. to intend. *n.* 1. an aiming. 2. the direction of a missile, blow, etc. 3. intention. —**take aim,** to aim a weapon, etc.
**aim'less,** *adj.* having no purpose.
**ain't** (ānt), [< *amn't*, contr. of *am not*], [Colloq.], am not: also a dialectal or substandard contraction for *is not*, *has not*, and *have not*.
**air** (âr), *n.* [< Gr. *aēr*], 1. the invisible mixture of gases surrounding the earth; atmosphere. 2. a breeze; wind. 3. an outward appearance: as, an *air* of dignity. 4. *pl.* affected, superior manners. 5. public expression. 6. a tune. *v.t.* 1. to let air into. 2. to publicize. *adj.* of aviation. —**in the air,** prevalent. —**on the air,** in *radio & TV*, broadcasting. —**up in the air,** 1. not settled. 2. [Colloq.], angry, excited, etc.
**air base,** a base for military aircraft.
**air'borne',** *adj.* carried by or through air.
**air brake,** a brake operated by the action of compressed air on a piston.
**air conditioning,** the process of cleaning

the air and controlling its humidity and temperature in buildings, etc. —**air′-con·di′tion,** *v.t.* —**air′-con·di′tioned,** *adj.*

**air′-cool′,** *v.t.* to cool by passing air over, into, or through. —**air′-cooled′,** *adj.*

**air′craft′** (-kraft′), ***n. sing. & pl.*** any machine or machines for flying; airplanes, etc.

**aircraft carrier,** a ship with a large, flat deck for carrying aircraft.

**air·drome** (âr′drōm′), ***n.*** [< *air* + Gr. *dromos*, course], an airport.

**Aire·dale** (âr′dāl′), ***n.*** [< *Airedale*, valley in England], a large terrier with a wiry coat.

**air′field′,** ***n.*** a field where aircraft can take off and land.

**air′foil′** (-foil′), ***n.*** a wing, rudder, etc. of an aircraft.

**air force,** the aviation branch of the armed forces.

**air lift,** a system of transporting troops, supplies, etc. by aircraft.

**air line,** 1. a system of air transport. 2. an organization providing such transport.

**air liner,** a large aircraft for passengers.

**air lock,** an airtight compartment, with adjustable air pressure, between places of unequal pressure.

**air mail,** mail transported by aircraft. —**air′-mail′,** *adj.*

**air′man** (-mən), ***n.*** [*pl.* -MEN], 1. an aviator. 2. an enlisted person in the U.S. Air Force.

**air′-mind′ed,** *adj.* interested in aviation.

**air′plane′,** ***n.*** a motor-driven or jet-propelled aircraft kept aloft by the forces of air upon its wings: also **aeroplane.**

**air′port′,** ***n.*** a place where aircraft can take off and land, with facilities for repair, etc.

**air pressure,** the pressure of the atmosphere.

**air raid,** an attack by aircraft. —**air′-raid′,** *adj.*

**air rifle,** a rifle operated by compressed air.

**air′ship′,** ***n.*** a self-propelled aircraft that is lighter than air and can be steered.

**air′sick′,** *adj.* sick or nauseated because of air travel. —**air′sick′ness,** ***n.***

**air′strip′,** ***n.*** a temporary airfield.

**air′tight′,** *adj.* 1. too tight for air or gas to enter or escape. 2. impregnable: as, an *airtight* alibi.

**air′y,** *adj.* [-IER, -IEST], 1. of air. 2. open to the air; breezy. 3. unsubstantial as air; visionary. 4. light as air; graceful. 5. lighthearted; gay. 6. flippant. 7. [Colloq.], putting on airs. —**air′i·ly,** *adv.* —**air′i·ness,** ***n.***

**aisle** (īl), ***n.*** [< L. *ala*, wing], a passageway, as between rows of seats. —**aisled** (īld), *adj.*

**a·jar** (ə-jär′), *adv. & adj.* [< AS. *cyrr*, a turn], slightly open, as a door.

**a·kim·bo** (ə-kim′bō), *adv. & adj.* [< ON. *keng*, bent + *bogi*, a bow], with hands on hips and elbows bent outward.

**a·kin** (ə-kin′), *adj.* [*a-*, of + *kin*], 1. of one kin; related. 2. having similar qualities.

**-al,** [< L.], a suffix meaning: 1. *of, like,* or *suitable for*, as in *comical.* 2. *the act or process of*, as in *denial.*

**Al,** in *chem.*, aluminum.

**à la** (ä′ lä), [Fr.], in the style of.

**al·a·bas·ter** (al′ə-bas′tẽr), ***n.*** [< name of Egypt. town], 1. a translucent, whitish variety of gypsum. 2. a banded variety of calcite. *adj.* of or like alabaster.

**à la carte** (ä′lə kärt′), [Fr.], with a separate price for each item on the menu.

**a·lack** (ə-lak′), *interj.* [*ah* + *lack*], [Archaic], an exclamation of regret, surprise, etc.

**a·lac·ri·ty** (ə-lak′rə-ti), ***n.*** [< L. *alacer*, lively], 1. quick willingness. 2. lively action; briskness. —**a·lac′ri·tous,** *adj.*

**A·lad·din** (ə-lad′′n), ***n.*** a boy in the *Arabian Nights* who found a magic lamp.

**à la king** (ä′lä kiŋ′), served in a sauce containing mushrooms, pimientos, etc.

**à·la·mode** (ä′lə-mōd′, al′ə-), *adj.* [< Fr.], 1. in fashion. 2. served in a certain style, as pie with ice cream. Also **à la mode, a la mode.**

**a·lar** (ā′lẽr), *adj.* [< L. *ala*, a wing], 1. of a wing. 2. having wings.

**a·larm** (ə-lärm′), ***n.*** [< It. *all'arme*, to arms], 1. a sudden call to arms. 2. a warning of danger. 3. a mechanism that warns of danger, arouses from sleep, etc. 4. fear caused by danger. ***v.t.*** 1. to warn of danger. 2. to frighten.

**alarm clock,** a clock with a device that sounds at a predetermined time.

**a·larm′ing,** *adj.* frightening.

**a·larm′ist,** ***n.*** 1. one who habitually spreads alarming rumors. 2. one who anticipates the worst. *adj.* of an alarmist.

**a·las** (ə-las′, ə-läs′), *interj.* an exclamation of sorrow, pity, regret, etc.

**alb** (alb), ***n.*** [< L. *albus*, white], a long, white linen robe worn by a priest at Mass.

**al·ba·core** (al′bə-kôr′), ***n.*** [< Ar. *al*, the + *bukr*, young camel], any of various saltwater fishes of the mackerel family, including the tuna.

**al·ba·tross** (al′bə-trôs′), ***n.*** [< Sp. < Ar. *al qādūs*, water container], a large, web-footed sea bird related to the petrel.

**al·be·it** (ôl-bē′it), *conj.* [ME. *al be it*, al(though) it be], although; even though.

**al·bi·no** (al-bī′nō), ***n.*** [*pl.* -NOS], [< L. *albus*, white], a person, animal, or plant lacking normal coloration: human albinos have white skin, whitish hair, and pink eyes. —**al·bi·nism** (al′bə-niz′m), ***n.***

**al·bum** (al′bəm), ***n.*** [< L. *albus*, white], 1. a book with blank pages for mounting pictures, stamps, etc. 2. a booklike holder for phonograph records.

**al·bu·men** (al-bū′mən), ***n.*** 1. the white of an egg. 2. [Rare], albumin.

**al·bu·min** (al-bū′min), ***n.*** [< L. *albus*, white], any of a class of water-soluble proteins found in egg, milk, blood, vegetable tissues, etc. —**al·bu′mi·nous** (-mi-nəs), *adj.*

**al·che·my** (al′kə-mi), ***n.*** [< Ar.; ? ult. < Gr. *cheein*, to pour], the chemistry of the Middle Ages, the chief aim of which was to change the baser metals into gold. —**al·chem·ic** (al-kem′ik), *adj.* —**al′che·mist,** ***n.***

**al·co·hol** (al′kə-hôl′, -hol′), ***n.*** [< Ar. *al kohl*, powder of antimony], 1. a colorless, volatile, pungent liquid: it can be burnt as fuel and, in one form, is the intoxicating ingredient in fermented liquors. 2. any such intoxicating liquor. 3. any of a series of similarly organic compounds, as methyl (or wood) alcohol.

**al′co·hol′ic,** *adj.* 1. of alcohol. 2. suffering from alcoholism. ***n.*** one who has chronic alcoholism. —**al′co·hol′i·cal·ly,** *adv.*

**al′co·hol′ism,** ***n.*** a diseased condition caused by habitually drinking too much alcohol.

**al·cove** (al′kōv), ***n.*** [< Ar. *al*, the + *qobbah*, an arch], a recessed section of a room.

**al·de·hyde** (al′də-hīd′), ***n.*** [< *alcohol* + L. *de*, without; + *hydrogen*], a colorless fluid obtained from alcohol by oxidation.

**al·der** (ôl′dẽr), ***n.*** [AS. *alor*], a small tree or shrub of the birch family.

**al·der·man** (ôl′dẽr-mən), ***n.*** [*pl.* -MEN], [< AS. *eald*, old + *man*], in many cities, a municipal officer representing a certain district or ward. —**al′der·man·ship′,** ***n.***

**Al·der·ney** (ôl′dẽr-ni), ***n.*** [*pl.* -NEYS], any of a breed of small dairy cattle.

**ale** (āl), ***n.*** [AS. *ealu*], a fermented drink made from malt and hops: it is like beer but contains more alcohol.

**a·lem·bic** (ə-lem′bik), ***n.*** [< Ar. *al*, the + *anbīq*, a still < Gr. *ambix*, a cup], 1. an apparatus of glass or metal, formerly used for distilling. 2. anything that refines or purifies.

**a·lert** (ə-lũrt′), *adj.* [< L. *erigere*, to erect], 1. watchful; vigilantly ready. 2. active; nimble. *n.* an alarm; warning signal. *v.t.* to warn, as to be ready: as, the troops were *alerted.* —**on the alert,** watchful; vigilant.

**Al·ex·an·drine** (al′ig-zan′drin), *n.* in *prosody,* an iambic line having normally six feet. *adj.* of an Alexandrine.

**al·fal·fa** (al-fal′fə), *n.* [< Ar. *al-fachfacha*, good fodder], a plant of the pea family, used for fodder, pasture, and as a cover crop.

**al·gae** (al′jē), *n.pl.* [*sing.* -GA (-gə)], [pl. of L. *alga*, seaweed], a group of primitive plants, one-celled or many-celled, containing chlorophyll and found in water or damp places.

**al·ge·bra** (al′jə-brə), *n.* [< Ar. *al*, the + *jabara*, reunite], the branch of mathematics that uses positive and negative numbers, letters, etc. to express the relationship between quantities. —**al′ge·bra′ic** (-brā′ik), **al′ge·bra′i·cal,** *adj.* —**al′ge·bra′i·cal·ly,** *adv.*

**-algia,** [< Gr. *algos*], a suffix meaning *pain*, as in *neuralgia.*

**Al·gon·qui·an** (al-goŋ′ki-ən, -kwi-ən), *adj.* designating or of a widespread family of North American Indian languages. *n.* this family of languages.

**al·go·rithm** (al′gə-rith'm), *n.* [< *algorism*, Arabic system of numerals], any special method of solving a certain kind of mathematical problem, as finding the greatest common divisor of two numbers.

**a·li·as** (ā′li-əs), *n.* [*pl.* ALIASES], [L., other], an assumed name. *adv.* otherwise named: as, Bell *alias* Jones.

**A·li Ba·ba** (al′i bab′ə, ä′li bä′bə), in the *Arabian Nights*, a poor man who found the treasure of forty thieves.

**al·i·bi** (al′ə-bī′), *n.* [*pl.* -BIS], [L. < *alius ibi*, elsewhere], 1. in *law*, the plea that an accused person was elsewhere than at the scene of the offense. 2. [Colloq.], any excuse. *v.i.* [-BIED, -BIING], [Colloq.], to offer an excuse.

**al·ien** (āl′yən, ā′li-ən), *adj.* [< L. *alius*, other], foreign; strange. *n.* 1. a foreigner. 2. a foreign-born resident who is not naturalized. —**alien to,** not in harmony with.

**al′ien·ate′** (-āt′), *v.t.* [-ATED, -ATING], 1. to transfer the ownership of (property) to another. 2. to make unfriendly. 3. to cause a transference of (affection). —**al′ien·a′tion,** *n.*

**al′ien·ist,** *n.* a psychiatrist: used in law.

**a·light** (ə-līt′), *v.i.* [ALIGHTED or ALIT, ALIGHTING], [AS. *alihtan*], 1. to get down or off. 2. to come down after flight.

**a·light′,** *adj.* lighted up; burning.

**a·lign** (ə-līn′), *v.t.* [< Fr. *à*, to + *ligne*, line], 1. to bring into a straight line. 2. to bring into agreement, etc.: often reflexive. *v.i.* to line up. Also sp. **aline.** —**a·lign′ment,** *n.*

**a·like** (ə-līk′), *adj.* [AS. *gelic*], like one another; similar. *adv.* 1. similarly. 2. equally.

**al·i·ment** (al′ə-mənt), *n.* [< L. *alere*, nourish], nourishment; food.

**al′i·men′ta·ry** (-men′tə-ri), *adj.* 1. of food or nutrition. 2. nourishing.

**alimentary canal** (or **tract**), the passage in the body (from the mouth to the anus) that food goes through.

**al·i·mo·ny** (al′ə-mō′ni), *n.* [< L. *alere*, nourish], money a judge orders paid to a woman by her legally separated or divorced husband.

**a·lit** (ə-lit′), alt. pt. and pp. of **alight.**

**a·live** (ə-līv′), *adj.* [< AS. *on*, in + *life*, life], 1. having life; living. 2. in existence, operation, etc. 3. lively; alert. —**alive to,** aware of. —**alive with,** teeming with.

**al·ka·li** (al′kə-lī′), *n.* [*pl.* -LIS, -LIES], [< Ar. *al*, the + *qaliy*, ashes of a certain plant], 1. any base, as soda, that is soluble in water and can neutralize acids. 2. any mineral that can neutralize acids. *adj.* alkaline.

**al′ka·line′** (-līn′, -lin), *adj.* of, like, or containing an alkali.—**al′ka·lin′i·ty** (-lin′ə-ti), *n.*

**al′ka·lize′** (-līz′), *v.t.* & *v.i.* [-LIZED, -LIZING], to make alkaline.

**al′ka·loid′** (-loid′), *n.* an organic alkaline substance containing nitrogen: some plant alkaloids are used as drugs, as cocaine.

**all** (ôl), *adj.* [AS. *eall*], 1. the whole quantity of: as, *all* the gold. 2. every one of: as, *all* men. 3. the greatest possible: as, in *all* sincerity. 4. any: as, beyond *all* doubt. 5. alone; only: as, *all* work and no play. *pron.* 1. [construed as pl.], everyone: as, *all* are going. 2. everything. 3. every part. *n.* a totality; whole. *adv.* 1. wholly; quite: as, *all* worn out. 2. apiece: as, a score of two *all.* —**above all,** most of all. —**after all,** nevertheless. —**all but,** 1. all except. 2. almost. —**all in,** [Colloq.], fatigued. —**all in all,** 1. as a whole. 2. everything. —**at all,** 1. in the least. 2. in any way. 3. under any considerations.

**all-,** a prefix meaning: 1. *wholly, entirely,* as in *all-absorbing.* 2. *for every,* as in *all-purpose.*

**Al·lah** (al′ə, ä′lə), *n.* God: the Moslem name.

**all′-A·mer′i·can,** *adj.* chosen as the best in the U.S. *n.* 1. an imaginary football team, etc. of the best U.S. college players of the year. 2. a player on such a team.

**all′-a·round′,** *adj.* having many abilities, talents, or uses; versatile.

**al·lay** (ə-lā′), *v.t.* [-LAYED, -LAYING], [< AS. *a-*, down + *lecgan*, lay], 1. to calm. 2. to lessen or relieve (pain, etc.).

**al·le·ga·tion** (al′ə-gā′shən), *n.* 1. an alleging. 2. an assertion. 3. an assertion without proof.

**al·lege** (ə-lej′), *v.t.* [-LEGED, -LEGING], [< L. *ex-* out of + *litigare*, to dispute], 1. to declare; affirm. 2. to declare without proof.

**al·leg′ed·ly,** *adv.* according to allegation.

**al·le·giance** (ə-lē′jəns), *n.* [< L. *ad-*, to + *ligare*, bind], 1. the duty of being loyal to one's ruler, country, etc. 2. loyalty; devotion, as to a cause.

**al·le·go·rize** (al′ə-gə-rīz′), *v.t.* [-RIZED, -RIZING], to treat as an allegory. *v.i.* to use allegories. —**al′le·go·riz′er,** *n.*

**al·le·go·ry** (al′ə-gôr′i), *n.* [*pl.* -RIES], [< Gr. *allos*, other + *agoreuein*, speak], a story in which people, things, and happenings have another meaning, often instructive, as in a fable. —**al′le·gor′i·cal,** *adj.*

**al·le·gret·to** (al′ə-gret′ō), *adj.* & *adv.* [It., dim. of *allegro*], in *music*, moderately fast.

**al·le·gro** (ə-lā′grō, -leg′rō), *adj.* & *adv.* [It.], in *music*, fast.

**al·le·lu·ia** (al′ə-lōō′yə), *interj.* [see HALLELUJAH], praise ye the Lord!

**al·ler·gen** (al′ẽr-jən), *n.* [*allergy* + *-gen*], a substance inducing an allergic state.

**al·ler·gic** (ə-lũr′jik), *adj.* of, caused by, or having an allergy.

**al·ler·gy** (al′ẽr-ji), *n.* [*pl.* -GIES], [< Gr. *allos*, other + *ergon*, action], a hypersensitivity to a specific substance (as a food, pollen, etc.) or condition (as heat or cold).

**al·le·vi·ate** (ə-lē′vi-āt′), *v.t.* [-ATED, -ATING], [< L. *ad-*, to + *levis*, light], to lessen or relieve (pain, etc.). —**al·le′vi·a′tion,** *n.*

**al·ley** (al′i), *n.* [*pl.* -LEYS], [< OFr. *aler*, go], 1. a narrow street. 2. a long, narrow, wooden lane for bowling.

**al′ley·way′,** *n.* an alley between buildings.

**al·li·ance** (ə-lī′əns), *n.* 1. an allying or being allied. 2. a close association, as of nations for a common objective or of families by marriage. 3. the countries, persons, etc. in such association.

**al·lied** (ə-līd′, al′īd), *adj.* 1. united by kinship, treaty, etc. 2. closely related.

**al·li·ga·tor** (al′ə-gā′tẽr), *n.* [< Sp. < L. *lacertus*, lizard], a large lizard of the U.S., similar to the crocodile but having a short, blunt snout.

**al·lit·er·ate** (ə-lit′ẽr-āt′), *v.i.* [-ATED, -ATING], to have or use alliteration.

**al·lit·er·a·tion** (ə-lit′ẽr-ā′shən), *n.* [< L. *ad*, to + *littera*, letter], repetition of an initial sound in two or more words of a phrase, etc.

**al·lo·cate** (al′ə-kāt′), *v.t.* [-CATED, -CATING], [< L. *ad*, to + *locus*, a place], 1. to set apart for a specific purpose. 2. to distribute, or allot. —**al′lo·ca′tion,** *n.*

**al·lot** (ə-lot′), *v.t.* [-LOTTED, -LOTTING], [< OFr. *a-*, to + *lot*, lot], 1. to distribute in shares; apportion. 2. to assign (a share). —**al·lot′ment,** *n.*

**al·lot·ro·py** (ə-lot′rə-pi), *n.* [< Gr. *allos*, other + *tropos*, manner], the property that certain chemical elements have of existing in two or more different forms, as carbon in charcoal, diamonds, etc.: also **al·lot′ro·pism.**

**all′-out′,** *adj.* [Colloq.], complete or wholehearted: as, an *all-out* effort.

**al·low** (ə-lou′), *v.t.* [< L. *ad-*, to + *locus*, a place], 1. to permit; let: as, I'm not *allowed* to go. 2. to let have: as, she *allowed* herself no sweets. 3. to acknowledge as valid. 4. to provide (an extra quantity), as for shrinkage, waste, etc. —**allow for,** to leave room, time, etc. for. —**al·low′a·ble,** *adj.*

**al·low′ance** (-əns), *n.* 1. an allowing. 2. something allowed. 3. an amount of money, food, etc. given regularly to a child, soldier, etc. 4. a reduction in price, as for a trade-in. —**make allowance(s) for,** to excuse because of mitigating factors.

**al·loy** (al′oi, ə-loi′), *n.* [< L. *ad-*, to + *ligare*, bind], 1. a metal that is a mixture of two or more metals. 2. a less valuable metal mixed with a more valuable one. *v.t.* (ə-loi′), to make into an alloy.

**all right,** 1. satisfactory. 2. unhurt. 3. correct. 4. yes; very well.

**all′-round′,** *adj.* all-around.

**all·spice** (ôl′spīs′), *n.* a spice, combining the tastes of several spices, made from the berry of a West Indian tree.

**all′-star′,** *adj.* made up entirely of outstanding or star performers.

**al·lude** (ə-lo͞od′), *v.i.* [-LUDED, -LUDING], [< L. *ad-*, to + *ludere*, to play], to refer indirectly (*to*).

**al·lure** (ə-loor′), *v.t. & v.i.* [-LURED, -LURING], [see AD- & LURE], to tempt with something desirable; attract. *n.* fascination; charm. —**al·lure′ment,** *n.* —**al·lur′ing,** *adj.*

**al·lu·sion** (ə-lo͞o′zhən), *n.* 1. an alluding. 2. indirect or casual reference. —**al·lu′sive** (-siv), *adj.* —**al·lu′sive·ly,** *adv.*

**al·lu·vi·um** (ə-lo͞o′vi-əm), *n.* [*pl.* -VIUMS, -VIA (-vi-ə)], [< L. *ad-*, to + *luere*, wash], sand, clay, etc. deposited by flowing water. —**al·lu′vi·al,** *adj.*

**al·ly** (ə-lī′), *v.t.* [-LIED, -LYING], [< L. *ad-*, to + *ligare*, bind], 1. to unite or join (*to* or *with*) for a specific purpose. 2. to relate by similarity of structure, etc. *v.i.* to become allied. *n.* (al′ī, ə-lī′), [*pl.* -LIES], 1. a country or person joined with another for a common purpose. 2. an associate.

**al·ma ma·ter, Al·ma Ma·ter** (al′mə mā′tẽr, äl′-, mä′-), [L., fostering mother], 1. the college or school that one attended. 2. its anthem.

**al·ma·nac** (ôl′mə-nak′), *n.* [< Ar. *al*, the + *manākh*, weather], a calendar with astronomical data, weather forecasts, etc.

**al·might·y** (ôl-mī′ti), *adj.* all-powerful. —**the Almighty,** God. —**al·might′i·ly,** *adv.*

**al·mond** (ä′mənd, am′ənd), *n.* [< Gr. *amygdalē*], 1. the edible, nutlike seed of a fruit like the peach. 2. the tree that it grows on.

**al·most** (ôl′mōst, ôl′mōst′), *adv.* very nearly.

**alms** (ämz), *n.* [*pl.* ALMS], [< Gr. *eleos*, pity], money, food, etc. given to poor people.

**alms′house′,** *n.* a poorhouse.

**al·oe** (al′ō), *n.* [*pl.* -OES], [< Gr. *aloē*], 1. a South African plant of the lily family. 2. *pl.* [construed as sing.], a laxative drug made from the juice of its fleshy leaves.

**a·loft** (ə-lôft′), *adv.* [*a-*, on + *loft*], 1. high up. 2. high above the deck of a ship.

**a·lo·ha** (ə-lō′ə, ä-lō′hä), *n. & interj.* [Haw.], love: a word used as a greeting or farewell.

**a·lone** (ə-lōn′), *adj. & adv.* [< *all* + *one*], 1. apart from anything or anyone else. 2. without any other person. 3. only. —**leave alone,** 1. to let be by oneself. 2. [Colloq.], to refrain from interfering with. —**let alone,** 1. to refrain from interfering with. 2. not to speak of: as, we hadn't a dime, *let alone* a dollar.

**a·long** (ə-lôŋ′), *prep.* [< AS. *and*, over against + *lang*, long], on or beside the length of. *adv.* 1. lengthwise. 2. progressively onward. 3. together (*with*). 4. with one: as, take me *along*.

**a·long′side′,** *adv.* at or by the side; side by side. *prep.* beside.

**a·loof** (ə-lo͞of′), *adv.* [< *a-*, on + D. *loef*, to windward], at a distance but in view; apart. *adj.* cool and reserved. —**a·loof′ness,** *n.*

**a·loud** (ə-loud′), *adv.* 1. loudly. 2. in an audible voice.

**alp** (alp), *n.* [< *Alps*, mts. in S Europe], a high mountain.

**al·pac·a** (al-pak′ə), *n.* [Sp. < Ar. *al*, the + Peruv. *paco*, animal], 1. a llama of Bolivia and Peru. 2. its long, silky wool. 3. a thin cloth woven from this wool.

**al·pha** (al′fə), *n.* 1. the first letter of the Greek alphabet (Α, α). 2. the beginning of anything.

**al·pha·bet** (al′fə-bet′), *n.* [< Gr. *alpha* + *beta*], the letters used in writing a language, esp. as arranged in their usual order. —**al′pha·bet′i·cal, al′pha·bet′ic,** *adj.*

**al·pha·bet·ize** (al′fə-bə-tīz′), *v.t.* [-IZED, -IZING], to arrange in alphabetical order.

**alpha particle,** a positively charged particle given off by certain radioactive substances.

**alpha rays,** rays of alpha particles.

**al·pine** (al′pīn, -pin), *adj.* of or like alps.

**al·read·y** (ôl-red′i), *adv.* by or before the given or implied time; previously.

**al·right** (ôl′rīt′), *adv.* all right: a spelling considered substandard.

**al·so** (ôl′sō), *adv.* [< AS. *eal*, all + *swa*, so], likewise; too; in addition.

**al′so-ran′** *n.* [Colloq.], a defeated contestant in a race, election, etc.

**alt.,** 1. alternate. 2. altitude. 3. alto.

**al·tar** (ôl′tẽr), *n.* [< L. *altus*, high], 1. a platform where sacrifices are made to a god, etc. 2. a table, etc. for sacred purposes in a place of worship. —**lead to the altar,** to marry.

**al·ter** (ôl′tẽr), *v.t. & v.i.* [< L. *alter*, other], to change; make or become different. —**al′ter·a·ble,** *adj.* —**al′ter·a·bil′i·ty,** *n.*

**al′ter·a′tion,** *n.* 1. an altering. 2. the result of this.

**al·ter·cate** (ôl′tẽr-kāt′), *v.i.* [-CATED, -CATING], [< L. *altercari*, to dispute], to quarrel.

**al′ter·ca′tion,** *n.* a quarrel; angry dispute.

**al·ter·nate** (ôl′tẽr-nit), *adj.* [< L. *alternus*, one after the other], 1. succeeding each other. 2. every other. *n.* a substitute. *v.t.* (-nāt′), [-NATED, -NATING], to do or use by turns. *v.i.* 1. to act, happen, etc. by turns. 2. to take turns regularly. —**al′ter·nate·ly,** *adv.* —**al′ter·na′tion,** *n.*

**alternating current,** an electric current that reverses its direction regularly and continually.

**al·ter·na·tive** (ôl-tũr′nə-tiv), *adj.* providing a choice between things. *n.* 1. a choice between things. 2. one of the things to be chosen. **—al·ter′na·tive·ly,** *adv.*

**al·though** (ôl-*th*ō′), *conj.* in spite of the fact that; though: now sometimes sp. **altho.**

**al·tim·e·ter** (al-tim′ə-tẽr, al′tə-mē′-), *n.* [< L. *altus,* high; + *-meter*] an instrument for measuring altitude.

**al·ti·tude** (al′tə-tōōd′), *n.* [< L. *altus,* high], 1. the height of a thing, esp. above sea level. 2. a high place.

**al·to** (al′tō), *n.* [*pl.* -TOS], [It. < L. *altus,* high], 1. the range of the lowest female or highest male voice. 2. a singer with this range. *adj.* of, for, or in the alto.

**al·to·geth·er** (ôl′tə-ge*th*′ẽr), *adv.* 1. wholly; completely. 2. on the whole. *n.* a whole. **—in the altogether,** [Colloq.], nude.

**al·tru·ism** (al′trōō-iz′m), *n.* [< L. *alter,* other], unselfish concern for the welfare of others. **—al′tru·ist,** *n.* **—al′tru·is′tic** (-is′tik), *adj.* **—al′tru·is′ti·cal·ly,** *adv.*

**al·um** (al′əm), *n.* [< L. *alumen*], a double sulfate as of a univalent metal and a trivalent metal; esp., a double sulfate of potassium and aluminum, used in medicine, etc.

**al·u·min·i·um** (al′yōō-min′i-əm), *n.* [Brit.], aluminum.

**a·lu·mi·num** (ə-lōō′mi-nəm), *n.* [< L. *alumen,* alum], a silvery, lightweight, metallic chemical element: symbol, Al.

**a·lum·nus** (ə-lum′nəs), *n.* [*pl.* -NI (-nī)], [L., foster son], a boy or man who has attended or been graduated from a school, college, etc. **—a·lum′na** (-nə) [*pl.* -NAE (-nē)], *n.fem.*

**al·ways** (ôl′wiz, -wāz), *adv.* [< *all* + *way*], 1. at all times. 2. all the time; continually.

**a·lys·sum** (ə-lis′əm), *n.* [< Gr. *alyssos,* curing madness], 1. any of a number of plants of the mustard family, bearing white or yellow flowers. 2. sweet alyssum.

**am** (am, əm), [AS. *eom*], the first pers. sing., pres. indic., of **be.**

**Am.,** 1. America. 2. American.

**AM, A.M.,** amplitude modulation.

**A.M.,** Master of Arts: also **M.A.**

**A.M., a.m.,** *ante meridiem,* [L.], before noon: used to designate the time from midnight to noon.

**a·main** (ə-mān′), *adv.* [*a-,* on + *main,* strength], [Archaic], 1. forcefully. 2. at or with great speed.

**a·mal·gam** (ə-mal′gəm), *n.* [< Gr. *malagma,* an emollient], 1. any alloy of mercury with another metal: silver amalgam is used as a dental filling. 2. a mixture; blend.

**a·mal′gam·ate′** (-gə-māt′), *v.t.* & *v.i.* [-ATED, -ATING], to unite; mix; combine. **—a·mal′gam·a′tion,** *n.* **—a·mal′gam·a′tor,** *n.*

**a·man·u·en·sis** (ə-man′yoo-en′sis), *n.* [*pl.* -SES (-sēz)], [L. < *a-,* from + *manus,* hand + *-ensis,* relating to], a secretary; stenographer, copyist, etc.

**am·a·ranth** (am′ə-ranth′), *n.* [< Gr. *amarantos,* unfading], 1. any of a family of plants, some bearing showy flowers. 2. [Poetic], an imaginary flower that never dies.

**am·a·ryl·lis** (am′ə-ril′is), *n.* [< Gr. name for a shepherdess], a bulb plant with white to red lilylike flowers.

**a·mass** (ə-mas′), *v.t.* [< Fr. *à,* to + *masser,* pile up], to pile up; accumulate.

**am·a·teur** (am′ə-choor′, -toor′, -tyoor′), *n.* [Fr. < L. *amare,* to love], 1. one who does something for pleasure, not for pay. 2. one who is somewhat unskillful. *adj.* of or done by amateurs. **—am′ateur′ish,** *adj.* **—am′a·teur′ish·ly,** *adv.* **—am′a·teur·ism,** *n.*

**am·a·to·ry** (am′ə-tôr′i), *adj.* [< L. *amare,* to love], of or showing sexual love.

**a·maze** (ə-māz′), *v.t.* [AMAZED, AMAZING], [see MAZE], to fill with great surprise or wonder; astonish. **—a·mazed′,** *adj.*

**a·maze′ment,** *n.* great surprise or wonder.

**a·maz′ing,** *adj.* wonderful; astonishing.

**Am·a·zon** (am′ə-zon′), *n.* in *Gr. myth.,* one of a race of female warriors.

**am·bas·sa·dor** (am-bas′ə-dẽr), *n.* [< Pr. *ambaisat,* mission], the highest-ranking diplomatic representative of one country to another. **—am·bas′sa·do′ri·al** (-dôr′i-əl), *adj.* **—am·bas′sa·dor·ship′,** *n.*

**am·ber** (am′bẽr), *n.* [< Ar. *'anbar,* ambergris], 1. a brownish-yellow fossil resin used in jewelry, etc. 2. its color. *adj.* amberlike or amber-colored.

**am′ber·gris′** (-grēs′, -gris), *n.* [< Fr. *ambre gris,* gray amber], a waxy substance secreted by certain whales, used in making perfumes.

**ambi-,** [< L. *ambo*], a combining form meaning *both, around.*

**am·bi·dex·trous** (am′bə-dek′strəs), *adj.* [see AMBI- & DEXTEROUS], using both hands with equal ease. **—am′bi·dex·ter′i·ty** (-deks-ter′ə-ti), *n.* **—am′bi·dex′trous·ly,** *adv.*

**am·bi·ent** (am′bi-ənt), *adj.* [< L. *ambire,* to go around], on all sides. **—am′bi·ence,** *n.*

**am·bi·gu·i·ty** (am′bi-gū′ə-ti), *n.* 1. a being ambiguous. 2. [*pl.* -TIES], an ambiguous expression.

**am·big′u·ous** (-big′ū-əs), *adj.* [< L. *ambi-,* around + *agere,* go], 1. having two or more meanings. 2. not clear; vague. **—am·big′u·ous·ly,** *adv.* **—am·big′u·ous·ness,** *n.*

**am·bi·tion** (am-bish′ən), *n.* [< L. *ambitio,* a going around (to solicit votes)], 1. strong desire for fame, power, etc. 2. the thing so desired.

**am·bi′tious** (-bish′əs), *adj.* 1. full of or showing ambition. 2. showing great effort.

**am·biv·a·lence** (am-biv′ə-ləns), *n.* [*ambi-* + *valence*], simultaneous conflicting feelings. **—am·biv′a·lent,** *adj.*

**am·ble** (am′b'l), *v.i.* [-BLED, -BLING], [< L. *ambulare,* walk], 1. to move in an easy gait, as a horse. 2. to walk in a leisurely way. *n.* 1. a horse's ambling gait. 2. a leisurely walking pace. **—am′bler,** *n.*

**am·bro·sia** (am-brō′zhə), *n.* [< Gr. *a-,* not + *brotos,* mortal], 1. in *Gr. & Rom. myth.,* the food of the gods. 2. anything that tastes or smells delicious. **—am·bro′sial,** *adj.*

**am·bu·lance** (am′byoo-ləns), *n.* [< L. *ambulare,* walk], a vehicle equipped for carrying the sick or wounded.

**am′bu·late′** (-lāt′), *v.i.* [-LATED, -LATING], to move about; walk. **—am′bu·lant** (-lənt), *adj.* **—am′bu·la′tion,** *n.*

**am′bu·la·to′ry** (-lə-tôr′i), *adj.* 1. of or for walking. 2. able to walk.

**am·bus·cade** (am′bəs-kād′), *n., v.t. & v.i.* [-CADED, -CADING], ambush.

**am·bush** (am′boosh), *n.* [< ML. *in-,* in + *boscus,* a wood], 1. an arrangement of soldiers or others in hiding to make a surprise attack. 2. their hiding place. *v.t. & v.i.* to attack from hiding. **—am′bush·er,** *n.*

**a·me·ba** (ə-mē′bə), *n.* [*pl.* -BAS, -BAE (-bē)], an amoeba. **—a·me′bic,** *adj.*

**a·mel·io·rate** (ə-mēl′yə-rāt′), *v.t. & v.i.* [-RATED, -RATING], [< L. *ad,* to + *meliorare,* to better], to make or become better; improve. **—a·mel′io·ra′tion,** *n.*

**a·men** (ā′men′, ä′-), *interj.* [< Heb. *āmēn,* truly], may it be so!: used after a prayer or to express approval.

**a·me·na·ble** (ə-mē′nə-b'l, -men′ə-), *adj.* [< L. *ad,* to + *minare,* to drive], 1. responsible; answerable. 2. willing to follow advice· submissive. **—a·me′na·bil′i·ty,** *n.*

**a·mend** (ə-mend′), *v.t.* [< L. *emendare*], 1. to correct; emend. 2. to improve. 3. to change or revise, as a law. *v.i.* to improve one's conduct. **—a·mend′a·ble,** *adj.*

**a·mend′ment,** *n.* 1. a correction of errors, faults, etc. 2. improvement. 3. a revision proposed or made in a bill, law, etc.

**a·mends** (ə-mendz'), *n.pl.* [construed also as sing.], [see AMEND], payment made or satisfaction given for injury, loss, etc.
**a·men·i·ty** (ə-men'ə-ti, -mē'nə-), *n.* [*pl.* -TIES], [< L. *amoenus*, pleasant], 1. pleasantness. 2. *pl.* attractive features, as of a place. 3. *pl.* courteous acts; civilities.
**A·men-Ra** (ä'mən-rä'), *n.* the ancient Egyptian sun god.
**a·merce** (ə-mũrs'), *v.t.* [AMERCED, AMERCING], [< OFr. *a merci*, at the mercy of], to punish, esp. by imposing a fine.
**A·mer'i·can** (-kən), *adj.* 1. of or in America. 2. of the U.S., its people, etc. *n.* 1. a native or inhabitant of America. 2. a citizen of the U.S.
**A·mer'i·can·ism,** *n.* 1. a custom or belief originating in the U.S. 2. a word or idiom peculiar to American English. 3. devotion to the U.S., its customs, etc.
**A·mer'i·can·ize'** (-īz'), *v.t. & v.i.* [-IZED, -IZING], to make or become American in character, manners, etc. —**A·mer'i·can·i·za'tion,** *n.*
**American plan,** a system of hotel operation in which the price charged covers room, service, and meals.
**am·e·thyst** (am'ə-thist), *n.* [< Gr. *amethystos*, not drunken: the Greeks thought it prevented intoxication], 1. a purple variety of quartz or of corundum, used in jewelry. 2. purple; violet. *adj.* purple; violet.
**a·mi·a·ble** (ā'mi-ə-b'l), *adj.* [< L. *amicus*, friend], good-natured; friendly. —**a'mi·a·bil'i·ty,** *n.* —**a'mi·a·bly,** *adv.*
**am·i·ca·ble** (am'i-kə-b'l), *adj.* [see AMIABLE], friendly; peaceable. —**am'i·ca·bil'i·ty,** *n.* —**am'i·ca·bly,** *adv.*
**a·mid** (ə-mid'), *prep.* among; in the middle of: also **a·midst** (ə-midst').
**a·mid'ships,** *adv.* in or toward the middle of a ship: also **a·mid'ship.**
**a·mi·no acids** (am'i-nō', ə-mē'nō), [< *ammonia*], a group of nitrogenous organic compounds found in the proteins and essential to metabolism.
**Am·ish** (am'ish, ä'mish), *n. sing. & pl.* [< J. *Ammann*, the founder], Mennonites of a sect founded in the 17th c. *adj.* of this sect.
**a·miss** (ə-mis'), *adv.* [*a-*, at + *miss*], 1. astray. 2. wrongly. *adj.* improper; faulty.
**am·i·ty** (am'ə-ti), *n.* [*pl.* -TIES], [< L. *amicus*, friendly], friendship; peaceful relations.
**am·me·ter** (am'mē'tẽr), *n.* [*ampere* + *-meter*], an instrument for measuring an electric current in amperes.
**am·mo** (am'ō), *n.* [Slang], ammunition.
**am·mo·nia** (ə-mōn'yə), *n.* [from a salt found near Libyan shrine of Jupiter *Ammon*], 1. a colorless, pungent gas. 2. a water solution of this gas: also **ammonia water.**
**am·mu·ni·tion** (am'yoo-nish'ən), *n.* [< L. *munire*, to fortify], 1. bullets, gunpowder, bombs, and other missiles. 2. any means of attack or defense.
**am·ne·si·a** (am-nē'zhi-ə, -zhə), *n.* [< Gr. *a-*, not + *mnasthai*, to remember], partial or total loss of memory.
**am·nes·ty** (am'nəs-ti), *n.* [*pl.* -TIES], [< Gr. *amnēstia*, a forgetting], a general pardon, esp. for political offenses. *v.t.* [-TIED, -TYING], to pardon.
**a·moe·ba** (ə-mē'bə), *n.* [*pl.* -BAS, -BAE (-bē)], [< Gr. *ameibein*, to change], a microscopic, one-celled animal multiplying by fission. —**a·moe'bic, a·moe'boid,** *adj.*
**a·mok** (ə-muk', -mok'), *adj. & adv.* amuck.
**a·mong** (ə-muŋ'), *prep.* [< AS. *on*, in + *gemang*, a crowd], 1. surrounded by: as, *among* friends. 2. in the group of: as, best *among* books. 3. to or for each or several of. 4. by the joint action of.
**a·mongst** (ə-muŋst'), *prep.* among.
**a·mon·til·la·do** (ə-mon'ti-lä'dō), *n.* [Sp. < *Montilla*, Spain], a pale, dry Spanish sherry.
**a·mor·al** (ā-môr'əl), *adj.* not concerned with moral standards. —**a'mor·al'i·ty,** *n.*
**am·o·rous** (am'ə-rəs), *adj.* [< L. *amor*, love], 1. fond of making love. 2. full of love. 3. of sexual love or love-making.
**a·mor·phous** (ə-môr'fəs), *adj.* [< Gr. *a-*, without + *morphē*, form], 1. shapeless. 2. of no definite type. 3. in *chem.*, not crystalline. —**a·mor'phous·ly,** *adv.*
**a·mor·tize, a·mor·tise** (am'ẽr-tīz', ə-môr'-tīz), *v.t.* [-TIZED, -TIZING; -TISED, -TISING], [< L. *ad*, to + *mors*, death], to put money aside at intervals for payment of (a debt, etc.). —**a'mor·ti·za'tion, a'mor·ti·sa'tion,** *n.*
**a·mount** (ə-mount'), *v.i.* [< OFr. *amont*, upward < L. *ad*, to + *mons*, mountain], 1. to add up (*to* a sum). 2. to be equal (*to* something) in value or effect. *n.* 1. the sum of two or more quantities. 2. the whole value or effect. 3. a quantity.
**a·mour** (ə-moor'), *n.* [< L. *amor*, love], a love affair, esp. an illicit one.
**am·per·age** (am-pêr'ij, am'pêr'-), *n.* the strength of an electric current in amperes.
**am·pere** (am'pêr, am-pêr'), *n.* [< A.M. *Ampère*, 19th-c. Fr. physicist], the unit of electric current, the amount sent by one volt through a resistance of one ohm.
**am·per·sand** (am'pẽr-sand'), *n.* [< *and per se and*, & by itself (is) *and*], a sign (&) meaning *and*.
**am·phet·a·mine** (am-fet'ə-mēn', -min), *n.* a drug used to overcome mental depression, fatigue, etc., and to lessen the appetite.
**am·phib·i·an** (am-fib'i-ən), *n.* [see AMPHIBIOUS], 1. any animal or plant that lives both on land and in water. 2. an aircraft that can take off from or land on either land or water. 3. a tank, etc. that can travel on either land or water. *adj.* amphibious.
**am·phib'i·ous,** *adj.* [< Gr. *amphi-*, on both sides + *bios*, life], that can live or operate on land and in water.
**am·phi·the·a·ter, am·phi·the·a·tre** (am'fə-thē'ə-tẽr), *n.* [< Gr. *amphi-*, around + *theatron*, theater], a round or oval building with an open space surrounded by rising rows of seats.
**am·pho·ra** (am'fə-rə), *n.* [*pl.* -RAE (-rē'), -RAS (-rəz)], [< Gr. *amphi-*, on both sides + *pherein*, to bear], a tall jar with a narrow neck and two handles, used by ancient Greeks and Romans.
**am·ple** (am'p'l), *adj.* [-PLER, -PLEST], [< L. *amplus*], 1. large in size, scope, etc. 2. more than enough. 3. adequate. —**am'ply,** *adv.*
**am·pli·fi·er** (am'plə-fī'ẽr), *n.* one that amplifies; esp., an electronic tube, etc. for strengthening electrical impulses.
**am'pli·fy'** (-fī'), *v.t.* [-FIED, -FYING], [< L. *amplus*, large + *facere*, to make], 1. to make stronger; esp., to strengthen (electrical impulses). 2. to expand. *v.i.* to expatiate. —**am'pli·fi·ca'tion,** *n.*
**am·pli·tude** (am'plə-tōōd'), *n.* [see AMPLE], 1. extent; size. 2. abundance. 3. scope; breadth. 4. the range from the mean to the extreme, as of an alternating current.
**amplitude modulation,** the changing of the amplitude of the transmitting radio wave in accordance with the sound being broadcast.
**am·poule** (am'pōōl), *n.* [< L. *ampulla*, bottle], a small glass container for one dose of a hypodermic medicine: also **am'pule** (-pūl).
**am·pu·tate** (am'pyoo-tāt'), *v.t.* [-TATED, -TATING], [< L. *amb-*, about + *putare*, to prune], to cut off, esp. by surgery. —**am'pu·ta'tion,** *n.*
**am'pu·tee'** (-tē'), *n.* one who has had a limb or limbs amputated.
**amt.,** amount.
**a·muck** (ə-muk'), *adj. & adv.* [Malay *amoq*],

in a frenzy to kill. —**run amuck,** to lose control of oneself.

**am·u·let** (am′yoo-lit), *n.* [< L.], something worn to protect against evil.

**a·muse** (ə-mūz′), *v.t.* [AMUSED, AMUSING], [< Fr. à, to + OFr. *muser*, gaze at], 1. to keep agreeably occupied; entertain. 2. to make laugh, smile, etc. —**a·mus′ing,** *adj.*

**a·mused′,** *adj.* [pp. of *amuse*], 1. agreeably occupied. 2. caused to laugh, smile, etc. 3. showing amusement.

**a·muse′ment,** *n.* 1. a being amused. 2. something that amuses.

**amusement park,** an outdoor place with devices for entertainment, as a merry-go-round, etc.

**am·yl·ase** (am′i-lās′), *n.* [< Gr. *amylon*, starch], an enzyme that helps change starch into sugar, found in saliva, etc.

**an** (ən; *stressed*, an), *adj.*, *indefinite article* [< AS. *an*, one], 1. one; one sort of. 2. each; any one. 3. per: as, two *an* hour. *An* is used before words beginning with a vowel sound (*an* eye, *an* honor, *an* ultimatum). Cf. **a.**

**-an,** [< L. *-anus*], a suffix meaning: 1. *of, belonging to*, as in *diocesan*. 2. *born in, living in*, as in *American*. 3. *believing in*, as in *Mohammedan*.

**a·nab·a·sis** (ə-nab′ə-sis), *n.* [*pl.* -SES (-sēz′)], [Gr. < *ana-*, up + *bainein*, go], a military expedition.

**a·nach·ro·nism** (ə-nak′rə-niz′m), *n.* [< Gr. *ana-*, against + *chronos*, time], 1. anything out of its proper historical time. 2. the representation of this. —**a·nach′ro·nis′tic,** *adj.*

**an·a·con·da** (an′ə-kon′də), *n.* 1. a large South American snake of the boa family. 2. any similar snake that crushes its victim.

**a·nae·mi·a** (ə-nē′mi-ə), *n.* anemia.

**an·aes·the·si·a** (an′əs-thē′zhə), *n.* anesthesia. —**an′aes·thet′ic,** *adj. & n.* —**an·aes′the·tist,** *n.* —**an·aes′the·tize′,** *v.t.*

**an·a·gram** (an′ə-gram′), *n.* [< Gr. *anagrammatizein*, transpose letters], 1. a word or phrase made from another by rearranging its letters, as, *made—dame*. 2. *pl.* a game of making words by changing or adding letters.

**a·nal** (ā′n'l), *adj.* of the anus.

**an·al·ge·si·a** (an″l-jē′zi-ə, -si-ə), *n.* [< Gr. *an-*, without + *algēsia*, pain], a state of not feeling pain.

**an′al·ge′sic** (-zik, -sik), *adj.* of or causing analgesia. *n.* a drug producing analgesia.

**an·a·log computer** (an′ə-lôg′), a computer working on the basis of a physical, esp. electrical, analogy of the mathematical problem to be solved.

**a·nal·o·gize** (ə-nal′ə-jīz′), *v.i. & v.t.* [-GIZED, -GIZING], to use or explain by analogy. —**a·nal′o·gist,** *n.*

**a·nal′o·gous** (-gəs), *adj.* [see ANALOGY], similar or comparable in certain respects.

**an·a·logue, an·a·log** (an′ə-lôg′), *n.* a thing or part that is analogous.

**a·nal·o·gy** (ə-nal′ə-ji), *n.* [*pl.* -GIES], [< Gr. *ana-*, according to + *logos*, ratio], 1. similarity in some respects. 2. a comparing of something based on this.

**a·nal·y·sis** (ə-nal′ə-sis), *n.* [*pl.* -SES (-sēz′)], [Gr. < *ana-*, up + *lysis*, a loosing], 1. a breaking up of a whole into its parts to find out their nature, etc. 2. a statement of these findings. 3. in *chem.*, the separation of compounds and mixtures into their constituents to determine their nature or proportion. 4. psychoanalysis. —**an′a·lyt′i·cal,** *adj.*

**an·a·lyst** (an′ə-list), *n.* 1. one who analyzes. 2. a psychoanalyst.

**an′a·lyze′** (-līz′), *v.t.* [-LYZED, -LYZING], 1. to separate into parts so as to find out their nature, etc. 2. to examine the constituents of carefully. 3. to psychoanalyze. —**an′a·lyz′a·ble,** *adj.* —**an′a·lyz′er,** *n.*

**an·a·pest, an·a·paest** (an′ə-pest′), *n.* [< Gr. *ana-*, back + *paiein*, to strike], a metrical foot of three syllables, the first two unaccented and the third accented.

**an·arch·ism** (an′ẽr-kiz′m), *n.* 1. the theory that all forms of government are undesirable. 2. resistance to government.

**an′arch·ist** (-kist), *n.* 1. one who believes in anarchism. 2. a promoter of anarchy. —**an′ar·chis′tic,** *adj.*

**an′arch·y** (-ki), *n.* [< Gr. *an-*, without + *archos*, leader], 1. the absence of government and law. 2. political disorder and violence. 3. disorder; confusion. —**an·ar′chic** (-är′kik), **an·ar′chi·cal,** *adj.*

**a·nath·e·ma** (ə-nath′ə-mə), *n.* [*pl.* -MAS], [Gr., a thing devoted to evil], 1. a person or thing accursed. 2. anything greatly detested. 3. a formal curse, as in excommunicating a person. 4. any strong curse.

**a·nath′e·ma·tize′** (-tīz), *v.t. & v.i.* [-TIZED, -TIZING], to utter an anathema (against).

**a·nat·o·mize** (ə-nat′ə-mīz′), *v.t. & v.i.* [-MIZED, -MIZING], 1. to dissect (animals, etc.) in order to study the structure. 2. to analyze. —**a·nat′o·mist,** *n.*

**a·nat′o·my** (-mi), *n.* [*pl.* -MIES], [< Gr. *ana-*, up + *temnein*, to cut], 1. the dissecting of an organism to study its structure. 2. the science of the structure of plants or animals. 3. the structure of an organism. 4. any analysis. Abbrev. **anat.** —**an·a·tom·i·cal** (an′ə-tom′i-k'l), —**an′a·tom′ic,** *adj.*

**-ance,** [< L.], a suffix meaning: 1. *a —ing*, as in *utterance*. 2. *a being —ant*, as in *vigilance*. 3. *a thing that —s*, as in *conveyance*. 4. *a thing that is —ant*, as in *dissonance*. 5. a *thing that is —ed*, as in *inheritance*.

**an·ces·tor** (an′ses-tẽr), *n.* [< L. *ante-*, before + *cedere*, go], 1. a person from whom one is descended; forebear. 2. an early type of animal from which others have evolved.

**an·ces·tral** (an-ses′trəl), *adj.* of or inherited from ancestors. —**an·ces′tral·ly,** *adv.*

**an·ces·try** (an′ses-tri), *n.* [*pl.* -TRIES], 1. family lineage. 2. ancestors collectively.

**an·chor** (aŋ′kẽr), *n.* [< Gr. *ankyra*, a hook], 1. a heavy object, as a hooked iron weight, lowered into the water by cable to keep a ship from drifting. 2. anything giving security or stability. *v.t.* to hold secure as by an anchor. *v.i.* to lower the anchor; lie at anchor. —**at anchor,** anchored.

**an′chor·age** (-ij), *n.* 1. an anchoring or being anchored. 2. a place to anchor.

**an·cho·rite** (aŋ′kə-rīt′), *n.* [< Gr. *ana-*, back + *chōrein*, retire], 1. a religious recluse. 2. a hermit. Also **an′cho·ret** (-kẽr-it). —**an′cho·ress** (-is), *n.fem.*

**an·cho·vy** (an′chə-vi, an-chō′-), *n.* [*pl.* -VIES], [< Basque *anchova*], a very small fish of the herring family.

**an·cient** (ān′shənt), *adj.* [< L. *ante*, before], 1. of times long past. 2. very old. *n.* an aged person. —**the ancients,** the people who lived in ancient times.

**an·cil·lar·y** (an′sə-ler′i), *adj.* [< L. *ancilla*, maidservant], 1. subordinate (*to*). 2. auxiliary.

**and** (and, ənd, 'n), *conj.* [AS.], 1. also; in addition. 2. plus. 3. as a result. 4. [Colloq.], to: as, try *and* get it.

**an·dan·te** (an-dan′ti, än-dän′tā), *adj. & adv.* [< It. *andare*, to walk], in *music*, moderately slow.

**and·i·ron** (and′ī′ẽrn), *n.* [< OFr. *andier*], either of a pair of metal supports for holding logs in a fireplace: also called *firedog*.

**and/or,** either *and* or *or*: as, personal *and/or* real property.

**An·drew** (an′drōō), *n.* in the *Bible*, one of the twelve apostles.

**an·dro·gen** (an′drə-jən), *n.* [< Gr. *andros*, man; + *-gen*], a male sex hormone.

**an·ec·dote** (an'ik-dōt'), *n.* [< Gr. *anekdotos*, unpublished], a short, entertaining account of some event. —**an'ec·do'tal**, *adj.*
**a·ne·mi·a** (ə-nē'mi-ə), *n.* [< Gr. *a-*, without + *haima*, blood], a condition in which there is a reduction in the number of red corpuscles in the blood stream. —**a·ne'mic**, *adj.*
**an·e·mom·e·ter** (an'ə-mom'ə-tēr), *n.* [< Gr. *anemos*, the wind; + *-meter*], a gauge for measuring pressure or velocity of the wind.
**a·nem·o·ne** (ə-nem'ə-nē'), *n.* [Gr. < *anemos*, the wind], 1. a plant with white to red, cup-shaped flowers. 2. a sea anemone.
**a·nent** (ə-nent'), *prep.* [< AS. *on efen*, on even (with)], as regards; concerning.
**an·es·the·si·a** (an'əs-thē'zhə), *n.* [< Gr. *an-*, without + *aisthēsis*, feeling], a partial or total loss of the sense of pain, touch, etc.
**an'es·thet'ic** (-thet'ik), *adj.* 1. of or with anesthesia. 2. producing anesthesia. *n.* a drug, gas, etc. that produces anesthesia.
**an·es·the·tist** (ə-nes'thə-tist), *n.* a person trained to administer anesthetics.
**an·es'the·tize'** (-tīz'), *v.t.* [-TIZED, -TIZING], to cause anesthesia in; give anesthetics to.
**an·eu·rysm, an·eu·rism** (an'yoor-iz'm), *n.* [< Gr. *ana-*, up + *eurys*, broad], a sac formed by enlargement of an artery wall, caused by disease or injury.
**a·new** (ə-nōō', ə-nū'), *adv.* again.
**an·gel** (ān'jəl), *n.* [< Gr. *angelos*, messenger], 1. *a*) a messenger of God. *b*) an immortal spirit. 2. a person regarded as beautiful, good, etc. 3. [Slang], one who pays for the production of a play, etc. —**an·gel·ic** (an-jel'ik), **an·gel'i·cal**, *adj.*
**an·gel·fish** (ān'jəl-fish'), *n.* [*pl.* see FISH], a bright-colored tropical fish with spiny fins.
**angel (food) cake,** a light, spongy, white cake made without shortening or egg yolks.
**an·ger** (aŋ'gēr), *n.* [< ON. *angr*, distress], a hostile feeling of displeasure because of injury, opposition, etc. *v.t.* to make angry.
**an·gi·na pec·to·ris** (an-jī'nə pek'tə-ris), [L., choking of the breast], a heart disease with chest pains and feelings of suffocation.
**an·gle** (aŋ'g'l), *n.* [< Gr. *ankylos*, bent], 1. the shape or space formed by two straight lines or plane surfaces that meet. 2. the degrees of difference in direction between them. 3. a sharp corner. 4. a point of view. *v.t. & v.i.* [-GLED, -GLING], 1. to move or bend at an angle. 2. [Colloq.], to give a specific point of view to (a story, etc.).
**an·gle** (aŋ'g'l), *v.i.* [-GLED, -GLING], [AS. *angul*, fishhook], 1. to fish with a hook and line. 2. to use tricks to get something: as, to *angle* for a promotion. —**an'gler**, *n.*
**angle iron,** an angled piece of iron or steel as for joining or reinforcing two beams.
**An·gles** (aŋ'g'lz), *n.pl.* a Germanic people that settled in England in the 5th c. A.D.
**an'gle·worm'**, *n.* an earthworm.
**An·gli·can** (aŋ'gli-kən), *adj.* [< L. *Anglicus*, of the Angles], of the Church of England or other church with the same faith and forms. *n.* a member of an Anglican church.
**An·gli·cism** (aŋ'glə-siz'm), *n.* a word, idiom, trait, etc. peculiar to the English.
**An'gli·cize', an'gli·cize'** (-sīz'), *v.t. & v.i.* [-CIZED, -CIZING], to change to English idiom, pronunciation, customs, etc. —**An'gli·ci·za'tion, an'gli·ci·za'tion** (-si-zā'shən), *n.*
**Anglo-,** a combining form meaning *English* or *English and*, as in *Anglo-Norman*.
**An'glo-Sax'on** (-sak's'n), *n.* 1. a member of the Germanic peoples living in England before the 12th century. 2. their language; Old English. 3. a person of English nationality or descent. *adj.* of Anglo-Saxon or the Anglo-Saxons.
**An·go·ra** (aŋ-gôr'ə), *n.* [former name of *Ankara*, Turkey], 1. a kind of cat with long, silky fur. 2. *a*) a kind of goat raised for its long, silky hair. *b*) cloth made from this.
**an·gry** (aŋ'gri), *adj.* [-GRIER, -GRIEST], 1. feeling or showing anger. 2. wild and stormy. —**an'gri·ly**, *adv.*
**an·guish** (aŋ'gwish), *n.* [< L. *angere*, choke], great mental or physical pain; agony. *v.t. & v.i.* to feel or make feel anguish.
**an·gu·lar** (aŋ'gyoo-lēr), *adj.* 1. having or forming an angle or angles; sharp-cornered. 2. lean; gaunt. 3. without ease or grace; stiff. —**an'gu·lar'i·ty** (-lar'ə-ti) [*pl.* -TIES], *n.*
**an·hy·drous** (an-hī'drəs), *adj.* [< Gr. *an-*, without + *hydōr*, water], 1. without water. 2. having no water of crystallization.
**an·i·line** (an''l-ēn', -in), *n.* [< Ar. *al*, the + *nīl*, blue; + *-ine*], a colorless, oily liquid derivative of benzene, used in making dyes. *adj.* made from aniline. Also **an'i·lin** (-in).
**an·i·mad·ver·sion** (an'ə-mad-vũr'zhən), *n.* an unfavorable remark; blame.
**an'i·mad·vert'** (-vũrt'), *v.i.* [< L. *animus*, mind + *ad-*, to + *vertere*, to turn], to comment unfavorably (*on* or *upon*); criticize.
**an·i·mal** (an'ə-m'l), *n.* [< L. *anima*, breath, soul], 1. any living organism typically capable of moving about: cf. **plant.** 2. any four-footed creature; beast. 3. a brutish person. *adj.* 1. of or like an animal. 2. gross, bestial, etc. —**an'i·mal'i·ty**, *n.*
**an·i·mal·cule** (an'ə-mal'kyool), *n.* [< L. dim. of *animal*], a very small or microscopic animal.
**an·i·mal·ism** (an'ə-m'l-iz'm), *n.* 1. the activity, appetites, nature, etc. of animals. 2. the doctrine that man is a mere animal with no soul. —**an'i·mal·ist**, *n.*
**an·i·mate** (an'ə-māt'), *v.t.* [-MATED, -MATING], [see ANIMAL], 1. to give life or motion to. 2. to make gay or spirited. 3. to inspire. *adj.* (-mit), 1. living. 2. lively. —**an'i·mat'ed**, *adj.* —**an'i·mat'er, an'i·ma'tor**, *n.*
**an'i·ma'tion,** *n.* 1. an animating or being animated. 2. life. 3. vivacity.
**an·i·mos·i·ty** (an'ə-mos'ə-ti), *n.* [*pl.* -TIES], [see ANIMUS], strong hatred; ill will.
**an·i·mus** (an'ə-məs), *n.* [L., passion], a grudge; animosity; hostility.
**an·i·on** (an'ī'ən), *n.* [< Gr. *ana-*, up + *ienai*, to go], a negative ion.
**an·ise** (an'is), *n.* [< Gr. *anēson*], 1. a plant of the carrot family. 2. its fragrant seed, used for flavoring: also **an·i·seed** (an'i-sēd').
**an·kle** (aŋ'k'l), *n.* [AS. *ancleow*], 1. the joint that connects the foot and leg. 2. the part of the leg between the foot and calf.
**an'kle·bone',** *n.* the bone of the ankle.
**an·klet** (aŋ'klit), *n.* 1. an ornament, etc. worn around the ankle. 2. a short sock.
**an·nals** (an''lz), *n.pl.* [< L. *annus*, year], 1. a written account of events year by year. 2. historical records; history. —**an'nal·ist**, *n.*
**an·neal** (ə-nēl'), *v.t.* [< AS. *an-*, on + *æl*, fire], to heat (glass, metals, etc.), and then cool slowly to prevent brittleness.
**an·nex** (ə-neks'), *v.t.* [< L. *ad-*, to + *nectere*, to tie], 1. to attach, esp. to something larger. 2. to incorporate into a state the territory of (another state). *n.* (an'eks), something annexed, esp. to a building. —**an·nex'a·ble**, *adj.* —**an'nex·a'tion**, *n.*
**an·ni·hi·late** (ə-nī'ə-lāt'), *v.t.* [-LATED, -LATING], [< L. *ad-*, to + *nihil*, nothing], to destroy entirely. —**an·ni'hi·la'tion**, *n.*
**an·ni·ver·sa·ry** (an'ə-vũr'sēr-i), *n.* [*pl.* -RIES], [< L. *annus*, year + *vertere*, to turn], 1. the yearly return of the date of some event. 2. its celebration. *adj.* of an anniversary.
**an·no·tate** (an'ō-tāt'), *v.t. & v.i.* [-TATED, -TATING], [< L. *ad-*, to + *nota*, a sign], to provide explanatory notes for. —**an'no·ta'tion**, *n.* —**an'no·ta'tor**, *n.*
**an·nounce** (ə-nouns'), *v.t.* [-NOUNCED, -NOUNCING], [< L. *ad-*, to + *nuntiare*, to

report], 1. to declare publicly; proclaim. 2. to say. 3. to make known the arrival of. 4. to be an announcer for. ***v.i.*** to act as an announcer. **—an·nounce′ment, *n.***

**an·nounc′er, *n.*** 1. one who announces. 2. one who introduces radio or television programs, identifies the station, etc.

**an·noy** (ə-noi′), ***v.t.*** [< L. *in odio*, in aversion], 1. to bother; vex. 2. to make angry. 3. to harm; molest. **—an·noy′ing, *adj.***

**an·noy′ance** (-əns), ***n.*** 1. an annoying or being annoyed. 2. that which annoys.

**an·nu·al** (an′yoo-əl), ***adj.*** [< L. *annus*, year], 1. of or measured by a year. 2. yearly. 3. alive only one year or season. ***n.*** 1. a periodical published once a year. 2. a plant that lives one season. **—an′nu·al·ly, *adv.***

**an·nu·i·ty** (ə-nōō′ə-ti, -nū′-), ***n.*** [*pl.* -TIES], [see ANNUAL], 1. an investment yielding fixed annual payments. 2. such a payment.

**an·nul** (ə-nul′), ***v.t.*** [-NULLED, -NULLING], [< L. *annullare*, bring to nothing], to make null and void; cancel. **—an·nul′ment, *n.***

**an·nu·lar** (an′yoo-lẽr), ***adj.*** [< L. *anulas*, a ring], like or forming a ring.

**an·num** (an′əm), ***n.*** [L.], a year.

**an·nun·ci·a·tion** (ə-nun′si-ā′shən), ***n.*** 1. an announcing. 2. [A-], *a*) the angel Gabriel's announcement to Mary that she would bear Jesus. *b*) the festival commemorating this.

**an·ode** (an′ōd), ***n.*** [< Gr. *ana-*, up + *hodos*, way], a positive electrode.

**an·o·dyne** (an′ə-dīn′), ***n.*** [< Gr. *an-*, without + *odynē*, pain], anything that relieves or lessens pain. ***adj.*** lessening pain.

**a·noint** (ə-noint′), ***v.t.*** [< L. *in-*, on + *ungere*, to smear], to put oil on, as in consecrating. **—a·noint′ment, *n.***

**a·nom·a·lous** (ə-nom′ə-ləs), ***adj.*** [< Gr. *an-*, not + *homos*, the same], deviating from the general rule; abnormal.

**a·nom′a·ly** (-li), ***n.*** [*pl.* -LIES], 1. departure from the usual. 2. anything anomalous.

**a·non** (ə-non′), ***adv.*** [AS. *on an*, in one], 1. soon; shortly. 2. at another time. —**ever and anon**, now and then.

**a·non·y·mous** (ə-non′ə-məs), ***adj.*** [< Gr. *an-*, without + *onoma*, name], 1. with no name known or acknowledged. 2. given, written, etc. by one whose name is withheld or unknown. Abbrev. **anon. —an·o·nym·i·ty** (an′ə-nim′ə-ti), ***n.*** **—a·non′y·mous·ly, *adv.***

**a·noph·e·les** (ə-nof′ə-lēz′), ***n.*** [Gr. *anōphelēs*, harmful], the mosquito that can transmit malaria.

**an·oth·er** (ə-nuth′ẽr), ***adj.*** 1. an additional; one more. 2. a different. ***pron.*** 1. one additional. 2. a different one. 3. one of the same kind.

**an·swer** (an′sẽr), ***n.*** [< AS. *and-*, against + *swerian*, swear], 1. a reply to a question, letter, etc. 2. any retaliation. 3. a solution to a problem. ***v.i.*** 1. to reply. 2. to be sufficient. 3. to be responsible (*to* a person *for*). 4. to conform (with *to*): as, he *answers* to the description. ***v.t.*** 1. to reply to. 2. to serve: as, to *answer* a purpose. 3. to atone for. 4. to suit: as, he *answers* the description. Abbrev. **ans. —answer back,** [Colloq.], to reply insolently. **—an′swer·a·ble, *adj.***

**ant** (ant), ***n.*** [AS. *æmete*], any of a group of insects, generally wingless, that live in colonies, commonly in the ground.

**-ant,** [ult. < L.], a suffix meaning: 1. *—ing*, as in *defiant*. 2. *a person* or *thing that —s*, as in *occupant*.

**ant·ac·id** (ant-as′id), ***adj.*** [< *anti-* + *acid*], counteracting acidity. ***n.*** an antacid substance, such as sodium bicarbonate.

**an·tag·o·nism** (an-tag′ə-niz′m), ***n.*** 1. active opposition (*to* or *against*); hostility. 2. an opposing force, principle, etc.

**an·tag′o·nist, *n.*** an adversary; opponent.

**an·tag′o·nis′tic, *adj.*** 1. opposing; hostile. 2. counteracting.

**an·tag·o·nize** (an-tag′ə-nīz′), ***v.t.*** [-NIZED, -NIZING], [< Gr. *anti-*, against + *agōn*, a contest], 1. to oppose. 2. to incur the dislike of.

**ant·arc·tic** (ant-ärk′tik), ***adj.*** [see ANTI- & ARCTIC], of or near the South Pole or the region around it.

**an·te** (an′ti), ***n.*** [L., before], in *poker*, the stake that each player must put into the pool before receiving cards. ***v.t. & v.i.*** [-TEED or -TED (-tid), -TEEING], in *poker*, to put in (one's stake): also **ante up.**

**ante-,** [see ANTE], a prefix meaning *before*, as in *antecedent*.

**ant′eat′er, *n.*** a mammal with a long snout, that feeds mainly on ants.

**an·te·bel·lum** (an′ti-bel′əm), ***adj.*** [L.], before the war; specif., before the American Civil War.

**an·te·ced·ent** (an′tə-sēd′'nt), ***adj.*** [< L. *ante-*, before + *cedere*, go], prior; previous. ***n.*** 1. any thing prior to another. 2. *pl.* one's ancestry, past life, etc. 3. in *grammar*, the word or phrase to which a pronoun refers. **—an′te·ced′ence, an′te·ced′en·cy** (-'n-si), ***n.***

**an·te·cham·ber** (an′ti-chām′bẽr), ***n.*** a smaller room leading into a larger room.

**an·te·date** (an′ti-dāt′), ***v.t.*** [-DATED, -DATING], 1. to assign too early a date to. 2. to come before in time.

**an·te·di·lu·vi·an** (an′ti-di-lōō′vi-ən), ***adj.*** [< *ante-* + L. *diluvium*, a flood], 1. of the time before the Flood. 2. very old; old-fashioned. ***n.*** one that is antediluvian.

**an·te·lope** (an′t'l-ōp′), ***n.*** [< Gr. *antholops*, deer], a swift, cud-chewing, horned animal resembling the deer.

**‡an·te me·ri·di·em** (an′ti mə-rid′i-əm), [L.], before noon: abbrev. **A.M., a.m.**

**an·ten·na** (an-ten′ə), ***n.*** [L., sail yard], 1. [*pl.* -NAE (-ē), -NAS], either of a pair of feelers on the head of an insect, crab, etc. 2. [*pl.* -NAS], in *radio & TV*, a wire or wires for sending and receiving the electromagnetic waves.

**an·te·pe·nult** (an′ti-pē′nəlt), ***n.*** the second syllable from the last in a word.

**an·te·ri·or** (an-têr′i-ẽr), ***adj.*** [< L. *ante*, before], 1. toward the front: cf. **posterior.** 2. earlier; previous. **—an·te′ri·or·ly, *adv.***

**an·te·room** (an′ti-rōōm′), ***n.*** [*ante-* + *room*], a room through which another room is entered; waiting room.

**an·them** (an′thəm), ***n.*** [< Gr. *anti-*, over against + *phōnē*, voice], 1. a religious choral song. 2. the official song of a country.

**an·ther** (an′thẽr), ***n.*** [< Gr. *anthos*, a flower], the part of a stamen that contains the pollen.

**an·thol·o·gist** (an-thol′ə-jist), ***n.*** one who compiles an anthology.

**an·thol·o·gy** (an-thol′ə-ji), ***n.*** [*pl.* -GIES], [< Gr. *anthos*, flower + *legein*, gather], a collection of poems, stories, etc.

**an·thra·cite** (an′thrə-sīt′), ***n.*** [< Gr. *anthrax*, coal], hard coal, which gives much heat and little smoke. **—an′thra·cit′ic** (-sit′ik), ***adj.***

**an·thrax** (an′thraks), ***n.*** [*pl.* -THRACES (-thrə-sēz′)], [Gr., coal, carbuncle], 1. a boil. 2. an infectious disease of cattle, etc. which can be transmitted to man.

**anthropo-,** [Gr. *anthrōpos*], a combining form meaning *man, human.*

**an·thro·poid** (an′thrə-poid′), ***adj.*** [< *anthropo-* + *-oid*], manlike; esp., designating or of any of the most highly developed apes, as the chimpanzee. ***n.*** an anthropoid ape.

**an·thro·pol·o·gy** (an′thrə-pol′ə-ji), ***n.*** [*anthropo-* + *-logy*], the study of the origin, distribution, characteristics, customs, etc. of mankind. **—an′thro·po·log′i·cal** (-pə-loj′i-k'l), ***adj.*** **—an′thro·pol′o·gist, *n.***

**an·thro·po·mor·phism** (an'thrə-pə-môr'-fiz'm), ***n.*** [< *anthropo-* + Gr. *morphē*, form], the attributing of human shape or characteristics to gods, objects, animals, etc. **—an'thro·po·mor'phic,** ***adj.***

**an·ti** (an'ti, -ti), ***n.*** [*pl.* -TIS], [see ANTI-], [Colloq.], a person opposed to something. ***adj.*** [Colloq.], opposed.

**anti-,** [< Gr. *anti*, against], a prefix meaning: 1. *against; hostile to.* 2. *that operates against.* 3. *that prevents, cures,* or *neutralizes.* 4. *opposite; reverse.* 5. *rivaling.*

**an·ti·air·craft** (an'ti-âr'kraft), ***adj.*** used for defense against enemy aircraft.

**an·ti·bac·te·ri·al** (an'ti-bak-têr'i-əl), ***adj.*** that checks the growth or effect of bacteria.

**an·ti·bi·ot·ic** (an'ti-bī-ot'ik), ***n.*** [*anti-* + Gr. *biōsis*, way of life], any of certain substances, as penicillin or streptomycin, produced by some microorganisms and capable of destroying or weakening bacteria, etc.

**an·ti·bod·y** (an'ti-bod'i), ***n.*** [*pl.* -IES], [*anti-* + *body*], a protein produced in the body to neutralize the antigen.

**an·tic** (an'tik), ***n.*** [< L.; see ANTIQUE], a ludicrous act, gesture, etc.; caper. ***v.i.*** [-TICKED, -TICKING], to do antics; caper.

**An·ti·christ** (an'ti-krīst'), ***n.*** 1. in the *Bible*, the great antagonist of Christ: I John 2:18. 2. [a-], an opponent of Christ.

**an·tic·i·pate** (an-tis'ə-pāt'), ***v.t.*** [-PATED, -PATING], [< L. *ante*, before + *capere*, take], 1. to look forward to; expect. 2. to make happen earlier than due. 3. to forestall. 4. to foresee (a wish) and perform in advance. 5. to do something before (someone else). **—an·tic'i·pa'tion,** ***n.*** **—an·tic'i·pa'tive,** ***adj.*** **—an·tic'i·pa·to'ry** (-pə-tôr'i), ***adj.***

**an·ti·cler·i·cal** (an'ti-kler'i-k'l), ***adj.*** opposed to the clergy or church.

**an·ti·cli·max** (an'ti-klī'maks), ***n.*** [*anti-* + *climax*], 1. a sudden drop from the important to the trivial. 2. a descent which is in disappointing contrast to a preceding rise. **—an'ti·cli·mac'tic** (-klī-mak'tik), ***adj.***

**an·ti·cy·clone** (an'ti-sī'klōn), ***n.*** an atmospheric condition in which spiraling winds move away from a center of high pressure.

**an·ti·dote** (an'ti-dōt'), ***n.*** [< Gr. *anti-*, against + *dotos*, given], 1. a remedy to counteract a poison. 2. anything that tends to counteract an evil. **—an'ti·dot'al,** ***adj.***

**an·ti·freeze** (an'ti-frēz'), ***n.*** a substance used, as in automobile radiators, to prevent freezing.

**an·ti·gen** (an'tə-jən), ***n.*** [*anti-* + *-gen*], a substance which causes the production of an antibody when introduced directly into the body, as into the blood stream.

**an·ti·his·ta·mine** (an'ti-his'tə-mēn', -min), ***n.*** any of several drugs used in treating allergic conditions, as hay fever, etc.

**an'ti·knock'** (-nok'), ***n.*** a substance added to the fuel of internal-combustion engines to do away with or reduce noise made by too rapid combustion.

**an·ti·ma·cas·sar** (an'ti-mə-kas'ẽr), ***n.*** [*anti-* + *macassar*, a hair oil], a small cover on the back or arms of a chair, sofa, etc. to prevent soiling.

**an·ti·mo·ny** (an'tə-mō'ni), ***n.*** [< ML.], a silvery-white, metallic chemical element used in alloys to harden them: symbol, Sb.

**‡an·ti·pas·to** (än'tē-päs'tô), ***n.*** [It.; *anti-*, before + *pasto*, food], an appetizer of salted fish, meat, olives, etc.

**an·tip·a·thy** (an-tip'ə-thi), ***n.*** [*pl.* -THIES], [< Gr. *anti-*, against + *pathein*, feel], 1. strong dislike; aversion. 2. an object of such dislike. **—an·ti·pa·thet·ic** (an'ti-pə-thet'ik), **an'ti·pa·thet'i·cal,** ***adj.***

**an·ti·phon** (an'tə-fon'), ***n.*** [see ANTHEM], a hymn, etc. sung in responsive, alternating parts. **—an·tiph'o·nal** (-tif'ə-n'l), ***adj.***

**an·tip·o·des** (an-tip'ə-dēz'), ***n.pl.*** [< Gr. *anti-*, opposite + *pous*, foot], two places directly opposite each other on the earth.

**an·ti·pope** (an'ti-pōp'), ***n.*** a pope set up against the one chosen by church laws.

**an·ti·quar·i·an** (an'ti-kwâr'i-ən), ***adj.*** 1. of antiques. 2. of antiquaries. ***n.*** an antiquary.

**an'ti·quar'y** (-kwer'i), ***n.*** [*pl.* -IES], a collector or student of antiquities.

**an'ti·quate'** (-kwāt'), ***v.t.*** [-QUATED, -QUATING], to make old or obsolete.

**an·tique** (an-tēk'), ***adj.*** [< L. *antiquus*, ancient], 1. of ancient times; old. 2. out-of-date; old-fashioned. 3. of or in the style of a former period. ***n.*** 1. an ancient relic. 2. a piece of furniture, etc. of a former period. ***v.t.*** [-TIQUED, -TIQUING], to make look antique.

**an·tiq·ui·ty** (an-tik'wə-ti), ***n.*** [*pl.* -TIES], 1. the ancient period of history. 2. great age; oldness. 3. *usually in pl.* a relic, etc. of the distant past.

**an'ti-Sem'i·tism** (-sem'ə-tiz'm), ***n.*** 1. prejudice against Jews. 2. discrimination against or persecution of Jews. **—an'ti-Sem'ite** (-īt), ***n.*** **—an'ti-Se·mit'ic** (-sə-mit'-ik), ***adj.***

**an'ti·sep'sis** (-sep'sis), ***n.*** 1. a being antiseptic. 2. the use of antiseptics.

**an'ti·sep'tic** (-sep'tik), ***adj.*** [*anti-* + *septic*], 1. preventing infection, decay, etc.; effective against bacteria, etc. 2. using antiseptics. ***n.*** any antiseptic substance, as alcohol. **—an'ti·sep'ti·cal·ly,** ***adv.***

**an'ti·so'cial,** ***adj.*** 1. not sociable. 2. against the people's welfare.

**an'ti·spas·mod'ic** (-spaz-mod'ik), ***adj.*** relieving spasms. ***n.*** a remedy for spasms.

**an·tith·e·sis** (an-tith'ə-sis), ***n.*** [*pl.* -SES (-sēz')], [Gr. < *anti-*, against + *tithenai*, to place], 1. a contrast or opposition, as of ideas. 2. the exact opposite. **—an·ti·thet·ic** (an'ti-thet'ik), **an'ti·thet'i·cal,** ***adj.***

**an·ti·tox·in** (an'ti-tok'sin), ***n.*** [*anti-* + *toxin*], 1. a substance formed in the blood to act against a specific toxin. 2. a serum containing an antitoxin, injected to prevent a disease. **—an'ti·tox'ic,** ***adj.***

**an'ti·trust',** ***adj.*** opposed to or regulating trusts (business monopolies).

**ant·ler** (ant'lẽr), ***n.*** [< L. *ante-*, before + *ocularis*, of the eyes], the branched, deciduous horn of any animal of the deer family. **—ant'lered,** ***adj.***

**an·to·nym** (an'tə-nim'), ***n.*** [Gr. < *anti-*, opposite + *onyma*, name], a word meaning the opposite of another word.

**an·trum** (an'trəm), ***n.*** [*pl.* -TRUMS, -TRA (-trə)], [< Gr. *antron*, cave], a cavity; esp., a sinus of the upper jaw.

**a·nus** (ā'nəs), ***n.*** [*pl.* -NUSES, -NI (-nī)], [L.], the opening at the lower end of the alimentary canal.

**an·vil** (an'vil), ***n.*** [AS. *onfilte*], 1. a block on which metal objects are hammered into shape. 2. a bone in the ear.

**anx·i·e·ty** (aŋ-zī'ə-ti), ***n.*** [*pl.* -TIES], 1. worry or uneasiness about what may happen. 2. an eager desire.

**anx·ious** (aŋk'shəs, aŋ'-), ***adj.*** [< L. *angere*, choke], 1. worried; uneasy. 2. causing anxiety. 3. eagerly wishing. **—anx'ious·ly,** ***adv.*** **—anx'ious·ness,** ***n.***

**an·y** (en'i), ***adj.*** [AS. *ænig*], 1. one (no matter which) of more than two: as, *any* boy may go. 2. some: as, has he *any* gas? 3. every: as, *any* child can tell. ***pron. sing. & pl.*** any person or persons; any amount. ***adv.*** to any degree or extent.

**an'y·bod'y** (-bud'i, -bod'i), ***pron.*** 1. any person. 2. an important person.

**an'y·how',** ***adv.*** 1. in any way. 2. at any rate; in any case. 3. carelessly.

**an'y·one',** ***pron.*** any person; anybody.

**any one,** any single (person or thing).
**an'y·thing',** *pron.* any thing, event, fact, etc. *n.* a thing, no matter of what kind. *adv.* in any way. **—anything but,** not at all.
**an'y·way',** *adv.* 1. in any manner. 2. at any rate; at least. 3. haphazardly.
**an'y·where,** *adv.* 1. in, at, or to any place. 2. [Colloq.], at all. **—get anywhere,** [Colloq.], to achieve anything.
**an'y·wise',** *adv.* in any manner at all.
**a/o, A/O.,** account of.
**A-OK** (ā'ō-kā'), *adj.* [*A*ll *OK*], [Colloq.], excellent, in working order, etc.: also **A-Okay.**
**A one** (ā'wun'), [Colloq.], superior; first-class: also **A 1, A number 1.**
**a·or·ta** (ā-ôr'tə), *n.* [*pl.* -TAS, -TAE (-tē)], [< Gr. *aeirein,* to raise], the main artery of the body, carrying blood from the heart.
**a·pace** (ə-pās'), *adv.* at a fast pace; swiftly.
**A·pach·e** (ə-pach'i), *n.* [*pl.* -ES (-iz), APACHE], a member of a tribe of fierce, nomadic Indians of the southwestern U.S.
**a·part** (ə-pärt'), *adv.* [< L. *ad,* to + *pars,* part], 1. aside. 2. away in place or time. 3. away from one another. 4. in or to pieces. *adj.* separated. **—apart from,** other than; besides. **—take apart,** to reduce (a whole) to its parts.
**a·part·heid** (ə-pärt'hīt), *n.* [S.Afr.D., apartness] in South Africa, the policy of strict racial segregation.
**a·part'ment** (-mənt), *n.* [see APART], a room or suite of rooms to live in.
**apartment house,** a building in which the rooms are rented as apartments.
**ap·a·thet·ic** (ap'ə-thet'ik), *adj.* [< *apathy*], 1. feeling no emotion. 2. indifferent. Also **ap'a·thet'i·cal. —ap'a·thet'i·cal·ly,** *adv.*
**ap·a·thy** (ap'ə-thi), *n.* [*pl.* -THIES], [< Gr. *a-,* without + *pathos,* emotion], 1. lack of emotion. 2. indifference.
**ape** (āp), *n.* [AS. *apa*], 1. a chimpanzee, gorilla, orangutan, or gibbon. 2. any monkey. 3. a mimic. *v.t.* [APED (āpt), APING], to imitate. **—ape'like',** *adj.*
**‡a·pé·ri·tif** (ä'pā'rē'tēf'), *n.* [Fr.], an alcoholic drink taken before meals.
**ap·er·ture** (ap'ēr-chēr), *n.* [< L. *aperire,* open], an opening; hole; gap.
**a·pex** (ā'peks), *n.* [*pl.* -PEXES, -PICES (ap'i-sēz, ā'pi-)], [L.], 1. the highest point of anything; tip; peak. 2. a climax.
**a·pha·si·a** (ə-fā'zhə), *n.* [Gr. < *a-,* not + *phanai,* speak], a total or partial loss of the power to use or understand words.
**a·phe·li·on** (ə-fē'li-ən), *n.* [*pl.* -ONS, -A (-ə)], [< Gr. *apo,* from + *hēlios,* sun], the point farthest from the sun in the orbit of a planet or comet: cf. **perihelion.**
**a·phid** (ā'fid, af'id), *n.* [< Mod. L. *aphis*], an insect that lives on plants by sucking their juice.
**aph·o·rism** (af'ə-riz'm), *n.* [< Gr. *apo-,* from + *horizein,* to bound], 1. a concise statement of a principle. 2. a maxim; adage. **—aph'o·ris'tic,** *adj.*
**aph·ro·dis·i·ac** (af'rə-diz'i-ak'), *adj.* [< Gr. *Aphroditē*], arousing sexual desire. *n.* an aphrodisiac drug, food, etc.
**Aph·ro·di·te** (af'rə-dī'ti), *n.* the Greek goddess of love and beauty.
**a·pi·ar·y** (ā'pi-er'i), *n.* [*pl.* -IES], [< L. *apis,* bee], a place where bees are kept. **—a'pi·a·rist** (-ə-rist), *n.*
**a·piece** (ə-pēs'), *adv.* [*a* + *piece*], to or for each.
**ap·ish** (āp'ish), *adj.* 1. like an ape. 2. stupidly imitative. **—ap'ish·ly,** *adv.*
**a·plomb** (ə-plom'), *n.* [< Fr.; see PLUMB], self-possession; poise.
**A.P.O., APO,** Army Post Office.
**a·poc·a·lypse** (ə-pok'ə-lips'), *n.* [< Gr. *apokalyptein,* disclose], 1. [A-], the last book of the New Testament; book of Revelation. 2. a revelation. **—a·poc'a·lyp'tic** (-lip'tik), **a·poc'a·lyp'ti·cal,** *adj.*
**A·poc·ry·pha** (ə-pok'rə-fə), *n.pl.* [< Gr. *apo-,* away + *kryptein,* hide], fourteen books of the Septuagint rejected in Protestantism and Judaism: eleven are accepted in the Roman Catholic Biblical canon.
**a·poc'ry·phal,** *adj.* 1. of doubtful authenticity. 2. not genuine; spurious.
**ap·o·gee** (ap'ə-ji), *n.* [< Gr. *apo-,* from + *gē,* earth], 1. the point farthest from the earth in the orbit of the moon or of a man-made satellite: opposed to *perigee.* 2. an apex.
**A·pol·lo** (ə-pol'ō), *n.* 1. the Greek and Roman god of music, poetry, prophecy, medicine, and of the sun. 2. [*pl.* -LOS], a handsome young man.
**a·pol·o·get·ic** (ə-pol'ə-jet'ik), *adj.* showing apology; expressing regret: also **a·pol'o·get'i·cal. —a·pol'o·get'i·cal·ly,** *adv.*
**a·pol'o·get'ics,** *n.pl.* [construed as sing.], [see APOLOGY], the branch of theology dealing with the defense of Christianity.
**ap·o·lo·gi·a** (ap'ə-lō'ji-ə), *n.* an apology.
**a·pol·o·gist** (ə-pol'ə-jist), *n.* one who defends or attempts to justify a doctrine, faith, action, etc.
**a·pol'o·gize'** (-jīz'), *v.i.* [-GIZED, -GIZING], to make an apology; express regret.
**a·pol·o·gy** (ə-pol'ə-ji), *n.* [*pl.* -GIES], [< Gr. *apo-,* from + *logos,* word], 1. a formal defense of an idea, doctrine, etc. 2. an expressing of regret for a fault, insult, etc. 3. an inferior substitute: a humorous usage.
**ap·o·plec·tic** (ap'ə-plek'tik), *adj.* of, like, causing, or having apoplexy.
**ap·o·plex·y** (ap'ə-plek'si), *n.* [< Gr. *apo-,* down + *plēssein,* to strike], sudden paralysis caused by the breaking or obstruction of a blood vessel in the brain.
**a·pos·ta·sy** (ə-pos'tə-si), *n.* [*pl.* -SIES], [< Gr. *apo-,* away + *stasis,* standing], an abandoning of what one believed in.
**a·pos'tate** (-tāt, -tit), *n.* a person guilty of apostasy; renegade. *adj.* guilty of apostasy.
**a pos·te·ri·o·ri** (ā' pos-têr'i-ō'rī), [L.], 1. from effect to cause. 2. based on observation or experience.
**A·pos·tle** (ə-pos''l), *n.* [< Gr. *apo-,* from + *stellein,* send], 1. [occas. a-], any of the disciples of Jesus, esp. the original twelve. 2. [usually a-], the leader of a new reform.
**ap·os·tol·ic** (ap'əs-tol'ik), *adj.* 1. of the Apostles, their teachings, works, etc. 2. [often A-], of the Pope; papal.
**a·pos·tro·phe** (ə-pos'trə-fi), *n.* [< Gr. *apo-,* from + *strephein,* to turn], the sign (') indicating: 1. the omission of a letter or letters from a word, as in *isn't.* 2. the possessive case, as in *Mary's* dress. 3. certain plural forms, as in *6's, t's.*
**a·poth·e·car·y** (ə-poth'ə-ker'i), *n.* [*pl.* -IES], [< Gr. *apothēkē,* storehouse], a pharmacist.
**ap·o·thegm** (ap'ə-them'), *n.* [< Gr. *apo-,* from + *phthengesthai,* to utter], a short, terse saying; maxim: also sp. **apophthegm.**
**a·poth·e·o·sis** (ə-poth'i-ō'sis, ap'ə-thē'ə-), *n.* [*pl.* -SES, (-sēz, -sēz')], [< Gr. *apo-,* from + *theos,* god], 1. the deifying of a person. 2. the glorification of a person or thing.
**a·poth·e·o·size** (ə-poth'i-ə-sīz', ap'ə-thē'-), *v.t.* [-SIZED, -SIZING], 1. to deify. 2. to glorify; idealize.
**ap·pall, ap·pal** (ə-pôl'), *v.t.* [-PALLED, -PALLING], [< OFr. *a-,* to + *pale,* pale], to horrify; shock; dismay. **—ap·pal'ling,** *adj.*
**ap·pa·ra·tus** (ap'ə-rā'təs, -rat'əs), *n.* [*pl.* -TUS, -TUSES], [< L. *ad-,* to + *parare,* prepare], 1. the materials, tools, etc. for a specific use. 2. any complex device, etc.
**ap·par·el** (ə-par'əl), *n.* [< OFr. *a-,* to + *pareiller,* put like things together], clothing; attire. *v.t.* [-ELED or -ELLED, -ELING or -ELLING], to clothe; dress.

**ap·par·ent** (ə-par′ənt, -pâr′-), *adj.* [see APPEAR], 1. visible; readily seen. 2. evident; obvious. 3. appearing to be real or true.

**ap·par′ent·ly,** *adv.* 1. clearly. 2. seemingly.

**ap·pa·ri·tion** (ap′ə-rish′ən), *n.* [see APPEAR], 1. anything that appears unexpectedly. 2. a ghost; phantom.

**ap·peal** (ə-pēl′), *v.t.* [< L. *ad-*, to + *pellere*, drive], to make an appeal of (a law case). *v.i.* 1. to make an appeal in a law case. 2. to make an urgent request (*for* a decision, help, etc.). 3. to be interesting or attractive. *n.* 1. a request for the transference of a law case to a higher court for rehearing. 2. a request for help, etc. 3. interest; attraction. **—ap·peal′ing,** *adj.* **—ap·peal′ing·ly,** *adv.*

**ap·pear** (ə-pêr′), *v.i.* [< L. *ad-*, to + *parere*, become visible], 1. to come into sight. 2. to become understood: as, it *appears* I lost. 3. to seem; look. 4. to present oneself formally in court. 5. to come before the public.

**ap·pear′ance,** *n.* 1. an appearing. 2. the outward aspect of anything. 3. an apparition. 4. a pretense or show. **—keep up appearances,** to maintain an outward show of what is proper, etc.

**ap·pease** (ə-pēz′), *v.t.* [-PEASED, -PEASING], [ult. < L. *ad*, to + *pax*, peace], to pacify or quiet, esp. by giving in to the demands of. **—ap·pease′ment,** *n.* **—ap·peas′er,** *n.*

**ap·pel·lant** (ə-pel′ənt), *adj.* appellate. *n.* one who appeals, esp. to a higher court.

**ap·pel·late** (ə-pel′it), *adj.* in *law*, relating to appeals; that appeals or is appealed to.

**appellate court,** a court that can review appeals and reverse the decisions of lower courts.

**ap·pel·la·tion** (ap′ə-lā′shən), *n.* [see APPEAL], a naming or name; title.

**ap·pend** (ə-pend′), *v.t.* [< L. *ad-*, to + *pendere*, suspend], to affix; attach; add.

**ap·pend′age,** *n.* 1. anything appended; adjunct. 2. an external part, as a tail.

**ap·pen·dec·to·my** (ap′ən-dek′tə-mi), *n.* [*pl.* -MIES], [see -ECTOMY], the surgical removal of the vermiform appendix.

**ap·pen·di·ci·tis** (ə-pen′də-sī′tis), *n.* inflammation of the vermiform appendix.

**ap·pen·dix** (ə-pen′diks), *n.* [*pl.* -DIXES, -DICES (-də-sēz′)], [see APPEND], 1. additional material at the end of a book. 2. the vermiform appendix.

**ap·per·cep·tion** (ap′ẽr-sep′shən), *n.* perception. **—ap′per·cep′tive,** *adj.*

**ap·per·tain** (ap′ẽr-tān′), *v.i.* [< L. *ad-*, to + *pertinere*, to reach], to belong as a function, part, etc.; pertain; relate.

**ap·pe·tite** (ap′ə-tīt′), *n.* [< L. *ad-*, to + *petere*, seek], a desire, esp. for food.

**ap′pe·tiz′er** (-tīz′ẽr), *n.* a tasty food that stimulates the appetite.

**ap′pe·tiz′ing,** *adj.* stimulating the appetite; savory; delicious. **—ap′pe·tiz′ing·ly,** *adv.*

**ap·plaud** (ə-plôd′), *v.t.* & *v.i.* [< L. *ad-*, to + *plaudere*, to strike], 1. to show approval (of) by clapping the hands, etc. 2. to praise; approve.

**ap·plause** (ə-plôz′), *n.* approval or praise, esp. as shown by clapping hands, etc.

**ap·ple** (ap′′l), *n.* [AS. *æppel*], 1. a round, firm, edible fruit. 2. the tree it grows on.

**ap′ple·jack′** (-jak′), *n.* a brandy distilled from apple cider.

**apple polisher,** [Slang], one who seeks favor by gifts, flattery, etc.

**ap′ple·sauce′** (-sôs′), *n.* apples sweetened and cooked to a pulp in water.

**ap·pli·ance** (ə-plī′əns), *n.* a device or machine, esp. one for household use.

**ap·pli·ca·ble** (ap′li-kə-b′l), *adj.* that can be applied; appropriate. **—ap′pli·ca·bly,** *adv.*

**ap′pli·cant** (-kənt), *n.* one who applies, as for employment, help, etc.

**ap·pli·ca·tion** (ap′li-kā′shən), *n.* 1. an applying. 2. anything applied, as a remedy. 3. a method of using. 4. a request: as, a job *application.* 5. continued exertion. 6. relevance.

**ap′pli·ca′tor,** *n.* any device for applying or inserting medicine, etc.

**ap·plied** (ə-plīd′), *adj.* used in actual practice: as, *applied* science.

**ap·pli·qué** (ap′li-kā′), *n.* [Fr.], decoration made of one material attached by sewing, etc. to another. *v.t.* [-QUÉD,- QUÉING], to decorate with appliqué.

**ap·ply** (ə-plī′), *v.t.* [-PLIED, -PLYING], [< L. *ad-*, to + *plicare*, to fold], 1. to put on: as, *apply* glue. 2. to use practically: as, *apply* your knowledge. 3. to devote (oneself or one's faculties) diligently. *v.i.* 1. to make a request. 2. to be suitable, or relevant. **—ap·pli′er,** *n.*

**ap·point** (ə-point′), *v.t.* [< L. *ad-*, to + *punctum*, a point], 1. to ordain; set (a date, place, etc.). 2. to name for an office, etc.: as, I *appoint* him chairman. 3. to furnish: as, *well-appointed.* **—ap·point′ee,** *n.*

**ap·poin·tive** (ə-poin′tiv), *adj.* of or filled by appointment: as, an *appointive* office.

**ap·point·ment** (ə-point′mənt), *n.* 1. an appointing or being appointed. 2. a position filled by appointing. 3. an engagement to meet a person. 4. *pl.* furniture.

**ap·por·tion** (ə-pôr′shən), *v.t.* [see AD- & PORTION], to portion out; allot.

**ap·pose** (ə-pōz′), *v.t.* [-POSED, -POSING], [see APPOSITE], to put side by side or opposite. **—ap·pos′a·ble,** *adj.*

**ap·po·site** (ap′ə-zit), *adj.* [< L. *ad-*, to + *ponere*, put], fitting; apt.

**ap·po·si·tion** (ap′ə-zish′ən), *n.* 1. an apposing, or the position resulting from this. 2. the placing of a word or phrase beside another in explanation, as in *Jim, my son,* is here. **—ap·pos·i·tive** (ə-poz′ə-tiv), *adj.* & *n.*

**ap·prais·al** (ə-prāz′′l), *n.* 1. an appraising. 2. an appraised value; estimate.

**ap·praise** (ə-prāz′), *v.t.* [-PRAISED, -PRAISING], [< L. *ad*, to + *pretium*, value], 1. to set a price for. 2. to estimate the quantity or quality of. **—ap·prais′er,** *n.*

**ap·pre·ci·a·ble** (ə-prē′shi-ə-b′l), *adj.* enough to be perceived; noticeable.

**ap·pre·ci·ate** (ə-prē′shi-āt′), *v.t.* [-ATED, -ATING], [see APPRAISE], 1. to think well of; value. 2. to recognize gratefully. 3. to estimate the quality of. 4. to estimate rightly. 5. to be fully or sensitively aware of.

**ap·pre′ci·a′tion,** *n.* 1. grateful recognition, as of benefits. 2. sensitive awareness.

**ap·pre′ci·a′tive** (-ā′tiv, -ə-tiv), *adj.* feeling or showing appreciation.

**ap·pre·hend** (ap′ri-hend′), *v.t.* [< L. *ad-*, to + *prehendere*, seize], 1. to arrest (a suspect, etc.). 2. to perceive. 3. to fear; dread.

**ap′pre·hen′sion** (-hen′shən), *n.* 1. arrest. 2. understanding. 3. fear; dread; anxiety.

**ap′pre·hen′sive** (-siv), *adj.* anxious; uneasy.

**ap·pren·tice** (ə-pren′tis), *n.* [see APPREHEND], 1. a person working under a skilled craftsman to learn the trade. 2. any beginner. *v.t.* [-TICED, -TICING], to place or accept as an apprentice. **—appren′ticeship′,** *n.*

**ap·prise, ap·prize** (ə-prīz′), *v.t.* [-PRISED, -PRISING; -PRIZED, -PRIZING], [< L. *ad-*, to + *prehendere*, seize], to inform; notify.

**ap·prize, ap·prise** (ə-prīz′), *v.t.* [-PRIZED, -PRIZING; -PRISED, -PRISING], to appraise.

**ap·proach** (ə-prōch′), *v.i.* [< L. *ad*, to + *prope*, near], to come or go near or nearer. *v.t.* 1. to come near or nearer to. 2. to come to resemble; approximate. 3. to bring near (*to* something). 4. to make a proposal or request to. *n.* 1. a coming near. 2. an approximation; resemblance. 3. *often in pl.*

an advance or overture (*to* someone). 4. a way of reaching. —**ap·proach'a·ble,** *adj.*
**ap·pro·ba·tion** (ap'rə-bā'shən), *n.* [see APPROVE], approval or consent.
**ap·pro·pri·ate** (ə-prō'pri-āt'), *v.t.* [-ATED, -ATING], [< L. *ad-*, to + *proprius*, one's own], 1. to take for one's own use. 2. to steal. 3. to set aside for a specific use; as, to *appropriate* money for roads. *adj.* (-it), suitable; fit; proper. —**ap·pro'pri·ate·ly,** *adv.*
**ap·pro'pri·a'tion,** *n.* 1. an appropriating or being appropriated. 2. money, etc. set aside for a specific use.
**ap·prov·al** (ə-prōōv''l), *n.* 1. an approving or being approved. 2. favorable opinion. 3. consent. —**on approval,** for one to examine and decide whether to buy or return.
**ap·prove** (ə-prōōv'), *v.t.* [-PROVED, -PROVING], [< L. *ad-*, to + *probus*, good], 1. to consent to. 2. to consider to be good, satisfactory, etc. *v.i.* to have a favorable opinion (*of*). —**ap·prov'ing·ly,** *adv.*
**ap·prox·i·mate** (ə-prok'sə-mit), *adj.* [< L. *ad*, to + *prope*, near], 1. near in position. 2. much like. 3. more or less correct. *v.t.* (-māt'), [-MATED, -MATING], to come near to: as, to *approximate* reality.
**ap·prox'i·ma'tion** (-mā'shən), *n.* a close estimate; near likeness.
**ap·pur·te·nance** (ə-pũr't'n-əns), *n.* [see APPERTAIN], 1. something added to a more important thing. 2. an additional, subordinate right or privilege.
**ap·pur'te·nant,** *adj.* appertaining.
**a·pri·cot** (ā'pri-kot', ap'ri-), *n.* [< L. *praecoquus*, early matured fruit], 1. a small, yellowish-orange, peachlike fruit. 2. the tree that it grows on.
**A·pril** (ā'prəl), *n.* [< L.], the fourth month of the year, having 30 days: abbrev. **Apr.**
**a pri·o·ri** (ā' pri-ō'ri, ä' pri-ôr'i), [L.], 1. from cause to effect. 2. based on theory instead of experience or experiment.
**a·pron** (ā'prən), *n.* [< L. *mappa*, napkin], 1. a garment worn over the front part of the body to protect one's clothes. 2. anything like this in appearance or use, as the front part of a stage. *v.t.* to put an apron on.
**ap·ro·pos** (ap'rə-pō'), *adv.* [Fr. *à propos*, to the purpose], at the right time; opportunely. *adj.* relevant; apt. —**apropos of,** in connection with.
**apse** (aps), *n.* [see APT], a semicircular or polygonal projection of a church, usually domed or vaulted.
**apt** (apt), *adj.* [< Gr. *haptein*, fasten], 1. appropriate; fitting. 2. tending; inclined. 3. quick to learn. —**apt'ly,** *adv.* —**apt'ness,** *n.*
**apt.,** [*pl.* APTS.], apartment.
**ap·ti·tude** (ap'tə-tōōd', -tūd'), *n.* [see APT], 1. suitability; fitness. 2. a natural tendency, ability, etc. 3. quickness to learn.
**aq·ua** (ak'wə, ā'kwə), *n.* [*pl.* -UAS, -UAE (-wē, -kwē)], [L.], water. *adj.* bluish-green.
**aq·ua·ma·rine** (ak'wə-mə-rēn'), *n.* [L. *aqua marina*, sea water], 1. a transparent, pale bluish-green beryl. 2. its color. *adj.* bluish-green.
**aq·ua·plane** (ak'wə-plān'), *n.* [coined after *airplane*], a board on which one rides erect as it is pulled by a boat. *v.i.* [-PLANED, -PLANING], to ride on such a board.
**a·quar·i·um** (ə-kwâr'i-əm), *n.* [*pl.* -IUMS, -IA (-i-ə)], [< L. *aquarius*, of water], 1. a tank, etc. for keeping live water animals and plants. 2. a place exhibiting these.
**A·quar·i·us** (ə-kwâr'i-əs), *n.* [L., water carrier], the eleventh sign of the zodiac.
**a·quat·ic** (ə-kwat'ik, -kwät'-), *adj.* 1. growing or living in water. 2. done in or on the water: as, *aquatic* sports.
**aq·ue·duct** (ak'wi-dukt'), *n.* [< L. *aqua*, water + *ducere*, to lead], 1. a large pipe for bringing water from a distant source. 2. an elevated structure supporting such a pipe.
**a·que·ous** (ā'kwi-əs, ak'wi-), *adj.* of, like, or formed by water; watery.
**aq·ui·line** (ak'wə-lin', -lin), *adj.* [< L. *aquila*, eagle], 1. of or like an eagle. 2. like an eagle's beak, as a hooked nose.
**-ar,** [ult. < L.], 1. a suffix meaning *of, relating to, like*, as in *polar*. 2. a suffix showing *agency*, as in *vicar*.
**Ar.,** 1. Arabic. 2. Aramaic.
**Ar·ab** (ar'əb), *n.* 1. a native of Arabia. 2. any of a Semitic people originating in Arabia; commonly, a Bedouin. *adj.* of the Arabs. —**A·ra·bi·an** (ə-rā'bi-ən), *adj.* & *n.*
**ar·a·besque** (ar'ə-besk'), *n.* [< It. *Arabo*, Arab], an elaborate, intertwined design.
**Arabian Nights,** a collection of ancient stories from Arabia, India, Persia, etc.
**Ar·a·bic** (ar'ə-bik), *adj.* 1. of Arabia. 2. of the Arabs. *n.* the Semitic language of the Arabs, used from Iraq to northern Africa.
**Arabic numerals,** the figures 1, 2, 3, 4, 5, 6, 7, 8, 9, and the 0 (zero).
**ar·a·ble** (ar'ə-b'l), *adj.* [< L. *arare*, to plow], suitable for plowing.
**a·rach·nid** (ə-rak'nid), *n.* [< Gr. *arachnē*, spider], any of a group of small animals with eight legs, including spiders and scorpions.
**Ar·a·ma·ic** (ar'ə-mā'ik), *n.* a group of Semitic languages spoken in Biblical times.
**ar·bi·ter** (är'bi-tẽr), *n.* [L., a witness], arbitrator; judge; umpire.
**ar·bit·ra·ment** (är-bit'rə-mənt), *n.* 1. arbitration. 2. an arbitrator's verdict.
**ar·bi·trar·y** (är'bə-trer'i), *adj.* [see ARBITER], 1. based on one's preference or whim. 2. capricious. 3. absolute; despotic. —**ar'bi·trar'i·ly,** *adv.* —**ar'bi·trar'i·ness,** *n.*
**ar·bi·trate** (är'bə-trāt'), *v.t.* & *v.i.* [-TRATED, -TRATING], [see ARBITER], 1. to submit (a dispute) to arbitration. 2. to decide (a dispute) as an arbitrator.
**ar'bi·tra'tion,** *n.* settlement of a dispute by an arbitrator.
**ar'bi·tra'tor** (-tẽr), *n.* a person selected to judge a dispute.
**ar·bor** (är'bẽr), *n.* [< L. *herba*, grass], a place shaded by trees, shrubs, etc.; bower.
**ar·bor** (är'bẽr), *n.* [*pl.* ARBORES (-bə-rēz')], [L.], a tree. —**Arbor Day,** in most States, a day in spring observed by planting trees.
**ar·bo·re·al** (är-bôr'i-əl), *adj.* 1. of or like a tree. 2. living in trees.
**ar·bo·re·tum** (är'bə-rē'təm), *n.* [*pl.* -TUMS, -TA (-tə)], [L.], a place where many kinds of trees and shrubs are grown, as for study.
**ar·bor·vi·tae** (är'bẽr-vi'tē), *n.* [L., tree of life], any of various pine trees having soft, scalelike leaves: also **arbor vitae.**
**ar·bour** (är'bẽr), *n.* arbor (bower): Brit. sp.
**ar·bu·tus** (är-bū'təs), *n.* [L.], 1. a tree or shrub with dark-green leaves and strawberrylike berries. 2. a trailing plant with white or pink flower clusters.
**arc** (ärk), *n.* [< L. *arcus*, a bow, arch], 1. a bowlike curved line or object. 2. the band of incandescent light formed when a current leaps a short gap between electrodes. 3. a part of a curved line, as of a circle. *v.i.* [ARCED or ARCKED (ärkt), ARCING or ARCKING], to form an electric arc.
**ar·cade** (är-kād'), *n.* [see ARC], 1. a covered passageway, esp. one lined with shops. 2. a line of arches and their supporting columns.
**ar·cane** (är-kān'), *adj.* [< L.; see ARCANUM], 1. hidden or secret. 2. esoteric.
**ar·ca·num** (är-kā'nəm), *n.* [*pl.* -NUMS, -NA (-nə)], [L. < *arca*, chest], a secret; mystery.
**arch** (ärch), *n.* [see ARC], 1. a curved structure used as a support over an open space, as in a doorway. 2. the form of an arch. 3. anything shaped like an arch. *v.t.* & *v.i.* 1. to span with or as an arch. 2. to form (into) an arch. —**arched** (ärcht), *adj.*

**arch** (ärch), *adj.* [< *arch-*], 1. chief; principal. 2. gaily mischievous; pert.
**arch-,** [< Gr. *archos*, ruler], a prefix meaning *chief, principal*, as in *archbishop*.
**-arch,** [see ARCH-], a suffix meaning *ruler*, as in *matriarch*.
**arch.,** 1. archaic. 2. architecture.
**ar·chae·ol·o·gy** (är'ki-ol'ə-ji), *n.* [< Gr. *archaios*, ancient; + *-logy*], the study of the life of ancient peoples, as by excavation of ancient cities, etc.: also sp. **archeology.** —**ar'chae·o·log'i·cal** (-ə-loj'i-k'l), *adj.* —**ar'chae·ol'o·gist** *n.*
**ar·cha·ic** (är-kā'ik), *adj.* [< Gr. *archaios*, ancient], 1. ancient. 2. old-fashioned. 3. no longer used except in poetry, the Bible, etc. —**ar'cha·ism,** *n.*
**arch·an·gel** (ärk'ān'jəl), *n.* an angel of the highest rank.
**arch·bish·op** (ärch'bish'əp), *n.* a bishop of the highest rank.
**arch'dea'con** (-dē'k'n), *n.* a chief deacon, ranking just below a bishop.
**arch'duke'** (-do͞ok', -dūk'), *n.* a prince of the former Austrian royal family.
**arch'en'e·my,** *n.* [*pl.* -MIES], a chief enemy.
**Ar·che·o·zo·ic** (är'ki-ə-zō'ik), *adj.* [< Gr. *archos*, first; + *zoo-* + *-ic*], designating or of the earliest known geological era beginning about two billion years ago.
**arch·er** (ärch'ẽr), *n.* [< L. *arcus*, a bow], one who shoots with bow and arrow.
**arch'er·y,** *n.* the practice or art of shooting with bow and arrow.
**ar·che·type** (är'kə-tīp'), *n.* [< Gr. *arche-*, first + *typos*, a mark], an original pattern, or model; prototype. —**ar'che·typ'al,** *adj.*
**ar·chi·pel·a·go** (är'kə-pel'ə-gō'), *n.* [*pl.* -GOES, -GOS], [< Gr. *archi-*, chief + *pelagos*, sea], 1. a sea with many islands. 2. such a group of islands.
**ar·chi·tect** (är'kə-tekt'), *n.* [< Gr. *archi-*, chief + *tektōn*, worker], 1. a person who designs buildings and supervises their construction. 2. any builder or creator.
**ar'chi·tec'ture** (-tek'chẽr), *n.* 1. the science or profession of designing and constructing buildings. 2. a style of construction. 3. design and construction. —**ar'chi·tec'tur·al,** *adj.* —**ar'chi·tec'tur·al·ly,** *adv.*
**ar·chives** (är'kīvz), *n.pl.* [< Gr. *archē*, the beginning], 1. a place where public records are kept. 2. the records kept there.
**ar·chi·vist** (är'kə-vist), *n.* a person having charge of archives.
**arch·way** (ärch'wā'), *n.* a passage under an arch.
**-archy,** [< Gr. *archos*, ruler], a suffix meaning *ruling*, as in *monarchy*.
**arc·tic** (ärk'tik, är'tik), *adj.* [< Gr. *arktikos*, northern], 1. of or near the North Pole. 2. very cold; frigid.
**arc'tics,** *n.pl.* [< *arctic*], warmly lined, waterproof overshoes.
**-ard,** [< MHG. *hart*, bold], a suffix meaning *one who does* (something not admirable) *too much*, as in *drunkard*.
**ar·den·cy** (är'd'n-si), *n.* a being ardent.
**ar·dent** (är'd'nt), *adj.* [< L. *ardere*, to burn], 1. glowing; beaming. 2. passionate; eager.
**ar·dor** (är'dẽr), *n.* [see ARDENT], 1. emotional warmth; passion; zeal. 2. intense heat. Also, Brit. sp., **ardour.**
**ar·du·ous** (är'jo͞o-əs), *adj.* [L. *arduus*, steep], 1. difficult to do; laborious. 2. energetic; working hard. —**ar'du·ous·ly,** *adv.*
**are** (är), [AS. *aron*], pl. and 2d pers. sing., pres. indic., of **be.**
**ar·e·a** (âr'i-ə), *n.* [L., level piece of ground], 1. an expanse of land; region. 2. a total outside surface, measured in square units. 3. scope. —**ar'e·al,** *adj.*
**a·re·na** (ə-rē'nə), *n.* [*pl.* -NAS, -NAE (-nē)], [L., sandy place], 1. the center of an ancient Roman amphitheater, where contests were held. 2. any place or sphere of struggle.
**aren't** (ärnt), are not.
**Ar·es** (âr'ēz), *n.* in *Gr. myth.*, the god of war.
**ar·gent** (är'jənt), *adj.* [< Gr. *argos*, white], silvery. —**ar·gen'te·ous** (-jen'ti-əs), *adj.*
**Ar·gen·tine** (är'jən-tēn', -tīn'), *adj.* of Argentina, its people, etc. *n.* a native or inhabitant of Argentina.
**ar·gon** (är'gon), *n.* [Gr., inert], a chemical element, a colorless, odorless gas found in the atmosphere and used in radio tubes, etc.: symbol, A.
**Ar·go·naut** (är'gə-nôt'), *n.* [< Gr. *Argo*, Jason's ship + *nautēs*, sailor], in *Gr. legend*, any of those who sailed with Jason in search of the Golden Fleece.
**ar·go·sy** (är'gə-si), *n.* [*pl.* -SIES], [< It. *Ragusea*, ship of *Ragusa*, a Sicilian city], [Poetic], a large merchant ship or a fleet of such ships.
**ar·got** (är'gō, -gət), *n.* [Fr.], the specialized vocabulary of a particular group, as of criminals, tramps, etc.
**ar·gue** (är'gū), *v.i.* [-GUED, -GUING], [< L. *arguere*, prove], 1. to give reasons (*for* or *against*). 2. to dispute (*with* or *about*). *v.t.* 1. to dispute about; debate. 2. to maintain. 3. to persuade with reasons.
**ar'gu·ment** (-gyoo-mənt), *n.* 1. an arguing; debate. 2. a reason or reasons offered in arguing. 3. a summary.
**ar'gu·men·ta'tion** (-men-tā'shən), *n.* the process of arguing; debate.
**ar'gu·men'ta·tive** (-tə-tiv), *adj.* 1. controversial. 2. apt to argue.
**ar·gy·rol** (är'jə-rôl'), *n.* [< Gr. *argyros*, silver], an antiseptic made with silver: a trademark (**Argyrol**).
**a·ri·a** (ä'ri-ə, âr'i-ə), *n.* [It. < L. *aer*, air], a melody in an opera, etc., esp. for solo voice.
**-arian,** [< L.], a suffix denoting variously *age, sect, social belief, occupation*, as in *octogenarian*.
**ar·id** (ar'id), *adj.* [< L. *arere*, be dry], 1. dry. 2. barren. 3. uninteresting; dull. —**a·rid·i·ty** (ə-rid'ə-ti), *n.* —**ar'id·ly,** *adv.*
**Ar·i·es** (âr'ēz, -i-ēz'), *n.* [L., the Ram], the first sign of the zodiac.
**a·right** (ə-rīt'), *adv.* correctly.
**ar·il** (ar'il), *n.* [ML. *arillus*, dried grape], an additional covering on certain seeds.
**a·rise** (ə-rīz'), *v.i.* [AROSE (-rōz'), ARISEN (-riz''n), ARISING], [AS. < *a-*, out + *risan*, rise], 1. to get up, as from bed. 2. to rise; ascend. 3. to come into being. 4. to result (*from* something).
**ar·is·toc·ra·cy** (ar'ə-stok'rə-si), *n.* [*pl.* -CIES], [< Gr. *aristos*, best + *kratein*, to rule], 1. government by a privileged minority, usually of inherited wealth. 2. a country with such government. 3. a privileged ruling class; upper class.
**a·ris·to·crat** (ə-ris'tə-krat', ar'is-), *n.* 1. a member of the aristocracy. 2. one with the tastes, manners, etc. of the upper class. —**a·ris'to·crat'ic, a·ris'to·crat'i·cal,** *adj.*
**a·rith·me·tic** (ə-rith'mə-tik'), *n.* [< Gr. *arithmos*, number], the science of computing by positive, real numbers. *adj.* (ar'ith-met'ik), of arithmetic: also **ar'ith·met'i·cal.** —**a·rith'me·ti'cian** (-tish'ən), *n.*
**ark** (ärk), *n.* [< L. *arcere*, enclose], 1. the ark of the covenant. 2. in the *Bible*, the boat in which Noah, his family, and two of every kind of creature survived the Flood.
**ark of the covenant,** in the *Bible*, the chest containing the tablets inscribed with the Ten Commandments.
**arm** (ärm), *n.* [AS. *earm*], 1. *a*) an upper limb of the human body. *b*) anything commonly in contact with this, as a sleeve, the support for the arm on a chair, etc. 2. anything like an arm in shape, function, position, etc. —

**keep at arm's length,** to keep at a distance. **—with open arms,** cordially. **—arm'less,** *adj.*

**arm** (ärm), *n.* [< L. *arma,* weapons], 1. any weapon: see **arms.** 2. any branch of the military forces. *v.i.* to prepare for war.

**ar·ma·da** (är-mä'də), *n.* [Sp. < *arma,* weapons], a fleet of warships or warplanes.

**ar·ma·dil·lo** (är'mə-dil'ō), *n.* [*pl.* -LOS], [< Sp.; see ARMADA], a small burrowing mammal of Texas and Central and South America, covered with bony plates.

**Ar·ma·ged·don** (är'mə-ged''n), *n.* 1. in the *Bible,* the place where the last decisive battle between the forces of good and evil will be fought. 2. any decisive battle.

**ar·ma·ment** (är'mə-mənt), *n.* 1. *often pl.* all the military forces and equipment of a nation. 2. all the military equipment of a warship, fortification, etc. 3. an arming or being armed for war.

**ar·ma·ture** (är'mə-chẽr), *n.* [< L. *armare,* to arm], 1. an armorlike covering. 2. flat wire wound around a cable. 3. the part that revolves in an electric motor or dynamo: it consists of an iron core wound with wire.

**arm'chair',** *n.* a chair with supports at the sides for one's arms.

**armed forces,** all the military, naval, and air forces of a country.

**arm'ful'** (-fool'), *n.* [*pl.* -FULS], as much as the arms or an arm can hold.

**arm'hole',** *n.* an opening for the arm in a garment.

**ar·mis·tice** (är'mə-stis), *n.* [< L. *arma,* arms + *stare,* stand still], a temporary stopping of war by truce.

**Armistice Day,** see **Veterans' Day.**

**arm'let** (-lit), *n.* an ornamental band worn around the upper arm.

**ar·mor** (är'mẽr), *n.* [< L. *armare,* to arm], any defensive or protective covering. *v.t. & v.i.* to put armor on. Brit. sp. **armour.**

**ar·mor·er** (är'mẽr-ẽr), *n.* 1. formerly, one who made or repaired armor. 2. a maker of firearms.

**ar·mo·ri·al** (är-môr'i-əl), *adj.* of coats of arms; heraldic.

**ar·mor·y** (är'mẽr-i), *n.* [*pl.* -IES], [see ARMOR], 1. an arsenal. 2. an armaments factory.

**arm'pit',** *n.* the hollow under the arm at the shoulder.

**arms** (ärmz), *n.pl.* 1. weapons. 2. warfare; fighting. 3. heraldic symbols. **—up in arms,** 1. prepared to fight. 2. indignant.

**ar·my** (är'mi), *n.* [*pl.* -MIES], [< L. *armare,* to arm], 1. a large, organized body of soldiers for waging war, esp. on land. 2. any large number of persons, animals, etc.

**ar·ni·ca** (är'ni-kə), *n.* a medicine made from a plant of the aster family, for treating sprains, bruises, etc.

**a·ro·ma** (ə-rō'mə), *n.* [< Gr. *arōma,* spice], a pleasant odor; fragrance.

**ar·o·mat·ic** (ar'ə-mat'ik), *adj.* of or having an aroma: also **ar'o·mat'i·cal.**

**a·rose** (ə-rōz'), pt. of **arise.**

**a·round** (ə-round'), *adv.* 1. in a circle. 2. in every direction. 3. to the opposite direction. 4. [Colloq.], near by: as, stay *around.* *prep.* 1. so as to encircle or envelop. 2. on the border of. 3. in various places in or on. 4. [Colloq.], about: as, *around* 1890.

**a·rouse** (ə-rouz'), *v.t.* [AROUSED, AROUSING], 1. to stir up, as to action. 2. to wake.

**ar·peg·gio** (är-pej'ō, -i-ō'), *n.* [*pl.* -GIOS], [< It. *arpa,* a harp], the playing of the notes of a chord in quick succession.

**ar·raign** (ə-rān'), *v.t.* [< L. *ad,* to + *ratio,* reason], 1. to bring before a law court to stand trial. 2. to call to account; accuse. **—ar·raign'ment,** *n.*

**ar·range** (ə-rānj'), *v.t.* [-RANGED, -RANGING], [see AD- & RANGE], 1. to put in the correct order. 2. to classify. 3. to settle (a dispute); adjust (a claim, etc.). 4. in *music,* to adapt (a work) to particular instruments or voices.

**ar·range'ment,** *n.* 1. an arranging. 2. a result or manner of arranging. 3. *usually in pl.* a plan. 4. a settlement. 5. in *music, a)* an arranging of a composition. *b)* the composition as thus arranged.

**ar·rant** (ar'ənt), *adj.* [var. of *errant*], out-and-out; unmitigated; notorious.

**ar·ras** (ar'əs), *n.* [< *Arras,* Fr. city], 1. a kind of tapestry. 2. a wall hanging of tapestry.

**ar·ray** (ə-rā'), *v.t.* [ult. < L. *ad-,* to + Gmc. base *raid-,* order], 1. to place in order. 2. to dress in finery. *n.* 1. an orderly grouping. 2. an impressive display. 3. clothes.

**ar·rears** (ə-rêrz'), *n.pl.* [< L. *ad,* to + *retro,* behind], overdue debts. **—in arrears,** behind in paying a debt, in one's work, etc.

**ar·rest** (ə-rest'), *v.t.* [< L. *ad,* to + *restare,* to stop], 1. to stop or check. 2. to seize by authority of the law. 3. to catch and keep. *n.* an arresting or being arrested. **—under arrest,** in legal custody.

**ar·rest'ing,** *adj.* attracting attention.

**ar·riv·al** (ə-rīv''l), *n.* 1. an arriving. 2. a person or thing that arrives.

**ar·rive** (ə-rīv'), *v.i.* [-RIVED, -RIVING], [< L. *ad,* to + *ripa,* shore], 1. to reach one's destination. 2. to come. 3. to attain fame, etc. **—arrive at,** to reach by thinking, etc.

**ar·ro·gance** (ar'ə-gəns), *n.* a being arrogant; haughtiness: also **ar'ro·gan·cy.**

**ar'ro·gant,** *adj.* [see ARROGATE], full of or due to pride; haughty. **—ar'ro·gant·ly,** *adv.*

**ar·ro·gate** (ar'ə-gāt'), *v.t.* [-GATED, -GATING], [< L. *ad-,* for + *rogare,* ask], to claim or seize without right. **—ar'ro·ga'tion,** *n.*

**ar·row** (ar'ō), *n.* [AS. *arwe*], 1. a slender, usually pointed shaft, shot from a bow. 2. a sign (←) used to indicate direction.

**ar·row·head** (ar'ō-hed'), *n.* 1. the pointed tip of an arrow. 2. a plant with arrow-shaped leaves.

**ar'row·root',** *n.* [< use as antidote for poisoned arrows], 1. a tropical American plant with starchy roots. 2. a starch made from its roots.

**ar·roy·o** (ə-roi'ō), *n.* [*pl.* -OS], [Sp. < L. *arrugia,* mine pit], 1. a dry gully. 2. a rivulet.

**ar·se·nal** (är's'n-əl), *n.* [< Ar. *dār aṣ-ṣinā'ah,* workshop], a place for making or storing weapons and other munitions.

**ar·se·nic** (är's'n-ik), *n.* [< L. < Gr.; ult. < Per. *zar,* gold], a silvery-white, very poisonous chemical element, compounds of which are used in insecticides, medicines, etc.: symbol, As. *adj.* (är-sen'ik), of or containing arsenic: also **ar·sen'i·cal.**

**ar·son** (är's'n), *n.* [< L. *ardere,* to burn], the crime of purposely setting fire to a building. **—ar'son·ist,** *n.*

**art** (ärt), *n.* [< L. *ars*], 1. creativeness. 2. skill. 3. any specific skill or its application. 4. a making of things that have form or beauty. 5. any branch of this, as painting, sculpture, etc. 6. paintings, statues, etc. 7. *usually in pl.* any of certain branches of academic learning, as music. 8. any craft or its principles. 9. cunning. 10. *usually in pl.* a trick; wile.

**art** (ärt), archaic 2d pers. sing., pres. indic., of **be.**

**art.,** 1. article. 2. artificial. 3. artillery.

**Ar·te·mis** (är'tə-mis), *n.* the Greek goddess of the moon and hunting.

**ar·te·ri·o·scle·ro·sis** (är-têr'i-ō-skli-rō'sis), *n.* [see ARTERY & SCLEROSIS], a hardening of the walls of the arteries, as in old age.

**ar·ter·y** (är'tẽr-i), *n.* [*pl.* -IES], [< Gr. *aeirein,* raise], 1. any of the tubes carrying blood from the heart. 2. a main road or channel. **—ar·te'ri·al** (-têr'i-əl), *adj.*

**ar·te·sian well** (är-tē'zhən), [< Fr. *Artois,* former Fr. province], a deep well in which

water is forced up by underground pressure.
**art·ful** (ärt′fəl), *adj.* 1. skillful or clever; adroit. 2. crafty; cunning. —**art′ful·ly,** *adv.*
**ar·thri·tis** (är-thri′tis), *n.* [< Gr. *arthron,* a joint; + *-itis*], inflammation of a joint or joints. —**ar·thrit′ic** (-thrit′ik), *adj.*
**ar·thro·pod** (är′thrə-pod′), *n.* [< Gr. *arthron,* a joint; + *-pod*], any of a group of invertebrate animals with jointed legs and a segmented body.
**Ar·thur** (är′thẽr), *n.* a legendary king of Britain in the 6th c. A.D. —**Ar·thu′ri·an** (-thoor′i-ən), *adj.*
**ar·ti·choke** (är′ti-chōk′), *n.* [ult. < Ar. *alkharshuf*], 1. a thistlelike plant. 2. its flower head, cooked as a vegetable.
**ar·ti·cle** (är′ti-k'l), *n.* [< L. *artus,* joint], 1. one of the sections of a document. 2. a separate piece of writing, as in a newspaper, magazine, etc. 3. a single item: as, an *article* of luggage. 4. in *grammar,* any one of the words *a, an,* or *the,* used as adjectives. *v.t.* [-CLED, -CLING], 1. to accuse. 2. to bind by the articles of an agreement.
**ar·tic·u·lar** (är-tik′yoo-lẽr), *adj.* [< L. *artus,* a joint], of the joints.
**ar·tic·u·late** (är-tik′yoo-lit), *adj.* [< L. *artus,* joint], 1. jointed. 2. spoken distinctly. 3. expressing oneself clearly. 4. able to speak. *v.t.* (-lāt′), [-LATED, -LATING], 1. to put together by joints. 2. to pronounce distinctly; enunciate. 3. to express clearly. *v.i.* 1. to speak distinctly. 2. to be jointed. —**ar·tic′u·late·ly,** *adv.* —**ar·tic′u·la′tion,** *n.*
**ar·ti·fact** (är′ti-fakt′), *n.* [see ARTIFICE], any object made by human work or skill.
**ar·ti·fice** (är′tə-fis), *n.* [< L. *ars,* art + *facere,* make], 1. skill. 2. trickery. 3. a trick.
**ar·tif·i·cer** (är-tif′ə-sẽr), *n.* 1. a skillful craftsman. 2. an inventor.
**ar·ti·fi·cial** (är′tə-fish′əl), *adj.* [see ARTIFICE], 1. made by human work or art; not natural. 2. simulated: as, *artificial* teeth. 3. affected: as, an *artificial* smile. —**ar′ti·fi′ci·al′i·ty** (-fish′i-al′ə-ti) [*pl.* -TIES], *n.*
**ar·til·ler·y** (är-til′ẽr-i), *n.* [< OFr. *atilier,* equip], 1. mounted guns, as cannon. 2. the science of guns; gunnery. —**the artillery,** the military branch using heavy mounted guns. —**ar·til′ler·y·man** [*pl.* -MEN (-mən)], *n.*
**ar·ti·san** (är′tə-z'n), *n.* [< L. *artire,* instruct in arts], a skilled craftsman.
**art·ist** (är′tist), *n.* 1. one who is skilled in any of the fine, esp. graphic, arts. 2. one who does anything very well.
**ar·tis·tic** (är-tis′tik), *adj.* 1. of art or artists. 2. done skillfully. 3. fond of the fine arts. —**ar·tis′ti·cal·ly,** *adv.*
**ar·tist·ry** (är′tis-tri), *n.* artistic quality, ability, work, or workmanship.
**art·less** (ärt′lis), *adj.* 1. lacking skill or art. 2. simple; natural. —**art′less·ly,** *adv.*
**art·y** (är′ti), *adj.* [-IER, -IEST], [Colloq.], affectedly artistic. —**art′i·ness,** *n.*
**-ary,** [< L.], a suffix meaning *relating to, connected with,* as in *auxiliary.*
**Ar·y·an** (âr′i-ən, är′yən), *n.* [< Sans. *ārya,* a tribal name], 1. the parent language of the Indo-European family. 2. a person supposed to be a descendant of the prehistoric people who spoke this language. *Aryan* has no validity as a racial term, although it has been so used by the Nazis.
**as** (az, əz), *adv.* [< *also*], 1. to the same amount or degree; equally: e.g., I am *as* good as he. 2. for instance: e.g., some colors, *as* green and blue, seem cool. *conj.* 1. in the same manner that: e.g., do *as* he does. 2. while: e.g., she wept *as* she spoke. 3. because: e.g., *as* you object, we won't go. 4. that the consequence is: e.g., a question so obvious *as* to need no reply. 5. though: e.g., tall *as* he is, he can't reach it. *pron.* 1. a fact that: e.g., he is tired, *as* you can see. 2. that: e.g., it's the same color *as* yours (is). *prep.* in the role or function of: e.g., he poses *as* a friend. —**as for** (or **to**), concerning. —**as if** (or **though**), as it (or one) would if. —**as is,** [Slang], just as it is.
**As,** in *chem.,* arsenic.
**AS.,** Anglo-Saxon: also **A.S., A.-S.**
**as·a·fet·i·da, as·a·foet·i·da** (as′ə-fet′i-də), *n.* [< Per. *azā,* gum + L. *f(o)etidus,* fetid], a bad-smelling resin used in medicine.
**as·bes·tos, as·bes·tus** (as-bes′təs, az-), *n.* [< Gr. *a-,* not + *sbennynai,* extinguish], a fire-resistant, fibrous mineral used in fireproofing, insulation, etc.
**as·cend** (ə-send′), *v.i.* & *v.t.* [< L. *ad-,* to + *scandere,* climb], to go or climb up; mount. —**as·cend′a·ble,** *adj.* —**as·cend′er,** *n.*
**as·cend·an·cy, as·cend·en·cy** (ə-sen′dən-si), *n.* controlling influence; domination.
**as·cend′ant, as·cend′ent,** *adj.* 1. ascending. 2. controlling; predominant. *n.* ascendancy. —**in the ascendant,** at or nearing the height of power, fame, etc.
**as·cen·sion** (ə-sen′shən), *n.* 1. an ascending. 2. [A-], the fortieth day after Easter, celebrating the Ascension: also **Ascension Day.** —**the Ascension,** in the *Bible,* the bodily ascent of Jesus into heaven.
**as·cent** (ə-sent′), *n.* 1. an ascending or rising. 2. an upward slope.
**as·cer·tain** (as′ẽr-tān′), *v.t.* [see AD- & CERTAIN], to find out with certainty. —**as′cer·tain′a·ble,** *adj.* —**as′cer·tain′ment,** *n.*
**as·cet·ic** (ə-set′ik), *adj.* [< Gr. *askein,* to exercise], self-denying. *n.* one who leads a life of rigorous self-denial, esp. for religious purposes. —**as·cet′i·cism** (-ə-siz'm), *n.*
**a·scor·bic acid** (ə-skôr′bik), [*a-,* not + *scorbutic* + *-ic*], vitamin C.
**as·cot** (as′kət), *n.* a necktie with very broad ends hanging from the knot.
**as·cribe** (ə-skrīb′), *v.t.* [-CRIBED, -CRIBING], [< L. *ad-,* to + *scribere,* write], 1. to assign (*to* a supposed cause or source). 2. to regard as belonging (*to* something) as an attribute. —**as·crip·tion** (ə-skrip′shən), *n.*
**a·sep·sis** (ə-sep′sis, ā-), *n.* a being aseptic.
**a·sep·tic** (ə-sep′tik, ā-), *adj.* not septic; free from disease-producing germs.
**a·sex·u·al** (ā-sek′shoo-əl), *adj.* 1. having no sex; sexless. 2. designating or of reproduction without the union of male and female germ cells. —**a·sex′u·al·ly,** *adv.*
**ash** (ash), *n.* [AS. *æsce*], 1. the grayish powder left after something has burned. 2. the gray color of wood ash. See also **ashes.**
**ash** (ash), *n.* [AS. *æsc*], 1. a shade tree of the olive family. 2. its tough wood.
**a·shamed** (ə-shāmd′), *adj.* 1. feeling shame. 2. reluctant because fearing shame beforehand. —**a·sham′ed·ly** (-id-li), *adv.*
**ash·en** (ash′'n), *adj.* 1. of ashes. 2. like ashes, esp. in color; pale.
**ash′en,** *adj.* of the ash tree or its wood.
**ash·es** (ash′iz), *n.pl.* 1. the substance remaining after a thing has burned. 2. human remains. 3. fine volcanic lava.
**a·shore** (ə-shôr′), *adv.* & *adj.* 1. to or on shore. 2. to or on land.
**Ash·to·reth** (ash′tə-rith), *n.* Astarte.
**ash tray,** a container for smokers' tobacco ashes.
**Ash Wednesday,** the first day of Lent: from the putting of ashes on the forehead in penitence.
**ash′y,** *adj.* [-IER, -IEST], 1. of, like, or covered with ashes. 2. ashen; pale.
**A·sian** (ā′zhən, -shən), *adj.* of Asia, its people, etc. *n.* a native or inhabitant of Asia. —**A·si·at·ic** (ā′zhi-at′ik, -shi-), *adj.* & *n.*
**a·side** (ə-sīd′), *adv.* 1. on or to one side. 2. away; on reserve: as, put one ticket *aside.* 3. out of one's thoughts, etc. 4. apart; notwithstanding: as, joking *aside.* *n.* words

spoken aside; actor's words supposedly heard only by the audience. **—aside from,** 1. with the exception of. 2. apart from.

**as·i·nine** (as′ə-nīn′), *adj.* [< L. *asinus*, ass], like an ass; stupid; silly. **—as′i·nine′ly,** *adv.* **—as′i·nin′i·ty** (-nin′ə-ti) [*pl.* -TIES], *n.*

**ask** (ask, äsk), *v.t.* [AS. *ascian*], 1. to use words in seeking an answer to (a question). 2. to put a question to (a person). 3. to request or demand. 4. to invite. *v.i.* 1. to make a request (*for*). 2. to inquire (*about*).

**a·skance** (ə-skans′), *adv.* 1. with a sidewise glance. 2. with suspicion, etc. Also **a·skant′.**

**a·skew** (ə-skū′), *adv.* to one side; awry. *adj.* on one side; awry.

**a·slant** (ə-slant′), *adv.* on a slant. *prep.* slantingly across. *adj.* slanting.

**a·sleep** (ə-slēp′), *adj.* 1. sleeping. 2. inactive; dull. 3. numb: as, her arm is *asleep.* 4. dead. *adv.* into a sleeping condition.

**a·so·cial** (ā-sō′shəl), *adj.* not social; avoiding contact with others.

**asp** (asp), *n.* [< Gr. *aspis*], a small, poisonous snake of Africa and Europe.

**as·par·a·gus** (ə-spar′ə-gəs), *n.* [< Gr. *asparagos*, sprout], 1. any of a group of plants with edible shoots. 2. these shoots.

**as·pect** (as′pekt), *n.* [< L. *ad-*, to + *specere*, look], 1. the way one appears; looks. 2. the appearance of a thing or idea from a specific viewpoint. 3. a side facing in a given direction.

**as·pen** (as′pən), *n.* [AS. *æspe*], a poplar tree whose leaves flutter in the least breeze. *adj.* fluttering; trembling.

**as·per·i·ty** (as-per′ə-ti), *n.* [*pl.* -TIES], [< L. *asper*, rough], 1. roughness or harshness. 2. sharpness of temper.

**as·perse** (ə-spũrs′), *v.t.* [-PERSED, -PERSING], [< L. *ad-*, to + *spargere*, sprinkle], to slander. **—as·pers′er,** *n.*

**as·per·sion** (ə-spũr′zhən), *n.* a damaging or disparaging remark; slander.

**as·phalt** (as′fôlt), *n.* [< Gr.; prob. < Sem.], a brown or black tarlike substance mixed with sand or gravel, for paving, roofing, etc. *v.t.* to pave, roof, etc. with asphalt.

**as·pho·del** (as′fə-del′), *n.* [< Gr.; cf. DAFFODIL], a plant of the lily family with white or yellow flowers.

**as·phyx·i·a** (as-fik′si-ə), *n.* [Gr. < *a-*, not + *sphyzein*, to throb], loss of consciousness from too little oxygen and too much carbon dioxide in the blood. **—as·phyx′i·ant,** *adj.* & *n.*

**as·phyx′i·ate′** (-āt′), *v.t.* [-ATED, -ATING], to cause asphyxia in, as by suffocating. **—as·phyx′i·a′tion,** *n.* **—as·phyx′i·a′tor,** *n.*

**as·pic** (as′pik), *n.* [< OFr. *aspe*], 1. an asp (snake). 2. a jelly of meat juice, tomato juice, etc. used as a relish, etc.

**as·pir·ant** (ə-spīr′ənt, as′pə-rənt), *adj.* aspiring. *n.* one who aspires.

**as·pi·rate** (as′pə-rāt′; *for adj. & n.*, -pẽr-it), *v.t.* [-RATED, -RATING], [< L.; see ASPIRE], 1. to begin (a syllable, etc.) with the sound of English *h*. 2. to follow (a consonant) with an audible puff of breath. *n.* an aspirated sound. *adj.* aspirated.

**as′pi·ra′tion,** *n.* 1. act of breathing. 2. an aspiring; ambition. 3. an aspirate.

**as·pire** (ə-spīr′), *v.i.* [-PIRED, -PIRING], [< L. *ad-*, to + *spirare*, breathe], to be ambitious (*to* get or do something); seek.

**as·pi·rin** (as′pẽr-in), *n.* a white crystalline powder used for reducing fever, pain, etc.

**ass** (as), *n.* [< L. *asinus*], 1. a donkey. 2. a stupid or silly person.

**as·sail** (ə-sāl′), *v.t.* [< L. *ad*, to + *salire*, to leap], 1. to attack physically and violently. 2. to attack with arguments, etc.

**as·sail′ant** (-ənt), *n.* an attacker.

**as·sas·sin** (ə-sas′in), *n.* [< Ar. *ḥashshāshīn*, hashish eaters], a murderer who strikes suddenly; often, a hired killer.

**as·sas′si·nate′** (-ə-nāt′), *v.t.* [-NATED, -NATING], to murder as assassins do. **—as·sas′si·na′tion,** *n.* **—as·sas′si·na′tor,** *n.*

**as·sault** (ə-sôlt′), *n.* [< L. *ad*, to + *saltare*, leap], 1. a violent attack. 2. rape: a euphemism. 3. in *law*, a threat or attempt to harm another physically. *v.t.* & *v.i.* to make an assault (upon). **—as·sault′er,** *n.*

**assault and battery,** in *law*, the carrying out of threatened physical harm.

**as·say** (ə-sā′, as′ā), *n.* [< L. *ex*, out + *agere*, to deal], 1. a testing. 2. the analysis of an ore, etc. to determine the nature and proportion of the ingredients. *v.t.* (ə-sā′), to make an assay of; test. **—as·say′er,** *n.*

**as·sem·blage** (ə-sem′blij), *n.* 1. an assembling. 2. a group of persons or things. 3. a fitting together of parts.

**as·sem·ble** (ə-sem′b'l), *v.t.* & *v.i.* [-BLED, -BLING], [< L. *ad-*, to + *simul*, together], 1. to gather into a group; collect. 2. to put or fit together. **—as·sem′bler,** *n.*

**as·sem′bly,** *n.* [*pl.* -BLIES], 1. an assembling. 2. a group of persons gathered together. 3. [A-], a legislative body. 4. a fitting together of parts to form a unit.

**assembly line,** an arrangement whereby workers in succession perform special operations on the work as it moves along.

**as·sent** (ə-sent′), *v.i.* [< L. *ad-*, to + *sentire*, feel], 1. to consent. 2. to agree. *n.* 1. consent. 2. agreement.

**as·sert** (ə-sũrt′), *v.t.* [< L. *ad-*, to + *serere*, join], 1. to declare; affirm. 2. to maintain or defend (rights, etc.). **—assert oneself,** 1. to insist on one's rights. 2. to thrust oneself forward. **—as·sert′er, as·ser′tor,** *n.*

**as·ser·tion** (ə-sũr′shən), *n.* 1. an asserting. 2. a positive statement.

**as·ser′tive** (-tiv), *adj.* 1. positive. 2. unduly confident or insistent.

**as·sess** (ə-ses′), *v.t.* [< L. *ad-*, to + *sedere*, sit], 1. to set an estimated value on (property, etc.) for taxation. 2. to set the amount of (damages, a fine, etc.). 3. to impose a fine, tax, etc. on. **—as·ses′sor,** *n.*

**as·set** (as′et), *n.* [< L. *ad-*, to + *sedere*, sit], 1. anything owned that has value. 2. a desirable thing: as, charm is an *asset*. 3. *pl.* all the property, accounts receivable, cash, etc. of a person or business. 4. *pl.* in *law*, property usable to pay debts.

**as·sev·er·ate** (ə-sev′ə-rāt′), *v.t.* [-ATED, -ATING], [< L. *ad-*, to + *severus*, severe], to state positively. **—as·sev′er·a′tion,** *n.*

**as·sid·u·ous** (ə-sij′o͞o-əs), *adj.* [< L. *ad-*, to + *sedere*, sit], diligent; persevering; careful. **—as·si·du·i·ty** (as′ə-dū′ə-ti) [*pl.* -TIES], *n.*

**as·sign** (ə-sīn′), *v.t.* [< L. *ad-*, to + *signum*, a mark], 1. to set or fix for a specific purpose; designate. 2. to appoint, as to a duty. 3. to give out as a task; allot. 4. in *law*, to transfer, as a right, property, etc. **—as·sign′a·ble,** *adj.* **—as·sign′er, as·sign′or,** *n.*

**as·sig·na·tion** (as′ig-nā′shən), *n.* 1. an assignment. 2. an appointment to meet, esp. one made secretly by lovers.

**as·sign·ment** (ə-sīn′mənt), *n.* 1. an assigning or being assigned. 2. anything assigned.

**as·sim·i·late** (ə-sim′'l-āt′), *v.t.* [-LATED, -LATING], [< L. *ad-*, to + *similis*, like], 1. to absorb and incorporate as part of itself; digest. 2. to make like or alike. *v.i.* 1. to become like. 2. to be absorbed and incorporated. **—as·sim′i·la′tion,** *n.*

**as·sist** (ə-sist′), *v.t.* & *v.i.* [< L. *ad-*, to + *stare*, to stand], to help; aid. *n.* an instance or act of helping.

**as·sist′ance** (-əns), *n.* help; aid.

**as·sist′ant,** *adj.* assisting. *n.* a helper.

**as·siz·es** (ə-sīz′iz), *n.pl.* [see ASSESS], 1. court sessions held periodically in each county of England. 2. the time or place of these.

**as·so·ci·ate** (ə-sō′shi-āt′), *v.t.* [-ATED, -AT-

ING], [< L. *ad-*, to + *socius*, companion], 1. to connect; combine; join. 2. to bring into relationship as partner, etc. 3. to connect in the mind. ***v.i.*** to unite or join (*with*) as a partner, friend, etc. ***n.*** (-it), 1. a partner, colleague, friend, etc. 2. anything joined with another. ***adj.*** (-it), 1. united by the same interests, purposes, etc. 2. having secondary status or privileges.

**as·so'ci·a'tion** (-si-ā'shən), ***n.*** 1. an associating or being associated. 2. fellowship; partnership. 3. an organization of persons having common purposes, etc.; society. 4. a connection between ideas, etc.

**association football,** soccer.

**as·so·nance** (as'ə-nəns), ***n.*** [< L. *ad-*, to + *sonare*, to sound], likeness of sound without actual rhyme. **—as'so·nant,** ***adj. & n.***

**as·sort** (ə-sôrt'), ***v.t.*** [< L. *ad-*, to + *sors*, lot], to separate into classes according to kind; classify. ***v.i.*** to harmonize (*with*).

**as·sort'ed,** ***adj.*** 1. various; miscellaneous. 2. classified. 3. matched.

**as·sort'ment,** ***n.*** 1. classification. 2. a miscellaneous collection; variety.

**asst.,** assistant.

**as·suage** (ə-swāj'), ***v.t.*** [-SUAGED, -SUAGING], [< L. *ad*, to + *suavis*, sweet], 1. to lessen (pain, etc.); allay; calm. 2. to satisfy or quench (thirst, etc.). **—as·suage'ment,** ***n.***

**as·sume** (ə-sōōm', -sūm'), ***v.t.*** [-SUMED, -SUMING], [< L. *ad-*, to + *sumere*, take], 1. to take on (the appearance, role, etc. of). 2. to seize; usurp. 3. to undertake. 4. to take for granted; suppose. 5. to feign.

**as·sum'ing,** ***adj.*** presumptuous.

**as·sump·tion** (ə-sump'shən), ***n.*** 1. [A-], in the *R.C. Church*, *a)* the ascent of the Virgin Mary into heaven. *b)* the festival celebrating this (Aug. 15). 2. an assuming. 3. a supposition. 4. presumption.

**as·sur·ance** (ə-shoor'əns), ***n.*** 1. an assuring or being assured. 2. sureness; confidence. 3. promise, guarantee, etc. 4. self-confidence. 5. [Brit.], insurance.

**as·sure** (ə-shoor'), ***v.t.*** [-SURED, -SURING], [< L. *ad*, to + *securus*, secure], 1. to make (a person) sure of something; convince. 2. to give confidence to. 3. to promise confidently. 4. to guarantee. 5. to insure.

**as·sured',** ***adj.*** 1. sure; guaranteed. 2. confident. **—as·sur·ed·ly** (ə-shoor'id-li), ***adv.***

**As·tar·te** (as-tär'ti), ***n.*** the Phoenician goddess of fertility and sexual love.

**as·ter** (as'tēr), ***n.*** [< Gr. *astēr*, star], any of several plants of the composite family with variously colored flowers like daisies.

**as·ter·isk** (as'tēr-isk), ***n.*** [< Gr. dim. of *astēr*, star], a starlike sign (*) used in printing to mark footnotes, etc.

**a·stern** (ə-stūrn'), ***adj. & adv.*** 1. behind a ship. 2. at or toward the rear. 3. backward.

**as·ter·oid** (as'tēr-oid'), ***n.*** [see ASTER & -OID], any of the small planets between Mars and Jupiter. **—as'ter·oid'al,** ***adj.***

**asth·ma** (az'mə), ***n.*** [Gr. < *azein*, breathe hard], a chronic disorder characterized by wheezing, coughing, difficult breathing, etc. **—asth·mat'ic** (-mat'ik), ***adj.***

**a·stig·ma·tism** (ə-stig'mə-tiz'm), ***n.*** [< Gr. *a-*, without + *stigma*, a mark; + *-ism*], a defect of a lens or the eyes that prevents light rays from meeting in a single focal point. **—as·tig·mat·ic** (as'tig-mat'ik), ***adj.***

**a·stir** (ə-stūr'), ***adv. & adj.*** 1. in motion. 2. out of bed.

**as·ton·ish** (ə-ston'ish), ***v.t.*** [< L. *ex-*, out + *tonare*, to thunder], to fill with sudden surprise; amaze. **—as·ton'ish·ing,** ***adj.*** **—as·ton'ish·ing·ly,** ***adv.*** **—as·ton'ish·ment,** ***n.***

**as·tound** (ə-stound'), ***v.t.*** [see ASTONISH], to astonish greatly. **—as·tound'ing,** ***adj.***

**as·tra·khan** (as'trə-kən), ***n.*** the tightly curled wool pelt of lambs from Astrakhan.

**as·tral** (as'trəl), ***adj.*** [< Gr. *astron*, star], of, from, or like the stars.

**a·stray** (ə-strā'), ***adv. & adj.*** off the right path.

**a·stride** (ə-strīd'), ***adv. & adj.*** with a leg on either side. ***prep.*** with a leg on either side of.

**as·trin·gent** (ə-strin'jənt), ***adj.*** [< L. *ad-*, to + *stringere*, draw], 1. that contracts body tissue and blood vessels, checking blood flow. 2. harsh; severe. ***n.*** an astringent substance. **—as·trin'gen·cy,** ***n.***

**as·tro·labe** (as'trə-lāb'), ***n.*** [< Gr. *astron*, star + *lambanein*, take], an instrument formerly used to find the altitude of a star, etc.

**as·trol·o·gy** (ə-strol'ə-ji), ***n.*** [< Gr. *astron*, star + *legein*, speak], a pseudo science claiming to foretell the future by studying the supposed influence of the moon, sun, etc. on human affairs. **—as·trol'o·ger,** ***n.*** **—as·tro·log·i·cal** (as'trə-loj'i-k'l), ***adj.***

**as·tro·naut** (as'trə-nôt'), ***n.*** [< *astronautics*], one trained to make flights in space.

**as·tro·nau·tics** (as'trə-nô'tiks), ***n.pl.*** [construed as sing.], [< Fr.; ult. < Gr. *astron*, star + *nautēs*, sailor], the science dealing with travel through outer space.

**as·tro·nom·i·cal** (as'trə-nom'i-k'l), ***adj.*** 1. of astronomy. 2. huge, as numbers.

**as·tron·o·my** (ə-stron'ə-mi), ***n.*** [< Gr. *astron*, star + *nemein*, arrange], the science of the stars, planets, etc., their motion, size, etc. **—as·tron'o·mer** (-mēr), ***n.***

**as·tute** (ə-stōōt', -stūt'), ***adj.*** [< L. *astus*, craft], shrewd; keen. **—as·tute'ness,** ***n.***

**a·sun·der** (ə-sun'dēr), ***adv. & adj.*** [AS. *on sundran*], 1. in or into pieces. 2. in different directions; apart.

**a·sy·lum** (ə-sī'ləm), ***n.*** [< Gr. *a-*, without + *sylē*, right of seizure], 1. place of safety; refuge. 2. an institution for the care of the mentally ill, or the aged, poor, etc.

**a·sym·me·try** (ā-sim'i-tri, as-im'-), ***n.*** lack of symmetry. **—a'sym·met'ri·cal** (-met'ri-k'l), ***adj.*** **—a'sym·met'ri·cal·ly,** ***adv.***

**at** (at, ət), ***prep.*** [AS. *æt*], 1. on; in; near; by: as, *at* the office. 2. to or toward: as, look *at* her. 3. attending: as, *at* the party. 4. busy with: as, *at* work. 5. in the state or manner of: as, *at* war, *at* a trot. 6. because of: as, sad *at* his death. 7. in the amount, price, etc. of. 8. on or near the time of.

**at·a·brine** (at'ə-brin, -brēn'), ***n.*** [Gr. *atebrin*], a synthetic drug used in treating malaria: a trademark **(Atabrine).**

**at·a·vism** (at'ə-viz'm), ***n.*** [< L. *atavis*, ancestor], resemblance or reversion to a remote or primitive type. **—at'a·vis'tic,** ***adj.***

**a·tax·i·a** (ə-tak'si-ə), ***n.*** [< Gr. *a-*, not + *tassein*, arrange], inability to co-ordinate bodily or muscular movements: also **a·tax'y.**

**ate** (āt; *Brit.* et), pt. of **eat.**

**-ate,** [< L. *-atus*, pp. ending], a suffix meaning: 1. *to become, cause to become, produce, provide with*, as in *refrigerate, evaporate.* 2. *of* or *characteristic of, characterized by*, as in *passionate.*

**-ate,** [< L. *-atus*, noun ending], a suffix denoting *a function, official*, or *agent*, as in *potentate.*

**at·el·ier** (at''l-yā'), ***n.*** [Fr.], a studio.

**a·the·ism** (ā'thē-iz'm), ***n.*** [< Gr. *a-*, without + *theos*, god], the belief that there is no God. **—a'the·ist,** ***n.*** **—a'the·is'tic,** ***adj.***

**A·the·na** (ə-thē'nə), ***n.*** the Greek goddess of wisdom and skills: also **A·the'ne** (-nē).

**ath·e·nae·um, ath·e·ne·um** (ath'ə-nē'əm), ***n.*** 1. a literary or scientific club. 2. any library or reading room.

**a·thirst** (ə-thūrst'), ***adj.*** 1. [Archaic], thirsty. 2. eager.

**ath·lete** (ath'lēt), ***n.*** [< Gr. *athlon*, a prize], a person trained in exercises or games requiring physical strength, skill, etc.

**athlete's foot,** ringworm of the feet.

**ath·let'ic** (-let'ik), ***adj.*** 1. of or like athletes

or athletics. 2. physically strong, skillful, etc. —**ath·let'i·cal·ly,** ***adv.***

**ath·let'ics,** ***n.pl.*** [sometimes construed as sing.], athletic sports, games, etc.

**a·thwart** (ə-thwôrt'), ***prep.*** 1. across. 2. against. ***adv.*** crosswise.

**-atic,** [< Gr.], a suffix meaning *of, of the kind of,* as in *dramatic.*

**a·tilt** (ə-tilt'), ***adj. & adv.*** tilted.

**a·tin·gle** (ə-tiŋ'g'l), ***adj.*** tingling.

**-ation,** [< Fr. or L.], a suffix meaning: 1. *a —ing* or *being —ed,* as in *activation.* 2. *a thing that is —ed,* as in *quotation.*

**-ative,** [< Fr. or L.], a suffix meaning *of, like,* or *relating to,* as in *correlative.*

**At·lan·tis** (at-lan'tis), ***n.*** a legendary submerged continent in the Atlantic.

**At·las** (at'ləs), ***n.*** 1. in *Gr. myth.,* a giant whose shoulders supported the heavens. 2. [a-], a book of maps.

**at·mos·phere** (at'məs-fêr'), ***n.*** [< Gr. *atmos,* vapor + *sphaira,* sphere], 1. all the air surrounding the earth. 2. social environment. 3. a general tone or effect. 4. a unit of pressure equal to 14.69 pounds per square inch. —**at'mos·pher'ic** (-fer'ik), ***adj.***

**at·oll** (at'ôl, ə-tol'), ***n.*** [? < Malayalam], a coral island surrounding a lagoon.

**at·om** (at'əm), ***n.*** [< Gr. *atomos,* uncut], 1. a tiny particle; jot. 2. in *chem. & physics,* any of the smallest particles of an element that form compounds with similar particles of other elements.

**at'om·bomb',** ***n.*** an atomic bomb: also **atom bomb.** ***v.t.*** to attack with such bombs.

**a·tom·ic** (ə-tom'ik), ***adj.*** 1. of an atom or atoms. 2. of atomic energy. 3. tiny. Also **a·tom'i·cal.** —**a·tom'i·cal·ly,** ***adv.***

**atomic bomb,** a very destructive bomb, whose immense power derives from a chain reaction of nuclear fission.

**atomic energy,** the energy released from an atom in nuclear reactions, esp. in nuclear fission and nuclear fusion.

**atomic theory,** the theory that all material objects and substances are composed of atoms.

**at·om·ize** (at'əm-īz'), ***v.t.*** [-IZED, -IZING], 1. to separate into atoms. 2. to reduce a liquid to a fine spray.

**at·om·iz·er** (at'əm-īz'ẽr), ***n.*** a device for breaking a liquid, as a perfume, into tiny particles and spraying these out.

**a·to·nal·i·ty** (ā'tō-nal'ə-ti), ***n.*** in *music,* lack of tonality through intentional disregard of key. —**a·ton·al** (ā-tōn''l), ***adj.***

**a·tone** (ə-tōn'), ***v.i.*** [ATONED, ATONING], [< *atonement*], to make amends (*for* wrongdoing, etc.). —**a·ton'er,** ***n.***

**a·tone'ment,** ***n.*** [*at* + *one* + *-ment*], 1. an atoning. 2. amends; expiation. 3. [A-], in *theology,* the redeeming of mankind through Jesus' death.

**a·top** (ə-top'), ***adj. & adv.*** on the top; at the top. ***prep.*** on the top of.

**-atory,** [< L.], a suffix meaning *of, characterized by,* as in *exclamatory.*

**a·tro·cious** (ə-trō'shəs), ***adj.*** [< L. *atrox,* fierce; + *-ious*], 1. very cruel, evil, etc. 2. [Colloq.], in bad taste.

**a·troc·i·ty** (ə-tros'ə-ti), ***n.*** [*pl.* -TIES], 1. atrocious behavior or act. 2. [Colloq.], a thing in bad taste.

**at·ro·phy** (at'rə-fi), ***n.*** [< Gr. *a-,* not + *trephein,* nourish], a wasting away or failure to grow, due to poor nutrition. ***v.i.*** [-PHIED, -PHYING], to waste away or fail to grow.

**at·ro·pine** (at'rə-pēn', -pin), ***n.*** [< Gr. *Atropos,* one of the Fates; + *-ine*], a poisonous alkaloid obtained from belladonna, used to relieve spasms: also **at'ro·pin** (-pin).

**at·tach** (ə-tach'), ***v.t.*** [< OFr. *a-,* to + *tach,* a nail], 1. to fasten by tying, etc. 2. to join (often used reflexively). 3. to connect by ties of affection, etc. 4. to affix, as a signature. 5. to ascribe (with *to*). 6. in *law,* to take (property, etc.) by writ. ***v.i.*** to be joined; belong. —**at·tach'a·ble,** ***adj.***

**at·ta·ché** (at'ə-shā', ə-tash'ā), ***n.*** [Fr.; see ATTACH], a member of the diplomatic staff of an ambassador. —**at'ta·ché'ship,** ***n.***

**at·tach'ment,** ***n.*** 1. an attaching or being attached. 2. anything that attaches; fastening. 3. devotion. 4. anything attached. 5. an accessory for an electrical appliance, etc. 6. in *law,* a taking of a person, property, etc. into custody.

**at·tack** (ə-tak'), ***v.t.*** [< It.; akin to *attach*], 1. to use force against in order to harm. 2. to speak or write against. 3. to undertake vigorously. 4. to begin acting upon harmfully. ***v.i.*** to make an assault. ***n.*** 1. an attacking. 2. an onset of a disease.

**at·tain** (ə-tān'), ***v.t.*** [< L. *ad-,* to + *tangere,* to touch], 1. to gain; accomplish; achieve. 2. to arrive at. —**at·tain'a·ble,** ***adj.***

**at·tain·der** (ə-tān'dẽr), ***n.*** [< OFr. *ataindre,* to convict], loss of civil rights, property, etc. of one sentenced to death or outlawed.

**at·tain'ment,** ***n.*** 1. an attaining or being attained. 2. anything attained, as a skill.

**at·taint** (ə-tānt'), ***v.t.*** 1. to convict of crime punishable by attainder. 2. to disgrace; dishonor. ***n.*** an attainder.

**at·tar** (at'ẽr), ***n.*** [< Ar. *'itr,* perfume], a perfume made from flower petals.

**at·tempt** (ə-tempt'), ***v.t.*** [< L. *ad-,* to + *temptare,* try], to try to do, get, etc. ***n.*** 1. a try. 2. an attack, as on a person's life.

**at·tend** (ə-tend'), ***v.t.*** [< L. *ad-,* to + *tendere,* stretch], 1. to take care of. 2. to go with. 3. to accompany as a result. 4. to be present at. ***v.i.*** 1. to pay attention. 2. to wait (*on* or *upon*). —**attend to,** 1. to apply oneself to. 2. to take care of. —**at·tend'er,** ***n.***

**at·tend'ance,** ***n.*** 1. an attending. 2. the number of persons attending.

**at·tend'ant,** ***adj.*** 1. attending or serving. 2. being present. 3. accompanying. ***n.*** one who attends or serves.

**at·ten·tion** (ə-ten'shən), ***n.*** 1. an attending; a giving heed. 2. the ability to give heed. 3. heed; notice. 4. *usually in pl.* act of courtesy. 5. the erect posture of soldiers ready for a command.

**at·ten'tive** (-tiv), ***adj.*** 1. paying attention. 2. courteous, devoted, etc.

**at·ten·u·ate** (ə-ten'ū-āt'), ***v.t.*** [-ATED, -ATING], [< L. *ad-,* to + *tenuis,* thin], 1. to make thin or slender. 2. to dilute. 3. to lessen or weaken. ***v.i.*** to become thin, weak, etc. ***adj.*** (-it), attenuated.

**at·test** (ə-test'), ***v.t.*** [< L. *ad-,* to + *testari,* bear witness], 1. to declare to be true or genuine. 2. to certify, as by oath. 3. to serve as proof of. ***v.i.*** to bear witness. —**at·tes·ta·tion** (at'es-tā'shən), ***n.***

**at·tic** (at'ik), ***n.*** [< Gr. *Attikos,* of Attica (ancient Gr. state): with reference to architectural style], the space or rooms just below the roof of a house; garret.

**at·tire** (ə-tīr'), ***v.t.*** [-TIRED, -TIRING], [< OFr. *a,* to + *tire,* order], to clothe; dress up. ***n.*** clothes; finery. —**at·tire'ment,** ***n.***

**at·ti·tude** (at'ə-tōōd', -tūd'), ***n.*** [see APT], 1. a bodily posture showing mood. 2. a manner showing one's disposition, opinion, etc. 3. one's disposition, etc.

**at·tor·ney** (ə-tũr'ni), ***n.*** [*pl.* -NEYS], [< OFr. *a-,* to + *torner,* to turn], a person legally empowered to act for another; esp., a lawyer: abbrev. **atty.**

**attorney at law,** a lawyer.

**attorney general,** [*pl.* ATTORNEYS GENERAL, ATTORNEY GENERALS], the chief law officer of a government.

**at·tract** (ə-trakt'), ***v.t.*** [< L. *ad-,* to + *trahere,* draw], 1. to draw to itself or one-

self. 2. to get the admiration, attention, etc. of; allure. *v.i.* to be attractive.
**at·trac·tion** (ə-trak′shən), *n.* 1. an attracting. 2. power of attracting. 3. charm; fascination. 4. anything that attracts. 5. in *physics*, the mutual action by which bodies, particles, etc. tend to cohere.
**at·trac′tive** (-tiv), *adj.* 1. that attracts. 2. pleasing, charming, pretty, etc. **—at·trac′tive·ly,** *adv.* **—at·trac′tive·ness,** *n.*
**at·tri·bute** (ə-trib′yoot), *v.t.* [-BUTED, -BUTING], [< L. *ad-*, to + *tribuere*, assign], to think of as belonging to; ascribe (*to*). *n.* (at′-rə-būt′), a characteristic or quality of a person or thing. **—at·trib′u·ta·ble,** *adj.* **—at·trib′u·ter,** *n.* **—at′tri·bu′tion,** *n.*
**at·trib·u·tive** (ə-trib′yoo-tiv), *adj.* 1. attributing. 2. preceding the noun it modifies: said of an adjective. *n.* an attributive word.
**at·tri·tion** (ə-trish′ən), *n.* [L. < *ad-*, to + *terere*, rub], a wearing away by friction.
**at·tune** (ə-tōōn′, -tūn′), *v.t.* [-TUNED, -TUNING], 1. to tune. 2. to bring into harmony.
**a·typ·i·cal** (ā-tip′i-k'l), *adj.* not typical.
**Au,** *aurum*, [L.], in *chem.*, gold.
**au·burn** (ô′bẽrn), *adj.* & *n.* [< L. *albus*, white; infl. by ME. *brun*, brown], reddish brown.
**auc·tion** (ôk′shən), *n.* [< L. *augere*, to increase], a public sale where items are sold to the highest bidders. *v.t.* to sell at auction.
**auc′tion·eer′** (-êr′), *n.* one who auctions things. *v.t.* to auction.
**au·da·cious** (ô-dā′shəs), *adj.* [< L. *audere*, to dare], 1. reckless; bold. 2. too bold; insolent. **—au·da′cious·ly,** *adv.*
**au·dac·i·ty** (ô-das′ə-ti), *n.* 1. bold courage; daring. 2. insolence; impudence. 3. [*pl.* -TIES], an audacious act, etc.
**au·di·ble** (ô′də-b'l), *adj.* [< L. *audire*, hear], loud enough to be heard. **—au′di·bil′i·ty, au′di·ble·ness,** *n.* **—au′di·bly,** *adv.*
**au·di·ence** (ô′di-əns), *n.* [< L. *audire*, hear], 1. those gathered to hear and see something. 2. all those reached by a radio or television program, book, etc. 3. the act of hearing. 4. a formal interview.
**au·di·o** (ô′di-ō′), *adj.* [L., I hear], in *electricity*, of frequencies corresponding to normally audible sound waves.
**au·dit** (ô′dit), *n.* [< L. *audire*, hear], an examination and adjustment of financial accounts. *v.t.* & *v.i.* to examine and check (accounts, etc.).
**au·di·tion** (ô-dish′ən), *n.* 1. the act or sense of hearing. 2. a hearing to try out an actor, etc. *v.t.* & *v.i.* to try out in an audition.
**au·di·tor** (ô′də-tẽr), *n.* 1. a hearer. 2. one who audits accounts.
**au·di·to·ri·um** (ô′də-tôr′i-əm), *n.* [*pl.* -RIUMS, -RIA (-ə)], 1. a room where an audience sits. 2. a building or hall for speeches, concerts, etc
**au·di·to·ry** (ô′də-tôr′i), *adj.* of hearing or the sense of hearing
**Au·ge·an** (ô-jē′ən), *adj.* in *Gr. legend*, of King Augeas or his filthy stable, which Hercules cleaned in one day.
**au·ger** (ô′gẽr), *n.* [< AS. *nafogar* < *nafu*, hub + *gar*, a spear], a tool for boring holes.
**aught** (ôt), *n.* [< AS. *a*, one + *wiht*, thing], 1. anything whatever. 2. a naught. *adv.* in any way.
**aug·ment** (ôg-ment′; *for n.*, ôg′ment), *v.t.* & *v.i.* [< L. *augere*, to increase], to make or become greater. *n.* an increase. **—aug·ment′a·ble,** *adj.* **—aug′men·ta′tion,** *n.*
**au gra·tin** (ō grä′t'n, gra′-), [Fr.], with a browned crust of grated cheese, etc.
**au·gur** (ô′gẽr), *n.* [L.; ? < *augere*, to increase], a fortuneteller; soothsayer. *v.t.* & *v.i.* 1. to foretell. 2. to be an omen (of).
**au·gu·ry** (ô′gyẽr-i), *n.* [*pl.* -RIES], 1. the rite of divination. 2. an omen.
**Au·gust** (ô′gəst), *n.* [L. < *Augustus*, Roman emperor], the eighth month of the year, having 31 days: abbrev. **Aug.**
**au·gust** (ô-gust′), *adj.* [L. < *augere*, to increase], inspiring awe; imposing.
**‡au jus** (ō′ zhū′), [Fr.], served in its natural juice or gravy: said of meat.
**auk** (ôk), *n.* [< ON. *alka*], any of various diving birds of northern seas, with webbed feet and short wings.
**auld** (ôld), *adj.* [Dial. & Scot.], old.
**auld lang syne** (ôld′ laŋ sīn′), [Scot., old long since], the good old days.
**aunt** (ant, änt), *n.* [< L. *amita*], 1. the sister of one's father or mother. 2. the wife of one's uncle. Also **aunt′ie, aunt′y.**
**au·ra** (ô′rə), *n.* [*pl.* -RAS, -RAE (-rē)], [Gr., air], 1. an invisible emanation. 2. an invisible atmosphere supposedly surrounding a person or thing. **—au′ral,** *adj.*
**au·ral** (ô′rəl), *adj.* [< L. *auris*, ear], of or received through the sense of hearing.
**au·re·ole** (ô′ri-ōl′), *n.* [< L. *aurum*, gold], 1. a halo. 2. a sun's corona.
**au·re·o·my·cin** (ô′ri-ō-mī′sin), *n.* [< L. *aureus*, golden + Gr. *mykēs*, fungus], an antibiotic effective against bacteria, etc.
**au re·voir** (ō′ rə-vwär′), [Fr.], good-by.
**au·ri·cle** (ô′ri-k'l), *n.* [< L. dim. of *auris*, ear], 1. the outer part of the ear 2. either of two upper chambers of the heart. 3. an earlike part. **—au′ri·cled,** *adj.*
**au·ric·u·lar** (ô-rik′yoo-lẽr), *adj.* 1. of the ear or the sense of hearing. 2. said into the ear. 3. ear-shaped. 4. of an auricle of the heart. **—au·ric′u·lar·ly,** *adv.*
**au·rif·er·ous** (ô-rif′ẽr-əs), *adj.* [< L. *aurum*, gold + *ferre*, to bear], bearing gold.
**Au·ro·ra** (ô-rôr′ə), *n.* 1. the Roman goddess of dawn. 2. [a-], [*pl.* -RAS, -RAE (-ē)], *a*) the dawn. *b*) any early period. **—au·ro′ral,** *adj.*
**aurora aus·tra·lis** (ô-strā′lis), [L. < *auster*, south wind], luminous bands seen in the night sky of the Southern Hemisphere.
**aurora bo·re·a·lis** (bôr′i-al′is), [L. < *boreas*, north wind], luminous bands seen in the night sky of the Northern Hemisphere.
**aus·pice** (ôs′pis), *n.* [*pl.* -PICES], [L. *auspicium*, omen], 1. an omen. 2. a prophecy, esp. when favorable. 3. *usually pl.* patronage.
**aus·pi·cious** (ôs-pish′əs), *adj.* 1. favorable; propitious. 2. successful.
**aus·tere** (ô-stêr′), *adj.* [< Gr. < *auos*, dry], 1. stern; harsh. 2. morally strict. 3. unadorned. 4. grave; sober. **—aus·tere′ly,** *adv.*
**aus·ter·i·ty** (ô-ster′ə-ti), *n.* [*pl.* -TIES], 1. sternness; harshness. 2. *in pl.* an austere habit or practice.
**au·tarch·y** (ô′tär-ki), *n.* [*pl.* -IES], [< Gr. *autos*, self + *archos*, ruler], 1. absolute rule; despotism. 2. a country under such rule. **—au·tar′chic, au·tar′chi·cal,** *adj.*
**au·then·tic** (ô-then′tik), *adj.* [< Gr. *authentēs*, autocrat], 1. authoritative; reliable. 2. genuine; real. **—au·then′ti·cal·ly.** *adv.*
**au·then′ti·cate′** (-ti-kāt′), *v.t.* [-CATED, -CATING], 1. to make valid. 2. to verify; prove to be genuine. **—au·then′ti·ca′tion,** *n.*
**au·then·tic·i·ty** (ô′then-tis′ə-ti), *n.* authoritativeness or genuineness.
**au·thor** (ô′thẽr), *n.* [< L. *augere*, to increase], 1. one who makes or originates something. 2. the writer (*of* a book, etc.). 3. one who writes books, etc. **—au′thor·ess,** *n.fem.*
**au·thor·i·tar·i·an** (ə-thôr′ə-târ′i-ən), *adj.* believing in or characterized by unquestioning obedience to authority rather than individual freedom. *n.* an authoritarian person. **—au·thor′i·tar′i·an·ism,** *n.*
**au·thor′i·ta′tive** (-tā′tiv), *adj.* 1. asserting authority; dictatorial. 2. having authority; official. 3. based on competent authority; reliable. **—au·thor′i·ta′tive·ly,** *adv.*

**au·thor·i·ty** (ə-thôr′ə-ti), *n.* [*pl.* -TIES], [see AUTHOR], 1. the power or right to give commands, take action, etc.; jurisdiction. 2. *pl.* government officials, etc. having this right. 3. influence resulting from knowledge, prestige, etc. 4. a person, writing, etc. cited in support of an opinion. 5. an expert.

**au·thor·ize** (ô′thə-rīz′), *v.t.* [-IZED, -IZING], 1. to give official approval to. 2. to give power or authority to; commission. 3. to justify. —**au′thor·i·za′tion,** *n.*

**au·thor·ship** (ô′thẽr-ship′), *n.* 1. the profession of a writer. 2. the origin (of a book, idea, etc.).

**au·to** (ô′tō), *n.* [*pl.* -TOS], [Colloq.], an automobile. —**au′to·ist,** *n.*

**auto-,** [< Gr. *autos*], a combining form meaning *self, self-propelled.*

**au·to·bi·og·ra·phy** (ô′tə-bī-og′rə-fi), *n.* [*pl.* -PHIES], [*auto-* + *bio-* + *-graphy*], the story of one's own life written by oneself. —**au′to·bi′o·graph′i·cal,** *adj.*

**auto court,** a motel.

**au·toc·ra·cy** (ô-tok′rə-si), *n.* [*pl.* -CIES], [see AUTOCRAT], government in which one person has supreme power.

**au·to·crat** (ô′tə-krat′), *n.* [< Gr. *autos*, self + *kratos*, power], 1. a ruler with supreme power. 2. any domineering person. —**au′to·crat′ic, au′to·crat′i·cal,** *adj.*

**au·to·gi·ro, au·to·gy·ro** (ô′tə-jī′rō), *n.* [*pl.* -ROS], [< *auto-* + Gr. *gyros*, circle], a propeller-driven aircraft supported in the air by another, horizontal propeller above the fuselage: a trademark **(Autogiro).**

**au·to·graph** (ô′tə-graf′, -gräf′), *n.* [< Gr. *autos*, self + *graphein*, write], a person's own signature or handwriting. *v.t.* to write one's signature on or in.

**au·to·in·tox·i·ca·tion** (ô′tō-in-tok′sə-kā′shən), *n.* [*auto-* + *intoxication*], poisoning by toxic substances formed within the body.

**au·to·mat** (ô′tə-mat′), *n.* [G.; see AUTOMATIC], a restaurant in which patrons get food from coin-operated compartments.

**au·to·mat·ic** (ô′tə-mat′ik), *adj.* [Gr. *automatos*, self-moving], 1. done without conscious thought or volition. 2. moving, operating, etc. by itself. *n.* an automatic rifle or pistol. —**au′to·mat′i·cal·ly,** *adv.*

**au·to·ma·tion** (ô′tə-mā′shən), *n.* a manufacturing system in which many or all of the processes are automatically performed or controlled, as by electronic devices.

**au·tom·a·ton** (ô-tom′ə-ton′, -tən), *n.* [*pl.* -TONS, -TA (-tə)], [see AUTOMATIC], 1. anything that can move or act of itself. 2. a person acting in a mechanical way.

**au·to·mo·bile** (ô′tə-mə-bēl′, ô′tə-mō′bēl), *n.* [*auto-* + *mobile*], a car propelled by an engine that is part of it, and meant for traveling on streets or roads.

**au·to·mo·tive** (ô′tə-mō′tiv), *adj.* [*auto-* + *motive*], 1. self-propelling. 2. having to do with automobiles.

**au·ton·o·my** (ô-ton′ə-mi), *n.* 1. self-government. 2. [*pl.* -MIES], any state that governs itself. —**au·ton′o·mous,** *adj.*

**au·top·sy** (ô′top-si), *n.* [*pl.* -SIES], [< Gr. *autos*, self + *opsis*, sight], an examination of a dead body to find the cause of death, etc.

**au·tumn** (ô′təm), *n.* [< L. *autumnus*], the season between summer and winter: also called *fall.* —**au·tum·nal** (ô-tum′n'l), *adj.*

**aux·il·ia·ry** (ôg-zil′yə-ri), *adj.* [< L. *augere*, to increase], 1. helping; assisting. 2. subsidiary. 3. additional. *n.* [*pl.* -RIES], an auxiliary person, group, thing, etc.

**auxiliary verb,** a verb that helps form tenses, moods, voices, etc. of other verbs, as *will* in "I will go."

**a·vail** (ə-vāl′), *v.i.* & *v.t.* [< L. *ad*, to + *valere*, be strong], to be of use, help, worth, or advantage (to). *n.* use or help; benefit. —**avail oneself of,** to take advantage of.

**a·vail′a·ble,** *adj.* 1. that can be used. 2. that can be got or had; handy. —**a·vail′a·bil′i·ty,** *n.* —**a·vail′a·bly,** *adv.*

**av·a·lanche** (av′ə-lanch′), *n.* [Fr. < L. *labi*, to slip], a large mass of loosened snow, earth, etc. sliding down a mountain.

**‡a·vant-garde** (ä′vän′gärd′), *n.* [Fr.], vanguard.

**av·a·rice** (av′ə-ris), *n.* [< L. *avere*, wish], greed for money. —**av′a·ri′cious** (-rish′əs), *adj.* —**av′a·ri′cious·ness,** *n.*

**a·vast** (ə-vast′), *interj.* [< D. *houd vast*, hold fast], in *naut. usage*, stop! cease!

**av·a·tar** (av′ə-tär′), *n.* [Sans. *avatāra*, descent], 1. in *Hinduism*, a god's coming to earth in bodily form. 2. an embodiment.

**a·vaunt** (ə-vônt′), *interj.* [< L. *ab*, from + *ante*, before], [Archaic], begone! go away!

**A·ve Ma·ri·a** (ä′vi mə-rē′ə), [L.], in the *R.C. Church*, 1. "Hail, Mary," the first words of a prayer. 2. this prayer.

**a·venge** (ə-venj′), *v.t.* & *v.i.* [AVENGED, AVENGING], [< L. *ad*, to + *vindicare*, avenge], 1. to get revenge for (an injury, etc.). 2. to take vengeance on behalf of, as for a wrong. —**a·veng′er,** *n.*

**a·ve·nue** (av′ə-nōō′, -nū′), *n.* [< L. *ad-*, to + *venire*, come], 1. a way of approach or departure. 2. a street, path, etc.: abbrev. **Ave., ave.**

**a·ver** (ə-vũr′), *v.t.* [AVERRED, AVERRING], [< L. *ad*, to + *verus*, true], 1. to declare to be true; assert. 2. in *law*, to prove; justify.

**av·er·age** (av′rij, -ẽr-ij), *n.* [< Fr. *avarie*, damage to ship; hence, equal sharing of the loss among the owners], 1. the result of dividing the sum of two or more quantities by the number of quantities. 2. the usual kind, amount, etc. *adj.* 1. constituting an average. 2. usual; normal. *v.t.* [-AGED, -AGING], 1. to calculate the average of. 2. to do, take, etc. on an average: as, to *average* six sales a day. 3. to divide proportionately among more than two. *v.i.* to be or amount to an average. —**on the average,** as an average quantity, rate, etc.

**a·verse** (ə-vũrs′), *adj.* [see AVERT], unwilling.

**a·ver·sion** (ə-vũr′zhən), *n.* 1. an averting. 2. intense or definite dislike. 3. the object disliked. 4. reluctance.

**a·vert** (ə-vũrt′), *v.t.* [< L. *ab-*, from + *vertere*, to turn], 1. to turn away or aside. 2. to prevent. —**a·vert′i·ble,** *adj.*

**a·vi·ar·y** (ā′vi-er′i), *n.* [*pl.* -IES], [< L. *avis*, bird], a large cage for keeping many birds.

**a·vi·a·tion** (ā′vi-ā′shən, av′i-), *n.* [see AVIARY], the art or science of flying airplanes.

**a′vi·a′tor,** *n.* an airplane pilot. —**a′vi·a′trix** (-triks), **a′vi·a′tress** (-tris), *n.fem.*

**av·id** (av′id), *adj.* [< L. *avere*, to desire], very eager or greedy. —**a·vid·i·ty** (ə-vid′ə-ti), *n.*

**av·o·ca·do** (av′ə-kä′dō, ä′və-), *n.* [*pl.* -DOS], [< Mex. Sp. < Aztec], 1. a thick-skinned, pear-shaped tropical fruit with yellow, buttery flesh. 2. the tree it grows on.

**av·o·ca·tion** (av′ə-kā′shən), *n.* [< L. *ab-*, away + *vocare*, call], work done in addition to regular work; hobby.

**a·void** (ə-void′), *v.t.* [< L. *ex*, out + *vuidier*, to empty], to keep away from; shun; shirk. —**a·void′a·ble,** *adj.* —**a·void′ance,** *n.*

**av·oir·du·pois** (av′ẽr-də-poiz′), *n.* [< OFr. *aveir de peis*, goods having weight], 1. an English and American system of weighing in which 16 oz. = 1 lb.: also **avoirdupois weight.** 2. [Colloq.], weight, esp. of a person.

**a·vouch** (ə-vouch′), *v.t.* [see ADVOCATE], 1. to guarantee. 2. to declare the truth of; affirm. *v.i.* to give assurance.

**a·vow** (ə-vou′), *v.t.* [see ADVOCATE], to declare openly; confess. —**a·vow′al,** *n.*

**aw** (ô), *interj.* a sound of protest, etc.

**a·wait** (ə-wāt'), *v.t.* [< OFr. *a-*, to + *waitier*, to watch], 1. to wait for; expect. 2. to be in store for.

**a·wake** (ə-wāk'), *v.t. & v.i.* [AWOKE or AWAKED, AWAKED or AWOKE, AWAKING], [< AS. *awac(i)an*], 1. to rouse from sleep; wake. 2. to rouse from inactivity. *adj.* 1. not asleep. 2. active; alert.

**a·wak·en** (ə-wāk'ən), *v.t. & v.i.* to awake.

**a·wak'en·ing,** *n. & adj.* (an) awaking.

**a·ward** (ə-wôrd'), *v.t.* [< OFr. *es-*, out + *garder*, to guard], 1. to give, as by legal decision. 2. to give as the result of judging; grant: as, to *award* a prize. *n.* 1. a decision, as by judges. 2. a prize.

**a·ware** (ə-wâr'), *adj.* [< AS. *wær*, cautious], conscious; knowing. **—a·ware'ness,** *n.*

**a·wash** (ə-wäsh', -wôsh'), *adv. & adj.* on a level so that water just washes over.

**a·way** (ə-wā'), *adv.* [< AS. *on*, on + *weg*, way], 1. from any given place: as, he ran *away*. 2. off; aside. 3. far: as, *away* behind. 4. from one's possession: as, give it *away*. 5. at once: as, fire *away*. 6. continuously: as, work *away* at it. *adj.* 1. absent; gone. 2. at a distance: as, a mile *away*. *interj.* begone! **—away with,** go, come, or take away. **—do away with,** to get rid of or kill.

**awe** (ô), *n.* [ON. *agi*], a mixed feeling of reverence, fear, and wonder. *v.t.* [AWED, AWING], to inspire awe in; fill with awe.

**a·weigh** (ə-wā'), *adj.* being weighed, or hoisted: said of an anchor.

**awe·some** (ô'səm), *adj.* full of or inspiring awe. **—awe'some·ness,** *n.*

**awe-struck** (ô'struk'), *adj.* filled with awe: also **awe'-strick'en** (-strik''n).

**aw·ful** (ô'fool), *adj.* 1. inspiring awe. 2. terrifying. 3. (ô'f'l), [Colloq.], very bad. *adv.* [Colloq.], very. **—aw'ful·ness,** *n.*

**aw·ful·ly** (ô'fool-i), *adv.* 1. in a way to inspire awe. 2. (ô'fli), [Colloq.], very.

**a·while** (ə-hwīl'), *adv.* for a short time.

**awk·ward** (ôk'wẽrd), *adj.* [< ON. *afug*, turned backward + Eng. *-ward*], 1. clumsy; bungling. 2. unwieldy: as, an *awkward* tool. 3. uncomfortable: as, an *awkward* pose. 4. embarrassing; inopportune. **—awk'ward·ly,** *adv.* **—awk'ward·ness,** *n.*

**awl** (ôl), *n.* [AS. *æl*], a small, pointed tool for making holes in wood, leather, etc.

**awn** (ôn), *n.* [ON. *ögn*], the bristly fibers on a head of barley, oats, etc.

**awn·ing** (ôn'iŋ), *n.* [? < MFr. *auvent*, window shade], a piece of canvas stretched on a frame before a window, etc. as a protection from sun or rain.

**a·woke** (ə-wōk'), pt. and occas. pp. of **awake.**

**A.W.O.L., a.w.o.l.** (*often* ā'wôl'), absent (or absence) without leave.

**a·wry** (ə-rī'), *adv. & adj.* [see A- (on) & WRY], 1. with a twist to a side; askew. 2. wrong; amiss: as, our plans went *awry*.

**ax, axe** (aks), *n.* [*pl.* AXES (ak'siz)], [AS. *æx*], a tool with a long handle and bladed head, for chopping wood, etc. *v.t.* [AXED, AXING], to trim with an ax. **—get the ax,** [Slang], to be discharged from one's job. **—have an ax to grind,** [Colloq.], to have a purpose of one's own to promote.

**ax·i·al** (ak'si-əl), *adj.* 1. of, like, or forming an axis. 2. around or along an axis.

**ax·i·om** (ak'si-əm), *n.* [< Gr. *axios*, worthy], 1. a maxim; truism. 2. an established principle or law. 3. a statement that needs no proof because its truth is obvious. **—ax'i·o·mat'ic,** *adj.* **—ax'i·o·mat'i·cal·ly,** *adv.*

**ax·is** (ak'sis), *n.* [*pl.* AXES (-sēz)], [L.], 1. a straight line about which an object rotates. 2. a central line around which the parts of a thing are regularly arranged. **—the Axis,** Germany, Italy, and Japan, aligned against the United Nations in World War II.

**ax·le** (ak's'l), *n.* [< ON. *oxull*], 1. a rod or spindle on or with which a wheel revolves. 2. the bar connecting two opposite wheels of a wagon, carriage, etc.: also **ax'le·tree'.**

**aye** (ā), *adv.* [ON. *ei*], [Archaic], always; ever: also sp. **ay.**

**aye** (ī), *adv.* [? < prec.], yes; yea. *n.* an affirmative vote or voter. Also sp. **ay.**

**a·zal·ea** (ə-zāl'yə), *n.* [< Gr. *azaleos*, dry: it thrives in dry soil], a shrub with variously colored, usually fragrant flowers.

**az·i·muth** (az'ə-məth), *n.* [< Ar. *al*, the + *samt*, way], in *astronomy*, etc., distance in angular degrees in a clockwise direction from the north point or, in the Southern Hemisphere, south point.

**Az·tec** (az'tek), *n.* 1. a member of a people who had an advanced civilization in Mexico before the Spanish conquest in 1519. 2. their language. *adj.* of the Aztecs.

**az·ure** (azh'ẽr, ā'zhẽr), *adj.* [< Per. *lāzhuward*, lapis lazuli], sky-blue. *n.* 1. sky blue. 2. [Poetic], the blue sky.

# B

**B, b** (bē), *n.* [*pl.* B's, b's, Bs, bs], the second letter of the English alphabet.

**B,** *n.* 1. in *chem.*, boron. 2. in *music*, the seventh tone in the scale of C major.

**B., b.,** 1. base. 2. bass. 3. bay. 4. born.

**Ba,** in *chem.*, barium.

**B.A.,** Bachelor of Arts: also **A.B.**

**baa** (bä), *v.i. & n.* [echoic], bleat.

**Ba·al** (bā'əl, bāl), *n.* [*pl.* BAALIM (-im), BAALS], 1. an ancient Semitic sun god. 2. a false god; idol. **—Ba'al·ism,** *n.*

**bab·bitt, Bab·bitt** (bab'it), *n.* [< the novel by Sinclair Lewis], a smug, conventional, anti-intellectual person eager for business success; etc. **—bab'bitt·ry, Bab'bitt·ry,** *n.*

**bab·ble** (bab''l), *v.i.* [-BLED, -BLING], [echoic], 1. to talk like a small child; prattle. 2. to talk unwisely or too much. 3. to murmur: as, a *babbling* brook. *v.t.* to say incoherently or foolishly. *n.* 1. confused, incoherent vocal sounds. 2. foolish talk. 3. a continuous murmur. **—bab'bler,** *n.*

**babe** (bāb), *n.* 1. a baby. 2. [Slang], a girl or young woman.

**Ba·bel** (bā'b'l, bab''l), *n.* 1. in the *Bible*, a city whose inhabitants God made talk in different languages, as a punishment. 2. [also b-], *a)* a confusion of voices, etc.; tumult. *b)* a place of such confusion.

**ba·boon** (ba-bōōn'), *n.* [OFr. *babuin*], a fierce ape of Africa and Asia, with a doglike snout, cheek pouches, and a short tail.

**ba·bush·ka** (bə-boosh'kə), *n.* [Russ., grandmother], a scarf worn on the head by women.

**ba·by** (bā'bi), *n.* [*pl.* -BIES], [ME. *babi*], 1. a very young child; infant. 2. one who behaves like an infant. 3. the youngest in a group. 4. [Slang], a girl or young woman. *adj.* 1. of or for an infant. 2. very young. 3. small of its kind. 4. childish. *v.t.* [-BIED, -BYING], to pamper; coddle. **—ba'by·hood',** *n.* **—ba'by·ish,** *adj.* **—ba'by-like',** *adj.*

**ba'by-sit',** *v.i.* [-SAT, -SITTING], to act as a baby sitter.

**baby sitter,** a person hired to care for children, as when the parents are away.

**bac·ca·lau·re·ate** (bak'ə-lô'ri-it), *n.* [see BACHELOR], 1. the degree of bachelor of

arts, bachelor of science, etc. 2. a sermon delivered at commencement.
**bac·cha·nal** (bak'ə-n'l), *n.* 1. a worshiper of Bacchus. 2. a drunken carouser. 3. a drunken orgy. —**bac'cha·na'li·an** (-nā'li-ən), *adj. & n.*
**Bac·chus** (bak'əs), *n.* the Greek and Roman god of wine and revelry.
**bach·e·lor** (bach'ə-lẽr, bach'lẽr), *n.* [< L. hyp. *baccalaris,* young fellow], 1. one who has received a baccalaureate degree. 2. an unmarried man. —**bach'e·lor·hood',** *n.*
**Bachelor of Arts** (or **Science,** etc.), 1. a degree given by a college or university to one who has completed a prescribed course in the arts or sciences. 2. one who has this degree.
**bach·e·lor's-but·ton** (bach'ə-lẽrz-but''n, bach'lẽrz-), *n.* any of several plants with flowers shaped like buttons; cornflower.
**ba·cil·lus** (bə-sil'əs), *n.* [*pl.* -LI (-ī)], [< L. *baculus,* a stick], 1. any of a genus of rod-shaped bacteria. 2. any of the bacteria.
**back** (bak), *n.* [AS. *bæc*], 1. the hind part of the body from the base of the neck to the end of the spine. 2. the backbone. 3. the rear part of anything. 4. the reverse. 5. in *football,* a player behind the front line. *adj.* 1. at the rear. 2. distant. 3. of or for the past: as, *back* pay. 4. backward. *adv.* 1. at, to, or toward the rear. 2. to or toward a former condition, time, etc. 3. in concealment. 4. in return: as, pay him *back.* *v.t.* 1. to move backward. 2. to support. 3. to bet on. 4. to provide or be a back for. *v.i.* to go backward.—**back and forth,** from side to side.—**back down,** [Colloq.], to withdraw an opinion, claim, etc. —**back out,** [Colloq.], 1. to withdraw from an enterprise. 2. to break a promise. —**go back on,** [Colloq.], 1. to back out. 2. to desert; fail. —**turn one's back on,** to desert; fail.
**back'bite'** (-bīt'), *v.t. & v.i.* [-BIT, -BITTEN or -BIT, -BITING], to slander (an absent person or persons). —**back'bit'ing,** *n.*
**back'bone',** *n.* 1. the spinal column. 2. a main support. 3. courage.—**back'boned',** *adj.*
**back'break'ing,** *adj.* very tiring.
**back'drop',** *n.* a curtain, often scenic, hung at the back of a stage.
**back'er,** *n.* 1. a patron; supporter. 2. one who bets on a contestant.
**back'field',** *n.* in *football,* the quarterback, two halfbacks, and fullback.
**back'fire',** *n.* a premature explosion in a cylinder, or an explosion in an exhaust or intake pipe, of a gasoline or oil engine. *v.i.* 1. to explode as a backfire. 2. to go awry: as, the plan *backfired.*
**back'gam'mon** (-gam'ən), *n.* [prob. *back* + *gammon,* a game], a game played by two people on a special board with pieces that are moved according to the throw of dice.
**back'ground',** *n.* 1. the distant part of a landscape, etc. 2. surroundings behind or subordinate to something. 3. the whole of one's study, experience, etc. 4. events leading up to something.
**back'hand',** *n.* a way of stroking, as in tennis, with a backhanded motion. *adj.* backhanded. *adv.* with a backhanded stroke.
**back'hand'ed,** *adj.* 1. performed with the back of the hand turned forward, as a stroke in tennis. 2. slanting up to the left: said of handwriting. 3. insincere; sarcastic.
**back'ing,** *n.* 1. something forming a back for support. 2. support given to a person or cause. 3. supporters.
**back'log'** (-lôg'), *n.* an accumulation or reserve. *v.i. & v.t.* [-LOGGED, -LOGGING], to accumulate in reserve.
**back'slide'** (-slīd'), *v.i.* [-SLID, -SLIDDEN or -SLID, -SLIDING], to slide backward in morals, religion, etc. —**back'slid'er,** *n.*
**back'stage',** *adv.* 1. in the wings or dressing rooms of a theater. 2. upstage.
**back talk,** [Colloq.], insolent retorts.
**back'track',** *v.i.* 1. to return by the same path. 2. to retreat.
**back'ward** (-wẽrd), *adv.* 1. toward the back. 2. with the back foremost. 3. in a way opposite to normal. 4. into the past. Also **back'wards.** *adj.* 1. turned toward the rear or in the opposite way. 2. reluctant; shy. 3. retarded; slow. —**back'ward·ness,** *n.*
**back'wa'ter,** *n.* 1. water moved or held back by a dam, tide, etc. 2. a place or condition considered stagnant, backward, etc. *adj.* stagnant; backward.
**back'woods',** *n.pl.* 1. heavily wooded, remote areas. 2. [Colloq.], any remote, thinly populated place. *adj.* of or like the backwoods. —**back'woods'man** [*pl.* -MEN], *n.*
**ba·con** (bā'kən), *n.* [< OHG. *bahho,* side of bacon], salted and smoked meat from the back or sides of a hog. —**bring home the bacon,** [Colloq.], to earn a living.
**bac·te·ri·a** (bak-têr'i-ə), *n.pl.* [*sing.* -RIUM (-əm)], [< Gr. dim. of *baktron,* staff], microorganisms which have no chlorophyll and multiply by simple division: some bacteria cause diseases, but others are necessary for fermentation, etc. —**bac·te'ri·al,** *adj.*
**bac·te·ri·cide** (bak-têr'ə-sīd'), *n.* an agent that destroys bacteria.
**bac'te'ri·ol'o·gy** (-i-ol'ə-ji), *n.* the science that deals with bacteria. —**bac'te'ri·o·log'i·cal** (-i-ə-loj'i-k'l), *adj.*—**bac'te'ri·ol'o·gist,** *n.*
**bad** (bad), *adj.* [WORSE (wũrs), WORST (wũrst)], [ME. *badde*], 1. not as it should be; not good. 2. unfit. 3. unfavorable: as, *bad* news. 4. rotted; spoiled. 5. incorrect; faulty. 6. wicked; immoral. 7. harmful; injurious. 8. severe: as, a *bad* storm. 9. ill; in pain. 10. sorry; distressed. 11. offensive: as, a *bad* smell. 12. in *law,* not valid. *adv.* [Colloq.], badly. *n.* anything that is bad. —**in bad,** [Colloq.], in trouble or disfavor.
**bad** (bad), archaic pt. of **bid.**
**bad blood,** a feeling of mutual enmity.
**bade** (bad), 1. pt. of **bid.** 2. alt. pt. of **bide.**
**badge** (baj), *n.* [ME. *bage*], 1. a device worn to show rank, membership, etc. 2. any distinctive sign, etc.
**badg·er** (baj'ẽr), *n.* [? < obs. *badger,* corn dealer], 1. a burrowing animal with a broad back and short legs. 2. its fur. *v.t.* to nag.
**bad·i·nage** (bad''n-ij, bad'i-näzh'), *n.* [Fr. < ML. *badare,* gape], playful, teasing talk; banter. *v.t.* [-NAGED, -NAGING], to tease.
**bad·lands** (bad'landz'), *n.pl.* any section of barren land where rapid erosion has cut the soil or soft rocks into strange shapes.
**bad'ly,** *adv.* 1. in a bad manner. 2. [Colloq.], very much; greatly.
**bad·min·ton** (bad'min-tən), *n.* [< *Badminton,* Eng. estate], a game in which a feathered cork (shuttlecock) is batted back and forth with rackets across a net.
**bad'-tem'pered,** *adj.* having a bad temper or cranky disposition; irritable.
**baf·fle** (baf''l), *v.t.* [-FLED, -FLING], [< ?], 1. to frustrate by puzzling; confound. 2. to hinder. *n.* a screen to deflect the flow of liquids, gases, etc. —**baf'fle·ment,** *n.* —**baf'fler,** *n.* —**baf'fling,** *adj.* —**baf'fling·ly,** *adv.*
**bag** (bag), *n.* [ON. *baggi*], 1. a container made of fabric, paper, etc., with an opening that can be closed. 2. a suitcase. 3. a purse. 4. game taken in hunting. 5. in *baseball,* a base. *v.t.* [BAGGED, BAGGING], 1. to make bulge. 2. to capture. 3. to kill in hunting. 4. [Slang], to get. *v.i.* 1. to swell. 2. to hang loosely. —**be left holding the bag,** [Colloq.], to be left to suffer the bad consequences. —**in the bag,** [Colloq.], certain; assured. —**bag'like,** *adj.*
**bag·a·telle** (bag'ə-tel'), *n.* [Fr.], a trifle.

**ba·gel** (bā′g'l), *n.* [Yid.], a small, doughnut-shaped bread roll.

**bag·gage** (bag′ij), *n.* [< ML. *baga*, leather bag], 1. the bags, etc. of a traveler; luggage. 2. a lively girl.

**bag·gy** (bag′i), *adj.* [-GIER, -GIEST], 1. puffed in a baglike way. 2. hanging loosely.

**bag′pipe′,** *n. often pl.* a shrill-toned musical instrument with a bag from which air is forced into reed pipes to produce the sound: played chiefly in Scotland.

**bah** (bä, ba), *interj.* an exclamation of contempt, scorn, or disgust.

**bail** (bāl), *n.* [< L. *bajulare*, bear a burden], 1. money deposited with the court to get an arrested person temporarily released. 2. such a release. 3. the person giving bail. *v.t.* to have (an arrested person) set free by giving bail. **—bail′a·ble,** *adj.*

**bail** (bāl), *n.* [< LL. hyp. *bajula*, vessel], a bucket for dipping up water from a boat. *v.i. & v.t.* to dip out (water) from (a boat). **—bail out,** to parachute from an aircraft.

**bail** (bāl), *n.* [ON. *beygla*, hoop], a hoop-shaped handle for a bucket, etc.

**bail·iff** (bāl′if), *n.* [< L. *bajulus*, porter], 1. a sheriff's assistant. 2. a court officer who has charge of prisoners and guards the jurors. 3. in England, a district administrative official. 4. a steward of an estate.

**bail·i·wick** (bāl′ə-wik′), *n.* [ME. *bailie*, bailiff + *wick* < AS. *wic*, village], 1. a bailiff's district. 2. one's special field of interest or authority.

**bairn** (bârn), *n.* [Scot.], a child.

**bait** (bāt), *v.t.* [ON. *beita*, make bite], 1. to set dogs on for sport: as, to *bait* bears. 2. to torment, esp. by verbal attacks. 3. to put food on (a hook or trap) as a lure for game. 4. to lure; entice. *n.* 1. food, etc. put on a hook or trap as a lure. 2. anything used as a lure; enticement. **—bait′er,** *n.*

**baize** (bāz), *n.* [< L. *badius*, brown], a coarse woolen cloth used on pool tables, etc.

**bake** (bāk), *v.t.* [BAKED, BAKING], [AS. *bacan*], 1. to cook (food) by dry heat, as in an oven. 2. to harden by heat, as pottery. *v.i.* 1. to bake bread, etc. 2. to become baked.

**ba·ke·lite** (bā′kə-līt′), *n.* [after L. H. *Baekeland* (1863-1944), Belgian chemist], a synthetic resin used like hard rubber, celluloid, etc.: a trademark **(Bakelite).**

**bak·er** (bāk′ẽr), *n.* one whose work or business is baking bread, etc.

**baker's dozen,** thirteen.

**bak′er·y,** *n.* [*pl.* -IES], a place where bread, pastries, etc. are baked or sold.

**bak′ing,** *n.* 1. the act of one who bakes. 2. the amount baked at a single time.

**baking powder,** a leavening agent containing baking soda and an acid substance.

**baking soda,** sodium bicarbonate, used as an antacid and, in baking, as a leaven.

**bak·sheesh, bak·shish** (bak′shēsh′), *n.* [< Hind. & Per. *bakhshidan*, give], in Turkey, Egypt, etc., a tip; gratuity.

**bal·a·lai·ka** (bal′ə-lī′kə), *n.* [Russ.], a Russian stringed instrument of the guitar family.

**bal·ance** (bal′əns), *n.* [< L. *bilanx*, with two scales], 1. an instrument for weighing, esp. one with two matched hanging scales. 2. a state of equilibrium in weight, force, etc. 3. bodily or mental equilibrium. 4. the harmonious proportion of elements in a design, etc. 5. a weight, force, etc. that counteracts another. 6. equality of debits and credits, or the difference between them. 7. a wheel that regulates the movement of a watch, etc.: also **balance wheel.** 8. [Colloq.], a remainder. *v.t.* [-ANCED, -ANCING], 1. to weigh as in a balance. 2. to compare as to relative value, etc. 3. to counterpoise or counteract; offset. 4. to put or keep in a state of equilibrium; poise. 5. to find the difference between, or to equalize, the debits and credits of (an account). *v.i.* 1. to be in equilibrium. 2. to be equal in value, weight, etc. 3. to have the credits and debits equal. **—in the balance,** not settled.

**balance sheet,** a statement showing the financial status of a business.

**bal·brig·gan** (bal-brig′ən), *n.* [after *Balbriggan*, Ireland], a knitted cotton material used for hosiery, underwear, etc.

**bal·co·ny** (bal′kə-ni), *n.* [*pl.* -NIES], [< It. < OHG. *balcho*, a beam], 1. a platform projecting from an upper story and enclosed by a railing. 2. in a theater, etc., a tier of seats projecting over the main floor.

**bald** (bôld), *adj.* [? < W. *bal*, white spot], 1. having white on the head, as some animals and birds. 2. lacking hair on the head. 3. lacking the natural covering. 4. plain.

**bal·der·dash** (bôl′dẽr-dash′), *n.* [< 16th-c. slang], nonsense.

**bale** (bāl), *n.* [< OHG. *balla*, ball], a large bundle, esp. a standardized quantity of goods, as raw cotton, compressed and bound. *v.t.* [BALED, BALING], to make into bales. **—bal′er,** *n.*

**bale** (bāl), *n.* [AS. *bealu*], [Poetic], 1. evil; harm. 2. sorrow; woe.

**bale·ful** (bāl′fəl), *adj.* deadly; harmful; evil.

**balk** (bôk), *n.* [AS. *balca*, ridge], 1. an obstruction; thwarting. 2. a blunder; error. 3. in *baseball*, an uncompleted pitch, entitling base runners to advance one base. *v.t.* to obstruct; thwart. *v.i.* to stop and refuse to move or act. **—balk′er,** *n.*

**Bal·kan** (bôl′kən), *adj.* of the Balkans, their people, etc.

**balk·y** (bôk′i), *adj.* [-IER, -IEST], balking or likely to balk, as a mule. **—balk′i·ness,** *n.*

**ball** (bôl), *n.* [ON. *böllr*], 1. any round object; sphere; globe. 2. a round or egg-shaped object used in various games. 3. any of several such games, esp. baseball. 4. a missile for a cannon, rifle, etc. 5. in *baseball*, a pitched ball that is not hit and is not a strike. *v.i. & v.t.* to form into a ball. **—ball up,** [Slang], to muddle; confuse. **—on the ball,** [Slang], alert; efficient.

**ball** (bôl), *n.* [< Fr. < Gr. *ballizein*, to dance], a formal social dance.

**bal·lad** (bal′əd), *n.* [Fr. *ballade*, dancing song], 1. a sentimental song with the same melody for each stanza. 2. a narrative song or poem, usually anonymous and characterized by simple words, short stanzas, and a refrain. **—bal′lad·eer′,** *n.* **—bal′lad·ry,** *n.*

**bal·last** (bal′əst), *n.* [< D. *bar*, bare + *last*, a load], 1. anything heavy carried in a ship or vehicle to give stability. 2. crushed rock or gravel, used in railroad beds, etc. *v.t.* to furnish with ballast.

**ball bearing,** 1. a bearing in which the parts turn on freely rolling metal balls. 2. one of these balls.

**bal·le·ri·na** (bal′ə-rē′nə), *n.* [It. < L.; see BALL (dance)], a woman ballet dancer.

**bal·let** (bal′ā, ba′lā′), *n.* [< Fr.; see BALL (dance)], 1. an intricate group dance using pantomime and conventionalized movements. 2. dancers of ballet.

**bal·lis·tic missile** (bə-lis′tik), a kind of long-range missile.

**bal·lis′tics** (-tiks), *n.pl.* [construed as sing.], the science dealing with the motion and impact of projectiles. **—bal·lis′tic,** *adj.*

**bal·loon** (bə-lo͞on′), *n.* [< Fr. < It. *balla*, ball], 1. a large, airtight bag that rises when filled with a gas lighter than air. 2. an airship with such a bag. 3. an inflatable rubber bag, used as a toy. *v.i.* to swell; expand. *adj.* like a balloon. **—bal·loon′ist,** *n.*

**bal·lot** (bal′ət), *n.* [< It. *balla*, ball], 1. a ticket, paper, etc. by which a vote is registered. 2. act or method of voting, as by ballots. 3. the total number of votes cast. 4. a list of candidates for office. *v.i.* to vote.

**ball point pen,** a fountain pen with a small ball bearing instead of a point.

**ball′room′,** *n.* a large room for dancing.

**bal·ly·hoo** (bal′i-hōō′), *n.* [< *Ballyhooly,* village in Ireland], [Colloq.], 1. loud talk; uproar. 2. loud or sensational advertising, etc. *v.t. & v.i.* [-HOOED, -HOOING], [Colloq.], to advertise or promote with ballyhoo.

**balm** (bäm), *n.* [< Gr. *balsamon*], 1. a fragrant, healing ointment or oil. 2. anything healing or soothing. 3. fragrance.

**balm′y,** *adj.* [-IER, -IEST], 1. soothing, fragrant, mild, etc. 2. [Slang], crazy; foolish.

**ba·lo·ney** (bə-lō′ni), *n.* [< *bologna*], 1. bologna. 2. [Slang], nonsense.

**bal·sa** (bôl′sə), *n.* [Sp.], 1. the very lightweight wood of a tropical American tree, used for rafts, etc. 2. the tree.

**bal·sam** (bôl′səm), *n.* [see BALM], 1. an aromatic resin obtained from certain trees. 2. any of various aromatic, resinous oils. 3. any of various trees yielding balsam.

**Bal·tic** (bôl′tik), *adj.* of or near the Baltic Sea.

**bal·us·ter** (bal′əs-tẽr), *n.* [< Gr. *balaustion,* flower of the wild pomegranate: from the shape], any of the small posts of a railing, as on a staircase.

**bal·us·trade** (bal′ə-strād′), *n.* a row of balusters supporting a rail.

**bam·boo** (bam-bōō′), *n.* [Malay *bambu*], a treelike tropical grass with hollow, jointed stems that are used for furniture, canes, etc.

**bam·boo·zle** (bam-bōō′z′l), *v.t.* [-ZLED, -ZLING], [? < *bombast*], [Colloq.], 1. to trick; cheat. 2. to confuse. —**bam·boo′zler,** *n.*

**ban** (ban), *v.t.* [BANNED, BANNING], [AS. *bannan,* summon], to prohibit; forbid. *n.* 1. a condemnation by church authorities. 2. a curse. 3. a formal or authoritative prohibition. 4. a sentence of outlawry.

**ba·nal** (bā′n′l, bə-nal′), *adj.* [Fr.; see BAN], trite; hackneyed. —**ba·nal′i·ty** [*pl.* -TIES], *n.*

**ba·nan·a** (bə-nan′ə), *n.* [Sp. & Port.], 1. a treelike tropical plant with large clusters of edible fruit. 2. the narrow, somewhat curved fruit, having a creamy flesh and a yellow or red skin.

**band** (band), *n.* [ON.], 1. something that binds or ties together, as a strip of wood, metal, rubber, etc. 2. a stripe. 3. a narrow strip of cloth used for decoration. 4. in *radio,* a range of broadcasting wave lengths. *v.t.* to put a band on or around.

**band** (band), *n.* [< Fr.; prob. < Goth. *bandwa,* a sign], 1. a group of people united for a common purpose. 2. a group of musicians playing together, esp. upon wind and percussion instruments. *v.i. & v.t.* to join (*together*) for some purpose.

**band·age** (ban′dij), *n.* [Fr. < *bande,* a strip], a strip of cloth used to bind or cover an injury. *v.t.* [-AGED, -AGING], to bind with a bandage. —**band′ag·er,** *n.*

**ban·dan·na, ban·dan·a** (ban-dan′ə), *n.* [Hind. *bāndhnū,* method of dyeing], a large, colored handkerchief, usually figured.

**band·box** (band′boks′), *n.* a light pasteboard box to hold hats, etc.

**ban·deau** (ban-dō′, ban′dō), *n.* [*pl.* -DEAUX (-dōz′, -dōz)], [Fr.], a narrow ribbon worn around the head.

**ban·dit** (ban′dit), *n.* [< It. *bandito*], a robber; highwayman. —**ban′dit·ry,** *n.*

**band′mas′ter,** *n.* the conductor of a band of musicians.

**ban·do·leer, ban·do·lier** (ban′də-lêr′), *n.* [< It. *banda,* a band], a broad shoulder belt with pockets for carrying ammunition, etc.

**band saw,** a saw made as an endless belt on pulleys.

**bands·man** (bandz′mən, banz′-), *n.* [*pl.* -MEN (-mən)], one of a band of musicians.

**band′stand′,** *n.* an outdoor, usually roofed platform for a band or orchestra.

**band′wag′on,** *n.* a wagon for the band to ride in, as in a parade. —**on the bandwagon,** [Colloq.], on the winning or popular side.

**ban·dy** (ban′di), *v.t.* [-DIED, -DYING], [Fr. *bander,* bandy at tennis], 1. to toss or pass back and forth. 2. to pass (gossip, etc.) carelessly. *adj.* [? < Fr. *bander,* bend], curved outward.

**ban′dy-leg′ged** (-leg′id, -legd′), *adj.* having bandy legs; bowlegged.

**bane** (bān), *n.* [AS. *bana,* slayer], 1. the cause of harm, death, etc. 2. deadly poison: obs. except in **ratsbane,** etc. —**bane′ful,** *adj.*

**bang** (baŋ), *v.t.* [< ON. *banga,* to pound], to hit, close, etc. hard and noisily. *v.i.* 1. to make a loud noise. 2. to hit noisily or violently. *n.* 1. a hard, noisy blow. 2. a loud, sudden noise. 3. [Slang], pleasure. *adv.* 1. noisily. 2. abruptly. —**bang up,** to damage.

**bang** (baŋ), *v.t.* [< dial. *bangled,* flapping], to cut (hair) short and straight. *n. pl.* banged hair worn across the forehead.

**ban·gle** (baŋ′g′l), *n.* [Hind. *bangrī*], a decorative bracelet or anklet.

**ban·ish** (ban′ish), *v.t.* [< ML. *bannum,* a ban], 1. to exile. 2. to send or put away.

**ban·is·ter** (ban′is-tẽr), *n.* [< *baluster*], 1. a baluster. 2. *pl.* a balustrade.

**ban·jo** (ban′jō), *n.* [*pl.* -JOS, -JOES], [ult. < Gr. *pandoura,* musical instrument], a stringed musical instrument having a circular body covered with taut skin.

**bank** (baŋk), *n.* [ult. < OHG. *bank,* a (money changer's) bench], 1. an establishment for receiving or lending money. 2. any fund held in reserve. *v.t. & v.i.* to deposit (money) in a bank. —**bank on,** [Colloq.], to rely on.

**bank** (baŋk), *n.* [? < ON. *bakki*], 1. a long mound or heap. 2. a steep slope. 3. a stretch of rising land at the edge of a river, etc. 4. a shallow place, as in a sea. 5. the sloping of an airplane laterally on a turn. *v.t.* 1. to cover (a fire) with ashes and fuel so that it will burn longer. 2. to pile up so as to form a bank. 3. to slope (a curve in the road, etc.). 4. to slope (an airplane) laterally on a turn. 5. to cause (a billiard ball) to recoil from a cushion.

**bank** (baŋk), *n.* [< OHG. *bank,* bench], 1. a row of oars. 2. a row or tier, as of keys in a keyboard. *v.t.* to arrange in a bank.

**bank′book′,** *n.* the book in which a depositor's account in a bank is recorded.

**bank′er,** *n.* a person or company that owns or manages a bank.

**bank note,** a promissory note issued by a bank: a form of paper money.

**bank·rupt** (baŋk′rupt), *n.* [< Fr. < It. *banca,* bench + *rotta,* broken], a person legally declared unable to pay his debts. *adj.* 1. legally declared a bankrupt. 2. lacking in some quality. *v.t.* to make bankrupt. —**bank′rupt·cy** (-si) [*pl.* -CIES], *n.*

**ban·ner** (ban′ẽr), *n.* [< Goth. *bandwa,* a sign], 1. a flag. 2. a headline extending across a newspaper page. *adj.* foremost.

**banns, bans** (banz), *n.pl.* [see BAN], the proclamation, usually made in church three times, of an intended marriage.

**ban·quet** (baŋ′kwit), *n.* [Fr. < *banc,* table], 1. a feast. 2. a formal dinner. *v.t.* to honor with a banquet. —**ban′quet·er,** *n.*

**ban·shee, ban·shie** (ban′shē), *n.* [< Ir. *bean,* woman + *sith,* fairy], in *Ir. & Scot. folklore,* a female spirit whose wailing warns of impending death.

**ban·tam** (ban′təm), *n.* [< *Bantam,* former province in Java], 1. [B-], any of several breeds of small fowl. 2. a small aggressive person. *adj.* like a bantam.

**ban′tam·weight′**, *n.* a boxer or wrestler weighing between 113 and 118 lbs.
**ban·ter** (ban′tẽr), *v.t.* [17th-c. slang], to tease playfully. *v.i.* to exchange banter (*with* someone). *n.* genial teasing. —**ban′ter·er**, *n.*
**ban·yan** (ban′yən), *n.* [ult. < Sans.], an East Indian fig tree whose branches take root and become trunks.
**bap·tism** (bap′tiz'm), *n.* [< Gr. *baptizein*, immerse], 1. the rite of admitting a person into a Christian church by dipping him in water or sprinkling water on him. 2. an initiating experience. —**bap·tis′mal** (-tiz′-m'l), *adj.*
**Bap′tist** (-tist), *n.* a member of a Protestant denomination practicing baptism by immersion: abbrev. **Bap., Bapt.**
**bap′tis·ter·y** (-tis-tri), *n.* [*pl.* -IES], a place, usually in a church, used for baptizing: also **bap′tist·ry** [*pl.* -RIES].
**bap·tize** (bap-tīz′, bap′tīz), *v.t.* [-TIZED, -TIZING], 1. to administer baptism to. 2. to initiate. 3. to christen. —**bap·tiz′er**, *n.*
**bar** (bär), *n.* [< LL. *barra*], 1. any long, narrow piece of wood, metal, etc., often used as a barrier, lever, etc. 2. an oblong piece, as of soap. 3. anything that obstructs or hinders. 4. a band or strip. 5. a law court, esp. that part, enclosed by a railing, where the lawyers sit. 6. lawyers collectively. 7. the legal profession. 8. a counter as for serving alcoholic drinks. 9. a place with such a counter. 10. in *music*, *a*) a vertical line dividing a staff into measures. *b*) a measure. *v.t.* [BARRED, BARRING], 1. to fasten as with a bar. 2. to obstruct; close. 3. to oppose; prevent. 4. to exclude. *prep.* excluding. —**cross the bar**, to die.
**barb** (bärb), *n.* [< L. *barba*, beard], 1. a beardlike growth. 2. a sharp point projecting backward from the main point of a fishhook, etc. *v.t.* to provide with a barb.
**bar·bar·i·an** (bär-bâr′i-ən), *n.* [see BARBAROUS], 1. a member of a people considered primitive, savage, etc. 2. a cruel person; brute. *adj.* uncivilized, cruel, etc. —**bar-bar′i·an·ism**, *n.*
**bar·bar′ic** (-bar′ik), *adj.* 1. primitive; uncivilized. 2. wild, crude, etc.
**bar·bar·ism** (bär′bə-riz'm), *n.* 1. the state of being primitive or uncivilized. 2. a barbarous act, custom, etc.
**bar·bar·i·ty** (bär-bar′ə-ti), *n.* [*pl.* -TIES], 1. cruelty; brutality. 2. a cruel or brutal act. 3. a barbaric taste, manner, etc.
**bar·ba·rous** (bär′bə-rəs), *adj.* [< Gr. *barbaros*, foreign], 1. uncivilized. 2. crude, coarse, etc. 3. cruel; brutal.
**bar·be·cue** (bär′bə-kū′), *n.* [< Sp. < Haitian *barbacoa*, framework], 1. a hog, steer, etc. roasted whole over an open fire. 2. an entertainment, usually outdoors, at which such meat is served. *v.t.* [-CUED, -CUING], 1. to roast (an animal) whole. 2. to broil (meat or fish), often in a highly seasoned sauce **(barbecue sauce)**.
**barbed wire**, wire with sharp points along it, used for barriers: also **barb′wire′**, *n.*
**bar·ber** (bär′bẽr), *n.* [see BARB], a person whose work is cutting hair, shaving beards, etc. *v.t.* & *v.i.* to cut the hair (of), shave, etc.
**bar·ber·ry** (bär′ber′i), *n.* [*pl.* -RIES], [< ML. *barberis*], 1. a spiny shrub with sour, oblong, red berries. 2. the berry.
**bar·bi·tu·rate** (bär′bə-tyoor′it, bär-bich′-ẽr-it), *n.* [< Mod. L. *Usnea barbata*, lit., bearded moss], any of certain drugs used as sedatives, etc.
**bar·ca·role, bar·ca·rolle** (bär′kə-rōl′), *n.* [Fr. < It. *barca*, boat], 1. a song sung by Venetian gondoliers. 2. a piece of music imitating this.
**bard** (bärd), *n.* [Gael. & Ir. *bardh*], 1. an ancient Celtic poet. 2. a poet.
**bare** (bâr), *adj.* [AS. *bær*], 1. not covered or clothed; naked. 2. exposed; revealed. 3. without furnishings; empty. 4. simple; plain. 5. mere: as, *bare* needs. *v.t.* [BARED, BARING], to make bare; uncover. —**lay bare**, to uncover; expose. —**bare′ness**, *n.*
**bare′back′**, *adv.* & *adj.* on a horse with no saddle. —**bare′backed′**, *adj.*
**bare′faced′**, *adj.* 1. with the face uncovered. 2. open; shameless.
**bare′foot′**, *adj.* & *adv.* without shoes and stockings: also **bare′foot′ed.**
**bare′head′ed**, *adj.* & *adv.* without a hat, etc. on the head. —**bare′head′ed·ness**, *n.*
**bare′ly**, *adv.* 1. openly. 2. nakedly. 3. only just; scarcely.
**bar·gain** (bär′g'n), *n.* [< OFr. *bargaignier*, haggle], 1. an agreement to exchange, sell, or buy goods. 2. any mutual agreement. 3. something sold at a price favorable to the buyer. *v.i.* 1. to haggle. 2. to make a bargain (*with*). —**bargain for**, to expect; count on. —**into the bargain**, in addition; besides. —**strike a bargain**, to agree on terms.
**barge** (bärj), *n.* [< LL. *barga*], 1. a large, flat-bottomed boat for carrying freight on rivers, etc. 2. any similar boat, as a houseboat. *v.i.* [BARGED, BARGING], 1. to move slowly and clumsily. 2. [Colloq.], to enter rudely or abruptly (*into*).
**bar·i·tone** (bar′ə-tōn′), *n.* [< Gr. *barys*, deep + *tonos*, tone], 1. a male singing voice with a range between tenor and bass. 2. a singer or a brass-wind instrument having such a range. 3. a part for a baritone.
**bar·i·um** (bâr′i-əm), *n.* [< Gr. *barys*, heavy], a silvery-white, metallic chemical element: symbol, Ba.
**bark** (bärk), *n.* [ON. *börkr*], the outside covering of trees and some plants. *v.t.* 1. to take the bark off (a tree, etc.). 2. [Colloq.], to scrape; skin: as, he *barked* his knees.
**bark** (bärk), *v.i.* [AS. *beorcan*], 1. to make the sharp, abrupt cry of a dog or a similar sound. 2. to speak sharply; snap. *n.* the characteristic cry of a dog or any noise like this. —**bark up the wrong tree**, to attack or pursue the wrong thing.
**bark** (bärk), *n.* [< L. *barca*], a sailing vessel with its two forward masts square-rigged and its rear mast rigged fore-and-aft.
**bark′er**, *n.* one who attracts customers to a side show, etc. by loud talking.
**bar·ley** (bär′li), *n.* [< AS. *bere*], 1. a cereal grass. 2. its seed or grain.
**bar′maid′**, *n.* a woman bartender.
**barn** (bärn), *n.* [< AS. *bere*, barley + *ærn*, a building], a farm building for sheltering harvested crops, livestock, etc.
**bar·na·cle** (bär′nə-k'l), *n.* [Fr. *bernicle*], a shell-bearing sea animal that attaches itself to rocks, ship bottoms, etc.
**barn·storm** (bärn′stôrm′), *v.i.* to tour in small towns and rural districts, performing plays, making speeches, etc.
**barn swallow**, a swallow with a long, deeply forked tail: it usually nests in barns.
**barn′yard′**, *n.* the yard near a barn. *adj.* of, like, or fit for a barnyard.
**ba·rom·e·ter** (bə-rom′ə-tẽr), *n.* [< Gr. *baros*, weight; + *-meter*], 1. an instrument for measuring atmospheric pressure and thus forecasting weather. 2. anything that marks change. —**bar·o·met·ric** (bar′ə-met′-rik), *adj.*
**bar·on** (bar′ən), *n.* [< base of OHG. *baro*, a man], 1. a member of the lowest rank of British nobility. 2. a powerful capitalist; magnate. —**bar′on·ess**, *n.fem.* —**ba·ro·ni·al** (bə-rō′ni-əl), *adj.*
**bar′on·et** (-ə-nit, -net′), *n.* 1. a man holding the lowest hereditary British rank of honor, below a baron. 2. the title that shows this rank —**bar′on·et·cy** (-si) [*pl.* -CIES], *n.*

**ba·roque** (bə-rōk′), *adj.* [Fr.; Port. *barroco*, imperfect pearl], 1. of or like a style of art and architecture characterized by much ornamentation and curved rather than straight lines. 2. fantastically overdecorated. *n.* baroque style, art, etc.

**bar·racks** (bar′əks), *n.pl.* [< LL. hyp. *barrum*, clay], 1. a building or buildings for housing soldiers. 2. any large, plain building.

**bar·ra·cu·da** (bar′ə-kōō′də), *n.* [*pl.* -DA, -DAS], [Sp.], a ferocious, edible, pikelike, tropical fish.

**bar·rage** (bə-räzh′), *n.* [Fr. < *barrer*, to stop], 1. a curtain of artillery fire for defensive or offensive purposes. 2. any prolonged attack. *v.t. & v.i.* [-RAGED, -RAGING], to lay down a barrage (against).

**barred** (bärd), *adj.* 1. having bars or stripes. 2. closed off with bars. 3. not allowed.

**bar·rel** (bar′əl), *n.* [? < LL. *barra*, a stave], 1. a large, wooden, cylindrical container with slightly bulging sides and flat ends. 2. the capacity of a standard barrel (31½ gals.). 3. any somewhat similar cylinder, as the straight tube of a gun. *v.t.* [-RELED or -RELLED, -RELING or -RELLING], to put or pack in barrels.

**barrel organ,** a mechanical musical instrument played by turning a crank.

**bar·ren** (bar′ən), *adj.* [< OFr. *baraigne*], 1. that cannot bear offspring; sterile. 2. without vegetation; unfruitful. 3. unproductive; unprofitable. 4. boring; dull.

**bar·rette** (bə-ret′), *n.* a bar or clasp for holding a girl's or woman's hair in place.

**bar·ri·cade** (bar′ə-kād′; *also, for n.*, bar′ə-kād′), *n.* [Fr. < It. *barra*, a bar], a barrier, esp. one thrown up hastily for defense. *v.t.* [-CADED, -CADING], to block with a barricade.

**bar·ri·er** (bar′i-ēr), *n.* [see BAR], 1. an obstruction, as a fence, wall, etc. 2. anything that holds apart: as, shyness was a *barrier* between them. 3. a boundary or limitation.

**bar·ring** (bär′iŋ), *prep.* excepting.

**bar·ris·ter** (bar′is-tēr), *n.* [< *bar* (law court)], in England, a lawyer who pleads cases in court.

**bar′room′,** *n.* a room with a bar where alcoholic drinks are sold.

**bar·row** (bar′ō), *n.* [< AS. *beran*, to bear], 1. a traylike frame with two handles at each end, used for carrying loads. 2. a wheelbarrow.

**Bart.,** Baronet.

**bar′tend′er** (-ten′dēr), *n.* a man who mixes and serves alcoholic drinks at a bar.

**bar·ter** (bär′tēr), *v.i. & v.t.* [< ON. *baratta*], to trade by exchanging (goods) without money. *n.* a bartering. —**bar′ter·er,** *n.*

**bas·al** (bā′s'l), *adj.* 1. of or at the base. 2. basic; fundamental. —**bas′al·ly,** *adv.*

**basal metabolism,** the quantity of energy used by any organism at rest.

**ba·salt** (bə-sôlt′, bas′ôlt), *n.* [L. *basaltes*, dark marble], a hard, heavy, dark volcanic rock. —**ba·sal′tic,** *adj.*

**bas·cule bridge** (bas′kūl), [Fr. *bascule*, a seesaw], a drawbridge counterweighted so that it can be raised and lowered easily.

**base** (bās), *n.* [see BASIS], 1. the part of a thing that the thing rests on. 2. the most important element, as of a system. 3. the part of a word to which affixes are added. 4. a basis. 5. a goal or station in certain games, as baseball. 6. a headquarters or a source of supply. 7. in *chem.*, a substance that forms a salt when it reacts with an acid. *adj.* forming a base. *v.t.* [BASED, BASING], 1. to make a base for. 2. to put on a base; establish.

**base** (bās), *adj.* [< LL. *bassus*, low], 1. morally low; disgraceful. 2. menial; servile. 3. inferior in quality. 4. not precious: as, iron is a *base* metal. —**base′ly,** *adv.*

**base′ball′,** *n.* 1. a game played with ball and bat by two opposing teams on a field with four bases forming a diamond. 2. the ball used in this game.

**base′board′,** *n.* a molding covering a plaster wall where it meets the floor.

**base hit,** in *baseball*, a fair hit by which the batter gets safely on base.

**base′less,** *adj.* having no basis in fact.

**base′ment** (-mənt), *n.* the story of a building just below the main floor.

**bash** (bash), *v.t.* [echoic], [Colloq.], to strike with a violent blow.

**bash·ful** (bash′fəl), *adj.* [< ME. *baschen*, abash; + *-ful*], showing social timidity; shy.

**bas·ic** (bās′ik), *adj.* 1. of or at the base; fundamental. 2. in *chem.*, of, like, or containing a base; alkaline. —**bas′i·cal·ly,** *adv.*

**bas·il** (baz′'l), *n.* [< Gr. *basilikos*, royal], a fragrant herb of the mint family.

**ba·sil·i·ca** (bə-sil′i-kə), *n.* [*pl.* -CAS], [< Gr. *basilikē* (*stoa*), royal (portico)], an early Christian church with a nave and side aisles.

**bas·i·lisk** (bas′ə-lisk′), *n.* [< Gr. *basileus*, king], a mythical, lizardlike monster whose glance and breath were fatal.

**ba·sin** (bā′s'n), *n.* [< LL. *bacca*, water vessel], 1. a wide, shallow container for liquid. 2. its contents or capacity. 3. a sink. 4. a large hollow containing water, as a pond, bay, etc. 5. a river basin.

**ba·sis** (bā′sis), *n.* [*pl.* -SES (-sēz)], [Gr., a step], 1. a base or foundation. 2. a principal constituent. 3. a basic principle.

**bask** (bask, bäsk), *v.i. & v.t.* [ME. *basken*, to beat], to expose (oneself) pleasantly to warmth: often figuratively.

**bas·ket** (bas′kit, bäs′-), *n.* [< OCelt. *bascauda*, crock with woven pattern], 1. a container made of interwoven cane, wood strips, etc. 2. its contents. 3. in *basketball*, *a*) the goal, a basket-shaped net open at the bottom. *b*) a scoring toss of the ball through it. —**bas′ket·like′,** *adj.*

**bas′ket·ball′,** *n.* 1. a game played by two opposing teams on a floor with a raised basket at either end through which an inflated ball must be tossed. 2. the ball used.

**Basque** (bask), *n.* 1. a member of a people living in the W Pyrenees. 2. their language. *adj.* of the Basques or their language.

**bas-re·lief** (bä′ri-lēf′), *n.* [Fr. < It.; see BASS & RELIEF], sculpture in which the figures project a little from the background.

**bass** (bās), *n.* [< LL. *bassus*, low], 1. the lowest male singing voice. 2. the lowest part in music. 3. a singer or instrument having a very low range; specif., a bass viol. *adj.* of, for, or in the bass.

**bass** (bas), *n.* [*pl.* BASS, BASSES], [AS. *bears*], an edible perchlike fish found in fresh or salt water.

**bass clef** (bās), in *music*, a sign indicating that the notes on the staff are below middle C.

**bas·set** (bas′it), *n.* [< OFr. *bas*, low], a hunting hound with a long body, short legs, and long ears: also **basset hound.**

**bas·si·net** (bas′ə-net′), *n.* [see BASIN], a large basket used as a baby's bed, often hooded and on wheels.

**bas·so** (bas′ō), *n.* [*pl.* -SOS], [It.], a bass voice or singer. *adj.* bass.

**bas·soon** (ba-sōōn′, bə-), *n.* [< Fr.], a double-reed bass musical instrument of the wood-wind class. —**bas·soon′ist,** *n.*

**bass viol** (bās), the largest, deepest-toned instrument of the viol group.

**bast** (bast), *n.* [AS. *bæst*], plant fiber, used in ropes, mats, etc.

**bas·tard** (bas′tērd), *n.* [< Goth. *bansts*, barn], an illegitimate child. *adj.* 1. of illegitimate birth. 2. inferior, sham, etc. —**bas′tard·ly,** *adv.* —**bas′tar·dy,** *n.*

**bas′tard·ize′,** *v.t.* [-IZED, -IZING], 1. to make, declare, or show to be a bastard. 2. to misuse; corrupt.

**baste** (bāst), *v.t.* [BASTED, BASTING], [< OHG. *bastjan,* sew with bast], to sew temporarily with long, loose stitches. —**bast′er,** *n.*

**baste** (bāst), *v.t.* [BASTED, BASTING], [< OFr. *bassiner,* moisten], to moisten (roasting meat) with drippings, etc.

**bas·tille, bas·tile** (bas-tēl′), *n.* [Fr.; see BASTION], a prison. —**the Bastille,** a prison in Paris destroyed July 14, 1789.

**bas·tion** (bas′chən), *n.* [Fr. < Gmc. *bastjan,* make with bast, build], 1. a projection from a fortification. 2. any strong defense.

**bat** (bat), *n.* [AS. *batt*], 1. a stout club. 2. a club used in striking the ball in baseball and cricket. 3. [Colloq.], a blow or hit. *v.t.* [BATTED, BATTING], to strike as with a bat. *v.i.* to take a turn at batting. —**at bat,** having a turn at batting. —**go to bat for,** [Slang], to defend.

**bat** (bat), *n.* [< ON.], a nocturnal, mouse-like, flying mammal with membranous wings. —**blind as a bat,** entirely blind.

**bat** (bat), *v.t.* [BATTED, BATTING], [see BATTER (to beat)], [Colloq.], to wink. —**not bat an eye,** [Colloq.], not show surprise.

**batch** (bach), *n.* [AS. *bacan,* bake], 1. the amount (of bread, etc.) in one baking. 2. a quantity or number of anything taken made, etc. in one lot.

**bate** (bāt), *v.t. & v.i.* [BATED, BATING], [< *abate*], to reduce. —**with bated breath,** with the breath held in, as in fear, etc.

**bath** (bath, bäth), *n.* [AS. *bæth*], 1. a washing, esp. of the body, in water. 2. water, etc. for bathing or for soaking something. 3. a bathtub. 4. a bathroom.

**bathe** (bāth), *v.t.* [BATHED (bāthd), BATHING] [see BATH], 1. to put into a liquid; immerse. 2. to give a bath to. 3. to cover as with liquid: as, *bathed* in light. *v.i.* 1. to take a bath. 2. to soak oneself in something. —**bath·er** (bāth′ẽr), *n.*

**bath′house′,** *n.* 1. a building equipped for bathing. 2. a building used by bathers for changing clothes.

**bath′i·nette′** (-ə-net′), *n.* [after *bassinet*], a portable folding bathtub for babies: a trademark **(Bathinette).**

**ba·thos** (bā′thos), *n.* [Gr., depth], 1. change from the exalted to the trivial. 2. false pathos. —**ba·thet·ic** (bə-thet′ik), *adj.*

**bath′robe′,** *n.* a loose-fitting robe worn to and from the bath, etc.

**bath′room′,** *n.* 1. a room to bathe in, etc. 2. a toilet.

**bath′tub′,** *n.* a tub to bathe in.

**bath·y·sphere** (bath′i-sfêr′), *n.* [< Gr. *bathys,* deep; + *sphere*], a round, watertight chamber with windows, from which men can study undersea life.

**ba·tiste** (ba-tēst′, bə-), *n.* [Fr. < supposed orig. maker, *Baptiste*], a fine cotton fabric.

**ba·ton** (ba-ton′), *n.* [< Fr. < LL. *bastum,* a stick], 1. a staff serving as a symbol of office. 2. a slender stick used in directing an orchestra, etc.

**bat·tal·ion** (bə-tal′yən), *n.* [see BATTLE], a tactical military unit, a subdivision of a regiment: it is made up of several companies.

**bat·ten** (bat′′n), *n.* [see BATON], 1. a sawed strip of wood. 2. a strip of wood put over a seam between boards as a fastening or covering. *v.t.* to fasten or supply with battens (with *down*).

**bat·ten** (bat′′n), *v.i.* [ON. *batna,* improve], to grow fat; thrive. *v.t.* to fatten up.

**bat·ter** (bat′ẽr), *v.t.* [< L. *battuere,* to beat], 1. to strike with blow after blow. 2. to injure by hard wear. *v.i.* to pound noisily.

**bat·ter** (bat′ẽr), *n.* in *baseball & cricket,* the player whose turn it is to bat.

**bat·ter** (bat′ẽr), *n.* [see BATTER (to beat)], a thin mixture of flour, milk, etc., for making cakes, waffles, etc.

**bat′ter·ing-ram′** (-ram′), *n.* an ancient military device having a heavy beam for battering down walls, etc.

**bat·ter·y** (bat′ẽr-i), *n.* [*pl.* -IES], [see BATTER (to beat)], 1. a battering; beating. 2. any set of devices arranged or used together. 3. in *baseball,* the pitcher and the catcher. 4. in *electricity,* a cell or group of cells storing an electrical charge and able to furnish a current. 5. in *law,* an illegal beating of another person: see **assault and battery.** 6. in *military science,* a set of artillery pieces, used together.

**bat·ting** (bat′iŋ), *n.* [see BAT (club)], cotton or wool fiber wadded in sheets.

**bat·tle** (bat′′l), *n.* [< L. *battuere,* to beat], 1. a large-scale fight between armed forces. 2. armed fighting. 3. any fight or conflict. *v.t. & v.i.* [-TLED, -TLING], to fight. —**give (or do) battle,** to fight. —**bat′tler,** *n.*

**bat′tle-ax′, bat′tle-axe′,** *n.* 1. a heavy ax formerly used as a weapon. 2. [Slang], a harsh, domineering woman.

**bat·tle·dore** (bat′′l-dôr′), *n.* [? < Pr. *batedor,* beater], a racket used to hit a shuttlecock in a game like badminton.

**bat′tle·field′,** *n.* 1. the place where a battle takes place or took place. 2. any area of conflict. Also **bat′tle·ground′.**

**bat·tle·ment** (bat′′l-mənt), *n.* [< OFr. *batailler,* fortify], a low wall, as on top of a tower, with open spaces for shooting.

**bat′tle·ship′,** *n.* any of a class of large warships with the biggest guns and very heavy armor.

**bat·ty** (bat′i), *adj.* [-TIER, -TIEST], [< *bat* (the mammal)], [Slang]. 1. insane. 2. odd.

**bau·ble** (bô′b′l), *n.* [< L. *bellus,* pretty], a showy trifle; trinket.

**baux·ite** (bôk′sīt, bō′zīt), *n.* [Fr. < *Baux,* town in France], the claylike ore from which aluminum is obtained.

**bawd** (bôd), *n.* [< OHG. *bald,* bold], a woman who keeps a brothel.

**bawd·y** (bô′di), *adj.* [-IER, -IEST], indecent; obscene. —**bawd′i·ness,** *n.*

**bawl** (bôl), *v.i. & v.t.* [< ON. *baula,* to bellow], 1. to shout noisily; bellow. 2. [Colloq.], to weep noisily. *n.* 1. a bellow. 2. [Colloq.], a noisy weeping. —**bawl out,** [Slang], to scold.

**bay** (bā), *n.* [< LL. *baia*], a wide inlet of a sea or lake, indenting the shoreline.

**bay** (bā), *n.* [< LL. *badare,* gape], 1. an alcove marked off by columns, etc. 2. a recess in a wall line, as for a window. 3. a bay window.

**bay** (bā), *v.i.* [< LL. *badare,* gape], to bark in long, deep tones. *n.* 1. a baying. 2. the situation of a hunted animal forced to turn and fight. —**at bay,** 1. with escape cut off. 2. held off. —**bring to bay,** to force into a situation that makes escape impossible.

**bay** (bā), *n.* [< L. *baca,* berry], 1. the laurel tree. 2. *pl.* honor; fame.

**bay** (bā), *adj.* [< L. *badius*], reddish-brown: said esp. of horses. *n.* 1. reddish brown. 2. a horse, etc. of this color.

**bay·ber·ry** (bā′ber′i), *n.* [*pl.* -RIES], 1. the wax myrtle. 2. any of its wax-coated berries.

**bay leaf,** the aromatic leaf of the bay tree, dried and used as seasoning.

**bay·o·net** (bā′ə-nit), *n.* [< Fr. < *Bayonne,* city in France], a detachable blade put on a rifle, for hand-to-hand fighting. *v.t. & v.i.* [-NETED, -NETING], to stab with a bayonet.

**bay·ou** (bī′ōō), *n.* [prob. < Am. Ind.], in the southern U.S., a marshy inlet or outlet of a lake, river, etc.

**bay window,** 1. a window or set of windows

jutting out from a wall. 2. [Slang], a large, protruding belly.

**ba·zaar, ba·zar** (bə-zär′), *n.* [Per. *bāzār*], 1. in Oriental countries, a market place. 2. a benefit sale for a club, church, etc.

**ba·zoo·ka** (bə-zōō′kə), *n.* [< name of a comic horn], a portable weapon of metal tubing, for launching armor-piercing rockets.

**bbl.,** [*pl.* BBLS.], barrel.

**BB (shot)** (bē′bē′), [designation of size], a size of shot (diameter, .18 in.) for an air rifle **(BB gun).**

**B.C.,** before Christ.

**bd.,** [*pl.* BDS.], 1. board. 2. bond.

**be** (bē, bi), *v.i.* [WAS or WERE, BEEN, BEING], [AS. *beon*], 1. to exist; live. 2. to happen; occur. 3. to remain or continue. *Note: be* is used to link its subject to a predicate complement (he *is* handsome, let x *be* y) or as an auxiliary: (1) with a past participle: *a*) to form the passive voice (he will *be* whipped). *b*) to form the perfect tense (Christ *is* risen). (2) with a present participle to express continuation (the player *is* running). (3) with a present participle or infinitive to express futurity, possibility, obligation, intention, etc. (he *is* going next week, she *is* to scrub the floor). *Be* is conjugated, in the present indicative: (I) *am,* (he, she, it) *is,* (we, you, they) *are;* in the past indicative: (I, he, she, it) *was,* (we, you, they) *were.*

**be-,** [AS. < *be,* about], a prefix meaning: 1. *around,* as in *beset.* 2. *completely,* as in *bedeck.* 3. *away,* as in *betake.* 4. *about,* as in *bemoan.* 5. *make,* as in *besot.* 6. *furnish with, affect by,* as in *becloud.*

**beach** (bēch), *n.* [Eng. dial., pebbles], a level stretch of sandy shore. *v.i. & v.t.* to ground (a boat) on a beach. **—beach′less,** *adj.*

**beach′comb′er** (-kōm′ẽr), *n.* 1. a long wave rolling ashore. 2. one who lives on what he finds on beaches, etc.

**beach′head′,** *n.* a position established by invading troops on an enemy shore.

**bea·con** (bē′kən), *n.* [AS. *beacen*], 1. a light for warning or guiding: often used figuratively. 2. a tower, as a lighthouse, for signaling. *v.t. & v.i.* to guide.

**bead** (bēd), *n.* [< AS. *biddan,* pray: cf. *n.* 3], 1. a small ball of glass, etc., pierced for stringing. 2. *pl.* a string of beads. 3. *pl.* a rosary. 4. any small, round object, as the front sight of a rifle. 5. a drop or bubble. *v.t.* to decorate with beads. **—count** (or **tell** or **say**) **one's beads,** to say prayers with a rosary. **—bead′y** [-IER, -IEST], *adj.*

**bea·dle** (bē′d'l), *n.* [< Frankish *bidal,* messenger], formerly, a minor parish officer in the Church of England.

**bea·gle** (bē′g'l), *n.* [? < OFr. *begueule,* wide-throat], a small hound with a smooth coat, short legs, and drooping ears.

**beak** (bēk), *n.* [< L. *beccus*], 1. a bird's bill. 2. the beaklike mouth part of various insects, fishes, etc. **—beak′like′,** *adj.*

**beak·er** (bēk′ẽr), *n.* [< Gr. *bikos,* wine jar], 1. a goblet. 2. a glass or metal container used by chemists, etc.

**beam** (bēm), *n.* [AS., tree], 1. a long, thick piece of timber, metal, etc. 2. the crossbar of a balance. 3. a ship's breadth at its widest. 4. a slender shaft of light, etc. 5. a radiant look, smile, etc. 6. a radio signal sent continuously as a guide for aircraft. *v.t.* 1. to give out (shafts of light). 2. to direct (a radio signal, etc.). *v.i.* 1. to shine brightly. 2. to smile warmly.

**bean** (bēn), *n.* [AS.], 1. the edible, kidney-shaped seed of certain plants. 2. a pod with such seeds. 3. a plant bearing these. 4. [Slang], the head or brain.

**bear** (bâr), *v.t.* [BORE (bôr), BORNE or BORN (bôrn), BEARING], [AS. *beran*], 1. to carry. 2. to have or show: as, it *bore* his signature. 3. to give birth to. 4. to support or sustain. 5. to withstand or endure: as, to *bear* torture. 6. to permit of: as, it will *bear* investigation. 7. to carry or conduct (oneself). 8. to supply: as, to *bear* witness. *v.i.* 1. to be productive. 2. to extend or move in a given direction. 3. to be oppressive (*on*). **—bear down (on),** 1. to exert pressure or effort (on). 2. to approach. **—bear on,** to have relation to. **—bear out,** to confirm. **—bear up,** to endure. **—bear with,** to tolerate. **—bear′a·ble,** *adj.* **—bear′er,** *n.*

**bear** (bâr), *n.* [AS. *bera*], 1. a large, clumsy, heavy mammal with shaggy fur and a very short tail. 2. [B-], either of two constellations in the Northern Hemisphere **(Great Bear** and **Little Bear).** 3. one who is clumsy, rude, etc. 4. a speculator who sells stocks, etc. hoping to buy them back later at a lower price. *adj.* of or favorable to such speculators: as, a *bear* market.

**beard** (bêrd), *n.* [AS.], 1. the hair on the chin and cheeks of a man. 2. any beard-like part, as the awn on certain grains. *v.t.* 1. to oppose bravely; defy. 2. to provide with a beard. **—beard′ed,** *adj.*

**bear·ing** (bâr′iŋ), *n.* 1. the way of carrying and conducting oneself. 2. a supporting part. 3. a producing or the ability to produce. 4. endurance. 5. *often in pl.* relative position or direction. 6. relation; relevance. 7. a part of a machine on which another part revolves, slides, etc.

**bear′ish,** *adj.* 1. like a bear; rude, surly, etc. 2. directed toward or causing a lowering of prices in the stock exchange, etc.

**beast** (bēst), *n.* [< L. *bestia*], 1. any large, four-footed animal. 2. one who is brutal, gross, etc. **—beast′like,** *adj.*

**beast′ly,** *adj.* [-LIER, -LIEST], 1. of or like a beast; brutal, etc. 2. [Colloq.], disagreeable; disgusting. **—beast′li·ness,** *n.*

**beast of burden,** any animal used for carrying things.

**beast of prey,** any animal that hunts and kills other animals for food.

**beat** (bēt), *v.t.* [BEAT, BEATEN, BEATING], [AS. *beatan*], 1. to strike repeatedly. 2. to punish by so striking. 3. to dash repeatedly against. 4. to make (a path) by treading. 5. to mix by stirring. 6. to move (wings, etc.) up and down. 7. to outdo or defeat. 8. to mark (time) as by tapping. 9. [Colloq.], to baffle. *v.i.* 1. to strike repeatedly. 2. to throb or pulsate. 3. [Colloq.], to win. *n.* 1. a beating, as of the heart. 2. any of a series of strokes. 3. a throb. 4. a habitual route. 5. the unit of musical rhythm. *adj.* [Slang], 1. tired; exhausted. 2. of a group in the U.S. who reject social conventions, affect extreme slang speech, etc. **—beat a retreat,** to retreat. **—beat down,** to suppress. **—beat it!** [Slang], go away! **—beat off,** to drive back. **—beat up (on),** [Slang], to give a beating to. **—beat′er,** *n.*

**beat′en** (-'n), *adj.* 1. struck with repeated blows. 2. shaped by hammering. 3. flattened by treading. 4. defeated.

**be·a·tif·ic** (bē′ə-tif′ik), *adj.* 1. making blissful or blessed. 2. very happy; blissful.

**be·at·i·fy** (bi-at′ə-fī′), *v.t.* [-FIED, -FYING], [< L. *beatus,* happy + *facere,* make], 1. to make blissfully happy. 2. in the *R.C. Church,* to declare one who has died to be among the blessed in heaven. **—be·at′i·fi·ca′tion,** *n.*

**beat′ing,** *n.* 1. the act of one that beats. 2. a whipping. 3. a throbbing. 4. a defeat.

**be·at·i·tude** (bi-at′ə-tōōd′, -tūd′), *n.* [< L. *beatus,* happy], 1. perfect blessedness or happiness. 2. a blessing. **—the Beatitudes,** the pronouncements in the Sermon on the Mount.

**beat·nik** (bēt′nik), *n.* [Slang], a member of the beat group.
**beau** (bō), *n.* [*pl.* BEAUS, BEAUX (bōz)], [Fr. < L. *bellus*, pretty], 1. a dandy; fop. 2. a woman's sweetheart.
**beau·te·ous** (bū′ti-əs), *adj.* beautiful.
**beau·ti·cian** (bū-tish′ən), *n.* one who works in a beauty shop.
**beau·ti·ful** (bū′tə-fəl), *adj.* having beauty.
**beau′ti·fy′** (-fī′), *v.t.* & *v.i.* [-FIED, -FYING], to make or become beautiful. —**beau′ti·fi·ca′tion,** *n.* —**beau′ti·fi′er,** *n.*
**beau·ty** (bū′ti), *n.* [*pl.* -TIES], [< L. *bellus*, pretty], 1. the quality of being very pleasing, as in form, color, tone, behavior, etc. 2. a thing having this quality. 3. good looks. 4. a very good-looking woman.
**beauty shop** (or **salon** or **parlor**), a place where women can get a permanent wave, manicure, etc.
**bea·ver** (bē′vẽr), *n.* [AS. *beofor*], 1. an amphibious animal with webbed hind feet and a flat, broad tail. 2. its soft, brown fur. 3. a man's high silk hat.
**be·calm** (bi-käm′), *v.t.* 1. to make calm. 2. to make (a ship) motionless from lack of wind.
**be·came** (bi-kām′), pt. of **become.**
**be·cause** (bi-kôz′), *conj.* [< ME. *bi*, by + *cause*], for the reason or cause that. —**because of,** on account of.
**beck** (bek), *n.* a beckoning gesture of the hand, head, etc. —**at the beck and call of,** at the service of.
**beck·on** (bek′'n), *v.i.* & *v.t.* [< AS. *beacen*, a sign], to summon by a gesture, nod, etc.
**be·cloud** (bi-kloud′), *v.t.* to cloud over.
**be·come** (bi-kum′), *v.i.* [-CAME, -COME, -COMING], [AS. *becuman*], to come or grow to be. *v.t.* to suit; be suitable to: as, that hat *becomes* her. —**become of,** to happen to.
**be·com′ing,** *adj.* 1. appropriate; seemly. 2. suitable (to the wearer).
**bed** (bed), *n.* [AS. *bedd*], 1. a piece of furniture for sleeping on. 2. a plot of soil where plants are raised. 3. the bottom of a river, lake, etc. 4. any flat surface used as a foundation. 5. a layer; stratum. *v.t.* [BEDDED, BEDDING], 1. to put to bed. 2. to embed. 3. to plant in a bed of earth. 4. to arrange in layers. *v.i.* 1. to go to bed; sleep. 2. to stratify.
**be·daz·zle** (bi-daz′'l), *v.t.* [-ZLED, -ZLING], to bewilder; confuse.
**bed′bug′,** *n.* a small, wingless, reddish-brown biting insect that infests beds, etc.
**bed′cham′ber,** *n.* a bedroom.
**bed′clothes′** (-klōz′, -klōthz′), *n.pl.* sheets, blankets, bedspreads, etc.
**bed·ding** (bed′iŋ), *n.* 1. mattresses and bedclothes. 2. any foundation.
**be·deck** (bi-dek′), *v.t.* to adorn.
**be·dev·il** (bi-dev′'l), *v.t.* [-ILED or -ILLED, -ILING or -ILLING], 1. to plague; torment. 2. to worry; bewilder. —**be·dev′il·ment,** *n.*
**bed′fast′** (-fast′), *adj.* bedridden.
**bed′fel′low,** *n.* 1. a person who shares one's bed. 2. any associate.
**be·dim** (bi-dim′), *v.t.* [-DIMMED, -DIMMING], to make dim; darken or obscure.
**bed·lam** (bed′ləm), *n.* [< (the London hospital of St. Mary of) *Bethlehem*], 1. an insane asylum. 2. any noisy, confused place or situation.
**Bed·ou·in** (bed′oo-in), *n.* [< Ar. *badāwin*, desert dwellers], 1. an Arab of the desert tribes of Arabia, Syria, or North Africa. 2. any wanderer.
**bed′pan′,** *n.* a shallow pan used as a toilet by one bedridden.
**be·drag·gle** (bi-drag′'l), *v.t.* [-GLED, -GLING], to make wet, limp, and dirty, as by dragging through mire. —**be·drag′gled,** *adj.*
**bed′rid′den** (-rid′'n), *adj.* having to stay in bed, usually for a long time, because of illness, infirmity, etc.: also **bed′rid′.**
**bed′rock′,** *n.* 1. solid rock beneath the soil and superficial rock. 2. a secure foundation. 3. basic principles.
**bed′room′,** *n.* a room to sleep in.
**bed′side′,** *n.* the space beside a bed. *adj.* beside a bed.
**bed′sore′,** *n.* a body sore on a bedridden person, caused by chafing or pressure.
**bed′spread′,** *n.* an ornamental cover spread over the blanket on a bed.
**bed′spring′,** *n.* a framework of springs in a bed to support the mattress.
**bed′stead′** (-sted′), *n.* a framework for supporting the spring and mattress of a bed.
**bed′time′,** *n.* the time to go to bed.
**bee** (bē), *n.* [AS. *beo*], 1. a four-winged insect which feeds on the nectar of flowers. 2. a meeting of people to work together or to compete. —**have a bee in one's bonnet,** to be obsessed with one notion.
**beech** (bēch), *n.* [AS. *bece*], 1. a tree with smooth, gray bark, hard wood, and edible nuts. 2. its wood. *adj.* of this tree.
**beech′nut′,** *n.* the three-cornered nut of the beech tree.
**beef** (bēf), *n.* [*pl.* BEEVES (bēvz), BEEFS], [< L. *bos*, ox], 1. a full-grown cow, bull, or steer, esp. one bred for meat. 2. meat from such animals. 3. [Colloq.], human muscle; strength. 4. [Slang], a complaint. *v.i.* [Slang], to complain. —**beef′y** [-IER, -IEST], *adj.*
**beef′steak′** (-stāk′), *n.* a slice of beef to be broiled or fried.
**bee·hive** (bē′hīv′), *n.* 1. a shelter for domestic bees. 2. [Colloq.], a place of great activity.
**bee′line′,** *n.* a straight line or route from one place to another. —**make a beeline for,** [Colloq.], to go straight toward.
**been** (bin, ben, bēn), pp. of **be.**
**beep** (bēp), *n.* [echoic], 1. the brief, sharp sound of a horn, as on an automobile. 2. a similar-sounding electronic signal, used in warning, direction-finding, etc. *v.i.* & *v.t.* to make or cause to make such a sound.
**beer** (bêr), *n.* [AS. *beor*], 1. a mildly alcoholic drink made from malt, hops, etc. 2. a soft drink made from extracts of roots, etc.
**bees′wax′,** *n.* wax secreted by honeybees, used by them in making their honeycomb.
**beet** (bēt), *n.* [< L. *beta*], 1. a plant with a thick white or red root. 2. this root, used as a vegetable or as a source of sugar.
**bee·tle** (bē′t'l), *n.* [< AS. *bitan*, to bite], an insect with hard front wings used to cover the membranous hind wings when these are folded.
**bee·tle** (bē′t'l), *n.* [AS. *betel*], a heavy mallet or pestle, usually wooden.
**bee·tle** (bē′t'l), *v.i.* [-TLED, -TLING], [prob. < *beetle-browed*], to project or jut; overhang. *adj.* jutting; overhanging: also **bee′tling.**
**bee′tle-browed′,** *adj.* [see BEETLE (insect) & BROW], 1. having bushy or overhanging eyebrows. 2. frowning; scowling.
**beeves** (bēvz), *n.* pl. of **beef.**
**be·fall** (bi-fôl′), *v.i.* & *v.t.* [-FELL, -FALLEN, -FALLING], [AS. < *be-* + *feallan*, fall], to happen or occur (to).
**be·fit** (bi-fit′), *v.t.* [-FITTED, -FITTING], to be suitable or fit for. —**be·fit′ting,** *adj.*
**be·fog** (bi-fôg′, -fog′), *v.t.* [-FOGGED, -FOGGING], 1. to envelop in fog. 2. to confuse.
**be·fore** (bi-fôr′), *adv.* [< AS. *be-* + *foran*, before], 1. ahead; in front. 2. up to now. 3. earlier; sooner. *prep.* 1. ahead of in time, space, or order. 2. in the sight or presence of: as, he appeared *before* the court. 3. earlier than. 4. rather than: as, I'd take that book *before* this. *conj.* 1. in advance of the time that: as, call *before* you go. 2. sooner than: as, I'd die *before* I'd tell.

**be·fore′hand′** (-hand′), ***adv. & adj.*** ahead of time; in anticipation.
**be·foul** (bi-foul′), ***v.t.*** 1. to make filthy. 2. to cast aspersions on.
**be·friend** (bi-frend′), ***v.t.*** to act as a friend to.
**be·fud·dle** (bi-fud′'l), ***v.t.*** [-DLED, -DLING], to stupefy or confuse.
**beg** (beg), ***v.t. & v.i.*** [BEGGED, BEGGING], [< OFr. *begard*], 1. to ask for (alms): as, he *begged* a dime. 2. to ask earnestly; entreat. **—beg off,** to ask to be released from. **—go begging,** to be unwanted.
**be·gan** (bi-gan′), pt. of **begin.**
**be·get** (bi-get′), ***v.t.*** [-GOT or *archaic* -GAT (-gat′), -GOTTEN or -GOT, -GETTING], [< AS. *begitan*, acquire], 1. to become the father of. 2. to cause. **—be·get′ter, *n.***
**beg·gar** (beg′ẽr), ***n.*** 1. one who lives by begging. 2. one who is very poor. ***v.t.*** 1. to make a beggar of. 2. to make appear useless: as, her wit *beggars* description.
**beg′gar·ly,** ***adj.*** very poor, mean, etc.
**be·gin** (bi-gin′), ***v.i.*** [-GAN, -GUN, -GINNING], [AS. *beginnan*], 1. to start. 2. to come into being. ***v.t.*** 1. to cause to start. 2. to originate.
**be·gin′ner,** ***n.*** one who is just beginning to do or learn something; novice.
**be·gin′ning,** ***n.*** 1. a start. 2. the time or place of starting. 3. the first part or stage.
**be·gone** (bi-gôn′, -gon′), ***interj. & v.i.*** (to) be gone; go away; get out.
**be·go·ni·a** (bi-gōn′yə, -gō′ni-ə), ***n.*** [after M. *Bégon* (1638–1710), Fr. botanist], a plant with showy white, pink, or red flowers.
**be·got** (bi-got′), pt. and alt. pp. of **beget.**
**be·got·ten** (bi-got′'n), pp. of **beget.**
**be·grime** (bi-grīm′), ***v.t.*** [-GRIMED, -GRIMING], to cover with grime; soil.
**be·grudge** (bi-gruj′), ***v.t.*** [-GRUDGED, -GRUDGING], 1. to envy (another) the possession of. 2. to give with reluctance: as, he *begrudges* her every cent. **—be·grudg′ing·ly, *adv.***
**be·guile** (bi-gīl′), ***v.t.*** [-GUILED, -GUILING], 1. to mislead or deprive (*of*) by guile; deceive. 2. to pass (time) pleasantly. 3. to charm or delight. **—be·guile′ment, *n.***
**be·gun** (bi-gun′), pp. of **begin.**
**be·half** (bi-haf′, -häf′), ***n.*** [< AS. *be*, by + *healf*, side], support, side, interest, etc. **—in** (or **on**) **behalf of,** in the interest of; for.
**be·have** (bi-hāv′), ***v.t. & v.i.*** [-HAVED, -HAVING], [see BE- & HAVE], 1. to conduct (oneself), esp. in a proper way. 2. to act or react.
**be·hav·ior** (bi-hāv′yẽr), ***n.*** manner of behaving; conduct: also, Brit. sp., **behaviour.**
**be·hav′ior·ism,** ***n.*** the doctrine that observed behavior provides the only valid data of psychology: it rejects the concept of *mind*. **—be·hav′ior·ist, *n. & adj.***
**be·head** (bi-hed′), ***v.t.*** to cut off the head of.
**be·held** (bi-held′), pt. and pp. of **behold.**
**be·he·moth** (bi-hē-məth, bē′ə-), ***n.*** [<Heb.], 1. in the *Bible*, a huge animal, assumed to be the hippopotamus. 2. any huge animal.
**be·hest** (bi-hest′), ***n.*** [AS. *behæs*, a vow], an order; command.
**be·hind** (bi-hīnd′), ***adv.*** [AS. *behindan*], 1. in the rear. 2. in a former time, place, etc. 3. into arrears. 4. slow; late. 5. to or toward the back: as, look *behind*. ***prep.*** 1. in the rear of: as, sit *behind* me. 2. inferior to. 3. later than: as, *behind* schedule. 4. beyond: as, *behind* the hill. 5. supporting: as, he is *behind* the plan. 6. hidden by: as, what's *behind* his smile? ***adj.*** 1. that follows: as, the person *behind*. 2. in arrears.
**be·hind′hand′** (-hand′), ***adv. & adj.*** behind in payment, time, etc.; late.
**be·hold** (bi-hōld′), ***v.t.*** [-HELD, -HELD or *archaic* -HOLDEN, -HOLDING], [AS. *bihealdan*], to see; look at. ***interj.*** look! see! **—be·hold′er, *n.***
**be·hold·en** (bi-hōl′d'n), ***adj.*** held under obligation; indebted.
**be·hoof** (bi-hōōf′), ***n.*** [AS. *behof*, profit], behalf, benefit, interest, sake, etc.
**be·hoove** (bi-hōōv′), ***v.t. & v.i.*** [-HOOVED, -HOOVING], [AS. *behofian*, to need], 1. to be necessary (for): as, it *behooves* me to reply. 2. to be fitting (for). Also **be·hove′** (-hōv′) [-HOVED, -HOVING].
**beige** (bāzh), ***n.*** [Fr.], grayish tan. ***adj.*** grayish-tan.
**be·ing** (bē′iŋ), ***n.*** [see BE], 1. existence; life. 2. one's fundamental nature. 3. one that lives or exists: as, a human *being*. ***adj.*** at hand: as, for the time *being*, I'll stay.
**be·la·bor** (bi-lā′bẽr), ***v.t.*** 1. to beat severely. 2. to attack verbally.
**be·lat·ed** (bi-lāt′id), ***adj.*** too late; tardy.
**be·lay** (bi-lā′), ***v.t. & v.i.*** [-LAYED, -LAYING], [< AS. *belecgan*, make fast], 1. in *naut. usage*, to make (a rope) secure by winding around a pin, etc. 2. [Colloq.], to hold; stop.
**belch** (belch), ***v.i. & v.t.*** [AS. *bealcian*], 1. to expel (gas) through the mouth from the the stomach. 2. to throw forth violently: as, the volcano *belched* flames. ***n.*** a belching.
**bel·dam** (bel′dəm), ***n.*** [see BELLE & DAME], 1. any old woman. 2. a haggish old woman.
**be·lea·guer** (bi-lē′gẽr), ***v.t.*** [< D. < *leger*, a camp], 1. to besiege by encircling. 2. to surround; beset. **—be·lea′guered, *adj.***
**bel·fry** (bel′fri), ***n.*** [*pl.* -FRIES], [< OHG. *bergfrid*, lit., protector of peace: orig., a movable tower for military assaults], 1. a bell tower. 2. the part of a tower that holds the bell(s).
**Belg.,** 1. Belgian. 2. Belgium.
**Bel·gian** (bel′jən), ***adj.*** of Belgium, its people, etc. ***n.*** a native of Belgium.
**be·lie** (bi-lī′), ***v.t.*** [-LIED, -LYING], 1. to disguise or misrepresent. 2. to leave unfulfilled. 3. to prove false.
**be·lief** (bə-lēf′), ***n.*** [< AS. *geleafa*], 1. conviction; faith, esp. religious faith. 2. trust; confidence. 3. acceptance as trustworthy, real, etc. 4. an opinion. 5. a creed or doctrine.
**be·lieve** (bə-lēv′), ***v.t.*** [-LIEVED, -LIEVING], [< AS. *geliefan*], 1. to take as true, real, etc. 2. to have confidence in a statement or promise of. 3. to assume. ***v.i.*** to have faith (*in*). **—be·liev′a·ble, *adj.* —be·liev′er, *n.***
**be·lit·tle** (bi-lit′'l), ***v.t.*** [-TLED, -TLING], to make seem little, less important, etc.
**bell** (bel), ***n.*** [AS. *belle*], 1. a hollow, cuplike object as of metal, which rings when struck. 2. the sound of a bell. 3. anything shaped like a bell. 4. in *naut. usage*, a bell rung to mark the periods of the watch. ***v.t.*** to attach a bell to. ***v.i.*** to become bell-shaped.
**bel·la·don·na** (bel′ə-don′ə), ***n.*** [It., beautiful lady: from use as cosmetic], 1. a poisonous plant with reddish flowers. 2. a drug obtained from this plant.
**bell′boy′,** ***n.*** a boy or man employed by a hotel, etc. to carry luggage and do errands: also [Slang], **bell′hop′.**
**bell buoy,** a buoy with a warning bell rung by the motion of the waves.
**belle** (bel), ***n.*** [Fr., fem. of *beau*], a pretty woman or girl; esp., the prettiest one.
**belles-let·tres** (bel′let′rə), ***n.pl.*** [Fr.], nontechnical literature, as fiction, poetry, drama, etc. **—bel·let·rist** (bel′let′rist), ***n.***
**bel·li·cose** (bel′ə-kōs′), ***adj.*** [< L. *bellum*, war], quarrelsome; warlike. **—bel′li·cose′ly, *adv.* —bel′li·cos′i·ty** (-kos′ə-ti), ***n.***
**bel·lig·er·ent** (bə-lij′ẽr-ənt), ***adj.*** [< L. *bellum*, war + *gerere*, carry on], 1. at war. 2. of war. 3. warlike. ***n.*** any person or nation at war. **—bel·lig′er·ence, bel·lig′er·en·cy, *n.* —bel·lig′er·ent·ly, *adv.***
**bel·low** (bel′ō), ***v.i.*** [AS. *bylgan*], 1. to roar with a reverberating sound, as a bull. 2. to make a sound like this. ***v.t.*** to utter loudly or powerfully. ***n.*** a bellowing sound.
**bel·lows** (bel′ōz), ***n. sing. & pl.*** [see BELLY],

1. a device for producing a stream of air, used for blowing fires, in pipe organs, etc. 2. anything collapsible like a bellows.

**bell·weth·er** (bel'we*th*'ẽr), *n.* a male sheep wearing a bell, usually leading the flock.

**bel·ly** (bel'i), *n.* [*pl.* -LIES], [AS. *belg*, leather bag], 1. the part of the body between the chest and thighs; abdomen. 2. the stomach. 3. the deep interior (of a thing). *v.t. & v.i.* [-LIED, -LYING], to bulge.

**bel'ly·ache'** (-āk'), *n.* [Colloq.], pain in the abdomen. *v.i.* [-ACHED, -ACHING], [Slang], to complain. —**bel'ly·ach'er,** *n.*

**be·long** (bi-lôŋ'), *v.i.* [< AS. *langian*, to go along with], to have a proper place: as, it *belongs* in this room. —**belong to,** 1. to be a part of. 2. to be owned by.

**be·long'ings,** *n.pl.* possessions.

**be·lov·ed** (bi-luv'id, -luvd'), *adj.* dearly loved. *n.* a dearly loved person.

**be·low** (bi-lō'), *adv. & adj.* [see BE- & LOW], 1. in or to a lower place; beneath. 2. later (in a book, etc.). 3. in hell. 4. on earth. *prep.* 1. lower than, as in position, value, etc. 2. not worthy of: as, *below* my dignity.

**Bel·shaz·zar** (bel-shaz'ẽr), *n.* in the *Bible*, the last king of Babylon.

**belt** (belt), *n.* [< L. *balteus*, a belt], 1. a band of leather, etc. worn around the waist. 2. any encircling thing like this. 3. an endless band, as for transferring motion from one wheel to another. 4. a distinctive area: as, the corn *belt*. *v.t.* 1. to surround or fasten as with a belt; girdle. 2. to strike as with a belt.

**be·moan** (bi-mōn'), *v.t. & v.i.* to lament.

**be·muse** (bi-mūz'), *v.t.* [-MUSED, -MUSING], [*be-* + *muse*], to confuse; preoccupy.

**bench** (bench), *n.* [AS. *benc*], 1. a long seat made of wood, stone, etc. 2. a worktable. 3. the place where judges sit in a court. 4. [occas. B-], *a*) the status of a judge. *b*) judges collectively. *c*) a law court. *v.t.* in *sports*, to take (a player) out of a game. —**on the bench,** 1. serving in court as a judge. 2. in *sports*, not taking part in the game.

**bend** (bend), *v.t.* [BENT, BENDING], [< AS. *bendan*, bind], 1. to make curved or crooked. 2. to turn from a straight line. 3. to make submit. *v.i.* 1. to turn from a straight line; swerve. 2. to yield by curving, as from pressure. 3. to curve the body; stoop (often with *over*). 4. to give in; yield: as, he *bent* to her wishes. *n.* 1. a bending or being bent. 2. a bent part. —**bend'a·ble,** *adj.*

**bend'er,** *n.* 1. a person or thing that bends. 2. [Slang], a drinking bout; spree.

**be·neath** (bi-nēth'), *adv. & adj.* [< AS. *be-* + *neothan*, down], in a lower place; below; underneath. *prep.* 1. below; lower than. 2. underneath. 3. unworthy of: as, it is *beneath* him to cheat.

**ben·e·dict** (ben'ə-dikt'), *n.* [< *Benedick*, in Shakespeare's *Much Ado About Nothing*], a recently married man, especially one who seemed a confirmed bachelor.

**ben·e·dic·tion** (ben'ə-dik'shən), *n.* [< L. *bene*, well + *dicere*, speak], 1. a blessing. 2. an invocation of divine blessing at the end of a church service.

**ben·e·fac·tion** (ben'ə-fak'shən), *n.* [< L. *bene*, well + *facere*, do], 1. a benefiting, esp. as an act of charity. 2. a benefit given.

**ben·e·fac·tor** (ben'ə-fak'tẽr), *n.* one who has given financial or other help; patron. —**ben'e·fac'tress** (-tris), *n.fem.*

**ben·e·fice** (ben'ə-fis), *n.* [see BENEFACTION], an endowed church office providing a living for a vicar, etc. *v.t.* [-FICED, -FICING], to provide with a benefice.

**be·nef·i·cence** (bə-nef'ə-s'ns), *n.* [see BENEFACTION], 1. a being kind or doing good. 2. a kindly action or gift.

**be·nef'i·cent** (-s'nt), *adj.* showing beneficence; doing or resulting in good: also **be·nef'ic.** —**be·nef'i·cent·ly,** *adv.*

**ben·e·fi·cial** (ben'ə-fish'əl), *adj.* productive of benefits; advantageous; favorable.

**ben·e·fi·ci·ar·y** (ben'ə-fish'ẽr-i, -i-er'i), *n.* [*pl.* -ARIES], 1. anyone receiving benefit. 2. a person named to receive an inheritance, income from an insurance policy, etc.

**ben·e·fit** (ben'ə-fit), *n.* [see BENEFACTION], 1. a kindly, charitable act; favor. 2. anything contributing to improvement; advantage. 3. a public performance, bazaar, etc. the proceeds of which are to help some person or cause. *v.t.* [-FITED, -FITING], to help; aid. *v.i.* to receive advantage; profit.

**be·nev·o·lence** (bə-nev'ə-ləns), *n.* [L. *bene*, well + *volere*, to wish], 1. an inclination to do good; kindness. 2. a kindly, charitable act. —**be·nev'o·lent,** *adj.*

**be·night·ed** (bi-nīt'id), *adj.* 1. surrounded by darkness. 2. unenlightened; ignorant.

**be·nign** (bi-nīn'), *adj.* [< L. *bene*, well + *genus*, type], 1. good-natured; kindly. 2. favorable; beneficial. 3. in *medicine*, not malignant. —**be·nign'ly,** *adv.*

**be·nig·nant** (bi-nig'nənt), *adj.* [< *benign*], 1. kindly; gracious, esp. to inferiors. 2. benign; beneficial. —**be·nig'nan·cy,** *n.*

**be·nig'ni·ty** (-nə-ti), *n.* [*pl.* -TIES], 1. kindliness. 2. a kind act; favor.

**ben·i·son** (ben'ə-z'n, -s'n), *n.* [< L.; see BENEDICTION], a blessing.

**Ben·ja·min** (ben'jə-mən), *n.* in the *Bible*, 1. Jacob's youngest son and his favorite. 2. the tribe of Israel descended from him.

**bent** (bent), pt. and pp. of **bend.** *adj.* 1. curved; crooked. 2. strongly determined (*on*). *n.* 1. a tendency. 2. a mental leaning; propensity: as, a *bent* for music.

**bent** (bent), *n.* [AS. *beonot*], any of various low-growing grasses: in full, **bent grass.**

**be·numb** (bi-num'), *v.t.* 1. to make numb. 2. to deaden mentally; stupefy.

**ben·ze·drine** (ben'zə-drēn'), *n.* a drug used as an inhalant to relieve nasal congestion, and as a stimulant of the central nervous system: a trademark **(Benzedrine).**

**ben·zene** (ben'zēn), *n.* [< *benzoin*], an inflammable liquid obtained from coal tar and used as a solvent, in dyes, etc.

**ben·zine** (ben'zēn), *n.* [< *benzoin*], an inflammable liquid obtained from petroleum and used as a motor fuel, in dry cleaning, etc.

**ben·zo·ate** (ben'zō-it, -āt'), *n.* a salt or ester of benzoic acid.

**ben·zo·ic acid** (ben-zō'ik), [< *benzoin*], a white, crystalline acid used as an antiseptic and preservative.

**ben·zo·in** (ben'zō-in, -zoin), *n.* [< Ar. *lubān jāwi*, incense of Java], a resin from certain trees of Sumatra and Java, used in medicine, perfumery, etc.

**ben·zol** (ben'zōl, -zol), *n.* benzene.

**Be·o·wulf** (bā'ə-woolf'), *n.* the hero of the Anglo-Saxon folk epic of that name, a poem probably composed c. 700 A.D.

**be·queath** (bi-kwē*th*', -kwēth'), *v.t.* [AS. < *be-* + *cewthan*, say], 1. to leave (property, etc.) to another by one's will. 2. to hand down; pass on. —**be·queath'al** (-kwē*th*'əl), *n.*

**be·quest** (bi-kwest'), *n.* 1. a bequeathing. 2. a legacy.

**be·rate** (bi-rāt'), *v.t.* [-RATED, -RATING], [*be-* + *rate* (to scold)], to scold severely.

**be·reave** (bi-rēv'), *v.t.* [-REAVED or -REFT, -REAVING], [< AS. *be-* + *reafian*, rob], 1. to deprive, as of hope. 2. to leave destitute, as by death. —**be·reave'ment,** *n.*

**be·reft** (bi-reft'), alt. pt. and pp. of **bereave.** *adj.* 1. deprived. 2. left sad and lonely, as by a death.

**be·ret** (bə-rā'), *n.* [< Fr. < L. *birrus*, hood], a flat, round, soft cap of felt, wool, etc.

**ber·i·ber·i** (ber'i-ber'i), *n.* [Singh. *beri*, weakness], a disease caused by lack of vitamin $B_1$ and characterized by extreme weakness, paralysis, and anemia.
**berke·li·um** (bũrk'li-əm), *n.* [< *Berkeley*, Calif.], a radioactive chemical element: symbol, Bk.
**Ber·mu·da shorts** (bẽr-mū'də), [< *Bermuda* Islands], knee-length tailored shorts for informal wear.
**ber·ry** (ber'i), *n.* [*pl.* -RIES], [AS. *berie*], 1. any small fleshy fruit with seeds, as a strawberry. 2. the dry seed of various plants, as a coffee bean. *v.i.* [-RIED, -RYING], 1. to bear berries. 2. to pick berries.
**ber·serk** (bũr'sẽrk, bẽr-sũrk'), *adj. & adv.* [ON. *berserkr*, warrior], in or into a violent rage or frenzy.
**berth** (bũrth), *n.* [< base of *bear* (carry)], 1. a ship's place of anchorage. 2. a position, duty, etc. 3. a built-in bed, as in a ship's cabin or pullman car. *v.t.* to put into or furnish with a berth. *v.i.* to occupy a berth.
**ber·yl** (ber'il), *n.* [< Gr. *bēryllos*], a very hard mineral, of which emerald is a variety.
**be·ryl·li·um** (bə-ril'i-əm), *n.* [< *beryl*], a rare, metallic chemical element: symbol, Be.
**be·seech** (bi-sēch'), *v.t.* [-SOUGHT or -SEECHED, -SEECHING], [< AS. *be-* + *secan*, seek], to ask (for) earnestly; entreat; beg.
**be·seem** (bi-sēm'), *v.i.* to be suitable (to).
**be·set** (bi-set'), *v.t.* [-SET, -SETTING], [< AS. *be-* + *settan*, set], 1. to set thickly with. 2. to attack from all sides. 3. to surround.
**be·set'ting,** *adj.* constantly harassing or attacking: as, a *besetting* temptation.
**be·shrew** (bi-shrōō'), *v.t.* [< ME. *be-* + *schrewen*, curse], [Archaic], to curse.
**be·side** (bi-sīd'), *prep.* [< ME. *be-*, by + *side*], 1. at the side of; near. 2. in comparison with: as, *beside* his grief hers seems small. 3. in addition to. 4. aside from: as, that's *beside* the point. *adv.* besides. **—beside oneself**, mad, as with fear, rage, etc.
**be·sides** (bi-sīdz'), *adv.* 1. in addition. 2. except for that mentioned. 3. moreover. *prep.* 1. in addition to. 2. other than.
**be·siege** (bi-sēj'), *v.t.* [-SIEGED, -SIEGING], 1. to hem in with armed forces; lay siege to. 2. to close in on. 3. to overwhelm, as with requests, etc. **—be·sieg'er,** *n.*
**be·smear** (bi-smêr'), *v.t.* to smear over; soil.
**be·smirch** (bi-smũrch'), *v.t.* [*be-* + *smirch*], to soil; sully. **—be·smirch'er,** *n.*
**be·som** (bē'zəm), *n.* [AS. *besema*, rod], a broom, esp. one made of twigs.
**be·sot** (bi-sot'), *v.t.* [-SOTTED, -SOTTING], to make a sot of; stupefy, as with liquor.
**be·sought** (bi-sôt'), pt. and pp. of **beseech.**
**be·spat·ter** (bi-spat'ẽr), *v.t.* 1. to spatter, as with mud. 2. to defame.
**be·speak** (bi-spēk'), *v.t.* [-SPOKE, -SPOKEN or -SPOKE, -SPEAKING], 1. to speak for in advance; reserve. 2. to be indicative of; show. 3. [Archaic or Poetic], to speak to.
**Bes·se·mer process** (bes'ə-mẽr), [< H. *Bessemer*, 19th-c. Eng. inventor], a method of making steel (**Bessemer steel**) by blasting air through molten iron.
**best** (best), *adj.* [superl. of *good*], [AS. *betst*], 1. most excellent. 2. most suitable, desirable, etc. 3. largest: as, the *best* part of a day. 4. most healthy. *adv.* [superl. of *well*], 1. in the most excellent manner. 2. in the highest degree. *n.* 1. the most excellent person, thing, condition, etc. 2. the utmost. 3. one's finest clothes. *v.t.* to defeat; excel. **—all for the best,** ultimately good. **—at best,** under the most favorable conditions. **—get** (or **have**) **the best of,** 1. to defeat. 2. to outwit. **—had best,** ought to. **—make the best of,** to adapt oneself to as well as possible.
**bes·tial** (bes'chəl, -tyəl), *adj.* [< L. *bestia*, beast], 1. of beasts. 2. like a beast; savage, brutal, etc. **—bes'ti·al'i·ty** (-chi-al'ə-ti, -ti-al'-) [*pl.* -TIES], *n.* **—bes'tial·ly,** *adv.*
**be·stir** (bi-stũr'), *v.t.* [-STIRRED, -STIRRING], to stir up; busy (oneself).
**best man,** the principal attendant of the bridegroom at a wedding.
**be·stow** (bi-stō'), *v.t.* [see BE- & STOW], 1. to present as a gift (often with *on* or *upon*). 2. to apply; devote. **—be·stow'al,** *n.*
**be·strew** (bi-strōō'), *v.t.* [-STREWED, -STREWED or -STREWN, -STREWING], to strew or scatter about.
**be·stride** (bi-strīd'), *v.t.* [-STRODE (-strōd') or -STRID (-strid'), -STRIDDEN (-strid''n) or -STRID, -STRIDING], 1. to sit on, mount, or stand astride. 2. to stride over or across.
**best-sell·er** (best'sel'ẽr), *n.* a book, phonograph record, etc. currently outselling most others.
**bet** (bet), *n.* [prob. < *abet*], 1. an agreement that the party proved wrong about something will do or pay what is stipulated. 2. the thing or sum thus staked. *v.t. & v.i.* [BET or BETTED, BETTING], 1. to declare as in a bet. 2. to stake (money, etc.) in a bet.
**be·ta** (bā'tə, bē'-), *n.* the second letter of the Greek alphabet (Β, β).
**be·take** (bi-tāk'), *v.t.* [-TOOK, -TAKEN, -TAKING], [see BE- & TAKE], to go (used reflexively): as, he *betook* himself home.
**beta rays,** a stream of electrons given off by a radioactive substance.
**be·tel nut** (bē't'l), the orange-colored, nutlike fruit of a tropical palm of the Far East.
**be·think** (bi-thiŋk'), *v.t.* [-THOUGHT, -THINKING], to think of, consider, recollect, etc.
**be·tide** (bi-tīd'), *v.i. & v.t.* [-TIDED, -TIDING], [< ME.; see BE- & TIDE], to happen (to).
**be·times** (bi-tīmz'), *adv.* 1. early. 2. promptly; quickly.
**be·to'ken,** *v.t.* 1. to be a token or sign of. 2. to indicate; denote.
**be·took** (bi-took'), pt. of **betake.**
**be·tray** (bi-trā'), *v.t.* [ult. < L. *tradere*, deliver], 1. to help the enemy of (one's country, etc.). 2. to fail to uphold: as, to *betray* a trust. 3. to deceive. 4. to seduce and fail to marry. 5. to reveal unknowingly. **—be·tray'al,** *n.* **—be·tray'er,** *n.*
**be·troth** (bi-trôth', -trōth'), *v.t.* [-TROTHED, -TROTHING], [< ME.; see BE- & TRUTH], to promise in marriage. **—be·troth'al,** *n.*
**be·trothed** (bi-trôtht', -trōthd'), *adj.* engaged to be married. *n.* a betrothed person.
**bet·ter** (bet'ẽr), *adj.* [compar. of *good*], [AS. *betera*], 1. more excellent. 2. more suitable, desirable, etc. 3. larger: as, the *better* part of a day. 4. improved in health. *adv.* [compar. of *well*], 1. in a more excellent manner. 2. in a higher degree. *n.* 1. a person superior in position, etc. 2. a more excellent thing, condition, etc. *v.t.* 1. to outdo; surpass. 2. to improve. **—better off,** in better circumstances. **—get** (or **have**) **the better of,** 1. to defeat. 2. to outwit. **—had better,** ought to; should. **—think better of,** to reconsider.
**bet'ter, bet'tor,** *n.* one who bets.
**better half,** [Colloq.], a spouse.
**bet'ter·ment** (-mənt), *n.* a bettering; improvement.
**be·tween** (bi-twēn'), *prep.* [< AS. *be*, by + *twegen*, two], 1. in the space, time, etc. separating (two things). 2. involving: as, a struggle *between* powers. 3. connecting: as, a bond *between* friends. 4. in the combined possession or action of. 5. one or the other of: as, choose *between* us. *adv.* in an intermediate space, time, etc.
**be·twixt** (bi-twikst'), *prep. & adv.* [AS. *betwix*], between: archaic except in **betwixt and between,** not altogether one nor altogether the other.

**bev·el** (bev′'l), *n.* [< ?], 1. a tool for measuring or marking angles, etc. 2. an angle other than a right angle. 3. an angled part or surface. *v.t.* [-ELED or -ELLED, -ELING or -ELLING], to cut to an angle other than a right angle. *v.i.* to slope at an angle. *adj.* sloped; beveled.

**bev·er·age** (bev′rij, -ẽr-ij), *n.* [< L. *bibere*, to drink], any drink, as milk, coffee, etc.

**bev·y** (bev′i), *n.* [*pl.* -IES], [? < OFr. *bevee*, drink; ? hence, a drinking group], 1. a group, esp. of girls or women. 2. a flock, esp. of quail.

**be·wail** (bi-wāl′), *v.t. & v.i.* to wail (over); lament; mourn; complain (about).

**be·ware** (bi-wâr′), *v.i. & v.t.* [-WARED, -WARING], [prob. < AS. *bewarian*, to guard], to be wary or careful (of).

**be·wil·der** (bi-wil′dẽr), *v.t.* [ult. < AS. *wilde*, wild], to confuse hopelessly; befuddle. **—be·wil′dered,** *adj.* **—be·wil′der·ment,** *n.*

**be·witch** (bi-wich′), *v.t.* [< AS. *wicce*, witch], 1. to cast a spell over. 2. to enchant; fascinate; charm. **—be·witch′ing,** *adj.*

**bey** (bā), *n.* [Turk.], 1. the governor of a Turkish district. 2. formerly, the native ruler of Tunis (now called *Tunisia*).

**be·yond** (bi-yond′), *prep.* [< AS. *be-* + *geond*, yonder], 1. farther on than; past. 2. later than. 3. outside the reach of: as, *beyond* help. 4. more or better than. *adv.* farther away. **—the (great) beyond,** whatever follows death.

**bi-,** [< L. < *bis*, twice], a prefix meaning: 1. *having two.* 2. *doubly.* 3. *happening every two.* 4. *happening twice during every.* 5. *using two.* 6. *joining* or *involving two.*

**Bi,** in *chem.*, bismuth.

**bi·an·nu·al** (bī-an′yoo-əl), *adj.* coming twice a year; semiannual. **—bi·an′nu·al·ly,** *adv.*

**bi·as** (bī′əs), *n.* [Fr. *biais*, a slant], 1. a slanting or diagonal line, cut or sewn in cloth. 2. a mental leaning; partiality; prejudice. *adj.* slanting; diagonal. *adv.* diagonally. *v.t.* [BIASED or BIASSED, BIASING or BIASSING], to prejudice. **—on the bias,** diagonally.

**bib** (bib), *n.* [< L. *bibere*, to drink], 1. an apronlike cloth tied around a child's neck at meals. 2. the top part of an apron.

**Bib.,** 1. Bible. 2. Biblical.

**Bi·ble** (bī′b'l), *n.* [< Gr. *biblos*, papyrus bark < Egypt.], 1. the sacred book of Christianity; Old Testament and New Testament. 2. the sacred book of Judaism; Old Testament. 3. [b-], any book regarded as authoritative. **—Bib·li·cal, bib·li·cal** (bib′li-k'l), *adj.*

**biblio-,** [< Gr. *biblion*, book], a combining form meaning *book, of books.*

**bib·li·og·ra·phy** (bib′li-og′rə-fi), *n.* [*pl.* -PHIES], a list of writings on a given subject or by a given author. **—bib′li·og′ra·pher,** *n.* **—bib′li·o·graph′i·cal** (-ə-graf′i-k'l), *adj.*

**bib′li·o·phile′** (-ə-fil′), *n.* one who loves or collects books.

**bib·u·lous** (bib′yoo-ləs), *adj.* [< L. *bibere*, to drink], addicted to alcoholic liquor.

**bi·cam·er·al** (bī-kam′ẽr-əl), *adj.* [< *bi-* + L. *camera*, chamber], having two legislative chambers.

**bi·car·bon·ate** (bī-kär′bə-nit, -nāt′), *n.* an acid salt of carbonic acid.

**bicarbonate of soda,** baking soda.

**bi·cen·ten·ni·al** (bī′sen-ten′i-əl), *adj.* happening once every 200 years. *n.* a 200th anniversary.

**bi·ceps** (bī′seps), *n.* [*pl.* -CEPSES], [< L. *bis*, two + *caput*, head], a muscle with two points of origin; esp., the large muscle in the front of the upper arm.

**bi·chlo·ride (of mercury)** (bī-klôr′īd), a poisonous compound used as a disinfectant.

**bick·er** (bik′ẽr), *v.i. & n.* [< ON. *bikkja*], squabble; quarrel. **—bick′er·er,** *n.*

**bi·cus·pid** (bī-kus′pid), *adj.* [< *bi-* + L. *cuspis*, pointed end], having two points. *n.* any of the eight adult teeth with two-pointed crowns.

**bi·cy·cle** (bī′si-k'l), *n.* [Fr. < *bi-* + Gr. *kyklos*, wheel], a vehicle consisting of a metal frame on two wheels, and having handle bars and a saddlelike seat. *v.i. & v.t.* [-CLED, -CLING], to ride or travel on a bicycle. **—bi′cy·clist** (-klist), *n.*

**bid** (bid), *v.t.* [BADE (bad) or BID, BIDDEN or BID, BIDDING], [< AS. *biddan*, beg & *beodan*, offer], 1. to command or ask. 2. to declare; say: as, *bid* defiance to him. 3. [pt. & pp. BID], *a*) to offer (an amount) as the price for. *b*) in *card games*, to state (a number of tricks) and declare (trump). *v.i.* [pt. & pp. BID], to make a bid. *n.* 1. a bidding; offer; proposal. 2. an amount, etc. bid. 3. an attempt or try (*for*). 4. [Colloq.], an invitation. **—bid fair,** to seem likely. **—bid′der,** *n.*

**bid′ding,** *n.* 1. a command or request. 2. an invitation or summons.

**bid·dy** (bid′i), *n.* [*pl.* -DIES], a hen.

**bide** (bīd), *v.i.* [BODE or BIDED or BADE (bad), BIDED, BIDING], [AS. *bidan*], [Archaic or Dial.], 1. to stay; continue. 2. to dwell. 3. to wait. *v.t.* to endure. **—bide one's time,** to wait patiently for an opportunity.

**bi·en·ni·al** (bī-en′i-əl), *adj.* [< L. *bis*, twice + *annus*, year], 1. happening every two years. 2. lasting for two years. *n.* 1. a biennial event. 2. in *botany*, a plant that lives two years. **—bi·en′ni·al·ly,** *adv.*

**bier** (bêr), *n.* [AS. *bær*], a portable framework on which a coffin is put.

**bi·fo·cal** (bī′fō′k'l), *adj.* adjusted or ground to two different focal lengths. *n.* a lens with one part ground for close focus and the other for distant focus.

**bi′fo′cals,** *n.pl.* eyeglasses with bifocal lenses.

**big** (big), *adj.* [BIGGER, BIGGEST], [akin to L. *bucca*, swollen cheek], 1. of great size; large. 2. full-grown. 3. loud. 4. important. 5. extravagant; pompous. 6. noble: as, a *big* heart. *adv.* [Colloq.], 1. boastfully: as, he talks *big.* 2. impressively. **—big′ness,** *n.*

**big·a·my** (big′ə-mi), *n.* [< LL. *bis*, twice + Gr. *gamos*, marriage], in *law*, the crime of marrying a second time while a previous marriage is still in effect. **—big′a·mist,** *n.* **—big′a·mous,** *adj.*

**big′-heart′ed,** *adj.* generous; kind.

**big′horn′,** *n.* a Rocky Mountain wild sheep with long, curved horns.

**bight** (bīt), *n.* [AS. *byht*], 1. a bending; corner; fork. 2. a loop in a rope. 3. a curve in a river, coast line, etc. 4. a bay.

**big·ot** (big′ət), *n.* [prob. < Sp. *hombre de bigote*, man with a mustache, hence man of spirit], one who holds blindly and intolerantly to a particular creed, opinion, etc. **—big′ot·ed,** *adj.* **—big′ot·ry** (-ri) [*pl.* -RIES], *n.*

**big shot,** [Slang], an important or influential person: also [Colloq.], **big′wig′,** *n.*

**bike** (bīk), *n., v.t. & v.i.* [BIKED, BIKING], [Colloq.], bicycle.

**bi·lat·er·al** (bī-lat′ẽr-əl), *adj.* 1. of, having, or on two sides. 2. affecting both sides equally; reciprocal. **—bi·lat′er·al·ism,** *n.*

**bile** (bīl), *n.* [L. *bilis*], 1. the bitter, greenish fluid secreted by the liver: it helps in digestion. 2. bad temper; anger.

**bilge** (bilj), *n.* [var. of *bulge*], 1. the rounded, lower part of a ship's hold. 2. stagnant water that gathers there: also **bilge water.** 3. [Slang], nonsense.

**bil·i·ar·y** (bil′i-er′i), *adj.* 1. of the bile. 2. bile-carrying. 3. bilious.

**bi·lin·gual** (bī-liŋ′gwəl), *adj.* [< L. *bis*, two + *lingua*, tongue], of, in, or speaking two languages. **—bi·lin′gual·ly,** *adv.*

**bil·ious** (bil′yəs), *adj.* 1. of the bile. 2. having or resulting from some ailment of the liver. 3. bad-tempered; cross.

**-bility,** a suffix used to form nouns from adjectives ending in *-ble*, as *capability*.

**bilk** (bilk), *v.t.* [? < *balk*], to deceive; swindle; defraud. *n.* a bilking or being bilked.

**bill** (bil), *n.* [< ML. *bulla*, sealed document], 1. a statement of charges for goods or services. 2. a list of things offered, as a menu or theater program. 3. an advertising poster or handbill. 4. a draft of a proposed law. 5. a bill of exchange. 6. a piece of paper money. 7. in *law*, a written declaration of charges against a defendant. *v.t.* 1. to make out a bill of (items). 2. to present a statement of charges to. 3. to advertise by bills. **—fill the bill,** [Colloq.], to meet the requirements. **—bill'a·ble,** *adj.*

**bill** (bil), *n.* [AS. *bile*], 1. a bird's beak. 2. a beaklike mouth part, as of a turtle. *v.i.* to touch bills together. **—bill and coo,** to kiss, talk softly, etc. in love-making.

**bill'board',** *n.* a signboard for advertising posters, etc.

**bil·let** (bil'it), *n.* [Fr.; see BILL (an account)], 1. a written order to provide lodging for military personnel. 2. lodging; quarters. 3. a position or job. *v.t.* to assign (soldiers, etc.) to lodging by billet.

**bil·let-doux** (bil'i-dōō'), *n.* [*pl.* BILLETS-DOUX (-dōōz')], [Fr.], a love letter.

**bill'fold'** (-fōld'), *n.* a wallet.

**bil·liards** (bil'yẽrdz), *n.* [< Fr. *billiard*, orig., a cue], a game played with hard balls driven by a cue on an oblong table with raised, cushioned edges.

**bil·lings·gate** (bil'iŋz-gāt'), *n.* [< a London fish market], foul, vulgar, abusive talk.

**bil·lion** (bil'yən), *n.* [Fr. < L. *bis*, twice + *million*, million], 1. in the U.S. and France, a thousand millions. 2. in Great Britian and Germany, a million millions. **—bil'lionth,** *adj. & n.*

**bill of exchange,** a written order to pay a certain sum of money to the person named.

**bill of fare,** a menu.

**bill of lading,** a receipt issued to a shipper by a carrier, listing the goods received for shipment.

**Bill of Rights,** the first ten amendments to the U.S. Constitution, which guarantee civil liberties.

**bill of sale,** a written statement transferring ownership by sale.

**bil·low** (bil'ō), *n.* [ON. *bylgja*], 1. a large wave. 2. any large swelling mass or surge, as of smoke. *v.i.* to surge or swell like a billow. **—bil'low·y** [-IER, -IEST], *adj.*

**bil·ly** (bil'i), *n.* [*pl.* -LIES], [ult. < OFr. *bille*, tree trunk], a club, esp. a policeman's truncheon.

**billy goat,** [Colloq.], a male goat.

**bi·met·al·lism** (bī-met''l-iz'm), *n.* the use of two metals, esp. gold and silver, as the monetary standard, with fixed values in relation to each other. **—bi·met'al·list,** *n.*

**bi·month·ly** (bī-munth'li), *adj. & adv.* 1. once every two months. 2. loosely, twice a month. *n.* [*pl.* -LIES], a bimonthly publication.

**bin** (bin), *n.* [AS. *binn*, manger], a box or enclosed space for storing foods, fuels, etc. *v.t.* [BINNED, BINNING], to store in a bin.

**bi·na·ry** (bī'nə-ri), *adj.* [< L. *bis*, double], made up of two parts; twofold. *n.* [*pl.* -RIES], a set of two.

**bind** (bīnd), *v.t.* [BOUND, BINDING], [AS. *bindan*], 1. to tie together, as with rope. 2. to hold; restrain. 3. to encircle with (a belt, etc.). 4. to bandage (often with *up*). 5. to make stick together. 6. to constipate. 7. to reinforce with a band, as of tape. 8. to fasten together and protect with a cover, as a book. 9. to obligate by duty, love, etc.: as, he is *bound* to help. 10. to put under legal restraint. *v.i.* to be obligatory.

**bind'er,** *n.* 1. one who binds. 2. a binding substance, as tar. 3. a cover for holding sheets of paper together.

**bind'er·y,** *n.* [*pl.* -IES], a place where books are bound.

**bind'ing,** *n.* 1. anything that binds, as a band, tape, tar, etc. 2. the covers and backing of a book. *adj.* that binds; esp., that holds one to an agreement, promise, etc. **—bind'ing·ly,** *adv.*

**binge** (binj), *n.* [Slang], a spree.

**bin·go** (biŋ'gō), *n.* a gambling game resembling lotto.

**bin·na·cle** (bin'ə-k'l), *n.* [ult. < L. *habitaculum*, dwelling], the case enclosing a ship's compass.

**bin·oc·u·lar** (bī-nok'yə-lẽr, bi-), *adj.* [< L. *bini*, double + *oculus*, eye], using, or for, both eyes. *n.* a binocular instrument; esp., *pl.*, field glasses.

**bi·no·mi·al** (bī-nō'mi-əl), *n.* [< LL. *bi-*, two + Gr. *nomos*, law], in *math.*, an expression consisting of two terms connected by a plus or minus sign.

**bio-,** [Gr. < *bios*, life], a combining form meaning *life, of living things*, as in *biology*.

**bi·o·chem·is·try** (bī'ō-kem'is-tri), *n.* the branch of chemistry that deals with the life processes of plants and animals. **—bi'o-chem'i·cal,** *adj.* **—bi'o·chem'ist,** *n.*

**bi·o·cide** (bī'ə-sīd'), *n.* [*bio-* + *-cide*], a poisonous chemical substance that can kill living organisms.

**biog.,** 1. biographical. 2. biography.

**bi·og·ra·phy** (bī-og'rə-fi, bi-), *n.* [*pl.* -PHIES], [< Gr. *bios*, life + *graphein*, write], an account of a person's life written by another. **—bi·og'ra·pher,** *n.* **—bi·o·graph·i·cal** (bī'ə-graf'i-k'l), **bi'o·graph'ic,** *adj.*

**biol.,** 1. biological. 2. biology.

**bi·ol·o·gy** (bī-ol'ə-ji), *n.* [*bio-* + *-logy*], the science that deals with the origin, history, characteristics, habits, etc. of plants and animals. **—bi·o·log·i·cal** (bī'ə-loj'i-k'l), *adj.* **—bi'o·log'i·cal·ly,** *adv.* **—bi·ol'o·gist,** *n.*

**bi·par·ti·san** (bī-pär'tə-z'n), *adj.* of or representing two parties. **—bi·par'ti·san·ship',** *n.*

**bi·par·tite** (bī-pär'tīt), *adj.* [< L. *bi-*, two + *partire*, divide], having two (corresponding) parts. **—bi·par'tite·ly,** *adv.*

**bi·ped** (bī'ped), *n.* [< L. *bi-*, two + *pes*, foot], any two-footed animal.

**bi·plane** (bī'plān'), *n.* an airplane with two wings, one above the other.

**birch** (būrch), *n.* [AS. *beorc*], 1. a tree having hard, close-grained wood and smooth bark in layers. 2. its wood. 3. a bunch of birch twigs used for whipping. *v.t.* to flog. *adj.* of birch: also **birch·en** (būr'chən).

**bird** (būrd), *n.* [AS. *bridd*, young bird], 1. any of a group of warm-blooded vertebrates with feathers and wings. 2. [Slang], a person: as, he's a queer *bird*. **—bird in the hand,** something sure because already in one's possession: opposed to **bird in the bush,** something unsure. **—birds of a feather,** people with like traits or tastes.

**bird·ie** (būr'di), *n.* in *golf*, a score of one under par for any hole.

**bird'lime'** (-līm'), *n.* a sticky substance spread on twigs to catch birds.

**bird's'-eye',** *n.* a cotton or linen cloth with a diamond-shaped weave. *adj.* 1. seen from above; general: as, a *bird's-eye* view. 2. having markings that resemble birds' eyes: as, *bird's-eye* maple.

**birth** (būrth), *n.* [< AS. *beran*, to bear], 1. the act of bringing forth offspring. 2. a being born. 3. descent or origin. 4. the beginning of anything. 5. natural inclination: as, an actor by *birth*. **—give birth to,** 1. to bring forth (offspring). 2. to originate.

**birth'day',** *n.* the anniversary of the day of a person's birth or a thing's beginning.

**birth′mark′**, *n.* a skin blemish present at birth.
**birth′place′**, *n.* the place of one's birth.
**birth rate,** the number of births per year per 1,000 of population in a given group.
**birth′right′**, *n.* any rights that a person has by birth.
**bis·cuit** (bis′kit), *n.* [*pl.* -CUITS, -CUIT], [< L. *bis*, twice + *coquere*, to cook], 1. [Chiefly Brit.], a crisp wafer; cracker or cooky. 2. a quick bread, made light with baking powder or soda and baked in small pieces.
**bi·sect** (bī-sekt′), *v.t.* [< *bi-* + L. *secare*, to cut], 1. to cut in two. 2. in *geometry*, to divide into two equal parts. *v.i.* to divide; fork. **—bi·sec′tion,** *n.* **—bi·sec′tor,** *n.*
**bish·op** (bish′əp), *n.* [< Gr. *episkopos*, overseer], 1. a high-ranking clergyman, the head of a church district or diocese. 2. a chessman that can move only diagonally.
**bish′op·ric** (-rik), *n.* the district, position, rank, etc. of a bishop.
**bis·muth** (biz′məth), *n.* [< G.], a pinkish-gray, brittle, metallic element, used in alloys of low melting point: symbol, Bi.
**bi·son** (bī′s'n), *n.* [*pl.* BISON], [ult. < Gmc.], a four-legged mammal with a shaggy mane and a humped back, as the American buffalo.
**bisque** (bisk), *n.* [Fr.], a thick creamed soup made from shellfish, vegetables, etc.
**bis·tro** (bis′trō), *n.* [Fr. slang], a small café.
**bit** (bit), *n.* [< AS. *bite*, a bite], 1. a metal mouthpiece on a bridle, acting as a control. 2. anything that curbs or controls. 3. a drilling or boring tool for use in a brace, etc. *v.t.* [BITTED, BITTING], 1. to put a bit into the mouth of (a horse). 2. to curb.
**bit** (bit), *n.* [< AS. *bita*, piece], 1. a small piece or quantity. 2. somewhat: as, he's a *bit* of a bore. 3. [Colloq.], 12½ cents, as in **two bits** (a quarter). 4. [Colloq.], a short time; moment. *adj.* very small: as, a *bit* part. **—bit by bit,** gradually. **—do one's bit,** to do one's share.
**bitch** (bich), *n.* [AS. *bicce*], 1. the female of the dog, fox, etc. 2. a bad or bad-tempered woman: vulgar term of contempt. *v.i.* [Slang], to complain.
**bite** (bīt), *v.t.* [BIT (bit), BITTEN or BIT, BITING], [AS. *bitan*], 1. to seize or cut with or as with the teeth. 2. to cut into, as with a sharp weapon. 3. to sting, as a snake. 4. to cause to smart. 5. to eat into; corrode. *v.i.* 1. to press or snap the teeth (*into*, *at*, etc.). 2. to cause a biting, or smarting, sensation. 3. to swallow a bait. 4. to be caught, as by a trick. *n.* 1. a biting. 2. biting quality; smart. 3. a wound or sting from biting. 4. a mouthful. 5. [Colloq.], a light meal. **—bite the dust,** 1. to fall dead. 2. to be defeated. **—bit′er,** *n.*
**bit·ing** (bīt′iŋ), *adj.* 1. cutting; sharp. 2. sarcastic. **—bit′ing·ly,** *adv.*
**bitt** (bit), *n.* [? < ON. *biti*, beam], in *naut. usage*, any of the deck posts, often in pairs, to which ropes, etc. are fastened. *v.t.* to wind (ropes, etc.) around a bitt.
**bit·ter** (bit′ẽr), *adj.* [AS. < base of *bitan*, to bite], 1. having a sharp and disagreeable taste. 2. causing or showing sorrow, pain, etc. 3. sharp and disagreeable; harsh. **—bit′ter·ish,** *adj.* **—bit′ter·ly,** *adv.*
**bit·tern** (bit′ẽrn), *n.* [< L. *butio*], a heronlike bird with a booming cry.
**bit′ters,** *n.pl.* a liquor containing bitter herbs, etc., used in some cocktails.
**bit′ter·sweet′**, *n.* a poisonous vine with purple flowers and red berries that taste bitter and sweet. *adj.* both bitter and sweet; both painful and pleasant.
**bi·tu·men** (bi-tōō′mən, -tū′-), *n.* [L.], any of several substances obtained as residue in the distillation of coal tar, petroleum, etc., or occurring as natural asphalt. **—bi·tu′mi·nous** (-mə-nəs), *adj.*
**bituminous coal,** coal that yields pitch or tar when it burns; soft coal.
**bi·valve** (bī′valv′), *n.* any mollusk having two valves or shells hinged together, as a clam. *adj.* having two hinged shells.
**biv·ou·ac** (biv′ōō-ak′, biv′wak), *n.* [Fr. < OHG. *bi-*, by + *wacht*, a guard], a temporary encampment (as of soldiers) in the open. *v.i.* [-ACKED, -ACKING], to encamp in the open.
**bi·week·ly** (bī-wēk′li), *adj. & adv.* 1. (occurring) once every two weeks. 2. semiweekly. *n.* [*pl.* -LIES], a biweekly publication.
**bi·zarre** (bi-zär′), *adj.* [Fr. < Basque *bizar*, beard], odd; eccentric; grotesque.
**Bk,** in *chem.*, berkelium.
**bk.,** [*pl.* BKS.], 1. bank. 2. book.
**bl.,** 1. bale(s). 2. barrel(s).
**B/L,** [*pl.* BS/L], bill of lading.
**blab** (blab), *v.t. & v.i.* [BLABBED, BLABBING], 1. to reveal (secrets). 2. to gossip. *n.* 1. gossip. 2. one who blabs: also **blab′ber.**
**black** (blak), *adj.* [AS. *blæc*], 1. opposite to white: see **color.** 2. dark-complexioned. 3. Negro. 4. without light; dark. 5. dirty. 6. evil; wicked. 7. sad; dismal. 8. sullen. *n.* 1. black pigment: opposite of *white*. 2. dark clothing, as for mourning. 3. a Negro. *v.t. & v.i.* to blacken. **—black out,** to lose consciousness. **—black′ly,** *adv.* **—black′ness,** *n.*
**black′-and-blue′**, *adj.* discolored, as by a bruise.
**black′ball′**, *n.* a vote against. *v.t.* 1. to vote against. 2. to ostracize.
**black′ber′ry,** *n.* [*pl.* -RIES], 1. the small, edible, dark fruit of any of various brambles of the rose family. 2. the bush or vine it grows on.
**black′bird′**, *n.* any of various birds the male of which is almost all black.
**black′board′**, *n.* a smooth surface, usually of slate, on which one can write with chalk.
**black′en** (-'n), *v.i.* to become black or dark. *v.t.* 1. to make black; darken. 2. to slander.
**black eye,** a discoloration of the skin around an eye, caused by a blow.
**black′-eyed′ Su′san** (-īd′ sōō′z'n), a yellow, daisylike flower with a dark center.
**black flag,** the flag of piracy, usually black with a white skull and crossbones.
**black·guard** (blag′ẽrd, -ärd), *n.* a scoundrel; villain. **—black′guard·ly,** *adj. & adv.*
**black′head′**, *n.* a dark plug of dried fatty matter in a pore of the skin.
**black′-heart′ed,** *adj.* wicked; evil.
**black′ing,** *n.* black shoe polish.
**black′jack′** (-jak′), *n.* 1. a small, leather-covered bludgeon with a flexible handle. 2. the black flag of piracy. 3. a card game in which the object is to total 21 points. Also **black jack.** *v.t.* to hit with a blackjack.
**black list,** a list of those to be punished, refused employment, etc. **—black′-list′**, *v.t.*
**black magic,** sorcery.
**black′mail′** (-māl′), *n.* [lit., black rent < OFr. *maille*, a coin], payment extorted to prevent disclosure of information that could bring disgrace. *v.t.* to get or try to get blackmail from. **—black′mail′er,** *n.*
**black mark,** a mark of failure, etc.
**black market,** a place or system for selling goods illegally, esp. in violation of rationing or price control. **—black mar·ket·eer** (mär′kə-têr′).
**black′out′**, *n.* 1. an extinguishing of all stage lights to end a scene, etc. 2. an extinguishing or concealing of lights that might be visible to enemy aircraft. 3. momentary unconsciousness.
**black sheep,** a person regarded as disgraceful by his family or group.
**black′smith′**, *n.* a man who works and repairs iron, and shoes horses.

**black′thorn′,** ***n.*** a thorny shrub with purple or black, plumlike fruit; sloe.

**black widow,** a black female spider with red underneath: it has a poisonous bite and eats its mate.

**blad·der** (blad′ẽr), ***n.*** [AS. *blæddre*], 1. a sac in the pelvic cavity, which holds urine flowing from the kidneys. 2. a thing resembling this: as, a football *bladder.*

**blade** (blād), ***n.*** [AS. *blæd*], 1. the leaf of a grass or a cereal. 2. the flat part of any leaf. 3. a broad, flat surface, as of an oar. 4. the cutting part of a knife, tool, etc. 5. a sword or swordsman. 6. a gay young man.

**blame** (blām), ***v.t.*** [BLAMED, BLAMING], [see BLASPHEME], 1. to accuse of being at fault; condemn (*for*). 2. to put the responsibility of (an error, etc. *on*). ***n.*** 1. a blaming. 2. responsibility for a fault. **—be to blame,** to deserve blame. **—blame′less,** ***adj.***

**blame′wor′thy** (-wũr′*th*i), ***adj.*** deserving to be blamed. **—blame′wor′thi·ness,** ***n.***

**blanch** (blanch, blänch), ***v.t.*** [see BLANK], 1. to make white; bleach. 2. to make pale. ***v.i.*** to turn pale.

**bland** (bland), ***adj.*** [L. *blandus*], 1. agreeable; suave. 2. mild; soothing. **—bland′ly,** ***adv.***

**blan·dish** (blan′dish), ***v.t. & v.i.*** [see BLAND], to flatter; coax; cajole. **—blan′dish·ment,** ***n.***

**blank** (blaŋk), ***adj.*** [< OHG. *blanch*, white], 1. not written on: as, *blank* paper. 2. empty; vacant. 3. empty of thought: as, a *blank* mind. 4. utter; complete: as, a *blank* denial. ***n.*** 1. an empty space, esp. one to be filled out in a printed form. 2. such a printed form. 3. an empty place or time. 4. a powder-filled cartridge without a bullet. ***v.t.*** 1. to conceal by covering over. 2. to hold (an opponent) scoreless. **—draw a blank,** [Colloq.], to be unsuccessful. **—blank′ly,** ***adv.*** **—blank′ness,** ***n.***

**blan·ket** (blaŋ′kit), ***n.*** [see BLANK], 1. a large, soft piece of cloth used for warmth, esp. as a bed cover. 2. anything like this: as, a *blanket* of snow. ***adj.*** including many or all items: as, a *blanket* insurance policy. ***v.t.*** 1. to cover, as with a blanket. 2. to overlie; obscure.

**blare** (blâr), ***v.t. & v.i.*** [BLARED, BLARING], [ME. *bleren*, cry noisily], to sound or exclaim loudly. ***n.*** a loud, trumpetlike sound.

**blar·ney** (blär′ni), ***n.*** [< *Blarney* stone in Ireland, traditionally kissed to gain skill in flattery], flattery. ***v.t. & v.i.*** [-NEYED, -NEYING], to flatter; coax.

**bla·sé** (blä-zā′), ***adj.*** [Fr.], satiated and bored.

**blas·pheme** (blas-fēm′), ***v.t.*** [-PHEMED, -PHEMING], [< Gr. *blasphēmein*, speak evil of], 1. to speak profanely of or to (God or sacred things). 2. to curse. ***v.i.*** to utter blasphemy. **—blas·phem′er,** ***n.***

**blas′phe·my** (-fi-mi), ***n.*** [*pl.* -MIES], 1. profane abuse of God or sacred things. 2. contempt for God. **—blas′phe·mous,** ***adj.***

**blast** (blast, bläst), ***n.*** [< AS. *blæst*], 1. a strong rush of air. 2. the sound of a sudden rush of air, as through a horn. 3. a blight. 4. an explosion, as of dynamite. ***v.t.*** 1. to blight; wither. 2. to explode. **—blast off,** [Colloq.], to take off with explosive force and begin its flight, as a rocket.

**blast furnace,** a smelting furnace in which a blast of air produces the intense heat.

**blast′-off′, blast′off′,** ***n.*** [Colloq.], the launching of a rocket, ballistic missile, etc.

**bla·tant** (blā′t'nt), ***adj.*** [prob. < L. *blaterare*, to babble], 1. disagreeably loud; noisy. 2. obtrusive; gaudy. **—bla′tan·cy** [*pl.* -CIES], ***n.***

**blath·er** (bla*th*′ẽr), ***n.*** [ON. *blathr*], foolish talk. ***v.i. & v.t.*** to talk foolishly.

**blaze** (blāz), ***n.*** [AS. *blæse*], 1. a brilliant burst of flame; fire. 2. any bright light. 3. a spectacular outburst. 4. a vivid display. ***v.i.*** [BLAZED, BLAZING], 1. to burn rapidly or shine brightly. 2. to be excited, as with anger. **—blaze away,** to shoot.

**blaze** (blāz), ***n.*** [prob. < D. *bles*], 1. a white spot on an animal's face. 2. a mark made on a tree by cutting off a piece of bark. ***v.t.*** [BLAZED, BLAZING], to mark (a tree, trail, etc.) with blazes.

**blaze** (blāz), ***v.t.*** [BLAZED, BLAZING], [ON. *blasa*, to blow], to make known; proclaim.

**blaz·er** (blāz′ẽr), ***n.*** a kind of sports jacket, usually brightly colored.

**bla·zon** (blā′z'n), ***n.*** [OFr. *blason*, a shield], 1. a coat of arms. 2. showy display. ***v.t.*** to proclaim. **—bla′zon·ry,** ***n.***

**bldg.,** building.

**bleach** (blēch), ***v.t. & v.i.*** [< AS. *blac*, pale], to make or become white or colorless. ***n.*** a chemical for bleaching. **—bleach′er,** ***n.***

**bleach′ers,** ***n.pl.*** seats, usually roofless, for spectators at outdoor events.

**bleak** (blēk), ***adj.*** [prob. < ON. *bleikr*, pale], 1. exposed to wind and cold; bare. 2. cold; harsh. 3. cheerless; gloomy. **—bleak′ly,** ***adv.***

**blear** (blêr), ***adj.*** [ME. *bleren*], 1. made dim by tears, mucus, etc., as the eyes. 2. blurred. ***v.t.*** 1. to dim with tears, mucus, etc. 2. to blur. **—blear′y** [-IER, -IEST], ***adj.***

**bleat** (blēt), ***v.i.*** [AS. *blætan*], to make the cry of a sheep, goat, or calf. ***n.*** a bleating.

**bleed** (blēd), ***v.i.*** [BLED (bled), BLEEDING], [< AS. *blod*, blood], 1. to emit or lose blood. 2. to feel pain, grief, or sympathy. 3. to ooze sap, juice, etc. ***v.t.*** 1. to draw blood from. 2. to ooze (sap, juice, etc.). 3. [Colloq.], to extort money from.

**blem·ish** (blem′ish), ***v.t.*** [< OFr. *ble(s)me*, pale], to mar; injure. ***n.*** a defect; fault.

**blench** (blench), ***v.t. & v.i.*** to blanch.

**blench** (blench), ***v.i.*** [AS. *blencan*, deceive], to shrink back; flinch.

**blend** (blend), ***v.t.*** [BLENDED or BLENT, BLENDING], [AS. *blendan*], 1. to mix or mingle varieties of (tea, tobacco, etc.). 2. to mix thoroughly. ***v.i.*** 1. to mix; merge. 2. to shade gradually into each other, as colors. 3. to harmonize. ***n.*** 1. a blending. 2. a mixture of varieties: as, a *blend* of coffee.

**bless** (bles), ***v.t.*** [BLESSED or BLEST, BLESSING], [< AS. *bletsian*, consecrate with blood], 1. to make holy. 2. to ask divine favor for. 3. to wish well to. 4. to endow (*with*). 5. to make happy. 6. to praise. 7. to guard.

**bless·ed** (bles′id, blest), ***adj.*** 1. holy; sacred. 2. blissful; fortunate. 3. beatified. 4. bringing comfort. **—bless′ed·ness,** ***n.***

**bless′ing,** ***n.*** 1. a benediction. 2. an invoking of divine favor. 3. a wish for prosperity, success, etc. 4. approval. 5. anything that gives happiness.

**blew** (blōō), pt. of **blow.**

**blight** (blīt), ***n.*** [? < AS. *blieian*, turn pale], 1. any insect, disease, etc. that destroys plants. 2. anything that destroys, frustrates, etc. ***v.t.*** 1. to wither. 2. to destroy.

**blimp** (blimp), ***n.*** [Colloq.], a small, nonrigid or semirigid airship.

**blind** (blīnd), ***adj.*** [AS.], 1. without the power of sight. 2. of or for sightless persons. 3. lacking insight. 4. hard to see; hidden. 5. having no opening. 6. closed at one end: as, a *blind* alley. 7. not controlled by reason: as, *blind* fate. 8. in *aeronautics*, by the use of instruments only: as, *blind* flying. ***n.*** 1. anything that obscures sight or keeps out light, as a window shade. 2. a place of concealment. 3. a decoy. **—blind′ing,** ***adj.*** **—blind′ly,** ***adv.*** **—blind′ness,** ***n.***

**blind date,** [Slang], a date with a stranger, arranged by a third person.

**blind·ers** (blīn′dẽrz), ***n.pl.*** blinkers for a horse.

**blind′fold′** (-fōld′), ***v.t.*** [< ME. *blindfeld*, struck blind], to cover the eyes of, as with a cloth. ***n.*** something used to cover the eyes. ***adj.*** 1. having the eyes covered. 2. reckless.

**blink** (bliŋk), *v.i.* [? < D. *blinken*, shine], 1. to wink rapidly. 2. to flash on and off; twinkle. *v.t.* to cause (eyes, light, etc.) to wink or blink. *n.* 1. a blinking. 2. a glimmer. 3. a glimpse. —**blink at**, to ignore. —**on the blink**, [Slang], out of order.

**blink'er**, *n.* 1. *pl.* flaps on a bridle that shut out a horse's side view. 2. a flashing warning light.

**bliss** (blis), *n.* [AS. *bliths*], 1. great joy or happiness. 2. spiritual joy. —**bliss'ful**, *adj.*

**blister** (blis'tẽr), *n.* [< ON. *blastr*], 1. a little swelling of the skin, filled with watery matter and caused by burning or rubbing. 2. anything like a blister. *v.t.* 1. to raise blisters on. 2. to lash with words. *v.i.* to form blisters. —**blis'ter·y**, *adj.*

**blithe** (blīth), *adj.* [AS.], gay; joyful.

**blithe'some** (-səm), *adj.* blithe.

**blitz·krieg** (blits'krēg'), *n.* [G. *blitz*, lightning + *krieg*, war], sudden, swift, large-scale offensive warfare.

**bliz·zard** (bliz'ẽrd), *n.* [< dial. *bliz*, violent blow + *-ard*], a severe snowstorm with high wind.

**bloat** (blōt), *v.t.* & *v.i.* [< ON. *blautr*, soft], 1. to swell, as with water or air. 2. to puff up, as with pride.

**blob** (blob), *n.* [echoic], a small drop or mass.

**bloc** (blok), *n.* [Fr. < LG. *block*, lump], a group of persons, as of different political parties, combined for a common purpose.

**block** (blok), *n.* [see BLOC], 1. a solid piece of wood, stone, metal, etc. 2. a heavy stand on which chopping, etc. is done. 3. an auctioneer's platform. 4. an obstruction or hindrance. 5. a pulley in a frame. 6. a city square. 7. a group or row of buildings. 8. a number of things regarded as a unit. 9. in *printing*, a piece of engraved wood, etc. with a design. *v.t.* 1. to obstruct; hinder. 2. to mount or mold on a block. —**block in** (or **out**), to sketch roughly; outline. —**on the block**, up for sale or auction.

**block·ade** (blo-kād'), *n.* [*block* + *-ade*], 1. a shutting off of a place by troops or ships to prevent passage. 2. any strategic barrier. *v.t.* [-ADED, -ADING], to subject to a blockade.

**block and tackle**, pulley blocks and ropes, used for lifting heavy objects.

**block'head'**, *n.* a stupid person.

**block'house'**, *n.* a strong wooden fort with a projecting second story.

**bloke** (blōk), *n.* [Slang], a fellow.

**blond** (blond), *adj.* [Fr. < LL. *blondus*], 1. having light-colored hair and skin. 2. light-colored. Also sp. **blonde**. *n.* a blond man or boy. —**blonde**, *n.fem.*

**blood** (blud), *n.* [AS. *blod*], 1. the red fluid circulating in the arteries and veins of animals. 2. bloodshed. 3. the essence of life; life. 4. the sap of a plant. 5. passion, temperament, etc. 6. parental heritage; lineage. 7. kinship. 8. a dandy. —**bad blood**, anger; hatred. —**in cold blood**, 1. with cruelty. 2. deliberately. —**make one's blood boil**, to make one angry.

**blood bank**, a supply of blood stored for future use in transfusion.

**blood count**, the number of red and white corpuscles in a given volume of blood.

**blood'cur'dling** (-kũr'dliŋ), *adj.* very frightening; causing terror or horror.

**blood'ed** (-id), *adj.* of fine breed.

**blood'hound'**, *n.* any of a breed of large, keen-scented tracking dogs.

**blood'less**, *adj.* 1. without bloodshed. 2. anemic or pale. —**blood'less·ly**, *adv.*

**blood'let'ting**, *n.* the opening of a vein to remove blood; bleeding.

**blood'mo·bile'** (-mə-bēl'), *n.* a mobile unit for collecting blood from donors for blood banks.

**blood money**, money paid for a murder.

**blood plasma**, the fluid part of blood, as distinguished from the corpuscles.

**blood poisoning**, a diseased condition of the blood, due to certain microorganisms, etc.

**blood pressure**, the pressure of the blood against the inner walls of the blood vessels.

**blood relation**, a person related by birth.

**blood'shed'**, *n.* killing; slaughter.

**blood'shot'**, *adj.* tinged with blood; red and hurting: said of the eyes.

**blood'suck'er**, *n.* an animal that sucks blood; esp., a leech.

**blood'thirst'y**, *adj.* murderous; cruel.

**blood vessel**, a vein, artery, or capillary.

**blood'y**, *adj.* [-IER, -IEST], 1. of, containing, or covered with blood. 2. involving bloodshed. 3. bloodthirsty. 4. [Brit. Slang], cursed; damned. *adv.* [Brit. Slang], very. *v.t.* [-IED, -YING], to cover or stain with blood. —**blood'i·ly**, *adv.* —**blood'i·ness**, *n.*

**bloom** (bloom), *n.* [< ON. *blomi*, flowers], 1. a flower; blossom. 2. the state or time of flowering. 3. a period of most health, vigor, etc. 4. a youthful, healthy glow. 5. the powdery coating on some fruits or leaves. *v.i.* 1. to flower. 2. to be in one's prime. 3. to glow with health, etc.

**bloom·ers** (bloom'ẽrz), *n.pl.* [< Amelia *Bloomer*, Am. feminist], 1. baggy trousers gathered at the knee, worn by women for athletics. 2. a similar undergarment.

**bloom'ing**, *adj.* 1. blossoming. 2. flourishing. 3. [Colloq.], utter.

**blos·som** (blos'əm), *n.* [AS. *blostma*], 1. a flower, esp. of a fruit-bearing plant. 2. a state or time of flowering. *v.i.* 1. to have or open into blossoms; bloom. 2. to begin to thrive or flourish; develop.

**blot** (blot), *n.* [< AS. *plott*, clod], 1. a spot or stain, esp. of ink. 2. a moral sin. *v.t.* [BLOTTED, BLOTTING], 1. to spot; stain. 2. to disgrace. 3. to erase or cancel (with *out*). 4. to obscure (with *out*). 5. to dry with blotting paper. *v.i.* 1. to make blots. 2. to become blotted. 3. to be absorbent.

**blotch** (bloch), *n.* [< OFr. *bloche*, clod], 1. a discoloration or eruption on the skin. 2. any large, irregular stain. *v.t.* to mark with blotches. —**blotch'y**, *adj.*

**blot'ter**, *n.* 1. a piece of blotting paper. 2. a book for recording events as they occur: as, a police *blotter*.

**blotting paper**, a soft, absorbent paper used to dry a surface freshly written on in ink.

**blouse** (blous, blouz), *n.* [Fr., workman's smock], 1. a kind of shirtwaist worn by women and children. 2. a coat or tunic worn by soldiers, etc. 3. a sailor's jumper. *v.i.* & *v.t.* [BLOUSED, BLOUSING], to gather in at the waistline. —**blouse'like'**, *adj.*

**blow** (blō), *v.i.* [BLEW, BLOWN (blōn), BLOWING], [AS. *blawan*], 1. to stir or move, as the wind. 2. to send forth air, as with the mouth. 3. to pant. 4. to sound by blowing. 5. to spout water and air: as, whales *blow*. 6. to be carried by the wind. 7. to storm. 8. [Colloq.], to brag. 9. [Slang], to go away. *v.t.* 1. to force air from, into, onto, or through. 2. to drive by blowing. 3. to sound by blowing. 4. to inflate. 5. to burst by an explosion (with *up* or *out*). 6. to melt (a fuse, etc.). 7. [Colloq.], to spend (money) freely. *n.* 1. a blowing or being blown. 2. a blast or gale. —**blow off**, [Colloq.], to release emotions, as by shouting. —**blow over**, to pass over or by. —**blow up**, [Colloq.], to lose one's temper. —**blow'er**, *n.*

**blow** (blō), *n.* [prob. < *blow*, *v.i.*], 1. a hit, as with the fist. 2. a sudden attack. 3. a sudden calamity; shock. —**come to blows**, to begin fighting.

**blow** (blō), *v.i.* [BLEW, BLOWN (blōn), BLOWING], [AS. *blowan*], to bloom. *v.t.* to cause to bloom. *n.* a mass of blossoms.

**blow′fly′**, *n.* [*pl.* -FLIES], a fly that lays its eggs on meat, in wounds, etc.
**blow′out′**, *n.* 1. the bursting of a tire. 2. [Slang], a party, banquet, etc.
**blow′pipe′**, *n.* a tube for forcing air into a flame to intensify its heat.
**blow′torch′**, *n.* a small gasoline torch that shoots out a hot flame.
**blub·ber** (blub′ẽr), *n.* [ME., a bubble], the fat of the whale. *v.i.* to weep loudly. *v.t.* to say while blubbering. **—blub′ber·y**, *adj.*
**blu·cher** (blōō′chẽr, -kẽr), *n.* [< von *Blücher*, Prussian general (1742–1819)], a kind of shoe in which the vamp is of one piece with the tongue.
**bludg·eon** (bluj′ən), *n.* [? < MFr. *bouge*, club], a short club with a thick, heavy end. *v.t. & v.i.* 1. to strike with a bludgeon. 2. to threaten; coerce. **—bludg′eon·er**, *n.*
**blue** (blōō), *adj.* [< OHG. *blao*], 1. of the color of the clear sky. 2. livid: said of the skin. 3. gloomy. 4. puritanical: as, *blue* laws. *n.* 1. the color of the clear sky. 2. any blue pigment. 3. anything colored blue. *v.t.* [BLUED, BLUING or BLUEING], 1. to make blue. 2. to use bluing in or on. *v.i.* to become blue. **—out of the blue**, unexpected. **—the blue**, 1. the sky. 2. the sea. **—the blues**, 1. [Colloq.], a depressed, unhappy feeling. 2. a type of Negro folk song, having slow jazz rhythm, melancholy words, etc.
**Blue′beard′**, *n.* a legendary man who married and then murdered six wives.
**blue′bell′**, *n.* any of various plants with blue, bell-shaped flowers.
**blue′ber′ry**, *n.* [*pl.* -RIES], 1. a small, edible, blue-black berry. 2. the shrub it grows on.
**blue′bird′**, *n.* a small N. American songbird with a bluish back.
**blue blood**, 1. descent from nobility. 2. a person of such descent.
**blue book**, a book listing socially prominent people: also **blue′book′**, *n.*
**blue′bot′tle**, *n.* 1. a plant bearing blue, white, pink, or purple flowers with bottle-shaped rays; cornflower. 2. a large blowfly with a steel-blue abdomen.
**blue′fish′**, *n.* [*pl.* see FISH], a blue-and-silver food fish of the Atlantic coast.
**blue′grass′**, *n.* a type of grass with bluish-green stems; esp., **Kentucky bluegrass.**
**blue′jack′et**, *n.* an enlisted man in the U.S. or British navy.
**blue′jay′**, *n.* a noisy, crested bird with a blue back: also **blue jay.**
**blue′-pen′cil**, *v.t.* to edit: from the blue pencils used by editors.
**blue′print′**, *n.* 1. a photographic reproduction in white on a blue background, as of architectural plans. 2. any detailed plan or outline. *v.t.* to make a blueprint of.
**blue′stock′ing**, *n.* a learned, bookish, or pedantic woman.
**bluff** (bluf), *v.t. & v.i.* [prob. < D. *bluffen*, baffle], to mislead or frighten by a false, bold front. *n.* 1. a bluffing. 2. one who bluffs. **—bluff′er**, *n.*
**bluff** (bluf), *adj.* [< D. *blaf*, flat], 1. ascending steeply with a broad, flat front. 2. having a rough, frank manner. *n.* a high, steep bank or cliff. **—bluff′ly**, *adv.*
**blu·ing** (blōō′iŋ), *n.* a blue rinse used on white fabrics to prevent yellowing: also sp. **blueing.**
**blu·ish** (blōō′ish), *adj.* somewhat blue.
**blun·der** (blun′dẽr), *v.i.* [< ON. *blunda*, shut the eyes], 1. to move clumsily. 2. to make a foolish mistake. *v.t.* 1. to say stupidly. 2. to do clumsily or poorly; bungle. *n.* a foolish mistake.
**blun′der·buss′** (-bus′), *n.* [D. *donderbus*, thunder box], 1. an obsolete short gun with a broad muzzle. 2. one who blunders.
**blunt** (blunt), *adj.* [prob. < ON.], 1. slow to perceive; dull. 2. having a dull edge, etc. 3. plain-spoken. *v.t. & v.i.* to make or become dull. **—blunt′ly**, *adv.* **—blunt′ness**, *n.*
**blur** (blũr), *v.t. & v.i.* [BLURRED, BLURRING], [? < *blear* + *blot*], 1. to smear; blot. 2. to make or become indistinct in shape, etc. 3. to dim. *n.* 1. a being blurred. 2. an obscuring stain. 3. anything indistinct. **—blur′ry**, *adj.*
**blurb** (blũrb), *n.* [arbitrary coinage], [Colloq.], an exaggerated advertisement.
**blurt** (blũrt), *v.t.* [? < *bl*ow, *bl*ast, etc. + sp*urt*], to say impulsively (with *out*).
**blush** (blush), *v.i.* [< AS. *blyscan*, to shine], 1. to become red in the face, as from embarrassment. 2. to be ashamed (*at* or *for*). 3. to become rosy. *n.* 1. a reddening of the face, as from shame. 2. a rosy color. *adj.* rosy. **—at first blush**, at first sight.
**blus·ter** (blus′tẽr), *v.i.* [< LG. *blüstern*], 1. to blow stormily: said of wind. 2. to speak in a noisy or swaggering manner. *n.* 1. noisy commotion. 2. noisy or swaggering talk. **—blus′ter·er**, *n.* **—blus′ter·y**, *adj.*
**blvd.**, boulevard.
**BM**, [Colloq.], bowel movement.
**bo·a** (bō′ə), *n.* [L.], 1. a large, nonpoisonous, tropical snake that crushes its prey in its coils, as the python. 2. a woman's long scarf of fur or feathers.
**boar** (bôr), *n.* [AS. *bar*], 1. an uncastrated male pig. 2. a wild hog.
**board** (bôrd), *n.* [AS. *bord*, plank], 1. a long, thin, flat piece of sawed wood. 2. a flat piece of wood, etc. for some special use: as, a bulletin *board*. 3. pasteboard. 4. a table, esp. for meals. 5. meals, esp. as provided regularly for pay. 6. a group of administrators; council. *v.t.* 1. to cover with boards (often with *up*). 2. to provide with meals regularly for pay. *v.i.* to receive meals regularly for pay. **—the boards**, the stage (of a theater).
**board** (bôrd), *n.* [AS. *bord*], 1. the side of a ship. 2. a rim or border, as in *seaboard*. *v.t.* 1. to come onto the deck of (a ship). 2. to get on (a train, bus, etc.). **—on board**, on a ship, aircraft, etc.
**board′er**, *n.* one who gets his meals, or room and meals, regularly for pay.
**board′ing·house′**, *n.* a house where meals, or lodging and meals, can be had for pay.
**board′walk′**, *n.* a walk made of thick boards, especially along a beach.
**boast** (bōst), *v.i.* [< Anglo-Fr.], to talk, esp. about oneself, with too much pride; brag. *v.t.* to brag or glory in. *n.* 1. a boasting. 2. anything boasted of. **—boast′er**, *n.* **—boast′ful**, *adj.* **—boast′ful·ly**, *adv.*
**boat** (bōt), *n.* [AS. *bat*], 1. a small, open water craft. 2. a ship: landsman's term. 3. a boat-shaped dish. *v.i.* to go in a boat. **—in the same boat**, in the same situation. **—boat′man** [*pl.* -MEN], *n.*
**boat′ing**, *n.* rowing, sailing, etc.
**boat·swain** (bō′s'n, bōt′swān′), *n.* a ship's officer in charge of the deck crew, the rigging, etc.: also **bosun.**
**bob** (bob), *n.* [< ME. *bobbe*, hanging cluster; 3 & 4 < the *v.*], 1. any knoblike hanging weight. 2. a woman's or girl's short haircut. 3. a quick, jerky motion. 4. a float on a fishing line. *v.t.* [BOBBED, BOBBING], [ME. *bobben*, to knock against], 1. to make move with a jerky motion. 2. to cut (hair, a tail, etc.) short. *v.i.* to move with a jerky motion. **—bob up**, to appear unexpectedly.
**bob·bin** (bob′in), *n.* [Fr. *bobine*], a reel or spool for thread, etc. used in spinning, machine sewing, etc.
**bob·by** (bob′i), *n.* [*pl.* -BIES], [after Sir Robert (*Bobby*) Peel (1788–1850), who remodeled the London police force], [Brit. Slang], a policeman.

**bobby pin,** [from use with *bobbed* hair], a small metal hairpin with the ends pressing close together.

**bobby socks,** [< *bob*, to cut short], [Colloq.], girls' ankle-length socks.

**bobby sox·er** (sok′sẽr), [Colloq.], a girl in her teens: also **bob′by-sox′er,** ***n.***

**bob′cat′,** ***n.*** the American lynx.

**bob·o·link** (bob″'l-iŋk′), ***n.*** [echoic], a migratory songbird of N. America.

**bob′sled′,** ***n.*** a long racing sled.

**bob·white** (bob′hwit′), ***n.*** [echoic], a small N. American quail.

**bock** (bok), ***n.*** [< *Eimbeck*, German city where first brewed], a dark beer usually made in the spring: also **bock beer.**

**bode** (bōd), ***v.t.*** [BODED, BODING], [< AS. *boda*, messenger], to be an omen of. **—bode ill** (or **well**), to be a bad (or good) omen.

**bode** (bōd), pt. of **bide.**

**bod·ice** (bod′is), ***n.*** [alt. < *bodies*, pl. of *body*], the closefitting upper part of a woman's dress.

**bod·i·ly** (bod″'l-i), ***adj.*** 1. physical. 2. of, in, or for the body. ***adv.*** 1. in person. 2. as a single group.

**bod·kin** (bod′kin), ***n.*** [? < Celt.], 1. a pointed instrument for making holes in cloth. 2. a thick, blunt needle. 3. [Obs.], a dagger.

**bod·y** (bod′i), ***n.*** [*pl.* -IES], [< AS. *bodig*], 1. the whole physical substance of a man, animal, or plant. 2. the trunk of a man or animal. 3. the main part of anything. 4. a corpse. 5. a distinct mass: as, a ***body*** of water. 6. a distinct group of people or things. 7. strength or consistency, as of wine. 8. [Colloq.], a person.

**bod′y·guard′,** ***n.*** a person or persons, usually armed, assigned to guard someone.

**body politic,** people constituting a political unit with a government; state.

**Boer** (bōr, bôr, boor), ***n.*** [< D. *boer*, peasant], a descendant of Dutch colonists in South Africa. ***adj.*** of the Boers.

**bog** (bog, bôg), ***n.*** [< Gael. *bog*, soft, moist], wet, spongy ground; small marsh or swamp. ***v.t. & v.i.*** [BOGGED, BOGGING], to sink in or as in a bog (often with *down*). **—bog′gy,** ***adj.***

**bo·gey** (bō′gi), ***n.*** [*pl.* -GEYS], 1. a bogy. 2. [after an imaginary Colonel *Bogey*], in *golf*, one stroke over par on a hole.

**bog·gle** (bog″'l), ***v.i.*** [-GLED, -GLING], [< Scot. *bogle*, specter], 1. to be startled; shy away (with *at*). 2. to hesitate or have scruples (with *at*). 3. to bungle. ***v.t.*** to bungle or botch. ***n.*** a boggling.

**bo·gus** (bō′gəs), ***adj.*** not genuine; spurious.

**bo·gy** (bō′gi), ***n.*** [*pl.* -GIES], [< Scot. *bogle*, specter], an imaginary evil spirit; goblin.

**Bo·he·mi·an** (bō-hē′mi-ən), ***n.*** 1. a native of Bohemia. 2. the Czech language. 3. one who lives unconventionally. ***adj.*** 1. of Bohemia, its people, etc. 2. like a Bohemian.

**boil** (boil), ***v.i.*** [< L. *bulla*, a bubble], 1. to bubble up and vaporize over direct heat. 2. to seethe like boiling liquids. 3. to be agitated, as with rage. 4. to cook by boiling. ***v.t.*** 1. to heat to the boiling point. 2. to cook by boiling. ***n.*** the act or state of boiling. **—boil down,** 1. to lessen in quantity by boiling. 2. to abridge; condense.

**boil** (boil), ***n.*** [AS. *byle*], an inflamed, pus-filled swelling on the skin.

**boil′er,** ***n.*** 1. a container in which things are boiled or heated. 2. a strong container in which water is turned to steam for heating or power. 3. a tank to hold hot water.

**boil′ing point,** the temperature at which a liquid boils: for water, usually 212°F.

**bois·ter·ous** (bois′tẽr-əs), ***adj.*** [< OFr. *boisteus*, rough], 1. rough; violent; turbulent. 2. loud and exuberant.

**bold** (bōld), ***adj.*** [AS. *b(e)ald*], 1. daring; fearless. 2. very free in behavior or manner; impudent. 3. steep; abrupt. 4. prominent and clear. **—make bold,** to be so bold as (to do something). **—bold′ly,** ***adv.*** **—bold′ness,** ***n.***

**bold′-faced′** (-fāst′), ***adj.*** impudent.

**bole** (bōl), ***n.*** [ON. *bolr*], a tree trunk.

**bo·le·ro** (bō-lâr′ō), ***n.*** [*pl.* -ROS], [Sp.], 1. a Spanish dance in ¾ time. 2. the music for this. 3. a short, open vest.

**boll** (bōl), ***n.*** [< AS. *bolla*, bowl], the pod of a plant, esp. of flax or cotton.

**boll weevil,** a small beetle whose larvae do damage to cotton bolls.

**bo·lo·gna** (bə-lō′nə, -ni), ***n.*** [< *Bologna*, It. city], a seasoned, smoked sausage.

**Bol·she·vik, bol·she·vik** (bol′shə-vik′, bōl′-), ***n.*** [*pl.* -VIKS, -VIKI (-vē′ki)], [Russ. < *bolshe*, the majority], 1. a member of the majority party that came into power in Russia in 1917. 2. a member of the Communist Party of the Soviet Union. ***adj.*** of or like the Bolsheviks or Bolshevism.

**Bol′she·vism, bol′she·vism,** ***n.*** the policies and practices of the Bolsheviks. **—Bol′she·vist, bol′she·vist,** ***n. & adj.***

**bol·ster** (bōl′stẽr), ***n.*** [AS.], 1. a long, narrow pillow. 2. any bolsterlike object or support. ***v.t.*** to prop (*up*) as with a bolster.

**bolt** (bōlt), ***n.*** [AS.], 1. a short, blunt arrow used with a crossbow. 2. a flash of lightning. 3. a sliding bar for locking a door, etc. 4. a threaded metal rod used with a nut to hold parts together. 5. a roll of cloth, paper, etc. ***v.t.*** 1. to say suddenly; blurt. 2. to swallow (food) hurriedly. 3. to fasten as with a bolt. 4. to abandon (a party, group, etc.). ***v.i.*** 1. to start suddenly; spring away. 2. to withdraw support from one's party, etc. **—bolt upright,** very straight upright.

**bolt** (bōlt), ***v.t.*** [< OFr. *bure*, coarse cloth], to sift (flour, grain, etc.).

**bomb** (bom), ***n.*** [< Gr. *bombos*, hollow sound], an explosive, incendiary, or gas-filled container, for dropping, hurling, etc. ***v.t. & v.i.*** to attack or destroy with bombs.

**bom·bard** (bom-bärd′), ***v.t.*** [Fr. < *bombarde*, cannon], 1. to attack with artillery or bombs. 2. to attack with questions, etc.

**bom′bard·ier′** (-bẽr-dêr′), ***n.*** one who releases the bombs in a bomber.

**bom·bast** (bom′bast), ***n.*** [ult. < Per. *pambak*, cotton], high-sounding, pompous speech. **—bom·bas′tic,** ***adj.***

**bomb·er** (bom′ẽr), ***n.*** an airplane designed for dropping bombs.

**bomb′shell′,** ***n.*** 1. a bomb. 2. any sudden, unforeseen occurrence.

**bo·na fi·de** (bō′nə fī′di *or* fīd′), [L.], in good faith; without fraud or deceit.

**bo·nan·za** (bō-nan′zə), ***n.*** [Sp. < L. *bonus*, good], 1. a rich vein of ore. 2. [Colloq.], any source of wealth.

**bon·bon** (bon′bon′), ***n.*** [Fr. *bon*, good], a small piece of candy.

**bond** (bond), ***n.*** [AS. *bindan*, bind], 1. anything that binds, fastens, or unites. 2. *pl.* shackles. 3. a binding agreement. 4. a duty or obligation imposed by a contract, promise, etc. 5. the status of goods kept in a warehouse until taxes are paid. 6. an interest-bearing certificate issued by a government or business, redeemable on a specified date. 7. *a*) surety against theft, absconding, etc. *b*) a payer of bail. *c*) the amount paid as surety or bail. ***v.t.*** 1. to join; bind. 2. to furnish a bond (sense 7*a*) for (another). 3. to place or hold (goods) in bond. 4. to put under bonded debt.

**bond·age** (bon′dij), ***n.*** [ult. < ON. *bua*, dwell], serfdom; slavery.

**bond′man** (-mən), ***n.*** [*pl.* -MEN], a slave. **—bond′wom′an** [*pl.* -WOMEN], ***n.fem.***

**bonds·man** (bondz′mən), ***n.*** [*pl.* -MEN],

1. a bondman. 2. one who furnishes bond, or surety, for another.
**bone** (bōn), *n.* [AS. *ban*], 1. any of the pieces of hard tissue forming the skeleton of most vertebrates. 2. this hard tissue. 3. *pl.* the skeleton. 4. a bonelike substance or thing. *v.t.* [BONED, BONING], to remove the bones from. *v.i.* [Slang], to study hard (often with *up*). **—feel in one's bones,** to be certain without any real reason. **—have a bone to pick,** to have cause to quarrel. **—make no bones about,** [Colloq.], to admit freely. **—bone′less,** *adj.*
**bone′dry′,** *adj.* very dry.
**bon·er** (bōn′ẽr), *n.* [Slang], a blunder.
**bon·fire** (bon′fīr′), *n.* [ME. *banfir,* bone fire (pyre)], an outdoor fire.
**bon·go** (boŋ′gō), *n.* [*pl.* -GOS (-gōz)], [Am. Sp. < ?], either of a pair of small, tuned drums: in full, **bongo drums.**
**bo·ni·to** (bə-nē′tō), *n.* [*pl.* -TOS, -TOES], [Sp.], any of several salt-water food fishes of the mackerel family.
‡**bon jour** (bōn′ zhōōr′), [Fr.], good day; hello.
**bon·net** (bon′it), *n.* [< OFr. *bonet*], a brimless hat with a chin ribbon, worn by children and women. *v.t.* to put a bonnet on.
**bon·ny, bon·nie** (bon′i), *adj.* [-NIER, -NIEST], [< Fr. *bon,* good], 1. handsome; pretty. 2. healthy-looking; robust.
**bon·sai** (bon-sī′), *n.* [Japan., lit., tray arrangement], 1. the art of dwarfing and shaping trees, shrubs, etc. 2. such a tree or shrub.
**bo·nus** (bō′nəs), *n.* [*pl.* -NUSES], [L., good], anything given in addition to the customary or required amount.
‡**bon voy·age** (bōn′ vwä′yäzh′), [Fr.], pleasant journey.
**bon·y** (bōn′i), *adj* [-IER, -IEST], 1. of, like, or having bones. 2. thin; emaciated.
**boo** (bōō), *interj. & n.* [*pl.* BOOS], a sound made to express disapproval, etc., or to startle. *v.i. & v.t.* [BOOED, BOOING], to shout "boo" (at).
**boo·by** (bōō′bi), *n.* [*pl.* -BIES], [Sp. *bobo*], a fool: also **boob** (bōōb).
**booby trap,** any scheme or device for tricking a person unawares.
**boo·dle** (bōō′d'l), *n.* [? < D. *boedel,* property], [Slang], 1. something given as a bribe; graft. 2. loot. **—boo′dler,** *n.*
**boo·gie·woo·gie** (boo′gi-woo′gi), *n.* [echoic], jazz music characterized by repeated bass figures in 8/8 rhythm.
**book** (book), *n.* [AS. *boc*], 1. a printed work on sheets of paper bound together, usually between hard covers. 2. a main division of a literary work. 3. a record; account. 4. a libretto. 5. a booklike package, as of matches. *v.t.* 1. to record in a book; list. 2. to engage ahead of time, as rooms, etc. 3. to record charges against on a police record. **—bring to book,** to force to explain. **—by the book,** according to the rules. **—the (Good) Book,** the Bible.
**book′bind′er,** *n.* a person whose work is binding books. **—book′bind′ing,** *n.*
**book′case′** (-kās′), *n.* a set of shelves for holding books.
**book end,** a weight or bracket that keeps a row of books upright.
**book′ie** (-i), *n.* [Slang], a bookmaker.
**book′ish,** *adj.* 1. inclined to read and study. 2. pedantic. **—book′ish·ness,** *n.*
**book′keep′ing,** *n.* the work of keeping a systematic record of business transactions. **—book′keep′er,** *n.*
**book′let** (-lit), *n.* a small book; pamphlet.
**book′mak′er,** *n.* a person in the business of taking bets, esp. on horses.
**book′mark′,** *n.* anything put between the pages of a book to mark the place.
**book′plate′,** *n.* a label with the owner's name, etc. for pasting in a book.
**book′worm′,** *n.* 1. an insect larva that feeds on the binding, paste, etc. of books. 2. one who spends much time reading.
**boom** (bōōm), *v.i.* [echoic], to make a deep, hollow sound. *v.t.* to say with such a sound. *n.* such a sound.
**boom** (bōōm), *n.* [D., a beam], 1. a spar extending from a mast to hold the bottom of a sail outstretched. 2. a long beam on a derrick for supporting and guiding anything lifted. 3. a barrier, as of logs, to prevent floating logs from dispersing. *v.i.* to sail at top speed.
**boom** (bōōm), *v.i.* [< prec. *v.i.*], to increase or grow rapidly. *v.t.* to cause to flourish; support vigorously. *n.* a prosperous period.
**boom·er·ang** (bōōm′ẽr-aŋ), *n.* [< Australian native name], 1. a flat, curved stick that can be thrown so that it will return to the thrower. 2. a scheme, etc. that goes awry and results in disadvantage. *v.i.* to act as a boomerang.
**boon** (bōōn), *n.* [ON. *bon,* petition], 1. a welcome benefit. 2. [Archaic], a request.
**boon** (bōōn), *adj.* [< L. *bonus,* good], merry; convivial: in *boon companion.*
**boon·docks** (bōōn′doks′), *n.pl.* [orig. military slang < Tag. *bundok,* mountain], [Colloq.], a wild, often wooded area; wilderness.
**boon·dog·gle** (bōōn′dôg″l, -dog″l), *v.i.* [-GLED, -GLING], to do trifling, valueless work. *n.* trifling, valueless work.
**boor** (boor), *n.* [D. *boer,* a peasant], a rude, awkward, ill-mannered person. **—boor′ish,** *adj.* **—boor′ish·ly,** *adv.*
**boost** (bōōst), *v.t.* [prob. naut. *bouse,* haul up], [Colloq.], 1. to raise as by a push from below. 2. to speak in favor of. *n.* [Colloq.], 1. a push upward or forward. 2. an increase. **—boost′er,** *n.*
**boot** (bōōt), *n.* [OFr. *bote*], 1. a covering of leather, rubber, etc. for the foot and part of the leg. 2. a patch for the inside of a tire casing. 3. a kick. *v.t.* 1. to put boots on. 2. to kick. 3. [Slang], to dismiss. **—the boot,** [Slang], dismissal; discharge.
**boot** (bōōt), *n., v.t. & v.i.* [AS. *bot,* advantage], [Obs.], profit. **—to boot,** besides; in addition.
**boot′black′,** *n.* one whose work is shining shoes or boots.
**boot·ee** (bōō-tē′, bōō′ti), *n.* a baby's soft, knitted shoe.
**booth** (bōōth), *n.* [< ON. *bua,* dwell], 1. a stall for the sale of goods. 2. a small enclosure for voting at elections. 3. a small structure for housing a public telephone, etc.
**boot′leg′,** *v.t. & v.i.* [-LEGGED, -LEGGING], [< hiding liquor in a boot], to make or sell (liquor, etc.) illegally. *adj.* 1. made or sold illegally. 2. of bootlegging. *n.* bootlegged liquor. **—boot′leg′ger,** *n.*
**boot′less,** *adj.* [< *boot* (profit)], useless.
**boot·lick** (bōōt′lik′), *v.t. & v.i.* [Slang], to seek favor with by fawning, servility, etc.
**boo·ty** (bōō′ti), *n.* [*pl.* -TIES], [< MLG. *bute*], 1. spoils of war. 2. plunder. 3. any prize.
**booze** (bōōz), *v.i.* [BOOZED, BOOZING], [D. *buizen*], [Colloq.], to drink too much liquor. *n.* [Colloq.], liquor.
**bo·rac·ic acid** (bô-ras′ik), boric acid.
**bo·rate** (bôr′āt), *n.* a salt or ester of boric acid. *v.t.* [-RATED, -RATING], to treat with borax or boric acid. **—bo′rat·ed,** *adj.*
**bo·rax** (bôr′aks), *n.* [< Per. *būrah*], a white, crystalline salt, used in glass, soaps, etc.
**bor·der** (bôr′dẽr), *n.* [< OHG. *bord,* margin], 1. an edge or part near an edge; margin. 2. a dividing line between two countries, etc. 3. a narrow strip along an edge. *v.t.* 1. to provide with a border. 2. to extend along the edge of. *adj.* of or near a border. **—border on** (or **upon**), to be next to.

**bor′der·land′,** *n.* 1. land near a border. 2. a vague condition, place, etc.
**bor′der·line′,** *n.* a boundary. *adj.* 1. on a boundary. 2. indefinite; doubtful.
**bore** (bôr), *v.t.* [BORED, BORING], [< AS. *bor,* auger], 1. to make a hole in with a drill, etc. 2. to make (a well, etc.) as by drilling. 3. to weary by being dull. *v.i.* to bore a hole or passage. *n.* 1. a hole made as by boring. 2. *a*) the hollow part of a tube or gun barrel. *b*) its inside diameter. 3. a tiresome, dull person or thing. —**bor′er,** *n.*
**bore** (bôr), pt. of **bear.**
**bore·dom** (bôr′dəm), *n.* the condition of being bored or uninterested.
**bo·ric acid** (bôr′ik), a white, crystalline, acid compound, used as a mild antiseptic.
**born** (bôrn), pp. of **bear** (to give birth). *adj.* 1. brought into life or existence. 2. by nature: as, a *born* musician.
**borne** (bôrn), pp. of **bear** (to carry).
**bo·ron** (bô′ron), *n.* [< *borax*], a nonmetallic chemical element occurring in borax, etc.: symbol, B.
**bor·ough** (bũr′ō), *n.* [AS. *burg,* town], 1. a self-governing, incorporated town. 2. one of the five administrative units of New York City.
**bor·row** (bor′ō, bôr′ō), *v.t. & v.i.* [< AS. *borh,* a pledge], 1. to take or receive (something) intending to return it. 2. to adopt (an idea, etc.) as one's own. —**bor′row·er,** *n.*
**borsch** (bôrsh), *n.* [Russ. *borshch*], beet soup, served usually with sour cream.
**bosh** (bosh), *n. & interj.* [Turk., empty], [Colloq.], nonsense.
**bosk·y** (bos′ki), *adj.* 1. wooded. 2. shady.
**bos·om** (booz′əm, bōō′zəm), *n.* [AS. *bosm*], 1. the human breast. 2. the breast regarded as the source of feelings. 3. the interior; midst: as, the *bosom* of one's family. 4. the part of a garment that covers the breast. *adj.* 1. of the bosom. 2. close; intimate.
**boss** (bôs), *n.* [D. *baas,* a master], [Colloq.], 1. an employer or supervisor. 2. one who controls a political organization. *v.t. & v.i.* [Colloq.], 1. to be the boss (of). 2. to exercise undue authority (over). *adj.* [Colloq.], chief.
**boss** (bôs, bos), *n.* [< OFr. *boce,* a swelling], a protruding ornament or projecting knob. *v.t.* to stud.
**boss′y,** *adj.* [-IER, -IEST], [Colloq.], domineering.
**Bos·ton terrier** (or **bull**) (bôs′t'n, bos′-), [< *Boston,* Mass.], a small dog having a smooth, dark coat with white markings.
**bo·sun** (bō′s'n), *n.* a boatswain.
**bot·a·ny** (bot′ə-ni), *n.* [< Gr. *botanē,* a plant], the science that deals with plants and plant life: abbrev. **bot.** —**bo·tan·i·cal** (bə-tan′i-k'l), **bo·tan′ic,** *adj.* —**bot′a·nist,** *n.*
**botch** (boch), *v.t.* [prob. < D. *botsen,* to patch], 1. to patch or repair clumsily. 2. to bungle. *n.* a bungled piece of work.
**both** (bōth), *adj. & pron.* [< ON. *bathir*], the two: as, *both* (birds) sang loudly. *conj. & adv.* together; equally (with *and*): as, I am *both* tired and hungry.
**both·er** (both′ẽr), *v.t. & v.i.* [prob. < *pother*], 1. to annoy; worry. 2. to trouble (oneself). *n.* 1. worry; trouble. 2. one who gives trouble. —**both′er·some** (-səm), *adj.*
**bot·tle** (bot′'l), *n.* [< LL. *buttis,* a vat], 1. a narrow-necked container for liquids, usually of glass. 2. its contents. *v.t.* [-TLED, -TLING], 1. to put into a bottle. 2. to restrain (with *up*). —**bot′tler,** *n.*
**bot′tle·neck′,** *n.* 1. a narrow passage or road. 2. any hindrance to progress.
**bot·tom** (bot′əm), *n.* [AS. *botm*], 1. the lowest part of anything. 2. the part on which something rests. 3. the side underneath. 4. the seat of a chair. 5. the ground beneath a body of water. 6. a ship's keel. 7. basis; cause; origin. *adj.* lowest; last; basic. —**at bottom,** fundamentally. —**bot′tom·less,** *adj.*
**bot·u·lism** (boch′ə-liz'm), *n.* [< L. *botulus,* sausage], poisoning resulting from the toxin produced by a bacillus often found in improperly preserved foods.
**bou·doir** (bōō′dwär), *n.* [Fr., pouting room], a woman's private room.
**bouf·fant** (bōō-fänt′), *adj.* [< Fr. *bouffer,* swell up], puffed out; full.
**bough** (bou), *n.* [AS. *boh,* shoulder], a branch of a tree; esp., a main branch.
**bought** (bôt), pt. and pp. of **buy.**
**bouil·lon** (bool′yon, -yən), *n.* [Fr. < *bouillir,* to boil], a clear broth.
**boul·der** (bōl′dẽr), *n.* [< ME. *bulderstan*; cf. Sw. *bullersten,* noise stone], a large rock worn by weather and water.
**boul·e·vard** (bool′ə-värd′, bōō′lə-), *n.* [Fr. < G. *bollwerk,* bulwark], a broad street, often lined with trees.
**bounce** (bouns), *v.i.* [BOUNCED, BOUNCING], [< D. *bonzen,* to thump], 1. to spring back, as upon impact; rebound. 2. to spring; leap. *v.t.* 1. to bump. 2. to cause to bound or rebound, as a ball. 3. [Slang], to put (a person) out as by force. *n.* 1. a bouncing; rebound. 2. a leap; jump. 3. capacity for bouncing. 4. [Slang], spirit; dash. —**get the bounce,** [Slang], to be dismissed.
**bounc′er,** *n.* [Slang], anyone hired to remove disorderly people from a night club, restaurant, etc.
**bounc′ing,** *adj.* 1. big; heavy. 2. healthy.
**bound** (bound), *v.i.* [Fr. *bondir,* to leap], 1. to move with a leap or leaps. 2. to bounce; rebound. *v.t.* to cause to bound or bounce. *n.* 1. a jump; leap. 2. a bounce; rebound.
**bound** (bound), pt. and pp. of **bind.** *adj.* 1. tied. 2. closely connected. 3. certain: as, *bound* to win. 4. obliged: as, legally *bound* to do it. 5. having a binding, as a book. 6. [Colloq.], determined; resolved.
**bound** (bound), *adj.* [< ON. *bua,* prepare], going; headed: as, *bound* for home.
**bound** (bound), *n.* [< LL. *butina*], 1. a boundary. 2. *pl.* an area near a boundary. *v.t.* 1. to limit. 2. to be a limit or boundary to. 3. to name the boundaries of. —**out of bounds,** 1. beyond the boundaries. 2. prohibited. —**bound′less,** *adj.*
**bound·a·ry** (boun′də-ri), *n.* [*pl.* -RIES], anything marking a limit; bound; border.
**bound′en** (-dən), *adj.* [old pp. of *bind*], 1. obligated; indebted. 2. obligatory: as, one's *bounden* duty.
**bound′er** (-dẽr), *n.* [< *bound* (leap)], [Colloq.], a rude person; cad.
**boun·te·ous** (boun′ti-əs), *adj.* [see BOUNTY], 1. generous. 2. abundant.
**boun′ti·ful** (-ti-fəl), *adj.* bounteous.
**boun′ty,** *n.* [*pl.* -TIES], [< L. *bonus,* good], 1. generosity. 2. a generous gift. 3. a reward or premium.
**bou·quet** (bō-kā′, bōō-), *n.* [Fr.], 1. a bunch of flowers. 2. (bōō-kā′), aroma, esp. of a wine, etc.
**bour·bon** (bũr′bən), *n.* [< *Bourbon* County, Kentucky], a corn whiskey.
**bour·geois** (boor-zhwä′), *n.* [*pl.* -GEOIS], [Fr. < OHG. *burg,* town], a member of the bourgeoisie. *adj.* of the bourgeoisie: used variously to mean commonplace, smug, etc.
**bour·geoi·sie** (boor′zhwä-zē′), *n.* [construed as sing. or pl.], the social class between the very wealthy and the working class; middle class.
**bourn, bourne** (bôrn, boorn), *n.* [< LL. *bodina,* limit], a goal; objective.
**bout** (bout), *n.* [< AS. *bugan,* to bend], 1. a struggle or contest: as, a boxing *bout.* 2. a period spent in some activity; spell or term.

**bou·tique** (bōō-tēk′), *n.* [Fr. < Gr. *apothēkē*; see APOTHECARY], a small shop where fashionable, usually expensive, articles are sold.

**bou·ton·niere, bou·ton·nière** (bōō′t'n-yer′), *n.* [Fr., buttonhole], a flower worn in the buttonhole.

**bo·vine** (bō′vīn), *adj.* [< L. *bos*, ox], 1. of or like an ox or cow. 2. slow, patient, stupid, etc. *n.* an ox, cow, etc.

**bow** (bou), *v.i.* [< AS. *bugan*, to bend], 1. to bend the head or body in respect, agreement, etc. 2. to submit; yield. *v.t.* 1. to bend (the head or body) in agreement, etc. 2. to weigh (*down*); overwhelm. *n.* a bending of the head or body, as in greeting, etc. —**take a bow**, to acknowledge applause, etc.

**bow** (bō), *n.* [< AS. *bugan*, to bend], 1. anything curved, as a rainbow. 2. a curve; bend. 3. a flexible, curved strip of wood with a cord connecting the ends, for shooting arrows. 4. a slender stick strung with horsehairs, for playing a violin, etc. 5. a bowknot. *adj.* curved. *v.t.* & *v.i.* 1. to bend; curve. 2. to play (a violin, etc.) with a bow.

**bow** (bou), *n.* [< LG. or Scand.], the front part of a ship, etc. *adj.* of or near the bow.

**bowd·ler·ize** (boud′lẽr-īz′), *v.t.* [-IZED, -IZING], [< Dr. T. *Bowdler*, who published an expurgated Shakespeare (1818)], to expurgate. —**bowd′ler·ism**, *n.*

**bow·el** (bou′əl), *n.* [< L. *botulus*, sausage], 1. an intestine, esp. of a human being. 2. *pl.* the inside: as, the *bowels* of the earth. —**move one's bowels**, to defecate.

**bow·er** (bou′ẽr), *n.* [< AS. *bur*, dwelling], a place enclosed by leafy boughs or vines; arbor. *v.t.* to enclose in a bower.

**bow·ie knife** (bō′i, bōō′i), [< Col. J. *Bowie*, its inventor], a long, single-edged hunting knife.

**bow·knot** (bō′not′), *n.* a slipknot with one or two loops.

**bowl** (bōl), *n.* [AS. *bolla*], 1. a hollow, rounded dish. 2. a large drinking cup. 3. a bowllike thing or part. 4. an amphitheater. 5. the contents of a bowl.

**bowl** (bōl), *n.* [< L. *bulla*, a bubble], 1. a heavy ball used in the game of bowls. 2. a delivery of the ball in bowling. *v.i.* & *v.t.* 1. to roll (a ball) or participate in bowling. 2. to move swiftly and smoothly. —**bowl over**, 1. to knock over. 2. [Colloq.], to astonish. —**bowl′er**, *n.*

**bowl·der** (bōl′dẽr), *n.* a boulder.

**bow·leg** (bō′leg′), *n.* a leg with outward curvature. —**bow′leg′ged** (-leg′id, -legd′), *adj.*

**bowl′ing**, *n.* 1. a game in which a heavy ball is bowled along a wooden lane (**bowling alley**) at ten wooden pins; tenpins. 2. the game of bowls. *adj.* of or for bowling.

**bowls** (bōlz), *n.* a bowling game played on a smooth lawn (**bowling green**).

**bow·man** (bō′mən), *n.* [*pl.* -MEN], an archer.

**bow·sprit** (bou′sprit′, bō′-), *n.* [prob. < D.], a tapered pole extending forward from the bow of a sailing vessel.

**bow tie** (bō), a necktie tied in a bow.

**box** (boks), *n.* [< Gr. *pyxos*, box (shrub)], 1. a container, usually one with four sides and a lid; case. 2. the contents of a box. 3. a boxlike thing or space: as, a jury *box*. 4. a small, enclosed group of seats, as in a theater. 5. a booth. 6. in *baseball*, the place where a player must stand: as, a batter's *box*. *v.t.* to put into a box. —**box in** (or **up**), to shut in or keep in.

**box** (boks), *n.* [< ?], a blow struck with the hand, esp. on the ear. *v.t.* 1. to strike such a blow. 2. to fight by boxing with. *v.i.* to fight with the fists.

**box** (boks), *n.* [< Gr. *pyxos*], an evergreen shrub with small leaves: also **box′wood′**.

**box′car′**, *n.* an enclosed railroad freight car.

**box′er**, *n.* a man who boxes; prize fighter.

**box′ing**, *n.* the skill or occupation of fighting with the fists, esp. in special padded mittens (**boxing gloves**).

**box office**, 1. a place where admission tickets are sold, as in a theater. 2. appeal as measured by ticket sales.

**boy** (boi), *n.* [ME. *boie*], 1. a male child. 2. any man: familiar term. 3. a male servant. *interj.* an exclamation of pleasure, surprise, etc. —**boy′hood**, *n.* —**boy′ish**, *adj.*

**boy·cott** (boi′kot′), *v.t.* [< Capt. *Boycott*, Irish land agent so treated], to join together in refusing to deal with, buy, etc., so as to coerce, etc. *n.* a boycotting. —**boy′cott′er**, *n.*

**Boy Scouts**, a boys' club that stresses outdoor life and service to others.

**boy·sen·ber·ry** (boi′s'n-ber′i, -z'n-), *n.* [*pl.* -RIES], [< R. *Boysen*, Am. horticulturist], a purple berry obtained by crossing the raspberry, loganberry, and blackberry.

**Br**, in *chem.*, bromine.

**Br.**, 1. Britain. 2. British.

**br.**, 1. branch. 2. brother. 3. brown.

**bra** (brä), *n.* [Colloq.], a brassiere.

**brace** (brās), *v.t.* [BRACED, BRACING], [< L. *brachium*, arm], 1. to bind. 2. to strengthen by supporting the weight of, etc. 3. to make ready for an impact, shock, etc. 4. to stimulate. *n.* 1. a couple; pair. 2. a thing that clamps or connects; fastener. 3. *pl.* [Brit.], suspenders. 4. a device for setting up or maintaining tension. 5. either of the signs { }, used to connect words, lines, etc. 6. any propping device. 7. *a*) a device for supporting a weak part of the body. *b*) a wire device for straightening the teeth. 8. a tool for holding a drilling bit. —**brace up**, [Colloq.], to call forth one's courage, etc.

**brace and bit**, a boring tool consisting of a removable drill (bit) in a rotating handle (brace).

**brace·let** (brās′lit), *n.* [< L. *brachium*, arm], 1. an ornamental band or chain worn on the wrist or arm. 2. [Colloq.], a handcuff.

**brack·en** (brak′ən), *n.* [ON.], 1. any large, coarse fern. 2. a growth of such ferns.

**brack·et** (brak′it), *n.* [< Fr. *brague*, kind of mortise], 1. a support or shelf projecting from a wall, etc. 2. any angle-shaped support. 3. either of the signs [ ], used to enclose a word, etc. 4. a classification: as, high income *brackets*. *v.t.* 1. to support with brackets. 2. to enclose within brackets. 3. to classify together.

**brack·ish** (brak′ish), *adj.* [Scot. < MD.], 1. salty. 2. nauseous. —**brack′ish·ness**, *n.*

**bract** (brakt), *n.* [L. *bractea*, thin metal plate], a modified leaf growing at the base of a flower. —**brac′te·al** (-ti-əl), *adj.*

**brad** (brad), *n.* [ON. *broddr*, a spike], a thin wire nail.

**brae** (brā), *n.* [ON. *bra*, brow], [Scot.], a sloping bank; hillside.

**brag** (brag), *v.t.* & *v.i.* [BRAGGED, BRAGGING], [prob. < OFr. *braguer*], to boast. *n.* a boast; boasting. —**brag′ger**, *n.*

**brag′gart** (-ẽrt), *n.* an offensively boastful person. *adj.* boastful.

**Brah·ma** (brä′mə), *n.* the chief member of the Hindu trinity (Brahma, Vishnu, and Siva), regarded as the creator of the universe.

**Brah′man**, *n.* [*pl.* -MANS], a member of the priestly Hindu caste. —**Brah′man·ism**, *n.*

**braid** (brād), *v.t.* [AS. *bregdan*, to twist], 1. to interweave three or more strands of (hair, straw, etc.). 2. to decorate with braid. *n.* 1. a strip, as of hair, formed by braiding. 2. a band of cloth, tape, etc. used to bind or decorate clothing.

**Braille, braille** (brāl), *n.* [< L. *Braille*, its 19th-c. Fr. inventor], a system of printing for the blind, using raised dots for letters.

**brain** (brān), *n.* [AS. *brægen*], 1. the mass

of nerve tissue in the cranium of vertebrates. 2. *often pl.* intelligence. *v.t.* to dash out the brains of.

**brain child,** [Colloq.], an idea, plan, etc. produced by one's mental labor.

**brain′less,** *adj.* foolish; stupid.

**brain′sick′,** *adj.* having or caused by a mental disorder. —**brain′sick′ness,** *n.*

**brain storm,** [Colloq.], a sudden inspiration.

**brain trust,** [Slang], a group of advisers with expert or special knowledge.

**brain′wash′,** *v.t.* [Colloq.], to indoctrinate so thoroughly as to effect a radical change of beliefs. —**brain′wash′ing,** *n.*

**brain′y,** *adj.* [-IER, -IEST], [Colloq.], intelligent; mentally acute. —**brain′i·ness,** *n.*

**braise** (brāz), *v.t.* [BRAISED, BRAISING], [< Fr. *braise*, live coals], to brown (meat) and then simmer slowly in a covered pan.

**brake** (brāk), *n.* [< MLG. *breken*, to break], any device for slowing or stopping a vehicle or machine, as by pressing a block against a moving part. *v.t. & v.i.* [BRAKED, BRAKING], to slow down or stop as with a brake.

**brake** (brāk), *n.* [prob. < MLG. *brake*, stumps], a clump of briers, etc.; thicket.

**brake′man,** *n.* [*pl.* -MEN], an operator of brakes or assistant to the conductor on a railroad train.

**bram·ble** (bram′b'l), *n.* [< AS. *brom*, broom], a prickly shrub of the rose family, as the raspberry, blackberry, etc. —**bram′bly,** *adj.*

**bran** (bran), *n.* [OFr. *bren*], the skin or husk of grains of wheat, rye, etc. separated from the flour, as by sifting.

**branch** (branch, bränch), *n.* [< LL. *branca*, a claw], 1. any woody extension from a tree or shrub; limb. 2. any offshoot or division. 3. a tributary stream. 4. a division of a family. 5. a separately located unit of a business, etc. *v.i.* 1. to put forth branches. 2. to come out from the main part as a branch. —**branch off,** 1. to separate into branches. 2. to diverge. —**branch out,** to extend one's interests, activities, etc.

**brand** (brand), *n.* [AS. < *biernan*, to burn], 1. a burning or partially burned stick. 2. a mark burned on the skin, formerly used to punish criminals, now used on cattle to show ownership. 3. the iron used in branding. 4. a stigma. 5. an identifying mark, label, etc. 6. the make of a commodity: as, a *brand* of cigars. *v.t.* 1. to mark with a brand. 2. to put a stigma on.

**bran·dish** (bran′dish), *v.t.* [< OHG. *brand*, sword], to wave menacingly, as a sword.

**brand′-new′,** *adj.* [orig., fresh from the fire; see BRAND], entirely new.

**bran·dy** (bran′di), *n.* [*pl.* -DIES], [< D. *brandewijn*, distilled wine], an alcoholic liquor distilled from wine or from fruit juice.

**brant** (brant), *n.* [*pl.* BRANTS, BRANT], [? < *brand*, because of the bird's burnt color], a small, dark wild goose.

**brash** (brash), *adj.* [prob. < *break* + *dash*], 1. rash; too hasty. 2. insolent; impudent.

**brass** (bras, bräs), *n.* [AS. *bræs*], 1. a yellowish metal, an alloy of copper and zinc. 2. *pl.* brass-wind musical instruments. 3. [Colloq.], bold impudence. 4. [Slang], military officers of high rank. —**brass′y,** *adj.*

**brass band,** a band in which mainly brass winds are played.

**brass·ie** (bras′i, bräs′i), *n.* [orig. with a brass-bottomed head], a golf club with a wooden head and medium loft: also sp. **brassy** [*pl.* -IES].

**bras·siere, bras·sière** (brə-zêr′), *n.* [Fr. < *bras*, an arm], an undergarment worn by women to support the breasts.

**brass knuckles,** linked metal rings or a metal bar with holes, worn on the hand for rough fighting.

**brass tacks,** [Colloq.], basic facts.

**brass winds,** musical instruments made of coiled metal tubes extending from a cup-shaped mouthpiece. —**brass′-wind′,** *adj.*

**brat** (brat), *n.* [< Gael. *bratt*, a rag: from a ragamuffin's clothes], a child, esp. an impudent, unruly one: scornful or playful term.

**bra·va·do** (brə-vä′dō, -vā′-), *n.* [*pl.* -DOES, -DOS], [Sp. < *bravo*, brave], pretended courage or feigned confidence.

**brave** (brāv), *adj.* [Fr. < It. *bravo*], 1. not afraid; having courage. 2. having a fine appearance. *n.* 1. any brave man. 2. a North American Indian warrior. *v.t.* [BRAVED, BRAVING], 1. to defy; dare. 2. to meet or undergo with courage.

**brav·er·y** (brāv′ēr-i), *n.* [*pl.* -IES], 1. courage; valor. 2. fine appearance, show, etc.

**bra·vo** (brä′vō), *interj.* [It.], well done! excellent! *n.* [*pl.* -VOS], a shout of "bravo!"

**brawl** (brôl), *v.i.* [< OFr. *brailler*, to shout], to quarrel or fight noisily. *n.* a noisy quarrel, fight, etc. —**brawl′er,** *n.*

**brawn** (brôn), *n.* [< OFr. *braon*, muscle], 1. strong, well-developed muscles. 2. muscular strength. —**brawn′y** [-IER, -IEST], *adj.*

**bray** (brā), *v.i.* [< LL. *bragire*, cry out], to make a loud, harsh sound, as a donkey. *n.* 1. the harsh cry of a donkey. 2. a sound like this.

**bra·zen** (brā′z'n), *adj.* [< AS. *bræs*, brass], 1. of brass. 2. like brass in color, etc. 3. shameless. 4. harsh and piercing. —**brazen out** (or **through**), to behave as if not ashamed of. —**bra′zen·ly,** *adv.*

**bra·zier** (brā′zhēr), *n.* [see BRAISE], a metal container to hold burning coals.

**bra·zier** (brā′zhēr), *n.* a person who works in brass.

**Bra·zil·ian** (brə-zil′yan), *adj.* of Brazil, its people, etc. *n.* a native of Brazil.

**Bra·zil nut** (brə-zil′), the edible, oily, three-sided seed of a tree of tropical America.

**breach** (brēch), *n.* [< AS. *brecan*, to break], 1. an opening made by breaking something; gap. 2. a failure to observe a law, promise, etc. 3. a break in friendship. *v.t.* to make a breach in. —**breach of promise,** a breaking of a promise to marry.

**bread** (bred), *n.* [AS.], 1. a baked food made of flour or meal mixed with water, etc. 2. a livelihood: as, he earns his *bread*. *v.t.* to cover with bread crumbs before cooking. —**break bread,** to eat. —**bread′less,** *adj.*

**breadth** (bredth), *n.* [< AS. *brad*, broad], 1. width. 2. scope; extent.

**bread′win′ner,** *n.* one who supports dependents by his earnings.

**break** (brāk), *v.t.* [BROKE, BROKEN, BREAKING], [< AS. *brecan*], 1. to separate into pieces by force; smash. 2. to cut the surface of (soil, the skin, etc.). 3. to make unusable by cracking or disrupting. 4. to tame as with force. 5. to demote. 6. to make poor or bankrupt. 7. to surpass (a record). 8. to violate, as a promise. 9. to disrupt the order of: as, the troops *broke* formation. 10. to interrupt (a journey, electric circuit, etc.). 11. to reduce the effect of by interrupting (a fall, etc.). 12. to penetrate (silence, darkness, etc.). 13. to stop or give up (a habit, etc.). 14. to disclose. 15. to bring to an end by force, as a strike. *v.i.* 1. to divide into separate pieces; burst. 2. to stop associating (often with *up* or *with*). 3. to become unusable. 4. to change suddenly: as, his voice *broke*. 5. to escape (often with *out*). 6. to begin suddenly: as, he *broke* into song. 7. to come into being, notice, etc.: as, the story *broke*. *n.* 1. a breaking. 2. a broken place. 3. a beginning to appear: as, the *break* of day. 4. an interrupting of regularity. 5. an interval; omission. 6. a sudden change. 7. [Slang], a chance piece of luck. —**break**

**down,** 1. to go out of working order. 2. to have a physical or emotional collapse. —**break in,** 1. to enter forcibly. 2. to interrupt. 3. to train. —**break off,** to stop abruptly. —**break out,** to become covered with pimples, etc. —**break up,** 1. to separate; disperse. 2. to stop. 3. [Colloq.], to distress; upset. —**break′a·ble,** *adj.*
**break′age** (-ij), *n.* 1. a breaking. 2. things broken. 3. loss due to breaking. 4. the sum allowed for such loss.
**break′down′,** *n.* 1. a breaking down. 2. a failure of health. 3. an analysis.
**break′er,** *n.* 1. a thing that breaks. 2. a wave that breaks into foam.
**break·fast** (brek′fəst), *n.* the first meal of the day. *v.i.* to eat breakfast.
**break·neck** (brāk′nek′), *adj.* dangerous to life and limb.
**break′through′,** *n.* the act or place of breaking through against resistance.
**break′up′,** *n.* 1. a dispersion. 2. disintegration. 3. collapse. 4. an ending.
**break′wa′ter,** *n.* a barrier to break the impact of waves, as before a harbor.
**breast** (brest), *n.* [AS. *breost*], 1. either of two milk-secreting glands at the upper, front part of a woman's body. 2. the upper, front part of the body. 3. the part of a garment, etc. over the breast. 4. the breast regarded as the source of emotions. *v.t.* to face firmly; oppose. —**make a clean breast of,** to confess fully.
**breast′bone′,** *n.* the sternum.
**breast′-feed′,** *v.t.* [-FED, -FEEDING], to feed (a baby) milk from the breast.
**breast′pin′,** *n.* an ornamental pin worn on a dress, near the throat.
**breast′plate′,** *n.* armor for the breast.
**breast stroke,** a swimming stroke in which both arms are brought out sideways from the chest.
**breast′work′,** *n.* a low, quickly constructed barrier to protect gunners.
**breath** (breth), *n.* [AS. *bræth*, odor], 1. air taken into and let out of the lungs. 2. respiration. 3. the power to breathe easily. 4. life; spirit. 5. a fragrant odor. 6. a slight breeze. 7. a whisper; murmur. —**below** (or **under**) **one's breath,** in a whisper.
**breathe** (brēth), *v.i. & v.t.* [BREATHED, BREATHING], 1. to take (air) into the lungs and let it out again; inhale and exhale. 2. to live. 3. to speak softly; whisper. 4. to rest. —**not breathe a word,** to keep a secret.
**breath·er** (brēth′ẽr), *n.* 1. one who breathes. 2. [Colloq.], a pause or rest.
**breath·less** (breth′lis), *adj.* 1. without breath. 2. dead. 3. panting; gasping. 4. unable to breathe normally because of excitement, fear, etc. 5. stifling.
**breath′-tak′ing,** *adj.* very exciting.
**bred** (bred), pt. and pp. of **breed.**
**breech** (brēch), *n.* [AS. *brec*], 1. the buttocks. 2. the back part of a thing. 3. the part of a gun behind the barrel.
**breech′cloth′,** *n.* a loincloth.
**breech·es** (brich′iz), *n.pl.* 1. trousers reaching to the knees. 2. [Colloq.], any trousers.
**breed** (brēd), *v.t.* [BRED, BREEDING], [< AS. *brod*, brood], 1. to bring forth (offspring). 2. to be the source of; produce. 3. to raise (animals). 4. to rear; train. *v.i.* 1. to be produced; originate. 2. to reproduce. *n.* 1. a race; stock. 2. a sort; type. —**breed′er,** *n.*
**breed′ing,** *n.* 1. the producing of young. 2. good manners. 3. the producing of plants and animals, esp. for improving the stock.
**breeze** (brēz), *n.* [< Sp. *brisa*, northeast wind], a gentle wind. *v.i.* [BREEZED, BREEZING], [Slang], to move or go briskly.
**breez·y** (brēz′i), *adj.* [-IER, -IEST], 1. having a breeze. 2. brisk; lively. —**breez′i·ly,** *adv.*

**breve** (brēv), *n.* [It. < L. *brevis*, short], 1. a curved mark (˘) put over a short vowel. 2. in *music*, a double whole note.
**bre·vi·ar·y** (brē′vi-er′i, brev′i-), *n.* [*pl.* -IES], [< L. *brevis*, short], a book of daily offices and prayers, esp. of the R. C. Church.
**brev·i·ty** (brev′ə-ti), *n.* [*pl.* -TIES], [< L. *brevis*, short], 1. briefness. 2. conciseness.
**brew** (broo), *v.t.* [< AS. *breowan*], 1. to make (beer, ale, etc.) from malt and hops by boiling and fermenting. 2. to steep (tea, etc.). 3. to plot; contrive. *v.i.* 1. to brew beer, ale, etc. 2. to gather, as a storm. *n.* a beverage brewed. —**brew′er,** *n.*
**brew·er·y** (broo′ẽr-i), *n.* [*pl.* -IES], a place where beer, ale, etc. are brewed.
**bri·ar** (brī′ẽr), *n.* brier. —**bri′ar·y,** *adj.*
**bribe** (brīb), *n.* [< OFr. *briber*, beg], anything given or promised as an inducement, esp. to do something illegal or wrong. *v.t.* [BRIBED, BRIBING], to offer or give a bribe to. —**brib·er·y** (brīb′ẽr-i) [*pl.* -IES], *n.*
**bric-a-brac, bric-à-brac** (brik′ə-brak′), *n.* [< Fr. *à bric et à brac*, by hook or crook], small, rare, or artistic objects used to ornament a room.
**brick** (brik), *n.* [< OFr. *briche*, fragment], 1. an oblong block of baked clay, used in building, etc. 2. anything shaped like a brick. *adj.* built or paved with brick. *v.t.* to build or cover with brick.
**brick′bat′,** *n.* 1. a piece of brick, esp. one used as a missile. 2. an unfavorable remark.
**brick′lay′ing,** *n.* the work of building with bricks. —**brick′lay′er,** *n.*
**brid·al** (brīd′'l), *n.* [< AS. *brydealo*, bride feast], a wedding. *adj.* 1. of a bride. 2. of a wedding.
**bride** (brīd), *n.* [AS. *bryd*], a woman just married or about to be married.
**bride′groom′,** *n.* [< AS. *bryd*, bride + *guma*, man], a man just married or about to be married.
**brides·maid** (brīdz′mād′), *n.* a woman attending the bride during a wedding.
**bridge** (brij), *n.* [AS. *brycg*], 1. a structure built over a river, etc. to provide a way across. 2. a thing like a bridge in shape or function. 3. the bony part of the nose. 4. a raised platform on a ship. 5. a fixed or removable mounting for false teeth. *v.t.* to build or be a bridge over. —**burn one's bridges,** to cut off all one's ways to retreat.
**bridge** (brij), *n.* [prob. < Russ.], a card game for two pairs of players in which they bid for the right to name the trump suit or declare no-trump.
**bridge′head′,** *n.* a fortified position established by an attacking force on the enemy's side of a bridge, etc.
**bri·dle** (brī′d'l), *n.* [< AS. *bregdan*, pull], 1. a head harness for guiding a horse. 2. anything that controls or restrains. *v.t.* [-DLED, -DLING], 1. to put a bridle on. 2. to curb; control. *v.i.* to draw one's head back as an expression of scorn, pride, etc.
**bridle path,** a path for horseback riding.
**brief** (brēf), *adj.* [< L. *brevis*], 1. short; terse; concise. 2. curt. *n.* a summary, specif. of the main points of a law case. *v.t.* 1. to summarize. 2. to give (a person) all the pertinent facts on a matter. —**brief′ly,** *adv.* —**brief′ness,** *n.*
**brief case,** a small, flat case for carrying papers, books, etc.
**bri·er** (brī′ẽr), *n.* [AS. *brer*], any thorny bush, as a bramble. —**bri′er·y,** *adj.*
**bri·er** (brī′ẽr), *n.* [Fr. *bruyère*], a variety of heath, whose root is used for tobacco pipes.
**brig** (brig), *n.* [< *brigantine*], 1. a two-masted ship with square sails. 2. a prison on a warship.
**bri·gade** (bri-gād′), *n.* [< LL. *briga*, strife], 1. a military unit comprising two or more

regiments. 2. a group of people organized to do something: as, a fire *brigade.* ***v.t.*** [-GADED, -GADING], to gather into a brigade.

**brig·a·dier** (brig'ə-dêr'), ***n.*** a brigadier general.

**brigadier general,** a military officer ranking just above a colonel.

**brig·and** (brig'ənd), ***n.*** [see BRIGADE], a bandit, esp. one of a roving band.

**brig·an·tine** (brig'ən-tēn', -tīn'), ***n.*** [< ML. *brigantinus*, fighting vessel], a ship with a fore-and-aft-rigged mainmast and a square-rigged foremast.

**bright** (brīt), ***adj.*** [AS. *bryht*], 1. shining; giving light. 2. brilliant in color or sound; vivid. 3. lively; cheerful. 4. mentally quick; clever. 5. illustrious. 6. favorable. **—bright'ly,** ***adv.*** **—bright'ness,** ***n.***

**bright'en** (-'n), ***v.t. & v.i.*** to make or become bright or brighter.

**bril·liant** (bril'yənt), ***adj.*** [< Fr. < It. *brillare*, to sparkle], 1. shining brightly. 2. vivid. 3. splendid; magnificent. 4. very able; keenly intelligent. ***n.*** a diamond or other gem cut with many facets to increase its sparkle. **—bril'liance, bril'lian·cy,** ***n.***

**brim** (brim), ***n.*** [AS. *brim*, sea], 1. the topmost edge of a cup, glass, etc. 2. a projecting rim, as of a hat. ***v.t.*** [BRIMMED, BRIMMING], to fill to the brim. ***v.i.*** to be full to the brim. **—brim'ful,** ***adj.***

**brim·stone** (brim'stōn'), ***n.*** [< ME. *brinnen*, burn + *ston*, stone], sulfur.

**brin·dle** (brin'd'l), ***n.*** a brindled color.

**brin'dled** (-d'ld), ***adj.*** [prob. < ME. *brennen*, to burn], streaked or spotted with a darker color: said of a gray or tawny animal.

**brine** (brīn), ***n.*** [AS. *bryne*], 1. water full of salt. 2. the ocean. ***v.t.*** [BRINED, BRINING], to put into brine, as in pickling. **—brin'y** [-IER, -IEST], ***adj.***

**bring** (briŋ), ***v.t.*** [BROUGHT, BRINGING], [AS. *bringan*], 1. to cause (a person or thing) to come along with oneself. 2. to cause to happen. 3. to lead to an action or belief. 4. to sell for: as, to *bring* a good price. **—bring about,** to cause; make happen. **—bring forth,** to give birth to; produce. **—bring off,** to accomplish. **—bring out,** 1. to expose; reveal. 2. to offer (a play, book, etc.) to the public. **—bring to,** 1. to revive from unconsciousness, etc. 2. to cause (a ship) to stop. **—bring up,** 1. to rear (children). 2. to introduce, as into discussion. 3. to cough or vomit up.

**brink** (briŋk), ***n.*** [< ON. *brekka*, hillside], the edge, esp. at the top of a steep place; verge.

**brink·man·ship** (briŋk'mən-ship'), ***n.*** the policy of pursuing a course of action to the brink of catastrophe.

**bri·oche** (brē'ōsh, -osh), ***n.*** [Fr.], a light roll made with butter, eggs, and yeast.

**bri·quette, bri·quet** (bri-ket'), ***n.*** [< Fr. *brique*, brick], a brick of pressed coal dust, used for fuel.

**brisk** (brisk), ***adj.*** [prob. < Fr. *brusque*, brusque], 1. quick in manner; energetic. 2. sharp; invigorating. **—brisk'ly,** ***adv.***

**bris·ket** (bris'kit), ***n.*** [prob. < OFr. *bruschet*], meat from the breast of an animal.

**bris·tle** (bris''l), ***n.*** [AS. *byrst*], any short, stiff hair. ***v.i.*** [-TLED, -TLING], 1. to be stiff and erect. 2. to have one's hair stand up. 3. to stiffen with fear, anger, etc. 4. to be thick as with bristles. **—bris'tly** (-li), ***adj.***

**Brit.,** 1. Britain. 2. British.

**Brit·i·cism** (brit'ə-siz'm), ***n.*** a word or idiom peculiar to the British.

**Brit·ish** (brit'ish), ***adj.*** of Great Britain or its people. ***n.*** English as spoken and written in England. **—the British,** the people of Great Britain.

**Brit·on** (brit''n), ***n.*** 1. a native or inhabitant of Great Britain or the British Commonwealth. 2. a member of an early Celtic people of S Britain.

**brit·tle** (brit''l), ***adj.*** [< AS. *breotan*, break], easily broken or shattered; fragile. ***n.*** a crisp candy. **—brit'tle·ness,** ***n.***

**broach** (brōch), ***n.*** [< LL. *brocca*, spike], a tapered bit for boring holes. ***v.t.*** 1. to make a hole in so as to let out liquid. 2. to start a discussion of. **—broach'er,** ***n.***

**broad** (brôd), ***adj.*** [AS. *brod*], 1. wide; of large extent from side to side. 2. extending about; clear: as, *broad* daylight. 3. obvious: as, a *broad* hint. 4. outspoken; unreserved. 5. tolerant; liberal: as, a *broad* view. 6. extensive; general; main. ***n.*** the broad part of anything. **—broad'ly,** ***adv.*** **—broad'ness,** ***n.***

**broad'cast'** (-kast', -käst'), ***v.t. & v.i.*** [-CAST or, *in radio*, -CASTED, -CASTING], 1. to scatter or spread widely. 2. to transmit by radio. ***adj.*** 1. widely scattered. 2. of or for radio broadcasting. ***n.*** 1. a sowing by broadcasting. 2. a radio program. ***adv.*** far and wide. **—broad'cast'er,** ***n.***

**broad'cloth',** ***n.*** a fine, smooth cloth.

**broad'en** (-'n), ***v.t. & v.i.*** to widen.

**broad jump,** a jump for distance.

**broad'loom',** ***adj.*** woven on a wide loom: said of rugs and carpets.

**broad'-mind'ed,** ***adj.*** tolerant of unconventional behavior, etc.; liberal.

**broad·side** (brôd'sīd'), ***n.*** 1. the side of a ship above the water line. 2. the firing of all guns on one side of a ship. 3. their simultaneous fire. 4. a large printed sheet, as with advertising. ***adv.*** with the side facing.

**broad'sword',** ***n.*** a broad-bladed sword, for slashing rather than thrusting.

**bro·cade** (brō-kād'), ***n.*** [< Sp. < LL. *brocare*, embroider], a rich cloth with a raised design woven into it. ***v.t.*** [-CADED, -CADING], to weave a raised design into (cloth).

**broc·co·li** (brok'ə-li), ***n.*** [It. < LL. *brocca*, spike], a kind of cauliflower.

**bro·chure** (brō-shoor'), ***n.*** [Fr. < *brocher*, to stitch], a pamphlet.

**brogue** (brōg), ***n.*** [prob. < Ir. *barrōg*, a grip], a dialectal pronunciation, esp. that of English by the Irish.

**brogue** (brōg), ***n.*** [< Ir. *brōg*, shoe], a man's heavy oxford shoe: also **bro·gan** (brō'gən).

**broil** (broil), ***v.t. & v.i.*** [< OFr. *bruir*, burn], to cook by exposure to direct heat. ***n.*** 1. a broiling; great heat. 2. anything broiled.

**broil'er,** ***n.*** 1. a pan, part of a stove, etc. for broiling. 2. a chicken for broiling.

**broke** (brōk), pt. of **break.** ***adj.*** [Slang], having no money; bankrupt.

**bro·ken** (brō'kən), pp. of **break.** ***adj.*** 1. splintered, fractured, etc. 2. violated; as, a *broken* vow. 3. ruined. 4. interrupted; discontinuous. 5. imperfectly spoken: as, *broken* English. 6. tamed. **—bro'ken·ly,** ***adv.***

**bro'ken·heart'ed,** ***adj.*** crushed by grief or despair; heartbroken.

**bro·ker** (brō'kẽr), ***n.*** [< OFr. *brochier*, to tap; orig. sense "wine dealer"], a person paid a fee as an agent in selling stocks, etc.

**bro'ker·age** (-ij), ***n.*** 1. the business of a broker. 2. a broker's fee.

**bro·mide** (brō'mīd, -mid), ***n.*** 1. a compound of bromine with another element or radical. 2. potassium bromide, used as a sedative. 3. a trite saying.

**bro·mine** (brō'mēn, -min), ***n.*** [< Gr. *bromos*, stench], a chemical element, usually a reddish-brown, corrosive liquid: symbol, Br.

**bron·chi** (broŋ'kī), ***n.pl.*** [*sing.* -CHUS], the two main branches of the windpipe. **—bron'chi·al** (-ki-əl), ***adj.***

**bron·chi'tis** (-kī'tis), ***n.*** inflammation of the bronchial tubes.

**bron·co** (broŋ'kō), ***n.*** [*pl.* -COS], [Sp., rough], a small, wild or partly tamed horse of the western U.S.: also **bron'cho** [*pl.* -CHOS].

**bron′co·bust′er,** *n.* [Slang], a tamer of broncos: also **bron′cho·bust′er.**

**bron·to·sau·rus** (bron′tə-sô′rəs), *n.* [< Gr. *brontē*, thunder + *sauros*, lizard], a huge, extinct American dinosaur.

**bronze** (bronz), *n.* [Fr. < It. *bronzo*], 1. an alloy of copper and tin. 2. a reddish-brown color. *adj.* of or like bronze. *v.t. & v.i.* [BRONZED, BRONZING], to make or become bronze in color. —**bronz′y,** *adj.*

**brooch** (brōch, brōōch), *n.* [see BROACH], a large, ornamental pin with a clasp.

**brood** (brōōd), *n.* [AS. *brod*], 1. a group of birds hatched at one time. 2. the children in a family. *v.t.* to sit on and hatch (eggs). *v.i.* 1. to brood eggs. 2. to think deeply about something, with unhappiness, etc.

**brood′er,** *n.* 1. one that broods. 2. a heated shelter for raising fowl.

**brook** (brook), *n.* [AS. *broc*], a small stream.

**brook** (brook), *v.t.* [AS. *brucan*, to use], to put up with; endure.

**broom** (brōōm, broom), *n.* [AS. *brom*, brushwood], 1. a shrub with small leaves and slender branches. 2. a long-handled brush used for sweeping.

**broom′stick′,** *n.* the handle of a broom.

**broth** (brôth, broth), *n.* [AS.], water in which meat has been boiled.

**broth·el** (brôth′əl, broth′-), *n.* [< AS. *breothan*, go to ruin], a house of prostitution.

**broth·er** (bruth ẽr), *n.* [*pl.* -ERS; *archaic* BRETHREN], [AS. *brothor*], 1. a male related to one by having the same parents. 2. a friend who is like a brother. 3. *a*) a lay member of a men's religious order. *b*) a fellow member of the same race, creed, etc.

**broth′er·hood′,** *n.* 1. the bond between brothers. 2. an association of men united in some interest, work, etc.

**broth′er-in-law′,** *n.* [*pl.* BROTHERS-], 1. the brother of one's spouse. 2. the husband of one's sister. 3. the husband of the sister of one's spouse.

**broth′er·ly,** *adj.* 1. of or like a brother. 2. friendly, kind, loyal, etc. *adv.* as a brother should. —**broth′er·li·ness,** *n.*

**brougham** (brōōm, brōō′əm), *n.* [< Lord *Brougham* (1779–1868)], a closed carriage (or automobile) with the driver's seat outside.

**brought** (brôt), pt. and pp. of **bring.**

**brou·ha·ha** (brōō′hä-hä′), *n.* [Fr.], a noisy stir or wrangle; hubbub.

**brow** (brou), *n.* [AS. *bru*], 1. the eyebrow. 2. the forehead. 3. the edge of a cliff.

**brow′beat′** (-bēt′), *v.t.* [-BEAT, -BEATEN, -BEATING], to intimidate with harsh looks and words; bully. —**brow′beat′er,** *n.*

**brown** (broun), *adj.* [AS. *brun*], 1. having the color of chocolate or coffee, a mixture of red, black, and yellow. 2. tanned; dark-skinned. *n.* brown color. *v.t. & v.i.* to make or become brown. —**brown′ish,** *adj.*

**brown·ie** (broun′i), *n.* 1. a small, helpful elf in stories. 2. [B-], a member of a branch of the Girl Scouts, for girls between the ages of 8 and 11. 3. a flat chocolate cake.

**brown′stone′,** *n.* a reddish-brown sandstone, used for building.

**brown sugar,** unrefined sugar.

**browse** (brouz), *n.* [< OS. *brustian*, to sprout], leaves, shoots, etc. which animals feed on. *v.t.* [BROWSED, BROWSING], 1. to nibble at. 2. to graze on. *v.i.* 1. to feed on leaves, shoots, etc. 2. to glance leisurely through a book, library, etc. —**brows′er,** *n.*

**bru·in** (brōō′in), *n.* [D., brown], a bear.

**bruise** (brōōz), *v.t.* [BRUISED, BRUISING], [< AS. *brysan*, crush], 1. to injure and discolor the surface of (the skin) without breaking it. 2. to injure slightly. *v.i.* to be bruised. *n.* a discoloration or injury of the skin.

**bruis′er,** *n.* [< *bruise*], a strong, pugnacious man.

**bruit** (brōōt), *n. & v.t.* [Fr. < *bruire*, roar], rumor.

**brunch** (brunch), *n.* [Colloq.], a combined breakfast and lunch.

**bru·nette** (brōō-net′), *adj.* [Fr., dim. of *brun*, brown], 1. having a dark or olive color. 2. having black or dark-brown hair and eyes, and a dark complexion. *n.* a brunette woman or girl. —**bru·net′,** *adj. & n.masc.*

**brunt** (brunt), *n.* [< ON. *bruncer*, heat], 1. shock (of an attack); impact (of a blow). 2. the main part of the shock or impact.

**brush** (brush), *n.* [< OFr. *broce*, bush], 1. a device for cleaning, painting, etc., having bristles, wires, etc. fastened into a back. 2. a bushy tail, as of a fox. 3. a brushing. 4. a light touch in passing. 5. brushwood. 6. sparsely settled country. *v.t.* 1. to clean, paint, etc. with a brush. 2. to touch or graze lightly. 3. to remove as with a brush. *v.i.* to graze past something. —**brush off,** to dismiss. —**brush up,** to refresh one's memory. —**brush′y,** *adj.*

**brush** (brush), *v.i.* [ME. *bruschen*], to rush; hurry. *n.* a short, quick fight.

**brush-off** (brush′ôf′), *n.* [Slang], dismissal. —**give the brush-off,** [Slang], to dismiss.

**brush′wood′,** *n.* 1. chopped-off tree branches. 2. underbrush.

**brusque** (brusk, broosk), *adj.* [Fr. < It. *brusco*], abrupt or blunt; curt.

**Brus·sels sprouts** (brus′'lz), 1. a kind of cabbage with small, cabbagelike heads on a stem. 2. its edible heads.

**bru·tal** (brōō′t'l), *adj.* like a brute; savage, cruel, etc. —**bru′tal·ly,** *adv.*

**bru·tal′i·ty** (-tal′ə-ti), *n.* 1. the quality of being brutal. 2. [*pl.* -TIES], a brutal act.

**brute** (brōōt), *adj.* [< L. *brutus*, irrational], 1. lacking the ability to reason: as, a *brute* beast. 2. of or like an animal. 3. cruel; stupid. *n.* 1. an animal. 2. a brutal person.

**brut·ish** (brōōt′ish), *adj.* like a brute; savage, stupid, etc. —**brut′ish·ly,** *adv.*

**B.S., B.Sc.,** Bachelor of Science.

**b.s., B/S,** bill of sale.

**bu.,** bushel; bushels.

**bub·ble** (bub′'l), *n.* [prob. echoic], 1. a film of liquid enveloping air or gas. 2. a globule of air or gas in a liquid or solid. 3. a plausible scheme that proves worthless. *v.i.* [-BLED, -BLING], 1. to rise in bubbles; boil; foam. 2. to make a gurgling sound. *v.t.* to form bubbles in. —**bub′bly,** *adj.*

**bu·bo** (bū′bō), *n.* [*pl.* -BOES], [< Gr. *boubon*, groin], an inflamed swelling of a lymph gland, esp. in the groin.

**bu·bon′ic plague** (-bon′ik), a contagious disease, usually fatal, characterized by buboes, chills, and fever.

**buc·ca·neer** (buk′ə-nêr′), *n.* [< Fr. *boucanier*], a pirate, or sea robber.

**buck** (buk), *n.* [AS. *bucca*, he-goat], 1. a male deer, goat, etc. 2. the act of bucking. 3. a dandy. 4. [Colloq.], a young man: patronizing term. 5. [Slang], a dollar. *v.i. & v.t.* 1. to rear upward quickly, as to throw off (a rider): said of a horse. 2. to charge (against), as in football. 3. [Colloq.], to resist stubbornly. —**buck for,** [Slang], to work hard for (a promotion, etc.). —**buck up,** [Colloq.], to cheer up. —**pass the buck,** [Colloq.], to throw the responsibility on another. —**buck′er,** *n.*

**buck** (buk), *n.* [D. *zaagbok*], 1. a sawbuck; sawhorse. 2. a gymnastic apparatus for vaulting over.

**buck·a·roo** (buk′ə-rōō, buk′ə-rōō′), *n.* [*pl.* -ROOS], [< Sp. *vaquero*], a cowboy.

**buck′board′,** *n.* [< *buck* (to rear upward)], an open carriage whose floor boards rest directly on the axles.

**buck·et** (buk′it), *n.* [< AS. *buc*, pitcher], 1. a container hung from a handle, for carrying water, etc.; pail. 2. a bucketful. 3. a thing like a bucket, as a dredge scoop. —**kick the bucket,** [Slang], to die.

**buck′et·ful′** (-fool′), *n.* [*pl.* -FULS], the amount that a bucket can contain.

**buck·eye** (buk′ī), *n.* [*buck* (male deer) + *eye*: alluding to the nut], 1. a horse chestnut with showy clusters of flowers, large leaves, and burs containing nuts. 2. the nut.

**buck·le** (buk′'l), *n.* [< L. *buccula*, cheek strap of a helmet], a clasp for fastening a strap, belt, etc. *v.t. & v.i.* [-LED, -LING], to fasten with a buckle. —**buckle down,** to apply oneself.

**buck·le** (buk′'l), *v.t. & v.i.* [-LED, -LING], [D. *bukken*, to bow], to bend or crumple. *n.* a bend, bulge, etc.

**buck·ler** (buk′lẽr), *n.* [OFr. *bocler*], a small, round shield worn on the arm.

**buck·ram** (buk′rəm), *n.* [? < *Bokhara*, in Asia Minor], a coarse, stiffened cloth used in bookbinding, etc.

**buck·saw** (buk′sô′), *n.* a wood-cutting saw set in a frame.

**buck′shot′**, *n.* a large lead shot for shooting deer and other large game.

**buck′skin′**, *n.* 1. a soft, yellowish-gray leather made from the skins of deer or sheep. 2. *pl.* clothes made of buckskin.

**buck′tooth′**, *n.* [*pl.* -TEETH], a projecting tooth. —**buck′-toothed′**, *adj.*

**buck′wheat′**, *n.* [< AS. *boc*, beech; + *wheat*], 1. a plant with beechnut-shaped seeds. 2. a dark flour made from the seeds.

**bu·col·ic** (bū-kol′ik), *adj.* [< Gr. *boukolos*, herdsman], 1. of shepherds; pastoral. 2. rural; rustic. —**bu·col′i·cal·ly,** *adv.*

**bud** (bud), *n.* [AS. *budda*, beetle], 1. a small swelling on a plant, from which a shoot, leaf, or flower develops. 2. an early stage of development. *v.i.* [BUDDED, BUDDING], 1. to put forth buds. 2. to begin to develop. *v.t.* 1. to cause to bud. 2. to insert a bud of (a plant) into the bark of another sort of plant. —**nip in the bud,** to check at the earliest stage.

**Bud·dhism** (bood′iz'm). *n.* [< *Buddha*, Hindu founder in 4th c. B.C.], a religion of Asia teaching that by right living one achieves Nirvana. —**Bud′dhist,** *n. & adj.*

**bud·dy** (bud′i), *n.* [*pl.* -DIES], [? < Brit. dial.], [Colloq.], a comrade; pal.

**budge** (buj), *v.t. & v.i.* [BUDGED, BUDGING], [< Fr. *bouger*, to move], to move slightly.

**budg·et** (buj′it), *n.* [< L. *bulga*, bag], 1. a collection of items; stock. 2. a plan adjusting expenses to income. 3. the estimated cost of living, operating, etc. *v.t.* 1. to put on a budget. 2. to schedule: as, *budget* your time. —**budg′et·ar′y,** *adj.*

**buff** (buf), *n.* [< Fr. *buffle*, buffalo], 1. a heavy, soft, brownish-yellow leather made from the skin of the buffalo or ox. 2. a military coat made of this. 3. a dull brownish yellow. 4. [Colloq.], the bare skin. *adj.* 1. made of buff. 2. of the color buff. *v.t.* to clean or shine with leather or a leather-covered wheel. —**buf′fer,** *n.*

**buf·fa·lo** (buf′'l-ō′), *n.* [*pl.* -LOES, -LOS, -LO], [< Port. < Gr. *bous*, ox], 1. any of various wild oxen, as the water buffalo of India. 2. popularly, the American bison. *v.t.* [Slang], to intimidate; overawe.

**buff·er** (buf′ẽr), *n.* [< OFr. *buffe*, a blow], anything that lessens shock, as of collision.

**buf·fet** (buf′it), *n.* [OFr. < *buffe*, a blow], a blow as with the hand. *v.t.* 1. to punch; slap. 2. to fight against. *v.i.* to fight.

**buf·fet** (bə-fā′, boo-), *n.* [Fr.], 1. a piece of furniture with drawers and cupboards for dishes, silver, etc. 2. a counter for serving refreshments.

**buffet supper** (or **lunch**), a meal at which guests serve themselves from a buffet, etc.

**buf·foon** (bu-fōōn′), *n.* [< Fr. < It. *buffare*, to jest], one who tries to amuse by jokes and tricks; clown. —**buf·foon′er·y** [*pl.* -IES], *n.*

**bug** (bug), *n.* [< AS. *budda*, beetle], 1. any crawling insect with sucking mouth parts. 2. any insect. 3. [Colloq.], a germ. 4. [Slang], a defect, as in a machine. 5. [Slang], a hidden microphone. *v.t.* [BUGGED, BUGGING], [Slang], 1. to annoy, bother, anger, etc. 2. to hide a microphone in (a room, etc.).

**bug′bear′**, *n.* [< earlier *bug* (bogey) + *bear* (the animal)], an imaginary terror: also **bug′a·boo′** (-ə-bōō′), *n.* [*pl.* -BOOS].

**bug·gy** (bug′i), *n.* [*pl.* -GIES], [< Fr. *bouger*, move], 1. a light, one-horse carriage with one seat. 2. a small carriage for a baby.

**bug′gy,** *adj.* [-GIER, -GIEST], infested or swarming with bugs.

**bu·gle** (bū′g'l), *n.* [< L. *buculus*, young ox], a wind instrument like a small trumpet, usually without valves. *v.i. & v.t.* [-GLED, -GLING], to signal by blowing a bugle.

**build** (bild), *v.t.* [BUILT (bilt), BUILDING], [< AS. *bold*, house], 1. to make by putting together materials, parts, etc.; construct. 2. to establish; base: as, *build* a theory on facts. *v.i.* 1. to put up a building or buildings. 2. to develop a plan, etc. (*on* or *upon*). *n.* the manner or form of construction: as, a stocky *build.* —**build up,** 1. to develop gradually. 2. to make strong or healthy.

**build′ing,** *n.* 1. anything that is built; structure. 2. the work or business of making houses, etc.

**build′-up′**, *n.* [Slang], favorable notice; praise.

**bulb** (bulb), *n.* [< Gr. *bolbos*], 1. an underground bud with roots and a short, scaly stem, as in a lily or onion. 2. a rhizome or tuber resembling a bulb, as in a crocus. 3. anything shaped like a bulb, as an incandescent lamp. —**bulb′ous,** *adj.*

**bulge** (bulj), *n.* [< L. *bulga*, leather bag], an outward swelling; protuberance. *v.i. & v.t.* [BULGED, BULGING], to swell out; protrude. —**bulg′y,** *adj.*

**bulk** (bulk), *n.* [ON. *bulki*, a heap], 1. size, mass, or volume, esp. if great. 2. the main mass; largest part. *v.i.* to have, or to increase in, size or importance. *adj.* 1. total; aggregate. 2. not packaged. —**bulk′y** [-IER, -IEST], *adj.* —**bulk′i·ly,** *adv.* —**bulk′i·ness,** *n.*

**bulk·head** (bulk′hed′), *n.* [< ON. *balkr*, partition; + *head*], 1. an upright partition, as in a ship, for protection against fire, leakage, etc. 2. a wall for holding back water, etc.

**bull** (bool), *n.* [< AS. *bula*, a steer], 1. the male of any bovine animal, as the ox, or of certain other large animals, as the elephant, whale, etc. 2. a large, noisy, or strong person. 3. [Slang], insincere talk; nonsense. *adj.* 1. male. 2. rising in price: as, a *bull* market. —**take the bull by the horns,** to deal boldly with a danger or difficulty.

**bull** (bool), *n.* [< L. *bulla*, a seal], an official document from the Pope.

**Bull, John** (bool), England, the English people, etc.: a personification.

**bull′dog′**, *n.* a short-haired, square-jawed, heavily built dog that has a stubborn grip. *adj.* like a bulldog; stubborn. *v.t.* to throw (a steer) by twisting its horns.

**bull·doze** (bool′dōz′), *v.t.* [-DOZED, -DOZING], [< ?], [Colloq.], to force or frighten by threatening; intimidate; bully.

**bull′doz′er** (-dōz′ẽr), *n.* a tractor with a large, shovellike blade in front for pushing earth, debris, etc.

**bul·let** (bool′it), *n.* [< Fr. *boule*, ball], a small, shaped piece of lead, steel, etc. to be shot from a firearm.

**bul·le·tin** (bool′ə-t'n), *n.* [< L. *bulla*, a seal], 1. a brief statement of late news. 2. a regular publication, as of an organization, etc.

**bul′let·proof′,** *adj.* that bullets cannot pierce. *v.t.* to make bulletproof.

**bull′fight′** (-fīt′), *n.* a spectacle in which a bull is provoked by men on horseback and afoot and then killed with a sword by the matador. —**bull′fight′er,** *n.*

**bull′finch′** (-finch′), *n.* a small European songbird with a short, rounded beak.

**bull′frog′,** *n.* a large North American frog with a deep, loud croak.

**bull′head′ed** (-hed′id), *adj.* stubborn; headstrong. —**bull′head′ed·ness,** *n.*

**bull′horn′** (-hôrn′), *n.* a portable electronic voice amplifier.

**bul·lion** (bool′yən), *n.* [< Fr. *billon,* small coin], unprocessed gold or silver.

**bull·ock** (bool′ək), *n.* [< AS. *bulluc,* young bull], a castrated bull; ox.

**bull's-eye** (boolz′ī′), *n.* 1. the central mark of a target. 2. a direct hit.

**bull terrier,** a strong, lean, white dog developed by crossbreeding the bulldog and the terrier.

**bul·ly** (bool′i), *n.* [*pl.* -LIES], [< MHG. *buole,* lover: infl. by *bull* (ox)], one who hurts or browbeats those who are weaker. *v.t. & v.i.* [-LIED, -LYING], to act the bully (toward). *adj. & interj.* [Colloq.], fine; very good.

**bul·ly** (bool′i), *n.* [< Fr. *bouillir,* to boil], canned or corned beef: also **bully beef.**

**bul·rush** (bool′rush′), *n.* [< AS. *bol,* tree trunk + *risc,* a rush], a tall plant of the sedge family, found in wet places.

**bul·wark** (bool′wẽrk), *n.* [< D. & MHG. *bolwerk*], 1. a defensive wall; rampart. 2. a defense; protection.

**bum** (bum), *n.* [prob. < G. *bummein,* go slowly], [Colloq.], a loafer; vagrant. *v.i.* [BUMMED, BUMMING], [Colloq.], 1. to loaf. 2. to live by begging. *v.t.* [Slang], to get by begging. *adj.* [BUMMER, BUMMEST], [Slang], poor in quality. —**on the bum,** [Colloq.], 1. living as a vagrant. 2. out of repair.

**bum·ble·bee** (bum′b'l-bē′), *n.* [< ME. *bumblen,* buzz], a large, hairy, yellow-and-black bee that buzzes in flight.

**bump** (bump), *v.t. & v.i.* [echoic], 1. to collide (with); hit against. 2. to move with jolts. *n.* 1. a light collision; jolt. 2. a swelling, esp. one caused by a blow. —**bump off,** [Slang], to murder. —**bump′y,** *adj.*

**bump′er,** *n.* a protective bar or pad used on a vehicle, ship, etc. to lessen the shock of a collision.

**bump′er,** *n.* [< *bump,* infl. by Fr. *bombé,* bulging], a cup or glass filled to the brim. *adj.* [Colloq.], unusually abundant.

**bump·kin** (bump′kin), *n.* [prob. < D. *boomkin,* short tree], an awkward or loutish person from the country.

**bump′tious** (-shəs), *adj.* [prob. < *bump*], disagreeably conceited or pushing.

**bun** (bun), *n.* [? < OFr. *bon,* good], 1. a small roll, usually somewhat sweetened. 2. hair worn in a roll or knot.

**bunch** (bunch), *n.* [ME. *bunche*], 1. a cluster of similar things growing or grouped together. 2. [Colloq.], a group (of people). *v.t. & v.i.* to collect into a bunch. —**bunch′y** [-IER, -IEST], *adj.*

**bun·combe** (buŋ′kəm), *n.* [< *Buncombe* county, N. Carolina, loquaciously represented in 16th Congress], [Colloq.], empty, insincere talk; humbug: also sp. **bunkum.**

**bun·dle** (bun′d'l), *n.* [MD. *bondel*], 1. a number of things bound together. 2. a package. 3. a bunch; collection. *v.t.* [-DLED, -DLING], 1. to make into a bundle. 2. to hustle (with *off, out,* etc.). —**bundle up,** to put on plenty of warm clothing.

**bung** (buŋ), *n.* a cork or other stopper for the hole of a barrel, cask, etc. *v.t.* 1. to close with a stopper. 2. [Slang], to bruise or damage (with *up*).

**bun·ga·low** (buŋ′gə-lō′), *n.* [< Hind. *bāṅglā,* thatched house], a small, one-storied house.

**bun·gle** (buŋ′g'l), *v.t. & v.i.* [-GLED, -GLING], [echoic], to do clumsily; spoil; botch. *n.* 1. a bungling. 2. a bungled piece of work.

**bun·ion** (bun′yən), *n.* [< Fr. *bouillon,* lump on horse's foot], an inflamed swelling at the base of the big toe.

**bunk** (buŋk), *n.* [< D. *bank,* a bench], 1. a shelflike bed built against a wall, as in a ship. 2. any narrow bed. *v.i.* to sleep in a bunk.

**bunk** (buŋk), *n.* [Slang], buncombe.

**bunk′er,** *n.* [Scot. < *bank* (bench)], 1. a large bin, as for storing fuel on a ship. 2. an underground fortification. 3. a mound serving as an obstacle on a golf course.

**bun·ny** (bun′i), *n.* [*pl.* -NIES], [dim. of *bun*], a rabbit: a child's term.

**Bun·sen burner** (bun′s'n), [< R. W. *Bunsen,* 19th-c. German chemist], a small, tubular gas burner that produces a hot, blue flame.

**bunt** (bunt), *v.t. & v.i.* [? < Bret. *bounta,* to butt], in *baseball,* to bat (a pitched ball) lightly so that it does not go beyond the infield. *n.* a bunted ball.

**bunt·ing** (bun′tiŋ), *n.* [? < ME. *bunten,* sift] 1. a thin cloth for making flags, etc. 2. flags collectively. 3. a soft, warm, baby's garment in the form of a hooded blanket.

**bunt′ing,** *n.* [< OFr. *bon,* good], a small bird of the finch family.

**buoy** (boi, bōō′i), *n.* [< L. *boia,* fetter], 1. a floating object anchored in water to warn of rocks, etc. or to mark a channel. 2. a life preserver. *v.t.* 1. to mark with a buoy. 2. to keep afloat. 3. to encourage.

**buoy·an·cy** (boi′ən-si, bōō′yən-), *n.* [? < Sp. *boyar,* to float], 1. the ability or tendency to float. 2. cheerfulness. —**buoy′ant,** *adj.*

**bur** (bũr), *n.* [< ON.], 1. a rough, prickly seedcase of certain plants. 2. a plant with burs. 3. a burr.

**bur·den** (bũr′d'n), *n.* [< AS. *beran,* to bear], 1. anything carried or endured; load. 2. something hard to bear. 3. the carrying capacity of a ship. *v.t.* to make bear a burden; oppress. —**bur′den·some,** *adj.*

**bur′den,** *n.* [< OFr. *bourdon,* a humming], 1. a chorus or refrain of a song. 2. a repeated, central idea; theme.

**bur·dock** (bũr′dok′), *n.* [*bur* + *dock* (plant)], a plant with large leaves, prickly burs, and a strong smell.

**bu·reau** (byoo′rō), *n.* [*pl.* -REAUS, -REAUX (-rōz)], [Fr., desk], 1. a chest of drawers for clothing, etc. 2. an office: as, information *bureau.* 3. a government department.

**bu·reauc·ra·cy** (byoo-rok′rə-si), *n.* [*pl.* -CIES], 1. government by departmental officials following an inflexible routine. 2. the officials collectively. 3. governmental officialism. 4. the concentration of authority in administrative bureaus. —**bu′reau·crat′** (-rə-krat′), *n.* —**bu′reau·crat′ic,** *adj.*

**bu·rette, bu·ret** (byoo-ret′), *n.* [Fr.], a graduated glass tube with a valve at the bottom, for measuring liquid or gas.

**burg** (bũrg), *n.* [earlier var. of *borough*], [Colloq.], a city or town.

**bur·geon** (bũr′jən), *v.i. & v.t.* [< OFr. *burjon,* a bud], to put forth (buds, etc.). *n.* a bud.

**-burger,** [< ham*burger*], [Slang], a combining form meaning *sandwich of ground meat, etc.* (*and*), as in *cheeseburger.*

**bur·gess** (bũr′jis), *n.* [see BOURGEOIS], a citizen of a borough.

**burgh** (bũrg; Scot. bur′ō), *n.* [Scot. var. of *borough*], 1. [Brit.], a borough. 2. in Scotland, a chartered town.

**burgh′er,** *n.* a citizen of a town.

**bur·glar** (bũr′glẽr), *n.* [< LL. *burgulator*], one who commits burglary.

**bur′glar·ize′,** *v.t.* [-IZED, -IZING], [Colloq.], to commit burglary in or upon.

**bur′gla·ry,** *n.* [*pl.* -RIES], the act of breaking into a building, esp. at night, to commit a felony, as theft.

**bur·go·mas·ter** (bũr′gə-mas′tẽr, -mäs′-), *n.* [< D. *burg*, city + *meester*, master], the mayor of a town in the Netherlands, Flanders, Austria, or Germany.

**Bur·gun·dy** (bũr′gən-di), *n.* [*pl.* -DIES], a red or white wine, orig. made in Burgundy, a former French province.

**bur·i·al** (ber′i-əl), *n.* a burying of a dead body in a grave, tomb, etc.

**burl** (bũrl), *n.* [< L. *burra*, coarse hair], 1. a knot in thread, yarn, etc. that gives a nubby appearance to cloth. 2. a kind of knot on some tree trunks. —**burled,** *adj.*

**bur·lap** (bũr′lap), *n.* [prob. < D.], a coarse cloth made of jute or hemp.

**bur·lesque** (bũr-lesk′), *n.* [Fr. < It. *burla*, a jest], 1. any broadly comic or satirical imitation; parody. 2. a sort of vaudeville characterized by low comedy and display of nudity. *adj.* 1. parodying. 2. of or connected with burlesque (vaudeville). *v.t. & v.i.* [-LESQUED (-leskt′), -LESQUING], to imitate comically.

**bur·ly** (bũr′li), *adj.* [-LIER, -LIEST], [prob. < ON.], big and strong. —**bur′li·ness,** *n.*

**burn** (bũrn), *v.t.* [BURNED or BURNT, BURNING], [AS. *bærnan*], 1. to destroy by fire. 2. to set on fire. 3. to injure by fire, friction, acid, etc. 4. to sunburn. 5. to cause (a hole, etc.) by fire. 6. to cause a sensation of heat in. *v.i.* 1. to be on fire. 2. to give out light or heat; glow. 3. to be destroyed or injured by fire or heat. 4. to feel hot. 5. to be excited. *n.* 1. an injury caused by fire, heat, etc. 2. a burned area. —**burn down,** to burn to the ground. —**burn up,** [Slang], to make or become angry.

**burn′er,** *n.* the part of a stove, lamp, etc. from which the flame comes.

**burn′ing,** *adj.* 1. glowing. 2. intense; critical: as a *burning* issue.

**bur·nish** (bũr′nish), *v.t. & v.i.* [< OFr. *brun*, brown], to make or become shiny by rubbing. *n.* gloss; polish. —**bur′nish·er,** *n.*

**burnt** (bũrnt), alt. pt. and pp. of **burn.**

**burp** (bũrp), *n. & v.i.* [echoic], [Slang], belch.

**burr** (bũr), *n.* 1. a bur. 2. a rough edge left on metal, etc. 3. a dentist's drill.

**burr** (bũr), *n.* [prob. echoic], 1. the trilling of *r*. 2. any rough pronunciation: as, a Scottish *burr*. 3. a whir.

**bur·ro** (bũr′ō), *n.* [*pl.* -ROS], [Sp. < L. *burricus*, small horse], a donkey.

**bur·row** (bũr′ō), *n.* [see BOROUGH], 1. a hole dug in the ground by an animal. 2. any similar hole. *v.i.* 1. to make a burrow. 2. to live or hide in a burrow. 3. to search.

**bur·sa** (bũr′sə), *n.* [*pl.* -SAE (-sē), -SAS], [Gr., a hide], in *anatomy*, a sac or cavity, esp. between joints. —**bur′sal,** *adj.*

**bur·sar** (bũr′sẽr), *n.* [see BURSA], a college treasurer.

**bur·si·tis** (bẽr-sī′tis), *n.* [< *bursa* + *-itis*], inflammation of a bursa.

**burst** (bũrst), *v.i.* [BURST, BURSTING], [AS. *berstan*], 1. to come apart suddenly and violently; explode. 2. to give sudden expression: as, to *burst* into tears. 3. to appear, enter, etc. suddenly. 4. to be abnormally full; bulge. *v.t.* to cause to burst. *n.* 1. a bursting. 2. a break; breach. 3. a sudden activity or spurt.

**bur·y** (ber′i), *v.t.* [-IED, -YING], [AS. *byrgan*], 1. to put (a dead body) into the earth, a tomb, etc. 2. to cover; conceal. 3. to put away. 4. to immerse.

**bus** (bus), *n.* [*pl.* BUSES, BUSSES], [< *omnibus*], a large motor coach for many passengers, usually following a regular route.

**bus boy,** a waiter's assistant who clears tables, brings water, etc.

**bush** (boosh), *n.* [< ON.], 1. a low, woody plant with spreading branches; shrub. 2. anything like a bush. 3. uncleared land. *v.i.* to grow thickly. —**beat around the bush,** to talk around a subject without getting to the point. —**bush′y** [-IER, -IEST], *adj.*

**bushed** (boosht), *adj.* [Colloq.], tired.

**bush·el** (boosh′əl), *n.* [< OFr. *boissil*, grain measure], a unit of dry measure equal to 4 pecks, or 32 quarts.

**bush·ing** (boosh′iŋ), *n.* [< D. *bos*, a box], a removable metal lining, for reducing friction on moving parts.

**bush league,** [Slang], in *baseball*, a small or second-rate minor league. —**bush leaguer.**

**bush′man,** *n.* [*pl.* -MEN], one who lives in the Australian bush.

**bush′mas′ter** (-mas′tẽr, -mäs′-), *n.* a large, poisonous snake of Central and South America.

**bush′whack′er** (-hwak′ẽr), *n.* [< D. *boschwachter*, forest watcher; now associated with *whack*], 1. a backwoodsman. 2. a guerrilla.

**bus·i·ly** (biz′'l-i), *adv.* in a busy manner.

**busi·ness** (biz′nis), *n.* [AS. *bisignes*; see BUSY], 1. one's work; occupation; profession. 2. one's rightful concern. 3. a matter or affair. 4. commerce; trade. 5. a commercial or industrial establishment. *adj.* of or for business. —**mean business,** [Colloq.], to be in earnest.

**business college** (or **school**), a school of typing, bookkeeping, etc.

**busi′ness·like′,** *adj.* efficient, methodical, systematic, etc.

**busi′ness·man′,** *n.* [*pl.* -MEN], a man in business, esp. as an owner or executive. —**busi′ness·wom′an** [*pl.* -WOMEN], *n.fem.*

**bus·kin** (bus′kin), *n.* [? < MD. *brosekin*, small boot], 1. a high, laced boot worn in ancient tragedy. 2. tragic drama.

**buss** (bus), *n., v.t. & v.i.* [< ?], [Archaic or Dial.], kiss.

**bust** (bust), *n.* [< It. *busto*], 1. a sculpture of a person's head and shoulders. 2. a woman's bosom.

**bust** (bust), *v.t. & v.i.* [< *burst*], [Slang], 1. to burst; break. 2. to make or become bankrupt or demoted. 3. to hit or punch. *n.* [Slang], 1. a failure. 2. a punch. 3. a spree.

**bus·tle** (bus′'l), *v.i. & v.t.* [-TLED, -TLING], [< ME. *busken*, prepare], to hurry busily and noisily. *n.* noisy, hurried activity.

**bus·tle** (bus′'l), *n.* [< G. *buschel*, pad], a framework or padding worn to fill out the upper back of a woman's skirt.

**bus·y** (biz′i), *adj.* [-IER, -IEST], [AS. *bisig*], 1. active; at work. 2. full of activity. 3. being used, as a telephone. 4. meddlesome. *v.t.* [-IED, -YING], to make or keep busy.

**bus′y·bod′y** (-bod′i), *n.* [*pl.* -IES], a meddler in the affairs of others.

**but** (but), *prep.* [< AS. *butan*, without], except; save: as, nobody goes *but* us. *conj.* 1. yet; still: as, it's bad, *but* not hopeless. 2. on the contrary: as, I am old, *but* he is young. 3. unless: as, it never rains *but* it pours. 4. that: as, I don't doubt *but* you're right. 5. that . . . not: as, I never gamble *but* I lose. 6. who . . . not; which . . . not: as, not a man *but* felt it. *adv.* 1. only: as, had I *but* known. 2. merely: as, he is *but* a boy. 3. just: as, they left *but* now. —**all but,** almost. —**but for,** if it were not for. —**cannot but,** have no choice except to.

**butch·er** (booch′ẽr), *n.* [< OFr. *boc*, he-goat], 1. one whose work is killing and dressing animals for meat. 2. one who sells meat. 3. a brutal killer. *v.t.* 1. to kill or dress (animals) for meat. 2. to kill brutally. 3. to botch. —**butch′er·y** [*pl.* -IES], *n.*

**but·ler** (but′lẽr), *n.* [< OFr. *bouteille*, a

bottle], the head manservant of a household, in charge of wines, pantry, etc.

**butt** (but), *n.* [< ?], 1. the thick end of anything. 2. a stub or stump, as of a cigar. 3. a target. 4. an object of ridicule or criticism. 5. [Slang], a cigarette. *v.t. & v.i.* to join end to end.

**butt** (but), *v.t. & v.i.* [< OHG. *bōzan*, to beat], 1. to ram with the head. 2. to project. *n.* a butting. **—butt in(to),** [Slang], to meddle or intrude (in). **—butt′er,** *n.*

**butt** (but), *n.* [< LL. *bottis*, cask], a large cask for wine or beer.

**butte** (būt), *n.* [Fr., mound], a steep hill standing alone in a plain.

**but·ter** (but′ẽr), *n.* [< L. *butryum* < Gr. *bous*, cow + *tyros*, cheese], 1. the thick, yellowish product that results from churning cream. 2. any substance somewhat like butter. *v.t.* 1. to spread with butter. 2. [Colloq.], to flatter (with *up*). **—but′ter·y** [-IER, -IEST], *adj.*

**but′ter·cup′,** *n.* 1. a plant with yellow, cup-shaped flowers. 2. its flower.

**but′ter·fat′,** *n.* the fatty part of milk, from which butter is made.

**but′ter·fly′,** *n.* [*pl.* -FLIES], [< AS. *buttorfleoge*], an insect with a slender body and four broad wings, usually bright-colored.

**but′ter·milk′,** *n.* the sour liquid left in milk after churning butter.

**but′ter·nut′,** *n.* 1. the white walnut tree. 2. its edible, oily nut.

**but′ter·scotch′** (-skoch′), *n.* a hard, sticky candy made from brown sugar and butter.

**but·tocks** (but′əks), *n.pl.* [< ME. *but*, thick end + dim. *-ock*], the fleshy, rounded parts of the hips; rump.

**but·ton** (but′'n), *n.* [OFr. *boton*], 1. any small disk or knob used as a fastening, ornament, etc., as on a garment. 2. anything small and shaped like a button. *v.t. & v.i.* to fasten with a button or buttons.

**but′ton·hole′,** *n.* a hole or slit into which a button is inserted. *v.t.* [-HOLED, -HOLING], 1. to make buttonholes in. 2. to detain and talk to; compel to listen.

**but·tress** (but′ris), *n.* [< OFr. *buter*, thrust against], 1. a structure built against a wall to support or reinforce it. 2. a support; prop. *v.t.* to prop up; bolster.

**bux·om** (buk′səm), *adj.* [ME. *buhsum*, flexible], healthy, comely, plump, etc.: said of a woman. **—bux′om·ness,** *n.*

**buy** (bī), *v.t.* [BOUGHT, BUYING], [AS. *bycgan*], 1. to get by paying money. 2. to get by a sacrifice: as, to *buy* fame with health. 3. to bribe. *n.* 1. anything bought. 2. [Colloq.], something worth its price. **—buy off,** to bribe. **—buy out,** to buy all the stock, rights, etc. of.

**buy·er** (bī′ẽr), *n.* 1. one who buys; consumer. 2. an employee whose work is to buy goods for a business firm, store, etc.

**buzz** (buz), *v.i.* [echoic], 1. to hum like a bee or fly. 2. to gossip. *v.t.* to fly an airplane low over. *n.* a sound like a bee's hum.

**buz·zard** (buz′ẽrd), *n.* [< L. *buteo*, kind of hawk], 1. any of various hawks that are slow and heavy in flight. 2. the turkey buzzard.

**buzz′er,** *n.* an electrical device that makes a buzzing noise, used as a signal.

**buzz saw,** a motor-driven circular saw.

**bx.,** [*pl.* BXS.], box.

**by** (bī), *prep.* [AS. *be*, *bi*], 1. near; at: as, sit *by* the fire. 2. *a*) in or during: as, travel *by* night. *b*) for a fixed time: as, he works *by* the hour. *c*) not later than: as, be home *by* midnight. 3. *a*) through: as, go *by* way of Rome. *b*) past; beyond: as, he walked right *by* me. 4. in behalf of: as, he did well *by* me. 5. through the agency of: as, made *by* human labor. 6. *a*) according to: as, go *by* the rules. *b*) in: as, to die *by* degrees. 7. *a*) in or to the amount of: as, apples *by* the peck. *b*) and in another dimension: as, two *by* four inches. 8. following: as, day *by* day. *adv.* 1. close at hand: as, stand *by*. 2. away; aside: as, to put money *by*. 3. past; beyond: as, he sped *by*. **—by and by,** after a while. **—by and large,** in most respects. **—by the by,** incidentally.

**by-,** a prefix meaning: 1. *near*. 2. *secondary*.

**by′-and-by′,** *n.* future time.

**bye′-bye′,** *n. & interj.* good-by.

**by′-e·lec′tion,** *n.* a special election held between regular elections.

**by·gone** (bī′gôn′, -gon′), *adj.* past; gone by. *n.* anything gone or past.

**by·law** (bī′lô′), *n.* [< ME. *by*, town; + *law*], a law of local application adopted by an organization or assembly.

**by′-line′,** *n.* a line above a newspaper article, etc., telling who wrote it.

**by′pass′,** *n.* a way, pipe, channel, etc. between two points that avoids or is auxiliary to the main way. *v.t.* 1. to detour. 2. to ignore. 3. to furnish with a by-pass.

**by′path′, by′-path′,** *n.* a side path; private or little-used path.

**by′-prod′uct,** *n.* anything produced in the course of making another thing.

**by′stand′er,** *n.* a person who stands near but does not participate; onlooker.

**by′way′,** *n.* a side road or path.

**by′word′,** *n.* 1. a proverb. 2. a person or thing proverbial as being contemptible.

**By·zan·tine** (biz′'n-tēn, -tin′), *adj.* of a style of architecture developed in Byzantium (modern Istanbul), characterized by domes, round arches, etc.

# C

**C, c** (sē), *n.* [*pl.* C's, c's, Cs, cs], the third letter of the English alphabet.

**C,** 1. a Roman numeral for 100. 2. in *chem.*, carbon. 3. in *music*, the first tone in the scale of C major. 4. central.

**C., c.,** 1. carton. 2. case. 3. cent; cents. 4. centigrade. 5. centimeter. 6. century. 7. circa. 8. copyright. 9. cubic.

**Ca,** in *chem.*, calcium.

**cab** (kab), *n.* [< *cabriolet*], 1. an automobile or carriage for public hire; taxicab. 2. the place in a locomotive, truck, etc. where the operator sits.

**ca·bal** (kə-bal′), *n.* [Fr., intrigue], 1. a small group joined in a secret scheme. 2. a secret scheme; plot.

**cab·a·la** (kab′ə-lə, kə-bä′lə), *n.* [< Heb. *qabbālāh*, received lore], 1. a religious philosophy developed by medieval rabbis, based on a mystical interpretation of the Bible. 2. mystical doctrine. **—cab′a·lism,** *n.* **—cab′a·list,** *n.* **—cab′a·list′ic,** *adj.*

**ca·ba·na** (kə-bä′nə), *n.* [< Sp. < LL. *capanna*], 1. a cabin. 2. a small shelter used as a bathhouse.

**cab·a·ret** (kab′ə-rā′), *n.* [Fr.], a café with dancing and singing as entertainment.

**cab·bage** (kab′ij), *n.* [< L. *caput*, head], a vegetable of the mustard family, with thick leaves compressed into a round head.

**cab·in** (kab′in), *n.* [< LL. *capanna*, hut], 1. a small, roughly constructed house; hut.

2. a room on a ship. 3. the space for passengers in an aircraft. *v.t.* to confine in or as in a cabin; cramp.

**cabin boy,** a boy whose work is to serve the officers and passengers aboard a ship.

**cab·i·net** (kab'ə-nit), *n.* [Fr. < Eng. *cabin*], 1. a case with drawers or shelves to hold or display things. 2. [C-], a body of official advisers to the chief executive of a nation. *adj.* 1. secret. 2. of a political cabinet.

**cab'i·net·mak'er,** *n.* a workman who makes fine furniture or woodwork.

**cab'i·net·work',** *n.* fine woodwork.

**ca·ble** (kā'b'l), *n.* [< L. *capere*, seize], 1. a thick, heavy rope, often of wire. 2. an insulated bundle of wires to carry an electric current. 3. a cablegram. *v.t.* [-BLED, -BLING] 1. to fasten with a cable. 2. to transmit by means of a cable under the sea. 3. to send a cablegram to. *v.i.* to send a cablegram.

**cable car,** a car drawn by a moving cable.

**ca'ble·gram'** (-gram'), *n.* a message sent overseas by telegraphic cable.

**ca·boo·dle** (kə-bo͞o'd'l), *n.* [< *kith* + D. *boedel*, property], [Slang], lot; group; as, the whole *caboodle*.

**ca·boose** (kə-bo͞os'), *n.* [< MD. *kaban huis*, cabin house], the trainmen's car at the rear of a freight train.

**cab·ri·o·let** (kab'ri-ə-lā'), *n.* [< Fr. *cabriole*, a leap]. 1. a light, two-wheeled, one-horse carriage. 2. a coupelike automobile with a folding top.

**cab·stand** (kab'stand'), *n.* a place where cabs are stationed for hire.

**ca·ca·o** (kə-kā'ō), *n.* [*pl.* -CAOS], [Sp. < Mex. *cacauatl*], 1. the seed of a tropical American evergreen tree, from which cocoa and chocolate are made: also **cacao bean.** 2. this tree.

**cache** (kash), *n.* [Fr. < L. *coacticare*, store up], 1. a place in which stores of food, supplies, etc. are hidden. 2. anything so stored or hidden. *v.t. & v.i.* [CACHED, CACHING], to place in a cache.

**ca·chet** (ka-shā', kash'ā), *n.* [Fr. < *cacher*, to hide], 1. originally, a seal on an official letter. 2. a distinguishing mark.

**cach·in·nate** (kak'ə-nāt'), *v.i.* [-NATED, -NATING], [< L. *cachinnare*; echoic], to laugh loudly or too much. **—cach'in·na'tion,** *n.*

**cack·le** (kak''l), *v.i.* [-LED, -LING], [echoic], to make the characteristic shrill sound of a hen. *n.* a cackling.

**ca·coph·o·ny** (kə-kof'ə-ni), *n.* [*pl.* -NIES]. [< Gr. *kakos*, bad + *phōnē*, voice], harsh, jarring sound; discord. **—ca·coph'o·nous,** *adj.***—ca·coph'o·nous·ly,** *adv.*

**cac·tus** (kak'təs), *n.* [*pl.* -TUSES, -TI (-tī)], [< Gr. *kaktos*, prickly], any of various plants growing in hot, arid regions, having fleshy stems and spines or scales.

**cad** (kad), *n.* [< *cadet*], a man whose behavior is not gentlemanly.

**ca·dav·er** (kə-dav'ẽr), *n.* [L. < *cadere*, to fall], a dead body; corpse, as for dissection.

**ca·dav'er·ous** (-əs), *adj.* of or like a cadaver; pale, ghastly, gaunt, etc.

**cad·die, cad·dy** (kad'i), *n.* [Scot. form of Fr. *cadet*; see CADET], one who attends a golf player, carrying his clubs, etc. *v.i.* [-DIED, -DYING], to act as a caddie.

**cad·dish** (kad'ish), *adj.* of or like a cad; ill-mannered. **—cad'dish·ly,** *adv.*

**cad·dy** (kad'i), *n.* [*pl.* -DIES], [< Malay *kati*, unit of weight], a small container for tea.

**-cade,** [< *cavalcade*], a suffix meaning *procession, parade*, as in *motorcade*.

**ca·dence** (kā'd'ns), *n.* [< L. *cadere*, to fall], 1. the fall of the voice in speaking. 2. flow of rhythm. 3. measured movement, as in marching. **—ca'denced,** *adj.*

**ca·den·za** (kə-den'zə), *n.* [It.; see CADENCE], an elaborate passage for the solo instrument in a concerto.

**ca·det** (kə-det'), *n.* [Fr. < L. *caput*, head + dim. suffix *-et*], a student in training to become an officer in the armed forces. **—ca·det'ship,** *n.*

**cadge** (kaj), *v.t. & v.i.* [CADGED, CADGING], [ME. *caggen*], [Colloq.], to beg or get by begging.

**cad·mi·um** (kad'mi-əm), *n.* [< L. *cadmia*, zinc ore (in which it occurs)], a blue-white, metallic chemical element used in alloys, pigment, etc.; symbol, Cd.

**ca·dre** (kad'ri), *n.* [Fr. < L. *quadrum* square], a nucleus around which an expanded organization, as a military unit, can be built.

**ca·du·ce·us** (kə-do͞o'si-əs) *n.* [*pl.* -CEI (-si-ī')], [L.], the winged staff with two serpents twined about it, carried by Mercury: now a symbol of the medical profession.

**cae·cum** (sē'kəm), *n.* [*pl.* -CA (-kə)], [L.], a cavity open at one end; esp., the pouch at the beginning of the large intestine.

**Cae·sar** (sē'zẽr), *n.* 1. the title of the Roman emperors from Augustus to Hadrian. 2. any emperor or dictator.

**Cae·sar·e·an operation** (or **section**) (si-zâr'i-ən), an operation for delivering a baby by cutting through the mother's abdominal and uterine walls: Julius Caesar was supposedly born thus.

**cae·su·ra** (si-zhoor'ə, -zyoor'ə), *n.* [*pl.* -RAS, -RAE (-ē)], [L. < *caedere*, to cut], a break or pause in a line of verse, usually in the middle.

**ca·fé** (ka-fā'), *n.* [Fr., lit., coffeehouse], 1. a restaurant. 2. a barroom, sometimes providing entertainment.

**café society**, a well-publicized set of habitual frequenters of cafés and night clubs.

**caf·e·te·ri·a** (kaf'ə-têr'i-ə), *n.* [Am. Sp., coffee store], a restaurant where patrons serve themselves.

**caf·feine. caf·fein** (kaf'ēn'), *n.* [< Fr. *café*, coffee], the alkaloid present in coffee, tea, etc.: it is a stimulant.

**cage** (kāj), *n.* [< L. *cavea*, hollow place], 1. a structure of wires, bars, etc. for confining animals. 2. any openwork frame or structure. 3. an elevator car. *v.t.* [CAGED, CAGING], to put in a cage.

**cage·y** (kāj'i), *adj.* [prob. < *cage*], [CAGIER, CAGIEST], [Slang], sly; tricky; cunning: also sp. **cagy.** **—cag'i·ly** *adv.* **—cag'i·ness,** *n.*

**ca·hoots** (kə-ho͞ots'), *n.pl.* [? < *cohort*], [Slang], partnership: implying scheming in phr. *in cahoots*.

**Cain** (kān), *n.* in the *Bible*, the oldest son of Adam and Eve: he killed his brother Abel. **—raise Cain**, [Slang], to create a great commotion.

**cairn** (kârn), *n.* [Scot.], a conical heap of stones built as a monument or landmark.

**cais·son** (kā'sən), *n.* [Fr. < *caisse*, box], 1. a two-wheeled wagon with a chest for ammunition. 2. a watertight box for underwater construction work.

**cai·tiff** (kā'tif), *n.* [< L. *captivus*, captive], a mean, evil, or cowardly person. *adj.* evil; mean; cowardly.

**ca·jole** (kə-jōl'), *v.t. & v.i.* [-JOLED, -JOLING], [< Fr.], to coax with false words, flattery, etc. **—ca·jol'er,** *n.* **—ca·jol'er·y** [*pl.* -IES], *n.*

**cake** (kāk), *n.* [< ON.], 1. a small, flat mass of baked or fried dough or batter. 2. a baked mixture of flour, eggs, sugar, etc., often with icing. 3. a small, flat, fried mass of hashed meat or fish. 4. a shaped, solid mass, as of soap. *v.t. & v.i.* [CAKED, CAKING], to form into a hard mass. **—take the cake,** [Slang], to win the prize.

**cake'walk',** *n.* a strutting dance developed by Negroes in the South competing for the prize of a cake. *v.i.* to perform a cakewalk.

**cal·a·bash** (kal′ə-bash′), *n.* [? < Per. *kharbuz*, melon], 1. the gourdlike fruit of a tropical American tree. 2. any of various gourds.
**cal·a·boose** (kal′ə-bōōs′), *n.* [Sp. *calabozo*], [Slang], a jail.
**cal·a·mine** (kal′ə-mīn′), *n.* [Fr. < L. *cadmia*, zinc ore], oxidized ores of zinc, used in skin lotions, etc.
**ca·lam·i·ty** (kə-lam′ə-ti), *n.* [*pl.* -TIES], [< L. *calamitas*], a great misfortune; disaster. **—ca·lam′i·tous,** *adj.* **—ca·lam′i·tous·ly,** *adv.*
**cal·car·e·ous** (kal-kâr′i-əs), *adj.* [< L. *calx*, lime], of or like limestone, calcium, or lime.
**cal·cif·er·ous** (kal-sif′ẽr-əs), *adj.* [< L. *calx*, lime; + *-ferous*], containing calcite.
**cal·ci·fy** (kal′sə-fī′), *v.t.* & *v.i.* [-FIED, -FYING], [< L. *calx*, lime; + *-fy*], to change into a hard, stony substance by the deposit of lime or calcium salts. **—cal′ci·fi·ca′tion,** *n.*
**cal·ci·mine** (kal′sə-mīn′), *n.* [< L. *calx*, lime], a white or colored liquid used as a wash for plastered walls, etc. *v.t.* [-MINED, -MINING], to cover with calcimine.
**cal·cine** (kal′sīn′), *v.t.* & *v.i.* [-CINED, -CINING], [< ML. *calcinare*], to change to an ashy powder by heat. **—cal′ci·na′tion,** *n.*
**cal·ci·um** (kal′si-əm), *n.* [< L. *calx*, lime], a soft, silver-white metallic chemical element found combined in limestone, chalk, etc.: symbol, Ca.
**calcium carbonate,** a white powder or crystalline compound found in limestone, chalk, bones, shells, etc.
**cal·cu·late** (kal′kyoo-lāt′), *v.t.* [-LATED, -LATING], [< L. *calculare*, reckon], 1. to determine by arithmetic; compute. 2. to determine by reasoning; estimate. 3. to plan; intend: used in the passive. *v.i.* to make a computation. **—cal′cu·la·ble** (-lə-b'l), *adj.* **—cal′cu·la·bly,** *adv.*
**cal′cu·lat′ing,** *adj.* 1. scheming; cunning. 2. shrewd; cautious.
**cal′cu·la′tion,** *n.* 1. a calculating. 2. something deduced by calculating. 3. forethought; prudence. **—cal′cu·la′tive,** *n.*
**cal′cu·la′tor,** *n.* 1. one who calculates. 2. a machine for doing arithmetic rapidly: also **calculating machine.**
**cal·cu·lous** (kal′kyoo-ləs), *adj.* caused by or having a calculus or calculi.
**cal·cu·lus** (kal′kyoo-ləs), *n.* [*pl.* -LI (-lī′), -LUSES], [L., pebble used in counting], 1. an abnormal stony mass in the body. 2. in *higher math.*, a method of calculation or analysis.
**cal·dron** (kôl′drən), *n.* [< L. *calidus*, warm], a large kettle or boiler.
**cal·en·dar** (kal′ən-dẽr), *n.* [< L. *calendarium*, account book], 1. a system of determining the length and divisions of a year. 2. a table that shows the days, weeks, and months of a given year. 3. a schedule, as of pending court cases. *v.t.* to schedule in a calendar.
**cal·en·der** (kal′ən-dẽr), *n.* [< Gr. *kylindros*, cylinder], a machine with rollers for giving paper or cloth a smooth or glossy finish. *v.t.* to press (paper, etc.) in a calender.
**cal·ends** (kal′əndz), *n.pl.* [< Gr. *kalein*, proclaim], the first day of each month in the ancient Roman calendar.
**calf** (kaf, käf), *n.* [*pl.* CALVES], [AS. *cealf*], 1. a young cow or bull. 2. the young of some other large animals, as the elephant, seal, etc. 3. leather from a calf's hide. 4. [Colloq.], an awkward, callow young person. **—kill the fatted calf,** to make a feast of welcome.
**calf** (kaf, käf), *n.* [*pl.* CALVES], [ON. *kalfr*], the fleshy back part of the leg from the knee to the ankle.
**calf′skin′,** *n.* 1. the skin of a calf. 2. leather made from this.
**cal·i·ber** (kal′ə-bẽr), *n.* [< Fr. & Sp.; prob. < Ar. *qālib*, a mold], 1. the diameter of a cylindrical body, esp. of a bullet or shell. 2. the diameter of the bore of a gun. 3. quality; ability. Also sp. **calibre.**
**cal·i·brate** (kal′ə-brāt′), *v.t.* [-BRATED, -BRATING], 1. to determine the caliber of. 2. to fix or correct the graduations of (a measuring instrument). **—cal′i·bra′tion,** *n.* **—cal′i·bra′tor,** *n.*
**cal·i·co** (kal′ə-kō′), *n.* [*pl.* -COES, -COS], [< *Calicut*, city in India], any of several kinds of cotton cloth, usually coarse and printed.
**Calif.,** California.
**cal·i·for·ni·um** (kal′ə-fôr′ni-əm), *n.* [< Univ. of *California*], a radioactive chemical element: symbol, Cf.
**cal·i·per** (kal′ə-pẽr), *n.* [var. of *caliber*], *usually pl.* an instrument consisting of a pair of hinged legs, for measuring thickness or diameter. *v.t.* & *v.i.* to measure with calipers.
**ca·liph, ca·lif** (kā′lif, kal′if), *n.* [< Ar. *khalīfa*], supreme ruler: the title taken by Mohammed's successors as heads of Islam.
**cal·is·then·ics** (kal′əs-then′iks), *n.pl.* [< Gr. *kallos*, beauty + *sthenos*, strength], athletic exercises. **—cal′is·then′ic,** *adj.*
**calk** (kôk), *n.* [< L. *calx*, heel], a metal plate on the bottom of a shoe to prevent slipping.
**calk** (kôk), *v.t.* [< L. *calcare*, to tread], 1. to make (a boat, etc.) watertight by filling the seams with oakum, tar, etc. 2. to stop up (cracks) with a filler. **—calk′er,** *n.*
**call** (kôl), *v.t.* [< ON. *kalla*], 1. to say in a loud tone; shout. 2. to summon. 3. to name; designate. 4. to awaken. 5. to telephone. 6. to consider as being. 7. to stop (a baseball game, etc.). 8. to demand payment of, as a loan. 9. in *poker*, to require a show of cards by equaling the bet of (another). *v.i.* 1. to shout. 2. to visit for a while (often with *on*). 3. to telephone. *n.* 1. a calling. 2. a loud utterance. 3. a summons; invitation. 4. a demand. 5. the distinctive cry of an animal or bird. 6. need: as, no *call* for tears. 7. a demand for payment. 8. a brief visit. **—call down,** [Slang], to scold. **—call for,** 1. to demand. 2. to come and get. **—call off,** [Colloq.], to cancel (a scheduled event). **—call on,** to ask (a person) to speak. **—call out,** to shout. **—call up,** 1. to recall. 2. to summon for duty. 3. to telephone. **—on call,** available when summoned. **—call′er,** *n.*
**cal·la** (kal′ə), *n.* [< Gr. *kallaia*, wattles of a cock], a plant with a large, white leaf surrounding a yellow flower spike: also **calla lily.**
**cal·lig·ra·phy** (kə-lig′rə-fi), *n.* [< Gr. *kallos*, beauty + *graphein*, write], 1. beautiful handwriting. 2. handwriting. **—cal·lig′rapher,** *n.*
**call′ing,** *n.* 1. act of one that calls. 2. a vocation; trade; profession.
**calling card,** a small card with one's name and, sometimes, address, used in making visits.
**cal·li·o·pe** (kə-lī′ə-pē′, kal′i-ōp′), *n.* [< Gr. *kallos*, beauty + *ops*, voice], a musical instrument with a series of steam whistles, played like an organ.
**cal·los·i·ty** (kə-los′ə-ti, ka-), *n.* 1. a being callous or hardened. 2. [*pl.* -TIES], a callus on the skin or the bark of a tree.
**cal·lous** (kal′əs), *adj.* [see CALLUS], 1. hardened. 2. unfeeling; insensitive. **—cal′lous·ly,** *adv.* **—cal′lous·ness,** *n.*
**cal·low** (kal′ō), *adj.* [AS. *calu*, bare, bald], undeveloped; inexperienced. **—cal′low·ness,** *n.*
**cal·lus** (kal′əs), *n.* [*pl.* -LUSES], [L., hard skin], a hardened, thickened place on the skin; callosity. *v.i.* to develop a callus.

**calm** (käm), *n.* [< Gr. *kauma*, heat], stillness; tranquillity. *adj.* undisturbed; tranquil; still. *v.t. & v.i.* to make or become calm. —**calm′ly,** *adv.* —**calm′ness,** *n.*
**cal·o·mel** (kal′ə-m'l, -mel′), *n.* [Fr. < Gr. *kalos*, beautiful + *melas*, black], a white, tasteless powder, used as a cathartic, etc.
**ca·lor·ic** (kə-lôr′ik, -lor′-), *n.* [see CALORIE], heat. *adj.* of heat. —**cal·o·ric·i·ty** (kal′ə-ris′ə-ti), *n.*
**cal·o·rie** (kal′ə-ri), *n.* [Fr. < L. *calor*, heat], a unit for measuring heat, esp. for measuring the energy produced by food when oxidized in the body: also sp. **calory** [*pl.* -RIES].
**cal′o·rif′ic** (-rif′ik), *adj.* [< L. *calor*, heat + *facere*, make], producing heat.
**cal′o·rim′e·ter** (-rim′ə-tēr), *n.* [< L. *calor*, heat; + *-meter*], an apparatus for measuring heat.
**cal·u·met** (kal′yoo-met′), *n.* [Fr. < L. *calamus*, reed], a long-stemmed tobacco pipe, smoked by North American Indians as a token of peace.
**ca·lum·ni·ate** (kə-lum′ni-āt′), *v.t. & v.i.* [-ATED, -ATING], [see CALUMNY], to slander. —**ca·lum′ni·a′tion,** *n.* —**ca·lum′ni·a′tor,** *n.*
**cal·um·ny** (kal′əm-ni), *n.* [*pl.* -NIES], [< L. *calumnia*, slander], a false and malicious statement; slander.
**Cal·va·ry** (kal′və-ri), *n.* in the *Bible*, the place where Jesus was crucified.
**calve** (kav, käv), *v.i. & v.t.* [CALVED, CALVING], to give birth to (a calf).
**calves** (kavz, kävz), *n.* pl. of **calf.**
**Cal·vin·ism** (kal′vin-iz'm), *n.* [< John *Calvin*, Fr. Protestant], the religious system of John Calvin and his followers, which emphasizes predestination. —**Cal′vin·ist,** *n. & adj.* —**Cal′vin·is′tic,** *adj.*
**ca·lyp·so** (kə-lip′sō), *n.* [< ?], a lively, rhythmic, topical ballad improvised and sung by natives of Trinidad.
**ca·lyx** (kā′liks kal′iks), *n.* [*pl.* -LYXES, -LYCES, (kal′ə-sēz′)], [L., pod], the outer whorl, or sepals, at a flower's base.
**cam** (kam), *n.* [AS. *camb*, comb], a wheel, projection on a wheel, etc. which gives an irregular motion as to a wheel or shaft, or receives such motion from it.
**ca·ma·ra·de·rie** (kä′mə-râ′dēr-i), *n.* [Fr.], good spirit among comrades.
**cam·ber** (kam′bēr), *n.* [< Fr. < L. *camur*, bent], a slight convex curve of a surface, as of a road. *v.t. & v.i.* to arch slightly.
**cam·bi·um** (kam′bi-əm), *n.* [LL., change], the layer of tissue between the bark and wood in woody plants, from which new wood and bark grow.
**cam·bric** (kām′brik), *n.* [< *Cambrai*, Fr. city], a fine linen or cotton cloth.
**came** (kām), pt. of **come.**
**cam·el** (kam′'l), *n.* [ult. < Heb. *gāmāl*], a large, domesticated animal with a humped back and long neck: because it can store water in its body, it is used in Asian and African deserts.
**ca·mel·lia** (kə-mēl′yə), *n.* [after G. J. *Kamel* (d. 1706), missionary to the Far East], 1. an evergreen shrub native to Asia, with shiny, dark-green leaves and white or red, rose-shaped flowers. 2. the flower.
**ca·mel·o·pard** (kə-mel′ə-pärd′), *n.* [< Gr. *kamelos*, camel + *pardalis*, leopard: from its neck and spots], a giraffe.
**camel's hair,** 1. the hair of the camel. 2. cloth made of this hair, sometimes mixed with wool, etc.
**Cam·em·bert (cheese)** (kam′əm-ber′), [< *Camembert*, Fr. district], a soft, creamy kind of cheese.
**cam·e·o** (kam′i-ō′, kam′yō), *n.* [*pl.* -OS], [< It. < ML. *camaeus*], a gem carved with a figure raised in relief.
**cam·er·a** (kam′ēr-ə), *n.* [L., a vault], 1. a device for taking photographs, a closed box containing a sensitized plate or film on which an image is formed when light enters through a lens. 2. in *TV*, that part of the transmitter which receives the image and transforms it into a flow of electrons for transmission. —**in camera,** 1. in a judge's private office. 2. privately.
**cam·i·sole** (kam′ə-sōl′), *n.* [Fr. < LL. *camisia*, shirt], a woman's loose underwaist or corset cover.
**cam·o·mile** (kam′ə-mil′), *n.* [< Gr. *chamai*, ground + *mēlon*, apple], a plant of the aster family whose leaves and flowers are used in medicine.
**cam·ou·flage** (kam′ə-fläzh′), *n.* [Fr. < *camoufler*, to disguise], 1. a disguising, as of ships or guns, to conceal them from the enemy. 2. a disguise; deception. *v.t. & v.i.* [-FLAGED, -FLAGING], to conceal by changing the appearance.
**camp** (kamp), *n.* [< L. *campus*, field], 1. *a*) a place where temporary tents, huts, etc. are put up. *b*) those in such a place. *c*) a group of such tents, etc. 2. the supporters of a particular cause. 3. a recreational place in the country, as for children or other vacationers. 4. military life. 5. [Slang], [orig., homosexual jargon], banality, mediocrity, etc. so extreme as to amuse or have a perversely sophisticated appeal. *v.i.* to set up a camp. —**break camp,** to dismantle a camp and depart. —**camp out,** to live in a camp or tent. —**camp′er,** *n.* —**camp′y,** *adj.*
**cam·paign** (kam-pān′), *n.* [< Fr. < L. *campus*, field], 1. a series of military operations with a particular objective. 2. a series of planned actions, as for electing a candidate. *v.i.* to participate in, or go on, a campaign. —**cam·paign′er,** *n.*
**cam·pa·ni·le** (kam′pə-nē′li), *n.* [*pl.* -LES, -LI (-lē)], [It. < LL. *campana*, a bell], a bell tower.
**camp′fire′,** *n.* 1. an outdoor fire at a camp. 2. a social gathering around such a fire.
**cam·phor** (kam′fēr), *n.* [ult. < Malay *kāpūr*, chalk], a crystalline substance with a strong odor, derived from an Oriental laurel: used in moth balls, in medicine as a stimulant, etc. —**cam·phor·ic** (kam-fôr′ik), *adj.* —**cam′phor·at′ed** (-āt′id), *adj.*
**camp meeting,** a religious gathering held outdoors or in a tent, etc.
**cam·pus** (kam′pəs), *n.* [*pl.* -PUSES], [L., field], the grounds of a school or college. *adj.* of the student body.
**can** (kan, kən), *v.i.* [pt. COULD (kood)], [< AS. *cunnan*, know], 1. to know how to. 2. to be able to. 3. to have the right to. 4. [Colloq.], to be permitted to; may. —**can but,** can only.
**can** (kan), *n.* [AS. *canne*, cup], 1. a metal container, esp. one in which liquids, foods, etc. are sealed for preservation. 2. the contents of a can. *v.t.* [CANNED, CANNING], 1. to put into airtight cans or jars for preservation. 2. [Slang], to dismiss; discharge.
**Ca·naan** (kā′nən), *n.* in the *Bible*, a region corresponding to Palestine, promised by God to Abraham.
**Ca·na·di·an** (kə-nā′di-ən), *adj.* of Canada, its people, etc. *n.* a native or inhabitant of Canada. Abbrev. **Can., Canad.**
**ca·naille** (kə-nāl′), *n.* [Fr. < It. < L. *canis*, dog], the mob; rabble.
**ca·nal** (kə-nal′), *n.* [< L. *canalis*, channel], 1. an artificial waterway for transportation or irrigation. 2. in *anatomy*, a tube or duct. *v.t.* [-NALLED or -NALED, -NALLING or -NALING], to make a canal through.
**ca·na·pé** (kan′ə-pi, -pā′), *n.* [Fr.], a cracker, etc. spread with spiced meat, cheese, etc., served as an appetizer.

**ca·nard** (kə-närd′), *n.* [Fr., a duck], an absurd report spread as a hoax.
**ca·nar·y** (kə-nâr′i), *n.* [*pl.* -IES], [< *Canary* Islands], 1. a yellow songbird of the finch family. 2. a light yellow: also **canary yellow.** *adj.* light-yellow: also **canary-yellow.**
**ca·nas·ta** (kə-nas′tə), *n.* [Sp., basket], a double-deck card game.
**can·can** (kan′kan′), *n.* [Fr.], a gay, wild dance, with much high kicking.
**can·cel** (kan′s'l), *v.t.* [-CELED or -CELLED, -CELING or -CELLING], [< L. *cancellus*, lattice], 1. to cross out, as with lines. 2. to make invalid. 3. to do away with; abolish. 4. to neutralize; balance (often with *out*). *n.* a canceling. **—can′cel·la′tion,** *n.*
**can·cer** (kan′sẽr), *n.* [L., a crab], 1. a malignant tumor. 2. anything evil that spreads and destroys. 3. [C-], the fourth sign of the zodiac. **—can′cer·ous,** *adj.*
**can·de·la·brum** (kan′d'l-ā′brəm, -ä′-), *n.* [*pl.* -BRA (-brə), -BRUMS], [L. < *candela*, candle], a large, branched candlestick: also **can′de·la′bra** (-brə), [*pl.* -BRAS].
**can·did** (kan′did), *adj.* [< L. *candidus*, white, sincere], 1. impartial. 2. honest; frank. **—can′did·ly,** *adv.* **—can′did·ness,** *n.*
**can·di·date** (kan′də-dāt′, -dit), *n.* [L. *candidatus*, white-robed, as office seekers], one seeking, or proposed for, an office, award, etc. **—can′di·da·cy** (-də-si), [*pl.* -CIES], *n.*
**can·died** (kan′did), *adj.* [pp. of *candy*], 1. cooked in sugar. 2. sugary.
**can·dle** (kan′d'l), *n.* [< L. *candela*], a cylinder of tallow or wax with a wick through it, which gives light when burned. *v.t.* [-DLED, -DLING], to examine (eggs) for freshness by holding in front of a light. **—burn the candle at both ends,** to work or play so much that one's energy is quickly dissipated. **—can′dler,** *n.*
**candle power,** a unit for measuring light, as of a lamp.
**can′dle·stick′,** *n.* a cupped or spiked holder for a candle or candles.
**can·dor** (kan′dẽr), *n.* [L., radiance], honesty in expressing oneself; frankness: also, Brit. spelling, **candour.**
**can·dy** (kan′di), *n.* [*pl.* -DIES], [< Per. *qand*, cane sugar], a solid confection of sugar or sirup with flavoring, nuts, fruits, etc. *v.t.* [-DIED, -DYING], 1. to preserve by cooking with sugar. 2. to crystallize into sugar. *v.i.* to become candied (sense 2).
**cane** (kān), *n.* [<Gr. *kanna*], 1. the slender, hollow, jointed stem of certain plants, as the bamboo. 2. a plant with such a stem. 3. a walking stick. 4. a stick used for beating. 5. sugar cane. 6. split rattan. *v.t.* [CANED, CANING], 1. to beat with a cane. 2. to make or furnish with cane.
**cane·brake** (kān′brāk′), *n.* a brake, or dense growth, of cane plants.
**cane sugar,** the sugar from sugar cane.
**ca·nine** (kā′nīn), *adj.* [< L. *canis*, dog], 1. of or like a dog. 2. of the family of animals that includes dogs, wolves, and foxes. 3. of a canine tooth. *n.* 1. a dog. 2. a canine tooth.
**canine tooth,** any of the four sharp-pointed teeth next to the incisors.
**can·is·ter** (kan′is-tẽr), *n.* [< Gr. *kanistron*, wicker basket], a box or can for coffee, tea, etc.
**can·ker** (kaŋ′kẽr), *n.* [< L.; see CANCER], an ulcerlike, spreading sore, usually in the mouth. **—can′ker·ous,** *adj.*
**canned** (kand), *adj.* 1. preserved, as in cans. 2. [Slang], recorded, as music. 3. [Slang], fired from work.
**can·nel coal** (kan′'l), [< *candle coal*], a variety of bituminous coal that burns with a bright flame.
**can·ner·y** (kan′ẽr-i), *n.* [*pl.* -IES], a factory where foods are canned.
**can·ni·bal** (kan′ə-b'l), *n.* [Sp. *canibal*], 1. a person who eats human flesh. 2. an animal that eats its own kind. *adj.* of or like cannibals. **—can′ni·bal·ism,** *n.* **—can′ni·bal·is′tic,** *adj.* **—can′ni·bal·is′ti·cal·ly,** *adv.*
**can·ning** (kan′iŋ), *n.* the process of preserving foods in cans or jars.
**can·non** (kan′ən), *n.* [*pl.* -NONS, -NON], [< L. *canna*, cane], a large mounted piece of artillery. *v.i.* to fire cannon.
**can′non·ade′** (-ād′), *n.* a continuous firing of artillery. *v.t.* & *v.i.* [-ADED, -ADING], to fire artillery (at).
**cannon ball,** a heavy metal ball, formerly used as a projectile in cannon.
**can·not** (kan′ot, ka-not′), can not. **—cannot but,** must; have no choice but to.
**can·ny** (kan′i), *adj.* [-NIER, -NIEST], [< *can* (be able)], [Scot.], 1. cautious; wary. 2. thrifty. 3. shrewd. **—can′ni·ly,** *adv.*
**ca·noe** (kə-nōō′), *n.* [Sp. *canoa* < Am. Ind.], a narrow, light boat moved with paddles. *v.i.* [-NOED, -NOEING], to paddle, or go in, a canoe. **—ca·noe′ist,** *n.*
**can·on** (kan′ən), *n.* [AS., a rule < L.], 1. a law or body of laws of a church. 2. any law or decree. 3. a criterion. 4. an official list, as of books of the Bible. 5. a clergyman serving in a cathedral. 6. in *music*, a round.
**cañ·on** (kan′yən), *n.* a canyon.
**ca·non·i·cal** (kə-non′i-k'l), *adj.* 1. of or according to church law. 2. of or belonging to a canon. *n.pl.* the prescribed clothes for a clergyman conducting services.
**can·on·ic·i·ty** (kan′ən-is′ə-ti), *n.* 1. the right to be included in the Biblical canon. 2. genuineness.
**can·on·ize** (kan′ən-īz′), *v.t.* [-IZED, -IZING], 1. to declare (a dead person) to be in the canon of saints. 2. to glorify. 3. to give church sanction to. **—can′on·i·za′tion,** *n.*
**can·o·py** (kan′ə-pi), *n.* [*pl.* -PIES], [< Gr. *kōnōpeion*, bed with mosquito nets], 1. a drapery, etc. fastened above a bed, throne, etc., or held over a person. 2. an overhanging shelter. *v.t.* [-PIED, -PYING], to place or form a canopy over; shelter.
**cant** (kant), *n.* [< L. *canere*, sing], 1. the secret slang of beggars, thieves, etc.; argot. 2. the special vocabulary of those in a certain occupation; jargon. 3. insincere talk, esp. when pious or moral. *v.i.* to use cant.
**cant** (kant), *n.* [< L. *cantus*, tire of a wheel], 1. an outside angle. 2. a beveled edge. 3. a tilt, slant, etc. *v.t.* & *v.i.* to bevel; slant; tilt. *adj.* slanting; oblique.
**can't** (kant, känt), cannot.
**can·ta·bi·le** (kän-tä′bi-lā′), *adj.* & *adv.* [< It. < L. *cantare*, sing], in *music*, in a flowing, songlike manner. *n.* music in this style.
**can·ta·loupe, can·ta·loup** (kan′tə-lōp′), *n.* [< It. < *Cantalupo*, estate near Rome, where first grown in Europe], 1. a melon with a hard, ribbed rind and sweet, juicy flesh. 2. any muskmelon.
**can·tan·ker·ous** (kan-taŋ′kẽr-əs), *adj.* [? < ME. *contac*, strife], bad-tempered; quarrelsome. **—can·tan′ker·ous·ly,** *adv.* **—can·tan′ker·ous·ness,** *n.*
**can·ta·ta** (kən-tä′tə), *n.* [< It.; see CANTABILE], a choral composition used as a setting for a story to be sung but not acted.
**can·teen** (kan-tēn′), *n.* [< Fr. < It. *cantina*, wine cellar], 1. a military shop where soldiers can buy refreshments and provisions. 2. a recreation center. 3. a small flask for carrying water.
**can·ter** (kan′tẽr), *n.* [< *Canterbury gallop*, a riding pace], an easy gallop. *v.i.* & *v.t.* to ride at this pace.
**can·ti·cle** (kan′ti-k'l), *n.* [< L. *canere*, sing], 1. a song or chant. 2. a hymn with words from the Bible, used in certain church services.

**can·ti·le·ver** (kan′t'l-ev′ẽr, -ē′vẽr), *n.* [< ?], a bracket or block projecting as a support; esp., a projecting structure anchored at one end to a pier and extending over a space to be bridged.

**can·to** (kan′tō), *n.* [*pl.* -TOS], [It. < L. *canere*, sing], any of the main divisions of a long poem.

**can·ton** (kan′tən, kan-ton′), *n.* [Fr. < L. *cantus*, corner], one of the political divisions of a country, esp. of Switzerland. *v.t.* to divide into cantons. **—can′ton·al,** *adj.*

**Can·ton·ese** (kan′tən-ēz′), *adj.* of Canton, China, its people, etc.

**can·ton·ment** (kan-ton′mənt, -tōn′-), *n.* [< Fr.: see CANTON], 1. the assignment of troops to temporary quarters. 2. the quarters assigned.

**can·tor** (kan′tẽr), *n.* [L., singer], a singer of liturgical solos in a synagogue.

**can·vas** (kan′vəs), *n.* [< L. *cannabis*, hemp], 1. a coarse cloth of hemp, cotton, etc., used for tents, sails, etc. 2. a sail, tent, etc. 3. an oil painting on canvas. *adj.* made of canvas. **—under canvas,** 1. in tents. 2. with sails unfurled.

**can′vas·back′,** *n.* a N. American wild duck with a grayish back.

**can·vass** (kan′vəs), *v.t. & v.i.* [< *canvas* (used for sifting)], to go through (places) or among (people) asking for votes, opinions, orders, etc. *n.* a canvassing or survey of votes, opinions, orders, etc. **—can′vass·er,** *n.*

**can·yon** (kan′yən), *n.* [Sp. *cañón*, tube <L. *canna*, reed], a long, narrow valley between high cliffs, often containing a stream.

**cap** (kap), *n.* [< LL. *cappa*], 1. any close-fitting head covering, visored or brimless. 2. a caplike thing, as a cover or top part. *v.t.* [CAPPED, CAPPING], 1. to put a cap on. 2. to cover (the top or end of). 3. to match or surpass. **—cap′per,** *n.*

**cap.,** [*pl.* CAPS.], capital.

**ca·pa·ble** (kā′pə-b'l), *adj.* [< L. *capere*, take], able; skilled; competent. **—capable of,** 1. admitting of. 2. having the qualities necessary for. **—ca′pa·bil′i·ty** (-bil′ə-ti), [*pl.* -TIES], *n.* **—ca′pa·bly,** *adv.*

**ca·pa·cious** (kə-pā′shəs), *adj.* [< L. *capere*, take], roomy; spacious. **—ca·pa′cious·ly,** *adv.* **—ca·pa′cious·ness,** *n.*

**ca·pac·i·ty** (kə-pas′ə-ti), *n.* [*pl.* -TIES], [< L. *capere*, take], 1. the ability to contain, absorb, or receive. 2. all that can be contained; volume. 3. ability. 4. position; function: as, in the *capacity* of adviser.

**ca·par·i·son** (kə-par′ə-s'n), *n.* [< LL. *cappa*, cape], an ornamented covering for a horse; trappings. *v.t.* to adorn.

**cape** (kāp), *n.* [< Sp. *capa*, hood < L. *caput*, head], a sleeveless garment fastened at the neck and hanging over the back and shoulders.

**cape** (kāp), *n.* [< L. *caput*, head], a piece of land projecting into water.

**ca·per** (kā′pẽr), *v.i.* [ult. < L. *caper*, goat], to skip about in a playful manner. *n.* 1. a gay, playful leap. 2. a prank. **—cut a caper** (or **capers**), 1. to caper. 2. to play silly tricks.

**ca·pers** (kā′pẽrz), *n.pl.* [< Gr. *kapparis*], the green flower buds of a Mediterranean bush, pickled and used as a seasoning.

**cap·il·lar·i·ty** (kap′'l-ar′ə-ti), *n.* the action by which liquids in contact with solids, as in a capillary tube, rise or fall.

**cap·il·lar·y** (kap′'l-er′i), *adj.* [< L. *capillus*, hair], very slender. *n.* [*pl.* -IES], 1. a tube with a very small bore: also **capillary tube.** 2. any of the tiny blood vessels connecting arteries with veins.

**cap·i·tal** (kap′ə-t'l), *adj.* [< L. *caput*, head], 1. involving or punishable by death. 2. chief; principal. 3. of, or being, the seat of government. 4. of or having to do with capital. 5. excellent. *n.* 1. a capital letter. 2. a city that is the seat of government of a state or nation. 3. money or property owned or used in business. 4. [often C-], capitalists collectively. 5. the top part of a column. **—make capital of,** to make the most of; exploit.

**cap′i·tal·ism** (-iz'm), *n.* 1. the economic system in which the means of production and distribution are privately owned and operated for profit. 2. the principles, power, etc. of capitalists.

**cap′i·tal·ist,** *n.* 1. an owner of wealth used in business. 2. an upholder of capitalism. 3. a wealthy person. **—cap′i·tal·is′tic,** *adj.* **—cap′i·tal·is′ti·cal·ly,** *adv.*

**cap′i·tal·ize′** (-īz′), *v.t.* [-IZED, -IZING] 1. to use as or convert into capital. 2. to use to one's advantage (with *on*). 3. to supply capital to or for. 4. to begin (a word) with a capital letter. **—cap′i·tal·i·za′tion,** *n.*

**capital letter,** a letter larger than, and often different from, the corresponding small letter, as A, B, C, etc.

**capital punishment,** the death penalty.

**capital stock,** the capital of a corporation, divided into shares.

**cap·i·ta·tion** (kap′ə-tā′shən), *n.* [< L. *caput*, head], a tax or fee of so much per head.

**Cap·i·tol** (kap′ə-t'l), *n.* [< L. *Capitolium*, temple of Jupiter], 1. the building in which the U.S. Congress meets, at Washington, D.C. 2. [usually c-], the building in which a State legislature meets.

**ca·pit·u·late** (kə-pich′ə-lāt′), *v.i.* [-LATED, -LATING], [< L. *capitulare*, to arrange terms], to give up (*to* an enemy) on prearranged conditions. **—ca·pit′u·la′tion,** *n.*

**ca·pon** (kā′pon), *n.* [< Gr. *kaptein*, to cut], a castrated rooster fattened for eating.

**ca·price** (kə-prēs′), *n.* [Fr. < It.], 1. a sudden turn of mind caused by a whim or impulse. 2. a capricious quality.

**ca·pri·cious** (kə-prish′əs), *adj.* subject to caprices; unpredictable. **—ca·pri′cious·ly,** *adv.* **—ca·pri′cious·ness,** *n.*

**Cap·ri·corn** (kap′ri-kôrn′), *n.* [< L. *caper*, goat + *cornu*, horn], the tenth sign of the zodiac.

**cap·si·cum** (kap′si-kəm), *n.* [prob. < L. *capsa*, a box], 1. any of various tropical plants with many-seeded, pungent pods. 2. these pods used as condiments or as a gastric stimulant.

**cap·size** (kap-sīz′), *v.t. & v.i.* [-SIZED, -SIZING], [< ?], to overturn; upset: said esp. of a boat.

**cap·stan** (kap′stən), *n.* [< L. *capere*, take], an upright drum, as on ships, around which cables are wound so as to haul them in.

**cap·stone** (kap′stōn′), *n.* the uppermost stone of a structure.

**cap·sule** (kap′s'l, -syool), *n.* [Fr. < L. *capsa*, chest], 1. a small, soluble gelatin container enclosing a dose of medicine. 2. a closed compartment for holding and protecting men, instruments, etc., as in a spaceship. 3. in *botany*, a seedcase.

**cap·tain** (kap′t'n), *n.* [< L. *caput*, head], 1. a chief or leader. 2. an army officer ranking just above lieutenant. 3. a navy officer ranking just above commander. 4. the master of a ship. 5. the leader of a team, as in sports. Abbrev. **Capt.** *v.t.* to be captain of; head. **—cap′tain·cy** [*pl.* -CIES], *n.*

**cap·tion** (kap′shən), *n.* [< L. *capere*, take], a title or subtitle, as of a newspaper article or picture. *v.t.* to supply a caption for.

**cap·tious** (kap′shəs), *adj.* [see CAPTION], 1. made for the sake of argument, as an objection. 2. quick to find fault.**— cap′tious·ly,** *adv.* **—cap′tious·ness,** *n.*

**cap·ti·vate** (kap′tə-vāt′), *v.t.* [-VATED, -VAT-

ING], to capture the attention or affection of. —**cap'ti·vat'ing,** *adj.* —**cap'ti·va'tion,** *n.* —**cap'ti·va'tor,** *n.*

**cap·tive** (kap'tiv), *n.* [< L. *capere,* take], a prisoner. *adj.* taken or held prisoner. —**cap·tiv'i·ty** [*pl.* -TIES], *n.*

**captive audience,** any group of people forced against their will to listen to something, as passengers on a bus having a radio loudspeaker.

**cap·tor** (kap'tər), *n.* one who captures.

**cap·ture** (kap'chēr), *v.t.* [-TURED, -TURING], [< L. *capere,* take], to take or seize by force, surprise, etc. *n.* 1. a capturing or being captured; seizure. 2. that which is captured.

**cap·u·chin** (kap'yoo-chin', -shin'), *n.* [< Fr. *capuce,* cowl], a S. American monkey with a hoodlike crown of black hair.

**car** (kär), *n.* [< L. *carrus,* chariot], 1. any vehicle on wheels. 2. a vehicle that moves on tracks. 3. an automobile. 4. an elevator cage.

**ca·ra·ba·o** (kä'rə-bä'ō), *n.* [*pl.* -OS], [Sp. < Malay], in the Philippines, a water buffalo.

**car·a·cul** (kar'ə-kəl), *n.* karakul.

**ca·rafe** (kə-raf', -räf'), *n.* [Fr.], a water bottle made of glass.

**car·a·mel** (kar'ə-m'l, kär'm'l), *n.* [Fr.], 1. burnt sugar used to color or flavor food. 2. chewy candy made from sugar, milk, etc. —**car'a·mel·ize'** (-īz'), [-IZED, -IZING], *v.t. & v.i.*

**car·a·pace** (kar'ə-pās'), *n.* [Fr. < Sp.], an upper shell, as of the turtle.

**car·at** (kar'ət), *n.* [Fr. < Gr. *keration*], 1. a unit of weight for precious stones, equal to about .2 gram. 2. one 24th part (of pure gold).

**car·a·van** (kar'ə-van'), *n.* [< Per. *kārwān*], 1. a company of people traveling together for safety, as through a desert. 2. a large closed vehicle; van.

**car·a·van·sa·ry** (kar'ə-van'sə-ri), *n.* [*pl.* -RIES], [< Per. *kārwān,* caravan + *sarāi,* palace], 1. in the Orient, an inn for caravans. 2. a large inn. Also **car'a·van'se·rai'** (-sə-rī', -sə-rā').

**car·a·way** (kar'ə-wā'), *n.* [< Ar. < Gr. *karon*], the spicy seeds of a plant, used to flavor bread, etc.

**car·bide** (kär'bīd), *n.* a compound of an element, usually a metal, with carbon.

**car·bine** (kär'bīn, -bēn), *n.* [< Fr. *scarabée,* beetle], 1. a short-barreled rifle. 2. in the *U.S. Army,* a light, semiautomatic, .30-caliber rifle.

**carbo-,** a combining form meaning *carbon*: also **carb-.**

**car·bo·hy·drate** (kär'bə-hī'drāt), *n.* [*carbo-* + *hydrate*], an organic compound composed of carbon, hydrogen, and oxygen, as a sugar or starch.

**car·bol·ic** (kär-bol'ik), *adj.* [< L. *carbo,* coal + *oleum,* oil], designating or of a poisonous acid, a coal-tar derivative, used in solution as an antiseptic, disinfectant, etc.

**car·bon** (kär'bən), *n.* [< L. *carbo,* coal], 1. a nonmetallic chemical element found esp. in all organic compounds: diamond and graphite are pure carbon: symbol, C. 2. carbon paper. 3. a copy made with carbon paper: in full, **carbon copy.** *adj.* of or like carbon.

**car·bo·na·ceous** (kär'bə-nā'shəs), *adj.* 1. of or containing carbon. 2. containing or like coal.

**car'bon·ate** (-it), *n.* a salt or ester of carbonic acid. *v.t.* (-āt'), [-ATED, -ATING], to charge with carbon dioxide.

**carbon dioxide,** a heavy, colorless, odorless gas: it passes out of the lungs in respiration.

**car·bon·ic acid** (kär-bon'ik), a weak acid formed by the solution of carbon dioxide in water.

**car·bon·if·er·ous** (kär'bə-nif'ēr-əs), *adj.* [< *carbon* + *-ferous*], containing carbon or coal.

**car'bon·ize'** (-īz'), *v.t.* [-IZED, -IZING], 1. to change into carbon, as by partial burning. 2. to treat or combine with carbon. —**car'bon·i·za'tion,** *n.*

**carbon monoxide,** a colorless, odorless, highly poisonous gas.

**carbon paper,** thin paper coated on one side with a carbon preparation, used to make copies of letters, etc.

**carbon tet·ra·chlo·ride** (tet'rə-klôr'īd), a noninflammable liquid used in fire extinguishers, cleaning mixtures, etc.

**car·bo·run·dum** (kär'bə-run'dəm), *n.* [*carbo-* + *corundum*], a hard abrasive made of carbon and silicon: a trademark (**Carborundum**).

**car·boy** (kär'boi), *n.* [< Per. *qarābah*], a large glass bottle enclosed in a framework: used as a container for corrosive liquids.

**car·bun·cle** (kär'buŋ-k'l), *n.* [< L. dim. of *carbo,* coal], a painful, pus-bearing inflammation of the tissue beneath the skin. —**car·bun'cu·lar** (-kyoo-lēr), *adj.*

**car·bu·re·tor** (kär'bə-rā'tər, -byoo-ret'ēr), *n.* a device for mixing air with gasoline spray to make an explosive mixture in an internal-combustion engine.

**car·cass, car·case** (kär kəs), *n.* [< Fr. < It. *carcassa*], 1. the dead body of any animal. 2. a framework or shell.

**car·cin·o·gen** (kär-sin'ə-jən), *n.* [*carcinoma* + *-gen*], any substance that produces cancer. —**car·cin'o·gen'ic,** *adj.*

**car·ci·no·ma** (kär'sə-nō'mə), *n.* [*pl.* -MAS, -MATA (-mə-tə)], [L. < Gr. *karkinos,* a crab], any of several kinds of epithelial cancer.

**card** (kärd), *n.* [L. *charta* < Gr. *chartēs,* leaf of paper], 1. a flat, stiff piece of paper or pasteboard; esp., *a*) one of a pack of playing cards. *b*) a post card. *c*) a card bearing a greeting. *d*) the printed program for sporting events, etc. 2. an attraction: as, a drawing *card.* 3. [Colloq.], a person notably funny, etc. —**put** (or **lay**) **one's cards on the table,** to reveal something frankly.

**card** (kärd), *n.* [< L. *carere,* to card], a metal comb, etc. for combing the fibers of wool, cotton, etc. *v.t.* to use such a tool on. —**card'ing,** *n.*

**card'board',** *n.* stiff, thick paper, or pasteboard, for cards, boxes, etc.

**car·di·ac** (kär'di-ak'), *adj.* [< Gr. *kardia,* heart], of or near the heart.

**car·di·gan** (kär'di-gən), *n.* [< 7th Earl of *Cardigan*], a knitted woolen jacket or jacket-like sweater.

**car·di·nal** (kär'd'n-əl), *adj.* [< L. *cardo,* pivot], 1. fundamental; chief. 2. bright-red. *n.* 1. a Roman Catholic official appointed by the Pope to his council. 2. bright red. 3. a bright-red American songbird, related to the finch: also **cardinal bird.** 4. a cardinal number.

**cardinal number,** any number used in counting or showing how many (e.g., two, forty, 627, etc.): cf. *ordinal.*

**cardinal points,** the four principal points of the compass; north, south, east, and west.

**cardio-,** [< Gr. *kardia,* heart], a combining form meaning *of the heart.*

**car·di·o·graph** (kär'di-ə-graf'), *n.* an electrocardiograph.

**cards** (kärdz), *n.pl.* any game played with a deck of cards, as poker.

**card'sharp',** *n.* a professional swindler at cards: also **card'sharp'er.**

**care** (kâr), *n.* [AS. *caru,* sorrow], 1. mental pain; worry. 2. watchfulness; heed. 3. a liking or regard (*for*). 4. charge; protection. 5. something to worry about, watch over, etc. *v.i.* [CARED, CARING], 1. to be concerned; mind. 2. to wish or like (*to* do something). —**care for,** 1. to love or like. 2. to look

after. **—care of,** at the address of. **—take care of,** 1. to attend to. 2. to provide for.
**ca·reen** (kə-rēn′), *v.t. & v.i.* [< L. *carina,* keel], to lean or cause to lean sideways; tip; tilt; lurch. *n.* a careening.
**ca·reer** (kə-rêr′), *n.* [ult. < L. *carrus;* see CAR], 1. full speed. 2. one's progress through life. 3. a profession or occupation. *v.i.* to rush wildly.
**ca·reer′ist,** *n.* a person excessively interested in his own professional ambitions.
**care′free′,** *adj.* without care or worry.
**care′ful,** *adj.* 1. watchful; cautious. 2. accurately or thoroughly done; painstaking. **—care′ful·ly,** *adv.* **—care′ful·ness,** *n.*
**care′less,** *adj.* 1. carefree; untroubled. 2. not paying enough attention; neglectful; reckless. 3. done or made without enough attention, precision, etc. **—care′less·ly,** *adv.* **—care′less·ness,** *n.*
**ca·ress** (kə-res′), *v.t.* [-RESSED, -RESSING], [ult. < L. *carus,* dear], to touch lovingly or gently. *n.* an affectionate touch, kiss, etc. **—ca·ress′ing·ly,** *adv.*
**car·et** (kar′it, kâr′-), *n.* [L., there is lacking], a mark (∧) used to show where something is to be added in a written or printed line.
**care′tak′er,** *n.* one whose work is to take care of some thing, place, or person.
**care′worn′,** *adj.* showing the effects of grief and worry; haggard; weary.
**car·fare** (kär′fâr′), *n.* the price of a ride on a streetcar, bus, etc.
**car·go** (kär′gō), *n.* [*pl.* -GOES, -GOS], [< Sp. *cargar,* to load], a load, esp. that carried by a ship; freight.
**car·hop** (kär′hop′), *n.* [*car* + bell*hop*], one who serves customers in cars at a drive-in restaurant.
**car·i·bou** (kar′ə-bōō′), *n.* [Canad. Fr.], a N. American reindeer.
**car·i·ca·ture** (kar′i-kə-chẽr), *n.* [Fr. < It. *caricare,* exaggerate], 1. the distorted imitating of a person, literary style, etc. by exaggeration for satirical effect. 2. a picture, etc. in which this is done. *v.t.* [-TURED, -TURING], to portray as in a caricature. **—car′i·ca·tur·ist,** *n.*
**car·ies** (kâr′ēz, -i-ēz′), *n.* [L., decay], decay of teeth, bones, etc.
**car·il·lon** (kar′ə-lon′), *n.* [Fr., chime of four bells < L. *quattuor,* four], 1. a set of bells tuned to the chromatic scale. 2. a melody played on such bells.
**car·i·ole** (kar′i-ōl′), *n.* [< It. *carro,* wagon], a small, one-horse carriage.
**car·i·ous** (kâr′i-əs), *adj.* [L. *cariosus*], 1. having caries; decayed. 2. corroded.
**car′load′,** *n.* a load that fills a car.
**car·min·a·tive** (kär-min′ə-tiv), *adj.* [< L. *carminare,* cleanse], expelling gas from the stomach and intestines. *n.* a carminative medicine.
**car·mine** (kär′min, -mīn), *n.* [ult. < Ar. *qirmiz,* crimson], a red or purplish-red color. *adj.* red or purplish-red.
**car·nage** (kär′nij), *n.* [Fr. < L. *caro,* flesh], bloody and extensive slaughter; massacre.
**car·nal** (kär′n'l), *adj.* [< L. *caro,* flesh], 1. of the flesh; material; worldly. 2. sensual; sexual. **—car·nal′i·ty** (-nal′ə-ti), *n.*
**car·na·tion** (kär-nā′shən), *n.* [< L. *caro,* flesh], 1. a variety of the pink. 2. its fragrant pink, white, or red flower.
**car·nel·ian** (kär-nēl′yən), *n.* [< OFr. *corneola*], a red variety of chalcedony, used in jewelry.
**car·ni·val** (kär′nə-v'l), *n.* [< Fr. or It.], 1. the period of feasting and revelry just before Lent. 2. a reveling; festivity. 3. an entertainment with rides, side shows, etc.
**car·ni·vore** (kär′nə-vôr′), *n.* a carnivorous animal: opposed to *herbivore.*
**car·niv·o·rous** (kär-niv′ə-rəs), *adj.* [< L. *caro,* flesh + *vorare,* eat], 1. flesh-eating: opposed to *herbivorous.* 2. of an order of flesh-eating mammals, including the dog, cat, etc. **—car·niv′o·rous·ly,** *adv.*
**car·ol** (kar′əl), *n.* [< OFr. *carole,* kind of dance], a song of joy or praise; esp., a Christmas song. *v.i. & v.t.* [-OLED or -OLLED, -OLING or -OLLING], to sing; warble. **—car′ol·er, car′ol·ler,** *n.*
**car·om** (kar′əm), *n.* [< Sp. *carambola,* red ball at billiards], 1. in *billiards,* a shot in which the cue ball hits two other balls in succession. 2. a hitting and rebounding. *v.i.* 1. to make a carom. 2. to hit and rebound.
**ca·rot·id** (kə-rot′id), *adj.* [< Gr. *karōtides,* pl.], designating, of, or near either of the two main arteries, one on each side of the neck, which convey blood to the head *n.* a carotid artery.
**ca·rous·al** (kə-rouz′'l), *n.* a carouse.
**ca·rouse** (kə-rouz′). *v.i.* [-ROUSED, -ROUSING], [< G. *gar aus*(*trinken*), (to drink) quite out], to participate in a lively drinking party. *n.* a carousing; lively drinking party. **—ca·rous′er,** *n.*
**carp** (kärp), *n.* [*pl.* CARP, CARPS], [< LL. *carpa*], an edible fresh-water fish living in ponds.
**carp** (kärp), *v.i.* [< ON. *karpa,* brag], to find fault pettily or unfairly. **—carp′ing,** *adj.*
**car·pel** (kär′p'l), *n.* [< Gr. *karpos,* fruit], a simple pistil, regarded as a modified leaf.
**car·pen·ter** (kär′pən-tẽr), *n.* [< L. *carpentum,* a cart], one who builds and repairs wooden articles, buildings, etc. *v.i.* to do a carpenter's work. **—car′pen·try** (-tri), *n.*
**car·pet** (kär′pit), *n.* [< L. *carpere,* to card], 1. a heavy fabric for covering a floor. 2. anything that covers like a carpet. *v.t.* to cover as with a carpet. **—on the carpet,** in the position of being reprimanded.
**car′pet·bag′,** *n.* an old-fashioned traveling bag, made of carpeting.
**car′pet·bag′ger,** *n.* a Northerner who went South to profit from the upheaval after the Civil War. **—car′pet·bag′ging,** *n.*
**car′pet·ing,** *n.* carpets; carpet fabric.
**car·port** (kär′pôrt′), *n.* a shelter for an automobile, usually just a roof extended from the side of a house.
**car·riage** (kar′ij), *n.* [< L. *carrus,* cart], 1. a carrying; transportation. 2. manner of carrying the head and body; bearing. 3. a four-wheeled passenger vehicle, usually horse-drawn. 4. a moving part (as on a typewriter) that supports and shifts something.
**car·ri·er** (kar′i-ẽr), *n.* 1. one that carries. 2. one in the business of transporting. 3. one that transmits disease germs. 4. an aircraft carrier.
**carrier pigeon,** a homing pigeon.
**car·ri·on** (kar′i-ən), *n.* [< L. *caro,* flesh], decaying flesh of a dead body.
**car·rot** (kar′ət), *n.* [< Gr. *karōton*], 1. a plant with an edible, fleshy, orange-red root. 2. the root.
**car′rot·y,** *adj.* orange-red, as hair.
**car·rou·sel** (kar′ə-zel′, kar′oo-sel′), *n.* [Fr.; ult. < L. *carrus,* car], a merry-go-round: also sp. **carousel.**
**car·ry** (kar′i), *v.t.* [-RIED, -RYING], [ult. < L. *carrus,* car], 1. to take from one place to another. 2. to lead or impel. 3. to transmit: as, air *carries* sounds. 4. to transfer or extend: as, *carry* the pipe to the sewer. 5. to win (an election, argument, etc.). 6. to hold or support. 7. to involve; imply. 8. to bear (oneself) in a specified way. 9. *a*) to keep in stock. *b*) to keep on one's account books, etc. *v.i.* 1. to act as a bearer, conductor, etc. 2. to cover a range, as a voice. *n.* [*pl.* -RIES], 1. the distance covered by a

gun, ball, etc. 2. a portage. **—carry away,** to excite great emotion in. **—carry on,** 1. to do; conduct. 2. to continue. 3. [Colloq.], to behave in a wild or childish way. **—carry out** (or **through**), 1. to put (plans, etc.) into practice. 2. to accomplish. **—carry over,** to postpone, continue, etc.

**car′ry·all′,** *n.* a large bag, basket, etc.

**carrying charge,** interest charged by brokers, merchants, etc. on the balance owed on a purchase.

**car′ry-o′ver,** *n.* 1. something carried over. 2. a remainder, as of crops or goods.

**cart** (kärt), *n.* [< ON. *kartr*], a small wagon. *v.t. & v.i.* to carry in a cart or other vehicle. **—cart′er,** *n.*

**cart·age** (kär′tij), *n.* 1. the work of carting. 2. the charge for this.

**carte blanche** (kärt′ blänsh′), [Fr., blank card], full authority.

**car·tel** (kär-tel′), *n.* [< G.; ult. < L. *charta*, writing], an association of business firms, etc. for establishing a national or international monopoly; trust.

**car·ti·lage** (kär′t'l-ij), *n.* [< L. *cartilago*], a tough, elastic tissue forming part of the skeleton. **—car′ti·lag′i·nous** (-aj′ə-nəs), *adj.*

**car·tog·ra·phy** (kär-tog′rə-fi), *n.* [see CHART & -GRAPHY], the art of making maps or charts. **—car·tog′ra·pher,** *n.*

**car·ton** (kär′t'n), *n.* [Fr. < It. *carta*, card], a cardboard box.

**car·toon** (kär-to͞on′), *n.* [< Fr.; see CARTON], 1. a drawing that caricatures some person or event. 2. a comic strip. 3. an animated cartoon. 4. a full-size design for a tapestry, etc. **—car·toon′ing,** *n.* **—car·toon′ist,** *n.*

**car·tridge** (kär′trij), *n.* [< Fr. < It. *carta*, card], 1. a cylindrical case as of cardboard or metal, containing the charge, and usually the projectile, for a firearm. 2. any similar container, as for camera film, etc.

**cart wheel,** 1. a wheel of a cart. 2. a handspring performed sidewise.

**carve** (kärv), *v.t.* [CARVED, CARVING], [AS. *ceorfan*], 1. to make by or as by cutting. 2. to shape or decorate by cutting. 3. to divide by cutting; slice. *v.i.* 1. to carve statues or designs. 2. to carve meat. **—carv′er,** *n.* **—carv′ing,** *n.*

**carving knife,** a large knife for cutting meat.

**car·y·at·id** (kar′i-at′id)], *n.* [*pl.* -IDS, -IDES (-i-dēz′)], [< Gr. *karyatides*, priestesses at Karyai, in ancient Greece], a supporting column having the form of a draped female figure.

**ca·sa·ba** (kə-sä′bə), *n.* [< *Kassaba*, town in Asia Minor], a kind of muskmelon, with a yellow rind: also **casaba melon.**

**cas·cade** (kas-kād′), *n.* [Fr. < L. *cadere*, to fall], 1. a small, steep waterfall. 2. a fall or shower, as of sparks, drapery, etc. *v.t. & v.i.* [-CADED, -CADING], to fall or drop in a cascade.

**cas·car·a** (kas-kâr′ə), *n.* [Sp., bark], 1. a buckthorn growing on the Pacific coast. 2. a laxative made from its bark.

**case** (kās), *n.* [< L. *casus*, what befalls < *cadere*, to fall]. 1. an example or instance: as, a *case* of measles. 2. a state of affairs; situation. 3. a statement of the facts, as in a law court. 4. convincing arguments: as, he has no *case*. 5. a lawsuit. 6. a form taken by a noun, pronoun, or adjective to show its relation to neighboring words. *v.t.* [Slang], to examine carefully. **—in any case,** anyhow. **—in case,** if; in the event that. **—in case of,** in the event of. **—in no case,** by no means.

**case** (kās), *n.* [< L. *capsa*, box], 1. a container, as a box. 2. a protective cover: as, a watch *case*. 3. a frame, as for a window. *v.t.* [CASED, CASING], 1. to put in a container. 2. to cover or enclose.

**case′hard′en,** *v.t.* 1. to form a hard, thin surface on (iron or steel). 2. to make callous or unfeeling.

**ca·se·in** (kā′si-in, -sēn), *n.* [< L. *caseus*, cheese], a protein that is one of the chief constituents of milk and the basis of cheese.

**case·ment** (kās′mənt), *n.* [< OFr. *encassement*, a frame], a hinged window frame that opens outward. **—case′ment·ed,** *adj.*

**cash** (kash), *n.* [Fr. *casse*, money box], 1. money that one actually has; esp., ready money. 2. money, a check, etc. paid at the time of purchase. *v.t.* to give or get cash for. *adj.* of or for cash. **—cash in,** 1. to turn into cash. 2. [Slang], to die.

**cash′-and-car′ry,** *adj.* with cash payments and no deliveries.

**cash′book′,** *n.* a book in which all receipts and payments of money are entered.

**cash discount,** a discount allowed to the purchaser if he pays within a specified period.

**cash·ew** (kash′o͞o, kə-sho͞o′), *n.* [< Fr. < Braz. name], 1. a tropical tree bearing kidney-shaped nuts. 2. the nut.

**cash·ier** (ka-shêr′), *n.* [Fr. *caissier*], a person in charge of the cash transactions of a bank or store.

**cash·ier** (ka-shêr′), *v.t.* [< LL. *cassare*, destroy], to dismiss in disgrace.

**cash·mere** (kash′mêr), *n.* [< *Kashmir*, region in India], 1. a fine carded wool from goats of N India and Tibet. 2. a soft, twilled cloth as of this wool.

**cash register,** a device, usually with a money drawer, used for automatically recording and adding the amounts of sales.

**cas·ing** (kās′iŋ), *n.* 1. the outer covering of a pneumatic tire. 2. the skin of a sausage. 3. a frame, as of a window or door.

**ca·si·no** (kə-sē′nō), *n.* [*pl.* -NOS, -NI (-nē)], [It. < L. *casa*, house], 1. a room or building for dancing, gambling, etc. 2. cassino.

**cask** (kask, käsk), *n.* [< Sp. < L. *quassare*, shatter], 1. a barrel of any size, esp. one for liquids. 2. a full cask or its contents.

**cas·ket** (kas′kit, käs′-), *n.* [prob. < OFr. *casse*, box], 1. a small box or chest, as for valuables. 2. a coffin.

**Cas·san·dra** (kə-san′drə), *n.* in *Gr. legend*, a Trojan prophetess of doom whose prophecies were never believed.

**cas·sa·va** (kə-sä′və), *n.* [< Fr. < Haitian *kasabi*], 1. a tropical plant with edible starchy roots. 2. a starch made from these roots, used in making bread and tapioca.

**cas·se·role** (kas′ə-rōl′), *n.* [Fr., dim. of *casse*, bowl], 1. a covered baking dish in which food can be cooked and then served. 2. food prepared in such a dish.

**cas·sette** (ka-set′), *n.* [Fr. < *casse*, a case], 1. a case with roll film in it, for loading a camera quickly. 2. a similar case with tape, for use in a tape recorder.

**cas·sia** (kash′ə), *n.* [ult. < Heb. *qātsa*, to strip off bark], 1. a tropical tree whose bark is used like cinnamon. 2. the bark. 3. any of various tropical plants whose leaves yield senna.

**cas·si·no** (kə-sē′nō), *n.* [see CASINO], a card game for two to four players.

**cas·sock** (kas′ək), *n.* [< Fr. < It. *casacca*], a long, closefitting vestment, worn by clergymen.

**cast** (kast, käst), *v.t.* [CAST, CASTING], [< ON. *kasta*], 1. to throw; fling; hurl. 2. to deposit (a ballot or vote). 3. to direct: as, to *cast* a light. 4. to throw off; shed, as a skin. 5. to shape (molten metal, etc.) by pouring into a mold. 6. to select (an actor) for (a role or play). *v.i.* to throw; hurl. *n.* 1. a casting; throw. 2. something formed in a mold. 3. a plaster form for immobilizing a limb. 4. the set of actors in a play. 5. an appearance, as of features. 6. kind; quality. 7. tinge; shade. —**cast about,** to search; look (*for*). —**cast aside** (or **away**), to discard; abandon. —**cast down,** 1. to turn downward. 2. to sadden; depress. —**cast off,** 1. to discard. 2. to free a ship from a dock, etc. —**cast up,** 1. to turn upward. 2. to add up.

**cas·ta·nets** (kas'tə-nets'), ***n.pl.*** [< Sp. < L. *castanea*, chestnut: from the shape], small, hollowed pieces of hard wood or ivory, held in the hand in pairs to beat time to music.

**cast'a·way',** ***n.*** 1. a person or thing cast off. 2. a shipwrecked person. ***adj.*** 1. discarded. 2. shipwrecked.

**caste** (kast, käst), ***n.*** [Fr. < L. *castus*, pure], 1. any of the hereditary Hindu social classes of a former segregated system of India. 2. any exclusive group. 3. class distinction based on birth, wealth, etc. —**lose caste,** to lose social status.

**cas·tel·lat·ed** (kas'tə-lā'tid), ***adj.*** [see CASTLE], built with turrets and battlements, like a castle. —**cas'tel·la'tion,** ***n.***

**cast'er,** ***n.*** 1. a person or thing that casts. 2. *a*) a container for vinegar, oil, etc. at the table. *b*) any of a set of small wheels for supporting and moving furniture: also sp. **castor.**

**cas·ti·gate** (kas'tə-gāt'), ***v.t.*** [-GATED, -GATING], [< L. *castigare*], to chastise; criticize severely. —**cas'ti·ga'tion,** ***n.*** —**cas'ti·ga'tor,** ***n.***

**Cas·tile (soap)** (kas'tēl), [< *Castile*, Spain, where first made], [also c-], a fine, hard soap made from olive oil.

**cast'ing,** ***n.*** 1. the action of one that casts. 2. a thing, esp. of metal, cast in a mold.

**cast'-i'ron,** ***adj.*** 1. made of cast iron. 2. very hard, stern, rigid, etc.

**cast iron,** a hard, brittle pig iron made by casting.

**cas·tle** (kas''l, käs'-), ***n.*** [< L. *castrum*, fort], 1. a large building or group of buildings fortified as a stronghold. 2. any massive dwelling like this. 3. a chessman shaped like a castle tower: it can move only horizontally or vertically: also called *rook*. ***v.t.*** [-TLED, -TLING], in *chess*, to move (a king) two squares, setting the castle in the square skipped by the king.

**cast'off',** ***adj.*** discarded; abandoned. ***n.*** a person or thing cast off.

**cas·tor-oil plant** (kas'tẽr-oil', käs'-), [< Gr. *kastōr*, beaver], a tropical plant with large seeds that yield a yellowish oil (**castor oil**) used as a cathartic and lubricant.

**cas·trate** (kas'trāt), ***v.t.*** [-TRATED, -TRATING], [< L. *castrare*], to remove the testicles of; emasculate. —**cas·tra'tion,** ***n.***

**cas·u·al** (kazh'ōō-əl), ***adj.*** [< L. *casus*, chance], 1. happening by chance; incidental; unplanned. 2. occasional: as, a *casual* worker. 3. careless; cursory. 4. nonchalant. 5. for informal wear. —**cas'u·al·ly,** ***adv.*** —**cas'u·al·ness,** ***n.***

**cas'u·al·ty** (-ti), ***n.*** [*pl.* -TIES], 1. an unfortunate or fatal accident. 2. a member of the armed forces killed, wounded, or captured. 3. anyone hurt or killed in an accident.

**cas'u·ist·ry** (kazh'ōō-is-ri), ***n.*** [*pl.* -RIES], [< L. *casus*, a case], the deciding of moral issues by subtle but false reasoning. —**cas'u·ist,** ***n.*** —**cas'u·is'tic,** ***adj.*** —**cas'u·is'ti·cal·ly,** ***adv.***

**cat** (kat), ***n.*** [< LL. *cattus*], 1. a small, soft-furred animal, often kept as a pet or for killing mice. 2. any flesh-eating mammal related to this, as the lion, tiger, leopard, etc. 3. a spiteful woman. 4. a cat-o'-nine-tails. —**let the cat out of the bag,** to let a secret be found out. —**cat'like,** ***adj.***

**cat·a·clysm** (kat'ə-kliz'm), ***n.*** [< Gr. *kata-*, down + *klyzein*, wash], 1. a great flood. 2. any sudden, violent change, as in war. —**cat'a·clys'mic** (-kliz'mik), ***adj.***

**cat·a·comb** (kat'ə-kōm'), ***n.*** [ult. < L. *cata*, by + *tumba*, tomb], *usually in pl.* a gallery in an underground burial place.

**cat·a·falque** (kat'ə-falk'), ***n.*** [Fr. < L. *cata-*, down + *fala*, scaffolding], a framework to hold the coffin of a dead person lying in state.

**cat·a·lep·sy** (kat'ə-lep'si), ***n.*** [< Gr. *katalēpsis*, a seizing], a condition of muscle rigidity and sudden, temporary loss of consciousness and feeling, as in epilepsy. —**cat'a·lep'tic,** ***adj. & n.***

**cat·a·logue, cat·a·log** (kat''l-ôg'), ***n.*** [< Gr. *kata-*, down + *legein*, to count], a complete list, as an alphabetical card file of the books in a library, a list of articles for sale, etc. ***v.t. & v.i.*** [-LOGUED, -LOGUING; -LOGED, -LOGING], to arrange in a catalogue. —**cat'a·logu'er, cat'a·log'er,** ***n.***

**ca·tal·pa** (kə-tal'pə), ***n.*** [< Am. Ind.], a tree with large, heart-shaped leaves, trumpet-shaped flowers, and air-borne seeds.

**ca·tal·y·sis** (kə-tal'ə-sis), ***n.*** [*pl.* -SES (-sēz')], [< Gr. *katalysis*, dissolution], the causing or speeding up of a chemical reaction by adding a substance which itself is not changed thereby. —**cat·a·lyt·ic** (kat''l-it'ik), ***adj. & n.*** —**cat'a·lyt'i·cal·ly,** ***adv.***

**cat·a·lyst** (kat''l-ist), ***n.*** a substance serving as the agent in catalysis.

**cat·a·mount** (kat'ə-mount'), ***n.*** [*cat* + *a*, of + *mount*], 1. a puma. 2. a lynx.

**cat·a·pult** (kat'ə-pult'), ***n.*** [< Gr. *kata-*, down + *pallein*, hurl], 1. an ancient military device for throwing stones, etc. 2. a device for launching an airplane from the deck of a ship. ***v.t.*** to shoot as from a catapult.

**cat·a·ract** (kat'ə-rakt'), ***n.*** [< Gr. *kata-*, down + *rēgnymi*, to break], 1. a large waterfall. 2. *a*) an eye disease in which the lens becomes opaque, causing partial or total blindness. *b*) the opaque area.

**ca·tarrh** (kə-tär'), ***n.*** [< Gr. *kata-*, down + *rhein*, to flow], inflammation of the mucous membrane of the nose or throat. —**ca·tarrh'al,** ***adj.***

**ca·tas·tro·phe** (kə-tas'trə-fi), ***n.*** [< Gr. *kata-*, down + *strephein*, to turn], 1. the culminating event of a drama, by which the plot is resolved; denouement. 2. any sudden, great disaster. —**cat·a·stroph·ic** (kat'ə-strof'ik), ***adj.*** —**cat'a·stroph'i·cal·ly,** ***adv.***

**cat'bird',** ***n.*** a slate-gray N. American songbird that makes a mewing sound like a cat.

**cat'boat',** ***n.*** a sailboat with a single sail and mast set well forward.

**cat'call',** ***n.*** a shrill noise or whistle expressing derision, etc.

**catch** (kach), ***v.t.*** [CAUGHT (kôt), CATCHING], [< L. *capere*, take], 1. to seize and hold; capture. 2. to take by or as by a trap. 3. to deceive. 4. to surprise. 5. to get to in time: as, he *caught* the bus. 6. to lay hold of; grab: as, *catch* the ball. 7. to become infected with: as, he *caught* a cold. 8. to understand. ***v.i.*** 1. to become held, fastened, etc. 2. to take hold, as fire. 3. to keep hold, as a lock. ***n.*** 1. a catching. 2. a thing that catches. 3. a person, thing, or amount caught. 4. one worth catching as a husband or wife. 5. a break in the voice. 6. [Colloq.], a tricky qualification. —**catch at,** to seize desperately. —**catch on,** [Colloq.], 1. to understand. 2. to become popular. —**catch up,** 1. to snatch. 2. to show to be in error. 3. to overtake.

**catch'all'** (-ôl'), ***n.*** a container for various sorts of things: as, most attics are *catchalls*.

**catch'er,** ***n.*** 1. one that catches. 2. in *baseball*, the player behind home plate, who catches pitched balls.

**catch′ing,** *adj.* 1. contagious. 2. attractive.
**catch′pen′ny** (-pen′i), *adj.* made merely to sell; cheap and flashy. *n.* a catchpenny commodity.
**catch·up** (kach′əp, kech′-), *n.* ketchup.
**catch′word′,** *n.* 1. a word so placed as to catch attention, as either of the words at the top of this page. 2. a word or phrase repeated so often that it becomes a slogan.
**catch′y,** *adj.* [-IER, -IEST], 1. easily caught up and remembered: as, a *catchy* tune. 2. tricky; deceiving.
**cat·e·chism** (kat′ə-kiz'm), *n.* [see CATECHIZE], 1. a handbook of questions and answers for teaching the tenets of a religion. 2. a close questioning.
**cat·e·chize** (kat′ə-kīz′), *v.t.* [-CHIZED, -CHIZING], [< Gr. *kata-*, thoroughly + *ēchein*, to sound], to question searchingly: also sp. **catechise.** —**cat′e·chi·za′tion** (-ki-zā′shən), —**cat′e·chi·sa′tion,** *n.*
**cat·e·gor·i·cal** (kat′ə-gôr′i-k'l), *adj.* 1. unqualified; positive; explicit: said of a statement, etc. 2. of, as, or in a category. —**cat′e·gor′i·cal·ly,** *adv.*
**cat·e·go·ry** (kat′ə-gôr′i), *n.* [*pl.* -RIES], [< Gr. *katēgorein*, assert], a class or division in a scheme of classification.
**ca·ter** (kā′tẽr), *v.i.* [< L. *ad-*, to + *capere*, take], 1. to provide food and service, as for parties. 2. to provide what is desired (with *to*). —**ca′ter·er,** *n.*
**cat·er-cor·nered** (kat′ẽr-kôr′nẽrd), *adj.* [< Fr. *quatre*, four; + *cornered*], diagonal. *adv.* diagonally. Also **cat′er-cor′ner.**
**cat·er·pil·lar** (kat′ẽr-pil′ẽr), *n.* [< L. *catta pilosa*, hairy cat], the wormlike larva of a butterfly, moth, etc.
**cat·er·waul** (kat′ẽr-wôl′), *v.i.* [prob. echoic], to make a shrill, howling sound like that of a cat; wail. *n.* such a sound.
**cat′fish′,** *n.* [*pl.* see FISH], a scaleless fish with long, whiskerlike feelers about the mouth.
**cat′gut′,** *n.* a tough thread made from dried intestines, as of sheep, and used for surgical sutures, etc.
**Cath.,** Catholic.
**ca·thar·sis** (kə-thär′sis), *n.* [< Gr. *katharos*, pure], 1. a purging, esp. of the bowels. 2. a relieving of the emotions, as through the arts or psychotherapy.
**ca·thar′tic,** *adj.* purging. *n.* a medicine for purging the bowels; laxative.
**ca·the·dral** (kə-thē′drəl), *n.* [< Gr. *kata-*, down + *hedra*, a seat], 1. the main church of a bishop's see. 2. any large church.
**cath·e·ter** (kath′ə-tẽr), *n.* [< Gr. *kata-*, down + *hienai*, to send], a slender tube inserted into a body cavity for drawing off fluid, esp. urine from the bladder. —**cath′e·ter·ize′** (-īz′) [-IZED, -IZING], *v.t.*
**cath·ode** (kath′ōd), *n.* [< Gr. *kata-*, down + *hodos*, way], a negatively charged electrode. —**ca·thod·ic** (kə-thod′ik), *adj.*
**cathode rays,** streams of electrons projected from a cathode: they produce X rays on striking solids.
**cath·o·lic** (kath′ə-lik, kath′lik), *adj.* [< Gr. *kata-*, completely + *holos*, whole], 1. universal; all-inclusive. 2. having broad sympathies; liberal. 3. [C-], of the Christian church headed by the Pope; Roman Catholic. *n.* [C-], a member of the Roman Catholic Church. —**ca·thol·i·cism** (kə-thol′ə-siz'm), *n.*
**cath·o·lic·i·ty** (kath′ə-lis′ə-ti), *n.* 1. broadness of taste, sympathy, understanding, etc. 2. universality.
**cat·kin** (kat′kin), *n.* [dim. of *cat*], a spike of closely clustered, small flowers without petals, as on a willow.
**cat nap,** a short, light sleep; doze. —**cat′nap′** [-NAPPED, -NAPPING], *v.i.*
**cat′nip,** *n.* [< *cat* + obs. *nep*, catnip], a plant of the mint family: cats like its odor: also **cat′mint′.**
**cat-o′-nine-tails** (kat′ə-nīn′tālz′), *n. sing. & pl.* a whip made of nine knotted cords attached to a handle.
**cat's-paw** (kats′pô′), *n.* a person used by another to do distasteful or unlawful work; dupe.
**cat·sup** (kech′əp, kat′səp), *n.* ketchup.
**cat·tail** (kat′tāl′), *n.* a tall marsh plant with long, brown, fuzzy spikes.
**cat′tish,** *adj.* 1. like a cat; feline. 2. catty.
**cat·tle** (kat′'l), *n.* [ult. < L. *caput*, the head], 1. farm animals; livestock. 2. cows, bulls, steers, or oxen.
**cat′tle·man** (-mən), *n.* [*pl.* -MEN], a man who raises cattle for the market.
**cat·ty** (kat′i), *adj.* [-TIER, -TIEST], 1. of or like cats. 2. spiteful; mean; subtly malicious. —**cat′ti·ly,** *adv.* —**cat′ti·ness,** *n.*
**cat·walk** (kat′wôk′), *n.* a narrow pathway, as along a bridge or over an engine room.
**Cau·ca·sian** (kô-kā′zhən), *adj.* 1. of the Caucasus, its people, etc. 2. designating or of one of the main ethnic divisions of the human race: loosely called the *white race*. *n.* 1. a native of the Caucasus. 2. a member of the Caucasian division of mankind.
**cau·cus** (kô′kəs), *n.* [< ?], a meeting of a party to decide choice of policy, candidates, etc. *v.i.* to hold a caucus.
**cau·dal** (kô′d'l), *adj.* [< L. *cauda*, tail], of, like, at, or near the tail.
**cau·date** (kô′dāt), *adj.* [< L. *cauda*, tail], having a tail or taillike part: also **cau′dat·ed.**
**caught** (kôt), pt. and pp. of **catch.**
**caul** (kôl), *n.* [OFr. *cale*, kind of cap], a membrane sometimes enveloping the head of a child at birth.
**caul·dron** (kôl′drən), *n.* a caldron.
**cau·li·flow·er** (kô′lə-flou′ẽr), *n.* [< Fr., after L. *caulis*, cabbage], 1. a variety of cabbage with a compact white head of fleshy stalks bearing small flowers and buds. 2. this head, used as a vegetable.
**caulk** (kôk), *v.t.* to calk. —**caulk′er,** *n.*
**caus·al** (kôz′'l), *adj.* 1. of, like, being, or expressing a cause. 2. relating to cause and effect. —**cau·sal·i·ty** (kô-zal′ə-ti), *n.* —**caus′al·ly,** *adv.*
**cau·sa·tion** (kô-zā′shən), *n.* 1. a causing or being caused. 2. a causal agency; anything producing an effect. —**caus·a·tive** (kôz′ə-tiv), *adj.*
**cause** (kôz), *n.* [< L. *causa*], 1. anything bringing about an effect or result. 2. a reason or motive for producing a given effect. 3. any activity or movement that people are interested in and support. 4. a case to be decided by a court; lawsuit. *v.t.* [CAUSED (kôzd), CAUSING], to be the cause of; bring about. —**cause′less,** *adj.*
**cause·way** (kôz′wā′), *n.* [ult. < L. *calx*, limestone; + *way*], 1. a raised way or road, as across wet ground. 2. a paved way or road; highway.
**caus·tic** (kôs′tik), *adj.* [< Gr. *kaiein*, to burn], 1. that can burn or destroy living tissue by chemical action; corrosive. 2. biting; sarcastic. *n.* a caustic substance. —**caus′ti·cal·ly,** *adv.*
**cau·ter·ize** (kô′tẽr-īz′), *v.t.* [-IZED, -IZING], [< Gr. *kautēr*, branding iron], to burn with a hot iron or needle, or with a caustic, so as to destroy dead tissue, etc. —**cau′ter·i·za′tion,** *n.*
**cau′ter·y,** *n.* [*pl.* -IES], 1. an instrument or substance for cauterizing. 2. a cauterizing.
**cau·tion** (kô′shən), *n.* [< L., akin to L. *cavere*, take care], 1. a warning. 2. prudence; wariness. *v.t.* to warn.
**cau′tion·ar′y** (-er′i), *adj.* urging caution.
**cau·tious** (kô′shəs), *adj.* full of caution;

careful to avoid danger; wary. —**cau′tious·ly,** *adv.* —**cau′tious·ness,** *n.*

**cav·al·cade** (kav″l-kād′), *n.* [Fr. < It. *cavalcare*, to ride], a procession, as of horsemen, carriages, etc.

**cav·a·lier** (kav′ə-lêr′), *n.* [Fr. < L. *caballus*, horse], 1. an armed horseman; knight. 2. a gallant gentleman, esp. one serving as a lady's escort. *adj.* 1. gay; offhand. 2. arrogant. —**cav′a·lier′ly,** *adj. & adv.*

**cav·al·ry** (kav″l-ri), *n.* [*pl.* -RIES], [< Fr.; see CAVALIER], combat troops mounted originally on horses but now often on motorized armored vehicles. —**cav′al·ry·man** [*pl.* -MEN], *n.*

**cave** (kāv), *n.* [< L. *cavus*, hollow], a hollow place inside the earth; cavern. *v.t. & v.i.* [CAVED, CAVING], to collapse or make collapse (with *in*).

‡**ca·ve·at emp·tor** (kā′vi-at′ emp′tôr), [L.], let the buyer beware.

**cave man,** 1. a prehistoric human being of the Stone Age who lived in caves: also **cave dweller.** 2. a man who is rough and crudely direct.

**cav·ern** (kav′ẽrn), *n.* [< L. *cavus*, hollow], a cave, esp. a large cave.

**cav′ern·ous** (-əs), *adj.* 1. full of caverns. 2. of or like a cavern.

**cav·i·ar, cav·i·are** (kav′i-är′), *n.* [Fr. < Turk. *khāvyār*], a salty relish prepared from the eggs of sturgeon, salmon, etc.

**cav·il** (kav″l), *v.i.* [-ILED or -ILLED, -ILING or -ILLING], [< L. *cavilla*, a jest], to object unnecessarily; carp. *n.* a captious criticism; quibble. —**cav′il·er, cav′il·ler,** *n.*

**cav·i·ty** (kav′ə-ti), *n.* [*pl.* -TIES], [< L. *cavus*, hollow], a hole; hollow place, as in a tooth.

**ca·vort** (kə-vôrt′), *v.i.* [< ?], to prance; leap about; caper.

**caw** (kô), *n.* [echoic], the harsh cry of a crow or raven. *v.i.* to make this sound.

**cay·enne** (kī-en′, kā-), *n.* [< native Braz. *kynnha*], a very hot red pepper made from the dried seeds or fruit of a pepper plant: also **cayenne pepper.**

**cay·use** (kī-ūs′), *n.* [< Am. Ind.], an Indian pony.

**cc., c.c.,** cubic centimeter(s).

**Cd,** in *chem.*, cadmium.

**cease** (sēs), *v.t. & v.i.* [CEASED, CEASING], [< L. *cedere*, to yield], to end; stop; discontinue.

**cease·less** (sēs′lis), *adj.* unceasing; always going on; continual. —**cease′less·ly,** *adv.*

**ce·dar** (sē′dẽr), *n.* [< Gr. *kedros*], 1. an evergreen tree having fragrant, durable wood. 2. its wood.

**cedar waxwing,** a brownish-gray, crested American bird with red, waxlike tips on its wing feathers; also **ce′dar·bird′,** *n.*

**cede** (sēd), *v.t.* [CEDED, CEDING], [< L. *cedere*, to yield], to give up; transfer the ownership of.

**ce·dil·la** (si-dil′ə), *n.* [Sp., dim. of *zeda*, the zeta], a mark put under *c* in some French words (e.g., *garçon*), to show that it has an *s* sound.

**ceil** (sēl), *v.t.* [< Fr. < L. *caelum*, heaven], 1. to build a ceiling in or over. 2. to cover the ceiling or walls of (a room).

**ceil·ing** (sēl′iŋ), *n.* [< L. *caelum*, heaven], 1. the inside top part of a room, opposite the floor. 2. an upper limit: as, a wage *ceiling*. 3. in *aeronautics*, the upper limit of visibility. —**hit the ceiling,** [Slang], to become angry.

**cel·e·brate** (sel′ə-brāt′), *v.t.* [-BRATED, -BRATING], [< L *celebrare*, to honor], 1. to perform (a ritual, etc.). 2. to commemorate (an anniversary, holiday, etc.) with festivity. 3. to honor publicly. *v.i.* [Colloq.], to have a good time. —**cel′e·brant** (-brənt), *n.*

**cel′e·brat′ed,** *adj.* famous; renowned.

**cel′e·bra′tion,** *n.* 1. a celebrating. 2. that which is done to celebrate.

**ce·leb·ri·ty** (sə-leb′rə-ti), *n.* [*pl.* -TIES], 1. fame. 2. a famous person.

**ce·ler·i·ty** (sə-ler′ə-ti), *n.* [< L. *celer*, quick], swiftness; speed.

**cel·er·y** (sel′ẽr-i), *n.* [< Gr. *selinon*, parsley], a plant whose crisp, blanched stalks are eaten as a vegetable.

**ce·les·ta** (sə-les′tə), *n.* [< Fr.; see CELESTIAL], a small keyboard instrument with bell-like tones produced by hammers striking metal plates.

**ce·les·tial** (sə-les′chəl), *adj.* [< L. *caelum*, heaven], 1. of the heavens, or sky. 2. heavenly; divine. *n.* any being thought to live in heaven. —**ce·les′tial·ly,** *adv.*

**cel·i·ba·cy** (sel′ə-bə-si), *n.* [*pl.* -CIES], the state of being unmarried; single life.

**cel·i·bate** (sel′ə-bit), *adj.* [< L. *caelebs*], 1. unmarried; single. 2. bound by a vow to remain unmarried. *n.* an unmarried person.

**cell** (sel), *n.* [< L. *cella*], 1. a small room, as in a prison. 2. a small hollow, as in a honeycomb. 3. a small unit of protoplasm: all plants and animals are made up of one or more cells. 4. a receptacle for generating electricity by chemical reactions. 5. a small unit of an organization.

**cel·lar** (sel′ẽr), *n.* [see CELL], a room or rooms below ground and usually under a building.

**cel′lar·et′** (-et′), *n.* [*cellar* + *-et*], a cabinet for wine, liquor, glasses, etc.

**cel·lo, 'cel·lo** (chel′ō), *n.* [*pl.* -LOS, -LI (-ē)], [< *violoncello*], an instrument of the violin family, between the viola and bass viol in size and pitch. —**cel′list, 'cel′list,** *n.*

**cel·lo·phane** (sel′ə-fān′), *n.* [< *cellulose* + Gr. *phanein*, to seem], a thin, transparent material made from cellulose, used as a moistureproof wrapping.

**cel·lu·lar** (sel′yoo-lẽr), *adj.* of, like, or containing a cell or cells.

**cel·lu·loid** (sel′yoo-loid′), *n.* [*cellulose* + *-oid*], a thin, inflammable plastic substance made from cellulose nitrate and camphor: a trademark **(Celluloid).**

**cel·lu·lose** (sel′yoo-lōs′), *n.* [< L. *cella*, cell], the chief substance in the cell walls of plants, used in making paper, rayon, etc.

**Celt** (selt, kelt), *n.* [< L.], a Celtic-speaking person.

**Cel·tic** (sel′tik, kel′-), *adj.* of the Celts, their languages, etc. *n.* a family of languages including Gaelic and Welsh.

**ce·ment** (sə-ment′), *n.* [< L. *caementum*, rough stone], 1. a substance of powdered lime and clay, mixed with water and used to fasten stones or bricks together, or as paving: it hardens upon drying. 2. any adhesive substance, as glue. *v.t.* 1. to unite as with cement. 2. to cover with cement. *v.i.* to be cemented. —**ce·ment′er,** *n.*

**cem·e·ter·y** (sem′ə-ter′i), *n.* [*pl.* -IES], [< Gr. *koiman*, put to sleep], a place for the burial of the dead; graveyard.

**cen·o·bite** (sen′ə-bit′, sē′nə-), *n.* [< Gr. *koinos*, common + *bios*, life], a member of a religious order in a convent or monastery.

**cen·o·taph** (sen′ə-taf′), *n.* [< Gr. *kenos*, empty + *taphos*, tomb], a monument honoring a dead person whose body is somewhere else.

**cen·ser** (sen′sẽr), *n.* [see INCENSE, *n.*], a container in which incense is burned.

**cen·sor** (sen′sẽr), *n.* [L. < *censere*, to value], 1. one whose task is to examine literature, mail, etc. and to remove or prohibit anything considered unsuitable. 2. a faultfinder. *v.t.* to act as a censor of (literature, etc.). —**cen′sor·ship′,** *n.*

**cen·so·ri·ous** (sen-sôr′i-əs), *adj.* inclined to find fault; critical. —**cen·so′ri·ous·ly,** *adv.*

**cen·sure** (sen′shẽr), *n.* [see CENSOR], a blaming; condemnation. *v.t.* [-SURED, -SURING], to blame; condemn as wrong. —**cen′sur·a·ble,** *adj.* —**cen′sur·er,** *n.*
**cen·sus** (sen′səs), *n.* [L. < *censere*, enroll], any official count of population and recording of age, sex, etc.
**cent** (sent), *n.* [Fr. < L. *centum*, hundred], 1. a hundred, as in *per cent.* 2. a 100th part of a dollar or a coin of this value; penny.
**cent.,** 1. centigrade. 2. century.
**cen·taur** (sen′tôr), *n.* [< Gr. *Kentauros*], in *Gr. myth.*, a monster with a man's head and trunk and a horse's body.
**cen·ta·vo** (sen-tä′vō), *n.* [*pl.* -vos], [Sp.; see CENT], a small coin of the Philippines, Mexico, and some S. American countries; one 100th of a peso.
**cen·te·nar·i·an** (sen′tə-nâr′i-ən), *n.* a person at least 100 years old.
**cen·te·nar·y** (sen′tə-ner′i, sen-ten′ə-ri), *n.* [*pl.* -IES], [< L. *centum*, hundred], 1. a century. 2. a centennial. *adj.* 1. of a century. 2. of a centennial.
**cen·ten·ni·al** (sen-ten′i-əl), *n.* [< L. *centum*, hundred + *annus*, year], 1. a 100th anniversary. 2. its celebration. *adj.* 1. of or lasting 100 years. 2. of a centennial. —**cen·ten′ni·al·ly,** *adv.*
**cen·ter** (sen′tẽr), *n.* [< Gr. *kentron*, a point], 1. the point equally distant from all points on the circumference of a circle or surface of a sphere. 2. a pivot. 3. the approximate middle point or part of anything. 4. a focal point of activity. 5. [often C-], a political party between left (liberals) and right (conservatives). 6. in *sports*, a player at the center of a line, floor, etc. *v.i.* to be at a center. *v.t.* 1. to place in or near the center. 2. to gather to one place.
**cen′ter·board′,** *n.* a movable keellike board lowered through a slot in the floor of a sailboat to prevent drifting.
**center of gravity,** that point in a thing around which its weight is evenly balanced.
**cen′ter·piece′,** *n.* an ornament, bowl of flowers, etc. for the center of a table.
**centi-,** [L], a combining form meaning: 1. *hundred.* 2. *a 100th part of.*
**cen·ti·grade** (sen′tə-grād′), *adj.* [Fr.; see CENTI- & GRADE], of or by a thermometer (**centigrade thermometer**) on which 0° is the freezing point and 100° is the boiling point of water.
**cen·ti·gram, cen·ti·gramme** (sen′tə-gram′), *n.* [Fr.; see CENTI- & GRAM], a unit of weight, equal to 1/100 gram.
**cen·time** (sän′tēm), *n.* [Fr.], the 100th part of a franc.
**cen·ti·meter, cen·ti·me·tre** (sen′tə-mē′tẽr), *n.* [Fr.; see CENTI- & METER], a unit of measure, equal to 1/100 meter.
**cen·ti·pede** (sen′tə-pēd′), *n.* [Fr. < L. *centum*, hundred + *pes*, foot], a wormlike animal with a pair of legs for each body segment.
**cen·tral** (sen′trəl), *adj.* 1. in or near the center. 2. from the center. 3. equally accessible from various points. 4. main; chief; basic. *n.* a telephone exchange or operator. —**cen′tral·ly,** *adv.* —**cen′tral·ness** *n.*
**cen′tral·ize′** (-īz′), *v.t.* [-IZED, -IZING], 1. to make central; bring to a center. 2. to organize under one control. *v.i.* to become centralized. —**cen′tral·i·za′tion,** *n.*
**centri-,** [< Gr. *kentron*], a combining form meaning *center.*
**cen·trif·u·gal** (sen-trif′yoo-g′l), *adj.* [< *centri-* + L. *fugere*, flee], 1. moving or tending to move away from the center. 2. using or acted upon by centrifugal force. —**cen·trif′u·gal·ly,** *adv.*
**centrifugal force,** the force tending to make rotating bodies move away from the center of rotation.
**cen·trip·e·tal** (sen-trip′ə-t'l), *adj.* [< *centri-* + L. *petere*, seek], 1. moving or tending to move toward the center. 2. using or acted upon by centripetal force. —**cen·trip′e·tal·ly,** *adv.*
**centripetal force,** the force tending to make rotating bodies move toward the center of rotation.
**cen·tu·ple** (sen′too-p'l, sen-tōō′-), *adj.* [< L. *centuplus*], a hundred times as much or as many. *v.t.* [-PLED, -PLING], to increase a hundredfold.
**cen·tu·ri·on** (sen-tyoor′i-ən), *n.* [see CENTURY], in ancient Rome, the commander of a military unit, originally of 100 men.
**cen·tu·ry** (sen′chə-ri), *n.* [*pl.* -RIES], [< L. *centum*, hundred], any period of 100 years, esp. as reckoned from 1 A.D.
**ce·phal·ic** (sə-fal′ik), *adj.* [< Gr. *kephalē*, head], 1. of the head or skull. 2. in, on, or near the head.
**ce·ram·ic** (sə-ram′ik), *adj.* [< Gr. *keramos*, clay], 1. of pottery, porcelain, etc. 2. of ceramics.
**ce·ram′ics** (-iks), *n.pl.* 1. [construed as sing.], the art or work of making pottery, porcelain, etc. 2. objects made of these materials.
**ce·re·al** (sêr′i-əl), *adj.* [< L. *Cerealis*, of Ceres], of grain. *n.* 1. any grain used for food, as wheat, oats, etc. 2. any grass producing such grain. 3. food made from grain.
**cer·e·bel·lum** (ser′ə-bel′əm), *n.* [*pl.* -LUMS, -LA], [L., dim. of *cerebrum*], the section of the brain behind and below the cerebrum.
**cer·e·bral** (ser′ə-brəl, sə-rē′-), *adj.* of the brain or the cerebrum.
**cerebral palsy,** paralysis due to a lesion of the brain, characterized chiefly by spasms.
**cer·e·brate** (ser′ə-brāt′), *v.i.* [-BRATED, -BRATING], [< *cerebrum* + *-ate*], to use one's brain; think. —**cer′e·bra′tion,** *n.*
**cer·e·brum** (ser′ə-brəm, sə-rē′-), *n.* [*pl.* -BRUMS, -BRA], [L.], the upper main part of the brain.
**cere·ment** (sêr′mənt), *n.* [< Gr. *kēros*, wax], 1. a shroud for a dead person. 2. *usually pl.* any burial clothes.
**cer·e·mo·ni·al** (ser′ə-mō′ni-əl), *adj.* of or consisting of ceremony; formal. *n.* 1. a set system of forms or rites. 2. a rite. —**cer′e·mo′ni·al·ism,** *n.* —**cer′e·mo′ni·al·ly,** *adv.*
**cer′e·mo′ni·ous** (-əs), *adj.* 1. full of ceremony. 2. very polite or formal. —**cer′e·mo′ni·ous·ly,** *adv.*
**cer·e·mo·ny** (ser′ə-mō′ni), *n.* [*pl.* -NIES], [L. *caerimonia*], 1. a set of formal acts proper to a special occasion, as a religious rite. 2. behavior that follows rigid etiquette. 3. formality. 4. empty formality.
**Ce·res** (sêr′ēz), *n.* [L.], the Roman goddess of agriculture.
**ce·rise** (sə-rēz′, -rēs′), *n. & adj.* [Fr., a cherry], bright red; cherry red.
**cer·tain** (sũr′t'n), *adj.* [< L. *cernere*, decide], 1. fixed; settled. 2. inevitable. 3. reliable; dependable. 4. sure; positive. 5. specific, but unnamed: as, a *certain* person. 6. some: as, to a *certain* extent. —**for certain,** without doubt.
**cer′tain·ly,** *adv.* surely; undoubtedly.
**cer′tain·ty** (-ti), *n.* 1. the state of being certain. 2. [*pl.* -TIES], anything certain.
**cer·tif·i·cate** (sẽr-tif′ə-kit), *n.* [< L. *certus*, certain + *facere*, make], a written statement testifying to a fact, qualification, etc. *v.t.* (-kāt′), [-CATED, -CATING], to issue a certificate to or for.
**cer·ti·fied** (sũr′tə-fīd′), *adj.* 1. guaranteed. 2. having a certificate.
**cer·ti·fy** (sũr′tə-fī′), *v.t.* [-FIED, -FYING], [see CERTIFICATE], 1. to declare (a thing) true,

accurate, etc. by formal statement. 2. to guarantee: as, to *certify* a check. 3. to grant a certificate to. **—cer'ti·fi·ca'tion,** *n.*

**cer·ti·tude** (sũr'tə-tōōd', -tūd'), *n.* certainty; assurance.

**ce·ru·le·an** (sə-rōō'li-ən), *adj.* [< L. *caelum*, sky], sky-blue; azure.

**cer·vix** (sũr'viks), *n.* [*pl.* -VICES (-və-sēz), -VIXES], [L., neck], a necklike part, as of the uterus. **—cer'vi·cal** (-vi-k'l), *adj.*

**ce·si·um** (sē'zi-əm), *n.* [< L. *caesius*, bluish-gray], a soft, bluish-gray, metallic chemical element: symbol, Cs.

**ces·sa·tion** (se-sā'shən), *n.* [< L. *cessare*, to cease], a ceasing; stop; pause.

**ces·sion** (sesh'ən), *n.* [< L. *cedere*, to yield], a ceding (of rights, etc.) to another.

**cess·pool** (ses'pōōl'), *n.* [prob. < It. *cesso*, privy], a deep hole in the ground to receive drainage or sewage from sinks, toilets, etc.

**ce·ta·cean** (si-tā'shən), *adj.* [< L. *cetus*, whale], of the group of water mammals that includes whales and dolphins. *n.* any such animal.

**cf.,** *confer*, [L.], compare.

**Cf,** in *chem.*, californium.

**cg.,** centigram; centigrams.

**ch.,** [*pl.* CHS.], chapter.

**chafe** (chāf), *v.t.* [CHAFED, CHAFING], [< L. *calefacere*, make warm], 1. to rub so as to make warm. 2. to wear away or make sore by rubbing. 3. to annoy; irritate. *v.i.* 1. to rub (often with *on* or *against*). 2. to be angry. **—chafe at the bit,** to be impatient.

**chaff** (chaf, chäf), *n.* [AS. *ceaf*], 1. threshed or winnowed husks of grain. 2. anything worthless. 3. teasing talk; banter. *v.t. & v.i.* to tease; banter. **—chaff'y** [-IER, -IEST], *adj.*

**chaf·ing dish** (chāf'iŋ), a pan with a heating device beneath it, to cook food at the table or to keep food hot.

**cha·grin** (shə-grin'), *n.* [Fr.], a feeling of disappointment, humiliation, etc. *v.t.* [-GRINED, -GRINING], to cause to feel chagrin.

**chain** (chān), *n.* [< L. *catena*], 1. a flexible series of joined links. 2. *pl.* bonds; fetters. 3. *pl.* captivity. 4. a chainlike measuring instrument: a *surveyor's chain* is 66 feet long; an *engineer's chain* is 100 feet. 5. a connected series of things or events. *v.t.* 1. to fasten with chains. 2. to restrain.

**chain gang,** a gang of prisoners chained together, as when working.

**chain reaction,** 1. a series of nuclear reactions in which the products of each reaction activate additional particles of the reacting substances, thus causing new reactions, as in nuclear fission. 2. any sequence of events, each of which results in the following.

**chair** (châr), *n.* [< L. *cathedra;* see CATHEDRAL], 1. a seat, usually with legs and a back, for one person. 2. an office or position of authority, as a professorship. 3. a chairman.

**chair'man** (-mən), *n.* [*pl.* -MEN], a person who presides at a meeting or heads a committee, etc. **—chair'man·ship',** *n.*

**chaise** (shāz), *n.* [Fr.], a lightweight carriage, having two or four wheels.

**chaise longue** (lôŋ), [*pl.* CHAISE LONGUES (lôŋz)], [Fr., long chair], a couchlike chair with a long seat.

**chal·ced·o·ny** (kal-sed''n-i, kal'sə-dō'ni), *n.* [*pl.* -NIES], [< Gr.], a kind of colored quartz with the luster of wax.

**cha·let** (sha-lā', shal'i), *n.* [Swiss Fr.], 1. a Swiss cottage with overhanging eaves. 2. any house like this.

**chal·ice** (chal'is), *n.* [< L. *calix*], 1. a cup; goblet. 2. the cup for the wine of Holy Communion. 3. a cup-shaped flower.

**chalk** (chôk), *n.* [< L. *calx*, limestone], 1. a soft, whitish limestone. 2. a piece of chalk or chalklike substance used for writing on a blackboard. *adj.* made with chalk. *v.t.* to mark with chalk. **—chalk up,** 1. to make a record of. 2. to charge to (an account). **—chalk'i·ness,** *n.* **—chalk'y** [-IER, -IEST], *adj.*

**chal·lenge** (chal'ənj), *n.* [< L. *calumnia*, false accusation], 1. a demand for identification: as, a sentry gave the *challenge*. 2. a calling into question: as, a *challenge* to an assertion. 3. a call to a fight, contest, etc. 4. a demand; claim upon. *v.t.* [-LENGED, -LENGING], 1. to make a challenge to (a person). 2. to make objection to; question. 3. to call to a fight, contest, etc. 4. to call for; demand: as, this idea *challenges* attention. **—chal'leng·er,** *n.*

**chal·lis, chal·lie** (shal'i), *n.* [? < *Calais*, Fr. town], a lightweight, usually printed fabric.

**cham·ber** (chām'bẽr), *n.* [< L. *camera*, a vault], 1. a room in a house, esp. a bedroom. 2. *pl.* a judge's office near the courtroom. 3. an assembly hall. 4. a legislative or judicial body. 5. a council: as, a *chamber* of commerce. 6. an enclosed space. 7. the part of a gun that holds the cartridge.

**cham·ber·lain** (chām'bẽr-lin), *n.* [< OHG. *chamarlinc*], 1. an officer in charge of the household of a ruler or lord. 2. a high official in certain royal courts. 3. a treasurer.

**cham'ber·maid'** (-mād'), *n.* a woman whose work is taking care of bedrooms.

**chamber music,** music suitable for performance in a room or small hall, as trios, quartets, etc.

**cham·bray** (sham'brā), *n.* [< *Cambrai*, in France], a gingham made by weaving white threads across a colored warp.

**cha·me·le·on** (kə-mē'li-ən, -mēl'yən), *n.* [< Gr. *chamai*, on the ground + *leōn*, lion], any of various lizards that can change the color of their skin.

**cham·ois** (sham'i), *n.* [*pl.* CHAMOIS], [Fr.], 1. a small, goatlike antelope of the mountains of Europe and SW Asia. 2. a soft leather made from the skin of chamois, sheep, etc.: also sp. **shammy, chammy.**

**champ** (champ), *v.t. & v.i.* [prob. echoic], to chew or bite hard and noisily.

**champ** (champ), *n.* [Slang], a champion.

**cham·pagne** (sham-pān'), *n.* 1. an effervescent white wine, specif. one from Champagne, a region in NE France: a symbol of luxury. 2. pale yellow.

**cham·pi·on** (cham'pi-ən), *n.* [< LL. *campio*, gladiator], 1. one who fights for another or for a cause; defender. 2. a winner of first place in a competition. *adj.* excelling over all others. *v.t.* to fight for; defend; support. **—cham'pi·on·ship',** *n.*

**chance** (chans, chäns), *n.* [< L. *cadere*, to fall], 1. the way things happen. 2. luck; fortune. 3. a happening. 4. a risk or gamble. 5. a share in a lottery. 6. an opportunity: as, a *chance* to go. 7. a possibility or probability. *adj.* accidental. *v.i.* [CHANCED, CHANCING], to happen by chance. *v.t.* to risk. **—by chance,** accidentally. **—chance on** (or **upon**), to find by chance.

**chan·cel** (chan's'l, chän'-), *n.* [< L. *cancelli*, lattices], that part of a church around the altar reserved for the clergy and the choir.

**chan·cel·ler·y** (chan'sə-lẽr-i, chän'-), *n.* [*pl.* -IES], the position or office of a chancellor.

**chan·cel·lor** (chan'sə-lẽr, chän'-), *n.* [< LL. *cancellarius*, secretary], 1. a high state or church official. 2. the title of the head of some universities. 3. the prime minister in certain countries. 4. a chief judge of a court of chancery or equity in some States. **—chan'cel·lor·ship',** *n.*

**chan·cer·y** (chan'sẽr-i, chän'-), *n.* [*pl.* -IES], [< LL. *cancellaria*], 1. a court of equity. 2. a court of record. 3. a chancellery.

**chan·cre** (shaŋ'kẽr), *n.* [Fr.; see CANCER], a sore or ulcer of syphilis.

**chan·de·lier** (shan'də-lêr'), *n.* [Fr. < L. *candela*, torch], a fixture with branches for candles, electric bulbs, etc., usually hanging from a ceiling.
**chan·dler** (chan'dlẽr, chän'-), *n.* [< L. *candela*, candle], 1. a maker of candles. 2. a retailer of supplies and groceries. **—chan'dler·y** [*pl.* -IES], *n.*
**change** (chānj), *v.t.* [CHANGED, CHANGING], [< L. *cambire*, to barter], 1. to put or take (a thing) in place of something else; substitute: as, he *changed* his clothes. 2. to exchange: as, they *changed* places. 3. to make different; alter. *v.i.* 1. to alter; vary: as, the scene *changes*. 2. to leave one train, bus, etc. and board another. 3. to put on other clothes. 4. to make an exchange. *n.* 1. a substitution, alteration, or variation. 2. variety. 3. another set of clothes. 4. money returned as the difference between the purchase price and the sum given in payment. 5. small coins. **—ring the changes,** 1. to ring a set of bells with all variations. 2. to do or say a thing in many ways. **—change'a·ble,** *adj.* **—change'less,** *adj.* **—chang'er,** *n.*
**change'ling,** *n.* [*change* + *-ling*], a child secretly exchanged for another.
**change of life,** menopause.
**chan·nel** (chan''l), *n.* [see CANAL], 1. the bed of a river, etc. 2. the deeper part of a harbor, etc. 3. a body of water joining two larger ones. 4. any means of passage. 5. the official course of action: as, to request through *channels*. 6. a long groove. 7. a frequency band assigned to a radio or television station. *v.t.* [-NELED or -NELLED, -NELING or -NELLING], 1. to make a channel in. 2. to send through a channel.
**chant** (chant, chänt), *n.* [< L. *canere*, sing], 1. a song, esp. one in which a number of words are sung to each tone. 2. a singsong mode of speaking. *v.i. & v.t.* to sing or say in a chant.
‡**chan·teuse** (shän'töz'), *n.* [Fr.], a woman singer.
**chant·ey** (shan'ti, chan'-), *n.* [*pl.* -TEYS], a song that sailors sing in rhythm with their motions while working: also sp. **chanty.**
**chan·ti·cleer** (chan'ti-klêr'), *n.* [see CHANT & CLEAR], a rooster.
**chan·try** (chan'tri, chän'-), *n.* [*pl.* -TRIES], a chapel or altar endowed for the saying of Masses and prayers.
**cha·os** (kā'os), *n.* [Gr. < *chainein*, gape], any great confusion or disorder. **—cha·ot'ic** (-ot'ik), *adj.* **—cha·ot'i·cal·ly,** *adv.*
**chap** (chap, chop), *n.* [ON. *kjapir*], 1. a jaw. 2. a cheek.
**chap** (chap), *n.* [< Brit. *chapman*, peddler], [Colloq.], a man; fellow.
**chap** (chap), *v.t. & v.i.* [CHAPPED or CHAPT, CHAPPING], [ME. *chappen*, cut], to split; crack open; roughen, as skin. *n.* a chapped place in the skin.
**cha·peau** (sha-pō'), *n.* [*pl.* -PEAUX, -PEAUS (-pōz')], [Fr. < LL. *cappa*, hood], a hat.
**chap·el** (chap''l), *n.* [< LL. *cappa*, hood], 1. a church. 2. a small or private place of worship in a church, school, etc.
**chap·er·on, chap·er·one** (shap'ə-rōn'), *n.* [Fr., hood], a person, esp. an older woman, who accompanies young unmarried people in public for propriety. *v.t.* [-ONED, -ONING], to act as chaperon to.
**chap·lain** (chap'lin), *n.* [see CHAPEL], 1. a clergyman attached to a chapel. 2. a clergyman serving in a religious capacity with the armed forces. **—chap'lain·ship',** *n.*
**chap·let** (chap'lit), *n.* [< LL. *cappa*, cap], 1. a garland for the head. 2. a string of beads, esp. prayer beads.
**chaps** (chaps), *n.pl.* [Mex. Sp. *chaparajos*], leather trousers worn over ordinary trousers by cowboys to protect their legs.
**chap·ter** (chap'tẽr), *n.* [< L. *caput*, head], 1. a main division, as of a book. 2. a local branch of an organization.
**char** (chär), *v.t. & v.i.* [CHARRED, CHARRING], [< *charcoal*], to scorch.
**char·ac·ter** (kar'ik-tẽr), *n.* [< Gr. *charattein*, engrave], 1. a conventional mark, letter, or symbol, as 7, A, ?, etc. 2. a distinctive trait. 3. kind or sort. 4. one's personality. 5. moral strength. 6. reputation. 7. status; position. 8. a person in a play, novel, etc. 9. [Colloq.], an eccentric person. **—in character,** appropriate. **—out of character,** inappropriate.
**char'ac·ter·is'tic** (-is'tik), *adj.* typical; distinctive. *n.* a distinguishing trait or quality. **—char'ac·ter·is'ti·cal·ly,** *adv.*
**char'ac·ter·ize'** (-īz'), *v.t.* [-IZED, -IZING], 1. to describe the particular traits of. 2. to be a characteristic of. **—char'ac·ter·i·za'tion,** *n.* **—char'ac·ter·iz'er,** *n.*
**cha·rade** (shə-rād'), *n.* [Fr. < Pr. *charrar*, to gossip], a game in which words to be guessed are acted out in pantomime.
**char·coal** (chär'kōl), *n.* [prob. < ME. *charren*, turn + *cole*, coal], 1. a black form of carbon made by partially burning wood in the absence of air. 2. a very dark gray.
**chard** (chärd), *n.* [< L. *carduus*, thistle], a kind of beet with edible leaves and stalks.
**chare** (châr), *n.* [< AS *cierran*, turn], an odd job; chore. *v.i.* [CHARED, CHARING], 1. to do odd chores. 2. to do housework for pay.
**charge** (chärj), *v.t.* [CHARGED, CHARGING], [ult. < L. *carrus*, car], 1. to load or fill (*with* something). 2. to add an electrical charge to (a battery, etc.). 3. to give as a duty, command, etc. to. 4. to accuse; blame: as, *charged* with burglary. 5. to make liable for (an error, etc.). 6. to ask as a price. 7. to put as a debt: as, *charge* it to my account. 8. to attack vigorously. *v.i.* 1. to ask payment (*for*): as, we *charge* for this service. 2. to attack vigorously. *n.* 1. a load; burden. 2. responsibility or care (*of*). 3. instruction; command. 4. accusation; indictment. 5. cost. 6. a debt. 7. an onslaught; onset. 8. the signal for this. **—in charge,** having the responsibility or control. **—charge'a·ble,** *adj.*
**charge account,** an arrangement by which a customer may pay for purchases within a specified future period.
**charg'er,** *n.* 1. a person or thing that charges. 2. a war horse.
**char·i·ot** (char'i-ət), *n.* [see CAR], a horse-drawn, two-wheeled cart used in ancient times for war, racing, etc.
**char'i·ot·eer'** (-ə-têr'), *n.* a chariot driver.
**cha·ris·ma** (kə-riz'mə), *n.* [*pl.* -MATA (-mə-tə)], [Gr.], 1. in *Christian theology*, a divinely inspired gift, as for prophesying, healing, etc. 2. a special, inspiring quality of leadership.
**char·i·ta·ble** (char'ə-tə-b'l), *adj.* 1. generous to those in need. 2. of or for charity. 3. kindly in judging others; lenient. **—char'i·ta·bly,** *adv.*
**char'i·ty** (-ti), *n.* [*pl.* -TIES], [< L. *caritas*, affection], 1. in *Christianity*, love for one's fellow men. 2. leniency in judging others. 3. a giving of help to those in need. 4. an institution, fund, etc. for giving such help.
**cha·ri·va·ri** (shə-riv'ə-rē', shä'ri-vä'ri), *n.* [Fr.], a mock serenade; shivaree.
**char·la·tan** (shär'lə-t'n), *n.* [Fr. < It. < LL. *cerretanus*, seller of papal indulgences], a quack; imposter. **—char'la·tan·ism,** *n.* **—char'la·tan·ry** [*pl.* -RIES], *n.*
**char·ley horse** (chär'li), [Colloq.], a cramp in the leg or arm muscles, caused by a strain.
**charm** (chärm), *n.* [< L. *carmen*], 1. an action, object, or words assumed to have magic power. 2. a trinket worn on a brace-

let, etc. 3. fascination, allure, etc. ***v.t.* & *v.i.*** 1. to act on as though by magic. 2. to please greatly; fascinate; delight. **—charm′er, *n.* —charm′ing, *adj.***

**char·nel (house)** (chär′n'l), [< L. *caro*, flesh], any place where there are corpses, bones, etc.

**Cha·ron** (kâr′ən), ***n.*** in *Gr. myth.*, the boatman who ferried dead souls across the river Styx to Hades.

**chart** (chärt), ***n.*** [< Gr. *chartēs*, leaf of paper], 1. a map, specif. one for use by navigators. 2. an information sheet with tables, diagrams, etc.; also, a graph. 3. a table, graph, etc. ***v.t.*** 1. to make a chart of. 2. to show as by a chart.

**char·ter** (chär′tẽr), ***n.*** [see CHART], 1. a franchise given by a government to a person, company, etc. 2. permission from a society for a local chapter. ***v.t.*** 1. to grant a charter to. 2. to hire for exclusive use.

**charter member,** any of the original members of an organization.

**char·treuse** (shär-tröz′), ***n.*** [Fr.], pale, yellowish green. ***adj.*** of this color.

**char′wom′an** (chär′-), ***n.*** [*pl.* -WOMEN], [see CHORE], a cleaning woman.

**char·y** (châr′i), ***adj.*** [-IER, -IEST], [< AS. *caru*, care], careful; cautious. **—char′i·ly, *adv.***

**chase** (chās), ***v.t.*** [CHASED, CHASING], [ult. < L. *capere*, take], 1. to follow in order to catch. 2. to run after; follow. 3. to drive away. 4. to hunt. ***v.i.*** 1. to go in pursuit. 2. [Colloq.], to rush: as, I *chased* around town. ***n.*** 1. a chasing; pursuit. 2. the hunting of game for sport. 3. anything hunted; quarry. **—give chase,** to pursue.

**chase** (chās), ***n.*** [ult. < L. *capsa*, a box], 1. a groove or furrow. 2. a rectangular metal frame in which pages or columns of type are locked. ***v.t.*** [CHASED, CHASING], to make a groove or furrow in.

**chase** (chās), ***v.t.*** [CHASED, CHASING], [< Fr. *enchasser*, encase], to ornament (metal) by engraving, cutting, etc.

**chas′er, *n.*** [Colloq.], a mild drink, as water, taken after whisky, etc.

**chasm** (kaz'm), ***n.*** [< Gr. *chasma*], 1. a deep crack in the earth's surface; abyss. 2. any break or gap; rift. **—chas′mal, *adj.***

**chas·sis** (shas′i, chas′i), ***n.*** [*pl.* -SIS (-iz)], [Fr. < L. *capsa*, a box], 1. the lower frame, wheels, and engine of a motor vehicle. 2. *a*) a supporting frame or framework, as for the parts of a radio or television set. *b*) the assembled frame and parts.

**chaste** (chāst), ***adj.*** [< L. *castus*, pure], 1. not indulging in unlawful sexual activity. 2. decent; modest. 3. simple in style.

**chas·ten** (chās′'n), ***v.t.*** [< L. *castigare*, punish], 1. to punish in order to correct; chastise. 2. to restrain from excess; subdue.

**chas·tise** (chas-tīz′), ***v.t.*** [-TISED, -TISING], [see CHASTEN], to punish in order to correct, usually by beating. **—chas·tise′ment, *n.***

**chas·ti·ty** (chas′tə-ti), ***n.*** 1. abstention from unlawful sexual activity. 2. celibacy or virginity. 3. decency.

**chat** (chat), ***v.i.*** [CHATTED, CHATTING], [< *chatter*], to talk in a light, informal manner. ***n.*** light, informal talk.

**châ·teau** (sha-tō′), ***n.*** [*pl.* -TEAUX (-tōz′)], [Fr. < L. *castellum*, castle], 1. a French feudal castle. 2. a large country house.

**chat·tel** (chat′'l), ***n.*** [see CATTLE], an article of movable property.

**chattel mortgage,** a mortgage on personal property.

**chat·ter** (chat′ẽr), ***v.i.*** [echoic], 1. to make short, rapid, indistinct sounds, as birds, apes, etc. 2. to talk much and foolishly. 3. to click together rapidly, as teeth do from fright or cold. ***n.*** 1. rapid, indistinct sounds. 2. foolish talk. **—chat′ter·er, *n.***

**chat·ter·box** (chat′ẽr-boks′), ***n.*** one who talks incessantly.

**chat·ty** (chat′i), ***adj.*** [-TIER, -TIEST], fond of chatting. **—chat′ti·ly, *adv.***

**chauf·feur** (shō′fẽr, shō-fũr′), ***n.*** [Fr., lit., stoker], one whose work is to drive an automobile for someone else. ***v.t.*** to act as chauffeur to.

**chau·vin·ism** (shō′vin-iz'm), ***n.*** [< N. *Chauvin*, fanatical Fr. patriot], 1. militant and fanatical patriotism. 2. unreasoning devotion to one's race, sex, etc. **—chau′vin·ist, *n.* & *adj.* —chau′vin·is′tic, *adj.***

**cheap** (chēp), ***adj.*** [< AS. *ceap*, bargain], 1. low in price. 2. charging low prices. 3. worth more than the price. 4. got with little effort. 5. of little value. 6. held in low esteem; common. ***adv.*** at a low cost. **—cheap′ly, *adv.* —cheap′ness, *n.***

**cheap′en, *v.t.* & *v.i.*** to make or become cheap or cheaper.

**cheat** (chēt), ***n.*** [< L. *es-*, out + *cadere*, fall], 1. a fraud; swindle. 2. a swindler. ***v.t.*** 1. to deceive; defraud. 2. to foil; escape: as, to *cheat* death. ***v.i.*** to practice fraud or deception. **—cheat′er, *n.***

**check** (chek), ***n.*** [< OFr. *eschec*, a check at chess], 1. a sudden stop. 2. any restraint of action. 3. one that restrains. 4. a supervision or test of accuracy, etc. 5. a mark (✓) to show verification of something. 6. a token to show ownership: as, a hat *check*. 7. one's bill, as at a restaurant. 8. a written order to a bank to pay the amount of money stated. 9. a pattern of squares like that of a chessboard. 10. in *chess*, the state of a king that is in danger. ***interj.*** [Colloq.], agreed! right! ***v.t.*** 1. to stop suddenly. 2. to restrain; curb. 3. to test, verify, etc. by investigation or comparison. 4. to mark with a check. 5. to deposit temporarily. 6. in *chess*, to place (an opponent's king) in check. ***v.i.*** to agree with one another item for item. ***adj.*** 1. used to verify. 2. having a crisscross pattern. **—check in** (or **out**), to register at (or pay and leave) a hotel, etc. **—in check,** in restraint. **—check′er, *n.***

**check′book′, *n.*** a book containing blank checks, issued by a bank.

**check′er·board′, *n.*** a board marked off into 64 squares of two alternating colors.

**check′ered** (-ẽrd), ***adj.*** 1. having a pattern of colored squares. 2. varied.

**check′ers** (-ẽrz), ***n.pl.*** [construed as sing.], a game played on a checkerboard by two players.

**check′mate′** (-māt′), ***n.*** [< Per. *shāh māt*, the king is dead], 1. in *chess*, a check of an opponent's king from which it cannot be removed, ending the game. 2. hopeless defeat. ***v.t.*** [-MATED, -MATING], 1. to place in checkmate. 2. to defeat completely.

**check′up′, *n.*** an examination.

**Ched·dar** (ched′ẽr), ***n.*** [< *Cheddar*, England, where it was first made], a kind of hard, smooth cheese: also **Cheddar cheese.**

**cheek** (chēk), ***n.*** [AS. *ceace*, jaw], 1. either side of the face below the eye. 2. [Colloq.], sauciness; impudence. **—tongue in cheek,** without sincerity.

**cheek′bone′, *n.*** the bone of the upper cheek, just below the eye.

**cheek′y, *adj.*** [-IER, -IEST], saucy; impudent. **—cheek′i·ness, *n.***

**cheep** (chēp), ***n.*** [echoic], the short, shrill sound of a young bird. ***v.t.* & *v.i.*** to chirp.

**cheer** (chêr), ***n.*** [< Gr. *kara*, the head], 1. a state of mind or of feeling. 2. gladness; joy. 3. food, entertainment, etc. that makes one happy. 4. an excited shout to urge on, welcome, etc. ***v.t.*** 1. to fill with cheer; gladden. 2. to urge, encourage, salute, etc. with cheers. ***v.i.*** to shout cheers. **—be of**

**good cheer,** to be cheerful. —**cheer up,** to make or become glad. —**cheer′er,** *n.*
**cheer′ful,** *adj.* 1. full of cheer; gay. 2. bright and attractive. 3. willing: as, a *cheerful* helper. —**cheer′ful·ly,** *adv.* —**cheer′ful·ness,** *n.*
**cheer′less,** *adj.* not cheerful; joyless; dreary. —**cheer′less·ly,** *adv.* —**cheer′less·ness,** *n.*
**cheer′y,** *adj.* [-IER, -IEST], cheerful; lively; bright. —**cheer′i·ly,** *adv.* —**cheer′i·ness,** *n.*
**cheese** (chēz), *n.* [ult. < L. *caseus*], a solid food made from milk curds.
**cheese′cake′,** *n.* 1. a cake made of sweetened curds, eggs, milk, etc. 2. [Slang], display of the figure of a pretty girl, as in a photograph.
**cheese′cloth′,** *n.* [from its use for wrapping cheese], a thin, cotton cloth with a loose weave.
**chees·y,** *adj.* [-IER, -IEST], 1. like cheese. 2. [Slang], inferior; poor. —**chees′i·ness,** *n.*
**chee·tah** (chē′tə), *n.* [< Hind. < Sans. *citra*, spotted], a leopardlike animal of Africa and S Asia: it can be trained to hunt.
**chef** (shef), *n.* [Fr. < *chef de cuisine*], 1. a head cook. 2. any cook.
‡**chef-d'oeu·vre** (she′dë′vr′), *n.* [*pl.* CHEFS-D'OEUVRE (she′dë′vr′)], [Fr., principal work], a masterpiece, as in art or literature.
**chem·i·cal** (kem′i-k'l), *adj.* 1. of chemistry. 2. made by or used in chemistry. 3. operated by the use of chemicals. *n.* any substance used in or obtained by a chemical process. —**chem′i·cal·ly,** *adv.*
**che·mise** (shə-mēz′), *n.* [Fr. < LL. *camisia*, shirt], a woman's undergarment somewhat like a long, loose undershirt.
**chem·ist** (kem′ist), *n.* [< *alchemist*], 1. a student of or specialist in chemistry. 2. [Brit.], a druggist.
**chem·is·try** (kem′is-tri), *n.* [< *chemist*], the science dealing with the composition and properties of substances, and with the reactions by which substances are produced from or converted into other substances.
**chem·ur·gy** (kem′ẽr-ji), *n.* [*chemist* + *-urgy*], the branch of chemistry dealing with the use of farm products in manufacturing products other than food or clothing.
**che·nille** (shə-nēl′), *n.* [Fr., caterpillar], 1. a tufted, velvety cord used for embroidery, etc. 2. a fabric filled or woven with chenille.
**cheque** (chek), *n.* a (bank) check: Brit. spelling.
**cher·ish** (cher′ish), *v.t.* [< L. *carus*, dear], 1. to hold dear. 2. to treat tenderly; nurture. 3. to harbor in the mind.
**Cher·o·kee** (cher′ə-kē), *n.* [*pl.* -KEE, -KEES], a member of a tribe of Indians of the SW.
**che·root** (shə-ro͞ot′), *n.* [< Fr. < Tamil *shuruttu*, a roll], a cigar with both ends cut square.
**cher·ry** (cher′i), *n.* [*pl.* -RIES], [< Gr. *kerasion*], 1. a small, fleshy fruit with a smooth, hard seed. 2. the tree that it grows on. 3. the wood of this tree. 4. bright red.
**cher·ub** (cher′əb), *n.* [*pl.* -UBS; also, for 1, -UBIM (-ə-bim, -yoo-bim)], [< Heb. *kerūbh*], 1. any of an order of angels, usually represented as a chubby, rosy-faced child with wings. 2. an innocent or lovely child. —**che·ru·bic** (chə-ro͞o′bik), *adj.*
**cher·vil** (chũr′vil), *n.* [< Gr. *chairein*, rejoice + *phyllon*, leaf], a plant of the carrot family, with parsleylike leaves.
**chess** (ches), *n.* [< OFr. *eschec*, a check at chess], a game played on a checkerboard by two players, using 16 pieces (**chessmen**).
**chest** (chest), *n.* [< Gr. *kiste*, a box], 1. a box with a lid. 2. a piece of furniture with drawers; bureau. 3. the part of the body enclosed by the ribs and breastbone.
**ches·ter·field** (ches′tẽr-fēld′), *n.* [< a 19th-c. Earl of *Chesterfield*], a single-breasted topcoat, usually with a velvet collar.
**chest·nut** (ches′nət, -nut′), *n.* [< Gr. *kastanea*; + *nut*], 1. the edible nut of a tree of the beech family. 2. this tree, or its wood. 3. reddish brown. 4. [Colloq.], a trite joke, phrase, etc. *adj.* reddish-brown.
**che·val glass** (shə-val′), [Fr. *cheval*, horse, support], a full-length mirror on swivels in a frame.
**chev·a·lier** (shev′ə-lêr′), *n.* [see CAVALIER], 1. a chivalrous man. 2. [Archaic], a knight.
**chev·i·ot** (shev′i-ət), *n.* [< *Cheviot* Hills, on the Scottish-English border], a close-napped wool fabric in a twill weave.
**chev·ron** (shev′rən), *n.* [Fr., rafter], a V-shaped bar on the sleeves of a uniform, showing rank.
**chew** (cho͞o), *v.t.* & *v.i.* [< AS. *ceowan*], to bite and crush with the teeth. *n.* 1. a chewing. 2. something chewed or for chewing.
**chewing gum,** a sweet, flavored, preparation of chicle, used for chewing.
**chg.,** [*pl.* CHGS.], charge.
**chi** (kī, kē,) *n.* the 22d letter of the Greek alphabet (Χ, χ).
**Chi·an·ti** (ki-an′ti, -än′-), *n.* [It.], a dry, red wine.
**chi·a·ro·scu·ro** (ki-är′ə-skyoor′ō), *n.* [*pl.* -ROS], [< It. < L. *clarus*, clear + *obscurus*, dark], a style of painting, drawing, etc. using only light and shade.
**chic** (shēk, shik), *n.* [Fr. < MHG. *schicken*, arrange], smart elegance of style and manner. *adj.* [CHICQUER, CHICQUEST], stylish.
**chi·can·er·y** (shi-kān′ẽr-i), *n.* [*pl.* -IES], [< Fr.], 1. trickery; sophistry. 2. a trick.
**Chi·ca·no** (chi-kä′nō), *n.* [*pl.* -NOS], [prob. < Am.Sp. (*Mé*)*jicano*, a Mexican] a U.S. citizen or inhabitant of Mexican descent.
**chick** (chik), *n.* [< *chicken*], 1. a young chicken or bird. 2. a child.
**chick·a·dee** (chik′ə-dē′), *n.* [echoic], a small bird of the titmouse family.
**chick·en** (chik′ən), *n.* [< AS. *cycen*, little cock], 1. a hen or rooster, esp. a young one. 2. the edible flesh of the chicken. 3. any young bird. *adj.* 1. made of chicken. 2. small and tender: as, *chicken* lobster. 3. [Slang], timid; cowardly.
**chick′en-heart′ed,** *adj.* cowardly; timid.
**chicken pox,** an infectious virus disease, usually of children, characterized by slight fever and a skin eruption.
**chick′weed′,** *n.* any of various weeds with seeds and leaves that birds eat.
**chic·le** (chik′'l), *n.* [< Mex. Ind.], a gumlike substance from a tropical American tree, used in chewing gum: also **chicle gum.**
**chic·o·ry** (chik′ə-ri), *n.* [*pl.* -RIES], [< Gr. *kichora*], 1. a plant whose leaves are used for salad. 2. its root, ground for mixing with coffee or as a coffee substitute.
**chide** (chīd), *v.t.* & *v.i.* [CHIDED or CHID (chid), CHIDED or CHID or CHIDDEN, CHIDING], [AS. *cidan*], to scold; rebuke. —**chid′ing·ly,** *adv.*
**chief** (chēf), *n.* [< L. *caput*, head], 1. the head or top part. 2. the head of any group; leader. *adj.* 1. foremost; highest. 2. main; most important.
**chief′ly,** *adv.* 1. most of all. 2. mainly.
**chief′tain** (-tən), *n.* [< L. *caput*, head], 1. a chief of a clan or tribe. 2. any leader of a group. —**chief′tain·cy** [*pl.* -CIES], *n.*
**chif·fon** (shi-fon′), *n.* [Fr. < *chiffe*, rag], a sheer silk cloth. *adj.* 1. made of chiffon. 2. fluffy from being whipped.
**chif·fo·nier, chif·fon·nier** (shif′ə-nêr′), *n.* [Fr. < *chiffon*], a narrow, high chest of drawers, often with a mirror attached.
**chig·ger** (chig′ẽr), *n.* [of W. Ind. origin], the tiny, red larva of certain mites, whose bite causes itching.
**chi·gnon** (shēn′yon), *n.* [Fr. < L. *catena*,

chain], a coil of hair worn at the back of the neck by women.

**Chi·hua·hua** (chi-wä′wä), *n.* [< *Chihuahua*, a Mex. state], a breed of tiny dog with large, pointed ears, originally from Mexico.

**chil·blain** (chil′blān′) *n.* [*chill* + *blain* < AS. *blegen*, a sore], an inflamed sore on the feet or hands, caused by exposure to cold.

**child** (child), *n.* [*pl.* CHILDREN], [AS. *cild*], 1. an infant. 2. a boy or girl in the period before puberty. 3. a son or daughter. **—with child**, pregnant. **—child′like,** *adj.*

**child′birth′**, *n.* the act of giving birth to a child.

**child′hood′**, *n.* the state or time of being a child.

**child·ish,** *adj.* 1. of or like a child. 2. immature; silly. **—child′ish·ly,** *adv.* **—child′-ish·ness,** *n.*

**chil·dren** (chil′drən), *n.* pl. of **child.**

**Chil·e·an** (chil′i-ən), *adj.* of Chile, its people, etc. *n.* a native or inhabitant of Chile.

**chil·e** (or **chil·i) con car·ne** (chil′i kon kär′ni), [Sp.], a Mexican dish of red peppers, spices, beans, and meat.

**chil·i** (chil′i), *n.* [*pl.* -IES], [< native Mex. name], 1. the very hot dried pod of red pepper. 2. chile con carne.

**chili sauce,** a tomato sauce with chilies.

**chill** (chil), *n.* [AS. *ciele*], 1. a bodily coldness with shivering. 2. a moderate coldness. 3. a sudden fear, etc. *adj.* 1. uncomfortably cool. 2. cool in manner. *v.i. & v.t.* to make or become cool; cause a chill (in). **—chil′ly** [-LIER, -LIEST], *adj.*

**chime** (chīm), *n.* [< Gr. *kymbalon*, bell], 1. *usually pl.* *a)* a set of tuned bells. *b)* the musical sounds produced by these. 2. harmony. *v.i.* [CHIMED, CHIMING], 1. to sound as a chime. 2. to sound in harmony. 3. to harmonize; agree. *v.t.* to give (the time) by striking bells. **—chime in,** 1. to join in. 2. to agree. **—chim′er,** *n.*

**chi·me·ra, chi·mae·ra** (kə-mêr′ə, ki-), *n.* [< Gr. *chimaira*, orig., goat], 1. [C-], in *Gr. myth.*, a fire-breathing monster with a lion's head, goat's body, and serpent's tail. 2. an impossible or foolish fancy.

**chi·mer′i·cal** (-i-k'l), *adj.* 1. imaginary; unreal. 2. visionary. Also **chi·mer′ic.**

**chim·ney** (chim′ni), *n.* [*pl.* -NEYS], [ult. < Gr. *kaminos*, oven], 1. the passage or structure through which smoke from a fire escapes, often extending above the roof. 2. a glass tube around the flame of a lamp.

**chimney sweep,** one who cleans soot from chimneys.

**chim·pan·zee** (chim′pan-zē′, chim-pan′zi), *n.* [< Afr. native name], a medium-sized anthropoid ape of Africa.

**chin** (chin), *n.* [AS. *cin*], the part of the face below the lower lip; projecting part of the lower jaw. *v.t.* [CHINNED, CHINNING], to pull (oneself) up, when hanging by the hands from a bar, until the chin is level with the bar. *v.i.* [Slang], to talk volubly.

**chi·na** (chī′nə), *n.* 1. a fine porcelain originally made in China. 2. dishes, etc. made of this porcelain. 3. any earthenware dishes, etc. Also **chi′na·ware′.**

**chinch (bug)** (chinch), [< Sp. < L. *cimex*, bug], a small, white-winged, black bug that damages grain plants.

**chin·chil·la** (chin-chil′ə), *n.* [Sp. < Peruvian *sinchi*, strong], 1. a small rodent of S. America. 2. the expensive, soft, pale-gray fur of this animal. 3. a heavy wool cloth used for making overcoats.

**Chi·nese** (chī-nēz′), *n.* 1. [*pl.* -NESE], a native of China or a descendant of the people of China. 2. the language of the Chinese. *adj.* of China, its people, etc.

**chink** (chiŋk), *n.* [AS. *cinu*], a crack; fissure. *v.t.* to close up the chinks in.

**chink** (chiŋk), *n.* [echoic], a sharp, clinking sound. *v.i. & v.t.* to make or cause to make this sound.

**Chi·nook** (chi-no͝ok′, -nook′), *n.* 1. [*pl.* -NOOK, -NOOKS], any of various Indian tribes formerly inhabiting the Columbia River valley. 2. [c-], any of various winds.

**chintz** (chints), *n.* [< Hind. *chhīnt*], a cotton cloth printed in various colors and usually glazed.

**chintz′y,** *adj.* [-IER, -IEST], 1. like chintz. 2. [Colloq.], cheap, stingy, petty, etc.

**chip** (chip), *v.t.* [CHIPPED, CHIPPING], [< AS.], to break or cut off small fragments from. *v.i.* to break off in small pieces. *n.* 1. a small piece of wood, etc., cut or broken off. 2. a place where a small piece has been chipped off. 3. a small disk used in gambling games as a counter. 4. *pl.* thin slices of food: as, potato *chips.* **—chip in,** [Colloq.], to contribute (money, etc.). **—chip off the old block,** a person much like his father. **—chip on one's shoulder,** [Colloq.], an inclination to fight. **—in the chips,** [Slang], wealthy.

**chip·munk** (chip′muŋk), *n.* [< Am. Ind.], a small, striped N. American squirrel.

**Chip·pen·dale** (chip′ən-dāl′), *adj.* designating or of furniture made by, or in the graceful, rococo style of, Thomas Chippendale, 18th-c. English cabinetmaker.

**chip·per** (chip′ẽr), *adj.* [< Brit. dial.], [Colloq.], in good spirits; lively.

**chiro-,** [< Gr. *cheir*, hand], a combining form meaning *hand.*

**chi·rop·o·dist** (kī-rop′ə-dist, ki-), *n.* [*chiro-* + *-pod* + *-ist*], a podiatrist. **—chi·rop′o-dy,** *n.*

**chi·ro·prac·tic** (kī′rə-prak′tik), *n.* [< *chiro-* + Gr. *praktikos*, practical], a method of treating disease by manipulation of the joints of the body, esp. the spinal column. **—chi′ro·prac′tor,** *n.*

**chirp** (chũrp), *v.i. & v.t.* [echoic], to make, or utter in, short, shrill tones, as some birds or insects do. *n.* a short, shrill sound.

**chir·rup** (chir′əp), *v.i.* [-RUPED, -RUPING], [< *chirp*], to chirp repeatedly. *n.* a chirruping sound. **—chir′rup·er,** *n.*

**chis·el** (chiz′'l), *n.* [< L. *caedere*, to cut], a sharp-edged tool for cutting or shaping wood, stone, etc. *v.i. & v.t.* [-ELED or -ELLED, -ELING or -ELLING], 1. to cut or engrave with a chisel. 2. [Colloq.], to swindle or get by swindling. **—chis′el·er, chis′el·ler,** *n.*

**chit** (chit), *n.* [< Hind.], a voucher of a sum owed for drink, food, etc.

**chit·chat** (chit′chat′), *n.* [< *chat*], 1. light, informal talk. 2. gossip.

**chi·tin** (kī′tin), *n.* [< Gr. *chitōn*, tunic], the horny, outer covering of insects, crustaceans, etc. **—chi′tin·ous,** *adj.*

**chit·ter·lings** (chit′ẽr-liŋz), *n.pl.* [ME.], the small intestines of pigs, used for food.

**chiv·al·rous** (shiv′'l-rəs), *adj.* 1. having the attributes of an ideal knight; gallant, courteous, etc. 2. of chivalry. Also **chiv′al·ric** (-rik, shi-val′rik).

**chiv′al·ry,** *n.* [< OFr. *chevaler*, knight], 1. the medieval system of knighthood. 2. the qualifications of a knight, as courage, fairness, courtesy, etc.

**chive** (chīv), *n.* [< L. *cepa*, onion], a plant of the onion family, with small leaves used to flavor soups, stews, salads, etc.

**chlo·ral** (klôr′əl), *n.* 1. a thin, oily, colorless liquid prepared by the action of chlorine on alcohol. 2. chloral hydrate.

**chloral hydrate,** a colorless, crystalline compound, prepared from chloral, used chiefly as a sedative.

**chlor·dane** (klôr′dān, klōr′-), *n.* [< Gr. *chlōros*, pale green; + in*dane*, a coal-tar derivative], a poisonous volatile oil used as an insecticide.

**chlo·ride** (klôr′īd), *n.* a compound of chlorine and another element or radical.

**chlo·rin·ate** (klôr′ə-nāt′), *v.t.* [-ATED, -ATING], to treat (water or sewage) with chlorine for purification. —**chlo′rin·a′tion,** *n.*

**chlo·rine** (klôr′ēn, -in), *n.* [< Gr. *chlōros*, pale green], a greenish-yellow, poisonous, gaseous chemical element with a disagreeable odor, used in bleaching, water purification, etc.: symbol, Cl.

**chlo·ro·form** (klôr′ə-fôrm′), *n.* [< Fr.; see CHLORINE & FORMIC], a sweetish, colorless, volatile liquid used as an anesthetic and solvent. *v.t.* 1. to anesthetize with chloroform. 2. to kill with chloroform.

**chlo·ro·phyll, chlo·ro·phyl** (klôr′ə-fil′), *n.* [< Gr. *chlōros*, green + *phyllon*, leaf], the green coloring matter in plants, which converts carbon dioxide and water into carbohydrates.

**chock** (chok), *n.* [ONorm.Fr. *choque*, a block], a block or wedge placed under a wheel, etc. to prevent motion. *v.t.* to provide or wedge fast as with chocks. *adv.* completely, so as to be full: as, *chock* full of grain.

**chock′-full′,** *adj.* as full as possible.

**choc·o·late** (chôk′lit, chok′ə-), *n.* [< Mex. Ind. *chocolatl*], 1. a substance made from roasted and ground cacao seeds. 2. a drink made with chocolate. 3. candy made of chocolate. 4. reddish brown. *adj.* 1. made of or with chocolate. 2. reddish-brown.

**choice** (chois), *n.* [< OFr. *choisir*, choose < OHG.], 1. a choosing; selection. 2. the right or power to choose. 3. a person or thing chosen. 4. the best part. 5. a variety from which to choose. 6. an alternative. *adj.* 1. of special excellence. 2. carefully chosen.

**choir** (kwīr), *n.* [< OFr. < L.; see CHORUS], 1. a group of singers, esp. in a church. 2. the part of a church where the choir sings.

**choke** (chōk), *v.t.* [CHOKED, CHOKING], [< AS. *aceocian*], 1. to prevent from breathing by blocking the windpipe; strangle; suffocate. 2. to obstruct by clogging. 3. to hinder the growth or action of. 4. to fill up. 5. to cut off air from the carburetor of (a gasoline engine) so as to make a richer gasoline mixture. *v.i.* 1. to be suffocated. 2. to be obstructed. *n.* 1. a choking. 2. a sound of choking. 3. the valve that chokes a gasoline engine. —**choke back,** to hold back (feelings, sobs, etc.).

**choke′cher′ry,** *n.* [*pl.* -RIES], 1. a wild cherry tree of N. America. 2. its astringent fruit.

**chok′er,** *n.* a closely fitting necklace.

**chol·er** (kol′ẽr), *n.* [< Gr. *cholē*, bile], anger.

**chol·er·a** (kol′ẽr-ə), *n.* [see CHOLER], an infectious disease, usually fatal, characterized by violent diarrhea, vomiting, etc.

**chol′er·ic,** *adj.* [see CHOLER], easily angered.

**cho·les·ter·ol** (kə-les′tə-rōl′), *n.* [< Gr. *cholē*, bile + *stereos*, solid], a crystalline alcohol found especially in animal fats, blood, and bile.

**choose** (chōōz), *v.t.* & *v.i.* [CHOSE, CHOSEN, CHOOSING], [AS. *ceosan*], 1. to take as a choice; select. 2. to prefer; decide.

**choos′y,** *adj.* [-IER, -IEST], [Colloq.], very particular; fussy. —**choos′i·ness,** *n.*

**chop** (chop), *v.t.* [CHOPPED, CHOPPING], [ME. *choppen*], 1. to cut by blows with a sharp tool. 2. to cut into small bits. *v.i.* to make quick, cutting strokes as with a sharp tool. *n.* 1. a short, sharp blow. 2. a slice of lamb, pork, veal, etc. from the rib, loin, or shoulder. 3. a short, broken movement of waves. —**chop′per,** *n.*

**chop·py** (chop′i), *adj.* [-PIER, -PIEST], [< *chop* (cut)], 1. rough with short, broken waves, as the sea. 2. with sharp, abrupt movements. —**chop′pi·ness,** *n.*

**chops** (chops), *n.pl.* [< ON. *kjaptr*, a jaw], 1. the jaws. 2. the flesh about the mouth.

**chop·sticks** (chop′stiks′), *n.pl.* [Pid. Eng.], two small sticks held together in one hand and used by the Chinese and Japanese to lift food to the mouth.

**chop su·ey** (chop′ sōō′i), [< Chin. *tsa-sui*, various pieces], a Chinese-American dish of meat, bean sprouts, celery, etc. in a sauce, served with rice.

**cho·ral** (kôr′əl), *adj.* [Fr.], of, for, or sung by a choir or chorus. —**cho′ral·ly,** *adv.*

**cho·ral, cho·rale** (kô-ral′), *n.* a simple hymn tune, often sung in unison.

**chord** (kôrd), *n.* [Eng. *cord;* sp. after L. *chorda*], 1. [Poetic], the string of a musical instrument. 2. a responsive emotional element: as, his speech struck a sympathetic *chord.* 3. a straight line joining any two points on an arc.

**chord** (kôrd), *n.* [< *accord*], in *music*, a combination of three or more tones sounded together in harmony.

**chore** (chôr), *n.* [< AS. *cerr*, a job], 1. a small, routine task. 2. a hard task.

**cho·re·a** (kô-rē′ə), *n.* [< Gr. *choriea*, choral dance], a nervous disease characterized by involuntary muscular contractions.

**chor·e·og·ra·phy** (kô′ri-og′rə-fi), *n.* [< Gr. *choreia*, dance; + *-graphy*], 1. ballet dancing. 2. the art of devising ballets. —**chor′e-og′ra·pher,** *n.*

**chor·is·ter** (kôr′is-tẽr), *n.* [see CHORUS], a member of a choir.

**chor·tle** (chôr′t'l), *v.i.* & *v.t.* [-TLED, -TLING], [coined by Lewis Carroll, prob. < *chuckle* + *snort*], to make, or utter with, a gleeful chuckling or snorting sound. *n.* such a sound.

**cho·rus** (kôr′əs), *n.* [< Gr. *choros*], 1. a group of dancers and singers performing together. 2. the part of a drama, song, etc. performed by a chorus. 3. a group singing or speaking something together. 4. music written for group singing. 5. the refrain of a song, following the verse. *v.i.* & *v.t.* to sing or recite all together and simultaneously. —**in chorus,** in unison.

**chose** (chōz), pt. of **choose.**

**cho·sen** (chō′z'n), pp. of **choose.** *adj.* selected; choice.

**chow** (chou), *n.* [? < Chin.], 1. any of a Chinese breed of medium-sized dog. 2. [Slang], food.

**chow·der** (chou′dẽr), *n.* [< Fr. *chaudière*, pot], a dish consisting of fresh fish, clams, etc. stewed with vegetables, often in milk.

**chow mein** (chou′ mān′), [Chin. *ch'ao*, fry + *mien*, flour], a Chinese-American stew of meat, onions, bean sprouts, etc., served with fried noodles.

**Christ** (krīst), *n.* [< Gr. *Christos*, the Anointed], Jesus of Nazareth, regarded by Christians as the prophesied Messiah.

**chris·ten** (kris′'n), *v.t.* 1. to take into a Christian church by baptism; baptize. 2. to give a name to, esp. at baptism. —**chris′ten·ing,** *n.*

**Chris·ten·dom** (kris′'n-dəm), *n.* 1. Christians collectively. 2. countries where most of the inhabitants profess Christianity.

**Chris·tian** (kris′chən), *n.* a believer in Jesus as the Christ, or in the religion based on the teachings of Jesus. *adj.* 1. of Jesus Christ. 2. of or professing the religion based on the teachings of Jesus. 3. having the qualities taught by Jesus, as love, kindness, etc. 4. of Christians or Christianity.

**Chris·ti·an·i·ty** (kris′chi-an′ə-ti), *n.* 1. Christians collectively. 2. the Christian religion. 3. the state of being a Christian.

**Chris·tian·ize** (kris′chən-īz′), *v.t.* [-IZED, -IZING], 1. to convert to Christianity. 2. to cause to conform with Christian character.

**Christian name,** the baptismal name, as distinguished from the family name.

**Christian Science,** a religion and system of healing: official name, **Church of Christ, Scientist. —Christian Scientist.**

**Christ·mas** (kris′məs), *n.* [see CHRIST & MASS (rite)], the yearly celebration, December 25, of the birth of Jesus Christ.

**chro·mat·ic** (krō-mat′ik), *adj.* [< Gr. *chrōma*, color], 1. of or containing color or colors. 2. in *music*, using or progressing by half tones. **—chro·mat′i·cal·ly,** *adv.*

**chrome** (krōm), *n.* [Fr. < Gr. *chrōma*, a color], chromium. *adj.* designating any of various pigments (**chrome red, chrome yellow,** etc.) made from chromium compounds.

**-chrome,** [< Gr. *chrōma*, a color], a suffix meaning: 1. *color, coloring agent.* 2. *chromium.*

**chro·mi·um** (krō′mi-əm), *n.* [see CHROME], a hard, metallic chemical element resistant to corrosion: symbol, Cr.

**chromo-,** [< Gr. *chrōma*], a combining form meaning *color, pigment,* as in *chromosome.*

**chro·mo·some** (krō′mə-sōm′), *n.* [*chromo-* + *-some* (body)], any of the microscopic rod-shaped bodies which carry the genes that convey hereditary characteristics.

**chron·ic** (kron′ik), *adj.* [< Gr. *chronos*, time], 1. lasting a long time or recurring: said of a disease. 2. having had an ailment or habit for a long time. **—chron′i·cal·ly,** *adv.*

**chron·i·cle** (kron′i-k'l), *n.* [< Gr. *chronika*, annals], 1. a historical record of events in the order in which they happened. 2. a narrative or history. *v.t.* [-CLED, -CLING], to tell the history of. **—chron′i·cler,** *n.*

**chrono-,** [< Gr. *chronos*], a combining form meaning *time;* also **chron-.**

**chron·o·log·i·cal** (kron′ə-loj′i-k'l), *adj.* arranged in the order of occurrence. **—chron′o·log′i·cal·ly,** *adv.*

**chro·nol·o·gy** (krə-nol′ə-ji), *n.* [*pl.* -GIES], [*chrono-* + *-logy*], 1. the science of measuring time and of dating events. 2. the arrangement of events, dates, etc. in the order of occurrence. **—chro·nol′o·gist,** *n.*

**chro·nom·e·ter** (krə-nom′ə-tẽr), *n.* [*chrono-* + *-meter*], a highly accurate kind of clock or watch.

**chrys·a·lis** (kris′'l-is), *n.* [*pl.* -LISES, CHRYSALIDES (kri-sal′ə-dēz′)], [< Gr. *chrysallis*], 1. the form of an insect when in a cocoon; pupa. 2. the cocoon.

**chrys·an·the·mum** (kris-an′thə-məm), *n.* [< Gr. *chrysos*, gold + *anthemon*, flower], a late-blooming plant of the composite family, with showy, ball-shaped flowers.

**chrys·o·lite** (kris′'l-īt′), *n.* [< Gr. *chrysos*, gold + *lithos*, stone], a green or yellow semi-precious stone.

**chrys·o·prase** (kris′ə-prāz′), *n.* [< Gr. *chrysos*, gold + *prason*, leek], a light-green quartz, often used as a semiprecious stone.

**chub** (chub), *n.* [ME. *chubbe*], a fresh-water fish related to the carp.

**chub′by,** *adj.* [-BIER, -BIEST], [< *chub*], round and plump. **—chub′bi·ness,** *n.*

**chuck** (chuk), *v.t.* [? < Fr. *choquer*, strike against], 1. to tap playfully, esp. under the chin. 2. to throw; toss. 3. [Colloq.], to get rid of. *n.* a chucking.

**chuck** (chuk), *n.* [? var. of *chock*], 1. a cut of beef from around the neck and the shoulder blade. 2. a clamplike device, as on a lathe, by which the tool or work is held.

**chuck′hole′,** *n.* [< dial. *chock*, a bump + *hole*], a rough hole in pavement.

**chuck·le** (chuk′'l), *v.i.* [-LED, -LING], [prob. var. of *cluck*], to laugh softly in a low tone. *n.* a soft, low-toned laugh. **—chuck′ler,** *n.*

**chuck wagon,** [Slang], a portable kitchen cart for feeding ranch hands.

**chug** (chug), *n.* [echoic], a short, abrupt, explosive sound, as of an engine. *v.i.* [CHUGGED, CHUGGING], to make such sounds.

**chuk′ka boot** (chuk′ə), [ult. < Sans. *cakra*, wheel], a man's ankle-high shoe.

**chum** (chum), *n.* [prob. < *chamber mate*], [Colloq.], 1. orig., a roommate. 2. an intimate friend. *v.i.* [CHUMMED, CHUMMING], [Colloq.], to be intimate friends. **—chum′my** [-MIER, -MIEST], *adj.*

**chump** (chump), *n.* [? < *chunk* + *lump*], [Colloq.], a stupid person.

**chunk** (chuŋk), *n.* [? var. of *chuck* (a block)], [Colloq.], a short, thick piece.

**chunk′y,** *adj.* [-IER, -IEST], [Colloq.], 1. short and thick. 2. stocky; thickset.

**church** (chũrch), *n.* [< Late Gr. *kyriakē* (*dōma*), Lord's (house)], 1. a building for public worship, esp. one for Christian worship. 2. religious service. 3. all Christians. 4. [usually C-], a particular sect or denomination of Christians. **—church′like′,** *adj.*

**church′ly,** *adj.* of or fit for a church.

**church′man** (-mən), *n.* [*pl.* -MEN], 1. a clergyman. 2. a church member.

**church′ward′en** (-wôr′d'n), *n.* a lay officer attending to secular affairs of a church.

**church′yard′,** *n.* the yard adjoining a church, often used as a cemetery.

**churl** (chũrl), *n.* [AS. *ceorl*, freeman], 1. a peasant. 2. a surly, ill-bred person; boor. **—churl′ish,** *adj.* **—churl′ish·ness,** *n.*

**churn** (chũrn), *n.* [AS. *cyrin*], a container in which milk or cream is shaken to form butter. *v.t.* & *v.i.* 1. to shake (milk or cream) in a churn. 2. to make (butter) thus. 3. to stir up or move vigorously.

**chute** (shōōt), *n.* [Fr., a fall], an inclined trough or passage down which things may slide or be sent: as, a coal *chute.*

**chut·ney** (chut′ni), *n.* [*pl.* -NEYS], [Hind. *chaṭnī*], a spicy relish of fruits, spices, etc.

**CIA, C.I.A.,** Central Intelligence Agency.

**ci·ca·da** (si-kā′də), *n.* [*pl.* -DAS, -DAE (-dē)], [L.], a large locust with transparent wings: the male makes a loud, shrill sound.

**cic·a·trix** (sik′ə-triks), *n.* [*pl.* CICATRICES (sik′ə-trī′sēz)], [L.], the contracted tissue at the place where a wound heals; scar.

**cic·a·trize** (sik′ə-trīz′), *v.t.* & *v.i.* [-TRIZED, -TRIZING], to heal with the formation of a scar. **—cic′a·tri·za′tion,** *n.*

**-cide,** [< L. *caedere*, kill], a suffix meaning *killer* or *killing.*

**ci·der** (sī′dẽr), *n.* [ult. < Heb. *shēkar*, sweet liquor], the juice pressed from apples, used as a beverage or for making vinegar.

**ci·gar** (si-gär′), *n.* [Sp. *cigarro*], a compact roll of tobacco leaves for smoking.

**cig·a·rette, cig·a·ret** (sig′ə-ret′), *n.* [Fr. dim. of *cigare*, cigar], a cylinder of finely cut smoking tobacco rolled in thin paper.

**cil·i·a** (sil′i-ə), *n.pl.* [sing. CILIUM (-əm)], [L.], 1. the eyelashes. 2. in *biology*, small hairlike processes. **—cil′i·ate** (-it, -āt′), *adj.*

**cil′i·ar′y** (-er′i), *adj.* of, like, or having cilia.

**cinch** (sinch), *n.* [< Sp. < L. *cingulum*, girdle], 1. a saddle or pack girth. 2. [Slang], a thing easy to do. *v.t.* 1. to tighten a saddle girth on. 2. [Slang], to make sure of.

**cin·cho·na** (sin-kō′nə), *n.* [< 17th-c. Peruvian Countess del *Chinchon*], 1. a tropical tree with a bitter bark. 2. the bark, from which quinine is made.

**cinc·ture** (siŋk′chẽr), *n.* [L. *cinctura*], a belt or girdle. *v.t.* [-TURED, -TURING], to encircle with a belt.

**cin·der** (sin′dẽr), *n.* [AS. *sinder*], 1. a minute piece of partly burned coal or wood. 2. *pl.* ashes from wood or coal.

**Cin·der·el·la** (sin′dẽr-el′ə), *n.* in a fairy tale, a household drudge who eventually marries a prince.

**cin·e·ma** (sin′ə-mə), *n.* [< Gr. *kinēma*, motion], 1. a motion picture. 2. a motion-picture theater. **—the cinema,** motion pictures collectively. **—cin′e·mat′ic,** *adj.*

**cin·e·ra·ri·um** (sin′ə-râr′i-əm), *n.* [*pl.* -RIA (-ə)], [L. < *cinis*, ashes], a place to keep the ashes of cremated bodies.

**cin·na·bar** (sin′ə-bär′), *n.* [ult. < Persian], 1. mercuric sulfide, a heavy, bright-red mineral. 2. brilliant red.

**cin·na·mon** (sin′ə-mən), *n.* [< Heb. *qinnāmōn*], 1. the light-brown spice made from the inner bark of a laurel tree of the East Indies. 2. this bark.

**ci·pher** (sī′fẽr), *n.* [< Ar. *sifr*, nothing], 1. a naught; zero; 0. 2. a nonentity. 3. secret writing based on a key; code. 4. the key to such a code. *v.i.* to solve arithmetical problems. *v.t.* to solve by arithmetic.

**cir·ca** (sũr′kə), *prep.* [L.], about: used to indicate an approximate date.

**Cir·ce** (sũr′si), *n.* in the *Odyssey*, an enchantress who turned men to swine.

**cir·cle** (sũr′k'l), *n.* [< Gr. *kirkos*], 1. a plane figure bounded by a curved line every point of which is equally distant from the center. 2. this curved line. 3. anything like a circle, as a ring. 4. a cycle; complete or recurring series. 5. a group of people with common interests. *v.t.* [-CLED, -CLING], 1. to form a circle around. 2. to move around, as in a circle. *v.i.* to go around in a circle.

**cir′clet** (-klit), *n.* 1. a small circle. 2. a circular band for the finger, etc.

**cir·cuit** (sũr′kit), *n.* [< L. *circum-*, around + *ire*, go], 1. a boundary line or its length. 2. a going around something. 3. the regular journey through a district of a person in his work. 4. a chain of theaters. 5. a path over which electric current may flow.

**circuit breaker,** a device that automatically interrupts the flow of electric current.

**cir·cu·i·tous** (sẽr-kū′i-təs), *adj.* roundabout; indirect. **—cir·cu′i·tous·ly,** *adv.*

**cir·cuit·ry** (sũr′kə-tri), *n.* the system of an electric circuit, or the elements comprising such a circuit, as in a computer.

**cir·cu·lar** (sũr′kyoo-lẽr), *adj.* 1. in the shape of a circle; round. 2. moving in a circle. 3. roundabout; circuitous. *n.* a letter, advertisement, etc. intended for a number of people. **—cir′cu·lar·ly,** *adv.*

**cir′cu·lar·ize′** (-īz′), *v.t.* [-IZED, -IZING], 1. to make round. 2. to send circulars to.

**cir·cu·late** (sũr′kyoo-lāt′), *v.i.* [-LATED, -LATING], [< LL. *circulari*, form a circle], 1. to move in a circle or circuit and return, as the blood. 2. to move around from person to person or from place to place, as money. *v.t.* to cause to circulate. **—cir′cu·la′tor,** *n.* **—cir′cu·la·to′ry** (-lə-tôr′i), *adj.*

**cir′cu·la′tion,** *n.* 1. a circulating. 2. the movement of the blood in the veins and arteries throughout the body. 3. the distribution of newspapers, magazines, etc. among readers. **—cir′cu·la′tive,** *adj.*

**circum-,** [< L. *circum*], a prefix meaning *around, about, surrounding.*

**cir·cum·cise** (sũr′kəm-sīz′), *v.t.* [-CISED, -CISING], [< L. *circum-*, around + *caedere*, to cut], to cut off all or part of the foreskin of. **—cir′cum·ci′sion** (-sizh′ən), *n.*

**cir·cum·fer·ence** (sẽr-kum′fẽr-əns), *n.* [< L. *circum-*, around + *ferre*, carry], 1. the line bounding a circle or other rounded surface. 2. the measurement of this line; distance around.

**cir·cum·flex** (sũr′kəm-fleks′), *n.* [< L. *circum-*, around + *flectere*, to bend], a mark (^, ⌒, ~) used over a vowel to indicate a particular pronunciation.

**cir′cum·lo·cu′tion** (-lō-kū′shən), *n.* [< L. *circum-*, around + *loqui*, speak], a roundabout way of expressing something.

**cir′cum·nav′i·gate′** (-nav′ə-gāt′), *v.t.* [-GATED, -GATING], [< L.; see CIRCUM- & NAVIGATE], to sail around (the earth, etc.). **—cir′cum·nav′i·ga′tion,** *n.*

**cir′cum·scribe′** (-skrīb′), *v.t.* [-SCRIBED, -SCRIBING], [< L.; see CIRCUM- & SCRIBE], 1. to trace a line around; encompass. 2. to limit; confine. **—cir′cum·scrip′tion,** *n.*

**cir′cum·spect′** (-spekt′), *adj.* [< L. *circum-*, around + *specere*, look], cautious; discreet. **—cir′cum·spec′tion,** *n.*

**cir′cum·stance′** (-stans′), *n.* [< L. *circum-*, around + *stare*, stand], 1. a fact or event accompanying another or involved in a situation. 2. *pl.* conditions affecting one, esp. financial conditions: as, in tight *circumstances*. 3. ceremony; show: as, pomp and *circumstance*. **—under no circumstances,** never. **—under the circumstances,** conditions being what they are.

**cir′cum·stan′tial** (-stan′shəl), *adj.* 1. having to do with, or depending on, circumstances. 2. full of details; complete.

**circumstantial evidence,** in *law*, proof of attendant circumstances used as evidence to infer a principal fact.

**cir′cum·vent′** (-vent′), *v.t.* [< L. *circum-*, around + *venire*, come], to get the better of or prevent by skill or trickery. **—cir′cum·ven′tion,** *n.*

**cir·cus** (sũr′kəs), *n.* [< Gr. *kirkos*, a circle], 1. in ancient Rome, an amphitheater. 2. a traveling show of acrobats, wild animals, clowns, etc. 3. [Colloq.], any riotously entertaining person, thing, etc.

**cir·rho·sis** (si-rō′sis), *n.* [< Gr. *kirrhos*, tawny: after the yellowish diseased liver], a degenerative disease, esp. of the liver, marked by excess formation of connective tissue. **—cir·rhot′ic** (-rot′ik), *adj.*

**cir·rus** (sir′əs), *n.* [*pl.* -RI (-ī)], [L., a curl], 1. in *biology*, *a*) a plant tendril. *b*) a threadlike appendage, as a feeler. 2. a formation of filmy, fleecy clouds, generally whitish. **—cir′rose** (-ōs), **cir′rous** (-əs), *adj.*

**cis·tern** (sis′tẽrn), *n.* [< L. *cista*, chest], a large tank for storing water, esp. rain water.

**cit·a·del** (sit′ə-d'l, -del′), *n.* [< L. *civitas*, state], 1. a fortress. 2. a refuge.

**ci·ta·tion** (sī-tā′shən), *n.* 1. a citing; quoting. 2. a passage cited; quotation. 3. honorable mention for meritorious service.

**cite** (sīt), *v.t.* [CITED, CITING], [< L. *citare*, summon], 1. to summon before a court of law. 2. to quote. 3. to mention by way of example, proof, etc. 4. to mention in an official report for meritorious service.

**cit·i·fied** (sit′i-fīd′), *adj.* having the ways, dress, etc. of city people.

**cit·i·zen** (sit′ə-z'n), *n.* [< L. *civis*, citizen], a member of a state or nation who owes allegiance to it by birth or naturalization and is entitled to full civil rights. **—cit′i·zen·ship′,** *n.*

**cit′i·zen·ry** (-ri), *n.* [*pl.* -RIES], citizens collectively.

**cit·ric** (sit′rik), *adj.* designating or of an acid obtained from citrus fruits.

**cit·ron** (sit′rən), *n.* [Fr., lemon; see CITRUS], 1. a yellow, thick-skinned fruit resembling a lemon. 2. the candied rind of this fruit.

**cit·ron·el·la** (sit′rə-nel′ə), *n.* [see CITRON], a sharp-smelling oil used to keep insects away.

**cit·rus** (sit′rəs), *n.* [L.], 1. any of the trees that bear oranges, lemons, limes, etc. 2. any such fruit. *adj.* of these trees: also **cit′rous.**

**cit·y** (sit′i), *n.* [*pl.* -IES], [< L. *civis*, citizen], 1. a large, important town. 2. in the U.S., an incorporated municipality whose boundaries, powers, etc. are defined by State charter. 3. all the people of a city.

**city hall,** a building housing a municipal government.

**civ·et** (siv′it), *n.* [< Ar. *zabād*], a yellowish, fatty secretion of a catlike, flesh-eating animal (**civet cat**) of Africa and S Asia: used in making perfume.

**civ·ic** (siv′ik), *adj.* [< L. *civis,* citizen], 1. of a city. 2. of citizens. 3. of citizenship.
**civ′ics** (-iks), *n.pl.* [construed as sing.], the study of civic affairs and the rights and duties of citizenship.
**civ·il** (siv′'l, -il), *adj.* [see CIVIC], 1. of a citizen or citizens. 2. of a community of citizens. 3. polite. 4. civilized. 5. not military or ecclesiastical. **—civ′il·ly,** *adv.*
**civil engineering,** engineering dealing with the construction of bridges, roads, etc. **—civil engineer.**
**ci·vil·ian** (sə-vil′yən), *n.* [see CIVIC], a person not in the armed forces. *adj.* of civilians.
**ci·vil·i·ty** (sə-vil′ə-ti), *n.* [*pl.* -TIES], 1. courtesy; consideration. 2. a civil, or polite, act.
**civ·i·li·za·tion** (siv′'l-i-zā′shən), *n.* 1. a civilizing or becoming civilized. 2. the total culture of a people, period, etc. 3. the peoples considered to have reached a high state of cultural and social development.
**civ·i·lize** (siv′'l-iz′), *v.t.* [-LIZED, -LIZING], [see CIVIC], to bring out of a condition of savagery or barbarism.
**civ′i·lized′,** *adj.* 1. advanced in social organization and the arts and sciences. 2. cultured; refined.
**civil law,** the body of law having to do with private rights.
**civil liberties,** liberties guaranteed to the individual by law; rights of thinking, speaking, and acting without hindrance except in the interests of the public welfare.
**civil rights,** those rights guaranteed to the individual, esp. by the 13th and 14th amendments to the U.S. Constitution.
**civil service,** all those employed in government administration except in the armed forces, legislature, or judiciary. **—civil servant.**
**civil war,** war between different factions of the same nation. **—the Civil War,** the war between the North and the South in the U.S. (1861-1865).
**Cl,** in *chem.,* chlorine.
**clack** (klak), *v.i. & v.t.* [echoic], to make or cause to make an abrupt, sharp sound. *n.* this sound. **—clack′er,** *n.*
**clad** (klad), occas. pt. and pp. of **clothe.** *adj.* clothed; dressed.
**claim** (klām), *v.t.* [< L. *clamare,* cry out], 1. to demand as rightfully belonging to one. 2. to require; deserve: as, this problem *claims* our attention. 3. to assert; maintain. *n.* 1. a claiming. 2. a right to something. 3. something claimed. **—claim′a·ble,** *adj.* **—claim′ant, claim′er,** *n.*
**clair·voy·ance** (klâr-voi′əns), *n.* [Fr. < *clair,* clear + *voir,* see], the supposed ability to perceive things that are not in sight. **—clair·voy′ant,** *n. & adj.*
**clam** (klam), *n.* [< earlier *clam,* a clamp], a hard-shelled bivalve mollusk. *v.i.* [CLAMMED, CLAMMING], to dig for clams.
**clam·ber** (klam′bẽr), *v.i. & v.t.* [ME. *clamberen*], to climb by using both hands and feet, esp. in a clumsy way.
**clam·my** (klam′i), *adj.* [-MIER, -MIEST], [< AS. *clam,* clay], moist, cold, and sticky. **—clam′mi·ness,** *n.*
**clam·or** (klam′ẽr), *n.* [< L. *clamare,* cry out], 1. a loud outcry; uproar. 2. a noisy demand or complaint. *v.i.* to make a clamor. **—clam′or·ous,** *adj.*
**clamp** (klamp), *n.* [< LG. *klampe*], a device for clasping or fastening things together. *v.t.* to fasten or brace with a clamp. **—clamp down (on),** [Colloq.], to be stricter (with).
**clan** (klan), *n.* [< Gael. < L. *planta,* offshoot], 1. a group of families claiming descent from a common ancestor. 2. a group of people with interests in common; clique. **—clan′nish,** *adj.* **—clans·man** (klanz′mən) [*pl.* -MEN], *n.*
**clan·des·tine** (klan-des′tin), *adj.* [< L. *clam,* secret], secret or hidden; underhand.
**clang** (klaŋ), *v.i. & v.t.* [echoic], to make or cause to make a loud, sharp, ringing sound, as by striking metal. *n.* this sound.
**clan·gor** (klaŋ′gẽr), *n.* [L. < *clangere*], 1. a clang. 2. a persistent clanging.
**clank** (klaŋk), *n.* [echoic], a sharp, metallic sound. *v.i. & v.t.* to make or cause to make this sound.
**clap** (klap), *v.i.* [CLAPPED, CLAPPING], [AS. *clæppan,* to beat], 1. to make the explosive sound of two flat surfaces struck together. 2. to strike the hands together, as in applause. *v.t.* 1. to strike together briskly. 2. to strike with an open hand. 3. to put, move, etc. abruptly: as, *clapped* into jail. *n.* the sound or act of clapping; sharp blow.
**clap·board** (klab′ẽrd, klap′bôrd′), *n.* [transl. of G. *klapholz* < *klappen,* fit + *holz,* wood], a thin board with one thicker edge, used as siding for frame houses.
**clap′per,** *n.* a thing that makes a clapping sound, as the tongue of a bell.
**clap′trap′,** *n.* [*clap* (applause) + *trap*], insincere, empty talk intended to get applause. *adj.* showy and cheap.
**claque** (klak), *n.* [Fr. < *claquer,* to clap], a group of people paid to applaud.
**clar·et** (klar′ət), *n.* [< L. *clarus,* clear], 1. a dry red wine. 2. purplish red: also **claret red.** *adj.* purplish-red.
**clar·i·fy** (klar′ə-fī′), *v.t. & v.i.* [-FIED, -FYING], [< L. *clarus,* clear + *facere,* make], to make or become clear. **—clar′i·fi·ca′tion,** *n.* **—clar′i·fi′er,** *n.*
**clar·i·net** (klar′ə-net′), *n.* [< Fr.; ult. < L. *clarus,* clear], a single-reed, wood-wind instrument played by means of holes and keys. **—clar′i·net′ist, clar′i·net′tist,** *n.*
**clar·i·on** (klar′i-ən), *adj.* [< L. *clarus,* clear], clear, sharp, and shrill: as, a *clarion* call.
**clar·i·ty** (klar′ə-ti), *n.* [< L. *clarus,* clear], clearness (in various senses).
**clash** (klash), *v.t.* [echoic], to strike with a loud, harsh, metallic noise. *v.i.* 1. to collide, making such a noise. 2. to conflict; disagree. *n.* 1. the sound of clashing. 2. conflict; disagreement.
**clasp** (klasp, kläsp), *n.* [ME. *claspe*], 1. a fastening, as a hook, to hold things together. 2. a grasping; embrace. 3. a grip of the hand. *v.t.* 1. to fasten with a clasp. 2. to hold or embrace tightly. 3. to grip with the hand. **—clasp′er,** *n.*
**class** (klas, kläs), *n.* [< L. *classis*], 1. a number of people or things grouped together because of likenesses; kind; sort. 2. social rank: as, the working *class.* 3. a group of students meeting together for instruction; also, a group graduating together. 4. grade or quality: as, first *class.* 5. [Slang], excellence, as of style. *v.t.* to classify. *v.i.* to be classed.
**clas·sic** (klas′ik), *adj.* [< L. *classis,* class], 1. most representative of the excellence of its kind. 2. of the art, literature, etc. of the ancient Greeks and Romans. 3. balanced, formal, simple, etc. 4. [Colloq.], famous as traditional or typical. *n.* 1. a literary or artistic work of the highest excellence. 2. a creator of such works. 3. [Colloq.], a famous traditional or typical event. **—the classics,** ancient Greek and Roman literature.
**clas′si·cal** (-i-k'l), *adj.* 1. classic (senses 1, 2, 3). 2. versed in Greek and Roman literature, etc. 3. designating or of music conforming to certain standards of form, complexity, etc. 4. standard and traditional: as, *classical* economics. **—clas′si·cal′i·ty** (-kal′ə-ti), *n.* **—clas′si·cal·ly,** *adv.*
**clas′si·cism** (-ə-siz'm), *n.* 1. the aesthetic principles and methods characteristic of ancient Greece and Rome. 2. adherence to

these principles. Also **clas′si·cal·ism.** —**—clas′si·cist, clas′si·cal·ist,** ***n.***
**clas·si·fy** (klas′ə-fī′), ***v.t.*** [-FIED, -FYING], 1. to arrange in classes according to a system. 2. to designate (a government document) as secret or restricted. **—clas′si·fi·ca′tion,** ***n.***
**class′mate′,** ***n.*** a member of the same class at a school or college.
**clat·ter** (klat′ẽr), ***n.*** [AS. *clatrung*], 1. a rapid succession of loud, sharp noises. 2. a tumult; hubbub. ***v.i. & v.t.*** to make or cause to make a clatter.
**clause** (klôz), ***n.*** [< L. *claudere*, to close], 1. a group of words containing a subject and verb: cf. **main clause, subordinate clause.** 2. a particular article in a document.
**claus·tro·pho·bi·a** (klôs′trə-fō′bi-ə), ***n.*** [< L. *claustrum*, enclosure; + *-phobia*], a fear of being in enclosed places.
**clav·i·chord** (klav′ə-kôrd′), ***n.*** [< L. *clavis*, key + *chorda*, string], a stringed musical instrument with a keyboard: predecessor of the piano.
**clav·i·cle** (klav′ə-k′l), ***n.*** [< L. *clavis*, key], a bone connecting the sternum with the shoulder blade; collarbone.
**claw** (klô), ***n.*** [AS. *clawu*], 1. a sharp, hooked nail on an animal's or bird's foot. 2. the pincers of a crab, etc. ***v.t. & v.i.*** to scratch, clutch, etc. as with claws.
**clay** (klā), ***n.*** [AS. *clæg*], 1. a firm, plastic earth, used in making pottery, etc. 2. *a*) earth. *b*) the human body. **—clay′ey** [CLAYIER, CLAYIEST], ***adj.*** **—clay′ish,** ***adj.***
**-cle,** [< L. dim. suffix *-culus, -cula, -culum*], a diminutive suffix, as in *particle*.
**clean** (klēn), ***adj.*** [AS. *clæne*], 1. free from dirt and impurities; unsoiled. 2. morally pure. 3. habitually avoiding filth. 4. free from flaws; clear. 5. entire; complete. ***adv.*** completely. ***v.t. & v.i.*** to make clean. **—clean up,** 1. to make clean or neat. 2. [Colloq.], to finish. 3. [Slang], to make much profit. **—come clean,** [Slang], to confess. **—clean′ness,** ***n.***
**clean′-cut′,** ***adj.*** 1. clearly outlined. 2. well-formed. 3. trim, neat, etc.
**clean′er,** ***n.*** a person or thing that cleans; esp., one who dry-cleans.
**clean·ly** (klen′li), ***adj.*** [-LIER, -LIEST], 1. having clean habits. 2. always kept clean. ***adv.*** (klēn′li), in a clean manner. **—clean′li·ness** (klen′-), ***n.***
**cleanse** (klenz), ***v.t.*** [CLEANSED, CLEANSING], [AS. *clænsian*], to make clean or pure. **—cleans′er,** ***n.***
**clear** (klêr), ***adj.*** [< L. *clarus*], 1. bright; free from clouds. 2. transparent. 3. easily seen or heard; distinct. 4. orderly: as, a *clear* mind. 5. not obscure; obvious. 6. certain; positive. 7. free from guilt. 8. free from charges; net. 9. free from obstruction; open. 10. free from debt. ***adv.*** in a clear manner. ***v.t.*** 1. to make clear. 2. to free from impurities, obstructions, etc. 3. to make lucid. 4. to open: as, to *clear* a path. 5. to get rid of. 6. to prove the innocence of. 7. to pass or leap over, by, etc. 8. to make as profit. ***v.i.*** to become clear. **—clear away** (or **off**), 1. to remove so as to leave a cleared space. 2. to go away. **—clear out,** [Colloq.], to depart. **—clear up,** to make or become clear. **—in the clear,** 1. in the open. 2. [Colloq.], guiltless. **—clear′ly,** ***adv.*** **—clear′ness,** ***n.***
**clear′ance** (-əns), ***n.*** 1. the clear space between an object and that which it is passing. 2. in *banking*, the adjustment of accounts in a clearinghouse.
**clear′-cut′,** ***adj.*** 1. clearly outlined. 2. distinct; plain.
**clear′ing,** ***n.*** a plot of land cleared of trees.
**clear′ing·house′,** ***n.*** an office maintained by several banks as a center for exchanging checks, balancing accounts, etc.
**clear′sight′ed,** ***adj.*** 1. seeing clearly. 2. understanding or thinking clearly.
**cleat** (klēt), ***n.*** [< AS.], a piece of wood or metal fastened to something to strengthen it or give secure footing.
**cleav·age** (klēv′ij), ***n.*** 1. a cleaving; splitting; dividing. 2. a cleft; fissure.
**cleave** (klēv), ***v.t. & v.i.*** [CLEFT or CLEAVED or CLOVE, CLEFT or CLEAVED or CLOVEN, CLEAVING], [AS. *cleofan*], 1. to divide by a blow; split; sever. 2. to pierce.
**cleave** (klēv), ***v.i.*** [CLEAVED, CLEAVING], [AS. *cleofian*], 1. to adhere; cling. 2. to be faithful (*to*).
**cleav′er,** ***n.*** a heavy, sharp-edged cleaving tool used by butchers.
**clef** (klef), ***n.*** [Fr. < L. *clavis*, key], a symbol used in music to indicate the pitch of the notes on the staff.
**cleft** (kleft), pt. and pp. of **cleave** (to split). ***adj.*** split; divided. ***n.*** an opening made by cleaving; crack; fissure.
**clem·a·tis** (klem′ə-tis), ***n.*** [< Gr. *klēma*, vine], a vine of the crowfoot family with bright-colored flowers.
**clem·en·cy** (klem′ən-si), ***n.*** [*pl.* -CIES], [see CLEMENT], 1. leniency; mercy. 2. mildness, as of weather.
**clem·ent** (klem′ənt), ***adj.*** [L. *clemens*], 1. lenient; merciful. 2. mild, as weather.
**clench** (klench), ***v.t.*** [< AS. (*be*) *clencan*, make cling], 1. to close firmly, as the teeth or fist. 2. to grip tightly. ***n.*** a firm grip.
**clere·sto·ry** (klêr′stôr′i), ***n.*** [*pl.* -RIES], [*clere* (for *clear*) + *story* (floor)], the wall of a church rising above the roofs of the flanking aisles and containing windows.
**cler·gy** (klũr′ji), ***n.*** [*pl.* -GIES], [see CLERK], ministers, priests, etc., collectively.
**cler′gy·man** (-mən), ***n.*** [*pl.* -MEN], a member of the clergy; minister, priest, etc.
**cler·ic** (kler′ik), ***n.*** [see CLERK], a clergyman. ***adj.*** of a clergyman or the clergy.
**cler′i·cal** (-i-k′l), ***adj.*** 1. of a clergyman or the clergy. 2. of an office clerk or clerks; of office work. **—cler′i·cal·ly,** ***adv.***
**clerk** (klũrk), ***n.*** [< Gr. *klēros*, clergy], 1. a layman with minor duties in a church. 2. an office worker who keeps accounts and records: in public service, other duties may be involved. 3. a salesperson in a store. ***v.i.*** to work as a clerk. **—clerk′ing,** ***n.***
**clev·er** (klev′ẽr), ***adj.*** [? < AS. *clifian*, cleave], 1. skillful; adroit; dexterous. 2. intelligent; smart. **—clev′er·ly,** ***adv.*** **—clev′er·ness,** ***n.***
**clew** (kloo͞), ***n.*** [< AS. *cleowen*], 1. a ball of thread or yarn. 2. something that leads out of a maze or helps to solve a problem: usually sp. **clue.**
**cli·ché** (klē-shā′), ***n.*** [*pl.* -CHÉS (-shāz′)], [Fr. < *clicher*, to stereotype], a trite expression or idea.
**click** (klik), ***n.*** [echoic], a slight, sharp sound like that of a door latch snapping into place. ***v.i. & v.t.*** to make or cause to make a click.
**cli·ent** (klī′ənt), ***n.*** [< L. *cliens*, follower], 1. a person or company in whose behalf a lawyer, accountant, etc. acts. 2. a customer.
**cli·en·tele** (klī′ən-tel′), ***n.*** [Fr. < L. *clientela*], clients or customers, collectively.
**cliff** (klif), ***n.*** [AS. *clif*], a high, steep rock or face of rock.
**cli·mac·ter·ic** (klī-mak′tẽr-ik), ***n.*** [< Gr. *klimax*, ladder], a crucial period in life, esp. the menopause in women. ***adj.*** crucial.
**cli·mate** (klī′mit), ***n.*** [< Gr. *klima*, region], 1. the prevailing weather conditions of a place. 2. a region with reference to its prevailing weather.—**cli·mat′ic** (-mat′ik), ***adj.***
**cli·max** (klī′maks), ***n.*** [< Gr. *klimax*, ladder], 1. a series of ideas or events progressively increasing in force. 2. the final, culminating element in such a series. 3. the highest point, as of interest; culmination. ***v.i. & v.t.*** to

reach, or bring to, a climax. **—cli·mac'tic** (-mak'tik), *adj.*
**climb** (klīm), *v.i. & v.t.* [CLIMBED, CLIMBING], [AS. *climban*], 1. to move up, esp. by using the hands and feet. 2. to ascend gradually. 3. to grow upward. *n.* 1. a climbing. 2. a thing or place to be climbed. **—climb down,** to descend. **—climb'er,** *n.*
**clime** (klīm), *n.* [see CLIMATE], [Poetic], a region; realm; climate.
**clinch** (klinch), *v.t.* [var. of *clench*], 1. to fasten (a driven nail, bolt, etc.) by bending the projecting end. 2. to settle (an argument, bargain, etc.) definitely. *v.i.* in *boxing*, to grip the opponent with the arms so as to hinder his punching. *n.* a clinching.
**clinch'er,** *n.* 1. one who clinches. 2. [Colloq.], a decisive point, as in argument.
**cling** (kliŋ), *v.i.* [CLUNG, CLINGING], [AS. *clingan*], 1. to adhere; hold fast, as by embracing. 2. to be or stay near. **—cling'er,** *n.* **—cling'ing,** *adj. & n.* **—cling'y,** *adj.*
**clin·ic** (klin'ik), *n.* [< Gr. *klinē*, bed], 1. the teaching of medicine by treating patients in the presence of students. 2. a place where medical specialists practice as a group. 3. an outpatient department, as of a hospital, often offering free treatment.
**clin'i·cal** (-i-k'l), *adj.* 1. of or connected with a clinic. 2. having to do with the treatment and observation of disease in patients, as distinguished from theoretical study.
**clink** (kliŋk), *v.i. & v.t.* [echoic], to make or cause to make a slight, sharp sound, as of glass struck. *n.* 1. such a sound. 2. [Colloq.], a jail.
**clink·er** (kliŋk'ẽr), *n.* [D. *klinker*], 1. a very hard brick. 2. a hard mass of fused matter, as from burned coal.
**clip** (klip), *v.t.* [CLIPPED, CLIPPING], [< ON. *klippa*], 1. to cut as with shears. 2. to cut short. 3. to cut the hair of. 4. [Colloq.], to hit sharply. 5. [Slang], to swindle. *v.i.* [Colloq.], to move rapidly. *n.* 1. a clipping. 2. a thing clipped. 3. [Colloq.], a quick, sharp punch. 4. [Colloq.], rapid pace.
**clip** (klip), *v.i. & v.t.* [CLIPPED, CLIPPING], [AS. *clyppan*, to embrace], to grip tightly; fasten. *n.* anything that clips or fastens.
**clip·per** (klip'ẽr), *n.* 1. *often pl.* a tool for cutting or shearing. 2. a sailing ship built and rigged for great speed.
**clip'ping,** *n.* a piece cut out or off, as an item cut from a newspaper.
**clique** (klēk), *n.* [Fr. < *cliquer*, make a noise], a small, exclusive circle of people; coterie. **—cli'quish,** *adj.* **—cli'quish·ly,** *adv.*
**cloak** (klōk), *n.* [< LL. *clocca*, bell: from its shape], 1. a loose, usually sleeveless outer garment. 2. something that covers or conceals; disguise. *v.t.* 1. to cover with a cloak. 2. to conceal; hide.
**cloak'room',** *n.* a room where hats, coats, etc. can be left temporarily.
**clob·ber** (klob'ẽr), *v.t.* [< ?], [Slang], to beat repeatedly; maul.
**cloche** (klōsh; Fr. klôsh), *n.* [Fr. < LL. *clocca*, bell], a closefitting, bell-shaped hat for women.
**clock** (klok), *n.* [ME. *clocke*, orig., clock with bells < LL. *clocca*, bell], a device for measuring time, usually by means of pointers moving over a dial. *v.t.* to record the time of (a race, etc.) with a stop watch.
**clock** (klok), *n.* [prob. < prec., because orig. bell-shaped], a woven or embroidered ornament on the side of a stocking, going up from the ankle.
**clock'wise'** (-wīz'), *adv. & adj.* in the direction in which the hands of a clock rotate.
**clock'work'** (-wũrk'), *n.* 1. the mechanism of a clock. 2. any similar mechanism, with springs and gears. **—like clockwork,** regularly and precisely.
**clod** (klod), *n.* [AS. *clott*, var. of *clot*], 1. a lump, esp. of earth or clay. 2. a dull, stupid fellow. **—clod'dish,** *adj.*
**clod'hop'per,** *n.* [*clod* + *hopper*], 1. a plowman. 2. a clumsy fellow; boor. 3. a coarse, heavy shoe.
**clog** (klog), *n.* [ME. *clogge*, lump of wood], 1. anything that hinders or obstructs. 2. a heavy shoe, usually with a wooden sole. *v.t.* [CLOGGED, CLOGGING], 1. to hinder; impede. 2. to obstruct (a passage); block up. *v.i.* to become blocked up.
**clois·ter** (klois'tẽr), *n.* [< L. *claudere*, to close], 1. a place of religious seclusion; monastery or convent. 2. a covered walk along an inside wall with a columned opening along one side. *v.t.* to confine as in a cloister. **—clois'tered,** *adj.* **—clois'tral** *adj.*
**close** (klōs), *adj.* [CLOSER, CLOSEST], [see CLOSE, *v.*], 1. confined or confining: as, *close* quarters. 2. hidden; secluded. 3. secretive; reserved. 4. stingy; niggardly. 5. confined in circulation; humid; stuffy. 6. with little space between; near together. 7. compact; dense: as, a *close* weave. 8. near to the surface: as, a *close* shave. 9. intimate; familiar: as, a *close* friend. 10. strict; thorough; careful: as, *close* attention. 11. nearly alike: as, a *close* resemblance. 12. nearly equal in balance, outcome, etc.: as, a *close* contest. *adv.* in a close manner or position. *n.* an enclosed place. **—close'ly,** *adv.* **—close'ness,** *n.*
**close** (klōz), *v.t.* [CLOSED, CLOSING], [< L. *claudere*, to close], 1. to shut. 2. to stop up (an opening). 3. to finish; conclude. *v.i.* 1. to become shut. 2. to end; finish. 3. to come close, as in order to attack. *n.* an end; conclusion. **—close down** (or **up**), to shut or stop entirely. **—close in,** to draw near from various directions.
**close call** (klōs), [Colloq.], a narrow escape from danger or misfortune: also **close shave.**
**close·fist·ed** (klōs'fis'tid), *adj.* stingy.
**close-mouthed** (klōs'mouthd', -moutht'), *adj.* not talking much; taciturn.
**clos·et** (kloz'it), *n.* [< L. *claudere*, to close], 1. a small room or cupboard for clothes, supplies, etc. 2. a small room for privacy. *v.t.* to shut up in a private room for confidential talk.
**close-up** (klōs'up'), *n.* a photograph taken at very close range.
**clo·sure** (klō'zhẽr), *n.* [< L. *claudere*, to close], 1. a closing or being closed. 2. a finish; end. 3. anything that closes. 4. the parliamentary procedure by which debate is closed and the measure brought up for immediate vote.
**clot** (klot), *n.* [AS. *clott*], a thick, coagulated mass, as of blood. *v.t. & v.i.* [CLOTTED, CLOTTING], to become or cause to become a clot; coagulate.
**cloth** (klôth), *n.* [*pl.* CLOTHS (klô*th*z, klôths)], [AS. *clath*], 1. a woven, knitted, or pressed fabric of fibrous material, as cotton, wool, silk, etc. 2. a tablecloth, washcloth, dustcloth, etc. 3. the identifying dress of a profession. *adj.* made of cloth. **—the cloth,** the clergy.
**clothe** (klō*th*), *v.t.* [CLOTHED or CLAD, CLOTHING], [see CLOTH], 1. to provide with or dress in clothes. 2. to cover: as, *clothed* in glory.
**clothes** (klōz, klō*th*z), *n.pl.* [see CLOTH], 1. clothing; wearing apparel. 2. bedclothes.
**clothes'pin',** *n.* a small clip of wood or plastic, for fastening clothes on a line.
**cloth·ier** (klō*th*'yẽr), *n.* a dealer in clothes or cloth.
**cloth·ing** (klō*th*'iŋ), *n.* 1. clothes; wearing apparel. 2. a covering.
**clo·ture** (klō'chẽr), *n.* closure: applied to parliamentary debate.
**cloud** (kloud), *n.* [AS. *clud*, mass of rock], 1. a visible mass of vapor in the sky. 2. a

mass of smoke, dust, steam, etc. 3. a great number of moving things: as, a *cloud* of locusts. 4. anything that darkens, obscures, etc. ***v.t.*** 1. to darken or obscure as with clouds. 2. to make gloomy. 3. to sully. ***v.i.*** 1. to become cloudy. 2. to become gloomy. **—in the clouds,** 1. fanciful; impractical. 2. in a reverie. **—under a cloud,** under suspicion. **—cloud′less,** ***adj.*** **—cloud′y** [-IER, -IEST], ***adj.***
**cloud′burst′** (-bũrst′), ***n.*** a sudden, unusually heavy rain.
**clout** (klout), ***n.*** [AS. *clut*, a patch], [Colloq.], a blow, as with the hand. ***v.t.*** [Colloq.], to strike, as with the hand; hit.
**clove** (klōv), ***n.*** [< L. *clavus*, nail: from its shape], 1. the dried flower bud of a tropical evergreen tree. 2. a pungent, fragrant spice obtained from these buds. 3. the tree.
**clove** (klōv), ***n.*** [AS. *clufu*], a segment of a bulb, as of garlic.
**clove** (klōv), alt. pt. of **cleave** (split).
**clo·ven** (klō′v'n), alt. pp. of **cleave** (split). ***adj.*** divided; split.
**clo·ver** (klō′vẽr), ***n.*** [AS. *clafre*], any of various herbs with leaves in three parts and small flowers in dense heads: some are used for forage. **—in clover,** living a luxurious, carefree life.
**clo′ver·leaf′** (-lēf′), ***n.*** [*pl.* -LEAVES (-lēvz′)], a multiple highway intersection in the form of a four-leaf clover, permitting traffic to move unhindered in any of four directions.
**clown** (kloun), ***n.*** [< LG. source], 1. a clumsy, rude person; boor. 2. a man who entertains by antics, jokes, etc., as in a circus. ***v.i.*** 1. to perform as a clown. 2. to joke, act silly, etc. **—clown′ish,** ***adj.***
**cloy** (kloi), ***v.t.*** [ME. *acloien*, stop up (with a nail); ult. < L. *clavus*, nail], to surfeit by too much, esp. of anything too sweet, rich, etc.
**club** (klub), ***n.*** [< ON. *klubba*, mass], 1. a heavy stick used as a weapon. 2. any stick used in a game, as golf, polo, etc. 3. *a*) a group of people associated for a common purpose. *b*) its meeting place. 4. any of a suit of playing cards marked with a black trefoil (♣). 5. *pl.* this suit. ***v.t.*** [CLUBBED, CLUBBING], to strike as with a club. ***v.i.*** to unite for a common purpose.
**club′foot′,** ***n.*** [*pl.* -FEET], a congenitally misshapen, often clublike, foot. **—club′-foot′ed,** ***adj.***
**cluck** (kluk), ***v.i.*** [echoic], to make the sound of a hen calling her chicks. ***n.*** this sound.
**clue** (kloo), ***n.*** a clew (sense 2).
**clump** (klump), ***n.*** [< LG. *klump*], 1. a lump; mass. 2. a cluster, as of trees. 3. the sound of heavy footsteps. ***v.i.*** 1. to tramp heavily. 2. to form clumps. **—clump′ish,** ***adj.*** **—clump′y** [-IER, -IEST], ***adj.***
**clum·sy** (klum′zi), ***adj.*** [-SIER, -SIEST], [ME. *clumsid*, numb with cold], 1. lacking grace or skill; awkward. 2. awkwardly shaped or made. **—clum′si·ly,** ***adv.*** **—clum′si·ness,** ***n.***
**clung** (kluŋ), pt. and pp. of **cling.**
**clus·ter** (klus′tẽr), ***n.*** [AS. *clyster*], a number of persons or things grouped together. ***v.i.* & *v.t.*** to gather or grow in a cluster.
**clutch** (kluch), ***v.t.*** [AS. *clyccan*, clench], to snatch with a hand or claw. ***v.i.*** to snatch or seize (*at*). ***n.*** 1. *usually pl.* power; control. 2. a grasp; grip. 3. a device for engaging and disengaging a motor or engine.
**clutch** (kluch), ***n.*** [< ON. *klekja*, hatch], 1. a nest of eggs. 2. a brood of chicks.
**clut·ter** (klut′ẽr), ***n.*** [< *clot*], a jumble; confusion. ***v.t.*** to put into disorder; litter.
**Cm,** in *chem.*, curium.
**cm.,** centimeter(s).
**co-,** a shortened form of *com-*, meaning: 1. *together, with*, as in *co-operation*. 2. *joint*, as in *co-owner*. 3. *equally*, as in *coextensive*.
**Co,** in *chem.*, cobalt.
**Co., co.,** [*pl.* COS.], 1. company. 2. county.
**C.O.,** Commanding Officer.
**c/o, c.o.,** care of.
**coach** (kōch), ***n.*** [< *Kócs*, city in Hungary], 1. a large, covered, four-wheeled carriage. 2. a railroad passenger car. 3. a bus. 4. one who instructs and trains students, athletes, dramatic groups, etc. ***v.t.*** to instruct and train (students, etc.). ***v.i.*** to act as a coach. **—coach′man** (-mən) [*pl.* -MEN], ***n.***
**co·ad·ju·tor** (kō-aj′ə-tẽr), ***n.*** [< L. *co-*, together + *adjuvare*, help], an assistant, esp. to a bishop.
**co·ag·u·late** (kō-ag′yoo-lāt′), ***v.t.*** [-LATED, -LATING], [< L. *co-*, together + *agere*, move], to cause (a liquid) to become semisolid; clot. ***v.i.*** to become coagulated. **—co·ag′u·la′-tion,** ***n.***
**coal** (kōl), ***n.*** [AS. *col*], 1. a black, combustible mineral used as fuel. 2. a piece of coal. 3. an ember. ***v.t.*** to provide with coal. ***v.i.*** to take in a supply of coal.
**co·a·lesce** (kō′ə-les′), ***v.i.*** [-LESCED, -LESCING], [< L. *co-*, together + *alescere*, grow up], to unite into a single body or group. **—co′-a·les′cence,** ***n.***
**co·a·li·tion** (kō′ə-lish′ən), ***n.*** [see COALESCE], a combination or union, esp. if temporary.
**coal oil,** kerosene.
**coal tar,** a black, thick liquid obtained by the distillation of coal: used in dyes, etc.
**coarse** (kôrs), ***adj.*** [< *course* in sense of "usual"], 1. common; of poor quality. 2. consisting of rather large particles: as, *coarse* sand. 3. rough; harsh. 4. vulgar; unrefined; crude. **—coarse′ly,** ***adv.*** **—coarse′ness,** ***n.***
**coars′en,** ***v.t.* & *v.i.*** to make or become coarse.
**coast** (kōst), ***n.*** [< L. *costa*, rib, side], 1. land alongside the sea; seashore. 2. a slide down an incline, as on a sled. ***v.i.*** 1. to sail near or along the coast. 2. to go down an incline, as on a sled. 3. to continue in motion on momentum. **—coast′al,** ***adj.***
**coast′er,** ***n.*** 1. a person or thing that coasts. 2. a small tray placed under a glass, etc. to protect a table.
**coast guard,** a group of men employed by a government to defend its coasts, aid vessels in distress, etc.
**coast line,** the outline of a coast.
**coat** (kōt), ***n.*** [< LL. *cota*, tunic], 1. a sleeved outer garment opening down the front. 2. the natural covering of a plant or animal. 3. a layer, as of paint, over a surface. ***v.t.*** to cover with a layer.
**coat·ing** (kōt′iŋ), ***n.*** something covering or spread over a surface.
**coat of arms,** a shield marked with the insignia of a family.
**coat′tail′** (-tāl′), ***n.*** either half of the skirt of a coat divided in the back.
**coax** (kōks), ***v.t.* & *v.i.*** [< obs. slang *cokes*, a fool], 1. to urge by soothing words, flattery, etc. 2. to get by coaxing.
**co·ax·i·al** (kō-ak′si-əl), ***adj.*** having a common axis: also **co·ax′al.**
**cob** (kob) ***n.*** [prob. < LG.], 1. a corncob. 2. a male swan. 3. a short, thickset horse.
**co·balt** (kō′bôlt), ***n.*** [< G. < *kobold*, demon of the mines], a hard, steel-gray metallic chemical element, used in alloys: symbol, Co. **—co·bal′tic, co·bal′tous,** ***adj.***
**cobalt blue,** dark blue.
**cob·ble** (kob′'l), ***v.t.*** [< ?], [-BLED, -BLING], 1. to mend (shoes, etc.). 2. to mend or make clumsily.
**cob·ble** (kob′'l), ***n.*** [< ?], a cobblestone. ***v.t.*** [-BLED, -BLING], to pave with cobblestones.
**cob′bler** (-lẽr), ***n.*** 1. one who mends shoes. 2. a deep-dish fruit pie.
**cob′ble·stone′,** ***n.*** a rounded stone formerly used for paving streets.
**co·bra** (kō′brə), ***n.*** [Port.], a very poisonous snake of Asia and Africa.

**cob·web** (kob′web′), *n.* [< ME. *coppe*, spider; + *web*], 1. a web spun by a spider. 2. anything flimsy, gauzy, etc. like this.
**co·ca** (kō′kə), *n.* [Peruv. *cuca*], a tropical shrub of S. America and the West Indies from whose dried leaves cocaine is extracted.
**co·caine, co·cain** (kō-kān′), *n.* [< *coca*], an alkaloid drug, used as a narcotic and local anesthetic.
**coc·cyx** (kok′siks), *n.* [*pl.* COCCYGES (kok-sī′jēz)], [< Gr. *kokkyx*, cuckoo: so called because shaped like a cuckoo's beak], a small, triangular bone at the end of the vertebral column.
**coch·i·neal** (koch′ə-nēl′), *n.* [ult. < L. *coccum*, a (red) berry], a red dye made from the dried bodies of a tropical insect.
**coch·le·a** (kok′li-ə), *n.* [*pl.* -AE (-ē′)], [< Gr. *kochlias*, snail], the spiral-shaped part of the internal ear. —**coch′le·ar,** *adj.*
**cock** (kok), *n.* [AS. *coc*], 1. the male of the chicken; rooster. 2. a male bird. 3. a faucet or valve. 4. *a*) the hammer of a firearm. *b*) its position when set for firing. 5. a jaunty set, as of a hat. *v.t.* 1. to turn on one side; tilt. 2. to raise or turn alertly. 3. to set the hammer of (a gun) in firing position.
**cock** (kok), *n.* [ME. *cokke*], a small cone-shaped pile, as of hay. *v.t.* to pile in cocks.
**cock·ade** (kok-ād′), *n.* [< Fr. *coq*, a cock], a rosette, knot of ribbon, etc. worn on the hat as a badge. —**cock·ad′ed,** *adj.*
**cock-and-bull story** (kok′′n-bool′), an absurd, improbable story.
**cock·a·too** (kok′ə-tōō′), *n.* [*pl.* -TOOS], [< Malay *kakatua*], a large, bright-colored, crested parrot of Australia.
**cock·crow** (kok′krō′), *n.* dawn.
**cock·er·el** (kok′ēr-əl), *n.* a young rooster, not above a year old.
**cock·er (spaniel)** (kok′ēr), [< use in hunting woodcock], a small spaniel with long, silky hair and drooping ears.
**cock·eyed** (kok′īd′), *adj.* [< *cock* (turn on one side)], 1. cross-eyed. 2. [Slang], *a*) lopsided; awry. *b*) fantastically absurd.
**cock·fight** (kok′fīt′), *n.* a fight between gamecocks wearing metal spurs.
**cock′horse′,** *n.* a hobbyhorse.
**cock·le** (kok′′l), *n.* [< Gr. *konchē*, mussel], an edible shellfish with two heart-shaped shells. —**cockles of one's heart,** the depth of one's emotions.
**cock·le** (kok′′l), *n.* [< AS. *coccel*], any of various weeds in grain fields.
**cock′le·shell′,** *n.* the shell of a cockle.
**cock·ney** (kok′ni), *n.* [*pl.* -NEYS], [ME. *cokenei*, fop, townsman], 1. a native of the East End of London, England, speaking a characteristic dialect. 2. this dialect.
**cock·pit** (kok′pit′), *n.* 1. an enclosed space for cockfights. 2. in some airplanes, the space where the pilot sits.
**cock·roach** (kok′rōch′), *n.* [Sp. *cucaracha*], an insect with a flat, brown or black body, a common kitchen pest.
**cocks·comb** (koks′kōm′), *n.* 1. the red, fleshy growth on a rooster's head. 2. a plant with flowers like this.
**cock·sure** (kok′shoor′), *adj.* [*cock* (see COCKY) + *sure*], absolutely sure or too sure.
**cock·tail** (kok′tāl′), *n.* [< ?], 1. a short mixed alcoholic drink, usually iced. 2. an appetizer, as diced fruits, sea food with a sharp sauce, etc.
**cock·y** (kok′i), *adj.* [-IER, IEST], [< *cock* (male bird)], [Colloq.], jauntily conceited. —**cock′i·ly,** *adv.* —**cock′i·ness,** *n.*
**co·co** (kō′kō), *n.* [*pl.* -COS], [Sp. < Gr. *kokkos*, berry], 1. the coconut palm. 2. a coconut.
**co·coa** (kō′kō), *n.* [see CACAO], 1. powder made from roasted cacao seeds. 2. a hot drink made of this powder. 3. reddish-yellow brown.
**co·co·nut, co·coa·nut** (kō′kə-nut′), *n.* the fruit of a tropical tree (**coconut palm**), a thick, brown, oval husk enclosing a layer of edible white meat and a milky fluid.
**co·coon** (kə-kōōn′), *n.* [< L. *coccum*, seed], the silky case which the larvae of some insects spin about themselves as a shelter during the pupa stage.
**cod** (kod), *n.* [*pl.* COD, CODS], [ME.], an important food fish found in the N. Atlantic.
**C.O.D., c.o.d.,** collect on delivery.
**co·da** (kō′də), *n.* [It. < L. *cauda*, tail], in *music*, a final passage.
**cod·dle** (kod′′l), *v.t.* [-DLED, -DLING], [< ?], 1. to cook gently in water not quite boiling. 2. to pamper.
**code** (kōd), *n.* [< L. *codex*, wooden tablet], 1. a body of laws of a nation, etc., arranged systematically. 2. any set of principles: as, a moral *code*. 3. a set of signals for sending messages, as by telegraph, etc. 4. a system of secret writing, using symbols. *v.t.* [CODED, CODING], to put in a code.
**co·de·ine** (kō′di-ēn′, -dēn), *n.* [< Gr. *kodeia*, poppy head], a sedative and pain-reliever derived from opium: also **co′de·in** (-di-in).
**co·dex** (kō′deks), *n.* [*pl.* -DICES (-də-sēz′)], [see CODE], a manuscript volume, esp. of the Scriptures, etc.
**cod′fish′,** *n.* [*pl.* see FISH], the cod.
**codg·er** (koj′ēr), *n.* [< ?], [Colloq.], a queer or peculiar person.
**cod·i·cil** (kod′ə-s'l), *n.* [< L. dim.; see CODE], an addition to a will.
**cod·i·fy** (kod′ə-fī′, kō′də-), *v.i.* [-FIED, -FYING], to arrange (laws, etc.) systematically. —**cod′i·fi·ca′tion,** *n.* —**cod′i·fi′er,** *n.*
**co·ed, co-ed** (kō′ed′), *n.* [Colloq.], a girl attending a coeducational college.
**co·ed·u·ca·tion** (kō′ej-oo-kā′shən), *n.* the educational system in which students of both sexes attend classes together. —**co′ed·u·ca′tion·al,** *adj.*
**co·ef·fi·cient** (kō′ə-fish′ənt), *adj.* [see CO- & EFFECT], co-operating. *n.* 1. a factor that helps to produce a result. 2. in *math.*, a number or symbol prefixed as a multiplier: as, *6* is a *coefficient* in *6ab*.
**co·e·qual** (kō-ē′kwəl), *adj.* & *n.* equal.
**co·erce** (kō-ũrs′), *v.t.* [-ERCED, -ERCING], [< L. *co-*, together + *arcere*, confine], 1. to restrain by force; curb. 2. to force; compel. —**co·er′cion** (-ũr′shən), *n.* —**co·er′ci·ble,** *adj.* —**co·er′cive,** *adj.*
**co·e·val** (kō-ē′v'l), *adj.* & *n.* [< L. *co-*, together + *aevum*, age], contemporary.
**co·ex·ist** (kō′ig-zist′), *v.i.* to exist together, at the same time or in the same place. —**co′ex·ist′ence,** *n.* —**co′ex·ist′ent,** *adj.*
**cof·fee** (kôf′i), *n.* [< Ar. *qahwah*], 1. an aromatic drink made from the roasted and ground beanlike seeds of a tropical shrub of the madder family. 2. the seeds, whole or ground, or the shrub. 3. light brown.
**coffee break,** a brief respite from work when coffee, etc. is taken.
**coffee shop,** a restaurant where coffee and light refreshments are served.
**coffee table,** a small, low table for serving refreshments.
**cof·fer** (kôf′ēr), *n.* [see COFFIN], 1. a chest in which money or valuables are kept. 2. *pl.* a treasury; funds. *v.t.* to enclose in a coffer.
**cof·fin** (kôf′in), *n.* [< Gr. *kophinos*, basket], a case to put a dead person into for burial.
**cog** (kog), *n.* [< Scand.], 1. one of the teeth on a cogwheel. 2. a cogwheel. —**slip a cog,** to make an error.
**co·gent** (kō′jənt), *adj.* [< L. *co-*, together + *agere*, drive], compelling; convincing. —**co′gen·cy,** *n.* —**co′gent·ly,** *adv.*
**cog·i·tate** (koj′ə-tāt′), *v.i.* [-TATED, -TATING], [< L. *cogitare*, ponder], to think seriously; ponder. *v.t.* to think about.—**cog′i·ta′tion,** *n.*

**co·gnac** (kō′nyak), ***n.*** [Fr.], a French brandy.
**cog·nate** (kog′nāt), ***adj.*** [< L. *co-*, together + *(g)nasci*, be born], 1. related by family. 2. derived from a common original form, as two words. 3. having the same nature. ***n.*** 1. a person related to another. 2. a cognate word, language, or thing.
**cog·ni·tion** (kog-nish′ən), ***n.*** [< L. *co-*, together + *(g)noscere*, know], 1. the process of knowing or perceiving; perception. 2. anything that is known or perceived.
**cog·ni·za·ble** (kog′ni-zə-b'l), ***adj.*** 1. that can be recognized, perceived, etc. 2. in *law*, within the jurisdiction of a court.
**cog·ni·zance** (kog′ni-zəns), ***n.*** 1. a being aware; perception; knowledge. 2. notice; heed. **—take cognizance of,** to notice.
**cog′ni·zant** (-zənt), ***adj.*** aware (with *of*).
**cog·no·men** (kog-nō′mən), ***n.*** [L. < *co-*, with + *nomen*, name], 1. a surname. 2. any name; esp., a nickname.
**cog′wheel′,** ***n.*** a wheel rimmed with teeth which mesh with those of another wheel to transmit or receive motion.
**co·hab·it** (kō-hab′it), ***v.i.*** [< L. *co-*, together + *habitare*, dwell], to live together as husband and wife, esp. when not legally married. **—co·hab′i·ta′tion,** ***n.***
**co·heir** (kō-âr′), ***n.*** one who inherits jointly with another or others.
**co·here** (kō-hêr′), ***v.i.*** [-HERED, -HERING], [< L. *co-*, together + *haerere*, to stick], 1. to stick together. 2. to be connected logically.
**co·her′ent** (-ənt), ***adj.*** 1. sticking together. 2. logically connected and intelligible. **—co·her′ence,** ***n.*** **—co·her′ent·ly,** ***adv.***
**co·he·sion** (kō-hē′zhən), ***n.*** a cohering; tendency to stick together. **—co·he′sive** (-siv), ***adj.*** **—co·he′sive·ly,** ***adv.***
**co·hort** (kō′hôrt), ***n.*** [< L. *cohors*, enclosure], 1. a band of soldiers. 2. a group; band. 3. now, often, an associate.
**coif** (koif), ***n.*** [< LL. *cofea*, cap], a cap that fits the head closely.
**coif·fure** (kwä-fyoor′), ***n.*** [< Fr.; see COIF], 1. a headdress. 2. a hair style.
**coil** (koil), ***v.t. & v.i.*** [< L. *com-*, together + *legere*, gather], to wind in a spiral form. ***n.*** 1. anything wound into a series of rings or spirals. 2. such a series or a single turn of it. 3. in *electricity*, a spiral of wire.
**coin** (koin), ***n.*** [< L. *cuneus*, a wedge], a piece of stamped metal, issued by a government as money. ***v.t.*** 1. to make (coins) by stamping (metal). 2. to make up, as a new word. **—coin′er,** ***n.***
**coin′age** (-ij), ***n.*** 1. the act or process of coining. 2. the thing coined. 3. an invented word or expression.
**co·in·cide** (kō′in-sīd′), ***v.i.*** [-CIDED, -CIDING], [< L. *co-*, together + *in-*, in + *cadere*, to fall], 1. to take up the same place in space. 2. to occur at the same time. 3. to agree; match exactly.
**co·in·ci·dence** (kō-in′sə-dəns), ***n.*** 1. a coinciding. 2. an accidental and remarkable occurrence of related or identical events, ideas, etc. at the same time.
**co·in′ci·dent,** ***adj.*** 1. coinciding in space or time. 2. in exact agreement; identical.
**co·in·ci·den·tal** (kō-in′sə-den′t'l), ***adj.*** characterized by coincidence. **—co·in′ci·den′tal·ly,** ***adv.***
**co·i·tus** (kō′i-təs), ***n.*** [< L. *co-*, together + *ire*, go], sexual intercourse: also **co·i·tion** (kō-ish′ən).
**coke** (kōk), ***n.*** [prob. < ME. *colke*, a core], coal from which most of the gases have been removed by heating: used as a fuel.
**col-,** com-: used before *l.*
**Col.,** 1. Colonel. 2. Colorado.
**col·an·der** (kul′ən-dẽr, kol′-), ***n.*** [prob. < L. *colum*, strainer], a perforated pan for draining off liquids.
**cold** (kōld), ***adj.*** [AS. *cald*], 1. of a temperature much lower than that of the human body. 2. chilled or chilling. 3. not cordial: as, a *cold* reception. 4. objective; calm: as, *cold* logic. 5. *a*) faint, as a scent in hunting. *b*) off the track. 6. [Slang], perfectly memorized. 7. [Slang], insensible: as, knocked *cold.* ***n.*** 1. absence of heat or warmth. 2. the sensation produced by this. 3. a virus infection of the respiratory tract, causing sneezing, coughing, etc. **—catch cold,** to become ill with a cold. **—have cold feet,** [Colloq.], to be timid. **—in the cold,** neglected. **—cold′ish,** ***adj.*** **—cold′ly,** ***adv.*** **—cold′ness,** ***n.***
**cold′-blood′ed,** ***adj.*** 1. having blood that varies in temperature with the surrounding air, water, etc., as fishes and reptiles. 2. cruel; callous. **—cold′-blood′ed·ly,** ***adv.***
**cold cream,** a creamy preparation for softening and cleansing the skin.
**cold shoulder,** [Colloq.], a slight; snub. **—cold′-shoul′der,** ***v.t.***
**cold sore,** little blisters about the mouth during a cold or fever.
**cold war,** critical conflict in diplomacy, economics, etc. between states.
**cold wave,** 1. a period of very cold weather. 2. a kind of permanent wave.
**cole** (kōl), ***n.*** [< L. *caulis*, cabbage], any of various plants of the mustard family, to which cabbage belongs; esp., rape.
**cole′slaw′** (-slô′), ***n.*** [< D.; see COLE & SLAW], a salad made of shredded raw cabbage: also **cole slaw.**
**cole·wort** (kōl′wũrt′), ***n.*** [*cole* + *wort*], any cabbage whose leaves do not form a compact head.
**col·ic** (kol′ik), ***n.*** [< Gr. *kōlon*, colon], acute abdominal pain caused by any abnormal condition in the bowels. **—col′ick·y,** ***adj.***
**col·i·se·um** (kol′ə-sē′əm), ***n.*** [< L. *colosseus*, huge], a large building or stadium.
**co·li·tis** (kō-lī′tis), ***n.*** [< *colon* + *-itis*], inflammation of the colon.
**col·lab·o·rate** (kə-lab′ə-rāt′), ***v.i.*** [-RATED, -RATING], [< L. *com-*, with + *laborare*, to work], 1. to work together, esp. in literary or scientific work. 2. to co-operate with the enemy. **—col·lab′o·ra′tion,** ***n.*** **—col·lab′o·ra′tive,** ***adj.*** **—col·lab′o·ra′tor,** ***n.***
**col·lapse** (kə-laps′), ***v.i.*** [-LAPSED, -LAPSING], [< L. *com-*, together + *labi*, to fall], 1. to fall in or together; cave in. 2. to break down suddenly. 3. to fail suddenly in health. 4. to fold together compactly. ***v.t.*** to cause to collapse. ***n.*** 1. a sudden caving in. 2. a failure. 3. a sudden breakdown in health. **—col·laps′i·ble,** ***adj.***
**col·lar** (kol′ẽr), ***n.*** [< L. *collum*, neck], 1. the part of a dress, shirt, etc. that encircles the neck. 2. band for a dog's neck. 3. anything like a collar, as the harness for a horse's neck. ***v.t.*** 1. to put a collar on. 2. to seize, as by the collar.
**col′lar·bone′,** ***n.*** the clavicle.
**col·late** (ko-lāt′), ***v.t.*** [-LATED, -LATING], [< L. *com-*, together + *latus*, brought], 1. to compare (texts) carefully. 2. to put (pages) in proper order. **—col·la′tor,** ***n.***
**col·lat·er·al** (kə-lat′ẽr-əl), ***adj.*** [< L. *com-*, together + *latus*, a side], 1. parallel. 2. accompanying. 3. of a similar but subordinate nature. 4. of the same ancestors but in a different line. 5. designating or of security given as a pledge for the repayment of a loan, etc. ***n.*** 1. a collateral relative. 2. something used for collateral security.
**col·la·tion** (ko-lā′shən), ***n.*** 1. the act, process or result of collating. 2. a light meal.
**col·league** (kol′ēg), ***n.*** [< Fr. < L. *com-*, with + *legare*, appoint as deputy], a fellow worker; associate in office.
**col·lect** (kə-lekt′), ***v.t.*** [< L. *com-*, together + *legere*, gather], 1. to gather together. 2. to

gather (stamps, etc.) as a hobby. 3. to obtain payment for (bills, etc.). 4. to regain control of (oneself). ***v.i.*** to assemble or accumulate. ***adj. & adv.*** with payment to be made by the receiver: as, he telephoned *collect.* ***n.*** (kol′ekt), a short prayer.
**col·lect′ed,** ***adj.*** 1. gathered together. 2. in control of oneself; calm.
**col·lec′tion,** ***n.*** 1. a collecting. 2. things collected. 3. money collected.
**col·lec′tive,** ***adj.*** 1. formed by collecting. 2. of or as a group: as, our *collective* effort. 3. designating a noun which in the singular denotes a collection of individuals (e.g., army). ***n.*** 1. any collective enterprise, or the people in it. 2. a collective noun. **—col·lec′tive·ly,** ***adv.***
**col·lec′tor,** ***n.*** one that collects; esp., one hired to collect money due.
**col·leen** (kol′ēn, kə-lēn′), ***n.*** [< Ir. *caile,* girl], [Irish], a girl.
**col·lege** (kol′ij), ***n.*** [see COLLEAGUE], 1. a group of individuals having certain powers and duties: as, the electoral *college.* 2. an institution of higher education that grants degrees. 3. any of the schools of a university. 4. a school offering specialized instruction: as, a business *college.*
**col·le·gian** (kə-lē′jən), ***n.*** a college student.
**col·le′gi·ate** (-jit, -ji-it), ***adj.*** of or like a college or college students.
**col·lide** (kə-līd′), ***v.i.*** [-LIDED, -LIDING], [< L. *com-,* together + *laedere,* to strike], 1. to come into violent contact; crash. 2. to conflict; clash.
**col·lie** (kol′i), ***n.*** [< ?], a large, long-haired Scottish sheep dog.
**col·lier** (kol′yẽr), ***n.*** [ME. < *col,* coal], 1. a coal miner. 2. a ship for carrying coal.
**col′lier·y,** ***n.*** [*pl.* -IES], a coal mine.
**col·li·sion** (kə-lizh′ən), ***n.*** 1. a colliding. 2. a clash; conflict.
**col·lo·cate** (kol′ō-kāt′), ***v.t.*** [-CATED, -CATING], [< L. *com-* together + *locare,* to place], 1. to arrange. 2. to place side by side. **—col′lo·ca′tion,** ***n.***
**col·lo·di·on** (kə-lō′di-ən), ***n.*** [< Gr. *kolla,* glue + *eidos,* form], an inflammable solution that dries into a tough, elastic film: used to protect wounds, photographic plates, etc.
**col·loid** (kol′oid), ***n.*** [< Gr. *kolla,* glue; + *-oid*], a gelatinous substance formed of insoluble particles suspended in a fluid. **—col·loi·dal** (kə-loi′d'l), ***adj.***
**Colloq., colloq.,** colloquial.
**col·lo·qui·al** (kə-lō′kwi-əl), ***adj.*** [see COLLOQUY], 1. having to do with conversation. 2. belonging to or containing the words and idioms characteristic of conversation and informal writing; informal. **—col·lo′qui·al·ism,** ***n.*** **—col·lo′qui·al·ly,** ***adv.***
**col·lo·quy** (kol′ə-kwi), ***n.*** [*pl.* -QUIES], [<L. *com-,* together + *loqui,* speak], a conversation; conference. **—col′lo·quist,** ***n.***
**col·lu·sion** (kə-lōō′zhən), ***n.*** [< L. *com-,* with + *ludere,* to play], a secret agreement for fraudulent or illegal purpose; conspiracy. **—col·lu′sive** (-siv), ***adj.***
**Colo.,** Colorado.
**co·logne** (kə-lōn′), ***n.*** [< *eau de Cologne,* lit., water of Cologne], a fragrant liquid made of alcohol and various aromatic oils.
**co·lon** (kō′lən), ***n.*** [< Gr. *kōlon,* limb, clause], a mark of punctuation (:) used before a long quotation, explanation, example, series, etc., and after the salutation of a formal letter.
**co·lon** (kō′lən), ***n.*** [*pl.* -LONS, -LA (-lə)], [< Gr. *kolon*], that part of the large intestine extending from the caecum to the rectum. **—co·lon·ic** (kə-lon′ik), ***adj.***
**colo·nel** (kũr′n'l), ***n.*** [< It. *colonna,* (military) column], an army officer ranking just above a lieutenant colonel. **—colo′nel·cy** [*pl.* -CIES], **colo′nel·ship′,** ***n.***
**co·lo·ni·al** (kə-lō′ni-əl), ***adj.*** of or living in a colony. ***n.*** an inhabitant of a colony.
**col·o·nist** (kol′ə-nist), ***n.*** 1. one of the original settlers of a colony. 2. a colonial.
**col′o·nize′** (-nīz′), ***v.t. & v.i.*** [-NIZED, -NIZING], 1. to found a colony (in). 2. to settle in a colony. **—col′o·ni·za′tion,** ***n.***
**col·on·nade** (kol′ə-nād′), ***n.*** [< L. *columna,* column], in *architecture,* a series of regularly spaced columns.
**col·o·ny** (kol′ə-ni), ***n.*** [*pl.* -NIES], [< L. *colere,* cultivate], 1. a group of settlers in a distant land, under the jurisdiction of their native land. 2. a region thus settled. 3. a community of people of the same nationality or pursuits in a section of a city, etc.
**col·o·phon** (kol′ə-fon′, -fən), ***n.*** [< Gr. *kolophōn,* finishing stroke], a publisher's inscription or emblematic device, put on the last page or title page of a book.
**col·or** (kul′ẽr), ***n.*** [L.], 1. the property of reflecting light waves of a particular length: the *primary colors of the spectrum* as seen by the eye are red, orange, yellow, green, blue, indigo, and violet. 2. any coloring matter; pigment: in this sense the preceding colors are sometimes distinguished from black, white, and gray (*achromatic colors*). 3. color of the face or skin. 4. ***pl.*** a colored badge, etc. that shows the wearer's affiliation. 5. *pl.* a flag. 6. outward appearance. 7. picturesque quality. ***v.t.*** 1. to give color to; paint; dye. 2. to change the color of. 3. to alter, esp. by distortion: as, to *color* a story. ***v.i.*** 1. to become colored. 2. to change color. 3. to blush or flush. **—show one's colors,** to reveal one's true self. **—with flying colors,** with great success. **—col′or·a′tion,** ***n.***
**col·o·ra·tu·ra (soprano)** (kul′ẽr-ə-tyoor′ə), [It.], a soprano of high range, adept at brilliant ornamental runs, trills, etc.
**col′or-blind′,** ***adj.*** unable to distinguish certain colors or any colors. **—color blindness.**
**col′ored** (-ẽrd), ***adj.*** 1. having color. 2. of a race other than the Caucasian; specif. Negro. 3. altered or distorted.
**col′or·ful,** ***adj.*** 1. full of color. 2. picturesque, vivid, etc. **—col′or·ful·ly,** ***adv.***
**col′or·ing,** ***n.*** 1. anything applied to impart color; pigment, etc.: also **coloring matter.** 2. appearance with reference to color. 3. false appearance.
**col′or·less,** ***adj.*** 1. without color. 2. lacking variety or interest; dull.
**color line,** the barrier of social, political, and economic restrictions imposed on any of the colored races.
**co·los·sal** (kə-los′'l), ***adj.*** like a colossus in size; huge; gigantic. **—co·los′sal·ly,** ***adv.***
**co·los·sus** (kə-los′əs), ***n.*** [*pl.* -SI (-ī), -SUSES], [< Gr. *kolossos*], 1. a gigantic statue. 2. any huge or important person or thing.
**col·our** (kul′ẽr), ***n., v.t. & v.i.*** color: Brit. spelling.
**colt** (kōlt), ***n.*** [< AS.], a young horse, donkey, zebra, etc.; specif., a young male horse.
**col·ter** (kōl′tẽr), ***n.*** [< L. *culter,* knife], a blade or disk on a plow, for making vertical cuts in the soil.
**col·um·bine** (kol′əm-bīn′), ***n.*** [< L. *columba,* dove], a plant of the crowfoot family, with showy, spurred flowers.
**col·umn** (kol′əm), ***n.*** [< L. *columna*], 1. a slender, upright structure, usually a supporting member in a building. 2. anything like a column: as, the spinal *column.* 3. any of the vertical sections of printed matter on a page. 4. a regular feature article in a newspaper, etc., usually by a special writer. 5. a formation of troops or ships placed one behind another. **—col·umnar** (kə-lum′nẽr), ***adj.*** **—col′umned,** ***adj.***
**col′um·nist** (-nist, ist), ***n.*** one who writes a column (sense 4).

**com-,** [L. < *cum*, with], a prefix meaning: 1. *with, together*, as in *combine*. 2. *intensification*, as in *command*.
**co·ma** (kō′mə), ***n.*** [*pl.* -MAS], [< Gr. *koiman*, put to sleep], a state of deep, prolonged unconsciousness, caused by injury or disease; stupor.
**com·a·tose** (kom′ə-tōs′, kō′mə-), ***adj.*** 1. of, like, or in a coma. 2. lethargic.
**comb** (kōm), ***n.*** [AS. *camb*], 1. a thin strip of bone, metal, plastic, etc. with teeth, used to arrange, clean, or set the hair. 2. a tool for carding wool, cotton, etc. 3. the red, fleshy outgrowth on the head of a rooster, etc. 4. a thing like this, as the crest of a wave. 5. a honeycomb. ***v.t.*** 1. to clean or arrange with a comb. 2. to search thoroughly.
**com·bat** (kom′bat; *also, for v.*, kəm-bat′), ***v.t. & v.i.*** [-BATED or -BATTED, -BATING or -BATTING], [< L. *com-*, together + *battuere*, to beat], to fight; oppose by force. ***n.*** 1. armed fighting; battle. 2. struggle; conflict. **—com′bat·ant** (bə-tənt), ***adj. & n.***
**com·ba·tive** (kəm-bat′iv, kom′bə-tiv), ***adj.*** ready or eager to fight.
**comb·er** (kōm′ẽr), ***n.*** 1. one that combs wool etc. 2. a large breaking wave.
**com·bi·na·tion** (kom′bə-nā′shən), ***n.*** 1. a combining or being combined. 2. a thing made by combining. 3. an association of people for a common purpose. 4. the series of numbers to which a dial is turned on a lock (**combination lock**) to open it.
**com·bine** (kəm-bīn′), ***v.t. & v.i.*** [-BINED, -BINING], [< L. *com-*, together + *bini*, two by two], to come or bring into union; join. ***n.*** 1. (kom′bīn), a machine for harvesting and threshing grain. 2. (kom′bīn, kəm-bīn′), [Colloq.], an association for commercial or political purposes.
**combining form,** a word or word base used as an element in word formation, as *tele-* in *telephone*.
**com·bus·ti·ble** (kəm-bus′tə-b'l), ***adj.*** capable of taking fire; inflammable.
**com·bus·tion** (kəm-bus′chən), ***n.*** [Fr. < L. *com*, intens. + *urere*, to burn], 1. the act or process of burning. 2. oxidation.
**come** (kum), ***v.i.*** [CAME (kām), COME, COMING], [AS *cuman*], 1. to move from "there" to "here." 2. to arrive or appear. 3. to extend; reach. 4. to happen; occur: as, success *came* to him. 5. to exist in a certain order: as, 9 *comes* after 8. 6. to be descended. 7. to be caused; result. 8. to become: as, it *came* loose. 9. to be available: as, it *comes* in four sizes. 10. to amount: as, the bill *comes* to $5.68. **—come about,** 1. to happen. 2. to turn about. **—come across** (or **upon**), to find by chance. **—come around** (or **round**), 1. to revive; recover. 2. to make a turn. 3. [Colloq.], to concede. **—come between,** to estrange; divide. **—come by,** to get; gain. **—come in,** to enter. **—come into,** 1. to join. 2. to inherit. **—come off,** 1. to become detached. 2. to occur. **—come out,** 1. to be disclosed. 2. to be offered for public sale, etc. 3. to end up. **—come through,** 1. to complete something successfully. 2. [Slang], to do or give what is wanted. **—come to,** to recover consciousness. **—come up,** to arise, as in discussion. **—come up to,** 1. to reach to. 2. to equal. **—how come?** [Colloq.], why?
**come′back′,** ***n.*** 1. [Colloq.], a return to a previous position, as of power. 2. [Slang], a witty answer; a retort.
**co·me·di·an** (kə-mē′di-ən), ***n.*** an actor of comic parts. **—co·me′di·enne′** (-en′), ***n.fem.***
**com·e·dy** (kom′ə-di), ***n.*** [*pl.* -DIES], [< Gr. *kōmos*, festival + *aeidein*, sing], 1. a humorous play, etc. with a nontragic ending. 2. an amusing incident.
**come·ly** (kum′li), ***adj.*** [-LIER, -LIEST], [AS. *cymlic*], 1. attractive. 2. seemly; proper. **—come′li·ness,** ***n.***
**come′-on′,** ***n.*** [Slang], an inducement.
**co·mes·ti·ble** (kə-mes′tə-b'l), ***adj.*** [< L. *com-*, intens. + *edere*, eat], eatable; edible. ***n.*** *usually in pl.* food.
**com·et** (kom′it), ***n.*** [< Gr. *komē*, hair], a heavenly body having a starlike nucleus and, usually, a long, luminous tail: comets move in orbits around the sun.
**come·up·pance** (kum′up′'ns), ***n.*** [Slang], deserved punishment.
**com·fit** (kum′fit), ***n.*** [< L. *com-*, with + *facere*, do], a candy; sweetmeat.
**com·fort** (kum′fẽrt), ***v.t.*** [< L. *com-*, intens. + *fortis*, strong], to soothe in distress or sorrow; console. ***n.*** 1. relief from distress, etc. 2. one that comforts. 3. a state of, or thing that provides, ease and quiet enjoyment. **—com′fort·ing,** ***adj. & n.*** **—com′fort·less,** ***adj.***
**com·fort·a·ble** (kum′fẽr-tə-b'l, kumf′tẽr-b'l), ***adj.*** 1. providing comfort: as, *comfortable* shoes. 2. at ease in body or mind. 3. [Colloq.], sufficient to satisfy: as, a *comfortable* salary. **—com′fort·a·bly,** ***adv.***
**com′fort·er,** ***n.*** 1. one that comforts. 2. a quilted bed covering.
**com·ic** (kom′ik), ***adj.*** 1. of comedy. 2. amusing; funny. ***n.*** 1. a comedian. 2. the humorous part of art or life. 3. *usually in pl.* [Colloq.], comic strips.
**com′i·cal** (-i-k'l), ***adj.*** causing amusement; humorous; funny. **—com′i·cal·ly,** ***adv.***
**comic strip,** a series of cartoons telling a humorous or adventurous story, as in a newspaper or in a magazine (**comic book**).
**com·ing** (kum′iŋ), ***adj.*** [ppr. of *come*], 1. approaching. 2. next. 3. [Colloq.], showing promise of being a success. ***n.*** arrival; approach; advent.
**com·i·ty** (kom′ə-ti), ***n.*** [*pl.* -TIES], [< L. *comis*, polite], civility; courtesy.
**com·ma** (kom′ə), ***n.*** [< Gr. *komma*, clause], a mark of punctuation (,) used to indicate a slight separation of sentence elements.
**com·mand** (kə-mand′, -mänd′), ***v.t.*** [< L. *com-*, intens. + *mandare*, commit], 1. to give an order to; direct. 2. to have authority over; control. 3. to have for use: as, to *command* a fortune. 4. to deserve and get: as, to *command* respect. 5. to control (a position); overlook. ***v.i.*** to be in authority. ***n.*** 1. an order; direction. 2. authority to command. 3. power to control by position. 4. mastery. 5. a military or naval force, or a district, under someone's authority.
**com·man·dant** (kom′ən-dant′, -dänt′), ***n.*** a commanding officer, as of a fort.
**com·man·deer** (kom′ən-dêr′), ***v.t.*** [see COMMAND], to seize (property) for military or governmental use.
**com·mand′er,** ***n.*** one who commands; leader; officer; specif., in the *U.S. Navy*, an officer just above a lieutenant commander.
**commander in chief,** [*pl.* COMMANDERS IN CHIEF], the supreme commander of the armed forces of a nation.
**com·mand′ing,** ***adj.*** 1. in command. 2. controlling; dominating. 3. impressive.
**com·mand′ment,** ***n.*** a command; law.
**com·man·do** (kə-man′dō, -män′-), ***n.*** [*pl.* -DOS, -DOES], [D.; Port.], a member of a small force trained to raid enemy territory.
**com·mem·o·rate** (kə-mem′ẽr-āt′), ***v.t.*** [-RATED, -RATING], [< L. *com-*, intens. + *memorare*, remind], 1. to honor the memory of as by a ceremony. 2. to serve as a memorial to. **—com·mem′o·ra′tion,** ***n.*** **—com·mem′o·ra′tive,** ***adj.***
**com·mence** (kə-mens′), ***v.i. & v.t.*** [-MENCED, -MENCING], [< L. *com-*, together + *initiare*, begin], to begin; start.
**com·mence′ment,** ***n.*** 1. a beginning;

start. 2. the ceremony of conferring degrees or diplomas at a school or college.

**com·mend** (kə-mend′), *v.t.* [see COMMAND], 1. to put in the care of another; entrust. 2. to recommend. 3. to praise. —**com·mend′a·ble,** *adj.* —**com·mend′a·bly,** *adv.* —**com·men·da·tion** (kom′ən-dā′-shən), *n.*

**com·men·su·ra·ble** (kə-men′shoor-ə-b'l), *adj.* [see COMMENSURATE], measurable by the same standard or measure.

**com·men·su·rate** (kə-men′shoor-it), *adj.* [< L. *com-*, with + *mensura*, measurement], 1. equal in measure or size. 2. proportionate; corresponding. 3. commensurable.

**com·ment** (kom′ent), *n.* [< L. *com-*, intens. + *meminisse*, remember], 1. an explanatory or critical note on something written or said. 2. a remark or observation. 3. talk; gossip. *v.i.* to make comments.

**com·men·tar·y** (kom′ən-ter′i), *n.* [*pl.* -IES], a series of explanatory notes or remarks.

**com·men·ta·tor** (kom′ən-tā′tẽr), *n.* one who reports and analyzes events, trends, etc: as, a news *commentator*.

**com·merce** (kom′ẽrs), *n.* [< L. *com-*, together + *merx*, merchandise], trade on a large scale, as between countries.

**com·mer·cial** (kə-mũr′shəl), *adj.* 1. of or connected with commerce. 2. made or done for sale or profit. *n.* in *radio & TV*, a paid advertisement. —**com·mer′cial·ly,** *adv.*

**com·mer′cial·ism,** *n.* the practices and spirit of commerce or business.

**com·mer′cial·ize′** (-īz′), *v.t.* [-IZED, -IZING], to put on a business basis, esp. so as to make profit. —**com·mer′cial·i·za′tion,** *n.*

**com·min·gle** (kə-miŋ′g'l), *v.t. & v.i.* [-GLED, -GLING], to mingle together.

**com·mis·er·ate** (kə-miz′ẽr-āt′), *v.t.* [-ATED, -ATING], [< L. *com-*, intens. + *miserari*, to pity], to feel or show pity for. *v.i.* to condole (*with*). —**com·mis′er·a′tion,** *n.*

**com·mis·sar** (kom′ə-sär′), *n.* [< Russ.; see COMMISSARY], formerly, the head of a government department in the U.S.S.R.

**com′mis·sar′i·at** (-sâr′i-ət), *n.* 1. those branches of an army that provide food and supplies. 2. formerly, a government department in the U.S.S.R.: now called *ministry*.

**com·mis·sar·y** (kom′ə-ser′i), *n.* [*pl.* -IES], [< L. *committere*, commit], 1. formerly, an army officer in charge of supplies. 2. a store in an army camp, lumber camp, etc., where food and supplies are sold.

**com·mis·sion** (kə-mish′ən), *n.* [see COMMIT], 1. a document authorizing certain duties or powers. 2. authority to act for another, or that which one is authorized to do. 3. a group of people chosen to do something. 4. a committing; doing. 5. the thing done. 6. a percentage of money from sales, allotted to the agent. 7. a certificate conferring military or naval rank as an officer. *v.t.* 1. to give a commission to. 2. to authorize. 3. to put into service, as a naval vessel. —**in** (or **out of**) **commission,** (not) fit to be used.

**com·mis′sion·er,** *n.* 1. a member of a commission. 2. an official in charge of a governmental department.

**com·mit** (kə-mit′), *v.t.* [-MITTED, -MITTING], [< L. *com-*, together + *mittere*, send], 1. to give in charge; consign. 2. to put in custody or confinement: as, *committed* to prison. 3. to do or perpetrate, as a crime. 4. to pledge; bind. —**com·mit′ment,** *n.*

**com·mit·tee** (kə-mit′i), *n.* [see COMMIT], a group of people chosen to act upon a certain matter. —**com·mit′tee·man** [*pl.* -MEN], *n.*—**com·mit′tee·wom′an**[*pl.*-WOMEN], *n.fem.*

**com·mode** (kə-mōd′), *n.* [Fr.; see COM- & MODE], 1. a chest of drawers. 2. a movable washstand. 3. a toilet.

**com·mo·di·ous** (kə-mō′di-əs), *adj.* [see COMMODE], spacious; roomy.

**com·mod·i·ty** (kə-mod′ə-ti), *n.* [*pl.* -TIES], [see COMMODE], 1. any useful thing. 2. anything bought and sold.

**com·mo·dore** (kom′ə-dôr′), *n.* [< Sp. or Fr.; see COMMAND], a naval officer ranking just above a captain.

**com·mon** (kom′ən), *adj.* [< L. *com-*, with + *munus*, duties], 1. shared by all. 2. belonging to the community; public. 3. general; widespread. 4. familiar; usual. 5. ordinary. 6. having no rank: as, a *common* soldier. 7. vulgar; coarse. 8. designating a noun that refers to any of a group, as *book*. *n.* *sometimes pl.* land owned or used by all the inhabitants of a place. —**in common,** equally with all concerned. —**com′mon·ly,** *adv.* —**com′mon·ness,** *n.*

**com′mon·al·ty** (-əl-ti), *n.* [*pl.* -TIES], the common people; public.

**com′mon·er,** *n.* a person not of the nobility.

**common law,** the unwritten law of a country based on custom, usage, and judicial decisions.

**common people,** the people who are not of the upper classes.

**com′mon·place′,** *n.* 1. a trite remark; platitude. 2. anything common or ordinary. *adj.* ordinary; usual.

**common pleas,** in *law*, civil suits between private parties.

**com·mons** (kom′ənz), *n.pl.* 1. the common people. 2. a dining room, as at a college. —**the Commons,** the House of Commons.

**common sense,** practical judgment or intelligence. —**com′mon-sense′,** *adj.*

**com′mon·weal′** (-wēl′), *n.* the public welfare: also **common weal.**

**com′mon·wealth′** (-welth′), *n.* 1. the people of a nation or state. 2. a democracy or republic.

**com·mo·tion** (kə-mō′shən), *n.* [< L. *com-*, together + *movere*, move], violent motion; turmoil; confusion; agitation.

**com·mu·nal** (kom′yoo-n'l, kə-mū′-), *adj.* 1. of a commune. 2. of or belonging to the community; public. —**com′mu·nal·ly,** *adv.*

**com·mune** (kə-mūn′), *v.i.* [-MUNED, -MUNING], [< OFr. *comuner*, to share], to converse intimately.

**com·mune** (kom′ūn), *n.* [< Fr. < L.; see COMMON], the smallest administrative district of local government in some European countries, esp. France.

**com·mu·ni·ca·ble** (kə-mū′ni-kə-b'l), *adj.* that can be communicated, as a thought or a disease. —**com·mu′ni·ca·bil′i·ty,** *n.*

**com·mu·ni·cant** (kə-mū′ni-kənt), *n.* 1. one who receives Holy Communion. 2. one who communicates information.

**com·mu·ni·cate** (kə-mū′nə-kāt′), *v.t.* [-CATED, -CATING], [< L. *communicare*], 1. to impart; transmit. 2. to give (information, etc.). *v.i.* 1. to give and receive information. 2. to be connected, as rooms.

**com·mu′ni·ca′tion,** *n.* 1. a transmitting. 2. a giving and receiving of information by talk, writing, etc. 3. the information so given. 4. *often in pl.* a means of communicating. —**com·mu′ni·ca′tive,** *adj.*

**com·mun·ion** (kə-mūn′yən), *n.* [see COMMON], 1. possession in common. 2. a communing. 3. a group of people of the same religious faith. 4. [C-], a celebrating of the Eucharist.

**com·mu·ni·qué** (kə-mū′nə-kā′), *n.* [Fr.], an official communication.

**com·mu·nism** (kom′yoo-niz'm), *n.* [see COMMON], 1. a theory or system of the ownership of the means of production by the community, with all members sharing in the work and the products. 2. [often C-], a movement for establishing such a system.

**com·mu·nist** (kom′yoo-nist), *n.* 1. an advocate or supporter of communism. 2. [C-], a member of a Communist party. *adj.* of or like communism. **—com'mu·nis'tic,** *adj.*

**com·mu·ni·ty** (kə-mū'nə-ti), *n.* [*pl.* -TIES], [see COMMON], 1. a body of people living in the same place. 2. the public. 3. ownership or participation in common.

**com·mute** (kə-mūt'), *v.t.* [-MUTED, -MUTING], [< L. *com-*, intens. + *mutare*, to change], 1. to exchange; substitute. 2. to change (an obligation. punishment, etc.) to one that is less severe. *v.i.* 1. to be a substitute. 2. to travel as a commuter. **—commu'ta·ble,** *adj.* **—com'mu·ta'tion,** *n.*

**com·mut'er,** *n.* one who travels regularly, as by train, between a suburb and his place of work in the city.

**comp.,** 1. comparative. 2. compound.

**com·pact** (kəm-pakt'), *adj.* [< L. *com-*, together + *pangere*, fasten], 1. closely and firmly packed; solid. 2. brief; terse. *v.t.* to pack firmly together. *n.* (kom'pakt'), 1. a small case containing a mirror, face powder, etc. 2. an agreement; covenant. **—compact'ly,** *adv.* **—com·pact'ness,** *n.*

**com·pan·ion** (kəm-pan'yən), *n.* [< L. *com-*, with + *panis*, bread], 1. an associate; comrade. 2. a person paid to live or travel with another. 3. a thing that matches another in sort, color, etc. **—com·pan'ion·ship',** *n.*

**com·pan'ion·a·ble,** *adj.* sociable; warm and friendly. **—com·pan'ion·a·bil'i·ty,** *n.*

**com·pan'ion·way',** *n.* the stairway from the deck of a ship to the hold.

**com·pa·ny** (kum'pə-ni), *n.* [*pl.* -NIES], 1. companionship; society. 2. a group of people; esp., a group associated for some purpose: as, a business *company*. 3. a ship's crew. 4. a military unit, subdivision of a regiment. 5. [Colloq.], a guest or guests.

**com·pa·ra·ble** (kom'pēr-ə-b'l), *adj.* 1. that can be compared. 2. worthy of comparison. **—com'pa·ra·bly,** *adv.*

**com·par·a·tive** (kəm-par'ə-tiv), *adj.* 1. involving comparison. 2. relative. 3. in *grammar*, designating the second degree of comparison of adjectives and adverbs. *n.* in *grammar*, the comparative degree: as, *finer* is the *comparative* of *fine*. **—com·par'a·tive·ly,** *adv.*

**com·pare** (kəm-pâr'), *v.t.* [-PARED, -PARING], [< L. *com-*, with + *par*, equal], 1. to liken (*to*). 2. to examine for similarities or differences. 3. in *grammar*, to form the degrees of comparison of. *v.i.* to be worth comparing (*with*). **—beyond** (or **past**) **compare,** without equal.

**com·par·i·son** (kəm-par'ə-s'n), *n.* 1. a comparing or being compared. 2. similarity; likeness. 3. in *grammar*, change in an adjective or adverb to show the three degrees (*positive*, *comparative*, and *superlative*). **—in comparison with,** compared with.

**com·part·ment** (kəm-pärt'mənt), *n.* [< L. *com-*, with + *partiri*, divide], any of the divisions into which a space is partitioned.

**com·pass** (kum'pəs), *v.t.* [< L. *com-*, together + *passus*, a step], 1. to go around. 2. to surround. 3. to achieve; contrive. *n.* 1. *often pl.* an instrument with two pivoted legs, for drawing circles, measuring, etc. 2. a boundary. 3. an enclosed area. 4. range; extent. 5. an instrument for showing direction, usually with a swinging magnetic needle that points to north.

**com·pas·sion** (kəm-pash'ən), *n.* [< L. *com-*, together + *pati*, suffer], pity; deep sympathy. **—com·pas'sion·ate,** *adj.*

**com·pat·i·ble** (kəm-pat'ə-b'l), *adj.* [see COMPASSION], getting along harmoniously; in agreement. **—com·pat'i·bil'i·ty,** *n.*

**com·pa·tri·ot** (kəm-pā'tri-ət), *n.* [< L.; see COM- & PATRIOT], a fellow countryman.

**com·peer** (kəm-pêr'), *n.* [see COMPARE], 1. an equal; peer. 2. a companion; comrade.

**com·pel** (kəm-pel'), *v.t.* [-PELLED, -PELLING], [< L. *com-*, together + *pellere*, drive], to force or get by force.

**com·pen·di·ous** (kəm-pen'di-əs), *adj.* containing all the essentials in a brief form; concise. **—com·pen'di·ous·ly,** *adv.*

**com·pen·di·um** (kəm-pen'di-əm), *n.* [*pl.* -UMS, -A (-ə)], [< L. *com-*, together + *pendere*, weigh], a concise, comprehensive summary.

**com·pen·sate** (kom'pən-sāt'), *v.t.* [-SATED, -SATING], [ult. < L. *com-*, with + *pendere*, weigh], 1. to make up for; counterbalance. 2. to pay; recompense. *v.i.* to make amends (*for*). **—com·pen·sa·to·ry** (kəm-pen'sə-tôr'i), *adj.*

**com'pen·sa'tion,** *n.* 1. a compensating or being compensated. 2. anything given as an equivalent, or to make amends; pay.

**com·pete** (kəm-pēt'), *v.i.* [-PETED, -PETING], [< L. *com-*, together + *petere*, seek], 1. to strive in opposition; vie. 2. to participate (*in* a contest, etc.).

**com·pe·tence** (kom'pə-təns), *n.* 1. sufficient means for one's needs. 2. ability; fitness. Also **com'pe·ten·cy** [*pl.* -CIES].

**com·pe·tent** (kom'pə-tənt), *adj.* [see COMPETE], 1. capable; able; fit. 2. sufficient; adequate. **—com'pe·tent·ly,** *adv.*

**com·pe·ti·tion** (kom'pə-tish'ən), *n.* 1. a competing rivalry, esp. in business. 2. a contest; match. **—com·pet·i·tive** (kəm-pet'ə-tiv), *adj.*

**com·pet'i·tor** (-tēr), *n.* one who competes, as a business rival.

**com·pile** (kəm-pīl'), *v.t.* [-PILED, -PILING], [< L. *com-*, together + *pilare*, to compress], 1. to gather together (writings, facts, etc.) from various sources. 2. to compose (a book, etc.) in this manner. **—com·pi·la·tion** (kom'p'l-ā'shən), *n.* **—com·pil'er,** *n.*

**com·pla·cen·cy** (kəm-plā's'n-si), *n.* [*pl.* -CIES], [< L. *com-*, with + *placere*, please], 1. contentment. 2. self-satisfaction; smugness. Also **com·pla'cence. —com·pla'cent,** *adj.* **—com·pla'cent·ly,** *adv.*

**com·plain** (kəm-plān'), *v.i.* [< L. *com-*, with + *plangere*, strike (the breast)], 1. to express pain, dissatisfaction, etc. 2. to find fault. 3. to make an accusation or a formal charge. **—com·plain'ant,** *n.*

**com·plaint'** (-plānt'), *n.* 1. an utterance of pain, dissatisfaction, etc. 2. an illness; ailment. 3. in *law*, a formal charge.

**com·plai·sant** (kəm-plā'z'nt, -s'nt), *adj.* [see COMPLACENCY], willing to please; obliging. **—com·plai'sance,** *n.*

**com·ple·ment** (kom'plə-mənt), *n.* [see COMPLETE], 1. that which completes or perfects. 2. the amount needed to fill or complete. 3. an entirety. *v.t.* (-ment'), to make complete. **—com'ple·men'ta·ry,** *adj.*

**com·plete** (kəm-plēt'), *adj.* [< L. *com-*, intens. + *plere*, fill], 1. lacking no parts. 2. finished. 3. thorough; perfect. *v.t.* [-PLETED, -PLETING], 1. to finish. 2. to make entire or perfect. **—com·plete'ly,** *adv.* **—complete'ness,** *n.* **—com·ple'tion,** (-plē'shən), *n.*

**com·plex** (kəm-pleks', kom'pleks), *adj.* [< L. *com-*, with + *plectere*, to weave], 1. consisting of two or more related parts. 2. complicated. *n.* (kom'pleks), 1. a complex whole. 2. in *psychiatry*, a group of partly unconscious emotional attitudes toward some thing, strongly influencing behavior. **—com·plex'i·ty** [*pl.* -TIES], *n.*

**com·plex·ion** (kəm-plek'shən), *n.* [see COMPLEX], 1. the color, texture, etc. of the skin, esp. of the face. 2. character; nature; aspect.

**com·pli·a·ble** (kəm-plī'ə-b'l), *adj.* complying. **—com·pli'a·bly,** *adv.*

**com·pli·ance** (kəm-plī'əns), *n.* 1. a complying with a request, demand, etc. 2. a tendency to give in to others. Also **compli'an·cy. —com·pli'ant,** *adj.*

**com·pli·cate** (kom'plə-kāt'), ***v.t. & v.i.*** [-CATED, -CATING], [< L. *com-*, together + *plicare*, to fold], to make or become intricate, difficult, or involved. **—com'pli·cat'ed,** ***adj.*** **—com'pli·ca'tion,** ***n.***

**com·plic·i·ty** (kəm-plis'ə-ti), ***n.*** [*pl.* -TIES], [see COMPLEX], partnership in wrongdoing.

**com·pli·ment** (kom'plə-mənt), ***n.*** [Fr. < L.; akin to COMPLEMENT], 1. a formal act of courtesy; esp., something said in praise. 2. *pl.* respects. ***v.t.*** (-ment'), to pay a compliment to.

**com'pli·men'ta·ry** (-men'tẽr-i), ***adj.*** 1. paying or containing a compliment. 2. given free as a courtesy.

**com·ply** (kəm-plī'), ***v.i.*** [-PLIED, -PLYING], [see COMPLETE], to act in accordance with a request, order, etc. **—com·pli'er,** ***n.***

**com·po·nent** (kəm-pō'nənt), ***adj.*** [< L. *com-*, together + *ponere*, put], serving as one of the parts of a whole. ***n.*** a part; ingredient.

**com·port** (kəm-pôrt'), ***v.t.*** [< L. *com-*, together + *portare*, bring], to behave (oneself) in a specified manner. ***v.i.*** to agree or accord (*with*). **—com·port'ment,** ***n.***

**com·pose** (kəm-pōz'), ***v.t.*** [-POSED, -POSING], [< Fr. *com-*, with + *poser*, to place], 1. to make up; constitute. 2. to put in proper form. 3. to create (a musical or literary work). 4. to settle; make calm. 5. to set (type) for printing. ***v.i.*** 1. to create musical or literary works. 2. to set type.

**com·posed',** ***adj.*** calm; self-possessed.

**com·pos'er,** ***n.*** a person who composes, esp. one who composes music.

**com·pos·ite** (kəm-poz'it), ***adj.*** [< L. *com-*, together + *ponere*, put], 1. formed of distinct parts. 2. in *botany*, of a group of plants, including the daisy, aster, etc., having flower heads consisting of clusters of small flowers. ***n.*** a composite thing.

**com·po·si·tion** (kom'pə-zish'ən), ***n.*** 1. a composing. 2. the creation of literary or musical works. 3. the make-up of a thing. 4. something composed.

**com·pos·i·tor** (kəm-poz'i-tẽr), ***n.*** a typesetter.

**com·post** (kom'pōst), ***n.*** [see COMPOSITE], a mixture of decomposing vegetation, manure, etc. for fertilizing soil.

**com·po·sure** (kəm-pō'zhẽr), ***n.*** [see COMPOSE], calmness; self-possession.

**com·pote** (kom'pōt), ***n.*** [Fr.; see COMPOSITE], 1. a dish of stewed fruits. 2. a long-stemmed dish for candy, fruit, etc.

**com·pound** (kom-pound'), ***v.t.*** [see COMPOSITE], 1. to mix; combine. 2. to make by combining parts. ***adj.*** (kom'pound, kompound'), made up of two or more parts. ***n.*** (kom'pound), 1. a thing formed by combining parts. 2. in *chem.*, a substance containing two or more elements combined. **—compound a felony** (or **crime**), to agree, for payment, not to prosecute a felony (or crime).

**com·pound** (kom'pound), ***n.*** [Malay *kampun*], in the Orient, an enclosed space with one or more buildings in it.

**compound fracture,** a fracture in which the broken bone pierces the skin.

**compound interest,** interest paid on both the principal and the accumulated interest.

**com·pre·hend** (kom'pri-hend'), ***v.t.*** [< L. *com-*, with + *prehendere*, seize], 1. to grasp mentally; understand. 2. to include; comprise. **—com'pre·hen'si·ble** (-hen'sə-b'l), ***adj.*** **—com'pre·hen'si·bly,** ***adv.***

**com'pre·hen'sion** (-hen'shən), ***n.*** 1. a comprehending or comprising. 2. the act or capacity of understanding.

**com'pre·hen'sive,** ***adj.*** 1. including much; inclusive. 2. understanding. **—com'pre·hen'sive·ly,** ***adv.*** **—com'pre·hen'sive·ness,** ***n.***

**com·press** (kəm-pres'), ***v.t.*** [< L. *com-*, together + *premere*, press], to press together and make more compact. ***n.*** (kom'pres), a pad of folded cloth, often wet or medicated, applied to a part of the body as to lessen inflammation. **—com·pressed', com·pres'si·ble,** ***adj.*** **—com·pres'sion,** ***n.***

**com·pres'sor** (-ẽr), ***n.*** a machine for compressing, air, gas, etc.

**com·prise, com·prize** (kəm-prīz'), ***v.t.*** [-PRISED, -PRISING; -PRIZED, -PRIZING], [see COMPREHEND], 1. to include; contain. 2. to consist of. **—com·pris'al, com·priz'al,** ***n.***

**com·pro·mise** (kom'prə-mīz'), ***n.*** [< L. *com-*, together + *promittere*, to promise], 1. a settlement in which each side makes concessions. 2. the result of such a settlement; something midway. ***v.t. & v.i.*** [-MISED, -MISING], 1. to settle by compromise. 2. to lay open to danger, suspicion, disrepute, etc.

**comp·tom·e·ter** (komp-tom'ə-tẽr), ***n.*** [see COMPUTE & -METER], a calculator (sense 2): a trademark (**Comptometer**).

**comp·trol·ler** (kən-trōl'ẽr), ***n.*** [< *controller*, after Fr. *compte*, account], a controller (sense 1). **—comp·trol'ler·ship',** ***n.***

**com·pul·sion** (kəm-pul'shən), ***n.*** a compelling or being compelled; force. **—com·pul'sive** (-siv), ***adj.*** **—com·pul'sive·ly,** ***adv.***

**com·pul'so·ry** (-sẽr-i), ***adj.*** 1. compelled; required. 2. compelling.

**com·punc·tion** (kəm-puŋk'shən), ***n.*** [< L. *com-*, intens. + *pungere*, to prick], a feeling of slight regret for some wrong done. **—com·punc'tious,** ***adj.***

**com·pute** (kəm-pūt'), ***v.t. & v.i.*** [-PUTED, -PUTING], [< L. *com-*, with + *putare*, reckon], to determine, as an amount, by reckoning; calculate. **—com·put'a·ble,** ***adj.*** **—com·pu·ta·tion** (kom'pyoo-tā'shən) ***n.***

**com·put·er** (kəm-pū'tẽr), ***n.*** a person or thing that computes; specif., an electronic machine that performs rapid, often complex calculations or compiles, correlates, and selects data.

**com·put·er·ize** (kəm-pū'tẽr-īz'), ***v.t.*** [-IZED, -IZING], to equip with, or operate, etc. by or as if by means of, electronic computers.

**com·rade** (kom'rad), ***n.*** [< Sp. *camarada*, chamber mate < L. *camera*, room], 1. a friend; close companion. 2. an associate. **—com'rade·ly,** ***adj.*** **—com'rade·ship',** ***n.***

**con** (kon), ***adv.*** [< L. *contra*], against: as, pro and *con*. ***n.*** a vote, person, etc. in opposition.

**con** (kon), ***v.t.*** [CONNED, CONNING], [< AS. *cunnan*, know], to study carefully.

**con** (kon), ***v.t.*** [CONNED, CONNING], [see CONDUCE], to direct the course of (a vessel).

**con** (kon), ***adj.*** [Slang], confidence: as, a *con* man. ***v.t.*** [CONNED, CONNING], [Slang], to swindle.

**con-,** com-: used before certain consonants.

**con·cat·e·na·tion** (kon'kat-'n-ā'shən), ***n.*** [< L. *com-*, together + *catena*, chain], a connected series, as of events.

**con·cave** (kon-kāv', kon'kāv), ***adj.*** [< L. *com-*, intens. + *cavus*, hollow], hollow and curved like a section of the inside of a sphere. **—con·cave'ly,** ***adv.*** **—con·cav'i·ty** (-kav'ə-ti) [*pl.* -TIES], ***n.***

**con·ceal** (kən-sēl'), ***v.t.*** [< L. *com-*, together + *celare*, hide], 1. to hide. 2. to keep secret. **—con·ceal'ment,** ***n.***

**con·cede** (kən-sēd'), ***v.t.*** [-CEDED, -CEDING], [< L. *com-*, with + *cedere*, cede], 1. to admit the truth of. 2. to grant as a right.

**con·ceit** (kən-sēt'), ***n.*** [see CONCEIVE], 1. an exaggerated opinion of oneself, one's merits, etc.; vanity. 2. a fanciful or witty expression or notion. 3. imagination.

**con·ceit'ed,** ***adj.*** vain.

**con·ceiv·a·ble** (kən-sēv'ə-b'l), ***adj.*** that can be imagined. **—con·ceiv'a·bly,** ***adv.***

**con·ceive** (kən-sēv'), ***v.t.*** [-CEIVED, -CEIVING],

[< L. *com-*, together + *capere*, take], 1. to become pregnant with. 2. to form in the mind; imagine. 3. to understand. ***v.i.*** 1. to become pregnant. 2. to form an idea (*of*).

**con·cen·trate** (kon′s'n-trāt′), ***v.t.*** [-TRATED, -TRATING], [< *con-* + L. *centrum*, center; + *-ate*], 1. to focus (one's thoughts, efforts, etc.). 2. to increase the strength or density of. ***v.i.*** to fix one's attention (*on* or *upon*). ***n.*** a substance that has been concentrated. **—con′cen·tra′tion,** ***n.***

**concentration camp,** a place of confinement for prisoners, political foes, etc.

**con·cen·tric** (kən-sen′trik), ***adj.*** [< L. *com-*, together + *centrum*, center], having a center in common, as circles: also **con·cen′tri·cal. —con·cen′tri·cal·ly,** ***adv.***

**con·cept** (kon′sept), ***n.*** [see CONCEIVE], an idea; general notion.

**con·cep·tion** (kən-sep′shən), ***n.*** 1. a conceiving or being conceived in the womb. 2. the beginning, as of a process. 3. the formulation of ideas. 4. a concept. 5. an original idea or design. **—con·cep′tive,** ***adj.***

**con·cep′tu·al** (-choo͞-əl), ***adj.*** of conception or concepts. **—con·cep′tu·al·ly,** ***adv.***

**con·cern** (kən-sûrn′), ***v.t.*** [< L. *com-*, with + *cernere*, sift], 1. to have a relation to. 2. to involve or interest. ***n.*** 1. a matter; affair. 2. interest in or regard for a person or thing. 3. relation; reference. 4. worry; anxiety. 5. a business firm. **—as concerns,** in regard to. **—concern oneself,** 1. to busy oneself. 2. to be worried.

**con·cerned′,** ***adj.*** 1. involved or interested (*in*). 2. uneasy or anxious.

**con·cern′ing,** ***prep.*** relating to.

**con·cert** (kon′sērt), ***n.*** [< L. *com-*, with + *certare*, strive], 1. mutual agreement; concord. 2. a performance of music. **—in concert,** in unison.

**con·cert·ed** (kən-sũr′tid), ***adj.*** mutually arranged or agreed upon; combined.

**con·cer·ti·na** (kon′sẽr-tē′nə), ***n.*** [< *concert*], a small accordion.

**con·cer·to** (kən-cher′tō), ***n.*** [*pl.* -TOS, -TI (-tē)], [It.], a musical composition for one or more solo instruments and an orchestra.

**con·ces·sion** (kən-sesh′ən), ***n.*** 1. a conceding. 2. a thing conceded; acknowledgment. 3. a privilege granted by a government, company, etc., as the right to sell food at a park. **—con·ces′sive** (-ses′iv), ***adj.***

**con·ces′sion·aire′** (-âr′), ***n.*** [< Fr.], the holder of a concession (sense 3).

**conch** (koŋk, konch), ***n.*** [*pl.* CONCHS (koŋks), CONCHES (kon′chiz)], [< Gr. *konchē*], the spiral, one-piece shell of certain sea mollusks.

**con·cil·i·ate** (kən-sil′i-āt′), ***v.t.*** [-ATED, -ATING], [see COUNCIL], to win over; make friendly. **—con·cil′i·a′tion,** ***n.*** **—con·cil′i·a′tor,** ***n.*** **—con·cil′i·a·to′ry** (-ə-tôr′i), ***adj.***

**con·cise** (kən-sīs′), ***adj.*** [< L. *com-*, intens. + *caedere*, cut], stating much in few words; terse; succinct. **—con·cise′ly,** ***adv.***

**con·clave** (kon′klāv, koŋ′-), ***n.*** [< L. *com-*, with + *clavis*, key], a private meeting; specif., one held by cardinals to elect a pope.

**con·clude** (kən-klo͞od′), ***v.t.*** & ***v.i.*** [-CLUDED, -CLUDING], [< L. *com-*, together + *claudere*, to shut], 1. to bring or come to an end; finish. 2. to reason; deduce. 3. to decide; determine. 4. to arrange (a treaty, etc.).

**con·clu·sion** (kən-klo͞o′zhən), ***n.*** 1. the end. 2. a judgment or opinion formed after thought. 3. an outcome. 4. a concluding (*of* a treaty, etc.). **—in conclusion,** lastly.

**con·clu′sive** (-siv), ***adj.*** decisive; final. **—con·clu′sive·ly,** ***adv.***

**con·coct** (kon-kokt′, kən-), ***v.t.*** [< L. *com-*, together + *coquere*, cook], 1. to make by combining ingredients. 2. to devise; plan. **—con·coct′er,** ***n.*** **—con·coc′tion,** ***n.***

**con·com·i·tant** (kon-kom′ə-tənt), ***adj.*** [< L. *com-*, together + *comes*, companion], accompanying; attendant. ***n.*** a concomitant condition, thing, etc. **—con·com′i·tant·ly,** ***adv.*** **—con·com′i·tance** (-təns), ***n.***

**con·cord** (kon′kôrd, koŋ′-), ***n.*** [< L. *com-*, together + *cor*, heart], 1. agreement; harmony. 2. peaceful relations, as between nations. 3. a treaty establishing this.

**con·cord·ance** (kon-kôr′d'ns, kən-), ***n.*** 1. agreement; harmony. 2. an alphabetical list of the words in a book, with references to the passages where they occur.

**con·cord′ant,** ***adj.*** agreeing; harmonious.

**con·cor·dat** (kon-kôr′dat), ***n.*** [see CONCORD], a compact; formal agreement.

**con·course** (kon′kôrs, koŋ′-), ***n.*** [see CONCUR], 1. a crowd; throng. 2. an open space where crowds gather, as in a park.

**con·crete** (kon′krēt, kon-krēt′), ***adj.*** [< L. *com-*, together + *crescere*, grow], 1. having a material existence; real; actual. 2. specific, not general. 3. made of concrete. ***n.*** 1. anything concrete. 2. a hard building material made of sand, gravel, cement, and water. ***v.t.*** [-CRETED, -CRETING], 1. (kon-krēt′), to solidify. 2. (kon′krēt), to cover with concrete. ***v.i.*** to solidify. **—con·crete′ly,** ***adv.***

**con·cre′tion** (-krē′shən), ***n.*** 1. a solidifying or being solidified. 2. a solidified mass.

**con·cu·bine** (koŋ′kyoo-bīn′, kon′-), ***n.*** [< L. *com-*, with + *cubare*, to lie down], in some societies, a secondary wife having inferior status.

**con·cu·pis·cence** (kon-kū′pə-s'ns), ***n.*** [< L. *com-*, together + *cupere*, to desire], strong, sexual desire; lust. **—con·cu′pis·cent,** ***adj.***

**con·cur** (kən-kũr′), ***v.i.*** [-CURRED, -CURRING], [< L. *com-*, together + *currere*, to run], 1. to occur at the same time; coincide. 2. to act together. 3. to agree.

**con·cur′rence,** ***n.*** a concurring; esp., agreement.

**con·cur′rent,** ***adj.*** 1. occurring at the same time. 2. acting together; co-operating. 3. in *law*, having equal jurisdiction.

**con·cus·sion** (kən-kush′ən), ***n.*** [< L. *com-*, together + *quatere*, to shake], 1. a violent shaking; shock, as from impact. 2. an impaired condition, esp. of the brain, caused by a violent blow or impact.

**con·demn** (kən-dem′), ***v.t.*** [< L. *com-*, intens. + *damnare*, to harm], 1. to disapprove of strongly. 2. to declare guilty. 3. to inflict a penalty upon. 4. to appropriate (property) for public use. 5. to declare unfit for use. **—con·dem·na·tion** (kon′dem-nā′shən), ***n.***

**con·dense** (kən-dens′), ***v.t.*** & ***v.i.*** [-DENSED, -DENSING], [< L. *com-*, intens. + *densus*, dense], 1. to make or become more dense or compact. 2. to express in fewer words. 3. to change to a denser form, as from gas to a liquid. **—con·densed′,** ***adj.*** **—con·den·sa·tion** (kon′den-sā′shən), ***n.***

**con·dens′er,** ***n.*** one that condenses; specif., *a*) an apparatus for liquefying gases or vapors. *b*) a lens for concentrating light rays on an area. *c*) a device for receiving and storing an electric charge.

**con·de·scend** (kon′di-send′), ***v.i.*** [< LL. *com-*, together + *descendere*, climb down], 1. to be gracious or affable toward those regarded as of inferior rank. 2. to deal with others patronizingly. **—con′de·scen′sion,** ***n.***

**con·dign** (kən-dīn′), ***adj.*** [< L. *com-*, intens. + *dignus*, worthy], suitable; deserved: said esp. of punishment.

**con·di·ment** (kon′də-mənt), ***n.*** [ult. < L. *condire*, to pickle], a seasoning or relish for food as pepper, mustard, etc.

**con·di·tion** (kən-dish′ən), ***n.*** [< L. *com-*, together + *dicere*, speak], 1. anything required for the existence, completion, performance, etc. of something else; provision or prerequisite. 2. state of being: as, a critical *condition.* 3. proper or healthy state: as, athletes must be in *condition.* 4. social position; rank. ***v.t.*** 1. to stipulate. 2. to subject to a condition. 3. to bring into fit condition. 4. to develop a pattern of behavior in; make accustomed (*to*). **—on condition that**, provided that.

**con·di′tion·al,** ***adj.*** 1. dependent on a condition; qualified. 2. expressing a condition. **—con·di′tion·al·ly,** ***adv.***

**con·dole** (kən-dōl′), ***v.i.*** [-DOLED, -DOLING], [< L. *com-*, with + *dolere*, grieve], to express sympathy; commiserate. **—con·do′lence, con·dole′ment,** ***n.***

**con·do·min·i·um** (kon′də-min′i-əm), ***n.*** [Mod. L.; see COM- & DOMAIN], 1. an arrangement under which a tenant in an apartment building holds full title to his unit and joint ownership in the common grounds. 2. [*pl.* -IUMS, -IA (-ə)], such a building.

**con·done** (kən-dōn′), ***v.t.*** [-DONED, -DONING], [< L. *com-*, intens. + *donare*, give], to forgive, pardon, or overlook (an offense). **—con·do·na·tion** (kon′dō-nā′shən), ***n.***

**con·dor** (kon′dēr), ***n.*** [Sp. < Peruv. *cuntur*], a large vulture of the S. American Andes with a bare head; also, a similar vulture of California.

**con·duce** (kən-dōōs′), ***v.i.*** [-DUCED, -DUCING], [< L. *com-*, together + *ducere*, to lead], to tend; contribute; lead (*to* or *toward*). **—con·du′cive,** ***adj.***

**con·duct** (kon′dukt; *for v.*, kən-dukt′), ***n.*** [see CONDUCE], 1. guidance. 2. management. 3. behavior. ***v.t. & v.i.*** 1. to lead. 2. to manage. 3. to direct (an orchestra, etc.). 4. to behave (oneself). 5. to be a channel for; transmit. **—con·duc′tion,** ***n.*** **—con·duct′i·ble,** ***adj.*** **—con·duc′tive,** ***adj.***

**con·duc·tiv·i·ty** (kon′duk-tiv′ə-ti), ***n.*** the power of transmitting heat, electricity, etc.

**con·duc′tor,** ***n.*** 1. one who conducts; leader. 2. the director of an orchestra, choir, etc. 3. one who has charge of the passengers on a streetcar or train. 4. a thing that conducts electricity, heat, etc.

**con·duit** (kon′dit, -doo-it), ***n.*** [see CONDUCE], 1. a pipe or channel for conveying fluids. 2. a tube for electric wires.

**cone** (kōn), ***n.*** [< Gr. *kōnos*], 1. a solid figure with a circle for its base and a curved surface tapering to a point. 2. any object shaped like a cone. 3. the woody, scaly fruit of evergreen trees.

**con·fab** (kon′fab), ***n.*** [Colloq.], a chat.

**con·fab·u·late** (kən-fab′yoo-lāt′), ***v.i.*** [-LATED, -LATING], [< L. *com-*, together + *fabulari*, to talk], to talk together informally. **—con·fab′u·la′tion,** ***n.***

**con·fec·tion** (kən-fek′shən), ***n.*** [< L. *com-*, with + *facere*, make], a bonbon, candy, ice cream, preserve, etc.

**con·fec′tion·er,** ***n.*** one who makes or sells candy and other confections.

**con·fec′tion·er′y** (-er′i), ***n.*** [*pl.* -IES], the shop of a confectioner.

**con·fed·er·a·cy** (kən-fed′ēr-ə-si), ***n.*** [*pl.* -CIES], a league or alliance. **—the Confederacy,** the eleven Southern States that seceded from the U.S. in 1860 and 1861.

**con·fed·er·ate** (kən-fed′ēr-it), ***adj.*** [< L. *com-*, together + *foedus*, league], 1. united in an alliance. 2. [C-], of the Confederacy. ***n.*** 1. an ally. 2. an accomplice. 3. [C-], a Southerner who supported the Confederacy. ***v.t. & v.i.*** (-āt′), [-ATED, -ATING], to unite in a confederacy; ally.

**con·fed′er·a′tion** (-ā′shən), ***n.*** an alliance.

**con·fer** (kən-fūr′), ***v.t.*** [-FERRED, -FERRING], [< L. *com-*, together + *ferre*, bring], to give; bestow. ***v.i.*** to have a conference.

**con·fer·ee** (kon′fēr-ē′), ***n.*** a participant in a conference: also sp. **conferree.**

**con·fer·ence** (kon′fēr-əns), ***n.*** 1. a formal meeting for discussion. 2. an association of churches, schools, etc. for a common purpose.

**con·fess** (kən-fes′), ***v.t. & v.i.*** [< L. *com-*, together + *fateri*, acknowledge], 1. to admit or acknowledge (a fault, crime, belief, etc.). 2. to tell (one's sins) to a priest.

**con·fes·sion** (kən-fesh′ən), ***n.*** 1. a confessing. 2. something confessed. 3. a creed. 4. a sect; denomination.

**con·fes′sion·al,** ***n.*** an enclosure in a church where a priest hears confessions.

**con·fes′sor,** ***n.*** 1. one who confesses. 2. a priest authorized to hear confessions.

**con·fet·ti** (kən-fet′i), ***n.pl.*** [It.], [construed as sing.], bits of colored paper scattered about at carnivals and celebrations.

**con·fi·dant** (kon′fə-dant′), ***n.*** a close, trusted friend. **—con′fi·dante′,** ***n.fem.***

**con·fide** (kən-fīd′), ***v.i.*** [-FIDED, -FIDING], [< L. *com-*, intens. + *fidere*, to trust], to trust (*in* someone); share secrets. ***v.t.*** 1. to tell about as a secret. 2. to entrust (*to*).

**con·fi·dence** (kon′fə-dəns), ***n.*** 1. trust; reliance. 2. assurance; certainty. 3. belief in one's own abilities. 4. the belief that another will keep a secret. 5. a secret.

**confidence game,** a swindle effected by one (**confidence man**) who first gains the confidence of his victim.

**con′fi·dent** (-dənt), ***adj.*** full of confidence; specif., *a*) certain. *b*) sure of oneself; bold. **—con′fi·dent·ly,** ***adv.***

**con′fi·den′tial** (-den′shəl), ***adj.*** 1. told in confidence; secret. 2. of or showing confidence. 3. entrusted with private matters. **—con′fi·den′tial·ly,** ***adv.***

**con·fid·ing** (kən-fīd′iŋ), ***adj.*** trustful or inclined to trust.

**con·fig·u·ra·tion** (kən-fig′yoo-rā′shəŋ), ***n.*** [< L. *com-*, together + *figurare*, to form], form; contour; outline.

**con·fine** (kon′fīn′; *for v.*, kən-fīn′), ***n.*** [< L. *com-*, with + *finis*, an end], *usually in pl.* a boundary or bounded region. ***v.t.*** [-FINED, -FINING], 1. to keep within limits; restrict. 2. to keep shut up, as in prison, a sickbed, etc. **—con·fine′ment,** ***n.***

**con·firm** (kən-fūrm′), ***v.t.*** [< L. *com-*, intens. + *firmus*, firm], 1. to strengthen. 2. to give formal approval to. 3. to prove to be true. 4. to admit to full membership in a church.

**con·fir·ma·tion** (kon′fēr-mā′shən), ***n.*** 1. a confirming. 2. something that confirms. 3. a ceremony admitting a person to full membership in a church.

**con·firmed′,** ***adj.*** 1. firmly established; habitual. 2. corroborated; proved.

**con·fis·cate** (kon′fis-kāt′), ***v.t.*** [-CATED, -CATING], [< L. *com-*, together + *fiscus*, treasury], 1. to seize (private property) for the public treasury. 2. to seize as by authority; appropriate. **—con′fis·ca′tion,** ***n.***

**con·fis·ca·to·ry** (kən-fis′kə-tôr′i), ***adj.*** 1. of or effecting confiscation. 2. confiscating.

**con·fla·gra·tion** (kon′flə-grā′shən), ***n.*** [< L. *com-*, intens. + *flagrare*, to burn], a big, destructive fire.

**con·flict** (kən-flikt′; *for n.*, kon′flikt), ***v.i.*** [< L. *com-*, together + *fligere*, to strike], to clash; be antagonistic, incompatible, etc. ***n.*** 1. a fight; struggle. 2. sharp disagreement, as of interests or ideas.

**con·flu·ence** (kon′flōō-əns), ***n.*** [< L. *com-*, together + *fluere*, flow], 1. a flowing together, as of streams. 2. the place of this. 3. a flocking together. 4. a crowd. **—con′flu·ent,** ***adj.***

**con·form** (kən-fôrm′), ***v.t.*** [< L. *com-*, together + *formare*, to form], 1. to make similar. 2. to bring into agreement; adapt. ***v.i.*** 1. to be or become similar. 2. to be in agreement. 3. to act in accordance with rules, customs, etc. **—con·form′ist,** ***n.***

**con·form′a·ble,** *adj.* 1. that conforms; specif., *a*) similar. *b*) in agreement. *c*) adapted. 2. quick to conform; obedient.

**con·for·ma·tion** (kon′fôr-mā′shən), *n.* 1. a symmetrical arrangement of the parts of a thing. 2. the structure or form of a thing.

**con·form·i·ty** (kən-fôr′mə-ti), *n.* [*pl.* -TIES], 1. a being in agreement; correspondence; similarity. 2. a conforming to rules, customs, etc. Also **con·form′ance.**

**con·found** (kən-found′, kon-), *v.t.* [< L. *com-*, together + *fundere*, pour], 1. to confuse; bewilder. 2. to damn: used as a mild oath. **—con·found′ed,** *adj.*

**con·frere** (kon′frâr), *n.* [Fr.], a colleague.

**con·front** (kən-frunt′), *v.t.* [< L. *com-*, together + *frons*, front], 1. to face, esp. boldly or defiantly. 2. to bring face to face (*with*). **—con·fron·ta·tion** (kon′frun-tā′shən), *n.*

**con·fuse** (kən-fūz′), *v.t.* [-FUSED, -FUSING], [see CONFOUND], 1. to mix up; put into disorder. 2. to bewilder; embarrass. 3. to mistake the identity of. **—con·fus′ed·ly,** *adv.*

**con·fu′sion** (-fū′zhən), *n.* a confusing or being confused; disorder, bewilderment, etc.

**con·fute** (kən-fūt′), *v.t.* [-FUTED, -FUTING], [< L. *confutare*], to prove to be false or in error. **—con·fu·ta·tion** (kon′fyoo-tā′shən), *n.* **—con·fut′er,** *n.*

**con·geal** (kən-jēl′), *v.t. & v.i.* [< L. *com-*, together + *gelare*, freeze], 1. to freeze. 2. to thicken; coagulate. **—con·geal′ment,** *n.*

**con·gen·ial** (kən-jēn′yəl), *adj.* [see COM- & GENIAL], 1. kindred; compatible. 2. of the same temperament; friendly; agreeable. **—con·ge′ni·al′i·ty** (-jē′ni-al′ə-ti), *n.*

**con·gen·i·tal** (kən-jen′ə-t'l), *adj.* [< L.; see COM- & GENITAL], existing as such at birth. **—con·gen′i·tal·ly,** *adv.*

**con·ger (eel)** (koŋ′gẽr), [< Gr. *gongros*], a large, edible salt-water eel.

**con·gest** (kən-jest′), *v.t.* [< L. *com-*, together + *gerere*, carry], 1. to cause too much blood to accumulate in (a part of the body). 2. to overcrowd; fill to excess. **—con·ges′tion,** *n.*

**con·glom·er·ate** (kən-glom′ẽr-āt′; *for adj. & n.*, -it), *v.t. & v.i.* [-ATED, -ATING], [< L. *com-*, together + *glomus*, ball], to form into a rounded mass. *adj.* 1. formed into a rounded mass. 2. formed of substances collected into a single mass. *n.* 1. a conglomerate mass. 2. rock made up of fragments or pebbles cemented together in clay and sand. 3. a large corporation formed by merging many companies in unrelated industries. **—con·glom′er·a′tion,** *n.*

**con·grat·u·late** (kən-grach′ə-lāt′), *v.t.* [-LATED, -LATING], [< L. *com-*, together + *gratulari*, wish joy], to rejoice with (a person who has been fortunate, etc.); felicitate. **—con·grat′u·la·to′ry** (-lə-tôr′i), *adj.*

**con·grat′u·la′tion,** *n.* 1. a congratulating. 2. *pl.* expressions of pleasure over another's good fortune, etc.

**con·gre·gate** (kon′grə-gāt′), *v.t. & v.i.* [-GATED, -GATING], [< L. *com-*, together + *grex*, a flock], to gather into a mass or crowd; assemble. **—con′gre·ga′tive,** *adj.*

**con′gre·ga′tion,** *n.* 1. a gathering; assemblage. 2. an assembly of people for religious worship.

**con′gre·ga′tion·al,** *adj.* 1. of or like a congregation. 2. [C-], of a Protestant denomination of self-governing churches.

**con·gress** (koŋ′grəs), *n.* [< L. *com-*, together + *gradi*, to step], 1. an assembly or conference. 2. a legislature, esp. of a republic. 3. [C-], the U.S. legislature, consisting of the Senate and the House of Representatives. **—con·gres·sion·al** (kən-gresh′ən-'l), *adj.*

**con′gress·man,** *n.* [*pl.* -MEN], a member of Congress, esp. of the House of Representatives.

**con·gru·ent** (koŋ′groo-ənt), *adj.* [< L. *congruere*, agree], corresponding; harmonious. **—con′gru·ence, con′gru·en·cy,** *n.*

**con·gru·ous** (koŋ′groo-əs), *adj.* 1. congruent. 2. fitting; suitable; appropriate. **—con·gru·i·ty** (kən-groo′ə-ti) [*pl.* -TIES], *n.*

**con·i·cal** (kon′i-k'l), *adj.* 1. of a cone. 2. resembling or shaped like a cone. Also **con′ic. —con′i·cal·ly,** *adv.*

**co·ni·fer** (kō′nə-fẽr, kon′ə-), *n.* [< L. *conus*, cone + *ferre*, to bear], any of a large group of cone-bearing trees and shrubs, mostly evergreens, as the pine, fir, etc. **—co·nif·er·ous** (kō-nif′ẽr-əs), *adj.*

**conj.,** conjunction.

**con·jec·ture** (kən-jek′chẽr), *n.* [< L. *conjicere*, to guess], 1. guesswork; inferring, theorizing, or predicting from incomplete evidence. 2. a guess. *v.t. & v.i.* [-TURED, -TURING], to guess. **—con·jec′tur·al,** *adj.*

**con·join** (kən-join′), *v.t. & v.i.* [< L. *conjungere*], to join together; unite. **—con·joint′,** *adj.* **—con·joint′ly,** *adv.*

**con·ju·gal** (kon′joo-gəl), *adj.* [< L. *conjunx*, spouse], of marriage or the relation between husband and wife.

**con·ju·gate** (kon′joo-git, -gāt′), *adj.* [< L. *com-*, together + *jugare*, join], joined together, esp. in a pair. *v.t.* (-gāt′), [-GATED, -GATING], 1. to join together; couple. 2. in *grammar*, to give in order the inflectional forms of (a verb). **—con′ju·ga′tion,** *n.* **—con′ju·ga′tive,** *adj.*

**con·junc·tion** (kən-juŋk′shən), *n.* [see CONJOIN], 1. a joining together; union; combination. 2. coincidence. 3. a word used to connect words, phrases, or clauses (e.g., *and, but, if*, etc.). **—con·junc′tive,** *adj.*

**con·junc·ti·vi·tis** (kən-juŋk′tə-vī′tis), *n.* [see -ITIS], inflammation of the mucous membrance lining the eyelids.

**con·jure** (kun′jẽr, kon′-; *for v.t. 1*, kən-joor′), *v.i.* [-JURED, -JURING], [< L. *com-*, together + *jurare*, swear], 1. to summon a demon, spirit, etc. by magic. 2. to practice magic. *v.t.* 1. to entreat solemnly. 2. to make appear, come (*up*), etc. as by magic. **—con·ju·ra·tion** (kon′joo-rā′shən), *n.*

**con·jur·er, con·jur·or** (kun′jẽr-ẽr, kon′-), *n.* a magician; sorcerer.

**conk** (koŋk), *n. & v.t.* [< *conch*], [Slang], hit on the head. **—conk out,** [Slang], to fail suddenly in operation.

**con·nect** (kə-nekt′), *v.t.* [< L. *com-*, together + *nectere*, fasten], 1. to join (two things together, or one thing *with* or *to* another). 2. to show or think of as related; associate. *v.i.* to join or be joined. **—con·nec′tor, con·nect′er,** *n.*

**con·nect′ed,** *adj.* 1. joined together. 2. coherent. 3. related. **—con·nect′ed·ly,** *adv.*

**con·nec·tion** (kə-nek′shən), *n.* 1. a connecting or being connected; union. 2. a thing that connects. 3. a relation; association. 4. *usually in pl. a*) a relative, esp. by marriage. *b*) an associate, etc. 5. *usually in pl.* the meeting of trains, etc. at points of transfer. Brit. sp., **connexion.**

**con·nec′tive** (-tiv), *adj.* connecting. *n.* that which connects; esp., a word connecting words, phrases, or clauses.

**con·nip·tion (fit)** (kə-nip′shən), [pseudo-Latin], [Colloq.], a fit of anger, hysteria, etc.

**con·nive** (kə-nīv′), *v.i.* [-NIVED, -NIVING], [< L. *connivere*, to wink, connive], 1. to pretend not to look (*at* crime, etc.), thus giving tacit consent. 2. to co-operate secretly (*with* someone), esp. in wrongdoing. **—con·niv′ance,** *n.* **—con·niv′er,** *n.*

**con·nois·seur** (kon′ə-sũr′), *n.* [< Fr. < L. *cognoscere*, know], one who has expert knowledge and keen discrimination, esp. in the fine arts.

**con·note** (kə-nōt′), *v.t.* [-NOTED, -NOTING], [< L. *com-*, together + *notare*, to mark], to suggest or convey (associations, overtones, etc.) in addition to the explicit, or denoted, meaning. —**con·no·ta·tion** (kon′ə-tā′shən), *n.* —**con′no·ta′tive,** *adj.*

**con·nu·bi·al** (kə-nōō′bi-əl, -nū′-), *adj.* [< L. *com-*, together + *nubere*, marry], of marriage; conjugal.

**con·quer** (koŋ′kẽr), *v.t.* [< L. *com-*, intens. + *quaerere*, seek], 1. to get control of as by winning a war. 2. to overcome; defeat. *v.i.* to win; be victorious. —**con′quer·a·ble,** *adj.* —**con′quer·or,** *n.*

**con·quest** (koŋ′kwest, kon′-), *n.* 1. a conquering. 2. something conquered.

**con·quis·ta·dor** (kon-kwis′tə-dôr′), *n.* [*pl.* -DORS, -DORES], [Sp., conqueror], any of the Spanish conquerors of Mexico, Peru, or other parts of America in the 16th century.

**con·san·guin·e·ous** (kon′saŋ-gwin′i-əs), *adj.* [see COM- & SANGUINE], related by blood. —**con′san·guin′i·ty,** *n.*

**con·science** (kon′shəns), *n.* [< L. *com-*, with + *scire*, know], an awareness of right and wrong, with a compulsion to do right.

**con·sci·en·tious** (kon′shi-en′shəs), *adj.* governed by one's conscience; scrupulous. —**con′sci·en′tious·ly,** *adv.*

**conscientious objector,** one who for reasons of conscience refuses to take part in warfare.

**con·scious** (kon′shəs), *adj.* [< L.; see CONSCIENCE], 1. having an awareness (*of* or *that*). 2. able to feel and think; awake. 3. aware of oneself as a thinking being. 4. intentional: as, *conscious* humor. 5. known to or felt by oneself. —**con′scious·ly,** *adv.*

**con′scious·ness,** *n.* 1. the state of being conscious; awareness. 2. the totality of one's thoughts and feelings; mind.

**con·script** (kən-skript′ *for v;* kon′skript *for adj & n.*), *v.t.* [< L. *com-*, with + *scribere*, write], to enroll for compulsory service in the armed forces; draft. *adj.* conscripted. *n.* a draftee. —**con·scrip′tion,** *n.*

**con·se·crate** (kon′sə-krāt′), *v.t.* [-CRATED, -CRATING], [< L. *com-*, together + *sacer*, sacred], to set apart as holy; devote to religious use. —**con′se·cra′tion,** *n.*

**con·sec·u·tive** (kən-sek′yoo-tiv), *adj.* [see CONSEQUENCE], following in uninterrupted order; successive. —**con·sec′u·tive·ly,** *adv.*

**con·sen·sus** (kən-sen′səs), *n.* [see CONSENT], 1. agreement in opinion. 2. general opinion.

**con·sent** (kən-sent′), *v.i.* [< L. *com-*, with + *sentire*, feel], to agree, permit, or assent. *n.* 1. permission; approval. 2. agreement.

**con·se·quence** (kon′si-kwens′), *n.* [< L. *com-*, with + *sequi*, follow], 1. a result; effect. 2 a logical result or conclusion. 3. importance. —**take the consequences,** to accept the results of one's actions.

**con′se·quent′** (-kwent′), *adj.* following as a result; resulting.

**con′se·quen′tial** (-kwen′shəl), *adj.* 1. consequent. 2. acting important.

**con′se·quent′ly,** *adv.* as a result; by logical inference; therefore.

**con·ser·va·tion** (kon′sẽr-vā′shən), *n.* 1. a conserving. 2. the official care and protection of natural resources, as forests. —**con′ser·va′tion·ist,** *n.*

**con·serv·a·tive** (kən-sũr′və-tiv), *adj.* 1. tending to conserve. 2. tending to preserve established institutions, etc.; opposed to change. 3. moderate; prudent. *n.* a conservative person. —**con·serv′a·tism,** *n.* —**con·serv′a·tive·ly,** *adv.*

**con·serv·a·to·ry** (kən-sũr′və-tôr′i), *n.* [*pl.* -RIES], 1. a greenhouse. 2. a school for teaching music, art, etc.

**con·serve** (kən-sũrv′; *for n., usually* kon′-sũrv), *v.t.* [-SERVED, -SERVING], [< L. *com-*, with + *servare*, to guard], 1. to keep from being damaged, lost, or wasted. 2. to make (fruit) into preserves. *n. often in pl.* a preserve of two or more fruits.

**con·sid·er** (kən-sid′ẽr), *v.t.* [< L. *considerare*, observe], 1. to think about in order to understand or decide. 2. to have or keep in mind. 3. to have regard for (others). 4. to believe to be. *v.i.* to think seriously.

**con·sid′er·a·ble,** *adj.* 1. worth considering; important. 2. much or large. —**con·sid′er·a·bly,** *adv.*

**con·sid′er·ate** (-it), *adj.* having or showing regard for others and their feelings.

**con·sid′er·a′tion** (-ā′shən), *n.* 1. act of considering; deliberation. 2. thoughtful regard for others. 3. something considered in making a decision. 4. a recompense; fee. —**take into consideration,** to keep in mind. —**under consideration,** being thought over.

**con·sid′ered** (-ẽrd), *adj.* 1. arrived at after careful thought. 2. respected.

**con·sid′er·ing,** *prep.* in view of; taking into account.

**con·sign** (kən-sīn′), *v.t.* [< L. *consignare*, to seal], 1. to hand over; deliver. 2. to entrust. 3. to assign; set apart. 4. to send or deliver (goods). —**con·sign′a·ble,** *adj.*

**con·sign′ment** (-mənt), *n.* 1. a consigning or being consigned. 2. a shipment of goods sent to an agent for sale or safekeeping.

**con·sist** (kən-sist′), *v.i.* [< L. *com-*, together + *sistere*, to stand], 1. to be made up or composed (*of*). 2. to be contained or inherent (*in*). 3. to exist in harmony (*with*).

**con·sist′en·cy** (-sis′tən-si), *n.* [*pl.* -CIES], 1. firmness or thickness, as of a liquid. 2. agreement; harmony. 3. conformity with previous practice or principle.

**con·sist′ent** (-tənt), *adj.* 1. in harmony; compatible. 2. holding to the same principles or practice. —**con·sist′ent·ly,** *adv.*

**con·sis·to·ry** (kən-sis′tə-ri), *n.* [*pl.* -RIES], [see CONSIST], 1. a church council, as the papal senate. 2. a session of such a body.

**con·so·la·tion** (kon′sə-lā′shən), *n.* 1. comfort; solace. 2. one that consoles.

**con·sole** (kən-sōl′), *v.t.* [-SOLED, -SOLING], [< L. *com-*, with + *solari*, to solace], to comfort; cheer (a person) up, as at the time of a loss. —**con·sol′a·ble,** *adj.*

**con·sole** (kon′sōl), *n.* [Fr.], 1. the desklike frame containing the keys, stops, etc. of an organ. 2. a radio, television, or phonograph cabinet meant to stand on the floor.

**con·sol·i·date** (kən-sol′ə-dāt′), *v.t. & v.i.* [-DATED, -DATING], [< L. *com-*, together + *solidus*, solid], 1. to combine into one; unite. 2. to make or become strong or stable. —**con·sol′i·da′tion,** *n.* —**con·sol′i·da′tor,** *n.*

**con·som·mé** (kon′sə-mā′), *n.* [Fr.], a clear, strained meat soup.

**con·so·nance** (kon′sə-nəns), *n.* [< L. *com-*, with + *sonus*, sound], agreement; harmony, esp. of musical tones.

**con′so·nant** (-nənt), *adj.* 1. in harmony or accord. 2. harmonious in tone. *n.* a letter representing a speech sound made by obstructing the breath stream, as *p, t, l,* etc. —**con·so·nan·tal** (kon′sə-nan′t'l), *adj.*

**con·sort** (kon′sôrt); *for v.,* kən-sôrt′), *n.* [< L. *com-*, with + *sors*, a share], 1. a companion. 2. a wife or husband, esp. of a reigning monarch. *v.i. & v.t.* to associate.

**con·spec·tus** (kən-spek′təs), *n.* [see CONSPICUOUS], 1. a general view; survey. 2. a summary.

**con·spic·u·ous** (kən-spik′ū-əs), *adj.* [< L. *com-*, intens. + *specere*, see], 1. easy to see; obvious. 2. outstanding; remarkable. —**con·spic′u·ous·ly,** *adv.*

**con·spir·a·cy** (kən-spir′ə-si), *n.* [*pl.* -CIES], 1. a conspiring. 2. an unlawful plot. 3. the group taking part in such a plot.

**con·spire** (kən-spīr′), *v.i.* [-SPIRED, -SPIRING],

[< L. *com-*, together + *spirare*, breathe], 1. to plan together secretly, esp. in order to commit a crime. 2. to work together toward one end. —**con·spir'a·tor** (-spir'ə-tēr), *n.*

**con·sta·ble** (kon'stə-b'l, kun'-), *n.* [< LL. *comes stabuli*, lit., count of the stable], a policeman.

**con·stab·u·lar·y** (kən-stab'yoo-ler'i), *n.* [*pl.* -IES], constables collectively.

**con·stant** (kon'stənt), *adj.* [< L. *com-*, together + *stare*, to stand], 1. not changing; fixed; regular. 2. resolute. 3. loyal; faithful. 4. continual; persistent. *n.* anything that does not change or vary. —**con'stan·cy**, *n.* —**con'stant·ly**, *adv.*

**con·stel·la·tion** (kon'stə-lā'shən), *n.* [< L. *com-*, with + *stella*, star], 1. a group of fixed stars. 2. any brilliant cluster.

**con·ster·na·tion** (kon'stēr-nā'shən), *n.* [< L. *consternare*, terrify], great alarm; dismay.

**con·sti·pate** (kon'stə-pāt'), *v.t.* [-PATED, -PATING], [< L. *com-*, together + *stipare*, cram], to cause constipation in.

**con'sti·pa'tion**, *n.* infrequent and difficult movement of the bowels.

**con·stit·u·en·cy** (kən-stich'ōō-ən-si), *n.* [*pl.* -CIES], the voters in a district.

**con·stit'u·ent** (-ənt), *adj.* [see CONSTITUTE], 1. necessary to the whole; component. 2. that elects. 3. authorized to make or revise a constitution. *n.* 1. a voter in a district. 2. a component.

**con·sti·tute** (kon'stə-tōōt', -tūt'), *v.t.* [-TUTED, -TUTING], [< L. *com-*, together + *statuere*, to set], 1. to establish (a law, government, etc.). 2. to set up (an assembly, etc.) in a legal form. 3. to appoint or ordain. 4. to make up; compose.

**con'sti·tu'tion** (-tōō'shən, -tū'-), *n.* 1. a constituting; establishment. 2. structure; organization. 3. *a*) the system of basic laws and principles of a government, society, etc. *b*) a document stating these.

**con'sti·tu'tion·al**, *adj.* 1. of or in one's constitution, or structure; basic. 2. of or in accordance with the constitution of a government, society, etc. *n.* [Colloq.], a walk or other exercise taken for one's health. —**con'sti·tu'tion·al'i·ty** (-al'ə-ti), *n.* —**con'sti·tu'tion·al·ly**, *adv.*

**con·strain** (kən-strān'), *v.t.* [< L. *com-*, together + *stringere*, draw tight], 1. to confine; restrain. 2. to force; compel.

**con·straint'**, *n.* 1. confinement; restriction. 2. force; compulsion. 3. forced, unnatural quality of manner.

**con·strict** (kən-strikt'), *v.t.* [see CONSTRAIN], to make smaller or narrower by squeezing, etc.; contract. —**con·stric'tion**, *n.* —**con·stric'tor**, *n.* —**con·stric'tive**, *adj.*

**con·struct** (kən-strukt'), *v.t.* [< L. *com-*, together + *struere*, pile up], to build, devise, etc. —**con·struc'tor**, *n.*

**con·struc·tion** (kən-struk'shən), *n.* 1. a constructing or manner of being constructed. 2. a structure. 3. an interpretation, as of a statement. 4. the arrangement of words in a sentence.

**con·struc'tive**, *adj.* helping to construct; leading to improvements: as, *constructive* criticism. —**con·struc'tive·ly**, *adv.*

**con·strue** (kən-strōō'), *v.t. & v.i.* [-STRUED, -STRUING], [see CONSTRUCT], 1. to analyze the grammatical construction of (a sentence, etc.). 2. to translate. 3. to explain; interpret. —**con·stru'a·ble**, *adj.*

**con·sul** (kon's'l), *n.* [< L. *consulere*, to deliberate], 1. a chief magistrate of ancient Rome. 2. a government official appointed to live in a foreign city and look after his country's citizens and business there. —**con'su·lar**, *adj.* —**con'sul·ship'**, *n.*

**con'su·late** (-s'l-it), *n.* 1. the position, powers, etc. of a consul. 2. the office or residence of a consul. 3. his term of office.

**con·sult** (kən-sult'), *v.i.* [< L. *consulere*, ask advice], to talk things over; confer. *v.t.* 1. to seek information or instruction from. 2. to consider; have regard for.

**con·sult'ant**, *n.* 1. a person who consults another. 2. one who gives professional or technical advice.

**con·sul·ta·tion** (kon's'l-tā'shən), *n.* 1. a consulting. 2. a conference. —**con·sul·ta·tive** (kən-sul'tə-tiv), *adj.*

**con·sume** (kən-sōōm'), *v.t.* [-SUMED, -SUMING], [< L. *com-*, together + *sumere*, to take], 1. to destroy, as by fire. 2. to use up or waste (time, money, etc.). 3. to eat or drink up. —**con·sum'a·ble**, *adj.*

**con·sum'er**, *n.* a person or thing that consumes; specif., one who uses goods or services to satisfy his needs rather than to produce other goods.

**con·sum·mate** (kən-sum'it), *adj.* [< L. *com-*, together + *summa*, a sum], complete; perfect. *v.t.* (kon'sə-māt'), [-MATED, -MATING], 1. to complete; finish. 2. to make (marriage) actual by sexual intercourse. —**con'summa'tion**, *n.*

**con·sump·tion** (kən-sump'shən), *n.* 1. a consuming or being consumed. 2. a wasting disease; esp., tuberculosis of the lungs. 3. *a*) the using up of goods or services. *b*) the amount used up.

**con·sump'tive** (-tiv), *adj.* 1. consuming or tending to consume. 2. of or having tuberculosis of the lungs. *n.* one who has tuberculosis of the lungs.

**cont., contd.**, continued.

**con·tact** (kon'takt), *n.* [< L. *com-*, together + *tangere*, to touch], 1. a touching or meeting. 2. the state of being in association (*with*). 3. connection. *v.t.* 1. to place in contact. 2. [Colloq.], to get in touch with. *v.i.* to come into contact.

**con·ta·gion** (kən-tā'jən), *n.* [see CONTACT], 1. the spreading of disease by contact. 2. a contagious disease. 3. the spreading of an emotion, idea, etc.

**con·ta·gious** (kən-tā'jəs), *adj.* 1. spread by contact: said of diseases. 2. carrying the causative agent of a contagious disease. 3. spreading from person to person.

**con·tain** (kən-tān'), *v.t.* [< L. *com-*, together + *tenere*, to hold], 1. to have in it; hold; include. 2. to have the capacity for holding. 3. to hold back or restrain within fixed limits. —**con·tain'a·ble**, *adj.*

**con·tain'er**, *n.* a thing for containing something, as a box, can, etc.

**con·tam·i·nate** (kən-tam'ə-nāt'), *v.t.* [-NATED, -NATING], [< L. *com-*, together + base of *tangere*, to touch], to make impure, corrupt, etc. by contact; pollute. —**contam'i·na'tion**, *n.*

**con·temn** (kən-tem'), *v.t.* [< L. *com-*, intens. + *temnere*, to scorn], to treat with contempt; scorn.

**con·tem·plate** (kon'təm-plāt'), *v.t.* [-PLATED, -PLATING], [< L. *contemplari*, observe], 1. to gaze at intently. 2. to think about intently; study. 3. to expect or intend. *v.i.* to muse. —**con'tem·pla'tion**, *n.* —**con'tem·pla'tive**, *adj.*

**con·tem·po·ra·ne·ous** (kən-tem'pə-rā'ni-əs), *adj.* contemporary.

**con·tem·po·ra·ry** (kən-tem'pə-rer'i), *adj.* [< L. *com-*, with + *tempus*, time], 1. living or occurring in the same period. 2. of about the same age. *n.* [*pl.* -RIES], one living in the same period as another or others.

**con·tempt** (kən-tempt'), *n.* [see CONTEMN], 1. the feeling one has toward something he considers worthless or vile; scorn. 2. the condition of being despised. 3. in *law*, a showing disrespect for the dignity of a court (or legislature).

**con·tempt′i·ble** (-temp′tə-b'l), *adj.* deserving contempt. —**con·tempt′i·bly,** *adv.*
**con·temp·tu·ous** (kən-temp′cho͞o-əs), *adj.* showing contempt; scornful. —**con·temp′tu·ous·ly,** *adv.*
**con·tend** (kən-tend′), *v.i.* [< L. *com-*, together + *tendere*, stretch], 1. to fight. 2. to argue. 3. to strive in competition; vie. *v.t.* to assert. —**con·tend′er,** *n.*
**con·tent** (kən-tent′), *adj.* [see CONTAIN], 1. satisfied. 2. willing; assenting. *v.t.* to satisfy. *n.* contentment; satisfaction.
**con·tent** (kon′tent), *n.* [see CONTAIN], 1. *usually pl. a)* all that is contained in something. *b)* all that is expressed in a writing or speech. 2. substance or meaning. 3. capacity, volume, or area. 4. the amount contained.
**con·tent′ed,** *adj.* satisfied. —**con·tent′ed·ly,** *adv.* —**con·tent′ed·ness,** *n.*
**con·ten·tion** (kən-ten′shən), *n.* [see CONTEND], 1. argument; dispute. 2. a point that one argues for. 3. strife; struggle. —**con·ten′tious,** *adj.*
**con·tent′ment,** *n.* a being contented.
**con·test** (kən-test′), *v.t.* [< L. *com-*, together + *testari*, bear witness], 1. to try to disprove; dispute. 2. to fight for. *v.i.* to struggle (*with* or *against*). *n.* (kon′test), 1. a struggle; fight. 2. a dispute. 3. any race, game, etc. in which there is competition.
**con·test′ant,** *n.* [Fr.], one who contests or competes in a contest.
**con·text** (kon′tekst), *n.* [< L. *com-*, together + *texere*, weave], the parts just before and after a word or passage, that determine its meaning. —**con·tex·tu·al** (kən-teks′cho͞o-əl), *adj.*
**con·tig·u·ous** (kən-tig′ū-əs), *adj.* [see CONTINGENT], 1. in contact; touching. 2. near; adjoining. —**con·ti·gu·i·ty** (kon′ti-gū′ə-ti) [*pl.* -TIES], *n.* —**con·tig′u·ous·ly,** *adv.*
**con·ti·nence** (kon′tə-nəns), *n.* [see CONTAIN], 1. self-restraint. 2. self-restraint in sexual activity, esp. complete abstinence. Also **con′ti·nen·cy** [*pl.* -CIES]. —**con′ti·nent,** *adj.* —**con′ti·nent·ly,** *adv.*
**con·ti·nent** (kon′tə-nənt), *n.* [see CONTAIN], any of the six largest land masses of the earth.
**con′ti·nen′tal** (-nen′t'l), *adj.* 1. of a continent. 2. [often C-], European. 3. [C-], of the American colonies at the time of the American Revolution.
**con·tin·gen·cy** (kən-tin′jən-si), *n.* [*pl.* -CIES], 1. dependence on chance. 2. a possible or chance event.
**con·tin′gent,** *adj.* [< L. *com-*, together + *tangere*, to touch], 1. possible. 2. accidental. 3. dependent (*on* or *upon* an uncertainty); conditional. *n.* 1. a chance happening. 2. a quota, as of troops. 3. a part of a large group. —**con·tin′gent·ly,** *adv.*
**con·tin·u·al** (kən-tin′ū-əl), *adj.* 1. repeated often. 2. continuous. —**con·tin′u·al·ly,** *adv.*
**con·tin′u·ance,** *n.* 1. a continuing. 2. duration. 3. an unbroken succession. 4. in *law*, postponement to a later date.
**con·tin′u·a′tion** (-ā′shən), *n.* 1. a continuing or being continued. 2. a beginning again; resumption. 3. a part added; sequel.
**con·tin·ue** (kən-tin′ū), *v.i.* [-UED, -UING], [< L. *continuare*, join], 1. to last; endure. 2. to go on in a specified condition or action. 3. to stay. 4. to keep on; persist. 5. to resume after an interruption. *v.t.* 1. to go on with. 2. to extend. 3. to resume. 4. to cause to remain, as in office; retain. 5. in *law*, to postpone or adjourn to a later date.
**con·ti·nu·i·ty** (kon′tə-no͞o′ə-ti, -nū′-), *n.* [*pl.* -TIES], 1. a continuous state or quality. 2. an unbroken, coherent whole. 3. the script for a movie, radio program, etc.
**con·tin·u·ous** (kən-tin′ū-əs), *adj.* going on without interruption; unbroken; connected. —**con·tin′u·ous·ly,** *adv.*
**con·tort** (kən-tôrt′), *v.t.* [< L. *com-*, together + *torquere*, to twist], to force out of shape as by twisting. —**con·tor′tion,** *n.*
**con·tor′tion·ist,** *n.* one who can twist his body into unnatural positions.
**con·tour** (kon′toor), *n.* [Fr. < L. *com-*, intens. + *tornare*, to turn], the outline of a figure, land, etc.
**contra-,** [< L. *contra*], a prefix meaning *against, opposite, opposed to.*
**con·tra·band** (kon′trə-band′), *n.* [< Sp. < It. *contra-*, against + *bando*, proclamation], smuggled goods. *adj.* forbidden by law to be imported or exported.
**con·tra·bass** (kon′trə-bās′), *n.* [< L. *contra*, opposite + *bassus*, low], an instrument or voice having the lowest bass tone; specif., the largest and deepest-toned instrument of the viol class.
**con·tra·cep·tion** (kon′trə-sep′shən), *n.* [*contra-* + *conception*], prevention of the fertilization of the human ovum. —**con′tra·cep′tive,** *adj. & n.*
**con·tract** (kon′trakt; *for v.*, kən-trakt′, *except v.t. 1, usually* kon′trakt), *n.* [< L. *com-*, together + *trahere*, draw], an agreement, esp. a written one, enforceable by law. *v.t.* 1. to undertake by contract. 2. to get; incur. 3. to reduce in size; shrink. 4. to shorten (a word or phrase). *v.i.* 1. to make a contract. 2. to become reduced in size or bulk. —**con·tract′i·ble,** *adj.*
**con·trac·tile** (kən-trak′t'l), *adj.* having the power of contracting.
**con·trac·tion** (kən-trak′shən), *n.* 1. a contracting or being contracted. 2. a shortened form, as *don't* for *do not.*
**con·trac·tor** (kon′trak-tẽr, kən-trak′-), *n.* one who contracts to supply certain materials or do certain work for a stipulated sum.
**con·trac·tu·al** (kən-trak′cho͞o-əl), *adj.* of or constituting a contract.
**con·tra·dict** (kon′trə-dikt′), *v.t.* [< L. *contra-*, against + *dicere*, speak], 1. to assert the opposite of (a statement). 2. to deny the statement of (a person). —**con′tra·dic′tion,** *n.* —**con′tra·dic′to·ry,** *adj.*
**con·tra·dis·tinc·tion** (kon′trə-dis-tiŋk′shən), *n.* distinction by contrast: usually in *in contradistinction to.*
**con·tral·to** (kən-tral′tō), *n.* [*pl.* -TOS, -TI (-ti)], [It.; see CONTRA- & ALTO], 1. a female voice of the lowest range. 2. a woman with such a voice. *adj.* of or for a contralto.
**con·trap·tion** (kən-trap′shən), *n.* [< ?], [Colloq.], a contrivance; gadget.
**con·tra·pun·tal** (kon′trə-pun′t'l), *adj.* [< It. *contrapunto*, counterpoint], of or characterized by counterpoint.
**con·tra·ri·e·ty** (kon′trə-rī′ə-ti), *n.* 1. a being contrary. 2. [*pl.* -TIES], anything that is contrary.
**con·tra·ri·wise** (kon′trer-i-wiz′), *adv.* 1. on the contrary. 2. in the opposite way, etc.
**con·tra·ry** (kon′trer-i; *for 4, often* kən-trâr′i), *adj.* [< L. *contra*, against], 1. opposed; altogether different. 2. opposite in nature, order, etc. 3. unfavorable. 4. perverse; obstinate. *n.* [*pl.* -RIES], the opposite. —**on the contrary,** as opposed to what has been said. —**con′tra·ri·ly,** *adv.* —**con′tra·ri·ness,** *n.*
**con·trast** (kən-trast′), *v.t.* [< L. *contra*, against + *stare*, to stand], to compare so as to point out the differences. *v.i.* to show differences on comparison. *n.* (kon′trast), 1. a contrasting or being contrasted. 2. a striking difference between things being compared. 3. a person or thing showing differences when compared with another.
**con·tra·vene** (kon′trə-vēn′), *v.t.* [-VENED, -VENING], [< L. *contra*, against + *venire*,

come], 1. to go against; violate. 2. to contradict. —**con'tra·ven'tion** (-ven'shən), *n.*
**con·trib·ute** (kən-trib'yoot), *v.t.* & *v.i.* [-UTED, -UTING], [< L.; see COM- & TRIBUTE], 1. to give jointly with others to a common fund. 2. to write (an article, etc.) as for a magazine. 3. to furnish (ideas, etc.). —**contribute to,** to have a share in bringing about. —**con·trib'u·tor,** *n.* —**con·trib'u·to'ry** (-yoo-tôr'i), *adj.*
**con·tri·bu·tion** (kon'trə-bū'shən), *n.* 1. a contributing. 2. money, aid, etc. contributed.
**con·trite** (kən-trīt'), *adj.* [< L. *conterere,* grind], full of or showing remorse or guilt. —**con·tri'tion** (-trish'ən), *n.*
**con·triv·ance** (kən-trīv'əns), *n.* 1. the act or way of contriving. 2. something contrived, as a device, plan, etc.
**con·trive** (kən-trīv'), *v.t.* [-TRIVED, -TRIVING], [< OFr. *con-,* intens. + *trover,* find], 1. to devise; plan. 2. to invent; design. 3. to bring about; manage. —**con·triv'er,** *n.*
**con·trol** (kən-trōl'), *v.t.* [-TROLLED, -TROLLING], [< ML. *contrarotulum,* a register], 1. to regulate (financial affairs). 2. to exercise authority over; direct. 3. to restrain. *n.* 1. authority to direct or regulate. 2. a means of restraint; check. 3. *often in pl.* an apparatus to regulate a mechanism. —**con·trol'la·ble,** *adj.*
**con·trol'ler,** *n.* 1. an official in charge of expenditures: also sp. **comptroller.** 2. one who controls. 3. a device for controlling speed, power, etc. of a machine.
**con·tro·ver·sial** (kon'trə-vūr'shəl), *adj.* subject to controversy; debatable. —**con'tro·ver'sial·ly,** *adv.*
**con·tro·ver·sy** (kon'trə-vūr'si), *n.* [*pl.* -SIES], [< L. *contra,* against + *vertere,* to turn], 1. a discussion in which opinions clash; debate. 2. a quarrel.
**con'tro·vert'** (-vūrt'), *v.t.* 1. to argue against; deny. 2. to argue about; debate. —**con'tro·vert'i·ble,** *adj.*
**con·tu·ma·cy** (kon'too-mə-si, -tyoo-), *n.* [*pl.* -CIES], [< L. *contumax,* stubborn], stubborn refusal to submit to authority. —**con'tu·ma'cious** (-mā'shəs), *adj.*
**con·tu·me·ly** (kon'too-mə-li, -tyoo-), *n.* [*pl.* -LIES], [< L. *contumelia,* reproach], 1. humiliating treatment; scornful insolence. 2. a scornful insult. —**con'tu·me'li·ous** (-mē'li-əs), *adj.*
**con·tu·sion** (kən-tōō'zhən, -tū'-), *n.* [< L. *com-,* intens. + *tundere,* to beat], a bruise.
**co·nun·drum** (kə-nun'drəm), *n.* [pseudo-L.], 1. a riddle whose answer is a pun. 2. any puzzling problem.
**con·va·lesce** (kon'və-les'), *v.i.* [-LESCED, -LESCING], [< L. *com-,* intens. + *valere,* be strong], to regain health and strength.
**con'va·les'cence,** *n.* 1. gradual recovery after illness. 2. the period of this. —**con'va·les'cent,** *adj.* & *n.*
**con·vec·tion** (kən-vek'shən), *n.* [< L. *com-,* together + *vehere,* carry], a transmitting; esp., the transmission of heat by the movement of the heated particles, as in air currents. —**con·vec'tion·al,** *adj.*
**con·vene** (kən-vēn') *v.i.* & *v.t.* [-VENED, -VENING], [< L. *com-,* together + *venire,* come], to assemble for a meeting.
**con·ven·ience** (kən-vēn'yəns), *n.* [see CONVENE], 1. the quality of being convenient. 2. comfort. 3. anything that adds to one's comfort or saves work. —**at one's convenience,** at a time or place suitable to one.
**con·ven'ient** (-yənt), *adj.* favorable to one's comfort; easy to do, use, or get to; handy. —**convenient to,** [Colloq.], easily accessible to; near. —**con·ven'ient·ly,** *adv.*
**con·vent** (kon'vənt, -vent), *n.* [see CONVENE], a community of nuns.
**con·ven·ti·cle** (kən-ven'ti-k'l), *n.* [see CONVENE], a religious assembly, esp. an illegal or secret one.
**con·ven·tion** (kən-ven'shən), *n.* 1. a convening or being convened. 2. an assembly, often periodical, or the delegates to it. 3. an agreement between nations, persons, etc. 4. custom; usage.
**con·ven·tion·al** (kən-ven'shən-'l), *adj.* 1. having to do with a convention. 2. sanctioned by or following custom or usage; customary. 3. formal; not natural, original, or spontaneous. —**con·ven'tion·al'i·ty** (-al'ə-ti) [*pl.* -TIES], *n.* —**con·ven'tion·al·ly,** *adv.*
**con·verge** (kən-vūrj'), *v.i.* [-VERGED, -VERGING], [< L. *com-,* together + *vergere,* turn], to tend to come together at a point. —**con·ver'gence,** *n.* —**con·ver'gent,** *adj.*
**con·ver·sant** (kon'vēr-s'nt, kən-vūr'-), *adj.* familiar or acquainted (*with*).
**con·ver·sa·tion** (kon'vēr-sā'shən), *n.* a talking together; informal talk. —**con'ver·sa'tion·al,** *adj.*
**con·verse** (kən-vūrs'), *v.i.* [-VERSED, -VERSING], [< L. *conversari,* to live with], to hold a conversation; talk. *n.* (kon'vērs), conversation.
**con·verse** (kən-vūrs', kon'vērs), *adj.* [see CONVERT], reversed in position, order, etc.; opposite. *n.* (kon'vērs), a converse thing; the opposite. —**con·verse'ly,** *adv.*
**con·ver·sion** (kən-vūr'zhən), *n.* a converting or being converted.
**con·vert** (kən-vūrt'), *v.t.* [< L. *com-,* together + *vertere,* turn], 1. to change; transform. 2. to change from one religion, opinion, etc. to another. 3. to exchange for something equal in value. 4. to misappropriate. *v.i.* to be converted. *n.* (kon'vērt), a person converted, as to a religion. —**con·vert'er, con·ver'tor,** *n.*
**con·vert·i·ble** (kən-vūr'tə-b'l), *adj.* that can be converted. *n.* an automobile with a folding top. —**con·vert'i·bil'i·ty,** *n.*
**con·vex** (kon-veks', kon'veks), *adj.* [< L. *com-,* together + *vehere,* bring], curving outward, like the surface of a sphere. —**con·vex'i·ty** [*pl.* -TIES], *n.*
**con·vey** (kən-vā'), *v.t.* [< L. *com-,* together + *via,* way], 1. to take from one place to another; carry. 2. to transmit. —**con·vey'a·ble,** *adj.* —**con·vey'er, con·vey'or,** *n.*
**con·vey'ance,** *n.* 1. a conveying. 2. means of conveying, esp. a vehicle.
**con·vict** (kən-vikt'), *v.t.* [see CONVINCE], to prove or find (a person) guilty. *n.* (kon'vikt), a convicted person serving a prison sentence.
**con·vic'tion** (-vik'shən), *n.* 1. a convicting or being convicted. 2. a convincing or being convinced. 3. strong belief.
**con·vince** (kən-vins'), *v.t.* [-VINCED, -VINCING], [< L. *com-,* intens. + *vincere,* conquer], to persuade by argument or evidence; make feel certain. —**con·vinc'er,** *n.* —**con·vinc'ing,** *adj.* —**con·vinc'ing·ly,** *adv.*
**con·viv·i·al** (kən-viv'i-əl), *adj.* [< L. *com-,* together + *vivere,* live], 1. festive. 2. fond of eating, drinking, and good company; sociable. —**con·viv'i·al'i·ty** (-al'ə-ti), *n.*
**con·vo·ca·tion** (kon'və-kā'shən), *n.* 1. a convoking. 2. an assembly.
**con·voke** (kən-vōk'), *v.t.* [-VOKED, -VOKING], [< L. *com-,* together + *vocare,* call], to call together; assemble. —**con·vok'er,** *n.*
**con·vo·lu·tion** (kon'və-lōō'shən), *n.* [< L. *com-,* together + *volvere,* to roll], 1. a twisting, coiling, or winding together. 2. a fold, twist, or coil. 3. any of the irregular folds on the surface of the brain.
**con·voy** (kən-voi'), *v.t.* [see CONVEY], to escort in order to protect. *n.* (kon'voi), 1. a convoying or being convoyed. 2. a protecting escort, as ships or troops. 3. ships, troops, etc. being convoyed.

**con·vulse** (kən-vuls′), *v.t.* [-VULSED, -VULSING], [< L. *com-*, together + *vellere*, to pluck], 1. to shake violently; agitate. 2. to cause to shake as with laughter, rage, etc.

**con·vul′sion** (-vul′shən), *n.* 1. *usually in pl.* a violent, involuntary contraction or spasm of the muscles. 2. a fit of laughter. 3. a violent disturbance. **—con·vul′sive,** *adj.*

**co·ny** (kō′ni), *n.* [*pl.* -NIES], [< L. *cuniculus*], a rabbit or rabbit fur.

**coo** (ko͞o), *v.i.* [echoic], to make the soft, murmuring sound of pigeons. *n.* this sound.

**cook** (kook), *v.t.* [ult. < L. *coquere*], to prepare (food) by boiling, baking, frying, etc. *v.i.* 1. to be a cook. 2. to undergo cooking. *n.* one who prepares meals. **—cook up,** [Colloq.], to devise. **—cook′er,** *n.*

**cook′er·y,** *n.* [*pl.* -IES], the art or practice of cooking.

**cook′out′,** *n.* a meal cooked and eaten outdoors.

**cook·y, cook·ie** (kook′i), *n.* [*pl.* -IES], [prob. < D. *koek*, cake], a small, sweet, flat cake.

**cool** (ko͞ol), *adj.* [AS. *col*], 1. moderately cold. 2. tending to reduce the effects of heat: as, *cool* clothes. 3. not excited; composed. 4. showing dislike or indifference. 5. calmly bold. 6. [Colloq.], without exaggeration: as, he lost a *cool* thousand. *n.* a cool place, time, etc.: as, the *cool* of the evening. *v.t. & v.i.* to make or become cool. **—cool′ly,** *adv.* **—cool′ness,** *n.*

**cool·ant** (ko͞ol′ənt), *n.* a substance used for cooling, as a circulating fluid in an engine.

**cool′er,** *n.* 1. a place for keeping things cool. 2. anything that cools. 3. [Slang], a jail.

**coo·lie, coo·ly** (ko͞o′li), *n.* [*pl.* -LIES], [Hind. *qūlī*, servant], in the Orient, an unskilled native laborer.

**coon** (ko͞on), *n.* [Colloq.], a raccoon.

**coop** (ko͞op), *n.* [ult. < L. *cupa*, cask], 1. a small cage or pen for poultry, etc. 2. a place of confinement. *v.t.* to confine as in a coop.

**co-op, co-öp** (kō′op′), *n.* [Colloq.], a co-operative society, store, etc.

**coop′er,** *n.* [see COOP], one whose work is making or repairing barrels and casks.

**co-op·er·ate** (kō-op′ẽr-āt′), *v.i.* [-ATED, -ATING], [< L. *co-*, with + *opus*, work], to act or work together with another or others: also **coöperate, cooperate. —co-op′er·a′tion,** *n.* **—co-op′er·a′tor,** *n.*

**co-op′er·a′tive** (-ẽr-ā′tiv, -rə-tiv), *adj.* 1. co-operating or inclined to co-operate. 2. designating or of an organization owned collectively by members who share its profits. *n.* such an organization. Also **coöperative, cooperative.**

**co-or·di·nate** (kō-ôr′də-nit, -nāt′), *adj.* [< L. *co-*, with + *ordo*, order], 1. of equal order or importance: as, the *co-ordinate* clauses of a compound sentence. 2. of co-ordination or co-ordinates. *n.* a co-ordinate person or thing. *v.t.* (-nāt′), [-NATED, -NATING], 1. to make co-ordinate. 2. to bring into proper order or relation; adjust. Also **coördinate, coordinate. —co-or′di·na′tor,** *n.*

**co-or′di·na′tion,** *n.* 1. a co-ordinating or being co-ordinated. 2. the harmonious functioning, as of muscles. Also **coördination, coordination.**

**coot** (ko͞ot), *n.* [MD. *koet*], 1. a web-footed water bird. 2. [Colloq.], a fool.

**coot·ie** (ko͞ot′i), *n.* [Slang], a louse.

**cop** (kop), *v.t.* [COPPED, COPPING], [? ult. < L. *capere*, take], [Slang], to seize; steal. *n.* [Slang], a policeman.

**co·part·ner** (kō-pärt′nẽr), *n.* an associate; partner. **—co·part′ner·ship′,** *n.*

**cope** (kōp), *v.i.* [COPED, COPING], [< OFr. *coup*, a blow], to fight or contend (*with*) successfully.

**cope** (kōp), *n.* [< L. *cappa*], a large, capelike vestment worn by priests.

**co·pi·lot** (kō′pī′lət), *n.* the assistant pilot of an aircraft.

**cop·ing** (kōp′iŋ), *n.* [< *cope* (cloak)], the top layer of a masonry wall.

**co·pi·ous** (kō′pi-əs), *adj.* [< L. *copia*, abundance], abundant; plentiful. **—co′pi·ous·ly,** *adv.* **—co′pi·ous·ness,** *n.*

**cop·per** (kop′ẽr), *n.* [< LL. *cuprum*], 1. a reddish-brown, ductile, metallic element: symbol, Cu. 2. a thing made of this metal. 3. a penny. 4. a reddish brown. *adj.* 1. of copper. 2. reddish-brown. **—cop′per·y,** *adj.*

**cop′per·head′,** *n.* a poisonous snake of N. America.

**cop·ra** (kop′rə), *n.* [Port. < Hind. *khoprā*], dried coconut meat.

**copse** (kops), *n.* [< OFr. *coper*, cut], a thicket of small trees: also **cop·pice** (kop′is).

**cop·u·la** (kop′yoo-lə), *n.* [*pl.* -LAS], [L. < *co-*, together + *apere*, join], 1. something that links together. 2. a weakened verbal form, as a form of *be*, *seem*, etc., linking a subject with a predicate complement.

**cop′u·late′** (-lāt′), *v.i.* [-LATED, -LATING], [see COPULA], to unite in sexual intercourse. **—cop′u·la′tion,** *n.*

**cop′u·la′tive** (-lā′tiv, -lə-), *adj.* 1. coupling. 2. of connected words or clauses. 3. being a copula: as, a *copulative* verb. 4. of or for copulating. *n.* a copulative word.

**cop·y** (kop′i), *n.* [*pl.* -IES], [< L. *copia*, abundance], 1. a thing made just like another. 2. any of a number of books, magazines, etc. having the same contents. 3. a model or pattern. 4. a manuscript to be set in type. *v.t. & v.i.* [-IED, -YING], 1. to make a copy of. 2. to imitate. **—cop′y·ist,** *n.*

**cop′y·right′,** *n.* the exclusive legal right to the publication, sale, etc. of a literary or artistic work. *v.t.* to protect (a book, etc.) by copyright. *adj.* protected by copyright.

**cop′y·writ′er,** *n.* a writer of copy, esp. for advertisements.

**co·quet** (kō-ket′), *v.i.* [-QUETTED, -QUETTING], [< Fr. *coc*, rooster], 1. to flirt. 2. to trifle (*with*). **—co·quet·ry** (kō′kə-tri, kō-ket′ri) [*pl.* -RIES], *n.*

**co·quette** (kō-ket′), *n.* [Fr.; see COQUET], a girl or woman flirt. *v.i.* [-QUETTED, -QUETTING], to flirt. **—co·quet′tish,** *adj.*

**cor-,** com-: used before *r*.

**cor·al** (kôr′əl), *n.* [< Gr. *korallion*], 1. a hard substance made up of the skeletons of certain marine animals: reefs and atolls of coral occur in tropical seas. 2. a yellowish red. *adj.* 1. of coral. 2. yellowish-red.

**cord** (kôrd), *n.* [< Gr. *chordē*], 1. thick string. 2. a measure of wood cut for fuel (128 cu. ft.). 3. a rib on the surface of a fabric. 4. corduroy. 5. a small insulated electric cable. 6. in *anatomy*, any part like a cord. *v.t.* 1. to fasten with a cord. 2. to stack (wood) in cords.

**cord·age** (kôr′dij), *n.* cords and ropes collectively.

**cor·dial** (kôr′jəl), *adj.* [Fr. < L. *cor*, heart], hearty; warm and genuine. *n.* 1. a medicine, food, or drink that stimulates the heart. 2. an aromatic alcoholic drink. **—cor·dial·i·ty** (kôr′ji-al′ə-ti, kôr-jal′-) [*pl.* -TIES], *n.* **—cor′dial·ly,** *adv.*

**cord·ite** (kôr′dīt), *n.* [< *cord:* it is stringy], a smokeless explosive made of nitroglycerin, guncotton, etc.

**cor·don** (kôr′d'n), *n.* [Fr. < *corde*, cord], 1. a line or circle of people, ships, etc. guarding an area. 2. a cord, ribbon, or braid worn as a decoration.

**cor·do·van** (kôr′də-vən), *n.* [< *Córdoba*, Spain], 1. a soft, colored leather. 2. *pl.* shoes made of this. *adj.* made of cordovan.

**cor·du·roy** (kôr′də-roi′), *n.* [prob. < *cord* + obs. *duroy*, coarse fabric], 1. a heavy, ribbed cotton fabric. 2. *pl.* trousers made of this. *adj.* 1. made of corduroy. 2. ribbed.

**core** (kôr), *n.* [prob. < L. *cor*, heart], 1. the central part of an apple, pear, etc. 2. the central part of anything. 3. the most important part. *v.t.* [CORED, CORING], to remove the core of. —**cor'er,** *n.*

**co·re·spond·ent** (kō'ri-spon'dənt), *n.* [*co-* + *respondent*], in *law*, a person charged with having committed adultery with the husband or wife from whom a divorce is sought.

**cork** (kôrk), *n.* [< Sp. < Ar. *alcorque*], 1. light, thick, elastic outer bark of a kind of oak tree (the **cork oak**). 2. a piece of cork, esp. one used as a stopper for a bottle, etc. 3. any stopper. *v.t.* to stop with a cork.

**cork'er,** *n.* [Slang], a remarkable person or thing.

**cork'ing,** *adj. & interj.* [Slang], very good.

**cork'screw',** *n.* a spiral-shaped device for pulling corks out of bottles. *adj.* like a corkscrew in shape; spiral.

**corm** (kôrm), *n.* [< Gr. *kormos*, a log], the bulblike, underground stem of certain plants, as the crocus.

**cor·mo·rant** (kôr'mə-rənt), *n.* [< L. *corvus* (raven) *marinus* (< *mare*, the sea)], 1. a large, voracious sea bird. 2. a greedy person; glutton. *adj.* greedy; gluttonous.

**corn** (kôrn), *n.* [< AS.], 1. a small, hard seed, esp. of any cereal plant; kernel. 2. a kind of grain that grows in kernels on large ears; maize. 3. in England, wheat. 4. in Scotland and Ireland, oats. 5. [Slang], ideas, humor, etc. regarded as old-fashioned, trite, etc. *v.t.* to pickle (meat, etc.) in brine.

**corn** (kôrn), *n.* [< L. *cornu*, a horn], a horny thickening of the skin, esp. on the toes.

**corn'cob'** (-kob'), *n.* 1. the woody core of an ear of corn. 2. a tobacco pipe (**corncob pipe**) with a bowl made of corncob.

**cor·ne·a** (kôr'ni-ə), *n.* [< L. *cornu*, a horn], the transparent outer coat of the eyeball. —**cor'ne·al,** *adj.*

**cor·ner** (kôr'nẽr), *n.* [< L. *cornu*, a horn], 1. the point or place where lines or surfaces join and form an angle. 2. the angle so formed. 3. the place where two streets meet. 4. a remote, secluded place. 5. a region; quarter. 6. an awkward position, from which escape is difficult. 7. a speculative monopoly formed in some stock or commodity so as to raise the price. *v.t.* 1. to furnish with corners. 2. to force into a corner (sense 6). 3. to form a corner (sense 7) in. *adj.* at, on, or used in a corner. —**cut corners,** to cut down expenses, time required, etc. —**cor'nered,** *adj.*

**cor'ner·stone',** *n.* 1. a stone at the corner of a building: often laid at a ceremony beginning the erection of a building. 2. the basic or main part; foundation.

**cor·net** (kôr-net'), *n.* [< L. *cornu*, a horn], a brass-wind musical instrument of the trumpet family. —**cor·net'tist, cor·net'ist,** *n.*

**corn'flow'er,** *n.* the bachelor's-button.

**cor·nice** (kôr'nis), *n.* [? < Gr. *korōnis*, wreath], a horizontal molding projecting along the top of a wall, etc.

**corn'starch',** *n.* a starchy flour made from Indian corn, used in cooking.

**cor·nu·co·pi·a** (kôr'nə-kō'pi-ə, kôr'nyoo-), *n.* [L. *cornu copiae*, horn of plenty], 1. a horn-shaped container overflowing with fruits, flowers, and grain. 2. an abundance.

**corn·y** (kôr'ni), *adj.* [-IER, -IEST], [Slang], unsophisticated, trite, etc. —**corn'i·ness,** *n.*

**co·rol·la** (kə-rol'ə), *n.* [< L. *corona*, crown], the petals, or inner leaves, of a flower.

**cor·ol·lar·y** (kôr'ə-ler'i), *n.* [*pl.* -IES], [< L. *corollarium*, gratuity], 1. a proposition following from one already proved. 2. an inference or deduction. 3. a normal result.

**co·ro·na** (kə-rō'nə), *n.* [*pl.* -NAS, -NAE (-nē)], [L. < Gr. *korōnē*, wreath], 1. a crown. 2. a circle of light around the sun or moon; esp., the halo around the sun during a total eclipse. —**co·ro·nal** (kə-rō'n'l, kôr'ə-), *adj.*

**cor·o·nar·y** (kôr'ə-ner'i), *adj.* 1. of or like a crown. 2. of the arteries supplying blood to the heart tissues.

**coronary thrombosis,** the formation of an obstructing clot in a coronary artery.

**cor·o·na·tion** (kôr'ə-nā'shən), *n.* the crowning of a sovereign.

**cor·o·ner** (kôr'ə-nẽr), *n.* [ME., officer of the crown], a public officer who must determine the cause of any death not obviously due to natural causes.

**cor·o·net** (kôr'ə-net'), *n.* [< OFr. *corone*, crown], 1. a small crown worn by nobility. 2. a band of jewels, etc. for the head.

**corp., corpn.,** corporation.

**cor·po·ral** (kôr'pẽr-əl), *n.* [< It. *capo* (< L. *caput*), head], in the *U.S. armed forces*, the lowest-ranking noncommissioned officer: abbrev. **Corp., Cpl.**

**cor·po·ral** (kôr'pẽr-əl), *adj.* [< L. *corpus*, body], of the body. —**cor'po·ral'i·ty,** *n.*

**corporal punishment,** punishment inflicted directly on the body.

**cor·po·rate** (kôr'pẽr-it), *adj.* [< L. *corpus*, body], 1. united; combined. 2. of, like, or being a corporation. —**cor'po·rate·ly,** *adv.*

**cor·po·ra·tion** (kôr'pə-rā'shən), *n.* a group organized, as to operate a business, under a charter granting them as a body some of the legal rights, etc. of an individual.

**cor·po·re·al** (kôr-pôr'i-əl), *adj.* [< L. *corpus*, body], 1. of or for the body. 2. of a material nature; physical. —**cor·po're·al'i·ty,** *n.*

**corps** (kôr), *n.* [*pl.* CORPS (kôrz)], [Fr. < L. *corpus*, body], 1. a body of people associated under common direction. 2. *a*) a specialized branch of the armed forces: as, the Medical *Corps*. *b*) a tactical subdivision of an army.

**corpse** (kôrps), *n.* [see CORPS], a dead body, esp. of a person.

**cor·pu·lence** (kôr'pyoo-ləns), *n.* [< L. *corpus*, body], fatness; obesity: also **cor'pu·len·cy.** —**cor'pu·lent,** *adj.*

**cor·pus** (kôr'pəs), *n.* [*pl.* -PORA (-pẽr-ə)], [L], 1. a body, esp. a dead one: used humorously. 2. a body of laws, writings, etc.

**cor·pus·cle** (kôr'pəs-'l, -pus-'l), *n.* [< L. *corpus*, body], 1. a very small particle. 2. any of the red cells or white cells in the blood, lymph, etc. of vertebrates.

**cor·ral** (kə-ral'), *n.* [Sp. < L. *currere*, run], an enclosure for horses, cattle, etc.; pen. *v.t.* [-RALLED, -RALLING], 1. to drive into or confine in a corral. 2. to surround or capture.

**cor·rect** (kə-rekt'), *v.t.* [< L. *com-*, together + *regere*, lead straight], 1. to make right. 2. to mark the errors of. 3. to punish or discipline. 4. to cure or counteract (a defect). *adj.* 1. conforming with a conventional standard. 2. true; accurate; right. —**cor·rec'tive,** *adj. & n.* —**cor·rect'ly,** *adv.* —**cor·rect'ness,** *n.*

**cor·rec·tion** (kə-rek'shən), *n.* 1. a correcting or being corrected. 2. rectification substituted for a mistake. 3. punishment to correct faults. —**cor·rec'tion·al,** *adj.*

**cor·re·late** (kôr'ə-lāt'), *v.i. & v.t.* [-LATED, -LATING], [*cor-* + *relate*], to be in or bring into mutual relation. —**cor're·la'tion,** *n.*

**cor·rel·a·tive** (kə-rel'ə-tiv), *adj.* 1. having a mutual relation. 2. in *grammar*, expressing mutual relation and used in pairs, as the conjunctions *neither* . . . *nor*. *n.* a correlative word.

**cor·re·spond** (kôr'ə-spond'), *v.i.* [< L. *com-*, together + *respondere*, to answer], 1. to be in agreement (*with* something); match. 2. to be similar or equal (*to*). 3. to communicate by letters. —**cor're·spond'ing,** *adj.* —**cor're·spond'ing·ly,** *adv.*

**cor're·spond'ence,** *n.* 1. agreement. 2. similarity; analogy. 3. communication by exchange of letters. 4. the quantity of letters normally received or written.
**cor're·spond'ent,** *adj.* corresponding. *n.* 1. a thing that corresponds. 2. one who exchanges letters with another. 3. one hired as by a newspaper to furnish news regularly from an area.
**cor·ri·dor** (kôr'ə-dẽr, -dôr'), *n.* [< L. *currere,* to run], a long hall or passageway.
**cor·rob·o·rate** (kə-rob'ə-rāt'), *v.t.* [-RATED, -RATING], [< L. *com-,* intens. + *robur,* strength], to strengthen; confirm (a report, etc.); support. **—cor·rob'o·ra'tion,** *n.* **—cor·rob'o·ra'tive,** *adj.*
**cor·rode** (kə-rōd'), *v.t. & v.i.* [-RODED, -RODING], [< L. *com-,* intens. + *rodere,* gnaw], to wear away gradually; rust.
**cor·ro'sion** (-rō'zhən), *n.* a corroding or being corroded.**—cor·ro'sive** (-siv), *adj. & n.*
**cor·ru·gate** (kôr'ə-gāt'), *v.t. & v.i.* [-GATED, -GATING], [< L. *com-,* intens. + *rugare,* to wrinkle], to make folds or wrinkles in; furrow. **—cor'ru·ga'tion,** *n.*
**cor·rupt** (kə-rupt'), *adj.* [< L. *com-,* together + *rumpere,* break in pieces], 1. rotten. 2. evil; depraved. 3. taking bribes. *v.t. & v.i.* to make or become corrupt. **—cor·rupt'i·ble,** *adj.* **—cor·rup'tive,** *adj.*
**cor·rup'tion** (-rup'shən), *n.* 1. a making, becoming, or being corrupt. 2. depravity. 3. bribery. 4. decay.
**cor·sage** (kôr-säzh'), *n.* [see CORPS & -AGE], a small bouquet for a woman to wear, as at the waist or shoulder.
**cor·sair** (kôr'sâr), *n.* [Fr. < ML. *cursus,* a raid], a pirate or pirate ship.
**corse·let** (kôr's'l-et'), *n.* [see CORPS], a woman's lightweight corset.
**cor·set** (kôr'sit), *n.* [see CORPS], *sometimes pl.* a closefitting undergarment worn, chiefly by women, to give support to or shape the torso. *v.t.* to dress in a corset.
**cor·tege** (kôr-tāzh', -tezh'), *n.* [< Fr. < It. *corteggio*], 1. a number of attendants; retinue. 2. a ceremonial procession.
**cor·tex** (kôr'teks), *n.* [*pl.* -TICES (-ti-sēz')], [L., bark of a tree], 1. the outer part of an internal organ; esp., the layer of gray matter over most of the brain. 2. in *botany,* the bark. **—cor'ti·cal** (-ti-k'l), *adj.*
**cor·ti·sone** (kôr'tə-sōn', -zōn'), *n.* a hormone used in the treatment of arthritis and certain other diseases.
**co·run·dum** (kə-run'dəm), *n.* [< Sans. *kuruvinda,* ruby], a very hard mineral used for grinding and polishing.
**cor·us·cate** (kôr'əs-kāt'), *v.i.* [-CATED, -CATING], [< L. *coruscus,* vibrating], to glitter; sparkle. **—cor'us·ca'tion,** *n.*
**cor·vette, cor·vet** (kôr-vet'), *n.* [Fr. < L. *corbis,* basket], a small, fast warship used for antisubmarine and convoy duty.
**cos·met·ic** (koz-met'ik), *adj.* [< Gr. *kosmos,* order], beautifying or designed to beautify. *n.* any preparation designed to beautify the skin, hair, etc.
**cos·mic** (koz'mik), *adj.* [< Gr. *kosmos,* order], 1. of the cosmos. 2. vast. **—cos'mi·cal·ly,** *adv.*
**cosmic rays,** rays of great penetrating power, which bombard the earth from beyond its atmosphere.
**cos·mog·o·ny** (koz-mog'ə-ni), *n.* [*pl.* -NIES], [< Gr. *kosmos,* universe + *gignesthai,* produce], 1. the origin of the universe. 2. a theory of this.
**cos·mol·o·gy** (koz-mol'ə-ji), *n.* [< Gr. *kosmos,* world; + *-logy*], theory or philosophy of the nature and principles of the universe.
**cos·mo·naut** (koz'mə-nôt'), *n.* [< Russ.; ult. < Gr. *kosmos,* universe + *nautēs,* sailor], an astronaut.
**cos·mo·pol·i·tan** (koz'mə-pol'ə-t'n), *adj.* [< Gr. *kosmos,* world + *polis,* city], 1. belonging to the whole world. 2. not bound by local or national prejudices; at home in all countries. *n.* a cosmopolitan person.
**cos·mop·o·lite** (koz-mop'ə-līt'), *n.* a cosmopolitan person.
**cos·mos** (koz'məs, -mos), *n.* [Gr. *kosmos,* world], 1. the universe considered as an orderly system. 2. any orderly system.
**Cos·sack** (kos'ak, -ək), *n.* a member of a people of the S Soviet Union, famous as horsemen.
**cost** (kôst), *v.i.* [COST, COSTING], [< L. *com-,* together + *stare,* to stand], 1. to be obtained for (a certain price). 2. to require the expenditure, loss, etc. of. *n.* 1. the amount of money, labor, etc. required to get a thing; price. 2. loss; sacrifice **—at all costs,** by any means required.
**cost'ly,** *adj.* [-LIER, -LIEST], 1. costing much; dear. 2. very valuable; sumptuous. **—cost'li·ness,** *n.*
**cost of living,** the average cost of the necessities of life, as food, shelter, and clothes.
**cos·tume** (kos'tōōm, -tūm), *n.* [Fr. < L. *consuetudo,* custom], 1. style of dress in general, esp. the style typical of a certain period, people, etc. 2. a complete set of clothes. *v.t.* (kos-tōōm', -tūm'), [-TUMED, -TUMING], to provide with a costume.
**cos·tum'er,** *n.* one who makes, sells, or rents costumes, as for theaters, balls, etc.
**co·sy** (kō'zi), *adj.* [-SIER, -SIEST], *& n.* [*pl.* -SIES], cozy. **—co'si·ly,** *adv.* **—co'si·ness,** *n.*
**cot** (kot), *n.* [< Hind. *khāṭ*], a narrow bed, esp. one made of canvas on a folding frame.
**cote** (kōt), *n.* [AS., cottage], a small shelter for birds, sheep, etc.
**co·te·rie** (kō'tẽr-i, -tə-rē'), *n.* [Fr. < *cote,* hut], a social set; clique.
**co·til·lion** (kō-til'yən), *n.* [Fr. *cotillon,* a petticoat], 1. a kind of square dance of the 19th century. 2. the music for this dance.
**cot·tage** (kot'ij), *n.* [< OFr. *cote,* hut], a small house, as one used for vacations.
**cottage cheese,** a soft, white cheese made from the curds of sour milk.
**cot·ter pin** (kot'ẽr), a split pin fastened in place by spreading apart its ends after insertion.
**cot·ton** (kot''n), *n.* [< Ar. *quṭun*], 1. the soft, white, fibrous matter around the seeds of a plant of the mallow family. 2. this plant. 3. the crop of such plants. 4. thread or cloth made of cotton. *adj.* of cotton. **—cotton·y,** *adj.*
**cot'ton·mouth',** *n.* [from its whitish mouth], a water moccasin.
**cot'ton·seed',** *n.* the seed of the cotton plant, yielding an oil (**cottonseed oil**).
**cot'ton·tail',** *n.* a common American rabbit with a fluffy tail.
**cot'ton·wood',** *n.* 1. a poplar that has seeds covered with cottony hairs. 2. its wood.
**cot·y·le·don** (kot''l-ē'd'n), *n.* [< Gr. *kotylē,* cavity], the earliest leaf or one of the earliest leaves growing out of a seed.
**couch** (kouch), *n.* [< OFr. *coucher,* lie down], an article of furniture on which one may lie down; sofa. *v.t.* 1. to lay as on a couch. 2. to put in words; state. *v.i.* to recline.
**cou·gar** (kōō'gẽr), *n.* [< Fr. < S. American Indian name], a tawny-brown wild animal of the cat family: also called *puma.*
**cough** (kôf), *v.i.* [ME. *coughen*], to expel air suddenly and noisily from the lungs. *v.t.* to expel by coughing. *n.* 1. a coughing. 2. a condition of coughing frequently.
**could** (kood), 1. pt. of. **can.** 2. an auxiliary equivalent to *can,* expressing especially a shade of doubt (e.g., it *could* be so).
**could·n't** (kood''nt), could not.
**cou·lomb** (kōō-lom'), *n.* [after C. A. de

*Coulomb*, 18th-c. Fr. physicist], the amount of electricity provided by a current of one ampere in one second.
**coun·cil** (koun′s'l), ***n.*** [< L. *com-*, with + base of *calare*, call together], 1. a group of people called together for discussion, advice, etc. 2. an administrative or legislative body: as, a city *council*.
**coun′cil·man** (-mən), ***n.*** [*pl.* -MEN], a member of a city council.
**coun′ci·lor, coun′cil·lor** (-ẽr), ***n.*** a member of a council.
**coun·sel** (koun′s'l), ***n.*** [< L. *consilium*], 1. mutual exchange of ideas, etc.; discussion. 2. advice. 3. a plan; resolution. 4. a lawyer or group of lawyers. ***v.t.*** [-SELED or -SELLED, -SELING or -SELLING], 1. to give advice to. 2. to recommend (an action, plan, etc.). ***v.i.*** to give or take advice.
**coun′se·lor, coun′sel·lor** (-ẽr), ***n.*** 1. an adviser. 2. a lawyer.
**count** (kount), ***v.t.*** [see COMPUTE], 1. to name, unit by unit, to reach a total. 2. to take account of; include. 3. to consider; believe to be. ***v.i.*** 1. to name numbers or things in order. 2. to be taken into account. 3. to have importance. ***n.*** 1. a counting or adding up. 2. the total number. 3. a reckoning. 4. in *law*, any of the charges in an indictment. **—count on** (or **upon**), to rely on. **—count out**, to disregard.
**count** (kount), ***n.*** [< L. *comes*, companion], a European nobleman equal in rank to an English earl.
**count′down′, count′-down′,** ***n.*** the schedule for preparing to fire a rocket, detonate a nuclear blast, etc.: it is counted off in units of time going down to zero.
**coun·te·nance** (koun′tə-nəns), ***n.*** [< L. *continentia*, bearing], 1. the facial expression. 2. the face; visage. 3. approval; support. ***v.t.*** [-NANCED, -NANCING], to approve; give support to.
**count′er,** ***n.*** 1. a small device or token for keeping count, as in games. 2. an imitation coin. 3. a long table in a store or restaurant, for serving customers, displaying goods, etc. 4. one who counts.
**coun·ter** (koun′tẽr), ***adv.*** [< L. *contra*, against], in a contrary direction, manner, etc. ***adj.*** contrary; opposed. ***n.*** 1. the opposite. 2. a stiff leather piece around the heel of a shoe. ***v.t. & v.i.*** to act, do, etc. counter to; oppose.
**counter-,** a combining form meaning: 1. *contrary to*, as in *counterclockwise*. 2. *in retaliation*, as in *counterattack*. 3. *complementary*, as in *counterpart*.
**coun′ter·act′,** ***v.t.*** to act against; neutralize the effect of. **—coun′ter·ac′tion,** ***n.***
**coun′ter·at·tack′,** ***n.*** an attack made in opposition to another attack. ***v.t. & v.i.*** to attack in opposition.
**coun·ter·bal·ance** (koun′tẽr-bal′əns), ***n.*** a weight, force, or influence that balances another. ***v.t. & v.i.*** (koun′tẽr-bal′əns), [-ANCED, -ANCING], to be a counterbalance (to); offset.
**coun′ter·clock′wise′,** ***adj. & adv.*** in a direction opposite to that in which the hands of a clock move.
**coun′ter·cul′ture,** ***n.*** the culture of many young people manifested by a life style that is opposed to the prevailing culture.
**coun′ter·es′pi·on·age,** ***n.*** actions to prevent or thwart enemy espionage.
**coun·ter·feit** (koun′tẽr-fit), ***adj.*** [< OFr. *contre-*, counter + *faire*, make], 1. made in imitation of the genuine with intent to defraud; forged: as, *counterfeit* money. 2. pretended; sham. ***n.*** an imitation made to deceive. ***v.t. & v.i.*** 1. to make an imitation of (money, etc.) in order to defraud. 2. to pretend. **—coun′ter·feit′er,** ***n.***
**coun·ter·mand** (koun′tẽr-mand′, -mänd′), ***v.t.*** [< L. *contra*, opposite + *mandare*, to command], 1. to cancel (a command). 2. to order back by a contrary order.
**coun′ter·march′,** ***n.*** a march back or in the opposite direction. ***v.i. & v.t.*** to march back.
**coun′ter·pane′** (-pān′), ***n.*** [ult. < L. *culcita puncta*, embroidered quilt], a bedspread.
**coun′ter·part′,** ***n.*** a person or thing that closely resembles another.
**coun′ter·point′,** ***n.*** [< It.; see COUNTER- & POINT], the art of adding related but distinct melodies to a basic melody, according to the rules of harmony.
**coun′ter·poise′,** ***n.*** [see COUNTER, *adv.* & POISE], 1. a weight, force, influence, etc. that balances another. 2. a state of balance. ***v.t. & v.i.*** [-POISED, -POISING], to be a counterpoise (to).
**coun′ter·rev′o·lu′tion,** ***n.*** a movement to restore the system overthrown by a revolution.
**coun′ter·sign′,** ***n.*** 1. a signature added to a previously signed writing in order to confirm it. 2. a secret signal which must be given to a sentry in order to pass. ***v.t.*** to confirm with a signature.
**coun′ter·sink′,** ***v.t.*** [-SUNK, -SINKING], 1. to enlarge the top part of (a hole in metal, wood, etc.) so that it will receive the head of a bolt, screw, etc. 2. to sink (a bolt, screw, etc.) into such a hole.
**coun′ter·weight′,** ***n.*** a weight equal to another. ***v.t.*** to counterbalance.
**count·ess** (koun′tis), ***n.*** the wife or widow of a count or earl.
**count′less** (-lis), ***adj.*** too many to count.
**coun·tri·fied** (kun′tri-fīd′), ***adj.*** 1. rural; rustic. 2. having the appearance, etc. of country people. Also sp. **countryfied.**
**coun·try** (kun′tri), ***n.*** [*pl.* -TRIES], [< LL. *contrata*, that which is beyond], 1. an area; region. 2. the whole territory, or the people, of a nation. 3. the land of one's birth or citizenship. 4. land with few houses; rural region. ***adj.*** rural; rustic.
**country club,** a club in the outskirts of a city, with a clubhouse, golf course, etc.
**coun′try·man** (-mən), ***n.*** [*pl.* -MEN], 1. a man living in the country. 2. a man of one's own country; compatriot.
**coun′try·side′,** ***n.*** 1. a rural region or district. 2. its people.
**coun·ty** (koun′ti), ***n.*** [*pl.* -TIES], [< LL. *comitatus*, office of a count], 1. a small administrative district of a country; esp., a subdivision of a State. 2. the people of a county. ***adj.*** of a county.
**coup** (kōō), ***n.*** [*pl.* COUPS (kōōz)], [Fr. < L. *colaphus*, a blow], 1. literally, a blow. 2. a sudden brilliant stroke or stratagem.
‡**coup de grâce** (kōō′ də gräs′), [Fr., lit., stroke of mercy], the blow, shot, etc. that brings death to a sufferer.
‡**coup d'é·tat** (kōō′ dā′tä′), [Fr., lit., stroke of state], the sudden overthrow of a government.
**coupe** (kōōp, kōō-pā′), ***n.*** [< Fr. < *couper*, to cut], a closed, two-door automobile.
**cou·ple** (kup′'l), ***n.*** [< L. *copula*, a link], 1. anything joining two things together; link. 2. two similar things joined together; pair. 3. a man and woman who are engaged, married, etc. 4. [Colloq.], a few. ***v.t.*** [-PLED, -PLING], to link; connect. ***v.i.*** 1. to pair. 2. to join in marriage.
**cou·plet** (kup′lit), ***n.*** two successive, rhyming lines of poetry.
**cou·pling** (kup′liŋ), ***n.*** 1. a joining together. 2. a mechanical device for joining parts.
**cou·pon** (kōō′pon, kū′-), ***n.*** [Fr. < *couper*, to cut], 1. a detachable certificate on a bond, to be presented for payment of the interest due at a certain time. 2. a certificate,

ticket, etc. redeemable for cash or gifts, or to be used in ordering goods, samples, etc.

**cour·age** (kũr′ij), *n.* [< L. *cor*, heart], the quality of being brave; valor.

**cou·ra·geous** (kə-rā′jəs), *adj.* having courage; brave. —**cou·ra′geous·ly,** *adv.*

**cou·ri·er** (koor′i-ẽr, kũr′-), *n.* [< L. *currere*, to run], 1. a messenger sent in haste. 2. an attendant hired to accompany tourists.

**course** (kôrs), *n.* [< L. *currere*, to run], 1. an onward movement; progress. 2. a way, path, or channel. 3. the direction taken. 4. a regular mode of action: as, the law takes its *course*. 5. a number of like things in order; series. 6. a part of a meal served at one time. 7. in *education*, *a*) a complete series of studies. *b*) any of the studies. *v.i.* [COURSED, COURSING], to run, chase, or race. —**in due course,** in the usual sequence (of events). —**in the course of,** during. —**of course,** 1. naturally. 2. certainly.

**court** (kôrt), *n.* [< L. *cohors*, enclosure], 1. an uncovered space surrounded by buildings or walls. 2. a short street. 3. a playing area, as for tennis. 4. a royal palace. 5. the family, advisers, etc. of a sovereign. 6. a sovereign and his councilors as a governing body. 7. courtship. 8. in *law*, *a*) a judge or judges. *b*) a place where trials are held, investigations made, etc. *c*) a judicial assembly. *v.t.* 1. to pay attention to (a person) in order to get something. 2. to try to get the love of; woo. 3. to seek: as, to *court* favor.

**cour·te·ous** (kũr′ti-əs), *adj.* [< *court*, *n.* 5], polite and gracious. —**cour′te·ous·ly,** *adv.*

**cour·te·san, cour·te·zan** (kôr′tə-z′n), *n.* [ult. < *court*, *n.* 5], a prostitute.

**cour·te·sy** (kũr′tə-si), *n.* [*pl.* -SIES], 1. courteous behavior. 2. a polite or considerate act or remark. 3. a favor.

**court′house′,** *n.* 1. a building in which law courts are held. 2. a building housing the offices of a county government.

**cour·ti·er** (kôr′ti-ẽr, -tyẽr), *n.* an attendant at a royal court.

**court′ly,** *adj.* [-LIER, -LIEST], suitable for a king's court; dignified; elegant. *adv.* in a courtly manner. —**court′li·ness,** *n.*

**court′-mar′tial** (-mär′shəl), *n.* [*pl.* COURTS-MARTIAL], 1. a military or naval court to try offenses against military law. 2. a trial by such a court. *v.t.* [-TIALED or -TIALLED, -TIALING or -TIALLING], to try by such a court.

**court′room′,** *n.* a room in which a law court is held.

**court′ship,** *n.* the act, process, or period of courting a woman.

**court′yard′,** *n.* a space enclosed by walls, adjoining or in a large building.

**cous·in** (kuz′′n), *n.* [? ult. < L. *com-*, with + *soror*, sister], the son or daughter of one's uncle or aunt. —**cous′in·ly,** *adj.* & *adv.*

‡**cou·tu·ri·er** (kōō′tü′ryā′), *n.* [Fr.], a man dressmaker. —**cou′tu′rière′** (-ryâr′), *n.fem.*

**cove** (kōv), *n.* [AS. *cofa*, cave], a small bay.

**cov·e·nant** (kuv′ə-nənt), *n.* [see CONVENE], 1. a binding agreement made by two or more persons, parties, etc.; compact. 2. a legal contract. 3. the promises made by God to man, as recorded in the Bible. *v.i.* & *v.t.* to promise by or in a covenant.

**cov·er** (kuv′ẽr), *v.t.* [< L. *co-*, intens. + *operire*, to hide], 1. to place something on or over. 2. to extend over. 3. to clothe. 4. to conceal; hide. 5. to protect as by shielding. 6. to protect financially: as, to *cover* a loss. 7. to travel over. 8. to include; deal with: as, to *cover* a subject. 9. to point a firearm at. 10. in *journalism*, to get news, pictures, etc. of. *v.i.* to overspread, as a liquid. *n.* 1. anything that covers, as a lid, top, etc. 2. a shelter for protection. 3. a tablecloth and setting. 4. a pretense. —**take cover,** to seek shelter. —**under cover,** 1. in secret. 2. by pretense. 3. hidden.

**cov′er·age** (-ij), *n.* the amount, extent, etc. covered by something.

**cov′er·all′,** *n. usually pl.* a one-piece work garment for mechanics, etc.

**cover crop,** a crop, as red clover, grown to protect soil from erosion and leaching.

**cov′er·ing,** *n.* anything that covers.

**cov·er·let** (kuv′ẽr-lit), *n.* [< OFr. *couvrir*, to cover + *lit*, bed], a bedspread.

**cov·ert** (kuv′ẽrt), *adj.* [see COVER], concealed; hidden; disguised. *n.* 1. a protected place; shelter. 2. in *hunting*, a hiding place for game. —**cov′ert·ly,** *adv.*

**covert cloth,** a smooth, twilled cloth of wool with cotton, rayon, or silk.

**cov·et** (kuv′it), *v.t.* & *v.i.* [< L. *cupiditas*, cupidity], to desire ardently (something that another person has).

**cov·et·ous** (kuv′i-təs), *adj.* greedy; avaricious. —**cov′et·ous·ly,** *adv.*

**cov·ey** (kuv′i), *n.* [*pl.* -EYS], [< OFr. *cover*, to hatch], a small flock of birds, esp. partridges or quail.

**cow** (kou), *n.* [< AS. *cu*], 1. the mature female of any animal of the ox family, esp. one domesticated for its milk. 2. the female of certain other animals, as the elephant.

**cow** (kou), *v.t.* [< ON. *kūga*, subdue], to frighten; make timid; overawe.

**cow·ard** (kou′ẽrd), *n.* [ult. < L. *cauda*, tail], one who lacks courage; one easily frightened. *adj.* cowardly.

**cow′ard·ice** (-is), *n.* lack of courage.

**cow′ard·ly,** *adj.* of or like a coward. *adv.* in the manner of a coward.

**cow′boy′,** *n.* a ranch worker who herds cattle: also **cow′hand′, cow hand.**

**cow′catch′er,** *n.* a metal frame on the front of a locomotive for clearing the tracks.

**cow·er** (kou′ẽr), *v.i.* [prob. < ON.], to crouch or huddle up, as from fear or cold; cringe.

**cow′hide′,** *n.* 1. the hide of a cow. 2. leather made from it. 3. a leather whip. *v.t.* [-HIDED, -HIDING], to flog with a cowhide.

**cowl** (koul), *n.* [< L. *cucullus*, hood], 1. a monk's hood. 2. a monk's cloak with a hood. 3. the top front part of an automobile body to which the windshield is attached. *v.t.* to cover as with a cowl.

**cow′lick′,** *n.* [< its looking as if licked by a cow], a tuft of hair that cannot easily be combed flat.

**cowl′ing,** *n.* [see COWL], a detachable metal covering for an airplane engine.

**cow·pox** (kou′poks′), *n.* a disease of cows: its virus is used in vaccination against smallpox.

**cow·slip** (kou′slip′), *n.* 1. the marsh marigold. 2. a kind of primrose.

**cox** (koks), *n.* [*pl.* COXES], [Colloq.], a coxswain. *v.t.* & *v.i.* to be coxswain to (a boat).

**cox·comb** (koks′kōm′), *n.* [for *cock's comb*], a silly, vain, conceited fellow; fop; dandy.

**cox·swain** (kok′s′n, -swān′), *n.* [< *cock* (a small boat) + *swain*], one who steers a boat or racing shell: also sp. **cockswain.**

**coy** (koi), *adj.* [ME., quiet; see QUIET], 1. shy; bashful. 2. pretending to be shy. —**coy′ly,** *adv.* —**coy′ness,** *n.*

**coy·ote** (kī′ōt, kī-ō′ti), *n.* [< Mex. Ind. *coyotl*], a small wolf of the prairies of W North America.

**coz·en** (kuz′′n), *v.t.* & *v.i.* [Fr. *cousiner*, lit., act as a cousin], to cheat; deceive.

**co·zy** (kō′zi), *adj.* [-ZIER, -ZIEST], [Scot. < ?], warm and comfortable; snug. *n.* [*pl.* -ZIES], a padded cover for a teapot, to keep the tea hot. —**co′zi·ly,** *adv.* —**co′zi·ness,** *n.*

**C.P.A., c.p.a.,** Certified Public Accountant.

**Cpl.,** Corporal.

**C.P.O.,** Chief Petty Officer.

**Cr,** in *chem.*, chromium.

**crab** (krab), ***n.*** [< AS. *crabba*, lit., scratcher], 1. a shellfish with four pairs of legs and a pair of pincers. 2. [C-], Cancer. 3. a crab apple. 4. one who is always cross or complaining. ***v.i.*** [CRABBED, CRABBING], [Colloq.], to complain.
**crab apple,** 1. a small, very sour apple. 2. the tree it grows on.
**crab·bed** (krab'id), ***adj.*** [< *crab*], 1. crabby. 2. hard to read; illegible.
**crab'by,** ***adj.*** [-BIER, -BIEST], [< *crab*], peevish; morose; cross. **—crab'bi·ly,** ***adv.***
**crab grass,** a coarse grass that spreads quickly.
**crack** (krak), ***v.i.*** [< AS. *cracian*, resound], 1. to make a sudden, sharp noise, as in breaking. 2. to break or split, usually without complete separation of parts. 3. to rasp, as the voice. 4. [Slang], to have a mental breakdown. 5. [Slang], to joke. ***v.t.*** 1. to cause to make a sudden, sharp noise. 2. to break, or cause a narrow split in. 3. to break down (petroleum) by heat and pressure into gasoline, etc. 4. [Colloq.], to solve. 5. [Slang], to break into (a safe, etc.). 6. [Slang], to make (a joke). ***n.*** 1. a sudden, sharp noise. 2. a break; partial fracture. 3. a chink; crevice. 4. a cracking of the voice. 5. [Colloq.], a sharp, resonant blow. 6. [Slang], an attempt; try. 7. [Slang], a joke or gibe. ***adj.*** [Colloq.], excelling; first-rate. **—crack down (on)**, [Colloq.], to become strict (with). **—cracked up to be,** [Colloq.], believed to be. **—crack up** [Colloq.], 1. to crash. 2. to break down physically or mentally.
**cracked** (krakt), ***adj.*** 1. broken without complete separation into parts. 2. harsh or strident: said of a voice. 3. [Colloq.], crazy.
**crack'er,** ***n.*** 1. a firecracker. 2. a thin, crisp wafer of unleavened dough.
**crack'er·jack',** ***adj.*** [Slang], excellent; first-rate. ***n.*** [Slang], a first-rate person or thing.
**crack'le** (-'l), ***v.i.*** [-LED, -LING], [< *crack*], to make a succession of slight, sharp sounds. ***v.t.*** to break with such sounds. ***n.*** 1. a succession of such sounds. 2. a finely cracked surface found on some pottery, etc.
**crack'ling,** ***n.*** 1. a crackle. 2. the browned, crisp rind of roast pork.
**crack'pot',** ***n.*** [Colloq.], an extreme fanatic.
**crack'-up',** ***n.*** 1. a crash. 2. a mental or physical breakdown.
**-cracy,** [< Gr. *kratos*, rule], a suffix meaning *a* (specified) *type of government, rule by*, as in *autocracy*.
**cra·dle** (krā'd'l), ***n.*** [AS. *cradol*], 1. a baby's small bed, usually on rockers. 2. infancy. 3. the place of a thing's beginning. 4. a framework for support or protection. 5. a box on rockers for washing gold out of gold-bearing sand. ***v.t.*** [-DLED, -DLING], 1. to place or rock in or as in a cradle. 2. to take care of in infancy. 3. to wash (sand) in a cradle.
**craft** (kraft, kräft), ***n.*** [AS. *cræfte*, power], 1. some special skill or art. 2. guile; slyness. 3. an occupation requiring special manual skill. 4. the members of a skilled trade. 5. [*pl.* CRAFT], a boat, ship, or aircraft.
**crafts'man** (-mən), ***n.*** [*pl.* -MEN], a skilled workman; artisan. **—crafts'man·ship',** ***n.***
**craft'y,** ***adj.*** [-IER, -IEST], subtly deceitful; sly; cunning. **—craft'i·ly,** ***adv.*** **—craft'i·ness,** ***n.***
**crag** (krag), ***n.*** [< Celt.], a steep rock projecting from a rock mass. **—crag'gy** [-GIER, -GIEST], ***adj.*** **—crag'gi·ness,** ***n.***
**cram** (kram), ***v.t.*** [CRAMMED, CRAMMING], [AS. *crammian*], 1. to pack full or too full. 2. to stuff; force. 3. to stuff to excess with food. ***v.i.*** 1. to eat too much or too quickly. 2. [Colloq.], to prepare for an examination in a hurried, intensive way.
**cramp** (kramp), ***n.*** [< OFr. *crampe*, bent], 1. a sudden, painful contraction of muscles, as from chill or strain. 2. *pl.* intestinal griping and pain. ***v.t.*** to confine; hamper.
**cran·ber·ry** (kran'ber'i, -bẽr-i), ***n.*** [*pl.* -RIES], [for D. *kranebere*], a firm, sour, edible, red berry, the fruit of a marsh shrub.
**crane** (krān), ***n.*** [AS. *cran*], 1. a large wading bird with very long legs and neck. 2. a machine for lifting and moving heavy weights, using a movable projecting arm or a horizontal traveling beam. ***v.t. & v.i.*** [CRANED, CRANING], 1. to raise or move as by a crane. 2. to stretch (the neck).
**cra·ni·om·e·try** (krā'ni-om'ə-tri), ***n.*** [< Gr. *kranion*, skull + *metron*, measure], the science of measuring skulls.
**cra·ni·um** (krā'ni-əm), ***n.*** [*pl.* -NIUMS, -NIA (-ni-ə)], [Gr. *kranion*], the skull, esp. the part containing the brain. **—cra'ni·al,** ***adj.***
**crank** (kraŋk), ***n.*** [AS. *cranc*], 1. a handle, etc. connected at right angles to a shaft of a machine to transmit motion. 2. [Colloq.], an eccentric or irritable person. ***v.t.*** to start or operate by a crank.
**crank'case',** ***n.*** the metal casing that encloses the crankshaft of an engine.
**crank'shaft',** ***n.*** a shaft turning a crank or turned by a crank.
**crank'y,** ***adj.*** [-IER, -IEST], irritable; cross; queer; eccentric. **—crank'i·ly,** ***adv.*** **—crank'i·ness,** ***n.***
**cran·ny** (kran'i), ***n.*** [*pl.* -NIES], [< LL. *crena*, notch], a crevice; crack.
**crape** (krāp), ***n.*** crepe; esp., black crepe as a sign of mourning.
**craps** (kraps), ***n.pl.*** [construed as sing.], a gambling game played with two dice: also **crap'shoot'ing.** **—crap'shoot'er,** ***n.***
**crash** (krash), ***v.i.*** [prob. echoic], 1. to fall, collide, break, etc. with a loud noise; smash. 2. to collapse; fail. ***v.t.*** 1. to cause (a car, airplane, etc.) to crash. 2. to force with a crashing noise (*in, out, through*, etc.). 3. [Colloq.], to get into (a party, etc.) without an invitation. ***n.*** 1. a loud, sudden noise. 2. a crashing, as of a car, etc. 3. a sudden collapse, as of business. ***adj.*** [Colloq.], using speed and all possible resources: as, a *crash* program.
**crash** (krash), ***n.*** [prob. < Russ. *krashenina*], a coarse linen cloth.
**crass** (kras), ***adj.*** [L. *crassus*], grossly stupid or dull. **—crass'ly,** ***adv.***
**-crat,** [< Gr. *kratos*, rule], a combining form meaning *member* or *supporter of* (a specified kind of) *government*.
**crate** (krāt), ***n.*** [L. *cratis*], a packing case made of slats of wood. ***v.t.*** [CRATED, CRATING], to pack in a crate.
**cra·ter** (krā'tẽr), ***n.*** [< Gr. *kratẽr*, bowl], 1. the bowl-shaped cavity at the mouth of a volcano. 2. a pit, as one made by a bomb explosion.
**cra·vat** (krə-vat'), ***n.*** [< Fr. < *Cravate*, Croatian: from scarves worn by Croatian soldiers], a necktie.
**crave** (krāv), ***v.t.*** [CRAVED, CRAVING], [AS. *crafian*], 1. to ask for earnestly; beg. 2. to long for eagerly. 3. to be in great need of. ***v.i.*** to have an eager longing (*for*).
**cra·ven** (krā'vən), ***adj.*** [< L. *crepare*, creak], cowardly. ***n.*** a coward.
**crav·ing** (krāv'iŋ), ***n.*** intense and prolonged desire, as for food.
**craw** (krô), ***n.*** [ME. *crawe*], 1. the crop of a bird. 2. the stomach of any animal.
**craw·fish** (krô'fish'), ***n.*** [*pl.* see FISH], a crayfish.
**crawl** (krôl), ***v.i.*** [< ON. *krafla*], 1. to move slowly by dragging the body along the ground, as a worm does. 2. to go on hands and knees; creep. 3. to move slowly or feebly. 4. to swarm with crawling things.

5. to feel as if insects were crawling on one. *n.* 1. the act of crawling. 2. an overarm swimming stroke.

**cray·fish** (krā′fish′), *n.* [*pl.* see FISH], [< OHG.], 1. a fresh-water crustacean somewhat like a little lobster. 2. a sea shellfish like a lobster without pincers.

**cray·on** (krā′ən, -on), *n.* [Fr. < L. *Creta*, Crete], 1. a small stick of white or colored chalk, waxy material, etc., used for drawing or writing. 2. a drawing made with crayons. *v.t.* to draw with crayons.

**craze** (krāz), *v.t. & v.i.* [CRAZED, CRAZING], [ME. *crasen*, to crack < ON.], to make or become insane. *n.* a fad. **—crazed,** *adj.*

**cra·zy** (krā′zi), *adj.* [-ZIER, -ZIEST], [< *craze*], 1. unsound of mind; insane, mad, frantic, etc. 2. of or fit for an insane person. **—cra′zi·ly,** *adv.* **—cra′zi·ness,** *n.*

**crazy quilt,** a patchwork quilt with no regular design.

**creak** (krēk), *v.i.* [see CROAK], to make a harsh, squeaking sound. *n.* such a sound. **—creak′y** [-IER, -IEST], *adj.*

**cream** (krēm), *n.* [< Gr. *chrisma*, ointment], 1. the oily, yellowish part of milk. 2. a creamlike cosmetic ointment. 3. the finest part. 4. a yellowish white. *adj.* 1. made of or with cream. 2. yellowish-white. *v.t.* 1. to add cream to. 2. to beat into a soft, smooth consistency. **—cream of,** creamed purée of. **—cream′y** [-IER, -IEST], *adj.*

**cream cheese,** a soft, white cheese made of cream or of milk and cream.

**cream′er,** *n.* a pitcher for cream.

**cream′er·y** (-ẽr-i), *n.* [*pl.* -IES], a place where dairy products are processed or sold.

**cream of tartar,** a white, acid, crystalline substance, used in medicine and cooking.

**crease** (krēs), *n.* [see CREST], 1. a line made by folding and pressing. 2. a fold; wrinkle. *v.t.* [CREASED, CREASING], 1. to make a crease in. 2. to wrinkle. *v.i.* to become creased.

**cre·ate** (krē-āt′), *v.t.* [-ATED, -ATING], [< L. *creare*], 1. to cause to come into existence; originate. 2. to cause; produce; bring about.

**cre·a·tion** (krē-ā′shən), *n.* 1. a creating or being created. 2. the universe. 3. anything created. **—cre·a′tion·al,** *adj.*

**cre·a′tive** (-tiv), *adj.* 1. creating or able to create. 2. inventive. **—cre·a′tive·ly,** *adv.*

**cre·a′tor** (-tẽr), *n.* 1. one that creates. 2. [C-], God.

**crea·ture** (krē′chẽr), *n.* [< L. *creatura*], 1. a living being, animal or human. 2. a person dominated by another.

**cre·dence** (krē′d'ns), *n.* [< L. *credere*, believe], belief, as in another's testimony.

**cre·den·tial** (kri-den′shəl), *n.* [see CREDENCE], *usually in pl.* a paper showing one's right to a certain position or authority.

**cre·den·za** (kri-den′zə), *n.* [*pl.* -ZAS], [It.], a type of buffet, or sideboard.

**cred·i·ble** (kred′ə-b'l), *adj.* [< L. *credere*, believe], that can be believed; reliable. **—cred′i·bil′i·ty,** *n.* **—cred′i·bly,** *adv.*

**cred·it** (kred′it), *n.* [< L. *credere*, believe], 1. belief; confidence. 2. trustworthiness. 3. favorable reputation. 4. praise or approval. 5. a person or thing bringing approval. 6. *usually pl.* acknowledgment of work done, as on a motion picture. 7. the amount of money in one's bank account, etc. 8. the entry in an account of payment on a debt. 9. trust in one's ability to meet payments. 10. the time allowed for payment. 11. a completed unit of study in a school. *v.t.* 1. to believe; trust. 2. to give credit or acknowledgment for. 3. to give credit in a bank account, etc. **—on credit,** with the agreement to pay later.

**cred′it·a·ble,** *adj.* bringing approval or honor; praiseworthy. **—cred′it·a·bly,** *adv.*

**cred·i·tor** (kred′i-tẽr), *n.* one to whom another owes a debt.

**cre·do** (krē′dō, krā′-), *n.* [*pl.* -DOS], [L., I believe], a creed.

**cre·du·li·ty** (krə-dōō′lə-ti, -dū′-), *n.* [*pl.* -TIES], a tendency to believe too readily.

**cred·u·lous** (krej′oo-ləs), *adj.* [< L. *credere*, believe], tending to believe too readily. **—cred′u·lous·ly,** *adv.* **—cred′u·lous·ness,** *n.*

**creed** (krēd), *n.* [< L. *credo*, lit., I believe], 1. a brief statement of religious belief, esp. one accepted as authoritative by a church. 2. any statement of belief, principles, etc.

**creek** (krēk, krik), *n.* [< ON. *kriki*, a winding], 1. a small stream, somewhat larger than a brook. 2. a narrow inlet or bay.

**creel** (krēl), *n.* [< L. *cratis*, wickerwork], a wicker basket for holding fish.

**creep** (krēp), *v.i.* [CREPT, CREEPING], [AS. *creopan*], 1. to move with the body close to the ground, as on hands and knees. 2. to move slowly, stealthily, or timidly. 3. to grow along the ground or a wall, as ivy. 4. to feel as if insects were creeping on one's skin. **—the creeps,** [Colloq.], a feeling of horror or repugnance. **—creep′er,** *n.*

**creep′y,** *adj.* [-IER, -IEST], 1. creeping. 2. having or causing a feeling of fear or repugnance. **—creep′i·ness,** *n.*

**cre·mate** (krē′māt, kri-māt′), *v.i.* [-MATED, -MATING], [< L. *cremare*, to burn], to burn (a dead body) to ashes. **—cre·ma′tion,** *n.*

**cre·ma·to·ry** (krē′mə-tôr′i), *n.* [*pl.* -RIES], a furnace for cremating: also **cre′ma·to′ri·um** (-tôr′i-əm). *adj.* of or for cremation.

**cre·nate** (krē′nāt), *adj.* [< LL. *crena*, a notch], having a notched or scalloped edge, as certain leaves: also **cre′nat·ed.**

**Cre·ole** (krē′ōl), *n.* [< Fr. < L. *creare*, create], 1. a person of French or Spanish descent born in Latin America. 2. a person descended from the original French settlers of Louisiana. 3. [c-], loosely, a person with both Creole and Negro ancestors.

**cre·o·sote** (krē′ə-sōt′), *n.* [< Gr. *kreas*, flesh + *sōzein*, save], an oily liquid with a pungent odor, distilled from wood tar or coal tar: used as an antiseptic and as a wood preservative. *v.t.* [-SOTED, -SOTING], to treat with creosote.

**crepe, crêpe** (krāp), *n.* [< Fr. < L. *crispus*, curly], 1. a thin, crinkled cloth of silk, rayon, wool, etc.; crape. 2. black crepe as a sign of mourning: usually sp. **crape** 3. thin paper crinkled like crepe: also **crepe paper.**

**crept** (krept), pt. and pp. of **creep.**

**cre·pus·cu·lar** (kri-pus′kyoo-lẽr), *adj.* [< L. *creper*, dark], of or like twilight; dim.

**cre·scen·do** (krə-shen′dō), *adj. & adv.* [It. < *crescere*, to increase], in *music*, gradually increasing in loudness. *n.* [*pl.* -DOS], a gradual increase in loudness.

**cres·cent** (kres′'nt), *n.* [< L. *crescere*, grow], 1. the shape of the moon in its first or last quarter. 2. anything shaped like this. *adj.* 1. [Poetic], increasing. 2. shaped like a crescent.

**cress** (kres), *n.* [AS. *cresse*, lit., creeper], a plant of the mustard family, as water cress, whose leaves are used in salads.

**crest** (krest), *n.* [< L. *crista*], 1. a comb, tuft, etc. on the head of an animal or bird. 2. a heraldic device, as on note paper, etc. 3. the top line or surface; summit: as, the *crest* of a wave. **—crest′ed,** *adj.*

**crest·fall·en** (krest′fôl′'n), *adj.* 1. with drooping crest. 2. dejected; disheartened.

**cre·tin** (krē′tin), *n.* [< Fr. *chrétien*, Christian, hence human being], a person suffering from cretinism. **—cre′tin·ous,** *adj.*

**cre′tin·ism,** *n.* a congenital thyroid deficiency, with resulting deformity and idiocy.

**cre·tonne** (kri-ton′, krē′ton), *n.* [Fr. < *Creton*, village in Normandy], a heavy cot-

ton or linen cloth with printed patterns.
**cre·vasse** (krə-vas′), *n.* [Fr., crevice], 1. a deep crack, esp. in a glacier. 2. a break in the levee of a river.
**crev·ice** (krev′is), *n.* [< L. *crepare*, to crack], a narrow opening caused by a crack or split; fissure.
**crew** (kro͞o), *n.* [< L. *crescere*, grow], a group of people working together, as all the seamen on a ship.
**crew** (kro͞o), alt. pt. of **crow**.
**crew·el** (kro͞o′əl), *n.* [prob. via MLG. or MD.], a loosely twisted, worsted yarn used in embroidery (**crewelwork**).
**crib** (krib), *n.* [AS. *cribb*], 1. a rack, box, etc. for fodder. 2. a small bed with high sides, for a baby. 3. a wooden enclosure for storing grain, etc. 4. [Colloq.], a literal translation or other aid used unethically in doing schoolwork. *v.t.* [CRIBBED, CRIBBING], 1. to confine. 2. to furnish with a crib. 3. [Colloq.], to plagiarize. *v.i.* [Colloq.], to do schoolwork by using a crib.
**crib′bage** (-ij), *n.* [< *crib* + *-age*], a card game in which the object is to form various combinations that count for points.
**crick** (krik), *n.* [prob. < ON.], a painful cramp in the neck or back.
**crick·et** (krik′it), *n.* [< OFr. *criquer*, creak], a leaping insect related to the grasshoppers.
**crick·et** (krik′it), *n.* [prob. < MD. *cricke*, a stick], 1. an outdoor game played with a ball, bats, and wickets, by two teams of eleven men each. 2. [Colloq.], fair play.
**cried** (krīd), pt. and pp. of **cry**.
**cri·er** (krī′ẽr), *n.* 1. one who cries. 2. one who shouts out news, proclamations, etc.
**crime** (krīm), *n.* [< L. *crimen*, offense], 1. an act that violates a law. 2. a sin.
**crim·i·nal** (krim′ə-n'l), *adj.* 1. having the nature of crime. 2. relating to or guilty of crime. *n.* a person guilty of a crime. **—crim′i·nal′i·ty** (-ə-nal′-ə-ti) [*pl.* -TIES], *n.*
**crim·i·nol·o·gy** (krim′ə-nol′ə-ji), *n.* the scientific study of crime and criminals. **—crim′i·nol′o·gist,** *n.*
**crimp** (krimp), *v.t.* [< MD. *crimpen*, to contract], 1. to press into narrow, regular folds; pleat. 2. to curl (the hair). *n.* 1. a crimping. 2. anything crimped. **—put a crimp in,** [Slang], to hinder.
**crim·son** (krim′z'n), *n.* [< Sans. *kṛmi*, insect], deep red. *adj.* deep-red. *v.t. & v.i.* to make or become crimson.
**cringe** (krinj), *v.i.* [CRINGED, CRINGING], [AS. *cringan*, fall (in battle, etc.)], 1. to draw back, crouch, etc., as when afraid; cower. 2. to act in a servile manner; fawn.
**crin·kle** (kriŋ′k'l), *v.i. & v.t.* [-KLED, -KLING], [< AS. *cringan* (see CRINGE)], 1. to wrinkle; ripple. 2. to rustle, as paper. *n.* a wrinkle. **—crin′kly** [-KLIER, -KLIEST], *adj.*
**crin·o·line** (krin′'l-in), *n.* [Fr. < L. *crinis*, hair + *linum*, thread], 1. a coarse, stiff cloth used as a lining in garments. 2. a hoop skirt.
**crip·ple** (krip′'l), *n.* [< AS. *creopan*, to creep], one who is lame or otherwise disabled. *v.t.* [-PLED, -PLING], 1. to lame. 2. to disable; impair. **—crip′pler,** *n.*
**cri·sis** (krī′sis), *n.* [*pl.* -SES (-sēz)], [< Gr. *krinein*, to separate], 1. the turning point in a disease, when it becomes clear whether the patient will recover or die. 2. any crucial situation.
**crisp** (krisp), *adj.* [< L. *crispus*, curly], 1. brittle; easily crumbled. 2. sharp and clear. 3. bracing; fresh: as, *crisp* air. 4. curly and wiry. *v.t. & v.i.* to make or become crisp. **—crisp′ly,** *adv.* **—crisp′ness,** *n.*
**crisp′y,** *adj.* [-IER, -IEST], crisp.
**criss·cross** (kris′krôs′), *n.* [earlier *Christcross*], a mark or pattern made of crossed lines. *adj.* marked by crossings. *v.t.* to mark with crossing lines. *v.i.* to move crosswise. *adv.* 1. crosswise. 2. awry.
**cri·ter·i·on** (krī-têr′i-ən), *n.* [*pl.* -IA (-ə), -IONS], [< Gr. *kritēs*, judge], a standard, rule, or test by which a judgment can be formed.
**crit·ic** (krit′ik), *n.* [< Gr. *krinein*, discern], 1. one who writes judgments of books, music, etc. professionally. 2. one who finds fault.
**crit′i·cal** (-i-k'l), *adj.* 1. tending to find fault. 2. of critics or criticism. 3. of or forming a crisis; crucial. **—crit′i·cal·ly,** *adv.*
**crit·i·cism** (krit′ə-siz'm), *n.* 1. the act of making judgments, esp. of literary or artistic work. 2. a review, etc. expressing such judgment. 3. a finding fault. 4. the art, principles, or methods of critics.
**crit·i·cize** (krit′ə-sīz′), *v.i. & v.t.* [-CIZED, -CIZING], 1. to analyze and judge as a critic. 2. to find fault (with); censure. Brit. spelling, **criticise. —crit′i·ciz′er,** *n.*
**cri·tique** (kri-tēk′), *n.* [Fr.], a critical analysis or review.
**croak** (krōk), *v.i.* [echoic], 1. to make a deep, hoarse sound: as, frogs *croak.* 2. [Slang], to die. *v.t.* to utter in deep, hoarse tones. *n.* a croaking sound. **—croak′y,** *adj.*
**cro·chet** (krō-shā′), *n.* [Fr., small hook], a kind of knitting done with one hooked needle. *v.t. & v.i.* [-CHETED (-shād′), -CHETING (-shā′iŋ)], to knit with such a needle.
**crock** (krok), *n.* [AS. *crocc(a)*], an earthenware pot or jar.
**crock′er·y** (-ẽr-i), *n.* [< *crock*], pots, jars, etc. made of baked clay.
**croc·o·dile** (krok′ə-dīl′), *n.* [< Gr. *krokē*, pebble + *drilos*, worm], a large, lizardlike reptile of tropical streams, having a long, narrow head with massive jaws.
**cro·cus** (krō′kəs), *n.* [*pl.* -CUSES, -CI (-sī)], [< Gr. *krokos*, saffron], a small plant of the iris family, with a yellow, purple, or white flower: it blooms early in the spring.
**Cro-Ma·gnon** (krō-mag′non), *adj.* [< *Cro-Magnon* cave in France], of a prehistoric race of men who lived on the European continent. *n.* a member of this race.
**crone** (krōn), *n.* [prob. < MD. *kronje*, old ewe], a withered old woman.
**cro·ny** (krō′ni), *n.* [*pl.* -NIES], [< Gr. *chronios*, contemporary], a close friend.
**crook** (krook), *n.* [< ON. *krōkr*, hook], 1. a hook; hooked or curved staff, etc. 2. a bend or curve. 3. [Colloq.], a swindler; thief. *v.t. & v.i.* [CROOKED (krookt), CROOKING], to bend or curve.
**crook·ed** (krook′id *for 2 & 3*; krookt *for 1*), *adj.* 1. having a crook. 2. not straight; bent. 3. dishonest. **—crook′ed·ly,** *adv.*
**croon** (kro͞on), *v.i. & v.t.* [< MLG.], 1. to sing in a low, gentle tone. 2. to sing (popular songs) in a soft, sentimental manner. *n.* a low, gentle singing. **—croon′er,** *n.*
**crop** (krop), *n.* [AS. *cropp*, bunch], 1. a saclike part of a bird's gullet, in which food is softened for digestion; craw. 2. any agricultural product, growing or harvested. 3. the yield of any product in one season or place. 4. a group. 5. the handle of a whip. 6. a riding whip. 7. hair cut close to the head. *v.t.* [CROPPED or *occas.* CROPT, CROPPING], 1. to cut or bite off the ends of. 2. to reap. 3. to cut short. **—crop out** (or **up**), to appear unexpectedly.
**crop′per,** *n.* 1. one that crops. 2. [Colloq.], a heavy fall; hence, a failure.
**crop rotation,** a system of growing different crops successively, to prevent soil depletion, etc.
**cro·quet** (krō-kā′), *n.* [Fr.; see CROTCHET], an outdoor game in which the players use mallets to drive a wooden ball through hoops in the ground.

**cro·quette** (krō-ket′), *n.* [Fr. < *croquer*, to crunch], a small mass of chopped meat, fish, etc. fried in deep fat.
**cro·sier** (krō′zhēr), *n.* [< OFr. *croce*], the staff of a bishop or abbot, symbol of his office: also sp. **crozier.**
**cross** (krôs), *n.* [< L. *crux*], 1. an upright post with another across it, on which criminals were once executed. 2. a representation of this as a symbol of the crucifixion of Jesus, and hence of Christianity. 3. any trouble or affliction. 4. any mark or symbol made by intersecting lines, bars, etc. 5. a crossing of varieties or breeds. *v.t.* & *v.i.* 1. to make the sign of the cross upon. 2. to place across or crosswise. 3. to intersect. 4. to draw a line or lines across. 5. to go or extend across. 6. to meet (each other) in passing. 7. to thwart; oppose. 8. to interbreed (animals or plants). *adj.* 1. lying or passing across. 2. contrary; opposed. 3. cranky; irritable. 4. of mixed variety or breed. **—cross off** (or **out**), to cancel as by drawing lines across. **—cross one's mind,** to suggest itself to one. **—the Cross,** 1. the cross on which Jesus died. 2. Christianity.
**cross′bar′,** *n.* a bar, line, or stripe placed crosswise.
**cross′beam′,** *n.* a beam placed across another or from one wall to another.
**cross′bones′,** *n.* a representation of two bones placed across each other, usually under a skull, used to symbolize death.
**cross′bow′** (-bō′), *n.* a medieval weapon consisting of a bow set transversely on a wooden stock. **—cross′bow′man** [*pl.* -MEN], *n.*
**cross′breed′,** *v.t.* & *v.i.* [-BRED, -BREEDING], to hybridize; cross. *n.* a hybrid.
**cross′-coun′try,** *adj.* & *adv.* across open country or fields, not by roads.
**cross′cut′,** *adj.* 1. used for cutting across: as, a *crosscut* saw. 2. cut across. *n.* a cut across. *v.t.* & *v.i.* [-CUT, -CUTTING], to cut across.
**cross′-ex·am′ine,** *v.t.* & *v.i.* in *law,* to question (a witness already questioned by the opposing side) to determine the validity of his testimony. **—cross′-ex·am′i·na′tion,** *n.*
**cross′-eye′,** *n.* an abnormal condition in which the eyes are turned toward each other. **—cross′-eyed′,** *adj.*
**cross′hatch′** (-hach′), *v.t.* & *v.i.* to shade with two sets of crossing parallel lines.
**cross′ing,** *n.* 1. the act of passing across, thwarting, interbreeding, etc. 2. an intersection, as of lines or streets. 3. a place where a street, river, etc. may be crossed.
**cross′piece′,** *n.* a piece lying across something else.
**cross′-pol′li·nate′,** *v.t.* & *v.i.* [-NATED, -NATING], to transfer pollen from the anther of (one flower) to the stigma of (another).
**cross reference,** a reference from one part of a book, index, etc. to another part.
**cross′road′,** *n.* 1. a road that crosses another. 2. *usually pl.* the place where roads intersect.
**cross section,** 1. a cutting across something. 2. a piece so cut off. 3. a representative part of the whole.
**cross′-stitch′,** *n.* 1. a stitch made by crossing two stitches in the form of an X. 2. needlework made with this stitch. *v.t.* & *v.i.* to sew or embroider with this stitch.
**cross′-town′,** *adj.* going across the main avenues of a city.
**cross′walk′,** *n.* a lane marked off across a street, for pedestrians' use.
**cross′wise′** (-wīz′), *adv.* across; so as to cross: also **cross′ways′** (-wāz′).
**cross′word′ puzzle,** an arrangement of numbered squares to be filled in with words whose definitions are given as clues.
**crotch** (kroch), *n.* [Fr. *croche,* a hook], 1. a pole forked on top. 2. a place where two branches fork from a tree. 3. the place where the legs fork from the human body.
**crotch·et** (kroch′it), *n.* [< OFr. *croc,* a hook], a peculiar whim. **—crotch′et·y,** *adj.*
**crouch** (krouch), *v.i.* [< OFr. *croc,* a hook], 1. to stoop low. 2. to cringe. *n.* a crouching.
**croup** (kro͞op), *n.* [< obs. *croup,* speak hoarsely], an inflammation of the respiratory passages, with labored breathing and hoarse coughing. **—croup′y,** *adj.*
**crou·pi·er** (kro͞o′pyā′), *n.* [Fr.], a person in charge of a gambling table.
**crou·ton** (kro͞o-ton′, kro͞o′ton), *n.* [< Fr.; see CRUST], a small piece of toasted bread served in soup.
**crow** (krō), *n.* [AS. *crawa*], a large, glossy-black bird with a harsh call. **—as the crow flies,** in a direct line. **—eat crow** [Colloq.], to admit an error, recant, etc.
**crow** (krō), *v.i.* [CROWED or, for 1, CREW (kro͞o), CROWED, CROWING], [echoic], 1. to make the shrill cry of a rooster. 2. to utter a cry of victory, pleasure, etc.; exult. *n.* the cry of a rooster.
**crow·bar** (krō′bär′), *n.* a long, metal bar used as a lever for prying, etc.
**crowd** (kroud), *v.i.* [AS. *crudan*], to throng. *v.t.* 1. to press; push. 2. to pack or fill too full. *n.* 1. a large number of people or things gathered closely together. 2. [Colloq.], a set; clique. **—crowd′ed,** *adj.*
**crow′foot′,** *n.* [*pl.* -FOOTS], a plant of the buttercup family, with leaves resembling a crow's foot.
**crown** (kroun), *n.* [< Gr. *korōnē,* wreath], 1. a wreath worn on the head in victory. 2. a reward; honor. 3. the head covering of a monarch. 4. *a*) the power of a monarch. *b*) the monarch. 5. a thing like a crown in shape, position, etc., as the top of the head. 6. a British silver coin equal to five shillings. 7. the highest point, quality, state, etc. of anything. 8. the part of a tooth projecting beyond the gum line. *v.t.* 1. to put a crown on. 2. to make (a person) a monarch. 3. to give honor, etc. to. 4. to be the highest part of. 5. to put the finishing touch on.
**crown prince,** the heir apparent to a throne.
**crow's-foot** (krōz′foot′), *n.* [*pl.* -FEET (-fēt′)], *usually in pl.* any of the wrinkles that often develop at the outer corners of the eyes.
**crow's-nest** (krōz′nest′), *n.* a lookout platform high on a ship's mast.
**cro·zier** (krō′zhēr), *n.* a crosier.
**cru·cial** (kro͞o′shəl), *adj.* [< L. *crux,* a cross], 1. decisive; critical. 2. extremely trying.
**cru·ci·ble** (kro͞o′sə-b'l), *n.* [< ML. *crucibulum,* lamp], 1. a heat-resistant container for melting ores, etc. 2. a severe test.
**cru·ci·fix** (kro͞o′sə-fiks′), *n.* [< L. *crux,* a cross + *figere,* fasten], a representation of a cross with Jesus crucified on it.
**cru′ci·fix′ion** (-fik′shən), *n.* 1. a crucifying. 2. [C-], the crucifying of Jesus, or a representation of this.
**cru′ci·form′** (-fôrm′), *adj.* cross-shaped.
**cru′ci·fy′** (-fī′), *v.t.* [-FIED, -FYING], [see CRUCIFIX], 1. to execute by suspending from a cross, with the hands and feet fastened to it. 2. to torment; torture.
**crude** (kro͞od), *adj.* [L. *crudus,* raw], 1. in a raw or natural state. 2. lacking grace, taste, etc. 3. roughly made. **—crude′ly,** *adv.* **—cru·di·ty** (kro͞o′də-ti), **crude′ness,** *n.*
**cru·el** (kro͞o′əl), *adj.* [see CRUDE], causing pain and suffering; without mercy or pity. **—cru′el·ly,** *adv.* **—cru′el·ty** [*pl.* -TIES], *n.*
**cru·et** (kro͞o′it), *n.* [< OFr. *crue,* earthen pot], a small glass bottle to hold vinegar, oil, etc., for the table.
**cruise** (kro͞oz), *v.i.* [CRUISED, CRUISING], [< D. *kruisen,* to cross], to sail or drive about from place to place, without a set destina-

tion. ***v.t.*** to sail or journey over or about. ***n.*** a cruising voyage.

**cruis′er,** ***n.*** 1. anything that cruises, as a police car. 2. a fast warship smaller than a battleship.

**crul·ler** (krul′ẽr), ***n.*** [D. < *krullen*, to curl], a doughnut made of twisted strips of dough.

**crumb** (krum), ***n.*** [AS. *cruma*], 1. a small piece broken off, as of bread. 2. a bit; scrap: as, *crumbs* of knowledge. ***v.t. & v.i.*** to break into crumbs. **—crumb′y** [-IER, -IEST], ***adj.***

**crum·ble** (krum′b'l), ***v.t.*** [-BLED, -BLING], [freq. of *crumb*], to break into crumbs. ***v.i.*** to fall to pieces; decay. **—crum′bly,** ***adj.***

**crum·my** (krum′i), ***adj.*** [-MIER, -MIEST], [Slang], poor, shabby, mean, etc.

**crum·pet** (krum′pit), ***n.*** [< AS. *crump*, bent], a batter cake baked on a griddle.

**crum·ple** (krum′p'l), ***v.t. & v.i.*** [-PLED, -PLING], [< dial. *crump*, curl up], to crush together into wrinkles.

**crunch** (krunch), ***v.i. & v.t.*** [echoic], to chew, press, grind, etc. with a noisy, crackling sound. ***n.*** the act or sound of crunching. **—crunch′y** [-IER, -IEST], ***adj.***

**crup·per** (krup′ẽr, kroop′-), ***n.*** [< OFr. *crope*, rump], a leather strap attached to a harness and passed under a horse's tail.

**cru·sade** (kro͞o-sād′), ***n.*** [ult. < L. *crux*, cross], 1. [often C-], any of the military expeditions of Christians from the 11th to the 13th centuries to recover the Holy Land from the Moslems. 2. vigorous, concerted action for some cause or against some abuse. ***v.i.*** [-SADED, -SADING], to engage in a crusade. **—cru·sad′er,** ***n.***

**cruse** (kro͞oz, kro͞os), ***n.*** [< MD. *cruyse* or ON. *krūs*], a small container for liquids.

**crush** (krush), ***v.t.*** [< OFr. *cruisir*], 1. to press with force so as to break or put out of shape. 2. to grind or pound into small bits. 3. to subdue; overwhelm. 4. to extract by squeezing. ***v.i.*** to become crushed. ***n.*** 1. a crushing. 2. a crowded mass of people. 3. [Colloq.], an infatuation. **—crush′er,** ***n.***

**crust** (krust), ***n.*** [< L. *crusta*], 1. the hard, outer part of bread. 2. any dry, hard piece of bread. 3. the pastry shell of a pie. 4. any hard surface layer, as of snow. 5. [Slang], insolence. ***v.t. & v.i.*** to cover or become covered with a crust.

**crus·ta·cean** (krus-tā′shən), ***n.*** [see CRUST], any of a class of invertebrates having a hard outer shell, as shrimps, crabs, lobsters, etc.

**crust′y,** ***adj.*** [-IER, -IEST], 1. having a crust. 2. bad-tempered; surly.

**crutch** (kruch), ***n.*** [AS. *crycc*], 1. a staff with a top crosspiece that fits under the armpit, used to aid the lame in walking. 2. any prop, support, etc.

**crux** (kruks), ***n.*** [L., a cross], 1. a difficult problem. 2. a crucial or essential point.

**cry** (krī), ***v.i.*** [CRIED, CRYING], [< L. *quiritare*, to wail], 1. to make a loud sound, as in pain, fright, etc. 2. to shed tears; sob; weep. 3. to utter its characteristic call: said of an animal. ***v.t.*** 1. to utter loudly; shout. 2. to announce loudly, as wares for sale. ***n.*** [*pl.* CRIES], 1. a crying; call; shout. 2. an entreaty. 3. a fit of weeping. 4. the characteristic vocal sound of an animal. **—a far cry,** a great distance or difference. **—cry for,** 1. to plead for. 2. to need greatly.

**cry′ba′by,** ***n.*** [*pl.* -BIES], one who complains constantly, in a childish way.

**cry·o·gen·ics** (krī′ə-jen′iks), ***n.*** [< Gr. *kryos*, cold; + *-gen* + *-ics*], the science that deals with production of very low temperatures and their effect on matter.

**crypt** (kript), ***n.*** [< Gr. *kryptein*, hide], an underground vault, esp. one used for burial.

**cryp·tic** (krip′tik), ***adj.*** secret; occult: also **cryp′ti·cal.** **—cryp′ti·cal·ly,** ***adv.***

**cryp·to·gram** (krip′tə-gram′), ***n.*** [< Gr. *kryptos*, hidden; + *-gram*], something written in code or cipher: also **cryp′to·graph′.**

**cryp·tog·ra·phy** (krip-tog′rə-fi), ***n.*** [< Gr. *kryptos*, hidden + *graphein*, write], the art of writing or deciphering secret code.

**crys·tal** (kris′t'l), ***n.*** [< Gr. *kryos*, frost], 1. a clear, transparent quartz. 2. a very clear, brilliant glass. 3. anything clear like crystal, as the covering over a watch face. 4. a solidified form of a substance having plane faces symmetrically grouped. ***adj.*** 1. of crystal. 2. like crystal; clear.

**crys·tal·line** (kris′t'l-in), ***adj.*** 1. made of or formed in crystal(s). 2. like crystal.

**crys′tal·lize′** (-īz′), ***v.i. & v.t.*** [-LIZED, -LIZING], 1. to become or cause to become crystalline. 2. to take on or cause to take on a definite form. **—crys′tal·li·za′tion,** ***n.***

**Cs,** in *chem.*, cesium.

**cs.,** case; cases.

**C.S.T.,** Central Standard Time.

**ct.,** 1. [*pl.* CTS.], cent. 2. court.

**Cu,** *cuprum*, [L.], in *chem.*, copper.

**cu.,** cubic.

**cub** (kub), ***n.*** [prob. < Celt.], 1. a young fox, bear, lion, etc. 2. an inexperienced youth.

**cub·by·hole** (kub′i-hōl′), ***n.*** [< Brit. dial. *cub*, little shed; + *hole*], a small, enclosed space.

**cube** (kūb), ***n.*** [< Gr. *kybos*], 1. a solid with six equal, square sides. 2. the product obtained by multiplying a given number by its square: as, the *cube* of 3 is 27. ***v.t.*** [CUBED, CUBING], 1. to obtain the cube of (a number). 2. to form into the shape of cubes.

**cube root,** the number of which a given number is the cube: as, the *cube root* of 8 is 2.

**cu·bic** (kū′bik), ***adj.*** 1. having the shape of a cube: also **cu′bi·cal.** 2. having three dimensions: a cubic foot is the volume of a cube one foot in length, width, and breadth.

**cu·bi·cle** (kū′bi-k'l), ***n.*** [< L. *cubare*, lie down], a small compartment.

**cub·ism** (kūb′iz'm), ***n.*** a school of modern art characterized by the use of cubes and other geometric forms. **—cub′ist,** ***adj. & n.***

**cu·bit** (kū′bit), ***n.*** [L. *cubitum*], an ancient measure of length, about 18 to 22 inches.

**cuck·old** (kuk′'ld), ***n.*** [see CUCKOO], a man whose wife has committed adultery. ***v.t.*** to make a cuckold of.

**cuck·oo** (kook′o͞o′, ko͞o′ko͞o′), ***n.*** [< OFr. *cucu*; echoic], 1. a brown bird with a long, slender body: the European species lays its eggs in the nests of other birds. 2. its call. ***adj.*** [Slang], crazy; silly.

**cu·cum·ber** (kū′kum-bẽr), ***n.*** [< L. *cucumis*], a long, green-skinned vegetable with firm, white flesh, pickled or used in salads.

**cud** (kud), ***n.*** [AS. *cwudu*], a mouthful of swallowed food regurgitated from the first stomach of cattle and other ruminants and chewed again.

**cud·dle** (kud′'l), ***v.t.*** [-DLED, -DLING], [< ?], to embrace and fondle. ***v.i.*** to lie close and snug; nestle. **—cud′dly** [-DLIER, -DLIEST], ***adj.***

**cudg·el** (kuj′əl), ***n.*** [AS. *cycgel*], a short, thick stick or club. ***v.t.*** [-ELED or -ELLED, -ELING or -ELLING], to beat with a cudgel. **—cudgel one's brains,** to think hard.

**cue** (kū), ***n.*** [< *q* (? for L. *quando*, when), found on 16th-c. plays], 1. a signal in dialogue, etc. for an actor's entrance or speech. 2. any signal to begin or enter. 3. a hint; suggestion. ***v.t.*** [CUED, CUING], [Colloq.], to give a cue to.

**cue** (kū), ***n.*** [< *queue*], 1. a queue. 2. a long, tapering rod used in billiards, etc.

**cuff** (kuf), ***n.*** [< ME. *cuffe*, glove], 1. a band at the wrist end of a sleeve. 2. a turned-up fold at the bottom of a trouser leg. 3. a slap. ***v.t.*** to slap.

**cuff links,** a pair of linked buttons, etc. for fastening a shirt cuff.

**cui·rass** (kwi-ras′), *n.* [ult. < L. *corium*, leather], a piece of armor for the upper torso.

**cui·sine** (kwi-zēn′), *n.* [Fr. < L. *coquere*, to cook], 1. a style of cooking or preparing food. 2. the food prepared.

**cul-de-sac** (kul′də-sak′), *n.* [*pl.* -SACS], [Fr., lit., bottom of a sack], a blind alley.

**-cule,** [< Fr. or L.], a suffix added to nouns to form diminutives.

**cu·li·nar·y** (kū′lə-ner′i), *adj.* [< L. *culina*, kitchen], of cookery.

**cull** (kul), *v.t.* [< L. *colligere*, collect], to pick out; select and gather: *n.* something picked out for rejection as not up to standard.

**cul·mi·nate** (kul′mə-nāt′), *v.i.* [-NATED, -NATING], [< L. *culmen*, peak], to reach its highest point or climax. **—cul′mi·na′tion,** *n.*

**cul·pa·ble** (kul′pə-b'l), *adj.* [< L. *culpa*, fault], deserving blame. **—cul′pa·bil′i·ty,** *n.*

**cul·prit** (kul′prit), *n.* [< early law Fr. *culpable*, guilty + *prit*, ready (to prove)], a person accused, or found guilty, of a crime.

**cult** (kult), *n.* [< L. *cultus*, care], 1. a system of religious worship. 2. devoted attachment to a person, principle, etc. 3. a sect.

**cul·ti·vate** (kul′tə-vāt′), *v.t.* [-VATED, -VATING], [see CULT], 1. to prepare (land) for growing crops; till. 2. to grow or develop (plants). 3. to seek to develop or improve, as the mind. 4. to seek to become familiar with. **—cul′ti·va·ble** (-və-b'l), *adj.* **—cul′ti·vat′ed,** *adj.* **—cul′ti·va′tor,** *n.*

**cul′ti·va′tion,** *n.* 1. the cultivating of land, plants, etc. 2. the development or advancement of something. 3. culture; training.

**cul·ture** (kul′chēr), *n.* [see CULT], 1. the cultivation of soil. 2. a growth of bacteria, etc. in a prepared substance (**culture medium**). 3. improvement by study or training. 4. the training of the mind, taste, etc. 5. the skills, arts, etc. of a given people in a given period; civilization. *v.t.* [-TURED, -TURING], to cultivate. **—cul′tur·al,** *adj.*

**cul·vert** (kul′vērt), *n.* [< ?], a drain or waterway under a road or embankment.

**cum·ber** (kum′bēr), *v.t.* [< LL. *combrus*, barrier], to hinder; hamper.

**cum′ber·some** (-səm), *adj.* burdensome; unwieldy: also **cum′brous** (-brəs).

**cu·mu·late** (kūm′yə-lāt′; *for adj., usually* -lit), *v.t. & v.i.* [-LATED, -LATING], [< L. *cumulus*, a heap], to gather into a heap; accumulate. *adj.* gathered into a heap.

**cu′mu·la′tive** (-lā′tiv, -lə-tiv), *adj.* increasing in effect, size, etc. by successive additions. **—cu′mu·la′tive·ly,** *adv.*

**cu·mu·lus** (kūm′yə-ləs), *n.* [*pl.* -LI (-lī′)], [L., a heap], a thick cloud formation with rounded masses piled up.

**cu·ne·i·form** (kū-nē′ə-fôrm′), *adj.* [< L. *cuneus*, a wedge; + *-form*], wedge-shaped, as the characters used in ancient Assyrian inscriptions. *n.* cuneiform characters.

**cun·ning** (kun′iŋ), *adj.* [< ME. *cunnen*, know], 1. skillful; clever. 2. sly; crafty. 3. pretty in a delicate way, as a child. 4. created with skill. *n.* 1. slyness; craftiness. 2. [Archaic], skill. **—cun′ning·ly,** *adv.*

**cup** (kup), *n.* [AS. *cuppe*], 1. a small, bowl-shaped container for beverages, often with a handle. 2. a cup and its contents. 3. a cupful. 4. anything shaped like a cup. *v.t.* [CUPPED, CUPPING], to shape like a cup.

**cup·board** (kub′ērd), *n.* a closet or cabinet fitted with shelves for dishes, food, etc.

**cup′cake′,** *n.* a small cake.

**cup′ful′,** *n.* [*pl.* -FULS], as much as a cup will hold; specif., half a pint.

**Cu·pid** (kū′pid), *n.* 1. the Roman god of love. 2. [c-], a representation of Cupid as a winged boy with bow and arrow.

**cu·pid·i·ty** (kū-pid′ə-ti), *n.* [< L. *cupere*, to desire], strong desire for wealth; greed.

**cu·po·la** (kū′pə-lə), *n.* [It. < L. *cupa*, a tub], 1. a rounded roof or ceiling. 2. a small dome or similar structure on a roof.

**cu·pre·ous** (kū′pri-əs), *adj.* [< L. *cuprum*, copper], of, like, or containing copper.

**cur** (kūr), *n.* [prob. < ON. *kurra*, to growl], 1. a dog of mixed breed; mongrel. 2. a contemptible person.

**cur·a·ble** (kyoor′ə-b'l), *adj.* that can be cured. **—cur′a·bil′i·ty,** *n.* **—cur′a·bly,** *adv.*

**cu·rate** (kyoor′it), *n.* [< L. *cura*, care (of souls)], a clergyman who assists a vicar or rector. **—cu′ra·cy** (-ə-si) [*pl.* -CIES], *n.*

**cur·a·tive** (kyoor′ə-tiv), *adj.* having the power to cure. *n.* a remedy.

**cu·ra·tor** (kyoo-rā′tēr), *n.* [< L. *curare*, take care of], one who has charge, as of a museum or library.

**curb** (kūrb), *n.* [< L. *curvus*, bent], 1. a chain or strap attached to a horse's bit, used to check the horse. 2. anything that checks or restrains. 3. a stone or concrete edging of a sidewalk or pavement. 4. a market dealing in stocks and bonds not listed on the exchange. *v.t.* 1. to restrain; control. 2. to provide with a curb.

**curb′ing,** *n.* 1. material for curbstones. 2. a curb or part of a curb (sense 3).

**curb′stone′,** *n.* the stones making up a curb.

**curd** (kūrd), *n.* [< AS. *crudan*, to press], the coagulated part of soured milk from which cheese is made. *v.t. & v.i.* to curdle.

**cur·dle** (kūr′d'l), *v.t. & v.i.* [-DLED, -DLING], to form into curd; congeal. **—curdle one's blood,** to horrify or terrify one.

**cure** (kyoor), *n.* [< L. *cura*, care], 1. a healing or being healed. 2. a remedy. 3. a method of medical treatment. *v.t.* [CURED, CURING], 1. to restore to health. 2. to remedy (an ailment, evil, etc.). 3. to preserve (meat) by salting, smoking, etc.

**cur·few** (kūr′fū), *n.* [< OFr. *covrir*, to hide + *feu*, fire: orig., a nightly signal for people to cover fires and retire], a time in the evening beyond which children, etc. may not appear on the streets.

**cu·rie** (kyoor′i, kyoo-rē′), *n.* [< Marie *Curie*, (1867–1934), Pol. chemist in France], the unit used in measuring radioactivity.

**cu·ri·o** (kyoor′i-ō′), *n.* [*pl.* -OS], [contr. of *curiosity*], an art object valued as a curiosity.

**cu·ri·os·i·ty** (kyoor′i-os′ə-ti), *n.* [*pl.* -TIES], 1. a desire to learn or know. 2. anything curious or rare.

**cu·ri·ous** (kyoor′i-əs), *adj.* [< L. *curiosus*, careful], 1. eager to learn or know; inquisitive or prying. 2. strange; unusual.

**cu·ri·um** (kyoor′i-əm), *n.* [see CURIE], an element produced by atomic fission: symbol, Cm.

**curl** (kūrl), *v.t.* [< ME. *crull*, curly], 1. to twist (hair, etc.) into ringlets. 2. to cause to bend around. *v.i.* to become curled. *n.* 1. a ringlet of hair. 2. anything with a curled shape. **—curl up,** 1. to gather into spirals or curls. 2. to sit or lie with the legs drawn up. **—curl′y** [-IER, -IEST], *adj.*

**cur·lew** (kūr′lōō, -lū), *n.* [echoic], a large, brownish wading bird with long legs and a long, curved bill.

**curl·i·cue** (kūr′li-kū′), *n.* [< *curly* + *cue*], a fancy curve, flourish, etc.

**curl·ing** (kūr′liŋ), *n.* a game played on ice by sliding a flat, heavy stone at a mark.

**cur·mudg·eon** (kēr-muj′ən), *n.* [< ?], a surly, ill-mannered person.

**cur·rant** (kūr′ənt), *n.* [ult. < *Corinth*, ancient Gr. city], 1. a small, seedless raisin from the Mediterranean region. 2. the sour berry of a large group of hardy shrubs.

**cur·ren·cy** (kūr′ən-si), *n.* [*pl.* -CIES], [see CURRENT], 1. circulation. 2. the money in circulation in any country. 3. general use or acceptance.

**cur·rent** (kũr'ənt), *adj.* [< L. *currere*, to run], 1. of this day, week, etc. 2. circulating. 3. commonly accepted; in general use. *n.* 1. a flow of water or air in a definite direction. 2. a running or flowing. 3. a general tendency or drift. 4. the flow or rate of flow of electricity in a conductor.

**cur·ric·u·lum** (kə-rik'yoo-ləm), *n.* [*pl.* -LUMS, -LA (-lə)], [L., a course], a course of study in a school. **—cur·ric'u·lar** (-lẽr), *adj.*

**cur·ry** (kũr'i), *v.t.* [-RIED, -RYING], [OFr. *correier*, put in order], 1. to rub down and clean the coat of (a horse, etc.) with a comb or brush. 2. to prepare (tanned leather). **—curry favor,** to try to get favor by flattery, fawning, etc. **—cur'ri·er,** *n.*

**cur·ry** (kũr'i), *n.* [*pl.* -RIES], [Tamil *kari*], 1. a powder prepared from various spices, or a sauce made with this, used esp. in India. 2. a stew made with curry. *v.t.* [-RIED, -RYING], to flavor with curry.

**curse** (kũrs), *n.* [AS. *curs*], 1. a calling on God or the gods to bring evil on some person or thing. 2. a blasphemous oath. 3. evil that seems to come in answer to a curse. *v.t.* [CURSED or CURST, CURSING], 1. to call evil down on. 2. to swear at. 3. to bring evil or injury on; afflict. *v.i.* to swear; blaspheme.

**curs·ed** (kũr'sid, kũrst), *adj.* 1. under a curse. 2. deserving to be cursed; evil.

**cur·sive** (kũr'siv), *adj.* [ult. < L. *currere*, to run], designating or of writing in which the letters are joined.

**cur·so·ry** (kũr'sẽr-i), *adj.* [< L. *cursor*, runner], hastily, hence often superficially, done.

**curt** (kũrt), *adj.* [L. *curtus*], 1. short; shortened. 2. so brief as to be rude: as, a *curt* reply.

**cur·tail** (kẽr-tāl'), *v.t.* [< L. *curtus*, short], to cut short; reduce. **—cur·tail'ment,** *n.*

**cur·tain** (kũr't'n), *n.* [< L. *cors*, a court], a piece of cloth, etc., hung at a window, in front of a stage, etc. to decorate or conceal. *v.t.* to provide as with a curtain.

**curt·sy** (kũrt'si), *n.* [*pl.* -SIES], [var. of *courtesy*], a woman's salutation made as a mark of respect by bending the knees and dipping the body slightly. *v.i.* [-SIED, -SYING], to make a curtsy. Also sp. **curtsey.**

**cur·va·ture** (kũr'və-chẽr), *n.* 1. a curving or being curved. 2. a curve or curved part.

**curve** (kũrv), *n.* [L. *curvus*, bent], 1. a line having no straight part; bend with no angles. 2. something shaped like, or moving in, a curve. *v.t. & v.i.* [CURVED, CURVING], 1. to form a curve. 2. to move in a curve.

**cur·vi·lin·e·ar** (kũr'və-lin'i-ẽr), *adj.* consisting of or enclosed by curved lines.

**cush·ion** (koosh'ən), *n.* [< LL. *coxinum*], 1. a pillow or pad. 2. a thing like this in shape or use, as something that absorbs shock. *v.t.* to provide with a cushion.

**cusp** (kusp), *n.* [L. *cuspis*, point], a point, as on the surface of a tooth.

**cus·pid** (kus'pid), *n.* a tooth with one cusp; canine tooth.

**cus·pi·dor** (kus'pə-dôr'), *n.* [< Port. *cuspir*, to spit], a spittoon.

**cuss** (kus), *n.* [Colloq.], 1. a curse. 2. a person or animal regarded as queer, perverse, etc. *v.t. & v.i.* [Colloq.], to curse. **—cuss'ed,** *adj.*

**cus·tard** (kus'tẽrd), *n.* [prob. ult. < OFr. *croustade*, dish with a crust], a mixture of eggs, milk, sugar, etc., boiled or baked.

**cus·to·di·an** (kus-tō'di-ən), *n.* 1. one who has the custody or care of something; caretaker. 2. a janitor. **—cus·to'di·an·ship',** *n.*

**cus·to·dy** (kus'tə-di), *n.* [*pl.* -DIES], [< L. *custos*, a guard], 1. a guarding or keeping safe; care. 2. imprisonment. **—cus·to'di·al** (-tō'di-əl), *adj.*

**cus·tom** (kus'təm), *n.* [< L. *com-*, intens. + *suere*, be accustomed], 1. a usual practice; habit. 2. social conventions carried on by tradition. 3. *pl.* duties or taxes imposed on imported goods. 4. the regular patronage of a business. *adj.* 1. made to order. 2. making things to order.

**cus'tom·ar'y** (-tə-mer'i), *adj.* according to or established by custom, or usage; usual. **—cus'tom·ar'i·ly,** *adv.*

**cus'tom·er,** *n.* a person who buys, esp. one who buys regularly.

**cus'tom-made',** *adj.* made to order, to the customer's specifications.

**cut** (kut), *v.t.* [CUT, CUTTING], [ME. *cutten*], 1. to make an opening in with a sharp-edged instrument; gash. 2. to pierce sharply so as to hurt. 3. to have (a new tooth) grow through the gum. 4. to divide into parts with a sharp-edged instrument; sever. 5. to hew. 6. to reap. 7. to trim or pare. 8. to pass across; intersect. 9. to reduce; curtail: as, prices were *cut*. 10. to make or do by or as by cutting. 11. [Colloq.], to pretend not to recognize (a person). 12. [Colloq.], to be absent from (a school class, etc.). *v.i.* 1. to pierce, sever, gash, etc. 2. to take cutting: as, wood *cuts* easily. 3. to swing a bat, etc., as at a ball. *adj.* 1. that has been cut. 2. made or formed by cutting. *n.* 1. a cutting or being cut. 2. a stroke or opening made by a sharp-edged instrument. 3. a piece cut off, as of meat. 4. a reduction. 5. a passage or channel cut out. 6. the style in which a thing is cut. 7. an act, remark, etc. that hurts one's feelings. 8. *a*) a block or plate engraved for printing. *b*) the impression from this. 9. [Colloq.], a snub. 10. [Colloq.], an unauthorized absence. 11. [Slang], a share, as of profits. **—a cut above,** [Colloq.], somewhat better than. **—cut and dried,** 1. arranged beforehand. 2. lifeless; boring. **—cut down (on),** to reduce; curtail. **—cut it out,** [Colloq.], to stop what one is doing. **—cut off,** 1. to sever. 2. to stop abruptly; shut off. **—cut out,** 1. to remove; omit. 2. to eliminate and take the place of (a rival). **—cut out for,** suited for. **—cut up,** 1. to cut into pieces. 2. [Slang], to clown, joke, etc.

**cu·ta·ne·ous** (kū-tā'ni-əs), *adj.* [< L. *cutis*, skin], of or on the skin.

**cut'a·way',** *n.* a man's formal coat cut so as to curve back to the tails.

**cute** (kūt), *adj.* [CUTER, CUTEST], [< *acute*], [Colloq.], 1. clever; shrewd. 2. pretty or attractive, esp. in a dainty way.

**cu·ti·cle** (kū'ti-k'l), *n.* [L. *cuticula*, skin], 1. the outer layer of the skin. 2. hardened skin, as at the base and sides of a fingernail.

**cut·lass, cut·las** (kut'ləs), *n.* [< L. *culter*, knife], a short, thick, curved sword.

**cut·ler·y** (kut'lẽr-i), *n.* [< L. *culter*, knife], 1. cutting instruments, as knives. 2. table knives, forks, and spoons.

**cut·let** (kut'lit), *n.* [< L. *costa*, a rib], 1. a small slice of meat from the ribs or leg, for frying or broiling. 2. a small, flat croquette of chopped meat or fish.

**cut'off',** *n.* 1. a road, etc. that is a short cut. 2. a device for shutting off the flow of steam, etc.

**cut'-rate',** *adj.* selling at a lower price.

**cut·ter** (kut'ẽr), *n.* 1. a person or thing that cuts. 2. a small, swift vessel. 3. a small, light sleigh.

**cut'throat',** *n.* a murderer. *adj.* 1. murderous. 2. merciless; relentless.

**cut·ting** (kut'iŋ), *n.* a shoot cut away from a plant for rooting or grafting. *adj.* 1. that cuts; sharp. 2. chilling or piercing. 3. sarcastic; harsh. **—cut'ting·ly,** *adv.*

**cut·tle·fish** (kut''l-fish'), *n.* [*pl.* see FISH], [AS. *cudele*], a sea mollusk with ten sucker-bearing arms and a hard internal shell.

**cut'worm',** *n.* any of various caterpillars which attack young plants of cabbage, corn, etc., cutting them off at ground level.

**cwt.,** hundredweight.

**-cy,** [< Gr. *-kia*], a suffix meaning: 1. *quality, condition, state,* or *fact of being,* as in *hesitancy.* 2. *position, rank,* or *office of,* as in *curacy.*
**cy·a·nide** (sī'ə-nīd'), ***n.*** a highly poisonous, white, crystalline compound.
**cy·an·o·gen** (sī-an'ə-jən), ***n.*** [< Gr. *kyanos,* blue; + *-gen*], a colorless, poisonous, inflammable gas.
**cy·ber·net·ics** (sī'bēr-net'iks), ***n.pl.*** [construed as sing.], [< Gr. *kybernētēs,* helmsman], the comparative study of electronic computers and the human nervous system.
**cy·cla·mate** (sī'klə-māt', sik'lə-), ***n.*** a sodium or calcium salt used as an artificial sweetener.
**cyc·la·men** (sik'lə-mən, -men'), ***n.*** [*pl.* -MENS], [< Gr. *kyklaminos*], a plant of the primrose family, with heart-shaped leaves.
**cy·cle** (sī'k'l), ***n.*** [< Gr. *kyklos,* circle], 1. *a*) a period of time within which a round of regularly recurring events is completed. *b*) a complete set of such events. 2. a very long period of time. 3. a series of poems or songs on the same theme. 4. a bicycle, tricycle, etc. ***v.i.*** [CYCLED, CYCLING], 1. to occur in cycles. 2. to ride a bicycle, etc. **—cy·clic** (sī'klik), **cy'cli·cal,** ***adj.***
**cy·clist** (sī'klist), ***n.*** one who rides a cycle.
**cyclo-,** [< Gr. *kyklos,* circle], a combining form meaning *of a circle* or *wheel, circular.*
**cy·clom·e·ter** (sī-klom'ə-tēr), ***n.*** [*cyclo-* + *-meter*], an instrument that records the revolutions of a wheel for measuring distance traveled.
**cy·clone** (sī'klōn), ***n.*** [< Gr. *kyklos,* circle], a storm with heavy rainfall and winds rotating about a center of low pressure.
**cy·clo·pe·di·a, cy·clo·pae·di·a** (sī'klə-pē'di-ə), ***n.*** an encyclopedia.
**Cy·clops** (sī'klops), ***n.*** [*pl.* CYCLOPES (sī-klō'pēz)], [< Gr. *kyklos,* circle + *ōps,* eye], in *Gr. myth.,* any of a race of one-eyed giants.
**cy·clo·tron** (sī'klə-tron'), ***n.*** [*cyclo-* + *electron*], an apparatus for giving high energy to particles, as protons, etc.: used in atomic research.
**cyg·net** (sig'nit), ***n.*** [< Gr. *kyknos,* swan], a young swan.
**cyl·in·der** (sil'in-dēr), ***n.*** [< Gr. *kylindein,* to roll], 1. a solid figure described by the edge of a rectangle rotated around the parallel edge as axis. 2. anything with this shape; specif., *a*) the turning point of a revolver. *b*) the piston chamber in an engine. **—cy·lin·dri·cal** (si-lin'dri-k'l), ***adj.***
**cym·bal** (sim'b'l), ***n.*** [< Gr. *kymbē,* hollow of a vessel], in *music,* either of a pair of concave brass plates struck together to produce a sharp, ringing sound. **—cym'bal·ist,** ***n.***
**cyn·ic** (sin'ik), ***n.*** [see CYNICAL], a cynical person. ***adj.*** cynical.
**cyn'i·cal** (-i-k'l), ***adj.*** [< Gr. *kyōn,* dog], 1. inclined to question the sincerity and goodness of people. 2. morose, sarcastic, etc. **—cyn'i·cal·ly,** ***adv.***
**cyn'i·cism** (-ə-siz'm), ***n.*** 1. the attitude or beliefs of a cynic. 2. a cynical expression or view.
**cy·no·sure** (sī'nə-shoor', sin'ə-), ***n.*** [< Gr. *kynosoura,* dog's tail], a center of attention.
**cy·press** (sī'prəs), ***n.*** [L. *cypressus*], 1. an evergreen, cone-bearing tree of the pine family. 2. its hard wood.
**cyst** (sist), ***n.*** [< Gr. *kystis,* sac], any of certain saclike structures in plants or animals, esp. one filled with diseased matter. **—cyst'ic,** ***adj.***
**cy·tol·o·gy** (sī-tol'ə-ji), ***n.*** [< Gr. *kytos,* a hollow; + *-logy*], the branch of biology dealing with the study of cells.
**cy·to·plasm** (sī'tə-plaz'm), ***n.*** [< Gr. *kytos,* a hollow; + *-plasm*], the protoplasm of a cell exclusive of the nucleus: also **cy'to·plast'.**
**czar** (zär), ***n.*** [< Russ. < L. *Caesar*], 1. the title of any of the former emperors of Russia. 2. an autocrat. **—cza·ri·na** (zä-rē'nə), ***n.fem.***
**Czech** (chek), ***n.*** 1. a member of a Slavic people of central Europe. 2. the West Slavic language of the Czechs; Bohemian. ***adj.*** of Czechoslovakia, its people, or their language. **—Czech·o·slo·va·ki·an** (chek'ə-slō-vä'ki-ən), ***n. & adj.***

# D

**D, d** (dē), ***n.*** [*pl.* D's, d's, Ds, ds], the fourth letter of the English alphabet.
**D,** ***n.*** 1. a Roman numeral for 500. 2. in *chem.,* deuterium. 3. in *music,* the second tone in the scale of C major.
**D.,** 1. December. 2. Dutch.
**d.,** 1. day(s). 2. degree. 3. [L.], *denarii,* pence: as, 6*d.* 4. diameter. 5. died.
**'d,** 1. abbreviation of *had* or *would,* as in *I'd.* 2. -ed, as in *foster'd.*
**D.A.,** District Attorney.
**dab** (dab), ***v.t. & v.i.*** [DABBED, DABBING], [ME. *dabben,* to strike], 1. to touch lightly and quickly; pat. 2. to put on (paint, etc.) with light, quick strokes. ***n.*** 1. a tap; pat. 2. a soft or moist bit of something.
**dab** (dab), ***n.*** [see DAB, ***v.***], a small, edible flatfish.
**dab·ble** (dab''l), ***v.i.*** [-BLED, -BLING], [< D. *dabben,* to strike], 1. to play in water, as with the hands. 2. to do something superficially (with *in* or *at*). **—dab'bler,** ***n.***
**dace** (dās), ***n.*** [*pl.* DACE, DACES], [< ML. *darsus*], a small fresh-water fish of the carp family.
**dachs·hund** (däks'hoond'), ***n.*** [G. *dachs,* badger + *hund,* dog], a small dog with a long body and short legs.
**da·cron** (dā'kron), ***n.*** a synthetic fabric that resists wrinkles: a trademark (**Dacron**).
**dac·tyl** (dak'til), ***n.*** [< Gr. *daktylos,* finger], a metrical foot of three syllables, the first accented. **—dac·tyl'ic,** ***adj.***
**dad** (dad), ***n.*** [< child's cry *dada*], [Colloq.], father: also **dad'dy** [*pl.* -DIES].
**dad'dy-long'legs',** ***n.*** [*pl.* DADDY-LONGLEGS], an arachnid with long legs.
**da·do** (dā'dō), ***n.*** [*pl.* -DOES], [< L. *datum,* a die], 1. the part of a pedestal between the cap and the base. 2. the lower part of a wall if decorated unlike the upper part.
**dae·mon** (dē'mən), ***n.*** [< Gr. *daimōn*], 1. in *Gr. myth.,* a secondary deity. 2. a guardian spirit. 3. a demon; devil.
**daf·fo·dil** (daf'ə-dil'), ***n.*** [< Gr. *asphodelos*], a narcissus that has yellow flowers.
**daf·fy** (daf'i), ***adj.*** [-FIER, -FIEST], [< ?], [Colloq.], crazy; silly.
**daft** (daft, däft), ***adj.*** [< AS. (*ge*)*dæfte,* gentle], 1. silly; foolish. 2. insane.
**dag·ger** (dag'ēr), ***n.*** [ME. as if < *daggen,* to slit], 1. a short weapon with a sharp point. 2. in *printing,* a reference mark (†).
**da·guerre·o·type** (də-ger'ə-tīp'), ***n.*** [< L. J. M. *Daguerre,* 19th-c. Fr. inventor], a photograph made by an early method on a chemically treated plate.
**dahl·ia** (dal'yə, däl'-), ***n.*** [< A. *Dahl,* 18th-c. Swed. botanist], 1. a perennial plant with large, showy flowers. 2. the flower.

**dai·ly** (dā′li), ***adj.*** done, happening, or published every day or every weekday. ***n.*** [*pl.* -LIES], a daily newspaper. ***adv.*** every day.
**daily dozen,** [Colloq.], gymnastic exercises (orig. twelve) done daily.
**dain·ty** (dān′ti), ***n.*** [*pl.* -TIES], [< L. *dignitas*, worth], a delicacy. ***adj.*** [-TIER, -TIEST], 1. delicious and choice. 2. delicately pretty. 3. of delicate and refined taste. 4. fastidious; squeamish. **—dain′ti·ness,** ***n.***
**dair·y** (dâr′i), ***n.*** [*pl.* -IES], [AS. *deie*, dairymaid], 1. a place where milk and cream are made into butter, cheese, etc. 2. a store where milk and milk products are sold. 3. a farm that produces and sells milk and milk products. **—dair′y·maid′,** ***n.*** **—dair′y·man,** [*pl.* -MEN], ***n.***
**da·is** (dā′is), ***n.*** [*pl.* DAISES], [< L. *discus*, platter], a raised platform.
**dai·sy** (dā′zi), ***n.*** [*pl.* -SIES], [AS. *dæges eage*, day's eye], a plant of the composite family, bearing flowers with white rays around a yellow disk.
**Da·lai La·ma** (dä-lī′ lä′mə), [Mong. *dalai*, ocean + *blama*, high priest], the high priest of the Lamaist religion.
**dale** (dāl), ***n.*** [AS. *dæl*], a small valley.
**dal·ly** (dal′i), ***v.i.*** [-LIED, -LYING], [< OFr. *dalier*, to trifle], 1. to play, esp. in making love. 2. to toy or flirt: as, he *dallied* with the idea. 3. to loiter. **—dal′li·ance** (-i-əns), ***n.***
**Dal·ma·tian** (dal-mā′shən), ***n.*** a large, lean, short-haired dog with a black-and-white coat.
**dam** (dam), ***n.*** [< MD. *damm*], a barrier, esp. one built to hold back flowing water. ***v.t.*** [DAMMED, DAMMING], 1. to put a dam in. 2. to keep back or confine.
**dam** (dam), ***n.*** [see DAME], the female parent of any four-footed animal.
**dam·age** (dam′ij), ***n.*** [< L. *damnum*], 1. injury; harm causing a loss. 2. *pl.* money compensating for injury, loss, etc. ***v.t.*** [-AGED, -AGING], to do damage to. **—dam′age·a·ble,** ***adj.*** **—dam′ag·ing·ly,** ***adv.***
**dam·ask** (dam′əsk), ***n.*** [< It. < *Damascus*, Syria], 1. a reversible fabric in figured weave. 2. a fine twilled table linen. 3. deep pink or rose. 4. steel decorated with wavy markings. ***adj.*** 1. like or made of damask. 2. deep-pink.
**dame** (dām), ***n.*** [< L. *domina*, lady], 1. a lady. 2. [D-], in Great Britain, a woman's title of honor equivalent to *Sir*. 3. [Slang], any woman.
**damn** (dam), ***v.t.*** [DAMNED, DAMNING], [< L. *damnare*, condemn], 1. to condemn as bad, inferior, etc. 2. to swear at by saying "damn." 3. to condemn to hell. ***n.*** the saying of "damn" as a curse. ***adj. & adv.*** [Colloq.], damned. ***interj.*** an expression of anger, etc. **—not care** (or **give**) **a damn,** [Colloq.], not care at all.
**dam·na·ble** (dam′nə-b'l), ***adj.*** 1. deserving damnation. 2. deserving to be sworn at.
**dam·na′tion** (-nā′shən), ***n.*** 1. a damning or being damned. 2. eternal punishment. ***interj.*** an expression of anger, etc.
**damned** (damd), ***adj.*** 1. condemned, as to hell. 2. [Colloq.], cursed; outrageous. ***adv.*** [Colloq.], very.
**Dam·o·cles** (dam′ə-klēz′), ***n.*** in *Gr. legend*, a man whose king demonstrated to him the dangers of a ruler's life by seating him under a sword hanging by a hair.
**Da·mon and Pyth·i·as** (dā′mən ən pith′-i-əs), in *Rom. legend*, two very devoted friends.
**damp** (damp), ***n.*** [MD., vapor], 1. moisture; wetness. 2. a harmful gas sometimes found in mines. ***adj.*** slightly wet; moist. ***v.t.*** 1. to make damp. 2. to stifle. 3. to check or reduce. **—damp′ness,** ***n.***
**damp′-dry′,** ***v.t.*** [-DRIED, -DRYING], to dry (laundry) so that some moisture is kept. ***adj.*** designating laundry so dried.
**damp′en,** ***v.t.*** 1. to make damp; moisten. 2. to depress. 3. to deaden or reduce. ***v.i.*** to become damp. **—damp′en·er,** ***n.***
**damp′er,** ***n.*** 1. one that depresses or disheartens. 2. a valve in a flue to control the draft. 3. a device to check vibration in piano strings.
**dam·sel** (dam′z'l), ***n.*** [see DAME], [Archaic], a girl; maiden.
**dam·son** (dam′z'n), ***n.*** [< *Damascus*, Syria], a variety of small, purple plum.
**Dan.,** Danish.
**dance** (dans, däns), ***v.i.*** [DANCED, DANCING], [< OFr. *danser*], 1. to move the body, esp. the feet, in rhythm, usually to music. 2. to move lightly, rapidly, gaily, etc. ***v.t.*** 1. to perform (a dance). 2. to cause to dance. ***n.*** 1. rhythmic movement, usually to music. 2. a particular kind of dance. 3. the art of dancing. 4. a party at which people dance. 5. a piece of music for dancing. 6. rapid, lively movement. **—danc′er,** ***n.***
**dan·de·li·on** (dan′di-lī′ən), ***n.*** [< Fr. *dent*, tooth + *de*, of + *lion*, lion], a common weed with yellow flowers.
**dan·der** (dan′dẽr), ***n.*** [< ?], [Colloq.], 1. anger. 2. temper. **—get one's dander up,** [Colloq.], to become angry.
**dan·dle** (dan′d'l), ***v.t.*** [-DLED, -DLING], [It. *dondolare*], to dance (a child) up and down as on the knee.
**dan·druff** (dan′drəf), ***n.*** [< earlier *dandro* + dial. *hurf*, scab], little scales of dead skin on the scalp.
**dan·dy** (dan′di), ***n.*** [*pl.* -DIES], [Scot. var. of *Andy* < *Andrew*], 1. a man overly attentive to his clothes and appearance; fop. 2. [Slang], something very good. ***adj.*** [-DIER, -DIEST], [Slang], very good.
**Dane** (dān), ***n.*** a native of Denmark.
**dan·ger** (dān′jẽr), ***n.*** [ult. < L. *dominus*, a master: from idea of being at his mercy], 1. liability to injury, damage, loss, etc.; peril. 2. a thing that may cause injury, pain, etc.
**dan′ger·ous,** ***adj.*** full of danger; unsafe.
**dan·gle** (daŋ′g'l), ***v.i.*** [-GLED, -GLING], [< ON.], to hang swinging loosely. ***v.t.*** to cause to dangle.
**Dan·iel** (dan′yəl), ***n.*** in the *Bible*, a Hebrew prophet whose faith saved him in the lions' den.
**Dan·ish** (dān′ish), ***adj.*** of Denmark, the Danes, or their language. ***n.*** their language.
**dank** (daŋk), ***adj.*** [? < ON.], disagreeably damp. **—dank′ness,** ***n.***
**dap·per** (dap′ẽr), ***adj.*** [? < MD.], 1. small and active. 2. trim; spruce.
**dap·ple** (dap′'l), ***adj.*** [<ON. *depill*, a spot], spotted; mottled: also **dappled.** ***v.t.*** [-PLED, -PLING], to cover with spots.
**dare** (dâr), ***v.t. & v.i.*** [DARED or *archaic* DURST, DARED, DARING], [AS. *durran*], 1. to have enough courage for (some act). 2. to oppose and defy. 3. to challenge (someone) to do something. ***n.*** a challenge. **—dare say,** to consider probable.
**dare′dev′il** (-dev′'l), ***adj.*** reckless; foolhardy. ***n.*** a daredevil person.
**dar′ing,** ***adj.*** fearless; bold. ***n.*** bold courage.
**dark** (därk), ***adj.*** [< AS. *deorc*], 1. entirely or partly without light. 2. almost black. 3. not light in color. 4. hidden. 5. gloomy. 6. evil; sinister. 7. ignorant. ***n.*** 1. the state of being dark. 2. night. 3. secrecy. 4. ignorance. **—dark′ly,** ***adv.*** **—dark′ness,** ***n.***
**Dark Ages,** [< *dark*, *adj.* 7], the Middle Ages, esp. the earlier part.
**dark′en,** ***v.i. & v.t.*** to make or become dark.
**dark horse,** [Colloq.], an unexpected, almost unknown winner or contestant.
**dark′room′,** ***n.*** a darkened room for developing photographs.

**dar·ling** (där′liŋ), *n.* [AS. *deorling*], a person much loved by another. *adj.* very dear; beloved.

**darn** (därn), *v.t. & v.i.* [< MFr. dial. *darner*, mend], to mend by sewing a network of stitches across the gap. *n.* 1. a darning. 2. a darned place in fabric.

**darn** (därn), *v.t., n., adj., adv. & interj.* [Colloq.], damn: a euphemism.

**dar·nel** (där′n'l), *n.* [< Fr. *darnelle*], a poisonous weed resembling rye.

**dart** (därt), *n.* [OFr. < Gmc.], 1. a small, pointed weapon for throwing or shooting. 2. a sudden, quick movement. *v.t. & v.i.* to throw, shoot, move, etc. suddenly and fast.

**Dar·win·i·an** (där-win′i-ən), *adj.* [< Charles *Darwin*, 19th-c. Eng. naturalist], of Charles Darwin or his theory of evolution. *n.* a believer in this theory. **—Dar′win·ism,** *n.*

**dash** (dash), *v.t.* [ME. *daschen*], 1. to smash; destroy. 2. to strike violently against. 3. to throw or thrust (*away, down,* etc.). 4. to splash. 5. to do, write, etc. hastily (with *off*). *v.i.* 1. to strike violently against. 2. to rush. *n.* 1. a smash. 2. a splash. 3. a bit of something. 4. a rush. 5. a short, swift race. 6. vigor; spirit. 7. the mark of punctuation (—) used to indicate a break or omission. **—dash′er,** *n.*

**dash′board′,** *n.* a panel with instruments and gauges, as in an automobile.

**dash′ing,** *adj.* 1. full of dash or spirit. 2. showy.

**das·tard** (das′tẽrd), *n.* [ME., a craven], a mean, skulking coward. *adj.* dastardly.

**das′tard·ly,** *adj.* cowardly and brutal.

**dat.,** dative.

**da·ta** (dā′tə, dat′ə), *n.pl.* [often construed as sing.], [see DATUM], facts from which conclusions can be drawn.

**data processing,** the recording and handling of information by mechanical means or computer.

**date** (dāt), *n.* [< L. *dare*, give], 1. the time at which a thing happens. 2. the day of the month. 3. an appointment or social engagement. *v.t.* [DATED, DATING], 1. to mark (a letter, etc.) with a date. 2. to find out or give the date of. *v.i.* 1. to be dated (*from*). 2. to belong to a definite period in the past. **—out of date,** old-fashioned. **—up to date,** modern.

**date** (dāt), *n.* [< Gr. *daktylos*, lit., a finger], the sweet, fleshy fruit of a tall palm tree.

**date line,** 1. a line on which the date is given, as in a letter, etc. 2. an imaginary line through the Pacific, largely along the 180th meridian, at which, by international agreement, each calendar day begins at midnight: when it is Sunday just west of the line, it is Saturday just east of it.

**da·tive** (dā′tiv), *adj.* [< L. *dare*, give], denoting that case which expresses the indirect object of a verb. *n.* 1. the dative case. 2. a word or phrase in this case.

**da·tum** (dā′təm, dat′əm), *n.* [L., what is given], sing. of **data.**

**daub** (dôb), *v.t. & v.i.* [< L. *de-*, intens. + *albus*, white], 1. to cover or smear with sticky, soft stuff. 2. to paint badly. *n.* 1. anything daubed on. 2. a daubing stroke. 3. a poorly painted picture.

**daugh·ter** (dô′tẽr), *n.* [AS. *dohtor*], 1. a girl or woman in her relationship to either or both parents. 2. a female descendant.

**daugh′ter-in-law′,** *n.* [*pl.* DAUGHTERS-IN-LAW], the wife of one's son.

**daunt** (dônt), *v.t.* [< L. *domare*, to tame], 1. to frighten; intimidate. 2. to dishearten.

**daunt′less,** *adj.* that cannot be daunted or intimidated; brave. **—daunt′less·ly,** *adv.*

**dau·phin** (dô′fin), *n.* [Fr., dolphin], the eldest son of the king of France: a title used from 1349 to 1830.

**dav·en·port** (dav′ən-pôrt′), *n.* [< the manufacturer's name], a large sofa.

**Da·vid** (dā′vid), *n.* in the *Bible*, the second king of Israel.

**dav·it** (dav′it), *n.* [< OFr. dim. of *David*], 1. either of a pair of uprights curving over the side of a ship for suspending or lowering a small boat. 2. a crane used to raise or lower a ship's anchor.

**Da·vy Jones** (dā′vi jōnz′), the spirit of the sea: humorous name given by sailors.

**daw·dle** (dô′d'l), *v.i. & v.t.* [-DLED, -DLING], [< dial. *daddle*], to waste (time) in trifling; loiter. **—daw′dler,** *n.*

**dawn** (dôn), *v.i.* [< AS. *dæg*, day], 1. to begin to be day. 2. to begin to appear, develop, etc. 3. to begin to be clear to the mind. *n.* 1. daybreak. 2. the beginning (*of* something).

**day** (dā), *n.* [AS. *dæg*], 1. the period of light between sunrise and sunset. 2. the time (24 hours) that it takes the earth to revolve once on its axis. 3. *often pl.* a period; era; time. 4. a period of power, glory, etc. 5. hours of work: as, an eight-hour *day.* **—call it a day,** [Colloq.], to stop working for the day. **—day after day,** every day.

**day′break′,** *n.* the time in the morning when light first appears; dawn.

**day coach,** a regular passenger car of a railroad train.

**day′dream′,** *n.* 1. a pleasant, dreamy thought. 2. a pleasing but visionary idea. *v.i.* to have daydreams. **—day′dream′er,** *n.*

**day′light′,** *n.* 1. the light of day. 2. dawn. 3. daytime. 4. understanding.

**day′light′-sav′ing time,** time that is one hour later than standard time.

**day nursery,** a nursery for taking care of small children during the daytime.

**day′time′,** *n.* the time between dawn and sunset.

**daze** (dāz), *v.t.* [DAZED, DAZING], [< ON. *dasi*, tired], 1. to stun or bewilder. 2. to dazzle. *n.* a dazed condition. **—daz′ed·ly,** *adv.*

**daz·zle** (daz′'l), *v.t. & v.i.* [-ZLED, -ZLING], [freq. of *daze*], 1. to overpower or be overpowered by the glare of bright light. 2. to surprise or arouse admiration with brilliant qualities, display, etc. *n.* a dazzling.

**D.C., d.c.,** direct current.

**D.D.,** Doctor of Divinity.

**D.D.S.,** Doctor of Dental Surgery.

**DDT,** [from its chemical name], a powerful insecticide.

**de-,** [< Fr. *de-* or L. *de*], a prefix meaning: 1. *away from, off,* as in *detrain.* 2. *down,* as in *decline.* 3. *entirely,* as in *derelict.* 4. *reverse the action of,* as in *decode.*

**dea·con** (dē′k'n), *n.* [< Gr. *diakonos*, servant], a clergyman or layman who assists a minister. **—dea′con·ess,** *n.fem.*

**dead** (ded), *adj.* [AS.], 1. no longer living. 2. without life. 3. lacking feeling, energy, warmth, etc. 4. no longer used; obsolete. 5. lacking in activity, interest, color, etc.; dull. 6. unerring: as, a *dead* shot. 7. complete: as, a *dead* loss. 8. [Colloq.], very tired. *n.* the time of most cold, most darkness, etc.: as, the *dead* of night. *adv.* 1. completely. 2. directly. **—the dead,** those who have died. **—dead′ness,** *n.*

**dead·beat** (ded′bēt′), *n.* [Slang], one who tries to evade paying for things.

**dead·en** (ded′'n), *v.t.* 1. to lessen the vigor or intensity of; dull. 2. to make numb. 3. to make soundproof.

**dead end,** a street, alley, etc. closed at one end. **—dead′-end′,** *adj.*

**dead heat,** a race in which two or more contestants finish even.

**dead letter,** an unclaimed letter.

**dead′line′** (-līn′), *n.* a time limit, as for a payment, news story, etc.

**dead′lock′** (-lok′), *n.* a standstill resulting from the action of equal and opposed forces. *v.t. & v.i.* to bring or come to a deadlock.
**dead′ly,** *adj.* [-LIER, -LIEST], 1. causing or liable to cause death; fatal. 2. until death. 3. as in death: as, *deadly* pale. 4. [Colloq.], unbearable. *adv.* 1. like death. 2. as if dead. 3. extremely. **—dead′li·ness,** *n.*
**dead pan,** [Slang], an expressionless face.
**dead weight,** the weight of an inert person or thing.
**dead·wood** (ded′wood′), *n.* 1. dead wood on trees. 2. anything useless or burdensome.
**deaf** (def), *adj.* [AS.], 1. unable to hear. 2. unwilling to respond, as to a plea.
**deaf′en** (-′n), *v.t.* 1. to make deaf. 2. to overwhelm with noise. **—deaf′en·ing,** *adj.*
**deaf′-mute′** (-mūt′), *n.* a person who is deaf and has not learned to speak.
**deal** (dēl), *v.t.* [DEALT (delt), DEALING], [AS. *dælan*], 1. to portion out; distribute. 2. to administer, as a blow. 3. to distribute (playing cards) to the players. *v.i.* 1. to have to do (*with*): as, science *deals* with facts. 2. to conduct oneself: as, *deal* fairly with others. 3. to do business, trade (*with* or *in*). *n.* 1. a dealing. 2. the distribution of playing cards. 3. [Colloq.], *a*) a business transaction. *b*) an agreement or arrangement. **—deal′er,** *n.*
**deal** (dēl), *n.* [AS. *dæl*, a part], an indefinite amount. **—a good** (or **great**) **deal,** 1. a large amount. 2. very much: as, *a good deal* faster.
**deal′ing,** *n.* 1. distribution. 2. behavior. 3. *usually pl.* transactions or relations.
**dean** (dēn), *n.* [< LL. *decanus*, head of ten (monks, etc.)], 1. the presiding official of a cathedral. 2. a college official in charge of the students or faculty. 3. the member of a group who has belonged to it the longest.
**dear** (dêr), *adj.* [AS. *deore*], 1. much loved. 2. esteemed: a polite form of address, as, *Dear* Sir. 3. high-priced; costly. 4. earnest: as, our *dearest* hope. *n.* a loved person; darling. *interj.* an expression of surprise, etc.
**dearth** (dũrth), *n.* [< ME. *deere*, dear], 1. famine. 2. scarcity; lack.
**death** (deth), *n.* [AS.], 1. the act or fact of dying; ending of life. 2. the state of being dead. 3. any ending resembling dying: as, the *death* of fascism. 4. the cause of death. **—put to death,** to kill; execute.
**death′bed′,** *n.* 1. the bed on which a person dies. 2. one's last hours.
**death′blow′,** *n.* 1. a blow that kills. 2. a thing fatal (*to* something).
**death′less,** *adj.* that cannot die; immortal: as, *deathless* words. **—death′less·ly,** *adv.*
**death′ly,** *adj.* 1. fatal. 2. like or characteristic of death. *adv.* 1. in a deathlike way. 2. extremely: as, *deathly* ill.
**death′trap′,** *n.* any unsafe structure.
**death′watch′,** *n.* a vigil beside a dead or dying person.
**de·ba·cle** (dā-bä′k'l, di-bak′'l), *n.* [< Fr. *débâcler*, break up], 1. an overthrow; rout. 2. a sudden disaster.
**de·bar** (di-bär′), *v.t.* [-BARRED, -BARRING], [< Fr.; see DE- & BAR], 1. to exclude (*from* something). 2. to prevent or prohibit.
**de·bark** (di-bärk′), *v.t. & v.i.* [< Fr.; see DE- & BARK (ship)], to disembark. **—de·bar·ka·tion** (dē′bär-kā′shən), *n.*
**de·base** (di-bās′), *v.t.* [-BASED, -BASING], [*de-* + *base* (low)], to make lower in value, quality, dignity, etc. **—de·base′ment,** *n.*
**de·bate** (di-bāt′), *v.i. & v.t.* [-BATED, -BATING], [< OFr.; see DE- & BATTER, *v.t.*], to engage in dispute (about); argue formally. *n.* 1. discussion of opposing reasons. 2. a formal contest of skill in reasoned argument between opposing teams. **—de·bat′a·ble,** *adj.* **—de·bat′er,** *n.*
**de·bauch** (di-bôch′), *v.t.* [< OFr. *desbaucher*, to draw away from work], to lead astray morally; corrupt. *v.i.* to dissipate. *n.* an orgy. **—de·bauch′er·y** [*pl.* -IES], *n.*
**de·ben·ture** (di-ben′chẽr), *n.* [Fr. < L.; see DEBT], 1. a voucher acknowledging a debt. 2. an interest-bearing bond.
**de·bil·i·tate** (di-bil′ə-tāt′), *v.t.* [-TATED, -TATING], [< L. *debilis*, weak], to make weak; enervate. **—de·bil′i·ta′tion,** *n.*
**de·bil·i·ty** (di-bil′ə-ti), *n.* [*pl.* -TIES], [< L. *debilis*, weak], weakness; feebleness.
**deb·it** (deb′it), *n.* [< L. *debere*, owe], 1. an entry in an account of money owed. 2. the left-hand side of an account, where such entries are made. *v.t.* to charge with, or enter as, a debt.
**deb·o·nair, deb·o·naire** (deb′ə-nâr′), *adj.* [< OFr. *de bon aire*, of good breed], 1. affable; courteous. 2. gay; jaunty. Also **deb′on·nair′.** **—deb′o·nair′ly,** *adv.*
**de·brief** (dē′brēf′), *v.t.* [*de-* + *brief*, *v.*], to question and instruct (a pilot, emissary, etc.) following a flight or mission.
**de·bris, dé·bris** (də-brē′, dā′brē), *n.* [< OFr. *desbrisier*, break apart], 1. broken, scattered remains; rubbish. 2. rubble.
**debt** (det), *n.* [< L. *debere*, owe], 1. something owed to another 2. the state of owing: as, to be in *debt.* 3. in *theology*, a sin.
**debt′or** (-ẽr), *n.* one who owes a debt.
**de·bunk** (di-buŋk′), *v.t.* [*de-* + *bunk* (nonsense)], [Colloq.], to expose the false or exaggerated claims, etc. of.
**de·but, dé·but** (di-bū′, dā′bū), *n.* [Fr. < *débuter*, to lead off (at bowls, etc.)], 1. a first appearance before the public, as of an actor. 2. the formal introduction of a girl to society.
**deb·u·tante, dé·bu·tante** (deb′yoo-tänt′, deb′yə-tant′), *n.* [Fr.], a girl making her debut into society.
**deca-,** [< Gr. *deka*, ten], a combining form meaning *ten:* also **dec-.**
**dec·ade** (dek′ād), *n.* [< Gr. *deka*, ten], 1. a group of ten. 2. a period of ten years.
**de·ca·dence** (di-kā′d'ns, dek′ə-dəns), *n.* [< L. *de-*, from + *cadere*, to fall], process, condition, or period of decline, as in morals, art, etc.; deterioration: also **de·ca′den·cy** (-d'n-si). **—de·ca′dent,** *adj. & n.*
**dec·a·gon** (dek′ə-gon′), *n.* [see DECA- & -GON], a plane figure with ten sides and ten angles.
**dec·a·he·dron** (dek′ə-hē′drən), *n.* [*pl.* -DRONS, -DRA (drə)], [see DECA- & -HEDRON], a solid figure with ten plane surfaces.
**de·cal·co·ma·ni·a** (di-kal′kə-mā′ni-ə), *n.* [< Fr. *décalquer*, counterdraw + Gr. *mania*, madness], a picture or design transferred from prepared paper to glass, wood, etc.: also **de·cal** (di-kal′).
**Dec·a·logue, Dec·a·log** (dek′ə-lôg′), *n.* [< Gr.; see DECA- & -LOGUE], [sometimes d-], the Ten Commandments.
**de·camp** (di-kamp′), *v.i.* [< Fr.; see DE- & CAMP], 1. to break camp. 2. to go away suddenly and secretly.
**de·cant** (di-kant′), *v.t.* [< L. *de-*, from + *cantus;* see CANT (edge)], to pour off (a liquid) without stirring up the sediment.
**de·cant′er,** *n.* a decorative glass bottle for serving wine, etc.
**de·cap·i·tate** (di-kap′ə-tāt′), *v.t.* [-TATED, -TATING], [< L. *de-*, off + *caput*, head], to behead. **—de·cap′i·ta′tion,** *n.*
**dec·a·pod** (dek′ə-pod′), *adj.* [*deca-* + *-pod*], ten-legged. *n.* any crustacean with ten legs.
**dec·a·syl·la·ble** (dek′ə-sil′ə-b'l), *n.* a line of verse having ten syllables.
**de·cath·lon** (di-kath′lon), *n.* [< *deca-* + Gr. *athlon*, contest], an athletic contest consisting of ten events in various track sports.
**de·cay** (di-kā′), *v.i.* [< L. *de-*, down + *cadere*, to fall], 1. to lose strength, pros-

perity, etc. gradually; deteriorate. 2. to rot. *v.t.* to cause to decay. *n.* 1. deterioration. 2. a rotting or rottenness.

**de·cease** (di-sēs′), *n.* [< L. *de-*, from + *cedere*, go], death. *v.i.* [-CEASED, -CEASING], to die.

**de·ceased′,** *adj.* dead. —**the deceased,** the dead person or persons.

**de·ceit** (di-sēt′), *n.* 1. the act of deceiving or lying. 2. a lie. 3. deceitful quality.

**de·ceit′ful,** *adj.* 1. apt to lie or cheat. 2. deceiving; false. —**de·ceit′ful·ly,** *adv.*

**de·ceive** (di-sēv′), *v.t.* [-CEIVED, -CEIVING], [< L. *decipere*], to make (a person) believe what is not true; mislead. *v.i.* to use deceit.

**de·cel·er·ate** (dē-sel′ẽr-āt′), *v.t.* & *v.i.* [-ATED, -ATING], [*de-* + *accelerate*], to slow down.

**De·cem·ber** (di-sem′bẽr), *n.* [< L. *decem*, ten: tenth month in Rom. calendar], the twelfth and last month of the year, having 31 days: abbrev. **Dec.**

**de·cen·cy** (dē′s'n-si), *n.* [*pl.* -CIES], a being decent; proper modesty, conduct, etc.

**de·cen·ni·al** (di-sen′i-əl), *adj.* [< L. *decem*, ten + *annus*, year], 1. of or lasting ten years. 2. occurring every ten years. *n.* a tenth anniversary.

**de·cent** (dē′s'nt), *adj.* [< L. *decere*, befit], 1. proper and fitting. 2. not obscene. 3. respectable. 4. adequate: as, *decent* wages. 5. kind; generous. —**de′cent·ly,** *adv.*

**de·cen·tral·ize** (dē-sen′trəl-iz′), *v.t.* [-IZED, -IZING], to break up the centralization of authority, as in a government, and distribute, as to local authorities. —**de·cen′tral·i·za′tion,** *n.*

**de·cep·tion** (di-sep′shən), *n.* 1. a deceiving or being deceived. 2. an illusion or fraud. —**de·cep′tive,** *adj.*

**dec·i·bel** (des′ə bel′), *n.* [< L. *decem*, ten; + *bel* (after A. G. *Bell* [1847–1922], U.S. inventor)], a unit for measuring the volume of a sound.

**de·cide** (di-sīd′), *v.t.* [-CIDED, -CIDING], [< L. *de-*, off + *caedere*, to cut], to end (a contest, argument, etc.) by giving one side the victory. *v.i.* 1. to pass judgment. 2. to reach a decision.

**de·cid′ed** (-id), *adj.* 1. definite; unquestionable. 2. unhesitating. —**de·cid′ed·ly,** *adv.*

**de·cid·u·ous** (di-sij′o͞o-əs), *adj.* [< L. *de-*, off + *cadere*, fall], 1. falling off at a certain season, as some leaves or antlers. 2. shedding leaves annually.

**dec·i·mal** (des′ə-m'l), *adj.* [< L. *decem*, ten], relating to or based upon the number ten. *n.* a fraction with a denominator of ten or some power of ten, shown by a point before the numerator, as .5 = 5/10.

**dec·i·mate** (des′ə-māt′), *v.t.* [-MATED, -MATING], [< L. *decem*, ten], to destroy or kill a large part of (lit., a tenth part of). —**dec′i·ma′tion,** *n.* —**dec′i·ma′tor,** *n.*

**de·ci·pher** (di-sī′fẽr), *v.t.* [*de-* + *cipher*], 1. to translate from secret writing or code. 2. to make out the meaning of (a scrawl, etc.). —**de·ci′pher·a·ble,** *adj.*

**de·ci·sion** (di-sizh′ən), *n.* 1. the act of deciding or settling a dispute or question. 2. the act of making up one's mind. 3. a judgment or conclusion. 4. determination.

**de·ci·sive** (di-sī′siv), *adj.* 1. that settles a dispute, question, etc. 2. showing decision.

**deck** (dek), *n.* [MD. *decke*, a covering], 1. a floor of a ship. 2. a pack of playing cards. *v.t.* to adorn; trim.

**deck hand,** a sailor, usually one who works on deck.

**deck·le, deck·el** (dek′'l), *n.* [< G. *decke*, a cover], in *papermaking*, 1. a frame to guide the pulp into a desired width. 2. a deckle edge.

**deckle edge,** the untrimmed edge of paper made in a deckle. —**deck′le-edged′,** *adj.*

**de·claim** (di-klām′), *v.i.* & *v.t.* [< L. *de-*, intens. + *clamare*, to cry], to speak or recite loudly and rhetorically. —**dec·la·ma·tion** (dek′lə-mā′shən), *n.*

**dec·la·ra·tion** (dek′lə-rā′shən), *n.* 1. a declaring; announcement. 2. a formal statement.

**de·clar·a·tive** (di-klar′ə-tiv), *adj.* making a statement or assertion.

**de·clare** (di-klâr′), *v.t.* [-CLARED, -CLARING], [< L. *de-*, intens. + *clarus*, clear], 1. to announce openly or formally. 2. to show; reveal. 3. to say emphatically. 4. in *bridge*, to make the winning bid in (a suit). —**declare oneself,** to state strongly one's opinion.

**de·clas·si·fy** (dē-klas′ə-fī′), *v.t.* [-FIED, -FYING], to make (secret documents) available to the public.

**de·clen·sion** (di-klen′shən), *n.* [see DECLINE], 1. a descent. 2. a decline. 3. in *grammar*, the inflection of nouns, pronouns, or adjectives.

**de·cline** (di-klīn′), *v.i.* [-CLINED, -CLINING], [< L. *de-*, from + *clinare*, bend], 1. to bend or slope downward. 2. to deteriorate. 3. to refuse something. *v.t.* 1. to cause to bend or slope downward. 2. to refuse politely. 3. in *grammar*, to give the inflected forms of (a noun, pronoun, or adjective). *n.* 1. a declining; a dropping, failing, decay, etc. 2. a period of decline. 3. a downward slope. —**dec·li·na·tion** (dek′lə-nā′shən), *n.*

**de·cliv·i·ty** (di-kliv′ə-ti), *n.* [*pl.* -TIES], [< L. *de-*, down + *clivus*, a slope], a downward slope.

**de·coct** (di-kokt′), *v.t.* [< L. *de-*, down + *coquere*, to cook], to extract the essence of by boiling. —**de·coc′tion,** *n.*

**de·code** (dē-kōd′), *v.t.* [-CODED, -CODING], to translate (something in code) into comprehensible language.

**dé·colle·té** (dā′kol-tā′), *adj.* [Fr. < L. *de*, from + *collum*, neck], cut low so as to bare the neck and shoulders.

**de·com·pose** (dē′kəm-pōz′), *v.t.* & *v.i.* [-POSED, -POSING], [< Fr.], 1. to break up into basic parts. 2. to rot; decay. —**de′com·po·si′tion** (-kom-pə-zish′ən), *n.*

**de·con·gest·ant** (dē′kən-jes′tənt), *n.* a medication or treatment that relieves congestion, as in the nasal passages.

**de·con·tam·i·nate** (dē′kən-tam′ə-nāt′), *v.t.* [-NATED, -NATING], to rid of a harmful substance, as poison gas.

**dé·cor** (dā-kôr′), *n.* [Fr.], a decorative scheme, as of a room.

**dec·or·ate** (dek′ə-rāt′), *v.t.* [-ATED, -ATING], [< L. *decus*, an ornament], 1. to adorn; ornament. 2. to paint or wallpaper. 3. to give a medal or similar honor to. —**dec′o·ra′tive** (-rā′tiv, -rə-tiv), *adj.* —**dec′o·ra′tive·ly,** *adv.* —**dec′o·ra′tor,** *n.*

**dec′o·ra′tion,** *n.* 1. a decorating. 2. an ornament. 3. a medal or similar honor.

**Decoration Day,** Memorial Day.

**dec·o·rous** (dek′ə-rəs, di-kôr′əs), *adj.* having or showing decorum, good taste, etc.

**de·co·rum** (di-kôr′əm), *n.* [*pl.* -RUMS, -RA (-ə)], [L. < *decere*, be suitable], 1. whatever is suitable or proper. 2. propriety in behavior, speech, etc.

**de·coy** (di-koi′; *also, for n.*, dē′koi), *n.* [< D. *de kooi*, the cage], 1. an artificial or trained bird, etc. used to lure game into gun range. 2. a thing or person used to lure into danger. *v.t.* & *v.i.* to lure or be lured into a trap.

**de·crease** (di-krēs′), *v.i.* & *v.t.* [-CREASED, -CREASING], [< L. *de-*, from + *crescere*, grow], to become or make gradually less, smaller, etc.; diminish. *n.* (dē′krēs), 1. a decreasing; lessening. 2. amount of decreasing.

**de·cree** (di-krē′), *n.* [< L. *de-*, from + *cernere*, see], an official order or decision. *v.t.* [-CREED, -CREEING], to order by decree.

**de·crep·it** (di-krep'it), ***adj.*** [< L. *de-*, intens. + *crepare*, creak], broken down or worn out by old age or long use. **—de·crep'i·tude'** (-ə-tōōd'), ***n.***

**de·cry** (di-krī'), ***v.t.*** [-CRIED, -CRYING], [< Fr.; see DE- & CRY], to denounce; censure.

**ded·i·cate** (ded'ə-kāt'), ***v.t.*** [-CATED, -CATING], [< L. *de-*, intens. + *dicare*, proclaim], 1. to set apart for some purpose, esp. a religious one; devote. 2. to address (a book, etc.) to someone as a sign of honor. **—ded'i·ca'tion, *n.* —ded'i·ca'tor, *n.***

**de·duce** (di-dōōs', -dūs'), ***v.t.*** [-DUCED, -DUCING], [< L. *de-*, down + *ducere*, to lead], to infer by reasoning. **—de·duc'i·ble, *adj.***

**de·duct** (di-dukt'), ***v.t.*** [see DEDUCE], to take away or subtract (an amount or quantity). **—de·duct'i·ble, *adj.***

**de·duc'tion** (-duk'shən), ***n.*** 1. a deducting. 2. the amount deducted. 3. reasoning from the general to the specific. 4. a conclusion. **—de·duc'tive, *adj.***

**deed** (dēd), ***n.*** [ME. *dede*], 1. a thing done; act. 2. a feat of courage, skill, etc. 3. a legal document that states a contract, transfer of property, etc. ***v.t.*** to transfer by such a document. **—in deed,** in fact; really.

**deem** (dēm), ***v.t. & v.i.*** [AS. *deman*, to judge], to think; believe; suppose.

**deep** (dēp), ***adj.*** [AS. *deop*], 1. extending far downward, inward, or backward. 2. hard to understand; abstruse. 3. wise. 4. dark and rich: said of colors. 5. absorbed by: as, *deep* in thought. 6. intense; profound. 7. of low pitch: said of sound. ***n.*** 1. a deep place. 2. the part that is darkest, etc.: as, the *deep* of night. ***adv.*** far down, far back, etc. **—the deep,** [Poetic], the sea or ocean.

**deep'en** (-'n), ***v.t. & v.i.*** to make or become deep or deeper.

**deep'freeze',** ***n.*** a refrigerator for storing foods at a very low temperature: a trademark (**Deepfreeze**).

**deep'-fry',** ***v.t.*** [-FRIED, -FRYING], to fry in a deep pan of boiling fat.

**deep'-root'ed,** ***adj.*** 1. having deep roots. 2. firmly established.

**deep'-seat'ed,** ***adj.*** 1. buried deep. 2. firmly established.

**deer** (dêr), ***n.*** [*pl.* DEER, *occas.* DEERS], [AS. *deor*, wild animal], a hoofed, cud-chewing animal, the male of which bears antlers that are shed annually.

**de-es·ca·late** (dē-es'kə-lāt'), ***v.i. & v.t.*** [-LATED, -LATING], to reduce or lessen in scope, magnitude, etc.

**de·face** (di-fās'), ***v.t.*** [-FACED, -FACING], [see DE- & FACE], to spoil the appearance of; mar. **—de·face'a·ble, *adj.* —de·face'ment, *n.***

**de·fal·cate** (di-fal'kāt), ***v.i.*** [-CATED, -CATING], [< L. *defalcare*, to cut off], to embezzle. **—de·fal·ca·tion** (dē'fal-kā'shən), ***n.***

**de·fame** (di-fām'), ***v.t.*** [-FAMED, -FAMING], [< L. *dis-*, from + *fama*, fame], to attack the reputation of; slander or libel. **—def·a·ma·tion** (def'ə-mā'shən), ***n.* —de·fam·a·to·ry** (di-fam'ə-tôr'i), ***adj.* —de·fam'er, *n.***

**de·fault** (di-fôlt'), ***n.*** [< L. *de-*, away + *fallere*, fail], 1. failure to do or appear as required. 2. failure to pay money due. ***v.i. & v.t.*** 1. to fail to do or pay when required. 2. to lose (a contest) by default.

**de·feat** (di-fēt'), ***v.t.*** [< L. *dis-*, from + *facere*, do], 1. to win victory over. 2. to bring to nothing; frustrate. ***n.*** a defeating or being defeated.

**de·feat'ist,** ***n.*** one who too readily accepts defeat. **—de·feat'ism, *n.***

**def·e·cate** (def'ə-kāt'), ***v.i.*** [-CATED, -CATING], [< L. *de-*, from + *faex*, dregs], to excrete waste matter from the bowels. **—def'e·ca'tion, *n.***

**de·fect** (di-fekt', dē'fekt), ***n.*** [< L. *de-*, from + *facere*, do], 1. lack of something necessary for completeness. 2. an imperfection; fault. ***v.i.*** (di-fekt'), to forsake a party, cause, etc.; desert. **—de·fec'tion, *n.* —de·fec'tor, *n.***

**de·fec·tive** (di-fek'tiv), ***adj.*** having defects; incomplete; faulty. **—de·fec'tive·ly, *adv.***

**de·fend** (di-fend'), ***v.t.*** [< L. *de-*, away + *fendere*, to strike], 1. to guard from attack; protect. 2. to support by speech or act. 3. in *law*, *a*) to oppose (an action, etc.). *b*) to act for (an accused). **—de·fend'er, *n.***

**de·fend·ant** (di-fen'dənt), ***n.*** in *law*, the person sued or accused.

**de·fense** (di-fens'), ***n.*** 1. a defending against attack. 2. something that defends. 3. justification by speech or writing. 4. *a*) the arguments of a defendant. *b*) the defendant and his counsel. Brit. sp., **defence. —de·fense'less, *adj.* —de·fen'si·ble, *adj.***

**de·fen'sive,** ***adj.*** 1. defending. 2. of or for defense. ***n.*** attitude, position, etc. of defense.

**de·fer** (di-fũr'), ***v.i. & v.t.*** [-FERRED, -FERRING], [see DIFFER], to postpone; delay. **—de·fer'ment, *n.***

**de·fer** (di-fũr'), ***v.i.*** [-FERRED, -FERRING], [< L. *de-*, down + *ferre*, to bear], to yield in opinion or judgment.

**def·er·ence** (def'ẽr-əns), ***n.*** 1. a yielding in opinion, judgment, etc. 2. courteous respect.

**def'er·en'tial** (-en'shəl), ***adj.*** showing deference; very respectful.

**de·fi·ance** (di-fī'əns), ***n.*** a defying; open, bold resistance to authority. **—de·fi'ant, *adj.* —de·fi'ant·ly, *adv.***

**de·fi·cien·cy** (di-fish'ən-si), ***n.*** 1. a being deficient. 2. [*pl.* -CIES], a shortage.

**de·fi'cient** (-ənt), ***adj.*** [see DEFECT], 1. lacking in some essential; incomplete. 2. inadequate in amount.

**def·i·cit** (def'ə-sit), ***n.*** [L. < *deficere*, to lack], the amount by which a sum of money is less than expected, due, etc.

**de·file** (di-fīl'), ***v.t.*** [-FILED, -FILING], [< OFr. *defouler*, tread underfoot], 1. to make filthy. 2. to profane; sully. **—de·file'ment, *n.***

**de·file** (di-fīl', dē'fīl), ***v.i.*** [-FILED, -FILING], [< Fr. *de-*, from + *file*, a line], to march in a line. ***n.*** a narrow passage, valley, etc.

**de·fine** (di-fīn'), ***v.t.*** [-FINED, -FINING], [< L. *de-*, from + *finis*, boundary], 1. to determine the limits or nature of; describe exactly. 2. to state the meaning of (a word, etc.). **—de·fin'a·ble, *adj.***

**def·i·nite** (def'ə-nit), ***adj.*** [see DEFINE], 1. having exact limits. 2. precise in meaning; explicit. 3. certain; positive. 4. in *grammar*, limiting or specifying: as, *the* is the *definite* article. **—def'i·nite·ly, *adv.***

**def·i·ni·tion** (def'ə-nish'ən), ***n.*** 1. a defining or being defined. 2. an explanation of what a word, etc. means.

**de·fin·i·tive** (di-fin'ə-tiv), ***adj.*** 1. conclusive; final. 2. most nearly complete. 3. serving to define. **—de·fin'i·tive·ly, *adv.***

**de·flate** (di-flāt'), ***v.t. & v.i.*** [-FLATED, -FLATING], [< L. *de-*, from + *flare*, to blow], 1 to collapse by letting out air or gas. 2. to lessen in amount, size, importance, etc.

**de·fla'tion,** ***n.*** 1. a deflating. 2. a lessening of the amount of money in circulation, making it rise in value.

**de·flect** (di-flekt'), ***v.t. & v.i.*** [< L. *de-*, from + *flectere*, to bend], to bend or turn to one side. **—de·flec'tion, *n.* —de·flec'tive, *adj.***

**de·flow·er** (di-flou'ẽr), ***v.t.*** [see DE- & FLOWER], 1. to take away the virginity of (a woman). 2. to ravish; spoil.

**de·fo·li·ant** (di-fō'li-ənt), ***n.*** [< L. *de-*, from + *folium*, leaf], a chemical spray that strips growing plants of their leaves. **—de·fo'li·ate'** (-āt'), ***v.t.*** [-ATED, -ATING].

**de·for·est** (di-fôr'ist, -for'-), ***v.t.*** to clear (land) of forests or trees.

**de·form** (di-fôrm'), ***v.t.*** [< L. *de-*, from + *forma*, form], 1. to mar the form of. 2. to make ugly; disfigure. —**de·for·ma·tion** (dē′fôr-mā′shən, def′ẽr-), *n.* —**de·form′er**, *n.*

**de·formed′**, *adj.* misshapen.

**de·form·i·ty** (di-fôr′mə-ti), *n.* [*pl.* -TIES], 1. a deformed part, as of the body. 2. ugliness; depravity.

**de·fraud** (di-frôd′), *v.t.* to take property, rights, etc. from by fraud; cheat.

**de·fray** (di-frā′), *v.t.* [< OFr. *de-*, off + *frai*, expense], to pay (the cost or expenses). —**de·fray′a·ble**, *adj.* —**de·fray′al**, *n.*

**de·frost** (dē-frôst′), *v.t.* & *v.i.* to rid or become rid of frost or ice. —**de·frost′er**, *n.*

**deft** (deft), *adj.* [see DAFT], skillful; dexterous.

**de·funct** (di-fuŋkt′), *adj.* [< L. *defungi*, to finish], no longer existing; dead.

**de·fy** (di-fī′), *v.t.* [-FIED, -FYING], [< L. *dis-*, from + *fidus*, faithful], 1. to resist boldly or openly. 2. to dare to do or prove something.

**de·gen·er·ate** (di-jen′ẽr-it), *adj.* [< L. *de-*, from + *genus*, race], having sunk below a former or normal condition, etc.; deteriorated. *n.* a degenerate person. *v.i.* (-āt′), [-ATED, -ATING], to lose former, normal, or higher qualities. —**de·gen′er·a·cy** (-ə-si), *n.* —**de·gen′er·a′tion**, *n.*

**de·grade** (di-grād′), *v.t.* [-GRADED, -GRADING], [< L. *de-*, down + *gradus*, a step], 1. to demote. 2. to lower in quality, moral character, etc. 3. to dishonor; debase. —**deg·ra·da·tion** (deg′rə-dā′shən), *n.*

**de·gree** (di-grē′), *n.* [see DEGRADE], 1. any of the successive steps in a process. 2. social or official rank. 3. intensity, extent, or amount. 4. a rank given by a college or university to one who has completed a course of study, or to a distinguished person as an honor. 5. a grade of comparison of adjectives and adverbs: as, the superlative *degree*. 6. in *law*, the seriousness of a crime: as, murder in the first *degree*. 7. a unit of measure for angles or arcs, 1/360 of the circumference of a circle. 8. a unit of measure for temperature. —**by degrees**, gradually. —**to a degree**, 1. to a great extent. 2. somewhat.

**de·hu·mid·i·fy** (dē′hū-mid′ə-fī′), *v.t.* [-FIED, -FYING], to remove moisture from (the air, etc.). —**de′hu·mid′i·fi′er**, *n.*

**de·hy·drate** (dē-hī′drāt), *v.t.* [-DRATED, -DRATING], [< *de-* + Gr. *hydōr*, water; + *-ate*], in *chem.*, etc., to remove water from; dry. *v.i.* to lose water. —**de′hy·dra′tion**, *n.*

**de·i·fy** (dē′ə-fī′), *v.t.* [-FIED, -FYING], [< L. *deus*, god + *facere*, make], 1. to make a god of. 2. to look upon as a god; worship. —**de′i·fi·ca′tion** (-fi-kā′shən), *n.*

**deign** (dān), *v.i.* & *v.t.* [< L. *dignus*, worthy], to condescend (to do or give).

**de·ism** (dē′iz'm), *n.* [< L. *deus*, god], the belief that God exists and created the world but thereafter assumed no control over it.

**de·i·ty** (dē′ə-ti), *n.* [*pl.* -TIES], [< L. *deus*, god], 1. the state of being a god. 2. a god or goddess. —**the Deity**, God.

**de·ject** (di-jekt′), *v.t.* [< L. *de-*, down + *jacere*, to throw], to dishearten; depress. —**de·jec′tion**, *n.*

**de·ject′ed**, *adj.* depressed; downcast.

**de·lay** (di-lā′), *v.t.* [< OFr. *de-*, from + *laier*, to leave], 1. to put off; postpone. 2. to make late; detain. *v.i.* to stop for a while. *n.* a delaying or being delayed.

**de·le** (dē′li), *v.t.* [DELED (-lid), DELEING (-li-iŋ)], [see DELETE], in *printing*, to delete. *n.* a mark (ȹ) showing that a letter, etc. is to be taken out.

**de·lec·ta·ble** (di-lek′tə-b'l), *adj.* [see DELIGHT], enjoyable; delightful.

**de·lec·ta·tion** (dē′lek-tā′shən), *n.* [see DELIGHT], delight; entertainment.

**del·e·gate** (del′ə-gāt′, *also, for n.*, -git), *n.* [< L. *de-*, from + *legare*, send], a person authorized to act for others; representative. *v.t.* [-GATED, -GATING], 1. to appoint as a delegate. 2. to entrust (authority, etc.) to another.

**del′e·ga′tion**, *n.* 1. a delegating or being delegated. 2. a group of delegates.

**de·lete** (di-lēt′), *v.t.* & *v.i.* [-LETED, -LETING], [< L. *delere*, destroy], to take out or erase (a letter, word, etc.). —**de·le′tion**, *n.*

**del·e·te·ri·ous** (del′ə-têr′i-əs), *adj.* [< Gr. *dēleisthai*, injure], harmful to health, well-being, etc.; injurious.

**delft·ware** (delft′wâr′), *n.* [< *Delft*, city in Holland], 1. a kind of glazed pottery, usually blue. 2. a brown earthenware. Also **delft.**

**de·lib·er·ate** (di-lib′ẽr-it; *for v.*, -āt′), *adj.* [< L. *de-*, intens. + *librare*, weigh], 1. carefully thought out; done on purpose. 2. not rash or hasty. 3. slow; unhurried. *v.i.* & *v.t.* [-ATED, -ATING], to consider carefully. —**de·lib′er·ate·ly**, *adv.* —**de·lib′er·a′tive** (-ā′tiv), *adj.* —**de·lib′er·a′tor** (-tẽr), *n.*

**de·lib′er·a′tion**, *n.* 1. a deliberating. 2. *often pl.* consideration and debate. 3. carefulness.

**del·i·ca·cy** (del′i-kə-si), *n.* [*pl.* -CIES], 1. the quality or state of being delicate; fineness, weakness, sensitiveness, tact, etc. 2. a choice food or dainty.

**del′i·cate** (-kit), *adj.* [< L. *delicatus*, delightful], 1. deliciously mild or soft. 2. beautifully fine in texture, workmanship, etc. 3. slight and subtle. 4. easily damaged, disordered, etc. 5. frail in health. 6. needing careful handling. 7. finely sensitive. 8. considerate and tactful. —**del′i·cate·ly**, *adv.*

**del·i·ca·tes·sen** (del′i-kə-tes′'n), *n.pl.* [< G. pl. < Fr. *délicatesse*, delicacy], 1. [often construed as sing.], prepared cooked meats, fish, cheeses, salads, etc. 2. [construed as sing.], a shop where such foods are sold.

**de·li·cious** (di-lish′əs), *adj.* [see DELIGHT], 1. delightful. 2. very pleasing to taste or smell. *n.* [D-], a sweet winter apple. —**de·li′cious·ly**, *adv.* —**de·li′cious·ness**, *n.*

**de·light** (di-līt′), *v.t.* & *v.i.* [< L. *de-*, from + *lacere*, entice], to give great pleasure (to). *n.* 1. great pleasure. 2. something giving great pleasure. —**de·light′ed**, *adj.*

**de·light′ful**, *adj.* giving delight; very pleasing. —**de·light′ful·ly**, *adv.*

**De·li·lah** (di-lī′lə), *n.* in the *Bible*, the mistress and betrayer of Samson.

**de·lin·e·ate** (di-lin′i-āt′), *v.t.* [-ATED, -ATING], [< L. *de-*, from + *linea*, a line], 1. to draw; sketch. 2. to depict in words. —**de·lin′e·a′tion**, *n.* —**de·lin′e·a′tive**, *adj.*

**de·lin·quent** (di-liŋ′kwənt), *adj.* [< L. *de-*, from + *linquere*, leave], 1. failing to do what duty or law requires. 2. overdue, as taxes. *n.* a delinquent person; esp., a juvenile guilty of misdemeanors, etc. —**de·lin′quen·cy** [*pl.* -CIES], *n.*

**del·i·quesce** (del′ə-kwes′), *v.i.* [-QUESCED, -QUESCING], [< L. *de-*, from + *liquere*, be liquid], 1. to melt. 2. to become liquid by absorbing moisture from the air. —**del′i·ques′cence**, *n.* —**del′i·ques′cent**, *adj.*

**de·lir·i·ous** (di-lir′i-əs), *adj.* 1. in a state of delirium or wild excitement. 2. of or caused by delirium. —**de·lir′i·ous·ly**, *adv.*

**de·lir′i·um** (-əm), *n.* [*pl.* -UMS, -A (-ə)], [ult. < L. *de-*, from + *lira*, a line], 1. a temporary mental disturbance, as during a fever, marked by confused speech and hallucinations. 2. an uncontrollably wild excitement.

**delirium tre·mens** (trē′mənz), [Mod. L., lit., trembling delirium], a violent delirium resulting from excessive alcoholic liquor.

**de·liv·er** (di-liv′ẽr), *v.t.* [< L. *de-*, from + *liberare*, to free], 1. to set free or rescue. 2. to assist at the birth of. 3. to utter, as a speech. 4. to hand over. 5. to distribute, as mail. 6. to strike (a blow). 7. to throw, as a ball. —**de·liv′er·a·ble**, *adj.*

**de·liv′er·ance,** ***n.*** 1. a freeing or being freed. 2. expression of opinion, judgment, etc.

**de·liv′er·y,** ***n.*** [*pl.* -IES], 1. a handing over; transfer. 2. a distributing, as of mail. 3. a giving birth; childbirth. 4. any giving forth. 5. a striking (of a blow). 6. a throwing (of a ball). 7. the manner of delivering. 8. something delivered.

**dell** (del), ***n.*** [AS. *dell*], a small, secluded valley, glen, etc., usually a wooded one.

**del·phin·i·um** (del-fin′i-əm), ***n.*** [< Gr. *delphin*, dolphin], a tall plant bearing spikes of flowers, usually blue; larkspur.

**del·ta** (del′tə), ***n.*** 1. the fourth letter of the Greek alphabet (Δ, δ). 2. a deposit of soil, usually triangular, formed at the mouth of some rivers.

**de·lude** (di-lo͞od′), ***v.t.*** [-LUDED, -LUDING], [< L. *de-*, from + *ludere*, to play], to mislead; deceive. **—de·lud′er,** ***n.***

**del·uge** (del′ūj), ***n.*** [< L. *dis-*, off + *luere*, to wash], 1. a great flood. 2. a heavy rainfall. ***v.t.*** [-UGED, -UGING], 1. to flood. 2. to overwhelm.

**de·lu·sion** (di-lo͞o′zhən), ***n.*** 1. a deluding or being deluded. 2. a false belief, specif. one that persists psychotically. **—de·lu′sive,** ***adj.***

**de luxe** (di looks′, di luks′), [Fr., of luxury], of extra good quality; elegant.

**delve** (delv), ***v.i.*** [DELVED, DELVING], [AS. *delfan*], 1. [Archaic or Brit. Dial.], to dig. 2. to investigate; search. **—delv′er,** ***n.***

**Dem.,** 1. Democrat. 2. Democratic.

**dem·a·gogue, dem·a·gog** (dem′ə-gôg′), ***n.*** [< Gr. *dēmos*, the people + *agōgos*, leader], one who tries to stir up people's emotions, in order to accomplish selfish ends. **—dem′a·gog′y** (-gō′ji, -gôg′i), **dem′a·gog′uer·y** (-gôg′ẽr-i), ***n.***

**de·mand** (di-mand′, -mänd′), ***v.t.*** [< L. *de-*, from + *mandare*, entrust], 1. to ask for boldly or urgently. 2. to ask for as a right. 3. to ask to know. 4. to require; need. ***v.i.*** to make a demand. ***n.*** 1. a demanding. 2. a thing demanded. 3. a strong request. 4. a requirement. 5. in *economics*, *a*) the desire for a commodity with the ability to pay for it. *b*) the amount people are ready to buy at a certain price. **—in demand,** demanded or sought. **—on demand,** when presented for payment.

**de·mar·ca·tion, de·mar·ka·tion** (dē′mär-kā′shən), ***n.*** [Fr. < Sp. *de-*, from + *marcar*, to mark], 1. the act of setting and marking boundaries. 2. a boundary line.

**de·mean** (di-mēn′), ***v.t.*** [*de-* + *mean* (low)], to degrade; humble.

**de·mean** (di-mēn′), ***v.t.*** [see DEMEANOR], to behave or conduct (oneself).

**de·mean·or** (di-mēn′ẽr), ***n.*** [< OFr. *demener*, to lead], outward behavior; conduct.

**de·ment·ed** (di-men′tid), ***adj.*** [< *dementia*], mentally ill. **—de·ment′ed·ly,** ***adv.***

**de·men·ti·a** (di-men′shə, -shi-ə), ***n.*** [< L. *de-*, away + *mens*, the mind], loss or impairment of mental powers.

**dementia prae·cox** (prē′koks), [L., lit., precocious dementia], a form of dementia, usually beginning in late adolescence, characterized by withdrawal, hallucinations, etc.

**de·mer·it** (dē-mer′it), ***n.*** [ult. < L. *demerere*, deserve well, with *de-* mistaken as negative], 1. a fault; defect. 2. a mark recorded against a student, etc. for poor work or conduct.

**de·mesne** (di-mān′, -mēn′), ***n.*** [see DOMAIN], region; domain; realm.

**De·me·ter** (di-mē′tẽr), ***n.*** in *Gr. myth.*, the goddess of agriculture.

**demi-,** [Fr.], a prefix meaning: 1. *half.* 2. *less than usual in size, power*, etc., as in *demigod.*

**dem·i·god** (dem′i-god′), ***n.*** 1. a minor deity. 2. a person regarded as partly divine.

**dem′i·john′** (-jon′), ***n.*** [Fr. *dame-jeanne*], a large bottle of glass or earthenware in a wicker casing.

**de·mil·i·ta·rize** (dē-mil′ə-tə-rīz′), ***v.t.*** [-RIZED, -RIZING], to free from military control or militarism.

**dem·i·monde** (dem′i-mond′), ***n.*** [Fr.; *demi-* + *monde*, world], the class of women who have lost social standing because of sexual promiscuity.

**de·mise** (di-mīz′), ***n.*** [< L. *de-*, down + *mittere*, send], 1. the transfer of an estate by will or lease. 2. death. ***v.t. & v.i.*** [-MISED, -MISING], to transfer (an estate) by will or lease.

**dem·i·tasse** (dem′i-tas′, -täs′), ***n.*** [Fr.; *demi-* + *tasse*, cup], a small cup of or for after-dinner coffee.

**de·mo·bi·lize** (dē-mō′b'l-īz′), ***v.t. & v.i.*** [-LIZED, -LIZING], to disband (troops). **—de·mo′bi·li·za′tion,** ***n.***

**de·moc·ra·cy** (də-mok′rə-si), ***n.*** [*pl.* -CIES], [< Gr. *dēmos*, the people + *kratein*, to rule], 1. government by the people, directly or through representatives. 2. a country, etc. with such government. 3. equality of rights, opportunity, and treatment.

**dem·o·crat** (dem′ə-krat′), ***n.*** 1. one who believes in democracy. 2. one who practices the principle of equality of rights, etc. 3. [D-], a member of the Democratic Party.

**dem′o·crat′ic,** ***adj.*** 1. of or upholding democracy. 2. of or for all the people. 3. treating others as one's equals. 4. [D-], of or belonging to the Democratic Party.

**Democratic Party,** one of the two major political parties in the U.S.

**de·mol·ish** (di-mol′ish), ***v.t.*** [< L. *de-*, down + *moliri*, build], to tear down; destroy. **—dem·o·li·tion** (dem′ə-lish′ən, dē′mə-), ***n.***

**de·mon** (dē′mən), ***n.*** [< L. *daemon*], 1. a daemon. 2. a devil; evil spirit. 3. a person or thing regarded as evil, cruel, etc. **—de·mon·ic** (dē-mon′ik), ***adj.***

**de·mon·e·tize** (dē-mon′ə-tīz′, -mun′-), ***v.t.*** [-TIZED, -TIZING], 1. to deprive (currency) of its standard value. 2. to stop using as money. **—de·mon′e·ti·za′tion,** ***n.***

**de·mo·ni·ac** (di-mō′ni-ak′), ***adj.*** 1. possessed by a demon. 2. of a demon or demons. 3. devilish. 4. frenzied; frantic. Also **de·mo·ni·a·cal** (dē′mə-nī′ə-k'l).

**de·mon·stra·ble** (di-mon′strə-b'l), ***adj.*** that can be demonstrated, or proved. **—de·mon′stra·bly,** ***adv.***

**dem·on·strate** (dem′ən-strāt′), ***v.t.*** [-STRATED, -STRATING], [< L. *de-*, from + *monstrare*, to show], 1. to show by reasoning; prove. 2. to explain by using examples, etc. 3. to exhibit as by showing the working of. ***v.i.*** to show feelings or ideas by public meetings, parades, etc. **—dem′on·stra′tor,** ***n.***

**dem′on·stra′tion,** ***n.*** 1. a proving. 2. an explanation by example, etc. 3. a showing of how something works. 4. a display, as of public opinion.

**de·mon·stra·tive** (di-mon′strə-tiv), ***adj.*** 1. showing clearly. 2. giving proof (*of*). 3. showing feelings openly. 4. in *grammar*, pointing out: as, *that* is a *demonstrative* pronoun. ***n.*** a demonstrative pronoun or adjective. **—de·mon′stra·tive·ly,** ***adv.***

**de·mor·al·ize** (di-môr′ə-līz′), ***v.t.*** [-IZED, -IZING], 1. to corrupt the morals of. 2. to lower the morale of. 3. to throw into confusion. **—de·mor′al·i·za′tion,** ***n.***

**de·mote** (di-mōt′), ***v.t.*** [-MOTED, -MOTING], [*de-* + pro*mote*], to reduce to a lower grade; lower in rank. **—de·mo′tion,** ***n.***

**de·mul·cent** (di-mul′s'nt), ***adj.*** [< L. *de-*, down + *mulcere*, to stroke], soothing. ***n.*** a soothing ointment.

**de·mur** (di-mũr′), ***v.i.*** [-MURRED, -MURRING], [< L. *de-*, from + *mora*, a delay], to hesitate; have scruples (with *at*). ***n.*** an objection.

**de·mure** (di-myoor′), *adj.* [*de-* (prob. intens.) + OFr. *meür*, mature], 1. sober; serious. 2. coy. **—de·mure′ness,** *n.*
**de·mur·rage** (di-mũr′ij), *n.* 1. the delaying of a ship, freight car, etc., as by failure to load, unload, etc. within the time allowed. 2. the compensation paid for this.
**den** (den), *n.* [AS. *denn*], 1. the lair of a wild animal. 2. a haunt, as of thieves. 3. a small, cozy room where one can be alone to read, work, etc.
**de·na·ture** (dē-nā′chẽr), *v.t.* [-TURED, -TURING], 1. to change the nature of. 2. to make (alcohol) unfit to drink.
**de·ni·al** (di-nī′əl), *n.* 1. a denying; saying "no" (to a request, etc.). 2. a contradiction. 3. a refusal to believe or accept (a doctrine, etc.). 4. abstinence from desired things.
**de·nier** (də-nêr′, den′yẽr), *n.* [Fr. < L. *deni*, by tens], a unit of weight for measuring the fineness of threads of silk, nylon, etc.
**den·im** (den′im), *n.* [< Fr. *serge de Nîmes*, serge of Nîmes, town in France], a coarse, twilled cotton cloth.
**den·i·zen** (den′i-z'n), *n.* [< LL. *de intus*, from within], an inhabitant.
**de·nom·i·nate** (di-nom′ə-nāt′), *v.t.* [-NATED, -NATING], [< L. *de-*, intens. + *nominare*, to name], to name; call. **—de·nom′i·na′tive** (-nā′tiv, -nə-tiv), *adj.*
**de·nom′i·na′tion** (-nā′shən), *n.* 1. the act of naming. 2. a name. 3. a class or kind having a specific name or value: as, coins of various *denominations*. 4. a religious sect.
**de·nom′i·na′tion·al,** *adj.* of, or under the control of, a religious sect.
**de·nom′i·na′tor** (-tẽr), *n.* 1. one that denominates. 2. in *math.*, the term below the line in a fraction.
**de·note** (di-nōt′), *v.t.* [-NOTED, -NOTING], [< L. *de-*, down + *notare*, to mark], 1. to indicate; designate. 2. to mean; signify explicitly. **—de·no·ta·tion** (dē′nō-tā′shən), *n.*
**de·noue·ment, dé·noue·ment** (dā-nōō′-män), *n.* [Fr.], the outcome or unraveling of a plot in a drama, story, etc.
**de·nounce** (di-nouns′), *v.t.* [-NOUNCED, -NOUNCING], [see DENUNCIATION], 1. to accuse publicly; inform against. 2. to condemn strongly. 3. to give formal notice of the ending of (a treaty, armistice, etc.). **—de·nounce′ment,** *n.* **—de·nounc′er,** *n.*
**dense** (dens), *adj.* [DENSER, DENSEST], [L. *densus*, compact], 1. packed tightly together. 2. thick; impenetrable. 3. stupid.
**den·si·ty** (den′sə-ti), *n.* [*pl.* -TIES], 1. a being dense or crowded. 2. stupidity. 3. number per unit, as of area. 4. the ratio of the mass of an object to its volume.
**dent** (dent), *n.* [ME., dial. var. of *dint*], a slight hollow made in a surface by a blow. *v.t.* to make a dent in. *v.i.* to become dented.
**den·tal** (den′t'l), *adj.* [< L. *dens*, tooth], of or for the teeth or dentistry.
**den·tate** (den′tāt), *adj.* [see DENTAL], having teeth or toothlike projections.
**den·ti·frice** (den′tə-fris), *n.* [< L. *dens*, tooth + *fricare*, rub], any preparation for cleaning teeth, as a powder, paste, or liquid.
**den·tine** (den′tēn), *n.* [see DENTAL], the hard tissue under the enamel of a tooth.
**den·tist** (den′tist), *n.* one whose profession is the care and repair of teeth. **—den′tistry,** *n.*
**den·ti·tion** (den-tish′ən), *n.* [see DENTAL], the number, sort, and arrangement of the teeth.
**den·ture** (den′chẽr), *n.* [see DENTAL], a set of artificial teeth.
**de·nude** (di-nōōd′, -nūd′), *v.t.* [-NUDED, -NUDING], [< L. *de-*, off + *nudare*, to strip], to make bare; strip.
**de·nun·ci·a·tion** (di-nun′si-ā′shən), *n.* [< L. *de-*, intens. + *nuntiare*, announce], a denouncing; specif., *a*) strong public condemnation. *b*) a notice by a nation of its intention to end a treaty, etc.
**de·ny** (di-nī′), *v.t.* [-NIED, -NYING], [< L. *de-*, intens. + *negare*, to refuse], 1. to declare (a statement) untrue; contradict. 2. to refuse to accept as true or right. 3. to refuse to recognize; repudiate. 4. to refuse to give. 5. to refuse a request of. **—deny oneself,** to do without desired things.
**de·o·dor·ant** (dē-ō′dẽr-ənt), *adj.* that can destroy or counteract undesired odors. *n.* any deodorant preparation.
**de·part** (di-pärt′), *v.i.* [< L. *dis-*, apart + *partire*, divide], 1. to go away; leave. 2. to die. 3. to deviate (*from*).
**de·part′ed,** *adj.* 1. gone away. 2. dead. **—the departed,** dead person(s).
**de·part·ment** (di-pärt′mənt), *n.* 1. a separate part or division: as, the police *department*. 2. a field of knowledge or activity. **—de·part·men·tal** (dē′pärt-men′t'l), *adj.*
**department store,** a retail store for the sale of various goods arranged in departments.
**de·par·ture** (di-pär′chẽr), *n.* 1. a departing. 2. a starting out, as on a trip. 3. a deviation (*from* something).
**de·pend** (di-pend′), *v.i.* [< L. *de-*, down + *pendere*, hang], 1. to be determined by something else; be contingent (*on*). 2. to rely. 3. to rely for support or aid.
**de·pend′a·ble,** *adj.* trustworthy; reliable. **—de·pend′a·bil′i·ty,** *n.*
**de·pend′ence,** *n.* 1. a being dependent. 2. reliance for support or aid. 3. reliance; trust.
**de·pend′en·cy,** *n.* [*pl.* -CIES], 1. dependence. 2. something dependent. 3. a territory geographically distinct from the country governing it.
**de·pend′ent,** *adj.* 1. hanging down. 2. influenced or determined by something else. 3. relying (*on* another) for support or aid. 4. subordinate. *n.* one who relies on another for support, etc. Also sp. **de·pend′ant.**
**de·pict** (di-pikt′), *v.t.* [< L. *de-*, intens. + *pingere*, to paint], 1. to represent by drawing, painting, etc. 2. to picture in words; describe. **—de·pict′er,** *n.* **—de·pic′tion,** *n.*
**de·pil·a·to·ry** (di-pil′ə-tôr′i), *adj.* [< L. *de-*, from + *pilus*, hair], serving to remove unwanted hair. *n.* [*pl.* -RIES], a depilatory substance or device.
**de·plane** (di-plān′), *v.i.* [-PLANED, -PLANING], to get out of an airplane after it lands.
**de·plete** (di-plēt′), *v.t.* [-PLETED, -PLETING], [< L. *de-*, from + *plere*, fill], 1. to empty wholly or partly. 2. to exhaust. **—de·ple′tion,** *n.*
**de·plor·a·ble** (di-plôr′ə-b'l), *adj.* to be deplored; lamentable. **—de·plor′a·bly,** *adv.*
**de·plore** (di-plôr′), *v.t.* [-PLORED, -PLORING], [< L. *de-*, intens. + *plorare*, weep], to be regretful or sorry about; lament.
**de·ploy** (di-ploi′), *v.t. & v.i.* [< L. *dis-*, from + *plicare*, to fold], in *military usage*, to spread out so as to form a wider front. **—de·ploy′ment,** *n.*
**de·pon·ent** (di-pō′nənt), *n.* [< L. *de-*, down + *ponere*, set], in *law*, one who gives written testimony under oath.
**de·pop·u·late** (dē-pop′yoo-lāt′), *v.t.* [-LATED, -LATING], to reduce the population of. **—de·pop′u·la′tion,** *n.*
**de·port** (di-pôrt′), *v.t.* [< L. *de-*, from + *portare*, carry], 1. to behave (oneself) in a specified way. 2. to banish from a country. **—de·por·ta·tion** (dē′pôr-tā′shən), *n.*
**de·port′ment,** *n.* conduct; behavior.
**de·pose** (di-pōz′), *v.t.* [-POSED, -POSING], [< OFr. *de-*, from + *poser*, cease], 1. to remove from office; oust. 2. to testify.
**de·pos·it** (di-pos′it), *v.t.* [< L. *deponere*, lay down], 1. to place for safekeeping, as money in a bank. 2. to give as a pledge or

partial payment. 3. to set down. 4. to leave lying, as sediment. *n.* 1. something placed for safekeeping, as money in a bank. 2. a pledge or part payment. 3. something left lying. —**de·pos'i·tor**, *n.*

**dep·o·si·tion** (dep'ə-zish'ən), *n.* 1. a deposing or being deposed. 2. a testifying. 3. something deposited.

**de·pos·i·to·ry** (di-poz'ə-tôr'i), *n.* [*pl.* -RIES], 1. a place where things are put for safekeeping. 2. a trustee.

**de·pot** (dē'pō; *Brit. or military*, dep'ō), *n.* [< Fr.; see DEPOSIT], 1. a warehouse. 2. a railroad station. 3. a storage place for military supplies.

**de·prave** (di-prāv'), *v.t.* [-PRAVED, -PRAVING], [< L. *de-*, intens. + *pravus*, crooked], to make morally bad; corrupt. —**de·praved'**, *adj.* —**de·prav'i·ty** (-prav'ə-ti) [*pl.* -TIES], *n.*

**dep·re·cate** (dep'rə-kāt'), *v.t.* [-CATED, -CATING], [< L. *de-*, off + *precari*, pray], to express disapproval of. —**dep're·ca'tion**, *n.* —**dep're·ca·to'ry** (-kə-tôr'i), *adj.*

**de·pre·ci·ate** (di-prē'shi-āt'), *v.t. & v.i.* [-ATED, -ATING], [< L. *de-*, from + *pretium*, price], 1. to lessen in value. 2. to belittle. —**de·pre'ci·a'tion**, *n.* —**de·pre'ci·a'tor**, *n.*

**dep·re·da·tion** (dep'ri-dā'shən), *n.* [< L. *de-*, intens. + *praedari*, rob], a plundering.

**de·press** (di-pres'), *v.t.* [< L. *de-*, down + *premere*, press], 1. to press down. 2. to sadden. 3. to weaken. 4. to lower in value, price, etc. —**de·pressed'**, *adj.* —**de·press'ing**, *adj.* —**de·pres'sor** (-ẽr), *n.*

**de·pres·sion** (di-presh'ən), *n.* 1. a depressing or being depressed. 2. a hollow or low place. 3. low spirits; dejection. 4. a decrease in force, activity, etc. 5. a period of reduced business activity, much unemployment, etc. —**de·pres'sive** (-pres'iv), *adj.*

**de·prive** (di-prīv'), *v.t.* [-PRIVED, -PRIVING], [< L. *de-*, intens. + *privare*, to separate], 1. to take away from forcibly. 2. to keep from having, etc. —**dep·ri·va·tion** (dep'rə-vā'shən), **de·priv·al** (di-prīv''l), *n.*

**dept.**, department.

**depth** (depth), *n.* [ME. < *dep*, deep; + *-th*], 1. the distance from the top downward, or from front to back. 2. deepness. 3. intensity. 4. profundity. 5. *usually pl.* the deepest or inmost part.

**dep·u·ta·tion** (dep'yoo-tā'shən), *n.* 1. a deputing or being deputed. 2. a group of deputies; delegation.

**de·pute** (di-pūt'), *v.t.* [-PUTED, -PUTING], [< L. *de-*, from + *putare*, cleanse], 1. to give (authority, etc.) to a deputy. 2. to appoint as one's substitute.

**dep·u·tize** (dep'yoo-tīz'), *v.t.* [-TIZED, -TIZING], to appoint as deputy.

**dep·u·ty** (dep'yoo-ti), *n.* [*pl.* -TIES], [see DEPUTE], a person appointed to act for another or others.

**de·rail** (dē-rāl'), *v.t. & v.i.* to run off the rails, as a train. —**de·rail'ment**, *n.*

**de·range** (di-rānj'), *v.t.* [-RANGED, -RANGING], [< OFr. *des-*, apart + *rengier*, to range], 1. to upset the arrangement or working of. 2. to make insane. —**de·ranged'**, *adj.* —**de·range'ment**, *n.*

**Der·by** (dũr'bi; *Brit.* där'-), *n.* [*pl.* -BIES], 1. any of several established horse races, orig., the one in England founded by an Earl of Derby. 2. [d-], a stiff felt hat with a round crown.

**der·e·lict** (der'ə-likt'), *adj.* [< L. *de-*, intens. + *relinquere;* see RELINQUISH], 1. deserted by the owner; abandoned. 2. negligent. *n.* 1. a ship deserted at sea. 2. a person or thing abandoned as worthless.

**der'e·lic'tion** (-lik'shən), *n.* 1. a forsaking or being forsaken. 2. a neglect of duty.

**de·ride** (di-rīd'), *v.t.* [-RIDED, -RIDING], [< L. *de-*, down + *ridere*, to laugh], to laugh at in contempt or scorn; ridicule. —**de·ri'sion** (-rizh'ən), *n.* —**de·ri'sive** (-rī'siv), *adj.*

**der·i·va·tion** (der'ə-vā'shən), *n.* 1. a deriving or being derived. 2. the source or origin of something. 3. the origin and development of a word.

**de·riv·a·tive** (də-riv'ə-tiv), *adj.* derived; not original. *n.* something derived.

**de·rive** (də-rīv'), *v.t.* [-RIVED, -RIVING], [< L. *de-*, from + *rivus*, a stream], 1. to get or receive (*from* a source). 2. to deduce or infer. 3. to trace from or to a source. *v.i.* to proceed (*from* a source); originate.

**der·ma·tol·o·gy** (dũr'mə-tol'ə-ji), *n.* [< Gr. *derma*, skin; + *-logy*], the branch of medicine dealing with the skin and its diseases. —**der'ma·tol'o·gist**, *n.*

**der·mis** (dũr'mis), *n.* [see EPIDERMIS], 1. the layer of skin just below the epidermis. 2. the skin. —**der'mic**, *adj.*

**der·o·gate** (der'ə-gāt'), *v.i. & v.t.* [-GATED, -GATING], [< L. *de-*, from + *rogare*, ask], to detract. —**der'o·ga'tion**, *n.*

**de·rog·a·to·ry** (di-rog'ə-tôr'i), *adj.* [see DEROGATE], 1. detracting. 2. disparaging; belittling. Also **de·rog'a·tive**.

**der·rick** (der'ik), *n.* [after *Derrick*, 17th-c. London hangman: orig. applied to a gallows], 1. a large apparatus for moving heavy objects. 2. a tall framework, as over an oil well, to support drilling machinery, etc.

**der·rin·ger** (der'in-jẽr), *n.* [< name of the U.S. inventor], a short-barreled pistol of large caliber.

**der·vish** (dũr'vish), *n.* [< Per. *darvīsh*, beggar], a member of any of various Moslem ascetic orders.

**des·cant** (des-kant'), *v.i.* [< L. *dis-*, apart + *cantus*, song], 1. to discourse. 2. to sing.

**de·scend** (di-send'), *v.i.* [< L. *de-*, down + *scandere*, climb], 1. to move down to a lower place. 2. to pass from earlier to later time, from greater to less, etc. 3. to slope downward. 4. to come down (*from* a source). 5. to stoop (*to* some act). 6. to make a sudden visit or attack (*on*). *v.t.* to move down along. —**de·scend'ent**, *adj.*

**de·scend'ant**, *n.* an offspring of a certain ancestor, family, group, etc.

**de·scent** (di-sent'), *n.* 1. a coming or going down. 2. ancestral line. 3. a downward slope. 4. a way down. 5. a sudden attack. 6. a decline.

**de·scribe** (di-skrīb'), *v.t.* [-SCRIBED, -SCRIBING], [< L. *de-*, from + *scribere*, write], 1. to tell or write about. 2. to picture in words. 3. to trace the form or outline of.

**de·scrip·tion** (di-skrip'shən), *n.* 1. the act or technique of describing. 2. a statement or passage that describes. 3. sort; kind. 4. a tracing or outlining. —**de·scrip'tive**, *adj.*

**de·scry** (di-skrī'), *v.t.* [-SCRIED, -SCRYING], [< OFr. *descrier*, proclaim], 1. to catch sight of (distant or obscure objects). 2. to detect.

**des·e·crate** (des'i-krāt'), *v.t.* [-CRATED, -CRATING], [< L. *dis-*, apart + *sacer*, sacred], to violate the sacredness of; profane. —**des'e·cra'tion**, *n.*

**de·seg·re·gate** (dē-seg'ri-gāt'), *v.t. & v.i.* [-GATED, -GATING], to abolish racial segregation in (public schools, housing, etc.). —**de'seg·re·ga'tion**, *n.*

**de·sert** (di-zũrt'), *v.t. & v.i.* [< L. *de-*, from + *serere*, join], 1. to abandon; forsake. 2. to leave (one's military post, etc.) without permission and with no intent to return. —**de·sert'er**, *n.* —**de·ser'tion** (-zũr'shən), *n.*

**des·ert** (dez'ẽrt), *n.* [see DESERT, *v.*], 1. an uninhabited regon; wilderness. 2. a dry, barren, sandy region.

**de·sert** (di-zũrt'), *n.* [see DESERVE], *often pl.* deserved reward or punishment.

**de·serve** (di-zũrv′), *v.i. & v.t.* [-SERVED, -SERVING], [< L. *de-*, intens. + *servire*, serve], to be worthy (of); merit. **—de·serv′ed·ly,** *adv.* **—de·serv′ing,** *adj.*
**des·ic·cate** (des′i-kāt′), *v.t. & v.i.* [-CATED, -CATING], [< L. *de-*, intens. + *siccus*, dry], to dry up completely. **—des′ic·ca′tion,** *n.*
**de·sid·er·a·tum** (di-sid′ēr-ā′təm), *n.* [*pl.* -TA (-tə)], [see DESIRE], something needed and wanted.
**de·sign** (di-zīn′), *v.t.* [< L. *de-*, out + *signum*, a mark], 1. to plan; sketch an outline for. 2. to contrive. 3. to plan to do; intend. *v.i.* to make original plans, etc. *n.* 1. a plan; scheme. 2. purpose; intention. 3. a working plan; pattern. 4. the arrangement of parts, form, color, etc. in a work of art. —**by design,** purposely. **—de·sign′er,** *n.*
**des·ig·nate** (dez′ig-nāt′), *v.t.* [-NATED, -NATING], [see DESIGN], 1. to point out; specify. 2. to name. 3. to appoint. **—des′ig·na′tion,** *n.* **—des′ig·na′tor,** *n.*
**de·sign′ing,** *adj.* scheming; artful. *n.* the art of making designs, etc.
**de·sir·a·ble** (di-zīr′ə-b'l), *adj.* worth having; pleasing. **—de·sir′a·bil′i·ty,** *n.*
**de·sire** (di-zīr′), *v.t.* [-SIRED, -SIRING], [< L. *desiderare*], 1. to long for; crave. 2. to ask for. *n.* 1. a wish or craving. 2. sexual appetite. 3. a request. 4. anything desired.
**de·sir′ous** (-əs), *adj.* desiring.
**de·sist** (di-zist′), *v.i.* [< L. *de-*, from + *stare*, to stand], to cease; stop.
**desk** (desk), *n.* [see DISK], a table for writing, drawing, or reading.
**des·o·late** (des′ə-lit), *adj.* [< L. *de-*, intens. + *solus*, alone], 1. lonely; solitary. 2. uninhabited. 3. laid waste. 4. forlorn. *v.t.* (-lāt′), [-LATED, -LATING], 1. to rid of inhabitants. 2. to lay waste. 3. to make forlorn.
**des′o·la′tion,** *n.* 1. a making desolate. 2. a desolate condition or place. 3. misery. 4. loneliness.
**de·spair** (di-spâr′), *v.i.* [< L. *de-*, without + *sperare*, to hope], to lose hope. *n.* 1. loss or lack of hope. 2. a person or thing causing despair. **—de·spair′ing,** *adj.*
**des·patch** (di-spach′), *v.t. & n.* dispatch.
**des·per·a·do** (des′pə-rā′dō, -rā′-), *n.* [*pl.* -DOES, -DOS], [< OSp.; see DESPAIR], a dangerous criminal; bold outlaw.
**des·per·ate** (des′pēr-it), *adj.* 1. rash or violent because of despair. 2. so hopeless as to cause despair. **—des′per·ate·ly,** *adv.*
**des·per·a·tion** (des′pēr-ā′shən), *n.* 1. a being desperate. 2. recklessness resulting from despair.
**des·pi·ca·ble** (des′pik-ə-b'l, di-spik′-), *adj.* that is or should be despised; contemptible. **—des′pi·ca·bly,** *adv.*
**de·spise** (di-spīz′), *v.t.* [-SPISED, -SPISING], [< L. *de*, down + *specere*, look at], to be contemptuous of; scorn.
**de·spite** (di-spīt′), *prep.* [see DESPISE], in spite of; notwithstanding.
**de·spoil** (di-spoil′), *v.t.* [< L. *de-*, intens. + *spoliare*, to strip], to rob; plunder.
**de·spond** (di-spond′), *v.i.* [< L. *de-*, from + *spondere*, to promise], to lose courage or hope.
**de·spond′en·cy,** *n.* loss of courage or hope; dejection. **—de·spond′ent,** *adj.*
**des·pot** (des′pət), *n.* [< Gr. *despotēs*, a master], 1. an absolute ruler. 2. a tyrant. **—des·pot·ic** (di-spot′ik), *adj.* **—des′pot·ism,** *n.*
**des·sert** (di-zũrt′), *n.* [Fr. < *desservir*, clear the table], a course, usually sweet, served at the end of a meal.
**des·ti·na·tion** (des′tə-nā′shən), *n.* 1. the end or purpose for which something or someone is destined. 2. the place toward which one is going.
**des·tine** (des′tin), *v.t.* [-TINED, -TINING], [< L. *de-*, intens. + *stare*, to stand], 1. to predetermine, as by fate. 2. to intend. —**destined for,** 1. bound for. 2. intended for.
**des·tin·y** (des′tə-ni), *n.* [*pl.* -IES], 1. the inevitable succession of events. 2. (one's) fortune, or fate.
**des·ti·tute** (des′tə-to͞ot′, -tūt′), *adj.* [< L. *de*, down + *statuere*, to set], 1. lacking (with *of*). 2. lacking the necessities of life. **—des′ti·tu′tion,** *n.*
**de·stroy** (di-stroi′), *v.t.* [< L. *de-*, down + *struere*, build], 1. to tear down; demolish. 2. to spoil completely; ruin. 3. to kill.
**de·stroy′er,** *n.* 1. one that destroys. 2. a small, fast, heavily armed warship.
**de·struct·i·ble** (di-struk′tə-b'l), *adj.* that can be destroyed. **—de·struct′i·bil′i·ty,** *n.*
**de·struc·tion** (di-struk′shən), *n.* 1. a destroying or being destroyed; ruin. 2. the cause or means of destroying. **—de·struc′tive,** *adj.* **—de·struc′tive·ly,** *adv.*
**des·ue·tude** (des′wi-to͞od′, -tūd′), *n.* [Fr. < L. *de-*, from + *suescere*, be accustomed], disuse.
**des·ul·to·ry** (des′'l-tôr′i), *adj.* [< L. *de-*, from + *salire*, to leap], 1. disconnected; not methodical. 2. random. **—des′ul·to′ri·ly,** *adv.*
**de·tach** (di-tach′), *v.t.* [< Fr.; see DE- & ATTACH], 1. to unfasten and remove; disconnect. 2. to send on a special task, as troops. **—de·tach′a·ble,** *adj.*
**de·tached′,** *adj.* 1. disconnected; separate. 2. aloof; disinterested; impartial.
**de·tach′ment,** *n.* 1. a detaching; separation. 2. a unit of troops or ships sent on special service. 3. impartiality or aloofness.
**de·tail** (di-tāl′), *v.t.* [< Fr. *dé-*, from + *tailler*, to cut], 1. to give the particulars of. 2. in *military usage*, to choose for a special task. *n.* (*also* dē′tāl), 1. a dealing with things item by item. 2. a minute account. 3. a small part; item. 4. in *military usage*, *a*) persons chosen for a special task. *b*) the special task.
**de·tain** (di-tān′), *v.t.* [< L. *de-*, off + *tenere*, hold], 1. to keep in custody. 2. to delay. **—de·tain′er,** *n.* **—de·tain′ment,** *n.*
**de·tect** (di-tekt′), *v.t.* [< L. *de-*, from + *tegere*, to cover], to discover (anything hidden, not clear, etc.). **—de·tect′a·ble, de·tec·ti′ble,** *adj.* **—de·tec′tion,** *n.* **—de·tec′tor,** *n.*
**de·tec′tive,** *n.* a person, often a policeman, whose work is investigating crimes, getting information, etc.
**de·ten·tion** (di-ten′shən), *n.* 1. a detaining or being detained. 2. an enforced delay.
**de·ter** (di-tũr′), *v.t.* [-TERRED, -TERRING], [< L, *de-*, from + *terrere*, frighten], to keep (a person) from doing something through fear, doubt, etc.; discourage. **—de·ter′ment,** *n.*
**de·ter·gent** (di-tũr′jənt), *adj.* [< L. *de-*, off + *tergere*, wipe], cleansing. *n.* a cleansing substance.
**de·te·ri·o·rate** (di-têr′i-ə-rāt′), *v.t. & v.i.* [-RATED, -RATING], [< L. *deterior*, worse], to make or become worse; depreciate. **—de·te′ri·o·ra′tion,** *n.*
**de·ter·mi·nate** (di-tũr′mə-nit), *adj.* [see DETERMINE], 1. having exact limits; definite. 2. settled; conclusive. 3. resolute.
**de·ter′mi·na′tion** (-nā′shən), *n.* 1. a determining or being determined. 2. a firm intention. 3. firmness of purpose.
**de·ter·mine** (di-tũr′min), *v.t.* [-MINED, -MINING], [< L. *de-*, from + *terminus*, a limit], 1. to set limits to; define. 2. to settle conclusively; resolve; decide. 3. to be the deciding factor in; direct. 4. to find out exactly. *v.i.* to decide; resolve.
**de·ter′mined,** *adj.* 1. having one's mind made up. 2. resolute; unwavering.
**de·ter′min·ism** (-iz'm), *n.* the doctrine that one's choice of action is not free but determined independent of his will.

**de·ter·rent** (di-tũr′ənt), *adj.* deterring. *n.* something that deters. —**de·ter′rence,** *n.*
**de·test** (di-test′), *v.t.* [< L. *detestari*, to curse by the gods], to dislike intensely; hate. —**de·test′a·ble,** *adj.* —**de·tes·ta·tion** (dē′-tes-tā′shən), *n.*
**de·throne** (dē-thrōn′), *v.t.* [-THRONED, -THRONING], to remove from a throne; depose. —**de·throne′ment,** *n.*
**det·o·nate** (det′ə-nāt′, dē′tō-), *v.i. & v.t.* [-NATED, -NATING], [< L. *de-*, intens. + *tonare*, to sound], to explode noisily. —**det′o·na′tion,** *n.* —**det′o·na′tor,** *n.*
**de·tour** (dē′toor, di-toor′), *n.* [< Fr.; see DE- & TURN], 1. a roundabout way. 2. a route used when the regular route is closed. *v.i. & v.t.* to use or cause to use a detour.
**de·tract** (di-trakt′), *v.t.* [< L. *de-*, from + *trahere*, draw], to take away. *v.i.* to take something desirable (*from*). —**de·trac′tion,** *n.* —**de·trac′tor,** *n.*
**de·train** (dē-trān′), *v.i. & v.t.* to get off or cause to get off a railroad train.
**det·ri·ment** (det′rə-mənt), *n.* [< L. *de-*, off + *terere*, rub], 1. damage; injury. 2. anything that causes this. —**det′ri·men′tal,** *adj.*
**de·tri·tus** (di-trī′təs), *n.* [< L. *deterere*, wear away], fragments of rock, etc. produced by disintegration or erosion; debris.
**deuce** (do͞os, dūs), *n.* [< L. *duo*, two], 1. a playing card or side of a die with two spots. 2. in *tennis*, a tie score after which one side must score twice in a row to win. 3. the devil: a mild curse or exclamation.
**deu·te·ri·um** (do͞o-têr′i-əm, dū-), *n.* [Mod. L.], a heavy isotope of hydrogen: symbol, D.
**Deu·ter·on·o·my** (do͞o′tẽr-on′ə-mi, dū′-), *n.* [< Gr. *deuteros*, second + *nomos*, law], the fifth book of the Old Testament.
**de·val·u·ate** (dē-val′ū-āt′), *v.t.* [-ATED, -ATING], to lessen the value of. —**de·val′u·a′tion,** *n.*
**dev·as·tate** (dev′əs-tāt′), *v.t.* [-TATED, -TATING], [< L. *de-*, intens. + *vastus*, empty], to lay waste; ravage. —**dev′as·ta′tion,** *n.*
**de·vel·op** (di-vel′əp), *v.t.* [< Fr. *de-*, apart + OFr. *voluper*, wrap], 1. to make fuller, better, etc. 2. to show or work out by degrees; disclose. 3. in *photography*, to put (a film, etc.) in chemical solutions to make the picture visible. *v.i.* 1. to come into being or activity. 2. to become developed; grow. 3. to be disclosed. —**de·vel′op·er,** *n.*
**de·vel′op·ment,** *n.* 1. a developing or being developed. 2. a thing that is developed. 3. a happening. —**de·vel′op·men′tal,** *adj.*
**de·vi·ate** (dē′vi-āt′), *v.i.* [-ATED, -ATING], [see DEVIOUS], to turn aside (*from* a course, standard, etc.); diverge. —**de′vi·a′tion,** *n.*
**de·vice** (di-vīs′), *n.* [see DEVISE], 1. a thing devised; plan. 2. a scheme; trick. 3. a mechanical contrivance; invention. 4. an ornamental design, esp. on a coat of arms. 5. a motto or emblem. —**leave to one's own devices,** to allow to do as one wishes.
**dev·il** (dev′'l), *n.* [ult. < Gr. *diabolos*, lit., slanderer], 1. [often D-], in *theology*, *a*) the chief evil spirit; Satan (with *the*). *b*) any demon of hell. 2. a wicked person. 3. a sprightly, mischievous person. 4. a printer's apprentice. *v.t.* [-ILED or -ILLED, -ILING or -ILLING], 1. to prepare (food) with strong seasoning. 2. to annoy. —**dev′il·ish,** *adj.*
**dev′il-may-care′,** *adj.* reckless; careless.
**dev′il·ment,** *n.* mischievous action.
**dev′il's-food′ cake,** reddish-brown chocolate cake.
**dev′il·try** (-tri), *n.* [*pl.* -TRIES], reckless mischief, fun, etc.
**de·vi·ous** (dē′vi-əs), *adj.* [< L. *de-*, off + *via*, road], 1. roundabout; rambling. 2. going astray; crooked. —**de′vi·ous·ly,** *adv.*
**de·vise** (di-vīz′), *v.t. & v.i.* [-VISED, -VISING], [< L. *dividere*, divide], 1. to contrive; plan; invent. 2. to bequeath (real property) by will. *n.* a gift of real property by will.
**de·void** (di-void′), *adj.* [see DE- & VOID], completely without; empty (*of*).
**de·volve** (di-volv′), *v.t. & v.i.* [-VOLVED, -VOLVING], [< L. *de-*, down + *volvere*, to roll], to pass (*on*) to another, as duties, rights, etc. —**de·volve′ment,** *n.*
**de·vote** (di-vōt′), *v.t.* [-VOTED, -VOTING], [< L. *de-*, from + *vovere*, to vow], 1. to dedicate. 2. to apply (oneself, etc.) to some purpose.
**de·vot′ed,** *adj.* 1. dedicated. 2. very loyal; faithful. —**de·vot′ed·ly,** *adv.*
**dev·o·tee** (dev′ə-tē′), *n.* one warmly devoted to something or someone.
**de·vo′tion,** *n.* 1. a devoting or being devoted. 2. piety; devoutness. 3. religious worship. 4. *pl.* prayers. 5. loyalty; deep affection. —**de·vo′tion·al,** *adj.*
**de·vour** (di-vour′), *v.t.* [< L. *de-*, intens. + *vorare*, swallow whole], 1. to eat (up) hungrily. 2. to consume; destroy; engulf. 3. to take in greedily with the eyes or ears.
**de·vout** (di-vout′), *adj.* [see DEVOTE], 1. very religious; pious. 2. earnest; sincere.
**dew** (do͞o, dū), *n.* [AS. *deaw*], 1. atmospheric moisture that condenses in drops on cool surfaces at night. 2. anything refreshing, pure, etc., like dew. *v.t.* to wet, as with dew; make moist. —**dew′y** [-IER, -IEST], *adj.*
**dew′drop′,** *n.* a drop of dew.
**dew·lap** (do͞o′lap′, dū′-), *n.* [< ME. *dew*, dew + *lappe*, a fold], a loose fold of skin under the throat of cattle, etc.
**dex·ter·i·ty** (dek-ster′ə-ti), *n.* [see DEXTEROUS], skill in using one's hands, body, or mind; adroitness.
**dex·ter·ous** (dek′strəs, -stẽr-əs), *adj.* [< L. *dexter*, right], having or showing skill in using the hands, body, or mind. Also **dex′trous.** —**dex′ter·ous·ly,** *adv.*
**dex·trose** (dek′strōs), *n.* a sugar found in plants and animals; glucose.
**di-,** [Gr. *di-* < *dis*, twice], a prefix meaning *twice, double, twofold.*
**di-,** dis-.
**di·a·be·tes** (dī′ə-bē′tis, -tēz), *n.* [< Gr. *dia-*, through + *bainein*, go], a disease characterized by excess sugar in the blood and urine, hunger, thirst, etc.: also **sugar diabetes.** —**di′a·bet′ic** (-bet′ik, -bē′tik), *adj. & n.*
**di·a·bol·ic** (dī′ə-bol′ik), *adj.* [see DEVIL], very wicked or cruel; devilish: also **di′a·bol′i·cal.** —**di′a·bol′i·cal·ly,** *adv.*
**di·a·crit·ic** (dī′ə-krit′ik), *adj.* [< Gr. *dia-*, across + *krinein*, to separate], diacritical. *n.* a diacritical mark.
**di′a·crit′i·cal,** *adj.* used to distinguish.
**diacritical mark,** a mark added to a letter to show pronunciation, etc.: e.g., ä, ā, â, é.
**di·a·dem** (dī′ə-dem′), *n.* [< Gr. *dia-*, through + *dein*, bind], 1. a crown. 2. a jeweled or ornamented headband.
**di·ag·nose** (dī′əg-nōs′, -nōz′), *v.t. & v.i.* [-NOSED, -NOSING], to make a diagnosis (of).
**di′ag·no′sis** (-nō′sis), *n.* [*pl.* -NOSES (-sēz)], [< Gr. *dia-*, between + *gignōskein*, know], 1. the act or fact of deciding the nature of a disease (hence, of any situation) by examination and observation. 2. the resulting decision. —**di′ag·nos′tic** (-nos′tik), *adj.*
**di·ag·o·nal** (dī-ag′ə-n'l), *adj.* [< Gr. *dia-*, through + *gōnia*, an angle], 1. extending slantingly between opposite corners. 2. slanting; oblique. 3. having slanted markings, lines, etc. *n.* a diagonal line, plane, course, part, etc. —**di·ag′o·nal·ly,** *adv.*
**di·a·gram** (dī′ə-gram′), *n.* [< Gr. *dia-*, across + *graphein*, write], a sketch, plan, graph, etc. that helps explain something, as by outlining its parts. *v.t.* [-GRAMED or -GRAMMED, -GRAMING or -GRAMMING], to make a diagram of. —**di′a·gram·mat′ic** (-grə-mat′ik), **di′a·gram·mat′i·cal,** *adj.*

**di·al** (dī′əl, dīl), *n.* [< L. *dies*, day], 1. a sundial. 2. the face of a clock, etc. 3. the face of a meter, etc. for indicating, as by a pointer, the amount of something. 4. a graduated disk, as on a radio, for tuning in stations. 5. a rotating disk on a telephone, for making connections automatically. *v.t. & v.i.* [-ALED or -ALLED, -ALING or -ALLING], 1. to show on or measure with a dial. 2. to tune in (a radio station). 3. to call by using a telephone dial.
**dial.,** 1. dialect. 2. dialectal.
**di·a·lect** (dī′ə-lekt′), *n.* [< Gr. *dia-*, between + *legein*, to talk], the form of a spoken language peculiar to a region, social group, etc.
**di′a·lec′tal,** *adj.* of a dialect.
**di′a·lec′tic** (-lek′tik), *n.* 1. the art or practice of examining ideas logically for their validity: also **dialectics.** 2. logical argumentation. *adj.* 1. of or using dialectic. 2. dialectal. Also **di′a·lec′ti·cal.**
**di·a·logue, di·a·log** (dī′ə-lôg′), *n.* [see DIALECT], 1. a conversation. 2. the passages of talk in a play, story, etc.
**di·am·e·ter** (dī-am′ə-tẽr), *n.* [< Gr. *dia-*, through + *metron*, a measure], 1. a straight line passing through the center of a circle, sphere, etc. from one side to the other. 2. the length of such a line.
**di·a·met·ri·cal** (dī′ə-met′ri-k'l), *adj.* 1. of or along a diameter. 2. directly opposite; contrary. Also **di′a·met′ric.**
**di·a·mond** (dī′mənd, dī′ə-), *n.* [< Gr. *adamas*, adamant], 1. nearly pure carbon in crystalline form: it is the hardest mineral known and has great brilliance. 2. a piece of this, used as a gem, etc. 3. a figure shaped like this: ◆. 4. a playing card marked with this figure. 5. in *baseball*, *a*) the infield. *b*) the whole playing field.
**Di·an·a** (dī-an′ə), *n.* in *Rom. myth.*, the goddess of the moon and of hunting.
**di·a·pa·son** (dī′ə-pā′z'n), *n.* [< Gr. *dia*, through + *pas*, all (tones)], 1. the entire range of a voice or instrument. 2. either of two principal organ stops covering the entire range.
**di·a·per** (dī′ə-pẽr), *n.* [< Gr. *dia-*, through + *aspros*, white], 1. a white cotton or linen cloth woven in a pattern of repeated figures. 2. (*also* dī′pẽr), a small cloth used as a baby's breechcloth. *v.i.* to put a diaper on (a baby).
**di·aph·a·nous** (dī-af′ə-nəs), *adj.* [< Gr. *dia-*, through + *phainein*, to show], transparent or translucent.
**di·a·phragm** (dī′ə-fram′), *n.* [< Gr. *dia-*, through + *phragma*, fence], 1. the partition of muscles and tendons between the chest and the abdomen; midriff. 2. a device to regulate the amount of light entering a camera lens, etc. 3. a vibrating disk that produces sound waves, as in an earphone. —**di′a·phrag·mat′ic** (-frag-mat′ik), *adj.*
**di·ar·rhe·a, di·ar·rhoe·a** (dī′ə-rē′ə), *n.* [< Gr. *dia-*, through + *rheein*, to flow], excessive frequency and looseness of bowel movements.
**di·a·ry** (dī′ə-ri), *n.* [*pl.* -RIES], [< L. *dies*, day], a daily written record of the writer's experiences, etc.
**di·as·to·le** (dī-as′tə-lē′), *n.* [< Gr. *dia-*, apart + *stellein*, put], the usual rhythmic dilatation of the heart.
**di·a·ther·my** (dī′ə-thũr′mi), *n.* [< Gr. *dia-*, through + *thermē*, heat], medical treatment in which heat is generated in the tissues beneath the skin by a high-frequency electric current. —**di′a·ther′mic,** *adj.*
**di·a·ton·ic** (dī′ə-ton′ik), *adj.* [< Gr. *diatonikos*, stretched through (the notes)], in *music*, designating or of any standard major or minor scale of eight tones.
**di·a·tribe** (dī′ə-trīb′), *n.* [< Gr. *dia-*, through + *tribein*, to rub], a bitter denunciation.
**dib·ble** (dib′'l), *n.* [var. of *dabble*], a pointed tool for making holes in the soil for seeds, bulbs, etc. *v.t.* [-BLED, -BLING], to make a hole in (the soil) with a dibble.
**dice** (dīs), *n.pl.* [*sing.* DIE (dī), DICE], [see DIE, *n.*], small cubes marked on each side with from one to six spots and used in gambling. *v.i.* [DICED, DICING], to play with dice. *v.t.* to cut into small cubes.
**di·chot·o·my** (dī-kot′ə-mi), *n.* [*pl.* -MIES], [< Gr. *dicha*, in two + *temnein*, to cut], division into two parts.
**dick** (dik), *n.* [Slang], a detective.
**dick·er** (dik′ẽr), *v.i. & v.t.* [< *dicker*, ten hides], to barter; haggle. *n.* a dickering.
**dick·ey** (dik′i), *n.* [*pl.* -EYS], [< nickname *Dick*], 1. a detachable collar or shirt front. 2. a small bird: also **dick′ey·bird′.** 3. a back seat in a carriage. Also sp. **dicky** [*pl.* -IES].
**di·cot·y·le·don** (dī′kot-'l-ē′d'n), *n.* a plant with two seed leaves (cotyledons). —**di′cot·y·le′don·ous,** *adj.*
**dict.,** 1. dictator. 2. dictionary.
**dic·ta·phone** (dik′tə-fōn′), *n.* [< *dictate* + *-phone*], a machine for recording and reproducing words spoken into it: a trademark (**Dictaphone**).
**dic·tate** (dik′tāt′; *also, for v.*, dik-tāt′), *v.t. & v.i.* [-TATED, -TATING], [< L. *dicere*, speak], 1. to speak (something) aloud for someone else to write down. 2. to command expressly. 3. to give (orders) with authority. *n.* an authoritative order. —**dic·ta′tion,** *n.*
**dic′ta·tor,** *n.* 1. a ruler with absolute power and authority. 2. one who speaks aloud words for another to write. —**dic·ta·to·ri·al** (dik′tə-tôr′i-əl), *adj.* —**dic·ta′tor·ship′,** *n.*
**dic·tion** (dik′shən), *n.* [< L. *dicere*, say], 1. manner of expression in words; wording. 2. enunciation.
**dic′tion·ar′y** (-er′i), *n.* [*pl.* -IES], [see DICTION], a book of alphabetically listed words in a language, with definitions, pronunciations, etc.
**dic·to·graph** (dik′tə-graf′, -gräf′), *n.* [< L. *dicere*, speak; + *-graph*], a telephonic instrument used for secretly listening to or recording conversations: a trademark (**Dictograph**).
**dic·tum** (dik′təm), *n.* [*pl.* -TUMS, -TA (-tə)], [L. < *dicere*, speak], a formal statement of opinion; pronouncement.
**did** (did), pt. of **do.**
**di·dac·tic** (dī-dak′tik), *adj.* [< Gr. *didaskein*, teach], 1. intended for instruction. 2. morally instructive. Also **di·dac′ti·cal.**
**did·dle** (did′'l), *v.t. & v.i.* [-DLED, -DLING], [< ?], [Colloq.], 1. to cheat. 2. to waste (time) in trifling. —**did′dler,** *n.*
**did·n't** (did′'nt), did not.
**Di·do** (dī′dō), *n.* in *Rom. legend*, founder and queen of Carthage.
**di·do** (dī′dō), *n.* [*pl.* -DOS, -DOES], [< ?], a mischievous trick; prank.
**die** (dī), *v.i.* [DIED, DYING], [< ON. *deyja*], 1. to stop living. 2. to stop functioning; end. 3. to lose force or activity. 4. to wither; become extinct. 5. [Colloq.], to wish very much: as, I'm *dying* to go. —**die away** (or **down**), to cease gradually. —**die off,** to die one by one until all are gone. —**die out,** 1. to die away. 2. to go out of existence.
**die** (dī), *n.* [*pl.*, for 1, DICE; for 2, DIES], [< L. *dare*, give], 1. either of a pair of dice. 2. any of various devices for molding, stamping, cutting, etc. *v.t.* [DIED, DYING], to mold, stamp, etc. with a die. —**the die is cast,** the decision made is irrevocable.
**die casting,** 1. the process of making a casting by forcing molten metal into a metallic mold, or die. 2. a casting so made.
**die′-hard′, die′hard′,** *n.* a stubborn, resistant person; esp., a conservative.

**di·e·lec·tric** (dī'ə-lek'trik), ***n.*** [< *dia-*, across + *electric*], in *electricity*, a nonconducting material. ***adj.*** nonconducting.

**di·er·e·sis** (dī-er'ə-sis), ***n.*** [*pl.* -SES (-sēz')], [< Gr. *dia-*, apart + *hairein*, take], the mark (¨), placed over the second of two consecutive vowels to show that it is pronounced separately.

**Die·sel** (dē'z'l, -s'l), ***n.*** [< R. *Diesel*, G. inventor], an internal-combustion engine that burns crude oil ignited by the heat from air compression: also **diesel, Diesel engine** (or **motor**).

**di·et** (dī'ət), ***n.*** [< Gr. *diaita*, manner of living], 1. the usual food and drink of a person or animal. 2. special, limited food and drink taken for health or to gain or lose weight. ***v.i. & v.t.*** to adhere to or place on a diet. **—di'e·tar'y** (-ə-ter'i), ***adj.***

**di·et** (dī'ət), ***n.*** [< ML. *dieta*, assembly], a formal assembly.

**di'e·tet'ic** (-ə-tet'ik), ***adj.*** of diet (food).

**di'e·tet'ics,** ***n.pl.*** [construed as sing.], the study of the kinds and quantities of food needed for health.

**di'e·ti'tian, di'e·ti'cian** (-tish'ən), ***n.*** an expert in dietetics.

**dif-,** dis-: used before *f*, as in *differ*.

**dif·fer** (dif'ẽr), ***v.i.*** [< L. *dis-*, apart + *ferre*, carry], 1. to be different (*from*). 2. to be of opposite or different opinions; disagree.

**dif'fer·ence** (dif'ẽr-əns, dif'rəns), ***n.*** 1. a being different. 2. the way in which people or things are different. 3. a differing in opinion; disagreement; quarrel. 4. the amount by which one quantity is greater or less than another.

**dif'fer·ent,** ***adj.*** 1. not alike (with *from*, or, colloquially, *than*). 2. distinct; separate. 3. unusual. **—dif'fer·ent·ly,** ***adv.***

**dif'fer·en'tial** (-en'shəl), ***adj.*** of, showing, or constituting a difference. ***n.*** 1. a differential gear. 2. in *math.*, a minute difference between values of a variable quantity.

**differential gear,** an arrangement of gears used in automobiles to allow one axle to turn faster than the other, as on curves.

**dif'fer·en'ti·ate'** (-en'shi-āt'), ***v.t.*** [-ATED, -ATING], 1. to constitute a difference in or between. 2. to make unlike. 3. to distinguish between. ***v.i.*** 1. to become different or differentiated. 2. to note a difference. **—dif'fer·en'ti·a'tion,** ***n.***

**dif·fi·cult** (dif'i-kəlt, -kult'), ***adj.*** 1. hard to do, understand, etc. 2. hard to satisfy, deal with, etc.

**dif'fi·cul'ty,** ***n.*** [*pl.* -TIES], [< L. *dis-*, not + *facilis*, easy], 1. a being difficult. 2. something difficult; obstacle or objection. 3. trouble. 4. a disagreement or quarrel.

**dif·fi·dent** (dif'i-dənt), ***adj.*** [< L. *dis-*, not + *fidere*, to trust], lacking self-confidence; shy. **—dif'fi·dence,** ***n.*** **—dif'fi·dent·ly,** ***adv.***

**dif·frac'tion,** ***n.*** [< L. *dis-*, apart + *frangere*, to break], 1. the breaking up of a ray of light into dark and light bands or into the colors of the spectrum. 2. a similar breaking up of other waves, as of sound.

**dif·fuse** (di-fūs'), ***adj.*** [< L. *dis-*, apart + *fundere*, pour], 1. spread out; not concentrated. 2. using more words than are needed. ***v.t. & v.i.*** (-fūz'), [-FUSED, -FUSING], to pour in every direction; spread widely. **—dif-fuse'ly** (-fūs'li), ***adv.*** **—dif·fu'sion,** ***n.*** **—dif·fu'sive,** ***adj.***

**dig** (dig), ***v.t.*** [DUG, DIGGING], [< OFr. *diguer*, excavate], 1. to turn up or remove (ground), as with a spade, the hands, claws, etc. 2. to make (a hole, etc.) by digging. 3. to get out by digging. 4. to find out, as by careful study. ***v.i.*** 1. to excavate. 2. [Colloq.], to work or study hard. ***n.*** 1. [Colloq.], a poke, nudge, etc.; hence, a sarcastic comment. 2. an archaeological excavation. **—dig'ger,** ***n.***

**di·gest** (dī'jest), ***n.*** [< L. *di-*, apart + *gerere*, to bear], a body of condensed, systematic information; summary. ***v.t.*** (di-jest', dī-), 1. to summarize. 2. to change (food) in the mouth, stomach, and intestines so that it can be absorbed by the body. 3. to think over; absorb mentally. **—di·gest'i·ble,** ***adj.***

**di·ges'tion,** ***n.*** 1. a digesting or being digested. 2. the ability to digest. **—di·ges'tive,** ***adj.***

**dig·it** (dij'it), ***n.*** [L. *digitus*], 1. a finger or toe. 2. any number from 0 to 9. **—dig'it·al,** ***adj.***

**digital computer,** a computer using numbers to perform logical and numerical calculations.

**dig·i·ta·lis** (dij'i-tal'is), ***n.*** [see DIGIT: from its thimblelike flowers], 1. the foxglove. 2. a medicine made from the leaves of the purple foxglove, used as a heart stimulant.

**dig·ni·fied** (dig'nə-fīd'), ***adj.*** having and showing dignity. **—dig'ni·fied'ly,** ***adv.***

**dig·ni·fy** (dig'nə-fī'), ***v.t.*** [-FIED, -FYING], [< L. *dignus*, worthy + *facere*, make], to give dignity to; make worthy; honor; exalt.

**dig·ni·tar·y** (dig'nə-ter'i), ***n.*** [*pl.* -IES], [< L. *dignitas*, dignity; + *-ary*], a person holding a high, dignified position.

**dig·ni·ty** (dig'nə-ti), ***n.*** [*pl.* -TIES], [< L. *dignus*, worthy], 1. worthiness; nobility. 2. high repute; honor. 3. the degree of worth or honor. 4. loftiness of manner; stateliness. 5. calm self-possession and self-respect.

**di·gress** (də-gres', dī-), ***v.i.*** [< L. *dis-*, apart + *gradi*, go], to turn aside from the main subject in talking or writing. **—di·gres'sion** (-gresh'ən), ***n.*** **—di·gres'sive,** ***adj.***

**dike** (dīk), ***n.*** [AS. *dic*, ditch], an embankment or dam made to prevent flooding by the sea or by a stream: also sp. **dyke.**

**di·lap·i·dat·ed** (di-lap'ə-dāt'id), ***adj.*** [< L. *dis-*, apart + *lapidare*, throw stones at], falling to pieces. **—di·lap'i·da'tion,** ***n.***

**di·late** (dī-lāt', di-), ***v.t. & v.i.*** [-LATED, -LATING], [< L. *dis-*, apart + *ferre*, bring], 1. to make or become wider or larger. 2. to speak or write at length (*on* or *upon* a subject). **—di·la'tion, dil·a·ta·tion** (dil'ə-tā'shən), ***n.***

**dil·a·to·ry** (dil'ə-tôr'i), ***adj.*** [see DILATE], 1. causing delay. 2. inclined to delay; slow.

**di·lem·ma** (di-lem'ə), ***n.*** [< Gr. *di-*, two + *lēmma*, assumption], any situation necessitating a choice between unpleasant alternatives.

**dil·et·tan·te** (dil'ə-tan'ti, -tänt'), ***n.*** [*pl.* -TES, -TI (-ti)], [It. < L. *delectare*, to delight], one who dabbles in art, literature, etc. in a superficial way. ***adj.*** of or like a dilettante.

**dil·i·gent** (dil'ə-jənt), ***adj.*** [< L. *dis-*, apart + *legare*, select], 1. persevering and careful in work; hardworking. 2. done carefully. **—dil'i·gence,** ***n.*** **—dil'i·gent·ly,** ***adv.***

**dill** (dil), ***n.*** [AS. *dile*], 1. a plant of the carrot family, with aromatic seeds used to flavor pickles, etc. 2. the seeds of this plant.

**dil·ly·dal·ly** (dil'i-dal'i), ***v.i.*** [-LIED, -LYING], [redupl. of *dally*], to waste time; loiter.

**di·lute** (di-lōōt', dī-), ***v.t.*** [-LUTED, -LUTING], [< L. *dis-*, off + *luere*, to wash], to thin down or weaken as by mixing with water. ***adj.*** diluted. **—di·lu'tion,** ***n.***

**dim** (dim), ***adj.*** [DIMMER, DIMMEST], [AS. *dimm*], 1. not bright, clear, or distinct; dull, obscure, etc. 2. not clearly seeing, hearing, or understanding. ***v.t. & v.i.*** [DIMMED, DIMMING], to make or grow dim.

**dim.,** 1. diminuendo. 2. diminutive.

**dime** (dīm), ***n.*** [< L. *decem*, ten], a coin of the U.S. and Canada equal to ten cents.

**di·men·sion** (də-men'shən), ***n.*** [< L. *dis-*, off + *metiri*, to measure], 1. any measurable extent, as length, breadth, etc. 2. *pl.* measurement in length, breadth, and, often, height. 3. scope. **—di·men'sion·al,** ***adj.***

**dime store,** a store where a wide variety of low-priced articles is sold.

**di·min·ish** (də-min′ish), ***v.t. & v.i.*** [< L. *deminuere*, make smaller], to make smaller in size, degree, importance, etc.; lessen. **—dim·i·nu·tion** (dim′ə-nū′shən), ***n.***

**di·min·u·en·do** (də-min′ū-en′dō), ***adj. & adv.*** [It.; see DIMINISH], in *music*, with gradually diminishing volume.

**di·min·u·tive** (də-min′yoo-tiv), ***adj.*** [see DIMINISH], very small; tiny. ***n.*** 1. a tiny person or thing. 2. a word formed from another by adding a suffix expressing smallness or endearment. **—di·min′u·tive·ly,** ***adv.***

**dim·i·ty** (dim′ə-ti), ***n.*** [*pl.* -TIES], [< Gr. *dis-*, two + *mitos*, thread], a thin, strong, corded cotton cloth, often figured.

**dim′mer,** ***n.*** a device for dimming electric lights.

**dim·ple** (dim′p'l), ***n.*** [ME. *dimpul*], a small, natural hollow, as on the cheek. ***v.t. & v.i.*** [-PLED, -PLING], to form dimples (in).

**din** (din), ***n.*** [AS. *dyne*], a loud, continuous noise; confused clamor. ***v.t.*** [DINNED, DINNING], 1. to strike with a din. 2. to repeat insistently or noisily. ***v.i.*** to make a din.

**dine** (dīn), ***v.i.*** [DINED, DINING], [ult. < L. *dis-*, away + *jejunus*, fasting], to eat dinner. ***v.t.*** to entertain at dinner.

**din·er** (dīn′ẽr), ***n.*** 1. a person eating dinner. 2. a railroad car equipped to serve meals. 3. a restaurant built to look like such a car.

**di·nette** (dī-net′), ***n.*** an alcove or small space used as a dining room.

**ding** (diŋ), ***n.*** [< ON. *dengja*, to hammer], the sound of a bell: also **ding′-dong′** (-dôŋ′).

**din·ghy** (diŋ′gi), ***n.*** [*pl.* -GHIES], [Hind. *dingī*], 1. a rowboat. 2. any small boat used as a tender, etc. Also **din′gey** [*pl.* -GEYS], **din′gy** [*pl.* -GIES].

**din·gy** (din′ji), ***adj.*** [-GIER, -GIEST], [? < *dung* + *-y*], 1. dirty-colored. 2. dismal; shabby.

**dink·y** (diŋ′ki), ***adj.*** [-KIER, -KIEST], [Scot. dial. *dink*, trim], [Slang], small.

**din·ner** (din′ẽr), ***n.*** [see DINE], 1. the chief meal of the day. 2. a formal meal honoring a person or event.

**di·no·saur** (dī′nə-sôr′), ***n.*** [< Gr. *deinos*, terrible + *sauros*, lizard], any of a group of huge extinct reptiles.

**dint** (dint), ***n.*** [AS. *dynt*, a blow], 1. force; exertion. 2. a dent. ***v.t.*** to dent.

**di·o·cese** (dī′ə-sēs′, -sis), ***n.*** [< Gr. *dioikein*, keep house], the district under a bishop's jurisdiction. **—di·oc′e·san** (-os′ə-s'n), ***adj.***

**di·oe·cious** (dī-ē′shəs), ***adj.*** [< *di-* + Gr. *oikos*, house], in *biology*, having the male and female reproductive organs in separate individuals.

**Di·o·ny·sus, Di·o·ny·sos** (dī′ə-nī′səs), ***n.*** the Greek god of vegetation and wine.

**di·ox·ide** (dī-ok′sīd), ***n.*** an oxide with two atoms of oxygen per molecule.

**dip** (dip), ***v.t.*** [DIPPED, DIPPING], [AS. *dyppan*], 1. to put into liquid for only a moment. 2. to take out as by scooping up. 3. to lower (a flag, etc.) and immediately raise again. ***v.i.*** 1. to plunge into water, etc. and quickly come out. 2. to sink down suddenly. 3. to slope down. 4. to lower a container, the hand, etc. as into water. 5. to read or study at random (with *into*). ***n.*** 1. a dipping or being dipped. 2. a plunge into water, etc. 3. a liquid into which something is dipped. 4. whatever is removed by dipping. 5. a downward slope or plunge. 6. [Colloq.], liquid sauce.

**diph·the·ri·a** (dif-thêr′i-ə, dip-), ***n.*** [< Gr. *diphthera*, leather], an acute infectious disease characterized by high fever and the formation of a membrane in the air passages.

**diph·thong** (dif′thôŋ, dip′-), ***n.*** [< Gr. *di-*, two + *phthongos*, sound], a sound made by gliding from one vowel to another in one syllable, as in *oil*, *out*. **—diph·thon′gal,** ***adj.***

**di·plo·ma** (di-plō′mə), ***n.*** [< Gr. *diplōma*, folded letter], a certificate issued by a school, college, etc. indicating graduation or conferring a degree.

**di·plo′ma·cy** (-si), ***n.*** [*pl.* -CIES], [< L. *diploma*, official document; see DIPLOMA], 1. the conducting of relations between nations. 2. tact.

**dip·lo·mat** (dip′lə-mat′), ***n.*** 1. a representative of a government who conducts relations with another government. 2. a tactful person.

**dip′lo·mat′ic,** ***adj.*** 1. of diplomacy. 2. tactful. **—dip′lo·mat′i·cal·ly,** ***adv.***

**dip′per,** ***n.*** 1. a long-handled cup, etc. for dipping. 2. [D-], either of two groups of stars in the shape of a dipper (**Big Dipper** and **Little Dipper**).

**dip·so·ma·ni·a** (dip′sə-mā′ni-ə), ***n.*** [< Gr. *dipsa*, thirst + *mania*, madness], an abnormal craving for alcoholic drink. **—dip′so·ma′ni·ac** (-ak), ***n.***

**dire** (dīr), ***adj.*** [DIRER, DIREST], [L. *dirus*], dreadful; terrible.

**di·rect** (də-rekt′, dī-), ***adj.*** [< L. *dis-*, apart + *regere*, to rule], 1. straight; not deviating or interrupted. 2. straightforward; frank. 3. immediate. 4. with nothing between. 5. lineal. 6 exact; complete: as, the *direct* opposite. ***v.t.*** 1. to manage; guide; conduct. 2. to order; command. 3. to turn or point; aim; head. 4. to tell (a person) the way to a place. 5. to address (a letter, etc.). 6. to supervise the action and effects of (a play, etc.). ***adv.*** directly. **—di·rect′ness,** ***n.***

**direct current,** an electric current flowing in one direction.

**di·rec·tion** (də-rek′shən, dī-), ***n.*** 1. a directing; management; control. 2. the address on a letter, etc. 3. *pl.* instructions for doing, using, etc. 4. an order; command. 5. the point toward which one is moving or facing. 6. the line leading to a place: as, in the *direction* of Berlin. **—di·rec′tion·al,** ***adj.***

**di·rec′tive** (-tiv), ***adj.*** directing. ***n.*** a general order issued by a central office, military unit, etc.

**di·rect′ly,** ***adv.*** 1. in a direct way or line; straight. 2. with nothing coming between. 3. exactly: as, *directly* opposite. 4. instantly.

**direct object,** the word or words that denote the receiver of the action of a verb, as *me* in *he hit me*.

**di·rec′tor,** ***n.*** 1. one who directs, as a play, etc. 2. a member of a board directing the affairs of a corporation, etc.

**di·rec′to·rate** (-tə-rit), ***n.*** 1. the office of director. 2. a board of directors.

**di·rec′to·ry** (-tə-ri), ***adj.*** directing; advising. ***n.*** [*pl.* -RIES], a book or list of the names and addresses of a specific group.

**dire·ful** (dīr′fəl), ***adj.*** dire.

**dirge** (dũrj), ***n.*** [< L. *dirige* (direct), first word of a funeral hymn], a song, poem, etc. of grief or mourning.

**dir·i·gi·ble** (dir′i-jə-b'l), ***adj.*** [see DIRECT & -IBLE], that can be steered. ***n.*** a long, cigar-shaped balloon that can be steered.

**dirk** (dũrk), ***n.*** [< ?], a short dagger.

**dirt** (dũrt), ***n.*** [< ON. *drītr*, excrement], 1. any unclean matter, as mud, trash, etc.; filth. 2. earth; soil. 3. dirtiness; uncleanness; obscenity. 4. malicious talk; gossip.

**dirt′y,** ***adj.*** [-IER, -IEST], 1. soiled; unclean. 2. obscene. 3. contemptible; mean. 4. rough: as, *dirty* weather. ***v.t. & v.i.*** [-IED, -YING], to make or become dirty; soil.

**dis-,** [< L.], a prefix denoting *separation*, *negation*, or *reversal*, as in *disperse*, *dishonest*, *disown*.

**dis·a·bil·i·ty** (dis′ə-bil′ə-ti), ***n.*** [*pl.* -TIES], 1. a disabled condition. 2. that which disables or disqualifies.

**dis·a′ble** (-ā′b'l), *v.t.* [-BLED, -BLING], 1. to make unable or unfit; cripple. 2. to disqualify legally. **—dis·a′ble·ment,** *n.*

**dis·a·buse** (dis′ə-būz′), *v.t.* [-BUSED, -BUSING], to rid of false ideas.

**dis·ad·van·tage** (dis′əd-van′tij), *n.* 1. an unfavorable situation; drawback; handicap. 2. loss; injury. **—dis·ad′van·ta′geous** (-ad′vən-tā′jəs), *adj.* **—dis·ad′van·ta′geous·ly,** *adv.*

**dis·af·fect** (dis′ə-fekt′), *v.t.* to make unfriendly, discontented, or disloyal. **—dis′af·fec′tion,** *n.*

**dis·a·gree** (dis′ə-grē′), *v.i.* [-GREED, -GREEING], 1. to be unlike; differ. 2. to differ in opinion. 3. to quarrel or dispute. 4. to be unsuitable or harmful (with *with*).

**dis′a·gree′a·ble,** *adj.* 1. unpleasant; offensive. 2. quarrelsome. **—dis′a·gree′a·bly,** *adv.*

**dis′a·gree′ment,** *n.* 1. a disagreeing. 2. difference; incongruity; discrepancy. 3. difference of opinion. 4. a quarrel or dispute.

**dis·al·low** (dis′ə-lou′), *v.t.* to refuse to allow (a claim, etc.).

**dis·ap·pear** (dis′ə-pêr′), *v.i.* 1. to cease to be seen; vanish. 2. to cease being. **—dis′ap·pear′ance,** *n.*

**dis·ap·point** (dis′ə-point′), *v.t.* 1. to fail to satisfy the hopes or expectations of. 2. to balk; thwart. **—dis′ap·point′ment,** *n.*

**dis·ap·pro·ba·tion** (dis′ap-rə-bā′shən), *n.* disapproval; unfavorable opinion.

**dis·ap·prove** (dis′ə-proov′), *v.t.* & *v.i.* [-PROVED, -PROVING], 1. to have or express an unfavorable opinion (of). 2. to refuse to approve. **—dis′ap·prov′al,** *n.*

**dis·arm** (dis-ärm′), *v.t.* 1. to take away weapons from. 2. to make harmless. 3. to make friendly. *v.i.* to reduce armed forces and armaments. **—dis·ar′ma·ment,** *n.*

**dis·arm′ing,** *adj.* removing hostility.

**dis·ar·range** (dis′ə-rānj′), *v.t.* [-RANGED, -RANGING], to put out of order; disorder. **—dis′ar·range′ment,** *n.*

**dis·ar·ray** (dis′ə-rā′), *v.t.* to throw into disorder or confusion. *n.* disorder; confusion.

**dis·as·sem·ble** (dis′ə-sem′b'l), *v.t.* [-BLED, -BLING], to take apart. **—dis′as·sem′bly,** *n.*

**dis·as·ter** (di-zas′tēr), *n.* [< L. *dis-* + *astrum,* star], any event causing great harm or damage; calamity. **—dis·as′trous** (-trəs), *adj.*

**dis·a·vow** (dis′ə-vou′), *v.t.* to deny any knowledge of or responsibility for; disclaim. **—dis′a·vow′al,** *n.*

**dis·band** (dis-band′), *v.i.* & *v.t.* to stop existing as an organization.

**dis·bar** (dis-bär′), *v.t.* [-BARRED, -BARRING], to deprive (a lawyer) of the right to practice law. **—dis·bar′ment,** *n.*

**dis′be·lieve′,** *v.t.* & *v.i.* [-LIEVED, -LIEVING], to fail to believe (*in*). **—dis′be·lief′,** *n.*

**dis·burse** (dis-būrs′), *v.t.* [-BURSED, -BURSING], [< OFr. *desbourser*], to pay out; expend. **—dis·burse′ment,** *n.*

**disc** (disk), *n.* a disk.

**dis·card** (dis-kärd′), *v.t.* [< OFr.; see DIS- & CARD], 1. in *card games,* to throw away (undesired cards). 2. to get rid of as no longer useful. *n.* (dis′kärd), 1. a discarding or being discarded. 2. something discarded.

**dis·cern** (di-zūrn′, -sūrn′), *v.t.* [< L. *dis-*, apart + *cernere,* to separate], to perceive or recognize clearly. **—dis·cern′i·ble,** *adj.*

**dis·cern′ing,** *adj.* keenly perceptive; shrewd.

**dis·charge** (dis-chärj′), *v.t.* [-CHARGED, -CHARGING], [< L. *dis-*, from + *carrus,* wagon], 1. to release or dismiss: as, *discharged* from the army. 2. to unload (a cargo). 3. to shoot (a gun or projectile). 4. to emit: as, the sore *discharges* pus. 5. to pay (a debt) or perform (a duty). 6. in *electricity,* to remove stored energy from (a battery, etc.). *v.i.* 1. to get rid of a load, etc. 2. to be released or thrown off. 3. to go off, as a gun. *n.* (*also* dis′chärj′), 1. a discharging or being discharged. 2. that which discharges or is discharged.

**dis·ci·ple** (di-sī′p'l), *n.* [orig. prob. < L. *dis-*, apart + *capere,* hold], 1. a pupil or follower of any teacher or school. 2. an early follower of Jesus, esp. any of the twelve sent out to teach the gospel. **—dis·ci′ple·ship′,** *n.*

**dis·ci·pli·nar·i·an** (dis′ə-pli-nâr′i-ən), *n.* one who enforces discipline.

**dis·ci·pline** (dis′ə-plin), *n.* [see DISCIPLE], 1. training that develops self-control, character, etc. 2. orderly conduct. 3. treatment that corrects or punishes. *v.t.* [-PLINED, -PLINING], 1. to train; control. 2. to punish. **—dis′ci·pli·nar′y** (-pli-ner′i), *adj.*

**dis·claim** (dis-klām′), *v.t.* 1. to give up any claim to; disown. 2. to repudiate.

**dis·claim′er,** *n.* a denial or renunciation, as of a claim or title.

**dis·close** (dis-klōz′), *v.t.* [-CLOSED, -CLOSING], 1. to uncover; bring into the open. 2. to reveal. **—dis·clos′ure** (-klō′zhēr), *n.*

**dis·col′or,** *v.t.* & *v.i.* to change in color; stain; tarnish: also, Brit. sp., **discolour.**

**dis·com·fit** (dis-kum′fit), *v.t.* [< L. *dis-* + *conficere,* prepare], 1. to frustrate the plans of. 2. to embarrass. **—dis·com′fi·ture** (-fi-chēr), *n.*

**dis·com′fort,** *n.* 1. lack of comfort; uneasiness. 2. anything causing this. *v.t.* to cause discomfort to.

**dis·com·mode** (dis′kə-mōd′), *v.t.* [-MODED, -MODING], [< *dis-* + L. *commodare,* make suitable], to inconvenience; disturb.

**dis·com·pose** (dis′kəm-pōz′), *v.t.* [-POSED, -POSING], 1. to disturb; disconcert. 2. to disorder. **—dis′com·po′sure** (-pō′zhēr), *n.*

**dis·con·cert** (dis′kən-sūrt′), *v.t.* to upset; confuse. **—dis′con·cert′ed,** *adj.*

**dis·con·nect** (dis′kə-nekt′), *v.t.* to break the connection between. **—dis′con·nec′tion,** *n.*

**dis′con·nect′ed,** *adj.* 1. separated. 2. incoherent. **—dis′con·nect′ed·ly,** *adv.*

**dis·con·so·late** (dis-kon′sə-lit), *adj.* [see DIS- & CONSOLE, *v.*], 1. inconsolable; hopeless. 2. cheerless. **—dis·con′so·late·ly,** *adv.*

**dis·con·tent** (dis′kən-tent′), *adj.* discontented. *n.* dissatisfaction with one's situation: also **dis′con·tent′ment.** *v.t.* to make discontented.

**dis′con·tent′ed,** *adj.* not contented; dissatisfied; restless. **—dis′con·tent′ed·ly,** *adv.*

**dis·con·tin·ue** (dis′kən-tin′ū), *v.t.* & *v.i.* [-UED, -UING], to stop; cease; give up. **—dis′con·tin′u·ance, dis′con·tin′u·a′tion,** *n.*

**dis·cord** (dis′kôrd), *n.* [< L. *dis-*, apart + *cor,* heart], 1. disagreement. 2. a harsh or confused noise. **—dis·cord′ant,** *adj.*

**dis·co·thèque** (dis′kə-tek), *n.* [Fr. < *disque,* record + *bibliothèque,* library], a café, etc. for dancing to recorded popular music.

**dis·count** (dis′kount; *for v., also* dis-kount′), *v.t.* [< L. *dis-*, apart + *computare,* compute], 1. to deduct, as from an original price or debt. 2. to pay or receive the value of (a bill, promissory note, etc.) minus a deduction for interest. 3. to allow for exaggeration, bias, etc. in (a story, etc.). 4. to disregard. 5. to lessen the effect of by anticipating. *n.* 1. a deduction. 2. the rate of interest charged on a discounted bill, etc.

**dis·cour·age** (dis-kūr′ij), *v.t.* [-AGED, -AGING], 1. to deprive of courage; dishearten. 2. to persuade (a person) to refrain. 3. to try to prevent by disapproving. **—dis·cour′age·ment,** *n.* **—dis·cour′ag·ing·ly,** *adv.*

**dis·course** (dis′kôrs), *n.* [< L. *dis-*, from + *currere,* to run], 1. talk; conversation. 2. a formal treatment of a subject, spoken or written. *v.i.* (dis-kôrs′), [-COURSED, -COURSING], to talk; converse.

**dis·cour·te·ous** (dis-kūr′ti-əs), *adj.* impolite; ill-mannered. **—dis·cour′te·ous·ly,** *adv.*

**dis·cour′te·sy** (-tə-si), *n.* 1. impoliteness;

rudeness. 2. [*pl.* -SIES], a rude or impolite act or remark.

**dis·cov·er** (dis-kuv′ẽr), ***v.t.*** [see DIS- & COVER], 1. to be the first to find, see, etc. 2. to learn of the existence of. **—dis·cov′er-a·ble,** ***adj.*** **—dis·cov′er·er,** ***n.***

**dis·cov′er·y,** ***n.*** [*pl.* -IES], 1. a discovering. 2. anything discovered.

**dis·cred·it** (dis-kred′it), ***v.t.*** 1. to disbelieve. 2. to cast doubt on. 3. to disgrace. ***n.*** 1. loss of belief; doubt. 2. disgrace. **—dis·cred′it·a·ble,** ***adj.***

**dis·creet** (dis-krēt′), ***adj.*** [see DISCERN], careful about what one says or does; prudent.

**dis·crep·an·cy** (dis-krep′ən-si), ***n.*** [*pl.* -CIES], [< L. *dis-*, from + *crepare*, to rattle], disagreement; inconsistency.

**dis·crete** (dis-krēt′), ***adj.*** [see DISCERN], 1. separate and distinct. 2. made up of distinct parts. **—dis·crete′ly,** ***adv.***

**dis·cre·tion** (dis-kresh′ən), ***n.*** 1. the freedom to make decisions. 2. the quality of being discreet; prudence. **—dis·cre′tion·ar′y** (-ə-ner′i), ***adj.***

**dis·crim·i·nate** (dis-krim′ə-nāt′), ***v.i.*** [-NATED, -NATING], [< L. *dis-*, apart + *crimen*, verdict], 1. to distinguish. 2. to make distinctions in treatment. **—dis·crim′i·nat′ing,** ***adj.*** **—dis·crim′i·na′tion,** ***n.***

**dis·crim′i·na·to′ry** (-nə-tôr′i), ***adj.*** showing discrimination or bias.

**dis·cur·sive** (dis-kũr′siv), ***adj.*** [see DISCOURSE], wandering from one topic to another; rambling. **—dis·cur′sive·ness,** ***n.***

**dis·cus** (dis′kəs), ***n.*** [*pl.* -CUSES, -CI (dis′ī)], [< Gr. *diskos*], a heavy disk of metal, etc., thrown in a contest of strength and skill.

**dis·cuss** (dis-kus′), ***v.t.*** [< L. *dis-*, apart + *quatere*, shake], to talk or write about; consider the pros and cons of. **—dis·cus′sion** (-kush′ən), ***n.***

**dis·dain** (dis-dān′), ***v.t.*** [< L. *dis-*, not + *dignari*, deign], to regard as beneath one's dignity or status; scorn. ***n.*** aloof contempt. **—dis·dain′ful,** ***adj.*** **—dis·dain′ful·ly,** ***adv.***

**dis·ease** (di-zēz′), ***n.*** [see DIS- & EASE], 1. illness in general. 2. a particular destructive process in an organism. **—dis·eased′,** ***adj.***

**dis·em·bark** (dis′im-bärk′), ***v.t. & v.i.*** to put or go ashore from a ship; land. **—dis′em-bar·ka′tion,** ***n.***

**dis·em·bod·y** (dis′im-bod′i), ***v.t.*** [-BODIED, -BODYING], to free (a spirit, etc.) from bodily existence.

**dis·em·bow·el** (dis′im-bou′əl), ***v.t.*** [-ELED or -ELLED, -ELING or -ELLING], to take out the bowels of; eviscerate.

**dis·en·chant** (dis′in-chant′, -chänt′), ***v.t.*** to free from an enchantment or illusion.

**dis′en·gage′,** ***v.t. & v.i.*** [-GAGED, -GAGING], to release or get loose from something that engages, holds, etc. **—dis′en·gage′ment,** ***n.***

**dis′en·tan′gle,** ***v.t.*** [-GLED, -GLING], to free from something that entangles, confuses, etc.; extricate. **—dis′en·tan′gle·ment,** ***n.***

**dis′es·tab′lish,** ***v.t.*** to deprive of the status of being established.

**dis·fa·vor** (dis-fā′vẽr), ***n.*** 1. an unfavorable opinion; dislike; disapproval. 2. the state of being disliked, etc. ***v.t.*** to regard or treat unfavorably. Also, Brit. sp., **disfavour.**

**dis·fig·ure** (dis-fig′yẽr), ***v.t.*** [-URED, -URING], to hurt the appearance of; deface.

**dis·gorge** (dis-gôrj′), ***v.t. & v.i.*** [-GORGED, -GORGING], [< OFr.; see DIS- & GORGE], 1. to vomit. 2. to pour forth (its contents).

**dis·grace** (dis-grās′), ***n.*** [< It. *dis-*, not + *grazia*, favor], 1. loss of favor or respect; shame; disrepute. 2. a person or thing bringing shame. ***v.t.*** [-GRACED, -GRACING], to bring shame upon.

**dis·grace′ful,** ***adj.*** causing or characterized by disgrace; shameful.

**dis·grun·tle** (dis-grun′t'l), ***v.t.*** [-TLED, -TLING], [ult. < *dis-* + *grunt*], to make peevishly discontented; make sulky.

**dis·guise** (dis-gīz′), ***v.t.*** [-GUISED, -GUISING], [< OFr.; see DIS- & GUISE], 1. to make appear, sound, etc. so different as to be unrecognizable. 2. to hide the real nature of. ***n.*** 1. anything used for disguising. 2. a being disguised. **—dis·guis′ed·ly,** ***adv.***

**dis·gust** (dis-gust′), ***n.*** [< *dis-* + L. *gustus*, taste], a sickening dislike; loathing; repugnance. ***v.t.*** to cause to feel disgust. **—dis-gust′ed,** ***adj.*** **—dis·gust′ing,** ***adj.***

**dish** (dish), ***n.*** [see DISK], 1. a shallow, concave container for holding food, as a plate, bowl, etc. 2. as much as a dish holds. 3. a particular kind of food: as, a tasty *dish*. ***v.t.*** to serve in a dish (with *up* or *out*).

**dis·ha·bille** (dis′ə-bēl′), ***n.*** [< Fr. < *dés-*, dis- + *habiller*, to dress], the state of being dressed only partially or in night clothes.

**dis·har′mo·ny,** ***n.*** [*pl.* -NIES], absence of harmony.

**dis·heart·en** (dis-här′t'n), ***v.t.*** to discourage; depress. **—dis·heart′en·ment,** ***n.***

**di·shev·el** (di-shev′'l), ***v.t.*** [-ELED or -ELLED, -ELING or -ELLING], [< OFr. *des-*, apart + *chevel*, hair], to cause (hair, clothes, etc.) to become disarranged; rumple.

**dis·hon′est,** ***adj.*** not honest; not to be trusted. **—dis·hon′est·ly,** ***adv.***

**dis·hon′es·ty,** ***n.*** 1. a being dishonest. 2. [*pl.* -TIES], a dishonest act.

**dis·hon′or,** ***n.*** 1. loss of honor or respect; shame; disgrace. 2. a cause of dishonor. ***v.t.*** to insult or disgrace. **—dis·hon′or·a·ble,** ***adj.*** **—dis·hon′or·a·bly,** ***adv.***

**dis′il·lu′sion,** ***v.t.*** to free from illusion; disenchant. ***n.*** a disillusioning or being disillusioned; also **dis′il·lu′sion·ment.**

**dis·in·cline** (dis′in-klīn′), ***v.t. & v.i.*** to make or be unwilling. **—dis′in·cli·na′tion,** ***n.***

**dis·in·fect** (dis′in-fekt′), ***v.t.*** to destroy the harmful bacteria, viruses, etc. in; sterilize. **—dis′in·fec′tant,** ***adj.*** **—dis′in·fec′tion,** ***n.***

**dis·in·her·it** (dis′in-her′it), ***v.t.*** to deprive of an inheritance. **—dis′in·her′i·tance,** ***n.***

**dis·in·te·grate** (dis-in′tə-grāt′), ***v.t. & v.i.*** [-GRATED, -GRATING], to separate into parts or fragments; break up. **—dis·in′te·gra·ble** (-grə-b'l), ***adj.*** **—dis·in′te·gra′tion,** ***n.***

**dis·in·ter** (dis′in-tũr′), ***v.t.*** [-TERRED, -TERRING], to dig up from a grave, etc.

**dis·in·ter·est·ed** (dis-in′tẽr-is-tid, -tris-tid), ***adj.*** 1. impartial; unbiased. 2. [Colloq.], uninterested. **—dis·in′ter·est·ed·ly,** ***adv.***

**dis·joint′,** ***v.t.*** 1. to put out of joint; dislocate. 2. to dismember. 3. to destroy the unity, connections, etc. of. ***v.i.*** to come apart at the joints. **—dis·joint′ed,** ***adj.***

**dis·junc·tive** (dis-juŋk′tiv), ***adj.*** 1. separating or causing to separate. 2. in *grammar*, indicating a contrast or an alternative: as, *either . . . or*, *but*, and *although* are *disjunctive* conjunctions.

**disk** (disk), ***n.*** [Gr. *diskos*], 1. any thin, flat, circular thing. 2. a phonograph record. Also sp. **disc.**

**disk jockey,** one who conducts a radio program of recorded music.

**dis·like′,** ***v.t.*** [-LIKED, -LIKING], to have a feeling of not liking. ***n.*** a feeling of not liking; distaste.

**dis·lo·cate** (dis′lō-kāt′), ***v.t.*** [-CATED, -CATING], 1. to put out of joint. 2. to disarrange. **—dis′lo·ca′tion,** ***n.***

**dis·lodge′,** ***v.t. & v.i.*** [-LODGED, -LODGING], to remove or go from a position or place of lodgment. **—dis·lodg′ment,** ***n.***

**dis·loy′al,** ***adj.*** not loyal; perfidious. **—dis-loy′al·ty** [*pl.* -TIES], ***n.*** **—dis·loy′al·ly,** ***adv.***

**dis·mal** (diz′m'l), ***adj.*** [< L. *dies mali*, evil days], 1. causing gloom or misery. 2. dark and gloomy; dreary. **—dis′mal·ly,** ***adv.***

**dis·man·tle** (dis-man′t'l), ***v.t.*** [-TLED,

-TLING], [see DIS- & MANTLE], 1. to strip of covering. 2. to strip (a house, etc.) as of furniture. 3. to take apart.
**dis·may** (dis-mā′), ***v.t.*** [< Anglo-Fr.], to make afraid at the prospect of trouble; daunt. ***n.*** a loss of courage.
**dis·mem·ber** (dis-mem′bẽr), ***v.t.*** [see DIS- & MEMBER], 1. to cut or tear the limbs from. 2. to cut or pull to pieces.
**dis·miss** (dis-mis′), ***v.t.*** [< L. *dis-*, from + *mittere*, send], 1. to request or allow to leave. 2. to discharge from an office, employment, etc. 3. to put aside mentally. **—dis·miss′al, *n.***
**dis·mount′,** ***v.i.*** to get off, as from a horse. ***v.t.*** 1. to remove (a thing) from its mounting. 2. to cause to get off. 3. to take (a machine) apart.
**dis·o·be·di·ence** (dis′ə-bē′di-əns), ***n.*** refusal to obey. **—dis′o·be′di·ent, *adj.***
**dis′o·bey′,** ***v.t. & v.i.*** to refuse or fail to obey.
**dis′o·blige′,** ***v.t.*** [-BLIGED, -BLIGING], to refuse to oblige. **—dis′o·blig′ing, *adj.***
**dis·or′der,** ***n.*** 1. lack of order; confusion. 2. a breach of public peace; riot. 3. irregularity. 4. an upset of normal function; disease. ***v.t.*** 1. to throw into disorder. 2. to upset the normal functions of.
**dis·or′der·ly,** ***adj.*** 1. not orderly; untidy; unsystematic. 2. unruly; riotous. 3. violating public peace, safety, etc. ***adv.*** in a disorderly manner. **—dis·or′der·li·ness, *n.***
**dis·or·gan·ize** (dis-ôr′gə-nīz′), ***v.t.*** [-IZED, -IZING], to break up the order or system of; throw into confusion. **—dis·or′gan·i·za′tion, *n.* —dis·or′gan·i′zer, *n.***
**dis·own′,** ***v.t.*** to refuse to acknowledge as one's own; cast off.
**dis·par·age** (dis-par′ij), ***v.t.*** [-AGED, -AGING], [< OFr. *des-* (see DIS-) + *parage*, rank], 1. to discredit. 2. to belittle. **—dis·par′age·ment, *n.* —dis·par′ag·er, *n.***
**dis·pa·rate** (dis′pə-rit), ***adj.*** [< L. *dis-*, not + *par*, equal], distinct or different in kind. **—dis·par′i·ty** (-par′ə-ti) [*pl.* -TIES], ***n.***
**dis·pas′sion·ate,** ***adj.*** free from passion, emotion, or bias; calm; impartial. **—dis·pas′sion, *n.* —dis·pas′sion·ate·ly, *adv.***
**dis·patch** (dis-pach′), ***v.t.*** [< Sp. *despachar*, to expedite], 1. to send off, or on an errand. 2. to kill. 3. to finish quickly. ***n.*** 1. a sending off. 2. a killing. 3. speed; haste. 4. a message. 5. a news story sent to a paper. **—dis·patch′er, *n.***
**dis·pel** (dis-pel′), ***v.t.*** [-PELLED, -PELLING], [< L. *dis-*, away + *pellere*, to drive], to scatter and drive away. **—dis·pel′ler, *n.***
**dis·pen·sa·ble** (dis-pen′sə-b'l), ***adj.*** 1. that can be given out. 2. that can be dispensed with; not needed.
**dis·pen′sa·ry** (-sə-ri), ***n.*** [*pl.* -RIES], 1. a room where medicines are made up and given out. 2. a place where medical treatment is given free or cheaply.
**dis·pen·sa·tion** (dis′pən-sā′shən), ***n.*** 1. a dispensing. 2. anything distributed. 3. an administrative system. 4. a release from an obligation. 5. in *theology*, *a*) the ordering of events under divine authority. *b*) any religious system. **—dis′pen·sa′tor, *n.***
**dis·pense** (dis-pens′), ***v.t.*** [-PENSED, -PENSING], [< L. *dis-*, out + *pendere*, weigh], 1. to give out; distribute. 2. to prepare and give out (medicines, etc.). 3. to administer: as, to *dispense* the law. 4. to exempt; excuse. **—dispense with,** 1. to get rid of. 2. to do without. **—dis·pens′er, *n.***
**dis·perse** (dis-pũrs′), ***v.t.*** [-PERSED, -PERSING], [< L. *dis-*, out + *spargere*, strew], 1. to break up and scatter. 2. to dispel (mist, etc.). ***v.i.*** to scatter. **—dis·per′sal, *n.* —dis·per′sion, *n.* —dis·pers′er, *n.***
**dis·pir·it** (di-spir′it), ***v.t.*** to depress; dishearten. **—dis·pir′it·ed, *adj.***
**dis·place′,** ***v.t.*** [-PLACED, -PLACING], 1. to move from its customary place. 2. to remove from office. 3. to replace.
**dis·placed′ person,** a person left homeless in a foreign country by war.
**dis·place′ment,** ***n.*** 1. a displacing or being displaced. 2. the weight or volume of air, water, etc. displaced by a floating object.
**dis·play** (dis-plā′), ***v.t.*** [< L. *dis-*, apart + *plicare*, to fold], 1. to unfold; spread out. 2. to show off; exhibit. ***n.*** 1. an exhibition. 2. anything displayed. 3. ostentation; show.
**dis·please′,** ***v.t. & v.i.*** [-PLEASED, -PLEASING], to fail to please; offend.
**dis·pleas′ure** (-plezh′ẽr), ***n.*** a being displeased; dissatisfaction.
**dis·port** (dis-pôrt′), ***v.i.*** [< OFr. *des-* (see DIS-) + *porter*, carry], to play; frolic. ***v.t.*** to amuse (oneself).
**dis·pose** (dis-pōz′), ***v.t.*** [-POSED, -POSING], [see DIS- & POSE], 1. to arrange. 2. to settle (affairs). 3. to make use of. 4. to incline mentally. **—dispose of,** 1. to deal with; settle. 2. to give away. 3. to sell. 4. to get rid of. **—dis·pos′a·ble, *adj.* —dis·pos′al, *n.***
**dis·po·si·tion** (dis′pə-zish′ən), ***n.*** 1. orderly arrangement. 2. management of affairs. 3. a giving away (*of*). 4. a tendency. 5. one's temperament.
**dis′pos·sess′,** ***v.t.*** to deprive of the possession of land, a house, etc.; oust.
**dis′pro·por′tion,** ***n.*** a lack of proportion. **—dis′pro·por′tion·ate, *adj.***
**dis·prove′,** ***v.t.*** [-PROVED, -PROVING], to prove to be false or in error. **—dis·proof′, *n.***
**dis·pu·ta·tion** (dis′pyoo-tā′shən), ***n.*** 1. a disputing; dispute. 2. debate. **—dis′pu·ta′tious** (-shəs), ***adj.***
**dis·pute** (dis-pūt′), ***v.i.*** [-PUTED, -PUTING], [< L. *dis-*, apart + *putare*, think], 1. to argue; debate. 2. to quarrel. ***v.t.*** 1. to argue or debate (a question). 2. to doubt. 3. to oppose in any way. ***n.*** 1. a disputing; argument; debate. 2. a quarrel. **—in dispute,** not settled. **—dis·pu′ta·ble, *adj.* —dis·pu·tant** (dis′pyoo-tənt), ***adj. & n.***
**dis·qual′i·fy′,** ***v.t.*** [-FIED, -FYING], to make or declare unqualified, unfit, or ineligible. **—dis·qual′i·fi·ca′tion, *n.***
**dis·qui·et** (dis-kwī′ət), ***v.t.*** to make anxious or restless; disturb. ***n.*** restlessness; anxiety: also **dis·qui′e·tude′** (-ə-tōōd′, -tūd′).
**dis·qui·si·tion** (dis′kwə-zish′ən), ***n.*** [< L. *dis-*, apart + *quaerere*, seek], a formal discourse; treatise.
**dis′re·gard′,** ***v.t.*** 1. to pay little or no attention to. 2. to treat without due respect; slight. ***n.*** 1. lack of attention. 2. lack of due regard or respect. **—dis′re·gard′ful, *adj.***
**dis′re·pair′,** ***n.*** the condition of needing repairs; state of neglect.
**dis·rep′u·ta·ble,** ***adj.*** 1. not reputable; discreditable. 2. not respectable.
**dis′re·pute′,** ***n.*** lack or loss of repute; bad reputation; disgrace.
**dis′re·spect′,** ***n.*** lack of respect; rudeness. **—dis′re·spect′ful, *adj.***
**dis·robe** (dis-rōb′), ***v.t. & v.i.*** [-ROBED, -ROBING], to undress; strip.
**dis·rupt** (dis-rupt′), ***v.t. & v.i.*** [< L. *dis-*, apart + *rumpere*, to break], to break apart; split up. **—dis·rup′tion, *n.***
**dis·sat′is·fy′,** ***v.t.*** [-FIED, -FYING], to fail to satisfy. **—dis′sat·is·fac′tion, *n.***
**dis·sect** (di-sekt′), ***v.t.*** [< L. *dis-*, apart + *secare*, to cut], 1. to cut apart piece by piece, as a body for purposes of study. 2. to analyze closely. **—dis·sec′tion, *n.***
**dis·sem·ble** (di-sem′b'l), ***v.t.*** [-BLED, -BLING], [< L. *dissimulare*], to conceal (one's true feelings, motives, etc.) under a false appearance. **—dis·sem′blance, *n.***
**dis·sem·i·nate** (di-sem′ə-nāt′), ***v.t.*** [-NATED, -NATING], [< L. *dis-*, apart + *seminare*, to

sow], to scatter about; spread widely. **—dis·sem'i·na'tion,** *n.* **—dis·sem'i·na'tor,** *n.*
**dis·sen·sion** (di-sen'shən), *n.* 1. a dissenting; disagreement. 2. strife; quarreling.
**dis·sent** (di-sent'), *v.i.* [< L. *dis-*, apart + *sentire*, feel], 1. to disagree. 2. to reject the doctrines of an established church. *n.* a dissenting; difference of opinion.
**dis·ser·ta·tion** (dis'ẽr-tā'shən), *n.* [< L. *dis-*, apart + *serere*, join], a formal discourse; treatise; thesis.
**dis·serv·ice** (dis-sũr'vis), *n.* harm; injury.
**dis·si·dence** (dis'ə-dəns), *n.* [< L. *dis-*, apart + *sidere*, sit], disagreement; dissent. **—dis'si·dent** (-dənt), *adj.* & *n.*
**dis·sim·i·lar** (di-sim'ə-lẽr, dis-sim'-), *adj.* not similar; different. **—dis·sim'i·lar'i·ty** (-lar'ə-ti), *n.* **—dis·sim'i·lar·ly,** *adv.*
**dis·sim·u·late** (di-sim'yoo-lāt'), *v.t.* & *v.i.* [-LATED, -LATING], [see DIS- & SIMULATE], to dissemble. **—dis·sim'u·la'tion,** *n.*
**dis·si·pate** (dis'ə-pāt'), *v.t.* [-PATED, -PATING], [< L. *dis-*, apart + *sipare*, to throw], 1. to scatter. 2. to make disappear. 3. to waste; squander. *v.i.* 1. to vanish. 2. to indulge in pleasure to the point of harming oneself. **—dis'si·pat'ed,** *adj.* **—dis'si·pa'tion,** *n.* **—dis'si·pat'er, dis'si·pa'tor,** *n.*
**dis·so·ci·ate** (di-sō'shi-āt'), *v.t.* & *v.i.* [-ATED, -ATING], [< L. *dis-*, apart + *sociare*, join], to sever association (with); disunite. **—dis·so'ci·a'tion,** *n.*
**dis·sol·u·ble** (di-sol'yoo-b'l), *adj.* that can be dissolved. **—dis·sol'u·bil'i·ty,** *n.*
**dis·so·lute** (dis'ə-lōōt'), *adj.* [see DISSOLVE], dissipated and immoral; debauched.
**dis·so·lu·tion** (dis'ə-lōō'shən), *n.* 1. a dissolving or being dissolved. 2. a breaking up or into parts. 3. an ending. 4. death.
**dis·solve** (di-zolv'), *v.t.* & *v.i.* [-SOLVED, -SOLVING], [< L. *dis-*, apart + *solvere*, loosen], 1. to make or become liquid; melt. 2. to pass or make pass into solution. 3. to break up; decompose. 4. to end as by breaking up; terminate. 5. to disappear or make disappear.
**dis·so·nance** (dis'ə-nəns), *n.* [< L. *dis-*, apart + *sonare*, to sound], 1. an inharmonious combination of sounds. 2. any lack of harmony or agreement. **—dis'so·nant,** *adj.*
**dis·suade** (di-swād'), *v.t.* [-SUADED, -SUADING], [< L. *dis-*, away + *suadere*, persuade], to cause to turn aside (*from* a course, etc.) by persuasion or advice. **—dis·sua'sion,** *n.*
**dis·taff** (dis'taf), *n.* [< AS. *dis-*, flax + *stæf*, staff], 1. a staff on which flax, wool, etc. is wound for use in spinning. 2. women's work or concerns. 3. women in general.
**dis·tance** (dis'təns), *n.* [< L. *dis-*, apart + *stare*, to stand], 1. a being separated in space or time; remoteness. 2. an interval between two points in space or time. 3. a remoteness in behavior; reserve. 4. a faraway place. *v.t.* [-TANCED, -TANCING], to do better or more than; outdo.
**dis·tant** (dis'tənt), *adj.* 1. far apart in space or time. 2. away: as, ten miles *distant*. 3. far apart in relationship: as, a *distant* cousin. 4. aloof; reserved. 5. from or at a distance. **—dis'tant·ly,** *adv.*
**dis·taste** (dis-tāst'), *n.* dislike; aversion. **—dis·taste'ful,** *adj.*
**dis·tem·per** (dis-tem'pẽr), *n.* [< ML. *distemperare*, to mix up], an infectious virus disease of young dogs.
**dis·tend** (di-stend'), *v.t.* & *v.i.* [< L. *dis-*, apart + *tendere*, to stretch], 1. to stretch out. 2. to make or become swollen. **—dis·ten'si·ble,** *adj.* **—dis·ten'tion,** *n.*
**dis·till, dis·til** (di-stil'), *v.t.* & *v.i.* [-TILLED, -TILLING], [< L. *de-*, down + *stillare*, to drop], 1. to fall or let fall in drops. 2. to undergo, subject to, or obtain by distillation. **—dis·till'er,** *n.*
**dis·til·la·tion** (dis't'l-ā'shən), *n.* the process of heating a mixture and condensing the resulting vapor to produce a more nearly pure substance.
**dis·till'er·y,** *n.* [*pl.* -IES], a place where distilling is carried on.
**dis·tinct** (di-stiŋkt'), *adj.* [see DISTINGUISH], 1. not alike; different. 2. separate. 3. clearly marked off; plain. 4. unmistakable.
**dis·tinc·tion** (di-stiŋk'shən), *n.* 1. the act of making or keeping distinct. 2. a particular quality or feature that differentiates. 3. fame. 4. the quality that makes one seem superior. 5. a mark of honor.
**dis·tinc'tive,** *adj.* making distinct; characteristic. **—dis·tinc'tive·ness,** *n.*
**dis·tin·guish** (di-stiŋ'gwish), *v.t.* [< L. *dis-*, apart + *stinguere*, to prick], 1. to perceive or show the difference in. 2. to characterize. 3. to perceive clearly. 4. to classify. 5. to make famous. *v.i.* to make a distinction (*between* or *among*). **—dis·tin'guish·a·ble,** *adj.* **—dis·tin'guish·a·bly,** *adv.*
**dis·tin'guished,** *adj.* celebrated; famous.
**dis·tort** (di-stôrt'), *v.t.* [< L. *dis-*, intens. + *torquere*, to twist], 1. to twist out of shape. 2. to misrepresent (facts, etc.). **—dis·tor'tion,** *n.*
**dis·tract** (di-strakt'), *v.t.* [< L. *dis-*, apart + *trahere*, draw], 1. to draw (the mind, etc.) away in another direction; divert. 2. to harass; confuse. 3. to derange.
**dis·trac'tion,** *n.* 1. a distracting or being distracted; confusion. 2. anything that distracts; diversion. 3. great mental agitation.
**dis·trait** (di-strā'), *adj.* [Fr.; see DISTRACT], absent-minded; inattentive.
**dis·traught** (di-strôt'), *adj.* [prob. < *distrait*], 1. distracted; harassed. 2. driven mad; crazed.
**dis·tress** (di-stres'), *v.t.* [ult. < L. *dis-*, apart + *stringere*, stretch], to cause misery or suffering to. *n.* 1. pain; anxiety; suffering. 2. an affliction. 3. a state of danger or trouble. **—dis·tress'ful,** *adj.*
**dis·trib·ute** (di-strib'yoot), *v.t.* [-UTED, -UTING], [< L. *dis-*, apart + *tribuere*, allot], 1. to deal out in shares. 2. to spread out. 3. to classify. 4. to put (things) in various distinct places. **—dis'tri·bu'tion.** *n.*
**dis·trib'u·tor,** *n.* one that distributes; esp., *a*) a dealer who distributes goods to consumers. *b*) a device for distributing electric current to the spark plugs of a gasoline engine.
**dis·trict** (dis'trikt), *n.* [< L. *dis-*, apart + *stringere*, stretch], 1. a division of a state, city, etc. made for a specific purpose. 2. any region.
**district attorney,** the prosecuting attorney for the State in a specified district.
**dis·trust',** *n.* a lack of trust; doubt. *v.t.* to have no trust in; doubt. **—dis·trust'ful,** *adj.*
**dis·turb** (di-stũrb'), *v.t.* [< L. *dis-*, intens. + *turbare*, to disorder], 1. to break up the quiet or settled order of. 2. to make uneasy. 3. to interrupt.
**dis·turb'ance,** *n.* 1. a disturbing or being disturbed. 2. anything that disturbs. 3. commotion; disorder.
**dis·u·nite** (dis'yoo-nīt'), *v.t.* [-NITED, -NITING], to make disagree; separate.
**dis·use** (dis-ūs'), *n.* lack of use.
**ditch** (dich), *n.* [AS. *dic*], a long, narrow cut in the earth, as for carrying water. *v.t.* 1. to make a ditch in. 2. [Slang], to get rid of.
**dith·er** (di*th*'ẽr), *n.* [var. of dial. *didder*, tremble], an excited state.
**dit·to** (dit'ō), *n.* [*pl.* -TOS], [It. < L. *dicere*, say], 1. the same (as above or before). 2. a ditto mark. *adv.* as said above.
**ditto mark,** a mark (″) used in lists or tables to show that the item above is to be repeated.

**dit·ty** (dit′i), *n.* [*pl.* -TIES], [< L. *dictare*, dictate], a short, simple song.
**di·u·ret·ic** (dī′yoo-ret′ik), *adj.* [< Gr. *dia-*, through + *ourein*, urinate], increasing the flow of urine. *n.* a diuretic drug.
**di·ur·nal** (dī-ũr′n'l), *adj.* [< L. *dies*, day], 1. daily. 2. of the daytime.
**div.,** 1. divide. 2. dividend. 3. division.
**di·va** (dē′və), *n.* [*pl.* -VAS], [It. < L., goddess], a prima donna.
**di·van** (dī-van′, di-van′), *n.* [< Per. *dīvān*], a large, low couch or sofa.
**dive** (dīv), *v.i.* [DIVED or DOVE, DIVED, DIVING], [AS. *dyfan*], 1. to plunge head first into water. 2. to submerge. 3. to plunge suddenly into a place. 4. in *aviation*, to make a steep descent. *n.* 1. a diving. 2. any sudden plunge. 3. in *aviation*, a sharp descent. 4. [Colloq.], a cheap, disreputable saloon, etc. **—div′er,** *n.*
**dive bomber,** an airplane that releases bombs while diving at the target.
**di·verge** (də-vũrj′, dī-), *v.i.* [-VERGED, -VERGING], [< L. *dis-*, apart + *vergere*, to incline], 1. to go or be in different directions; branch off. 2. to vary from a norm; deviate. **—di·ver′gence,** *n.* **—di·ver′gent,** *adj.*
**di·vers** (dī′vẽrz), *adj.* [< L. *dis-*, apart + *vertere*, to turn], various.
**di·verse** (də-vũrs′, dī-), *adj.* [see DIVERS], 1. different. 2. varied. **—di·verse′ly,** *adv.*
**di·ver·si·fy** (də-vũr′sə-fī′, dī-), *v.t.* [-FIED, -FYING], to make diverse; vary. **—di·ver′si·fi·ca′tion,** *n.*
**di·ver·sion** (də-vũr′zhən, dī-), *n.* 1. a diverting; turning aside. 2. distraction of attention. 3. a pastime.
**di·ver·si·ty** (də-vũr′sə-ti, dī-), *n.* [*pl.* -TIES], 1. dissimilarity. 2. variety.
**di·vert** (də-vũrt′, dī-), *v.t.* [see DIVERS], 1. to turn aside (*from* a course). 2. to amuse.
**di·ver·tisse·ment** (dē′ver′tēs′män′), *n.* [Fr.], a diversion; entertainment.
**di·vest** (də-vest′, dī-), *v.t.* [< L. *dis-*, from + *vestire*, to dress], 1. to strip (*of* clothing, etc.). 2. to deprive (*of* rank, rights, etc.).
**di·vide** (də-vīd′), *v.t.* [-VIDED, -VIDING], [< L. *dividere*], 1. to separate into parts; sever. 2. to classify. 3. to make or keep separate. 4. to apportion. 5. to cause to disagree. 6. to mark off the divisions of. 7. in *math.*, to separate into equal parts by a divisor. *v.i.* 1. to be or become separate. 2. to disagree. 3. to share. *n.* a ridge that divides two drainage areas. **—di·vid′er,** *n.*
**div·i·dend** (div′ə-dend′), *n.* 1. the number or quantity to be divided. 2. *a*) a sum to be divided among stockholders, etc. *b*) a single share of this.
**di·vid′ers** (-ẽrz), *n.pl.* an instrument for dividing lines, etc.; compasses.
**div·i·na·tion** (div′ə-nā′shən), *n.* [< *divine*, *v.*], 1. the practice of trying to foretell the future or the unknown. 2. a prophecy.
**di·vine** (də-vīn′), *adj.* [< L. *divus*, a god], 1. of, like, or from God or a god; holy. 2. devoted to God; religious. 3. supremely great, good, etc. *n.* a clergyman. *v.t.* [-VINED, -VINING], 1. to prophesy. 2. to guess. 3. to find out by intuition. **—di·vin′er,** *n.*
**divining rod,** a forked stick allegedly useful in discovering water, minerals, etc.
**di·vin·i·ty** (də-vin′ə-ti), *n.* [*pl.* -TIES], 1. a being divine. 2. a god. 3. theology.
**di·vis·i·ble** (də-viz′ə-b'l), *adj.* that can be divided, esp. without leaving a remainder. **—di·vis′i·bil′i·ty,** *n.* **—di·vis′i·bly,** *adv.*
**di·vi·sion** (də-vizh′ən), *n.* 1. a dividing or being divided. 2. a difference of opinion. 3. a sharing. 4. anything that divides; partition. 5. a segment, group, etc. 6. the process of finding how many times a number (the *divisor*) is contained in another (the *dividend*). 7. a section of an army corps.
**di·vi·sor** (də-vī′zẽr). *n.* in *math.*, the number by which the dividend is divided.
**di·vorce** (də-vôrs′), *n.* [< L. *dis-*, apart + *vertere*, to turn], 1. legal dissolution of a marriage. 2. complete separation. *v.t.* [-VORCED, -VORCING], 1. to dissolve legally a marriage between. 2. to separate from (one's spouse) by divorce. 3. to separate.
**di·vor·cée** (də-vôr′sā′), *n.* [Fr.], a divorced woman. **—di·vor′cé′,** *n.masc.*
**div·ot** (div′ət), *n.* [Scot.], a lump of turf dislodged by a golf club in making a stroke.
**di·vulge** (də-vulj′), *v.t.* [-VULGED, -VULGING], [< L. *dis-*, apart + *vulgare*, make public], to make known; reveal. **—di·vul′gence,** *n.*
**Dix·ie** (dik′si), *n.* [< ?], the Southern States of the U.S.: also **Dixie Land.**
**Dix′ie·land′,** *adj.* in, of, or like the style of jazz associated with New Orleans.
**diz·zy** (diz′i), *adj.* [-ZIER, -ZIEST], [AS. *dysig*, foolish], 1. feeling giddy or unsteady. 2. causing dizziness. 3. confused. 4. [Colloq.], silly. **—diz′zi·ly,** *adv.* **—diz′zi·ness,** *n.*
**DNA,** [from its chemical name], an essential component of all living matter and a basic element in chromosomes, transmitting the hereditary pattern.
**do** (do͞o), *v.t.* [DID, DONE, DOING], [AS. *don*], 1. to perform (an action, etc.). 2. to finish; complete. 3. to cause: as, it *does* no harm. 4. to exert: as, *do* your best. 5. to deal with as required: as, *do* the ironing. 6. to work at; have as one's occupation. 7. [Colloq.], to cheat. 8. [Colloq.], to serve (a jail term). *v.i.* 1. to behave: as, *do* as you please. 2. to be active: as, *do*, don't talk. 3. to get along; fare: as, how is he *doing?* 4. to be adequate: as, the red hat will *do*. *Auxiliary uses* of *do*: 1. to give emphasis: as, please *do* stay. 2. to ask a question: as, *did* you go? 3. to serve as a substitute verb: as, act as I *do* (act). **—do away with,** 1. to get rid of. 2. to kill. **—do in,** [Slang], to kill. **—do over,** [Colloq.], to redecorate. **—do up,** [Colloq.], to wrap up. **—do with,** to make use of. **—do without,** to get along without. **—have to do with,** to have relation with or to. **—make do,** to get along with what is available.
**do** (dō), *n.* [It.], in *music*, the first or last tone of the diatonic scale.
**dob·bin** (dob′in), *n.* [rhyme alteration from *Robin*], a horse; esp., a plodding horse.
**doc·ile** (dos′'l), *adj.* [< L. *docere*, teach], easy to teach or discipline; tractable. **—doc′ile·ly,** *adv.* **—do·cil·i·ty** (dō-sil′ə-ti, do-), *n.*
**dock** (dok), *n.* [< ML. *ductia*, channel], 1. a large excavated basin for receiving ships between voyages. 2. a landing pier; wharf. 3. the water between two piers. *v.t.* to pilot (a ship) to a dock. *v.i.* to come into a dock.
**dock** (dok), *n.* [< Fl. *dok*, cage], the place where the accused stands or sits in a court.
**dock** (dok), *n.* [AS. *docce*], a coarse weed of the buckwheat family, with large leaves.
**dock** (dok), *n.* [< ON. *dockr*], the solid part of an animal's tail. *v.t.* 1. to cut off the end of (a tail, etc.); bob. 2. to deduct from (wages, etc.).
**dock·et** (dok′it), *n.* [< *cocket*, a seal + obs. *doggette*, register], a list of cases to be tried by a law court. *v.t.* to enter in a docket.
**dock′yard′,** *n.* a place with docks, machinery, etc. for repairing or building ships.
**doc·tor** (dok′tẽr), *n.* [< L., teacher], 1. a person on whom a university has conferred a high degree: as, a *Doctor* of Philosophy. 2. a physician or surgeon. 3. a person licensed to practice any of the healing arts. *v.t.* [Colloq.], 1. to try to heal. 2. to mend. 3. to tamper with. **—doc′tor·al,** *adj.*
**doc′tor·ate** (-it), *n.* the degree of doctor conferred by a university.
**doc·tri·naire** (dok′tri-nâr′), *adj.* [Fr.], adhering to a doctrine in a dogmatic way.

**doc·trine** (dok′trin), ***n.*** [see DOCTOR], something taught, esp. as the principles of a religion, political party, etc.; tenet or tenets; dogma. **—doc′tri·nal,** ***adj.***
**doc·u·ment** (dok′yoo-mənt), ***n.*** [< L. *documentum*, proof], anything printed, written, etc. relied upon to record or prove something. ***v.t.*** (-ment′), to provide with or support by documents. **—doc′u·men·ta′tion,** ***n.***
**doc′u·men′ta·ry** (-men′tə-ri), ***adj.*** 1. of or supported by documents. 2. recording news events or social conditions in nonfictional, but dramatic form. ***n.*** [*pl.* -RIES], a documentary motion picture, radio program, etc.
**dod·der** (dod′ẽr), ***v.i.*** [< *dither*], 1. to shake or tremble as from old age. 2. to totter.
**dodge** (doj), ***v.i.* & *v.t.*** [DODGED, DODGING], [? < Scot. *dod*, to jog], 1. to move quickly aside, or avoid by so moving. 2. to use tricks or evasions, or evade by so doing. ***n.*** 1. a dodging. 2. a trick used in evading or cheating. **—dodg′er,** ***n.***
**do·do** (dō′dō), ***n.*** [*pl.* -DOS, -DOES], [Port. *doudo*, lit., stupid], a large, flightless bird, now extinct.
**doe** (dō), ***n.*** [AS. *da*], the female of the deer, antelope, rabbit, etc.
**do·er** (do͞o′ẽr), ***n.*** 1. one who does something. 2. one who gets things done.
**does** (duz), 3d pers. sing., pres. indic., of **do.**
**doe′skin′,** ***n.*** 1. leather from the skin of a female deer. 2. a soft wool cloth.
**does·n't** (duz′'nt), does not.
**doff** (dof, dôf), ***v.t.*** [< *do* + *off*], 1. to take off (one's hat, etc.). 2. to put aside.
**dog** (dôg), ***n.*** [AS. *docga*], 1. a domesticated animal related to the fox, wolf, and jackal. 2. a low, contemptible fellow. 3. a mechanical device for holding or grappling. 4. *pl.* [Slang], feet. ***v.t.*** [DOGGED, DOGGING], to follow or hunt like a dog. ***adv.*** very. **—dog eat dog,** ruthless competition. **—go to the dogs** [Colloq.], to deteriorate.
**doge** (dōj), ***n.*** [It. < L. *dux*, leader], the chief magistrate in the former republics of Venice and Genoa. **—doge′ship′,** ***n.***
**dog′-ear′,** ***n.*** a turned-down corner of the leaf of a book. **—dog′eared′,** ***adj.***
**dog′fish′,** ***n.*** [*pl.* see FISH], any of various small sharks.
**dog·ged** (dôg′id), ***adj.*** persistent; stubborn.
**dog·ger·el** (dôg′ẽr-əl), ***n.*** [prob. < It. *doga*, barrel stave], trivial, usually comic verse.
**dog′-gone′,** ***interj.*** damn! darn! ***v.t.*** [-GONED, -GONING], [Colloq.], to damn.
**dog′house′,** ***n.*** a dog's shelter. **—in the doghouse,** [Slang], in disfavor.
**do·gie, do·gy** (dō′gi), ***n.*** [*pl.* -GIES], [< ?], in the western U.S., a stray calf.
**dog·ma** (dôg′mə), ***n.*** [*pl.* -MAS, -MATA (-mə-tə)], [< Gr. *dokein*, think], a doctrine; belief; esp., a body of theological doctrines strictly adhered to.
**dog·mat′ic** (-mat′ik), ***adj.*** 1. of or like dogma. 2. asserted without proof. 3. positive or arrogant in stating opinion. Also **dog·mat′i·cal. —dog·mat′i·cal·ly,** ***adv.***
**dog′ma·tism** (-tiz'm), ***n.*** dogmatic assertion of opinion. **—dog′ma·tist,** ***n.***
**dog tag,** 1. a license tag for a dog. 2. [Slang], a military identification tag worn about the neck.
**dog′-tired′,** ***adj.*** [Colloq.], very tired.
**dog′tooth′,** ***n.*** [*pl.* -TEETH], a canine tooth: also **dog tooth.**
**dog′trot′,** ***n.*** a slow, easy trot.
**dog′watch′,** ***n.*** in *naut. usage*, either of two duty periods, from 4 to 6 P.M. and 6 to 8 P.M.
**dog′wood′,** ***n.*** a tree bearing pink or white flowers early in the spring.
**doi·ly** (doi′li), ***n.*** [*pl.* -LIES], [after a 17th-c. London draper], a small mat, as of linen or paper, used as protection for a table, etc.
**do·ings** (do͞o′iŋz), ***n.pl.*** actions.
**dol·drums** (dol′drəmz), ***n.pl.*** [? < *dull*], 1. low spirits. 2. equatorial ocean regions noted for dead calms.
**dole** (dōl), ***n.*** [AS. *dal*], 1. money or food given in charity. 2. anything given sparingly. 3. money paid by a government to the unemployed. ***v.t.*** [DOLED, DOLING], to give sparingly or as a dole.
**dole·ful** (dōl′fəl), ***adj.*** [< L. *dolere*, suffer], sad; sorrowful; dismal. **—dole′ful·ly,** ***adv.***
**doll** (dol), ***n.*** [< nickname for *Dorothy*], a child's toy made to resemble a child or grown person. ***v.t.* & *v.i.*** [Slang], to dress stylishly or showily (with *up*).
**dol·lar** (dol′ẽr), ***n.*** [< G. *thaler*], 1. the monetary unit of the U.S., equal to 100 cents. 2. the monetary unit of certain other countries, as Canada. 3. a coin or paper bill of the value of a dollar.
**doll·y** (dol′i), ***n.*** [*pl.* -IES], 1. a doll: child's term. 2. a low, flat, wheeled frame for moving heavy objects.
**dol·man** (dol′mən), ***n.*** [*pl.* -MANS], [< Fr. < Turk. *dōlāmān*, long robe], a woman's coat or wrap with capelike arm pieces instead of sleeves.
**dol·or·ous** (dol′ẽr-əs, dō′lẽr-), ***adj.*** [< L. *dolere*, suffer], 1. sorrowful; sad. 2. painful.
**dol·phin** (dol′fin), ***n.*** [< Gr. *delphis*], a mammal of the whale family, with a beaklike snout.
**dolt** (dōlt), ***n.*** [? < *dull*], a stupid, slow-witted person. **—dolt′ish,** ***adj.***
**-dom,** [AS. < *dom*, state], a suffix meaning: 1. *the position* or *domain of*, as in *kingdom*. 2. *the fact* or *state of being*, as in *martyrdom*. 3. *a body of*, as in *officialdom*.
**do·main** (dō-mān′), ***n.*** [< L. *dominus*, master], 1. territory under one government or ruler. 2. land belonging to one person; estate. 3. field of activity or influence.
**dome** (dōm), ***n.*** [< L. *domus*, house], 1. a large, rounded roof or ceiling. 2. any dome-shaped object.
**do·mes·tic** (də-mes′tik), ***adj.*** [see DOME], 1. of the home or family. 2. of or made in one's country. 3. tame: said of animals. 4. home-loving. ***n.*** a maid, cook, etc.: also **domestic worker. —do·mes′ti·cal·ly,** ***adv.***
**do·mes′ti·cate′** (-tə-kāt′), ***v.t.*** [-CATED, -CATING], 1. to accustom to home life. 2. to tame for man's use. **—do·mes′ti·ca′tion,** ***n.***
**do·mes·tic·i·ty** (dō′mes-tis′ə-ti), ***n.*** home life, or devotion to it.
**dom·i·cile** (dom′ə-sil, -sīl′), ***n.*** [Fr. < L. *domus*, home], a home; residence. ***v.t.*** [-CILED, -CILING], to establish in a domicile.
**dom·i·nant** (dom′ə-nənt), ***adj.*** dominating. **—dom′i·nance,** ***n.*** **—dom′i·nant·ly,** ***adv.***
**dom·i·nate** (dom′ə-nāt′), ***v.t.* & *v.i.*** [-NATED, -NATING], [< L. *dominus*, a master], 1. to rule or control by superior power. 2. to rise high above (the surroundings). **—dom′i·na′tion,** ***n.***
**dom·i·neer** (dom′ə-nêr′), ***v.i.*** [< D.; see DOMINATE], to rule (*over*) in a harsh or arrogant way; tyrannize.
**dom′i·neer′ing,** ***adj.*** overbearing.
**dom·i·nie** (dom′ə-ni), ***n.*** [see DOMINATE], 1. in Scotland, a schoolmaster. 2. [Colloq.], a clergyman.
**do·min·ion** (də-min′yən), ***n.*** [see DOMAIN], 1. rule or power to rule. 2. a governed or, sometimes, a self-governing territory.
**dom·i·no** (dom′ə-nō′), ***n.*** [*pl.* -NOES, -NOS], [Fr. & It.], 1. a loose cloak with a hood and mask, worn at masquerades. 2. a mask for the eyes. 3. a small, oblong tile marked with dots. 4. *pl.* [construed as sing.], a game played with such tiles.
**don** (don), ***n.*** [Sp. < L. *dominus*, lord], 1. [D-], Sir; Mr.: a Spanish title of respect.

2. a Spanish gentleman. 3. [Colloq.], a tutor at a British college.

**don** (don), *v.t.* [DONNED, DONNING], [contr. of *do on*], to put on (clothes).

‡**Do·ña** (dô′nyä), *n.* [Sp. < L. *domina*, mistress], 1. Lady; Madam: a Spanish title of respect. 2. [d-], a Spanish lady.

**do·nate** (dō′nāt), *v.t.* [-NATED, -NATING], [< L. *donus*, gift], to give or contribute.

**do·na′tion,** *n.* 1. a donating or giving. 2. a gift or contribution.

**done** (dun), pp. of **do.** *adj.* 1. completed. 2. sufficiently cooked.

**Don Ju·an** (don jōō′ən, dôn hwän′), in *Spanish legend*, a dissolute nobleman and seducer of women.

**don·key** (doŋ′ki, duŋ′), *n.* [*pl.* -KEYS], [< ?], 1. a small domestic animal like the horse but with longer ears; ass. 2. a stupid or foolish person.

**do·nor** (dō′nẽr), *n.* one who donates.

**Don Quix·ote** (don kwik′sət, ki-hō′ti), 1. a satirical romance by Cervantes. 2. its chivalrous, unrealistic hero.

**don't** (dōnt), do not.

**doo·dle** (dōō′d'l), *v.i.* [-DLED, -DLING], [G. *dudeln*, to trifle], to scribble aimlessly. *n.* a mark made in aimless scribbling.

**doom** (dōōm), *n.* [AS. *dom*], 1. a judgment; sentence. 2. fate. 3. ruin or death. *v.t.* 1. to pass judgment on; condemn. 2. to destine to a tragic fate.

**dooms·day** (dōōmz′dā′), *n.* Judgment Day.

**door** (dôr), *n.* [AS. *duru*], 1. a movable structure for opening or closing an entrance. 2. a doorway. 3. a means of access. —**out of doors,** outdoors.

**door′bell′,** *n.* a bell inside that is rung by an outside push button.

**door′man′** (-man′, -mən), *n.* [*pl.* -MEN], 1. a man whose work is opening the door of a public building, hailing taxicabs, etc. 2. a man who guards an entrance.

**door mat,** a mat to wipe the shoes on before entering a house, etc.

**door′nail′,** *n.* a large-headed nail used in studding doors. —**dead as a doornail,** absolutely dead.

**door′step′,** *n.* a step leading from an outer door to a path, lawn, etc.

**door′way′,** *n.* 1. an opening in a wall that can be closed by a door. 2. a means of access; passage.

**door′yard′,** *n.* a yard onto which a door of a house opens.

**dope** (dōp), *n.* [< D. *doop*, sauce], 1. any thick liquid used as a lubricant, varnish, filler, etc. 2. [Slang], *a*) information. *b*) a narcotic. *c*) a stupid person. *v.t.* [DOPED, DOPING], 1. to drug. 2. [Slang], to figure (*out*).

**dope·y** (dō′pi), *adj.* [DOPIER, DOPIEST], [Slang], 1. in a drugged stupor. 2. lethargic or stupid.

**Dor·ic** (dôr′ik, dor′-), *adj.* [< Gr. *Dōris*, ancient region of Greece], designating or of the oldest order of Greek architecture, characterized by fluted columns with simple capitals.

**dorm** (dôrm), *n.* [Colloq.], a dormitory.

**dor·mant** (dôr′mənt), *adj.* [< L. *dormire*, to sleep], 1. sleeping. 2. quiet; still; inactive. —**dor′man·cy,** *n.*

**dor·mer** (dôr′mẽr), *n.* [orig., dormitory; see DORMANT], a window set upright in a structure projecting from a sloping roof: also **dormer window.**

**dor·mi·to·ry** (dôr′mə-tôr′i), *n.* [*pl.* -RIES], [see DORMANT], 1. a room with beds for a number of people. 2. a building, as at a college, with many rooms providing sleeping and living accommodations.

**dor·mouse** (dôr′mous′), *n.* [*pl.* -MICE (-mis′)], [< Eng. dial. *dorm*, to doze + *mouse*], a small, hibernating European rodent that resembles a squirrel.

**dor·sal** (dôr′s'l), *adj.* [< L. *dorsum*, the back], of, on, or near the back. —**dor′sal·ly,** *adv.*

**do·ry** (dôr′i), *n.* [*pl.* -RIES], [< Central Am. Ind. *dori*, dugout], a small, flat-bottomed fishing boat with high sides.

**dose** (dōs), *n.* [< Gr. *dosis*, gift], an amount of medicine to be taken at one time. *v.t.* [DOSED, DOSING], to give doses to. —**dos′age,** *n.*

**dos·si·er** (dos′i-ā′, -i-ẽr), *n.* [Fr.], a collection of documents about some person or matter.

**dost** (dust) archaic 2d pers. sing., pres. indic., of **do**: used with *thou*.

**dot** (dot), *n.* [AS. *dott*, head of boil], 1. a tiny speck or mark. 2. a small, round spot. *v.t.* [DOTTED, DOTTING], to mark as with a dot or dots. —**on the dot,** [Colloq.], at the exact time.

**dot·age** (dōt′ij), *n.* [ME. < *doten*, to dote], 1. feeble and childish state due to old age. 2. excessive affection.

**do·tard** (dō′tẽrd), *n.* [see DOTAGE], a foolish and doddering old person.

**dote** (dōt), *v.i.* [DOTED, DOTING], [ME. *doten*], 1. to be weak-minded, esp. in old age. 2. to be excessively fond (with *on* or *upon*).

**doth** (duth), archaic 3d pers. sing., pres. indic., of **do,** in auxiliary uses.

**Dou·ay Bible** (dōō′ā′), [< *Douay*, France, where one part was first published], an English version of the Bible for the use of Roman Catholics.

**dou·ble** (dub′'l), *adj.* [< L. *duplus*], 1. twofold. 2. having two layers. 3. having two of one kind. 4. being of two kinds: as, a *double* standard. 5. having two meanings. 6. twice as much, as many, etc. *adv.* twofold or twice. *n.* 1. anything twice as much, as many, etc. as normal. 2. a duplicate; counterpart. 3. a fold. 4. in *baseball*, a hit on which the batter reaches second base. 5. in *bridge*, the doubling of an opponent's bid. 6. *pl.* a game of tennis, etc. with two players on each side. *v.t.* [-BLED, -BLING], 1. to make twice as much or many. 2. to fold. 3. to repeat or duplicate. 4. to be the double of. 5. in *bridge*, to increase the point value or penalty of (an opponent's bid). *v.i.* 1. to become double. 2. to turn sharply backward: as, to *double* on one's tracks. 3. to serve as a double, serve two purposes, etc. —**double up,** 1. to clench (one's fist). 2. to bend over, as in pain. 3. to share a room, etc. with someone.

**dou′ble-bar′reled,** *adj.* 1. having two barrels, as a kind of shotgun. 2. having a double purpose or meaning.

**double bass,** the bass viol.

**double bed,** a bed big enough for two.

**double boiler,** a utensil having one pan for food fitting into another in which water is boiled.

**dou′ble-breast′ed,** *adj.* overlapping across the breast, as a coat.

**dou′ble-cross′,** *v.t.* [Slang], to betray. —**dou′ble-cross′er,** *n.*

**double date,** [Colloq.], a social engagement in which two couples are together. —**dou′ble-date′** [-DATED, -DATING], *v.i.*

**dou′ble-deal′ing,** *n.* duplicity.

**dou′ble-edged′,** *adj.* 1. having two cutting edges. 2. applicable both ways, as an argument.

‡**dou·ble-en·ten·dre** (dōō′bl′-än′tän′dr′), *n.* [Fr., prob. < *double entente*, double meaning], a word or phrase with two meanings, esp. when one is risqué.

**dou′ble-head′er,** *n.* two baseball games played in succession on the same day.

**dou′ble-joint′ed,** *adj.* having joints that permit limbs, fingers, etc. to bend at other than the usual angles.

**dou′ble-park′,** ***v.t. & v.i.*** to park (an automobile), usually unlawfully, beside another parked at a curb.
**double play,** in *baseball*, a play by which two players are put out.
**dou′ble-reed′,** ***adj.*** designating or of a woodwind instrument, as the oboe, having two reeds separated by a narrow opening. ***n.*** a double-reed instrument.
**double standard,** the moral code imposing a more restrictive standard of behavior on women than on men, esp. in matters of sex.
**dou·blet** (dub′lit), ***n.*** [< OFr. *double*, orig., something folded], 1. a man's closefitting jacket of the 14th to the 16th centuries. 2. either of a pair. 3. a pair.
**double take,** a delayed, startled reaction to the unexpected, preceded by placid, unthinking acceptance.
**double talk,** 1. ambiguous and deceptive talk. 2. meaningless syllables like talk.
**double time,** a marching cadence of 180 three-foot steps a minute.
**dou·bloon** (du-blo͞on′), ***n.*** [< Fr. < Sp. < L. *duplus*, double], an obsolete Spanish coin.
**dou·bly** (dub′li), ***adv.*** 1. twice. 2. two at a time.
**doubt** (dout), ***v.i.*** [< L. *dubitare*], to be uncertain or undecided. ***v.t.*** 1. to be uncertain about. 2. to tend to disbelieve. ***n.*** 1. a wavering of opinion or belief. 2. a condition of uncertainty. 3. an unsettled point or matter. **—no doubt,** 1. certainly. 2. probably. **—without doubt,** certainly.
**doubt′ful,** ***adj.*** 1. uncertain. 2. giving rise to doubt. 3. feeling doubt; undecided.
**doubt′less,** ***adv.*** 1. certainly. 2. probably.
**douche** (do͞osh), ***n.*** [Fr. < It. *doccia*], 1. a jet of liquid applied externally or internally to the body. 2. a device for douching. ***v.t. & v.i.*** [DOUCHED, DOUCHING], to apply a douche (to).
**dough** (dō), ***n.*** [AS. *dag*], 1. a mixture of flour, liquid, etc. worked into a soft, thick mass for baking. 2. [Slang], money.
**dough·boy** (dō′boi′), ***n.*** [Colloq.], formerly, a U.S. infantryman.
**dough′nut′,** ***n.*** a small, usually ring-shaped cake, fried in deep fat.
**dough·ty** (dou′ti), ***adj.*** [-TIER, -TIEST], [< AS. *dugan*, to avail], [Archaic], valiant; strong: now humorous. **—dough′ti·ly,** ***adv.***
**dough′y,** ***adj.*** [-IER, -IEST], of or like dough; soft, pasty, etc.
**dour** (do͞or, door, dour), ***adj.*** [< L. *durus*, hard], 1. [Scot.], severe; stern. 2. sullen; gloomy. **—dour′ly,** ***adv.*** **—dour′ness,** ***n.***
**douse** (dous), ***v.t.*** [DOUSED, DOUSING], [prob. < LG.], 1. to thrust suddenly into liquid. 2. to drench. 3. [Colloq.], to extinguish, as a light. ***v.i.*** to be immersed or drenched.
**dove** (duv), ***n.*** [< ON. *dūfa*], a bird of the pigeon family, with a cooing cry: a symbol of peace.
**dove** (dōv), alt. pt. of **dive.**
**dove·cote** (duv′kōt′), ***n.*** a small box with compartments for nesting pigeons: also **dove′cot′** (-kot′).
**dove·tail** (duv′tāl′), ***n.*** a projecting part that fits into a corresponding indentation to form a joint. ***v.t. & v.i.*** to join or fit together closely or by means of dovetails.
**dow·a·ger** (dou′ə-jẽr), ***n.*** [see DOWER], 1. a widow with a title or property derived from her dead husband. 2. [Colloq.], an elderly, dignified woman of wealth.
**dow·dy** (dou′di), ***adj.*** [-DIER, -DIEST], [< ME. *doude*, a slut], not neat in dress; shabby.
**dow·el** (dou′əl), ***n.*** [prob. < MLG. *dövel*], a peg of wood, etc., usually fitted into corresponding holes in two pieces to fasten them together.
**dow·er** (dou′ẽr), ***n.*** [ult. < L. *dare*, give], 1. that part of a husband's property which his widow inherits for life. 2. a dowry.
**down** (doun), ***adv.*** [AS. *adun*, from the hill], 1. to, in, or on a lower place or level. 2. in or to a low or lower condition, amount, etc. 3. from an earlier to a later period. 4. in a serious manner: as, get *down* to work. 5. in cash: as $5 *down* and $80 on account. 6. in writing: as, take *down* notes. ***adj.*** 1. descending. 2. in a lower place. 3. gone, brought, paid, etc. down. 4. dejected; discouraged. ***prep.*** down toward, along, through, into, or upon. ***v.t.*** to put or throw down. ***n.*** 1. a descent. 2. a misfortune: as, ups and *downs*. 3. in *football*, one of a series of plays by which a team tries to advance the ball. **—down and out,** penniless, ill, etc. **—down on,** [Colloq.], angry with.
**down** (doun), ***n.*** [< ON. *dūnn*], 1. soft, fine feathers. 2. soft, fine hair.
**down** (doun), ***n.*** [AS. *dun*, hill], ***usually in pl.*** open, high grassy land.
**down′cast′,** ***adj.*** 1. directed downward. 2. sad; dejected.
**down′-east′,** ***adj.*** [Colloq.], of New England.
**down′fall′,** ***n.*** 1. a sudden fall, as from power. 2. a heavy fall of rain or snow. **—down′fall′en,** ***adj.***
**down′grade′,** ***n.*** a downward slope. ***adv. & adj.*** downward. ***v.t.*** [-GRADED, -GRADING], to demote. **—on the downgrade,** declining.
**down′heart′ed,** ***adj.*** discouraged.
**down′hill′,** ***adv. & adj.*** toward the bottom of a hill. **—go downhill,** to decline.
**down′pour′,** ***n.*** a heavy rain.
**down′right′,** ***adv.*** thoroughly. ***adj.*** 1. absolute; utter. 2. plain; frank.
**down′stairs′,** ***adv.*** 1. down the stairs. 2. on or to a lower floor. ***adj.*** on a lower floor. ***n.*** a lower floor.
**down′stream′,** ***adv. & adj.*** in the direction of the current of a stream.
**down′town′,** ***adj. & adv.*** in or toward the main business section of a city.
**down′trod′den,** ***adj.*** oppressed.
**down′ward** (-wẽrd), ***adv. & adj.*** toward a lower place, position, etc.: also **down′wards,** ***adv.***
**down·y** (doun′i), ***adj.*** [-IER, -IEST], 1. covered with soft, fine feathers or hair. 2. soft and fluffy, like down. **—down′i·ness,** ***n.***
**dow·ry** (dou′ri), ***n.*** [*pl.* -RIES], [see DOWER], 1. the property that a woman brings to her husband at marriage. 2. a natural talent.
**dowse** (douz), ***v.i.*** [DOWSED, DOWSING], [< ?], to search for water or minerals with a divining rod (**dowsing rod**).
**dox·ol·o·gy** (doks-ol′ə-ji), ***n.*** [*pl.* -GIES], [< Gr. *doxa*, praise + *legein*, speak], a hymn of praise to God.
**doze** (dōz), ***v.i.*** [DOZED, DOZING], [orig., stupefy < LG.], to sleep fitfully; nap. ***n.*** a light sleep; nap.
**doz·en** (duz′'n), ***n.*** [*pl.* -ENS; *when preceded by a number*, -EN], [< L. *duo*, two + *decem*, ten], a set of twelve: abbrev. **doz., dz.**
**D.P.,** displaced person.
**Dr.,** Doctor.
**drab** (drab), ***n.*** [< LL. *drappus*, cloth], a dull yellowish brown. ***adj.*** [DRABBER, DRABBEST], 1. dull yellowish-brown. 2. dull. **—drab′ly,** ***adv.*** **—drab′ness,** ***n.***
**drach·ma** (drak′mə), ***n.*** [*pl.* -MAS, -MAE (-mē)], [< Gr. *drachma*, handful], 1. an ancient Greek silver coin. 2. a modern Greek monetary unit.
**draft** (draft, dräft), ***n.*** [< AS. *dragan*, to draw]. 1. a drawing, as of a vehicle or load. 2. a drawing in of a fish net. 3. the amount of fish caught in a net. 4. a drink or the amount taken at one drink. 5. a drawing, as of beer, from a cask. 6. a rough sketch of a writing. 7. a plan or drawing of a work to be done. 8. a current of air, as in a room. 9. a device for regulating the current of air

in a heating system. 10. a written order for payment of money; check. 11. the taking of persons for compulsory military service. 12. those thus taken. 13. the depth of water that a ship displaces. *v.t.* 1. to take, as for military service, by drawing from a group. 2. to make a sketch of or plans for. *adj.* 1. used for pulling loads. 2. drawn from a cask: as, *draft* beer. Also sp. **draught**.

**draf·tee** (draf-tē′, dräf-), *n.* a person drafted for military service.

**drafts·man** (drafts′mən, dräfts′-), *n.* [*pl.* -MEN], one who draws plans of structures or machinery: also sp. **draughtsman.** —**drafts′man·ship′**, *n.*

**draft′y**, *adj.* [-IER, -IEST], 1. in a draft (*n.* 8). 2. causing or having a draft or drafts: as, a *drafty* house. —**draft′i·ness**, *n.*

**drag** (drag), *v.t. & v.i.* [DRAGGED, DRAGGING], [< AS. *dragan* or ON. *draga*], 1. to pull or be pulled with effort, esp. along the ground. 2. to search (a river bottom, etc.), as with a net. 3. to draw (something) out over a period of time; move or pass slowly. *n.* 1. something dragged along the ground; specif., a harrow. 2. a grapnel, dragnet, etc. 3. anything that hinders. 4. a dragging. 5. [Slang], influence. 6. [Slang], a puff of a cigarette, etc. —**drag on** (or **out**), to prolong or be prolonged tediously.

**drag·gle** (drag′'l), *v.t. & v.i.* [-GLED, -GLING], [< *drag*], to make or become wet and dirty by dragging in mud or water.

**drag′net′**, *n.* 1. a net dragged along the bottom of a lake, etc. for catching fish. 2. an organized system or network for catching criminals, etc.

**drag·on** (drag′ən), *n.* [< Gr. *drakōn*], a mythical monster, usually a large, winged reptile breathing out fire and smoke.

**drag′on·fly′**, *n.* [*pl.* -FLIES], a large, harmless insect with a long body and four wings.

**dra·goon** (drə-gōōn′), *n.* [see DRAGON], a heavily armed cavalryman. *v.t.* to persecute or force by persecution.

**drain** (drān), *v.t.* [< AS. *dryge*, dry], 1. to draw off (liquid, etc.) gradually. 2. to draw liquid from gradually. 3. to exhaust gradually: said of strength, etc. *v.i.* 1. to flow off gradually. 2. to become dry by the flowing off of liquid. 3. to discharge its waters. *n.* 1. a channel, tube, etc. for draining. 2. a draining. —**drain′er**, *n.*

**drain′age** (-ij), *n.* 1. a draining. 2. a system of pipes, etc. for carrying off waste matter. 3. that which is drained off.

**drake** (drāk), *n.* [< ?], a male duck.

**dram** (dram), *n.* [< Gr. *drachma*, handful], 1. in *apothecaries' weight*, a unit equal to 1/8 oz. 2. in *avoirdupois weight*, a unit equal to 1/16 oz.

**dra·ma** (drä′mə, dram′ə), *n.* [Gr., action], 1. a literary composition to be performed on a stage; play. 2. the art of writing, acting, or producing plays. 3. a series of events so interesting, etc. as to resemble those of a play. 4. dramatic quality.

**dra·mat·ic** (drə-mat′ik), *adj.* 1. of or connected with drama. 2. like a play. 3. vivid, exciting, etc. —**dra·mat′i·cal·ly**, *adv.*

**dra·mat′ics**, *n.pl.* [construed as sing.], the performing or producing of plays.

**dram·a·tis per·so·nae** (dram′ə-tis pẽr-sō′nē), [L.], the characters in a play.

**dram·a·tist** (dram′ə-tist), *n.* one who writes plays; playwright.

**dram′a·tize′** (-tīz′), *v.t.* [-TIZED, -TIZING], 1. to make into a drama. 2. to regard or show dramatically. —**dram′a·ti·za′tion**, *n.*

**dram·a·tur·gy** (dram′ə-tũr′ji), *n.* [< Fr. < Gr. *drama* + *ergon*, work], the art of writing or producing plays.

**drank** (draŋk), pt. and archaic pp. of **drink**.

**drape** (drāp), *v.t.* [DRAPED, DRAPING], [< LL. *drappus*, cloth], 1. to cover or hang as with cloth in loose folds. 2. to arrange (a garment, etc.) in folds or hangings. *v.i.* to hang or fall in folds. *n. usually in pl.* cloth hanging in loose folds; curtain.

**drap·er** (drāp′ẽr), *n.* [Brit.], a dealer in cloth and dry goods.

**dra′per·y**, *n.* [*pl.* -IES], 1. cloth; fabric. 2. hangings or clothing arranged in loose folds. 3. *pl.* curtains.

**dras·tic** (dras′tik), *adj.* [< Gr. *drastikos*, active], having a violent effect; severe; harsh. —**dras′ti·cal·ly**, *adv.*

**draught** (draft, dräft), *n., v.t., adj.* draft.

**draughts** (drafts, dräfts), *n.pl.* [Brit.], the game of checkers: also sp. **drafts.**

**draughts′man** (-mən), *n.* [*pl.* -MEN], a draftsman.

**draw** (drô), *v.t.* [DREW, DRAWN, DRAWING], [AS. *dragon*], 1. to make move toward one; pull. 2. to pull up, down, back, in, or out. 3. to need (a specified depth of water) to float in: said of a ship. 4. to attract. 5. to breathe in. 6. to elicit, as a reply. 7. to cause to happen. 8. to receive: as, to *draw* a salary. 9. to withdraw (money) held in an account. 10. to write (a check or draft). 11. to deduce. 12. to stretch. 13. to make (lines, pictures, etc.), as with a pencil. *v.i.* 1. to draw something (in various senses of the *v.t.*). 2. to be drawn. 3. to come; move. 4. to shrink. 5. to allow a draft, as of smoke, to move through. *n.* 1. a drawing or being drawn. 2. the result of drawing. 3. a thing drawn. 4. a tie; stalemate. 5. a thing that attracts. 6. the movable part of a drawbridge. —**draw out**, 1. to extend. 2. to get (a person) to talk. —**draw up**, 1. to arrange in order. 2. to draft (a document). 3. to stop.

**draw′back′**, *n.* anything that hinders; shortcoming; disadvantage.

**draw′bridge′**, *n.* a bridge that can be raised, lowered, or drawn aside.

**draw·er** (drô′ẽr), *n.* 1. one that draws. 2. (drôr), a sliding box in a table, chest, etc.

**draw·ers** (drôrz), *n.pl.* an undergarment for the lower part of the body.

**draw′ing**, *n.* 1. the act of one that draws. 2. the art of making pictures, etc. as with a pencil. 3. a picture, etc. thus made. 4. a lottery.

**drawing card**, an entertainer, show, etc. that draws a large audience.

**drawing room**, [< *withdrawing room:* guests withdrew there after dinner], 1. a room where guests are received or entertained. 2. a private compartment on a railroad sleeping car.

**drawl** (drôl), *n.* [prob. < *draw*, *v.*], a slow, prolonged manner of speech. *v.t. & v.i.* to speak with a drawl. —**drawl′ing·ly**, *adv.*

**drawn** (drôn), pp. of **draw.** *adj.* 1. disemboweled. 2. tense; haggard.

**drawn butter**, melted butter.

**dray** (drā), *n.* [< AS. *dragan*, to draw], a wagon for heavy loads. —**dray′age** (-ij), *n.*

**dread** (dred), *v.t. & v.i.* [AS. *on-drædan*], to anticipate with fear or distaste. *n.* 1. intense fear. 2. fear mixed with awe. *adj.* 1. dreaded or dreadful. 2. inspiring awe.

**dread′ful**, *adj.* 1. inspiring dread; terrible. 2. [Colloq.], very bad, offensive, etc. —**dread′ful·ly**. *adv.* —**dread′ful·ness**, *n.*

**dread′nought′**, **dread′naught′** (-nôt′), *n.* a large battleship with big guns.

**dream** (drēm), *n.* [< ON. *draum*], 1. a sequence of images, thoughts, etc. passing through a sleeping person's mind. 2. a daydream; reverie. 3. a fond hope. 4. anything dreamlike. *v.i. & v.t.* [DREAMED or DREAMT (dremt), DREAMING], 1. to have a dream or dreams (of). 2. to have vague notions (*of*). —**dream′er**, *n.*

**dream′y,** ***adj.*** [-IER, -IEST], 1. filled with dreams. 2. visionary; impractical. 3. shadowy; vague. 4. soothing. **—dream′i·ly,** ***adv.***
**drear** (drêr), ***adj.*** [Poetic], dreary.
**drear′y,** ***adj.*** [-IER, -IEST], [AS. *dreorig*, sad], gloomy; dismal. **—drear′i·ness,** ***n.***
**dredge** (drej), ***n.*** [see DRAW], an apparatus for scooping up mud, etc., as in deepening channels. ***v.t. & v.i.*** [DREDGED, DREDGING], to enlarge or clean out with a dredge.
**dredge** (drej), ***v.t.*** [DREDGED, DREDGING], [< ME. *dragge*, sweetmeat], to sprinkle with flour, etc.
**dregs** (dregz), ***n.pl.*** [< ON. *dregg*], 1. the particles of solid matter that go to the bottom in a liquid. 2. the most worthless part. **—dreg′gy** [-GIER, -GIEST], ***adj.***.
**drench** (drench), ***v.t.*** [< AS. *drincan*, to drink], to wet all over; soak.
**dress** (dres), ***v.t.*** [DRESSED or DREST, DRESSING], [< L. *dirigere*, lay straight], 1. to put clothes on; clothe. 2. to trim; adorn. 3. to arrange or do up (the hair). 4. to arrange (troops, etc.) in straight lines. 5. to apply medicines and bandages to (a wound, etc.). 6. to prepare: as, to *dress* a fowl. 7. to smooth or finish (leather, stone, etc.). ***v.i.*** 1. to put on clothes. 2. to wear formal clothes. 3. to get into a straight line. ***n.*** 1. clothes. 2. the common, one-piece, skirted garment of women. **—dress up,** to dress in formal or elegant clothes.
**dress′er,** ***n.*** 1. one who dresses (in various senses). 2. a chest of drawers for clothes.
**dress′ing,** ***n.*** 1. the act of one that dresses. 2. bandages for wounds, etc. 3. a sauce for salads, etc. 4. a stuffing for roast fowl.
**dress′ing-down′,** ***n.*** [Colloq.], a reprimand.
**dressing gown,** a loose robe for wear when one is undressed or lounging.
**dress′mak′er,** ***n.*** one who makes dresses, etc.; seamstress. ***adj.*** not tailored on mannish lines. **—dress′mak′ing,** ***n.***
**dress rehearsal,** a final rehearsal, as of a play, with costumes, etc.
**dress′y,** ***adj.*** [-IER, -IEST], [Colloq.], 1. wearing showy clothes. 2. elegant. **—dress′i·ness,** ***n.***
**drew** (drōō), pt. of **draw.**
**drib·ble** (drib′'l), ***v.i. & v.t.*** [-BLED, -BLING], [< *drip*], 1. to flow, or let flow, in drops. 2. to drool. 3. in certain games, to move (the ball) along by repeated bouncing or kicking. ***n.*** a driblet; dribbling flow.
**drib·let, drib·blet** (drib′lit), ***n.*** [*drib*, drip + *-let*], a small amount; bit.
**dried** (drīd), pt. and pp. of **dry.**
**dri·er** (drī′ẽr), ***n.*** 1. a person or thing that dries. 2. an apparatus for drying by heating, etc. 3. a substance added to paint, etc. to make it dry fast. ***adj.*** comparative of **dry.**
**dri′est** (-ist), ***adj.*** superlative of **dry.**
**drift** (drift), ***n.*** [< AS. *drifan*, to drive], 1. a being driven along, as by a current. 2. the course on which something is driven. 3. a tendency; trend. 4. meaning; intent. 5. a heap of snow, etc. piled up by wind. 6. rocks, gravel, etc. carried by a river or glacier. ***v.i.*** 1. to be carried along, as by a current. 2. to go along aimlessly. 3. to accumulate in heaps by force of wind or water. ***v.t.*** to cause to drift. **—drift′er,** ***n.***
**drift′wood′,** ***n.*** wood drifting in the water or washed ashore: often figurative.
**drill** (dril), ***n.*** [< D. *drillen*, to drill], 1. a tool for boring holes in wood, metal, etc. 2. systematic military or physical training. 3. the method or practice of teaching by repeated exercises. ***v.t. & v.i.*** 1. to bore with a drill. 2. to train in military, physical, or mental exercises. **—drill′er,** ***n.***
**drill** (dril), ***n.*** [< ?], a machine for making holes and dropping seeds into them.
**drill** (dril), ***n.*** [< L. *trilix*, three-threaded], a coarse, twilled linen or cotton cloth.
**drink** (driŋk), ***v.t.*** [DRANK, DRUNK, DRINKING], [AS. *drincan*], 1. to swallow (liquid). 2. to absorb (liquid). 3. to swallow the contents of. ***v.i.*** 1. to swallow liquid. 2. to drink alcoholic liquor, esp. to excess. ***n.*** 1. any liquid for drinking. 2. alcoholic liquor. **—drink in,** to take in eagerly with the senses or mind. **—drink to,** to drink a toast to. **—drink′a·ble,** ***adj.*** **—drink′er,** ***n.***
**drip** (drip), ***v.i. & v.t.*** [DRIPPED or DRIPT, DRIPPING], [AS. *dryppan*], to fall, or let fall, in drops. ***n.*** 1. a falling in drops. 2. [Slang], a person regarded as unpleasant.
**drip′-dry′,** ***adj.*** designating or of fabrics or garments that dry quickly when hung soaking wet. ***v.i.*** [-DRIED, -DRYING], to launder as a drip-dry fabric does.
**drip′ping,** ***adj.*** thoroughly wet. ***n.*** *usually pl.* anything that drips, as fat from roasting meat.
**drive** (drīv), ***v.t.*** [DROVE, DRIVEN, DRIVING], [AS. *drifan*], 1. to force to go; impel. 2. to force into or from a state or act. 3. to force to work, usually to excess. 4. to hit (a ball) hard. 5. to make penetrate. 6. to control the movement of (an automobile, etc.). 7. to transport as in an automobile. 8. to push (a bargain, etc.) through. ***v.i.*** 1. to advance violently. 2. to drive a blow, ball, etc. 3. to be driven: said of an automobile. 4. to go in a vehicle. 5. to operate a motor vehicle. ***n.*** 1. a driving. 2. a trip in a vehicle. 3. a road for automobiles, etc. 4. a rounding up of animals. 5. a campaign to achieve some purpose. 6. energy; push. 7. a strong impulse or urge. 8. the propelling mechanism of a machine, etc. 9. [Colloq.], a driveway. **—drive at,** to mean.
**drive′-in′,** ***n.*** a place where people can be served food, see a motion picture, etc. while seated in their cars.
**driv·el** (driv′'l), ***v.i. & v.t.*** [-ELED or -ELLED, ELING or -ELLING], [AS. *dreflian*], 1. to let (saliva) run from the mouth; slobber. 2. to speak or say in a silly or stupid manner. ***n.*** 1. saliva running from the mouth. 2. silly, stupid talk.
**driv′er,** ***n.*** 1. one who drives an automobile, horse, etc. 2. a wooden-headed golf club used in hitting the ball from the tee.
**drive·way** (drīv′wā′), ***n.*** a path, as for automobiles, from a garage to the street.
**driz·zle** (driz′'l), ***v.i.*** [-ZLED, -ZLING], [< ME. *dresen*, to fall], to rain in fine, mistlike drops. ***n.*** a rain of this kind. **—driz′zly,** ***adj.***
**droll** (drōl), ***adj.*** [< Fr. < D. *drol*, stout fellow], amusing in a quaint way. **—droll′er·y** [*pl.* -IES], ***n.*** **—drol′ly,** ***adj.***
**drom·e·dar·y** (drom′ə-der′i), ***n.*** [*pl.* -IES], [< LL. *dromedarius* (*camelus*), running (camel)], the one-humped Arabian camel.
**drone** (drōn), ***n.*** [AS. *dran*], 1. a male honeybee which does no work. 2. an idler who lives by the work of others.
**drone** (drōn), ***v.i.*** [DRONED, DRONING], [prob. < *drone* (bee)], 1. to make a continuous humming sound. 2. to talk in a monotonous voice. ***v.t.*** to utter in a monotonous tone. ***n.*** a continuous humming sound.
**drool** (drōōl), ***v.i.*** [< *drivel*], 1. to let saliva flow from one's mouth. 2. to flow from the mouth, as saliva.
**droop** (drōōp), ***v.i.*** [< ON. *drūpa*], 1. to sink, hang, or bend down. 2. to lose vitality. 3. to become dejected. ***v.t.*** to let sink or hang down. ***n.*** a drooping. **—droop′y,** ***adj.***
**drop** (drop), ***n.*** [AS. *dropa*], 1. a small quantity of liquid that is roundish, as when falling. 2. anything like a drop in shape, size, etc. 3. a very small quantity. 4. a sudden fall, slump, descent, etc. 5. something that drops, as a curtain or trap door. 6. the distance between a higher and lower

level. *v.i.* [DROPPED or DROPT, DROPPING], 1. to fall in drops. 2. to fall. 3. to sink to the ground exhausted, wounded, or dead. 4. to fall into a specified state: as, she *dropped* off to sleep. 5. to come to an end: as, let the matter *drop*. *v.t.* 1. to let fall in drops. 2. to let fall. 3. to utter (a hint, etc.) casually. 4. to send (a letter). 5. to dismiss; have done with. 6. to lower. 7. [Colloq.], to deposit at a specified place. **—drop behind,** to be outdistanced. **—drop in,** to pay a casual visit. **—drop out,** to stop being a participant. **—drop′per,** *n.*

**drop curtain,** a theater curtain that can be lowered and raised.

**drop kick,** in *football,* a kick in which the ball is dropped to the ground and kicked just as it rebounds. **—drop′-kick′,** *v.t. & v.i.*

**drop·let** (drop′lit), *n.* a very small drop.

**drop′out′,** *n.* a student who withdraws from school before graduating.

**drop·sy** (drop′si), *n.* [< Gr. *hydrōps* < *hydōr,* water], an abnormal accumulation of serous fluid in the body. **—drop′si·cal** (-k'l), *adj.*

**dross** (drôs, dros), *n.* [< AS. *dreosan,* to fall], 1. a scum on molten metal. 2. refuse.

**drought** (drout), *n.* [< AS. *drugoth,* dryness], prolonged dry weather: also **drouth** (drouth).

**drove** (drōv), *n.* [< AS. *draf*], 1. a number of cattle, sheep, etc. driven or moving along as a group; flock; herd. 2. a moving crowd of people.

**drove** (drōv), pt. of **drive.**

**dro·ver** (drō′vẽr), *n.* 1. one who drives animals to market. 2. a cattle dealer.

**drown** (droun), *v.i.* [< ON. *drukkna*], to die by suffocation in water. *v.t.* 1. to kill by such suffocation. 2. to flood; soak. 3. to deaden or muffle (sound, etc.): with *out.*

**drowse** (drouz), *v.i.* [DROWSED, DROWSING], [< D. *droosen*], to be sleepy or almost asleep; doze. *n.* the fact or state of drowsing.

**drow′sy,** *adj.* [-SIER, -SIEST], being or making sleepy or half asleep. **—drow′si·ly,** *adv.*

**drub** (drub), *v.t.* [DRUBBED, DRUBBING], [< Ar. *daraba,* to cudgel], 1. to beat with a stick. 2. to defeat soundly. **—drub′bing,** *n.*

**drudge** (druj), *n.* [< ?], a person who does hard, menial, or unpleasant work. *v.i.* [DRUDGED, DRUDGING], to do such work. **—drudg′er·y,** [*pl.* -IES], *n.*

**drug** (drug), *n.* [< OFr. *drogue*], 1. any substance used as or in a medicine. 2. a narcotic. *v.t.* [DRUGGED, DRUGGING], 1. to put a harmful drug in (a beverage, etc.). 2. to stupefy or poison as with a drug. **—drug on the market,** a commodity in much greater supply than demand.

**drug′gist** (-ist), *n.* 1. a dealer in drugs, medical equipment, etc. 2. a pharmacist.

**drug′store′,** *n.* a store selling drugs, medical supplies, and various other commodities.

**dru·id, Dru·id** (drōō′id), *n.* [< Celt.], a member of a Celtic religious order in ancient Britain, Ireland, and France.

**drum** (drum), *n.* [< D. *trom* or MLG. *trumme*], 1. a percussion instrument consisting of a hollow cylinder with a membrane stretched over the end or ends. 2. the sound produced by beating a drum. 3. any drumlike cylindrical object. 4. the eardrum. *v.i.* [DRUMMED, DRUMMING], 1. to beat a drum. 2. to tap continually, as with the fingers. **—drum into,** to make known to by continued repetition. **—drum out of,** to expel from in disgrace.

**drum major,** one who twirls a baton at the head of a marching band. **—drum ma′jor·ette′,** *fem.*

**drum′mer,** *n.* 1. a drum player. 2. [Colloq.], a traveling salesman.

**drum′stick′,** *n.* 1. a stick for beating a drum. 2. the lower half of the leg of a cooked fowl.

**drunk** (druŋk), pp. of **drink.** *adj.* overcome by alcoholic liquor; intoxicated. *n.* [Slang], 1. a drunken person. 2. a drinking spree.

**drunk·ard** (druŋ′kẽrd), *n.* a person who often gets drunk; inebriate.

**drunk′en,** *adj.* (used before the noun) 1. intoxicated. 2. caused by or in a drunken state. **—drunk′en·ness,** *n.*

**drupe** (drōōp), *n.* [< Gr. *dryppa,* overripe olive], any fruit with a soft, fleshy part around an inner stone that contains the seed, as an apricot or cherry.

**dry** (drī), *adj.* [DRIER, DRIEST], [AS. *dryge*], 1. not under water: as, *dry* land. 2. not wet or moist. 3. lacking rain or water; arid. 4. thirsty. 5. not yielding milk. 6. solid; not liquid. 7. not sweet: as, *dry* wine. 8. prohibiting or opposed to the use or sale of alcoholic liquors: as, a *dry* county. 9. matter-of-fact: as, *dry* wit. 10. boring; uninteresting. *n.* [*pl.* DRYS], [Colloq.], a prohibitionist. *v.t. & v.i.* [DRIED, DRYING], to make or become dry. **—dry up,** 1. to make or become thoroughly dry. 2. [Slang], to stop talking. **—dry′ly,** *adv.* **—dry′ness,** *n.*

**dry·ad, Dry·ad** (drī′əd), *n.* [< Gr. *drys,* tree], in *Gr. myth.,* a tree nymph.

**dry battery,** 1. an electric battery made up of several connected dry cells. 2. a dry cell.

**dry cell,** a voltaic cell containing an absorbent so that its contents cannot spill.

**dry′-clean′,** *v.t.* to clean (garments, etc.) with a solvent other than water, as naphtha. **—dry cleaner. —dry cleaning.**

**dry dock,** a dock from which the water can be emptied, used for building ships.

**dry′er,** *n.* a drier.

**dry goods,** cloth, cloth products, etc.

**dry ice,** carbon dioxide highly compressed and in a solid state, used as a refrigerant.

**dry rot,** a fungous decay causing seasoned timber to crumble to powder.

**dry run,** [Slang], practice for some event.

**D.S.C.,** Distinguished Service Cross.

**D.S.T.,** Daylight Saving Time.

**D.T.'s, d.t.'s** (dē′tēz′), [Slang], delirium tremens.

**du·al** (dōō′əl, dū′-), *adj.* [< L. *duo,* two], 1. of two. 2. double; twofold. **—du′al·ism,** *n.* **—du·al·i·ty** (dōō-al′ə-ti, dū-), *n.*

**dub** (dub), *v.t.* [DUBBED, DUBBING], [< AS. *dubbian,* to strike], 1. to confer a title or name upon. 2. to make smooth, as by hammering, scraping, etc. 3. [Slang], to bungle.

**dub** (dub), *v.t.* [DUBBED, DUBBING], [< *double*], to insert (dialogue, music, etc.) in the sound track of a movie: usually with *in.*

**du·bi·e·ty** (dōō-bī′ə-ti, dū-), *n.* 1. uncertainty. 2. [*pl.* -TIES], a thing that is doubtful.

**du·bi·ous** (dōō′bi-əs, dū′-), *adj.* [< L. *dubius,* uncertain], 1. causing doubt. 2. skeptical. 3. questionable. **—du′bi·ous·ly,** *adv.*

**du·cal** (dōō′k'l, dū′-), *adj.* [LL. *ducalis,* of a leader], of a duke or dukedom.

**duc·at** (duk′ət), *n.* [see DUCHY], any of several former European coins.

**duch·ess** (duch′is), *n.* 1. the wife or widow of a duke. 2. a woman who holds a duchy in her own right.

**duch·y** (duch′i), *n.* [*pl.* -IES], [< L. *dux,* leader], the territory ruled by a duke or duchess.

**duck** (duk), *n.* [< AS. *duce,* lit., diver], 1. a swimming bird with a flat bill, short neck, and webbed feet. 2. the flesh of a duck as food. **—like water off a duck's back,** with no effect.

**duck** (duk), *v.t. & v.i.* [ME, *duken*], 1. to plunge or dip under water for a moment. 2. to lower or bend (the head, body, etc.) suddenly, as to avoid a blow. 3. [Colloq.], to avoid (a task, person, etc.). *n.* a ducking.

**duck** (duk), *n.* [D. *doek*], a cotton or linen cloth like canvas but finer and lighter.

**duck'bill'**, *n.* a small, egg-laying water mammal with webbed feet and a bill like a duck's.
**duck'ling**, *n.* a young duck.
**duck'pins'**, *n.pl.* [construed as sing.], 1. a game like tenpins, played with smaller pins and balls. 2. the pins used.
**duck'weed'**, *n.* a small flowering plant that floats on fresh water like a green scum.
**duck'y**, *adj.* [-IER, -IEST], [Slang], excellent, pleasing, delightful, etc.
**duct** (dukt), *n.* [< L. *ducere*, to lead], a tube or channel through which a fluid moves. **—duct'less**, *adj.*
**duc·tile** (duk't'l, -til), *adj.* [see DUCT], 1. that can be drawn or hammered thin without breaking: said of metals. 2. easily led; tractable. **—duc·til'i·ty** (-til'ə-ti), *n.*
**ductless gland**, a gland, as the thyroid, which has no excretory ducts and sends its secretions directly into the lymph or blood.
**dud** (dud), *n.* [ult. < D. *dood*, dead], [Slang], 1. a bomb or shell that fails to explode. 2. a failure.
**dude** (dood, dūd), *n.* [< ?], 1. a dandy; fop. 2. [Western Slang], a city fellow or tourist.
**dudg·eon** (duj'ən), *n.* [prob. < Anglo-Fr. (*en*) *digeon*, (at) the dagger hilt], an angry or offended feeling. **—in high dudgeon**, very angry, offended, or resentful.
**duds** (dudz), *n.pl.* [prob. < ON. *dutha*, wrap up], [Slang], 1. clothes. 2. belongings.
**due** (doo, dū), *adj.* [< L. *debere*, owe], 1. owed or owing as a debt; payable. 2. suitable; proper. 3. enough: as, *due* care. 4. expected or scheduled to arrive. *adv.* exactly; directly: as, *due* west. *n.* anything due. **—due to**, 1. caused by. 2. [Colloq.], because of.
**du·el** (doo'əl, dū'-), *n.* [ult. < L. *duo*, two], 1. a prearranged fight between two persons armed with deadly weapons. 2. any contest like this. *v.i. & v.t.* [-ELED or -ELLED, -ELING or -ELLING], to fight a duel with. **—du'el·ist, du'el·list, du'el·er, du'el·ler**, *n.*
**du·en·na** (doo-en'ə, dū-), *n.* [< L. *domina*, mistress], a chaperon or governess.
**dues** (dooz, dūz), *n.pl.* [see DUE], 1. a fee or tax. 2. the sum of money paid, or to be paid, by a member to an organization.
**du·et** (doo-et', dū-), *n.* [< L. *duo*, two], 1. a musical composition for two voices or instruments. 2. the two performers.
**duf·fel bag** (duf''l), [< *Duffel*, town in Belgium], a large cloth bag for carrying clothing and personal belongings.
**duf·fer** (duf'ẽr), *n.* [< thieves' slang *duff*, to fake], [Slang], an incompetent person.
**dug** (dug), pt. and pp. of **dig**.
**dug** (dug), *n.* [< Dan. *dægge*, to suckle], a female animal's nipple or teat.
**dug'out'** (-out'), *n.* 1. a boat hollowed out of a log. 2. a large hole dug in the ground or in a hillside, used as a shelter. 3. in *baseball*, either of two covered shelters with benches, for the opposing teams.
**duke** (dook, dūk), *n.* [< L. *dux*, leader], 1. the ruler of a duchy. 2. a nobleman next in rank to a prince. **—duke'dom**, *n.*
**dul·cet** (dul'sit), *adj.* [< L. *dulcis*, sweet], soothing or pleasant to hear; melodious.
**dul·ci·mer** (dul'sə-mẽr), *n.* [< L. *dulcis*, sweet + *melos*, song], a musical instrument with metal strings, played with hammers.
**dull** (dull), *adj.* [< AS. *dol*, stupid], 1. mentally slow; stupid. 2. physically slow; sluggish. 3. boring; tedious. 4. not sharp; blunt. 5. not feeling or felt keenly. 6. not vivid or bright. *v.t. & v.i.* to make or become dull. **—dull'ness**, *n.* **—dul'ly**, *adv.*
**dull'ard** (-ẽrd), *n.* a stupid person.
**du·ly** (doo'li, dū'-), *adv.* 1. in a due manner; rightfully; properly. 2. when due.
**dumb** (dum), *adj.* [AS.], 1. lacking the power of speech; mute. 2. silent. 3. [< G. *dumm*], [Colloq.], stupid. **—dumb'ly**, *adv.*
**dumb·bell** (dum'bel'), *n.* 1. a device consisting of two heavy weights joined by a short bar, used in exercises to develop the muscles. 2. [Slang], a stupid person.
**dumb show**, 1. formerly, a part of a play done in pantomime. 2. silent gestures.
**dumb'-wait'er**, *n.* a small elevator for sending food, etc. from one floor to another.
**dum·dum** (**bullet**) (dum'dum), [< *Dumdum*, arsenal near Calcutta], a soft-nosed bullet that expands when it hits.
**dum·found, dumb·found** (dum'-found'), *v.t.* [< *dumb* + *confound*], to make speechless by surprising; amaze.
**dum·my** (dum'i), *n.* [*pl.* -MIES], 1. a figure made in human form, used for displaying clothing, etc. 2. an imitation; sham. 3. [Slang], a stupid person. 4. in *card games*, the successful bidder's partner, whose hand is exposed on the board and played by the successful bidder. *adj.* sham.
**dump** (dump), *v.t.* [prob. < ON.], 1. to unload in a heap or mass. 2. to throw away as rubbish. *n.* 1. a rubbish pile. 2. a place for dumping. 3. a temporary supply center. **—in the dumps**, in low spirits.
**dump·ling** (dump'liŋ), *n.* [dim. of dial. *dump*, shapeless lump], 1. a small piece of dough, steamed or boiled and served with meat or soup. 2. a crust of baked dough filled with fruit.
**dump truck**, a truck that is unloaded by tilting the truck bed backward.
**dump·y** (dump'i), *adj.* [-IER, -IEST], short and thick; squat. **—dump'i·ness**, *n.*
**dun** (dun), *adj. & n.* [AS. *dunn*], dull grayish brown.
**dun** (dun), *v.t. & v.i.* [DUNNED, DUNNING], [prob. dial. var. of *din*], to ask (a debtor) repeatedly for payment. *n.* an insistent demand for payment.
**dunce** (duns), *n.* [< *Dunsman*, a follower of John *Duns* Scotus, 13th-c. Scot. scholar], a stupid or ignorant person.
**dun·der·head** (dun'dẽr-hed'), *n.* [< D. *donder*, thunder], a stupid person; dunce.
**dune** (doon, dūn), *n.* [< OD. *duna*], a rounded hill or ridge of drifted sand.
**dung** (duŋ), *n.* [AS.], animal excrement.
**dun·ga·ree** (duŋ'gə-rē'), *n.* [Hind. *dungrī*], 1. a coarse cotton cloth used for tents, etc. 2. *pl.* work trousers or overalls of this cloth.
**dun·geon** (dun'jən), *n.* [OFr. *donjon*], a dark underground cell or prison.
**dung'hill'** (duŋ'-), *n.* 1. a heap of dung. 2. anything vile or filthy.
**dunk** (duŋk), *v.t. & v.i.* [G. *tunken*, to dip], to dip (bread, cakes, etc.) into coffee, etc. before eating it.
**du·o** (doo'ō, dū'ō), *n.* [*pl.* -OS, -I (-ē)], [It.], a duet (esp. in sense 2).
**du·o·dec·i·mal** (doo'ə-des'ə-m'l, dū'-), *adj.* [< L. *duo*, two + *decem*, ten], relating to twelve or twelfths. *n.* one twelfth.
**du·o·de·num** (doo'ə-dē'nəm, dū'-), *n.* [*pl.* -NA (-nə)], [< L. *duodeni*, twelve each: its length is about twelve fingers' breadth], the first section of the small intestine, below the stomach. **—du'o·de'nal**, *adj.*
**dupe** (doop, dūp), *n.* [< L. *upupa*, species of bird], a person easily tricked or fooled. *v.t.* [DUPED, DUPING], to deceive; cheat.
**du·plex** (doo'pleks, dū'-), *adj.* [L.], double. *n.* 1. an apartment with rooms on two floors. 2. a house consisting of two separate family units.
**du·pli·cate** (doo'plə-kit, dū'-; *for v.*, -kāt'), *adj.* [< L. *duplicare*, to double], 1. double. 2. corresponding exactly. *n.* an exact copy; facsimile. *v.t.* [-CATED, -CATING], 1. to make an exact copy of. 2. to cause to happen again. Abbrev. **dup.** **—du'pli·ca'tion**, *n.*

**du'pli·ca'tor** (-kā'tẽr), *n.* a machine for making exact copies of written matter.
**du·plic·i·ty** (doo-plis'ə-ti, dū-), *n.* [*pl.* -TIES], [< LL. *duplicitas*], hypocritical cunning or deception; double-dealing.
**du·ra·ble** (door'ə-b'l, dyoor'-), *adj.* [< L. *durare*, to last], 1. lasting in spite of hard wear or use. 2. stable. —**du'ra·bil'i·ty**, *n.*
**dur·ance** (door'əns, dyoor'-), *n.* [see DURABLE], imprisonment.
**du·ra·tion** (doo-rā'shən, dyoo-), *n.* [see DURABLE], the time that a thing continues.
**du·ress** (doo-res', dyoo-), *n.* [< L. *durus*, hard], 1. imprisonment. 2. coercion.
**dur·ing** (door'iŋ, dyoor'-), *prep.* [see DURABLE], 1. throughout the entire time of. 2. in the course of.
**durst** (dũrst), archaic pt. of **dare.**
**dusk** (dusk), *n.* [AS. *dosc*, *dox*, dark-colored], 1. the dark part of twilight. 2. gloom; darkness; dimness. —**dusk'y** [-IER, -IEST], *adj.*
**dust** (dust), *n.* [AS.], 1. powdery earth or any finely powdered matter. 2. earth. 3. disintegrated mortal remains. 4. anything worthless. *v.t.* 1. to sprinkle with dust, powder, etc. 2. to rid of dust.
**dust bowl,** an area where droughts and dust storms are common.
**dust'er,** *n.* 1. one that dusts. 2. a brush or cloth for removing dust from furniture, etc.
**dust jacket,** a removable paper covering folded around the binding of a book.
**dust'pan',** *n.* a shovellike receptacle into which floor dust is swept.
**dust'y,** *adj.* [-IER, -IEST], 1. covered with or full of dust. 2. like dust; powdery. 3. dust-colored. —**dust'i·ness**, *n.*
**Dutch** (duch), *adj.* 1. of the Netherlands, its people, language, etc. 2. [Slang], German. *n.* 1. the language of the Netherlands. 2. [construed as pl.], the people of the Netherlands. —**go Dutch**, [Colloq.], to have each pay his own expenses. —**in Dutch**, [Slang], in difficulties.
**Dutch door,** a door with upper and lower halves opening separately.
**Dutch oven,** an iron kettle for baking, with a convex lid.
**Dutch treat,** [Colloq.], any entertainment, etc. in which each pays his own expenses.
**Dutch uncle,** [Colloq.], one who bluntly and sternly lectures another.
**du·te·ous** (doo'ti-əs, dū'-), *adj.* dutiful.
**du·ti·a·ble** (doo'ti-ə-b'l, dū'-), *adj.* necessitating payment of a duty.
**du·ti·ful** (doo'ti-fəl, dū'-), *adj.* showing, or resulting from, a sense of duty; obedient.
**du·ty** (doo'ti, dū'-), *n.* [*pl.* -TIES], [see DUE & -TY], 1. conduct owed to one's parents, elders, etc.; respect. 2. any action necessary in one's position. 3. conduct resulting from a sense of justice, morality, etc. 4. a sense of obligation: as, *duty* calls. 5. a tax on imports, exports, etc.
**dwarf** (dwôrf), *n.* [AS. *dweorh*], any living being or thing that is much smaller than the usual one of its kind. *v.t.* 1. to stunt the growth of. 2. to make seem small in comparison. *v.i.* to become dwarfed. *adj.* undersized; stunted. —**dwarf'ish**, *adj.*
**dwell** (dwel), *v.i.* [DWELT or DWELLED, DWELLING], [AS. *dwellan*, deceive, hence hinder], to reside; make one's home. —**dwell on** (or **upon**), to linger over in thought or speech. —**dwell'er**, *n.*
**dwell'ing (place),** a place to live in; abode.
**dwin·dle** (dwin'd'l), *v.i. & v.t.* [-DLED, -DLING], [< AS. *dwinan*, waste away], to make or become smaller or less; diminish.
**dye** (dī), *n.* [AS. *deah*], 1. color; tint; hue. 2. a substance used to color fabric, hair, etc. *v.t. & v.i.* [DYED, DYEING], to color as with a dye. —**dye'ing**, *n.* —**dy'er**, *n.*
**dyed'-in-the-wool',** *adj.* thoroughgoing; unchangeable.
**dye'stuff',** *n.* any substance constituting or yielding a dye.
**dy·ing** (dī'iŋ), ppr. of **die.** *adj.* 1. at the point of death. 2. about to end. *n.* a ceasing to live or exist.
**dyke** (dīk), *n.* a dike.
**dy·nam·ic** (dī-nam'ik), *adj.* [< Gr. *dynamis*, power], 1. relating to energy or physical force in motion. 2. energetic; vigorous; forceful. —**dy·nam'i·cal·ly**, *adv.*
**dy·nam'ics,** *n.pl.* 1. [construed as sing.], the branch of physics dealing with the action of force on bodies in motion or at rest. 2. the various forces operating in any field.
**dy·na·mite** (dī'nə-mīt'), *n.* [see DYNAMIC], a powerful explosive made with nitroglycerin. *v.t.* [-MITED, -MITING], to blow up with dynamite.
**dy·na·mo** (dī'nə-mō'), *n.* [*pl.* -MOS], [see DYNAMIC], a device for converting mechanical energy into electrical energy.
**dy·nas·ty** (dī'nəs-ti), *n.* [*pl.* -TIES], [< Gr. *dynasthai*, be strong], a succession of rulers who are members of the same family. —**dy·nas'tic** (-nas'tik), *adj.*
**dys-,** [< Gr.], a prefix meaning *bad, ill, difficult*, etc.
**dys·en·ter·y** (dis''n-ter'i), *n.* [< Gr. *dys-*, bad + *entera*, bowels], an intestinal disease characterized by inflammation and bloody diarrhea. —**dys'en·ter'ic**, *adj.*
**dys·pep·sia** (dis-pep'shə, -si-ə), *n.* [< Gr. *dys-*, bad + *peptein*, to digest], indigestion. —**dys·pep'tic**, *adj. & n.*
**dz.,** dozen; dozens.

# E

**E, e** (ē), *n.* [*pl.* E's, e's, Es, es], the fifth letter of the English alphabet.
**E,** *n.* in *music*, the third tone in the scale of C major.
**e-,** ex-: used before *b, d, l, m, n, r*, and *v.*
**E, E., e, e.,** 1. east. 2. eastern.
**each** (ēch), *adj. & pron.* [< AS. *a*, ever + *gelic*, alike], every one of two or more considered separately. *adv.* apiece. Abbrev. **ea.**
**ea·ger** (ē'gẽr), *adj.* [< L. *acer*, keen], keenly desiring; wanting very much; impatient or anxious. —**ea'ger·ly**, *adv.* —**ea'ger·ness**, *n.*
**ea·gle** (ē'g'l), *n.* [< L. *aquila*], 1. a large, strong bird of prey, with sharp vision and powerful wings. 2. a representation of the eagle, esp. as the emblem of the U.S. 3. a former ten-dollar gold coin of the U.S. 4. in *golf*, a score of two below par on a hole.
**ea·glet** (ē'glit), *n.* a young eagle.
**ear** (êr), *n.* [< AS. *eare*], 1. the part of the body that perceives sound. 2. the external part of the ear. 3. the sense of hearing. 4. attention; heed. 5. anything like an ear. —**be all ears**, to listen attentively. —**play by ear**, to play (music) without using notation. —**up to the ears**, deeply involved.
**ear** (êr), *n.* [AS.], the grain-bearing spike of a cereal plant. *v.i.* to sprout ears.
**ear'ache',** *n.* an ache or pain in the ear.
**ear'drum,** *n.* the thin membrane inside the ear that vibrates when struck by sound waves.
**earl** (ũrl), *n.* [AS. *eorl*, warrior], a British nobleman ranking just above a viscount.

**ear·ly** (ũr'li), *adv. & adj.* [-LIER, -LIEST], [< AS. *ær*, before + *-lice*, -ly], 1. near the beginning. 2. before the expected or usual time. 3. in the distant past. 4. in the near future. —**ear'li·ness**, *n.*

**ear'mark'**, *n.* 1. an identifying mark put on the ear of cattle. 2. any identifying mark or feature. *v.t.* 1. to set a distinctive mark upon. 2. to reserve for a special purpose.

**ear'muffs'** (-mufs'), *n.pl.* coverings for the ears, worn in cold weather.

**earn** (ũrn), *v.t.* [AS. *earnian*], 1. to receive (wages, etc.) for one's work. 2. to get as deserved. 3. to gain (interest, etc.) as profit.

**ear·nest** (ũr'nist), *adj.* [AS. *eornoste*], 1. serious and intense; not joking. 2. important. —**in earnest**, 1. serious. 2. with determination. —**ear'nest·ly**, *adv.* —**ear'nest·ness**, *n.*

**ear·nest** (ũr'nist), *n.* [ult. < Heb. *'ērābōn*], money, etc. given as a pledge in binding a bargain.

**earn'ings**, *n.pl.* 1. wages or other recompense. 2. profits, interest, etc.

**ear'ring'**, *n.* a ring or other small ornament for the lobe of the ear.

**ear'shot'** (-shot'), *n.* the distance within which a sound can be heard.

**earth** (ũrth), *n.* [AS. *eorthe*], 1. the planet we live on, the fifth largest of the solar system: cf. **planet**. 2. this world as distinguished from heaven and hell. 3. land. 4. ground; soil. —**down to earth**, practical.

**earth'-bound', earth'bound'**, *adj.* confined to or by the earth and earthly things.

**earth'en**, *adj.* 1. made of earth. 2. made of baked clay.

**earth'en·ware'**, *n.* the coarser sort of containers, tableware, etc. made of baked clay.

**earth'ly**, *adj.* 1. terrestrial. 2. worldly. 3. temporal. 4. conceivable. —**earth'li·ness**, *n.*

**earth'nut'**, *n.* a root or tuber, or underground pod, as of the peanut.

**earth'quake'** (-kwāk'), *n.* a shaking of the crust of the earth, caused by underground shifting of rock.

**earth'work'**, *n.* a fortification made by piling up earth.

**earth'worm'**, *n.* a round, segmented worm that burrows in the soil.

**earth·y** (ũr'thi), *adj.* [-IER, -IEST], 1. of or like earth or soil. 2. *a*) coarse; gross. *b*) simple and natural. —**earth'i·ness**, *n.*

**ease** (ēz), *n.* [< L. *adjacens*, lying near-by], 1. freedom from pain or trouble; comfort. 2. poise; natural manner. 3. freedom from difficulty; facility. *v.t.* [EASED, EASING], 1. to free from pain or trouble; comfort. 2. to lessen (pain, anxiety, etc.). 3. to facilitate. 4. to reduce the strain or pressure of. 5. to move by careful shifting, etc. *v.i.* to lessen in tension, pain, etc. —**eas'er**, *n.*

**ea·sel** (ē'z'l), *n.* [< D. *ezel*, ass], an upright frame to hold an artist's canvas, etc.

**ease·ment** (ēz'mənt), *n.* 1. an easing or being eased. 2. in *law*, a right that one may have in another's land.

**eas·i·ly** (ē'z'l-i), *adv.* 1. with ease. 2. without a doubt. 3. very likely.

**east** (ēst), *n.* [AS.], 1. the direction in which sunrise occurs (90° on the compass, opposite west). 2. a region in or toward this direction. *adj.* 1. in, of, or toward the east. 2. from the east. *adv.* in or toward the east.

**East·er** (ēs'tẽr), *n.* [< AS. *Eastre*, dawn goddess], an annual Christian festival in the spring celebrating the resurrection of Jesus.

**east'er·ly**, *adj. & adv.* 1. toward the east. 2. from the east.

**east'ern**, *adj.* 1. in, of, or toward the east. 2. from the east. —**east'ern·most'**, *adj.*

**east'ern·er**, *n.* a native or inhabitant of the east.

**east'ward** (-wẽrd), *adv. & adj.* toward the east: also **east'wards**, *adv.*

**eas·y** (ēz'i), *adj.* [-IER, -IEST], [see EASE], 1. not difficult. 2. free from anxiety, pain, etc. 3. comfortable; restful. 4. free from constraint; not stiff. 5. not strict or severe. 6. unhurried; moderate. *adv.* [Colloq.], easily. —**take it easy**, [Colloq.], 1. to refrain from anger, haste, etc. 2. to relax; rest.

**easy chair**, a stuffed or padded armchair.

**eas'y·go'ing, eas'y-go'ing**, *adj.* dealing with things in an easy, carefree way.

**eat** (ēt), *v.t.* [ATE, EATEN, EATING], [AS. *etan*], 1. to chew and swallow (food). 2. to consume or ravage (with *away* or *up*). 3. to destroy, as acid does; corrode. 4. to make by eating: as, acid *eats* holes in cloth. *v.i.* to eat food; have a meal. —**eat'er**, *n.*

**eat'a·ble**, *adj.* fit to be eaten. *n. usually in pl.* a thing fit to be eaten.

**eats** (ēts), *n.pl.* [Colloq.], food; meals.

**eau de Co·logne** (ō' də kə-lōn'), [Fr., lit., water of Cologne], cologne.

**eaves** (ēvz), *n.pl.* [AS. *efes*], the edge of a roof, usually projecting beyond the walls.

**eaves'drop'** (-drop'), *v.i.* [-DROPPED, -DROPPING], [orig., to stand under eaves to overhear], to listen secretly to a conversation. —**eaves'drop'per**, *n.*

**ebb** (eb), *n.* [AS. *ebba*], 1. the flowing of the tide back toward the sea. 2. a lessening; decline. *v.i.* 1. to recede, as the tide. 2. to lessen; decline.

**eb·on** (eb'ən), *adj. & n.* [< Gr. *ebenos*], [Poetic], ebony.

**eb'on·y** (-i), *n.* [*pl.* -IES], [see EBON], the hard, heavy, dark wood of certain tropical trees. *adj.* 1. of ebony. 2. like ebony; black.

**e·bul·lient** (i-bul'yənt), *adj.* [< L. *e-*, out + *bullire*, to boil], 1. bubbling; boiling. 2. enthusiastic; exuberant. —**e·bul'lience**, *n.*

**e·bul·li·tion** (eb'ə-lish'ən), *n.* 1. a boiling or bubbling up. 2. a sudden outburst, as of emotion.

**ec-**, ex-: used before *c* or *s*.

**ec·cen·tric** (ik-sen'trik), *adj.* [< Gr. *ek-*, out of + *kentron*, center], 1. not having the same center, as two circles. 2. having its axis off center. 3. not exactly circular. 4. odd in conduct; peculiar. *n.* 1. a disk set off center on a shaft, for converting circular motion into back-and-forth motion. 2. an eccentric person. —**ec·cen'tri·cal·ly**, *adv.* —**ec·cen·tric·i·ty** (ek'sən-tris'ə-ti) [*pl.* -TIES], *n.*

**Ec·cle·si·as·tes** (i-klē'zi-as'tēz), *n.* [Gr., preacher], a book of the Old Testament.

**ec·cle·si·as·tic** (i-klē'zi-as'tik), *adj.* [< Gr. *ekklēsia*, citizens' assembly], ecclesiastical. *n.* a clergyman.

**ec·cle'si·as'ti·cal**, *adj.* [see prec. entry], of the church or the clergy.

**ech·e·lon** (esh'ə-lon'), *n.* [< Fr. < L. *scala*, ladder], 1. a steplike formation of units of troops, ships, aircraft, etc. 2. any subdivision of a military command in the direction of depth: as, a rear *echelon*.

**ech·o** (ek'ō), *n.* [*pl.* -OES], [< Gr. *ēchē*, a sound], 1. the repeating of a sound by reflection of sound waves from a surface. 2. a sound so produced.

**e·cho·ic** (e-kō'ik), *adj.* imitative in sound, as the word *buzz*. —**ech'o·ism**, *n.*

**é·clair** (ā-klâr', i-), *n.* [Fr., lit., lightning], a frosted pastry filled with custard, etc.

**é·clat** (ā-klä'), *n.* [< Fr. *éclater*, to burst (out)], 1. brilliant success. 2. acclaim; fame.

**ec·lec·tic** (ik-lek'tik, ek-), *adj.* [< Gr. *ek-*, out + *legein*, to pick], selecting or selected from various systems, doctrines, or sources.

**e·clipse** (i-klips'), *n.* [< Gr. *ek-*, out + *leipein*, to leave], 1. the obscuring of the sun when the moon comes between it and the earth (**solar eclipse**), or of the moon when the earth's shadow is cast upon it (**lunar eclipse**). 2. any obscuring of light, or of fame, glory, etc. *v.t.* [ECLIPSED, ECLIPSING],

1. to cause an eclipse of. 2. to surpass.
**e·clip·tc** (i-kl ip'tik), *n.* the sun's apparent annual path, or orbit; great circle of the celestial sphere. *adj.* of the ecliptic.
**ec·logue** (ek'lôg), *n.* [see ECLECTIC], a short pastoral poem.
**e·col·o·gy** (ē-kol'ə-ji), *n.* [< Gr. *oikos*, house; + *-logy*], the branch of biology dealing with the relations between living organisms and their environment. **—e·col'o·gist,** *n.*
**econ.,** 1. economics. 2. economy.
**e·co·nom·ic** (ē'kə-nom'ik, ek'ə-), *adj.* 1. of the management of income, expenditures, etc., as of a community or government. 2. of economics. 3. of the satisfaction of the material needs of people.
**e'co·nom'i·cal,** *adj.* 1. not wasting money, time, etc.; thrifty. 2. of economics.
**e'co·nom'ics,** *n.pl.* [construed as sing.], the science that deals with the production, distribution, and consumption of wealth.
**e·con·o·mist** (i-kon'ə-mist), *n.* a specialist in economics.
**e·con'o·mize'** (-mīz'), *v.i.* [-MIZED, -MIZING], to reduce waste or expenses.
**e·con·o·my** (i-kon'ə-mi), *n.* [*pl.* -MIES], [< Gr. *oikos*, house + *nomos*, managing], 1. the management of the income, expenditures, etc. of a household, government, etc. 2. careful management of wealth, etc.; thrift. 3. an instance of thrift. 4. a system of producing, distributing, and using wealth.
**ec·ru** (ek'rōō), *adj. & n.* [< Fr. < L. *ex*, out + *crudus*, raw], light tan; beige.
**ec·sta·sy** (ek'stə-si), *n.* [*pl.* -SIES], [< Gr. *ekstasis*, distraction], a state or feeling of overpowering joy; rapture. **—ec·stat·ic** (ik-stat'ik), *adj.* **—ec·stat'i·cal·ly,** *adv.*
**-ectomy,** [< Gr. *ek-*, out + *temnein*, to cut], a combining form meaning *surgical excision of*, as in *appendectomy*.
**ec·to·plasm** (ek'tə-plaz'm), *n.* [< Gr. *ektos*, outside; + *-plasm*], 1. the outer layer of the cytoplasm of a cell. 2. in *spiritualism*, a substance supposed to emanate from the medium's body during a trance.
**ec·u·men·i·cal** (ek'yoo-men'i-k'l), *adj.* [< Gr. *oikoumenē* (*gē*), the inhabited (world)], 1. general; universal; esp., of the Christian Church as a whole. 2. furthering religious unity, esp. among Christian churches.
**ec'u·men·ism** (-mə-niz'm, e-kyōō'-), *n.* the ecumenical movement, esp. among Christian churches.
**ec·ze·ma** (ek'sə-mə, eg'zi-, eg-zē'-), *n.* [< Gr. *ek-*, out of + *zeein*, to boil], a skin disease characterized by inflammation, itching, and scaliness.
**-ed,** [AS.], a suffix used: 1. to form the past tense and past participle of many verbs. 2. to form adjectives from nouns or verbs, as in *cultured*.
**ed.,** [*pl.* EDS.], 1. edition. 2. editor.
**ed·dy** (ed'i), *n.* [*pl.* -DIES], [prob. < ON. *itha*], a little whirlpool or whirlwind. *v.i.* [-DIED, -DYING], to whirl.
**e·del·weiss** (ā'd'l-vis'), *n.* [G.; *edel*, noble + *weiss*, white], a small, flowering Alpine plant with white, woolly leaves.
**e·de·ma** (i-dē'mə), *n.* [< Gr. *oidein*, to swell], dropsy.
**E·den** (ē'd'n), *n.* 1. in the *Bible*, the garden where Adam and Eve first lived; Paradise. 2. any delightful place.
**edge** (ej), *n.* [AS. *ecg*], 1. the sharp, cutting part of a blade. 2. sharpness; keenness. 3. the brink, as of a cliff; verge. 4. a border; margin. 5. [Colloq.], advantage: as, he has the *edge* on me. *v.t. & v.i.* [EDGED, EDGING], 1. to form an edge (on). 2. to make (one's way) sideways. 3. to move gradually. **—on edge,** 1. very tense; irritable. 2. impatient.
**edge'ways'** (-wāz'), *adv.* with the edge foremost: also **edge'wise'** (-wiz').
**edg'ing,** *n.* trimming, fringe, etc. for a border.
**edg·y** (ej'i), *adj.* [-IER, -IEST], irritable; nervous; on edge.
**ed·i·ble** (ed'ə-b'l), *adj.* [< L. *edere*, eat], fit to be eaten. *n. usually pl.* food. **—ed'i·bil'i·ty,** *n.*
**e·dict** (ē'dikt), *n.* [< L. *e-*, out + *dicere*, speak], a public order; decree.
**ed·i·fice** (ed'ə-fis), *n.* [see EDIFY], a building, esp. a large, imposing one.
**ed·i·fy** (ed'ə-fī'), *v.t.* [-FIED, -FYING], [< L. *aedificare*, build], to instruct; esp., to instruct or improve morally. **—ed'i·fi·ca'tion,** *n.* **—ed'i·fi'er,** *n.*
**ed·it** (ed'it), *v.t.* [< L. *e-*, out + *dare*, give], 1. to prepare (a manuscript, etc.) for publication, as by selection, revision, etc. 2. to govern the policy and contents of (a newspaper, etc.).
**edit.,** 1. edited. 2. edition. 3. editor.
**e·di·tion** (i-dish'ən), *n.* [see EDIT], 1. the size or form in which a book is published. 2. the total number of copies of a book, newspaper, etc. published at one time.
**ed·i·tor** (ed'i-tēr), *n.* [L.], 1. one who edits. 2. a writer of editorials.
**ed·i·to·ri·al** (ed'ə-tôr'i-əl), *adj.* of or written by an editor. *n.* a newspaper or magazine article explicitly stating opinions held by the editor or publisher. **—ed'i·to'ri·al·ly,** *adv.*
**ed'i·to'ri·al·ize'** (-īz'), *v.t. & v.i.* [-IZED, -IZING], to put editorial opinions into (a newspaper article, etc.).
**educ.,** 1. education. 2. educational.
**ed·u·ca·ble** (ej'oo-kə-b'l), *adj.* that can be educated or trained. **—ed'u·ca·bil'i·ty,** *n.*
**ed·u·cate** (ej'oo-kāt'), *v.t.* [-CATED, -CATING], [< L. *e-*, out + *ducere*, to lead], 1. to develope the knowledge, skill, or character of, esp. by formal schooling; teach. 2. to pay for the schooling of. **—ed'u·ca'tor,** *n.*
**ed'u·ca'tion,** *n.* 1. the process of educating; teaching. 2. knowledge, etc. thus developed. 3. formal schooling. **—ed'u·ca'tion·al,** *adj.*
**e·duce** (i-dōōs', ē-dūs'), *v.t.* [EDUCED, EDUCING], [see EDUCATE], 1. to draw out; elicit. 2. to deduce.
**-ee,** [< Anglo-Fr. pp. ending], a suffix designating: 1. *the recipient of an action*, as in *appointee*. 2. *one in a specified condition*, as in *refugee*.
**eel** (ēl), *n.* [AS. *æl*], a long, slippery, snakelike fish. **—eel'like',** *adj.*
**e'er** (âr), *adv.* [Poetic], ever.
**-eer,** [< L. *-arius*], a suffix denoting *a person involved with* or *an action involving*, as in *engineer*, *profiteer*.
**ee·rie, ee·ry** (êr'i), *adj.* [-RIER, -RIEST], [< AS. *earg*, timid], inspiring fear; weird; uncanny. **—ee'ri·ness,** *n.*
**ef-,** ex-: used before *f*, as in *efferent*.
**ef·face** (i-fās'), *v.t.* [-FACED, -FACING], [< L. *ex*, out + *facies*, form], 1. to erase; blot out. 2. to make (oneself) inconspicuous.
**ef·fect** (ə-fekt', i-), *n.* [< L. *ex-*, out + *facere*, do], 1. anything brought about by a cause; result. 2. the power to cause results. 3. influence or action. 4. meaning: as, he spoke to this *effect*. 5. a being operative or in force. 6. *pl.* belongings; property. *v.t.* 1. to bring about; accomplish. 2 .to make. **—in effect,** 1. actually. 2. virtually. 3. in practice. **—take effect,** to begin to act.
**ef·fec'tive,** *adj.* 1. producing a desired effect; efficient. 2. operative; in practice. 3. striking; impressive. **—ef·fec'tive·ly,** *adv.*
**ef·fec·tu·al** (ə-fek'chōō-əl, i-), *adj.* 1. producing, or capable of producing, the desired effect. 2. having legal force; valid.
**ef·fem·i·nate** (ə-fem'ə-nit, i-), *adj.* [< L. *ex-*, out + *femina*, woman], showing qualities attributed to women, as weakness, delicacy, etc.; unmanly. **—ef·fem'i·na·cy** (-nə-si), *n.*
**ef·fer·ent** (ef'ēr-ənt), *adj.* [< L. *ex-*, out +

*ferre*, to bear], carrying away from a center, as nerves: cf. **afferent.**
**ef·fer·vesce** (ef'ẽr-ves'), ***v.i.*** [-VESCED, -VESCING], [< L. *ex-*, out + *fervere*, to boil], 1. to give off gas bubbles; bubble; foam. 2. to be lively and vivacious. **—ef'fer·ves'cence, *n.* —ef'fer·ves'cent, *adj.***
**ef·fete** (e-fēt', i-), ***adj.*** [< L. *ex-*, out + *fetus*, exhausted], no longer able to produce; spent and sterile.**—ef·fete'ly, *adv.*—ef·fete'ness, *n.***
**ef·fi·ca·cious** (ef'ə-kā'shəs), ***adj.*** [see EFFECT & -OUS], that produces the desired effect; effective. **—ef'fi·ca'cious·ly, *adv.* —ef'fi·ca·cy** (-kə-si) [*pl.* -CIES], ***n.***
**ef·fi·cient** (ə-fish'ənt, i-), ***adj.*** [see EFFECT], producing the desired result with a minimum of effort, expense, or waste. **—ef·fi'cien·cy** [*pl.* -CIES], ***n.*** **—ef·fi'cient·ly, *adv.***
**ef·fi·gy** (ef'ə-ji), ***n.*** [*pl.* -GIES], [< L. *ex-*, out + *fingere*, to form], a statue or other image; esp., a crude representation (for hanging or burning) of one who is hated.
**ef·flo·resce** (ef'lô-res'), ***v.i.*** [-RESCED, -RESCING], [< L. *ex-*, out + *florescere*, to blossom], 1. to flower. 2. in *chem.*, to change from a crystalline to a powdery state through loss of the water of crystallization.
**ef·flu·vi·um** (e-flōō'vi-əm, i-), ***n.*** [*pl.* -VIA (-ə), -VIUMS], [< L. *ex-*, out + *fluere*, flow], 1. an aura. 2. a noxious vapor or odor.
**ef·fort** (ef'ẽrt), ***n.*** [< L. *ex-*, intens. + *fortis*, strong], 1. the use of energy to do something. 2. a try; attempt. 3. a result of effort; achievement. **—ef'fort·less, *adj.***
**ef·fron·ter·y** (e-frun'tẽr-i, i-), ***n.*** [*pl.* -IES], [< L. *ex-*, from + *frons*, forehead], impudence; unashamed boldness; audacity.
**ef·ful·gent** (e-ful'jənt, i-), ***adj.*** [< L. *ex-*, forth + *fulgere*, to shine], brightly shining; radiant. **—ef·ful'gence, *n.***
**ef·fuse** (e-fūz', i-), ***v.t. & v.i.*** [-FUSED, -FUSING], [< L. *ex-*, out + *fundere*, pour], 1. to pour out or forth. 2. to spread; diffuse.
**ef·fu'sion** (-fū'zhən), ***n.*** 1. a pouring forth. 2. unrestrained expression in words.
**ef·fu'sive** (-siv), ***adj.*** 1. pouring forth. 2. expressing emotion gushingly; overly demonstrative. **—ef·fu'sive·ness, *n.***
**e.g.,** *exempli gratia*, [L.], for example.
**e·gad** (i-gad', ē-), ***interj.*** [prob. < *ah God*], a softened oath.
**egg** (eg), ***n.*** [ON.], 1. the oval body laid by a female bird, fish, etc., containing the germ of a new individual. 2. a female reproductive cell; ovum. 3. a hen's egg, raw or cooked. 4. a thing resembling a hen's egg. 5. [Slang], a person: as, he's a bad *egg*.
**egg** (eg), ***v.t.*** [< ON. *eggja*, give edge to], to urge or incite (with *on*).
**egg'head',** ***n.*** [Slang], an intellectual.
**egg'nog'** (-nog'), ***n.*** [*egg* + *nog*, strong beer], a drink made of eggs, milk, sugar, and, often, whisky.
**egg'plant',** ***n.*** 1. a plant with a large, pear-shaped, purple-skinned fruit, eaten as a vegetable. 2. the fruit.
**e·gis** (ē'jis), ***n.*** aegis.
**eg·lan·tine** (eg'lən-tīn', -tēn'), ***n.*** [< L. *aculeus*, a prickle], a sweet-smelling wild rose with pink flowers; sweetbrier.
**e·go** (ē'gō, eg'ō), ***n.*** [*pl.* -GOS], [L., I], 1. the individual as aware of himself; the self. 2. [Colloq.], conceit. 3. in *psychoanalysis*, that part of the psyche which consciously controls the impulses of the id.
**e'go·cen'tric** (-sen'trik), ***adj.*** viewing everything in relation to oneself. ***n.*** an egocentric person.
**e'go·ism,** ***n.*** 1. selfishness; self-interest. 2. conceit. **—e'go·ist, *n.* —e'go·is'tic, *adj.***
**e'go·tism** (-tiz'm), ***n.*** 1. excessive reference to oneself in speaking or writing. 2. self-conceit. **—e'go·tist, *n.* —e'go·tis'tic, *adj.***
**e·gre·gious** (i-grē'jəs), ***adj.*** [< L. *e-*, out + *grex*, a herd], remarkably bad; flagrant.
**e·gress** (ē'gres), ***n.*** [< L. *e-*, out + *gradi*, go], a way out; exit.
**e·gret** (ē'grit, eg'ret), ***n.*** [< Fr. *aigrette* < OHG.], 1. a heron having long, white plumes. 2. such a plume: usually **aigrette.**
**E·gyp·tian** (i-jip'shən, ē-), ***adj.*** of Egypt, its people, etc. ***n.*** 1. a native of Egypt. 2. the language of the ancient Egyptians.
**eh** (ā, e), ***interj.*** a sound expressing: 1. surprise. 2. doubt or inquiry.
**ei·der** (ī'dẽr), ***n.*** [ON. *œthr*], 1. a large sea duck of the northern regions: often **eider duck.** 2. its soft, fine down used to stuff pillows, quilts, etc.: also **eider down.**
**eight** (āt), ***adj. & n.*** [AS. *eahta*], one more than seven; 8; VIII. **—eighth** (ātth, āth), ***adj. & n.***
**eight·een** (ā'tēn'), ***adj. & n.*** eight more than ten; 18; XVIII. **—eight'eenth', *adj. & n.***
**eight·y** (ā'ti), ***adj. & n.*** [*pl.* -IES], eight times ten; 80; LXXX. **—the eighties,** the years from 80 through 89 (of a century or a person's age). **—eight'i·eth** (-ith), ***adj. & n.***
**ei·ther** (ē'*th*ẽr, ī'-), ***adj.*** [AS. *agewæther*], 1. one or the other (of two). 2. each (of two). ***pron.*** one or the other. ***conj.*** a correlative used with *or* to denote a choice of alternatives: as, *either* go or stay. ***adv.*** any more than the other; also: as, if I don't go, he won't *either.*
**e·jac·u·late** (i-jak'yoo-lāt'), ***v.t.*** [-LATED, -LATING], [see EJECT], 1. to eject (fluids) suddenly. 2. to utter suddenly; exclaim. **—e·jac'u·la'tion, *n.* —e·jac'u·la'tor** (-tẽr), ***n.***
**e·ject** (i-jekt'), ***v.t.*** [< L. *e-*, out + *jacere*, throw], to throw or drive out; expel; discharge. **—e·jec'tion, *n.* —e·jec'tor, *n.***
**eke** (ēk), ***v.t.*** [EKED, EKING], [< AS. *eacan*, to increase], to manage to make (a living) with difficulty: with *out.*
**e·lab·o·rate** (i-lab'ẽr-it; *for v.*, -ə-rāt'), ***adj.*** [< L. *e-*, out + *labor*, work], developed in great detail; complicated. ***v.t.*** [-RATED, -RATING], to work out in detail. ***v.i.*** to state something in detail (with *on* or *upon*). **—e·lab'o·rate·ly, *adv.* —e·lab'o·ra'tion, *n.***
**‡é·lan** (ā'län'), ***n.*** [Fr. < *élancer*, to dart], ardor; enthusiasm; vigor.
**e·lapse** (i-laps'), ***v.i.*** [ELAPSED, ELAPSING], [< L. *e-*, out + *labi*, glide], to slip away; pass, as time.
**e·las·tic** (i-las'tik), ***adj.*** [< Gr. *elaunein*, to drive], 1. able to return immediately to its original size, shape, etc. after being stretched, squeezed, etc.; flexible. 2. able to recover easily as from dejection; buoyant. 3. adaptable. ***n.*** an elastic band or fabric. **—e·las'tic'i·ty** (-tis'ə-ti), ***n.***
**e·late** (i-lāt', ē-), ***v.t.*** [ELATED, ELATING], [< L. *ex-*, out + *ferre*, to bear], to raise the spirits of; make proud, happy, etc. **—e·lat'ed, *adj.* —e·la'tion, *n.***
**el·bow** (el'bō), ***n.*** [< AS. *eln*, forearm + *boga*, a bow], 1. the joint between the upper and lower arm; esp., the outer curve of a bent arm. 2. anything bent like an elbow. ***v.t. & v.i.*** to shove as with the elbows.
**elbow grease,** [Colloq.], hard work.
**el'bow·room ,** ***n.*** ample space or room.
**eld·er** (el'dẽr), ***adj.*** [< AS. *ald*, old], 1. older. 2. superior in rank, position, etc. 3. earlier; former. ***n.*** 1. an older or aged person. 2. an ancestor. 3. any of certain church officials.
**el·der** (el'dẽr), ***n.*** [AS. *ellern*], a shrub or tree of the honeysuckle family, with red or blackish berries.
**el'der·ber'ry,** ***n.*** [*pl.* -RIES], 1. the elder. 2. its berry, used for making wine.
**eld'er·ly,** ***adj.*** somewhat old.
**eld·est** (el'dist), ***adj.*** [< AS. *ald*, old], oldest.
**El Do·ra·do** (el' də-rä'dō), [*pl.* -DOS], [Sp., the gilded], any fabulously rich place: also sp. **Eldorado.**

**e·lect** (i-lekt′), *adj.* [< L. *e-*, out + *legere*, choose], 1. chosen. 2. elected but not yet installed in office: as, mayor-*elect*. 3. in *theology*, chosen by God for salvation and eternal life. *v.t.* & *v.i.* 1. to select for an office by voting. 2. to choose. **—the elect,** 1. the persons in a specially privileged group. 2. in *theology*, those who are elect.

**e·lec·tion** (i-lek′shən), *n.* 1. a choosing or choice. 2. a choosing by vote.

**e·lec′tion·eer′** (-êr′), *v.i.* to canvass votes in an election.

**e·lec′tive,** *adj.* 1. filled by election: as, an *elective* office. 2. chosen by election. 3. having the power to choose. 4. optional. *n.* an optional course in a school curriculum.

**e·lec·tor** (i-lek′tẽr), *n.* 1. one who elects; specif., a qualified voter. 2. a member of the electoral college. **—e·lec′tor·al,** *adj.*

**electoral college,** an assembly elected by the voters to perform the formal duty of electing the president and vice-president of the U.S.

**e·lec′tor·ate** (-it), *n.* all those qualified to vote in an election.

**E·lec·tra** (i-lek′trə), *n.* in *Gr. legend*, the daughter of a murdered king, who plotted the death of her mother in revenge.

**e·lec·tric** (i-lek′trik), *adj.* [< Gr. *ēlektron*, amber: from the effect of friction upon amber], 1. of or charged with electricity. 2. producing, or produced by, electricity. 3. operated by electricity. 4. electrifying; exciting. Also **e·lec′tri·cal.** **—e·lec′tri·cal·ly,** *adv.*

**electric chair,** a chair used in electrocuting those condemned to death.

**e·lec·tri·cian** (i-lek′trish′ən, ē′lek-), *n.* a person whose work is the construction, repair, or installation of electric apparatus.

**e·lec·tric·i·ty** (i-lek′tris′ə-ti, ē′lek-), *n.* 1. a form of energy generated by friction, induction, or chemical change, and having magnetic, chemical, and radiant effects. 2. an electric current. 3. electric current as a public utility for lighting, etc.

**e·lec·tri·fy** (i-lek′trə-fī′), *v.t.* [-FIED, -FYING], 1. to charge with electricity. 2. to excite; thrill; shock. 3. to equip for the use of electricity. **—e·lec′tri·fi·ca′tion,** *n.*

**electro-,** a combining form meaning *electric, electricity.*

**e·lec·tro·car·di·o·gram** (i-lek′trō-kär′di-ə-gram′), *n.* [*electro-* + *cardio-* + *-gram*], a tracing showing the changes in electric potential produced by heart contractions.

**e·lec′tro·car′di·o·graph′** (-graf′), *n.* an instrument for making electrocardiograms.

**e·lec·tro·cute** (i-lek′trə-kūt′), *v.t.* [-CUTED, -CUTING], [*electro-* + *execute*], to execute or kill by electricity. **—e·lec′tro·cu′tion,** *n.*

**e·lec·trode** (i-lek′trōd), *n.* [*electro-* + *-ode*], either of the two terminals of an electric source.

**e·lec·tro·dy·nam·ics** (i-lek′trō-dī-nam′iks), *n.pl.* [construed as sing.], the branch of physics dealing with the phenomena of electric currents and associated magnetic forces. **—e·lec′tro·dy·nam′ic,** *adj.*

**e·lec·trol·y·sis** (i-lek′trol′ə-sis), *n.* [*electro-* + *-lysis*], 1. the decomposition into ions of a chemical compound in solution by the action of an electric current. 2. the removal of hair from the body by destroying the hair roots with an electric needle.

**e·lec·tro·lyte** (i-lek′trə-līt′), *n.* [*electro-* + *-lyte*], any substance which in solution is dissociated into ions and thus made capable of conducting an electric current. **—e·lec′tro·lyt′ic** (-lit′ik), **e·lec′tro·lyt′i·cal,** *adj.*

**e·lec′tro·mag′net,** *n.* a soft iron core that becomes a magnet when an electric current flows through a coil surrounding it.

**e·lec·tro·mo·tive** (i-lek′trə-mō′tiv), *adj.* producing an electric current through differences in potential.

**e·lec·tron** (i-lek′tron), *n.* [see ELECTRIC], any of the nonnuclear, negatively charged particles that form a part of all atoms.

**e·lec·tron·ic** (i-lek′tron′ik), *adj.* 1. of electrons. 2. operating, produced, or done by the action of electrons.

**e·lec′tron′ics,** *n.pl.* [construed as sing.], the science that deals with electronic action, as in vacuum tubes, photoelectric cells, etc.

**e·lec·tro·plate** (i-lek′trə-plāt′), *v.t.* [-PLATED, -PLATING], to deposit a coating of silver, nickel, etc. on by electrolysis. *n.* anything so plated.

**e·lec′tro·type′** (-tīp′), *n.* in *printing*, a facsimile plate made by electroplating a wax impression of the original plate.

**el·ee·mos·y·nar·y** (el′ə-mos′′n-er′i, el′i-ə-), *adj.* [< Gr. *eleēmosynē*, alms], of, for, or supported by charity.

**el·e·gant** (el′ə-gənt), *adj.* [< L. *e-*, out + *legare*, choose], 1. having dignified richness and grace, as of manner, dress, design, etc.; tastefully luxurious. 2. [Colloq.], excellent. **—el′e·gance,** *n.* **—el′e·gant·ly,** *adv.*

**el·e·gi·ac** (el′ə-jī′ək, i-lē′ji-ak′), *adj.* 1. of, like, or fit for an elegy. 2. sad; mournful.

**el·e·gy** (el′ə-ji), *n.* [*pl.* -GIES], [< Gr. *elegos*, a lament], a mournful poem, esp. of lament and praise for the dead.

**el·e·ment** (el′ə-mənt), *n.* [< L. *elementum*], 1. the natural or fitting environment for a person or thing. 2. a component or principle of something; basic part. 3. in *chem.*, any substance that cannot be separated into different substances except by nuclear disintegration: all matter is composed of such substances. **—the elements,** 1. the first principles; rudiments. 2. wind, rain, etc.

**el·e·men·tal** (el′ə-men′t'l), *adj.* 1. of or like natural forces; primal. 2. of first principles; basic. 3. being an essential part or parts.

**el′e·men′ta·ry** (-tẽr-i, -tri), *adj.* elemental; esp., of first principles or fundamentals.

**elementary school,** a school of the first six (or eight) grades, where basic subjects are taught.

**el·e·phant** (el′ə-fənt), *n.* [< Gr. *elephas*], a huge, thick-skinned mammal with a long, flexible snout, or trunk, and two ivory tusks.

**el·e·phan·ti·a·sis** (el′ə-fən-tī′ə-sis), *n.* a chronic disease of the skin characterized by the enlargement of bodily parts.

**el·e·phan·tine** (el′ə-fan′tēn, -tin, -tīn), *adj.* like an elephant in size or gait; huge, slow, clumsy, etc.

**el·e·vate** (el′ə-vāt′), *v.t.* [-VATED, -VATING], [< L. *e-*, out + *levare*, to lift], 1. to raise; lift up. 2. to raise in rank. 3. to raise to a higher moral level. 4. to elate; exhilarate.

**el′e·va′tion,** *n.* 1. an elevating or being elevated. 2. a high place or position. 3. height above the surface of the earth or above sea level. 4. a scale drawing of the front, rear, or side of a structure.

**el′e·va′tor,** *n.* 1. one that elevates, or lifts. 2. a suspended cage for hoisting or lowering goods or people. 3. a warehouse for storing and discharging grain. 4. a device like a horizontal rudder, for making an aircraft go up or down.

**e·lev·en** (i-lev′'n), *adj.* & *n.* [AS. *endleofan*], one more than ten; 11; XI. **—e·lev′enth** (-'nth), *adj.* & *n.*

**elf** (elf), *n.* [*pl.* ELVES (elvz)], [AS. *ælf*], 1. in *folklore*, a small fairy or sprite. 2. a mischievous child or small person. **—elf′in, elf′ish,** *adj.*

**e·lic·it** (i-lis′it), *v.t.* [< L. *e-*, out + *lacere*, to entice], to draw forth (a response, etc.).

**e·lide** (i-līd′), *v.t.* [ELIDED, ELIDING], [< L. *e-*, out + *laedere*, to strike], to leave out; esp., to slur over (a vowel, letter, etc.) in

pronunciation. —**e·li·sion** (i-lizh′ən), *n.*
**el·i·gi·ble** (el′i-jə-b'l), *adj.* [see ELECT], fit to be chosen; qualified. *n.* an eligible person. —**el′i·gi·bil′i·ty,** *n.*
**e·lim·i·nate** (i-lim′ə-nāt′), *v.t.* [-NATED, -NATING], [< L. *e-*, out + *limen*, threshold], 1. to remove; get rid of. 2. to leave out of consideration; omit. 3. to excrete. —**e·lim′i·na′tion,** *n.* —**e·lim′i·na′tor,** *n.*
**e·lite, é·lite** (i-lēt′, ā-), *n.* [< Fr. < L.; see ELECT], [also construed as pl.], the choice or select part of a group, as of a society.
**e·lix·ir** (i-lik′sẽr), *n.* [< Ar. *al-iksīr*], 1. a hypothetical substance sought for by medieval alchemists to prolong life indefinitely: also **elixir of life.** 2. a panacea. 3. a medicine made of drugs in alcoholic solution.
**E·liz·a·be·than** (i-liz′ə-bē′thən, -beth′ən), *adj.* of or characteristic of the time of Elizabeth I (1558–1603). *n.* an English person, esp. a writer, of that time.
**elk** (elk), *n.* [*pl.* ELK, ELKS], [< AS. *elh*], 1. a large, mooselike deer of N Europe and Asia, with broad antlers. 2. the wapiti.
**ell** (el), *n.* something shaped like an L; specif., an extension or wing at right angles to the main structure.
**ell** (el), *n.* [AS. *eln*], a former measure of length (in England, 45 inches).
**el·lipse** (i-lips′), *n.* [*pl.* -LIPSES (-lip′siz)], [< Gr. *elleipein*, to fall short], a closed curve in the form of a symmetrical oval.
**el·lip·sis** (i-lip′sis), *n.* [*pl.* -SES (-sēz)], [see ELLIPSE], 1. the omission of a word or words understood in the context; e.g., (you) come if (it is) possible. 2. a mark (. . . or ***) indicating an omission of words or letters.
**el·lip·ti·cal** (i-lip′ti-k'l), *adj.* 1. of, or having the form of, an ellipse. 2. of or characterized by ellipsis. Also **el·lip′tic.**
**elm** (elm), *n.* [AS.], 1. a tall, hardy shade tree. 2. its hard, heavy wood.
**el·o·cu·tion** (el′ə-kū′shən), *n.* [see ELOQUENT], the art of public speaking or declaiming. —**el′o·cu′tion·ist,** *n.*
**e·lon·gate** (i-lôŋ′gāt), *v.t.* & *v.i.* [-GATED, -GATING], [< LL. *elongare*], to lengthen; extend. *adj.* lengthened; stretched. —**e·lon·ga·tion** (i-lôŋ′gā′shən, ē′loŋ-), *n.*
**e·lope** (i-lōp′), *v.i.* [ELOPED, ELOPING], [prob. < AS. *a-*, away + *hleapan*, run], to run away secretly, esp. in order to get married. —**e·lope′ment,** *n.* —**e·lop′er,** *n.*
**el·o·quent** (el′ə-kwənt), *adj.* [< L. *e-*, out + *loqui*, speak], vivid, forceful, fluent, etc. in speech or writing. —**el′o·quence** (-kwəns), *n.* —**el′o·quent·ly,** *adv.*
**else** (els), *adj.* [AS. *elles*], 1. different; other: as, somebody *else.* 2. in addition: as, is there anything *else?* *adv.* 1. differently; otherwise: as, where *else* can I go? 2. if not: as, study, (or) *else* you will fail.
**else′where′** (-hwâr′), *adv.* in, at, or to some other place; somewhere else.
**e·lu·ci·date** (i-lōō′sə-dāt′), *v.t.* [-DATED, -DATING], [< L. *e-*, out + *lucidus*, light, clear], to make clear. —**e·lu′ci·da′tion,** *n.*
**e·lude** (i-lōōd′), *v.t.* [ELUDED, ELUDING], [< L. *e-*, out + *ludere*, to play], 1. to avoid or escape from by quickness, cunning, etc. 2. to escape detection by; evade; baffle.—**e·lud′er,** *n.* —**e·lu·sion** (i-lōō′zhən), *n.*
**e·lu·sive** (i-lōō′siv), *adj.* 1. tending to elude. 2 hard to grasp mentally; baffling.
**elves** (elvz), *n.* pl. of **elf.**
**E·ly·si·um** (i-lizh′i-əm, i-liz′-), *n.* 1. in *Gr. myth.*, the place where virtuous people went after death. 2. any state of ideal bliss; paradise.—**E·ly′sian** (-lizh′ən, -lizh′i-ən), *adj.*
**em** (em), *n.* [< the letter *M*], in *printing*, a unit of measure, as of column width.
**'em** (əm, 'm), *pron.* [Colloq.], them.
**em-,** en-: used before *p*, *b*, or *m*.
**e·ma·ci·ate** (i-mā′shi-āt′), *v.t.* [-ATED, -ATING], [< L. *e-*, out + *macies*, leanness], to cause to become abnormally lean; make lose much weight. —**e·ma′ci·at′ed,** *adj.* —**e·ma′ci·a′tion** (-shi-ā′shən, -si-), *n.*
**em·a·nate** (em′ə-nāt′), *v.i.* [-NATED, -NATING], [< L. *e-*, out + *manare*, to flow], to come forth; issue. —**em′a·na′tion,** *n.*
**e·man·ci·pate** (i-man′sə-pāt′), *v.t.* [-PATED, -PATING], [< L. *manus*, the hand + *capere*, take], 1. to set free (a slave, etc.). 2. to free from restraint, etc. —**e·man′ci·pa′tion,** *n.* —**e·man′ci·pa′tor,** *n.*
**e·mas·cu·late** (i-mas′kyoo-lāt′), *v.t.* [-LATED, -LATING], [< L. *e-*, out + *masculus*, male], 1. to castrate. 2. to weaken. —**e·mas′cu·la′tion,** *n.*
**em·balm** (im-bäm′), *v.t.* [see EN- & BALM], to preserve (a dead body) with various chemicals. —**em·balm′er,** *n.*
**em·bank** (im-baŋk′), *v.t.* to protect, support, or enclose with a bank of earth, rubble, etc. —**em·bank′ment,** *n.*
**em·bar·go** (im-bär′gō), *n.* [*pl.* -GOES], [Sp. < L. *in*, in + *barra*, a bar], 1. a government prohibition of entry or departure of commercial ships at its ports. 2. any legal restriction of commerce. 3. restriction; restraint. *v.t.* to put an embargo upon.
**em·bark** (im-bärk′), *v.t.* [< L. *in*, in + LL. *barco*, small boat], to put or take aboard ship. *v.i.* 1. to go aboard a ship. 2. to begin a journey. 3. to engage in an enterprise.—**em·bar·ka·tion** (em′bär-kā′shən), *n.*
**em·bar·rass** (im-bar′əs), *v.t.* [< It. < *im-*, in + LL. *barra*, a bar], 1. to cause to feel self-conscious. 2. to hinder; impede. 3. to cause to be in debt. —**em·bar′rass·ment,** *n.*
**em·bas·sy** (em′bə-si), *n.* [*pl.* -SIES], [see AMBASSADOR], 1. the official residence or offices of an ambassador. 2. an ambassador and his staff. 3. a person or group sent as ambassadors.
**em·bat·tle** (em-bat′'l), *v.t.* [-TLED, -TLING], to provide with battlements.
**em·bat·tle** (em-bat′'l), *v.t.* [-TLED, -TLING], [< OFr.], [Rare, except in pp.], to prepare for battle.
**em·bed** (im-bed′), *v.t.* [-BEDDED, -BEDDING], to set or fix firmly in a surrounding mass.
**em·bel·lish** (im-bel′ish), *v.t.* [< OFr. *em-*, in + *bel* (< L. *bellus*), beautiful], 1. to decorate; adorn. 2. to improve (a story, etc.) by adding details, often fictitious. —**em·bel′lish·er,** *n.* —**em·bel′lish·ment,** *n.*
**em·ber** (em′bẽr), *n.* [< AS. *æmerge*], 1. a glowing piece of coal, wood, etc. 2. *pl.* the smoldering remains of a fire.
**em·bez·zle** (im-bez′'l), *v.t.* [-ZLED, -ZLING], [< OFr. *en-*, in + *besillier*, destroy], to steal (money, etc. entrusted to one). —**em·bez′zle·ment,** *n.* —**em·bez′zler,** *n.*
**em·bit·ter** (im-bit′ẽr), *v.t.* to make bitter or more bitter.
**em·bla·zon** (em-blā′z'n), *v.t.* [see BLAZON], 1. to decorate (*with* coats of arms, etc.). 2. to display brilliantly. 3. to extol.
**em·blem** (em′bləm), *n.* [< Gr. *en-*, in + *ballein*, to throw], a visible symbol of a thing, idea, etc.; sign; badge. —**em′blem·at′ic** (-blə-mat′ik), *adj.*
**em·bod·y** (im-bod′i), *v.t.* [-IED, -YING], 1. to give bodily form to. 2. to give definite form to. 3. to collect and include (material) in a book, system, etc. 4. to incorporate as part of a whole. —**em·bod′i·ment,** *n.*
**em·bold·en** (im-bōl′d'n), *v.t.* to give courage to; cause to be bold or bolder.
**em·bo·lism** (em′bə-liz'm), *n.* [< Gr. *en-*, in + *ballein*, throw], the obstruction of a blood vessel by a blood clot or air bubble.
**em·bos·om** (em-booz′əm, -bōō′zəm), *v.t.* 1. to embrace; cherish. 2. to enclose; shelter.
**em·boss** (im-bôs′), *v.t.* [see EN- & BOSS

(raised part)], 1. to decorate with raised designs, etc. 2. to raise in relief, as a design.

**em·bow·er** (em-bou'ẽr), ***v.t.*** to enclose or shelter in or as in a bower.

**em·brace** (im-brās'), ***v.t.*** [-BRACED, -BRACING], [< L. *im-*, in + *brachium*, an arm], 1. to clasp in the arms lovingly; hug. 2. to accept readily. 3. to take up, as a profession. 4. to encircle. 5. to include; contain. ***v.i.*** to clasp one another in the arms. ***n.*** an embracing; hug. —**em·brace'a·ble,** ***adj.***

**em·bra·sure** (em-brā'zhẽr), ***n.*** [Fr. < *embraser*, widen an opening], 1. an opening (for a door or window) wider on the inside than on the outside. 2. an opening in a wall for a gun, with the sides slanting outward.

**em·broi·der** (im-broi'dẽr), ***v.t. & v.i.*** [< OFr. *en-*, in + *brosder*, embroider], 1. to make (a design, etc.) on (fabric) with needlework. 2. to embellish (a story, etc.).

**em·broi'der·y,** ***n.*** [*pl.* -IES], 1. the art of embroidering. 2. embroidered work or fabric. 3. embellishment, as of a story.

**em·broil** (em-broil'), ***v.t.*** [see EN- & BROIL (to dispute)], 1. to confuse (affairs, etc.); entangle. 2. to involve (a person, government, etc.) in a dispute. —**em·broil'ment,** ***n.***

**em·bry·o** (em'bri-ō'), ***n.*** [*pl.* -OS], [< Gr. *en-*, in + *bryein*, to swell], 1. an animal in the earliest stages of its development in the uterus. 2. the rudimentary plant contained in a seed. 3. *a*) an undeveloped stage of something. *b*) anything in such a stage. —**em'bry·on'ic** (-on'ik), ***adj.***

**em'bry·ol'o·gy** (-ol'ə-ji), ***n.*** [*embryo* + *-logy*], the branch of biology dealing with the formation and development of embryos. —**em'bry·ol'o·gist,** ***n.***

**em·cee** (em'sē'), ***v.t. & v.i.*** [-CEED, -CEEING], [< *M.C.*, Master of Ceremonies], [Slang], to act as master of ceremonies (for). ***n.*** [Slang], a master of ceremonies.

**e·mend** (i-mend'), ***v.t.*** [< L. *e-*, out + *menda*, fault], to correct or improve, as a literary text. —**e·men·da·tion** (ē'men-dā'shən), ***n.***

**em·er·ald** (em'ẽr-əld), ***n.*** [< Gr. (*s*)*maragdos*], 1. a bright-green, transparent precious stone. 2. bright green. ***adj.*** bright-green.

**e·merge** (i-mũrj'), ***v.i.*** [EMERGED, EMERGING], [< L. *e-*, out + *mergere*, to dip], 1. to rise as from a fluid. 2. to become visible or apparent. —**e·mer'gence,** ***n.***

**e·mer·gen·cy** (i-mũr'jən-si), ***n.*** [*pl.* -CIES], [orig. sense, an emerging], a sudden, generally unexpected occurrence demanding immediate action.

**e·mer·i·tus** (i-mer'ə-təs), ***adj.*** [< L. *e-*, out + *mereri*, to serve], retired from active service, usually for age, but retaining one's rank or title: as, professor *emeritus*.

**em·er·y** (em'ẽr-i), ***n.*** [*pl.* -IES], [< Gr. *smyris*], a dark, hard, coarse variety of corundum used for grinding, polishing, etc.

**e·met·ic** (i-met'ik), ***adj.*** [< Gr. *emeein*, to vomit], causing vomiting. ***n.*** a medicine or other substance that causes vomiting.

**-emia,** [< Gr. *haima*, blood], a suffix meaning *a* (specified) *condition of the blood*, as in *leukemia*.

**em·i·grate** (em'ə-grāt'), ***v.i.*** [-GRATED, -GRATING], [< L. *e-*, out + *migrare*, to move], to leave a country or region to settle in another. —**em'i·grant** (-grənt), ***adj. & n.*** —**em'i·gra'tion,** ***n.***

**em·i·nence** (em'ə-nəns), ***n.*** [see EMINENT], 1. a high place, thing, etc. 2. superiority in rank, position, etc.; greatness. 3. [E-], a title of honor of a cardinal.

**em'i·nent,** ***adj.*** [< L. *eminere*, to project], 1. high. 2. projecting; prominent. 3. exalted; distinguished. 4. outstanding.

**e·mir** (ə-mêr'), ***n.*** [Ar. *amir*], 1. an Arabian ruler. 2. a Mohammedan or Turkish honorary title.

**em·is·sar·y** (em'ə-ser'i), ***n.*** [*pl.* -IES], [see EMIT], a person, esp. a secret agent, sent on a specific mission.

**e·mis·sion** (i-mish'ən), ***n.*** 1. an emitting. 2. something emitted; discharge. —**e·mis'sive** (-mis'iv), ***adj.***

**e·mit** (i-mit'), ***v.t.*** [EMITTED, EMITTING], [< L. *e-*, out + *mittere*, send], 1. to send out; give forth. 2. to utter (sounds, etc.).

**e·mol·li·ent** (i-mol'yənt), ***adj.*** [< L. *e-*, out + *mollire*, soften], softening; soothing. ***n.*** a medicine that softens or soothes surface tissues.

**e·mol·u·ment** (i-mol'yoo-mənt), ***n.*** [< L. *e-*, out + *molere*, grind], gain from employment; salary, fees, etc.

**e·mote** (i-mōt'), ***v.i.*** [EMOTED, EMOTING], [Colloq.], to display one's emotions dramatically.

**e·mo·tion** (i-mō'shən), ***n.*** [< L. *e-*, out + *movere*, to move], 1. strong, generalized feeling. 2. any specific feeling, as love, fear, anger, etc.

**e·mo'tion·al,** ***adj.*** 1. of or showing emotion. 2. easily aroused to emotion. 3. appealing to the emotions.

**em·pa·thy** (em'pə-thi), ***n.*** [< Gr. *en-*, in + *pathos*, feeling], intellectual or emotional identification with another.

**em·per·or** (em'pẽr-ẽr), ***n.*** [< L. *imperare*, to command], a man who rules an empire.

**em·pha·sis** (em'fə-sis), ***n.*** [*pl.* -SES (-sēz')], [< Gr. *en-*, in + *phasis*, appearance], 1. force of expression, action, etc. 2. special stress given to a syllable, word, etc. in speaking. 3. importance; stress.

**em·pha·size** (em'fə-sīz'), ***v.t.*** [-SIZED, -SIZING], to give emphasis to; stress.

**em·phat·ic** (im-fat'ik), ***adj.*** 1. felt or done with emphasis. 2. using emphasis in speaking, etc. 3. forcible. —**em·phat'i·cal·ly,** ***adv.***

**em·pire** (em'pīr), ***n.*** [see EMPEROR], 1. supreme rule. 2. government by an emperor or empress. 3. a group of states or territories under one sovereign power.

**em·pir·i·cal** (em-pir'i-k'l), ***adj.*** [< Gr. *en-*, in + *peira*, trial], 1. relying or based on experiment and observation. 2. relying on practical experience. Also **em·pir'ic.** —**em·pir'i·cism** (-ə-siz'm), ***n.***

**em·place·ment** (im-plās'mənt), ***n.*** the prepared position or platform from which a heavy gun is fired.

**em·ploy** (im-ploi'), ***v.t.*** [< L. *in-*, in + *plicare*, to fold], 1. to use. 2. to keep busy or occupied. 3. to engage the services of. ***n.*** employment.

**em·ploy·ee, emp·loy·e** (im-ploi'ē, em'ploi-ē'), ***n.*** a person employed by another for wages or salary: alsp sp. **employé.**

**em·ploy'er,** ***n.*** 1. one who employs others for wages or salary. 2. a user.

**em·ploy'ment,** ***n.*** 1. an employing or being employed. 2. work; occupation; job.

**em·po·ri·um** (em-pôr'i-əm), ***n.*** [*pl.* -RIUMS, -RIA (-ə)], [< Gr. *en-*, in + *poros*, way], a store with a wide variety of merchandise.

**em·power** (im-pou'ẽr), ***v.t.*** 1 to give power to; authorize. 2. to enable.

**em·press** (em'pris), ***n.*** 1. an emperor's wife. 2. a woman ruler of an empire.

**emp·ty** (emp'ti), ***adj.*** [-TIER, -TIEST], [< AS. *æmettig*, unoccupied], 1. having nothing or no one in it; unoccupied. 2. worthless: as, *empty* pleasures. 3. insincere: as, *empty* promises. ***v.t.*** [-TIED, -TYING], 1. to make empty. 2. to remove (the contents) of something. ***v.i.*** 1. to become empty. 2. to pour out; discharge. ***n.*** [*pl.* -TIES], an empty truck, bottle, etc. —**emp'ti·ness,** ***n.***

**emp'ty-hand'ed,** ***adj.*** bringing or carrying away nothing.

**em·pyr·e·al** (em-pir'i-əl, em'pə-rē'əl), ***adj.*** [< Gr. *en-*, in + *pyr*, a fire], of the empyrean.

**em·py·re·an** (em'pə-rē'ən), *n.* [see EMPYREAL], 1. the highest heaven. 2. the sky.

**e·mu** (ē'mū), *n.* [prob. < Port. *ema*, crane], a large, nonflying Australian bird, like the ostrich but smaller.

**em·u·late** (em'yoo-lāt'), *v.t.* [-LATED, -LATING], [< L. *aemulus*, trying to equal], 1. to try to equal or surpass. 2. to rival successfully. —**em'u·la'tion,** *n.* —**em'u·la'tor,** *n.*

**e·mul·si·fy** (i-mul'sə-fī'), *v.t. & v.i.* [-FIED, -FYING], to form into an emulsion. —**e·mul'si·fi·ca'tion,** *n.*

**e·mul·sion** (i-mul'shən), *n.* [< L. *e-*, out + *mulgere*, to milk], a fluid formed by the suspension of one liquid in another; specif., in *pharmacy*, a preparation of an oily substance suspended in a watery liquid.

**en** (en), *n.* [< the letter *N*], in *printing*, a space half the width of an em.

**en-,** [< L. *in*, in], a prefix meaning: 1. *to put into* or *on*, as in *enthrone*. 2. *to make*, as in *enfeeble*. 3. *in* or *into*, as in *enclose*.

**-en,** [< AS.], a suffix: 1. meaning: *a*) *to become* or *cause to be*, as in *weaken*. *b*) *to cause to have*, as in *hearten*. *c*) *made of*, as in *woolen*. 2. used to form plurals, as in *children*. 3. used to form diminutives, as in *chicken*.

**en·a·ble** (in-ā'b'l), *v.t.* [-BLED, -BLING], to make able; provide with means, power, etc. (*to* do something).

**en·act** (in-act'), *v.t.* 1. to make (a bill, etc.) into a law; pass (a law); decree. 2. to represent as in a play. —**en·act'ment,** *n.*

**en·am·el** (i-nam''l), *n.* [< OFr. *esmail*], 1. a glassy, opaque substance fused to metal or the like as a protective coating, etc. 2. the hard, white, glossy coating of teeth. 3. paint or varnish producing a hard, glossy surface. *v.t.* [-ELED or -ELLED, -ELING or -ELLING], to coat with enamel.

**en·am'el·ware'** (-wâr'), *n.* kitchen utensils, etc. of enameled metal.

**en·am·or, en·am·our** (in-am'ẽr), *v.t.* [ult. < L. *in*, in + *amor*, love], to fill with love and desire; charm. —**en·am'ored, en·am'oured,** *adj.*

**en·camp** (in-kamp'), *v.i. & v.t.* to lodge in a camp. —**en·camp'ment,** *n.*

**en·case** (in-kās'), *v.t.* [-CASED, -CASING], to enclose, as in a case: also **incase.**

**-ence,** [< L.], a suffix meaning *act*, *state*, or *result*, as in *conference*.

**en·ceph·a·li·tis** (en'sef-ə-lī'tis, en-sef'-), *n.* [< Gr. *enkephalos*, brain; + *-itis*], inflammation of the brain.

**en·chain** (en-chān'), *v.t.* 1. to put in chains; fetter. 2. to captivate.

**en·chant** (in-chant', -chänt'), *v.t.* [< L. *in-*, in + *cantare*, sing], 1. to cast a spell over. 2. to charm greatly; delight. —**en·chant'er,** *n.* —**en·chant'ing,** *adj.* —**en·chant'ment,** *n.*

**en·cir·cle** (in-sũr'k'l), *v.t.* [-CLED, -CLING], 1. to surround. 2. to move in a circle around. —**en·cir'cle·ment,** *n.*

**en·clave** (en'klāv), *n.* [< L. *in*, in + *clavis*, a key], foreign territory surrounded by a specified country.

**en·close** (in-klōz'), *v.t.* [-CLOSED, -CLOSING], 1. to shut in all around; surround; fence in. 2. to insert in an envelope, etc. together with a letter. 3. to contain. Also **inclose.**

**en·clo'sure** (-klō'zhẽr), *n.* 1. an enclosing or being enclosed. 2. something that encloses. 3. something enclosed. 4. an enclosed place. Abbrev. **enc., encl.**

**en·co·mi·um** (en-kō'mi-əm), *n.* [*pl.* -UMS, -A (-ə)], [< Gr. *en-*, in + *kōmos*, a revel], a formal expression of high praise; eulogy.

**en·com·pass** (in-kum'pəs), *v.t.* 1. to enclose; surround. 2. to contain; include.

**en·core** (än'kôr), *interj.* [Fr.], again; once more. *n.* 1. a demand by an audience, shown by applause, for further performance. 2. such further performance.

**en·coun·ter** (in-koun'tẽr), *v.t. & v.i.* [< L. *in*, in + *contra*, against], 1. to meet unexpectedly. 2. to meet in conflict. *n.* 1. a battle; fight. 2. an unexpected meeting.

**en·cour·age** (in-kũr'ij), *v.t.* [-AGED, -AGING], 1. to give courage, hope, or confidence to. 2. to help; give support to. —**en·cour'age·ment,** *n.* —**en·cour'ag·ing,** *adj.*

**en·croach** (in-krōch'), *v.i.* [< OFr. *en-*, in + *croc*, a hook], to trespass or intrude (*on* or *upon*). —**en·croach'ment,** *n.*

**en·crust** (in-krust'), *v.t. & v.i.* to incrust.

**en·cum·ber** (in-kum'bẽr), *v.t.* [see EN- & CUMBER], 1. to hold back the motion or action of; hinder. 2. to burden; load down. —**en·cum'brance** (-brəns), *n.*

**-ency,** [L. *-entia*], a suffix equivalent to *-ence*, as in *dependency*.

**ency., encyc., encycl.,** encyclopedia.

**en·cy·cli·cal** (en-sik'li-k'l, -sī'kli-), *n.* [< Gr. *en-*, in + *kyklos*, circle], a letter from the Pope to the clergy.

**en·cy·clo·pe·di·a, en·cy·clo·pae·di·a** (in-sī'klə-pē'di-ə), *n.* [< Gr. *enkyklios*, general + *paideia*, education], a book or set of books with alphabetically arranged articles on all branches of knowledge or a special field. —**en·cy'clo·pe'dic, en·cy'clo·pae'dic,** *adj.*

**en·cyst** (en-sist'), *v.t. & v.i.* to enclose or become enclosed in a cyst, capsule, or sac.

**end** (end), *n.* [AS. *ende*], 1. a boundary; limit. 2. the last part of anything; finish; conclusion. 3. a ceasing to exist; death or destruction. 4. the part at or near an extremity; tip. 5. an aim; purpose. 6. an outcome; result. 7. a remnant. 8. in *football*, a player at either end of the line. *v.t. & v.i.* to bring or come to an end; finish; stop. *adj.* at the end; final. —**at loose ends,** in an unsettled condition. —**end up,** to finish. —**make both ends meet,** to manage merely to exist on one's income. —**put an end to,** 1. to stop. 2. to do away with.

**en·dan·ger** (in-dān'jẽr), *v.t.* to expose to danger, harm, etc.; imperil.

**en·dear** (in-dêr'), *v.t.* to make dear or beloved. —**en·dear'ing·ly,** *adv.*

**en·dear'ment,** *n.* 1. affection. 2. an expression of affection.

**en·deav·or** (in-dev'ẽr), *v.i.* [< *en-* + OFr. *deveir*, duty], to try hard; strive. *n.* an earnest attempt to accomplish something. Also, Brit. sp., **endeavour.**

**en·dem·ic** (en-dem'ik), *adj.* [< Gr. *en-*, in + *dēmos*, people], prevalent in or restricted to a certain locality or group, as a disease.

**end·ing** (en'diŋ), *n.* 1. the last part; finish. 2. death.

**en·dive** (en'dīv, än'dēv), *n.* [Fr.; ult. < Gr. *entybon*], a kind of chicory with ragged, curly leaves used in salads.

**end'less,** *adj.* 1. having no end; eternal; infinite. 2. lasting too long: as, an *endless* speech. 3. with the ends joined to form a closed circle: as, an *endless* chain.

**end'most',** *adj.* at the end; farthest.

**endo-,** [< Gr. *endon*], a combining form meaning *within*, *inner:* also **end-.**

**en·do·crine** (en'də-krīn', -krin), *adj.* [< *endo-* + Gr. *krinein*, to separate], designating or of any gland producing an internal secretion carried by the blood or lymph to some part whose functions it regulates.

**en·do·derm** (en'də-dũrm'), *n.* [*endo-* + *-derm* < Mod.L. *derma*, skin], the inner layer of cells of the embyro in its early stage.

**en·do·plasm** (en'də-plaz'm), *n.* the inner part of the cytoplasm of a cell.

**en·dorse** (in-dôrs'), *v.t.* [-DORSED, -DORSING], [< L. *in*, on + *dorsum*, back], 1. to write on the back of (a document); specif., to sign one's name as payee on the back of (a check, etc.). 2. to sanction. —**en·dorse'ment,** *n.* —**en·dors'er,** *n.*

**en·dow** (in-dou′), *v.t.* [ult. < L. *in*, in + *dotare*, give], 1. to provide with some talent, quality, etc.: as, he is *endowed* with courage. 2. to give money or property to a (college, etc.). —**en·dow′ment,** *n.*

**en·due** (in-do͞o′, -dū′), *v.t.* [-DUED, -DUING], [< L. *in-*, in + *ducere*, to lead], to provide (*with* qualities).

**en·dur·ance** (in-door′əns, -dyoor′-), *n.* 1. the ability to last. 2. the ability to stand pain, fatigue, etc. 3. duration.

**en·dure** (in-door′, -dyoor′), *v.t.* [-DURED, -DURING], [< L. *in-*, in + *durus*, hard], 1. to stand (pain, fatigue, etc.). 2. to tolerate. *v.i.* 1. to last; continue. 2. to bear pain, etc. without flinching. —**en·dur′a·ble,** *adj.*

**en·dur′ing,** *adj.* lasting; permanent.

**end′ways′** (-wāz′), *adv.* 1. on end; upright. 2. with the end foremost. 3. lengthwise. 4. end to end. Also **end′wise′** (-wīz′).

**-ene,** [after L. *-enus*, adj. suffix], a suffix used to form names for certain hydrocarbons, as in *acetylene*.

**en·e·ma** (en′ə-mə), *n.* [< Gr. *en-*, in + *hienai*, send], the injection of a liquid into the rectum either as a purgative or a medicine.

**en·e·my** (en′ə-mi), *n.* [*pl.* -MIES], [< L. *in-*, not + *amicus*, friend], 1. a person who hates another and wishes to injure him; also, one hostile to a cause, etc. 2. *a*) a nation hostile to another. *b*) a soldier, citizen, etc. of a hostile nation. 3. anything injurious. *adj.* of an enemy.

**en·er·get·ic** (en′ẽr-jet′ik), *adj.* having or showing energy; vigorous. —**en′er·get′i·cal·ly,** *adv.*

**en·er·gize** (en′ẽr-jīz′), *v.t.* [-GIZED, -GIZING], to give energy to. *v.i.* to show energy.

**en·er·gy** (en′ẽr-ji), *n.* [*pl.* -GIES], [< Gr. *en-*, in + *ergon*, work], 1. vigor of action, expression, etc. 2. effective power. 3. in *physics*, the capacity for doing work and overcoming resistance.

**en·er·vate** (en′ẽr-vāt′), *v.t.* [-VATED, -VATING], [< L. *enervis*, weak], to deprive of nerve, force, etc.; devitalize. —**en′er·va′tion,** *n.*

**en·fee·ble** (in-fē′b'l), *v.t.* [-BLED, -BLING], to make feeble; weaken.

**en·fold** (in-fōld′), *v.t.* 1. to wrap in folds; wrap up. 2. to embrace. —**en·fold′er,** *n.*

**en·force** (in-fôrs′), *v.t.* [-FORCED, -FORCING], 1. to give force to. 2. to impose by force: as, to *enforce* one's will. 3. to compel observance of (a law, etc.). —**en·force′a·ble,** *adj.* —**en·force′ment,** *n.* —**en·forc′er,** *n.*

**en·fran·chise** (en-fran′chīz), *v.t.* [-CHISED, -CHISING], 1. to free from slavery. 2. to admit to citizenship, esp. to the right to vote. —**en·fran′chise·ment** (-chiz-mənt), *n.*

**Eng.,** 1. England. 2. English.

**en·gage** (in-gāj′), *v.t.* [-GAGED, -GAGING], [< Fr.; see EN- & GAGE], 1. to pledge (oneself). 2. to bind by a promise of marriage. 3. to hire. 4. to attract and hold (the attention, etc.). 5. to enter into conflict with (the enemy). 6. to mesh together, as gears. *v.i.* 1. to pledge oneself. 2. to involve oneself: as, she *engaged* in dramatics. 3. to enter into conflict. 4. to mesh.

**en·gaged′,** *adj.* 1. pledged. 2. betrothed. 3. occupied; employed. 4. involved in combat, as troops. 5. meshed.

**en·gage′ment,** *n.* an engaging or being engaged; specif., *a*) a betrothal. *b*) an appointment, obligation, etc. *c*) employment. *d*) a conflict. *e*) an interlocking; being in gear.

**en·gag′ing,** *adj.* attractive; charming.

**en·gen·der** (in-jen′dẽr), *v.t.* [< L. *in-*, in + *generare*, to beget], to bring into being; cause; produce. —**en·gen′der·ment,** *n.*

**en·gine** (en′jən), *n.* [< L. *in-*, in + base of *gignere*, to produce], 1. any machine that uses energy to develop mechanical power. 2. a railroad locomotive. 3. any instrument or machine.

**en·gi·neer** (en′jə-nêr′), *n.* 1. one skilled in some branch of engineering. 2. the operator of an engine; esp., the driver of a railroad locomotive. *v.t.* 1. to plan, construct, etc. as an engineer. 2. to manage skillfully.

**en′gi·neer′ing,** *n.* the planning, designing, construction, or management of machinery, roads, bridges, etc.

**Eng·lish** (iŋ′glish), *adj.* 1. of England, its people, etc. 2. of their language. *n.* 1. the people of England. 2. the language of the English, spoken also in the U.S. and most parts of the British Commonwealth. 3. [often e-], a spinning motion given to a ball.

**English horn,** a double-reed instrument of the wood-wind family.

**Eng′lish·man** (-mən), *n.* [*pl.* -MEN], 1. a native or inhabitant of England. 2. a person of English ancestry. —**Eng′lish·wom′an** [*pl.* -WOMEN], *n.fem.*

**English sparrow,** the common sparrow, a small finch of European origin.

**en·gorge** (en-gôrj′), *v.t.* [-GORGED, -GORGING], 1. to gorge. 2. in *medicine*, to congest (a blood vessel, tissue, etc.) with blood or other fluid. *v.i.* to eat greedily.

**en·graft′,** *v.t.* to insert (a shoot from one tree, etc.) into another; graft.

**en·grave** (in-grāv′), *v.t.* [-GRAVED, -GRAVING], [*en-* + *grave* (to carve)], 1. to cut or etch (letters, designs, etc.) in or on (a metal plate, wooden block, etc.). 2. to print from such a plate, etc. 3. to make a deep impression on. —**en·grav′er,** *n.*

**en·grav′ing,** *n.* 1. the act or art of one who engraves metal plates, etc. for printing. 2. an engraved block, design, etc. 3. a printed impression made from an engraved surface.

**en·gross** (in-grōs′), *v.t.* [< OFr. *engrossier*, become thick], to take the entire attention of; occupy wholly. —**en·gross′ing,** *adj.*

**en·gulf** (in-gulf′), *v.t.* to swallow up.

**en·hance** (in-hans′, -häns′), *v.t.* [-HANCED, -HANCING], [ult. < L. *in*, in + *altus*, high], to make greater; intensify. —**en·hance′ment,** *n.* —**en·hanc′er,** *n.*

**e·nig·ma** (i-nig′mə), *n.* [*pl.* -MAS], [< Gr. *ainigma*], 1. a riddle. 2. a perplexing or baffling matter, person, etc. —**e·nig·mat·ic** (en′ig-mat′ik, ē′nig-), **e′nig·mat′i·cal,** *adj.*

**en·join** (in-join′), *v.t.* [< L. *in-*, in + *jungere*, join], 1. to command; order. 2. to prohibit, esp. by legal injunction.

**en·joy** (in-joi′), *v.t.* [< OFr. *enjoier*, give joy to], 1. to get joy or pleasure from; relish. 2. to have the use or benefit of. —**enjoy oneself,** to have a good time. —**en·joy′a·ble,** *adj.* —**en·joy′ment,** *n.*

**en·large** (in-lärj′), *v.t. & v.i.* [-LARGED, -LARGING], 1. to make or become larger; expand. 2. in *photography*, to reproduce on a larger scale. —**enlarge on** (or **upon**), to discuss at greater length. —**en·large′ment,** *n.*

**en·light·en** (in-līt′'n), *v.t.* 1. to free from ignorance, prejudice, etc. 2. to inform; instruct. —**en·light′en·ment,** *n.*

**en·list** (in-list′), *v.t. & v.i.* 1. to enroll in some branch of the armed forces. 2. to engage in a cause or movement; get (the support, etc. of someone). —**en·list′ment,** *n.*

**en·liv·en** (in-līv′ən), *v.t.* to make active, cheerful, etc.; liven up. —**en·liv′en·ment,** *n.*

**en masse** (en mas′), [Fr., lit., in mass], in a group; as a whole.

**en·mesh** (en-mesh′), *v.t.* to catch as in the meshes of a net; entangle.

**en·mi·ty** (en′mə-ti), *n.* [*pl.* -TIES], [see ENEMY], the attitude or feelings of an enemy or enemies; hostility.

**en·no·ble** (i-nō′b'l, en-nō′-), *v.t.* [-BLED, -BLING], to give nobility to; dignify

**en·nui** (än'wē), *n.* [*pl.* -NUIS], [Fr.; see ANNOY], weariness and boredom.
**e·nor·mi·ty** (i-nôr'mə-ti), *n.* [*pl.* -TIES], [< L. *enormis*, immense], 1. great wickedness. 2. an outrageous act.
**e·nor·mous** (i-nôr'məs), *adj.* [see ENORMITY], of great size, number, etc.; huge; vast.
**e·nough** (i-nuf'), *adj.* [AS. *genoh*], as much or as many as necessary; sufficient. *n.* the amount needed. *adv.* 1. sufficiently. 2. fully; quite: as, glad *enough* to go. 3. just adequately; tolerably. *interj.* no more!
**e·now** (i-nou'), *adj., n., adv.* [Archaic], enough.
**en·quire** (in-kwīr'), *v.t. & v.i.* [-QUIRED, -QUIRING], to inquire. **—en·quir'y** [*pl.* -IES], *n.*
**en·rage** (in-rāj'), *v.t.* [-RAGED, -RAGING], to put into a rage; infuriate.**—en·rage'ment,** *n.*
**en·rap·ture** (in-rap'chẽr), *v.t.* [-TURED, -TURING], to fill with delight; entrance.
**en·rich** (in-rich'), *v.t.* to make rich or richer; give greater value, better quality, etc. **—en·riched',** *adj.* **—en·rich'ment,** *n.*
**en·roll, en·rol** (in-rōl'), *v.t. & v.i.* [-ROLLED, -ROLLING], 1. to record or be recorded in a roll, or list. 2. to enlist. 3. to make or become a member. **—en·roll'ment, en·rol'ment,** *n.*
**en route** (än rōōt'), [Fr.], on the way.
**en·sconce** (en-skons'), *v.t.* [-SCONCED, -SCONCING], [*en-* + *sconce* (fortification)], 1. to hide; conceal; shelter. 2. to place or settle snugly.
**en·sem·ble** (än säm'b'l), *n.* [Fr. < LL. *in-*, in + *simul*, at the same time], 1. total effect. 2. a whole costume of matching parts. 3. *a*) the performance together of a group of musicians. *b*) a small band, chorus, etc.
**en·shrine** (in-shrīn'), *v.t.* [-SHRINED, -SHRINING], 1. to enclose in a shrine. 2. to hold as sacred; cherish. **—en·shrine'ment,** *n.*
**en·shroud** (en-shroud'), *v.t.* to cover as if with a shroud; hide; obscure.
**en·sign** (en'sīn), *n.* [< L. *in-*, in + *signum*, a sign], 1. a flag or banner. 2. (en's'n), in the *U.S. Navy*, a commissioned officer of the lowest rank.
**en·si·lage** (en's'l-ij), *n.* [Fr.], green fodder preserved in a silo.
**en·slave** (in-slāv'), *v.t.* [-SLAVED, -SLAVING], 1. to make a slave of. 2. to subjugate.
**en·snare** (en-snâr'), *v.t.* [-SNARED, -SNARING], to catch as in a snare; trap.
**en·sue** (en-sōō', -sū'), *v.i.* [-SUED, -SUING], [< L. *in-*, in + *sequi*, to follow], 1. to follow immediately. 2. to happen as a consequence; result.
**en·sure** (in-shoor'), *v.t. & v.i.* [-SURED, -SURING], to insure.
**-ent,** [< Fr. & L. ppr. ending], a suffix used to form adjectives or nouns from verbs, as *insistent, superintendent:* cf. **-ant.**
**en·tail** (in-tāl'), *v.t.* [< OFr. *taillier*, to cut], 1. in *law*, to limit the inheritance of (property) to a specific line of heirs. 2. to cause; require as necessary; necessitate.
**en·tan'gle** (in-), *v.t.* [-GLED, -GLING], 1. to involve in a tangle. 2. to involve in difficulty. 3. to confuse. 4. to complicate.
**en·tente** (än-tänt'), *n.* [Fr. < *entendre*, to understand], 1. an understanding or agreement, as between governments. 2. the parties to this.
**en·ter** (en'tẽr), *v.t.* [< L. *intra*, within], 1. to come or go into. 2. to penetrate. 3. to insert. 4. to write down in a list, etc. 5. to become a member of. 6. to get (someone) admitted. 7. to begin. *v.i.* 1. to come or go into some place. 2. to penetrate. **—enter into,** 1. to take part in. 2. to form a part of. **—enter on** (or **upon**), to begin.
**en·ter·ic** (en-ter'ik), *adj.* [< Gr. *enteron*, intestine], intestinal.
**en·ter·prise** (en'tẽr-prīz'), *n.* [ult. < L. *inter*, in + *prendere*, take], 1. an undertaking; esp., a bold, hard, or important one. 2. energy and initiative.
**en'ter·pris'ing,** *adj.* showing enterprise; full of energy and initiative; venturesome.
**en·ter·tain** (en'tẽr-tān'), *v.t.* [ult. < L. *inter*, between + *tenere*, to hold], 1. to amuse; interest. 2. to have as a guest. 3. to consider, as an idea. *v.i.* to have guests.
**en'ter·tain'er,** *n.* one who entertains; esp., one whose work is singing, dancing, etc.
**en'ter·tain'ing,** *adj.* interesting; diverting; amusing. **—en'ter·tain'ing·ly,** *adv.*
**en'ter·tain'ment,** *n.* 1. an entertaining or being entertained. 2. something that entertains, as a show or performance.
**en·thrall, en·thral** (in-thrôl'), *v.t.* [-THRALLED, -THRALLING], 1. to make a slave of; enslave. 2. to fascinate; enchant.
**en·throne** (in-thrōn'), *v.t.* [-THRONED, -THRONING], 1. to place on a throne. 2. to revere; exalt. **—en·throne'ment,** *n.*
**en·thuse** (in-thōōz', -thūz'), *v.t. & v.i.* [-THUSED, -THUSING], [Colloq.], 1. to make or become enthusiastic. 2. to show or cause to show enthusiasm.
**en·thu·si·asm** (in-thōō'zi-az'm, -thū'-), *n.* [< Gr. *enthous*, inspired], intense or eager interest; zeal; fervor. **—en·thu'si·ast** (-ast), *n.* **—en·thu'si·as'tic,** *adj.*
**en·tice** (in-tīs'), *v.t.* [-TICED, -TICING], [< L. *in*, in + *titio*, a burning brand], to tempt with hope of reward or pleasure.
**en·tire** (in-tīr'), *adj.* [< L. *integer*, whole], not lacking any parts; complete; whole; intact. **—en·tire'ly,** *adv.*
**en·tire'ty** (-ti), *n.* [*pl.* -TIES], 1. the state or fact of being entire; wholeness. 2. an entire thing; whole. **—in its entirety,** as a whole; completely.
**en·ti·tle** (in-tī't'l), *v.t.* [-TLED, -TLING], 1. to give a title or name to. 2. to give a right or claim to.
**en·ti·ty** (en'tə-ti), *n.* [*pl.* -TIES], [ult. < L. *esse*, to be], 1. existence. 2. a thing that has real and individual existence.
**en·tomb** (in-tōōm'), *v.t.* to place in a tomb; bury. **—en·tomb'ment,** *n.*
**en·to·mol·o·gy** (en'tə-mol'ə-ji), *n.* [< Gr. *entomon*, insect; + *-logy*], the branch of zoology that deals with insects. **—en'to·mo·log'i·cal** (-mə-loj'i-k'l), *adj.* **—en'to·mol'o·gist,** *n.*
**en·tou·rage** (än'too-räzh'), *n.* [Fr. < *entourer*, surround], a group of associates or attendants; retinue.
**en·tr'acte** (än-trakt'), *n.* [Fr. < *entre-*, between + *acte*, an act], 1. the interval between two acts of a play, opera, etc.; intermission. 2. music, a dance, etc. performed during this interval.
**en·trails** (en'trālz, -trəlz), *n.pl.* [< L. *interaneus*, internal], the inner organs of men or animals; specif., the intestines; viscera.
**en·train** (in-trān'), *v.t. & v.i.* to put or go aboard a train. **—en·train'ment,** *n.*
**en·trance** (en'trəns), *n.* 1. the act of entering. 2. a place for entering; door, gate, etc. 3. permission or right to enter.
**en·trance** (in-trans', -träns'), *v.t.* [-TRANCED, -TRANCING], 1. to put into a trance. 2. to delight; charm. **—en·trance'ment,** *n.*
**en·trant** (en'trənt), *n.* one who enters.
**en·trap** (in-trap'), *v.t.* [-TRAPPED, -TRAPPING], to catch as in a trap; ensnare.
**en·treat** (in-trēt'), *v.t. & v.i.* [< OFr. *en-*, in + *traiter;* see TREAT], to ask earnestly; beseech; implore. **—en·treat'ing·ly,** *adv.*
**en·treat'y,** *n.* [*pl.* -IES], an earnest request.
**en·tree, en·trée** (än'trā), *n.* [< Fr. *entrer;* see ENTER], 1. freedom to enter. 2. the main course of a meal. 3. in some countries, a dish served between the main courses.

**en·trench** (in-trench′), *v.t.* 1. to surround or fortify with a trench or trenches. 2. to establish securely. *v.i.* to encroach; trespass. Also **intrench.** —**en·trench′ment,** *n.*
**en·tre·pre·neur** (än′trə-prə-nūr′), *n.* [Fr.; see ENTERPRISE], one who organizes a business undertaking, assuming the risk for the sake of the profit.
**en·trust** (in-trust′), *v.t.* 1. to trust; charge with a trust or duty. 2. to assign the care of; turn over for safekeeping. Also **intrust.**
**en·try** (en′tri), *n.* [*pl.* -TRIES], [< OFr.; see ENTER], 1. an entering; entrance. 2. a way by which to enter. 3. an item or note entered in a list, journal, etc. 4. one entered in a race, competition, etc.
**en·twine** (in-twīn′), *v.t.* & *v.i.* [-TWINED, -TWINING], to twine together or around.
**e·nu·mer·ate** (i-nōō′mə-rāt′, -nū′-), *v.t.* [-ATED, -ATING], [<L. *e-*, out + *numerare*, to count], 1. to count. 2. to name one by one. —**e·nu′mer·a′tion,** *n.*
**e·nun·ci·ate** (i-nun′si-āt′, -shi-āt′), *v.t.* & *v.i.* [-ATED, -ATING], [< L. *e-*, out + *nuntiare*, announce], 1. to state definitely. 2. to announce. 3. to pronounce (words). —**e·nun′ci·a′tion,** *n.*
**en·vel·op** (in-vel′əp), *v.t.* [< OFr.; see EN- & DEVELOP], 1. to wrap up; cover completely. 2. to surround. —**en·vel′op·ment,** *n.*
**en·ve·lope** (en′və-lōp′, än′-), *n.* 1. a thing that envelops; covering. 2. a folded paper container for letters, etc., usually with a gummed flap.
**en·ven·om** (en-ven′əm), *v.t.* 1. to put venom or poison in. 2. to fill with bitterness.
**en·vi·a·ble** (en′vi-ə-b'l), *adj.* to be envied or desired. —**en′vi·a·bly,** *adv.*
**en·vi·ous** (en′vi-əs), *adj.* feeling or showing envy. —**en′vi·ous·ly,** *adv.*
**en·vi·ron·ment** (in-vī′rən-mənt, -ẽrn-mənt), *n.* [see ENVIRONS], 1. a surrounding or being surrounded. 2. surroundings. 3. all the conditions, circumstances, etc. surrounding, and affecting the development of, an organism. —**en·vi′ron·men′tal** (-men′t'l), *adj.*
**en·vi·rons** (in-vī′rənz), *n.pl.* [< OFr. *en-*, in + *viron*, a circuit], the districts surrounding a city; suburbs.
**en·vis·age** (en-viz′ij), *v.t.* [-AGED, -AGING], [see EN- & VISAGE], 1. to face; confront. 2. to form an image of in the mind; visualize.
**en·voy** (en′voi), *n.* [< Fr. < L. *in*, in + *via*, way], 1. a messenger; agent. 2. a diplomat ranking just below an ambassador.
**en·vy** (en′vi), *n.* [*pl.* -VIES], [< L. *invidia*], 1. discontent and ill will over another's advantages, possessions, etc. 2. desire for something belonging to another. 3. an object of such feeling. *v.t.* [-VIED, -VYING], to feel envy toward or because of.
**en·zyme** (en′zīm, -zim), *n.* [< Gr. *en-*, in + *zymē*, leaven], an organic substance produced in plant and animal cells that causes changes in other substances by catalysis: as, pepsin is a digestive *enzyme.*
**e·on** (ē′ən, ē′on), *n.* [see AEON], an extremely long, indefinite period of time.
**-eous,** [< L. *-eus*], a suffix meaning *having the nature of, like,* as in *beauteous.*
**ep·au·let, ep·au·lette** (ep′ə-let′), *n.* [< Fr.; see SPATULA], a shoulder ornament, as on military uniforms.
**e·pee, é·pée** (e-pā′), *n.* [Fr.; ult. < Gr. *spathē*, blade], a sword, especially one without a cutting edge, used in fencing.
**e·phed·rine** (e-fed′rin), *n.* [< L. *ephedra*, horsetail (a plant)], an alkaloid used to relieve nasal congestion, as in asthma, etc.
**e·phem·er·al** (ə-fem′ẽr-əl), *adj.* [< Gr. *epi-*, upon + *hēmera*, day], 1. lasting one day. 2. short-lived; transitory.
**e·phem·er·id** (ə-fem′ẽr-id), *n.* [see EPHEMERAL], a delicate insect with gauzy wings, which lives for a very short time; May fly.
**epi-,** [< Gr. *epi*, at, on], a prefix meaning *on, upon, over,* as in *epiglottis.*
**ep·ic** (ep′ik), *n.* [< Gr. *epos*, a word, tale], a long narrative poem in dignified style, about the deeds of a hero or heroes. *adj.* of or like an epic; heroic; grand: also **ep′i·cal.**
**ep·i·cen·ter** (ep′i-sen′tẽr), *n.* the area of the earth's surface directly above the place of origin of an earthquake.
**ep·i·cure** (ep′i-kyoor′), *n.* [< *Epicurus*, ancient Gr. philosopher], 1. one who has a discriminating taste for foods and liquors. 2. one who is fond of luxury and sensuous pleasure. —**ep′i·cu·re′an** (-kyoo-rē′ən), *adj.*
**ep·i·dem·ic** (ep′ə-dem′ik), *adj.* [< Gr. *epi-*, among + *dēmos*, people], prevalent and spreading rapidly among many people in a community, as a contagious disease. *n.* 1. an epidemic disease. 2. the spreading of such a disease. —**ep′i·dem′i·cal·ly,** *adv.*
**ep·i·der·mis** (ep′ə-dūr′mis), *n.* [< Gr. *epi-*, upon + *derma*, the skin], the outermost layer of the skin. —**ep′i·der′mal,** *adj.*
**ep·i·glot·tis** (ep′ə-glot′is), *n.* [< Gr. *epi-*, upon + *glotta*, tongue], the thin lid of cartilage that covers the windpipe during swallowing.
**ep·i·gram** (ep′ə-gram′), *n.* [< Gr. *epi-*, upon + *graphein*, write], a terse, witty, pointed statement. —**ep′i·gram·mat′ic** (-grə-mat′ik), *adj.*
**ep·i·lep·sy** (ep′ə-lep′si), *n.* [< Gr. *epi-*, upon + *lambanein*, seize], a chronic nervous disease, characterized by convulsions and unconsciousness.
**ep′i·lep′tic** (-tik), *adj.* of, like, or having epilepsy. *n.* one who has epilepsy.
**ep·i·logue, ep·i·log** (ep′ə-lôg′), *n.* [< Gr. *epi-*, upon + *legein*, speak], 1. a closing section of a novel, play, etc. providing further comment, esp. a speech to the audience by an actor. 2. the actor who speaks this.
**E·piph·a·ny** (i-pif′ə-ni), *n.* [< Gr. *epi-*, upon + *phainein*, to show], a Christian festival (Jan. 6) commemorating the revealing of Jesus as the Christ to the Gentiles.
**e·pis·co·pa·cy** (i-pis′kə-pə-si), *n.* [*pl.* -CIES], [< Gr. *epi-*, over + *skopein*, to look], 1. church government by bishops. 2. the position, rank, or term of office of a bishop. 3. bishops collectively.
**e·pis′co·pal** (-p'l), *adj.* 1. of or governed by bishops. 2. [E-], designating or of any of various churches governed by bishops.
**E·pis′co·pa′li·an** (-pā′li-ən), *adj.* Episcopal. *n.* a member of an Episcopal Church.
**e·pis′co·pate** (-pit, -pāt′), *n.* 1. the position, rank, or term of office of a bishop. 2. a bishop's see. 3. bishops collectively.
**ep·i·sode** (ep′ə-sōd′), *n.* [< Gr. *epeisodios*, coming in besides], 1. any part of a novel, poem, etc. that is complete in itself; incident. 2. an event or series of events complete in itself. —**ep′i·sod′ic** (-sod′ik), *adj.*
**e·pis·tle** (i-pis′'l), *n.* [< Gr. *epi-*, to + *stellein*, send], 1. a letter. 2. [E-], in the *Bible*, any of the letters of the Apostles. —**e·pis′to·lar′y** (-tə-ler′i), *adj.*
**ep·i·taph** (ep′ə-taf′, -täf′), *n.* [< Gr. *epi-*, upon + *taphos*, tomb], an inscription, as for a tomb, in memory of a dead person.
**ep·i·the·li·um** (ep′ə-thē′li-əm), *n.* [*pl.* -LIUMS, -LIA (-li-ə)], [< Gr. *epi-*, upon + *thēlē*, nipple], membranelike tissue that covers body surfaces and lines body cavities. —**ep′i·the′li·al** (-əl), *adj.*
**ep·i·thet** (ep′ə-thet′), *n.* [< Gr. *epi-*, on + *tithenai*, put], a word or phrase characterizing some person or thing.
**e·pit·o·me** (i-pit′ə-mi), *n.* [*pl.* -MES], [< Gr. *epi-*, upon + *temnein*, cut], 1. an abstract; summary. 2. a part or thing that is typical of the whole.

**e·pit'o·mize'** (-mīz'), *v.t.* [-MIZED, -MIZING], to make or be an epitome of.

‡**e plu·ri·bus u·num** (ē ploor'ə-bus ū'nəm), [L.], out of many, one: a motto of the U.S.

**ep·och** (ep'ək), *n.* [< Gr. *epi-*, upon + *echein*, hold], 1. the start of a new period of something: as, radio marked an *epoch* in communication. 2. a period of time in terms of notable events, men, etc. —**ep'och·al,** *adj.*

**ep·ox·y** (ep-ok'si), *adj.* [*ep*(*i*)- + *oxygen*], designating a compound, specif., a resin used in glues, etc., in which an oxygen atom is joined to each of two other connected atoms.

**ep·si·lon** (ep'sə-lon'), *n.* the fifth letter of the Greek alphabet (Ε, ε).

**Ep·som salts** (or **salt**) (ep'səm), [< *Epsom*, town in England], a white, crystalline salt, magnesium sulfate, used as a cathartic.

**eq·ua·ble** (ek'wə-b'l), *adj.* [see EQUAL], steady; uniform; even; tranquil. —**eq'ua·bil'i·ty, eq'ua·ble·ness,** *n.* —**eq'ua·bly,** *adv.*

**e·qual** (ē'kwəl), *adj.* [< L. *aequus*, even], 1. of the same quantity, size, value, etc. 2. having the same rights, ability, rank, etc. 3. evenly proportioned. *n.* any person or thing that is equal. *v.t.* [EQUALED or EQUALLED, EQUALING or EQUALLING], 1. to be equal to. 2. to do or make something equal to. —**equal to,** having enough ability, strength, etc. for. —**e'qual·ly,** *adv.*

**e·qual·i·ty** (i-kwäl'ə-ti, -kwôl'-), *n.* [*pl.* -TIES], state of being equal, esp. in political and social rights.

**e·qual·ize** (ē'kwəl-īz'), *v.t.* [-IZED, -IZING], to make equal or uniform. —**e'qual·i·za'tion,** *n.* —**e'qual·iz'er,** *n.*

**equal mark** (or **sign**), the arithmetical sign (=), indicating equality.

**e·qua·nim·i·ty** (ē'kwə-nim'ə-ti, ek'wə-), *n.* [< L. *aequus*, even + *animus*, mind], calmness of mind; composure.

**e·quate** (i-kwāt'), *v.t.* [-QUATED, -QUATING], to treat, regard, or express as equal.

**e·qua·tion** (i-kwā'zhən, -shən), *n.* 1. an equating or being equated. 2. an expression of equality between two quantities as shown by the equal mark: as, $x + 4x = 5x$.

**e·qua·tor** (i-kwā'tẽr), *n.* an imaginary circle around the earth, equally distant from both the North Pole and the South Pole.—**e·qua·to·ri·al** (ē'kwə-tôr'i-əl, ek'wə-), *adj.*

**eq·uer·ry** (ek'wẽr-i), *n.* [*pl.* -RIES], [Fr. *écurie*, a stable], 1. formerly, an officer in charge of the horses of a royal or noble household. 2. a personal attendant on some member of a sovereign's family.

**e·ques·tri·an** (i-kwes'tri-ən), *adj.* [< L. *equus*, horse], 1. of horses or horsemanship. 2. on horseback. *n.* a rider or circus performer on horseback.

**equi-**, a combining form meaning *equal, equally*, as in *equidistant*.

**e·qui·an·gu·lar** (ē'kwə-aŋ'gyoo-lẽr), *adj.* having all angles equal.

**e'qui·dis'tant,** *adj.* equally distant.

**e'qui·lat'er·al** (-lat'ẽr-əl), *adj.* [< L. *aequus*, equal + *latus*, side], having all sides equal. *n.* a figure having equal sides.

**e·qui·li·brate** (ē'kwə-lī'brāt, i-kwil'ə-brāt'), *v.t. & v.i.* [-BRATED, -BRATING], to bring into or be in equilibrium. —**e'qui·li·bra'tion,** *n.*

**e·qui·lib·ri·um** (ē'kwə-lib'ri-əm), *n.* [*pl.* -RIUMS, -RIA (-ri-ə)], [< L. *aequus*, equal + *libra*, balance], a state of balance between opposing forces.

**e·quine** (ē'kwīn), *adj.* [< L. *equus*, horse], of or like a horse. *n.* a horse.

**e·qui·nox** (ē'kwə-noks'), *n.* [< L. *aequus*, equal + *nox*, night], the time when the sun crosses the equator, making night and day of equal length in all parts of the earth.

**e·quip** (i-kwip'), *v.t.* [-QUIPPED, -QUIPPING], [< OFr. *e*(*s*)*quiper*, embark], to furnish with the necessities for an undertaking; fit out.

**eq·ui·page** (ek'wə-pij), *n.* a carriage with horses and liveried servants.

**e·quip·ment** (i-kwip'mənt), *n.* 1. an equipping or being equipped. 2. whatever one is equipped with; outfit, resources, etc.

**e·qui·poise** (ek'wə-poiz', ē'kwə-), *n.* [*equi-* + *poise*], 1. equal distribution of weight. 2. counterbalance.

**eq·ui·ta·ble** (ek'wi-tə-b'l), *adj.* [see EQUITY], fair; just. —**eq'ui·ta·bly,** *adv.*

**eq·ui·ty** (ek'wə-ti), *n.* [*pl.* -TIES], [< L. *aequus*, equal], 1. fairness; impartiality; justice. 2. the value of property beyond the amount owed on it. 3. in *law*, a system of doctrines supplementing common and statute law.

**e·quiv·a·lent** (i-kwiv'ə-lənt), *adj.* [< L. *aequus*, equal + *valere*, be strong], equal in quantity, value, force, meaning, etc. *n.* an equivalent thing. —**e·quiv'a·lence,** *n.*

**e·quiv·o·cal** (i-kwiv'ə-k'l), *adj.* [< L. *aequus*, equal + *vox*, voice], 1. having two or more meanings; purposely ambiguous. 2. uncertain; doubtful. 3. suspicious; questionable.

**e·quiv'o·cate'** (-kāt'), *v.i.* [-CATED, -CATING], to use equivocal terms in order to deceive or mislead. —**e·quiv'o·ca'tion,** *n.* —**e·quiv'o·ca'tor,** *n.*

**-er,** [< AS.], 1. a suffix meaning: *a*) a *person* or *thing having to do with*, as in *hatter*. *b*) *a person living in*, as in *New Yorker*. *c*) *a person* or *thing that*, as in *sprayer*. *d*) *repeatedly*, as in *flicker*. 2. a suffix forming the comparative degree, as in *greater*.

**e·ra** (er'ə), *n.* [LL. *aera*], 1. a period of time measured from some occurrence or date. 2. a period of time in terms of noteworthy events, men etc.

**e·rad·i·ca·ble** (i-rad'i-kə-b'l), *adj.* that can be eradicated.

**e·rad·i·cate** (i-rad'i-kāt'), *v.t.* [-CATED, -CATING], [< L. *e-*, out + *radix*, root], to uproot; wipe out; destroy. —**e·rad'i·ca'tion,** *n.* —**e·rad'i·ca'tor,** *n.*

**e·rase** (i-rās'), *v.t.* [ERASED, ERASING], [< L. *e-*, out + *radere*, scrape], 1. to rub, scrape, or wipe out, as writing 2. to obliterate, as from the mind. —**e·ras'a·ble,** *adj.*

**e·ras'er,** *n.* a thing that erases; specif., a rubber device for erasing pencil or ink marks, or a pad for removing chalk from a blackboard.

**e·ra·sure** (i-rā'shẽr), *n.* 1. an erasing. 2. the place where some word, mark, etc. has been erased.

**ere** (âr), *prep.* [AS. *ær*], [Archiac or Poetic], before (in time). *conj.* [Archaic or Poetic], 1. before. 2. rather than.

**e·rect** (i-rekt'), *adj.* [< L. *e-*, up + *regere*, make straight], upright. *v.t.* 1. to construct (a building, etc.). 2. to set in an upright position. 3. to put together. —**e·rec'tion,** *n.*

**ere·long** (âr'lôŋ'), *adv.* [Archaic], before long.

**er·e·mite** (er'ə-mīt'), *n.* [see HERMIT], a hermit; religious recluse.

**erg** (ũrg), *n.* [< Gr. *ergon*, work], a unit of work or energy.

‡**er·go** (ũr'gō), *conj.* [L.], therefore.

**Er·in** (âr'in), *n.* [Poetic], Ireland.

**er·mine** (ũr'min), *n.* [prob. < OHG. *harmo*, weasel], 1. weasel whose fur is white in winter. 2. its white fur.

**erne, ern** (ũrn), *n.* [AS. *earn*], a kind of eagle that lives near the sea.

**e·rode** (i-rōd'), *v.t.* [ERODED, ERODING], [< L. *e-*, out + *rodere*, gnaw], 1. to wear away. 2. to form by wearing away gradually: as, the stream *eroded* a gully. *v.i.* to become eroded.

**E·ros** (êr'os, er'-), *n.* in *Gr. myth.*, the god of love, son of Aphrodite.

**e·ro·sion** (i-rō'zhən), *n.* an eroding or being eroded: as, soil *erosion*. —**e·ro'sive,** *adj.*

**e·rot·ic** (i-rot′ik), ***adj.*** [< Gr. *erōs*, love], of or causing sexual feelings or desires; amatory. **—e·rot′i·cal·ly, *adv.***

**e·rot′i·cism** (-ə-siz'm), ***n.*** 1. erotic quality. 2. sexual behavior. 3. preoccupation with sex.

**err** (ũr), ***v.i.*** [< L. *errare*, wander], 1. to be wrong or mistaken. 2. to deviate from the established moral code. **—err′ing, *adj.***

**er·rand** (er′ənd), ***n.*** [AS. *ærende*], 1. a short trip to do a thing, as for another. 2. the thing to be done.

**er·rant** (er′ənt), ***adj.*** [see ERR], 1. roving in search of adventure. 2. erring; wrong.

**er′rant·ry** (-ri), ***n.*** the behavior of a knight-errant; deeds of chivalry.

**er·rat·ic** (ə-rat′ik), ***adj.*** [< L. *errare*, wander], 1. irregular; wandering. 2. eccentric; queer. ***n.*** an erratic person. **—er·rat′i·cal·ly, *adv.***

**er·ra·tum** (i-rā′təm, e-rä′-), ***n.*** [*pl.* -TA (-tə)], [L. < *errare*, wander], an error in printing or writing.

**er·ro·ne·ous** (ə-rō′ni-əs), ***adj.*** containing error; mistaken; wrong.

**er·ror** (er′ẽr), ***n.*** [< L. *errare*, wander], 1. the state of believing what is untrue. 2. a wrong belief. 3. something incorrect or wrong; mistake. 4. transgression. 5. in *baseball*, a misplay (by a fielder).

**er·satz** (er-zäts′), ***n. & adj.*** [G.], substitute: the word usually suggests inferior quality.

**Erse** (ũrs), ***adj. & n.*** [Scot. var. of *Irish*], Irish Gaelic.

**erst** (ũrst), ***adv.*** [< AS. *ær*, ere], [Archaic], formerly; long ago.

**erst′while′** (-hwīl′), ***adv.*** [Archaic], formerly; some time ago. ***adj.*** former.

**e·ruct** (i-rukt′), ***v.t. & v.i.*** [< L. *eructare*], to belch.

**er·u·dite** (er′yoo-dīt′, er′oo-), ***adj.*** [< L. *e-*, out + *rudis*, rude], learned; scholarly.

**er′u·di′tion** (-dish′ən), ***n.*** learning acquired by reading and study; scholarship.

**e·rupt** (i-rupt′) ***v.i.*** [< L. *e-*, out + *rumpere*, to break], 1. to burst forth or out, as lava from a volcano. 2. to throw forth lava, water, etc. 3. to break out in a rash.

**e·rup·tion** (i-rup′shən), ***n.*** 1. a bursting forth or out. 2. *a*) a breaking out in a rash. *b*) a rash **—e·rup′tive, *adj.***

**-ery,** [< LL. *-aria*], a suffix meaning: 1. *a place to*, as in *tannery*. 2. *a place for*, as in *nunnery*. 3. *act* or *practice of*, as in *robbery*. 4. *product of*, as in *pottery*. 5. *collection of*, as in *jewelry*. 6. *condition of*, as in *drudgery*.

**er·y·sip·e·las** (er′ə-sip′'l-əs, êr′ə-), ***n.*** [< Gr. *erythros*, red + *pella*, skin], an acute, infectious skin disease with local inflammation.

**-es,** [< AS.], a suffix used to form: 1. the plural of some nouns, as *fishes*. 2. the third person singular, present indicative, of verbs, as (he) *kisses*.

**E·sau** (ē′sô), ***n.*** in the *Bible*, Isaac's son, who sold his birthright to his brother, Jacob.

**es·ca·lade** (es′kə-lād′), ***n.*** [< L. *scala*, ladder], the act of scaling the walls of a fortified place by ladders. ***v.t.*** [-LADED, -LADING], to climb (a wall, etc.) or enter (a fortified place) by ladders.

**es·ca·late** (es′kə-lāt′), ***v.i.*** [-LATED, -LATING], 1. to rise as on an escalator. 2. to expand, as from a local conflict into a general war.

**es·ca·la·tor** (es′kə-lā′tẽr), ***n.*** [< L. *scala*, ladder], a moving stairway on an endless belt.

**es·cal·op, es·cal·lop** (e-skol′əp, -skal′-), ***n.*** scallop. ***v.t.*** to bake in a cream sauce.

**es·ca·pade** (es′kə-pād′), ***n.*** [Fr.], 1. an escaping. 2. a reckless adventure or prank.

**es·cape** (ə-skāp′, e-), ***v.i.*** [-CAPED, -CAPING], [< L. *ex-*, out of + *cappa*, cloak], 1. to get free. 2. to avoid harm, injury, etc. 3. to leak away: as, gas is *escaping*. ***v.t.*** 1. to get away from. 2. to avoid: as, he *escaped* death. 3. to slip away from: as, the date *escapes* me. ***n.*** 1. an escaping. 2. a means of escape. 3. a leakage. 4. a temporary mental release from reality. ***adj.*** providing an escape. **—es·cap′a·ble, *adj.* —es·cap′er, *n.***

**es·cap·ee** (ə-skā′pē′, e-), ***n.*** a person who has escaped.

**es·cape′ment,** ***n.*** a notched wheel with a detaining catch to regulate movement, as in a clockwork.

**es·cap′ism** (-iz'm), ***n.*** a tendency to escape from reality, responsibilities, etc., esp. through the imagination. **—es·cap′ist, *n.***

**es·ca·role** (es′kə-rōl′), ***n.*** [< L. *esca*, food], a plant whose leaves are used in salads.

**es·carp·ment** (e-skärp′mənt), ***n.*** [< It. *scarpa*], a steep slope or cliff.

**-escence,** a noun suffix corresponding to the adjective suffix *-escent*, as in *obsolescence*.

**-escent,** [< L. *-escens*], an adjective suffix meaning *starting to be*, *being*, or *becoming*, as in *obsolescent*.

**es·cheat** (es-chēt′), ***n.*** [< L. *es-*, out + *cadere*, to fall], 1. the reverting of property to the lord of the manor or to the government when there are no legal heirs. 2. property so reverting.

**es·chew** (es-chōō′, -chū′), ***v.t.*** [< OHG. *sciuhan*, to fear], to keep away from; shun.

**es·cort** (es′kôrt), ***n.*** [< L. *ex-*, out + *corrigere*, set right], 1. one or more persons (or cars, ships, etc.) accompanying another to protect or show honor. 2. a man accompanying a woman in public. ***v.t.*** (i-skôrt′), to go with as an escort.

**es·crow** (es′krō), ***n.*** [see SCROLL], in *law*, the state of a deed, etc. put in the care of a third party until certain conditions are met.

**es·cu·lent** (es′kyoo-lənt), ***adj.*** [< L. *esca*, food], edible. ***n.*** something fit for food.

**es·cutch·eon** (i-skuch′ən), ***n.*** [< L. *scutum*, shield], a shield on which a coat of arms is displayed.

**-ese,** [< L. *-ensis*], a suffix meaning: 1. (*an inhabitant*) *of*, as in *Portuguese*. 2. (*in*) *the language of*, as in *Chinese*.

**Es·ki·mo** (es′kə-mō′), ***n.*** 1. [*pl.* -MOS, -MO], a member of a race living in Greenland, arctic N.America, etc. 2. the language of the Eskimos. ***adj.*** of the Eskimos or their language. **—Es′ki·mo′an, *adj.***

**Eskimo dog,** a strong breed of dog used by the Eskimos to pull sleds.

**e·soph·a·gus** (i-sof′ə-gəs), ***n.*** [*pl.* -GI (-jī′)], [< Gr. *oisein* (fut. inf.), carry + *phagein*, eat], the passage for food from the pharynx to the stomach; gullet.

**es·o·ter·ic** (es′ə-ter′ik), ***adj.*** [< Gr. *esoteros*, inner], 1. understood by only a chosen few. 2. confidential. **—es′o·ter′i·cal·ly, *adv.***

**esp., espec.,** especially.

**es·pal·ier** (e-spal′yẽr), ***n.*** [< It. *spalla*, the shoulder], 1. a lattice or trellis on which trees and shrubs are trained to grow flat. 2. a plant, tree, etc. so trained.

**es·pe·cial** (ə-spesh′əl), ***adj.*** special; particular; chief. **—es·pe′cial·ly, *adv.***

**Es·pe·ran·to** (es′pə-rän′tō), ***n.*** [after pseudonym of its inventor], an artificial language for international use.

**es·pi·o·nage** (es′pi-ə-nij, es′pi-ə-näzh′), ***n.*** [< Fr. *espion*, a spy], the act or practice of spying.

**es·pla·nade** (es′plə-nād′, -näd′), ***n.*** [Fr.; ult. < L. *explanare*, to level], a level, open space of ground; esp., a public walk or roadway; promenade.

**es·pous·al** (i-spou′z'l), ***n.*** 1. *usually pl.* a wedding. 2. an espousing (of some cause, idea, etc.); advocacy.

**es·pouse** (i-spouz′), ***v.t.*** [-POUSED, -POUSING], [< L. *spondere*, betroth], 1. to marry. 2. to support or adopt (some cause, idea, etc.).

**es·pres·so** (es-pres′ō), ***n.*** [*pl.* -SOS], [It., pp. of *esprimere*, express], coffee made in a special machine from finely ground beans.

‡**es·prit** (es'prē'), *n.* [Fr.], 1. spirit. 2. lively wit.
‡**es'prit' de corps'** (də kôr'), [Fr.], group spirit; sense of pride, honor, etc. in common activities and interests.
**es·py** (ə-spī'), *v.t.* [-PIED, -PYING], [see SPY], to catch sight of; see; make out.
**-esque,** [Fr.], a suffix meaning: 1. *in the manner* or *style of.* 2. *like,* as in *statuesque.*
**es·quire** (ə-skwīr', es'kwīr), *n.* [< LL. *scutarius,* shield-bearer], 1. formerly, an attendant on a knight. 2. in England, a member of the gentry ranking just below a knight. 3. [E-], a title of courtesy, usually abbrev. **Esq., Esqr.,** placed after a man's surname: as, John Davis, *Esq.*
**-ess,** [ult. < Gr.], a suffix used to form feminine nouns, as in *lioness, actress.*
**es·say** (ə-sā', e-sā'), *v.t.* [< L. *exagium,* a weighing], to try. *n.* 1. (e-sā', es'ā), an attempt; trial. 2. (es'ā), a short, personal literary composition dealing with a single subject. —**es·say·ist** (es'ā-ist), *n.*
**es·sence** (es''ns), *n.* [< L. *esse,* to be], 1. the basic nature (of something). 2. a concentrated substance that keeps the flavor, fragrance, etc. of that from which it is extracted. 3. a perfume.
**es·sen·tial** (ə-sen'shəl), *adj.* 1. of or constituting the essence of something; basic. 2. necessary to make a thing what it is; indispensable. *n.* something necessary or fundamental. —**es·sen'tial·ly,** *adv.*
**E.S.T., EST,** Eastern Standard Time.
**es·tab·lish** (ə-stab'lish), *v.t.* [< L. *stabilis,* stable], 1. to ordain or appoint (officials, laws, etc.) permanently. 2. to found (a nation, business, etc.). 3. to set up in a business, a profession, etc. 4. to cause to be accepted. 5. to prove; demonstrate.
**es·tab'lish·ment,** *n.* 1. an establishing or being established. 2. a thing established, as a business, household, etc. —**the Establishment,** the ruling inner circle of any nation, institution, etc.
**es·tate** (ə-stāt'), *n.* [< L. *stare,* to stand], 1. a condition or stage of life. 2. one's property or possessions. 3. an individually owned piece of land containing a residence.
**es·teem** (ə-stēm'), *v.t.* [< L. *aestimare,* to value], 1. to value highly; prize. 2. to consider. *n.* favorable opinion; high regard.
**es·ter** (es'tēr), *n.* [G. < *äther,* ether + *säure,* acid], an organic compound, comparable to an inorganic salt, formed by the reaction of an acid and an alcohol.
**Es·ther** (es'tēr), *n.* in the *Bible,* the Jewish wife of a Persian king: she saved her people from slaughter.
**es·thete** (es'thēt), *n.* aesthete. —**es·thet'ic** (-thet'ik), *adj.*
**es·thet'ics** (-thet'iks), *n.pl.* aesthetics.
**es·ti·ma·ble** (es'tə-mə-b'l), *adj.* 1. that can be estimated or evaluated. 2. worthy of esteem.
**es·ti·mate** (es'tə-māt'; *for n.,* -mit), *v.t.* [-MATED, -MATING], [see ESTEEM], 1. to form an opinion about. 2. to determine roughly (the size, cost, etc.). *n.* 1. a rough calculation; esp., an approximate computation of probable cost. 2. an opinion or judgment.
**es'ti·ma'tion,** *n.* 1. an opinion or judgment. 2. esteem; regard; respect.
**es·trange** (ə-strānj'), *v.t.* [-TRANGED, -TRANGING], [< L. *extraneus,* foreign], 1. to alienate. 2. to turn (a person) from a friendly or affectionate attitude to an indifferent or unfriendly one. —**es·trange'ment,** *n.*
**es·tro·gen** (es'trə-jən), *n.* [< Gr. *oistros,* frenzy], any of several female sex hormones.
**es·tu·ar·y** (es'chōō-er'i), *n.* [*pl.* -IES], [< L. *aestus,* tide], the wide mouth of a river, where the tide meets the current.
**-et,** [< OFr.], a suffix meaning *little,* as in *islet.*
**e·ta** (ā'tə, ē'-), *n.* the seventh letter of the Greek alphabet (Η, η).
**et al.,** [L. *et alii*], and others.
**et cet·er·a** (et set'ēr-ə, set'rə), [L.], and others; and so forth: abbrev. **etc.**
**etch** (ech), *v.t.* [< MHG. *ezzen,* to eat], to make (a drawing, design, etc.) on (glass, metal plates, etc.) by the action of an acid.
**etch'ing,** *n.* 1. the art of producing drawings or designs on metal plates, etc. by the action of acid. 2. a print made from an etched plate.
**e·ter·nal** (i-tũr'n'l), *adj.* [< L. *aeternus*], 1. without beginning or end; everlasting. 2. forever the same. 3. seeming never to stop. —**the Eternal,** God. —**e·ter'nal·ly,** *adv.*
**e·ter·ni·ty** (i-tũr'nə-ti), *n.* [*pl.* -TIES], 1. the fact or state of being eternal. 2. infinite or endless time. 3. a long period of time that seems endless.
**e·ther** (ē'thēr), *n.* [< Gr. *aithein,* to burn], 1. the upper regions of space. 2. a colorless, volatile, highly inflammable liquid, used as an anesthetic and a solvent. 3. an invisible substance postulated as pervading space and serving to transmit light waves, etc.
**e·the·re·al** (i-thêr'i-əl), *adj.* 1. very light; airy; delicate. 2. heavenly; not earthly.
**eth·i·cal** (eth'i-k'l), *adj.* [< Gr. *ēthos,* character], 1. having to do with ethics or morality; of or conforming to moral standards. 2. conforming to professional standards of conduct. —**eth'i·cal·ly,** *adv.*
**eth·ics** (eth'iks), *n.pl.* 1. [construed as sing.], the study of standards of conduct and moral judgment. 2. the system of morals of a particular religion, group, etc.
**E·thi·o·pi·an** (ē'thi-ō'pi-ən), *adj.* of Ethiopia, its people, etc. *n.* a native or inhabitant of Ethiopia.
**eth·nic** (eth'nik), *adj.* [< Gr. *ethnos,* nation], of any of the basic divisions of mankind, as distinguished by customs, language, etc.: also **eth'ni·cal.** —**eth'ni·cal·ly,** *adv.*
**eth·nol·o·gy** (eth-nol'ə-ji), *n.* [< Gr. *ethnos,* nation; + *-logy*], the branch of anthropology that deals with the distribution, characteristics, culture, etc. of various peoples. —**eth'no·log'i·cal** (-nə-loj'i-k'l), *adj.* —**eth'no·log'i·cal·ly,** *adv.* —**eth·nol'o·gist,** *n.*
**eth·yl** (eth'əl), *n.* [< *ether*], a hydrocarbon radical, which forms the base of common alcohol, ether, etc.
**ethyl alcohol,** common alcohol.
**e·ti·ol·o·gy** (ē'ti-ol'ə-ji), *n.* [< Gr. *aitia,* cause + *logia,* description], 1. the cause assigned, as for a disease. 2. the science of causes or origins. —**e'ti·o·log'i·cal** (-ə-loj'i-k'l), *adj.*
**et·i·quette** (et'i-ket', -kət), *n.* [Fr. *etiquette,* a ticket], the forms, manners, etc. conventionally acceptable or required in society, a profession, etc.
**E·trus·can** (i-trus'kən), *adj.* of an ancient country (*Etruria*) in W Italy.
**et seq.,** [L. *et sequens*], and the following.
**-ette,** [Fr., fem. of *-et*], a suffix meaning: 1. *little,* as in *dinette.* 2. *female,* as in *suffragette.*
**é·tude** (ā'tōōd, ā'tūd), *n.* [Fr. < L. *studere,* to study], 1. a study. 2. a musical composition for a solo instrument, designed to give practice in some special technique.
**ETV,** educational television.
**et·y·mol·o·gy** (et'ə-mol'ə-ji), *n.* [*pl.* -GIES], [< Gr. *etymos,* true + *logos,* word], 1. the origin and development of a word. 2. scientific study of word origins. Abbrev. **etym.** —**et'y·mo·log'i·cal** (-mə-loj'i-k'l), *adj.* —**et'y·mol'o·gist,** *n.*
**eu-,** [Gr.], a prefix meaning *good, well,* as in *eulogy, eugenic.*

**eu·ca·lyp·tus** (ū'kə-lip'təs), *n.* [*pl.* -TUSES, -TI (-tī)], [< Gr. *eu-*, well + *kalyptos*, covered], a subtropical evergreen of the myrtle family, valued for timber and oil.

**Eu·cha·rist** (ū'kə-rist), *n.* [< Gr. *eucharistia*, gratitude], 1. Holy Communion; Lord's Supper. 2. the consecrated bread and wine used in this. **—Eu'cha·ris'tic,** *adj.*

**eu·chre** (ū'kẽr), *n.* [< ?], a card game, played with thirty-two cards. *v.t.* [-CHRED, -CHRING], [Colloq.], to outwit.

**eu·gen·ics** (yoo-jen'iks), *n.pl.* [construed as sing.], [see EU- & GENESIS], the science that deals with improving races and breeds, esp. the human race, by controlling heredity. **—eu·gen'ic,** *adj.* **—eu·gen'i·cal·ly,** *adv.*

**eu·lo·gize** (ū'lə-jīz'), *v.t.* [-GIZED, -GIZING], to compose a eulogy about. **—eu'lo·gist,** *n.*

**eu'lo·gy** (-ji), *n.* [*pl.* -GIES], [< Gr. *eulegein*, speak well of], 1. speech in praise of a person or thing; esp., a funeral oration. 2. high praise. **—eu'lo·gis'tic** (-jis'tik), *adj.*

**eu·nuch** (ū'nək), *n.* [< Gr. *eunē*, bed + *echein*, keep], a castrated man.

**eu·pep·si·a** (yoo-pep'shə, -si-ə), *n.* [< Gr. *eu*, well + *peptein*, digest], good digestion.

**eu·phe·mism** (ū'fə-miz'm), *n.* [< Gr. *eu-*, good + *phēmē*, voice], 1. the use of a less direct word or phrase for one considered offensive. 2. a word or phrase so substituted. **—eu'phe·mis'tic,** *adj.*

**eu·pho·ni·ous** (yoo-fō'ni-əs), *adj.* having a pleasant sound; harmonious.

**eu·pho·ny** (ū'fə-ni), *n.* [*pl.* -NIES], [< Gr. *eu-*, well + *phōnē*, voice], a pleasant combination of sounds, as in speech or music.

**eu·pho·ri·a** (yoo-fôr'i-ə), *n.* [< Gr. *eu-*, well + *pherein*, to bear], a feeling of well-being. **—eu·phor'ic,** *adj.*

**eu·phu·ism** (ū'fū-iz'm), *n.* [< *Euphues*, character in writings of J. Lyly, 16th-c. Eng. author], 1. any artificial, high-flown style of speech or writing. 2. an instance of this.

**Eur.,** 1. Europe. 2. European.

**Eur·a·sian** (yoo-rā'zhən, -shən), *adj.* 1. of Eurasia. 2. of mixed European and Asiatic descent. *n.* a person of mixed European and Asiatic descent.

**eu·re·ka** (yoo-rē'kə), *interj.* [< Gr., I have found (it)], an exclamation of triumphant achievement.

**Eu·ro·pe·an** (yoor'ə-pē'ən), *adj.* of Europe, its people, etc. *n.* a native of Europe.

**European plan,** a system of hotel operation in which guests are charged for rooms, and pay for meals separately.

**eu·ryth·mics** (yoo-rith'miks), *n.pl.* [construed as sing.], [< Gr. *eu-*, well + *rhythmos*, rhythm], the art of performing bodily movements in rhythm.

**Eu·sta·chi·an tube** (yoo-stā'ki-ən, -shən), [after B. *Eustachio*, 16th-c. It. anatomist], a slender tube between the middle ear and the pharynx.

**eu·tha·na·si·a** (ū'thə-nā'zhə), *n.* [< Gr. *eu-*, well + *thanatos*, death], 1. a painless death. 2. act of causing death painlessly to end suffering: advocated by some in cases of incurable diseases.

**e·vac·u·ate** (i-vak'ū-āt'), *v.t.* [-ATED, -ATING], [< L. *e-*, out + *vacuus*, empty], 1. to make empty. 2. to discharge (excrement, etc.). 3. to remove; send away. 4. to withdraw from. *v.i.* to withdraw. **—e·vac'u·a'tion,** *n.* **—e·vac'u·ee'** (-ē'), *n.*

**e·vade** (i-vād'), *v.i.* & *v.t.* [EVADED, EVADING], [< L. *e-*, out + *vadere*, go], 1. to avoid or escape (from) by deceit or cleverness. 2. to avoid doing or answering directly.

**e·val·u·ate** (i-val'ū-āt'), *v.t.* [-ATED, -ATING], [ult. < L. *ex-*, out + *valere*, be worth], to find the value or amount of; appraise. **—e·val'u·a'tion,** *n.*

**ev·a·nesce** (ev'ə-nes'), *v.i.* [-NESCED, -NESCING], [< L. *e-*, out + *vanescere*, vanish], to fade from sight; vanish.

**ev'a·nes'cent** (-nes''nt), *adj.* tending to fade from sight; ephemeral. **—ev'a·nes'cence,** *n.*

**e·van·gel·i·cal** (ē'van-jel'i-k'l, ev'ən-), *adj.* [< Gr. *evangelos*, bringing good news], 1. of or according to the Gospels or the New Testament. 2. of those Protestant churches that emphasize salvation by faith. Also **e'van·gel'ic.** **—e'van·gel'i·cal·ly,** *adv.*

**e·van'gel·ist,** *n.* 1. [E-], any of the four writers of the Gospels. 2. a preacher of the Gospel; esp., a traveling preacher who holds revival meetings. **—e·van'gel·ism,** *n.*

**e·vap·o·rate** (i-vap'ə-rāt'), *v.t.* [-RATED, -RATING], [< L. *e-*, out + *vaporare*, emit vapor], 1. to change (a liquid or solid) into vapor. 2. to remove moisture from (milk, etc.) as by heating, so as to get a concentrated product. *v.i.* 1. to become vapor. 2. to give off vapor. 3. to vanish. **—e·vap'o·ra'tion,** *n.* **—e·vap'o·ra'tor,** *n.*

**e·va·sion** (i-vā'zhən), *n.* 1. an evading; an avoiding of a duty, question, etc. by deceit or cleverness. 2. a means of doing this; subterfuge.

**e·va·sive** (i-vā'siv), *adj.* 1. tending or seeking to evade; not straightforward or definite. 2. elusive. **—e·va'sive·ness,** *n.*

**Eve** (ēv), *n.* in the *Bible*, Adam's wife, the first woman.

**eve** (ēv), *n.* [ME. < *even* (evening)], 1. [Poetic], evening. 2. the evening or day before a holiday. 3. the period just prior to some event.

**e·ven** (ē'vən), *adj.* [AS. *efne*], 1. flat; level; smooth. 2. not varying; constant: as, an *even* tempo. 3. calm; tranquil: as, an *even* temper. 4. in the same line or plane: as, *even* with the rim. 5. just; fair: as, an *even* trade. 6. equal in number, quantity, etc. 7. exactly divisible by two. 8. exact: as, an *even* mile. *adv.* 1. however improbable; indeed. 2. exactly; just: as, it happened *even* as I expected. 3. still; yet: as, he's *even* better. *v.t.* & *v.i.* to make or become even. **—break even,** [Slang], to finish as neither a winner nor a loser. **—even if,** though. **—e'ven·ly,** *adv.* **—e'ven·ness,** *n.*

**e'ven·hand'ed** (-han'did), *adj.* impartial.

**eve·ning** (ēv'niŋ), *n.* [< AS. *æfnung*], 1. the last part of the day and early part of night. 2. [Dial.], afternoon.

**e·vent** (i-vent'), *n.* [< L. *e-*, out + *venire*, come], 1. an occurrence, esp. one of importance. 2. a result. 3. a particular contest in a program of sports. **—in any event,** in any case. **—in the event of,** in case of.

**e·vent'ful,** *adj.* 1. full of outstanding events. 2. having an important outcome.

**e·ven·tide** (ē'vən-tīd'), *n.* [Archaic], evening.

**e·ven·tu·al** (i-ven'chōō-əl), *adj.* 1. depending on events; contingent. 2. happening at the end; final. **—e·ven'tu·al·ly,** *adv.*

**e·ven'tu·al'i·ty** (-al'ə-ti), *n.* [*pl.* -TIES], a possible event or outcome.

**e·ven'tu·ate'** (-āt'), *v.i.* [-ATED, -ATING], to happen in the end; result. **—e·ven'tu·a'tion,** *n.*

**ev·er** (ev'ẽr), *adv.* [AS. *æfre*], 1. always: as, *ever* the same. 2. at any time: as, do you *ever* see her? 3. at all; by any chance: as, if it *ever* starts, we can go. **—ever so,** [Colloq.], very.

**ev'er·glade'** (-glād'), *n.* swampland.

**ev'er·green'** (-grēn'), *adj.* having green leaves all year long, as most conifers. *n.* an evergreen plant or tree.

**ev'er·last'ing,** *adj.* lasting forever; eternal. *n.* eternity. **—the Everlasting,** God.

**ev'er·more',** *adv.* forever; always.

**e·vert** (ē-vũrt'), *v.t.* [< L. *e-*, out + *vertere*, to turn], to turn outward or inside out.

**ev·er·y** (ev'ri, ev'ẽr-i), *adj.* [AS. *æfre ælc*, lit.,

ever each], 1. all, taken individually and separately. 2. all possible: as, he was given *every* chance. 3. at each interval of: as, a dose *every* two hours. **—every now and then,** once in a while. **—every other,** each alternate, as the first, third, fifth, etc. **—every so often,** [Colloq.], once in a while.

**ev′er·y·bod′y** (-bod′i, -bud′i), ***pron.*** every person; everyone.

**ev′er·y·day′,** ***adj.*** 1. daily. 2. suitable for ordinary days: as, *everyday* shoes. 3. usual.

**ev′er·y·one′,** ***pron.*** everybody.

**every one,** 1. everyone. 2. every person or thing.

**ev′er·y·thing′,** ***pron.*** every thing; all.

**ev′er·y·where′,** ***adv.*** in every place.

**e·vict** (i-vikt′), ***v.t.*** [< L. *e-*, from + *vincere*, conquer], to put (a tenant) out by legal procedure. **—e·vic′tion,** ***n.***

**ev·i·dence** (ev′ə-dəns), ***n.*** 1. the state of being evident. 2. something that makes another thing evident; sign. 3. a statement of a witness, an exhibit, etc. bearing on or establishing the point in question in a court of law. ***v.t.*** [-DENCED, -DENCING], to make evident.

**ev·i·dent** (ev′ə-dənt), ***adj.*** [< L. *e-*, from + *videre*, see], easy to see or perceive; clear.

**e·vil** (ē′v'l), ***adj.*** [AS. *yfel*], 1. morally bad or wrong; wicked. 2. harmful; injurious. 3. unlucky; disastrous. ***n.*** 1. wickedness; sin. 2. anything causing harm, pain, etc.

**e′vil·do′er** (-do͞o′ēr), ***n.*** one who does evil.

**e·vince** (i-vins′), ***v.t.*** [EVINCED, EVINCING], [< L. *e-*, out + *vincere*, conquer], to show plainly (a quality, feeling, etc.). **—e·vin′ci·ble,** ***adj.***

**e·vis·cer·ate** (i-vis′ə-rāt′), ***v.t.*** [-ATED, -ATING], [< L. *e-*, out + *viscera;* see VISCERA], 1. to remove the entrails from. 2. to deprive of an essential part. **—e·vis′cer·a′tion,** ***n.***

**e·voke** (i-vōk′), ***v.t.*** [EVOKED, EVOKING], [< L. *e-*, out + *vox*, voice], to call forth; elicit, as a response. **—ev·o·ca·tion** (ev′ō-kā′shən), ***n.***

**ev·o·lu·tion** (ev′ə-lo͞o′shən), ***n.*** [see EVOLVE], 1. an unfolding; process of development or growth. 2. a thing evolved. 3. a movement that is part of a series. 4. in *biology*, *a)* the development of a species, organism, etc. from its original to its present state. *b)* the theory that all species developed from earlier forms. **—ev′o·lu′tion·ar′y,** ***adj.*** **—ev′o·lu′tion·ist,** ***n.***

**e·volve** (i-volv′), ***v.t.*** & ***v.i.*** [EVOLVED, EVOLVING], [< L. *e-*, out + *volere*, to roll], 1. to unfold; develop gradually. 2. to develop by evolution.

**ewe** (ū), ***n.*** [AS. *eowu*], a female sheep.

**ew·er** (ū′ēr), ***n.*** [< L. *aqua*, water], a large, wide-mouthed water pitcher.

**ex-,** [< L. < Gr. *ex*, out], a prefix meaning: 1. *from, out,* as in *expel.* 2. *beyond,* as in *excess.* 3. *thoroughly,* as in *exterminate.* 4. *upward,* as in *exalt.* 5. *former,* as in *ex-president.*

**Ex.,** Exodus.

**ex.,** 1. example. 2. except(ion).

**ex·ac·er·bate** (ig-zas′ēr-bāt′), ***v.t.*** [-BATED, -BATING], [< L. *ex-*, intens. + *acerbus*, sour], 1. to aggravate (disease, pain, etc.). 2. to exasperate; irritate. **—ex·ac′er·ba′tion,** ***n.***

**ex·act** (ig-zakt′), ***adj.*** [< L. *ex-*, out + *agere*, drive], 1. characterized by or requiring accuracy; methodical; correct; strict. 2. leaving no room for error or doubt; precise. ***v.t.*** 1. to extort. 2. to demand; require.

**ex·act′ing,** ***adj.*** 1. making severe demands; tyrannical. 2. requiring great care, effort, etc.; arduous. **—ex·act′ing·ly,** ***adv.***

**ex·ac′tion** (-zak′shən), ***n.*** 1. an exacting. 2. an extortion. 3. something exacted.

**ex·act′i·tude′** (-tə-to͞od′, -tūd′), ***n.*** the quality of being exact; accuracy.

**ex·ag·ger·ate** (ig-zaj′ə-rāt′), ***v.t.*** & ***v.i.*** [-ATED, -ATING], [< L. *ex-*, out + *agger*, a heap], to think or tell of (something) as greater than it is; overstate. **—ex·ag′ger·a′tion,** ***n.***

**ex·alt** (ig-zôlt′), ***v.t.*** [< L. *ex-*, up + *altus*, high], 1. to raise in status, dignity, etc. 2. to praise; glorify. 3. to fill with joy, pride, etc.; elate. **—ex·al·ta·tion** (eg′zôl-tā′shən), ***n.*** **—ex·alt′ed·ly,** ***adv.***

**ex·am** (ig-zam′), ***n.*** [Colloq.], an examination.

**ex·am·i·na·tion** (ig-zam′ə-nā′shən), ***n.*** 1. an examining or being examined. 2. a set of questions asked in testing.

**ex·am·ine** (ig-zam′in), ***v.t.*** [-INED, -INING] [< L. *examinare*, weigh], 1. to look at critically or methodically; investigate; inspect. 2. to test by questioning. **—ex·am′in·er,** ***n.*** **—ex·am′i·nee′,** ***n.***

**ex·am·ple** (ig-zam′p'l, -zäm′-), ***n.*** [< L. *eximere*, take out], 1. something selected to show the character of the rest; sample. 2. a case that serves as a warning. 3. an instance that illustrates a principle. 4. a model; pattern. **—set an example,** to behave so as to be a model for others.

**ex·as·per·ate** (ig-zas′pə-rāt′), ***v.t.*** [-ATED, -ATING], [< L. *ex-*, out + *asper*, rough], to irritate; anger; aggravate. **—ex·as′per·at′ing·ly,** ***adv.*** **—ex·as′per·a′tion,** ***n.***

**ex·ca·vate** (eks′kə-vāt′), ***v.t.*** [-VATED, -VATING], [< L. *ex-*, out + *cavus*, hollow], 1. to make a hole or cavity in. 2. to form by hollowing out, as a tunnel. 3. to unearth. 4. to dig out; remove (earth, etc.). **—ex′ca·va′tion,** ***n.*** **—ex′ca·va′tor,** ***n.***

**ex·ceed** (ik-sēd′), ***v.t.*** & ***v.i.*** [< L. *ex-*, out + *cedere*, go], 1. to go or be beyond (a limit, etc.). 2. to surpass.

**ex·ceed·ing** (ik-sēd′iŋ), ***adj.*** surpassing; extreme. **—ex·ceed′ing·ly,** ***adv.***

**ex·cel** (ik-sel′), ***v.i.*** & ***v.t.*** [-CELLED, -CELLING], [< L. *ex-*, out of + *-cellere*, rise], to be better or greater than (another or others).

**ex·cel·lence** (ek′s'l-əns), ***n.*** the fact or state of excelling; superiority.

**ex′cel·len·cy** (-ən-si), ***n.*** [*pl.* -CIES], 1. [E-], a title of honor for certain dignitaries, as an ambassador. 2. [Archaic], excellence.

**ex′cel·lent,** ***adj.*** unusually good of its kind; of exceptional merit. **—ex′cel·lent·ly,** ***adv.***

**ex·cel·si·or** (ek-sel′si-ôr′), ***adj.*** & ***interj.*** [see EXCEL], always upward. ***n.*** (ik-sel′si-ēr), long, thin wood shavings used for packing.

**ex·cept** (ik-sept′), ***v.t.*** [< L. *ex-*, out + *capere*, take], to leave out or take out; exclude. ***v.i.*** to object. ***prep.*** leaving out; but.

**ex·cept′ing,** ***prep.*** except.

**ex·cep′tion,** ***n.*** 1. an excepting. 2. a person or thing omitted, excluded, or different from others of the same class; case to which a rule does not apply. 3. an objection.

**ex·cep′tion·a·ble,** ***adj.*** liable to exception.

**ex·cep′tion·al,** ***adj.*** unusual; extraordinary.

**ex·cerpt** (ik-sũrpt′), ***v.t.*** [< L. *ex-*, out + *carpere*, to pick], to select or quote (passages from a book, etc.); extract. ***n.*** (ek′sẽrpt), a passage selected or quoted; extract.

**ex·cess** (ik-ses′), ***n.*** [see EXCEED], 1. action that goes beyond a reasonable limit. 2. an amount greater than is necessary. 3. the amount by which one thing is more than another; surplus. ***adj.*** (*usually* ek′ses′), extra; surplus. **—in excess of,** more than.

**ex·ces′sive,** ***adj.*** too much; immoderate.

**ex·change** (iks-chānj′), ***v.t.*** & ***v.i.*** [-CHANGED, -CHANGING], [see EX- & CHANGE], 1. to give or receive (*for* another thing); trade; barter. 2. to interchange, as gifts. ***n.*** 1. an exchanging; interchange, trade, etc. 2. a thing exchanged. 3. a place for exchanging: as, a stock *exchange.* 4. a central office providing telephone service. 5. the value of one currency in terms of another. **—ex·change′a·ble,** ***adj.***

**ex·cheq·uer** (iks-chek′ẽr, eks′chek-), *n.* [< LL. *scaccarium*, chessboard: accounts of revenue were kept on a square board], 1. a national treasury. 2. funds; finances.
**ex·cise** (ek′sīz, ik-sīz′), *n.* [prob. < L. *ad-*, to + *census*, a tax], a tax on various commodities within a country, as liquor, tobacco, etc.: also **excise tax.** —**ex·cis′a·ble,** *adj.*
**ex·cise** (ik-sīz′), *v.t.* [-CISED, -CISING], [< L. *ex-*, out + *caedere*, to cut], to cut out. —**ex·cis′a·ble,** *adj.* —**ex·ci′sion** (-sizh′ən), *n.*
**ex·cit·a·ble** (ik-sīt′ə-b'l), *adj.* easily excited. —**ex·cit′a·bil′it·y,** *n.* —**ex·cit′a·bly,** *adv.*
**ex·cite** (ik-sīt′), *v.t.* [-CITED, -CITING], [< L. *ex-*, out + *ciere*, to call], 1. to make active; stimulate. 2. to arouse; provoke. 3. to arouse the feelings of. —**ex·ci·ta·tion** (ek′sī-tā′shən), *n.* —**ex·cit′ed,** *adj.*
**ex·cite′ment,** *n.* 1. an exciting or being excited. 2. that which excites.
**ex·cit′ing,** *adj.* causing excitement; stirring; thrilling. —**ex·cit′ing·ly,** *adv.*
**ex·claim** (iks-klām′), *v.i. & v.t.* [< L. *ex-*, out + *clamare*, to shout], to cry out; say suddenly and vehemently.
**ex·cla·ma·tion** (eks′klə-mā′shən), *n.* 1. an exclaiming. 2. something exclaimed; interjection. —**ex·clam·a·to·ry** (iks-klam′ə-tôr′i), *adj.*
**exclamation mark** (or **point**), a mark (!) used in punctuating to show surprise, strong emotion, etc.
**ex·clude** (iks-klōōd′), *v.t.* [-CLUDED, -CLUDING], [< L. *ex-*, out + *claudere*, shut], 1. to refuse to admit, consider, etc.; reject. 2. to put or force out; expel. —**ex·clud′a·ble,** *adj.* —**ex·clu′sion** (-klōō′zhən), *n.*
**ex·clu′sive** (-klōō′siv), *adj.* 1. excluding all others. 2. not shared or divided; sole: as, an *exclusive* right. 3. excluding certain people for social reasons; snobbish. —**exclusive of,** not including. —**ex·clu′sive·ly,** *adv.*
**ex·com·mu·ni·cate** (eks′kə-mū′nə-kāt′), *v.t.* [-CATED, -CATING], to exclude from communion with a church. —**ex′com·mu′ni·ca′tion,** *n.*
**ex·co·ri·ate** (ik-skôr′i-āt′), *v.t.* [-ATED, -ATING], [< L. *ex-*, off + *corium*, skin], 1. to strip or scratch off the skin of. 2. to denounce strongly. —**ex·co′ri·a′tion,** *n.*
**ex·cre·ment** (eks′krə-mənt), *n.* waste matter excreted from the bowels.
**ex·cres·cence** (iks-kres″ns), *n.* [< L. *ex-*, out + *crescere*, grow], 1. a normal outgrowth, as hair. 2. an abnormal outgrowth, as a bunion. —**ex·cres′cent,** *adj.*
**ex·cre·ta** (eks-krē′tə), *n.pl.* waste matter excreted from the body, as urine or feces.
**ex·crete** (iks-krēt′), *v.t. & v.i.* [-CRETED, -CRETING], [< L. *ex-*, out of + *cernere*, sift], to eliminate (waste matter) from the body. —**ex·cre′tion,** *n.* —**ex·cre·to·ry** (eks′kri-tôr′i), *adj.*
**ex·cru·ci·at·ing** (iks-krōō′shi-āt′iŋ), *adj.* [< L. *ex-*, intens. + *cruciare*, crucify], intensely painful; agonizing.
**ex·cul·pate** (eks′kəl-pāt′), *v.t.* [-PATED, -PATING], [< L. *ex*, out + *culpa*, fault], to free from blame; prove guiltless. —**ex′cul·pa′tion,** *n.*
**ex·cur·sion** (ik-skũr′zhən, -shən), *n.* [< L. *ex-*, out + *currere*, to run], 1. a short trip, as for pleasure. 2. a round trip at reduced rates. 3. a deviation or digression. *adj.* for an excursion. —**ex·cur′sion·ist,** *n.*
**ex·cur′sive** (-siv) *adj.* rambling; digressing.
**ex·cuse** (ik-skūz′), *v.t.* [-CUSED, -CUSING], [< L. *ex-*, from + *causa*, a charge], 1. to apologize, or give reasons, for. 2. to overlook (an offense or fault). 3. to release from an obligation, etc. 4. to permit to leave. 5. to justify. *n.* (-skūs′), 1. a defense of one's conduct; apology. 2. something that excuses. 3. a pretext. —**excuse oneself,** 1. to apologize. 2. to ask for permission to leave. —**ex·cus′a·ble,** *adj.*
**ex·e·cra·ble** (ek′si-krə-b'l), *adj.* [L. *execrabilis*], detestable. —**ex′e·cra·bly,** *adv.*
**ex·e·crate** (ek′si-krāt′), *v.t.* [-CRATED, CRATING], [< L. *ex-*, out + *sacrare*, consecrate], 1. to curse. 2. to loathe; abhor. *v.i.* to curse. —**ex′e·cra′tion,** *n.*
**ex·e·cute** (ek′si-kūt′), *v.t.* [-CUTED, -CUTING], [< L. *ex-*, out + *sequi*, follow], 1. to carry out; do. 2. to administer (laws, etc.). 3. to put to death by a legal sentence. 4. to create in accordance with a plan, etc. 5. to make valid (a deed, will, etc.).
**ex′e·cu′tion,** *n.* 1. an executing; a performing, administering, etc. 2. a putting to death by a legal sentence. 3. the manner of doing or producing something.
**ex′e·cu′tion·er,** *n.* one who carries out a court-imposed death penalty.
**ex·e·cu·tive** (ig-zek′yoo-tiv), *adj.* 1. of or capable of carrying out duties, functions, etc. 2. empowered to administer (laws, government affairs, etc.). *n.* 1. the branch of government administering the laws and affairs of a nation. 2. one who administers or manages affairs. —**ex·ec′u·tive·ly,** *adv.*
**ex·ec·u·tor** (ig-zek′yoo-tẽr), *n.* a person appointed to carry out the provisions of another's will.
**ex·e·ge·sis** (ek′sə-jē′sis), *n.* [*pl.* -SES (-sēz)], [< Gr. *ex-*, out + *hēgeisthai*, to guide], analysis or interpretation of a word, passage, etc., esp. of the Bible. —**ex′e·get′ic** (-jet′ik), *adj.*
**ex·em·plar** (ig-zem′plẽr), *n.* [< L. *exemplum*, a copy], 1. a model; pattern. 2. a sample.
**ex·em′pla·ry** (-plə-ri), *adj.* serving as a model or example: as, *exemplary* behavior.
**ex·em·pli·fy** (ig-zem′plə-fī′), *v.t.* [-FIED, -FYING], [< L. *exemplum*, example + *facere*, make], to show by example. —**ex·em′pli·fi·ca′tion,** *n.*
**ex·empt** (ig-zempt′), *v.t.* [< L. *ex-*, out + *emere*, take], to free from a rule or obligation which others must observe. *adj.* freed from a rule, obligation, etc. —**ex·empt′i·ble,** *adj.* —**ex·emp′tion,** *n.*
**ex·er·cise** (ek′sẽr-sīz′), *n.* [< L. *exercere*, to cause to work], 1. active use or operation. 2. activity for developing the body or mind. 3. a task to be practiced for developing some skill. 4. *pl.* a program of speeches, etc. *v.t.* [-CISED, -CISING], 1. to use. 2. to put into action for the purpose of developing; train. 3. to perform (duties, etc.). 4. to exert (influence, etc.). *v.i.* to take exercise.
**ex·ert** (ig-zũrt′), *v.t.* [< L. *exerere*, stretch out], to put into action: as, *exert* your will. —**exert oneself,** to try or work hard.
**ex·er′tion,** *n.* 1. the act, fact, or process of exerting. 2. effort.
**ex·e·unt** (ek′si-ənt), [L.], they go off (the stage): a stage direction to actors.
**ex·hale** (eks-hāl′), *v.t. & v.i.* [-HALED, -HALING], [< L. *ex-*, out + *halare*, breathe], 1. to breathe forth (air or smoke). 2. to give off (vapor, etc.). —**ex·ha·la·tion** (eks′-hə-lā′shən), *n.*
**ex·haust** (ig-zôst′), *v.t.* [< L. *ex-*, out + *haurire*, draw], 1. to use up. 2. to empty completely; drain. 3. to tire out. 4. to deal with thoroughly. *n.* 1. the discharge of used steam, gas, etc. from an engine. 2. the pipe through which it is discharged. 3. the used gas, steam, etc. discharged. —**ex·haust′i·bil′i·ty,** *n.* —**ex·haust′i·ble,** *adj.*
**ex·haus·tion** (ig-zôs′chən), *n.* 1. an exhausting. 2. the state of being exhausted; esp., great fatigue.
**ex·haus′tive,** *adj.* complete; thorough.
**ex·hib·it** (ig-zib′it), *v.t.* [< L. *ex-*, out + *habere*, hold], 1. to show; display. 2. to present to public view. *v.i.* to put art objects, etc. on public display. *n.* 1. a display.

2. a thing exhibited. 3. in *law*, an object produced as evidence in a court. **—ex·hib′i·tor, ex·hib′it·er,** *n.*
**ex·hi·bi·tion** (ek′sə-bish′ən), *n.* 1. an exhibiting or showing. 2. that which is shown. 3. a public showing.
**ex′hi·bi′tion·ism,** *n.* a tendency to call attention to oneself or show off one's skill, etc. **—ex′hi·bi′tion·ist,** *n.*
**ex·hil·a·rate** (ig-zil′ə-rāt′), *v.t.* [-RATED, -RATING], [< L. *ex-*, intens. + *hilaris*, glad], to make merry; stimulate. **—ex·hil′a·rat′ing,** *adj.* **—ex·hil′a·ra′tion,** *n.*
**ex·hort** (ig-zôrt′), *v.t. & v.i.* [< L. *ex-*, out + *hortari*, to urge], to urge earnestly; entreat. **—ex·hor·ta·tion** (eg′zôr-tā′shən, ek′sẽr-), *n.*
**ex·hume** (iks-hūm′, ig-zūm′), *v.t.* [-HUMED, -HUMING], [< L. *ex-*, out + *humus*, the ground], to dig out of the earth; disinter. **—ex·hu·ma·tion** (eks′hyoo-mā′shən), *n.*
**ex·i·gen·cy** (ek′sə-jən-si), *n.* [*pl.* -CIES], [< L. *ex-*, out + *agere*, to drive], 1. urgency. 2. a situation calling for immediate attention. 3. *pl.* pressing needs. **—ex′i·gent,** *adj.*
**ex·ile** (eg′zīl, ek′sīl), *n.* [< L. *ex(s)ul*, an exile], 1. a prolonged, often enforced, living away from one's country; banishment. 2. a person in exile. *v.t.* (*also* ig-zīl′), [-ILED, -ILING], to banish.
**ex·ist** (ig-zist′), *v.i.* [< L. *ex-*, forth + *sistere*, to stand], 1. to be; have reality or being. 2. to occur; be present (*in*). 3. to continue being; live.
**ex·ist′ence,** *n.* 1. the state or fact of being. 2. life; living. 3. occurrence. **—ex·ist′ent,** *adj.*
**ex·is·ten·tial·ism** (eg′zis-ten′shəl-iz′m), *n.* a literary-philosophic movement which stresses the individual's responsibility to exercise free will in a purposeless universe.
**ex·it** (eg′zit, ek′sit), *n.* [< L. *ex-*, out + *ire*, go], 1. an actor's departure from the stage. 2. a going out; departure. 3. a way out.
‡**ex li·bris** (eks lī′bris, lē′-), [L.], from the library of: abbrev. **ex lib.**
**exo-,** [< Gr. *exō*], a prefix meaning *outside, outer, outer part*: also **ex-.**
**ex·o·dus** (ek′sə-dəs), *n.* [< Gr. *ex-*, out + *hodos*, way], 1. a going out or forth. 2. [E-], the departure of the Israelites from Egypt (with *the*). 3. [E-], the second book of the Old Testament, which describes this.
**ex of·fi·ci·o** (eks ə-fish′i-ō′), [L., lit., from office], by virtue of one's office, or position.
**ex·og·e·nous** (eks-oj′ə-nəs), *adj.* [*exo-* + *-genous*], 1. originating externally. 2. in *biology*, growing or developing from or on the outside.
**ex·on·er·ate** (ig-zon′ə-rāt′), *v.t.* [-ATED, -ATING], [< L. *ex-*, out + *onerare*, to load], to declare or prove blameless. **—ex·on′er·a′tion,** *n.*
**ex·or·bi·tant** (ig-zôr′bə-tənt), *adj.* [< L. *ex-*, out + *orbita*, a track], going beyond what is reasonable, just, etc.; excessive. **—ex·or′bi·tance,** *n.* **—ex·or′bi·tant·ly,** *adv.*
**ex·or·cise, ex·or·cize** (ek′sôr-sīz′), *v.t.* [-CISED, -CISING; -CIZED, -CIZING], [< Gr. *ex-*, out + *horkos*, oath], 1. to expel (a supposed evil spirit) by ritual or incantation. 2. to free from such a spirit. **—ex′or·cis′er, ex′or·ciz′er,** *n.* **—ex′or·cism** (-siz′m), *n.*
**ex·ot·ic** (ig-zot′ik), *adj.* [< Gr. *exō*, outside], 1. foreign. 2. strangely beautiful, enticing, etc. **—ex·ot′i·cism,** *n.*
**ex·pand** (ik-spand′), *v.t. & v.i.* [< L. *ex-*, out + *pandere*, to spread], 1. to spread out; unfold. 2. to increase in size, etc.; enlarge.
**ex·panse** (ik-spans′), *n.* 1. a large area or unbroken surface; wide extent. 2. expansion.
**ex·pan′sion,** *n.* 1. an expanding or being expanded; enlargement. 2. an expanded thing or part. 3. the extent or degree of expansion.
**ex·pan′sive,** *adj.* 1 that can expand. 2. broad; extensive. 3. sympathetic; demonstrative. **—ex·pan′sive·ly,** *adv.*
**ex·pa·ti·ate** (ik-spā′shi-āt′), *v.i.* [-ATED, -ATING], [< L. *ex(s)patiari*, wander], to speak or write at length (*on* or *upon*). **—ex·pa′ti·a′tion,** *n.* **—ex·pa′ti·a′tor,** *n.*
**ex·pa·tri·ate** (eks-pā′tri-āt′; *for n., also* -it), *v.t.* [-ATED, -ATING], [< L. *ex*, out of + *patria*, fatherland], to exile or banish. *n.* an expatriated person. **—ex·pa′tri·a′tion,** *n.*
**ex·pect** (ik-spekt′), *v.t.* [< L. *ex-*, out + *spectare*, to look], 1. to look for as likely to occur or appear. 2. to look for as proper or necessary. 3. [Colloq.], to suppose; guess. **—be expecting,** [Colloq.], to be pregnant.
**ex·pect′an·cy,** *n.* [*pl.* -CIES], 1. expectation. 2. that which is expected, esp. on a statistical basis. Also **ex·pect′ance.**
**ex·pect′ant,** *adj.* expecting.
**ex·pec·ta·tion** (ek′spek-tā′shən), *n.* 1. an expecting or being expected. 2. a thing looked forward to. 3. *also pl.* a reason for expecting something; prospect.
**ex·pec·to·rant** (ik-spek′tə-rənt), *adj.* stimulating expectoration. *n.* any expectorant medicine.
**ex·pec·to·rate** (ik-spek′tə-rāt′), *v.t. & v.i.* [-RATED, -RATING], [< L. *ex-*, out + *pectus*, breast], to spit. **—ex·pec′to·ra′tion,** *n.*
**ex·pe·di·en·cy** (ik-spē′di-ən-si), *n.* [*pl.* -CIES], 1. a being expedient; suitability for a given purpose. 2. the doing of what is selfish rather than what is right or just; self-interest. Also **ex·pe′di·ence.**
**ex·pe′di·ent** (-ənt), *adj.* [see EXPEDITE], 1. useful for effecting a desired result; convenient. 2. based on or guided by self-interest. *n.* an expedient thing; means to an end. **—ex·pe′di·ent·ly,** *adv.*
**ex·pe·dite** (ek′spi-dīt′), *v.t.* [-DITED, -DITING], [< L. *expedire*, lit., to free the foot], 1. to speed up the progress of. 2. to do quickly.
**ex′pe·dit′er,** *n.* one employed to expedite urgent or involved projects.
**ex′pe·di′tion** (-dish′ən), *n.* [see EXPEDITE], 1. a voyage, march, etc., as for exploration or battle. 2. those on such a journey. 3. efficient speed.
**ex′pe·di′tion·ar′y** (-er′i), *adj.* of or constituting an expedition.
**ex′pe·di′tious** (-dish′əs), *adj.* efficient and speedy; prompt. **—ex′pe·di′tious·ly,** *adv.*
**ex·pel** (ik-spel′), *v.t.* [-PELLED, -PELLING], [< L. *ex-*, out + *pellere*, thrust], 1. to drive out by force. 2. to dismiss by authority: as, *expelled* from school. **—ex·pel′ler,** *n.*
**ex·pend** (ik-spend′), *v.t.* [< L. *ex-*, out + *pendere*, weigh], to spend; use up.
**ex·pend′a·ble,** *adj.* 1. that can be expended. 2. in *military usage*, designating equipment (or men) expected to be used up (or sacrificed) in service.
**ex·pend·i·ture** (ik-spen′di-chẽr), *n.* 1. an expending of money, time, etc. 2. the amount of money, etc. expended.
**ex·pense** (ik-spens′), *n.* 1. an expending of money. 2. cost; charge. 3. *pl.* charges met with in one's work. 4. loss; sacrifice.
**ex·pen′sive,** *adj.* costly; high-priced.
**ex·pe·ri·ence** (ik-spêr′i-əns), *n.* [< L. *experiri*, to try], 1. an actual living through an event. 2. anything or everything observed or lived through. 3. training and personal participation. 4. knowledge or skill resulting from this. *v.t.* [-ENCED, -ENCING], to have experience of; undergo.
**ex·pe′ri·enced,** *adj.* 1. having had much experience. 2. having learned from experience.
**ex·per·i·ment** (ik-sper′ə-mənt), *n.* [see EXPERIENCE], a test or trial undertaken to discover or demonstrate something. *v.i.* to make an experiment. **—ex·per′i·men·ta′tion** (-men-tā′shən), *n.*
**ex·per′i·men′tal,** *adj.* 1. based on experi-

ence. 2. based on or tested by experiment. 3. used for experiments.

**ex·pert** (ek′spẽrt, ik-spũrt′), *adj.* [see EXPERIENCE], 1. very skillful. 2. of or from an expert. *n.* (ek′spẽrt), one who is very skillful or well-informed in some special field. —**ex·pert′ly,** *adv.* —**ex·pert′ness,** *n.*

**ex·pert·ise** (ek′spẽr-tēz′), *n.* [Fr.], the skill or knowledge of an expert.

**ex·pi·ate** (ek′spi-āt′), *v.t.* [-ATED, -ATING], [< L. *ex-*, out + *pius*, devout], to make amends for (wrongdoing or guilt); atone for. —**ex′pi·a·ble,** *adj.* —**ex′pi·a′tion,** *n.*

**ex·pire** (ik-spīr′), *v.i.* [-PIRED, -PIRING], [< L. *ex-*, out + *spirare*, breathe], 1. to breathe out; exhale. 2. to die. 3. to come to an end; stop. —**ex·pi·ra·tion** (ek′spə-rā′shən), *n.*

**ex·plain** (iks-plān′), *v.t.* [< L. *ex-*, out + *planus*, level], 1. to make plain or understandable. 2. to give the meaning of; expound. 3. to account for. *v.i.* to give an explanation. —**ex·plain′a·ble,** *adj.*

**ex·pla·na·tion** (eks′plə-nā′shən), *n.* 1. an explaining. 2. something that explains; interpretation, meaning, etc.

**ex·plan·a·to·ry** (iks-plan′ə-tôr′i), *adj.* explaining.

**ex·ple·tive** (eks′pli-tiv), *n.* [< L. *ex-*, out + *plere*, to fill], an oath or exclamation.

**ex·pli·ca·ble** (eks′pli-kə-b'l), *adj.* that can be explained.

**ex·pli·cate** (eks′pli-kāt′), *v.t.* [-CATED, -CATING], [< L. *ex-*, out + *plicare*, to fold], to make clear or explicit (something obscure or implied); explain. —**ex′pli·ca′tion,** *n.*

**ex·plic·it** (iks-plis′it), *adj.* [< L. *ex-*, out + *plicare*, to fold], 1. clearly stated; definite. 2. outspoken. —**ex·plic′it·ly,** *adv.*

**ex·plode** (iks-plōd′), *v.t.* [-PLODED, -PLODING], [orig., to drive off the stage < L. *ex-*, off + *plaudere*, applaud], 1. to discredit; expose as fake. 2. to make burst with a loud noise. *v.i.* to burst or break forth noisily.

**ex·ploit** (eks′ploit), *n.* [see EXPLICIT], a daring act; bold deed. *v.t.* (iks-ploit′), 1. to make use of. 2. to make unethical use of for one's own profit. —**ex′ploi·ta′tion,** *n.*

**ex·plore** (iks-plôr′), *v.t. & v.i.* [-PLORED, -PLORING], [< L. *ex-*, out + *plorare*, cry out], 1. to look into closely; investigate. 2. to travel in (a little known region) for discovery. —**ex′plo·ra′tion** (-plô-rā′shən), *n.* —**ex·plor′a·to′ry** (-ə-tôr′i), *adj.* —**ex·plor′er,** *n.*

**ex·plo·sion** (iks-plō′zhən), *n.* 1. an exploding; esp., a blowing up. 2. the noise made by exploding. 3. a noisy outburst.

**ex·plo′sive** (-siv), *adj.* 1. of, causing, or like an explosion. 2. tending to explode. *n.* a substance that can explode, as gun powder.

**ex·po·nent** (ik-spō′nənt), *n.* [see EXPOUND], 1. one who expounds, or interprets. 2. a person or thing that is an example or symbol (*of* something). 3. in *math.*, a symbol placed at the upper right of another to show how many times the latter is to be multiplied by itself (e.g., $b^2 = b \times b$).

**ex·port** (ik-spôrt′, ek′spôrt), *v.t.* [< L. *ex-*, out + *portare*, carry], to send (goods, etc.) to another country, esp. for sale. *n.* (ek′spôrt), 1. an exporting. 2. something exported. Also **ex′por·ta′tion.** —**ex·port′er,** *n.*

**ex·pose** (ik-spōz′), *v.t.* [-POSED, -POSING], [see EXPOUND], 1. to lay open (*to* danger, attack, etc.). 2. to reveal; exhibit; make known. 3. in *photography*, to subject (a sensitized film or plate) to actinic rays.

**ex·po·sé** (ek′spō-zā′), *n.* [Fr.], a public disclosure of a scandal, etc.

**ex·po·si·tion** (ek′spə-zish′ən), *n.* [see EXPOUND], 1. a detailed explanation. 2. writing or speaking that explains. 3. a large public exhibition or show.

**ex·pos·i·tor** (ik-spoz′ə-tẽr), *n.* one who expounds or explains.

**ex·pos′i·to′ry** (-tôr′i), *adj.* of or containing exposition; explanatory.

**ex post fac·to** (eks pōst fak′tō), [L., from the (thing) done afterward], done after something, but having retroactive effect.

**ex·pos·tu·late** (ik-spos′chə-lāt′), *v.i.* [-LATED, -LATING], [< L. *ex-*, intens. + *postulare*, to demand], to reason with a person earnestly, opposing his actions or intentions. —**ex·pos′tu·la′tion,** *n.* —**ex·pos′tu·la′tor,** *n.*

**ex·po·sure** (ik-spō′zhẽr), *n.* 1. an exposing or being exposed. 2. facing position: as, a southern *exposure*. 3. the time during which a photographic film is exposed. 4. a section of film for one picture.

**ex·pound** (ik-spound′), *v.t.* [< L. *ex-*, out + *ponere*, put], 1. to set forth; state in detail. 2. to explain. —**ex·pound′er,** *n.*

**ex·press** (iks-pres′), *v.t.* [< L. *ex-*, out + *pressare*, to press], 1. to squeeze out (juice, etc.). 2. to put into words; state. 3. to reveal; show. 4. to signify or symbolize. 5. to send by express. *adj.* 1. expressed; stated; explicit. 2. exact. 3. special. 4. fast and direct: as, an *express* bus, highway, etc. 5. of express (transportation). *adv.* by express. *n.* 1. an express train, bus, etc. 2. a service for transporting things rapidly. 3. the things sent by express.

**ex·pres′sion** (-presh′ən), *n.* 1. a putting into words; stating. 2. a manner of expressing, esp. with eloquence. 3. a particular word or phrase. 4. a showing of feeling, character, etc. 5. a look, intonation, etc. that conveys meaning. 6. an algebraic symbol or symbols. —**ex·pres′sion·less,** *adj.*

**ex·pres′sion·ism,** *n.* a modern movement in the arts, drama, etc. to express inner experience by using symbols, stylization, etc. —**ex·pres′sion·ist,** *adj. & n.*

**ex·pres′sive,** *adj.* 1. expressing. 2. full of expression. —**ex·pres′sive·ness,** *n.*

**ex·press′ly,** *adv.* 1. plainly; definitely. 2. especially; particularly.

**ex·press′way′,** *n.* a highway for fast traffic, usually of limited access.

**ex·pro·pri·ate** (eks-prō′pri-āt′), *v.t.* [-ATED, -ATING], [< L. *ex*, out + *proprius*, one's own], to take (land, property, etc.) from its owner, esp. for public use. —**ex·pro′pri·a′tion,** *n.* —**ex·pro′pri·a′tor,** *n.*

**ex·pul·sion** (ik-spul′shən), *n.* an expelling or being expelled. —**ex·pul′sive,** *adj.*

**ex·punge** (ik-spunj′), *v.t.* [-PUNGED, -PUNGING], [< L. *ex-*, out + *pungere*, to prick], to blot or strike out; erase. —**ex·pung′er,** *n.*

**ex·pur·gate** (ek′spẽr-gāt′), *v.t.* [-GATED, -GATING], [< L. *ex-*, out + *purgare*, cleanse], to remove passages considered obscene, etc. from (a book, etc.). —**ex′pur·ga′tion,** *n.*

**ex·qui·site** (eks′kwi-zit, ik-skwiz′it), *adj.* [< L. *ex-*, out + *quaerere*, ask], 1. carefully or elaborately done. 2. very beautiful, delicate, etc. 3. of highest quality. 4. very keen or sharp. —**ex′qui·site·ly,** *adv.*

**ex·tant** (ek′stənt, ik-stant′), *adj.* [< L. *ex-*, out + *stare*, stand], still existing.

**ex·tem·po·ra·ne·ous** (ik-stem′pə-rā′ni-əs), *adj.* [< L. *ex*, out + *tempus*, time], done, spoken, or speaking with little advance thought. —**ex·tem′po·ra′ne·ous·ly,** *adv.*

**ex·tem·po·re** (ik-stem′pə-rē′), *adv. & adj.* [L.; see prec. entry], without preparation; offhand.

**ex·tem′po·rize′** (-rīz′), *v.i. & v.t.* [-RIZED, -RIZING], to speak, perform, etc. extempore; improvise. —**ex·tem′po·ri·za′tion,** *n.*

**ex·tend** (ik-stend′), *v.t.* [< L. *ex-*, out + *tendere*, stretch], 1. to draw out; prolong. 2. to enlarge in area, scope, etc.; expand. 3. to stretch forth. 4. to offer; grant. *v.i.* to be extended. —**ex·tend′ed,** *adj.*

**ex·ten′si·ble** (-sten′sə-b'l), *adj.* that can be extended. —**ex·ten′si·bil′i·ty,** *n.*

**ex·ten′sion** (-sten′shən), *n.* 1. an extending or being extended. 2. extent; range. 3. an extended part or branch; addition.
**ex·ten′sive** (-siv), *adj.* having great extent; vast; comprehensive. **—ex·ten′sive·ly,** *adv.*
**ex·tent** (ik-stent′), *n.* 1. the space, amount, degree, etc. to which a thing extends; size. 2. scope; limits. 3. an extended space.
**ex·ten·u·ate** (ik-sten′ū-āt′), *v.t.* [-ATED, -ATING], [< L. *ex-*, out + *tenuis*, thin], to lessen the seriousness of (an offense, etc.).
**ex·te·ri·or** (ik-stêr′i-ẽr), *adj.* [see EXTERNAL], 1. outer; on the outside. 2. coming from without. *n.* an outside or outside surface.
**ex·ter·mi·nate** (ik-stũr′mə-nāt′), *v.t.* [-NATED, -NATING], [< L. *ex-*, out + *terminus*, boundary], to destroy entirely; wipe out. **—ex·ter′mi·na′tion,** *n.* **—ex·ter′mi·na′tor,** *n.*
**ex·ter·nal** (ik-stũr′n'l), *adj.* [< L. *externus*], 1. on the outside; outer. 2. material; existing apart from the mind. 3. coming from without. 4. superficial. 5. foreign. *n.* an outward surface or part. **—ex·ter′nal·ly,** *adv.*
**ex·tinct** (ik-stiŋkt′), *adj.* [see EXTINGUISH], 1. having died down; extinguished. 2. no longer in existence.
**ex·tinc′tion,** *n.* 1. an extinguishing. 2. a dying out, as of a race, species of animal, etc. 3. a destroying or being destroyed.
**ex·tin·guish** (ik-stiŋ′gwish), *v.t.* [prob. < L. *ex-*, intens. + *ting(u)ere*, to wet], 1. to put out (a fire, etc.). 2. to destroy. **—ex·tin′guish·a·ble,** *adj.* **—ex·tin′guish·er,** *n.*
**ex·tir·pate** (ek′stẽr-pāt′, ik-stũr′pāt), *v.t.* [-PATED, -PATING], [< L. *ex-*, out + *stirps*, root], 1. to pull up by the roots. 2. to destroy completely; abolish. **—ex′tir·pa′tion,** *n.*
**ex·tol, ex·toll** (ik-stōl′), *v.t.* [-TOLLED, -TOLLING], [< L. *ex-*, up + *tollere*, raise], to praise highly; laud.
**ex·tort** (ik-stôrt′), *v.t.* [< L. *ex-*, out + *torquere*, twist], to get (money, etc.) by violence, threats, etc.; exact (*from*).
**ex·tor′tion,** *n.* 1. an extorting. 2. something extorted. **—ex·tor′tion·ate,** *adj.*
**ex·tra** (eks′trə), *adj.* [< L. *extra*, more than], more or better than normal, expected, necessary, etc.; additional. *n.* an extra person or thing; specif., *a*) a special edition of a newspaper. *b*) an actor hired by the day for a minor part. *adv.* more than usually; especially: as, *extra* good quality.
**extra-,** [see EXTERNAL], a prefix meaning *outside, beyond, besides.*
**ex·tract** (iks-trakt′), *v.t.* [< L. *ex-*, out + *trahere*, draw], 1. to draw out by effort. 2. to obtain by pressing, distilling, etc. 3. to deduce; derive. 4. to select or quote (a passage, etc.). *n.* (eks′trakt), something extracted; specif., *a*) a concentrate: as, vanilla *extract.* *b*) an excerpt. **—ex·trac′tor,** *n.*
**ex·trac′tion,** *n.* 1. an extracting or being extracted. 2. origin; descent.
**ex·tra·cur·ric·u·lar** (eks′trə-kə-rik′yoo-lẽr), *adj.* not part of the regular curriculum.
**ex·tra·dite** (eks′trə-dīt′), *v.t.* [-DITED, -DITING], [< L. *ex*, out + *tradere*, give up], to turn over (an alleged criminal, fugitive, etc.) to the jurisdiction of another country, state, etc. **—ex′tra·di′tion** (-dish′ən), *n.*
**ex·tra·ne·ous** (iks-trā′ni-əs), *adj.* [see EXTRA- & STRANGE], 1. coming from outside; foreign. 2. not pertinent.
**ex·tra·or·di·nar·y** (iks-trôr′d'n-er′i), *adj.* [< L. *extra ordinem*, out of order], 1. not ordinary. 2. going far beyond the ordinary; unusual. **—ex·tra·or′di·nar′i·ly,** *adv.*
**ex·trap·o·late** (eks-trap′ə-lāt′), *v.t.* & *v.i.* [-LATED, -LATING], [*extra* + *interpolate*], to estimate (a value, quantity, etc. beyond the known range) by using known variables.
**ex·tra·sen·so·ry** (eks′trə-sen′sə-ri), *adj.* apart from normal sense perception.
**ex′tra·ter′ri·to′ri·al,** *adj.* outside the territorial limits or jurisdiction of the country, state, etc.
**ex·trav·a·gant** (iks-trav′ə-gənt), *adj.* [< L. *extra*, beyond + *vagari*, wander], 1. going beyond the limits of reason or moderation; excessive. 2. spending unnecessarily; wasteful. **—ex·trav′a·gance,** *n.*
**ex·trav·a·gan·za** (iks-trav′ə-gan′zə), *n.* [< It. *estravaganza*, extravagance], a spectacular theatrical production.
**ex·treme** (iks-trēm′), *adj.* [< L. *exterus*, outer], 1. farthest away; utmost. 2. last; final. 3. very great; excessive. 4. radical: as, *extreme* views. 5. very severe. *n.* 1. either of two things that are as different or far as possible from each other. 2. an extreme degree, act, state, etc. **—go to extremes,** to be immoderate in speech or actions. **—ex·treme′ly,** *adv.* **—ex·treme′ness,** *n.*
**ex·trem′ist,** *n.* one who goes to extremes or holds extreme views. **—ex·trem′ism,** *n.*
**ex·trem·i·ty** (iks-trem′ə-ti), *n.* [*pl.* -TIES], 1. the outermost part; end. 2. the greatest degree. 3. a state of extreme necessity, danger, etc. 4. *pl.* the hands and feet.
**ex·tri·cate** (eks′tri-kāt′), *v.t.* [-CATED, -CATING], [< L. *ex-*, out + *tricae*, vexations], to set free; disentangle (*from* a net, difficulty, etc.). **—ex′tri·ca′tion,** *n.*
**ex·trin·sic** (eks-trin′sik), *adj.* [< L. *exter*, without + *secus*, besides], 1. not essential; not inherent. 2. external. **—ex·trin′si·cal·ly,** *adv.*
**ex·tro·vert** (eks′trō-vũrt′), *n.* [< *extra-* + L. *vertere*, to turn], one who is interested in phenomena outside himself rather than his own feelings. **—ex′tro·ver′sion,** *n,*
**ex·trude** (iks-trōōd′), *v.t.* [-TRUDED, -TRUDING], [< L. *ex-*, out + *trudere*, to thrust], to push or force out, as through a small opening. *v.i.* to stick out; project. **—ex·tru′sion** (-trōō′zhən), *n.* **—ex·tru′sive,** *adj.*
**ex·u·ber·ance** (ig-zōō′bẽr-əns, -zū′-), *n.* [< L. *ex-*, intens + *uberare*, bear abundantly], 1. the state or quality of being exuberant. 2. an instance of this; esp., high spirits in action or speech. Also **ex·u′ber·an·cy.**
**ex·u′ber·ant,** *adj.* 1. growing profusely. 2. overflowing; lavish; effusive. 3. overflowing with good health and spirits.
**ex·ude** (ig-zōōd′, ik-sūd′), *v.i.* & *v.t.* [-UDED, -UDING], [< L. *ex-*, out + *sudare*, to sweat], to pass out in drops, as through pores, an incision, etc.; ooze. **—ex·u·da·tion** (eks′-yoo-dā′shən), *n.*
**ex·ult** (ig-zult′), *v.i.* [< L. *ex-*, intens. + *saltare*, to leap], to rejoice greatly; be jubilant. **—ex·ult′ant,** *adj.* **—ex′ul·ta′tion,** *n.*
**eye** (ī), *n.* [AS. *eage*], 1. organ of sight in man and animals. 2. the eyeball. 3. the iris: as, blue *eyes.* 4. the area around the eye: as, a black *eye.* 5. sight; vision. 6. a look; glance. 7. attention; observation. 8. the power of judging, etc. by eyesight: as, an *eye* for distances. 9. *often in pl.* judgment; opinion: as, in the *eyes* of the law. 10. a thing like an eye in appearance or function. *v.t.* [EYED, EYING or EYEING], 1. to look at; observe. 2. to provide with eyes. **—have an eye for,** to be discerningly appreciative of. **—keep an eye on,** to look after. **—lay** (or **set** or **clap**) **eyes on,** to look at. **—make eyes at,** to look at lovingly. **—see eye to eye,** to be in full agreement. **—with an eye to,** paying attention to; considering.
**eye′ball′,** *n.* the ball-shaped part of the eye, enclosed by the socket and eyelids.
**eye′brow′,** *n.* the bony arch over each eye, or the hair growing on this.
**eye′ful′,** *n.* [Slang], one that looks striking.
**eye′glass′,** *n.* 1. a lens to help faulty vision. 2. *pl.* a pair of such lenses in a frame.
**eye′lash′,** *n.* any of the hairs on the eyelid.
**eye′let** (-lit), *n.* 1. a small hole for receiving

a cord, hook, etc. 2. a metal ring, etc. for lining it. 3. a small hole edged by stitching in embroidery.
**eye'lid'**, *n.* either of the two movable folds of flesh that cover and uncover the eyeball.
**eye opener,** something that causes the eyes to open in astonishment or realization.
**eye'piece'**, *n.* in a telescope, microscope, etc., the lens nearest the viewer's eye.
**eye'sight'**, *n.* 1. the power of seeing; sight. 2. the range of vision.
**eye'sore'**, *n.* a thing disagreeable to look at.
**eye'strain'**, *n.* a strained condition of the eye muscles, caused by too much or incorrect use of the eyes, faulty vision, etc.
**eye'tooth'**, *n.* [*pl.* -TEETH], a canine tooth of the upper jaw. **—cut one's eyeteeth,** to become experienced or sophisticated.
**eye'wash'**, *n.* a lotion for the eyes.
**eye'wit'ness,** *n.* one who has himself seen a specific thing happen.
**ey·rie, ey·ry** (âr'i, êr'i), *n.* [*pl.* -RIES], an aerie.

# F

**F, f** (ef), *n.* [*pl.* F's, f's, Fs, fs], the sixth letter of the English alphabet.
**F,** *n.* 1. in *chem.*, fluorine. 2. in *music*, the fourth tone in the scale of C major.
**F.,** 1. Fahrenheit. 2. February. 3. France. 4. French. 5. Friday.
**F., f.,** 1. feminine. 2. folio(s). 3. following. 4. franc. 5. in *music*, forte.
**fa** (fä), *n.* [It.], in *music*, the fourth tone of the diatonic scale.
**fa·ble** (fā'b'l), *n.* [< L. *fabula*, a story], 1. a fictitious story, usually about animals, meant to teach a moral lesson. 2. a myth or legend. 3. a falsehood. **—fa'bled,** *adj.*
**fab·ric** (fab'rik), *n.* [< L. *fabrica*, workshop], 1. a framework; structure. 2. any woven, knitted, or felted cloth.
**fab·ri·cate** (fab'ri-kāt'), *v.t.* [-CATED, -CATING], [see FABRIC], 1. to make; construct; manufacture. 2. to make up (a story, reason, etc.); invent. **—fab'ri·ca'tion,** *n.*
**fab·u·lous** (fab'yoo-ləs), *adj.* [see FABLE], 1. of or like a fable; fictitious. 2. incredible; astounding. **—fab'u·lous·ly,** *adv.*
**fa·çade** (fə-säd'), *n.* [Fr.; see FACE], the front or main face of a building.
**face** (fās), *n.* [< L. *facies*], 1. the front of the head. 2. the expression of the countenance. 3. the main or front surface. 4. the surface that is marked, etc., as of a clock, fabric, etc. 5. appearance; outward aspect. 6. dignity; self-respect: as, to lose *face*. 7. [Colloq.], a grimace. 8. [Colloq.], audacity. *v.t.* [FACED, FACING], 1. to turn, or have the face turned, toward. 2. to confront with boldness, etc. 3. to cover with a new surface. *v.i.* to turn, or have the face turned, in a specified direction. **—face to face,** 1. confronting one another. 2. in the presence of (with *with*). **—in the face of,** 1. in the presence of. 2. in spite of. **—on the face of it,** apparently.
**fac·et** (fas'it), *n.* [see FACE], 1. any of the polished plane surfaces of a cut gem. 2. any of a number of sides or aspects, as of a personality. **—fac'et·ed,** *adj.*
**fa·ce·tious** (fə-sē'shəs), *adj.* [< L. *facetus*, witty], lightly joking; jocular, esp. at an inappropriate time. **—fa·ce'tious·ly,** *adv.*
**face value,** 1. the value written on a bill, bond, etc. 2. the seeming value.
**fa·cial** (fā'shəl), *adj.* of or for the face. *n.* [Colloq.], a cosmetic treatment for the face.
**fac·ile** (fas''l), *adj.* [Fr. < L. *facere*, do], 1. not hard to do; easy. 2. moving or working easily; fluent. **—fac'ile·ly,** *adv.*
**fa·cil·i·tate** (fə-sil'ə-tāt'), *v.t.* [-TATED, -TATING], [see FACILE], 1. to make easy or easier. 2. to assist. **—fa·cil'i·ta'tion,** *n.*
**fa·cil'i·ty** (-ti), *n.* [*pl.* -TIES], 1. absence of difficulty. 2. a ready ability; skill. 3. *pl.* the means by which something can be easily done; conveniences.
**fac·ing** (fās'iŋ), *n.* 1. a lining or trimming on the edge of a dress, coat, etc. 2. a covering of contrasting material on a building.
**fac·sim·i·le** (fak-sim'ə-li), *n.* [< L. *facere*, make + *simile*, like], an exact likeness, reproduction, or copy. *adj.* of, or having the nature of, a facsimile.
**fact** (fakt), [< L. *facere*, do], 1. a thing that has actually happened or is true. 2. reality; truth. 3. something stated as being true. **—as a matter of fact,** really: also **in fact.**
**fac·tion** (fak'shən), *n.* [< L. *facere*, do], 1. a group of people in an organization who have common aims, usually dissident from the main body. 2. dissension.
**fac'tious** (-shəs), *adj.* of, produced by, or tending to produce faction.
**fac·ti·tious** (fak-tish'əs), *adj.* [< L. *facere*, do], forced or artificial.
**fac·tor** (fak'tēr), *n.* [< L. *facere*, do], 1. one who transacts business for another. 2. any of the conditions, etc. that bring about a result. 3. in *math.*, any of the quantities which form a product when multiplied together. *v.t.* in *math.*, to resolve into factors.
**fac·to·ry** (fak'tə-ri), *n.* [*pl.* -RIES], [see FACTOR], a building or buildings in which things are manufactured.
**fac·to·tum** (fak-tō'təm), *n.* [< L. *facere*, do + *totum*, all], one hired to do all sorts of work; handy man.
**fac·tu·al** (fak'chōō-əl), *adj.* of or containing facts; real; actual. **—fac'tu·al·ly,** *adv.*
**fac·ul·ty** (fak''l-ti), *n.* [*pl.* -TIES], [see FACILE], 1. any natural or specialized power of a living organism: as, the *faculty* of hearing. 2. special aptitude. 3. any of the departments of learning in a university. 4. all the teachers in a school, college, etc.
**fad** (fad), *n.* [< Brit. dial.], a style, etc. that interests many people for a short time.
**fade** (fād), *v.i.* [FADED, FADING], [< OFr. *fade*, pale], 1. to lose color or brilliance; dim. 2. to lose freshness or strength. 3. to disappear slowly; die out. *v.t.* to cause to fade.
**fa·er·ie, fa·er·y** (fâr'i), *n.* [*pl.* -IES], [Archaic], a fairy.
**fag** (fag), *v.t. & v.i.* [FAGGED, FAGGING], [< *flag* (to droop)], to make or become very tired by hard work.
**fag** (fag), *n.* [< *fag end*], [Slang], a cigarette.
**fag·ot, fag·got** (fag'ət), *n.* [ult. < Gr. *phakelos*, a bundle], a bundle of sticks or twigs, esp. for use as fuel.
**Fahr·en·heit** (far'ən-hīt'), *adj.* [< G. D. *Fahrenheit*, 18th-c. G. physicist], designating or of a thermometer on which the boiling point of water is 212° and the freezing point is 32°. *n.* this thermometer or its scale.
**fail** (fāl), *v.i.* [< L. *fallere*, deceive], 1. to be insufficient; fall short. 2. to weaken; die away. 3. to be negligent in a duty, expectation, etc. 4. to be unsuccessful. 5. to become bankrupt. *v.t.* 1. to be of no help to; disappoint. 2. to leave; abandon. 3. to neglect: as, to *fail* to go. 4. in *education*, *a*) to give a grade of failure to. *b*) to get a grade of failure in. **—without fail,** without failing (to do, occur, etc.).

**fail'ing,** *n.* 1. a failure. 2. a fault or defect.

**faille** (fāl, fīl), *n.* [Fr.], a ribbed, soft fabric of silk or rayon, for dresses, etc.

**fail·ure** (fāl'yẽr), *n.* 1. a being insufficient. 2. a weakening. 3. neglect. 4. a not succeeding. 5. one that does not succeed. 6. a becoming bankrupt. 7. in *education*, a failing to pass.

**fain** (fān), *adj.* [AS. *fæg(e)n*, glad], [Archaic], 1. glad; ready. 2. reluctantly willing. 3. eager. *adv.* with eagerness.

**faint** (fānt), *adj.* [see FEIGN], 1. weak; feeble. 2. timid. 3. feeling weak and dizzy. 4. dim; indistinct. *n.* a state of temporary unconsciousness. *v.i.* to fall into a faint.

**faint'heart'ed,** *adj.* cowardly; timid.

**fair** (fâr), *adj.* [AS. *fæger*], 1. attractive; beautiful: as, *fair* women. 2. unblemished: as, a *fair* reputation. 3. blond: as, *fair* hair. 4. clear and sunny: as, *fair* weather. 5. clear and open: as, a *fair* view. 6. just and honest. 7. according to the rules. 8. likely. 9. average: as, in *fair* condition. *adv.* 1. in a fair manner. 2. squarely. **—fair and square,** [Colloq.], with justice and honesty. **—fair'ish,** *adj.* **—fair'ly,** *adv.* **—fair'ness,** *n.*

**fair** (fâr), *n.* [< L. *feriae*, *pl.*, holidays], 1. a regular gathering for barter and sale of goods. 2. a carnival or bazaar, often for charity. 3. a competitive exhibition of farm, household, and manufactured products, with various amusements and educational displays.

**fair'-haired',** *adj.* 1. having blond hair. 2. [Colloq.], favorite: as, the teacher's *fair-haired* boy.

**fair'-spo'ken,** *adj.* speaking or spoken politely.

**fair'-trade',** *adj.* designating or of an agreement whereby a distributor of a product charges no less than the minimum price set by the producer.

**fair'way'** (-wā'), *n.* the mowed part of a golf course between the tees and the greens.

**fair'-weath'er,** *adj.* 1. suitable only for fair weather. 2. dependable only in easy circumstances: as, *fair-weather* friends.

**fair·y** (fâr'i), *n.* [*pl.* -IES], [< OFr. *faerie*], 1. in *folklore*, a tiny, graceful being in human form, with magic powers. 2. [Slang], a male homosexual. *adj.* 1. of fairies. 2. fairylike.

**fair'y·land',** *n.* 1. the imaginary land where fairies live. 2. a lovely, enchanting place.

**fairy tale,** 1. a story about fairies. 2. an unbelievable or untrue story.

**faith** (fāth), *n.* [< L. *fidere*, to trust], 1. unquestioning belief, esp. in God, religion, etc. 2. a particular religion. 3. complete trust or confidence. 4. loyalty. **—good** (or **bad**) **faith,** (in)sincerity; (dis)honesty.

**faith'ful** (-fəl), *adj.* 1. loyal. 2. reliable. 3. accurate; exact. **—faith'ful·ness,** *n.*

**faith'less** (-lis), *adj.* untrue, disloyal, or dishonest. **—faith'less·ness,** *n.*

**fake** (fāk), *v.t. & v.i.* [FAKED, FAKING], [< ?], [Colloq.], to make (something) seem real, etc. by deception. *n.* [Colloq.], a fraud; counterfeit. *adj.* [Colloq.], sham; false.

**fa·kir** (fə-kêr', fā'kẽr), *n.* [Ar. *faqīr*, lit., poor], one of a Moslem holy sect who lives by begging.

**fal·con** (fôl'k'n, fô'k'n), *n.* [prob. < L. *falx*, sickle], a hawk trained to hunt small game. **—fal'con·er,** *n.* **—fal'con·ry,** *n.*

**fal·de·ral** (fal'də-ral'), *n.* mere nonsense: also **fal'de·rol'** (-rol'), **fol'de·rol'** (fol'-).

**fall** (fôl), *v.i.* [FELL, FALLEN, FALLING], [AS. *feallan*], 1. to come down by gravity; drop; descend. 2. to come down suddenly from an upright position; tumble; collapse. 3. to be wounded or killed in battle. 4. to take a downward direction; become lower; lessen. 5. to lose power, status, etc. 6. to do wrong; sin. 7. to be captured. 8. to pass into a particular state: as, to *fall* ill. 9. to take place; occur. 10. to come by chance or as a right. *n.* 1. a dropping; descending. 2. a coming down suddenly from an upright position. 3. a downward direction. 4. a becoming less. 5. a capture. 6. a loss of status, virtue, etc. 7. autumn. 8. the amount of what has fallen: as, a six-inch *fall* of snow. 9. the distance something falls. 10. *pl.* water falling over a cliff, etc. *adj.* of, for, or in the autumn. **—fall back,** to withdraw; retreat. **—fall for,** [Slang], 1. to fall in love with. 2. to be tricked by. **—fall in,** to line up in formation. **—fall off,** to become smaller, worse, etc. **—fall on,** to attack. **—fall out,** 1. to quarrel. 2. to leave one's place in line. **—fall through,** to fail.

**fal·la·cious** (fə-lā'shəs), *adj.* [see FALLACY], 1. erroneous. 2. misleading; deceptive.

**fal·la·cy** (fal'ə-si), *n.* [*pl.* -CIES], [< L. *fallere*, deceive], 1. aptness to mislead. 2. a mistaken idea; error. 3. false reasoning.

**fall·en** (fôl''n), *adj.* that fell; dropped, prostrate, ruined, degraded, captured, etc.

**fal·li·ble** (fal'ə-b'l), *adj.* [< L. *fallere*, deceive], liable to be deceived, mistaken, or erroneous.**—fal'li·bil'i·ty,** *n.***—fal'li·bly,** *adv.*

**Fal·lo·pi·an tube** (fə-lō'pi-ən), [< G. *Fallopio*, 16th-c. It. anatomist], either of the two tubes that carry ova to the uterus.

**fall'out',** *n.* 1. the descent to earth of radioactive particles following a nuclear explosion. 2. these particles.

**fal·low** (fal'ō), *adj.* [< AS. *fealh*], 1. plowed but left unplanted. 2. untrained; inactive, as the mind.

**false** (fôls), *adj.* [FALSER, FALSEST], [< L. *fallere*, deceive], 1. not true; incorrect. 2. untruthful; lying. 3. unfaithful. 4. misleading. 5. not real; artificial. *adv.* in a false manner. **—false'ly,** *adv.* **—false'ness,** *n.*

**false'heart'ed,** *adj.* deceitful; treacherous.

**false'hood,** *n.* 1. falsity. 2. a lie. 3. lying.

**fal·set·to** (fôl-set'ō), *n.* [*pl.* -TOS], an artificial way of singing in which the voice is much higher-pitched than normal. *adj.* of or singing in falsetto. *adv.* in falsetto.

**fal·si·fy** (fôl'sə-fī'), *v.t.* [-FIED, -FYING], 1. to misrepresent. 2. to alter (a record, etc.) fraudulently. *v.i.* to tell falsehoods.**—fal'si·fi·ca'tion,** *n.* **—fal'si·fi'er,** *n.*

**fal·si·ty** (fôl'sə-ti), *n.* [*pl.* -TIES], 1. the quality of being false. 2. a lie.

**Fal·staff,** Sir **John** (fôl'staf, -stäf), a character in Shakespeare's plays, a fat, blustering, witty knight.

**fal·ter** (fôl'tẽr), *v.i.* [prob. < ON.], 1. to move unsteadily; stumble. 2. to stammer. 3. to act hesitantly; waver.

**fame** (fām), *n.* [< L. *fama*], 1. reputation, esp. for good. 2. the state of being well known. **—famed,** *adj.*

**fa·mil·ial** (fə-mil'yəl), *adj.* of or common to a family.

**fa·mil·iar** (fə-mil'yẽr), *adj.* [see FAMILY], 1. friendly; intimate. 2. too friendly; unduly intimate. 3. closely acquainted (*with*). 4. common. **—fa·mil'iar·ly,** *adv.*

**fa·mil'i·ar'i·ty** (-i-ar'ə-ti), *n.* [*pl.* -TIES], 1. intimacy. 2. free and intimate behavior. 3. undue intimacy. 4. close acquaintance (*with* something).

**fa·mil'iar·ize'** (-yə-rīz'), *v.t.* [-IZED, -IZING], 1. to make commonly known. 2. to make (another or oneself) fully acquainted.

**fam·i·ly** (fam'ə-li), *n.* [*pl.* -LIES], [< L. *famulus*, servant], 1. all the people living in the same house. 2. parents and their children. 3. relatives. 4. all those descended from a common ancestor. 5. descent; lineage. 6. a group of similar or related things.

**family name,** a surname.

**fam·ine** (fam'in), *n.* [< L. *fames*, hunger],

1. an acute and general shortage of food. 2. starvation. 3. an acute and general lack of anything.

**fam·ish** (fam′ish), *v.t. & v.i.* [see FAMINE], 1. to be or make very hungry. 2. to starve.

**fa·mous** (fā′məs), *adj.* having fame; renowned. **—fa′mous·ly,** *adv.*

**fan** (fan), *n.* [< L. *vannus*, basket for winnowing grain], any device used to set up a current of air for ventilating or cooling. *v.t. & v.i.* [FANNED, FANNING], 1. to move (air) as with a fan. 2. to direct air toward as with a fan. 3. to stir up; excite. 4. to spread (*out*). 5. in *baseball*, to strike out.

**fan** (fan), *n.* [prob. < *fanatic*], [Colloq.], a person enthusiastic about a specified sport, performer, etc.

**fa·nat·ic** (fə-nat′ik), *adj.* [< L. *fanum*, temple], unreasonably enthusiastic; overly zealous: also **fa·nat′i·cal.** *n.* a fanatic person. **—fa·nat′i·cal·ly,** *adv.* **—fa·nat′i·cism,** *n.*

**fan·ci·er** (fan′si-ẽr), *n.* a person with a special interest in something, esp. plant or animal breeding.

**fan·ci·ful** (fan′si-fəl), *adj.* 1. full of fancy; imaginative. 2. not real; imaginary. 3. quaint: as, *fanciful* costumes.

**fan·cy** (fan′si), *n.* [*pl.* -CIES], [contr. < *fantasy*], 1. imagination, esp. when light, playful, etc. 2. a mental image. 3. a whim; caprice; notion. 4. an inclination or fondness. *adj.* [-CIER, -CIEST], 1. whimsical; capricious. 2. extravagant: as, a *fancy* price. 3. ornamental; elaborate: as, a *fancy* necktie. 4. of superior skill or quality. *v.t.* [-CIED, -CYING], 1. to imagine. 2. to be fond of. 3. to suppose. **—fan′cied,** *adj.*

**fan′cy-free′,** *adj.* 1. free to fall in love; not married or engaged. 2. carefree.

**fan·dan·go** (fan-daŋ′gō), *n.* [*pl.* -GOS], [Sp.], a lively Spanish dance in rhythm varying from slow to quick ¾ time.

**fan·fare** (fan′fâr′), *n.* [< Fr. *fanfaron*, braggart], 1. a loud blast of trumpets. 2. noisy or showy display.

**fang** (faŋ), *n.* [AS. < *fon*, seize], 1. any of the long, pointed teeth of meat-eating mammals. 2. any of the long, hollow teeth through which some snakes inject venom.

**fan·ta·si·a** (fan-tā′zi-ə, -zhə), *n.* [see FANTASY], 1. a musical composition of no fixed form. 2. a medley of familiar tunes.

**fan·tas·tic** (fan-tas′tik), *adj.* [see FANTASY], 1. imaginary; unreal. 2. grotesque; odd. 3. extravagant. **—fan·tas′ti·cal·ly,** *adv.*

**fan·ta·sy** (fan′tə-si), *n.* [*pl.* -SIES], [< Gr. *phainein*, to show], 1. imagination or fancy. 2. an illusion or reverie. 3. an imaginative poem, play, etc.

**far** (fär), *adj.* [FARTHER, FARTHEST], [AS. *feor*], 1. distant in space or time: as, a *far* land. 2. more distant: as, the *far* side. *adv.* 1. very distant in space, time, or degree. 2. to or from a distance in time or position. 3. very much: as, *far* better. **—as far as,** to the distance or degree that. **—by far,** considerably. **—far and away,** very much. **—(in) so far as,** to the extent that. **—so far,** up to that or this point.

**far′a·way′,** *adj.* 1. distant in time or place. 2. dreamy: as, a *faraway* look.

**farce** (färs), *n.* [< L. *farcire*, to stuff], 1. (an) exaggerated comedy based on broadly humorous situations. 2. something absurd or ridiculous. **—far·ci·cal** (fär′si-k'l), *adj.*

**far cry,** a great distance or extent.

**fare** (fâr), *v.i.* [FARED, FARING], [< AS. *faran*, go], 1. to happen; result. 2. to be in a specified condition: as, to *fare* well. 3. to eat. *n.* 1. the charge for transportation. 2. a passenger in a train, bus, etc. 3. food.

**fare·well** (fâr′wel′), *interj.* good-by. *n.* 1. good wishes at parting. 2. a departure. *adj.* parting: as, a *farewell* gesture.

**far·fetched** (fär′fecht′), *adj.* not reasonable; strained, as a comparison.

**far′-flung′** (-fluŋ′), *adj.* extending for a great distance.

**fa·ri·na** (fə-rē′nə), *n.* [L., meal], flour or meal made from cereal grains, potatoes, etc., eaten as a cooked cereal.

**farm** (färm), *n.* [< ML. *firma*, fixed payment], a piece of land (with house, barns, etc.) on which crops or animals are raised; orig., such land let out to tenants. *v.t.* 1. to cultivate (land). 2. to let out (work or workers) on contract to outsiders. *v.i.* to work on or operate a farm.

**farm′er,** *n.* one who manages or operates a farm.

**farm′house′,** *n.* a house on a farm.

**farm′ing,** *n.* the business of operating a farm; agriculture.

**farm′yard′,** *n.* the yard surrounding or enclosed by farm buildings.

**far·o** (fâr′ō), *n.* [? < *pharaoh*], a gambling game played with cards.

**far-off** (fär′ôf′), *adj.* distant; remote.

**far·ra·go** (fə-rā′gō, -rä′-), *n.* [*pl.* -GOES], [< L. *far*, kind of grain], a confused mixture.

**far′-reach′ing,** *adj.* having a wide range, extent, influence, etc.

**far·ri·er** (far′i-ẽr), *n.* [< L. *ferrum*, iron], a blacksmith.

**far·row** (far′ō), *n.* [AS. *fearh*, young pig], a litter of pigs. *v.t. & v.i.* to give birth to (a litter of pigs).

**far′sight′ed,** *adj.* 1. planning ahead; provident. 2. seeing distant objects more clearly than near ones. **—far′sight′ed·ness,** *n.*

**far·ther** (fär′thẽr), *adj.* [compar. of *far*], 1. more distant. 2. additional; more. *adv.* 1. at or to a greater distance. 2. to a greater degree. 3. in addition. Cf. **further.**

**far′ther·most′,** *adj.* most distant; farthest.

**far·thest** (fär′thist), *adj.* [superl. of *far*], 1. most distant. 2. longest. *adv.* at or to the greatest distance or degree.

**far·thing** (fär′thiŋ), *n.* [AS. *feorthing*], a small British coin, equal to half of a halfpenny: no longer in use.

**fas·ces** (fas′ēz), *n.pl.* [L., pl. of *fascis*, bundle], a bundle of rods bound about an ax, a symbol of authority of ancient Roman magistrates.

**fas·ci·nate** (fas′'n-āt′), *v.t.* [-NATED, -NATING], [< L. *fascinum*, witchcraft], 1. to hold motionless, as by inspiring terror. 2. to attract by delightful qualities; charm. **—fas′ci·nat′ing,** *adj.* **—fas′ci·na′tion,** *n.*

**fas·cism** (fash′iz'm), *n.* [< It. < L.; see FASCES], 1. [F-], the doctrines, methods, etc. of the Italian dictatorship (1922-1943) under Mussolini. 2. a system of government characterized by dictatorship, belligerent nationalism and racism, glorification of war, etc. **—fas′cist, Fas′cist,** *n. & adj.*

**fash·ion** (fash′ən), *n.* [ult. < L. *facere*, make], 1. the form or shape of a thing. 2. kind; sort. 3. way; manner. 4. the current style of dress, conduct, etc. *v.t.* 1. to make; form. 2. to adapt (with *to*). **—after** (or **in**) **a fashion,** to some extent. **—fash′ion·er,** *n.*

**fash′ion·a·ble,** *adj.* 1. stylish. 2. of or used by people who follow fashion. **—fash′ion·a·ble·ness,** *n.* **—fash′ion·a·bly,** *adv.*

**fast** (fast, fäst), *adj.* [AS. *fæst*], 1. firm; firmly fastened. 2. loyal; devoted. 3. unfading: said of colors. 4. swift; quick. 5. ahead of time: as, a *fast* clock. 6. having loose morals; promiscuous. *adv.* 1. firmly; fixedly. 2. thoroughly: as, *fast* asleep. 3. rapidly; swiftly. **—fast′ness,** *n.*

**fast** (fast, fäst), *v.i.* [AS. *fæstan*], 1. to abstain from all or certain foods. 2. to eat very little. *n.* 1. a fasting. 2. a period of fasting.

**fast′back′,** *n.* an automobile body whose

roof forms an unbroken curve from windshield to rear bumper.
**fas·ten** (fas'n, fäs'-), *v.t.* [see FAST (*adj.*)], 1. to attach; connect. 2. to make secure, as by locking, buttoning, etc. 3. to direct (the attention, etc. *on*). *v.i.* to become fastened. —**fas'ten·er,** *n.*
**fas'ten·ing,** *n.* anything used to fasten; bolt clasp, hook, etc.
**fas·tid·i·ous** (fas-tid'i-əs), *adj.* [< L. *fastus,* disdain], 1. not easy to please. 2. daintily refined; oversensitive. —**fas·tid'i·ous·ly,** *adv.*
**fast·ness** (fast'nis, fäst'-), *n.* 1. the quality or condition of being fast. 2. a stronghold.
**fat** (fat), *adj.* [FATTER, FATTEST], [AS. *fætt*], 1. containing fat; oily. 2. *a*) fleshy; plump. *b*) too plump. 3. thick; broad. 4. fertile: as, *fat* land. 5. profitable: as, a *fat* job. 6. plentiful. *n.* 1. an oily, yellow or white substance formed in animal tissue. 2. the richest part of anything. —**fat'ness,** *n.*
**fa·tal** (fā't'l), *adj.* 1. fateful; decisive. 2. resulting in death. 3. destructive; ruinous.
**fa'tal·ism,** *n.* the belief that all events are determined by fate and are therefore inevitable. —**fa'tal·ist,** *n.* —**fa'tal·is'tic,** *adj.*
**fa·tal·i·ty** (fə-tal'-ə-ti, fā-), *n.* [*pl.* -TIES], an event resulting in death; death.
**fate** (fāt), *n.* [< L. *fatum,* oracle], 1. the power supposed to determine the outcome of events; destiny. 2. one's lot or fortune. 3. final outcome. 4. death; destruction. —**the Fates,** in *Gr. & Rom. myth.,* the three goddesses who control human destiny and life.
**fat·ed** (fāt'id), *adj.* 1. destined. 2. doomed.
**fate'ful** (-fəl), *adj.* 1. prophetic. 2. significant; decisive. 3. controlled as if by fate. 4. bringing death or destruction.
**fat·head** (fat'hed'), *n.* a stupid person.
**fa·ther** (fä'*th*ẽr), *n.* [AS. *fæder*], 1. a male parent. 2. [F-], God. 3. an ancestor. 4. an originator; founder; inventor. 5. in the *R.C. Church, a*) a priest. *b*) his title. *v.t.* 1. to be the father of or a father to. 2. to originate; invent. —**fa'ther·hood',** *n.* —**fa'ther·less,** *adj.*
**fa'ther-in-law',** *n.* [*pl.* FATHERS-IN-LAW], the father of one's wife or husband.
**fa'ther·land',** *n.* one's native land.
**fa'ther·ly,** *adj.* of or like a father; kindly.
**fath·om** (fa*th*'əm), *n.* [AS. *fæthm,* the two arms outstretched], a nautical unit of depth or length, equal to 6 feet. *v.t.* 1. to measure the depth of. 2. to understand thoroughly. —**fath'om·a·ble,** *adj.* —**fath'om·less,** *adj.*
**fa·tigue** (fə-tēg'), *n.* [< L. *fatigare,* to weary], 1. exhaustion; weariness. 2. a weakening in metal caused by strain. *v.t.* [-TIGUED, -TIGUING], to tire out; weary.
**fat·ten** (fat''n), *v.t. & v.i.* to make or become fat (in various senses).
**fat'ty,** *adj.* [-TIER, -TIEST], 1. of or containing fat. 2. like fat; greasy. —**fat'ti·ness,** *n.*
**fa·tu·i·ty** (fə-tū'ə-ti, -tōō'-), *n.* [*pl.* -TIES], 1. smug stupidity. 2. something fatuous.
**fat·u·ous** (fach'ōō-əs), *adj.* [L. *fatuus*], complacently stupid; foolish. —**fat'u·ous·ly,** *adv.*
**fau·cet** (fô'sit), *n.* [prob. < OFr. *faulser,* to breach], a device with a valve for regulating the flow of a liquid from a pipe, etc.; tap.
**fault** (fôlt), *n.* [< L. *fallere,* deceive], 1. something that mars; flaw; defect. 2. a misdeed or mistake. 3. blame for something wrong. 4. a break in rock strata. —**at fault,** in the wrong. —**find fault (with),** to criticize. —**to a fault,** too much.
**fault'find'ing,** *n. & adj.* criticizing.
**fault'less,** *adj.* perfect. —**fault'less·ly,** *adv.*
**fault'y,** *adj.* [-IER, -IEST], having a fault or faults; defective. —**fault'i·ly,** *adv.*
**faun** (fôn), *n.* [L. *Faunus*], any of a class of Roman rural deities, half man and half goat.
**fau·na** (fô'nə), *n.* [< LL. *Fauna,* Rom. goddess], the animals of a specified region or time.
**Faust** (foust), *n.* a man in legend (and literature) who sells his soul to the devil for knowledge and power.
**faux pas** (fō' pä'), [*pl.* FAUX PAS (päz')], [Fr., false step], a social blunder.
**fa·vor** (fā'vẽr), *n.* [< L. *favere,* to favor], 1. friendly regard; approval. 2. partiality. 3. a kind or obliging act. 4. a small gift or token. *v.t.* 1. to approve; like. 2. to be partial to. 3. to support; advocate. 4. to make easier; help. 5. to do a kindness for. 6. to resemble: as, he *favors* his father. Also, Brit. sp., **favour.** —**in favor of,** 1. approving. 2. to the advantage of.
**fa'vor·a·ble,** *adj.* favoring; approving; helpful. —**fa'vor·a·bly,** *adv.*
**fa'vored,** *adj.* 1. treated with favor. 2. having (specified) features: as, *ill-favored.*
**fa·vor·ite** (fā'vẽr-it), *n.* 1. a person or thing regarded with special liking. 2. a contestant regarded as most likely to win. *adj.* highly regarded; preferred.
**fa'vor·it·ism,** *n.* partiality; bias.
**fawn** (fôn), *v.i.* [< AS. *fægen,* fain], 1. to show affection by licking the hand, etc.: said of a dog. 2. to cringe and flatter.
**fawn** (fôn), *n.* [< L. *fetus,* fetus], 1. a deer less than one year old. 2. a pale, yellowish brown. *adj.* of this color.
**fay** (fā), *n.* [see FATE], a fairy.
**faze** (fāz), *v.t.* [FAZED, FAZING], [< AS. *fes(i)an,* to drive], [Colloq.], to disturb.
**FBI, F.B.I.,** Federal Bureau of Investigation.
**FCC, F.C.C.,** Federal Communications Commission.
**Fe,** *ferrum,* [L.], in *chem.,* iron.
**fe·al·ty** (fē'əl-ti), *n.* [*pl.* -TIES], [< L. *fidelitas,* fidelity], loyalty, esp. to a feudal lord.
**fear** (fêr), *n.* [AS. *fær,* danger], 1. anxious anticipation of danger, pain, etc.; fright. 2. awe; reverence. 3. anxiety; concern. 4. a cause for fear. *v.t. & v.i.* 1. to be afraid (of). 2. to be in awe (of). 3. to expect with misgiving. —**fear'less,** *adj.* —**fear'less·ly,** *adv.*
**fear'ful,** *adj.* 1. causing, feeling, or showing fear. 2. [Colloq.], very bad, great, etc.
**fear'some,** *adj.* causing fear; frightful.
**fea·si·ble** (fē'zə-b'l), *adj.* [< OFr. *faire,* do], 1. capable of being done; possible. 2. likely; probable. 3. suitable. —**fea'si·bil'i·ty** [*pl.* -TIES], *n.* —**fea'si·bly,** *adv.*
**feast** (fēst), *n.* [< L. *festus,* festal], 1. a religious festival. 2. a rich and elaborate meal. *v.i.* to have a feast. *v.t.* 1. to give a feast to. 2. to delight: as, he *feasted* his eyes on her.
**feat** (fēt), *n.* [< L. *factum,* a deed], an act or deed showing unusual daring, skill, etc.
**feath·er** (fe*th*'ẽr), *n.* [AS. *fether*], 1. any of the soft, light outgrowths covering the body of a bird. 2. *pl. a*) plumage. *b*) attire. 3. class; kind: as, birds of a *feather. v.t.* to provide or adorn with feathers. —**feather in one's cap,** an achievement worthy of pride. —**in fine** (or **high** or **good**) **feather,** in good spirits. —**feath'er·y,** *adj.*
**feath'er·brain',** *n.* a foolish, silly, frivolous person. —**feath'er·brained',** *adj.*
**feath'er·stitch',** *n.* an embroidery stitch forming a zigzag line.
**feath'er·weight',** *n.* a boxer or wrestler weighing between 119 and 126 pounds.
**fea·ture** (fē'chẽr), *n.* [< L. *facere,* make], 1. *a*) *pl.* the form or cast of the face. *b*) any of the parts of the face. 2. a distinct or outstanding part or quality of something. 3. a special story, article, etc. as in a newspaper. 4. a full-length motion picture. *v.t.* [-TURED, -TURING], to make a feature or specialty of. —**fea'ture·less,** *adj.*
**fe·brile** (fē'brəl, feb'rəl), *adj.* [< L. *febris,* fever], feverish.

**Feb·ru·ar·y** (feb′roo-er′i, feb′yoo-), ***n.*** [L. *Februarius* (*menses*), orig. month of expiation], the second month of the year, having 28 days (or 29 days in leap years): abbrev. **Feb., F.**

**fe·ces** (fē′sēz), ***n.pl.*** [< L. *faeces*, dregs], 1. excrement. 2. dregs. **—fe′cal** (-kəl), ***adj.***

**feck·less** (fek′lis), ***adj.*** [Scot. < *effect* + *-less*], 1. weak; ineffective. 2. careless.

**fe·cund** (fē′kənd, fek′ənd), ***adj.*** [< L. *fecundus*], fertile; productive. **—fe·cun·di·ty** (fi-kun′də-ti), ***n.***

**fed** (fed), pt. and pp. of **feed. —fed up,** [Slang], having had enough to become disgusted, bored, etc.

**Fed.,** Federal.

**fed·er·al** (fed′ēr-əl), ***adj.*** [< L. *foedus*, a league], 1. designating or of a union of states, groups, etc. in which each member subordinates its power to a central authority. 2. designating or of a central government of this sort; esp., [usually F-], the central government of the U.S. 3. [F-], of or supporting a former U.S. political party **(Federalist Party)** which favored a strong centralized government. 4. [F-], of or supporting the central government of the U.S. in the Civil War. ***n.*** [F-], a supporter of the Federal government in the Civil War. **—fed′er·al·ism, *n.* —fed′er·al·ist, *n.***

**fed·er·ate** (fed′ēr-āt′), ***v.t. & v.i.*** [-ATED, -ATING], to unite in a federation.

**fed·er·a·tion** (fed′ə-rā′shən), ***n.*** [see FEDERAL], 1. a union of states, groups, etc. in which each subordinates its power to that of the central authority. 2. a federated organization.

**fe·do·ra** (fi-dôr′ə), ***n.*** [Fr.], a soft felt hat worn by men.

**fee** (fē), ***n.*** [ult. < Gmc.], 1. a charge for professional services, licenses, tuition, etc. 2. a gift of money; tip. 3. an inheritance in land. ***v.t.*** to give a fee to.

**fee·ble** (fē′b'l), ***adj.*** [-BLER, -BLEST], [< L. *flere*, weep], 1. weak; infirm: as, a *feeble* old man. 2. without force or effectiveness: as, a *feeble* light. **—fee′bly, *adv.***

**fee′ble-mind′ed,** ***adj.*** mentally weak; subnormal in intelligence.

**feed** (fēd), ***v.t.*** [FED, FEEDING], [< AS. *fod*, food], 1. to give food to. 2. to provide something necessary for the growth, operation, etc. of; nourish. 3. to gratify: as, to *feed* one's vanity. ***v.i.*** to eat: said of animals. ***n.*** 1. food for animals; fodder. 2. material supplied to a machine. 3. the part of a machine supplying this material. **—feed on** (or **upon**), to be nourished or gratified by.

**feed′back′,** ***n.*** the transfer of part of the output back to the input, as of electricity or of information.

**feel** (fēl), ***v.t.*** [FELT, FEELING], [AS. *felan*], 1. to touch; examine by handling. 2. to be aware of through physical sensation. 3. to be influenced or moved by. 4. to be aware of: as, I *feel* his sincerity. 5. to think; believe. ***v.i.*** 1. to have physical sensation. 2. to appear to be to the senses: as, it *feels* warm. 3. to grope. 4. to be aware of being: as, I *feel* sad. 5. to be moved to sympathy, pity, etc. ***n.*** 1. the act of feeling. 2. the sense of touch. 3. the nature of a thing perceived through touch. **—feel like,** [Colloq.], to have a desire for. **—feel out,** to try cautiously to find out the opinions of. **—feel up to,** [Colloq.], to feel capable of.

**feel′er,** ***n.*** 1. a specialized organ of touch in an animal or insect, as an antenna. 2. a remark, etc. made to feel another out.

**feel′ing,** ***n.*** 1. the sense of touch. 2. the ability to experience physical sensation. 3. an awareness; sensation. 4. an emotion. 5. *pl.* sensitivities: as, hurt *feelings*. 6. sympathy; pity. 7. an opinion or sentiment.

**feet** (fēt), ***n.*** pl. of **foot. —on one's feet,** firmly established. **—stand on one's own feet,** to be independent.

**feign** (fān), ***v.t. & v.i.*** [< L. *fingere*, to shape], 1. to make up (an excuse, etc.). 2. to pretend; dissemble. **—feigned, *adj.***

**feint** (fānt), ***n.*** [see FEIGN], 1. a false show; pretense. 2. a pretended attack intended to take the opponent off his guard, as in boxing. ***v.i.*** to deliver such an attack.

**feld·spar** (feld′spär′), ***n.*** [< G. *feld*, field + *spat(h)*, a mineral], any of several hard, crystalline minerals.

**fe·lic·i·tate** (fə-lis′ə-tāt′), ***v.t.*** [-TATED, -TATING], [< L. *felix*, happy], to congratulate; wish happiness to. **—fe·lic′i·ta′tion, *n.***

**fe·lic′i·tous** (-təs), ***adj.*** [< *felicity*], used or expressed in a way suitable to the occasion.

**fe·lic′i·ty,** ***n.*** [*pl.* -TIES], [< L. *felix*, happy], 1. happiness; bliss. 2. anything producing happiness. 3. apt and pleasing expression in writing, etc.

**fe·line** (fē′līn), ***adj.*** [< L. *felis*, cat], 1. of a cat or the cat family. 2. catlike; sly. ***n.*** any animal of the cat family.

**fell** (fel), pt. of **fall.**

**fell** (fel), ***v.t.*** [AS. *fellan*], 1. to knock down. 2. to cut down (a tree).

**fell** (fel), ***adj.*** [< OFr.], fierce; cruel.

**fell** (fel), ***n.*** [AS. *fel*], an animal's hide or skin.

**fel·low** (fel′ō, -ə), ***n.*** [< ON. *fēlagi*, partner], 1. an associate. 2. one of the same rank; equal. 3. one of a pair; mate. 4. one holding a fellowship in a college, etc. 5. a member of a learned society. 6. [Colloq.], a man or boy. ***adj.*** having the same position, work, etc.: as, *fellow* workers.

**fel′low·ship′,** ***n.*** 1. companionship. 2. a mutual sharing. 3. a group of people with the same interests. 4. an endowment for the support of a graduate student in a university or college.

**fellow traveler,** a nonmember who supports the cause of a party.

**fel·on** (fel′ən), ***n.*** [< OFr.], a person guilty of a major crime; criminal. ***adj.*** wicked.

**fel·on** (fel′ən), ***n.*** [ME.], a painful infection at the end of a finger or toe, near the nail.

**fel·o·ny** (fel′ə-ni), ***n.*** [*pl.* -NIES], [< OFr.], a major crime, as murder, arson, etc.**—fe·lo·ni·ous** (fə-lō′ni-əs), ***adj.***

**felt** (felt), ***n.*** [AS.], a fabric of wool, often mixed with fur or hair, worked together by pressure, heat, etc. ***v.t.*** to make into felt.

**felt** (felt), pt. and pp. of **feel.**

**fem.,** feminine.

**fe·male** (fē′māl), ***adj.*** [< L. *femina*, woman], 1. designating or of the sex that bears offspring. 2. of, like, or suitable to women or girls; feminine. 3. in *mechanics*, having a hollow part for receiving an inserted part. ***n.*** a female person, animal, or plant.

**fem·i·nine** (fem′ə-nin), ***adj.*** [< L. *femina*, woman], 1. of women or girls. 2. having qualities suitable to or characteristic of women; gentle, delicate, etc. 3. in *grammar*, designating or of the gender of words referring to females or things originally regarded as female. **—fem′i·nin′i·ty, *n.***

**fem′i·nism,** ***n.*** the movement to win political, economic, and social equality for women. **—fem′i·nist, *n. & adj.***

**fe·mur** (fē′mēr), ***n.*** [L., thigh], the thighbone.**—fem·o·ral** (fem′ēr-əl), ***adj.***

**fen** (fen), ***n.*** [AS.], low, marshy land; bog.

**fence** (fens), ***n.*** [abbrev. of *defence*], 1. a protective or confining barrier of posts, wire, etc. 2. one who buys and sells stolen goods. ***v.t.*** [FENCED, FENCING], to enclose as with a fence. ***v.i.*** 1. to practice the art of fencing. 2. to avoid giving a direct reply; evade. 3. to buy or sell stolen goods.

**fenc′ing** ***n.*** the art of fighting with a foil or other sword.

**fend** (fend), *v.i.* [< *defend*], to resist; parry.—**fend for oneself**, to manage by oneself. —**fend off**, to ward off; repel.
**fend'er**, *n.* anything that fends off or protects something else, as the guard over an automobile wheel.
**fen·nel** (fen''l), *n.* [< L. *fenum*, hay], a tall herb of the carrot family, with yellow flowers: its aromatic seeds are used in cooking.
**FEPC,** Fair Employment Practices Committee.
**fe·ral** (fêr'əl), *adj.* [< L. *ferus*, wild], 1. untamed; wild. 2. brutal; savage.
**fer·ment** (fũr'mənt; *for v.*, fẽr-ment'), *n.* [< L. *fervere*, to boil], 1. a substance causing fermentation, as yeast. 2. excitement; agitation. *v.t.* 1. to cause fermentation in. 2. to excite; agitate. *v.i.* 1. to undergo fermentation. 2. to be agitated; seethe.
**fer·men·ta·tion** (fũr'mən-tā'shən, -men-), *n.* 1. the breakdown of complex molecules in organic compounds, caused by the influence of a ferment: as, bacteria curdle milk by *fermentation*. 2. agitation.
**fern** (fũrn), *n.* [AS. *fearn*], any of a large group of shrubby, nonflowering plants having roots, stems, and fronds, and reproducing by spores. —**fern'y,** *adj.*
**fe·ro·cious** (fi-rō'shəs), *adj.* [< L. *ferus*, fierce], fierce; savage; violently cruel. —**fe·ro'cious·ly,** *adv.* —**fe·roc·i·ty** (-ros'ə-ti), *n.*
**-ferous,** [< L. *ferre*, to bear], a suffix meaning *bearing, yielding*, as in *coniferous*.
**fer·ret** (fer'it), *n.* [< L. *fur*, thief], a kind of weasel, tamed for hunting rabbits, rats, etc. *v.t.* 1. to force out of hiding with a ferret. 2. to search out.
**Fer·ris wheel** (fer'is), [after G. *Ferris*, 19th-c. U.S. inventor], a large upright wheel revolving on a fixed axle and having suspended seats: used in amusement parks, etc.
**ferro-,** [< L. *ferrum*, iron], a combining form meaning: 1. *iron, connection with iron*. 2. *iron and*.
**fer·ro·con·crete** (fer'ō-kon'krēt), *n.* concrete having an iron or steel framework embedded in it: also called *reinforced concrete*.
**fer·rous** (fer'əs), *adj.* [< L. *ferrum*, iron], of, containing, or derived from iron.
**fer·rule** (fer'əl, -ool), *n.* [< L. *viriae*, bracelets], a metal ring or cap put around the end of a tool, cane, etc. to give added strength.
**fer·ry** (fer'i), *v.t. & v.i.* [-RIED, -RYING], [AS. *ferian*, carry], to take across or cross (a river, etc.) in a boat. *n.* [*pl.* -RIES], 1. a system for transporting people, goods, etc. across a river, etc. 2. a boat (in full, **ferryboat**) used for ferrying.
**fer·tile** (fũr't'l), *adj.* [< L. *ferre*, to bear], 1. producing abundantly; fruitful. 2. able to produce young, seeds, fruit, etc. 3. fertilized. —**fer·til·i·ty** (fẽr-til'ə-ti), *n.*
**fer'ti·lize'** (-īz'), *v.t.* [-LIZED, -LIZING], 1. to make fertile. 2. to spread fertilizer on. 3. to make (an ovum or a female) fruitful by introducing a male germ cell; impregnate. —**fer'ti·li·za'tion,** *n.*
**fer'ti·liz'er,** *n.* manure, chemicals, etc. used to enrich the soil.
**fer·ule** (fer'əl, -o͞ol), *n.* [L. *ferula*, rod], a flat stick or ruler used for punishing children.
**fer·vent** (fũr'vənt), *adj.* [< L. *fervere*, to glow], 1. hot; burning. 2. showing great warmth of feeling; intensely earnest. —**fer'ven·cy,** *n.*—**fer'vent·ly,** *adv.*
**fer·vid** (fũr'vid), *adj.* [see FERVENT], impassioned; fervent. —**fer'vid·ly,** *adv.*
**fer·vor** (fũr'vẽr), *n.* [see FERVENT], 1. intense heat. 2. great warmth of emotion; ardor; zeal. Also, Brit. sp., **fervour.**
**fes·tal** (fes't'l), *adj.* [< L. *festum*, feast], of or like a feast; gay. —**fes'tal·ly,** *adv.*
**fes·ter** (fes'tẽr), *n.* [< L. *fistula*, ulcer], a small sore producing pus. *v.i.* 1. to form pus; ulcerate. 2. to grow embittered; rankle.
**fes·ti·val** (fes'tə-v'l), *n.* [see FESTIVE], 1. a time or day of feasting or celebration. 2. a celebration or entertainment. 3. merrymaking. *adj.* of, for, or fit for a festival.
**fes·tive** (fes'tiv), *adj.* [< L. *festum*, feast], of or for a feast or festival; joyous; gay.
**fes·tiv·i·ty** (fes-tiv'ə-ti), *n.* [*pl.* -TIES], 1. gaiety; merrymaking. 2. a festival. 3. *pl.* festive proceedings.
**fes·toon** (fes-to͞on'), *n.* [< It. *festa*, feast], a garland of flowers, etc. hanging in a curve. *v.t.* to adorn with festoons.
**fe·tal** (fē't'l), *adj.* of a fetus.
**fetch** (fech), *v.t.* [AS. *feccan*], 1. to go after and bring back; get. 2. to cause to come. 3. to sell for. *n.* 1. a fetching. 2. a trick.
**fetch'ing,** *adj.* [Colloq.], attractive.
**fete, fête** (fāt), *n.* [Fr.; see FEAST], a festival; entertainment. *v.t.* [FETED, FETING, FÊTED, FÊTING], to honor with festivities.
**fet·id** (fet'id, fē'tid), *adj.* [< L. *f(o)etere*, to stink], having a bad smell; stinking.
**fe·tish, fe·tich** (fē'tish, fet'ish), *n.* [< Port. *feitiço*], 1. any object believed to have magic power. 2. anything held in unreasoning devotion. 3. any nonsexual object that excites erotic feelings.
**fe'tish·ism, fe'tich·ism,** *n.* worship of or belief in fetishes.—**fe'tish·ist, fe'tich·ist,** *n.*
**fet·lock** (fet'lok'), *n.* [prob. < MLG.], 1. a tuft of hair on the back of a horse's leg above the hoof. 2. the projection bearing this tuft.
**fet·ter** (fet'ẽr), *n.* [< AS. *fot*, foot], 1. *usually pl.* a shackle for the feet. 2. any check or restraint. *v.t.* 1. to bind with fetters. 2. to restrain.
**fet·tle** (fet''l), *n.* [ME. *fetlen*, make ready], condition; state: as, he is in fine *fettle*.
**fe·tus** (fē'təs), *n.* [*pl.* -TUSES], [L., a bringing forth], the unborn young of an animal.
**feud** (fūd), *n.* [< OFr.], a deadly quarrel, esp. between families for several generations. *v.i.* to carry on a feud.
**feu·dal** (fū'd'l), *adj.* [< ML. *feudum*, a fief], of or relating to feudalism.
**feu'dal·ism,** *n.* the social organization of medieval Europe, in which land worked by serfs was held by vassals in exchange for military and other services to overlords.
**fe·ver** (fē'vẽr), *n.* [< L. *febris*], 1. an abnormally increased body temperature. 2. any disease marked by fever. 3. a restless excitement. *v.t.* to cause fever in.—**fe'vered,** *adj.* —**fe'ver·ish,** *adj.*—**fe'ver·ish·ly,** *adv.*
**few** (fū), *adj.* [AS. *feawe*, *pl.*], not many. *pron. & n.* a small number.—**quite a few,** [Colloq.], a good many.—**some few,** a few.
**fey** (fā), *adj.* [ME. *feie* < AS. *fæge*, fated], 1. in an unusually excited state, formerly believed to portend sudden death. 2. strange or unusual, as eccentric, whimsical, etc.
**fez** (fez), *n.* [*pl.* FEZZES], [< *Fez*, city in Morocco], a red, tapering felt cap, formerly worn by Turkish men.
**ff.** 1. folios. 2. following (pages).
**FHA, F.H.A.,** Federal Housing Administration.
**fi·an·cé** (fē'än-sā'), *n.* [Fr. < *fiance*, a promise], the man to whom a woman is engaged to be married.
**fi·an·cée** (fē'än-sā'), *n.* [Fr.], the woman to whom a man is engaged to be married.
**fi·as·co** (fi-as'kō), *n.* [*pl.* -COES, -COS], [It., lit., a flask], a complete, ridiculous failure.
**fi·at** (fī'ət, -at), *n.* [L., let it be done], 1. a decree. 2. a sanction.
**fib** (fib), *n.* [? < *fable*], a lie about something unimportant. *v.i.* [FIBBED, FIBBING], to tell a fib.—**fib'ber,** *n.*
**fi·ber, fi·bre** (fī'bẽr), *n.* [< L. *fibra*], 1. a threadlike structure combining with others to form animal or vegetable tissue. 2. any

substance that can be separated into threadlike parts for weaving, etc. 3. texture. 4. character; nature. —**fi′brous,** *adj.*
**fi′ber·board′,** *n.* a boardlike material made from pressed fibers, used in building.
**fi′ber·glas′** (-glas′, -gläs′), *n.* finely spun filaments of glass made into textiles or insulating material: a trademark **(Fiberglas).**
**fi·bril** (fī′brəl), *n.* a small fiber.
**fi·broid** (fī′broid), *adj.* like or composed of fibrous tissue, as a tumor.
**fib·u·la** (fib′yoo-lə), *n.* [*pl.* -LAE (-lē′), -LAS], [L., a clasp], the long, thin outer bone of the lower leg.
**-fic,** [< L. *facere*, make], a suffix meaning *making, creating*, as in *terrific*.
**-fication,** [see -FIC], a suffix meaning *a making, creating*, as in *glorification*.
**fich·u** (fish′ōō), *n.* [Fr.], a triangular cape worn over the shoulders by women.
**fick·le** (fik′'l), *adj.* [AS. *ficol*], changeable; capricious; inconstant.
**fic·tion** (fik′shən), *n.* [< L. *fingere*, to form], 1. an imaginary statement, story, etc. 2. any literary work with imaginary characters and events. 3. such works collectively; esp., novels and stories. —**fic′tion·al,** *adj.*
**fic·ti·tious** (fik-tish′əs), *adj.* 1. of or like fiction; imaginary. 2. false; assumed for deception, as a name. —**fic·ti′tious·ly,** *adv.*
**fid·dle** (fid′'l), *n.* [< L. *vitula*], [Colloq.], a violin. *v.i.* [-DLED, -DLING], 1. [Colloq.], to play on a violin. 2. to fidget. —**play second fiddle,** to act in a subordinate position.
**fiddler crab,** a small, burrowing crab of the Atlantic coast.
**fid′dle·sticks′,** *interj.* nonsense!
**fi·del·i·ty** (fi-del′ə-ti, fə-), *n.* [*pl.* -TIES], [< L. *fides*, faith], 1. faithful devotion to duty; loyalty. 2. accuracy of reproduction.
**fidg·et** (fij′it), *n.* [< ON. *fikja*], *often in pl.* a restless or nervous state. *v.i.* to make restless or nervous movements. —**fidg′et·y,** *adj.*
**fi·du·ci·ar·y** (fi-dōō′shi-er′i), *adj.* [< L. *fiducia*, trust], holding or held in trust. *n.* [*pl.* -IES], a trustee.
**fie** (fī), *interj.* shame!: now often humorous.
**fief** (fēf), *n.* [ult. < Gmc.], in feudalism, heritable land held by a vassal.
**field** (fēld), *n.* [AS. *feld*], 1. *often pl.* a wide stretch of open land; plain. 2. a piece of cleared land for crops or pasture. 3. a piece of land for a particular purpose: as, a football *field*. 4. any wide, unbroken space: as, a *field* of ice. 5. *a*) a battlefield. *b*) a battle. 6. a sphere of knowledge or activity. 7. the background, as on a flag. 8. all the entrants in a contest. 9. in *physics*, a space within which magnetic or electrical lines of force are active. *v.t.* 1. to stop or catch and return (a baseball, etc.). 2. to put (a player or a team) into active play.—**play the field,** to take a broad area of operations.
**field′er,** *n.* in *baseball*, etc., a player occupying a defensive position.
**field glass, field glasses,** a small, portable, binocular telescope.
**field gun,** a mobile artillery piece for use in battle: also called **field′piece′,** *n.*
**field marshal,** in some European armies, an officer ranking just below the commander in chief.
**field work,** the work done by a scientist, social worker, etc. in performing his functions away from his headquarters. —**field′work′er,** *n.*
**fiend** (fēnd), *n.* [AS. *feond*], 1. an evil spirit; devil. 2. an inhumanly wicked person. 3. [Colloq.], an addict: as, a dope *fiend*, golf *fiend*, etc. —**fiend′ish,** *adj.*
**fierce** (fêrs), *adj.* [FIERCER, FIERCEST], [< L. *ferus*, wild], 1. violently cruel; savage. 2. violent; uncontrolled. 3. intensely eager. —**fierce′ly,** *adv.* —**fierce′ness,** *n.*
**fi·er·y** (fī′ri, fī′ẽr-i), *adj.* [-IER, -IEST], 1. like fire; glaring, hot, etc. 2. ardent. 3. excitable. —**fi′er·i·ness,** *n.*
**fi·es·ta** (fi-es′tə), *n.* [Sp. < L. *festus*, festal], 1. a religious festival. 2. any gala celebration; holiday.
**fife** (fīf), *n.* [< ?], a small, shrill musical instrument like a flute. *v.t. & v.i.* [FIFED, FIFING], to play on a fife.
**fif·teen** (fif′tēn′), *adj. & n.* [AS. *fiftene*], five more than ten; 15; XV. —**fif′teenth′** (-tēnth′), *adj. & n.*
**fifth** (fifth), *adj.* [< AS. *fif*, five], preceded by four others in a series; 5th. *n.* 1. the one following the fourth. 2. any of the five equal parts of something; ⅕. 3. a fifth of a gallon.
**fifth column,** [orig. (1936) applied to those inside Madrid sympathetic to four columns besieging it], a group of people within a country who secretly aid the enemy.
**fif·ty** (fif′ti), *adj. & n.* [*pl.* -TIES], [AS. *fiftig*], five times ten; 50; L.—**the fifties,** the years from 50 through 59 (of a century or a person's age).—**fif′ti·eth** (-ith), *adj. & n.*
**fif′ty-fif′ty,** *adj.* [Colloq.], equal; even. *adv.* [Colloq.], equally.
**fig** (fig), *n.* [< L. *ficus*], 1. a small, sweet, pear-shaped fruit, usually dried for eating. 2. the tree it grows on. 3. a trifle.
**fig.,** 1. figurative(ly). 2. figure(s).
**fight** (fīt), *v.i.* [FOUGHT, FIGHTING], [AS. *feohtan*], 1. to take part in a physical struggle or battle. 2. to contend. *v.t.* 1. to oppose physically or in battle. 2. to struggle against. 3. to engage in (a war, etc.). 4. to gain by struggle: as, he *fought* his way up. *n.* 1. any struggle, contest, or quarrel. 2. readiness to fight.
**fight′er,** *n.* 1. one that fights; esp., a prizefighter. 2. a small, light airplane for aerial combat: often **fighter plane.**
**fig·ment** (fig′mənt), *n.* [< L. *fingere*, make], something imagined or made up in the mind.
**fig·ur·a·tive** (fig′yoor-ə-tiv), *adj.* 1. representing by means of a figure or symbol. 2. not in its usual or exact sense; metaphorical. 3. using figures of speech.
**fig·ure** (fig′yoor), *n.* [< L. *fingere*, to form], 1. an outline; shape; form. 2. the human form. 3. a person thought of in a specified way: as, a historical *figure*. 4. a likeness of a person or thing. 5. an illustration; diagram. 6. a design. 7. a pattern of musical notes. 8. the symbol for a number: as, the *figure* 5. 9. *pl.* arithmetic. 10. a sum of money. 11. a surface or space bounded by lines or planes. *v.t.* [-URED, -URING], 1. to represent in definite form. 2. to imagine. 3. to ornament with a design. 4. to compute with figures. 5. [Colloq.], to believe; predict. *v.i.* 1. to be conspicuous. 2. to do arithmetic.—**figure on,** to count on.—**figure out,** 1. to solve. 2. to understand. —**figure up,** to total.
**fig′ure·head′,** *n.* 1. a carved figure on the bow of a ship. 2. one in a position of ostensible leadership who has no real power or authority.
**figure of speech,** an expression using words in an unusual or nonliteral sense; metaphor, simile, etc.
**fig·u·rine** (fig′yoo-rēn′), *n.* [Fr.], a small sculptured or molded figure.
**fil·a·ment** (fil′ə-mənt), *n.* [< L. *filum*, thread], a very slender thread or threadlike part; specif., the fine wire in a light bulb, etc.
**fil·bert** (fil′bẽrt), *n.* [after a St. *Philibert*], the hazelnut or the tree it grows on.
**filch** (filch), *v.t.* [< slang *filch*, hooked staff], to steal (something trivial); pilfer.
**file** (fīl), *n.* [< L. *filum*, thread], 1. a folder, cabinet, etc. for keeping papers in order. 2.

an orderly arrangement of papers, etc. 3. a line of persons or things situated one behind another. *v.t.* [FILED, FILING], 1. to put (papers, etc.) in order. 2. to put into official records. *v.i.* to move or march in a line.

**file** (fīl), *n.* [AS. *feol*], a steel tool with a ridged surface for smoothing or grinding. *v.t.* [FILED FILING], to smooth or grind, as with a file. —**fil′er,** *n.*

**fi·let mi·gnon** (fi-lā′ min-yon′), [Fr.], a round cut of lean beefsteak broiled.

**fil·i·al** (fil′i-əl, fil′yəl), *adj.* [< L. *filius*, son], of, suitable to, or due from a son or daughter.

**fil·i·bus·ter** (fil′ə-bus′tẽr), *n.* [< Sp. < D. *vrijbuiter*, freebooter], 1. a member of a legislature who obstructs a bill by making long speeches. 2. such obstruction of a bill. *v.i. & v.t.* to obstruct (a bill) by such methods. —**fil′i·bus′ter·er,** *n.*

**fil·i·gree, fil·a·gree** (fil′ə-grē′), *n.* [< L. *filum*, thread + *granum*, grain], lacelike ornamental work of intertwined wire of gold, silver, etc. *v.t.* [-GREED, -GREEING], to ornament with filigree.

**fil·ing** (fīl′iŋ), *n.* *usually in pl.* a small piece of metal, etc. scraped off with a file.

**Fil·i·pi·no** (fil′ə-pē′nō), *n.* [*pl.* -NOS], [Sp.], a native of the Philippines. *adj.* Philippine.

**fill** (fil), *v.t.* [AS. *fyllan*], 1. to put as much as possible into. 2. to occupy wholly: as, the mob *filled* the room. 3. to occupy (a position, etc.). 4. to put a person into (a position, etc.). 5. to supply the things called for in (an order, etc.). 6. to close or plug (holes, cracks, etc.). 7. to satisfy the hunger of. 8. to be plentiful in. *v.i.* to become full. *n.* 1. enough to make full or to satisfy. 2. anything that fills. —**fill in,** 1. to complete by supplying something. 2. to supply for completion. 3. to be a substitute. —**fill out,** 1. to make or become larger, etc. 2. to complete (a document, etc.) with data. —**fill′er,** *n.*

**fil·let** (fil′it), *n.* [< L. *filum*, thread], 1. a thin strip or band. 2. (fil′ā, fi-lā′), a boneless, lean piece of fish or meat. *v.t.* (fi-lā′), to bone and slice (meat or fish).

**fill′ing,** *n.* a thing used to fill something else, as gold, etc. in a cavity in a tooth.

**fil·lip** (fil′əp), *n.* [< *flip*], 1. a snap of the fingers. 2. anything stimulating. *v.t.* 1. to toss with a fillip. 2. to stimulate.

**fil·ly** (fil′i), *n.* [*pl.* -LIES], [ON. *fylja*], 1. a young mare. 2. [Colloq.], a vivacious girl.

**film** (film), *n.* [AS. *filmen*], 1. a fine, thin skin or coating. 2. a flexible cellulose material covered with a substance sensitive to light and used in photography. 3. a haze or blur. 4. a motion picture. *v.t. & v.i.* 1. to cover or be covered as with a film. 2. to photograph or be photographed for motion pictures. —**film′y** [-IER, -IEST], *adj.*

**film′strip′,** *n.* a strip of film with stills of pictures, diagrams, charts, etc., arranged in sequence for projection separately and used as a teaching aid.

**fil·ter** (fil′tẽr), *n.* [< LL. *filtrum*, felt], 1. a device for straining out solid particles, etc. from a fluid. 2. any porous substance so used, as sand, etc. 3. a device for absorbing certain light rays: as, a lens *filter*. *v.t.* 1. to pass (fluids) through a filter. 2. to remove (solid particles, etc.) from a fluid with a filter. *v.i.* 1. to be filtered. 2. to pass slowly. —**fil′ter·a·ble, fil′tra·ble** (-trə-b'l), *adj.*

**filth** (filth), *n.* [< AS. *ful*, foul], 1. foul dirt. 2. obscenity. —**filth′y** [-IER, -IEST], *adj.*

**fil·trate** (fil′trāt), *v.t.* [-TRATED, -TRATING], to filter. —**fil·tra′tion,** *n.*

**fin** (fin), *n.* [AS. *finn*], 1. any of several winglike membranous organs on the body of a fish, dolphin, etc. 2. anything like this in shape or use.

**fi·na·gle** (fi-nā′g'l), *v.i. & v.t.* [-GLED, -GLING], [prob. < *Feinagel*, G. whist expert], to cheat; use, or get by, trickery. —**fi·na′gler,** *n.*

**fi·nal** (fī′n'l), *adj.* [< L. *finis*, end], 1. of or coming at the end; last. 2. deciding; conclusive. *n.* 1. anything final. 2. *pl.* the last of a series of contests. —**fi·nal′i·ty** (-nal′ə-ti), *n.* —**fi′nal·ly,** *adv.*

**fi·na·le** (fi-nä′li), *n.* [It.], the concluding part of a musical work, etc.

**fi′nal·ist,** *n.* one who competes in the finals.

**fi·nance** (fə-nans′, fī′nans), *n.* [< L. *finis*, end], 1. *pl.* money resources, income, etc. 2. the science of managing money matters. *v.t.* [-NANCED, -NANCING], to supply money for. —**fi·nan′cial** (-shəl), *adj.*

**fin·an·cier** (fin′ən-sêr′, fī′nən-), *n.* [Fr.], one skilled in finance.

**finch** (finch), *n.* [AS. *finc*], any of a group of small, short-beaked songbirds, including the canary, sparrow, etc.

**find** (fīnd), *v.t.* [FOUND, FINDING], [AS. *findan*], 1. to discover by chance; come upon. 2. to get by searching. 3. to perceive; learn. 4. to recover (something lost). 5. to reach; attain. 6. to decide. *v.i.* to reach a decision: as, the jury *found* for the accused. *n.* 1. a finding. 2. something found. —**find out,** to discover; learn.

**find′er,** *n.* 1. a person or thing that finds. 2. a camera device that shows what will appear in the photograph.

**find′ing,** *n.* 1. discovery. 2. something found. 3. the verdict of a judge or jury.

**fine** (fīn), *adj.* [FINER, FINEST], [ult. < L. *finis*, end], 1. superior; excellent. 2. with no impurities; refined. 3. clear and bright, as the weather. 4. not heavy, thick, or coarse: as, *fine* sand. 5. sharp: as, a *fine* edge. 6. discriminating: as, *fine* distinctions. 7. handsome; elegant. *adv.* [Colloq.], very well. *n.* money paid as punishment for an offense. *v.t.* [FINED, FINING], 1. to make fine. 2. to require to pay a fine.

**fine arts,** any of certain art forms, esp. painting, sculpture, architecture, etc.

**fin·er·y** (fīn′ẽr-i), *n.* [*pl.* -IES], showy, gay clothes, jewelry, etc.

**fi·nesse** (fi-nes′), *n.* [Fr.; see FINE], 1. skill; adroitness. 2. the ability to handle delicate situations diplomatically. 3. cunning.

**fin·ger** (fiŋ′gẽr), *n.* [AS.], 1. any of the five parts at the end of the hand; esp., any other than the thumb. 2. anything like a finger in shape or use. *v.t.* 1. to touch with the fingers; handle. 2. to play (an instrument) by using the fingers on strings, keys, etc.

**fin′ger·ling** (-liŋ), *n.* a small fish about the size of a finger.

**fin′ger·nail′,** *n.* the horny substance on the upper part of the end joint of a finger.

**fin′ger·print′,** *n.* an impression of the lines and whorls on the tip of a finger, used to identify a person. *v.t.* to take the fingerprints of.

**fin·i·al** (fin′i-əl, fī′ni-), *n.* [< *finis* + *-ial*], an ornament at the top of a spire, lamp, etc.

**fin·i·cal** (fin′i-k'l), *adj.* [< *fine*], too particular; fussy: also **fin′ick·y** (-i-ki), **fin′ick·ing.**

**fi·nis** (fī′nis, fin′is), *n.* [*pl.* -NISES], [L.], the end, as of a book; conclusion.

**fin·ish** (fin′ish), *v.t.* [< L. *finis*, end], 1. to come to the end of; end. 2. to complete; accomplish. 3. to use up. 4. to perfect. 5. to give a desired surface to, as by polishing. *v.i.* to come to an end. *n.* 1. the last part; end. 2. anything used to finish a surface, etc. 3. perfection. 4. the manner of completion. 5. the way in which a surface is finished. 6. polish in manners, speech, etc. —**finish off,** 1. to end. 2. to kill. —**finish up,** 1. to end. 2. to consume all of. —**finish with,** to end. —**fin′ished,** *adj.* —**fin′ish·er,** *n.*

**fi·nite** (fī′nīt), *adj.* [see FINISH], 1. having definable limits; not infinite. 2. in *grammar*, having limits of person, number, and tense: said of a verb that can be used to form a predicate. —**fi′nite·ly,** *adv.*

**fink** (fiŋk), *n.* [< ?], [Slang], an informer or strikebreaker.

**Finn** (fin), *n.* a native of Finland.

**fin·nan had·die** (fin′ən had′i), [prob. < *Findhorn* (Scotland) *haddock*], smoked haddock: also **finnan haddock.**

**Finn·ish** (fin′ish), *adj.* of Finland, its people, their language, etc. *n.* the language of the Finns. Abbrev. **Finn., Fin.**

**fiord** (fyôrd), *n.* [Norw. < ON. *fjörthr*], a narrow inlet of the sea bordered by steep cliffs: also sp. **fjord.**

**fir** (fũr), *n.* [AS. *fyrh*], 1. a cone-bearing evergreen somwhat like a pine. 2. its wood.

**fire** (fir), *n.* [AS. *fyr*], 1. the flame, heat, and light of combustion. 2. something burning, as fuel in a furnace. 3. a destructive burning: as, a forest *fire.* 4. excitement; ardor. 5. a discharge of firearms. *v.t. & v.i.* [FIRED, FIRING], 1. to start burning. 2. to supply with fuel. 3. to bake in a kiln, as bricks. 4. to excite or become excited; inflame. 5. to shoot (a gun, bullet, etc.). 6. [Colloq.], to hurl: as, *fire* questions. 7. [Colloq.], to dismiss from a position; discharge. —**catch fire,** to ignite. —**hang fire,** to delay or be delayed. —**on fire,** 1. burning. 2. greatly excited. —**under fire,** under attack.

**fire′arm′,** *n.* any hand weapon from which a shot is fired by explosive force, as a rifle.

**fire′brand′,** *n.* 1. a piece of burning wood. 2. one who stirs up strife, etc.

**fire′bug′,** *n.* [Colloq.], one who deliberately sets fire to buildings, etc.

**fire′crack′er,** *n.* a roll of paper containing an explosive, set off at celebrations, etc.

**fire′damp′,** *n.* a gas formed in coal mines, explosive when mixed with air.

**fire′dog′,** *n.* an andiron.

**fire engine,** a motor truck with equipment for fighting fires.

**fire escape,** a ladder, outside stairway, etc. for escape from a burning building.

**fire′fly′,** *n.* [*pl.* -FLIES], a winged beetle whose abdomen glows with a phosphorescent light; lightning bug.

**fire′man** (-mən), *n.* [*pl.* -MEN], 1. a man whose work is fighting fires. 2. a man who tends a fire in a furnace, etc.

**fire′place′,** *n.* a place for a fire, esp. an open place built in a wall.

**fire′plug′,** *n.* a street hydrant to which a hose can be attached for fighting fires.

**fire′proof′,** *adj.* not easily destroyed by fire. *v.t.* to make fireproof.

**fire′side′,** *n.* 1. the space around a fireplace. 2. home or home life.

**fire′trap′,** *n.* a building hard to escape from in case of fire.

**fire′wa′ter,** *n.* [Colloq.], alcoholic liquor.

**fire′wood′,** *n.* wood used as fuel.

**fire′works′,** *n.pl.* firecrackers, rockets, etc., used for noisy or brilliant displays.

**firm** (fũrm), *adj.* [< L. *firmus*], 1. solid; hard. 2. not moved easily; fixed. 3. not fluctuating; steady. 4. resolute; constant: as, a *firm* faith. 5. positive: as, a *firm* command. *v.t. & v.i.* to make or become firm.

**firm** (fũrm), *n.* [< It. < L. *firmus,* firm], a business company.

**fir·ma·ment** (fũr′mə-mənt), *n.* [< L. *firmus,* firm], the sky, viewed poetically as a solid arch or vault.

**first** (fũrst), *adj.* [AS. *fyrst*], 1. before any others; 1st. 2. earliest. 3. foremost in rank, importance, etc. *adv.* 1. before any other person or thing. 2. for the first time. 3. sooner; preferably. *n.* 1. any person, thing, class, etc. that is first. 2. the beginning. 3. the winning place, as in a race.

**first aid,** emergency treatment for injury, etc., before regular medical aid is available. —**first′-aid′,** *adj.*

**first′-born′,** *adj.* born first in a family; oldest. *n.* the first-born child.

**first′-class′,** *adj.* 1. of the highest class, quality, etc. 2. designating or of the best accommodations. *adv.* with the best accommodations.

**first′hand′,** *adj. & adv.* from the original producer or source; direct.

**first lieutenant,** an army officer ranking just above a second lieutenant.

**first person,** that form of a pronoun or verb which refers to the speaker.

**first′-rate′** (-rāt′), *adj.* 1. of the highest quality, etc. 2. [Colloq.], excellent. *adv.* [Colloq.], very well.

**firth** (fũrth), *n.* [< ON. *fjörthr*], a narrow arm of the sea, esp. in Scotland.

**fis·cal** (fis′k'l), *adj.* [< L. *fiscus,* money bag], 1. relating to the public treasury or revenues. 2. financial. —**fis′cal·ly,** *adv.*

**fish** (fish), *n.* [*pl.* FISH; in referring to different species, FISHES], [AS. *fisc*], 1. any of a large group of cold-blooded animals living in water and having backbones, gills for breathing, and fins. 2. the flesh of a fish used as food. *v.i.* 1. to catch or try to catch fish. 2. to try to get something indirectly. *v.t.* to find and bring to view; pull (*out*). —**fish′er,** *n.*

**fish′er·man** (-mən), *n.* [*pl.* -MEN], 1. a person who fishes for sport or for a living. 2. a ship used in fishing.

**fish′er·y,** *n.* [*pl.* -IES], 1. the business of catching fish. 2. a place where fish are caught or bred.

**fish′hook′,** *n.* a hook, usually barbed, for catching fish.

**fish′ing,** *n.* the catching of fish for sport or for a living.

**fish story,** [Colloq.], an exaggerated story.

**fish′wife′** (-wīf′), *n.* [*pl.* -WIVES], a coarse, scolding woman.

**fish′y,** *adj.* [-IER, -IEST], 1. like a fish in odor, taste, etc. 2. dull; without expression: as, a *fishy* stare. 3. [Colloq.], questionable.

**fis·sion** (fish′ən), *n.* [< L. *findere,* to split], a splitting apart; cleavage: see also **nuclear fission.**

**fis′sion·a·ble,** *adj.* designating a substance, as uranium, whose nuclei can undergo fission.

**fis·sure** (fish′ẽr), *n.* [see FISSION], a cleft or crack. *v.t. & v.i.* [-SURED, -SURING], to crack or split apart.

**fist** (fist), *n.* [AS. *fyst*], a hand with the fingers clenched into the palm.

**fist·ic** (fis′tik), *adj.* [Colloq.], having to do with boxing; pugilistic.

**fis·ti·cuffs** (fis′ti-kufs′), *n.pl.* a fight, or the art of fighting, with the fists.

**fis·tu·la** (fis′choo-lə), *n.* [*pl.* -LAS, -LAE (-lē′)], [L.], an abnormal hollow passage as from an abscess, cavity, etc. to the skin.

**fit** (fit), *v.t.* [FITTED, FITTING], [prob. ult. < L. *facere,* do], 1. to be suitable to. 2. to be the proper size, shape, etc. for. 3. to adjust so as to fit. 4. to equip; outfit. *v.i.* 1. to be suitable or proper. 2. to be as specified in size, shape, etc. *adj.* [FITTER, FITTEST], 1. suited to some purpose, function, etc. 2. proper; right. 3. prepared; ready. 4. in good physical condition; healthy. *n.* the manner of fitting: as, a tight *fit.* —**fit′ly,** *adv.* —**fit′ness,** *n.* —**fit′ter,** *n.*

**fit** (fit), *n.* [AS. *fitt,* conflict], 1. any sudden, uncontrollable attack: as, a *fit* of coughing. 2. a temporary outburst, as of feeling. 3. a convulsion with loss of consciousness. —**by fits and starts,** in an irregular way.

**fit′ful** (-fəl), *adj.* characterized by intermittent bursts of activity; spasmodic; irregular.

**fit′ting,** *adj.* suitable; proper. *n.* 1. an ad-

justment or trying on of clothes, etc. for fit. 2. *pl.* fixtures. **—fit′ting·ly,** *adv.*
**five** (fīv), *adj.* & *n.* [AS. *fif*], one more than four; 5; V.
**five′-and-ten′-cent′ store,** a dime store: also **five-and-ten,** *n.*
**fix** (fiks), *v.t.* [FIXED or FIXT, FIXING], [< ML. *figere*, fasten], 1. to fasten firmly. 2. to set firmly in the mind. 3. to direct steadily, as one's eyes. 4. to make rigid. 5. to make permanent. 6. to establish, as a price. 7. to determine definitely. 8. to set in order. 9. to repair. 10. to prepare (food, etc.). 11. [Colloq.], to influence the result or action of (a race, jury, etc.) as by bribery. 12. [Colloq.], to punish. *v.i.* 1. to become fixed. 2. [Colloq.], to prepare or intend. *n.* 1. [Colloq.], a predicament. 2. [Slang], a situation that is fixed (sense 11). 3. [Slang], an injection of a narcotic by an addict. **—fix up,** [Colloq.], 1. to repair. 2. to set in order.
**fix·a·tion** (fik-sā′shən), *n.* 1. a fixing or being fixed. 2. in *psych.*, an obsession.
**fix·a·tive** (fik′sə-tiv), *adj.* that can, or tends to, make permanent, prevent fading, etc. *n.* a fixative substance.
**fixed** (fikst), *adj.* 1. firm. 2. established; set. 3. resolute. 4. obsessive: as, a *fixed* idea. **—fix·ed·ly** (fik′sid-li), *adv.*
**fix·ings** (fik′siŋz), *n.pl.* [Colloq.], furnishings; accessories; trimmings.
**fix·ture** (fiks′chẽr), *n.* [see FIX], 1. anything firmly in place. 2. *usually in pl.* any of the attached fittings of a house, store, etc. 3. [Colloq.], a person long established in a place or in a job.
**fizz** (fiz), *n.* [echoic], 1. a hissing, sputtering sound. 2. a drink that hisses and bubbles. *v.i.* [FIZZED, FIZZING], to make a hissing or bubbling sound.
**fiz·zle** (fiz′'l), *v.i.* [-ZLED, -ZLING], [echoic], 1. to fizz. 2. [Colloq.], to fail, esp. after a good start. *n.* 1. a hissing sound. 2. [Colloq.], a failure.
**fjord** (fyôrd), *n.* a fiord.
**Fl,** in *chem.*, fluorine.
**fl.,** 1. *floruit*, [L.], (he or she) flourished. 2. fluid.
**flab·ber·gast** (flab′ẽr-gast′), *v.t.* [? < *flabby* + *aghast*], [Colloq.], to amaze.
**flab·by** (flab′i), *adj.* [-BIER, -BIEST], [< *flap*], 1. limp and soft. 2. weak. **—flab′bi·ness,** *n.*
**flac·cid** (flak′sid), *adj.* [< L. *flaccus*], flabby.
‡**fla·con** (flä′kōn′), *n.* [Fr.], a small bottle with a stopper, for perfume, etc.
**flag** (flag), *n.* [prob. < *flag*, to flutter], 1. a cloth with colors, patterns, etc., used as a symbol of a nation, organization, etc. or as a signal. 2. an iris (flower). *v.t.* [FLAGGED, FLAGGING], 1. to signal as with a flag. 2. to send (a message) by signaling.
**flag** (flag), *n.* [< ON. *flaga*], a flagstone. *v.t.* [FLAGGED, FLAGGING], to pave with flags.
**flag** (flag), *v.i.* [FLAGGED, FLAGGING], [prob. < ME. *flacken*, to flutter], 1. to become limp; droop. 2. to grow weak; tire.
**flag·el·late** (flaj′ə-lāt′), *v.t.* [-LATED, -LATING], [< L. *flagellum*, a whip], to whip; flog. *adj.* having flagella or shaped like a flagellum: also **flag′el·lat′ed. —flag′el·la′tion,** *n.*
**fla·gel·lum** (flə-jel′əm), *n.* [*pl.* -LA (-ə), -LUMS], [L., a whip], in *biology*, a whiplike part serving as an organ of locomotion in bacteria and certain cells.
**flag·on** (flag′ən), *n.* [see FLASK], a container for liquids, usually with a handle, spout, and lid.
**flag′pole′,** *n.* a pole on which a flag is flown: also **flag′staff′.**
**fla·grant** (flā′grənt), *adj.* [< L. *flagrare*, to blaze], glaringly bad; notorious; outrageous. **—fla′gran·cy** (-grən-si), **fla′grance,** *n.*
**flag′ship′,** *n.* the ship that carries the commander of a fleet or squadron.
**flag′stone′,** *n.* a large, flat paving stone.
**flail** (flāl), *n.* [< L. *flagellum*, a whip], an implement used to thresh grain by hand. *v.t.* 1. to thresh with a flail. 2. to beat.
**flair** (flâr), *n.* [< OFr. *flairer*, emit an odor], a natural talent; aptitude; knack.
**flak** (flak), *n.* [G. abbrev.], antiaircraft fire.
**flake** (flāk), *n.* [< ON. *flaki*], 1. a small, soft, thin mass. 2. a chip or peeling. *v.t.* & *v.i.* [FLAKED, FLAKING], 1. to form into flakes. 2. to chip off in flakes. **—flak′y,** *adj.*
**flam·boy·ant** (flam-boi′ənt), *adj.* [< Fr. < L. *flamma*, a flame], 1. flamelike or brilliant. 2. ornate; gaudy. **—flam·boy′ance,** *n.*
**flame** (flām), *n.* [< L. *flamma*], 1. the burning gas of a fire, appearing as a tongue of light. 2. the state of burning with a blaze. 3. a thing like a flame. 4. an intense emotion. 5. [Slang], a sweetheart. *v.i.* [FLAMED, FLAMING], 1. to burst into flame. 2. to act like a flame. 3. to become excited.
**flame′-throw′er,** *n.* a military weapon that shoots flaming liquid.
**fla·min·go** (flə-miŋ′gō), *n.* [*pl.* -GOS, -GOES], [Port. < Sp. *flama*, flame], a tropical wading bird with long legs, and pink or red feathers.
**flam·ma·ble** (flam′ə-b'l), *adj.* easily set on fire; inflammable.
**flange** (flanj), *n.* [prob. < OFr. *flangir*, to turn], a projecting rim on a wheel, etc., as to hold it in place, give it strength, or attach it to something else. *v.t.* [FLANGED, FLANGING], to put a flange on.
**flank** (flaŋk), *n.* [< OFr. *flanc*], 1. the side of an animal between the ribs and the hip. 2. the side of anything. 3. the right or left side of a military force. *v.t.* 1. to be at the side of. 2. to attack, or pass around, the side of (enemy troops). **—flank′er,** *n.*
**flan·nel** (flan′'l), *n.* [prob. < W. *gwlan*, wool], 1. a lightweight woolen cloth. 2. *pl.* clothes made of this cloth. 3. flannelette.
**flan·nel·ette, flan·nel·et** (flan''l-et′), *n.* a soft cotton cloth like flannel.
**flap** (flap), *n.* [ME. *flap(pe)*], 1. anything flat and broad hanging loose from one end. 2. the motion or sound of a swinging flap. 3. a slap. *v.t.* & *v.i.* [FLAPPED, FLAPPING], 1. to strike with something flat. 2. to move back and forth or up and down; flutter.
**flap′jack′,** *n.* a large pancake.
**flap·per** (flap′ẽr), *n.* 1. one that flaps. 2. [Colloq.], in the 1920's, a bold, unconventional young girl.
**flare** (flâr), *v.i.* [FLARED, FLARING], [? < D. *vlederen*, flutter], 1. to blaze brightly and unsteadily. 2. to spread outward, as a bell. *n.* 1. a bright, unsteady blaze. 2. a brief, dazzling signal light. 3. a sudden outburst, as of emotion. 4. a spreading outward. **—flare up** (or **out**), to burst into flame or anger, violence, etc.
**flare′-up′,** *n.* a sudden outburst of flame or of emotion, violence, etc.
**flash** (flash), *v.i.* [ME. *flaschen*, to splash], 1. to send out a sudden, brief light. 2. to sparkle. 3. to come or pass suddenly. *v.t.* 1. to cause to flash. 2. to send (news, etc.) swiftly. *n.* 1. a sudden, brief light. 2. a brief moment. 3. a sudden, brief display. 4. a brief news item sent by radio, etc. 5. a gaudy display. **—flash′er,** *n.*
**flash′-back′,** *n.* an interruption in the continuity of a story, etc. by the narration of some earlier episode.
**flash′bulb′,** *n.* a light bulb that gives a brief, dazzling light, for taking photographs.
**flash′cube′,** *n.* a small rotating cube containing a flashbulb in each of four sides.
**flash flood,** a sudden flood.
**flash′ing,** *n.* sheets of metal used to weatherproof roof joints or edges.
**flash′light′,** *n.* 1. a light that shines in flashes, used for signaling. 2. a portable

electric light, usually operated by a battery.

**flash'y,** *adj.* [-IER, -IEST], 1. dazzling for a little while. 2. gaudy; showy.—**flash'i·ness,** *n.*

**flask** (flask, fläsk), *n.* [< ML. *flasca*, wine bottle], 1. any of various bottles used in laboratories, etc. 2. a small, flat pocket container for liquor, etc.

**flat** (flat), *adj.* [FLATTER, FLATTEST], [< ON. *flatr*], 1. having a smooth, level surface. 2. lying spread out. 3. broad, even, and thin. 4. absolute: as, a *flat* denial. 5. not fluctuating: as, a *flat* rate. 6. tasteless; insipid: as, a *flat* drink. 7. of little interest; dull. 8. emptied of air: as, a *flat* tire. 9. in *music*, below the true pitch. *adv.* 1. in a flat manner or position. 2. exactly. 3. in *music*, below the true pitch. *n.* 1. a flat surface or part. 2. an expanse of level land. 3. a deflated tire. 4. in *music*, *a*) a note one half step below another. *b*) the symbol (♭) for such a note. *v.t. & v.i.* [FLATTED, FLATTING], to make or become flat.—**fall flat,** to arouse no response. —**flat'ness,** *n.*

**flat** (flat), *n.* [< Scot. *flet*, a floor], an apartment or suite of rooms.

**flat'boat',** *n.* a flat-bottomed boat for carrying freight on rivers, etc.

**flat'fish',** *n.* [*pl.* see FISH], a flat-bodied fish with both eyes on the upper side, as the flounder or sole.

**flat'foot',** *n.* 1. a condition of the foot in which the instep arch is flattened. 2. [Slang], a policeman. —**flat'foot'ed,** *adj.*

**flat'i'ron,** *n.* an iron (sense 2).

**flat'ten** (-'n), *v.t. & v.i.* to make or become flat or flatter.

**flat·ter** (flat'ẽr), *v.t.* [prob. < OFr. *flater*, to smooth], 1. to praise insincerely. 2. to try to please, as by praise. 3. to make seem more attractive than is so. 4. to gratify the vanity of. *v.i.* to use flattery.

**flat'ter·y,** *n.* [*pl.* -IES], a flattering; excessive or insincere praise.

**flat·top, flat-top** (flat'top'), *n.* [Slang], an aircraft carrier.

**flat·u·lent** (flach'ə-lənt, -yoo-lənt), *adj.* [ult. < L. *flare*, to blow], 1. having or producing gas in the stomach or intestines. 2. pompous; vain. —**flat'u·lence,** *n.*

**flaunt** (flônt), *v.i. & v.t.* [prob. < ON.], to show off gaudily or impudently.

**fla·vor** (flā'vẽr), *n.* [? ult. < L. *flare*, to blow + *foetor*, stench], 1. that quality of a substance which gives it a characteristic taste. 2. flavoring. 3. characteristic quality. *v.t.* to give flavor to. Also, Brit. sp., **flavour.**

**fla'vor·ing,** *n.* an added essence, extract, etc. that flavors food or drink.

**flaw** (flô), *n.* [prob. < ON. *fla*, break in a cliff], 1. a crack, as in a gem. 2. a defect; fault. *v.t. & v.i.* to make or become faulty.

**flax** (flaks), *n.* [AS. *fleax*], 1. a slender, erect plant with delicate blue flowers: its seed (**flaxseed**) is used to make linseed oil. 2. the fibers of this plant, spun into linen thread.

**flax·en** (flak's'n), *adj.* 1. of or made of flax. 2. pale-yellow.

**flay** (flā), *v.t.* [AS. *flean*], 1. to strip off the skin of. 2. to criticize harshly. —**flay'er,** *n.*

**flea** (flē), *n.* [AS. *fleah*], a small, wingless, jumping insect that is parasitic and bloodsucking.

**flea'bit'ten,** *adj.* 1. bitten by fleas. 2. infested with fleas. 3. wretched; decrepit.

**fleck** (flek), *n.* [ON. *flekkr*], a spot; speck; flake. *v.t.* to spot; speckle. —**flecked,** *adj.*

**fled** (fled), pt. and pp. of **flee.**

**fledge** (flej), *v.i.* [FLEDGED, FLEDGING], [AS. (*un*)*flycge*, (un)fledged], to grow the feathers necessary for flying. *v.t.* to rear (a young bird) until it is able to fly.

**fledg·ling, fledge·ling** (flej'liŋ), *n.* [< ME. *flegge*, fit to fly], 1. a young bird just able to fly. 2. a young, inexperienced person.

**flee** (flē), *v.i. & v.t.* [FLED, FLEEING], [AS. *fleon*], to go swiftly or escape.

**fleece** (flēs), *n.* [AS. *fleos*], the wool covering a sheep or similar animal. *v.t.* [FLEECED, FLEECING], 1. to shear the fleece from. 2. to swindle. —**fleec'er,** *n.*

**fleec'y,** *adj.* [-IER, -IEST], of or like fleece; soft and light. —**fleec'i·ness,** *n.*

**fleet** (flēt), *n.* [AS. *fleotan*, to float], 1. a number of warships under one command. 2. any group of ships, trucks, etc. under one control.

**fleet** (flēt), *adj.* [< AS. *fleotan*, to float], swift; rapid. —**fleet'ness,** *n.*

**fleet'ing,** *adj.* passing swiftly.

**Flem·ish** (flem'ish), *adj.* of Flanders, its people, or their language. *n.* the Low German language of Flanders.

**flesh** (flesh), *n.* [AS. *flæsc*], 1. the soft substance of the body; esp., the muscular tissue. 2. the pulpy part of fruits and vegetables. 3. meat. 4. the body as distinct from the soul. 5. the color of a white person's skin. —**in the flesh,** 1. alive. 2. in person. —**one's (own) flesh and blood,** one's close relatives. —**flesh'y** [-IER, -IEST], *adj.*

**flesh'pot',** *n.* 1. a pot for cooking meat. 2. *pl.* bodily comforts; luxury.

**fleur-de-lis** (flũr'də-lē'), *n.* [*pl.* FLEURS-DE-LIS (-lēz')], [Fr., flower of the lily], 1. the iris. 2. a lilylike emblem, formerly the French royal coat of arms.

**flew** (flōō), pt. of **fly.**

**flex** (fleks), *v.t. & v.i.* [< L. *flectere*, to bend], 1. to bend, as an arm. 2. to contract, as a muscle.

**flex·i·ble** (flek'sə-b'l), *adj.* 1. able to bend without breaking; pliant. 2. easily influenced. 3. adjustable to change. —**flex'i·bil'i·ty,** *n.* —**flex'i·bly,** *adv.*

**flex·ure** (flek'shẽr), *n.* 1. a bending, curving, or flexing. 2. a bend; curve.

**flick** (flik), *n.* [prob. echoic], a light, quick stroke. *v.t.* to strike, throw, etc. with a light, quick stroke.

**flick·er** (flik'ẽr), *v.i.* [AS. *flicorian*], 1. to move with a quick, light, wavering motion. 2. to burn or shine unsteadily. *n.* 1. a flickering. 2. a dart of flame or light.

**fli·er** (flī'ẽr), *n.* 1. a thing that flies. 2. an aviator. 3. a train, etc. with a fast schedule. 4. [Slang], a reckless gamble.

**flight** (flīt), *n.* [AS. *flyht*], 1. the act, manner, or power of flying. 2. the distance flown. 3. a group of things flying together. 4. an airplane scheduled to fly a certain trip. 5. a trip by airplane. 6. a soaring above the ordinary: as, a *flight* of fancy. 7. a set of stairs, esp. between landings.

**flight** (flīt), *n.* [< AS. *fleon*, flee], a fleeing, as from danger. —**put to flight,** to force to flee.

**flight'less,** *adj.* not able to fly.

**flight'y,** *adj.* [-IER, -IEST], given to sudden whims; frivolous. —**flight'i·ness,** *n.*

**flim·sy** (flim'zi), *adj.* [-SIER, -SIEST], [prob. < W. *llymsi*], 1. easily broken or damaged; frail. 2. ineffectual: as, a *flimsy* excuse. *n.* a thin kind of paper. —**flim'si·ness,** *n.*

**flinch** (flinch), *v.i.* [< OFr. *flenchir*], to draw back from a blow or anything difficult or painful. *n.* a flinching.

**fling** (fliŋ), *v.t.* [FLUNG, FLINGING], [prob. < ON.], 1. to throw, esp. with force; hurl. 2. to put abruptly or violently. 3. to move (one's arms, legs, etc.) suddenly. *n.* 1. a flinging. 2. a brief time of wild actions. 3. a spirited dance. 4. [Colloq.], a try.

**flint** (flint), *n.* [AS.], a very hard, grayish or brown quartz, which produces sparks when struck against steel. —**flint'y,** *adj.*

**flip** (flip), *v.t.* [FLIPPED, FLIPPING], [echoic], 1. to toss with a quick jerk; flick. 2. to snap (a coin, etc.) into the air with the thumb. *v.i.* to move jerkily. *n.* a flipping. *adj.*

[FLIPPER, FLIPPEST], [Colloq.], flippant; pert.
**flip** (flip), *n.* [prob. < *flip*, to toss], a sweetened drink of beer, cider, etc.
**flip'pant** (-ənt), *adj.* [prob. < *flip*], frivolous and disrespectful; saucy. —**flip'pan·cy,** *n.*
**flip·per** (flip'ẽr), *n.* a broad, flat limb adapted for swimming, as in seals.
**flirt** (flũrt), *v.t.* [? echoic], to move quickly: as, the bird *flirted* its tail. *v.i.* 1. to make love without serious intentions. 2. to trifle; play: as, to *flirt* with an idea. *n.* 1. a quick, jerky movement. 2. one who plays at love.
**flir·ta·tion** (flũr-tā'shən), *n.* a superficial love affair. —**flir·ta'tious,** *adj.*
**flit** (flit), *v.i.* [FLITTED, FLITTING], [ON. *flytja*], to move lightly and rapidly.
**float** (flōt), *n.* [< AS. *fleotan*, to float], 1. anything that stays on the surface of a liquid, as a raft, a cork on a fishing line, etc. 2. a low, flat vehicle decorated for exhibit in a parade. *v.i.* 1. to stay on the surface of a liquid. 2. to drift gently on water, in air, etc. 3. to move about vaguely. *v.t.* 1. to cause to float. 2. to put into circulation: as, to *float* a bond issue.
**flock** (flok), *n.* [AS. *flocc*], 1. a group of certain animals, as birds, sheep, etc., living or feeding together. 2. a group of people or things. *v.i.* to assemble or travel in a flock.
**floe** (flō), *n.* [ON. *flo*, layer], a large field or sheet of floating ice.
**flog** (flog, flôg), *v.t.* [FLOGGED, FLOGGING], [? < L. *flagellare*], to beat with a stick, whip, etc. —**flog'ger,** *n.*
**flood** (flud), *n.* [AS. *flod*], 1. an overflowing of water on land usually dry. 2. the rising tide: also **flood tide.** 3. a great outpouring, as of words. *v.t.* to cover or fill as with a flood. *v.i.* to gush out in a flood. —**the Flood,** in the *Bible*, the great flood in Noah's time.
**flood'light',** *n.* 1. a lamp that casts a broad beam of bright light. 2. such a beam of light. *v.t.* [-LIGHTED or -LIT, -LIGHTING], to illuminate by a floodlight.
**floor** (flôr), *n.* [AS. *flor*], 1. the inside bottom surface of a room. 2. any corresponding surface, as of the ocean. 3. a story in a building. 4. the right to speak in an assembly. *v.t.* 1. to furnish with a floor. 2. to knock down. 3. [Colloq.], to defeat; puzzle.
**floor'ing,** *n.* 1. a floor or floors. 2. material for making a floor.
**floor show,** an entertainment presented in a restaurant or night club.
**floor'walk'er,** *n.* a person employed by a department store to direct customers, supervise sales, etc.
**flop** (flop), *v.t.* [FLOPPED, FLOPPING], [var. of *flap*], to flap or throw noisily and clumsily. *v.i.* 1. to move, drop, or flap around loosely or clumsily. 2. [Colloq.], to fail. *n.* 1. a flopping. 2. the sound of flopping. 3. [Colloq.], a failure. —**flop'py** [-PIER, -PIEST], *adj.*
**flop'house',** *n.* a cheap hotel.
**flo·ra** (flôr'ə), *n.* [L. < *flos*, a flower], the plants of a specified region or time.
**flo·ral** (flôr'əl), *adj.* of, made of, or like flowers. —**flo'ral·ly,** *adv.*
**flo·res·cence** (flô-res''ns), *n.* [< L. *florere*, to bloom], 1. a blooming. 2. the condition or period of blooming. —**flo·res'cent,** *adj.*
**flo·ret** (flôr'it), *n.* [< L. *flos*, a flower], 1. a small flower. 2. any of the small flowers making up the head of a composite flower.
**flor·id** (flôr'id), *adj.* [< L. *flos*, a flower], 1. ruddy: said of the complexion. 2. ornate; showy; gaudy. —**flor'id·ly,** *adv.*
**flor·in** (flôr'in), *n.* [< L. *flos*, a flower], any of various European silver or gold coins.
**flo·rist** (flôr'ist), *n.* [< L. *flos*, a flower], one who grows or sells flowers.
**floss** (flôs, flos), *n.* [prob. < L. *floccus*, tuft of wool], 1. the short, downy waste fibers of silk. 2. soft, untwisted silk fibers, used in embroidery. 3. a soft, silky substance like this. —**floss'y** [-IER, -IEST], *adj.*
**flo·ta·tion** (flō-tā'shən), *n.* 1. a floating or launching. 2. the act of financing a business by selling an entire issue of bonds, etc.
**flo·til·la** (flō-til'ə), *n.* [Sp., dim. of *flota*, a fleet], 1. a small fleet. 2. a fleet of boats or small ships.
**flot·sam** (flot'səm), *n.* [< AS. *flotian*, to float], the wreckage of a ship or its cargo found floating on the sea: also **flotsam and jetsam.**
**flounce** (flouns), *v.i.* [FLOUNCED, FLOUNCING], [prob. < Scand.], to move with quick, flinging motions of the body, as in anger. *n.* a flouncing.
**flounce** (flouns), *n.* [< OFr. *froncir*, to wrinkle], a wide ruffle sewed to a skirt, sleeve, etc. *v.t.* [FLOUNCED, FLOUNCING], to trim with a flounce.
**floun·der** (floun'dẽr), *v.i.* [prob. < *founder*], 1. to struggle awkwardly, as in deep snow. 2. to speak or act in an awkward, confused manner.
**floun·der** (floun'dẽr), *n.* [< OFr. *flondre*], any of various flatfishes caught for food, as the halibut.
**flour** (flour), *n.* [orig., flower (i.e., best) of meal], 1. a fine, powdery substance produced by grinding and sifting grain. 2. any finely powdered substance. *v.t.* to put flour in or on. —**flour'y,** *adj.*
**flour·ish** (flũr'ish), *v.i.* [< L. *flos*, a flower], 1. to grow vigorously; thrive. 2. to be at the peak of development, etc. *v.t.* to brandish (a sword, etc.). *n.* 1. anything done in a showy way. 2. a brandishing. 3. decorative lines in writing. 4. a musical fanfare.
**flout** (flout), *v.t. & v.i.* [? < ME. *flouten*, play the flute], to mock or scorn. *n.* a scornful act or remark.
**flow** (flō), *v.i.* [AS. *flowan*], 1. to move as a liquid does. 2. to move gently and smoothly. 3. to proceed; issue. 4. to hang loose: as, *flowing* hair. *v.t.* to overflow; flood. *n.* 1. a flowing. 2. the rate of flow. 3. anything that flows. 4. the rising of the tide.
**flow·er** (flou'ẽr, flour), *n.* [< L. *flos*], 1. the part of a plant with the reproductive organs; blossom. 2. a plant cultivated for its blossoms. 3. the best or finest part. *v.i.* 1. to produce blossoms. 2. to reach the best stage. —**in flower,** flowering.
**flow'er·pot',** *n.* a container to hold earth for a plant to grow in.
**flow'er·y,** *adj.* [-IER, -IEST], 1. covered or decorated with flowers. 2. full of ornate expressions and fine words.
**flown** (flōn), pp. of **fly.**
**flu** (flo͞o), *n.* influenza.
**fluc·tu·ate** (fluk'cho͞o-āt'), *v.i.* [-ATED, -ATING], [< L. *fluctus*, a wave], to be continually varying irregularly. —**fluc'tu·a'tion,** *n.*
**flue** (flo͞o), *n.* [? < OFr. *flue*, a flowing], a shaft for the passage of smoke, hot air, etc., as in a chimney.
**flu·ent** (flo͞o'ənt), *adj.* [< L. *fluere*, to flow], 1. flowing smoothly. 2. able to write or speak easily, expressively, etc. —**flu'en·cy,** *n.* —**flu'ent·ly,** *adv.*
**fluff** (fluf), *n.* [? < rare *flue*, soft mass & *puff*], 1. soft, light down. 2. a loose, soft mass, as of fur. *v.t.* 1. to shake or pat until loose and fluffy. 2. to bungle (one's lines), as in acting.
**fluf·fy** (fluf'i), *adj.* [-FIER, -FIEST], like or covered with fluff; soft and light.
**flu·id** (flo͞o'id), *adj.* [< L. *fluere*, to flow], 1. that can flow as a liquid or gas does. 2. that can change rapidly or easily. *n.* a liquid or gas. —**flu·id'i·ty,** *n.* —**flu'id·ly,** *adv.*
**fluke** (flo͝ok), *n.* [AS. *floc*], any of a number of flat, parasitic worms.
**fluke** (flo͝ok), *n.* [< ?], 1. any of the pointed

blades on an anchor, which catch in the ground. 2. a barb of an arrow, harpoon, etc. 3. [Slang], a stroke of luck.

**flume** (flo͞om), *n.* [< L. *flumen*, river], an inclined chute for carrying water to transport logs, furnish power, etc.

**flung** (fluŋ), pt. and pp. of **fling.**

**flunk** (fluŋk), *v.t. & v.i.* [< ?], [Colloq.], to fail, as in schoolwork.

**flunk·y** (fluŋ′ki), *n.* [*pl.* -IES], [orig. Scot.], 1. a liveried manservant. 2. a toady. Also **flunk′ey** [*pl.* -EYS].

**flu·o·res·cence** (flo͞o′ə-res′′ns), *n.* [ult. < L. *fluor*, flux], 1. the property some substances have of producing light when acted upon by radiant energy. 2. the light so produced. **—flu′o·res′cent,** *adj.*

**fluorescent lamp,** a glass tube coated on the inside with a fluorescent substance that gives off light **(fluorescent light)** when acted upon by a stream of electrons.

**flu·o·ri·date** (flo͞o′ə-ri-dāt′), *v.t.* [-DATED, -DATING], to add fluorides to (a water supply) in order to reduce tooth decay. **—flu′o·ri·da′tion,** *n.*

**flu·o·ride** (flo͞o′ə-rīd′), *n.* any of various compounds of fluorine.

**flu·o·rine** (flo͞o′ə-rēn′, -rin), *n.* [< L. *fluor*, flux], a corrosive, greenish-yellow, gaseous chemical element: symbol, F.

**flu·o·ro·scope** (floor′ə-skōp′), *n.* a machine for examining internal structures by viewing the shadows cast on a fluorescent screen by objects through which X rays are directed.

**flur·ry** (flũr′i), *n.* [*pl.* -RIES], [prob. echoic], 1. a sudden gust of wind, rain, or snow. 2. a sudden commotion. *v.t.* [-RIED, -RYING], to confuse; agitate.

**flush** (flush), *v.i.* [blend of *flash*, *v.* & ME. *flusschen*, fly up suddenly], 1. to blush. 2. to glow. 3. to start up from cover: said of birds. *v.t.* 1. to wash out with a flow of water. 2. to make blush or glow. 3. to excite. 4. to drive (birds) from cover. *n.* 1. a rapid flow, as of water. 2. a sudden, vigorous growth. 3. sudden excitement. 4. a blush; glow. 5. a sudden feeling of heat, as in a fever. *adj.* 1. well supplied, as with money. 2. abundant. 3. level or even (*with*). 4. direct; full.

**flush** (flush), *n.* [< L. *fluere*, to flow], a hand of cards all in the same suit.

**flus·ter** (flus′tẽr), *v.t. & v.i.* [prob. < ON.], to make or be confused. *n.* a flustered state.

**flute** (flo͞ot), *n.* [< Pr. *flăut*], 1. a high-pitched wind instrument consisting of a long, slender tube with finger holes and keys. 2. a groove in the shaft of a column. **—flut′ed,** *adj.* **—flut′ing,** *n.* **—flut′ist,** *n.*

**flut·ter** (flut′ẽr), *v.i.* [< AS. *fleotan*, to float], 1. to flap the wings rapidly, without flying. 2. to wave, move, or beat rapidly and irregularly. *v.t.* to cause to flutter. *n.* 1. a fluttering movement. 2. an excited or confused state. **—flut′ter·y,** *adj.*

**flu·vi·al** (flo͞o′vi-əl), *adj.* [< L. *fluere*, to flow], of, found in, or produced by a river.

**flux** (fluks), *n.* [< L. *fluere*, to flow], 1. a flowing. 2. a coming in of the tide. 3. a continual change. 4. any abnormal discharge from the body. 5. a substance used to help metals to fuse, as in soldering.

**fly** (flī), *v.i.* [FLEW, FLOWN, FLYING], [AS. *fleogan*], 1. to move through the air by using wings, as a bird, or in an aircraft. 2. to wave or float in the air. 3. to move swiftly. 4. to flee. 5. [FLIED, FLYING], in *baseball*, to hit a fly. *v.t.* 1. to cause to float in the air. 2. to operate (an aircraft). 3. to flee from. *n.* [*pl.* FLIES], 1. a flap that conceals buttons, etc. in a garment. 2. a flap serving as a door of a tent. 3. in *baseball*, a ball batted high in the air. **—fly into,** to have a violent outburst of. **—let fly (at),** 1. to hurl (at). 2. to direct a verbal attack (at). **—on the fly,** [Slang], while in a hurry.

**fly** (flī), *n.* [*pl.* FLIES], [AS. *fleoge*], 1. any of a large group of insects with two transparent wings; esp., the housefly. 2. an artificial fly used as fishing bait.

**fly′-by-night′,** *adj.* financially unsound. *n.* an absconding debtor.

**fly′er,** *n.* a flier.

**fly′ing,** *adj.* 1. that flies or can fly. 2. moving swiftly. 3. of or for aircraft or aviators.

**flying fish,** a fish with winglike fins used in leaping through the air.

**flying saucer,** any of various unidentified flying objects reported seen, variously regarded as light phenomena, missiles, etc.

**fly′leaf′,** *n.* [*pl.* -LEAVES], a blank leaf at the beginning or end of a book.

**fly′pa′per,** *n.* a sticky paper set out to catch flies: also **fly paper.**

**fly′weight′,** *n.* a boxer who weighs 112 pounds or less.

**fly′wheel′,** *n.* a heavy wheel for regulating the speed of the machine to which it is attached.

**FM,** frequency modulation.

**foal** (fōl), *n.* [AS. *fola*], a young horse, mule, etc.; colt or filly. *v.t. & v.i.* to give birth to (a foal).

**foam** (fōm), *n.* [AS. *fam*], 1. the froth formed on liquids by violent shaking, etc. 2. something like foam, as frothy saliva. *v.i.* to froth. **—foam at the mouth,** to rage. **—foam′y** [-IER, -IEST], *adj.*

**fob** (fob), *n.* [prob. < dial. G. *fuppe*, a pocket], 1. a short ribbon or chain attached to a pocket watch. 2. any ornament worn on such a chain, etc.

**F.O.B., f.o.b.,** free on board.

**fo·cal** (fō′k'l), *adj.* of or placed at a focus.

**focal distance,** the distance from the optical center of a lens to the point where the light rays converge.

**fo·cus** (fō′kəs), *n.* [*pl.* -CUSES, -CI (-sī)], [L., hearth], 1. the point where rays of light, heat, etc. come together; specif., the point where rays of reflected or refracted light meet. 2. focal distance. 3. an adjustment of this distance to make a clear image: as, move the lens into *focus*. 4. any center of activity, attention, etc. *v.t.* [-CUSED or -CUSSED, -CUSING or -CUSSING], 1. to bring into focus. 2. to adjust the focal distance of (the eye, a lens, etc.) so as to produce a clear image. 3. to concentrate. **—in focus,** clear; distinct. **—out of focus,** indistinct; blurred.

**fod·der** (fod′ẽr), *n.* [< AS. *foda*, food], coarse food for cattle, horses, etc., as hay.

**foe** (fō), *n.* [AS. *fah*, hostile], an enemy; opponent.

**foe·tus** (fē′təs), *n.* a fetus. **—foe′tal,** *adj.*

**fog** (fôg, fog), *n.* [< *foggy*], 1. a large mass of water vapor condensed to fine particles, just above the earth's surface. 2. a state of mental confusion. *v.i.* [FOGGED, FOGGING], to make or become foggy.

**fog′gy,** *adj.* [-GIER, -GIEST], [orig., covered with *fog* (long, rank grass)], 1. full of fog; misty. 2. dim; blurred. 3. confused.

**fog′horn′,** *n.* a horn blown to give warning to ships in a fog.

**fo·gy** (fō′gi), *n.* [*pl.* -GIES], [< ?], one who is old-fashioned in ideas and actions: also **fo′gey** [*pl.* -GEYS].

**foi·ble** (foi′b'l), *n.* [< Fr. *faible*, feeble], a small weakness in character; frailty.

**foil** (foil), *v.t.* [< OFr. *f(o)uler*, trample], to baffle; thwart. *n.* a long, thin, blunted fencing sword.

**foil** (foil), *n.* [< L. *folium*, a leaf], 1. a very thin sheet of metal: as, gold *foil*. 2. a person or thing that sets off another by contrast.

**foist** (foist), ***v.t.*** [prob. < dial. D. *vuisten*, to hide in the hand], to impose by fraud; palm off.

**fold** (fōld), ***v.t.*** [AS. *faldan*], 1. to double (material) up on itself. 2. to draw together and intertwine: as, *fold* your arms. 3. to embrace. 4. to wrap up; envelop. ***v.i.*** 1. to be or become folded. 2. [Slang], to fail, as a play, business, etc. ***n.*** a folded layer.

**fold** (fōld), ***n.*** [AS. *falod*], 1. a pen for sheep. 2. a flock of sheep. 3. *a*) the members of a church. *b*) a church.

**-fold,** [AS. *-feald*], a suffix meaning: 1. *having* (a specified number of) *parts.* 2. (a specified number of) *times as many* or *as much,* as in *tenfold.*

**fold'er,** ***n.*** 1. a sheet of heavy paper folded as a holder for papers. 2. a booklet of folded, unstitched sheets.

**fo·li·age** (fō'li-ij), ***n.*** [< L. *folia*], leaves, as of a plant or tree.

**fo·li·ate** (fō'li-āt'; *for adj., usually* -it), ***v.i.*** [-ATED, -ATING], [< L. *folium*, leaf], to send out leaves. ***adj.*** having leaves.

**fo'li·a'tion,** ***n.*** 1. a being in leaf. 2. the consecutive numbering of leaves of a book.

**fo·li·o** (fō'li-ō), ***n.*** [*pl.* -OS], [< L. *folium*, leaf], 1. a large sheet of paper folded once. 2. a book (the largest regular size) made of sheets so folded. 3. the number of a page in a book. ***adj.*** having sheets folded once. ***v.t.*** [-OED, -OING], to number the pages of (a book, etc.).

**folk** (fōk), ***n.*** [*pl.* FOLK, FOLKS], [AS. *folc*], 1. a people; nation. 2. *pl.* people; persons. ***adj.*** of the common people. **—(one's) folks,** [Colloq.], (one's) family.

**folk'lore',** ***n.*** the traditional beliefs, legends, etc. of a people.

**folk'sy** (-si), ***adj.*** [Colloq.], 1. of or like the common people. 2. sociable.

**fol·li·cle** (fol'i-k'l), ***n.*** [< L. *follis*, bellows], any small sac, gland, etc.: as, a hair *follicle.*

**fol·low** (fol'ō), ***v.t.*** [AS. *folgian*], 1. to come or go after. 2. to chase. 3. to go along: as, *follow* the road. 4. to take up, as a trade. 5. to result from. 6. to take as a model; imitate. 7. to obey. 8. to watch or listen to closely. 9. to understand. ***v.i.*** 1. to come or go after something else in place, time, etc. 2. to result. **—follow out** (or **up**), to carry out fully. **—follow through,** to continue and finish a stroke or action.

**fol'low·er,** ***n.*** one that follows; specif., *a*) one who follows another's teachings; disciple. *b*) an attendant.

**fol'low·ing,** ***adj.*** that follows; next after. ***n.*** a group of followers.

**fol'low-up',** ***n.*** a letter, visit, etc. that follows as a repetition or addition.

**fol·ly** (fol'i), ***n.*** [*pl.* -LIES], [see FOOL], 1. a lack of sense; a being foolish. 2. a foolish action or belief.

**fo·ment** (fō-ment'), ***v.t.*** [< L. *fovere*, keep warm], to stir up; arouse; incite. **—fo'men·ta'tion,** ***n.***

**fond** (fond), ***adj.*** [< ME. *fonnen*, be foolish], 1. foolishly tender; doting. 2. loving; tender: as, *fond* caresses. **—fond of,** having a liking for. **—fond'ly,** ***adv.*** **—fond'ness,** ***n.***

**fon·dant** (fon'dənt), ***n.*** [Fr. < *fondere*, melt], a soft, creamy candy made of sugar.

**fon·dle** (fon'd'l), ***v.t.*** [-DLED, -DLING], [< *fond*], to caress; pet.

**fon·due** (fon'dōō), ***n.*** [Fr. < *fondre*, melt], a dish made of cheese, eggs, etc.

**font** (font), ***n.*** [< L. *fons*, spring], 1. a bowl to hold the water used in baptism. 2. a basin for holy water. 3. a source; origin.

**font** (font), ***n.*** [see FOUND (to cast)], in *printing*, a complete assortment of type in one size or style.

**food** (fōōd), ***n.*** [AS. *foda*], 1. any substance, esp. a solid, taken in by a plant or animal to enable it to live and grow. 2. anything that nourishes: as, *food* for thought.

**food'stuff',** ***n.*** any material made into or used as food.

**fool** (fōōl), ***n.*** [< L. *follis*, windbag], 1. a silly person; simpleton. 2. a jester. 3. a dupe. ***v.i.*** 1. to act like a fool. 2. to joke. ***v.t.*** trick; deceive. **—fool around,** [Colloq.], trifle. **—fool away,** [Colloq.], to squander. **—fool with,** [Colloq.], to meddle with.— **fool'er·y** [*pl.* -IES], ***n.***

**fool'har'dy,** ***adj.*** [-DIER, -DIEST], foolishly daring; rash. **—fool'har'di·ness,** ***n.***

**fool'ish,** ***adj.*** silly; unwise; absurd.

**fool'proof',** ***adj.*** so harmless, simple, etc. as not to be mishandled, injured, etc. even by a fool.

**fools·cap** (fōōlz'kap'), ***n.*** [from a watermark of a jester's cap], a size of writing paper varying from 12 by 15 inches to 13½ by 17 inches.

**foot** (foot), ***n.*** [*pl.* FEET], [AS. *fot*], 1. the end part of the leg, on which one stands. 2. the base or bottom: as, the *foot* of a page. 3. a measure of length, equal to 12 inches: symbol, ′. 4. infantry. 5. a group of syllables serving as a unit of meter in verse. ***v.t.*** 1. to add up (a column of figures). 2. [Colloq.], to pay (costs, etc.). **—foot it,** [Colloq.], to dance or walk. **—on foot,** walking. **—put one's foot down,** [Colloq.], to be firm. **—under foot,** in the way.

**foot'age** (-ij), ***n.*** measurement in feet.

**foot'-and-mouth' disease,** a contagious disease of cattle, deer, etc., characterized by fever and blisters in the mouth and around the hoofs.

**foot'ball',** ***n.*** 1. a field game played with an inflated leather ball by two teams. 2. the ball used.

**foot'-can'dle,** ***n.*** a unit of illumination, equal to the amount of direct light thrown by one standard candle on a surface one foot away.

**foot'fall'** (-fôl'), ***n.*** a footstep.

**foot'hill',** ***n.*** a low hill at the foot of a mountain or mountain range.

**foot'hold',** ***n.*** 1. a place for the feet, as in climbing. 2. a secure position.

**foot'ing,** ***n.*** 1. a secure placing of the feet. 2. a foothold. 3. a secure position or basis. 4. a basis for relationship.

**foot'lights',** ***n.pl.*** a row of lights along the front of a stage floor.

**foot'-loose'** (-lōōs'), ***adj.*** free to go where or do as one likes.

**foot'man** (-mən), ***n.*** [*pl.* -MEN], a manservant who waits on table, opens the door, etc.

**foot'note',** ***n.*** a note of comment or reference at the bottom of a page.

**foot'path',** ***n.*** a narrow path for use by pedestrians only.

**foot'-pound',** ***n.*** a unit of energy, equal to the amount of energy required to raise a one-pound weight a distance of one foot.

**foot'print',** ***n.*** a mark left by a foot.

**foot'sore',** ***adj.*** having sore or tender feet, as from much walking.

**foot'step',** ***n.*** 1. the distance covered in a step. 2. the sound of a step. 3. a footprint.

**foot'stool',** ***n.*** a low stool for supporting the feet of a seated person.

**foot'work',** ***n.*** the manner of using the feet, as in boxing, dancing, tennis, etc.

**fop** (fop), ***n.*** [ME. *foppe*, a fool], a man who pays too much attention to his clothes, appearance, etc. **—fop'per·y** [*pl.* -IES], ***n.*** **—fop'pish,** ***adj.*** **—fop'pish·ly,** ***adv.***

**for** (fôr, fẽr), ***prep.*** [< AS. *fore*, before], 1. in place of: as, use blankets *for* coats. 2. in the interest of: as, his agent acted *for* him. 3. in favor of: as, vote *for* her. 4. in honor of: as, the banquet was *for* him. 5. with the purpose or object of: as, a gun *for* protection. 6. in search of: as, look *for* his dog. 7. meant to be received by: as, flowers *for* a girl. 8. suitable to: as, a room *for* sleeping. 9. with a feeling toward: as, an ear *for* music. 10. in its effect on: as, milk is good *for* you. 11. as being: as, we left him *for* dead. 12. considering the nature of: as, it is cool *for* July. 13. because of: as, he cried *for* pain. 14. to the length, amount, or duration of. 15. at the price of: as, two *for* a dollar. ***conj.*** because.

**for-**, [AS.], a prefix meaning *away, apart, off*, as in *forbid, forgo*.

**for·age** (fôr′ij, for′-), ***n.*** [< Frank. *fodr*, food], 1. food for domestic animals. 2. a search for food. ***v.i.*** [-AGED, -AGING], to search for food. ***v.t.*** to get or take food from; raid.

**fo·ra·men** (fō-rā′mən), ***n.*** [*pl.* -MENS, -MINA (-ram′i-nə)], [< L. *forare*, to bore], a small opening, esp. in a bone.

**for·ay** (fôr′ā, for′ā), ***v.t. & v.i.*** [< OFr. *forrer*, to forage], to plunder. ***n.*** a raid, as for spoils.

**for·bear** (fôr-bâr′), ***v.t.*** [-BORE, -BORNE, -BEARING], [see FOR- & BEAR (to carry)], to refrain from (doing, saying, etc.). ***v.i.*** 1. to refrain or abstain. 2. to control oneself.

**for·bear** (fôr′bâr′), ***n.*** a forebear.

**for·bear′ance,** ***n.*** 1. the act of forbearing. 2. self-restraint; patient restraint.

**for·bid** (fẽr-bid′, fôr-), ***v.t.*** [-BADE (-bad′) or -BAD, -BIDDEN, -BIDDING], [see FOR- & BID], to rule against; prohibit; not permit.

**for·bid′ding,** ***adj.*** looking dangerous or disagreeable; frightening. **—for·bid′ding·ly,** ***adv.***

**force** (fôrs), ***n.*** [< L. *fortis*, strong], 1. strength; power. 2. physical coercion against a person or thing. 3. the power to control, persuade, etc.; effectiveness. 4. military power. 5. any group of people organized for some activity: as, a sales *force*. ***v.t.*** [FORCED, FORCING], 1. to make do something by force; compel. 2. to break open, into, or through by force. 3. to take by force; extort. 4. to impose as by force (with *on* or *upon*). 5. to produce as by force: as, she *forced* a smile. 6. to cause (plants, etc.) to develop faster by artificial means. **—in force,** 1. in full strength. 2. in effect; valid.

**forced** (fôrst), ***adj.*** 1. compulsory: as, *forced* labor. 2. not natural; strained: as, a *forced* smile. **—forc·ed·ly** (fôr′sid-li), ***adv.***

**force′ful** (-fəl), ***adj.*** full of force; powerful; vigorous; effective. **—force′ful·ly,** ***adv.***

**for·ceps** (fôr′səps, -seps), ***n.*** [*pl.* -CEPS], [L. < *formus*, hot + *capere*, take], small tongs or pincers for grasping, pulling, etc.

**for·ci·ble** (fôr′sə-b'l), ***adj.*** 1. done by force. 2. having force. **—for′ci·bly,** ***adv.***

**ford** (fôrd), ***n.*** [AS.], a shallow place in a stream, etc. that can be crossed by walking. ***v.t.*** to cross at a ford. **—ford′a·ble,** ***adj.***

**fore** (fôr), ***adv. & adj.*** [AS.], at, in, or toward the front part, as of a ship. ***n.*** the front. ***interj.*** in *golf*, a shout warning those ahead that one is about to drive the ball.

**fore-**, [AS.], a prefix meaning: 1. *before in time, place*, etc., as in *forenoon*. 2. *the front part of*, as in *forearm*.

**fore′-and-aft′,** ***adj.*** from the bow to the stern; set lengthwise, as a rig.

**fore′arm′,** ***n.*** the part of the arm between the elbow and the wrist.

**fore·arm′,** ***v.t.*** to arm in advance.

**fore′bear′** (-bâr′), ***n.*** [< *fore* + *be* + *-er*], an ancestor: also sp. **forbear.**

**fore·bode′** (-bōd′), ***v.t. & v.i.*** [-BODED, -BODING], [< AS.], 1. to foretell; predict. 2. to have a presentiment of (something evil). **—fore·bod′ing,** ***n.***

**fore′cast′,** ***v.t.*** [-CAST or -CASTED, -CASTING], 1. to foresee. 2. to predict; prophesy. 3. to serve as a prediction of. ***n.*** a prediction.

**fore·cas·tle** (fōk′s'l, fôr′kas′'l, -käs′-), ***n.*** 1. the upper deck of a ship in front of the foremast. 2. the front part of a merchant ship, where the sailors' quarters are located.

**fore·close** (fôr-klōz′), ***v.t. & v.i.*** [-CLOSED, -CLOSING], [<OFr. *fors*, outside + *clore*, to close], to take away the right to redeem (a mortgage, etc.). **—fore·clo′sure** (-zhẽr), ***n.***

**fore·doom′,** ***v.t.*** to doom in advance.

**fore′fa′ther,** ***n.*** an ancestor.

**fore′fin′ger,** ***n.*** the finger nearest the thumb.

**fore′foot′,** ***n.*** [*pl.* -FEET], either of the front feet of an animal.

**fore′front′,** ***n.*** 1. the extreme front. 2. the position of most activity, importance, etc.

**fore·go′,** ***v.t. & v.i.*** [-WENT, -GONE, -GOING], 1. to precede. 2. to forgo.

**fore′go′ing,** ***adj.*** preceding; previously said, written, etc.

**fore·gone′,** ***adj.*** 1. previous. 2. previously determined.

**fore′ground′,** ***n.*** the part of a scene, etc. nearest the viewer.

**fore′hand′,** ***adj.*** made with the palm of the hand forward, as a stroke in tennis. ***n.*** a forehand stroke.

**fore′hand′ed,** ***adj.*** 1. making provision for the future; thrifty. 2. done beforehand.

**fore·head** (fôr′id, for′əd, fôr′hed′), ***n.*** the part of the face between the eyebrows and the hairline.

**for·eign** (fôr′in, for′ən), ***adj.*** [< L. *foras*, out-of-doors], 1. situated outside one's own country, locality, etc. 2. of, from, or having to do with other countries. 3. not characteristic or belonging.**—for′eign·ness,** ***n.***

**for′eign-born′,** ***adj.*** born in another country.

**for′eign·er,** ***n.*** a person born in another country; alien.

**fore·know′,** ***v.t.*** [-KNEW, -KNOWN, -KNOWING], to know beforehand. **—fore′knowl′edge** (-nol′ij), ***n.***

**fore′leg′,** ***n.*** either of the front legs of an animal.

**fore′lock′,** ***n.*** a lock of hair growing just above the forehead.

**fore′man** (-mən), ***n.*** [*pl.* -MEN], 1. the chairman of a jury. 2. a man in charge of a group of workers, as in a factory.

**fore′mast′,** ***n.*** the mast nearest the bow of a ship.

**fore′most′** (-mōst′, -məst), ***adj.*** first in place, time, rank, etc. ***adv.*** first.

**fore′named′,** ***adj.*** named before.

**fore′noon′,** ***n.*** the time from sunrise to noon.

**fo·ren·sic** (fə-ren′sik), ***adj.*** [< L. *forum*, market place], of or suitable for public debate. **—fo·ren′si·cal·ly,** ***adv.***

**fore′or·dain′,** ***v.t.*** to ordain beforehand; predestine. **—fore′or·di·na′tion** (-d'n-ā′shən), **fore′or·dain′ment,** ***n.***

**fore′paw′,** ***n.*** a front paw.

**fore′quar′ter,** ***n.*** the front half of a side of beef, pork, etc.

**fore′run′ner,** ***n.*** 1. a herald. 2. a sign that tells or warns of something to follow. 3. a predecessor; ancestor.

**fore′sail′** (-sāl′, -s'l), ***n.*** the main sail on the foremast.

**fore·see′,** ***v.t.*** [-SAW, -SEEN, -SEEING], to see or know beforehand. **—fore·see′a·ble,** ***adj.***

**fore·shad′ow,** ***v.t.*** to indicate or suggest beforehand; presage. **—fore·shad′ow·er,** ***n.***

**fore·short′en,** ***v.t.*** in *drawing, painting*, etc., to shorten some lines of (an object) to give the illusion of proper relative size.

**fore·show′,** ***v.t.*** [-SHOWED, -SHOWN or -SHOWED, -SHOWING], to show or indicate beforehand; foretell.

**fore′sight′,** ***n.*** 1. *a*) a foreseeing. *b*) the power to foresee. 2. prudent regard or provision for the future. **—fore′sight′ed,** ***adj.***

**fore′skin′,** ***n.*** the fold of skin that covers the end of the penis.

**for·est** (fôr′ist, for′-), ***n.*** [< L. *foris*, out-of-

doors], a large tract of land covered with trees; woodland. *adj.* of or in a forest. *v.t.* to plant with trees. —**for′est·ed,** *adj.*
**fore·stall** (fôr-stôl′), *v.t.* [AS. *foresteall*, ambush], 1. to prevent by doing something beforehand. 2. to act in advance of.
**for′est·ry,** *n.* the science of planting and taking care of forests.
**fore′taste′,** *n.* a preliminary taste; anticipation.
**fore·tell′,** *v.t.* [-TOLD, -TELLING], to tell or indicate beforehand; prophesy; predict.
**fore′thought′,** *n.* 1. a thinking or planning beforehand. 2. foresight; prudence.
**fore·to·ken** (fôr′tō′kən), *n.* a prophetic sign; omen. *v.t.* (fôr-tō′kən), to foreshadow.
**for·ev·er** (fẽr-ev′ẽr, fôr-), *adv.* 1. for always; endlessly. 2. always; at all times. Also **for·ev′er·more′.**
**fore·warn,** *v.t.* to warn beforehand.
**fore′word′,** *n.* a brief or simple preface.
**for·feit** (fôr′fit), *n.* [< OFr. *forfaire*, transgress], 1. a fine or penalty for some crime, fault, or neglect. 2. the act of paying a forfeit. *adj.* lost or taken away as a forfeit. *v.t.* to lose or be deprived of as a forfeit.
**for′fei·ture** (-fi-chẽr), *n.* 1. a forefeiting. 2. anything forfeited; penalty or fine.
**for·gath·er** (fôr-gath′ẽr), *v.i.* to come together; assemble: also **fore·gath′er.**
**for·gave** (fẽr-gāv′, fôr-), pt. of **forgive.**
**forge** (fôrj), *n.* [< L. *faber*, workman], 1. a furnace for heating metal to be wrought. 2. a place where metal is heated and wrought; smithy. *v.t.* & *v.i.* [FORGED, FORGING], 1. to shape (metal) by heating and hammering. 2. to form; shape. 3. to imitate (a signature, etc.) fraudulently; counterfeit (a check, etc.). —**forg′er,** *n.*
**forge** (fôrj), *v.t.* & *v.i.* [FORGED, FORGING], [prob. alt. < *force*], to move forward consistently but slowly, as if against difficulties.
**for′ger·y,** *n.* [*pl.* -IES], 1. the act or legal offense of forging documents, signatures, etc. to deceive. 2. anything forged.
**for·get** (fẽr-get′, fôr-), *v.t.* & *v.i.* [-GOT, -GOTTEN or -GOT, -GETTING], [AS. *forgeitan*], 1. to be unable to remember. 2. to overlook or neglect. —**forget oneself,** to act in an improper manner. —**for·get′ter,** *n.*
**for·get′ful,** *adj.* 1. apt to forget. 2. negligent. —**for·get′ful·ness,** *n.*
**for·get′-me-not′,** *n.* a plant with hairy leaves and clusters of small, blue flowers.
**for·give** (fẽr-giv′, fôr-), *v.t.* & *v.i.* [-GAVE, -GIVEN, -GIVING], [AS. *forgiefan*], to give up resentment against or the desire to punish; pardon (an offense or offender). —**for·giv′a·ble,** *adj.* —**for·give′ness,** *n.*
**for·giv′ing,** *adj.* inclined to forgive.
**for·go** (fôr-gō′), *v.t.* [-WENT, -GONE, -GOING], [AS. *forgan*], to do without; abstain from.
**for·got** (fẽr-got′, fôr-), pt. and alt. pp. of **forget.**
**for·got′ten** (-′n), pp. of **forget.**
**fork** (fôrk), *n.* [< L. *furca*], 1. an instrument with prongs at one end, for picking up or spearing. 2. something like a fork in shape. 3. the place where a road, etc. divides into branches. 4. one of these branches. *v.i.* to divide into branches. *v.t.* to use a fork on. —**fork over** (or **out, up**), [Colloq.], to pay out; hand over.
**for·lorn** (fẽr-lôrn′, fôr-), *adj.* [< AS. *forleosan*, lose utterly], 1. left behind; deserted. 2. wretched; miserable. 3. without hope.
**form** (fôrm), *n.* [< L. *forma*], 1. shape; general structure. 2. the figure of a person or animal. 3. a mold. 4. the combination of qualities making something what it is. 5. arrangement; style. 6. a way of doing something. 7. a customary way of behaving; ceremony. 8. a printed document with blanks to be filled in. 9. a particular kind or type. 10. condition of mind or body. 11. any of the changes in a word to show inflection, etc. 12. type, etc. locked in a frame for printing. *v.t.* 1. to shape; fashion. 2. to train; instruct. 3. to develop (habits). 4. to make up; constitute. *v.i.* to be formed.
**-form,** [< L. *-formis*], a suffix meaning *having the form of*, as in *cuneiform.*
**for·mal** (fôr′m'l), *adj.* [L. *formalis*], 1. according to fixed customs, rules, etc. 2. stiff; ceremonious. 3. designed for wear at ceremonies, etc. 4. done or made in explicit, definite form: as, a *formal* contract. *n.* [Colloq.], 1. a dance requiring formal clothes. 2. a woman's long, evening dress.
**form·al·de·hyde** (fôr-mal′də-hīd′), *n.* [< *formic* + *aldehyde*], a colorless, pungent gas, used in solution as a disinfectant and preservative.
**for′mal·ism,** *n.* strict attention to outward forms and customs.
**for·mal·i·ty** (fôr-mal′ə-ti), *n.* [*pl.* -TIES], 1. *a*) an observing of customs, rules, etc.; propriety. *b*) excessive attention to regularity, convention, etc.; stiffness. 2. a formal act; ceremony.
**for′mal·ize′** (-īz′), *v.t.* [-IZED, -IZING], 1. to shape. 2. to make formal. *v.i.* to be formal.
**for·mat** (fôr′mat), *n.* [< L. (*liber*) *formatus*, (a book) formed], the shape, size, and arrangement of a book, etc.
**for·ma·tion** (fôr-mā′shən), *n.* 1. a forming or being formed. 2. a thing formed. 3. the way in which something is formed; structure; arrangement.
**form·a·tive** (fôr′mə-tiv), *adj.* helping or involving formation or development.
**for·mer** (fôr′mẽr), *adj.* [< ME. *formest*, foremost], 1. previous; earlier; past. 2. being the first mentioned of two.
**for′mer·ly,** *adv.* in the past.
**for·mic** (fôr′mik), *adj.* [< L. *formica*, ant], designating a colorless acid found in ants, spiders, etc.
**for·mi·da·ble** (fôr′mi-də-b'l), *adj.* [< L. *formidare*, to dread], 1. causing dread, fear, or awe. 2. hard to handle or overcome.
**form′less,** *adj.* shapeless; amorphous.
**for·mu·la** (fôr′myoo-lə), *n.* [*pl.* -LAS, -LAE (-lē′)], [L. < *forma*, form], 1. a fixed form of words, esp. a conventional expression. 2. any conventional rule for doing something. 3. a prescription for a baby's food, a medicine, etc. 4. a set of symbols expressing a mathematical rule. 5. in *chem.*, an expression of the composition, as of a compound, using symbols and figures.
**for′mu·late′** (-lāt′), *v.t.* [-LATED, -LATING], 1. to express in a formula. 2. to express in a definite way. —**for′mu·la′tion,** *n.*
**for·ni·cate** (fôr′ni-kāt′), *v.i.* [-CATED, -CATING], [< L. *fornix*, brothel], to commit fornication. —**for′ni·ca′tor,** *n.*
**for′ni·ca′tion,** *n.* voluntary sexual intercourse between unmarried persons.
**for·sake** (fẽr-sāk′, fôr-), *v.t.* [-SOOK (-sook′), -SAKEN, -SAKING], [< AS. *for-* + *sacan*, strive], 1. to give up (a habit, etc.). 2. to abandon; desert. —**for·sak′en,** *adj.*
**for·sooth** (fẽr-so͞oth′, fôr-), *adv.* [AS. *forsoth*], [Archaic], no doubt; indeed.
**for·swear** (fôr-swâr′), *v.t.* [-SWORE, -SWORN, -SWEARING], to deny or renounce on oath. *v.i.* to commit perjury.
**for·syth·i·a** (fẽr-sith′i-ə, fôr-), *n.* [< Wm. *Forsyth*, 18th-c. Eng. botanist], a shrub with yellow bell-shaped flowers, which appear in early spring before the leaves.
**fort** (fôrt), *n.* [< L. *fortis*, strong], a fortified place for military defense.
**forte** (fôrt), *n.* [< Fr.; see FORT], that which one does particularly well.
**for·te** (fôr′ti, -tā), *adj.* & *adv.* [It. < L. *fortis*, strong], in *music*, loud.

**forth** (fôrth), ***adv.*** [AS.], 1. forward; onward. 2. out; into view.
**forth'com'ing,** ***adj.*** 1. approaching; about to appear. 2. ready when needed.
**forth'right',** ***adj.*** straightforward. ***adv.*** 1. straight ahead. 2. at once.
**forth'with',** ***adv.*** without delay.
**for·ti·fi·ca·tion** (fôr'tə-fi-kā'shən), ***n.*** 1. the act or science of fortifying. 2. a fort, etc. 3. a fortified place.
**for·ti·fy** (fôr'tə-fī'), ***v.t.*** [-FIED, -FYING], [< L. *fortis*, strong + *facere*, make], 1. to strengthen physically, emotionally, etc. 2. to strengthen against attack, as with forts. 3. to support; corroborate. 4. to strengthen (liquor, etc.) by adding alcohol.
**for·tis·si·mo** (fôr-tis'ə-mō'), ***adj. & adv.*** [It. superl. of *forte*, strong], in *music*, very loud.
**for·ti·tude** (fôr'tə-to͞od', -tūd'), ***n.*** [< L. *fortis*, strong], firm courage; patient endurance of trouble, pain, etc.
**fort·night** (fôrt'nīt, -nit), ***n.*** [lit., fourteen nights], [Chiefly Brit.], two weeks.
**for·tress** (fôr'tris), ***n.*** [< L. *fortis*, strong], a fortified place; fort.
**for·tu·i·tous** (fôr-to͞o'ə-təs, -tū'-), ***adj.*** [< L. *fors*, luck], happening by chance; accidental. **—for·tu'i·tous·ly,** ***adv.***
**for·tu'i·ty,** ***n.*** [*pl.* -TIES], [see FORTUITOUS], chance; accident.
**for·tu·nate** (fôr'chə-nit), ***adj.*** 1. having good luck. 2. coming by good luck; favorable. **—for'tu·nate·ly,** ***adv.***
**for·tune** (fôr'chən), ***n.*** [< L. *fors*, luck], 1. luck; chance; fate. 2. one's future lot, good or bad. 3. good luck; success. 4. wealth; riches.
**for'tune·tell'er,** ***n.*** one who professes to foretell events in other people's lives.
**for·ty** (fôr'ti), ***adj. & n.*** [*pl.* -TIES], [AS. *feowertig*], four times ten; 40; XL. **—the forties,** the years from 40 through 49 (of a century or a person's age).**—for'ti·eth** (-ith), ***adj. & n.***
**fo·rum** (fôr'əm), ***n.*** [L.], 1. the public square of an ancient Roman city. 2. an assembly for the discussion of public matters.
**for·ward** (fôr'wẽrd), ***adj.*** [AS. *foreweard*], 1. at, toward, or of the front. 2. advanced. 3. onward. 4. prompt; ready. 5. bold; presumptuous. 6. of or for the future. ***adv.*** toward the front; ahead. ***n.*** in *basketball*, *hockey*, etc., a player in a front position. ***v.t.*** 1. to promote. 2. to send on.
**for'wards,** ***adv.*** forward.
**fos·sil** (fos''l), ***n.*** [< L. *fossilis*, dug up], 1. any hardened remains or traces of a plant or animal of a previous geological age, preserved in the earth's crust. 2. [Colloq.], a person who has outmoded, fixed ideas. ***adj.*** 1. of or like a fossil. 2. antiquated.
**fos·ter** (fôs'tẽr), ***v.t.*** [AS. *fostrian*, nourish], 1. to bring up; rear. 2. to help to develop; promote. 3. to cherish. ***adj.*** having a specified status in a family but not by birth: as, a *foster* brother.
**fought** (fôt), pt. and pp. of **fight.**
**foul** (foul), ***adj.*** [AS. *ful*], 1. stinking; loathsome. 2. extremely dirty. 3. indecent; profane. 4. wicked; abominable. 5. stormy: as, *foul* weather. 6. tangled: as, a *foul* rope. 7. not within the limits or rules set. 8. designating lines setting limits on the playing field. 9. dishonest. 10. [Colloq.], unpleasant, disagreeable, etc. ***n.*** in *sports*, a hit, blow, move, etc. that is foul (sense 7). ***v.t.*** 1. to make filthy. 2. to dishonor; disgrace. 3. to obstruct: as, grease *fouls* sink drains. 4. to entangle, as a rope. 5. to make a foul against, as in a game. 6. in *baseball*, to bat (the ball) foul. ***v.i.*** to be or become fouled. **—foul up,** [Colloq.], to bungle. **—foul'ly,** ***adv.***
**fou·lard** (fo͞o-lärd'), ***n.*** [Fr.], a lightweight fabric of silk, rayon, etc., usually figured.
**foul play,** 1. unfair play. 2. treacherous action or violence, as in assault, murder, etc.
**found** (found), ***v.t.*** [< L. *fundus*, bottom], 1. to base: as, *founded* on fact. 2. to begin the construction or organization of; establish. **—found'er,** ***n.***
**found** (found), ***v.t.*** [< L. *fundere*, pour], 1. to melt and pour (metal) into a mold. 2. to make by founding metal; cast.
**found** (found), pt. and pp. of **find.**
**foun·da·tion** (foun-dā'shən), ***n.*** 1. a founding or being founded; establishment. 2. an endowment to maintain an institution. 3. an institution so endowed. 4. basis. 5. the base of a wall, house, etc.
**foun·der** (foun'dẽr), ***v.i.*** [< L. *fundus*, bottom], 1. to stumble, fall, or go lame. 2. to fill with water and sink: said of a ship. 3. to break down.
**found·ling** (found'liŋ), ***n.*** a child found after desertion by its parents.
**found·ry** (foun'dri), ***n.*** [*pl.* -RIES], a place where metal is cast.
**fount** (fount), ***n.*** [< L. *fons*], 1. a fountain; spring. 2. a source.
**foun·tain** (foun't'n), ***n.*** [< L. *fons*], 1. a natural spring of water. 2. a source. 3. *a*) an artificial jet or flow of water: as, a drinking *fountain*. *b*) the basin, pipes, etc. where this flows. 4. a reservoir, as for ink.
**foun'tain·head',** ***n.*** the source, as of a stream.
**fountain pen,** a pen which is fed writing fluid from its own reservoir.
**four** (fôr), ***adj. & n.*** [AS. *feower*], one more than three; 4; IV.
**four'flush'er** (-flush'ẽr), ***n.*** [< *flush* in poker], [Slang], one who bluffs.
**four'-in-hand',** ***n.*** a necktie tied in a slipknot with the ends left hanging.
**four'score',** ***adj. & n.*** [Archaic or Poetic], four times twenty; eighty.
**four'some** (-səm), ***n.*** a group of four people.
**four'square',** ***adj.*** 1. square. 2. unyielding; firm. 3. frank; forthright. ***adv.*** in a square form or manner.
**four'teen'** (-tēn'), ***adj. & n.*** [AS. *feowertyne*], four more than ten; 14; XIV. **—four'teenth',** ***adj. & n.***
**fourth** (fôrth), ***adj.*** [AS. *feortha*], preceded by three others in a series; 4th. ***n.*** 1. the one following the third. 2. any of the four equal parts of something; $^1/_4$.
**Fourth of July,** Independence Day.
**fowl** (foul), ***n.*** [AS. *fugal*], 1. any bird: as, wild *fowl*. 2. any of the domestic birds used as food, as the chicken, duck, etc. 3. the flesh of these birds used for food.
**fox** (foks), ***n.*** [AS.], 1. a small, wild animal of the dog family, considered sly and crafty. 2. its fur. 3. a sly, crafty person. ***v.t.*** to trick by craftiness.
**fox'glove',** ***n.*** a plant with long spikes full of thimblelike flowers.
**fox'hole',** ***n.*** a hole dug in the ground as protection against enemy gunfire.
**fox terrier,** a small, active terrier, sometimes wire-haired, formerly trained to drive foxes out of hiding.
**fox trot,** a ballroom dance in 4/4 time, or music for it. **—fox'-trot',** ***v.i.***
**foy·er** (foi'ẽr, foi'ā), ***n.*** [Fr. < L. *focus*, hearth], an entrance hall or lobby.
**Fr.,** 1. Father. 2. French. 3. Friday.
**fr.,** 1. fragment. 2. franc. 3. from.
**fra·cas** (frā'kəs), ***n.*** [< It. *fracassare*, smash], a noisy dispute; brawl.
**frac·tion** (frak'shən), ***n.*** [< L. *frangere*, to break], 1. a small part, amount, etc.; fragment. 2. in *math.*, a quantity less than a whole, expressed as a decimal or with a numerator and denominator. **—frac'tion·al,** ***adj.*** **—frac'tion·al·ly,** ***adv.***
**frac·tious** (frak'shəs), ***adj.*** [< ?], 1. unruly;

rebellious. 2. irritable. —**frac'tious·ly**, *adv.*
**frac·ture** (frak'chẽr), *n.* [< L. *frangere*, to break], a breaking or break, esp. of a bone. *v.t. & v.i.* [-TURED, -TURING], to break; crack.
**frag·ile** (fraj'əl), *adj.* [< L. *frangere*, to break], easily broken; delicate; brittle.
**frag·ment** (frag'mənt), *n.* [< L. *frangere*, to break], 1. a part broken away. 2. an incomplete part, as of a novel.
**frag'men·tar'y** (-mən-ter'i), *adj.* made up of fragments; not complete.
**fra·grant** (frā'grənt), *adj.* [< L. *fragrare*, emit a smell], having a pleasant odor. —**fra'grance, fra'gran·cy** [*pl.* -CIES], *n.*
**frail** (frāl), *adj.* [see FRAGILE], 1. easily broken; fragile. 2. slender and delicate. 3. easily tempted; morally weak.
**frail'ty** (-ti), *n.* 1. a being frail; esp., moral weakness. 2. [*pl.* -TIES], a fault arising from such weakness.
**frame** (frām), *v.t.* [FRAMED, FRAMING], [< AS. *framian*, be helpful], 1. to form according to a pattern; design: as, to *frame* laws. 2. to construct. 3. to enclose in a border, as a picture, etc. 4. [Slang], to make appear guilty, as by falsifying evidence. *n.* 1. anything made of parts fitted together; framework, as of a house. 2. body structure; build. 3. the structural case into which a window, door, etc. is set. 4. an ornamental border, as of a picture. 5. the way that anything is constructed; form. 6. mood; temper: also **frame of mind.** 7. in *bowling*, etc., any of the divisions of a game.
**frame house,** a house with a wooden framework.
**frame'-up',** *n.* [Colloq.], a secret, deceitful scheme, as a falsifying of evidence to make a person seem guilty.
**frame'work',** *n.* 1. a structure to hold together or to support something. 2. a basic structure, etc.
**franc** (fraŋk), *n.* [Fr. < L. *Francorum rex* (king of the French), formerly on the coin], the monetary unit of France, Belgium, or Switzerland.
**fran·chise** (fran'chīz), *n.* [< OFr. *franc*, free], 1. any special right or privilege granted by a government. 2. the right to vote; suffrage. —**fran'chised,** *adj.*
**Franco-,** a combining form meaning: 1. *of France, of the French.* 2. *France and.*
**fran·gi·ble** (fran'jə-b'l), *adj.* [< L. *frangere*, to break], breakable. —**fran'gi·bil'i·ty,** *n.*
**Frank** (fraŋk), *n.* a member of the Germanic tribes whose 9th-c. empire extended over what is now France, Germany, and Italy.
**frank** (fraŋk), *adj.* [< OFr. *franc*, free], free in expressing oneself; candid. *v.t.* to send (mail) free of postage. *n.* 1. the right to send mail free. 2. a mark indicating this.
**Frank·en·stein** (fraŋk'ən-stīn'), *n.* 1. the title character in a 19th-c. novel, creator of a monster that destroys him. 2. popularly, the monster.
**frank·furt·er** (fraŋk'fẽr-tẽr), *n.* [G. < *Frankfurt*, Germany], a smoked sausage of beef or beef and pork; wiener.
**frank·in·cense** (fraŋk'in-sens'), *n.* [see FRANK & INCENSE], a gum resin burned as incense.
**Frank·ish** (fraŋk'ish), *n.* the West Germanic language of the Franks.
**fran·tic** (fran'tik), *adj.* [< Gr. *phrenitis*, madness], wild with anger, worry, etc. —**fran'ti·cal·ly,** *adv.*
**frap·pé** (fra-pā'), *n.* [< Fr. *frapper*, to strike], 1. a dessert made of partly frozen fruit juices, etc. 2. a beverage poured over shaved ice.
**fra·ter·nal** (frə-tũr'n'l), *adj.* [< L. *frater*, brother], 1. of brothers; brotherly. 2. designating or of a society organized for fellowship.
**fra·ter·ni·ty** (frə-tũr'nə-ti), *n.* [*pl.* -TIES], 1. brotherliness. 2. a group of men joined together by common interests, for fellowship, etc., as in some colleges. 3. a group of people with the same beliefs, work, etc.
**frat·er·nize** (frat'ẽr-nīz'), *v.i. & v.t.* [-NIZED, -NIZING], to associate in a brotherly way. —**frat'er·ni·za'tion,** *n.* —**frat'er·niz'er,** *n.*
**frat·ri·cide** (frat'rə-sīd'), *n.* [< L. *frater*, brother + *caedere*, to kill], the act of killing one's own brother or sister.
‡**Frau** (frou), *n.* [*pl.* FRAUEN (frou'ən); Eng. FRAUS], [G.], a wife: as a title, equivalent to *Mrs.*
**fraud** (frôd), *n.* [< L. *fraus*], 1. deceit; trickery. 2. an intentional dishonesty. 3. [Colloq.], a person who is not what he pretends to be.
**fraud·u·lent** (frô'jə-lənt), *adj.* 1. based on or using fraud. 2. done or obtained by fraud. —**fraud'u·lence,** *n.*
**fraught** (frôt), *adj.* [< MD. *vracht*, a load], filled (*with*): as, *fraught* with danger.
‡**Fräu·lein** (froi'līn), *n.* [*pl.* FRÄULEIN; Eng. -LEINS], [G.], an unmarried woman: as a title, equivalent to *Miss.*
**fray** (frā), *n.* [< *affray*], 1. a noisy quarrel. 2. a fight; conflict.
**fray** (frā), *v.t. & v.i.* [< L. *fricare*, rub], to make or become worn or ragged.
**fraz·zle** (fraz''l), *v.t. & v.i.* [-ZLED, -ZLING], [? < LG.], [Colloq.], 1. to wear to tatters. 2. to tire out. *n.* [Colloq.], a being frazzled.
**freak** (frēk), *n.* [< ?], 1. an odd notion; whim. 2. any abnormal animal, person, or plant. *adj.* queer; abnormal. —**freak'ish,** *adj.*
**freck·le** (frek''l), *n.* [< ON.], a small, yellowish-brown spot on the skin. *v.t. & v.i.* [-LED, -LING], to make or become spotted with freckles. —**freck'led,** *adj.* —**freck'ly,** *adv.*
**free** (frē), *adj.* [FREER, FREEST], [AS. *freo*], 1. not under the control or power of another; having liberty; independent. 2. having civil liberties. 3. able to move in any direction; loose. 4. not burdened by obligations, discomforts, constraints, etc. 5. not confined to the usual rules: as, *free* verse. 6. not exact: as, a *free* translation. 7. generous; profuse: as, *free* spending. 8. without cost or payment. 9. exempt from taxes, duties, etc. 10. clear of obstructions: as, a *free* road. *adv.* 1. without cost. 2. in a free manner. *v.t.* [FREED, FREEING], to make free; specif., *a*) to release from bondage or arbitrary power, obligation, etc. *b*) to clear of obstruction, etc. —**free from** (or **of**), without. —**make free with,** to use freely. —**set free,** to release; liberate. —**free'ly,** *adv.*
**free'boot'er** (-bōōt'ẽr), *n.* [< D. *vrij*, free + *buit*, plunder], a pirate.
**freed·man** (frēd'mən), *n.* [*pl.* -MEN], a man legally freed from slavery.
**free·dom** (frē'dəm), *n.* 1. a being free. 2. a political liberty: as, *freedom* of speech. 3. exemption from a specified obligation, discomfort, etc. 4. a being able to act, use, etc. without hindrance. 5. ease of movement; facility. 6. frankness.
**free'-for-all',** *n.* a disorganized, general fight; brawl. *adj.* open to anyone.
**free'hand',** *adj.* drawn by hand without the use of instruments, etc.
**free'hold',** *n.* 1. the holding of a piece of land, etc. for life or with the right to pass it on by inheritance. 2. an estate, etc. so held. —**free'hold'er,** *n.*
**free lance,** a writer, actor, etc. who sells his services to individual buyers. —**free'-lance',** *adj. & v.i.* [-LANCED, -LANCING].
**free'man** (-mən), *n.* [*pl.* -MEN], 1. a person not in slavery. 2. a citizen.
**Free·ma·son** (frē'mā's'n), *n.* a member of a secret society based on brotherliness and mutual aid. —**Free'ma'son·ry,** *n.*

**free on board,** delivered (by the seller) aboard the train, ship, etc. at the point of shipment, at no extra charge.
**free′stone′,** *n.* a peach, etc. in which the pit does not cling to the pulp.
**free′think′er,** *n.* one who forms his opinions about religion independently.
**free trade,** trade conducted without protective tariffs, duties, etc.
**free verse,** poetry not adhering to regular metrical, rhyming, or stanzaic forms.
**free′way′,** *n.* a multiple-lane highway designed to move traffic quickly.
**free′will′,** *adj.* voluntary; spontaneous.
**freeze** (frēz), *v.i.* [FROZE, FROZEN, FREEZING], [AS. *freosan*], 1. to be formed into, or become covered with, ice. 2. to become very cold. 3. to be damaged or killed by cold. 4. to become motionless. 5. to be chilled by a strong emotion. 6. to become formal or unfriendly. *v.t.* 1. to change into, or cover with, ice. 2. to make very cold. 3. to preserve (food) by rapid refrigeration. 4. to kill or damage by cold. 5. to make motionless. 6. to make formal or unfriendly. 7. [Colloq.], to fix (prices, etc.) at a given level by authority. *n.* 1. a freezing or being frozen. 2. a period of freezing weather.
**freeze′-dry′,** *v.t.* [-DRIED, -DRYING], to quick-freeze (food, vaccines, etc.) and then dry under high vacuum at low temperature.
**freez′er,** *n.* 1. a machine for making ice cream and sherbet. 2. a refrigerator for freezing foods or storing frozen foods.
**freezing point,** the temperature at which a liquid freezes: for water, it is 32° F, or 0° C.
**freight** (frāt), *n.* [< MD. *vraht*, a load], 1. the transporting of goods by water, land, or air. 2. the cost for such transportation. 3. the goods transported. 4. a railroad train for transporting goods: in full, **freight train.** *v.t.* 1. to load with freight. 2. to send by freight.
**freight′er,** *n.* a ship for carrying freight.
**French** (french), *adj.* of France, its people, language, etc. *n.* the language of France. —**the French,** the people of France. —**French′man** [*pl.* -MEN], *n.*
**French cuff,** a shirt-sleeve cuff turned back on itself and fastened with a link.
**French dressing,** a salad dressing made of vinegar, oil, and various seasonings.
**French fried,** fried in very hot, deep fat.
**French horn,** a brass-wind instrument with a coiled tube ending in a wide, flaring bell.
**French leave,** an unauthorized departure.
**French toast,** sliced bread dipped in a batter of egg and milk and fried.
**fre·net·ic** (frə-net′ik), *adj.* [< Gr. *phrenētikos*, mad], frantic; frenzied.
**fren·zy** (fren′zi), *n.* [*pl.* -ZIES], [< Gr. *phrenitis*, madness], wild excitement; brief delirium. —**fren′zied,** *adj.*
**fre·quen·cy** (frē′kwən-si), *n.* [*pl.* -CIES], 1. frequent occurrence. 2. the number of times any event recurs in a given period; rate of occurrence. 3. in *physics*, the number of vibrations or cycles in a unit of time.
**frequency modulation,** the changing of the frequency of the transmitting radio wave in accordance with the sound being broadcast.
**fre·quent** (frē′kwənt), *adj.* [< L. *frequens*, crowded], 1. occurring often. 2. constant; habitual. *v.t.* (fri-kwent′), to go to or be in habitually. —**fre′quent·ly,** *adv.*
**fres·co** (fres′kō), *n.* [*pl.* -COES, -COS], [It., fresh], 1. the art of painting with water colors on wet plaster. 2. a painting or design so made. *v.t.* to paint in fresco.
**fresh** (fresh), *adj.* [AS. *fersc*], 1. recently made, grown, etc.: as, *fresh* coffee. 2. not spoiled. 3. not tired; lively. 4. not worn, faded, etc. 5. new; recent. 6. additional: as, a *fresh* start. 7. inexperienced. 8. cool and refreshing: as, a *fresh* day. 9. brisk: said of wind. 10. not salt: said of water.
**fresh** (fresh), *adj.* [< G. *frech*, bold], [Slang], saucy; impudent.
**fresh′en** (-ən), *v.t.* & *v.i.* to make or become fresh. —**fresh′en·er,** *n.*
**fresh·et** (fresh′it), *n.* a flooding of a stream, as because of melting snow.
**fresh′man** (-mən), *n.* [*pl.* -MEN], 1. a beginner. 2. a first-year student in a high school or college.
**fresh′-wa′ter,** *adj.* 1. of or living in water that is not salty. 2. sailing only on inland waters. 3. unskilled.
**fret** (fret), *v.t.* & *v.i.* [FRETTED, FRETTING], [AS. *fretan*, eat up], 1. to gnaw, chafe, wear away, etc. 2. to make or become rough: as, water *fretted* by the wind. 3. to irritate or be irritated; worry. *n.* irritation; worry. —**fret′ter,** *n.*
**fret** (fret), *n.* [< OFr. *frete* & AS. *frætwa*], an ornamental pattern of straight bars joining one another at right angles.
**fret** (fret), *n.* [Fr., a band], any of the ridges on the finger board of a banjo, guitar, etc. to regulate fingering.
**fret′ful,** *adj.* irritable; peevish.
**fret′work′,** *n.* work ornamented with frets.
**Freud·i·an** (froi′di-ən), *adj.* of or according to Sigmund Freud, Austrian psychiatrist, or his theories and practice. *n.* one who believes in Freud's theories or uses his methods.
**fri·a·ble** (frī′ə-b'l), *adj.* [< L. *friare*, to rub], easily crumbled. —**fri′a·bil′i·ty,** *n.*
**fri·ar** (frī′ēr), *n.* [< L. *frater*, brother], in the *R. C. Church*, a member of any of certain religious orders.
**fri′ar·y,** *n.* [*pl.* -IES], 1. a monastery where friars live. 2. a brotherhood of friars.
**fric·as·see** (frik′ə-sē′), *n.* [< Fr. *fricasser*, cut up and fry], meat cut into pieces and stewed or fried. *v.t.* [-SEED, -SEEING], to prepare as a fricassee.
**fric·tion** (frik′shən), *n.* [< L. *fricare*, to rub], 1. a rubbing of one object against another. 2. conflict, as because of differing opinions. 3. the resistance to motion of surfaces that touch. —**fric′tion·al,** *adj.*
**Fri·day** (frī′di), *n.* [after *Frig*, Germanic goddess], 1. the sixth day of the week. 2. the devoted servant of Robinson Crusoe: also **man Friday.**
**fried** (frīd), pt. and pp. of **fry.** *adj.* cooked by frying.
**friend** (frend), *n.* [AS. *freond*], 1. a person whom one knows well and is fond of. 2. an ally, supporter, or sympathizer. 3. [F-], a member of a Christian sect, the Society of Friends; Quaker. —**friend′less,** *adj.*
**friend′ly,** *adj.* [-LIER, -LIEST], 1. of or like a friend; kindly. 2. not hostile; amicable. 3. supporting; helping. —**friend′li·ness,** *n.*
**friend′ship,** *n.* 1. the state of being friends. 2. friendly feeling.
**frieze** (frēz), *n.* [< Frank.], a decoration forming an ornamental band around a room, building, etc.
**frig·ate** (frig′it), *n.* [< It. *fregata*], a fast, medium-sized sailing warship of the 18th and 19th centuries.
**fright** (frīt), *n.* [AS. *fyrhto*], 1. sudden fear; alarm. 2. [Colloq.], an ugly or startling person or thing.
**fright′en,** *v.t.* 1. to make suddenly afraid; scare. 2. to drive (*away*, *off*, etc.) by frightening. —**fright′ened,** *adj.*
**fright′ful,** *adj.* 1. causing fright; alarming. 2. disgusting. 3. [Colloq.], unpleasant.
**frig·id** (frij′id), *adj.* [< L. *frigus*, coldness], 1. extremely cold. 2. without warmth of feeling or manner. —**fri·gid′i·ty,** *n.*
**frill** (fril), *n.* [? < OFr. *fraise*, a ruff], 1. a

ruffle. 2. [Colloq.], any unnecessary ornament. *v.t.* to decorate with a ruffle. —**frill'er**, *n.* —**frill'y** [-IER, -IEST], *adj.*

**fringe** (frinj), *n.* [< L. *fimbria*], 1. a border of threads or cords, hanging loose or tied in bunches at the top. 2. an outer edge; border. *v.t.* [FRINGED, FRINGING], 1. to decorate with fringe. 2. to be a fringe for; edge.

**frip·per·y** (frip'ẽr-i), *n.* [*pl.* -IES], [< OFr. *frepe*, rag], 1. cheap, gaudy clothes. 2. showy display in dress, manners, etc.

**fri·sé** (fri-zā'), *n.* [Fr. < *friser*, to curl], a type of upholstery fabric with a thick pile of loops.

**Fri·sian** (frizh'ən), *n.* the Low German language of a chain of islands **(Frisian Islands)** off the coast of the Netherlands and Germany.

**frisk** (frisk), *v.i.* [prob. < OHG. *frisc*, lively], to frolic. *v.t.* [Slang], to search (a person) for weapons, etc. by passing the hands over his clothing. —**frisk'er**, *n.*

**frisk'y**, *adj.* [-IER, -IEST], lively; frolicsome.

**frit·ter** (frit'ẽr), *v.t.* [< L. *frangere*, to break], to waste (money, time, etc.) bit by bit on petty things.

**frit·ter** (frit'ẽr), *n.* [< LL. *frigere*, fry], a small cake of fried batter, usually containing corn, fruit, or other filling.

**fri·vol·i·ty** (fri-vol'ə-ti), *n.* 1. a frivolous quality. 2. [*pl.* -TIES], a frivolous act or thing.

**friv·o·lous** (friv'ə-ləs), *adj.* [L. *frivolus*], 1. trifling; trivial. 2. silly and light-minded.

**friz, frizz** (friz), *v.t. & v.i.* [FRIZZED, FRIZZING], [Fr. *friser*], to form into small, tight curls, as hair. *n.* something frizzed, as hair. —**friz'zi·ness**, *n.* —**friz'zly, friz'zy**, *adj.*

**friz·zle** (friz''l), *v.t. & v.i.* [-ZLED, -ZLING], [prob. < *fry*], to make or cause to make a sputtering, hissing noise, as in frying.

**friz·zle** (friz''l), *n., v.t. & v.i.* [-ZLED, -ZLING], friz.

**fro** (frō), *adv.* [ON. *frā*], backward; back: now only in *to and fro*, back and forth.

**frock** (frok), *n.* [< OHG. *hroc*, cloak], 1. a robe worn by friars, monks, etc. 2. a dress; gown. *v.t.* to clothe in a frock.

**frog** (frôg, frog), *n.* [AS. *frogga*], 1. a small, four-legged leaping animal with webbed feet and no tail: it lives either in water or on land. 2. a braided loop used as a fastener on clothing. 3. a device for keeping railroad cars on the proper rails at switches. —**frog in the throat**, hoarseness.

**frol·ic** (frol'ik), *n.* [< MD. *vrō*, merry], 1. a gay party or game. 2. merriment; fun. *v.i.* [-ICKED, -ICKING], to make merry; have fun. —**frol'ick·er**, *n.*

**frol'ic·some** (-səm), *adj.* playful; merry; gay.

**from** (frum, from), *prep.* [AS.], 1. beginning at; starting with: as, he walked *from* the door. 2. out of: as, *from* a closet. 3. originating with: as, a letter *from* me. 4. out of the possibility or use of: as, he kept me *from* going. 5. as not being like: as, to know good *from* evil. 6. because of: as, to shake *from* fear.

**frond** (frond), *n.* [L. *frons*, leafy branch], the leaflike, spore-bearing organ of a fern.

**front** (frunt), *n.* [< L. *frons*, forehead], 1. outward behavior: as, a bold *front*. 2. the part facing forward. 3. the first part; beginning. 4. the place directly before one. 5. the land bordering a street, ocean, etc. 6. the advanced battle area in warfare. 7. [Colloq.], an appearance of social standing, wealth, etc. *adj.* at, to, in, on, or of the front. *v.t. & v.i.* to face. —**in front of**, before. —**fron'tal**, *adj.* —**fron'tal·ly**, *adv.*

**front·age** (frun'tij), *n.* 1. the front part of a building. 2. the front boundary line of a lot or the length of this line. 3. land bordering a street, river, etc.

**fron·tier** (frun-têr'), *n.* [see FRONT], 1. that part of a country which borders another country or an unexplored region. 2. any new field of learning, etc. *adj.* of or on the frontier. —**fron·tiers'man** (-têrz'mən) [*pl.* -MEN], *n.*

**fron·tis·piece** (frun'tis-pēs'), *n.* [< L. *frons*, front + *specere*, look], an illustration facing the title page of a book.

**frost** (frôst, frost), *n.* [AS. < *freosan*, freeze], 1. a freezing or being frozen. 2. temperature below the freezing point of water. 3. frozen dew or vapor. *v.t.* 1. to cover with frost. 2. to hurt or kill by frost. 3. to cover with frosting. —**frost'y** [-IER, -IEST], *adj.*

**frost'bite'**, *v.t.* [-BIT, -BITTEN, -BITING], to injure (body tissues) by exposure to intense cold. *n.* injury caused by such exposure.

**frost'ing**, *n.* 1. a mixture of sugar, butter, etc. for covering a cake; icing. 2. a dull, frostlike finish on glass, metal, etc.

**froth** (frôth, froth), *n.* [ON. *frotha*], 1. foam. 2. foaming saliva. 3. any light, trifling thing. *v.i. & v.t.* to foam or cause to foam. —**froth'y** [-IER, -IEST], *adj.*

**fro·ward** (frō'ẽrd, -wẽrd), *adj.* [< *fro* + *-ward*], not easily controlled; willful; contrary. —**fro'ward·ness**, *n.*

**frown** (froun), *v.i.* [< OFr. *frognier*], 1. to contract the brows, as in displeasure or concentration. 2. to look with disapproval (*on* or *upon*). *n.* a frowning.

**frow·zy** (frou'zi), *adj.* [-ZIER, -ZIEST], [< ?], dirty and untidy; slovenly. Also sp. **frowsy**. —**frow'zi·ness, frow'si·ness**, *n.*

**froze** (frōz), pt. of **freeze**.

**fro·zen** (frō'z'n), pp. of **freeze**. *adj.* 1. turned into or covered with ice. 2. damaged or killed by freezing. 3. as if turned into ice. 4. preserved by freezing.

**fruc·ti·fy** (fruk'tə-fī'), *v.i. & v.t.* [-FIED, -FYING], [< L. *fructificare*], to be or cause to be fruitful.

**fru·gal** (froo͞'g'l), *adj.* [< L. *frugi*, fit for food], 1. not wasteful; thrifty or sparing. 2. not costly; inexpensive. —**fru·gal'i·ty** (-gal'ə-ti) [*pl.* -TIES], *n.* —**fru'gal·ly**, *adv.*

**fruit** (froo͞t), *n.* [< L. *fructus*], 1. *usually in pl.* any plant product, as grain, vegetables, etc. 2. the edible part of a plant or tree, consisting of the seeds and pulpy surrounding tissues: often distinguished from *vegetable*. 3. result or product of any action. *v.i. & v.t.* to bear or cause to bear fruit.

**fruit'ful**, *adj.* 1. bearing much fruit. 2. productive. 3. profitable. —**fruit'ful·ly**, *adv.*

**fru·i·tion** (froo͞-ish'ən), *n.* 1. the bearing of fruit. 2. a coming to fulfillment.

**fruit'less**, *adj.* 1. without results; unsuccessful. 2. bearing no fruit.

**fruit'y**, *adj.* [-IER, -IEST], 1. like fruit in taste or smell. 2. [Colloq.], rich in interest.

**frump** (frump), *n.* [< D. *rompelen*, rumple], a dowdy woman. —**frump'ish, frump'y**, *adj.*

**frus·trate** (frus'trāt), *v.t.* [-TRATED, -TRATING], [< L. *frustra*, in vain], 1. to bring to nothing; nullify. 2. to prevent from achieving a goal or gratifying a desire. —**frustra'tion**, *n.*

**frus·tum** (frus'təm), *n.* [*pl.* -TUMS, -TA (-tə)], [L., piece], the solid figure formed when the top of a cone or pyramid is cut off by a plane parallel to the base.

**fry** (frī), *v.t. & v.i.* [FRIED, FRYING], [< L. *frigere*], to cook or be cooked in hot fat or oil. —**fry'er**, *n.*

**fry** (frī), *n.* [*pl.* FRY], [? < Gmc.], 1. young fish. 2. young; offspring.

**ft.**, foot; feet.

**fuch·si·a** (fū'shə, -shi-ə), *n.* [< L. *Fuchs*, 16th-c. G. botanist], 1. a shrubby plant with pink, red, or purple flowers. 2. purplish red.

**fud·dle** (fud''l), *v.t.* [-DLED, -DLING], [? < D.],

to confuse or stupefy as with alcoholic liquor. *n.* a fuddled state.
**fud·dy-dud·dy** (fud'i-dud'i), *n.* [*pl.* -DIES], [Slang], a fussy, critical, or old-fashioned person.
**fudge** (fuj), *interj.* [< ?], nonsense! *n.* 1. nonsense. 2. a soft candy made of butter, milk, sugar, flavoring, etc.
**fu·el** (fū'əl), *n.* [ult. < L. *focus*, fireplace], 1. coal, oil, gas, wood, etc. burned to supply heat or power. 2. anything that maintains or intensifies strong feeling. *v.t. & v.i.* [-ELED or -ELLED, -ELING or -ELLING], to supply with or get fuel.
**fu·gi·tive** (fū'jə-tiv), *adj.* [< L. *fugere*, flee], 1. fleeing or having fled. 2. passing quickly; fleeting. *n.* one who flees or has fled from danger, justice, etc.
**fugue** (fūg), *n.* [< L. *fugere*, flee], a musical work in which a theme is taken up successively and developed by the various instruments or voices in counterpoint.
**Fuh·rer** (fū'rēr), *n.* [G.], leader: title assumed by Adolf Hitler: also sp. **Fuehrer.**
**-ful,** [< *full*, *adj.*], a suffix meaning: 1. *full of, having*, as in *joyful*. 2. *having the qualities of* or *the tendency to*, as in *helpful*. 3. *the quantity that will fill*, as in *handful*.
**ful·crum** (ful'krəm), *n.* [L. < *fulcire*, to prop], the support on which a lever turns in raising something.
**ful·fill, ful·fil** (fool-fil'), *v.t.* [-FILLED, -FILLING], [AS. *fullfyllan*], 1. to carry out, as a promise. 2. to do, as a duty. 3. to satisfy (a condition). 4. to bring to an end; complete. —**ful·fill'ment, ful·fil'ment,** *n.*
**ful·gent** (ful'jənt), *adj.* [< L. *fulgere*, shine], [Poetic], very bright; radiant.
**full** (fool), *adj.* [AS.], 1. having in it all there is space for; filled. 2. having eaten all that one wants. 3. having a great deal of. 4. complete: as, a *full* load. 5. having reached the greatest size, extent, etc. 6. plump; chubby. 7. with plenty of material: as, a *full* skirt. *n.* the greatest amount, extent, etc. *adv.* 1. completely; to the greatest degree. 2. directly; exactly. —**full'ness, ful'ness,** *n.*
**full** (fool), *v.t. & v.i.* [< L. *fullo*, cloth fuller], to clean, shrink, and thicken (cloth).
**full'back',** *n.* in *football*, one of the backs, originally the one farthest behind the scrimmage line.
**full'-blood'ed,** *adj.* 1. vigorous. 2. of unmixed breed or race.
**full'-blown',** *adj.* 1. in full bloom. 2. fully developed; matured.
**full dress,** formal clothes.
**full'-fledged',** *adj.* completely developed or trained; of full status.
**full'-grown',** *adj.* fully grown.
**full moon,** the moon seen as a circle when its whole disk reflects the sun's light.
**full'y,** *adv.* 1. completely; entirely. 2. exactly. 3. amply. 4. at least.
**ful·mi·nate** (ful'mə-nāt'), *v.i. & v.t.* [-NATED, -NATING], [< L. *fulmen*, lightning], 1. to explode; detonate. 2. to shout forth (denunciations, etc.). —**ful'mi·na'tion,** *n.*
**ful·some** (fool'səm, ful'-), *adj.* [see FULL, *adj.* & -SOME; but infl. by *foul*], disgusting or offensive, esp. because of excess or insincerity. —**ful'some·ly,** *adv.*
**fum·ble** (fum'b'l), *v.i. & v.t.* [-BLED, -BLING], [? < ON. *famla*, grope], 1. to grope or handle clumsily. 2. in *football*, etc., to fail to catch or handle (the ball) properly. *n.* a fumbling.
**fume** (fūm), *n.* [< L. *fumus*], a gas, smoke, or vapor, esp. if offensive or suffocating. *v.i.* [FUMED, FUMING], 1. to give off fumes. 2. to show anger. *v.t.* to expose to fumes.
**fu·mi·gate** (fū'mə-gāt'), *v.t.* [-GATED, -GATING], [< L. *fumus*, smoke + *agere*, make], to expose to fumes, esp. to disinfect or kill the vermin in. —**fu'mi·ga'tion,** *n.* —**fu'mi·ga'tor,** *n.*
**fun** (fun), *n.* [< obs. *fon*, act foolishly], 1. lively, gay play or playfulness; amusement. 2. a source of merriment. —**make fun of,** to ridicule.
**func·tion** (fuŋk'shən), *n.* [< L. *fungi*, perform], 1. the normal or characteristic action of anything. 2. a special duty required in work. 3. a formal ceremony or social occasion. 4. in *math.*, a quantity whose value varies with that of another quantity or quantities. *v.i.* to act in a required manner; work; be used.
**func'tion·al,** *adj.* 1. of a function. 2. performing a function. 3. affecting a function of some bodily organ without apparent organic changes. —**func'tion·al·ly,** *adv.*
**func'tion·ar'y** (-er'i), *n.* [*pl.* -IES], an official performing some function.
**fund** (fund), *n.* [L. *fundus*, bottom], 1. a supply that can be drawn upon; store: as, a *fund* of jokes. 2. *a)* a sum of money set aside for a purpose. *b)* *pl.* ready money. *v.t.* to put or convert into a long-term debt.
**fun·da·men·tal** (fun'də-men't'l), *adj.* [see FUND], of or forming a foundation or basis; basic. *n.* a principle, law, etc. serving as a basis. —**fun'da·men'tal·ly,** *adv.*
**fun'da·men'tal·ism,** *n.* [occas. F-], orthodox religious beliefs based on a literal interpretation of the Bible. —**fun'da·men'tal·ist,** *n. & adj.*
**fu·ner·al** (fū'nēr-əl), *n.* [< L. *funus*], the ceremonies connected with burial or cremation of the dead. *adj.* of or suitable for these ceremonies.
**fu·ne·re·al** (fū-nêr'i-əl), *adj.* suitable for a funeral; sad and solemn; dismal.
**fun·gi·cide** (fun'jə-sīd'), *n.* [see -CIDE], any substance that kills fungi.
**fun·gus** (fuŋ'gəs), *n.* [*pl.* -GI (fun'jī), -GUSES], [< Gr. *sp(h)ongos*, sponge], any of various plants, as mildews, molds, mushrooms, etc., that have no leaves, flowers, or green color and reproduce by spores. —**fun'gous,** *adj.*
**fu·nic·u·lar** (fū-nik'yoo-lēr), *n.* [ult. < L. *funis*, a rope; + *-ar*], a mountain railway on which the cars are moved by cables.
**funk** (fuŋk), *n.* [? < Fl. *fonck*, dismay], [Colloq.], a cowering through fear; panic.
**fun·nel** (fun''l), *n.* [ult. < L. *fundere*, pour], 1. a slender tube with a cone-shaped mouth, for pouring things into narrow-mouthed containers. 2. a smokestack, as of a ship. 3. a flue. *v.i. & v.t.* [-NELED or -NELLED, -NELING or -NELLING], to move or pour as through a funnel.
**fun·ny** (fun'i), *adj.* [-NIER, -NIEST], 1. causing laughter; humorous. 2. [Colloq.], strange; queer. *n.* [*pl.* -NIES], *usually in pl.* [Colloq.], a comic strip. —**fun'ni·ness,** *n.*
**funny bone,** a place on the elbow where a sharp impact on a nerve causes a painful tingling: also **crazy bone.**
**fur** (fũr), *n.* [< OFr. *forre*, sheath], 1. the soft, thick hair covering certain animals. 2. a processed skin bearing such hair. *adj.* of fur.
**fur·be·low** (fũr'bə-lō'), *n.* [var. of Fr. *falbala*], 1. a flounce or ruffle. 2. *usually pl.* showy trimming.
**fur·bish** (fũr'bish), *v.t.* [< OHG. *furban*, to clean], 1. to polish; burnish. 2. to renovate.
**Fu·ries** (fyoor'iz), *n.pl.* in *Gr. & Rom. myth.*, the three female spirits who punished unavenged crimes.
**fu·ri·ous** (fyoor'i-əs), *adj.* full of fury.
**furl** (fũrl), *v.t. & v.i.* [< L. *firmum*, firm + *ligare*, to lay], to roll up tightly and securely, as a flag. *n.* a roll of something furled.
**fur·long** (fũr'loŋ), *n.* [< AS. *furh*, a furrow + *lang*, long], a measure of distance equal to 1/8 of a mile, or 220 yards.

**fur·lough** (fũr′lō), *n.* [< D. *verlof*], a leave of absence, esp. for enlisted military personnel. *v.t.* to grant a furlough to.
**fur·nace** (fũr′nis), *n.* [< L. *fornus*, oven], 1. an enclosed structure in which heat is produced. 2. any very hot place.
**fur·nish** (fũr′nish), *v.t.* [< Gmc.], 1. to fit out with furniture, etc.; equip. 2. to supply; provide. —**fur′nish·er,** *n.*
**fur′nish·ings,** *n.pl.* 1. furniture and fixtures, as for a house. 2. things to wear.
**fur·ni·ture** (fũr′ni-chẽr), *n.* [Fr. *fourniture*], 1. the movable things in a room, etc. which equip it for living, as chairs, beds, etc. 2. necessary equipment of a ship, trade, etc.
**fu·ror** (fyoor′ôr), *n.* [< Fr. *fureur* & L. *furor*], 1. fury; frenzy. 2. a widespread outburst of enthusiasm; craze; rage.
**fur·ri·er** (fũr′i-ẽr), *n.* one who processes furs or deals in fur garments.
**fur·ring** (fũr′iŋ), *n.* thin strips of wood or metal fixed on a wall, floor, etc. before adding the laths or boards.
**fur·row** (fũr′ō), *n.* [AS. *furh*], 1. a narrow groove made in the ground by a plow. 2. anything like this, as a wrinkle. *v.t.* to make furrows in. *v.i.* to become wrinkled.
**fur·ry** (fũr′i), *adj.* [-RIER, -RIEST], 1. of or like fur. 2. covered with fur. —**fur′ri·ness,** *n.*
**fur·ther** (fũr′*th*ẽr), *adj.* [< AS.], 1. more distant; farther. 2. additional; more. *adv.* 1. at or to a greater distance. 2. to a greater degree or extent. 3. in addition. *Further* is now interchangeable with *farther* in senses 1 & 2 of the *adv.* and 1 of the *adj.*, though *farther* is often preferred in reference to space, and *further* in reference to time, degree, and addition. *v.t.* to promote; give aid to.
**fur′ther·ance,** *n.* 1. a furthering, or helping forward. 2. an aid.
**fur′ther·more′,** *adv.* besides; moreover.
**fur·thest** (fũr′*th*ist), *adj.* most distant; farthest: also **fur′ther·most′.** *adv.* at or to the greatest distance or degree.
**fur·tive** (fũr′tiv), *adj.* [< L. *fur*, thief], done or acting in a stealthy manner; sly; shifty.
**fu·ry** (fyoor′i), *n.* [*pl.* -RIES], [< L. *furere*, to rage], 1. violent anger; wild rage. 2. violence; vehemence; fierceness.
**furze** (fũrz), *n.* [AS. *fyrs*], a prickly evergreen shrub with yellow flowers, common in Europe, esp. on wastelands.
**fuse** (fūz), *v.t.* & *v.i.* [FUSED, FUSING], [< L. *fundere*, to shed], 1. to melt. 2. to unite as if by melting together.
**fuse** (fūz), *n.* [< L. *fusus*, spindle], 1. a tube or wick filled with combustible material for setting off an explosive charge. 2. a strip of easily melted metal placed in an electrical circuit: it melts and breaks the circuit when the current becomes too strong.
**fu·se·lage** (fū′z'l-ij, fū′zə-läzh′), *n.* [Fr.], the body of an airplane, exclusive of the wings and tail.
**fu·si·ble** (fū′zə-b'l), *adj.* that can be fused.
**fu·sil·lade** (fū′z'l-ād′), *n.* [< Fr. *fusiller*, to shoot], a simultaneous discharge of many firearms.
**fu·sion** (fū′zhən), *n.* 1. a fusing; melting together: see also **nuclear fusion.** 2. a blending; coalition. 3. anything made by fusing.
**fuss** (fus), *n.* [prob. echoic], a nervous, excited state; bother. *v.i.* to bustle about or worry over trifles. —**fuss′y** [-IER, -IEST], *adj.*
**fus·tian** (fus′chən), *n.* [< L. *fustis*, wooden stick], pompous, pretentious talk or writing; bombast. *adj.* of fustian.
**fust·y** (fus′ti), *adj.* [-IER, -IEST], [< dial. *fust*, moldiness], 1. musty; moldy. 2. old-fashioned. —**fust′i·ly,** *adv.* —**fust′i·ness,** *n.*
**fu·tile** (fū′t'l), *adj.* [< L. *futilis*, that easily pours out], useless; vain. —**fu′tile·ly,** *adv.* —**fu·til′i·ty** (-til′ə-ti) [*pl.* -TIES], *n.*
**fu·ture** (fū′chẽr), *adj.* [< L. *futurus*, about to be], 1. that is to be or come. 2. indicating time to come: as, *future* tense. *n.* 1. the time that is to come. 2. what is going to be; prospects. Abbrev. **fut.**
**fu·tu·ri·ty** (fū-toor′ə-ti, -tyoor′-), *n.* [*pl.* -TIES], 1. the future. 2. a future condition or event. 3. the quality of being future.
**fuze** (fūz), *n.*, *v.t.* & *v.i.* [FUZED, FUZING], to fuse.
**fuzz** (fuz), *n.* [? echoic], loose, light particles; fine hairs or fibers. —**fuzz′y** [-IER, -IEST], *adj.* —**fuzz′i·ly,** *adv.* —**fuzz′i·ness,** *n.*
**-fy,** [< L. *facere*, do], a suffix meaning: 1. *to make*, as in *liquefy*. 2. *to cause to have*, as in *glorify*. 3. *to become*, as in *putrefy*.

# G

**G, g** (jē), *n.* [*pl.* G's, g's, Gs, gs], the seventh letter of the English alphabet.
**G,** *n.* in *music*, the fifth tone in the scale of C major.
**G.,** German.
**G., g.,** 1. gauge. 2. gram. 3. gulf.
**gab** (gab), *n.* & *v.i.* [GABBED, GABBING], [prob. < ON. *gabba*, mock], [Colloq.], chatter.
**gab·ar·dine, gab·er·dine** (gab′ẽr-dēn′), *n.* [< MHG. *walvart*, pilgrimage], a twilled cloth of wool, cotton, etc. with a fine, diagonal weave.
**gab·ble** (gab′'l), *v.i.* & *v.t.* [-BLED, -BLING], [< *gab*], to talk or utter rapidly and incoherently. *n.* such talk.
**gab·by** (gab′i), *adj.* [-BIER, -BIEST], [Colloq.], talkative.
**ga·ble** (gā′b'l), *n.* [prob. < ON. *gafl*], the triangular wall enclosed by the sloping ends of a ridged roof. —**ga′bled,** *adj.*
**Ga·bri·el** (gā′bri-əl), *n.* in the *Bible*, the angel herald of good news.
**Gad, gad** (gad), *interj.* a mild oath: a euphemism for *God*.
**gad** (gad), *v.i.* [GADDED, GADDING], [? < AS. *gædeling*, companion], to roam about aimlessly or restlessly. —**gad′der,** *n.*
**gad′a·bout′,** *n.* [Colloq.], one who gads about, looking for fun, excitement, etc.
**gad′fly′,** *n.* [*pl.* -FLIES], [cf. GOAD & FLY], 1. a large fly that stings cattle, etc. 2. one who annoys or irritates others.
**gadg·et** (gaj′it), *n.* [? < *gauge*], any small mechanical contrivance.
**Gael** (gāl), *n.* a Celt of Scotland, Ireland, or the Isle of Man.
**Gael·ic** (gāl′ik), *adj.* of the Gaels or any of their Celtic languages. *n.* any Celtic language spoken by the Gaels: abbrev. **Gael.**
**gaff** (gaf), *n.* [prob. < Celt.], 1. a large hook on a pole for landing large fish. 2. a spar supporting a fore-and-aft sail. —**stand the gaff,** [Slang], to bear up well under pain, punishment, etc.
**gag** (gag), *v.t.* [GAGGED, GAGGING], [echoic], 1. to cause to retch. 2. to keep from speaking, as by stopping the mouth of. *v.i.* to retch. *n.* 1. something put into the mouth to prevent talking, etc. 2. any restraint of free speech. 3. [Slang], a joke.
**gage** (gāj), *n.* [< OFr. *g(u)age*], 1. something given as a pledge. 2. a glove, etc. thrown down as a challenge to fight. 3. a challenge.
**gage** (gāj), *n.* & *v.t.* [GAGED, GAGING], gauge.

**gai·e·ty** (gā'ə-ti), *n.* [*pl.* -TIES], 1. the quality of being gay; cheerfulness. 2. merrymaking.
**gai·ly** (gā'li), *adv.* in a gay manner; specif., *a*) merrily. *b*) with bright display.
**gain** (gān), *n.* [< OFr. *gaaignier*], 1. an increase in advantage. 2. acquisition. *v.t.* 1. to earn. 2. to win. 3. to get as an addition, profit, or advantage. 4. to get to; reach. *v.i.* to make progress. **—gain on,** to draw nearer to (an opponent in a race).
**gain'ful,** *adj.* producing gain; profitable.
**gain·say** (gān'sā'), *v.t.* [-SAID, -SAYING], [*gain-* < AS. *gegn*, against], 1. to deny. 2. to contradict. 3. to speak or act against.
**gait** (gāt), *n.* [< ON. *gata*, path], 1. manner of walking or running. 2. any of the various foot movements of a horse, as a trot, canter, etc. **—gait'ed,** *adj.*
**gai·ter** (gā'tẽr), *n.* [Fr. *guêtre*], a cloth or leather covering for the instep, ankle, and lower leg.
**gal** (gal), *n.* [Slang], a girl.
**gal.,** gallon; gallons.
**ga·la** (gā'lə, gal'ə), *adj.* [< OFr. *gale*, enjoyment], festive. *n.* a festival.
**ga·lac·tic** (gə-lak'tik), *adj.* [< Gr. *gala*, milk], of the Milky Way, or Galaxy.
**Gal·a·had** (gal'ə-had'), *n.* in *Arthurian legend*, the knight who, because of his purity, found the Holy Grail.
**gal·ax·y** (gal'ək-si), *n.* [< Gr. *gala*, milk], 1. [often G-], the Milky Way. 2. [*pl.* -IES], any similar group of stars. 3. an assembly of illustrious people.
**gale** (gāl), *n.* [< ?], 1. a strong wind. 2. an outburst, as of laughter.
**ga·le·na** (gə-lē'nə), *n.* [L., lead ore], native lead sulfide, a lead-gray mineral with metallic luster: it is the principal ore of lead.
**gall** (gôl), *n.* [AS. *galla*], 1. a bitter, greenish fluid secreted by the liver; bile. 2. something bitter or distasteful. 3. bitter feeling. 4. [Colloq.], impudence.
**gall** (gôl), *n.* [AS. *gealla*], a sore on the skin caused by chafing. *v.t.* 1. to make (the skin) sore by chafing. 2. to irritate; annoy; vex.
**gall** (gôl), *n.* [< L. *galla*], a tumor on plant tissue caused by irritation due to fungi, insects, or bacteria.
**gal·lant** (gal'ənt), *adj.* [< OFr. *gale*, enjoyment], 1. stately; grand. 2. brave and noble; daring. 3. (gə-lant', gal'ənt), polite and attentive to women. *n.* (gal'ənt, gə-lant'), 1. a brave, noble man. 2. a man attentive and polite to women.
**gal'lant·ry,** *n.* [*pl.* -RIES], 1. heroic courage. 2. the behavior of a gallant. 3. *usually in pl.* an act or speech characteristic of a gallant.
**gall bladder,** a membranous sac attached to the liver, in which gall, or bile, is stored.
**gal·le·on** (gal'i-ən), *n.* [ult. < MGr. *galaia*, kind of ship], a large, 15th- and 16th-c. Spanish ship, with three or four decks.
**gal·ler·y** (gal'ẽr-i), *n.* [*pl.* -IES], [< ML. *galeria*], 1. a covered walk or porch open at one side. 2. a long, narrow balcony on the outside of a building. 3. a balcony in a theater, etc.; esp., the highest balcony with the cheapest seats. 4. the people occupying these seats. 5. an establishment for exhibitions, etc.: as, an art *gallery*.
**gal·ley** (gal'i), *n.* [*pl.* -LEYS], [< MGr. *galaia*, kind of ship], 1. a long, low ship of ancient times, propelled by oars and sails. 2. a large rowboat. 3. a ship's kitchen. 4. in *printing*, *a*) a shallow tray for holding composed type. *b*) proof printed from such type: in full, **galley proof.**
**Gal·lic** (gal'ik), *adj.* 1. of ancient Gaul or its people. 2. French.
**Gal·li·cize** (gal'ə-sīz'), *v.t.* & *v.i.* [-CIZED, -CIZING], to make or become French or like the French in thought, language, etc.
**gal·li·na·ceous** (gal'ə-nā'shəs), *adj.* [< L. *gallus*, a cock], of or belonging to a group of birds that nest on the ground, as grouse.
**gal·li·vant** (gal'ə-vant'), *v.i.* [arbitrary elaboration of *gallant*], to go about in search of amusement. **—gal'li·vant'er,** *n.*
**gal·lon** (gal'ən), *n.* [< LL. *galleta*, jug], a liquid measure, equal to 4 quarts.
**gal·lop** (gal'əp), *n.* [< OFr. *galoper*, to gallop], the fastest gait of a horse, etc., consisting of a succession of leaping strides. *v.i.* to go at a gallop. *v.t.* to cause to gallop.
**gal·lows** (gal'ōz), *n.* [*pl.* -LOWSES, -LOWS], [AS. *galga*], an upright frame with a crossbeam, for hanging condemned persons.
**gall·stone** (gôl'stōn'), *n.* a small, solid mass sometimes formed in the gall bladder or bile duct.
**gal·lus·es** (gal'əs-iz), *n.pl.* [< *gallows*], [Colloq.], suspenders.
**ga·lore** (gə-lôr'), *adv.* [Ir. *go leōr*, enough], in abundance; plentifully.
**ga·losh, ga·loshe** (gə-losh'), *n.* [OFr. *galoche*], *usually in pl.* a high overshoe of rubber and waterproof fabric.
**gal·van·ic** (gal-van'ik), *adj.* 1. of or producing an electric current, esp. from a battery. 2. startling. Also **gal·van'i·cal.**
**gal·va·nism** (gal'və-niz'm), *n.* [< L. *Galvani*, 18th-c. It. physicist], electricity produced by chemical action.
**gal'va·nize'** (-nīz'), *v.t.* [-NIZED, -NIZING], 1. to apply an electric current to. 2. to startle; excite. 3. to plate (metal) with zinc.
**galvanized iron,** iron coated with zinc as a protection against rust.
**gal'va·nom'e·ter** (-nom'ə-tẽr), *n.* an instrument for determining the intensity and direction of an electric current.
**gam·bit** (gam'bit), *n.* [< Sp. *gambeta*, a tripping], in *chess*, an opening in which a pawn or other piece is sacrificed to get an advantage in position.
**gam·ble** (gam'b'l), *v.i.* [-BLED, -BLING], [AS. *gamenian*, to play], 1. to play games of chance for money, etc. 2. to take a risk in order to gain some advantage. *v.t.* 1. to lose in gambling (with *away*). 2. to bet; wager. *n.* an undertaking involving risk.
**gam·bol** (gam'bəl), *v.i.* [-BOLED or -BOLLED, -BOLING or -BOLLING], [< It. *gamba*, leg], to jump and skip about in play; frolic. *n.* a gamboling; frolic.
**game** (gām), *n.* [AS. *gamen*], 1. any form of play; amusement; specif., an amusement or sport involving competition under rules. 2. a single contest in such a competition. 3. the number of points required for winning. 4. a scheme; plan. 5. wild birds, fish, or animals hunted for sport or food. *v.i.* [GAMED, GAMING], to play cards, etc. for stakes; gamble. *adj.* 1. designating or of wild animals, etc. hunted for sport or food. 2. [Colloq.], plucky; courageous. **—the game is up,** failure is certain.
**game** (gām), *adj.* [< ?], [Colloq.], lame.
**game'cock',** *n.* a specially bred rooster trained for cockfighting.
**game·ster** (gām'stẽr), *n.* one who gambles.
**gam·ete** (gam'ēt, gə-mēt'), *n.* [< Gr. *gamos*, marriage], a reproductive cell that unites with another to form the cell that develops into a new individual.
**game warden,** an official in charge of enforcing the game laws.
**gam·in** (gam'in), *n.* [Fr.], a homeless or neglected child who roams the streets.
**gam·ing** (gām'iŋ), *n.* gambling.
**gam·ma** (gam'ə), *n.* the third letter of the Greek alphabet (Γ, γ).
**gamma rays,** one of the three kinds of rays emitted by radioactive substances: they are similar to, but shorter than, X rays.
**gam·mon** (gam'ən), *n.* [< Gr. *kampē*, joint], a ham, smoked or cured.

**gam·ut** (gam′ət), *n.* [< Gr. *gamma* (the letter), designating the lowest note of the medieval scale], 1. an entire musical scale or range. 2. the entire range of anything.
**gam·y** (gām′i), *adj.* [-IER, -IEST], 1. having the strong flavor of cooked game. 2. slightly tainted. 3. plucky. —**gam′i·ly,** *adv.*
**gan·der** (gan′dẽr), *n.* [AS. *gan(d)ra*], 1. a male goose. 2. [Slang], a look.
**gang** (gaŋ), *n.* [AS. *gang*, a going], a group of people working or acting together: as, a *gang* of criminals, a neighborhood *gang*.
**gan·gling** (gaŋ′gliŋ), *adj.* [< ?], thin, tall, and awkward; lanky: also **gan′gly.**
**gan·gli·on** (gaŋ′gli-ən), *n.* [*pl.* -GLIA (-ə), -GLIONS], [< Gr. *ganglion*, tumor], a mass of nerve cells from which nerve impulses are transmitted.
**gang′plank′,** *n.* a movable ramp by which to board or leave a ship.
**gan·grene** (gaŋ′grēn), *n.* [< Gr. *grainein*, gnaw], decay of body tissue when the blood supply is obstructed by injury, disease, etc. —**gan′gre·nous** (-gri-nəs), *adj.*
**gang·ster** (gaŋ′stẽr), *n.* 1. a member of a gang of criminals. 2. any criminal.
**gang′way′,** *n.* [AS. *gangweg*], a passageway; specif., *a*) an opening in a ship's side. *b*) a gangplank. *interj.* clear the way!
**gan·net** (gan′it), *n.* [AS. *ganot*], a large, web-footed water bird.
**gant·let** (gônt′lit, gant′-), *n.* [< Sw. *gata*, lane + *lopp*, a run], 1. a former punishment in which the offender ran between two rows of men who struck him. 2. a series of troubles or difficulties.
**gaol** (jāl), *n.* a jail: Brit. sp.
**gap** (gap), *n.* [< ON. *gapa*, to gape], 1. a hole or opening made by breaking or parting. 2. a mountain pass or ravine. 3. a blank space; hiatus.
**gape** (gāp), *v.i.* [GAPED, GAPING], [< ON. *gapa*], 1. to open the mouth wide, as in yawning. 2. to stare with the mouth open. 3. to open wide. *n.* 1. a gaping. 2. a wide opening. —**gap′er,** *n.*
**gar** (gär), *n.* [*pl.* GAR, GARS], [AS. *gar*, a spear], a long fish with a beaklike snout: also **gar′fish′.**
**ga·rage** (gə-räzh′, -räj′), *n.* [Fr. < *garer*, protect], 1. a shelter for automobiles. 2. a place where automobiles are stored, repaired, etc. *v.t.* [-RAGED, -RAGING], to put or keep in a garage.
**garb** (gärb), *n.* [< OHG. *garawi*, dress], 1. clothing; style of dress. 2. external appearance. *v.t.* to clothe.
**gar·bage** (gär′bij), *n.* [ME., entails of fowls], waste parts of food.
**gar·ble** (gär′b'l), *v.t.* [-BLED, -BLING], [< Ar. *ghirbāl*, a sieve], to distort or confuse (a story, etc.) so as to mislead or misrepresent.
**gar·den** (gär′d'n), *n.* [< Frank. *gardo*], 1. a piece of ground for growing flowers, vegetables, or fruits. 2. an area of fertile land. 3. a public parklike place, often having displays of animal and plant life. *v.i.* to make or work in a garden. *adj.* of, for, or grown in a garden. —**gar′den·er,** *n.*
**gar·de·ni·a** (gär-dēn′yə), *n.* [< A. *Garden*, 18th-c. Am. botanist], a fragrant flower with waxy, white petals.
**Gar·gan·tu·a** (gär-gan′choo͞-ə), *n.* a giant king in a satire by Rabelais. —**Gar·gan′tu·an,** *adj.*
**gar·gle** (gär′g'l), *v.i.* & *v.t.* [-GLED, -GLING], [< L. *gurgulio*, throat], to rinse (the throat) with a liquid kept in motion by the expulsion of air from the lungs. *n.* a liquid for gargling.
**gar·goyle** (gär′goil), *n.* [see GARGLE], a waterspout in the form of a fantastic creature, projecting from the gutter of a building.
**gar·ish** (gâr′ish), *adj.* [prob. < ME. *gauren*, to stare], too bright or gaudy; glaring.
**gar·land** (gär′lənd), *n.* [< OFr. *garlande*], a wreath of flowers, leaves, etc. *v.t.* to decorate with garlands.
**gar·lic** (gär′lik), *n.* [< AS. *gar*, a spear + *leac*, a leek], 1. a plant of the lily family. 2. its strong-smelling bulb, used as seasoning. —**gar′lick·y,** *adj.*
**gar·ment** (gär′mənt), *n.* [see GARNISH], any article of clothing. *v.t.* to clothe.
**gar·ner** (gär′nẽr), *v.t.* [< L. *granum*, grain], to gather up and store. *n.* a granary.
**gar·net** (gär′nit), *n.* [< L. *granum*, a grain], 1. a hard, glasslike mineral of various colors: the most precious variety, used as a gem, is of a deep red. 2. deep red.
**gar·nish** (gär′nish), *v.t.* [prob. < MHG. *warnen*, prepare], 1. to decorate, trim. 2. to decorate (food) to add color or flavor. 3. to garnishee. *n.* 1. a decoration. 2. something used to garnish food, as parsley.
**gar·nish·ee** (gär′ni-shē′), *v.t.* [-EED, -EEING], in *law*, to attach (a debtor's property, wages, etc.) so that it can be used to pay the debt.
**gar·ni·ture** (gär′ni-chẽr), *n.* garnish.
**gar·ret** (gar′it), *n.* [< OFr. *garite*, watchtower], an attic.
**gar·ri·son** (gar′i-s'n), *n.* [< OFr. *garir*, to watch], 1. troops stationed in a fort. 2. a fortified place with troops, guns, etc. *v.t.* to station (troops) in (a fortified place) for its defense.
**gar·rote** (gə-rot′, -rōt′), *n.* [Sp.], 1. any device used in strangling a person. 2. a disabling by strangling. *v.t.* [-ROTED, -ROTING], to execute or attack by strangling.
**gar·ru·lous** (gar′oo-ləs, -yoo-), *adj.* [< L. *garrire*, to chatter], talking much, often about unimportant things. —**gar·ru·li·ty** (gə-roo͞′lə-ti), *n.* —**gar′ru·lous·ly,** *adv.*
**gar·ter** (gär′tẽr), *n.* [< OFr. *garet*, the back of the knee], an elastic band or strap for holding a stocking in place. *v.t.* to fasten with a garter.
**garter snake,** a small, harmless, yellow-striped snake, common in N.America.
**gas** (gas), *n.* [coined < Gr. *chaos*, chaos], 1. the fluid form of a substance in which it can expand indefinitely; vapor. 2. any mixture of inflammable gases used for lighting or heating. 3. any gas used as an anesthetic. 4. [Colloq.], gasoline. *v.t.* [GASSED, GASSING], to attack or kill by gas. *adj.* of or using gas.
**gas·e·ous** (gas′i-əs), *adj.* of, like, or in the form of, gas. —**gas′e·ous·ness,** *n.*
**gash** (gash), *v.t.* [< OFr. *garser*], to make a long, deep cut in. *n.* a long, deep cut.
**gas·ket** (gas′kit), *n.* [prob. < It. *gaschetta*, rope end], a piece or ring of rubber, metal, etc. used to make a joint leakproof.
**gas mask,** a filtering mask to protect against breathing in poisonous gases.
**gas·o·line, gas·o·lene** (gas′'l-ēn′), *n.* [< *gas* + L. *oleum*, oil], a volatile, inflammable liquid distilled from petroleum and used chiefly as a fuel in motor vehicles.
**gasp** (gasp), *v.i.* [< ON. *geispa*, to yawn], to catch the breath suddenly or with effort. *v.t.* to say with gasps. *n.* a gasping.
**gas station,** a place for the sale of gasoline, oil, etc. for motor vehicles.
**gas′sy,** *adj.* [-SIER, -SIEST], 1. full of or containing gas. 2. like gas.
**gas·tric** (gas′trik), *adj.* [< *gastro-* + *-ic*], of, in, or near the stomach.
**gastric juice,** the digestive fluid produced by glands in the stomach lining.
**gas·tri·tis** (gas-trī′tis), *n.* [< *gastro-* + *-itis*], inflammation of the stomach.
**gastro-,** [< Gr. *gastēr*], a combining form meaning *the stomach (and)*.
**gas·tron·o·my** (gas-tron′ə-mi), *n.* [< Gr. *gastēr*, stomach + *nomos*, law], the art of

good eating. —**gas'tro·nom'i·cal** (-trə-nom'-i-k'l), *adj.* —**gas'tro·nom'i·cal·ly**, *adv.*
**gas·tro·pod** (gas'trə-pod'), *n.* [*gastro-* + *-pod*], any of a large group of mollusks having single spiral shells, as the snail, or no shell, as certain slugs: gastropods move by means of a broad, muscular, ventral disk.
**gate** (gāt), *n.* [< AS. *geat*], 1. a movable structure controlling passage through an opening in a fence or wall. 2. a gateway. 3. a structure controlling the flow of water, as in a canal. 4. the total paid admissions to a performance or exhibition. —**give the gate,** [Slang], to get rid of.
**gate'way',** *n.* 1. an entrance in a wall, etc. fitted with a gate. 2. a means of getting at something.
**gath·er** (gath'ēr), *v.t.* [AS. *gad(e)rian*], 1. to bring together in one place or group. 2. to get gradually; accumulate. 3. to collect by picking, as a harvest. 4. to infer; conclude. 5. to draw into folds or pleats. *v.i.* 1. to assemble. 2. to increase. *n.* a pleat.
**gath'er·ing,** *n.* 1. the act of one that gathers. 2. what is gathered; specif., a meeting.
**gauche** (gōsh), *adj.* [Fr. < MFr. *gauchir*, become warped], awkward; tactless.
**gaud** (gôd), *n.* [prob. < OFr. *gaudir*, make merry], a cheap, showy ornament; trinket.
**gaud'y,** *adj.* [-IER, -IEST], bright and showy, but in bad taste. —**gaud'i·ness,** *n.*
**gauge** (gāj), *n.* [< ONorm.Fr. *gauger*, to gauge], 1. a standard measure. 2. any device for measuring. 3. the distance between the rails of a railway. 4. the size of the bore of a shotgun. *v.t.* [GAUGED, GAUGING], 1. to measure the size, amount, etc. of. 2. to estimate; judge. —**gaug'er,** *n.*
**Gaul** (gôl), *n.* 1. an ancient division of the Roman Empire, in W Europe. 2. any of the people of Gaul.
**Gaul'ish,** *n.* the Celtic language spoken in ancient Gaul.
**gaunt** (gônt, gänt), *adj.* [ME. *gawnte*], 1. thin and bony; haggard, as from great hunger or age. 2. looking grim or forbidding. —**gaunt'ly,** *adv.* —**gaunt'ness,** *n.*
**gaunt·let** (gônt'lit, gänt'-), *n.* [< OFr. *gant*, glove], 1. a knight's armored glove. 2. a long glove with a flaring cuff. —**throw down the gauntlet,** to challenge, as to combat.
**gaunt·let** (gônt'lit, gänt'-), *n.* a gantlet.
**gauze** (gôz), *n.* [Fr. *gaze*], any very thin, transparent, loosely woven material, as of cotton, silk, etc. —**gauz'y** [-IER, -IEST], *adj.*
**gave** (gāv), pt. of **give.**
**gav·el** (gav''l), *n.* [< ?], s small mallet used by a presiding officer in calling for attention.
**ga·votte** (gə-vot'), *n.* [Fr.], a 17th-c. dance like the minuet, but livelier.
**gawk** (gôk), *v.i.* [prob. < *gowk*, stupid person], [Colloq.], to stare stupidly.
**gawk·y** (gôk'i), *adj.* [-IER, -IEST], clumsy; ungainly. —**gawk'i·ly,** *adv.* —**gawk'i·ness,** *n.*
**gay** (gā), *adj.* [OFr. *gai*], 1. joyous and lively; merry. 2. bright; brilliant: as, *gay* colors.
**gay·e·ty** (gā'ə-ti), *n.* [*pl.* -TIES], gaiety.
**gay·ly** (gā'li), *adv.* gaily.
**gaze** (gāz), *v.i.* [GAZED, GAZING], [prob. < ON.], to look steadily; stare. *n.* a steady look. —**gaz'er,** *n.*
**ga·zelle** (gə-zel'), *n.* [< Ar. *ghazāl*], a small, swift antelope of Africa and Asia, with large, lustrous eyes.
**ga·zette** (gə-zet'), *n.* [Fr. < It. dial. *gazeta*, a small coin (price of the paper)], 1. a newspaper. 2. in England, an official government publication. *v.t.* [-ZETTED, -ZETTING], to announce or list in a gazette.
**gaz·et·teer** (gaz'ə-têr'), *n.* a dictionary of geographical names.
**Ge,** in *chem.*, germanium.
**gear** (gêr), *n.* [< ON. *gervi*, preparation], 1. clothing and personal equipment. 2. equipment for some task. 3. *a*) a system of toothed wheels meshed together so that the motion of one is passed on to the others. *b*) a gearwheel. *c*) proper working order: as, out of *gear*. *d*) a specific adjustment in motor-vehicle transmissions. *e*) a part of a mechanism performing a specific function: as, a steering *gear*. *v.t.* to connect by or furnish with gears. *v.i.* to be in proper working order. —**geared,** *adj.*
**gear'shift',** *n.* a device for connecting any of several sets of transmission gears to a motor, etc.
**gear'wheel',** *n.* a toothed wheel designed to mesh with another: also **gear wheel.**
**gee** (jē), *interj.* & *n.* a word of command to a horse, etc., meaning "turn right!" *v.t.* & *v.i.* [GEED, GEEING], to turn to the right.
**gee** (jē), *interj.* [< *Je*sus], [Slang], an exclamation of surprise, etc.
**geese** (gēs), *n.* pl. of **goose.**
**gee·zer** (gē'zēr), *n.* [ult. < *guise*], [Slang], an eccentric old man.
**Gei·ger counter** (gī'gēr), [< H. *Geiger*, G. physicist], an instrument for detecting and counting ionizing particles, as from radioactive ores.
**gei·sha** (gā'shə), *n.* [*pl.* -SHA, -SHAS], [Japan.], a Japanese professional singing and dancing girl.
**gel** (jel), *n.* [< *gelatin*], a jellylike substance formed by a colloidal solution. *v.i.* [GELLED, GELLING], to form a gel.
**gel·a·tin, gel·a·tine** (jel'ə-t'n), *n.* [< L. *gelare*, freeze], a tasteless, odorless substance extracted by boiling bones, hoofs, etc., or a similar vegetable substance: dissolved and cooled, it forms a jellylike substance used in food, photographic film, etc. —**ge·lat·i·nous** (ji-lat''n-əs), *adj.*
**geld** (geld), *v.t.* [GELDED or GELT, GELDING], [< ON. *geldr*, barren], to castrate (a horse, etc.).
**geld'ing,** *n.* a gelded animal, esp. a horse.
**gel·id** (jel'id), *adj.* [< L. *gelu*, frost], frozen; very cold. —**ge·lid·i·ty** (jə-lid'ə-ti), *n.*
**gem** (jem), *n.* [< L. *gemma*], 1. a precious stone, cut for use as a jewel. 2. anything prized for its beauty and value. *v.t.* [GEMMED, GEMMING], to adorn with gems.
**Gem·i·ni** (jem'ə-nī'), *n.pl.* [L., twins], the third sign of the zodiac.
**-gen,** [ult. < Gr. *gignesthai*, be born], a suffix meaning: 1. *something that produces*, as in *oxygen*. 2. *something produced* (in a specified way).
**Gen.,** 1. General. 2. Genesis.
**gen·darme** (zhän'därm), *n.* [Fr. < *gens d'armes*, men-at-arms], a policeman.
**gen·der** (jen'dēr), *n.* [< L. *genus*, origin], 1. in *grammar*, the classification by which words are grouped as masculine, feminine, or neuter. 2. [Colloq.], sex.
**gene** (jēn), *n.* [see -GEN], any of the elements in a chromosome by which hereditary characters are transmitted.
**gen·e·al·o·gy** (jē'ni-al'ə-ji), *n.* [*pl.* -GIES], [< Gr. *genea*, race + *legein*, speak], 1. a recorded history of one's ancestry. 2. the study of family descent. 3. descent from an ancestor; lineage. —**gen'e·a·log'i·cal** (-ə-loj'-i-k'l), *adj.* —**gen'e·al'o·gist,** *n.*
**gen·er·a** (jen'ēr-ə), *n.* pl. of **genus.**
**gen·er·al** (jen'ēr-əl), *adj.* [< L. *genus*, class], 1. of, for, or from all; not local or special. 2. of or for a whole genus, kind, etc. 3. widespread: as, *general* unrest. 4. most common; usual. 5. not specific or precise: as, in *general* terms. 6. highest in rank: as, attorney *general*. *n.* 1. an army officer ranking just above a lieutenant general: also **full general.** 2. any army officer ranking above a colonel. —**in general,** 1. usually. 2. without specific details. —**gen'er·al·ness,** *n.*

**General Assembly,** the United Nations legislative assembly.
**gen′er·al·is′si·mo′** (-is′ə-mō′), *n.* [*pl.* -MOS], [It.], the commander in chief of all the armed forces of a country.
**gen·er·al·i·ty** (jen′ə-ral′ə-ti), *n.* [*pl.* -TIES], 1. the quality of being general. 2. a nonspecific statement, idea, etc. 3. the majority.
**gen′er·al·ize′** (-īz′), *v.t.* [-IZED, -IZING], 1. to state in terms of a general law. 2. to infer from particular instances. *v.i.* 1. to formulate general principles. 2. to make vague statements. **—gen′er·al·i·za′tion,** *n.*
**gen′er·al·ly,** *adv.* 1. widely; popularly. 2. usually. 3. not specifically.
**General of the Army,** the highest rank in the U.S. Army.
**gen·er·ate** (jen′ə-rāt′), *v.t.* [-ATED, -ATING], [< L. *genus*, race], 1. to produce (offspring); beget. 2. to bring into being; produce. **—gen′er·a′tive,** *adj.*
**gen′er·a′tion,** *n.* 1. a generating; production. 2. a single stage in the succession of descent. 3. the average time (c. 30 years) between human generations. 4. all the people born at about the same time.
**gen′er·a′tor,** *n.* a machine for changing mechanical energy into electrical energy; dynamo.
**ge·ner·ic** (jə-ner′ik), *adj.* [< L. *genus*, race, kind], 1. inclusive or general; not specific. 2. of or characteristic of a genus. **—ge·ner′i·cal·ly,** *adv.*
**gen·er·os·i·ty** (jen′ə-ros′ə-ti), *n.* 1. the quality of being generous. 2. [*pl.* -TIES], a generous act.
**gen·er·ous** (jen′ēr-əs), *adj.* [< L. *generosus*, noble], 1. noble-minded; magnanimous. 2. willing to give or share; unselfish. 3. large; ample. **—gen′er·ous·ly,** *adv.*
**gen·e·sis** (jen′ə-sis), *n.* [Gr.], 1. [G-], the first book of the Old Testament. 2. [*pl.* -SES (-sēz′)], a beginning; origin; creation.
**ge·net·ics** (jə-net′iks), *n.pl.* [construed as sing.], [< *genesis*], the branch of biology dealing with heredity and variation in animal and plant species. **—ge·net′ic,** *adj.* **—ge·net′i·cal·ly,** *adv.* **—ge·net′i·cist** (-ə-sist), *n.*
**gen·ial** (jēn′yəl), *adj.* [see GENIUS], 1. good for life and growth: as, a *genial* climate. 2. cordial and kindly; amiable. **—ge·ni·al·i·ty** (jē′ni-al′ə-ti), *n.* **—gen′ial·ly,** *adv.*
**ge·nie** (jē′ni), *n.* [< Fr. < Ar. *jinni*], in *Moslem legend*, a supernatural being having magic power.
**gen·i·tal** (jen′ə-t'l), *adj.* [< L. *genere*, to beget], of reproduction or the sexual organs.
**gen′i·tals,** *n.pl.* the reproductive organs; esp., the external sex organs.
**gen·i·tive** (jen′ə-tiv), *adj.* [< Gr. *genos*, genus], designating or in the grammatical case expressing possession, origin, etc. *n.* the genitive case.
**gen·ius** (jēn′yəs), *n.* [L., guardian spirit], 1. particular spirit of a nation, place, age, etc. 2. natural ability; strong inclination (*to* or *for*). 3. great mental capacity and inventive ability. 4. a person having this.
**gen·o·cide** (jen′ə-sīd), *n.* [< Gr. *genos*, race; + *-cide*], the systematic killing of a whole people or nation. **—gen′o·cid′al,** *adj.*
**gen·re** (zhän′rə), *n.* [Fr. < L. *genus*, class], 1. a kind; sort; type. 2. painting in which ordinary subjects are treated realistically.
**gent** (jent), *n.* [Slang], a gentleman.
**gen·teel** (jen-tēl′), *adj.* [< Fr. *gentil*], 1. formerly, gentlemanly or ladylike. 2. affectedly well-bred, polite, etc.
**gen·tian** (jen′shən), *n.* [< *Genitus*, an ancient king], a plant with blue, white, red, or yellow flowers.
**gen·tile, Gen·tile** (jen′tīl), *n.* [< L. *gentilis*, of the same clan], any person not a Jew. *adj.* not Jewish.
**gen·til·i·ty** (jen-til′ə-ti), *n.* [*pl.* -TIES], [see GENTLE], 1. orig., the position of a person in the upper classes. 2. politeness; refinement.
**gen·tle** (jen′t'l), *adj.* [-TLER, -TLEST], [< L. *gentilis*, of the same clan], 1. of good birth. 2. refined; polite. 3. generous; kind. 4. tame: as, a *gentle* dog. 5. kindly; patient. 6. mild; moderate: as, a *gentle* tap. 7. gradual: as, a *gentle* slope. **—the gentle sex,** women. **—gen′tle·ness,** *n.* **—gen′tly,** *adv.*
**gen′tle·folk′,** *n.pl.* people of good birth and social standing: also **gentlefolks.**
**gen′tle·man** (-mən), *n.* [*pl.* -MEN], 1. a man of good birth and social standing. 2. a well-bred, courteous man. 3. *often in pl.* any man: polite term. **—gen′tle·man·ly,** *adj.* **—gen′tle·wom′an** [*pl.* -WOMEN], *n.fem.*
**gentleman's** (or **gentlemen's**) **agreement,** an unwritten agreement secured only by the parties' pledge of honor.
**gen·try** (jen′tri), *n.* [see GENTEEL], 1. people of good birth and social standing. 2. people of a particular class or group.
**gen·u·flect** (jen′yoo-flekt′), *v.i.* [< L. *genu*, knee + *flectere*, bend], to bend the knee, as in worship. **—gen′u·flec′tion, gen′u·flex′ion,** *n.*
**gen·u·ine** (jen′ū-in), *adj.* [< L. *genuinus*, inborn], 1. really being what it is said to be; true. 2. sincere. **—gen′u·ine·ly,** *adv.*
**ge·nus** (jē′nəs), *n.* [*pl.* GENERA (jen′ēr-ə), GENUSES], [L., race, class], 1. a class; kind; sort. 2. a classification of related plants or animals.
**geo-,** [< Gr. *gē*], a prefix meaning *earth, of the earth*, as in *geology*.
**ge·od·e·sy** (jē-od′ə-si), *n.* [< Gr. *gē*, the earth + *daiein*, to divide], the branch of mathematics concerned with measuring the earth and its surface. **—ge′o·det′ic,** (-ə-det′ik), *adj.*
**ge·og·ra·phy** (jē-og′rə-fi), *n.* [*pl.* -PHIES], [< Gr. *gē*, earth + *graphein*, write], 1. the science dealing with the earth's surface, continents, climates, plants, animals, resources, etc. 2. the physical features of a region. **—ge·og′ra·pher,** *n.* **—ge′o·graph′i·cal** (-ə-graf′i-k'l), **ge′o·graph′ic,** *adj.*
**ge·ol·o·gy** (jē-ol′ə-ji), *n.* [*pl.* -GIES], [*geo-* + *-logy*], the science dealing with the earth's crust and the development of its layers, including the study of rocks and fossils. **—ge′o·log′i·cal** (-ə-loj′i-k'l), *adj.* **—ge′o·log′i·cal·ly,** *adv.* **—ge·ol′o·gist,** *n.*
**ge·om·e·try** (jē-om′ə-tri), *n.* [*pl.* -TRIES], [< Gr. *gē*, earth + *metrein*, measure], the branch of mathematics dealing with the properties, measurement, and relationships of points, lines, planes, and solids. **—ge′o·met′ric** (-ə-met′rik), **ge′o·met′ri·cal,** *adj.*
**ge·o·phys·ics** (jē′ō-fiz′iks), *n.pl.* [construed as sing.], the science dealing with the effects of weather, winds, tides, etc. on the earth. **—ge′o·phys′i·cal,** *adj.*
**ge·o·pol·i·tics** (jē′ō-pol′ə-tiks), *n.pl.* [construed as sing.], [< G. *geopolitik*], the study of the relation of a nation's policies to geography.
**ge·ra·ni·um** (ji-rā′ni-əm), *n.* [< Gr. *geranos*, a crane], 1. a wild plant with pink or purple flowers and many-lobed leaves. 2. a related cultivated plant with showy flowers.
**ger·i·at·rics** (jer′i-at′riks), *n.pl.* [construed as sing.], [< Gr. *gēras*, old age; + *-iatrics*], the study of the diseases of old age.
**germ** (jũrm), *n.* [< L. *germen*, sprout], 1. the rudimentary form from which a new organism is developed; seed, bud, etc. 2. any microscopic, disease-causing organism, esp. one of the bacteria. 3. an origin.
**Ger·man** (jũr′mən), *adj.* of Germany, its people, language, etc. *n.* 1. a native of Germany. 2. the language of the Germans.

**ger·mane** (jẽr-mān′), *adj.* [see GERM], closely related; relevant.
**Ger·man·ic** (jẽr-man′ik), *adj.* 1. German. 2. designating or of the original language of the German peoples or the languages descended from it. *n.* the Germanic branch of languages.
**ger·ma·ni·um** (jẽr-mā′ni-əm), *n.* [< L. *Germania,* Germany], a rare, metallic chemical element: symbol, Ge.
**ger·mi·cide** (jũr′mə-sīd′), *n.* [< *germ* + *-cide*], anything used to destroy germs. —**ger′mi·cid′al,** *adj.*
**ger·mi·nal** (jũr′mə-n'l), *adj.* 1. of or like germs or germ cells. 2. in the first stage.
**ger·mi·nate** (jũr′mə-nāt′), *v.i. & v.t.* [-NATED, -NATING], [< L. *germen,* a sprout], to start developing; sprout, as from a seed. —**ger′mi·na′tion,** *n.*
**ger·on·tol·o·gy** (jer′ən-tol′ə-jē), *n.* [< Gr. *gerōn,* old man; +*-logy*], the scientific study of aging and the problems of the aged.
**ger·ry·man·der** (ger′i-man′dẽr, jer′-), *v.t. & v.i.* [< E. *Gerry,* governor of Mass. (1812) + *salamander,* from shape of the county redistricted then], to divide (a voting area) so as to give unfair advantage to one political party. *n.* redistricting of this kind.
**ger·und** (jer′ənd), *n.* [< L. *gerere,* to do], in *grammar,* a verbal noun ending in *-ing.*
**Ge·sta·po** (gə-stä′pō; G. -shtä′-), *n.* [< G. *Ge*heime *Sta*ats*po*lizei, secret state police], in Nazi Germany, the terrorist secret state police.
**ges·tate** (jes′tāt), *v.t.* [-TATED, -TATING], [< L. *gerere,* to bear], to carry in the uterus during pregnancy. —**ges·ta′tion,** *n.*
**ges·tic·u·late** (jes-tik′yoo-lāt′), *v.i.* [-LATED, -LATING], [see GESTURE], to make or use gestures.—**ges·tic′u·la′tion,** *n.*
**ges·ture** (jes′chẽr), *n.* [< L. *gerere,* to bear], 1. movement of part of the body, to express or emphasize ideas, emotions, etc. 2. any act or remark conveying a state of mind or intention, sometimes made only for effect. *v.i.* [-TURED, -TURING], to make gestures.
**get** (get), *v.t.* [GOT, GOT or GOTTEN, GETTING], [< ON. *geta*], 1. to come into the state of having; receive; obtain; acquire. 2. to arrive at: as, we *got* home early. 3. to go and bring: as, *get* your books. 4. to persuade: as, *get* him to go. 5. to cause to be: as, he *got* his hands dirty. 6. to prepare: as, I'll *get* dinner. 7. [Colloq.], to be compelled or obliged (with *have* or *has*): as, he's *got* to pass. 8. [Colloq.], to possess (with *have* or *has*): as, he's *got* red hair. 9. [Colloq.], to baffle or defeat: as, this problem *gets* me. 10. [Colloq.], to understand. 11. [Slang], to cause an emotional response in: as, that singer *gets* me. *v.i.* 1. to come or arrive (with *from, to,* etc.). 2. to come to be: as, I *got* into trouble. *Get* is used as an auxiliary for emphasis in passive constructions: as, we *got* beaten. *n.* the young of an animal. —**get along,** to manage or succeed. —**get around,** 1. to move from place to place. 2. to circumvent. 3. to influence as by flattery. —**get away,** 1. to go away. 2. to escape. —**get away with,** [Slang], to succeed in doing or taking without being discovered or punished. —**get by,** [Colloq.], to survive; manage. —**get off,** 1. to come off, down, or out of. 2. to leave or start. 3. to escape or help to escape. —**get on,** 1. to go on or into. 2. to put on. 3. to proceed. 4. to grow older. 5. to manage or succeed. —**get out,** 1. to go out or away. 2. to take out. 3. to be disclosed. 4. to publish. —**get over,** 1. to recover from. 2. to forget. —**get through,** 1. to finish. 2. to manage to survive. —**get together,** 1. to assemble. 2. [Colloq.], to reach an agreement. —**get up,** 1. to rise (from sleep, etc.). 2. to contrive; organize.
**get′a·way′,** *n.* 1. the act of starting, as in a race. 2. the act of escaping.
**Geth·sem·a·ne** (geth-sem′ə-ni), *n.* in the *Bible,* a garden outside of Jerusalem, scene of the agony, betrayal, and arrest of Jesus.
**get′-up′,** *n.* [Colloq.], costume; dress.
**gew·gaw** (gū′gô), *n.* [ME.], a trinket.
**gey·ser** (gī′zẽr, -sẽr), *n.* [< ON. *göysa,* to gush], a spring from which boiling water and steam gush into the air at intervals.
**ghast·ly** (gast′li, gäst′-), *adj.* [-LIER, -LIEST], [AS. *gastlic,* ghostly], 1. horrible; frightful. 2. ghostlike; pale. 3. [Colloq.], very unpleasant. —**ghast′li·ness,** *n.*
**gher·kin** (gũr′kin), *n.* [< D. *agurk*], a small pickled cucumber.
**ghet·to** (get′ō), *n.* [*pl.* -TOS], [It.], 1. a section of some European cities to which Jews were restricted. 2. any section of a city in which many members of an ethnic or racial group live.
**ghost** (gōst), *n.* [AS. *gast*], 1. the supposed disembodied spirit of a dead person, appearing as a pale, shadowy apparition. 2. a faint semblance: as, not a *ghost* of a chance. —**give up the ghost,** to die.
**ghost′ly,** *adj.* [-LIER, -LIEST], 1. of or like a ghost. 2. spiritual. —**ghost′li·ness,** *n.*
**ghost writer,** one who writes speeches, articles, etc. for another who professes to be the author.
**ghoul** (gōōl), *n.* [< Ar. *ghūla,* seize], in *Oriental folklore,* an evil spirit that robs graves and feeds on the dead. —**ghoul′ish,** *adj.* —**ghoul′ish·ly,** *adv.* —**ghoul′ish·ness,** *n.*
**GHQ, G.H.Q.,** General Headquarters.
**GI, G.I.** (jē′ī′), *adj.* 1. government issue: designating clothing, etc. issued to military personnel. 2. [Colloq.], of or characteristic of the U.S. armed forces. *n.* [Colloq.], an enlisted soldier.
**gi·ant** (jī′ənt), *n.* [< Gr. *gigas*], 1. an imaginary being of human form but of superhuman size. 2. a person or thing of great size, strength, intellect, etc. *adj.* like a giant. —**gi′ant·ess,** *n.fem.*
**gib·ber** (jib′ẽr, gib′-), *v.i. & v.t.* [echoic], to speak or utter rapidly and incoherently.
**gib′ber·ish,** *n.* unintelligible chatter.
**gib·bet** (jib′it), *n.* [< Frankish *gibb,* forked stick], 1. a gallows. 2. a structure from which bodies of executed criminals were hung and exposed to public scorn. *v.t.* to hang on a gibbet.
**gib·bon** (gib′ən), *n.* [Fr.], a small, slender, long-armed ape of India, S China, and the East Indies.
**gibe** (jīb), *n., v.i. & v.t.* [GIBED, GIBING], [? < OFr. *giber,* handle roughly], jeer; taunt.
**gib·let** (jib′lit), *n.* [< OFr. *gibelet,* stew made of game], *usually in pl.* any of the edible internal parts of a fowl, as the gizzard.
**gid·dy** (gid′i), *adj.* [-DIER, -DIEST], [< AS. *gydig,* insane], 1. having or causing a whirling, dazed sensation; dizzy. 2. frivolous.
**Gid·e·on** (gid′i-ən), *n.* in the *Bible,* a hero of Israel who led his people victoriously in battle.
**gift** (gift), *n.* [< AS. *giefan,* give], 1. something given; present. 2. the act of giving. 3. a natural ability; talent.
**gift′ed,** *adj.* having a natural ability or aptitude; talented. —**gift′ed·ness,** *n.*
**gig** (gig), *n.* [prob. < ON.], 1. a light, two-wheeled open carriage drawn by one horse. 2. a long, light ship's boat with oars and sail.
**gi·gan·tic** (jī-gan′tik), *adj.* [see GIANT], huge; enormous; immense. —**gi·gan′ti·cal·ly,** *adv.*
**gig·gle** (gig′'l), *v.i.* [-GLED, -GLING], [? < MD.], to laugh with uncontrollable, rapid, high-pitched sounds, suggestive of foolishness, etc. *n.* such a laugh. —**gig′gler,** *n.*
**gig·o·lo** (jig′ə-lō′), *n.* [*pl.* -LOS], [Fr.], a man paid to be a woman's escort.

**Gi·la monster** (hē′lə), [< the *Gila* River, Ariz.], a stout, poisonous, black-and-orange lizard found in desert regions of the Southwest.

**gild** (gild), *v.t.* [GILDED OR GILT, GILDING], [AS. *gyldan*], 1. to overlay with a thin layer of gold. 2. to make (something) seem more attractive or valuable than it is.

**gill** (gil), *n.* [ME. *gile*], the organ for breathing of most animals that live in water, as fish, etc.

**gill** (jil), *n.* [< L. *gillo*, cooling vessel], a liquid measure, equal to ¼ pint.

**gilt** (gilt), alt. pt. and pp. of **gild.** *adj.* gilded. *n.* a thin layer of gold, or a substance like gold, covering a surface.

**gilt′-edged′,** *adj.* 1. having the edge gilded. 2. of the highest quality or value: said of bonds, securities, etc. Also **gilt′-edge′.**

**gim·bals** (jim′b'lz, gim′-), *n.pl.* [< L. *geminus*, twin], a device consisting of a pair of rings pivoted so that one is free to swing within the other: a ship's compass suspended in gimbals will stay horizontal.

**gim·let** (gim′lit), *n.* [< MD. *wimpel*], a small boring tool with a spiral cutting edge.

**gim·mick** (gim′ik), *n.* [? < G. *gemach*, convenience], [Slang], any tricky or deceptive device.

**gin** (jin), *n.* [< L. *juniperus*, juniper], a strong alcoholic liquor distilled from grain and usually flavored with juniper berries.

**gin** (jin), *n.* [ME., abbrev. of *engin*; see ENGINE], 1. a snare or trap, as for game. 2. a machine for separating cotton from the seeds. *v.t.* [GINNED, GINNING], 1. to trap. 2. to run (cotton) through a gin.

**gin·ger** (jin′jẽr), *n.* [< LL. *zingiber*], 1. a tropical herb whose rootstalks are used for flavoring and in medicine. 2. a spice made from the rootstalk. 3. [Colloq.], vigor; spirit. **—gin′ger·y,** *adj.*

**ginger ale,** an effervescent, nonalcoholic drink flavored with ginger.

**gin′ger·bread′,** *n.* 1. a cake flavored with ginger. 2. showy ornamentation.

**gin′ger·ly,** *adv.* carefully; timidly. *adj.* careful; timid. **—gin′ger·li·ness,** *n.*

**ging·ham** (giŋ′əm), *n.* [< Malay *gingan*, striped], a cotton cloth, usually woven in stripes, checks, or plaids.

**gin·gi·vi·tis** (jin′jə-vi′tis), *n.* [< L. *gingiva*, the gum; + *-itis*], inflammation of the gums.

**gin rummy,** a variety of the card game rummy, for two or more players.

**gin·seng** (jin′seŋ), *n.* [Chin. *jen shen*], an herb with a thick, aromatic root, used medicinally.

**gip** (jip), *n., v.t. & v.i.* gyp.

**gip·sy** (jip′si), *n.* [*pl.* -SIES], a gypsy.

**gi·raffe** (jə-raf′, -räf′), *n.* [Fr.; ult. < Ar. *zarāfah*], a large, cud-chewing animal of Africa, with a very long neck and legs.

**gird** (gũrd), *v.t.* [GIRT OR GIRDED, GIRDING], [AS. *gyrdan*], 1. to encircle or fasten with a belt. 2. to encircle. 3. to prepare (oneself) for action.

**gird·er** (gũr′dẽr), *n.* a large wooden or steel beam for supporting the joists of a floor, a framework, etc.

**gir·dle** (gũr′d'l), *n.* [AS. *gyrdel*], 1. a belt for the waist. 2. anything that surrounds. 3. a light, corsetlike garment, for supporting the waist and hips. *v.t.* [-DLED, -DLING], 1. to bind as with a girdle. 2. to encircle.

**girl** (gũrl), *n.* [ME. *girle*, youngster], 1. a female child. 2. a young, unmarried woman. 3. a female servant. 4. [Colloq.], a sweetheart. **—girl′hood,** *n.* **—girl′ish,** *adj.*

**Girl Scouts,** a club to provide character-building activities for girls.

**girt** (gũrt), pt. and pp. of **gird.**

**girt** (gũrt), *v.t.* 1. to gird. 2. to fasten with a girdle, belt, etc.

**girth** (gũrth), *n.* [< ON. *gyrtha*, encircle], 1. a band put around the belly of a horse, etc. to hold a saddle or pack. 2. the circumference, as of a tree trunk or person's waist.

**gist** (jist), *n.* [< OFr. *giste*, point at issue], the essence or main point, as of an article or argument.

**give** (giv), *v.t.* [GAVE, GIVEN, GIVING], [AS. *giefan*], 1. to hand over as a present. 2. to hand over; deliver: as, he *gave* the boy his bag. 3. to pay, as money. 4. to cause to have: as, oil *gives* a wave to hair. 5. to grant; allow. 6. to produce; supply: as, cows *give* milk. 7. to yield; concede. 8. to offer: as, *give* advice. 9. to utter (words, etc.): as, *give* a reply. 10. to perform: as, we *gave* a concert. 11. to inflict (a whipping, etc.). *v.i.* to bend, move, etc. from force or pressure. *n.* a bending, moving, etc. under pressure. **—give away,** 1. to make a gift of. 2. to give (the bride) to the bridegroom. 3. [Colloq.], to expose. **—give forth** (or **off**), to emit. **—give in,** to yield. **—give it to,** [Colloq.], to beat or scold. **—give out,** 1. to make public. 2. to distribute. 3. to become worn out, etc. **—give up,** 1. to relinquish. 2. to stop. 3. to stop trying. 4. to lose hope for. 5. to devote wholly. **—giv′er,** *n.*

**give′a·way′,** *n.* [Colloq.], 1. an unintentional revelation. 2. anything given free or as a bargain. *adj.* [Colloq.], being or involving a giveaway.

**giv·en** (giv′'n), pp. of **give.** *adj.* 1. bestowed. 2. accustomed, as from habit: as, *given* to drink. 3. stated. 4. in *logic & math.*, assumed; granted.

**given name,** a person's first name.

**giz·zard** (giz′ẽrd), *n.* [< L. *gigeria*, cooked entrails of poultry], the muscular second stomach of a bird.

**Gk.,** Greek.

‡**gla·cé** (glă′sā′), *adj.* [Fr.], 1. having a smooth, glossy surface. 2. covered with icing or sugar. 3. frozen; iced.

**gla·cial** (glā′shəl), *adj.* 1. of ice or glaciers. 2. of or produced by a glacial epoch.

**glacial epoch,** any period when much of the earth was covered with glaciers.

**gla·ci·ate** (glā′shi-āt′), *v.t.* [-ATED, -ATING], 1. to cover over with ice or a glacier. 2. to expose to or change by glacial action.

**gla·cier** (glā′shẽr), *n.* [< L. *glacies*, ice], a large mass of ice and snow moving slowly down a mountain or valley.

**glad** (glad), *adj.* [GLADDER, GLADDEST], [AS. *glæd*], 1. happy. 2. causing joy; making happy. 3. pleased; willing. 4. bright; gay.

**glad** (glad), *n.* [Slang], a gladiolus.

**glad′den** (-'n), *v.t. & v.i.* to make or become glad. **—glad′den·er,** *n.*

**glade** (glād), *n.* [prob. akin to *glad*], an open space in a forest.

**glad·i·a·tor** (glad′i-ā′tẽr), *n.* [L. < *gladius*, sword], 1. in ancient Rome, a slave or paid performer who fought in an arena as a public show. 2. any person involved in a fight, etc. **—glad′i·a·to′ri·al** (-ə-tôr′i-əl), *adj.*

**glad·i·o·lus** (glad′i-ō′ləs), *n.* [*pl.* -LUSES, -LI (-lī)], [L. < *gladius*, sword], a plant of the iris family with swordlike leaves and tall spikes of funnel-shaped flowers in various colors: also **glad′i·o′la.**

**glad′some** (-səm), *adj.* 1. giving joy; delightful. 2. joyful; cheerful.

**Glad·stone (bag)** (glad′stōn′), [after W. *Gladstone*, Brit. statesman], a traveling bag hinged to open flat.

**glair** (glâr), *n.* [< L. *clarus*, clear], raw white of egg, used in sizing. **—glair′y,** *adj.*

**glam·our, glam·or** (glam′ẽr), *n.* [Scot. var. of *grammer*, magic], seemingly mysterious allure; bewitching charm. **—glam′or·ous, glam′our·ous,** *adj.*

**glance** (glans, gläns), ***v.i.*** [GLANCED, GLANCING], [< OFr. *glacier*, to slip], 1. to strike obliquely and go off at an angle. 2. to flash; gleam. 3. to look suddenly and briefly. ***n.*** 1. a glancing off. 2. a flash; gleam. 3. a quick glimpse.

**gland** (gland), ***n.*** [< L. *glans*, acorn], any organ that separates certain elements from the blood and secretes them for the body to use or throw off. **—glan·du·lar** (glan′joo-lẽr), ***adj.***

**glare** (glâr), ***v.i.*** [GLARED, GLARING], [ME. *glaren*], 1. to shine with a steady, dazzling light. 2. to stare fiercely. ***v.t.*** to express with a glare. ***n.*** 1. a steady, dazzling light. 2. a fierce or angry stare. 3. a bright, glassy surface, as of ice.

**glar′ing,** ***adj.*** 1. dazzlingly bright. 2. too showy. 3. staring fiercely. 4. flagrant: as, a *glaring* mistake. Also **glar′y.**

**glass** (glas, gläs), ***n.*** [AS. *glæs*], 1. a hard, brittle substance, usually transparent, made by fusing silicates with soda, lime, etc. 2. glassware. 3. *a*) an article made of glass, as a drinking container, mirror, etc. *b*) *pl.* eyeglasses or binoculars. 4. the quantity contained in a drinking glass. ***v.t.*** to enclose in glass. ***adj.*** of or made of glass. **—glass′ful′** [*pl.* -FULS], ***n.***

**glass′ware′,** ***n.*** articles made of glass.

**glass′y,** ***adj.*** [-IER, -IEST], 1. like glass; smooth; transparent. 2. expressionless or lifeless: as, a *glassy* stare. **—glass′i·ness,** ***n.***

**glau·co·ma** (glô-kō′mə), ***n.*** [see GLAUCOUS], a disease of the eye, with hardening of the eyeball.

**glau·cous** (glô′kəs), ***adj.*** [< Gr. *glaukos*, gleaming], 1. green with a grayish-blue cast. 2. covered with a whitish bloom that can be rubbed off, as grapes, plums, etc.

**glaze** (glāz), ***v.t.*** [GLAZED, GLAZING], [ME. *glasen*], 1. to furnish (windows, etc.) with glass. 2. to give a hard, glossy finish to (pottery, etc.). 3. to cover (food) with a sugary coating. ***v.i.*** to become glassy or glossy. ***n.*** a glassy coating, as on pottery.

**gla·zier** (glā′zhẽr), ***n.*** 1. one whose work is fitting glass in windows. 2. one whose work is glazing pottery.

**gleam** (glēm), ***n.*** [AS. *glæm*], 1. a flash or beam of light. 2. a faint light. 3. a faint manifestation, as of hope, etc. ***v.i.*** 1. to shine with a gleam. 2. to appear suddenly.

**glean** (glēn), ***v.t. & v.i.*** [< Celt.], 1. to collect (grain left by reapers). 2. to collect (facts, etc.) gradually. **—glean′er,** ***n.***

**glee** (glē), ***n.*** [AS. *gleo*], 1. gaiety; joy; merriment. 2. a part song for three or more voices. **—glee′ful,** ***adj.*** **—glee′ful·ly,** ***adv.***

**glee club,** a group singing part songs.

**glen** (glen), ***n.*** [< Scot. Gael. *glenn*], a narrow, secluded valley.

**glib** (glib), ***adj.*** [GLIBBER, GLIBBEST], [cf. D. *glibberig*, slippery], 1. speaking or spoken fluently. 2. speaking or spoken too easily to be convincing. **—glib′ly,** ***adv.***

**glide** (glīd), ***v.i.*** [GLIDED, GLIDING], [AS. *glidan*], 1. to move smoothly and easily. 2. to descend slowly in an airplane without using an engine. ***v.t.*** to cause to glide. ***n.*** 1. a smooth, easy flow. 2. a slow descent in an airplane without using an engine.

**glid′er,** ***n.*** 1. one that glides. 2. an engineless airplane flown by being manipulated into air currents that keep it aloft. 3. a porch swing suspended in a frame.

**glim·mer** (glim′ẽr), ***v.i.*** [< AS. *glæm*, gleam], 1. to give a faint, flickering light. 2. to appear faintly. ***n.*** 1. a faint, flickering light. 2. a dim perception; glimpse.

**glimpse** (glimps), ***v.t.*** [GLIMPSED, GLIMPSING], [< *glimmer*], to catch a brief, quick view of. ***v.i.*** to look quickly. ***n.*** 1. a flash. 2. a slight trace; inkling. 3. a brief, quick view.

**glint** (glint), ***v.i.*** [prob. < ON.], to gleam; flash. ***n.*** a gleam.

**glis·san·do** (gli-sän′dō), ***n.*** [*pl.* -DI (-di)], [as if It. < Fr. *glisser*, to slide], in *music*, a gliding effect.

**glis·ten** (glis′′n), ***v.i. & n.*** [AS. *glisnian*], shine; sparkle; gleam.

**glit·ter** (glit′ẽr), ***v.i.*** [prob. < ON. *glitra*], 1. to shine; sparkle. 2. to be showy and bright. ***n.*** 1. a sparkling light. 2. showiness; brilliance. **—glit′ter·ing, glit′ter·y,** ***adj.***

**gloam·ing** (glōm′iŋ), ***n.*** [< AS. *glom*, twilight], evening dusk; twilight.

**gloat** (glōt), ***v.i.*** [prob. < ON. *glotta*, grin scornfully], to gaze or meditate with malicious pleasure. **—gloat′er,** ***n.***

**glob·al** (glō′b'l), ***adj.*** world-wide.

**globe** (glōb), ***n.*** [< L. *globus*, ball], 1. a ball-shaped thing; sphere. 2. the earth; world. 3. a spherical model of the earth. 4. anything shaped somewhat like a globe, as a light bulb. **—glo′bate,** (-bāt), ***adj.***

**globe′-trot′ter,** ***n.*** one who travels widely about the world, especially for pleasure.

**glob·u·lar** (glob′yoo-lẽr), ***adj.*** 1. shaped like a globe. 2. made up of globules.

**glob·ule** (glob′yool), ***n.*** [< L. *globus*, ball], a tiny ball; very small drop.

**glock·en·spiel** (glok′ən-spēl′), ***n.*** [G. < *glocke*, bell + *spiel*, play], a musical instrument with tuned metal bars in a frame, played with hammers.

**glom·er·ate** (glom′ẽr-it), ***adj.*** [< L. *glomus*, ball], formed into a rounded mass.

**gloom** (gloom), ***n.*** [prob. < AS. *glom*, twilight], 1. darkness; dimness. 2. a dark or dim place. 3. sadness; dejection. **—gloom′y** [-IER, -IEST], ***adj.*** **—gloom′i·ness,** ***n.***

**glo·ri·fy** (glôr′ə-fī′), ***v.t.*** [-FIED, -FYING], [< L. *gloria*, glory + *facere*, make], 1. to give glory to. 2. to exalt in worship. 3. to honor; extol. 4. to make, or make seem, better, greater, etc. **—glo′ri·fi·ca′tion,** ***n.***

**glo′ri·ous** (-i-əs), ***adj.*** 1. full of glory. 2. receiving or deserving glory. 3. splendid; magnificent. **—glo′ri·ous·ly,** ***adv.***

**glo·ry** (glôr′i), ***n.*** [*pl.* -RIES], [< L. *gloria*], 1. great honor; fame. 2. anything bringing this. 3. worship. 4. the height of prosperity, pleasure, pride, etc. 5. splendor. 6. heavenly bliss. 7. a halo (sense 2). ***v.i.*** [-RIED, -RYING], to be proud; exult (*in*).

**gloss** (glôs), ***n.*** [? < ON.], 1. the luster of a polished surface. 2. a deceiving outward show. ***v.t.*** 1. to give a shiny surface to. 2. to make (an error, etc.) appear right or trivial. **—gloss′y** [-IER, -IEST], ***adj.***

**gloss** (glôs), ***n.*** [< Gr. *glōssa*, tongue], a note of comment or explanation, as in a footnote. ***v.t.*** 1. to annotate. 2. to interpret falsely.

**glos·sa·ry** (glos′ẽr-i, glôs′-), ***n.*** [*pl.* -RIES], [< Gr. *glōssa*, tongue], a list of difficult terms with explanations, as for a book, author, subject, etc.

**glot·tal** (glot′'l), ***adj.*** of or articulated at the glottis, as English *h*.

**glot·tis** (glot′is), ***n.*** [< Gr. *glōssa*, tongue], the opening between the vocal cords.

**glove** (gluv), ***n.*** [AS. *glof*], 1. a covering for the hand, with separate sheaths for the fingers and thumb. 2. a baseball player's mitt. 3. a boxing glove. ***v.t.*** [GLOVED, GLOVING], to cover as with a glove.

**glow** (glō), ***v.i.*** [AS. *glowan*], 1. to give off a bright light due to great heat. 2. to give out a steady light. 3. to be or feel hot. 4. to be enlivened by emotion. 5. to be bright with color. ***n.*** 1. light given off as a result of great heat. 2. any steady, even light. 3. brightness, warmth, etc.

**glow·er** (glou′ẽr), ***v.i.*** [prob. < ON.], to stare with sullen anger. ***n.*** a sullen, angry stare; scowl. **—glow′er·ing·ly,** ***adv.***

**glow′worm′,** ***n.*** a wingless insect or insect

larva that gives off a phosphorescent glow.

**glu·cose** (glōō'kōs), *n.* [< Gr. *glykys*, sweet], 1. a crystalline sugar, occurring naturally in fruits and honey: also *dextrose*. 2. a sweet sirup prepared by the hydrolysis of starch.

**glue** (glōō), *n.* [< LL. *glus*, glue], 1. a sticky, viscous liquid prepared from animal gelatin and used to stick things together. 2. any substance so used. *v.t.* [GLUED, GLUING], to stick together as with glue. **—glue'y,** *adj.*

**glum** (glum), *adj.* [GLUMMER, GLUMMEST], [< ME. *gloum(b)en*, look morose], gloomy; sullen. **—glum'ly,** *adv.* **—glum'ness,** *n.*

**glut** (glut), *v.i.* [GLUTTED, GLUTTING], [< L. *glutire*, to swallow], to overindulge. *v.t.* 1. to feed, fill, etc. to excess. 2. to supply (the market) beyond demand. *n.* 1. a glutting or being glutted. 2. a supply that is greater than the demand.

**glu·ten** (glōō't'n), *n.* [L., glue], a gray, sticky, nutritious substance found in wheat flour. **—glu'te·nous,** *adj.*

**glu·ti·nous** (glōō'ti-nəs), *adj.* [< L. *gluten*, glue], gluey; sticky. **—glu'ti·nous·ly,** *adv.*

**glut·ton** (glut''n), *n.* [< L. *glutire*, devour], one who eats too much. **—glut'ton·ous,** *adj.*

**glut·ton·y,** *n.* [*pl.* -IES], the habit or act of eating too much.

**glyc·er·in, glyc·er·ine** (glis'ẽr-in), *n.* [< Gr. *glykeros*, sweet], a colorless, sirupy liquid prepared from fats and oils: used in skin lotion, explosives, etc.

**gly·co·gen** (gli'kə-jən), *n.* [< Gr. *glykeros*, sweet], a starchlike substance produced in animal tissues that is changed into a simple sugar as needed by the body.

**gm.,** gram; grams.

**Gmc.,** Germanic.

**gnarl** (närl), *n.* [< ME. *knarre*], a knot on a tree trunk or branch. *v.t.* to twist; make knotted. **—gnarled, gnarl'y,** *adj.*

**gnash** (nash), *v.i. & v.t.* [prob. < ON.], to grind (the teeth) together, as in anger.

**gnat** (nat), *n.* [AS. *gnæt*], any of various small, two-winged insects that bite or sting.

**gnaw** (nô), *v.t. & v.i.* [GNAWED, GNAWED or GNAWN, GNAWING], [AS. *gnagen*], 1. to bite and wear away bit by bit; consume. 2. to torment, as by constant pain.

**gneiss** (nīs), *n.* [< OHG. *gneisto*, a spark], a granitelike rock formed of layers of feldspar, quartz, mica, etc. **—gneiss'ic,** *adj.*

**gnome** (nōm), *n.* [ult. < Gr. *gnōmē*, thought], in *folklore*, a dwarf who dwells in the earth and guards its treasures.

**gno·mon** (nō'mon), *n.* [< Gr. *gignōskein*, know], a column, pin on a sundial, etc. that casts a shadow indicating the time of day.

**gnos·tic** (nos'tik), *adj.* [< Gr. *gnōsis*, knowledge], of or having knowledge.

**gnu** (nōō), *n.* [< the native name], a large African antelope with an oxlike head and horns and a horselike mane and tail.

**go** (gō), *v.i.* [WENT, GONE, GOING], [AS. *gan*], 1. to move along; travel; proceed. 2. to depart; leave. 3. to work; operate: as, the motor won't *go*. 4. to result; turn out. 5. to pass: said of time. 6. to become: as, to *go* wild. 7. to be expressed, sung, etc.: as, how does the song *go*? 8. to be in harmony: as, blue *goes* with gold. 9. to fail: as, his hearing *went* first. 10. to be given or sold. 11. to belong: as, the socks *go* in this drawer. *n.* [*pl.* GOES], 1. a success. 2. [Colloq.], a try; attempt. **—go back on,** [Colloq.], 1. to betray. 2. to break (a promise, etc.). **—go for,** 1. to try to get. 2. [Slang], to be attracted by. **—go hard with,** to cause trouble to. **—go in for,** [Colloq.], to engage or indulge in. **—go off,** 1. to depart. 2. to explode. **—go out,** 1. to be extinguished, become outdated, etc. 2. to attend social affairs, etc. **—go over,** 1. to examine thoroughly. 2. to do again. 3. [Colloq.], to be successful. **—go through,** 1. to endure; experience. 2. to search. **—go through with,** to complete. **—go up,** 1. to ascend. 2. to increase. **—let go,** 1. to let escape. 2. to release one's hold. **—let oneself go,** to be unrestrained. **—on the go,** [Colloq.], in constant motion or action.

**goad** (gōd), *n.* [AS. *gad*], 1. a sharp-pointed stick used in driving oxen. 2. any driving impulse; spur. *v.t.* to drive as with a goad.

**go'-a·head',** *n.* permission or an order to proceed: usually with *the*.

**goal** (gōl), *n.* [ME. *gol*, boundary], 1. the place at which a race, trip, etc. is ended. 2. an end that one strives to attain. 3. in some games, *a*) the line, net, etc. over or into which the ball or puck must go to score. *b*) the score made.

**goal'keep'er,** *n.* in some games, a player stationed at a goal to block the ball or puck: also [Colloq.], **goal'ie** (-i).

**goat** (gōt), *n.* [AS. *gat*], 1. a cud-chewing mammal with hollow, backward-curving horns, related to the sheep. 2. [Slang], a scapegoat. **—get one's goat,** [Slang], to irritate one.

**goat·ee** (gō-tē'), *n.* a pointed beard.

**goat'herd',** *n.* one who herds goats.

**goat'skin',** *n.* the hide of a goat, used as a garment, wine bottle, etc.

**gob** (gob), *n.* [< OFr. *gobe*, mouth], [Colloq.], a lump, chunk, or mass.

**gob** (gob), *n.* [< ?], [Slang], a sailor in the U.S. Navy.

**gob·ble** (gob''l), *n.* [echoic], the throaty sound made by a male turkey. *v.i.* [-BLED, -BLING], to make this sound. **—gob'bler,** *n.*

**gob·ble** (gob''l), *v.t. & v.i.* [-BLED, -BLING], [prob. < OFr. *gobe*, mouth], 1. to eat fast and greedily. 2. [Slang], to seize eagerly.

**gob'ble·dy·gook'** (-di-gook'), *n.* [Slang], pompous and wordy talk or writing.

**go-be·tween** (gō'bi-twēn'), *n.* one who passes back and forth between others with messages, etc.

**gob·let** (gob'lit), *n.* [ult. < LL. *cuppa*, cup], a drinking glass with a base and stem.

**gob·lin** (gob'lin), *n.* [< ML. *gobelinus*], in *folklore*, an evil or mischievous spirit.

**go-by** (gō'bi'), *n.* [Colloq.], an intentional disregard or slight.

**god** (god), *n.* [AS.], 1. any of various beings conceived of as supernatural, immortal, and having special powers over people and nature. 2. an idol. 3. a person or thing deified. 4. [G-], in *monotheism*, the creator and ruler of the universe, eternal and all-powerful; Supreme Being. **—god'like',** *adj.*

**god'child',** *n.* [*pl.* -CHILDREN], the person for whom a godparent is sponsor.

**god'daugh'ter,** *n.* a female godchild.

**god'dess,** *n.* 1. a female god. 2. a woman of very great charm or beauty.

**god'fa'ther,** *n.* a male godparent.

**god'head** (-hed), *n.* 1. the state or quality of being a god: also **god'hood.** 2. [G-], God.

**Go·di·va** (gə-di'və), *n.* in *English legend*, an 11th-century noblewoman who rode naked through the streets on condition that her husband abolish a heavy tax.

**god'less,** *adj.* 1. irreligious. 2. wicked.

**god'ly,** *adj.* [-LIER, -LIEST], devoted to God; devout. **—god'li·ness,** *n.*

**god'moth'er,** *n.* a female godparent.

**god'par'ent,** *n.* a person who sponsors a newborn child and assumes responsibility for its faith.

**god'send',** *n.* anything that comes unexpectedly and when needed or desired, as if sent by God.

**god'son',** *n.* a male godchild.

**God'speed',** *n.* [contr. of *God speed you*], success; good luck: a wish made for travelers.

**go-get·ter** (gō′get′ẽr), *n.* [Slang], an active, aggressive person who usually gets what he wants.

**gog·gle** (gog′'l), *v.i.* [-GLED, -GLING], [ME. *gogelen*], to stare with bulging eyes. *n. pl.* large spectacles to protect the eyes against dust, wind, etc. *adj.* bulging: said of the eyes. —**gog′gle-eyed′** (-īd′), *adj.*

**go·ing** (gō′iŋ), *n.* 1. a departure. 2. the condition of the ground or land with reference to the ease with which it can be traveled. *adj.* moving; working. —**be going to**, will or shall.

**goi·ter, goi·tre** (goi′tẽr), *n.* [< L. *guttur*, throat], a diseased condition of the thyroid gland, seen as a swelling in the front of the neck.

**gold** (gōld), *n.* [AS.], 1. a heavy, yellow, metallic chemical element: it is a precious metal and is used in coins, jewelry, etc.: symbol, Au. 2. money; wealth. 3. bright yellow. *adj.* 1. made of or like gold. 2. bright yellow.

**gold′en,** *adj.* 1. made of or containing gold. 2. bright-yellow. 3. very valuable; excellent. 4. flourishing.

**Golden Fleece,** in *Gr. legend*, the fleece of gold captured by Jason.

**gold′en·rod′,** *n.* a North American plant with long, branching stalks bearing clusters of small, yellow flowers.

**golden rule,** the precept that one should act toward others as he would want them to act toward him.

**gold′-filled′,** *adj.* made of a base metal overlaid with gold.

**gold′finch′,** *n.* [AS. *goldfinc*], a small American songbird the male of which has a yellow body with black markings.

**gold′fish′,** *n.* [*pl.* see FISH], a small, golden-yellow fish, often kept in aquariums.

**gold leaf,** gold beaten into very thin sheets, used for gilding. —**gold′-leaf′**, *adj.*

**gold rush,** a rush of people to territory where gold has recently been discovered.

**gold′smith′,** *n.* a skilled worker who makes articles of gold.

**gold standard,** a monetary standard in which the basic currency unit equals a specified quantity of gold.

**golf** (gôlf, golf), *n.* [? < D. *kolf*, club], an outdoor game played on a large tract of land (**golf course** or **golf links**) with a small, hard rubber ball and a set of slender-handled clubs, the object being to drive the ball into a series of small holes with the fewest possible strokes. *v.i.* to play golf. —**golf′er**, *n.*

**Go·li·ath** (gə-lī′əth), *n.* in the *Bible*, the Philistine giant killed by David with a sling.

**gol·ly** (gol′i), *interj.* an exclamation of surprise, etc.: a euphemism for *God.*

**-gon,** [< Gr. *gōnia*, an angle], a combining form meaning *a figure having* (a specified number of) *angles.*

**gon·ad** (gon′ad, gō′nad), *n.* [< Gr. *gonē*, seed], a gland that produces reproductive cells; ovary or testis.

**gon·do·la** (gon′də-lə), *n.* [It.], 1. a long, narrow boat used on the canals of Venice. 2. a railroad freight car with low sides and no top: in full, **gondola car.** 3. a cabin suspended under a dirigible or balloon.

**gon′do·lier′** (-lêr′), *n.* a man who rows or poles a gondola.

**gone** (gôn, gon), pp. of **go.** *adj.* 1. departed. 2. ruined. 3. lost. 4. dead. 5. consumed. 6. ago; past. —**far gone,** deeply involved.

**gon′er,** *n.* [Colloq.], a person or thing certain to die, be ruined, etc.

**gon·fa·lon** (gon′fə-lən), *n.* [< OHG. *gund*, battle + *fano*, banner], a flag or ensign hanging from a crosspiece.

**gong** (gôŋ, goŋ), *n.* [echoic], a slightly convex metallic disk that gives a loud resonant tone when struck.

**gon·or·rhe·a, gon·or·rhoe·a** (gon′ə-rē′ə), *n.* [< Gr. *gonos*, semen + *rheein*, to flow], a venereal disease with inflammation of the genital organs.

**goo** (go͞o), *n.* [Slang], anything sticky, or sticky and sweet. —**goo′ey**, *adj.*

**goo·ber** (go͞o′bẽr), *n.* [? < Afr. *nguba*], a peanut.

**good** (good), *adj.* [BETTER, BEST], [AS. *god*], 1. having the proper qualities: as, a *good* road, a *good* mayor. 2. beneficial: as, milk is *good* for you. 3. valid; real: as, *good* money. 4. healthy: as, *good* eyesight. 5. honorable. 6. enjoyable, happy, etc. 7. morally sound or excellent; virtuous, kind, dutiful, etc. 8. skilled: as, a *good* bowler. 9. considerable: as, a *good* many. *n.* something good; specif., *a*) worth; virtue: as, there is *good* in him. *b*) benefit: as, for the *good* of all. *interj.* an exclamation of satisfaction, pleasure, etc. *adv.* [Dial. or Colloq.], well; fully. —**as good as,** virtually; nearly. —**good for,** 1. able to endure or work for (a period of time). 2. worth. —**make good,** 1. to repay or replace. 2. to fulfill. 3. to succeed. —**no good,** useless; worthless. —**to the good,** as a profit, benefit, etc.

**good′-by′, good′-bye′** (-bī′), *interj. & n.* [*pl.* -BYS, -BYES], [contr. of *God be with ye*], farewell: also written **goodby, goodbye.**

**Good Friday,** Friday before Easter, commemorating the Crucifixion.

**good′-heart′ed,** *adj.* kind; generous.

**good humor,** a cheerful, agreeable mood. —**good′-hu′mored**, *adj.*

**good′-look′ing,** *adj.* handsome.

**good′ly,** *adj.* [-LIER, -LIEST], 1. pleasing. 2. ample; rather large. —**good′li·ness**, *n.*

**good′-na′tured,** *adj.* pleasant; amiable.

**good′ness,** *n.* the state or quality of being good; virtue, kindness, etc. *interj.* an exclamation of surprise.

**goods** (goodz), *n.pl.* 1. movable personal property. 2. merchandise; wares. 3. fabric; cloth. —**get** (or **have**) **the goods on,** [Slang], to discover (or know) something incriminating about.

**good Sa·mar·i·tan** (sə-mar′ə-t'n), anyone who helps others unselfishly: Luke 10:30–37.

**good′-sized′,** *adj.* ample; fairly big.

**good′-tem′pered,** *adj.* amiable.

**good turn,** a friendly, helpful act.

**good will,** 1. benevolence. 2. willingness. 3. the value of a business in patronage, reputation, etc., beyond its tangible assets. —**good′-will′**, *adj.*

**good′y,** *n.* [*pl.* -IES], [Colloq.], *often in pl.* something good to eat, as a candy. *interj.* [Colloq.], a child's exclamation of delight.

**goof** (go͞of), *n.* [Slang], a stupid or silly person. *v.i.* [Slang], to err, fail, etc. —**goof′y** [-IER, -IEST], *adj.* —**goof′i·ness**, *n.*

**goon** (go͞on), *n.* [Slang], 1. an awkward, stupid person. 2. a thug. 3. a strikebreaker.

**goose** (go͞os), *n.* [AS. *gos*], [*pl.* GEESE], 1. a long-necked, web-footed bird like a duck but larger, esp. the female. 2. its flesh as food. 3. a silly person. 4. [*pl.* GOOSES], a tailor's pressing iron with a gooseneck handle. —**cook one's goose,** [Colloq.], to spoil one's chances. —**goose′like**, *adj.*

**goose′ber′ry,** *n.* [*pl.* -RIES], 1. a small, sour berry, like a currant but larger, used for preserves, pies, etc. 2. the shrub it grows on.

**goose flesh** (or **pimples** or **skin**), a roughened condition of the skin, caused by cold, shock, etc.

**goose′neck′,** *n.* any of various mechanical devices shaped like a goose's neck, as a flexible support for a desk lamp.

**goose step,** a marching step in which the legs are kept unbent.

**G.O.P.,** Grand Old Party (the Republican Party).

**go·pher** (gō'fẽr), *n.* [Fr. *gaufre,* honeycomb: from its burrowing], 1. a burrowing rodent with wide cheek pouches. 2. a striped ground squirrel of the prairies.

**Gor·di·an knot** (gôr'di-ən), in *Gr. legend,* a knot tied by King Gordius, to be undone only by the future master of Asia: Alexander the Great cut it with his sword.

**gore** (gôr), *n.* [AS. *gor,* filth], blood from a wound; esp., clotted blood.

**gore** (gôr), *n.* [< AS. *gar,* a spear], a tapering piece of cloth inserted in a garment, sail, etc. to give it further width. *v.t.* [GORED, GORING], 1. to insert gores in. 2. to pierce as with a tusk. **—gored,** *adj.*

**gorge** (gôrj), *n.* [< L. *gurges,* whirlpool], 1. the gullet. 2. what has been swallowed. 3. a deep, narrow pass between steep heights. *v.i. & v.t.* [GORGED, GORGING], to eat greedily; stuff. **—gorg'er,** *n.*

**gor·geous** (gôr'jəs), *adj.* [< OFr. *gorgias,* beautiful], 1. brilliantly colored; magnificent. 2. [Slang], beautiful; delightful.

**go·ril·la** (gə-ril'ə), *n.* [< W. Afr.], the largest and most powerful of the manlike apes, native to Africa.

**gor·mand·ize** (gôr'mən-dīz'), *v.i.* [-IZED, -IZING], [< Fr. *gourmandise,* gluttony], to eat like a glutton. **—gor'mand·iz'er,** *n.*

**gorse** (gôrs), *n.* [AS. *gorst*], furze.

**gor·y** (gôr'i), *adj.* [-IER, -IEST], 1. covered with gore; bloody. 2. with much bloodshed.

**gosh** (gosh), *interj.* [< *God*], an exclamation of surprise, etc.

**gos·hawk** (gos'hôk', gôs'-), *n.* [< AS.; see GOOSE & HAWK], a large, swift hawk.

**gos·ling** (goz'liŋ), *n.* a young goose.

**gos·pel** (gos'p'l), *n.* [AS. *gōdspel,* good news], 1. the teachings of Jesus and the Apostles. 2. [G-], any of the first four books of the New Testament. 3. a belief proclaimed as absolutely true. 4. any doctrine widely held.

**gos·sa·mer** (gos'ə-mẽr), *n.* [ME. *gosesomer,* lit., goose summer], 1. a filmy cobweb. 2. a very thin, filmy cloth. *adj.* light and filmy: also **gos'sa·mer·y.**

**gos·sip** (gos'əp), *n.* [< AS. *godsibbe,* godparent], 1. one who chatters idly about others. 2. such talk. *v.i.* [-SIPED, -SIPING], to indulge in gossip. **—gos'sip·y,** *adj.*

**got** (got), pt. and pp. of **get.**

**Goth** (goth), *n.* any member of a Germanic people that conquered most of the Roman Empire in the 3d–5th centuries A.D.

**Goth'ic,** *adj.* 1. of the Goths or their language. 2. designating or of a style of architecture developed in W Europe between the 12th and 16th centuries, with flying buttresses, pointed arches, etc. 3. [also g-], uncivilized. *n.* 1. the East Germanic language of the Goths. 2. Gothic architecture.

**got·ten** (got''n), alt. pp. of **get.**

‡**gouache** (gwäsh), *n.* [Fr. < L. *agua,* water], 1. a way of painting with opaque water colors mixed with gum. 2. such a pigment or a picture so painted.

**gouge** (gouj), *n.* [< LL. *gu(l)bia*], 1. a chisel for cutting grooves or holes in wood. 2. [Colloq.], a groove or hole made as with a gouge. *v.t.* [GOUGED, GOUGING], 1. to scoop out as with a gouge. 2. [Colloq.], to defraud or overcharge. **—goug'er,** *n.*

**gou·lash** (gōō'läsh), *n.* [< Hung. *gulyás,* shepherds' food], a beef or veal stew seasoned with paprika: also **Hungarian goulash.**

**gourd** (gôrd, goord), *n.* [< L. *cucurbita*], 1. any trailing or climbing plant of a family that includes the squash, melon, etc. 2. the bulb-shaped fruit of one species of this family. 3. the dried, hollowed-out shell of such a fruit, used as a cup, dipper, etc.

**gour·mand** (goor'mənd), *n.* [Fr.], a person who likes fine foods.

**gour·met** (goor'mā), *n.* [OFr., wine taster], a person who likes and is a judge of fine foods and drinks; epicure.

**gout** (gout), *n.* [< L. *gutta,* a drop], a disease characterized by painful swelling of the joints, esp. in the big toe. **—gout'y,** *adj.*

**gov., Gov.,** 1. government. 2. governor.

**gov·ern** (guv'ẽrn), *v.t. & v.i.* [< Gr. *kybernan,* to steer], 1. to exercise authority over; control; rule. 2. to influence the action or conduct of; guide. 3. to determine. **—gov'ern·a·ble,** *adj.*

**gov·ern·ess** (guv'ẽr-nis), *n.* a woman employed in a private home to train and teach the children.

**gov·ern·ment** (guv'ẽr-mənt, guv'ẽrn-), *n.* 1. the exercise of authority over an organization, state, etc.; control; rule. 2. a system of ruling, political administration, etc. 3. those who direct the affairs of a state, etc.; administration. **—gov'ern·men'tal,** *adj.*

**gov·er·nor** (guv'ẽr-nẽr, guv'ə-), *n.* 1. one who governs; esp., *a)* one appointed to govern a province, etc. *b)* the elected head of any State of the U.S. 2. a mechanical device for automatically controlling the speed of an engine. **—gov'er·nor·ship',** *n.*

**govt., Govt.,** government.

**gown** (goun), *n.* [< ML. *gunna*], 1. a woman's dress. 2. a long, flowing robe worn by judges, clergymen, etc., and by graduates receiving degrees. *v.t.* to clothe in a gown.

**Gr.,** Greek.

**gr.,** 1. grain(s). 2. gram(s). 3. gross.

**grab** (grab), *v.t.* [GRABBED, GRABBING], [prob. < MLG. *grabben*], 1. to snatch suddenly. 2. to get by unscrupulous methods. *n.* a grabbing. **—grab'ber,** *n.*

**grace** (grās), *n.* [< L. *gratus,* pleasing], 1. beauty or charm of form, movement, or expression. 2. favor; good will. 3. mercy. 4. a delay granted for payment of an obligation. 5. a short prayer of thanks before or after a meal. 6. [G-], a title of an archbishop, duke, or duchess. 7. love and favor of God toward man. *v.t.* [GRACED, GRACING], to dignify or adorn. **—in the good** (or **bad**) **graces of,** in favor (or disfavor) with. **—grace'less,** *adj.*

**grace'ful,** *adj.* having beauty of form, movement, or expression. **—grace'ful·ly,** *adv.*

**grace note,** a musical note not necessary to the melody, added only for ornamentation.

**Grac·es** (grās'iz), *n.pl.* in *Gr. myth.,* three sister goddesses who controlled pleasure, charm, elegance, etc.

**gra·cious** (grā'shəs), *adj.* 1. having or showing kindness, charm, etc. 2. compassionate. 3. indulgent or polite to supposed inferiors.

**grack·le** (grak''l), *n.* [L. *graculus,* jackdaw], any of various blackbirds somewhat smaller than a crow.

**grad.,** 1. graduate. 2. graduated.

**gra·da·tion** (grā-dā'shən), *n.* 1. an arranging in grades, or steps. 2. a gradual change by stages. 3. a step or degree in a graded series.

**grade** (grād), *n.* [< L. *gradus*], 1. a stage or step in a progression. 2. *a)* a degree in a scale of quality, rank, etc. *b)* a group of people of the same rank, merit, etc. 3. the degree of slope. 4. a sloping part. 5. one of the divisions by years in a school curriculum. 6. a mark or rating in evaluation. *v.t.* [GRADED, GRADING], 1. to classify by steps or stages; sort. 2. to give a grade (sense 6) to. 3. to make (ground) level or slope (ground) evenly for a roadway, etc. *v.i.* to change gradually. **—make the grade,** to succeed.

**grade crossing,** a place where two railroads or a railroad and roadway intersect.

**grade school,** elementary, or grammar, school.
**gra·di·ent** (grā′di-ənt), *n.* [< L. *gradi*, to step], 1. a slope, as of a road. 2. the degree of slope.
**grad·u·al** (graj′o͞o-əl), *adj.* [< L. *gradus*, a step], taking place by degrees; little by little.
**grad·u·ate** (graj′o͞o-it), *n.* [< L. *gradus*, a step], one who has completed a course of study at a school or college. *v.t.* (-āt′), [-ATED, -ATING], 1. to give a degree or diploma to upon completion of a course of study. 2. to mark with degrees for measuring. 3. to classify into grades, according to size, quality, etc. *v.i.* to become a graduate of a school, etc. *adj.* (-it), 1. being a graduate of a school, etc. 2. of or for graduates.
**grad′u·a′tion,** *n.* 1. a graduating from a school or college. 2. the ceremony connected with this.
**graft** (graft, gräft), *n.* [< Gr. *grapheion*, stylus], 1. a shoot or bud of one plant or tree inserted into another, where it grows permanently. 2. the inserting of such a shoot. 3. a piece of skin, bone, etc. transplanted by surgery. 4. *a*) dishonest use of one's position to gain money, etc., as in politics. *b*) anything so gained. *v.t. & v.i.* 1. to insert (a graft). 2. to obtain (money, etc.) by graft. **—graft′er,** *n.*
**gra·ham** (grā′əm), *adj.* [< S. *Graham*, 19th-c. Am. physician], designating or made of unsifted, whole-wheat flour.
**Grail** (grāl), *n.* [< ML. *gradalis*, cup], in *medieval legend*, the cup used by Jesus at the Last Supper: also **Holy Grail.**
**grain** (grān), *n.* [< L. *granum*], 1. a small, hard seed of any cereal plant, as wheat, corn, etc. 2. cereal plants. 3. a tiny, solid particle, as of salt or sand. 4. a tiny bit. 5. the smallest unit of weight. 6. *a*) the arrangement of fibers, particles, etc. of wood, leather, etc. *b*) the markings or texture due to this. 7. disposition; nature. **—against the grain,** contrary to one's feelings, nature, etc.
**gram** (gram), *n.* [< Gr. *gramma*, small weight], the basic unit of weight in the metric system, equal to about 1/28 of an ounce: also sp. **gramme.**
**-gram,** [< Gr. *gramma*, writing], a combining form meaning *something written*, as in *telegram*.
**gram·mar** (gram′ẽr), *n.* [< Gr. *gramma*, writing], 1. language study dealing with the forms of words and with their arrangement in sentences. 2. a system of rules for speaking and writing a given language. 3. one's manner of speaking or writing as judged by such rules. **—gram·mar·i·an** (grə-mâr′i-ən), *n.* **—gram·mat·i·cal** (grə-mat′i-k'l), *adj.*
**grammar school,** elementary school.
**gram·o·phone** (gram′ə-fōn′), *n.* [< Gr. *gramma*, something written; + *-phone*], a phonograph: a trademark **(Gramophone).**
**gran·a·ry** (gran′ẽr-i, grā′nẽr-i), *n.* [*pl.* -RIES], [< L. *granum*, grain], a building for storing grain.
**grand** (grand), *adj.* [< L. *grandis*, large], 1. higher in rank than others: as, a *grand* duke. 2. most important; main: as, the *grand* ballroom. 3. imposing in size, beauty, extent, etc. 4. distinguished; illustrious. 5. complete; over-all: as, the *grand* total. 6. [Colloq.], delightful; very satisfactory. *n.* [Slang], a thousand dollars. **—grand′ly,** *adv.*
**grand-,** a combining form meaning *of the generation older* (or *younger*) *than*, as in *grandfather, grandson*.
**gran·dam** (gran′dam, -dəm), *n.* [see GRAND- & DAME], [Archaic], 1. a grandmother. 2. an old woman.
**grand′child′,** *n.* [*pl.* -CHILDREN], a child of one's son or daughter.
**grand′daugh′ter,** *n.* a daughter of one's son or daughter.
**gran·dee** (gran-dē′), *n.* [< Sp. & Port.; see GRAND], a person of high rank.
**gran·deur** (gran′jẽr), *n.* [see GRAND], 1. greatness of position. 2. splendor. 3. nobility; dignity.
**grand′fa′ther,** *n.* 1. the father of one's father or mother. 2. a forefather.
**gran·dil·o·quent** (gran-dil′ə-kwənt), *adj.* [< L. *grandis*, grand + *loqui*, speak], using pompous, bombastic language. **—gran·dil′o·quence,** *n.* **—gran·dil′o·quent·ly,** *adv.*
**gran·di·ose** (gran′di-ōs′), *adj.* [< L. *grandis*, great], 1. having grandeur; imposing. 2. pompous and showy. **—gran′di·ose′ly,** *adv.*
**grand jury,** a jury that investigates accusations and indicts persons for trial if there is sufficient evidence.
**grand′ma** (-mä), *n.* [Colloq.], grandmother.
**grand′moth′er,** *n.* 1. the mother of one's father or mother. 2. a female ancestor.
**grand opera,** opera in which the whole text is set to music.
**grand′pa** (-pä), *n.* [Colloq.], grandfather.
**grand′par′ent,** *n.* a grandfather or grandmother.
**grand piano,** a large piano with a horizontal, harp-shaped case.
**grand′son′,** *n.* a son of one's son or daughter.
**grand′stand′,** *n.* the main seating structure for spectators as at a sporting event.
**grange** (grānj), *n.* [< L. *granum*, grain], 1. a farm. 2. [G-], an association of farmers or a local lodge of this.
**gran·ite** (gran′it), *n.* [< L. *granum*, grain], a hard, igneous rock composed chiefly of quartz, feldspar, and mica.
**gran·ny, gran·nie** (gran′i), *n.* [*pl.* -NIES], [Colloq.], 1. a grandmother. 2. an old woman. 3. any fussy person.
**grant** (grant, gränt), *v.t.* [< L. *credere*, believe], 1. to give (what is requested), as permission, etc. 2. to give or transfer by legal procedure. 3. to admit as true. *n.* 1. a granting. 2. something granted, as property, etc. **—take for granted,** to consider as a fact.
**gran·u·lar** (gran′yoo-lẽr), *adj.* 1. containing or consisting of grains. 2. like grains or granules.
**gran′u·late′** (-lāt′), *v.t. & v.i.* [-LATED, -LATING], to form into grains or granules. **—gran′u·lat′ed,** *adj.* **—gran′u·la′tion,** *n.*
**gran·ule** (gran′yool), *n.* [< L. *granum*, a grain], a small grain or particle.
**grape** (grāp), *n.* [< OFr. dial. *crape*, bunch of grapes], 1. a small, round, juicy fruit, growing in clusters on a woody vine. 2. a grapevine. 3. a dark purplish red.
**grape′fruit′,** *n.* a large, round citrus fruit with a yellow rind and a sourish taste.
**grape′vine′,** *n.* 1. a woody vine bearing grapes. 2. a secret means of spreading information. 3. a rumor.
**graph** (graf, gräf), *n.* [short for *graphic formula*], a diagram representing the successive changes in the value of a variable quantity or quantities. *v.t.* to represent by a graph.
**-graph,** [< Gr. *graphein*, write], a combining form meaning *something that writes* or *describes*, as in *telegraph*.
**graph·ic** (graf′ik), *adj.* [< Gr. *graphein*, write], 1. described in realistic detail. 2. of the graphic arts. Also **graph′i·cal.**
**graphic arts,** any form of visual artistic representation, as painting, drawing, etc.
**graph·ite** (graf′īt), *n.* [< Gr. *graphein*, write], a soft, black form of carbon used in pencils, for lubricants, etc.
**graph·ol·o·gy** (gra-fol′ə-ji), *n.* [< Gr. *graphein*, write; + *-logy*], the study of handwriting, esp. as it is supposed to indicate character, etc. **—graph·ol′o·gist,** *n.*
**-graphy,** [< Gr. *graphein*, write], a combin-

ing form meaning: 1. *a process* or *manner of writing*, or *graphically representing*, as in *lithography*. 2. *a descriptive science*, as in *geography*.

**grap·nel** (grap′n'l), *n.* [< Pr. *grapa*, a hook], 1. a small anchor with several claws. 2. a grappling iron.

**grap·ple** (grap′'l), *n.* [OFr. *grappil*], 1. a grappling iron. 2. a seizing; grip, as in wrestling. *v.t.* [-PLED, -PLING], to grip and hold. *v.i.* to struggle. —**grap′pler,** *n.*

**grappling iron** (or **hook**), a device with claws for grasping and holding things.

**grasp** (grasp, gräsp), *v.t.* [ME. *graspen*], 1. to grip, as with the hand. 2. to take hold of eagerly; seize. 3. to comprehend. *n.* 1. a grasping; grip. 2. control; possession. 3. the power to hold or seize. 4. comprehension. —**grasp at,** 1. to try to seize. 2. to take eagerly. —**grasp′er,** *n.*

**grasp′ing,** *adj.* 1. that grasps. 2. greedy; eager for gain; avaricious.

**grass** (gras, gräs), *n.* [AS. *græs*], 1. any of various green plants with bladelike leaves growing densely in fields, lawns, etc. 2. a plant with narrow leaves, jointed stems, and seedlike fruit, as wheat, rye, etc. 3. pasture. —**grass′y** [-IER, -IEST], *adj.*

**grass′hop′per,** *n.* any of a group of insects with two pairs of wings and powerful hind legs for jumping.

**grass′land′,** *n.* land with grass growing on it, used for grazing; pasture land.

**grass′-roots′,** *adj.* [Colloq.], in *politics*, originating among or carried on by the common people.

**grass widow,** a woman divorced or separated from her husband. —**grass widower.**

**grate** (grāt), *v.t.* [GRATED, GRATING], [< OFr. *grater*], 1. to grind into particles by scraping. 2. to rub against (an object) or rub together with a harsh sound. 3. to irritate. *v.i.* 1. to rub with or make a rasping sound. 2. to be irritating. —**grat′er,** *n.*

**grate** (grāt), *n.* [< L. *cratis*, a hurdle], 1. a framework of bars in a window, etc. 2. a frame of metal bars for holding fuel in a fireplace. 3. a fireplace.

**grate·ful** (grāt′fəl), *adj.* [obs. *grate* (< L. *gratus*), pleasing], 1. thankful. 2. welcome.

**grat·i·fy** (grat′ə-fī′), *v.t.* [-FIED, -FYING], [< L. *gratus*, pleasing + *facere*, make], 1. to please or satisfy. 2. to indulge; humor. —**grat′i·fi·ca′tion,** *n.* —**grat′i·fi′er** *n.*

**grat·ing** (grāt′iŋ), *n.* a framework of bars in a window, door, etc.; grate.

**grat′ing,** *adj.* sounding harsh.

**gra·tis** (grā′tis, grat′is), *adv.* & *adj.* [L. < *gratia*, a favor], free of charge.

**grat·i·tude** (grat′ə-tōōd′, -tūd′), *n.* [< L. *gratus*, thankful], a feeling of thankful appreciation for favors received.

**gra·tu·i·tous** (grə-tōō′ə-təs, -tū′-), *adj.* [< L. *gratus*, pleasing], 1. given free of charge. 2. uncalled-for. —**gra·tu′i·tous·ly,** *adv.*

**gra·tu·i·ty** (grə-tōō′ə-ti, -tū′-), *n.* [*pl.* -TIES], a gift of money, etc., esp. for service; tip.

**grave** (grāv), *adj.* [< L. *gravis*, heavy], 1. important. 2. serious: as, a *grave* illness. 3. solemn. 4. somber; dull. —**grave′ly,** *adv.*

**grave** (grāv), *n.* [< AS. *grafan*, dig], 1. a hole in the ground in which to bury a dead body. 2. any burial place. 3. death. *v.t.* [GRAVED, GRAVEN or GRAVED, GRAVING], to sculpture or engrave. —**grav′er,** *n.*

**grav·el** (grav′'l), *n.* [< OFr. *grave*, coarse sand], a loose mixture of pebbles and rock fragments coarser than sand. *v.t.* [-ELED or -ELLED, -ELING or -ELLING], to cover (a walk, etc.) with gravel. —**grav′el·ly,** *adj.*

**grav·en** (grāv′'n), alt. pp. of **grave.** *adj.* 1. engraved; sculptured. 2. sharply impressed.

**grave′stone′,** *n.* a tombstone.

**grave′yard′,** *n.* a cemetery.

**grav·i·tate** (grav′ə-tāt′), *v.i.* [-TATED, -TATING], 1. to move or tend to move in accordance with the force of gravity. 2. to be attracted (*toward*).

**grav′i·ta′tion,** *n.* 1. a gravitating. 2. in *physics*, the force by which every mass attracts and is attracted by every other mass. —**grav′i·ta′tion·al,** *adj.*

**grav·i·ty** (grav′ə-ti), *n.* [*pl.* -TIES], [< L. *gravis*, heavy], 1. graveness; seriousness; danger or menace. 2. weight: as, specific *gravity*. 3. in *physics*, gravitation; esp., the pull on all bodies in the earth's sphere toward the earth's center.

**gra·vy** (grā′vi), *n.* [*pl.* -VIES], [< ?], 1. the juice given off by meat in cooking. 2. a sauce made from this. 3. [Slang], easy profit.

**gray** (grā), *n.* [< AS. *græg*], a color made by mixing black and white. *adj.* 1. of the color gray. 2. having hair this color. 3. *a*) darkish. *b*) dreary. 4. old. *v.t.* & *v.i.* to make or become gray. Brit. sp. **grey.** —**gray′ish,** *adj.*

**gray·ling** (grā′liŋ), *n.* [*pl.* -LING, -LINGS], a fresh-water game fish of the trout family.

**gray matter,** 1. grayish nerve tissue of the brain and spinal cord. 2. [Colloq.], intelligence.

**graze** (grāz), *v.t.* [GRAZED, GRAZING], [< AS. *græs*, grass], to put (livestock) to feed on (a pasture, etc.). *v.i.* to feed on growing grass, etc. —**graz′er,** *n.*

**graze** (grāz), *v.t.* & *v.i.* [GRAZED, GRAZING], [prob. < prec.], to scrape or rub lightly in passing. *n.* a grazing. —**graz′ing·ly,** *adv.*

**Gr. Brit., Gr. Br.,** Great Britain.

**grease** (grēs), *n.* [< L. *crassus*, fat], 1. melted animal fat. 2. any thick, oily substance or lubricant. *v.t.* (grēs, grēz), [GREASED, GREASING], to smear or lubricate with grease.

**grease paint,** greasy coloring matter used by actors in making up for the stage.

**greas·y** (grēs′i, grēz′i), *adj.* [-IER, -IEST], 1. soiled with grease. 2. containing or like grease; oily. —**greas′i·ness,** *n.*

**great** (grāt), *adj.* [AS.], 1. of much more than ordinary size, extent, etc. 2. much above the average; esp., *a*) intense: as, *great* pain. *b*) eminent: as, a *great* writer. 3. most important; main. 4. designating a relationship one generation removed: as, *great*-grandparent. 5. [Colloq.], excellent; fine. —**great′ly,** *adv.* —**great′ness,** *n.*

**great Dane,** [also G-], a large, powerful dog with short, smooth hair.

**great′-grand′child′,** *n.* a child of any of one's grandchildren.

**great′-grand′par′ent,** *n.* a parent of any of one's grandparents.

**great′heart′ed,** *adj.* 1. brave; fearless. 2. generous; unselfish.

**grebe** (grēb), *n.* [Fr. *grèbe*], a diving and swimming bird of the loon family.

**Gre·cian** (grē′shən), *adj.* & *n.* Greek.

**Greco-,** a combining form meaning *Greek* or *Greek and.*

**greed** (grēd), *n.* [< *greedy*], excessive desire for having; avarice.

**greed′y,** *adj.* [-IER, -IEST], [AS. *grædig*], 1. wanting excessively to have or acquire. 2. wanting to eat and drink too much; gluttonous. —**greed′i·ly,** *adv.* —**greed′i·ness,** *n.*

**Greek** (grēk), *n.* 1. a native or inhabitant of Greece. 2. the language of Greece. *adj.* of Greece, its people, language, or culture.

**green** (grēn), *adj.* [AS. *grene*], 1. of the color of growing grass. 2. sickly or bilious. 3. unripe. 4. inexperienced or naive. 5. not dried or seasoned. 6. [Colloq.], jealous. *n.* 1. the color of growing grass. 2. *pl.* green leafy vegetables, as spinach, etc. 3. an area of smooth turf: as, a putting *green*.

**green′back′,** *n.* any U.S. paper money printed in green on the back.

**green′er·y,** *n.* [*pl.* -IES], green vegetation.

**green·gage** (grēn′gāj′), *n.* [after Wm. *Gage,* who introduced it into England, c. 1725], a large golden-green plum.
**green′horn′**(-hôrn′), *n.* a beginner; novice.
**green′house′,** *n.* a building with glass roof and sides, artificially heated for growing plants.
**green onion,** an immature onion with a long stalk and green leaves.
**green pepper,** the green, immature fruit of the sweet red pepper.
**green′sward′** (-swôrd′), *n.* green turf.
**green′wood′,** *n.* a forest in leaf.
**greet** (grēt), *v.t.* [AS. *gretan*], 1. to address with friendliness, etc. 2. to meet or receive (a person, event, etc.) in a specified way. 3. to present itself to. —**greet′er,** *n.*
**greet′ing,** *n.* 1. the act or words of one who greets. 2. *often pl.* a message of regards.
**gre·gar·i·ous** (gri-gâr′i-əs), *adj.* [< L. *grex,* herd], 1. living in herds. 2. fond of the company of others; sociable.
**Gre·go·ri·an calendar** (gri-gôr′i-ən), the calendar now widely used, introduced by Pope Gregory XIII in 1582.
**gre·nade** (gri-nād′), *n.* [< Fr. < L. *granum,* seed], a small bomb detonated by a fuse and usually thrown by hand.
**gren·a·dier** (gren′ə-dêr′), *n.* 1. originally, a soldier who threw grenades. 2. a member of a special regiment.
**gren·a·dine** (gren′ə-dēn′, gren′ə-dēn′), *n.* [Fr.], a sirup made from pomegranate juice.
**grew** (grōō), pt. of **grow.**
**grey** (grā), *adj., n., & v.* gray: Brit. sp.
**grey′hound′,** *n.* a tall, slender, swift hound.
**grid** (grid), *n.* [< *gridiron*], 1. a gridiron or grating. 2. a lead plate in a storage battery. 3. an electrode of wire mesh in a vacuum tube to control the flow of electrons.
**grid·dle** (grid′'l), *n.* [< L. *craticula,* gridiron], a heavy, flat metal pan for cooking pancakes, etc.
**grid′dle·cake′,** *n.* a pancake.
**grid·i·ron** (grid′ī′ērn), *n.* [see GRIDDLE], 1. a framework of metal bars or wires for broiling; grill. 2. anything suggesting this, as a football field.
**grief** (grēf), *n.* [see GRIEVE], 1. intense emotional suffering caused by loss, disaster, etc.; deep sorrow. 2. a cause of such suffering. —**come to grief,** to meet with failure.
**griev·ance** (grēv′əns), *n.* 1. a circumstance thought to be unjust and ground for complaint. 2. complaint against a wrong, real or imagined.
**grieve** (grēv), *v.i. & v.t.* [GRIEVED, GRIEVING], [< L. *gravis,* heavy], to feel or cause to feel grief.
**griev·ous** (grēv′əs), *adj.* 1. causing grief. 2. showing or full of grief. 3. severe. 4. deplorable; atrocious. —**griev′ous·ly,** *adv.*
**grif·fin** (grif′in), *n.* [< Gr.], a mythical animal, part eagle and part lion.
**grill** (gril), *n.* [see GRIDDLE], 1. a gridiron. 2. grilled food. 3. a restaurant that specializes in grilled foods: also **grill′room′.** *v.t.* 1. to broil. 2. to question relentlessly.
**grille** (gril), *n.* [see GRIDDLE], an open grating forming a screen. —**grilled,** *adj.*
**grim** (grim), *adj.* [GRIMMER, GRIMMEST], [AS. *grimm*], 1. fierce; cruel. 2. hard and unyielding; stern. 3. appearing threatening, forbidding, etc. 4. hideous; ghastly.
**gri·mace** (gri-mās′), *n.* [Fr.], a wry or ugly expression of pain, contempt, etc. *v.i.* [-MACED, -MACING], to make grimaces.
**gri·mal·kin** (gri-mal′kin, -môl′-), *n.* [< ?], a cat; esp., an old female cat.
**grime** (grīm), *n.* [< D. or LG.], sooty dirt rubbed into a surface, as of the skin. *v.t.* [GRIMED, GRIMING], to make very dirty. —**grim′y** [-IER, -IEST], *adj.*
**grin** (grin), *v.i.* [GRINNED, GRINNING], [AS. *grennian*], to smile broadly, showing the teeth. *n.* such a smile.
**grind** (grīnd), *v.t.* [GROUND, GRINDING], [AS. *grindan*], 1. to crush into fine particles; pulverize. 2. to oppress. 3. to sharpen or smooth by friction. 4. to rub together harshly or gratingly: as, he *ground* his teeth. 5. to operate by turning the crank of. *n.* 1. a grinding. 2. a long, difficult task or study. —**grind′er,** *n.*
**grind′stone′,** *n.* a revolving stone disk for sharpening tools or polishing things. —**keep** (or **have** or **put**) **one's nose to the grindstone,** to work hard and steadily.
**grin·go** (griŋ′gō), *n.* [*pl.* -GOS], [Mex. Sp.; Sp., gibberish], in Latin America, a foreigner, esp. an American: hostile term.
**grip** (grip), *n.* [< AS. *gripan,* seize], 1. a secure grasp; firm hold. 2. any special manner of clasping hands: as, Freemasons have a secret *grip.* 3. the power of grasping firmly. 4. mental grasp. 5. firm control; mastery. 6. a handle. 7. a valise. *v.t.* [GRIPPED or GRIPT, GRIPPING], to take firmly and hold fast. *v.i.* to get a grip. —**come to grips,** to struggle (*with*). —**grip′per,** *n.*
**gripe** (grīp), *v.t.* [GRIPED, GRIPING], [AS. *gripan,* seize], 1. to distress; afflict. 2. to cause sharp pain in the bowels of. 3. [Slang], to annoy. *v.i.* [Slang], to complain. *n.* 1. *pl.* pains in the bowels. 2. [Slang], a complaint.
**grippe** (grip), *n.* [Fr. < Russ. *chripu,* huskiness], influenza: also sp. **grip.**
**gris·ly** (griz′li), *adj.* [-LIER, -LIEST], [AS. *grislic*], terrifying; ghastly. —**gris′li·ness,** *n.*
**grist** (grist), *n.* [AS.], grain that is to be or has been ground. —**grist to one's mill,** anything one can use profitably.
**gris·tle** (gris′'l), *n.* [AS.], cartilage. —**gris′tly** [-TLIER, -TLIEST], *adj.*
**grit** (grit), *n.* [AS. *greot*], 1. rough, hard particles of sand, etc. 2. a coarse sandstone. 3. obstinate courage; pluck. *v.t.* [GRITTED, GRITTING], to grind (the teeth) in anger, etc. *v.i.* to grate or grind. —**grit′ty** [-TIER, -TIEST], *adj.* —**grit′ti·ness,** *n.*
**grits** (grits), *n.pl.* [AS. *grytt(e)*], coarse hominy.
**griz·zled** (griz′'ld), *adj.* [< OHG. *gris,* gray], 1. gray or steaked with gray. 2. having gray hair.
**griz·zly** (griz′li), *adj.* [-ZLIER, -ZLIEST], grayish; grizzled. *n.* [*pl.* -ZLIES], a grizzly bear.
**grizzly bear,** a large, ferocious, yellow-brown bear of W North America.
**groan** (grōn), *v.i. & v.t.* [AS. *granian*], to utter (with) a deep sound expressing pain, distress, etc. *n.* such a sound. —**groan′er,** *n.*
**groat** (grōt), *n.* [< MD. *groot,* thick], an obsolete English silver coin worth fourpence.
**gro·cer** (grō′sēr), *n.* [< ML. *grossarius,* wholesale dealer], a storekeeper who sells food and household supplies.
**gro′cer·y,** *n.* [*pl.* -IES], 1. the business or store of a grocer. 2. *pl.* the goods sold by a grocer.
**grog** (grog), *n.* [after Old *Grog,* nickname of an 18th-c. Brit. admiral], 1. originally, rum diluted with water. 2. any alcoholic liquor.
**grog′gy,** *adj.* [-GIER, -GIEST], [< *grog*], [Colloq.], 1. intoxicated. 2. shaky or dizzy.
**groin** (groin), *n.* [? < AS. *grynde,* abyss], 1. the fold where the abdomen joins either thigh. 2. in *architecture,* the sharp, curved edge at the intersection of two vaults.
**groom** (grōōm), *n.* [ME. *grome,* boy], 1. a man or boy whose work is tending horses. 2. a bridegroom. *v.t.* 1. to tend (horses). 2. to make neat and tidy. 3. to train (a person) for a particular purpose.
**groove** (grōōv), *n.* [< ON. *grof,* a pit], 1. a long, narrow furrow cut with a tool. 2. any channel or rut. 3. a habitual way of doing things. *v.t.* [GROOVED, GROOVING], to make a groove in. —**groove′less,** *adj.*

**grope** (grōp), *v.i.* [GROPED, GROPING], [< AS. *grap*, a grasp], to feel or search about blindly or uncertainly. *v.t.* to seek or find by groping. —**grop′er,** *n.* —**grop′ing·ly,** *adv.*

**gros·beak** (grōs′bēk′), *n.* [< Fr.; see GROSS & BEAK], any of various finches with a thick, conical bill.

**gross** (grōs), *adj.* [< LL. *grossus*, thick], 1. too fat; burly. 2. flagrant; very wrong. 3. dense; thick. 4. coarse; vulgar. 5. total; with no deductions: as, his *gross* income. *n.* 1. the mass or bulk. 2. [*pl.* GROSS], twelve dozen. *v.t.* & *v.i.* [Colloq.], to make (a specified total amount) before expenses are deducted. —**gross′ly,** *adv.* —**gross′ness,** *n.*

**gro·tesque** (grō-tesk′), *adj.* [< It. *grotta*, grotto: from designs found in grottoes], 1. distorted or fantastic in appearance, shape, etc. 2. ridiculous; absurd.

**grot·to** (grot′ō), *n.* [*pl.* -TOES, -TOS], [< L. *crypta*, crypt], 1. a cave. 2. a cavelike shrine, summerhouse, etc.

**grouch** (grouch), *v.i.* [< OFr. *grouchier*], [Colloq.], to grumble or sulk. *n.* [Colloq.], 1. one who grouches. 2. a sulky mood. —**grouch′y** [-IER, -IEST], *adj.*

**ground** (ground), *n.* [AS. *grund*, bottom], 1. the solid surface of the earth. 2. soil; earth. 3. *often pl.* a tract of land: as, the *grounds* of an estate. 4. any area or distance. 5. basis; foundation. 6. *usually pl.* a valid reason: as, *grounds* for divorce. 7. the background, as in a design. 8. *pl.* dregs; sediment: as, coffee *grounds*. 9. the connection of an electrical conductor with the ground. *adj.* of, on, or near the ground. *v.t.* 1. to set on the ground. 2. to cause to run aground. 3. to base; found; establish. 4. to instruct in the first principles of. 5. in *aviation*, to keep from flying. 6. in *electricity*, to connect (a conductor) with the ground. *v.i.* 1. to strike or fall to the ground. 2. in *baseball*, to be put (*out*) on a grounder. —**gain** (or **lose**) **ground,** to gain (or lose) in achievement, popularity, etc. —**give ground,** to retreat; yield. —**hold** (or **stand**) **one's ground,** to remain firm, not yielding. —**run into the ground,** [Colloq.], to overdo.

**ground** (ground), pt. and pp. of **grind.**

**ground′er,** *n.* in *baseball*, a batted ball that travels along the ground.

**ground hog,** a woodchuck: also **ground′hog′,** *n.*

**ground′less** (-lis), *adj.* without reason or cause. —**ground′less·ly,** *adv.*

**ground′work′,** *n.* foundation; basis.

**group** (grōōp), *n.* [< It. *gruppo*], a number of persons or things gathered or classified together. *v.t.* & *v.i.* to form into groups.

**group·er** (grōōp′ẽr), *n.* [Port. *garoupa*], a large, tropical food fish.

**grouse** (grous), *n.* [*pl.* GROUSE], [< ?], a game bird with a round, plump body, feathered legs, and mottled feathers.

**grouse** (grous), *v.i.* [GROUSED, GROUSING], [< ?], [Slang], to complain. —**grous′er,** *n.*

**grove** (grōv), *n.* [AS. *graf*], a small wood; group of trees without undergrowth.

**grov·el** (gruv′'l, grov′'l), *v.i.* [-ELED or -ELLED, -ELING or -ELLING], [< ME. *grufelinge*, down on one's face], 1. to lie prone or crawl in a prostrate position, esp. abjectly. 2. to behave humbly or abjectly.

**grow** (grō), *v.i.* [GREW, GROWN, GROWING], [< AS. *growan*], 1. to come into being or be produced naturally. 2. to develop or thrive, as a living thing. 3. to increase in size, quantity, etc. 4. to become: as, he *grew* weary. *v.t.* to cause to or let grow; raise; cultivate. —**grow up,** to mature.

**growl** (groul), *n.* [prob. echoic], a rumbling, menacing sound, such as an angry dog makes. *v.i.* & *v.t.* to make, or express by, such a sound. —**growl′er,** *n.*

**grown** (grōn), pp. of **grow.** *adj.* having completed its growth; mature.

**grown′-up′,** *adj.* & *n.* adult: also, for *n.*, **grown′up′.**

**growth** (grōth), *n.* 1. a growing or developing. 2. *a*) increase in size, etc. *b*) the amount of this. 3. something that grows or has grown. 4. an abnormal mass of tissue, as a tumor.

**grub** (grub), *v.i.* [GRUBBED, GRUBBING], [ME. *grubben*], 1. to dig in the ground. 2. to work hard. *v.t.* 1. to clear (ground) of roots. 2. to uproot. *n.* 1. a wormlike larva, esp. of a beetle. 2. [Slang], food. —**grub′ber,** *n.*

**grub′by,** *adj.* [-BIER, -BIEST], dirty; untidy.

**grub′stake′** (-stāk′), *n.* [*grub* (food) + *stake*], [Colloq.], money or supplies advanced to a prospector, etc. as an investment.

**grudge** (gruj), *v.t.* [GRUDGED, GRUDGING], [< ME. *grucchen*, to grouch], 1. to envy (a person) because of his possession of (something). 2. to give or allow with reluctance. *n.* resentment; ill will. —**grudg′ing·ly,** *adv.*

**gru·el** (grōō′əl), *n.* [< ML. *grutum*, meal], a thin broth of meal cooked in water or milk. *v.t.* [-ELED or -ELLED, -ELING or -ELLING], to subject to intense strain; exhaust. —**gru′el·ing, gru′el·ling,** *adj.*

**grue·some** (grōō′səm), *adj.* [< obs. *grue*, to shudder + *-some*], causing fear and loathing; horrifying. —**grue′some·ly,** *adv.*

**gruff** (gruf), *adj.* [D. *grof*], 1. rough or surly; rude. 2. harsh and throaty; hoarse.

**grum·ble** (grum′b'l), *v.i.* [-BLED, -BLING], [prob. < D. *grommelen*], 1. to growl. 2. to mutter in discontent; complain. 3. to rumble. *v.t.* to express by grumbling. *n.* 1. a grumbling, as in discontent. 2. a rumble.

**grump·y** (grum′pi), *adj.* [-IER, -IEST], [prob. < *grumble*], peevish; surly. —**grump′i·ly,** *adv.*

**grunt** (grunt), *v.i.* & *v.t.* [< AS. *grunian*], to utter (with) the deep sound of a hog.

**guar·an·tee** (gar′ən-tē′), *n.* 1. a guaranty (sense 1). 2. *a*) a pledge to replace something if it is not as represented. *b*) assurance that something will be done as specified. 3. a guarantor. *v.t.* [-TEED, -TEEING], 1. to give a guarantee for. 2. to promise; affirm.

**guar·an·tor** (gar′ən-tẽr, -tôr′), *n.* one who gives a guaranty or guarantee.

**guar·an·ty** (gar′ən-ti), *n.* [*pl.* -TIES], [< OFr. *guarant*, a warrant], 1. a pledge or security for another's debt or obligation. 2. an agreement that secures the existence or maintenance of something.

**guard** (gärd), *v.t.* [< OFr. *guarder*], 1. to watch over and protect; defend. 2. to keep from escape or trouble. *v.i.* 1. to keep watch; take precautions. 2. to act as a guard. *n.* 1. defense; protection. 2. caution; safeguard. 3. any device that protects against injury or loss. 4. a person or group that guards. —**on (one's) guard,** vigilant.

**guard′ed,** *adj.* 1. kept safe; defended. 2. careful; restrained: as, *guarded* speech.

**guard′house′,** *n.* in *military usage*, 1. a building used by a guard when he is not walking a post. 2. a jail for temporary confinement.

**guard·i·an** (gär′di-ən), *n.* 1. one who guards or cares for another person, property, etc.; custodian. 2. a person legally in charge of the affairs of a minor or of someone incapable of taking care of his own affairs. *adj.* protecting. —**guard′i·an·ship′,** *n.*

**gua·va** (gwä′və), *n.* [< native name], the yellow, pear-shaped fruit of a tropical American tree or shrub.

**gu·ber·na·to·ri·al** (gōō′bẽr-nə-tôr′i-əl, gū′-), *adj.* [L. *gubernator*, governor], of a governor or his office.

**guer·don** (gũr′d'n), *n.* [< OHG. *widar*, again + L. *donum*, gift], [Poetic], a reward; recompense. *v.t.* [Poetic], to reward.

**Guern·sey** (gũrn′zi), *n.* [*pl.* -SEYS], [< *Guernsey*, one of the Channel Islands], a breed of dairy cattle, usually fawn-colored with white markings.

**guer·ril·la, gue·ril·la** (gə-ril′ə), *n.* [Sp. dim. of *guerra*, war], a member of a small defensive force of irregular soldiers, making surprise raids. *adj.* of or by guerrillas.

**guess** (ges), *v.t. & v.i.* [prob. < ON.], 1. to form a judgment or estimate of without actual knowledge; surmise. 2. to judge correctly by doing this. 3. to think or suppose. *n.* 1. a guessing. 2. something guessed.

**guess′work′**, *n.* 1. a guessing. 2. a view, work, etc. based on guessing.

**guest** (gest), *n.* [AS. *giest*], 1. a person entertained at the home, club, etc. of another. 2. one paying for his lodgings, meals, etc., as at a hotel. *adj.* 1. for guests. 2. performing by invitation: as, a *guest* artist.

**guf·faw** (gə-fô′), *n. & v.i.* [echoic], laugh in a loud, coarse burst.

**guid·ance** (gīd′′ns), *n.* 1. a guiding; direction; leadership. 2. something that guides.

**guide** (gīd), *v.t.* [GUIDED, GUIDING], [< OFr. *guier*], 1. to point out the way for; lead. 2. to direct the course of; control; manage. *n.* 1. one whose work is conducting tours, etc. 2. a guiding or controlling device. 3. a book of basic information on a place, subject, etc. —**guid′a·ble**, *adj.*

**guide′book′**, *n.* a book containing directions and information for tourists.

**guided missile,** a military missile whose course is directed by radar, etc.

**guide′post′**, *n.* a post, as at a roadside, with a sign and directions for travelers.

**guild** (gild), *n.* [< AS. *gieldan*, to pay], any association for mutual aid and the promotion of common interests.

**guil·der** (gil′dẽr), *n.* [< D. *gulden*, golden], the unit of currency and a silver coin in the Netherlands.

**guile** (gīl), *n.* [< OFr. *guile*], crafty, deceitful talk or conduct; cunning. —**guile′ful**, *adj.*

**guil·lo·tine** (gil′ə-tēn′), *n.* [Fr. < J. *Guillotin*, who advocated its use in 18th c.], an instrument for beheading, having a heavy blade dropped between two grooved uprights. *v.t.* (gil′ə-tēn′), [-TINED, -TINING], to behead with a guillotine.

**guilt** (gilt), *n.* [AS. *gylt*, a sin], the act or fact of having done a wrong or committed an offense. —**guilt′less**, *adj.*

**guilt′y**, *adj.* [-IER, -IEST], 1. having guilt. 2. legally judged an offender. 3. of, involving, or showing guilt: as, a *guilty* look.

**guin·ea** (gin′i), *n.* [first coined of gold from Guinea], 1. a former English gold coin equal to 21 shillings. 2. a guinea fowl.

**guinea fowl** (or **hen**), [first imported from Guinea], a domestic fowl with a rounded body and speckled feathers.

**guinea pig,** [orig. carried from S. America by ships in the Guinea slave trade], 1. a small, fat rodent with a short tail, used in biological experiments. 2. any person or thing used in an experiment.

**Guin·e·vere** (gwin′ə-vêr′), *n.* in *legend*, the wife of King Arthur: also **Guin′e·ver** (-vẽr).

**guise** (gīz), *n.* [< OHG. *wisa*, manner], 1. manner of dress; garb. 2. semblance. 3. a false appearance; pretense.

**gui·tar** (gi-tär′), *n.* [< Sp. < Gr. *kithara*, lyre], a musical instrument of the lute family, with usually six strings plucked with the fingers or a plectrum. —**gui·tar′ist**, *n.*

**gulch** (gulch), *n.* [prob. < dial. *gulch*, swallow greedily], a steep-walled valley cut by a swift stream.

**gulf** (gulf), *n.* [ult. < Gr. *kolpos*, bosom], 1. a large area of ocean partially enclosed by land. 2. a wide, deep chasm or abyss. 3. a vast or impassable separation.

**gull** (gul), *n.* [< Celt.], a gray and white sea bird with large wings and webbed feet.

**gull** (gul), *n.* [prob. < obs. *gull*, to swallow], a person easily tricked; dupe. *v.t.* to cheat.

**gul·let** (gul′it), *n.* [< L. *gula*, throat], 1. the esophagus. 2. the throat.

**gul·li·ble** (gul′ə-b'l), *adj.* easily gulled, or tricked; credulous. —**gul′li·bil′i·ty**, *n.*

**gul·ly** (gul′i), *n.* [*pl.* -LIES], [see GULLET], a channel or narrow ravine worn by water.

**gulp** (gulp), *v.t. & v.i.* [prob. < MD.], 1. to swallow hastily or greedily. 2. to choke back as if swallowing. *n.* 1. a gulping. 2. a swallow. —**gulp′er**, *n.*

**gum** (gum), *n.* [< Gr. *kommi*], 1. a sticky substance given off by certain trees and plants. 2. an adhesive; mucilage; glue. 3. chewing gum. *v.t.* [GUMMED, GUMMING], to coat or unite with gum. *v.i.* to become sticky or clogged. —**gum up**, [Slang], to cause to go awry. —**gum′my** [-MIER, -MIEST], *adj.* —**gum′mi·ness**, *n.*

**gum** (gum), *n.* [AS. *goma*], *often pl.* the firm flesh surrounding the base of the teeth.

**gum·bo** (gum′bō), *n.* [*pl.* -BOS], [prob. of Negro origin], a soup thickened with unripe okra pods.

**gum′drop′**, *n.* a small, firm candy made of sweetened gum arabic or gelatin.

**gump·tion** (gump′shən), *n.* [< Scot.], [Colloq.], courage and initiative; enterprise.

**gum′shoe′**, *n.* 1. a rubber overshoe. 2. [Slang], a detective.

**gun** (gun), *n.* [prob. < *Gunna*, pet name given to a weapon in 1330], 1. a weapon with a metal tube from which a projectile is discharged by the explosion of gunpowder. 2. any similar device not discharged by an explosive: as, an air *gun*. *v.i.* [GUNNED, GUNNING], to shoot or hunt with a gun. *v.t.* [Slang], to advance the throttle of (an engine). —**gun for**, [Slang], to seek.

**gun′boat′**, *n.* a small armed ship.

**gun′cot′ton**, *n.* an explosive made of cotton treated with nitric and sulfuric acids.

**gun′fire′**, *n.* firing of a gun or guns.

**gun′man** (-mən), *n.* [*pl.* -MEN], a gangster or thug armed with a gun.

**gun′ner**, *n.* 1. soldier, etc. who helps fire artillery. 2. a naval warrant officer in charge of a ship's guns.

**gun′ner·y**, *n.* the science of making or firing heavy guns or projectiles.

**gun·ny** (gun′i), *n.* [*pl.* -NIES], [< Sans. *goni*, sack], 1. a sack made of a coarse, heavy fabric of jute or hemp: also **gunny sack** (or **bag**). 2. this fabric.

**gun′pow′der**, *n.* an explosive powder used in guns, for blasting, etc.

**gun′run′ning**, *n.* the smuggling of guns and ammunition. —**gun′run′ner**, *n.*

**gun′shot′**, *n.* shot fired from a gun.

**gun′smith′**, *n.* one who makes or repairs small guns.

**gun·wale** (gun′′l), *n.* [< supporting a ship's guns], the upper edge of the side of a ship or boat: also sp. **gunnel**.

**gup·py** (gup′i), *n.* [*pl.* -PIES], [< R. *Guppy*, of Trinidad], a tiny fresh-water fish of the West Indies, etc.

**gur·gle** (gũr′g'l), *v.i.* [-GLED, -GLING], [< L. *gurgulio*, gullet], to make, or flow with, a bubbling sound. *n.* a gurgling sound.

**gush** (gush), *v.i.* [prob. < ON. *gusa*], 1. to flow out plentifully. 2. [Colloq.], to express exaggerated feeling. *v.t.* to cause to gush. *n.* a gushing. —**gush′ing·ly**, *adv.*

**gush′er**, *n.* 1. one who gushes. 2. an oil well from which oil spouts forth.

**gush′y**, *adj.* [-IER, -IEST], given to or full of exaggerated feeling; effusive.

**gus·set** (gus′it), *n.* [< OFr. *gousse*, husk], a triangular piece inserted to strengthen or enlarge a garment, glove, etc.

**gust** (gust), *n.* [< ON. *gjosa*, gush], 1. a sudden, strong rush of air. 2. a sudden outburst of rain, laughter, rage, etc. —**gust'y** [-IER, -IEST], *adj.* —**gus'ti·ly,** *adv.*
**gus·ta·to·ry** (gus'tə-tôr'i), *adj.* [< L. *gustus*, taste], of the sense of taste.
**gus·to** (gus'tō), *n.* [*pl.* -TOS], [< L. *gustus*, taste], 1. taste; liking. 2. zest; relish.
**gut** (gut), *n.* [< AS. *geotan*, pour], 1. *pl.* the bowels. 2. an intestine. 3. tough cord made of animal intestines. 4. *pl.* [Slang], pluck; courage. *v.t.* [GUTTED, GUTTING], 1. to remove the intestines from. 2. to destroy the interior of, as by fire.
**gut·ta·per·cha** (gut'ə-pūr'chə), *n.* [Malay *gĕtah*, gum + *pĕrca*, the tree], a rubberlike substance formed by the juice of certain Malay trees.
**gut·ter** (gut'ēr), *n.* [< L. *gutta*, a drop], a trough or channel to carry off water, as along the eaves of a roof or the side of a street. *v.i.* to flow in a stream.
**gut'ter·snipe'** (-snīp'), *n.* [Colloq.], a poor child who lives mainly in the streets.
**gut·tur·al** (gut'ēr-'l), *adj.* [< L. *guttur*, throat], 1. of the throat. 2. produced in the throat; rasping. —**gut'tur·al·ly,** *adv.*
**guy** (gī), *n.* [< OFr. *guier*, to guide], a rope, wire, etc. used to steady or guide something. *v.t.* [GUYED, GUYING], to use a guy.
**guy** (gī), *n.* [< *Guy* Fawkes, Eng. conspirator in a plot to blow up Parliament (1605)], [Slang], a boy or man. *v.t.* [GUYED, GUYING], [Colloq.], to tease.
**guz·zle** (guz''l), *v.i.* & *v.t.* [-ZLED, -ZLING], [? < OFr. *gosier*, throat], to drink greedily or immoderately. —**guz'zler,** *n.*
**gym** (jim), *n.* [Colloq.], gymnasium.
**gym·na·si·um** (jim-nā'zi-əm), *n.* [*pl.* -SIUMS, -SIA (-zi-ə)], [< Gr. *gymnos*, naked], a room or building equipped for physical training and sports.
**gym·nas'tics,** *n.pl.* exercises to develop and train the muscles. —**gym'nast,** *n.* —**gym·nas'tic,** *adj.* —**gym·nas'ti·cal·ly,** *adv.*
**gyn·e·col·o·gy** (jī'ni-kol'ə-ji, gī'-, jin'i-), *n.* [< Gr. *gynē*, woman; + *-logy*], the study and treatment of women's diseases. —**gyn'e·col'o·gist,** *n.*
**gyp** (jip), *n.* [prob. < *gypsy*], [Slang], 1. a swindle. 2. a swindler. *v.t.* & *v.i.* [GYPPED, GYPPING], [Slang], to swindle. —**gyp'per,** *n.*
**gyp·sum** (jip'səm), *n.* [< Gr. *gypsos*], a sulfate of calcium used for making plaster of Paris, in treating soil, etc.
**gyp·sy** (jip'si), *n.* [*pl.* -SIES], [< *Egipcien*, Egyptian: formerly thought to be from Egypt], 1. [often G-], a member of a wandering Caucasian people, originally from India, with dark skin and black hair. 2. [G-], their Indo-European language. 3. one who looks or lives like a gypsy.
**gy·rate** (jī'rāt, jī-rāt'), *v.i.* [-RATED, -RATING], [ult. < Gr. *gyros*, a circle], to move in a circular or spiral path; whirl. —**gy·ra'tion,** *n.* —**gy·ra·to·ry** (jī'rə-tôr'i), *adj.*
**gyro-,** [< Gr. *gyros*, a circle], a combining form meaning: 1. *gyrating*, as in *gyroscope*. 2. *gyroscope*.
**gy·ro·scope** (jī'rə-skōp'), *n.* [*gyro-* + *-scope*], a wheel mounted in a ring so that its axis is free to turn in any direction: when the wheel is spun rapidly, it will tend to keep its original plane of rotation.
**gyve** (jīv), *n.* & *v.t.* [GYVED, GYVING], [ME. *give*], [Archaic], fetter; shackle.

# H

**H, h** (āch), *n.* [*pl.* H's, h's, Hs, hs], the eighth letter of the English alphabet.
**H,** in *chem.*, hydrogen.
**H., h.,** 1. height. 2. high. 3. hour(s).
**ha** (hä), *interj.* an exclamation of wonder, surprise, anger, triumph, etc.
‡**ha·be·as cor·pus** (hā'bi-əs kôr'pəs), [L., (that) you have the body], in *law*, a writ requiring that a prisoner be brought before a court to decide the legality of his detention.
**hab·er·dash·er** (hab'ēr-dash'ēr), *n.* [ME.], a dealer in men's hats, shirts, neckties, etc. —**hab'er·dash'er·y** [*pl.* -IES], *n.*
**ha·bil·i·ment** (hə-bil'ə-mənt), *n.* [< Fr. *habiller*, clothe], 1. a garment. 2. *pl.* clothing.
**hab·it** (hab'it), *n.* [< L. *habere*, have], 1. a distinctive costume or dress, as of a religious order. 2. disposition. 3. a thing done often and, hence, easily; custom. 4. a usual way of doing. 5. an addiction. *v.t.* to dress.
**hab'it·a·ble,** *adj.* fit to be lived in. —**hab'it·a·bil'i·ty,** *n.* —**hab'it·a·bly,** *adv.*
**hab·i·tat** (hab'ə-tat'), *n.* [L., it inhabits], 1. the region where a plant or animal naturally lives. 2. a place regularly frequented by someone.
**hab'i·ta'tion** (-tā'shən), *n.* 1. an inhabiting. 2. a dwelling; home.
**ha·bit·u·al** (hə-bich'o͞o-əl), *adj.* 1. done or caused by habit. 2. steady; inveterate: as, a *habitual* smoker. 3. much seen, done, or used; usual. —**ha·bit'u·al·ly,** *adv.*
**ha·bit'u·ate'** (-āt'), *v.t.* [-ATED, -ATING], to accustom (*to*). —**ha·bit'u·a'tion,** *n.*
**hab'i·tude'** (-to͞od'), *n.* 1. habitual condition of mind or body; disposition. 2. custom.
**ha·bit·u·é** (hə-bich'o͞o-ā'), *n.* [Fr.], one who frequents a certain place.
**ha·ci·en·da** (hä'si-en'də), *n.* [Sp. < L. *facere*, do], in Spanish America, a large estate or plantation.
**hack** (hak), *v.t.* [AS. *haccian*], to chop or cut roughly. *v.i.* 1. to make rough cuts. 2. to give harsh, dry coughs. *n.* 1. a tool for hacking. 2. a gash or notch. 3. a harsh, dry cough. —**hack'er,** *n.* —**hack'ing,** *adj.*
**hack** (hak), *n.* [< *hackney*], 1. a horse for hire. 2. an old, worn-out horse. 3. a literary drudge. 4. a coach for hire. 5. a taxicab. *adj.* 1. employed as a hack. 2. trite.
**hack·le** (hak''l), *n.* [ME. *hakell*], neck feathers of a rooster, pigeon, etc.
**hack·ney** (hak'ni), *n.* [*pl.* -NEYS], [< *Hackney*, England], 1. a horse for driving or riding. 2. a carriage for hire. 3. a drudge. *adj.* 1. hired out. 2. stale; trite. *v.t.* to make trite by overuse. —**hack'neyed,** *adj.*
**hack saw,** a fine-toothed saw for cutting metal: also **hack'saw',** *n.*
**had** (had), pt. and pp. of **have.**
**had·dock** (had'ək), *n.* [*pl.* -DOCK, -DOCKS], [prob. < OFr. *hadot*], a small, Atlantic food fish, related to the cod.
**Ha·des** (hā'dēz), *n.* 1. in *Gr. myth.*, the resting place of the dead. 2. hell.
**had·n't** (had''nt), had not.
**hadst** (hadst), [Archaic], had: with *thou.*
**haft** (haft, häft), *n.* [AS. *hæft*], the handle or hilt of a knife, sword, etc.
**hag** (hag), *n.* [< AS. *hægtes*], 1. a witch. 2. an ugly old woman, esp. an evil one.
**hag·gard** (hag'ērd), *adj.* [< MFr. *hagard*, untamed (hawk)], having a wild, wasted, worn look; gaunt. —**hag'gard·ness,** *n.*
**hag·gle** (hag''l), *v.i.* [-GLED, -GLING], [< Scot. *hag*, to hack], to argue about terms, price, etc. *n.* a haggling. —**hag'gler,** *n.*

**hag'rid'den,** *adj.* harassed, as by fears, etc.
**hah** (hä), *interj.* ha.
**hail** (hāl), *v.t.* [< ON. *heill*, whole, sound], 1. to greet with a shout; cheer. 2. to shout to or after. *n.* a greeting. *interj.* an exclamation of tribute, greeting, etc. **—hail from,** to be from.
**hail** (hāl), *n.* [AS. *hægel*], 1. frozen raindrops falling during thunderstorms. 2. a shower of or like hail. *v.t. & v.i.* to pour down like hail.
**hail'stone',** *n.* a piece of hail.
**hail'storm',** *n.* a storm with hail.
**hair** (hâr), *n.* [AS. *hær*], 1. any of the threadlike outgrowths from the skin. 2. a growth of these, as on the human head. 3. a very small space, degree, etc. 4. a threadlike growth on a plant. *adj.* of or for hair. **—get in one's hair,** [Slang], to annoy one. **—split hairs,** to quibble. **—hair'less,** *adj.*
**hair'breadth'** (-bredth'), *n.* a very short distance. *adj.* very narrow; close. Also **hairs'breadth', hair's'breadth'.**
**hair'cloth',** *n.* cloth woven from horsehair or camel's hair.
**hair'cut',** *n.* a cutting of, or a style of cutting, the hair. **—hair'cut'ter,** *n.*
**hair'-do',** *n.* the style in which (a woman's) hair is arranged; coiffure.
**hair'dress'er,** *n.* one whose work is dressing (women's) hair.
**hair'line',** *n.* 1. a very thin line. 2. the outline of the hair on the head.
**hair'pin',** *n.* a small, bent piece of wire, etc. for keeping the hair in place. *adj.* U-shaped: as, a *hairpin* turn.
**hair'-rais'ing,** *adj.* [Colloq.], horrifying.
**hair'split'ting,** *adj. & n.* making petty distinctions; quibbling. **—hair'split'ter,** *n.*
**hair'spring',** *n.* a slender, hairlike coil spring, as in a watch.
**hair'y,** *adj.* [-IER, -IEST], 1. covered with hair. 2. of or like hair. **—hair'i·ness,** *n.*
**hake** (hāk), *n.* [*pl.* HAKE, HAKES], [prob. < ON.], an edible sea fish related to the cod.
**hal·berd** (hal'bẽrd), *n.* [< MHG. *helmbarte*], a combination spear and battle-ax of the 15th and 16th centuries.
**hal·cy·on** (hal'si-ən), *adj.* [< Gr. *alkyōn*, kingfisher (fabled calmer of the sea)], tranquil; happy; calm: as, *halcyon* days.
**hale** (hāl), *adj.* [HALER, HALEST], [AS. *hal*], vigorous and healthy. **—hale'ness,** *n.*
**hale** (hāl), *v.t.* [HALED, HALING], [< OFr. *haler*], to drag; haul; force to go.
**half** (haf, häf), *n.* [*pl.* HALVES], [AS. *healf*], 1. either of the two equal parts of anything. 2. either of the two equal periods of some games. *adj.* 1. being a half. 2. incomplete; partial. *adv.* 1. to the extent of a half. 2. partially. **—not half bad,** rather good.
**half'-and-half',** *n.* something that is half one thing and half another, as a mixture of equal parts of porter and ale, etc.
**half'back',** *n.* in *football*, either of two backs, in addition to the fullback and the quarterback.
**half'-baked',** *adj.* 1. only partly baked. 2. not completely thought out.
**half'-breed',** *n.* one whose parents are of different races: also **half'-caste'.**
**half brother,** a brother related through one parent only.
**half cocked,** [cf. *cock*, *n.* 4], ill-prepared; rashly: in *go off half cocked.*
**half dollar,** a silver coin of the U.S. and Canada, worth 50 cents.
**half'heart'ed,** *adj.* with little enthusiasm, determination, interest, etc.
**half'-mast',** *n.* the position of a flag halfway down its staff, as in token of mourning.
**half'-moon',** *n.* 1. the moon when only half its disk is seen. 2. anything shaped like this. *adj.* shaped like a half-moon.
**half note,** in *music*, a note having one half the duration of a whole note.
**half·pen·ny** (hā'pən-i, hāp'ni), *n.* [*pl.* -PENCE (hā'pəns), -PENNIES], a British bronze coin equal to half a penny.
**half sister,** a sister related through one parent only.
**half sole,** a sole (of a shoe or boot) from the arch to the toe.
**half'-track',** *n.* an army truck, armored vehicle, etc. with caterpillar treads instead of rear wheels.
**half'way',** *adj.* 1. midway between two points, etc. 2. partial: as, *halfway* measures. *adv.* 1. to the midway point. 2. partially. **—meet halfway,** to be willing to compromise with.
**half'-wit',** *n.* 1. a feeble-minded person. 2. a stupid, silly person. **—half'-wit'ted,** *adj.*
**hal·i·but** (hal'ə-bət, häl'-), *n.* [*pl.* -BUT, -BUTS], [ME. *hali*, holy + *butt*, a flounder: eaten on holidays], a large, edible flatfish found in northern seas.
**hal·i·to·sis** (hal'ə-tō'sis), *n.* [< L. *halitus*, breath], bad-smelling breath.
**hall** (hôl), *n.* [AS. *heall*], 1. the main dwelling on an estate. 2. a public building with offices, etc. 3. a large room for meetings, entertainments, eating, etc. 4. a college or university building. 5. a vestibule at the entrance of a building. 6. a passageway.
**hal·le·lu·jah, hal·le·lu·iah** (hal'ə-lōō'yə), *interj.* [< Heb. *hallelū*, praise + *yāh*, Jehovah], praise (ye) the Lord! *n.* a hymn of praise to God.
**hall·mark** (hôl'märk'), *n.* [< the mark stamped on gold and silver articles at Goldsmiths' Hall in London], a mark or symbol of genuineness or high quality.
**hal·loo** (hə-lōō'), *interj. & n.* a shout to attract attention. *v.i. & v.t.* [-LOOED, -LOOING], to shout or call.
**hal·low** (hal'ō), *v.t.* [< AS. *halig*, holy], to make or regard as holy or sacred.
**hal·lowed** (hal'ōd; *in liturgy, often* hal'ō-id), *adj.* holy; sacred.
**Hal·low·een, Hal·low·e'en** (hal'ō-ēn', häl'-), *n.* [contr. < *all hallow even*], the evening of October 31, followed by All Saints' Day.
**hal·lu·ci·na·tion** (hə-lōō'sə-nā'shən), *n.* [< L. *hallucinari*, to wander mentally], the apparent perception of sights, sounds, etc. that are not actually present.
**hal·lu'ci·no·gen** (-nə-jen, hal'yoo-sin'ə-jen), *n.* a drug or other substance that produces hallucinations. **—hal·lu'ci·no·gen'ic,** *adj.*
**hall·way** (hôl'wā'), *n.* a corridor.
**ha·lo** (hā'lō), *n.* [*pl.* -LOS, -LOES], [< Gr. *halōs*, threshing floor on which oxen trod in a circle], 1. a ring of light, as around the sun. 2. a symbolic ring of light shown around the head of a saint in pictures.
**hal·o·gen** (hal'ə-jən), *n.* [< Gr. *hals*, salt], any of the chemical elements fluorine, chlorine, bromine, and iodine.
**halt** (hôlt), *n., v.t. & v.i.* [< G. *halten*], stop.
**halt** (hôlt), *v.i.* [< AS. *healtian*], 1. to limp. 2. to hesitate. *adj.* [Archaic], lame. **—the halt,** those who are lame. **—halt'ing·ly,** *adv.*
**hal·ter** (hôl'tẽr), *n.* [AS. *hælfire*], 1. a rope or strap for tying or leading an animal. 2. a hangman's noose. 3. a woman's upper garment, held up by a loop around the neck.
**halve** (hav, häv), *v.t.* [HALVED, HALVING], 1. to divide into two equal parts. 2. to reduce to half.
**halves** (havz, hävz), *n.* pl. of **half. —by halves,** halfway; imperfectly. **—go halves,** to share expenses equally.
**hal·yard** (hal'yẽrd), *n.* [< ME. *halien* (see HALE, *v.*)], a rope or tackle for raising or lowering a flag, sail, etc.: also sp. **halliard.**

**ham** (ham), *n.* [AS. *hamm*], 1. the back of the thigh. 2. the upper part of a hog's hind leg, salted, smoked, etc. 3. [Slang], *a*) an actor who overacts. *b*) an amateur radio operator. —**ham'my,** *adj.* [Slang].

**ham·burg·er** (ham'bũr'gẽr), *n.* [< *Hamburg*, Germany], 1. ground beef. 2. a cooked patty of such meat, often in a sandwich. Also **ham'burg.**

**Ham·let** (ham'lit), *n.* the title hero of a tragedy by Shakespeare.

**ham·let** (ham'lit), *n.* [< LG. *hām*, home], a very small village.

**ham·mer** (ham'ẽr), *n.* [AS. *hamor*], 1. a tool for pounding, having a metal head and a handle. 2. a thing like this in shape or use, as the part of a gun that strikes the firing pin. *v.t. & v.i.* 1. to strike repeatedly, as with a hammer. 2. to drive, shape, or fasten, as with hammer blows. —**hammer (away) at,** to keep emphasizing.

**ham·mock** (ham'ək), *n.* [Sp. *hamaca;* of W. Ind. origin], a bed of canvas, etc. swung from ropes at both ends.

**ham·per** (ham'pẽr), *v.t.* [ME. *hampren*], to hinder; impede; encumber.

**ham·per** (ham'pẽr), *n.* [< OFr. *hanap*, a cup], a large basket, usually with a cover.

**ham·ster** (ham'stẽr), *n.* [G.], a ratlike animal of Europe and Asia, often used in scientific experiments.

**ham·string** (ham'striŋ'), *n.* a tendon at the back of the knee. *v.t.* [-STRUNG, -STRINGING], to disable, as by cutting a hamstring.

**hand** (hand), *n.* [AS.], 1. the part of the arm below the wrist, used for grasping. 2. a side or direction: as, at my right *hand.* 3. possession: as, the papers are in my *hands.* 4. control: in *in* (or *out of*) *hand*, etc. 5. an active part: as, take a *hand* in the work. 6. a promise to marry. 7. skill. 8. one having a special skill. 9. handwriting. 10. applause. 11. help: as, lend me a *hand.* 12. a hired worker: as, a farm *hand.* 13. a source: as, I got the news at first *hand.* 14. anything like a hand, as a pointer on a clock. 15. the breadth of a hand. 16. in *card games*, *a*) the cards held by a player at one time. *b*) a round of play. *adj.* of, for, or controlled by the hand. *v.t.* 1. to give as with the hand. 2. to help or conduct with the hand. —**at hand,** near. —**change hands,** to pass to another's ownership. —**from hand to mouth,** with nothing saved for the future. —**hand in hand,** together. —**hand it to,** [Slang], to give deserved credit to. —**hand over fist,** [Colloq.], easily and in large amounts. —**hands down,** easily. —**on hand,** 1. near. 2. available. 3. present. —**on the one** (or **other**) **hand,** from one (or the opposed) point of view. —**upper hand,** the advantage.

**hand'bag',** *n.* 1. a woman's purse. 2. a small satchel.

**hand'ball',** *n* a game in which players bat a small rubber ball against a wall or walls with the hand.

**hand'bill',** *n.* a small printed notice to be passed out by hand.

**hand'book',** *n.* 1. a compact reference book; manual. 2. a guidebook.

**hand'breadth',** *n.* the breadth of the human palm, about 4 inches, used as a unit of measurement.

**hand'cart',** *n.* a small cart, often with only two wheels, pushed or pulled by hand.

**hand'clasp',** *n.* a clasping of hands in greeting, promise, etc.

**hand'cuff',** *n. usually in pl.* either of a pair of connected rings for shackling the wrists of a prisoner. *v.t.* to put handcuffs on.

**hand'ed,** *adj.* having or involving (a specified kind or number of) hands, as in *left-handed, two-handed.*

**hand'ful',** *n.* [*pl.* -FULS], 1. as much or as many as the hand will hold. 2. a few; not many. 3. [Colloq.], someone or something hard to control.

**hand·i·cap** (han'di-kap'), *n.* [< *hand in cap*, former kind of lottery], 1. a competition in which difficulties are imposed on, or advantages given to, the various contestants to equalize their chances. 2. such a difficulty or advantage. 3. any hindrance. *v.t.* [-CAPPED, -CAPPING], 1. to give a handicap to. 2. to hinder.

**hand·i·craft** (han'di-kraft', -kräft'), *n.* 1. skill with the hands. 2. work calling for this, as weaving.

**hand'i·work',** *n.* 1. work done by a person himself. 2. the result of one's actions.

**hand·ker·chief** (haŋ'kẽr-chif), *n.* [*hand* + *kerchief*], 1. a small cloth for wiping the nose, face, etc. 2. a kerchief.

**han·dle** (han'd'l), *n.* [AS. < *hand*], 1. that part of a tool, etc. by which it is held or lifted. 2. occasion; pretext. *v.t.* [-DLED, -DLING], 1. to touch, lift, operate, etc. with the hand. 2. to manage; control. 3. to deal with; treat. 4. to trade or deal in. *v.i.* to respond to control.

**handle bar,** *often in pl.* a curved metal bar with handles on the end, for steering a bicycle, etc.

**hand'made',** *adj.* made by hand, not by machine.

**hand'maid',** *n.* a woman or girl servant.

**hand'-me-down',** *n.* [Colloq.], a used garment, etc. passed on to one.

**hand organ,** a barrel organ.

**hand'out',** *n.* a gift of food, clothing, etc., as to a beggar or tramp.

**hand'shake',** *n.* a gripping of each other's hand in greeting, promise, etc.

**hand·some** (han'səm), *adj.* [orig., easily handled], 1. considerable: as, a *handsome* sum. 2. proper; gracious. 3. good-looking in a manly or impressive way.

**hand'spring',** *n.* a spring in which one turns over in mid-air with one or both hands touching the ground.

**hand'-to-hand',** *adj.* at close quarters: said of fighting.

**hand'-to-mouth',** *adj.* with nothing saved for the future.

**hand'writ'ing,** *n.* 1. writing done by hand, as with a pen. 2. a style of such writing.

**hand'y,** *adj.* [-IER, -IEST], 1. close at hand; easily reached. 2. easily used; convenient. 3. clever with the hands. —**hand'i·ly,** *adv.*

**handy man,** a man who does odd jobs.

**hang** (haŋ), *v.t.* [HUNG, HANGING; for *v.t.* 3 & *v.i.* 3, HANGED is preferred pt. & pp.], [AS. *hangian*], 1. to attach from above with no support from below; suspend. 2. to attach, as a door, so as to swing freely. 3. to kill by suspending from a rope about the neck. 4. to attach (wallpaper, etc.) to walls. 5. to deadlock (a jury). *v.i.* 1. to be attached above with no support from below. 2. to swing freely. 3. to die by hanging. 4. to droop; bend. *n.* 1. the way a thing hangs. 2. the way a thing is done. 3. meaning; general idea. —**hang around** (or **about**), [Colloq.], to loiter around. —**hang back,** to hesitate, as from shyness. —**hang on,** 1. to depend on. 2. to listen attentively to. —**hang out,** [Slang], to frequent.

**hang·ar** (haŋ'ẽr), *n.* [Fr.], a shed or shelter, esp. one for aircraft.

**hang'dog',** *adj.* sneaking or abject.

**hang'er,** *n.* 1. one who hangs things. 2. that on which something is hung.

**hang'ing,** *adj.* that hangs. *n.* 1. a killing by hanging. 2. *usually in pl.* something hung on a wall, etc., as drapery.

**hang'man** (-mən), *n.* [*pl.* -MEN], a man who hangs condemned persons.

**hang′nail′**, *n.* [< AS. *hangnægl*, sore nail], torn skin hanging next to a fingernail.
**hang′o′ver**, *n.* 1. a survival. 2. sickness resulting from drinking much alcoholic liquor.
**hang′-up′**, *n.* [Slang], a personal or emotional problem, apparently not resolvable.
**hank** (haŋk), *n.* [? < ON. *hönk*], a skein of yarn or thread.
**hank·er** (haŋ′kẽr), *v.i.* [prob. < D.], to long (*for*); yearn. **—hank′er·ing,** *n.*
**hank·y-pank·y** (haŋ′ki-paŋ′ki), *n.* [redupl. < *hand*], [Colloq.], trickery; deception.
**han·som** (han′səm), *n.* [< J. A. *Hansom*, Eng. inventor], a two-wheeled covered carriage pulled by one horse.
**hap** (hap), *n.* [< ON. *happ*], [Archaic], chance; luck. *v.i.* [HAPPED, HAPPING], [Archaic], to happen. **—hap′ly,** *adv.*
**hap·haz·ard** (hap′haz′ẽrd), *adj.* not planned; random. *adv.* by chance.
**hap·less,** (hap′lis), *adj.* unlucky.
**hap·pen** (hap′′n), *v.i.* [ME. *happenen*], 1. to take place; occur. 2. to be, occur, or come by chance. 3. to have the luck or occasion: as, I *happened* to see it. **—happen on,** to meet or find by chance.
**hap′pen·ing,** *n.* an occurrence; event.
**hap·py** (hap′i), *adj.* [-PIER, -PIEST], [< *hap*], 1. lucky; fortunate. 2. having or showing great pleasure or joy; glad. 3. suitable and clever; apt: as, a *happy* suggestion. **—hap′pi·ly,** *adv.* **—hap′pi·ness,** *n.*
**hap′py-go-luck′y,** *adj.* easygoing; trusting to luck. *adv.* by chance.
**ha·ra-ki·ri** (har′ə-kêr′i), *n.* [Japan. *hara*, belly + *kiri*, cutting], ritual suicide by ripping out the bowels.
**ha·rangue** (hə-raŋ′), *n.* [< ML. *harenga*], a long, blustering speech; tirade. *v.i. & v.t.* [-RANGUED, -RANGUING], to deliver a harangue (to). **—ha·rangu′er,** *n.*
**har·ass** (har′əs, hə-ras′), *v.t.* [< OFr. *harer*, set a dog on], 1. to worry or torment. 2. to trouble (an enemy) by constant attacks. **—har′ass·ment,** *n.*
**har·bin·ger** (här′bin-jẽr), *n.* [< OFr. *herberge*, shelter], a forerunner; herald.
**har·bor** (här′bẽr), *n.* [< AS. *here*, army + *beorg*, shelter], 1. a shelter. 2. a protected inlet for anchoring ships; port. *v.t.* 1. to shelter; house. 2. to hold in the mind: as, to *harbor* envy. *v.i.* to take shelter. Brit. sp. **harbour.** **—har′bor·less,** *adj.*
**hard** (härd), *adj.* [AS. *heard*], 1. firm and unyielding to the touch; solid, compact, etc. 2. powerful: as, a *hard* blow. 3. difficult to do, understand, or deal with. 4. unfeeling: as, a *hard* heart. 5. harsh; severe. 6. energetic: as, a *hard* worker. 7. having mineral salts that interfere with lathering: said of water. 8. containing much alcohol: said of liquors. *adv.* 1. energetically: as, work *hard*. 2. with strength: as, hit *hard*. 3. with difficulty: as, *hard*-earned. 4. firmly. 5. close; near: as, we live *hard* by. 6. so as to be solid: as, frozen *hard*. **—hard and fast,** invariable; strict. **—hard up,** [Colloq.], in great need of money. **—hard′ness,** *n.*
**hard′-bit′ten,** *adj.* tough; dogged.
**hard′-boiled′,** *adj.* 1. boiled until solid: said of eggs. 2. [Colloq.], unfeeling; callous.
**hard′-core′,** *adj.* absolute; unqualified.
**hard·en** (här′d′n), *v.t. & v.i.* to make or become hard. **—hard′en·er,** *n.*
**hard′head′ed,** *adj.* 1. shrewd and unsentimental; practical. 2. stubborn.
**hard′heart′ed,** *adj.* unfeeling; cruel.
**har·di·hood** (här′di-hood′), *n.* boldness.
**hard·ly** (härd′li), *adv.* 1. not easily. 2. severely; harshly. 3. barely; only just: often ironic for "not at all." 4. improbably.
**hard′pan′,** *n.* a layer of hard subsoil difficult to work.
**hard′ship′,** *n.* 1. hard circumstances of life. 2. a thing hard to bear, as poverty, pain, etc.
**hard′tack′** (-tak′), *n.* unleavened bread made in hard, large wafers.
**hard′ware′** (-wâr′), *n.* 1. articles made of metal, as tools, nails, fittings, etc. 2. the mechanical, magnetic, and electronic devices of a computer.
**hard′wood′,** *n.* tough, heavy timber with a compact texture.
**har·dy** (här′di), *adj.* [-DIER, -DIEST], [< OHG. *hartjan*, make hard], 1. bold and resolute. 2. too bold; rash. 3. robust; enduring.
**hare** (hâr), *n.* [AS. *hara*], 1. a swift animal of the rodent family, like the rabbit but larger. 2. the common American rabbit.
**hare′brained′,** *adj.* senseless, rash, etc.
**hare′lip′,** *n.* a congenital deformity consisting of a cleft of the upper lip.
**ha·rem** (hâr′əm), *n.* [< Ar. *harīm*, prohibited (place)], 1. that part of a Moslem's house in which the women live. 2. the women in a harem. Also **ha·reem** (hä-rēm′).
**hark** (härk), *v.i.* [ME. *herkien*], to listen carefully: usually in the imperative. **—hark back,** to go back in thought or speech.
**hark·en** (här′k′n), *v.i. & v.t.* hearken.
**Har·le·quin** (här′lə-kwin, -kin), *n.* 1. a comic character in pantomime, who wears a mask and gay, spangled tights. 2. [h-], a clown; buffoon.
**har·lot** (här′lət), *n.* [OFr., rogue], a prostitute. **—har′lot·ry** (-ri), *n.*
**harm** (härm), *n.* [AS. *hearm*], hurt; injury; damage. *v.t.* to do harm to; hurt.
**harm′ful,** *adj.* causing harm; hurtful.
**harm′less,** *adj.* causing no harm.
**har·mon·ic** (här-mon′ik), *adj.* in *music*, of or in harmony. *n.* an overtone.
**har·mon·i·ca** (här-mon′i-kə), *n.* a small wind instrument with a series of metal reeds that vibrate and produce tones when air is blown or sucked across them.
**har·mon′ics,** *n.pl.* [construed as sing.], the science of musical sounds.
**har·mo·ni·ous** (här-mō′ni-əs), *adj.* 1. having parts combined in an orderly or pleasing arrangement. 2. having conforming ideas, interests, etc. 3. having musical tones combined to give a pleasing effect.
**har·mo·nize** (här′mə-nīz′), *v.i.* [-NIZED, -NIZING], to be, sing, or play in harmony. *v.t.* to make harmonious.
**har·mo·ny** (här′mə-ni), *n.* [*pl.* -NIES], [ult. < Gr. *harmozein*, fit together], 1. pleasing agreement of parts in color, size, shape, etc. 2. agreement in action, ideas, etc.; a being peaceable or friendly. 3. in *music*, the pleasing combination of tones in a chord.
**har·ness** (här′nis), *n.* [OFr. *harneis*, armor], the leather straps and metal pieces by which a horse, mule, etc. is fastened to a vehicle, plow, etc. *v.t.* 1. to put harness on. 2. to control so as to use the power of.
**harp** (härp), *n.* [AS. *hearpe*], a musical instrument with strings stretched across a triangular frame, played by plucking. *v.i.* 1. to play a harp. 2. to persist in talking or writing tediously (*on* or *upon*). **—harp′ist,** *n.*
**har·poon** (här-po͞on′), *n.* [< Fr. *harpe*, a claw], a barbed spear with an attached line, used for spearing whales, etc. *v.t.* to strike or kill with a harpoon. **—har·poon′er,** *n.*
**harp·si·chord** (härp′si-kôrd′), *n.* [< obs. Fr.; see HARP & CORD], a stringed musical instrument with a keyboard, like the piano.
**Har·py** (här′pi), *n.* [*pl.* -PIES], [< Gr. *harpazein*, seize], 1. in *Gr. myth.*, any of several hideous, winged monsters who carried off the souls of the dead. 2. [h-], a greedy person.
**har·ri·dan** (har′i-dən), *n.* [< OFr. *haridelle*, worn-out horse], a disreputable, shrewish old woman.
**har·row** (har′ō), *n.* [prob. < ON.], a heavy

frame with spikes or disks, used for leveling and breaking up plowed ground, etc. *v.t.* 1. to draw a harrow over (land). 2. to hurt. 3. distress; vex. —**har′row·ing,** *adj.*

**har·ry** (har′i), *v.t.* [-RIED, -RYING], [< AS. *here,* army], 1. to raid and destroy or rob. 2. to torment; worry.

**harsh** (härsh), *adj.* [prob. < ON.], 1. unpleasantly rough to the eye, ear, taste, or touch. 2. unpleasantly crude or severe. 3. stern; cruel. —**harsh′ly,** *adv.*—**harsh′ness,** *n.*

**hart** (härt), *n.* [AS. *heor(o)t*], a male deer, esp. a red deer after its fifth year; stag.

**har·um-scar·um** (hâr′əm-skâr′əm), *adj.* [prob. < *hare* + *scare* + *'em*], reckless; rash; wild. *n.* a reckless person or rash action.

**har·vest** (här′vist), *n.* [AS. *hærfest*], 1. the time of the year when grain, fruit, etc. are gathered in. 2. a season's crop. 3. the gathering in of a crop. 4. the outcome of any effort. *v.t. & v.i.* to gather in (a crop, etc.). —**har′vest·er,** *n.* —**har′vest·ing,** *n.*

**has** (haz), the 3d pers. sing., pres. indic., of **have.**

**has′-been′,** *n.* [Colloq.], a person or thing whose popularity is past.

**hash** (hash), *v.t.* [< Fr. *hache,* hatchet], 1. to chop up (meat and vegetables) for cooking. 2. [Colloq.], to bungle. *n.* 1. a chopped mixture of cooked meat and vegetables, usually baked. 2. a mixture. 3. a muddle.

**hash·ish** (hash′ēsh, -ish), *n.* [Ar. *ḥashīsh,* hemp], a narcotic made from Indian hemp, used in the Orient.

**has·n't** (haz′′nt), has not.

**hasp** (hasp, häsp), *n.* [AS. *hæspe*], a fastening for a door, etc.; esp., a metal piece fitted over a staple and fastened by a padlock, bolt, etc. *v.t.* to fasten as with a hasp.

**has·sle, has·sel** (has′′l), *n.* [< ?], [Slang], a heated discussion; squabble.

**has·sock** (has′ək), *n.* [AS. *hassuc,* (clump of) coarse grass], a firmly stuffed cushion used as a footstool or seat.

**hast** (hast), [Archaic], have: with *thou.*

**haste** (hāst), *n.* [OFr.], quickness of motion; hurrying. *v.t. & v.i.* [Rare], to hasten. —**make haste,** to hurry.

**has·ten** (hās′′n), *v.t.* to make hurry. *v.i.* to move swiftly; be quick. —**has′ten·er,** *n.*

**hast·y** (hās′ti), *adj.* [-IER, -IEST], 1. done with haste; hurried. 2. done or acting too quickly or rashly. 3. impetuous or impatient. —**hast′i·ly,** *adv.* —**hast′i·ness,** *n.*

**hat** (hat), *n.* [AS. *hætt*], a head covering, usually with a brim and a crown. —**pass the hat,** to take up a collection. —**talk through one's hat,** [Colloq.], to talk nonsense.

**hat′band′,** *n.* a band of cloth around the crown of a hat, above the brim.

**hatch** (hach), *v.t.* [ME. *hacchen*], 1. to bring forth (young) from (an egg or eggs). 2. to contrive (a plan, plot, etc.). *v.i.* 1. to bring forth young: said of eggs. 2. to emerge from the egg. —**hatch′er,** *n.*

**hatch** (hach), *n.* [AS. *hæc,* grating], 1. a hatchway. 2. a lid for a hatchway.

**hatch** (hach), *v.t.* [< OFr. *hache,* an ax], to mark or engrave with fine, crossed or parallel lines. —**hatch′ing,** *n.*

**hatch′er·y,** *n.* [*pl.* -IES], a place for hatching eggs, as of fish or poultry.

**hatch·et** (hach′it), *n.* [< OFr. *hache,* ax], a small ax with a short handle. —**bury the hatchet,** to make peace.

**hatch′way′,** *n.* an opening in a ship's deck, or in a floor or roof.

**hate** (hāt), *v.t.* [HATED, HATING], [AS. *hatian*], 1. to have strong dislike or ill will for. 2. to wish to avoid: as, he *hates* work. *v.i.* to feel hatred. *n.* 1. a strong feeling of dislike or ill will. 2. a person or thing hated. —**hat′er,** *n.*

**hate′ful,** *adj.* 1. [Rare], feeling or showing hate. 2. deserving hate. —**hate′ful·ly,** *adv.*

**hath** (hath), archaic 3d pers. sing., pres. indic., of **have.**

**hat′rack′,** *n.* a rack to hold hats.

**ha·tred** (hā′trid), *n.* strong dislike or ill will; hate.

**hat·ter** (hat′ẽr), *n.* one who makes or sells hats.

**hau·berk** (hô′bẽrk), *n.* [< OHG. *hals,* neck + *bergan,* protect], a medieval coat of armor.

**haugh·ty** (hô′ti), *adj.* [-TIER, -TIEST], [< OFr. *haut,* high], having or showing great pride in oneself and contempt for others. —**haugh′ti·ly,** *adv.* —**haugh′ti·ness,** *n.*

**haul** (hôl), *v.t. & v.i.* [< OFr. *haler,* draw], 1. to move by pulling; drag. 2. to transport by wagon, truck, etc. *n.* 1. the act of hauling. 2. the amount gained, caught, etc. at one time; catch. 3. the distance over which something is transported. 4. the load transported. —**haul off,** [Colloq.], to draw the arm back before hitting. —**haul′er,** *n.*

**haunch** (hônch, hänch), *n.* [< OFr. *hanche* < Gmc.], 1. the hip, buttock, and upper thigh together. 2. an animal's loin and leg together.

**haunt** (hônt, hänt), *v.t.* [< OFr. *hanter,* to frequent], 1. to visit often or continually. 2. to recur frequently to: as, memories *haunt* me. *n.* a place often visited.

**haunt′ed,** *adj.* supposedly frequented by ghosts: as, a *haunted* house.

**haunt′ing,** *adj.* recurring often to the mind.

**hau·teur** (hō-tũr′), *n.* [Fr. < *haut,* proud], haughtiness; disdainful pride.

**have** (hav), *v.t.* [HAD, HAVING], [AS. *habban*], 1. to hold; own; possess: as, he *has* money, a week *has* 7 days. 2. to experience: as, *have* a good time. 3. to grasp or hold mentally, as an idea. 4. to get; take: as, *have* a drink. 5. to beget (offspring). 6. to engage in: as, we *had* a fight. 7. to cause to; cause to be: as, he *had* us sing. 8. to permit; tolerate: as, I won't *have* this noise! 9. [Colloq.], to hold in a position of disadvantage. *Have* is used as an auxiliary to express completed action (e.g., I *had* left), and with infinitives to express obligation or necessity (e.g., we *have* to go). *Have got* often replaces *have. Have* is conjugated in the present indicative (I) *have,* (he, she, it) *has,* (we, you, they) *have.* —**have it in for,** [Colloq.], to bear a grudge against. —**have it out,** to settle a conflict, as by fighting. —**have on,** to be wearing. —**have to do with,** 1. to be related to. 2. to deal with.

**ha·ven** (hā′v'n), *n.* [AS. *hæfen*], 1. a port or harbor. 2. a place of shelter; refuge.

**have·n't** (hav′′nt), have not.

**hav·er·sack** (hav′ẽr-sak′), *n.* [< G. *habersack,* lit., sack of oats], a canvas bag for provisions, worn on the back by soldiers, hikers, etc.

**hav·oc** (hav′ək), *n.* [< OFr. *havot,* plunder], great destruction and devastation. —**play havoc with,** to ruin.

**haw** (hô), *n.* [AS. *haga*], 1. the berry of the hawthorn. 2. the hawthorn.

**haw** (hô), *interj. & n.* a command to a horse, etc., meaning "turn left!"

**haw** (hô), *v.i.* [echoic], to hesitate in speaking: in *hem and haw.*

**hawk** (hôk), *n.* [AS. *hafoc*], a bird of prey with short, rounded wings, a long tail, and a hooked beak. *v.i.* to hunt birds with the help of hawks. —**hawk′ing,** *n.*

**hawk** (hôk), *v.t. & v.i.* [< *hawker*], to advertise or peddle (goods) in the streets by shouting.

**hawk** (hôk), *v.i.* [echoic], to clear the throat audibly. *n.* an audible clearing of the throat.

**hawk′er,** *n.* [prob. < MLG. *hoker*], a street peddler; huckster.

**hawk′-eyed′,** *adj.* keen-sighted as a hawk.

**haw·ser** (hô′zẽr), *n.* [OFr. *haulser* < L. *altus,*

high], a rope or cable by which a ship is anchored, towed, etc.

**haw·thorn** (hô′thôrn′), *n.* [< AS. *haga*, hedge + *thorn*], a spiny shrub or small tree of the rose family, with red berries.

**hay** (hā), *n.* [AS. *hieg*], grass, clover, etc. cut and dried for fodder. *v.i.* to cut and dry grass, etc. for hay.

**hay′cock′** (-kok′), *n.* a small heap of hay drying in a field.

**hay fever,** acute inflammation of the eyes and respiratory tract: an allergic reaction to some kinds of pollen.

**hay′loft′,** *n.* a loft, or upper story, in a barn or stable, for storing hay.

**hay′mow′** (-mou′), *n.* a hayloft.

**hay′stack′,** *n.* a large heap of hay piled up outdoors: also **hay′rick′** (-rik′).

**hay′wire′,** *adj.* [Slang], 1. out of order; wrong. 2. crazy.

**haz·ard** (haz′ẽrd), *n.* [OFr., game of dice], 1. chance. 2. risk; danger. 3. any obstacle on a golf course. *v.t.* to chance; risk.

**haz′ard·ous,** *adj.* risky; dangerous.

**haze** (hāz), *n.* [prob. < LG. dial.], 1. a thin vapor of fog, smoke, dust, etc. in the air. 2. slight vagueness of mind. **—ha′zy** [-IER, -IEST], *adj.* **—ha′zi·ly,** *adv.* **—ha′zi·ness,** *n.*

**haze** (hāz), *v.t.* [HAZED, HAZING], [OFr. *haser*, irritate], to force (fellow students) to undergo humiliating or painful ordeals, as in initiation. **—haz′er,** *n.* **—haz′ing,** *n.*

**ha·zel** (hā′z'l), *n.* [AS. *hæsel*], 1. a tree or shrub of the birch family, with edible nuts. 2. a reddish brown. *adj.* light reddish-brown.

**ha′zel·nut′,** *n.* the small, edible, roundish nut of the hazel; filbert.

**H-bomb** (āch′bom′), *n.* hydrogen bomb.

**he** (hē), *pron.* [for *pl.* see THEY], [AS.], 1. the man, boy, or male animal previously mentioned. 2. anyone: as, *he* who laughs last laughs best. *n.* a man, boy, or male animal.

**He,** in *chem.*, helium.

**head** (hed), *n.* [AS. *heafod*], 1. the part of the body containing the brain, and the eyes, ears, nose and mouth. 2. the mind; intelligence. 3. [*pl.* HEAD], a unit of counting: as, ten *head* of cattle. 4. the main side of a coin. 5. the uppermost part or thing; top. 6. the topic or title of a section, chapter, etc. 7. the foremost or projecting part; front. 8. the part designed for holding, striking, etc.: as, the *head* of a nail. 9. the membrane across the end of a drum, etc. 10. the source of a river, etc. 11. pressure: as, a *head* of steam. 12. a position of leadership. 13. a leader, ruler, etc. 14. a crisis or culmination: as, things may soon come to a *head*. *adj.* 1. most important; principal. 2. at the top or front. 3. striking against the front: as, *head* winds. *v.t.* 1. to be chief of; command. 2. to lead; precede. 3. to cause to go in a specified direction. *v.i.* to set out; go: as, he *headed* eastward. **—go to one's head,** 1. to confuse or intoxicate one. 2. to make one vain. **—head off,** to get ahead of and intercept. **—head over heels,** deeply; completely. **—keep** (or **lose) one's head,** to keep (or lose) one's poise, self-control, etc. **—lay** (or **put) heads together,** to consult or scheme together. **—not make head or tail of,** not to understand. **—out of** (or **off) one's head,** [Colloq.], crazy. **—over one's head,** 1. too difficult for one to understand. 2. to a higher authority. **—turn one's head,** to make one vain. **—head′less,** *adj.*

**head′ache′** (-āk′), *n.* 1. a continuous pain in the head. 2. [Colloq.], a cause of worry, trouble, etc.

**head′dress′,** *n.* a covering for the head.

**head′ed,** *adj.* having a head or heads: used in compounds, as, *clearheaded.*

**head′first′,** *adv.* 1. with the head in front; headlong. 2. recklessly; rashly.

**head′gear′,** *n.* a hat, cap, bonnet, etc.

**head′-hunt′er,** *n.* a member of any of certain primitive tribes who remove and preserve the heads of slain enemies.

**head′ing,** *n.* 1. something forming the head, top, or front. 2. the title, topic, etc. as of a chapter.

**head′land′,** *n.* a point of land reaching out into the water; cape.

**head′light′,** *n.* a light with a reflector and lens, at the front of a vehicle.

**head′line′,** *n.* printed lines at the top of a newspaper article, giving the topic. *v.t.* [-LINED, -LINING], to give featured billing or notice to. **—head′lin′er,** *n.*

**head′long′** (-lôŋ′), *adv.* & *adj.* [< ME. *hedelinge(s)*], 1. with the head first. 2. with uncontrolled speed and force. 3. reckless(ly); rash(ly).

**head′mas′ter,** *n.* in certain schools, the principal. **—head′mis′tress,** *n.fem.*

**head′-on′,** *adj.* & *adv.* with the head or front foremost: as, hit *head-on.*

**head′phone′,** *n.* 1. a telephone or radio receiver held to the ear by a band over the head. 2. *usually pl.* a pair of such receivers.

**head′piece′,** *n.* 1. a helmet, cap, or other covering for the head. 2. a headphone.

**head′quar′ters** (-kwôr′tẽrz), *n.pl.* [sometimes construed as sing.], 1. the main office, or center of operations, of one in command, as in an army. 2. any main office.

**heads·man** (hedz′mən), *n.* [*pl.* -MEN], one who executes by beheading.

**head′stone′,** *n.* a stone marker placed at the head of a grave.

**head′strong′,** *adj.* determined to do as one pleases; obstinate. **—head′strong′ness,** *n.*

**head′wa′ters,** *n.pl.* the small streams that are the sources of a river.

**head′way′,** *n.* 1. motion forward. 2. progress. 3. clearance overhead.

**head·y** (hed′i), *adj.* [-IER, -IEST], 1. impetuous; rash. 2. intoxicating. **—head′i·ness,** *n.*

**heal** (hēl), *v.t.* & *v.i.* [AS. *hælan*], 1. to make or become well or healthy again. 2. to cure (a disease); mend, as a wound. **—heal′er,** *n.*

**health** (helth), *n.* [AS. *hælth*], 1. physical and mental well-being; freedom from disease, etc. 2. physical condition: as, poor *health.* 3. a wish for one's health and happiness, as in a toast.

**health′ful,** *adj.* helping to produce or maintain health. **—health′ful·ly,** *adv.*

**health·y** (hel′thi), *adj.* [-IER, -IEST], 1. having good health. 2. showing or resulting from good health: as, a *healthy* appetite. 3. healthful. **—health′i·ness,** *n.*

**heap** (hēp), *n.* [< AS. *heap*, a troop], 1. many things together in a pile; mass. 2. [Colloq.], a large amount. *v.t.* 1. to make a heap of. 2. to give in large amounts. 3. to fill (a plate, etc.) full or to overflowing. *v.i.* to form a heap.

**hear** (hêr), *v.t.* [HEARD (hûrd), HEARING], [AS. *hieran*], 1. to become aware of (sounds) by the ear. 2. to listen to. 3. to conduct a hearing of (a law case, etc.). 4. to be informed of; learn. *v.i.* to be able to hear sounds. **—hear from,** to get a letter, etc. from. **—not hear of,** not assent to.

**hear′ing,** *n.* 1. the act or process of perceiving sounds. 2. the ability to hear. 3. opportunity to be heard. 4. an investigation or trial before a judge, etc. 5. the distance a sound will carry: as, within *hearing.*

**heark·en** (här′k'n), *v.i.* [AS. *heorcnian*], to listen carefully; give heed. **—heark′en·er,** *n.*

**hear·say** (hêr′sā′), *n.* gossip; rumor.

**hearse** (hûrs), *n.* [< L. *hirpex*, a harrow], a vehicle for carrying a dead body to a grave.

**heart** (härt), *n.* [AS. *heorte*], 1. the hollow, muscular organ that circulates the blood by alternate dilation and contraction. 2.

the central, vital, or main part; core. 3. the human heart considered as the center of emotions, personal attributes, etc.; specif., *a*) inmost thoughts and feelings. *b*) love, sympathy, etc. *c*) spirit or courage. 4. a conventionalized design of a heart (♥). 5. any of a suit of playing cards marked with such symbols in red. **—after one's own heart,** that pleases one perfectly. **—at heart,** in one's inmost nature. **—by heart,** by memorizing or from memory. **—set one's heart on,** to have a fixed desire for. **—take to heart,** 1. to consider seriously. 2. to be troubled by.

**heart′ache′** (-āk′), *n.* sorrow; grief.

**heart′break′,** *n.* overwhelming sorrow or grief. **—heart′bro′ken,** *adj.*

**heart′burn′,** *n.* a burning, acid sensation in the stomach.

**heart·en** (här′t'n), *v.t.* to encourage.

**heart′felt′,** *adj.* sincere; genuine.

**hearth** (härth), *n.* [AS. *heorth*], 1. the stone or brick floor of a fireplace. 2. *a*) the fireside. *b*) the home.

**hearth′stone′,** *n.* 1. the stone forming a hearth. 2. fireside; home.

**heart′less,** *adj.* unkind; unfeeling.

**heart′-rend′ing,** *adj.* causing much grief or mental anguish. **—heart′-rend′ing·ly,** *adv.*

**heart′sick′,** *adj.* sick at heart; extremely unhappy; despondent. **—heart′sick′ness,** *n.*

**heart′string′,** *n. usually pl.* deepest feelings or affections.

**heart′-to-heart′,** *adj.* intimate and candid.

**heart·y** (här′ti), *adj.* [-IER, -IEST], 1. warm and sincere; cordial. 2. strongly felt; vigorous: as, a *hearty* dislike. 3. strong and healthy. 4. nourishing: as, a *hearty* meal. *n.* [*pl.* -IES], comrade: sailor's term. **—heart′i·ly,** *adv.* **—heart′i·ness,** *n.*

**heat** (hēt), *n.* [AS. *hætu*], 1. the quality of being hot; hotness, or the perception of this. 2. much hotness. 3. hot weather or climate. 4. the warming of a house, etc. 5. *a*) intensity of feeling; ardor, anger, etc. *b*) a period of such feeling. 6. a single effort, bout, or trial. 7. the period of sexual excitement in animals. 8. [Slang], intense activity. *v.t. & v.i.* 1. to make or become warm or hot. 2. to make or become excited.

**heat′ed·ly,** *adv.* with anger, vehemence, or excitement.

**heat′er,** *n.* an apparatus for giving heat; stove, furnace, radiator, etc.

**heath** (hēth), *n.* [AS. *hæth*], 1. a tract of open wasteland, esp. in the British Isles. 2. any of various shrubs growing on heaths; esp., heather.

**hea·then** (hē′*th*ən), *n.* [*pl.* -THENS, -THEN], [AS. *hæthen*], 1. anyone not a Jew, Christian, or Moslem. 2. a person regarded as uncivilized, irreligious, etc. *adj.* 1. pagan. 2. irreligious. **—hea′then·ish,** *adj.*

**heath·er** (he*th*′ẽr), *n.* [ME. *haddyr*], a low-growing plant of the heath family, esp. common in the British Isles, with small, purplish flowers.

**heave** (hēv), *v.t.* [HEAVED or HOVE, HEAVING], [< AS. *hebban*], 1. to lift, esp. with effort. 2. to lift in this way and throw. 3. to make (a sigh, etc.) with effort. 4. in *naut. usage*, to raise, haul, etc. by pulling with a rope, etc. *v.i.* 1. to swell up. 2. to rise and fall rhythmically; as, his chest *heaved* with sobs. 3. *a*) to vomit. *b*) to pant; gasp. 4. in *naut. usage*, to haul (*on* or *at* a rope, etc.). *n.* the act or effort of heaving. **—heave to,** to stop going forward, as a ship.

**heav·en** (hev′'n), *n.* [AS. *heofon*], 1. *usually pl.* the visible sky; firmament. 2. [H-], God. 3. any place or state of great happiness. 4. in *theology*, the place where God and his angels are and where the blessed go after death.

**heav′en·ly,** *adj.* 1. of the visible heavens. 2. causing or characterized by great happiness, etc. 3. in *theology*, of or in heaven; holy.

**heav′en·ward,** *adv. & adj.* toward heaven: also **heav′en·wards,** *adv.*

**heav·y** (hev′i), *adj.* [-IER, -IEST], [AS. *hefig*], 1. hard to lift because of its weight. 2. of more than the usual, expected, or defined weight. 3. larger, greater, or more intense than usual: as, a *heavy* blow, a *heavy* vote, *heavy* applause. 4. to an unusual extent: as, a *heavy* drinker. 5. hard to do: as, *heavy* work. 6. sorrowful: as, a *heavy* heart. 7. burdened with sleep, etc.: as, *heavy* eyelids. 8. hard to digest: as, a *heavy* meal. 9. cloudy; gloomy: as, a *heavy* sky. *adv.* in a heavy manner. *n.* [*pl.* -IES], in the *theater*, a villain. **—heavy with child,** pregnant. **—heav′i·ly,** *adv.* **—heav′i·ness,** *n.*

**heav′y-du′ty,** *adj.* that can resist great strain, weather, wear, etc.

**heav′y-hand′ed,** *adj.* 1. clumsy; tactless. 2. cruel; tyrannical. **—heav′y-hand′ed·ness,** *n.*

**heav′y-heart′ed,** *adj.* sad; unhappy.

**heav′y·weight′,** *n.* a boxer or wrestler who weighs 176 pounds or more.

**Heb., Hebr.,** Hebrew.

**He·bra·ic** (hi-brā′ik), *adj.* of or characteristic of the Hebrews, their language, or culture; Hebrew.

**He·brew** (hē′brōō), *n.* 1. a member of an ancient Semitic people who settled in Canaan; Israelite. 2. a Jew. 3. *a*) the ancient Semitic language of the Israelites. *b*) its modern form. *adj.* of Hebrew or the Hebrews.

**heck** (hek), *interj. & n.* [Slang], hell: a euphemism.

**heck·le** (hek′'l), *v.t.* [-LED, -LING], [< ME. *hekelin*], to interrupt (a speaker) with annoying questions or taunts. **—heck′ler,** *n.*

**hec·tare** (hek′târ), *n.* [Fr.], metric measure of area, 10,000 square meters.

**hec·tic** (hek′tik), *adj.* [< Gr. *hektikos*, habitual], 1. feverish; flushed. 2. [Colloq.], frenzied; turbulent.

**hec·to·graph** (hek′tə-graf′, -gräf′), *n.* [< Gr. *hekaton*, hundred], a duplicating device by which copies are taken from a sheet of gelatin.

**Hec·tor** (hek′tẽr), *n.* in the *Iliad*, a Trojan hero killed by Achilles.

**he'd** (hēd), 1. he had. 2. he would.

**hedge** (hej), *n.* [AS. *hecg*], 1. a dense row of shrubs, etc. forming a boundary. 2. any fence or barrier. 3. a hedging. *v.t.* [HEDGED, HEDGING], 1. to put a hedge around. 2. to hinder or guard as with a barrier. 3. to try to avoid loss in (a bet, etc.) as by making counterbalancing bets. *v.i.* to refuse to commit oneself; avoid direct answers.

**hedge′hog′,** *n.* 1. a small insect-eating mammal of Europe, with sharp spines on the back. 2. the American porcupine.

**hedge′hop′,** *v.i.* [-HOPPED, -HOPPING], [Slang], in *aviation*, to fly very close to the ground. **—hedge′hop′per,** *n.*

**he·don·ism** (hē′d'n-iz'm), *n.* [< Gr. *hēdonē*, pleasure], the doctrine that pleasure is the principal good. **—he′don·ist,** *n.*

**-hedron,** [< Gr.], a combining form meaning *a figure* or *crystal with a* (specified) *number of surfaces.*

**heed** (hēd), *v.t. & v.i.* [AS. *hedan*], to pay careful attention (to). *n.* careful attention. **—heed′ful,** *adj.* **—heed′less,** *adj.*

**hee·haw** (hē′hô′), *n. & v.i.* [echoic], bray.

**heel** (hēl), *n.* [AS. *hela*], 1. the back part of the foot, under the ankle. 2. that part of a stocking or shoe at the heel. 3. anything like a heel in location, shape, etc. 4. [Slang], a contemptible person. *v.t.* 1. to furnish with a heel. 2. to follow closely; chase. 3. [Slang], to furnish with money, etc. *v.i.* to go along at the heels of someone. —**down at the heel** (or **heels**), shabby; rundown. —**heel′less**, *adj.*

**heel** (hēl), *v.i.* [AS. *hieldan*], to lean to a side; list: said esp. of a ship. *v.t.* to make (a ship) list. *n.* the act of heeling.

**heft** (heft), *n.* [< base of *heave*], [Colloq.], 1. weight; heaviness. 2. importance; influence. *v.t.* [Colloq.], to try to judge the weight of by lifting. *v.i.* [Colloq.], to weigh.

**heft·y** (hef′ti), *adj.* [-IER, -IEST], [Colloq.], 1. heavy. 2. large and strong.

**he·gem·o·ny** (hi-jem′ə-ni), *n.* [*pl.* -NIES], [< Gr. *hēgemōn*, leader], leadership or dominance, esp. that of one nation in a league.

**He·gi·ra** (hi-jī′rə), *n.* [< Ar. *hijrah*, flight], the flight of Mohammed from Mecca in 622 A.D.

**heif·er** (hef′ēr), *n.* [AS. *heahfore*], a young cow that has not borne a calf.

**height** (hīt), *n.* [< AS. *heah*, high], 1. the topmost point or part. 2. the highest limit; extreme. 3. the distance from the bottom to the top. 4. elevation above a given level; altitude. 5. a relatively great distance above a given level, etc. 6. *pl.* an eminence; hill.

**height′en** (-'n), *v.t. & v.i.* 1. to bring or come to a higher position. 2. to make or become larger, greater, etc.

**hei·nous** (hā′nəs), *adj.* [< OFr. *haine*, hatred], hateful; odious; outrageous.

**heir** (âr), *n.* [< L. *heres*], one who inherits or is entitled to inherit another's property, title, etc.

**heir apparent,** the heir whose right to inherit cannot be denied if he outlives the ancestor.

**heir′ess** (-is), *n.* a woman or girl who is an heir, esp. of great wealth.

**heir′loom′** (-lōōm′), *n.* [*heir* + *loom*, *n.*], any possession handed down from generation to generation.

**held** (held), pt. and pp. of **hold.**

**Helen (of Troy),** in *Gr. legend*, the beautiful wife of the king of Sparta: the Trojan War was started by her elopement with Paris to Troy.

**hel·i·cal** (hel′i-k'l), *adj.* of, or having the form of, a helix; spiral. —**hel′i·cal·ly**, *adv.*

**hel·i·cop·ter** (hel′i-kop′tēr, hē′li-), *n.* [< Gr. *helix*, a spiral + *pteron*, wing], a kind of aircraft lifted and moved by a large propeller mounted horizontally above the fuselage.

**he·li·o·trope** (hē′li-ə-trōp′), *n.* [< Gr. *hēlios*, the sun + *trepein*, to turn], 1. a plant with fragrant clusters of small, reddish-purple or white flowers. 2. reddish purple. *adj.* reddish-purple.

**hel·i·port** (hel′i-pôrt′), *n.* a flat place, often on a roof, for helicopters to land and take off.

**he·li·um** (hē′li-əm), *n.* [< Gr. *hēlios*, sun], a chemical element, a very light, inert, noninflammable gas, used to inflate balloons, etc.: symbol, He.

**he·lix** (hē′liks), *n.* [*pl.* -LIXES, -LICES (hel′i-sēz′)], [Gr., a spiral], 1. any spiral, as the thread of a screw, bolt, etc. 2. the folded rim of cartilage around the outer ear.

**hell** (hel), *n.* [< AS. *helan*, to hide], 1. in *Christianity*, the place to which sinners and unbelievers go after death for torment. 2. any place or state of misery, cruelty, etc. —**catch** (or **get**) **hell,** [Slang], to be severely scolded, punished, etc. —**raise hell,** [Slang], to cause trouble, uproar, etc.

**he'll** (hēl), 1. he will. 2. he shall.

**hell′cat′**, *n.* an evil, spiteful woman.

**Hel·len·ic** (he-len′ik, -lē′nik), *adj.* 1. Greek. 2. of the language, culture, etc. of the ancient Greeks.

**hel·lion** (hel′yən), *n.* [Colloq.], a person fond of deviltry; troublemaker.

**hell′ish,** *adj.* 1. devilish; fiendish. 2. [Colloq.], very unpleasant. —**hell′ish·ly**, *adv.*

**hel·lo** (he-lō′, hel′ō), *interj.* an exclamation of greeting.

**helm** (helm), *n.* [AS. *halma*], 1. the wheel or tiller by which a ship is steered. 2. the control or leadership of an organization, enterprise, etc. *v.t.* to guide; steer.

**hel·met** (hel′mit), *n.* [< OFr. *helme*], a protective head covering of metal, etc., variously designed for use in combat, certain sports, etc.

**helms·man** (helmz′mən), *n.* [*pl.* -MEN], the man who steers a ship.

**he·lot** (hel′ət, hē′lət), *n.* [prob. < Gr. *helein*, seize], a serf or slave.

**help** (help), *v.t.* [AS. *helpan*], 1. to make it easier for (a person) to do something or for (a thing) to happen; aid; assist. 2. to remedy: as, it will *help* your cough. 3. to keep from; avoid: as, I can't *help* liking him. 4. to prevent: as, I can't *help* his cheating. 5. to serve or wait on: said of waiters, clerks, etc. *v.i.* to give assistance; be useful. *n.* 1. a helping; aid; assistance. 2. remedy. 3. one that helps. 4. a hired helper or helpers; servant(s), farm hand(s), etc. —**help oneself to,** to take without asking. —**help out,** to help in getting or doing something. —**help′er**, *n.*

**help·ful** (help′fəl), *adj.* giving help; useful.

**help·ing** (hel′piŋ), *n.* 1. a portion of food served to one person. 2. a giving of aid.

**help′less,** *adj.* 1. without power to help oneself; weak. 2. without help or protection.

**help′mate′**, *n.* [< *helpmeet*], a companion and helper, as a wife or husband.

**help′meet′**, *n.* [misreading of "an *help meet* for him" (Gen. 2:18)], a helpmate.

**hel·ter-skel·ter** (hel′tēr-skel′tēr), *adv.* in a disorderly, hurried manner.

**helve** (helv), *n.* [AS. *hielfe*], the handle of an ax, etc.

**hem** (hem), *n.* [AS.], the border on a garment or piece of cloth, made by folding and sewing down the edge. *v.t.* [HEMMED, HEMMING], 1. to fold back the edge of and sew down. 2. *a*) to surround. *b*) to confine (with *in*, *around*, or *about*). —**hem′mer**, *n.*

**hem** (hem), *interj. & n.* an expression of the sound made in clearing the throat, as to attract attention. *v.i.* [HEMMED, HEMMING], to make this sound. —**hem and haw,** to hesitate in speaking.

**hemi-,** [Gr. *hēmi-*], a prefix meaning *half*, as in *hemisphere.*

**hem·i·sphere** (hem′ə-sfêr′), *n.* 1. half of a sphere or globe. 2. any of the halves (northern, southern, eastern, or western) of the earth. —**hem′i·spher′i·cal** (-sfer′i-k'l), *adj.*

**hem·lock** (hem′lok), *n.* [AS. *hymlic*], 1. a poisonous weed of the carrot family, with small, white flowers. 2. poison made from this weed. 3. an evergreen tree of the pine family. 4. the wood of this tree.

**hemo-,** [< Gr. *haima*], a combining form meaning *blood.*

**he·mo·glo·bin** (hē′mə-glō′bin), *n.* [< *hemo-* + *globule*], the red coloring matter of the red blood corpuscles.

**he·mo·phil·i·a** (hē′mə-fil′i-ə), *n.* [see HEMO- & -PHILE], a hereditary condition in which the blood fails to clot normally, causing prolonged bleeding.

**hem·or·rhage** (hem′ēr-ij), *n.* [< Gr. *haima*, blood + *rhēgnynai*, to break], the escape of blood from its vessels; bleeding. *v.i.* [-RHAGED, -RHAGING], to suffer a hemorrhage. —**hem·or·rhag·ic** (hem′ə-raj′ik), *adj.*

**hem·or·rhoid** (hem′ə-roid′), *n.* [< Gr. *haima*, blood + *rhein*, to flow], *usually in pl.* a painful swelling or tumor of a vein in the region of the anus: also called, in the plural, *piles.* —**hem′or·rhoi′dal** (-roi′d'l), *adj.*

**hemp** (hemp), *n.* [AS. *henep*], 1. a tall Asiatic plant of the nettle family, having tough fiber. 2. the fiber, used to make rope, sailcloth, etc. —**hemp′en,** *adj.*
**hem·stitch** (hem′stich′), *n.* an ornamental stitch, used esp. at a hem, made by pulling out several parallel threads and tying the cross threads into small bunches. *v.t.* to put hemstitches on.
**hen** (hen), *n.* [AS. *henn*], 1. the female of the chicken, or domestic fowl. 2. the female of various other birds.
**hence** (hens), *adv.* [< AS. *heonan*, from here], 1. from this place; away: as, go *hence*. 2. from this time: as, a year *hence*. 3. from this origin or source. 4. as a result; therefore. *interj.* go away!
**hence′forth′,** *adv.* from this time on: also **hence′for′ward.**
**hench·man** (hench′mən), *n.* [*pl.* -MEN], [AS. *hengest*, horse + *-man*], a trusted helper or follower.
**hen·na** (hen′ə), *n.* [Ar. *hinnā′*], 1. an ornamental tropical shrub of Asia. 2. a dye extracted from its leaves, used to tint the hair auburn. 3. reddish brown. *adj.* reddish-brown. *v.t.* [-NAED, -NAING], to tint with henna.
**hen·peck** (hen′pek′), *v.t.* to domineer over (one's husband). —**hen′pecked′,** *adj.*
**hep** (hep), *adj.* [Slang], informed.
**hep·a·ti·tis** (hep′ə-tī′tis), *n.* [< Gr. *hēpar*, liver; + *-itis*], inflammation of the liver.
**her** (hũr), *pron.* [AS. *hire*], the objective case of she. *poss. pronominal adj.* of, belonging to, or done by her.
**He·ra** (hêr′ə), *n.* in *Gr. myth.*, the wife of Zeus and queen of the gods.
**her·ald** (her′əld), *n.* [< OFr. *heralt*], 1. formerly, an official who made proclamations, carried state messages, etc. 2. one who announces significant news; messenger. 3. a harbinger. *v.t.* to announce; foretell.
**he·ral·dic** (he-ral′dik), *adj.* of heraldry or heralds. —**he·ral′di·cal·ly,** *adv.*
**her′ald·ry,** *n.* [*pl.* -RIES], 1. the science dealing with coats of arms, genealogies, etc. 2. ceremony or pomp.
**herb** (ũrb, hũrb), *n.* [< L. *herba*], 1. any seed plant whose stem withers away annually. 2. any such plant used as a medicine, seasoning, etc., as mint and sage. —**her·ba·ceous** (hẽr-bā′shəs), *adj.*
**herb·age** (ũr′bij, hũr′-), *n.* herbs collectively; esp., pasturage; grass.
**herb·al** (hũr′b'l, ũr′-), *adj.* of herbs. *n.* formerly, a book about herbs or plants.
**her·bi·cide** (hũr′bə-sīd′, ũr′-), *n.* any chemical substance used to destroy plants, esp. weeds. —**her′bi·ci′dal,** *adj.*
**her·biv·o·rous** (hẽr-biv′ẽr-əs), *adj.* [< L. *herba*, herb + *vorare*, devour], feeding chiefly on grass or plants.
**her·cu·le·an** (hẽr-kū′li-ən, hũr′kyoo-lē′-), *adj.* [sometimes H-], 1. having the great size and strength of Hercules. 2. calling for great strength, size, or courage.
**Her·cu·les** (hũr′kyoo-lēz′), *n.* 1. in *Gr. & Rom. myth.*, a hero renowned for feats of strength. 2. [h-], any very large, strong man.
**herd** (hũrd), *n.* [AS. *heord*], 1. a number of cattle or other large animals feeding or living together. 2. the common people; public: contemptuous term. *v.t. & v.i.* to form into a herd, group, etc. —**herd′er,** *n.*
**herd** (hũrd), *n.* [AS. *h(i)erde*], a herdsman: now only in combination, as in *cowherd*. *v.t.* to tend or drive as a herdsman.
**herds·man** (hũrdz′mən), *n.* [*pl.* -MEN], one who tends or drives a herd.
**here** (hêr), *adv.* [AS. *her*], 1. at or in this place: often used as an intensive, as, John *here* is an actor. 2. to or into this place: as, come *here*. 3. at this point; now. 4. on earth. *n.* 1. this place (where the speaker is). 2. this life or time. —**neither here nor there,** irrelevant.
**here′a·bout′,** *adv.* in this general vicinity: also **here′a·bouts′.**
**here·af′ter,** *adv.* from now on; in the future. *n.* 1. the future. 2. the state after death.
**here·by′,** *adv.* by this means.
**he·red·i·tar·y** (hə-red′ə-ter′i), *adj.* 1. *a*) of, or passed down by, inheritance from an ancestor. *b*) having title, etc. by inheritance. 2. of or passed down by heredity.
**he·red·i·ty** (hə-red′ə-ti), *n.* [*pl.* -TIES], [< L. *heres*, heir], the transmission from parent to offspring of certain characteristics.
**here·in** (hêr-in′), *adv.* 1. in here. 2. in this writing, container, etc.
**here·of′,** *adv.* of or concerning this.
**her·e·sy** (her′ə-si), *n.* [*pl.* -SIES], [< Gr. *hairesis*, selection, sect], 1. a religious belief opposed to the orthodox doctrines of a church. 2. any opinion opposed to established views.
**her·e·tic** (her′ə-tik), *n.* one who professes a heresy; esp., a church member who holds beliefs opposed to the official church doctrines. —**he·ret·i·cal** (hə-ret′i-k'l), *adj.*
**here′to·fore′,** *adv.* up to now; before this.
**here′up·on′,** *adv.* 1. immediately following this. 2. concerning this point.
**here·with′,** *adv.* 1. along with this. 2. by this method or means.
**her·it·a·ble** (her′i-tə-b'l), *adj.* that can be inherited. —**her′it·a·bil′i·ty,** *n.*
**her·it·age** (her′ə-tij), *n.* 1. property that is or can be inherited. 2. a tradition, etc. derived from one's ancestors or the past.
**her·maph·ro·dite** (hẽr-maf′rə-dīt′), *n.* [< Gr. *Hermaphroditos*, son of Hermes and Aphrodite, united in a single body with a nymph], a person, animal, or plant with the sexual organs of both the male and the female. *adj.* of or like a hermaphrodite.
**Her·mes** (hũr′mēz), *n.* a Greek god who was messenger of the other gods.
**her·met·ic** (hẽr-met′ik), *adj.* [< *Hermes* (reputed founder of alchemy)], airtight: also **her·met′i·cal.** —**her·met′i·cal·ly,** *adv.*
**her·mit** (hũr′mit), *n.* [< Gr. *erēmos*, solitary], one who lives alone in seclusion; recluse.
**her·mit·age** (hũr′mə-tij), *n.* the place where a hermit lives.
**her·ni·a** (hũr′ni-ə), *n.* [*pl.* -AS, -AE (-ē′)], [L.], the protrusion of an organ, esp. a part of the intestine, through a tear in the wall of the surrounding structure; rupture.
**he·ro** (hêr′ō), *n.* [*pl.* -ROES], [< Gr. *hērōs*], 1. a man of great courage, nobility, etc., or one admired for his exploits. 2. the central male character in a novel, play, etc.
**he·ro·ic** (hi-rō′ik), *adj.* 1. of or like a hero. 2. of or about heroes and their deeds; epic. 3. daring and risky. 4. exalted; eloquent. Also **he·ro′i·cal.** *n.pl.* extravagant talk or action. —**he·ro′i·cal·ly,** *adv.*
**her·o·in** (her′ō-in), *n.* [G.], a habit-forming narcotic derived from morphine.
**her·o·ine** (her′ō-in), *n.* a girl or woman hero in life or literature.
**her·o·ism** (her′ō-iz'm), *n.* the qualities and actions of a hero or heroine.
**her·on** (her′ən), *n.* [< OFr. *hairon*], a wading bird with long legs, neck, and bill.
**her·pes** (hũr′pēz), *n.* [< Gr. *herpein*, to creep], a skin disease causing small blisters.
**her·pe·tol·o·gy** (hũr′pi-tol′ə-ji), *n.* [< Gr. *herpeton*, reptiles; + *-logy*], the branch of zoology dealing with reptiles.
**‡Herr** (her), *n.* [*pl.* HERREN (-ən)], [G.], 1. a man; gentleman. 2. Mr.; Sir.
**her·ring** (her′iŋ), *n.* [AS. *hæring*], any of a group of small food fishes of the N Atlantic.
**her′ring·bone′,** *n.* 1. the spine of a herring with the ribs extending in rows of parallel,

slanting lines. 2. anything made in this pattern. *adj.* having this pattern.
**hers** (hũrz), *pron.* that or those belonging to her: as, *hers* are better.
**her·self** (hẽr-self'), *pron.* 1. the intensive form of **she**: as, she went *herself*. 2. the reflexive form of **she**: as, she hurt *herself*. 3. her true self: as, she's not *herself* today.
**hertz** (hũrts), *n.* [*pl.* HERTZ], [after H.R. *Hertz*, 19th-c. G. physicist], the international unit of frequency, equal to one cycle per second.
**he's** (hēz), 1. he is. 2. he has.
**hes·i·tant** (hez'ə-tənt), *adj.* hesitating; undecided; doubtful. —**hes'i·tan·cy** [*pl.* -CIES], **hes'i·tance,** *n.* —**hes'i·tant·ly,** *adv.*
**hes·i·tate** (hez'ə-tāt'), *v.i.* [-TATED, -TATING], [< L. *haerere*, to stick], 1. to stop in indecision; feel unsure; waver. 2. to pause. 3. to be reluctant. 4. to pause continually in speaking. —**hes'i·ta'tion,** *n.*
**Hes·sian** (hesh'ən), *adj.* of Hesse, Germany. *n.* 1. a native of Hesse. 2. any of the Hessian mercenaries who fought for the British in the Revolutionary War.
**hetero-,** [< Gr. *heteros*, the other], a combining form meaning *other, another, different.*
**het·er·o·dox** (het'ẽr-ə-doks'), *adj.* [< Gr. *hetero-*, other + *doxa*, opinion], opposed to the usual beliefs, esp. in religion; unorthodox. —**het'er·o·dox'y** (-dok'si) [*pl.* -IES], *n.*
**het·er·o·ge·ne·ous** (het'ẽr-ə-jē'ni-əs), *adj.* [< Gr. *hetero-*, other + *genos*, a kind], 1. differing in structure, quality, etc.; dissimilar. 2. composed of unlike parts.
**het'er·o·sex'u·al** (-sek'shōō-əl), *adj.* 1. of or having sexual desire for those of the opposite sex. 2. of different sexes. *n.* a heterosexual individual.
**het up** (het), [*het*, dial. pt. & pp. of *heat*], [Slang], excited.
**HEW,** Department of Health, Education, and Welfare.
**hew** (hū), *v.t.* [HEWED, HEWED or HEWN, HEWING], [AS. *heawan*], 1. to chop or cut with an ax, knife, etc. 2. to make or shape thus. —**hew'er,** *n.*
**hex** (heks), *n.* [< G. *hexe*, witch], [Colloq.], something supposed to bring bad luck; jinx. *v.t.* [Colloq.], to bewitch; cause bad luck to.
**hexa-,** [< Gr. *hex*, six], a combining form meaning *six.*
**hex·a·gon** (hek'sə-gon'), *n.* [< Gr. *hex*, six + *gōnia*, an angle], a plane figure with six angles and six sides. —**hex·ag'o·nal** (-sag'ə-n'l), *adj.*
**hex·am·e·ter** (hek-sam'ə-tẽr), *n.* [< Gr. *hex*, six + *metron*, measure], 1. a line of verse containing six metrical feet. 2. verse consisting of hexameters.
**hey** (hā), *interj.* an exclamation used to attract attention, express surprise, etc.
**hey·day** (hā'dā'), *n.* the time of greatest health, vigor, prosperity, etc.; prime.
**Hg,** *hydrargyrum*, [L.], in *chem.*, mercury.
**hi** (hī), *interj.* an exclamation of greeting.
**hi·a·tus** (hī-ā'təs), *n.* [*pl.* -TUSES, -TUS], [L. < *hiare*, to gape], a break or gap where a part is missing; blank space; lacuna.
**hi·ber·nate** (hī'bẽr-nāt'), *v.i.* [-NATED, -NATING], [< L. *hibernus*, wintry], to spend the winter in a dormant state. —**hi'ber·na'tion,** *n.*
**hi·bis·cus** (hī-bis'kəs, hi-), *n.* [Gr. *hibiskos*], a plant, shrub, or small tree of the mallow family, with large, colorful flowers.
**hic·cup, hic·cough** (hik'əp), *n.* [< ?], 1. an involuntary contraction of the diaphragm that closes the glottis at the moment of breathing in. 2. the sharp sound made by this. *v.i.* to make a hiccup.
**hick** (hik), *n.* [< *Richard*], [Colloq.], a country person, regarded as unsophisticated, simple, etc.: somewhat contemptuous term. *adj.* [Colloq.], of or like a hick.
**hick·o·ry** (hik'ẽr-i), *n.* [*pl.* -RIES], [< Am. Ind. *powcohicora*], 1. an American tree of the walnut family. 2. its hard, tough wood. 3. its smooth-shelled, edible nut.
**hide** (hīd), *v.t.* [HID (hid), HIDDEN (hid''n) or HID, HIDING], [AS. *hydan*], 1. to put or keep out of sight; conceal. 2. to keep secret. 3. to obstruct the view of. *v.i.* 1. to be concealed. 2. to conceal oneself. —**hid'er,** *n.*
**hide** (hīd), *n.* [AS. *hyd*], an animal skin or pelt, either raw or tanned.
**hide'bound',** *adj.* obstinately conservative and narrow-minded.
**hid·e·ous** (hid'i-əs), *adj.* [< OFr. *hide*, fright], horrible; very ugly; revolting.
**hide'-out',** *n.* [Colloq.], a hiding place for gangsters or the like.
**hie** (hī), *v.i. & v.t.* [HIED, HIEING or HYING], [AS. *higian*], to speed; hasten.
**hi·er·arch·y** (hī'ẽr-är'ki), *n.* [*pl.* -IES], [< Gr. *hieros*, sacred + *archos*, ruler], 1. church government by clergy in graded ranks. 2. the officials in such a system. 3. a group of persons or things arranged in order of rank, grade, etc. —**hi'er·ar'chi·cal,** *adj.*
**hi·er·at·ic** (hī'ə-rat'ik), *adj.* [< Gr. *hieros*, sacred], of or used by priests; priestly.
**hi·er·o·glyph·ic** (hī'ẽr-ə-glif'ik, hī'rə-), *n.* [< Gr. *hieros*, sacred + *glyphein*, carve], 1. a picture or symbol representing a word, sound, etc. in a system used by ancient Egyptians and others. 2. a symbol, etc. hard to understand. *adj.* of or like hieroglyphics: also **hi'er·o·glyph'i·cal.**
**hi-fi** (hī'fī'), *adj.* of or having high fidelity of sound reproduction.
**hig·gle** (hig''l), *v.i.* [-GLED, -GLING], [prob. < *haggle*], to haggle.
**high** (hī), *adj.* [AS. *heah*], 1. lofty; tall. 2. extending upward a (specified) distance. 3. reaching to, situated at, or done from a height. 4. above others in rank, position, etc.; superior: as, *high* priest. 5. grave: as, *high* treason. 6. greater in size, amount, cost, etc. than usual: as, *high* stakes. 7. luxurious: as, *high* living. 8. raised or acute in pitch; shrill. 9. slightly tainted, as meat. 10. elated: as, *high* spirits. 11. [Slang], drunk. *adv.* in or to a high level, degree, rank, etc. *n.* 1. a high level, degree, etc. 2. an area of high barometric pressure. 3. an arrangement of gears giving the greatest speed. —**high and low,** everywhere. —**on high,** in heaven.
**high'ball',** *n.* whisky or brandy mixed with soda water, ginger ale, etc.
**high'born',** *adj.* of noble birth.
**high'boy',** *n.* a high chest of drawers mounted on legs.
**high'bred',** *adj.* 1. of superior stock or breed. 2. showing good breeding; well-mannered.
**high'brow',** *n.* [Slang], one having or affecting highly cultivated tastes; intellectual. *adj.* [Slang], of or for highbrows.
**high·fa·lu·tin(g)** (hī'fə-lōō't'n), *adj.* [Colloq.], high-flown; pretentious.
**high fidelity,** in radio, sound recording, etc., nearly exact reproduction of a wide range of sound waves.
**high'fli'er, high'fly'er,** *n.* 1. a person or thing that flies high. 2. one who acts or talks in an extravagant manner.
**high'flown'** (-flōn'), *adj.* 1. extravagantly ambitious. 2. trying to be eloquent; bombastic.
**high'-fre'quen·cy,** *adj.* designating or of an alternating electric current or oscillation with a high frequency, usually more than 20,000 cycles per second.
**High German,** the Germanic dialect spoken in central and southern Germany.
**high'-grade',** *adj.* excellent.
**high'hand'ed,** *adj.* overbearing; arrogant.

**high′-hat′,** *adj.* [Slang], snobbish. *v.t.* [-HATTED, -HATTING], [Slang], to snub.
**high′land** (-lənd), *n.* a region with many hills and mountains.
**high′light′,** *v.t.* 1. to put high lights on. 2. to give prominence to.
**high light,** 1. a part on which light is brightest. 2. the most important or interesting part, scene, etc.
**high′ly,** *adv.* 1. very much. 2. favorably. 3. at a high level, wage, rank, etc.
**high′-mind′ed,** *adj.* having high ideals, principles, and feelings.
**high′ness,** *n.* 1. height. 2. [H-], a title used in speaking to or of royalty.
**high′-pres′sure,** *adj.* 1. having or withstanding high pressure. 2. using strongly persuasive methods. *v.t.* [-SURED, -SURING], [Colloq.], to urge with such methods.
**high′-rise′** (-rīz′), *n.* a tall apartment house, office building, etc. of many stories.
**high′road′,** *n.* 1. a main road; highway. 2. an easy or direct way.
**high school,** a school offering academic or vocational subjects to students in grades 8 (or 9) through 12.
**high seas,** ocean waters not under the jurisdiction of any country.
**high′-spir′it·ed,** *adj.* 1. courageous. 2. lively; spirited. —**high′-spir′it·ed·ly,** *adv.*
**high′-strung′,** *adj.* highly sensitive; nervous and tense; excitable.
**high′-ten′sion,** *adj.* having or carrying a high voltage.
**high tide,** 1. the highest level to which the tide rises. 2. any culminating point.
**high time,** time beyond the proper time but before it is too late.
**high′-toned′,** *adj.* 1. high in tone; high-pitched. 2. [Colloq.], stylish; fashionable.
**high′way′,** *n.* 1. a public road. 2. a main road; thoroughfare.
**high′way′man** (-mən), *n.* [*pl.* -MEN], one who robs travelers on a highway.
**hi·jack** (hī′jack′), *v.t.* [Colloq.], to steal (goods in transit, esp. bootlegged liquor) by force: also sp. **highjack.** —**hi′jack′er,** *n.*
**hike** (hīk), *v.i.* [HIKED, HIKING], [< dial. *heik*], to take a long, vigorous walk; tramp or march. *v.t.* [Colloq.], 1. to pull up; hoist. 2. to raise (prices, etc.). *n.* a hiking; march.
**hi·lar·i·ous** (hi-lâr′i-əs, hī-), *adj.* [< Gr. *hilaros*, cheerful], very gay; noisily merry. —**hi·lar′i·ty** (-lar′ə-ti), *n.*
**hill** (hil), *n.* [AS. *hyll*], 1. a natural raised part of the earth's surface, smaller than a mountain. 2. a small pile, heap, or mound: as, an ant*hill*. 3. a mound of soil heaped around plant roots: as, a *hill* of corn.
**hill′bill′y,** *n.* [*pl.* -IES], [< nickname *Billy*], [Colloq.], one who lives in or comes from the mountains or backwoods, esp. of the South. *adj.* [Colloq.], of hillbillies.
**hill′ock** (-ək), *n.* a small hill; mound.
**hill′side′,** *n.* the side of a hill.
**hill′top′,** *n.* the top of a hill.
**hill′y,** *adj.* [-IER, -IEST], 1. full of hills. 2. like a hill; steep. —**hill′i·ness,** *n.*
**hilt** (hilt), *n.* [AS.], the handle of a sword, tool, etc. —**(up) to the hilt,** entirely.
**him** (him), *pron.* [AS.], objective case of **he.**
**him·self′,** *pron.* 1. the intensive form of **he:** as, he went *himself*. 2. the reflexive form of **he:** as, he hurt *himself*. 3. his true self: as, he is not *himself* today.
**hind** (hīnd), *adj.* [HINDER, HINDMOST or HINDERMOST], [prob. < *hinder, adj.*], back; rear; posterior.
**hind** (hīnd), *n.* [AS.], the female of the red deer in and after its third year.
**hin·der** (hin′dẽr), *v.t.* [AS. *hindrian*], 1. to keep back; obstruct; stop. 2. to thwart.
**hind·er** (hīn′dẽr), *adj.* [AS.], rear; posterior.
**hind′most′,** *adj.* farthest back; last.
**hind′quar′ter,** *n.* the hind half of a side of veal, beef, lamb, etc.
**hin·drance** (hin′drəns), *n.* 1. a hindering. 2. a person or thing that hinders; obstacle.
**hind′sight′,** *n.* an understanding, after the event, of what should have been done.
**Hin·du** (hin′dōō), *n.* 1. a member of the largest native group of India. 2. a follower of Hinduism. *adj.* 1. of the Hindus, their language, culture, etc. 2. of Hinduism.
**Hin′du·ism,** *n.* the principal religion and social system of India.
**hinge** (hinj), *n.* [< ME. *hengen*, hang], 1. a joint on which a door, lid, etc. swings. 2. a natural joint, as of the shell of a clam. *v.t.* [HINGED, HINGING], to attach by a hinge. *v.i.* 1. to swing as on a hinge. 2. to depend. —**hinged,** *adj.*
**hint** (hint), *n.* [< AS. *hentan*, seize], a slight indication; indirect allusion. *v.t.* & *v.i.* to give a hint (of); intimate. —**hint′er,** *n.*
**hin·ter·land** (hin′tẽr-land′), *n.* [G.], 1. the land behind that bordering on a coast or river. 2. a remote area; back country.
**hip** (hip), *n.* [AS. *hype*], 1. the part of the body around the joint formed by each thigh bone and the pelvis. 2. the angle formed by the meeting of two sloping sides of a roof. —**hipped,** *adj.*
**hip** (hip), *n.* [AS. *heop*], the small, fleshy, ripened fruit of a rosebush.
**hip** (hip), *adj.* [? < *hep*], [Slang], 1. informed, aware, sophisticated, etc. 2. of hippies.
**hipped** (hipt), *adj.* [< *hypochondria*], [Colloq.], 1. depressed. 2. obsessed (with *on*).
**hip·pie** (hip′ē), *n.* [Slang], a young person who, in his alienation from conventional society, has turned to mysticism, psychedelic drugs, communal living, etc.
**hip·po** (hip′ō), *n.* [*pl.* -POS], [Colloq.], a hippopotamus.
**Hip·po·crat·ic oath** (hip′ə-krat′ik), the oath, attributed to Hippocrates, ancient Greek physician, generally taken by medical graduates: it sets forth their ethical code.
**hip·po·drome** (hip′ə-drōm′), *n.* [< Gr. *hippos*, horse + *dromos*, course], an arena for a circus, games, etc.
**hip·po·pot·a·mus** (hip′ə-pot′ə-məs), *n.* [*pl.* -MUSES, -MI (-mī′), -MUS], [< Gr. *hippos*, horse + *potamos*, river], a large, plant-eating mammal with a heavy, thick-skinned body: it lives in or near rivers in Africa.
**hire** (hīr), *v.t.* [HIRED, HIRING], [< AS. *hyr*], to pay for the services of (a person) or the use of (a thing). *n.* 1. a hiring. 2. the amount paid in hiring. —**hire out,** to give one's work in return for payment.
**hire′ling,** *n.* one who will follow anyone's orders for pay; mercenary.
**hir·sute** (hũr′sōōt, hẽr-sūt′), *adj.* [L. *hirsutus*], hairy; shaggy.
**his** (hiz), *pron.* [AS.], that or those belonging to him: as, *his* are better. *poss. pronominal adj.* of, belonging to, or done by him.
**hiss** (his), *v.i.* [echoic], 1. to make a sound like that of a prolonged *s*. 2. to show disapproval by hissing. *v.t.* to say or indicate by hissing. *n.* a sound like a prolonged *s*.
**hist** (st, hist), *interj.* be quiet!
**hist.,** 1. historical. 2. history.
**his·ta·mine** (his′tə-mēn′), *n.* [< Gr. *histos*, tissue; + *ammonia*], an ammonia derivative discharged by tissue in allergic reactions.
**his·tol·o·gy** (his-tol′ə-ji), *n.* [< Gr. *histos*, tissue; + *-logy*], the branch of biology concerned with the microscopic study of the structure of tissues. —**his·tol′o·gist,** *n.*
**his·to·ri·an** (his-tôr′i-ən), *n.* a writer of, or authority on, history.
**his·tor′ic** (-ik), *adj.* historical; esp., famous in history.
**his·tor′i·cal,** *adj.* 1. of or concerned with history. 2. based on people or events of the

past. 3. established by history; factual.
**his·to·ry** (his′tə-ri), *n.* [*pl.* -RIES], [< Gr. *histōr*, learned], 1. an account of what has happened, esp. in the life of a people, country, etc. 2. all recorded past events. 3. the branch of knowledge that deals with the recording, analyzing, etc. of past events. 4. a known past: as, my coat has a *history*.
**his·tri·on·ic** (his′tri-on′ik), *adj.* [< L. *histrio*, actor], 1. of acting or actors. 2. overacted or overacting.—**his′tri·on′i·cal·ly**, *adv.*
**his′tri·on′ics**, *n.pl.* 1. [construed as sing.], dramatics. 2. an artificial or affected manner.
**hit** (hit), *v.t.* & *v.i.* [HIT, HITTING], [< ON. *hitta*, meet with], 1. to come against (something) with force; bump; knock; collide. 2. to give a blow (to); strike. 3. to strike with a missile. 4. to affect (one) strongly: as, we are hard *hit* by poverty. 5. to come (*on* or *upon*) or find by accident or after search. 6. [Slang], to arrive at: as, to *hit* town. 7. in *baseball*, to get (a base hit). *n.* 1. a blow that strikes its mark. 2. a collision. 3. a successful and popular song, play, etc. 4. in *baseball*, a base hit. —**hit it off**, to get along well together. —**hit or miss**, in a haphazard way. —**hit′ter**, *n.*
**hit′-and-run′**, *adj.* hitting accidentally with a vehicle and then fleeing: also **hit′skip′**.
**hitch** (hich), *v.i.* [prob. < OFr. *hocier*], 1. to move jerkily. 2. to become fastened or caught. *v.t.* 1. to move, pull, etc. with jerks. 2. to fasten with a hook, knot, etc. 3. [Slang], to get (a ride) in hitchhiking. *n.* 1. a tug; jerk. 2. a limp. 3. a hindrance; obstacle. 4. a catching or fastening. 5. [Military Slang], a period of enlistment. 6. in *naut. usage*, a kind of knot. —**hitch′er**, *n.*
**hitch·hike** (hich′hīk′), *v.i.* [-HIKED, -HIKING], to travel by asking for rides from motorists on the road. —**hitch′hik′er**, *n.*
**hith·er** (hith′ẽr), *adv.* [AS. *hider*], to this place; here. *adj.* nearer.
**hith′er·to′**, *adv.* until this time.
**hive** (hīv), *n.* [AS. *hyf*], 1. a shelter for a colony of domestic bees; beehive. 2. the bees of a hive. 3. a crowd of busy people. 4. a place of great activity. *v.t.* [HIVED, HIVING], to gather (bees) into a hive. *v.i.* to enter a hive.
**hives** (hīvz), *n.* [orig. Scot. dial.], an allergic skin condition characterized by itching and smooth raised patches.
**H.M.S.**, 1. His (or Her) Majesty's Service. 2. His (or Her) Majesty's Ship.
**hoar** (hôr), *adj.* [AS. *har*], hoary.
**hoard** (hôrd), *n.* [AS. *hord*], a supply stored up and hidden or reserved. *v.t.* & *v.i.* to accumulate and store away (money, goods, etc.). —**hoard′er**, *n.*
**hoar′frost′**, *n.* white, frozen dew on the ground, leaves, etc.; rime.
**hoarse** (hôrs), *adj.* [HOARSER, HOARSEST], [AS. *has*], 1. harsh and grating in sound. 2. having a rough, husky voice. —**hoarse′ness**, *n.*
**hoar′y**, *adj.* [-IER, -IEST], 1. white or gray. 2. having white or gray hair from old age. 3. very old. —**hoar′i·ness**, *n.*
**hoax** (hōks), *n.* [< *hocus-pocus*], a trick or fraud; esp., a practical joke. *v.t.* to deceive with a hoax. —**hoax′er**, *n.*
**hob** (hob), *n.* [< ?], a ledge at the back or side of a fireplace, for keeping a kettle, pan, etc. warm.
**hob** (hob), *n.* [< *Robin* Goodfellow, an elf], an elf; goblin. —**play** (or **raise**) **hob**, to cause mischief.
**hob·ble** (hob′'l), *v.i.* [-BLED, -BLING], [ME. *hobelin*], to go haltingly; limp. *v.t.* 1. to cause to limp. 2. to hamper the movement of (a horse, etc.) by tying two legs together. 3. to hinder. *n.* 1. a limp. 2. a rope, etc. used to hobble a horse.
**hob·ble·de·hoy** (hob′'l-di-hoi′), *n.* [prob. < Eng. dial. *hob*, a rustic], a gawky youth.
**hob·by** (hob′i), *n.* [*pl.* -BIES], [< *Hob* (nickname for *Robin*): formerly applied to horses], 1. [Rare], a hobbyhorse. 2. a thing that a person likes to do in his spare time.
**hob′by·horse′**, *n.* 1. a child's toy consisting of a stick with a horse's head. 2. a rocking horse.
**hob·gob·lin** (hob′gob′lin), *n.* [< *hob*, an elf + *goblin*], 1. an elf; goblin. 2. a bugbear.
**hob·nail** (hob′nāl′), *n.* [*hob*, a peg + *nail*], a broad-headed nail put on the soles of heavy shoes to prevent wear, etc. *v.t.* to put hobnails on. —**hob′nailed′**, *adj.*
**hob·nob** (hob′nob′), *v.i.* [-NOBBED, -NOBBING], [< ME. *habben*, have + *nabben*, not have], to be on close terms (*with*).
**ho·bo** (hō′bō), *n.* [*pl.* -BOS, -BOES], 1. a migratory worker. 2. a vagrant; tramp.
**hock** (hok), *n.* [AS. *hoh*, the heel], the joint bending backward in the hind leg of a horse, ox, etc.
**hock** (hok), *v.t.* & *n.* [? < D. *hok*, prison, debt], [Slang], pawn.
**hock·ey** (hok′i), *n.* [prob. < OFr. *hoquet*, bent stick], 1. a team game played on ice skates, with curved sticks and a rubber disk (*puck*). 2. a similar game played on a field, with a small ball.
**hock′shop′**, *n.* [Slang], a pawnshop.
**ho·cus-po·cus** (hō′kəs-pō′kəs), *n.* [imitation L.], 1. meaningless words used as a formula by conjurers. 2. sleight of hand. 3. trickery.
**hod** (hod), *n.* [< MD. *hodde*], 1. a long-handled wooden trough used for carrying bricks, mortar, etc. on the shoulder. 2. a coal scuttle.
**hodge·podge** (hoj′poj′), *n.* [< OD. *hutspot*, a stew], a jumbled mixture; mess.
**hoe** (hō), *n.* [< OHG. *houwan*, hew], a tool with a thin blade set across the end of a long handle, for weeding, loosening soil, etc. *v.t.* & *v.i.* [HOED, HOEING], to dig, cultivate, weed, etc. with a hoe. —**ho′er**, *n.*
**hoe′cake′** (-kāk′), *n.* a thin bread made of corn meal.
**hog** (hôg, hog), *n.* [AS. *hogg*], 1. a pig; esp., a full-grown pig raised for its meat. 2. [Colloq.], a selfish, greedy, or filthy person. *v.t.* [HOGGED, HOGGING], [Slang], to take all of or an unfair share of. —**go the whole hog**, [Slang], to go all the way. —**hog′gish**, *adj.*
**hogs·head** (hôgz′hed′, hogz′-), *n.* 1. a large barrel or cask, esp. one holding from 100 to 140 gallons. 2. a liquid measure, esp. one equal to 63 gallons.
**hog′tie′**, *v.t.* [-TIED, -TYING or -TIEING], 1. to tie the four feet or the hands and feet of. 2. [Colloq.], to make incapable of effective action.
**hog′wash′**, *n.* 1. refuse fed to hogs; swill. 2. empty talk, writing, etc.
‡**hoi pol·loi** (hoi′ pə-loi′), [Gr., the many], the common people; the masses.
**hoist** (hoist), *v.t.* [< LG. *hissen*], to raise aloft; lift, esp. with a pulley, crane, etc. *n.* 1. a hoisting. 2. an apparatus for lifting; elevator or tackle.
**ho·kum** (hō′kəm), *n.* [< *hocus-pocus*], [Slang], 1. mawkish sentiment in a play, story, etc. 2. nonsense; humbug.
**hold** (hōld), *v.t.* [HELD, HOLDING], [AS. *haldan*], 1. to keep in the hands, arms, etc.; grasp. 2. to keep in a certain position or condition. 3. to restrain or control; keep back. 4. to be in possession of; occupy: as, to *hold* an office. 5. to guard; defend: as, *hold* the fort. 6. to carry on (a meeting, etc.). 7. to contain: as, the jar *holds* a pint. 8. to regard; consider: as, I *hold* the story to be true. *v.i.* 1. to go on being firm, loyal, etc. 2. to remain unbroken or unyielding: as, the rope *held*. 3. to be true or valid: as,

this rule *holds* for most cases. 4. to continue: as, the wind *held* steady. ***n.*** 1. a grasping or seizing; grip. 2. a thing to hold on by. 3. a thing for holding something else. 4. a strong influence: as, she has a *hold* over him. 5. a prison. **—get (catch, lay,** or **take) hold of,** to take, seize, acquire, etc. **—hold forth,** 1. to preach; lecture. 2. to offer. **—hold out,** 1. to last; endure. 2. to stand firm. 3. to offer. 4. [Slang], to refuse to hand over something. **—hold over,** 1. to postpone. 2. to stay for an additional period. **—hold up,** 1. to prop up. 2. to show. 3. to last; endure. 4. to stop; delay. 5. to stop forcibly and rob. **—hold′er,** ***n.***

**hold** (hōld), ***n.*** [< *hole* or MD. *hol*], the interior of a ship below decks, in which the cargo is carried.

**hold′ing,** ***n.*** 1. land, esp. a farm, rented from another. 2. *often pl.* property owned, esp. stocks and bonds.

**hold′o′ver,** ***n.*** [Colloq.], one staying on from a previous period.

**hold′up′,** ***n.*** 1. a delay. 2. the act of stopping forcibly and robbing.

**hole** (hōl), ***n.*** [AS. *hol*], 1. a hollow place; cavity. 2. an animal's burrow. 3. a small, dingy, squalid place. 4. an opening in anything; gap; tear; rent. 5. in *golf, a*) a small cavity into which the ball is to be hit. *b*) the tee, fairway, etc. leading to this. ***v.t.*** [HOLED, HOLING], 1. to make holes in. 2. to put or drive into a hole. **—hole up,** to hibernate, as in a hole. **—in the hole,** [Colloq.], financially embarrassed or behind. **—hole′y,** ***adj.***

**hol·i·day** (hol′ə-dā′), ***n.*** 1. a religious festival; holy day. 2. a day of freedom from labor, often one set aside by law to celebrate some event. 3. *often pl.* [Chiefly Brit.], a vacation. ***adj.*** of or suited to a holiday; joyous; gay.

**ho·li·ness** (hō′li-nis), ***n.*** 1. a being holy. 2. [H-], a title of the Pope: used with *his* or *your.*

**hol·ler** (hol′ẽr), ***v.i. & v.t., n.*** shout; yell: often considered substandard.

**hol·low** (hol′ō), ***adj.*** [AS. *holh*], 1. having a cavity within it; not solid. 2. shaped like a bowl; concave. 3. sunken: as, *hollow* cheeks. 4. empty, insincere, etc.: as, *hollow* praise. 5. hungry. 6. deep-toned and dull. ***adv.*** in a hollow manner. ***n.*** 1. a hollow place; cavity. 2. a valley. ***v.t. & v.i.*** to make or become hollow. **—hol′low·ness,** ***n.***

**hol·ly** (hol′i), ***n.*** [*pl.* -LIES], [AS. *holegn*], an evergreen shrub with glossy leaves and red berries.

**hol·ly·hock** (hol′i-hok′), ***n.*** [< ME. *holi*, holy + *hoc*, mallow], a tall, hardy plant of the mallow family, with large, showy flowers of various colors.

**Holmes, Sher·lock** (shũr′lok), a fictitious British detective in stories by A. Conan Doyle (1859–1930) of England.

**hol·o·caust** (hol′ə-kôst′), ***n.*** [< Gr. *holos*, whole + *kaustos*, burnt], 1. complete destruction of people or animals by fire. 2. great destruction.

**hol·o·graph** (hol′ə-graf′, -grāf′), ***adj.*** [< Gr. *holos*, whole + *graphein*, write], written in the handwriting of the person under whose name it appears. ***n.*** a holograph document.

**Hol·stein** (hōl′stīn, -stēn), ***n.*** [< Schleswig-*Holstein*, in Germany, where first bred], a breed of large, black-and-white dairy cattle.

**hol·ster** (hōl′stẽr), ***n.*** [ult. < ON. *hulstr*, sheath], a leather pistol case, often attached to a belt.

**ho·ly** (hō′li), ***adj.*** [-LIER, -LIEST], [AS. *halig*], 1. dedicated to religious use; sacred. 2. spiritually pure; sinless. 3. deserving reverence or worship.

**Holy Communion,** any of various church rites in which bread and wine are consecrated and received as (symbols of) the body and blood of Jesus.

**Holy Ghost,** the third person of the Trinity; spirit of God: also **Holy Spirit.**

**hom·age** (hom′ij, om′-), ***n.*** [ult. < L. *homo*, man], anything given or done to show reverence, honor, etc.

**home** (hōm), ***n.*** [AS. *ham*], 1. the place where one lives. 2. the city, state, etc. where one was born or reared. 3. a place thought of as home. 4. the household or the life around it. 5. an institution for orphans, the aged, etc. 6. the natural environment of an animal, plant, etc. 7. home plate. ***adj.*** 1. of one's home or country; domestic. 2. central: as, a *home* office. ***adv.*** 1. at, to, or in the direction of home. 2. to the point aimed at: as, he drove the nail *home.* ***v.i.*** [HOMED, HOMING], to go to one's home. **—at home,** 1. in one's home. 2. at ease. **—bring home to,** to impress upon. **—home′less,** ***adj.*** **—home′like′,** ***adj.***

**home economics,** the science and art of managing a home, including nutrition, clothing, budgeting, etc.

**home′land′,** ***n.*** the country in which one was born or makes one's home.

**home′ly,** ***adj.*** [-LIER, -LIEST], 1. suitable for home life; simple; everyday. 2. crude; unpolished. 3. plain; ugly. **—home′li·ness,** ***n.***

**home′made′,** ***adj.*** made, or as if made, at home.

**home′mak′er** (-māk′ẽr), ***n.*** a woman who manages a home; housewife.

**home plate,** in *baseball*, the slab that the batter stands beside: it is the last of the four bases that a runner must touch in succession to score a run.

**hom·er** (hōm′ẽr), ***n.*** [Colloq.], a home run.

**home run,** in *baseball*, a safe hit that permits the batter to touch all the bases and score a run.

**home′sick′,** ***adj.*** longing for home. **—home′sick′ness,** ***n.***

**home′spun′,** ***n.*** 1. cloth made of yarn spun at home. 2. coarse cloth like this. ***adj.*** 1. spun at home. 2. made of homespun. 3. plain; homely.

**home′stead′** (-sted′), ***n.*** 1. a place for a family's home, including the land and buildings. 2. a 160-acre tract of U.S. public land, granted as a farm. **—home′stead′er,** ***n.***

**home′stretch′** (-strech′), ***n.*** the part of a race track between the last turn and the finish line.

**home′ward** (-wẽrd), ***adv. & adj.*** toward home: also **home′wards,** ***adv.***

**home′work′,** ***n.*** 1. work done at home. 2. schoolwork to be done outside the classroom.

**hom·i·cide** (hom′ə-sīd′), ***n.*** [< L. *homo*, man + *caedere*, kill], 1. the killing of one person by another. 2. a person who kills another. **—hom′i·cid′al,** ***adj.***

**hom·i·let·ics** (hom′ə-let′iks), ***n.pl.*** [construed as sing.], [see HOMILY], the art of writing and preaching sermons. **—hom′i·let′ic,** ***adj.***

**hom·i·ly** (hom′′l-i), ***n.*** [*pl.* -LIES], [< Gr. *homilos*, assembly], 1. a sermon. 2. a solemn moral talk or writing.

**homing pigeon,** a pigeon trained to find its way home from distant places, and hence used to carry messages.

**hom·i·ny** (hom′ə-ni), ***n.*** [< Am. Ind.], dry corn hulled and coarsely ground: it is boiled for food.

**homo-,** [< Gr. *homos*], a combining form meaning *same, equal, like.*

**ho·mo·ge·ne·ous** (hō′mə-jē′ni-əs, hom′ə-), ***adj.*** [< Gr. *homos*, the same + *genos*, a kind], 1. the same in structure, quality, etc.; similar. 2. composed of similar parts. **—ho′mo·ge·ne′i·ty** (-jə-nē′ə-ti), ***n.***

**ho·mo·gen·ize** (hə-moj′ə-nīz′), *v.t.* [-IZED, -IZING], to make homogeneous, or more uniform throughout.
**homogenized milk,** milk in which the fat particles are so well emulsified that the cream does not separate on standing.
**hom·o·graph** (hom′ə-graf′, -gräf′), *n.* [< Gr. *homos,* same + *graphein,* write], a word spelled the same as another but different in meaning and origin.
**ho·mol·o·gous** (hō-mol′ə-gəs), *adj.* [< Gr. *homos,* same + *legein,* speak], matching in structure, position, character, origin, etc.
**hom·o·nym** (hom′ə-nim′), *n.* [< Gr. *homos,* same + *onyma,* name], a word with the same pronunciation as another but with a different meaning, origin, and, usually, spelling (e.g., *bore* and *boar*).
**Ho·mo sa·pi·ens** (hō′mō sā′pi-enz′), [L.; *homo,* man & *sapiens,* ppr. of *sapere,* to know], man; human being.
**ho·mo·sex·u·al** (hō′mə-sek′shoo-əl), *adj.* of or having sexual desire for those of the same sex. *n.* a homosexual person. **—ho′mo·sex′u·al′i·ty,** *n.*
**Hon., hon.,** 1. honorable. 2. honorary.
**hone** (hōn), *n.* [< AS. *han,* a stone], a whetstone used to sharpen cutting tools, esp. razors. *v.t.* [HONED, HONING], to sharpen on a hone.
**hon·est** (on′ist), *adj.* [< L. *honor,* honor], 1. trustworthy; truthful. 2. *a*) showing fairness and sincerity: as, an *honest* effort. *b*) gained by fair methods: as, an *honest* living. 3. being what it seems; genuine. 4. frank and open: as, an *honest* face. 5. [Archaic], chaste. **—hon′est·ly,** *adv.*
**hon·es·ty** (on′is-ti), *n.* a being honest; truthfulness, sincerity, etc.
**hon·ey** (hun′i), *n.* [*pl.* -EYS], [AS. *hunig*], 1. a thick, sweet, sirupy substance that bees make as food from the nectar of flowers. 2. anything like honey. 3. darling.
**hon′ey·bee′,** *n.* a bee that makes honey.
**hon′ey·comb′** (-kōm′), *n.* 1. the structure of six-sided wax cells made by bees to hold their honey, eggs, etc. 2. anything like this. *v.t.* to fill with holes like a honeycomb. *adj.* of or like a honeycomb.
**hon′ey·dew′** (-doo′, -dū′), *n.* 1. a sweet fluid exuded from the leaves of some plants in summer. 2. a variety of muskmelon with a smooth, whitish rind and sweet, green flesh: in full **honeydew melon.**
**hon·eyed** (hun′id), *adj.* 1. sweetened with honey. 2. sweet as honey; flattering.
**hon′ey·moon′,** *n.* the vacation spent together by a newly married couple. *v.i.* to have or spend a honeymoon.
**hon′ey·suck′le** (-suk′′l), *n.* any of a group of climbing, twining vines with small, fragrant flowers of red, yellow, or white.
**honk** (hôŋk, hoŋk), *n.* [echoic], 1. the call of a wild goose. 2. a similar sound, as of an automobile horn. *v.i. & v.t.* to make or cause to make such a sound.
**hon·ky-tonk** (hôŋ′ki-tôŋk′, hoŋ′ki-toŋk′), *n.* [prob. echoic], [Slang], a cheap, disreputable saloon, etc.
**hon·or** (on′ẽr), *n.* [L.], 1. high regard or respect; esp., *a*) glory; fame. *b*) good reputation. 2. adherence to principles considered right; integrity. 3. chastity. 4. high rank or distinction. 5. [H-], a title of certain officials, as judges (with *his, her,* or *your*). 6. something done or given as a token of respect. 7. a source of respect and fame. *v.t.* 1. to respect greatly. 2. to show high regard for. 3. to confer an honor on. 4. to accept and pay: as, to *honor* a check. **—do the honors,** to function as a host. Also, Brit. sp., **honour.**
**hon′or·a·ble,** *adj.* 1. worthy of being honored. 2. honest; upright. 3. bringing honor: as, *honorable* mention. **—hon′or·a·ble·ness,** *n.* **—hon′or·a·bly,** *adv.*
**hon·o·rar·ium** (on′ə-rar′i-əm), *n.* [LL.], [*pl.* -IUMS, -IA (-i-ə)], a payment to a professional man for services on which no fee is set.
**hon′or·ar′y** (-rer′i), *adj.* 1. done or given as an honor. 2. designating or in an office held as an honor, without service or pay.
**hood** (hood), *n.* [AS. *hod*], 1. a covering for the head and neck, often part of a cloak. 2. anything like a hood, as the metal cover over an automobile engine. *v.t.* to cover as with a hood. **—hood′ed,** *adj.*
**-hood,** [< AS. *had*], a suffix meaning: 1. *state* or *quality,* as in *childhood.* 2. *the whole group of,* as in *priesthood.*
**hood·lum** (hōōd′ləm), *n.* [? < *huddle 'em*], [Colloq.], a rowdy or ruffian.
**hoo·doo** (hōō′dōō), *n.* [*pl.* -DOOS], [var. of *voodoo*], 1. voodoo. 2. [Colloq.], bad luck or a person or thing that causes it. *v.t.* [Colloq.], to bring bad luck to.
**hood·wink** (hood′wiŋk′), *v.t.* [*hood* + *wink*], 1. to blindfold. 2. to deceive.
**hoo·ey** (hōō′i), *interj. & n.* [echoic], [Slang], nonsense; bunk.
**hoof** (hoof, hōōf), *n.* [*pl.* HOOFS, rarely HOOVES], [AS. *hof*], the horny covering on the feet of cattle, horses, etc., or the entire foot. *v.t. & v.i.* [Colloq.], to walk.
**hook** (hook), *n.* [AS. *hoc*], 1. a bent piece of metal, etc. used to catch, hold, or pull something. 2. a fishhook. 3. something shaped like a hook. 4. in *baseball,* a curve. 5. a stroke, blow, etc. in which a curving motion is involved. *v.t.* to catch, fasten, throw, hit, etc. with a hook. *v.i.* 1. to curve as a hook does. 2. to be fastened with or caught by a hook. **—by hook or by crook,** by any means, honest or dishonest. **—hook up,** to connect (a radio, etc.)
**hook·ah, hook·a** (hook′ə), *n.* [Ar. *ḥuqqah*], an Oriental pipe with a long tube by means of which the smoke is drawn through water so as to be cooled.
**hooked rug,** a rug made by drawing strips of cloth or yarn back and forth through canvas or burlap.
**hook′up′,** *n.* the arrangement and connection of parts, circuits, etc., as in (a) radio.
**hook′worm′,** *n.* a small, parasitic roundworm with hooks around the mouth, infesting the small intestine.
**hoo·li·gan** (hōō′li-gən), *n.* [< *Hooligan,* a family name], a hoodlum.
**hoop** (hōōp, hoop), *n.* [AS. *hop*], 1. a circular band for holding together the staves of a barrel. 2. anything like this, as a ring in a hoop skirt. *v.t.* to bind or fasten with a hoop.
**hoop skirt,** a woman's skirt worn over a framework of hoops to make it spread out.
**hoo·ray** (hoo-rā′, hōō-), *interj., n., v.i. & v.t.* hurrah.
**hoose·gow, hoos·gow** (hōōs′gou), *n.* [prob. < Sp. *juzgado,* a court], [Slang], a jail.
**Hoo·sier** (hōō′zhẽr), *n.* a native or inhabitant of Indiana: a nickname.
**hoot** (hōōt), *n.* [echoic], 1. the sound that an owl makes. 2. any sound like this, as a shout of scorn. *v.i.* to utter a hoot. *v.t.* to express (scorn) of (someone) by hooting.
**hop** (hop), *v.i.* [HOPPED, HOPPING], [AS. *hoppian*], 1. to make a short leap or leaps on one foot. 2. to leap with all feet at once, as a frog, etc. 3. [Slang], to go. *v.t.* 1. to jump over. 2. to jump onto. *n.* 1. a hopping. 2. [Colloq.], *a*) a dance. *b*) a flight in an airplane.
**hop** (hop), *n.* [< MD. *hoppe*], 1. a climbing vine with cone-shaped flowers. 2. *pl.* its dried ripe cones, used for flavoring beer, ale, etc.
**hope** (hōp), *n.* [AS. *hopa*], 1. a feeling that what is wanted will happen. 2. the object of this. 3. a person or thing from which

something is hoped. *v.t.* [HOPED, HOPING], to want and expect. *v.i.* to have hope (*for*).

**hope′ful,** *adj.* feeling or inspiring hope. *n.* a young person who seems likely to succeed.

**hope′ful·ly,** *adv.* 1. in a hopeful manner. 2. it is to be hoped that: regarded by some as a loose usage.

**hope′less,** *adj.* 1. without hope. 2. arousing no hope. —**hope′less·ly,** *adv.*

**hop·per** (hop′ẽr), *n.* 1. one that hops. 2. a hopping insect. 3. a container from which material is fed into something else.

**hop′scotch′,** *n.* [*hop* + *scotch*, line], a game in which children hop about in figures drawn on the ground.

**horde** (hôrd), *n.* [ult. < Turk. *ordū*, a camp], a crowd; pack; swarm.

**hore·hound** (hôr′hound′), *n.* [< AS. *har*, white + *hune*, horehound], 1. a plant of the mint family, with white, downy leaves that contain a bitter juice. 2. cough medicine or candy made with this juice.

**ho·ri·zon** (hə-rī′z'n), *n.* [< Gr. *horos*, boundary], 1. the line where the sky seems to meet the earth. 2. the limit of one's experience, interest, etc.

**hor·i·zon·tal** (hôr′ə-zon′t'l, hor′-), *adj.* 1. parallel to the plane of the horizon. 2. flat and even; level. —**hor′i·zon′tal·ly,** *adv.*

**hor·mone** (hôr′mōn), *n.* [< Gr. *hormē*, impulse], a chemical substance formed in some organ of the body and carried to another part, where it takes effect.

**horn** (hôrn), *n.* [AS.], 1. a hard, bonelike projection growing on the head of a cow, goat, etc. 2. anything like a horn in position, shape, etc., as the end of a crescent. 3. the substance horns are made of. 4. any brass-wind instrument. 5. a device sounded to give warning. *adj.* made of horn. —**horn in,** [Slang], to intrude or meddle. —**horned,** *adj.* —**horn′less,** *adj.*

**horn′book′,** *n.* a sheet of parchment with the alphabet, numbers, etc. on it, mounted on a small board with a handle and protected by a thin, clear plate of horn: formerly used as a children's primer.

**hor·net** (hôr′nit), *n.* [AS. *hyrnet*], a large wasp whose sting is very painful.

**horn of plenty,** a cornucopia.

**horn′pipe′,** *n.* 1. a lively dance formerly popular with sailors. 2. music for this.

**horn′y,** *adj.* [-IER, -IEST], 1. made of horn. 2. having horns. 3. hard like horn; callous and tough. —**horn′i·ness,** *n.*

**ho·rol·o·gy** (hô-rol′ə-ji), *n.* [< Gr. *hōra*, hour; + *-logy*], the science of measuring time or making timepieces. —**hor·o·log·ic** (hôr′ə-loj′ik, hor′-), *adj.* —**ho·rol′o·gist,** *n.*

**hor·o·scope** (hôr′ə-skōp′, hor′-), *n.* [< Gr. *hōra*, hour + *skopein*, to view], a chart of the zodiacal signs and the positions of the planets, etc., by which astrologers profess to tell a person's future. —**cast a horoscope,** to calculate the supposed influence of the stars and planets on a person's life.

**hor·ren·dous** (hô-ren′dəs), *adj.* [see HORRIBLE], horrible; dreadful.

**hor·ri·ble** (hôr′i-b'l, hor′-), *adj.* [< L. *horrere*, to bristle], 1. causing horror; terrible; dreadful. 2. [Colloq.], very bad, ugly, shocking, unpleasant, etc. —**hor′ri·bly,** *adv.*

**hor·rid** (hôr′id, hor′-), *adj.* 1. causing horror; terrible. 2. [Colloq.], very bad, unpleasant, etc. —**hor′rid·ly,** *adv.*

**hor·ri·fy** (hôr′ə-fī′, hor′-), *v.t.* [-FIED, -FYING], 1. to cause to feel horror. 2. [Colloq.], to shock greatly. —**hor′ri·fi·ca′tion,** *n.*

**hor·ror** (hôr′ẽr, hor′-), *n.* [< L. *horrere*, to bristle], 1. the strong feeling caused by something frightful or shocking. 2. strong dislike. 3. something that causes horror.

**hors d'oeu·vre** (ôr′dũrv′, -duv′), [*pl.* D'OEUVRES], [Fr., lit., outside of work], *usually in pl.* any of a variety of appetizers, as canapés, olives, etc.

**horse** (hôrs), *n.* [AS. *hors*], 1. a large, four-legged, solid-hoofed animal with flowing mane and tail, domesticated for drawing loads, carrying riders, etc. 2. a frame on legs to support something. *v.t.* [HORSED, HORSING], to supply with a horse or horses; put on horseback. *adj.* of or on horses. —**hold one's horses,** [Slang], to curb one's impatience. —**horse around,** [Slang], to engage in horseplay.

**horse′back′,** *n.* the back of a horse. *adv.* on horseback.

**horse chestnut,** 1. a flowering tree with glossy brown nuts. 2. its nut.

**horse′fly′,** *n.* [*pl.* -FLIES], a large fly that sucks the blood of horses, etc.; gadfly.

**horse′hair′,** *n.* 1. hair from the mane or tail of a horse. 2. a stiff fabric made from this hair.

**horse′laugh′,** *n.* a boisterous laugh; guffaw.

**horse′man** (-mən), *n.* [*pl.* -MEN], a man skilled in the riding or care of horses.

**horse′play′,** *n.* rough, boisterous play.

**horse′pow′er,** *n.* a unit for measuring the power output of engines, etc., equal to 33,000 foot-pounds per minute.

**horse′rad′ish,** *n.* 1. a plant of the mustard family, with a pungent, white root. 2. a relish made by grating this root.

**horse sense,** [Colloq.], common sense.

**horse′shoe′,** *n.* 1. a flat, U-shaped, protective metal plate nailed to a horse's hoof. 2. anything shaped like this. 3. *pl.* a game in which horseshoes are tossed at a stake.

**horse′whip′,** *n.* a whip for driving horses. *v.t.* [-WHIPPED or -WHIPT, -WHIPPING], to lash with a horsewhip.

**hors′y** (hôr′si), *adj.* [-IER, -IEST], 1. of, like, or suggesting a horse. 2. of or like people who are fond of horses, fox hunting, or horse racing. —**hors′i·ness,** *n.*

**hor·ta·to·ry** (hôr′tə-tôr′i), *adj.* [< L. *hortari*, incite], exhorting; advising.

**hor·ti·cul·ture** (hôr′ti-kul′chẽr), *n.* [< L. *hortus*, garden + *cultura*, culture], the art or science of growing flowers, fruits, and vegetables. —**hor′ti·cul′tur·ist,** *n.*

**ho·san·na** (hō-zan′ə), *n.* & *interj.* [< Heb. *hōshi'āh nnā*, save, we pray], an exclamation of praise to God.

**hose** (hōz), *n.* [*pl.* HOSE], [AS. *hosa*], 1. *pl.* *a*) stockings. *b*) socks. 2. [*pl.* HOSE, HOSES], a flexible tube, used to convey fluids, esp. water from a hydrant. *v.t.* [HOSED, HOSING], to water with a hose.

**ho·sier** (hō′zhẽr), *n.* one who makes or sells hosiery or similar knitted or woven goods.

**ho·sier·y** (hō′zhẽr-i), *n.* stockings.

**hos·pice** (hos′pis), *n.* [< L. *hospes*, host, guest], a shelter for travelers.

**hos·pi·ta·ble** (hos′pi-tə-b'l, hos-pit′ə-), *adj.* [< L. *hospes*, host, guest], characterized by generosity and friendliness to guests. —**hos′pi·ta·bly,** *adv.*

**hos·pi·tal** (hos′pi-t'l), *n.* [< L. *hospes*, host, guest], an institution where the ill or injured may receive medical or surgical treatment, nursing, etc.

**hos·pi·tal·i·ty** (hos′pi-tal′ə-ti), *n.* [*pl.* -TIES], the act, practice, or quality of being hospitable.

**hos′pi·tal·ize′** (-īz′), *v.t.* [-IZED, -IZING], to put in a hospital. —**hos′pi·tal·i·za′tion,** *n.*

**Host, host** (hōst), *n.* [< L. *hostia*, sacrifice], the bread of the Eucharist.

**host** (hōst), *n.* [< L. *hospes*, host, guest], 1. a man who entertains guests, esp. in his own home. 2. a man who keeps an inn or hotel. 3. an organism on or in which another (called a *parasite*) lives.

**host** (hōst), *n.* [< L. *hostis*, enemy], 1. an army. 2. a great number.

**hos·tage** (hos′tij), ***n.*** [OFr.], a person kept or given as a pledge for the fulfillment of certain terms.

**hos·tel** (hos′t'l), ***n.*** [see HOSPITAL], a lodging place; inn: also **hos′tel·ry** [*pl.* -RIES]. —**hos′tel·er,** ***n.***

**host·ess** (hōs′tis), ***n.*** 1. a woman who entertains guests in her home; often, the host's wife. 2. a woman employed in a restaurant to supervise the waitresses, seating, etc.

**hos·tile** (hos′t'l), ***adj.*** [< L. *hostis*, enemy], 1. of or characteristic of an enemy. 2. unfriendly; antagonistic. —**hos′tile·ly,** ***adv.***

**hos·til·i·ty** (hos-til′ə-ti), ***n.*** [*pl.* -TIES], 1. a feeling of enmity, ill will, etc. 2. *a*) active opposition. *b*) *pl.* warfare.

**hos·tler** (hos′lẽr, os′-) ***n.*** [contr. of *hosteler*], one who takes care of horses at an inn, stable, etc.

**hot** (hot), ***adj.*** [HOTTER, HOTTEST], [AS. *hat*], 1. *a*) having a temperature higher than that of the human body. *b*) having a relatively high temperature. 2. producing a burning sensation: as, a *hot* pepper. 3. full of intense feeling; impetuous: as, a *hot* temper. 4. violent: as, a *hot* battle. 5. lustful. 6. following closely: as, *hot* pursuit. 7. [Slang], *a*) recent; fresh: as, *hot* news. *b*) recently stolen or smuggled. *c*) excellent; good. ***adv.*** in a hot manner. —**make it hot for,** [Colloq.], to make things uncomfortable for. —**hot′ly,** ***adv.*** —**hot′ness,** ***n.***

**hot air,** [Slang], empty or pretentious talk.

**hot′bed′,** ***n.*** 1. a bed of earth covered with glass and heated by manure, for forcing plants. 2. any place that fosters rapid growth.

**hot′-blood′ed,** ***adj.*** easily excited.

**hot cake,** a griddle cake. —**sell like hot cakes,** [Colloq.], to be sold rapidly and in large quantities.

**hot dog,** [Colloq.], 1. a wiener. 2. a wiener served in a soft roll.

**ho·tel** (hō-tel′), ***n.*** [see HOSPITAL], an establishment providing lodging, and often food, for travelers, etc.

**hot′head′ed,** ***adj.*** 1. quick-tempered. 2. impetuous. —**hot′head′,** ***n.***

**hot′house′,** ***n.*** a greenhouse.

**hot plate,** a small stove for cooking.

**hot rod,** [Slang], an automobile, usually a jalopy, whose motor has been supercharged.

**hot′-tem′pered,** ***adj.*** easily angered.

**Hot·ten·tot** (hot′'n-tot′), ***n.*** 1. a member of a Negroid race of S. Africa. 2. the language of the Hottentots.

**hound** (hound), ***n.*** [AS. *hund*, dog], 1. any of several breeds of hunting dog. 2. any dog. ***v.t.*** 1. to hunt or chase with or as with hounds. 2. to urge on. —**hound′ed,** ***adj.***

**hour** (our), ***n.*** [< Gr. *hōra*], 1. one of the twenty-four equal parts of a day; sixty minutes. 2. the time for a particular activity, etc.: as, the dinner *hour*. 3. the period of time in a classroom. 4. *pl.* a special period for work, etc.: as, office *hours*. 5. the time of day: as, the *hour* is 2:30. —**after hours,** after the regular hours for business, school, etc. —**hour after hour,** every hour.

**hour′glass′,** ***n.*** an instrument for measuring time by the trickling of sand, etc. from one part to another.

**hou·ri** (hoo′ri, hou′-), ***n.*** [*pl.* -RIS], [< Ar.], a nymph of the Moslem Paradise.

**hour′ly,** ***adj.*** 1. happening every hour. 2. done during an hour. 3. frequent. ***adv.*** 1. once an hour. 2. often; frequently.

**house** (hous), ***n.*** [*pl.* HOUSES (houz′iz)], [AS. *hus*], 1. a building to live in; specif., a building occupied by one family. 2. the people who live in a house; household. 3. a family as including kin, ancestors, and descendants. 4. a building for storing things. 5. *a*) a theater. *b*) the audience in a theater. 6. a business firm. 7. a legislative assembly. ***v.t.*** (houz), [HOUSED, HOUSING], 1. to provide a house or lodgings for. 2. to cover, shelter, etc. —**keep house,** to take care of the affairs of a home. —**on the house,** given free at the expense of the establishment. —**house′ful′,** ***n.***

**house′boat′,** ***n.*** a large, flat-bottomed boat used as a dwelling place.

**house′bro′ken,** ***adj.*** trained to live in a house (i.e., to void in the proper place): said of a dog, cat, etc.: also **house′broke′.**

**house′fly′,** ***n.*** [*pl.* -FLIES], a two-winged fly found in and around houses.

**house′hold′,** ***n.*** 1. all the persons who live in one house. 2. the home and its affairs. ***adj.*** of a household; domestic.

**house′hold′er,** ***n.*** 1. one who owns or maintains a house. 2. the head of a household.

**house′keep′er,** ***n.*** a woman who runs a home, does the housework. etc.

**House of Commons,** the lower branch of the legislature of Great Britain or Canada.

**House of Lords,** the upper branch of the legislature of Great Britain.

**House of Representatives,** the lower branch of the legislature of the United States, or of most of the States of the U.S.

**house′warm′ing,** ***n.*** a party for one who has moved into a new home.

**house′wife′,** ***n.*** [*pl.* -WIVES], a woman in charge of her own household.

**house′work′,** ***n.*** the work involved in housekeeping; cleaning, cooking, etc.

**hous·ing** (houz′iŋ), ***n.*** 1. the providing of shelter or lodging. 2. shelter or lodging. 3. houses collectively. 4. an enclosing frame, box, etc.

**hove** (hōv), alt. pt. and pp. of **heave.**

**hov·el** (huv′'l, hov′'l), ***n.*** [ME.], any small, miserable dwelling; hut.

**hov·er** (huv′ẽr, hov′-), ***v.i.*** [< ME. *hoven*, to stay]. 1. to flutter in the air near one place. 2. to linger close by. 3. to waver (*between*).

**how** (hou), ***adv.*** [AS. *hu*], 1. in what manner or way. 2. in what state or condition. 3. for what reason. 4. to what effect. 5. to what extent, degree, amount, etc. 6. at what price. 7. [Colloq.], what? *How* is also used as an intensive. ***n.*** the way of doing.

**how·be·it** (hou-bē′it), ***adv.*** [Archaic], however it may be; nevertheless.

**how·e'er′** (-er′), ***adv. & conj.*** however.

**how·ev′er,** ***adv.*** 1. by whatever means. 2. to whatever degree or extent. ***conj.*** nevertheless; yet; but.

**how·itz·er** (hou′it-sẽr), ***n.*** [< Czech. *haufnice*, orig., a sling], a short cannon, firing shells in a relatively high trajectory.

**howl** (houl), ***v.i.*** [ME. *houlen*], 1. to utter the long, wailing cry of wolves, dogs, etc. 2. to utter a similar cry of pain, anger, etc. 3. to make a sound like this: as, the wind *howls*. 4. to shout or laugh in scorn, mirth, etc. ***v.t.*** 1. to utter with a howl. 2. to drive by howling. ***n.*** 1. the wailing cry of a wolf, etc. 2. any similar cry. —**howl down,** to drown out with shouts of scorn, etc.

**howl′er,** ***n.*** 1. one who howls. 2. [Colloq.], a ridiculous blunder.

**how·so·ev·er** (hou′sō-ev′ẽr), ***adv.*** 1. to whatever degree or extent. 2. by whatever means.

**hoy·den** (hoi′d'n), ***n.*** [< ?], a bold, boisterous girl; tomboy. —**hoy′den·ish,** ***adj.***

**Hoyle** (hoil), ***n.*** a book of rules for card games, first compiled by E. Hoyle (1672–1769). —**according to Hoyle,** according to the rules and regulations.

**H.P., HP, h.p., hp,** horsepower.

**H.Q., Hq.,** Headquarters.

**hr.,** [*pl.* HRS.], hour; hours.

**H.R.,** House of Representatives.

**H.R.H.,** His (or Her) Royal Highness.

**ht.,** 1. heat. 2. [*pl.* HTS.], height; heights.
**HUAC, H.U.A.C.,** House Un-American Activities Committee.
**hub** (hub), *n.* [prob. < *hob*, a peg], 1. the center part of a wheel. 2. a center of interest, activity, etc.
**hub·bub** (hub'ub), *n.* [said to be < Ir. cry], an uproar; tumult.
**huck·le·ber·ry** (huk''l-ber'i), *n.* [*pl.* -RIES], [? < AS. *wyrtil*, shrub + *berie*, berry], 1. a shrub having dark-blue berries. 2. this berry.
**huck·ster** (huk'stẽr), *n.* [prob. < MD. *hoek*, a corner], a peddler, esp. of fruits, vegetables, etc. *v.t.* to peddle.
**hud·dle** (hud''l), *v.i. & v.t.* [-DLED, -DLING], [? < ME. *hoderen*, cover up], 1. to crowd close together. 2. to draw (oneself) up tightly. *n.* 1. a confused crowd or heap. 2. in *football*, a grouping of a team to get signals before a play. 3. [Slang], a secret discussion.
**hue** (hū), *n.* [AS. *heow*], 1. color. 2. a particular shade of color; tint. **—hued,** *adj.*
**hue** (hū), *n.* [< OFr. *hu*, hunting cry], a shouting: now only in *hue and cry*, a loud outcry or clamor.
**huff** (huf), *v.t.* [prob. echoic], to make angry; offend. *v.i.* to blow; puff. *n.* a burst of anger or resentment. **—huff'y,** *adj.*
**hug** (hug), *v.t.* [HUGGED, HUGGING], [prob. < ON. *hugga*, to comfort], 1. to clasp closely and fondly in the arms; embrace. 2. to cling to (a belief, etc.). 3. to keep close to: as, the bus *hugged* the curb. *v.i.* to embrace one another. *n.* a close embrace.
**huge** (hūj), *adj.* [OFr. *ahuge*], very large; immense. **—huge'ly,** *adv.* **—huge'ness,** *n.*
**Hu·gue·not** (hū'gə-not'), *n.* a French Protestant of the 16th or 17th century.
**huh** (hu), *interj.* an exclamation used to express contempt, surprise, etc., or to ask a question.
**hu·la-hu·la** (ho͞o'lə-ho͞o'lə), *n.* [Haw.], a native Hawaiian dance: also **hula.**
**hulk** (hulk), *n.* [AS. *hulc*], 1. the body of a ship, esp. if old and dismantled. 2. a big, clumsy person or thing. *v.i.* to rise bulkily (usually with *up*).
**hulk'ing,** *adj.* bulky and clumsy.
**hull** (hul), *n.* [AS. *hulu*], 1. the outer covering of a seed or fruit, as the husk of grain, shell of nuts, etc. 2. the frame or main body of a ship or of a flying boat. *v.t.* to remove the hulls from (nuts, etc.).
**hul·la·ba·loo** (hul'ə-bə-lo͞o'), *n.* [echoic], clamor; uproar.
**hum** (hum), *v.i.* [HUMMED, HUMMING], [echoic], 1. to make a low, murmuring, continuous sound. 2. to sing with closed lips. 3. [Colloq.], to be full of activity. *v.t.* to sing (a tune, etc.) with closed lips. *n.* a continuous murmuring sound.
**hu·man** (hū'mən), *adj.* [< L. *humanus*], 1. of or characteristic of a person or people. 2. having the form or nature of a person. *n.* a person: usually **human being.**
**hu·mane** (hyoo-mān'), *adj.* [var. of *human*], 1. kind, merciful, considerate, etc. 2. civilizing; refining. **—hu·mane'ly,** *adv.*
**hu·man·ism** (hū'mən-iz'm), *n.* 1. any system of thought concerned with human interests and ideals. 2. [H-], the intellectual movement that stemmed from the study of Greek and Latin classics during the Middle Ages. **—hu'man·ist,** *n. & adj.*
**hu·man·i·tar·i·an** (hyoo-man'ə-târ'-i-ən), *n.* a person devoted to promoting the welfare of humanity; philanthropist. *adj.* helping humanity; philanthropic. **—hu-man'i·tar'i·an·ism,** *n.*
**hu·man·i·ty** (hyoo-man'ə-ti), *n.* [*pl.* -TIES], 1. the fact or quality of being human. 2. the human race. 3. the fact or quality of being humane; kindness, sympathy, etc. **—the humanities,** the branches of learning concerned with human thought and relations, esp. literature, philosophy, etc.
**hu·man·ize** (hū'mə-niz'), *v.t. & v.i.* [-IZED, -IZING], to make or become human or humane. **—hu'man·i·za'tion,** *n.*
**hu'man·kind',** *n.* the human race.
**hu'man·ly,** *adv.* 1. in a human manner. 2. by human means.
**hum·ble** (hum'b'l, um'-), *adj.* [-BLER, -BLEST], [< L. *humilis*, low], 1. having or showing awareness of one's defects; modest. 2. lowly; unpretentious. *v.t.* [-BLED, -BLING], 1. to lower in condition or rank. 2. to make humble in mind. **—hum'bly,** *adv.*
**hum·bug** (hum'bug'), *n.* [< ?], 1. fraud; sham; hoax. 2. an impostor. *v.t.* [-BUGGED, -BUGGING], to dupe; cheat.
**hum·drum** (hum'drum'), *adj.* [echoic], dull; monotonous.
**hu·mer·us** (hū'mẽr-əs), *n.* [*pl.* -MERI (-mẽr-ī')], [L.], the bone of the upper arm or forelimb.
**hu·mid** (hū'mid), *adj.* [< L. *umere*, be moist], damp; moist.
**hu·mid·i·fy** (hyoo-mid'ə-fī'), *v.t.* [-FIED, -FYING], to make humid. **—hu·mid'i·fi'er,** *n.*
**hu·mid'i·ty,** *n.* 1. moistness; dampness. 2. the amount of moisture in the air.
**hu·mi·dor** (hū'mi-dôr'), *n.* a jar or case for keeping tobacco, etc. moist.
**hu·mil·i·ate** (hyoo-mil'i-āt'), *v.t.* [-ATED, -ATING], [< L. *humilis*, humble], to lower the pride or dignity of; mortify. **—hu·mil'i·at'ing·ly,** *adv.* **—hu·mil'i·a'tion,** *n.*
**hu·mil'i·ty** (-ə-ti), *n.* [*pl.* -TIES], the state or quality of being humble of mind or spirit.
**hum·ming·bird** (hum'iŋ-bũrd'), *n.* a very small, brightly colored bird with narrow wings that vibrate rapidly, making a humming sound in flight.
**hum·mock** (hum'ək), *n.* [< ?], 1. a low, rounded hill; knoll. 2. a ridge in an ice field.
**hu·mor** (hū'mẽr, ū'-), *n.* [< L. *humor*, fluid: after former belief in four body humors (fluids) held responsible for one's disposition], 1. a mood; state of mind. 2. whim; caprice. 3. a comical quality. 4. *a*) the ability to appreciate or express what is funny, amusing, etc. *b*) the expression of this. *v.t.* to comply with the mood or whim of. Also, Brit. sp., **humour.**
**hu'mor·ist,** *n.* 1. a person with a well-developed sense of humor. 2. a professional writer or teller of amusing stories, etc.
**hu'mor·ous,** *adj.* amusing; comical.
**hump** (hump), *n.* [< ?], 1. a rounded, protruding lump, as on a camel's back. 2. a hummock. *v.t.* to arch; hunch.
**hump'back',** *n.* 1. a humped back, caused by a deformity of the spine. 2. a person having a humped back.
**hu·mus** (hū'məs), *n.* [L., earth], the dark part of the soil, resulting from the partial decay of leaves and other vegetable matter.
**Hun** (hun), *n.* a member of a savage Asiatic people who invaded Europe in the 4th and 5th centuries A.D.
**hunch** (hunch), *v.t.* [< *hunchback*], to form into a hump. *v.i.* to move forward jerkily; push; shove. *n.* 1. a hump. 2. [Colloq.], a feeling that something is going to happen.
**hunch'back',** *n.* a humpback.
**hun·dred** (hun'drid), *adj. & n.* [AS.], ten times ten; 100; C. **—hun'dredth** (-dridth), *adj. & n.*
**hun'dred·fold',** *adj. & adv.* a hundred times as much or as many.
**hun'dred·weight',** *n.* a unit of weight, equal to 100 pounds in the U.S. and 112 pounds in England.
**hung** (huŋ), pt. and pp. of **hang.**
**Hung.,** 1. Hungarian. 2. Hungary.

**Hun·gar·i·an** (huŋ-gâr′i-ən), ***adj.*** of Hungary, its people, etc. ***n.*** 1. a native of Hungary. 2. the language of the Hungarians.
**hun·ger** (huŋ′gẽr), ***n.*** [AS. *hungor*], 1. the discomfort caused by a need for food. 2. a need or appetite for food. 3. any strong desire. ***v.i.*** 1. to be hungry. 2. to crave.
**hun·gry** (huŋ′gri), ***adj.*** [-GRIER, -GRIEST], 1. wanting or needing food. 2. craving; eager. **—hun′gri·ly,** ***adv.*** **—hun′gri·ness,** ***n.***
**hunk** (huŋk), ***n.*** [? < Fl. *hunke*], [Colloq.], a large piece, lump, etc.
**hunt** (hunt), ***v.t. & v.i.*** [AS. *huntian*], 1. to chase (game) for food or sport. 2. to try to find; search; seek. 3. to chase; harry. ***n.*** 1. a hunting. 2. a group of people who hunt together. 3. a search. **—hunt′er, hunts′man** [*pl.* -MEN], ***n.***
**hur·dle** (hũr′d'l), ***n.*** [*AS. hyrdel*], 1. a framelike barrier for runners or horses to jump over in a race. 2. an obstacle. ***v.t.*** [-DLED, -DLING], 1. to jump over. 2. to overcome (an obstacle). **—hur′dler,** ***n.***
**hur·dy-gur·dy** (hũr′di-gũr′di), ***n.*** [*pl.* -DIES], [prob. echoic], popularly, a barrel organ.
**hurl** (hũrl), ***v.t.*** [prob. < ON.], 1. to throw with force or violence. 2. to cast down. 3. to utter vehemently. ***n.*** a hurling; throw.
**hurl·y-burl·y** (hũr′li-bũr′li), ***n.*** [*pl.* -IES], a turmoil; uproar.
**hur·rah** (hoo-rô′, hə-rä′), ***interj. & n.*** [echoic], a shout of joy, approval, etc. ***v.i. & v.t.*** to shout "hurrah" (for).
**hur·ray** (hoo-rā′, hə-), ***interj., n., v.t. & v.i.*** hurrah.
**hur·ri·cane** (hũr′i-kān′), ***n.*** [< W. Ind. *huracan*], a violent storm like a cyclone, originating in the tropics.
**hur·ried** (hũr′id), ***adj.*** 1. forced to do, act, etc. in a hurry. 2. done in a hurry.
**hur·ry** (hũr′i), ***v.t.*** [-RIED, -RYING], [prob. akin to *hurl*], 1. to move or send with haste. 2. to cause to occur or be done more rapidly or too rapidly. 3. to urge to act soon or too soon. ***v.i.*** to move or act with haste. ***n.*** 1. rush; haste. 2. eagerness to do, go, etc.
**hurt** (hũrt), ***v.t.*** [HURT, HURTING], [< OFr. *hurter*, to hit], 1. to cause pain or injury to. 2. to harm. 3. to offend. ***v.i.*** 1. to cause pain, harm, etc. 2. to have pain. ***n.*** 1. a pain or injury. 2. harm; damage.
**hurt′ful,** ***adj.*** causing hurt; harmful.
**hur·tle** (hũr′t'l), ***v.i.*** [-TLED, -TLING], [ME. *hurtlen*], 1. to come with a crash; collide (*against* or *together*). 2. to move violently and swiftly. ***v.t.*** to throw with violence.
**hus·band** (huz′bənd), ***n.*** [< ON. *hūs*, house + *bondi*, freeholder], a married man. ***v.t.*** to manage economically.
**hus′band·man** (-mən), ***n.*** [*pl.* -MEN], [Archaic or Poetic], a farmer.
**hus′band·ry,** ***n.*** 1. careful, thrifty management. 2. farming.
**hush** (hush), ***v.t. & v.i.*** [< ME. *huscht*, quiet], 1. to make or become quiet or silent. 2. to soothe; lull. ***n.*** quiet; silence. ***interj.*** an exclamation calling for silence.
**husk** (husk), ***n.*** [prob. < MD. *huus*, house], 1. the dry outer covering of various fruits or seeds, as of corn. 2. any dry or useless covering. ***v.t.*** to remove the husk from.
**Hus·ky, hus·ky** (hus′ki), ***n.*** [*pl.* -KIES], [? < *Eskimo*], an Eskimo dog.
**husk′y,** ***adj.*** [-IER, -IEST], 1. dry in the throat; hoarse. 2. big and strong. **—husk′i·ly,** ***adv.*** **—husk′i·ness,** ***n.***
**hus·sar** (hoo-sär′), ***n.*** [< Serb. *husar*], a European light-armed cavalryman, usually with a brilliant dress uniform.
**hus·sy** (huz′i, hus′i), ***n.*** [*pl.* -SIES], [< ME. *huswife*, housewife], 1. a woman of low morals. 2. a saucy, pert girl.
**hus·tle** (hus′'l), ***v.t.*** [-TLED, -TLING], [D. *husselen*, shake up], 1. to push about; jostle. 2. to force in a rough, hurried manner. ***v.i.*** 1. to move hurriedly. 2. [Colloq.], to work energetically. ***n.*** 1. a hustling. 2. [Colloq.], energetic action. **—hus′tler,** ***n.***
**hut** (hut), ***n.*** [< OHG. *hutta*], a small, shedlike house or cabin. **—hut′like,** ***adj.***
**hutch** (huch), ***n.*** [< LL. *hutica*, chest], 1. a chest or cupboard. 2. a pen or coop for animals or poultry. 3. a hut.
**huz·za** (hə-zä′, hoo-), ***interj., n., v.t. & v.i.*** hurrah.
**hy·a·cinth** (hī′ə-sinth′), ***n.*** [< Gr. *hyakinthos*], a plant of the lily family, with spikes of bell-shaped flowers.
**hy·brid** (hī′brid), ***n.*** [L. *hybrida*, offspring of tame sow and wild boar], 1. the offspring of two animals or plants of different species, etc. 2. anything of mixed origin. ***adj.*** of or like a hybrid. **—hy′brid·ism,** ***n.***
**hy·brid·ize** (hī′bri-dīz′), ***v.t.*** [-IZED, -IZING], to produce or cause to produce hybrids; cross. **—hy′brid·i·za′tion,** ***n.***
**hy·dran·ge·a** (hī-drān′jə, -dran′ji-ə), ***n.*** [< *hydro-* + Gr. *angeion*, vessel], a shrub with large, showy clusters of white, blue, or pink flowers.
**hy·drant** (hī′drənt), ***n.*** [< Gr. *hydōr*, water], a large pipe with a valve for drawing water from a water main.
**hy·drate** (hī′drāt), ***n.*** [< *hydr*(o)- + *-ate*], a chemical compound of water and some other substance. ***v.t. & v.i.*** [-DRATED, -DRATING], to combine with water.
**hy·drau·lic** (hī-drô′lik), ***adj.*** [ult. < Gr. *hydōr*, water + *aulos*, tube], 1. of hydraulics. 2. operated by the movement and force of liquid, as a brake. **—hy·drau′li·cal·ly,** ***adv.***
**hy·drau′lics,** ***n.pl.*** [construed as sing.], the science dealing with the mechanical properties of liquids, as water, and their application in engineering.
**hydro-,** [< Gr. *hydōr*, water], a combining form meaning: 1. *water*, as in *hydrometer*. 2. *hydrogen*, as in *hydrocarbon*.
**hy·dro·car·bon** (hī′drə-kär′bən), ***n.*** any compound containing only hydrogen and carbon.
**hy·dro·chlo·ric** (hī′drə-klôr′ik), ***adj.*** designating or of an important commercial acid, produced by the combination of hydrogen and chlorine.
**hy·dro·e·lec·tric** (hī′drō-i-lek′trik), ***adj.*** producing, or relating to the production of, electricity by water power.
**hy·dro·gen** (hī′drə-jən), ***n.*** [see HYDRO- & -GEN], an inflammable, colorless, gaseous chemical element: the lightest known substance: symbol, H.
**hydrogen bomb,** an extremely destructive atomic bomb in which atoms of hydrogen are fused into helium by explosion of a nuclear-fission unit in the bomb.
**hydrogen peroxide,** an unstable liquid used as a bleach or disinfectant.
**hy·drol·y·sis** (hī-drol′ə-sis), ***n.*** [*pl.* -SES (-sēz′)], [*hydro-* + *-lysis*], a chemical reaction in which a compound reacts with the ions of water to produce a weak acid, a weak base, or both.
**hy·drom·e·ter** (hī-drom′ə-tẽr), ***n.*** [*hydro-* + *-meter*], an instrument for determining the specific gravity of liquids.
**hy·dro·pho·bi·a** (hī′drə-fō′bi-ə), ***n.*** [see HYDRO- & -PHOBIA], 1. an abnormal fear of water. 2. [from the symptomatic inability to swallow liquids], rabies (esp. in man).
**hy·dro·plane** (hī′drə-plān′), ***n.*** [*hydro-* + *plane*], 1. a small, flat-bottomed motorboat, capable of high speeds. 2. a seaplane.
**hy·dro·pon·ics** (hī′drə-pon′iks), ***n.pl.*** [construed as sing.], [< *hydro-* + Gr. *ponos*, labor], the science of growing plants in liquid mineral solutions.
**hy·dro·ther·a·py** (hī′drə-ther′ə-pi), ***n.*** [*hy-*

*dro-* + *therapy*], the treatment of disease by the internal or external use of water.

**hy·drous** (hī′drəs), *adj.* [< *hydr*(*o*)- + *-ous*], containing water, esp. in chemical combination.

**hy·drox·ide** (hī-drok′sīd, -sid), *n.* [< *hydr*(*o*)- + *oxide*], a compound consisting of an element or radical combined with the radical OH.

**hy·e·na** (hī-ē′nə), *n.* [< Gr. *hyaina*], a wolflike, flesh-eating animal of Africa and Asia, with a shrill cry.

**hy·giene** (hī′jēn), *n.* [< Gr. *hygiēs*, healthy], a system of principles for the preservation of health. **—hy′gi·en·ist** (-ji-ən-ist), *n.*

**hy·gi·en·ic** (hī′ji-en′ik, hī-jē′nik), *adj.* 1. of hygiene or health. 2. sanitary. **—hy′gi·en′i·cal·ly,** *adv.*

**Hy·men** (hī′mən), *n.* 1. the ancient Greek god of marriage. 2. [h-], *a*) marriage. *b*) a wedding song.

**hy·men** (hī′mən), *n.* [Gr. *hymēn*, skin], the thin mucous membrane that usually covers part of the opening of the vagina in a virgin.

**hy·me·ne·al** (hī′mə-nē′əl), *adj.* [see HYMEN], of a wedding or marriage.

**hymn** (him), *n.* [< Gr. *hymnos*], 1. a song in praise or honor of God. 2. any song of praise. *v.t.* & *v.i.* to praise in a hymn.

**hym·nal** (him′nəl), *n.* a collection of hymns: also **hymn′book′**.

**hyper-,** [Gr. < *hyper*], a prefix meaning *over, above, excessive.*

**hy·per·bo·la** (hī-pũr′bə-lə), *n.* [*pl.* -LAS], [< Gr. *hyper-*, over + *ballein*, to throw], a curve formed by the section of a cone cut by a plane that makes a greater angle with the base than the side of the cone makes.

**hy·per·bo·le** (hī-pũr′bə-li), *n.* [< Gr. *hyper-*, over + *ballein*, to throw], exaggeration for effect, not to be taken literally. **—hy·per·bol·ic** (hī′pẽr-bol′ik), *adj.*

**hy·per·crit·i·cal** (hī′pẽr-krit′i-k'l), *adj.* too critical.

**hy·per·sen·si·tive** (hī′pẽr-sen′sə-tiv), *adj.* excessively sensitive.**—hy′per·sen′si·tiv′i·ty,** *n.*

**hy·per·ten·sion** (hī′pẽr-ten′shən), *n.* abnormally high blood pressure.

**hy·per·thy·roid·ism** (hī′pẽr-thī′roid-iz'm), *n.* excessive activity of the thyroid gland, causing rapid pulse, sleeplessness, etc. **—hy′per·thy′roid,** *adj.* & *n.*

**hy·per·tro·phy** (hī-pũr′trə-fi), *n.* [< *hyper-* + Gr. *trophein*, to nourish], abnormal increase in the size of an organ or tissue. *v.i.* & *v.t.* [-PHIED, -PHYING], to increase abnormally in size.

**hy·phen** (hī′f'n), *n.* [< Gr. *hypo-*, under + *heis*, one], a mark (-) used between the parts of a compound word or the syllables of a divided word, as at the end of a line. *v.t.* to hyphenate.

**hy′phen·ate′** (-āt′), *v.t.* [-ATED, -ATING], to join or write with a hyphen.

**hyp·no·sis** (hip-nō′sis), *n.* [*pl.* -SES (-sēz)], [< Gr. *hypnos*, sleep; + *-osis*], a sleeplike condition psychically induced, in which the subject responds to the suggestions of the hypnotist.

**hyp·not·ic** (hip-not′ik), *adj.* 1. causing sleep; soporific. 2. of, like, or inducing hypnosis. 3. easily hypnotized. *n.* a drug causing sleep. **—hyp·not′i·cal·ly,** *adv.*

**hyp·no·tism** (hip′nə-tiz'm), *n.* the act or practice of inducing hypnosis. **—hyp′no·tist,** *n.*

**hyp·no·tize** (hip′nə-tīz′), *v.t.* [-TIZED, -TIZING], to induce hypnosis in.

**hypo-,** [< Gr. *hypo*, less than], a prefix meaning: 1. *under, beneath*, as in *hypodermic.* 2. *less than, deficient in*, as in *hypothyroid.*

**hy·po·chon·dri·a** (hī′pə-kon′dri-ə, hip′ə-), *n.* [LL. *pl.*, abdomen (supposed seat of this condition)], abnormal anxiety over one's health, often with imaginary illnesses.

**hy′po·chon′dri·ac′** (-ak′), *n.* one who has hypochondria.

**hy·poc·ri·sy** (hi-pok′rə-si), *n.* [*pl.* -SIES], [< Gr. *hypokrisis*, acting a part], a pretending to be what one is not, or to feel what one does not; esp., a pretense of virtue, etc.

**hyp·o·crite** (hip′ə-krit), *n.* [see HYPOCRISY], one who pretends to be pious, virtuous, etc., without really being so. **—hyp′o·crit′i·cal,** *adj.* **—hyp′o·crit′i·cal·ly,** *adv.*

**hy·po·der·mic** (hī′pə-dũr′mik), *adj.* [< *hypo-* + Gr. *derma*, skin], injected under the skin. *n.* 1. a hypodermic injection. 2. a hypodermic syringe or needle.

**hypodermic injection,** the injection of a medicine or drug under the skin.

**hypodermic syringe,** a glass syringe attached to a hollow needle (**hypodermic needle**), used for giving hypodermic injections.

**hy·pot·e·nuse** (hī-pot′'n-ōōs′, -ūs′), *n.* [< Gr. *hypo-*, under + *teinein*, stretch], the side of a right-angled triangle opposite the right angle: also **hy·poth′e·nuse′** (-poth′-).

**hy·poth·e·sis** (hī-poth′ə-sis, hi-), *n.* [*pl.* -SES (-sēz′)], [< Gr. *hypo-*, under + *tithenai*, to place], an unproved theory, etc. tentatively accepted to explain certain facts. **—hy·poth′e·size′** (-sīz′) [-SIZED, -SIZING], *v.i.* & *v.t.*

**hy·po·thet·i·cal** (hī′pə-thet′i-k'l), *adj.* based on a hypothesis; assumed; supposed: also **hy′po·thet′ic. —hy′po·thet′i·cal·ly,** *adv.*

**hy·po·thy·roid·ism** (hī′pō-thī′roid-iz'm), *n.* deficient activity of the thyroid gland, causing sluggishness, goiter, etc.**—hy′po·thy′roid,** *adj.* & *n.*

**hys·sop** (his′əp), *n.* [< Heb. *ēzōb*, aromatic plant], a fragrant, blue-flowered plant of the mint family.

**hys·ter·ec·to·my** (his′tẽr-ek′tə-mi), *n.* [*pl.* -MIES], [< Gr. *hystera*, uterus; + *-ectomy*], surgical removal of all or part of the uterus.

**hys·te·ri·a** (his-têr′i-ə, -ter′-), *n.* [< Gr. *hystera*, uterus: orig. attributed to disturbances of the uterus], 1. a psychiatric condition characterized by excitability, anxiety, the simulation of organic disorders, etc. 2. any outbreak of wild, uncontrolled excitement.

**hys·ter·ic** (his-ter′ik), *adj.* hysterical. *n.* 1. *usually pl.* [occas. construed as sing.], a hysterical fit. 2. a person subject to hysteria.

**hys·ter′i·cal,** *adj.* 1. of or like hysteria. 2. having or subject to hysteria.

# I

**I, i** (ī), *n.* [*pl.* I's, i's, Is, is], the ninth letter of the English alphabet.

**I** (ī), *n.* 1. a Roman numeral for 1. 2. in *chem., the symbol for* iodine.

**I** (ī), *pron.* [for *pl.* see WE], [AS. *ic*], the person speaking or writing.

**I., i.,** 1. island(s). 2. isle(s).

**-ial,** [L. *-ialis*], an adjective-forming suffix, as in *artificial.*

**i·amb** (ī′amb), *n.* iambic.

**i·am·bic** (ī-am′bik), *n.* [< Gr. *iambos*], 1. a metrical foot of two syllables, the first unaccented and the other accented. 2. an iambic verse. *adj.* in iambics.

**-iatrics,** [< Gr. *iatros*, physician], a combining form meaning *treatment of disease*, as in *geriatrics*.
**-iatry,** [< Gr. *iatreia*, healing], a combining form meaning *medical treatment*, as in *psychiatry*.
**i·bex** (ī′beks), *n.* [*pl.* IBEXES, IBICES (ib′ə-sēz′)], [L.], a wild goat of Europe, Asia, or Africa, with large, backward-curved horns.
‡**i·bi·dem** (i-bī′dem), *adv.* [L.], in the same place, i.e., the book, chapter, etc. cited just before: abbrev. **ibid., ib.**
**-ibility,** [*pl.* -TIES], [< L. *-ibilitas*], a suffix used to form nouns from adjectives ending in *-ible*, as in *sensibility*.
**i·bis** (ī′bis), *n.* [< Gr. *ibis*], a large wading bird related to the herons.
**-ible,** [L. *-ibilis*], -able, as in *legible*.
**-ic,** [< Gr. *-ikos*], a suffix meaning: 1. *of, having to do with*, as in *volcanic*. 2. *like*, as in *angelic*. 3. *produced by*, as in *photographic*. 4. *made up of, containing*, as in *alcoholic*.
**-ical,** a suffix corresponding to *-ic*, used to form adjectives, as in *physical, poetical*.
**ICBM,** intercontinental ballistic missile.
**I.C.C., ICC,** Interstate Commerce Commission.
**ice** (īs), *n.* [AS. *is*], 1. water frozen solid by cold. 2. a frozen dessert of fruit juice, sugar, etc. 3. [Slang], diamonds. *v.t.* [ICED, ICING], 1. to change into ice; freeze. 2. to cool with ice. 3. to cover with icing. *v.i.* to freeze (often with *up* or *over*). —**break the ice,** to make a start, as in getting acquainted. —**cut no ice,** [Colloq.], to have no influence.
**Ice.,** 1. Iceland. 2. Icelandic.
**ice age,** the glacial epoch.
**ice′berg′** (-bŭrg′), *n.* [prob. < D. *ijsberg*, lit., ice mountain], a great mass of ice broken off from a glacier and floating in the sea.
**ice′boat′,** *n.* 1. a light, often triangular frame, equipped with runners and propelled over ice by a sail. 2. an icebreaker.
**ice′bound′,** *adj.* 1. held fast by ice, as a boat. 2. blocked up by ice, as a coast.
**ice′box′** (-boks′), *n.* a refrigerator, esp. one in which ice is used.
**ice′break′er,** *n.* a sturdy boat for breaking a channel through ice.
**ice′cap′,** *n.* a large, permanent ice sheet with a raised center, as on a mountain top.
**ice cream,** a food made of cream or milk, sweetened, flavored, and frozen.
**ice field** (or **floe**), a large sheet of ice floating in the sea.
**Ice·lan·dic** (īs-lan′dik), *adj.* of Iceland, its people, etc. *n.* the Germanic language of the Icelanders.
**ice′man′** (-man′, -mən), *n.* [*pl.* -MEN], one who sells or delivers ice.
**ich·thy·ol·o·gy** (ik′thi-ol′ə-ji), *n.* [< Gr. *ichthys*, a fish; + *-logy*], the branch of zoology dealing with fishes. —**ich′thy·ol′o·gist,** *n.*
**i·ci·cle** (ī′si-k'l), [< AS. *is*, ice + *gicel*, piece of ice], a hanging piece of ice, formed when dripping water freezes.
**ic·ing** (īs′iŋ), *n.* a mixture of sugar, water, flavoring, whites of eggs, etc. for covering a cake; frosting.
**i·con** (ī′kon), *n.* [*pl.* ICONS, ICONES (ī′kə-nēz′)], [< Gr. *eikon*, image], 1. an image or picture. 2. in the *Orthodox Eastern Church*, a sacred image or picture of Jesus, Mary, etc. —**i·con′ic, i·con′i·cal,** *adj.*
**i·con·o·clast** (ī-kon′ə-klast′), *n.* [< Gr. *eikon*, image + *klaein*, to break], one who attacks venerated institutions or ideas. —**i·con′o·clasm,** *n.* —**i·con′o·clas′tic,** *adj.*
**-ics,** [see -IC], a suffix meaning (a specified) *art* or *science*, as in *physics*.
**i·cy** (ī′si), *adj.* [ICIER, ICIEST], 1. full of or covered with ice. 2. of ice. 3. like ice; slippery or very cold. 4. cold in manner; unfriendly. —**i′ci·ly,** *adv.* —**i′ci·ness,** *n.*
**id** (id), *n.* [L., it], in *psychoanalysis*, that part of the psyche which is the source of instinctive energy.
**I'd** (īd), 1. I had. 2. I would. 3. I should.
**i·de·a** (ī-dē′ə), *n.* [< Gr. *idea*, appearance of a thing], 1. a thought; mental conception or image. 2. an opinion or belief. 3. a plan; scheme. 4. a vague impression.
**i·de·al** (ī-dē′əl, ī-dēl′), *adj.* [see IDEA], 1. existing as an idea, model, etc. 2. thought of as perfect. 3. existing only in the mind; imaginary. 4. of idealism. *n.* 1. a conception of something in its most excellent form. 2. a perfect model. —**i·de′al·ness,** *n.*
**i·de′al·ism,** *n.* 1. behavior or thought based on a conception of things as one thinks they should be. 2. a striving to achieve one's ideals. 3. in *philos.*, any theory which holds that the objects of perception are actually ideas of the perceiving mind. —**i·de′al·ist,** *n.* —**i′de·al·is′tic,** *adj.* —**i′de·al·is′ti·cal·ly,** *adv.*
**i·de·al·ize** (ī-dē′ə-līz′), *v.t.* [-IZED, -IZING], to regard or show as perfect or more nearly perfect than is true. —**i·de′al·i·za′tion,** *n.*
**i·de′al·ly,** *adv.* 1. in an ideal manner; perfectly. 2. in theory or idea.
**i·den·ti·cal** (ī-den′ti-k'l), *adj.* [< L. *idem*, the same], 1. the very same. 2. exactly alike. —**i·den′ti·cal·ly,** *adv.*
**i·den·ti·fi·ca·tion** (ī-den′tə-fi-kā′shən), *n.* 1. an identifying or being identified. 2. anything by which one can be identified.
**i·den·ti·fy** (ī-den′tə-fī′), *v.t.* [-FIED, -FYING], 1. to make identical; treat as the same. 2. to show to be a certain person or thing. 3. to join or associate closely (*with*).
**i·den·ti·ty** (ī-den′tə-ti), *n.* [*pl.* -TIES], 1. the state or fact of being the same. 2. *a*) the state or fact of being some specific person or thing; individuality. *b*) the state of being as described.
**id·e·ol·o·gy** (ī′di-ol′ə-ji, id′i-), *n.* [*pl.* -GIES], [< Gr. *idea*, idea + *logos*, word], the doctrines, opinions, etc. of an individual, class, etc. —**id′e·o·log′i·cal** (-ə-loj′i-k'l), *adj.*
**ides** (īdz), *n.pl.* [< L. *idus*], in the ancient Roman calendar, the 15th day of March, May, July, or October, or the 13th of the other months.
**id·i·o·cy** (id′i-ə-si), *n.* [*pl.* -CIES], 1. the state of being an idiot. 2. great foolishness or stupidity.
**id·i·om** (id′i-əm), *n.* [< Gr. *idios*, one's own], 1. the dialect of a people, region, etc. 2. the usual way in which words of a language are joined together to express thought. 3. a conventional phrase or expression having a meaning different from the literal. 4. a characteristic style.
**id·i·o·mat·ic** (id′i-ə-mat′ik), *adj.* 1. characteristic of a particular language. 2. of, like, or using idioms. Also **id′i·o·mat′i·cal.**
**id·i·o·syn·cra·sy** (id′i-ə-siŋ′krə-si), *n.* [*pl.* -SIES], [< Gr. *idio-*, one's own + *synkrasis*, mixture], any personal peculiarity, mannerism, etc.
**id·i·ot** (id′i-ət), *n.* [< Gr. *idiōtēs*, ignorant person], 1. a person in the lowest grade of mental deficiency. 2. a very foolish or stupid person.
**id′i·ot′ic** (-ot′ik), *adj.* very foolish or stupid.
**i·dle** (ī′d'l), *adj.* [IDLER, IDLEST], [AS. *idel*, empty], 1. useless; futile. 2. unfounded: as *idle* rumors. 3. *a*) unemployed; not busy. *b*) inactive; not used. 4. lazy. *v.i.* [IDLED, IDLING], 1. to move slowly or aimlessly. 2. to be unemployed or inactive. 3. to operate slowly without transmitting power: said of machinery. *v.t.* 1. to squander (time). 2. to cause (a motor, etc.) to idle. —**i′dle·ness,** *n.* —**i′dler,** *n.* —**i′dly,** *adv.*

**i·dol** (ī'd'l), *n.* [< Gr. *eidōlon*, image], 1. an image of a god, used as an object of worship. 2. any object of ardent or excessive devotion.

**i·dol·a·try** (ī-dol'ə-tri), *n.* [*pl.* -TRIES], 1. worship of idols. 2. excessive devotion to or reverence for some person or thing. —**i·dol'a·ter,** *n.* —**i·dol'a·trous,** *adj.*

**i·dol·ize** (ī'd'l-īz'), *v.t.* [-IZED, -IZING], 1. to make an idol of. 2. to love or admire excessively. —**i'dol·i·za'tion,** *n.*

**i·dyl, i·dyll** (ī'd'l), *n.* [< Gr. *eidos*, a form], 1. a short poem or prose work describing a simple, pleasant scene of rural or pastoral life. 2. a scene suitable for such a work.

**i·dyl·lic** (ī-dil'ik), *adj.* pleasing and simple.

**i.e.,** *id est*, [L.], that is (to say).

**-ier,** [< L. *-arius*], a suffix meaning *a person concerned with* (a specified action or thing), as in *bombardier*.

**if** (if), *conj.* [AS. *gif*], 1. on condition that; in case that: as, *if* I come, I'll see him. 2. although: as, *if* I was wrong, at least I tried. 3. whether: as, I don't know *if* I can go. —**as if,** as it would be if.

**ig·loo** (ig'lōō), *n.* [*pl.* -LOOS], [Esk. *igdlu*], an Eskimo hut, dome-shaped and usually built of blocks of packed snow: also sp. **iglu.**

**ig·ne·ous** (ig'ni-əs), *adj.* [< L. *ignis*, a fire], 1. of fire. 2. produced by volcanic action of great heat: as, *igneous* rock.

**ig·nite** (ig-nīt'), *v.t.* [-NITED, -NITING], [< L. *ignis*, a fire], to set fire to. *v.i.* to catch on fire. —**ig·nit'a·ble, ig·nit'i·ble,** *adj.*

**ig·ni·tion** (ig-nish'ən), *n.* 1. an igniting or being ignited. 2. the electrical system for igniting the explosive mixture in the cylinder of an internal-combustion engine.

**ig·no·ble** (ig-nō'b'l), *adj.* [< L. *in-*, not + (*g*)*nobilis*, known], not noble; base; mean.

**ig·no·min·i·ous** (ig'nə-min'i-əs), *adj.* marked by ignominy; shameful, contemptible, humiliating, etc. —**ig'no·min'i·ous·ly,** *adv.*

**ig·no·min·y** (ig'nə-min'i), *n.* [*pl.* -IES], [< L. *in-*, without + *nomen*, name], loss of reputation; shame; disgrace.

**ig·no·ra·mus** (ig'nə-rā'mus), *n.* [*pl.* -MUSES], an ignorant person.

**ig·no·rance** (ig'nẽr-əns), *n.* a being ignorant; lack of knowledge.

**ig'no·rant,** *adj.* [see IGNORE], 1. lacking knowledge or experience. 2. caused by or showing lack of knowledge. 3. uninformed (*in*) or unaware (*of*). —**ig'no·rant·ly,** *adv.*

**ig·nore** (ig-nôr'), *v.t.* [-NORED, -NORING], [< L. *in-*, not + *gnarus*, knowing], to disregard deliberately; pay no attention to.

**i·gua·na** (i-gwä'nə), *n.* [< W. Ind.], a large tropical American lizard.

**il-,** in-: used before *l*.

**Il·i·ad** (il'i-əd), *n.* [< Gr. *Ilios*, Troy], a Greek epic poem, ascribed to Homer, about the Trojan War.

**-ility,** [< L. *-ilitas*], a suffix used to form nouns from adjectives ending in *-ile*, *-il*, *-able*, *-ible*.

**ilk** (ilk), *n.* [< AS. *ilca*, same], [Colloq.], a family; kind; sort. —**of that ilk,** of the same sort.

**ill** (il), *adj.* [WORSE, WORST], [< ON. *illr*], 1. bad: as, *ill* repute, *ill* will, an *ill* omen, etc. 2. not well; sick. *n.* an evil or disease. *adv.* [WORSE, WORST], 1. badly. 2. scarcely: as, I can *ill* afford it. —**ill at ease,** uncomfortable.

**I'll** (il), 1. I shall. 2. I will.

**ill'-bred',** *adj.* rude; impolite.

**il·le·gal** (i-lē'gəl), *adj.* prohibited by law; against the law. —**il·le·gal·i·ty** (il'ē-gal'ə-ti) [*pl.* -TIES], *n.* —**il·le'gal·ly,** *adv.*

**il·leg·i·ble** (i-lej'ə-b'l), *adj.* difficult or impossible to read because badly written or printed. —**il'leg·i·bil'i·ty,** *n.* —**il·leg'i·bly,** *adv.*

**il·le·git·i·mate** (il'i-jit'ə-mit), *adj.* 1. born of parents not married to each other. 2. contrary to law, rules, or logic. —**il'le·git'i·ma·cy** (-mə-si), *n.* —**il'le·git'i·mate·ly,** *adv.*

**ill'fat'ed,** *adj.* 1. certain to have an evil fate or unlucky end. 2. unlucky.

**ill'fa'vored,** *adj.* 1. ugly. 2. unpleasant.

**ill'got'ten,** *adj.* obtained by evil, unlawful, or dishonest means: as, *ill-gotten* gains.

**ill'-hu'mor,** *n.* a disagreeable or sullen mood: also **ill humor.** —**ill'-hu'mored,** *adj.*

**il·lib·er·al** (i-lib'ẽr-əl), *adj.* 1. without culture. 2. narrow-minded. 3. miserly; stingy.

**il·li·cit** (i-lis'it), *adj.* [< L. *illicitus*, not allowed], unlawful; improper. —**il·lic'it·ly,** *adv.*

**il·lim·it·a·ble** (i-lim'i-tə-b'l), *adj.* without limit; immeasurable; endless.

**il·lit·er·ate** (i-lit'ẽr-it), *adj.* uneducated; esp., unable to read or write. *n.* an illiterate person. —**il·lit'er·a·cy** (-ə-si), *n.*

**ill'-man'nered,** *adj.* having bad manners; rude; impolite. —**ill'-man'nered·ly,** *adv.*

**ill nature,** an unpleasant, disagreeable disposition. —**ill'-na'tured,** *adj.*

**ill'ness,** *n.* an unhealthy condition of the body or mind; sickness.

**il·log·i·cal** (i-loj'i-k'l), *adj.* not logical or reasonable. —**il·log'i·cal·ly,** *adv.*

**ill'-starred',** *adj.* unlucky.

**ill'-tem'pered,** *adj.* cross; sullen.

**ill'-timed',** *adj.* inappropriate.

**ill'-treat',** *v.t.* to treat unkindly, unfairly, etc. —**ill'-treat'ment,** *n.*

**il·lu·mi·nate** (i-lōō'mə-nāt'), *v.t.* [-NATED, -NATING], [< L. *in-*, in + *luminare*, to light], 1. to give light to; light up. 2. *a*) to make clear; explain. *b*) to inform. 3. to decorate, as with light. *v.i.* to light up.

**il·lu'mi·na'tion,** *n.* 1. an illuminating. 2. light; intensity of light.

**il·lu'mine** (-min), *v.t. & v.i.* [-MINED, -MINING], to light up.

**illus., illust.,** illustration.

**ill-us·age** (il'ūs'ij, -ūz'-), *n.* unfair, unkind, or cruel treatment: also **ill usage.**

**ill-use** (il'ūz'; *for n.*, -ūs'), *v.t.* to abuse. *n.* ill-usage.

**il·lu·sion** (i-lōō'zhən), *n.* [< L. *illudere*, to mock], 1. a false idea or conception. 2. an unreal or misleading appearance or image. —**il·lu'sive** (-siv), **il·lu'so·ry** (-sẽr-i), *adj.*

**il·lus·trate** (il'əs-trāt', i-lus'trāt), *v.t.* [-TRATED, -TRATING], [< L. *in-*, in + *lustrare*, illuminate], 1. to explain; make clear, as by examples, comparisons, etc. 2. to furnish (books, etc.) with explanatory or decorative pictures, etc. —**il'lus·tra'tor,** *n.*

**il'lus·tra'tion,** *n.* 1. an illustrating or being illustrated. 2. an example, etc. used to help explain. 3. a picture, diagram, etc. used to decorate or explain.

**il·lus·tra·tive** (i-lus'trə-tiv), *adj.* illustrating or tending to illustrate.

**il·lus·tri·ous** (i-lus'tri-əs), *adj.* [< L. *illustris*, bright], distinguished; famous.

**ill will,** hostility; hate; dislike.

**I'm** (īm), I am.

**im-,** in-: used before *b*, *m*, and *p*.

**im·age** (im'ij), *n.* [< L. *imago*], 1. a representation of a person or thing; esp., a statue. 2. the visual impression of something in a lens, mirror, etc. 3. a copy; likeness. 4. a mental picture; idea. 5. a figure of speech. *v.t.* [-AGED, -AGING], 1. to make a representation of. 2. to reflect. 3. to imagine.

**im·age·ry** (im'ij-ri), *n.* [*pl.* -RIES], 1. images generally; esp., statues. 2. mental images. 3. descriptions and figures of speech.

**im·ag·i·na·ble** (i-maj'i-nə-b'l), *adj.* that can be imagined. —**im·ag'i·na·bly,** *adv.*

**im·ag'i·nar'y** (-ner'i), *adj.* existing only in the imagination; unreal.

**im·ag'i·na'tion** (-nā'shən), *n.* 1. *a*) the act or power of forming mental images of what is not present. *b*) the act or power of creating new ideas as by combining previous experiences. 2. anything imagined. 3. an empty fancy.

**im·ag'i·na'tive** (-nā'tiv, -nə-tiv), *adj.* 1. having, using, or showing imagination. 2. of or resulting from imagination.

**im·ag·ine** (i-maj'in), *v.t.* & *v.i.* [-INED, -INING], [< L. *imago*, image], 1. to make a mental image (of); conceive in the mind. 2. to suppose; think.

**im·ag·ism** (im'əj-iz'm), *n.* a movement in modern poetry (c. 1912–1924) using precise, concrete images and extensive free verse.

**im·be·cile** (im'bə-s'l), *adj.* [< L. *imbecilis*, feeble], 1. feeble-minded. 2. very foolish or stupid. *n.* 1. a person in the second lowest grade of mental deficiency: cf. **idiot.** 2. a foolish or stupid person. **—im'be·cil'ic** (-sil'ik), *adj.* **—im'be·cil'i·ty,** *n.*

**im·bed** (im-bed'), *v.t.* [-BEDDED, -BEDDING], to embed.

**im·bibe** (im-bīb'), *v.t.* [-BIBED, -BIBING], [< L. *in-*, in + *bibere*, to drink], 1. to drink or drink in. 2. to absorb into the mind. *v.i.* to drink. **—im·bib'er,** *n.*

**im·bro·glio** (im-brōl'yō), *n.* [*pl.* -GLIOS], [It. < *broglio*, confusion], 1. an involved, confusing situation. 2. a confused misunderstanding.

**im·bue** (im-bū'), *v.t.* [-BUED, -BUING], [< L. *imbuere*], 1. to saturate. 2. to dye. 3. to fill (the mind, etc.).

**im·i·tate** (im'ə-tāt'), *v.t.* [-TATED, -TATING], [< L. *imitari*], 1. to try to be the same as. 2. to mimic. 3. to reproduce in form, color, etc. 4. to resemble. **—im'i·ta'tor,** *n.*

**im'i·ta'tion,** *n.* 1. an imitating. 2. the result of imitating; copy. *adj.* made to resemble something specified: as, *imitation* leather. **—im'i·ta'tive,** *adj.*

**im·mac·u·late** (i-mak'yoo-lit), *adj.* [< L. *in-*, not + *macula*, a spot], 1. perfectly clean. 2. without a flaw or error. 3. pure; innocent; sinless. **—im·mac'u·late·ly,** *adv.*

**im·ma·nent** (im'ə-nənt), *adj.* [< LL. *in-*, in + *manere*, remain], remaining within; inherent. **—im'ma·nence,** *n.*

**im·ma·te·ri·al** (im'ə-têr'i-əl), *adj.* 1. spiritual. 2. unimportant.

**im·ma·ture** (im'ə-tyoor', -choor'), *adj.* 1. not mature; not completely developed; not ripe. 2. not finished or perfected. **—im'ma·ture'ly,** *adv.* **—im'ma·tu'ri·ty,** *n.*

**im·meas·ur·a·ble** (i-mezh'ēr-ə-b'l), *adj.* that cannot be measured; boundless; vast. **—im·meas'ur·a·bly,** *adv.*

**im·me·di·ate** (i-mē'di-it), *adj.* [see IN- (not) & MEDIATE], 1. not separated in space or time; closest; nearest. 2. without delay; instant. 3. next in order. 4. directly or closely related. **—im·me'di·a·cy,** *n.*

**im·me·mo·ri·al** (im'ə-môr'i-əl), *adj.* extending back beyond the reach of memory or record; very old.

**im·mense** (i-mens'), *adj.* [< L. *in-*, not + *metiri*, to measure], very large; vast; huge.

**im·men'si·ty,** *n.* [*pl.* -TIES], 1. vastness. 2. infinite space or being.

**im·merse** (i-mũrs'), *v.t.* [-MERSED, -MERSING], [< L. *immergere*], 1. to plunge into or as if into a liquid. 2. to baptize by dipping under water. 3. to involve deeply; engross, as in thought. **—im·mer'sion,** *n.*

**im·mi·grant** (im'ə-grənt), *n.* one who immigrates. *adj.* immigrating.

**im·mi·grate** (im'ə-grāt'), *v.i.* [-GRATED, -GRATING], [see IN- (in) & MIGRATE], to come into a new country, etc. in order to settle there: cf. **emigrate.**

**im'mi·gra'tion,** *n.* 1. an immigrating. 2. the immigrants of a specified period.

**im·mi·nent** (im'ə-nənt), *adj.* [< L. *in-*, on + *minere*, to project], likely to happen without delay; impending. **—im'mi·nence,** *n.*

**im·mis·ci·ble** (i-mis'ə-b'l), *adj.* [*im-* (not) + *miscible*], that cannot be mixed or blended.

**im·mo·bile** (i-mō'b'l), *adj.* 1. firmly placed; stable. 2. motionless. **—im'mo·bil'i·ty,** *n.* **—im·mo'bi·lize'** (-īz') [-LIZED, -LIZING], *v.t.*

**im·mod·er·ate** (i-mod'ēr-it), *adj.* without restraint; excessive. **—im·mod'er·ate·ly,** *adv.*

**im·mod·est** (i-mod'ist), *adj.* 1. indecent; improper. 2. bold; impudent. **—im·mod'est·ly,** *adv.* **—im·mod'es·ty,** *n.*

**im·mo·late** (im'ə-lāt'), *v.t.* [-LATED, -LATING], [< L. *immolare*, sprinkle with sacrificial meal], to kill as a sacrifice. **—im'mo·la'tion,** *n.*

**im·mor·al** (i-môr'əl, i-mor'-), *adj.* not moral; esp., unchaste; lewd. **—im·mor'al·ly,** *adv.*

**im·mo·ral·i·ty** (im'ə-ral'ə-ti), *n.* 1. a being immoral. 2. [*pl.* -TIES], an immoral act; vice.

**im·mor·tal** (i-môr't'l), *adj.* 1. not mortal; living forever; enduring. 2. having lasting fame. *n.* an immortal being. **—im·mor·tal·i·ty** (im'ôr-tal'ə-ti), *n.*

**im·mor'tal·ize'** (-īz'), *v.t.* [-IZED, -IZING], to make immortal, as in fame.

**im·mov·a·ble** (i-mōōv'ə-b'l), *adj.* 1. firmly fixed. 2. unyielding.

**im·mune** (i-mūn'), *adj.* [< L. *in-*, without + *munus*, duty], exempt from or protected against something disagreeable or harmful; esp., protected against a disease, as by inoculation. **—im'mu·ni·za'tion,** *n.* **—im'mu·nize'** [-NIZED, -NIZING], *v.t.*

**im·mu·ni·ty** (i-mū'nə-ti), *n.* [*pl.* -TIES], 1. exemption from taxes, military service, etc. 2. resistance to a specified disease.

**im·mure** (i-myoor'), *v.t.* [-MURED, -MURING], [< L. *im-*, in + *murus*, wall], to shut up within walls; confine.

**im·mu·ta·ble** (i-mū'tə-b'l), *adj.* unchangeable. **—im·mu'ta·bly,** *adv.*

**imp** (imp), *n.* [< Gr. *em-*, in + *phyein*, to produce], 1. a young demon. 2. a mischievous child.

**im·pact** (im-pakt'), *v.t.* [< L. *impingere*, press firmly together], to force tightly together. *n.* (im'pakt), 1. a striking together. 2. the force of a collision; shock.

**im·pair** (im-pâr'), *v.t.* [< L. *in-*, intens. + *pejor*, worse], to make worse, less, etc.; damage. **—im·pair'ment,** *n.*

**im·pale** (im-pāl'), *v.t.* [-PALED, -PALING], [< L. *in-*, on + *palus*, pole], to pierce through with, or fix on, something pointed.

**im·pal·pa·ble** (im-pal'pə-b'l), *adj.* 1. not perceptible to the touch. 2. too subtle to be easily understood. **—im·pal'pa·bly,** *adv.*

**im·pan·el** (im-pan''l), *v.t.* [-ELED or -ELLED, -ELING or -ELLING], 1. to enter the name or names of on a jury list. 2. to choose (a jury) from such a list.

**im·part** (im-pärt'), *v.t.* [see IN- (in) & PART], 1. to give a share of; give. 2. to make known; reveal. **—im'par·ta'tion,** *n.*

**im·par·tial** (im-pär'shəl), *adj.* fair; just. **—im'par·ti·al'i·ty** (-shi-al'ə-ti), *n.*

**im·pass·a·ble** (im-pas'ə-b'l), *adj.* that cannot be passed or traveled over.

**im·passe** (im'pas, im-pas'), *n.* [Fr.], a situation from which there is no escape.

**im·pas·si·ble** (im-pas'ə-b'l), *adj.* [< L. *im-*, not + *pati*, suffer], 1. that cannot feel pain. 2. that cannot be aroused emotionally.

**im·pas·sioned** (im-pash'ənd), *adj.* passionate; fiery; ardent. **—im·pas'sioned·ly,** *adv.*

**im·pas·sive** (im-pas'iv), *adj.* 1. not feeling pain. 2. not feeling or showing emotion; calm; serene. **—im·pas'sive·ly,** *adv.*

**im·pa·tient** (im-pā'shənt), *adj.* lacking patience; specif., *a*) annoyed because of delay, opposition, etc. *b*) restlessly eager to do something, etc. **—im·pa'tience,** *n.*

**im·peach** (im-pēch'), *v.t.* [< L. *in-*, in + *pedica*, a fetter], 1. to discredit (a person's honor, etc.). 2. to bring (a public official) before the proper tribunal on a charge of wrongdoing. —**im·peach′ment,** *n.*

**im·pec·ca·ble** (im-pek′ə-b'l), *adj.* [< L. *in-*, not + *peccare*, to sin], without defect or error; flawless. —**im·pec'ca·bil′i·ty,** *n.*

**im·pe·cu·ni·ous** (im′pi-kū′ni-əs), *adj.* [< L. *in-*, not + *pecunia*, money], having no money. —**im′pe·cu′ni·os′i·ty** (-os′ə-ti), *n.*

**im·pede** (im-pēd′), *v.t.* [-PEDED, -PEDING], [< L. *in-*, in + *pes*, foot], to hinder progress of; obstruct. —**im·ped′ing·ly,** *adv.*

**im·ped·i·ment** (im-ped′ə-mənt), *n.* 1. an impeding. 2. anything that impedes; specif., a speech defect.

**im·pel** (im-pel′), *v.t.* [-PELLED, -PELLING], [< L. *in-*, on + *pellere*, to drive], 1. to drive or move forward. 2. to force, compel, or urge.

**im·pend** (im-pend′), *v.i.* [< L. *in-*, in + *pendere*, hang], 1. to hang (*over*). 2. to be about to happen. —**im·pend′ing,** *adj.*

**im·pen·e·tra·ble** (im-pen′i-trə-b'l), *adj.* 1. that cannot be penetrated. 2. that cannot be solved or understood. —**im·pen′a·tra·bil′i·ty,** *n.* —**im·pen′a·tra·bly,** *adv.*

**im·pen·i·tent** (im-pen′i-tənt), *adj.* not penitent; without regret, shame, or remorse.

**im·per·a·tive** (im-per′ə-tiv), *adj.* [< L. *imperare*, to order], 1. indicating authority or command. 2. necessary; urgent. 3. designating or of the mood of a verb that expresses a command, etc. *n.* a command.

**im·per·cep·ti·ble** (im′pĕr-sep′tə-b'l), *adj.* not easily perceived by the senses or the mind; very slight, subtle, etc. —**im′per·cep′ti·bly,** *adv.*

**im·per·fect** (im-pũr′fikt), *adj.* 1. not complete. 2. not perfect. 3 indicating a past action or state as incomplete or continuous: "was singing" is in the imperfect tense.

**im·per·fec·tion** (im′pĕr-fek′shən), *n.* 1. a being imperfect. 2. a defect; fault.

**im·per·fo·rate** (im-pũr′fĕr-it), *adj.* 1. having no openings. 2. having a straight edge without perforations, as a postage stamp.

**im·pe·ri·al** (im-pêr′i-əl), *adj.* [< L. *imperium*, empire], 1. of an empire, emperor, or empress. 2. having supreme authority. 3. majestic; magnificent. 4. of great size or superior quality. *n.* a small, pointed chin beard. —**im·pe′ri·al·ly,** *adv.*

**im·pe′ri·al·ism,** *n.* 1. imperial state, authority, or government. 2. the policy of forming and maintaining an empire, as by subjugating territories, establishing colonies, etc. —**im·pe′ri·al·ist,** *n.* & *adj.*

**im·per·il** (im-per′əl), *v.t.* [-ILED or -ILLED, -ILING or -ILLING], to put in peril; endanger.

**im·pe·ri·ous** (im-pêr′i-əs), *adj.* [< L. *imperium*, command], 1. overbearing; domineering. 2. urgent; imperative.

**im·per·ish·a·ble** (im-per′ish-ə-b'l), *adj.* not perishable; indestructible.

**im·per·me·a·ble** (im-pũr′mi-ə-b'l), *adj.* not permeable; not permitting passage, esp. of fluids. —**im·per′me·a·bil′i·ty,** *n.*

**im·per·son·al** (im-pũr′s'n-əl), *adj.* 1. without reference to any particular person: as, an *impersonal* attitude. 2. not existing as a person. 3. designating or of a verb occurring only in the third person singular, with *it* as the subject. —**im·per′son·al·ly,** *adv.*

**im·per·son·ate** (im-pũr′sə-nāt′), *v.t.* [-NATED, -NATING], to assume the role of, theatrically or fraudulently; mimic. —**im′per·son·a′tion,** *n.* —**im·per′son·a′tor,** *n.*

**im·per·ti·nent** (im-pũr′t'n-ənt), *adj.* 1. not pertinent. 2. impudent; insolent. —**im·per′ti·nence,** *n.*

**im·per·turb·a·ble** (im′pĕr-tũr′bə-b'l), *adj.* that cannot be perturbed; calm.

**im·per·vi·ous** (im-pũr′vi-əs), *adj.* 1. incapable of being penetrated, as by moisture. 2. not affected or influenced by (with *to*).

**im·pe·ti·go** (im′pi-tī′gō), *n.* [< L. *in-*, in + *petere*, to assault], a skin disease with eruption of pustules.

**im·pet·u·ous** (im-pech′o͞o-əs), *adj.* [see IMPETUS], acting suddenly and with little thought; impulsive. —**im′pet·u·os′i·ty** (-os′ə-ti) [*pl.* -TIES], *n.* —**im·pet′u·ous·ly,** *adv.*

**im·pe·tus** (im′pə-təs), *n.* [*pl.* -TUSES], [< L. *in-*, in + *petere*, rush at], 1. the force with which a body moves against resistance. 2. motivating force; incentive.

**im·pi·e·ty** (im-pī′ə-ti), *n.* 1. lack of reverence for God. 2. disrespect.

**im·pinge** (im-pinj′), *v.i.* [-PINGED, -PINGING], [< L. *in-*, in + *pangere*, to strike], 1. to strike, hit, etc. (*on* or *upon*). 2. to encroach (*on* or *upon*).

**im·pi·ous** (im′pi-əs), *adj.* not pious; lacking in reverence for God. —**im′pi·ous·ly,** *adv.*

**im·pla·ca·ble** (im-plā′kə-b'l, -plak′ə-), *adj.* not to be placated or appeased; relentless.

**im·plant** (im-plant′, -plänt′), *v.t.* 1. to plant firmly and deeply. 2. to fix firmly in the mind; instill. —**im′plan·ta′tion,** *n.*

**im·plau·si·ble** (im-plô′zə-b'l), *adj.* not plausible. —**im·plau′si·bly,** *adv.*

**im·ple·ment** (im′plə-mənt), *n.* [< L. *in-*, in + *plere*, to fill], something used in a given activity; tool, instrument, etc. *v.t.* (-ment′), 1. to fulfill; accomplish. 2. to provide with implements. —**im′ple·men·ta′tion,** *n.*

**im·pli·cate** (im′pli-kāt′), *v.t.* [-CATED, -CATING], [< L. *in-*, in + *plicare*, to fold], 1. to imply. 2. to show to be a party to a crime, etc. 3. to entangle.

**im′pli·ca′tion,** *n.* 1. an implying or being implied. 2. something implied, from which an inference may be drawn.

**im·plic·it** (im-plis′it), *adj.* [see IMPLICATE], 1. suggested though not plainly expressed; implied. 2. necessarily involved though not apparent; inherent. 3. without reservation; absolute. —**im·plic′it·ly,** *adv.*

**im·plore** (im-plôr′), *v.t.* [-PLORED, -PLORING], [< L. *in-*, intens. + *plorare*, cry out], 1. to ask earnestly for. 2. to beg (a person) to do something. —**im·plor′er,** *n.*

**im·ply** (im-plī′), *v.t.* [-PLIED, -PLYING], [< L. *implicare*, involve], 1. to have as a necessary part, condition, etc. 2. to indicate without saying openly; hint.

**im·po·lite** (im′pə-līt′), *adj.* not polite; ill-mannered; discourteous.

**im·pol·i·tic** (im-pol′ə-tik), *adj.* not politic; unwise. —**im·pol′i·tic·ly,** *adv.*

**im·pon·der·a·ble** (im-pon′dĕr-ə-b'l), *adj.* that cannot be weighed or measured. *n.* anything imponderable.

**im·port** (im-pôrt′), *v.t.* [< L. *in-*, in + *portare*, bring], 1. to bring (goods) into one country from another in commerce. 2. to mean; signify. *v.i.* to be of importance; matter. *n.* (im′pôrt), 1. something imported. 2. meaning; signification. 3. importance. —**im′por·ta′tion,** *n.* —**im·port′er,** *n.*

**im·por·tant** (im-pôr′t'nt), *adj.* [see IMPORT], 1. meaning a great deal; having much significance or consequence. 2. having, or acting as if having, power, authority, etc. —**im·por′tance,** *n.* —**im·por′tant·ly,** *adv.*

**im·por·tu·nate** (im-pôr′chə-nit), *adj.* persistent in asking or demanding.

**im·por·tune** (im′pôr-to͞on′, -tūn′), *v.t.* & *v.i.* [-TUNED, -TUNING], [< L. *importunus*, troublesome], to urge or entreat persistently and repeatedly. —**im′por·tu′ni·ty** [*pl.* -TIES], *n.* —**im′por·tune′ly,** *adv.*

**im·pose** (im-pōz′), *v.t.* [-POSED, -POSING], [see IN- (in) & POSE], 1. to place (a burden, tax, etc. *on* or *upon*). 2. to force (oneself) on others. —**impose on** (or **upon**), 1. to take advantage of. 2. to deceive; cheat.

**im·pos′ing,** *adj.* impressive because of great size, strength, dignity, etc.

**im'po·si'tion** (-pə-zish'ən), *n.* an imposing or imposing on; specif., a taking advantage of friendship.
**im·pos·si·ble** (im-pos'ə-b'l), *adj.* 1. not capable of being, being done, or happening. 2. [Colloq.], not capable of being endured, used, etc. because disagreeable or unsuitable. —**im·pos'si·bil'i·ty** [*pl.* -TIES], *n.* —**im·pos'si·bly,** *adv.*
**im·post** (im'pōst), *n.* [< L. *in-*, in + *ponere*, to place], a tax; esp., a duty on imports.
**im·pos·tor** (im-pos'tẽr), *n.* [see IMPOSE], one who deceives by pretending to be what he is not; cheat.
**im·pos'ture** (-chẽr), *n.* the act or practice of an impostor; fraud.
**im·po·tent** (im'pə-tənt), *adj.* 1. lacking physical strength. 2. ineffective; powerless. 3. unable to engage in sexual intercourse: said of males. —**im'po·tence, im'po·ten·cy,** *n.* —**im'po·tent·ly,** *adv.*
**im·pound** (im-pound'), *v.t.* 1. to shut up (an animal) in a pound. 2. to take into legal custody. —**im·pound'er,** *n.*
**im·pov·er·ish** (im-pov'ẽr-ish), *v.t.* [< L. *in*, in + *pauper*, poor], 1. to make poor. 2. to deprive of strength, resources, etc.
**im·prac·ti·ca·ble** (im-prak'ti-kə-b'l), *adj.* not capable of being carried out in practice.
**im·prac·ti·cal** (im-prak'ti-k'l), *adj.* not practical. —**im'prac·ti·cal'i·ty** [*pl.* -TIES], *n.*
**im·pre·cate** (im'pri-kāt'), *v.t.* [-CATED, -CATING], [< L. *in-*, on + *prex*, prayer], to invoke (evil, a curse, etc.). —**im'pre·ca'tion,** *n.*
**im·preg·na·ble** (im-preg'nə-b'l), *adj.* 1. that cannot be overcome or entered by force. 2. unyielding. —**im'preg·na·bil'i·ty,** *n.* —**im·preg'na·bly,** *adv.*
**im·preg·nate** (im-preg'nāt), *v.t.* [-NATED, -NATING], 1. to make pregnant; fertilize. 2. to saturate. 3. to imbue (with ideas, etc.). *adj.* impregnated. —**im·preg'na·ble,** *adj.* —**im'preg·na'tion,** *n.*
**im·pre·sa·ri·o** (im'pri-sä'ri-ō'), *n.* [*pl.* -OS], [It.], the manager of an opera, concert series, etc.
**im·press** (im-pres'), *v.t.* [*im-* (in) + *press* (force into service)], 1. to force into military service. 2. to seize for public use.
**im·press** (im-pres'), *v.t.* [see IN- (in) & PRESS (squeeze)], 1. to stamp; imprint. 2. to affect strongly the mind or emotions of. 3. to fix in the memory. *n.* (im'pres), 1. an impressing. 2. an imprint, etc.
**im·pres·sion** (im-presh'ən), *n.* 1. an impressing. 2. *a*) a mark, imprint, etc. *b*) an effect produced on the mind. 3. a vague notion.
**im·pres'sion·a·ble,** *adj.* easily impressed or influenced; sensitive.
**im·pres'sion·ism,** *n.* a theory of art, music, etc. whose aim is to reproduce the immediate, over-all impression. —**im·pres'sion·ist,** *adj.* & *n.* —**im·pres'sion·is'tic,** *adj.*
**im·pres·sive** (im-pres'iv), *adj.* tending to impress the mind or emotions.
**im·pri·ma·tur** (im'pri-mā'tẽr), *n.* [Mod. L., let it be printed], license to publish or print a book, article, etc.; esp., sanction given by the Roman Catholic Church.
**im·print** (im-print'), *v.t.* [< L. *im-*, in + *premere*, to press], to mark or fix as by pressing or stamping. *n.* (im'print), 1. a mark made by printing or pressing. 2. a characteristic effect. 3. a note in a book giving facts of its publication.
**im·pris·on** (im-priz''n), *v.t.* to put in or as in prison. —**im·pris'on·ment,** *n.*
**im·prob·a·ble** (im-prob'ə-b'l), *adj.* not probable; unlikely. —**im'prob·a·bil'i·ty,** *n.* —**im·prob'a·bly,** *adv.*
**im·promp·tu** (im-promp'tōō), *adj.* & *adv.* [< L. *in promptu*, in readiness], without preparation; offhand.
**im·prop·er** (im-prop'ẽr), *adj.* 1. not suitable; unfit. 2. incorrect. 3. contrary to good taste. —**im·prop'er·ly,** *adv.*
**im·pro·pri·e·ty** (im'prə-pri'ə-ti), *n.* [*pl.* -TIES], 1. a being improper. 2. an improper act, usage, etc.
**im·prove** (im-prōōv'), *v.t.* [-PROVED, -PROVING], [ult. < L. *in-*, in + *prodesse*, to profit], 1. to use (time) well. 2. to make better. 3. to add value to, as by cultivation. *v.i.* to become better. —**im·prov'a·ble,** *adj.*
**im·prove'ment,** *n.* 1. an improving or being improved. 2. a change that improves or adds value to something.
**im·prov·i·dent** (im-prov'ə-dənt), *adj.* lacking foresight or thrift. —**im·prov'i·dence,** *n.*
**im·pro·vise** (im'prə-vīz'), *v.t.* & *v.i.* [-VISED, -VISING], [< L. *in-*, not + *providere*, foresee], 1. to compose and perform without preparation. 2. to make or do with whatever is at hand. —**im'pro·vi·sa'tion,** *n.*
**im·pru·dent** (im-prōō'd'nt), *adj.* not prudent; rash. —**im·pru'dence,** *n.*
**im·pu·dent** (im'pyoo-dənt), *adj.* [< L. *in-*, not + *pudere*, feel shame], shamelessly bold; insolent. —**im'pu·dence,** *n.*
**im·pugn** (im-pūn'), *v.t.* [< L. *in-*, against + *pugnare*, to fight], to oppose as false.
**im·pulse** (im'puls), *n.* [see IMPEL], 1. *a*) a driving forward. *b*) an impelling force; impetus. *c*) the motion or effect of such a force. 2. *a*) incitement to action by a stimulus. *b*) a sudden inclination to act.
**im·pul·sive** (im-pul'siv), *adj.* 1. driving forward. 2. given to acting on impulse.
**im·pu·ni·ty** (im-pū'nə-ti), *n.* [< L. *in-*, without + *poena*, punishment], freedom from punishment, penalty, harm, etc.
**im·pure** (im-pyoor'), *adj.* 1. unclean; dirty. 2. immoral; obscene. 3. mixed with foreign matter; adulterated.
**im·pu'ri·ty,** *n.* 1. a being impure. 2. [*pl.* -TIES], an impure thing or part.
**im·pute** (im-pūt'), *v.t.* [-PUTED, -PUTING], [< L. *in-*, to + *putare*, to charge], to attribute (something, esp. a crime or fault) to another. —**im'pu·ta'tion** (-pyoo-tā'-shən), *n.*
**in-,** [L. *in-*], a prefix meaning *no, not, lacking.* The following list includes some common compounds formed with *in-* that do not have special meanings; they will be understood if *not* or *lack of* is used with the meaning of the base word.

**inability**
**inaccurate**
**inactive**
**inadequate**
**inadmissible**
**inadvisable**
**inapplicable**
**inappropriate**
**inartistic**
**inaudible**
**inauspicious**
**incapable**
**incautious**
**incombustible**
**incommensurable**
**incommensurate**
**incommodious**
**incommunicable**
**incomprehensible**
**inconceivable**
**inconclusive**
**incontrovertible**
**incorrect**
**incurable**
**indecipherable**
**indecorous**
**indefinable**
**indiscernible**
**indisputable**
**indistinct**
**indistinguishable**
**indivisible**
**inedible**
**ineffective**
**ineffectual**
**inefficacy**
**ineligible**
**inequality**
**inequitable**
**inequity**
**inessential**
**inexact**
**inexcusable**
**inexpressive**
**infertile**
**inharmonious**
**inhospitable**
**inhumane**
**inoperable**
**inopportune**
**inquietude**
**insensitive**
**inseparable**
**insobriety**
**insoluble**
**insolvable**
**insufficient**
**insurmountable**
**insusceptible**
**invariable**

**in-,** [< Eng. or L. *in*, in], a prefix used: 1. to mean *in, into, within, on, toward*, as in *infer, induct*. 2. as an intensifier, as in *instigate*.
**in** (in), *prep.* [AS.], 1. contained by: as, *in* the room. 2. wearing: as, *in* formal dress. 3. during: as, done *in* a day. 4. at the end of: as, due *in* an hour. 5. not beyond: as, *in* sight. 6. amidst: as, *in* a storm. 7. affected by: as, *in* trouble. 8. employed at: as, a man *in* business. 9. with regard to: as, *in* my opinion. 10. using: as, speak *in* French. 11. because of; for: as, he cried *in* pain. 12. into: as, come *in* the house. ***adv.*** 1. to the inside: as, he went *in*. 2. so as to be contained by a certain space, condition, etc. ***adj.*** 1. that is in power: as, the *in* group. 2. inner; inside. 3. [Colloq.], currently smart, popular, etc. ***n.*** 1. *usually in pl.* one that is in power. 2. [Colloq.], special access, favor, etc. **—have it in for,** [Colloq.], to hold a grudge against. **—ins and outs,** all the parts, details, and intricacies. **—in that,** because. **—in with,** associated with.
**-in,** a combining form used in forming words analogous to *sit-in* to describe similar demonstrations: as, *teach-in, be-in*.
**in.,** [*pl.* IN., INS.], inch; inches.
**in·ac·ces·si·ble** (in'ək-ses'ə-b'l), ***adj.*** 1. impossible to reach or enter. 2. that cannot be seen, talked to, etc.**—in'ac·ces'si·bly,** ***adv.***
**in·ad·vert·ent** (in'əd-vũr't'nt), ***adj.*** 1. not attentive; negligent. 2. due to oversight. **—in'ad·vert'ence,** ***n.*** **—in'ad·vert'ent·ly,** ***adv.***
**in·al·ien·a·ble** (in-āl'yən-ə-b'l), ***adj.*** [see ALIEN], that cannot be taken away or transferred. **—in·al'ien·a·bly,** ***adv.***
**in·am·o·ra·ta** (in-am'ə-rä'tə), ***n.*** [< It.], one's sweetheart or mistress.
**in·ane** (in-ān'), ***adj.*** [L. *inanis*], 1. empty. 2. lacking sense; silly. **—in·an·i·ty** (in-an'ə-ti), ***n.***
**in·an·i·mate** (in-an'ə-mit), ***adj.*** 1. not animate. 2. not animated; dull.
**in·ar·tic·u·late** (in'är-tik'yoo-lit), ***adj.*** 1. without the articulation of normal speech: as, an *inarticulate* cry. 2. unable to speak clearly or expressively.
**in·as·much** (in'əz-much'), ***conj.*** because; since (followed by *as*).
**in·at·ten·tion** (in'ə-ten'shən), ***n.*** failure to give attention; negligence. **—in'at·ten'tive,** ***adj.*** **—in'at·ten'tive·ly,** ***adv.***
**in·au·gu·ral** (in-ô'gyoo-rəl), ***adj.*** [Fr.], of an inauguration. ***n.*** a speech made at an inauguration.
**in·au·gu·rate** (in-ô'gyoo-rāt'), ***v.t.*** [-RATED, -RATING], [< L. *inaugurare*, to practice augury], 1. to induct into office with a formal ceremony. 2. to make a formal beginning of. **—in·au'gu·ra'tion,** ***n.***
**in·board** (in'bôrd'), ***adv. & adj.*** inside the hull of a ship or boat. ***n.*** a marine motor mounted inboard.
**in·born** (in'bôrn'), ***adj.*** present in the organism at birth; innate; natural.
**in·bred** (in'bred'), ***adj.*** 1. inborn; natural. 2. resulting from inbreeding.
**in·breed** (in'brēd', in'brēd'), ***v.t.*** [-BRED, -BREEDING], to breed by continual mating of individuals of the same or closely related stocks.
**inc.,** 1. inclosure. 2. inclusive. 3. incorporated: also **Inc.**
**In·ca** (iŋ'kə), ***n.*** a member of the highly civilized Indian people that dominated Peru until the Spanish conquest.
**in·cal·cu·la·ble** (in-kal'kyoo-lə-b'l), ***adj.*** 1. that cannot be calculated; too great or too many to be counted. 2. unpredictable.
**in·can·des·cent** (in'kən-des''nt), ***adj.*** [< L. *in-*, in + *candere*, to shine], 1. glowing with intense heat; red-hot or, esp., white-hot. 2. very bright. **—in'can·des'cence,** ***n.***
**in·can·ta·tion** (in'kan-tā'shən), ***n.*** [< L. *in-*, in + *cantare*, to chant], words chanted in magic spells or rites.
**in·ca·pac·i·tate** (in'kə-pas'ə-tāt'), ***v.t.*** [-TATED, -TATING], 1. to make unable or unfit; disable. 2. in *law*, to disqualify.
**in'ca·pac'i·ty** (-ti), ***n.*** [*pl.* -TIES], 1. lack of capacity, power, or fitness. 2. legal ineligibility.
**in·car·cer·ate** (in-kär'sə-rāt'), ***v.t.*** [-ATED, -ATING], [< L. *in-*, in + *carcer*, prison], to imprison. **—in·car'cer·a'tion,** ***n.***
**in·car·nate** (in-kär'nit), ***adj.*** [< L. *in-*, in + *caro*, flesh], endowed with a human body; personified. ***v.t.*** (-nāt), [-NATED, -NATING], 1. to give bodily form to; embody. 2. to be the type or embodiment of.
**in·cen·di·ar·y** (in-sen'di-er'i), ***adj.*** [< L. *incendium*, a fire], 1. having to do with willful destruction of property by fire. 2. designed to cause fires, as certain bombs. 3. willfully stirring up strife, riot, etc. ***n.*** [*pl.* -IES], 1. an arsonist. 2. one who willfully stirs up strife, riot, etc.
**in·cense** (in'sens), ***n.*** [see INCENSE (to anger)], 1. any substance burned to produce a pleasant odor. 2. the fragrance from this. 3. any pleasant odor.
**in·cense** (in-sens'), ***v.t.*** [-CENSED, -CENSING], [< L. *in-*, in + *candere*, to glow], to make very angry; enrage.
**in·cen·tive** (in-sen'tiv), ***adj.*** [< L. *in-*, on + *canere*, sing], stimulating to action. ***n.*** a stimulus; encouragement; motive.
**in·cep·tion** (in-sep'shən), ***n.*** [see INCIPIENT], a beginning; start.
**in·ces·sant** (in-ses''nt), ***adj.*** [< L. *in-*, not + *cessare*, cease], never ceasing; continuing without interruption; constant.
**in·cest** (in'sest), ***n.*** [< L. *in-*, not + *castus*, chaste], sexual intercourse between persons too closely related to marry legally. **—in·ces·tu·ous** (in-ses'choo-əs), ***adj.***
**inch** (inch), ***n.*** [< L. *uncia*, twelfth part], a measure of length, equal to 1/12 foot: symbol, ". ***v.t. & v.i.*** to move very slowly by degrees. **—within an inch of,** very near.
**in·cho·ate** (in-kō'it), ***adj.*** [< L. *inchoare*, begin], just begun; rudimentary.
**in·ci·dence** (in'si-dəns), ***n.*** the degree or range of occurrence or effect.
**in·ci·dent** (in'si-dənt), ***adj.*** [< L. *in-*, on + *cadere*, to fall], 1. likely to happen in connection with. 2. falling upon or affecting. ***n.*** something that happens; event.
**in'ci·den'tal** (-den't'l), ***adj.*** 1. happening in connection with something more important; casual. 2. secondary or minor. ***n.*** 1. something incidental. 2. *pl.* miscellaneous items.
**in'ci·den'tal·ly,** ***adv.*** 1. in an incidental manner; accidentally. 2. by the way.
**in·cin·er·ate** (in-sin'ə-rāt'), ***v.t. & v.i.*** [-ATED, -ATING], [< L. *in*, to + *cinis*, ashes], to burn to ashes; burn up. **—in·cin'er·a'tion,** ***n.***
**in·cin'er·a'tor,** ***n.*** a furnace for burning trash.
**in·cip·i·ent** (in-sip'i-ənt), ***adj.*** [< L. *in-*, on + *capere*, take], just beginning to exist or appear. **—in·cip'i·ence,** ***n.***
**in·cise** (in-sīz'), ***v.t.*** [-CISED, -CISING], [< L. *in-*, into + *caedere*, to cut], 1. to cut into with a sharp tool. 2. to engrave; carve.
**in·ci·sion** (in-sizh'ən), ***n.*** 1. an incising. 2. a cut; gash. 3. incisive quality.
**in·ci·sive** (in-sī'siv), ***adj.*** 1. cutting into. 2. sharp; piercing; acute: as, an *incisive* mind.
**in·ci·sor** (in-sī'zẽr), ***n.*** any of the front cutting teeth between the canines in either jaw.
**in·cite** (in-sīt'), ***v.t.*** [-CITED, -CITING], [< L. *in-*, on + *citare*, urge], to urge to action; rouse. **—in·cite'ment,** ***n.*** **—in·cit'er,** ***n.***
**in·clem·ent** (in-klem'ənt), ***adj.*** [< L. *in-*, not + *clemens*, lenient], 1. rough; stormy. 2. lacking mercy; harsh. **—in·clem'en·cy,** ***n.***

**in·cli·na·tion** (in'klə-nā'shən), *n.* 1. an inclining, bending, or sloping. 2. bend; slope. 3. *a*) a bias; tendency. *b*) a preference.
**in·cline** (in-klīn'), *v.i.* [-CLINED, -CLINING], [< L. *in-*, on + *clinare*, lean], 1. to lean; slope. 2. to have a tendency. 3. to have a preference or liking. *v.t.* 1. to cause to lean, slant, etc. 2. to make willing; influence. *n.* (in'klīn, in-klīn'), a slope; grade.
**in·close** (in-klōz'), *v.t.* [-CLOSED, -CLOSING], to enclose. —**in·clo'sure** (-klō'zhẽr), *n.*
**in·clude** (in-klōōd'), *v.t.* [-CLUDED, -CLUDING], [< L. *in-*, in + *claudere*, to close], 1. to enclose. 2. to have as part of a whole; contain. —**in·clu'sion** (-klōō'-zhən), *n.*
**in·clu'sive** (-klōō'siv), *adj.* 1. taking everything into account. 2. including the terms or limits mentioned: as, the first to the tenth *inclusive*. —**in·clu'sive·ly**, *adv.*
**in·cog·ni·to** (in-kog'ni-tō', in'kəg-nē'tō), *adv.* & *adj.* [< L. *in-*, not + *cognitus*, known], disguised under an assumed name, rank, etc. *n.* [*pl.* -TOS], 1. a person who is incognito. 2. *a*) the state of being incognito. *b*) the disguise assumed.
**in·co·her·ent** (in'kō-hêr'ənt), *adj.* 1. not logically connected; disjointed. 2. characterized by incoherent speech, etc. —**in'co·her'ence**, *n.* —**in'co·her'ent·ly**, *adv.*
**in·come** (in'kum), *n.* the money or other gain received for labor or services, or from property, investments, etc.
**income tax,** a tax on income or on that part of income which exceeds a certain amount.
**in'com'ing,** *adj.* coming in or about to come in.
**in·com·mode** (in'kə-mōd'), *v.t.* [-MODED, -MODING], [< L. *in-*, not + *commodus*, convenient], to inconvenience; put out; bother.
**in·com·mu·ni·ca·do** (in'kə-mū'ni-kä'dō), *adj.* [Sp.], not allowed to communicate with others.
**in·com·pa·ra·ble** (in-kom'pẽr-ə-b'l), *adj.* 1. having no basis of comparison. 2. beyond comparison; matchless.
**in·com·pat·i·ble** (in'kəm-pat'ə-b'l), *adj.* not compatible; specif., unable to live together harmoniously. —**in'com·pat'i·bil'i·ty**, *n.*
**in·com·pe·tent** (in-kom'pə-tənt), *adj.* without adequate ability, knowledge, fitness, etc. *n.* an incompetent person. —**in·com'pe·tence**, *n.* —**in·com'pe·tent·ly**, *adv.*
**in·com·plete** (in'kəm-plēt'), *adj.* 1. lacking a part or parts. 2. unfinished; not concluded. 3. not perfect.
**in·con·gru·ous** (in-koŋ'grōō-əs), *adj.* 1. lacking harmony or agreement of parts, etc. 2. unsuitable; inappropriate. —**in'con·gru'i·ty** (-kən-grōō'ə-ti), *n.*
**in·con·se·quen·tial** (in'kon-si-kwen'shəl), *adj.* of no consequence; unimportant.
**in·con·sid·er·a·ble** (in'kən-sid'er-ə-b'l), *adj.* trivial; small.
**in·con·sid·er·ate** (in'kən-sid'ẽr-it), *adj.* without thought or consideration for others.
**in·con·sist·ent** (in'kən-sis'tənt), *adj.* 1. not in harmony or accord. 2. self-contradictory: as, an *inconsistent* tale. 3. changeable. —**in'con·sist'en·cy** [*pl.* -CIES], *n.*
**in·con·sol·a·ble** (in'kən-sōl'ə-b'l), *adj.* that cannot be consoled. —**in'con·sol'a·bly**, *adv.*
**in·con·spic·u·ous** (in'kən-spik'ū-əs), *adj.* attracting little attention.
**in·con·stant** (in-kon'stənt), *adj.* not constant; changeable, fickle, irregular, etc.
**in·con·test·a·ble** (in'kən-tes'tə-b'l), *adj.* unquestionable; indisputable.
**in·con·ti·nent** (in-kon'tə-nənt), *adj.* without self-restraint, esp. in regard to sexual activity. —**in·con'ti·nence**, *n.*
**in·con·ven·ience** (in'kən-vēn'yəns), *n.* 1. lack of comfort, ease, etc. 2. anything inconvenient. *v.t.* [-IENCED, -IENCING], to cause inconvenience to; trouble; bother.
**in'con·ven'ient,** *adj.* not favorable to one's comfort; causing bother, etc.
**in·cor·po·rate** (in-kôr'pə-rāt'), *v.t.* [-RATED, -RATING], [see IN- (in) & CORPORATE], 1. to combine; include; embody. 2. to bring together into a single whole; merge. 3. to form into a corporation. *v.i.* to unite into one group or substance; form a corporation. —**in·cor'po·ra'tion**, *n.*
**in·cor·ri·gi·ble** (in-kôr'i-jə-b'l, -kor'-), *adj.* [see IN- (not) & CORRECT], that cannot be corrected or reformed, esp. because set in bad habits. —**in·cor'ri·gi·bil'i·ty**, *n.*
**in·cor·rupt·i·ble** (in'kə-rup'tə-b'l), *adj.* 1. that cannot be bribed. 2. not liable to decay or destruction. —**in'cor·rupt'i·bil'i·ty**, *n.*
**in·crease** (in-krēs'), *v.i.* [-CREASED, -CREASING], [< L. *in-*, in + *crescere*, grow], to become greater in size, amount, number, etc. *v.t.* to make greater in size, etc. *n.* (in'krēs), 1. an increasing or becoming increased. 2. the result or amount of an increasing. —**on the increase**, increasing.
**in·creas'ing·ly,** *adv.* more and more.
**in·cred·i·ble** (in-kred'ə-b'l), *adj.* not credible; seeming too unusual to be possible. —**in·cred'i·bil'i·ty**, *n.* —**in·cred'i·bly**, *adv.*
**in·cred·u·lous** (in-krej'oo-ləs), *adj.* 1. unwilling to believe; doubting. 2. showing doubt or disbelief. —**in·cre·du·li·ty** (in'krə-dōō'lə-ti, -dū'-), *n.* —**in·cred'u·lous·ly**, *adv.*
**in·cre·ment** (in'krə-mənt, iŋ'-), *n.* [< L. *incrementum*], 1. a becoming greater or larger; increase. 2. amount of increase.
**in·crim·i·nate** (in-krim'ə-nāt'), *v.t.* [-NATED, -NATING], [< L. *in-*, in + *crimen*, offense], 1. to accuse of a crime. 2. to involve in, or make appear guilty of, a crime or fault. —**in·crim'i·na'tion**, *n.*
**in·crust** (in-krust'), *v.t.* to cover as with a crust, or hard outer layer. *v.i.* to form into a crust. Also **encrust**. —**in'crus·ta'tion**, *n.*
**in·cu·bate** (in'kyoo-bāt'), *v.t.* [-BATED, -BATING], [< L. *in-*, on + *cubare*, to lie], 1. to sit on and hatch (eggs). 2. to keep (eggs, embryos, etc.) in a favorable environment for hatching or developing. —**in'cu·ba'tion**, *n.*
**in'cu·ba'tor,** *n.* 1. a heated container for hatching eggs. 2. a similar apparatus in which premature babies are kept for a period.
**in·cu·bus** (in'kyoo-bəs), *n.* [LL.], 1. a nightmare. 2. anything oppressive; burden.
**in·cul·cate** (in-kul'kāt, in'kul-kāt'), *v.t.* [-CATED, -CATING], [< L. *in-*, in + *calcare*, trample underfoot], to impress upon the mind, as by insistent urging. —**in'cul·ca'tion**, *n.*
**in·cul·pate** (in-kul'pāt, in'kul-pāt'), *v.t.* [-PATED, -PATING], [< L. *in-*, on + *culpa*, blame], to incriminate.
**in·cum·ben·cy** (in-kum'bən-si), *n.* [*pl.* -CIES], 1. a duty or obligation. 2. a term of office.
**in·cum·bent** (in-kum'bənt), *adj.* [< L. *in-*, on + *cubare*, lie down], resting (*on* or *upon* one) as a duty or obligation. *n.* the holder of an office, etc.
**in·cum·ber** (in-kum'bẽr), *v.t.* to encumber. —**in·cum'brance** (-brəns), *n.*
**in·cur** (in-kũr'), *v.t.* [-CURRED, -CURRING], [< L. *in-*, in + *currere*, to run], to meet with or bring upon oneself (something undesirable).
**in·cur·sion** (in-kũr'zhən), *n.* [see INCUR], an invasion or raid; inroad.
**Ind.,** 1. India. 2. Indian. 3. Indiana.
**ind.,** 1. independent. 2. index.
**in·debt·ed** (in-det'id), *adj.* 1. in debt. 2. obliged; owing gratitude.
**in·debt'ed·ness,** *n.* 1. a being indebted. 2. the amount owed; all one's debts.
**in·de·cent** (in-dē's'nt), *adj.* not decent; specif., *a*) improper. *b*) morally offensive. —**in·de'cen·cy**, *n.* —**in·de'cent·ly**, *adv.*

**in·de·ci·sion** (in′di-sizh′ən), *n.* inability to decide; vacillation.

**in′de·ci′sive** (-sī′siv), *adj.* 1. not decisive. 2. showing indecision.

**in·deed** (in-dēd′), *adv.* certainly; truly. *interj.* an exclamation of surprise, doubt, sarcasm, etc.

**in·de·fat·i·ga·ble** (in′di-fat′i-gə-b'l), *adj.* [< L. *in-*, not + *defatigare*, tire out], not tiring.

**in·de·fen·si·ble** (in′di-fen′sə-b'l), *adj.* 1. that cannot be defended. 2. that cannot be justified.

**in·def·i·nite** (in-def′ə-nit), *adj.* 1. having no exact limits. 2. not precise in meaning; vague. 3. not certain; unsure. 4. not clear in outline; blurred. 5. in *grammar*, not limiting or specifying: as, *a* and *an* are *indefinite* articles. —**in·def′i·nite·ly**, *adv.*

**in·del·i·ble** (in-del′ə-b'l), *adj.* [< L. *in-*, not + *delere*, destroy], 1. that cannot be erased, washed out, etc. 2. leaving an indelible mark. —**in·del′i·bly**, *adv.*

**in·del·i·cate** (in-del′i-kit), *adj.* lacking propriety or modesty; coarse. —**in·del′i·ca·cy** [*pl.* -CIES], *n.* —**in·del′i·cate·ly**, *adv.*

**in·dem·ni·fy** (in-dem′nə-fī′), *v.t.* [-FIED, -FYING], [< L. *indemnis*, unhurt; + *-fy*], 1. to insure against loss, damage, etc. 2. to repay for (loss or damage). —**in·dem′ni·fi·ca′tion**, *n.*

**in·dem′ni·ty**, *n.* [*pl.* -TIES], 1. insurance against loss, damage, etc. 2. repayment for loss, damage, etc.

**in·dent** (in-dent′), *v.t. & v.i.* [< L. *in*, in + *dens*, tooth], 1. to notch. 2. to make jagged in outline. 3. to space (the beginning of a paragraph, etc.) in from the regular margin. —**in′den·ta′tion**, *n.*

**in·den·ture** (in-den′chẽr), *n.* 1. a written contract. 2. *usually pl.* a contract binding one person to work for another. *v.t.* [-TURED, -TURING], to bind by indenture.

**in·de·pend·ence** (in′di-pen′dəns), *n.* a being independent; freedom from the control of another.

**Independence Day**, the Fourth of July, the anniversary of the American colonies' adoption of the Declaration of Independence on July 4, 1776.

**in·de·pend·ent** (in′di-pen′dənt), *adj.* 1. free from the influence or control of others; specif., *a*) self-governing. *b*) self-determined, self-reliant, etc. *c*) not connected with any political party. *d*) not connected with others: as, an *independent* grocer. 2. not depending on another for financial support. *n.* one who is independent in thinking, action, etc.

**in·de·scrib·a·ble** (in′di-skrīb′ə-b'l), *adj.* beyond the power of description.

**in·de·struct·i·ble** (in′di-struk′tə-b'l), *adj.* that cannot be destroyed.

**in·de·ter·mi·na·ble** (in′di-tũr′mi-nə-b'l), *adj.* that cannot be decided or ascertained.

**in·de·ter·mi·nate** (in′di-tũr′mə-nit), *adj.* 1. indefinite; vague. 2. unsettled; inconclusive. —**in′de·ter′mi·na′tion** (-nā′shən), *n.*

**in·dex** (in′deks), *n.* [*pl.* -DEXES, -DICES (-də-sēz′)], [L.; see INDICATE], 1. the forefinger: also **index finger**. 2. a pointer, as the needle on a dial. 3. an indication: as, an *index* of ability. 4. an alphabetical list of names, subjects, etc. indicating pages where found, as in a book. 5. a figure showing ratio or relative change. 6. [I-], in the *R.C. Church*, a list of books forbidden to be read. *v.t.* to make an index of or for.

**In·di·a ink** (in′di-ə), a black liquid ink.

**In′di·an**, *n.* 1. a native of India or the East Indies. 2. a member of any of the aboriginal races of the Americas: also **American Indian**. 3. any of the languages spoken by the American Indians. *adj.* 1. of India or the East Indies, their people, etc. 2. of the American Indians or their culture.

**Indian corn**, 1. a kind of grain that grows in kernels on large ears. 2. its ears. 3. its seeds or kernels.

**Indian summer**, mild, warm weather after the first frosts of late autumn.

**in·di·cate** (in′də-kāt′), *v.t.* [-CATED, -CATING], [< L. *in-*, in + *dicare*, declare], 1. to direct attention to; point out. 2. to be a sign of. 3. to show the need for. 4. to express briefly or generally. —**in′di·ca′tion**, *n.*

**in·dic·a·tive** (in-dik′ə-tiv), *adj.* 1. giving an indication. 2. designating that mood of a verb used to express an act, state, etc. as actual, or to ask a question. *n.* the indicative mood. Abbrev. **indic.**

**in′di·ca′tor**, *n.* a person or thing that indicates; specif., a gauge, dial, etc. that measures something.

**in·dict** (in-dīt′), *v.t.* [ult. < L. *in*, against + *dicere*, speak], to charge with a crime. —**in·dict′ment**, *n.*

**in·dif·fer·ent** (in-dif′ẽr-ənt), *adj.* 1. having or showing no bias; neutral. 2. unconcerned; apathetic. 3. of no importance. 4. fair; average. —**in·dif′fer·ence**, *n.*

**in·dig·e·nous** (in-dij′ə-nəs), *adj.* [< OL. *indu*, in + L. *gignere*, be born], born or growing naturally in a region or country; native.

**in·di·gent** (in′di-jənt), *adj.* [< OL. *indu*, in + *egere*, to need], poor; needy. —**in′di·gence**, *n.*

**in·di·gest·i·ble** (in′də-jes′tə-b'l), *adj.* not easily digested. —**in′di·gest′i·bil′i·ty**, *n.*

**in·di·ges·tion** (in′də-jes′chən), *n.* difficulty in digesting food.

**in·dig·nant** (in-dig′nənt), *adj.* [< L. *in-*, not + *dignus*, worthy], feeling or expressing anger, esp. at unjust or mean action.

**in·dig·na·tion** (in′dig-nā′shən), *n.* righteous anger.

**in·dig·ni·ty** (in-dig′nə-ti), *n.* [*pl.* -TIES], an insult or affront to one's dignity or self-respect.

**in·di·go** (in′di-gō′), *n.* [*pl.* -GOS, -GOES], [< Sp. *indico*, Indian], 1. a blue dye obtained from certain plants or made synthetically. 2. a deep violet-blue. *adj.* of this color.

**in·di·rect** (in′də-rekt′), *adj.* 1. not straight. 2. not straight to the point. 3. dishonest: as, *indirect* dealing. 4. not immediate; secondary: as, an *indirect* result.

**in′di·rec′tion**, *n.* 1. roundabout act, procedure, or means. 2. deceit; dishonesty.

**indirect object**, in *grammar*, the person or thing indirectly affected by the action of the verb (e.g., *us* in *give us time*).

**in·dis·creet** (in′dis-krēt′), *adj.* lacking prudence; unwise. —**in′dis·creet′ly**, *adv.*

**in′dis·cre′tion** (-kresh′ən), *n.* 1. lack of discretion. 2. an indiscreet act or remark.

**in·dis·crim·i·nate** (in′dis-krim′ə-nit), *adj.* 1. confused; random. 2. making no distinctions. —**in′dis·crim′i·nate·ly**, *adv.*

**in·dis·pen·sa·ble** (in′dis-pen′sə-b'l), *adj.* absolutely necessary.

**in·dis·posed** (in′dis-pōzd′), *adj.* 1. slightly ill. 2. unwilling; disinclined. —**in′dis·po·si′tion** (-pə-zish′ən), *n.*

**in·dis·sol·u·ble** (in′di-sol′yoo-b'l), *adj.* that cannot be dissolved or destroyed; lasting.

**in·dite** (in-dīt′), *v.t.* [-DITED, -DITING], [see INDICT], to compose and write.

**in·di·vid·u·al** (in′də-vij′oo-əl), *adj.* [< L. *individuus*, not divisible], 1. existing as a separate thing or being; single. 2. of, for, by, or characteristic of a single person or thing. *n.* 1. a single thing or being. 2. a person.

**in′di·vid′u·al·ism**, *n.* 1. the leading of one's life in one's own way. 2. individuality. 3. the doctrine that the state exists for the individual. —**in′di·vid′u·al·ist**, *n.* —**in′di·vid′u·al·is′tic**, *adj.*

**in′di·vid′u·al′i·ty** (-al′ə-ti), *n.* [*pl.* -TIES],

1. the sum of the characteristics that set one person or thing apart. 2. existence as an individual.

**in'di·vid'u·al·ize'** (-ə-līz'), *v.t.* [-IZED, -IZING], to consider individually; particularize.

**in'di·vid'u·al·ly,** *adv.* 1. as individuals; separately. 2. showing individual characteristics; distinctively.

**in·doc·tri·nate** (in-dok'tri-nāt'), *v.t.* [-NATED, -NATING], to instruct in doctrines, theories, beliefs, etc. —**in·doc'tri·na'tion,** *n.*

**In·do-Eu·ro·pe·an** (in'dō-yoor'ə-pē'ən), *adj.* designating a family of languages including most of those of Europe and some of those in Asia. *n.* this family of languages.

**in·do·lent** (in'də-lənt), *adj.* [< L. *in-*, not + *dolere*, feel pain], idle; lazy. —**in'do·lence,** *n.*

**in·dom·i·ta·ble** (in-dom'i-tə-b'l), *adj.* [< L. *in-*, not + *domere*, to tame], not easily discouraged or defeated.—**in·dom'i·ta·bly,** *adv.*

**in·door** (in'dôr'), *adj.* living, belonging, etc. in a building.

**in·doors** (in'dôrz'), *adv.* in or into a building.

**in·dorse** (in-dôrs'), *v.t.* [-DORSED, -DORSING], to endorse. —**in·dorse'ment,** *n.*

**in·du·bi·ta·ble** (in-dōō'bi-tə-b'l, in-dū'-), *adj.* that cannot be doubted; unquestionable. —**in·du'bi·ta·bly,** *adv.*

**in·duce** (in-dōōs', -dūs'), *v.t.* [-DUCED, -DUCING], [< L. *in-*, in + *ducere*, to lead], 1. to persuade. 2. to bring on: as, indigestion *induced* by overeating. 3. to draw (a conclusion) from particular facts. 4. to bring about (an electric or magnetic effect) in a body by placing it within a field of force.

**in·duce'ment,** *n.* 1. an inducing or being induced. 2. a motive; incentive.

**in·duct** (in-dukt'), *v.t.* [see INDUCE], 1. to bring in. 2. to place formally in an office, a society, etc. 3. to bring formally into the armed forces.

**in·duct·ee** (in-duk'tē'), *n.* one being inducted.

**in·duc·tion** (in-duk'shən), *n.* 1. an inducting or being inducted. 2. reasoning from particular facts to a general conclusion. 3. the inducing of an electric or magnetic effect by the influence of a field of force. —**in·duc'tive,** *adj.*

**in·due** (in-dōō', -dū'), *v.t.* [-DUED, -DUING], to endue.

**in·dulge** (in-dulj'), *v.t.* [-DULGED, -DULGING], [< L. *indulgere*, be kind to], 1. to satisfy (a desire). 2. to gratify the wishes of; humor. *v.i.* to give way to one's desires.

**in·dul·gence** (in-dul'jəns), *n.* 1. an indulging or being indulgent. 2. what is indulged in. 3. a favor or privilege. 4. in the *R.C. Church*, a remission of punishment still due for a sin after the guilt has been forgiven.

**in·dul'gent,** *adj.* indulging or inclined to indulge; kind or lenient, often to excess.

**in·du·rate** (in'doo-rāt', in'dyōō-), *v.t.* & *v.i.* [-RATED, -RATING], [< L. *in-*, in + *durus*, hard], 1. to harden. 2. to make or become callous or unfeeling.

**in·dus·tri·al** (in-dus'tri-əl), *adj.* 1. of, connected with, or resulting from industries. 2. of or concerned with people working in industries. —**in·dus'tri·al·ly,** *adv.*

**in·dus'tri·al·ism,** *n.* economic organization characterized by large industries, etc.

**in·dus'tri·al·ist,** *n.* one who owns or manages an industrial enterprise.

**in·dus'tri·al·ize'** (-īz'), *v.t.* [-IZED, -IZING], 1. to develop industrialism in. 2. to organize as an industry.

**in·dus·tri·ous** (in-dus'tri-əs), *adj.* characterized by earnest, steady effort; hardworking. —**in·dus'tri·ous·ly,** *adv.*

**in·dus·try** (in'dəs-tri), *n.* [*pl.* -TRIES], [< L. *industrius*, active], 1. earnest, steady effort. 2. any branch of trade, production, or manufacture, or all of these collectively. 3. the owners and managers of industry.

**-ine,** [< L. *-inus*], a suffix meaning *of, having the nature of, like*, as in *divine, crystalline.*

**-ine,** [< L. *-ina*], a suffix used to form certain abstract nouns, as in *medicine, doctrine.*

**-ine,** [< L. *-inus*], a suffix used to form the chemical names of: 1. *halogens*, as in *iodine*. 2. *alkaloids* or *nitrogen bases*, as in *morphine.*

**in·e·bri·ate** (in-ē'bri-āt'; *for n., usually* -it), *v.t.* [-ATED, -ATING], [ult. < L. *in-*, intens. + *ebrius*, drunk], to make drunk; intoxicate. *n.* a drunkard. —**in·e'bri·a'tion,** *n.*

**in·ef·fa·ble** (in-ef'ə-b'l), *adj.* [< L. *in-*, not + *effabilis*, utterable], inexpressible in words.

**in·ef·fi·cient** (in'ə-fish'ənt), *adj.* 1. not producing the desired effect with a minimum of energy, time, etc. 2. incapable. —**in'ef·fi'cien·cy,** *n.*

**in·ept** (in-ept'), *adj.* [< L. *in-*, not + *aptus*, fit], 1. unsuitable; unfit. 2. absurd. 3. awkward; clumsy. —**in·ept'ly,** *adv.*

**in·ept·i·tude** (in-ep'tə-tōōd', -tūd'), *n.* 1. a being inept. 2. an inept act, remark, etc.

**in·ert** (in-ũrt'), *adj.* [< L. *in-*, not + *ars*, skill], 1. without power to move or to resist. 2. inactive; dull; slow. 3. with few or no active properties. —**in·ert'ly,** *adv.*

**in·er·tia** (in-ũr'shə), *n.* [see INERT], 1. in *physics*, the tendency of matter to remain at rest (or continue in a fixed direction) unless affected by an outside force. 2. disinclination to move or act.

**in·es·cap·a·ble** (in'ə-skāp'ə-b'l), *adj.* that cannot be escaped. —**in'es·cap'a·bly,** *adv.*

**in·es·ti·ma·ble** (in-es'ti-mə-b'l), *adj.* too great to be properly estimated.

**in·ev·i·ta·ble** (in-ev'i-tə-b'l), *adj.* [< L. *in-*, not + *evitabilis*, avoidable], that cannot be avoided; certain to happen. —**in'ev·i·ta·bil'i·ty,** *n.* —**in·ev'i·ta·bly,** *adv.*

**in·ex·haust·i·ble** (in'ig-zôs'tə-b'l), *adj.* 1. that cannot be exhausted or used up. 2. tireless.

**in·ex·o·ra·ble** (in-ek'sẽr-ə-b'l), *adj.* [< L. *in-*, not + *exorare*, move by entreaty], that cannot be influenced by persuasion or entreaty; unrelenting. —**in·ex'o·ra·bly,** *adv.*

**in·ex·pen·sive** (in'ik-spen'siv), *adj.* not expensive; cheap. —**in'ex·pen'sive·ly,** *adv.*

**in·ex·pe·ri·ence** (in'ik-sper'i-əns), *n.* lack of experience or of the knowledge or skill resulting from experience. —**in'ex·pe'ri·enced,** *adj.*

**in·ex·pert** (in'ik-spũrt', in-ek'spẽrt), *adj.* not expert; unskillful. —**in'ex·pert'ly,** *adv.*

**in·ex·pi·a·ble** (in-ek'spi-ə-b'l), *adj.* that cannot be expiated or atoned for: as, an *inexpiable* sin. —**in·ex'pi·a·bly,** *adv.*

**in·ex·pli·ca·ble** (in-eks'pli-kə-b'l), *adj.* that cannot be explained. —**in·ex'pli·ca·bly,** *adv.*

**in·ex·press·i·ble** (in'iks-pres'ə-b'l), *adj.* that cannot be expressed.

**in·ex·tin·guish·a·ble** (in'ik-stiŋ'gwish-ə-b'l), *adj.* that cannot be put out or suppressed.

‡**in ex·tre·mis** (in iks-trē'mis), [L., in extremity], at the point of death.

**in·ex·tri·ca·ble** (in-eks'tri-kə-b'l), *adj.* 1. that one cannot extricate himself from. 2. that cannot be disentangled or untied. 3. insolvable. —**in·ex'tri·ca·bly,** *adv.*

**inf.,** 1. infantry. 2. infinitive.

**in·fal·li·ble** (in-fal'ə-b'l), *adj.* [see IN- (not) & FALLIBLE], 1. incapable of error. 2. not liable to fail, go wrong, etc.; reliable. —**in·fal'li·bil'i·ty,** *n.* —**in·fal'li·bly,** *adv.*

**in·fa·mous** (in'fə-məs), *adj.* 1. having a bad reputation; notorious. 2. causing a bad reputation; scandalous.

**in·fa·my** (in'fə-mi), *n.* [*pl.* -MIES], 1. very bad reputation; disgrace. 2. great wickedness. 3. an infamous act.

**in·fan·cy** (in′fən-si), *n.* [*pl.* -CIES], 1. the state or period of being an infant. 2. the earliest stage of anything.
**in·fant** (in′fənt), *n.* [< L. *in-*, not + *fari*, speak], a very young child; baby. *adj.* 1. of or for infants. 2. in a very early stage.
**in·fan·tile** (in′fən-tīl′, -til), *adj.* 1. of infants. 2. like an infant; babyish.
**infantile paralysis,** poliomyelitis.
**in·fan·try** (in′fən-tri), *n.* [*pl.* -TRIES], [< Sp. & Port. *infante*, a youth], that branch of an army consisting of soldiers trained to fight on foot. —**in′fan·try·man,** [*pl.* -MEN], *n.*
**in·fat·u·ate** (in-fach′ōō-āt′), *v.t.* [-ATED, -ATING], [< L. *in-*, intens. + *fatuus*, foolish], to inspire with unreasoning passion. —**in·fat′u·at′ed,** *adj.* —**in·fat′u·a′tion,** *n.*
**in·fect** (in-fekt′), *v.t.* [< L. *inficere*, to strain], 1. to contaminate, or cause to become diseased, with a germ or virus. 2. to imbue with one's feelings or beliefs, esp. so as to corrupt.
**in·fec·tion** (in-fek′shən), *n.* 1. an infecting or being infected. 2. an infectious disease.
**in·fec′tious** (-shəs), *adj.* 1. likely to cause infection. 2. designating a disease caused by the presence in the body of certain microorganisms. 3. tending to spread to others.
**in·fer** (in-fũr′), *v.t.* [-FERRED, -FERRING], [< L. *in-*, in + *ferre*, bring], 1. to conclude by reasoning from something known or assumed. 2. to imply: generally regarded as a loose usage. —**in′fer·ence,** *n.*
**in·fe·ri·or** (in-fêr′i-ẽr), *adj.* [< L. *inferus*, low], 1. lower in space. 2. lower in order, status, quality, etc. (with *to*). 3. poor in quality; below average. *n.* an inferior person or thing. —**in·fe′ri·or′i·ty** (-ôr′ə-ti), *n.*
**in·fer·nal** (in-fũr′n'l), *adj.* [< L. *inferus*, below], 1. of hell or Hades. 2. hellish; fiendish.
**in·fer·no** (in-fũr′nō), *n.* [*pl.* -NOS], [It. < L.; see INFERNAL], hell.
**in·fest** (in-fest′), *v.t.* [< L. *infestus*, hostile], to overrun in large numbers, usually so as to be harmful. —**in′fes·ta′tion,** *n.*
**in·fi·del** (in′fə-d'l), *adj.* [< L. *in-*, not + *fidelis*, faithful], 1. not believing in religion. 2. not believing in a certain, esp. the prevailing, religion. *n.* an infidel person.
**in·fi·del·i·ty** (in′fə-del′ə-ti), *n.* [*pl.* -TIES], unfaithfulness, esp. in marriage.
**in·field** (in′fēld′), *n.* 1. the square area enclosed by the four base lines on a baseball field. 2. the players (*infielders*) whose field positions are there.
**in·fil·trate** (in-fil′trāt, in′fil-trāt′), *v.t. & v.i.* [-TRATED, -TRATING], 1. to filter, or cause (a fluid) to filter, through. 2. to pass through, as in filtering. —**in′fil·tra′tion,** *n.*
**in·fi·nite** (in′fə-nit), *adj.* [see IN- (not) & FINITE], 1. lacking limits; endless; immeasurable. 2. very great; vast. *n.* that which is infinite. —**the Infinite (Being),** God.
**in·fin·i·tes·i·mal** (in′fin-ə-tes′ə-m'l), *adj.* [< L. *infinitus*, infinite], too small to be measured; very minute.
**in·fin·i·tive** (in-fin′ə-tiv), *n.* [see INFINITE], the form of a verb without reference to person, number, or tense: usually following *to*, as, *to go*.
**in·fin′i·tude′** (-tōōd′, -tūd′), *n.* 1. a being infinite. 2. an infinite quantity or extent.
**in·fin′i·ty** (-ti), *n.* [*pl.* -TIES], [< L. *infinitas*], 1. the quality of being infinite. 2. unlimited space, time, etc. 3. an indefinitely large quantity.
**in·firm** (in-fũrm′), *adj.* 1. weak; feeble. 2. not firm; unstable. —**in·firm′ly,** *adv.*
**in·fir·ma·ry** (in-fũr′mə-ri), *n.* [*pl.* -RIES], a place for the care of the sick, injured, etc.; hospital.
**in·fir·mi·ty** (-mə-ti), *n.* [*pl.* -TIES], 1. physical weakness or defect. 2. moral weakness.
**in·flame** (in-flām′), *v.t. & v.i.* [-FLAMED, -FLAMING], [see IN- (in) & FLAME], 1. to arouse, excite, etc. or become roused, excited, etc. 2. to undergo or cause to undergo inflammation. —**in·flam′er,** *n.*
**in·flam·ma·ble** (in-flam′ə-b'l), *adj.* 1. easily set on fire. 2. easily excited.
**in·flam·ma·tion** (in′flə-mā′shən), *n.* 1. an inflaming or being inflamed. 2. a diseased condition of a part of the body, characterized by redness, pain, heat, and swelling.
**in·flam·ma·to·ry** (in-flam′ə-tôr′i), *adj.* 1. rousing or likely to rouse excitement, anger, etc. 2. of or caused by inflammation.
**in·flate** (in-flāt′), *v.t.* [-FLATED, -FLATING], [< L. *in-*, in + *flare*, blow], 1. to blow full with air or gas. 2. to raise in spirits. 3. to increase, as prices, currency in circulation, etc. beyond normal. *v.i.* to become inflated. —**in·flat′a·ble,** *adj.*
**in·fla′tion,** *n.* 1. an inflating or being inflated. 2. an increase in the currency in circulation or a marked expansion of credit, resulting in a fall in currency value and a sharp rise in prices. —**in·fla′tion·ar′y,** *adj.*
**in·flect** (in-flekt′), *v.t.* [< L. *in-*, in + *flectere*, to bend], 1. to vary the tone of (the voice). 2. to change the form of (a word) by inflection.
**in·flec·tion** (in-flek′shən), *n.* 1. a change in the tone of the voice. 2. the change of form in a word to indicate number, case, gender, tense, etc. Also sp. **in·flex′ion.** —**in·flec′tion·al,** *adj.*
**in·flex·i·ble** (in-flek′sə-b'l), *adj.* 1. not flexible; specif., *a*) rigid. *b*) firm in mind; stubborn. 2. unalterable. —**in·flex′i·bil′i·ty,** *n.*
**in·flict** (in-flikt′), *v.t.* [< L. *in-*, against + *fligere*, to strike], 1. to cause (pain, wounds, etc.) as by striking. 2. to impose (a punishment, etc.). —**in·flic′tion** (-flik′shən), *n.*
**in·flu·ence** (in′flōō-əns), *n.* [< L. *in-*, in + *fluere*, to flow], 1. power to affect others. 2. power to produce effects because of wealth, position, ability, etc. 3. one that has influence. *v.t.* [-ENCED, -ENCING], to have influence or effect on.
**in′flu·en′tial** (-en′shəl), *adj.* exerting influence, esp. great influence.
**in·flu·en·za** (in′flōō-en′zə), *n.* [It., an influence], an acute, contagious virus infection, characterized by inflammation of the respiratory tract, fever, muscular pain, etc.
**in·flux** (in′fluks′), *n.* [see INFLUENCE], a flowing in.
**in·fold** (in-fōld′), *v.t.* 1. to wrap in folds; wrap up. 2. to embrace.
**in·form** (in-fôrm′), *v.t.* [see IN- (in) & FORM], to give knowledge of something to. *v.i.* to give information, esp. in accusing another. —**in·form′er,** *n.*
**in·for·mal** (in-fôr′m'l), *adj.* not formal; specif., *a*) not according to fixed customs, rules, etc. *b*) casual, relaxed, etc. *c*) not requiring formal dress. *d*) colloquial. —**in′for·mal′i·ty** (-mal′ə-ti), [*pl.* -TIES], *n.*
**in·form·ant** (in-fôr′mənt), *n.* a person who gives information.
**in·for·ma·tion** (in′fẽr-mā′shən), *n.* 1. an informing or being informed. 2. news; tidings. 3. knowledge acquired in any manner; data; facts. —**in′for·ma′tion·al,** *adj.*
**in·for·ma·tive** (in-fôr′mə-tiv), *adj.* giving information; instructive.
**infra-,** [< L.], a prefix meaning *below*.
**in·frac·tion** (in-frak′shən), *n.* [see IN- (in) & FRACTION], a violation of a law, pact, etc.
**in·fra·red** (in′frə-red′), *adj.* [*infra-* + *red*], designating or of those invisible rays just beyond the red of the visible spectrum: they have a penetrating heating effect.
**in·fre·quent** (in-frē′kwənt), *adj.* not frequent; happening seldom; rare. —**in·fre′quen·cy,** *n.* —**in·fre′quent·ly,** *adv.*
**in·fringe** (in-frinj′), *v.t.* [-FRINGED, -FRING-

ING], [< L. *in-*, in + *frangere*, to break], to break or violate (a law or pact). **—infringe on** (or **upon**), to encroach on (the rights, etc. of others). **—in·fringe′ment,** *n.*
**in·fu·ri·ate** (in-fyoor′i-āt′), *v.t.* [-ATED, -ATING], [< L. *in-*, in + *furia*, rage], to make very angry; enrage. **—in·fu′ri·a′tion,** *n.*
**in·fuse** (in-fūz′), *v.t.* [-FUSED, -FUSING], [< L. *in-*, in + *fundere*, pour], 1. to instill or impart (qualities, etc.). 2. to fill; inspire. 3. to steep, as tea, to extract certain qualities. **—in·fus′er,** *n.* **—in·fu′sion** (-fū′zhən), *n.*
**-ing,** [< AS.], a suffix used to form the present participle or verbal nouns, as *talking, painting*.
**in·gen·ious** (in-jēn′yəs), *adj.* [< L. *in-*, in + *gignere*, to produce], 1. clever, resourceful, etc. 2. cleverly or originally made or done.
**in·gé·nue** (an′zhi-nōō′), *n.* [Fr., ingenuous], the role of an inexperienced young woman in a play.
**in·ge·nu·i·ty** (in′jə-nōō′ə-ti), *n.* a being ingenious; cleverness, originality, etc.
**in·gen·u·ous** (in-jen′ū-əs), *adj.* [< L. *in-*, in + *gignere*, to produce], 1. frank; open. 2. simple; naive. **—in·gen′u·ous·ly,** *adv.*
**in·gest** (in-jest′), *v.t.* [< L. *in-*, into + *gerere*, carry], to take (food, etc.) into the body for digestion. **—in·ges′tion,** *n.*
**in·glo·ri·ous** (in-glôr′i-əs), *adj.* 1. shameful; disgraceful. 2. not famous.
**in·got** (iŋ′gət), *n.* [ME. < *in*, in + *goten*, poured], a mass of metal cast into a bar or other convenient shape.
**in·grained** (in-grānd′), *adv.* 1. worked into the grain; firmly established. 2. inveterate: as, an *ingrained* liar.
**in·grate** (in′grāt), *n.* an ungrateful person.
**in·gra·ti·ate** (in-grā′shi-āt′), *v.t.* [-ATED, -ATING], [< L. *in*, in + *gratia*, favor], to bring (oneself) into another's favor. **—in·gra′ti·at′ing·ly,** *adv.* **—in·gra′ti·a′tion,** *n.*
**in·grat·i·tude** (in-grat′ə-tōōd′), *n.* lack of gratitude; ungratefulness.
**in·gre·di·ent** (in-grē′di-ənt), *n.* [see INGRESS], any of the component parts of a mixture.
**in·gress** (in′gres), *n.* [< L. *in-*, into + *gradi*, go], 1. the right to enter. 2. an entrance.
**in·grown** (in′grōn′), *adj.* grown inward, esp. into the flesh, as a toenail.
**in·hab·it** (in-hab′it), *v.t.* [< L. *in-*, in + *habitare*, dwell], to live in.
**in·hab′it·ant,** *n.* a person or animal that inhabits a specified place.
**in·hal·ant** (in-hāl′ənt), *adj.* used in inhalation. *n.* a medicine to be inhaled.
**in·hale** (in-hāl′), *v.t. & v.i.* [-HALED, -HALING], [< L. *in-*, in + *halare*, breathe], to breathe in (air or smoke). **—in·ha·la·tion** (in′hə-lā′shən), *n.*
**in·here** (in-hêr′), *v.i.* [-HERED, -HERING], [< L. *in-*, in + *haerere*, to stick], to exist (*in*) as a quality, right, etc.
**in·her·ent** (in-hêr′ənt, -her′-), *adj.* [see INHERE], existing in someone or something as a natural and inseparable quality, right, etc. **—in·her′ence,** *n.* **—in·her′ent·ly,** *adv.*
**in·her·it** (in-her′it), *v.t. & v.i.* [ult. < L. *in*, in + *heres*, heir], 1. to receive (property) as an heir. 2. to have (certain characteristics) by heredity. **—in·her′i·tor,** *n.*
**in·her′it·ance,** *n.* 1. the action of inheriting. 2. something inherited or to be inherited; legacy. 3. right to inherit.
**in·hib·it** (in-hib′it), *v.t.* [< L. *in-*, in + *habere*, to hold], 1. to forbid. 2. to restrain; suppress; check.
**in·hi·bi·tion** (in′hi-bish′ən, in′i-), *n.* 1. an inhibiting or being inhibited. 2. a mental process that restrains an action, emotion, or thought.
**in·hu·man** (in-hū′mən), *adj.* not having normal human characteristics; esp., cruel, brutal, etc. **—in′hu·man′i·ty** (-man′ə-ti), *n.*
**in·im·i·cal** (in-im′i-k'l), *adj.* [< L. *in-*, not + *amicus*, friend], 1. hostile; unfriendly. 2. in opposition; adverse.
**in·im·i·ta·ble** (in-im′i-tə-b'l), *adj.* that cannot be imitated; matchless.
**in·iq·ui·ty** (in-ik′wə-ti), *n.* [< L. *in-*, not + *aequus*, equal], 1. wickedness; sin. 2. [*pl.* -TIES], a wicked or unjust act. **—in·iq′ui·tous,** *adj.* **—in·iq′ui·tous·ly,** *adv.*
**in·i·tial** (i-nish′əl), *adj.* [< L. *in-*, in + *ire*, go], of or at the beginning; first. *n.* the first letter of a name. *v.t.* [-TIALED or -TIALLED, -TIALING or -TIALLING], to mark with (one's) initials. **—in·i′tial·ly,** *adv.*
**Initial Teaching Alphabet,** an alphabet of 44 characters devised by Sir James Pitman (1901– ) of England, for teaching beginners to read English: abbrev. **i/t/a, I.T.A.**
**in·i·ti·ate** (i-nish′i-āt′), *v.t.* [-ATED, -ATING], [see INITIAL], 1. to bring into practice or use. 2. to teach the fundamentals of a subject to. 3. to admit as a member into a fraternity, club, etc., as by secret ceremony. **—in·i′ti·a′tor,** *n.* **—in·i′ti·a′tion,** *n.*
**in·i·ti·a·tive** (i-nish′i-ə-tiv), *n.* 1. the action of taking the first step or move. 2. ability in originating new ideas or methods. 3. the introduction of proposed legislation, as to popular vote, by voters' petitions.
**in·ject** (in-jekt′), *v.t.* [< L. *in-*, in + *jacere*, throw], 1. to force (a fluid) as into a vein, tissue, etc. by means of a syringe, etc. 2. to introduce (a remark, etc.). **—in·jec′tion,** *n.*
**in·junc·tion** (in-juŋk′shən), *n.* [see IN- (in) & JUNCTION], 1. a command; order. 2. a court order prohibiting, or ordering, a given action.
**in·jure** (in′jēr), *v.t.* [-JURED, -JURING], 1. to do physical harm to; hurt. 2. to wrong or offend. **—in′jur·er,** *n.*
**in·ju·ri·ous** (in-joor′i-əs), *adj.* injuring or likely to injure; harmful.
**in·ju·ry** (in′jēr-i), *n.* [*pl.* -RIES], [< L. *in-*, not + *jus*, right], 1. physical harm. 2. unjust treatment; wrong. 3. an injurious act.
**in·jus·tice** (in-jus′tis), *n.* 1. a being unjust. 2. an unjust act; injury.
**ink** (iŋk), *n.* [< Gr. *enkauston*, red ink], a colored liquid used for writing, printing, etc. *v.t.* to cover, mark, or color with ink.
**ink·ling** (iŋk′liŋ), *n.* 1. a hint; suggestion. 2. a vague notion.
**ink′well′,** *n.* a container for ink.
**ink′y,** *adj.* [-IER, -IEST], 1. like ink in color; dark; black. 2. covered with ink.
**in·laid** (in′lād′, in-lād′), pt. and pp. of **inlay.** *adj.* set in a surface as a decoration.
**in·land** (in′lənd), *adj.* of, located in, or confined to the interior of a country. *n.* (*also* -land′), the interior of a country. *adv.* (*also* -land′), into or toward the interior.
**in-law** (in′lô′), *n.* [< *mother-in-law*, etc.], [Colloq.], a relative by marriage.
**in·lay** (in-lā′, in′lā′), *v.t.* [-LAID, -LAYING], 1. to set (pieces of wood, etc.) in a surface to form a decoration. 2. to decorate thus. *n.* (in′lā′), [*pl.* -LAYS], 1. inlaid decoration or material. 2. a filling of metal, etc. cemented into a cavity in a tooth.
**in·let** (in′let), *n.* a narrow strip of water extending into a body of land.
**in·mate** (in′māt′), *n.* a person confined with others in an institution, hospital, etc.
**in·most** (in′mōst′), *adj.* 1. located farthest within; innermost. 2. most secret.
**inn** (in), *n.* [AS., lodging], 1. a small hotel. 2. a restaurant or tavern.
**in·nate** (in′āt, i-nāt′), *adj.* [< L. *in-*, in + *nasci*, be born], inborn; natural; not acquired. **—in·nate′ly,** *adv.*
**in·ner** (in′ēr), *adj.* 1. located farther within; interior. 2. more intimate or secret: as,

*inner* emotions. 3. of the mind or spirit.
**in′ner·most′,** *adj.* inmost.
**in·ning** (in′iŋ), *n.* [< AS. *innung*, getting in], in *baseball*, etc., 1. a team's turn at bat. 2. a numbered round of play in which both teams have a turn at bat.
**inn′keep′er,** *n.* the owner of an inn.
**in·no·cent** (in′ə-s'nt), *adj.* [< L. *in-*, not + *nocere*, do wrong to], 1. free from sin, evil, etc.; specif., not guilty of a specific crime. 2. harmless. 3. knowing no evil. 4. without guile or cunning; artless. *n.* an innocent person, as a child. **—in′no·cence,** *n.*
**in·noc·u·ous** (i-nok′ū-əs), *adj.* [< L. *in-*, not + *nocere*, harm], harmless.
**in′no·va′tion** (-vā′shən), *n.* [< L. *in-*, in + *novus*, new], 1. the process of making changes. 2. a new method, custom, device, etc. **—in′no·va′tor,** *n.*
**in·nu·en·do** (in′ū-en′dō), *n.* [*pl.* -DOES], [< L. *in-*, in + *-nuere*, to nod], an indirect remark, gesture, etc., usually disparaging.
**in·nu·mer·a·ble** (i-nōō′mẽr-ə-b'l), *adj.* too numerous to be counted.
**in·oc·u·late** (in-ok′yoo-lāt′), *v.t.* [-LATED, -LATING], [< L. *in-*, in + *oculus*, eye], to inject a serum into, esp. in order to make immune by causing a mild form of the disease. **—in·oc′u·la′tion,** *n.* **—in·oc′u·la′tor,** *n.*
**in·of·fen·sive** (in′ə-fen′siv), *adj.* causing no harm or annoyance; unobjectionable.
**in·op·er·a·tive** (in-op′ə-rā′tiv, -ẽr-ə-tiv), *adj.* not working or functioning.
**in·or·di·nate** (in-ôr′d'n-it), *adj.* [< L. *in-*, not + *ordo*, an order], excessive; immoderate. **—in·or′di·nate·ly,** *adv.*
**in·or·gan·ic** (in′ôr-gan′ik), *adj.* not organic; specif., designating or of matter not animal or vegetable; not living.
**in·put** (in′poot′), *n.* what is put in, as power put into a machine.
**in·quest** (in′kwest), *n.* [see INQUIRE], a judicial inquiry, esp. when held before a jury, as a coroner's investigation of a death.
**in·quire** (in-kwīr′), *v.i.* [-QUIRED, -QUIRING], [< L. *in-*, into + *quaerere*, seek], 1. to ask a question or questions. 2. to investigate (often with *into*). *v.t.* to seek information about. **—in·quir′er,** *n.* **—in·quir′ing·ly,** *adv.*
**in·quir·y** (in-kwīr′i, in′kwə-ri), *n.* [*pl.* -IES], 1. an inquiring; investigation. 2. a question.
**in·qui·si·tion** (in′kwə-zish′ən), *n.* 1. an inquiry or investigation. 2. [I-], in the *R.C. Church*, the tribunal for suppressing heresy and heretics. 3. any arbitrary suppression of nonconformity.
**in·quis·i·tive** (in-kwiz′ə-tiv), *adj.* 1. inclined to ask many questions. 2. unnecessarily curious; prying. **—in·quis′i·tive·ness,** *n.*
**in·quis′i·tor,** *n.* 1. an investigator. 2. [I-], an official of the Inquisition. **—in·quis′i·to′ri·al** (-tôr′i-əl), *adj.*
‡**in re** (in rē′), [L.], in the matter (of).
**in·road** (in′rōd′), *n.* 1. a raid. 2. *usually in pl.* any injurious encroachment.
**in′rush′,** *n.* a rushing in.
**in·sane** (in-sān′), *adj.* 1. mentally ill or deranged; crazy. 2. of or for insane people. 3. very foolish; senseless. **—in·san′i·ty** (-san′ə-ti), [*pl.* -TIES], *n.* **—in·sane′ly,** *adv*
**in·sa·ti·a·ble** (in-sā′shə-b'l, -shi-ə-b'l), *adj.* that cannot be satisfied. **—in·sa′ti·a·bly,** *adv.*
**in·scribe** (in-skrīb′), *v.t.* [-SCRIBED, -SCRIBING], [< L. *in-*, in + *scribere*, write], 1. to mark or engrave (words, symbols, etc.) on (a surface). 2. to add (a person's name) to a list. 3. to fix in the mind.
**in·scrip′tion** (-skrip′shən), *n.* 1. an inscribing. 2. something inscribed.
**in·scru·ta·ble** (in-skrōō′tə-b'l), *adj.* [< L. *in-*, not + *scrutari*, example], that cannot be learned or understood; enigmatic.**—in·scru′ta·bil′i·ty,** *n.* **—in·scru′ta·bly,** *adv.*
**in·sect** (in′sekt), *n.* [L. *insectum*], any of a large group of small, often winged, invertebrates, as beetles, flies, wasps, etc., having three pairs of legs.
**in·sec′ti·cide′** (-sek′tə-sīd′), *n.* [see INSECT & -CIDE], any substance used to kill insects.
**in′sec·tiv′o·rous** (-tiv′ẽr-əs), *adj.* [< *insect* + L. *vorare*, devour], feeding chiefly on insects. **—in·sec′ti·vore′** (-tə-vôr′), *n.*
**in·se·cure** (in′si-kyoor′), *adj.* 1. not safe; unprotected. 2. feeling anxiety. 3. not firm or dependable. **—in′se·cu′ri·ty,** *n.*
**in·sem·i·nate** (in-sem′ə-nāt′), *v.t.* [-NATED, -NATING], [< L. *in-*, in + *semen*, seed], 1. to impregnate with semen. 2. to sow seeds in. **—in·sem′i·na′tion,** *n.*
**in·sen·sate** (in-sen′sāt, -sit), *adj.* 1. not feeling sensation. 2. stupid. 3. without regard or feeling; cold. **—in·sen′sate·ly,** *adv.*
**in·sen·si·ble** (in-sen′sə-b'l), *adj.* 1. unable to perceive with the senses. 2. unconscious. 3. unaware; indifferent. 4. so slight as to be virtually imperceptible. **—in·sen′si·bil′i·ty,** *n.* **—in·sen′si·bly,** *adv.*
**in·sert** (in-sũrt′), *v.t.* [< L. *in-*, into + *serere*, join], to put or fit (something) into something else. *n.* (in′sẽrt), anything inserted or to be inserted. **—in·ser′tion,** *n.*
**in·set** (in-set′; *for n.*, in′set′), *v.t.* [-SET, -SETTING], to set in; insert. *n.* something inserted.
**in·side** (in′sīd′), *n.* 1. the inner side, surface, or part. 2. *pl.* [Colloq.], the viscera. *adj.* 1. internal. 2. known only to insiders; secret. *adv.* 1. on or in the inside; within. 2. indoors. *prep.* (in′sīd′), inside of; in.
**in′sid′er,** *n.* 1. a person inside a given place or group. 2. one having secret or confidential information.
**in·sid·i·ous** (in-sid′i-əs), *adj.* [< L. *insidiae*, an ambush], 1. characterized by treachery or slyness. 2. more dangerous than seems evident. **—in·sid′i·ous·ly,** *adv.*
**in·sight** (in′sīt′), *n.* 1. the ability to see and understand clearly the inner nature of things; intuition. 2. an instance of this.
**in·sig·ni·a** (in-sig′ni-ə), *n.pl.* [*sing.* -NE (-nē)], [ult. < L. *in-*, in + *signum*, a mark], distinguishing marks, as emblems of rank, membership, etc.
**in·sig·nif·i·cant** (in′sig-nif′ə-kənt), *adj.* 1. meaningless. 2. unimportant; trivial. 3. small; unimposing. **—in′sig·nif′i·cance,** *n.*
**in·sin·cere** (in′sin-sêr′), *adj.* not sincere; deceptive or hypocritical. **—in′sin·cere′ly,** *adv.* **—in′sin·cer′i·ty** (-ser′ə-ti), *n.*
**in·sin·u·ate** (in-sin′ū-āt′), *v.t.* [-ATED, -ATING], [< L. *in-*, in + *sinus*, a curve], 1. to get in or introduce slowly, indirectly, etc. 2. to suggest (a thing) indirectly; hint. **—in·sin′u·a′tion,** *n.*
**in·sip·id** (in-sip′id), *adj.* [< L. *in-*, not + *sapidus*, savory], 1. without flavor; tasteless. 2. not exciting; dull. **—in′si·pid′i·ty,** *n.*
**in·sist** (in-sist′), *v.i.* [< L. *in-*, in + *sistere*, to stand], to take and maintain a stand (often with *on* or *upon*). *v.t.* to demand strongly.
**in·sist′ent,** *adj.* 1. insisting or demanding. 2. compelling attention. **—in·sist′ence,** *n.*
**in·so·far** (in′sō-fär′), *adv.* to the degree that (with *as*): often **in so far**.
**in·sole** (in′sōl′), *n.* the inside sole of a shoe.
**in·so·lent** (in′sə-lənt), *adj.* [< L. *in-*, not + *solere*, be accustomed], disrespectful of custom or authority; impudent. **—in′so·lence,** *n.* **—in′so·lent·ly,** *adv.*
**in·sol·vent** (in-sol′vənt), *adj.* not solvent; unable to pay debts; bankrupt. *n.* an insolvent person. **—in·sol′ven·cy,** *n.*
**in·som·ni·a** (in-som′ni-ə), *n.* [< L. *in-*, without + *somnus*, sleep], abnormal inability to sleep. **—in·som′ni·ac′** (-ak′), *n.*
**in·so·much** (in′sō-much′), *adv.* 1. to such a degree or extent; so (with *as* or *that*). 2. inasmuch (with *as*).

**in·sou·ci·ant** (in-sōō′si-ənt), *adj.* [Fr.], unbothered; carefree. —**in·sou′ci·ance,** *n.*
**in·spect** (in-spekt′), *v.t.* [< L. *in-*, at + *specere*, to look], 1. to look at carefully. 2. to examine or review officially. —**in·spec′tion,** *n.*
**in·spec′tor,** *n.* 1. one who inspects; official examiner. 2. an officer on a police force, ranking next below a superintendent.
**in·spi·ra·tion** (in′spə-rā′shən), *n.* 1. an inhaling. 2. an inspiring or being inspired mentally or emotionally. 3. any stimulus to creative thought or action. 4. an inspired idea, action, etc. —**in′spi·ra′tion·al,** *adj.*
**in·spire** (in-spīr′), *v.t.* [-SPIRED, -SPIRING], [< L. *in-*, in + *spirare*, breathe], 1. to inhale. 2. to stimulate or impel, as to some creative effort. 3. to motivate by divine influence. 4. to arouse (a feeling): as, kindness *inspires* love. *v.i.* 1. to inhale. 2. to give inspiration.
**in·spir·it** (in-spir′it), *v.t.* to put spirit or life into; hearten. —**in·spir′it·ing·ly,** *adv.*
**Inst.,** 1. Institute. 2. Institution.
**inst.,** instant (of the present month).
**in·sta·bil·i·ty** (in′stə-bil′ə-ti), *n.* lack of firmness, determination, etc.
**in·stall** (in-stôl′), *v.t.* [< ML. *in-*, in + *stallum*, a place], 1. to place (a person) in an office, etc., with formality. 2. to establish in a place. 3. to fix in position for use: as, to *install* light fixtures. —**in·stal·la·tion** (in′stə-lā′shən), *n.*
**in·stall·ment, in·stal·ment** (in-stôl′mənt), *n.* 1. an installing or being installed. 2. any of the parts of a sum of money to be paid at regular specified times. 3. any of several parts, as of a magazine serial.
**in·stance** (in′stəns), *n.* [see INSTANT], 1. a request; suggestion. 2. an example; case. 3. a step in processing; occasion: as, in the first *instance*. *v.t.* [-STANCED, -STANCING], to give as an example; cite.
**in·stant** (in′stənt), *adj.* [< L. *in-*, upon + *stare*, to stand], 1. urgent; pressing. 2. of the current month: as, your letter of the 8th *instant*. 3. imminent. 4. immediate. 5. that can be prepared quickly, as by adding water: as, *instant* coffee. *n.* 1. a moment. 2. a particular moment.
**in·stan·ta·ne·ous** (in′stən-tā′ni-əs), *adj.* done or happening in an instant; immediate.
**in′stant·ly,** *adv.* immediately.
**in·stead** (in-sted′), *adv.* [*in* + *stead*], in place of the other: as, since we had no sugar, we used honey *instead*. —**instead of,** in place of.
**in·step** (in′step′), *n.* the upper surface of the arch of the foot, between the ankle and the toes.
**in·sti·gate** (in′stə-gāt′), *v.t.* [-GATED, -GATING], [< L. *in-*, on + *stigare*, to prick], 1. to urge on to some action. 2. to foment, as rebellion. —**in′sti·ga′tion,** *n.* —**in′sti·ga′tor,** *n.*
**in·still, in·stil** (in-stil′), *v.t.* [-STILLED, -STILLING], [< L. *in-*, in + *stilla*, a drop], 1. to put in drop by drop. 2. to put (a feeling, etc.) *into* gradually.
**in·stinct** (in′stiŋkt), *n.* [< L. *instinguere*, impel], 1. (an) inborn tendency to behave in a way characteristic of a species. 2. a natural or acquired tendency; knack. —**in·stinc′tive,** *adj.* —**in·stinc′tive·ly,** *adv.*
**in·sti·tute** (in′stə-tōōt′, -tūt′), *v.t.* [-TUTED, -TUTING], [< L. *in-*, in + *statuere*, set up], 1. to set up; establish. 2. to start; initiate. *n.* something instituted, as an organization for the promotion of art, science, etc.
**in′sti·tu′tion** (-tōō′shən, -tū′-), *n.* 1. an instituting or being instituted. 2. an established law, custom, etc. 3. an organization having some social, educational, or religious purpose. 4. the building housing it. 5. [Colloq.], a familiar person or thing. —**in′sti·tu′tion·al,** *adj.*
**in·struct** (in-strukt′), *v.t.* [< L. *in-*, in + *struere*, pile up], 1. to teach; educate. 2. to inform. 3. to direct or order.
**in·struc′tion** (-struk′shən), *n.* 1. an instructing; education. 2. something taught. 3. *pl.* directions; orders.
**in·struc′tive,** *adj.* instructing; giving knowledge. —**in·struc′tive·ly,** *adv.*
**in·struc′tor,** *n.* 1. a teacher. 2. a college teacher of the lowest rank.
**in·stru·ment** (in′stroo-mənt), *n.* [see INSTRUCT], 1. a thing by means of which something is done; means. 2. a tool or implement. 3. any of various devices producing musical sound. 4. in *law*, a formal document.
**in′stru·men′tal** (-men′t'l), *adj.* 1. serving as a means; helpful. 2. of, performed on, or written for a musical instrument or instruments. —**in′stru·men′tal·ly,** *adv.*
**in′stru·men′tal·ist,** *n.* one who performs on a musical instrument.
**in′stru·men·tal′i·ty** (-tal′ə-ti), *n.* [*pl.* -TIES], a means; agency.
**in′stru·men·ta′tion** (-tā′shən), *n.* the arrangement of music for instruments.
**in·sub·or·di·nate** (in′sə-bôr′d'n-it), *adj.* not submitting to authority; disobedient. —**in′sub·or′di·na′tion,** *n.*
**in·sub·stan·tial** (in′səb-stan′shəl), *adj.* not substantial; specif., *a*) unreal; imaginary. *b*) flimsy.
**in·suf·fer·a·ble** (in-suf′ẽr-ə-b'l), *adj.* not sufferable; intolerable. —**in·suf′fer·a·bly,** *adv.*
**in·su·lar** (in′sə-lẽr, -syoo-), *adj.* [< L. *insula*, island], 1. of or like an island or islanders. 2. narrow-minded; limited. —**in′su·lar′i·ty** (-lar′ə-ti), *n.* —**in′su·lar·ly,** *adv.*
**in·su·late** (in′sə-lāt′, -syoo-), *v.t.* [-LATED, -LATING], [< L. *insula*, island], 1. to set apart; isolate. 2. to protect with a nonconducting material in order to prevent the leakage of electricity, heat, or sound. —**in′su·la′tor,** *n.*
**in′su·la′tion,** *n.* 1. an insulating or being insulated. 2. material used to insulate.
**in·su·lin** (in′sə-lin, -syoo-), *n.* [< L. *insula*, island: referring to islands of tissue in the pancreas], an extract from the pancreas of sheep and oxen used in the treatment of diabetes: a trademark (**Insulin**).
**in·sult** (in′sult), *n.* [< L. *in-*, on + *salire*, to leap], an act, remark, etc. meant to hurt one's feelings or self-respect. *v.t.* (in-sult′), to subject to an insult; affront.
**in·su·per·a·ble** (in-sōō′pẽr-ə-b'l, -sū′-), *adj.* [< L. *in-*, not + *superare*, overcome], that cannot be overcome. —**in·su′per·a·bly,** *adv.*
**in·sup·port·a·ble** (in′sə-pôr′tə-b'l), *adj.* not supportable; unbearable.
**in·sur·ance** (in-shoor′əns), *n.* 1. an insuring or being insured. 2. a contract (**insurance policy**) whereby a person or company guarantees payment for a specified loss by fire, death, etc. 3. the amount for which something is insured. 4. the business of insuring against loss.
**in·sure** (in-shoor′), *v.t.* [-SURED, -SURING], [see IN- (in) & SURE], 1. to make sure; guarantee. 2. to protect: as *insured* against error. 3. to take out or issue insurance on. —**in·sur′a·ble,** *adj.*
**in·sur·gent** (in-sũr′jənt), *adj.* [< L. *in-*, upon + *surgere*, rise], rising up against governmental authority; rebellious. *n.* an insurgent person. —**in·sur′gence,** *n.*
**in·sur·rec·tion** (in′sə-rek′shən), *n.* [see INSURGENT], a rising up against established authority; rebellion; revolt. —**in′sur·rec′tion·ist,** *n.*
**int.,** 1. interest. 2. international.
**in·tact** (in-takt′), *adj.* [< L. *in-*, not + *tactus*, touched], untouched or uninjured; kept or left whole.

**in·tagl·io** (in-tal'yō), *n.* [*pl.* -IOS], [It. < *in-*, in + *tagliare*, to cut], a design carved or engraved below the surface.
**in·take** (in'tāk'), *n.* 1. a taking in. 2. amount taken in. 3. the place in a pipe, etc. where a fluid is taken in.
**in·tan·gi·ble** (in-tan'jə-b'l), *adj.* 1. that cannot be touched; incorporeal. 2. that cannot be easily defined; vague. *n.* something intangible. —**in·tan'gi·bil'i·ty**, *n.*
**in·te·ger** (in'tə-jẽr), *n.* [L., whole], a whole number (e.g., 5, 11, 748).
**in·te·gral** (in'tə-grəl), *adj.* [see INTEGER], 1. necessary for completeness; essential. 2. whole or complete. —**in'te·gral·ly**, *adv.*
**in·te·grate** (in'tə-grāt), *v.t. & v.i.* [-GRATED, -GRATING], [< L. *integer*, whole], 1. to make or become whole or complete. 2. to bring (parts) together into a whole. 3. to remove barriers imposing segregation upon (racial groups). —**in'te·gra'tion**, *n.*
**in·teg·ri·ty** (in-teg'rə-ti), *n.* [see INTEGER], 1. completeness; wholeness. 2. unimpaired condition. 3. honesty, sincerity, etc.
**in·teg·u·ment** (in-teg'yoo-mənt), *n.* [< L. *in-*, upon + *tegere*, to cover], an outer covering; skin, shell, etc.
**in·tel·lect** (in'tə-lekt'), *n.* [< L. *inter-*, between + *legere*, choose], 1. the ability to reason or understand. 2. high intelligence. 3. a person of (high) intelligence.
**in·tel·lec·tu·al** (in'tə-lek'chōō-əl), *adj.* 1. of, done by, or appealing to the intellect. 2. requiring intelligence. 3. showing high intelligence. *n.* one who has intellectual interests. —**in'tel·lec'tu·al'i·ty**, *n.*
**in·tel·li·gence** (in-tel'ə-jəns), *n.* [see INTELLECT], 1. *a*) the ability to learn or understand. *b*) the ability to cope with a new situation. 2. news; information. 3. those engaged in gathering secret information.
**in·tel'li·gent** (-jənt), *adj.* having or showing intelligence; quick to learn.
**in·tel'li·gent'si·a** (-jent'si-ə), *n.* [< Russ.], intellectuals collectively.
**in·tel·li·gi·ble** (in-tel'i-jə-b'l), *adj.* [see INTELLECT], that can be understood; clear; comprehensible. —**in·tel'li·gi·bil'i·ty**, *n.*
**in·tem·per·ate** (in-tem'pẽr-it), *adj.* 1. not temperate or moderate; excessive. 2. drinking too much alcoholic liquor. —**in·tem'perance**, *n.* —**in·tem'per·ate·ly**, *adv.*
**in·tend** (in-tend'), *v.t.* [< L. *in-*, at + *tendere*, stretch], 1. to plan; purpose. 2. to mean (something) to be or be used for. 3. to mean; signify. *v.i.* to have a purpose.
**in·tend'ed**, *n.* [Colloq.], one's prospective wife or husband.
**in·tense** (in-tens'), *adj.* [see INTEND], 1. very strong: as, an *intense* light. 2. strained to the utmost; strenuous: as, *intense* thought. 3. characterized by much action, emotion, etc. —**in·tense'ly**, *adv.*
**in·ten·si·fy** (in-ten'sə-fī'), *v.t. & v.i.* [-FIED, -FYING], to make or become more intense; increase. —**in·ten'si·fi·ca'tion**, *n.*
**in·ten'si·ty**, *n.* [*pl.* -TIES], 1. a being intense. 2. great energy or vehemence, as of emotion. 3. the amount of force or energy of heat, light, sound, etc.
**in·ten'sive**, *adj.* 1. of or characterized by intensity; thorough. 2. in *grammar*, giving force or emphasis: as, *oneself* is often *intensive*. *n.* in *grammar*, an intensive word, prefix, etc. —**in·ten'sive·ly**, *adv.*
**in·tent** (in-tent'), *adj.* [see INTEND], 1. firmly directed; earnest. 2. having one's attention or purpose firmly fixed: as, *intent* on going. *n.* 1. an intending. 2. something intended; a purpose. —**to all intents and purposes**, in almost every respect.
**in·ten·tion** (in-ten'shən), *n.* 1. a determination to act in a specified way. 2. anything intended; purpose.
**in·ten'tion·al**, *adj.* done purposely.
**in·ter** (in-tũr'), *v.t.* [-TERRED, -TERRING], [< L. *in*, in + *terra*, earth], to put (a dead body) into the ground or a tomb; bury.
**inter-**, [L.], a combining form meaning: 1. *between*, *among*, as in *intercede*. 2. *with* or *on each other* (or *one another*), *mutual*, as in *intermarry*.
**in'ter·act'**, *v.i.* to act on each other.
**in'ter·breed'**, *v.t.* [-BRED, -BREEDING], to cross different varieties of (animals or plants) in breeding. *v.i.* to breed in this way.
**in·ter·cede** (in'tẽr-sēd'), *v.i.* [-CEDED, -CEDING], [< L. *inter-*, between + *cedere*, go], 1. to plead in behalf of another. 2. to act as an intermediary; mediate.
**in·ter·cept** (in'tẽr-sept'), *v.t.* [< L. *inter-*, between + *capere*, take], 1. to seize or interrupt on the way: as, to *intercept* a message. 2. to stop or prevent. 3. to cut off communication with, sight of, etc. —**in'ter·cep'tion**, *n.* —**in'ter·cep'tor**, **in'ter·cept'er**, *n.*
**in'ter·ces'sion** (-sesh'ən), *n.* an interceding; mediation in behalf of another. —**in'ter·ces'sor** (-ses'ẽr), *n.* —**in'ter·ces'so·ry**, *adj.*
**in'ter·change'**, *v.t.* [-CHANGED, -CHANGING], 1. to give and take mutually; exchange. 2. to put (each of two things) in the other's place. 3. to alternate. *n.* (in'tẽr-chānj'), 1. a mutual giving in exchange. 2. alternation. 3. a place on a freeway where traffic enters or departs. —**in'ter·change'a·ble**, *adj.*
**in'ter·col·le'gi·ate**, *adj.* between or among colleges and universities.
**in·ter·com** (in'tẽr-kom'), *n.* [Slang], an intercommunication system, as in an airplane.
**in'ter·com·mu'ni·cate**, *v.t. & v.i.* [-CATED, -CATING], to communicate with or to each other or one another. —**in'ter·com·mu'ni·ca'tion**, *n.*
**in'ter·cos'tal** (-kos't'l), *adj.* [< *inter-*; + L. *costa*, a rib], between the ribs.
**in·ter·course** (in'tẽr-kôrs'), *n.* [see INTER- & COURSE], 1. communication or dealings between people, countries, etc. 2. the sexual joining of two individuals; copulation: usually **sexual intercourse**.
**in'ter·de·pend'ence**, *n.* mutual dependence. —**in'ter·de·pend'ent**, *adj.*
**in·ter·dict** (in'tẽr-dikt'), *v.t.* [< L. *inter-*, between + *dicere*, say], 1. to prohibit (an action). 2. to restrain from doing or using something. *n.* (in'tẽr-dikt'), an official prohibition or restraint. —**in'ter·dic'tion**, *n.*
**in·ter·est** (in'tẽr-ist, in'trist), *n.* [< L. *inter-*, between + *esse*, be], 1. a right to, or share in, something. 2. anything in which one has a share. 3. *often pl.* welfare; benefit. 4. those having a common concern in some industry, cause, etc.: as, the steel *interest*. 5. *a*) a feeling of concern, curiosity, etc. about something. *b*) the power of causing this feeling. *c*) something causing this feeling. 6. *a*) money paid for the use of money. *b*) the rate of such payment. *v.t.* 1. to involve or excite the interest or attention of. 2. to cause to have an interest, or share, in. —**in the interest of**, for the sake of.
**in'ter·est·ed**, *adj.* 1. having an interest or share. 2. influenced by personal interest. 3. feeling or showing interest.
**in'ter·est·ing**, *adj.* exciting interest, curiosity, or attention. —**in'ter·est·ing·ly**, *adv.*
**in·ter·fere** (in'tẽr-fêr'), *v.i.* [-FERED, -FERING], [< L. *inter*, between + *ferire*, to strike], 1. to clash; collide. 2. *a*) to come between; intervene. *b*) to meddle. 3. in *football*, to obstruct opposing tacklers to clear the way for the ball carrier. —**interfere with**, to hinder. —**in'ter·fer'ence**, *n.*
**in·ter·im** (in'tẽr-im), *n.* [< L. *inter*, between], the period of time between; meantime. *adj.* temporary.

**in·te·ri·or** (in-têr′i-ẽr), *adj.* [< L. *inter*, between], 1. situated within; inner. 2. inland. 3. private. *n.* 1. the interior part, as of a room, country, etc. 2. the domestic affairs of a country. —**in·te′ri·or·ly,** *adv.*

**in·ter·ject** (in′tẽr-jekt′), *v.t.* [< L. *inter-*, between + *jacere*, to throw], to throw in between; insert. —**in′ter·jec′tor,** *n.*

**in′ter·jec′tion** (-jek′shən), *n.* 1. an interjecting. 2. something interjected. 3. in *grammar*, an exclamation. Abbrev. **interj.**

**in′ter·lace′,** *v.t.* & *v.i.* [-LACED, -LACING], to lace or weave together.

**in′ter·lard′** (-lärd′), *v.t.* [see INTER- & LARD], to intersperse; diversify: as, to *interlard* a talk with quotations.

**in′ter·line′,** *v.t.* [-LINED, -LINING], to write or print (something) between the lines of (a text, etc.). —**in′ter·lin′e·ar** (-lin′i-ẽr), *adj.*

**in′ter·line′,** *v.t.* [-LINED, -LINING], to put an inner lining under the ordinary lining of (a garment).

**in′ter·lock′,** *v.t.* & *v.i.* to lock together; join with one another.

**in·ter·loc·u·tor** (in′tẽr-lok′yoo-tẽr), *n.* [< L. *inter*, between + *loqui*, to talk], 1. an entertainer in a minstrel show who acts as master of ceremonies. 2. a person taking part in a conversation.

**in′ter·loc′u·to′ry** (-tôr′i), *adj.* 1. in *law*, not final, as a decree. 2. conversational.

**in·ter·lop·er** (in′tẽr-lōp′ẽr), *n.* [prob. ult. < Fr. *entre*, between + D. *loopen*, to run], one who intrudes in others' affairs for his own gain.

**in·ter·lude** (in′tẽr-lōōd′), *n.* [< L. *inter*, between + *ludus*, play], anything that fills time between two events, as music between acts of a play.

**in′ter·mar′ry,** *v.i.* [-RIED, -RYING], 1. to become connected by marriage: said of different families, races, etc. 2. to marry: said of closely related persons. —**in′ter·mar′riage,** *n.*

**in·ter·me·di·ar·y** (in′tẽr-mē′di-er′i), *adj.* 1. acting as a go-between or mediator. 2. intermediate. *n.* [*pl.* -IES], a go-between.

**in·ter·me·di·ate** (in′tẽr-mē′di-it), *adj.* [< L. *inter*, between + *medius*, middle], in the middle; in between. *n.* an intermediary.

**in·ter·ment** (in-tũr′mənt), *n.* [see INTER], burial.

**in·ter·mez·zo** (in′tẽr-met′sō), *n.* [*pl.* -ZOS, -ZI (-si, -zi)], [It.], 1. a short, light entertainment between the acts of a play or opera. 2. in *music*, a short piece; esp., one connecting the main parts of a composition.

**in·ter·mi·na·ble** (in-tũr′mi-nə-b'l), *adj.* lasting, or seeming to last, forever; endless.

**in′ter·min′gle,** *v.t.* & *v.i.* [-GLED, -GLING], to mix together; mingle.

**in·ter·mis·sion** (in′tẽr-mish′ən), *n.* [< L. *inter-*, between + *mittere*, send], an interval of time between periods of activity, as between acts of a play.

**in′ter·mit′tent** (-mit′'nt), *adj.* [see INTERMISSION], stopping and starting again at intervals; periodic. —**in′ter·mit′tent·ly,** *adv.*

**in′ter·mix′,** *v.t.* & *v.i.* to mix together; blend.

**in·tern** (in′tẽrn), *n.* [< L. *internus*, internal], a doctor serving as assistant resident in a hospital, usually just after graduation from medical school: also sp. **interne.** *v.i.* to serve as an intern. *v.t.* (in-tũrn′), to detain and confine within an area: as, to *intern* aliens in wartime. —**in·tern′ment,** *n.*

**in·ter·nal** (in-tũr′n'l), *adj.* [< L. *internus*], 1. of or on the inside; inner. 2. intrinsic: as, *internal* evidence. 3. domestic: as, *internal* revenue. 4. to be taken inside the body: as, *internal* remedies. *n.* 1. *pl.* the internal organs of the body. 2. inner or essential quality. —**in·ter′nal·ly,** *adv.*

**in·ter′nal-com·bus′tion engine,** an engine, as in an automobile, powered by the explosion of a fuel-and-air mixture within the cylinders.

**internal revenue,** governmental income from taxes on income, profits, etc.

**in·ter·na·tion·al** (in′tẽr-nash′ən-'l), *adj.* 1. between or among nations. 2. concerned with the relations between nations. 3. for the use of all nations. —**in′ter·na′tion·al·ize′** [-IZED, -IZING], *v.t.*

**in·ter·ne·cine** (in′tẽr-nē′sin), *adj.* [< L. *inter-*, between + *necare*, kill], extremely destructive to both sides.

**in′ter·pen′e·trate,** *v.t.* [-TRATED, -TRATING], to penetrate thoroughly. *v.i.* to penetrate each other. —**in′ter·pen′e·tra′tion,** *n.*

**in′ter·plan′e·tar′y** (-plan′ə-ter′i), *adj.* between planets.

**in′ter·play′,** *n.* action, effect, or influence on each other.

**in·ter·po·late** (in-tũr′pə-lāt′), *v.t.* [-LATED, -LATING], [< L. *inter-*, between + *polire*, to polish], 1. to change (a text, etc.) by inserting new material. 2. to insert between or among others. —**in·ter′po·la′tion,** *n.*

**in·ter·pose** (in′tẽr-pōz′), *v.t.* & *v.i.* [-POSED, -POSING], 1. to place or come between. 2. to intervene (with). 3. to interrupt (with). —**in′ter·po·si′tion** (-pə-zish′ən), *n.*

**in·ter·pret** (in-tũr′prit), *v.t.* [< L. *interpres*, negotiator], 1. to explain or translate. 2. to construe. 3. to give one's own conception of, as a role in a play. *v.i.* to translate. —**in·ter′pre·ta′tion,** *n.* —**in·ter′pret·er,** *n.*

**in·ter·ra·cial** (in′tẽr-rā′shəl), *adj.* between, among, or for persons of different races.

**in·ter·reg·num** (in′tẽr-reg′nəm), *n.* [*pl.* -NUMS, -NA (-nə)], [< L. *inter-*, between + *regnum*, rule], 1. an interval between two successive reigns, when the country has no sovereign. 2. any interval.

**in′ter·re·lat′ed,** *adj.* having a close connection with one another. —**in′ter·re·la′tion,** *n.*

**in·ter·ro·gate** (in-ter′ə-gāt′), *v.t.* & *v.i.* [-GATED, -GATING], [< L. *inter-*, between + *rogare*, ask], to question, esp. formally. —**in·ter′ro·ga′tion,** *n.* —**in·ter′ro·ga′tor,** *n.*

**interrogation mark** (or **point**), a question mark.

**in·ter·rog·a·tive** (in′tə-rog′ə-tiv), *adj.* asking a question. *n.* an interrogative word, element, etc. (e.g., what?).

**in·ter·rupt** (in′tə-rupt′), *v.t.* [< L. *inter-*, between + *rumpere*, to break], 1. to break into (a discussion, etc.) or break in upon (a person speaking, etc.). 2. to make a break in the continuity of. —**in′ter·rup′tion,** *n.*

**in′ter·scho·las′tic,** *adj.* between or among schools.

**in·ter·sect** (in′tẽr-sekt′), *v.t.* [< L. *inter-*, between + *secare*, to cut], to divide into two parts by passing through. *v.i.* to cross each other.

**in′ter·sec′tion,** *n.* 1. an intersecting. 2. the point or line where two lines, surfaces, roads, etc. meet or cross.

**in·ter·sperse** (in′tẽr-spũrs′), *v.t.* [-SPERSED, -SPERSING], [< L. *inter-*, among + *spargere*, scatter], to scatter among other things; put here and there.

**in′ter·state′,** *adj.* between or among states of a federal government.

**in·ter·stice** (in-tũr′stis), *n.* [*pl.* -STICES], [< L. *inter-*, between + *sistere*, to set], a crevice; crack. —**in·ter·sti·tial** (in′tẽr-stish′əl), *adj.*

**in′ter·twine′,** *v.t.* & *v.i.* [-TWINED, -TWINING], to twine together.

**in·ter·ur·ban** (in′tẽr-ũr′bən), *adj.* between cities or towns. *n.* an interurban railway, train, etc.

**in·ter·val** (in′tẽr-v'l), *n.* [< L. *inter-*, between + *vallum*, wall], 1. a space between things. 2. the time between events. 3. the difference in pitch between two tones. —**at in-**

tervals, 1. now and then. 2. here and there.
**in·ter·vene** (in'tẽr-vēn'), *v.i.* [-VENED, -VENING], [< L. *inter-*, between + *venire*, come], 1. to come or be between. 2. to occur between two events, etc. 3. to come in to modify, settle, or hinder some action, etc.
**in'ter·ven'tion** (-ven'shən), *n.* 1. an intervening. 2. interference of one state in the affairs of another. **—in'ter·ven'tion·ist,** *n.*
**in'ter·view'** (-vū'), *n.* 1. a meeting of people face to face to confer. 2. a meeting between a reporter and a person whose views, etc. are to be the subject of an article. 3. such an article. *v.t.* to have an interview with.
**in'ter·weave',** *v.t. & v.i.* [-WOVE, -WOVEN, -WEAVING], 1. to weave together. 2. to connect closely.
**in·tes·tate** (in-tes'tāt, -tit), *adj.* [< L. *in-*, not + *testari*, make a will], having made no will. *n.* one who dies intestate.
**in·tes·tine** (in-tes'tin), *n.* [< L. *intus*, within], *usually pl.* the lower part of the alimentary canal extending from the stomach to the anus; bowel(s). **—in·tes'ti·nal,** *adj.*
**in·ti·mate** (in'tə-mit), *adj.* [< L. *intus*, within], 1. most private or personal. 2. closely associated; very familiar. *n.* an intimate friend. **—in'ti·ma·cy** (-mə-si) [*pl.* -CIES], *n.* **—in'ti·mate·ly,** *adv.*
**in·ti·mate** (in'tə-māt'), *v.t.* [-MATED, -MATING], [< L. *intimare*], 1. to hint or imply. 2. to announce. **—in'ti·ma'tion,** *n.*
**in·tim·i·date** (in-tim'ə-dāt'), *v.t.* [-DATED, -DATING], [< L. *in-*, in + *timidus*, afraid], to make afraid, as with threats. **—in·tim'i·da'tion,** *n.*
**in·to** (in'too, -too, -tə), *prep.* [AS.], 1. toward and within: as, *into* a room. 2. advancing to the midst of: as, to talk *into* the night. 3. to the form, substance, etc. of: as, divided *into* parts.
**in·tol·er·a·ble** (in-tol'ẽr-ə-b'l), *adj.* unbearable; too severe, painful, etc. to be endured.
**in·tol·er·ant** (in-tol'ẽr-ənt), *adj.* unwilling to tolerate others' beliefs, etc. **—intolerant of,** not able or willing to tolerate. **—in·tol'er·ance,** *n.* **—in·tol'er·ant·ly,** *adv.*
**in·to·na·tion** (in'tō-nā'shən), *n.* 1. an intoning. 2. the manner of utterance with regard to rise and fall in pitch.
**in·tone** (in-tōn'), *v.t. & v.i.* [-TONED, -TONING], to speak or recite in a singing tone; chant.
‡**in to·to** (in tō'tō), [L.], as a whole.
**in·tox·i·cant** (in-tok'sə-kənt), *n.* something that intoxicates, as alcoholic liquor.
**in·tox·i·cate** (in-tok'sə-kāt'), *v.t.* [-CATED, -CATING], [< L. *in-*, in + *toxicum*, poison], 1. to make drunk. 2. to excite greatly. **—in·tox'i·ca'tion,** *n.*
**intra-,** [L., within], a combining form meaning *within, inside of.*
**in·trac·ta·ble** (in-trak'tə-b'l), *adj.* hard to manage; unruly; stubborn. **—in·trac'ta·bil'i·ty,** *n.* **—in·trac'ta·bly,** *adv.*
**in·tra·mu·ral** (in'trə-myoor'əl), *adj.* within the walls or limits of a city, college, etc.
**in·tran·si·gent** (in-tran'si-jənt), *adj.* [ult. < L. *in-*, not + *transigere*, to settle], refusing to compromise. *n.* one who is intransigent, esp. in politics. **—in·tran'si·gence,** *n.* **—in·tran'si·gent·ly,** *adv.*
**in·tran·si·tive** (in-tran'sə-tiv), *adj.* not transitive; not used with an object to complete its meaning; said of certain verbs.
**in·tra·ve·nous** (in'trə-vē'nəs), *adj.* [*intra-* + *venous*], into or within a vein: as, an *intravenous* injection.
**in·trench** (in-trench'), *v.t. & v.i.* to entrench.
**in·trep·id** (in-trep'id), *adj.* [< L. *in-*, not + *trepidus*, alarmed], bold; fearless; brave. **—in'tre·pid'i·ty,** *n.* **—in·trep'id·ly,** *adv.*
**in·tri·cate** (in'tri-kit), *adj.* [< L. *in-*, in + *tricae*, vexations], hard to follow or understand because complicated, perplexing, etc. **—in'tri·ca·cy** (-kə-si) [*pl.* -CIES], *n.*
**in·trigue** (in-trēg'), *v.i.* [-TRIGUED, -TRIGUING], [see INTRICATE], to plot secretly or underhandedly. *v.t.* to get by secret plotting. *n.* 1. secret or underhanded plotting. 2. a secret or underhanded plot or scheme. 3. a secret love affair. **—in·tri'guer,** *n.*
**in·trin·sic** (in-trin'sik), *adj.* [< L. *intrinsecus*, inwardly], belonging to the real nature of a thing; inherent. **—in·trin'si·cal·ly,** *adv.*
**in·tro·duce** (in'trə-dōōs', -dūs'), *v.t.* [-DUCED, -DUCING], [< L. *intro-*, in + *ducere*, to lead], 1. to put in; insert. 2. to bring in as a new feature. 3. to bring into use or fashion. 4. *a*) to make acquainted with; present to: as, *introduce* me to her. *b*) to give experience of: as, they *introduced* him to music. 5. to start; begin: as, *introduce* the speech with a joke.
**in'tro·duc'tion** (-duk'shən), *n.* 1. an introducing or being introduced. 2. the preliminary section of a book, speech, etc.; preface.
**in'tro·duc'to·ry** (-tẽr-i), *adj.* serving to introduce; preliminary: also **in'tro·duc'tive.**
**in·tro·spec·tion** (in'trə-spek'shən), *n.* [< L. *intro-*, within + *specere*, to look], a looking into one's own mind, feelings, etc. **—in'tro·spec'tive,** *adj.*
**in·tro·vert** (in'trə-vũrt'), *n.* [< L. *intro-*, within + *vertere*, to turn], one who is more interested in his own thoughts, feelings, etc. than in external objects or events. *v.t.* 1. to direct (one's interest, etc.) upon oneself. 2. to bend (something) inward. **—in'tro·ver'sion** (-vũr'zhən), *n.*
**in·trude** (in-trōōd'), *v.t. & v.i.* [-TRUDED, -TRUDING], [< L. *in-*, in + *trudere*, to thrust], to force (oneself) upon others without being asked or welcomed. **—in·trud'er,** *n.*
**in·tru·sion** (in-trōō'zhən), *n.* an intruding. **—in·tru'sive** (-siv), *adj.*
**in·trust** (in-trust'), *v.t.* to entrust.
**in·tu·i·tion** (in'tōō-ish'ən, -tū-), *n.* [< L. *in-*, in + *tueri*, look at], the immediate knowing or learning of something without the conscious use of reasoning. **—in·tu'i·tive** (-i-tiv), *adj.* **—in·tu'i·tive·ly,** *adv.*
**in·un·date** (in'ən-dāt'), *v.t.* [-DATED, -DATING], [< L. *in-*, in + *undare*, to flood], to flood; overflow or overwhelm. **—in'un·da'tion,** *n.*
**in·ure** (in-yoor'), *v.t.* [-URED, -URING], [*in-*, in + obs. *ure* (< OFr.), work], to accustom to pain, trouble, etc. *v.i.* to take effect.
**in·vade** (in-vād'), *v.t.* [-VADED, -VADING], [< L. *in-*, in + *vadere*, go], 1. to enter forcibly, as to conquer. 2. to intrude upon; violate. **—in·vad'er,** *n.*
**in·va·lid** (in'və-lid), *adj.* [< L. *in-*, not + *validus*, strong], 1. weak and sickly. 2. of or for invalids. *n.* one who is ill or disabled. *v.t.* to dismiss, as a soldier, from active service as because of illness.
**in·val·id** (in-val'id), *adj.* not valid; having no force; null and void.
**in·val'i·date'** (-ə-dāt'), *v.t.* [-DATED, -DATING], to make invalid; deprive of legal force.
**in·val·u·a·ble** (in-val'ū-ə-b'l), *adj.* too valuable to be measured; precious.
**in·va·sion** (in-vā'zhən), *n.* an invading or being invaded, as by an army.
**in·vec·tive** (in-vek'tiv), *n.* [see INVEIGH], a violent verbal attack; denunciation.
**in·veigh** (in-vā'), *v.i.* [< L. *in-*, in + *vehere*, carry], to make a violent verbal attack; rail (*against*). **—in·veigh'er,** *n.*
**in·vei·gle** (in-vē'g'l, -vā'-), *v.t.* [-GLED, -GLING], [prob. < Fr. *aveugler*, to blind], to entice or trick into doing something.
**in·vent** (in-vent'), *v.t.* [< L. *in-*, on + *venire*, come], 1. to think up: as, *invent* an

alibi. 2. to think out or produce (a new device, etc.); originate. —**in·ven'tor,** *n.*
**in·ven'tion** (-ven'shən), *n.* 1. an inventing. 2. the power of inventing; ingenuity. 3. something invented.
**in·ven'tive** (-tiv), *adj.* 1. of invention. 2. skilled in inventing. —**in·ven'tive·ly,** *adv.*
**in·ven·to·ry** (in'vən-tôr'i), *n.* [*pl.* -RIES], [see INVENT], 1. an itemized list of goods, property, etc., as of a business. 2. the store of goods, etc. for such listing; stock. *v.t.* [-RIED, -RYING], to make an inventory of.
**in·verse** (in-vūrs'; *also, for adj.*, in'vūrs'), *adj.* inverted; directly opposite. *n.* an inverse thing: as, love is the *inverse* of hate.
**in·ver·sion** (in-vūr'zhən), *n.* 1. an inverting or being inverted. 2. something inverted.
**in·vert** (in-vūrt'), *v.t.* [< L. *in-*, to + *vertere*, to turn], 1. to turn upside down. 2. to reverse the order, position, direction, etc. of.
**in·ver·te·brate** (in-vūr'tə-brit, -brāt'), *adj.* not vertebrate; having no backbone, or spinal column. *n.* any invertebrate animal.
**in·vest** (in-vest'), *v.t.* [< L. *in-*, in + *vestis*, clothing], 1. [Rare], to clothe. 2. to install in office with ceremony. 3. to furnish with power, authority, etc. 4. to put (money) into business, bonds, etc., in order to get a profit. *v.i.* to invest money. —**in·ves'tor,** *n.*
**in·ves·ti·gate** (in-ves'tə-gāt'), *v.t. & v.i.* [-GATED, -GATING], [< L. *in-*, in + *vestigare*, to track], to search (into); examine. —**in·ves'ti·ga'tive,** *adj.* —**in·ves'ti·ga'tor,** *n.*
**in·ves'ti·ga'tion,** *n.* an investigating; careful search; systematic inquiry.
**in·ves·ti·ture** (in-ves'tə-chẽr), *n.* a formal investing with an office, power, etc.
**in·vest·ment** (in-vest'mənt), *n.* 1. an investing or being invested. 2. *a*) money invested. *b*) anything in which money is or may be invested.
**in·vet·er·ate** (in-vet'ẽr-it), *adj.* [< L. *inveterare*, to age], firmly established; habitual. —**in·vet'er·a·cy,** *n.*
**in·vid·i·ous** (in-vid'i-əs), *adj.* [< L. *invidia*, envy], such as to excite ill will; giving offense, as by discriminating unfairly.
**in·vig·or·ate** (in-vig'ə-rāt'), *v.t.* [-ATED, -ATING], to give vigor to; fill with energy.
**in·vin·ci·ble** (in-vin'sə-b'l), *adj.* [< L. *in-*, not + *vincere*, overcome], that cannot be overcome; unconquerable. —**in·vin'ci·bil'i·ty,** *n.* —**in·vin'ci·bly,** *adv.*
**in·vi·o·la·ble** (in-vī'ə-lə-b'l), *adj.* 1. not to be violated; not to be profaned or injured; sacred. 2. indestructible. —**in·vi'o·la·bil'i·ty,** *n.* —**in·vi'o·la·bly,** *adv.*
**in·vi'o·late** (-lit, -lāt'), *adj.* not violated; kept sacred or unbroken.
**in·vis·i·ble** (in-viz'ə-b'l), *adj.* 1. not visible; that cannot be seen. 2. out of sight. 3. imperceptible. —**in·vis'i·bil'i·ty,** *n.*
**in·vi·ta·tion** (in'və-tā'shən), *n.* 1. an inviting. 2. a message or note used in inviting.
**in·vite** (in-vīt'), *v.t.* [-VITED, -VITING], [< L. *invitare*], 1. to ask (a person) to come somewhere or do something. 2. to make a request for. 3. to give occasion for: as, his conduct *invites* scandal. 4. to tempt; entice.
**in·vit'ing,** *adj.* tempting; enticing.
**in·vo·ca·tion** (in'və-kā'shən), *n.* an invoking of God, the Muses, etc.
**in·voice** (in'vois), *n.* [< Fr. *envoi*, a sending], an itemized list of goods shipped to a buyer, stating prices, etc. *v.t.* [-VOICED, -VOICING], to make an invoice of.
**in·voke** (in-vōk'), *v.t.* [-VOKED, -VOKING], [< L. *in-*, on + *vocare*, to call], 1. to call on (God, the Muses, etc.) for blessing, help, etc. 2. to conjure. 3. to beg for; implore.
**in·vol·un·tar·y** (in-vol'ən-ter'i), *adj.* 1. not done by choice. 2. unintentional. 3. not consciously controlled: as, digestion is *involuntary*. —**in·vol'un·tar'i·ly,** *adv.*
**in·vo·lute** (in'və-lōōt'), *adj.* [see INVOLVE], 1. intricate; involved. 2. rolled up or curled in a spiral. —**in'vo·lu'tion,** *n.*
**in·volve** (in-volv'), *v.t.* [-VOLVED, -VOLVING], [< L. *in-*, in + *volere*, to roll], 1. to make intricate; complicate. 2. to entangle in difficulty, danger, etc.; implicate. 3. to affect or include: as, the parade *involved* 400. 4. to require: as, saving *involves* thrift. 5. to occupy the attention of: as, *involved* in study. —**in·volve'ment,** *n.*
**in·vul·ner·a·ble** (in-vul'nẽr-ə-b'l), *adj.* 1. that cannot be wounded or injured. 2. proof against attack. —**in·vul'ner·a·bil'i·ty,** *n.* —**in·vul'ner·a·bly,** *adv.*
**in·ward** (in'wẽrd), *adj.* 1. situated within; internal. 2. mental or spiritual. 3. directed toward the inside. *adv.* 1. toward the inside. 2. into the mind or soul. Also **in'wards,** *adv.*
**in'ward·ly,** *adv.* 1. in or on the inside. 2. in the mind or spirit. 3. toward the inside.
**i·o·dine** (ī'ə-dīn', -din), *n.* [< Gr. *iōdēs*, violetlike], 1. a nonmetallic chemical element used in medicine, etc.: symbol, I. 2. [Colloq.], tincture of iodine, used as an antiseptic. Also **i'o·din** (-din).
**i·on** (ī'ən, ī'on), *n.* [< Gr. *ienai*, to go], an electrically charged atom or group of atoms.
**-ion,** [< L. *-io*], a noun-forming suffix meaning *the act* or *state of*, or *the result of*, as in *fusion, translation, correction*.
**I·on·ic** (ī-on'ik), *adj.* of a Greek order of architecture characterized by ornamental scrolls on the capitals.
**i·on·ize** (ī'ə-nīz'), *v.t. & v.i.* [-IZED, -IZING], to dissociate into ions, as a salt dissolved in water, or become electrically charged, as a gas under radiation. —**i'on·i·za'tion,** *n.*
**i·on·o·sphere** (ī-on'ə-sfêr'), *n.* the outer layers of the earth's atmosphere, containing ionized air particles.
**i·o·ta** (ī-ō'tə), *n.* 1. the ninth letter of the Greek alphabet (Ι, ι). 2. a very small quantity; jot.
**IOU, I.O.U.,** (ī'ō'ū'), 1. I owe you. 2. a signed note bearing these letters, acknowledging a debt.
**-ious,** [see -OUS], a suffix used to form adjectives meaning *having, characterized by*, as in *furious*.
**ip·e·cac** (ip'i-kak), *n.* [< S. Am. Indian name], an emetic made from the dried roots of a South American plant.
‡**ip·so fac·to** (ip'sō fak'tō), [L.], by the fact (or act) itself.
**IQ, I.Q.,** [*i*ntelligence *q*uotient], a number indicating a person's level of intelligence, based on a text.
**ir-,** in-: used before *r*.
**Ir.,** 1. Ireland. 2. Irish.
**I·ra·ni·an** (ī-rā'ni-ən), *adj.* of Iran, its people, language, etc. *n.* 1. a native or inhabitant of Iran; Persian. 2. a group of languages, including Persian.
**I·ra·qi** (ē-rä'ki), *adj.* of Iraq, its people, language, etc. *n.* 1. a native of Iraq. 2. the Arabic dialect of the Iraqis.
**i·ras·ci·ble** (i-ras'ə-b'l), *adj.* [see IRATE], easily angered; hot-tempered.
**i·rate** (ī'rāt, ī-rāt'), *adj.* [< L. *ira*, anger], angry; wrathful; incensed. —**i'rate·ly,** *adv.*
**ire** (īr), *n.* [< L. *ira*], anger; wrath.
**Ire.,** Ireland.
**ir·i·des·cent** (ir'ə-des''nt), *adj.* [< Gr. *iris*, rainbow], having or showing an interplay of rainbowlike colors. —**ir'i·des'cence,** *n.*
**i·ris** (ī'ris), *n.* [*pl.* IRISES, IRIDES (ī'rə-dēz')], [Gr., rainbow], 1. the round, pigmented membrane surrounding the pupil of the eye. 2. a plant with sword-shaped leaves and a showy flower.
**I·rish** (ī'rish), *adj.* of Ireland, its people, language, etc. *n.* 1. the Celtic language of Ireland. 2. the English dialect of Ireland.

—**the Irish,** the people of Ireland. —**I′rish·man** [*pl.* -MEN], *n.* —**I′rish·wom′an** [*pl.* -WOMEN], *n.fem.*

**irk** (ũrk), *v.t.* [ME. *irken*, be weary of], to make tired; annoy; vex.

**irk′some** (-səm), *adj.* tiresome; tedious.

**i·ron** (ī′ẽrn), *n.* [AS. *ise(r)n*], 1. a metallic chemical element, the most common of all the metals: symbol, Fe. 2. any tool, etc. made of iron, as a device with a flat undersurface, used, when heated, for pressing cloth. 3. *pl.* iron shackles. 4. firm strength; power. 5. a golf club with a metal head. *adj.* 1. of iron. 2. like iron; strong; firm. *v.t. & v.i.* to press (clothes, etc.) with a hot iron. —**iron out,** to smooth out; eliminate.

**i′ron·clad′,** *adj.* 1. covered with iron. 2. difficult to change or break: as, an *ironclad* lease.

**iron curtain,** secrecy and censorship regarded as forming a barrier, esp. around the Soviet Union.

**i·ron·i·cal** (ī-ron′i-k'l), *adj.* 1. meaning the contrary of what is expressed. 2. using irony. 3. opposite to what might be expected. Also **i·ron′ic.** —**i·ron′i·cal·ly,** *adv.*

**iron lung,** a large respirator enclosing all of the body but the head.

**i′ron·ware′,** *n.* things made of iron.

**i·ro·ny** (ī′rə-ni), *n.* [*pl.* -NIES], [< Gr. *eirōn*, dissembler in speech], 1. expression in which the intended meaning of the words is the opposite of their usual sense. 2. an event or result that is the opposite of what is expected.

**Ir·o·quois** (ir′ə-kwoi′), *n.* [*pl.* -QUOIS], a member of a tribe of American Indians that lived in W and N New York. *adj.* of the Iroquois. —**Ir′o·quoi′an,** *adj. & n.*

**ir·ra·di·ate** (i-rā′di-āt′), *v.t.* [-ATED, -ATING], 1. to shine upon; light up. 2. to enlighten. 3. to radiate. 4. to expose to X rays, ultraviolet rays, etc. *v.i.* to emit rays; shine. —**ir·ra′di·a′tion,** *n.*

**ir·ra·tion·al** (i-rash′ən-'l), *adj.* 1. lacking the power to reason. 2. senseless; unreasonable; absurd. —**ir·ra′tion·al′i·ty,** *n.*

**ir·rec·on·cil·a·ble** (i-rek′ən-sīl′ə-b'l), *adj.* that cannot be brought into agreement; incompatible. —**ir·rec′on·cil′a·bly,** *adv.*

**ir·re·cov·er·a·ble** (ir′i-kuv′ẽr-ə-b'l), *adj.* that cannot be recovered, regained, or remedied. —**ir′re·cov′er·a·bly,** *adv.*

**ir·re·deem·a·ble** (ir′i-dēm′ə-b'l), *adj.* 1. that cannot be redeemed. 2. that cannot be converted into coin, as certain paper money. 3. that cannot be changed or reformed. —**ir′re·deem′a·bly,** *adv.*

**ir·ref·u·ta·ble** (i-ref′yoo-tə-b'l, ir′ri-fū′-), *adj.* indisputable. —**ir·ref′u·ta·bly,** *adv.*

**ir·re·gard·less** (ir′i-gärd′lis), *adj. & adv.* regardless: a substandard or humorous redundancy.

**ir·reg·u·lar** (i-reg′yoo-lẽr), *adj.* 1. not conforming to established rule, standard, etc. 2. not straight or even; not uniform in shape, design, etc. 3. in *grammar*, not inflected in the normal manner: as, *go* is an *irregular* verb. —**ir·reg′u·lar′i·ty** (-lar′ə-ti), *n.* —**ir·reg′u·lar·ly,** *adv.*

**ir·rel·e·vant** (i-rel′ə-vənt), *adj.* not pertinent; not to the point. —**ir·rel′e·vance, ir·rel′e·van·cy,** *n.* —**ir·rel′e·vant·ly,** *adv.*

**ir·re·li·gious** (ir′i-lij′əs), *adj.* 1. indifferent or hostile to religion. 2. profane; impious.

**ir·re·me·di·a·ble** (ir′i-mē′di-ə-b'l), *adj.* that cannot be remedied; incurable.

**ir·rep·a·ra·ble** (i-rep′ẽr-ə-b'l), *adj.* that cannot be repaired, mended, remedied, etc. —**ir·rep′a·ra·bly,** *adv.*

**ir·re·place·a·ble** (ir′i-plās′ə-b'l), *adj.* that cannot be replaced.

**ir·re·press·i·ble** (ir′i-pres′ə-b'l), *adj.* that cannot be repressed. —**ir′re·press′i·bly,** *adv.*

**ir·re·proach·a·ble** (ir′i-prōch′ə-b'l), *adj.* blameless; faultless. —**ir′re·proach′a·bly,** *adv.*

**ir·re·sist·i·ble** (ir′i-zis′tə-b'l), *adj.* that cannot be resisted; too strong, fascinating, etc. to be withstood. —**ir′re·sist′i·bly,** *adv.*

**ir·res·o·lute** (i-rez′ə-lōōt′), *adj.* not resolute; wavering; indecisive. —**ir·res′o·lu′tion,** *n.*

**ir·re·spec·tive** (ir′i-spek′tiv), *adj.* regardless (*of*). —**ir′re·spec′tive·ly,** *adv.*

**ir·re·spon·si·ble** (ir′i-spon′sə-b'l), *adj.* 1. not responsible for actions. 2. lacking a sense of responsibility. —**ir′re·spon′si·bil′i·ty,** *n.* —**ir′re·spon′si·bly,** *adv.*

**ir·re·triev·a·ble** (ir′i-trēv′ə-b'l), *adj.* that cannot be retrieved, recovered, restored, etc.

**ir·rev·er·ent** (i-rev′ẽr-ənt), *adj.* not reverent; showing disrespect. —**ir·rev′er·ence,** *n.*

**ir·re·vers·i·ble** (ir′i-vũr′sə-b'l), *adj.* that cannot be reversed; esp., that cannot be repealed or annulled. —**ir′re·vers′i·bly,** *adv.*

**ir·rev·o·ca·ble** (i-rev′ə-kə-b'l), *adj.* that cannot be revoked or undone.

**ir·ri·gate** (ir′ə-gāt′), *v.t.* [-GATED, -GATING], [< L. *in-*, in + *rigare*, to water], 1. to supply (land) with water as by means of artificial ditches. 2. in *medicine*, to wash out (a cavity or canal). —**ir′ri·ga′tion,** *n.*

**ir·ri·ta·ble** (ir′ə-tə-b'l), *adj.* 1. easily irritated or provoked. 2. in *medicine*, excessively sensitive to a stimulus. —**ir′ri·ta·bil′i·ty,** *n.* —**ir′ri·ta·bly,** *adv.*

**ir·ri·tant** (ir′ə-tənt), *adj.* causing irritation. *n.* a thing that irritates.

**ir·ri·tate** (ir′ə-tāt′), *v.t.* [-TATED, -TATING], [< L. *irritare*, excite], 1. to provoke to anger; annoy. 2. to make inflamed or sore. —**ir′ri·ta′tion,** *n.*

**ir·rup·tion** (i-rup′shən), *n.* [< L. *in-*, in + *rumpere*, to break], 1. a bursting in. 2. a violent invasion. —**ir·rup′tive,** *adj.*

**IRS, I.R.S.,** Internal Revenue Service.

**is** (iz), [AS.], the 3d pers. sing., pres. indic., of **be.** —**as is,** as it is now.

**is.,** 1. island. 2. isle.

**I·saac** (ī′zək), *n.* in the *Bible*, one of the patriarchs, son of Abraham, and father of Jacob and Esau.

**I·sa·iah** (ī-zā′ə), *n.* 1. a Hebrew prophet of the 8th century B.C. 2. a book of the Old Testament with his teachings.

**-ise,** -ize.

**-ish,** [AS. *-isc*], a suffix meaning: 1. *of* (a specified people), as in *Spanish*. 2. *like*, as in *devilish*. 3. *somewhat*, as in *tallish*. 4. [Colloq.], *approximately*, as in *thirtyish*.

**Ish·tar** (ish′tär), *n.* the Babylonian and Assyrian goddess of love and fertility.

**i·sin·glass** (ī′ziŋ-glas′, -gläs′), *n.* [< MD. *huizen*, sturgeon + *blas*, bladder], 1. a gelatin prepared from fish bladders. 2. mica, esp. in thin sheets.

**I·sis** (ī′sis), *n.* the Egyptian goddess of fertility.

**isl.,** [*pl.* ISLS.], 1. island. 2. isle.

**Is·lam** (is′ləm, iz′-, is-läm′), *n.* [Ar. *islām*, lit., submission (to God's will)], 1. the Moslem religion, a monotheistic religion founded by Mohammed. 2. Moslems collectively or the lands in which they predominate.

**is·land** (ī′lənd), *n.* [< AS. *igland*, lit., island land: sp. after *isle*], 1. a land mass not as large as a continent, surrounded by water. 2. anything like an island in position or isolation.

**is′land·er,** *n.* a native or inhabitant of an island.

**isle** (īl), *n.* [< L. *insula*], an island, esp. a small island.

**is·let** (ī′lit), *n.* a very small island.

**ism** (iz'm), *n.* any doctrine, theory, system, etc. whose name ends in *-ism*.

**-ism,** [< Gr. *-ismos*], a suffix meaning: 1. *act* or *result of*, as in *terrorism*. 2. *condition*, *conduct*, or *qualities of*, as in *patriotism*. 3. *theory of*, as in *socialism*. 4. *devotion to*, as in *nationalism*. 5. *an instance of*, as in *witticism*.

**is·n't** (iz'nt), is not.

**iso-**, [< Gr. *isos*], a combining form meaning *equal, similar, alike:* also **is-**.

**i·so·bar** (ī'sə-bär'), *n.* [< *iso-* + Gr. *baros*, weight], a line on a map connecting points of equal barometric pressure.

**i·so·late** (ī'sə-lāt'), *v.t.* [-LATED, -LATING], [< It. *isola* (< L. *insula*), island], to set apart from others; place alone. —**i'so·la'tion**, *n.*

**i'so·la'tion·ist**, *n.* one who wants his country to take no part in international leagues, etc. *adj.* of isolationists. —**i'so·la'tion·ism**, *n.*

**i·so·mer** (ī'sə-mẽr), *n.* [< *iso-* + Gr. *meros*, a part], any of two or more chemical compounds whose molecules contain the same atoms but in different arrangements. —**i'so·mer'ic** (-mer'ik), *adj.*

**i·so·met·ric** (ī'sə-met'rik), *adj.* [< Gr. *isos*, equal + *metron*, measure], 1. of or having equality of measure: also **i'so·met'ri·cal.** 2. designating or of isometrics. *n.pl.* exercise in which one set of muscles is briefly tensed in opposition to another set of muscles or to an immovable object.

**i·sos·ce·les** (ī-sos'ə-lēz'), *adj.* [< Gr. *isos*, equal + *skelos*, leg], designating a triangle with two equal sides.

**i·so·tope** (ī'sə-tōp'), *n.* [< *iso-* + Gr. *topos*, place], any of two or more forms of an element having the same atomic number but different atomic weights.

**Is·ra·el** (iz'ri-əl), *n.* 1. in the *Bible*, Jacob. 2. the Jewish people.

**Is·rae·li** (iz-rā'li), *adj.* of modern Israel or its people. *n.* a native or inhabitant of modern Israel.

**Is·ra·el·ite** (iz'ri-əl-īt'), *n.* any of the people of ancient Israel.

**is·su·ance** (ish'ōō-əns), *n.* an issuing; issue.

**is·sue** (ish'ōō), *n.* [< L. *ex-*, out + *ire*, go], 1. an outgoing; outflow. 2. an outlet; exit. 3. a result; consequence. 4. offspring. 5. a point under dispute. 6. a sending or giving out. 7. the entire amount put forth at one time. 8. in *medicine*, a discharge of blood, etc. *v.i.* [-SUED, -SUING], 1. to go or flow out; emerge. 2. to result (*from*) or end (*in*). 3. to be published. *v.t.* 1. to let out; discharge. 2. to give or deal out, as supplies. 3. to publish. —**at issue**, in dispute. —**take issue**, to disagree. —**is'su·er**, *n.*

**-ist**, [< Gr. *-istēs*], a suffix meaning: 1. *one who practices* or *is occupied with*, as in *satirist, violinist*. 2. *an adherent of*, as in *anarchist*.

**isth·mus** (is'məs), *n.* [*pl.* -MUSES, -MI (-mī)], [< Gr. *isthmos*, a neck], a narrow strip of land connecting two larger bodies of land.

**it** (it), *pron.* [for *pl.* see THEY], [AS. *hit*], the animal or thing previously mentioned. *It* is also used as: *a*) the subject of an impersonal verb: as, *it* is snowing. *b*) a subject or object of indefinite sense in various idiomatic constructions: as, *it's* all right, he lords *it* over us. *n.* in the game of "tag," etc., the player who must do some specific thing.

**i/t/a, I.T.A.**, Initial Teaching Alphabet.

**Ital., It.**, 1. Italian. 2. Italy.

**ital., it.**, italic; italics.

**I·tal·ian** (i-tal'yən), *adj.* of Italy, its people, language, etc. *n.* 1. a native or inhabitant of Italy. 2. the Romance language of Italy.

**i·tal·ic** (i-tal'ik), *adj.* [< its early use in *Italy*], designating a type in which the letters slant upward to the right: *this is italic type.* *n.* italic type or print: also **italics**, *pl.* (sometimes construed as sing.).

**i·tal·i·cize** (i-tal'ə-sīz'), *v.t.* [-CIZED, -CIZING], to print in italics.

**itch** (ich), *v.i.* [AS. *giccan*], 1. to feel a tingling of the skin, with the desire to scratch. 2. to have a restless desire. *n.* 1. an itching of the skin. 2. a skin disease accompanied by itching (with *the*). 3. a restless desire; hankering. —**itch'y** [-IER, -IEST], *adj.*

**-ite**, [< Gr. *-itēs*], a suffix meaning: 1. *an inhabitant of*, as in *Akronite*. 2. *an adherent of*, as in *laborite*. 3. *a manufactured product*, as in *dynamite*.

**i·tem** (ī'təm), *adv.* [L.], also: used before each article in a series being enumerated. *n.* 1. an article; unit; separate thing. 2. a bit of news or information.

**i'tem·ize'** (-īz'), *v.t.* [-IZED, -IZING], to specify the items of; set down by items.

**it·er·ate** (it'ə-rāt'), *v.t.* [-ATED, -ATING], [< L. *iterum*, again], to utter or do again; repeat. —**it'er·a'tion**, *n.*

**i·tin·er·ant** (ī-tin'ẽr-ənt), *adj.* [< L. *iter*, a walk], traveling from place to place. *n.* a traveler.

**i·tin·er·ar·y** (ī-tin'ə-rer'i), *n.* [*pl.* -IES], 1. a route. 2. a record of a journey. 3. a plan or outline of a journey or route.

**-itis**, [Gr. *-itis*], a suffix meaning *inflammation of* (a specified part or organ), as in *neuritis*.

**its** (its), *pron.* that or those belonging to it. *poss. pronominal adj.* of, belonging to, or done by it.

**it's** (its), 1. it is. 2. it has.

**it·self** (it-self'), *pron.* 1. the intensive form of **it**: as, the frame *itself* is valuable. 2. the reflexive form of **it**: as, the dog scratched *itself*.

**-ity**, [< L. *-itas*], a suffix meaning *state* or *quality*, as in *chastity*.

**I've** (īv), I have.

**-ive**, [L. *-ivus*], a suffix meaning: 1. *of*, or *having the nature of*, as in *substantive*. 2. *tending to*, as in *creative*.

**i·vo·ry** (ī'vẽr-i), *n.* [*pl.* -RIES], [< L. *ebur*], 1. the hard, white substance forming the tusks of elephants, walruses, etc. 2. a substance like ivory. 3. creamy white. 4. *pl.* [Slang], *a*) piano keys. *b*) dice. *adj.* 1. of or like ivory. 2. creamy-white.

**ivory tower**, figuratively, a place of mental withdrawal from reality or action.

**i·vy** (ī'vi), *n.* [*pl.* IVIES], [AS. *ifig*], 1. a climbing vine with a woody stem and evergreen leaves. 2. any of various similar climbing plants.

**-ize**, [< Gr. *-izein*], a suffix meaning: 1. *to cause to be*, as in *sterilize*. 2. *to become* (*like*), as in *crystallize*. 3. *to combine with*, as in *oxidize*. 4. *to engage in*, as in *theorize*.

# J

**J, j** (jā), *n.* [*pl.* J's, j's, Js, js], the tenth letter of the English alphabet.

**jab** (jab), *v.t.* & *v.i.* [JABBED, JABBING], [< ME. *jobben*, to peck], 1. to poke, as with a sharp instrument. 2. to punch with short, straight blows. *n.* a quick thrust or blow.

**jab·ber** (jab'ẽr), *v.i.* & *v.t.* [prob. echoic], to talk quickly, incoherently, or foolishly; chatter. *n.* chatter. —**jab'ber·er**, *n.*

**ja·bot** (zha'bō'), *n.* [*pl.* -BOTS (-bōz')], [Fr., bird's crop], a trimming or frill, often of lace, on the neck of a woman's blouse.

**jack** (jak), *n.* [< the name *Jack*], 1. [often J-], a man or boy. 2. any of various machines used to lift something heavy a short distance: as, an automobile *jack*. 3. a playing card with a page boy's picture on it. 4. a small flag flown on a ship's bow as a signal or to show nationality. 5. a plug-in receptacle used to make electric contact. 6. [Slang], money. *v.t.* to raise by means of a jack. —**jack up**, [Colloq.], to raise (prices, wages, etc.).

**jack-**, [see JACK], a combining form meaning: 1. *male*, as in *jackass*. 2. *large* or *strong*, as in *jackknife*. 3. *boy, fellow*, as in *jack-o'-lantern*.

**jack·al** (jak'ôl, -əl), *n.* [< Sans.], a yellowish-gray wild dog of Asia and N Africa.

**jack·ass** (jak'as'), *n.* [*jack-* + *ass*], 1. a male donkey. 2. a fool.

**jack·daw** (jak'dô'), *n.* [< *jack-* + ME. *dawe*, a jackdaw], a European black bird like a small crow.

**jack·et** (jak'it), *n.* [< Sp. *jaco*, coat], 1. a short coat. 2. an outer covering, as the removable paper cover on a book, the skin of a potato, etc. *v.t.* to put a jacket on.

**jack'-in-the-box'**, *n.* [*pl.* -BOXES], [see JACK-], a toy consisting of a box from which a figure on a spring jumps up when the lid is lifted.

**jack'-in-the-pul'pit** (-pool'pit), *n.* [*pl.* -PITS], [see JACK-], an American plant of the lily family, with a flower spike partly arched over by a hoodlike covering.

**jack'knife'**, *n.* [*pl.* -KNIVES], a large pocketknife. *v.i.* to bend at the middle, in the form of a half-open jackknife.

**jack'-of-all'-trades'**, *n.* [*pl.* JACKS-], [see JACK-], [often J-], one who can do many kinds of work acceptably.

**jack-o'-lan·tern** (jak'ə-lan'tẽrn), *n.* [*pl.* -TERNS], [see JACK-], a hollow pumpkin cut to look like a face and used as a lantern.

**jack'pot'**, *n.* [*jack*, playing card + *pot*], cumulative stakes, as in a poker game, slot machine, etc.: also **jack pot**.

**jack rabbit**, a large hare of W North America, with long ears and strong hind legs.

**Ja·cob** (jā'kəb), *n.* in the *Bible*, a son of Isaac: Gen. 25–50.

**jade** (jād), *n.* [< Sp. *piedra de ijada*, stone of the side: supposed to cure pains in the side], 1. a hard, ornamental stone, usually green. 2. the green color of this stone.

**jade** (jād), *n.* [? < ON. *jalda*, mare], 1. a worn-out, worthless horse. 2. a disreputable woman. *v.t. & v.i.* [JADED, JADING], to tire, weary, or satiate.

**jae·ger** (yā'gẽr), *n.* [< G. *jäger*, huntsman], a bird of the gull family, which robs weaker birds of their prey: also sp. **jäger**.

**jag** (jag), *n.* [ME. *jagge*], a sharp, toothlike projection.

**jag** (jag), *n.* [Slang], a drunken spree.

**jag·ged** (jag'id), *adj.* having sharp projecting points; raggedly torn. —**jag'ged·ly**, *adv.*

**jag·uar** (jag'wär), *n.* [Port. < S. Am. Ind.], a wild animal, like a large leopard, found from N Mexico to S Brazil.

**jai-a-lai** (hī'ə-lī'), *n.* [< Basque *jai*, celebration + *alai*, merry], a Latin-American game like handball, played with a basketlike racket fastened to the arm.

**jail** (jāl), *n.* [ult. < L. *cavea*, a cage], a prison for those convicted of minor offenses or awaiting trial. *v.t.* to put or keep in jail.

**jail'bird'** (-bũrd'), *n.* [Colloq.], 1. a prisoner in jail. 2. a person often put in jail.

**jail'er, jail'or**, *n.* a person in charge of a jail or of prisoners.

**ja·lop·y** (jə-lop'i), *n.* [*pl.* -IES], [prob. < Fr. *chaloupe*, skiff], [Slang], an old, ramshackle automobile or airplane: also sp. **jallopy**.

**jal·ou·sie** (jal'oo-sē'), *n.* [Fr.], a window, shade, door, etc. of wooden, metal, or glass slats arranged as in a Venetian blind.

**jam** (jam), *v.t.* [JAMMED, JAMMING], [< ?], 1. to squeeze into a confined space. 2. to crush. 3. to crowd. 4. to crowd into and block (a passageway, etc.). 5. to wedge so that it cannot move. 6. in *radio*, to make (signals) unintelligible by sending out others on the same wave length. *v.i.* 1. *a*) to become wedged fast. *b*) to become unworkable because of jammed parts. 2. to become squeezed into a confined space. 3. [Slang], in *jazz*, to improvise. *n.* 1. a jamming or being jammed: as, a traffic *jam*. 2. [Colloq.], a difficult situation.

**jam** (jam), *n.* [? < prec.], fruit boiled with sugar to a thick mixture.

**jamb, jambe** (jam), *n.* [< OFr. *jambe*, leg], a side post of a doorway, etc.

**jam·bo·ree** (jam'bə-rē'), *n.* [coined word], [Colloq.], a noisy revel.

**jan·gle** (jaŋ'g'l), *v.i.* [-GLED, -GLING], [< OFr. *jangler*], 1. to make a harsh, inharmonious sound. 2. to quarrel. *v.t.* to cause to make a harsh sound. *n.* 1. a harsh sound. 2. a quarrel.

**jan·i·tor** (jan'i-tẽr), *n.* [L., doorkeeper], one who takes care of a building, office, etc.

**Jan·u·ar·y** (jan'ū-er'i), *n.* [*pl.* -IES], [< L. < *Janus*], the first month of the year, having 31 days: abbrev. **Jan.**

**Ja·nus** (jā'nəs), *n.* in *Rom. myth.*, the god who was guardian of portals and patron of beginnings and endings.

**Jap.**, 1. Japan. 2. Japanese.

**ja·pan** (jə-pan'), *n.* [< *Japan*], a hard lacquer giving a glossy finish. *v.t.* [-PANNED, -PANNING], to varnish with japan.

**Jap·a·nese** (jap'ə-nēz'), *adj.* of Japan, its people, language, etc. *n.* 1. [*pl.* -NESE], a native of Japan. 2. the language of Japan.

**Japanese beetle**, a green-and-brown beetle, orig. from Japan, which eats leaves, fruits, and grasses.

**jape** (jāp), *n., v.t. & v.i.* [JAPED, JAPING], [ME. *japen*], joke; trick.

**jar** (jär), *v.i.* [JARRED, JARRING], [ult. echoic], 1. to make a harsh sound; grate. 2. to have an irritating effect (*on* one). 3. to vibrate from an impact. 4. to clash; conflict. *v.t.* to jolt, shock, etc. *n.* 1. a harsh, grating sound. 2. a vibration due to an impact. 3. a jolt; shock. 4. a clash; quarrel.

**jar** (jär), *n.* [< Ar. *jarrah*, earthen vessel], 1. a container made of glass, earthenware, etc., with a large opening. 2. as much as a jar will hold.

**jar·di·niere** (jär'd'n-êr'), *n.* [Fr. < *jardin*, a garden], an ornamental pot or stand for flowers or plants.

**jar·gon** (jär'gən), *n.* [OFr., a chattering], 1. unintelligible talk. 2. the specialized vocabulary of those in the same work, way of life, etc.

**jas·mine, jas·min** (jas'min, jaz'-), *n.* [< Per. *yāsamin*], a shrub with fragrant flowers of yellow, red, or white.

**Ja·son** (jā's'n), *n.* in *Gr. legend*, the leader of the Argonauts in the search for the Golden Fleece.

**jas·per** (jas'pẽr), *n.* [< Gr. *iaspis*], an opaque variety of colored quartz.

**jaun·dice** (jôn'dis), *n.* [ult. < L. *galbus*, yellow], a diseased condition in which the eyeballs, skin, and urine become abnormally yellow, caused by bile in the blood. *v.t.* [-DICED, -DICING], 1. to cause to have jaundice. 2. to make prejudiced through envy, etc.

**jaunt** (jônt), *v.i.* [< ?], to take a short pleasure trip. *n.* a short trip for pleasure.

**jaun·ty** (jôn'ti), *adj.* [-TIER, -TIEST], [< Fr. *gentil*, genteel], 1. stylish. 2. easy and careless; sprightly. —**jaun'ti·ly**, *adv.*

**Ja·va** (jä′və, jav′ə), ***n.*** [< *Java*, Indonesia], [often j-], [Slang], coffee.
**jave·lin** (jav′lin, -ə-lin), ***n.*** [< Fr. *javeline*], a light spear, esp. one thrown for distance in a contest.
**jaw** (jô), ***n.*** [< OFr. *joue*, cheek], 1. either of the two bony parts that hold the teeth and frame the mouth. 2. either of two movable parts that grasp or crush something, as in a vise. ***v.i.*** [Slang], to talk.
**jaw′bone′**, ***n.*** a bone of a jaw. ***v.t. & v.i.*** [-BONED, -BONING], to attempt to persuade by using one's high office to apply pressure.
**jay** (jā), ***n.*** [< LL. *gaius*, jay], 1. any of several birds of the crow family. 2. a bluejay.
**jay′walk′**, ***v.i.*** [< slang *jay*, stupid person + *walk*], [Colloq.], to cross a street without regard to traffic rules or signals.
**jazz** (jaz), ***n.*** [< Creole patois *jass*], 1. a kind of music of American Negro origin, characterized by syncopation, melodic variations, unusual tonal effects, etc. 2. [Slang], lively spirit. ***adj.*** of, in, or like jazz. ***v.t.*** to play or arrange as jazz. **—jazz up**, [Slang], to enliven. **—jazz′y** [-IER, -IEST], ***adj.***
**jeal·ous** (jel′əs), ***adj.*** [see ZEAL], 1. watchful in guarding: as, he is *jealous* of his rights. 2. resentfully suspicious: as, a *jealous* lover. 3. resulting from such a feeling: as, a *jealous* rage. 4. resentfully envious.
**jeal′ous·y**, ***n.*** [*pl.* -IES], a jealous quality, state of mind, or feeling.
**jean** (jēn), ***n.*** [< L. *Genua*, Genoa], 1. a durable, twilled cotton cloth. 2. *pl.* trousers or overalls of this.
**jeep** (jēp), ***n.*** [< an animal in a comic strip by E. C. Segar], a small, rugged, military automobile.
**jeer** (jêr), ***v.i. & v.t.*** [? < *cheer*], to make fun of in a rude, sarcastic manner; scoff (at). ***n.*** a jeering remark. **—jeer′ing·ly**, ***adv.***
**Je·ho·vah** (ji-hō′və), ***n.*** [< Heb. sacred name for God], God.
**je·june** (ji-jōōn′), ***adj.*** [L. *jejunus*, empty], not satisfying or interesting.
**jell** (jel), ***v.i. & v.t.*** [< *jelly*], [Colloq.], 1. to become, or make into, jelly. 2. to crystallize, as a plan. ***n.*** [Colloq.], jelly.
**jel·ly** (jel′i), ***n.*** [*pl.* -LIES], [< L. *gelare*, freeze], 1. a soft, gelatinous food made from cooked fruit sirup or meat juice. 2. any substance like this. ***v.i. & v.t.*** [-LIED, -LYING], to become, or make into, jelly.
**jel′ly·fish′**, ***n.*** [*pl.* see FISH], 1. a sea animal with an umbrella-shaped body of jellylike substance and long tentacles. 2. [Colloq.], a weak-willed person.
**jeop·ard·ize** (jep′ẽr-dīz′), ***v.t.*** [-IZED, -IZING], to put into jeopardy; endanger.
**jeop·ard·y** (jep′ẽr-di), ***n.*** [*pl.* -IES], [< OFr. *jeu parti*, lit., a game with even chances], risk; danger.
**Jer·e·mi·ah** (jer′ə-mī′ə), ***n.*** in the *Bible*, a Hebrew prophet.
**jerk** (jũrk), ***n.*** [< ?], 1. a sharp, abrupt pull, twist, etc. 2. a sudden muscular contraction; twitch. 3. [Slang], a person regarded as stupid, dull, etc. ***v.t. & v.i.*** 1. to move with a jerk; pull sharply. 2. to twitch.
**jerk** (jũrk), ***v.t.*** [< Sp. *charqui*, dried meat], to preserve (meat) by drying sliced strips of it in the sun.
**jer·kin** (jũr′kin), ***n.*** [cf. OFr. *jergot*, doublet], a short, closefitting jacket, often sleeveless.
**jerk′wa′ter**, ***adj.*** [Colloq.], small, unimportant, etc.: as, a *jerkwater* town.
**jerk·y** (jũr′ki), ***adj.*** [-IER, -IEST], characterized by jerks; spasmodic. **—jerk′i·ly**, ***adv.***
**Jer·sey** (jũr′zi), ***n.*** [< *Jersey*, one of the Channel Islands], 1. any of a breed of reddish-brown dairy cattle. 2. [j-], *a*) a soft, knitted cloth. *b*) [*pl.* -SEYS], a closefitting, knitted upper garment.
**jest** (jest), ***n.*** [< L. *gerere*, perform], 1. a mocking remark; taunt. 2. a joke. 3. ridicule. 4. something to be laughed at. ***v.i.*** 1. to jeer; banter. 2. to joke.
**jest′er**, ***n.*** one who jests; esp., a fool employed to amuse a ruler in the Middle Ages.
**Jes·u·it** (jezh′ōō-it, jez′ū-), ***n.*** a member of the Society of Jesus, a R.C. religious order, founded 1534. ***adj.*** of the Jesuits.
**Je·sus** (jē′zəs), ***n.*** the founder of the Christian religion: also **Jesus Christ.**
**jet** (jet), ***v.t. & v.i.*** [JETTED, JETTING], [< L. *jacere*, to throw], to gush out in a stream. ***n.*** 1. a stream of liquid or gas suddenly emitted. 2. a spout for emitting a jet. 3. a jet-propelled airplane: also **jet (air)plane.**
**jet** (jet), ***n.*** [< Gr. *Gagas*, town in Asia Minor], 1. a hard, black mineral like coal, used in jewelry. 2. a lustrous black. ***adj.*** 1. black. 2. made of jet.
**jet′lin′er**, ***n.*** a commercial jet aircraft for carrying passengers.
**jet′port′**, ***n.*** an airport with long runways, for use by jet airplanes.
**jet propulsion**, a method of propelling airplanes, boats, etc. by causing gases to be emitted under pressure from a rear vent. **—jet-pro·pelled** (jet′prə-peld′), ***adj.***
**jet·sam** (jet′səm), ***n.*** [see JETTISON], 1. cargo thrown overboard to lighten a ship in danger. 2. such cargo washed ashore.
**jet·ti·son** (jet′ə-s'n), ***v.t.*** [< L. *jactare*, to throw], 1. to throw (goods) overboard so as to lighten a ship in danger. 2. to discard.
**jet·ty** (jet′i), ***n.*** [*pl.* -TIES], [see JET, *v.*], 1. a wall built out into the water to restrain currents, protect a harbor, etc. 2. a landing pier.
**Jew** (jōō), ***n.*** [< Heb. *yehūdi*, citizen of Judah], 1. a person descended, or regarded as descended, from the ancient Hebrews. 2. a person whose religion is Judaism.
**jew·el** (jōō′əl), ***n.*** [ult. < L. *jocus*, a joke], 1. a precious stone; gem. 2. any person or thing very dear to one. 3. a small gem used as a bearing in a watch. ***v.t.*** [-ELED or -ELLED, -ELING or -ELLING], to decorate or set with jewels.
**jew·el·er, jew·el·ler** (jōō′əl-ẽr), ***n.*** one who makes or deals in jewelry.
**jew′el·ry**, ***n.*** jewels collectively.
**Jew·ish** (jōō′ish), ***adj.*** of or characteristic of the Jews. ***n.*** popularly, Yiddish.
**Jew·ry** (jōō′ri), ***n.*** the Jewish people.
**Jez·e·bel** (jez′ə-b'l), ***n.*** in the *Bible*, a wicked queen of Israel.
**j.g., jg.**, junior grade.
**jib** (jib), ***n.*** [< ?], a triangular sail projecting ahead of the foremast.
**jibe** (jīb), ***v.i.*** [JIBED, JIBING], [< D. *gijpen*], 1. to shift from one side of a ship to the other, as a fore-and-aft sail. 2. to change the course of a ship so that the sails jibe. 3. [Colloq.], to be in agreement or accord.
**jibe** (jīb), ***n., v.i. & v.t.*** [JIBED, JIBING], gibe.
**jif·fy** (jif′i), ***n.*** [*pl.* -FIES], [Colloq.], a very short time: also **jiff.**
**jig** (jig), ***n.*** [< OFr. *gigue*], 1. a fast, springy dance in triple time, or music for this. 2. a device used to guide a tool, as a drill. ***v.i. & v.t.*** [JIGGED, JIGGING], to dance (a jig).
**jig·ger** (jig′ẽr), ***n.*** 1. a small glass, usually of 1½ ozs., used to measure liquor. 2. the contents of a jigger.
**jig·gle** (jig′'l), ***v.t. & v.i.*** [-GLED, -GLING], [< *jig*], to move in quick, slight jerks. ***n.*** a jiggling.
**jig·saw** (jig′sô′), ***n.*** a saw consisting of a narrow blade set in a frame, used for cutting along wavy or irregular lines: also **jig saw.**
**jigsaw puzzle**, a puzzle consisting of irregularly cut pieces of pasteboard, etc. which when fitted together form a picture.
**jilt** (jilt), ***v.t.*** [? < *Jill*, sweetheart], to reject

or cast off (a lover or sweetheart) after encouraging him.

**Jim Crow** (jim′ krō′), [name of an early Negro minstrel song], [Colloq.], discrimination against or segregation of Negroes. —**jim′-crow′**, *adj. & v.t.*

**jim·my** (jim′i), *n.* [*pl.* -MIES], [< *James*], a short crowbar, used by burglars to pry open windows, etc. *v.t.* [-MIED, -MYING], to pry open with or as with a jimmy.

**jin·gle** (jiŋ′g'l), *v.i.* [-GLED, -GLING], [echoic], 1. to make light, ringing sounds, as small bells. 2. to have easy rhythm, simple rhymes, etc., as some poetry. *v.t.* to cause to jingle. *n.* a jingling sound, verse, etc.

**jin·go** (jiŋ′gō), *n.* [*pl.* -GOES], [< phr. *by jingo* in a patriotic Brit. song], one who favors an aggressive, warlike foreign policy. —**jin′go·ism**, *n.*

**jin·ni** (ji-nē′), *n.* [*pl.* JINN], [Ar.], in *Moslem legend*, a supernatural being that can influence human affairs; genie.

**jin·rik·i·sha** (jin-rik′shô), *n.* [< Japan. *jin*, a man + *riki*, power + *sha*, carriage], a small, two-wheeled oriental carriage, pulled by one or two men: also sp. **jinricksha.**

**jinx** (jiŋks), *n.* [? < Gr. *iynx*, the wryneck, bird used in casting spells], [Slang], a person or thing supposed to cause bad luck. *v.t.* [JINXED, JINXING], [Slang], to cause bad luck to.

**jit·ney** (jit′ni), *n.* [*pl.* -NEYS], [? < Fr. *jeton*, a token], [Slang], 1. a five-cent coin. 2. a bus or car carrying passengers for a small fare, orig. five cents.

**jit·ter** (jit′ẽr), *v.i.* [? echoic], [Slang], to be nervous; fidget. —**the jitters**, [Slang], a nervous feeling; fidgets. —**jit′ter·y**, *adj.*

**jit′ter·bug′**, *n.* [*jitter* + *bug*], [Slang], one who dances in a fast, acrobatic manner to jazz music. *v.i.* [-BUGGED, -BUGGING], [Slang], to dance thus.

**jiu·jit·su** (jōō-jit′sōō), *n.* jujitsu.

**jive** (jiv), *n.* [< ?], [Slang], jazz or its jargon.

**Job** (jōb), *n.* in the *Bible*, a man who endured much suffering but did not lose his faith in God.

**job** (job), *n.* [< ME. *gobbe*, portion], 1. a piece of work done for pay. 2. task; duty. 3. the thing or material being worked on. 4. employment; work. *adj.* hired or done by the job. *v.t. & v.i.* [JOBBED, JOBBING], 1. to handle (goods) as middleman. 2. to sublet (work, etc.). —**job′less**, *adj.*

**job·ber** (job′ẽr), *n.* 1. one who buys goods in quantity and sells them to dealers. 2. one who does piecework.

**job lot,** goods, often of various sorts, for sale as one quantity.

**jock·ey** (jok′i), *n.* [*pl.* -EYS], [< Scot. dim. of *Jack*], one whose job is to ride a horse in a race. *v.t. & v.i.* [-EYED, -EYING], 1. to cheat; swindle. 2. to maneuver for position or advantage.

**jo·cose** (jō-kōs′), *adj.* [< L. *jocus*, a joke], humorous; facetious. —**jo·cos′i·ty** (-kos′ə-ti) [*pl.* -TIES], *n.*

**joc·u·lar** (jok′yoo-lẽr), *adj.* [< L. *jocus*, a joke], joking; full of fun. —**joc′u·lar′i·ty** (-lar′ə-ti) [*pl.* -TIES], *n.* —**joc′u·lar·ly**, *adv.*

**joc·und** (jok′ənd), *adj.* [< L. *jucundus*, pleasant], cheerful; genial; gay. —**jo·cun·di·ty** (jō-kun′di-ti), *n.*

**jodh·purs** (jod′pẽrz), *n.pl.* [after *Jodhpur*, India], riding breeches made loose and full above the knees and closefitting below.

**jog** (jog), *v.t.* [JOGGED, JOGGING], [ME. *joggen*], 1. to give a little shake to. 2. to nudge. *v.i.* to move along at a slow, steady, jolting pace (with *on* or *along*). *n.* 1. a little shake or nudge. 2. a slow, steady, jolting motion: also **jog trot.**

**jog** (jog), *n.* [var. of *jag*], a projecting or notched part in a surface or line.

**jog·gle** (jog′'l), *v.t. & v.i.* [-GLED, -GLING], [< *jog*], to shake or jolt slightly. *n.* a slight jolt.

**John** (jon), *n.* in the *Bible*, 1. a Christian apostle, the reputed author of the fourth Gospel. 2. this book.

**John Bull** (bool), England, or an Englishman, personified.

**John Doe** (dō), a fictitious name used in legal papers for an unknown person.

**john·ny·cake** (jon′i-kāk′), *n.* [origin unc.], a kind of corn bread.

**John the Baptist,** in the *Bible*, the forerunner and baptizer of Jesus.

**join** (join), *v.t. & v.i.* [< L. *jungere*], 1. to bring or come together (with); connect; combine; unite. 2. to become a part or member of (a club, etc.). 3. to participate (*in* a conversation, etc.).

**join′er**, *n.* 1. a carpenter who finishes interior woodwork. 2. [Colloq.], one who joins many organizations.

**joint** (joint), *n.* [< L. *jungere*, join], 1. a place where, or way in which, two things are joined. 2. one of the parts of a jointed whole. 3. a large cut of meat with the bone still in it. 4. in *anatomy*, a place where two bones, etc. are joined, usually so that they can move. 5. a point where a branch or leaf grows out of a stem. 6. [Slang], a saloon, cheap restaurant, etc. *adj.* 1. common to two or more: as, a *joint* declaration. 2. sharing with another: as, a *joint* owner. *v.t.* 1. to fasten together by a joint or joints. 2. to cut (meat) into joints. —**out of joint,** 1. dislocated. 2. disordered.

**joint′ly,** *adv.* in common.

**joist** (joist), *n.* [< OFr. *giste*, bed], any of the parallel timbers that hold up the planks of a floor or the laths of a ceiling.

**joke** (jōk), *n.* [L. *jocus*], 1. anything said or done to arouse laughter, as a funny anecdote. 2. something not meant to be taken seriously. 3. a person or thing to be laughed at. *v.i.* [JOKED, JOKING], to make jokes.

**jok′er,** *n.* 1. one who jokes. 2. a hidden provision, as in a legal document, etc., to make it different from what it seems to be. 3. an extra playing card used in some games.

**jol·li·ty** (jol′ə-ti), *n.* a being jolly; gaiety.

**jol·ly** (jol′i), *adj.* [-LIER, -LIEST], [OFr. *joli*], 1. full of high spirits and good humor; merry. 2. [Colloq.], enjoyable. *v.t. & v.i.* [-LIED, -LYING], [Colloq.], 1. to try to make (a person) feel good, as by flattering. 2. to make fun of. —**jol′li·ly**, *adv.* —**jol′li·ness**, *n.*

**jol′ly-boat′** (jol′i-), *n.* [prob. < D. *jol*, yawl], a ship's small boat: also **jolly boat.**

**jolt** (jōlt), *v.t.* [< earlier *jot*], to shake up, as a vehicle running on a rough road. *v.i.* to move along in a bumpy manner. *n.* 1. a sudden jerk, bump, etc. 2. a shock or surprise.

**Jo·nah** (jō′nə), *n.* 1. in the *Bible*, a Hebrew prophet: thrown overboard in a storm, he was swallowed by a big fish, but later cast up unharmed. 2. any person said to bring bad luck by his presence.

**jon·quil** (joŋ′kwil, jon′-), *n.* [< L. *juncus*, a rush], a variety of narcissus with yellow or white flowers.

**Jo·seph** (jō′zəf), *n.* in the *Bible*, 1. one of Jacob's sons, who became a high official in Egypt. 2. the husband of Mary, mother of Jesus.

**josh** (josh), *v.t. & v.i.* [? *joke* and *bosh*], [Slang], to ridicule in a good-humored way.

**Josh·u·a** (josh′oo-ə), *n.* in the *Bible*, Moses' successor, and leader of the Israelites into the Promised Land.

**joss** (jos), *n.* [Pid. Eng.; ult. < L. *deus*, god], a figure of a Chinese god.

**jos·tle** (jos′'l), *v.t. & v.i.* [-TLED, -TLING], [see JOUST], to push, as in a crowd; shove roughly. *n.* a jostling. —**jos′tle·ment,** *n.*

**jot** (jot), *n.* [< Gr. *iōta*, the smallest letter], a very small amount. *v.t.* [JOTTED, JOTTING], to make a brief note of (usually with *down*). —**jot'ter**, *n.*

**jounce** (jouns), *v.t.* & *v.i.* [JOUNCED, JOUNCING], [prob. < *jaunt*], to jolt or bounce. *n.* a jolt.

**jour·nal** (jũr'n'l), *n.* [< L. *diurnalis*, daily], 1. a daily record of happenings. 2. a diary. 3. a record of the transactions of a club, etc. 4. a newspaper, magazine, etc. 5. in *bookkeeping*, a book of original entry for recording transactions. 6. in *mechanics*, the part of an axle, etc. that turns in a bearing.

**jour'nal·ese'** (-ēz', -ēs'), *n.* a facile style of newspaper writing with characteristic hackneyed expressions.

**jour'nal·ism** (-iz'm), *n.* the work of gathering news for, or producing, a newspaper or other journal. —**jour'nal·ist**, *n.* —**jour'nal·is'tic**, *adj.*

**jour·ney** (jũr'ni), *n.* [*pl.* -NEYS], [< OFr. *journee*; ult. < L. *dies*, day], a traveling from one place to another; trip. *v.i.* [-NEYED, -NEYING], to travel.

**jour'ney·man** (-mən), *n.* [*pl.* -MEN], [archaic *journey*, day's work + *man*], a worker who has learned his trade.

**joust** (just, joust), *n.* [ult. < L. *juxta*, close to], 1. a combat with lances between two knights on horseback. 2. *pl.* a tournament. *v.i.* to engage in a joust. —**joust'er**, *n.*

**Jove** (jōv), *n.* [Poetic], Jupiter.

**jo·vi·al** (jō'vi-əl), *adj.* [< LL. *Jovialis*, of Jupiter: from astrological notion of planet's influence], full of hearty, playful good humor; gay. —**jo'vi·al'i·ty** (-al'ə-ti), *n.*

**jowl** (joul), *n.* [AS. *ceafl*, jaw], 1. the lower jaw. 2. the cheek.

**jowl** (joul), *n.* [AS. *ceole*, throat], a fleshy, hanging part under the jaw.

**joy** (joi), *n.* [ult. < L. *gaudium*, joy], 1. a very glad feeling; happiness; delight. 2. anything causing this. —**joy'less**, *adj.*

**joy'ful**, *adj.* 1. full of joy. 2. feeling, expressing, or causing joy; glad. —**joy'ful·ly**, *adv.*

**joy'ous** (-əs), *adj.* joyful; happy; gay.

**joy ride**, [Colloq.], an automobile ride merely for pleasure, often with reckless speed.

**J.P.**, Justice of the Peace.

**Jr., jr.**, junior.

**ju·bi·lant** (jōō'b'l-ənt), *adj.* [< L. *jubilum*, wild shout], joyful and triumphant; rejoicing; elated. —**ju'bi·lant·ly**, *adv.*

**ju·bi·la·tion** (jōō'b'l-ā'shən), *n.* 1. a rejoicing. 2. a happy celebration.

**ju·bi·lee** (jōō'b'l-ē'), *n.* [< Heb. *yōbēl*, a ram's horn (trumpet)], 1. a 50th or 25th anniversary. 2. a time or occasion of rejoicing. 3. jubilation; rejoicing.

**Ju·dah** (jōō'də), *n.* in the *Bible*, one of Jacob's sons.

**Ju·da·ism** (jōō'di-iz'm), *n.* the Jewish religion.

**Ju·das (Is·car·i·ot)** (jōō'dəs is-kar'i-ət), 1. the disciple who betrayed Jesus for pay. 2. a betrayer; informer.

**judge** (juj), *n.* [< L. *jus*, law + *dicere*, say], 1. a public official with authority to hear and decide cases in a court of law. 2. a person designated to determine the winner, settle a controversy, etc. 3. a person qualified to decide on the relative worth of anything. *v.t.* & *v.i.* [JUDGED, JUDGING], 1. to hear and pass judgment (on) in a court of law. 2. to determine the winner of (a contest) or settle (a controversy). 3. to form an opinion about. 4. to criticize or censure. 5. to think; suppose. —**judge'ship**, *n.*

**judg'ment, judge'ment**, *n.* 1. a judging; deciding. 2. a legal decision; order given by a judge, etc. 3. an opinion or estimate. 4. the ability to come to an opinion. 5. [J-], the Last Judgment.

**Judgment Day**, in *theology*, the day of God's final judgment of all people.

**ju·di·ca·to·ry** (jōō'di-kə-tôr'i), *adj.* [see JUDGE], having to do with administering justice. *n.* [*pl.* -RIES], a law court, or law courts collectively.

**ju'di·ca·ture** (-chẽr), *n.* 1. the administering of justice. 2. jurisdiction of a judge or court. 3. judges or courts collectively.

**ju·di·cial** (jōō-dish'əl), *adj.* 1. of judges, courts, or their functions. 2. allowed, enforced, etc. by a court. 3. befitting a judge. 4. fair; impartial. —**ju·di'cial·ly**, *adv.*

**ju·di·ci·ar·y** (jōō-dish'i-er'i), *adj.* of judges or courts. *n.* [*pl.* -IES], 1. the part of government that administers justice. 2. judges collectively.

**ju·di·cious** (jōō-dish'əs), *adj.* [see JUDGE], having, applying, or showing sound judgment. —**ju·di'cious·ly**, *adv.*

**ju·do** (jōō'dō), *n.* a form of jujitsu developed as a sport and as a means of self-defense.

**jug** (jug), *n.* [a pet form of *Judith* or *Joan*], 1. a container for liquids, with a small opening and a handle. 2. [Slang], a jail.

**jug·gle** (jug''l), *v.t.* & *v.i.* [-GLED, -GLING], [< L. *jocus*, a joke], 1. to perform tricks of skill or sleight of hand with (balls, etc.). 2. to use trickery on so as to deceive. —**jug'gler**, *n.* —**jug'gler·y**, *n.*

**Ju·go·slav, Ju·go-Slav** (ū'gō-släv'), *n.* & *adj.* Yugoslav. —**Ju'go·slav'ic**, *adj.*

**jug·u·lar** (jug'yoo-lẽr), *adj.* [< L. *jugum*, a yoke], of the neck or throat. *n.* either of two large veins in the neck carrying blood from the head: in full, **jugular vein.**

**juice** (jōōs), *n.* [< L. *jus*, soup], 1. the liquid part of a plant, fruit, etc. 2. a liquid in or from animal tissue. 3. [Slang], electricity. *v.t.* [JUICED, JUICING], [Colloq.], to extract juice from.

**juic'er**, *n.* a device or appliance for extracting juice from fruit.

**juic·y** (jōō'si), *adj.* [-IER, -IEST], 1. full of juice. 2. full of interest. —**juic'i·ness**, *n.*

**ju·jit·su, ju·jut·su** (jōō-jit'sōō), *n.* [< Japan. *jū*, pliant + *jutsu*, art], a Japanese system of wrestling in which the strength and weight of an opponent are used against him.

**juke box** (jōōk), [< Am. Negro *jook-house*, roadhouse], [Colloq.], an electric phonograph operated by a coin.

**ju·lep** (jōō'lip), *n.* [< Per. *gūl*, rose + *āb*, water], an iced drink of whisky or brandy, sugar, and fresh mint: also **mint julep.**

**Jul·ian calendar** (jōōl'yən), the calendar introduced by Julius Caesar in 46 B.C. and used until the Gregorian calendar was introduced.

**ju·li·enne** (jōō'li-en'), *adj.* [< *Julien*, a Fr. caterer], cut into strips: said of vegetables.

**Ju·li·et** (jōōl'yət, jōō'li-et'), *n.* the heroine of Shakespeare's tragedy *Romeo and Juliet.*

**Ju·ly** (jōō-lī'), *n.* [*pl.* -LIES], [< L. < *Julius* Caesar], the seventh month of the year, having 31 days.

**jum·ble** (jum'b'l) *v.t.* & *v.i.* [-BLED, -BLING], [merging of *jump* & *tumble*], to mix or be mixed in a confused, disorderly heap. *n.* a confused mixture or heap.

**jum·bo** (jum'bō), *n.* [*pl.* -BOS], [< *Jumbo*, P. T. Barnum's elephant], a large person, animal, or thing. *adj.* very large.

**jump** (jump), *v.i.* [< ?], 1. to spring from the ground, etc.; leap. 2. to jerk; bob. 3. to start in surprise. 4. to move abruptly, as to a new topic. 5. to rise suddenly, as prices. *v.t.* 1. to leap over. 2. to cause to leap. 3. to spring aboard or leap from (a train, etc.). 4. to cause (prices, etc.) to rise. 5. [Slang], to attack suddenly. 6. [Slang], to leave suddenly: as, to *jump* town. *n.* 1. a jumping. 2. a distance jumped. 3. a sudden transition. 4. a sudden rise, as in prices. 5. a sudden, nervous start; twitch. **—get** (or **have**) **the jump on,** [Slang], to get (or have) an advantage over.**—jump at,** to accept eagerly. **—jump bail,** to forfeit one's bail by running away. **—jump the gun,** [Slang], to begin something before the right time. **—jump'er,** *n.*

**jump·er** (jum'pẽr), *n.* [< dial. *jump*, short coat], 1. a loose jacket. 2. a sleeveless dress for wearing over a blouse, etc.

**jump'y,** *adj.* [-IER, -IEST], 1. moving in jumps, etc. 2. easily made nervous.

**Jun.,** Junior.

**junc·tion** (juŋk'shən), *n.* [< L. *jungere*, join], 1. a joining or being joined. 2. a place of joining, as of roads.

**junc·ture** (juŋk'chẽr), *n.* 1. a junction. 2. a point of time. 3. a crisis.

**June** (jōōn), *n.* [< L. *Junius* (a Roman family)], the sixth month of the year, having 30 days.

**jun·gle** (juŋ'g'l), *n.* [< Sans. *jangala*, wasteland], land densely covered with trees, vines, etc., as in the tropics.

**jun·ior** (jōōn'yẽr), *adj.* [L. < *juvenis*, young], 1. the younger: written *Jr.* after a son's name if it is the same as his father's. 2. of more recent position or lower status: as, a *junior* partner. 3. of juniors. *n.* 1. one who is younger, of lower rank, etc. 2. a third-year student in a high school or college.

**junior college,** a school offering only the first two years of a college course.

**junior high school,** a school teaching the 7th, 8th, and 9th grades.

**ju·ni·per** (jōō'nə-pẽr), *n.* [L. *juniperus*], a small evergreen shrub or tree with berry-like cones.

**junk** (juŋk), *n.* [< ?], 1. old metal, paper, rags, etc. 2. [Colloq.], rubbish. *v.t.* [Colloq.], to discard.

**junk** (juŋk), *n.* [< Malay *dgong*], a Chinese flat-bottomed ship.

**Jun·ker, jun·ker** (yooŋ'kẽr), *n.* [G.], a German of the landowning class.

**jun·ket** (juŋ'kit), *n.* [< It. *giuncata*, cream cheese], 1. milk sweetened, flavored, and thickened into curd. 2. a picnic. 3. an excursion; esp., an excursion by an official, at public expense. *v.i.* to go on a junket. *v.t.* to entertain, as on a junket.

**Ju·no** (jōō'nō), *n.* in *Rom. myth.*, the wife of Jupiter and queen of the gods.

**jun·to** (jun'tō), *n.* [*pl.* -TOS], [< Sp. < L. *jungere*, join], a group of political intriguers.

**Ju·pi·ter** (jōō'pə-tẽr), *n.* 1. the chief Roman god. 2. the largest planet in the solar system: cf. **planet.**

**ju·rid·i·cal** (joo-rid'i-k'l), *adj.* [< L. *jus*, law + *dicere*, declare], of judicial proceedings, or of law. **—ju·rid'i·cal·ly,** *adv.*

**ju·ris·dic·tion** (joor'is-dik'shən), *n.* [< L. *jus*, law + *dicere*, declare], 1. the administering of justice. 2. authority. 3. the range of authority. **—ju'ris·dic'tion·al,** *adj.*

**ju·ris·pru·dence** (joor'is-prōō'd'ns), *n.* [< L. *jus*, law + *prudentia*, a foreseeing], 1. the science or philosophy of law. 2. a system of laws.

**ju·rist** (joor'ist), *n.* [< L. *jus*, law], an expert in law; writer on law.

**ju·ror** (joor'ẽr), *n.* a member of a jury: also **ju'ry·man** [*pl.* -MEN], *n.*

**ju·ry** (joor'i), *n.* [*pl.* -RIES], [< L. *jurare*, swear], 1. a group of people sworn to hear evidence in a law case and to give a decision. 2. a committee that decides winners in a contest.

**just** (just), *adj.* [< L. *jus*, law], 1. right or fair: as, a *just* decision. 2. righteous: as, a *just* man. 3. deserved: as, a *just* rebuke. 4. lawful. 5. right; proper. 6. correct; true. 7. accurate; exact. *adv.* 1. exactly: as, *just* one o'clock. 2. almost exactly. 3. only: as, *just* a simple man. 4. barely: as, *just* missed him. 5. a very short time ago: as, she's *just* left. 6. [Colloq.], quite; really: as, *just* beautiful. **—just now,** a moment ago. **—just the same,** [Colloq.], nevertheless.

**jus·tice** (jus'tis), *n.* 1. a being righteous. 2. fairness. 3. rightfulness. 4. reward or penalty as deserved. 5. the use of authority to uphold what is just. 6. the administration of law. 7. a judge. 8. a justice of the peace. **—do justice to,** to treat fairly or with due appreciation. **—jus'tice·ship,** *n.*

**justice of the peace,** a local magistrate, who decides minor cases, performs marriages, etc.

**jus·ti·fy** (jus'tə-fī'), *v.t.* [-FIED, -FYING], [< L. *justus*, just + *facere*, make], 1. to show to be just, right, etc. 2. to free from blame or guilt. 3. to supply good grounds for. **—jus'ti·fi'a·ble,** *adj.* **—jus'ti·fi'a·bly,** *adv.* **—jus'ti·fi·ca'tion** (-fi-kā'shən), *n.*

**jut** (jut), *v.i.* [JUTTED, JUTTING], [< *jet*, *v.*], to stick out; project. *n.* a part that juts.

**Jute** (jōōt), *n.* a member of any of several early Germanic tribes in Jutland: Jutes settled in England in the 5th century A.D.

**jute** (jōōt), *n.* [< Sans. *juta*, matted hair], 1. a strong fiber used for making burlap, rope, etc. 2. an East Indian plant having this fiber.

**ju·ven·ile** (jōō'və-n'l, -nil'), *adj.* [< L. *juvenis*, young], 1. young; immature. 2. of or for young persons. *n.* 1. a young person. 2. an actor who takes youthful roles. 3. a book for children.

**jux·ta·pose** (juks'tə-pōz'), *v.t.* [-POSED, -POSING], [< L. *juxta*, beside; + *pose*, *v.*], to put side by side; place close together. **—jux'ta·po·si'tion** (-pə-zish'ən), *n.*

# K

**K, k** (kā), *n.* [*pl.* K's, k's, Ks, ks], the eleventh letter of the English alphabet.

**K,** *kalium*, [Mod. L.], in *chem.*, potassium.

**K., k.,** 1. karat (carat). 2. kilogram. 3. king. 4. knight. 5. in *naut. usage*, knot.

**kaf·fir** (kaf'ẽr), *n.* a grain sorghum grown in dry regions for grain and fodder.

**kai·ser** (kī'zẽr), *n.* [< L. *Caesar*], emperor: the title [K-] of the former rulers of Austria and Germany.

**kale, kail** (kāl), *n.* [Scot. var. of *cole*], 1. a hardy cabbage with spreading, curled leaves. 2. [Slang], money.

**ka·lei·do·scope** (kə-lī'də-skōp'), *n.* [< Gr. *kalos*, beautiful + *eidos*, form; + *-scope*], 1. a small tube containing bits of colored glass reflected by mirrors to form symmetrical patterns as the tube is rotated. 2. anything that constantly changes. **—ka·lei'do·scop'ic** (-skop'ik), *adj.*

**ka·liph, ka·lif** (kā'lif), *n.* a caliph.

**kal·so·mine** (kal'sə-mīn'), *n.* & *v.t.* calcimine.

**Kan·a·ka** (kə-nak'ə, kan'ə-kə), *n.* [Haw., man], a Hawaiian.

**kan·ga·roo** (kaŋ'gə-rōō'), *n.* [< ?], a leaping, plant-eating mammal of Australia and nearby islands, with short forelegs and strong, large hind legs: the female has a pouch for carrying her young.

**kangaroo court,** [Colloq.], a mock court illegally passing and executing judgment, as among frontiersmen.
**ka·o·lin, ka·o·line** (kā'ə-lin), *n.* [Fr. < Chin. name of hill where found], a white clay used in porcelain, etc.
**ka·pok** (kā'pok), *n.* [Malay *kapoq*], the silky fibers around the seeds of a tropical tree (**kapok tree**), used for stuffing pillows, mattresses, etc.
**kap·pa** (kap'ə), *n.* the tenth letter of the Greek alphabet (Κ, κ).
**ka·put** (kä-po͞ot'), *adj.* [G.], [Colloq.], lost, ruined, destroyed, etc.
**kar·a·kul** (kar'ə-kəl), *n.* [< *Kara Kul*, lake in the U.S.S.R.], 1. a sheep of C Asia. 2. the curly black fur from the fleece of its newborn lambs. Also sp. **caracul, karakule.**
**kar·at** (kar'ət), *n.* a carat.
**ka·ra·te** (kä-rä'tē), *n.* [Japan. lit., open hand], a Japanese system of self-defense using the side of the open hand.
**ka·ty·did** (kā'ti-did'), *n.* [echoic of its shrill sound], a large, green, tree insect resembling the grasshopper.
**kay·ak** (kī'ak), *n.* [Esk.], an Eskimo canoe made of skins covering a wooden frame.
**kay·o** (kā'ō'), *n.* & *v.t.* [-OED, -OING], [< *k*nock *o*ut], [Slang], in *boxing*, KO; knockout.
**kc.,** kilocycle; kilocycles.
**keel** (kēl), *n.* [< ON. *kjölr*], the chief timber or steel piece extending along the length of the bottom of a boat or ship. **—keel over,** [Colloq.], 1. to turn upside down. 2. to fall over suddenly. **—on an even keel,** in an upright, level position.
**keen** (kēn), *adj.* [AS. *cene*, wise], 1. having a sharp edge or point: as, a *keen* knife. 2. cutting; piercing: as, a *keen* wind. 3. very perceptive: as, *keen* eyes. 4. sharp-witted; shrewd. 5. eager 6. strong; vivid. **—keen'ly,** *adv.*
**keen** (kēn), *n.* [< Ir. *caoinim*, I wail], [Irish], a wailing for the dead. *v.t.* & *v.i.* [Irish], to lament or wail for (the dead).
**keep** (kēp), *v.t.* [KEPT, KEEPING], [AS. *cepan*, behold], 1. to celebrate; observe: as, *keep* the Sabbath. 2. to fulfill (a promise, etc.). 3. to protect; guard; take care of; tend. 4. to preserve. 5. to provide for; support. 6. to make regular entries in: as, to *keep* books. 7. to maintain in a specified state, action, etc.: as, *keep* the engine running. 8. to hold for the future; retain. 9. to hold and not let go; detain, withhold, restrain, etc. 10. to stay in or on (a course, place, etc.). *v.i.* 1. to stay in a specified state, action, etc. 2. to continue; go on. 3. to refrain: as, to *keep* from drinking. 4. to stay fresh; not spoil. *n.* 1. care or custody. 2. food and shelter; support. 3. the inner stronghold of a castle. **—for keeps,** [Colloq.], 1. with the winner keeping what he wins. 2. permanently. **—keep to oneself,** 1. to avoid others. 2. to refrain from telling.
**keep'er,** *n.* one that keeps; specif., *a*) a guard, as of prisoners. *b*) a guardian. *c*) a custodian.
**keep'ing,** *n.* 1. observance (of a rule, etc.). 2. care; charge. 3. agreement; conformity: as, in *keeping* with custom.
**keep'sake',** *n.* something kept, or to be kept, in memory of the giver.
**keg** (keg), *n.* [< ON. (*vin*)*kaggr*, (wine) barrel], 1. a small barrel. 2. a unit of weight for nails (100 lbs.).
**kelp** (kelp), *n.* [ME. *culp*(*e*)], a large, brown seaweed, rich in iodine.
**Kelt** (kelt), *n.* a Celt. **—Kel'tic,** *adj.* & *n.*
**ken** (ken) *v.t.* & *v.i.* [KENNED, KENNING], [AS. *cennan*, cause to know], [Scot.], to know. *n.* 1. [Rare], range of vision. 2. range of knowledge.
**ken·nel** (ken''l), *n.* [< L. *canis*, dog], 1. a doghouse. 2. *often pl.* a place where dogs are bred or kept. *v.t.* & *v.i.* [-NELED or -NELLED, -NELING or -NELLING], to keep or live in a kennel.
**kept** (kept), pt. & pp. of **keep.**
**ker·a·tin** (ker'ə-tin), *n.* [< Gr. *keras*, horn], an albuminous substance forming the principal matter of hair, nails, horn, etc.
**kerb** (kũrb), *n.* curb (of a pavement): Brit. sp.
**ker·chief** (kũr'chif), *n.* [< OFr. *covrir*, to cover + *chef*, head], 1 a piece of cloth worn over the head or around the neck. 2. a handkerchief. **—ker'chiefed,** *adj.*
**ker·nel** (kũr'n'l), *n.* [AS. *cyrnel*], 1. a grain or seed, as of corn. 2. the inner, softer part of a nut, etc. 3. the central, most important part; gist.
**ker·o·sene** (ker'ə-sēn'), *n.* [< Gr. *kēros*, wax], a thin oil distilled from petroleum, used in lamps, stoves, etc.
**kes·trel** (kes'trəl), *n.* [echoic], a small European falcon that can hover in the air against the wind.
**ketch** (kech), *n.* [? akin to *catch*], a fore-and-aft rigged sailing vessel.
**ketch·up** (kech'əp), *n.* [Malay *kēchap*, taste], a sauce for meat, fish, etc.; esp., a thick sauce (**tomato ketchup**) of tomatoes, onions, spices, etc.: also **catsup, catchup.**
**ket·tle** (ket''l), *n.* [< L. *catinus*, bowl], 1. a metal container for boiling liquids, etc. 2. a teakettle.
**ket'tle·drum',** *n.* a hemispheric drum of copper with a parchment top that can be tightened or loosened to change the pitch.
**key** (kē), *n.* [*pl.* KEYS], [AS. *cæge*], 1. a device for moving the bolt of a lock and thus locking or unlocking something. 2. any somewhat similar device, as a lever pressed in operating a piano, typewriter, etc. 3. a thing that explains or solves, as a code, the legend of a map, etc. 4. a controlling person or thing. 5. style or mood of expression. 6. in *music*, a system of related tones based on a keynote and forming a given scale. *adj.* controlling; important. *v.t.* [KEYED, KEYING], 1. to furnish with a key. 2. to regulate the tone or pitch of. 3. to bring into harmony. **—key up,** to make nervous.
**key** (kē), *n.* [*pl.* KEYS], [Sp. *cayo*, small island], a reef or low island.
**key'board',** *n.* the row or rows of keys of a piano, typewriter, etc.
**key'hole',** *n.* an opening (in a lock) into which a key is inserted.
**key'note',** *n.* 1. the lowest, basic note or tone of a musical scale. 2. the basic idea or principle, as of a speech, policy, etc.
**key punch,** a machine with a keyboard for recording data by punching holes in cards for use in computers, etc.
**key'stone',** *n.* 1. the central, topmost stone of an arch, which holds the others in place. 2. the main part or principle.
**kg.,** 1. kilogram(s). 2. keg(s).
**kha·ki** (kak'i, kä'ki), *adj.* [< Persian *khāk*, dust], 1. dull yellowish-brown. 2. made of khaki cloth. *n.* [*pl.* -KIS], 1. a dull yellowish brown. 2. strong, twilled cloth of this color. 3. *often pl.* a khaki uniform.
**khan** (kän, kan), *n.* [Turki *khān*, lord], 1. a title of Tatar or Mongol rulers in the Middle Ages. 2. a title of various dignitaries in India, Iran, etc.
**kib·butz** (ki-bo͞ots', -boots'), *n.* [*pl.* -BUTZIM (kē'bo͞o-tsēm')], [Mod. Heb.], an Israeli collective settlement, esp. a collective farm.
**kib·itz·er** (kib'it-sẽr), *n.* [Yid. < G. *kiebitz*], [Colloq.], an onlooker, as at a card game, who volunteers advice. **—kib'itz,** *v.i.*
**ki·bosh** (kī'bosh, ki-bosh'), *n.* [prob. < Yid.], [Slang], nonsense: now usually in *put the kibosh on*, to put an end to; veto.

**kick** (kik), *v.i.* [? < ON. *kika*, bend at the knee], 1. to strike out with the foot. 2. to recoil, as a gun. 3. [Colloq.], to complain. *v.t.* 1. to strike with the foot. 2. to drive, force, etc. as by kicking. 3. to score (a goal, etc.) by kicking. *n.* 1. a kicking. 2. a sudden recoil. 3. [Colloq.], a complaint. 4. [Colloq.], a stimulating or pleasurable effect. **—kick in,** [Slang], to pay (one's share).

**kick'back',** *n.* [Slang], 1. a giving back of part of money received as payment. 2. the money so returned.

**kick'off',** *n.* in *football*, a place kick that puts the ball into play.

**kid** (kid), *n.* [prob. < ON. *kith*], 1. a young goat. 2. leather from the skin of young goats: also **kid'skin'**. 3. [Colloq.], a child. *adj.* 1. made of kidskin. 2. [Colloq.], younger: as, my *kid* sister. *v.t. & v.i.* [KIDDED, KIDDING], [Slang], to tease or hoax. **—kid'der,** *n.*

**kid'dy, kid'die,** *n.* [*pl.* -DIES], [dim. of *kid*], [Colloq.], a child.

**kid·nap** (kid'nap), *v.t.* [-NAPED or -NAPPED, -NAPING or -NAPPING], [< *kid*, child + *nab*, snatch], 1. to steal (a child). 2. to seize and hold (a person) by force or fraud, as for ransom. **—kid'nap'er, kid'nap'per,** *n.*

**kid·ney** (kid'ni), *n.* [*pl.* -NEYS], [? < ME. *kid*, young goat + *ei*, egg], 1. either of a pair of glandular organs which separate water and waste products from the blood and excrete them as urine. 2. an animal's kidneys, used as food. 3. *a*) disposition. *b*) class; kind.

**kidney stone,** a hard, mineral deposit sometimes formed in the kidney.

**kill** (kil), *v.t.* [prob. < AS. *cwellan*], 1. to cause the death of; slay. 2. to destroy; put an end to. 3. to defeat or veto (legislation). 4. to spend (time) on trivial matters. *n.* 1. the act of killing. 2. an animal or animals killed. **—kill'er,** *n.*

**kill'ing,** *adj.* 1. causing death; deadly. 2. exhausting; fatiguing. 3. [Colloq.], very comical. *n.* 1. slaughter; murder. 2. [Colloq.], a sudden great profit.

**kill'-joy',** *n.* one who destroys or lessens other people's enjoyment.

**kiln** (kil, kiln), *n.* [< L. *culina*, cookstove], a furnace or oven for drying, burning, or baking bricks, lime, etc.

**ki·lo** (kē'lō, kil'ō), *n.* [*pl.* -LOS], [Fr.], 1. a kilogram. 2. a kilometer.

**kilo-,** [< Gr. *chilioi*, thousand], a combining form meaning *one thousand*.

**kil·o·cy·cle** (kil'ə-sī'k'l), *n.* 1. 1,000 cycles. 2. 1,000 cycles per second: used in radio to express the frequency of the waves of electric energy.

**kil·o·gram, kil·o·gramme** (kil'ə-gram'), *n.* a unit of weight and mass, equal to 1,000 grams (2.2046 lbs.).

**kil·o·li·ter, kil·o·li·tre** (kil'ə-lē'tēr), *n.* a unit of capacity, equal to 1,000 liters, or one cubic meter (264.18 gallons).

**kil·o·me·ter, kil·o·me·tre** (kil'ə-mē'tēr, ki-lom'ə-), *n.* a unit of length or distance, equal to 1,000 meters (3,280.8 feet).

**kil·o·watt** (kil'ə-wot'), *n.* a unit of electrical power, equal to 1,000 watts.

**kilt** (kilt), *n.* [prob. < ON.], a short, pleated skirt worn by men of the Scottish Highlands.

**kil·ter** (kil'tēr), *n.* [Colloq.], good condition; proper order: now always preceded by *in* or *out of*.

**ki·mo·no** (kə-mō'nə), *n.* [*pl.* -NOS], [Japan.], 1. a loose outer garment with a sash, worn, esp. formerly, by the Japanese. 2. a woman's loose dressing gown like this.

**kin** (kin), *n.* [AS. *cynn*], 1. relatives; family; kindred. 2. family relationship. *adj.* related, as by blood; kindred. **—of kin,** related.

**-kin,** [prob. < MD. *-ken*], a noun suffix meaning *little*, as in *lambkin*.

**kind** (kīnd), *n.* [AS. (*ge*)*cynd*], 1. a natural group or division; race. 2. sort; variety; class. *adj.* 1. sympathetic, gentle, benevolent, etc. 2. cordial: as, *kind* regards. **—in kind,** in the same way. **—kind of,** [Colloq.], somewhat; rather. **—of a kind,** alike.

**kin·der·gar·ten** (kin'dēr-gär't'n), *n.* [G.; *kinder*, children + *garten*, garden], a school or class for young children, usually four to six years old, that develops basic skills and social behavior by games, handicraft, etc.

**kind'heart'ed,** *adj.* kind; sympathetic.

**kin·dle** (kin'd'l), *v.t.* [-DLED, -DLING], [< ON. *kynda*], 1. to set on fire; ignite. 2. to excite (interest, feelings, etc.). *v.i.* 1. to catch fire. 2. to become aroused or excited.

**kin·dling** (kin'dliŋ), *n.* material, as bits of wood, for starting a fire.

**kind'ly,** *adj.* [-LIER, -LIEST], 1. kind; gracious. 2. agreeable; pleasant. *adv.* 1. in a kind, gracious manner. 2. agreeably.

**kind'ness,** *n.* 1. the state, quality, or habit of being kind. 2. a kind act.

**kin·dred** (kin'drid), *n.* [< AS. *cynn*, kin + *-ræden*, condition], 1. relationship by birth or, sometimes, by marriage. 2. relatives or family; kin. *adj.* 1. related by birth or origin. 2. similar: as, *kindred* spirits.

**kine** (kīn), *n.pl.* [< AS. *cy*, cows], [Archaic or Dial.], cows; cattle.

**ki·ne·tic** (ki-net'ik), *adj.* [< Gr. *kinein*, move], of or resulting from motion.

**ki·net'ics,** *n.pl.* [construed as sing.], the science dealing with the motion of masses in relation to the forces acting on them.

**king** (kiŋ), *n.* [AS. *cyning*], 1. a male ruler of a state. 2. a man who is supreme in some field. 3. something supreme in its class. 4. a playing card with a picture of a king on it. 5. in *chess*, the chief piece. *adj.* chief (in size, importance, etc.). **—king'ly,** *adj.* **—king'ship,** *n.*

**king'dom** (-dəm), *n.* 1. a country headed by a king or queen; monarchy. 2. a realm; domain: as, the *kingdom* of poetry. 3. any of the three divisions into which all natural objects have been classified (the *animal*, *vegetable*, and *mineral kingdoms*).

**king'fish'er,** *n.* a bright-colored, short-tailed diving bird that feeds on fish.

**King James Version,** the revised English translation of the Bible, published (1611) with the authorization of King James I.

**King Lear** (lêr), the title character of a tragedy by Shakespeare.

**king'pin',** *n.* 1. the pin at the apex in bowling, tenpins, etc. 2. [Colloq.], the main or essential person or thing.

**kink** (kiŋk), *n.* [prob. < D. or Sw.], 1. a short twist or curl in a rope, hair, etc. 2. a painful cramp in the neck, back, etc. 3. a mental twist; queer notion; whim. *v.t. & v.i.* to form or cause to form a kink or kinks. **—kink'y** [-IER, -IEST], *adj.*

**kins·folk** (kinz'fōk'), *n.pl.* family; relatives: also, [Dial.], **kin'folk'**.

**kin·ship** (kin'ship), *n.* 1. family relationship. 2. close connection.

**kins·man** (kinz'mən), *n.* [*pl.* -MEN], a relative; esp., a male relative. **—kins'wom'an** [*pl.* -WOMEN], *n.fem.*

**ki·osk** (ki-osk', kī'osk), *n.* [< Per. *kūshk*, palace], a small, open structure, used as a newsstand, etc.

**kip·per** (kip'ēr), *v.t.* [< ?], to cure (herring, salmon, etc.) by salting and drying or smoking. *n.* a kippered herring, etc.

**kirk** (kūrk; Scot. kirk), *n.* [Scot. & North Eng.], a church.

**kis·met** (kiz'met, kis'-), *n.* [< Ar. *qasama*, divide], fate; destiny.

**kiss** (kis), *v.t. & v.i.* [AS. *cyssan*], 1. to touch or caress with the lips as an act of affection, greeting, etc. 2. to touch lightly or gently. *n.* 1. an act of kissing. 2. a light, gentle touch. 3. any of various candies.
**kiss'er,** *n.* 1. a person who kisses. 2. [Slang], *a*) the mouth or lips. *b*) the face.
**kit** (kit), *n.* [ME. *kyt*, tub], 1. *a*) a soldier's equipment; pack. *b*) a set of tools. *c*) equipment for some particular activity, etc. 2. a box, bag, etc. for carrying such tools or equipment. **—the whole kit and caboodle,** [Colloq.], the whole lot.
**kitch·en** (kich'ən), *n.* [ult. < L. *coquere*, to cook], a room or place for the preparation and cooking of food.
**kitch'en·ette', kitch'en·et'** (-et'), *n.* a small, compact kitchen.
**kitch'en·ware'** (-wâr'), *n.* kitchen utensils.
**kite** (kīt), *n.* [AS. *cyta*], 1. a bird of the hawk family. 2. a light, wooden frame covered with paper or cloth, to be flown in the wind at the end of a string. *v.i.* [KITED, KITING], [Colloq.], to soar or glide.
**kith** (kith), *n.* [< AS. *cyth*], [Archaic], friends, acquaintances, etc.: now only in *kith and kin* (friends, acquaintances, and relatives).
**kit·ten** (kit''n), *n.* [< OFr. dim. of *chat*, cat], a young cat.
**kit'ten·ish** (-ish), *adj.* like a kitten; playful; often, playfully coy. **—kit'ten·ish·ly,** *adv.*
**kit·ty** (kit'i), *n.* [*pl.* -TIES], 1. a kitten. 2. a pet name for a cat.
**kit·ty** (kit'i), *n.* [*pl.* -TIES], [< ?], 1. the stakes in a poker game. 2. money pooled for some particular purpose.
**K.K.K., KKK,** Ku Klux Klan.
**klep·to·ma·ni·a** (klep'tə-mā'ni-ə), *n.* [< Gr. *kleptēs*, thief; + *mania*], an abnormal, persistent impulse to steal. **—klep'to·ma'ni·ac'** (-ak'), *n.*
**km.,** kilometer(s).
**knack** (nak), *n.* [ME. *knak*, sharp blow], 1. a trick; device. 2. ability to do something easily; dexterity.
**knap·sack** (nap'sak'), *n.* [< D. *knappen*, eat + *zak*, a sack], a leather or canvas bag for carrying equipment, etc. on the back.
**knave** (nāv), *n.* [AS. *cnafa*, boy], 1. a dishonest, deceitful person; rogue. 2. a jack (playing card). **—knav'ish,** *adj.*
**knav·er·y** (nāv'ẽr-i), *n.* [*pl.* -IES], rascality.
**knead** (nēd), *v.t.* [AS. *cnedan*], 1. to work (dough, clay, etc.) into a plastic mass by pressing and squeezing. 2. to massage.
**knee** (nē), *n.* [AS. *cneow*], 1. the joint between the thigh and the lower leg. 2. anything shaped like a knee, esp. a bent knee. **—bring to one's knees,** to force to submit.
**knee'cap',** *n.* a movable bone at the front of the human knee.
**kneel** (nēl), *v.i.* [KNELT or KNEELED, KNEELING], [< AS. *cneow*, knee], to bend or rest on one's knee or knees. **—kneel'er,** *n.*
**knell** (nel), *v.i.* [AS. *cnyllan*], 1. to ring slowly; toll. 2. to sound ominously. *v.t.* to call or announce as by a knell. *n.* 1. the sound of a bell rung slowly, as at a funeral. 2. an omen of death, failure, etc.
**knelt** (nelt), pt. and pp. of **kneel.**
**knew** (nōō, nū), pt. of **know.**
**knick·ers** (nik'ẽrz), *n.pl.* [< D. *Knickerbocker*, fictitious D. author of W. Irving's *History of New York*], short, loose trousers gathered just below the knees: also **knick'er·bock'ers** (-bok'ẽrz).
**knick·knack** (nik'nak'), *n.* [< *knack*], a small ornamental article; trinket.
**knife** (nīf), *n.* [*pl.* KNIVES (nīvz)], [AS. *cnif*], 1. a cutting instrument with a sharp-edged blade set in a handle. 2. a cutting blade, as in a machine. *v.t.* [KNIFED, KNIFING], 1. to cut or stab with a knife. 2. [Colloq.], to injure or defeat by treachery.
**knight** (nīt), *n.* [AS. *cniht*, boy], 1. in medieval times, a man formally raised to honorable military rank and pledged to chivalrous conduct. 2. in Britain, a man who for some achievement is given honorary, nonhereditary rank entitling him to use *Sir* before his given name. 3. a chessman shaped like a horse's head. *v.t.* to make (a man) a knight.
**knight'-er'rant** (-er'ənt), *n.* [*pl.* KNIGHTS-ERRANT], 1. a medieval knight wandering in search of adventure. 2. a chivalrous or quixotic person.**—knight'-er'rant·ry** (-ri), *n.*
**knight'hood** (-hood), *n.* 1. the rank, status, or vocation of a knight. 2. chivalry. 3. knights collectively.
**knight'ly,** *adj.* of or like a knight; chivalrous, brave, etc. **—knight'li·ness,** *n.*
**knit** (nit), *v.t. & v.i.* [KNITTED or KNIT, KNITTING], [< AS. *cnotta*, a knot], 1. to make (a fabric) by looping together yarn by means of special needles. 2. to fasten together closely or grow together, as a broken bone. 3. to draw or become drawn together in wrinkles, as the brows.
**knit'ting,** *n.* knitted work.
**knob** (nob), *n.* [prob. < MLG. *knobbe*, a knot], 1. a rounded lump or protuberance. 2. a handle, usually round, of a door, drawer, etc. **—knobbed,** *adj.*
**knob'by,** *adj.* [-BIER, -BIEST], 1. covered with knobs. 2. like a knob.
**knock** (nok), *v.i.* [< AS. *cnocian*], 1. to strike a blow. 2. to rap on a door. 3. to bump; collide. 4. to make a thumping noise: said of an engine, etc. *v.t.* 1. to hit; strike. 2. to hit so as to cause to fall (with *down* or *off*). 3. to make by hitting: as, he *knocked* a hole in the screen. 4. [Colloq.], to find fault with. *n.* 1. a knocking. 2. a hit; rap. 3. a thumping noise in an engine, etc. 4. [Colloq.], an adverse criticism. **—knock about** (or **around**), [Colloq.], to wander about. **—knock down,** 1. to take apart. 2. to indicate the sale of (an article) at an auction. **—knock off,** [Colloq.], 1. to stop working. 2. to deduct. 3. to kill, overcome, etc. **—knock out,** to make unconscious or exhausted. **—knock together,** to make or compose hastily.
**knock'er,** *n.* one that knocks; esp., a small ring, knob, etc. on a door, for use in knocking.
**knock'-kneed'** (-nēd'), *adj.* having legs which bend inward at the knee.
**knock'out',** *n.* 1. a knocking out or being knocked out. 2. [Slang], a person or thing that is very attractive or striking. 3. in *boxing*, a victory won when an opponent is unable to continue the fight, as by being knocked unconscious.
**knoll** (nōl), *n.* [AS. *cnoll*], a little rounded hill or hilltop; mound.
**knot** (not), *n.* [AS. *cnotta*], 1. a lump in a thread, etc. as formed by a tangle. 2. a fastening made by tying together pieces of string, rope, etc. 3. an ornamental bow of ribbon, etc. 4. a small group or cluster. 5. something that ties closely; esp., the bond of marriage. 6. a problem; difficulty. 7. a hard lump on a tree where a branch grows out, or a cross section of such a lump in a board. 8. in *naut. usage*, a unit of speed of one nautical mile an hour. *v.t. & v.i.* [KNOTTED, KNOTTING], 1. to make or form a knot (in). 2. to entangle or become entangled.
**knot'hole',** *n.* a hole in a board, etc. where a knot has fallen out.
**knot'ty,** *adj.* [-TIER, -TIEST], 1. full of knots: as, *knotty* pine. 2. hard to solve; puzzling: as, a *knotty* problem. **—knot'ti·ness,** *n.*
**know** (nō), *v.t.* [KNEW, KNOWN, KNOWING], [AS. (*ge*)*cnawan*], 1. to be well-informed

about. 2. to be aware of: as, he *knew* why we left. 3. to be acquainted with. 4. to distinguish: as, to *know* right from wrong. *v.i.* 1. to have knowledge. 2. to be sure or aware. —**know′a·ble,** *adj.*

**know′-how′,** *n.* [Colloq.], technical skill.

**know′ing,** *adj.* 1. having knowledge. 2. shrewd; clever. 3. implying shrewd or secret understanding: as, a *knowing* look.

**knowl·edge** (nol′ij), *n.* 1. the fact or state of knowing. 2. range of information or understanding. 3. what is known; learning. 4. the body of facts accumulated by mankind. —**knowl′edge·a·ble,** *adj.*

**known** (nōn), pp. of **know.**

**knuck·le** (nuk′'l), *n.* [prob. < LG.], 1. a joint of the finger; esp., the joint connecting a finger to the rest of the hand. 2. the knee or hock joint of an animal, used as food. —**knuckle down,** 1. to work hard. 2. to yield; give in: also **knuckle under.**

**KO** (kā′ō′), *v.t.* [KO'D, KO'ING], [Slang], in *boxing*, to knock out. *n.* [*pl.* KO's], [Slang], in *boxing*, a knockout. Also **K.O., k.o.**

**ko·a·la** (kō-ä′lə), *n.* [< native name], an Australian tree-dwelling marsupial with thick, gray fur.

**kohl·ra·bi** (kōl′rä′bi), *n.* [*pl.* -BIES], [< It. *cavolo rapa*], a kind of cabbage with an edible, turniplike stem.

**ko·la** (kō′lə), *n.* [< W. Afr. name], 1. a tropical tree with brown nuts containing caffeine. 2. the nut. 3. an extract made from the nuts. Also sp. **cola.**

**ko·peck, ko·pek** (kō′pek), *n.* [Russ. *kopeika*], a Russian coin of bronze or copper, equal to 1/100 ruble.

**Ko·ran** (kō-rän′, kō′ran), *n.* [< Ar. *qur'ān*, book], the sacred book of the Moslems.

**ko·sher** (kō′shẽr), *adj.* [Heb. *kāsher*, proper], in *Judaism*, clean or fit to eat according to the dietary laws.

**kow·tow** (kou′tou′, kō′-), *v.i.* [Chin. *k'o-t'ou*, lit., knock head], to show great deference, submissive respect, etc. (*to* a person).

**KP, K.P.,** kitchen police, a detail to assist the cooks in an army kitchen.

**Kr,** in *chem.*, krypton.

**kraal** (kräl), *n.* [S. Afr. D.], 1. a village of South African natives. 2. an enclosure for cattle or sheep in South Africa.

**Krem·lin** (krem′lin), *n.* [< Russ. *kreml'*], a citadel in Moscow formerly housing many Soviet government offices.

**Krish·na** (krish′nə), *n.* a Hindu god, an incarnation of Vishnu.

**kro·na** (krō′nə), *n.* [*pl.* -NOR (-nôr)], [ult. < L. *corona*, crown], the monetary unit and a silver coin of Sweden.

**kro·ne** (krō′nə), *n.* [*pl.* -NER (-nẽr)], [see KRONA], 1. the monetary unit and a silver coin of Denmark or Norway. 2. [*pl.* -NEN], a former coin of Germany or Austria.

**kryp·ton** (krip′ton), *n.* [< Gr. *kryptein*, to hide], a rare chemical element, an inert gas: symbol, Kr.

**ku·chen** (kōō′khən), *n.* [G., cake], a cake made of yeast dough, often filled with raisins, nuts, etc.

**ku·dos** (kū′dos), *n.* [Gr. *kydos*], credit for an achievement; glory; fame.

**Ku Klux Klan** (kū′kluks′klan′, kōō′), [< Gr. *kyklos*, circle], a U.S. secret society that is anti-Negro, anti-Semitic, anti-Catholic, etc. and uses terrorist methods.

**küm·mel** (kim′'l), *n.* [G.], a liqueur flavored with caraway seeds, anise, etc.

**kum·quat** (kum′kwot), *n.* [< Chin. *chin-chü*, golden orange], 1. a small, orange-colored, oval fruit, with a sour pulp and a sweet rind. 2. the tree that it grows on.

**kw.,** kilowatt.

**kwh., K.W.H., kw-h, kw-hr,** kilowatt-hour.

# L

**L, l** (el), [*pl.* L's, l's, Ls, ls], the twelfth letter of the English alphabet.

**L** (el), *n.* 1. a Roman numeral for 50. 2. an extension forming an L with the main structure.

**L., l.,** 1. lake. 2. latitude. 3. left. 4. length. 5. [L.], *libra(e)*, pound(s). 6. [*pl.* LL.], line. 7. liter(s).

**L.,** Latin.

**la** (lä), *n.* [< L.], in *music*, the sixth tone of the diatonic scale.

**lab** (lab), *n.* [Colloq.], a laboratory.

**la·bel** (lā′b'l), *n.* [< OHG. *lappa*, rag], 1. a card, paper, etc. marked and attached to an object to indicate its contents, destination, ownership, etc. 2. a term of generalized classification. *v.t.* [-BELED or -BELLED, -BELING or -BELLING], 1. to attach a label to. 2. to classify as; call.

**la·bi·al** (lā′bi-əl), *adj.* [< L. *labium*, lip], 1. of the lips. 2. in *phonetics*, formed mainly with the lips, as *b*, *m*, and *p*.

**la′bi·ate′** (-āt′, -it), *adj.* [see LABIAL], having, or formed like, a lip or lips.

**la·bor** (lā′bẽr), *n.* [L.], 1. physical or mental exertion; work. 2. a specific task. 3. all wage-earners, esp. manual workers. 4. the process of childbirth. *v.i.* 1. to work. 2. to work hard. 3. to move slowly and with difficulty. 4. to be in childbirth. *v.t.* to develop in too great detail: as, to *labor* a point. —**labor under,** to suffer from (a false idea, etc.). Also, Brit. sp., **labour.** —**la′bor·ing·ly,** *adv.*

**lab·o·ra·to·ry** (lab′rə-tôr′i, lab′ẽr-ə-), *n.* [*pl.* -RIES], [see LABOR], a room or building for scientific work or research.

**Labor Day,** the first Monday in September, a legal holiday honoring labor.

**la·bored** (lā′bẽrd), *adj.* made or done with great effort; strained: Brit. sp. **laboured.**

**la′bor·er,** *n.* one who labors; esp., a wage-earning worker whose work is characterized by physical exertion.

**la·bo·ri·ous** (lə-bôr′i-əs), *adj.* 1. involving much labor; difficult. 2. hard-working.

**la′bor·ite′** (-īt′), *n.* a member or supporter of a labor party, esp., [L-], of the British Labor Party.

**labor party,** 1. a political party organized to protect and further the rights of workers. 2. [L- P-], such a party in Great Britain.

**labor union,** an association of workers to promote and protect the welfare, interests, and rights of its members.

**la·bur·num** (lə-bũr′nəm), *n.* [L.], a small tree or shrub of the pea family, with drooping clusters of yellow flowers.

**lab·y·rinth** (lab′ə-rinth′), *n.* [< Gr. *labyrinthos*], a structure containing winding passages hard to follow without losing one's way; maze. —**lab′y·rin′thine** (-rin′thin), *adj.*

**lac** (lak), *n.* [< Sans. *lākshā*], a resinous substance formed on certain Asiatic trees: source of shellac.

**lace** (lās), *n.* [< L. *laqueus*, noose], 1. a string, etc. used to draw together and fasten the parts of a shoe, corset, etc. 2. an openwork fabric of linen, silk, etc., woven in ornamental designs. *v.t.* [LACED, LACING], 1. to fasten with a lace. 2. to weave together; intertwine. 3. to thrash; whip.

**lac·er·ate** (las'ə-rāt'), *v.t.* [-ATED, -ATING], [< L. *lacer*, mangled], to tear jaggedly; mangle. —**lac'er·a'tion,** *n.*

**lace'work',** *n.* 1. lace. 2. any openwork decoration like lace.

**lach·ry·mal** (lak'rə-m'l), *adj.* [< L. *lacrima*, a tear], of, for, or producing tears.

**lac·ing** (lās'iŋ), *n.* 1. the act of one who laces. 2. a thrashing. 3. a cord or lace.

**lack** (lak), *n.* [prob. < MLG. *lak*], 1. the fact or state of not having enough or of not having any. 2. the thing that is needed. *v.i. & v.t.* to be deficient (in) or entirely without.

**lack·a·dai·si·cal** (lak'ə-dā'zi-k'l), *adj.* [< archaic *alackaday*, an exclamation of regret, etc.], showing lack of interest or spirit; listless. —**lack'a·dai'si·cal·ly,** *adv.*

**lack·ey** (lak'i), *n.* [*pl.* -EYS], [< Sp. *lacayo*], 1. a male servant of low rank. 2. a servile follower; toady. *v.t. & v.i.* [-EYED, -EYING], to serve as a lackey.

**lack·lus·ter, lack·lus·tre** (lak'lus'tẽr), *adj.* lacking brightness; dull.

**la·con·ic** (lə-kon'ik), *adj.* [< Gr. *Lakōn*, a Spartan], stating much in few words; concise. —**la·con'i·cal·ly,** *adv.*

**lac·quer** (lak'ẽr), *n.* [< Fr. & Port. *laca*, lac], 1. a clear varnish made of shellac or gum resins dissolved in alcohol. 2. a resinous varnish obtained from certain Oriental trees. 3. a wooden article coated with this. *v.t.* to coat with lacquer.

**la·crosse** (lə-krôs'), *n.* [Fr. < *la*, the + *crosse*, crutch], a ball game played by two teams using long-handled webbed rackets.

**lac·tate** (lak'tāt), *v.i.* [-TATED, -TATING], [< L. *lac*, milk], to secrete milk. *n.* any salt or ester of lactic acid.

**lac·ta'tion,** *n.* 1. the secretion of milk by a mammary gland. 2. the period of such secretion.

**lac·te·al** (lak'ti-əl), *adj.* [< L. *lac*, milk], of or like milk; milky.

**lac·tic** (lak'tik), *adj.* [< L. *lac*, milk], 1. of or obtained from milk. 2. designating or of a clear, sirupy acid formed when milk sours.

**lac·tose** (lak'tōs), *n.* [< L. *lac*, milk], a white, crystalline sugar found in milk: also **milk sugar.**

**la·cu·na** (lə-kū'nə), *n.* [*pl.* -NAS, -NAE (-nē)], [L., a ditch], a blank space; gap; hiatus.

**lac·y** (lās'i), *adj.* [-IER, -IEST], of or like lace.

**lad** (lad), *n.* [ME. *ladde*], a boy; youth.

**lad·der** (lad'ẽr), *n.* [AS. *hlæd(d)er*], 1. a framework of two sidepieces connected by a series of rungs, for use in climbing up or down. 2. any means of climbing.

**lad·die** (lad'i), *n.* [Chiefly Scot.], a lad.

**lade** (lād), *v.t. & v.i.* [LADED, LADEN or LADED, LADING], [AS. *hladan*], 1. to load. 2. to bail; ladle.

**lad'en,** pp. of **lade.** *adj.* 1. loaded. 2. burdened; afflicted.

**lad'ing,** *n.* 1. a loading. 2. a load; cargo.

**la·dle** (lā'd'l), *n.* [AS. *hlædel*], a long-handled, cuplike spoon for dipping. *v.t.* [-DLED, -DLING], to dip out with, or carry in, a ladle.

**la·dy** (lā'di), *n.* [*pl.* -DIES], [< AS. *hlaf*, loaf + base of *dæge*, kneader], 1. a woman of good breeding or social position: corresponding to *gentleman*. 2. any woman. 3. a wife. 4. [L-], a British title given to women of certain ranks. *adj.* female.

**la'dy·bug',** *n.* a small, roundish beetle with a spotted back: also **ladybird.**

**la'dy·fin'ger,** *n.* a small spongecake shaped somewhat like a finger.

**lady in waiting,** a woman attending, or waiting upon, a queen or princess.

**la'dy·like',** *adj.* like or suitable for a lady; refined; well-bred.

**la'dy·ship',** *n.* 1. the rank or position of a lady. 2. [often L-], the form used in speaking to or of a titled Lady: with *your* or *her*.

**lag** (lag), *v.i.* [LAGGED, LAGGING], [prob. < *lack*, *v.t.*], to fall behind; move slowly; loiter. *n.* 1. a falling behind or being retarded. 2. the amount of this.

**la·ger (beer)** (lä'gẽr, lô'-), [G. *lager bier*, storehouse beer], a beer that is aged for several months after it has been brewed.

**lag·gard** (lag'ẽrd), *n.* [< *lag* (loiter) + *-ard*], a slow person; one who falls behind. *adj.* backward; slow; hanging back.

**la·goon** (lə-gōōn'), *n.* [< L. *lacuna*, pond], 1. a shallow lake or pond, esp. one connected with a larger body of water. 2. the water enclosed by a circular coral reef. 3. shallow water separated from the sea by sand dunes. Also sp. **lagune.**

**la·ic** (lā'ik), *adj.* [< Gr. *laos*, the people], secular; lay: also **la'i·cal.** *n.* a layman.

**laid** (lād), pt. and pp. of **lay.** —**laid up,** 1. stored away; out of use. 2. [Colloq.], so ill or injured as to be confined or disabled.

**lain** (lān), pp. of **lie** (to recline).

**lair** (lâr), *n.* [AS. *leger*], a resting place, esp. of a wild animal; den.

**laird** (lârd), *n.* [Scot. form of *lord*], in Scotland, a landowner, esp. a wealthy one.

**lais·sez faire** (les'ā fâr'), [Fr., allow to do], noninterference; esp., absence of governmental control over industry and business.

**la·i·ty** (lā'ə-ti), *n.* [*pl.* -TIES], [< *lay*, *adj.*], laymen collectively.

**lake** (lāk), *n.* [< L. *lacus*, pond], 1. a large inland body of water. 2. a pool of oil or other liquid.

**lake** (lāk), *n.* [see LAC (resin)], 1. a dark-red pigment made from cochineal. 2. its color.

**lam** (lam), *v.t.* [LAMMED, LAMMING], [< ?], [Slang], to beat; thrash.

**lam** (lam), *n.* [< ?], [Slang], headlong flight. *v.i.* [LAMMED, LAMMING], [Slang], to flee. —**on the lam,** [Slang], in headlong flight.

**la·ma** (lä'mə), *n.* [Tibetan *blama*], a Buddhist priest or monk in Tibet and Mongolia.

**La·ma·ism** (lä'mə-iz'm), *n.* the religious system of the lamas, a form of Buddhism.

**la·ma·ser·y** (lä'mə-ser'i), *n.* [*pl.* -IES], [< Fr.], a monastery of lamas.

**lamb** (lam), *n.* [AS.], 1. a young sheep. 2. its flesh used as food. 3. a gentle, innocent, or gullible person. *v.i.* to give birth: said of a ewe. —**the Lamb,** Jesus.

**lam·baste** (lam-bāst'), *v.t.* [-BASTED, -BASTING], [*lam* (to beat) + *baste*], [Slang], 1. to beat soundly. 2. to scold severely.

**lamb·da** (lam'də), *n.* the eleventh letter of the Greek alphabet (Λ, λ).

**lam·bent** (lam'bənt), *adj.* [< L. *lambere*, to lick], 1. playing lightly over a surface: said of a flame. 2. giving off a soft radiance. 3. light and graceful: as, *lambent* wit.

**lamb'kin,** *n.* a little lamb.

**lamb'skin',** *n.* the skin of a lamb, esp. with the fleece left on it.

**lame** (lām), *adj.* [AS. *lama*], 1. crippled; esp., unable to walk well because of a disabled leg or foot. 2. stiff and painful. 3. poor; ineffectual: as, a *lame* excuse. *v.t. & v.i.* [LAMED, LAMING], to make or become lame.

**la·mé** (la-mā'), *n.* [< Fr. *lame*, metal plate], a cloth made of or with metal threads, esp. of gold or silver.

**lame duck,** a legislator whose term extends beyond the time of his defeat for re-election.

**la·ment** (lə-ment'), *v.i. & v.t.* [< L. *lamentum*, a wailing], to feel or express deep sorrow (for); mourn. *n.* 1. a lamenting; wail. 2. an elegy, dirge, etc. mourning some loss or calamity. —**lam·en·ta·tion** (lam'ən-tā'shən), *n.*

**lam·en·ta·ble** (lam'ən-tə-b'l), *adj.* 1. to be lamented; deplorable. 2. expressing sorrow.

**lam·i·na** (lam'ə-nə), *n.* [*pl.* -NAE (-nē'), -NAS], [L.], a thin scale or layer, as of metal.
**lam·i·nate** (lam'ə-nāt'), *v.t.* [-NATED, -NATING], to make by building up in layers, as plywood. *v.i.* to split into thin layers. *adj.* (-nit), in thin sheets or layers: also **lam'i·nat'ed.** —**lam'i·na'tion,** *n.*
**lamp** (lamp), *n.* [< Gr. *lampein*, to shine], 1. a container with a wick for burning oil, etc. to produce light or heat. 2. any device for producing light or therapeutic rays.
**lamp'black',** *n.* fine soot formed by burning tars, oils, etc., used as a black pigment.
**lam·poon** (lam-pōōn'), *n.* [< Fr. *lampons*, let us drink: used as a refrain], a satirical writing attacking someone. *v.t.* to attack in a lampoon. —**lam·poon'er,** *n.*
**lamp'post',** *n.* a post supporting a street lamp.
**lam·prey** (lam'pri), *n.* [*pl.* -PREYS], [< ML. *lampreda*], an eellike water animal with a funnel-shaped, sucking mouth.
**lance** (lans, läns), *n.* [< L. *lancea*], 1. a thrusting weapon consisting of a long wooden shaft with a sharp metal head. 2. a lancer. 3. any instrument like a lance. 4. a lancet. *v.t.* [LANCED, LANCING], 1. to pierce with a lance. 2. to cut open with a lancet.
**Lan·ce·lot** (lan'sə-lot'), *n.* the most celebrated of the knights of the Round Table.
**lan·cer** (lan'sẽr, län'-), *n.* a cavalry soldier armed with a lance.
**lan·cet** (lan'sit, län'-), *n.* [< OFr. dim. of *lance*], a small, pointed surgical knife, usually two-edged.
**land** (land), *n.* [AS.], 1. the solid part of the earth's surface. 2. a country or nation. 3. ground or soil. 4. real estate. *v.t.* 1. to put on shore from a ship. 2. to bring to a particular place: as, it *landed* him in jail. 3. to set (an aircraft) down on land or water. 4. to catch or get; secure. 5. [Colloq.], to deliver (a blow). *v.i.* 1. to leave a ship and go on shore. 2. to come to a port, etc.: said of a ship. 3. to arrive at a specified place. 4. to come to rest.
**land·ed** (lan'did), *adj.* 1. owning land. 2. consisting of land or real estate: as, a *landed* estate.
**land'fall',** *n.* 1. a sighting of land from a ship at sea. 2. the land sighted.
**land grant,** a grant of public land by the government for a college, railroad, etc.
**land'hold'er,** *n.* an owner or occupant of land. —**land'hold'ing,** *adj. & n.*
**land'ing,** *n.* 1. the act of coming to shore. 2. the place where a ship is loaded or unloaded. 3. a platform at the end of a flight of stairs. 4. the act of alighting.
**landing gear,** the undercarriage of an aircraft, including wheels, etc.
**land'la'dy,** *n.* [*pl.* -DIES], 1. a woman who leases land, houses, etc. to others. 2. a woman who keeps a rooming house, inn, etc.
**land'locked',** *adj.* 1. surrounded by land, as a bay. 2. cut off from the sea and confined to fresh water: as, the *landlocked* salmon.
**land'lord',** *n.* 1. a man who leases land, houses, etc. to others. 2. a man who keeps a rooming house, inn, etc.
**land'lub'ber** (-lub'ẽr), *n.* one who has had little experience at sea.
**land'mark',** *n.* 1. an object that marks the boundary of a piece of land. 2. any prominent feature of the landscape, marking a locality. 3. an important event of a period.
**land office,** a government office that handles the sales of public lands. —**land'-of'fice business,** [Colloq.], a booming business.
**land'scape'** (-skāp'), *n.* [< D. *land*, land + *-schap*, -ship], 1. a picture representing natural, inland scenery. 2. an expanse of natural scenery seen in one view. *v.t.* [-SCAPED, -SCAPING], to make (a plot of ground) more attractive, as by adding lawns, bushes, etc. —**land'scap'er,** *n.*
**land'slide',** *n.* 1. the sliding of a mass of rocks or earth down a slope. 2. the mass sliding down. 3. an overwhelming victory.
**land'ward** (-wẽrd), *adv. & adj.* toward the land: also **land'wards,** *adv.*
**lane** (lān), *n.* [AS. *lanu*], 1. a narrow way, path, road, etc. 2. a path or course designated, for reasons of safety, for ships, aircraft, automobiles, etc.
**lan·guage** (laŋ'gwij), *n.* [< L. *lingua*, tongue], 1. human speech or the written symbols for speech. 2. any means of communicating. 3. the speech of a particular nation, etc.: as, the English *language*. 4. style of expression. 5. the particular words and phrases of a profession, group, etc.
**lan·guid** (laŋ'gwid), *adj.* [< L. *languere*, be faint], 1. without vigor or vitality; weak. 2. listless; indifferent. 3. slow; dull.
**lan·guish** (laŋ'gwish), *v.i.* [< L. *languere*], 1. to become weak; droop. 2. to become slack or dull. 3. to long; pine. 4. to put on a wistful air. —**lan'guish·ment,** *n.*
**lan'guish·ing,** *adj.* 1. becoming weak; drooping. 2. lingering. 3. pining; longing. 4. wistfully amorous.
**lan·guor** (laŋ'gẽr), *n.* [see LANGUID], lack of vigor or vitality; weakness; listlessness; sluggishness. —**lan'guor·ous,** *adj.*
**lank** (laŋk), *adj.* [AS. *hlanc*], 1. long and slender. 2. straight and flat: said of hair.
**lank'y,** *adj.* [-IER, -IEST], awkwardly tall and lean. —**lank'i·ly,** *adv.* —**lank'i·ness,** *n.*
**lan·o·lin** (lan'ə-lin), *n.* [< L. *lana*, wool + *oleum*, oil], a fatty substance obtained from wool and used in ointments, cosmetics, etc.
**lan·tern** (lan'tẽrn), *n.* [ult. < Gr. *lampein*, to shine], a transparent case for holding and shielding a light.
**lan'tern-jawed',** *adj.* having long, thin jaws and sunken cheeks.
**lan·yard** (lan'yẽrd), *n.* [< OFr. *lasne*, noose], a short rope used on board ship for holding, fastening, etc.: also sp. **laniard.**
**lap** (lap), *n.* [AS. *læppa*], 1. the front part from the waist to the knees of a sitting person. 2. the part of the clothing covering this. 3. that in which one is cared for: as, the *lap* of luxury. 4. *a*) an overlapping. *b*) a part that overlaps. 5. one complete circuit of a race track. *v.t.* [LAPPED, LAPPING], 1. to fold (*over* or *on*). 2. to wrap; enfold. 3. to overlap. 4. to get a lap ahead of (an opponent) in a race. *v.i.* 1. to overlap. 2. to extend beyond something in space or time (with *over*).
**lap** (lap), *v.i. & v.t.* [LAPPED, LAPPING], [AS. *lapian*], 1. to drink (a liquid) by dipping it up with the tongue as a dog does. 2. to strike gently with a light splash, as waves. *n.* 1. a lapping. 2. the sound of lapping. —**lap up,** [Colloq.], to take in eagerly.
**la·pel** (lə-pel'), *n.* [dim. of *lap* (a fold)], the front part of a coat folded back and forming a continuation of the collar.
**lap·i·dar·y** (lap'ə-der'i), *n.* [*pl.* -IES], [< L. *lapis*, a stone], a workman who cuts and polishes precious stones.
**lap·is laz·u·li** (lap'is laz'yoo-lī'), [< L. *lapis*, stone + ML. *lazulus*, azure], an azure, opaque, semiprecious stone.
**Lapp** (lap), *n.* a member of a Mongoloid people living in Lapland.
**lap·pet** (lap'it), *n.* [dim. of *lap* (a fold)], 1. a small loose fold of a garment. 2. any fleshy part hanging loosely, as an ear lobe.
**lapse** (laps), *n.* [< L. *labi*, to slip], 1. a small error. 2. a moral slip. 3. a falling into a lower condition. 4. a passing, as of time. 5. the termination, as of a privilege through

failure to meet requirements. *v.i.* [LAPSED, LAPSING], 1. to fall into a specified state: as, he *lapsed* into silence. 2. to deviate from virtue. 3. to elapse. 4. to become void because of failure to meet requirements.

**lar·board** (lär′bẽrd), *n. & adj.* [< AS. *hladan*, lade + *bord*, side], port; left.

**lar·ce·ny** (lär′sə-ni), *n.* [*pl.* -NIES], [ult. < L. *latro*, robber], the unlawful taking of another's property; theft.—**lar′ce·nous,** *adj.*

**larch** (lärch), *n.* [< L. *larix*], 1. a cone-bearing pine tree. 2. its tough wood.

**lard** (lärd), *n.* [< L. *lardum*], the fat of hogs, melted and clarified. *v.t.* 1. to stuff (meat, etc.) with bacon or fat pork before cooking. 2. to smear with lard, etc.; grease. 3. to embellish: as, to *lard* a speech with oaths.

**lard′er,** *n.* 1. a place where food supplies are kept. 2. food supplies.

**la·res and pe·na·tes** (lâr′ēz and pi-nā′tēz), household gods of the ancient Romans.

**large** (lärj), *adj.* [LARGER, LARGEST], [< L. *largus*], 1. of great extent or amount; big, bulky, spacious, etc. 2. bigger than others of its kind. 3. operating on a big scale: as, a *large* producer. *adv.* in a large way: as, write *large*. —**at large,** 1. free; not imprisoned. 2. fully; in detail. 3. representing no particular district: as, a congressman *at large*. —**large′ness,** *n.* —**larg′ish,** *adj.*

**large′ly,** *adv.* 1. much; in great amounts. 2. for the most part; mainly.

**lar·gess, lar·gesse** (lär′jis, -jes), *n.* [see LARGE], 1. generous giving. 2. a gift generously given.

**lar·go** (lär′gō), *adj. & adv.* [It., slow], in *music*, slow and stately.

**lar·i·at** (lar′i-ət), *n.* [Sp. *la reata*, the rope], 1. a rope used for tethering grazing horses, etc. 2. a lasso.

**lark** (lärk), *n.* [AS. *lāwerce*], any of various songbirds found throughout the world; esp., the English skylark.

**lark** (lärk), *v.i.* [< ON.], [Colloq.], to play or frolic. *n.* a frolic.

**lark·spur** (lärk′spũr′), *n.* a plant with spurred, usually blue flowers.

**lar·rup** (lar′əp), *v.t.* [-RUPED, -RUPING], [prob. < D. *larpen*], [Colloq.], to whip; flog.

**lar·va** (lär′və), *n.* [*pl.* -VAE (-vē)], [L., ghost], 1. an insect in the earliest stage after hatching, before it becomes a pupa. 2. the early form of any animal that changes structurally, as the tadpole. —**lar′val,** *adj.*

**lar·yn·gi·tis** (lar′in-jī′tis), *n.* inflammation of the larynx, often with loss of voice.

**lar·ynx** (lar′iŋks), *n.* [*pl.* -YNGES (lə-rin′jēz), -YNXES], [Gr. *larynx*], the structure at the upper end of the trachea, containing the vocal cords.

**las·civ·i·ous** (lə-siv′i-əs), *adj.* [< L. *lascivus*, wanton], 1. characterized by or expressing lust. 2. exciting lustful desires.

**la·ser** (lā′zẽr), *n.* [*l*ight *a*mplification by *s*timulated *e*mission of *r*adiation], a device that amplifies light waves and concentrates them in a narrow, very intense beam.

**lash** (lash), *n.* [? akin to OFr. *laz*, lace], 1. the flexible striking part of a whip. 2. a stroke as with a whip. 3. an eyelash. *v.t.* 1. to strike or drive as with a lash. 2. to switch energetically: as, the cat *lashed* her tail. 3. to censure, rebuke, etc. *v.i.* to make strokes as with a whip. —**lash out,** 1. to strike out violently. 2. to speak angrily.

**lash** (lash), *v.t.* [see LACE], to fasten or tie with a rope, etc.

**lass** (las), *n.* [? < N.], a young woman.

**las′sie,** *n.* [Scot.] a young girl.

**las·si·tude** (las′ə-to͞od′, -tūd′), *n.* [< L. *lassus*, faint], a state or feeling of being tired or weak.

**las·so** (las′ō), *n.* [*pl.* -SOS, -SOES], [< Sp. < L. *laqueus*, noose], a long rope with a sliding noose at one end, used in catching cattle, etc. *v.t.* [-SOED, -SOING], to catch with a lasso. —**las′so·er,** *n.*

**last** (last, läst), *adj.* [alt. superl. of *late*], 1. being or coming after all others in place or time; final. 2. only remaining: as, my *last* dime. 3. most recent: as, *last* month. 4. least likely: as, the *last* person I would suspect. 5. conclusive: as, the *last* word. *adv.* 1. after all others. 2. at the most recent time or occasion. 3. finally. *n.* the one coming last. —**at last,** finally.

**last** (last, läst), *v.i.* [AS. *læstan*], 1. to remain in existence, operation, use, etc.; continue; endure. 2. to be enough (*for*).

**last** (last, läst), *n.* [< AS. *last*, footstep], a form shaped like a foot, used in building or repairing shoes.

**las·tex** (las′teks), *n.* fine rubber thread wound with cotton, nylon, etc., for use in elastic fabric: a trademark (**Lastex**).

**last′ing,** *adj.* that lasts a long time; durable; permanent. —**last′ing·ly,** *adv.*

**Last Judgment,** in *theology*, the final judgment of mankind at the end of the world.

**last′ly,** *adv.* in conclusion; finally.

**last straw,** [< the straw that broke the camel's back in the fable], the final, crushing blow or misfortune.

**Last Supper,** the last supper eaten by Jesus with his disciples before the Crucifixion.

**lat.,** latitude.

**latch** (lach), *n.* [< AS. *læccan*], a fastening for a door, gate, or window, esp. one consisting of a bar, etc. that is thrust into a notch. *v.t. & v.i.* to fasten with a latch.

**latch′key′,** *n.* a key for drawing back or unfastening the latch of a door.

**late** (lāt), *adj.* [LATER or LATTER, LATEST or LAST], [AS. *læt*], 1. happening, coming, etc. after the usual or expected time, or at a time far advanced in a period: as, *late* to class, *late* Victorian. 2. *a*) recent. *b*) recently dead. *adv.* [LATER, LATEST or LAST], 1. after the expected time. 2. at or until an advanced time in the day, year, etc. 3. toward the end of a period. 4. recently: also **late′ly.** —**of late,** recently. —**late′ness,** *n.*

**la·tent** (lā′t'nt), *adj.* [< L. *latere*, lurk], lying hidden and undeveloped in a person or thing. —**la′ten·cy,** *n.* —**la′tent·ly,** *adv.*

**lat·er·al** (lat′ẽr-əl), *adj.* [< L. *latus*, side], of, at, from, or toward the side; sideways. *n.* in *football*, a short pass more or less parallel to the goal line: also **lateral pass.**

**la·tex** (lā′teks), *n.* [L., a fluid], a milky liquid in certain plants and trees: latex is the basis of rubber.

**lath** (lath, läth), *n.* [*pl.* LATHS (la*th*z, läths)], [AS. *lætt*], any of the thin, narrow strips of wood used as a groundwork for plastering, etc. *v.t.* to cover with laths.

**lathe** (lā*th*), *n.* [prob. < MD. *lade*], a machine for shaping wood, metal, etc. by holding and turning it rapidly against a cutting tool.

**lath·er** (la*th*′ẽr), *n.* [AS. *leathor*, soap], 1. the foam formed by soap and water. 2. foamy sweat. *v.t. & v.i.* to cover with or form lather.

**Lat·in** (lat′'n), *adj.* [< *Latium*, ancient country in C Italy], 1. of ancient Rome, its people, their language, etc. 2. designating or of the languages derived from Latin, the peoples who speak them, their countries, etc. *n.* 1. an inhabitant of ancient Rome. 2. the language of ancient Rome. 3. a person, as a Spaniard or Italian, whose language is derived from Latin.

**lat·i·tude** (lat′ə-to͞od′, -tūd′), *n.* [< L. *latus*, wide], 1. extent; scope; range. 2. freedom from restrictions. 3. distance north or south from the equator, measured in degrees. 4. a region with reference to this distance. —**lat′i·tu′di·nal,** *adj.*

**lat′i·tu′di·nar′i·an** (-tōō′d'n-âr′i-ən, -tū′-), *adj.* liberal in one's views, esp. in religious matters. *n.* one who is latitudinarian.

**la·trine** (lə-trēn′), *n.* [< L. *lavare*, wash], a toilet for the use of many people, as in an army camp.

**lat·ter** (lat′ẽr), *adj.* [alt. compar. of *late*], 1. *a*) later; more recent. *b*) nearer the end or close. 2. being the last mentioned of two.

**lat′ter·ly,** *adv.* lately; recently.

**lat·tice** (lat′is), *n.* [< MHG. *latte*, lath], 1. an openwork structure of crossed strips of wood, metal, etc. used as a screen, support, etc. 2. a window, door, etc. screened by such a structure. *v.t.* [-TICED, -TICING], 1. to arrange like a lattice. 2. to furnish with a lattice.

**lat′tice·work′,** *n.* 1. a lattice. 2. lattices collectively. Also **lat′tic·ing.**

**laud** (lôd), *n.* [< L. *laus*], praise. *v.t.* to praise; extol.

**laud′a·ble,** *adj.* praiseworthy.

**laud·a·num** (lôd′'n-əm), *n.* [< L. *ladanum*, a yellowish resin], 1. formerly, any of various opium preparations. 2. a tincture of opium.

**laud·a·to·ry** (lôd′ə-tôr′i), *adj.* expressing praise; commendatory.

**laugh** (laf, läf), *v.i.* [AS. *hleahhan*], to make the sounds and facial movements that express mirth, ridicule, etc. *n.* 1. the act or sound of laughing. 2. a cause of laughter. **—laugh at,** 1. to be amused by. 2. to make fun of.

**laugh′a·ble,** *adj.* amusing; ridiculous.

**laugh′ing,** *adj.* 1. that laughs. 2. causing laughter: as, a *laughing* matter.

**laughing gas,** nitrous oxide, used as an anesthetic, esp. in dentistry.

**laugh′ing·stock′** (-stok′), *n.* an object of ridicule.

**laugh′ter** (-tẽr), *n.* the action or sound of laughing.

**launch** (lônch), *v.t.* [see LANCE], 1. to hurl or discharge (a weapon, etc.). 2. to slide (a vessel) into the water. 3. to set in operation; start: as, to *launch* an attack. 4. to start (a person) on some course. *v.i.* 1. *a*) to put to sea. *b*) to begin something new: with *out* or *forth*. 2. to plunge (*into*).

**launch** (lônch), *n.* [prob. ult. < Malay *lancār*, speedy], 1. the largest boat carried by a warship. 2. a large, open motorboat.

**launching pad** (or **platform**), the platform from which a rocket, guided missile, etc. is launched.

**laun·der** (lôn′dẽr), *v.t.* [< L. *lavare*, to wash], to wash or wash and iron (clothes, etc.). **—laund′er·er,** *n.* **—laun′dress** (-dris), *n.fem.*

**laun·dro·mat** (lôn′drə-mat′), *n.* a self-service laundry with coin-operated washers and dryers: a trademark **(Laundromat).**

**laun·dry** (lôn′dri), *n.* [*pl.* -DRIES], 1. a place for laundering. 2. clothes, etc. laundered or to be laundered.

**laun′dry·man** (-mən), *n.* [*pl.* -MEN], a man who collects and delivers laundry.

**lau·re·ate** (lô′ri-it), *adj.* [< L. *laurus*, laurel], honored, as with a crown of laurel. *n.* a poet laureate. **—lau′re·ate·ship′,** *n.*

**lau·rel** (lô′rəl), *n.* [< L. *laurus*], 1. an evergreen tree or shrub of S Europe, with large, glossy leaves. 2. its foliage, esp. as woven into crowns. 3. *pl.* *a*) fame; honor. *b*) victory. 4. any of a family of trees and shrubs including the bay, cinnamon, etc.

**la·va** (lä′və, lav′ə), *n.* [< L. *lavare*, to wash], 1. melted rock issuing from a volcano. 2. such rock when solidified by cooling.

**lav·a·liere, lav·a·lier** (lav′ə-lêr′), *n.* [< Fr.], an ornament hanging from a chain, worn around the neck.

**lav·a·to·ry** (lav′ə-tôr′i), *n.* [*pl.* -RIES], [< L. *lavare*, to wash], 1. a bowl or basin for washing the face and hands. 2. a washroom.

**lave** (lāv), *v.t. & v.i.* [LAVED, LAVING], [< L. *lavare*], [Poetic], to wash; bathe.

**lav·en·der** (lav′ən-dẽr), *n.* [< ML. *lavendula*], 1. a fragrant European mint with spikes of pale-purplish flowers. 2. the dried flowers and leaves, used to perfume clothes, etc. 3. a pale purple. *adj.* pale-purple.

**lav·ish** (lav′ish), *adj.* [< OFr. *lavasse*, downpour], 1. very generous; prodigal. 2. very abundant. *v.t.* to give or spend liberally.

**law** (lô), *n.* [AS. *lagu*], 1. all the rules of conduct established by the authority or custom of a nation, etc. 2. any one of such rules. 3. obedience to such rules. 4. the study of such rules; jurisprudence. 5. the seeking of justice in courts under such rules. 6. the profession of lawyers, judges, etc. 7. any rule expected to be observed. 8. *a*) a sequence of natural events occurring with unvarying uniformity under the same conditions. *b*) the stating of such a sequence. **—the Law,** 1. the Mosaic code, or the part of the Old Testament containing it. 2. [l-], [Colloq.], a policeman, or the police.

**law′-a·bid′ing,** *adj.* obeying the law.

**law′break′er,** *n.* one who violates the law.

**law′ful,** *adj.* 1. in conformity with the law. 2. recognized by law: as, *lawful* debts.

**law′giv′er,** *n.* one who draws up a code of laws for a nation or people; lawmaker.

**law′less,** *adj.* 1. not regulated by the authority of law. 2. not in conformity with law; illegal. 3. not obeying the law; unruly.

**law′mak′er,** *n.* one who makes or helps to make laws; esp., a legislator.

**lawn** (lôn), *n.* [< OFr. *launde*, heath], a piece of ground covered with grass kept closely mowed, as around a house.

**lawn** (lôn), *n.* [< *Laon*, city in France], a fine, sheer cloth of linen or cotton.

**lawn mower,** a hand-propelled or power-driven machine for cutting the grass of a lawn.

**law′suit′** (-sōōt′, -sūt′), *n.* a case before a civil court for decision.

**law·yer** (lô′yẽr), *n.* one whose profession is advising others in matters of law or representing them in lawsuits.

**lax** (laks), *adj.* [L. *laxus*], 1. loose; slack; not tight. 2. not strict or exact. **—lax′ness,** *n.*

**lax·a·tive** (lak′sə-tiv), *adj.* [see LAX], making the bowels loose and relieving constipation. *n.* any laxative medicine.

**lax′i·ty,** *n.* lax quality or condition.

**lay** (lā), *v.t.* [LAID, LAYING], [AS. *lecgan*], 1. to cause to fall with force; knock down. 2. to place or put in a horizontal position (*on* or *in*): as, *lay* the book on the table. 3. to put down in the correct position, as bricks, etc. 4. to place, situate, put, etc.: as, he *lays* great trust in me. 5. to produce (an egg), as a hen. 6. to allay, suppress, etc. 7. to bet (a specified sum, etc.). 8. to devise: as, to *lay* plans. 9. to present or assert: as, he *laid* claim to the mill. *n.* the way or position in which something is situated: as, the *lay* of the land. **—lay aside,** to set aside for future use; save: also **lay by, lay away. —lay in,** to get and store away. **—lay off,** 1. to put aside. 2. to discharge (employees), esp. temporarily. **—lay open,** 1. to cut open. 2. to expose. **—lay out,** 1. to spend. 2. to arrange according to a plan. 3. to set out (clothes, etc.) ready for wear or use. **—lay over,** to stop a while in a place before continuing a journey. **—lay up,** 1. to store for future use. 2. to confine to a sick bed.

**lay** (lā), pt. of **lie** (to recline).

**lay** (lā), *adj.* [ult. < Gr. *laos*, the people], 1. of

a layman. 2. not belonging to a given profession.

**lay** (lā), *n.* [< OFr. *lai*], 1. a short poem, esp. one for singing. 2. [Archaic], a song.

**lay′er,** *n.* 1. a person or thing that lays. 2. a single thickness, coat, fold, etc.

**lay·ette** (lā-et′), *n.* [< MD. *lade*, chest], a complete outfit of clothes, bedding, etc. for a newborn baby.

**lay·man** (lā′mən), *n.* [*pl.* -MEN], a person not belonging to the clergy or one not belonging to a given profession.

**lay·off** (lā′ôf′), *n.* a putting out of work temporarily or the period of this.

**lay′out′,** *n.* 1. the manner in which anything is laid out; specif., the make-up of a newspaper, advertisement, etc. 2. the thing laid out.

**lay·o·ver** (lā′ō′vẽr), *n.* a stopping for a while in some place during a journey.

**Laz·a·rus** (laz′ə-rəs), *n.* in the *Bible*, a man raised from the dead by Jesus.

**laze** (lāz), *v.i.* & *v.t.* [LAZED, LAZING], to idle.

**la·zy** (lā′zi), *adj.* [-ZIER, -ZIEST], [prob. < MLG. or MD.], 1. not eager or willing to work or exert oneself; slothful. 2. slow and heavy; sluggish. **—la′zi·ness,** *n.*

**lb.,** [L.], 1. *libra*, pound. 2. *librae*, pounds: also **lbs.**

**l.c.,** 1. *loco citato*, [L.], in the place cited. 2. in *typography*, lower case.

**lea** (lē), *n.* [AS. *leah*], [Chiefly Poetic], a meadow or grassy field.

**leach** (lēch), *v.t.* [prob. < AS. *leccan*, to water], 1. to wash (wood ashes, etc.) with a filtering liquid. 2. to extract (a soluble substance) from some material. *v.i.* to lose soluble matter through a filtering liquid.

**lead** (lēd), *v.t.* [LED, LEADING], [AS. *lædan*], 1. to direct, as by going before or along with, by physical contact, pulling a rope, etc.; guide. 2. to direct by influence: as, he *led* us to victory. 3. to be the head of (an expedition, orchestra, etc.). 4. to be or go at the head of: as, she *leads* the class. 5. to live; spend: as, he *leads* a fast life. *v.i.* 1. to show the way, as by going before. 2. to tend in a certain direction; go (with *to*, *from*, etc.). 3. to bring as a result (with *to*): as, one thing *led* to another. 4. to be first, chief, etc. 5. to make the first move in a game, etc. *n.* 1. leadership; example: as, follow his *lead*. 2. first or front place. 3. the extent of distance ahead: as, we have a safe *lead*. 4. anything that leads, as a clue. 5. a leading role or actor in a play. 6. in *card games*, the right of playing first or the card played. **—lead off,** to begin. **—lead on,** to lure. **—lead up to,** to prepare the way for.

**lead** (led), *n.* [AS.], 1. a heavy, soft, bluish-gray metallic chemical element used for piping, etc.: symbol, Pb. 2. a weight for sounding depths at sea, etc. 3. bullets. 4. a thin stick of graphite, used in pencils. *adj.* made of or containing lead. *v.t.* to cover, line, or weight with lead.

**lead·en** (led′′n), *adj.* 1. made of lead. 2. heavy. 3. sluggish. 4. gloomy. 5. of a dull gray.

**lead·er** (lēd′ẽr), *n.* one that leads; guiding head. **—lead′er·ship′,** *n.*

**lead·ing** (lēd′iŋ), *n.* direction; guidance. *adj.* 1. that leads; guiding. 2. principal; chief.

**leading question,** a question put so as to suggest the answer sought.

**leaf** (lēf), *n.* [*pl.* LEAVES (lēvz)], [AS. *leaf*], 1. any of the flat, thin parts, usually green, growing from the stem of a plant. 2. a petal. 3. a sheet of paper. 4. a thin sheet of metal. 5. a hinged or removable section of a table top. *v.i.* to bear leaves (often with *out*). *v.t.* to turn the pages of (a book, etc.): often with *through*. **—turn over a new leaf,** to make a new start. **—leaf′less,** *adj.*

**leaf′let** (-lit), *n.* 1. a small or young leaf. 2. a separate sheet of printed matter, often folded.

**leaf′y,** *adj.* [-IER, -IEST], 1. of or like a leaf. 2. having many leaves. **—leaf′i·ness,** *n.*

**league** (lēg), *n.* [< L. *ligare*, bind], an association of nations, groups, etc. for promoting common interests. *v.t.* & *v.i.* [LEAGUED, LEAGUING], to form into a league.

**league** (lēg), *n.* [ult. < Celt.], a measure of distance, about 3 miles.

**League of Nations,** an association of nations (1920–1946) to promote international co-operation and peace.

**Le·ah** (lē′ə), *n.* in the *Bible*, the elder of the two wives of Jacob.

**leak** (lēk), *v.i.* [< ON. *leka*, to drip], 1. to let a fluid out or in accidentally. 2. to enter or escape in this way, as a fluid. 3. to become known gradually: as, the truth *leaked* out. *v.t.* to allow to leak. *n.* 1. an accidental crack, etc. that lets a fluid out or in. 2. any accidental means of escape. 3. leakage. **—leak′y,** *adj.*

**leak′age** (-ij), *n.* 1. a leaking in or out; leak. 2. something that leaks in or out. 3. the amount that leaks.

**lean** (lēn), *v.i.* [LEANED or LEANT (lent), LEANING], [AS. *hlinian*], 1. to bend or slant from an upright position. 2. to bend the body and rest part of one's weight on something. 3. to rely (*upon* or *on*). 4. to tend: as, to *lean* toward crime. *v.t.* to cause to stand slanting or to rest against something.

**lean** (lēn), *adj.* [AS. *hlæne*], 1. with little flesh or fat; thin; spare. 2. meager. *n.* meat containing little or no fat. **—lean′ness,** *n.*

**lean′ing,** *n.* 1. the act of one that leans. 2. tendency; inclination.

**lean′-to′,** *n.* [*pl.* -TOS], a structure whose sloping roof abuts a wall, etc.

**leap** (lēp), *v.i.* [LEAPED or LEAPT (lept, lēpt), LEAPING], [AS. *hleapan*], to jump; spring; bound. *v.t.* 1. to pass over by a jump. 2. to cause to leap. *n.* 1. a jump; spring; bound. 2. the distance covered by a jump. 3. a place that is, or is to be, leaped over or from.

**leap year,** every fourth year, containing an extra day in February.

**learn** (lũrn), *v.t.* & *v.i.* [LEARNED (lũrnd) or LEARNT (lũrnt), LEARNING], [AS. *leornian*], 1. to get knowledge of or skill in (an art, trade, etc.) by study, experience, etc. 2. to come to know; hear (*of*). 3. to memorize. **—learn′er,** *n.*

**learn·ed** (lũr′nid), *adj.* 1. having or showing much learning; erudite. 2. characterized by or requiring study.

**learn′ing,** *n.* 1. the acquiring of knowledge or skill. 2. acquired knowledge or skill.

**lease** (lēs), *n.* [< L. *laxus*, loose], a contract by which a landlord rents lands, buildings, etc. to a tenant for a specified time. *v.t.* [LEASED, LEASING], to give or get by a lease. **—leas′a·ble,** *adj.* **—leas′er,** *n.*

**leash** (lēsh), *n.* [< L. *laxus*, loose], a cord, strap, etc. by which a dog or the like is held in check. *v.t.* to check or hold as by a leash. **—hold in leash,** to control.

**least** (lēst), *adj.* [alt. superl. of *little*], [AS. *læst*], smallest in size, degree, etc. *adv.* in the smallest degree. *n.* the smallest in amount, importance, etc. **—at (the) least,** 1. with no less. 2. at any rate. **—not in the least,** not at all.

**least′wise′** (-wīz′), *adv.* [Colloq.], at least; at any rate: also **least′ways′** (-wāz′).

**leath·er** (leth′ẽr), *n.* [AS. *lether-*], animal skin prepared for use by removing the hair and tanning. *adj.* of leather.

**leath′er·neck′** (-nek′), *n.* [Slang], a U.S. marine.

**leath′er·y,** *adj.* like leather; tough and flexible.

**leave** (lēv), *v.t.* [LEFT, LEAVING], [AS. *læfan*, let remain], 1. to allow to remain: as, *leave* some cake for me, *leave* it open. 2. to have remaining after one: as, he *leaves* a widow. 3. to bequeath. 4. to go away from. 5. to abandon. 6. [Slang], to let: as, *leave* us go now. *v.i.* to go away or set out. **—leave off,** 1. to stop. 2. to stop doing or using. **—leave out,** to omit.

**leave** (lēv), *n.* [AS. *leaf*], 1. permission. 2. permission to be absent from duty. 3. the period for which this is granted. **—take leave of,** to say good-by to. **—take one's leave,** to depart.

**leave** (lēv), *v.i.* [LEAVED, LEAVING], to put forth, or bear, leaves; leaf.

**leav·en** (lev′'n), *n.* [< L. *levare*, raise], 1. a substance, such as yeast, producing fermentation in dough. 2. any influence causing a gradual change. *v.t.* 1. to make (dough) rise. 2. to spread through, causing a gradual change.

**leav′en·ing,** *n.* 1. a causing to ferment by leaven. 2. a leaven.

**leaves** (lēvz), *n.* pl. of **leaf.**

**leav·ing** (lēv′iŋ), *n.* 1. *usually in pl.* a leftover; remnant. 2. *pl.* refuse.

**lech·er** (lech′ẽr), *n.* [OFr. *leicheor*, glutton], a lewd, grossly sensual man.

**lech′er·ous,** *adj.* lustful; lewd.

**lech′er·y,** *n.* gross sensuality; lewdness.

**lec·i·thin** (les′ə-thin), *n.* [< Gr. *lekithos*, egg yolk], a nitrogenous, fatty substance found in animal tissue, egg yolk, and some plants.

**lec·tern** (lek′tẽrn), *n.* [< L. *legere*, read], a reading stand.

**lec·ture** (lek′chẽr), *n.* [< L. *legere*, read], 1. an informative talk given before an audience, class, etc. 2. a lengthy scolding. *v.t. & v.i.* [-TURED, -TURING], 1. to give a lecture (to). 2. to scold. **—lec′tur·er,** *n.*

**led** (led), pt. and pp. of **lead** (guide).

**ledge** (lej), *n.* [ME. *legge*], 1. a shelf. 2. a projecting ridge of rocks.

**ledg·er** (lej′ẽr), *n.* [< ME. *leggen*, lay], in *bookkeeping*, the book of final entry, in which a record of debits, credits, and all money transactions is kept.

**lee** (lē), *n.* [AS. *hleo*, shelter], 1. shelter. 2. in *naut. usage*, the side or part away from the wind. *adj.* of or on the side sheltered from the wind.

**leech** (lēch), *n.* [AS. *læce*], 1. a bloodsucking worm living in water and used, esp. formerly, to bleed patients. 2. a person who clings to another to get some gain out of him.

**leek** (lēk), *n.* [AS. *leac*], a vegetable that resembles a thick green onion.

**leer** (lêr), *n.* [AS. *hleor*], a sly, sidelong look showing ill will, lustfulness, etc. *v.i.* to look with a leer. **—leer′ing·ly,** *adv.*

**leer·y** (lêr′i), *adj.* [Colloq.], wary; suspicious.

**lees** (lēz), *n.pl.* [< ML. *lia*], dregs; sediment, as of wine.

**lee·ward** (lē′wẽrd; *naut.*, lōō′ẽrd), *adj.* in the direction toward which the wind blows. *n.* the lee part or side. *adv.* toward the lee.

**lee·way** (lē′wā′), *n.* 1. the leeward drift of a ship or aircraft from its course. 2. [Colloq.], *a*) margin of time, money, etc. *b*) room for freedom of action.

**left** (left), *adj.* [< ME. *lift*], 1. of or designating that side toward the west when one faces north. 2. closer to the left side of one facing the thing mentioned. *n.* 1. the left side. 2. [often L-], in *politics*, a liberal or radical position, party, etc. (often with *the*). *adv.* on or toward the left hand or side.

**left** (left), pt. and pp. of **leave** (to go away).

**left′-hand′,** *adj.* 1. on or directed toward the left. 2. of, for, or with the left hand.

**left′-hand′ed,** *adj.* 1. using the left hand more skillfully than the right. 2. done with or made for use with the left hand. 3. insincere; dubious: as, a *left-handed* compliment. *adv.* with the left hand: as, he writes *left-handed.*

**left′ist,** *n. & adj.* in *politics*, liberal or radical.

**left′o′ver,** *n.* something left over, as from a meal. *adj.* remaining unused, etc.

**left wing,** in *politics*, the more liberal or radical section of a party, group, etc. **—left′-wing′,** *adj.* **—left′-wing′er,** *n.*

**leg** (leg), *n.* [ON. *leggr*], 1. one of the parts of the body by means of which men and animals stand and walk. 2. the part of a garment covering the leg. 3. anything like a leg in shape or use. *v.i.* [LEGGED, LEGGING], [Colloq.], to walk or run (usually with *it*). **—pull one's leg,** [Colloq.], to make fun of or fool one. **—leg′less,** *adj.*

**leg·a·cy** (leg′ə-si), *n.* [*pl.* -CIES], [ult. < L. *lex*, law], 1. money or property left to someone by a will. 2. anything handed down as from an ancestor.

**le·gal** (lē′g'l), *adj.* [< L. *lex*, law], 1. of or on law. 2. permitted by law. 3. of or for lawyers. **—le′gal·ly,** *adv.*

**le·gal·i·ty** (li-gal′ə-ti), *n.* [*pl.* -TIES], quality, condition, or instance of being legal or lawful.

**le·gal·ize** (lē′g'l-īz′), *v.t.* [-IZED, -IZING], to make legal or lawful. **—le′gal·i·za′tion,** *n.*

**legal tender,** money acceptable by law in payment of a debt.

**leg·ate** (leg′it), *n.* [< L. *lex*, law], an envoy, esp. one officially representing the Pope.

**leg·a·tee** (leg′ə-tē′), *n.* one to whom a legacy is bequeathed.

**le·ga·tion** (li-gā′shən), *n.* a legate and his staff and headquarters.

**le·ga·to** (li-gä′tō), *adj. & adv.* [< It. *legare*, to tie], in *music*, in a smooth, even style.

**leg·end** (lej′ənd), *n.* [< L. *legere*, read], 1. a story or body of stories handed down for generations and popularly regarded as history. 2. an inscription on a coin, etc. 3. a title, key, etc. accompanying an illustration or map.

**leg·end·ar·y** (lej′ən-der′i), *adj.* of, based on, or presented in a legend or legends; traditional.

**leg·er·de·main** (lej′ẽr-di-mān′), *n.* [Fr. *leger de main*, light of hand], 1. sleight of hand; tricks of a stage magician. 2. trickery.

**leg·ged** (leg′id, legd), *adj.* having (a specified number or kind of) legs: as, *long-legged.*

**leg·ging** (leg′iŋ), *n. usually in pl.* a covering of canvas, etc. for protecting the leg below the knee.

**leg·gy** (leg′i), *adj.* [-GIER, -GIEST], having long, or long and awkward, legs.

**leg·horn** (leg′ẽrn, leg′hôrn), *n.* [< *Leghorn*, It. seaport], 1. [often L-], any of a breed of small chicken. 2. a hat made of Italian wheat straw.

**leg·i·ble** (lej′ə-b'l), *adj.* [< L. *legere*, read], that can be read, esp. easily. **—leg′i·bil′i·ty,** *n.* **—leg′i·bly,** *adv.*

**le·gion** (lē′jən), *n.* [< L. *legere*, to select], 1. a large group of soldiers; army. 2. a large number; multitude. **—le′gion·ar′y,** *adj. & n.*

**le′gion·naire′** (-âr′), *n.* [< Fr.], a member of a legion.

**leg·is·late** (lej′is-lāt′), *v.i.* [-LATED, -LATING], [< L. *lex*, law + *lator*, proposer], to make or pass a law or laws. *v.t.* to cause to become, go, etc. by making laws. **—leg′is·la′tor,** *n.*

**leg′is·la′tion,** *n.* 1. the making of laws. 2. the law or laws made.

**leg′is·la′tive,** *adj.* 1. of legislation. 2. having the power to make laws.

**leg′is·la′ture** (-chẽr), *n.* a body of persons given the power to make laws.

**le·git·i·mate** (li-jit′ə-mit), *adj.* [< L. *lex*, law], 1. born of parents married to each other. 2. lawful; allowed. 3. reasonable; logically correct. 4. of stage plays, as distinguished from motion pictures, etc. ***v.t.*** (-māt′), [-MATED, -MATING], 1. to make or declare legitimate. 2. to justify or authorize. —**le·git′i·ma·cy** (-mə-si), ***n.***

**le·git′i·ma·tize′** (-mə-tīz′), ***v.t.*** [-TIZED, -TIZING], to legitimate: also **le·git′i·mize′**.

**leg-of-mut·ton** (leg′ə-mut′′n, leg′əv-), ***adj.*** shaped like a leg of mutton; much larger at one end than at the other, as a sleeve.

**leg·ume** (leg′ūm, li-gūm′), ***n.*** [< L. *legere*, gather], 1. any plant of the pea family, characterized by true pods enclosing seeds. 2. the edible fruit of such plants; pod or its seeds. —**le·gu·mi·nous**, (li-gū′mi-nəs), ***adj.***

**le·i** (lā, lā′i), ***n.*** [*pl.* -IS], [Haw.], a garland or wreath of flowers and leaves.

**lei·sure** (lē′zhẽr, lezh′ẽr), ***n.*** [< L. *licere*, be permitted], free time during which one may indulge in rest, recreation, etc. ***adj.*** free and unoccupied: as, *leisure* time.

**lei′sure·ly, *adj.*** without haste; deliberate; slow. ***adv.*** in an unhurried manner.

**leit·mo·tiv, leit·mo·tif** (līt′mō-tēf′), ***n.*** [< G. *leiten*, to lead + *motiv*, motif], a short musical phrase recurring with a given character, situation, etc. in an opera.

**lem·on** (lem′ən), ***n.*** [< Per. *līmūn*], 1. a small, sour, pale-yellow citrus fruit. 2. the spiny, semitropical tree that it grows on. 3. [Slang], an undesirable thing. ***adj.*** 1. pale-yellow. 2. made with lemons.

**lem′on·ade′** (-ād′), ***n.*** a drink made of lemon juice, sugar, and water.

**le·mur** (lē′mẽr), ***n.*** [< L. *lemures*, ghosts], a small mammal related to the monkey.

**lend** (lend), ***v.t.*** [LENT, LENDING], [< AS. *læn*, a loan], 1. to let another use or have (a thing) temporarily. 2. to let out (money) at interest. 3. to impart: as, to *lend* an air of mystery. ***v.i.*** to make a loan or loans. —**lend itself** (or **oneself**) **to**, to be useful for or open to. —**lend′er, *n.***

**length** (leŋkth), ***n.*** [< AS. *lang*, long], 1. the distance from end to end of a thing. 2. extent in space or time. 3. a long stretch or extent. 4. a piece of a certain length. —**at length**, 1. finally. 2. in full.

**length′en, *v.t.* & *v.i.*** to make or become longer.

**length′wise′** (-wīz′), ***adv.* & *adj.*** in the direction of the length: also **length′ways′** (-wāz′).

**length′y, *adj.*** [-IER, -IEST], long; esp., too long. —**length′i·ly, *adv.***

**le·ni·ent** (lē′ni-ənt, lēn′yənt), ***adj.*** [< L. *lenis*, soft], not harsh or severe; merciful; mild. —**le′ni·en·cy, *n.*** —**le′ni·ent·ly, *adv.***

**lens** (lenz), ***n.*** [L., lentil: < its shape], 1. a curved piece of glass, plastic, etc. for bringing together or spreading rays of light passing through it: used in optical instruments to form an image. 2. a similar transparent part of the eye: it focuses upon the retina light rays entering the pupil.

**Lent** (lent), ***n.*** [AS. *lengten*, the spring < *lang*, long], in *Christianity*, the forty weekdays of fasting and penitence, from Ash Wednesday to Easter. —**Lent′en, lent′en, *adj.***

**lent** (lent), pt. & pp. of **lend.**

**len·til** (len′t'l, -til), ***n.*** [< L. *lens*], 1. a plant of the pea family, with small, edible seeds. 2. this seed.

**Le·o** (lē′ō), ***n.*** [L., lion], the fifth sign of the zodiac.

**le·o·nine** (lē′ə-nīn′), ***adj.*** [< L. *leo*, lion], of or like a lion.

**leop·ard** (lep′ẽrd), ***n.*** [< Gr. *leōn*, lion + *pardos*, panther], 1. a large, wild animal of the cat family, with a black-spotted tawny coat, found in Africa and Asia. 2. the jaguar.

**lep·er** (lep′ẽr), ***n.*** [< Gr. *lepros*, scaly], a person having leprosy.

**lep·re·chaun** (lep′rə-kôn′), ***n.*** [OIr. *lu*, little + *corp*, body], in *Irish folklore*, a fairy who can reveal hidden treasures to anyone who catches him.

**lep·ro·sy** (lep′rə-si), ***n.*** [see LEPER], a chronic infectious disease of the skin, tissues, or nerves, characterized by ulcers, white scaly scabs, deformities, etc. —**lep′rous, *adj.***

**Les·bi·an** (lez′bi-ən), ***n.*** [< *Lesbos*, island of ancient Greece, where the poetess Sappho lived], a homosexual woman. —**Les′bi·an·ism, *n.***

**lese majesty** (lēz), [< Fr.], a crime against the sovereign; treason.

**le·sion** (lē′zhən), ***n.*** [< L. *laedere*, to harm], an injury of an organ or tissue resulting in impairment of function.

**less** (les), ***adj.*** [alt. compar. of *little*], [AS. *læs(sa)*], not so much, so great, etc.; smaller, fewer, of lower rank, etc. ***adv.*** [compar. of *little*], to a smaller extent. ***n.*** a smaller amount. ***prep.*** minus.

**-less**, [AS. *leas*, free], a suffix meaning: 1. *without, lacking*, as in *valueless*. 2. *not ——ing* or *——ed*, as in *tireless, dauntless.*

**les·see** (les-ē′), ***n.*** [< OFr. *lesser*, to lease], one to whom a lease is given; tenant.

**less·en** (les′′n), ***v.t.* & *v.i.*** to make or become less; decrease, belittle, etc.

**less·er** (les′ẽr), ***adj.*** [alt. compar. of *little*], smaller, less, or less important.

**les·son** (les′′n), ***n.*** [< L. *legere*, read], 1. an exercise for a student to learn. 2. something learned for one's safety, etc. 3. *pl.* course of instruction. 4. a selection read from the Bible. 5. a lecture; rebuke.

**les·sor** (les′ôr), ***n.*** [see LEASE], one who gives a lease; landlord.

**lest** (lest), ***conj.*** [< AS. *thy læs the*, by the less that], for fear that: as, speak low *lest* he hear.

**let** (let), ***v.t.*** [LET, LETTING], [AS. *lætan*, leave behind], 1. to leave: now only in *let alone, let be.* 2. *a)* to rent. *b)* to assign (a contract). 3. to cause to escape: as, *let* blood. 4. to allow; permit. Also used as an auxiliary in commands or suggestions: as, *let* us go. ***v.i.*** to be rented. —**let down**, 1. to lower. 2. to slow up. 3. to disappoint. —**let off**, 1. to give forth. 2. to deal leniently with. —**let on**, [Colloq.], 1. to pretend. 2. to indicate one's awareness of a fact. —**let out**, 1. to release. 2. to rent out. 3. to make a garment larger. —**let up**, 1. to relax. 2. to cease.

**let** (let), ***n.*** [< AS. *lettan*, make late], an obstacle; hindrance: usually in *without let or hindrance.*

**-let**, [< Fr. *-el* + *-et*, dim. suffixes], a suffix meaning *small*, as in *ringlet.*

**let′down′, *n.*** 1. a slowing up. 2. [Colloq.], a disappointment.

**le·thal** (lē′thəl), ***adj.*** [< L. *let(h)um*, death], causing death; fatal.

**leth·ar·gy** (leth′ẽr-ji), ***n.*** [*pl.* -GIES], [< Gr. *lēthē*, oblivion], 1. an abnormal drowsiness. 2. total indifference; apathy. —**le·thar·gic** (li-thär′jik), ***adj.*** —**le·thar′gi·cal·ly, *adv.***

**let's** (lets), let us.

**let·ter** (let′ẽr), ***n.*** [< L. *littera*], 1. any character of the alphabet. 2. a written or printed message, usually sent by mail. 3. literal meaning. ***v.t.*** to mark with letters. —**letters**, 1. literature. 2. learning; knowledge.

**let′tered, *adj.*** 1. literate. 2. well educated. 3. marked with letters.

**let′ter·head′, *n.*** 1. the name, address, etc. of a person or firm as a heading on letter paper. 2. stationery with such a heading.

**let′ter·ing, *n.*** 1. the act of making letters or inscribing in or with letters. 2. letters so made or inscribed.

**let′ter-per′fect, *adj.*** correct in every respect.

**let′ter·press′, *n.*** printed words; esp., reading matter, as distinguished from illustrations.

**let·tuce** (let′is), *n.* [< L. *lac*, milk], 1. a plant with crisp, green leaves. 2. the leaves, much used for salads.

**let·up** (let′up′), *n.* [Colloq.], 1. a slackening. 2. a stop; pause.

**leu·co·cyte** (lo͞o′kə-sīt′), *n.* [< Gr. *leukos*, white + *kytos*, hollow], a white blood corpuscle: it destroys disease-causing organisms.

**leu·ke·mi·a, leu·kae·mi·a** (lo͞o-kē′-mi-ə), *n.* [see LEUCOCYTE & -EMIA], a disease characterized by abnormal increase in the number of leucocytes.

**lev·ee** (lev′i), *n.* [ult. < L. *levare*, raise], an embankment to prevent a river from flooding bordering land.

**lev·ee** (lev′i, lə-vē′), *n.* [< Fr. *se lever*, to rise], a morning reception held by a sovereign.

**lev·el** (lev′'l), *n.* [< L. *libra*, a balance], 1. an instrument for determining the horizontal. 2. a horizontal plane or line: as, sea *level*. 3. a horizontal area. 4. height; altitude. 5. position, rank, etc.: as, *levels* of reading. *adj.* 1. perfectly flat and even. 2. not sloping. 3. even in height (*with*). 4. equal in importance, advancement, quality, etc. *adv.* on a level line. *v.t. & v.i.* [-ELED or -ELLED, -ELING or -ELLING], 1. to make or become level, even, flat, equal, etc. 2. to demolish. 3. to raise and aim (a gun, etc.).

**lev′el-head′ed,** *adj.* having an even temper and sound judgment.

**lev·er** (lev′ẽr, lē′vẽr), *n.* [< L. *levare*, raise], 1. a bar used as a pry. 2. a device consisting of a bar turning about a fixed point, using force at a second point to lift a weight at a third. *v.t.* to lift with a lever.

**lev′er·age** (-ij), *n.* the action or mechanical power of a lever.

**le·vi·a·than** (lə-vī′ə-thən), *n.* [< Heb. *liwyāthān*, sea monster], any huge thing.

**lev·i·ta·tion** (lev′ə-tā′shən), *n.* [< L. *levis*, light], the illusion of raising a body in the air with no support.

**Le·vit·i·cus** (lə-vit′i-kəs), *n.* the third book of the Old Testament.

**lev·i·ty** (lev′ə-ti), *n.* [*pl.* -TIES], [< L. *levis*, light], frivolity; improper gaiety.

**lev·y** (lev′i), *n.* [*pl.* -IES], [< L. *levare*, to raise], 1. an imposing and collecting of a tax, fine, etc. 2. the amount collected. 3. compulsory enlistment for military service. 4. a group so enlisted. *v.t.* [-IED, -YING], 1. to impose (a tax, fine, etc.). 2. to enlist (troops). 3. to wage (war).

**lewd** (lo͞od), *adj.* [AS. *læwede*, lay, hence vulgar], indecent; lustful; obscene.

**lex·i·cog·ra·phy** (lek′sə-kog′rə-fi), *n.* [see LEXICON & -GRAPHY], the act, art, or work of writing or compiling a dictionary. —**lex′i·cog′ra·pher,** *n.* —**lex′i·co·graph′ic** (-si-kə-graf′ik), **lex′i·co·graph′i·cal,** *adj.*

**lex′i·con** (lek′si-kən), *n.* [< Gr. *lexis*, word], 1. a dictionary. 2. a special vocabulary.

**LG., L.G.,** Low German.

**LGr.,** Late Greek.

**Li,** in *chem.*, lithium.

**li·a·bil·i·ty** (lī′ə-bil′ə-ti), *n.* [*pl.* -TIES], 1. the state of being liable. 2. anything for which a person is liable. 3. *usually in pl.* a debt: opposed to *asset*. 4. something that works to one's disadvantage.

**li·a·ble** (lī′ə-b'l), *adj.* [< L. *ligare*, bind], 1. legally bound or responsible. 2. subject to: as, *liable* to suspicion. 3. *a*) disagreeably likely: as, he's *liable* to suffer. *b*) [Colloq.], likely.

**li·ai·son** (lē′ā-zōn′, -ə-zon′, li-ā′z'n), *n.* [< L. *ligare*, bind], 1. intercommunication, as between units of a military force. 2. an illicit love affair.

**li·ar** (lī′ẽr), *n.* one who tells lies.

**li·ba·tion** (lī-bā′shən), *n.* [< L. *libare*, pour out], 1. the ritual of pouring out wine or oil in honor of a god. 2. the liquid poured out.

**li·bel** (lī′b'l), *n.* [< L. *liber*, book], 1. any written or printed matter tending to injure a person's reputation unjustly. 2. the act or crime of publishing such a thing. *v.t.* [-BELED or -BELLED, -BELING or -BELLING], to make a libel against. —**li′bel·er, li′bel·ler,** *n.* —**li′bel·ous, li′bel·lous,** *adj.*

**lib·er·al** (lib′ẽr-əl), *adj.* [< L. *liber*, free], 1. generous. 2. ample; abundant. 3. not literal or strict. 4. tolerant; broad-minded. 5. favoring reform or progress; specif., [also L-], favoring political reforms. *n.* 1. one who favors reform or progress. 2. [L-], a member of a liberal political party, esp. that of England. —**lib′er·al·ism,** *n.* —**lib′er·al·ly,** *adv.* —**lib′er·al·ness,** *n.*

**liberal arts,** literature, philosophy, languages, history, etc. as courses of study.

**lib′er·al′i·ty** (-ə-ral′ə-ti), *n.* [*pl.* -TIES], 1. generosity. 2. broad-mindedness.

**lib′er·al·ize′** (-ẽr-ə-līz′), *v.t. & v.i.* [-IZED, -IZING], to make or become liberal. —**lib′er·al·i·za′tion,** *n.*

**lib·er·ate** (lib′ə-rāt′), *v.t.* [-ATED, -ATING], [< L. *liber*, free], to release from slavery, enemy occupation, etc. —**lib′er·a′tion,** *n.* —**lib′er·a′tor,** *n.*

**lib·er·tine** (lib′ẽr-tēn′), *n.* [< L. *liber*, free], a man who is sexually promiscuous. *adj.* licentious. —**lib′er·tin·ism,** *n.*

**lib·er·ty** (lib′ẽr-ti), *n.* [*pl.* -TIES], [< L. *liber*, free], 1. freedom from slavery, captivity, etc. 2. a particular right, freedom, etc. 3. *usually pl.* excessive freedom or familiarity. 4. leave given to a sailor to go ashore. See also **civil liberties.** —**at liberty,** 1. not confined. 2. permitted (*to*). 3. not busy or in use.

**li·bid·i·nous** (li-bid′'n-əs), *adj.* [see LIBIDO], lustful; lascivious. —**li·bid′i·nous·ly,** *adv.*

**li·bi·do** (li-bī′dō, -bē′-), *n.* [L., desire], 1. the sexual urge. 2. in *psychoanalysis*, psychic energy generally; force behind all human action. —**li·bid′i·nal** (-bid′'n-əl), *adj.*

**Li·bra** (lī′brə), *n.* [L., a balance, pair of scales], the seventh sign of the zodiac.

**li·brar·i·an** (lī-brâr′i-ən), *n.* a person in charge of a library.

**li·brar·y** (lī′brer′i), *n.* [*pl.* -IES], [< L. *liber*, book], 1. a room or building where a collection of books, etc. is kept. 2. an institution in charge of the care and circulation of such a collection. 3. a collection of books.

**li·bret·to** (li-bret′ō), *n.* [*pl.* -TOS, -TI (-i)], [It. < L. *liber*, book], the words, or text, of an opera, oratorio, etc. —**li·bret′tist,** *n.*

**lice** (līs), *n.* pl. of **louse.**

**li·cense, li·cence** (lī′s'ns), *n.* [< L. *licere*, be permitted], 1. formal or legal permission to do something specified. 2. a document indicating such permission. 3. freedom to deviate from rule, practice, etc.: as, poetic *license*. 4. excessive freedom, constituting an abuse of liberty. *v.t.* [-CENSED, -CENSING; -CENCED, -CENCING], to permit formally.

**li′cen·see′, li′cen·cee′** (-sē′), *n.* a person to whom a license is granted.

**li·cen·ti·ate** (lī-sen′shi-it, -āt′), *n.* a person licensed to practice a specified profession.

**li·cen·tious** (lī-sen′shəs), *adj.* [see LICENSE], morally unrestrained; lascivious.

**li·chen** (lī′kən), *n.* [< Gr. *leichein*, to lick], a mosslike plant growing in patches on rocks and tree trunks.

**lic·it** (lis′it), *adj.* [< L. *licere*, be permitted], permitted; lawful.

**lick** (lik), *v.t.* [AS. *liccian*], 1. to pass the tongue over. 2. to pass lightly over like a tongue. 3. [Colloq.], *a*) to whip. *b*) to vanquish. *n.* 1. a licking with the tongue. 2. a small quantity. 3. a salt lick. 4. [Colloq.],

*a*) a sharp blow. *b*) a short, rapid burst of activity. **—lick up**, to consume by or as by licking.
**lic·o·rice** (lik′ēr-is, lik′rish), ***n.*** [< Gr. *glykys*, sweet + *rhiza*, root], 1. a black flavoring extract made from the root of a European plant. 2. candy flavored with this extract.
**lid** (lid), ***n.*** [AS. *hlid*], 1. a movable cover, as for a box, etc. 2. an eyelid. 3. [Slang], a hat.
**lie** (lī), ***v.i.*** [LAY, LAIN, LYING], [AS. *licgan*], 1. to be or put oneself in a horizontal or reclining position. 2. to rest on a support in a horizontal position. 3. to be in a specified condition. 4. to be situated: as, Canada *lies* to the north. 5. to exist: as, the fault *lies* in me. 6. to be buried. ***n.*** the way in which something is situated; lay.
**lie** (lī), ***v.i.*** [LIED, LYING], [AS. *leogan*], to make a statement that one knows to be false. ***v.t.*** to bring, put, accomplish, etc. by lying. ***n.*** a thing said in lying; falsehood.
**lief** (lēf), ***adv.*** [AS. *leof*], [Rare], willingly; gladly: only in *would* (or *had*) *as lief*, etc.
**liege** (lēj), ***adj.*** [< OFr.], loyal; faithful. ***n.*** in *feudal law*, 1. a lord or sovereign. 2. a subject.
**li·en** (lēn, lē′ən), ***n.*** [Fr.; ult. < L. *ligare*, to bind], a legal claim on another's property as security against the payment of a debt.
**lieu** (lōō), ***n.*** [< L. *locus*, place], stead; place. **—in lieu of**, instead of.
**lieu·ten·ant** (lōō-ten′ənt), ***n.*** [OFr. < *lieu*, place + *tenant*, holding], 1. one who acts for a superior. 2. a commissioned military officer: see **first lieutenant, second lieutenant.** 3. a naval officer ranking just above a lieutenant junior grade. Abbrev. **Lieut., Lt. —lieu·ten′an·cy** [*pl.* -CIES], ***n.***
**lieutenant colonel,** a military officer ranking just above a major.
**lieutenant commander,** a naval officer ranking just above a lieutenant.
**lieutenant general,** a military officer ranking just above a major general.
**lieutenant governor,** an elected official of a State who ranks below and substitutes for the governor: abbrev. **Lt. Gov., Lieut. Gov.**
**lieutenant junior grade,** a naval officer ranking just above an ensign.
**life** (līf), ***n.*** [*pl.* LIVES], [AS. *lif*], 1. that property of plants and animals (ending at death) which makes it possible for them to take in food, get energy from it, grow, etc. 2. the state of having this property. 3. a human being: as, 100 *lives* were lost. 4. living things collectively: as, plant *life*. 5. the time a person or thing is alive or flourishing. 6. one's manner of living: as, a *life* of poverty. 7. the people and activities of a given time, place, etc.: as, military *life*. 8. human existence: as, to learn from *life*. 9. a biography. 10. the source of liveliness: as, the *life* of the party. 11. vigor; liveliness.
**life belt,** a life preserver in the form of a belt.
**life′blood′,** ***n.*** 1. the blood necessary to life. 2. the vital part of anything.
**life′boat′,** ***n.*** one of the small rescue boats carried by a ship.
**life buoy,** a life preserver.
**life′guard′,** ***n.*** a swimmer employed at beaches, etc. to prevent drownings.
**life insurance,** insurance in which a stipulated sum is paid at the death of the insured.
**life′less,** ***adj.*** 1. without life; specif., *a*) inanimate. *b*) dead. 2. dull. **—life′less·ly,** ***adv.***
**life′like′,** ***adj.*** resembling real life or a real person or thing.
**life line,** 1. the rope by means of which a diver is raised and lowered. 2. a vital transport line.
**life′long′,** ***adj.*** lasting, or remaining as such, for all one's life.
**life preserver,** any device for saving a person from drowning by keeping him afloat.
**life′sav′er,** ***n.*** 1. a life preserver. 2. a lifeguard. **—life′sav′ing,** ***adj. & n.***
**life′-size′,** ***adj.*** as big as the person or thing represented, as a statue, etc.
**life style,** the consistent, integrated way of life of an individual as typified by his manner, attitudes, possessions, etc.
**life′time′,** ***n.*** the length of one's life. ***adj.*** lasting for such a period.
**life′work′,** ***n.*** the work or task to which a person devotes his life.
**lift** (lift), ***v.t.*** [< AS. *lyft*, air], 1. to bring up to a higher position; raise. 2. to raise in rank, condition, etc.; exalt. 3. to pay off (a mortgage). 4. [Slang], to steal. ***v.i.*** 1. to exert strength in raising something. 2. to rise; go up. ***n.*** 1. a lifting or rising. 2. the amount lifted. 3. the distance something is lifted. 4. lifting force, influence, etc. 5. elevation of mood, etc. 6. elevated position or carriage. 7. a ride in the direction one is going. 8. help of any kind. 9. [Brit.], an elevator. **—lift one's voice,** to call or speak out loudly.
**lift′off′, lift′-off′,** ***n.*** the launching of a rocket or spacecraft.
**lig·a·ment** (lig′ə-mənt), ***n.*** [< L. *ligare*, bind], a band of tissue connecting bones or holding organs in place.
**lig·a·ture** (lig′ə-chēr), ***n.*** [< L. *ligare*, bind], 1. a tying or binding together. 2. a tie, bond, bandage, etc. 3. in *surgery*, a thread used to tie up an artery, etc. 4. in *printing*, two or more letters united, as æ.
**light** (līt), ***n.*** [AS. *leoht*], 1. *a*) a form of radiant energy acting on the retina of the eye to make sight possible. *b*) infrared or ultraviolet radiation. 2. brightness; illumination. 3. the source of light, as a lamp, the sun, etc. 4. daylight. 5. a thing used to ignite something. 6. a means by which light is let in; window. 7. knowledge; enlightenment. 8. public view. 9. aspect: as, viewed in another *light*. 10. an outstanding person. ***adj.*** 1. having light; bright. 2. pale in color; fair. ***adv.*** palely: as, a *light* blue color. ***v.t.*** [LIGHTED or LIT, LIGHTING], 1. to set on fire; ignite: as, to *light* a bonfire. 2. to cause to give off light. 3. to furnish with light. 4. to brighten; animate. ***v.i.*** 1. to catch fire. 2. to be lighted (usually with *up*). **—bring** (or **come**) **to light,** to reveal (or be revealed). **—in the light of,** considering.
**light** (līt), ***adj.*** [AS. *leoht*], 1. having little weight; not heavy, esp. for its size. 2. less than usual in weight, amount, force, etc.: as, a *light* blow. 3. of little importance. 4. easy to bear: as, a *light* tax. 5. easy to do: as, *light* work. 6. gay; happy. 7. dizzy; giddy. 8. not serious: as, *light* reading. 9. moderate: as, a *light* meal. 10. moving with ease: as, *light* on her feet. ***adv.*** lightly. ***v.i.*** [LIGHTED or LIT, LIGHTING], 1. to come to rest after traveling through the air. 2. to happen (*on* or *upon*). 3. to strike suddenly, as a blow. **—light out,** [Slang], to depart suddenly. **—make light of,** to treat as unimportant.
**light′en,** ***v.t. & v.i.*** to make or become light or brighter; shine; flash.
**light′en,** ***v.t. & v.i.*** 1. to make or become lighter in weight. 2. to make or become more cheerful.
**light′er,** ***n.*** a person or thing that lights something or starts it burning.
**light′er,** ***n.*** [< D. *licht*, light], a large barge used in loading or unloading ships lying offshore. **—light′er·age** (-ij), ***n.***
**light′-fin′gered,** ***adj.*** skillful at stealing, especially by picking pockets.
**light′-foot′ed,** ***adj.*** stepping lightly and gracefully. **—light′-foot′ed·ness,** ***n.***
**light′head′ed,** ***adj.*** 1. delirious. 2. giddy; dizzy. 3. flighty; frivolous.

**light'heart'ed,** *adj.* free from care; gay.
**light heavyweight,** a boxer or wrestler weighing between 161 and 175 lbs.
**light'house',** *n.* a tower with a bright light to guide ships at night.
**light'ing,** *n.* the act, manner, or art of giving light, or illuminating.
**light'ly,** *adv.* 1. with little weight or pressure. 2. gently. 3. to a small degree or amount: as, to spend *lightly*. 4. nimbly; deftly. 5. cheerfully. 6. with indifference.
**light'-mind'ed,** *adj.* flighty; thoughtless.
**light'ning** (-niŋ), *n.* a flash of light in the sky caused by the discharge of atmospheric electricity.
**lightning bug,** a firefly.
**lightning rod,** a metal rod placed high on a building and grounded to divert lightning from the structure.
**lights,** *n.pl.* [from their light weight], the lungs of animals, used as food.
**light'ship',** *n.* a ship with a bright light, moored in a dangerous place to warn other ships.
**light'some,** *adj.* 1. graceful; lively. 2. cheerful; gay. **—light'some·ly,** *adv.*
**light'weight',** *adj.* light in weight. *n.* a boxer or wrestler weighing between 127 and 135 lbs.
**light'-year',** *n.* the distance that light travels in one year, nearly 6 trillion miles.
**lig·ne·ous** (lig'ni-əs), *adj.* [< L. *lignum*, wood], of, or having the nature of, wood.
**lig·nite** (lig'nīt), *n.* [< L. *lignum*, wood], a soft, brownish-black coal with the texture of the original wood.
**lik·a·ble, like·a·ble** (līk'ə-b'l), *adj.* attractive, pleasant, genial, etc.
**like** (līk), *adj.* [AS. *gelic*], similar; having the same characteristics; equal. *adv.* 1. in the manner of one that is: as, to work *like* mad. 2. [Colloq.], likely: as, *like* as not, he'll go. *prep.* 1. similar to. 2. similarly to: as, to sing *like* a bird. 3. characteristic of: as, it's not *like* him to cry. 4. in the mood for: as, I feel *like* eating. 5. indicative of: as, it looks *like* rain. *conj.* [Colloq.], 1. as: as, it's just *like* he said. 2. as if: as, he looks *like* he's dying. *n.* an equal; counterpart: as, the *like* of it. **—and the like,** and others of the same kind. **—like anything** (or **blazes, crazy, the devil, mad,** etc.), [Colloq. or Slang], with furious energy, speed, etc.
**like** (līk), *v.i.* [LIKED, LIKING], [AS. *lician*], to be so inclined: as, do as you *like*. *v.t.* 1. to be pleased with; enjoy. 2. to wish: as, I'd *like* to go. *n.pl.* preferences; tastes.
**-like,** a suffix meaning *like, characteristic of*, as in *ball-like, homelike*.
**like·li·hood** (līk'li-hood'), *n.* (a) probability.
**like·ly** (līk'li), *adj.* [-LIER, -LIEST], [AS. *geliclic*], 1. credible: as, a *likely* account. 2. reasonably to be expected: as, *likely* to happen. 3. suitable: as, a *likely* place to swim. *adv.* probably: as, *likely* he'll win.
**lik·en** (līk''n), *v.t.* to compare.
**like'ness,** *n.* 1. a being like. 2. (the same) form. 3. a picture, portrait, etc.
**like'wise',** *adv.* [< *in like wise*], 1. in the same manner. 2. also; too.
**lik'ing,** *n.* 1. fondness; affection. 2. preference; taste; pleasure.
**li·lac** (lī'lək), *n.* [< Per. *nīlak*, bluish], 1. a shrub with large clusters of tiny, fragrant flowers. 2. a pale-purple color. *adj.* pale-purple.
**Lil·li·pu·tian** (lil'ə-pū'shən), *adj.* [< *Lilliput*, place in J. Swift's *Gulliver's Travels*], tiny; dwarfed. *n.* a very small person.
**lilt** (lilt), *n.* [ME. *lilten*, to sound], a light, swingy rhythm or tune. *v.t. & v.i.* to sing or speak with a light, graceful rhythm.
**lil·y** (lil'i), *n.* [*pl.* -IES], [< Gr. *leirion*, lily], 1. a plant grown from a bulb and having trumpet-shaped flowers. 2. its flower. 3. any similar plant: as, the water *lily*. *adj.* like a lily, as in whiteness.
**lil'y-liv'ered** (-liv'ẽrd), *adj.* cowardly.
**lily of the valley,** [*pl.* LILIES OF THE VALLEY], a low plant with a spike of fragrant, small, white, bell-shaped flowers.
**Li·ma bean** (lī'mə), [< *Lima*, Peru], 1. a bean plant with broad pods. 2. its broad, flat, edible bean.
**limb** (lim), *n.* [AS. *lim*], 1. an arm, leg, or wing. 2. a large branch of a tree. **—out on a limb,** [Colloq.], in a precarious position.
**lim·ber** (lim'bẽr), *adj.* [prob. < *limb*], 1. easily bent; flexible. 2. able to bend the body easily. *v.t. & v.i.* to make or become limber.
**lim·bo** (lim'bō), *n.* [< L. (*in*) *limbo*, (on) the border], 1. [often L-], in some Christian theologies, the abode after death of unbaptized children, etc. 2. a place or condition of neglect or oblivion.
**Lim·burg·er (cheese)** (lim'bẽr-gẽr), [< *Limb(o)urg*, Belgian province], a soft, white cheese with a strong odor.
**lime** (līm), *n.* [AS. *lim*], a white substance, calcium oxide, obtained by the action of heat on limestone and used in mortar and cement and to neutralize acid soil. *v.t.* [LIMED, LIMING], 1. to smear or catch with birdlime. 2. to treat with lime.
**lime** (līm), *n.* [< Per. *līmūn*, lemon], 1. a small, lemon-shaped, greenish-yellow fruit with a juicy, sour pulp. 2. the semitropical tree it grows on.
**lime'light',** *n.* 1. a brilliant light created by the oxidation of lime: formerly used in theaters. 2. a prominent position before the public.
**lim·er·ick** (lim'ẽr-ik), *n.* [prob. < *Limerick*, Ir. county], a rhymed, nonsense poem of five lines.
**lime'stone',** *n.* rock consisting mainly of calcium carbonate.
**lim·ey** (līm'i), *n.* [< *lime* juice formerly served to Brit. sailors to prevent scurvy], [Slang], an Englishman, esp. a soldier or sailor.
**lim·it** (lim'it), *n.* [< L. *limes*], 1. the point, line, etc. where something ends or must end; boundary. 2. *pl.* bounds. 3. the greatest amount allowed. *v.t.* to set a limit to or for; restrict. **—lim'i·ta'tion,** *n.* **—lim'it·less,** *adj.*
**lim'it·ed,** *adj.* 1. confined within bounds; restricted. 2. making a restricted number of stops: said of a train, bus, etc. *n.* a limited train, bus, etc.
**limn** (lim), *v.t.* [< L. *illuminare*, make light], 1. to paint or draw. 2. to describe.
**lim·ou·sine** (lim'ə-zēn'), *n.* [Fr., lit., a hood], a large, luxury automobile to be driven by a chauffeur.
**limp** (limp), *v.i.* [< AS. *limpan*], to walk with or as with a lame leg. *n.* a halt or lameness in walking. *adj.* lacking firmness; wilted.
**limp·et** (lim'pit), *n.* [< LL. *lempreda*], a shellfish which clings to rocks and timbers.
**lim·pid** (lim'pid), *adj.* [< L. *limpidus*], perfectly clear; transparent. **—lim·pid'i·ty,** *n.*
**lim·y** (līm'i), *adj.* [-IER, -IEST], 1. covered with, of, or like birdlime; sticky. 2. of, like, or containing lime.
**lin·age** (līn'ij), *n.* 1. alignment. 2. the number of written or printed lines on a page.
**lin·den** (lin'dən), *n.* [AS.], a tree with heart-shaped leaves and yellowish flowers.
**line** (līn), *n.* [< L. *linea*, linen thread], 1. a cord, rope, wire, etc. 2. any wire, pipe, etc., or system of these, conducting fluid, electricity, etc. 3. a thin, threadlike mark. 4. a border; boundary; limit. 5. outline; contour. 6. a row of persons or things, as of printed letters across a page. 7. *a*) alignment. *b*) agreement; conformity. 8. a suc-

cession of persons or things. 9. lineage. 10. a transportation system of buses, ships, etc. 11. the course a moving thing takes. 12. a course of conduct, action, explanation, etc. 13. a person's trade or occupation. 14. a stock of goods. 15. a short letter, note, etc. 16. a verse of poetry. 17. *pl.* all the speeches of a character in a play. 18. the forward combat position in warfare. 19. in *football*, the players in the forward row. 20. in *math.*, the path of a moving point. *v.t.* [LINED, LINING], 1. to mark with lines. 2. to bring into alignment (with *up*). 3. to form a line along. *v.i.* to form a line (with *up*). **—draw the** (or **a**) **line,** to set a limit. **—hold the line,** to stand firm. **—toe the line,** to do exactly as told.

**line** (līn), *v.t.* [LINED, LINING], [< L. *linum*, flax], to put, or serve as, a lining in.

**lin·e·age** (lin′i-ij), *n.* [see LINE, *n.*], 1. direct descent from an ancestor. 2. ancestry.

**lin·e·al** (lin′i-əl), *adj.* 1. in the direct line of descent from an ancestor. 2. hereditary. 3. linear. **—lin′e·al·ly,** *adv.*

**lin·e·a·ment** (lin′i-ə-mənt), *n.* [< L. *linea*, a line], *usually in pl.* a distinctive feature, esp. of the face.

**lin·e·ar** (lin′i-ẽr), *adj.* 1. of, made of, or using a line or lines. 2. narrow and long.

**linear measure,** a system of measuring length in which 12 in. = 1 ft.

**line·man** (līn′mən), *n.* [*pl.* -MEN], 1. a man who sets up and repairs telephone or electric wires, etc. 2. in *football*, a player in the line. Also **lines′man** [*pl.* -MEN].

**lin·en** (lin′ən), *n.* [AS. < *lin*, flax], 1. thread or cloth made of flax. 2. articles made of linen, or of cotton, etc., as tablecloths, sheets, etc.

**lin·er** (līn′ẽr), *n.* a steamship, airplane, etc. in regular service for a specific line.

**line′-up′, line′up′,** *n.* an arrangement of persons or things in or as in a line.

**-ling,** [AS.], a suffix meaning: 1. *small*, as in *duckling*. 2. *contemptible*, as in *hireling*.

**lin·ger** (liŋ′gẽr), *v.i.* [< ME. *lengen*, to delay], 1. to continue to stay as though reluctant to leave. 2. to loiter.

**lin·ge·rie** (lăn′zhə-rē′; Fr. lan′zh′-rē′), *n.* [Fr.], women's underwear.

**lin·go** (liŋ′gō), *n.* [*pl.* -GOES], [< L. *lingua*, tongue], language; esp., a dialect, jargon, etc. one is not familiar with.

**lin·gual** (liŋ′gwəl), *adj.* [< L. *lingua*, tongue], of, or pronounced by using, the tongue. *n.* a sound pronounced by using the tongue especially, as *l*.

**lin·guist** (liŋ′gwist), *n.* [< L. *lingua*, tongue], 1. one who can speak, read, and write several languages. 2. a specialist in linguistics.

**lin·guis′tics,** *n.pl.* [construed as sing.], 1. the science of language. 2. the study of a particular language. **—lin·guis′tic,** *adj.*

**lin·i·ment** (lin′ə-mənt), *n.* [< L. *linere*, to smear], a medicated liquid to be rubbed on the skin for soothing sore or inflamed areas.

**lin·ing** (līn′iŋ), *n.* the material covering an inner surface.

**link** (liŋk), *n.* [< ON.], 1. any of the series of loops forming a chain. 2. *a*) a section of something resembling a chain: as, a *link* of sausage. *b*) an element in a series: as, a weak *link* in the evidence. 3. anything that connects: as, a *link* with the past. *v.t.* & *v.i.* to join; connect.

**link′age,** *n.* 1. a linking or being linked. 2. a series or system of links.

**links** (liŋks), *n.pl.* [AS. *hlinc*, a slope], a golf course.

**lin·net** (lin′it), *n.* [< L. *linum*, flax: it feeds on flaxseed], a small finch.

**li·no·le·um** (li-nō′li-əm), *n.* [< L. *linum*, flax + *oleum*, oil], a hard floor covering made of a mixture of ground cork and linseed oil over a burlap or canvas backing.

**lin·o·type** (līn′ə-tīp′), *n.* [< *line of type*], a keyboard-operated typesetting machine that casts a line of type in one bar: a trademark (**Linotype**).

**lin·seed** (lin′sēd′), *n.* [AS. *linsæd*], flaxseed.

**linseed oil,** a yellowish oil extracted from flaxseed, used in oil paints, etc.

**lin·sey-wool·sey** (lin′zi-wool′zi), *n.* [*pl.* -WOOLSEYS], [ME. < *lin*, flax + *wool*], a coarse cloth made of linen and wool or cotton and wool.

**lint** (lint), *n.* [< L. *linum*, flax], 1. scraped and softened linen. 2. fine bits of thread, fluff, etc. from cloth or yarn. **—lint′y,** *adj.*

**lin·tel** (lin′t'l), *n.* [< L. *limes*, border], the horizontal crosspiece over a door or window.

**li·on** (lī′ən), *n.* [< Gr. *leōn*], 1. a large, powerful mammal of the cat family, found in Africa and SW Asia. 2. a person of great strength or courage. 3. a celebrity. **—li′on·ess** (-is), *n.fem.*

**li′on·ize′** (-īz′), *v.t.* [-IZED, -IZING], to treat as a celebrity.

**lip** (lip), *n.* [AS. *lippa*], 1. either of the two fleshy folds forming the edges of the mouth. 2. anything like a lip, as the rim of a pitcher. 3. [Slang], insolent talk. *adj.* superficial; not sincere: as, *lip* service. **—keep a stiff upper lip,** [Colloq.], to bear pain or distress bravely.

**lipped** (lipt), *adj.* having a lip or lips: often in compounds, as, *tight-lipped*.

**lip reading,** recognition of a speaker's words, as by the deaf, by watching the movement of his lips. **—lip′-read′,** *v.t.* & *v.i.*

**lip′stick′,** *n.* a small stick of rouge for coloring the lips.

**liq·ue·fy** (lik′wə-fī′), *v.t.* & *v.i.* [-FIED, -FYING], [< L. *liquere*, be liquid + *facere*, make], to change to a liquid. **—liq′ue·fac′tion** (-fak′shən), *n.*

**li·queur** (li-kũr′), *n.* [Fr.], any of certain sweet, sirupy, flavored alcoholic liquors.

**liq·uid** (lik′wid), *adj.* [< L. *liquidus*], 1. readily flowing; fluid. 2. clear; transparent. 3. flowing smoothly and musically, as verse. 4. readily convertible into cash. *n.* a substance that, unlike a solid, flows readily but, unlike a gas, does not tend to expand indefinitely. **—li·quid′i·ty,** *n.*

**liq·ui·date** (lik′wi-dāt′), *v.t.* [-DATED, -DATING], [see LIQUID], 1. to settle the accounts of (a business), by apportioning assets and debts. 2. to pay (a debt). 3. to convert into cash. 4. to get rid of, as by killing. **—liq′ui·da′tion,** *n.* **—liq′ui·da′tor,** *n.*

**liq·uor** (lik′ẽr), *n.* [L.], 1. any liquid. 2. an alcoholic drink, esp. a distilled drink, as whisky or rum.

**li·ra** (lêr′ə), *n.* [*pl.* LIRE (-ā), -RAS], [< L. *libra*, pound], the monetary unit and a silver coin of Italy.

**lisle** (līl), *n.* [< *Lisle* (now *Lille*), France], 1. a fine, hard, extra-strong cotton thread. 2. a fabric, stockings, etc. woven of this.

**lisp** (lisp), *v.i.* [< AS. *wlisp*, a lisping], 1. to substitute the sounds (th) and (*th*) for the sounds of *s* and *z*. 2. to speak imperfectly. *v.t.* to utter with a lisp. *n.* the act, habit, or sound of lisping. **—lisp′er,** *n.*

**lis·some** (lis′əm), *adj.* [< *lithesome*], 1. supple. 2. nimble. **—lis′some·ness,** *n.*

**list** (list), *n.* [< AS. *liste*, border], a series of names, words, etc. set forth in order. *v.t.* to set forth or enter in a list, directory, etc.

**list** (list), *v.t.* & *v.i.* [< AS. *lystan*, to incline], to tilt to one side, as a ship. *n.* a tilting.

**list** (list), *v.t.* & *v.i.* [< AS. *hlyst*, hearing], [Archaic], to listen (to).

**lis·ten** (lis′'n), *v.i.* [AS. *hlysnan*], 1. to make a conscious effort to hear. 2. to give heed; take advice. **—lis′ten·er,** *n.*

**list·less** (list′lis), *adj.* [*list* (var. of *lust*) + *-less*], indifferent because of illness, dejection, etc.; languid. —**list′less·ly,** *adv.*
**lists** (lists), *n.pl.* [< ME. *liste*, border], an arena in which knights jousted.
**lit** (lit), pt. and pp. of **light.**
**lit.,** 1. liter(s). 2. literal(ly). 3. literature.
**lit·a·ny** (lit′'n-i), *n.* [*pl.* -NIES], [< Gr. *litaneia*], prayer in which the congregation participates with responses.
**li·ter** (lē′tẽr), *n.* [< Gr. *litra*, a pound], the basic unit of capacity in the metric system, equal to 1.0567 liquid quarts or .908 dry quart: also sp. **litre.**
**lit·er·a·cy** (lit′ẽr-ə-si), *n.* the ability to read and write.
**lit·er·al** (lit′ẽr-əl), *adj.* [< L. *lit(t)era*, a letter], 1. following the exact words of the original: as, a *literal* translation. 2. in a basic or strict sense: as, the *literal* meaning. 3. prosaic; matter-of-fact: as, a *literal* mind. 4. restricted to fact: as, the *literal* truth.
**lit′er·al·ism,** *n.* the tendency to take words, statements, etc. in their literal sense.
**lit·er·ar·y** (lit′ə-rer′i), *adj.* 1. of or dealing with literature. 2. skilled in learning and literature. —**lit′er·ar′i·ly,** *adv.*
**lit·er·ate** (lit′ẽr-it), *adj.* [< L. *lit(t)era*, a letter], educated; esp., able to read and write. *n.* a literate person.
**lit·e·ra·ti** (lit′ə-rā′ti, -rä′ti), *n.pl.* [L.], scholarly or literary people.
**lit·er·a·ture** (lit′ẽr-ə-chẽr), *n.* [< L. *lit(t)era*, a letter], 1. *a)* all the writings of a particular time, country, etc., esp. those valued for excellence of form and expression. *b)* all the writings on a particular subject. 2. [Colloq.], any printed matter.
**lithe** (lith), *adj.* [AS. *lithe*, soft], bending easily; flexible; supple. —**lithe′ness,** *n.*
**lithe′some** (-səm), *adj.* lithe; lissome.
**lith·i·um** (lith′i-əm), *n.* [< Gr. *lithos*, stone], a soft, silver-white, metallic chemical element, the lightest known metal; symbol, Li.
**lith·o·graph** (lith′ə-graf′, -gräf′), *n.* a print made by lithography.
**li·thog·ra·phy** (li-thog′rə-fi), *n.* [< Gr. *lithos*, stone; + *-graphy*], printing from a flat stone or metal plate, parts of which have been treated to repel ink. —**li·thog′ra·pher,** *n.* —**lith·o·graph·ic** (lith′ə-graf′ik), *adj.*
**lit·i·gant** (lit′ə-gənt), *n.* [see LITIGATE], a party to a lawsuit.
**lit·i·gate** (lit′ə-gāt′), *v.t. & v.i.* [-GATED, -GATING], [< L. *lis*, dispute + *agere*, do], to contest in a lawsuit.
**lit′i·ga′tion,** *n.* 1. the carrying on of a lawsuit. 2. a lawsuit.
**lit·mus** (lit′məs), *n.* [< ON. *litr*, color + *mosi*, moss], a purple coloring matter obtained from lichens: paper treated with it (**litmus paper**) turns blue in bases and red in acids.
**Litt. D.,** Doctor of Letters: also **Lit. D.**
**lit·ter** (lit′ẽr), *n.* [< L. *lectus*, a couch], 1. a framework enclosing a couch on which a person can be carried. 2. a stretcher for carrying the sick or wounded. 3. straw, hay, etc. used as bedding for animals. 4. the young borne at one time by a dog, cat, etc. 5. things lying about in disorder. *v.t.* 1. to make untidy (often with *up*). 2. to scatter about carelessly.
**lit·tle** (lit′'l), *adj.* [LITTLER or LESS or LESSER, LITTLEST or LEAST], [AS. *lytel*], 1. small in size, amount, degree, etc. 2. short in duration; brief. 3. small in importance or power: as, the *little* man. 4. narrow-minded: as, a *little* mind. *adv.* [LESS, LEAST], 1. slightly; not much. 2. not in the least. *n.* a small amount, degree, etc. —**little by little,** gradually. —**make** (or **think) little of,** to consider as not very important. —**lit′tleness,** *n.*
**lit·to·ral** (lit′ə-rəl), *adj.* [< L. *littus*, seashore], of, on, or along the shore. *n.* the region along the shore.
**lit·ur·gy** (lit′ẽr-ji), *n.* [*pl.* -GIES], [ult. < Gr. *leōs*, people + *ergon*, work], prescribed ritual for public worship. —**li·tur·gi·cal** (li-tũr′ji-k'l), *adj.*
**liv·a·ble** (liv′ə-b'l), *adj.* 1. fit or pleasant to live in, as a house. 2. endurable. 3. agreeable to live with. Also sp. **liveable.**
**live** (liv), *v.i.* [LIVED, LIVING], [AS. *lifian*], 1. to have life. 2. *a)* to remain alive. *b)* to endure. 3. to pass life in a specified manner. 4. to enjoy a full life. 5. to feed: as, bats *live* on insects. 6. to reside. *v.t.* 1. to carry out in one's life: as, he *lives* his faith. 2. to spend; pass: as, she *lived* a useful life. —**live down,** to live so as to wipe out the shame of (a fault, etc.). —**live up to,** to act in accordance with (one's ideals, promises, etc.).
**live** (līv), *adj.* [< *alive*], 1. having life. 2. of the living state or living beings. 3. energetic: as, a *live* executive. 4. of present interest: as, a *live* issue. 5. still burning: as, a *live* spark. 6. unexploded: as, a *live* shell. 7. carrying electrical current: as, a *live* wire.
**-lived** (līvd; *occas.* livd), a combining form meaning *having* (a specified kind of) *life*, as in *short-lived.*
**live·li·hood** (līv′li-hood′), *n.* [< AS. *lif*, life + *-lad*, course], means of living or of supporting life.
**live·long** (liv′lôŋ′), *adj.* [ME. *lefe longe*, lief long: *lief* is merely intens.], long in passing; whole; entire: as, the *livelong* day.
**live·ly** (līv′li), *adj.* [-LIER, -LIEST], [AS. *liflic*], 1. full of life; vigorous. 2. full of spirit; exciting. 3. gay; cheerful. 4. vivid; keen. 5. bounding back with great resilience: as, a *lively* ball. —**live′li·ness,** *n.*
**liv·en** (līv′ən), *v.t. & v.i.* to make or become lively or gay; cheer (*up*). —**liv′en·er,** *n.*
**liv·er** (liv′ẽr), *n.* [AS. *lifer*], 1. the largest glandular organ in vertebrate animals: it secretes bile and is important in metabolism. 2. this organ of an animal used as food.
**liv·er·ied** (liv′ẽr-id), *adj.* wearing a livery.
**liv·er·wort** (liv′ẽr-wũrt′), *n.* any of a group of green, red, purple, or yellow-brown plants resembling the mosses.
**liv·er·wurst** (liv′ẽr-wũrst′), *n.* [*liver* + G. *wurst*, sausage], a sausage containing ground liver.
**liv·er·y** (liv′ẽr-i), *n.* [*pl.* -IES], [< OFr. *livree*, gift of clothes to a servant], 1. an identifying uniform as of a servant. 2. *a)* the care and feeding of horses for a fee. *b)* the keeping of horses or vehicles for hire. *c)* a stable providing these services: also **livery stable.**
**liv·er·y·man** (liv′ẽr-i-mən), *n.* [*pl.* -MEN], one who owns or works in a livery stable.
**lives** (līvz), *n.* pl. of **life.**
**live·stock** (līv′stok′), *n.* domestic animals kept for use on a farm or raised for sale.
**live wire,** 1. a wire carrying electric current. 2. [Colloq.], an energetic person.
**liv·id** (liv′id), *adj.* [< L. *lividus*], 1. discolored by a bruise: said of the flesh. 2. grayish-blue: as, *livid* with rage.
**liv·ing** (liv′iŋ), *adj.* 1. alive; having life. 2. in active operation or use: as, a *living* language. 3. of persons alive: as, within *living* memory. 4. true; lifelike. 5. *a)* of life: as, *living* conditions. *b)* enough to maintain a reasonable standard of existence: as, a *living* wage. *n.* 1. a being alive. 2. livelihood. 3. the manner of existence. —**the living,** those that are still alive.
**living room,** a room (in a home) furnished with sofas, soft chairs, etc., for lounging, entertaining, etc.
**liz·ard** (liz′ẽrd), *n.* [< L. *lacertus*], any of a large group of reptiles with long slender

bodies and tails, a scaly skin, and four legs.
**LL.,** Late Latin.
**ll.,** lines.
**lla·ma** (lä′mə), *n.* [< Peruv. native name], a South American beast of burden related to the camel but smaller and without humps.
**lla·no** (lä′nō), *n.* [*pl.* -NOS], [Sp. < L. *planus*, plain], any of the level, grassy plains of Spanish America.
**LL.D.,** Doctor of Laws.
**lo** (lō), *interj.* [AS. *la*], look! see!
**load** (lōd), *n.* [AS. *lad*, a course], 1. an amount carried at one time. 2. a varying measure of weight or quantity: as, a *load* of wood. 3. something borne with difficulty. *v.t.* 1. to put (something to be carried) into or upon (a carrier). 2. to burden; oppress. 3. to put a charge of ammunition into (a firearm). *v.i.* to supply or take a load.
**load′stone′,** *n.* [*load*, lode + *stone*], a strongly magnetic iron ore.
**loaf** (lōf), *n.* [*pl.* LOAVES (lōvz)], [AS. *hlaf*], 1. a portion of bread baked in one piece. 2. any mass of food shaped like a loaf and baked.
**loaf** (lōf), *v.i.* [< *loafer*], 1. to loiter or lounge about doing nothing. 2. to work in a lazy way. *v.t.* to spend (time) idly (often with *away*).
**loaf′er,** *n.* [cf. D. *landlooper*, vagabond], 1. one who loafs; idler. 2. a moccasinlike sport shoe.
**loam** (lōm), *n.* [AS. *lam*], a rich soil, esp. one composed of clay, sand, and some organic matter. **—loam′y** [-IER, -IEST], *adj.*
**loan** (lōn), *n.* [< ON. *lān*], 1. the act of lending. 2. something lent; esp., a sum of money lent, often at interest. *v.t.* & *v.i.* to lend. **—loan′er,** *n.*
**loath** (lōth), *adj.* [AS. *lath*, hostile], unwilling; reluctant.
**loathe** (lō*th*), *v.t.* [LOATHED, LOATHING], [AS. *lathian*, be hateful], to feel intense dislike or disgust for; abhor.
**loath·ing** (lō*th*′iŋ), *n.* intense dislike, disgust, or hatred.
**loath·some** (lō*th*′səm), *adj.* causing loathing; disgusting. **—loath′some·ness,** *n.*
**loaves** (lōvz), *n.* pl. of **loaf.**
**lob** (lob), *n.* [ME. *lobbe*, *lob-*, lit., "heavy, thick"], in *tennis*, a stroke in which the ball is sent high into the air. *v.t.* [LOBBED, LOBBING], to send (a ball) in a lob. *v.i.* to move clumsily.
**lo·bar** (lō′bẽr), *adj.* of a lobe or lobes.
**lob·by** (lob′i), *n.* [*pl.* -BIES], [ML. *lobium*], 1. an entrance hall, as of a hotel, theater, etc. 2. a group of lobbyists representing the same interest. *v.i.* [-BIED, -BYING], to act as a lobbyist.
**lob′by·ist,** *n.* one who tries to get legislators to support certain measures.
**lobe** (lōb), *n.* [< Gr. *lobos*], a rounded projection, as the lower end of the ear or any of the divisions of the lung. **—lobed,** *adj.*
**lob·ster** (lob′stẽr), *n.* [< L. *locusta*, locust, lobster], an edible sea crustacean with four pairs of legs and a pair of large pincers.
**lo·cal** (lō′k'l), *adj.* [< L. *locus*, a place], 1. relating to place. 2. of, characteristic of, or confined to a particular place. 3. of or for a particular part of the body. 4. making all stops along its run: as, a *local* train. *n.* 1. a local train, bus, etc. 2. a branch, as of a labor union. **—lo′cal·ly,** *adv.*
**lo·cale** (lō-kal′), *n.* [Fr. *local*], a locality, esp. with reference to associated events, etc.
**lo·cal·i·ty** (lō-kal′ə-ti), *n.* [*pl.* -TIES], 1. position with regard to surrounding objects, etc. 2. a place.
**lo·cal·ize** (lō′k'l-īz′), *v.t.* [-IZED, -IZING], to limit, confine, or trace to a particular place or locality. **—lo′cal·i·za′tion,** *n.*
**lo·cate** (lō′kāt, lō-kāt′), *v.t.* [-CATED, -CATING], [< L. *locus*, a place], 1. to establish in a certain place: as, the office is *located* downtown. 2. to discover the position of. 3. to show the position of: as, *locate* Guam on this map. *v.i.* [Colloq.], to settle: as, he *located* in Cleveland. **—lo′ca·tor,** *n.*
**lo·ca′tion,** *n.* 1. a locating or being located. 2. position; place. 3. an area marked off for a specific purpose.
**loc. cit.,** *loco citato*, [L.], in the place cited.
**loch** (lok, lokh), *n.* [Gael. & OIr.], [Scot.], 1. a lake. 2. an inlet of the sea.
**lock** (lok), *n.* [AS. *loc*, a bolt], 1. a mechanical device for fastening a door, strongbox, etc. as with a key or combination. 2. an enclosed part of a canal, etc. equipped with gates so that the level of the water can be raised or lowered. 3. the mechanism of a firearm that explodes the charge. *v.t.* 1. to fasten with a lock. 2. to shut (*up*, *in*, or *out*); confine. 3. to fit; link: as, to *lock* arms. 4. to jam together so as to make immovable. *v.i.* 1. to become locked. 2. to interlock.
**lock** (lok), *n.* [AS. *loc*], 1. a curl of hair. 2. *pl.* [Poetic], the hair of the head. 3. a tuft of wool, etc.
**lock′er,** *n.* a chest, closet, etc. which can be locked, esp. one for individual use.
**lock′et** (lok′it), *n.* [< OFr. *loc*, a lock], a small, hinged case of gold, silver, etc., for holding a picture, lock of hair, etc.: it is usually worn on a necklace.
**lock′jaw′,** *n.* a form of tetanus, in which the jaws become firmly closed.
**lock′out′,** *n.* the refusal by an employer to allow his employees to come in to work unless they accept his terms.
**lock′smith′,** *n.* one whose work is making or repairing locks and keys.
**lock·up** (lok′up′), *n.* a jail.
**lo·co·mo·tion** (lō′kə-mō′shən), *n.* [< L. *locus*, a place; + *motion*], motion, or the power of moving, from one place to another.
**lo′co·mo′tive** (-tiv), *adj.* of locomotion. *n.* an electric, steam, or Diesel engine on wheels, designed to push or pull a train.
**lo·cus** (lō′kəs), *n.* [*pl.* -CI (-sī)], [L.], 1. a place. 2. in *math.*, a line, plane, etc. every point of which satisfies a given condition.
**lo·cust** (lō′kəst), *n.* [< L. *locusta*], 1. a large, winged insect related to the grasshopper and cricket. 2. a cicada. 3. a tree of the eastern U.S., with clusters of fragrant white flowers: also called *black locust*.
**lo·cu·tion** (lō-kū′shən), *n.* [< L. *loqui*, speak], a particular style of speech.
**lode** (lōd), *n.* [< AS. *lad*, course], a vein, stratum, etc. of metallic ore.
**lode′star′,** *n.* a star by which one directs his course; esp., the North Star.
**lode′stone′,** *n.* a loadstone.
**lodge** (loj), *n.* [< OFr. *loge*, arbor], 1. a small house for special or seasonal use: as, a hunting *lodge*. 2. the local chapter or hall of a fraternal society. *v.t.* [LODGED, LODGING], 1. to house, esp. temporarily. 2. to put, drive, etc. into a place; deposit. 3. to bring (a complaint, etc.) before legal authorities. 4. to confer (powers) upon (with *in*). *v.i.* 1. to live in a place for a time. 2. to live (*with* or *in*) as a paying guest. 3. to come to rest (*in*): as, a bone *lodged* in her throat.
**lodg′er,** *n.* one who rents a room in another's home.
**lodg′ing,** *n.* 1. a place to live in, esp. temporarily. 2. *pl.* a room or rooms rented in a private home.
**loft** (lôft, loft), *n.* [< ON. *loft*, upper room, air], 1. the space just below the roof of a house, barn. etc. 2. an upper story of a warehouse or factory. 3. a gallery: as, a choir *loft*. 4. in *golf*, height given to a ball, as by certain clubs. *v.t.* & *v.i.* to give (a ball) loft.

**loft'y,** *adj.* [-IER, -IEST], 1. very high. 2. elevated; noble. 3. haughty; arrogant.

**log** (lôg), *n.* [ME. *logge*], 1. a section of the trunk of a felled tree. 2. a device for measuring the speed of a ship. 3. a daily record of a ship's speed, progress, etc. 4. any record of progress, etc. *v.t.* [LOGGED, LOGGING], 1. to saw (trees) into logs. 2. to enter in a ship's log. *v.i.* to cut down trees and remove the logs. **—log'ger,** *n.*

**log,** logarithm.

**lo·gan·ber·ry** (lō'gən-ber'i), *n.* [*pl.* -RIES], [< J.H. *Logan*, who developed it], 1. a hybrid bramble developed from the blackberry and the red raspberry. 2. its purplish-red fruit.

**log·a·rithm** (lôg'ə-rith'm, log'-), *n.* [< Gr. *logos*, ratio + *arithmos*, number], the exponent of the power to which a fixed number must be raised to produce a given number. **—log'a·rith'mic,** *adj.*

**log·book** (lôg'book'), *n.* a log (sense 3).

**loge** (lōzh), *n.* [Fr.; see LODGE], a box in a theater, etc.

**log·ger·head** (lôg'ẽr-hed'), *n.* [< *log* + *head*], a stupid fellow. **—at loggerheads,** in disagreement.

**log·gia** (loj'i-ə, lô'jə), *n.* [*pl.* -GIAS], [It.; see LODGE], a roofed gallery projecting from the side of a building.

**log'ging,** *n.* the work of felling trees, cutting them into logs, and transporting them to the sawmill.

**log·ic** (loj'ik), *n.* [ult. < Gr. *logos*, word], 1. the science of correct reasoning. 2. correct reasoning. 3. way of reasoning: as, bad *logic*. 4. what is expected by the working of cause and effect.

**log'i·cal** (-i-k'l), *adj.* 1. of or used in the science of logic. 2. according to the principles of logic. 3. expected because of what has gone before. 4. using correct reasoning.

**lo·gi·cian** (lō-jish'ən), *n.* an expert in logic.

**lo·gis·tics** (lə-jis'tiks), *n.pl.* [construed as sing.], [< Fr. *loger*, to quarter], the branch of military science having to do with moving, supplying, and quartering troops.

**log'roll'ing,** *n.* 1. mutual exchange of favors, esp. among politicians. 2. the sport of balancing oneself while revolving a floating log with one's feet.

**-logue,** [see LOGIC], a combining form meaning *a* (specified kind of) *speaking* or *writing*, as in *monologue*: also **-log.**

**lo·gy** (lō'gi), *adj.* [-GIER, -GIEST], [? < D. *log*, dull], [Colloq.], dull or sluggish.

**-logy,** [see LOGIC], a combining form meaning: 1. *a* (specified kind of) *speaking*, as in *eulogy*. 2. *science, doctrine, theory of*, as in *geology*.

**loin** (loin), *n.* [< L. *lumbus*], 1. *usually in pl.* the lower part of the back between the hipbones and the ribs. 2. the front part of the hindquarters of beef, lamb, etc. 3. *pl.* the hips and the lower abdomen regarded as the region of strength, etc.

**loin'cloth',** *n.* a cloth worn about the loins, as by some tropical tribes.

**loi·ter** (loi'tẽr), *v.i.* [< MD. *loteren*], 1. to spend time idly; linger. 2. to move slowly and indolently. *v.t.* to spend (time) idly.

**loll** (lol), *v.i.* [< MD. *lollen*], 1. to lean or lounge about in a lazy manner. 2. to droop. *v.t.* to let hang loosely, as the tongue. *n.* a lolling.

**lol·li·pop, lol·ly·pop** (lol'i-pop'), *n.* [prob. < *lolly*, the tongue + *pop*], a piece of hard candy on the end of a stick.

**lone** (lōn), *adj.* [< *alone*], 1. by oneself; solitary. 2. isolated.

**lone'ly,** *adj.* [-LIER, -LIEST], 1. alone. 2. *a*) isolated. *b*) unfrequented. 3. unhappy at being alone. **—lone'li·ness,** *n.*

**lone'some,** *adj.* 1. having or causing a lonely feeling. 2. unfrequented.

**long** (lôŋ), *adj.* [AS.], 1. measuring much in space or time. 2. in length: as, six feet *long*. 3. of greater than usual length, quantity, etc.: as, a *long* list. 4. tedious; slow. 5. far-reaching: as, a *long* view of the matter. 6. well supplied: as, *long* on excuses. *adv.* 1. for a long time. 2. for the duration of: as, all day *long*. 3. at a remote time: as, it happened *long* ago. **—as** (or **so**) **long as,** 1. during the time that. 2. since. 3. provided that. **—before long,** soon.

**long** (lôŋ), *v.i.* [AS. *langian*], to feel a strong yearning; wish earnestly.

**long.,** longitude.

**long distance,** a telephone exchange or operator that puts through calls to and from distant places. **—long'-dis'tance,** *adj.*

**long'-drawn',** *adj.* prolonged.

**lon·gev·i·ty** (lon-jev'ə-ti), *n.* [< L. *longus*, long + *aevum*, age], long life.

**long'-faced',** *adj.* glum.

**long'hair',** *adj.* [Colloq.], of intellectuals or intellectual tastes.

**long'hand',** *n.* ordinary handwriting: distinguished from *shorthand*.

**long'horn',** *n.* any of a breed of long-horned cattle of the Southwest.

**long'ing,** *n.* earnest desire. *adj.* feeling or showing a yearning. **—long'ing·ly,** *adv.*

**lon·gi·tude** (lon'jə-tōōd', -tūd'), *n.* [< L. *longus*, long], angular distance, measured in degrees, east or west from the prime meridian.

**lon'gi·tu'di·nal** (-tōō'di-n'l), *adj.* 1. of or in length. 2. running or placed lengthwise. 3. of longitude.

**long'-lived'** (-līvd'), *adj.* having or tending to have a long life span.

**long'-range',** *adj.* taking the future into consideration.

**long·shore·man** (lôŋ'shôr'mən), *n.* [*pl.* -MEN], [< *alongshore* + *man*], a person whose work is loading and unloading ships.

**long shot,** [Colloq.], in betting, a choice that is little favored and, hence, carries great odds.

**long'-stand'ing,** *adj.* having continued for a long time.

**long'-suf'fer·ing,** *adj.* bearing trouble, etc. patiently for a long time. *n.* long and patient endurance.

**long ton,** 2,240 pounds.

**long'-wind'ed,** *adj.* 1. speaking or writing at great length. 2. tiresomely long.

**long'wise',** *adv.* lengthwise: also **long'ways'.**

**look** (look), *v.i.* [AS. *locian*], 1. to direct one's eyes in order to see. 2. to search. 3. to appear; seem. 4. to be facing in a specified direction. *v.t.* 1. to direct one's eyes on. 2. to express by one's looks: as, he *looked* his despair. *n.* 1. the act of looking. 2. appearance; aspect. 3. *pl.* [Colloq.], *a*) appearance. *b*) personal appearance. *interj.* 1. see! 2. pay attention! **—look after,** to take care of. **—look down on** (or **upon**), to regard with contempt. **—look for,** to expect. **—look forward to,** to anticipate. **—look in (on),** to pay a brief visit (to). **—look into,** to investigate. **—look out,** to be careful. **—look over,** to examine. **—look to,** 1. to take care of. 2. to rely on. **—look up,** to search for as in a dictionary. **—look up to,** to admire. **—look'er,** *n.*

**look'er-on',** *n.* [*pl.* LOOKERS-ON], an observer or spectator.

**look'ing glass,** a (glass) mirror.

**look'out',** *n.* 1. a careful watching. 2. a place for keeping watch. 3. a person detailed to watch.

**loom** (lōōm), *n.* [AS. (*ge*)*loma*, tool], a machine for weaving thread or yarn into cloth.

**loom** (lōōm), *v.i.* [prob. < LG. or Scand.], to come into sight indistinctly, esp. in a large or threatening form.

**loon** (lo͞on), *n.* [< ON. *lomr*], a fish-eating, diving bird, somewhat like a duck.

**loon** (lo͞on), *n.* [Scot.], a clumsy, stupid person; dolt.

**loon·y** (lo͞on′i), *adj.* [-IER, -IEST], [< *lunatic*], [Slang], crazy; demented.

**loop** (lo͞op), *n.* [< ON.], 1. the figure of a line, thread, etc. that curves back to cross itself. 2. anything forming this figure. *v.t.* 1. to make a loop of. 2. to fasten with a loop. *v.i.* to form a loop or loops.

**loop·hole** (lo͞op′hōl′), *n.* [prob. < MD. *lupen*, to peer; + *hole*], 1. a hole or slit in a wall. 2. a means of evading something unpleasant.

**loose** (lo͞os), *adj.* [< ON.], 1. not confined or restrained; free. 2. not firmly fastened. 3. not tight or compact. 4. not precise; inexact. 5. sexually immoral. *adv.* loosely. *v.t.* [LOOSED, LOOSING], 1. to set free; unbind. 2. to make less tight, compact, etc. 3. to relax. 4. to release: as, he *loosed* the arrow. *v.i.* to become loose. **—loose′ly,** *adv.*

**loos·en** (lo͞os′'n), *v.t.* & *v.i.* to make or become loose or looser. **—loos′en·er,** *n.*

**loot** (lo͞ot), *n.* [Hind. *lūt*], goods stolen or taken by force; plunder. *v.t.* & *v.i.* to plunder. **—loot′er,** *n.*

**lop** (lop), *v.t.* [LOPPED, LOPPING], [ME. *loppen*], 1. to trim (a tree, etc.) by cutting off branches, etc. 2. to remove as by cutting off.

**lop** (lop), *v.i.* [LOPPED, LOPPING], [? var. of *lob*], to hang down loosely.

**lope** (lōp), *v.i.* [LOPED, LOPING], [< ON. *hlaupa*, to leap], to move with a long, swinging stride, as in galloping. *v.t.* to cause to lope. *n.* a loping stride.

**lop·sid·ed** (lop′sīd′id), *adj.* noticeably heavier, bigger, or lower on one side.

**lo·qua·cious** (lō-kwā′shəs), *adj.* [< L. *loqui*, speak], very talkative. **—lo·qua′cious·ly,** *adv.* **—lo·quac′i·ty** (-kwas′ə-ti), *n.*

**Lor·an, lor·an** (lôr′an), *n.* [< *Lo*ng *Ra*nge *N*avigation], a system by which a ship or aircraft can determine its position by radio signals sent from known stations.

**lord** (lôrd), *n.* [< AS. *hlaf*, loaf + *weard*, keeper], 1. a ruler; master. 2. the head of a feudal estate. 3. [L-], *a)* God. *b)* Jesus Christ. 4. in Great Britain, a titled nobleman. **—lord it (over),** to be overbearing (toward).

**lord′ly,** *adj.* [-LIER, -LIEST], 1. noble; magnificent. 2. haughty. *adv.* in the manner of a lord. **—lord′li·ness,** *n.*

**lord′ship,** *n.* 1. the rank or authority of a lord. 2. rule; dominion. 3. a title used in speaking of or to a lord: with *his* or *your*.

**Lord's Prayer,** the prayer beginning *Our Father*: Matt. 6:9–13.

**lore** (lôr), *n.* [AS. *lar*], knowledge; learning, esp. of a traditional nature.

**lor·gnette** (lôr-nyet′), *n.* [Fr. < OFr. *lorgne*, squinting], a pair of eyeglasses, or an opera glass, attached to a handle.

**lorn** (lôrn), *adj.* [ME. < *losen*, lose], [Archaic], forsaken, forlorn, etc.

**lor·ry** (lôr′i, lor′i), *n.* [*pl.* -RIES], [prob. < dial. *lurry*, to lug], [Brit.], a motor truck.

**lose** (lo͞oz), *v.t.* [LOST, LOSING], [< AS. *leosan*], 1. to become unable to find: as, he *lost* his keys. 2. to have taken from one by accident, death, removal, etc. 3. to fail to keep: as, to *lose* one's temper. 4. to fail to see, hear, or understand. 5. to fail to have, get, etc.: as, he *lost* his chance. 6. to fail to win. 7. to cause the loss of. 8. to wander from (one's way, etc.). 9. to squander. *v.i.* to suffer (a) loss. **—los′er,** *n.*

**loss** (lôs), *n.* [AS. *los*, ruin], 1. a losing or being lost. 2. the damage, trouble, etc. caused by losing. 3. the person, thing, or amount lost. **—at a loss (to),** uncertain (how to).

**lost** (lôst), pt. and pp. of **lose.** *adj.* 1. ruined; destroyed. 2. not to be found; missing. 3. no longer held, seen, heard, etc. 4. not gained or won. 5. having wandered from the way. 6. wasted.

**lot** (lot), *n.* [AS. *hlot*], 1. the deciding of a matter by chance, as by drawing counters. 2. the decision thus arrived at. 3. one's share by lot. 4. fortune: as, his unhappy *lot*. 5. a plot of ground. 6. a group of persons or things. 7. *often pl.* [Colloq.], a great amount. 8. [Colloq.], sort: as, he's a bad *lot*. *adv.* very much. **—draw** (or **cast**) **lots,** to decide by lot.

**Lo·thar·i·o** (lō-thâr′i-ō′), *n.* [*pl.* -OS], [< the rake in the play *The Fair Penitent*], a gay seducer of women.

**lo·tion** (lō′shən), *n.* [< L. *lavare*, wash], a liquid preparation used, as on the skin, for washing, healing, etc.

**lot·ter·y** (lot′ẽr-i), *n.* [*pl.* -IES], [see LOTTO], a game of chance in which people buy numbered chances on prizes, winners being chosen by lot.

**lot·to** (lot′ō), *n.* [It., lot], a game of chance played on cards with numbered squares: counters are placed on numbers chosen by lot.

**lo·tus, lo·tos** (lō′təs), *n.* [< Gr. *lotos*], 1. in *Gr. legend*, a plant whose fruit induced forgetfulness. 2. any of several tropical water lilies. 3. a plant of the pea family with yellow, purple, or white flowers.

**loud** (loud), *adj.* [AS. *hlud*], 1. strongly audible: said of sound. 2. sounding with great intensity. 3. noisy. 4. emphatic: as, *loud* denials. 5. [Colloq.], *a)* flashy. *b)* vulgar. *adv.* in a loud manner. **—loud′ness,** *n.*

**loud′-speak′er,** *n.* in *radio*, etc., a device for converting electrical energy to sound and amplifying it.

**lounge** (lounj), *v.i.* [LOUNGED, LOUNGING], [? < Scot. dial. *lungis*, laggard], 1. to move, sit, lie, etc. in a relaxed way. 2. to spend time in idleness. *n.* 1. a room with comfortable furniture for lounging. 2. a couch.

**louse** (lous), *n.* [*pl.* LICE], [AS. *lus*], 1. a small, wingless insect parasitic on man and other animals. 2. any similar insect parasitic on plants. 3. [*pl.* LOUSES], [Slang], a mean, contemptible person. **—louse up,** [Slang], to botch; bungle.

**lous·y** (lou′zi), *adj.* [-IER, -IEST], 1. infested with lice. 2. [Slang], *a)* disgusting. *b)* poor; inferior. *c)* well supplied (*with*).

**lout** (lout), *n.* [? < ME. *lowt*, rag], a clumsy, stupid fellow. **—lout′ish,** *adj.*

**lou·ver** (lo͞o′vẽr), *n.* [OFr. *lover*], 1. an opening in a turret, etc. fitted with louver boards. 2. any ventilating slit.

**louver board,** any of a series of sloping slats set in an opening to let in air and light but shed rain.

**Lou·vre** (lo͞o′vrə, lo͞ov), *n.* an ancient palace in Paris, now an art museum.

**love** (luv), *n.* [AS. *lufu*], 1. strong affection or liking for someone or something. 2. a passionate affection for one of the opposite sex. 3. the object of such affection; sweetheart. 4. in *tennis*, a score of zero. *v.t.* & *v.i.* [LOVED, LOVING], to feel love (for). **—in love,** feeling love. **—make love,** to woo, embrace, etc. **—lov′a·ble, love′a·ble,** *adj.*

**love′bird′,** *n.* a small bird of the parrot family, often kept as a cage bird: the mates appear to be greatly attached to each other.

**love′lorn′,** *adj.* pining from love.

**love′ly,** *adj.* [-LIER, -LIEST], 1. very pleasing in looks or character; beautiful. 2. [Colloq.], highly enjoyable. **—love′li·ness,** *n.*

**lov·er** (luv′ẽr), *n.* one who loves; specif., *a)* a sweetheart. *b) pl.* a man and a woman in love with each other. **—lov′er·ly,** *adj.* & *adv.*

**love seat,** a small sofa for two.

**love'sick'**, *adj.* 1. so much in love as to be incapable of normal behavior. 2. expressive of such a condition. **—love'sick'ness**, *n.*

**lov'ing**, *adj.* feeling or expressing love.

**loving cup**, a large drinking cup with two handles, often given as a prize.

**low** (lō), *adj.* [AS. *lah*], 1. not high or tall. 2. below the normal or usual surface or level: as, *low* ground. 3. shallow. 4. less in size, degree, etc. than usual: as, *low* speed. 5. deep in pitch. 6. depressed in spirits. 7. not of high rank; humble. 8. vulgar; coarse. 9. poor; inferior. 10. not loud. *adv.* in or to a low level, degree, etc. *n.* 1. a low level, degree, etc. 2. an arrangement of gears giving the lowest speed and greatest power. **—lay low**, to overcome or kill. **—lie low**, to keep oneself hidden.

**low** (lō), *v.i.* [AS. *hlowan*], to make the characteristic sound of a cow; moo. *n.* this sound.

**low'born'**, *adj.* of humble birth.

**low'boy'**, *n.* a chest of drawers mounted on short legs.

**low'-brow', low'brow'**, *n.* [Slang], one considered to lack cultivated tastes. *adj.* [Slang], of or for low-brows.

**low'-down'**, *n.* [Slang], the pertinent facts (with *the*). *adj.* (lō'doun'), [Colloq.], mean; contemptible.

**low·er** (lō'ẽr), *adj.* [compar. of *low*], below in place, rank, etc. *v.t.* 1. to let or put down: as, to *lower* a window. 2. to reduce in height, amount, etc.: as, to *lower* prices. 3. to cause to be less respected. *v.i.* to become lower; sink, fall, etc.

**low·er** (lou'ẽr), *v.i.* [ME. *l(o)uren*], 1. to scowl or frown. 2. to appear black and threatening. *n.* a frowning or threatening look.

**lower case**, small-letter type used in printing, as distinguished from capital letters (*upper case*). **—low'er-case'**, *adj.*

**Low German**, 1. the Germanic dialects spoken in the northern lowlands of Germany, the Netherlands, etc. 2. the branch of Germanic languages including English, Dutch, Flemish, etc.

**low'-grade'**, *adj.* of inferior quality.

**low'land** (-lənd), *n.* land below the level of the surrounding land.

**low'ly**, *adj.* [-LIER, -LIEST], 1. of low position or rank. 2. humble; meek. *adv.* humbly.

**low'-mind'ed**, *adj.* having or showing a coarse, vulgar mind.**—low'-mind'ed·ly**, *adv.*

**low'-spir'it·ed**, *adj.* sad; melancholy.

**low tide**, the lowest level reached by the ebbing tide.

**lox** (loks), *n.* [< Yid. < G. *lachs*, salmon], a variety of salty smoked salmon.

**loy·al** (loi'əl), *adj.* [see LEGAL], 1. faithful to one's country, friends, ideals, etc. 2. of or indicating loyalty. **—loy'al·ly**, *adv.*

**loy'al·ist**, *n.* one who supports the established government of his country during a revolt. **—loy'al·ism**, *n.*

**loy'al·ty**, *n.* [*pl.* -TIES], quality, state, or instance of being loyal.

**loz·enge** (loz'inj), *n.* [< Pr. *lausa*, slab], 1. a diamond-shaped figure. 2. a cough drop, candy, etc., orig. in this shape.

**LP**, *adj.* [*L*ong *P*laying], designating or of a phonograph record with microgrooves. *n.* an LP record: a trademark.

**LSD**, [*l*ysergic acid *d*iethylamide], a crystalline compound used in the study of mental disorders: it produces hallucinations, etc. that occur spontaneously in a person suffering from certain psychoses.

**Lt.**, Lieutenant.

**Ltd., ltd.**, limited.

**lub·ber** (lub'ẽr), *n.* [< ME. *lobbe*, heavy], 1. a big, slow, clumsy person. 2. an inexperienced, clumsy sailor.**—lub'ber·li·ness**, *n.*

**lu·bri·cant** (lōō'bri-kənt), *adj.* reducing friction by providing a smooth surface film over parts coming into contact. *n.* a lubricant oil, grease, etc.

**lu'bri·cate'** (-kāt'), *v.t.* [-CATED, -CATING], [< L. *lubricus*, smooth], 1. to make slippery or smooth. 2. to apply a lubricant to (machinery, etc.). **—lu'bri·ca'tion**, *n.* **—lu'bri·ca'tor**, *n.*

**lu·cerne** (lōō-sũrn'), *n.* [< L. *lucere*, to shine: ? from seed's glowing appearance], alfalfa.

**lu·cid** (lōō'sid), *adj.* [< L. *lucere*, shine], 1. shining. 2. transparent. 3. sane. 4. clear; readily understood. **—lu·cid'i·ty**, *n.*

**Lu·ci·fer** (lōō'sə-fẽr), *n.* [L. *lux*, light + *ferre*, to bear], 1. [Poetic], the planet Venus when it is the morning star. 2. Satan, esp. as the leader of the angels' revolt before his fall. 3. [l-], a match ignited by friction.

**lu·cite** (lōō'sīt), *n.* [< L. *lux*, light], a crystal-clear synthetic resin, plastic under heat: a trademark (**Lucite**).

**luck** (luk), *n.* [prob. < D. (*ge*)*luk*], 1. the seemingly chance happening of events which affect one; fortune. 2. good fortune. **—in luck**, lucky. **—out of luck**, unlucky.

**luck'y**, *adj.* [-IER, -IEST], 1. having good luck. 2. resulting fortunately. 3. believed to bring good luck. **—luck'i·ly**, *adv.*

**lu·cra·tive** (lōō'krə-tiv), *adj.* [< L. *lucrum*, riches], producing wealth or profit; profitable. **—lu'cra·tive·ly**, *adv.*

**lu·cre** (lōō'kẽr), *n.* [< L. *lucrum*], riches; money: chiefly derogatory.

**lu·cu·brate** (lōō'kyoo-brāt'), *v.i.* [-BRATED, -BRATING], [< L. *lucubrare*, work by candlelight], to work or study laboriously, esp. late at night. **—lu'cu·bra'tion**, *n.*

**lu·di·crous** (lōō'di-krəs), *adj.* [< L. *ludus*, a game], causing laughter because absurd or ridiculous. **—lu'di·crous·ly**, *adv.*

**luff** (luf), *v.i.* [prob. < Old D.], to turn the bow of a ship toward the wind.

**lug** (lug), *v.t.* [LUGGED, LUGGING], [prob. < ON.], to carry or drag with effort. *n.* 1. an earlike projection by which a thing is held or supported. 2. [Slang], a stupid fellow.

**lug·gage** (lug'ij), *n.* [< *lug*, *v.*], suitcases, trunks, etc.; baggage.

**lu·gu·bri·ous** (loo-gōō'bri-əs, -gū'-), *adj.* [< L. *lugere*, mourn], mournful: usually implying ridiculously excessive grief.

**Luke** (look), *n.* in the *Bible*, 1. a Christian apostle, the reputed author of the third Gospel. 2. this book.

**luke·warm** (look'wôrm'), *adj.* [< ME. *leuke*, tepid; + *warm*], 1. barely warm; tepid. 2. lacking enthusiasm.

**lull** (lul), *v.t.* [ME. *lullen*], 1. to calm by gentle sound or motion. 2. to bring into a specified condition by soothing and reassuring. 3. to allay. *v.i.* to become calm. *n.* a short period of calm.

**lull'a·by'** (-ə-bī'), *n.* [*pl.* -BIES], a song for lulling a baby to sleep.

**lum·ba·go** (lum-bā'gō), *n.* [< L. *lumbus*, loin], pain in the lower back.

**lum·bar** (lum'bẽr), *adj.* [< L. *lumbus*, loin], of or near the loins.

**lum·ber** (lum'bẽr), *n.* [< pawnbrokers of *Lombardy* in Italy; hence, stored articles], 1. discarded household articles, furniture, etc. 2. timber sawed into beams, boards, etc. *v.i.* to cut down timber and saw it into lumber. **—lum'ber·er**, *n.* **—lum'ber·ing**, *n.*

**lum·ber** (lum'bẽr), *v.i.* [< ON.], to move heavily and noisily. **—lum'ber·ing**, *adj.*

**lum·ber·jack** (lum'bẽr-jak'), *n.* [*lumber* + *jack* (man)], a man whose work is cutting down timber and preparing it for the sawmill.

**lum'ber·man**, *n.* [*pl.* -MEN], 1. a lumberjack. 2. one who deals in lumber.

**lu·mi·nar·y** (lo͞o′mə-ner′i), *n.* [*pl.* -IES], [< L. *lumen*, light], 1. a body that gives off light, as the sun. 2. a famous intellectual.
**lu·mi·nes·cence** (lo͞o′mə-nes″ns), *n.* [< L. *lumen*, a light; + *-escence*], any giving off of light caused by the absorption of radiant energy, etc. and not by incandescence.
**lu·mi·nous** (lo͞o′mə-nəs), *adj.* [< L. *lumen*, a light], 1. giving off light; bright. 2. clear; readily understood. —**lu′mi·nos′i·ty** (-nos′ə-ti), *n.* —**lu′mi·nous·ly**, *adv.*
**lump** (lump), *n.* [ME. *lumpe*], 1. an indefinitely shaped mass of something. 2. a swelling. 3. aggregate; collection. *adj.* in a lump or lumps. *v.t.* 1. to put together in a lump or lumps. 2. to treat or deal with in a mass. *v.i.* to become lumpy.
**lump** (lump), *v.t.* [Early Mod. Eng., look sour], [Colloq.], to put up with (something disagreeable).
**lump′y**, *adj.* [-IER, -IEST], 1. full of lumps. 2. covered with lumps. 3. like a lump; heavy; clumsy. —**lump′i·ness**, *n.*
**lu·na·cy** (lo͞o′nə-si), *n.* [*pl.* -CIES], [< *lunatic*], 1. insanity. 2. utter foolishness.
**lu·nar** (lo͞o′nẽr), *adj.* [< L. *luna*, the moon], 1. of or like the moon. 2. measured by the moon's revolutions.
**lu·na·tic** (lo͞o′nə-tik), *adj.* [< L. *luna*, the moon], 1. insane. 2. of or for insane persons. 3. utterly foolish. *n.* an insane person.
**lunch** (lunch), *n.* [? < Sp. *lonja*, slice of ham], a light meal; esp., the midday meal between breakfast and dinner. *v.i.* to eat lunch.
**lunch·eon** (lun′chən), *n.* a lunch; esp., a formal lunch.
**lunch′eon·ette′** (-et′), *n.* a small restaurant where light lunches can be had.
**lung** (luŋ), *n.* [AS. *lungen*], either of the two spongelike breathing organs in the thorax of vertebrates.
**lunge** (lunj), *n.* [< Fr. *allonger*, lengthen], 1. a sudden thrust as with a sword. 2. a sudden plunge forward. *v.i.* & *v.t.* [LUNGED, LUNGING], to move, or cause to move, with a lunge. —**lung′er**, *n.*
**lu·pine** (lo͞o′pīn), *adj.* [< L. *lupus*, wolf], of or like a wolf.
**lurch** (lũrch), *v.t.* [ult. < Fr. *lâcher*, let go], to pitch or sway suddenly to one side. *n.* a lurching movement.
**lurch** (lũrch), *n.* [prob. < OFr. *lourche*, duped], a difficult situation: only in phr. *leave in the lurch.*
**lure** (loor), *n.* [< OFr. *leurre*], 1. anything that tempts or entices: as, the *lure* of the stage. 2. a bait used in fishing. *v.t.* [LURED, LURING], to attract; tempt; entice.
**lu·rid** (loor′id), *adj.* [L. *luridus*], 1. glowing through a haze, as flames enveloped by smoke. 2. startling; shocking; sensational.
**lurk** (lũrk), *v.i.* [ME. *lurken*], 1. to stay hidden, ready to attack, etc. 2. to move furtively. —**lurk′er**, *n.* —**lurk′ing·ly**, *adv.*
**lus·cious** (lush′əs), *adj.* [ME. *lucius*], 1. highly gratifying to taste or smell; delicious. 2. delighting any of the senses.
**lush** (lush), *adj.* [< OFr. *lasche*, lax], 1. tender and full of juice. 2. of or characterized by luxuriant growth. —**lush′ness**, *n.*
**lush** (lush), *n.* [Slang], a drunkard.
**lust** (lust), *n.* [AS., pleasure], 1. bodily appetite; esp., excessive sexual desire. 2. overmastering desire: as, a *lust* for power. *v.i.* to feel an intense desire. —**lust′ful**, *adj.*
**lus·ter** (lus′tẽr), *n.* [< L. *lustrare*, illumine], 1. gloss; sheen. 2. brightness; radiance. 3. brilliant beauty or fame; glory. Also sp. **lustre.**
**lus·trous** (lus′trəs), *adj.* having luster; shining. —**lus′trous·ly**, *adv.*
**lust·y** (lus′ti), *adj.* [-IER, -IEST], [ME. *lusti*, joyful], full of youthful vigor; robust.
**lute** (lo͞ot), *n.* [ult. < Ar. *al'ūd*, the wood], an old stringed instrument like the guitar, with a rounded body.
**Lu·ther·an** (lo͞o′thẽr-ən), *adj.* of the Protestant denomination founded by Martin Luther (1483–1546), leader of the German Reformation. *n.* a member of the Lutheran Church. —**Lu′ther·an·ism**, *n.*
**lux·u·ri·ant** (lug-zhoor′i-ənt), *adj.* [see LUXURY], 1. growing with vigor and in abundance; lush. 2. having rich ornamentation, etc. —**lux·u′ri·ance**, *n.*
**lux·u′ri·ate′** (-āt′), *v.i.* [-ATED, -ATING], 1. to live in great luxury. 2. to revel (with *in*).
**lux·u′ri·ous**, *adj.* 1. fond of or indulging in luxury. 2. constituting luxury; rich, comfortable, etc. —**lux·u′ri·ous·ly**, *adv.*
**lux·u·ry** (luk′shə-ri, lug′zhə-), *n.* [*pl.* -RIES], [< L. *luxus*], 1. the enjoyment of the best and most costly things. 2. anything contributing to such enjoyment, esp. when not really necessary.
**-ly**, [< AS. *-lic*], a suffix meaning: 1. *like* or *characteristic of*, as in *manly*. 2. *in* (a specified) *manner*, *to* (a specified) *extent* or *direction*, *in* or *at* (a specified) *time* or *place*, as in *harshly*, *outwardly*, *hourly*. 3. *in sequence*, as in *thirdly*. 4. *happening* (*once*) *every* (specified period), as in *monthly*.
**ly·ce·um** (lī-sē′əm, lī′si-), *n.* [< Gr. *Lykeion*, grove at Athens where Aristotle taught], 1. a lecture hall. 2. an organization providing public lectures, etc.
**lye** (lī), *n.* [AS. *leag*], any strongly alkaline substance, used in cleaning and in making soap.
**ly·ing** (lī′iŋ), ppr. of **lie** (to tell lies). *adj.* false; not truthful. *n.* the telling of a lie.
**ly·ing** (lī′iŋ), ppr. of **lie** (to recline).
**ly′ing-in′**, *n.* confinement in childbirth. *adj.* of or for childbirth.
**lymph** (limf), *n.* [< Gr. *nymphē*; see NYMPH], a clear, yellowish body fluid, like blood plasma but containing colorless corpuscles.
**lym·phat·ic** (lim-fat′ik), *adj.* 1. of, containing, or conveying lymph. 2. sluggish.
**lymph gland**, any of the glandlike structures lying in groups in the lymphatic vessels.
**lymph·oid** (lim′foid), *adj.* of or like lymph or the tissue of the lymph glands.
**lynch** (linch), *v.t.* [< a Virginia magistrate *Lynch*, who exceeded his jurisdiction], to kill (an accused person) by mob action and without lawful trial. —**lynch′ing**, *n.*
**lynx** (liŋks), *n.* [Gr. *lynx*], a wildcat found throughout the N Hemisphere, having long legs, a short tail, and tufted ears.
**ly·on·naise** (lī′ə-nāz′), *adj.* [Fr., of Lyon], prepared with finely sliced, fried onions: as, *lyonnaise* potatoes.
**lyre** (līr), *n.* [< Gr. *lyra*], a small stringed instrument of the harp family, used by the ancient Greeks.
**lyr·ic** (lir′ik), *adj.* [< Gr. *lyrikos*], 1. suitable for singing; songlike; specif., designating or of poetry expressing the poet's personal emotion. 2. of or having a relatively high voice with a light, flexible quality: as, a *lyric* tenor. *n.* 1. a lyric poem. 2. *usually pl.* the words of a song.
**lyr·i·cal** (lir′i-k'l), *adj.* 1. lyric. 2. expressing enthusiasm, etc. in strong, emotional language. —**lyr′i·cal·ly**, *adv.*
**lyr·i·cism** (lir′i-siz'm), *n.* lyric quality, style, expression, etc.
**lyr·i·cist** (lir′i-sist), *n.* a writer of lyrics, esp. for popular songs.
**-lysis**, [< Gr. *lysis*, a loosening], a combining form meaning *a loosing*, *dissolution*, *dissolving*, *destruction*, as in *electrolysis*, *paralysis*.
**-lyte**, [see -LYSIS], a combining form meaning a *substance undergoing decomposition*, as in *electrolyte*.

# M

**M, m** (em), *n.* [*pl.* M's, m's, Ms, ms], the thirteenth letter of the English alphabet.
**M** (em), *n.* a Roman numeral for 1,000.
**M.,** 1. Monday. 2. [*pl.* MM.], Monsieur.
**M., m.,** 1. male. 2. married. 3. masculine. 4. meter(s). 5. mile(s). 6. minute(s). 7. month.
**ma** (mä), *n.* [Colloq.], mother.
**M.A.,** Master of Arts: also **A.M.**
**ma'am** (mam, mäm, məm), *n.* [Colloq.], madam: used in direct address.
**ma·ca·bre** (mə-kä′brə, -bẽr), *adj.* [< OFr. (*danse*) *Macabré*, (dance) of death], gruesome; grim and horrible.
**mac·ad·am** (mə-kad′əm), *n.* [< J. L. *MacAdam* (1756—1836), Scot. engineer], 1. small broken stones, used in making roads. 2. a road made by rolling successive layers of such stones, often with tar or asphalt. **—mac·ad′am·ize′** [-IZED -IZING], *v.t.*
**mac·a·ro·ni** (mak′ə-rō′ni), *n.* [*pl.* -NIS, -NIES], [It. *maccaroni*, pl.], long, thin, hollow tubes made of dried flour paste, to be cooked for food.
**mac·a·roon** (mak′ə-rōōn′), *n.* [see MACARONI], a small, sweet cooky made with crushed almonds or coconut.
**ma·caw** (mə-kô′), *n.* [prob. < Braz. native name], a large, bright-colored, harsh-voiced parrot of Central and South America.
**Mac·beth** (mək-beth′), *n.* the title hero of a tragedy by Shakespeare.
**mace** (mās), *n.* [< OFr.], 1. a heavy, spiked war club, used in the Middle Ages. 2. a staff used as a symbol of authority by certain officials.
**mace** (mās), *n.* [< Gr. *maker*, bark from India], a spice, usually ground, made from the dried husk of the nutmeg.
**mac·er·ate** (mas′ə-rāt′), *v.t.* [-ATED, -ATING], [< L. *macerare*, soften], 1. to soften or separate the parts of by soaking in liquid. 2. to cause to waste away. *v.i.* to waste away; grow thin. **—mac′er·a′tion,** *n.*
**mach.,** 1. machine. 2. machinery.
**ma·che·te** (mä-chā′tā, mə-shet′, -shet′i), *n.* [Sp. < L. *marcus*, hammer], a large, heavy-bladed knife used, as in S. America, for cutting sugar cane, etc., or as a weapon.
**Mach·i·a·vel·li·an** (mak′i-ə-vel′i-ən), *adj.* of or like Machiavelli (1469—1527), Italian statesman, or his political principles of craftiness and duplicity.
**mach·i·nate** (mak′ə-nāt′), *v.i. & v.t.* [-NATED, -NATING], [< L. *machinari*, to plot], to plan or plot artfully, esp. to do evil.
**mach′i·na′tion,** *n. usually in pl.* an artful or secret plot or scheme, esp. an evil one.
**ma·chine** (mə-shēn′), *n.* [< Gr. *mēchos*, contrivance], 1. a mechanical vehicle; specif., an automobile. 2. a structure consisting of a framework with various moving parts, for doing some kind of work. 3. a person or organization regarded as acting like a machine. 4. the controlling group in a political party. 5. in *mechanics*, a device, as the lever or screw, that transmits, or changes the application of, energy. *adj.* 1. of machines. 2. done by machinery. *v.t.* [-CHINED, -CHINING], to make, shape, etc. by machinery.
**machine gun,** an automatic gun, firing a rapid stream of bullets.
**ma·chin·er·y** (mə-shēn′ẽr-i, -shēn′ri), *n.* [*pl.* -IES], 1. machines collectively. 2. the working parts of a machine. 3. any means by which something is kept in action: as, *machinery* of government.
**ma·chin′ist,** *n.* one who makes, repairs, or operates machinery.
**mack·er·el** (mak′ẽr-əl), *n.* [*pl.* -EL, -ELS], [< ML. *macarellus*], an edible fish of the North Atlantic.
**Mack·i·naw coat** (mak′ə-nô′), [< *Mackinac* Is. in N Lake Huron], a short, heavy, double-breasted coat of wool, often plaid: also **mackinaw.**
**mack·in·tosh** (mak′in-tosh′), *n.* [< C. *Macintosh* (1766—1843), the Scot. inventor], a raincoat of rubberized cloth.
**macro-,** [< Gr. *makros*, long], a combining form meaning *long, large.*
**mac·ro·cosm** (mak′rə-koz′m), *n.* [see MACRO- & COSMOS], the universe.
**ma·cron** (mā′krən, mak′ron), *n.* [< Gr. *makros*, long], a mark (¯) placed over a vowel to indicate its pronunciation.
**mad** (mad), *adj.* [MADDER, MADDEST], [< AS. (*ge*)*mædan*, drive mad], 1. mentally ill; insane. 2. frantic: as, *mad* with fear. 3. foolish and rash. 4. infatuated: as, she's *mad* about him. 5. wildly gay. 6. having rabies: as, a *mad* dog. 7. [Colloq.], angry. **—like mad,** with furious energy, speed, etc.
**mad·am** (mad′əm), *n.* [*pl.* -AMS; *for 1, usually* MESDAMES (mā-däm′)], [< Fr., orig. *ma dame*, my lady], 1. a woman; lady; a polite title: often **ma'am.** 2. a woman in charge of a brothel.
**mad·ame** (mad′əm; Fr. mä′däm′), *n.* [*pl.* MESDAMES (mā-däm′)], [Fr.], a married woman: French title equivalent to *Mrs.*
**mad′cap′,** *n.* [*mad* + *cap*, fig. for head], a reckless, impulsive person, esp. a girl. *adj.* reckless and impulsive.
**mad·den** (mad′'n), *v.t. & v.i.* to make or become mad; make or become insane, angry, or wildly excited. **—mad′den·ing,** *adj.*
**mad·der** (mad′ẽr), *n.* [AS. *mædere*], 1. any of various plants; esp., a vine with yellow flowers and berries. 2. a red dye made from its root. 3. crimson.
**made** (mād), pt. and pp. of **make.** *adj.* 1. constructed. 2. produced artificially. 3. sure of success.
**ma·de·moi·selle** (mad′ə-mə-zel′; Fr. mäd′-mwä′zel′), *n.* [*pl.* MESDEMOISELLES (mād′-)], [Fr.; *ma*, my + *demoiselle*, young lady], an unmarried woman or girl: French title equivalent to *Miss.*
**made′-to-or′der,** *adj.* made to conform to the customer's specifications.
**made′-up′,** *adj.* 1. put together. 2. invented; false: as, a *made-up* story. 3. with cosmetics applied.
**mad′house′,** *n.* 1. an insane asylum. 2. any place of turmoil, noise, etc.
**mad′ly,** *adv.* 1. insanely. 2. wildly; furiously. 3. foolishly.
**mad′man′,** *n.* [*pl.* -MEN], an insane person; lunatic. **—mad′wom′an** [*pl.* -WOMEN], *n.fem.*
**mad′ness,** *n.* 1. insanity. 2. great anger; fury. 3. great folly.
**Ma·don·na** (mə-don′ə), *n.* [It. < *ma*, my + *donna*, lady], 1. Mary, mother of Jesus. 2. a picture or statue of Mary.
**ma·dras** (mad′rəs, mə-dras′), *n.* [< *Madras*, India], a fine, firm cotton cloth, usually striped.
**mad·ri·gal** (mad′ri-g'l), *n.* [< LL. *matricalis*, of the womb], a part song, without accompaniment, popular in the 15th to 17th centuries.
**mael·strom** (māl′strəm), *n.* [< D. *malen*, grind + *stroom*, a stream], 1. a large or

violent whirlpool. 2. an agitated state of mind, affairs, etc.

**ma·es·tro** (mīs′trō, mā-es′-), *n.* [*pl.* -TROS, -TRI (-tri)], [It. < L. *magister*, master], a master in any art; esp., a great composer, conductor, or teacher of music.

**mag.,** 1. magazine. 2. magnetic.

**mag·a·zine** (mag′ə-zēn′), *n.* [< Ar. *makhzan*, granary], 1. a warehouse or military supply depot. 2. a space in which explosives are stored, as in a fort. 3. a supply chamber, as in a rifle, camera, etc. 4. a periodical publication containing stories, articles, etc.

**ma·gen·ta** (mə-jen′tə), *n.* [< *Magenta*, town in Italy], 1. a purplish-red dye. 2. purplish red. *adj.* purplish-red.

**mag·got** (mag′ət), *n.* [ME. *magotte*], 1. a wormlike larva, as of the housefly. 2. an odd notion; whim. —**mag′got·y,** *adj.*

**Ma·gi** (mā′jī), *n.pl.* [*sing.* -GUS (-gəs)], [< OPer. *magu*], 1. the priestly caste in ancient Persia. 2. in the *Bible*, the wise men who came bearing gifts to the infant Jesus.

**mag·ic** (maj′ik), *n.* [< Gr. *magikos*, of the Magi], 1. the pretended art of producing effects by charms, spells, etc.; sorcery. 2. any mysterious power: as, the *magic* of love. 3. the art of producing illusions by sleight of hand, etc. *adj.* 1. of, produced by, or using magic. 2. producing extraordinary results, as if by magic. —**mag′i·cal,** *adj.*

**ma·gi·cian** (mə-jish′ən), *n.* [OFr. *magicien*], an expert in magic.

**magic lantern,** an instrument for projecting on a screen a magnified image of a picture on a slide.

**mag·is·te·ri·al** (maj′is-têr′i-əl), *adj.* 1. of or suitable for a magistrate. 2. authoritative. —**mag′is·te′ri·al·ly,** *adv.*

**mag·is·trate** (maj′is-trāt′), *n.* [< L. *magister*, a master], 1. a civil officer empowered to administer the law. 2. a minor official, as a justice of the peace. —**mag′is·tra·cy** (-trə-si), *n.*

**mag·ma** (mag′mə), *n.* [*pl.* -MAS, -MATA (-mə-tə)], [< Gr. *massein*, to knead], molten rock deep in the earth, from which igneous rock is formed.

**Mag·na Char·ta** (or **Car·ta**) (mag′nə kär′tə), [ML., great charter], the charter (1215) that guaranteed certain civil and political liberties to the English people.

**mag·na·nim·i·ty** (mag′nə-nim′ə-ti), *n.* 1. a magnanimous quality or state. 2. [*pl.* -TIES], a magnanimous act.

**mag·nan·i·mous** (mag-nan′ə-məs), *adj.* [< L. *magnus*, great + *animus*, soul], generous in overlooking injury or insult; rising above pettiness; noble.

**mag·nate** (mag′nāt), *n.* [< L. *magnus*, great], a very influential person.

**mag·ne·sia** (mag-nē′shə, -zhə), *n.* [< Gr. *Magnēsia lithos*, stone of Magnesia (district in ancient Greece)], a white powder, an oxide of magnesium, used as a laxative.

**mag·ne′si·um** (-shi-əm, -zhi-), *n.* [< *magnesia*], a light, silvery metallic chemical element: symbol, Mg.

**mag·net** (mag′nit), *n.* [see MAGNESIA], 1. any piece of iron, steel, or loadstone that has the property of attracting iron or steel. 2. anything that attracts.

**mag·net·ic** (mag-net′ik), *adj.* 1. having the properties of a magnet. 2. of, producing, or caused by magnetism. 3. of the earth's magnetism. 4. that can be magnetized. 5. powerfully attractive. —**mag·net′i·cal·ly,** *adv.*

**magnetic field,** the space around a magnet in which the magnetic force exerted is appreciable.

**mag·net·ism** (mag′nə-tiz'm), *n.* 1. the property, quality, or condition of being magnetic. 2. the force to which this is due. 3. personal charm.

**mag′net·ite′** (-tīt′), *n.* a black iron oxide: called *loadstone* when magnetic.

**mag′net·ize′** (-tīz′), *v.t.* [-IZED, -IZING], 1. to give magnetic properties to (steel, iron, etc.). 2. to charm (a person).

**mag·ne·to** (mag-nē′tō), *n.* [*pl.* -TOS], a small generator in which one or more permanent magnets produce the magnetic field.

**mag·nif·i·cence** (mag-nif′ə-s'ns), *n.* [< L. *magnus*, great + *facere*, do], richness and splendor; imposing beauty; grandeur.

**mag·nif′i·cent,** *adj.* 1. splendid; stately; grand, as in construction. 2. exalted: said of ideas, etc. —**mag·nif′i·cent·ly,** *adv.*

**mag·nif·i·co** (mag-nif′ə-kō′), *n.* [*pl.* -COES], [see MAGNIFICENCE], a person of high rank.

**mag·ni·fy** (mag′nə-fī′), *v.t. & v.i.* [-FIED, -FYING], [see MAGNIFICENCE], 1. to exaggerate. 2. to increase the apparent size of (an object), as (with) a lens. —**mag′ni·fi·ca′tion** (-fi-kā′shən), *n.* —**mag′ni·fi′er,** *n.*

**mag·nil·o·quent** (mag-nil′ə-kwənt), *adj.* [< L. *magnus*, great + *loqui*, to speak], pompous or grandiose in talking or writing.

**mag·ni·tude** (mag′nə-tōōd′, -tūd′), *n.* [< L. *magnus*, great], 1. greatness of size, extent, power, etc. 2. *a*) size. *b*) importance. 3. the degree of brightness of a fixed star.

**mag·no·li·a** (mag-nō′li-ə, -nōl′yə), *n.* [< P. *Magnol* (1638–1715), Fr. botanist], 1. a tree with large, fragrant flowers of white, pink, or purple. 2. the flower.

**mag·num** (mag′nəm), *n.* [< L. *magnus*, great], a bottle holding two quarts, used for wine, etc.

‡**mag·num o·pus** (mag′nəm ō′pəs), [L.], 1. a masterpiece. 2. a person's greatest work.

**mag·pie** (mag′pī), *n.* [< *Mag*, dim. of *Margaret* + *pie*, magpie], 1. a noisy, black-and-white bird of the crow family. 2. one who chatters.

**Mag·yar** (mag′yär; Hung. môd′-), *n.* 1. a member of the main ethnic group in Hungary. 2. the Hungarian language.

**ma·ha·ra·jah, ma·ha·ra·ja** (mä′hə-rä′jə), *n.* [< Sans. *maha*, great + *rājā*, king], in India, a prince, formerly the sovereign of a native state. —**ma′ha·ra′ni, ma′ha·ra′nee** (-nē), *n.fem.*

**ma·hat·ma** (mə-hat′mə, -hät′-), *n.* [< Sans. *maha*, great + *ātman*, soul], in *Buddhism*, one of a class of wise and holy persons having unusual powers.

**mah-jongg, mah·jong** (mä′jôŋ′), *n.* [< Chin. *mach'iao*, sparrow (a figure on one of the tiles)], a game of Chinese origin, played with small tiles.

**ma·hog·a·ny** (mə-hog′ə-ni, -hôg′-), *n.* [*pl.* -NIES], [< native W. Ind. name], 1. *a*) the reddish-brown hard wood of a tropical American tree. *b*) the tree. 2. reddish brown. *adj.* reddish-brown.

**maid** (mād), *n.* 1. a maiden. 2. any unmarried woman. 3. a girl or woman servant.

**maid′en** (-'n), *n.* [AS. *mægden*], 1. a girl or young unmarried woman. 2. a virgin. *adj.* 1. of or suitable for a maiden. 2. unmarried. 3. untried; new. 4. first or earliest: as, a *maiden* voyage. —**maid′en·hood′,** *n.* —**maid′en·ly,** *adj. & adv.*

**maid′en·hair′,** *n.* a fern with delicate fronds and slender stalks.

**maiden name,** the surname that a woman had when not yet married.

**maid of honor,** an unmarried woman acting as chief attendant to a bride.

**mail** (māl), *n.* [< OHG. *malha*, wallet], 1. letters, packages, etc. transported and delivered by the post office. 2. the postal system. *adj.* of mail. *v.t.* to send by mail; put into a mailbox. —**mail′er,** *n.*

**mail** (māl), *n.* [< L. *macula*, mesh of a net], a flexible body armor made of small metal rings, scales, etc. *v.t.* to cover as with mail.
**mail′box′**, *n.* 1. a box into which mail is put when delivered. 2. a box, as on a street, into which mail is put for collection. Also **mail box.**
**mail′man′**, *n.* [*pl.* -MEN], a man who carries or delivers mail; postman.
**mail′-or′der house,** a business that takes orders and sends goods by mail.
**maim** (mām), *v.t.* [OFr. *mahaigner*], to cripple; mutilate; disable.
**main** (mān), *n.* [AS. *mægen*, strength], 1. a principal pipe in a distributing system for water, gas, etc. 2. [Poetic], the ocean. *adj.* chief in size, importance, etc.; principal. —**by main force** (or **strength**), by sheer force (or strength). —**in the main,** mostly; chiefly. —**with might and main,** with all one's strength.
**main clause,** a clause that can function as a complete sentence by itself.
**main·land** (mān′land′, -lənd), *n.* the principal land mass of a continent, as distinguished from near-by islands.
**main′ly,** *adv.* chiefly; principally.
**main·mast** (mān′məst, -mast′), *n.* the principal mast of a vessel.
**main·sail** (mān′s'l, -sāl′), *n.* the principal sail of a vessel, set from the mainmast.
**main′spring′**, *n.* 1. the principal spring in a clock, watch, etc. 2. the chief motive, incentive, etc.
**main′stay′** (-stā′), *n.* 1. the supporting line extending forward from the mainmast. 2. a chief support.
**main·tain** (mān-tān′), *v.t.* [< L. *manu tenere*, hold in the hand], 1. to keep or keep up; carry on. 2. to keep in continuance or in a certain state, as of repair. 3. to defend. 4. to declare to be true. 5. to support by aid, etc. 6. to provide the means of existence for: as, to *maintain* a family.
**main·te·nance** (mān′tə-nəns), *n.* 1. a maintaining or being maintained. 2. means of support or sustenance.
‡**mai·tre d'hô·tel** (me′tr′ dô′tel′), [Fr., master of the house], 1. a butler. 2. a hotel manager. 3. a headwaiter.
**maize** (māz), *n.* [< W. Ind. *mahiz*], 1. a grain that grows in kernels on large ears: also called *Indian corn* or *corn*. 2. its yellowish color. *adj.* yellow.
**Maj.,** Major.
**ma·jes·tic** (mə-jes′tik), *adj.* grand; noble: also **ma·jes′ti·cal.** —**ma·jes′ti·cal·ly,** *adv.*
**maj·es·ty** (maj′is-ti), *n.* [*pl.* -TIES], [< L. *magnus*, great], 1. [M-], a title used in speaking to or of a sovereign: with *His, Her,* or *Your.* 2. grandeur; dignity.
**ma·jor** (mā′jẽr), *adj.* [L. compar. of *magnus*, great], 1. greater in size, amount, importance, rank, etc. 2. of full legal age. 3. in *music*, higher than the corresponding minor by a half tone. *v.i.* in *education*, to specialize (*in* a field of study). *n.* 1. a military officer ranking just above a captain. 2. in *education*, a principal field of study.
**ma′jor-do′mo** (-dō′mō), *n.* [*pl.* -MOS], [< L. *major*, great + *domus*, house], a man in charge of a great household.
**major general,** [*pl.* MAJOR GENERALS], a military officer ranking just above a brigadier general.
**ma·jor·i·ty** (mə-jôr′ə-ti, -jor′-), *n.* [*pl.* -TIES], [see MAJOR], 1. the greater number; more than half. 2. the excess of the larger number of votes cast for one candidate, etc. over the rest of the votes. 3. full legal age. 4. the military rank of a major.
**make** (māk), *v.t.* [MADE, MAKING], [AS. *macian*], 1. to bring into being; build, create, cause, etc. 2. to cause to be or become: as, I *made* him angry. 3. to prepare for use: as, *make* the beds. 4. to amount to: as, two pints *make* a quart. 5. to have the qualities of: as, he *made* a good doctor. 6. to acquire; earn. 7. to cause the success of: as, this venture *made* him. 8. to understand: as, what do you *make* of that? 9. to execute, do, etc.: as, to *make* a speech. 10. to cause or force to: as, *make* him go. 11. to arrive at; reach: as, the ship *made* port. 12. [Colloq.], to get a position on, etc.: as, he *made* the team. *v.i.* 1. to go; proceed: as, he *made* for the door. 2. to behave as specified: as, *make* merry. 3. to cause something to be as specified: as, *make* ready. *n.* 1. the act or process of making. 2. the way in which something is made; style; build. 3. type; sort; brand. —**make away with,** 1. to steal. 2. to kill. —**make believe,** to pretend. —**make for,** 1. to head for. 2. to attack. 3. to help effect. —**make out,** 1. to see with difficulty. 2. to understand. 3. to fill out (a blank form, etc.). 4. to (try to) show or prove to be. 5. to succeed; get along. —**make over,** 1. to change; renovate. 2. to transfer the ownership of. —**make up,** 1. to put together. 2. to form; constitute. 3. to invent. 4. to provide (what is lacking). 5. to compensate (*for*). 6. to become friends again after a quarrel. 7. to put on cosmetics, etc. 8. to decide (one's mind). 9. to arrange (type, illustrations, etc.) as for a book. —**make up to,** to flatter. —**mak′er,** *n.*
**make′-be·lieve′**, *n.* 1. pretense; feigning. 2. a pretender. *adj.* pretended; feigned.
**make′shift′** (-shift′), *n.* a temporary substitute or expedient. *adj.* that will do as a temporary substitute.
**make′-up′**, *n.* 1. the way something is put together; composition. 2. nature; disposition. 3. the cosmetics, etc. used by an actor. 4 cosmetics generally. 5. the arrangement of type, illustrations, etc., as in a book.
**mal-,** [< L. *malus*, bad], a prefix meaning *bad* or *badly, wrong, ill.*
**mal·ad·just·ed** (mal′ə-jus′tid), *adj.* poorly adjusted, esp. to the environment. —**mal′ad·just′ment,** *n.*
**mal·ad·min·is·ter** (mal′əd-min′ə-stẽr), *v.t.* to administer without efficiency or honesty.
**mal·a·droit** (mal′ə-droit′), *adj.* [Fr.; see MAL- & ADROIT], awkward; clumsy; bungling.
**mal·a·dy** (mal′ə-di), *n.* [*pl.* -DIES], [< L. *male habitus*, badly kept], an ailment; disease; illness.
**ma·laise** (ma-lāz′), *n.* [Fr. < *mal*, bad + *aise*, ease], a vague feeling of physical discomfort.
**mal·a·prop·ism** (mal′ə-prop-iz'm), *n.* [< Mrs. *Malaprop* in Sheridan's *The Rivals* (1775)], a ridiculous misuse of words, esp. through confusion caused by resemblance in sound.
**ma·lar·i·a** (mə-lâr′i-ə), *n.* [It. < *mala aria*, bad air], an infectious disease transmitted by the anopheles mosquito, characterized by intermittent chills and fever. —**ma·lar′i·al, ma·lar′i·ous,** *adj.*
**Ma·lay** (mā′lā, mə-lā′), *n.* 1. a member of a group of brown-skinned peoples living chiefly in the Malay Peninsula and the Malay Archipelago. 2. their language. *adj.* of the Malays, their language, etc. Also **Ma·lay′an.**
**Mal·a·ya·lam** (mal′ə-yä′ləm), *n.* a language of the SW coast of India.
**mal·con·tent** (mal′kən-tent′), *adj.* [Fr.; see MAL- & CONTENT], dissatisfied; rebellious. *n.* a malcontent person.
**male** (māl), *adj.* [< L. *mas*, a male], 1. designating or of the sex that fertilizes the ovum. 2. of, like, or suitable to men or boys; masculine. 3. in *mechanics*, having a part shaped to fit into a corresponding hollow part. *n.* a male person, animal, or plant.

**mal·e·dic·tion** (mal'ə-dik'shən), *n.* [< L. *male*, evil + *dicere*, speak], 1. a curse. 2. a speaking of evil. —**mal'e·dic'to·ry**, *adj.*
**mal·e·fac·tor** (mal'ə-fak'tēr), *n.* [< L. *male*, evil + *facere*, do], an evildoer; criminal. —**mal'e·fac'tress**, *n.fem.* —**mal'e·fac'tion**, *n.*
**ma·lev·o·lent** (mə-lev'ə-lənt), *adj.* [< L. *male*, evil + *velle*, to wish], wishing evil or harm to others. —**ma·lev'o·lence**, *n.*
**mal·fea·sance** (mal-fē'z'ns), *n.* [< Fr. *mal*, evil + *faire*, do], wrongdoing, esp. in handling public affairs.
**mal·for·ma·tion** (mal'fôr-mā'shən), *n.* faulty or abnormal formation of a body or part. —**mal·formed'**, *adj.*
**mal·ice** (mal'is), *n.* [< L. *malus*, bad], 1. active ill will; desire to harm others. 2. in *law*, evil intent.
**ma·li·cious** (mə-lish'əs), *adj.* having, showing, or caused by malice; spiteful.
**ma·lign** (mə-līn'), *v.t.* [< L. *male*, ill + *genus*, born], to speak evil of; slander. *adj.* 1. malevolent. 2. evil; sinister. 3. very harmful.
**ma·lig·nant** (mə-lig'nənt), *adj.* [see MALIGN], 1. having an evil influence. 2. wishing evil. 3. very harmful. 4. causing or likely to cause death: as, a *malignant* tumor. —**ma·lig'nan·cy, ma·lig'nance**, *n.*
**ma·lig·ni·ty** (mə-lig'nə-ti), *n.* 1. great malice. 2. the quality of being very harmful. 3. [*pl.* -TIES], a malignant act, event, or feeling.
**ma·lin·ger** (mə-liŋ'gēr), *v.i.* [< Fr. *malingre*, sickly], to feign illness in order to escape duty or work. —**ma·lin'ger·er**, *n.*
**mall** (môl, mal), *n.* [< *maul*, mallet: from use in a game on outdoor lanes], a shaded walk or public promenade.
**mal·lard** (mal'ērd), *n.* [OFr. *mal(l)art*], the common wild duck.
**mal·le·a·ble** (mal'i-ə-b'l), *adj.* [< L. *malleus*, a hammer], 1. that can be hammered, pounded, or pressed into various shapes without breaking. 2. adaptable. —**mal'le·a·bil'i·ty**, *n.*
**mal·let** (mal'it), *n.* [see MALLEABLE], 1. a short-handled hammer with a wooden head, for driving a chisel, etc. 2. any similar long-handled hammer, as for use in croquet.
**mal·low** (mal'ō), *n.* [< L. *malva*], any of a family of plants, including the hollyhock, cotton, and okra, with large, showy flowers.
**mal·nu·tri·tion** (mal'nōō-trish'ən, -nū-), *n.* faulty or inadequate nutrition; undernourishment.
**mal·o·dor·ous** (mal-ō'dēr-əs), *adj.* having a bad odor; stinking.
**mal·prac·tice** (mal-prak'tis), *n.* professional misconduct or improper practice, esp. by a physician.
**malt** (môlt), *n.* [AS. *mealt*], 1. barley or other grain soaked and then kiln-dried: used in brewing and distilling certain alcoholic liquors. 2. such liquor; beer, ale, etc. *adj.* made with malt. *v.t.* to change (barley, etc.) into malt.
**Mal·tese** (môl'tēz'), *adj.* of Malta, its inhabitants, etc. *n.* 1. [*pl.* -TESE], a native of Malta. 2. the language spoken in Malta.
**mal·treat** (mal-trēt'), *v.t.* [see MAL- & TREAT], to treat roughly or brutally; abuse. —**mal·treat'ment**, *n.*
**mam·ma, ma·ma** (mä'mə; *occas.* mə-mä'), *n.* mother: a child's word.
**mam·ma** (mam'ə), *n.* [*pl.* -MAE (-ē)], [AS. < L., breast], a gland for secreting milk, found in all female mammals.
**mam·mal** (mam'əl), *n.* [< L. *mamma*, breast], any of a group of vertebrates the females of which have milk-secreting glands for feeding their offspring. —**mam·ma·li·an** (ma-mā'li-ən), *adj.* & *n.*
**mam·ma·ry** (mam'ə-ri), *adj.* designating or of the milk-secreting glands, or mammae.
**mam·mon** (mam'ən), *n.* [< Aram. *māmōnā*, riches], 1. [usually M-], the false god of riches and avarice. 2. riches regarded as an object of greedy pursuit.
**mam·moth** (mam'əth), *n.* [Russ. *mammot'*], a huge, extinct elephant with a hairy skin and long tusks. *adj.* very big; huge.
**man** (man), *n.* [*pl.* MEN], [AS. *mann*], 1. a human being; person. 2. the human race; mankind. 3. an adult male person. 4. an adult male servant, employee, etc. 5. a husband. 6. a manly person. 7. any of the pieces used in chess, checkers, etc. *v.t.* [MANNED, MANNING], 1. to furnish with men for work, defense, etc.: as, to *man* a ship. 2. to strengthen; brace. —**as a** (or **one**) **man**, in unison; unanimously. —**to a man**, with no exception.
**-man**, a combining form meaning: 1. *a member of a* (specified) *nation*, as in *Frenchman*. 2. *one doing a* (specified) *kind of work*, as in *laundryman*.
**man·a·cle** (man'ə-k'l), *n.* [< L. *manus*, hand], *usually in pl.* a handcuff; fetter or shackle for the hand. *v.t.* [-CLED, -CLING], 1. to put handcuffs on. 2. to restrain.
**man·age** (man'ij), *v.t.* [-AGED, -AGING], [< L. *manus*, hand], 1. to control the action, use, working, etc. of; handle; guide. 2. to have charge of; direct: as, he *manages* a hotel. 3. to succeed in accomplishing. *v.i.* 1. to carry on business. 2. to contrive to get along. —**man'age·a·ble**, *adj.*
**man'age·ment**, *n.* 1. a managing or being managed; control, direction, etc. 2. the persons managing a business, institution, etc. 3. skillful managing.
**man'ag·er**, *n.* one who manages; esp., one who manages a business, institution, etc.
**man·a·ge·ri·al** (man'ə-jêr'i-əl), *adj.* of a manager or management.
**man·a·tee** (man'ə-tē'), *n.* [< native (Carib) name], a large, plant-eating aquatic mammal of shallow tropical waters.
**Man·chu, Man·choo** (man-chōō'), *n.* 1. a member of a Mongolian people of Manchuria who ruled China from 1644 to 1912. 2. their language. *adj.* of Manchuria, the Manchus, their language, etc.
**man·da·mus** (man-dā'məs), *n.* [L., we command], a writ requiring that a specified thing be done, issued by a higher court to a lower one, or to a person, city, etc.
**man·da·rin** (man'də-rin), *n.* [< Sans. *mantra*, counsel], 1. a high official of the former Chinese Empire. 2. [M-], the main dialect of Chinese. 3. a small orange with a loose rind; tangerine.
**man·date** (man'dāt, -dit), *n.* [< L. *mandare*, to command], 1. an order or command. 2. *a*) formerly, a commission from the League of Nations to a country to administer some region, colony, etc. *b*) the area so administered. 3. the will of constituents expressed to their representative, etc.
**man·da·to·ry** (man'də-tôr'i), *adj.* 1. of, like, or containing a mandate. 2. commanded; obligatory.
**man·di·ble** (man'də-b'l), *n.* [< L. *mandere*, chew], 1. the jaw; esp., the lower jaw. 2. either part of a bird's beak, an insect's biting jaws, etc.
**man·do·lin** (man'd'l-in'), *n.* [ult. < Gr. *pandoura*, kind of lute], a musical instrument with from eight to twelve metal strings, usually paired, and a deep, rounded sound box.
**man·drake** (man'drāk), *n.* [< Gr. *mandragoras*], 1. a poisonous plant of the nightshade family. 2. its thick root, used in medicine as a narcotic.
**man·drill** (man'dril), *n.* [*man* + *drill* (baboon)], a large, fierce baboon of W Africa.
**mane** (mān), *n.* [AS. *manu*], the long hair

growing from the top or sides of the neck of the horse, lion, etc. —**maned,** *adj.*

**man'-eat'er,** *n.* an animal that eats, or is thought to eat, human flesh.

**ma·nège, ma·nege** (ma-nezh', mə-nāzh'), *n.* [Fr.; ult. < L. *manus*, hand], the art of riding and training horses.

**ma·neu·ver** (mə-nōō'vẽr, -nū'-), *n.* [< L. *manu operare*, to work by hand], 1. a planned and controlled movement of troops, warships, etc. 2. a stratagem; scheme. *v.i.* & *v.t.* 1. to perform or cause to perform maneuvers. 2. to manage or plan skillfully; scheme. 3. to move, get, make, etc. by some scheme. —**ma·neu'ver·a·ble,** *adj.*

**man·ful** (man'fəl), *adj.* manly.

**man·ga·nese** (maŋ'gə-nēs', maŋ'gə-nēz'), *n.* [< It.; ult. < ML. *magnesia*], a grayish-white metallic chemical element, used in alloys: symbol, Mn.

**mange** (mānj), *n.* [< OFr. *mangeue*, an itch], a skin disease of animals, esp. one causing a loss of hair.

**man·ger** (mān'jẽr), *n.* [< L. *mandere*, to chew], a box or trough to hold hay, etc. for horses or cattle to eat.

**man·gle** (maŋ'g'l), *v.t.* [-GLED, -GLING], [< OFr. *mehaigner*, maim], 1. to mutilate by roughly cutting, hacking, etc. 2. to spoil; botch; mar. —**man'gler,** *n.*

**man·gle** (maŋ'g'l), *n.* [< Gr. *manganon*, war machine], a machine for pressing sheets and other flat pieces of cloth between rollers. *v.t.* [-GLED, -GLING], to press in a mangle. —**man'gler,** *n.*

**man·go** (maŋ'gō), *n.* [*pl.* -GOES, -GOS], [< Tamil *mān-kāy*], 1. the yellow-red, somewhat acid fruit of a tropical tree. 2. the tree.

**man·grove** (maŋ'grōv), *n.* [< W. Ind. name], a tropical tree with branches that spread and send down roots, thus forming more trunks.

**man·gy** (mān'ji), *adj.* [-GIER, -GIEST], 1. having the mange. 2. shabby and filthy. 3. mean and low. —**man'gi·ness,** *n.*

**man'han'dle,** *v.t.* [-DLED, -DLING], to handle roughly.

**man'hole',** *n.* a hole through which a man can enter a sewer, conduit, etc.

**man'hood,** *n.* 1. the state or time of being a man. 2. virility, courage, etc. 3. men collectively.

**man'-hour',** *n.* a unit of work, equal to that done by one man in one hour.

**ma·ni·a** (mā'ni-ə), *n.* [Gr.], 1. wild or violent insanity. 2. an excessive enthusiasm; obsession; craze.

**-mania,** [see MANIA], a combining form meaning *a* (specified) *type of mental disorder*, as in *kleptomania*.

**ma·ni·ac** (mā'ni-ak'), *adj.* wildly insane; raving. *n.* a violently insane person; lunatic. —**ma·ni·a·cal** (mə-nī'ə-k'l), *adj.*

**man·ic** (man'ik, mā'nik), *adj.* of, having, or characterized by mania.

**man'ic-de·pres'sive,** *adj.* designating, of, or having a psychosis characterized by alternating periods of mania and melancholia. *n.* a person who has this psychosis.

**man·i·cure** (man'ə-kyoor'), *n.* [< L. *manus*, a hand + *cura*, care], care of the hands and, esp., the fingernails. *v.t.* & *v.i.* [-CURED, -CURING], to take care of (the hands and fingernails). —**man'i·cur'ist,** *n.*

**man·i·fest** (man'ə-fest'), *adj.* [< L. *manifestus*, lit., struck by the hand], apparent to the senses or the mind; obvious. *v.t.* 1. to make clear or evident; reveal. 2. to prove; be evidence of. *n.* an itemized list of a ship's cargo. —**man'i·fest'ly,** *adv.*

**man·i·fes·ta·tion** (man'ə-fes-tā'shən), *n.* 1. a manifesting or being manifested. 2. something that manifests.

**man·i·fes·to** (man'ə-fes'tō), *n.* [*pl.* -TOES], [It. < L.; see MANIFEST], a public declaration of intention by an important person or group.

**man·i·fold** (man'ə-fōld'), *adj.* [see MANY & -FOLD], 1. having many forms, parts, etc. 2. of many sorts. 3. being such in many ways: as, a *manifold* villain. 4. operating several parts of one kind. *n.* a pipe with several outlets, as for conducting cylinder exhaust from an engine. *v.t.* to make several copies of, as with carbon paper.

**man·i·kin** (man'ə-kin), *n.* [< D. *manneken*], 1. a little man. 2. a mannequin. Also sp. **mannikin.**

**Ma·nil·a hemp** (mə-nil'ə), a strong fiber from the leafstalk of a Philippine tree, used for making rope, paper, etc.

**Manila paper,** a strong, brownish paper.

**ma·nip·u·late** (mə-nip'yoo-lāt'), *v.t.* [-LATED, -LATING], [ult. < L. *manus*, a hand + *plere*, to fill], 1. to work or handle skillfully. 2. to manage artfully or shrewdly, esp. in an unfair way. 3. to alter (figures, etc.) for one's own purposes. —**ma·nip'u·la'tion,** *n.* —**ma·nip'u·la'tor,** *n.*

**man'kind',** *n.* 1. the human race. 2. (man'-kind'), all human males.

**man'ly,** *adj.* [-LIER, -LIEST], having the qualities regarded as suitable for a man; virile, brave, etc. *adv.* in a manly way.

**man·na** (man'ə), *n.* [< Heb. *mān*], 1. in the *Bible*, food miraculously provided for the Israelites in the wilderness. 2. any needed sustenance that seems miraculously supplied.

**man·ne·quin** (man'ə-kin), *n.* [see MANIKIN], 1. a model of the human body, used by tailors, etc. 2. a woman who models clothes in stores, etc.

**man·ner** (man'ẽr), *n.* [< L. *manus*, a hand], 1. a way of doing something; mode of procedure. 2. a way, esp. a usual way, of acting; habit. 3. *pl.* *a*) ways of social behavior: as, bad *manners*. *b*) polite ways of social behavior: as, he has no *manners*. 4. kind; sort. —**by no manner of means,** definitely not.

**man'nered,** *adj.* 1. having manners of a specified sort: as, ill-*mannered*. 2. affected: as, a *mannered* literary style.

**man'ner·ism,** *n.* 1. excessive use of some distinctive manner in art, literature, etc. 2. a peculiarity of manner in behavior, speech, etc. —**man'ner·ist,** *n.*

**man'ner·ly,** *adj.* polite. *adv.* politely.

**man'nish,** *adj.* masculine.

**ma·noeu·vre** (mə-nōō'vẽr, -nū'-), *n.*, *v.i.* & *v.t.* [-VRED, -VRING], maneuver.

**man of the world,** a man of wide experience who is broad-minded.

**man'-of-war',** *n.* [*pl.* MEN-OF-WAR], an armed naval vessel; warship.

**man·or** (man'ẽr), *n.* [< L. *manere*, dwell], in England, a landed estate. —**ma·no·ri·al** (mə-nôr'i-əl), *adj.*

**man'pow'er,** *n.* 1. power furnished by human strength. 2. the collective strength, ability to work, etc. of the people in a given area, nation, etc. Also **man power.**

**man·sard** (man'särd), *n.* [< F. *Mansard*, 17th-c. Fr. architect], a roof with two slopes on each side, the lower steeper than the upper: also **mansard roof.**

**manse** (mans), *n.* [< L. *manere*, dwell], a parsonage.

**man'ser'vant,** *n.* [*pl.* MENSERVANTS], a male servant: also **man servant.**

**man·sion** (man'shən), *n.* [< L. *manere*, dwell], a large, imposing house.

**man'slaugh'ter** (-slô'tẽr), *n.* the killing of a human being by another, esp. when unlawful but without malice.

**man·tel** (man't'l), *n.* [see MANTLE], 1. the facing about a fireplace, including a projecting shelf. 2. this shelf: also **man′tel-piece′.**

**man·til·la** (man-til′ə), *n.* [Sp. < LL. *mantellum*, a cloak], a woman's scarf worn over the hair and shoulders.

**man·tis** (man′tis), *n.* [*pl.* -TISES, -TES (-tēz)], [< Gr. *mantis*, prophet], an insect that holds its forelegs folded as if praying: often **praying mantis.**

**man·tle** (man′t'l), *n.* [< L. *mantellum*], 1. a loose, sleeveless cloak. 2. anything that envelops or conceals. 3. a small, meshwork hood which when placed over a flame becomes white-hot and gives off light. *v.t.* [-TLED, -TLING], to cover as with a mantle. *v.i.* 1. to be or become covered. 2. to blush or flush.

**man·u·al** (man′ū-əl), *adj.* [< L. *manus*, a hand], of the hands; made, done, or worked by the hands. *n.* 1. a handy book for use as a guide, reference, etc. 2. prescribed drill in the handling of a weapon, esp. a rifle: also **manual of arms.**

**man·u·fac·ture** (man′yoo-fak′chẽr), *n.* [< L. *manus*, hand + *facere*, make], 1. the making of goods by hand or, esp., by machinery, often on a large scale. 2. anything so made. *v.t.* [-TURED, -TURING], 1. to make, esp. by machinery. 2. to work (wool, steel, etc.) into usable form. 3. to make up (excuses, etc.); invent.

**man′u·fac′tur·er,** *n.* a person or company in the business of manufacturing.

**man·u·mit** (man′yoo-mit′), *v.t.* [-MITTED, -MITTING], [< L. *manus*, a hand + *mittere*, send], to free from slavery. **—man′u·mis′sion** (-mish′ən), *n.*

**ma·nure** (mə-nyoor′, -noor′), *v.t.* [-NURED, -NURING], [< OFr. *manouvrer*, work with the hands], to put manure on or into. *n.* animal excrement used to fertilize soil.

**man·u·script** (man′yoo-skript′), *adj.* [< L. *manus*, hand + *scriptus*, written], written by hand or typewritten. *n.* a written or typewritten document, book, etc., esp. one submitted to a publisher.

**Manx** (maŋks), *adj.* of the Isle of Man, its people, etc. *n.* the Gaelic language spoken on the Isle of Man.

**man·y** (men′i), *adj.* [MORE, MOST], [AS. *manig*], numerous. *n.* a large number (of persons or things). *pron.* many persons or things.

**man′y-sid′ed,** *adj.* 1. having many sides or faces. 2. having many possibilities, qualities, etc.

**map** (map), *n.* [ult. < L. *mappa*, napkin, cloth], 1. a representation of all or part of the earth's surface, showing countries, bodies of water, etc. 2. a representation of the sky, showing the stars, etc. *v.t.* [MAPPED, MAPPING], 1. to make a map of. 2. to plan: as, to *map* out an idea.

**ma·ple** (mā′p'l), *n.* [AS. *mapel*], 1. any of a large group of trees grown for wood, sap, or shade. 2. its hard, light-colored wood. 3. the flavor of the sirup or the sugar made from its sap.

**mar** (mär), *v.t.* [MARRED, MARRING], [AS. *merran*, hinder], to injure so as to make imperfect, etc.; spoil.

**Mar.,** March.

**mar·a·bou** (mar′ə-bōō′), *n.* [Fr. < Ar. *murābit*, hermit], 1. a large stork of Africa or India. 2. its plumes, used in millinery.

**ma·ra·ca** (mə-rä′kə), *n.* [< the Braz. native name], a percussion instrument made of a dried gourd or gourd-shaped rattle with pebbles in it.

**mar·a·schi·no** (mar′ə-skē′nō), *n.* [It. < *marasca*, cherry], a liqueur or cordial made from a kind of black wild cherry.

**maraschino cherries,** cherries in a sirup flavored with maraschino.

**mar·a·thon** (mar′ə-thon′), *n.* [< *Marathon*, in ancient Greece], 1. a foot race of 26 miles, 385 yards. 2. any long-distance or endurance contest.

**ma·raud** (mə-rôd), *v.i. & v.t.* [< Fr. *maraud*, vagabond], to raid and plunder.

**mar·ble** (mär′b'l), *n.* [< Gr. *marmaros*, white stone], 1. a hard limestone, white or colored, which takes a high polish. 2. a piece of this stone, used in sculpture, etc. 3. anything like marble in hardness, coldness, etc. 4. a little ball of stone, glass, etc. 5. *pl.* [construed as sing.], a children's game played with such balls. *adj.* of or like marble. *v.t.* [-BLED, -BLING], to make (paper, etc.) look mottled like marble.

**mar·cel** (mär-sel′), *n.* [< M. *Marcel*, 19th-c. Fr. hairdresser], a series of even waves put in the hair. *v.t.* [-CELLED, -CELLING], to put such waves in (hair).

**March** (märch), *n.* [< L. *Mars*, Mars], the third month of the year, having 31 days.

**march** (märch), *v.i.* [Fr. *marcher*, orig., trample], 1. to walk with regular steps, as in military formation. 2. to go, advance, or progress steadily. *v.t.* to cause to march. *n.* 1. a marching. 2. a steady advance; progress. 3. a regular, steady step. 4. the distance covered in marching. 5. a piece of music for marching. **—on the march,** marching. **—steal a march on,** to get an advantage over secretly. **—march′er,** *n.*

**march** (märch), *n.* [< Gmc. *mark*], a border or frontier of a country.

**mar·chion·ess** (mär′shən-is), *n.* 1. the wife or widow of a marquis. 2. a lady of the rank of a marquis.

**Mar·di gras** (mär′di grä′), [Fr., fat Tuesday], the last day before Lent: a day of carnival in New Orleans, etc.

**mare** (mâr), *n.* [< AS. *mearh*, horse], a female horse, mule, donkey, etc.

**mar·ga·rine** (mär′jə-rin, -rēn′), *n.* [Fr.], a blend of refined, edible, usually vegetable oil churned with skim milk: it is used like butter: also **mar′ga·rin** (-jə-rin).

**mar·gin** (mär′jin), *n.* [L. *margo*], 1. a border; edge. 2. the blank border of a printed or written page. 3. an amount beyond what is needed. 4. provision for increase, error, etc. 5. the difference between the cost and the selling price of a commodity. **—mar′gi·nal,** *adj.*

**mar·i·gold** (mar′i-gōld′), *n.* [< Virgin *Mary* + *gold*], a plant of the composite family, with red, yellow, or orange flowers.

**ma·ri·jua·na, ma·ri·hua·na** (mä′ri-hwä′nə), *n.* [Am. Sp.], 1. the hemp plant. 2. a narcotic obtained from it, smoked in cigarettes by addicts.

**ma·rim·ba** (mə-rim′bə), *n.* [< native Afr. name], a kind of xylophone with resonant tubes beneath the wooden bars.

**ma·ri·na** (mə-rē′nə), *n.* [It. & Sp., seacoast < L. *mare*, sea], a small harbor with docks, services, etc. for pleasure craft.

**mar·i·nade** (mar′ə-nād′), *n.* [Fr. < Sp. *marinar*, to pickle], 1. spiced vinegar or wine in which meats and fish are pickled. 2. meat or fish so pickled. *v.t.* (mar′ə-nād′), [-NADED, -NADING], to marinate.

**mar·i·nate** (mar′ə-nāt′), *v.t.* [-NATED, -NATING], [< *marinade* + *-ate*], 1. to soak (meat or fish) in marinade; steep in brine. 2. to steep in oil and vinegar.

**ma·rine** (mə-rēn′), *adj.* [< L. *mare*, sea], 1. of or found in the sea. 2. *a*) maritime; nautical. *b*) naval. *n.* 1. a soldier trained for service at sea. 2. [often M-], a member of the Marine Corps. 3. naval or merchant ships collectively.

**Marine Corps,** a branch of the U.S. armed forces trained for land, sea, and aerial combat.

**mar·i·ner** (mar′ə-nẽr), *n.* a sailor; seaman.

**mar·i·o·nette** (mar′i-ə-net′), *n.* [Fr. < *Marie*, Mary], a little jointed doll moved by strings or wires.

**mar·i·tal** (mar′ə-t'l), *adj.* [< L. *maritus*, a husband], of marriage. —**mar′i·tal·ly**, *adv.*

**mar·i·time** (mar′ə-tīm′), *adj.* [< L. *mare*, sea], 1. on, near, or living near the sea. 2. of navigation, shipping, etc.: as, *maritime* law.

**mar·jo·ram** (mär′jẽr-əm), *n.* [? ult. < Gr. *amarakos*], a fragrant plant of the mint family, used in cooking.

**Mark** (märk), *n.* in the *Bible*, 1. a Christian apostle, the reputed author of the second Gospel. 2. this book.

**mark** (märk), *n.* [AS. *mearc*, boundary], 1. a spot, scratch, etc. on a surface. 2. a printed or written symbol: as, punctuation *marks*. 3. a brand or label on an article showing the maker, etc. 4. an indication of some quality, character, etc. 5. a grade: as, a *mark* of B in Latin. 6. a standard of quality. 7. impression; influence. 8. an object of known position, serving as a guide. 9. a line, dot, etc. indicating position, as on a graduated scale. 10. a target; goal. *v.t.* 1. to put or make a mark or marks on. 2. to identify as by a mark. 3. to indicate by a mark. 4. to show plainly: as, her smile *marked* her joy. 5. to set off; characterize. 6. to pay attention to: as, *mark* my words. 7. to grade; rate. —**make one's mark**, to achieve fame. —**mark down** (or **up**), to mark for sale at a reduced (or an increased) price. —**mark time**, 1. to keep time while at a halt by lifting the feet as if marching. 2. to suspend progress for a time. —**mark′er**, *n.*

**mark** (märk), *n.* [AS. *marc*], the basic monetary unit of Germany.

**marked** (märkt), *adj.* 1. having a mark or marks. 2. noticeable; obvious: as, a *marked* change. —**mark·ed·ly** (mär′kid-li), *adv.*

**mar·ket** (mär′kit), *n.* [ult. < L. *merx*, merchandise], 1. a gathering of people for buying and selling things. 2. an open space or building where goods are shown for sale: also **market place**. 3. a shop for the sale of provisions: as, a meat *market*. 4. a region in which goods can be bought and sold: as, the European *market*. 5. trade; buying and selling. 6. demand for (goods, etc.): as, a good *market* for tea. *v.t.* 1. to offer for sale. 2. to sell. *v.i.* to buy provisions. —**mar′ket·a·bil′i·ty**, *n.* —**mar′ket·a·ble**, *adj.*

**mark′ing**, *n.* 1. a mark or marks. 2. the characteristic arrangement of marks, as on fur or feathers.

**mark·ka** (märk′kä), *n.* [*pl.* -KAA (-kä)], [Finn.], the monetary unit of Finland.

**marks·man** (märks′mən), *n.* [*pl.* -MEN], a person who shoots, esp. one who shoots well. —**marks′man·ship′**, *n.*

**mark′up′**, *n.* the amount added to the cost to cover overhead and profit in setting the selling price.

**marl** (märl), *n.* [< L. *marga*], a crumbly soil, mainly clay, sand, and calcium carbonate, used as a fertilizer and in making cement or bricks. *v.t.* to fertilize with marl.

**mar·lin** (mär′lin), *n.* [< *marlinespike*], a large, slender deep-sea fish.

**mar·line·spike, mar·lin·spike** (mär′lin-spīk′), *n.* a pointed iron instrument used in splicing rope.

**mar·ma·lade** (mär′mə-lād′), *n.* [ult. < Gr. *meli*, honey + *mēlon*, apple], a jamlike preserve of oranges or some other fruits and sugar.

**mar·mo·set** (mär′mə-zet′), *n.* [< OFr. *marmouset*, grotesque figure], a small monkey of S. and C. America.

**mar·mot** (mär′mət), *n.* [prob. < L. *mus montanus*, mountain mouse], any of a group of thick-bodied rodents, as the woodchuck.

**ma·roon** (mə-rōōn′), *n.* & *adj.* [Fr. *marron*, chestnut], dark brownish red.

**ma·roon** (mə-rōōn′), *v.t.* [< Sp. *cimarrón*, wild], 1. to put (a person) ashore in a desolate place and leave him there. 2. to leave abandoned, helpless, etc.

**mar·quee** (mär-kē′), *n.* [< Fr. *marquise*, orig. a shelter for a marquise], a rooflike projection over the entrance to a theater, hotel, etc.

**mar·que·try** (mär′kə-tri), *n.* [< Fr. *marque*, a mark], decorative inlaid work, as in furniture.

**mar·quis** (mär′kwis; Fr. mär′kē′), *n.* [< ML. *marchensis*, a prefect], in some European countries, a nobleman ranking above an earl or count.

**mar·quise′** (-kēz′), *n.* 1. the wife or widow of a marquis. 2. a lady of the rank of a marquis.

**mar·qui·sette** (mär′ki-zet′, -kwi-), *n.* [< Fr. *marquise*, awning], a thin, lightweight fabric with square, open meshes, used for curtains, etc.

**mar·riage** (mar′ij), *n.* 1. the state of being married; wedlock. 2. a wedding. 3. any intimate union. —**mar′riage·a·ble**, *adj.*

**mar′ried**, *adj.* 1. being husband and wife. 2. having a husband or wife. 3. of marriage.

**mar·row** (mar′ō), *n.* [AS. *mearg*], 1. the soft, fatty tissue that fills the cavities of bones. 2. the innermost or essential part.

**mar·ry** (mar′i), *v.t.* [-RIED, -RYING], [< L. *maritus*, a husband], 1. to join as husband and wife. 2. to take as husband or wife. 3. to give in marriage (often with *off*). 4. to unite. *v.i.* to get married.

**Mars** (märz), *n.* 1. the Roman god of war. 2. a planet of the solar system: cf. **planet**.

**marsh** (märsh), *n.* [AS. *mersc*], a tract of low, wet, soft land; swamp. —**marsh′y** [-IER, -IEST], *adj.* —**marsh′i·ness**, *n.*

**mar·shal** (mär′shəl), *n.* [< OHG. *marah*, horse + *scalh*, servant], 1. in various foreign armies, a general officer of the highest rank. 2. an official in charge of ceremonies, parades, etc. 3. in the U.S., *a*) a Federal officer appointed to a judicial district with duties like those of a sheriff. *b*) the head of some police or fire departments. *v.t.* [-SHALED or -SHALLED, -SHALING or -SHALLING], 1. to arrange (troops, ideas, etc.) in order. 2. to direct as a marshal; guide.

**marsh·mal·low** (märsh′mal′ō), *n.* [orig. made from the root of a mallow growing in marshes], a soft, spongy candy of sugar, gelatin, etc.

**mar·su·pi·al** (mär-sōō′pi-əl), *adj.* [< Gr. *marsypos*, a pouch], of a group of lower mammals that carry their young in an external pouch on the abdomen. *n.* an animal of this kind, as a kangaroo.

**mart** (märt), *n.* [D. *markt*], a market.

**mar·ten** (mär′t'n), *n.* [< OFr. *martre*], 1. a small mammal like a weasel but larger, with soft, thick fur. 2. the fur: also called *sable*.

**mar·tial** (mär′shəl), *adj.* [< L. *martialis*, of Mars], 1. of or suitable for war. 2. warlike; bold. 3. military. —**mar′tial·ly**, *adv.*

**martial law**, temporary rule by military authorities over civilians, as in time of war.

**Mar·tian** (mär′shən), *adj.* of Mars. *n.* a hypothetical inhabitant of Mars.

**mar·tin** (mär′t'n), *n.* [Fr.], any of various birds of the swallow family.

**mar·ti·net** (mär′t'n-et′), *n.* [after *Martinet*, 17th-c. Fr. general], a very strict disciplinarian.

**mar·tyr** (mär′tẽr), *n.* [< Gr. *martyr*, a witness], 1. one who chooses to suffer or die for his faith or principles. 2. one who suffers misery for a long time. *v.t.* to kill or persecute for adherence to a belief. —**mar′tyr·dom**, *n.*

**mar·vel** (mär′v'l), *n.* [< L. *mirari*, admire], a wonderful or astonishing thing. *v.i. & v.t.* [-VELED or -VELLED, -VELING or -VELLING], to become full of wonder (often followed by a clause).

**mar·vel·ous, mar·vel·lous** (mär′v'l-əs), *adj.* 1. causing wonder; extraordinary, etc. 2. improbable; incredible. 3. [Colloq.], fine; splendid. **—mar′vel·ous·ly, mar′vel·lous·ly,** *adv.*

**Marx·ism** (märk′siz'm), *n.* the system of thought developed by Karl Marx and Friedrich Engels, serving as a basis for socialism and communism. **—Marx′ist, Marx′i·an,** *adj. & n.*

**Mar·y** (mâr′i), *n.* in the *Bible*, the mother of Jesus.

**Mary Mag·da·lene** (mag′də-lēn′), in the *Bible*, a woman out of whom Jesus cast seven devils.

**masc., mas.,** masculine.

**mas·ca·ra** (mas-kar′ə), *n.* [< Ar. *maskharah*, buffoon], a cosmetic for coloring the eyelashes.

**mas·cot** (mas′kot), *n.* [< Fr. *masco*, sorcerer], any person, animal, or thing supposed to bring good luck.

**mas·cu·line** (mas′kyoo-lin), *adj.* [< L. *mas*, male]. 1. male; of men or boys. 2. suitable to or characteristic of men; strong, vigorous, mannish, etc. 3. in *grammar*, designating or of the gender of words referring to males or things originally regarded as male. **—mas′cu·lin′i·ty,** *n.*

**ma·ser** (mā′zẽr), *n.* [*m*icrowave *a*mplification by *s*timulated *e*mission], an electronic device that amplifies microwaves, infrared waves, etc. and emits them in a very intense beam.

**mash** (mash), *n.* [< AS. *mascwyrt*, infused malt], 1. crushed malt or grain soaked in hot water and used in brewing and distilling. 2. a mixture of bran, meal, etc. in warm water, for feeding horses, etc. 3. any soft mixture or mass. *v.t.* to change into a soft mass by beating, crushing, etc.

**mask** (mask, mäsk), *n.* [ult. < Ar. *maskharah*, buffoon], 1. a covering to conceal or protect the face. 2. anything that conceals or disguises. 3. a masquerade: often sp. **masque.** 4. *a*) a molded likeness of the face. *b*) a grotesque representation of a face, worn to amuse or frighten. *v.t.* to cover, conceal, or protect as with a mask.

**mas·och·ism** (mas′ə-kiz'm), *n.* [< L. von Sacher-*Masoch*, 19th-c. Austrian writer], the abnormal getting of pleasure from being hurt or humiliated. **—mas′och·ist,** *n.* **—mas′och·is′tic,** *adj.*

**ma·son** (mā′s'n), *n.* [< ML. *matio*], 1. one whose work is building with stone, brick, etc. 2. [M-], a Freemason.

**Ma·son·ic** (mə-son′ik), *adj.* of Freemasons or Freemasonry.

**ma·son·ry** (mā′s'n-ri), *n.* [*pl.* -RIES], 1. the trade of a mason. 2. something built by a mason; brickwork or stonework. 3. [usually M-], Freemasonry.

**masque** (mask, mäsk), *n.* [see MASK], 1. a masquerade (sense 1). 2. a former kind of dramatic entertainment, with a mythical or allegorical theme.

**mas·quer·ade** (mas'kə-rād′, mäs'-), *n.* [see MASK], 1. a ball or party at which masks and fancy costumes are worn. 2. *a*) a disguise. *b*) an acting under false pretenses. *v.i.* [-ADED, -ADING], 1. to take part in a masquerade. 2. to act under false pretenses.

**Mass, mass** (mas), *n.* [< L. *missa* in *ite, missa est* (go, you are dismissed)], in the *R. C. Church*, the service of the Eucharist.

**mass** (mas), *n.* [< Gr. *maza*, barley cake], 1. a quantity of matter of indefinite shape and size; lump. 2. a large quantity or number: as, a *mass* of bruises. 3. bulk; size. 4. the main part. 5. in *physics*, the quantity of matter in a body as measured in its relation to inertia. *v.t. & v.i.* to gather or assemble into a mass. **—the masses,** the common people.

**mas·sa·cre** (mas′ə-kẽr), *n.* [< OFr. *maçacre*, shambles], the indiscriminate, merciless killing of human beings or animals. *v.t.* [-CRED, -CRING], to kill (many people or animals).

**mas·sage** (mə-säzh′), *n.* [Fr. < Port. *amassar*, knead], a rubbing, kneading, etc. of part of the body, as to stimulate circulation. *v.t.* [-SAGED, -SAGING], to give a massage to. **—mas·sag′er,** *n.*

**mas·seur** (ma-sũr′), *n.* [Fr.], a man whose work is massaging. **—mas·seuse′** (-sooz′), *n.fem.*

**mas·sive** (mas′iv), *adj.* 1. forming or consisting of a large mass; big and heavy. 2. large and imposing. **—mas′sive·ly,** *adv.*

**mass meeting,** a large public meeting to discuss public affairs, etc.

**mass production,** quantity production of goods, esp. by machinery and division of labor.

**mast** (mast), *n.* [AS. *mæst*], a tall vertical spar used to support the sails, yards, etc. on a ship. *v.t.* to put masts on.

**mas·ter** (mas′tẽr, mäs′-), *n.* [< L. *magister*], 1. a man who rules others or has control over something; specif., *a*) one who is head of a household. *b*) an employer. *c*) the owner of an animal or slave. *d*) the captain of a merchant ship. *e*) [Chiefly Brit.], a man teacher. 2. an expert; specif., *a*) a workman skilled in his trade. *b*) an artist regarded as great. 3. [M-], a title applied to: *a*) a boy too young to be addressed as *Mr.* *b*) a person holding any of certain advanced academic degrees: as, *Master* of Arts. *adj.* 1. being master. 2. of a master. 3. chief; main; controlling. *v.t.* 1. to be or become master of. 2. to become an expert in (an art, etc.).

**mas′ter·ful,** *adj.* 1. acting the part of a master; domineering. 2. expert; skillful.

**mas′ter·ly,** *adj.* expert; skillful. *adv.* in a masterly manner. **—mas′ter·li·ness,** *n.*

**mas′ter·mind′,** *v.t.* to plan or direct (a group project, etc.).

**master of ceremonies,** a person who presides over an entertainment.

**mas′ter·piece′,** *n.* 1. a thing made or done with masterly skill. 2. the greatest work of a person or group. Also **mas′ter·work′.**

**master sergeant,** in the *U.S. armed forces*, a noncommissioned officer of the highest rank.

**mas′ter·y,** *n.* [*pl.* -IES], 1. control as by a master. 2. ascendancy or victory. 3. expert skill or knowledge. Also **mas′ter·dom.**

**mast′head′,** *n.* 1. the top part of a ship's mast. 2. that part of a newspaper or magazine stating its address, publishers, etc.

**mas·ti·cate** (mas′tə-kāt′), *v.t.* [-CATED, -CATING], [ult. < Gr. *mastax*, mouth], to chew up. **—mas′ti·ca′tion,** *n.*

**mas·tiff** (mas′tif, mäs′-), *n.* [< L. *mansuetus*, tame], a large, smooth-coated dog with powerful jaws and drooping ears.

**mas·to·don** (mas′tə-don′), *n.* [< Gr. *mastos*, breast + *odous*, tooth: from the nipplelike processes on its molars], an extinct animal resembling the elephant but larger.

**mas·toid** (mas′toid), *adj.* [< Gr. *mastos*, breast + *eidos*, form], designating, of, or near a projection of the temporal bone behind the ear. *n.* the mastoid projection.

**mas′toid·i′tis** (-ī′tis), *n.* inflammation of the mastoid.

**mas·tur·ba·tion** (mas'tẽr-bā′shən), *n.* [< L. *masturbari*], genital self-excitation. **—mas′tur·bate′** [-BATED, -BATING], *v.i.*

**mat** (mat), *n.* [< LL. *matta*], 1. a flat piece

of cloth, woven straw, etc., variously used for protection, as under a vase, etc. or on the floor. 2. anything growing or interwoven in a thick tangle. *v.t.* [MATTED, MATTING], 1. to cover as with a mat. 2. to interweave. *v.i.* to be interwoven.

**mat** (mat), *adj.* [ult. < Ar. *māt*, he is dead], not glossy; dull. *n.* 1. a dull surface or finish. 2. a border, as of cardboard, put around a picture. 3. in *printing*, a matrix.

**mat·a·dor** (mat'ə-dôr'), *n.* [< Sp. *matar*, to kill], the bullfighter who kills the bull with a sword.

**match** (mach), *n.* [< L. *myxa*, candlewick], a slender piece of wood, cardboard, etc. tipped with a composition that catches fire by friction.

**match** (mach), *n.* [AS. *gemæcca*, mate], 1. any person or thing equal or similar to another. 2. two persons or things that go well together. 3. a contest or game. 4. a marriage or mating. *v.t.* 1. to join in marriage; mate. 2. to put in opposition (*with*, *against*). 3. to be equal or similar to. 4. to make or get a counterpart or equivalent to: as, *match* this cloth. 5. to suit (one thing) to another. *v.i.* to be equal, similar, suitable, etc.

**match'less,** *adj.* having no equal.

**match'mak'er,** *n.* 1. one who arranges marriages for others. 2. one who arranges prize fights, wrestling matches, etc.

**mate** (māt), *n.* [prob. < MLG. *mate*], 1. a companion or fellow worker. 2. one of a matched pair. 3. *a*) a husband or wife. *b*) the male or female of paired animals. 4. an officer of a merchant ship, ranking below the captain. *v.t. & v.i.* [MATED, MATING], 1. to join as a pair. 2. to couple in marriage or sexual union.

**mate** (māt), *n. & v.t.* [MATED, MATING], checkmate.

**ma·te·ri·al** (mə-têr'i-əl), *adj.* [< L. *materia*, matter], 1. of matter; physical: as, a *material* object. 2. of the body or bodily needs, comfort, etc.; not spiritual. 3. important, essential, etc. *n.* 1. what a thing is, or may be, made of; elements or parts. 2. cloth.

**ma·te'ri·al·ism** (-iz'm), *n.* 1. the doctrine that everything in the world, including thought, can be explained only in terms of matter. 2. the tendency to be more concerned with material than with spiritual values. **—ma·te'ri·al·ist,** *adj. & n.* **—ma·te'ri·al·is'tic,** *adj.*

**ma·te'ri·al·ize'** (-ə-līz'), *v.t.* [-IZED, -IZING], to give material form to. *v.i.* 1. to become fact; be realized. 2. to take on bodily form: said of spirits, etc. **—ma·te'ri·al·i·za'tion,** *n.*

**ma·te'ri·al·ly,** *adv.* 1. physically. 2. to a great extent; substantially.

**ma·te·ri·el, ma·té·ri·el** (mə-têr'i-el'), *n.* [Fr.; see MATERIAL], the necessary materials and tools; specif., military weapons, supplies, etc.

**ma·ter·nal** (mə-tũr'n'l), *adj.* [< L. *mater*, mother], 1. of, like, or from a mother. 2. on the mother's side of the family.

**ma·ter·ni·ty** (mə-tũr'nə-ti), *n.* [*pl.* -TIES], the state of being a mother; motherhood. *adj.* for pregnant women.

**math** (math), *n.* [Colloq.], mathematics.

**math·e·mat·i·cal** (math'ə-mat'i-k'l), *adj.* 1. of, like, or concerned with mathematics. 2. very precise, accurate, etc.

**math·e·mat·ics** (math'ə-mat'iks), *n.pl.* [construed as sing.], [< Gr. *manthenein*, learn], the science dealing with quantities, forms, etc. and their relationships by the use of numbers and symbols. **—math'e·ma·ti'cian** (-mə-tish'ən), *n.*

**mat·in** (mat'in), *n.* [< L. *matutinus*, of the morning], 1. *pl.* [often M-], a service of morning prayer. 2. [Poetic], a morning song.

**mat·i·nee, mat·i·née** (mat''n-ā'), *n.* [< Fr. *matin*, morning], an afternoon performance of a play, etc.

**matri-,** [< L. *mater*], a combining form meaning *mother*.

**ma·tri·arch** (mā'tri-ärk'), *n.* [*matri-* + patri*arch*], 1. a woman who rules her family or tribe. 2. an aged, dignified woman. **—ma'tri·ar'chal, ma'tri·ar'chic,** *adj.*

**ma·tri·cide** (mā'trə-sīd', mat'rə-), *n.* [< L. *mater*, mother + *caedere*, kill], 1. the murder of a woman by her child. 2. one who kills his own mother.

**ma·tric·u·late** (mə-trik'yoo-lāt'), *v.t. & v.i.* [-LATED, -LATING], [see MATRIX], to enroll, esp. as a student in a college. **—ma·tric'u·la'tion,** *n.*

**mat·ri·mo·ny** (mat'rə-mō'ni), *n.* [*pl.* -NIES], [< L. *mater*, mother], 1. the act or rite of marriage. 2. the married state. **—mat'ri·mo'ni·al,** *adj.* **—mat'ri·mo'ni·al·ly,** *adv.*

**ma·trix** (mā'triks, mat'riks), *n.* [*pl.* -TRICES (-trə-sēz'), -TRIXES], [LL., womb < L. *mater*, mother], that within which something originates, takes form, etc.; specif., a mold for the face of a type or for a printing plate.

**ma·tron** (mā'trən), *n.* [< L. *mater*, mother], 1. a wife or widow. 2. a woman manager of the domestic arrangements of a hospital, prison, etc. **—ma'tron·ly,** *adj. & adv.*

**mat·ted** (mat'id), *adj.* closely tangled in a dense mass.

**mat·ter** (mat'ẽr), *n.* [< L. *materia*], 1. what a thing is made of; material. 2. whatever occupies space and is perceptible to the senses. 3. any specified substance: as, coloring *matter*. 4. content of thought or expression. 5. an amount or quantity. 6. *a*) a thing or affair: as, business *matters*. *b*) cause or occasion: as, no laughing *matter*. 7. importance; significance: as, it's of no *matter*. 8. trouble; difficulty: as, what's the *matter?* 9. pus. *v.i.* 1. to be of importance. 2. to form pus. **—as a matter of fact,** in fact; really. **—no matter,** regardless of.

**mat'ter-of-fact',** *adj.* sticking to facts; literal, practical, etc.

**Mat·thew** (math'ū), *n.* in the *Bible*, 1. a Christian apostle, the reputed author of the first Gospel. 2. this book.

**mat·ting** (mat'iŋ), *n.* 1. a fabric of straw, hemp, etc. for mats, floor covering, etc. 2. mats collectively.

**mat·tock** (mat'ək), *n.* [AS. *mattuc*], a tool like a pickax, for loosening the soil, digging up roots, etc.

**mat·tress** (mat'ris), *n.* [< Ar. *maṭraḥ*, cushion], a casing of strong cloth filled with cotton, foam rubber, coiled springs, etc. and used on a bed.

**mat·u·rate** (mach'oo-rāt', mat'yoo-), *v.i.* [-RATED, -RATING], [see MATURE], 1. to suppurate; discharge pus. 2. to ripen; mature. **—mat'u·ra'tion,** *n.*

**ma·ture** (mə-tyoor', -choor'), *adj.* [< L. *maturus*, ripe], 1. full-grown; ripe. 2. fully developed, perfected, etc. 3. due: said of a note, bond, etc. *v.t. & v.i.* [-TURED, -TURING], to make or become mature. **—ma·ture'ly,** *adv.* **—ma·tu'ri·ty,** *n.*

**matz·oth** (mät'sōth, -sōs), *n.pl.* [*sing.* MATZO (-sô)], [< Heb. *matstsāh*, unleavened], flat, thin pieces of unleavened bread, eaten during the Passover: also **matz'os** (-sōs).

**maud·lin** (môd'lin), *adj.* [< ME. *Maudeleyne*, (Mary) Magdalene (often represented as weeping)], foolishly, often tearfully sentimental.

**maul** (môl), *n.* [< L. *malleus*, a hammer], a heavy hammer for driving stakes, etc. *v.t.* 1. to bruise or lacerate. 2. to handle roughly. **—maul'er,** *n.*

**maun·der** (môn'dẽr), *v.i.* [prob. < obs. *maund*, beg], to move, act, or talk in an

aimless or rambling way. —**maun′der·er**, *n.*
**mau·so·le·um** (mô′sə-lē′əm), *n.* [*pl.* -LEUMS, -LEA (-ə)], [< the tomb of King *Mausolus*, in ancient Asia Minor], a large, imposing tomb.
**mauve** (mōv), *n.* [Fr. < L. *malva*, mallow], any of several shades of delicate purple. *adj.* of such a color.
**mav·er·ick** (mav′ẽr-ik), *n.* [after S. *Maverick*, 19th-c. Texan whose cattle had no brand], 1. an unbranded animal, esp. a lost calf. 2. [Colloq.], a person who acts independently of any organization, political party, etc.
**maw** (mô), *n.* [AS. *maga*], 1. orig., the stomach. 2. the crop of a bird. 3. the throat, gullet, jaws, etc.
**mawk·ish** (môk′ish), *adj.* [< ON. *mathkr*, maggot], 1. sickening. 2. sentimental in a weak, sickly way. —**mawk′ish·ly**, *adv.*
**max·il·la** (mak-sil′ə), *n.* [*pl.* -LAE (-ē)], [L.], a jaw or jawbone, esp. the upper one. —**max·il·lar·y** (mak′sə-ler′i, mak-sil′ə-ri), *adj.*
**max·im** (mak′sim), *n.* [< L. *maxima* (*propositio*), the greatest (premise)], a concise rule of conduct; adage.
**max·i·mum** (mak′sə-məm), *n.* [*pl.* -MUMS, -MA (-mə)], [< L. superl. of *magnus*, great], 1. the greatest quantity, number, etc. possible. 2. the highest degree or point reached. *adj.* greatest or highest possible or reached.
**May** (mā), *n.* [< L. *Maius*], the fifth month of the year, having 31 days.
**may** (mā), *v.* [pt. MIGHT], [ME. *mai*], an auxiliary expressing: 1. possibility: as, it *may* rain. 2. permission: as, you *may* go: see also **can.** 3. contingency: as, be quiet so that we *may* hear. 4. wish or hope: as, *may* he win!
**Ma·ya** (mä′yə), *n.* 1. a member of a race of Indians of SE Mexico and Central America, who had a highly developed civilization. 2. their language. *adj.* of the Mayas or Maya. —**Ma′yan**, *adj. & n.*
**may·be** (mā′bi, -bē), *adv.* [ME. (for *it may be*)], perhaps; possibly.
**May Day**, May 1: celebrated as a traditional spring festival: in many countries, a labor holiday.
**May·flow·er** (mā′flou′ẽr), *n.* 1. an early spring flower; esp., the trailing arbutus. 2. the ship on which the Pilgrims came to America (1620).
**may·hem** (mā′hem, -əm), *n.* [see MAIM], in *law*, the offense of maiming a person intentionally.
**may·on·naise** (mā′ə-nāz′), *n.* [< *Mahon*, port on a Sp. island], a creamy salad dressing made of egg yolks, olive oil, seasoning, etc.
**may·or** (mā′ẽr, mâr), *n.* [< L. *major*, greater], the chief administrative official of a municipality.
**may′or·al·ty** (-əl-ti), *n.* [*pl.* -TIES], the office or term of office of a mayor.
**May′pole′**, *n.* a high pole around which merrymakers dance on May Day.
**mayst** (māst), [Archaic], may: with *thou*.
**maze** (māz), *n.* [< AS. *amazian*, amaze], 1. a confusing, intricate network of pathways; labyrinth. 2. a state of confusion.
**M.C.**, Master of Ceremonies.
**MD.**, Middle Dutch.
**M.D.**, Doctor of Medicine.
**me** (mē), *pron.* [AS.], the objective case of **I.**
**ME.**, Middle English.
**mead** (mēd), *n.* [AS. *meodu*], an alcoholic liquor made of fermented honey.
**mead** (mēd), *n.* [Poetic], a meadow.
**mead·ow** (med′ō), *n.* [< AS. *mæd*], 1. a piece of land where grass is grown for hay. 2. low, level grassland near a stream, etc.
**meadow lark**, any of various N. American songbirds with a yellow breast.
**mea·ger, mea·gre** (mē′gẽr), *adj.* [< L. *macer*, lean], 1. thin; lean. 2. poor; not rich or fertile. —**mea′ger·ly**, *adv.*
**meal** (mēl), *n.* [AS. *mæl*], 1. any of the times for eating; lunch, dinner, etc. 2. the food served or eaten at one time.
**meal** (mēl), *n.* [AS. *melu*], 1. any edible grain, coarsely ground: as, corn *meal*. 2. any substance similarly ground or powdered. —**meal′y** [-IER, -IEST], *adj.*
**meal′time′**, *n.* the usual time for serving or eating a meal.
**meal·y-mouthed** (mēl′i-mouthd′, -moutht′), *adj.* not willing to state the facts in simple, direct words.
**mean** (mēn), *v.t.* [MEANT (ment), MEANING], [AS. *mænan*], 1. to have in mind; intend: as, he *means* to go. 2. to intend to express: as, what do you *mean*? 3. to signify; denote: as, the word *means* "yes." *v.i.* to have a (specified) degree of importance, effect, etc.: as, she *means* little to him. —**mean well**, to have good intentions.
**mean** (mēn), *adj.* [AS. (*ge*)*mæne*], 1. low in quality or grade. 2. low in social status. 3. trivial; paltry. 4. poor in appearance; shabby. 5. ignoble; petty. 6. stingy. 7. [Colloq.], contemptibly selfish, bad-tempered, etc. —**mean′ly**, *adv.* —**mean′ness**, *n.*
**mean** (mēn), *adj.* [< L. *medius*, middle], 1. halfway between extremes. 2. average. *n.* 1. what is between extremes. 2. in *math.*, a quantity intermediate in value between other quantities; esp., an average.
**me·an·der** (mi-an′dẽr), *v.i.* [< Gr. *Maiandros*, a winding river in Asia Minor], 1. to take a winding course: said of a stream. 2. to wander idly. —**me·an′der·er**, *n.*
**mean′ing**, *n.* what is meant; what is intended to be signified, indicated, etc.; import: as, a look full of *meaning*. *adj.* 1. significant. 2. intending. —**mean′ing·ful**, *adj.* —**mean′ing·less**, *adj.*
**means** (mēnz), *n.pl.* 1. [construed as sing. or pl.], that by which something is done or obtained: as, a *means* to an end. 2. resources; property. —**by all means**, 1. without fail. 2. certainly. —**by means of**, by using. —**by no means**, certainly not.
**meant** (ment), pt. and pp. of **mean.**
**mean′time′**, *adv.* in the intervening time; at the same time. *n.* the intervening time. Also **mean′while′**.
**mea·sles** (mē′z'lz), *n.pl.* [construed as sing.], [ME. *maseles*], 1. an acute, infectious, communicable virus disease, usually of children, characterized by a skin eruption, high fever, etc. 2. a similar but milder disease: in full, **German measles.**
**mea·sly** (mēz′li), *adj.* [-SLIER, -SLIEST], 1. having measles. 2. [Colloq.], contemptibly slight or worthless.
**meas·ure** (mezh′ẽr), *n.* [< L. *metiri*, to measure], 1. the extent, dimensions, capacity, etc. of anything. 2. a determining of this; measurement. 3. *a*) a unit of measurement. *b*) any standard of valuation. 4. a system of measurement. 5. an instrument for measuring. 6. a definite quantity measured out. 7. a course of action: as, reform *measures*. 8. a statute; law. 9. a rhythmical pattern or unit; specif., the notes and rests between two bars on a musical staff. *v.t.* [-URED, -URING], 1. to find out or estimate the extent, dimensions, etc. of, esp. by a standard. 2. to mark off by measuring. 3. to be a measure of. *v.i.* 1. to take measurements. 2. to be of specified measurements. —**beyond measure**, exceedingly. —**in a measure**, to some extent. —**meas′ur·a·ble**, *adj.* —**meas′ure·less**, *adj.*
**meas′ure·ment**, *n.* 1. a measuring or being measured. 2. extent or quantity determined by measuring. 3. a system of measuring.

**meat** (mēt), *n.* [AS. *mete*], 1. food: now esp. in phr. *meat and drink.* 2. the flesh of animals, usually of mammals, used as food. 3. the edible part: as, the *meat* of a nut. 4. the substance or essence. —**meat'less,** *adj.* —**meat'y** [-IER, -IEST], *adj.*

**me·chan·ic** (mə-kan'ik), *n.* [< Gr. *mēchanē*, machine], a worker skilled in using tools or repairing machines.

**me·chan'i·cal,** *adj.* 1. having to do with machinery or tools. 2. produced or operated by machinery. 3. of the science of mechanics. 4. machinelike; spiritless.

**me·chan'ics,** *n.pl.* [construed as sing.], 1. the science of motion and the action of forces on bodies. 2. knowledge of machinery. 3. the technical aspect: as, the *mechanics* of poetry.

**mech·a·nism** (mek'ə-niz'm), *n.* [see MECHANIC], 1. the working parts of a machine. 2. any system of interrelated parts. 3. any physical or mental process by which a result is produced. 4. the mechanical aspect.

**mech'a·nize'** (-nīz'), *v.t.* [-NIZED, -NIZING], 1. to make mechanical. 2. to equip (an industry) with machinery or (an army, etc.) with motor vehicles, tanks, etc. —**mech'a·ni·za'tion,** *n.*

**med·al** (med''l), *n.* [< L. *metallum*, metal], a small, flat piece of metal having an inscription commemorating some event, or awarded for some distinguished action, merit, etc.

**med·al·ist, med·al·list** (med''l-ist), *n.* 1. one who makes medals. 2. one who has been awarded a medal.

**me·dal·lion** (mə-dal'yən), *n.* [< Fr.], 1. a large medal. 2. a design, portrait, etc. shaped like a medal.

**med·dle** (med''l), *v.i.* [-DLED, -DLING], [< L. *miscere*, mix], to interfere with another's affairs. —**med'dler,** *n.* —**med'dle·some,** *adj.*

**me·di·a** (mē'di-ə), *n.* alt. pl. of **medium.**

**me·di·al** (mē'di-əl), *adj.* [< L. *medius*], 1. middle. 2. average; ordinary.

**me·di·an** (mē'di-ən), *adj.* 1. middle; intermediate. 2. designating the middle number in a series. *n.* a median number, point, or line.

**me·di·ate** (mē'di-āt'), *v.i.* [-ATED, -ATING], 1. to be in an intermediate position. 2. to be an intermediary. *v.t.* to settle (differences) between persons, nations, etc. by intercession. *adj.* (-it), 1. intermediate. 2. dependent on an intervening agency. —**me'di·a'tion,** *n.* —**me'di·a'tor,** *n.*

**med·ic** (med'ik), *n.* [Colloq.], 1. a physician or surgeon. 2. a member of a military medical corps.

**med·i·cal** (med'i-k'l), *adj.* of or connected with the practice or study of medicine.

**me·dic·a·ment** (mə-dik'ə-mənt), *n.* a medicine.

**Med·i·care** (med'i-kâr'), *n.* a system of Federal government insurance to provide medical and hospital care for the aged.

**med·i·cate** (med'i-kāt'), *v.t.* [-CATED, -CATING], [< L. *medicari*, heal], to treat with medicine. —**med'i·ca'tion,** *n.*

**me·dic·i·nal** (mə-dis''n-'l), *adj.* of, or having the properties of, medicine.

**med·i·cine** (med'ə-s'n), *n.* [< L. *medicus*, physician], 1. the science and art of treating and preventing disease. 2. any substance, as a drug, used in treating disease, relieving pain, etc.

**med'i·co'** (-kō'), *n.* [*pl.* -COS], [It.], [Colloq.], a physician.

**me·di·e·val** (mē'di-ē'v'l), *adj.* [< L. *medius*, middle + *aevum*, age], of, like, or characteristic of the Middle Ages. —**me'di·e'val·ism,** *n.* —**me'di·e'val·ist,** *n.*

**me·di·o·cre** (mē'di-ō'kēr), *adj.* [< L. *medius*, middle + *ocris*, peak], of middle quality; ordinary. —**me'di·oc'ri·ty** (-ok'rə-ti) [*pl.* -TIES], *n.*

**med·i·tate** (med'ə-tāt'), *v.t.* [-TATED, -TATING], [< L. *meditari*], to plan; intend. *v.i.* to think deeply; reflect. —**med'i·ta'tion,** *n.* —**med'i·ta'tive,** *adj.*

**Med·i·ter·ra·ne·an** (med'ə-tə-rā'ni-ən), *adj.* [< L. *medius*, middle + *terra*, land], of the Mediterranean Sea or near-by regions.

**me·di·um** (mē'di-əm), *n.* [*pl.* -DIUMS, -DIA], [L. < *medius*, middle], 1. *a*) something intermediate. *b*) a middle state or degree; mean. 2. an intervening thing through which a force acts. 3. any means, agency, etc.: as, a *medium* of communication. 4. any surrounding substance or environment. 5. one through whom messages are supposedly sent from the dead. *adj.* intermediate in quantity, quality, etc.

**med·ley** (med'li), *n.* [*pl.* -LEYS], [ult. < L. *miscere*, mix], 1. a mixture of dissimilar things. 2. a musical piece made up of passages from other songs, etc. *adj.* mixed.

**me·dul·la** (mi-dul'ə), *n.* [*pl.* -LAE (-ē)], [L., the marrow], in *anatomy*, 1. the marrow of bones. 2. the inner substance of an organ. 3. a widening of the spinal cord forming the lowest part of the brain: in full, **medulla ob·lon·ga·ta** (ob'lôŋ-gā'tə).

**Me·du·sa** (mə-dōō'sə, -dū'zə), *n.* 1. in *Gr. myth.*, a monster with snakes for hair: slain by Perseus. 2. [m-], [*pl.* -SAS, -SAE (-sē, -zē)], a jellyfish.

**meek** (mēk), *adj.* [< ON. *miukr*, gentle], 1. patient and mild. 2. tamely submissive; spiritless. —**meek'ly,** *adv.* —**meek'ness,** *n.*

**meer·schaum** (mêr'shəm, -shôm'), *n.* [G. < *meer*, sea + *schaum*, foam], 1. a white, claylike mineral used for tobacco pipes. 2. a tobacco pipe made of this.

**meet** (mēt), *v.t.* [MET, MEETING], [AS. *metan*], 1. to come upon; confront. 2. to be present at the arrival of: as, to *meet* a bus. 3. to come into contact with. 4. to be introduced to. 5. to oppose or contend with. 6. to experience: as, to *meet* disaster. 7. to be perceived by (the eye, etc.). 8. *a*) to satisfy (a demand, etc.). *b*) to pay (a bill, etc.). *v.i.* 1. to come together. 2. to come into contact, etc. 3. to be introduced. 4. to assemble. *n.* a meeting: as, a track *meet.* —**meet with,** 1. to experience. 2. to receive.

**meet** (mēt), *adj.* [< AS. (*ge*)*mæte*, fitting], suitable; appropriate. —**meet'ly,** *adv.*

**meet'ing,** *n.* 1. a coming together. 2. a gathering of people. 3. a point of contact; junction. 4. a duel.

**mega-,** [Gr. < *megas*, great], a combining form meaning: 1. *large, great, powerful.* 2. *a million of.*

**meg·a·cy·cle** (meg'ə-sī'k'l), *n.* [*mega-* + *cycle*], in *physics*, one million cycles.

**meg·a·lo·ma·ni·a** (meg'ə-lə-mā'ni-ə), *n.* [< Gr. *megas*, large; + *-mania*], a mental disorder characterized by delusions of grandeur, power, etc. —**meg'a·lo·ma'ni·ac** (-ak), *adj.* & *n.*

**meg·a·lop·o·lis** (meg'ə-lop'ə-lis), *n.* [Gr., great city], a vast, populous, continuously urban area.

**meg·a·phone** (meg'ə-fōn'), *n.* [*mega-* + *-phone*], a funnel-shaped device for increasing the volume of the voice.

**meg·a·ton** (meg'ə-tun'), *n.* [*mega-* + *ton*], the explosive force of a million tons of TNT.

**mel·an·cho·li·a** (mel'ən-kō'li-ə), *n.* a mental disorder characterized by extreme depression of spirits.

**mel·an·chol·y** (mel'ən-kol'i), *n.* [< Gr. *melas*, black + *cholē*, bile], sadness and depression of spirits. *adj.* 1. sad or depressed; gloomy. 2. causing sadness.

**Mel·a·ne·sian** (mel'ə-nē'zhən), *adj.* of Melanesia, a group of islands in the South

Pacific, its people, languages, etc. *n.* 1. a member of the dark-skinned native people of Melanesia. 2. any of their languages.
‡**mé·lange** (mā'länzh'), *n.* [Fr. < *mêler*, to mix], a mixture; medley.
**Mel·ba toast** (mel'bə), [< N. *Melba* (1861?–1931), Australian soprano], very thinly sliced, crisp toast.
**meld** (meld), *v.t. & v.i.* [G. *melden*, announce], in *pinochle*, etc., to declare (a combination of cards in one's hand) for inclusion in one's score. *n.* 1. a melding. 2. the score made by melding.
**me·lee, mê·lée** (mā-lā', mā'lā), *n.* [Fr.], a confused, general hand-to-hand fight between groups.
**mel·io·rate** (mēl'yə-rāt'), *v.t. & v.i.* [-RATED, -RATING], [< L. *melior*, better], to make or become better. —**mel'io·ra'tion**, *n.*
**mel·lif·lu·ous** (mə-lif'lo͞o-əs), *adj.* [< L. *mel*, honey + *fluere*, to flow], flowing sweetly and smoothly; honeyed: said of words, sounds, etc.: also **mel·lif'lu·ent.** —**mel·lif'lu·ence**, *n.* —**mel·lif'lu·ous·ly**, *adv.*
**mel·low** (mel'ō), *adj.* [prob. < AS. *melu*, meal (ground grain)], 1. soft, sweet, etc. because ripe: said of fruit. 2. full-flavored: said of wine, etc. 3. full, rich, soft, etc.: said of sound, light, etc. 4. made gentle and understanding by experience. *v.t. & v.i.* to make or become mellow.
**me·lo·de·on** (mə-lō'di-ən), *n.* [pseudo-Gr. form < *melody*], a small reed organ.
**me·lo·di·ous** (mə-lō'di-əs), *adj.* 1. containing or producing melody. 2. pleasing to hear; tuneful. —**me·lo'di·ous·ly**, *adv.*
**mel·o·dra·ma** (mel'ə-drä'mə, -dram'ə), *n.* [< Gr. *melos*, song + *drama*, drama], a drama with sensational action, extravagant emotions, and, generally, a happy ending. —**mel'o·dra·mat'ic** (-drə-mat'ik), *adj.*
**mel·o·dy** (mel'ə-di), *n.* [*pl.* -DIES], [< Gr. *melos*, song + *aedein*, sing], 1. pleasing sounds in sequence. 2. in *music*, *a*) a tune, song, etc. *b*) the leading part in a harmonic composition. —**me·lod·ic** (mə-lod'ik), *adj.*
**mel·on** (mel'ən), *n.* [< Gr. *mēlon*, apple], the large, juicy, many-seeded fruit of certain trailing plants of the gourd family, as the watermelon, cantaloupe, etc.
**melt** (melt), *v.t. & v.i.* [AS. *m(i)eltan*], 1. to change from a solid to a liquid state, generally by heat. 2. to dissolve. 3. to disappear or cause to disappear gradually (often with *away*). 4. to merge gradually. 5. to soften: as, her grief *melted* our hearts.
**mem·ber** (mem'bẽr), *n.* [< L. *membrum*], 1. a limb or other part of a person, animal, or plant. 2. a distinct part of a whole. 3. any of the persons constituting an organization or group.
**mem'ber·ship'**, *n.* 1. the state of being a member. 2. all the members of a group. 3. the number of members.
**mem·brane** (mem'brān'), *n.* [< L. *membrum*, member], a thin, soft layer of animal or plant tissue, that covers or lines an organ or part. —**mem'bra·nous** (-brə-nəs), *adj.*
**me·men·to** (mi-men'tō), *n.* [*pl.* -TOS, -TOES], [L. < *meminisse*, remember], a reminder; souvenir.
**mem·o** (mem'ō), *n.* [*pl.* -OS], [Colloq.], a memorandum.
**mem·oirs** (mem'wärz), *n.pl.* [< L. *memoria*], a record of events that is based on the writer's personal experience and knowledge; often, an autobiography.
**mem·o·ra·bil·i·a** (mem'ẽr-ə-bil'i-ə), *n.pl.* [*sing.* -ORABILE (-ə-rab'ə-lē'), [L.], noteworthy events.
**mem·o·ra·ble** (mem'ẽr-ə-b'l), *adj.* worth remembering; notable. —**mem'o·ra·bly**, *adv.*
**mem·o·ran·dum** (mem'ə-ran'dəm), *n.* [*pl.* -DUMS, -DA (-də)], [L.], 1. a short note written to remind oneself of something. 2. an informal written communication, as in a business office.
**me·mo·ri·al** (mə-môr'i-əl), *adj.* [see MEMORY], serving as a remembrance. *n.* anything meant to help people remember a person, event, etc., as a monument, holiday, etc. —**me·mo'ri·al·ize'** [-IZED, -IZING], *v.t.*
**Memorial Day,** a U.S. holiday, on May 30 in most States, for honoring the dead of the armed forces; Decoration Day.
**mem·o·rize** (mem'ə-rīz'), *v.t.* [-RIZED, -RIZING], to commit to memory.
**mem·o·ry** (mem'ẽr-i), *n.* [*pl.* -RIES], [< L. *memor*, mindful], 1. the power or act of remembering. 2. all that one remembers. 3. something remembered. 4. the period over which remembering extends: as, not within my *memory*. 5. commemoration.
**men** (men), *n.* pl. of **man.**
**men·ace** (men'is), *n.* [< L. *minari*, threaten], a threat or threatening. *v.t. & v.i.* [-ACED, -ACING], to threaten.
**mé·nage, me·nage** (mā-näzh'), *n.* [< Fr. < L. *mansio*, house], a household.
**me·nag·er·ie** (mə-naj'ẽr-i), *n.* [see MÉNAGE], a collection of wild animals kept in cages, etc., esp. for exhibition.
**mend** (mend), *v.t.* [see AMEND], 1. to repair. 2. to make better; reform: as, *mend* your manners. *v.i.* to improve, esp. in health. *n.* 1. a mending. 2. a mended place. —**on the mend**, improving, esp. in health.
**men·da·cious** (men-dā'shəs), *adj.* [< L. *mendax*], lying; untruthful. —**men·da'cious·ly**, *adv.* —**men·dac'i·ty** (-das'ə-ti), *n.*
**men·di·cant** (men'di-kənt), *adj.* [< L. *mendicus*, needy], begging. *n.* 1. a beggar. 2. a mendicant friar. —**men'di·can·cy**, *n.*
**Men·e·la·us** (men'ə-lā'əs), *n.* in *Gr. legend*, a king of Sparta and husband of Helen.
**men'folk'**, *n.pl.* [Dial.], men: also **menfolks.**
**me·ni·al** (mē'ni-əl), *adj.* [< L. *mansio*, house], 1. of or fit for servants. 2. servile; low. *n.* 1. a domestic servant. 2. a servile, low person. —**me'ni·al·ly**, *adv.*
**me·nin·ges** (mə-nin'jēz), *n.pl.* [< Gr. *mēninx*, a membrane], the three membranes that envelop the brain and spinal cord.
**men·in·gi·tis** (men'in-ji'tis), *n.* inflammation of the meninges.
**Men·non·ite** (men'ən-īt'), *n.* [< *Menno* Simons, 16th-c. D. reformer], a member of an evangelical Christian sect opposed to military service, taking of oaths, etc.
**men·o·pause** (men'ə-pôz'), *n.* [< Gr. *mēn*, month + *pauein*, to end], the permanent, natural cessation of menstruation.
**men·ses** (men'sēz), *n.pl.* [L., pl. of *mensis*, month], the periodic flow, usually monthly, of blood from the uterus.
**men·stru·al** (men'stro͞o-əl), *adj.* 1. of the menses. 2. in *astron.*, monthly.
**men·stru·ate** (men'stro͞o-āt'), *v.i.* [-ATED, -ATING], [< L. *mensis*, month], to have a discharge of the menses. —**men'stru·a'tion**, *n.*
**men·su·ra·tion** (men'shə-rā'shən), *n.* [< L. *mensura*, measure], a measuring.
**-ment,** [< L. *-mentum*], a suffix meaning: 1. *a result of*, as in *improvement*. 2. *a means for*, as in *adornment*. 3. *the act of*, as in *movement*. 4. *the state of being*, as in *bereavement*.
**men·tal** (men't'l), *adj.* [< L. *mens*, the mind], 1. of, for, by, or in the mind. 2. mentally ill: as, a *mental* patient. 3. for the mentally ill: as, a *mental* hospital.
**mental deficiency,** subnormality of intelligence.
**men·tal·i·ty** (men-tal'ə-ti), *n.* [*pl.* -TIES], mental capacity or power; mind.
**men'tal·ly**, *adv.* 1. in, with, or by the mind. 2. as regards the mind.
**men·thol** (men'thol, -thôl), *n.* [G. < L. *mentha*, mint], a white, waxy, crystalline

alcohol obtained from oil of peppermint and used in medicine and perfumery. —**men'tho·lat'ed** (-thə-lā'tid), *adj.*
**men·tion** (men'shən), *n.* [< L. *mens*, the mind], a brief reference. *v.t.* to refer to briefly or incidentally. —**make mention of,** to mention. —**men'tion·a·ble,** *adj.*
**men·tor** (men'tẽr), *n.* [< *Mentor*, friend of Odysseus], a wise, loyal adviser.
**men·u** (men'ū, mā'nū), *n.* [*pl.* -US], [Fr. < L. *minutus*, small], a detailed list of the foods served at a meal.
**me·ow, me·ou** (mi-ou'), *n.* [echoic], the characteristic vocal sound made by a cat. *v.i.* to make this sound.
**me·phit·ic** (me-fit'ik), *adj.* [< L. *mephitis*, a stench], 1. bad-smelling. 2. poisonous.
**mer·can·tile** (mũr'kən-til, -til'), *adj.* [see MERCHANT], 1. of or characteristic of merchants or trade. 2. of mercantilism.
**mer·can·til·ism** (mũr'kən-til-iz'm, -tīl-), *n.* 1. the doctrine or policy that a balance of exports over imports is desirable. 2. the practice of this policy. —**mer'can·til·ist,** *n.*
**mer·ce·nar·y** (mũr'sə-ner'i), *adj.* [< L. *merces*, wages], working or done for payment only. *n.* [*pl.* -IES], a soldier serving in a foreign army for pay.
**mer·cer** (mũr'sẽr), *n.* [< L. *merx*, wares], [Brit.], a dealer in textiles.
**mer·cer·ize** (mũr'sə-rīz'), *v.t.* [-IZED, -IZING], [< J. *Mercer*, 19th-c. Eng. calico dealer], to treat (cotton thread or fabric) with an alkali solution to strengthen it, give it a gloss, etc.
**mer·chan·dise** (mũr'chən-dīz'; *for n., also* -dīs'), *n.* [see MERCHANT], things bought and sold; wares. *v.t. & v.i.* [-DISED, -DISING], to buy and sell. —**mer'chan·dis'er,** *n.*
**mer·chant** (mũr'chənt), *n.* [ult. < L. *merx*, wares], 1. one whose business is buying and selling goods. 2. a dealer at retail; storekeeper. *adj.* mercantile.
**mer'chant·man** (-mən), *n.* [*pl.* -MEN], a vessel used in commerce.
**merchant marine,** all the ships of a nation that are used in commerce.
‡**mer·ci** (mâr'sē'), *interj.* [Fr.], thank you.
**mer·ci·ful** (mũr'si-fəl), *adj.* having or showing mercy. —**mer'ci·ful·ly,** *adv.*
**mer'ci·less,** *adj.* without mercy; pitiless.
**mer·cu·ri·al** (mẽr-kyoor'i-əl), *adj.* having qualities suggestive of mercury; quick, changeable, fickle, etc.—**mer·cu'ri·al·ly,** *adv.*
**mer·cu·ro·chrome** (mẽr-kyoor'ə-krōm'), *n.* [see MERCURY & -CHROME], a solution of a compound of mercury, used as an antiseptic: a trademark (**Mercurochrome**).
**Mer·cu·ry** (mũr'kyoo-ri), *n.* 1. a Roman god who was the messenger of the other gods. 2. the smallest planet in the solar system: cf. **planet.** 3. [m-], a heavy, silver-white metallic chemical element, liquid at ordinary temperatures, used in thermometers, dentistry, etc.; quicksilver: symbol, Hg.
**mer·cy** (mũr'si), *n.* [*pl.* -CIES], [< L. *merces*, payment], 1. a refraining from harming offenders, enemies, etc. 2. a disposition to forgive or be kind. 3. the power to forgive. 4. a fortunate thing. —**at the mercy of,** in the power of.
**mere** (mêr), *adj.* [superl. MEREST], [< L. *merus*, pure], nothing more or other than; only (as said to be).
**mere'ly,** *adv.* only; simply.
**mer·e·tri·cious** (mer'ə-trish'əs), *adj.* [< L. *meretrix*, a prostitute], alluring by false, showy charms; tawdry.
**mer·gan·ser** (mẽr-gan'sẽr), *n.* [< L. *mergus*, diver + *anser*, goose], a large, fish-eating, diving duck with a crested head.
**merge** (mũrj), *v.i. & v.t.* [MERGED, MERGING], [L. *mergere*, to dip], to lose or cause to lose identity by being absorbed, combined, etc.
**merg'er,** *n.* 1. a merging; specif., the combination of several companies in one. 2. something formed by merging.
**me·rid·i·an** (mə-rid'i-ən), *n.* [< L. *meridies*, noon], 1. the highest point reached by a heavenly body in its course. 2. the highest point of power, etc. 3. a great circle on the earth's surface passing through the geographical poles and any given point; specif., any of the lines of longitude.
**me·ringue** (mə-raŋ'), *n.* [Fr.], egg whites beaten stiff and mixed with sugar: used as a pie covering, etc.
**me·ri·no** (mə-rē'nō), *n.* [*pl.* -NOS], [Sp., shepherd], 1. one of a breed of sheep with long, fine wool. 2. the wool. 3. a soft yarn or cloth made of it.
**mer·it** (mer'it), *n.* [< L. *mereri*, earn], 1. worth; value; excellence. 2. something deserving reward, praise, etc. 3. *pl.* actual qualities or facts, good or bad. *v.t.* to deserve. —**mer'it·ed,** *adj.*
**mer·i·to·ri·ous** (mer'ə-tôr'i-əs), *adj.* having merit; deserving reward, praise, etc.
**Mer·lin** (mũr'lin), *n.* in *legend*, a magician and seer, helper of King Arthur.
**mer·maid** (mũr'mād'), *n.* [< AS. *mere*, sea; + *maid*], a legendary sea creature with the head and trunk of a woman and the tail of a fish. —**mer'man'** [*pl.* -MEN], *n.masc.*
**mer·ri·ment** (mer'i-mənt), *n.* gaiety and fun; mirth.
**mer·ry** (mer'i), *adj.* [-RIER, -RIEST], [AS. *myrge*], 1. full of fun and laughter; gay. 2. festive. —**make merry,** to be gay or festive. —**mer'ri·ly,** *adv.* —**mer'ri·ness,** *n.*
**mer'ry-go-round',** *n.* 1. a circular, revolving platform with wooden animals and seats on it, used as an amusement ride; carrousel. 2. a whirl.
**mer'ry·mak'ing,** *n.* a having fun; festivity.
**me·sa** (mā'sə), *n.* [Sp. < L. *mensa*, table], a high plateau or flat tableland with steep sides.
**mes·dames** (mā-däm'), *n.* [Fr.], pl. of **madame, madam** (sense 1), or **Mrs.**
**mesh** (mesh), *n.* [prob. < MD. *maesche*], 1. any of the open spaces of a net, screen, etc. 2. a net or network. *v.t. & v.i.* 1. to entangle or become entangled. 2. to engage or become engaged: said of gears, etc. —**in mesh,** with the gears engaged.
**mes·mer·ize** (mes'mə-rīz', mez'-), *v.t.* [-IZED, -IZING], [< F. A. *Mesmer*, 18th-c. G. physician], to hypnotize. —**mes'mer·ism,** *n.* —**mes'mer·ist,** *n.*
**mes·on** (mes'on, mē'son), *n.* [< Gr. *mesos*, middle; + electr*on*], an unstable particle, between the electron and the proton in mass, first observed in cosmic rays.
**mes·quite, mes·quit** (mes-kēt'), *n.* [< Mex. Ind. *mizquitl*], a spiny shrub growing in the Southwest and Mexico.
**mess** (mes), *n.* [< L. *missus*, course (at a meal)], 1. a serving, as of porridge. 2. a group of people who regularly eat together, as in the army. 3. the meal they eat. 4. a jumble. 5. a state of trouble. 6. a disorderly or dirty condition. *v.t.* 1. to make dirty or untidy. 2. to bungle; botch. Often with *up*. *v.i.* 1. to eat as one of a mess. 2. to make a mess. 3. to putter or meddle (often with *around* or *about*).
**mes·sage** (mes'ij), *n.* [< L. *mittere*, send], 1. any communication sent between persons. 2. a formal, official communication. 3. an inspired communication, as of a poet.
**mes·sen·ger** (mes'n-jẽr), *n.* 1. one who carries a message, does errands, etc. 2. [Archaic], a forerunner.
**Mes·si·ah** (mə-sī'ə), *n.* [< Heb. *māshīah*, anointed], 1. in *Judaism*, the expected deliverer of the Jews. 2. in *Christianity*, Jesus. —**Mes·si·an·ic** (mes'i-an'ik), *adj.*

**mes·sieurs** (mes'ẽrz; Fr. mā'syoo'), *n.* [Fr.], pl. of **monsieur.**
**Messrs.** (mes'ẽrz), Messieurs: now used chiefly as the plural of **Mr.**
**mess·y** (mes'i), *adj.* [-IER, -IEST], in or like a mess; untidy, dirty, etc. —**mess'i·ness,** *n.*
**mes·ti·zo** (mes-tē'zō), *n.* [*pl.* -ZOS, -ZOES], [Sp. < L. *miscere*, mix], a person of mixed parentage, esp. American Indian and Spanish. —**mes·ti'za** (-zə), *n.fem.*
**met** (met), pt. and pp. of **meet.**
**meta-,** [< Gr. *meta*, after], a prefix meaning: 1. *changed*, as in *metamorphosis*. 2. *after, beyond, higher*, as in *metaphysics*.
**me·tab·o·lism** (mə-tab'ə-liz'm), *n.* [< Gr. *meta*, beyond + *ballein*, throw], the processes in organisms by which protoplasm is formed from food and broken down into waste matter, with release of energy. —**met·a·bol·ic** (met'ə-bol'ik), *adj.*
**met·al** (met''l), *n.* [< Gr. *metallon*, mine], 1. *a*) any of a class of chemical elements, as iron, gold, copper, etc., that have luster, can conduct heat and electricity, etc. *b*) an alloy of such elements, as brass, bronze, etc. 2. anything consisting of metal. *adj.* made of metal. —**me·tal·lic** (mə-tal'ik), *adj.*
**met·al·lur·gy** (met''l-ũr'ji), *n.* [< Gr. *metallon*, metal + *-ergos*, working], the science of separating metals from their ores and preparing them for use, by refining, etc. —**met'al·lur'gi·cal,** *adj.* —**met'al·lur'gist,** *n.*
**met·a·mor·phism** (met'ə-môr'fiz'm), *n.* metamorphosis; change of form.
**met·a·mor·phose** (met'ə-môr'fōz, -fōs), *v.t. & v.i.* [-PHOSED, -PHOSING], to change in form; transform.
**met·a·mor·pho·sis** (met'ə-môr'fə-sis, -môr-fō'-), *n.* [*pl.* -SES (-sēz')], [< Gr. *meta*, over + *morphē*, form], 1. a change in form, structure, or function; specif., the physical change undergone by some animals, as of tadpole to frog. 2. any marked change, as in character. —**met'a·mor'phic,** *adj.*
**met·a·phor** (met'ə-fẽr, -fôr'), *n.* [< Gr. *meta*, over + *pherein*, carry], a figure of speech in which one thing is spoken of as if it were another (e.g., "all the world's a stage"). —**met'a·phor'i·cal** (-fôr'i-k'l), *adj.*
**met·a·phys·i·cal** (met'ə-fiz'i-k'l), *adj.* 1. of, or having the nature of, metaphysics. 2. very abstract; abstruse.
**met'a·phys'ics** (-iks), *n.pl.* [construed as sing.], [< Gr. *meta ta phsyika*, after the *Physics* (of Aristotle)], 1. the branch of philosophy that seeks to explain the nature of being and reality. 2. speculative philosophy in general.
**me·tas·ta·sis** (mə-tas'tə-sis), *n.* [*pl.* -SES (-sēz')], [< Gr. *meta-*, after + *histanai*, to place], the transfer, as of malignant cells, from one part of the body to another through the blood stream. —**me·tas'ta·size'** (-sīz') [-SIZED, -SIZING], *v.i.*
**met·a·tar·sus** (met'ə-tär'səs), *n.* [*pl.* -SI (-sī)], [< *meta-*, after + Gr. *tarsos*, flat of the foot], the part of the foot between the ankle and toes. —**met'a·tar'sal,** *adj. & n.*
**me·tath·e·sis** (mə-tath'ə-sis), *n.* [*pl.* -SES (-sēz')], [< Gr. *meta*, over + *tithenai*, to place], the transposition of letters or sounds in a word.
**mete** (mēt), *v.t.* [METED, METING], [AS. *metan*], to allot; portion (*out*).
**me·te·or** (mē'ti-ẽr), *n.* [< Gr. *meta*, beyond + *eōra*, a hovering], a small, solid body entering the earth's atmosphere from outer space at very great speed; shooting star.
**me·te·or·ic** (mē'ti-ôr'ik, -or'-), *adj.* 1. of a meteor. 2. like a meteor; momentarily brilliant, swift, etc. —**me'te·or'i·cal·ly,** *adv.*
**me·te·or·ite** (mē'ti-ẽr-it'), *n.* a stone or metal mass remaining from a meteor fallen to earth.
**me·te·or·ol·o·gy** (mē'ti-ə-rol'ə-ji), *n.* [see METEOR & -LOGY], the science of the atmosphere and its phenomena; study of weather and climate. —**me'te·or·o·log'i·cal,** (-ẽr-ə-loj'i-k'l), *adj.* —**me'te·or·o·log'i·cal·ly,** *adv.* —**me'te·or·ol'o·gist,** *n.*
**me·ter** (mē'tẽr), *n.* [< Gr. *metron*, measure], 1. rhythmic pattern in verse; measured arrangement of syllables according to stress and length. 2. the basic unit of length in the metric system, equal to 39.37 in. Also sp. **metre.**
**me·ter** (mē'tẽr), *n.* [< *mete*], an apparatus for measuring and recording the quantity or rate of flow of gas, water, etc. passing through it.
**-meter,** [< Gr. *metron*, a measure], a suffix meaning: 1. *a device for measuring*, as in *chronometer*. 2. *a*) (a specified number of) *meters*, as in *kilometer*. *b*) (a specified fraction of) *a meter*, as in *centimeter*.
**meth·ane** (meth'ān), *n.* [< *methyl*], a colorless, odorless, inflammable gas formed by the decomposition of vegetable matter.
**me·thinks** (mi-thiŋks'), *impersonal v.* [pt. -THOUGHT], [< AS. *me*, to me + *thyncth*, it seems], [Archaic], it seems to me: also **me-think'eth.**
**meth·od** (meth'əd), *n.* [ult. < Gr. *meta*, after + *hodos*, a way], 1. a way of doing anything; process. 2. system in doing things or handling ideas. 3. regular, orderly arrangement.
**me·thod·i·cal** (mə-thod'i-k'l), *adj.* characterized by method; orderly; systematic: also **me·thod'ic.** —**me·thod'i·cal·ly,** *adv.*
**Meth·od·ist** (meth'əd-ist), *n.* a member of a Protestant Christian denomination that developed from the teachings of John Wesley. —**Meth'od·ism,** *n.*
**Me·thu·se·lah** (mə-thōō'z'l-ə, -thū'-), *n.* in the *Bible*, a patriarch, said to have lived 969 years: Gen. 5:27.
**meth·yl** (meth'əl), *n.* [< Gr. *methy*, wine + *hylē*, wood], a hydrocarbon radical found in wood alcohol.
**methyl alcohol,** a poisonous alcohol used as a fuel, solvent, etc.; wood alcohol.
**me·tic·u·lous** (mə-tik'yoo-ləs), *adj.* [< L. *metus*, fear], very careful or too careful about details; scrupulous or finical.
**me·tier** (mā-tyā'), *n.* [Fr. < L.; see MINISTER], one's trade, profession, etc.
**me·ton·y·my** (mə-ton'ə-mi), *n.* [< Gr. *meta*, change + *onyma*, name], the use of the name of one thing for that of another associated with it (e.g., "the White House" for "the President").
**met·ric** (met'rik), *adj.* 1. of or used in measurement. 2. *a*) of the meter (unit of length). *b*) of the metric system. 3. metrical.
**met'ri·cal,** *adj.* 1. of or composed in meter or verse. 2. of measurement; metric.
**metric system,** a decimal system of weights and measures whose basic units are the gram (.0022046 pound), the meter (39.37 inches), and the liter (61.025 cubic inches).
**met·ro·nome** (met'rə-nōm'), *n.* [< Gr. *metron*, measure + *nomos*, law], a clockwork device with an inverted pendulum that beats time at a desired rate.
**me·trop·o·lis** (mə-trop''l-is), *n.* [*pl.* -LISES], [< Gr. *mētēr*, mother + *polis*, city], 1. the main city, often the capital, of a country, state, etc. 2. any large city or center of culture, etc.
**met·ro·pol·i·tan** (met'rə-pol'ə-t'n), *adj.* of or constituting a metropolis. *n.* 1. one who lives in and is wise in the ways of a metropolis. 2. an archbishop of a church province.
**met·tle** (met''l), *n.* [var. of *metal*], spirit; courage; ardor. —**on one's mettle,** prepared to do one's best. —**met'tle·some** (-səm), *adj.*
**mew** (mū), *n.* [< L. *mutare*, to change], 1. a

cage, as for hawks. 2. *pl.* [construed as sing.], a group of stables. *v.t.* to confine as in a cage.

**mew** (mū), *n.* [echoic], the characteristic vocal sound made by a cat. *v.i.* to make this sound.

**mewl** (mūl), *v.i.* [< *mew* (of a cat)], to cry weakly, like a baby; whimper.

**Mex.,** 1. Mexican. 2. Mexico.

**Mex·i·can** (mek′si-kən), *adj.* of Mexico, its people, language, etc. *n.* 1. a native of Mexico. 2. the language of the Mexicans.

**mez·za·nine** (mez′ə-nēn′), *n.* [< It. *mezzano*, middle], a low-ceilinged story between two main stories, often a balcony over the main floor.

**mez·zo** (met′sō, mez′ō), *adj. & adv.* [It.], in *music*, moderate(ly); half.

**mez′zo·so·pra′no,** *n.* [*pl.* -NOS, -NI (-ni)], [It.], a voice or singer between soprano and contralto.

**mfg.,** manufacturing.

**mfr.,** [*pl.* MFRS.], manufacturer.

**Mg,** in *chem.*, magnesium.

**mg.,** milligram(s).

**MGr.,** Medieval (or Middle) Greek.

**Mgr.,** 1. Manager. 2. Monsignor.

**MHG.,** Middle High German.

**mi** (mē), *n.* [It.], in *music*, the third tone of the diatonic scale.

**mi.,** 1. mile(s). 2. mill(s).

**mi·as·ma** (mī-az′mə), *n.* [*pl.* -MAS, -MATA (-mə-tə)], [< Gr. *miainein*, pollute], poisonous vapor formerly supposed to arise from swamps, etc. —**mi·as′mal, mi·as′mic,** *adj.*

**mi·ca** (mī′kə), *n.* [L., a crumb], a mineral that crystallizes in thin, flexible layers, resistant to heat.

**mice** (mīs), *n.* pl. of **mouse.**

**micro-,** [< Gr. *mikros*, small], a combining form meaning: 1. *little, small*, as in *microfilm*. 2. *enlarging what is small*, as in *microscope*.

**mi·crobe** (mī′krōb), *n.* [< Gr. *mikros*, small + *bios*, life], a very minute organism; esp., any of the bacteria that cause disease; germ.

**mi·cro·bi·ol·o·gy** (mī′krō-bī-ol′ə-ji), *n.* the branch of biology that deals with microorganisms.

**mi·cro·cosm** (mī′krə-koz′m), *n.* an organism or organization regarded as a world in miniature. —**mi′cro·cos′mic,** *adj.*

**mi·cro·film** (mī′krə-film′), *n.* film on which documents, etc. are photographed in a reduced size for convenience in storage and use. *v.t. & v.i.* to photograph on microfilm.

**mi·cro·groove** (mī′krə-grōōv′), *n.* a very narrow needle groove, as in a long-playing phonograph record: a trademark (**Microgroove**).

**mi·crom·e·ter** (mī-krom′ə-tēr), *n.* [< Fr.; see MICRO- & -METER], an instrument for measuring very small distances, angles, etc.

**mi·cron** (mī′kron), *n.* [*pl.* -CRONS, -CRA (-krə)], [< Gr. *mikros*, small], one millionth of a meter.

**Mi·cro·ne·sian** (mī′krə-nē′zhən), *adj.* of Micronesia, groups of islands in the Pacific, its people, languages, etc. *n.* 1. a native of Micronesia. 2. any of their languages.

**mi·cro·or·gan·ism, mi·cro·ör·gan·ism, mi·cro-or·gan·ism** (mī′krō-ôr′gən-iz′m), *n.* any microscopic animal or vegetable organism; esp., any of the bacteria, protozoa, etc.

**mi·cro·phone** (mī′krə-fōn′), *n.* [*micro-* + *-phone*], an instrument for intensifying weak sounds or for transforming sound waves into electrical impulses, as for transmission by radio.

**mi·cro·scope** (mī′krə-skōp′), *n.* [see MICRO- & -SCOPE], an instrument consisting of a combination of lenses, for making minute objects, as microorganisms, look larger.

**mi′cro·scop′ic** (-skop′ik), *adj.* 1. so small as to be invisible or obscure except through a microscope; minute. 2. of, with, or like a microscope. —**mi′cro·scop′i·cal·ly,** *adv.*

**mi·cros·co·py** (mī-kros′kə-pi, mī′krə-skō′-), *n.* the use of a microscope.

**mic·tu·rate** (mik′choo-rāt′), *v.i.* [-RATED, -RATING], [< L. *mingere*], to urinate.

**mid** (mid), *adj.* [superl. MIDMOST], [< AS. *midd*], middle.

**mid, 'mid** (mid), *prep.* [Poetic], amid.

**mid-,** a combining form meaning *middle* or *middle part of*.

**Mi·das** (mī′dəs), *n.* in *Gr. legend*, a king granted the power of turning everything that he touched into gold.

**mid·day** (mid′dā′), *n. & adj.* noon.

**mid·dle** (mid′'l), *adj.* [AS. *middel*], 1. halfway between two given points, times, etc. 2. intermediate; in between. 3. [M-], designating a stage in language development intermediate between *Old* and *Modern*: as, *Middle* English. *n.* 1. a point or part halfway between extremes; central point, time, etc. 2. something intermediate. 3. the middle part of the body; waist.

**middle age,** the time of life between youth and old age. —**mid′dle-aged′,** *adj.*

**Middle Ages,** the period of European history between ancient and modern times, c. 500 A.D.–1450 A.D.

**middle class,** the social class between the aristocracy or very wealthy and the working class, or proletariat.

**middle ear,** the tympanum.

**Middle English,** the English language between about 1125 and about 1475.

**mid′dle·man′** (-man′), *n.* [*pl.* -MEN], 1. a trader who buys from a producer and sells at wholesale or retail. 2. a go-between.

**mid′dle·weight′,** *n.* a boxer or wrestler weighing between 148 and 160 lbs.

**mid·dling** (mid′liŋ), *adj.* of middle size, quality, state, etc. *adv.* [Colloq.], somewhat.

**mid·dy** (mid′i), *n.* [*pl.* -DIES], 1. [Colloq.], a midshipman. 2. a loose blouse with a sailor collar, worn by women and children: also **middy blouse.**

**midge** (mij), *n.* [AS. *mycg*], 1. a small gnat or gnatlike insect. 2. a very small person.

**midg·et** (mij′it), *n.* 1. a very small person. 2. anything very small of its kind. *adj.* miniature.

**mid·land** (mid′lənd), *n.* the middle region of a country; interior. *adj.* in or of the midland; inland.

**mid·night** (mid′nīt′), *n.* twelve o'clock at night. *adj.* 1. of or at midnight. 2. like midnight; very dark.

**mid·riff** (mid′rif), *n.* [< AS. *midd*, mid + *hrif*, belly], 1. the diaphragm. 2. the middle part of the body, between the abdomen and the chest.

**mid·ship·man** (mid′ship′mən), *n.* [*pl.* -MEN], a student in training to be a naval officer.

**mid·ships** (mid′ships′), *adv.* amidships.

**midst** (midst), *n.* the middle; central part. —**in our** (or **your, their**) **midst,** among or with us (or you, them). —**in the midst of,** 1. in the middle of. 2. during.

**midst, 'midst** (midst), *prep.* [Poetic], in the midst of; amidst.

**mid′stream′,** *n.* middle of a stream.

**mid′sum′mer,** *n.* 1. the middle of summer. 2. the time of the summer solstice, about June 21. *adj.* of, in, or like midsummer.

**mid·way** (mid′wā′), *n.* that part of a fair where side shows, etc. are located. *adj. & adv.* in the middle; halfway.

**mid·wife** (mid′wīf′), *n.* [*pl.* -WIVES], [AS. *mid*, with + *wif*, wife], a woman who helps women in childbirth. —**mid′wife′ry** (-wīf′ēr-i, -wif′ri), *n.*

**mid′win′ter,** *n.* 1. the middle of winter.

2. the time of the winter solstice, about Dec. 22. *adj.* of, in, or like midwinter.
**mien** (mēn), *n.* [short for *demean*], one's conduct, bearing, or manner.
**miff** (mif), *v.t. & v.i.* [cf. G. *muffen*, sulk], [Colloq.], to offend or take offense.
**might** (mīt), *v.* [AS. *mihte*], 1. pt. of **may.** 2. an auxiliary generally equivalent to *may* (e.g., it *might* rain).
**might** (mīt), *n.* [AS. *miht*], great strength, power, force, or vigor.
**might·y** (mīt'i), *adj.* [-IER, -IEST], 1. powerful; strong. 2. great; remarkably large, etc. *adv.* [Colloq.], very. —**might'i·ness,** *n.*
**mi·gnon·ette** (min'yə-net'), *n.* [< Fr. *mignon*, small], a plant with spikes of small, fragrant flowers.
**mi·graine** (mī'grān), *n.* [ult. < Gr. *hēmi-*, half + *kranion*, skull], a periodic headache, usually limited to one side of the head.
**mi·grant** (mī'grənt), *adj.* migrating. *n.* a person, bird, or other animal that migrates.
**mi·grate** (mī'grāt), *v.i.* [-GRATED, -GRATING], [< L. *migrare*], 1. to settle in another country or region. 2. to move to another region with the change in season, as many birds. —**mi·gra·to·ry** (mī'grə-tôr-i), *adj.*
**mi·gra·tion** (mī-grā'shən), *n.* 1. a migrating 2. a group of people, birds, etc. migrating together. —**mi·gra'tion·al,** *adj.*
**mi·ka·do** (mi-kä'dō), *n.* [*pl.* -DOS], [< Japan. *mi*, exalted + *kado*, gate], [often M-], the emperor of Japan: title used by non-Japanese.
**mike** (mīk), *n.* [Slang], a microphone.
**mil** (mil), *n.* [< L. *mille*, thousand], a unit of length, .001 of an inch.
**mil.,** 1. military. 2. militia.
**milch** (milch), *adj.* [AS. *-milce*], giving milk; kept for milking: as, *milch* cows.
**mild** (mīld), *adj.* [AS. *milde*], 1. gentle or kind; not severe; moderate. 2. having a soft, pleasant flavor: said of tobacco, cheese, etc. —**mild'ly,** *adv.* —**mild'ness,** *n.*
**mil·dew** (mil'dōō', -dū'), *n.* [AS. *meledeaw*, lit., honeydew], a fungus that attacks various plants or appears on damp cloth, paper, etc. as a furry, whitish coating. *v.t. & v.i.* to affect or be affected with mildew.
**mile** (mīl), *n.* [< L. *milia* (*passuum*), thousand (paces)], a unit of linear measure, equal to 5,280 ft.: in full, **statute mile.** The **nautical** (or **air**) **mile** is 6,076.1 feet.
**mile·age** (mīl'ij), *n.* 1. an allowance per mile for traveling expenses. 2. total miles traveled. Also sp. **milage.**
**mile'stone',** *n.* 1. a stone set up to show the distance from some place. 2. a significant event.
**mi·lieu** (mēl-yoo'), *n.* [Fr. < L. *medius*, middle + *locus*, a place], surroundings; environment.
**mil·i·tant** (mil'i-tənt), *adj.* [< L. *miles*, soldier], 1. fighting. 2. ready and willing to fight. *n.* a militant person. —**mil'i·tan·cy,** *n.* —**mil'i·tant·ly,** *adv.*
**mil·i·ta·rism** (mil'i-tə-riz'm), *n.* 1. military spirit. 2. a continuous and belligerent maintenance of strong armed forces. —**mil'i·ta·rist,** *n.* —**mil'i·ta·ris'tic,** *adj.*
**mil·i·tar·y** (mil'ə-ter'i), *adj.* [< L. *miles*, soldier], 1. of, for, fit for, or done by soldiers. 2. of, for, or fit for war. 3. of the army. *n.* the army. —**mil'i·tar'i·ly,** *adv.*
**military police,** troops assigned to carry on police duties for the army.
**mil·i·tate** (mil'ə-tāt'), *v.i.* [-TATED, -TATING], [< L. *militare*, be a soldier], to operate or work (*against* or *for*).
**mi·li·tia** (mə-lish'ə), *n.* [< L. *miles*, a soldier], an army composed of citizens called out in time of emergency. —**mi·li'tia·man** [*pl.* -MEN], *n.*
**milk** (milk), *n.* [AS. *meolc*], 1. a white liquid secreted by the mammary glands of female mammals for suckling their young; esp., cow's milk. 2. any liquid like this, as coconut milk. *v.t.* 1. to draw milk from the mammary glands of (a cow, etc.). 2. to extract money, information, etc. from as if by milking. —**milk'er,** *n.* —**milk'ing,** *n.*
**milk'maid',** *n.* a girl or woman who milks cows or works in a dairy.
**milk'man',** *n.* [*pl.* -MEN], a man who sells or delivers milk.
**milk of magnesia,** a milky-white suspension of magnesium hydroxide in water, used as a laxative and antacid.
**milk shake,** a drink of milk, flavoring, and ice cream, mixed until frothy.
**milk'sop'** (-sop'), *n.* a sissy.
**milk'weed',** *n.* any of a group of plants with a milky juice.
**milk'y,** *adj.* [-IER, -IEST], 1. like milk; white as milk. 2. of or containing milk.
**Milky Way,** a broad, faintly luminous band of very distant stars and nebulae, seen across the sky at night.
**mill** (mil), *n.* [< L. *mola*, millstone], 1. a building with machinery for grinding grain into flour or meal. 2. any of various machines for grinding, crushing, cutting, etc. 3. a factory: as, a textile *mill.* *v.t.* to grind, form, etc. by or in a mill. *v.i.* to move (*around*) confusedly, as a crowd.
**mill** (mil), *n.* [< L. *millesimus*, thousandth], 1/10 of a cent: a unit used in calculating but not as a coin.
**mil·len·ni·um** (mi-len'i-əm), *n.* [*pl.* -NIUMS, -NIA (-ə)], [< L. *mille*, thousand + *annus*, year], 1. a thousand years. 2. in *theology*, the period of a thousand years during which Christ will reign on earth (with *the*): Rev. 20:1–5. 3. any period of great happiness, peace, etc. —**mil·len'ni·al,** *adj.*
**mill·er** (mil'ẽr), *n.* one who owns or operates a mill, esp. a flour mill.
**mil·let** (mil'it), *n.* [< L. *milium*], 1. a cereal grass used for hay. 2. its seed, sometimes used for food.
**milli-,** [< L. *mile*, thousand], a combining form meaning *one thousandth part of* (a specified unit).
**mil·li·gram, mil·li·gramme** (mil'ə-gram'), *n.* one thousandth of a gram.
**mil·li·me·ter, mil·li·me·tre** (mil'ə-mē'-tẽr) *n.* one thousandth of a meter.
**mil·li·ner** (mil'ə-nẽr), *n.* [< *Milaner*, importer of silks, etc. from Milan], one who makes or sells women's hats.
**mil·li·ner·y** (mil'ə-ner'i), *n.* 1. women's hats, headdresses, etc. 2. the work or business of a milliner.
**mil·lion** (mil'yən), *adj. & n.* [< L. *mille*, thousand], a thousand thousands; 1,000,000. —**mil'lionth,** *adj. & n.*
**mil'lion·aire'** (-âr'), *n.* 1. a person having at least a million dollars, pounds, etc. 2. a very wealthy person.
**mill'stone',** *n.* 1. either of a pair of flat, round stones for grinding grain, etc. 2. a heavy burden.
**mill'wright'** (-rīt'), *n.* a worker who installs or repairs the machinery in a mill.
**milque·toast** (milk'tōst'), *n.* [< a comic-strip character], any timid, shrinking, apologetic person.
**milt** (milt), *n.* [AS. *milte*], 1. the reproductive glands of male fishes, especially when filled with sperm. 2. such fish sperm.
**mime** (mīm), *n.* [< Gr. *mimos*], a clown or mimic. *v.t.* [MIMED, MIMING], to mimic.
**mim·e·o·graph** (mim'i-ə-graf', -gräf'), *n.* [< Gr. *mimeisthai*, imitate], a machine for making copies of written or typewritten matter by means of a stencil. *v.t.* to make (such copies) of.
**mim·ic** (mim'ik), *adj.* [< Gr. *mimos*, a

mime], 1. imitative. 2. make-believe. *n.* an imitator; esp., one skilled in mimicry. *v.t.* [-ICKED, -ICKING], 1. to imitate in speech or action, as in ridicule. 2. to copy closely. —**mim′ick·er,** *n.*

**mim′ic·ry,** *n.* [*pl.* -RIES], the practice, art, or way of mimicking.

**mi·mo·sa** (mi-mō′sə), *n.* [see MIME], a tree, shrub, or herb growing in warm regions and usually having spikes of white or pink flowers.

**min.,** 1. minimum. 2. minute(s).

**min·a·ret** (min′ə-ret′), *n.* [< Ar. *manārah*, lighthouse], a high, slender tower attached to a Moslem mosque.

**min·a·to·ry** (min′ə-tôr′i), *adj.* [< L. *minari*, threaten], menacing.

**mince** (mins), *v.t.* [MINCED, MINCING], [< L. *minutus*, small], 1. to cut up (meat, etc.) into small pieces. 2. to express or do with affected daintiness. 3. to lessen the force of: as, to *mince* no words. *v.i.* to speak, act, or walk with affected daintiness.

**mince′meat′,** *n.* a mixture of chopped apples, spices, suet, raisins, and (now rarely) meat, used as pie filling, etc.

**mince pie,** a pie made with mincemeat.

**minc′ing,** *adj.* affectedly dainty.

**mind** (mīnd), *n.* [AS. (*ge*)*mynd*], 1. memory: as, it brings to *mind* a story. 2. opinion: as, speak your *mind*. 3. what one intends or wills: as, to change one's *mind*. 4. that which thinks, feels, etc.; seat of consciousness. 5. the intellect. 6. the psyche (sense 2*b*). 7. reason; sanity. *v.t.* 1. to perceive; observe. 2. to pay attention to; obey. 3. to take care of: as, *mind* the baby. 4. to be careful about: as, *mind* the stairs. 5. to care about; object to: as, don't *mind* the noise. 6. [Dial.], to remember. *v.i.* 1. to pay attention. 2. to be obedient. 3. to be careful. 4. to care; object. —**bear** (or **keep**) **in mind,** to remember. —**be in one's right mind,** to be sane. —**have in mind,** to intend. —**make up one's mind,** to reach a decision. —**put in mind,** to remind.

**mind′ed,** *adj.* 1. having a (specified kind of) mind: as, *weak-minded*. 2. inclined: as, I am *minded* to go.

**mind′ful,** *adj.* having in mind; aware or careful (*of*). —**mind′ful·ly,** *adv.*

**mind′less,** *adj.* 1. without intelligence. 2. heedless (*of*). —**mind′less·ly,** *adv.*

**mind reader,** one who professes ability to perceive another's thoughts.

**mind's eye,** the imagination.

**mine** (mīn), *pron.* [AS. *min*], that or those belonging to me: as, this is *mine*.

**mine** (mīn), *n.* [OFr.], 1. a large excavation made in the earth, from which to extract ores, coal, etc. 2. a deposit of ore, coal, etc. 3. any great source of supply. 4. in *military science*, *a*) a tunnel dug under an enemy's fort, etc., in which an explosive is placed. *b*) an explosive charge hidden under the surface of the ground or placed in harbors, etc., as to destroy enemy tanks or ships. *v.t.* & *v.i.* [MINED, MINING], 1. to dig (ores, etc.) from (the earth). 2. to place explosive mines in (water, etc.). 3. to destroy, or try to destroy, with explosive mines. 4. to undermine.

**min′er,** *n.* one who digs ore, etc. in a mine.

**min·er·al** (min′ẽr-əl), *n.* [< ML. *minera*, a mine], 1. an inorganic substance found naturally in the earth, as metallic ore. 2. any naturally occurring substance neither vegetable nor animal. *adj.* of or containing minerals.

**min′er·al·ize′** (-ə-līz′), *v.t.* [-IZED, -IZING], 1. to convert (a metal) into an ore. 2. to impregnate (water, etc.) with minerals.

**min·er·al·o·gy** (min′ẽr-al′ə-ji, -äl′-), *n.* the science of minerals. —**min′er·al′o·gist,** *n.*

**mineral water,** water impregnated with mineral salts or gases.

**Mi·ner·va** (mi-nũr′və), *n.* the Roman goddess of wisdom and invention.

**mi·ne·stro·ne** (min′ə-strō′ni), *n.* [It.; ult. < L. *ministrare*, serve], a thick vegetable soup in a meat broth.

**min·gle** (miŋ′g'l), *v.t.* [-GLED, -GLING], [< AS. *mengan*, mix], to mix together; blend. *v.i.* 1. to become mixed, etc. 2. to join or unite with others. —**min′gler,** *n.*

**mini-,** [< *miniature*], a combining form meaning *miniature, very small, very short*, etc.

**min·i·a·ture** (min′i-ə-chẽr, min′i-chẽr), *n.* [< L. *miniare*, paint red], 1. a small painting, esp. a portrait. 2. a copy or model on a very small scale. *adj.* done on a very small scale.

**min′i·a·tur·ize′** (-īz′), *v.t.* [-IZED, -IZING], to make in a small and compact form.

**min·im** (min′im), *n.* [< L. *minimus*, least], 1. the smallest liquid measure, about a drop. 2. a tiny portion. *adj.* smallest.

**min·i·mize** (min′ə-mīz′), *v.t.* [-MIZED, -MIZING], to reduce to or estimate at a minimum.

**min·i·mum** (min′ə-məm), *n.* [*pl.* -MUMS, -MA (-mə)], [L., least], 1. the smallest quantity, number, etc. possible or permissible. 2. the lowest degree or point reached or recorded. *adj.* smallest possible, permissible, or reached. —**min′i·mal,** *adj.*

**min′ing,** *n.* the process or work of removing ores, coal, etc. from a mine.

**min·ion** (min′yən), *n.* [Fr. *mignon*, darling], a favorite, esp. one who is a servile follower: term of contempt.

**min·i·skirt** (min′i-skũrt′), *n.* a very short skirt ending well above the knee.

**min·is·ter** (min′is-tẽr), *n.* [L., a servant], 1. a person appointed to head a governmental department. 2. a diplomat representing his government in a foreign nation. 3. one authorized to conduct religious services in a church; pastor. *v.t.* to administer. *v.i.* 1. to act as an agent. 2. to give help; esp., to serve as a nurse. —**min′is·te′ri·al** (-têr′i-əl), *adj.* —**min′is·trant** (-trənt), *adj.* & *n.*

**min′is·tra′tion** (-trā′shən), *n.* service; help.

**min′is·try** (-tri), *n.* [*pl.* -TRIES], 1. the act of ministering, or serving. 2. the office or function of a clergyman. 3. the clergy. 4. *a*) the department under a minister of government. *b*) his term of office. *c*) such ministers collectively.

**mink** (miŋk), *n.* [< Scand.], 1. a weasellike mammal living on land and in water. 2. its valuable fur, soft, brown, and lustrous.

**min·now** (min′ō), *n.* [prob. < AS. *myne* & OFr. *menu*, small], 1. a very small freshwater fish of the carp family. 2. any small fish like this.

**mi·nor** (mī′nẽr), *adj.* [L.], 1. lesser in size, amount, importance, rank, etc. 2. under full legal age. 3. in *music*, lower than the corresponding major by a half tone: the minor key is often associated with sadness, melancholy, etc. *v.i.* in *education*, to specialize to a secondary degree (*in* a field of study). *n.* 1. a person under full legal age. 2. in *education*, a secondary field of study.

**mi·nor·i·ty** (mə-nôr′ə-ti, mī-nor′-), *n.* [*pl.* -TIES], 1. the lesser part or smaller number. 2. a racial, religious, or political group that differs from the larger, controlling group. 3. the state of being under full legal age.

**Min·o·taur** (min′ə-tôr′), *n.* in *Gr. myth.*, a monster with the body of a man and the head of a bull.

**min·ster** (min′stẽr), *n.* [AS. *mynster*], 1. the church of a monastery. 2. any of various large churches or cathedrals.

**min·strel** (min′strəl), *n.* [see MINISTER], 1. a traveling singer of the Middle Ages. 2. a member of a comic variety show (**minstrel show**) in which the performers are made up in blackface. —**min′strel·sy** (-si) [*pl.* -SIES]. *n.*

**mint** (mint), *n.* [< L. < Juno *Moneta*, whose temple was the mint], 1. a place where money is coined by the government. 2. a large amount. *adj.* new, as if freshly minted. *v.t.* 1. to coin (money). 2. to invent or create. —**mint′age**, *n.*

**mint** (mint), *n.* [< Gr. *mintha*], 1. an aromatic plant whose leaves are used for flavoring and in medicine. 2. a piece of mint-flavored candy.

**min·u·end** (min′ū-end′), *n.* [< L. *minuere*, lessen], the number from which another is to be subtracted.

**min·u·et** (min′ū-et′), *n.* [< Fr. *menu*, small], 1. a slow, stately dance. 2. music for this.

**mi·nus** (mī′nəs), *prep.* [L. < *minor*, less], 1. less: as, four *minus* two. 2. [Colloq.], without: as, *minus* a finger. *adj.* 1. involving subtraction: as, a *minus* sign. 2. negative. 3. less than: as, a grade of A *minus*. *n.* a sign (–) indicating subtraction or negative quantity: in full, **minus sign.**

**min·ute** (min′it), *n.* [see MINUTE, *adj.*], 1. the sixtieth part of an hour or of a degree of an arc. 2. a moment; instant. 3. a specific point in time. 4. *pl.* an official record of a meeting, etc. —**the minute (that)**, just as soon as.

**mi·nute** (mī-nōōt′, mi-nūt′), *adj.* [< L. *minor*, less], 1. very small. 2. of little importance. 3. of or attentive to tiny details; precise. —**mi·nute′ly**, *adv.*

**min′ute·man′**, *n.* [*pl.* -MEN], a member of the American citizen army at the beginning of the Revolutionary War.

**mi·nu·ti·ae** (mi-nū′shi-ē′), *n.pl.* [*sing.* -TIA (-shi-ə)], [see MINUTE, *adj.*], small or unimportant details.

**minx** (miŋks), *n.* [< LG.], a pert, saucy girl.

**mir·a·cle** (mir′ə-k'l), *n.* [< L. *mirus*, wonderful], 1. an event or action that apparently contradicts known scientific laws. 2. a remarkable thing.

**mi·rac·u·lous** (mi-rak′yoo-ləs), *adj.* 1. having the nature of, or like, a miracle. 2. able to work miracles.

**mi·rage** (mi-räzh′), *n.* [< LL. *mirare*, look at], an optical illusion caused by the reflection of light, by which a ship, oasis, etc. appears to be very near.

**mire** (mīr), *n.* [< ON. *myrr*], 1. an area of wet, soggy ground. 2. deep mud or slush. *v.t.* [MIRED, MIRING], 1. to cause to get stuck as in mire. 2. to soil with mud, etc. *v.i.* to sink in mud. —**mir′y** [-IER, -IEST], *adj.*

**mir·ror** (mir′ẽr), *n.* [< LL. *mirare*, look at], 1. a smooth surface that reflects images; esp., a silvered glass. 2. anything that gives a true representation. *v.t.* to reflect, as in a mirror.

**mirth** (mũrth), *n.* [< AS. *myrig*, pleasant], joyfulness or gaiety, esp. when marked by laughter. —**mirth′ful**, *adj.* —**mirth′less**, *adj.*

**mis-**, [< AS. *mis-* or OFr. *mes-*], a prefix meaning *wrong*(*ly*), *bad*(*ly*).

**mis·ad·ven·ture** (mis′əd-ven′chẽr), *n.* a mishap; bad luck.

**mis′al·li′ance**, *n.* an improper alliance; esp., an unsuitable marriage.

**mis·an·thrope** (mis′ən-thrōp′), *n.* [< Gr. *misein*, to hate + *anthrōpos*, man], one who hates or distrusts all people: also **mis·an′thro·pist** (-an′thrə-pist). —**mis′an·throp′ic** (-throp′ik), *adj.*

**mis·an·thro·py** (mis-an′thrə-pi), *n.* hatred or distrust of all people.

**mis′ap·ply′**, *v.t.* [-PLIED, -PLYING], to apply badly or improperly.

**mis·ap·pre·hend** (mis′ap-ri-hend′), *v.t.* to misunderstand. —**mis′ap·pre·hen′sion** (-hen′shən), *n.*

**mis′ap·pro′pri·ate′**, *v.t.* [-ATED, -ATING], to appropriate to a wrong or dishonest use. —**mis′ap·pro′pri·a′tion**, *n.*

**mis′be·got′ten**, *adj.* wrongly or unlawfully begotten; illegitimate.

**mis′be·have′**, *v.t.* & *v.i.* [-HAVED, -HAVING], to behave (oneself) wrongly. —**mis′be·hav′ior** (-yẽr), *n.*

**mis′be·lieve′**, *v.i.* [-LIEVED, -LIEVING], to hold wrong, false, or unorthodox beliefs, esp. in religion. —**mis′be·lief′**, *n.*

**misc.**, miscellaneous.

**mis·cal′cu·late′**, *v.t.* & *v.i.* [-LATED, -LATING], to calculate incorrectly; misjudge. —**mis′cal·cu·la′tion**, *n.*

**mis·call′**, *v.t.* to call by a wrong name.

**mis·car·riage** (mis-kar′ij), *n.* 1. failure to reach a proper end or destination. 2. the premature birth of a fetus, so that it does not live.

**mis·car′ry**, *v.i.* [-RIED, -RYING], 1. to go wrong: as, the plan *miscarried*. 2. to fail to arrive, as a letter. 3. to suffer a miscarriage of a fetus.

**mis·cast′**, *v.t.* [-CAST, -CASTING], to cast (an actor or a play) unsuitably.

**mis·ce·ge·na·tion** (mis′i-jə-nā′shən), *n.* [< L. *miscere*, mix + *genus*, race], marriage or interbreeding between members of different races.

**mis·cel·la·ne·ous** (mis′′l-ā′ni-əs), *adj.* [< L. *miscere*, mix], consisting of various kinds or qualities.

**mis·cel·la·ny** (mis′′l-ā′ni), *n.* [*pl.* -NIES], a collection of various kinds, esp. of literary works.

**mis·chance′**, *n.* bad luck.

**mis·chief** (mis′chif), *n.* [< OFr. *mes-*, mis- + *chief*, end], 1. harm or damage. 2. a cause of harm or annoyance. 3. *a*) a prank. *b*) gay teasing.

**mis′chief-mak′er**, *n.* one who causes mischief, as by gossiping.

**mis·chie·vous** (mis′chi-vəs), *adj.* 1. causing mischief; specif., *a*) harmful. *b*) prankish. 2. inclined to annoy with playful tricks.

**mis·ci·ble** (mis′ə-b'l), *adj.* [< L. *miscere*, to mix], that can be mixed. —**mis′ci·bil′i·ty**, *n.*

**mis·con·ceive** (mis′kən-sēv′), *v.t.* & *v.i.* to misunderstand. —**mis′con·cep′tion** (-sep′shən), *n.*

**mis·con′duct**, *n.* 1. bad or dishonest management. 2. improper conduct. *v.t.* (mis′kən-dukt′), 1. to manage badly. 2. to conduct (oneself) improperly.

**mis·con·strue** (mis′kən-strōō′), *v.t.* [-STRUED, -STRUING], to misinterpret. —**mis′con·struc′tion**, *n.*

**mis·count′**, *v.t.* & *v.i.* to count incorrectly.

**mis·cre·ant** (mis′kri-ənt), *adj.* [< OFr. *mes-*, mis- + *creire*, believe], villainous. *n.* a villain.

**mis·cue′**, *n.* a wrong cue, as on the stage.

**mis·deal′**, *v.t.* & *v.i.* [-DEALT, -DEALING], to deal (playing cards) wrongly. *n.* a wrong deal.

**mis·deed** (mis-dēd′), *n.* a wrong or wicked act; crime, sin, etc.

**mis·de·mean·or** (mis′di-mēn′ẽr), *n.* in *law*, any minor offense bringing a lesser punishment than a felony.

**mis′di·rect′**, *v.t.* to direct wrongly or badly. —**mis′di·rec′tion**, *n.*

**mi·ser** (mī′zẽr), *n.* [L., wretched], a greedy, stingy person who hoards money for its own sake. —**mi′ser·ly**, *adj.* —**mi′ser·li·ness**, *n.*

**mis·er·a·ble** (miz′ẽr-ə-b'l), *adj.* 1. in misery; wretched. 2. causing misery, discomfort, etc. 3. bad, inadequate, etc. 4. pitiable. —**mis′er·a·bly**, *adv.*

**mis·er·y** (miz′ẽr-i), *n.* [*pl.* -IES], [see MISER], 1. a condition of great suffering. 2. a cause of such suffering; pain, poverty, etc.

**mis·fea·sance** (mis-fē′z'ns), *n.* [< OFr. *mes-*, mis- + *faire*, do], in *law*, wrongdoing; specif., the doing of a lawful act in an unlawful manner.

**mis·fire** (mis-fīr′), *v.i.* [-FIRED, -FIRING], 1. to fail to ignite properly, as fuel in an engine. 2. to fail to be discharged, as a gun.

**mis·fit′,** *v.t. & v.i.* to fail to fit properly. *n.* 1. an improper fit. 2. (mis′fit′), a maladjusted person.

**mis·for′tune,** *n.* 1. ill fortune; trouble. 2. a mishap, calamity, etc.

**mis·give** (mis-giv′), *v.t.* [-GAVE, -GIVEN, -GIVING], to cause fear, doubt, etc. in: as, his heart *misgave* him. *v.i.* to feel fear, etc.

**mis·giv′ing,** *n. often in pl.* a disturbed feeling of fear, doubt, etc.

**mis·gov′ern,** *v.t.* to govern badly. **—mis·gov′ern·ment,** *n.*

**mis·guide′** (-gīd′), *v.t.* [-GUIDED, -GUIDING], to lead into error or misconduct; mislead.

**mis·han′dle,** *v.t.* [-DLED, -DLING], to handle badly or roughly; abuse.

**mis·hap** (mis′hap′), *n.* misfortune.

**mis′in·form′,** *v.t. & v.i.* to supply (with) false or misleading information. **— mis′in·for·ma′tion,** *n.*

**mis′in·ter′pret,** *v.t.* to interpret wrongly; understand or explain incorrectly. **—mis′in·ter′pre·ta′tion,** *n.*

**mis·judge′,** *v.t. & v.i.* [-JUDGED, -JUDGING], to judge wrongly or unfairly.

**mis·lay′,** (-lā′), *v.t.* [-LAID, -LAYING], 1. to put in a place afterward forgotten. 2. to put in a wrong place.

**mis·lead′** (-lēd′), *v.t.* [-LED, -LEADING], 1. to lead in a wrong direction. 2. to deceive; delude. 3. to lead into wrongdoing.

**mis·man′age,** *v.t. & v.i.* [-AGED, -AGING], to manage or administer badly. **—mis·man′age·ment,** *n.*

**mis·match′,** *v.t.* to match badly or unsuitably. *n.* a bad match.

**mis·mate′,** *v.t. & v.i.* [-MATED, -MATING], to mate badly or unsuitably.

**mis·name′,** *v.t.* [-NAMED, -NAMING], to call by a wrong name.

**mis·no·mer** (mis-nō′mẽr), *n.* [< *mis-* + L. *nomen*, name], a name wrongly applied.

**mi·sog·a·my** (mi-sog′ə-mi), *n.* [< Gr. *misein*, to hate + *gamos*, marriage], hatred of marriage. **—mi·sog′a·mist,** *n.*

**mi·sog·y·ny** (mi-soj′ə-ni), *n.* [< Gr. *misein*, to hate + *gynē*, woman], hatred of women. **—mi·sog′y·nist,** *n.*

**mis·place′,** *v.t.* [-PLACED, -PLACING], 1. to put in a wrong place. 2. to bestow (one's trust, etc.) unwisely. **—mis·place′ment,** *n.*

**mis·print′,** *v.t.* to print incorrectly. *n.* (*also* mis′print′), a printing error.

**mis′pro·nounce′,** *v.t. & v.i.* [-NOUNCED, -NOUNCING], to pronounce differently from the accepted pronunciations.

**mis·quote′,** *v.t. & v.i.* [-QUOTED, -QUOTING], to quote incorrectly. **—mis′quo·ta′tion,** *n.*

**mis·read′** (-rēd′), *v.t. & v.i.* [-READ (-red′), -READING], to read wrongly, esp. so as to misinterpret or misunderstand.

**mis′rep·re·sent′,** *v.t.* to represent falsely; give an untrue idea of. **—mis′rep·re·sen·ta′tion,** *n.*

**mis·rule′** (-rōōl′), *v.t.* [-RULED, -RULING], to misgovern. *n.* misgovernment.

**miss** (mis), *v.t.* [AS. *missan*], 1. to fail to hit, meet, catch, do, attend, see, hear, etc. 2. to let (a chance, etc.) go by. 3. to avoid: as, he *missed* being hit. 4. to notice or feel the absence or loss of. *v.i.* 1. to fail to hit. 2. to fail to be successful. *n.* a failure to hit, obtain, etc.

**miss** (mis), *n.* [*pl.* MISSES], [< *mistress*], 1. [M-], a title used before the name of an unmarried woman or girl. 2. a young unmarried woman or girl.

**mis·sal** (mis′'l), *n.* [< LL. *missa*, Mass], in the *R.C. Church*, a book of the prayers for celebrating Mass throughout the year.

**mis·shape** (mis-shāp′), *v.t.* [-SHAPED, -SHAPING], to deform; misform. **—mis·shap′en,** *adj.*

**mis·sile** (mis′'l), *n.* [< L. *mittere*, send], an object, as a spear, bullet, rocket, etc., designed to be hurled or launched toward a target; often, specif., a guided missile.

**mis′sile·ry, mis′sil·ry** (-rē), *n.* 1. the science of building and launching guided missiles. 2. such missiles.

**miss·ing** (mis′iŋ), *adj.* absent; lost.

**mis·sion** (mish′ən), *n.* [< L. *mittere*, send], 1. a sending out or being sent out to perform a special duty. 2. *a*) a group of missionaries. *b*) its headquarters. 3. a diplomatic delegation. 4. the special duty on which one is sent. 5. the special task for which one seems destined in life; calling.

**mis′sion·ar′y** (-er′i), *adj.* of religious missions or missionaries. *n.* [*pl.* -IES], a person sent out by his church to preach and make converts in a foreign country.

**mis·sive** (mis′iv), *n.* [Fr. < L. *mittere*, send], a letter or message.

**mis·spell** (mis-spel′), *v.t. & v.i.* [-SPELLED or -SPELT, -SPELLING], to spell incorrectly.

**mis·state′,** *v.t.* [-STATED, -STATING], to state incorrectly or falsely. **—mis·state′ment,** *n.*

**mis·step′,** *n.* 1. a wrong or awkward step. 2. a mistake in conduct.

**mist** (mist), *n.* [AS.], 1. a large mass of water vapor, less dense than a fog. 2. anything that dims or obscures. *v.t. & v.i.* to make or become misty.

**mis·take** (mis-tāk′), *v.t.* [-TOOK, -TAKEN, -TAKING], [< ON. *mistaka*, take wrongly], to understand or perceive wrongly. *v.i.* to make a mistake. *n.* a fault; error. **—mis·tak′a·ble,** *adj.*

**mis·tak′en,** *adj.* 1. wrong; having an incorrect understanding. 2. incorrect: said of ideas, etc. **—mis·tak′en·ly,** *adv.*

**mis·ter** (mis′tẽr), *n.* [< *master*], 1. [M-], a title used before the name of a man or his office and usually written *Mr.*: as, *Mr.* Hunt, *Mr.* Secretary. 2. [Colloq.], sir.

**mis·tle·toe** (mis′'l-tō′), *n.* [< AS. *mistel*, mistletoe + *tan*, a twig], a parasitic evergreen plant with yellowish flowers and waxy white berries.

**mis·took′** (-took′), pt. of **mistake.**

**mis·tral** (mis′trəl), *n.* [Fr.; Pr., master-wind], a cold, dry, north wind that blows over the Mediterranean coast of France.

**mis·treat′,** *v.t.* to treat wrongly or badly. **—mis·treat′ment,** *n.*

**mis·tress** (mis′tris), *n.* [< OFr. fem. of *maistre*, master], 1. a woman who is head of a household or institution. 2. a woman, nation, etc. that has control or power. 3. a woman who lives as a wife with a man to whom she is not married. 4. [Brit.], a woman schoolteacher. 5. [M-], formerly, a title used before the name of a woman: now replaced by **Mrs.** or **Miss.**

**mis·tri·al** (mis-trī′əl), *n.* in *law*, a trial made void because of an error or inability to reach a verdict.

**mis·trust′,** *n.* lack of trust or confidence. *v.t. & v.i.* to have mistrust; doubt. **—mis·trust′ful,** *adj.* **—mis·trust′ful·ly,** *adv.*

**mist·y** (mis′ti), *adj.* [-IER, -IEST], 1. of, like, or covered with mist. 2. blurred, as by mist; obscure; vague. **—mist′i·ness,** *n.*

**mis′un·der·stand′,** *v.t.* [-STOOD, -STANDING], to understand incorrectly; misinterpret.

**mis′un·der·stand′ing,** *n.* 1. a failure to understand correctly. 2. a quarrel.

**mis·us·age** (mis-ūs′ij, -ūz′-), *n.* 1. incorrect usage, as of words. 2. harsh treatment.

**mis·use** (mis-ūz′; *for n.*, -ūs′), *v.t.* [-USED, -USING], 1. to use improperly. 2. to treat badly or harshly; abuse. *n.* incorrect or improper use.

**mite** (mīt), *n.* [AS.], 1. a tiny arachnid living as a parasite upon animals or plants. 2. a very small sum of money. 3. a very small person, thing, or amount.
**mi·ter** (mī′tẽr), *n.* [< Gr. *mitra*, headband], 1. a tall, ornamented cap worn by bishops and abbots. 2. in *carpentry*, a joint formed by fitting together two pieces beveled so that they form a corner. Also sp. **mitre.**
**mit·i·gate** (mit′ə-gāt′), *v.t. & v.i.* [-GATED, -GATING], [< L. *mitis*, mild], to make or become less severe, less painful, etc. **—mit′i·ga′tion,** *n.* **—mit′i·ga′tor,** *n.*
**mitt** (mit), *n.* [< *mitten*], 1. a glove covering the hand and forearm but not the fingers. 2. a mitten. 3. a padded glove worn by fielders in baseball. 4. *usually in pl.* a padded mitten worn by boxers. 5. [Slang], a hand.
**mit·ten** (mit′'n), *n.* [< OFr. *mitaine*], a glove with a thumb but no separately divided fingers.
**mix** (miks), *v.t.* [MIXED or MIXT, MIXING], [< L. *miscere*], 1. to blend together in a single mass. 2. to make by blending ingredients: as, to *mix* a cake. 3. to combine: as, *mix* work and play. *v.i.* 1. to be mixed; blend. 2. to get along together. *n.* 1. a mixture. 2. a beverage for mixing with alcoholic liquor. **—mix up,** 1. to mix thoroughly. 2. to confuse. 3. to involve or implicate (*in*). **—mix′er,** *n.*
**mixed** (mikst), *adj.* 1. blended. 2. made up of different parts, classes, races, sexes, etc. 3. confused.
**mix′ture** (-chẽr), *n.* 1. a mixing or being mixed. 2. something mixed.
**mix′-up′,** *n.* confusion; tangle.
**miz·zen·mast** (miz′'n-məst, -mast′), *n.* [< L. *medius*, middle], the mast closest to the stern of the ship.
**ML., M.L.,** Medieval Latin.
**MLG., M.L.G.,** Middle Low German.
**Mlle.,** [*pl.* MLLES.], Mademoiselle.
**mm.,** millimeter(s).
**Mme.,** [*pl.* MMES.], Madame.
**Mn,** in *chem.*, manganese.
**mne·mon·ic** (ni-mon′ik), *adj.* [< Gr. *mnēmōn*, mindful], of or helping the memory.
**mne·mon′ics,** *n.pl.* [construed as sing.], the science or art of improving the memory.
**Mo,** in *chem.*, molybdenum.
**Mo.,** Monday.
**mo.,** [*pl.* MOS.], month.
**mo·a** (mō′ə), *n.* [< native name], any of an extinct group of large, flightless birds of New Zealand, related to the ostrich.
**moan** (mōn), *n.* [prob. < AS. *mænen*, complain], a low, mournful sound of sorrow or pain. *v.i. & v.t.* 1. to say with or utter a moan. 2. to complain.
**moat** (mōt), *n.* [OFr. *mote*], a deep, broad ditch dug around a fortress or castle, and often filled with water.
**mob** (mob), *n.* [< L. *mobile* (*vulgus*), movable (crowd)], 1. a disorderly, lawless crowd; rabble. 2. any crowd. 3. the masses: contemptuous term. 4. [Slang], a gang of criminals. *v.t.* [MOBBED, MOBBING], to crowd around and attack, annoy, etc.
**mo·bile** (mō′b'l, -bēl), *adj.* [< L. *movere*, to move], 1. movable. 2. readily movable. 3. easily expressing changes in emotion: as, *mobile* features. *n.* (-bēl), a piece of abstract sculpture which aims to depict movement, as by an arrangement of thin forms, rings, etc. suspended in mid-air. **—mo·bil′i·ty** (-bil′ə-ti), *n.*
**mo′bil·ize′** (-b'l-īz′), *v.t. & v.i.* [-IZED, -IZING], to make or become organized and ready, as for war. **—mo′bil·i·za′tion,** *n.*
**moc·ca·sin** (mok′ə-s'n), *n.* [< Am. Ind.], 1. a heelless slipper of soft, flexible leather. 2. a water moccasin.
**mo·cha** (mō′kə), *n.* a variety of coffee originally from Arabia. *adj.* flavored with coffee and, often, chocolate.
**mock** (mok), *v.t.* [OFr. *mocquer*], 1. to ridicule; deride. 2. to mimic, as in fun or derision. 3. to defy and make futile. *v.i.* to express scorn, ridicule, etc. *adj.* false; imitation. **—mock′er,** *n.* **—mock′ing,** *adj.*
**mock′er·y,** *n.* [*pl.* -IES], 1. a mocking. 2. one receiving or deserving ridicule. 3. a false or derisive imitation.
**mock′ing·bird′,** *n.* a small bird of the southern U.S. that imitates the calls of other birds.
**mod** (mod), *adj.* [*mod*ern], ultrastylish and sophisticated. *n.* a young person who is mod.
**mod·al** (mō′d'l), *adj.* of or indicating a mode or mood. **—mo·dal′i·ty** (-dal′ə-ti), *n.*
**mode** (mōd), *n.* [< L. *modus*], 1. a manner or way of acting, doing, or being. 2. customary usage, or current fashion. 3. in *grammar*, mood.
**mod·el** (mod′'l), *n.* [< L. *modus*, a measure], 1. a small representation of a planned or existing object. 2. a person or thing regarded as a standard of excellence to be imitated. 3. a style or design. 4. *a*) one who poses for an artist or photographer. *b*) one employed to display clothes by wearing them. *adj.* serving as a model. *v.t.* [-ELED or -ELLED, -ELING or -ELLING], 1. *a*) to make a model of. *b*) to plan or form after a model. 2. to display (clothes) by wearing. *v.i.* to serve as a model (sense 4).
**mod·er·ate** (mod′ẽr-it), *adj.* [< L. *moderare*, restrain], 1. within reasonable limits; avoiding extremes. 2. mild; calm. 3. of medium quality; mediocre. *n.* one holding moderate opinions, as in politics. *v.i. & v.t.* (-ə-rāt′), [-ATED, -ATING], 1. to become or make moderate. 2. to preside over (a meeting). **—mod′er·ate·ly,** *adv.*
**mod′er·a′tion,** *n.* 1. a moderating. 2. avoidance of extremes. 3. calmness.
**mod′er·a′tor,** *n.* one who presides at an assembly, debate, etc.
**mod·ern** (mod′ẽrn), *adj.* [< L. *modo*, just now], 1. of or characteristic of the present or recent times. 2. up-to-date. 3. [often M-], designating the current form of a language. *n.* a person living in modern times, having modern ideas, etc. **—mod′ern·ness,** *n.*
**Modern English,** the English language since about 1500.
**mod′ern·ism,** *n.* (a) modern usage, practice, thought, etc. **—mod′ern·ist,** *n.* **—mod′ern·is′tic,** *adj.*
**mo·der·ni·ty** (mo-dũr′nə-ti, mō-), *n.* a being modern.
**mod′ern·ize′** (-īz′), *v.t. & v.i.* [-IZED, -IZING], to make or become modern. **—mod′ern·i·za′tion,** *n.* **—mod′ern·iz′er,** *n.*
**mod·est** (mod′ist), *adj.* [< L. *modus*, measure], 1. having or showing humility; not vain. 2. shy; reserved. 3. decorous; decent. 4. not extreme; unpretentious. **—mod′est·ly,** *adv.* **—mod′es·ty,** *n.*
**mod·i·cum** (mod′i-kəm), *n.* [L., moderate], a small amount; bit.
**mod·i·fy** (mod′ə-fī′), *v.t.* [-FIED, -FYING], [< L. *modificare*, to limit], 1. to change slightly or partially in character, form, etc. 2. to limit or reduce slightly. 3. in *grammar*, to limit in meaning; qualify. **—mod′i·fi·ca′tion,** *n.* **—mod′i·fi′er,** *n.*
**mod·ish** (mōd′ish), *adj.* stylish; fashionable.
**mo·diste** (mō-dēst′), *n.* [Fr.; see MODE], a woman who makes or deals in fashionable clothes for women.
**Mod. L.,** Modern Latin.
**mod·u·late** (moj′oo-lāt′), *v.t.* [-LATED, -LATING], [< L. *modus*, measure], 1. to regulate or adjust. 2. to vary the pitch, intensity, etc. of (the voice). 3. to vary the frequency

of (radio waves, etc.). —**mod'u·la'tion,** *n.* —**mod'u·la'tor,** *n.*
**mod·ule** (moj'ōōl), *n.* [< L. *modus*, measure], 1. a standard or unit of measurement. 2. a detachable section or unit with a specific purpose or function, as in a spacecraft. 3. in *architecture*, the length of some part, used as a unit of measurement.
**mo·gul** (mō'gul), *n.* [Persian *Mughul*, Mongol], a powerful or important person.
**mo·hair** (mō'hâr'), *n.* [< Ar. *mukhayyar*], 1. the hair of the Angora goat. 2. a fabric made of this.
**Mo·ham·med·an** (mō-ham'ə-dən), *adj.* of Mohammed, Arabian founder and prophet of Islam, or Islam. *n.* an adherent of Islam. —**Mo·ham'med·an·ism,** *n.*
**moi·e·ty** (moi'ə-ti), *n.* [*pl.* -TIES], [< L. *medius*, middle], 1. a half. 2. an indefinite part.
**moire** (mwär), *n.* [Fr.], a fabric, esp. silk, having a watered, or wavy, pattern.
**moist** (moist), *adj.* [< L. *mucus*, mucus], damp; slightly wet. —**moist'ness,** *n.*
**mois·ten** (mois''n), *v.t. & v.i.* to make or become moist. —**mois'ten·er,** *n.*
**mois·ture** (mois'chẽr), *n.* water or other liquid causing a slight wetness.
**mo·lar** (mō'lẽr), *adj.* [< L. *mola*, millstone], designating a tooth adapted for grinding. *n.* a molar tooth.
**mo·las·ses** (mə-las'iz), *n.* [< L. *mel*, honey], a thick, dark sirup produced from sugar.
**mold** (mōld), *n.* [< L. *modus*, measure], 1. a hollow form for giving a certain shape to something plastic or molten. 2. a frame on which something is modeled. 3. a pattern; model. 4. something formed in or on a mold. 5. distinctive character. *v.t.* 1. to make in or on a mold. 2. to form or shape.
**mold** (mōld), *n.* [ME. *moul*], 1. a fungus producing a furry growth on the surface of organic matter. 2. this furry growth. *v.t. & v.i.* to make or become moldy.
**mold** (mōld), *n.* [AS. *molde*, earth], loose, soft soil rich in decayed organic matter.
**mold·er** (mōl'dẽr), *v.i. & v.t.* [< AS. *molde*, dust], to crumble to dust; decay.
**mold·ing** (mōl'diŋ), *n.* 1. the act of one that molds. 2. something molded. 3. a shaped strip of wood, etc., as around the upper walls of a room.
**mold·y** (mōl'di), *adj.* [-IER, -IEST], 1. covered or overgrown with mold (fungous growth). 2. musty or stale. —**mold'i·ness,** *n.*
**mole** (mōl), *n.* [AS. *mal*], a small, congenital spot on the human skin, usually dark-colored and raised.
**mole** (mōl), *n.* [ME. *molle*], a small, burrowing mammal with soft fur.
**mole** (mōl), *n.* [< L. *moles*, a mass], a breakwater.
**mol·e·cule** (mol'ə-kūl'), *n.* [< L. *moles*, a mass], 1. the smallest particle of an element or compound that can exist in the free state and still retain the characteristics of the substance. 2. a small particle. —**mo·lec·u·lar** (mə-lek'yoo-lẽr), *adj.*
**mole'hill',** *n.* a small ridge of earth formed by a burrowing mole.
**mole·skin** (mōl'skin'), *n.* 1. the fur of the mole. 2. a strong cotton fabric.
**mo·lest** (mə-lest'), *v.t.* [< L. *moles*, a burden], to annoy or meddle with so as to trouble or harm. —**mo·les·ta·tion** (mō'les-tā'shən), *n.*
**moll** (mol), *n.* [Slang], a gangster's mistress.
**mol·li·fy** (mol'ə-fī'), *v.t.* [-FIED, -FYING], [< L. *mollis*, soft + *facere*, make], 1. to soothe; appease. 2. to make less severe or violent.
**mol·lusk, mol·lusc** (mol'əsk), *n.* [< L. *mollis*, soft], any of a group of invertebrates, as oysters, clams, snails, etc., characterized by a soft body enclosed, usually, in a shell.
**mol·ly·cod·dle** (mol'i-kod''l), *n.* [< *Molly*, dim. of *Mary* + *coddle*], a man or boy used to being coddled. *v.t.* [-DLED, -DLING], to pamper; coddle.
**molt** (mōlt), *v.i.* [< L. *mutare*, to change], to shed hair, skin, horns, etc. prior to replacement by a new growth, as reptiles, birds, etc. —**molt'er,** *n.*
**mol·ten** (mōl't'n), *adj.* [archaic pp. of *melt*], 1. melted by heat. 2. made by being melted and cast in a mold.
**mo·lyb·de·num** (mə-lib'də-nəm), *n.* [< Gr. *molybdos*, lead], a silver-white metallic chemical element, used in alloys: symbol, Mo.
**mom** (mom), *n.* [Colloq.], mother.
**mo·ment** (mō'mənt), *n.* [< L. *momentum*, movement], 1. an indefinitely brief period of time; instant. 2. a definite point in time. 3. importance: as, business of great *moment*.
**mo·men·tar·i·ly** (mō'mən-ter'ə-li), *adv.* 1. for a short time. 2. from instant to instant.
**mo·men·tar·y** (mō'mən-ter'i), *adj.* lasting for only a moment; passing.
**mo·men·tous** (mō-men'təs), *adj.* of great moment; very important.
**mo·men·tum** (mō-men'təm), *n.* [*pl.* -TUMS, -TA (-tə)], [L.; see MOMENT], the impetus of a moving object, equal to the product of its mass and its linear velocity.
**Mon.,** 1. Monday. 2. Monsignor.
**mon·arch** (mon'ẽrk), *n.* [< Gr. *monos*, alone + *archein*, to rule], a hereditary ruler; king, queen, emperor, etc. —**mo·nar·chi·cal** (mə-när'ki-k'l), *adj.*
**mon·arch·ism** (mon'ẽr-kiz'm), *n.* 1. monarchical principles. 2. advocacy of such principles. —**mon'arch·ist,** *n. & adj.*
**mon·arch·y** (mon'ẽr-ki), *n.* [*pl.* -IES], 1. a state headed by a monarch. 2. government by a monarch.
**mon·as·ter·y** (mon'əs-ter'i), *n.* [*pl.* -IES], [< Gr. *monos*, alone], the residence of a group of monks or nuns, esp. of monks.
**mo·nas·tic** (mə-nas'tik), *adj.* of or characteristic of monks or nuns; ascetic: also **mo·nas'ti·cal.** *n.* a monk.
**mo·nas'ti·cism** (-tə-siz'm), *n.* the monastic state or way of life.
**mon·au·ral** (mon-ô'rəl), *adj.* [*mon*(*o*)- + *aural*], designating or of sound reproduction that uses only one source of sound.
**Mon·day** (mun'di), *n.* [AS. *mon*(*an*)*dæg*, moon's day], the second day of the week.
**mon·e·tar·y** (mon'ə-ter'i, mun'-), *adj.* [< L. *moneta*, place for coining money], 1. of the coinage or currency of a country. 2. of money; pecuniary. —**mon'e·tar'i·ly,** *adv.*
**mon·ey** (mun'i), *n.* [*pl.* -EYS, -IES], [< L. *moneta*, see MINT], 1. stamped pieces of metal, or any paper note, authorized by a government as a medium of exchange. 2. property; wealth. —**make money,** to gain profits; become wealthy. —**put money into,** to invest money in.
**mon·eyed** (mun'id), *adj.* rich; wealthy.
**money order,** an order for the payment of a specified sum of money, as one issued at one post office or bank and payable at another.
**mon·ger** (muŋ'gẽr), *n.* [< AS. *mangian*, to trade], [Chiefly Brit.], a dealer or trader (in a specified commodity): as, *fishmonger*.
**Mon·gol** (moŋ'gəl, -gōl), *n.* 1. a native of Mongolia. 2. a member of the Mongolian race. *adj.* Mongolian.
**Mon·go'li·an,** *adj.* 1. of Mongolia or its people, language, etc. 2. designating or of one of the three principal races of mankind, including most of the peoples of Asia, generally having a yellowish skin, slanting eyes, etc. *n.* a native of Mongolia or a member of the Mongolian race.
**Mon·gol·ism** (moŋ'gəl-iz'm), *n.* a type of congenital mental deficiency, accompanied with a flattened forehead, slanting eyes, etc.
**Mon·gol·oid** (moŋ'gəl-oid'), *adj.* 1. of or

characteristic of the Mongolian race. 2. having Mongolism.

**mon·goose, mon·goos** (moŋ′gōōs), *n.* [*pl.* -GOOSES], [< native name], a ferretlike, flesh-eating animal of India, that kills snakes, etc.

**mon·grel** (muŋ′grəl, moŋ′-), *n.* [< AS. *mengan*, mix], an animal or plant, esp. a dog, of mixed breed. *adj.* of mixed breed, race, character, etc.

**mon·ism** (mon′iz'm, mō′niz'm), *n.* [< Gr. *monos*, single], in *philos.*, the doctrine that there is only one ultimate substance or principle. **—mon′ist,** *n.*

**mo·ni·tion** (mō-nish′ən), *n.* [< L. *monere*, warn], admonition; warning.

**mon·i·tor** (mon′ə-tẽr), *n.* [< L. *monere*, warn], 1. [Rare], one who advises or warns. 2. in some schools, a student chosen to help keep order, record attendance, etc. 3. in *radio & TV*, a receiver used for checking on the operation of a transmitter. *v.t. & v.i.* to watch, or check on, as a radio broadcast.

**monk** (muŋk), *n.* [< Gr. *monos*, alone], a man who joins a religious order living in retirement under vows of poverty, chastity, and obedience. **—monk′ish,** *adj.*

**mon·key** (muŋ′ki), *n.* [*pl.* -KEYS], [? < MLG. *Moneke*, son of Martin the Ape in a medieval tale], any of the primates except man and the lemurs; specif., any of the smaller, long-tailed primates. *v.i.* [Colloq.], to play, trifle, or meddle.

**mon′key·shine′** (-shīn′), *n.* *usually in pl.* [Slang], a mischievous trick or prank.

**monkey wrench,** a wrench with an adjustable jaw.

**monks·hood** (muŋks′hood′), *n.* the aconite plant.

**mono-,** [< Gr. *monos*, single], a prefix meaning: *one, alone, single.*

**mon·o·chrome** (mon′ə-krōm′), *n.* [< Gr. *monos*, single + *chrōma*, color], a painting or drawing in one color or in different shades of one color.

**mon·o·cle** (mon′ə-k'l), *n.* [ult. < Gr. *monos*, single + L. *oculus*, eye], an eyeglass for one eye.

**mon·o·cot·y·le·don** (mon′ə-kot′'l-ē′d'n), *n.* any plant with only one cotyledon. **—mon′o·cot′y·le′don·ous** (-ē′d'n-əs, -ed′'n-), *adj.*

**mo·nog·a·my** (mə-nog′ə-mi), *n.* [< Gr. *monos*, single + *gamos*, marriage], the practice or state of being married to only one person at a time. **—mo·nog′a·mous,** *adj.*

**mon·o·gram** (mon′ə-gram′), *n.* [< Gr. *monos*, single + *gramma*, letter], the initials of a name, combined in a single design.

**mon·o·graph** (mon′ə-graf′, -gräf′), *n.* [*mono-* + *-graph*], a book, article, etc. about a single subject.

**mon·o·lith** (mon′ə-lith′), *n.* [< Gr. *monos*, single + *lithos*, stone], 1. a single large block of stone. 2. a pillar, statue, etc. made of such a block. **—mon′o·lith′ic,** *adj.*

**mon·o·logue, mon·o·log** (mon′ə-lôg′), *n.* [< Gr. *monos*, alone + *legein*, speak], 1. a long speech. 2. a soliloquy. 3. a skit, etc. for one actor only.

**mon·o·ma·ni·a** (mon′ə-mā′ni-ə), *n.* an excessive concern with or enthusiasm for some one thing; craze.

**mon·o·plane** (mon′ə-plān′), *n.* an airplane with only one pair of wings.

**mo·nop·o·list** (mə-nop′ə-list), *n.* one who has a monopoly or favors monopoly. **—mo·nop′o·lis′tic,** *adj.* **—mo·nop′o·lism,** *n.*

**mo·nop′o·lize′** (-līz′), *v.t.* [-LIZED, -LIZING], 1. to get, have, or exploit a monopoly of. 2. to get or occupy the whole of.

**mo·nop′o·ly** (-li), *n.* [*pl.* -LIES], [< Gr. *monos*, single + *pōlein*, sell], 1. exclusive control of a commodity or service in a given market. 2. such control granted by a government. 3. the subject of a monopoly. 4. a company that has a monopoly.

**mon·o·rail** (mon′ə-rāl′), *n.* a railway with a single track on which cars are suspended or balanced.

**mon·o·syl·la·ble** (mon′ə-sil′ə-b'l), *n.* a word of one syllable, as *cat.* **—mon′o·syl·lab′ic** (-si-lab′ik), *adj.*

**mon·o·the·ism** (mon′ə-thē-iz'm), *n.* [*mono-* + *theism*], the doctrine or belief that there is only one God. **—mon′o·the′ist,** *n.* **—mon′o·the·is′tic,** *adj.*

**mon·o·tone** (mon′ə-tōn′), *n.* [see MONO- & TONE], 1. utterance of successive words without change of pitch or key. 2. monotony of style, color, etc. 3. a single, unchanging tone. *adj.* monotonous.

**mo·not·o·nous** (mə-not′ə-nəs), *adj.* 1. going on in the same tone without variation. 2. having no variety. 3. tiresome because unvarying. **—mo·not′o·nous·ly,** *adv.*

**mo·not′o·ny** (-ni), *n.* 1. continuance of the same tone without variation. 2. lack of variety. 3. tiresome sameness.

**mon·o·type** (mon′ə-tīp′), *n.* [*mono-* + *-type*], in *printing*, either of a pair of machines for casting and setting up type in separate characters: a trademark (**Monotype**).

**mon·ox·ide** (mon-ok′sīd, mə-nok′-), *n.* an oxide with one atom of oxygen in each molecule.

**Monroe Doctrine,** the doctrine, stated by President James Monroe, that the U.S. would regard as an unfriendly act any interference by a European nation in the affairs of the Americas.

**mon·sieur** (mə-syũr′; Fr. mə-syoo′), *n.* [*pl.* MESSIEURS (mes′ẽrz; Fr. mā′syoo′)], [Fr., lit., my lord], a man; gentleman: French title [M-], equivalent to *Mr.* or *Sir.*

**Mon·si·gnor, mon·si·gnor** (mon-sēn′yẽr), *n.* [It., lit., my lord], a title given to certain Roman Catholic prelates.

**mon·soon** (mon-sōōn′), *n.* [< Ar. *mausim*, a season], 1. a seasonal wind of the Indian Ocean and S Asia. 2. the rainy season in India, etc., when this wind blows from the southwest.

**mon·ster** (mon′stẽr), *n.* [< L. *monere*, warn], 1. any plant or animal of abnormal shape or structure. 2. any very cruel or wicked person. 3. any huge animal or thing.

**mon·strance** (mon′strəns), *n.* [< L. *monstrare*, to show], in the *R. C. Church*, a receptacle in which the consecrated Host is exposed.

**mon·stros·i·ty** (mon-stros′ə-ti), *n.* 1. the state of being monstrous. 2. [*pl.* -TIES], a monstrous thing.

**mon·strous** (mon′strəs), *adj.* 1. horrible; hideous. 2. hideously evil. 3. huge. 4. highly abnormal. **—mon′strous·ly,** *adv.*

**mon·tage** (mon-täzh′), *n.* [Fr. < *monter*, to mount], a rapid sequence of photographic images, often superimposed, as to show associated ideas.

**month** (munth), *n.* [AS. *mona*, moon], 1. any of the twelve divisions of the calendar year. 2. a period of four weeks or 30 days. 3. one twelfth of the solar year: see **year** (sense 2).

**month′ly,** *adj.* 1. continuing for a month. 2. done, happening, payable, etc. every month. *n.* [*pl.* -LIES], a periodical published once a month. *adv.* once a month; every month.

**mon·u·ment** (mon′yoo-mənt), *n.* [< L. *monere*, remind], 1. something set up to keep alive the memory of a person or event, as a tablet, statue, etc. 2. a work of enduring significance.

**mon′u·men′tal** (-men′t'l), *adj.* 1. of or serving as a monument. 2. like a monument.

**moo** (mōō), *n.* [*pl.* MOOS], [echoic], the vocal sound made by a cow. *v.i.* [MOOED, MOOING], to make this sound; low.
**mood** (mōōd), *n.* [AS. *mod*, mind], a particular state of mind or feeling.
**mood** (mōōd), *n.* [< *mode*], in *grammar*, that aspect of verbs which indicates whether the action or state expressed is a fact, supposition, or command.
**mood′y,** *adj.* [-IER, -IEST], 1. subject to or characterized by gloomy or changing moods. 2. gloomy; sullen. **—mood′i·ness,** *n.*
**moon** (mōōn), *n.* [AS. *mona*], 1. the satellite of the earth, that revolves around it once about every 29½ days and shines by reflected sunlight. 2. anything shaped like the visible moon (i.e., orb or crescent). 3. any planetary satellite. *v.i.* to wander about in an idle, abstracted manner.
**moon′beam′,** *n.* a ray of moonlight.
**moon′light′,** *n.* the light of the moon. *adj.* 1. of moonlight. 2. moonlit. 3. done or occurring by moonlight, or at night.
**moon′light′ing,** *n.* the practice of holding another regular job, as at night, in addition to one's main job.
**moon′lit,** *adj.* lighted by the moon.
**moon′quake′,** *n.* a trembling of the surface of the moon, probably caused by internal rock slippage or meteorite impact.
**moon′shine′,** *n.* 1. moonlight. 2. [Colloq.], whisky, etc. unlawfully made or smuggled.
**moon′stone′,** *n.* a feldspar with a pearly luster, used as a gem.
**moon′struck′,** *adj.* crazed; lunatic; dazed.
**Moor** (moor), *n.* any of a Moslem people living in NW Africa. **—Moor′ish,** *adj.*
**moor** (moor), *n.* [AS. *mor*], [Brit.], a tract of open wasteland, usually covered with heather and often marshy: also **moor′land′**.
**moor** (moor), *v.t.* [cf. AS. *mærels*, mooring rope], 1. to hold (a ship, etc.) in place by cables from the shore, or by anchors. 2. to secure. *v.i.* to moor a ship, etc.
**moor′ings,** *n.pl.* 1. the lines, cables, etc. by which a ship is moored. 2. a place where a ship is moored.
**moose** (mōōs), *n.* [*pl.* MOOSE], [< Am. Ind.], the largest animal of the deer family, native to the northern U.S. and Canada.
**moot** (mōōt), *adj.* [AS. (*ge*)*mot*, a meeting], debatable. *v.t.* to debate or argue.
**mop** (mop), *n.* [earlier *mappe*], 1. a bundle of rags, a sponge, etc. at the end of a stick, as for washing floors. 2. anything suggesting this, as a thick head of hair. *v.t.* [MOPPED, MOPPING], to wash, wipe, or remove as with a mop (sometimes with *up*).
**mope** (mōp), *v.i.* [MOPED, MOPING], [< ?], to be gloomy and apathetic.
**mo·raine** (mə-rān′), *n.* [Fr.], a mass of rocks, sand, etc. left by a glacier.
**mor·al** (môr′əl, mor′-), *adj.* [< L. *mos*, pl. *mores*, morals], 1. dealing with, or able to distinguish between, right and wrong conduct. 2. of, teaching, or in accordance with, the principles of right and wrong. 3. good in conduct or character; specif., sexually virtuous. 4. involving sympathy without action: as, *moral* support. 5. virtually such because of its effects: as, a *moral* victory. *n.* 1. a moral lesson taught by a fable, event, etc. 2. *pl.* principles, standards, or conduct with respect to right and wrong; ethics.
**mo·rale** (mə-ral′, mô-räl′), *n.* moral or mental condition with respect to courage, discipline, confidence, etc.
**mo·ral·i·ty** (mô-ral′ə-ti, mə-), *n.* [*pl.* -TIES], 1. rightness or wrongness, as of an action. 2. a being in accord with moral principles; virtue.
**mor·al·ize** (môr′ə-līz′, mor′-), *v.i.* [-IZED, -IZING], to consider or discuss moral questions. **—mor′al·iz′er, mor′al·ist,** *n.*
**mor′al·ly,** *adv.* 1. in a moral manner. 2. as regards morals. 3. virtually.
**mo·rass** (mô-ras′, mə-), *n.* [< Frank.], a bog; swamp.
**mor·a·to·ri·um** (môr′ə-tôr′i-əm), *n.* [*pl.* -RIUMS, -RIA (-i-ə)], [< L. *mora*, a delay], 1. a legal authorization to delay payment of money due. 2. the effective period of such authorization.
**mo·ray** (môr′ā), *n.* [< L. *muraena*], a voracious, brilliantly colored eel.
**mor·bid** (môr′bid), *adj.* [< L. *morbus*, disease], 1. of or caused by disease; diseased. 2. resulting as from a diseased state of mind. **—mor·bid′i·ty,** *n.* **—mor′bid·ly,** *adv.*
**mor·dant** (môr′d′nt), *adj.* [< L. *mordere*, to bite], 1. caustic; sarcastic. 2. acting to fix colors in dyeing, etc. **—mor′dan·cy,** *n.*
**more** (môr), *adj.* [superl. MOST], [AS. *mara*], 1. greater in amount or degree (compar. of *much*). 2. greater in number (compar. of *many*). 3. additional: as, *more* news later. *n.* 1. a greater amount or degree. 2. [construed as pl.], a greater number (*of*). 3. something additional: as, *more* cannot be said. *adv.* 1. [superl. MOST], in or to a greater degree or extent: as, *more* useful. 2. in addition. **—more or less,** 1. somewhat. 2. approximately.
**more·o′ver** (-ō′vẽr), *adv.* in addition to what has been said; besides.
**mo·res** (mō′rēz, môr′ēz), *n.pl.* [L., customs], folkways so basic as to develop the force of law.
**mor·ga·nat·ic** (môr′gə-nat′ik), *adj.* [< OHG. *morgengeba*, morning gift (to the bride in lieu of a dower)], designating or of a marriage in which a man of high rank marries a woman of low rank without giving her or their offspring any claim to his rank or property.
**morgue** (môrg), *n.* [Fr.], 1. a place where the bodies of unknown dead or those dead of unknown causes are temporarily kept. 2. a newspaper office's reference file.
**mor·i·bund** (môr′ə-bund′), *adj.* [< L. *mori*, die], 1. dying. 2. coming to an end.
**Mor·mon** (môr′mən), *n.* a member of the Church of Jesus Christ of Latter-day Saints, founded in the U.S. in 1830.
**morn** (môrn), *n.* [Poetic], morning.
**morn·ing** (môr′niŋ), *n.* [< AS. *morgen*], 1. the first or early part of the day, from midnight, or esp. dawn, to noon. 2. dawn.
**morn′ing-glo′ry** (-glôr′i), *n.* [*pl.* -RIES], a twining plant with trumpet-shaped flowers.
**mo·ron** (môr′on), *n.* [< Gr. *mōros*, foolish], a person who is mentally deficient, but less so than an imbecile. **—mo·ron′ic,** *adj.*
**mo·rose** (mə-rōs′), *adj.* [< L. *mos*, manner], gloomy, sullen, surly, etc.
**Mor·pheus** (môr′fi-əs), *n.* in *Gr. myth.*, the god of dreams.
**mor·phine** (môr′fēn), *n.* [< *Morpheus*], an alkaloid derived from opium and used to induce sleep and relieve pain.
**mor·row** (mor′ō, môr′ō), *n.* [< AS. *morgen*, morning], [Poetic], 1. morning. 2. the following day.
**Morse code** (môrs), [after S. F. B. *Morse*, its inventor], a code, or alphabet, consisting of a system of dots, dashes, and spaces, used in telegraphy, etc.
**mor·sel** (môr′s′l), *n.* [< L. *morsum*, a bite], 1. a small portion of food. 2. a small piece.
**mor·tal** (môr′t′l), *adj.* [< L. *mors*, death], 1. that must eventually die. 2. of man as a being who must die. 3. of this world. 4. causing death; fatal. 5. dire: as, *mortal* terror. *n.* a human being. **—mor′tal·ly,** *adv.*
**mor·tal·i·ty** (môr-tal′ə-ti), *n.* 1. the mortal nature of man. 2. death on a large scale, as from war. 3. the ratio of deaths to population; death rate.

**mor·tar** (môr′tẽr), *n.* [< L. *mortarium*], 1. a bowl in which substances are pulverized with a pestle. 2. a short-barreled cannon which throws shells in a high trajectory. 3. a mixture of cement, sand, water, etc., used between bricks, stones, etc.

**mort·gage** (môr′gij), *n.* [< OFr. *mort*, dead + *gage*, pledge], 1. the pledging of property to a creditor as security for the payment of a debt. 2. the deed by which this is done. *v.t.* [-GAGED, -GAGING], 1. to pledge (property) by a mortgage. 2. to put an advance claim on: as, he *mortgaged* his future. —**mort′ga·gor, mort′gag·er,** *n.*

**mort·ga·gee** (môr′gi-jē′), *n.* one to whom property is mortgaged.

**mor·ti·cian** (môr-tish′ən), *n.* [< L. *mors*, death], an undertaker.

**mor·ti·fy** (môr′tə-fī′), *v.t.* [-FIED, -FYING], [< L. *mors*, death + *facere*, make], 1. to control (physical desires) by self-denial, fasting, etc. 2. to shame, humiliate, etc. 3. to make gangrenous. *v.i.* to become gangrenous. —**mor′ti·fi·ca′tion** (-fi-kā′shən), *n.*

**mor·tise** (môr′tis), *n.* [< Ar. *murtazza*, joined], a notch or hole cut in a piece of wood to receive a projecting part (*tenon*) shaped to fit.

**mor·tu·ar·y** (môr′chōō-er′i), *n.* [*pl.* -IES], [< L. *mortuus*, dead], a place where dead bodies are kept before burial or cremation.

**mos.,** months.

**Mo·sa·ic** (mō-zā′ik), *adj.* of Moses or the writings, laws, etc. attributed to him.

**mo·sa·ic** (mō-zā′ik), *n.* [ult. < Gr. *Mousa*, a Muse], 1. the making of pictures or designs by inlaying small bits of colored stone, etc. in mortar. 2. a picture or design so made.

**Mo·ses** (mō′ziz), *n.* in the *Bible*, the leader and lawgiver who brought the Israelites out of slavery in Egypt.

**mo·sey** (mō′zi), *v.i.* [-SEYED, -SEYING], [< *vamoose*], [Slang], to amble along.

**Mos·lem** (moz′ləm, mos′-), *n.* [*pl.* -LEMS, -LEM], [ult. < Ar. *aslama*, resign oneself (to God)], an adherent of Islam. *adj.* of Islam or the Moslems.

**mosque** (mosk), *n.* [ult. < Ar. *sajada*, pray], a Moslem place of worship.

**mos·qui·to** (mə-skē′tō), *n.* [*pl.* -TOES, -TOS], [Sp. < L. *musca*, a fly], a two-winged insect, the female of which bites animals and sucks blood.

**moss** (môs, mos), *n.* [AS. *mos*, a swamp], a very small, green plant that grows in velvety clusters on rocks, moist ground, etc. —**moss′y,** *adj.* —**moss′i·ness,** *n.*

**most** (mōst), *adj.* [compar. MORE], [AS. *mast*], 1. greatest in amount or degree (superl. of *much*). 2. greatest in number (superl. of *many*). 3. in the greatest number of instances. *n.* 1. the greatest amount or degree. 2. [construed as pl.], the greatest number (*of*). *adv.* [compar. MORE], in or to the greatest degree or extent: as, *most* horrible, *most* quickly. —**at (the) most,** not more than. —**for the most part,** in most instances.

**most′ly,** *adv.* 1. for the most part; in the main. 2. chiefly; principally.

**mot** (mō), *n.* [Fr., a word], a witticism or pithy remark.

**mote** (mōt), *n.* [AS. *mot*], a speck, as of dust.

**mo·tel** (mō-tel′), *n.* [*mo*torist + ho*tel*], a roadside hotel for motorists.

**moth** (môth), *n.* [*pl.* MOTHS (mô*th*z, môths)], [AS. *moththe*], 1. a four-winged, chiefly night-flying insect related to the butterfly. 2. a moth **(clothes moth)** whose larvae eat holes in woolens, furs, etc.

**moth′-eat′en,** *adj.* 1. gnawed away in patches by moths, as cloth. 2. worn out.

**moth·er** (mu*th*′ẽr), *n.* [AS. *modor*], 1. a female parent. 2. an origin or source. 3. a woman who is the head **(mother superior)** of a religious establishment. *adj.* 1. of or like a mother. 2. native: as, *mother* tongue. *v.t.* to be the mother of. —**moth′er·hood′,** *n.*

**Mother Goose,** the imaginary creator of a collection of English nursery rhymes.

**moth′er-in-law′,** *n.* [*pl.* MOTHERS-IN-LAW], the mother of one's husband or wife.

**moth′er·land′,** *n.* one's native land.

**moth′er·ly,** *adj.* of or like a mother; maternal. —**moth′er·li·ness,** *n.*

**moth′er-of-pearl′,** *n.* the hard internal layer of the shell of the pearl oyster, etc., used to make buttons, etc.

**mother tongue,** one's native language.

**mo·tif** (mō-tēf′), *n.* [Fr.; see MOTIVE], in *art, literature, & music*, a main theme or subject for development.

**mo·tile** (mō′t'l), *adj.* [< L. *movere*, to move], in *biology*, capable of or exhibiting spontaneous motion.

**mo·tion** (mō′shən), *n.* [< L. *movere*, to move], 1. a moving from one place to another. 2. a moving of a part of the body; specif., a gesture. 3. a proposal formally made in an assembly. *v.i.* to make a meaningful movement of the hand, etc. *v.t.* to direct by a meaningful gesture. —**in motion,** moving. —**mo′tion·less,** *adj.*

**motion picture,** a sequence of photographs or drawings projected on a screen in such rapid succession as to create the illusion of moving persons and objects.

**mo·ti·vate** (mō′tə-vāt′), *v.t.* [-VATED, -VATING], to provide with, or affect as, a motive; incite. —**mo′ti·va′tion,** *n.*

**mo·tive** (mō′tiv), *n.* [< L. *movere*, to move], 1. an inner drive, impulse, etc. that causes one to act; incentive. 2. a motif. *adj.* of or causing motion.

**-motive,** a suffix meaning *moving, of motion*, as in *locomotive*.

**mot·ley** (mot′li), *adj.* [prob. < OFr.], 1. of many colors. 2. of many different elements: as, a *motley* group. *n.* the many-colored costume of a jester.

**mo·tor** (mō′tẽr), *n.* [L. < *movere*, to move], 1. anything that produces motion. 2. an engine; esp., an internal-combustion engine. 3. an automobile. 4. a machine for converting electrical energy into mechanical energy. *adj.* 1. producing motion. 2. of or powered by a motor. 3. of, by, or for motor vehicles. *v.i.* to travel by automobile.

**mo′tor·boat′,** *n.* a boat propelled by a motor.

**mo′tor·cade′** (-kād′), *n.* [*motor*car + caval*cade*], an automobile procession.

**mo′tor·car′,** *n.* an automobile.

**motor court,** a motel.

**mo′tor·cy′cle** (-sī′k'l), *n.* a two-wheeled vehicle propelled by an internal-combustion engine. —**mo′tor·cy′clist,** *n.*

**mo′tor·ist,** *n.* one who drives an automobile or travels by automobile.

**mo·tor·ize** (mō′tẽr-īz′), *v.t.* [-IZED, -IZING], to equip with motor-driven vehicles.

**mo′tor·man** (-mən), *n.* [*pl.* -MEN], one who drives an electric streetcar.

**mot·tle** (mot′'l), *v.t.* [-TLED, -TLING], [< *motley*], to mark with blotches or streaks of different colors. —**mot′tled,** *adj.*

**mot·to** (mot′ō), *n.* [*pl.* -TOES, -TOS], [It., a word], 1. a word, phrase, etc. inscribed on something, as expressive of its character. 2. a maxim adopted as a principle of behavior.

**mould** (mōld), *n., v.t. & v.i.* mold (growth). —**mould′y** [-IER, -IEST], *adj.*

**mould** (mōld), *n. & v.t.* mold (form).

**mould′er,** *v.t. & v.i.* to molder.

**moult** (mōlt), *n., v.t. & v.i.* molt.

**mound** (mound), *n.* [prob. < MD. *mond*, protection], a heap or bank of earth, sand, etc. *v.i.* to heap up in a mound.

**mount** (mount), *n.* [< L. *mons*], a mountain.
**mount** (mount), *v.i.* [< L. *mons*, mountain], 1. to climb; ascend. 2. to climb up on something, as a horse. 3. to increase in amount. *v.t.* 1. to go up; ascend: as, to *mount* stairs. 2. to get up on (a platform, etc.). 3. to get on (a horse). 4. to set on or provide with a horse. 5. to place or fix on or in the proper support, backing, etc., as a gem in a setting. 6. to arrange (a dead animal, etc.) for exhibition. 7. to place (a gun) into position ready for use. *n.* 1. the act of mounting. 2. a horse for riding. 3. the support, setting, etc. on or in which a thing is mounted.
**moun·tain** (moun′t'n), *n.* [ult. < L. *mons*], 1. a natural raised part of the earth, larger than a hill. 2. a large pile, heap, etc, *adj.* 1. of or in mountains. 2. like a mountain.
**moun′tain·eer′** (-êr′), *n.* 1. one who lives in a mountainous region. 2. a mountain climber.
**mountain goat,** a long-haired, goatlike mammal of the Rocky Mountains.
**mountain lion,** the cougar; puma.
**moun′tain·ous,** *adj.* 1. full of mountains. 2. like a mountain; very large.
**moun·te·bank** (moun′tə-baŋk′), *n.* [< It. *montare*, to mount + *in*, on + *banco*, a bench], 1. one who sells quack medicines in a public place. 2. any charlatan, or quack. *v.i.* to act as a mountebank.
**mount′ed,** *adj.* serving on horseback.
**mount′ing,** *n.* something serving as a backing, support, setting, etc.
**mourn** (môrn), *v.i. & v.t.* [AS. *murnan*], 1. to feel or express sorrow for (something regrettable). 2. to grieve for (someone dead).
**mourn′ful,** *adj.* 1. feeling or expressing grief or sorrow. 2. causing sorrow.
**mourn′ing,** *n.* 1. a sorrowing; specif., the expression of grief at someone's death. 2. black clothes, etc., worn as a sign of grief for the dead. —**mourn′ing·ly,** *adv.*
**mouse** (mous), *n.* [*pl.* MICE (mis)], [AS. *mus*], 1. any of various small rodents, esp. one that infests human dwellings. 2. a timid person. 3. [Slang], a swollen bruise under the eye. *v.i.* (mouz), [MOUSED, MOUSING], to hunt for mice. —**mous′y** [-IER, -IEST], *adj.*
**mousse** (mo͞os), *n.* [Fr., foam], a light frozen dessert, made from whipped cream, gelatin, etc., sweetened and flavored.
**mous·tache** (məs-tash′, mus′tash), *n.* a mustache.
**mouth** (mouth), *n.* [*pl.* MOUTHS (mouthz)], [AS. *muth*], 1. the opening through which an animal takes in food and through which sounds are uttered. 2. any opening regarded as like the mouth: as, the *mouth* of a river. *v.t.* (mouth), 1. to say, esp. in an affected manner. 2. to caress or rub with the mouth. —**down in** (or **at**) **the mouth,** [Colloq.], depressed; unhappy.
**mouth·ful′,** *n.* [*pl.* -FULS], 1. as much as the mouth can hold. 2. the usual amount taken into the mouth. 3. a small amount. 4. [Slang], a pertinent remark: usually in **say a mouthful.**
**mouth organ,** a harmonica.
**mouth′piece′,** *n.* 1. a part, as of a musical instrument, placed at or in the mouth. 2. a person, periodical, etc. serving as a spokesman for others.
**mou·ton** (mo͞o′ton′), *n.* [Fr., sheep], the fur of any of certain sheep, dyed to resemble beaver, etc.
**mov·a·ble, move·a·ble** (mo͞ov′ə-b'l), *adj.* that can be moved from one place to another. *n.* 1. something movable. 2. *usually pl.* in *law*, personal property, esp. furniture.
**move** (mo͞ov), *v.t.* [MOVED, MOVING], [< L. *movere*], 1. to change the place or position of. 2. to set or keep in motion. 3. to cause (*to act, do, say*, etc.). 4. to arouse the emotions, etc. of. 5. to propose formally, as in a meeting. *v.i.* 1. to change place or position. 2. to change one's residence. 3. to be active. 4. to make progress. 5. to take action. 6. to be, or be set, in motion. 7. to make a formal application (*for*). 8. to be sold: said of goods. *n.* 1. act of moving. 2. an action toward some goal. 3. in *chess*, *checkers*, etc., the act of moving a piece, or one's turn to move. —**on the move,** [Colloq.], moving about from place to place.
**move′ment,** *n.* 1. a moving or manner of moving. 2. an evacuation of the bowels. 3. a change in the location of troops, ships, etc. 4. organized action by people working toward some goal. 5. the moving parts of a mechanism, as of a clock. 6. in *music*, *a*) rhythm. *b*) any of the principal divisions of an extended composition.
**mov′er,** *n.* one that moves; specif., one whose work is moving furniture, etc. for those changing residence.
**mov·ie** (mo͞ov′i), *n.* [< *moving picture*], [Colloq.], a motion picture.
**mow** (mō), *v.t.* [MOWED (mōd), MOWED or MOWN (mōn), MOWING], [AS. *mawan*], 1. to cut down (grass, etc.) from (a lawn, etc.) as with a sickle or lawn mower. 2. to cause to fall like cut grass; kill. —**mow′er,** *n.*
**mow** (mou), *n.* [AS. *muga*], 1. a heap of hay, esp. in a barn. 2. the part of a barn where hay, etc. is stored.
**MP, M.P.,** Military Police.
**mph, m.p.h.,** miles per hour.
**Mr.** (mis′tēr), [*pl.* MESSRS. (mes′ērz)], mister: before a man's name or title.
**Mrs.** (mis′iz), mistress: used before a married woman's name.
**MS., ms.,** [*pl.* MSS., MSS.], manuscript.
**M.S., M.Sc.,** Master of Science.
**Msgr.,** Monsignor.
**M.Sgt., M/Sgt.,** Master Sergeant.
**M.S.T.,** Mountain Standard Time.
**Mt., mt.,** [*pl.* MTS., MTS.], 1. mount. 2. mountain.
**mu** (mū, mo͞o), *n.* the twelfth letter of the Greek alphabet (M, μ).
**much** (much), *adj.* [MORE, MOST], [< AS. *mycel*], great in quantity, degree, etc. *adv.* 1. to a great degree or extent: as, *much* relieved. 2. nearly: as, *much* the same. *n.* 1. a great amount: as, *much* of it. 2. something great, important, etc.: as, is he *much* of a scholar? —**make much of,** to treat or consider as of great importance.
**mu·ci·lage** (mū′s'l-ij), *n.* [< L. *mucus*, mucus], 1. a thick, sticky substance found in certain plants. 2. any watery solution of gum, glue, etc. used as an adhesive. —**mu′ci·lag′i·nous** (-laj′i-nəs), *adj.*
**muck** (muk), *n.* [< ON. *myki*], 1. moist manure. 2. black earth with decaying matter, used as fertilizer. 3. dirt; filth. —**muck′y** [-IER, -IEST], *adj.*
**muck′rake′,** *v.i.* [-RAKED, -RAKING], [see MUCK & RAKE], to search for and expose corruption in politics, business, etc. —**muck′rak′er,** *n.*
**mu·cous** (mū′kəs), *adj.* 1. of, containing, or secreting mucus. 2. slimy.
**mucous membrane,** a mucus-secreting membrane lining body cavities, etc.
**mu·cus** (mū′kəs), *n.* [L.], the slimy secretion that moistens and protects the mucous membranes.
**mud** (mud), *n.* [prob. < a LG. source], wet, soft, sticky earth.
**mud·dle** (mud′'l), *v.t.* [-DLED, -DLING], [< *mud*], 1. to mix up; bungle. 2. to confuse, as with liquor. *v.i.* to act or think in a confused way. *n.* mess, confusion, etc.
**mud·dler** (mud′lẽr), *n.* a stick to stir mixed drinks.
**mud·dy** (mud′i), *adj.* [-DIER, -DIEST], 1. full

of or spattered with mud. 2. cloudy: as, *muddy* coffee. 3. confused, obscure, etc. ***v.t. & v.i.*** [-DIED, -DYING], to make or become muddy. —**mud′di·ness,** ***n.***

**mu·ez·zin** (mū-ez′in), ***n.*** [< Ar. *mu'adhdhin*, proclaiming], a Moslem crier who calls the people to prayer at the proper hours.

**muff** (muf), ***n.*** [< Fr. *moufle*, mitten], 1. a cylindrical covering of fur, etc. for keeping the hands warm. 2. in *baseball*, etc., a failure to hold a ball when catching it. 3. any bungling action. ***v.t. & v.i.*** 1. to miss (a catch, etc.). 2. to bungle.

**muf·fin** (muf′in), ***n.*** [< ?], a quick bread baked in a cup-shaped mold.

**muf·fle** (muf′'l), ***v.t.*** [-FLED, -FLING], [prob. < OFr. *moufle*, mitten], 1. to wrap or cover closely so as to keep warm, etc. 2. to cover so as to deaden sound. 3. to deaden (a sound). ***n.*** a wrap, etc. used for muffling.

**muf·fler** (muf′lẽr), ***n.*** 1. a scarf worn around the throat, as for warmth. 2. a device for silencing noises.

**muf·ti** (muf′ti), ***n.*** [*pl.* -TIS], [< Ar.], civilian clothes, esp. as distinguished from a uniform.

**mug** (mug), ***n.*** [prob. < ON.], 1. a cup of earthenware or metal with a handle. 2. as much as a mug will hold. 3. [Slang], the face. ***v.t.*** [MUGGED, MUGGING], [Slang], to assault from behind by strangling. ***v.i.*** [Slang], to grimace, esp. in overacting. —**mug′ger,** ***n.***

**mug·gy** (mug′i), ***adj.*** [-GIER, -GIEST], [< ME. *muggen*, to drizzle], hot, damp, and close: as, *muggy* weather. —**mug′gi·ness,** ***n.***

**mug·wump** (mug′wump′), ***n.*** [< Algonquian *mugquomp*, great man], an independent, esp. in politics.

**mu·lat·to** (mə-lat′ō, myoo-), ***n.*** [*pl.* -TOES], [Sp. & Port. *mulato*, of mixed breed], a person one of whose parents is a Negro and the other a Caucasian.

**mul·ber·ry** (mul′ber′i, -bẽr-i), ***n.*** [*pl.* -RIES], [< AS. *morberie*], 1. the purplish-red, edible, berrylike fruit of a tree on whose leaves silkworms feed. 2. this tree.

**mulch** (mulch), ***n.*** [ME. *molsh*, soft], leaves, peat, etc. spread on the ground around plants to prevent freezing of roots, etc. ***v.t.*** to apply mulch to.

**mulct** (mulkt), ***v.t.*** [< L. *mul(c)ta*, a fine], 1. to fine. 2. to deprive of something, as by fraud. ***n.*** a fine; penalty. —**mulct′er,** ***n.***

**mule** (mūl), ***n.*** [< L. *mulus*], 1. the (usually sterile) offspring of a male donkey and a female horse. 2. a machine that spins cotton fibers into yarn. 3. [Colloq.], a stubborn person.

**mule** (mūl), ***n.*** [< L. *mulleus*, red shoe], a lounging slipper that bares the heel.

**mu·le·teer** (mū′lə-têr′), ***n.*** [< Fr.], a mule driver.

**mul′ish,** ***adj.*** like a mule; stubborn.

**mull** (mul), ***v.t. & v.i.*** [ME. *mullen*, to grind], [Colloq.], to ponder (*over*).

**mull** (mul), ***v.t.*** [prob. < Fr. *mollir*, soften], to heat, sweeten, and flavor with spices, as beer, wine, etc.

**mul·lein, mul·len** (mul′in), ***n.*** [< OFr. *moleine*], a tall plant with downy leaves and variously colored flowers.

**mul·let** (mul′it), ***n.*** [< L. *mullus*], any of a group of edible salt- and fresh-water fishes.

**mul·li·gan (stew)** (mul′i-g'n), [< ?], [Slang], a stew made of odd bits of meat and vegetables.

**mul·li·ga·taw·ny** (mul′i-gə-tô′ni), ***n.*** [Tamil *milagutaṇṇir*, pepper water], an East Indian soup of meat, etc., flavored with curry.

**mul·lion** (mul′yən), ***n.*** [prob. < L. *medianus*, middle], a slender, vertical dividing bar between the lights of windows, screens, etc.

**multi-,** [L. < *multus*, much, many], a combining form meaning: 1. *having many.* 2. *more than two.* 3. *many times more than.*

**mul·ti·col·ored** (mul′ti-kul′ẽrd), ***adj.*** having many colors.

**mul·ti·far·i·ous** (mul′tə-fâr′i-əs), ***adj.*** [< L.], having many kinds of parts or elements; diverse.

**mul·ti·lat·er·al** (mul′ti-lat′ẽr-əl), ***adj.*** 1. many-sided. 2. involving more than two nations: as, a *multilateral* treaty.

**mul′ti·mil′lion·aire′,** ***n.*** a person whose wealth amounts to several millions of dollars, francs, etc.

**mul·ti·ple** (mul′tə-p'l), ***adj.*** [< L. *multus*, many + *plicare*, fold], having many parts, elements, etc. ***n.*** a number that is a product of a specified number and another number.

**mul·ti·pli·cand** (mul′tə-pli-kand′), ***n.*** a number that is to be multiplied by another.

**mul′ti·pli·ca′tion** (-pli-kā′shən), ***n.*** a multiplying or being multiplied; specif., the process of finding the quantity obtained by repeating a specified quantity a specified number of times.

**mul′ti·plic′i·ty** (-plis′ə-ti), ***n.*** 1. a being manifold or various. 2. a great number.

**mul′ti·pli′er** (-plī′ẽr), ***n.*** one that multiplies; specif., a number by which another is to be multiplied.

**mul·ti·ply** (mul′tə-plī′), ***v.t. & v.i.*** [-PLIED, -PLYING], [see MULTIPLE], 1. to increase in number, degree, etc. 2. to find the product (of) by multiplication.

**mul·ti·tude** (mul′tə-to͞od′, -tūd′), ***n.*** [< L. *multus*, many], a large number; crowd.

**mul′ti·tu′di·nous** (-to͞o′d'n-əs, -tū′-), ***adj.*** very numerous; many.

**mum** (mum), ***n.*** [Colloq.], a chrysanthemum.

**mum** (mum), ***adj.*** [ME. *momme*], silent; not speaking. —**mum's the word,** say nothing.

**mum·ble** (mum′b'l), ***v.t. & v.i.*** [-BLED, -BLING], [ME. *momelen*], to speak or say indistinctly; mutter. ***n.*** a mumbled utterance.

**mum·bo jum·bo** (mum′bō jum′bō), [< W. Afr.], 1. an idol or fetish. 2. meaningless ritual, etc.

**mum·mer** (mum′ẽr), ***n.*** [prob. < OFr. *momon*, a mask], one who wears a mask or disguise, as for acting out pantomimes.

**mum′mer·y,** ***n.*** [*pl.* -IES], 1. performance by mummers. 2. a hypocritical show or ceremony.

**mum·mi·fy** (mum′ə-fī′), ***v.t. & v.i.*** [-FIED, -FYING], to make into or become a mummy.

**mum·my** (mum′i), ***n.*** [*pl.* -MIES], [ult. < Ar. *mum*, wax], a well-preserved dead body, esp. one preserved by embalming, as by the ancient Egyptians.

**mumps** (mumps), ***n.pl.*** [construed as sing.], [< obs. *mump*, a grimace], an acute communicable disease characterized by swelling of the salivary glands.

**munch** (munch), ***v.t. & v.i.*** [echoic], to chew vigorously, often with a crunching sound.

**mun·dane** (mun′dān), ***adj.*** [< L. *mundus*, world], of the world; worldly.

**mu·nic·i·pal** (mū-nis′ə-p'l), ***adj.*** [< L. *municeps*, citizen of a free town], of or characteristic of a city, town, etc. or its local government. —**mu·nic′i·pal·ly,** ***adv.***

**mu·nic′i·pal′i·ty** (-pal′ə-ti), ***n.*** [*pl.* -TIES], a city, town, etc. having its own incorporated government.

**mu·nif·i·cent** (mū-nif′ə-s'nt), ***adj.*** [< L. *munus*, gift + *facere*, make], very generous in giving; lavish. —**mu·nif′i·cence,** ***n.***

**mu·ni′tions,** ***n.pl.*** [< L. *munire*, fortify], military supplies; esp., weapons and ammunition.

**mu·ral** (myoor′əl), ***adj.*** [< L. *murus*, wall], 1. of, on, or for a wall. 2. like a wall. ***n.*** a picture, esp. a large one, painted directly on a wall. —**mu′ral·ist,** ***n.***

**mur·der** (mũr′dẽr), ***n.*** [AS. *morthor*], the

unlawful and malicious or premeditated killing of a person. *v.t.* 1. to kill unlawfully and with malice. 2. to botch, as in performance: as, she *murdered* that song. —**mur′der·er,** *n.* —**mur′der·ess,** *n.fem.*

**mur′der·ous,** *adj.* 1. of or characteristic of murder; brutal. 2. capable or guilty of, or intending, murder.

**murk** (mũrk), *n.* [< ON. *myrkr,* dark], darkness; gloom. *adj.* dark or dim.

**murk·y** (mũr′ki), *adj.* [-IER, -IEST], dark or gloomy. —**murk′i·ly,** *adv.* —**murk′i·ness,** *n.*

**mur·mur** (mũr′mẽr), *n.* [echoic], 1. a low, indistinct, continuous sound. 2. a mumbled complaint. 3. an abnormal sound in the body, esp. in the region of the heart. *v.i.* to make a murmur. *v.t.* to say in a murmur. —**mur′mur·ing,** *adj.*

**mur·rain** (mũr′in), *n.* [< L. *mori,* die], a plague, esp. of cattle.

**mus·cat** (mus′kət), *n.* [Fr. < LL. *muscus,* musk], a sweet European grape.

**mus·ca·tel** (mus′kə-tel′), *n.* a rich, sweet wine made from the muscat.

**mus·cle** (mus′'l), *n.* [< L. *mus,* mouse], 1. the fibrous tissue making up the fleshy parts of the body. 2. any of these body parts that can be contracted and expanded to produce bodily movements. 3. muscular strength. *v.i.* [-CLED, -CLING], [Colloq.], to force one's way (*in*).

**mus′cle-bound′,** *adj.* having some of the muscles enlarged and less elastic, as from too much exercise.

**mus·cu·lar** (mus′kyoo-lẽr), *adj.* 1. of or done by muscles. 2. having well-developed muscles; strong. —**mus′cu·lar′i·ty,** *n.*

**mus′cu·la·ture** (-lə-chẽr), *n.* [Fr.], the arrangement of the muscles of a body, limb, etc.; muscular system.

**Muse** (mūz), *n.* [< Gr. *mousa*], 1. in *Gr. myth.,* any of the nine goddesses who presided over literature and the arts and sciences. 2. [m-], the spirit regarded as inspiring a poet or artist.

**muse** (mūz), *v.t. & v.i.* [MUSED, MUSING], [< OFr. *muser,* loiter], to think or consider deeply; meditate. —**mus′er,** *n.*

**mu·se·um** (mū-zē′əm), *n.* [ult. < Gr. *mousa,* Muse], a building, room, etc. for exhibiting artistic, historical, or scientific objects.

**mush** (mush), *n.* [var. of *mash*], 1. a porridge of boiled corn meal. 2. any thick, soft mass. 3. [Colloq.], maudlin sentiment. —**mush′y** [-IER, -IEST], *adj.*

**mush** (mush), *interj.* [? < Fr. *marcher,* go], a shout to start sled dogs or urge them on. *v.i.* to travel on foot over snow, usually with a dog sled.

**mush·room** (mush′rōōm), *n.* [< OFr. *mousse,* moss], any of various rapid-growing, fleshy fungi having a stalk with an umbrellalike top; esp., any edible variety. *adj.* of or like a mushroom. *v.i.* 1. to grow or spread rapidly. 2. to flatten out at the end so as to resemble a mushroom.

**mus·ic** (mū′zik), *n.* [< Gr. *mousikē* (*technē*), art of the Muses], 1. the art of combining tones to form expressive compositions. 2. such compositions, either as performed or scored. 3. any rhythmic sequence of pleasing sounds, as of birds. —**face the music,** [Colloq.], to accept the consequences.

**mu′si·cal,** *adj.* 1. of or for music. 2. melodious or harmonious. 3. fond of or skilled in music. 4. set to music. *n.* a musical comedy.

**musical comedy,** a theatrical production with musical numbers, dances, etc., centered upon a slight plot.

**mu·si·cale** (mū′zi-kal′), *n.* [Fr.], a social affair featuring music.

**mu·si·cian** (mū-zish′ən), *n.* one skilled in music, esp. a professional performer.

**mu·si·col·o·gy** (mū′zi-kol′ə-ji), *n.* [see -LOGY], the study of the science, history, and methods of music. —**mu′si·col′o·gist,** *n.*

**musk** (musk), *n.* [< Ar. *mushk*], a secretion having a strong odor, obtained from the male musk deer: used in making perfumes.

**musk deer,** a small, hornless deer of C Asia.

**mus·kel·lunge, mus·kal·lunge** (mus′kə-lunj′), *n.* [*pl.* -LUNGE], [< Algonquian], a very large, edible pike of N. America.

**mus·ket** (mus′kit), *n.* [< L. *musca,* a fly], a former kind of firearm, with a long barrel and a smooth bore.

**mus′ket·eer′** (-kə-têr′), *n.* a soldier armed with a musket.

**mus′ket·ry,** *n.* 1. the art or practice of firing muskets. 2. musketeers.

**musk′mel′on,** *n.* any of various sweet, juicy melons, as the cantaloupe.

**musk·rat** (musk′rat′), *n.* 1. a N. American water rodent with brown fir and a musky odor. 2. its fur.

**mus·lin** (muz′lin), *n.* [< *Mosul,* city in Iraq], a fine cotton cloth: a heavy type is used for sheets, etc.

**muss** (mus), *n.* [prob. var. of *mess*], [Colloq.], a mess; disorder. *v.t.* [Colloq.], to make messy. —**muss′y** [-IER, -IEST], *adj.*

**mus·sel** (mus′'l), *n.* [< L. *mus,* mouse], any of various bivalve mollusks, esp. an edible salt-water variety.

**must** (must), *v.* [pt. MUST], [AS. *moste*], an auxiliary expressing: 1. necessity: as, I *must* go. 2. probability: as, it *must* have been Joe. 3. certainty: as, all men *must* die. *n.* something that must be done, had, etc. *adj.* that must be done, etc.

**mus·tache** (məs-tash′, mus′tash), *n.* [ult. < Gr. *mastax,* a mouth], the hair on the upper lip of men.

**mus·tang** (mus′taŋ), *n.* [< Sp. *mestengo,* belonging to the graziers], a small wild horse of the Southwest plains.

**mus·tard** (mus′tẽrd), *n.* [< OFr.], 1. a plant with yellow flowers and slender pods. 2. the yellow powder made from its ground seeds, often prepared as a paste, used as a seasoning. 3. a dark yellow.

**mustard gas,** [< its mustardlike odor], a poison gas used in warfare.

**mus·ter** (mus′tẽr), *v.t.* [< L. *monere,* warn], 1. to assemble (troops, etc.). 2. to summon; collect: as, to *muster* up courage. *v.i.* to assemble, as troops. *n.* 1. a gathering or assembling, esp. of troops for inspection, etc. 2. the persons or things assembled. —**muster in** (or **out**). to enlist in (or discharge from) military service. —**pass muster,** to measure up to the required standard.

**must·n't** (mus′'nt), must not.

**mus·ty** (mus′ti), *adj.* [-TIER, -TIEST], [prob. ult. < *moist*], 1. having a stale, moldy smell or taste. 2. antiquated. —**mus′ti·ness,** *n.*

**mu·ta·ble** (mū′tə-b'l), *adj.* [< L. *mutare,* to change], 1. that can be changed. 2. inconstant; fickle. —**mu′ta·bil′i·ty,** *n.*

**mu·tate** (mū′tāt), *v.i. & v.t.* [-TATED, -TATING], [< L. *mutare,* to change], to change.

**mu·ta·tion** (mū-tā′shən), *n.* 1. a change, as in form, nature, etc. 2. a sudden variation in some inheritable characteristic of a plant or animal.

**mute** (mūt), *adj.* [< L. *mutus*], 1. not speaking; silent. 2. unable to speak. *n.* 1. a deaf-mute. 2. a device that softens the sound of a musical instrument. *v.t.* [MUTED, MUTING], to soften the sound of (a musical instrument). —**mute′ly,** *adv.* —**mute′ness,** *n.*

**mu·ti·late** (mū′t'l-āt′), *v.t.* [-LATED, -LATING], [< L. *mutilus,* maimed], to cut off or damage an important part of. —**mu′ti·la′tion,** *n.*

**mu·ti·neer** (mū′t'n-êr′), *n.* one guilty of mutiny.

**mu·ti·ny** (mū′t'n-i), *n.* [*pl.* -NIES], [ult. < L. *movere*, to move], forcible revolt against constituted authority; esp., rebellion of soldiers or sailors against their officers. *v.i.* [-NIED, -NYING], to revolt. —**mu′ti·nous,** *adj.*
**mutt** (mut), *n.* [Slang], a mongrel dog.
**mut·ter** (mut′ẽr), *v.i. & v.t.* [ME. *materen*], 1. to speak or say in low, indistinct tones. 2. to grumble. *n.* 1. a muttering. 2. something muttered. —**mut′ter·er,** *n.*
**mut·ton** (mut′'n), *n.* [< ML. *multo*, sheep], the flesh of (grown) sheep used as food.
**mu·tu·al** (mū′chōō-əl), *adj.* [< L. *mutare*, to change], 1. *a*) done, felt, etc. by each of two or more for or toward the other or others. *b*) of each other. 2. shared in common. —**mu′tu·al·ly,** *adv.*
**muz·zle** (muz′'l), *n.* [< ML. *musus*], 1. the nose and jaws of a dog, horse, etc. 2. a device put over the mouth of an animal to prevent its biting or eating. 3. the front end of the barrel of a firearm. *v.t.* [-ZLED, -ZLING], 1. to put a muzzle on (an animal). 2. to prevent from talking.
**my** (mī), *pron.* [AS. *min*], poss. form of **I.** *poss. pronominal adj.* of, belonging to, or done by me.
**my·e·li·tis** (mī′ə-lī′tis), *n.* [< Gr. *myelos*, marrow; + *-itis*], inflammation of the spinal cord or the bone marrow.
**my·na, my·nah** (mī′nə), *n.* [Hind. *mainā*], a tropical bird of SE Asia related to the starling: often kept as a pet.
**my·o·pi·a** (mī-ō′pi-ə), *n.* [< Gr. *myein*, to close + *ōps*, eye], nearsightedness. —**my·op′ic** (-op′ik), *adj.*
**myr·i·ad** (mir′i-əd), *n.* [< Gr. *myrias*, ten thousand], a large number of persons or things. *adj.* very many.
**myr·mi·don** (mũr′mi-don′, -dən), *n.* [after name of a Gr. tribe led by Achilles], an unquestioning follower.
**myrrh** (mũr), *n.* [ult. < Ar. *murr*], a fragrant gum resin exuded from a shrub of Arabia and E Africa, used in making incense, etc.
**myr·tle** (mũr′t'l), *n.* [< Gr. *myrtos*], 1. an evergreen shrub with white or pink flowers. 2. an evergreen creeping plant with white or blue flowers.
**my·self** (mī-self′), *pron.* 1. the intensive form of **I**: as, I went *myself*. 2. the reflexive form of **I**: as, I hurt *myself*. 3. my true self: as, I am not *myself* today.
**mys·te·ri·ous** (mis-têr′i-əs), *adj.* of, containing, or characterized by mystery. —**mys·te′ri·ous·ly,** *adv.* —**mys·te′ri·ous·ness,** *n.*
**mys·ter·y** (mis′tẽr-i), *n.* [*pl.* -IES], [< Gr. *mystērion*, secret worship of a deity], 1. something unexplained, unknown, or kept secret. 2. a novel or play about a secret or unexplained event: as, a murder *mystery*. 3. obscurity or secrecy.
**mys·tic** (mis′tik), *adj.* 1. of mystics or mysticism. 2. occult. 3. mysterious. *n.* a believer in mysticism.
**mys′ti·cal,** *adj.* 1. spiritually symbolic. 2. mystic (senses 1 & 2).
**mys·ti·cism** (mis′tə-siz'm), *n.* any doctrine that knowledge of spiritual truths may be attained intuitively.
**mys′ti·fy′** (-fī′), *v.t.* [-FIED, -FYING], 1. to puzzle or perplex. 2. to involve in mystery.
**mys·tique** (mis-tēk′), *n.* [Fr., mystic], a complex of quasi-mystical attitudes and feelings surrounding some person, institution, etc.
**myth** (mith), *n.* [< Gr. *mythos*], 1. a traditional story serving to explain some phenomenon, custom, etc. 2. mythology. 3. any fictitious story, person, or thing. —**myth′i·cal,** *adj.*
**my·thol·o·gy** (mi-thol′ə-ji), *n.* [*pl.* -GIES], 1. the study of myths. 2. myths collectively, esp. of a specific people. —**myth·o·log·i·cal** (mith′ə-loj′i-k'l), *adj.* —**my·thol′o·gist,** *n.*

# N

**N, n** (en), *n.* [*pl.* N's, n's, Ns, ns], the fourteenth letter of the English alphabet.
**N,** in *chem.*, nitrogen.
**N.,** Norse.
**N., n.,** 1. navy. 2. neuter. 3. new. 4. noon. 5. North. 6. noun.
**N, n,** northern.
**Na,** *natrium*, [L.], in *chem.*, sodium.
**N.A.,** North America.
**nab** (nab), *v.t.* [NABBED, NABBING], [prob. < dial. *nap*, snatch], [Colloq.], 1. to snatch or seize suddenly. 2. to arrest (a felon).
**na·bob** (nā′bob), *n.* [Hind. *navāb*], a very rich man. —**na′bob·ish,** *adj.*
**na·cre** (nā′kẽr), *n.* [Fr. < Ar.], mother-of-pearl. —**na′cre·ous** (-kri-əs), *adj.*
**na·dir** (nā′dẽr), *n.* [< Ar. *nazir*, opposite], 1. the point of the celestial sphere opposite the zenith, or directly beneath the observer. 2. the lowest point.
**nae** (nā), *adj. & adv.* [Scot.], 1. no. 2. not.
**nag** (nag), *v.i. & v.t.* [NAGGED, NAGGING], [< Scand.], to urge, scold, etc. constantly or annoy by scolding, etc. *n.* 1. the act of nagging. 2. [Colloq.], one who nags.
**nag** (nag), *n.* [ME. *nagge*], a horse, esp. an inferior one.
**nai·ad** (nā′ad, nī′-), *n.* [< Gr. *naein*, to flow], in *Gr. & Rom. myth.*, any of the nymphs who lived in springs, rivers, etc.
**nail** (nāl), *n.* [AS. *nægl*], 1. the thin, horny plate at the ends of the fingers and toes. 2. a slender, pointed piece of metal driven with a hammer to hold pieces of wood together. *v.t.* 1. to attach, fasten, etc. with nails. 2. to secure; fix. 3. [Colloq.], to catch.
**na·ive, na·ïve** (nä-ēv′), *adj.* [Fr. < L. *nativus*, natural], unaffectedly simple; artless; unsophisticated. —**na·ive′ly, na·ïve′ly,** *adv.* —**na·ïve′té, na·ïve′te** (-tā), *n.*
**na·ked** (nā′kid), *adj.* [AS. *nacod*], 1. completely unclothed; nude. 2. without covering: as, a *naked* sword. 3. without additions, disguises, etc.; plain: as, the *naked* truth. —**na′ked·ly,** *adv.* —**nak′ed·ness,** *n.*
**nam·by-pam·by** (nam′bi-pam′bi), *adj.* [< nickname of *Ambrose* Philips, 18th-c. Eng. poet], weakly sentimental; insipid.
**name** (nām), *n.* [AS. *nama*], 1. a word or phrase by which a person, thing, or class is known; title. 2. a word or phrase considered descriptive: as, we called him *names*. 3. fame or reputation. 4. appearance only, not reality: as, chief in *name* only. *adj.* well-known. *v.t.* [NAMED, NAMING], 1. to give a name to. 2. to mention by name. 3. to identify by the right name: as, *name* the States. 4. to appoint to an office, etc. 5. to specify (a date, price, etc.). —**in the name of,** 1. in appeal to. 2. by the authority of.
**name′less,** *adj.* 1. not having a name. 2. left unnamed. 3. not publicly known; obscure. 4. indescribable.
**name′ly** *adv.* that is to say; to wit.
**name′sake′** (-sāk′), *n.* a person with the same name as another; esp., one named after another.
**nan·keen, nan·kin** (nan-kēn′), *n.* [< *Nankin(g)*, China, where first made], a buff-colored, durable cotton cloth.

**nap** (nap), *v.i.* [NAPPED, NAPPING], [AS. *hnappian*], 1. to sleep lightly for a short time. 2. to be off one's guard. *n.* a brief, light sleep.

**nap** (nap), *n.* [AS. *-cnoppa*], the downy or hairy surface of cloth formed by short hairs or fibers. **—nap'py** [-PIER, -PIEST], *adj.*

**na·palm** (nā'päm), *n.* [< *na*phthenic and *palm*itic acids, its constituents], jellied gasoline used in flame-throwers, etc.

**nape** (nāp), *n.* [ME.], the back of the neck.

**naph·tha** (naf'thə, nap'-), *n.* [< Per. *naft*], an inflammable liquid distilled from petroleum, coal tar, etc.: it is used as a fuel, solvent, etc.

**naph'tha·lene', naph'tha·line'** (-lēn'), *n.* [*naptha* + *al*cohol + *-ene*], a white, crystalline hydrocarbon produced from coal tar: it is used in moth repellents, dyes, etc.

**nap·kin** (nap'kin), *n.* [< L. *mappa*, cloth], 1. a small piece of cloth or paper used at table for protecting the clothes and wiping the lips, etc. 2. a small towel.

**na·po·le·on** (nə-pō'li-ən), *n.* [< *Napoleon*], 1. a former gold coin of France. 2. a French pastry with a cream filling.

**Na·po'le·on'ic** (-on'ik), *adj.* of or like Napoleon I, emperor of France (1804–1815).

**nar·cis·sism** (när-sis'iz'm), *n.* [see NARCISSUS], self-love. **—nar·cis'sist,** *n.*

**Nar·cis·sus** (när-sis'əs), *n.* 1. in *Gr. myth.*, a youth who pined away for love of his own reflection in a spring and was changed into the narcissus. 2. [n-], [*pl.* -SUSES, -SI (-ī)], a bulbous plant with clusters of white, yellow, or orange flowers.

**nar·co·sis** (när-kō'sis), *n.* unconsciousness caused by a narcotic.

**nar·cot·ic** (när-kot'ik), *adj.* [< Gr. *narkē*, numbness], of or having to do with the effects of or addiction to narcotics. *n.* a drug, as morphine, that induces profound sleep, lethargy, and relief of pain.

**nard** (närd), *n.* [Gr. *nardos*], 1. an East Indian plant whose roots yield a fragrant ointment. 2. this ointment.

**nar·rate** (na-rāt', nar'āt), *v.t. & v.i.* [-RATED, -RATING], [< L. *narrare*, relate], to tell (a story), relate (events), etc. **—nar·ra'tor,** *n.*

**nar·ra·tion** (na-rā'shən), *n.* 1. a narrating. 2. a narrative.

**nar·ra·tive** (nar'ə-tiv), *adj.* in story form. *n.* 1. a story; account. 2. the art or practice of narrating.

**nar·row** (nar'ō), *adj.* [AS. *nearu*], 1. small in width; not wide. 2. limited in meaning, size, amount, etc.: as, a *narrow* majority. 3. limited in outlook; not liberal. 4. with limited margin; close: as, a *narrow* escape. *v.i. & v.t.* to decrease or limit in width, extent, or scope. *n. usually pl.* a narrow passage; strait. **—nar'row·ly,** *adv.*

**nar'row-mind'ed,** *adj.* limited in outlook; bigoted; prejudiced.

**nar·y** (nâr'i), *adj* [< *ne'er a*, never a], [Dial.], not any; no (with *a* or *an*).

**NASA** (nas'ə), National Aeronautics and Space Administration.

**na·sal** (nā'z'l), *adj.* [< L. *nasus*, nose], 1. of the nose. 2. uttered with the breath passing through the nose. **—na'sal·ly,** *adv.*

**nas·cent** (nas''nt, nā's'nt), *adj.* [< L. *nasci*, be born], 1. coming into being. 2. beginning to form or develop. **—nas'cen·cy,** *n.*

**na·stur·tium** (nə-stūr'shəm), *n.* [L. < *nasus*, nose + *torquere*, to twist], 1. a plant with red, orange, or yellow flowers of pungent odor. 2. the flowers.

**nas·ty** (nas'ti), *adj.* [-TIER, -TIEST], [< ?], 1. filthy; foul. 2. morally offensive; obscene. 3. very unpleasant: as, *nasty* weather. 4. malicious. **—nas'ti·ly,** *adv.* **—nas'ti·ness,** *n.*

**na·tal** (nā't'l), *adj.* [< L. *nasci*, be born], of or relating to one's birth.

**na·tion** (nā'shən), *n.* [< L. *nasci*, be born], 1. a stable community of people with a territory, history, culture, and language in common. 2. people united under a single government; country.

**na·tion·al** (nash'ən-'l), *adj.* of or affecting a nation as a whole. *n.* a citizen of a nation.

**National Guard,** in the U.S., the organized militia of the individual States: it can be activated as part of the U.S. Army.

**na'tion·al·ism,** *n.* 1. devotion to one's nation, its interests, etc.; patriotism or chauvinism. 2. the advocacy of national independence. **—na'tion·al·ist,** *adj. & n.* **—na'tion·al·is'tic** *adj.*

**na·tion·al·i·ty** (nash'ə-nal'ə-ti), *n.* [*pl.* -TIES], 1. national character. 2. the fact of belonging to a nation by birth or naturalization. 3. a nation or national group.

**na·tion·al·ize** (nash'ən-'l-īz'), *v.t.* [-IZED, -IZING], 1. to make national. 2. to transfer ownership or control of (land, industries, etc.) to the nation. **—na'tion·al·i·za'tion,** *n.*

**National Weather Service,** the division of the Department of Commerce that compiles data on weather conditions over the U.S., used in making weather forecasts.

**na·tive** (nā'tiv), *adj.* [< L. *nasci*, be born], 1. inborn; innate. 2. belonging to a locality or country by birth, production, or growth. 3. being, or associated with, the place of one's birth: as, one's *native* land, language, etc. 4. as found in nature; natural. 5. of or characteristic of the original inhabitants of a region. *n.* 1. a person born in the region indicated. 2. an original inhabitant. 3. an indigenous plant or animal.

**na'tive-born',** *adj.* born in a specified place or country.

**na·tiv·i·ty** (nə-tiv'ə-ti), *n.* [*pl.* -TIES], [see NATIVE], birth. **—the Nativity,** 1. the birth of Jesus. 2. Christmas Day.

**natl.,** national.

**NATO** (nā'tō), North Atlantic Treaty Organization.

**nat·ty** (nat'i), *adj.* [-TIER, -TIEST], [? < *neat*], trim and smart in appearance or dress.

**nat·u·ral** (nach'ẽr-əl), *adj.* [< L. *naturalis*, by birth], 1. of or dealing with nature. 2. produced or existing in nature; not artificial. 3. innate; not acquired 4. true to nature; lifelike. 5. normal: as, a *natural* result. 6. free from affectation; at ease. 7. in *music*, neither sharped nor flatted. *n.* [Colloq.], a person or thing sure to be successful. **—nat'u·ral·ness,** *n.*

**nat'u·ral·ism,** *n.* 1. action or thought based on natural desires. 2. in *literature*, *art*, etc., the picturing of people and things as they really are.

**nat'u·ral·ist,** *n.* 1. one who studies animals and plants. 2. an advocate of naturalism. **—nat'u·ral·is'tic,** *adj.*

**nat'u·ral·ize'** (-ə-līz'), *v.t.* [-IZED, -IZING], to confer citizenship upon (an alien). **—nat'u·ral·i·za'tion,** *n.*

**nat'u·ral·ly,** *adv.* 1. in a natural manner. 2. by nature; innately. 3. as one might expect; of course.

**natural resources,** those forms of wealth supplied by nature, as coal, oil, etc.

**natural science,** the systematized knowledge of nature, including biology, chemistry, physics, etc.

**na·ture** (nā'chẽr), *n.* [< L. *nasci*, be born], 1. the essential quality of a thing; essence. 2. inherent tendencies of a person. 3. kind; sort; type. 4. the entire physical universe. 5. [sometimes N-], the power, force, etc. that seems to regulate the universe. 6. the primitive state of man. 7. natural scenery. **—by nature,** inherently.

**-natured,** a combining form meaning *having* or *showing a* (specified kind of) *nature*,

*disposition*, or *temperament*, as *good-natured*.
**naught** (nôt), ***n.*** [< AS. *na wiht*, no person], 1. nothing. 2. a zero (0).
**naugh·ty** (nô′ti), ***adj.*** [-TIER, -TIEST], [< obs. *naught*, wicked], 1. mischievous; disobedient. 2. improper; obscene. **—naugh′ti·ly, *adv.* —naugh′ti·ness, *n.***
**nau·se·a** (nô′shə, -shi-ə), ***n.*** [< Gr. *nausia*, seasickness], 1. a feeling of sickness at the stomach, with an impulse to vomit. 2. disgust; loathing.
**nau·se·ate** (nô′shi-āt′, -zi-, -si-), ***v.i. & v.t.*** [-ATED, -ATING], to feel or cause to feel nausea.
**nau·seous** (nô′shəs, -shi-əs), ***adj.*** causing nausea; sickening; disgusting.
**nau·ti·cal** (nô′ti-k'l), ***adj.*** [< Gr. *naus*, ship], of sailors, ships, or navigation: abbrev. **naut. —nau′ti·cal·ly, *adv.***
**nau·ti·lus** (nô′t'l-əs), ***n.*** [*pl.* -LUSES, -LI (-ī′)], [< Gr. *naus*, ship], a tropical mollusk with a spiral shell: also **pearly nautilus.**
**na·val** (nā′v'l), ***adj.*** [< L. *navis*, ship], of, having, characteristic of, or for a navy, its ships, etc.
**nave** (nāv), ***n.*** [< L. *navis*, ship], the main part of a church, from the chancel to the main entrance.
**na·vel** (nā′v'l), ***n.*** [AS. *nefela*], the small scar in the abdomen, marking the place where the umbilical cord was attached to the fetus.
**nav·i·ga·ble** (nav′i-gə-b'l), ***adj.*** 1. wide or deep enough to be traveled on by ships. 2. that can be steered. **—nav′i·ga·bil′i·ty, *n.***
**nav·i·gate** (nav′ə-gāt′), ***v.t. & v.i.*** [-GATED, -GATING], [< L. *navis*, ship + *agere*, to lead], 1. to travel through or on (air, sea, etc.) in a ship or aircraft. 2. to steer (a ship or aircraft).
**nav′i·ga′tion** (-gā′shən), ***n.*** a navigating; esp., the science of locating the position and plotting the course of ships and aircraft.
**nav′i·ga′tor, *n.*** one skilled in the navigation of a ship or aircraft.
**na·vy** (nā′vi), ***n.*** [*pl.* -VIES], [< L. *navis*, ship], 1. all the warships of a nation. 2. [often N-], the entire sea force of a nation, including its vessels, personnel, administrators, etc. 3. very dark blue: also **navy blue.**
**navy bean,** [from its use in the U.S. Navy], a small, white bean related to the kidney bean.
**nay** (nā), ***adv.*** [< ON. *ne*, not + *ei*, ever], not only that, but also: as, I permit, *nay*, encourage it. ***n.*** 1. a denial. 2. a negative vote or voter. 3. a negative answer.
**Na·zi** (nä′tsi), ***adj.*** [G. contr. of the party name], designating or of the German fascist political party which ruled Germany under Hitler (1933–1945). ***n.*** a member or supporter of this party. **—Na′zism, Na′zi·ism, *n.***
**N.B., n.b.,** *nota bene*, [L.], note well.
**N.C.O.,** noncommissioned officer.
**N.D., n.d.,** no date.
**Ne,** in *chem.*, neon.
**NE, N.E., n.e.,** 1. northeast. 2. northeastern.
**Ne·an·der·thal** (ni-an′dẽr-täl′, -thôl′), ***adj.*** [< a G. valley], designating or of a race of early man of the Stone Age.
**neap** (nēp), ***adj.*** [AS. *nep-* in *nepflod*, neap tide], designating either of the two lowest high tides in the month.
**Ne·a·pol·i·tan** (nē′ə-pol′ə-t'n), ***adj.*** of Naples. ***n.*** a native or inhabitant of Naples.
**near** (nêr), ***adv.*** [AS. compar. of *neah*, nigh], 1. at a short distance in space or time. 2. almost; nearly: as, you are *near* right. 3. closely; intimately. ***adj.*** 1. close in distance or time. 2. close in relationship; akin. 3. close in friendship; intimate. 4. close in degree: as, a *near* escape. 5. short or quick: as, the *near* way. 6. stingy. ***prep.*** close to in space, time, degree, etc. ***v.t. & v.i.*** to draw near (to); approach. **—near′ness, *n.***
**near′-by′, near′by′, *adj. & adv.*** near; close at hand.
**near′ly, *adv.*** 1. almost; not quite. 2. closely: as, *nearly* related.
**near′sight′ed, *adj.*** seeing only near objects distinctly; myopic. **—near′sight′ed·ness, *n.***
**neat** (nēt), ***adj.*** [< L. *nitere*, to shine], 1. trim; tidy; clean. 2. skillful and precise. 3. well proportioned. 4. cleverly done or said. **—neat′ly, *adv.* —neat′ness, *n.***
**'neath, neath** (nēth, nē*th*), ***prep.*** [Poetic], beneath.
**neb** (neb), ***n.*** [AS. *nebb*], 1. the beak of a bird. 2. a nib; tip.
**neb·u·la** (neb′yoo-lə), ***n.*** [*pl.* -LAE (-lē′), -LAS], [L.], a cloudlike patch seen in the night sky, consisting of gaseous matter or of distant groups of stars. **—neb′u·lar, *adj.***
**neb′u·lous** (-ləs), ***adj.*** 1. of or like a nebula. 2. cloudy. 3. vague; indefinite.
**nec·es·sar·i·ly** (nes′ə-ser′ə-li, nes′ə-sâr′-), ***adv.*** 1. because of necessity. 2. as a necessary result.
**nec′es·sar′y** (-ser′i), ***adj.*** [< L. *ne-*, not + *cedere*, give away], 1. essential; indispensable. 2. inevitable. 3. required; not voluntary. ***n.*** [*pl.* -IES], something necessary.
**ne·ces·si·tate** (nə-ses′ə-tāt′), ***v.t.*** [-TATED, -TATING], 1. to make (something) necessary. 2. to compel. **—ne·ces′si·ta′tion, *n.***
**ne·ces·si·tous** (nə-ses′ə-təs), ***adj.*** in great need; destitute. **—ne·ces′si·tous·ly, *adv.***
**ne·ces′si·ty** (-ti), ***n.*** [*pl.* -TIES], [see NECESSARY], 1. natural causation; fate. 2. great need. 3. *often in pl.* something that cannot be done without. 4. poverty. **—of necessity,** necessarily.
**neck** (nek), ***n.*** [AS. *hnecca*], 1. that part of man or animal joining the head to the body. 2. that part of a garment nearest the neck. 3. a necklike part; specif., *a*) a narrow strip of land. *b*) the narrowest part of a bottle, etc. *c*) a strait. ***v.t. & v.i.*** [Slang], to kiss and caress in making love. **—neck and neck,** very close, as in a contest.
**neck·er·chief** (nek′ẽr-chif), ***n.*** [*neck* + *kerchief*], a handkerchief or scarf worn around the neck.
**neck′lace** (-lis), ***n.*** [*neck* + *lace* (string)], an ornamental string or chain of gold, beads, etc., worn around the neck.
**neck′tie′, *n.*** a band worn around the neck, tied in a bow or knotted in front.
**necro-,** [< Gr. *nekros*, dead body], a combining form meaning *death, corpse.*
**ne·crol·o·gy** (ne-krol′ə-ji), ***n.*** [*pl.* -GIES], [*necro-* + *-logy*], 1. a list of people who have died. 2. an obituary.
**nec·ro·man·cy** (nek′rə-man′si), ***n.*** [< Gr. *nekros*, corpse + *manteia*, divination], 1. divination by alleged communication with the dead. 2. sorcery. **—nec′ro·man′cer, *n.***
**ne·cro·sis** (ne-krō′sis), ***n.*** [< Gr. *nekros*, dead body], the death or decay of tissue in a part of the body.
**nec·tar** (nek′tẽr), ***n.*** [< Gr. *nektar*, lit., death-overcoming], 1. in *Gr. myth.*, the drink of the gods. 2. any very delicious beverage. 3. the sweetish liquid in many flowers.
**nec·tar·ine** (nek′tə-rēn′, nek′tə-rēn′), ***n.*** [< *nectar*], a kind of smooth-skinned peach.
**nee, née** (nā), ***adj.*** [Fr.], born: as, Mrs. Helen Jones, *nee* Smith.
**need** (nēd), ***n.*** [AS. *nied*], 1. necessity. 2. lack of something required or desired: as, the *need* of a rest. 3. something required or desired that is lacking: as, my daily *needs.* 4. *a*) a time or condition when help is required: as, a friend in *need.* *b*) poverty; want. ***v.t.*** 1. to have need of; require. 2. to be obliged: as, I *need* to be careful. ***v.i.*** to be in need. **—have need to,** to be required to. **—if need be,** if it is required.

**need′ful,** *adj.* necessary; needed; required.

**nee·dle** (nē′d'l), *n.* [AS. *nædl*], 1. a slender, pointed piece of steel with a hole for thread, used for sewing. 2. a slender rod of steel, bone, etc. used for crocheting or knitting. 3. the short, pointed piece that moves in the groove of a phonograph record and transmits vibrations. 4. the pointer of a compass, gauge, etc. 5. the thin, short leaf of the pine, spruce, etc. 6. the sharp slender metal tube at the end of a hypodermic syringe. *v.t.* [-DLED, -DLING], [Colloq.], 1. to goad; prod. 2. to tease.

**nee′dle-point′,** *adj.* designating lace made on a pattern with a needle.

**needle point,** 1. an embroidery of woolen threads upon canvas. 2. needle-point lace.

**need′less,** *adj.* not needed; unnecessary.

**nee′dle·work′,** *n.* work done with a needle; embroidery; sewing.

**need′n't** (-'nt), need not.

**need′y,** *adj.* [-IER, -IEST], in need; very poor; destitute. **—need′i·ness,** *n.*

**ne'er** (nâr), *adv.* [Poetic], never.

**ne'er′-do-well′,** *n.* a shiftless, irresponsible person. *adj.* good-for-nothing.

**ne·far·i·ous** (ni-fâr′i-əs), *adj.* [< L. *ne-*, not + *fas*, lawful], very wicked.

**ne·gate** (ni-gāt′), *v.t.* [-GATED, -GATING], [< L. *negare*, deny], 1. to deny. 2. to make ineffective; nullify.

**ne·ga·tion** (ni-gā′shən), *n.* 1. act or instance of denying; denial. 2. the lack or opposite of something positive.

**neg·a·tive** (neg′ə-tiv), *adj.* 1. expressing denial or refusal; saying "no." 2. opposite to or lacking in that which is positive: as, a *negative* force. 3. designating or of electricity made by friction on resin or wax, rather than on glass. 4. in *math.*, designating a quantity less than zero, or one to be subtracted. 5. in *photography*, reversing the light and shade of the original subject. *n.* 1. a negative word, reply, etc. 2. the point of view that opposes the positive. 3. the plate in a voltaic battery where the lower potential is. 4. an exposed and developed photographic plate or film on which light and shadow are reversed. *v.t.* [-TIVED, -TIVING], 1. to refuse; veto (a bill, etc.). 2. to deny. **—in the negative,** in refusal or denial of a plan, etc. **—neg′a·tiv′i·ty,** *n.*

**neg·lect** (ni-glekt′), *v.t.* [< L. *neg-*, not + *egere*, gather], 1. to ignore or disregard (something). 2. not to attend to (something) properly. 3. to leave undone. *n.* 1. a neglecting. 2. negligence. 3. a being neglected. **—neg·lect′ful,** *adj.*

**neg·li·gee** (neg′li-zhā′), *n.* [< Fr. *negliger*, to neglect], 1. a woman's loosely fitting dressing gown. 2. any informal attire.

**neg·li·gent** (neg′li-jənt), *adj.* 1. habitually failing to do the required thing; neglectful. 2. careless, inattentive, etc. **—neg′li·gence,** *n.* **—neg′li·gent·ly,** *adv.*

**neg′li·gi·ble** (-jə-b'l), *adj.* that can be neglected or disregarded; trifling.

**ne·go·ti·a·ble** (ni-gō′shi-ə-b'l, -shə-b'l), *adj.* that can be sold or transferred to a third person, as bonds, etc.

**ne·go′ti·ate′** (-āt′), *v.i.* [-ATED, -ATING], [< L. *negotium*, business], to discuss with a view to reaching agreement. *v.t.* 1. to settle (a transaction, treaty, etc.). 2. to transfer or sell (negotiable bonds, etc.). 3. [Colloq.], to succeed in crossing, passing, etc. **—ne·go′ti·a′tion,** *n.* **—ne·go′ti·a′tor,** *n.*

**Ne·gro** (nē′grō), *n.* [*pl.* -GROES], [< Sp. & Port. *negro*, black], 1. a member of any of the black races of Africa. 2. a person with some Negro ancestors. *adj.* of or for Negroes. **—Ne′groid** (-groid), *adj.*

**neigh** (nā), *v.i.* [AS. *hnægan*], to utter the characteristic cry of a horse. *n.* this cry.

**neigh·bor** (nā′bēr), *n.* [< AS. *neah*, nigh + hyp. *gebur*, farmer], 1. one that lives or is situated near another. 2. a fellow man. *adj.* near-by. *v.t.* & *v.i.* to live or be situated near or near-by. **—neigh′bor·ing,** *adj.*

**neigh′bor·hood′,** *n.* 1. a particular community, region, etc. 2. the people living near one another. **—in the neighborhood of,** [Colloq.], 1. near. 2. about; roughly.

**neigh′bor·ly,** *adj.* like or appropriate to neighbors; friendly, helpful, etc. **—neigh′bor·li·ness,** *n.*

**neigh·bour** (nā′bēr), *n., v.i.* & *v.t.* neighbor: Brit. sp. **—neigh′bour·hood′,** *n.* **—neigh′bour·ly,** *adj.*

**nei·ther** (nē′*th*ēr, nī′-), *adj.* [AS. *nahwæther*, not whether], not either: as, use *neither* hand. *pron.* not one or the other (of two). *conj.* 1. not either: as, I can *neither* go nor stay. 2. nor yet.

**nem·e·sis** (nem′ə-sis), *n.* [*pl.* -SES (-sēz′)], [Gr. < *nemein*, deal out], 1. just punishment. 2. one who imposes it.

**neo-,** [< Gr. *neos*], [sometimes N-], a combining form meaning *new, recent.*

**ne·o·clas·sic** (nē′ō-klas′ik), *adj.* designating or of a revival of classic style and form in art, literature, etc.: also **ne′o·clas′si·cal.**

**ne·o·lith·ic** (nē′ə-lith′ik), *adj.* [< *neo-* + Gr. *lithos*, stone; + *-ic*], designating or of the later part of the Stone Age.

**ne·ol·o·gism** (nē-ol′ə-jiz'm), *n.* [see NEO-, -LOGY, & -ISM], a new word or a new meaning for an established word.

**ne·on** (nē′on), *n.* [< Gr. *neos*, new], a rare, inert gaseous chemical element found in the earth's atmosphere: symbol, Ne.

**neon lamp,** a glass tube filled with neon, which glows when an electric current is sent through it.

**ne·o·phyte** (nē′ə-fīt′), *n.* [< Gr. *neos*, new + *phyein*, to produce], 1. a new convert, esp. to Christianity. 2. a beginner; novice.

**ne·pen·the** (ni-pen′thi), *n.* [< Gr. *ne-*, not + *penthos*, sorrow], anything that causes forgetfulness of sorrow.

**neph·ew** (nef′ū), *n.* [< L. *nepos*], 1. the son of one's brother or sister. 2. the son of one's brother-in-law or sister-in-law.

**ne·phri·tis** (ne-frī′tis), *n.* [< Gr. *nephros*, kidney; + *-itis*], disease of the kidneys, characterized by inflammation.

**nep·o·tism** (nep′ə-tiz'm), *n.* [< L. *nepos*, nephew], favoritism shown to relatives, esp. in appointment to jobs.

**Nep·tune** (nep′tōōn), *n.* 1. the Roman god of the sea. 2. the third largest planet in the solar system: cf. **planet.**

**nep·tu·ni·um** (nep-tōō′ni-əm), *n.* a chemical element produced from uranium: symbol, Np.

**Ne·re·id** (nêr′i-id), *n.* in *Gr. myth.*, a sea nymph.

**nerve** (nũrv), *n.* [< L. *nervus*], 1. any of the cordlike fibers carrying impulses between body organs and the central nervous system. 2. courage. 3. strength; energy. 4. *pl.* nervousness. 5. [Colloq.], impudent boldness. *v.t.* [NERVED, NERVING], to give strength or courage to. **—get on one's nerves,** [Colloq.], to make one irritable.

**nerve′less,** *adj.* 1. without strength, courage, etc. 2. in *anatomy, botany, & zoology*, having no nerve or nerves.

**nerve′-rack′ing, nerve′-wrack′ing** (-rak′iŋ), *adj.* very trying to one's patience or equanimity.

**nerv·ous** (nũr′vəs), *adj.* 1. vigorous in expression. 2. of or made up of nerves. 3. emotionally tense, restless, etc. 4. fearful.

**nervous system,** all the nerve cells and nervous tissues in an organism, including, in the vertebrates, the brain, spinal cord, nerves, etc.

**nerv′y,** *adj.* [-IER, -IEST], 1. courageous; bold. 2. [Slang], brazen; impudent.
**-ness,** [AS. *-nes(s)*], a suffix meaning: *condition, quality, state,* or *instance of being,* as in *sadness.*
**nest** (nest), *n.* [AS.], 1. the structure or place where a bird lays its eggs and shelters its young. 2. the place used by insects, fish, etc. for spawning or breeding. 3. a cozy place; retreat. 4. a resort or its frequenters: as, a *nest* of thieves. 5. a set of things, each fitting within the one next larger. *v.i.* to build or sit on a nest. *v.t.* to place as in a nest.
**nest egg,** money, etc. put aside as a reserve or to set up a fund.
**nes·tle** (nes′'l), *v.i.* [-TLED, -TLING], [AS. *nestlian*], 1. to settle down comfortably. 2. to press close for comfort or in affection. 3. to lie sheltered, as a house among trees. *v.t.* to press or rest snugly. **—nes′tler,** *n.*
**nest·ling** (nest′liŋ, nes′-), *n.* 1. a young bird not ready to leave the nest. 2. a baby.
**net** (net), *n.* [AS. *nett*], 1. an openwork fabric as of string, used to snare birds, fish, etc. 2. a trap; snare. 3. a meshed fabric, esp. one used to hold, protect, etc.: as, a hair *net.* *v.t.* [NETTED, NETTING], 1. to snare as with a net. 2. to enclose as with a net. *adj.* of or like net.
**net** (net), *adj.* [Fr., clear], left over after deductions or allowances have been made. *n.* a net amount, profit, weight, price, etc. *v.t.* [NETTED, NETTING], to gain.
**neth·er** (neth′ẽr), *adj.* [AS. *neothera*], lower or under: as, the *nether* world.
**neth′er·most′** (-mōst′), *adj.* lowest.
**net′ting,** *n.* netted material.
**net·tle** (net′'l), *n.* [AS. *netele*], a weed with stinging hairs. *v.t.* [-TLED, -TLING], 1. to sting as with nettles. 2. to annoy; vex.
**net′work′,** *n.* 1. an arrangement of parallel wires, threads, etc. intersected at intervals by others so as to leave open spaces. 2. any system of crossed or connected roads, canals, etc. 3. in *radio & TV,* a chain of transmitting stations.
**neu·ral** (noor′əl, nyoor′-), *adj.* [*neur(o)-* + *-al*], of a nerve, nerves, or the nervous system.
**neu·ral·gia** (noo-ral′jə, nyoo-), *n.* [*neur(o)-* + Gr. *algos,* pain], a severe pain along the course of a nerve. **—neu·ral′gic,** *adj.*
**neu·ras·the·ni·a** (noor′əs-thē′ni-ə, nyoor′-), *n.* [< *neur(o)-* + Gr. *astheneia,* weakness], a type of neurosis characterized by fatigue, worry, etc. **—neu′ras·then′ic** (-then′ik), *adj. & n.*
**neu·ri·tis** (noo-rī′tis, nyoo-), *n.* [*neur(o)-* + *-itis*], inflammation of a nerve or nerves, with pain and muscle tenderness. **—neu·rit′ic** (-rit′ik), *adj.*
**neuro-,** [< Gr. *neuron,* nerve], a combining form meaning *of a nerve, nerves,* or *the nervous system:* also **neur-.**
**neu·rol·o·gy** (noo-rol′ə-ji, nyoo-), *n.* [*neuro-* + *-logy*], the branch of medicine dealing with the nervous system and its diseases. **—neu·rol′o·gist,** *n.*
**neu·ron** (noor′on, nyoor′-), *n.* the nerve cell body and all its processes.
**neu·ro·sis** (noo-rō′sis, nyoo-), *n.* [*pl.* -SES (-sēz)], [< Gr. *neuron,* nerve], a mental disorder characterized by anxieties, compulsions, obsessions, etc. without apparent organic change.
**neu·rot′ic** (-rot′ik), *adj.* 1. of, characteristic of, or having a neurosis. 2. neural. *n.* a neurotic person.
**neu·ter** (nōō′tẽr, nū′-), *adj.* [< L. *ne-,* not + *uter,* either], 1. in *biology, a)* having no sexual organs. *b)* having undeveloped sexual organs in the adult. 2. in *grammar,* designating or of the gender that refers to things regarded as neither male nor female.
**neu·tral** (nōō′trəl, nū′-), *adj.* [see NEUTER], 1. supporting neither side in a quarrel or war. 2. not one thing or the other; indifferent. 3. having little or no decided color. *n.* 1. a neutral person or nation. 2. a neutral color. 3. in *mechanics,* the position of disengaged gears.
**neu·tral′i·ty** (-tral′ə-ti), *n.* 1. a being neutral. 2. the status or policy of a neutral nation.
**neu′tral·ize′** (-trə-līz′), *v.t.* [-IZED, -IZING], 1. to declare (a nation, etc.) neutral in war. 2. to destroy or counteract the effectiveness, force, etc. of. **—neu′tral·i·za′tion,** *n.*
**neu·tron** (nōō′tron, nū′-), *n.* [< *neutral*], one of the fundamental, uncharged particles of an atom.
**nev·er** (nev′ẽr), *adv.* [< AS. *ne,* not + *æfre* ever], 1. not ever; at no time. 2. not at all; in no case.
**nev′er·more′,** *adv.* never again.
**nev·er·the·less** (nev′ẽr-*th*ə-les′), *adv.* in spite of that; however.
**new** (nōō, nū), *adj.* [AS. *niwe*], 1. appearing, thought of, discovered, made, etc. for the first time. 2. different from (the) one in the past: as, a *new* hair-do. 3. strange; unfamiliar. 4. recently grown; fresh: as, *new* potatoes. 5. unused. 6. modern; recent. 7. more; additional. 8. starting as a repetition of a cycle, series, etc.: as, the *new* moon. 9. having just come: as, a *new* arrival. *adv.* 1. again. 2. newly; recently. **—new′ness,** *n.*
**new′born′,** *adj.* 1. just born. 2. reborn.
**new′com′er,** *n.* a recent arrival.
**New Deal,** the principles and policies adopted by President Franklin D. Roosevelt to advance the economic and social welfare of the American people.
**new·el** (nōō′əl, nū′-), *n.* [ult. < L. *nux,* nut], 1. the upright pillar around which the steps of a winding staircase turn. 2. the post that supports the handrail of a flight of stairs at the top or bottom: also **newel post.**
**new′fan′gled** (-faŋ′g'ld), *adj.* [< ME. *newe,* new + *-fangel* < AS. *fon,* to take], new; novel: contemptuous term.
**new′ly,** *adv.* 1. recently; lately. 2. anew.
**new′ly·wed′,** *n.* a recently married person.
**new moon,** the moon when it is between the earth and the sun: it appears as a thin crescent curving toward the right.
**news** (nōōz, nūz), *n.pl.* [construed as sing.], 1. new information; information previously unknown. 2. recent happenings. 3. reports of such events.
**news′boy′,** *n.* a boy who sells or delivers newspapers.
**news′cast′,** *n.* a radio or television news broadcast. **—news′cast′er,** *n.*
**news′pa′per,** *n.* a regular publication, usually daily or weekly, containing news, opinions, advertisements, etc.
**news′print′,** *n.* a cheap, thin paper used for newspapers, etc.
**news′reel′,** *n.* a motion picture of current news events.
**news′stand′,** *n.* a stand at which newspapers, magazines, etc. are sold.
**news′y,** *adj.* [-IER, -IEST], [Colloq.], containing much news.
**newt** (nōōt, nūt), *n.* [by merging of ME. *an eute,* a newt], any of various small, amphibious salamanders.
**New Testament,** the part of the Bible that contains the life and teachings of Jesus and his followers.
**new′-world′,** *adj.* of or from the New World, or Western Hemisphere.
**New Year's (Day),** January 1.
**New Year's Eve,** the evening before New Year's Day.
**next** (nekst), *adj.* [AS. *neahst,* superl. of *neah,* nigh], nearest; immediately preceding or

following. ***adv.*** 1. in the nearest time, place, rank, etc. 2. on the first subsequent occasion. ***prep.*** beside; nearest to.

**next′-door′**, ***adj.*** in or at the next house, building, etc.

**nex·us** (nek′səs), ***n.*** [*pl.* -USES, -US], [L.], 1. a link or connection. 2. a connected group or series.

**N.G., n.g.,** [Slang], no good.

**Ni,** in *chem.*, nickel.

**ni·a·cin** (nī′ə-s'n), ***n.*** [*ni*cotinic *ac*id + *-in*], nicotinic acid.

**nib** (nib), ***n.*** [< AS. *nebb*], 1. a bird's beak. 2. a point; esp., a pen point.

**nib·ble** (nib′'l), ***v.t.*** **&** ***v.i.*** [-BLED, -BLING], [cf. MLG. *nibbelen*], 1. to eat (food) with quick, small bites. 2. to bite at (food) lightly and intermittently. ***n.*** 1. a small bite. 2. a nibbling. **—nib′bler,** ***n.***

**nib·lick** (nib′lik), ***n.*** [< ?], an iron-headed golf club used for short lofts.

**nice** (nīs), ***adj.*** [NICER, NICEST], [< L. *nescius*, ignorant: etym. reflected in obs. senses], 1. fastidious; refined. 2. delicate; precise; subtle: as, a *nice* distinction. 3. calling for care, tact, etc. 4. finely discriminating or minutely accurate. 5. pleasant, attractive, kind, good, etc.: a generalized term of approval. **—nice′ly,** ***adv.*** **—nice′ness,** ***n.***

**ni·ce·ty** (nī′sə-ti), ***n.*** [*pl.* -TIES], 1. precision; accuracy. 2. fastidiousness; refinement. 3. a subtle or minute detail, distinction, etc. 4. something choice or dainty.

**niche** (nich), ***n.*** [Fr.; ult. < L. *nidus*, a nest], 1. a recess in a wall, for a statue, vase, etc. 2. an especially suitable place or position.

**nick** (nik), ***v.t.*** [prob. < MLG. *knicken*], 1. to make a small cut, chip, etc. on or in. 2. to strike or catch at the proper time. ***n.*** a cut, chip, etc. made by nicking. **—in the nick of time,** at the critical moment.

**nick·el** (nik′'l), ***n.*** [< G. *kupfernickel*, copper demon: the copperlike ore contains no copper], 1. a hard, silver-white, metallic chemical element, much used in alloys: symbol, Ni. 2. a nickel and copper coin of the U.S. and Canada equal to five cents. ***v.t.*** [-ELED or -ELLED, -ELING or -ELLING], to plate with nickel.

**nick·el·o·de·on** (nik′'l-ō′di-ən), ***n.*** [< *nickel* + Fr. *odéon*, concert hall], a coin-operated player piano or phonograph.

**nick·nack** (nik′nak′), ***n.*** a knickknack.

**nick·name** (nik′nām′), ***n.*** [by merging of ME. *an ekename*, a surname], 1. a substitute, often descriptive name given in fun, affection, etc. (e.g., "Shorty"). 2. a familiar form of a proper name (e.g., "Jim" for "James"). ***v.t.*** [-NAMED, -NAMING], to give a nickname to.

**nic·o·tine** (nik′ə-tēn′, -tin), ***n.*** [Fr. < J. *Nicot*, 16th-c. Fr. diplomat who introduced tobacco into France], a poisonous, oily liquid extracted from tobacco leaves.

**nic·o·tin·ic acid** (nik′ə-tin′ik), a member of the vitamin B complex.

**niece** (nēs), ***n.*** [< L. *neptis*], 1. the daughter of one's brother or sister. 2. the daughter of one's brother-in-law or sister-in-law.

**nif·ty** (nif′ti), ***adj.*** [-TIER, -TIEST], [prob. < *magnificent*], [Slang], attractive, smart, etc.

**nig·gard** (nig′ẽrd), ***n.*** [prob. ult. < ON.], a stingy person; miser. ***adj.*** stingy; miserly.

**nig·gle** (nig′'l), ***v.i.*** [-GLED, -GLING], [prob. < ON.], to work fussily; be finical.

**nigh** (nī), ***adj., adv., & prep.*** [AS. *neah*], [Chiefly Archaic or Dial.], near.

**night** (nīt), ***n.*** [AS. *niht*], 1. the period of darkness between sunset and sunrise. 2. any period or condition of darkness or gloom. **—make a night of it,** to celebrate all night.

**night′cap′,** ***n.*** 1. a cap worn in bed. 2. [Colloq.], an alcoholic drink taken just before going to bed.

**night club,** a place of entertainment for drinking, dancing, etc. at night.

**night′dress′,** ***n.*** a nightgown.

**night′fall′,** ***n.*** the close of the day.

**night′gown′,** ***n.*** a loose gown worn in bed by women or girls.

**night′hawk′,** ***n.*** 1. any of a group of night birds related to the whippoorwill. 2. a night owl.

**night·in·gale** (nīt′'n-gāl′), ***n.*** [< AS. *niht*, night + *galan*, sing], a small European thrush, the male of which sings melodiously, esp. at night.

**night letter,** a long telegram sent at night at a reduced rate.

**night′ly,** ***adj.*** 1. of or like the night. 2. done or occurring every night. ***adv.*** 1. at night. 2. every night.

**night′mare′** (-mâr′), ***n.*** [*night* + ME. *mare*, demon], 1. a frightening dream. 2. any frightening experience. **—night′mar′ish,** ***adj.***

**night owl,** a person who works at night or otherwise stays up late.

**night′shade′** (-shād′), ***n.*** any of various flowering plants related to the potato and tomato; esp., the belladonna.

**night′shirt′,** ***n.*** a kind of nightgown worn by men or boys.

**night′time′,** ***n.*** night (sense 1).

**ni·hil·ism** (nī′ə-liz'm), ***n.*** [< L. *nihil*, nothing], the general rejection of customary beliefs in morality, religion, etc. **—ni′hil·ist,** ***n.*** **—ni′hil·is′tic,** ***adj.***

**Ni·ke** (nī′kē), ***n.*** [< *Nike*, Gr. goddess of victory], a U.S. Army guided missile launched from the ground.

**nil** (nil), ***n.*** [L. < *nihil*], nothing.

**nim·ble** (nim′b'l), ***adj.*** [-BLER, -BLEST], [< AS. *niman*, to take], 1. quick-witted; alert. 2. moving quickly and lightly; agile. **—nim′ble·ness,** ***n.*** **—nim′bly,** ***adv.***

**nim·bus** (nim′bəs), ***n.*** [*pl.* -BUSES, -BI (-bī)], [L.], 1. a low, gray rain cloud. 2. a halo surrounding the head of a saint, etc., as on a picture.

**Nim·rod** (nim′rod), ***n.*** 1. in the *Bible*, a mighty hunter: Gen. 10:8–9. 2. a hunter.

**nin·com·poop** (nin′kəm-pōōp′), ***n.*** [< ?], a stupid, silly person; fool.

**nine** (nīn), ***adj.*** **&** ***n.*** [AS. *nigon*], one more than eight; 9; IX. **—ninth** (nīnth), ***adj.*** **&** ***n.***

**nine′pins′,** ***n.pl.*** [construed as sing.], a bowling game played with nine wooden pins.

**nine′teen′** (-tēn′), ***adj.*** **&** ***n.*** [AS. *nigontyne*]; nine more than ten; 19; XIX. **—nine′teenth′** (-tēnth′), ***adj.*** **&** ***n.***

**nine′ty** (-ti), ***adj.*** **&** ***n.*** [*pl.* -TIES], [AS. *nigontig*], nine times ten; 90; XC (or LXXXX). **—the nineties,** the years from 90 through 99 (of a century or a person's age). **—nine′ti·eth** (-ith), ***adj.*** **&** ***n.***

**nin·ny** (nin′i), ***n.*** [*pl.* -NIES], [prob. contr. of *an innocent*], a fool; dolt.

**nip** (nip), ***v.t.*** [NIPPED, NIPPING], [prob. < MLG. *nippen*], 1. to pinch or bite. 2. to sever (shoots, etc.) as by clipping. 3. to check the growth of. 4. to have a painful or injurious effect on, as cold or frost. ***n.*** 1. a nipping; pinch; bite. 2. a stinging quality, as in cold air. 3. stinging cold; frost. **—nip and tuck,** so close as to leave the outcome in doubt.

**nip** (nip), ***n.*** [prob. < D. *nippen*, to sip], a small drink of liquor.

**nip·per** (nip′ẽr), ***n.*** 1. anything that nips. 2. *pl.* pliers, pincers, etc. 3. the claw of a crab or lobster.

**nip·ple** (nip′'l), ***n.*** [prob. < *neb*, a beak], 1. the small protuberance on a breast or udder, through which the milk passes; teat. 2. a rubber cap with a teatlike part, for a baby's bottle.

**Nip·pon·ese** (nip′ə-nēz′), ***adj.*** **&** ***n.*** [*pl.* -ESE], [< Japan. *Nippon*, Japan], Japanese.

**nip·py** (nip'i), *adj.* [-PIER, -PIEST], sharp; biting. **—nip'pi·ness,** *n.*

**nir·va·na** (nẽr-van'ə, nir-vä'nə), *n.* [< Sans.], [also N-], in *Buddhism*, the state of perfect blessedness achieved by the absorption of the soul into the supreme spirit.

**ni·sei** (nē'sā'), *n.* [*pl.* -SEI, -SEIS], [Japan., lit., second generation], [also N-], a native U.S. citizen born of immigrant Japanese parents.

**nit** (nit), *n.* [AS. *hnitu*], 1. the egg of a louse or similar insect. 2. the young insect.

**ni·ter, ni·tre** (nī'tẽr), *n.* [< Gr. *nitron*], potassium nitrate or sodium nitrate, used in explosives, fertilizers, etc.; saltpeter.

**ni·trate** (nī'trāt), *n.* 1. a salt of nitric acid, as sodium nitrate. *v.t.* [-TRATED, -TRATING], to treat or combine with nitric acid or a nitrate. **—ni·tra'tion,** *n.*

**ni·tric** (nī'trik), *adj.* designating or of a colorless, corrosive acid containing nitrogen.

**ni·tro·cel·lu·lose** (nī'trə-sel'yoo-lōs'), *n.* a substance obtained by treating cellulose with nitric acid, used in making explosives, lacquers, etc.

**ni·tro·gen** (nī'trə-jən), *n.* [< Fr.; see NITER & -GEN], a colorless, odorless, gaseous chemical element forming nearly four fifths of the atmosphere: symbol, N. **—ni·trog'e·nous** (-troj'ə-nəs), *adj.*

**ni·tro·glyc·er·in, ni·tro·glyc·er·ine** (nī'trə-glis'ẽr-in), *n.* a thick, explosive oil, prepared by treating glycerin with nitric and sulfuric acids: it is used in dynamite.

**ni·trous oxide** (nī'trəs), a colorless gas containing nitrogen, used as an anesthetic.

**nit'wit',** *n.* [*nit* + *wit*], a stupid person.

**nix** (niks), *adv.* [G. *nichts*], [Slang], 1. nothing. 2. no. *interj.* 1. stop! 2. I forbid, disagree, etc.

**NLRB, N.L.R.B.,** National Labor Relations Board.

**no** (nō), *adv.* [< AS. *ne a*, not ever], 1. not at all: as, *no* worse. 2. nay; not so: used to deny, refuse, or disagree. *adj.* not a: as, he is *no* fool. *n.* [*pl.* NOES], 1. a refusal or denial. 2. a negative vote or voter.

**No., no.,** number.

**No·ah** (nō'ə), *n.* in the *Bible*, the patriarch commanded by God to build the ark: see **ark.**

**No·bel prizes** (nō-bel'), [after A.B. *Nobel*, 19th-c. Sw. inventor who established them], five annual prizes given for distinction in physics, chemistry, medicine, and literature, and for the promotion of peace.

**no·bil·i·ty** (nō-bil'ə-ti), *n.* [*pl.* -TIES], 1. a being noble. 2. high station in society. 3. the class of people of noble rank.

**no·ble** (nō'b'l), *adj.* [< L. *nobilis*, well-known], 1. famous or renowned. 2. having high moral qualities. 3. excellent. 4. grand; stately: as, a *noble* view. 5. of high rank or title. *n.* one having hereditary rank or title. **—no'ble·ness,** *n.* **—no'bly,** *adv.*

**no'ble·man** (-mən), *n.* [*pl.* -MEN], a member of the nobility; peer. **—no'ble·wom'an** [*pl.* -WOMEN], *n.fem.*

**no·body** (nō'bəd-i, -bod'i), *pron.* not anybody; no one. *n.* [*pl.* -IES], a person of no importance.

**noc·tur·nal** (nok-tũr'n'l), *adj.* [< L. *nox*, night], 1. of the night. 2. functioning, done, or happening in the night.

**noc·turne** (nok'tẽrn), *n.* [Fr.], a romantic or dreamy musical composition thought appropriate to night.

**nod** (nod), *v.i.* [NODDED, NODDING], [ME. *nodden*], 1. to bend the head forward quickly, as in agreement, greeting, etc. 2. to have the head fall forward because of drowsiness. *v.t.* 1. to bend (the head) forward quickly. 2. to signify (assent, etc.) by doing this. *n.* a nodding. **—nod'der,** *n.*

**node** (nōd), *n.* [L. *nodus*], 1. a knot; knob; swelling. 2. that part of a stem from which a leaf starts to grow. 3. a central point. 4. in *physics*, the point, line, or surface of a vibrating object where there is comparatively no vibration. **—no'dal** (nō'd'l), *adj.*

**nod·ule** (noj'ōōl, nod'ūl), *n.* a small knot or rounded lump.

**No·el, No·ël** (nō-el', nō'el), *n.* [Fr. < L. *natalis*, birthday], 1. Christmas. 2. [n-], a Christmas carol.

**nog·gin** (nog'in), *n.* [prob. < *nog*, strong ale], 1. a small cup or mug. 2. one fourth of a pint, as of liquor. 3. [Colloq.], the head.

**noise** (noiz), *n.* [< ?], 1. clamor; din. 2. sound; esp., any loud, disagreeable sound. *v.t.* [NOISED, NOISING], to spread (a report, rumor, etc.).

**noise'less,** *adj.* 1. without noise; silent. 2. with less noise than is expected: as, a *noiseless* typewriter. **—noise'less·ly,** *adv.*

**noi·some** (noi'səm), *adj.* [see ANNOY & -SOME], 1. injurious to health. 2. foul-smelling; offensive. **—noi'some·ly,** *adv.*

**nois'y,** *adj.* [-IER, -IEST], 1. making noise. 2. full of noise. **—nois'i·ly,** *adv.* **—nois'i·ness,** *n.*

**no·mad** (nō'mad), *n.* [< Gr. *nemein*, to pasture], 1. any of a people having no permanent home, but moving about constantly as in search of pasture. 2. a wanderer. *adj.* wandering. **—no·mad'ic,** *adj.*

**no man's land,** the area on a battlefield separating the combatants.

**nom de plume** (nom' də plōōm'), [pseudo Fr.], a pen name; pseudonym.

**no·men·cla·ture** (nō'mən-klā'chẽr), *n.* [< L. *nomen*, name + *calare*, call], the system of names used in a branch of learning, for parts of a device, etc.

**nom·i·nal** (nom'ə-n'l), *adj.* [< L. *nomen*, a name], 1. of or like a name. 2. in name only, not in fact: as, a *nominal* leader. 3. relatively very small: as, a *nominal* fee.

**nom·i·nate** (nom'ə-nāt'), *v.t.* [-NATED, -NATING], 1. to appoint to an office or position. 2. to name as a candidate for election. **—nom'i·na'tion,** *n.* **—nom'i·na'tor,** *n.*

**nom·i·na·tive** (nom'i-nə-tiv), *adj.* in *grammar*, designating or of the case of the subject of a verb and the words that agree with it. *n.* 1. this case. 2. a word in this case.

**nom·i·nee** (nom'ə-nē'), *n.* a person who is nominated.

**non-,** [< L. *non*], a prefix meaning *not:* less emphatic than *in-* and *un-*, which often give a word an opposite meaning. The following list includes some common compounds formed with *non-* that do not have special meanings; they will be understood if *not* is used before the meaning of the base word.

**nonabsorbent**
**nonacid**
**nonactive**
**nonadministrative**
**nonaggression**
**nonalcoholic**
**nonassignable**
**nonathletic**
**nonattendance**
**nonattributive**
**nonbasic**
**nonbeliever**
**nonbelligerent**
**nonblooming**
**nonbreakable**
**noncanonical**
**non-Catholic**
**nonchargeable**
**non-Christian**
**nonclerical**
**nonclinical**
**noncollectable**
**noncombining**
**noncombustible**
**noncommercial**
**non-Communist**
**noncompeting**
**noncompetitive**
**noncompliance**
**noncomplying**
**nonconducting**
**nonconflicting**
**nonconforming**
**nonconstructive**
**noncontagious**
**noncontiguous**
**noncontributory**
**noncontroversial**
**nonconvertible**
**noncorroding**
**noncritical**
**noncrystalline**
**noncumulative**
**nondelivery**
**nondepartmental**
**nondepreciating**

**nondestructive**
**nondetachable**
**nondisciplinary**
**nondiscrimination**
**nondramatic**
**noneducational**
**noneffective**
**nonelective**
**non-English**
**nonessential**
**nonexchangeable**
**nonexclusive**
**nonexempt**
**nonexistence**
**nonexistent**
**nonexperimental**
**nonexplosive**
**nonfactual**
**nonfading**
**nonfatal**
**nonfiction**
**nonfictional**
**nonflowering**
**nonfluctuating**
**nonflying**
**nonformal**
**nonfunctional**
**nongovernmental**
**nongranular**
**nonhazardous**
**nonhereditary**
**nonhuman**
**nonidentical**
**noninclusive**
**nonindependent**
**noninductive**
**nonindustrial**
**noninfected**
**noninfectious**
**noninflammable**
**noninjurious**
**noninstrumental**
**nonintellectual**
**noninterference**
**noninternational**
**nonintoxicating**
**nonirritating**
**non-Jewish**
**nonjudicial**
**nonlegal**
**nonliterary**
**nonmagnetic**
**nonmalignant**
**nonmember**
**nonmigratory**
**nonmilitant**
**nonmilitary**
**nonmortal**
**nonnegotiable**
**nonobligatory**
**nonobservance**
**nonobservant**
**nonoccupational**
**nonofficial**
**nonoperative**
**nonparticipation**
**nonpaying**
**nonpayment**
**nonperformance**
**nonperishable**
**nonphysical**
**nonpoetic**
**nonpoisonous**
**nonpolitical**
**nonporous**
**nonproducer**
**nonproductive**
**nonprofessional**
**nonprofitable**
**nonpunishable**
**nonracial**
**nonreciprocal**
**nonreciprocating**
**nonrecognition**
**nonrecoverable**
**nonrecurring**
**nonreigning**
**nonreligious**
**nonresidential**
**nonresidual**
**nonresistant**
**nonrestricted**
**nonreturnable**
**nonrhyming**
**nonrhythmic**
**nonrigid**
**nonrural**
**nonsalaried**
**nonscientific**
**nonscoring**
**nonseasonal**
**nonsecular**
**nonsensitive**
**nonshattering**
**nonshrinkable**
**nonsmoker**
**nonsocial**
**nonsolid**
**nonspecializing**
**nonspiritual**
**nonstaining**
**nonstarting**
**nonstatic**
**nonstrategic**
**nonstretchable**
**nonstriking**
**nonstructural**
**nonsubscriber**
**nonsuccessive**
**nonsupporting**
**nonsustaining**
**nonsymbolic**
**nonsympathizer**
**nontarnishable**
**nontaxable**
**nontechnical**
**nonterritorial**
**nonthinking**
**nontoxic**
**nontransferable**
**nontransparent**
**nontropical**
**nonuser**
**nonvenomous**
**nonviolation**
**nonviolence**
**nonviolent**
**nonvirulent**
**nonvocal**
**nonvocational**
**nonvolatile**
**nonvoter**
**nonvoting**
**nonwhite**

**non·age** (non′ij, nō′nij), *n.* [see NON- & AGE], the state of being under full legal age (usually 21).
**nonce** (nons), *n.* [by merging of ME. (*for then*) *ones*, (for the) once], the present use, occasion, or time: chiefly in *for the nonce*.
**non·cha·lant** (non′shə-lənt, non′shə-länt′), *adj.* [Fr.; ult. < L. *non*, not + *calere*, be warm], 1. without warmth or enthusiasm. 2. casually indifferent. **—non′cha·lance,** *n.*
**non·com** (non′kom′), *n.* [Colloq.], a noncommissioned officer.
**non·com·bat·ant** (non-kom′bə-tənt), *n.* 1. a civilian in wartime. 2. a member of the armed forces not involved in actual combat. *adj.* of noncombatants.
**non′com·mis′sioned officer,** an enlisted person in the armed forces holding any of the ranks above private first class and below warrant officer.
**non·com·mit·tal** (non′kə-mit′'l), *adj.* not committing one to a definite stand.
**non′con·duc′tor,** *n.* a substance that does not readily transmit electricity, sound, heat, etc.
**non′con·form′ist,** *n.* one who does not conform to prevailing attitudes, behavior, etc.; specif., one who dissents from an established church. **—non′con·form′i·ty,** *n.*
**non·de·script** (non′di-skript′), *adj.* [< L. *non*, not + *descriptus*, described], belonging to no definite class or type; hard to classify or describe.
**none** (nun), *pron.* [< AS. *ne*, not + *an*, one], 1. no one; not anyone. 2. not any: usually with a plural verb, as, *none* are his. *n.* no part; nothing: as, I want *none* of it. *adv.* not at all: as, *none* too soon. **—none the less,** nevertheless.
**non·en·ti·ty** (non-en′tə-ti), *n.* [*pl.* -TIES], a person considered of little importance.
**none·such** (nun′such′), *n.* a person or thing unrivaled or unequaled; paragon.
**non′in·ter·ven′tion,** *n.* refusal to intervene; esp., a refusal by one nation to interfere in another's affairs.
**non·metal** (non′met′'l), *n.* an element lacking the characteristics of a metal, as oxygen, carbon, fluorine, etc. **—non′me·tal′lic,** *adj.*
**non′pa·reil′** (-pə-rel′), *adj.* [Fr. < *non*, not + *pareil*, equal], unequaled; peerless.
**non·par′ti·san, non·par′ti·zan,** *adj.* not partisan; esp., not connected with any single political party.
**non·plus** (non-plus′, non′plus), *v.t.* [-PLUSED or -PLUSSED, -PLUSING or -PLUSSING], [L. *non*, not + *plus*, more], to cause to be so perplexed that one cannot go, speak, or act further.
**non·prof′it,** *adj.* not intending or intended to earn a profit.
**non·res′i·dent,** *adj.* not residing in the locality where one works, attends school, etc. *n.* a nonresident person.
**non′re·stric′tive** (-ri-strik′tiv), *adj. in grammar*, designating a clause, phrase, or word felt as not essential to the sense, usually set off by commas (e.g., John, *who is six feet tall*, is younger than Bill).
**non′sec·tar′i·an** (-sek-târ′i-ən), *adj.* not confined to any specific religion.
**non·sense** (non′sens, -səns), *n.* words, actions, etc. that are absurd or meaningless. **—non·sen′si·cal,** *adj.*
‡**non se·qui·tur** (non sek′wi-tẽr), [L., it does not follow], a conclusion that does not follow from the premises upon which it is based.
**non′stop′,** *adj.* & *adv.* without a stop.
**non′sup·port′,** *n.* failure to provide for a legal dependent.
**non·un′ion,** *adj.* 1. not belonging to a labor union. 2. not made or serviced under labor-union conditions. 3. not recognizing a labor union. **—non·un′ion·ism,** *n.*
**noo·dle** (nōō′d'l), *n.* [< ?], [Slang], the head.
**noo·dle** (nōō′d'l), *n.* [G. *nudel*, macaroni], a flat, narrow strip of dry dough, usually containing egg.
**nook** (nook), *n.* [ME. *nok*], 1. a corner. 2. a small recess or secluded spot.
**noon** (nōōn), *n.* [< L. *nona* (*hora*), ninth (hour): after a former period of worship, now observed at midday], twelve o'clock

in the daytime; midday. *adj.* of or at noon. Also **noon′day′**, **noon′tide′**, **noon′time′**.

**no one,** no person; not anybody; nobody: also **no′-one′**, *pron.*

**noose** (nōōs), *n.* [< L. *nodus*], a loop formed in a rope, etc. by means of a slipknot so that the loop tightens as the rope is pulled.

**nor** (nôr), *conj.* [ME., contr. of *nother*, neither], and not; and not either: as, I can neither go *nor* stay.

**Nor·dic** (nôr′dik), *adj.* [< G. or Fr. *nord*, north], designating or of a division of the Caucasian race found in Scandinavia, etc. *n.* a Nordic person.

**norm** (nôrm), *n.* [< L. *norma*, rule], a standard or model; esp., the standard of achievement of a large group.

**nor·mal** (nôr′m'l), *adj.* 1. conforming with an accepted standard or norm; natural; usual. 2. average in intelligence or emotional stability. *n.* 1. anything normal. 2. the usual state, amount, etc. **—nor′mal·cy, nor·mal′i·ty** (-mal′ə-ti), *n.*

**nor′mal·ize′**, *v.t.* [-IZED, -IZING], to make normal; bring into conformity with a standard. **—nor′mal·i·za′tion,** *n.*

**nor′mal·ly,** *adv.* 1. in a normal manner. 2. under normal circumstances; ordinarily.

**Nor·man** (nôr′mən), *n.* [< ON.], 1. any of the Scandinavians who occupied Normandy in the 10th century A.D. 2. a descendant of the Normans and French who conquered England in 1066. 3. a native of Normandy, France. *adj.* of Normandy, the Normans, their language, etc.

**Norse** (nôrs), *adj.* & *n.* [prob. < D. *noord*, north], 1. Scandinavian. 2. (of) those languages spoken in W Scandinavia. **—the Norse,** the Scandinavians.

**Norse′man** (-mən), *n.* [*pl.* -MEN], any of the ancient Scandinavian people.

**north** (nôrth), *n.* [AS.], 1. the direction to the right of one facing the sunset (0° or 360° on the compass). 2. a region in or toward this direction. 3. [often N-], the northern part of the earth. *adj.* 1. in, of, or toward the north. 2. from the north. *adv.* in or toward the north.

**north′east′,** *n.* 1. the direction halfway between north and east. 2. a region in or toward this direction. *adj.* 1. in, of, or toward the northeast. 2. from the northeast. *adv.* in, toward, or from the northeast. **—north′east′er·ly,** *adj.* & *adv.* **—north′east′ern,** *adj.* **—north′east′ward** (-wẽrd), *adv.* & *adj.* **—north′east′wards,** *adv.*

**north·east·er** (nôrth′ēs′tẽr, nôr-), *n.* a storm or wind from the northeast.

**north·er** (nôr′*th*ẽr), *n.* a storm or strong wind from the north.

**north·er·ly** (nôr′*th*ẽr-li), *adj.* & *adv.* 1. toward the north. 2. from the north.

**north·ern** (nôr′*th*ẽrn), *adj.* 1. in, of, or toward the north. 2. from the north. 3. [N-], of the North. **—north′ern·most′,** *adj.*

**north′ern·er,** *n.* a native or inhabitant of the north, esp. [N-], of the northern U.S.

**northern lights,** the aurora borealis.

**North Pole,** the northern end of the earth's axis.

**North Star,** the bright star above the North Pole.

**north′ward** (-wẽrd), *adv.* & *adj.* toward the north: also **north′wards,** *adv.*

**north′west′,** *n.* 1. the direction halfway between north and west. 2. a region in or toward this direction. *adj.* 1. in, of, or toward the northwest. 2. from the northwest. *adv.* in, toward, or from the northwest. **—north′west′er·ly,** *adj.* & *adv.* **—north′west′ern,** *adj.* **—north′west′ward** (-wẽrd), *adv.* & *adj.* **—north′west′wards,** *adv.*

**north·west·er** (nôrth′wes′tẽr, nôr-), *n.* a storm or wind from the northwest.

**Norw.,** 1. Norway. 2. Norwegian.

**Nor·we·gian** (nôr-wē′jən), *adj.* of Norway, its people, language, etc. *n.* 1. a native of Norway. 2. the language of Norway.

**nose** (nōz), *n.* [AS. *nosu*], 1. the part of the face between the mouth and the eyes, having two openings for breathing and smelling; in animals, the snout, or muzzle. 2. the sense of smell. 3. anything like a nose in shape or position. *v.t.* [NOSED, NOSING], 1. to discover as by smell; scent. 2. to push (a way, etc.) with the front forward. 3. to defeat by a very small margin (with *out*). *v.i.* 1. to pry inquisitively. 2. to move forward. **—on the nose,** [Slang], precisely; exactly. **—turn up one's nose at,** to scorn.

**nose dive,** 1. a swift, downward plunge of an airplane, nose first. 2. any sudden, sharp drop. **—nose′dive′** [-DIVED, -DIVING], *v.i.*

**nose·gay** (nōz′gā′), *n.* [*nose* + *gay* (in obs. sense of "gay object")], a bunch of flowers.

**nos·tal·gia** (nos-tal′jə), *n.* [< Gr. *nostos*, a return; + *-algia*], 1. homesickness. 2. a longing for something far away or long ago. **—nos·tal′gic,** *adj.* **—nos·tal′gi·cal·ly,** *adv.*

**nos·tril** (nos′trəl), *n.* [< AS. *nosu*, nose + *thyrel*, hole], either of the external openings of the nose.

**nos·trum** (nos′trəm), *n.* [L., ours], 1. a quack medicine. 2. a patent medicine.

**nos·y, nos·ey** (nōz′i), *adj.* [-IER, -IEST], [Colloq.], prying; inquisitive.

**not** (not), *adv.* [< ME. *nought*], in no way, degree, etc.: a word expressing negation or the idea of *no*.

**no·ta·ble** (nō′tə-b'l), *adj.* [< L. *notare*, to note], worthy of notice; remarkable; eminent. *n.* a person of distinction. **—no′ta·ble·ness,** *n.* **—no′ta·bly,** *adv.*

**no·ta·rize** (nō′tə-rīz′), *v.t.* [-RIZED, -RIZING], to certify or attest (a document) as a notary.

**no·ta·ry** (nō′tẽr-i), *n.* [*pl.* -RIES], [< L. *notare*, to note], an official authorized to certify or attest documents, take affidavits, etc.: in full, **notary public.**

**no·ta·tion** (nō-tā′shən), *n.* [< L. *notare*, to note], 1. the use of signs or symbols to represent words, quantities, etc. 2. any such system of signs or symbols, as in algebra, music, etc. 3. a noting. 4. a note.

**notch** (noch), *n.* [by merging of ME. *an oche*, a notch], 1. a V-shaped cut in an edge or surface. 2. a narrow pass with steep sides. 3. [Colloq.], a step; degree: as, a *notch* better. *v.t.* to cut a notch or notches in.

**note** (nōt), *n.* [< L. *nota*, a mark], 1. a distinguishing feature: as, a *note* of sadness. 2. importance, distinction, etc.: as, a person of *note*. 3. a brief writing to aid the memory; memorandum. 4. a comment or explanation; annotation. 5. notice; heed: as, take *note* of this. 6. a short letter. 7. a written acknowledgment of a debt. 8. a cry or call, as of a bird. 9. in *music*, *a*) a tone of definite pitch. *b*) a symbol for a tone, indicating its duration and pitch. *v.t.* [NOTED, NOTING], 1. to heed; observe. 2. to make a memorandum of. 3. to mention specially. **—compare notes,** to exchange views. **—not′er,** *n.*

**note′book′,** *n.* a book in which notes, or memorandums, are kept.

**not·ed** (nōt′id), *adj.* distinguished; eminent.

**note′wor′thy,** *adj.* worthy of note; outstanding; remarkable. **—note′wor′thi·ness,** *n.*

**noth·ing** (nuth′iŋ), *n.* [AS. *na thing*], 1. no thing; not anything. 2. nothingness. 3. a thing that does not exist. 4. a person or thing considered of little or no importance. 5. in *math.*, zero. *adv.* not at all; in no manner or degree. **—for nothing,** 1. free; at no cost. 2. in vain. 3. without reason.

**noth′ing·ness,** *n.* 1. nonexistence. 2. insignificance. 3. unconsciousness.

**no·tice** (nō′tis), *n.* [see NOTE], 1. announcement or warning. 2. a short article about a book, play, etc. 3. a sign giving some public information, warning, etc. 4. attention; heed. 5. a formal warning of intention to end an agreement or contract at a certain time. *v.t.* [-TICED, -TICING], 1. to mention; refer to. 2. to observe; pay attention to. **—take notice,** to observe.
**no′tice·a·ble,** *adj.* 1. easily seen; conspicuous. 2. significant. **—no′tice·a·bly,** *adv.*
**no·ti·fy** (nō′tə-fī′), *v.t.* [-FIED, -FYING], [< L. *noscere,* know + *facere,* make], to give notice to; inform. **—no′ti·fi·ca′tion** (-fi-kā′shən), *n.*
**no·tion** (nō′shən), *n.* [see NOTE], 1. a general idea. 2. a belief; opinion. 3. an inclination; whim. 4. *pl.* small, useful wares, as needles, thread, etc.
**no·to·ri·e·ty** (nō′tə-rī′ə-ti), *n.* [*pl.* -TIES], a being notorious.
**no·to·ri·ous** (nō-tôr′i-əs), *adj.* [see NOTE], widely known, esp. unfavorably.
**no′-trump′,** *n.* in *bridge,* 1. a bid to play with no suit being trumps. 2. the hand so played.
**not·with·stand·ing** (not′with-stan′diŋ, -with-), *prep.* in spite of. *adv.* nevertheless. *conj.* although.
**nought** (nôt), *n.* [< AS. *ne,* not + *awiht,* aught], naught. *adj.* worthless; useless.
**noun** (noun), *n.* [< L. *nomen,* a name], in *grammar,* a word that names or denotes a person, thing, action, etc.
**nour·ish** (nũr′ish), *v.t.* [< L. *nutrire*], 1. to feed or sustain with substances necessary to life and growth. 2. to stimulate; foster. **—nour′ish·ing,** *adj.*
**nour′ish·ment** (-mənt), *n.* 1. a nourishing or being nourished. 2. food.
**Nov.,** November.
**no·va** (nō′və), *n.* [*pl.* -VAS, -VAE (-vē)], [L., new (star)], in *astron.,* a star that suddenly increases greatly in brilliance and then gradually grows fainter.
**nov·el** (nov′'l), *adj.* [< L. dim. of *novus,* new] new; recent; unusual. *n.* a relatively long fictional prose narrative with a more or less complex plot.
**nov·el·ette** (nov′ə-let′), *n.* a short novel.
**nov′el·ist,** *n.* one who writes novels.
**nov′el·ty,** *n.* [*pl.* -TIES], 1. the quality of being novel; newness. 2. something new, fresh, or unusual. 3. *usually in pl.* a small, often cheap, cleverly made article.
**No·vem·ber** (nō-vem′bẽr), *n.* [< L. *novem,* nine: ninth month in Rom. calendar], the eleventh month of the year, having 30 days.
**no·ve·na** (nō-vē′nə), *n.* [*pl.* -NAS, -NAE (-nē)], [< L. *novem,* nine], in the *R. C. Church,* special prayers during a nine-day period.
**nov·ice** (nov′is), *n.* [< L. *novus,* new], 1. a person on probation in a religious order before taking the final vows. 2. a person new to a particular activity, etc.; beginner.
**no·vi·ti·ate, no·vi·ci·ate** (nō-vish′i-it), *n.* the condition or period of being a novice.
**no·vo·cain, no·vo·caine** (nō′və-kān′), *n.* [< L. *novus,* new; + *cocaine*], an alkaloid compound used as a local anesthetic: a trademark **(Novocain).**
**now** (nou), *adv.* [AS. *nu*], 1. *a*) at the present time. *b*) at once. 2. at the time referred to; then; next. 3. very recently: as, he left just *now.* 4. with things as they are: as, *now* we'll never know. *conj.* since; seeing that. *n.* the present time. **—now and then,** occasionally: also **now and again.**
**now′a·days′** (-ə-dāz′), *adv.* in these days; at the present time. *n.* the present time.
**no·where** (nō′hwâr′), *adv.* not in, at, or to any place. **—be** (or **get) nowhere,** to have no success; fail.
**no·wise** (nō′wīz′), *adv.* in no manner: also **no′way′, no′ways′.**
**nox·ious** (nok′shəs), *adj.* [< L. *nocere,* to hurt], harmful to health or morals; unwholesome. **—nox′ious·ly,** *adv.*
**noz·zle** (noz′'l), *n.* [dim. of *nose*], the small spout of a hose, pipe, etc.
**Np,** in *chem.,* neptunium.
**NT., N.T.,** New Testament.
**nth** (enth), *adj.* of the indefinitely large or small number represented by *n.* **—to the nth degree** (or **power**), 1. to an indefinite degree or power. 2. to an extreme.
**nu** (nōō, nū), *n.* the 13th letter of the Greek alphabet (N, ν).
**nu·ance** (nōō-äns′, nū′äns), *n.* [Fr. < *nuer,* to shade], a slight variation in tone, color, meaning, expression, etc.
**nub** (nub), *n.* [ult. var. of *knob*], 1. a knob; lump. 2. [Colloq.], the point of a story, etc.
**nub·bin** (nub′in), *n.* [dim. of *nub*], 1. a small lump. 2. a small or imperfect ear of corn.
**nu·cle·ar** (nōō′kli-ẽr, nū′-), *adj.* of, like, or forming a nucleus.
**nuclear fission,** the splitting of the nuclei of atoms, accompanied by conversion of part of the mass into energy, as in the atomic bomb.
**nuclear fusion,** the fusion of atomic nuclei, as of a heavy isotope of hydrogen, into a nucleus of heavier mass, as of helium, with a resultant loss in combined mass, which is converted into energy (as in the hydrogen bomb).
**nuclear physics,** the branch of physics dealing with the structure of atomic nuclei and the energies involved in nuclear changes.
**nu·cle·us** (nōō′kli-əs, nū′-), *n.* [*pl.* -CLEI (-kli-ī′), -CLEUSES], [L., kernel], 1. a central thing or part around which other things or parts are grouped. 2. any center of growth or development. 3. the central part of an atom. 4. the central mass of protoplasm in a cell.
**nude** (nōōd, nūd), *adj.* [L. *nudus*], naked; bare. *n.* a nude figure, esp. as in painting, etc. **—the nude,** a nude condition. **—nude′ly,** *adv.* **—nude′ness, nu′di·ty,** *n.*
**nudge** (nuj), *v.t.* [NUDGED, NUDGING], [< ?], to push gently, esp. with the elbow, in order to get attention. *n.* a gentle push; jog.
**nud′ism,** *n.* the practice or cult of going nude. **—nud′ist,** *adj.* & *n.*
**nug·get** (nug′it), *n.* [prob. < dial. *nug,* lump], a lump, esp. of native gold.
**nui·sance** (nōō′s'ns, nū′-), *n.* [< L. *nocere,* annoy], an act, thing, person, etc. causing trouble, annoyance, etc.
**null** (nul), *adj.* [< L. *nullus,* none], 1. without legal force; invalid: also **null and void.** 2. amounting to nought. 3. insignificant.
**nul·li·fy** (nul′ə-fī), *v.t.* [-FIED, -FYING], [< L. *nullus,* none + *facere,* make], 1. to make legally null. 2. to make valueless or useless. **—nul′li·fi′er,** *n.* **—nul′li·fi·ca′tion,** *n.*
**numb** (num), *adj.* [< ME. *nimen,* take], deadened; insensible: as, *numb* with grief. *v.t.* to make numb. **—numb′ly,** *adv.*
**num·ber** (num′bẽr), *n.* [< L. *numerus*], 1. a symbol or word showing how many or what place in a sequence (e.g., 2, 27, four, fifth, etc.). 2. *pl.* arithmetic. 3. the sum of a collection of persons or things; total. 4. *a*) *also pl.* many. *b*) *pl.* numerical superiority. 5. quantity. 6. *a*) a single issue of a periodical. *b*) a distinct part of a program of entertainment. 7. [Colloq.], a person or thing singled out: as, a smart *number.* 8. in *grammar,* the form of a word as indicating either singular or plural. *v.t.* 1. to enumerate. 2. to give a number to. 3. to include as one of a group, etc. 4. to limit the number of. 5. to comprise in number. 6. a total. *v.i.* to be numbered. **—beyond** (or **without) number,** too numerous to be counted. **—the numbers,** numbers pool.

**num′ber·less,** *adj.* 1. too many to be counted; countless. 2. without a number.
**Num·bers** (num′bẽrz), *n.pl.* [construed as sing.], the fourth book of the Old Testament: abbrev. **Num.**
**numbers pool** (or **game, racket**), an illegal lottery based on certain published numbers, as in newspaper financial reports.
**nu·mer·a·ble** (nōō′mẽr-ə-b'l, nū-), *adj.* that can be numbered or counted.
**nu·mer·al** (nōō′mẽr-əl, nū′-), *adj.* [< L. *numerus*, number], of or denoting a number or numbers. *n.* a figure, letter, or word expressing a number.
**nu·mer·a·tor** (nōō′mə-rā′tẽr, nū′-), *n.* that part of a fraction written above the line.
**nu·mer·i·cal** (nōō-mer′i-k'l, nū-), *adj.* 1. of, or having the nature of, number. 2. in or by numbers. 3. expressed by numbers.
**nu·mer·ous** (nōō′mẽr-əs, nū′-), *adj.* 1. of great number. 2. very many.
**nu·mis·mat·ic** (nōō′miz-mat′ik, nū′mis-), *adj.* [< L. *numisma*, a coin], 1. of coins or medals. 2. of numismatics.
**nu′mis·mat′ics,** *n.pl.* [construed as sing.], the study or collection of coins and medals. **—nu·mis′ma·tist** (-miz′mə-tist), *n.*
**num·skull** (num′skul′), *n.* [< *numb* + *skull*], a stupid person; dolt; dunce.
**nun** (nun), *n.* [< LL. *nonna*], a woman living in a convent under vows.
**nun·ci·o** (nun′shi-ō′), *n.* [*pl.* -os], [< It. < L. *nuntius*, messenger], a papal ambassador to a foreign state.
**nun′ner·y** (-ẽr-i), *n.* [*pl.* -IES], a community of nuns and the place in which they live.
**nup·tial** (nup′shəl, -chəl), *adj.* [< L. *nubere*, marry], of marriage or a wedding. *n. pl.* a wedding.
**nurse** (nũrs), *n.* [< L. *nutrire*, nourish], 1. a woman hired to care for another's children. 2. a person trained to care for the sick, assist surgeons, etc. *v.t.* [NURSED, NURSING], 1. to suckle (an infant). 2. to take care of (a child, invalid, etc.). 3. to nourish, foster, etc. 4. to try to cure: as, to *nurse* a cold. 5. to use or handle so as to protect or conserve. *v.i.* 1. to feed at the breast; suckle. 2. to serve as a nurse.
**nurse′maid′,** *n.* a girl or woman hired to care for a child or children.
**nurs·er·y** (nũr′sẽr-i), *n.* [*pl.* -IES], 1. a room in a home, set aside for the children. 2. a place where young trees or plants are raised for transplanting.
**nursery rhyme,** a poem for children.
**nursery school,** a prekindergarten school.
**nur·ture** (nũr′chẽr), *n.* [< L. *nutrire*, nourish], 1. food. 2. training; rearing. *v.t.* -TURED, -TURING], 1. to feed or nourish. 2. to train; educate; rear.
**nut** (nut), *n.* [AS. *hnutu*], 1. a dry, one-seeded fruit, consisting of a kernel, often edible, in a woody shell, as the walnut. 2. the kernel itself. 3. loosely, any hard-shelled, relatively nonperishable fruit, as the peanut. 4. a person, problem, etc. hard to understand. 5. a small metal block with a threaded hole, for screwing onto a bolt, etc. 6. [Slang], an eccentric or demented person.
**nut′crack′er,** *n.* 1. *sometimes pl.* an instrument for cracking nutshells. 2. a bird of the crow family that feeds on nuts.
**nut′hatch′** (-hach′), *n.* a small, nut-eating bird having a sharp beak.
**nut′meat′,** *n.* the kernel of a nut.
**nut′meg** (-meg), *n.* [< ME. *nut*, nut + OFr. *mugue*, musk], 1. the aromatic kernel of the seed of an East Indian tree, used as a spice. 2. this tree.
**nu·tri·ent** (nōō′tri-ənt, nū′-), *adj.* [< L. *nutrire*, nourish], nourishing. *n.* anything nutritious.
**nu·tri·ment** (nōō′trə-mənt, nū′-), *n.* anything that nourishes; food.
**nu·tri·tion** (nōō-trish′ən, nū-), *n.* [see NUTRIENT], 1. the process by which an organism takes in and assimilates food. 2. anything that nourishes; food. **—nu·tri′tion·al, nu′tri·tive,** *adj.* **—nu·tri′tion·ist,** *n.*
**nu·tri′tious,** *adj.* providing or promoting nutrition; nourishing. **—nu·tri′tious·ly,** *adv.*
**nuts,** *adj.* [Slang], crazy; foolish. *interj.* [Slang], an exclamation of disgust, scorn, etc.
**nut′shell′,** *n.* the shell enclosing the kernel of a nut. **—in a nutshell,** in concise form.
**nut′ty,** *adj.* [-TIER, -TIEST], 1. containing or producing nuts. 2. having a nutlike flavor. 3. [Slang], *a*) very enthusiastic. *b*) queer, demented, etc.
**nuz·zle** (nuz′'l), *v.t. & v.i.* [-ZLED, -ZLING], [< *nose*], 1. to push (against) or rub with the nose or snout. 2. to nestle; snuggle.
**NW, N.W., n.w.,** 1. northwest. 2. northwestern.
**ny·lon** (nī′lon), *n.* [arbitrary coinage], 1. an elastic, very strong, synthetic material made into thread, bristles, etc. 2. *pl.* stockings made of this.
**nymph** (nimf), *n.* [< Gr. *nymphē*], 1. in *Gr. & Rom. myth.*, any of a group of minor nature goddesses, living in rivers, trees, etc. 2. a lovely young woman. 3. the young of an insect without complete metamorphosis.
**nym·pho·ma·ni·a** (nim′fə-mā′ni-ə), *n.* uncontrollable sexual desire in a woman. **—nym′pho·ma′ni·ac′** (-ak′), *adj. & n.*

# O

**O, o** (ō), *n.* [*pl.* O's, o's, Os, os, oes], 1. the fifteenth letter of the English alphabet. 2. the numeral zero.
**O** (ō), *interj.* 1. an exclamation in direct address: as, *O* God, save us! 2. oh.
**O,** 1. in *chem.*, oxygen. 2. in *linguistics*, Old.
**O.,** 1. Ocean. 2. October.
**oaf** (ōf), *n.* [*pl.* OAFS, OAVES (ōvz)], [< ON. *alfr*, elf], a stupid, clumsy fellow; lout. **—oaf′ish,** *adj.* **—oaf′ish·ly,** *adv.*
**oak** (ōk), *n.* [AS. *ac*], 1. a large hardwood tree or shrub bearing nuts called *acorns*. 2. its wood. *adj.* of oak. **—oak′en,** *adj.*
**oa·kum** (ō′kəm), *n.* [< AS. *a-*, out + *camb*, a comb], hemp fiber got by taking apart old ropes: used to pack seams of boats, etc.
**oar** (ôr), *n.* [AS. *ar*], a long pole with a broad blade at one end, used in rowing. *v.t. & v.i.* to row. **—rest on one's oars,** to stop work in order to rest. **—oars′man** (ôrz′mən), [*pl.* -MEN], *n.* **—oars′man·ship′,** *n.*
**oar′lock′,** *n.* a device for holding the oar in place in rowing.
**o·a·sis** (ō-ā′sis), *n.* [*pl.* -SES (-sēz)], [< Gr. *ōasis*], a fertile place in a desert, due to the presence of water.
**oat** (ōt), *n.* [AS. *ate*], *usually in pl.* 1. a hardy cereal grass. 2. its edible grain. **—oaten,** *adj.*
**oath** (ōth), *n.* [*pl.* OATHS (ōthz, ōths)], [AS. *ath*], 1. a declaration based on an appeal to God that one will speak the truth, keep a promise, etc. 2. the profane use of God's name, as in anger. 3. a swearword; curse.
**oat′meal′,** *n.* 1. oats crushed into meal or flakes. 2. a porridge made from such oats.

**ob-,** [< L. *ob*], a prefix meaning: 1. *to, toward, before*, as in *object*. 2. *against*, as in *obnoxious*. 3. *upon, over*, as in *obfuscate*. 4. *completely*, as in *obsolete*.

**ob·bli·ga·to** (ob'li-gä'tō), *n.* [*pl.* -TOS, -TI (-ti)], [see OBLIGE], an elaborate musical accompaniment necessary to the proper performance of a piece.

**ob·du·rate** (ob'doo-rit, -dyoo-), *adj.* [< L. *ob-*, intens. + *durus*, hard], 1. hardhearted. 2. stubborn; obstinate. —**ob'du·ra·cy** *n.*

**o·be·di·ent** (ō-bē'di-ənt), *adj.* obeying or willing to obey. —**o·be'di·ence,** *n.*

**o·bei·sance** (ō-bā's'ns, ō-bē'-), *n.* [< OFr. *obeir*, obey], 1. a gesture of respect, as a bow. 2. homage; deference.—**o·bei'sant,** *adj.*

**ob·e·lisk** (ob''l-isk), *n.* [< Gr. *obelos*, needle], a tall, four-sided stone pillar tapering to a pyramidal top.

**O·ber·on** (ō'bə-ron'), *n.* in early folklore, the king of fairyland.

**o·bese** (ō-bēs'), *adj.* [< L. *ob-* (see OB-) + *edere*, eat], very fat; stout. —**o·bes·i·ty** (ō-bēs'ə-ti, -bes'-), *n.*

**o·bey** (ō-bā'), *v.t.* [< L. *ob-* (see OB-) + *audire*, hear], 1. to carry out the orders of. 2. to carry out (an order, etc.). 3. to be guided by: as, *obey* reason. *v.i.* to be obedient.

**ob·fus·cate** (ob-fus'kāt, ob'fəs-kāt'), *v.t.* [-CATED, -CATING], [< L. *ob-* (see OB-) + *fuscus*, dark], to obscure; confuse; bewilder. —**ob'fus·ca'tion,** *n.*

**o·bit** (ō'bit, ob'it), *n.* an obituary.

**o·bit·u·ar·y** (ō-bich'oo-er'i), *n.* [*pl.* -IES], [< L. *obitus*, death], a notice of someone's death, usually with a short biography.

**obj.,** 1. object. 2. objective.

**ob·ject** (ob'jikt), *n.* [< ML. *objectum*, thing thrown in the way < L. *ob-* (see OB-) + *jacere*, throw], 1. a thing that can be seen or touched. 2. a person or thing to which action, feeling, etc. is directed. 3. purpose; goal. 4. in *grammar*, a noun or substantive that receives the action of the verb or is governed by a preposition. *v.t.* (əb-jekt', ob-), to state in opposition or disapproval. *v.i.* to feel or express opposition or disapproval. —**ob·jec'tor,** *n.*

**ob·jec·tion** (əb-jek'shən, ob-), *n.* 1. a feeling or expression of opposition or disapproval. 2. a reason for objecting.

**ob·jec'tion·a·ble,** *adj.* 1. open to objection. 2. disagreeable; offensive.

**ob·jec'tive,** *adj.* 1. existing as an object or fact, independent of the mind; real. 2. concerned with the realities of the thing dealt with rather than the thoughts of the artist, writer, speaker, etc. 3. without bias or prejudice. 4. in *grammar*, designating or of the case of an object of a preposition or verb. *n.* something aimed at. —**ob·jec'tive·ly,** *adv.* —**ob·jec·tiv·i·ty** (ob'jek-tiv'ə-ti), *n.*

**ob·jur·gate** (ob'jēr-gāt'), *v.t.* [-GATED, -GATING], [< L. *ob-* (see OB-) + *jurgare*, chide], to upbraid sharply. —**ob'jur·ga'tion,** *n.*

**ob·late** (ob'lāt), *adj.* [< Mod. L. *oblatus*, thrust forward], flattened at the poles: as, an *oblate* spheroid. —**ob'late·ly,** *adv.*

**ob·la·tion** (ob-lā'shən), *n.* [< L. *oblatus*, offered], 1. an offering or sacrifice to God or a god. 2. the thing offered; esp., the bread and wine of the Eucharist.

**ob·li·gate** (ob'lə-gāt'), *v.t.* [-GATED, -GATING], [see OBLIGE], to bind by a contract, promise, sense of duty, etc.

**ob'li·ga'tion,** *n.* 1. an obligating or being obligated. 2. the contract, promise, responsibility, etc. binding one. 3. the binding power of a contract, promise, etc. 4. a being indebted for a favor, etc.

**ob·lig·a·to·ry** (ə-blig'ə-tôr'i, ob'li-gə-), *adj.* legally or morally binding; required.

**o·blige** (ə-blij', ō-), *v.t.* [OBLIGED, OBLIGING], [< L. *ob-* (see OB-) + *ligare*, bind], 1. to compel by moral, legal, or physical force. 2. to make indebted for a favor; do a favor for. —**o·blig'er,** *n.*

**o·blig'ing,** *adj.* ready to do favors; helpful.

**ob·lique** (ə-blēk'; *esp. military*, ō-blīk'), *adj.* [< L. *ob-* (see OB-) + *liquis*, awry], 1. slanting. 2. indirector or evasive. —**ob·lique'ly,** *adv.* —**ob·liq·ui·ty** (ə-blik'wə-ti), *n.*

**ob·lit·er·ate** (ə-blit'ə-rāt'), *v.t.* [-ATED, -ATING], [< L. *ob-* (see OB-) + *litera*, a letter], 1. to blot out; efface. 2. to do away with; destroy. —**ob·lit'er·a'tion,** *n.*

**ob·liv·i·on** (ə-bliv'i-ən), *n.* [< L. *oblivisci*, forget], 1. forgetfulness. 2. the state of being forgotten.

**ob·liv'i·ous,** *adj.* forgetful; unmindful (with *of* or *to*). —**ob·liv'i·ous·ness,** *n.*

**ob·long** (ob'lôŋ), *adj.* [< L. *ob-* (see OB-) + *longus*, long], longer than broad; specif., rectangular and longer in one direction. *n.* an oblong figure.

**ob·lo·quy** (ob'lə-kwi), *n.* [*pl.* -QUIES], [< L. *ob-* (see OB-) + *loqui*, speak], 1. widespread censure or calumny. 2. disgrace or infamy resulting from this.

**ob·nox·ious** (əb-nok'shəs, ob-), *adj.* [< L. *ob-* (see OB-) + *noxa*, harm], very unpleasant; offensive. —**ob·nox'ious·ly,** *adv.*

**o·boe** (ō'bō), *n.* [< Fr. *haut*, high (pitch) + *bois*, wood], a double-reed wood-wind instrument having a high, penetrating tone.

**Obs., obs.,** obsolete.

**ob·scene** (əb-sēn', ob-), *adj.* [< L. *obscenus*, filthy], offensive to modesty or decency; lewd. —**ob·scene'ly,** *adv.* —**ob·scen'i·ty** (-sen'ə-ti, -sē'nə-), [*pl.* -TIES], *n.*

**ob·scure** (əb-skyoor', ob-), *adj.* [< L. *obscurus*, covered over], 1. dim; dark; gloomy. 2. not easily seen; indistinct. 3. vague; ambiguous: as, an *obscure* answer. 4. inconspicuous; hidden. 5. not well known: as, an *obscure* actor. *v.t.* [-SCURED, -SCURING], to make obscure. —**ob·scu'ri·ty,** *n.*

**ob·se·qui·ous** (əb-sē'kwi-əs, ob-), *adj.* [< L. *obsequi*, comply with], excessively willing to serve or obey; servile.

**ob·se·quy** (ob'si-kwi), *n.* [*pl.* -QUIES], [< L. *obsequium*, service (by confusion with *exsequiae*, funeral)], *usually in pl.* a funeral rite or ceremony.

**ob·serv·ance** (əb-zũr'vəns, ob-), *n.* 1. the observing of a law, duty, custom, etc. 2. a customary act, rite, etc.

**ob·serv'ant,** *adj.* 1. strict in observing a rule, custom, etc. 2. paying careful attention. 3. perceptive or alert.

**ob·ser·va·tion** (ob'zẽr-vā'shən), *n.* 1. *a*) the act or power of observing. *b*) something noticed. 2. a being seen or noticed. 3. a noting and recording of facts, as for scientific study. 4. a comment; remark.

**ob·serv·a·to·ry** (əb-zũr'və-tôr'i, ob-), *n.* [*pl.* -RIES], a building equipped for astronomical or meteorological research.

**ob·serve** (əb-zũrv', ob-), *v.t.* [-SERVED, -SERVING], [< L. *ob-* (see OB-) + *servare*, keep], 1. to adhere to (a law, custom, etc.). 2. to celebrate (a holiday, etc.). 3. *a*) to notice (something). *b*) to pay attention to. 4. to say casually; remark. 5. to examine scientifically. —**ob·serv'er,** *n.*

**ob·sess** (əb-ses', ob-), *v.t.* [< L. *ob-* (see OB-) + *sedere*, sit], to haunt or trouble in mind; preoccupy. —**ob·ses'sive,** *adj.*

**ob·ses'sion,** *n.* 1. a being obsessed. 2. an idea, desire, etc. that obsesses one.

**ob·sid·i·an** (əb-sid'i-ən, ob-), *n.* [after one *Obsius*, its alleged discoverer], a dark, hard, glassy volcanic rock.

**ob·so·les·cent** (ob'sə-les''nt), *adj.* becoming obsolete. —**ob'so·les'cence,** *n.*

**ob·so·lete** (ob'sə-lēt'), *adj.* [< L. *ob-* (see OB-) + *solere*, become accustomed], 1. no longer in use; discarded. 2. out-of-date.

**ob·sta·cle** (ob'sti-k'l), *n.* [< L. *ob-* (see OB-) + *stare*, to stand], anything that stands in the way; obstruction.

**ob·ste·tri·cian** (ob'stə-trish'ən), *n.* a specialist in obstetrics.

**ob·stet·rics** (ob-stet'riks), *n.pl.* [construed as sing.], [< L. *obstetrix*, midwife], the branch of medicine concerned with the care and treatment of women in pregnancy and childbirth. **—ob·stet'ric, ob·stet'ri·cal,** *adj.*

**ob·sti·nate** (ob'sti-nit), *adj.* [< L. *obstinare*, resolve on], 1. unreasonably determined to have one's own way; stubborn. 2. resisting treatment: as, an *obstinate* fever. **—ob'sti·na·cy** (-nə-si), *n.* **—ob'sti·nate·ly,** *adv.*

**ob·strep·er·ous** (əb-strep'ẽr-əs, ob-), *adj.* [ult. < L. *ob-* (see OB-) + *strepere*, to roar], noisy or unruly, esp. in resisting.

**ob·struct** (əb-strukt', ob-), *v.t.* [ult. < L. *ob-* (see OB-) + *struere*, pile up], 1. to block or bar (a passage). 2. to hinder (progress, etc.). 3. *a*) to get in the way of. *b*) to block (the view). **—ob·struc'tive,** *adj.*

**ob·struc'tion,** *n.* 1. an obstructing. 2. anything that obstructs; obstacle.

**ob·tain** (əb-tān', ob-), *v.t.* [< L. *ob-* (see OB-) + *tenere*, to hold], to get possession of by trying; procure. *v.i.* to prevail: as, peace will *obtain*. **—ob·tain'a·ble,** *adj.*

**ob·trude** (əb-trōōd', ob-), *v.t.* [-TRUDED, -TRUDING], [< L. *ob-* (see OB-) + *trudere*, to thrust], 1. to push out; eject. 2. to force upon others without being asked. *v.i.* to obtrude oneself. **—ob·tru'sive,** *adj.*

**ob·tuse** (əb-tōōs', ob-), *adj.* [< L. *obtundere*, to strike upon, blunt], 1. not sharp; blunt. 2. greater than 90 degrees: said of an angle. 3. slow to understand or perceive.

**ob·verse** (əb-vũrs', ob'vẽrs), *adj.* [< L. *ob-* (see OB-) + *vertere*, to turn], 1. turned toward the observer: cf. *reverse*. 2. forming a counterpart. *n.* (ob'vẽrs), 1. the side, as of a coin or medal, bearing the main design. 2. a counterpart. **—ob·verse'ly,** *adv.*

**ob·vi·ate** (ob'vi-āt'), *v.t.* [-ATED, -ATING], [see OBVIOUS], to do away with or prevent by effective measures; make unnecessary. **—ob'vi·a'tion,** *n.* **—ob'vi·a'tor,** *n.*

**ob·vi·ous** (ob'vi-əs), *adj.* [L. *obvius*, in the way], easy to see or understand; evident.

**oc-,** ob-: used before *c*.

**oc·a·ri·na** (ok'ə-rē'nə), *n.* [It. < *auca*, goose: from its shape], a small wind instrument with finger holes and a mouthpiece.

**occas.,** occasional(ly).

**oc·ca·sion** (ə-kā'zhən), *n.* [< L. *ob-* (see OB-) + *cadere*, to fall], 1. a favorable time; opportunity. 2. an immediate cause of something. 3. *a*) a happening. *b*) a particular time. 4. a special time or event. 5. need arising from circumstances. *v.t.* to cause. **—on occasion,** sometimes.

**oc·ca'sion·al,** *adj.* 1. of or for special occasions. 2. happening now and then; infrequent. **—oc·ca'sion·al·ly,** *adv.*

**oc·ci·dent** (ok'sə-dənt), *n.* [< L. *occidere*, to fall: with reference to the setting sun], 1. [Poetic], the west. 2. [O-], Europe and the Western Hemisphere. Cf. *orient*. **—oc'ci·den'tal, Oc'ci·den'tal,** *adj. & n.*

**oc·ci·put** (ok'si-put'), *n.* [*pl.* OCCIPITA (ok-sip'ə-tə)], [L. < *ob-* (see OB-) + *caput*, head], the back part of the skull or head.

**oc·clude** (ə-klōōd'), *v.t.* [-CLUDED, -CLUDING], [< L. *ob-* (see OB-) + *claudere*, shut], 1. to close or block (a passage). 2. to shut in or out. *v.i.* in *dentistry*, to meet with the cusps fitting closely. **—oc·clu'sion** (-klōō'zhən), *n.*

**oc·cult** (ə-kult', ok'ult), *adj.* [< L. *occulere*, conceal], 1. hidden. 2. secret. 3. beyond human understanding. 4. of such mystic studies as astrology, etc. **—the occult,** anything occult. **—oc·cult'ism,** *n.*

**oc·cu·pan·cy** (ok'yoo-pən-si), *n.* [*pl.* -CIES], an occupying; a taking or keeping in possession.

**oc'cu·pant,** *n.* one who occupies.

**oc·cu·pa·tion** (ok'yoo-pā'shən), *n.* 1. an occupying or being occupied. 2. what occupies one's time; work; trade; vocation. **—oc'cu·pa'tion·al,** *adj.*

**occupational therapy,** therapy by work designed to divert the mind or to correct a physical defect.

**oc·cu·py** (ok'yoo-pī'), *v.t.* [-PIED, -PYING], [< L. *ob-* (see OB-) + *capere*, seize], 1. to take possession of by settlement or seizure. 2. to hold possession of; specif., *a*) to dwell in. *b*) to hold (a position or office). 3. to take up (space, time, etc.). 4. to employ (oneself, one's mind, etc.). **—oc'cu·pi'er,** *n.*

**oc·cur** (ə-kũr'), *v.i.* [-CURRED, -CURRING], [< L. *ob-* (see OB-) + *currere*, to run], 1. to be or be met with; exist. 2. to present itself; come to mind. 3. to happen.

**oc·cur'rence,** *n.* 1. the act or fact of occurring. 2. an event; incident.

**o·cean** (ō'shən), *n.* [< Gr. *ōkeanos*], 1. the body of salt water that covers more than two thirds of the earth's surface. 2. any of its five principal divisions; the Atlantic, Pacific, Indian, Arctic, or Antarctic Ocean. 3. a great quantity. **—o·ce·an·ic** (ō'shi-an'ik), *adj.*

**o·ce·a·nog·ra·phy** (ō'shi-ə-nog'rə-fi, ō'shən-og'-), *n.* the branch of geography dealing with the ocean. **—o'ce·a·nog'ra·pher,** *n.*

**o·cel·lus** (ō-sel'əs), *n.* [*pl.* -LI (-ī)], [L. < *oculus*, eye], the simple eye of certain invertebrates.

**o·ce·lot** (ō'sə-lot', os'ə-lət), *n.* [Fr. < Mex. *tlalli*, a field + *ocelotl*, jaguar], a large, spotted wild cat of N. and S. America.

**o·cher, o·chre** (ō'kẽr), *n.* [< Gr. *ōchros*, pale-yellow], 1. a yellow or reddish clay containing iron, used as a pigment. 2. the color of ocher; esp., dark yellow.

**-ock,** [AS. *-oc*, *-uc*, dim.], a suffix used originally to form the diminutive, as in ***hillock***.

**o'clock** (ə-klok', ō-), of or according to the clock.

**Oct.,** October.

**octa-,** [< Gr. *oktō*, eight], a combining form meaning *eight*, as in *octagon*: also **octo-, oct-.**

**oc·ta·gon** (ok'tə-gon', -gən), *n.* [< Gr.; see OCTA- & -GON], a plane figure with eight angles and eight sides. **—oc·tag'o·nal** (-tag'ə-n'l), *adj.*

**oc·tane number** (or **rating**) (ok'tān), a number representing the antiknock quality of a gasoline, etc.

**oc·tave** (ok'tāv, -tiv), *n.* [< L. *octavus*, eighth], in *music*, 1. the eighth full tone above or below a given tone. 2. the interval of eight degrees between a tone and either of its octaves. 3. the series of tones within this interval, or the keys of an instrument producing such a series.

**oc·ta·vo** (ok-tā'vō, -tä'-), *n.* [*pl.* -VOS], [< L. *in octavo*, in eight], 1. the page size (about 6 by 9 in.) of a book made up of printer's sheets folded into eight leaves. 2. a book of such pages.

**oc·tet, oc·tette** (ok-tet'), *n.* [< L. *octo*, eight; + *duet*], 1. a musical composition for eight voices or instruments. 2. the eight performers of this.

**Oc·to·ber** (ok-tō'bẽr), *n.* [< L. *octo-*, eight: eighth month in Rom. calendar], the tenth month of the year, having 31 days.

**oc·to·ge·nar·i·an** (ok'tə-ji-nâr'i-ən), *adj.* [< L. *octoginta*, eighty], between eighty and ninety years old. *n.* a person of this age.

**oc·to·pus** (ok'tə-pəs), *n.* [*pl.* -PUSES, -PI (-pī')], [< Gr. *oktō*, eight + *pous*, foot], a mollusk with a soft body and eight arms covered with suckers.

**oc·u·lar** (ok'yoo-lẽr), *adj.* [< L. *oculus*, eye],

1. of, for, or like the eye. 2. by eyesight.
**oc′u·list** (-list), *n.* a physician specializing in the treatment of diseases of the eye.
**odd** (od), *adj.* [< ON. *oddi*], 1. with the other of the pair missing: as, an *odd* glove. 2. having a remainder of one when divided by two. 3. left over after taking a round number. 4. with a few more: as, thirty *odd* years ago. 5. extra; occasional: as, *odd* jobs. 6. *a*) peculiar. *b*) queer; eccentric. **—odd′ly,** *adv.*
**odd′i·ty** (-ə-ti), *n.* 1. peculiarity. 2. [*pl.* -TIES], an odd person or thing.
**odds** (odz), *n.pl.* [occas. construed as sing.], 1. difference in favor of one side over the other; advantage. 2. advantage given to a bettor or competitor in proportion to the assumed chances against him. **—at odds,** quarreling. **—by (all) odds,** by far.
**odds and ends,** scraps; remnants.
**ode** (ōd), *n.* [< Gr. *ōidē*, song], a lyric poem characterized by lofty feeling and dignified style.
**-ode,** [< Gr. *hodos*], a suffix meaning *way, path.*
**O·din** (ō′din), *n.* in *Norse myth.*, the chief of the gods; god of art, war, and the dead.
**o·di·ous** (ō′di-əs), *adj.* [< L. *odium*, hatred], disgusting; offensive.
**o·di·um** (ō′di-əm), *n.* [< L. *odi*, I hate], 1. hatred. 2. the disgrace brought on by hateful action.
**o·dom·e·ter** (ō-dom′ə-tēr), *n.* [< Gr. *hodos*, way + *metron*, a measure], an instrument for measuring distance traveled, as by an automobile.
**odor** (ō′dēr), *n.* [L.], a smell; scent; aroma: also, Brit. spelling, **odour. —be in bad** (or **ill**) **odor,** to be in ill repute. **—o′dor·less,** *adj.* **—o′dor·ous,** *adj.*
**o·dor·if·er·ous** (ō′də-rif′ēr-əs), *adj.* [< L. *odor*, odor + *ferre*, to bear], giving off an odor, esp. a fragrant odor.
**O·dys·seus** (ō-dis′ūs, -i-əs), *n.* the hero of the *Odyssey*, one of the Greek leaders in the Trojan War.
**Od·ys·sey** (od′ə-si), *n.* 1. an ancient Greek epic poem, attributed to Homer, describing the wanderings of Odysseus after the fall of Troy. 2. [sometimes o-], [*pl.* -SEYS (-sēz′)], any extended journey.
**O.E.,** Old English (Anglo-Saxon).
**Oed·i·pus** (ed′ə-pəs, ē′də-), *n.* in *Gr. legend*, a king who unwittingly killed his father and married his mother.
**Oedipus complex,** in *psychoanalysis*, the unconscious tendency of a child, sometimes unresolved in adulthood, to be attached to the parent of the opposite sex and hostile toward the other parent.
**o'er** (ôr), *prep. & adv.* [Poetic], over.
**of** (uv, ov), *prep.* [AS.], 1. from; specif., *a*) coming from: as, men *of* Ohio. *b*) resulting from: as, he died *of* disease. *c*) at a distance from: as, a mile east *of* here. *d*) by: as, the stories *of* Poe. *e*) separated from: as, robbed *of* his money. *f*) from the whole constituting: as, two *of* us. *g*) made from: as, a house *of* wood. 2. belonging to. 3. *a*) possessing: as, a man *of* wealth. *b*) containing: as, a bag *of* peanuts. 4. specified as: as, a height *of* six feet. 5. characterized by: as, a man *of* honor. 6. concerning; about. 7. during.
**of-,** ob-: used before *f.*
**off** (ôf), *adv.* [ME. variant of *of*], 1. so as to be away, at a distance, etc. 2. so as to be no longer on, attached, etc.: as, take *off* his coat. 3. (a specified distance) away in space or time: as, 20 yards *off.* 4. so as to be no longer in operation, etc.: as, turn the motor *off.* 5. so as to be less, etc.: as, crops dropped *off.* 6. away from one's work. *prep.* 1. no longer (or not) on, attached, etc.: as, *off* the road. 2. from the substance of: as, to live *off* the land. 3. away from: as, miles *off* shore. 4. relieved from: as, *off* duty. 5. not up to the usual standard, etc. of: as, *off* one's game. *adj.* 1. not on, attached, in operation, etc. 2. on the way: as, he is *off* to school. 3. away from work: as, we are *off* today. 4. not up to the usual standard, etc. 5. more remote: as, on the *off* chance. 6. in (specified) circumstances: as, he is well *off.* 7. wrong: as, you are *off* by a cent. *interj.* go away! **—be** (or **take**) **off,** to go away. **—off and on,** now and then.
**of·fal** (ôf′′l, of′-), *n.* [ME. *ofall*, off-fall], 1. [construed as sing. or pl.], the entrails, etc. of a butchered animal. 2. refuse; garbage.
**off′-col′or,** *adj.* 1. varying from the standard color. 2. improper; risqué.
**of·fend** (ə-fend′), *v.i.* [< L. *ob-* (see OB-) + *fendere*, to hit], 1. to commit an offense; sin. 2. to create resentment, anger, etc. *v.t.* 1. to hurt the feelings of; make angry, etc. 2. to be displeasing to (the taste, sense, etc.). **—of·fend′er,** *n.*
**of·fense** (ə-fens′), *n.* 1. a sin or crime; wrongdoing. 2. a creating of resentment, anger, etc. 3. a feeling hurt, angry, etc. 4. something that causes anger, etc. 5. the act of attacking. 6. the person, army, etc. that is attacking. Also, Brit. sp., **offence. —take offense,** to become offended.
**of·fen′sive,** *adj.* 1. attacking or for attack. 2. unpleasant; disgusting. 3. causing anger, resentment, etc. *n.* attitude, position, or operation of attack. **—of·fen′sive·ly,** *adv.*
**of·fer** (ôf′ēr, of′-), *v.t.* [< L. *ob-* (see OB-) + *ferre*, bring], 1. to present to God or a god in worship: as, to *offer* prayers. 2. to present for acceptance: as, to *offer* help. 3. to suggest; propose. 4. to threaten or attempt: as, to *offer* resistance. 5. to bid (a price, etc.). *v.i.* to occur; present itself. *n.* the act of offering or thing offered.
**of′fer·ing,** *n.* 1. the act of making an offer. 2. something offered; specif., *a*) a gift. *b*) presentation in worship.
**of′fer·to′ry** (-tôr′i), *n.* [*pl.* -RIES], 1. the offering of the bread and wine to God in the Eucharist. 2. money collected at a church service, or a hymn sung during the collection.
**off′hand′,** *adv.* without prior preparation. *adj.* 1. said or done offhand. 2. casual, curt, etc. Also **off′hand′ed,** *adj.*
**of·fice** (ôf′is, of′-), *n.* [< L. *officium*], 1. a service done for another. 2. a duty, esp. as a part of one's work. 3. a position of authority or trust, as in government. 4. *a*) the place where the affairs of a business, etc. are carried on. *b*) the people working there. 5. a religious ceremony or rite.
**office boy,** a boy doing small tasks in an office.
**of′fice·hold′er,** *n.* a government official.
**of·fi·cer** (ôf′ə-sēr, of′-), *n.* 1. anyone holding an office, or position of authority, in a government, business, club, etc. 2. a policeman. 3. one holding a position of authority, esp. by commission, in the armed forces.
**of·fi·cial** (ə-fish′əl), *adj.* 1. of or holding an office, or position of authority. 2. authoritative; authorized. 3. formal. *n.* a person holding office. **—of·fi′cial·dom** (-dəm), **of·fi′cial·ism,** *n.* **—of·fi′cial·ly,** *adv.*
**of·fi·ci·ate** (ə-fish′i-āt′), *v.i.* [-ATED, -ATING], 1. to perform the duties of an office. 2. to perform the functions of a priest, minister, etc. **—of·fi′ci·a′tion,** *n.*
**of·fi·cious** (ə-fish′əs), *adj.* [see OFFICE], offering unwanted advice or services; meddlesome. **—of·fi′cious·ness,** *n.*
**of·fing** (ôf′iŋ), *n.* [< *off*], the distant part of the sea visible from the shore. **—in the offing,** 1. far but in sight. 2. at some vague future time.
**off·set** (ôf-set′), *v.t.* [-SET, -SETTING], to bal-

ance, compensate for, etc. ***n.*** (ôf′set′), 1. anything that offsets something else. 2. offset printing.

**offset printing,** a process in which the inked impression is first made on a rubber-covered roller, then transferred to paper.

**off′shoot′,** ***n.*** anything that derives from a main source; specif., a shoot growing from the main stem of a plant.

**off′shore′,** ***adj.*** 1. moving away from the shore. 2. at some distance from the shore. ***adv.*** away from the shore.

**off′side′,** ***adj.*** not in the proper position for play, as, in football, ahead of the ball before play has begun. ***n.*** an offside play.

**off′spring′,** ***n.*** [sometimes construed as pl.], a child or children; issue.

**OFr.,** Old French.

**oft** (ôft), ***adv.*** [AS.], [Poetic], often.

**of·ten** (ôf′′n), ***adv.*** [ME. < *oft(e)*], many times: also **of′ten·times′, oft′times′.**

**o·gle** (ō′g′l), ***v.i. & v.t.*** [OGLED, OGLING], [prob. < LG. *oog*, the eye], to keep looking (at) flirtatiously. ***n.*** an ogling look. —**o′gler,** ***n.***

**o·gre** (ō′gēr), ***n.*** [Fr.], 1. in fairy tales and folklore, a man-eating giant. 2. a hideous, cruel man. —**o′gre·ish, o′grish** (ō′grish), ***adj.***

**oh** (ō), ***interj. & n.*** [*pl.* OH'S, OHS], an exclamation of surprise, fear, wonder, pain, etc.

**OHG, O.H.G.,** Old High German.

**ohm** (ōm), ***n.*** [< G.S. *Ohm*, 19th-c. G. physicist], the unit of electrical resistance.

**-oid,** [< Gr. *eidos*, form], a suffix meaning *like, resembling*, as in *colloid*.

**oil** (oil), ***n.*** [< L. *oleum*], 1. any of various greasy, combustible, normally liquid substances obtained from animal, vegetable, and mineral matter: oils are insoluble in water. 2. petroleum. 3. an oil color. 4. an oil painting. ***v.t.*** 1. to lubricate or supply with oil. 2. to bribe. ***adj.*** of, from, or like oil. —**oil′er,** ***n.***

**oil′cloth′,** ***n.*** cloth made waterproof by being treated with oil or paint.

**oil color,** paint made by grinding a pigment in oil.

**oil painting,** 1. a picture painted in oil colors. 2. the art of painting in oil colors.

**oil′skin′,** ***n.*** 1. cloth made waterproof by treatment with oil. 2. *often in pl.* a garment made of this.

**oil well,** a well bored through layers of rock, etc. to a supply of petroleum.

**oil′y,** ***adj.*** [-IER, -IEST], 1. of, like, or containing oil. 2. greasy. 3. too suave or smooth; unctuous. —**oil′i·ness,** ***n.***

**oint·ment** (oint′mənt), ***n.*** [< L. *unguentum*; see UNGUENT], a fatty substance used on the skin as a salve, etc.

**O.K., OK** (ō′kā′), ***adj., adv., interj.*** [prob. < Democratic *O.K.* Club (1840)], all right; correct. ***n.*** approval. ***v.t.*** (ō′kā′), [O.K.'d, OK'd, O.K.'ing, OK'ing], to put an O.K. on; approve. Also sp. **okay.**

**o·kra** (ō′krə), ***n.*** [< W. Afr. name], 1. a plant with sticky green pods, used in soups, etc. 2. the pod of this plant.

**old** (ōld), ***adj.*** [OLDER or ELDER, OLDEST or ELDEST], [AS. *ald*], 1. having lived or existed for a long time. 2. of aged people. 3. of a certain age: as, two years *old*. 4. not new. 5. worn out by age or use. 6. former. 7. experienced: as, an *old* hand. 8. ancient. 9. of long standing. 10. designating the earlier or earliest of two or more: as, the *Old* Testament. ***n.*** time long past: as, days of *old*. —**the old,** old people. —**old′ish,** ***adj.***

**old·en** (ōl′d′n), ***adj.*** [Poetic], (of) old.

**Old English,** the Germanic language of the Anglo-Saxons, spoken in England from the 5th to the 12th centuries.

**old′-fash′ioned,** ***adj.*** in accordance with or favoring the ways, ideas, etc. of past times.

**Old French,** the French language as spoken from the 9th to the 16th centuries.

**Old Glory,** the flag of the U.S.

**old hat,** [Slang], old-fashioned; outmoded.

**Old High German,** the German language as spoken in S Germany from the 9th to the 12th centuries.

**Old Low German,** the language of N Germany and the Netherlands from the 8th to the 12th centuries.

**old maid,** 1. a woman who is unmarried and seems likely to remain so. 2. a prim, prudish, fussy person. —**old′maid′ish,** ***adj.***

**old master,** 1. any of the great painters before the 18th century. 2. a painting by any of these.

**Old Norse,** the language spoken in Norway, Denmark, and Iceland from the 8th to the 14th centuries.

**Old Saxon,** a low Germanic dialect common in part of N Germany in the 9th and 10th centuries.

**Old Testament,** the Bible of Judaism or the first of the two divisions of the Bible of Christianity.

**old′-tim′er,** ***n.*** [Colloq.], one who has been a resident, employee, member, etc. for a long time.

**old′-world′,** ***adj.*** 1. of or belonging to the ancient world or former times. 2. of the Old World: also **Old-World.**

**o·le·ag·i·nous** (ō′li-aj′i-nəs), ***adj.*** [< L. *olea*, the olive], oily; unctuous.

**o·le·an·der** (ō′li-an′dēr), ***n.*** [ML.], a poisonous evergreen shrub with fragrant white or red flowers.

**o·le·o·mar·ga·rine** (ō′li-ō-mär′jə-rin, -rēn′), ***n.*** [< L. *oleum*, an oil; + *margarine*], margarine: also **o′le·o′.**

**ol·fac′to·ry** (-tēr-i), ***adj.*** [< L. *olere*, have a smell + *facere*, make], of the sense of smell.

**ol·i·garch** (ol′i-gärk′), ***n.*** any of the rulers of an oligarchy.

**ol·i·garch·y** (ol′i-gär′ki), ***n.*** [*pl.* -IES], [< Gr. *oligos*, few + *archos*, ruler], 1. (a) government in which a few persons have the ruling power. 2. the ruling persons.

**ol·ive** (ol′iv), ***n.*** [< L. *oliva*], 1. an evergreen tree of S Europe and the Near East. 2. its small oval fruit, eaten green or ripe, or pressed to extract its oil. 3. the yellowish-green color of the unripe fruit. ***adj.*** 1. of the olive. 2. dull yellowish-green.

**olive branch,** the branch of the olive tree, a symbol of peace.

**olive oil,** a light-yellow oil pressed from ripe olives, used in cooking, etc.

**O·lym·pi·an** (ō-lim′pi-ən), ***n.*** 1. in *Gr. myth.*, any of the gods on Mount Olympus. 2. a participant in the Olympic games. ***adj.*** 1. godlike; majestic. 2. of the ancient Olympic games.

**O·lym′pic games** (-pik), 1. an ancient Greek festival with contests in athletics, music, etc., held every four years at Olympia, a plain in Greece. 2. an international athletic competition of modern times: also **the O·lym′pics** (-piks).

**om·buds·man** (om′bədz-mən), ***n.*** [*pl.* -MEN], [Swed.], an appointed public official who investigates activities of government agencies that may infringe on the rights of individuals.

**o·me·ga** (ō-meg′ə, -mē′gə, -mā′-), ***n.*** the twenty-fourth and final letter of the Greek alphabet (Ω, ω).

**om·e·let, om·e·lette** (om′lit, om′ə-let), ***n.*** [< L. *lamella*, small plate], eggs beaten up, often with water or milk, and cooked as a pancake in a pan.

**o·men** (ō′mən), ***n.*** [L.], a thing or happening supposed to foretell a future event; portent. ***v.t.*** to be an omen of.

**om·i·cron, om·i·kron** (om′i-kron′, ō′mi-),

*n.* the fifteenth letter of the Greek alphabet (O, ο).

**om·i·nous** (om'ə-nəs), *adj.* of or serving as an evil omen; threatening.

**o·mis·sion** (ō-mish'ən), *n.* 1. an omitting or being omitted. 2. anything omitted.

**o·mit** (ō-mit'), *v.t.* [OMITTED, OMITTING], [< L. *ob-* (see OB-) + *mittere*, send], 1. to leave out; fail to include. 2. to neglect; fail to do.

**omni-**, [L. < *omnis*, all], a combining form meaning *all, everywhere*.

**om·ni·bus** (om'ni-bus'), *n.* [*pl.* -BUSES], [L., for all], a bus. *adj.* providing for many things at once.

**om·nip·o·tent** (om-nip'ə-tənt), *adj.* [< L. *omnis*, all + *potens*, able], having unlimited power or authority; all-powerful. **—the Omnipotent**, God. **—om·nip'o·tence**, *n.*

**om·ni·pres·ent** (om'ni-prez''nt), *adj.* present in all places at the same time. **—om'ni·pres'ence**, *n.*

**om·nis·cient** (om-nish'ənt), *adj.* [< *omni-* + L. ppr. of *scire*, know], knowing all things. **—om·nis'cience**, *n.*

**om·niv·o·rous** (om-niv'ēr-əs), *adj.* [< L. *omnis*, all + *vorare*, devour], 1. eating any sort of food, esp. both animal and vegetable food. 2. taking in everything indiscriminately: as, an *omnivorous* reader.

**on** (on), *prep.* [AS.], 1. in contact with, supported by, or covering. 2. near to: as, *on* my left. 3. at the time of: as, *on* Monday. 4. connected with; engaged in: as, *on* the team, *on* a trip. 5. in a state of: as, *on* parole. 6. as a result of: as, a profit *on* the sale. 7. toward: as, light shone *on* us. 8. through the use of: as, to live *on* bread. 9. about: as, an essay *on* war. 10. [Colloq.], at the expense of, as a treat. *adv.* 1. in a situation of contacting, being supported by, or covering. 2. in a direction toward something: as, he looked *on*. 3. forward: as, move *on*. 4. continuously: as, she sang *on*. 5. into action or operation: as, turn *on* the light. *adj.* in action or operation: as, the play is *on*. **—and so on**, and more like the preceding. **—on and off**, intermittently.

**ON., O.N.**, Old Norse.

**once** (wuns), *adv.* [< AS. *an*, one], 1. one time only: as, he eats *once* a day. 2. at any time; ever. 3. formerly: as, a *once* famous man. *n.* one time: as, I'll go this *once*. **—at once**, 1. immediately. 2. at the same time. **—once (and) for all**, conclusively.

**on·com·ing** (on'kum'iŋ), *adj.* coming nearer in position or time. *n.* an approach.

**one** (wun), *adj.* [AS. *an*], 1. being a single thing. 2. united: as, with *one* accord. 3. designating a particular person or thing: as, from *one* day to another. 4. some or any: as, *one* day we'll win. 5. the same. *n.* 1. the first and lowest cardinal number; 1; I. 2. a single person or thing. *pron.* 1. a certain person or thing. 2. any person or thing. **—at one**, in accord. **—one by one**, one following the other.

**one'ness** (-nis), *n.* 1. singleness; unity. 2. unity of mind, feeling, etc. 3. sameness.

**on·er·ous** (on'ēr-əs), *adj.* [< L. *onus*, a load], burdensome; oppressive.**—on'er·ous·ly**, *adv.*

**one·self** (wun'self'), *pron.* a person's own self: also, **one's self**. **—be oneself**, 1. to function normally. 2. to be natural. **—by oneself**, alone; withdrawn.

**one'-sid'ed** (-sīd'id), *adj.* 1. on, having, or involving only one side. 2. unequal: as, a *one-sided* race. 3. favoring one side; partial.

**one'-track'**, *adj.* 1. having a single track. 2. [Colloq.], limited in scope: as, a *one-track* mind.

**one'-way'**, *adj.* moving, or allowing movement, in one direction only.

**on·ion** (un'yən), *n.* [< L. *unus*, one], 1. a plant of the lily family with an edible bulb. 2. this bulb, having a sharp smell and taste.

**on'ion·skin'**, *n.* a tough, thin, translucent paper of glossy surface.

**on'look'er**, *n.* a spectator.

**on·ly** (ōn'li), *adj.* [< AS. *an*, one + *-lic*, -ly], 1. alone of its or their kind; sole. 2. alone in superiority; best. *adv.* 1. and no other; solely. 2. merely. *conj.* [Colloq.], except that; but. **—only too**, very.

**on·o·mat·o·poe·ia** (on'ə-mat'ə-pē'ə), *n.* [< Gr. *onoma*, a name + *poiein*, make], the formation of words by imitating sounds (e.g., *buzz*). **—on'o·mat'o·poe'ic**, *adj.*

**on'rush'**, *n.* a headlong rush forward.

**on'set'**, *n.* 1. an attack. 2. a start.

**on'shore'**, *adj.* 1. moving onto or toward the shore. 2. situated or operating on land.

**on·slaught** (on'slôt'), *n.* [prob. < D. *slagen*, to strike], a violent attack.

**on·to** (on'tōō), *prep.* 1. to a position on. 2. [Slang], aware of. Also **on to**.

**o·nus** (ō'nəs), *n.* [L.], a burden; responsibility.

**on·ward** (on'wẽrd), *adv.* toward or at a position ahead: also **onwards**. *adj.* advancing.

**on·yx** (on'iks), *n.* [< Gr. *onyx*, fingernail], a type of agate with alternate layers of color.

**oo·dles** (ōō'd'lz), *n.pl.* [< ?], [Slang], a great amount.

**ooze** (ōōz), *n.* [AS. *wos*, sap], an oozing or something that oozes. *v.i.* [OOZED, OOZING], to flow or leak out slowly.

**ooze** (ōōz), *n.* [AS. *wase*], soft mud or slime, as at the bottom of a lake. **—oo·zy** (ōō'zi), [-ZIER, -ZIEST], *adj.* **—oo'zi·ly**, *adv.*

**op-**, ob-: used before *p*.

**o·pac·i·ty** (ō-pas'ə-ti), *n* 1. an opaque state or quality. 2. [*pl.* -TIES], an opaque thing.

**o·pal** (ō'p'l), *n.* [< Sans. *upala*, gem], a translucent silica of various colors that reflects light in a play of colors: some types are semiprecious.

**o·pal·esce** (ō'pə-les'), *v.i.* [-ESCED, -ESCING], to show a play of colors like an opal. **—o'pal·es'cence**, *n.* **—o'pal·es'cent**, *adj.*

**o·paque** (ō-pāk'), *adj.* [L. *opacus*, shady], 1. not transparent. 2. not reflecting light; dull; dark. **—o·paque'ly**, *adv.*

**op (art)** (op), a style of abstract painting using geometrical patterns to create various optical effects.

**op. cit.**, *opere citato*, [L.], in the work cited.

**o·pen** (ō'p'n), *adj.* [AS.], 1. not closed, covered, clogged, or shut: as, *open* doors. 2. not enclosed: as, *open* fields. 3. unfolded; spread out: as, an *open* book. 4. free to be entered, used, etc.: as, an *open* meeting. 5. not decided: as, an *open* question. 6. not closed to new ideas, etc.: as, an *open* mind. 7. generous. 8. free from restrictions: as, *open* season. 9. not already taken, etc.: as, the job is *open*. 10. not secret; public. 11. frank; candid: as, an *open* manner. *v.t. & v.i.* 1. to cause to be, or to become, open (senses 1, 2). 2. to spread out; expand; unfold. 3. to make or become available for use, etc. without restriction. 4. to begin; start. 5. to start operating: as, to *open* a store. **—open to**, 1. willing to receive, discuss, etc. 2. available to. **—o'pened**, *adj.* **—o'pen·er**, *n.*—**o'pen·ly**, *adv.*—**o'pen·ness**, *n.*

**o'pen-and-shut'**, *adj.* easily decided; obvious: as, an *open-and-shut* case.

**open door**, free and equal opportunity for all nations to trade with a given nation.

**o'pen·hand'ed**, *adj.* generous.

**o'pen·heart'ed**, *adj.* 1. not reserved; frank. 2. kindly; generous.

**o'pen-hearth'**, *adj.* designating or using a furnace with a wide hearth and low roof, for making steel.

**open house**, 1. a house extending welcome to all. 2. a time when an institution is open to visitors.

**o'pen·ing,** *n.* 1. a making or becoming open. 2. an open place; gap; hole. 3. a clearing. 4. a beginning. 5. start of operations. 6. a favorable chance. 7. an unfilled job.

**open letter,** a letter written to a specific person but published for all to read.

**o'pen-mind'ed,** *adj.* having a mind open to new ideas; unprejudiced.

**open season,** a period during which it is legal to hunt specified game.

**open shop,** a factory, business, etc. open to nonunion workers.

**o'pen·work',** *n.* ornamental work, as in cloth, with openings in it.

**op·er·a** (op'ẽr-ə), *n.* [< L. *opera*, a work], a play having its text set to music and sung to orchestral accompaniment.

**op·er·a** (op'ẽr-ə), *n.* pl. of **opus.**

**op·er·a·ble** (op'ẽr-ə-b'l), *adj.* [< L. *operari*, to work], 1. that can be treated by a surgical operation. 2. practicable.

**opera glasses,** a small binocular telescope used in theaters, etc.

**op·er·ate** (op'ə-rāt'), *v.i.* [-ATED, -ATING], [< L. *operari*, to work], 1. to be in action; act; work. 2. to bring about a certain effect. 3. to perform a surgical operation. *v.t.* to put or keep in action; manage.

**op·er·at·ic** (op'ə-rat'ik), *adj.* of or like the opera. **—op'er·at'i·cal·ly,** *adv.*

**op·er·a·tion** (op'ə-rā'shən), *n.* 1. the act or method of operating. 2. a being in action or at work. 3. any of a series of procedures in some work or plan, as in industry, military maneuvers, etc. 4. any surgical procedure to remedy a physical ailment. **—op'er·a'tion·al,** *adj.*

**op·er·a·tive** (op'ə-rā'tiv, -ẽr-ə-tiv), *adj.* 1. in operation; active. 2. efficient; effective. 3. connected with physical work or mechanical action. *n.* 1. a worker; esp., a skilled industrial worker. 2. a detective.

**op'er·a'tor** (-tẽr), *n.* one who operates; specif., *a*) a person who works a machine: as: a telephone *operator*. *b*) one engaged in business or industrial operations or enterprises.

**op·er·et·ta** (op'ə-ret'ə), *n.* [It. < *opera*], a short, amusing musical play.

**oph·thal·mic** (of-thal'mik), *adj.* [< Gr. *ophthalmos*, the eye], of or connected with the eyes.

**oph·thal·mol·o·gy** (of'thal-mol'ə-ji), *n.* the branch of medicine dealing with the structure, functions, and diseases of the eye. **—oph'thal·mol'o·gist,** *n.*

**o·pi·ate** (ō'pi-it, -āt'), *n.* 1. any medicine containing opium or any of its derivatives. 2. anything quieting.

**o·pine** (ō-pīne'), *v.t. & v.i.* [OPINED, OPINING], [< L. *opinari*, think], to think; suppose: usually humorous. **—o·pin'er,** *n.*

**o·pin·ion** (ə-pin'yən), *n.* [< L. *opinari*, think], 1. a belief based not on certainty but on what seems true or probable. 2. an estimation. 3. formal expert judgment.

**o·pin'ion·at'ed** (-ā'tid), *adj.* holding obstinately to one's opinions.

**o·pi·um** (ō'pi-əm), *n.* [< Gr. *opos*, vegetable juice], a narcotic drug prepared from the seed of a certain poppy.

**o·pos·sum** (ə-pos'əm), *n.* [N. Am. Ind.], a small, tree-dwelling mammal that carries its young in a pouch.

**op·po·nent** (ə-pō'nənt), *n.* [< L. *ob-* (see OB-) + *ponere*, to set], one who opposes, as in a fight, game, etc.; adversary.

**op·por·tune** (op'ẽr-tōōn', -tūn'), *adj.* [< L. *opportunus*, lit., before the port], 1. right for the purpose: said of time. 2. well-timed; timely. **—op'por·tune'ly,** *adv.*

**op'por·tun'ism,** *n.* the adapting of one's actions, thoughts, etc. to circumstances, as in politics, without regard for principles. **—op'por·tun'ist,** *n.*

**op·por·tu·ni·ty** (op'ẽr-tōō'nə-ti, -tū'-), *n.* [*pl.* -TIES], a combination of circumstances favorable for the purpose; good chance.

**op·pos·a·ble** (ə-pōz'ə-b'l), *adj.* 1. that can be opposed. 2. that can be placed opposite something else.

**op·pose** (ə-pōz'), *v.t.* [-POSED, -POSING], [< Fr. *poser*; see POSE, *v.*], 1. to place opposite, in balance or contrast. 2. to resist; contend with. **—op·posed',** *adj.*

**op·po·site** (op'ə-zit), *adj.* [see OPPONENT], 1. opposed to. 2. set against; in a contrary direction (*to*). 3. entirely different; exactly contrary. *n.* anything opposed. *prep.* across from. **—op'po·site·ly,** *adv.*

**op'po·si'tion** (-zish'ən), *n.* 1. an opposing or being opposed. 2. resistance; hostility. 3. anything that opposes. 4. [sometimes O-], a political party opposing the party in power.

**op·press** (ə-pres'), *v.t.* [< L. *ob-* (see OB-) + *primere*, to press], 1. to weigh heavily on the mind, spirits, etc. of; burden. 2. to keep down by the cruel or unjust use of authority. **—op·pres'sor,** *n.*

**op·pres·sion** (ə-presh'ən), *n.* 1. an oppressing or being oppressed. 2. a thing that oppresses. 3. physical or mental distress.

**op·pres·sive** (ə-pres'iv), *adj.* 1. burdensome. 2. tyrannical. 3. causing physical or mental distress. **—op·pres'sive·ly,** *adv.*

**op·pro·bri·ous** (ə-prō'bri-əs), *adj.* 1. expressing opprobrium; abusive. 2. deserving opprobrium; infamous.

**op·pro'bri·um** (-əm), *n.* [< L. *opprobare*, to reproach], 1. disgrace; scorn. 2. anything bringing shame.

**opt** (opt), *v.i.* [< Fr. < L. *optare*], to make a choice.

**op·tic** (op'tik), *adj.* [< Gr. *optikos*], of the eye or sense of sight. *n.* [Colloq.], the eye.

**op·ti·cal** (op'ti-k'l), *adj.* 1. of the sense of sight; visual. 2. of optics. 3. made to give help in seeing. **—op'ti·cal·ly,** *adv.*

**op·ti·cian** (op-tish'ən), *n.* one who makes or sells eyeglasses, etc.

**op·tics** (op'tiks), *n.pl.* [construed as sing.], the branch of physics dealing with light and vision.

**op·ti·mism** (op'tə-miz'm), *n.* [< L. *optimus*, best], 1. the belief that good ultimately prevails over evil. 2. the tendency to take the most hopeful or cheerful view of things. **—op'ti·mist,** *n.* **—op'ti·mis'tic,** *adj.*

**op·ti·mum** (op'tə-məm), *n.* [*pl.* -MUMS, -MA (-mə)], [see OPTIMISM], the best or most favorable degree, condition, etc. *adj.* best; most favorable: also **op'ti·mal.**

**op·tion** (op'shən), *n.* [< L. *optare*, to wish], 1. a choosing; choice. 2. the right of choosing. 3. something that is or can be chosen. 4. the right to buy or sell something at a set price within a set time. **—op'tion·al,** *adj.*

**op·tom·e·try** (op-tom'ə-tri), *n.* [< Gr. *optikos*, optic + *metron*, measure], the science or profession of testing the vision and fitting glasses to correct eye defects. **—op·tom'e·trist,** *n.*

**op·u·lent** (op'yoo-lənt), *adj.* [< L. *ops*, wealth], 1. wealthy; rich. 2. abundant. **—op'u·lence,** *n.* **—op'u·lent·ly,** *adv.*

**o·pus** (ō'pəs), *n.* [*pl.* OPERA (op'ẽr-ə); *now also* OPUSES], [L., a work], a work; composition; esp., any of the chronologically numbered musical works of a composer.

**or** (ôr, ẽr), *conj.* [< AS. *oththe*], a coordinating conjunction introducing: *a*) an alternative (red *or* blue) or the last in a series of choices. *b*) a synonymous word or phrase (oral, *or* spoken).

**-or,** [< L. *-or*], a suffix meaning: 1. *a person* or *thing that*, as in *inventor*. 2. *quality* or *condition*, as in *horror*, *favor*.

**or·a·cle** (ôr'ə-k'l, or'-), *n.* [< L. *orare*, pray],

1. in ancient Greece and Rome, the place where, or medium by which, deities were consulted. 2. the revelation of a medium or priest. 3. *a*) any person of great knowledge. *b*) statements of such a person. —**o·rac·u·lar** (ô-rak'yoo-lẽr), *adj.*

**o·ral** (ôr'əl), *adj.* [< L. *os*, mouth], 1. uttered; spoken. 2. of or near the mouth.

**or·ange** (ôr'ənj, or'-), *n.* [ult. < Ar. *naranj* & Per. *narang*], 1. a reddish-yellow, round citrus fruit with a sweet juicy pulp. 2. the evergreen tree it grows on. 3. reddish yellow. *adj.* 1. of oranges. 2. reddish-yellow.

**or'ange·ade'** (-ād'), *n.* a drink made of orange juice, water, and sugar.

**o·rang·u·tan** (ō-raŋ'oo-tan'), *n.* [< Malay *oran*, man + *utan*, forest], a large ape with reddish hair, found only in the jungles of Borneo and Sumatra: also **o·rang'**.

**o·rate** (ôr'āt, ô-rāt'), *v.i.* & *v.t.* [ORATED, ORATING], to make (an oration); say pompously: a humorously derogatory term.

**o·ra·tion** (ô-rā'shən), *n.* [< L. *orare*, speak], a formal speech, esp. one given at a ceremony.

**or·a·tor** (ôr'ə-tẽr, or'-), *n.* 1. one who delivers an oration. 2. an eloquent public speaker.

**or·a·to·ri·o** (ôr'ə-tôr'i-ō', or'-), *n.* [*pl.* -OS], [It., small chapel], a long, dramatic musical work, usually on a religious theme, presented without stage action.

**or·a·to·ry** (ôr'ə-tôr'i, or'-), *n.* [*pl.* -RIES], [L. *oratoria*], 1. skill in public speaking. 2. [< L. *orare*, pray], a small chapel, as for private prayer. —**or'a·tor'i·cal**, *adj.*

**orb** (ôrb), *n.* [< L. *orbis*, a circle], 1. a globe; sphere. 2. any heavenly sphere, as the sun.

**or·bit** (ôr'bit), *n.* [< L. *orbis*, a circle], 1. the eye socket. 2. the path of a heavenly body or artificial satellite in its revolution around another body. —**or'bit·al**, *adj.*

**or·chard** (ôr'chẽrd), *n.* [< AS. *ort*, a garden + *geard*, enclosure], 1. an area of land where fruit trees, etc. are grown. 2. such trees.

**or·ches·tra** (ôr'kis-trə), *n.* [< Gr. *orchēstra*, space for the chorus], 1. the space in front of the stage of a theater, where the musicians sit: also *orchestra pit*. 2. the main floor of a theater. 3. *a*) a group of musicians playing together. *b*) their instruments. —**or·ches'tral** (-kes'trəl), *adj.*

**or'ches·trate'** (-trāt'), *v.t.* & *v.i.* [-TRATED, -TRATING], to compose or arrange (music) for an orchestra. —**or'ches·tra'tion**, *n.*

**or·chid** (ôr'kid), *n.* [< Gr. *orchis*, testicle: from the shape of the roots], 1. a plant having flowers with three petals, one of which is enlarged. 2. this flower. 3. a light bluish red. *adj.* light bluish-red.

**or·dain** (ôr-dān'), *v.t.* [< L. *ordo*, an order], 1. to appoint; decree; establish; enact. 2. to appoint or admit to the position of minister, priest, etc. —**or·dain'er**, *n.*

**or·deal** (ôr-dēl', ôr'dēl), *n.* [< AS. *or-*, out + *dæl*, what is dealt], any trying or painful experience.

**or·der** (ôr'dẽr), *n.* [< L. *ordo*, straight row], 1. social position. 2. a state of peace; orderly conduct. 3. arrangement of things or events; series. 4. a definite plan; system. 5. a military, monastic, or fraternal brotherhood. 6. a condition in which everything is in its place and functioning properly. 7. condition in general: as, in poor *order*. 8. an authoritative command, instruction, etc. 9. a class; kind. 10. an established method, as of conduct in meetings, etc. 11. *a*) a request to supply something: as, my *order* for books. *b*) the goods supplied. 12. written instructions to pay money or surrender property. 13. *pl.* the position of ordained minister: as, he took holy *orders*. *v.t.* & *v.i.* 1. to put or keep (things) in order; arrange. 2. to command. 3. to request (something to be supplied). —**in** (or **out of**) **order**, 1. in (or out of) proper position. 2. in (or not in) working condition. —**in order that**, so that. —**in order to**, for the purpose of. —**on the order of**, similar to.

**or'der·ly**, *adj.* 1. neat; tidy. 2. well-behaved; law-abiding. *n.* [*pl.* -LIES], 1. a soldier who acts as the personal servant, messenger, etc. of an officer. 2. a male hospital attendant. —**or'der·li·ness**, *n.*

**or·di·nal** (ôr'd'n-əl), *adj.* [< L. *ordo*, order], expressing order in a series: the ordinal numbers are *first*, *second*, *third*, etc. *n.* 1. an ordinal number. 2. [often O-], a book of prescribed forms used in church services.

**or·di·nance** (ôr'di-nəns), *n.* [< L. *ordo*, an order], a statute, esp. one enacted by a city government.

**or·di·nar·i·ly** (ôr'd'n-er'ə-li), *adv.* usually; generally.

**or·di·nar·y** (ôr'd'n-er'i), *adj.* [< L. *ordo*, an order], 1. customary; usual. 2. familiar; unexceptional; common. *n.* [*pl.* -IES], a book containing the form for divine service. —**out of the ordinary**, unusual.

**or·di·na·tion** (ôr'də-nā'shən), *n.* an ordaining or being ordained.

**ord·nance** (ôrd'nəns), *n.* [< *ordinance*], 1. artillery. 2. all weapons and ammunition used in warfare.

**or·dure** (ôr'jẽr, -dyoor), *n.* [< OFr. *ord*, filthy], dung; excrement.

**ore** (ôr), *n.* [AS. *ar*, brass], a natural combination of minerals, esp. one from which a metal or metals can be profitably extracted.

**or·gan** (ôr'gən), *n.* [< Gr. *organon*, instrument], 1. a keyboard musical instrument with sets of graduated pipes through which compressed air is passed, causing sound by vibration. 2. in animals and plants, a part adapted to perform a specific function. 3. a means for performing some action. 4. a means of communicating ideas or opinions, as a periodical.

**or·gan·dy, or·gan·die** (ôr'gən-di), *n.* [*pl.* -DIES], [Fr. *organdi*], a very sheer, stiff cotton fabric.

**or·gan·ic** (ôr-gan'ik), *adj.* 1. of or having to do with a body organ; structural. 2. systematically arranged. 3. designating or of any chemical compound containing carbon. 4. of, like, or derived from living organisms. —**or·gan'i·cal·ly**, *adv.*

**or·gan·ism** (or'gən-iz'm), *n.* any living thing.

**or·gan·i·za·tion** (ôr'gən-i-zā'shən), *n.* 1. an organizing or being organized. 2. a group organized for some purpose, as a club, union, etc. —**or'gan·i·za'tion·al**, *adj.*

**or·gan·ize** (ôr'gən-īz'), *v.t.* [-IZED, -IZING], 1. to provide with an organic structure; systematize. 2. to arrange; establish. *v.i.* to become organized. —**or'gan·i'zer**, *n.*

**or·gasm** (ôr'gaz'm), *n.* [< Gr. *organ*, to swell], the climax of a sexual act.

**or·gy** (ôr'ji), *n.* [*pl.* -GIES], [< Gr. *orgia*, secret rites], 1. a wild merrymaking. 2. an overindulgence in any activity: as, an *orgy* of work. —**or'gi·as'tic** (-as'tik), *adj.*

**o·ri·ent** (ôr'i-ənt), *n.* [< L. *oriri*, arise: with reference to the rising sun], 1. [Poetic], the east. 2. [O-], *a*) the East; Asia. *b*) the Far East. Cf. *Occident*. *v.t.* & *v.i.* (-ent'), to adjust (oneself) to a particular situation.

**O'ri·en'tal** (-en't'l), *adj.* 1. of the Orient, its people, etc. 2. [o-], eastern. *n.* a member of a people native to the Orient.

**o'ri·en·ta'tion** (-tā'shən), *n.* 1. an orienting or being oriented. 2. adaptation to a situation or environment.

**or·i·fice** (ôr'ə-fis, or'-), *n.* [< L. *os*, mouth + *facere*, make], an opening; mouth or outlet.

**orig.,** 1. origin. 2. original. 3. originally.

**or·i·gin** (ôr′ə-jin, or′-), *n.* [< L. *oriri*, to rise], 1. a coming into existence or use; beginning. 2. parentage; birth. 3. source; root.

**o·rig·i·nal** (ə-rij′ə-n'l), *adj.* 1. first; earliest. 2. never having been before; new; novel. 3. capable of creating something new; inventive. 4. being that from which copies are made. *n.* 1. a primary type that has given rise to varieties or copies. 2. an original work, as of art or literature. —**o·rig′i·nal′i·ty** (-nal′ə-ti), *n.*

**o·rig·i·nate** (ə-rij′ə-nāt′), *v.t.* [-NATED, NATING], to bring into being; esp., to create; invent. *v.i.* to come into being; begin; start. —**o·rig′i·na′tion,** *n.* —**o·rig′i·na′tor,** *n.*

**o·ri·ole** (ôr′i-ōl′), *n.* [ult. < L. *aurum*, gold], any of a group of American birds, with bright-orange and black plumage, that build hanging nests.

**O·ri·on** (ō-rī′ən), *n.* an equatorial constellation supposedly outlining a hunter.

**or·i·son** (ôr′i-z'n, or′-), *n.* [< L. *orare*, pray], *usually in pl.* a prayer.

**or·lon** (ôr′lon), *n.* a synthetic fiber somewhat similar to nylon: a trademark **(Orlon).**

**or·mo·lu** (ôr′mə-lōō′), *n.* [Fr. *or moulu*, ground gold], an imitation gold consisting of an alloy of copper and tin.

**or·na·ment** (ôr′nə-mənt), *n.* [< L. *ornare*, adorn], 1. anything that adorns; decoration. 2. one whose character or talent adds luster to his society, etc. *v.t.* (-ment′), to decorate. —**or′na·men′tal,** *adj.* —**or′na·men′tal·ly,** *adv.* —**or′na·men·ta′tion,** *n.*

**or·nate** (ôr-nāt′), *adj.* [< L. *ornare*, adorn], heavily ornamented; showy.

**or·ner·y** (ôr′nẽr-i), *adj.* [-IER, -IEST], [< *ordinary*], [Chiefly Dial.], 1. having an ugly disposition. 2. obstinate.

**or·ni·thol·o·gy** (ôr′ni-thol′ə-ji), *n.* [< Gr. *ornis*, bird; + *-logy*], the branch of zoology dealing with birds. —**or′ni·thol′o·gist,** *n.*

**o·ro·tund** (ôr′ə-tund′), *adj.* [< L. *os*, mouth + *rotundus*, round], 1. full; resonant: said of the voice. 2. bombastic; showy.

**or·phan** (ôr′fən), *n.* [< Gr. *orphanos*], a child whose parents are dead. *adj.* 1. being an orphan. 2. of or for orphans. *v.t.* to cause to become an orphan.

**or′phan·age** (-ij), *n.* an institution for orphans.

**Or·phe·us** (ôr′fi-əs, -fūs), *n.* in *Gr. myth.*, a musician with magic ability on the lyre.

**or·ris** (ôr′is, or′-), *n.* [prob. < L. *iris*, iris], a plant of the iris family, having a fragrant rootstock, used in perfumery, etc.

**ortho-,** [< Gr. *orthos*, straight], a combining form meaning: 1. *straight*, as in *orthodontia*. 2. *proper, correct*, as in *orthography*.

**or·tho·don·ti·a** (ôr′thə-don′shə, -shi-ə), *n.* [< *orth(o)-* + Gr. *odōn*, tooth], the branch of dentistry concerned with correcting and preventing irregularities of the teeth. —**or′tho·don′tic,** *adj.* —**or′tho·don′tist,** *n.*

**or·tho·dox** (ôr′thə-doks′), *adj.* [< Gr. *orthos*, correct + *doxa*, opinion], conforming to the usual beliefs or established doctrines, esp. in religion; conventional. —**or′tho·dox′y,** *n.*

**Orthodox (Eastern) Church,** the dominant Christian church in E Europe, W Asia, and N Africa.

**or·thog·ra·phy** (ôr-thog′rə-fi), *n.* [*pl.* -PHIES], [see ORTHO- & -GRAPHY], 1. correct spelling. 2. spelling as a subject or science. —**or·tho·graph·ic** (ôr′thə-graf′ik), *adj.*

**or·tho·pe·dics** (ôr′thə-pē′diks), *n.pl.* [construed as sing.], [< *ortho-* + Gr. *paideia*, training of children], the branch of surgery concerned with deformities, diseases, and injuries of the bones and joints: also **or′tho·pe′dy.** —**or′tho·pe′dic,** *adj.* —**or′tho·pe′dist,** *n.*

**-ory,** [< L. *-orius*], a suffix meaning: 1. *of, having the nature of*, as in *commendatory*. 2. *a place* or *thing for*, as in *directory*.

**OS., O.S.,** Old Saxon.

**os·cil·late** (os′ə-lāt′), *v.i.* [-LATED, -LATING], [< L. *oscillare*, to swing], 1. to swing to and fro. 2. to fluctuate; vacillate. —**os′cil·la′tion,** *n.* —**os′cil·la′tor,** *n.*

**os·cu·late** (os′kyoo-lāt′), *v.t. & v.i.* [-LATED, -LATING], [< L. *osculum*, a kiss], to kiss.

**-ose,** [< L. *-osus*], a suffix meaning *full of, having the qualities of*, as in *bellicose, morose*.

**o·sier** (ō′zhẽr), *n.* [< ML. *ausaria*, bed of willows], a willow whose wood is used for baskets and furniture.

**O·si·ris** (ō-sī′ris), *n.* the ancient Egyptian god of the lower world.

**-osis,** [< Gr. *-osis*,], a suffix meaning: 1. *state, condition, action*, as in *osmosis*. 2 *an abnormal* or *diseased condition*, as in *neurosis*.

**-osity,** [< L. *-ositas*], a suffix used to form nouns corresponding to adjectives ending in *-ose* or *-ous*.

**OSlav.,** Old Slavic.

**os·mi·um** (oz′mi-əm), *n.* [< Gr. *osmē*, odor], a bluish metallic chemical element, occurring as an alloy with platinum: symbol, Os.

**os·mo·sis** (oz-mō′sis), *n.* [< Gr. *ōsmos*, impulse], the tendency of fluids to pass through a somewhat porous membrane so as to equalize concentrations on both sides.

**os·prey** (os′pri), *n.* [*pl.* -PREYS], [< L. *os*, a bone + *frangere*, to break], a large hawk that feeds solely on fish.

**os·se·ous** (os′i-əs), *adj.* [< L. *os*, bone], composed of, containing, or like bone; bony.

**os·si·fy** (os′ə-fī′), *v.t. & v.i.* [-FIED, -FYING], [< L. *os*, a bone; + *-fy*], to change or develop into bone. —**os′si·fi·ca′tion,** *n.*

**os·ten·si·ble** (os-ten′sə-b'l), *adj.* [< L. *ostendere*, to show], apparent; seeming; professed. —**os·ten′si·bly,** *adv.*

**os·ten·ta·tion** (os′ten-tā′shən), *n.* [see OSTENSIBLE], outright display; showiness. —**os′ten·ta′tious,** *adj.* —**os′ten·ta′tious·ly,** *adv.*

**osteo-,** [< Gr. *osteon*, bone], a combining form meaning *a bone* or *bones*, as in *osteopath*.

**os·te·op·a·thy** (os′ti-op′ə-thi), *n.* [< *osteo-* + *-pathy*], a system of treating ailments esp. by manipulation, on the theory that this will relieve the pressure of displaced bones on nerves, etc. —**os′te·o·path′** (-ə-path′), *n.*

**os·tra·cize** (os′trə-sīz′), *v.t.* [-CIZED, -CIZING], [< Gr. *ostrakon*, a shell (cast as a ballot)], to banish from society, etc. —**os′tra·cism,** *n.*

**os·trich** (ôs′trich, os′-), *n.* [< L. *avis*, bird + *struthio*, ostrich], a large, swift-running, nonflying bird of Africa and the Near East.

**O.T., OT, OT.,** Old Testament.

**O·thel·lo** (ə-thel′ō), *n.* a tragedy by Shakespeare in which the title character kills his wife because he wrongly believes her unfaithful.

**oth·er** (uth′ẽr), *adj.* [AS.], 1. being the remaining one or ones: as, use the *other* foot. 2. different or distinct from that or those implied: as, any *other* girl. 3. additional: as, he has no *other* coat. *pron.* 1. the other one. 2. some other person or thing: as, to do as *others* do. *adv.* otherwise: as, I can't do *other* than go. —**every other,** every alternate.

**oth′er·wise′** (-wīz′), *adv.* 1. in another manner; differently: as, I believe *otherwise*. 2. in all other respects: as, he is *otherwise* intelligent. 3. in other circumstances. *adj.* different.

**oth′er·world′ly** (-wũrld′li), *adj.* being apart from earthly interests.

**ot·ter** (ot′ẽr), *n.* [AS. *otor*], 1. a furry, swimming mammal related to the weasel and mink. 2. its fur.

**Ot·to·man** (ot′ə-mən), *n.* [ult. < Ar. *'Uthmāni*], 1. a Turk. 2. [o-], a low, cushioned seat or footstool. *adj.* Turkish.

**ouch** (ouch), *interj.* an exclamation of pain.

**ought** (ôt), *v.aux.* [< AS. *agan*, owe], an auxiliary used to express: 1. *obligation* or *duty*: as, he *ought* to pay rent. 2. *desirability*: as, you *ought* to rest. 3. *probability*: as, he *ought* to be here soon.

**ought** (ôt), *n.* a nought; cipher; zero.

‡**oui** (wē), *adv.* [Fr.], yes.

**ounce** (ouns), *n.* [< L. *uncia*, a twelfth], 1. a unit of weight, 1/16 pound avoirdupois or 1/12 pound troy. 2. a fluid ounce, 1/16 pint. 3. any small amount.

**ounce** (ouns), *n.* [ult. < Gr. *lynx*, lynx], the snow leopard of C Asia, having woolly, gray-white fur marked with black.

**our** (our), *pron.* [< AS. *ure*], possessive form of **we.** *poss. pronominal adj.* of, belonging to, or done by us.

**ours** (ourz), *pron.* that or those belonging to us: as, a friend of *ours*.

**our·self′** (-self′), *pron.* myself: used by a king, queen, etc., as in a formal speech.

**our·selves′** (-selvz′), *pron.* 1. the intensive form of **we**: as, we went *ourselves*. 2. the reflexive form of **we**: as, we hurt *ourselves*.

**-ous,** [< L. *-osus*], a suffix meaning *having*, *full of*, *characterized by*, as in *outrageous*.

**oust** (oust), *v.t.* [< OFr. *ouster*], to force out; expel; dispossess.

**ous′ter,** *n.* 1. one that ousts. 2. an ousting or being ousted; dispossession.

**out** (out), *adv.* [< AS. *ut*], 1. away or forth from a place, position, etc. 2. into the open air. 3. into existence or activity: as, disease broke *out*. 4. *a*) to a conclusion: as, argue it *out*. *b*) completely: as, tired *out*. 5. into sight or notice: as, the moon came *out*. 6. from existence or activity: as, fade *out*. 7. aloud: as, sing *out*. 8. beyond a regular surface, condition, etc.: as, stand *out*. 9. into disuse: as, long skirts went *out*. 10. from a number or stock: as, pick *out*. 11. [Slang], into unconsciousness. 12. in *baseball*, etc., in a manner producing an out: as, to fly *out*. *adj.* 1. external: usually in combination, as in *outpost*. 2. beyond regular limits. 3. away from work, etc. 4. in error: as, *out* in my estimates. 5. having suffered a loss: as, *out* five dollars. 6. not in operation, use, etc. 7. in *baseball*, having failed to get a hit. *prep.* out of: as, look *out* the window. *n.* 1. something that is out. 2. [Slang], a way out; excuse. 3. in *baesball*, retirement of a batter or runner from play. *v.i.* to go or come out. *interj.* get out! —**on the outs,** [Colloq.], on unfriendly terms. —**out for,** trying to get or do. —**out of,** 1. from inside of. 2. beyond. 3. from (material, etc.): as, made *out of* stone. 4. because of: as, *out of* spite. 5. no longer having: as, *out of* gas. 6. so as to deprive: as, cheat *out of* money. —**out to,** trying to.

**out-,** a combining form meaning: 1. *at* or *from a point away, outside*, as in *outpatient*. 2. *going away* or *forth, outward*, as in *outbound*. 3. *better* or *more than*, as in *outdo*.

**out′-and-out′,** *adj.* complete; thorough.

**out·bid′,** *v.t.* & *v.i.* [-BADE or -BID, -BIDDEN or -BID, -BIDDING], to bid more than (another).

**out′board′** (-bord′), *adj.* located on the outer surface of a watercraft: as, an *outboard* motor.

**out′bound′,** *adj.* outward bound.

**out′break′,** *n.* a breaking out; sudden occurrence, as of disease, anger, etc.

**out′build′ing,** *n.* a structure, as a barn, separate from the main building.

**out′burst′,** *n.* an outbreak; eruption.

**out′cast′,** *adj.* driven out; rejected. *n.* a person cast out or rejected.

**out·class′,** *v.t.* to surpass.

**out′come′,** *n.* result; consequence.

**out′crop′,** *n.* the emergence of a mineral so as to be exposed on the surface of the ground.

**out′cry′,** *n.* [*pl.* -CRIES], 1. a crying out. 2. a strong protest.

**out·dat′ed,** *adj.* out-of-date.

**out·dis′tance,** *v.t.* [-TANCED, -TANCING], to leave behind, as in a race.

**out·do′,** *v.t.* [-DID, -DONE, -DOING], to exceed; surpass. —**outdo oneself,** to do better than expected. —**out·do′er,** *n.*

**out′door′** (-dôr′), *adj.* 1. being outside of a building; open-air. 2. used or done outside.

**out′doors′** (-dôrz′), *adv.* in or into the open; outside. *n.* (out-dôrz′), the outdoor world.

**out′er,** *adj.* farther out; exterior.

**out′er·most′,** *adj.* & *adv.* farthest out.

**out′field′** (-fēld′), *n.* in *baseball*, 1. the playing area beyond the base lines. 2. the outfielders.

**out′field′er,** *n.* in *baseball*, a player whose position is in the outfield.

**out′fit,** *n.* 1. the equipment used in any craft or activity. 2. a group of people associated in some activity. *v.t.* [-FITTED, -FITTING], to equip. —**out′fit′ter,** *n.*

**out·flank′,** *v.t.* to go beyond, or cut off, the flank of (enemy troops).

**out′go′** (-gō′), *n.* [*pl.* -GOES], that which is paid out; expenditure. *v.t.* [-WENT, -GONE, -GOING], to go beyond; surpass.

**out′go′ing,** *adj.* 1. going out; leaving. 2. friendly; sociable.

**out·grow′,** *v.t.* [-GREW, -GROWN, -GROWING], 1. to exceed in growing. 2. to lose by becoming mature: as, he *outgrew* his credulity. 3. to grow too large for.

**out′growth′** (-grōth′), *n.* 1. a growing out. 2. consequence; result. 3. an offshoot.

**out·guess′** (-ges′), *v.t.* to outwit.

**out′house′,** *n.* an outdoor latrine.

**out′ing,** *n.* a pleasure trip or a holiday spent outdoors.

**out·land′ish** (-lan′dish), *adj.* 1. strange; alien. 2. fantastic; bizarre.

**out·last′,** *v.t.* to endure longer than.

**out′law′** (-lô′), *n.* 1. orig., a person deprived of legal rights and protection. 2. a notorious criminal. *v.t.* 1. orig., to declare to be an outlaw. 2. to declare illegal. —**out′law·ry** [*pl.* -RIES], *n.*

**out′lay′** (-lā′), *n.* 1. a spending (of money). 2. money spent.

**out′let′,** *n.* 1. a passage for letting something out. 2. a means of expression: as, an *outlet* for rage. 3. a market for goods.

**out′line′,** *n.* 1. a line bounding the limits of an object. 2. a sketch showing only the contours of an object. 3. an undetailed general plan, often in systematic form. *v.t.* [-LINED, -LINING], 1. to draw in outline. 2. to give or write an outline of.

**out·live′,** *v.t.* [-LIVED, -LIVING], to live longer than; survive.

**out′look′,** *n.* 1. the view from a place. 2. viewpoint. 3. prospect; probability.

**out′ly′ing** (-lī′iŋ), *adj.* relatively far out from a certain point; remote.

**out·mod′ed** (-mōd′id), *adj.* no longer in fashion or accepted; obsolete.

**out·num′ber** (-num′bẽr), *v.t.* to be more numerous than.

**out′-of-date′,** *adj.* not current; old-fashioned.

**out′-of-doors′,** *adj.* outdoor: also **out-of-door.** *n.* & *adv.* outdoors.

**out′-of-the-way′,** *adj.* 1. secluded. 2. unusual. 3. not conventional.

**out′pa′tient,** *n.* a patient, not an inmate, being treated at a hospital.

**out·play′,** *v.t.* to play better than.

**out′post′,** *n.* 1. *a*) a small group of troops stationed at a distance beyond the main force. *b*) the station so occupied. 2. a frontier settlement.

**out′put′,** *n.* the total quantity manufactured or produced, esp. in a given time.

**out·rage** (out′rāj′), *n.* [ult. < L. *ultra*, beyond], 1. an extremely violent or vicious act. 2. a deep insult or offense. 3. any serious breach of legal or moral codes. *v.t.* [-RAGED, -RAGING], 1. to commit an outrage upon. 2. to rape.

**out·ra′geous** (-rā′jəs), *adj.* 1. involving or doing great injury or wrong. 2. very offensive or shocking. **—out·ra′geous·ly,** *adv.*

**out·rank′,** *v.t.* to exceed in rank.

**out′rid′er,** *n.* an attendant on horseback who rides ahead of or beside a carriage.

**out′rig′ger,** *n.* 1. a timber rigged out from the side of a canoe to prevent tipping. 2. a canoe of this type.

**out′right′** (-rīt′), *adj.* 1. without reservation; downright. 2. complete; whole. *adv.* 1. entirely. 2. openly. 3. at once.

**out·run′,** *v.t.* [-RAN, -RUN, -RUNNING], 1. to run faster than. 2. to exceed.

**out·sell′,** *v.t.* [-SOLD, -SELLING], to sell more easily or in greater volume than.

**out′set′,** *n.* a setting out; beginning.

**out·shine′,** *v.t.* [-SHONE, -SHINING], 1. to shine brighter or longer than. 2. to surpass; excel. *v.i.* to shine forth.

**out′side′,** *n.* 1. the exterior; outer side. 2. the unenclosed part. 3. the most; absolute limit (with *the*). *adj.* 1. outer. 2. coming from or situated beyond the stated limits: as, *outside* help. 3. extreme. 4. slight: as, an *outside* chance. *adv.* 1. externally. 2. to or toward the exterior. 3. outdoors. *prep.* (*usually* out-sīd′), 1. on or to the outer side of. 2. outside the limits of. **—outside of,** 1. outside. 2. [Colloq.], other than.

**out·sid′er,** *n.* one not a member of a given group; alien.

**out′skirts′** (-skũrts′), *n.pl.* districts remote from the center, as of a city.

**out·smart′,** *v.t.* [Colloq.], to overcome by cunning or cleverness; outwit.

**out′spo′ken,** *adj.* 1. unrestrained in speech; frank. 2. spoken boldly or candidly.

**out·spread′** (*also for adj. and n.*, out′-spred′), *v.t. & v.i.* [-SPREAD, -SPREADING], to spread out; expand. *n.* a spreading out. *adj.* extended; expanded.

**out′stand′ing,** *adj.* 1. projecting. 2. distinguished; prominent. 3. unpaid.

**out·stretch′,** *v.t.* 1. to extend. 2. to stretch beyond. **—out·stretched′,** *adj.*

**out·strip′,** *v.t.* [-STRIPPED, -STRIPPING], 1. to go at a faster pace than. 2. to excel.

**out′ward** (-wẽrd), *adj.* 1. having to do with the outside; outer. 2. visible. 3. away from the interior. *adv.* 1. externally. 2. toward the outside. **—out′ward·ly,** *adv.*

**out·wear′,** *v.t.* [-WORE, -WORN, -WEARING], 1. to wear out. 2. to be more lasting than.

**out·weigh′,** *v.t.* 1. to weigh more than. 2. to be more important than.

**out·wit′,** *v.t.* [-WITTED, -WITTING], to get the better of by cunning or cleverness.

**o·va** (ō′və), *n.* pl. of **ovum.**

**o·val** (ō′v'l), *adj.* [< L. *ovum*, egg], 1. elliptical. 2. egg-shaped. *n.* anything oval in form.

**o·va·ry** (ō′vẽr-i), *n.* [*pl.* -RIES], [< L. *ovum*, egg], 1. the female reproductive gland, in which ova are formed. 2. in *botany*, the enlarged hollow part of the pistil, containing ovules. **—o·var′i·an** (ō-vâr′i-ən), *adj.*

**o·vate** (ō′vāt), *adj.* oval. **—o′vate·ly,** *adv.*

**o·va·tion** (ō-vā′shən), *n.* [< L. *ovare*, celebrate a triumph], an enthusiastic public welcome, burst of applause, etc.

**ov·en** (uv′ən), *n.* [AS. *ofen*], a receptacle or compartment for baking, drying, etc. by means of heat.

**o·ver** (ō′vẽr), *prep.* [AS. *ofer*], 1. in, at, or to a position above. 2. so as to cover; on or upon: as, put a board *over* the well. 3. upon, as an effect: as, he cast a spell *over* us. 4. above in authority, power, etc. 5. along the length of: as, go *over* this route. 6. to or on the other side of: as, fly *over* the lake. 7. through all parts of: as, *over* the whole state. 8. during: as, *over* the year. 9. more than: as, *over* ten cents. 10. in preference to. 11. concerning. *adv.* 1. *a*) above or across. *b*) across the brim. 2. more: as, three hours or *over*. 3. covering the whole area: as, it will heal *over*. 4. from start to finish: as, read it *over*. 5. *a*) from an upright position: as, to fall *over*. *b*) into an inverted position: as, to turn *over*. 6. again: as, do it *over*. 7. at or on the other side: as, *over* in Spain. 8. from one side, etc. to another: as, win him *over*. *adj.* 1. upper, outer, superior, or excessive. 2. finished; past. 3. having reached the other side. 4. [Colloq.], having a surplus.

**over-,** a combining form meaning: 1. *above in position, rank, etc.*, as in *overlord*. 2. *excessive*, as in *overrate*. 3. *passing across* or *beyond*, as in *overrun*. 4. *causing a change to a lower position*, as in *overwhelm*. The following list includes some common compounds formed with *over-*; they will be understood if *too much* or *excessively* is used with the meaning of the base word.

**overabundance**
**overactive**
**overambitious**
**overanxious**
**overbid**
**overburden**
**overbuy**
**overcapitalize**
**overcautious**
**overconfident**
**overcook**
**overcritical**
**overcrowd**
**overdevelop**
**overeager**
**overeat**
**overemphasize**
**overenthusiastic**
**overexercise**
**overexert**
**overexpose**
**overfond**
**overheat**
**overindulge**
**overload**
**overlong**
**overpay**
**overpopulate**
**overprecise**
**overproduce**
**overproduction**
**overrefined**
**overreligious**
**overripe**
**oversell**
**oversensitive**
**overspecialize**
**overstimulate**
**overstock**
**overstrict**
**oversubscribe**
**oversuspicious**
**overthrifty**
**overtire**
**overuse**
**overzealous**

**o′ver·act′,** *v.t. & v.i.* to act with exaggeration.

**o′ver·age′,** *adj.* over the age fixed as a standard.

**o′ver-all′, o′ver·all′,** *adj.* 1. from end to end. 2. total; including everything.

**o′ver·alls′** (-ôlz′), *n.pl.* loose trousers, often with an attached bib, worn over other clothes as a protection.

**o′ver·awe′,** *v.t.* [-AWED, -AWING], to overcome or subdue by inspiring awe.

**o′ver·bal′ance,** *v.t.* [-ANCED, -ANCING], 1. to weigh more than. 2. to throw off balance.

**o′ver·bear′ing,** *adj.* imposing one's own will; domineering.

**o′ver·board′** (-bôrd′), *adv.* over a ship's side; esp., from a ship into the water.

**o′ver·cast′** (-kast′, -käst′), *adj.* 1. cloudy; dark: said of the sky. 2. in *sewing*, sewn over an edge to prevent raveling.

**o′ver·charge′,** *v.t.* [-CHARGED, -CHARGING], 1. to charge too much for. 2. to overload. *n.* (ō′vẽr-chärj′), 1. an excessive charge. 2. too full a load.

**o′ver·cloud′,** *v.t. & v.i.* to make or become cloudy, gloomy, etc.

**o′ver·coat′,** *n.* a coat worn over the usual clothing, as a topcoat.

**o′ver·come′,** *v.t.* [-CAME, -COME, -COMING], 1. to get the better of in competition, etc. 2. to suppress, prevail over, overwhelm, etc.

**o′ver·do′**, *v.t.* [-DID, -DONE, -DOING], 1. to do too much. 2. to spoil by exaggerating. 3. to cook too long. *v.i.* to do too much.
**o′ver·dose′**, *n.* too large a dose.
**o′ver·draw′**, *v.t.* [-DREW, -DRAWN, -DRAWING], in *banking*, to draw on in excess of the amount credited to the drawer. —**o′ver·draft′**, *n.*
**o′ver·dress′**, *v.t.* & *v.i.* to dress extravagantly or in bad taste.
**o′ver·due′**, *adj.* beyond the time due for payment, arrival, etc.
**o′ver·es′ti·mate′** (-es′tə-māt′), *v.t.* to set too high an estimate on or for. *n.* (-mit), too high an estimate.
**o′ver·flow′**, *v.t.* 1. to flow across; flood. 2. to flow over the brim of. 3. to fill beyond capacity. *v.i.* 1. to run over. 2. to be superabundant. *n.* (o′vẽr-flō′), 1. an overflowing. 2. the amount that overflows. 3. a vent for overflowing liquids.
**o′ver·grow′**, *v.t.* [-GREW, -GROWN, -GROWING], to overspread so as to cover, as with foliage. *v.i.* to grow too fast or beyond normal size. —**o′ver-grown′**, *adj.* —**o′ver-growth′**, *n.*
**o′ver·hand′**, *adj.* done with the hand raised above the elbow. *adv.* in an overhand manner. —**o′ver·hand′ed**, *adj.*
**o′ver·hang′**, *v.t.* & *v.i.* [-HUNG, -HANGING], to hang over or project beyond (something). *n.* (ō′vẽr-haŋ′), the projection of one thing over another.
**o′ver·haul′** (-hôl′), *v.t.* 1. *a*) to check thoroughly for needed repairs, adjustments, etc. *b*) to make such repairs, etc., as on a motor. 2. to catch up with. *n.* (ō′vẽr-hôl′), an overhauling.
**o′ver·head′**, *adj.* 1. above the head. 2. in the sky. 3. on a higher level, with reference to related objects. *n.* the general, continuing costs of a business, as of rent, etc. *adv.* (ō′vẽr-hed′), aloft; above the head.
**o′ver·hear′**, *v.t.* [-HEARD, -HEARING], to hear (something spoken or a speaker) without the speaker's knowledge or intention.
**o′ver·joy′**, *v.t.* to give great joy to; delight.
**o′ver·kill′**, *n.* the capacity of a nuclear stockpile to kill more than the total population of any given nation.
**o′ver·land′**, *adv.* & *adj.* by, on, or across land.
**o′ver·lap′**, *v.t.* & *v.i.* [-LAPPED, -LAPPING], to lap over; to extend over (something or each other) so as to coincide in part.
**o′ver·lay′**, *v.t.* [-LAID, -LAYING], 1. to lay or spread over. 2. to cover, as with a decorative layer. *n.* (ō′vẽr-lā′), 1. a covering. 2. a decorative layer.
**o′ver·look′**, *v.t.* 1. to look at from above. 2. to give a view of from above. 3. to rise above. 4. *a*) to look beyond and not see. *b*) to ignore; neglect. 5. to excuse in an indulgent way. 6. to supervise.
**o′ver·lord′**, *n.* a lord ranking over other lords.
**o·ver·ly** (ō′vẽr-li), *adv.* too much.
**o′ver·much′**, *adj.*, *adv.*, & *n.* too much.
**o′ver·night′**, *adv.* during the night. *adj.* 1. done or lasting during the night. 2. for one night: as, an *overnight* guest. 3. of or for a short trip: as, an *overnight* bag.
**o′ver·pass′**, *n.* a bridge or other passageway over a road, railway, etc. *v.t.* (ō′vẽr-pas′), 1. to pass over, 2. to surpass.
**o′ver·pow′er**, *v.t.* 1. to subdue; overwhelm. 2. to furnish with too much power.
**o′ver·rate′**, *v.t.* [-RATED, -RATING], to rate or estimate too highly.
**o′ver·reach′**, *v.t.* 1. to reach beyond or above. 2. to reach too far for and miss. 3. to cheat. *v.i.* to reach too far.
**o′ver·ride′**, *v.t.* [-RODE, -RIDDEN, -RIDING], 1. to ride over. 2. to trample down. 3. to suppress or domineer over. 4. to disregard.
**o′ver·rule′**, *v.t.* [-RULED, -RULING], 1. to rule out or set aside, as by higher authority. 2. to prevail over. —**o′ver·rul′ing**, *adj.*
**o′ver·run′**, *v.t.* [-RAN, -RUN, -RUNNING], 1. to spread out over so as to cover. 2. to swarm over, as vermin. 3. to extend beyond (certain limits). *v.i.* to overflow.
**o′ver·seas′**, *adv.* over or beyond the sea. *adj.* 1. foreign. 2. from beyond the sea. 3. across the sea. Also **oversea.**
**o′ver·see′**, *v.t.* [-SAW, -SEEN, -SEEING], to supervise; superintend. —**o′ver·se′er**, *n.*
**o′ver·shad′ow**, *v.t.* 1. to cast a shadow over. 2. to darken. 3. to be more important, etc. than by comparison.
**o′ver·shoe′**, *n.* a boot of rubber or fabric worn over the regular shoe to protect from cold or dampness; galosh.
**o′ver·shoot′**, *v.t.* [-SHOT, -SHOOTING], 1. to shoot or pass over or beyond. 2. to go farther than (an intended limit). *v.i.* to shoot or go too far.
**o′ver·sight′**, *n.* 1. failure to see or notice. 2. a careless error or omission.
**o′ver·size′**, *adj.* 1. too large. 2. larger than the usual. *n.* (ō′vẽr-sīz′), a size larger than regular sizes.
**o′ver·sleep′**, *v.i.* [-SLEPT, -SLEEPING], to sleep longer than intended.
**o′ver·spread′**, *v.t.* & *v.i.* [-SPREAD, -SPREADING], to spread or cover over.
**o′ver·state′**, *v.t.* [-STATED, -STATING], to exaggerate. —**o′ver·state′ment**, *n.*
**o′ver·step′**, *v.t.* [-STEPPED, -STEPPING], to go beyond: usually figurative.
**o′ver·strung′**, *adj.* tense; jittery.
**o′ver·stuff′**, *v.t.* 1. to stuff with too much of something. 2. to upholster (furniture) with deep stuffing.
**o·vert** (ō′vẽrt, ō-vũrt′), *adj.* [< L. *aperire*, to open], 1. open; public. 2. in *law*, done openly, with evident intent. —**o·vert′ly**, *adv.*
**o·ver·take** (ō′vẽr-tāk′), *v.t.* [-TOOK, -TAKEN, -TAKING], 1. to catch up with. 2. to come upon suddenly.
**o′ver·tax′**, *v.t.* 1. to tax too heavily. 2. to make excessive demands on.
**o′ver·throw′**, *v.t.* [-THREW, -THROWN, -THROWING], 1. to throw or turn over. 2. to conquer. *n.* (ō′vẽr-thrō′), 1. an overthrowing or being overthrown. 2. destruction; end. —**o′ver·throw′er**, *n.*
**o′ver·time′**, *n.* 1. time beyond the established limit, as of working hours. 2. pay for work done in such time. *adj.* & *adv.* of, for, or during overtime.
**o′ver·tone′**, *n.* 1. a faint, higher tone accompanying a fundamental tone produced by a musical instrument. 2. *pl.* implications; connotations.
**o′ver·top′**, *v.t.* [-TOPPED, -TOPPING], 1. to rise beyond or above. 2. to excel; surpass.
**o·ver·ture** (ō′vẽr-chẽr), *n.* [see OVERT], 1. an introductory offer or proposal. 2. a musical introduction to an opera, etc.
**o′ver·turn′**, *v.t.* 1. to turn over. 2. to conquer. *v.i.* to tip over; capsize.
**o·ver·ween·ing** (ō′vẽr-wēn′iŋ), *adj.* [< AS. *ofer*, over + *wenan*, to hope], arrogant; conceited. —**o′ver·ween′ing·ly**, *adv.*
**o′ver·weight′**, *n.* 1. extra or surplus weight. 2. a preponderance. *adj.* (ō′vẽr-wāt′), above normal or legal weight.
**o′ver·whelm′** (-hwelm′), *v.t.* [see OVER- & WHELM], 1. to pour down on and bury beneath. 2. to crush; overpower. —**o′ver·whelm′ing**, *adj.* —**o′ver·whelm′ing·ly**, *adv.*
**o′ver·work′**, *v.t.* to work or use to excess. *v.i.* to work too hard or too long. *n.* severe or burdensome work.
**o′ver·wrought′** (-rôt′), *adj.* 1. overworked. 2. too nervous or excited. 3. too elaborate.
**ovi-**, [< L. *ovum*, egg], a combining form meaning *egg* or *ovum.*

**o·vi·duct** (ō′vi-dukt′), *n.* [*ovi-* + *duct*], a duct or tube through which the ova pass from the ovary to the uterus or to the outside.
**o·vip·a·rous** (ō-vip′ẽr-əs), *adj.* [< L. *ovum*, egg + *parere*, produce], producing eggs that hatch after leaving the body.
**o·void** (ō′void), *adj.* [< *ovi-* + *-oid*], egg-shaped. *n.* anything egg-shaped.
**o·vu·late** (ō′vyoo-lāt′), *v.i.* [-LATED, -LATING], [< *ovule* + *-ate*], to produce ova; discharge ova from the ovary. **—o′vu·la′tion,** *n.*
**o·vule** (ō′vūl), *n.* [Fr. < L. *ovum*, egg], 1. in *zoology*, an immature ovum. 2. in *botany*, the part of a plant which develops into a seed. **—o′vu·lar,** *adj.*
**o·vum** (ō′vəm), *n.* [*pl.* OVA (ō′və)], [L., an egg], a female germ cell.
**owe** (ō), *v.t.* [OWED, OWING], [AS. *agan*, to own], 1. to be indebted to (someone) for (a specified amount, etc.). 2. to be morally obligated to give. *v.i.* to be in debt.
**ow·ing** (ō′iŋ), *adj.* 1. that owes. 2. due; unpaid. **—owing to,** resulting from; caused by.
**owl** (oul), *n.* [AS. *ule*], 1. a night bird of prey, having a large head, large eyes, and a short, hooked beak. 2. a person of nocturnal habits, solemn appearance, etc.
**owl′et** (-it), *n.* a young or small owl.
**own** (ōn), *adj.* [< AS. *agan*, possess], belonging or relating to oneself or itself: as, his *own* car. *n.* that which belongs to oneself: as, that is his *own*. *v.t.* 1. to possess; have. 2. to admit; acknowledge. *v.i.* to confess (with *to*). **—on one's own,** [Colloq.], by one's own efforts. **—own′er,** *n.* **—own′er·ship′,** *n.*
**ox** (oks), *n.* [*pl.* OXEN (ok′s'n)], [AS. *oxa*], 1. any of the cattle family of domesticated cud-chewing mammals. 2. a castrated bull.
**ox′blood′,** *n.* a deep red color.
**ox′bow′** (-bō′), *n.* the U-shaped part of an ox yoke which passes under and around the animal's neck.
**ox·ford** (oks′fẽrd), *n.* [< *Oxford*, England], [sometimes O-], a low shoe laced over the instep: also **oxford shoe.**
**Oxford gray,** a very dark gray.
**ox·i·da·tion** (ok′sə-dā′shən), *n.* an oxidizing or being oxidized.
**ox·ide** (ok′sīd), *n.* [< Gr. *oxys*, sour + Fr. *acide*, acid], a compound of oxygen with another element or a radical.
**ox·i·dize** (ok′sə-dīz′), *v.t.* [-DIZED, -DIZING], to unite with oxygen; hence, to rust. *v.i.* to become oxidized. **—ox′i·diz′er,** *n.*
**oxy-,** [< Gr. *oxys*, sharp], a combining form meaning *sharp, pointed*, or *acid.*
**ox·y·a·cet·y·lene torch** (or **blowpipe**) (ok′si-ə-set′'l-ēn′), a blowpipe using the hot flame of an oxygen and acetylene mixture to cut and weld steel.
**ox·y·gen** (ok′si-jən), *n.* [see OXY- & -GEN], a colorless, odorless, gaseous chemical element, the most abundant of all elements: it is essential to life processes and to combustion: symbol, O.
**oxygen tent,** a boxlike enclosure supplied with oxygen, used, as in cases of pneumonia, to facilitate breathing.
**ox·y·mo·ron** (ok′si-môr′on), *n.* [*pl.* -RA (-rə)], [< Gr. *oxys*, sharp + *moros*, dull], a figure of speech in which contradictory terms are combined (e.g., sweet sorrow).
**o·yez, o·yes** (ō′yes, -yez), *interj.* [< L. *audire*, hear], hear ye! attention!: used to command attention in courtrooms.
**oys·ter** (ois′tẽr), *n.* [< Gr. *ostreon*], an edible marine mollusk with an irregular, hinged shell.
**oz.,** [*pl.* ozs.], ounce.
**o·zone** (ō′zōn), *n.* [Fr. < Gr. *ozein*, to smell], 1. a form of oxygen with a strong odor, formed by an electrical discharge in air and used as a bleaching agent, water purifier, etc. 2. [Slang], pure air.

# P

**P, p** (pē), *n.* [*pl.* P's, p's, Ps, ps], the sixteenth letter of the English alphabet. **—mind one's p's and q's,** to be careful of what one does.
**P,** in *chem.*, phosphorus.
**p.,** 1. [*pl.* PP.], page. 2. participle. 3. past. 4. per. 5. pint.
**pa** (pä), *n.* [Colloq.], father; papa.
**P.A.,** [Slang], public address (system).
**pab·u·lum** (pab′yoo-ləm), *n.* [L.], food.
**pace** (pās), *n.* [< L. *passus*, a step], 1. a step in walking, etc. 2. the length of a step or stride. 3. the rate of speed in walking, etc. 4. rate of progress, etc. 5. a gait. 6. a gait of a horse in which both legs on the same side are raised together. *v.t.* [PACED, PACING], 1. to walk back and forth across. 2. to measure by paces. 3. to set the pace for (a runner, etc.). *v.i.* 1. to walk with regular steps. 2. to move at a pace: said of a horse. **—put one through his paces,** to test one's abilities. **—pac′er,** *n.*
**pace′mak′er,** *n.* a runner, horse, etc. in the lead, as in a race. **—pace′mak′ing,** *n.*
**pach·y·derm** (pak′ə-dũrm′), *n.* [< Gr. *pachys*, thick + *derma*, skin], a large, thick-skinned, hoofed animal, as the elephant, rhinoceros, etc. **—pach′y·der′ma·tous,** *adj.*
**pa·cif·ic** (pə-sif′ik), *adj.* [see PACIFY], 1. making peace. 2. of a peaceful nature; calm; tranquil. **—pa·cif′i·cal·ly,** *adv.*
**pac·i·fi·er** (pas′ə-fī′ẽr), *n.* 1. a person or thing that pacifies. 2. a nipple or teething ring for babies.
**pac·i·fism** (pas′ə-fiz'm), *n.* belief that international disputes should be settled by peaceful means instead of war. **—pac′i·fist,** *n.*
**pac·i·fy** (pas′ə-fī′), *v.t.* [-FIED, -FYING], [< L. *pax*, peace + *facere*, make], to make peaceful or calm; appease. **—pac′i·fi·ca′tion,** *n.*
**pack** (pak), *n.* [< LG.], 1. a bundle of things tied up for carrying. 2. a package of a standard number: as, a *pack* of cigarettes or of playing cards. 3. a number of wild animals living together. 4. a mass of floating pieces of ice driven together. 5. *a*) treatment by wrapping a patient in wet or dry, hot or cold sheets, etc. *b*) the sheets so used. *v.t.* 1. to make a pack of. 2. *a*) to put together in a box, trunk, etc. *b*) to fill (a box, etc.). 3. to crowd; cram: as, the hall was *packed.* 4. to fill in (a joint, etc.) tightly, as for prevention of leaks. 5. to carry in a pack or on one's person. 6. to send (*off*): as, they *packed* him off to school. *v.i.* 1. to make up packs. 2. to put one's clothes, etc. into luggage for a trip. 3. to crowd together. 4. to settle into a compact mass.
**pack** (pak), *v.t.* to choose (a jury, etc.) dishonestly so as to get desired results.
**pack·age** (pak′ij), *n.* 1. a wrapped or boxed thing; parcel; bundle. *v.t.* [-AGED, -AGING], to put into a package.
**pack′er,** *n.* one who packs; esp., one who operates a packing house.
**pack·et** (pak′it), *n.* 1. a small package. 2. a boat that travels a regular route carrying passengers, freight, and mail.
**pack′ing,** *n.* 1. the act of one that packs. 2. any material used in packing, as to make watertight, etc.

**packing house,** a place where meats, fruits, etc. are processed for future sale.
**pact** (pakt), *n.* [< L. *pax*, peace], a compact or agreement.
**pad** (pad), *n.* [echoic], the dull sound of a footstep. *v.i.* [PADDED, PADDING], to walk, esp. with a soft step.
**pad** (pad), *n.* [prob. var. of *pod*], 1. anything soft used to protect from friction, blows, etc.; cushion. 2. the cushionlike sole of an animal's paw. 3. the floating leaf of a water lily. 4. a number of sheets of paper fastened along one edge; tablet. 5. [Slang], the apartment, room, etc. where one lives. *v.t.* [PADDED, PADDING], 1. to stuff or cover with soft material. 2. to lengthen (a speech, etc.) with unnecessary material. 3. to fill (an expense account, etc.) with fraudulent entries.
**pad′ding,** *n.* any material used to pad.
**pad·dle** (pad′'l), *n.* [prob. ult. < L. *patella*, small pan], 1. a short oar with a wide blade at one or both ends, used without an oarlock. 2. any similar implement used in flogging, etc. *v.t. & v.i.* [-DLED, -DLING], 1. to propel (a canoe, etc.) by a paddle. 2. to beat with a paddle; spank. **—pad′dler,** *n.*
**pad·dle** (pad′'l), *v.i.* [-DLED, -DLING], [prob. < *pad*, *v.i.*], to move the feet in shallow water; dabble. **—pad′dler,** *n.*
**paddle wheel,** a wheel with boards around it for propelling a steamboat.
**pad·dock** (pad′ək), *n.* [< AS. *pearruc*, enclosure], 1. a small enclosure near a stable, where horses are exercised. 2. an enclosure near a race track, where horses are assembled before a race.
**pad·dy** (pad′i), *n.* [*pl.* -DIES], [Malay *padi*], 1. rice in the husk. 2. rice. 3. a rice field.
**pad·lock** (pad′lok′), *n.* [< ?], a removable lock with a hinged link to be passed through a staple, chain, or eye. *v.t.* to fasten as with a padlock.
**pa·dre** (pä′dri), *n.* [< L. *pater*, father], 1. father: the title of a priest in Italy, Spain, etc. 2. [Military Slang], a chaplain.
**pae·an** (pē′ən), *n.* [< Gr. *Paian*, Apollo], a song of joy, triumph, etc.
**pa·gan** (pā′gən), *n.* [< L. *paganus*, peasant], 1. one who is not a Christian, Moslem, or Jew; heathen. 2. one who has no religion. *adj.* 1. of pagans. 2. not religious; heathen. **—pa′gan·ish,** *adj.* **—pa′gan·ism,** *n.*
**page** (pāj), *n.* [< L. *pangere*, fasten], 1. *a*) one side of a leaf of a book, newspaper, etc. *b*) loosely, the entire leaf. 2. *pl.* records; writing. *v.t.* [PAGED, PAGING], to number the pages of.
**page** (pāj), *n.* [< ML. *pagius*], a boy attendant, esp. one who runs errands, carries messages, etc., as in a hotel. *v.t.* [PAGED, PAGING], to try to find (a person) by calling his name, as a hotel page does.
**pag·eant** (paj′ənt), *n.* [prob. < ME. *pagend*, stage], 1. a spectacular exhibition, parade, etc. 2. an outdoor drama celebrating historical events.
**pag′eant·ry,** *n.* [*pl.* -RIES], 1. grand spectacle; gorgeous display. 2. empty display.
**pa·go·da** (pə-gō′də), *n.* [< Port.; prob. < Per. *but*, idol + *kadah*, house], in India, China, etc., a several-storied temple in the form of a pyramidal tower.
**paid** (pād), pt. and pp. of **pay.** *adj.* receiving pay; as, a *paid* advisor.
**pail** (pāl), *n.* [< L. *patella*, a pan], a cylindrical container, usually with a handle, for holding liquids, etc.; bucket.
**pail′ful′** (-fool′), *n.* [*pl.* -FULS], as much as a pail will hold.
**pain** (pān), *n.* [< Gr. *poinē*, penalty], 1. physical or mental suffering caused by injury, disease, tribulation, etc. 2. *pl.* great care: as, take *pains* with the work. *v.t.* to cause pain to; hurt. **—on** (or **upon, under**) **pain of,** with the threat of (penalty). **—pain′less,** *adj.* **—pain′less·ly,** *adv.*
**pain′ful,** *adj.* 1. causing or having pain; hurting. 2. irksome. **—pain′ful·ly,** *adv.*
**pains·tak·ing** (pānz′tāk′iŋ), *adj.* requiring or showing great care; very careful.
**paint** (pānt), *v.t.* [< L. *pingere*], 1. *a*) to make (a picture) using oil pigments, etc. *b*) to depict with paints. 2. to describe vividly. 3. to cover or decorate with paint. *v.i.* to paint pictures. *n.* a mixture of pigment with oil, water, etc. used as a covering or coloring. **—paint′a·ble,** *adj.*
**paint′er,** *n.* 1. an artist who paints pictures. 2. one whose work is covering surfaces, as walls with paint.
**paint′ing,** *n.* a painted picture.
**pair** (pâr), *n.* [*pl.* PAIRS, *occas., after a number,* PAIR], [< L. *par*, equal], 1. two corresponding things associated or used together: as, a *pair* of shoes. 2. a single unit of two corresponding parts: as, a *pair* of pants. 3. any two persons or animals regarded as a unit. *v.t. & v.i.* 1. to form a pair or pairs (of); match. 2. to mate.
**pa·ja·mas** (pə-jam′əz, -jä′məz), *n.pl.* [< Per. *pāi*, leg + *jāmah*, garment], a loosely fitting sleeping or lounging suit consisting of jacket and trousers.
**pal** (pal), *n.* [Eng. Gypsy, brother; ult. < Sans.], [Colloq.], a close friend.
**pal·ace** (pal′is), *n.* [< L. *Palatium*, one of the seven hills of Rome], 1. the official residence of a king, etc. 2. any large, magnificent building.
**pal·an·quin, pal·an·keen** (pal′ən-kēn′), *n.* [< Sans. *palyanka*], in the Orient, a covered litter for one person, carried by poles on men's shoulders.
**pal·at·a·ble** (pal′i-tə-b'l), *adj.* pleasant to the taste; savory. **—pal′at·a·bly,** *adv.*
**pal·ate** (pal′it), *n.* [< L. *palatum*], 1. the roof of the mouth. 2. taste. **—pal′a·tal,** *adj.*
**pa·la·tial** (pə-lā′shəl), *adj.* [see PALACE], 1. of, suitable for, or like a palace. 2. magnificent. **—pa·la′tial·ly,** *adv.*
**pa·lat·i·nate** (pə-lat′'n-āt′), *n.* the territory ruled by a palatine.
**pal·a·tine** (pal′ə-tīn′, -tin), *adj.* [see PALACE], having royal privileges. *n.* a nobleman having royal privileges in his own territory.
**pa·lav·er** (pə-lav′ēr), *n.* [< Port. *palavra*, word], talk; esp., profuse or idle talk. *v.i.* to talk glibly.
**pale** (pāl), *adj.* [< L. *pallere*, be pale], 1. of a whitish or colorless complexion. 2. lacking intensity, as color, light, etc. 3. feeble. *v.i. & v.t.* [PALED, PALING], to become or make pale. **—pale′ly,** *adv.* **—pale′ness,** *n.*
**pale** (pāl), *n.* [< L. *palus*, a stake], 1. a pointed stake used in fences. 2. a boundary; enclosure: now chiefly figurative.
**pale′face′,** *n.* a white person: a term allegedly first used by American Indians.
**pa·le·on·tol·o·gy** (pā′li-ən-tol′ə-ji), *n.* [< Gr. *palaios*, ancient + *ōn*, a being; + *-logy*], the branch of geology dealing with prehistoric life through the study of fossils. **—pa′le·on·tol′o·gist,** *n.*
**pal·ette** (pal′it), *n.* [< L. *pala*, a shovel], a thin, oblong board, on which an artist mixes his paints.
**pal·frey** (pôl′fri), *n.* [*pl.* -FREYS], [ult. < Gr. *para*, beside + L. *veredus*, post horse], [Archaic], a saddle horse, esp. one for a woman.
**pal·ing** (pāl′iŋ), *n.* 1. a fence made of pales. 2. a pale, or pales collectively.
**pal·i·sade** (pal′ə-sād′), *n.* [< Fr. < L. *palus*, a stake], 1. any of a row of large pointed stakes set in the ground to form a fence as for fortification. 2. such a fence. 3. *pl.* a line of steep cliffs.

**pall** (pôl), *v.i.* [PALLED, PALLING], [ME. *pallen*], 1. to become cloying, insipid, etc. 2. to become satiated.

**pall** (pôl), *n.* [< L. *pallium*, a cover], 1. a piece of velvet, etc. used to cover a coffin, hearse, etc. 2. a dark or gloomy covering.

**pal·la·di·um** (pə-lā′di-əm), *n.* [ult. < Gr. *Pallas*, the goddess Athena], a rare, silvery-white, metallic chemical element of the platinum group: it is used for jewelry or as a catalyst: symbol, Pd.

**pall·bear·er** (pôl′bâr′ẽr), *n.* [*pall* (cover) + *bearer*], one of the persons who attend the coffin at a funeral.

**pal·let** (pal′it), *n.* [< L. *palea*, chaff], a straw bed or mattress: often connoting an inferior bed.

**pal·li·ate** (pal′i-āt′), *v.t.* [-ATED, -ATING], [< L. *pallium*, a cloak], 1. to lessen the severity of without curing; alleviate. 2. to make (a crime, etc.) appear less serious than it is; excuse. —**pal′li·a′tion,** *n.* —**pal′li·a′tive,** *adj.* & *n.* —**pal′li·a′tor,** *n.*

**pal·lid** (pal′id), *adj.* [< L. *pallere*, become pale], faint in color; pale. —**pal′lid·ly,** *adv.*

**pal·lor** (pal′ẽr), *n.* [L. < *pallere*, be pale], unnatural paleness, as of the face.

**palm** (päm), *n.* [< L. *palma*: from its hand-like fronds], 1. any of several tropical or subtropical trees with a tall branchless trunk and a bunch of huge leaves at the top. 2. a leaf of this tree carried as a symbol of victory. 3. victory. —**palm′y,** *adj.*

**palm** (päm), *n.* [< L. *palma*], 1. the inner surface of the hand between the fingers and wrist. 2. a unit of measure equal to either the width (3–4 inches) or the length (7–9 inches) of the hand. 3. a broad, flat part at the end of an armlike part. *v.t.* to hide (something) in the palm, as in a sleight-of-hand trick. —**palm off,** to get (a thing) accepted, sold, etc. as by fraud.

**palm′er,** *n.* 1. a pilgrim who carried a palm leaf to show he had been to the Holy Land. 2. any pilgrim.

**pal·met·to** (pal-met′ō), *n.* [*pl.* -TOS, -TOES], a small palm tree with fan-shaped leaves.

**palm·is·try** (päm′is-tri), *n.* [prob. < ME. *paume*, the palm + *maistrie*, mastery], fortune-telling by means of the lines, etc. on the palm of a person's hand. —**palm′ist,** *n.*

**Palm Sunday,** the Sunday before Easter, commemorating Jesus' entry into Jerusalem, when palm branches were strewn before him.

**pal·o·mi·no** (pal′ə-mē′nō), *n.* [Am. Sp. dim. of *paloma*, dove: orig. said of horses of a dovelike color], a pale-yellow horse with a white mane and tail.

**pal·pa·ble** (pal′pə-b'l), *adj.* [< L. *palpare*, to touch], 1. that can be touched, felt, etc. 2. obvious; plain. —**pal′pa·bly,** *adv.*

**pal·pi·tate** (pal′pə-tāt′), *v.i.* [-TATED, -TATING], [< L. *palpare*, to feel], 1. to beat rapidly, as the heart. 2. to throb. —**pal′pi·tant,** *adj.* —**pal′pi·ta′tion,** *n.*

**pal·sy** (pôl′zi), *n.* [*pl.* -SIES], [see PARALYSIS], paralysis in any part of the body, sometimes accompanied by involuntary tremors. —**pal′sied,** *adj.*

**pal·try** (pôl′tri), *adj.* [-TRIER, -TRIEST], [prob. < LG. *palte*, rag], trifling; petty.

**pam·pas** (pam′pəz), *n.pl.* [< S. Am. Ind. *pampa*, plain], the extensive treeless plains of Argentina.

**pam·per** (pam′pẽr), *v.t.* [prob. < LG.], to be overindulgent with; coddle.

**pam·phlet** (pam′flit), *n.* [< OFr. *Pamphilet*, popular name of a ML. poem], a small, unbound booklet, often on some topic of current interest. —**pam′phlet·eer′** (-fli-têr′), *n.*

**Pan** (pan), *n.* in *Gr. myth.*, a god of fields, forests, flocks, and shepherds, represented with the legs of a goat.

**pan** (pan), *n.* [AS. *panne*], 1. any broad, shallow container used in cooking, etc. 2. a pan-shaped part or object. 3. [Slang], a face. *v.t.* & *v.i.* [PANNED, PANNING], 1. [Colloq.], to criticize unfavorably. 2. in *mining*, to wash (gravel) in a pan in order to separate (gold, etc.). —**pan out,** [Colloq.], to turn out; esp., to turn out well.

**pan-,** [< Gr. *pan*, all], a combining form meaning: 1. *all*, as in *pantheism*. 2. *of, comprising*, or *uniting every*, as in *Pan-American*.

**pan·a·ce·a** (pan′ə-sē′ə), *n.* [< Gr. *pan*, all + *akeisthai*, to cure], a supposed remedy for all diseases.

**Pan·a·ma hat,** (pan′ə-mä′, -mô′), a fine, hand-plaited hat made from leaves of a Central and South American palm tree.

**Pan′-A·mer′i·can,** *adj.* of the Americas or their peoples.

**pan·cake** (pan′kāk′), *n.* a thin, flat cake of batter fried on a griddle or in a pan.

**pan·chro·mat·ic** (pan′krō-mat′ik), *adj.* sensitive to light of all colors: as, *panchromatic* film.

**pan·cre·as** (pan′kri-əs, paŋ′-), *n.* [< Gr. *pan*, all + *kreas*, flesh], a large gland that secretes a digestive juice into the small intestine. —**pan′cre·at′ic** (-at′ik), *adj.*

**pan·da** (pan′də), *n.* [< native name], 1. a small, reddish-brown, raccoonlike animal of the Himalayas. 2. a white-and-black, bear-like animal of Asia: also **giant panda.**

**pan·dem·ic** (pan-dem′ik), *adj.* [< Gr. *pan*, all + *dēmos*, people], epidemic over a large region.

**pan·de·mo·ni·um** (pan′di-mō′ni-əm), *n.* [< name of demons' abode in Milton's *Paradise Lost*; < *pan-* + Gr. *daimōn*, demon], wild disorder or noise.

**pan·der** (pan′dẽr), *n.* [< *Pandarus*, lovers' go-between in a poem by Chaucer], 1. a procurer; pimp. 2. one who helps others to satisfy their vices, etc. Also **pan′der·er.** *v.i.* to act as a pander (*to*).

**Pan·do·ra** (pan-dôr′ə), *n.* [< Gr. *pan*, all + *dōron*, gift], in *Gr. myth.*, the first mortal woman: she opened a box letting all human ills into the world.

**pane** (pān), *n.* [< L. *pannus*, piece of cloth], a sheet of glass in a window, door, frame, etc.

**pan·e·gyr·ic** (pan′ə-jir′ik), *n.* [< Gr. *panēgyris*, public meeting], 1. a formal speech or writing praising a person or event. 2. high praise. —**pan′e·gyr′i·cal,** *adj.*

**pan·el** (pan′'l), *n.* [see PANE], 1. *a*) a section or division, usually rectangular, set off on a wall, door, etc. *b*) a board for instruments or controls. 2. a strip inserted in a skirt, etc. 3. a group of persons selected for judging, discussing, etc. 4. a list of persons summoned for jury duty. *v.t.* [-ELED or -ELLED, -ELING or -ELLING], to provide with panels.

**pan′el·ing, pan′el·ling,** *n.* panels collectively.

**pan′el·ist,** *n.* a member of a panel (*n.* 3).

**pang** (paŋ), *n.* [< ME. *prong*], a sudden, sharp, brief pain, physical or emotional.

**pan′han′dle,** *n.* [often P-], a strip of land like the handle of a pan.

**pan·han·dle** (pan′han′d'l), *v.t.* & *v.i.* [-DLED, -DLING], [Slang], to beg on the streets. —**pan′han′dler,** *n.*

**pan·ic** (pan′ik), *n.* [< Gr. *panikos*, of Pan, as inspirer of sudden fear], a sudden, unreasoning fear, often spreading quickly. *adj.* like, showing, or resulting from panic. *v.t.* [-ICKED, -ICKING], 1. to affect with panic. 2. [Slang], to delight as with comedy. —**pan′ick·y,** *adj.*

**pan′ic-strick′en,** *adj.* badly frightened.

**pan·nier** (pan′yẽr, -i-ẽr), *n.* [< L. *panis*, bread], a large basket for carrying loads on the back.

**pan·o·ply** (pan′ə-pli), *n.* [*pl.* -PLIES], [< Gr. *pan*, all + *hopla*, arms], 1. a complete suit of armor. 2. any magnificent array.

**pan·o·ra·ma** (pan′ə-ram′ə, -rä′mə), *n.* [< *pan-* + Gr. *horama*, a view], 1. an unlimited view in all directions. 2. a constantly changing scene. —**pan′o·ram′ic**, *adj.*

**pan·sy** (pan′zi), *n.* [*pl.* -SIES], [< Fr. *penser*, think], a small plant of the violet family, with velvety petals.

**pant** (pant), *v.i.* [ult. < L. *phantasia*, nightmare], 1. to breathe rapidly and heavily, as from running fast. 2. to yearn eagerly (with *for* or *after*). *v.t.* to gasp out. *n.* any of a series of rapid, heavy breaths; gasp.

**pan·ta·loons** (pan′tə-lōōnz′), *n.pl.* [< It.; ult. after St. *Pantolone*], trousers.

**pan·the·ism** (pan′thē-iz′m), *n.* [*pan-* + *theism*], the belief that all forces, manifestations, etc. of the universe are God. —**pan′the·ist**, *n.* —**pan′the·is′tic**, *adj.*

**pan·the·on** (pan′thē-on′), *n.* [< Gr. *pan*, all + *theos*, a god], 1. a temple for all the gods. 2. [often P-], a building in which the famous dead of a nation are entombed.

**pan·ther** (pan′thēr), *n.* [< Gr. *panthēr*], 1. a cougar. 2. a leopard. 3. a jaguar.

**pan·ties** (pan′tiz), *n.pl.* women's or children's short underpants.

**pan·to·mime** (pan′tə-mīm′), *n.* [< Gr.; see PAN- & MIME], 1. a drama without words, using actions and gestures only. 2. actions or gestures without words. *v.t.* & *v.i.* [-MIMED, -MIMING], to express or act in pantomime. —**pan′to·mim′ic** (-mim′ik), *adj.*

**pan·try** (pan′tri), *n.* [*pl.* -TRIES], [< L. *panis*, bread], a small room off the kitchen, where cooking ingredients, china, etc. are kept.

**pants** (pants), *n.pl.* [< *pantaloons*], 1. trousers. 2. drawers or panties.

**pant′suit′**, *n.* a woman's outfit consisting of a matched jacket and pants: also **pants suit.**

**panty hose**, a woman's one-piece undergarment combining panties with hose.

**pan·ty·waist** (pan′ti-wāst′), *n.* [Slang], a weakling; sissy.

**pan·zer** (pan′zēr; G. pän′tsēr), *adj.* [G., armor], armored: as, a *panzer* division.

**pap** (pap), *n.* [< ?], any soft food for babies or invalids.

**pa·pa** (pä′pə), *n.* father: a child's word.

**pa·pa·cy** (pā′pə-si), *n.* [*pl.* -CIES], [< ML. *papa*, pope], 1. the position or authority of the Pope. 2. the period during which a pope rules. 3. [P-], the government of the R. C. Church, headed by the Pope.

**pa·pal** (pā′p'l), *adj.* 1. of the Pope. 2. of the papacy. 3. of the R. C. Church.

**pa·paw** (pô′pô), *n.* [< S. Am. Ind. name], 1. a tree of the central and southern U.S., having a yellowish, edible fruit. 2. its fruit. Also **pawpaw.**

**pa·pa·ya** (pə-pä′yə), *n.* [Sp.], 1. a tropical tree with a large, yellowish-orange, edible fruit like a melon. 2. this fruit.

**pa·per** (pā′pēr), *n.* [see PAPYRUS (sense 2)], 1. a thin, flexible material in sheets, made from rags, wood pulp, etc., and used to write or print on, wrap, etc. 2. a single sheet of this. 3. an official document. 4. an essay, dissertation, etc. 5. a newspaper. 6. wallpaper. 7. *pl.* credentials. *adj.* 1. of, or made of, paper. 2. like paper; thin. *v.t.* to cover with wallpaper. —**pa′per·y**, *adj.*

**pa′per·back′**, *n.* a book bound in paper.

**pa′per·boy′**, *n.* a boy who sells or delivers newspapers.

**paper hanger**, a person whose work is to cover walls with wallpaper. —**paper hanging.**

**pa′per·weight′**, *n.* any small, heavy object to be placed on papers to keep them from being scattered.

**paper work**, the keeping of records, filing of reports, etc. incidental to some task.

**pa·pier-mâ·ché** (pā′pēr-mə-shā′), *n.* [Fr. < *papier*, paper + *mâcher*, to chew], a material made of paper pulp mixed with rosin, oil, etc. and molded into various objects when moist.

**pa·pil·la** (pə-pil′ə), *n.* [*pl.* -LAE (-ē)], [L. < *papula*, pimple], any small, nipplelike projection of tissue, as on the tongue. —**pap·il·lar·y** (pap′ə-ler′i), *adj.*

**pa·pist** (pā′pist), *n.* & *adj.* [< L. *papa*, pope], Roman Catholic: a hostile term.

**pa·poose** (pa-pōōs′), *n.* [< Am. Ind.], a North American Indian baby.

**pap·ri·ka, pap·ri·ca** (pa-prē′kə, pap′ri-), *n.* [ult. < Gr. *peperi*, a pepper], a mild red condiment ground from the fruit of certain peppers.

**Pap test** (pap), [< G. *Papanicolau* (1883–1962), U.S. anatomist who developed it], the examination of cells taken from the cervix of a woman: a test for uterine cancer.

**pa·py·rus** (pə-pī′rəs), *n.* [*pl.* -RI (-rī), -RUSES], [< Gr. *papyros*], 1. a tall water plant of Egypt. 2. a writing material made from the pith of this plant by the ancients.

**par** (pär), *n.* [L., an equal], 1. the established value of a currency in foreign-exchange rates. 2. an equal status, level, etc.: as, they are on a *par* in ability. 3. the average state, condition, etc.: as, his work is above *par*. 4. the face value of stocks, bonds, etc. 5. in *golf*, the number of strokes established as an expert score for a hole or course. *adj.* 1. of or at par. 2. average; normal.

**par·a·ble** (par′ə-b'l), *n.* [< Gr. *para-*, beside + *ballein*, to throw], a short, simple story teaching a moral lesson.

**pa·rab·o·la** (pə-rab′ə-lə), *n.* [*pl.* -LAS], [see PARABLE], in *geometry*, a curve formed by the intersection of a cone with a plane parallel to its side. —**par·a·bol·ic** (par′ə-bol′ik), *adj.*

**par·a·chute** (par′ə-shōōt′), *n.* [Fr. < *para-*, protecting + *chute*, fall], a large cloth contrivance, umbrella-shaped when unfolded, used to retard the speed of one dropping from an airplane, etc. *v.t.* & *v.i.* [-CHUTED, -CHUTING], to drop by parachute. —**par′a·chut′ist**, *n.*

**pa·rade** (pə-rād′), *n.* [< L. *parare*, prepare], 1. ostentatious display. 2. a review of troops. 3. any organized procession or march, as for display. 4. a public walk or promenade. *v.t.* [-RADED, -RADING], 1. to march or walk through (the streets, etc.), as for display. 2. to show off: as, he *parades* his knowledge. *v.i.* 1. to march in a parade. 2. to walk about ostentatiously. 3. to assemble in military formation for review.

**par·a·digm** (par′ə-dim, -dīm′), *n.* [< Gr. *para-*, beside + *deigma*, example], 1. an example or model. 2. in *grammar*, an example of a declension or conjugation, giving all the inflectional forms of a word.

**par·a·dise** (par′ə-dīs′), *n.* [< Gr. *paradeisos*, garden], 1. [P-], the garden of Eden. 2. heaven. 3. any place or state of great happiness.

**par·a·dox** (par′ə-doks′), *n.* [< Gr. *para-*, beyond + *doxa*, opinion], 1. a statement that seems contradictory, absurd, etc. but may be true in fact. 2. a statement that is self-contradictory and, hence, false. —**par′a·dox′i·cal**, *adj.* —**par′a·dox′i·cal·ly**, *adv.*

**par·af·fin** (par′ə-fin), *n.* [G. < L. *parum*, too little + *affinis*, akin: from its inertness], a white, waxy substance distilled from petroleum and used for making candles, sealing jars, etc.: also **par′af·fine** (-fin, -fēn′).

**par·a·gon** (par′ə-gon′, -gən), *n.* [< It. *paragone*, touchstone], a model of perfection or excellence.

**par·a·graph** (par′ə-graf′, -gräf′), *n.* [< Gr. *para-*, beside + *graphein*, write], 1. a distinct section of a writing, begun on a new line and often indented. 2. a sign (¶) used to indicate a new paragraph. 3. a brief item in a newspaper or magazine. *v.t.* to arrange in paragraphs.

**par·a·keet** (par'ə-kēt'), *n.* [see PARROT], a small, slender parrot with a long tail.

**par·al·lax** (par'ə-laks'), *n.* [< Gr. *para-*, beyond + *allassein*, to change], the apparent change in the position of an object resulting from a change in the viewer's position.

**par·al·lel** (par'ə-lel'), *adj.* [< Gr. *para-*, side by side + *allēlos*, one another], 1. extending in the same direction and at a constant distance apart, so as never to meet. 2. similar or corresponding. *n.* 1. a parallel line, surface, etc. 2. any person or thing similar to another; counterpart. 3. any comparison showing likeness. 4. any of the imaginary lines parallel to the equator and representing degrees of latitude. *v.t.* [-LELED or -LELLED, -LELING or -LELLING], 1. to be parallel with: as, the road *parallels* the river. 2. to compare. 3. to find or be a counterpart for. —**par'al·lel·ism** (-iz'm), *n.*

**par'al·lel'o·gram'** (-ə-gram'), *n.* a four-sided plane figure having the opposite sides parallel and equal.

**pa·ral·y·sis** (pə-ral'ə-sis), *n.* [*pl.* -SES (-sēz')], [< Gr. *para-*, beside + *lyein*, to loose], 1. (partial or complete) loss of the power of motion or sensation in part or all of the body. 2. a crippling of activities. —**par·a·lyt·ic** (par'ə-lit'ik), *adj. & n.*

**par·a·lyze** (par'ə-līz'), *v.t.* [-LYZED, -LYZING], 1. to cause paralysis in. 2. to make ineffective, powerless, etc.

**par·a·mount** (par'ə-mount'), *adj.* [< OFr. *par*, by + *amont*, uphill], ranking higher than any other; chief.

**par·a·mour** (par'ə-moor'), *n.* [< OFr. *par amour*, with love], a man's mistress or a woman's illicit lover.

**par·a·noi·a** (par'ə-noi'ə), *n.* [< Gr. *para-*, beside + *nous*, the mind], a mental disorder characterized by delusions, as of grandeur or, esp., persecution. —**par'a·noid'**, *adj.*

**par·a·pet** (par'ə-pit, -pet'), *n.* [< It. *parare*, to guard + *petto*, breast], 1. a wall or bank for screening troops from enemy fire. 2. a low wall or railing, as on a balcony.

**par·a·pher·na·li·a** (par'ə-fẽr-nā'li-ə, -fə-nāl'yə), *n.pl.* [< Gr. *para-*, beyond + *phernē*, dowry], 1. personal belongings. 2. equipment; apparatus.

**par·a·phrase** (par'ə-frāz'), *n.* [< Gr. *para-*, beyond + *phrazein*, tell], a rewording of the meaning of something spoken or written. *v.t. & v.i.* [-PHRASED, -PHRASING], to reword.

**par·a·ple·gi·a** (par'ə-plē'ji-ə), *n.* [< Gr. *para-*, beside + *plessein*, to strike], paralysis of the lower half of the body. —**par'a·pleg'ic** (-plej'ik, -plē'jik), *adj. & n.*

**par·a·site** (par'ə-sīt'), *n.* [< Gr. *para-*, beside + *sitos*, food], 1. one who lives at others' expense without making any useful return. 2. a plant or animal that lives on or within another. —**par'a·sit'ic** (-sit'ik), *adj.*

**par·a·sol** (par'ə-sôl'), *n.* [< It. *parare*, ward off + *sole*, the sun], a light umbrella used as a sunshade.

**par·a·troops** (par'ə-trōōps'), *n.pl.* a unit of soldiers trained to land behind enemy lines from airplanes, using parachutes.

**par·boil** (pär'boil'), *v.t.* [< L. *per*, through + *bullire*, to boil: meaning infl. by Eng. *part*], to boil until partly cooked.

**par·cel** (pär's'l), *n.* [see PARTICLE], 1. a small, wrapped bundle; package. 2. a piece (of land). *v.t.* [-CELED or -CELLED, -CELING or -CELLING], to separate into parts and distribute (with *out*).

**parcel post**, the post-office branch which carries and delivers parcels.

**parch** (pärch), *v.t.* [see PERISH], 1. to expose to great heat so as to dry or roast. 2. to make hot and dry. 3. to make very thirsty. *v.i.* to become very dry and hot.

**parch·ment** (pärch'mənt), *n.* [< LL. (*charta*) *Pergamenum*, (paper) of Pergamum, city in Asia Minor], 1. the skin of a sheep, goat, etc. prepared as a surface for writing. 2. a manuscript on parchment. 3. a fine paper like parchment.

**par·don** (pär'd'n), *v.t.* [< L. *per-*, through + *donare*, give], 1. to release from punishment. 2. to forgive (an offense). 3. to excuse (a person) for (a minor fault, etc.). *n.* 1. forgiveness. 2. an official document granting a pardon. —**par'don·a·ble**, *adj.*

**pare** (pâr), *v.t.* [PARED, PARING], [< L. *parare*, prepare], 1. to cut or trim away the rind, skin, etc. of; peel. 2. to reduce gradually.

**par·e·gor·ic** (par'ə-gôr'ik), *n.* [< Gr. *paregoros*, mitigating], a medicine which lessens pain; esp., camphorated tincture of opium, used to relieve diarrhea, etc.

**par·ent** (pâr'ənt), *n.* [< L. *parere*, beget], 1. a father or mother. 2. any organism in relation to its offspring. 3. a source or cause. —**pa·ren·tal** (pə-ren't'l), *adj.* —**pa·ren'tal·ly**, *adv.* —**par'ent·hood'**, *n.*

**par'ent·age** (-ij), *n.* descent from parents or ancestors; family.

**pa·ren·the·sis** (pə-ren'thə-sis), *n.* [*pl.* -SES (-sēz')], [< Gr. *para-*, beside + *entithenai*, insert], 1. a word, clause, etc. added as an explanation or comment within a sentence. 2. either or both of the curved lines ( ) used to set this off. —**par·en·thet·i·cal** (par'ən-thet'i-k'l), **par'en·thet'ic**, *adj.*

**pa·re·sis** (pə-rē'sis), *n.* [Gr. < *parienai*, relax], 1. partial paralysis. 2. a brain disease caused by syphilis of the central nervous system: also called *general paresis*.

**par·fait** (pär-fā'), *n.* [Fr., perfect], a frozen dessert of rich cream and eggs, or ice cream, fruit, etc., served in a tall, narrow glass.

**pa·ri·ah** (pə-rī'ə), *n.* [< Tamil *paraiyan*], 1. in India formerly, a member of one of the oppressed social castes. 2. any outcast.

**par·i·mu·tu·el** (par'i-mū'chōō-əl), *n.* [Fr., lit., mutual bets], a system of betting on races in which the winning bettors share the net of each pool in proportion to their wagers.

**par·ing** (pâr'iŋ), *n.* a piece pared off.

**Par·is** (par'is), *n.* in *Gr. legend*, a prince of Troy: see **Helen of Troy**.

**par·ish** (par'ish), *n.* [< Gr. *paroikia*, diocese], 1. *a*) a part of a diocese under the charge of a priest or minister. *b*) the congregation of a church. 2. a civil division in Louisiana, corresponding to a county.

**pa·rish·ion·er** (pə-rish'ən-ẽr), *n.* a member of a parish.

**par·i·ty** (par'ə-ti), *n.* [< L. *par*, equal], 1. equality in power, value, etc. 2. equality of value at a given ratio between different kinds of money, etc.

**park** (pärk), *n.* [ult. < Gmc.; cf. PADDOCK], 1. wooded land held as part of an estate or as a hunting preserve. 2. an area of public land, with playgrounds, etc., for recreation or rest. *v.t. & v.i.* 1. to leave (a vehicle) in a certain place temporarily. 2. to maneuver (a vehicle) into a space for parking.

**par·ka** (pär'kə), *n.* [Aleutian], a heavy jacket with an attached hood.

**park'way'**, *n.* a broad roadway edged or divided with plantings of trees, bushes, etc.

**parl·ance** (pär'ləns), *n.* [< OFr. *parler*, speak], 1. speech. 2. a style of speaking or writing; idiom: as, military *parlance*.

**par·lay** (pär'li, pär-lā'), *v.t. & v.i.* [< It. *paro*, a pair], to bet (an original wager plus its winnings) on another race, etc. *n.* a parlayed bet.

**par·ley** (pär′li), *v.i.* [< Fr. *parler*, speak], to confer, esp. with an enemy. *n.* [*pl.* -LEYS], a conference, as to settle a dispute.

**par·lia·ment** (pär′lə-mənt), *n.* [< OFr. *parler*, speak], 1. an official government council. 2. [P-], the national legislative body of certain countries, esp. Great Britain.

**par′lia·men·tar′i·an** (-men-târ′i-ən), *n.* one skilled in parliamentary rules or debate.

**par′lia·men′ta·ry** (-men′tə-ri), *adj.* 1. of or by a parliament. 2. conforming to the rules of a parliament.

**par·lor** (pär′lẽr), *n.* [< ML. *parlare*, speak], 1. a living room. 2. any of certain business establishments: as, a beauty *parlor*. Brit. sp., **parlour.**

**par·lous** (pär′ləs), *adj.* [Archaic], perilous.

**Par·me·san (cheese)** (pär′mə-zan′), [< *Parma*, an It. city], a hard, yellow Italian cheese, usually grated

**pa·ro·chi·al** (pə-rō′ki-əl), *adj.* [see PARISH], 1. of or in a parish or parishes. 2. narrow; provincial. —**pa·ro′chi·al·ism,** *n.*

**parochial school,** a school supported and controlled by a church.

**par·o·dy** (par′ə-di), *n.* [*pl.* -DIES], [< Gr. *parōidia*, counter song], 1. a farcical imitation of a literary or musical work. 2. a weak imitation. *v.t.* [-DIED, -DYING], to make a parody of. —**par′o·dist,** *n.*

**pa·role** (pə-rōl′), *n.* [Fr. < LL. *parabola*, word], the release of a prisoner before his sentence has expired, on condition of future good behavior. *v.t.* [-ROLED, -ROLING], to release on parole. —**on parole,** at liberty under conditions of parole.

**par·ox·ysm** (par′ək-siz′m), *n.* [< Gr. *para-*, beyond + *oxynein*, sharpen], 1. a sudden attack of a disease. 2. a sudden outburst, as of laughter. —**par′ox·ys′mal,** *adj.*

**par·quet** (pär-kā′), *n.* [Fr. < *parc*, a park], 1. the main floor of a theater: usually called *orchestra*. 2. a flooring of parquetry. *v.t.* [-QUETED (-kād′), -QUETING], to make (a floor) of parquetry.

**par·quet·ry** (pär′kit-ri), *n.* inlaid flooring in geometric forms.

**par·ri·cide** (par′ə-sīd′), *n.* [Fr. < L. *parri-*, kin + *caedere*, kill], 1. one who murders his parent or parents. 2. the act of a parricide.

**par·rot** (par′ət), *n.* [Fr. *perrot*], 1. a bird with a hooked bill and brightly colored feathers: some parrots can learn to repeat words. 2. a person who mechanically mimics others, without full understanding. *v.t.* to repeat or imitate without understanding.

**par·ry** (par′i), *v.t.* [-RIED, -RYING], [< L. *parare*, prepare], 1. to ward off, as a blow. 2. to evade, as a question. *v.i.* to make a parry. *n.* [*pl.* -RIES], a warding off or evasion.

**parse** (pärs), *v.t.* [PARSED, PARSING], [< L. *pars* (*orationis*), part (of speech)], to break (a sentence) down into its parts, explaining the grammatical form and function of each part.

**par·si·mo·ny** (pär′sə-mō′ni), *n.* [< L. *parcere*, to spare], stinginess; extreme frugality. —**par′si·mo′ni·ous,** *adj.*

**pars·ley** (pärs′li), *n.* [< Gr. *petros*, a rock + *selinon*, parsley], a plant with finely divided leaves used to flavor or garnish some foods.

**pars·nip** (pärs′nip), *n.* [< L. *pastinare*, dig up], 1. a plant with a long, thick, sweet, white root used as a vegetable. 2. the root.

**par·son** (pär′s'n), *n.* [see PERSON], 1. a minister in charge of a parish. 2. [Colloq.], any clergyman.

**par′son·age** (-ij), *n.* the dwelling provided for a parson by his church.

**part** (pärt), *n.* [< L. *pars*], 1. a portion, segment, etc. of a whole: as, *part* of a book. 2. an essential, separable element: as, an automobile *part*. 3. a portion or share; specif., *a*) duty: as, we do our *part*. *b*) *usually pl.* talent; ability: as, a man of *parts*. *c*) a role in a play. *d*) any of the voices or instruments in a musical ensemble, or the score for this. 4. *usually pl.* a region; district: as, he left these *parts*. 5. one of the sides in a conflict, etc. 6. a dividing line formed in combing the hair. *v.t.* 1. to break or divide into parts. 2. to comb (the hair) so as to leave a part. 3. to break or hold apart. *v.i.* 1. to break or divide into parts. 2. to separate and go different ways. 3. to cease associating. 4. to go away. *adj.* less than a whole. —**for one's part,** so far as one is concerned. —**for the most part,** mostly. —**in part,** partly. —**part from,** to separate from; leave. —**part with,** to give up; relinquish. —**take part,** to participate.

**par·take** (pär-tāk′), *v.i.* [-TOOK, -TAKEN, -TAKING], [< *part taker*], to eat or drink something, esp. with others. —**partake of,** to take or have a share in. —**par·tak′er,** *n.*

**par·terre** (pär-târ′), *n.* [Fr. < *par*, on + *terre*, earth], 1. an ornamental garden area. 2. the part of a theater under the balcony and behind the parquet.

**par·the·no·gen·e·sis** (pär′thə-nō-jen′ə-sis), *n.* [< Gr. *parthenos*, virgin + *genesis*, origin], reproduction by the development of an unfertilized ovum, seed, or spore, as in certain insects, algae, etc.

**Par·the·non** (pär′thə-non′), *n.* [< Gr. *parthenos*, a virgin (i.e., Athena)], the Doric temple of Athena on the Acropolis in Athens.

**par·tial** (pär′shəl), *adv.* [< L. *pars*, a part], 1. favoring one person, faction, etc. more than another; biased. 2. not complete. —**partial to,** fond of. —**par′ti·al′i·ty** (-shi-al′ə-ti), *n.* —**par′tial·ly,** *adv.*

**par·tic·i·pant** (pär-tis′ə-pənt), *n.* one who participates. *adj.* participating.

**par·tic′i·pate** (-pāt′), *v.i.* [-PATED, -PATING], [< L. *pars*, a part + *capere*, take], to have or take a share with others (*in* some activity). —**par·tic′i·pa′tion,** *n.* —**par·tic′i·pa·tor,** *n.*

**par·ti·ci·ple** (pär′tə-si-p'l), *n.* [see PARTICIPATE], a word derived from a verb and having the qualities of both verb and adjective. —**par′ti·cip′i·al** (-sip′i-əl, -sip′yəl), *adj.*

**par·ti·cle** (pär′ti-k'l), *n.* [< L. *pars*, part], 1. a tiny fragment or trace. 2. a short, indeclinable part of speech, as an article, preposition, etc.

**par·ti-col·ored** (pär′ti-kul′ẽrd), *adj.* [*parti* < Fr. *parti*, divided], 1. having different colors in different parts. 2. diversified.

**par·tic·u·lar** (pẽr-tik′yoo-lẽr), *adj.* [see PARTICLE], 1. of or belonging to a single group, person, or thing. 2. regarded separately; specific. 3. unusual. 4. exacting; hard to please. *n.* a distinct fact, item, detail, etc. —**in particular,** especially. —**par·tic′u·lar′i·ty** (-lar′ə-ti), *n.*

**par·tic′u·lar·ize′** (-īz′), *v.t.* & *v.i.* [-IZED, -IZING], to give particulars or details (of).

**par·tic′u·lar·ly,** *adv.* 1. in detail. 2. especially. 3. specifically.

**part′ing,** *adj.* 1. dividing; separating. 2. departing. 3. given, spoken, etc. at parting. *n.* 1. a breaking or separating. 2. a leave-taking. 3. a departure.

**par·ti·san** (pär′tə-z'n), *n.* [< L. *pars*, part], 1. a strong supporter of a faction, party, etc. 2. a guerrilla fighter. *adj.* of or like a partisan. Also sp. **partizan.** —**par′ti·san·ship′, par′ti·zan·ship′,** *n.*

**par·ti·tion** (pär-tish′ən), *n.* [< L. *partitio*], 1. division into parts; separation. 2. something that divides, as a wall separating rooms. *v.t.* 1. to divide into parts. 2. to divide by a partition.

**par·ti·tive** (pär′tə-tiv), *adj.* [Fr. < L. *partire*, to part], 1. making a division. 2. in *gram-*

*mar*, involving only a part of a whole. ***n.*** a partitive word (e.g., *few*, *any*).
**part′ly,** ***adv.*** not fully or completely.
**part·ner** (pärt′nẽr), ***n.*** [< ME.], 1. one who takes part in an activity with another or others; specif., one of two or more persons owning a business jointly. 2. a spouse. 3. either of two persons dancing together. 4. a player on the same side or team.
**part′ner·ship′,** ***n.*** 1. the state of being a partner. 2. the relationship of partners; joint interest.
**part of speech,** any of the classes to which the words of a language are assigned by form, function, etc., as noun, verb, etc.
**par·took** (pär-took′), pt. of **partake.**
**par·tridge** (pär′trij), ***n.*** [< Gr. *perdix*], any of several game birds, as the pheasant, quail, etc.
**part time,** a part of the customary time. **—part′-time′,** ***adj.***
**par·tu·ri·tion** (pär′choo-rish′ən), ***n.*** [< L. *parere*, to produce], childbirth.
**par·ty** (pär′ti), ***n.*** [*pl.* -TIES], [< L. *pars*, part], 1. a group of people working to promote a political platform or slate, a cause, etc. 2. a group acting together to accomplish a task. 3. a group assembled for social entertainment. 4. one concerned in an action, plan, lawsuit, etc.: as, he is a *party* to the affair. 5. [Colloq.], a person.
**party line,** a single circuit connecting two or more telephone users with the exchange.
**par·ve·nu** (pär′və-nōō′, -nū′), ***n.*** [*pl.* -NUS], [Fr. < L. *parvenire*, arrive], a newly rich person who is considered an upstart.
**pas·chal** (pas′k'l), ***adj.*** [< Heb. *pesah*, the Passover], of or connected with the Passover or with Easter.
**pa·sha** (pə-shä′, pash′ə), ***n.*** [< Turk. *bāshā*], a former Turkish title of rank or honor placed after the name.
**pass** (pas, päs), ***v.i.*** [< L. *passus*, a step], 1. to go; proceed. 2. to go from one place to another. 3. to go or be conveyed from one form, condition, owner, etc. to another. 4. *a*) to cease. *b*) to depart. 5. to die: usually with *away*. 6. to go by. 7. to elapse: as, an hour *passed*. 8. to make a way (*through* or *by*). 9. to be accepted without question. 10. to be approved, as by a legislative body. 11. to go through a test, course, etc. successfully. 12. to give a judgment, sentence, etc. 13. in *card games*, to decline a chance to bid. ***v.t.*** 1. to go by, behind, over, or through; specif., *a*) to leave beyond. *b*) to go through (a test, course, etc.) successfully. 2. to cause or allow to go, move, proceed, advance, qualify, etc. 3. to ratify; enact. 4. to spend (time). 5. to excrete. 6. to cause to move from place to place; circulate. 7. to give as an opinion or judgment. ***n.*** 1. an act of passing; passage. 2. a state; situation: as, a strange *pass*. 3. *a*) a ticket, etc. giving permission to come or go freely or without charge. *b*) a brief leave of absence given to a soldier. 4. a motion of the hand. 5. a narrow passage, etc., esp. between mountains. 6. [Slang], an overfamiliar attempt to embrace or kiss. 7. in *sports*, a transfer of a ball, etc. to another player during play. **—a pretty pass,** [Colloq.], a difficult situation. **—come** (or **bring**) **to pass,** to (cause to) happen. **—pass out,** [Slang], to faint. **—pass over,** to disregard; ignore. **—pass up,** [Slang], to refuse or let go. **—pass′er,** ***n.***
**pass.,** 1. passenger. 2. passive.
**pass′a·ble,** ***adj.*** 1. that can be passed, traveled over, etc. 2. moderate; adequate.
**pas·sage** (pas′ij), ***n.*** 1. a passing; specif., *a*) migration. *b*) transition. *c*) the enactment of a law. 2. permission or right to pass. 3. a voyage. 4. a way or means of passing; road, opening, passageway, etc. 5. interchange, as of blows. 6. a portion of something written, composed, etc.
**pas′sage·way′,** ***n.*** a narrow way for passage, as a hall, alley, etc.; passage.
**pass′book′,** ***n.*** a bankbook.
**pas·sé** (pa-sā′), ***adj.*** [Fr.], past; out-of-date.
**pas·sen·ger** (pas′'n-jẽr), ***n.*** [< OFr. *passage*, passage], a traveler in a train, boat, etc.
**pass′er-by′,** ***n.*** [*pl.* PASSERS-BY], one who passes by.
**pass′ing,** ***adj.*** 1. going by, beyond, etc. 2. fleeting. 3. casual: as, a *passing* remark. 4. allowing one to pass a test, etc.: as, a *passing* grade. 5. current. ***n.*** the act of one that passes. **—in passing,** incidentally.
**pas·sion** (pash′ən), ***n.*** [< L. *pati*, suffer], 1. [P-], the sufferings of Jesus on the cross or after the Last Supper. 2. any emotion, as hate, love, etc. 3. intense emotional excitement, as rage, enthusiasm, lust, etc. 4. the object of any strong desire.
**pas′sion·ate** (-it), ***adj.*** 1. having or showing strong emotions. 2. hot-tempered. 3. intense; ardent. 4. lustful. **—pas′sion·ate·ly,** ***adv.***
**pas·sive** (pas′iv), ***adj.*** [see PASSION], 1. not active, but acted upon. 2. offering no resistance; submissive. 3. in *grammar*, indicating the voice of a verb whose subject receives the action. ***n.*** the passive voice. **—pas′sive·ly,** ***adv.*** **—pas′sive·ness, pas·siv′i·ty,** ***n.***
**passive resistance,** opposition to a law, etc. by refusal to comply or by nonviolent acts, as fasting.
**Pass·o·ver** (pas′ō′vẽr, päs′-), ***n.*** a Jewish holiday commemorating the deliverance of the ancient Hebrews from slavery in Egypt.
**pass′port′,** ***n.*** a government document carried by a citizen traveling abroad, certifying identity and citizenship.
**pass′word′,** ***n.*** a secret word or phrase used by members of a group to identify themselves, as in passing a guard.
**past** (past, päst), ***adj.*** [rare pp. of *pass*], 1. gone by; ended. 2. of a former time. 3. immediately preceding: as, the *past* week. 4. in *grammar*, indicating time gone by: as, *past* tense. ***n.*** 1. the history of a person, group, etc. 2. a personal background that is hidden or questionable. ***prep.*** beyond in time, space, etc. ***adv.*** to and beyond.
**pas·ta** (päs′tə), ***n.*** [It.], 1. the flour paste of which spaghetti, ravioli, etc. is made. 2. any food made of this paste.
**paste** (pāst), ***n.*** [< Gr. *pastē*, porridge], 1. dough used in making rich pastry. 2. any soft, moist, smooth preparation: as, tooth *paste*, almond *paste*. 3. a mixture of flour or starch, water, etc. used as an adhesive. 4. a hard, brilliant glass used for artificial gems. ***v.t.*** [PASTED, PASTING], 1. to make adhere, as with paste. 2. [Slang], to hit.
**paste′board′,** ***n.*** a stiff material made of layers of paper pasted together.
**pas·tel** (pas-tel′), ***n.*** [< LL. *pasta*, paste], 1. a crayon of ground coloring matter. 2. a picture drawn with such crayons. 3. a soft, pale shade. **—pas′tel·ist, pas′tel·list,** ***n.***
**pas·tern** (pas′tẽrn), ***n.*** [< L. *pastor*, shepherd], the part of a horse's foot, between the fetlock and the hoof.
**pas·teur·ize** (pas′tẽr-īz′, -chẽr-), ***v.t.*** [-IZED, -IZING], [< L. *Pasteur*, 19th-c. Fr. bacteriologist], to destroy bacteria in (milk, etc.) by heating to 142°–145° for 30 minutes. **—pas′teur·i·za′tion,** ***n.***
**pas·tiche** (pas-tēsh′), ***n.*** [Fr.], 1. an artistic composition drawn from various sources. 2. a jumbled mixture; hodgepodge.
**pas·time** (pas′tīm′, päs′-), ***n.*** a way of spending spare time; diversion.
**pas·tor** (pas′tẽr, päs′-), ***n.*** [L., a shepherd], a clergyman in charge of a congregation.
**pas′to·ral,** ***adj.*** 1. of a pastor or his duties. 2. of shepherds. 3. of rustic life. 4. peace-

ful; simple. *n.* a poem, play, etc. with a rustic setting.

**pas'tor·ate** (-it), *n.* the position, duties, or term of office of a pastor.

**past participle,** a participle used to indicate a past time or state (e.g., *grown* in "it has grown well").

**pas·try** (pās'tri), *n.* [*pl.* -TRIES], [< *paste*], 1. pies, tarts, etc. with crusts baked from flour dough made with shortening. 2. all fancy baked goods.

**pas·tur·age** (pas'chēr-ij, päs'-), *n.* pasture.

**pas·ture** (pas'chēr, päs'-), *n.* [< L. *pascere*, to feed], 1. grass, etc. used as food by grazing animals. 2. ground suitable for grazing. *v.t.* [-TURED, -TURING], to put (cattle, etc.) out to graze in a pasture. *v.i.* to graze.

**past·y** (pās'ti), *adj.* [-IER, -IEST], of or like paste in color or texture. **—past'i·ness,** *n.*

**pat** (pat), *n.* [prob. echoic], 1. a gentle tap or stroke with a flat surface. 2. a sound made by this. 3. a small lump, as of butter. *v.t.* [PATTED, PATTING], to tap or stroke gently with the hand or a flat surface. *adj.* 1. apt; timely. 2. exactly suitable: as, a *pat* hand in poker. **—stand pat,** [Colloq.], to refuse to change an opinion, etc.

**pat.,** 1. patent. 2. patented.

**patch** (pach), *n.* [ME. *pacche*], 1. a piece of material applied to mend a hole, strengthen a weak spot, etc. 2. a dressing for a wound. 3. an area or spot: as, *patches* of blue sky. 4. a small plot of ground. 5. a scrap; bit. *v.t.* 1. to put a patch on. 2. to produce crudely or hurriedly (often with *up*). **—patch up,** to settle, as a quarrel. **—patch'y** [-IER, -IEST], *adj.*

**patch'work',** *n.* needlework, as a quilt, made of odd patches of cloth.

**pate** (pāt), *n.* [? < L. *patina*, pan], the top of the head: humorous use.

**pa·tel·la** (pə-tel'ə), *n.* [*pl.* -LAS, -LAE (-ē)], [L., plate], the kneecap. **—pa·tel'lar,** *adj.*

**pat·ent** (pat''nt; *also, for adj.* 1 & 2, pā't'nt), *adj.* [< L. *patere*, be open], 1. open to all. 2. obvious; plain. 3. protected by a patent. *n.* 1. a document granting the exclusive right to produce, use, or sell an invention, etc. for a certain time. 2. *a*) the right so granted. *b*) the thing protected by such a right. *v.t.* to secure a patent for. **—pat'ent·ee',** *n.*

**patent leather,** leather having a hard, glossy finish: formerly patented.

**patent medicine,** a trademarked medical preparation.

**pa·ter·nal** (pə-tũr'n'l), *adj.* [< L. *pater*, father], 1. fatherly. 2. inherited from a father. 3. on the father's side of the family.

**pa·ter'nal·ism,** *n.* the governing of subjects, employees, etc. in a manner suggesting a father's relationship with his children. **—pa·ter'nal·is'tic,** *adj.*

**pa·ter'ni·ty** (-nə-ti), *n.* 1. the state of being a father. 2. male parentage.

**pa·ter·nos·ter** (pā'tēr-nos'tēr), *n.* [L., our father], the Lord's Prayer, esp. in Latin: often **Pater Noster.**

**path** (path, päth), *n.* [AS. *pæth*], 1. a way worn by footsteps. 2. a walk for the use of people on foot. 3. a line of movement. 4. a course of conduct. **—path'less,** *adj.*

**pa·thet·ic** (pə-thet'ik), *adj.* [< Gr. *pathos*, suffering], arousing pity, sorrow, sympathy, etc.; pitiful. **—pa·thet'i·cal·ly,** *adv.*

**-pathic,** an adjective suffix corresponding to the noun suffix *-pathy.*

**path·o·gen·ic** (path'ə-jen'ik), *adj.* causing disease: also **path'o·ge·net'ic** (-jə-net'ik).

**pa·thol·o·gy** (pə-thol'ə-ji), *n.* [< Gr. *pathos*, suffering; + *-logy*], the branch of medicine that deals with the nature, course, etc. of disease. **—path·o·log·i·cal** (path'ə-loj'i-k'l), *adj.* **—pa·thol'o·gist,** *n.*

**pa·thos** (pā'thos), *n.* [Gr., suffering], the quality in something which arouses pity, sorrow, sympathy, etc.

**path'way',** *n.* a path.

**-pathy,** [< Gr. *pathos*, suffering], a suffix meaning *feeling* or *disease*, as in *antipathy, osteopathy.*

**pa·tience** (pā'shəns), *n.* a being patient; calm endurance, perseverance, etc.

**pa'tient** (-shənt), *adj.* [< L. *pati*, suffer], 1. enduring pain, trouble, insult, etc. without complaining. 2. calmly tolerating delay, confusion, etc. 3. diligent; persevering. *n.* one who is receiving medical care.

**pat·i·na** (pat''n-ə), *n.* [< It.], a fine greenish crust on bronze or copper, formed by oxidation.

**pa·ti·o** (pā'ti-ō', pa'-), *n.* [*pl.* -OS], [Sp.], 1. a courtyard open to the sky. 2. a terrace (sense 2).

**pat·ois** (pat'wä), *n.* [*pl.* -OIS (-wäz)], [Fr.], a nonstandard form of a language, as a provincial dialect.

**pat. pend.,** patent pending.

**patri-,** [< Gr. *patēr*], a combining form meaning *father.*

**pa·tri·arch** (pā'tri-ärk'), *n.* [< Gr. *patēr*, father + *archein*, rule], 1. the father and ruler of a family or tribe. 2. one regarded as a founder, as of a religion. 3. a man of great age and dignity. **—pa'tri·ar'chal,** *adj.*

**pa'tri·arch'y,** *n.* [*pl.* -IES], a form of social organization in which descent is traced through the father as head of the family.

**pa·tri·cian** (pə-trish'ən), *adj.* [< L. *pater*, father], of or like patricians; noble; aristocratic. *n.* an aristocrat.

**pat·ri·mo·ny** (pat'rə-mō'ni), *n.* [*pl.* -NIES], [< L. *pater*, father], property inherited from one's father or ancestors. **—pat'ri·mo'ni·al,** *adj.*

**pa·tri·ot** (pā'tri-ət), *n.* [< Gr. *patris*, fatherland], one who loves and zealously supports his country. **—pa'tri·ot'ic** (-ot'ik), *adj.* **—pa'tri·ot'i·cal·ly,** *adv.* **—pa'tri·ot·ism,** *n.*

**pa·trol** (pə-trōl'), *v.t.* & *v.i.* [-TROLLED, -TROLLING], [< Fr. *patouiller*, to paddle], to make a regular, repeated circuit of in guarding. *n.* 1. a patrolling. 2. a person or group patrolling. 3. a group of ships, airplanes, etc. used in patrolling.

**pa·trol'man** (-mən), *n.* [*pl.* -MEN], a policeman who patrols a certain area.

**pa·tron** (pā'trən), *n.* [< L. *pater*, father], 1. a protector; benefactor. 2. one who sponsors and supports some person, activity, etc. 3. a regular customer. **—pa'tron·al,** *adj.* **—pa'tron·ess,** *n.fem.*

**pa·tron·age** (pā'trən-ij, pat'rən-), *n.* 1. support, favor, etc. given by a patron. 2. *a*) customers. *b*) trade; business. 3. *a*) the power to grant political favors. *b*) such favors. 4. condescension.

**pa·tron·ize** (pā'trə-nīz', pat'rə-), *v.t.* [-IZED, -IZING], 1. to sponsor; support. 2. to show favor to in a condescending manner. 3. to be a regular customer of (a store, etc.).

**patron saint,** a saint looked upon as a special guardian.

**pat·ro·nym·ic** (pat'rə-nim'ik), *n.* [< Gr. *pater*, father + *onoma*, a name], a name showing descent from a given person (e.g., *Johnson*, son of John).

**pat·ter** (pat'ēr), *v.i.* & *v.t.* [< *pat*], to make or cause to make a patter. *n.* a series of light, rapid taps.

**pat·ter** (pat'ēr), *v.t.* & *v.i.* [< *paternoster*], to speak rapidly or glibly. *n.* glib, rapid speech, as of salesmen. **—pat'ter·er,** *n.*

**pat·tern** (pat'ērn), *n.* [< OFr. *patron*], 1. a person or thing worthy of imitation. 2. a model, plan, etc. used in making things. 3. a design or decoration. 4. definite tendency or characteristics. *v.t.* to make or do in imitation of a pattern (with *on* or *after*).

**pat·ty** (pat′i), *n.* [*pl.* -TIES], [Fr. *pâté*, pie], 1. a small pie. 2. a small, flat cake of ground meat, fish, etc., usually fried.

**pau·ci·ty** (pô′sə-ti), *n.* [< L. *paucus*, few], 1. fewness. 2. scarcity.

**Paul Bun·yan** (bun′yən), in *American legend*, a giant lumberjack who performed superhuman feats.

**paunch** (pônch), *n.* [< L. *pantex*, belly], the abdomen, or belly; esp., a potbelly. —**paunch′y**, *adj.* —**paunch′i·ness**, *n.*

**pau·per** (pô′pẽr), *n.* [L.], an extremely poor person, esp. one who lives on charity. —**pau′per·ism**, *n.* —**pau′per·ize′** [-IZED, -IZING], *v.t.* —**pau′per·i·za′tion**, *n.*

**pause** (pôz), *n.* [< Gr. *pauein*, to stop], 1. a temporary stop or rest. 2. in *music*, a sign (◡ or ⌒) placed below or above a note or rest that is to be prolonged. *v.i.* [PAUSED, PAUSING], to make a pause; stop; hesitate.

**pave** (pāv), *v.t.* [PAVED, PAVING], [< L. *pavire*, beat], to cover the surface of (a road, etc.) as with concrete or asphalt. —**pave the way (for)**, to prepare the way (for).

**pave′ment**, *n.* 1. a paved surface, as of concrete. 2. a paved street or road. 3. the material used in paving.

**pa·vil·ion** (pə-vil′yən), *n.* [<L. *papilio*, tent], 1. a large tent. 2. a building, often open-air, for exhibits, etc., as at a fair or park. 3. any of a group of related buildings.

**pav·ing** (pāv′iŋ), *n.* 1. a pavement. 2. material for a pavement.

**paw** (pô), *n.* [< OFr. *poue*], 1. the foot of a four-footed animal having claws. 2. [Colloq.], a hand. *v.t. & v.i.* 1. to touch, dig, strike, etc. with paws or feet. 2. to handle clumsily or roughly.

**pawl** (pôl), *n.* [? < D. *pal*], a device, as a hinged tongue which engages cogs in a wheel, allowing rotation in only one direction.

**pawn** (pôn), *n.* [< OFr. *pan*], 1. anything given as security, as for a debt. 2. the state of being pledged. *v.t.* 1. to give as security. 2. to wager or risk. —**pawn′er**, *n.*

**pawn** (pôn), *n.* [< LL. *pedo*, foot soldier], 1. a chessman of the lowest value. 2. a person subject to another's will.

**pawn′bro′ker**, *n.* a person licensed to lend money at interest on personal property left with him as security.

**pawn′shop′**, *n.* a pawnbroker's shop.

**pay** (pā), *v.t.* [PAID, PAYING], [< L. *pacare*, pacify], 1. to give to (a person) what is due, as for goods or services. 2. to give (what is due) in return, as for goods or services. 3. to settle (a debt, etc.). 4. to give (one's respects, etc.). 5. to make (a visit, etc.). 6. to be profitable to. *v.i.* 1. to give due compensation. 2. to be profitable. *n.* 1. a paying or being paid. 2. compensation; esp., wages or salary. *adj.* operated by inserting money: as, a *pay* telephone. —**in the pay of**, employed and paid by. —**pay off**, to pay all that is owed. —**pay out**, [pt., PAYED OUT], to let out (a rope, cable, etc.). —**pay up**, to pay in full or on time.

**pay′a·ble**, *adj.* 1. that can be paid. 2. due to be paid (on a specified date).

**pay dirt**, soil, ore, etc. rich enough in minerals to make mining profitable.

**pay·ee** (pā-ē′), *n.* one to whom a check, note, money, etc. is payable.

**pay′load′**, *n.* 1. a cargo. 2. the warhead of a ballistic missile, the instruments of an artificial satellite, etc., along with the compartment containing these.

**pay′mas′ter**, *n.* the official in charge of paying wages to employees.

**pay′ment**, *n.* 1. a paying or being paid. 2. something paid. 3. penalty or reward.

**pay′-off′**, *n.* [Colloq.], 1. settlement or reckoning. 2. an unexpected climax.

**pay·o·la** (pā-ō′lə), *n.* [Slang], 1. the practice of paying bribes for commercial advantage, as to a disk jockey for promoting a song unfairly. 2. such a bribe.

**pay roll**, 1. a list of employees to be paid, with the amount due to each. 2. the total amount needed for this.

**Pb**, *plumbum*, [L.], in *chem.*, lead.

**p.c., pct.**, per cent.

**Pd**, in *chem.*, palladium.

**pd.**, paid.

**pea** (pē), *n.* [*pl.* PEAS, or *archaic* PEASE], [< ME. *pese* (later misunderstood as pl.)], 1. a climbing plant with green seed pods. 2. its small, round seed, eaten as a vegetable.

**peace** (pēs), *n.* [< L. *pax*], 1. freedom from war or civil strife. 2. an agreement to end war. 3. law and order. 4. harmony. 5. serenity; calm; quiet. —**hold** (or **keep**) **one's peace**, to be silent. —**peace′a·ble**, *adj.*

**peace′ful**, *adj.* 1. not quarrelsome. 2. free from disturbance; calm. 3. of or characteristic of a time of peace. —**peace′ful·ly**, *adv.*

**peace′mak′er**, *n.* one who makes peace, as by settling the quarrels of others.

**peace′time′**, *n.* a time of peace. *adj.* of or characteristic of such a time.

**peach** (pēch), *n.* [< L. *Persicum* (*malum*), Persian (apple)], 1. a tree with round, juicy, orange-yellow fruit having a fuzzy skin and a rough pit. 2. its fruit. 3. the color of this fruit. 4. [Slang], any person or thing well-liked.

**pea·cock** (pē′kok′), *n.* [AS. *pawa*, peafowl + *cok*, a cock], any of a number of related large birds (technically, **pea′fowl′**), esp. the male with a long, showy tail which can be spread out like a fan. —**pea′hen′**, *n.fem.*

**pea jacket**, [prob. < D. *pij*, warm jacket], a short, heavy woolen coat worn by sailors.

**peak** (pēk), *n.* [var. of *pike* (summit)], 1. a pointed end or top, as of a cap, roof, etc. 2. the summit of a hill or mountain ending in a point. 3. a mountain with such a summit. 4. the highest point of anything.

**peak·ed** (pēk′id), *adj.* thin and drawn, as from illness.

**peal** (pēl), *n.* [< ME. *apele*, appeal], 1. the loud ringing of a bell or bells. 2. a set of bells. 3. a loud, prolonged sound, as of gunfire, laughter, etc. *v.t. & v.i.* to ring or resound.

**pea′nut′**, *n.* 1. a vine of the pea family, with underground pods containing edible seeds. 2. the pod or its seeds.

**peanut butter**, a paste or spread made by grinding roasted peanuts.

**pear** (pâr), *n.* [< L. *pirum*], 1. a tree bearing greenish-yellow fruit. 2. the soft, juicy fruit, round at the base and narrowing toward the stem.

**pearl** (pũrl), *n.* [< ML. *perla*], 1. a smooth, hard, usually white or bluish-gray, roundish growth, formed within the shell of some oysters and other mollusks: it is used as a gem. 2. mother-of-pearl. 3. anything pearl-like in shape, value, beauty, etc. 4. a bluish gray. *adj.* like a pearl in shape or color. —**pearl′y** [-IER, -IEST], *adj.*

**peas·ant** (pez′'nt), *n.* [< LL. *pagus*, district], in Europe, a farmer.

**peat** (pēt), *n.* [< ML. *peta*, a turf], partly decayed plant matter found in ancient swamps, dried and used as fuel.

**peb·ble** (peb′'l), *n.* [AS. *papol*(*stan*), pebble (stone)], a small stone worn smooth and round, as by running water. —**peb′bly**, *adj.*

**pe·can** (pi-kan′, -kän′), *n.* [< Am. Ind. name], 1. an edible nut with a thin, smooth shell. 2. the tree it grows on.

**pec·ca·dil·lo** (pek′ə-dil′ō), *n.* [*pl.* -LOES, -LOS], [Sp. < L. *peccare*, to sin], a minor or petty sin.

**pec·ca·ry** (pek′ə-ri), *n.* [*pl.* -RIES], [< S. Am.

native name], a piglike wild animal of tropical America, with sharp tusks.

**peck** (pek), *v.t.* [< ME. *pikken*, to pick], 1. to strike as with a beak. 2. to make by doing this: as, *peck* a hole. 3. to pick up or get by pecking. *v.i.* to make strokes as with a beak. *n.* 1. a stroke made as with a beak. 2. [Colloq.], a quick, casual kiss. —**peck at**, [Colloq.], to eat very little of.

**peck** (pek), *n.* [ME. *pekke*], 1. a unit of dry measure equal to ¼ bushel, or 8 quarts. 2. [Colloq.], a large amount, as of trouble.

**pec·tin** (pek′tin), *n.* [< Gr. *pēktos*, congealed], a carbohydrate obtained from certain fruits, which yields a gel that is the basis of fruit jellies.

**pec·to·ral** (pek′tə-rəl), *adj.* [< L. *pectus*, breast], of or located in or on the breast or chest. *n.* a pectoral muscle.

**pec·u·late** (pek′yoo-lāt′), *v.t. & v.i.* [-LATED, -LATING], [< L. *peculari*], to embezzle.

**pe·cul·iar** (pi-kūl′yẽr), *adj.* [< L. *peculium*, private property], 1. of only one person, thing, etc.; exclusive. 2. particular; special. 3. odd; strange. —**pe·cul′iar·ly**, *adv.*

**pe·cu·li·ar·i·ty** (pi-kū′li-ar′ə-ti), *n.* 1. a being peculiar. 2. [*pl.* -TIES], something that is peculiar, as a trait.

**pe·cu·ni·ar·y** (pi-kū′ni-er′i), *adj.* [< L. *pecunia*, money], 1. of or involving money. 2. involving a money penalty.

**ped·a·gogue** (ped′ə-gog′, -gôg′), *n.* [< Gr. *pais*, child + *agein*, to lead], a teacher; esp., a pedantic teacher: also **ped′a·gog′**.

**ped′a·go′gy** (-gō′ji, -goj′i), *n.* the art or science of teaching. —**ped′a·gog′ic** (-goj′ik), **ped′a·gog′i·cal**, *adj.*

**ped·al** (ped′′l), *adj.* [< L. *pes*, foot], of the foot or feet. *n.* a lever operated by the foot, as on a bicycle, organ, etc. *v.t. & v.i.* [-DALED or -DALLED, -DALING or -DALLING], to operate by pedals; use the pedals (of).

**ped·ant** (ped′′nt), *n.* [ult. prob. < L. *paedagogare*, educate], 1. one who emphasizes trivial points of learning. 2. a narrow-minded teacher who insists on exact adherence to rules. —**pe·dan·tic** (pi-dan′tik), *adj.* —**pe·dan′ti·cal·ly**, *adv.* —**ped′ant·ry**, *n.*

**ped·dle** (ped′′l), *v.i. & v.t.* [-DLED, -DLING], [< *peddler*, ult. < ME. *ped*, basket], to go from place to place selling (small articles). —**ped′dler**, **ped′lar**, *n.*

**-pede**, [< L. *pes*, foot], a combining form meaning *foot* or *feet*, as in *centipede*.

**ped·es·tal** (ped′is-t′l), *n.* [< It. *piè*, foot + *di*, of + *stal*, a rest], a bottom support or base, as of a column, statue, etc.

**pe·des·tri·an** (pə-des′tri-ən), *adj.* [< L. *pes*, foot], 1. going or done on foot. 2. lacking imagination; dull. *n.* one who goes on foot; walker. —**pe·des′tri·an·ism**, *n.*

**pe·di·at·rics** (pē′di-at′riks), *n.pl.* [construed as sing.], [< Gr. *pais*, child + *iatros*, physician], the branch of medicine dealing with the care of infants and children. —**pe′di·at′ric**, *adj.* —**pe′di·a·tri′cian** (-ə-trish′ən), *n.*

**ped·i·cure** (ped′i-kyoor′), *n.* [< L. *pes*, foot + *cura*, care], a trimming, cleaning, etc. of the toenails.

**ped·i·gree** (ped′ə-grē′), *n.* [< OFr. *piè de grue*, crane's foot], 1. a list of ancestors. 2. descent; lineage. 3. a known line of descent, as of a purebred animal. —**ped′i·greed′**, *adj.*

**ped·i·ment** (ped′ə-mənt), *n.* [< *periment* (alt. < *pyramid*)], a decorative gable or triangular piece on the front of a building, over a doorway, etc.

**pe·dom·e·ter** (pi-dom′ə-tẽr), *n.* [< L. *pes*, foot + Gr. *metron*, a measure], an instrument which measures the distance covered in walking.

**peek** (pēk), *v.i.* [prob. < ME. *kiken*, to peer], to glance or peer quickly and furtively. *n.* a glance or look.

**peel** (pēl), *v.t.* [< L. *pilare*, make bald], to cut away (the skin, rind, etc.) of. *v.i.* 1. to shed skin, etc. 2. to come off, as sunburned skin. *n.* the rind or skin of fruit. —**keep one's eyes peeled**, [Colloq.], to keep on the watch. —**peel′er**, *n.*

**peel′ing**, *n.* a rind, etc. peeled off.

**peep** (pēp), *v.i.* [prob. echoic], to make the short, high-pitched cry of a young bird. *n.* a peeping sound. —**peep′er**, *n.*

**peep** (pēp), *v.i.* [ME. *pepen*], 1. to look through a small opening or from a place of hiding. 2. to show gradually or partially. *n.* a brief look; furtive glimpse. —**peep′er**, *n.*

**peep′hole′**, *n.* a hole to peep through.

**peeping Tom**, [after the legendary English tailor who peeped at Lady Godiva], one who gets sexual pleasure from furtively watching others.

**peer** (pêr), *n.* [< L. *par*, equal], 1. a person or thing of the same rank, ability, etc.; equal. 2. a British duke, earl, etc. —**peer′ess**, *n.fem.* —**peer′age** (-ij), *n.*

**peer** (pêr), *v.i.* [prob. < *appear*], 1. to look closely, as in trying to see more clearly. 2. to show slightly. 3. [Poetic], to appear.

**peer′less**, *adj.* without equal.

**peeve** (pēv), *v.t. & v.i.* [PEEVED, PEEVING], [Colloq.], to make or become peevish. *n.* [Colloq.], an object of dislike; annoyance.

**pee′vish**, *adj.* [< ?], irritable; fretful; cross.

**pee·wee** (pē′wē′), *n.* [prob. < Am. Ind. *pewe*, little], [Colloq.], an unusually small person or thing.

**peg** (peg), *n.* [ME. *pegge*], 1. a short pin or bolt used to hold parts together, hang things on, mark the score in a game, etc. 2. a step or degree. *v.t.* [PEGGED, PEGGING], to fasten, fix, secure, mark, etc. as with pegs. *v.i.* to work, progress, etc. steadily (with *away*).

**Peg·a·sus** (peg′ə-səs), *n.* in *Gr. myth.*, a winged horse.

**pe·jo·ra·tion** (pē′jə-rā′shən, pej′ə-), *n.* [< L. *pejor*, worse], a worsening. —**pe′jo·ra′tive**, *adj. & n.*

**Pe·king·ese** (pē′kə-nēz′), *n.* [*pl.* -ESE], a small dog with long, silky hair, short legs, and a pug nose: also sp. **Pekinese**.

**pe·koe** (pē′kō), *n.* [< Chin. *pek-ho*, white down (on the young leaves used)], a black, small-leaved tea of Ceylon and India.

**pe·lag·ic** (pə-laj′ik), *adj.* [< Gr. *pelagos*, sea], of the open sea or ocean.

**pelf** (pelf), *n.* [ult. < OFr. *pelfre*, plunder], 1. [Rare], booty. 2. mere wealth: a term of contempt.

**pel·i·can** (pel′i-kən), *n.* [< Gr. *pelekan*], a large, web-footed water bird with an expandable pouch in the lower bill for scooping up fish.

**pel·la·gra** (pə-lā′grə, -lag′rə), *n.* [It. < *pelle*, skin + *agra*, hard], a chronic disease caused by lack of nicotinic acid in the diet and characterized by skin eruptions and nervous disorders. —**pel·la′grous**, *adj.*

**pel·let** (pel′it), *n.* [< L. *pila*, a ball], 1. a little ball, as of clay, medicine, etc. 2. a bullet, small lead shot, etc.

**pell-mell, pell·mell** (pel′mel′), *adv.* [ult. < OFr. *mesler*, to mix], 1. in a jumbled mass. 2. in reckless haste. *adj.* confused.

**pel·lu·cid** (pə-lōō′sid), *adj.* [< L. *per*, intens. + *lucidus*, bright], 1. transparent; clear. 2. clear and simple: as, a *pellucid* style.

**pelt** (pelt), *v.t.* [prob. ult. < L. *pillare*, to drive], 1. to throw things at. 2. to beat repeatedly. 3. to throw (missiles). *v.i.* to strike heavily or steadily, as rain.

**pelt** (pelt), *n.* [prob. < OFr. *pel*, a skin], 1. the skin of a fur-bearing animal, esp. when prepared for tanning.

**pel·vis** (pel′vis), *n.* [*pl.* -VES (-vēz)], [L., a basin], 1. the basinlike cavity in the posterior part of the trunk in man and many other vertebrates. 2. the bones forming this cavity: also **pelvic arch.** —**pel′vic,** *adj.*

**pem·mi·can, pem·i·can** (pem′i-kən), *n.* [< Am. Ind. *pemikkân*, fat meat], a concentrate of dried beef, suet, raisins, etc.

**pen** (pen), *n.* [< AS. *penn*], 1. a small enclosure for domestic animals. 2. any small enclosure. *v.t.* [PENNED or PENT, PENNING], to enclose as in a pen.

**pen** (pen), *n.* [< L. *penna*, feather], 1. a device used in writing or drawing with ink, often with a metal point split into two nibs. 2. the metal point. *v.t.* [PENNED, PENNING], to write as with a pen.

**pen** (pen), *n.* [Slang], a penitentiary.

**pe·nal** (pē′n'l), *adj.* [< L. *poena*, punishment], of, for, constituting, or deserving punishment. —**pe′nal·ly,** *adv.*

**pe·nal·ize** (pē′n'l-īz′, pen′'l-), *v.t.* [-IZED, -IZING], to impose a penalty on; punish.

**pen·al·ty** (pen′'l-ti), *n.* [*pl.* -TIES], 1. a punishment. 2. the handicap, etc. imposed on an offender, as a fine.

**pen·ance** (pen′əns), *n.* [see PENITENT], voluntary suffering or punishment to show repentance for wrongdoing.

**pence** (pens), *n.* [Brit.], pl. of **penny.**

**pen·chant** (pen′chənt; Fr. pän′shän′), *n.* [Fr. < L. *pendere*, hang], a strong liking.

**pen·cil** (pen′s'l), *n.* [< L. *penis*, tail], a pointed, rod-shaped instrument with a core of graphite or crayon, used for writing, drawing, etc. *v.t.* [-CILED or -CILLED, -CILING or -CILLING], to write, draw, etc. as with a pencil.

**pend** (pend), *v.i.* [< L. *pendere*, hang], to await judgment or decision.

**pend·ant** (pen′dənt), *n.* [< L. *pendere*, hang], 1. a hanging object, as an earring, used as an ornament. 2. a decorative piece suspended from a ceiling or roof.

**pend·ent** (pen′dənt), *adj.* [< L. *pendere*, hang], 1. suspended. 2. overhanging. 3. undecided; pending.

**pend′ing,** *adj.* 1. not decided. 2. impending. *prep.* 1. during. 2. while awaiting; until.

**pen·du·lous** (pen′joo-ləs), *adj.* [< L. *pendere*, hang], 1. hanging freely. 2. swinging.

**pen·du·lum** (pen′joo-ləm), *n.* [*pl.* -LUMS], [< L. *pendere*, hang], a body hung so that it can swing freely to and fro: used to regulate clock movements.

**Pe·nel·o·pe** (pə-nel′ə-pi), *n.* the faithful wife of Odysseus.

**pen·e·trate** (pen′ə-trāt′), *v.t. & v.i.* [-TRATED, -TRATING], [< L. *penitus*, inward], 1. to enter by piercing. 2. to have an effect throughout. 3. to affect deeply. 4. to understand. —**pen′e·tra′tion,** *n.*

**pen′e·trat′ing,** *adj.* 1. sharp; piercing. 2. acute; discerning. Also **pen′e·tra′tive.**

**pen·guin** (peŋ′gwin, pen′-), *n.* [cf. W. *pen*, head + *gwyn*, white], a flightless bird of the S Hemisphere with webbed feet and paddle-like flippers for swimming.

**pen·i·cil·lin** (pen′ə-sil′in), *n.* [< L. *penicillus*, brush], a powerful antibiotic obtained from fungi growing as green mold on stale bread, decaying fruit, etc.

**pen·in·su·la** (pə-nin′sə-lə, -syoo-lə), *n.* [< L. *paene*, almost + *insula*, isle], a land area almost entirely surrounded by water. —**pen·in′su·lar,** *adj.*

**pe·nis** (pē′nis), *n.* [*pl.* -NES (-nēz), -NISES], [L., orig., tail], the male organ of sexual intercourse.

**pen·i·tent** (pen′ə-tənt), *adj.* [< L. *paenitere*, repent], sorry for having done wrong and willing to atone. *n.* a penitent person. —**pen′i·tence,** *n.* —**pen′i·ten′tial** (-ten′shəl), *adj.* —**pen′i·tent·ly,** *adv.*

**pen·i·ten·tia·ry** (pən′ə-ten′shə-ri), *adj.* that makes one liable to imprisonment in a penitentiary. *n.* [*pl.* -RIES], a State or Federal prison for persons convicted of serious crimes.

**pen′knife′** (-nīf′), *n.* [*pl.* -KNIVES (-nīvz′)], a small pocketknife.

**pen′man** (-mən), *n.* [*pl.* -MEN], 1. one skilled in penmanship. 2. an author; writer.

**pen′man·ship′** (-ship′), *n.* 1. handwriting as an art or skill. 2. a style of handwriting.

**pen name,** a pseudonym.

**pen·nant** (pen′ənt), *n.* [< *pennon*], 1. any long, narrow flag or banner. 2. such a flag symbolizing a championship, as in baseball.

**pen·ni·less** (pen′i-lis), *adj.* without even a penny; extremely poor.

**pen·non** (pen′ən), *n.* [< L. *penna*, quill], 1. a flag or pennant. 2. a pinion; wing.

**pen·ny** (pen′i), *n.* [*pl.* -NIES; for 1 (esp. collective), PENCE], [< AS. *pening*], 1. a British bronze coin equal to 1/12 shilling. 2. a cent (sense 2). —**a pretty penny,** [Colloq.], a large sum of money.

**pen′ny·weight′,** *n.* a unit of weight, equal to 24 grains or 1/20 ounce troy weight.

**pe·nol·o·gy** (pē-nol′ə-ji), *n.* [< Gr. *poinē*, penalty; + *-logy*], the study of prisons and prison reform. —**pe·nol′o·gist,** *n.*

**pen·sion** (pen′shən), *n.* [< L. *pensio*, a paying], a regular payment, not wages, as to one who is retired or disabled. *v.t.* to grant a pension to. —**pen′sion·er,** *n.*

**pen·sive** (pen′siv), *adj.* [< L. *pensare*, consider], thoughtful or reflective, often in a melancholy way. —**pen′sive·ly,** *adv.*

**pent** (pent), alt. pt. and pp. of **pen** (to shut in). *adj.* held in; penned (often with *up*).

**penta-,** [< Gr. *pente*, five], a combining form meaning *five*: also **pent-.**

**pen·ta·gon** (pen′tə-gon′), *n.* [< Gr. *penta-*, five + *gōnia*, an angle], 1. a plane figure with five angles and five sides. 2. [P-], the pentagonal office building of the Defense Department, near Washington, D.C. —**pen·tag′o·nal** (-tag′ə-n'l), *adj.*

**pen·tam·e·ter** (pen-tam′ə-tēr), *n.* [see PENTA- & -METER], a line of verse containing five metrical feet.

**Pen·ta·teuch** (pen′tə-to͞ok′, -tūk′), *n.* [< Gr. *penta-*, five + *teuchos*, book], the first five books of the Old Testament.

**Pen·te·cost** (pen′ti-kôst′, -kost′), *n.* [< Gr. *pentēkostē* (*hēmera*), the fiftieth (day)], a Christian festival on the seventh Sunday after Easter. —**Pen′te·cos′tal,** *adj.*

**pent·house** (pent′hous′), *n.* [< L. *appendere*, append], a house or apartment built on the roof of a building.

**pe·nu·ri·ous** (pə-nyoor′-i-əs, -noor′-), *adj.* [see PENURY], miserly; stingy.

**pen·u·ry** (pen′yoo-ri), *n.* [< L. *penuria*, want], extreme poverty.

**pe·on** (pē′ən), *n.* [< Sp. < ML. *pedo*, foot soldier], 1. in Latin America, a member of the laboring class. 2. in the southwestern U.S., a person forced into servitude to work off a debt. —**pe′on·age** (-ij), *n.*

**pe·o·ny** (pē′ə-ni), *n.* [*pl.* -NIES], [< Gr. *Paiōn*, Apollo as god of medicine: from its former medicinal use], 1. a plant with large pink, white, red, or yellow, showy flowers. 2. the flower.

**peo·ple** (pē′p'l), *n.* [*pl.* -PLE; for 1, -PLES], [< L. *populus*, nation], 1. all the persons of a racial or ethnic group; nation, race, etc. 2. the persons of a certain place, group, or class. 3. the persons under the leadership of a particular person or body. 4. one's family; relatives 5. the populace. 6. persons considered indefinitely: as, what will *people* say? 7. human beings. *v.t.* [-PLED, -PLING], to populate.

**pep** (pep), *n.* [< *pepper*], [Slang], energy;

vigor. *v.t.* [PEPPED, PEPPING], [Slang], to fill with pep; invigorate (with *up*). —**pep′py** [-PIER, -PIEST], *adj.* —**pep′pi·ness,** *n.*

**pep·per** (pep′ẽr), *n.* [< Gr. *peperi*], 1. *a*) a tropical shrub with a many-seeded, red or green, sweet or hot fruit. *b*) the fruit. 2. *a*) a pungent condiment ground from the dried berries of an East Indian plant. *b*) this plant. *v.t.* 1. to season with ground pepper. 2. to pelt with small objects. 3. to sprinkle thickly.

**pep′per·corn′** (-kôrn′), *n.* the dried berry of the pepper plant.

**pep′per·mint′,** *n.* 1. a plant of the mint family, which yields a pungent oil used for flavoring. 2. the oil. 3. a candy flavored with this oil.

**pep′per·y,** *adj.* [-IER, -IEST], 1. of, like, or highly seasoned with pepper. 2. sharp; hot, as words. 3. hot-tempered.

**pep·sin** (pep′sin), *n.* [< Gr. *peptein*, to digest], an enzyme secreted in the stomach, aiding in the digestion of proteins.

**pep′tic** (-tik), *adj.* [see PEPSIN], 1. of or aiding digestion. 2. caused by digestive secretions: as, a *peptic* ulcer. *n.* anything that aids digestion.

**per** (pẽr), *prep.* [L.], 1. through; by; by means of. 2. for each: as, fifty cents *per* yard.

**per-,** [< L. *per*, through], a prefix meaning: 1. *through, throughout.* 2. *thoroughly, very.*

**Per.,** 1. Persia. 2. Persian.

**per·ad·ven·ture** (pũr′əd-ven′chẽr), *adv.* [< OFr. *par*, by + *aventure*, chance], [Archaic], possibly. *n.* [Archaic], chance.

**per·am·bu·late** (pẽr-am′byoo-lāt′), *v.t. & v.i.* [-LATED, -LATING], [< L. *per*, through + *ambulare*, to walk], to walk (through, over, etc.). —**per·am′bu·la′tion,** *n.*

**per·am′bu·la′tor** (-lā′tẽr), *n.* [Chiefly Brit.], a baby carriage.

**per annum,** [L.], by the year; yearly.

**per·cale** (pẽr-kāl′, -kal′), *n.* [Fr. < Per. *pargāl*], closely woven cotton cloth, used for sheets, etc.

**per cap·i·ta** (pẽr kap′ə-tə), [L., lit., by heads], for each person.

**per·ceive** (pẽr-sēv′), *v.t. & v.i.* [-CEIVED, -CEIVING], [< L. *per*, through + *capere*, take], 1. to grasp mentally. 2. to become aware (of) through the senses.

**per·cent** (pẽr-sent′), *n.* per cent.

**per cent,** [L. *per centum*], 1. in, to, or for every hundred: symbol, %. 2. [Colloq.], percentage.

**per·cent·age** (pẽr-sen′tij), *n.* 1. a rate or proportion per hundred. 2. part; portion: as, only a small *percentage* won.

**per·cept** (pũr′sept), *n.* [< L. *percipere*, perceive], an impression received by the mind through the senses.

**per·cep·ti·ble** (pẽr-sep′tə-b'l), *adj.* that can be perceived. —**per·cep′ti·bly,** *adv.*

**per·cep·tion** (pẽr-sep′shən), *n.* 1. the awareness of objects, etc. through the senses. 2. the faculty of perceiving. 3. knowledge, etc. gained by perceiving. 4. insight.

**per·cep′tive,** *adj.* 1. of perception. 2. capable of perceiving, esp. readily.

**perch** (pũrch), *n.* [*pl.* PERCH, PERCHES], [< Gr. *perkē*], 1. a small, spiny-finned, fresh-water food fish. 2. a similar marine fish.

**perch** (pũrch), *n.* [< L. *pertica*, pole], 1. a horizontal pole, etc. serving as a roost for birds. 2. any high resting place. 3. a measure of length, equal to 5½ yards. *v.i. & v.t.* to rest or place on or as on a perch.

**per·chance** (pẽr-chans′, -chäns′), *adv.* [< OFr. *par*, by + *chance*, chance], [Poetic], 1. by chance. 2. perhaps.

**per·cip·i·ent** (pẽr-sip′i-ənt), *adj.* perceiving, esp. keenly. *n.* one who perceives.

**per·co·late** (pũr′kə-lāt′), *v.t.* [-LATED, -LATING], [< L. *per*, through + *colare*, to strain], to pass (a liquid) through a porous substance; filter. *v.i.* to ooze through a porous substance. —**per′co·la′tion,** *n.*

**per′co·la′tor,** *n.* a coffeepot in which boiling water bubbles up through a tube and filters back down through coffee grounds.

**per·cus·sion** (pẽr-kush′ən), *n.* [< L. *percutere*, to strike], the hitting of one body against another, as the hammer of a firearm against a powder cap (**percussion cap**).

**percussion instrument,** a musical instrument producing a tone when struck, as a drum, cymbal, etc.

**per di·em** (pẽr dī′əm), [L.], daily.

**per·di·tion** (pẽr-dish′ən), *n.* [< L. *perdere*, lose], 1. complete loss. 2. in *theology*, *a*) the loss of the soul or of hope for salvation. *b*) hell.

**per·e·gri·nate** (per′ə-gri-nāt′), *v.t. & v.i.* [-NATED, -NATING], [see PILGRIM], to travel (about); journey. —**per′e·gri·na′tion,** *n.*

**per·emp·to·ry** (pẽr-emp′tẽr-i), *adj.* [< L. *perimere*, destroy], 1. in *law*, barring further action; final. 2. that cannot be denied, delayed, etc., as a command. 3. dogmatic; imperious. —**per·emp′to·ri·ness,** *n.*

**per·en·ni·al** (pə-ren′i-əl), *adj.* [< L. *per*, through + *annus*, year], 1. lasting throughout the whole year. 2. continuing for a long time. 3. living more than two years: said of plants. *n.* a perennial plant.

**per·fect** (pũr′fikt; *for v., usually* per-fekt′), *adj.* [< L. *per*, through + *facere*, do], 1. complete in all respects; flawless. 2. excellent, as in skill or quality. 3. completely accurate; exact. 4. sheer; utter: as, a *perfect* fool. 5. in *grammar*, expressing a state or action completed at the time of speaking. *v.t.* 1. to complete. 2. to make perfect or nearly perfect. *n.* 1. the perfect tense. 2. a verb form in this tense. —**per′fect·ly,** *adv.*

**per·fec·tion** (pẽr-fek′shən), *n.* 1. the act of perfecting. 2. a being perfect. 3. a person or thing that is the perfect embodiment of some quality. —**to perfection,** perfectly.

**per·fec′tion·ist,** *n.* a person who strives for perfection.

**per·fi·dy** (pũr′fə-di), *n.* [*pl.* -DIES], [< L. *per*, through + *fides*, faith], betrayal of trust; treachery. —**per·fid·i·ous** (pẽr-fid′i-əs), *adj.*

**per·fo·rate** (pũr′fə-rāt′), *v.t. & v.i.* [-RATED, -RATING], [< L. *per*, through + *forare*, to bore], 1. to make a hole or holes through, as by boring. 2. to pierce with holes in a row, as a pattern, etc. —**per′fo·ra′tion,** *n.*

**per·force** (pẽr-fôrs′), *adv.* [< OFr.; see PER & FORCE], of necessity; necessarily.

**per·form** (pẽr-fôrm′), *v.t.* [< L. *per-*, intens. + *fornir*, accomplish], 1. to do (a task, etc.). 2. to fulfill (a promise). 3. to render or enact (a piece of music, dramatic role, etc.). *v.i.* to execute an action or process, esp. in a performance (sense 4). —**per·form′er,** *n.*

**per·form′ance,** *n.* 1. the act of performing. 2. functional effectiveness. 3. deed or feat. 4. a formal exhibition of skill or talent, as a play.

**per·fume** (pẽr-fūm′), *v.t.* [-FUMED, -FUMING], [< L. *per-*, intens. + *fumare*, to smoke], to scent with perfume. *n.* (*usually* pũr′fūm), 1. a sweet scent; fragrance. 2. a substance producing a pleasing odor, as a liquid extract of the scent of flowers.

**per·fum′er·y** (-ẽr-i), *n.* [*pl.* -IES], 1. perfumes collectively. 2. a place where perfume is made or sold.

**per·func·to·ry** (pẽr-fuŋk′tẽr-i), *adj.* [< L. *per-*, intens. + *fungi*, perform], 1. done merely as a routine; superficial. 2. without concern; indifferent. —**per·func′to·ri·ly,** *adv.*

**per·go·la** (pũr′gə-lə), *n.* [It., arbor], a tunnel-shaped latticework structure.

**per·haps** (pẽr-haps′), *adv.* [*per-* + pl. of *hap*, chance], possibly; probably.

**peri-**, [< Gr. *peri-*], a prefix meaning: 1. *around, about.* 2. *near.*

**per·i·gee** (per'ə-jē'), *n.* [< Gr. *peri-*, around + *gē*, the earth], the point nearest to the earth in the orbit of the moon or of a man-made satellite: cf. **apogee.**

**per·il** (per'əl), *n.* [< L. *periculum*, danger], exposure to harm or injury; risk. *v.t.* [-ILED or -ILLED, -ILING or -ILLING], to expose to danger; risk.

**per'il·ous,** *adj.* involving peril or risk; dangerous. **—per'il·ous·ly,** *adv.*

**per·im·e·ter** (pə-rim'ə-tẽr), *n.* [< Gr. *peri-*, around + *metron*, a measure], 1. the outer boundary of a figure or area. 2. the total length of this.

**pe·ri·od** (pêr'i-əd), *n.* [< Gr. *periodos*, cycle], 1. the interval between successive occurrences of an event. 2. a portion of time distinguished by certain processes, etc.: as, a *period* of change. 3. any of the portions of time into which a game, school day, etc. is divided. 4. the menses. 5. an end or conclusion. 6. *a*) the pause in speaking or the mark of punctuation (.) used at the end of a sentence. *b*) the dot (.) following most abbreviations.

**pe·ri·od·ic** (pêr'i-od'ik), *adj.* 1. appearing or recurring at regular intervals. 2. intermittent.

**pe'ri·od'i·cal,** *adj.* 1. periodic. 2. of a periodical. 3. published at regular intervals of more than one day. *n.* a publication appearing at such intervals.

**per·i·pa·tet·ic** (per'i-pə-tet'ik), *adj.* [< Gr. *peri-*, around + *patein*, walk], 1. walking or moving about; itinerant. 2. [P-], of the philosophy or followers of Aristotle.

**pe·riph·er·y** (pə-rif'ẽr-i), *n.* [*pl.* -IES], [< Gr. *peri-*, around + *pherein*, to bear], 1. an outer boundary, esp. of a rounded object. 2. surrounding space or area. **—pe·riph'er·al,** *adj.*

**pe·riph·ra·sis** (pə-rif'rə-sis), *n.* [*pl.* -SES (-sēz')], [< Gr. *peri-*, around + *phrazein*, speak], the use of many words where a few would do.

**per·i·scope** (per'ə-skōp'), *n.* [*peri-* + *-scope*], an optical instrument that allows one to see around or over an obstacle: used on submarines, etc.

**per·ish** (per'ish), *v.i.* [< L. *per-*, intens. + *ire*, go], to be destroyed or ruined; specif., to die a violent or untimely death.

**per'ish·a·ble,** *adj.* that may perish; liable to spoil, as some foods.

**per·i·to·ne·um** (per'i-tə-nē'əm), *n.* [*pl.* -NEA (-nē'ə)], [< Gr. *peri-*, around + *teinein*, stretch], the serous membrane lining the abdominal cavity. **—per'i·to·ne'al,** *adj.*

**per'i·to·ni'tis** (-nī'tis), *n.* inflammation of the peritoneum.

**per·i·wig** (per'ə-wig'), *n.* [< Fr. *perruque*], a wig.

**per·i·win·kle** (per'ə-wiŋ'k'l), *n.* [< L. *pervinca*], a creeping evergreen plant with white or blue flowers; myrtle.

**per·i·win·kle** (per'ə-wiŋ'k'l), *n.* [AS. *perwynke*], a small salt-water snail with a thick, cone-shaped shell.

**per·jure** (pũr'jẽr), *v.t.* [-JURED, -JURING], [< L. *per*, through + *jurare*, swear], to make (oneself) guilty of perjury. **—per'jur·er,** *n.*

**per·ju·ry** (pũr'jẽr-i), *n.* [*pl.* -RIES], [< L. *perjurus*, false], the willful telling of a lie while under oath.

**perk** (pũrk), *v.t.* [ME. *perken*], 1. to raise, as the head, briskly. 2. to make (oneself) smart in appearance. Often with *up.* *v.i.* to become lively or gay (with *up*). **—perk'y** [-IER, -IEST], *adj.* **—perk'i·ness,** *n.*

**per·ma·nent** (pũr'mə-nənt), *adj.* [< L. *per*, through + *manere*, remain], lasting or intended to last indefinitely or for a relatively long time. *n.* [Colloq.], a permanent wave. **—per'ma·nence,** *n.* **—per'ma·nent·ly,** *adv.*

**permanent wave,** a hair wave produced by use of chemicals or heat and lasting for months.

**per·me·a·ble** (pũr'mi-ə-b'l), *adj.* that can be permeated, as by liquids. **—per'me·a·bil'i·ty,** *n.*

**per·me·ate** (pũr'mi-āt'), *v.t. & v.i.* [-ATED, -ATING], [< L. *per*, through + *meare*, to glide], to spread or diffuse; penetrate (*through* or *among*). **—per'me·a'tion,** *n.*

**per·mis·si·ble** (pẽr-mis'ə-b'l) *adj.* that can be permitted. **—per·mis'si·bly,** *adv.*

**per·mis·sion** (pẽr-mish'ən), *n.* the act of permitting; formal consent.

**per·mis·sive** (pẽr-mis'iv), *adj.* 1. that permits. 2. allowing freedom; indulgent; lenient.

**per·mit** (pẽr-mit'), *v.t.* [-MITTED, -MITTING], [< L. *per*, through + *mittere*, send], 1. to allow to be done; consent to. 2. to allow: as, *permit* me to go. *v.i.* to give opportunity: as, if time *permits.* *n.* (pũr'mit), 1. a document granting permission; license. 2. permission.

**per·mu·ta·tion** (pũr'myoo-tā'shən), *n.* 1. a change; alteration. 2. any one of the combinations or changes in position possible within a group.

**per·ni·cious** (pẽr-nish'əs), *adj.* [< L. *per*, thoroughly + *necare*, kill], causing injury, destruction, etc.; fatal.

**per·nick·e·ty** (pẽr-nik'ə-ti), *adj.* [< Scot. dial.], [Colloq.], too particular; fussy.

**per·o·ra·tion** (per'ə-rā'shən), *n.* [< L. *per*, through + *orare*, speak], the concluding part of a speech, including a summing up.

**per·ox·ide** (pẽr-ok'sīd), *n.* [< L. *per*, through; + *oxide*], any oxide containing the oxygen group linked by a single bond; specif., hydrogen peroxide. *v.t.* [-IDED, -IDING], to bleach with hydrogen peroxide.

**per·pen·dic·u·lar** (pũr'pen-dik'yoo-lẽr), *adj.* [< L. *perpendiculum*, plumb line], 1. at right angles to a given line or plane. 2. exactly upright; vertical. *n.* a line at right angles to another line or plane.

**per·pe·trate** (pũr'pə-trāt'), *v.t.* [-TRATED, -TRATING], [< L. *per*, thoroughly + *patrare*, to effect], to do (something evil, criminal, etc.); commit (a blunder), impose (a hoax), etc. **—per'pe·tra'tion,** *n.* **—per'pe·tra'tor,** *n.*

**per·pet·u·al** (pẽr-pech'ōō-əl), *adj.* [< L. *perpetuus*, constant], 1. lasting forever or for a long time. 2. continuing without interruption; constant. **—per·pet'u·al·ly,** *adv.*

**per·pet'u·ate'** (-āt'), *v.t.* [-ATED, -ATING], to make perpetual; cause to continue or be remembered. **—per·pet'u·a'tion,** *n.*

**per·pe·tu·i·ty** (pũr'pə-tōō'ə-ti, -tū'-), *n.* [*pl.* -TIES], unlimited time; eternity. **—in perpetuity,** forever.

**per·plex** (pẽr-pleks'), *v.t.* [< L. *per*, through + *plectere*, to twist], to make (a person) uncertain, hesitant, etc.; bewilder. **—per·plex'ing,** *adj.* **—per·plex'i·ty,** *n.*

**per·qui·site** (pũr'kwə-zit), *n.* [< L. *per-*, intens. + *quaerere*, seek], something in addition to one's regular pay for one's work, as a tip.

**per se** (pũr' sē'), [L.], by (or in) itself; inherently.

**per·se·cute** (pũr'sə-kūt'), *v.t.* [-CUTED, -CUTING], [< L. *per*, through + *sequi*, follow], to afflict constantly so as to injure or distress, as because of one's religion, beliefs, etc. **—per'se·cu'tion,** *n.* **—per'se·cu'tor,** *n.*

**Per·seph·o·ne** (pẽr-sef'ə-ni), *n.* in *Gr. myth.*, the daughter of Demeter, abducted by Pluto, the god of the lower world.

**Per·seus** (pũr'sūs, -si-əs), *n.* in *Gr. myth.*, the son of Zeus and slayer of Medusa.

**per·se·vere** (pũr'sə-vêr'), *v.i.* [-VERED, -VERING], [< L. *per-*, intens. + *severus*, severe], to continue doing something in spite of diffi-

culty, opposition, etc. —**per'se·ver'ance,** *n.*
**Per·sian** (pũr'zhən), *adj.* of Persia, its people, language, etc.; Iranian. *n.* 1. a native or inhabitant of Persia. 2. the Iranian language of the Persians.
**Persian lamb,** a fur with curly fleece, obtained from certain Asiatic lambs.
**per·si·flage** (pũr'si-fläzh'), *n.* [Fr. < L. *per* + Fr. *siffler*, to whistle], light, frivolous talk or writing; banter.
**per·sim·mon** (pẽr-sim'ən), *n.* [< Am. Ind.], 1. a hardwood tree with a plumlike fruit. 2. the fruit.
**per·sist** (pẽr-sist', -zist'), *v.i.* [< L. *per*, through + *sistere*, cause to stand], 1. to refuse to give up, esp. when faced with opposition. 2. to continue insistently. 3. to endure; remain; last.
**per·sist'ent,** *adj.* 1. continuing, esp. in the face of opposition, etc. 2. continuing to exist or endure. 3. constantly repeated. —**per·sist'ence, per·sist'en·cy,** *n.*
**per·son** (pũr's'n), *n.* [< L. *persona*], 1. a human being. 2. the human body. 3. personality; self. 4. in *grammar*, any of the three classes of pronouns (and corresponding verb forms) indicating the speaker (*first person, I* or *we*), the subject spoken to (*second person, you*), or the subject spoken of (*third person, he, she, it,* or *they*). —**in person,** in bodily presence.
**per'son·a·ble,** *adj.* having an attractive appearance and personality.
**per'son·age** (-ij), *n.* a person; esp., an important person; notable.
**per'son·al** (-əl), *adj.* 1. private; individual. 2. done in person. 3. of the body or physical appearance. 4. having to do with the character, conduct, etc. of a person: as, a *personal* remark. 5. inquisitive about the private affairs of others. 6. in *grammar*, indicating person (sense 4). 7. in *law*, of property **(personal property)** that is movable.
**per·son·al·i·ty** (pũr'sə-nal'ə-ti), *n.* [*pl.* -TIES], 1. the quality or fact of being a particular person. 2. distinctive individual qualities of a person, collectively. 3. a notable person. 4. *usually pl.* an offensive remark aimed at a person.
**per·son·al·ize** (pũr's'n-əl-iz'), *v.t.* [-IZED, -IZING], to make personal.
**per'son·al·ly,** *adv.* 1. directly by oneself. 2. as a person: as, I dislike him *personally.* 3. in one's own opinion. 4. as though directed at oneself.
**per·son·i·fy** (pẽr-son'ə-fi'), *v.t.* [-FIED, -FYING], 1. to think of or represent (a thing) as a person. 2. to be a perfect example of; typify. —**per·son'i·fi·ca'tion,** *n.*
**per·son·nel** (pũr'sə-nel'), *n.* [Fr.], persons employed in any work, enterprise, service, etc. *adj.* of or in charge of personnel.
**per·spec·tive** (pẽr-spek'tiv), *n.* [< L. *per*, through + *specere*, to look], 1. the art of picturing objects so as to show relative distance or depth. 2. the appearance of objects as determined by their relative distance and positions. 3. a sense of proportion.
**per·spi·ca·cious** (pũr'spi-kā'shəs), *adj.* [< L. *perspicere*, see through], having keen judgment; discerning. —**per'spi·ca'cious·ly,** *adv.* —**per'spi·cac'i·ty** (-kas'ə-ti), *n.*
**per·spic·u·ous** (pẽr-spik'ū-əs), *adj.* [< L. *perspicere*, see through], easily understood; lucid. —**per·spi·cu·i·ty** (pũr'spi-kū'ə-ti), *n.*
**per·spi·ra·tion** (pũr'spə-rā'shən), *n.* 1. a perspiring. 2. sweat.
**per·spire** (pẽr-spir'), *v.t. & v.i.* [-SPIRED, -SPIRING], [< L. *per*, through + *spirare*, breathe], to sweat.
**per·suade** (per-swād'), *v.t.* [-SUADED, -SUADING], [< L. *per-*, intens. + *suadere*, urge], to cause (someone) to do or believe something, esp. by reasoning, urging, etc.; induce.
**per·sua·sion** (pẽr-swā'zhən), *n.* 1. a persuading or being persuaded. 2. power of persuading. 3. a strong belief. 4. a particular religious belief.
**per·sua'sive,** *adj.* having the power, or tending, to persuade. —**per·sua'sive·ly,** *adv.*
**pert** (pũrt), *adj.* [< L. *apertus*, open], bold; impudent; saucy. —**pert'ly,** *adv.*
**per·tain** (pẽr-tān'), *v.i.* [< L. *per-*, intens. + *tenere*, to hold], 1. to belong; be connected or associated. 2. to be appropriate. 3. to have reference.
**per·ti·na·cious** (pũr'tə-nā'shəs), *adj.* [< L. *per-*, intens. + *tenax*, holding fast], 1. holding firmly to some purpose, belief, etc. 2. hard to get rid of. —**per'ti·na'cious·ly,** *adv.* —**per'ti·nac'i·ty** (-nas'ə-ti), *n.*
**per·ti·nent** (pũr't'n-ənt), *adj.* [see PERTAIN], of or connected with the matter at hand.—**per'ti·nence,** *n.*—**per'ti·nent·ly,** *adv.*
**per·turb** (pẽr-tũrb'), *v.t.* [< L. *per-*, intens. + *turbare*, disturb], to cause to be alarmed, agitated, or upset. —**per·turb'able,** *adj.* —**per·tur·ba·tion** (pũr'tẽr-bā'shən), *n.*
**pe·ru·sal** (pə-rōō'z'l), *n.* a perusing.
**pe·ruse** (pə-rōōz'), *v.t.* [-RUSED, -RUSING], [prob. < L. *per-*, intens.; + *use*, *v.*], 1. to read carefully; study. 2. to read.
**Pe·ru·vi·an** (pə-rōō'vi-ən), *adj.* of Peru, its people etc. *n.* a native of Peru.
**per·vade** (pẽr-vād'), *v.t.* [-VADED, -VADING], [< L. *per*, through + *vadere*, go], to spread or be prevalent throughout. —**per·va'sion** (-vā'zhən), *n.* —**per·va'sive** (-vā'siv), *adj.*
**per·verse** (pẽr-vũrs'), *adj.* [see PERVERT], 1. deviating from what is considered right or acceptable. 2. wicked. 3. stubbornly contrary. 4. obstinately disobedient. —**per·ver'si·ty** [*pl.* -TIES], *n.*
**per·ver·sion** (pẽr-vũr'zhən), *n.* 1. a perverting or being perverted. 2. something perverted. 3. any sexual act or practice considered abnormal.
**per·vert** (pẽr-vũrt'), *v.t.* [< L. *per-*, intens. + *vertere*, to turn], 1. to misdirect; corrupt. 2. to misuse. 3. to distort. 4. to debase. *n.* (pũr'vẽrt), a perverted person; esp., one who practices sexual perversions.
**pes·ky** (pes'ki), *adj.* [-KIER, -KIEST], [prob. var. of *pesty*], [Colloq.], annoying; troublesome. —**pes'ki·ness,** *n.*
**pe·so** (pā'sō), *n.* [*pl.* -SOS], [Sp. < L. *pensum*, something weighed], any of the monetary units and silver coins of several Spanish-speaking countries.
**pes·si·mism** (pes'ə-miz'm), *n.* [< L. *pejor*, worse], 1. the belief that evil ultimately prevails over good. 2. the tendency to expect the worst outcome. —**pes'si·mist,** *n.* —**pes'si·mis'tic,** *adj.*
**pest** (pest), *n.* [< L. *pestis*, plague], 1. a person or thing that causes trouble, annoyance, etc.; specif., vermin. 2. [Now Rare], a fatal epidemic disease.
**pes·ter** (pes'tẽr), *v.t.* [< OFr. *empestrer*, entangle], to annoy with petty irritations.
**pes·ti·cide** (pes'tə-sīd'), *n.* any chemical used for killing insects, weeds, etc.
**pes·tif·er·ous** (pes-tif'ẽr-əs), *adj.* [< L. *pestis*, plague + *ferre*, to bear], 1. carrying disease; infected with an epidemic disease. 2. [Colloq.], annoying.
**pes·ti·lence** (pes'tə-ləns), *n.* 1. any virulent or fatal contagious disease. 2. an epidemic of such disease. 3. anything regarded as harmful. —**pes'ti·len'tial** (-len'shəl), *adj.*
**pes'ti·lent,** *adj.* [< L. *pestis*, plague], 1. likely to cause death. 2. dangerous to morals; pernicious. 3. annoying.
**pes·tle** (pes''l), *n.* [< L. *pinsere*, to pound], a tool used to pound or grind substances, as in a mortar.

**pet** (pet), *n.* [orig. Scot. dial.], 1. an animal that is domesticated and kept as a companion or treated with affection. 2. a person treated with particular indulgence. *adj.* 1. kept or treated as a pet. 2. especially liked; favorite. 3. particular: as, a *pet* peeve. *v.t.* [PETTED, PETTING], to stroke or pat gently; caress. *v.i.* [Colloq.], to make love; kiss, embrace, etc.

**pet** (pet), *n.* [< obs. phr. *to take the pet*], a state of sulky ill-humor.

**pet·al** (pet''l), *n.* [< Gr. *petalos*, outspread], any of the leaflike parts of a blossom.

**pet·cock** (pet'kok'), *n.* [< ?], a small valve for draining pipes, etc.: also **pet cock.**

**pe·ter** (pē'tẽr), *v.i.* [< ?], [Colloq.], to become gradually smaller, weaker, etc. and then disappear (with *out*).

**pe·tite** (pə-tēt'), *adj.* [Fr.], small and trim in figure: said of a woman.

**pe·ti·tion** (pə-tish'ən), *n.* [< L. *petere*, ask], 1. a solemn, earnest request; entreaty. 2. a formal document embodying such a request. *v.t.* 1. to address a petition to. 2. to ask for. *v.i.* to make a petition.

**pet·rel** (pet'rəl), *n.* [? < St. *Peter*, who walked on the sea], a small, dark sea bird with long wings.

**pet·ri·fy** (pet'rə-fī'), *v.t.* [-FIED, -FYING], [< L. *petra*, a rock + *facere*, make], 1. to change into a stony substance. 2. to deaden; harden. 3. to stun, as with fear. *v.i.* to change into stone. —**pet'ri·fac'tion** (-fak'shən), **pet'ri·fi·ca'tion,** *n.*

**pet·rol** (pet'rəl), *n.* [see PETROLEUM], [Brit.], gasoline.

**pe·tro·le·um** (pə-trō'li-əm), *n.* [< L. *petra*, a rock + *oleum*, oil], an oily, liquid solution of hydrocarbons found in certain rock strata: it yields kerosene, gasoline, etc.

**pet·ti·coat** (pet'i-kōt'), *n.* [< *petty* + *coat*], 1. a skirt worn under a dress or outer skirt. 2. [Colloq.], a woman or girl.

**pet·ti·fog·ger** (pet'i-fog'ẽr, -fôg'-), *n.* [< *petty* + ? < obs. D. *focker*, cheater], a lawyer who handles petty cases, esp. in an unethical manner.

**pet·tish** (pet'ish), *adj.* [< *pet* (a fit)], peevish; petulant. —**pet'tish·ly,** *adv.*

**pet·ty** (pet'i), *adj.* [-TIER, -TIEST], [< OFr. *petit*], 1. relatively unimportant. 2. narrow-minded; mean. 3. relatively low in rank.

**petty cash,** a cash fund for incidental expenses.

**petty officer,** an enlisted man in the navy with the rank of a noncommissioned officer.

**pet·u·lant** (pech'oo-lənt), *adj.* [< L. *petere*, to attack], impatient or irritable, esp. over a petty annoyance. —**pet'u·lance,** *n.*

**pe·tu·ni·a** (pə-tōōn'yə, -tū'ni-ə), *n.* [< Braz. *petun*, tobacco], 1. a plant with funnel-shaped flowers. 2. the flower.

**pew** (pū), *n.* [< Gr. *podion*, balcony], any of the rows of fixed benches with a back, in a church.

**pe·wee** (pē'wē), *n.* [echoic of its call], the phoebe: also **pe·wit** (pē'wit, pū'it).

**pew·ter** (pū'tẽr), *n.* [OFr. *peutre*], 1. a grayish alloy of tin with lead, brass, or copper. 2. articles made of pewter.

**Pfc.,** Private First Class.

**pha·e·ton, pha·ë·ton** (fā'ə-t'n), *n.* [< *Phaëthon*, son of Helios, Gr. sun god: he almost set the world on fire with his father's sun chariot], 1. a light, four-wheeled carriage. 2. a kind of touring car.

**pha·lanx** (fā'laŋks, fal'aŋks), *n.* [*pl.* PHALANXES, PHALANGES (fə-lan'jēz)], [Gr., line of battle], 1. an ancient military formation of infantry in close ranks. 2. a massed group of individuals. 3. a group of individuals united for a common purpose. 4. [*pl.* -LANGES], any of the bones of the fingers or toes.

**phal·lus** (fal'əs), *n.* [*pl.* -LI (-ī)], [< Gr. *phallos*], an image of the penis, the generative organ. —**phal'lic,** *adj.*

**phan·tasm** (fan'taz'm), *n.* [< Gr. *phantazein*, to show], 1. a figment of the mind; esp., a specter. 2. a deceptive likeness.

**phan·tas·ma·go·ri·a** (fan-taz'mə-gôr'i-ə), *n.* [< Gr. *phantasma*, phantasm + (prob.) *agora*, assembly], a rapidly changing series of things seen or imagined, as in a dream.

**phan·ta·sy** (fan'tə-si), *n.* [*pl.* -SIES], a fantasy.

**phan·tom** (fan'təm), *n.* [see PHANTASM], 1. an apparition; specter. 2. an illusion. 3. any mental image. *adj.* of or like a phantom; unreal.

**Phar·aoh** (fâr'ō), *n.* the title of the rulers of ancient Egypt.

**Phar·i·see** (far'ə-sē'), *n.* 1. a member of an ancient Jewish sect that rigidly observed the written and oral law. 2. [p-], a self-righteous person.

**phar·ma·ceu·ti·cal** (fär'mə-sōō'ti-k'l, -sū'-), *adj.* [< Gr. *pharmakon*, a drug], 1. of pharmacy or pharmacists. 2. of or by drugs. Also **phar'ma·ceu'tic.**

**phar'ma·ceu'tics** (-tiks), *n.pl.* [construed as sing.], pharmacy (sense 1).

**phar·ma·cist** (fär'mə-sist), *n.* one licensed to practice pharmacy.

**phar'ma·col'o·gy** (-kol'ə-ji), *n.* [< Gr. *pharmakon*, a drug; + *-logy*], the study of the preparation and uses of drugs. —**phar'ma·col'o·gist,** *n.*

**phar'ma·co·poe'ia** (-kə-pē'ə), *n.* [< Gr. *pharmakon*, a drug + *poiein*, make], an official book listing drugs and medicines.

**phar·ma·cy** (fär'mə-si), *n.* [*pl.* -CIES], [< Gr. *pharmakon*, a drug], 1. the art or profession of preparing and dispensing drugs and medicines. 2. a drugstore.

**phar·yn·gi·tis** (far'in-jī'tis), *n.* inflammation of the pharynx; sore throat.

**phar·ynx** (far'iŋks), *n.* [*pl.* PHARYNXES, PHARYNGES (fə-rin'jēz)], [Gr.], the cavity leading from the mouth and nasal passages to the larynx and esophagus. —**pha·ryn·ge·al** (fə-rin'ji-əl), *adj.*

**phase** (fāz), *n.* [< Gr. *phasis*], 1. any stage in the illumination or appearance of the moon or a planet. 2. any stage in a series of changes, as in development or cyclic movement. 3. aspect or side, as of a subject. —**phase out,** to bring or come to an end, or withdraw from use, by stages.

**Ph.D.,** Doctor of Philosophy.

**pheas·ant** (fez''nt), *n.* [< Gr. *phasianos*, (bird) of *Phasis*, river in Asia], a chickenlike game bird with a long tail and brilliant feathers.

**phe·no·bar·bi·tal** (fē'nə-bär'bi-tôl'), *n.* a white crystalline powder used as a sedative and soporific.

**phe·nom·e·non** (fi-nom'ə-non'), *n.* [*pl.* -NA (-nə); also, esp. for 2 & 3, -NONS], [< Gr. *phainesthai*, appear], 1. any observable fact or event that can be scientifically described, as an eclipse. 2. anything extremely unusual. 3. [Colloq.], an extraordinary person; prodigy. —**phe·nom'e·nal,** *adj.*

**phew** (fū), *interj.* an exclamation of disgust, surprise, relief, etc.

**phi** (fī, fē), *n.* the twenty-first letter of the Greek alphabet (Φ, φ).

**phi·al** (fī'əl), *n.* [< Gr. *phialē*, shallow bowl], a small glass bottle; vial.

**phi·lan·der** (fi-lan'dẽr), *v.i.* [< Gr. *philos*, loving + *anēr*, man], to make love insincerely: said of a man. —**phi·lan'der·er,** *n.*

**phi·lan·thro·py** (fi-lan'thrə-pi), *n.* [< Gr. *philein*, to love + *anthrōpos*, man], 1. desire to help mankind as shown by acts of charity, etc. 2. [*pl.* -PIES], a philanthropic service, gift, institution, etc. —**phil·an-**

**throp·ic** (fil'ən-throp'ik), **phil'an·throp'i·cal,** *adj.* —**phi·lan'thro·pist,** *n.*

**phi·lat·e·ly** (fi-lat''l-i), *n.* [< Fr. < Gr. *philos*, loving + *ateleia*, exemption from tax: stamps show prepayment by sender], the collection and study of postage stamps, postmarks, etc. —**phi·lat'e·list,** *n.*

**-phile,** [< Gr. *philos*, loving], a combining form meaning *loving, liking.*

**phil·har·mon·ic** (fil'här-mon'ik), *adj.* [< Gr. *philos*, loving + *harmonia*, harmony], loving or devoted to music. *n.* [P-], a society that sponsors a symphony orchestra.

**Phi·lis·tine** (fə-lis'tin, fil'əs-tēn'), *n.* [after an ancient people in SW Palestine], one who is smugly conventional in ideas, tastes, etc. *adj.* smugly conventional.

**phil·o·den·dron** (fil'ə den'drən), *n.* [< Gr. *philos*, loving + *dendron*, tree], a tropical American climbing plant.

**phi·lol·o·gy** (fi-lol'ə-ji), *n.* [< Gr. *philein*, to love + *logos*, word], linguistics: former term. —**phil·o·log·i·cal** (fil'ə-loj'-i-k'l), *adj.* —**phi·lol'o·gist,** *n.*

**phi·los·o·pher** (fi-los'ə-fẽr), *n.* [< Gr. *philos*, loving + *sophos*, wise], 1. one who is learned in philosophy. 2. one who lives by a system of philosophy. 3. one who meets all events with calmness and composure.

**phil·o·soph·ic** (fil'ə-sof'ik), *adj.* 1. of a philosophy or a philosopher. 2. devoted to or learned in philosophy. 3. rational; calm. Also **phil'o·soph'i·cal.**

**phi·los·o·phize** (fi-los'ə-fīz'), *v.i.* [-PHIZED, -PHIZING], to think or reason like a philosopher. —**phi·los'o·phiz'er,** *n.*

**phi·los'o·phy** (-fi), *n.* [*pl.* -PHIES], [see PHILOSOPHER], 1. a study of the processes governing thought and conduct and of the principles that regulate the universe. 2. the general principles of a field of knowledge. 3. a particular system of ethics. 4. calmness; composure.

**phil·ter, phil·tre** (fil'tẽr), *n.* [< Gr. *philein*, to love], a magic potion, esp. one to induce love.

**phle·bi·tis** (fli-bī'tis), *n.* [< Gr. *phleps*, vein; + *-itis*], inflammation of a vein.

**phlegm** (flem), *n.* [< Gr. *phlegma*, inflammation], the secretion of mucus discharged from the throat, as during a cold.

**phleg·mat·ic** (fleg-mat'ik), *adj.* [see PHLEGM], 1. sluggish; dull. 2. calm; cool.

**phlox** (floks), *n.* [Gr., a flame], a plant with clusters of flowers of various colors.

**-phobe,** [< Gr. *phobos*, fear], a combining form meaning *fearing* or *hating.*

**pho·bi·a** (fō'bi-ə), *n.* [< Gr. *phobos*, a fear], an irrational, persistent fear of some thing or situation. —**pho'bic,** *adj.*

**-phobia,** a combining form meaning *fear, hatred*, as in *claustrophobia.*

**phoe·be** (fē'bi), *n.* [echoic; sp. infl. by *Phoebe*, Gr. goddess of the moon], a small, greenish-brown bird that catches insects in flight.

**phoe·nix** (fē'niks), *n.* [< Gr. *phoinix*], in *Egypt. myth.*, a bird which lived for 500 years and then consumed itself in fire, rising renewed from the ashes.

**phone** (fōn), *n., v.t. & v.i.* [PHONED, PHONING], [Colloq.], telephone.

**-phone,** [< Gr. *phōnē*, a sound], a combining form meaning *producing sound.*

**pho·net·ics** (fə-net'iks), *n.pl.* [< Gr. *phōnē*, a sound], [construed as sing.], the science dealing with the production and written representation of speech sounds. —**phonet'ic,** *adj.* —**pho·net'i·cal·ly,** *adv.* —**phone·ti·cian** (fō'nə-tish'ən), *n.*

**pho·no·graph** (fō'nə-graf', -gräf'), *n.* [< Gr. *phōnē*, a sound; + *-graph*], an instrument that reproduces sound from tracings made on a flat disk. —**pho'no·graph'ic,** *adj.*

**pho·ny** (fō'ni), *adj.* [-NIER, -NIEST], [< ?], [Slang], not genuine; false; fake. *n.* [*pl.* -NIES], [Slang], something or someone not genuine; fake. Also sp. **phoney.**

**phos·phate** (fos'fāt), *n.* [Fr.], 1. a salt or ester of phosphoric acid. 2. a fertilizer containing phosphates. 3. a flavored carbonated beverage.

**phos·pho·res·cence** (fos'fə-res''ns), *n.* 1. the property of giving off light without noticeable heat, as shown by phosphorus. 2. such a light. —**phos'pho·res'cent,** *adj.*

**phos·phor·ic** (fos-fôr'ik), *adj.* 1. of, like, or containing phosphorus. 2. designating any of three colorless, crystalline acids with a phosphorus and oxygen radical.

**phos·pho·rus** (fos'fẽr-əs), *n.* [*pl.* -RI (-ī')], [< Gr. *phōs*, a light + *pherein*, to bear], a nonmetallic chemical element, a phosphorescent, waxy solid: the white and yellow forms ignite spontaneously at room temperature: symbol, P. —**phos·pho·rous** (fos'fẽr-əs, fos-fôr'-), *adj.*

**pho·to** (fō'tō), *n.* [*pl.* -TOS], [Colloq.], a photograph.

**photo-,** [< Gr. *phōs*, a light], a combining form meaning: 1. *of* or *produced by light.* 2. *of photography.*

**pho'to·e·lec'tric cell,** any device in which light controls an electric circuit which operates a mechanical device, as for opening doors.

**pho·to·en·grave** (fō'tō-in-grāv'), *v.i.* [-GRAVED, -GRAVING], to reproduce by photoengraving. —**pho'to·en·grav'er,** *n.*

**pho'to·en·grav'ing,** *n.* 1. a process by which photographs are reproduced in relief on printing plates. 2. such a plate. 3. a print from such a plate.

**photo finish,** a race finish so close that the winner can be determined only from a photograph of the finish.

**pho·to·flash** (fō'tə-flash'), *adj.* designating an electric bulb which gives off a single bright flash of light: used in photography.

**pho·to·gen·ic** (fō'tə-jen'ik), *adj.* [*photo-* + *-gen* + *-ic*], 1. artistically suitable for being photographed. 2. in *biology*, phosphorescent.

**pho·to·graph** (fō'tə-graf', -gräf'), *n.* a picture made by photography. *v.t.* to take a photograph of. *v.i.* to undergo being photographed. —**pho·tog·ra·pher** (fə-tog'rə-fẽr), *n.*

**pho·tog·ra·phy** (fə-tog'rə-fi), *n.* [*photo-* + *-graphy*], the art or process of producing images of objects upon a surface sensitive to the chemical action of light, etc. —**pho·to·graph·ic** (fō'tə-graf'ik), *adj.* —**pho'to·graph'i·cal·ly,** *adv.*

**pho·to·off·set** (fō'tō-ôf'set'), *n.* a method of duplication in which the text or pictures are photographically transferred to a metal plate and then reproduced by offset printing.

**pho'to·play',** *n.* a screenplay.

**pho·to·stat** (fō'tə-stat'), *n.* [*photo-* + *-stat*], 1. a device for making photographic reproductions of printed matter, drawings, etc. directly upon special paper: a trademark (**Photostat**). 2. a reproduction so made. *v.t.* [-STATED or -STATTED, -STATING or -STATTING], to make a photostat of. —**pho'to·stat'ic,** *adj.*

**pho·to·syn·the·sis** (fō'tə-sin'thə-sis), *n.* the formation of carbohydrates in plants from water and carbon dioxide, by the action of sunlight on the chlorophyll.

**phrase** (frāz), *n.* [< Gr. *phrazein*, speak], 1. a short, colorful expression. 2. a group of words, not a full sentence or clause, conveying a single thought (e.g., *of mine*). 3. a short, distinct musical passage. *v.t. & v.i.* [PHRASED, PHRASING], to express in words or in a phrase. —**phras'al,** *adj.*

**phra·se·ol·o·gy** (frā'zi-ol'ə-ji), *n.* [*pl.* -GIES], choice or pattern of words.

**phre·net·ic** (fri-net′ik), *adj.* [< Gr. *phrenētikos*, mad], 1. insane; frenetic. 2. wildly excited; fanatic. *n.* a phrenetic person.
**phre·nol·o·gy** (fri-nol′ə-ji), *n.* [< Gr. *phrēn*, mind; + *-logy*], the alleged analysis of character and mental faculties by studying the form of the skull. —**phre·nol′o·gist**, *n.*
**phy·log·e·ny** (fī-loj′ə-ni), *n.* [*pl.* -NIES], [< Gr. *phylon*, tribe + *-geneia*, origin], the evolutionary development of any species.
**phy·lum** (fī′ləm), *n.* [*pl.* -LA (-lə)], [< Gr. *phylon*, tribe], any of the basic divisions of the plant or animal kingdom.
**phys·ic** (fiz′ik), *n.* [< Gr. *physis*, nature], a medicine, esp. a cathartic. *v.t.* [-ICKED, -ICKING], 1. to dose with medicine. 2. to cause to have a bowel movement.
**phys·i·cal** (fiz′i-k'l), *adj.* 1. of nature and all matter; material. 2. of or according to the laws of nature. 3. of, or produced by the forces of, physics. 4. of the body. *n.* [Colloq.], a physical examination.
**physical education,** instruction in the exercise and care of the body; esp., a course in gymnastics, etc.
**physical therapy,** the treatment of disease, injury, etc. by physical means, as by massage, exercise, infrared light, etc.
**phy·si·cian** (fə-zish′ən), *n.* [see PHYSIC], a doctor of medicine.
**phys·ics** (fiz′iks), *n.pl.* [construed as sing.], [< *physic*], the science dealing with the properties, changes, interaction, etc. of matter and energy. —**phys′i·cist** (-ə-sist), *n.*
**phys·i·og·no·my** (fiz′i-og′nə-mi), *n.* [*pl.* -MIES], [< Gr. *physis*, nature + *gnōmōn*, one who knows], the face; facial expression.
**phys·i·ol·o·gy** (fiz′i-ol′ə-ji), *n.* [< Gr. *physis*, nature + *logos*, a discourse], the science dealing with the functions and vital processes of living organisms. —**phys′i·o·log′i·cal** (-ə-loj′i-k'l), *adj.* —**phys′i·ol′o·gist**, *n.*
**phys·i·o·ther·a·py** (fiz′i-ō-ther′ə-pi), *n.* physical therapy. —**phys′i·o·ther′a·pist**, *n.*
**phy·sique** (fi-zēk′), *n.* [Fr.], the structure, strength, form, or appearance of the body.
**pi** (pī), *n.* [var. of *pie*], 1. a disordered collection of printing type. 2. any jumble. *v.t.* [PIED, PIEING], to make jumbled or disordered. Also sp. **pie.**
**pi** (pī), *n.* 1. the sixteenth letter of the Greek alphabet (Π, π). 2. the symbol (π) designating the ratio of the circumference of a circle to its diameter, about 3.1416.
**pi·a·nis·si·mo** (pē′ə-nis′ə-mō′), *adj.* & *adv.* [It.], in *music*, very soft.
**pi·an·ist** (pi-an′ist, pyan′-, pē′ə-nist), *n.* one who plays the piano esp. as a profession.
**pi·an·o** (pi-an′ō, pyan′-), *n.* [*pl.* -OS], [< *pianoforte*], a large, stringed, keyboard instrument: each key operates a felt-covered hammer that strikes and vibrates a corresponding steel wire.
**pi·an·o** (pi-ä′nō), *adj.* & *adv.* [It.], in *music*, soft.
**pi·an·o·for·te** (pi-an′ə-fôrt′, pyan′ə-fôr′ti), *n.* [It. < *piano*, soft + *forte*, strong], a piano.
**pi·as·ter, pi·as·tre** (pi-as′tēr), *n.* [ult. < L. *emplastrum*, plaster], a monetary unit and coin of Turkey and Egypt.
**pi·az·za** (pi-az′ə), *n.* [It.], 1. in Italy, a public square. 2. a veranda.
**pi·ca** (pī′kə), *n.* [ML., directory; hence prob. the type used in printing it], a size of type, 12 point.
**pic·a·resque** (pik′ə-resk′), *adj.* [< Sp. *picaro*, rascal], dealing with sharp-witted vagabonds: as, a *picaresque* novel.
**pic·a·yune** (pik′i-ūn′), *adj.* [Fr. *picaillon*, farthing], trivial; petty: also **pic′a·yun′ish.**
**pic·ca·lil·li** (pik′ə-lil′i), *n.* [prob. < *pickle*], a relish of vegetables, mustard, spices, etc.
**pic·co·lo** (pik′ə-lō′), *n.* [*pl.* -LOS], [It., small], a small flute, pitched an octave above the ordinary flute. —**pic′co·lo′ist**, *n.*
**pick** (pik), *n.* [< *pike* (weapon)], 1. any of several pointed tools for picking, esp. a heavy one used in breaking up soil, rock, etc. 2. a plectrum.
**pick** (pik), *v.t.* [ME. *picken*], 1. to pierce, dig up, etc. with something pointed. 2. to probe, scratch at, etc. in an attempt to remove, or to clear something from. 3. to gather (flowers, berries, etc.). 4. to pluck clean, as a fowl of its feathers. 5. to pull (*apart*). 6. to choose; select. 7. to provoke: as, to *pick* a fight. 8. to open (a lock) with a wire, etc. instead of a key. 9. to steal from: as, to *pick* pockets. *v.i.* 1. to eat sparingly (with *at*). 2. to use a pick. 3. to select, esp. in a fussy manner. *n.* 1. the act of choosing or a thing chosen. 2. the best. —**pick off,** 1. to remove by picking. 2. to hit with a carefully aimed shot. —**pick on,** [Colloq.], 1. to single out for criticism. 2. to tease; nag. —**pick out,** to choose. —**pick up,** 1. to grasp and lift. 2. to get; find; learn, esp. by chance. 3. to stop for and take along. 4. to gain (speed). 5. to improve. —**pick′y** [-IER, -IEST], *adj.*
**pick·a·back** (pik′ə-bak′), *adv.* [ult. < *pack*], on the shoulders or back: as, to carry *pickaback.*
**pick·ax, pick·axe** (pik′aks′), *n.* [< OFr. *picquois*], a pick with a point at one end of the head and a chisellike edge at the other.
**pick·er·el** (pik′ēr-əl), *n.* [*pl.* -EL, -ELS], [dim. of *pike* (fish)], a fish of the pike family, with a narrow, pointed snout.
**pick·et** (pik′it), *n.* [< Fr. *pic*, pike], 1. a pointed stake used in a fence, as a hitching post, etc. 2. a soldier or soldiers used to guard against surprise attack. 3. a person, as a member of a striking labor union, stationed outside a factory, etc. to demonstrate protest. *v.t.* 1. to enclose with a picket fence. 2. to hitch (an animal) to a picket. 3. to post as a military picket. 4. to place pickets, or serve as a picket, at (a factory, etc.).
**pick′ings,** *n.pl.* something picked; specif., *a*) small scraps. *b*) something got by dishonest means; spoils.
**pick·le** (pik′'l), *n.* [< MD. *pekel*], 1. any brine, vinegar, etc. used to preserve or flavor food. 2. a vegetable, specif. a cucumber, preserved in such a solution. 3. [Colloq.], an awkward situation. *v.t.* [-LED, -LING], to preserve in a pickle solution.
**pick′pock′et,** *n.* one who steals from pockets.
**pick′up′,** *n.* 1. a picking up. 2. the process or power of increasing in speed. 3. a small delivery truck. 4. [Colloq.], a casual acquaintance. 5. [Colloq.], improvement.
**pic·nic** (pik′nik), *n.* [< Fr.; prob. < *piquer*, to pick], a pleasure outing at which a meal is eaten outdoors. *v.i.* [-NICKED, -NICKING], to hold a picnic. —**pic′nick·er**, *n.*
**pi·cot** (pē′kō), *n.* [*pl.* -COTS (-kōz)], [< Fr. *pic*, a point], any of the small loops forming an ornamental edging on lace, ribbon, etc.
**pic·to·ri·al** (pik-tôr′i-əl), *adj.* 1. of, containing, or expressed in pictures. 2. suggesting a mental image; vivid.
**pic·ture** (pik′chēr), *n.* [< L. *pingere*, to paint], 1. a likeness of a person, scene, etc. produced by drawing, painting, photography, etc. 2. a typification or likeness: as, he's the *picture* of laziness. 3. anything admired for beauty. 4. a description. 5. a motion picture. *v.t.* [-TURED, -TURING], 1. to make a picture of. 2. to show visibly. 3. to describe. 4. to imagine.
**pic′tur·esque′** (-esk′), *adj.* like a picture; specif., *a*) having a natural beauty. *b*) pleasantly unfamiliar; quaint. *c*) vivid.
**picture window,** a large window that seems to frame the outside view.

**pid·dle** (pid′'l), *v.i. & v.t.* [-DLED, -DLING], [child's word for *urinate*], to dawdle; trifle.

**pidg·in** (pij′in), *n.* [Chin. pronun. of *business*], a jargon incorporating the vocabulary of one or more languages: *pidgin English* is simplified English with Chinese syntax.

**pie** (pī), *n.* [prob. same as *pie* (magpie)], a baked dish of fruit, meat, etc. with an upper or under crust, or both.

**pie·bald** (pī′bôld′), *adj.* [*pie* (magpie) + *bald*], covered with patches of two colors.

**piece** (pēs), *n.* [OFr. *pece*], 1. a part separated or broken from the whole. 2. a section of a whole regarded as complete in itself. 3. any single thing; specif., *a*) an artistic work. *b*) a firearm. *c*) a coin. *d*) one of a set, as of china. 4. a quantity, as of cloth, manufactured as a unit. *v.t.* [PIECED, PIECING], 1. to add pieces to, as in repairing. 2. to join (*together*) the pieces of. —**go to pieces**, 1. to fall apart. 2. to lose self-control.

**piece′meal′** (-mēl′), *adv.* [< ME. *pece*, piece + *-mele*, part], piece by piece. *adj.* made or done piecemeal.

**piece′work′**, *n.* work paid for at a fixed rate (**piece rate**) per piece of work done.

**pied** (pīd), *adj.* covered with spots of two or more colors; variegated.

**pier** (pêr), *n.* [< ML. *pera*], 1. a structure supporting the spans of a bridge. 2. a structure built out over water and supported by pillars: used as a landing place, pavilion, etc. 3. in *architecture*, a heavy column used to support weight.

**pierce** (pêrs), *v.t.* [PIERCED, PIERCING], [OFr. *percer*], 1. to pass into or through as a pointed instrument does; stab. 2. to make a hole in; bore. 3. to force a way into; break through. 4. to sound sharply through. 5. to penetrate with the sight or mind.

**pi·e·tism** (pī′ə-tiz'm), *n.* 1. a system which stresses devotion in religion. 2. exaggerated pious feeling. —**pi′e·tist**, *n.* —**pi′e·tis′tic**, *adj.*

**pi·e·ty** (pī′ə-ti), *n.* [*pl.* -TIES], [< L. *pius*, pious], 1. devotion to religious duties, etc. 2. loyalty and devotion to parents, family, etc. 3. a pious act, etc.

**pif·fle** (pif′'l), *n.* [Colloq.], anything considered trivial or nonsensical.

**pig** (pig), *n.* [ME. *pigge*], 1. a domesticated animal with a broad snout and a fat body; swine; hog. 2. a young pig. 3. [Colloq.], a greedy or filthy person. 4. an oblong casting of metal poured from the smelting furnace. *v.i.* [PIGGED, PIGGING], to bear pigs.

**pi·geon** (pij′ən), *n.* [< LL. *pipire*, to chirp], any of various related birds with a small head, plump body, and short legs.

**pi′geon·hole′** (-hōl′), *n.* a small open compartment, as in a desk, for filing papers, etc. *v.t.* [-HOLED, -HOLING], 1. to put in the pigeonhole of a desk, etc. 2. to put aside indefinitely; shelve.

**pi′geon-toed′** (-tōd′), *adj.* having the toes or feet turned in.

**pig·gish** (pig′ish), *adj.* like a pig; gluttonous; filthy. —**pig′gish·ness**, *n.*

**pig·gy** (pig′i), *n.* [*pl.* -GIES], a little pig.

**pig′gy·back′**, *adv. & adj.* 1. pickaback. 2. of or by a transportation system in which loaded truck trailers are carried on railroad flatcars.

**pig′head′ed**, *adj.* stubborn; obstinate.

**pig iron**, [see PIG, sense 4], crude iron, smelted for casting in molds.

**pig·ment** (pig′mənt), *n.* [< L. *pingere*, to paint], 1. coloring matter used to make paints. 2. any coloring matter in the cells and tissues of plants or animals.

**pig·men·ta·tion** (pig′mən-tā′shən), *n.* coloration in plants or animals due to pigment in the tissue.

**Pig·my** (pig′mi), *adj. & n.* [*pl.* -MIES], Pygmy.

**pig′skin′**, *n.* 1. leather made from the skin of a pig. 2. [Colloq.], a football.

**pig′sty′** (-stī′), *n.* [*pl.* -STIES], a pen where pigs are kept: also **pig′pen′**.

**pig′tail′** (-tāl′), *n.* a long braid of hair hanging at the back of the head.

**pike** (pīk), *n.* [< *turnpike*], a toll road.

**pike** (pīk), *n.* [< Fr. *pic*], a long wooden shaft with a metal spearhead: a former weapon.

**pike** (pīk), *n.* [*pl.* PIKE, PIKES], [akin to prec.: from the pointed head], a slender, fresh-water fish with a pointed snout.

**pik·er** (pī′kẽr), *n.* [< dial. var. of *pick*, in sense of "petty pilferer"], [Slang], one who does things in a petty or niggardly way.

**pi·las·ter** (pi-las′tẽr), *n.* [< L. *pila*, a pile], a rectangular supporting column projecting slightly from a wall.

**pile** (pīl), *n.* [< L. *pila*, pillar], 1. a mass of things heaped together. 2. a heap of wood, etc. on which a corpse or sacrifice is burned. 3. a large building. 4. [Colloq.], a large amount. 5. [Slang], a fortune. 6. in *physics*, a reactor. *v.t.* [PILED, PILING], 1. to heap up. 2. to accumulate (with *up*). *v.i.* 1. to form a pile. 2. to move confusedly in a mass (with *in*, *out*, etc.). 3. to accumulate (with *up*).

**pile** (pīl), *n.* [< L. *pilus*, a hair], 1. a raised surface of yarn loops, often sheared to produce a velvety surface, as on carpets. 2. soft, fine hair; down, fur, etc. —**piled**, *adj.*

**pile** (pīl), *n.* [< L. *pilum*, javelin], a long, heavy beam driven into the ground, sometimes under water, to support a bridge, dock, etc.

**pile driver**, a machine for driving piles by means of a heavy weight that is raised and then dropped on them.

**piles** (pīlz), *n.pl.* [< L. *pila*, a ball], hemorrhoids.

**pil·fer** (pil′fẽr), *v.t. & v.i.* [OFr. *pelfre*, booty], to steal (esp. small sums or petty objects).

**pil·grim** (pil′grim), *n.* [< L. *peregrinus*, foreigner], 1. a wanderer; sojourner. 2. one who travels to a shrine or holy place. 3. [P-], one of the band of English Puritans who founded Plymouth Colony in 1620.

**pil′grim·age** (-grə-mij), *n.* a journey made by a pilgrim, esp. to a holy place.

**pill** (pil), *n.* [< L. *pila*, ball], a pellet of medicine to be swallowed whole. —**the pill** (or **Pill**), [Colloq.], any contraceptive drug for women, taken in the form of a pill.

**pil·lage** (pil′ij), *n.* [< OFr. *piller*, rob], plunder; loot. *v.t. & v.i.* [-LAGED, -LAGING], to rob using violence; loot. —**pil′lag·er**, *n.*

**pil·lar** (pil′ẽr), *n.* [< L. *pila*, column], 1. a slender, vertical structure used as a support or a monument; column. 2. any person or thing that is a main support of something.

**pill′box′**, *n.* 1. a small box for pills. 2. an enclosed gun emplacement of concrete.

**pil·lion** (pil′yən), *n.* [< L. *pellis*, a skin], an extra seat behind the saddle on a horse or motorcycle.

**pil·lo·ry** (pil′ə-ri), *n.* [*pl.* -RIES], [< Pr. *espilori*], a device with holes for the head and hands, in which petty offenders were formerly locked and exposed to public scorn. *v.t.* [-RIED, -RYING], 1. to punish by placing in a pillory. 2. to lay open to public scorn.

**pil·low** (pil′ō), *n.* [< L. *pulvinus*], a cloth case filled with feathers, down, etc. to support the head as in sleeping. *v.t. & v.i.* to rest as on a pillow.

**pil′low·case′**, *n.* a removable covering for a pillow: also **pil′low·slip′**.

**pi·lot** (pī′lət), *n.* [< Gr. *pēdon*, oar], 1. a steersman; specif., one licensed to steer ships into or out of a harbor or through difficult waters. 2. one who flies an airplane, airship, etc. 3. a guide; leader. *v.t.* 1. to act as a pilot of, on, in, etc. 2. to lead.

**pi′lot·house′**, *n.* an enclosure for the helmsman on the upper deck of a ship.

**pilot light,** a small gas burner which is kept lighted to rekindle the principal burner when needed.
**pi·mien·to** (pi-myen'tō), *n.* [*pl.* -TOS], [Sp. < L. *pigmentum*, pigment], a variety of sweet, red pepper, used as a relish, etc.: also **pi·men'to** (-men'tō) [*pl.* -TOS].
**pimp** (pimp), *n.* [< ?], a prostitute's agent. *v.i.* to act as a pimp.
**pim·ple** (pim'p'l), *n.* [< ?], a small, often inflamed, swelling of the skin. **—pim'pled, pim'ply** [-PLIER, -PLIEST], *adj.*
**pin** (pin), *n.* [AS. *pinn*], 1. a peg of wood, metal, etc. used to hold things together, hang things on, etc. 2. a pointed piece of stiff wire for fastening things together. 3. anything like a pin in form, use, etc. 4. an ornament or badge fastened to the clothing with a pin or clasp. 5. in *bowling*, one of the wooden clubs at which the ball is rolled. *v.t.* [PINNED, PINNING], 1. to fasten as with a pin. 2. to hold firmly in one position. **—on pins and needles,** filled with anxiety. **—pin one down,** to get one to commit himself as to his plans, etc. **—pin (something) on one,** [Colloq.], to lay the blame of (something) on one.
**pin·a·fore** (pin'ə-fôr'), *n.* [*pin* + archaic *afore*, before], a sleeveless, apronlike garment for girls.
**pin boy,** in *bowling*, a boy who sets up the pins after each frame.
**pince-nez** (pans'nā', pins'-), *n.* [*pl.* PINCE-NEZ], [Fr., nose-pincher], eyeglasses kept in place by a spring gripping the bridge of the nose.
**pin·cers** (pin'sẽrz), *n.pl.* [occas. construed as sing.], [< OFr. *pincier*, to pinch], 1. a tool formed of two pivoted parts, used in gripping things. 2. a grasping claw, as of a crab.
**pinch** (pinch), *v.t.* [prob. < Gmc.], 1. to squeeze between two surfaces, edges, etc. 2. to press painfully upon (a toe, etc.). 3. to cause to become thin, cramped, etc. as by hunger, cold, etc. 4. [Slang], to steal. 5. [Slang], to arrest. *v.i.* 1. to squeeze painfully. 2. to be stingy. *n.* 1. a squeeze or nip. 2. as much as may be grasped between the finger and thumb. 3. hardship. 4. an emergency.
**pinch'ers,** *n.pl.* pincers.
**pinch'-hit',** *v.i.* [-HIT, -HITTING], 1. in *baseball*, to bat in place of the regular player. 2. to act as a substitute in an emergency (*for*). **—pinch hitter.**
**pin'cush'ion,** *n.* a small cushion to stick pins in to keep them handy.
**pine** (pīn), *n.* [< L. *pinus*], 1. an evergreen tree having cones and needle-shaped leaves. 2. its wood.
**pine** (pīn), *v.i.* [PINED, PINING], [< L. *poena*, a pain], 1. to waste (*away*) through grief, pain, etc. 2. to have an intense longing.
**pine'ap'ple,** *n.* [ME. *pinappel*, pine cone], 1. a juicy, edible tropical fruit somewhat resembling a pine cone. 2. the plant it grows on.
**pin'feath'er,** *n.* an undeveloped feather just emerging through the skin.
**ping** (piŋ), *n.* [echoic], the sound of a bullet striking something sharply. *v.i. & v.t.* to strike with a ping.
**ping-pong** (piŋ'poŋ', -pôŋ'), *n.* [echoic], a game somewhat like tennis, played on a table with a small celluloid ball: a trademark (**Ping-pong**).
**pin·ion** (pin'yən), *n.* [< L. *pinna*, a feather], 1. a small cogwheel which meshes with a larger one. 2. the end joint of a bird's wing. 3. a wing. 4. any wing feather. *v.t.* 1. to bind the wings or arms of. 2. to shackle.
**pink** (piŋk), *n.* [? < *pinkeye*, lit., little eye], 1. any of various plants with five-petaled, pale-red flowers. 2. the flower. 3. pale red. 4. the finest condition, example, etc. *adj.* pale-red. **—pink'ish,** *adj.*
**pink** (piŋk), *v.t.* [? < AS. *pyngan*, prick], 1. to cut a saw-toothed edge on (cloth, etc.). 2. to prick; stab. **—pink'er,** *n.*
**pink'eye',** *n.* a contagious eye infection causing inflammation of the eyeball and the inside of the eyelid: also **pink eye.**
**pink'ie, pink'y** (piŋk'i), *n.* [*pl.* -IES], the smallest finger.
**pin money,** a small sum of money for personal or minor expenses.
**pin·nace** (pin'is), *n.* [< L. *pinus*, a pine], 1. a small sailing ship. 2. a ship's boat.
**pin·na·cle** (pin'ə-k'l), *n.* [< L. *pinna*, wing], 1. a small turret or spire. 2. a slender, pointed formation, as a mountain peak. 3. the highest point.
**pin·nate** (pin'āt), *adj.* [< L. *pinna*, a feather], with leaflets on each side of a common stem. **—pin'nate·ly,** *adv.*
**pi·noch·le, pi·noc·le** (pē'nuk''l), *n.* [prob. < Fr.], a card game using a double deck of all cards above the eight.
**pin'point',** *v.t.* to show the precise location of.
**pint** (pīnt), *n.* [< MD.], a measure of capacity (liquid or dry) equal to ½ quart.
**pin·to** (pin'tō), *adj.* [Sp. < L. *pingere*, to paint], marked with spots of two or more colors; mottled; piebald. *n.* [*pl.* -TOS], a pinto horse or pony.
**pin'-up',** *adj.* 1. that is or can be fastened to a wall: as, a *pin-up* lamp. 2. [Slang], designating an attractive girl whose picture is displayed on a wall. *n.* [Slang], a pin-up picture, girl, etc.
**pin'wheel',** *n.* 1. a small wheel with colored vanes pinned to a stick so as to revolve in the wind. 2. a revolving firework.
**pi·o·neer** (pī'ə-nêr'), *n.* [< OFr. *peonier*, foot soldier], one who goes before, preparing the way for others, as an early settler. *v.i.* to act as a pioneer. *v.t.* 1. to open (a way, etc.). 2. to be a pioneer in or of.
**pi·ous** (pī'əs), *adj.* [< L. *pius*], 1. having or showing religious devotion. 2. pretending religious devotion. 3. sacred.
**pip** (pip), *n.* [< *pippin*], a small seed, as of an apple, orange, etc.
**pip** (pip), *n.* [< ?], any of the figures or spots on playing cards, dice, etc.
**pip** (pip), *n.* [< L. *pituita*, phlegm], a contagious disease of fowl.
**pipe** (pīp), *n.* [< L. *pipare*, chirp], 1. a tube of wood, metal, etc. for making musical sounds. 2. *pl.* the bagpipe. 3. a long tube for conveying water, gas, etc. 4. a tube with a small bowl at one end in which tobacco is smoked. 5. any tubular part, organ, etc. *v.i.* [PIPED, PIPING], 1. to play on a pipe. 2. to utter shrill sounds. *v.t.* 1. to play (a tune) on a pipe. 2. to utter in a shrill voice. 3. to bring, call, etc. by sounding a pipe. 4. to convey (water, gas, etc.) by pipes. **—pipe down,** [Slang], to become quiet. **—pip'er,** *n.*
**pipe dream,** [Colloq.], a fantastic idea or vain hope.
**pipe line,** 1. a line of pipes for conveying water, gas, oil, etc. 2. any means whereby something is conveyed.
**pipe organ,** an organ (sense 1).
**pip·ing** (pīp'iŋ), *n.* 1. music made by pipes. 2. a shrill sound. 3. a pipelike fold of material with which edges or seams are trimmed. *adv.* so as to sizzle: as, *piping* hot.
**pip·pin** (pip'in), *n.* [< OFr. *pepin*, seed], any of several varieties of apple.
**pip-squeak** (pip'skwēk'), *n.* anyone or anything regarded as insignificant.
**pi·quant** (pē'kənt), *adj.* [Fr. < *piquer*, to prick], 1. agreeably pungent to the taste.

2. exciting interest; stimulating. —**pi′quan·cy**, *n.* —**pi′quant·ly**, *adv.*
**pique** (pēk), *n.* [see PIQUANT], resentment at being slighted. *v.t.* [PIQUED, PIQUING], 1. to arouse such resentment in; offend. 2. to excite; arouse.
**pi·qué** (pi-kā′), *n.* [Fr.; see PIQUANT], a cotton fabric with vertical cords.
**pi·ra·cy** (pī′rə-si), *n.* [*pl.* -CIES], 1. robbery of ships on the high seas. 2. the unauthorized use of a copyrighted or patented work.
**pi·rate** (pī′rit), *n.* [< Gr. *peiran*, to attack], one who practices piracy. *v.t. & v.i.* [-RATED, -RATING], 1. to practice piracy (upon). 2. to use (a literary work, etc.) in violation of a copyright or patent. —**pi·rat′i·cal** (-rat′i-k'l), *adj.*
**pir·ou·ette** (pir′ōō-et′), *n.* [Fr., spinning top], in *dancing*, a whirling on the toes. *v.i.* [-ETTED, -ETTING], to do a pirouette.
**pis·ca·to·ri·al** (pis′kə-tôr′i-əl), *adj.* [< L. *piscator*, fisherman], of fishermen or fishing.
**Pis·ces** (pis′ēz), *n.* [< L. pl. of *piscis*, a fish], the twelfth sign of the zodiac.
**pis·mire** (pis′mīr′), *n.* [< ME. *pisse*, urine + *mire*, ant], an ant.
**pis·ta·chi·o** (pis-tä′shi-ō′, -tash′i-ō′), *n.* [*pl.* -OS], [< Gr. *pistakē*], 1. a small tree of the cashew family. 2. its edible, greenish seed (**pistachio nut**).
**pis·til** (pis′til, -t'l), *n.* [< L. *pistillum*, a pestle], the seed-bearing organ of a flower.
**pis·tol** (pis′t'l), *n.* [< Czech *pisk*, whistling sound], a small firearm held and fired with one hand. *v.t.* [-TOLED or -TOLLED, -TOLING or -TOLLING], to shoot with a pistol.
**pis·ton** (pis′t'n), *n.* [ult. < L. *pinsere*, to pound], a disk or short cylinder fitted in a hollow cylinder and moved back and forth by the pressure of a fluid so as to transmit motion to a rod (**piston rod**) or moved by the rod so as to exert pressure on the fluid.
**piston ring**, a split metal ring placed around a piston to make it fit the cylinder closely.
**pit** (pit), *n.* [D., kernel], the hard stone, as of the plum, peach, etc., which contains the seed. *v.t.* [PITTED, PITTING], to remove the pit from.
**pit** (pit), *n.* [< L. *puteus*, a well], 1. a hole in the ground. 2. an abyss. 3. a trap; pitfall. 4. any concealed danger. 5. an enclosed area in which animals are kept or made to fight. 6. a small hollow in a surface, as a scar left by smallpox. 7. the section for the orchestra in front of the stage. *v.t.* [PITTED, PITTING], 1. to put in a pit. 2. to make pits or scars in. 3. to set in competition (*against*). *v.i.* to become marked with pits.
**pit·a·pat** (pit′ə-pat′), *adv.* with rapid and strong beating. *n.* a rapid succession of beats. *v.i.* [-PATTED, -PATTING], to go pitapat.
**pitch** (pich), *n.* [< L. *pix*], 1. a black, sticky substance formed from coal tar, petroleum, etc. and used for roofing, pavements, etc. 2. any of certain bitumens, as asphalt.
**pitch** (pich), *v.t.* [ME. *picchen*], 1. to set up: as, *pitch* a tent. 2. to throw; toss. 3. to fix at a certain point, level, degree, etc. 4. in *baseball*, to throw (the ball) to the batter. *v.i.* 1. to pitch something, as a ball. 2. to plunge forward. 3. to incline downward; dip. 4. to rise and fall, as a ship in rough water. *n.* 1. act or manner of pitching. 2. a throw; toss. 3. anything pitched. 4. a point or degree: as, feelings are at a high *pitch*. 5. the degree of slope. 6. in *music*, etc., the highness or lowness of a sound determined by the frequency of vibration of the sound waves. —**pitch in**, [Colloq.], to set to work energetically.
**pitch′-black′**, *adj.* very black.
**pitch·blende** (pich′blend′), *n.* [< G. *pech*, pitch + *blenden*, dazzle], a dark, lustrous mineral containing radium, uranium, etc.
**pitch′-dark′**, *adj.* very dark.
**pitch·er** (pich′ẽr), *n.* [ult. < Gr. *bikos*, wine jar], a container, usually with a handle and lip, for holding and pouring liquids.
**pitch′er**, *n.* one who pitches; esp., in *baseball*, the player who pitches the ball to the batters.
**pitch′fork′**, *n.* a large, long-handled fork for lifting and tossing hay, etc.
**pitch′y**, *adj.* [-IER, -IEST], 1. full of or smeared with pitch. 2. like pitch; sticky, black, etc.
**pit·e·ous** (pit′i-əs), *adj.* arousing or deserving pity. —**pit′e·ous·ly**, *adv.*
**pit′fall′**, *n.* [< *pit* + AS. *fealle*, a trap], 1. a covered pit for trapping animals. 2. any concealed danger.
**pith** (pith), *n.* [AS. *pitha*], 1. the soft, spongy tissue in the center of certain plant stems. 2. the essential part; gist. 3. strength.
**pith·y** (pith′i), *adj.* [-IER, -IEST], 1. of, like, or full of pith. 2. full of meaning or force.
**pit·i·a·ble** (pit′i-ə-b'l), *adj.* 1. arousing or deserving pity. 2. deserving contempt. —**pit′i·a·ble·ness**, *n.* —**pit′i·a·bly**, *adv.*
**pit·i·ful** (pit′i-fəl), *adj.* 1. full of pity. 2. arousing or deserving pity. 3. deserving contempt. —**pit′i·ful·ly**, *adv.*
**pit·i·less** (pit′i-lis), *adj.* without pity; merciless. —**pit′i·less·ly**, *adv.* —**pit′i·less·ness**, *n.*
**pit·tance** (pit′əns), *n.* [< OFr. *pitance*, food allowed a monk], 1. a meager allowance of money. 2. a small amount or share.
**pit·ter-pat·ter** (pit′ẽr-pat′ẽr), *n.* [echoic], a rapid succession of light tapping sounds.
**pi·tu·i·tar·y** (pi-tōō′ə-ter′i, -tū′-), *adj.* [< L. *pituita*, phlegm], of a small, oval endocrine gland (**pituitary gland**) attached to the base of the brain: it secretes hormones affecting growth, etc.
**pit·y** (pit′i), *n.* [*pl.* -IES], [< L. *pietas*, piety], 1. sorrow for another's suffering or misfortune. 2. a cause for sorrow or regret. *v.t. & v.i.* [-IED, -YING], to feel pity (for).
**piv·ot** (piv′ət), *n.* [Fr.], 1. a point, shaft, etc. on which something turns. 2. a person or thing on which something depends. 3. a pivoting movement. *v.t.* to provide with a pivot. *v.i.* to turn as on a pivot. —**piv′ot·al**, *adj.* —**piv′ot·al·ly**, *adv.*
**pix·i·lat·ed** (pik′sə-lā′tid), *adj.* [< *pixy* + *titillated*], 1. slightly unbalanced mentally. 2. [Slang], drunk.
**pix·y, pix·ie** (pik′si), *n.* [*pl.* -IES], [< Brit. dial.], a fairy; sprite.
**piz·za** (pēt′sə), *n.* [It.], an Italian dish made of thin dough covered with tomatoes, cheese, etc. and baked.
**piz·zi·ca·to** (pit′sə-kä′tō), *adj.* [It.], in *music*, plucked: a direction to pluck the strings of a violin, etc. with the fingers.
**pk.**, [*pl.* PKS.], 1. pack. 2. park. 3. peck.
**pkg.**, [*pl.* PKGS.], package.
**pl.**, 1. place. 2. plural.
**pla·ca·ble** (plā′kə-b'l, plak′ə-), *adj.* capable of being placated; forgiving.
**plac·ard** (plak′ärd), *n.* [< Pr. *placa*, plaque], a notice for display in a public place. *v.t.* (plə-kärd′), to place placards on or in.
**pla·cate** (plā′kāt, plak′āt), *v.t.* [-CATED, -CATING], [< L. *placare*], to appease; pacify.
**place** (plās), *n.* [< Gr. *plateia*, street], 1. a court or short street in a city. 2. space; room. 3. a region. 4. *a*) the part of space occupied by a person or thing. *b*) situation. 5. a city, town, etc. 6. a residence. 7. a building or space devoted to a special purpose: as, a *place* of amusement. 8. a particular point, part, position, etc.: as, a sore *place* on the leg, a *place* in history. 9. a step or point in a sequence. 10. the cus-

tomary or proper position, time, etc. 11. a space, seat, etc. reserved or occupied by a person. 12. an office; employment. 13. the duties of any position. *v.t.* [PLACED, PLACING], 1. to put in a particular place, condition, or relation. 2. to find employment for. 3. to repose (trust) *in* a person or thing. 4. to identify by connecting with some event, etc. *v.i.* to finish second or among the first three in a race. —**take place,** to occur.

**place′ment,** *n.* 1. a placing or being placed. 2. the finding of employment for a person.

**pla·cen·ta** (plə-sen′tə), *n.* [*pl.* -TAE (-tē), -TAS], [ult. < Gr. *plax*, flat object], an organ within the uterus to which the fetus is connected and through which it is nourished.

**plac·er** (plas′ẽr), *n.* [Sp. < *plaza*, a place], a deposit of gravel or sand containing particles of gold, platinum, etc. that can be washed out.

**plac·id** (plas′id), *adj.* [< L. *placere*, to please], calm; quiet. —**pla·cid·i·ty** (plə-sid′ə-ti), **plac′id·ness,** *n.* —**plac′id·ly,** *adv.*

**plack·et** (plak′it), *n.* [< *placard*], a slit at the top of a skirt to make it easy to put on and take off: also **placket hole.**

**pla·gia·rize** (plā′jə-riz′), *v.t.* & *v.i.* [-RIZED, -RIZING], [< L. *plagiarius*, kidnaper], to take (ideas, writings, etc.) from (another) and offer them as one's own. —**pla′gia·rism** (-riz'm), *n.* —**pla′gia·rist, pla′gia·riz′er,** *n.*

**plague** (plāg), *n.* [< Gr. *plēgē*, misfortune], 1. any affliction or calamity. 2. any deadly epidemic disease. *v.t.* [PLAGUED, PLAGUING], to afflict, distress, torment, etc.

**plaid** (plad), *n.* [Gael. *plaide*, a blanket], 1. cloth with a checkered or crossbarred pattern. 2. any pattern of this kind.

**plain** (plān), *adj.* [< L. *planus*, flat], 1. flat; level. 2. open; clear: as, in *plain* view. 3. clearly understood; obvious. 4. outspoken; straightforward. 5. not luxurious. 6. not complicated; simple. 7. homely: as, a *plain* face. 8. unfigured, undyed, etc. 9. common; ordinary: as, a *plain* man. *n.* an extent of level country. *adv.* clearly.

**plain′-clothes′ man,** a police detective who wears civilian clothes on duty.

**plaint** (plānt), *n.* [< L. *plangere*, to lament], 1. a complaint. 2. a lament.

**plain·tiff** (plān′tif), *n.* [< L. *plangere*, to lament], one who brings a suit into a court of law.

**plain·tive** (plān′tiv), *adj.* [see PLAINTIFF], expressing sorrow or melancholy; sad.

**plait** (plāt; *occas.* plēt), *n.* [< L. *plicare*, to fold], 1. a pleat. 2. a braid of hair, etc. *v.t.* 1. to pleat. 2. to braid. —**plait′er,** *n.*

**plan** (plan), *n.* [ult. < L. *planta*, sole of the foot], 1. an outline; draft; map. 2. a diagram showing the arrangement of a structure, piece of ground, etc. 3. a scheme for making, doing, or arranging something. *v.t.* [PLANNED, PLANNING], 1. to make a plan of (a structure, etc.). 2. to devise a scheme for doing, etc. 3. to have in mind as a project or purpose. *v.i.* to make plans. —**plan′ner,** *n.*

**plane** (plān), *adj.* [< L. *planus*], flat; level. *n.* 1. a surface that wholly contains every straight line joining any two points lying on it. 2. a flat or level surface. 3. a level of achievement, etc. 4. an airplane.

**plane** (plān), *n.* [< L. *planus*, level], a carpenter's tool for leveling or smoothing wood. *v.t.* [PLANED, PLANING], to smooth or level with a plane. —**plan′er,** *n.*

**plan·et** (plan′it), *n.* [< Gr. *planan*, wander], any heavenly body that revolves about the sun: the major planets, in their order from the sun, are Mercury, Venus, Earth, Mars, Jupiter, Saturn, Uranus, Neptune, and Pluto. —**plan′e·tar′y** (-ə-ter′i), *adj.*

**plan·e·tar·i·um** (plan′ə-târ′i-əm), *n.* [*pl.* -UMS, -A (-ə)], a room with a large dome on which the images of the sun, planets, etc. are projected by a complex optical instrument that revolves to show the celestial motions.

**plank** (plaŋk), *n.* [< LL. *planca*], 1. a long, broad, thick board. 2. any of the principles in a platform, as of a political party. *v.t.* 1. to cover, lay, etc. with planks. 2. to broil and serve on a board, as steak. 3. [Colloq.], to set down with force.

**plank·ton** (plaŋk′tən), *n.* [< Gr. *plazesthai*, wander], the microscopic animals and plant life found floating in bodies of water.

**plant** (plant, plänt), *n.* [< L. *planta*], 1. any living thing that cannot move voluntarily, has no sense organs, and generally makes its own food by photosynthesis. 2. a soft-stemmed organism of this kind, as distinguished from a tree or shrub. 3. the machinery, buildings, etc. of a factory, etc. *v.t.* 1. to put into the ground to grow. 2. to set firmly in position. 3. to settle; establish. 4. to furnish; stock. 5. [Slang], to place (a person or thing) in such a way as to trick, trap, etc.

**plan·tain** (plan′tin), *n.* [< L. *plantago*], a plant with broad leaves at the bottom of the stem and spikes of tiny, greenish flowers.

**plan·tain** (plan′tin), *n.* [< W. Ind. native name], 1. a tropical plant yielding a kind of banana. 2. its fruit.

**plan·ta·tion** (plan-tā′shən), *n.* [< L. *plantare*, to plant], 1. an estate, as in the South, cultivated by workers living on it. 2. a cultivated planting of trees, etc.

**plant′er,** *n.* 1. the owner of a plantation. 2. a person or machine that plants. 3. a decorative container for plants.

**plaque** (plak), *n.* [< D. *plak*, disk], 1. any thin, flat piece of metal, wood, etc. used for ornamentation, as on a wall. 2. a platelike brooch or pin worn as a badge or ornament.

**plash** (plash), *n.*, *v.t.* & *v.i.* [echoic], splash.

**plas·ma** (plaz′mə), *n.* [< Gr. *plasma*, something molded], 1. the fluid part of blood, lymph, or milk. 2. protoplasm. Also **plasm.**

**plas·ter** (plas′tẽr, pläs′-), *n.* [< Gr. *emplassein*, to daub over], 1. a pasty mixture of lime, sand, and water, hard when dry, for coating walls, etc. 2. plaster of Paris. 3. a pasty preparation spread on cloth and applied to the body as a medicine. *v.t.* 1. to cover as with plaster. 2. to apply like a plaster: as, a wall *plastered* with posters. —**plas′ter·er,** *n.* —**plas′ter·ing,** *n.*

**plaster of Paris,** [from use of gypsum from Paris, France], a thick paste of gypsum and water that sets quickly: used for casts, etc.

**plas·tic** (plas′tik), *adj.* [< Gr. *plassein*, to form], 1. molding or shaping matter; formative. 2. that can be molded or shaped. *n.* any of various nonmetallic compounds, synthetically produced, which can be molded and hardened for commercial use. —**plas·tic′i·ty** (-tis′ə-ti), *n.*

**plastic surgery,** surgery dealing with the repair of deformed or destroyed parts of the body by transferring skin, bone, etc., as from other parts.

**plat** (plat), *n.* [var. of *plot*], 1. a small piece of ground. 2. a map; plan. *v.t.* [PLATTED, PLATTING], to make a map or plan of.

**plate** (plāt), *n.* [< Gr. *platys*, broad], 1. a smooth, flat, thin piece of metal, etc., specif. one on which an engraving is cut. 2. an impression taken from an engraved surface. 3. dishes, utensils, etc. of, or plated with, silver or gold. 4. a shallow dish. 5. the food in a dish or course. 6. a denture, specif. that part of it which fits to the mouth. 7. in *baseball*, home plate. 8. in *photography*, a sheet of glass, metal, etc.

coated with a film sensitive to light. 9. in *printing*, a cast made from a mold of set type. *v.t.* [PLATED, PLATING], to coat with gold, tin, etc.
**pla·teau** (pla-tō′), *n.* [*pl.* -TEAUS, -TEAUX (-tōz′)], [< Gr. *platys*, broad], 1. an elevated tract of level land. 2. a temporary halt in progress.
**plate glass,** polished, clear glass in thick sheets, for windows, mirrors, etc.
**plat·en** (plat′'n), *n.* [< OFr. *plat*, flat], 1. in a printing press, a flat metal plate or rotating cylinder that presses the paper against the inked type. 2. in a typewriter, the roller against which the keys strike.
**plat·form** (plat′fôrm′), *n.* [Fr. *plateforme*, lit., flat form], 1. a raised horizontal surface, as a stage for speakers, etc. 2. the statement of policy of a political party, etc.
**plat·i·num** (plat′'n-əm), *n.* [< Sp. *plata*, silver], a steel-gray metallic chemical element, resistant to corrosion: used for jewelry, etc.: symbol, Pt.
**plat·i·tude** (plat′ə-tōōd′, -tūd′), *n.* [Fr. < *plat*, flat, after *latitude*, etc.], a commonplace or trite remark.
**Pla·ton·ic** (plə-ton′ik), *adj.* 1. of Plato, an ancient Gr. philosopher, or his philosophy. 2. [also p-], not amorous but purely spiritual: as, *Platonic* love.
**Pla·ton·ism** (plā′t'n-iz'm), *n.* 1. the philosophy of Plato or his school: see **idealism.** 2. [also p-], the theory or practice of Platonic love. **—Pla′ton·ist,** *adj. & n.*
**pla·toon** (plə-tōōn′), *n.* [Fr. *pelaton*, a ball, group], 1. a military unit composed of two or more squads. 2. a group like this.
**plat·ter** (plat′ẽr), *n.* [< OFr. *plat*, flat], a large, shallow dish for serving food.
**plat·y·pus** (plat′ə-pəs), *n.* [*pl.* -PUSES, -PI (-pī′)], [< Gr. *platys*, flat + *pous*, foot], a duckbill.
**plau·dit** (plô′dit), *n.* [< L. *plaudere*, applaud], *usually in pl.* an expression of approval; esp., applause.
**plau·si·ble** (plô′zə-b'l), *adj.* [< L. *plaudere*, applaud], seemingly true, trustworthy, etc. **—plau′si·bil′i·ty,** *n.* **—plau′si·bly,** *adv.*
**play** (plā), *v.i.* [AS. *pleg(i)an*], 1. to move lightly, rapidly, etc.: as, sunlight *plays* on the water. 2. *a*) to have fun; frolic. *b*) to take part in a game or sport. 3. to gamble. 4. to perform on a musical instrument. 5. to act in a specified way: as, *play* fair. 6. to perform on the stage. *v.t.* 1. to take part in (a game or sport). 2. to engage in a game against. 3. to do in fun: as, to *play* tricks. 4. to bet (a sum) on. 5. to put into or keep in action; wield. 6. to cause: as, to *play* havoc. 7. to perform (music, a drama, etc.). 8. to perform on (an instrument). 9. to act the part of: as, to *play* Hamlet. *n.* 1. motion or activity, esp. when free or rapid. 2. freedom for motion or action. 3. recreation; sport. 4. fun; joking. 5. a move or act in a game. 6. gambling. 7. a dramatic composition or performance; drama. **—play down,** to attach little importance to. **—play up,** [Colloq.], to give prominence to. **—play up to,** [Colloq.], to try to please by flattery.
**play′bill′,** *n.* a program of a play.
**play′boy′,** *n.* [Colloq.], a rich man who spends much time in dissipation.
**play′er,** *n.* 1. one who plays a specified game, instrument, etc. 2. an actor.
**player piano,** a piano played mechanically.
**play′ful,** *adj.* 1. fond of play or fun; frisky. 2. humorous; merry. **—play′ful·ly,** *adv.*
**play′go′er,** *n.* one who goes to the theater frequently or regularly.
**play′ground′,** *n.* a place, often near a school, for outdoor recreation.
**play′house′,** *n.* 1. a theater. 2. a small house for children to play in. 3. a doll house.
**playing cards,** cards used in playing various games, arranged in decks of four suits.
**play′mate′,** *n.* a companion in games and recreation: also **play′fel′low.**
**play′-off′,** *n.* in *games*, a match played to break a tie.
**play on words,** a pun or punning.
**play′thing′,** *n.* a toy.
**play′wright′** (-rīt′), *n.* a person who writes plays; dramatist.
**pla·za** (plaz′ə, plä′zə), *n.* [Sp. < L.; see PLACE], a public square or market place in a city or town.
**plea** (plē), *n.* [< L. *placere*, please], 1. a statement in defense; excuse. 2. an appeal; request. 3. in *law*, a defendant's statement, answering the charges against him.
**plead** (plēd), *v.i.* [PLEADED, PLEADING; *colloq.* pt. & pp. PLEAD, PLED (pled)], 1. to present a plea in a law court. 2. to make an appeal; beg. *v.t.* 1. to argue (a law case). 2. to answer (guilty or not guilty) to a charge. 3. to offer as an excuse.
**pleas·ant** (plez′'nt), *adj.* [< OFr. *plaisir*, to please], 1. agreeable to the mind or senses; pleasing. 2. having an agreeable manner, look, etc. 3. gay or playful.
**pleas′ant·ry** (-'n-tri), *n.* [*pl.* -RIES], 1. pleasant jocularity in conversation. 2. a humorous remark; jest.
**please** (plēz), *v.t.* [PLEASED, PLEASING], [< L. *placere*], 1. to be agreeable to; satisfy. 2. to be the wish of: as, it *pleased* him to go. *v.i.* 1. to be agreeable; satisfy. 2. to have the wish; like: as, I'll do as I *please*. *Please* is also used in polite requests: as, *please* do it now. **—pleased,** *adj.*
**pleas′ing,** *adj.* giving pleasure; agreeable.
**pleas·ur·a·ble** (plezh′ẽr-ə-b'l), *adj.* pleasant; enjoyable. **—pleas′ur·a·bly,** *adv.*
**pleas·ure** (plezh′ẽr), *n.* 1. a pleased feeling; delight. 2. one's wish, will, or choice. 3. a thing that gives delight or satisfaction.
**pleat** (plēt), *n.* [ME. *pleten*], a flat double fold, as in cloth, pressed or stitched in place. *v.t.* to lay and press (cloth) in a pleat or pleats.
**ple·be·ian** (pli-bē′ən), *n.* [< L. *plebs*, common people], 1. one of the common people. 2. a vulgar, coarse person. *adj.* vulgar, coarse, or common. **—ple·be′ian·ism,** *n.*
**pleb·i·scite** (pleb′ə-sīt′), *n.* [< L. *plebs*, common people + *scitum*, decree], an expression of the people's will on a political issue by direct vote.
**plec·trum** (plek′trəm), *n.* [*pl.* -TRUMS, -TRA (-trə)], [< Gr. *plēssein*, to strike], a small, thin piece of metal, bone, etc. for plucking the strings of a banjo, guitar, etc.
**pled** (pled), colloq. pt. and pp. of **plead.**
**pledge** (plej), *n.* [< base of AS. *plegian*, to play], 1. the condition of being given or held as security for a contract, payment, etc. 2. a person or thing given or held as such security. 3. a drinking of a toast. 4. a promise or agreement. *v.t.* [PLEDGED, PLEDGING], 1. to give as security. 2. to drink a toast to. 3. to bind by a promise.
**ple·na·ry** (plē′nə-ri, plen′ə-), *adj.* [< L. *plenus*, full], 1. full; complete. 2. attended by all members, as an assembly.
**plen·i·po·ten·ti·ar·y** (plen′i-pə-ten′shi-er′i, -shə-ri), *adj.* [< L. *plenus*, full + *potens*, powerful], having or conferring full authority. *n.* [*pl.* -IES], one given full authority as an ambassador.
**plen·i·tude** (plen′ə-tōōd′, -tūd′), *n.* [< L. *plenus*, full], 1. fullness; completeness. 2. abundance; plenty.
**plen·te·ous** (plen′ti-əs), *adj.* plentiful.
**plen·ti·ful** (plen′ti-fəl), *adj.* 1. having or yielding plenty. 2. abundant.
**plen·ty** (plen′ti), *n.* [*pl.* -TIES], [< L. *plenus*,

full], 1. prosperity; opulence. 2. an ample amount. *adj.* plentiful; ample.

**pleth·o·ra** (pleth'ə-rə), *n.* [< Gr. *plēthos*, fullness], the state of being too full; overabundance.

**pleu·ra** (ploor'ə), *n.* [*pl.* -RAE (-ē)], [< Gr. *pleura*, a rib], a thin membrane lining each half of the chest cavity and enveloping the lungs. —**pleu'ral**, *adj.*

**pleu·ri·sy** (ploor'ə-si), *n.* inflammation of the pleura, characterized by painful breathing, fever, etc. —**pleu·rit·ic** (ploo-rit'ik), *adj.*

**plex·i·glass** (plek'si-glas', -gläs'), *n.* a lightweight, glasslike thermoplastic substance: a trademark (**Plexiglas**).

**plex·us** (plek'səs), *n.* [*pl.* -USES, -US], [< L. *plectere*, to twine], a network, as of blood vessels, nerves, etc.

**pli·a·ble** (plī'ə-b'l), *adj.* [< L. *plicare*, to fold], 1. easily bent; flexible. 2. easily influenced or persuaded. —**pli'a·bil'i·ty**, *n.*

**pli·ant** (plī'ənt), *adj.* 1. easily bent; pliable. 2. compliant. —**pli'an·cy**, *n.*

**pli·ers** (plī'ẽrz), *n.pl.* [< *ply* (to bend)], small pincers for handling small objects, cutting wire, etc.

**plight** (plīt), *n.* [< OFr. *ploit*, a fold], a condition, situation, etc.; esp., a dangerous or awkward situation.

**plight** (plīt), *v.t.* [< AS. *pliht*, danger], 1. to pledge or engage. 2. to bind (oneself) by a promise; betroth.

**plinth** (plinth), *n.* [< Gr. *plinthos*, tile], the square block at the base of a column, pedestal, etc.

**plod** (plod), *v.i.* [PLODDED, PLODDING], [prob. echoic], 1. to move heavily and laboriously; trudge. 2. to work steadily; drudge. —**plod'der**, *n.* —**plod'ding**, *adj.*

**plop** (plop), *v.t.* & *v.i.* [PLOPPED, PLOPPING], [echoic], to drop with a sound like that of something flat falling into water. *n.* such a sound. *adv.* with a plop.

**plot** (plot), *n.* [? < OFr. *pelote*, clod], 1. a small area of ground. 2. a diagram or map. 3. a secret, usually evil, scheme. 4. the plan of action of a play, novel, etc. *v.t.* [PLOTTED, PLOTTING], 1. to draw a map, plan, etc. of. 2. to make secret plans for. *v.i.* to scheme.

**plov·er** (pluv'ẽr, plō'vẽr), *n.* [< L. *pluvia*, rain], a shore bird of North America with a short tail and long, pointed wings.

**plow, plough** (plou), *n.* [AS. *ploh*], 1. a farm implement used to cut and turn up the soil. 2. any implement like this, as a snowplow. *v.t.* 1. to cut and turn up (soil) with a plow. 2. to make (one's way) through as if by plowing. *v.i.* 1. to use a plow. 2. to cut a way (*through* water, etc.). 3. to plod. —**plow into**, to begin work vigorously on.

**plow'man, plough'man** (-mən), *n.* [*pl.* -MEN], 1. one who plows. 2. a farm worker.

**plow'share', plough'share'** (-shâr'), *n.* the cutting blade of a plow.

**ploy** (ploi), *n.* [? < *employ*], an action or maneuver intended to outwit or disconcert another person.

**pluck** (pluk), *v.t.* [AS. *pluccian*], 1. to pull off or out; pick. 2. to drag. 3. to pull out the feathers of (a fowl). 4. to pull at and release quickly, as a taut string. *n.* 1. a pulling. 2. courage. —**pluck up**, to take heart.

**pluck'y**, *adj.* [-IER, -IEST], brave; resolute; spirited. —**pluck'i·ness**, *n.*

**plug** (plug), *n.* [MD. *plugge*], 1. an object used to stop up a hole, etc. 2. a cake of tobacco. 3. an electrical device for making contact or closing a circuit. 4. a fireplug. 5. [Slang], something inferior; esp., a worn-out horse. 6. [Slang], an advertisement or recommendation. *v.t.* [PLUGGED, PLUGGING], 1. to fill (a hole, etc.) with a plug. 2. to insert as a plug. 3. [Slang], to shoot or hit. 4. [Slang], to advertise insistently. *v.i.* [Colloq.], to work doggedly. —**plug'ger**, *n.*

**plum** (plum), *n.* [ult. < Gr. *proumnon*], 1. a tree bearing smooth-skinned fruit with a smooth pit. 2. the fruit. 3. a raisin. 4. the bluish-red color of some plums. 5. a choice or desirable object. —**plum'my**, *adj.*

**plum·age** (plōōm'ij), *n.* [OFr. < *plume*, a feather], a bird's feathers.

**plumb** (plum), *n.* [< L. *plumbum*, lead (metal)], a lead weight (**plumb bob**) hung at the end of a line (**plumb line**), used to determine how deep water is or whether a wall, etc. is vertical. *adj.* exactly perpendicular. *adv.* 1. straight down. 2. [Colloq.], entirely: as, *plumb* crazy. *v.t.* 1. to test with a plumb. 2. to discover the facts of. —**out of plumb**, not vertical.

**plumb·er** (plum'ẽr), *n.* [< L. *plumbum*, lead (metal)], a worker who fits and repairs water pipes and fixtures, etc.

**plumb·ing** (plum'iŋ), *n.* 1. the work of a plumber. 2. the pipes and fixtures with which a plumber works.

**plume** (plōōm), *n.* [< L. *pluma*], 1. a feather or a group of feathers. 2. an ornament made of feathers. *v.t.* [PLUMED, PLUMING], 1. to adorn with plumes. 2. to smooth its feathers: used reflexively, of a bird.

**plum·met** (plum'it), *n.* [see PLUMB], 1. a plumb. 2. a thing that weighs heavily. *v.i.* to fall straight downward.

**plump** (plump), *adj.* [< MD. *plomp*, bulky], full and rounded in form; chubby.

**plump** (plump), *v.i.* & *v.t.* [echoic], to drop or bump suddenly or heavily. *n.* 1. a falling, bumping, etc. 2. the sound of this. *adv.* 1. suddenly; heavily. 2. straight down. *adj.* blunt; downright.

**plun·der** (plun'dẽr), *v.t.* [< G. *plunder*, baggage], to rob or take by force. *v.i.* to steal. *n.* 1. the act of plundering. 2. goods taken by force; loot. —**plun'der·er**, *n.*

**plunge** (plunj), *v.t.* [PLUNGED, PLUNGING], [< L. *plumbum*, lead (metal)], to thrust or throw suddenly (*into*). *v.i.* 1. to dive or rush. 2. to move violently and rapidly downward or forward. 3. [Colloq.], to gamble heavily. *n.* 1. a dive or fall. 2. a swim.

**plung'er**, *n.* 1. one who plunges. 2. any cylindrical device that operates with a plunging motion, as a piston.

**plunk** (pluŋk), *v.t.* [echoic], 1. to strum (a banjo, etc.). 2. to throw or put down heavily; plump. *v.i.* 1. to give out a twanging sound. 2. to fall heavily. *n.* the sound made by plunking.

**plu·ral** (ploor'əl), *adj.* [< L. *plus*, more], more than one. *n.* in *grammar*, the form of a word designating more than one (e.g., *hands*, *men*).

**plu·ral·i·ty** (ploo-ral'ə-ti), *n.* [*pl.* -TIES], 1. a being plural or numerous. 2. a majority. 3. the excess of votes in an election that the leading candidate has over his nearest rival.

**plu·ral·ize** (ploor'əl-īz'), *v.t.* [-IZED, -IZING], to make plural.

**plus** (plus), *prep.* [L., more], 1. added to: as, two *plus* two. 2. and in addition. *adj.* 1. designating a sign (**plus sign**, +) indicating addition. 2. positive: as, a *plus* quantity. 3. higher than: as, a grade of B *plus*. 4. [Colloq.], and more: as, personality *plus*. *n.* 1. a plus sign. 2. something added.

**plush** (plush), *n.* [< L. *pilus*, hair], a fabric having a long, soft pile. *adj.* [Slang], luxurious. —**plush'y** [-IER, -IEST], *adj.*

**Plu·to** (plōō'tō), *n.* 1. in *Gr. & Rom. myth.*, the god of the lower world. 2. the outermost planet of the solar system: cf. **planet**.

**plu·toc·ra·cy** (plōō-tok'rə-si), *n.* [*pl.* -CIES], [< Gr. *ploutos*, wealth + *kratein*, to rule], 1. government by the wealthy. 2. a state so ruled. 3. the class of wealthy people who control a government.

**plu'to·crat'** (-tə-krat'), *n.* 1. a member of a plutocracy. 2. one whose wealth gives him control or influence.

**plu·to·ni·um** (plōō-tō'ni-əm), *n.* [< *Pluto* (planet)], a radioactive chemical element: symbol, Pu.

**ply** (plī), *v.t.* [PLIED, PLYING], [< L. *plicare*, to fold], to bend, twist, etc. *n.* [*pl.* PLIES], 1. a thickness or layer, as of cloth, plywood, etc. 2. a twisted strand in rope, etc.

**ply** (plī), *v.t.* [PLIED, PLYING], [contr. < *apply*], 1. to work with (a tool, faculty, etc.). 2. to work at (a trade). 3. to keep supplying, assailing, etc. (*with*). 4. to address (someone) urgently (*with* questions, etc.). 5. to sail back and forth across. *v.i.* 1. to keep busy. 2. to travel regularly (*between* places), as a ship or bus.

**ply'wood'**, *n.* [*ply* (*n.*) + *wood*], a construction material made of thin layers of wood glued and pressed together.

**P.M., PM, p.m.,** *post meridiem*, [L.], after noon: used to designate the time from noon to midnight.

**pneu·mat·ic** (nōō-mat'ik, nū-), *adj.* [< Gr. *pneuma*, air], 1. of or containing wind, air, or gases. 2. worked by or filled with compressed air. **—pneu·mat'i·cal·ly,** *adv.*

**pneu·mo·nia** (nōō-mō'nyə, nū-), *n.* [< Gr. *pneumōn*, a lung < *pnein*, breathe], a disease of the lungs in which tissue becomes inflamed, hardened, and watery.

**P.O., p.o.,** 1. post office. 2. petty officer.

**poach** (pōch), *v.t.* [< OFr. *poche*, a pocket: the yolk is "pocketed" in the white], to cook the unbroken contents of (an egg) in or over boiling water.

**poach** (pōch), *v.t. & v.i.* [< MHG. *puchen*, to plunder], 1. to trespass on (private property), esp. for hunting or fishing. 2. to hunt or catch (game or fish) illegally. 3. to steal.

**pock** (pok), *n.* [AS. *pocc*], 1. a pustule caused by smallpox, etc. 2. a pockmark.

**pock·et** (pok'it), *n.* [< OFr. *poke*, a bag], 1. a little bag or pouch, esp. when sewed into clothing for carrying small articles. 2. a pouchlike cavity or hollow. 3. an air pocket. 4. in *mining*, a cavity filled with ore. *adj.* 1. that can be carried in a pocket. 2. small. *v.t.* 1. to put into a pocket. 2. to envelop; enclose. 3. to take dishonestly, as money. 4. to suppress: as, to *pocket* one's pride. **—pock'et·ful'** [*pl.* -FULS], *n.*

**pock'et·book'**, *n.* 1. a woman's purse. 2. monetary resources.

**pock'et·knife'**, *n.* [*pl.* -KNIVES], a small knife whose blades fold into the handle.

**pock·mark** (pok'märk'), *n.* a scar or pit left by a pustule, as in smallpox.

**pod** (pod), *n.* [prob. < LG.], the seedcase of peas, beans, etc.

**-pod,** [*pl.* -PODA], [< Gr. *pous*, foot], a combining form meaning: 1. *foot.* 2. (*one*) *having* (a specified number or kind of) *feet.* Also **-pode.**

**po·di·a·try** (pō-dī'ə-tri), *n.* [< Gr. *pous*, foot; + *-iatry*], the profession dealing with the specialized care and treatment of the feet. **—po·di'a·trist,** *n.*

**po·di·um** (pō'di-əm), *n.* [*pl.* -DIA (-di-ə)], [< Gr. *pous*, foot], a raised platform for an orchestra conductor.

**po·em** (pō'im), *n.* [< Gr. *poiein*, compose], an arrangement of words, esp. a rhythmical composition, sometimes rhymed, in language more imaginative than ordinary speech.

**po·e·sy** (pō'i-si), *n.* [Archaic], poetry.

**po'et** (-it), *n.* 1. one who writes poems. 2. one who expresses himself with beauty of thought and language. **—po'et·ess,** *n.fem.*

**po'et·as'ter** (-as'tẽr), *n.* [< *poet* + L. *-aster*, dim. suffix], a writer of mediocre verse.

**po·et·ic** (pō-et'ik), *adj.* 1. of or for poets or poetry. 2. having the beauty, imagination, etc. of poetry. Also **po·et'i·cal.**

**poetic license,** the right to deviate, for artistic effect, from literal fact or rigid form.

**poet laureate,** the official poet of a nation, appointed to write poems celebrating national events, etc.

**po·et·ry** (pō'it-ri), *n.* 1. the writing of poems. 2. poems. 3. poetic quality.

**po·grom** (pō'grəm), *n.* [Russ., devastation], 1. an organized massacre of Jews, as in Czarist Russia. 2. any similar attack.

**poign·ant** (poin'ənt, -yənt), *adj.* [< L. *pungere*, to prick], 1. sharp to the smell or taste. 2. sharply painful to the feelings. 3. keen: as, *poignant* wit. **—poign'an·cy,** *n.*

**poin·ci·a·na** (poin'si-ā'nə, -an'ə), *n.* [< M. de *Poinci*, a governor of the Fr. West Indies], a small tropical tree with showy red, orange, or yellow flowers.

**poin·set·ti·a** (poin-set'i-ə, -set'ə), *n.* [< J. R. *Poinsett*, 19th-c. U.S. ambassador to Mexico], a tropical shrub with yellow flowers and petallike red leaves.

**point** (point), *n.* [< L. *pungere*, to prick], 1. a dot in writing, etc.: as, a decimal *point.* 2. position; location: as, all *points* south. 3. the exact moment. 4. a condition reached: as, boiling *point.* 5. an item; detail: as, *point* by *point.* 6. a distinguishing characteristic. 7. a unit, as of value, game scores, etc. 8. a sharp end. 9. a projecting piece of land; cape. 10. the essential fact or idea: as, the *point* of a joke. 11. a purpose; object. 12. a mark showing direction on a compass. 13. a unit of measure for printing type, about 1/72 inch. *v.t.* 1. to sharpen to a point. 2. to give (a story, etc.) emphasis (often with *up*). 3. to show (often with *out*): as, *point* the way. 4. to aim. *v.i.* 1. to direct one's finger (*at* or *to*). 2. to call attention (*to*). 3. to be directed (*to* or *toward*); face. **—at the point of,** very close to. **—beside the point,** irrelevant. **—to the point,** pertinent; apt: also **in point.**

**point'-blank',** *adj. & adv.* [*point* + *blank* (white center of a target)], 1. (aimed) straight at a mark. 2. direct(ly); blunt(ly).

**point'ed,** *adj.* 1. having a sharp end. 2. sharp; incisive. 3. aimed at someone, as a remark. 4. very evident.

**point'er,** *n.* 1. a long, tapered rod for pointing to things. 2. an indicator on a meter, etc. 3. a large, lean hunting dog with a smooth coat. 4. [Colloq.], a hint; clue.

**point'less,** *adj.* 1. without a point. 2. without meaning or force; senseless.

**point of view,** 1. the way in which something is viewed. 2. an attitude or opinion.

**poise** (poiz), *n.* [< L. *pendere*, weigh], 1. balance; stability. 2. ease and dignity of manner. 3. carriage, as of the body. *v.t. & v.i.* [POISED, POISING], to balance or be balanced; suspend or be suspended.

**poi·son** (poi'z'n), *n.* [< L. *potio*, potion], a substance which in small quantities can cause illness or death. *v.t.* 1. to harm or kill with poison. 2. to put poison into. 3. to influence wrongfully. *adj.* poisonous.

**poison ivy,** an American sumac with grayish berries and leaves that grow in groups of three and can cause a skin rash if touched.

**poi'son·ous,** *adj.* that can kill or injure by or as by poison. **—poi'son·ous·ly,** *adv.*

**poke** (pōk), *v.t.* [POKED, POKING], [< LG. *poken*], 1. to prod, as with a stick. 2. [Slang], to hit. 3. to make (a hole, etc.) by poking. *v.i.* 1. to jab (*at*). 2. to search (*about* or *around*). 3. to move slowly (*along*). *n.* 1. a jab; thrust. 2. [Slang], a blow with the fist. **—poke fun (at),** to ridicule.

**poke** (pōk), *n.* [OFr.], [Archaic & Dial.], 1. a sack; bag. 2. a pocket.

**pok·er** (pō′kẽr), *n.* [akin to G. *pochspiel* < *pochen*, to brag], a gambling game at cards.

**pok′er,** *n.* 1. a person or thing that pokes. 2. a bar, as of iron, for stirring a fire.

**poker face,** [Colloq.], an expressionless face, as of a poker player hiding the nature of his hand.

**pok·y, pok·ey** (pō′ki), *adj.* [-IER, -IEST], [< *poke* (push)], 1. slow; dull. 2. small and uncomfortable, as a room.

**Pol.,** 1. Poland. 2. Polish.

**po·lar** (pō′lẽr), *adj.* 1. of or near the North or South Pole. 2. of a pole or poles.

**polar bear,** a large white bear of arctic regions.

**Po·la·ris** (pō-lâr′is), *n.* the North Star.

**po·lar·i·za·tion** (pō′lẽr-i-zā′shən), *n.* 1. the producing or acquiring of polarity. 2. in *optics*, a condition, or the production of a condition, of light in which the rays assume different forms in different planes. —**po′lar·ize′** (-iz′), [-IZED, -IZING], *v.t.*

**po′lar·oid′** (-oid′), *n.* a thin, transparent, filmlike material that produces polarization of light: a trademark (**Polaroid**).

**Pole** (pōl), *n.* a native of Poland.

**pole** (pōl), *n.* [< L. *palus*, stake], a long, slender piece of wood, metal, etc. *v.t.* & *v.i.* [POLED, POLING], to propel (a boat or raft) with a pole.

**pole** (pōl), *n.* [< Gr. *polos*], 1. either end of any axis, as of the earth. 2. either of two opposed forces, parts, etc., as the ends of a magnet, terminals of a battery, etc.

**pole·cat** (pōl′kat′), *n.* [prob. < OFr. *po(u)le*, hen; + *cat*], 1. a small, bad-smelling, weasellike animal of Europe. 2. a skunk.

**po·lem·ic** (pō-lem′ik), *adj.* [< Gr. *polemos*, war], of or involving dispute: also **po·lem′i·cal.** *n.* a controversy.

**po·lem′ics,** *n.pl.* [construed as sing.], the art or practice of disputation.

**pole′star′,** *n.* the North Star.

**pole vault,** a leap for height by vaulting over a bar with the aid of a long pole. —**pole′-vault′,** *v.i.* —**pole′-vault′er,** *n.*

**po·lice** (pə-lēs′), *n.* [ult. < Gr. *polis*, city], 1. the governmental department (of a city, state, etc.) for keeping order and investigating crime. 2. [construed as pl.], the members of such a department. *v.t.* [-LICED, -LICING], 1. to control, protect, etc. with police or the like. 2. to keep (a military camp, etc.) clean and orderly.

**po·lice′man** (-mən), *n.* [*pl.* -MEN], a member of a police force. —**po·lice′wom′an** [*pl.* -WOMEN], *n.fem.*

**police state,** a government that seeks to suppress political opposition by means of a secret police force.

**pol·i·cy** (pol′ə-si), *n.* [*pl.* -CIES], [see POLICE], 1. political wisdom; prudence. 2. wise management. 3. any governing principle, plan, etc.

**pol·i·cy** (pol′ə-si), *n.* [*pl.* -CIES], [< Gr. *apodeixis*, proof], a written insurance contract.

**pol·i·o·my·e·li·tis** (pol′i-ō-mī′ə-lī′tis), *n.* [< Gr. *polios*, gray + *myelos*, marrow], an acute infectious disease caused by a virus inflammation of the gray matter of the spinal cord, often resulting in muscular paralysis: also **pol·i·o** (pō′li-ō′).

**Pol·ish** (pō′lish), *adj.* of Poland, its people, their language, etc. *n.* the Slavic language of the Poles.

**pol·ish** (pol′ish), *v.t.* [< L. *polire*], 1. to smooth and brighten, as by rubbing. 2. to refine (manners, style, etc.). *v.i.* to take a polish. *n.* 1. surface gloss. 2. elegance; refinement. 3. a substance used to polish. —**polish off,** [Colloq.], to finish (a meal, job, etc.) completely.

**po·lite** (pə-līt′), *adj.* [< L. *polire*, to polish], 1. cultured; refined. 2. having good manners. —**po·lite′ly,** *adv.* —**po·lite′ness,** *n.*

**pol·i·tic** (pol′ə-tik), *adj.* [see POLICE], 1. having practical wisdom; prudent. 2. expedient, as a plan. —**pol′i·tic·ly,** *adv.*

**po·lit·i·cal** (pə-lit′i-k'l), *adj.* 1. of, concerned with, or engaged in government, politics, etc. 2. of or characteristic of political parties or politicians.

**political science,** the science of the principles, organization, and methods of government.

**pol·i·ti·cian** (pol′ə-tish′ən), *n.* one actively engaged in politics: often used with implications of seeking personal or partisan gain, scheming, etc.

**pol′i·tics,** *n.pl.* [construed as sing., except in sense 4], 1. the science of government. 2. political affairs. 3. political methods, tactics, etc. 4. political opinions, principles, etc.

**pol′i·ty,** *n.* [*pl.* -TIES], [see POLICE], 1. governmental organization of a state, church, etc. 2. a society with a government; state.

**pol·ka** (pōl′kə), *n.* [prob. < Czech *pulka*, half step], 1. a fast dance for couples. 2. music for this dance. *v.i.* to dance the polka.

**pol·ka dot** (pō′kə), any of a pattern of small, round dots on cloth.

**poll** (pōl), *n.* [< MD. *polle*, head], 1. the head. 2. a counting, listing, etc. of persons, esp. of voters. 3. the number of votes recorded. 4. *usually in pl.* a place where votes are cast. 5. a selective canvassing of people's opinions on some question. *v.t.* 1. to cut off or cut short. 2. to register the votes of. 3. to receive (a certain number of votes). 4. to cast (a vote). 5. to canvass in a poll (sense 5).

**pol·len** (pol′ən), *n.* [L., dust], the yellow, powderlike male sex cells on the stamens of a flower.

**pol·li·nate** (pol′ə-nāt′), *v.t.* [-NATED, -NATING], to place pollen on the pistil of. —**pol′li·na′tion,** *n.*

**pol·li·wog** (pol′i-wog′), *n.* [cf. POLL (head) & WIGGLE], a tadpole: also sp. **pollywog.**

**poll tax,** a tax per head: in some States payment of a poll tax was formerly a prerequisite for voting.

**pol·lu·tant** (pə-lōō′tənt), *n.* something that pollutes; esp., a substance, as a chemical or waste material, discharged into the water or atmosphere.

**pol·lute** (pə-lōōt′), *v.t.* [-LUTED, -LUTING], [< L. *polluere*], to make unclean or impure; defile. —**pol·lu′tion,** *n.*

**Pol·ly·an·na** (pol′i-an′ə), *n.* [title heroine of a novel (1913)], a persistently optimistic person.

**po·lo** (pō′lō), *n.* [prob. < Tibet. *pulu*, ball], 1. a game played on horseback by two teams, using a wooden ball and long-handled mallets. 2. water polo.

**polo shirt,** a short-sleeved, usually knitted, pull-over sport shirt.

**pol·troon** (pol-trōōn′), *n.* [< It. *poltrone*, idler], a thorough coward.

**poly-,** [< Gr. *polys*], a combining form meaning *much, many.*

**pol·y·an·dry** (pol′i-an′dri), *n.* [< Gr. *poly-*, many + *anēr*, man], the practice of having two or more husbands at the same time. —**pol′y·an′drous,** *adj.*

**pol·y·clin·ic** (pol′i-klin′ik), *n.* [*poly-* + *clinic*], a clinic or hospital for the treatment of various kinds of diseases.

**pol·y·es·ter** (pol′i-es′tẽr), *n.* any of several resins used in making plastics, fibers, etc.

**po·lyg·a·my** (pə-lig′ə-mi), *n.* [< Gr. *poly-*, many + *gamos*, marriage], the practice of having two or more wives (or husbands) at the same time. —**po·lyg′a·mist,** *n.* —**po·lyg′a·mous,** *adj.*

**pol·y·glot** (pol′i-glot′), ***adj.*** [< Gr. *poly-*, many + *glōtta*, tongue], 1. speaking or writing several languages. 2. written in several languages.

**pol·y·gon** (pol′i-gon′), ***n.*** [< Gr.; see POLY- & -GON], a plane figure with several angles and sides, usually more than four. —**po·lyg·o·nal** (pə-lig′ə-n'l), ***adj.***

**pol·y·graph** (pol′i-graf′), ***n.*** [< Gr.; see POLY- & -GRAPH], an instrument for measuring changes in respiration, pulse rate, etc., used on persons suspected of lying.

**pol·y·he·dron** (pol′i-hē′drən), ***n.*** [*pl.* -DRONS, -DRA (-drə)], [< Gr.; see POLY- & -HEDRON], a solid figure with several plane surfaces, usually more than six. —**pol′y·he′dral,** ***adj.***

**Pol·y·ne·sian** (pol′ə-nē′zhən), ***adj.*** of Polynesia, a group of islands in the Pacific, its people, languages, etc. ***n.*** 1. a native of Polynesia. 2. the group of languages of Polynesia.

**pol·y·no·mi·al** (pol′i-nō′mi-əl), ***n.*** [*poly-* + bi*nomial*], in *algebra*, an expression consisting of two or more terms, as $x^2 - 2xy + y^2$.

**pol·yp** (pol′ip), ***n.*** [< Gr. *poly-*, many + *pous*, foot], 1. a small water animal with a fringe of tentacles at the top of a tubelike body. 2. a projecting growth of mucous membrane, as in the bladder.

**pol·y·syl·la·ble** (pol′i-sil′ə-b'l), ***n.*** a word of more than three syllables. —**pol′y·syl·lab′ic** (-si-lab′ik), ***adj.***

**pol·y·tech·nic** (pol′i-tek′nik), ***adj.*** [< Gr. *poly-*, many + *technē*, an art], of or providing instruction in many scientific and technical subjects.

**pol·y·the·ism** (pol′i-thē-iz'm), ***n.*** [< Gr. *poly-*, many + *theos*, god], belief in more than one god. —**pol′y·the·is′tic,** ***adj.***

**pol·y·un·sat·u·rat·ed** (pol′i-un-sach′oo-rāt′id), ***adj.*** designating any of certain plant and animal fats and oils with a low cholesterol content.

**po·made** (pō-mād′, -mäd′), ***n.*** [< L. *pomum*, apple (orig. an ingredient)], a perfumed ointment, esp. for the hair.

**pome·gran·ate** (pom′gran′it, pum′-), ***n.*** [ult. < L. *pomum*, apple + *granatum*, lit., having seeds], 1. a round, red, pulpy fruit with a hard rind and many seeds. 2. the tree it grows on.

**pom·mel** (pum′'l, pom′-), ***n.*** [< L. *pomum*, apple], the rounded, upward-projecting front part of a saddle. ***v.t.*** [-MELED or -MELLED, -MELING or -MELLING], to beat, as with the fists.

**pomp** (pomp), ***n.*** [< Gr. *pompē*, solemn procession], 1. stately display. 2. ostentatious or vain show.

**pom·pa·dour** (pom′pə-dôr′), ***n.*** [< Mme. *Pompadour*, mistress of Louis XV], a hair-do in which the hair is brushed up high from the forehead.

**pom·pa·no** (pom′pə-nō′), ***n.*** [*pl.* -NOS], [< Sp.], a spiny-finned food fish of N. America and the West Indies.

**pom·pon** (pom′pon), ***n.*** [Fr.], 1. an ornamental tuft, as of silk or wool, worn on hats, dresses, etc. 2. a chrysanthemum with small, round flowers.

**pom·pous** (pom′pəs), ***adj.*** 1. full of pomp. 2. pretentious; self-important. —**pom·pos′i·ty** (-pos′ə-ti), ***n.*** —**pom′pous·ly,** ***adv.***

**pon·cho** (pon′chō), ***n.*** [*pl.* -CHOS], [< S. Am. Ind.], a cloak like a blanket with a hole for the head, esp. one worn as a raincoat.

**pond** (pond), ***n.*** [< ME. *pound*, enclosure], a body of standing water smaller than a lake, often artificially formed.

**pon·der** (pon′dẽr), ***v.t. & v.i.*** [< L. *ponderare*, weigh], to think deeply (about); deliberate.

**pon′der·ous,** ***adj.*** 1. very heavy; unwieldy. 2. dull; labored, as in style.

**pone** (pōn), ***n.*** [< Am. Ind.], in the southern U.S., bread made of corn meal.

**pon·gee** (pon-jē′), ***n.*** [< Chin. dial. *pen-chi*, domestic loom], a soft, thin silk cloth, orig. in natural tan.

**pon·iard** (pon′yẽrd), ***n.*** [ult. < L. *pugnus*, fist], a dagger.

**pon·tiff** (pon′tif), ***n.*** [< L. *pontifex*, high priest], 1. a bishop. 2. the Pope. —**pon·tif′i·cal** (-i-k'l), ***adj.*** —**pon·tif′i·cal·ly,** ***adv.***

**pon·tif′i·cate** (-i-kit), ***n.*** the office or tenure of a pontiff. ***v.i.*** (-kāt′), [-CATED, -CATING], 1. to officiate as a pontiff. 2. to be dogmatic or pompous.

**pon·toon** (pon-to͞on′), ***n.*** [< L. *pons*, a bridge], 1. a flat-bottomed boat. 2. any of a row of boats, floating cylinders, etc., used to support a temporary bridge. 3. either of two boatlike floats on the landing gear of small airplanes, for landing on water.

**po·ny** (pō′ni), ***n.*** [*pl.* -NIES], [prob. < L. *pullus*, foal], 1. a horse of any small breed. 2. [Colloq.], a small liqueur glass. 3. [Colloq.], a literal translation of a foreign work, used in doing schoolwork, often dishonestly.

**pooch** (po͞och), ***n.*** [Slang], a dog.

**poo·dle** (po͞o′d'l), ***n.*** [G. *pudel*], any of a breed of curly-haired dogs.

**pooh** (po͞o), ***interj.*** an exclamation of contempt, disbelief, or impatience.

**pooh-pooh** (po͞o′po͞o′), ***v.t.*** to express contempt for; make light of.

**pool** (po͞ol), ***n.*** [AS. *pol*], 1. a small pond. 2. a puddle. 3. a swimming pool. 4. a deep, still spot in a river.

**pool** (po͞ol), ***n.*** [< LL. *pulla*, hen], 1. a game of billiards played on a table with six pockets. 2. a combination of resources, funds, etc. for some common purpose. 3. the parties forming such a combination. ***v.t. & v.i.*** to contribute to a common fund.

**poop** (po͞op), ***n.*** [< L. *puppis*, stern of a ship], a raised deck at the stern of a sailing ship.

**poop** (po͞op), ***v.t.*** [Slang], to tire; exhaust.

**poor** (poor), ***adj.*** [< L. *pauper*, poor], 1. having little or no means of support; needy. 2. lacking in some quality. 3. inadequate. 4. inferior. 5. mean-spirited. 6. worthy of pity; unfortunate. —**the poor,** poor, or needy, people. —**poor′ly,** ***adv.***

**poor′house′,** ***n.*** a house or institution for paupers, publicly supported.

**pop** (pop), ***n.*** [echoic], 1. a sudden, light, explosive sound. 2. any carbonated, nonalcoholic beverage. ***v.i.*** [POPPED, POPPING], 1. to make, or burst with, a pop. 2. to move, go, etc. suddenly. 3. to bulge: said of the eyes. ***v.t.*** 1. to cause to pop, as corn by roasting. 2. to put suddenly: as, he *popped* his head up. ***adv.*** with or like a pop.

**pop** (pop), ***n.*** [< *papa*], [Slang], father.

**pop.,** 1. popular. 2. population.

**pop (art),** an art style using commercial techniques and popular subjects, such as comic strips, posters, etc.

**pop·corn** (pop′kôrn′), ***n.*** 1. a variety of corn with hard grains which pop open into a white, puffy mass when heated. 2. the popped grains.

**pope** (pōp), ***n.*** [< Gr. *pappas*, father], [usually P-], in the *R.C. Church*, the bishop of Rome and head of the Church.

**pop′gun′,** ***n.*** a toy gun that shoots pellets by air compression, with a pop.

**pop·in·jay** (pop′in-jā′), ***n.*** [< Ar. *babagā*, parrot], a talkative, vain person; fop.

**pop·lar** (pop′lẽr), ***n.*** [< L. *populus*], 1. a tall, fast-growing tree with small leaves. 2. its wood.

**pop·lin** (pop′lin), ***n.*** [< It. *papalino*, papal: orig. made in Avignon, a Fr. papal town], a ribbed silk, cotton, or woolen cloth.

**pop·o·ver** (pop′ō′vẽr), ***n.*** a very light, puffy, hollow muffin.

**pop·py** (pop'i), *n.* [*pl.* -PIES], [< L. *papaver*], a plant with milky or colored juice and variously colored flowers.
**pop·py·cock** (pop'i-kok'), *n.* [Colloq.], nonsense.
**poppy seed,** the small, dark seed of the poppy, used in baking, etc.
**pop·u·lace** (pop'yoo-lis), *n.* [< L. *populus*], the common people; the masses.
**pop·u·lar** (pop'yoo-lẽr), *adj.* [< L. *populus*, the people], 1. of, carried on by, or intended for people generally. 2. liked by many people. 3. having many friends. 4. common; prevalent. **—pop'u·lar'i·ty** (-lar'ə-ti), *n.*
**pop·u·lar·ize** (pop'yoo-lə-rīz'), *v.t.* [-IZED, -IZING], to make popular.
**pop·u·late** (pop'yoo-lāt'), *v.t.* [-LATED, -LATING], [< L. *populus*, the people], 1. to inhabit. 2. to supply with inhabitants.
**pop'u·la'tion,** *n.* 1. the total of the people in a country, region, etc. 2. a populating or being populated.
**pop·u·lous** (pop'yoo-ləs), *adj.* full of people; thickly populated. **—pop'u·lous·ness,** *n.*
**por·ce·lain** (pôr's'l-in), *n.* [< It. *porcellana*], a fine, white, translucent baked clay; china.
**porch** (pôrch), *n.* [< L. *porta*, gate], 1. a covered entrance to a building. 2. an open or enclosed gallery or room on the outside of a building.
**por·cine** (pôr'sīn, -sin), *adj.* [< L. *porcus*, pig], of or like pigs or hogs.
**por·cu·pine** (pôr'kyoo-pīn'), *n.* [< L. *porcus*, pig + *spina*, spine], a gnawing animal having coarse hair mixed with long, stiff, sharp spines.
**pore** (pôr), *v.i.* [PORED, PORING], [ME. *pouren*], 1. to study minutely (with *over*). 2. to ponder (with *on* or *over*). **—por'er,** *n.*
**pore** (pôr), *n.* [< Gr. *poros*, passage], a tiny opening, as in plant leaves, the skin, etc., for absorbing or discharging fluids.
**pork** (pôrk), *n.* [< L. *porcus*, pig], the flesh of a pig used as food. **—pork'like',** *adj.*
**pork barrel,** [Slang], government appropriations for political patronage.
**por·nog·ra·phy** (pôr-nog'rə-fi), *n.* [< Gr. *pornē*, a prostitute; + *-graphy*], writings, pictures, etc. intended to arouse sexual desire. **—por'no·graph'ic** (-nə-graf'ik), *adj.*
**po·rous** (pôr'əs), *adj.* full of pores, or tiny holes through which fluids, air, or light may pass. **—po·ros·i·ty** (pô-ros'ə-ti), *n.*
**por·phy·ry** (pôr'fə-ri), *n.* [*pl.* -RIES], [< Gr. *porphyros*, purple], a hard rock having red and white crystals embedded in a fine-grained rock mass. **—por'phy·rit'ic,** *adj.*
**por·poise** (pôr'pəs), *n.* [< L. *porcus*, pig + *piscis*, a fish], 1. a small cetacean, dark above and white below, with a blunt snout. 2. a dolphin.
**por·ridge** (pôr'ij), *n.* [< *pottage* by confusion with LL. *porrata*, leek broth], [Chiefly Brit.], a soft food made of cereal or meal boiled in water or milk.
**por·rin·ger** (pôr'in-jẽr), *n.* [< Fr. *potager*, soup dish; infl. by *porridge*], a bowl for porridge, cereal, etc.
**port** (pôrt), *n.* [< L. *portus*, haven], 1. a harbor. 2. a city with a harbor where ships load or unload cargoes.
**port** (pôrt), *n.* [< *Oporto*, city in Portugal], a sweet, dark-red wine.
**port** (pôrt), *v.t.* [< L. *portare*, carry], to hold (a rifle, etc.) diagonally in front of one, as for inspection.
**port** (pôrt), *n.* [< *port* (harbor)], the left side of a ship, etc. as one faces the bow. *adj.* of or on the port. *v.t.* & *v.i.* to turn (the helm) to the left.
**port** (pôrt), *n.* [< L. *porta*, door], 1. a porthole. 2. an opening, as in a valve face, for the passage of steam, gas, etc.
**Port.,** 1. Portugal. 2. Portuguese.
**port·a·ble** (pôr'tə-b'l), *adj.* [< L. *portare*, carry], 1. that can be carried. 2. easily carried. **—port'a·bil'i·ty,** *n.*
**por·tage** (pôr'tij), *n.* [< L. *portare*, carry], 1. a carrying of boats and supplies overland between navigable rivers, lakes, etc. 2. any route over which this is done.
**por·tal** (pôr't'l), *n.* [< L. *porta*, gate], a doorway, gate, or entrance.
**port·cul·lis** (pôrt-kul'is), *n.* [< OFr. *porte*, gate + *coleïce*, sliding], a large iron grating lowered to bar the gateway of a castle or fortified town.
**por·tend** (pôr-tend'), *v.t.* [< L. *pro-*, forth + *tendere*, to stretch], to be an omen or warning of; foreshadow.
**por·tent** (pôr'tent), *n.* something that portends an event, usually evil; omen.
**por·ten·tous** (pôr-ten'təs), *adj.* 1. portending evil; ominous. 2. amazing.
**por·ter** (pôr'tẽr), *n.* [< L. *porta*, gate], a doorman; gatekeeper.
**por·ter** (pôr'tẽr), *n.* [< L. *portare*, carry], 1. a man who carries luggage, etc. for hire. 2. a man who sweeps, cleans, etc. in a bank, store, etc. 3. a railroad employee who waits on passengers in a parlor car or sleeper. 4. a dark-brown beer.
**por·ter·house** (pôr'tẽr-hous'), *n.* [orig., a tavern: cf. *porter*, *n.* 4], a choice cut of beef between the tenderloin and the sirloin: in full, **porterhouse steak.**
**port·fo·li·o** (pôrt-fō'li-ō'), *n.* [*pl.* -OS], [< L. *portare*, carry + *folium*, leaf], 1. a flat, portable case for loose papers, etc.; brief case. 2. the office of a minister of state. 3. a list of an investor's securities.
**port·hole** (pôrt'hōl'), *n.* an opening in a ship's side to admit light and air.
**por·ti·co** (pôr'ti-kō'), *n.* [*pl.* -COES, -COS], [< L. *porticus*], a porch or covered walk, consisting of a roof supported by columns.
**por·tiere, por·tière** (pôr-tyâr'), *n.* [Fr. < *porte*, door], a curtain hung in a doorway.
**por·tion** (pôr'shən), *n.* [< L. *portio*], 1. a part, esp. as allotted to a person; share. 2. a dowry. 3. one's lot; destiny. *v.t.* to divide into portions. **—por'tion·less,** *adj.*
**port·ly** (pôrt'li), *adj.* [-LIER, -LIEST], 1. dignified; stately. 2. stout; obese.
**port·man·teau** (pôrt-man'tō), *n.* [*pl.* -TEAUS, -TEAUX (-tōz)], [< Fr. *porter*, carry + *manteau*, cloak], a stiff suitcase that opens like a book into two compartments.
**por·trait** (pôr'trāt, -trit), *n.* [see PORTRAY], 1. a painting, photograph, etc. of a person, esp. of his face. 2. a description, portrayal, etc. **—por'trait·ist,** *n.*
**por·trai·ture** (pôr'tri-chẽr), *n.* 1. the practice or art of portraying. 2. a portrait.
**por·tray** (pôr-trā'), *v.t.* [< L. *pro-*, forth + *trahere*, draw], 1. to make a portrait of. 2. to describe graphically. 3. to represent on the stage. **—por·tray'al,** *n.*
**Por·tu·guese** (pôr'chə-gēz'), *adj.* of Portugal, its people, language, etc. *n.* 1. [*pl.* -GUESE], a native of Portugal. 2. the Romance language of Portugal and Brazil.
**pose** (pōz), *v.t.* [POSED, POSING], [< L. *pausare*, to pause], 1. to introduce, as a question. 2. to put (an artist's model, etc.) in a certain attitude. *v.i.* 1. to assume a certain attitude, as in being photographed. 2. to strike attitudes for effect. 3. to set oneself up: as, to *pose* as a scholar. *n.* 1. a bodily attitude, esp. one held for an artist. 2. an attitude assumed for effect.
**Po·sei·don** (pō-sī'd'n), *n.* the Greek god of the sea.
**pos·er** (pōz'ẽr), *n.* 1. one who poses; affected person; also **po·seur** (pō-zũr'). 2. a baffling question.
**posh** (posh), *adj.* [< obs. Brit. slang *posh*, a dandy], [Colloq.], luxurious and fashionable.

**po·si·tion** (pə-zish′ən), *n.* [< L. *ponere*, to place], 1. the way in which a person or thing is placed or arranged. 2. one's attitude or opinion. 3. the place where one is; location. 4. the usual or proper place. 5. rank; status; esp., high rank. 6. a post of employment; job; office. *v.t.* to put in a particular position. —**po·si′tion·al,** *adj.*

**pos·i·tive** (poz′ə-tiv), *adj.* [< L. *ponere*, to place], 1. definitely set; explicit: as, *positive* instructions. 2. having the mind set; confident. 3. overconfident; dogmatic. 4. showing agreement; affirmative. 5. constructive: as, *positive* criticism. 6. regarded as having real existence: as, a *positive* evil. 7. based on facts: as, *positive* proof. 8. concerned only with reality; practical. 9. in *electricity*, designating or of electricity generated on a glass rod rubbed with silk. 10. in *grammar*, of an adjective or adverb in its simple, uncompared degree. 11. in *math.*, greater than zero. 12. in *photography*, with the light and shade corresponding to those of the subject. *n.* something positive, as a degree, quality, quantity, photographic print, etc. —**pos′i·tive·ly,** *adv.*

**pos′i·tiv·ism,** *n.* 1. a being positive; certainty. 2. dogmatism.

**poss.,** possessive.

**pos·se** (pos′i), *n.* [ML., power], the body of men summoned by a sheriff to assist him in keeping the peace, etc.

**pos·sess** (pə-zes′), *v.t.* [< L. *possidere*], 1. to have as belonging to one; own. 2. to have as an attribute, quality, etc. 3. to gain control over: as, the idea *possessed* him. —**pos·ses′sor,** *n.*

**pos·sessed′,** *adj.* 1. owned. 2. controlled by a demon.

**pos·ses′sion** (-zesh′ən), *n.* 1. a possessing or being possessed. 2. anything possessed. 3. *pl.* property; wealth. 4. territory held by an outside country. 5. self-possession.

**pos·ses′sive,** *adj.* 1. of possession. 2. showing or desiring possession. 3. in *grammar*, designating or of a case, form, or construction indicating possession (e.g., *my*, *Bill's*). *n.* the possessive case, form, or construction. —**pos·ses′sive·ly,** *adv.*

**pos·si·ble** (pos′ə-b'l), *adj.* [< L. *posse*, be able], 1. that can be or exist. 2. that may or may not happen. 3. that can be done, gotten, etc. 4. potential. —**pos′si·bil′i·ty** (-bil′ə-ti) [*pl.* -TIES], *n.*

**pos′si·bly** (-bli), *adv.* 1. by any possible means. 2. perhaps; maybe.

**pos·sum** (pos′əm), *n.* [Colloq.], an opossum. —**play possum,** to feign ignorance, illness, etc.

**post** (pōst), *n.* [< L. *postis*], 1. a piece of wood, metal, etc. set upright, as to support a building, sign, etc. 2. the starting point in a horse race. *v.t.* 1. to put up (a poster, etc.) as on a wall. 2. to announce by posting notices. 3. to warn against trespassing on (grounds, etc.) by posted notices. 4. to put (a name) on a posted or published list.

**post** (pōst), *n.* [< LL. *postum* < L. *ponere*, to place], 1. the place where a soldier is stationed. 2. the place where troops are garrisoned. 3. the troops at such a place. 4. the place assigned to one. 5. a position or job. *v.t.* to assign to a post.

**post** (pōst), *n.* [< LL. *posta* < L. *ponere*, to place], (the) mail. *v.t.* 1. to mail. 2. to inform, as of events.

**post-,** [L. < *post*, after], a prefix meaning: 1. *after in time, later*, as in *postgraduate*. 2. *after in space, behind.*

**post·age** (pōs′tij), *n.* the amount charged for mailing a letter or package.

**postage stamp,** a government stamp to be put on mail to show that the proper postage has been prepaid.

**post·al** (pōs′t'l), *adj.* of mail or post offices.

**postal card,** a card with a printed postage stamp, for use in the mails.

**post card,** 1. a card, often a picture card, that can be sent through the mail when a postage stamp is affixed. 2. a postal card.

**post chaise,** a closed, four-wheeled carriage drawn by fast horses.

**post′date′,** *v.t.* [-DATED, -DATING], 1. to assign a later date to than the actual date. 2. to be subsequent to.

**post·er** (pōs′tẽr), *n.* a large advertisement or notice, often illustrated, posted publicly.

**pos·te·ri·or** (pos-têr′i-ẽr), *adj.* [L. < *post*, after], 1. later; following. 2. located behind; rear. *n.* the buttocks.

**pos·ter·i·ty** (pos-ter′ə-ti), *n.* [see POSTERIOR], 1. all of a person's descendants. 2. all future generations.

**pos·tern** (pōs′tẽrn, pos′-), *n.* [see POSTERIOR], a back door or gate.

**Post Exchange,** a nonprofit general store at an army post: abbrev. **PX** (no period).

**post′grad′u·ate,** *adj.* of or taking a course of study after graduation. *n.* a student taking such courses.

**post′haste′,** *adv.* with great haste.

**post horse,** formerly, a horse kept at an inn (**post house**), as for hire to travelers.

**post·hu·mous** (pos′choo-məs), *adj.* [< L. *postumus*, last], 1. born after the father's death. 2. published after the author's death. 3. arising or continuing after one's death.

**pos·til·ion, pos·til·lion** (pōs-til′yən, pos-), *n.* [Fr. < It. *posta*, a post], one who rides the leading left-hand horse of a team drawing a carriage.

**post·lude** (pōst′lōōd′), *n.* [*post-* + pre*lude*], a concluding musical piece.

**post′man** (-mən), *n.* [*pl.* -MEN], a mailman.

**post′mark′,** *n.* a post-office mark stamped on mail, canceling the postage stamp and recording the date, time, and place. *v.t.* to stamp with a postmark.

**post′mas′ter,** *n.* a person in charge of a post office. —**post′mis′tress,** *n.fem.*

**postmaster general,** [*pl.* POSTMASTERS GENERAL, POSTMASTER GENERALS], the head of a government's postal system.

‡**post me·ri·di·em** (pōst mə-rid′i-em′), [L.], after noon: abbrev. **P.M., PM, p.m.**

**post-mor·tem** (pōst′môr′təm), *adj.* [L.], 1. after death. 2. of or in an autopsy. *n.* an autopsy.

**post′na′tal** (-nā′t'l), *adj.* after birth.

**post office,** 1. the governmental department in charge of the mails. 2. a place where mail is sorted, postage stamps are sold, etc.

**post′paid′,** *adj.* with the postage prepaid.

**post·pone** (pōst-pōn′), *v.t.* [-PONED, -PONING], [< L. *post*, after + *ponere*, put], to put off until later. —**post·pone′ment,** *n.*

**post·script** (pōst′skript′), *n.* [< L. *post-*, after + *scribere*, write], a note added below the signature of a letter.

**pos·tu·late** (pos′choo-lāt′), *v.t.* [-LATED, -LATING], [< L. *postulare*, to demand], 1. to assume to be true, real, etc., esp. as a basis for argument. 2. to take as axiomatic. *n.* (-lit), 1. something postulated. 2. a prerequisite. 3. a basic principle.

**pos·ture** (pos′chẽr), *n.* [Fr. < *ponere*, to place], 1. the position of the body or its parts; carriage. 2. a position assumed as in posing. *v.i.* [-TURED, -TURING], to pose or assume an attitude. —**pos′tur·al,** *adj.*

**post′war′,** *adj.* after the (or a) war.

**po·sy** (pō′zi), *n.* [*pl.* -SIES], [< *poesy*], a flower or bouquet.

**pot** (pot), *n.* [AS. *pott*], 1. a round vessel for holding liquids, cooking, etc. 2. a pot with its contents; potful. 3. [Colloq.], all the money bet at a single time. 4. [Slang], marijuana. *v.t.* [POTTED, POTTING], 1. to put into a pot. 2. to cook or preserve in a pot. —**go to pot,** to go to ruin. —**pot'ful',** *n.*

**po·ta·ble** (pō'tə-b'l), *adj.* [Fr. < L. *potare*, to drink], drinkable. *n. usually in pl.* something drinkable. —**po'ta·bil'i·ty,** *n.*

**pot·ash** (pot'ash), *n.* [< D. *pot*, pot + *asch*, ash], a potassium compound derived from wood ashes, etc. and used in fertilizer, soaps, etc.

**po·tas·si·um** (pə-tas'i-əm), *n.* [see POTASH], a soft, silver-white, metallic chemical element: its salts are used in fertilizers, glass, etc.: symbol, K. —**po·tas'sic,** *adj.*

**po·ta·to** (pə-tā'tō), *n.* [*pl.* -TOES], [Sp. *patata* < W. Ind.], 1. the starchy tuber of a widely cultivated plant, used as a vegetable. 2. this plant.

**potato chip,** a very thin slice of potato fried crisp and then salted.

**pot'bel'ly,** *n.* [*pl.* -LIES], a protruding belly. —**pot'bel'lied,** *adj.*

**pot'boil'er,** *n.* a novel, painting, etc., often inferior, produced only to make money.

**po·tent** (pō't'nt), *adj.* [< L. *posse*, be able], 1. having authority or power. 2. convincing; cogent. 3. effective, as a drug. 4. able to perform sexual intercourse: said of a male. —**po'ten·cy** [*pl.* -CIES], **po'tence,** *n.*

**po·ten·tate** (pō't'n-tāt'), *n.* a potent, or powerful, person; ruler; monarch.

**po·ten·tial** (pə-ten'shəl), *adj.* [see POTENT], that can come into being; possible; latent. *n.* 1. something potential. 2. the relative voltage or degree of electrification at one point as referred to some other point in an electric circuit or field. —**po·ten'ti·al'i·ty** (-shi-al'ə-ti), [*pl.* -TIES], *n.*

**poth·er** (po*th*'ẽr), *n.* [< ?], a fuss; commotion. *v.t. & v.i.* to bother; worry.

**pot'hold'er,** *n.* a small pad or piece of cloth for handling hot pots, etc.

**pot'hook',** *n.* 1. an S-shaped hook for hanging a pot over a fire or for lifting a hot pot. 2. an S-shaped mark, as one made by children learning to write.

**po·tion** (pō'shən), *n.* [< L. *potare*, to drink], a drink, esp. of medicine or poison.

**pot'luck',** *n.* whatever the family meal happens to be: as, take *potluck* with us.

**pot'pie',** *n.* 1. a meat pie made in a pot or deep dish. 2. a stew with dumplings.

**pot·pour·ri** (pō'poo-rē', pot-poor'i), *n.* [Fr.; *pot*, a pot + *pourrir*, to rot], a medley or miscellany; mixture.

**pot·sherd** (pot'shūrd'), *n.* [< *pot* + *shard*], a piece of broken pottery.

**pot shot,** 1. an easy shot. 2. a random shot. 3. a haphazard attempt.

**pot·tage** (pot'ij), *n.* [< OFr. *pot*, a pot], a kind of stew or thick soup.

**pot'ter,** *n.* one who makes earthenware pots, dishes, etc.

**potter's field,** [cf. Matt. 27:7], a burial ground for persons who die poor or unknown.

**potter's wheel,** a rotating disk upon which clay pots, etc. are molded.

**pot'ter·y,** *n.* [*pl.* -IES], 1. a potter's workshop or factory. 2. the art of a potter. 3. pots, dishes, etc. made of clay hardened by heat; earthenware.

**pouch** (pouch), *n.* [< OFr. *po(u)che*], 1. a small sack or bag: as, a tobacco *pouch*. 2. a mailbag. 3. a saclike structure, as that on the abdomen of the kangaroo, etc. for carrying young. *v.i.* to form a pouch.

**poul·tice** (pōl'tis), *n.* [< L. *puls*, pap], a hot, soft, moist mass, as of mustard, applied to a sore part of the body. *v.t.* [-TICED, -TICING], to apply a poultice to.

**poul·try** (pōl'tri), *n.* [see PULLET], domestic fowls; chickens, ducks, geese, etc.

**pounce** (pouns), *n.* [? < OFr. *pounson;* see PUNCHEON], a pouncing. *v.i.* [POUNCED, POUNCING], to swoop down or leap (*on*, *upon*, or *at*) as if to seize.

**pound** (pound), *n.* [*pl.* POUNDS, collectively POUND], [< L. *pondus*, weight], 1. a unit of weight, equal to 16 ounces avoirdupois or 12 ounces troy. 2. the monetary unit of Great Britain and some other countries: symbol, £.

**pound** (pound), *v.t.* [AS. *punian*], 1. to beat to a pulp, powder, etc. 2. to hit hard. *v.i.* 1. to deliver repeated, heavy blows (*at* or *on*). 2. to move with heavy steps. 3. to throb.

**pound** (pound), *n.* [< AS. *pund-*], a municipal enclosure for stray animals.

**pour** (pôr), *v.t.* [ME. *pouren*], 1. to cause to flow in a continuous stream. 2. to emit, utter, etc. profusely or steadily. *v.i.* 1. to flow freely, continuously, etc. 2. to rain heavily. 3. to swarm. —**pour'er,** *n.*

**pout** (pout), *v.i.* [ME. *pouten*], 1. to thrust out the lips, as in sullenness. 2. to sulk. *n.* a pouting. —**pout'y** [-IER, -IEST], *adj.*

**pov·er·ty** (pov'ẽr-ti), *n.* [< L. *pauper*, poor], 1. the condition or quality of being poor; need. 2. inferiority; inadequacy. 3. scarcity.

**pov'er·ty-strick'en,** *adj.* very poor.

**POW, P.O.W.,** prisoner of war.

**pow·der** (pou'dẽr), *n.* [< L. *pulvis*], 1. any dry substance in the form of fine, dustlike particles, produced by crushing, grinding, etc. 2. a specific kind of powder: as, bath *powder*. *v.t.* 1. to sprinkle, dust, etc. with powder. 2. to make into powder. —**pow'der·y,** *adj.*

**powder puff,** a soft pad for applying cosmetic powder.

**powder room,** a lavatory for women.

**pow·er** (pou'ẽr), *n.* [ult. < L. *posse*, be able], 1. ability to do or act. 2. vigor; force; strength. 3. *a*) authority; influence. *b*) legal authority. 4. physical force or energy: as, electric *power*. 5. a person or thing having great influence, force, or authority. 6. a nation with influence over other nations. 7. the product of the multiplication of a quantity by itself. 8. the degree of magnification of a lens. *adj.* operated by electricity, etc.: as, *power* tools. —**pow'ered,** *adj.*

**pow'er·ful,** *adj.* strong; mighty; influential.

**pow'er·house',** *n.* a building where electric power is generated.

**pow'er·less,** *adj.* weak; impotent; unable.

**power of attorney,** legal authority to act for another person.

**pow·wow** (pou'wou'), *n.* [< Am. Ind.], 1. a conference of or with North American Indians. 2. [Colloq.], any conference.

**pox** (poks), *n.* [for *pocks;* see POCK], 1. any of various diseases characterized by skin eruptions, as smallpox. 2. syphilis.

**pp.,** 1. pages. 2. past participle.

**P.P., p.p.,** 1. parcel post. 2. postpaid.

**ppr.,** present participle.

**P.P.S., p.p.s.,** *post postscriptum*, [L.], an additional postscript.

**Pr.,** Provencal.

**pr.,** [*pl.* PRS.], 1. pair. 2. present. 3. price.

**prac·ti·ca·ble** (prak'ti-kə-b'l), *adj.* 1. that can be put into practice; feasible. 2. that can be used. —**prac'ti·ca·bil'i·ty,** *n.*

**prac·ti·cal** (prak'ti-k'l), *adj.* 1. of or obtained through practice or action. 2. useful. 3. concerned with the application of knowledge to useful ends: as, a *practical* mind. 4. given to actual practice: as, a *practical* farmer. 5. that is so in practice, if not in theory, intention, etc. 6. matter-of-fact. —**prac'ti·cal'i·ty** (-kal'ə-ti), *n.*

**practical joke,** a trick played in fun.

**prac'ti·cal·ly,** *adv.* 1. in a practical manner. 2. from a practical viewpoint. 3. in effect· virtually. 4. [Colloq.], almost; nearly.

**prac·tice** (prak′tis), *v.t.* [-TICED, -TICING], [< Gr. *prassein*, do], 1. to do or perform frequently; make a habit of. 2. to do repeatedly so as to become proficient. 3. to work at, esp. as a profession. *v.i.* 1. to do something repeatedly so as to become proficient. 2. to work at a profession. *n.* 1. a practicing; habit, custom, etc. 2. repeated action to acquire proficiency. 3. proficiency so acquired. 4. the actual doing of something. 5. the exercise of a profession. 6. a business based on this. —**prac′tic·er**, *n.*

**prac′ticed,** *adj.* skilled: also sp. **practised.**

**prac·tise** (prak′tis), *v.t. & v.i.* [-TISED, -TISING], to practice. —**prac′tis·er**, *n.*

**prac·ti·tion·er** (prak-tish′ən-ẽr), *n.* one who practices a profession, art, etc.

**prag·mat·ic** (prag-mat′ik), *adj.* [< Gr. *pragma*, thing done], 1. practical. 2. in *philos.*, testing the validity of all concepts by their practical results. Also **prag·mat′i·cal.** —**prag·mat′i·cal·ly,** *adv.* —**prag′ma·tism** (-mə-tiz'm), *n.* —**prag′ma·tist,** *n.*

**prai·rie** (prâr′i), *n.* [< L. *pratum*, meadow], a large area of level or rolling grassy land without many trees.

**prairie dog,** a small, squirrellike animal of North America, having a barking cry.

**prairie schooner,** a covered wagon.

**praise** (prāz), *v.t.* [PRAISED, PRAISING], [< L. *pretium*, worth], 1. to commend the worth of. 2. to glorify (God, etc.), as in song. *n.* a praising or being praised; commendation. —**prais′er,** *n.*

**praise′wor′thy,** *adj.* worthy of praise.

**pram** (pram), *n.* [Brit. Colloq.], a perambulator.

**prance** (prans, präns), *v.i.* [PRANCED, PRANCING], [prob. < OFr.], 1. to rise up, or move along, on the hind legs: said of a horse. 2. to caper or strut. *n.* a prancing. —**pranc′er,** *n.*

**prank** (praŋk), *n.* [< ?], a mischievous trick; practical joke. —**prank′ster** (-stẽr), *n.*

**prate** (prāt), *v.i.* [PRATED, PRATING], [< MD. *praten*], to talk on and on, foolishly.

**prat·tle** (prat′'l), *v.i. & v.t.* [-TLED, -TLING], [MLG. *pratelen*], to prate or babble. *n.* chatter or babble. —**prat′tler,** *n.*

**prawn** (prôn), *n.* [ME. *prayne*], an edible, shrimplike animal with a thin shell.

**pray** (prā), *v.t.* [< L. *prex*, prayer], 1. to implore: as, (I) *pray* (you) tell me. 2. to ask for by prayer. *v.i.* to say prayers, as to God.

**prayer** (prâr), *n.* 1. the act of praying. 2. an entreaty; supplication. 3. *a*) a humble entreaty, as to God. *b*) any set formula for this. 4. *often pl.* a devotional service chiefly of prayers. 5. something prayed for. —**prayer′ful,** *adj.* —**prayer′ful·ly,** *adv.*

**pre-,** [< L. *prae*, before], a prefix meaning *before in time, place, rank, etc.*

**preach** (prēch), *v.i.* [< L. *prae-*, before + *dicare*, proclaim], 1. to give a religious sermon. 2. to give moral advice, esp. in a tiresome manner. *v.t.* 1. to urge as by preaching. 2. to deliver (a sermon). —**preach′ing,** *n.* —**preach′ment,** *n.*

**preach′er,** *n.* one who preaches; esp., a clergyman.

**pre·am·ble** (prē′am′b'l), *n.* [< L. *prae-*, before + *ambulare*, go], an introduction, esp. one to a constitution, statute, etc., stating its purpose.

**pre·ar·range** (prē′ə-rānj′), *v.t.* [-RANGED, -RANGING], to arrange beforehand.

**pre·car·i·ous** (pri-kâr′i-əs), *adj.* [see PRAY], dependent upon circumstances or chance; uncertain; risky. —**pre·car′i·ous·ly,** *adv.*

**pre·cau·tion** (pri-kô′shən), *n.* [< L. *prae-*, before + *cavere*, take care], care taken beforehand, as against danger, failure, etc. —**pre·cau′tion·ar′y,** *adj.*

**pre·cede** (pri-sēd′), *v.t. & v.i.* [-CEDED, -CEDING], [< L. *prae-*, before + *cedere*, to move], to be, come, or go before in time, place, rank, etc.

**pre·ced·ence** (pri-sē′d'ns, pres′ə-dəns), *n.* the act, privilege, or fact of preceding in time, place, rank, etc.: also **pre·ced′en·cy.**

**pre·ced·ent** (pri-sē′d'nt; *for n.*, pres′ə-dent), *adj.* preceding. *n.* an act, statement, etc. that may serve as an example or justification for a later one.

**pre·ced′ing,** *adj.* that precedes.

**pre·cept** (prē′sept), *n.* [< L. *prae-*, before + *capere*, take], a rule of moral conduct.

**pre·cep·tor** (pri-sep′tẽr), *n.* a teacher.

**pre·cinct** (prē′siŋkt), *n.* [< L. *prae-*, before + *cingere*, surround], 1. an enclosure between buildings, walls, etc. 2. *usually pl.* environs. 3. a subdivision of a city, ward, etc. 4. a limited area. 5. a boundary.

**pre·ci·os·i·ty** (presh′i-os′ə-ti), *n.* [*pl.* -TIES], [see PRECIOUS], affectation in style.

**pre·cious** (presh′əs), *adj.* [< L. *pretium*, a price], 1. of great price or value; costly. 2. beloved; dear. 3. very fastidious, affected, etc. —**pre′cious·ly,** *adv.* —**pre′cious·ness,** *n.*

**prec·i·pice** (pres′ə-pis), *n.* [< L. *prae-*, before + *caput*, a head], a vertical or overhanging rock face.

**pre·cip·i·tant** (pri-sip′ə-tənt), *adj.* [see PRECIPICE], 1. falling steeply or rushing headlong. 2. acting rashly.

**pre·cip·i·tate** (pri-sip′ə-tāt′; *also, for adj. & n.*, -tit), *v.t.* [-TATED, -TATING], [see PRECIPICE], 1. to hurl downward. 2. to cause to happen before expected, needed, etc. 3. in *chem.*, to separate (a soluble substance) out from a solution. *v.i.* 1. in *chem.*, to be precipitated. 2. to condense from vapor and fall, as rain, snow, etc. *adj.* 1. falling steeply. 2. acting hastily or rashly. 3. very sudden; unexpected. *n.* a substance precipitated from a solution.

**pre·cip′i·ta′tion,** *n.* 1. a headlong fall or rush. 2. rash haste; impetuosity. 3. a bringing on suddenly. 4. *a*) rain, snow, etc. *b*) the amount of this. 5. in *chem.*, a precipitating or being precipitated from a solution.

**pre·cip′i·tous′** (-ə-təs), *adj.* 1. steep like a precipice. 2. rash. —**pre·cip′i·tous·ly,** *adv.*

**pré·cis** (prā-sē′, prā′sē), *n.* [*pl.* -CIS (-sēz′, -sēz)], [Fr.; see PRECISE], a concise abridgment; summary.

**pre·cise** (pri-sīs′), *adj.* [< L. *prae-*, before + *caedere*, to cut], 1. accurately stated; definite. 2. minutely exact. 3. strict; scrupulous. 4. overnice. —**pre·cise′ly,** *adv.*

**pre·ci·sion** (pri-sizh′ən), *n.* the quality of being precise; exactness. —**pre·ci′sion·ist,** *n.*

**pre·clude** (pri-klōōd′), *v.t.* [-CLUDED, -CLUDING], [< L. *prae-*, before + *claudere*, to shut], to shut out; make impossible, esp. in advance. —**pre·clu′sion** (-klōō′zhən), *n.*

**pre·co·cious** (pri-kō′shəs), *adj.* [ult. < L. *prae-*, before + *coquere*, to cook], developed earlier than usual, as a child. —**pre·co′cious·ness, pre·coc′i·ty** (-kos′ə-ti), *n.*

**pre·con·ceive** (prē′kən-sēv′), *v.t.* to form an idea or opinion of beforehand. —**pre′con·cep′tion** (-sep′shən), *n.*

**pre·cur·sor** (pri-kũr′sẽr), *n.* [< L. *praecurrere*, run ahead], 1. a forerunner. 2. a predecessor. —**pre·cur′so·ry** (-sə-ri), *adj.*

**pred·a·to·ry** (pred′ə-tôr′i), *adj.* [< L. *praeda*, a prey], 1. of or living by plundering or robbing. 2. preying on other animals.

**pred·e·ces·sor** (pred′ə-ses′ẽr, pred′ə-ses′ẽr), *n.* [< L. *prae-*, before + *decessus*, departure], a person preceding another, as in office.

**pre·des′ti·na′tion,** *n.* 1. in *theology*, *a*) the act by which God foreordained everything that would happen. *b*) God's foreordaining of souls to damnation or to salvation. 2. destiny.

**pre·des·tine** (pri-des′tin), *v.t.* [-TINED, -TINING], to destine or decree beforehand.

**pre·de·ter·mine** (prē'di-tũr'min), *v.t.* [-MINED, -MINING], to determine or decide beforehand. —**pre'de·ter'mi·na'tion,** *n.*

**pre·dic·a·ment** (pri-dik'ə-mənt), *n.* [see PREACH], a distressing or embarrassing situation.

**pred·i·cate** (pred'i-kāt'; *for n. and adj.*, -kit), *v.t.* [-CATED, -CATING], [see PREACH], 1. to affirm as a quality, attribute, etc. 2. to base upon facts, conditions, etc. *n.* in *grammar*, the word or words that make a statement about the subject. *adj.* in *grammar* of or involved in a predicate.

**pre·dict** (pri-dikt'), *v.t. & v.i.* [< L. *prae-*, before + *dicere*, tell], to make known beforehand; foretell; prophesy. —**pre·dict'a·ble,** *adj.* —**pre·dic'tion,** *n.*

**pre·di·gest** (prē'di-jest', -dī-), *v.t.* to make (food) more digestible by an artificial process before it is eaten. —**pre'di·ges'tion,** *n.*

**pre·di·lec·tion** (prē'də-lek'shən, pred''l-ek'-), *n.* [< L. *prae-*, before + *diligere*, prefer], a preconceived liking; partiality.

**pre·dis·pose** (prē'dis-pōz'), *v.t.* [-POSED, -POSING], to make susceptible (*to*); incline. —**pre'dis·po·si'tion,** *n.*

**pre·dom·i·nant** (pri-dom'ə-nənt), *adj.* 1. having influence or authority over others; superior. 2. most frequent; prevailing. —**pre·dom'i·nance,** *n.*

**pre·dom'i·nate'** (-nāt'), *v.i.* [-NATED, -NATING],. 1. to have influence or authority (*over* others); be superior. 2. to prevail; preponderate. —**pre·dom'i·na'tion,** *n.*

**pre-em·i·nent** (prē-em'ə-nənt), *adj.* eminent above others; surpassing: also **preëminent.** —**pre-em'i·nence,** *n.*

**pre-empt** (prē-empt'), *v.t.* [< L. *prae-*, before + *emere*, buy], 1. to settle on (public land) to establish purchasing priority. 2. to seize before anyone else can. Also **preëmpt.** —**pre-emp'tion,** *n.* —**pre-emp'tor,** *n.*

**preen** (prēn), *v.t.* [< *prune* ( to trim)], 1. to clean and trim (the feathers) with the beak: said of birds. 2. to dress up or adorn (oneself). *v.i.* to primp.

**pre-ex·ist** (prē'ig-zist'), *v.i. & v.t.* to exist previously or before (another person or thing): also **preëxist.** —**pre'-ex·ist'ence,** *n.*

**pre·fab·ri·cate** (prē-fab'ri-kāt'), *v.t.* [-CATED, -CATING], to build in standardized sections for shipment and quick assembly, as a house. —**pre'fab·ri·ca'tion,** *n.*

**pref·ace** (pref'is), *n.* [< L. *prae-*, before + *fari*, speak], an introduction to a book, speech, etc. *v.t.* [-ACED, -ACING], 1. to furnish with a preface. 2. to be a preface to. —**pref'a·to'ry** (-ə-tôr'i), *adj.*

**pre·fect** (prē'fekt), *n.* [< L. *praeficere*, to set over], any of various administrators. —**pre'fec·ture** (-fek-chēr), *n.*

**pre·fer** (pri-fũr'), *v.t.* [-FERRED, -FERRING], [< L. *prae-*, before + *ferre*, to bear], 1. to put before a court, etc. for consideration. 2. to promote; advance. 3. to like better.

**pref·er·a·ble** (pref'ēr-ə-b'l), *adj.* more desirable. —**pref'er·a·bly,** *adv.*

**pref·er·ence** (pref'ēr-əns), *n.* 1. a preferring or being preferred. 2. something preferred. 3. advantage given to one person, country, etc. over others. —**pref'er·en'tial** (-ə-ren'-shəl), *adj.* —**pref'er·en'tial·ly,** *adv.*

**pre·fer·ment** (pri-fũr'mənt), *n.* an advancement in rank, etc.; promotion.

**pre·fix** (prē-fiks'), *v.t.* [< L. *prae-*, before + *figere*, to fix], to fix to the beginning; place before. *n.* (prē'fiks), a syllable or group of syllables joined to the beginning of a word to alter its meaning.

**preg·na·ble** (preg'nə-b'l), *adj.* [< OFr. *prendre*, take], that can be assailed or captured; vulnerable. —**preg'na·bil'i·ty,** *n.*

**preg·nant** (preg'nənt), *adj.* [< L. *pregnans*], 1. bearing a fetus in the uterus; with young. 2. mentally fertile; inventive. 3. full of meaning, etc. 4. filled (*with*). —**preg'nan·cy** [*pl.* -CIES], *n.*

**pre·hen·sile** (pri-hen'sil), *adj.* [< L. *prehendere*, take], adapted for seizing or grasping, esp. by wrapping around something, as a monkey's tail.

**pre·his·tor·ic** (prē'his-tôr'ik), *adj.* of the period before recorded history: also **pre'his·tor'i·cal.** —**pre'his·tor'i·cal·ly,** *adv.*

**pre·judge** (prē-juj'), *v.t.* to judge beforehand, or without all the evidence.

**prej·u·dice** (prej'oo-dis), *n.* [< L. *prae-*, before + *judicium*, judgment], 1. a preconceived, usually unfavorable, idea. 2. a bias or opinion held in disregard of facts that contradict it. 3. hatred or intolerance of other races, etc. 4. injury or harm. *v.t.* [-DICED, -DICING], 1. to injure or harm. 2. to cause to have prejudice; bias. —**prej'u·di'cial** (-dish'əl), *adj.*

**prel·ate** (prel'it), *n.* [< L. *praelatus*, borne before], a high-ranking ecclesiastic, as a bishop. —**prel'a·cy** (-ə-si), *n.*

**pre·lim·i·nar·y** (pri-lim'ə-ner'i), *adj.* [< *pre-* + L. *limen*, threshold], leading up to the main action, etc.; preparatory. *n.* [*pl.* -IES], *often in pl.* a preliminary step, procedure, etc. —**pre·lim'i·nar'i·ly,** *adv.*

**prel·ude** (prel'ūd, prē'lōōd), *n.* [< L. *prae-*, before + *ludere*, to play], 1. a preliminary part; preface. 2. in *music*, an introductory section of a suite, etc. *v.i. & v.t.* [-UDED, -UDING], to serve as or be a prelude (to).

**pre·ma·ture** (prē'mə-tyoor', -choor'), *adj.* [< L. *prae-*, before + *maturus*, ripe], happening, done, arriving, etc. before the proper or usual time; too early.

**pre·med·i·tate** (prē-med'ə-tāt'), *v.t. & v.i.* [-TATED, -TATING], to think out or plan beforehand. —**pre'med·i·ta'tion,** *n.*

**pre·mi·er** (prē'mi-ēr; *for n., usually* primer'), *adj.* [< L. *primus*, first], first in importance; foremost. *n.* a chief official; specif., a prime minister. —**pre·mier'ship,** *n.*

**pre·mière** (pri-mer'; Fr. prə-myâr'), *n.* [Fr., fem. of *premier*], a first performance of a play, etc.

**pre·mise** (prem'is), *n.* [< L. *prae-*, before + *mittere*, send], 1. a previous statement serving as a basis for an argument. 2. *pl.* a piece of real estate. *v.t.* (*usually* pri-mīz'), [-MISED, -MISING], 1. to state as a premise. 2. to preface, as with explanatory remarks.

**pre·mi·um** (prē'mi-əm), *n.* [*pl.* -UMS], [< L. *prae-*, before + *emere*, take], 1. a reward or prize, esp. as an inducement to win, buy, etc. 2. an amount paid in addition to the regular charge, etc. 3. a payment, as for an insurance policy. 4. very high value: as, he put a *premium* on truth. —**at a premium,** very valuable because hard to get.

**pre·mo·ni·tion** (prē'mə-nish'ən), *n.* [< L. *prae-*, before + *monere*, warn], 1. a forewarning. 2. a foreboding. —**pre·mon·i·to·ry** (pri-mon'ə-tôr'i), *adj.*

**pre·na·tal** (prē-nā't'l), *adj.* [*pre-* + *natal*], before birth. —**pre·na'tal·ly,** *adv.*

**pre·oc·cu·py** (prē-ok'yoo-pi'), *v.t.* [-PIED, -PYING], [< L. *prae-*, before + *occupare*, seize], 1. to occupy the thoughts of; engross. 2. to take possession of before someone else or beforehand. —**pre·oc'cu·pa'tion** (-pā'shən), *n.* —**pre·oc'cu·pied',** *adj.*

**pre·or·dain** (prē'ôr-dān'), *v.t.* to ordain or decree beforehand.

**prep.,** 1. preparatory. 2. preposition.

**pre·paid** (prē-pād'), pt. & pp. of **prepay.**

**prep·a·ra·tion** (prep'ə-rā'shən), *n.* 1. a preparing or being prepared. 2. a preparatory measure. 3. something prepared, as a medicine, cosmetic, etc.

**pre·par·a·to·ry** (pri-par'ə-tôr'i), *adj.* serving to prepare; introductory.

**pre·pare** (pri-pâr′), *v.t.* [-PARED, -PARING], [< L. *prae-*, before + *parare*, get ready], 1. to make ready. 2. to equip or furnish. 3. to make by putting together parts or materials: as, *prepare* dinner. *v.i.* 1. to make things ready. 2. to make oneself ready.

**pre·par′ed·ness,** *n.* the state of being prepared, esp. for waging war.

**pre·pay** (prē-pā′), *v.t.* [-PAID, -PAYING], to pay or pay for in advance.

**pre·pon·der·ate** (pri-pon′də-rāt′), *v.i.* [-ATED, -ATING], [< L. *prae-*, before + *ponderare*, weigh], to surpass in amount, power, influence, etc.; predominate. —**pre·pon′der·ance,** *n.* —**pre·pon′der·ant,** *adj.*

**prep·o·si·tion** (prep′ə-zish′ən), *n.* [< L. *prae-*, before + *ponere*, to place], a relation word, as *in*, *by*, *to*, etc., that connects a noun or pronoun to another word. —**prep′o·si′tion·al,** *adj.*

**pre·pos·sess** (prē′pə-zes′), *v.t.* 1. to prejudice. 2. to impress favorably at once.

**pre′pos·sess′ing,** *adj.* that impresses favorably; pleasing. —**pre′pos·sess′ing·ly,** *adv.*

**pre·pos·ter·ous** (pri-pos′tēr-əs), *adj.* [< L. *prae-*, before + *posterus*, coming after], contrary to nature, reason, etc.; absurd.

**pre·req·ui·site** (prē-rek′wə-zit), *adj.* required beforehand as a necessary condition. *n.* something prerequisite.

**pre·rog·a·tive** (pri-rog′ə-tiv), *n.* [ult. < L. *prae-*, before + *rogare*, ask], an exclusive privilege, esp. one peculiar to a rank, class, etc.

**Pres.,** President.

**pres.,** present.

**pres·age** (pres′ij; *for v.*, pri-sāj′), *n.* [< L. *prae-*, before + *sagire*, perceive], 1. a warning or portent. 2. a foreboding. *v.t.* [-AGED, -AGING], 1. to give warning of. 2. to predict.

**pres·by·ter** (prez′bi-tēr), *n.* [see PRIEST], 1. in the Presbyterian Church, an elder. 2. in the Episcopal Church, a priest or minister.

**Pres·by·te·ri·an** (prez′bə-têr′i-ən), *adj.* designating or of a church of a Calvinistic denomination governed by presbyters. *n.* a member of a Presbyterian church.

**pre·sci·ence** (prē′shi-əns, presh′i-), *n.* [ult. < L. *prae-*, before + *scire*, know], foreknowledge; foresight. —**pre′sci·ent,** *adj.*

**pre·scribe** (pri-skrīb′), *v.t.* [-SCRIBED, -SCRIBING], [< L. *prae-*, before + *scribere*, write], 1. to order; direct. 2. to order or advise as a medicine or treatment: said of physicians.

**pre·scrip·tion** (pri-skrip′shən), *n.* 1. something prescribed; order. 2. a doctor's written direction for the preparation and use of a medicine. 3. a medicine so prescribed.

**pres·ence** (prez′'ns), *n.* 1. the fact or state of being present. 2. immediate surroundings: as, I was admitted to his *presence*. 3. one's bearing or appearance.

**presence of mind,** ability to think and act quickly in an emergency.

**pres·ent** (prez′'nt), *adj.* [< L. *prae-*, before + *esse*, be], 1. being at the specified place. 2. existing or happening now. 3. in *grammar*, indicating action or state now or action that is always true (e.g., man *is* mortal): as, *present* tense. *n.* 1. the present time or occasion. 2. the present tense. 3. a gift. *v.t.* (pri-zent′), 1. to introduce (a person). 2. to exhibit; show. 3. to offer for consideration. 4. to make a gift of (or to). —**present arms,** to hold a rifle vertically in front of the body.

**pre·sent·a·ble** (pri-zen′tə-b'l), *adj.* 1. suitable for presentation. 2. suitably groomed for meeting people.

**pres·en·ta·tion** (prez′'n-tā′shən, prē′zen-), *n.* 1. a presenting or being presented. 2. something presented.

**pre·sen·ti·ment** (pri-zen′tə-mənt), *n.* [see PRE- & SENTIMENT], a feeling that something, esp. of an unfortunate nature, is about to happen.

**pres′ent·ly,** *adv.* 1. soon. 2. now.

**pre·sent·ment** (pri-zent′mənt), *n.* presentation.

**present participle,** a participle of present meaning (e.g., *running* water).

**pre·serv·a·tive** (pri-zũr′və-tiv), *adj.* preserving. *n.* anything that preserves; esp., a substance added to food to keep it from spoiling.

**pre·serve** (pri-zũrv′), *v.t.* [-SERVED, -SERVING], [< L. *prae-*, before + *servare*, keep], 1. to protect from harm, damage, etc. 2. to keep from spoiling. 3. to prepare (food), as by canning, for future use. 4. to carry on; maintain. *n.* 1. *usually pl.* fruit preserved by cooking with sugar. 2. a place where game, fish, etc. are maintained. —**pres·er·va·tion** (prez′ēr-vā′shən), *n.*

**pre·side** (pri-zīd′), *v.i.* [-SIDED, -SIDING], [< L. *prae-*, before + *sedere*, sit], 1. to act as chairman. 2. to have control or authority.

**pres·i·dent** (prez′i-dənt), *n.* [see PRESIDE], 1. the highest officer of a company, club, etc. 2. [often P-], the chief executive, or formal head, of a republic. —**pres′i·den·cy** [*pl.* -CIES], *n.* —**pres′i·den′tial** (-den′shəl), *adj.* —**pres′i·den′tial·ly,** *adv.*

**press** (pres), *v.t.* [< L. *premere*], 1. to act on with steady force or weight; push against, squeeze, compress, etc. 2. to squeeze (juice, etc.) from. 3. to iron, as clothes. 4. to embrace closely. 5. to force; compel. 6. to urge persistently; entreat. 7. to try to force. 8. to emphasize. 9. to distress by an insufficiency: as, *pressed* for time. 10. to urge on. *v.i.* 1. to weigh down. 2. to go (*forward*) with determination. 3. to crowd. *n.* 1. pressure, urgency, etc. 2. a crowd. 3. any machine for crushing, stamping, smoothing, etc. 4. *a*) the art or business of printing. *b*) newspapers, magazines, etc., or the persons who write for them. 5. an upright closet for storing clothes, etc. —**go to press,** to start to be printed. —**press′er,** *n.*

**press** (pres), *v.t.* [< L. *prae-*, before + *stare*, to stand], to force into service, esp. military or naval service.

**press agent,** one whose work is to get publicity for his client.

**press′ing,** *adj.* calling for immediate attention; urgent. —**press′ing·ly,** *adv.*

**press′man** (-mən), *n.* [*pl.* -MEN], an operator of a printing press.

**pres·sure** (presh′ēr), *n.* 1. a pressing or being pressed. 2. a state of distress. 3. a compelling influence: as, social *pressure*. 4. urgent demands; urgency. 5. in *physics*, force expressed in weight per unit of area. *v.t.* [-SURED, -SURING], [Colloq.], to exert pressure on.

**pres′sur·ize′** (-īz′), *v.t.* [-IZED, -IZING], to keep nearly normal atmospheric pressure inside of (an airplane, etc.), as at high altitudes.

**pres·ti·dig·i·ta·tion** (pres′tə-dij′i-tā′shən), *n.* [Fr. < It. *presto*, quick + L. *digitus*, finger], sleight of hand. —**pres′ti·dig′i·ta′tor,** *n.*

**pres·tige** (pres-tēzh′), *n.* [Fr. < L. *praestigium*, delusion], 1. the power to command esteem. 2. reputation based on high achievement, character, etc.

**pres·ti·gious** (pres-tij′əs, -tē′jəs), *adj.* having or imparting prestige or distinction.

**pres·to** (pres′tō), *adv.* & *adj.* [It., quick], fast.

**pre·sume** (pri-zōōm′, -zūm′), *v.t.* [-SUMED, -SUMING], [< L. *prae-*, before + *sumere*, take], 1. to take upon oneself; venture. 2. to take for granted; suppose. *v.i.* to act presumptuously; take liberties. —**pre·sum′a·ble,** *adj.* —**pre·sum′a·bly,** *adv.*

**pre·sump·tion** (pri-zump′shən), *n.* 1. a presuming; specif., *a*) an overstepping of proper bounds. *b*) a taking of something for granted. 2. the thing presumed. 3. ground for presuming. —**pre·sump'tive**, *adj.*

**pre·sump'tu·ous** (-chōō-əs), *adj.* too bold or forward; taking liberties.

**pre·sup·pose** (prē'sə-pōz'), *v.t.* [-POSED, -POSING], 1. to suppose or assume beforehand. 2. to require or imply as a preceding condition. —**pre'sup·po·si'tion** (-sup-ə-zish'-ən), *n.*

**pre·tend** (pri-tend'), *v.t.* [< L. *prae-*, before + *tendere*, to reach], 1. to profess: as, to *pretend* infallibility. 2. to claim falsely: as, to *pretend* illness. 3. to suppose or make believe: as, *pretend* I'm you. *v.i.* to lay claim (with *to*). —**pre·tend'er**, *n.*

**pre·tense** (pri-tens', prē'tens), *n.* 1. a claim; pretension. 2. a false claim. 3. a false show of something. 4. something said or done for show. 5. a pretending, as at play. Also, Brit. sp., **pretence.**

**pre·ten·sion** (pri-ten'shən), *n.* 1. a pretext. 2. a claim. 3. assertion of a claim. 4. pretentiousness.

**pre·ten'tious** (-shəs), *adj.* [see PRETEND], 1. making claims to some distinction, importance, etc. 2. showy; ostentatious.

**pret·er·it, pret·er·ite** (pret'ẽr-it), *adj.* [< L. *praeter-*, beyond + *ire*, go], in *grammar*, expressing past action or state. *n.* 1. the past tense. 2. a verb in it.

**pre·ter·nat·u·ral** (prē'tẽr-nach'ẽr-əl), *adj.* [< L. *praeter-*, beyond + *naturalis*, natural], 1. out of the ordinary. 2. supernatural.

**pre·text** (prē'tekst), *n.* [< L. *prae-*, before + *texere*, weave], a false reason or motive put forth to hide the real one; excuse.

**pret·ty** (prit'i, pũr'ti), *adj.* [-TIER, -TIEST], [< AS. *prættig*, crafty], pleasing; attractive in a dainty, graceful way. *adv.* somewhat; to some degree. —**pret'ti·ly**, *adv.*

**pret·zel** (pret's'l), *n.* [< G. *brezel*], a hard, brittle biscuit sprinkled with salt, usually formed like a loose knot.

**pre·vail** (pri-vāl'), *v.i.* [< L. *prae-*, before + *valere*, be strong], 1. to be victorious (*over* or *against*). 2. to succeed. 3. to be or become stronger or more widespread; predominate. 4. to be prevalent. —**prevail on** (or **upon, with**), to persuade.

**pre·vail'ing,** *adj.* 1. being superior in strength or influence. 2. prevalent.

**prev·a·lent** (prev'ə-lənt), *adj.* [see PREVAIL], widely existing; generally accepted, used, etc. —**prev'a·lence**, *n.* —**prev'a·lent·ly**, *adv.*

**pre·var·i·cate** (pri-var'ə-kāt'), *v.i.* [-CATED, -CATING], [< L. *prae-*, before + *varicare*, straddle], 1. to evade the truth. 2. loosely, to lie. —**pre·var'i·ca'tion**, *n.* —**pre·var'i·ca'tor**, *n.*

**pre·vent** (pri-vent'), *v.t.* [< L. *prae-*, before + *venire*, come], to stop or keep from doing or happening, as by prior action; hinder. —**pre·vent'a·ble, pre·vent'i·ble**, *adj.*

**pre·ven'tion** (-ven'shən), *n.* 1. a preventing. 2. a means of preventing; hindrance.

**pre·ven'tive,** *adj.* preventing or serving to prevent. *n.* anything that prevents. Also **pre·ven'ta·tive** (-tə-tiv).

**pre·view** (prē'vū'), *n.* 1. an advance, often private, showing, as of a motion picture. 2. a showing of scenes from a motion picture to advertise it: also **pre'vue'** (-vū').

**pre·vi·ous** (prē'vi-əs), *adj.* [< L. *prae-*, before + *via*, a way], occurring or going before. —**previous to,** before.

**pre·war** (prē'wôr'), *adj.* before the war.

**prey** (prā), *n.* [< L. *praeda*, plunder], 1. an animal hunted for food by another animal. 2. a victim. 3. the act of seizing other animals for food: as, a bird of *prey*. *v.i.* 1. to plunder. 2. to hunt other animals for food. 3. to have a wearing influence. Usually used with *on* or *upon*.

**price** (prīs), *n.* [< L. *pretium*], 1. the amount of money, etc. asked or given for something; cost. 2. value; worth. 3. the cost, as in life, labor, etc., of obtaining some benefit. *v.t.* [PRICED, PRICING], 1. to fix the price of. 2. [Colloq.], to find out the price of. —**at any price,** no matter what the cost.

**price'less,** *adj.* of too great worth to be measured by price; invaluable.

**prick** (prik), *n.* [AS. *prica*, a dot], 1. a tiny puncture or dot made by a sharp point. 2. [Archaic], a pointed object. 3. a sharp pain caused as by being pricked. *v.t.* 1. to pierce slightly with a sharp point. 2. to make (a hole) with a sharp point. 3. to pain sharply. —**prick up one's** (or **its**) **ears,** 1. to raise the ears erect. 2. to listen closely.

**prick·le** (prik''l), *n.* [< AS. *prica*, prick], 1. a small, sharply pointed growth; thorn, etc. 2. a tingling sensation. *v.t. & v.i.* [-LED, -LING], to tingle. —**prick'ly** [-LIER, -LIEST], *adj.* —**prick'li·ness**, *n.*

**prickly heat,** an itching skin eruption caused by inflammation of the sweat glands.

**pride** (prīd), *n.* [< AS. *prut*, proud], 1. an overhigh opinion of oneself. 2. haughtiness; arrogance. 3. dignity and self-respect. 4. satisfaction in one's achievements. 5. a person or thing in which pride is taken. —**pride oneself on,** to be proud of.

**priest** (prēst), *n.* [< Gr. *presbys*, old], 1. a person authorized to perform certain religious rites. 2. any clergyman, minister, etc. —**priest'ess**, *n.fem.* —**priest'hood**, *n.* —**priest'like'**, *adj.* —**priest'ly**, *adj.*

**prig** (prig), *n.* [< 16th-c. cant], one who smugly affects great propriety or morality. —**prig'gish**, *adj.* —**prig'gish·ly**, *adv.*

**prim** (prim), *adj.* [PRIMMER, PRIMMEST], [prob. < OFr. *prim*, neat], stiffly formal, precise, or correct; proper. —**prim'ly**, *adv.*

**pri·ma·cy** (prī'mə-si), *n.* [*pl.* -CIES], [< L. *primus*, first], 1. a being first in time, rank, etc.; supremacy. 2. the rank of a primate.

**pri·ma don·na** (prē'mə don'ə), [*pl.* PRIMA DONNAS], [It., first lady], the principal woman singer in an opera.

**pri·ma-fa·ci·e** (prī'mə-fā'shi-ē'), *adj.* [L., at first view], adequate to establish a fact unless refuted: said of evidence.

**pri·mal** (prī'm'l), *adj.* [< L. *primus*, first], 1. first in time; original. 2. first in importance; chief. —**pri'mal·ly**, *adv.*

**pri·ma·ri·ly** (prī'mer'ə-li, prī-mâr'-), *adv.* 1. at first; originally. 2. principally.

**pri·ma·ry** (prī'mer'i, -mẽr-i), *adj.* [< L. *primus*, first], 1. first in time or order; original. 2. from which others are derived; fundamental. 3. first in importance; chief. 4. designating the basic colors, as red, green, and blue in color photography, or red, yellow, and blue in painting. *n.* [*pl.* -RIES], 1. something first in order, importance, etc. 2. *often in pl.* a preliminary election at which candidates are chosen for the final election.

**primary accent,** the heaviest accent (**'**) in pronouncing a word.

**pri·mate** (prī'mit, -māt), *n.* [< L. *primus*, first], 1. an archbishop, or the highest-ranking bishop in a province, etc. 2. any member of the most highly developed order of animals, composed of man, the apes, etc.

**prime** (prīm), *adj.* [< L. *primus*, first], 1. first in time; original. 2. first in rank or importance; chief; principal. 3. first in quality. 4. fundamental. 5. in *math.*, that can be divided by no other whole number than itself or 1. *n.* 1. the first or earliest part. 2. the best or most vigorous period. 3. the best part. *v.t.* [PRIMED, PRIMING], 1. to make ready; prepare. 2. to get (a pump) into operation by pouring water into it.

**prime meridian,** the meridian passing through Greenwich, England.

**prime minister,** in some countries, the chief executive of the government.

**prim·er** (prim′ẽr), ***n.*** [< L. *primus*, first], 1. a book for teaching spelling or reading to children. 2. any elementary textbook.

**prim·er** (prīm′ẽr), ***n.*** 1. a thing that primes. 2. an explosive cap, etc. used to fire the main charge.

**pri·me·val** (prī-mē′v'l), ***adj.*** [< L. *primus*, first + *aevum*, age], of the first age or ages; primitive. **—pri·me′val·ly, *adv.***

**prim·ing** (prīm′iŋ), ***n.*** the explosive used to fire a charge, as in a gun.

**prim·i·tive** (prim′ə-tiv), ***adj.*** [< L. *primus*, first], 1. of the earliest time; original. 2. crude; simple. 3. primary; basic. ***n.*** a primitive person or thing.

**pri·mo·gen·i·ture** (prī′mə-jen′i-chẽr), ***n.*** [< L. *primus*, first + *gignere*, beget], 1. the condition of being the first-born of the same parents. 2. the right of inheritance of the eldest son.

**pri·mor·di·al** (prī-môr′di-əl), ***adj.*** [< L. *primus*, first + *ordiri*, begin], primitive; fundamental; original.

**primp** (primp), ***v.t. & v.i.*** [< *prim*], to dress overcarefully or showily; prink.

**prim·rose** (prim′rōz′), ***n.*** [alt. (after *rose*), < ML. *primula*], a small plant with tubelike, often yellow flowers.

**prince** (prins), ***n.*** [< L. *princeps*, chief], 1. a monarch; esp., the head of a principality. 2. a son of a sovereign. 3. a person preeminent in a group. **—prince′dom, *n.***

**prince′ly,** ***adj.*** [-LIER, -LIEST], 1. of a prince. 2. magnificent; generous.

**prin·cess** (prin′sis, -ses), ***n.*** 1. orig., a woman sovereign. 2. a daughter of a sovereign. 3. the wife of a prince.

**prin·ci·pal** (prin′sə-p'l), ***adj.*** [see PRINCE], first in rank, importance, etc. ***n.*** 1. a principal person or thing. 2. a governing officer, as of a school. 3. the amount of a debt, etc. minus the interest. **—prin′ci·pal·ly, *adv.***

**prin′ci·pal′i·ty** (-pal′ə-ti), ***n.*** [*pl.* -TIES], a territory ruled by a prince.

**principal parts,** the principal inflected forms of a verb: in English, the present infinitive, the past tense, and the past participle (*drink, drank, drunk*).

**prin·ci·ple** (prin′sə-p'l), ***n.*** [see PRINCE], 1. a fundamental truth, law, etc. on which others are based. 2. a rule of conduct: as, the *principle* of equality. 3. adherence to such rules; integrity. 4. the law of nature by which a thing operates. 5. the method of a thing's operation.

**prink** (priŋk), ***v.t. & v.i.*** [< ?], to dress up; primp. **—prink′er, *n.***

**print** (print), ***n.*** [< L. *premere*, to press], 1. a mark made on a surface by pressing or stamping. 2. cloth printed with a design. 3. the impression of letters, designs, etc. made by inked type or from a plate, block, etc. 4. a photograph made by passing light through a negative onto sensitized paper. ***v.t. & v.i.*** 1. to stamp (a mark, letter, etc.) on a surface. 2. to produce on (paper, etc.) the impression of inked type, etc. 3. to produce (a book, etc.). 4. to write in letters resembling printed ones. 5. to produce (a photographic print). **—in** (or **out of**) **print,** still (or no longer) purchasable from the publisher: said of books, etc. **—print′er, *n.***

**print′ing,** ***n.*** 1. the act of one that prints. 2. something printed. 3. all the copies of a book, etc. printed at one time.

**printing press,** a machine for printing from inked type, plates, etc.

**pri·or** (prī′ẽr), ***adj.*** [L.], 1. earlier; previous. 2. preceding in order or importance. **—prior to,** before.

**pri·or** (prī′ẽr), ***n.*** [L., superior], the head of a priory. **—pri′or·ess, *n.fem.***

**pri·or·i·ty** (prī-ôr′ə-ti, -or′-), ***n.*** [*pl.* -TIES], 1. a being prior; precedence. 2. a prior right.

**pri′o·ry,** ***n.*** [*pl.* -RIES], a monastery governed by a prior, or a nunnery governed by a prioress.

**prism** (priz'm), ***n.*** [< Gr. *prizein*, to saw], 1. a solid figure whose ends are equal and parallel polygons and whose faces are parallelograms. 2. a transparent prism whose ends are triangles: used to disperse light into the spectrum. **—pris·mat·ic** (priz-mat′ik), ***adj.*** **—pris·mat′i·cal·ly, *adv.***

**pris·on** (priz′'n), ***n.*** [< L. *prendere*, take], a place where persons, esp. those convicted by or awaiting trial, are confined.

**pris′on·er,** ***n.*** one held captive or confined, esp. in prison.

**pris·sy** (pris′i), ***adj.*** [-SIER, -SIEST], [< *prim* + *sissy*], [Colloq.], very prim or prudish.

**pris·tine** (pris′tēn, -tin), ***adj.*** [< L. *pristinus*], 1. characteristic of the earliest period; original. 2. uncorrupted; unspoiled.

**prith·ee** (prith′i), ***interj.*** [< *pray thee*], [Archaic], I pray thee; please.

**pri·va·cy** (prī′və-si), ***n.*** [*pl.* -CIES], 1. a being private; seclusion. 2. secrecy.

**pri·vate** (prī′vit), ***adj.*** [< L. *privus*, separate], 1. of or concerning a particular person or group. 2. not open to or controlled by the public: as, a *private* school. 3. not holding public office: as, a *private* citizen. 4. secret: as, my *private* opinion. ***n.*** in the *U.S. armed forces*, the lowest rank of enlisted man. **—in private,** not publicly. **—pri′vate·ly, *adv.***

**pri·va·teer** (prī′və-têr′), ***n.*** 1. a privately owned ship commissioned in war to capture enemy ships, esp. merchant ships. 2. a commander or crew member of a privateer.

**pri·va·tion** (prī-vā′shən), ***n.*** the lack of usual necessities or comforts.

**priv·et** (priv′it), ***n.*** [earlier *primet*], an evergreen shrub of the olive family, used for hedges.

**priv·i·lege** (priv′'l-ij), ***n.*** [< L. *privus*, separate + *lex*, a law], a special right, favor, etc. granted to some person or group. ***v.t.*** [-LEGED, -LEGING], to grant a privilege to.

**priv·y** (priv′i), ***adj.*** private. ***n.*** [*pl.* -IES], a toilet, esp. in an outhouse. **—privy to,** privately informed about. **—priv′i·ly, *adv.***

**privy council,** a group of confidential counselors appointed by a ruler.

**prize** (prīz), ***v.t.*** [PRIZED, PRIZING], [var. of *price*], to value highly; esteem. ***n.*** 1. something offered or given to one winning a test, etc. 2. any valued possession. ***adj.*** 1. that has won or could win a prize. 2. given as a prize.

**prize** (prīz), ***n.*** [< L. *prehendere*, to take], something, esp. a warship, captured in war. ***v.t.*** [PRIZED, PRIZING], to pry, as with a lever.

**prize fight,** a professional boxing match.

**pro** (prō), ***adv.*** [L., for], on the affirmative side. ***n.*** [*pl.* PROS], 1. a person or vote on the affirmative side. 2. an argument for something.

**pro** (prō), ***adj. & n.*** [*pl.* PROS], [< *professional*], [Colloq.], professional.

**pro-,** [< Gr. *pro*, before], a prefix meaning *before in place, time*, etc.

**pro-,** [< L. *pro*, forward], a prefix meaning: 1. *moving forward*, as in *progress*. 2. *substituting for*, as in *pronoun*. 3. *favoring*, as in *pro-German*.

**prob.,** 1. probably. 2. problem.

**prob·a·bil·i·ty** (prob′ə-bil′ə-ti), ***n.*** [*pl.* -TIES], 1. a being probable; likelihood. 2. something probable.

**prob·a·ble** (prob′ə-b'l), ***adj.*** [< L. *probare*, to prove], likely to occur or to be so. **—prob′a·bly, *adv.***

**pro·bate** (prō′bāt), *n.* [see PROBE], the official establishing of the validity of a will. *adj.* having to do with such action: as, a *probate* court. *v.t.* [-BATED, -BATING], to establish officially the validity of (a will).

**pro·ba·tion** (prō-bā′shən), *n.* [see PROBE], 1. a testing or trial, as of character, ability, etc. 2. the conditional suspension of a convicted person's sentence. —**pro·ba′tion·al, pro·ba′tion·ar′y,** *adj.*

**pro·ba′tion·er,** *n.* a person on probation.

**probe** (prōb), *n.* [< L. *probare*, to test], 1. a surgical instrument for exploring a wound, etc. 2. a searching investigation. 3. a device, as an instrumented spacecraft exploring a celestial body, used to get information about an environment. *v.t.* [PROBED, PROBING], 1. to explore (a wound, etc.) with a probe. 2. to investigate thoroughly. *v.i.* to search (with *into*).

**prob·i·ty** (prō′bə-ti, prob′ə-), *n.* [< L. *probus*, good], integrity; honesty.

**prob·lem** (prob′ləm), *n.* [< Gr. *problēma*], 1. a question proposed for solution. 2. a perplexing or difficult matter, person, etc.

**prob·lem·at·i·cal** (prob′lə-mat′i-k'l), *adj.* 1. of the nature of a problem. 2. uncertain. Also **prob′lem·at′ic.**

**pro·bos·cis** (prō-bos′is), *n.* [*pl.* -CISES], [< Gr. *pro-*, before + *boskein*, to feed], 1. an elephant's trunk, or any similar long, flexible snout. 2. a person's nose: humorous usage.

**pro·ce·dure** (prə-sē′jẽr), *n.* the act or method of proceeding in an action.

**pro·ceed** (prə-sēd′), *v.i.* [< L. *pro-*, forward + *cedere*, go], 1. to go on, esp. after stopping. 2. to carry on some action. 3. to take legal action (*against*). 4. to issue; come forth.

**pro·ceed′ing,** *n.* 1. a going on with what one has been doing. 2. course of action. 3. *pl.* transactions, or a record of these. 4. *pl.* legal action.

**pro·ceeds** (prō′sēdz), *n.pl.* the sum derived from a sale, venture, etc.

**proc·ess** (pros′es), *n.* [see PROCEED], 1. the course of being done: chiefly in *in process*. 2. course, as of time. 3. a continuing development involving many changes: as, the *process* of digestion. 4. a method of doing something, with all the steps involved. 5. in *biology*, a projecting part. 6. in *law*, a court summons. *v.t.* to prepare by or subject to a special process.

**pro·ces·sion** (prə-sesh′ən), *n.* [see PROCEED], 1. the act of proceeding. 2. a number of persons or things moving forward in an orderly fashion, as in a parade.

**pro·ces′sion·al,** *n.* a hymn sung at the beginning of a church service during the entrance of the clergy.

**pro·claim** (prō-klām′), *v.t.* [< L. *pro-*, before + *clamare*, cry out], to announce officially; announce to be. —**pro·claim′er,** *n.*

**proc·la·ma·tion** (prok′lə-mā′shən), *n.* 1. a proclaiming. 2. something proclaimed.

**pro·cliv·i·ty** (prō-kliv′ə-ti), *n.* [*pl.* -TIES], [< L. *pro-*, before + *clivus*, a slope], a natural tendency; inclination.

**pro·cras·ti·nate** (prō-kras′tə-nāt′), *v.i.* [-NATED, -NATING], [< L. *pro-*, forward + *cras*, tomorrow], to postpone or defer taking action; delay. —**pro·cras′ti·na′tion,** *n.* —**pro·cras′ti·na′tor,** *n.*

**pro·cre·ate** (prō′kri-āt′), *v.t. & v.i.* [-ATED, -ATING], [< L. *pro-*, before + *creare*, create], to produce (young); beget. —**pro′cre·a′tion,** *n.* —**pro′cre·a′tive,** *adj.* —**pro′cre·a′tor,** *n.*

**proc·tor** (prok′tẽr), *n.* [see PROCURE], a college official who maintains order, supervises examinations, etc. —**proc·to′ri·al** (-tôr′i-əl), *adj.*

**proc·u·ra·tor** (prok′yoo-rā′tẽr), *n.* [see PROCURE], in the Roman Empire, a governor of a territory or province.

**pro·cure** (prō-kyoor′), *v.t.* [-CURED, -CURING], [< L. *pro*, for + *curare*, attend to], 1. to obtain; get. 2. to cause. —**pro·cur′a·ble,** *adj.* —**pro·cure′ment,** *n.*

**pro·cur′er,** *n.* a pimp. —**pro·cur′ess,** *n.fem.*

**prod** (prod), *n.* [< ? ], 1. a thrust with something pointed. 2. something that goads. *v.t.* [PRODDED, PRODDING], 1. to jab as with a pointed stick. 2. to urge or rouse.

**prod·i·gal** (prod′i-g'l), *adj.* [ult. < L. *pro-*, forth + *agere*, to drive], 1. exceedingly or recklessly wasteful. 2. extremely abundant. *n.* a spendthrift. —**prod′i·gal′i·ty** (-gal′ə-ti), *n.* —**prod′i·gal·ly,** *adv.*

**pro·di·gious** (prə-dij′əs), *adj.* [see PRODIGY], 1. wonderful; amazing. 2. enormous; huge.

**prod·i·gy** (prod′ə-ji), *n.* [*pl.* -GIES], [< L. *prodigium*, omen], an extraordinary person, thing, or act; specif., a child of genius.

**pro·duce** (prə-dōōs′, -dūs′), *v.t.* [-DUCED, -DUCING], [< L. *pro-*, forward + *ducere*, to lead], 1. to bring to view; show: as, *produce* your license. 2. to bear; bring forth. 3. to make; manufacture. 4. to cause. 5. to get (a play, etc.) ready for exhibition. *v.i.* to yield the usual product. *n.* (prod′ōōs, prō′dūs), something produced; esp., farm products collectively. —**pro·duc′er,** *n.*

**prod·uct** (prod′əkt), *n.* 1. something produced by nature, industry, or art. 2. result; outgrowth. 3. in *math.*, the number obtained by multiplying two or more numbers together.

**pro·duc·tion** (prə-duk′shən), *n.* a producing or something produced.

**pro·duc′tive,** *adj.* 1. fertile. 2. marked by abundant production. 3. bringing as a result (with *of*): as, waste is *productive* of many evils. —**pro·duc′tive·ly,** *adv.* —**pro·duc·tiv·i·ty** (prō′duk-tiv′ə-ti), *n.*

**Prof., prof.,** professor.

**pro·fane** (prə-fān′, prō-), *adj.* [< L. *pro-*, before + *fanum*, temple], 1. not concerned with religion; secular. 2. showing irreverence or contempt for sacred things. *v.t.* [-FANED, -FANING], to treat (sacred things) with irreverence or contempt. —**prof·a·na·tion** (prof′ə-nā′shən), *n.* —**pro·fane′ly,** *adv.*

**pro·fan·i·ty** (prə-fan′ə-ti), *n.* 1. a being profane. 2. [*pl.* -TIES], profane language; swearing.

**pro·fess** (prə-fes′), *v.t.* [< L. *pro-*, before + *fateri*, avow], 1. to declare openly; affirm. 2. to lay claim to (some feeling) insincerely. 3. to declare one's belief in.

**pro·fes·sion** (prə-fesh′ən), *n.* 1. a professing, or declaring; avowal. 2. an occupation requiring advanced academic training, as medicine, law, etc. 3. all the persons in such an occupation.

**pro·fes′sion·al,** *adj.* 1. of or engaged in a profession. 2. engaging in some activity, as a sport, mainly to earn one's livelihood. *n.* one who is professional (esp. in sense 2).

**pro·fes·sor** (prə-fes′ẽr), *n.* a teacher; esp., a college teacher of the highest rank. —**pro·fes·so·ri·al** (prō′fə-sôr′i-əl, prof′ə-), *adj.* —**pro·fes′sor·ship′,** *n.*

**prof·fer** (prof′ẽr), *v.t.* [< OFr.; see PRO- & OFFER], to offer (usually something intangible): as, to *proffer* friendship. *n.* an offer.

**pro·fi·cient** (prə-fish′ənt), *adj.* [< L. *proficere*, to advance], highly competent; skilled. —**pro·fi′cien·cy,** *n.*

**pro·file** (prō′fīl), *n.* [< It. *profilare*, to outline], 1. a side view of the face. 2. a drawing of this. 3. outline. 4. a short, vivid biography.

**prof·it** (prof′it), *n.* [< L. *pro-*, toward + *facere*, make], 1. advantage; gain. 2. *often pl.* financial gain; esp., net income, as of a business, after deducting costs. *v.t. & v.i.* 1. to be of advantage (to). 2. to benefit. —**prof′it·a·ble,** *adj.* —**prof′it·a·bly,** *adv.*

**prof·it·eer** (prof'ə-têr'), *n.* one who makes excessive profits by taking advantage of a shortage of supply to charge high prices. *v.i.* to be a profiteer. —**prof'it·eer'ing,** *n.*
**prof·li·gate** (prof'lə-git), *adj.* [< L. *pro-*, forward + *fligere*, to drive], 1. dissolute. 2. recklessly wasteful. *n.* a profligate person. —**prof'li·ga·cy** (-gə-si), *n.*
**pro·found** (prə-found'), *adj.* [< L. *pro-*, forward + *fundus*, bottom], 1. very deep: as, a *profound* lethargy. 2. marked by intellectual depth. 3. deeply felt: as, *profound* grief. 4. thoroughgoing. —**pro·found'ly,** *adv.* —**pro·fun'di·ty** (-fun'də-ti) [*pl.* -TIES], *n.*
**pro·fuse** (prə-fūs'), *adj.* [< L. *pro-*, forth + *fundere*, pour], giving or given freely and abundantly; lavish. —**pro·fu'sion** (-fū'zhən), *n.*
**pro·gen·i·tor** (prō-jen'ə-tẽr), *n.* [< L. *pro-*, forth + *gignere*, beget], a forefather; ancestor in direct line.
**prog·e·ny** (proj'ə-ni), *n.* [*pl.* -NIES], [see PROGENITOR], children; offspring.
**prog·no·sis** (prog-nō'sis), *n.* [*pl.* -SES (-sēz)], [< Gr. *pro-*, before + *gignōskein*, know], a prediction, esp. of the probable course of a disease. —**prog·nos'tic** (-nos'tik), *n.* & *adj.*
**prog·nos'ti·cate'** (-nos'tə-kāt'), *v.t.* [-CATED, -CATING], [see PROGNOSIS], to foretell; predict. —**prog·nos'ti·ca'tion,** *n.*
**pro·gram, pro·gramme** (prō'gram, -grəm), *n.* [< Gr. *pro-*, before + *graphein*, write], 1. a list of the events, pieces, performers, etc., as of an entertainment. 2. a plan of procedure. 3. *a*) a logical sequence of operations to be performed by an electronic computer, as in solving a problem. *b*) the coded data for this. *v.t.* [-GRAMED or -GRAMMED, -GRAMING or -GRAMMING], 1. to schedule in a program. 2. to furnish (a computer) with a program.
**prog·ress** (prog'res), *n.* [< L. *pro-*, before + *gradi*, to step], 1. a moving forward or onward. 2. development. 3. improvement. *v.i.* (prə-gres'), 1. to move forward or onward. 2. to continue toward completion. 3. to improve.
**pro·gres·sion** (prə-gresh'ən), *n.* 1. a moving forward. 2. a succession, as of events. 3. in *math.*, a series of numbers increasing or decreasing by proportional differences.
**pro·gres'sive** (-gres'iv), *adj.* 1. moving forward. 2. advancing by successive steps. 3. marked by or favoring progress, improvement, etc., as through political reform. *n.* one who is progressive.
**pro·hib·it** (prō-hib'it), *v.t.* [< L. *pro-*, before + *habere*, have], 1. to forbid, as by law. 2. to prevent; hinder. —**pro·hib'i·tive, pro·hib'i·to'ry,** *adj.*
**pro·hi·bi·tion** (prō'ə-bish'ən), *n.* 1. a prohibiting. 2. the forbidding by law of the manufacture or sale of alcoholic liquors. —**pro'hi·bi'tion·ist,** *n.*
**proj·ect** (proj'ekt; *for v.*, prə-jekt'), *n.* [< L. *pro-*, before + *jacere*, to throw], 1. a proposal; scheme. 2. an undertaking. *v.t.* 1. to propose (a plan). 2. to throw forward. 3. to cause to stick out. 4. to cause (a light, image, etc.) to fall upon a surface. *v.i.* to stick out. —**pro·jec'tion,** *n.*
**pro·jec·tile** (prə-jek't'l), *n.* 1. an object, as a bullet, etc., designed to be shot forward, as from a gun. 2. anything thrown forward.
**pro·jec'tor,** *n.* a person or thing that projects; specif., a machine for throwing images on a screen.
**pro·le·tar·i·at** (prō'lə-târ'i-ət), *n.* [< L. *proletarius*, a citizen of the lowest class], the working class; esp., the industrial working class. —**pro'le·tar'i·an,** *adj.* & *n.*
**pro·lif·ic** (prə-lif'ik), *adj.* [< L. *proles*, offspring + *facere*, make], 1. producing many young or much fruit. 2. creating many products of the mind.
**pro·lix** (prō-liks'), *adj.* [< L. *prolixus*, extended], so wordy as to be tiresome; long-winded. —**pro·lix'i·ty** [*pl.* -TIES], *n.*
**pro·logue** (prō'lôg), *n.* [< Gr. *pro-*, before + *logos*, a discourse], 1. an introduction to a poem, play, etc. 2. any preliminary act, event, etc. Also sp. **prolog.**
**pro·long** (prə-lôŋ'), *v.t.* [< L. *pro-*, forth + *longus*, long], to lengthen in time or space: also **pro·lon'gate** (-gāt) [-GATED, -GATING]. —**pro'lon·ga'tion** (prō'-), *n.*
**prom** (prom), *n.* [< *promenade*], [Colloq.], a dance given by a particular class of students at a college, high school, etc.
**prom·e·nade** (prom'ə-nād', -näd'), *n.* [Fr. < L. *pro-*, forth + *minare*, to herd], 1. a leisurely walk taken for pleasure, display, etc. 2. a public place for walking. 3. a ball or dance. *v.i.* & *v.t.* [-NADED, -NADING], to take a promenade (along or through).
**Pro·me·theus** (prə-mē'thūs, -thi-əs), *n.* in *Gr. myth.*, a Titan who taught mankind the use of fire, which he had stolen from heaven.
**prom·i·nent** (prom'ə-nənt), *adj.* [< L. *prominere*, to project], 1. sticking out; projecting. 2. noticeable; conspicuous. 3. widely and favorably known. —**prom'i·nence,** *n.* —**prom'i·nent·ly,** *adv.*
**pro·mis·cu·ous** (prə-mis'kū-əs), *adj.* [< L. *pro-*, forth + *miscere*, to mix], 1. consisting of different elements indiscriminately mingled. 2. characterized by a lack of discrimination, esp. in sexual liaisons. —**prom·is·cu·i·ty** (prom'is-kū'ə-ti), [*pl.* -TIES], *n.*
**prom·ise** (prom'is), *n.* [< L. *pro-*, forth + *mittere*, send], 1. an agreement to do or not to do something. 2. indication, as of a successful future. 3. anything promised. *v.t.* & *v.i.* [-ISED, -ISING], 1. to make a promise of (something). 2. to give a basis for expecting. —**prom'is·ing,** *adj.*
**Promised Land,** in the *Bible*, Canaan, promised by God to Abraham and his descendants: Gen. 15:18, 17:8.
**prom·is·so·ry** (prom'ə-sôr'i), *adj.* containing, or having the nature of, a promise.
**prom·on·to·ry** (prom'ən-tôr'i), *n.* [*pl.* -RIES], [prob. < L. *prominere*, to project], a peak of high land that juts out over an expanse of water; headland.
**pro·mote** (prə-mōt'), *v.t.* [-MOTED, -MOTING], [< L. *pro-*, forward + *movere*, to move], 1. to raise to a higher rank or position. 2. to further the growth, establishment, sale, etc. of. —**pro·mo'tion,** *n.*
**pro·mot'er,** *n.* one who organizes and furthers a new enterprise.
**prompt** (prompt), *adj.* [< L. *pro-*, forth + *emere*, take], 1. ready; instantly at hand. 2. done, spoken, etc. without delay. *v.t.* 1. to urge into action. 2. to remind (a person) of something he has forgotten; help with a cue. 3. to inspire. —**prompt'er,** *n.* —**prompt'ly,** *adv.* —**prompt'ness,** *n.*
**promp·ti·tude** (promp'tə-tōōd', -tūd'), *n.* the quality of being prompt.
**pro·mul·gate** (prō-mul'gāt), *v.t.* [-GATED, -GATING], [< L. *promulgare*, to publish], 1. to publish or make known officially. 2. to make widespread. —**pro'mul·ga'tion,** *n.*
**pron.,** 1. pronoun. 2. pronunciation.
**prone** (prōn), *adj.* [< L. *pronus*], 1. lying face downward or prostrate. 2. disposed or inclined: as, *prone* to err.
**prong** (prôŋ), *n.* [prob. < MLG. *prange*, pinching instrument], 1. any of the pointed ends of a fork. 2. any pointed projecting part. —**pronged,** *adj.*
**pro·noun** (prō'noun), *n.* [< L. *pro*, for + *nomen*, noun], a word used in place of a noun (e.g., *I*, *he*, *it*, etc.). —**pro·nom'i·nal** (-nom'ə-n'l), *adj.*
**pro·nounce** (prə-nouns'), *v.t.* [-NOUNCED, -NOUNCING], [< L. *pro-*, before + *nuntiare*,

announce], 1. to declare officially, solemnly, etc.: as, he was *pronounced* dead. 2. to utter or articulate (a sound or word). —**pro·nounce'a·ble,** *adj.*

**pro·nounced',** *adj.* clearly marked; decided: as, *pronounced* ideas.

**pro·nounce'ment,** *n.* a formal statement of a fact, opinion, or judgment.

**pron·to** (pron'tō), *adv.* [Sp.; see PROMPT], [Slang], at once; quickly; immediately.

**pro·nun·ci·a·tion** (prə-nun'si-ā'shən), *n.* 1. the act or manner of pronouncing words. 2. the transcription in phonetic symbols of the standard pronunciation(s) of a word.

**proof** (pro͞of), *n.* [*pl.* PROOFS], [< L. *probare*, prove], 1. a proving or testing of something. 2. evidence, etc. that establishes the truth of something. 3. the relative strength of an alcoholic liquor. 4. in *photography*, a trial print of a negative. 5. in *printing*, a trial impression, as from composed type, for checking errors, etc. *adj.* of tested strength; impervious to (with *against*).

**-proof,** a suffix meaning: 1. *impervious to*, as in *waterproof*. 2. *protected from*, as in *weatherproof*.

**proof'read',** *v.t. & v.i.* [-READ, -READING], to read (printers' proofs, etc.) in order to make corrections. —**proof'read'er,** *n.*

**prop** (prop), *n.* [< MD. *proppe*], a support, as a pole, placed under or against something: often used figuratively. *v.t.* [PROPPED, PROPPING], 1. to support, as with a prop (often with *up*). 2. to lean (something) *against* a support.

**prop** (prop), *n.* a property (sense 4).

**prop·a·gan·da** (prop'ə-gan'də), *n.* [< L.], 1. any movement or organization for the propagation of certain ideas, doctrines, etc. 2. the ideas, etc. spread in this way. —**prop'a·gan'dist,** *n. & adj.* —**prop'a·gan'dize** [-DIZED, -DIZING], *v.t. & v.i.*

**prop·a·gate** (prop'ə-gāt'), *v.t.* [-GATED, -GATING], [< L. *propago*, slip (of a plant)], 1. to cause (a plant or animal) to reproduce itself. 2. to reproduce (itself): said of a plant or animal. 3. to spread (ideas, customs, etc.). *v.i.* to reproduce, as plants or animals. —**prop'a·ga'tion,** *n.*

**pro·pel** (prə-pel'), *v.t.* [-PELLED, -PELLING], [< L. *pro-*, forward + *pellere*, drive], to drive onward or forward. —**pro·pel'lant,** *n.*

**pro·pel'ler,** *n.* a device having a series of blades mounted at an angle in a revolving hub for propelling a ship or aircraft.

**pro·pen·si·ty** (prə-pen'sə-ti), *n.* [pl. -TIES], [< L. *propendere*, hang forward], a natural inclination or tendency; bent.

**prop·er** (prop'ẽr), *adj.* [< L. *proprius*, one's own], 1. specially suitable; appropriate; fitting. 2. naturally belonging (*to*). 3. conforming to a standard; correct. 4. decent; decorous. 5. in the most restricted sense: as, Detroit *proper* (i.e., apart from its suburbs). 6. [Brit. Colloq.], complete; thorough. 7. designating a specific individual, place, etc.: *Jim*, *Paris*, etc. are *proper* nouns. —**prop'er·ly,** *adv.*

**proper fraction,** a fraction in which the numerator is less than the denominator, as 2/5.

**prop·er·ty** (prop'ẽr-ti), *n.* [*pl.* -TIES], [< L. *proprius*, one's own], 1. ownership. 2. something owned, esp. real estate. 3. any characteristic quality; trait. 4. any of the movable articles used in a stage setting.

**proph·e·cy** (prof'ə-si), *n.* [*pl.* -CIES], [see PROPHET], 1. prediction of the future. 2. something predicted.

**proph'e·sy'** (-sī'), *v.t. & v.i.* [-SIED, -SYING], 1. to predict as by divine guidance. 2. to predict in any way. —**proph'e·si'er,** *n.*

**proph'et** (prof'it), *n.* [< Gr. *pro-*, before + *phanai*, speak], 1. a religious leader regarded as, or claiming to be, divinely inspired. 2. one who predicts the future. —**proph'et·ess,** *n.fem.*

**pro·phet·ic** (prə-fet'ik), *adj.* 1. of or like a prophet. 2. of, like, or containing a prophecy. —**pro·phet'i·cal·ly,** *adv.*

**pro·phy·lac·tic** (prō'fə-lak'tik), *adj.* [< Gr. *pro-*, before + *phylassein*, to guard], preventive or protective; esp., preventing disease. *n.* a prophylactic medicine, device,etc.

**pro·pin·qui·ty** (prō-piŋ'kwə-ti), *n.* [< L. *propinquus*, near], nearness.

**pro·pi·ti·ate** (prə-pish'i-āt'), *v.t.* [-ATED, -ATING], [see PROPITIOUS], to win or regain the good will of; appease. —**pro·pi'ti·a'tion,** *n.* —**pro·pi'ti·a·to'ry** (-ə-tôr'i), *adj.*

**pro·pi·tious** (prə-pish'əs), *adj.* [< L. *pro-*, before + *petere*, seek], 1. favorably inclined. 2. favorable: as, a *propitious* omen.

**pro·po·nent** (prə-pō'nənt), *n.* [< L. *pro-*, forth + *ponere*, to place], 1. one who makes a proposal or proposition. 2. one who supports a cause.

**pro·por·tion** (prə-pôr'shən), *n.* [< L. *pro-*, before + *portio*, a part], 1. a part, share, etc. in its relation to the whole. 2. the comparative relation in size, amount, etc. between things; ratio. 3. balance or symmetry. 4. *pl.* dimensions. *v.t.* 1. to put in proper relation with something else. 2. to arrange the parts of (a whole) so as to be harmonious. —**pro·por'tion·al, pro·por'tion·ate** (-it), *adj.*

**pro·pos·al** (prə-pō'z'l), *n.* 1. a proposing. 2. a proposed plan or scheme. 3. an offer of marriage.

**pro·pose** (prə-pōz'), *v.t.* [-POSED, -POSING], [ult. < L. *pro-*, forth + *ponere*, to place], 1. to put forth for consideration, etc. 2. to plan; intend. 3. to present as a toast in drinking. 4. to nominate for office, etc. *v.i.* 1. to form a plan, etc. 2. to offer marriage.

**prop·o·si·tion** (prop'ə-zish'ən), *n.* 1. something proposed; plan. 2. [Colloq.], a project; business undertaking. 3. a subject to be debated. 4. in *math.*, a problem to be solved.

**pro·pound** (prə-pound'), *v.t.* [see PROPONENT], to put forth for consideration.

**pro·pri·e·tar·y** (prə-prī'ə-ter'i), *adj.* [see PROPERTY], belonging to a proprietor, as under a patent or copyright.

**pro·pri'e·tor,** *n.* an owner. —**pro·pri'e·tor·ship',** *n.* —**pro·pri'e·tress,** *n.fem.*

**pro·pri·e·ty** (prə-prī'ə-ti), *n.* [*pl.* -TIES], [see PROPER], 1. the quality of being proper, fitting, etc. 2. conformity with accepted standards of behavior.

**pro·pul·sion** (prə-pul'shən), *n.* [see PROPEL], 1. a propelling or being propelled. 2. something that propels. —**pro·pul'sive,** *adj.*

**pro·rate** (prō'rāt'), *v.t. & v.i.* [-RATED, -RATING], [< *pro rata*], to divide or assess proportionally. —**pro·rat'a·ble,** *adj.*

**pro·sa·ic** (prō-zā'ik), *adj.* [< L. *prosa*, prose], like prose; commonplace; dull.

**pro·sce·ni·um** (prō-sē'ni-əm), *n.* [*pl.* -NIA (-ni-ə)], [< Gr. *pro-*, before + *skēnē*, tent], the arch framing a conventional stage.

**pro·scribe** (prō-skrīb'), *v.t.* [-SCRIBED, -SCRIBING], [< L. *pro-*, before + *scribere*, write], 1. to outlaw; banish; exile. 2. to denounce and forbid. —**pro·scrip'tion** (-skrip'shən), *n.* —**pro·scrip'tive,** *adj.*

**prose** (prōz), *n.* [< L. *prosa*, direct], ordinary language, not poetry.

**pros·e·cute** (pros'i-kūt'), *v.t.* [-CUTED, -CUTING], [< L. *pro-*, before + *sequi*, follow], 1. to carry on; engage in. 2. to conduct legal proceedings against. —**pros'e·cu'tion,** *n.* —**pros'e·cu'tor,** *n.*

**pros·e·lyte** (pros''l-īt'), *n.* [< Gr. *prosēlytos*], one who has been converted from one reli-

gion, opinion, etc. to another. *v.t. & v.i.* [-LYTED, -LYTING], to proselytize.
**pros'e·lyt·ize'** (-i-tīz'), *v.t. & v.i.* [-IZED, -IZING], to make converts (of). —**pros'e·lyt·ism** (-i-tiz'm), *n.*
**Pro·ser·pi·na** (prō-sũr'pi-nə), *n.* in *Rom. myth.*, Persephone: also **Pro·ser'pi·ne'** (-nē', pros'ẽr-pīn').
**pros·o·dy** (pros'ə-di), *n.* [*pl.* -DIES], [< Gr. *prosōidia*, accent], versification; study of meter, rhyme, etc. —**pros'o·dist,** *n.*
**pros·pect** (pros'pekt), *n.* [< L. *pro-*, forward + *specere*, look], 1. a broad view; scene. 2. viewpoint; outlook. 3. anticipation. 4. something expected. 5. *usually in pl.* apparent chance for success, gain, etc. 6. a likely customer, candidate, etc. *v.t. & v.i.* to explore or search (*for*). —**pros'pec·tor,** *n.*
**pro·spec·tive** (prə-spek'tiv), *adj.* expected; likely. —**pro·spec'tive·ly,** *adv.*
**pro·spec·tus** (prə-spek'təs), *n.* [L.; see PROSPECT], a statement of the main features of a new work, business enterprise, etc.
**pros·per** (pros'pẽr), *v.i.* [< L. *prosperus*, favorable], to succeed; thrive.
**pros·per·i·ty** (pros-per'ə-ti), *n.* [*pl.* -TIES], prosperous condition; wealth.
**pros·per·ous** (pros'pẽr-əs), *adj.* 1. prospering; successful; flourishing. 2. wealthy. 3. favorable. —**pros'per·ous·ly,** *adv.*
**pros·tate** (pros'tāt), *adj.* [< Gr. *prostatēs*, one standing before], designating or of a gland surrounding the urethra at the base of the bladder in males.
**pros·ti·tute** (pros'tə-tōōt', -tūt'), *n.* [< L. *pro-*, before + *statuere*, cause to stand], a woman who engages in promiscuous sexual intercourse for pay. *v.t.* [-TUTED, -TUTING], 1. to offer (oneself) as a prostitute. 2. to sell (oneself, one's talents, etc.) for base purposes. —**pros'ti·tu'tion,** *n.*
**pros·trate** (pros'trāt), *adj.* [< L. *pro-*, before + *sternere*, stretch out], 1. lying face downward. 2. lying prone or supine. 3. laid low; overcome. *v.t.* [-TRATED, -TRATING], 1. to lay flat on the ground. 2. to lay low; subjugate. —**pros·tra'tion,** *n.*
**pros·y** (prō'zi), *adj.* [-IER, -IEST], like prose; prosaic, dull, tedious, etc.
**pro·tag·o·nist** (prō-tag'ə-nist), *n.* [< Gr. *prōtos*, first + *agōnistēs*, actor], the main character in a drama, novel, etc.
**pro·tect** (prə-tekt'), *v.t.* [< L. *pro-*, before + *tegere*, to cover], to shield from injury, danger, etc.; defend. —**pro·tec'tor,** *n.*
**pro·tec'tion,** *n.* 1. a protecting or being protected. 2. a person or thing that protects. 3. the system of protecting domestic products by taxing imports.
**pro·tec'tive,** *adj.* 1. protecting. 2. intended to guard domestic industry from foreign competition: as, *protective* tariffs.
**pro·tec'tor·ate** (-tẽr-it), *n.* a weak state under the control and protection of a strong state.
**pro·té·gé** (prō'tə-zhā'), *n.* [Fr.; see PROTECT], a person under the patronage or protection of another. —**pro'té·gée'** (-zhā'), *n.fem.*
**pro·te·in** (prō'tē-in, -tēn), *n.* [< Gr. *prōtos*, first], any of a class of complex nitrogenous substances occurring in all living matter and essential to diet.
**pro tem·po·re** (prō tem'pə-rē'), [L.], for the time being; temporarily: shortened to **pro tem.**
**pro·test** (prə-test'), *v.t.* [< L. *pro-*, forth + *testari*, affirm], 1. to state positively. 2. to speak strongly against. *v.i.* to express disapproval; object. *n.* (prō'test), 1. an objection. 2. a formal statement of objection. —**prot·es·ta·tion** (prot'əs-tā'shən), *n.*
**Prot·es·tant** (prot'is-tənt), *n.* [see PROTEST], any Christian not belonging to the Roman Catholic or Orthodox Eastern Church. —**Prot'es·tant·ism,** *n.*
**proto-,** [< Gr. *prōtos*, first], a combining form meaning: 1. *first in time, original.* 2. *first in importance, chief.*
**pro·to·col** (prō'tə-kol'), *n.* [< Late Gr. *prōtokollon*, contents page], 1. an original draft or record of a document, negotiation, etc. 2. the established ceremonial forms in official dealings, as between heads of states and their ministers.
**pro·ton** (prō'ton), *n.* [< Gr. *prōtos*, first], a fundamental particle of the nuclei of all atoms, carrying a unit positive charge of electricity.
**pro·to·plasm** (prō'tə-plaz'm), *n.* [< Gr. *prōtos*, first + *plassein*, to mold], a semifluid, viscous colloid, the essential living matter of all animal and plant cells. —**pro'to·plas'mic,** *adj.*
**pro·to·type** (prō'tə-tīp'), *n.* the first thing or being of its kind; original.
**pro·to·zo·an** (prō'tə-zō'ən), *n.* any of various one-celled microscopic animals: also **pro'to·zo'on** (-on) [*pl.* -ZOA (-ə)].
**pro·tract** (prō-trakt'), *v.t.* [< L. *pro-*, forward + *trahere*, draw], to draw out; prolong. —**pro·trac'tion,** *n.*
**pro·trac·tor** (prō-trak'tẽr), *n.* a graduated, semicircular instrument for drawing and measuring angles.
**pro·trude** (prō-trōōd'), *v.t. & v.i.* [-TRUDED, -TRUDING], [< L. *pro-*, forth + *trudere*, to thrust], to jut out; project. —**pro·tru'sion** (-trōō'zhən), *n.* —**pro·tru'sive,** *adj.*
**pro·tu·ber·ance** (prō-tōō'bẽr-əns, -tū'-), *n.* [< L. *pro-*, forth + *tuber*, a bump], a part or thing that protrudes; bulge. —**pro·tu'ber·ant,** *adj.* —**pro·tu'ber·ant·ly,** *adv.*
**proud** (proud), *adj.* [AS. *prud*], 1. having or showing a proper pride in oneself. 2. haughty; arrogant. 3. feeling or showing great pride or joy. 4. that is a cause of pride. 5. caused by pride. 6. stately; splendid: as, a *proud* fleet. —**proud of,** highly pleased with. —**proud'ly,** *adv.*
**proud flesh,** an abnormal growth of flesh around a healing wound.
**prove** (prōōv), *v.t.* [PROVED, PROVED or PROVEN, PROVING], [< L. *probare*, to test], 1. to test by experiment, standard, etc. 2. to establish as true. *v.i.* to be found by experience or trial. —**prov'a·ble,** *adj.*
**Pro·ven·çal** (prō'vən-säl', prov'ən-), *n.* the vernacular of S France, a distinct Romance language of literary importance in the Middle Ages.
**prov·en·der** (prov'ən-dẽr), *n.* [< L. *praebere*, give], 1. dry food for livestock. 2. [Colloq.], food.
**prov·erb** (prov'ẽrb), *n.* [< L. *pro-*, before + *verbum*, word], a short, popular saying that expresses an obvious truth. —**pro·ver·bi·al** (prə-vũr'bi-əl), *adj.* —**pro·ver'bi·al·ly,** *adv.*
**pro·vide** (prə-vīd'), *v.t.* [-VIDED, -VIDING], [< L. *pro-*, before + *videre*, see], 1. to get ready beforehand. 2. to make available; supply. 3. to furnish (*with*). *v.i.* 1. to prepare (*for* or *against*) a possible situation, etc. 2. to stipulate. 3. to furnish support (*for*).
**pro·vid'ed,** *conj.* on the condition or understanding (*that*).
**prov·i·dence** (prov'ə-dəns), *n.* [see PROVIDE], 1. preparation for the future. 2. skill in management; prudence. 3. the benevolent guidance of God or nature. 4. [P-], God.
**prov'i·dent,** *adj.* 1. providing for the future. 2. prudent; economical.
**prov'i·den'tial** (-den'shəl), *adj.* 1. decreed by Providence. 2. fortunate.
**pro·vid·ing** (prə-vīd'iŋ), *conj.* on the condition (*that*); provided.
**prov·ince** (prov'ins), *n.* [< L. *provincia*],

1. an administrative division of a country, esp. of Canada. 2. *a*) a region; district. *b*) *pl.* the parts of a country removed from the capital and the major cities. 3. proper duties. 4. a branch of learning.

**pro·vin·cial** (prə-vin′shəl), *adj.* 1. of the provinces. 2. having the ways, speech, etc. of people in a province. 3. countrified. 4. narrow; limited. —**pro·vin′cial·ism,** *n.*

**pro·vi·sion** (prə-vizh′ən), *n.* 1. a providing or preparing. 2. something provided for the future. 3. *pl.* a stock of food. 4. a clause, as in a legal document, stipulating some specific thing. *v.t.* to supply with provisions. —**pro·vi′sion·er,** *n.*

**pro·vi′sion·al,** *adj.* conditional or temporary: as, a *provisional* mayor.

**pro·vi·so** (prə-vī′zō), *n.* [*pl.* -SOS, -SOES], [L., it being provided], a clause, as in a document, making some condition; stipulation.

**prov·o·ca·tion** (prov′ə-kā′shən), *n.* 1. a provoking. 2. something that provokes; incitement.

**pro·voc·a·tive** (prə-vok′ə-tiv), *adj.* provoking or tending to provoke, as to action, thought, anger, etc. —**pro·voc′a·tive·ly,** *adv.*

**pro·voke** (prə-vōk′), *v.t.* [-VOKED, -VOKING], [< L. *pro-*, forth + *vocare*, to call], 1. to excite to some action or feeling. 2. to anger; irritate. 3. to stir up (action or feeling). 4. to evoke. —**pro·vok′ing,** *adj.*

**prov·ost** (prov′əst), *n.* [< L. *praepositus*, chief], a high executive official, as in some churches or colleges.

**pro·vost marshal** (prō′vō), an officer in charge of military police.

**prow** (prou), *n.* [< Gr. *prōira*], 1. the forward part of a ship. 2. something like this.

**prow·ess** (prou′is), *n.* [< L. *prodesse*, be of use], 1. bravery. 2. a valorous act. 3. superior ability, skill, etc.

**prowl** (proul), *v.i. & v.t.* [ME. *prollen*], to roam about furtively in search of prey. *n.* a prowling. —**on the prowl,** prowling about.

**prox·im·i·ty** (prok-sim′ə-ti), *n.* [< L. *prope*, near], nearness in space, time, etc.

**prox·y** (prok′si), *n.* [*pl.* -IES], [< ME. *procuracie*, office of a procurator], 1. the authority to act for another, as in voting. 2. a person so authorized.

**prude** (prōōd), *n.* [Fr.; prob. < *prudefemme*, excellent woman], one who is overly modest or proper in behavior, speech, etc. —**prud′er·y,** *n.* —**prud′ish,** *adj.*

**pru·dence** (prōō′d'ns), *n.* 1. a being prudent. 2. careful management. —**pru·den′tial** (-den′shəl), *adj.*

**pru·dent** (prōō′d'nt), *adj.* [< L. *providens*, provident], 1. exercising sound judgment in practical matters. 2. cautious in conduct; not rash. —**pru′dent·ly,** *adv.*

**prune** (prōōn), *n.* [< Gr. *prounon*, plum], a dried plum.

**prune** (prōōn), *v.t. & v.i.* [PRUNED, PRUNING], [< OFr.], 1. to remove branches, twigs, etc. from (a plant). 2. to cut out, as unnecessary parts. —**prun′er,** *n.*

**pru·ri·ent** (proor′i-ənt), *adj.* [< L. *prurire*, to itch], lustful; lewd. —**pru′ri·ence,** *n.*

**pry** (prī), *n.* [*pl.* PRIES], [< *prize*, a lever], a lever or crowbar. *v.t.* [PRIED, PRYING], 1. to raise or move with a lever, etc. 2. to draw forth with difficulty.

**pry** (prī), *v.i.* [PRIED, PRYING], [ME. *prien*, to peer], to look closely or inquisitively.

**P.S.,** Public School.

**PS., P.S., p.s.,** [*pl.* P.SS.], postscript.

**psalm** (säm), *n.* [< Gr. *psallein*, to pluck (a harp)], 1. a sacred song or poem. 2. any of the songs or hymns composing the Book of Psalms. —**psalm′ist,** *n.*

**psal·mo·dy** (säm′ə-di, sal′mə-), *n.* [*pl.* -DIES], [see PSALM], 1. the singing of psalms. 2. psalms collectively.

**Psalms** (sämz), *n.pl.* [construed as sing.], a book of the Old Testament, consisting of 150 psalms: abbrev. **Ps., Psa.**

**pseu·do** (sōō′dō, sū′-), *adj.* [see PSEUDO-], sham; false; spurious.

**pseudo-,** [< Gr. *pseudein*, deceive], a prefix meaning *sham, counterfeit.*

**pseu·do·nym** (sōō′də-nim′, sū′-), *n.* [< Gr. *pseudēs*, false + *onyma*, a name], a fictitious name, as assumed by an author; pen name.

**pshaw** (shô), *interj. & n.* an exclamation of impatience, disgust, etc.

**psi** (sī), *n.* the twenty-third letter of the Greek alphabet (Ψ, ψ).

**pso·ri·a·sis** (sō-rī′ə-sis), *n.* [< Gr. *psōra*, an itch], a chronic skin disease with scaly patches.

**psych.,** 1. psychological. 2. psychology.

**Psy·che** (sī′ki), *n.* [< Gr. *psychē*, soul], 1. in *Gr. & Rom. myth.*, the wife of Cupid: she personifies the soul. 2. [p-], *a*) the soul. *b*) the mind, esp. as an organic system adjusting the total organism to the environment.

**psy·che·del·ic** (sī′ki-del′ik), *adj.* [< *psyche* (mind) + Gr. *delein*, to make manifest], of or causing extreme changes in the conscious mind, such as inducing hallucinations, etc. *n.* a psychedelic drug.

**psy·chi·a·try** (sī-kī′ə-tri), *n.* [< *psych*(*o*)- + Gr. *iatreia*, healing], the branch of medicine dealing with disorders of the mind, including psychoses and neuroses. —**psy′chi·at′ric** (-ki-at′rik), *adj.* —**psy·chi′a·trist,** *n.*

**psy·chic** (sī′kik), *adj.* [< Gr. *psychē*, soul], 1. of the psyche, or mind. 2. beyond known physical processes. 3. apparently sensitive to forces beyond the physical world. Also **psy′chi·cal.** —**psy′chi·cal·ly,** *adv.*

**psycho-,** [< Gr. *psychē*, soul], a combining form meaning *the mind* or *mental processes*, as in *psychology*: also **psych-.**

**psy·cho·a·nal·y·sis** (sī′kō-ə-nal′ə-sis), *n.* a method of treating neuroses and some other mental disorders by analyzing emotional conflicts, repressions, etc. through the use of free association, dream analysis, etc. —**psy′cho·an′a·lyst** (-an′əl-ist), *n.*

**psy·cho·an·a·lyze** (-sī′kō-an′ə-līz′), *v.t.* [-LYZED, -LYZING], to treat by means of psychoanalysis.

**psy·chol·o·gy** (sī-kol′ə-ji), *n.* [*pl.* -GIES], [see PSYCHO- & -LOGY], 1. the science dealing with the mind and mental processes, feelings, etc. 2. the science of human and animal behavior. —**psy′cho·log′i·cal** (-kə-loj′i-k'l), *adj.* —**psy·chol′o·gist,** *n.*

**psy·cho·path·ic** (sī′kə-path′ik), *adj.* [*psycho-* + *-pathic*], of or characterized by mental disorder.

**psychopathic personality,** a person with serious personality defects, as emotional immaturity, impulsive (often criminal) behavior, asocial feelings, etc.: also **psy′cho·path′,** *n.*

**psy·cho·pa·thol·o·gy** (sī′kō-pə-thol′ə-ji), *n.* the pathology of the mind, its diseases, etc.

**psy·cho·sis** (sī-kō′sis), *n.* [*pl.* -SES (-sēz)], [< Gr. *psychē*, soul], any mental disorder in which the personality is very seriously disorganized. —**psy·chot′ic** (-kot′ik), *adj.*

**psy·cho·so·mat·ic** (sī′kō-sō-mat′ik), *adj.* [*psycho-* + *somatic*], designating or of a physical disorder originating in or aggravated by emotional processes.

**psy·cho·ther·a·py** (sī′kō-ther′ə-pi), *n.* [*psycho-* + *therapy*], the treatment of mental disorders by hypnosis, psychoanalysis, etc. —**psy′cho·ther′a·pist,** *n.*

**Pt,** in *chem.*, platinum.

**pt.,** [*pl.* PTS.], 1. part. 2. pint. 3. point.

**pt.,** past tense: also **p.t.**

**P.T.A.,** Parent-Teacher Association.

**ptar·mi·gan** (tär′mə-gən), *n.* [< Scot. *tarmachan*], a northern grouse.

**pto·maine, pto·main** (tō′mān), *n.* < Gr. *ptōma*, corpse], an alkaloid substance, often poisonous, found in decaying matter.

**Pu,** in *chem.*, plutonium.

**pub** (pub), *n.* [Brit. Slang], a bar; tavern: in full, **public house.**

**pu·ber·ty** (pū′bẽr-ti), *n.* [< L. *pubes*, adult], the state of physical development when it is first possible to beget or bear children.

**pu·bes·cent** (pū-bes′'nt), *adj.* [see PUBERTY], reaching, or having reached, puberty.

**pu·bic** (pū′bic), *adj.* [see PUBERTY], of or in the region of the genitals.

**pub·lic** (pub′lik), *adj.* [ult. < L. *populus*, the people], 1. of people as a whole. 2. for the use or benefit of all: as, a *public* building. 3. acting officially for the people: as, a *public* prosecutor. 4. known by most people. *n.* 1. the people as a whole. 2. a specific part of the people: as, the sporting *public*. **—in public,** in open view. **—pub′lic·ly,** *adv.*

**pub·li·can** (pub′li-kən), *n.* 1. in ancient Rome, a tax collector. 2. [Brit.], a saloonkeeper; innkeeper.

**pub·li·ca·tion** (pub′li-kā′shən), *n.* [see PUBLISH], 1. public notification. 2. the printing and distribution of books, magazines, etc. 3. something published, as a book, periodical, etc.

**public domain,** the condition of being free from copyright or patent.

**pub·li·cist** (pub′li-sist), *n.* a publicity agent.

**pub·lic·i·ty** (pub-lis′ə-ti), *n.* 1. a being commonly known. 2. any information which brings a person, thing, etc. to public notice. 3. notice by the public. 4. any procedure seeking this.

**pub·li·cize** (pub′li-sīz′), *v.t.* [-CIZED, -CIZING], to give publicity to.

**public relations,** relations of an organization with the general public through publicity.

**public school,** 1. in the U.S., an elementary or secondary school maintained by public taxes and supervised by local authorities. 2. in England, a private boarding school for boys. **—pub′lic-school′,** *adj.*

**pub′lic-spir′it·ed,** *adj.* having or showing zeal for the public welfare.

**public utility,** an organization supplying water, electricity, transportation, etc. to the public.

**pub·lish** (pub′lish), *v.t.* [< L. *publicare*], 1. to make publicly known; announce. 2. to issue (a printed work) for sale. **—pub′lish·a·ble,** *adj.* **—pub′lish·er,** *n.*

**puck** (puk), *n.* [akin to POKE], the hard rubber disk used in ice hockey.

**puck** (puk), *n.* [AS. *puca*], a mischievous sprite. **—puck′ish,** *adj.*

**puck·er** (puk′ẽr), *v.t. & v.i.* [< *poke* (bag)], to gather into wrinkles. *n.* a wrinkle or series of wrinkles. **—puck′er·y,** *adj.*

**pud·ding** (pood′iŋ), *n.* [prob. < AS. *puduc*, swelling], any of various soft foods made with flour or cereal, and eggs, milk, etc.

**pud·dle** (pud′'l), *n.* [dim. < AS. *pudd*, ditch], a small pool of water, esp. stagnant or spilled water. *v.t.* [-DLED, -DLING], 1. to make muddy. 2. to treat (iron) by puddling. **—pud′dler,** *n.*

**pud·dling** (pud′liŋ), *n.* the making of wrought iron from pig iron by heating and stirring it along with oxidizing agents.

**pudg·y** (puj′i), *adj.* [-IER, -IEST], [? < Scot. *pud*, belly], short and fat.

**pueb·lo** (pweb′lō), *n.* [*pl.* -LOS], [Sp. < L. *populus*, people], a type of communal Indian village in the Southwest, consisting of terraced structures, as of adobe, housing many families.

**pu·er·ile** (pū′ẽr-il), *adj.* [< L. *puer*, boy], childish; silly. **—pu′er·il′i·ty,** *n.*

**puff** (puf), *n.* [ult. echoic], 1. a short, sudden gust or expulsion of wind, breath, smoke, etc. 2. a draw at a cigarette, etc. 3. a light pastry filled with whipped cream, etc. 4. a soft pad: as, a powder *puff*. 5. a swelling. 6. a soft roll of hair on the head. 7. exaggerated praise, as of a book. *v.i.* 1. *a*) to blow in puffs. *b*) to breathe rapidly. 2. to swell (*out* or *up*). 3. to take puffs at a cigarette, etc. *v.t.* 1. to blow, smoke, etc. in or with puffs. 2. to swell; inflate. 3. to praise unduly. **—puff′y** [-IER, -IEST], *adj.*

**puff′ball′,** *n.* a round, mushroomlike plant that bursts at the touch.

**puf·fin** (puf′in), *n.* [ME. *poffin*], a northern seabird with a triangular beak.

**pug** (pug), *n.* [prob. < *puck* (sprite)], a small, short-haired dog with a snub nose.

**pu·gil·ism** (pū′jə-liz'm), *n.* [< L. *pugnus*, fist], the art or practice of boxing. **—pu′gil·ist,** *n.* **—pu′gil·is′tic,** *adj.*

**pug·na·cious** (pug-nā′shəs), *adj.* [< L. *pugnus*, fist], given to fighting; quarrelsome. **—pug·nac′i·ty** (-nas′ə-ti), *n.*

**puke** (pūk), *n., v.i. & v.t.* [PUKED, PUKING], [cf. G. *spucke*, spit], vomit.

**pul·chri·tude** (pul′krə-tōōd′, -tūd′), *n.* [< L. *pulcher*, beautiful], beauty.

**pull** (pool), *v.t.* [AS. *pullian*, to pluck], 1. to exert force on so as to move toward the source of the force. 2. to pluck out: as, to *pull* a tooth. 3. to rip; tear. 4. to strain, as a muscle. 5. [Colloq.], to perform; do: as, to *pull* a raid. 6. [Colloq.], to restrain: as, to *pull* a punch. *v.i.* 1. to exert force in dragging, tugging, etc. 2. to take a puff at a cigarette, etc. 3. to be capable of being pulled. 4. to move (*away*, *ahead*, etc.). *n.* 1. the act or force of pulling. 2. any difficult, continuous effort. 3. something to be pulled, as a handle. 4. [Slang], influence. **—pull for,** [Colloq.], to cheer on. **—pull off,** [Colloq.], to accomplish. **—pull oneself together,** [Colloq.], to get over (an illness, difficulty, etc.).

**pul·let** (pool′it), *n.* [< L. *pullus*, chicken], a young hen.

**pul·ley** (pool′i), *n.* [*pl.* -LEYS], [prob. < Gr. *polos*, axis], a small wheel with a grooved rim in which a rope or belt runs, as to raise weights or transmit power.

**Pull·man car** (pool′mən), [< G. *Pullman*, 19th-c. U.S. inventor], a railroad car having private compartments or berths for sleeping: also **Pullman,** *n.*

**pull′-o′ver,** *adj.* that is pulled on over the head. *n.* a pull-over sweater, shirt, etc.

**pul·mo·nar·y** (pul′mə-ner′i), *adj.* [< L. *pulmo*, a lung], of or affecting the lungs.

**pul·mo·tor** (pul′mō′tẽr, pool′-), *n.* [< L. *pulmo*, lung; + *motor*], an apparatus for applying artificial respiration: a trademark (**Pulmotor**).

**pulp** (pulp), *n.* [< L. *pulpa*, flesh], 1. a soft, moist, sticky mass. 2. the soft, juicy part of a fruit or soft pith of a plant stem. 3. the sensitive substance under the dentine of a tooth. 4. ground-up, moistened fibers of wood, rags, etc., used to make paper. *v.t.* to reduce to pulp. *v.i.* to become pulp. **—pulp′y** [-IER, -IEST], *adj.*

**pul·pit** (pool′pit), *n.* [< L. *pulpitum*, a stage], 1. a raised platform from which a clergyman preaches in a church. 2. preachers collectively. 3. preaching.

**pul·sar** (pul′sär), *n.* [< *pulse* + *-ar*], any of several small, heavenly objects in the Milky Way that emit radio pulses at regular intervals.

**pul·sate** (pul′sāt), *v.i.* [-SATED, -SATING], [< L. *pulsare*, to beat], 1. to beat or throb rhythmically, as the heart. 2. to vibrate; quiver. **—pul·sa′tion,** *n.* **—pul·sa′tor,** *n.*

**pulse** (puls), *n.* [< L. *pulsus*, a beating],

1. the regular beating in the arteries, caused by the contractions of the heart. 2. any regular beat. *v.i.* [PULSED, PULSING], to pulsate; throb.

**pulse** (puls), *n.* [< L. *puls*, a pottage], 1. the edible seeds of plants with pods, as peas, beans, etc. 2. any such plant.

**pul·ver·ize** (pul′və-rīz′), *v.t. & v.i.* [-IZED, -IZING], [< L. *pulvis*, dust], to grind or be ground into a powder.

**pu·ma** (pū′mə), *n.* [Sp.], the cougar.

**pum·ice** (pum′is), *n.* [< L. *pumex*], a light, porous, volcanic rock, used often as a powder, for removing stains, polishing, etc.

**pum·mel** (pum′'l), *n. & v.t.* [-MELED or -MELLED, -MELING or -MELLING], pommel.

**pump** (pump), *n.* [< Sp. *bomba*], a machine that forces a liquid or gas into, or draws it out of, something. *v.t.* 1. to move (fluids) with a pump. 2. to remove water, etc. from. 3. to inflate (a rubber tire) with air. 4. to draw out, move up and down, pour forth, etc. in the manner of a pump. 5. to question persistently. **—pump′er,** *n.*

**pump** (pump), *n.* [prob. < Fr. *pompe*, ornament], a low-cut shoe without straps or ties.

**pump·er·nick·el** (pum′pẽr-nik″'l), *n.* [G.], a coarse, dark rye bread.

**pump·kin** (pump′kin, puŋ′kin), *n.* [< Gr. *pepōn*, ripe], 1. a large, round, orange-yellow, edible gourdlike fruit that grows on a vine. 2. the vine.

**pun** (pun), *n.* [? < It. *puntiglio*, fine point], the humorous use of a word, or of different words sounded alike, so as to play on the various meanings. *v.i.* [PUNNED, PUNNING], to make puns. **—pun′ner,** *n.*

**punch** (punch), *n.* [see PUNCHEON], a tool driven against a surface that is to be pierced, shaped, or stamped. *v.t.* to pierce, stamp, etc. with a punch. **—punch′er,** *n.*

**punch** (punch), *v.t.* [ME. *punchen*], 1. to prod with a stick. 2. to herd (cattle) as by prodding. 3. to strike with the fist. 4. to make (a hole) with a punch. *n.* 1. a thrusting blow as with the fist. 2. [Colloq.], effective force. **—punch′er,** *n.*

**punch** (punch), *n.* [< Hind. *pāc*, five: it orig. had five ingredients], a sweet drink flavored with fruit juices, spices, etc., often mixed with wine or liquor.

**pun·cheon** (pun′chən), *n.* [ult. < L. *pungere*, to prick], 1. a short, upright wooden post used in framework. 2. a broad, roughly dressed timber. 3. a large cask, as for beer.

**punc·til′i·ous,** *adj.* [see PUNCTILIO], 1. careful in the observance of the nice points of conduct, etc. 2. very exact; scrupulous.

**punc·tu·al** (puŋk′chōō-əl), *adj.* [< L. *punctus*, a point], on time; prompt. **—punc′tu·al′i·ty** (-al′ə-ti), [*pl.* -TIES], *n.*

**punc·tu·ate** (puŋk′chōō-āt′), *v.t.* [-ATED, -ATING], [< L. *punctus*, a point], to use certain standardized marks, as the period, comma, colon, semicolon, etc., in (written or printed matter). **—punc′tu·a′tion,** *n.*

**punc·ture** (puŋk′chẽr), *n.* [< L. *pungere*, to pierce], 1. a piercing. 2. a hole made by a sharp point, as in a tire. *v.t. & v.i.* [-TURED, -TURING], to pierce or be pierced as with a sharp point.

**pun·dit** (pun′dit), *n.* [< Sans. *pandita*], a person of great learning.

**pun·gent** (pun′jənt), *adj.* [< L. *pungere*, to prick], 1. producing a sharp sensation of taste and smell. 2. biting: as, *pungent* language. 3. keenly clever; stimulating. **—pun′gen·cy,** *n.* **—pun′gent·ly,** *adv.*

**pun·ish** (pun′ish), *v.t.* [< L. *punire*], 1. to cause to undergo pain, loss, etc., as for a crime. 2. to impose a penalty for (an offense). **—pun′ish·a·ble,** *adj.*

**pun′ish·ment,** *n.* 1. a punishing or being punished. 2. the penalty imposed.

**pu·ni·tive** (pū′nə-tiv), *adj.* concerned with, or inflicting, punishment.

**punk** (puŋk), *n.* [< Am. Ind.], 1. decayed wood or dried fungus used for tinder. 2. any substance that smolders when ignited, used to light fireworks, etc.

**punk** (puŋk), *n.* [Slang], 1. a young gangster. 2. a young person regarded as inexperienced, insignificant, etc. *adj.* [Slang], poor in quality.

**pun·ster** (pun′stẽr), *n.* one who likes to make puns.

**punt** (punt), *n.* [? akin to *butt*], in *football*, a kick in which the ball is dropped from the hands and kicked before it strikes the ground. *v.t. & v.i.* to kick (a football) in a punt.

**punt** (punt), *n.* [< L. *pons*, a bridge], a flat-bottomed boat with square ends. *v.t. & v.i.* to propel (a punt) with a long pole.

**pu·ny** (pū′ni), *adj.* [-NIER, -NIEST], [< OFr. *puis*, after + *nê*, born], of inferior size, strength, or importance; weak.

**pup** (pup), *n.* 1. a young dog; puppy. 2. a young seal.

**pu·pa** (pū′pə), *n.* [*pl.* -PAE (-pē), -PAS], [L., doll], an insect in the stage between the larval and adult forms. **—pu′pal,** *adj.*

**pu·pil** (pū′p'l), *n.* [< L. *pupillus*, ward], a person taught under the supervision of a teacher or tutor, as in school.

**pu·pil** (pū′p'l), *n.* [< L. *pupilla*, figure reflected in the eye], the contractile circular opening in the center of the iris of the eye.

**pup·pet** (pup′it), *n.* [< L. *pupa*, doll], 1. a small, humanlike figure, esp. one moved by strings or the hands in a performance **(puppet show)**. 2. one whose actions, ideas, etc. are controlled by another.

**pup·py** (pup′i), *n.* [*pl.* -PIES], [< Fr. *poupée*, doll], a young dog.

**pup tent,** a small, portable tent.

**pur·blind** (pũr′blīnd′), *adj.* [ME. *pur blind*, quite blind], 1. partly blind. 2. slow in understanding. **—pur′blind′ly,** *adv.*

**pur·chase** (pũr′chis), *v.t.* [-CHASED, -CHASING], [< OFr. *pour*, for + *chacier*, to chase], to buy. *n.* 1. anything bought. 2. the act of buying. 3. a fast hold applied to move something heavy or to keep from slipping. **—pur′chas·a·ble,** *adj.* **—pur′chas·er,** *n.*

**pure** (pyoor), *adj.* [< L. *purus*], 1. free from anything that adulterates, taints, etc.; unmixed. 2. simple; mere. 3. faultless. 4. blameless. 5. virgin or chaste. 6. abstract or theoretical: as, *pure* physics.

**pu·rée** (pyoo-rā′, pyoor′ā), *n.* [Fr.; see PURE], 1. food prepared by straining the boiled pulp through a sieve. 2. a thick soup.

**pur·ga·tive** (pũr′gə-tiv), *adj.* purging. *n.* a substance that purges, as a cathartic.

**pur·ga·to·ry** (pũr′gə-tôr′i), *n.* [*pl.* -RIES], [see PURGE], in *R.C. theology*, a state or place after death for expiating sins by suffering. **—pur′ga·to′ri·al,** *adj.*

**purge** (pũrj), *v.t.* [PURGED, PURGING], [< L. *purus*, clean + *agere*, do], 1. to cleanse of impurities, etc. 2. to cleanse of sin. 3. to rid (a nation, party, etc.) of individuals held to be disloyal. 4. to empty (the bowels). *n.* 1. a purging. 2. that which purges; esp., a cathartic. **—purge′a·ble,** *adj.*

**pu·ri·fy** (pyoor′ə-fī′), *v.t.* [-FIED, -FYING], [< L. *purus*, pure + *facere*, make], 1. to rid of impurities, etc. 2. to free from guilt, sin, etc. *v.i.* to be purified. **—pu′ri·fi·ca′tion,** *n.*

**pur·ism** (pyoor′iz'm), *n.* strict or excessive observance of precise usage in language, style, etc. **—pur′ist,** *n.*

**Pu·ri·tan** (pyoor′ə-t'n), *n.* [see PURITY], 1. a member of a group originating in 16th-century England who wanted to purify the Church of England from elaborate ceremonies and forms. 2. [p-], a person regarded as very strict in morals and religion. —**pu'ri·tan'i·cal** (-tan'i-k'l), *adj.*

**pu·ri·ty** (pyoor'ə-ti), *n.* a being pure; specif., *a*) freedom from adulterating matter. *b*) cleanness. *c*) freedom from sin; chastity.

**purl** (pũrl), *v.t. & v.i.* [cf. It. *pirlare*, to twirl], to invert (stitches) in knitting. *n.* an inversion of stitches in knitting to give a ribbed effect.

**pur·lieu** (pũr'lo͞o), *n.* [< OFr. *pur-*, through + *aler*, go], 1. an outlying part, as of a city. 2. *pl.* environs.

**pur·loin** (pũr-loin'), *v.t. & v.i.* [< OFr. *pur-*, for + *loin*, far], to steal. —**pur·loin'er**, *n.*

**pur·ple** (pũr'p'l), *n.* [< Gr. *porphyra*, shellfish yielding purple dye], 1. a dark bluish red. 2. crimson cloth or clothing, esp. as a former emblem of royalty or high rank. *adj.* 1. bluish-red. 2. imperial; royal. 3. ornate; elaborate: as, *purple* prose. —**born to the purple**, of high or royal birth. —**pur'plish**, *adj.*

**pur·port** (pũr-pôrt'; *for n.*, pũr'pôrt), *v.t.* [< OFr. *pur-*, forth + *porter*, to bear], 1. to profess or claim as its meaning. 2. to give the appearance, often falsely, of being, intending, etc. *n.* meaning; sense.

**pur·pose** (pũr'pəs), *v.t. & v.i.* [-POSED, -POSING], [< OFr. *por*, for + *poser*, to place], to aim, intend, plan, etc. *n.* 1. something one intended to get or do; aim. 2. determination. 3. the object for which something exists or is done. —**on purpose**, intentionally. —**pur'pose·ful**, *adj.* —**pur'pose·less**, *adj.*

**pur'pose·ly**, *adv.* with a definite purpose; intentionally; deliberately.

**purr** (pũr), *n.* [echoic], a low, vibratory sound made by a cat when it seems to be pleased. *v.i.* to utter such a sound.

**purse** (pũrs), *n.* [< Gr. *byrsa*, a skin], 1. *a*) a small bag for carrying money. *b*) a woman's handbag. 2. finances; money. 3. a sum of money given as a present or prize. *v.t.* [PURSED, PURSING], to pucker.

**purs·er** (pũr'sẽr), *n.* [ME., purse bearer], an officer on a passenger ship, in charge of accounts, tickets, etc.

**pur·su·ance** (pẽr-so͞o'əns, -sū'-), *n.* a pursuing, or carrying out, as of a plan, etc.

**pur·su'ant**, *adj.* carrying out; following. —**pursuant to**, in accordance with.

**pur·sue** (pẽr-so͞o', -sū'), *v.t.* [-SUED, -SUING], [< L. *pro-*, forth + *sequi*, follow], 1. to follow in order to overtake or capture; chase. 2. to follow, as a specified course, action, etc. 3. to try to find; seek. 4. to continue to annoy or distress. —**pur·su'er**, *n.*

**pur·suit** (pẽr-so͞ot', -sūt'), *n.* 1. a pursuing. 2. an occupation.

**pu·ru·lent** (pyoor'ə-lənt, -yoo-lənt), *adj.* [< L. *pus*, pus], of, like, containing, or discharging pus. —**pu'ru·lence**, *n.*

**pur·vey** (pẽr-vā'), *v.t.* [see PROVIDE], to supply, as food or provisions. —**pur·vey'or**, *n.*

**pus** (pus), *n.* [L.], the yellowish-white matter produced by an infection. —**pus'sy**, *adj.*

**push** (poosh), *v.t.* [< L. *pulsare*, to beat], 1. to press against (a thing) so as to move it. 2. to press or urge forward. 3. to urge the use, sale, etc. of (something). *n.* 1. a pushing. 2. an advance against opposition. 3. [Colloq.], aggressiveness; enterprise.

**push'-o'ver**, *n.* [Slang], 1. anything easy to do. 2. a person, group, etc. easily persuaded, defeated, etc.

**pu·sil·lan·i·mous** (pū's'l-an'ə-məs), *adj.* [< L. *pusillus*, tiny + *animus*, the mind], cowardly; fainthearted. —**pu'sil·la·nim'i·ty** (-ə-nim'ə-ti), *n.*

**puss** (poos), *n.* [echoic of its spitting], a cat: pet name: also **puss'y** [*pl.* -IES].

**puss'y·foot'**, *v.i.* [Slang], 1. to move with stealth or caution, as a cat does. 2. to avoid committing oneself or making one's position clear.

**pussy willow**, a willow having silvery, velvetlike catkins.

**pus·tule** (pus'chool), *n.* [L. *pustula*], an inflamed, pus-filled pimple or blister.

**put** (poot), *v.t.* [PUT, PUTTING], [< AS. *putian*, to push], 1. to thrust; drive. 2. to cause to be in a specified position, place, condition, relation, etc.; place; set; lay. 3. to impose: as, *put* a tax on furs. 4. to attribute; ascribe. 5. to express: as, *put* it plainly. 6. to present for decision: as, *put* the question. *v.i.* to go (with *in*, *out*, etc.). *adj.* [Colloq.], fixed: as, stay *put*. —**put about**, to change a vessel's course. —**put across**, [Slang], to cause to be understood, accepted, successful, etc. —**put aside** (or **away, by**), to reserve for later use. —**put down**, to crush; repress. —**put it** (or **something**) **over on**, [Colloq.], to deceive; trick. —**put off**, 1. to delay; postpone. 2. to evade; divert. —**put on**, 1. to clothe oneself with. 2. to pretend. —**put out**, 1. to expel; dismiss. 2. to extinguish (a fire or light). 3. to disconcert; confuse. 4. to distress. 5. to inconvenience. 6. in *baseball*, to retire (a batter or runner). —**put through**, 1. to carry out. 2. to cause to do or undergo. —**put up**, 1. to offer; show. 2. to preserve, as fruits. 3. to provide lodgings for. 4. to provide (money). 5. [Colloq.], to incite (a person) *to* some action. —**put upon**, to impose on. —**put up with**, to tolerate.

**pu·tre·fy** (pū'trə-fī'), *v.t. & v.i.* [-FIED, -FYING], [< L. *putris*, putrid + *facere*, make], to make or become putrid; rot. —**pu'tre·fac'tion** (-fak'shən), *n.*

**pu·tres·cent** (pū-tres''nt), *adj.* putrefying; rotting. —**pu·tres'cence**, *n.*

**pu·trid** (pū'trid), *adj.* [< L. *putrere*, to rot], rotten and foul-smelling. —**pu·trid'i·ty**, *n.*

**putt** (put), *n.* [< *put*, *v.*], in *golf*, a light stroke made on the putting green to get the ball into the hole. *v.t. & v.i.* to hit (the ball) with a putt.

**put·tee** (pu-tē', put'i), *n.* [< Sans. *patta*, a strip of cloth], a covering for the lower leg in the form of a gaiter or a cloth strip wound spirally: also **puttie, putty** [*pl.* -TIES].

**putt·er** (put'ẽr), *n.* a straight-faced golf club used in putting.

**put·ter** (put'ẽr), *v.i.* [< AS. *potian*, to push], to busy oneself in an ineffective way (with *along*, *around*, etc.). *v.t.* to fritter (*away*).

**putt·ing green** (put'iŋ), in *golf*, the area of smooth turf around the hole.

**put·ty** (put'i), *n.* [< Fr. *potée*, lit., potful], a soft, plastic mixture of powdered chalk and linseed oil, used to fill cracks, etc. *v.t.* [-TIED, -TYING], to cement or fill with putty.

**puz·zle** (puz''l), *v.t.* [-ZLED, -ZLING], [prob. < ME. *posen*, pose (a question)], to perplex; bewilder. *v.i.* 1. to be perplexed, etc. 2. to exercise one's mind, as over a problem. *n.* 1. something that puzzles. 2. a toy or problem for exercising mental ingenuity. —**puzzle out**, to solve by deep study.

**Pvt.**, Private.

**PX** (pē'eks'), Post Exchange.

**Pyg·ma·li·on** (pig-māl'yən), *n.* in *Gr. legend*, a sculptor who fell in love with his statue of a maiden.

**Pyg·my** (pig'mi), *n.* [*pl.* -MIES], [< Gr. *pygmaios*, of the length of the forearm], 1. a member of any of several races of African and Asiatic dwarfs. 2. [p-], a dwarf. *adj.* 1. of the Pygmies. 2. [p-], dwarfish.

**py·ja·mas** (pə-jam'əz, -jä'məz), *n.pl.* pajamas: Brit. spelling.

**py·lon** (pī'lon), *n.* [Gr. *pylōn*, gateway], 1. a gateway, as of an Egyptian temple. 2. a towerlike structure supporting telegraph wires, marking a flight course, etc.

**py·lo·rus** (pī-lôr'əs), *n.* [*pl.* -RI (-ī)], [< Gr. *pylōros*, gatekeeper], the opening from the stomach into the duodenum. —**py·lor′ic,** *adj.*

**py·or·rhe·a, py·or·rhoe·a** (pī′ə-rē′ə), *n.* [< Gr. *pyon*, pus + *rhein*, to flow], an infection of the gums and tooth sockets, with formation of pus and loosening of the teeth.

**pyr·a·mid** (pir′ə-mid), *n.* [< Gr. *pyramis*], 1. a huge structure with a square base and four triangular sides meeting at a point, as the royal tombs of ancient Egypt. 2. in *geometry*, a solid figure having a polygonal base, the sides of which form the bases of triangular surfaces meeting at a common vertex. *v.t. & v.i.* to build up as in a pyramid. —**py·ram·i·dal** (pi-ram′ə-d'l), *adj.*

**pyre** (pīr), *n.* [< Gr. *pyr*, fire], a pile of wood for burning a dead body; funeral pile.

**py·rex** (pī′reks), *n.* [< *pie* + L. *rex*, king], a heat-resistant glassware for cooking, etc.: a trademark (**Pyrex**).

**py·rite** (pī′rīt), *n.* [*pl.* -RITES (pə-rī′tēz, pī′rīts)], [< Gr. *pyritēs*, flint], iron sulfide, a lustrous, yellow mineral: also called *iron pyrites, fool's gold.*

**pyro-,** [< Gr. *pyr*], a combining form meaning *fire, heat*: also **pyr-.**

**py·ro·ma·ni·a** (pī′rə-mā′ni-ə), *n.* [*pyro-* + *-mania*], a compulsion to start destructive fires. —**py′ro·ma′ni·ac′,** *n. & adj.*

**py·ro·tech·nics** (pī′rə-tek′niks), *n.pl.* [construed as sing.], [< *pyro-* + Gr. *technē*, art], 1. a display of fireworks: also **py′ro·tech′ny.** 2. a dazzling display, as of wit.

**Pyr·rhic victory** (pir′ik), [after *Pyrrhus*, a Gr. king who defeated the Romans but suffered heavy losses], a too costly victory.

**py·thon** (pī′thən, -thon), *n.* [< Gr. *Pythōn*, a serpent slain by Apollo], a large, nonpoisonous snake of SE Asia that crushes its prey to death.

# Q

**Q, q** (kū), *n.* [*pl.* Q's, q's, Qs, qs], the seventeenth letter of the English alphabet.

**q.,** 1. quart. 2. queen. 3. question.

**Q.E.D.,** *quod erat demonstrandum*, [L.], which was to be proved.

**QM,** Quartermaster.

**qt.,** [*pl.* QTS.], 1. quart. 2. quantity.

**quack** (kwak), *v.i.* [echoic], to utter the cry of a duck. *n.* this cry.

**quack** (kwak), *n.* [< earlier *quacksalver* (< MD. *quacken*, to brag + *zalf*, salve)], 1. an untrained person who practices medicine fraudulently. 2. any person who pretends to knowledge or skill he does not have. *adj.* fraudulent. —**quack′er·y** [*pl.* -IES], *n.*

**quad·ran·gle** (kwäd′raŋ′g'l), *n.* [see QUADRI- & ANGLE], 1. a plane figure with four angles and four sides. 2. an area surrounded on its four sides by buildings. —**quad·ran′gu·lar** (-gyoo-lẽr), *adj.*

**quad·rant** (kwäd′rənt), *n.* [< L. *quadrans*, fourth part], 1. a quarter section of a circle. 2. an arc of 90°. 3. an instrument for measuring altitudes in astronomy and navigation.

**quad·rate** (kwäd′rāt; *also, for adj. & n.*, -rit), *adj.* [< L. *quadrare*, to make square], square; rectangular. *n.* a square or rectangle. *v.i.* [-RATED, -RATING], to conform (*to*); square (*with*).

**quad·rat·ic** (kwäd-rat′ik), *adj.* in *algebra*, involving a quantity or quantities that are squared but none that are raised to a higher power.

**quad·ren·ni·al** (kwäd-ren′i-əl), *adj.* [< L. *quadri-* (see QUADRI-) + *annus*, a year], occurring once every four years. *n.* a quadrennial event.

**quadri-,** [L. < *quattuor*, four], a combining form meaning *four times*: also **quadr-.**

**quad·ri·lat·er·al** (kwäd′rə-lat′ẽr-əl), *adj.* [see QUADRI- & LATERAL], four-sided. *n.* a plane figure having four sides and four angles. —**quad′ri·lat′er·al·ly,** *adv.*

**qua·drille** (kwə-dril′, kə-), *n.* [Fr.; ult. < L. *quattuor*, four], 1. a square dance performed by four couples. 2. music for this dance.

**quad·ru·ped** (kwäd′roo-ped′), *n.* [< L. *quadru-*, four + *pes*, a foot], an animal, esp. a mammal, with four feet.

**quad·ru·ple** (kwäd′roo-p'l, kwäd-rōō′-), *adj.* [< L. *quadru-*, four + *-plus*, -fold], 1. consisting of four. 2. four times as much or as many. *adv.* fourfold. *n.* an amount four times as much or as many. *v.t. & v.i.* [-PLED, -PLING], to make or become four times as much or as many.

**quad′ru·plet** (-plit), *n.* 1. *pl.* four offspring born at a single birth. 2. any one of these.

**quad·ru·pli·cate** (kwäd-rōō′plə-kāt′; *for adj. & n., usually* -kit), *v.t.* [-CATED, -CATING], [< L. *quadru-*, four + *plicare*, to fold], to make four identical copies of. *adj.* fourfold. *n.* any of four identical copies.

**quaff** (kwäf, kwaf), *v.t. & v.i.* [prob. < LG. *quassen*, overindulge], to drink in large quantities. *n.* a quaffing.

**quag·mire** (kwag′mīr′, kwäg′-), *n.* [< *quake* + *mire*], wet, boggy ground.

**quail** (kwāl), *v.i.* [prob. ult. < L. *coagulare*, coagulate], to draw back in fear; lose courage; cower. —**quail′er,** *n.*

**quail** (kwāl), *n.* [< OFr.], a migratory game bird resembling domestic fowl.

**quaint** (kwānt), *adj.* [< OFr. *cointe* < L. *cognitus*, known], 1. pleasingly odd and antique. 2. unusual; curious. 3. fanciful; whimsical. —**quaint′ly,** *adv.* —**quaint′ness,** *n.*

**quake** (kwāk), *v.t.* [QUAKED, QUAKING], [< AS. *cwacian*], 1. to tremble; shake. 2. to shiver, as with fear or cold. *n.* 1. a quaking. 2. an earthquake.

**Quak·er** (kwāk′ẽr), *n.* [< founder's admonition to "quake" at the word of the Lord], a member of the Society of Friends: term not used by Friends. —**Quak′er·ess,** *n.fem.*

**qual·i·fi·ca·tion** (kwäl′ə-fi-kā′shən), *n.* 1. a qualifying or being qualified. 2. a modification; restriction. 3. any ability, etc. that fits one for a job, office, etc.

**qual·i·fied** (kwäl′ə-fīd′), *adj.* 1. fit; competent. 2. limited; modified.

**qual′i·fy′** (-fī′), *v.i.* [-FIED, -FYING], [< L. *qualis*, of what kind + *facere*, make], 1. to make fit for a job, etc. 2. to make legally capable. 3. to modify; restrict. 4. to moderate; soften. *v.i.* to be or become qualified. —**qual′i·fi′er,** *n.*

**qual·i·ta·tive** (kwäl′ə-tā′tiv), *adj.* having to do with quality. —**qual′i·ta′tive·ly,** *adv.*

**qual·i·ty** (kwäl′ə-ti), *n.* [*pl.* -TIES], [< L. *qualis*, of what kind], 1. that which makes something what it is; characteristic. 2. basic nature; kind. 3. the degree of excellence of a thing. 4. superiority.

**qualm** (kwäm), *n.* [AS. *cwealm*, disaster], 1. a sudden fit of sickness, faintness, etc. 2. a doubt; misgiving. 3. a scruple; twinge of conscience. —**qualm′ish,** *adj.*

**quan·da·ry** (kwän′dri, -də-ri), *n.* [*pl.* -RIES], [? < L. *quando*, when], a state of perplexity; dilemma.

**quan·ti·ta·tive** (kwän′tə-tā′tiv), *adj.* having to do with quantity.

**quan·ti·ty** (kwän′tə-ti), ***n.*** [*pl.* -TIES], [< L. *quantus*, how much], 1. an amount; portion. 2. any indeterminate bulk or number. 3. that property by which a thing can be measured. 4. a number or symbol expressing this property.

**quan·tum** (kwän′təm), ***n.*** [*pl.* -TA (-tə)], [L., how much], in *physics*, an elemental unit of energy: the **quantum theory** states that energy is radiated discontinuously, in quanta.

**quar·an·tine** (kwôr′ən-tēn′, kwär′-), ***n.*** [< L. *quadraginta*, forty], 1. the period, orig. forty days, during which a vessel suspected of carrying contagious disease is detained in port. 2. any isolation imposed to keep contagious diseases, etc. from spreading. 3. a place for such isolation. ***v.t.*** [-TINED, -TINING], to place under quarantine.

**quar·rel** (kwôr′əl, kwär′-), ***n.*** [< L. *queri*, complain], 1. a cause for dispute. 2. a dispute, esp. one marked by anger. ***v.i.*** [-RELED or -RELLED, -RELING or -RELLING], 1. to complain. 2. to dispute heatedly. 3. to have a breach in friendship. **—quar′rel·er, *n.***

**quar′rel·some** (-səm), ***adj.*** inclined to quarrel. **—quar′rel·some·ness, *n.***

**quar·ry** (kwôr′i, kwär′i), ***n.*** [*pl.* -RIES], [< OFr. *curer*, eviscerate], an animal, etc. being hunted down or pursued.

**quar·ry** (kwôr′i, kwär′i), ***n.*** [*pl.* -RIES], [< L. *quadrare*, to square], a place where stone or slate is excavated. ***v.t.*** [-RIED, -RYING], to excavate from a quarry. **—quar′ri·er, *n.***

**quart** (kwôrt), ***n.*** [< L. *quartus*, fourth], 1. a liquid measure, equal to ¼ gallon. 2. a dry measure equal to ⅛ peck.

**quar·ter** (kwôr′tẽr), ***n.*** [< L. *quartus*, fourth], 1. any of the four equal parts of something; fourth. 2. one fourth of a year. 3. one fourth of a dollar; 25 cents, or a coin of this value. 4. one leg of a four-legged animal, with the adjoining parts. 5. a region or district. 6. *pl.* lodgings. 7. a particular source: as, news from high *quarters*. 8. mercy. ***v.t.*** 1. to divide into four equal parts. 2. to provide lodgings for. ***adj.*** constituting a quarter. **—at close quarters,** at close range.

**quar′ter·back′,** ***n.*** in *football*, the back who generally calls signals.

**quar′ter-deck′, quar′ter·deck′,** ***n.*** the after part of the upper deck of a ship, usually for officers.

**quar′ter·ly,** ***adj.*** occurring regularly four times a year. ***adv.*** once every quarter of the year. ***n.*** [*pl.* -LIES], a publication issued quarterly.

**quar′ter·mas′ter,** ***n.*** 1. a military officer who provides troops with quarters, clothing, equipment, etc. 2. in *naut. usage*, a petty officer who attends to the steering, signals, etc.

**quarter note,** in *music*, a note (♩) having one fourth the duration of a whole note.

**quar·tet, quar·tette** (kwôr-tet′), ***n.*** [ult. < L. *quartus*, a fourth], 1. a group of four. 2. *a*) a musical composition for four voices or instruments. *b*) the four performers of this.

**quar·to** (kwôr′tō), ***n.*** [*pl.* -TOS], [< L. (*in*) *quarto*, (in) the fourth], 1. the page size (about 9 by 12 in.) of a book made up of sheets each of which is folded into four leaves, or eight pages. 2. a book of this size of page.

**quartz** (kwôrts), ***n.*** [G. *quarz*], a brilliant, crystalline mineral, usually colorless and transparent.

**qua·sar** (kwā′sär, -sər), ***n.*** [*quasi*stell*ar* radio source], a distant, starlike, celestial object that emits immense quantities of light or powerful radio waves, or both.

**quash** (kwäsh), ***v.t.*** [< L. *cassus*, empty], in *law*, to annul or set aside, as an indictment.

**quash** (kwäsh), ***v.t.*** [< L. *quatere*, to break], to put down; suppress, as an uprising.

**qua·si** (kwā′sī, -zī; kwä′si), ***adv.*** [< L. *quam*, as + *si*, if], as if; seemingly. ***adj.*** seeming. Often hyphenated as a prefix.

**quat·rain** (kwät′rān), ***n.*** [< L. *quattuor*, four], a stanza or poem of four lines.

**qua·ver** (kwā′vẽr), ***v.i.*** [ME. *cwafien*], 1. to shake or tremble. 2. to be tremulous: said of the voice. ***v.t.*** to utter in a tremulous voice. ***n.*** a tremulous quality in a voice, etc.

**quay** (kē), ***n.*** [< OFr. *cai*], a wharf, usually of concrete or stone.

**quea·sy** (kwē′zi), ***adj.*** [-SIER, -SIEST], [prob. < ON. or LG.], 1. causing or feeling nausea. 2. squeamish; easily nauseated. 3. embarrassed. **—quea′si·ly, *adv.* —quea′si·ness, *n.***

**queen** (kwēn), ***n.*** [AS. *cwen*], 1. the wife of a king. 2. a woman monarch in her own right. 3. a woman noted for her beauty or accomplishments. 4. the fully developed, reproductive female in a colony of bees, ants, etc. 5. a playing card with a picture of a queen on it. 6. in *chess*, the most powerful piece. **—queen′ly, *adj.***

**queer** (kwêr), ***adj.*** [prob. < G. *quer*, crosswise], 1. differing from the usual; odd; strange. 2. [Colloq.], eccentric. ***v.t.*** [Slang], to spoil the success of. **—queer′ness, *n.***

**quell** (kwel), ***v.t.*** [AS. *cwellan*, kill], 1. to crush; subdue. 2. to quiet; allay.

**quench** (kwench), ***v.t.*** [AS. *cwencan*, put out], 1. to extinguish: as, water *quenched* the fire. 2. to satisfy: as, he *quenched* his thirst. 3. to cool suddenly, as hot steel, by plunging into water, etc. **—quench′less, *adj.***

**quer·u·lous** (kwer′ə-ləs, -yoo-), ***adj.*** [< L. *queri*, complain], 1. inclined to find fault; fretful. 2. characterized by complaining.

**que·ry** (kwêr′i), ***n.*** [*pl.* -RIES], [< L. *quaerere*, ask], 1. a question; inquiry. 2. a question mark. ***v.t. & v.i.*** [-RIED, -RYING], to question.

**quest** (kwest), ***n.*** [< L. *quaerere*, seek], 1. a seeking; hunt. 2. a journey for adventure.

**ques·tion** (kwes′chən), ***n.*** [< L. *quaerere*, ask], 1. an asking; inquiry. 2. something asked. 3. doubt; uncertainty. 4. a matter open to discussion. 5. a matter of difficulty: as, it's not a *question* of money. 6. a point being debated, as before an assembly. ***v.t.*** 1. to ask questions of. 2. to express uncertainty about; doubt. 3. to dispute; challenge. ***v.i.*** to ask questions. **—out of the question,** impossible. **—ques′tion·er, *n.***

**ques′tion·a·ble,** ***adj.*** 1. that can be questioned. 2. suspected of being immoral, not respectable, etc. **—ques′tion·a·bly, *adv.***

**question mark,** a mark of punctuation (?) indicating that the sentence preceding it is a direct question, or showing doubt, uncertainty, etc.

**ques′tion·naire′** (-âr′), ***n.*** a written or printed list of questions used in gathering information from persons.

**queue** (kū), ***n.*** [< L. *cauda*, tail], 1. a pigtail. 2. a line, as of persons waiting to be served. ***v.i.*** [QUEUED, QUEUING], [Chiefly Brit.], to line up in a queue.

**quib·ble** (kwib′'l), ***n.*** [< L. *qui*, who], a petty evasion or cavil. ***v.i.*** [-BLED, -BLING], to evade the truth of a point under discussion by caviling. **—quib′bler, *n.***

**quick** (kwik), ***adj.*** [< AS. *cwicu*, living], 1. [Archaic], living. 2. *a*) rapid; swift: as, a *quick* walk. *b*) prompt: as, a *quick* reply. 3. prompt to understand or learn. 4. easily stirred: as, a *quick* temper. ***adv.*** quickly; rapidly. ***n.*** 1. the living: as, the *quick* and the dead. 2. the sensitive flesh under the nails. 3. the center of the feelings: as, her sarcasm cut him to the *quick*. **—quick′ly, *adv.* —quick′ness, *n.***

**quick bread,** any bread leavened with baking powder, soda, etc., and baked as soon as the batter is mixed.

**quick′en,** ***v.t. & v.i.*** 1. to enliven or become

enlivened. 2. to move more rapidly; hasten.

**quick'-freeze'**, *v.t.* [-FROZE, -FROZEN, -FREEZING], to subject (food) to sudden freezing for long storage at low temperatures.

**quick'ie** (-i), *n.* [Slang], anything done or made quickly and cheaply.

**quick'sand'**, *n.* [prob. < MD. or MLG.], a loose, wet, deep sand deposit, engulfing heavy objects easily.

**quick'set'** (-set'), *n.* a live slip, esp. of hawthorn, planted, as for a hedge.

**quick'sil'ver**, *n.* mercury (the metal).

**quick'-wit'ted**, *adj.* nimble of mind.

**quid** (kwid), *n.* [var. of *cud*], a piece, as of tobacco, to be chewed.

‡**quid pro quo** (kwid' prō kwō'), [L.], one thing in return for another.

**qui·es·cent** (kwī-es''nt), *adj.* [< L. *quiescere*, become quiet], quiet; still; inactive. —**qui·es'cence**, *n.* —**qui·es'cent·ly**, *adv.*

**qui·et** (kwī'ət), *adj.* [< L. *quies*, rest], 1. still; calm; motionless. 2. *a*) not noisy; hushed. *b*) not speaking; silent. 3. gentle; unobtrusive. 4. not easily excited. 5. not ostentatious: as, *quiet* clothes. *n.* 1. a quiet state; calmness, stillness, etc. 2. a quiet or peaceful quality. *v.t. & v.i.* to make or become quiet. —**qui'et·ly**, *adv.*

**qui·e·tude** (kwī'ə-tōōd', -tūd'), *n.* a state of being quiet; calmness.

**qui·e·tus** (kwī-ē'təs), *n.* [< ML. *quietus est*, he is quit], 1. discharge from debt, etc. 2. release from life; death.

**quill** (kwil), *n.* [prob. < MLG. or MD], 1. a large, stiff feather. 2. *a*) the hollow stem of a feather. *b*) anything made from this, as a pen. 3. a spine of a porcupine or hedgehog.

**quilt** (kwilt), *n.* [< L. *culcit(r)a*, bed], a bedcover filled with down, wool, etc. and stitched together in lines or patterns. *v.t.* to stitch as in making a quilt. *v.i.* to make a quilt. —**quilt'ed**, *adj.*

**quince** (kwins), *n.* [< Gr. *kydōnion*], 1. a yellowish, apple-shaped fruit, used in preserves. 2. the tree it grows on.

**qui·nine** (kwī'nīn), *n.* [< *quina*, cinchona bark], a bitter, crystalline alkaloid extracted from cinchona bark, used esp. in treating malaria: also **quin·in** (kwin'in).

**quin·sy** (kwin'zi), *n.* [< Gr. *kyōn*, dog + *anchein*, choke], inflammation of the tonsils, with formation of pus.

**quin·tes·sence** (kwin-tes''ns), *n.* [< ML. *quinta essentia*, fifth essence], 1. the pure, concentrated essence of anything. 2. the most perfect type or example of something.

**quin·tet, quin·tette** (kwin-tet'), *n.* [ult. < L. *quintus*, a fifth], 1. a group of five. 2. a musical composition for five voices or instruments. 3. the five performers of this.

**quin·tu·ple** (kwin'too-p'l, kwin-tū'-), *adj.* [< L. *quintus*, a fifth + *-plus*, -fold], 1. consisting of five. 2. five times as much or as many. *v.t. & v.i.* [-PLED, -PLING], to make or become five times as much or as many.

**quin·tu·plet** (kwin'too-plit, kwin-tū'-, -tup'-lit), *n.* [see QUINTUPLE], 1. *pl.* five offspring born at a single birth. 2. any one of these.

**quip** (kwip), *n.* [< L. *quippe*, indeed], a witty or sarcastic expression; jest. *v.t. & v.i.* [QUIPPED, QUIPPING], to make quips (at).

**quire** (kwīr), *n.* [< LL. *quaternum*, paper in sets of four], a set of 24 or 25 sheets of the same paper.

**quirk** (kwũrk), *n.* [< ?], a peculiarity or mannerism. —**quirk'y** [-IER, -IEST], *adj.*

**quirt** (kwũrt), *n.* [< Mex. Sp. *cuarta*], a riding whip with a braided leather lash and a short handle.

**quis·ling** (kwiz'liŋ), *n.* [< V. *Quisling*, Norw. collaborationist with the Nazis], one who betrays his country by helping its enemy invaders.

**quit** (kwit), *v.t.* [QUIT, QUITTED, QUITTING], [< LL. *quietare*, set free], 1. to free (oneself) *of.* 2. to give up. 3. to leave; depart from. 4. to stop, as work. *v.i.* 1. to go away. 2. to stop doing something. 3. [Colloq.], to give up one's job. *adj.* clear; free.

**quit·claim** (kwit'klām'), *v.t.* to give up a claim to (property, etc.). *n.* a document effecting such relinquishment.

**quite** (kwīt), *adv.* [< *quit*, *adj.*], 1. completely; entirely. 2. really; positively. 3. [Colloq.], to a considerable degree. —**quite a few**, [Colloq.], more than a few.

**quits** (kwits), *adj.* [< *quit*, *adj.*], on even terms, as by discharge of a debt, retaliation, etc.

**quit·tance** (kwit''ns), *n.* [see QUIT], 1. discharge from a debt, etc. 2. a receipt. 3. recompense; repayment.

**quit'ter**, *n.* [Colloq.], one who quits or gives up easily.

**quiv·er** (kwiv'ẽr), *v.i.* [prob. < base of *quaver*], to shake tremulously; tremble. *n.* a quivering; tremor. —**quiv'er·ing**, *adj.*

**quiv·er** (kwiv'ẽr), *n.* [< OFr. *quivre*], 1. a case for holding arrows. 2. its contents.

**quix·ot·ic** (kwik-sot'ik), *adj.* [< *Don Quixote*], extravagantly chivalrous or romantically idealistic; impractical.

**quiz** (kwiz), *n.* [*pl.* QUIZZES], [? < L. *quis*, who, which, what], a questioning; esp., an informal examination to test one's knowledge. *v.t.* [QUIZZED, QUIZZING], to ask questions of (a person); give a quiz to.

**quiz program** (or **show**), a type of radio or TV program in which a group of experts or members of an audience compete in answering questions.

**quiz·zi·cal** (kwiz'i-k'l), *adj.* 1. odd; comical. 2. perplexed. —**quiz'zi·cal·ly**, *adv.*

**quoin** (koin, kwoin), *n.* [var. of *coin*], 1. the external corner of a building; esp., any of the large stones at such a corner. 2. a wedge-shaped block.

**quoit** (kwoit, koit), *n.* [prob. < OFr. *coite*, a cushion], 1. a ring thrown, in a game, to encircle an upright peg. 2. *pl.* the game so played.

**quon·dam** (kwon'dəm), *adj.* [L.], former: as, my *quondam* companion.

**Quon·set hut** (kwon'sit), [< *Quonset*, R.I., where first made], a prefabricated, metal shelter, with a curved roof.

**quo·rum** (kwôr'əm), *n.* [< L. *qui*, who], the minimum number of members who must be present at an assembly before it can validly transact business.

**quot.**, quotation.

**quo·ta** (kwō'tə), *n.* [*pl.* -TAS], [< L. *quotus*, how many], a share or proportion assigned to each of a number.

**quo·ta·tion** (kwō-tā'shən), *n.* 1. a quoting. 2. the words or passage quoted. 3. *a*) a statement of the current price of a stock, bond, etc. *b*) the price itself.

**quotation mark**, either of a pair of punctuation marks (". . .") used to enclose a direct quotation.

**quote** (kwōt), *v.t.* [QUOTED, QUOTING], [< ML. *quotare*, to number (chapters)], 1. to repeat a passage from or statement of. 2. to repeat (a passage, statement, etc.). 3. to state (the price of something). *n.* [Colloq.], 1. a quotation. 2. a quotation mark. —**quot'a·ble**, *adj.*

**quoth** (kwōth), *v.t.* [< AS. *cwethan*, speak], [Archaic], said.

**quo·tid·i·an** (kwō-tid'i-ən), *adj.* [< L. *quotidie*], daily. *n.* anything, esp. a fever, that recurs daily.

**quo·tient** (kwō'shənt), *n.* [< L. *quot*, how many], the number obtained when one quantity is divided by another.

**q.v.**, [L.], *quod vide*, which see.

# R

**R, r** (är), *n.* [*pl.* R's, r's, Rs, rs], the eighteenth letter of the English alphabet.

**R** (är), *n.* in *math.*, radius. **—the three R's,** reading, writing, and arithmetic, regarded as the basic studies.

**R., r.,** 1. radius. 2. railroad. 3. right. 4. river. 5. road.

**Ra,** in *chem.*, radium.

**rab·bi** (rab′ī), *n.* [*pl.* -BIS, -BIES], [< Heb. *rabbī*, my master], an ordained teacher of the Jewish law. **—rab·bin·i·cal** (rə-bin′i-k'l), *adj.*

**rab·bit** (rab′it), *n.* [ME. *rabette*], 1. a burrowing rodent of the hare family, having soft fur and long ears. 2. its fur.

**rabbit punch,** in *boxing*, a short, sharp blow to the back of the neck.

**rab·ble** (rab′'l), *n.* [prob. < *rabble*, puddling bar], a disorderly crowd; mob.

**rab·id** (rab′id), *adj.* [< L. *rabere*, to rage], 1. violent; raging. 2. fanatical. 3. of or having rabies. **—rab′id·ly,** *adv.*

**ra·bies** (rā′bēz), *n.* [L., madness], an infectious disease of dogs, etc. transmitted to man by the bite of an infected animal: it is characterized by choking, convulsions, etc.: cf. **hydrophobia.**

**rac·coon** (ra-ko͞on′), *n.* [< Am. Ind. *arakunem*, hand-scratcher], 1. a small, tree-climbing mammal of N. America, having yellow-black fur and a black-ringed tail. 2. its fur.

**race** (rās), *n.* [< ON. *rās*, running], 1. a competition of speed, as in running. 2. any contest like a race: as, the *race* for mayor. 3. a swift current of water, or its channel. *v.i.* [RACED, RACING], 1. to take part in a race. 2. to go or move swiftly. *v.t.* 1. to compete with in a race. 2. to cause to engage in a race. 3. to cause to go or move swiftly or too swiftly. **—rac′er,** *n.*

**race** (rās), *n.* [It. *razza*], 1. any of the three primary divisions of mankind as distinguished esp. by skin color. 2. any geographical, national, or tribal ethnic grouping. 3. any distinct class of people.

**race track,** a course prepared for racing: also, esp. for horse races, **race′course′,** *n.*

**Ra·chel** (rā′chəl), *n.* in the *Bible*, the younger of the two wives of Jacob.

**ra·cial** (rā′shəl), *adj.* of or characteristic of a race (ethnic group). **—ra′cial·ly,** *adv.*

**ra′cial·ism** (-iz'm), *n.* racial prejudice, hatred, or discrimination.

**rac·ism** (rās′iz'm), *n.* 1. racialism. 2. the practice of racial discrimination, persecution, etc. **—rac′ist,** *adj. & n.*

**rack** (rak), *n.* [prob. < MD. *recken*, to stretch], 1. a framework, etc. for holding or displaying things, as a frame with hooks for hanging clothes. 2. a toothed bar into which a toothed gearwheel, etc. meshes. 3. an instrument of torture which stretches the victim's limbs. 4. any great torment. *v.t.* 1. to torture on a rack. 2. to torment. **—on the rack,** in a difficult situation. **—rack one's brains,** to try hard to think of something.

**rack** (rak), *n.* wrack: now only in **go to rack and ruin,** to become ruined.

**rack·et** (rak′it), *n.* [prob. echoic], 1. a noisy confusion. 2. [Slang], a dishonest or illegal scheme or business.

**rack·et** (rak′it), *n.* [< Fr. < Ar. *rāhah*, palm of the hand], a light bat for tennis, etc. with a network, as of catgut, in a frame attached to a handle: also sp. **racquet.**

**rack·et·eer** (rak′ə-têr′), *n.* one engaged in a racket; esp., one who obtains money illegally, as by fraud or threats of violence.

**rac·on·teur** (rak′on-tũr′), *n.* [Fr. < *raconter*, to recount], a person skilled at telling stories or anecdotes.

**rac·y** (rās′i), *adj.* [-IER, -IEST], [< *race* (tribe) + *-y*], 1. having the taste or quality associated with the genuine type: as, *racy* fruit. 2. lively; spirited. 3. pungent. 4. risqué.

**ra·dar** (rā′där), *n.* [*ra*dio *d*etecting *a*nd *r*anging], an instrument that sends out radio waves and picks them up after they have been reflected by a land mass, ship, etc.: used to indicate the position of the reflecting object.

**ra′dar·scope′,** *n.* an instrument that visually records the reflected radio beams picked up by radar.

**ra·di·al** (rā′di-əl), *adj.* [see RADIUS], of, like, or situated like a ray or rays; branching out from a center. **—ra′di·al·ly,** *adv.*

**ra·di·ant** (rā′di-ənt), *adj.* [see RADIUS], 1. shining brightly. 2. showing joy, etc.; beaming. 3. issuing (from a source) in or as in rays: as, *radiant* energy. **—ra′di·ance,** *n.* **—ra′di·ant·ly,** *adv.*

**ra·di·ate** (rā′di-āt′), *v.i.* [-ATED, -ATING], [see RADIUS], 1. to send out rays, as of heat or light. 2. to branch out in lines from a center. *v.t.* 1. to send out (heat, light, etc.) in rays. 2. to give forth (love, happiness, etc.). *adj.* having rays.

**ra′di·a′tion,** *n.* 1. a radiating. 2. the rays sent out. 3. the treatment of disease by radioactive material.

**ra′di·a′tor,** *n.* an apparatus for radiating heat, as into a room or from an automobile engine.

**rad·i·cal** (rad′i-k'l), *adj.* [< L. *radix*, root], 1. of or from the root; fundamental. 2. favoring extreme change, as of the social structure. *n.* 1. a person having radical views. 2. in *chem.*, a group of two or more atoms acting as a single atom. 3. in *math.*, the sign ($\sqrt{\phantom{x}}$) used with a quantity to show that its root is to be extracted. **—rad′i·cal·ism,** *n.* **—rad′i·cal·ly,** *adv.*

**ra·di·i** (rā′di-ī′), *n.* pl. of **radius.**

**ra·di·o** (rā′di-ō′), *n.* [*pl.* -OS], [< *radiotelegraphy*, etc.], 1. the transmission of sounds or signals by electric waves through space, without wires, to a receiving set. 2. such a receiving set. 3. broadcasting by radio as a business, entertainment, etc. *adj.* of, using, used in, or sent by radio. *v.t. & v.i.* [-OED, -OING], to transmit, or communicate with, by radio.

**radio-,** [see RADIUS], a combining form meaning: 1. *radical.* 2. *by radio.* 3. *by means of radiant energy*, as in *radiotherapy.*

**ra′di·o·ac′tive,** *adj.* giving off radiant energy in the form of particles or rays by the disintegration of atomic nuclei. **—ra′di·o·ac′tive·ly,** *adv.* **—ra′di·o·ac·tiv′i·ty,** *n.*

**ra′di·o·broad′cast′,** *n. & v.t.* [-CAST or -CASTED, -CASTING], broadcast by radio.

**ra′di·o·gram′** (-gram′), *n.* a message sent by radio: also **ra′di·o·tel′e·gram′.**

**ra′di·o·i′so·tope′,** *n.* an artificially created radioactive isotope of a chemical element normally nonradioactive.

**ra′di·ol′o·gy** (-ol′ə-ji), *n.* the study of radiant energy and its uses, as in X-ray therapy. **—ra′di·ol′o·gist,** *n.*

**ra′di·o·tel′e·graph′,** *n.* an instrument for sending radiograms. *v.t. & v.i.* to send (a message) by radiotelegraph. —**ra′di·o·te·leg′ra·phy,** *n.*

**ra′di·o·ther′a·py,** *n.* the treatment of disease by the use of X rays or rays from a radioactive substance, as radium.

**rad·ish** (rad′ish), *n.* [< L. *radix,* root], 1. a plant of the mustard family, with a red or white root. 2. the pungent root, eaten raw.

**ra·di·um** (rā′di-əm), *n.* [< L. *radius,* ray], a radioactive metallic chemical element, found in certain uranium minerals, which undergoes spontaneous atomic disintegration: symbol, Ra.

**ra·di·us** (rā′di-əs), *n.* [*pl.* -DII (-di-ī′), -DIUSES], [L., spoke (of a wheel), hence ray], 1. any straight line from the center to the periphery of a circle or sphere. 2. the circular area limited by the sweep of such a line: as, within a *radius* of two miles.

**R.A.F., RAF,** Royal Air Force.

**raf·fi·a** (raf′i-ə), *n.* [< native name], 1. a palm tree of Madagascar with large leaves. 2. fiber from its leaves, used for weaving.

**raff·ish** (raf′ish), *adj.* [riff*raff* + *-ish*], 1. disreputable. 2. tawdry; flashy.

**raf·fle** (raf′′l), *n.* [< OFr. *rafle,* dice game], a lottery in which each participant buys a chance to win the prize. *v.t.* [-FLED, -FLING], to offer as a prize in a raffle (often with *off*).

**raft** (raft, räft), *n.* [< ON. *raptr,* a log], a floating platform of logs, boards, etc. fastened together. —**raft′like,** *adj.*

**raft** (raft, räft), *n.* [Scot. *raff,* rubbish], [Colloq.], a large quantity.

**raft·er** (raf′tẽr, räf′-), *n.* [AS. *ræfter*], any of the beams that slope from the ridge of a roof to the eaves and support the roof.

**rag** (rag), *n.* [ult. < ON. *rögg,* tuft of hair], 1. a waste piece of cloth, esp. one torn or uneven. 2. a small piece of cloth for dusting, etc. 3. *pl.* old, worn clothes. *adj.* made of rags. —**chew the rag,** [Slang], to chat.

**rag** (rag), *v.t.* [RAGGED, RAGGING], [Slang], to tease or scold. *n.* [Slang], a ragging.

**rag·a·muf·fin** (rag′ə-muf′in), *n.* [ME. *Ragamofin,* name of a demon], a dirty, ragged person; esp., such a child.

**rage** (rāj), *n.* [< L. *rabies,* madness], 1. a furious, uncontrolled anger. 2. a great violence or intensity. 3. a craze; fad. *v.i.* [RAGED, RAGING], 1. to show violent anger, as in speech. 2. to be forceful, violent, etc. 3. to spread unchecked, as a disease.

**rag·ged** (rag′id), *adj.* 1. shabby or torn from wear. 2. wearing shabby or torn clothes. 3. uneven; rough. 4. shaggy: as, *ragged* hair.

**rag·lan** (rag′lən), *n.* [< Lord *Raglan,* 19th-c. Brit. general], a loose coat with sleeves that continue in one piece to the collar. *adj.* designating or of such a sleeve.

**ra·gout** (ra-gōō′), *n.* [< Fr. *ragoûter,* revive the appetite of], a stew of highly seasoned meat and vegetables.

**rag·time** (rag′tīm′), *n.* [< *ragged time*], 1. an early form of jazz characterized by strong syncopation in fast, even time. 2. its rhythm.

**rag′weed′,** *n.* [< the tattered appearance of the leaves], a common weed whose pollen is a cause of hay fever.

**rah** (rä, rô), *interj.* hurrah.

**raid** (rād), *n.* [North Eng. form of *road*], 1. a sudden, hostile attack, as by troops, aircraft, bandits, etc. 2. a sudden invasion of a place by police for discovering violations of the law. *v.t.* to make a raid on. *v.i.* to take part in a raid. —**raid′er,** *n.*

**rail** (rāl), *n.* [< L. *regula,* a rule], 1. a bar of wood, metal, etc. placed between posts as a guard or support. 2. any of the parallel metal bars forming a track, as for railroad cars. 3. a railroad. *v.t.* to supply with rails.

**rail** (rāl), *v.i.* [< Fr. *railler,* to banter], to speak bitterly; inveigh. —**rail′er,** *n.*

**rail** (rāl), *n.* [< OFr. *raale*], a small wading bird living in marshes.

**rail′ing,** *n.* 1. material for rails. 2. a fence or balustrade made of rails and posts.

**rail·ler·y** (rāl′ẽr-i), *n.* [*pl.* -IES], [see RAIL, *v.i.*], 1. light, good-natured ridicule. 2. a teasing remark.

**rail′road′,** *n.* 1. a road laid with parallel steel rails along which cars are drawn by locomotives. 2. a complete system of such roads. *v.t.* 1. to transport by railroad. 2. [Colloq.], to rush through quickly, so as to prevent careful consideration. *v.i.* to work on a railroad. —**rail′road′er,** *n.*

**rail′way′,** *n.* 1. [Brit.], a railroad. 2. any track with rails for guiding wheels.

**rai·ment** (rā′mənt), *n.* [< *arrayment*; see ARRAY], [Archaic], clothing.

**rain** (rān), *n.* [AS. *regn*], 1. water falling in drops condensed from the atmosphere. 2. the falling of such drops. 3. a rapid falling of many small objects. *v.i.* 1. to fall: said of rain. 2. to fall like rain. *v.t.* 1. to pour down (rain, etc.). 2. to give in large quantities. —**rain′y** [-IER, -IEST], *adj.*

**rain′bow′** (-bō′), *n.* the arc containing the colors of the spectrum formed in the sky by the refraction of the sun's rays in falling rain or mist. *adj.* of many colors.

**rain check,** the stub of a ticket to a baseball game, etc. entitling the holder to future admission if the event is halted because of rain.

**rain′coat′,** *n.* a waterproof coat for giving protection from rain.

**rain′drop′,** *n.* a single drop of rain.

**rain′fall′,** *n.* 1. a falling of rain. 2. the amount of water falling as rain, snow, etc. over a given area during a given time.

**rain′storm′,** *n.* a storm with a heavy rain.

**raise** (rāz), *v.t.* [RAISED, RAISING], [< ON. *reisa*], 1. to cause to rise; lift. 2. to construct; build. 3. to increase in amount, degree, intensity, etc.: as, *raise* prices, *raise* your voice. 4. to provoke; inspire. 5. to present for consideration: as, *raise* a question. 6. to collect (an army, money, etc.). 7. to end (a siege). 8. *a*) to cause to grow. *b*) to rear (children). *n.* 1. a raising. 2. an increase in amount, as in salary or wages.

**rai·sin** (rā′z′n), *n.* [< L. *racemus,* cluster of grapes], a sweet dried grape.

**ra·jah, ra·ja** (rä′jə), *n.* [< Sans. *rāj,* rule], a prince in India, etc.

**rake** (rāk), *n.* [AS. *raca*], a long-handled tool with teeth at one end, for gathering together hay, leaves, etc. *v.t.* [RAKED, RAKING], 1. to gather with a rake. 2. to search through minutely. 3. to direct gunfire along the length of (a line of troops, etc.).

**rake** (rāk), *n.* [< earlier *rakehell*], a dissolute, debauched man. —**rak′ish,** *adj.*

**rake** (rāk), *v.i.* & *v.t.* [RAKED, RAKING], [cf. Sw. *raka,* to project], to be or put at a slant. *n.* a slanting from the perpendicular.

**rake′-off′,** *n.* [Slang], a commission; esp., an illegitimate rebate.

**rak·ish** (rāk′ish), *adj.* [< *rake* (to slant) + *-ish*], 1. having a trim appearance, suggesting speed: said of a ship. 2. dashing; jaunty. —**rak′ish·ly,** *adv.* —**rak′ish·ness,** *n.*

**ral·ly** (ral′i), *v.t.* & *v.i.* [-LIED, -LYING], [< Fr. *re-,* again + *allier,* join], 1. to bring back together in or come back to a state of order, as troops. 2. to bring or come together for a common purpose. 3. to revive; recover. *n.* [*pl.* -LIES], a rallying or being rallied; esp., a gathering of people for some purpose.

**ral·ly** (ral′i), *v.t.* & *v.i.* [-LIED, -LYING], [see RAIL (complain)], to tease; ridicule; banter.

**ram** (ram), *n.* [AS. *ramm*], 1. a male sheep. 2. a battering-ram. *v.t.* [RAMMED, RAMMING], 1. to strike against with great force. 2. to force into place; press down.

**ram·ble** (ram′b′l), *v.i.* [-BLED, -BLING], [<

ME. *romen*, roam], 1. to move about idly; stroll; roam. 2. to talk or write aimlessly. 3. to spread in all directions, as vines. *n.* a rambling; stroll.

**ram'bler,** *n.* a person or thing that rambles; esp., any climbing rose.

**ram·bunc·tious** (ram-buŋk'shəs), *adj.* [< *robust*(*ious*)], [Colloq.], disorderly, boisterous, unruly, etc. **—ram·bunc'tious·ly,** *adv.*

**ram·e·kin, ram·e·quin** (ram'ə-kin), *n.* [< Fr.], a small, individual baking dish.

**ram·i·fy** (ram'ə-fī'), *v.t. & v.i.* [-FIED, -FYING], [< L. *ramus*, a branch + *facere*, make], to separate into branches or branchlike divisions. **—ram'i·fi·ca'tion,** *n.*

**ramp** (ramp), *n.* [< OFr. *ramper*, climb], a sloping passage joining different levels of a building, road, etc.

**ram·page** (ram-pāj'), *v.i.* [-PAGED, -PAGING], [see RAMP & RAGE], to rush violently about; rage. *n.* (ram'pāj), an outbreak of wild, raging behavior; usually in *on the* (or *a*) *rampage*.

**ramp·ant** (ram'pənt), *adj.* [see RAMP], 1. growing unchecked; widespread. 2. violent in action, speech, etc.

**ram·part** (ram'pärt, -pērt), *n.* [< Fr. *re-*, again + *emparer*, prepare], an embankment of earth surmounted by a parapet, for defending a fort, etc.

**ram'rod',** *n.* 1. a metal rod for ramming down the charge in a muzzle-loading gun. 2. a rod for cleaning a rifle bore.

**ram·shack·le** (ram'shak''l), *adj.* [< *ransack*], loose and rickety; likely to fall apart.

**ran** (ran), pt. of **run.**

**ranch** (ranch), *n.* [< Mex. Sp. *rancho*], a large farm, as in the western U.S., for raising cattle, horses, or sheep. **—ranch'er, ranch'man** [*pl.* -MEN], *n.*

**ran·cid** (ran'sid), *adj.* [< L. *rancere*, to be rank], having the bad smell or taste of stale fats or oils. **—ran·cid'i·ty,** *n.*

**ran·cor** (raŋ'kēr), *n.* [< L. *rancere*, to be rank], a continuing and bitter hate or ill will: Brit. sp. **rancour. —ran'cor·ous,** *adj.*

**ran·dom** (ran'dəm), *adj.* [< OFr. *randon*, impetuosity], lacking aim or method; haphazard. **—at random,** haphazardly.

**rang** (raŋ), pt. of **ring** (to sound).

**range** (rānj), *v.t.* [RANGED, RANGING], [< OHG. *hring*, a ring], 1. to arrange in order; set in a row or rows. 2. to place (oneself) with others in a cause, etc. 3. to roam about: as, to *range* the woods. *v.i.* 1. to extend in a given direction. 2. to wander about; roam. 3. to vary between stated limits. *n.* 1. a row, line, or series. 2. a series of connected mountains. 3. the distance that a gun can fire its projectile. 4. a place for shooting practice. 5. extent; scope. 6. a large, open area on which livestock graze. 7. the limits of possible variations of amount, degree, etc.: as, a wide *range* in price. 8. a cooking stove.

**rang'er,** *n.* 1. a wanderer. 2. a mounted trooper who patrols a region. 3. a warden who patrols forests.

**rang·y** (rān'ji), *adj.* [-IER, -IEST], long-limbed and slender. **—rang'i·ness,** *n.*

**rank** (raŋk), *n.* [< OHG. *hring*, a ring], 1. a row, line, or series. 2. a social class. 3. high position in society. 4. an official grade: as, the *rank* of major. 5. a degree of quality: as, a poet of the first *rank*. 6. *a*) a row of soldiers, etc. placed side by side. *b*) *pl.* the army; esp., enlisted soldiers. *v.t.* 1. to place in a rank. 2. to assign a position to. 3. to outrank. *v.i.* 1. to hold a certain position. 2. to hold the highest rank. **—rank and file,** 1. enlisted soldiers. 2. the common people.

**rank** (raŋk), *adj.* [AS. *ranc*, strong], 1. growing vigorously and coarsely: as, *rank* grass. 2. strong and offensive in smell or taste. 3. in bad taste. 4. extreme; utter: as, a *rank* fool. **—rank'ness,** *n.*

**ran·kle** (raŋ'k'l), *v.i.* [-KLED, -KLING], [< ML. *dracunculus*, ulcer], 1. to fester. 2. to cause continual mental pain, resentment, etc.

**ran·sack** (ran'sak), *v.t.* [< ON. *rann*, house + *sækja*, search], 1. to search thoroughly. 2. to plunder; pillage.

**ran·som** (ran'səm), *n.* [see REDEEM], 1. the redeeming of a captive by paying money or complying with demands. 2. the price paid or demanded for this. *v.t.* to obtain the release of (a captive, etc.) by paying the price demanded. **—ran'som·er,** *n.*

**rant** (rant), *v.i.* [MD. *ranten*], to talk in a loud, wild way; rave. **—rant'ing,** *n.*

**rap** (rap), *v.t.* [RAPPED, RAPPING], [prob. < Gmc.], 1. to strike quickly and sharply; tap. 2. to say sharply (with *out*). *v.i.* to knock sharply. *n.* 1. a quick, sharp knock. 2. [Slang], blame or punishment.

**ra·pa·cious** (rə-pā'shəs), *adj.* [< L. *rapere*, seize], greedy; voracious. **—ra·pa'cious·ly,** *adv.* **—ra·pac'i·ty** (-pas'ə-ti), *n.*

**rape** (rāp), *n.* [prob. < L. *rapere*, seize], 1. the crime of having sexual intercourse with a woman forcibly and without her consent. 2. a seizing and carrying away by force. *v.t.* [RAPED, RAPING], 1. to commit rape on; ravish. 2. to seize and carry away by force. **—rap'ist,** *n.*

**rape** (rāp), *n.* [< L. *rapa*, turnip], a plant of the mustard family, whose leaves are used for fodder.

**rap·id** (rap'id), *adj.* [< L. *rapere*, to rush], 1. swift; moving or done with speed. 2. steep: as, a *rapid* rise in the road. *n.* *usually in pl.* a part of a river where the water moves swiftly. **—ra·pid·i·ty** (rə-pid'ə-ti), **rap'id·ness,** *n.* **—rap'id·ly,** *adv.*

**ra·pi·er** (rā'pi-ēr), *n.* [Fr. *rapière*,] a light, sharp-pointed sword used for thrusting.

**rap·ine** (rap'in), *n.* [< L. *rapere*, seize], plunder; pillage.

**rap·port** (ra-pôrt'; Fr. rä'pôr'), *n.* [Fr. < L. *ad-*, to + *portare*, carry], sympathetic relationship; agreement; harmony.

**rapt** (rapt), *adj.* [< L. *rapere*, seize], 1. carried away with joy, love, etc.; enraptured. 2. completely engrossed (*in*).

**rap·ture** (rap'chēr), *n.* 1. the state of being carried away with joy, love, etc.; ecstasy. 2. an expression of this. **—rap'tur·ous,** *adj.*

**rare** (râr), *adj.* [RARER, RAREST], [< L. *rarus*], 1. not frequently found; scarce; uncommon. 2. unusually good; excellent. 3. not dense: as, *rare* atmosphere. **—rare'ness,** *n.*

**rare** (râr), *adj.* [RARER, RAREST], [AS. *hrere*], not completely cooked; partially raw.

**rare·bit** (râr'bit), *n.* Welsh rabbit.

**rar·e·fy** (râr'ə-fī'), *v.t. & v.i.* [-FIED, -FYING], [< L. *rarus*, rare + *facere*, make], to make or become less dense. **—rar'e·fac'tion** (-fak'shən), *n.* **—rar'e·fac'tive,** *adj.*

**rare·ly** (râr'li), *adv.* 1. infrequently; seldom. 2. uncommonly.

**rar·i·ty** (râr'ə-ti), *n.* 1. a being rare; specif., *a*) scarcity. *b*) lack of density; thinness. 2. [*pl.* -TIES], something remarkable or valuable because of its scarcity.

**ras·cal** (ras'k'l), *n.* [< OFr. *rasque*, filth], 1. a rogue. 2. a mischievous child. **—ras·cal'i·ty** (-kal'ə-ti), *n.* **—ras'cal·ly,** *adj. & adv.*

**rash** (rash), *adj.* [ME. *rasch*], too hasty in acting or speaking; reckless. **—rash'ly,** *adv.*

**rash** (rash), *n.* [see RASCAL], an eruption of red spots on the skin.

**rash·er** (rash'ēr), *n.* [< ?], a thin slice of bacon, etc. to be fried or broiled.

**rasp** (rasp, räsp), *v.t.* [< OHG. *raspon*, scrape together], 1. to scrape as with a file. 2. to grate upon; irritate. *v.i.* 1. to grate.

2. to make a rough, grating sound. *n.* 1. a type of rough file. 2. a rough, grating sound. —**rasp'y** [-IER, -IEST], *adj.*

**rasp·ber·ry** (raz'ber'i, -bẽr-), *n.* [*pl.* -RIES], [< earlier *rasp(is)*], 1. a prickly shrub of the rose family. 2. its small, edible, red, purple, or black berry. 3. [Slang], a sound of derision.

**rat** (rat), *n.* [AS. *ræt*], 1. a long-tailed rodent, resembling, but larger than, the mouse. 2. [Slang], a sneaky, contemptible person; informer, etc. *v.i.* [RATTED, RATTING], [Slang], to act as an informer.

**ratch·et** (rach'it), *n.* [< It. *rocca*, distaff], 1. a pawl that engages with a toothed wheel or bar, preventing backward motion. 2. such a wheel or bar.

**rate** (rāt), *n.* [< L. *reri*, reckon], 1. the amount, degree, etc. of anything in relation to units of something else: as, *rate* of pay. 2. price, esp. per unit of some commodity, service, etc. 3. a class; rank: as, of the first *rate*. *v.t.* [RATED, RATING], 1. to appraise. 2. to consider; esteem. 3. [Colloq.], to deserve: as, he *rates* the best. *v.i.* to have value, status, etc. —**at any rate,** 1. in any event. 2. anyway. —**rat'a·ble, rate'a·ble,** *adj.*

**rate** (rāt), *v.t. & v.i.* [RATED, RATING], [ME. *raten*], to scold; chide.

**rath·er** (rath'ẽr, rä'thẽr), *adv.* [< AS. *hrathe*, quickly], 1. more willingly; preferably. 2. with more justice, reason, etc.: as, I, *rather* than you, should pay. 3. more accurately: as, my son or, *rather*, stepson. 4. on the contrary. 5. somewhat: as, I *rather* like it.

**rat·i·fy** (rat'ə-fī'), *v.t.* [-FIED, -FYING], [< L. *ratus*, reckoned + *facere*, make], to approve; esp., to give formal sanction to. —**rat'i·fi·ca'tion,** *n.* —**rat'i·fi'er,** *n.*

**rat·ing** (rāt'iŋ), *n.* 1. a rank, or grade, as of enlisted men in an army. 2. a placement in a certain rank or class. 3. an evaluation.

**ra·tio** (rā'shō, -shi-ō'), *n.* [*pl.* -TIOS], [L., a reckoning], 1. a fixed relation in degree, number, etc. between two similar things; proportion. 2. in *math.*, a fraction.

**ra·ti·oc·i·nate** (rash'i-os'ə-nāt'), *v.i.* [-NATED, -NATING], [see RATIO], to reason, esp. using formal logic. —**ra'ti·oc'i·na'tion,** *n.*

**ra·tion** (rash'ən, rā'shən), *n.* [see RATIO], 1. a fixed portion; share. 2. a fixed allowance of food, as a daily allowance for one soldier. *v.t.* 1. to give rations to. 2. to distribute (food, clothing, etc.) in rations, as in times of scarcity. —**ra'tion·ing,** *n.*

**ra·tion·al** (rash'ən-'l), *adj.* [see RATIO], 1. of or based on reasoning. 2. able to reason. 3. sensible. —**ra'tion·al'i·ty** (-al'ə-ti), *n.*

**ra·tion·a·le** (rash'ə-nal', -nä'li, -nā'-), *n.* [L.; see RATIO], 1. the rational basis of something. 2. an explanation of reasons.

**ra·tion·al·ize** (rash'ən-'l-īz'), *v.t. & v.i.* [-IZED, -IZING], 1. to make or be rational or reasonable. 2. to devise plausible explanations for (one's acts, beliefs, etc.), usually in self-deceit. —**ra'tion·al·i·za'tion,** *n.*

**rat·line, rat·lin** (rat'lin), *n.* [prob. < ME. *raddle*, interlace], any of the small ropes which join the shrouds of a ship and serve as a ladder.

**rats·bane** (rats'bān'), *n.* [see BANE], rat poison.

**rat·tan** (ra-tan'), *n.* [< Malay *raut*, to strip], 1. a climbing palm with long, slender, tough stems. 2. these stems, used in wickerwork, canes, etc. Also sp. **ratan.**

**rat·tle** (rat''l), *v.i.* [-TLED, -TLING], [prob. echoic], 1. to make a series of sharp, short sounds. 2. to move with such sounds. 3. to chatter (often with *on*). *v.t.* 1. to cause to rattle. 2. [Colloq.], to confuse or upset. *n.* 1. a series of sharp, short sounds. 2. the series of horny rings at the end of a rattlesnake's tail. 3. a baby's toy, etc. that rattles when shaken. —**rat'tly** (-'l-i, -li), *adj.*

**rat'tle·brain',** *n.* a silly, talkative person.

**rat'tler,** *n.* a rattlesnake.

**rat'tle·snake',** *n.* a poisonous American snake with horny rings at the end of the tail that rattle when shaken.

**rat'tle·trap',** *n.* [*rattle* + *trap* (carriage)], a rickety wagon, automobile, etc.

**rat·ty** (rat'i), *adj.* [-TIER, -TIEST], [Slang], shabby, despicable, etc.

**rau·cous** (rô'kəs), *adj.* [L. *raucus*], hoarse; rough-sounding. —**rau'cous·ness,** *n.*

**rav·age** (rav'ij), *n.* [see RAVISH], destruction; ruin. *v.t.* [-AGED, -AGING], to destroy violently; ruin. *v.i.* to commit ravages.

**rave** (rāv), *v.i.* [RAVED, RAVING], [OFr. *raver*], 1. to talk incoherently or wildly. 2. to talk with extreme enthusiasm (*about*). *n.* [Slang], a very enthusiastic commendation.

**rav·el** (rav''l), *v.t. & v.i.* [-ELED or -ELLED, -ELING or -ELLING], [MD. *ravelen*], to separate into its parts, esp. threads; untwist; fray. —**rav'el·ing, rav'el·ling,** *n.*

**rav·en** (rā'vən), *n.* [AS. *hræfn*], a large bird of the crow family, with lustrous black feathers. *adj.* black and lustrous.

**rav·e·nous** (rav'ən-əs), *adj.* [see RAVISH], 1. greedily hungry. 2. rapacious.

**ra·vine** (rə-vēn'), *n.* [Fr., flood; ult. < L.], a long, deep hollow in the earth, worn by a stream; gorge.

**rav·ing** (rāv'iŋ), *adj.* 1. raging; delirious. 2. [Colloq.], exciting raving admiration: as, a *raving* beauty. *n.* wild, incoherent speech.

**ra·vi·o·li** (rav'i-ō'li), *n.pl.* [construed as sing.], [It.], small casings of dough containing chopped meat, cooked and served in a sauce.

**rav·ish** (rav'ish), *v.t.* [< L. *rapere*, seize], 1. to seize and carry away forcibly. 2. to rape. 3. to fill with great joy; delight. —**rav'ish·er,** *n.* —**rav'ish·ment,** *n.*

**rav'ish·ing,** *adj.* giving much delight.

**raw** (rô), *adj.* [AS. *hreaw*], 1. uncooked. 2. in its natural condition; unprocessed: as, *raw* silk. 3. inexperienced: as, a *raw* recruit. 4. with the skin rubbed off; sore and inflamed. 5. uncomfortably cold and damp: as, a *raw* wind. 6. [Colloq.], indecent; bawdy. 7. [Slang], harsh or unfair: as, *raw* treatment. —**raw'ly,** *adv.* —**raw'ness,** *n.*

**raw'boned'** (-bōnd'), *adj.* lean; gaunt.

**raw'hide',** *n.* 1. an untanned or partially tanned cattle hide. 2. a whip made of this.

**ray** (rā), *n.* [see RADIUS], 1. any of the thin lines, or beams, of light that appear to come from a bright source. 2. any of several lines or elements radiating from a center. 3. a stream of radiant energy, as heat, X rays, etc. 4. a tiny amount: as, a *ray* of hope.

**ray** (rā), *n.* [< L. *raia*], a fish with a broad, flat body, widely expanded fins at each side, and a whiplike tail.

**ray·on** (rā'on), *n.* [coined < *ray* (beam)], 1. a textile fiber produced by pressing a cellulose solution through very small holes and solidifying it in the form of filaments. 2. a fabric woven from such fibers.

**raze** (rāz), *v.t.* [RAZED, RAZING], [< L. *radere*, to scrape], to tear down completely; demolish: also sp. **rase.**

**ra·zor** (rā'zẽr), *n.* [see RAZE], a sharp-edged instrument for shaving.

**razz** (raz), *v.t. & v.i.* [< *raspberry*], [Slang], to tease, ridicule, etc.

**raz·zle-daz·zle** (raz''l-daz''l), *n.* [Slang], confusion, bustle, etc.

**r.b.i., rbi, RBI,** in *baseball*, run(s) batted in.

**R.C.,** 1. Red Cross. 2. Roman Catholic.

**Rd., rd.,** 1. road. 2. rod; rods.

**R.D.,** Rural Delivery.

**re** (rā), *n.* [It.], in *music*, a syllable representing the second tone of the diatonic scale.

**re** (rē), ***prep.*** [< L. *res*, thing], in the case or matter of; regarding.

**re-,** [< Fr. or L.], a prefix meaning: 1. *back*, as in *repay*. 2. *again, anew*, as in *reappear*. *Re-* is hyphenated: 1) to distinguish between a word in which it means *again* or *anew* and a word having a special meaning (e.g., *re-sound, resound*); 2) before elements beginning with *e*. The following list contains some common compounds formed with *re-* that do not have special meanings; they will be understood if *again* or *anew* is used before the meaning of the base word.

**readjust**
**readmit**
**reaffirm**
**reappoint**
**rearm**
**reassemble**
**reassign**
**reattempt**
**reawaken**
**reborn**
**rebroadcast**
**rebuild**
**recheck**
**recommence**
**reconduct**
**reconquer**
**reconstitute**
**reconvene**
**reconvert**
**recopy**
**re-cover**
**re-create**
**redecorate**
**rededicate**
**redeposit**
**redetermine**
**redirect**
**rediscover**
**redistribution**
**redo**
**redraw**
**re-edit**
**re-educate**
**re-elect**
**re-embark**
**re-embody**
**re-emerge**
**re-enact**
**re-engage**
**re-enlist**
**re-enter**
**re-establish**
**re-examine**
**re-experience**
**re-explain**
**refashion**
**refasten**
**reformulate**
**refuel**
**refurnish**
**rehear**
**reheat**
**rehire**
**reimpose**
**reinfect**
**reinoculate**
**reinsert**
**reinspect**
**reinvest**
**reinvestigate**
**reissue**
**rekindle**
**relearn**
**relive**
**reload**
**relocate**
**remake**
**remarry**
**rematch**
**remount**
**rename**
**renominate**
**renumber**
**reoffer**
**reopen**
**reorder**
**repaint**
**re-pay**
**rephrase**
**replant**
**replay**
**re-present**
**re-press**
**reprint**
**republish**
**repurchase**
**reread**
**resale**
**resell**
**resettle**
**reshape**
**re-sound**
**restudy**
**resupply**
**resurvey**
**retell**
**rethink**
**retold**
**retrain**
**retranslate**
**retrial**
**re-use**
**revaluate**
**revisit**
**revitalize**
**rewash**
**reweigh**
**rework**

**reach** (rēch), ***v.t.*** [AS. *ræcan*], 1. to thrust out (the hand, etc.). 2. to extend to by thrusting out, etc. 3. to obtain and hand over: as, *reach* me the salt. 4. to go as far as; attain. 5. to influence; affect. 6. to get in touch with, as by telephone. ***v.i.*** 1. to thrust out the hand, etc. 2. to extend in influence, space, etc. 3. to carry, as sight, sound, etc. 4. to try to get something. ***n.*** 1. a stretching or thrusting out. 2. the power of, or the extent covered in, stretching, obtaining, etc. 3. a continuous extent, as of water.

**re·act** (ri-akt′), ***v.i.*** 1. to act in return or reciprocally. 2. to return to a former condition, stage, etc. 3. to respond to a stimulus. 4. in *chem.*, to act with another substance in producing a chemical change.

**re·ac·tion** (ri-ak′shən), ***n.*** 1. a return or opposing action, etc. 2. a response, as to a stimulus. 3. a movement back to a former or less advanced condition. 4. a chemical change.

**re·ac′tion·ar′y** (-er′i), ***adj.*** of, characterized by, or advocating reaction. ***n.*** [*pl.* -IES], an advocate of reaction, esp. in politics.

**re·ac·tor** (ri-ak′tẽr), ***n.*** in *nuclear physics*, an apparatus in which there is controlled production of atomic energy from a nuclear chain reaction.

**read** (rēd), ***v.t.*** [READ (red), READING]. [< AS. *rædan*, to counsel], 1. to get the meaning of (writing) by interpreting the characters. 2. to utter aloud (written matter). 3. to understand or interpret. 4. to foretell (the future). 5. to study: as, to *read* law. 6. to register, as a gauge. ***v.i.*** 1. to read something written. 2. to learn by reading (with *about* or *of*). 3. to be phrased in certain words. **—read into** (or **in**), to interpret in a certain way. **—read out of**, to expel from (an organization).**—read′a·ble,** ***adj.***

**read** (red), ***adj.*** [pt. & pp. of *read*], informed from reading: as, well-*read*.

**read′er,** ***n.*** 1. one who reads. 2. a book for instruction in reading.

**read′ing,** ***n.*** 1. the act of one who reads. 2. the uttering aloud of written matter. 3. the study of books. 4. any material to be read. 5. a particular interpretation or formulation. 6. a recording of information by figures, etc., as on a barometer. ***adj.*** of, or for use in, reading.

**read·y** (red′i), ***adj.*** [-IER, -IEST], [AS. (*ge*)*ræde*], 1. prepared to act or be used immediately. 2. willing. 3. likely or liable; apt: as, *ready* to quibble. 4. dexterous. 5. prompt: as, a *ready* reply. 6. available immediately: as, *ready* cash. ***v.t.*** [-IED, -YING], to make ready; prepare. ***n.*** the position of a rifle just before aiming and firing. **—make ready**, to prepare. **—read′i·ly,** ***adv.*** **—read′i·ness,** ***n.***

**read′y-made′,** ***adj.*** made so as to be ready for immediate use or sale.

**re·a·gent** (rē-ā′jənt), ***n.*** in *chem.*, a substance used to detect, measure, or react with another substance.

**re·al** (rē′əl, rēl), ***adj.*** [< L. *res*, thing], 1. existing as or in fact; actual; true. 2. authentic; genuine. 3. in *law*, of or relating to immovable things: as, *real* property. ***adv.*** [Colloq.], very. **—re′al·ness,** ***n.***

**real estate,** land, including the buildings or improvements on it. **—re′al-es·tate′,** ***adj.***

**re′al·ism,** ***n.*** 1. a tendency to face facts and be practical. 2. in *art & literature*, portrayal of people and things as they really are. **—re′al·ist,** ***n.*** **—re′al·is′tic,** ***adj.***

**re·al·i·ty** (ri-al′ə-ti), ***n.*** [*pl.* -TIES], 1. the quality or state of being real. 2. a person or thing that is real; fact. **—in reality,** in fact; actually.

**re·al·ize** (rē′ə-līz′), ***v.t.*** [-IZED, -IZING], 1. to make real. 2. to understand fully. 3. to convert (assets, rights, etc.) into money. 4. to gain; obtain, as a profit. 5. to be sold for: said of property. **—re′al·i·za′tion,** ***n.***

**re′al·ly,** ***adv.*** 1. in reality; actually. 2. indeed. 3. truly or genuinely.

**realm** (relm), ***n.*** [see REGAL], 1. a kingdom. 2. a region; sphere.

**re·al·tor** (rē′əl-tẽr, -tôr′), ***n.*** a certified real-estate broker.

**re·al·ty** (rē′əl-ti), ***n.*** real estate.

**ream** (rēm), ***n.*** [< Ar. *rizmah*, a bale], 1. a quantity of paper varying from 480 to 516 sheets. 2. *pl.* [Colloq.], a great amount.

**ream** (rēm), ***v.t.*** [< AS. *ryman*, widen], to enlarge or taper (a hole) as with a reamer.

**ream·er** (rēm′ẽr), ***n.*** 1. a sharp-edged tool for enlarging or tapering holes. 2. a device for squeezing juice from oranges, etc.

**reap** (rēp), ***v.t. & v.i.*** [AS. *ripan*], 1. to cut (grain) with a scythe, machine, etc. 2. to gather (a harvest). 3. to obtain as a reward, payment, etc.

**reap′er,** ***n.*** 1. one who reaps. 2. a machine for reaping grain: also **reaping machine.**

**rear** (rêr), ***n.*** [< *arrear*], 1. the back part. 2. the position behind or at the back. 3. the part of an army, etc. farthest from the battle front. ***adj.*** of, at, or in the rear. **—bring up the rear,** to come at the end.

**rear** (rêr), ***v.t.*** [AS. *ræran*], 1. to put upright; elevate. 2. to build; erect. 3. to grow; breed. 4. to educate, nourish, etc.:

as, to *rear* children. ***v.i.*** 1. to rise on the hind legs, as a horse. 2. to rise up in anger, etc.
**rear admiral,** a naval officer next in rank above a captain.
**rear'most'** (-mōst'), ***adj.*** farthest in the rear.
**re'ar·range',** ***v.t.*** [-RANGED, -RANGING], to arrange again or in a different manner. —**re'ar·range'ment,** ***n.***
**rea·son** (rē'z'n), ***n.*** [ult. < L. *reri*, think], 1. an explanation of an act, idea, etc. 2. a cause; motive. 3. the ability to think, draw conclusions, etc. 4. good sense. 5. sanity. ***v.i.* & *v.t.*** 1. to think logically (about); analyze. 2. to argue or discuss. —**stand to reason,** to be logical. —**rea'son·ing,** ***n.***
**rea'son·a·ble,** ***adj.*** 1. able to reason. 2. just; fair. 3. sensible; wise. 4. not expensive. —**rea'son·a·bly,** ***adv.***
**re'as·sure',** ***v.t.*** [-SURED, -SURING], 1. to assure again. 2. to restore to confidence. —**re'as·sur'ance,** ***n.*** —**re'as·sur'ing·ly,** ***adv.***
**re·bate** (rē'bāt, ri-bāt'), ***v.t.*** [-BATED, -BATING], [< OFr.; see RE- & ABATE], to give back (part of a payment). ***n.*** return of part of a payment.
**Re·bec·ca, Re·bek·ah** (ri-bek'ə), ***n.*** in the *Bible*, the wife of Isaac.
**reb·el** (reb''l; *for v.*, ri-bel'), ***n.*** [< L. *re-*, again + *bellare*, to war], one who openly resists authority. ***adj.*** rebellious. ***v.i.*** [-ELLED, -ELLING], 1. to resist or oppose authority, government, etc. 2. to feel or show strong aversion.
**re·bel·lion** (ri-bel'yən), ***n.*** 1. armed, open resistance to the government. 2. defiance of any control.
**re·bel'lious** (-yəs), ***adj.*** 1. resisting authority. 2. opposing any control; defiant.
**re·birth',** ***n.*** 1. a new or second birth. 2. a reawakening; revival.
**re·bound** (ri-bound'), ***v.i.*** to spring back, as upon impact. ***n.*** (rē'bound'), a rebounding; recoil.
**re·buff** (ri-buf'), ***n.*** [< It. *rabbuffo*], 1. a blunt refusal of offered advice, help, etc. 2. any repulse. ***v.t.*** 1. to refuse bluntly; snub. 2. to check; repulse.
**re·buke** (ri-būk'), ***v.t.*** [-BUKED, -BUKING], [< OFr. *re-*, back + *bu(s)chier*, to beat], to address in sharp disapproval; reprimand. ***n.*** a sharp reprimand. —**re·buk'ing·ly,** ***adv.***
**re·bus** (rē'bəs), ***n.*** [L., lit., by things], a kind of puzzle consisting of pictures which suggest words or syllables.
**re·but** (ri-but'), ***v.t.*** [-BUTTED, -BUTTING], [< OFr. *re-*, back + *bouter*, to push], to contradict or oppose, esp. in a formal manner by argument, proof, etc. —**re·but'tal,** ***n.***
**re·cal·ci·trant** (ri-kal'si-trənt), ***adj.*** [< L. *re-*, back + *calcitrare*, to kick], refusing to obey authority, etc. —**re·cal'ci·trance,** ***n.***
**re·call** (ri-kôl'), ***v.t.*** 1. to call back. 2. to remember. 3. to take back; revoke. 4. to bring back in awareness or attention. ***n.*** (rē'kôl, ri-kôl'), 1. a recalling. 2. the removal of, or right to remove, an official from office by popular vote.
**re·cant** (ri-kant'), ***v.t.* & *v.i.*** [< L. *re-*, back + *canere*, to sing], to renounce formally (one's former beliefs, remarks, etc.). —**re·can·ta·tion** (rē'kan-tā'shən), ***n.***
**re·cap** (rē-kap'), ***v.t.*** [-CAPPED, -CAPPING], to vulcanize a strip of rubber on the outer surface of (a worn tire). ***n.*** (rē'kap'), a recapped tire. —**re·cap'pa·ble,** ***adj.***
**re·ca·pit·u·late** (rē'kə-pich'oo-lāt'), ***v.i.* & *v.t.*** [-LATED, -LATING], [see RE- & CAPITULATE], to summarize; restate briefly. —**re'ca·pit'u·la'tion,** ***n.***
**re·cap'ture,** ***v.t.*** [-TURED, -TURING], 1. to capture again; retake. 2. to remember. ***n.*** a recapturing or being recaptured.
**recd., rec'd.,** received.
**re·cede** (ri-sēd'), ***v.i.*** [-CEDED, -CEDING], [see RE- & CEDE], to go, move, or slope backward.
**re·ceipt** (ri-sēt'), ***n.*** [see RECEIVE], 1. a recipe. 2. a receiving or being received. 3. a written acknowledgment that something has been received. 4. *pl.* the amount, as of money, received. ***v.t.*** to mark (a bill) paid.
**re·ceiv·a·ble** (ri-sēv'ə-b'l), ***adj.*** 1. that can be received. 2. due; requiring payment.
**re·ceive** (ri-sēv'), ***v.t.*** [-CEIVED, -CEIVING], [< L. *re-*, back + *capere*, take], 1. to take (something given, sent, etc.). 2. to experience or undergo: as, to *receive* acclaim. 3. to learn: as, he *received* the news. 4. *a*) to let enter. *b*) to have room for. 5. to greet (visitors, etc.). ***v.i.*** to be a recipient.
**re·ceiv'er,** ***n.*** 1. one who receives. 2. one appointed to administer or hold in trust property in bankruptcy or in a lawsuit. 3. an apparatus that receives and converts electrical waves, signals, etc. into sound or light, as a radio or television receiving set, or that part of a telephone held to the ear.
**re·cent** (rē's'nt), ***adj.*** [< L. *recens*], 1. done, made, etc. just before the present; new. 2. of a time just before the present. —**re'cen·cy, re'cent·ness,** ***n.***—**re'cent·ly,** ***adv.***
**re·cep·ta·cle** (ri-sep'tə-k'l), ***n.*** [see RECEIVE], a container.
**re·cep·tion** (ri-sep'shən), ***n.*** 1. a receiving or being received. 2. the manner of this. 3. a social function, often formal, for the receiving of guests. 4. in *radio & TV*, the receiving of signals with reference to the quality of reproduction.
**re·cep'tion·ist,** ***n.*** an office employee who receives callers, gives information, etc.
**re·cep'tive,** ***adj.*** 1. receiving or tending to receive. 2. able or ready to receive requests, suggestions, new ideas, etc.
**re·cess** (ri-ses'; *also, for n., esp. sense 3,* rē'ses), ***n.*** [< L. *recedere*, recede], 1. a hollow place, as in a wall. 2. *usually in pl.* a withdrawn place. 3. a temporary halting of work, a session, etc. ***v.t.*** 1. to place in a recess. 2. to form a recess in. ***v.i.*** to take a recess.
**re·ces'sion,** ***n.*** 1. a going backward; withdrawal. 2. a temporary falling off of business activity. 3. the procession of the clergy and choir out of the sanctuary at the end of the service.
**re·ces'sion·al,** ***adj.*** of a recession. ***n.*** a hymn sung in church during the recession (sense 3).
**re·ces'sive,** ***adj.*** receding.
**rec·i·pe** (res'ə-pi), ***n.*** [L. < *recipere*, receive], 1. a list of materials and directions for preparing a dish or drink. 2. anything proposed for producing a desired result.
**re·cip·i·ent** (ri-sip'i-ənt), ***n.*** [see RECEIVE], one that receives. ***adj.*** able to receive.
**re·cip·ro·cal** (ri-sip'rə-k'l), ***adj.*** [< L. *reciprocus*, returning], 1. done, felt, etc. in return: as, *reciprocal* love. 2. mutual. 3. corresponding but reversed. 4. equivalent; complementary. ***n.*** 1. a complement; counterpart. 2. in *math.*, the quantity resulting from the division of 1 by a given quantity: as, the *reciprocal* of 7 is 1/7.
**re·cip·ro·cate** (ri-sip'rə-kāt'), ***v.t.* & *v.i.*** [-CATED, -CATING], 1. to move alternately back and forth. 2. to give and get reciprocally. 3. to do, feel, etc. in return. —**re·cip'ro·ca'tion,** ***n.***—**re·cip'ro·ca'tive,** ***adj.***
**rec·i·proc·i·ty** (res'ə-pros'ə-ti), ***n.*** 1. reciprocal state or relation. 2. mutual exchange; esp., exchange of special privileges between two countries.
**re·cit·al** (ri-sī't'l), ***n.*** 1. a reciting. 2. the account, story, etc. told. 3. a musical program, as by soloists. —**re·cit'al·ist,** ***n.***
**rec·i·ta·tion** (res'ə-tā'shən), ***n.*** 1. a recital (senses 1 & 2). 2. *a*) a speaking aloud in

public of something memorized. *b*) the piece so given. 3. a reciting by pupils of answers to questions on a prepared lesson.

**re·cite** (ri-sīt′), *v.t. & v.i.* [-CITED, -CITING], [see RE- & CITE], 1. to speak aloud as from memory, as school lessons. 2. to tell in detail; narrate. —**re·cit′er,** *n.*

**reck** (rek), *v.i. & v.t.* [AS. *reccan*], [Archaic], to have concern (for); heed.

**reck′less,** *adj.* heedless; rash.

**reck·on** (rek′ən), *v.t.* [AS. *-recenian*], 1. to count; compute. 2. to regard as being. 3. to estimate. 4. [Colloq.], to suppose. *v.i.* 1. to count up. 2. to rely (*on*).—**reckon with,** to take into consideration.

**reck′on·ing,** *n.* 1. count or computation. 2. the settlement of an account.

**re·claim** (ri-klām′), *v.t.* [see RE- & CLAIM], 1. to bring back from error, vice, etc. 2. to make (nonproductive land) usable. 3. to obtain (useful material) from waste products. —**rec·la·ma·tion** (rek′lə-mā′shən), *n.*

**re·cline** (ri-klīn′), *v.t. & v.i.* [-CLINED, -CLINING], [< L. *re-*, back + *clinare*, lean], to lie or cause to lie down. —**re·clin′er,** *n.*

**re·cluse** (rek′lo͞os, ri-klo͞os′), *n.* [< L. *re-*, back + *claudere*, shut], one who lives a secluded, solitary life. —**re·clu′sive,** *adj.*

**rec·og·ni·tion** (rek′əg-nish′ən), *n.* 1. a recognizing or being recognized. 2. *a*) identification of a person or thing as being known to one. *b*) a greeting.

**re·cog·ni·zance** (ri-kog′ni-zəns, -kon′i-), *n.* [< L. *re-*, again + *cognoscere*, know], in *law*, a bond binding one to some act, as to appear in court.

**rec·og·nize** (rek′əg-nīz′), *v.t.* [-NIZED, -NIZING], [< *recognizance*], 1. to identify as known before. 2. to know by some detail, as of appearance. 3. to perceive. 4. to accept; admit: as, to *recognize* defeat. 5. to acknowledge as worthy of commendation. 6. to acknowledge the sovereignty of (a state). 7. to grant the right to speak. —**rec′og·niz′a·ble,** *adj.* —**rec′og·niz′a·bly,** *adv.*

**re·coil** (ri-koil′), *v.i.* [< L. *re-*, back + *culus*, buttocks], 1. to draw back, as in fear, etc. 2. to spring or kick back, as a gun when fired. *n.* (*usually* rē′koil′), a recoiling.

**rec·ol·lect** (rek′ə-lekt′), *v.t. & v.i.* [see RE- & COLLECT], to remember, esp. with some effort. —**rec′ol·lec′tion,** *n.*

**rec·om·mend** (rek′ə-mend′), *v.t.* [see RE- & COMMEND], 1. to entrust. 2. to speak of favorably as suited to some position, etc. 3. to make acceptable. 4. to advise; counsel. —**rec′om·men·da′tion,** *n.*

**rec·om·pense** (rek′əm-pens′), *v.t.* [-PENSED, -PENSING], [see RE- & COMPENSATE], 1. to repay or reward. 2. to compensate, as a loss. *n.* 1. requital; reward. 2. compensation, as for a loss.

**rec·on·cile** (rek′ən-sīl′), *v.t.* [-CILED, -CILING], [see RE- & CONCILIATE], 1. to make friendly again. 2. to settle (a quarrel, etc.). 3. to make (facts, texts, etc.) consistent. 4. to make acquiescent (*to*). —**rec′on·cil′a·ble,** *adj.* —**rec′on·cil′i·a′tion** (-sil′i-ā′shən), *n.*

**rec·on·dite** (rek′ən-dīt′), *adj.* [< L. *re-*, back + *condere*, to hide], 1. beyond ordinary understanding; abstruse. 2. obscure.

**re′con·di′tion,** *v.t.* to put back in good condition by cleaning, repairing, etc.

**re·con·nais·sance, re·con·nois·sance** (ri-kon′ə-səns), *n.* [Fr.; see RECOGNIZANCE], the survey of a region, esp. for obtaining military information about an enemy.

**rec·on·noi·ter** (rek′ə-noi′tẽr, rē′kə-), *v.t. & v.i.* to survey or inspect (an enemy position, a region, etc.) in order to get information: also sp. **rec′on·noi′tre** [-TRED, -TRING].

**re·con·sid·er** (rē′kən-sid′ẽr), *v.t. & v.i.* to think over, as with a view to changing a decision. —**re′con·sid′er·a′tion,** *n.*

**re′con·struct′,** *v.t.* 1. to construct again; remake. 2. to build up, as from remains, an image of the original.

**re′con·struc′tion,** *n.* 1. a reconstructing. 2. [R-], the process or period, after the Civil War, of re-establishing the Southern States in the Union.

**re·cord** (ri-kôrd′; *for n. & adj.*, rek′ẽrd), *v.t.* [< L. *recordari*, remember], 1. to write down, so as to keep an account of. 2. to register, as on a graph. 3. to register (sound), as on a grooved disk, so that it can be reproduced. *n.* 1. a recording or being recorded. 2. any registered evidence of an event, etc. 3. the known facts about anything. 4. a grooved disk, etc. on which sound is recorded. 5. the best performance attained. *adj.* being the largest, fastest, etc. of its kind. —**on** (or **off the) record,** publicly (or privately) declared.

**re·cord′er,** *n.* 1. an official who keeps records. 2. a person, machine, etc. that records. 3. an early form of flute.

**re·cord′ing,** *n.* 1. what is recorded, as on a phonograph record. 2. the record.

**re·count** (ri-kount′), *v.t.* [see RE- & COUNT], to tell in detail; narrate.

**re-count** (rē′kount′), *v.t.* to count again. *n.* (rē′kount′), a second count, as of votes: also written **recount.**

**re·coup** (ri-ko͞op′), *v.t.* [< Fr. *re-*, again + *couper*, to cut], 1. to make up for: as, to *recoup* a loss. 2. to repay. *n.* a recouping.

**re·course** (rē′kôrs, ri-kôrs′), *n.* [see RE- & COURSE], 1. a turning for aid, protection, etc. 2. that to which one turns seeking aid, etc.

**re·cov·er** (ri-kuv′ẽr), *v.t.* [< L. *recuperare*], 1. to get back (something lost, etc.); regain (health, etc.). 2. to compensate for: as, *recover* losses. 3. to save (oneself) from a fall, etc. 4. to reclaim, as land from the sea. *v.i.* 1. to get back to a healthy condition, etc. 2. to save oneself as from a slip. —**re·cov′er·a·ble,** *adj.* —**re·cov′er·er,** *n.*

**re·cov′er·y,** *n.* [*pl.* -IES], 1. a recovering, regaining, etc. 2. a regaining of health, something lost, etc.

**rec·re·ant** (rek′ri-ənt), *adj.* [< OFr. *recreire*, surrender allegiance], cowardly. *n.* a coward. —**rec′re·ance, rec′re·an·cy,** *n.*

**rec·re·ate** (rek′ri-āt′), *v.t. & v.i.* [-ATED, -ATING], [< L. *recreare*, refresh], to refresh (oneself) in body or mind.

**rec·re·a·tion** (rek′ri-ā′shən), *n.* any play, amusement, etc. used for refreshment of body or mind. —**rec′re·a′tion·al,** *adj.*

**re·crim·i·nate** (ri-krim′ə-nāt′), *v.i.* [-NATED, -NATING], [< L. *re-*, back + *crimen*, offense], to reply to an accusation by accusing in return. —**re·crim′i·na′tion,** *n.*

**re·cruit** (ri-kro͞ot′), *v.t. & v.i.* [< L. *re-*, again + *crescere*, grow], 1. to enlist (personnel) into (an army or navy). 2. to enlist (new members) for an organization. *n.* 1. a recently enlisted soldier, sailor, etc. 2. a new member of any group. —**re·cruit′er,** *n.*

**rec·tal** (rek′t'l), *adj.* of, for, or near the rectum. —**rec′tal·ly,** *adv.*

**rec·tan·gle** (rek′taŋ′g'l), *n.* [< L. *rectus*, straight + *angulus*, a corner], a four-sided plane figure with four right angles. —**rec·tan′gu·lar** (-gyoo-lẽr), *adj.*

**rec·ti·fy** (rek′tə-fī′), *v.t.* [-FIED, -FYING], [< L. *rectus*, right + *facere*, make], to put right; correct. —**rec′ti·fi·ca′tion,** *n.*

**rec·ti·lin·e·ar** (rek′tə-lin′i-ẽr), *adj.* [< L. *rectus*, straight; + *linear*], 1. in or forming a straight line. 2. bounded by straight lines.

**rec·ti·tude** (rek′tə-to͞od′, -tūd′), *n.* [< L. *rectus*, straight], honesty; uprightness.

**rec·tor** (rek′tẽr), *n.* [< L. *regere*, to rule], 1. in various churches, the head of a parish. 2. the head of certain schools, colleges, etc.

**rec·to·ry** (rek′tẽr-i), *n.* [*pl.* -RIES], a rector's residence.

**rec·tum** (rek′təm), *n.* [*pl.* -TA (-tə)], [< L. *rectum* (*intestinum*), straight (intestine)], the lowest segment of the large intestine.

**re·cum·bent** (ri-kum′bənt), *adj.* [< L. *re-*, back + *cumbere*, lie down], lying down; reclining. —**re·cum′ben·cy,** *n.*

**re·cu·per·ate** (ri-kōō′pə-rāt′, -kū′-), *v.t. & v.i.* [-ATED, -ATING], [< L. *recuperare*, recover], 1. to get well again. 2. to recover (losses, health, etc.). —**re·cu′per·a′tion,** *n.* —**re·cu′per·a′tive,** *adj.*

**re·cur** (ri-kũr′), *v.i.* [-CURRED, -CURRING], [< L. *re-*, back + *currere*, run], 1. to return in thought, talk, etc.: as, to *recur* to a topic. 2. to occur again or at intervals. —**re·cur′rence,** *n.* —**re·cur′rent,** *adj.*

**re·curve** (ri-kũrv′), *v.t. & v.i.* [-CURVED, -CURVING], to curve back or backward.

**red** (red), *n.* [AS. *read*], 1. the color of blood. 2. any red pigment. 3. [often R-], a political radical; esp., a communist. *adj.* [REDDER, REDDEST], 1. of the color red. 2. [often R-], politically radical; esp., communist. —**in the red,** losing money. —**see red,** [Colloq.], to become angry. —**red′dish,** *adj.*

**re·dact** (ri-dakt′), *v.t.* [< L. *redigere*, to get in order], to edit. —**re·dac′tor,** *n.*

**red′cap′,** *n.* a porter in a railroad station, bus station, etc.

**red′coat′,** *n.* a British soldier (when a red coat was part of the British uniform).

**Red Cross,** an international society for the relief of suffering in time of war or disaster.

**red deer,** 1. a deer of Europe and Asia. 2. the American deer (in its summer coloring).

**red·den** (red′'n), *v.t.* to make red. *v.i.* to become red; esp., to blush or flush.

**re·deem** (ri-dēm′), *v.t.* [< L. *re*(*d*)-, back + *emere*, get], 1. to get or buy back; recover. 2. to pay off (a mortgage, etc.). 3. to turn in (coupons) for premiums. 4. to set free; rescue. 5. to deliver from sin. 6. to fulfill, as a promise. 7. to make amends for; atone for. —**re·deem′a·ble,** *adj.* —**re·deem′er,** *n.*

**re·demp·tion** (ri-demp′shən), *n.* 1. a redeeming or being redeemed. 2. something that redeems. —**re·demp′tive,** *adj.*

**red′-hand′ed,** *adj.* in the act, or fresh from the scene, of a crime.

**red′head′,** *n.* a person with red hair. —**red′head′ed,** *adj.*

**red herring,** [< herring drawn across the trace in hunting to divert the hounds], something used to divert attention or confuse.

**red′-hot′,** *adj.* 1. hot enough to glow. 2. very excited, as with anger. 3. very new, timely, etc.

**re·dis′trict,** *v.t.* to divide anew into districts.

**red′-let′ter,** *adj.* memorable; happy: as, a *red-letter* day.

**red man,** a N. American Indian.

**red·o·lent** (red′ə-lənt), *adj.* [< L. *re*(*d*)-, intens. + *olere*, to smell], 1. sweet-smelling. 2. smelling (*of*). 3. suggestive (*of*). —**red′o·lence, red′o·len·cy,** *n.*

**re·dou·ble** (rē-dub′'l), *v.t. & v.i.* [-BLED, -BLING], 1. to increase or be increased twofold; double. 2. to double back or again.

**re·doubt** (ri-dout′), *n.* [< L. *re-*, back + *ducere*, to lead], 1. a temporary fortification. 2. a stronghold.

**re·doubt·a·ble** (ri-dout′ə-b'l), *adj.* [< L. *re-*, intens. + *dubitare*, to doubt], 1. formidable. 2. deserving of respect.

**re·dound** (ri-dound′), *v.i.* [< L. *re*(*d*)-, intens. + *undare*, to surge], 1. to have a result (*to* the credit or discredit of). 2. to come back; react (*upon*).

**red pepper,** 1. a plant with a red, many-seeded fruit. 2. the fruit. 3. the ground fruit or seeds, used for seasoning.

**re·dress** (ri-dres′), *v.t.* [see RE- & DRESS], 1. to compensate for, as an evil. 2. to remedy, as a fault. 3. to make amends to. *n.* (*usually* rē′dres), 1. a compensation. 2. a redressing. —**re·dress′er,** *n.*

**red′skin′,** *n.* a N. American Indian.

**red snapper,** a salt-water food fish with a reddish body.

**red tape,** [< tape used for official papers], rigid adherence to routine and regulations, causing delay, etc. —**red′-tape′,** *adj.*

**re·duce** (ri-dōōs′, -dūs′), *v.t.* [-DUCED, -DUCING], [< L. *re-*, back + *ducere*, to lead], 1. to lessen, as in size, price, etc. 2. to change to a different form, as by melting, grinding, etc. 3. to lower, as in rank, state, etc.: as, *reduced* to poverty. 4. to subdue or conquer. *v.i.* to lose weight, as by dieting.

**re·duc·tion** (ri-duk′shən), *n.* 1. a reducing or being reduced. 2. anything made or brought about by reducing.

**re·dun′dant** (-dənt), *adj.* [see REDOUND], 1. excess; superfluous; esp., unnecessary to the meaning: said of words. 2. wordy. —**re·dun′dan·cy,** *n.* —**re·dun′dant·ly,** *adv.*

**red′wood′,** *n.* 1. a giant evergreen of the Pacific coast. 2. its reddish wood.

**re-ech·o, re·ech·o** (rē-ek′ō), *v.t. & v.i.* [-OED, -OING], to echo back. *n.* [*pl.* -OES], the echo of an echo.

**reed** (rēd), *n.* [AS. *hreod*], 1. a grass with a jointed, hollow stem. 2. a musical pipe made from such a stem. 3. in *music*, a thin strip of cane, etc. placed against the mouthpiece, as of a clarinet, and vibrated by the breath to produce tone. —**reed′y** [-IER, -IEST], *adj.*

**reef** (rēf), *n.* [< ON. *rif*, a rib], a ridge of rock or sand at or near the surface of the water.

**reef** (rēf), *n.* [ME. *riff*], a part of a sail which can be folded together and tied down to reduce the area exposed to the wind. *v.t. & v.i.* to reduce (a sail) by taking in part of it.

**reek** (rēk), *n.* [AS. *rec*], a strong, unpleasant smell. *v.i.* to emit a strong, offensive smell.

**reel** (rēl), *n.* [AS. *hreol*], 1. a spool on which thread, film, fishing line, etc. may be wound. 2. the quantity, esp. of motion-picture film, usually wound on one reel. *v.t.* 1. to wind on or off a reel (with *in* or *out*). 2. to pull in (a fish) by winding a reel (with *in*). 3. to tell, write, etc. fluently (with *off*). *v.i.* 1. to sway, stagger, etc., as from shock or drunkenness. 2. to spin; whirl.

**reel** (rēl), *n.* [< prec. *reel, v.i.*], a lively dance.

**reeve** (rēv), *v.t.* [REEVED or ROVE; also, for pp., ROVEN; REEVING], [prob. < D. *reven*], in *naut. usage*, 1. to slip (a rope, etc.) through (a block, pulley, etc.). 2. to fasten by passing through or around something.

**re·fec·tion** (ri-fek′shən), *n.* [< L. *re-*, again + *facere*, make], a light meal.

**re·fec′to·ry** (-tə-ri), *n.* [*pl.* -RIES], a dining hall, as in a monastery or college.

**re·fer** (ri-fũr′), *v.t.* [-FERRED, -FERRING], [< L. *re-*, back + *ferre*, to bear], 1. to submit (a quarrel, etc.) for settlement. 2. to direct (a person) *to* someone or something for aid, information, etc. *v.i.* 1. to relate or allude: with *to*, as, the book *referred* only to fish. 2. to direct attention (with *to*). 3. to turn for information, aid, etc. (with *to*).

**ref·er·ee** (ref′ə-rē′), *n.* 1. a person to whom anything is referred for decision. 2. in *sports*, a judge, as of a boxing match. *v.t. & v.i.* [-EED, -EEING], to act as referee (in).

**ref·er·ence** (ref′ẽr-əns), *n.* 1. a referring or being referred. 2. relation: as, with *reference* to his reply. 3. the directing of attention to a person or thing. 4. a casual mention. 5. *a*) an indication, as in a book, of some other source of information. *b*) such a source. 6. *a*) one who can offer information or recommendation. *b*) a statement of character, qualification, etc. given by such a person. **—make reference to,** to refer to; mention.

**ref·er·en·dum** (ref'ə-ren'dəm), *n.* [*pl.* -DUMS, -DA (-də)], [L., see REFER], 1. the submission of a law to a direct vote of the people. 2. the right of the people to vote on such laws. 3. the vote itself.

**re·fill** (rē-fil'), *v.t.* to fill again. *n.* (rē'fil'), a unit or supply to replace the contents of a container. **—re·fill'a·ble,** *adj.*

**re·fine** (ri-fīn'), *v.t. & v.i.* [-FINED, -FINING], [*re-* + *fine*, to make fine], 1. to free or become freed from impurities, etc. 2. to free or become freed from imperfection, vulgarity, etc.; polish. **—re·fin'er,** *n.*

**re·fined',** *adj.* 1. made free from impurities; purified. 2. cultivated; free from vulgarity.

**re·fine'ment,** *n.* 1. a refining or being refined. 2. the result of this. 3. delicacy or elegance of manners, speech, etc. 4. an improvement. 5. a fine distinction.

**re·fin'er·y,** *n.* [*pl.* -IES], a plant for purifying materials, as oil, sugar, etc.

**re·fit** (rē-fit'), *v.t. & v.i.* [-FITTED, -FITTING], to make or be made fit for use again by repairing, re-equipping, etc.

**re·flect** (ri-flekt'), *v.t. & v.i.* [< L. *re-*, back + *flectere*, to bend], 1. to throw back (light, heat, or sound). 2. to give back an image (of); mirror. 3. to bring or come back as a consequence: as, *reflected* glory. **—reflect on** (or **upon**), 1. to contemplate; ponder. 2. to cast blame or discredit. **—re·flec'tive,** *adv.*

**re·flec'tion,** *n.* 1. a reflecting or being reflected. 2. anything reflected. 3. contemplation. 4. an idea or remark. 5. blame; discredit.

**re·flec'tor,** *n.* a surface, device, etc. that reflects light, sound, heat, etc.

**re·flex** (rē'fleks), *adj.* [see REFLECT], designating or of an involuntary action, as a sneeze, due to the direct transmission of a stimulus to a muscle or gland.

**re·flex·ive** (ri-flek'siv), *adj.* 1. designating a verb whose subject and object are identical (e.g., I *wash* myself). 2. designating a pronoun used as the object of such a verb.

**re·for·est** (rē-fôr'ist, -for'-), *v.t. & v.i.* to plant new trees on (land once forested). **—re'for·est·a'tion,** *n.*

**re·form** (ri-fôrm'), *v.t.* [see RE- & FORM], 1. to make better as by stopping abuses; improve. 2. to cause (a person) to behave better. *v.i.* to become or behave better. *n.* an improvement; correction of faults.

**re-form** (rē'fôrm'), *v.t. & v.i.* to form again.

**ref·or·ma·tion** (ref'ẽr-mā'shən), *n.* 1. a reforming or being reformed. 2. [R-], the 16th-century religious movement that resulted in establishing the Protestant churches.

**re·form·a·to·ry** (ri-fôr'mə-tôr'i), *adj.* reforming or aiming at reform. *n.* [*pl.* -RIES], an institution for reforming young law offenders: also **reform school.**

**re·form·er** (ri-fôr'mẽr), *n.* one who seeks to reform morals, conditions, etc.

**re·fract** (ri-frakt'), *v.t.* [< L. *re-*, back + *frangere*, to break], to bend (a ray of light, heat, etc.) as it passes from one medium into another. **—re·frac'tion,** *n.*

**re·frac·to·ry** (ri-frak'tə-ri), *adj.* [see REFRACT], obstinate; hard to manage.

**re·frain** (ri-frān'), *v.i.* [< L. *re-*, back + *frenare*, to curb], to hold back; keep oneself (*from*).

**re·frain** (ri-frān'), *n.* [< L. *re-*, back + *frangere*, to break], a phrase or verse repeated at intervals in a song or poem.

**re·fran·gi·ble** (ri-fran'jə-b'l), *adj.* [< *re-* + L. *frangere*, to break; + *-ible*], that can be refracted, as light rays.

**re·fresh** (ri-fresh'), *v.t.* 1. to make fresh by cooling, airing, etc., as a room. 2. to make (a person) feel cooler, stronger, etc., as by food, sleep, etc. 3. to renew; replenish; revive. *v.i.* to become fresh again; revive.

**re·fresh'ment,** *n.* 1. a refreshing or being refreshed. 2. that which refreshes. 3. *pl.* food or drink or both.

**re·frig·er·ate** (ri-frij'ə-rāt'), *v.t.* [-ATED, -ATING], [< L. *re-*, intens. + *frigus*, cold], to make or keep cool or cold, as for preserving. **—re·frig'er·a'tion,** *n.* **—re·frig'er·ant,** *adj. & n.*

**re·frig'er·a'tor,** *n.* a box or room in which food etc. is kept cool.

**ref·uge** (ref'ūj), *n.* [< L. *re-*, back + *fugere*, flee], (a) shelter or protection from danger, etc.

**ref·u·gee** (ref'yoo-jē', ref'yoo-jē'), *n.* one who flees from his home or country to seek refuge elsewhere.

**re·ful·gent** (ri-ful'jənt), *adj.* [see RE- & FULGENT], shining; radiant; glowing. **—re·ful'gence, re·ful'gen·cy,** *n.*

**re·fund** (ri-fund'), *v.t. & v.i.* [< L. *re-*, back + *fundere*, pour], to give back (money, etc.); repay. *n.* (rē'fund'), a refunding or the amount refunded.

**re·fur·bish** (rē-fũr'bish), *v.t.* to freshen or polish up again; renovate.

**re·fuse** (ri-fūz'), *v.t. & v.i.* [-FUSED, -FUSING], [< L. *re-*, back + *fundere*, pour], 1. to decline to accept; reject. 2. to decline (*to* do, grant, etc.). **—re·fus'al,** *n.*

**ref·use** (ref'ūs, -ūz), *n.* [see REFUSE, *v.*], waste; rubbish. *adj.* of refuse.

**re·fute** (ri-fūt'), *v.t.* [-FUTED, -FUTING], [< L. *refutare*, repel], to prove to be false or wrong. **—ref·u·ta·tion** (ref'yoo-tā'shən), *n.*

**re·gain** (ri-gān'), *v.t.* 1. to get back again; recover. 2. to get back to.

**re·gal** (rē'g'l), *adj.* [< L. *rex*, king], of, like, or fit for a king; royal.

**re·gale** (ri-gāl'), *v.t. & v.i.* [-GALED, -GALING], [< Fr. *ré-* (see RE-) + OFr. *gale*, joy], to entertain as with a feast. **—re·gale'ment,** *n.*

**re·ga·li·a** (ri-gā'li-ə, -gāl'yə), *n.pl.* [see REGAL], 1. the insignia of kingship, as a crown, scepter, etc. 2. the decorations of any rank, society, etc. 3. fine clothes.

**re·gard** (ri-gärd'), *n.* [Fr.; see RE- & GUARD], 1. a firm, fixed look; gaze. 2. consideration; concern. 3. respect and affection. 4. reference; relation: as, in *regard* to your question. 5. *pl.* good wishes: as, give her my *regards*. *v.t.* 1. to look at attentively. 2. to hold in affection or respect. 3. to consider: as, I *regard* this as a bother. 4. to concern: as, this *regards* your welfare. **—as regards,** concerning. **—without regard to,** not taking into account. **—re·gard'ful,** *adj.*

**re·gard'ing,** *prep.* concerning; about.

**re·gard'less,** *adj.* without regard; careless (often with *of*). *adv.* [Colloq.], without regard for objections, etc.

**re·gat·ta** (ri-gat'ə), *n.* [It.], 1. a boat race. 2. a series of boat races.

**re·gen·er·ate** (ri-jen'ẽr-it), *adj.* [< L.; see RE- & GENERATE], 1. spiritually reborn. 2. renewed; restored; reformed. *v.t.* (-ə-rāt'), [-ATED, -ATING], 1. to cause to be spiritually reborn. 2. to cause to be completely reformed. 3. to bring into existence again; reproduce. **—re·gen'er·a'tive,** *adj.*

**re·gent** (rē'jənt), *n.* [< L. *regere*, to rule], 1. a person appointed to rule while a king, etc. is absent, too young, etc. 2. a member of a governing board, as of a college. **—re'gen·cy,** *n.* **—re'gent·ship',** *n.*

**re·gime, ré·gime** (ri-zhēm', rā-), *n.* [see REGIMEN], 1. political or ruling system. 2. a social system. 3. a regimen.

**reg·i·men** (rej'ə-men', -mən), *n.* [< L. *regere*, to rule], a system of diet, exercise, rest, etc. for promoting the health.

**reg·i·ment** (rej'ə-mənt), *n.* [< L. *regere*, to rule], a military unit, the basic component of a division. *v.t.* (-ment'), 1. to organize systematically. 2. to subject to strict discipline and conformity. **—reg'i·men'tal,** *adj.* **—reg'i·men·ta'tion,** *n.*

**re·gion** (rē'jən), *n.* [< L. *regere*, to rule], 1. a large and indefinite part of the earth's surface. 2. any division or part, as of an organism: as, the abdominal *region.* **—re'gion·al,** *adj.* **—re'gion·al·ly,** *adv.*

**reg·is·ter** (rej'is-tẽr), *n.* [< L. *regerere*, to record], 1. *a)* a list of names, items, etc. *b)* a book in which this is kept. 2. a device for recording: as, a cash *register.* 3. an opening of a heating duct into a room, by which the amount of passing air can be controlled. 4. in *music*, the range of a voice or instrument. *v.t.* 1. to enter in a list. 2. to indicate as on a scale. 3. to show, as by facial expression: as, to *register* joy. 4. to safeguard (mail) by having its committal to the postal system recorded, for a fee. *v.i.* 1. enter one's name in a list, as of voters. 2. [Colloq.], to make an impression.

**reg·is·trar** (rej'i-strär'), *n.* one who keeps records, as in a college.

**reg·is·tra·tion** (rej'i-strā'shən), *n.* 1. a registering or being registered. 2. an entry in a register. 3. the number of persons registered.

**reg'is·try** (-tri), *n.* [*pl.* -TRIES], 1. registration. 2. an office where registers are kept. 3. a register.

**re·gress** (rē'gres), *n.* [< L. *re-*, back + *gradi*, go], a going back. *v.i.* (ri-gres'), to go back. **—re·gres'sion,** *n.* **—re·gres'sive,** *adj.*

**re·gret** (ri-gret'), *v.t.* [-GRETTED, -GRETTING], [< OFr. *regreter*, mourn], to feel sorrow or remorse over (an occurrence, one's acts, etc.). *n.* sorrow, esp. over one's acts or omissions. **—regrets,** a polite expression of regret, as at declining an invitation. **—re·gret'ful,** *adj.* **—re·gret'ta·ble,** *adj.*

**reg·u·lar** (reg'yoo-lẽr), *adj.* [< L. *regula*, a rule], 1. conforming to a rule, type, etc.; orderly; symmetrical. 2. conforming to a fixed principle or procedure. 3. usual; customary. 4. consistent: as, a *regular* customer. 5. unchanging: as, a *regular* pulse. 6. properly qualified: as, a *regular* doctor. 7. [Colloq.], thorough; complete: as, a *regular* nuisance. 8. designating or of the standing army of a country. *n.* a regular soldier. **—reg'u·lar'i·ty** (-lar'ə-ti), *n.* **—reg'u·lar·ize'** [-IZED, -IZING], *v.t.* **—reg'u·lar·ly,** *adv.*

**reg·u·late** (reg'yoo-lāt'), *v.t.* [-LATED, -LATING], [< L. *regula*, a rule], 1. to control or direct according to a rule, principle, etc. 2. to adjust to a standard, rate, etc. 3. to adjust so as to make work accurately, as a clock. **—reg'u·la'tive,** *adj.* **—reg'u·la'tor,** *n.*

**reg'u·la'tion,** *n.* 1. a regulating or being regulated. 2. a rule or law by which conduct, etc. is regulated. *adj.* usual; regular.

**re·gur·gi·tate** (rē-gũr'jə-tāt'), *v.i.* & *v.t.* [-TATED, -TATING], [< ML. *re-*, back + LL. *gurgitare*, to surge], to bring (partly digested food) from the stomach back to the mouth. **—re·gur'gi·ta'tion,** *n.*

**re·ha·bil·i·tate** (rē'hə-bil'ə-tāt'), *v.t.* [-TATED, -TATING], [< ML. *re-*, again + *habilitare*, qualify], 1. to restore to rank, reputation, etc. which one has lost. 2. to put back in good condition. **—re'ha·bil'i·ta'tion,** *n.*

**re·hash** (rē-hash'), *v.t.* [*re-* + *hash*], to work up again or repeat, adding nothing new. *n.* (rē'hash'), 1. a rehashing. 2. a thing rehashed.

**re·hearse** (ri-hũrs'), *v.t.* & *v.i.* [-HEARSED, -HEARSING], [< OFr. *re-*, again + *herser*, to harrow], 1. to recite, esp. in detail. 2. to practice, as a play, for public performance. **—re·hears'al,** *n.* **—re·hears'er,** *n.*

**Reich** (rīk; G. rīkh), *n.* [G.], formerly, Germany or the German government.

**reign** (rān), *n.* [< L. *regere*, to rule], 1. royal power. 2. dominance; sway. 3. the period of a sovereign's rule. *v.i.* 1. to rule as a king or queen. 2. to prevail: as, peace *reigns.*

**re·im·burse** (rē'im-bũrs'), *v.t.* [-BURSED, -BURSING], [*re-* + archaic *imburse*, to pay], to pay back. **—re'im·burse'ment,** *n.*

**rein** (rān), *n.* [see RETAIN], 1. *usually in pl.* a narrow strap of leather attached in pairs to a horse's bit and manipulated to control the animal. 2. *pl.* a means of controlling, etc. *v.t.* to guide or control as with reins. **—give (free) rein to,** to free from restraint.

**re·in·car·na·tion** (rē'in-kär-nā'shən), *n.* [see INCARNATE], rebirth (of the soul) in another body. **—re'in·car'nate** [-NATED, -NATING], *v.t.*

**rein·deer** (rān'dêr'), *n.* [*pl.* -DEER, -DEERS], [< ON. *hreinn*, reindeer + *dyr*, deer], a large deer with branching antlers, found in northern regions and domesticated there as a beast of burden.

**re·in·force** (rē'in-fôrs'), *v.t.* [-FORCED, -FORCING], [*re-* + var. of *enforce*], 1. to strengthen (a military or naval force) by sending new troops or ships. 2. to strengthen, as by propping, adding new material, etc. Also sp. **re-enforce, reënforce.** **—re'in·force'ment,** *n.*

**re·in·state** (rē'in-stāt'), *v.t.* [-STATED, -STATING], to restore to a former condition, position, etc. **—re'in·state'ment,** *n.*

**re·it·er·ate** (rē-it'ə-rāt'), *v.t.* [-ATED, -ATING], [< L. *re-*, again + *itare*, to repeat], to say or do again or repeatedly. **—re·it'er·a'tion,** *n.* **—re·it'er·a'tive,** *adj.*

**re·ject** (ri-jekt'), *v.t.* [< L. *re-*, back + *jacere*, to throw], 1. to refuse to take, use, agree to, believe, etc. 2. to discard. *n.* (rē'jekt), something rejected. **—re·jec'tion,** *n.*

**re·joice** (ri-jois'), *v.i.* & *v.t.* [-JOICED, -JOICING], [< OFr. *re-*, again + *ējouir*, rejoice], to be or make glad or happy. **—re·joic'ing,** *n.*

**re·join** (rē-join'), *v.t.* & *v.i.* 1. to join again; reunite. 2. to answer.

**re·join·der** (ri-join'dẽr), *n.* [< Fr. *rejoindre*, to rejoin], 1. an answer to a reply. 2. any answer.

**re·ju·ve·nate** (ri-jōō'və-nāt'), *v.t.* [-NATED, -NATING], [< *re-* + L. *juvenis*, young], to make young or youthful again. **—re·ju've·na'tion,** *n.* **—re·ju've·na'tor,** *n.*

**re·lapse** (ri-laps'), *v.i.* [-LAPSED, -LAPSING], [see RE- & LAPSE], to slip back into a former state, esp. into illness after apparent recovery. *n.* a relapsing. **—re·laps'er,** *n.*

**re·late** (ri-lāt'), *v.t.* [-LATED, -LATING], [< L. *relatus*, brought back], 1. to tell the story of; narrate. 2. to connect, as in thought or meaning. *v.i.* to have reference or some connection (*to*). **—re·la'tor, re·lat'er,** *n.*

**re·lat'ed,** *adj.* connected, as by origin, kinship, marriage, etc.

**re·la'tion,** *n.* 1. a narrating. 2. a narrative; recital. 3. connection, as in thought, meaning, etc. 4. connection by origin or marriage; kinship. 5. a relative. 6. *pl.* the connections between or among persons, nations, etc. **—in** (or **with**) **relation to,** with reference to. **—re·la'tion·ship',** *n.*

**rel·a·tive** (rel'ə-tiv), *adj.* 1. related each to the other. 2. having to do with; relevant. 3. comparative: as, *relative* wages. 4. meaningful only in relationship: as, "cold" is a *relative* term. 5. in *grammar*, that refers to an antecedent: as, a *relative* pronoun. *n.* a person related by origin or marriage.

**rel·a·tiv·i·ty** (rel'ə-tiv'ə-ti), *n.* 1. a being relative. 2. in *physics*, the theory of the relative, rather than absolute, character of motion, velocity, mass, etc., and the interdependence of matter, time, and space.

**re·lax** (ri-laks'), *v.t.* & *v.i.* [< L. *re-*, back + *laxare*, loosen], 1. to make or become less firm, tense, etc. 2. to rest, as from work.

**re·lax·a·tion** (rē′lak-sā′shən), *n.* 1. a relaxing or being relaxed. 2. a lessening of or rest from work or effort. 3. recreation.
**re·lay** (rē′lā), *n.* [< OFr. *re-*, back + *laier*, to leave], 1. a fresh supply of horses, etc., as for a stage of a journey. 2. a relief crew of workers; shift. 3. a race (in full, **relay race**) between teams, each member of which goes a part of the distance. *v.t.* (ri-lā′), [-LAYED, -LAYING], to convey as by relays: as, to *relay* news.
**re·lease** (ri-lēs′), *v.t.* [-LEASED, -LEASING], [< OFr. *re-*, again + *laisser*, to leave], 1. to set free, as from prison, work, suffering, etc., 2. to let go, as something caught, etc. 3. to permit to be issued, published, etc. *n.* 1. a releasing, as from prison, work, etc. 2. a device to release a catch, etc., as on a machine. 3. a book, news item, etc. released to the public. 4. in *law*, a written surrender of a claim, etc.
**rel·e·gate** (rel′ə-gāt′), *v.t.* [-GATED, -GATING], [< L. *re-*, away + *legare*, send], 1. to exile; banish (*to*). 2. to consign or assign, esp. to an inferior position. 3. to refer, or hand over for decision. **—rel′e·ga′tion,** *n.*
**re·lent** (ri-lent′), *v.i.* [< L. *re-*, again + *lentus*, pliant], to soften in temper, resolution, etc.; become less stern or stubborn. **—re·lent′less,** *adj.* **—re·lent′less·ly,** *adv.*
**rel·e·vant** (rel′ə-vənt), *adj.* [see RELIEVE], relating to the matter in hand; pertinent. **—rel′e·vance, rel′e·van·cy,** *n.*
**re·li·a·ble** (ri-lī′ə-b'l), *adj.* that can be relied on; dependable. **—re·li′a·bil′i·ty,** *n.***—re·li′a·bly,** *adv.*
**re·li·ance** (re-lī′əns), *n.* 1. trust, dependence, or confidence. 2. what is relied on. **—re·li′ant,** *adj.*
**rel·ic** (rel′ik), *n.* [see RELINQUISH], 1. an object, custom, etc. surviving from the past. 2. a souvenir. 3. *pl.* ruins. 4. a sacred object, as the remains of a saint, reverenced as a memorial.
**rel·ict** (rel′ikt), *n.* [see RELINQUISH], [Rare], a widow.
**re·lief** (ri-lēf′), *n.* 1. a relieving, as of pain, anxiety, a burden, etc. 2. anything that eases tension or offers a pleasing change. 3. aid, esp. by a public agency to the needy. 4. *a*) release from work or duty. *b*) those bringing such release. 5. the projection of sculptured forms from a flat surface. 6. the differences in height, collectively, of land forms, shown as by lines on a map **(relief map)**. **—in relief,** carved or molded so as to project from a surface.
**re·lieve** (ri-lēv′), *v.t.* [-LIEVED, -LIEVING], [< L. *re-*, again + *levare*, to raise], 1. to ease, reduce, as pain, anxiety, etc. 2. to free from pain, distress, a burden, etc. 3. to give or bring aid to. 4. to set free from duty or work by replacing. 5. to make less tedious, etc. by providing a pleasing change. 6. to set off by contrast. **—re·liev′a·ble,** *adj.*
**re·li·gion** (ri-lij′ən), *n.* [< L. *religio*], 1. belief in God or gods to be worshiped, usually expressed in conduct and ritual. 2. any specific system of belief. worship, etc.
**re·li′gious** (-əs), *adj.* 1. devout; pious. 2. of or concerned with religion. 3 conscientiously exact; scrupulous.
**re·lin·quish** (ri-liŋ′kwish), *v.t.* [< L. *re-*, from + *linquere*, leave], 1. to give up, as a plan, or let go, as one's grasp. 2. to surrender (property, a right, etc.). **—re·lin′quish·er,** *n.* **—re·lin′quish·ment,** *n.*
**rel·i·quar·y** (rel′ə-kwer′i), *n.* [*pl.* -IES], [see RELIC], a small box for a relic or relics.
**rel·ish** (rel′ish), *n.* [< OFr. *reles*, something remaining], 1. an appetizing flavor. 2. enjoyment; zest: as, he eats with *relish*. 3. pickles, etc. served as an appetizer with meat, etc. *v.t.* to like; enjoy.
**re·luc·tant** (ri-luk′t'nt), *adj.* [< L. *re-*, against + *luctari*, to struggle], 1. unwilling; disinclined. 2. marked by unwillingness: as, a *reluctant* answer. **—re·luc′tance,** *n.*
**re·ly** (ri-lī′), *v.i.* [-LIED, -LYING], [< L. *re-*, back + *ligare*, bind], to trust; depend (with *on* or *upon*).
**re·main** (ri-mān′), *v.i.* [< L. *re-*, back + *manere*, to stay], 1. to be left over when the rest has been taken away, etc. 2. to stay. 3. to continue: as, he *remained* a cynic. 4. to be left to be dealt with, done, etc.
**re·main′der,** *n.* 1. those remaining. 2. what is left when a part is taken away. 3. what is left when a smaller number is subtracted from a larger. *adj.* left over.
**re·mains′,** *n.pl.* 1. what is left after use, destruction, etc. 2. a dead body.
**re·mand** (ri-mand′), *v.t.* [ult. < L. *re-*, back + *mandare*, to order], to send back, as a prisoner into custody.
**re·mark** (ri-märk′), *v.t. & v.i.* [see RE-MARK, *v.*], to notice, observe, or comment; make (as) an observation. *n.* a brief comment; casual observation.
**re·mark′a·ble,** *adj.* worthy of notice; extraordinary. **—re·mark′a·bly,** *adv.*
**re·me·di·al** (ri-mē′di-əl), *adj.* providing a remedy; corrective. **—re·me′di·al·ly,** *adv.*
**rem·e·dy** (rem′ə-di), *n.* [*pl.* -DIES], [< L. *re-*, again + *mederi*, heal], 1. any medicine or treatment for a disease. 2. something to correct a wrong or evil; relief. *v.t.* [-DIED, -DYING], to cure, correct, etc.
**re·mem·ber** (ri-mem′bẽr), *v.t.* [< L. *re-*, again + *memorare*, bring to mind], 1. to think of again. 2. to bring back to mind by an effort; recall. 3. to be careful not to forget. 4. to mention (a person) to another as sending regards. *v.i.* to bear in mind or call back to mind. **—re·mem′ber·a·ble,** *n.*
**re·mem′brance** (-brəns), *n.* 1. a remembering or being remembered. 2. the power to remember. 3. a souvenir. 4. *pl.* greetings.
**re·mind** (ri-mīnd′), *v.t. & v.i.* to put (a person) in mind (*of* something); cause to remember. **—re·mind′er,** *n.*
**rem·i·nisce** (rem′ə-nis′), *v.i.* [-NISCED, -NISCING], [< *reminiscence*], to think, talk, or write about past events.
**rem·i·nis·cence** (rem′ə-nis′'ns), *n.* [Fr. < L. *re-*, again + *memini*, remember], 1. a remembering. 2. memory. 3. *pl.* an account of remembered events. **—rem′i·nis′cent,** *adj.* **—rem′i·nis′cent·ly,** *adv.*
**re·miss** (ri-mis′), *adj.* [see REMIT], careless; negligent. **—re·miss′ness,** *n.*
**re·mis·sion** (ri-mish′ən), *n.* [see REMIT], 1. pardon; forgiveness. 2. release from a debt, tax, etc. 3. an abating, as of heat or pain.
**re·mit** (ri-mit′), *v.t.* [-MITTED, -MITTING], [< L. *re-*, back + *mittere*, send], 1. to forgive or pardon. 2. to refrain from exacting (a payment), inflicting (punishment), etc. 3. to let slacken. 4. to send or pay (money). *v.i.* 1. to slacken. 2. to send money, as in payment. **—re·mit′tance,** *n.*
**re·mit·tent** (ri-mit′'nt), *adj.* slackening for a while or at intervals, as a fever.
**rem·nant** (rem′nənt), *n.* [see REMAIN], what is left over, as a piece of cloth at the end of a bolt.
**re·mod·el** (rē-mod′'l), *v.t.* [-ELED or -ELLED, -ELING or -ELLING], 1. to model again. 2. to make over; rebuild. **—re·mod′el·er,** *n.*
**re·mon·strate** (ri-mon′strāt), *v.t.* [-STRATED, -STRATING], [< L. *re-*, again + *monstrare*, to show], to say in protest, objection, etc. *v.i.* to protest; object. **—re·mon′strance,** (-strəns), *n.* **—re·mon′strant,** *adj.*
**re·morse** (ri-môrs′), *n.* [< L. *re-*, again + *mordere*, to bite], a torturing sense of guilt

for one's actions. —**re·morse′ful,** *adj.* —**re-morse′less,** *adj.*

**re·mote** (ri-mōt′), *adj.* [< L. *remotus,* removed], 1. distant in space or time. 2. distant in relation, connection, etc. (*from*). 3. distantly related: as, a *remote* cousin. 4. slight: as, a *remote* chance. —**re·mote′ly,** *adv.*

**re·move** (ri-mōōv′), *v.t.* [-MOVED, -MOVING], [see RE- & MOVE], 1. to move (something) from where it is; take away or off. 2. to dismiss, as from office. 3. to get rid of. 4. to kill. *v.i.* to move away, as to another residence. *n.* 1. a removing. 2. a step; interval: as, only one *remove* from war. —**re·mov′a·ble,** *adj.* —**re·mov′al,** *n.*

**re·mu·ner·ate** (ri-mū′nə-rāt′), *v.t.* [-ATED, -ATING], [< L. *re-,* again + *munus,* gift], to pay (a person) for work done, a loss, etc. —**re·mu′ner·a′tion,** *n.* —**re·mu′ner·a′tive,** *adj.*

**Re·mus** (rē′məs), *n.* see **Romulus.**

**ren·ais·sance** (ren′ə-säns′, -zäns′), *n.* [Fr. < *re-,* again + *naître,* be born], 1. a rebirth; revival. 2. [R-], the great revival of art and learning in Europe in the 14th, 15th, and 16th centuries.

**re·nal** (rē′n'l), *adj.* [< L. *renes,* kidneys], of or near the kidneys.

**re·nas·cence** (ri-nas′'ns), *n.* a rebirth; revival. —**re·nas′cent,** *adj.*

**rend** (rend), *v.t. & v.i.* [RENT, RENDING], [AS. *rendan*], to tear or split apart with violence.

**rend·er** (ren′dẽr), *v.t.* [ult. < L. *re(d)-,* back + *dare,* give], 1. to submit, as an account for approval. 2. to give in return or pay as due: as, *render* thanks. 3. to cause to be. 4. to give (aid) or do (a service). 5. to play (music), act (a role), etc. 6. to translate. 7. to melt down; clarify, as lard.

**ren·dez·vous** (rän′də-vōō′), *n.* [*pl.* -VOUS (-vōōz′)], [< Fr. *rendez vous,* betake yourself], 1. a meeting place. 2. an agreement to meet. 3. such a meeting. *v.i. & v.t.* [-VOUSED (-vōōd′), -VOUSING], to assemble, as troops, at a prearranged time and place.

**ren·di·tion** (ren-dish′ən), *n.* a rendering; performance, translation, etc.

**ren·e·gade** (ren′ə-gād′), *n.* [< L. *re-,* again + *negare,* deny], one who abandons his party, principles, etc. to join the opposition; traitor.

**re·nege** (ri-nig′), *v.i.* [-NEGED, -NEGING], [see RENEGADE], 1. to play a card not of the suit called for. 2. [Colloq.], to go back on a promise.

**re·new** (ri-nōō′, -nū′), *v.t.* 1. to make new or fresh again. 2. to re-establish. 3. to resume. 4. to put in a fresh supply of. 5. to give or get an extension of: as, *renew* a lease. —**re·new′a·ble,** *adj.* —**re·new′al,** *n.*

**ren·net** (ren′it), *n.* [ME. < *rennen,* to run], an extract from the stomach lining of calves, etc., used to curdle milk.

**re·nounce** (ri-nouns′), *v.t.* [-NOUNCED, -NOUNCING], [< L. *re-,* back + *nuntiare,* tell], 1. to give up formally (a claim, etc.). 2. to give up, as a habit. 3. to disown. —**re·nounce′ment,** *n.*

**ren·o·vate** (ren′ə-vāt′), *v.t.* [-VATED, -VATING], [< L. *re-,* again + *novus,* new], to make new; repair; restore. —**ren′o·va′tion,** *n.* —**ren′o·va′tor,** *n.*

**re·nown** (ri-noun′), *n.* [< OFr. *re-,* again + *nom(m)er,* to name], fame; great reputation. —**re·nowned′,** *adj.*

**rent** (rent), *n.* [< L. *reddita,* paid], a stated payment at fixed intervals for the use of a house, land, etc. *v.t.* to get or give use of in return for rent. *v.i.* to be let for rent.

**rent** (rent), pt. & pp. of **rend.** *adj.* torn or split. *n.* a tear or rip, as in cloth.

**rent·al** (ren′t'l), *n.* 1. the rate paid as rent. 2. a house, automobile, etc. for rent. *adj.* of or for rent.

**re·nun·ci·a·tion** (ri-nun′si-ā′shən), *n.* a renouncing, as of a right.

**re·or·gan·ize** (rē-ôr′gə-nīz′), *v.t. & v.i.* [-IZED, -IZING], to organize anew, as a business. —**re′or·gan·i·za′tion,** *n.* —**re·or′gan·iz′er,** *n.*

**rep** (rep), *n.* [Fr. *reps* < Eng. *ribs*], a ribbed fabric of silk, wool, etc.: also sp. **repp.**

**Rep.,** 1. Representative. 2. Republican.

**re·paid** (ri-pād′), pt. & pp. of **repay.**

**re·pair** (ri-pâr′), *v.t.* [< L. *re-,* again + *parare,* prepare], 1. to put back in good condition; fix; renew. 2. to make amends for (a wrong, etc.). *n.* 1. a repairing. 2. *usually in pl.* an instance or result of repairing. 3. the state of being repaired: as, keep it in *repair.* —**re·pair′a·ble,** *adj.*

**re·pair** (ri-pâr′), *v.i.* [< L. *re-,* back + *patria,* native land], to go (*to* a place).

**rep·a·ra·ble** (rep′ẽr-ə-b'l), *adj.* that can be repaired. —**rep′a·ra·bly,** *adv.*

**rep·a·ra·tion** (rep′ə-rā′shən), *n.* [see REPAIR (to fix)], 1. a making of amends. 2. *usually pl.* compensation, as for war damage, payable in money, labor, etc.

**rep·ar·tee** (rep′ẽr-tē′), *n.* [< Fr. *re-,* back + *partir,* to part], 1. a quick, witty reply. 2. quick, witty conversation.

**re·past** (ri-past′, -päst′), *n.* [< LL. *re-,* again + *pascere,* to feed], food and drink; a meal.

**re·pa·tri·ate** (rē-pā′tri-āt′), *v.t. & v.i.* [-ATED, -ATING], [< L. *re-,* back + *patria,* native land], to return to the country of birth, citizenship, etc. —**re·pa′tri·a′tion,** *n.*

**re·pay** (ri-pā′), *v.t.* [-PAID, -PAYING], 1. to pay back. 2. to make return to for (a favor, etc.). —**re·pay′a·ble,** *adj.* —**re·pay′ment,** *n.*

**re·peal** (ri-pēl′), *v.t.* [see RE- & APPEAL], to revoke; cancel; annul, as a law. *n.* revocation, abrogation, etc. —**re·peal′a·ble,** *adj.*

**re·peat** (ri-pēt′), *v.t.* [< L. *re-,* again + *petere,* seek], 1. to say again. 2. to recite, as a poem. 3. to say after someone else. 4. to tell to someone else: as, *repeat* a secret. 5. to do, make, play, etc. again. *v.i.* to say or do again. *n.* 1. a repeating. 2. anything said or done again. 3. in *music, a*) a passage to be repeated. *b*) the symbol for this.

**re·peat′ed,** *adj.* said, made, or done again or often. —**re·peat′ed·ly,** *adv.*

**re·pel** (ri-pel′), *v.t.* [-PELLED, -PELLING] [< L. *re-,* back + *pellere,* to drive], 1. to drive or force back. 2. to refuse or reject. 3. to cause dislike in; disgust. 4. to be resistant to. *v.i.* to cause dislike, etc. —**re·pel′ler,** *n.*

**re·pel′lent,** *adj.* 1. repelling. 2. waterproof. *n.* something that repels.

**re·pent** (ri-pent′), *v.i. & v.t.* [< L. *re-,* again + *poena,* punishment], 1. to feel sorry for (a sin, error, etc.). 2. to feel such regret over (an action, intention, etc.) as to change one's mind. —**re·pent′ance,** *n.* —**re·pent′ant,** *adj.*

**re·per·cus·sion** (rē′pẽr-kush′ən), *n.* [see RE- & PERCUSSION], 1. a rebound. 2. reflection, as of sound; echo. 3. a reaction set in motion by some event or action.

**rep·er·toire** (rep′ẽr-twär′), *n.* [< Fr. < L. *reperire,* discover], the stock of plays, songs, etc. that one is prepared to perform.

**rep′er·to′ry** (-tôr′i), *n.* [*pl.* -RIES], a repertoire.

**rep·e·ti·tion** (rep′ə-tish′ən), *n.* [< L. *repetitio*], 1. a repeating. 2. something repeated. —**rep′e·ti′tious,** *adj.*

**re·pine** (ri-pīn′), *v.i.* [-PINED, -PINING], [*re-* + *pine, v.*], to feel or express discontent (*at*).

**re·place** (ri-plās′), *v.t.* [-PLACED, -PLACING], 1. to put back in a former place, condition, etc. 2. to take the place of. 3. to provide an equivalent for. —**re·place′ment,** *n.*

**re·plen·ish** (ri-plen′ish), *v.t.* [< L. *re-,* again + *plenus,* full], 1. to make full or complete again. 2. to supply again. —**re·plen′ish-ment,** *n.*

**re·plete** (ri-plēt′), *adj.* [< L. *re-*, again + *plere*, to fill], 1. filled; plentifully supplied. 2. stuffed, as with food. —**re·ple′tion,** *n.*

**rep·li·ca** (rep′li-kə), *n.* [It. < L.; see REPLY], in *art*, etc., an exact copy.

**re·ply** (ri-plī′), *v.i. & v.t.* [-PLIED, -PLYING], [< L. *re-*, back + *plicare*, to fold], to answer; respond. *n.* [*pl.* -PLIES], an answer.

**re·port** (ri-pôrt′), *v.t.* [< L. *re-*, back + *portare*, carry], 1. to give an account of, as for publication. 2. to carry and repeat (a message, etc.). 3. to announce formally. 4. to denounce (an offense or offender) to one in authority. *v.i.* 1. to make a report. 2. to present oneself, as for work. *n.* 1. rumor. 2. a statement or account. 3. a formal presentation of facts. 4. the noise of an explosion. —**re·port′ed·ly,** *adv.*

**re·port′er,** *n.* one who reports; esp., one who gathers information and writes reports for a newspaper, etc.

**re·pose** (ri-pōz′), *v.t.* [-POSED, -POSING], [< L. *re-*, again + *pausare*, to rest], to lay to rest. *v.i.* 1. to lie at rest. 2. to rest. *n.* 1. *a*) rest. *b*) sleep. 2. composure. 3. peace.

**re·pose** (ri-pōz′), *v.t.* [-POSED, -POSING], [see REPOSITORY], to place (trust, etc. *in* someone). —**re·pos′al,** *n.*

**re·pos·i·to·ry** (ri-poz′ə-tôr′i), *n.* [*pl.* -RIES], [< L. *re-*, back + *ponere*, to place], a box, room, etc. in which things may be put for safekeeping.

**re·pos·sess** (rē′pə-zes′), *v.t.* to get possession of again. —**re′pos·ses′sion,** *n.*

**rep·re·hend** (rep′ri-hend′), *v.t.* [< L. *re-*, back + *prehendere*, take], 1. to reprimand; rebuke. 2. to blame.

**rep′re·hen′si·ble** (-hen′sə-b'l), *adj.* deserving to be reprehended.

**rep′re·hen′sion,** *n.* a reprehending; censure.

**rep·re·sent** (rep′ri-zent′), *v.t.* [see RE- & PRESENT, *v.*], 1. to present to the mind. 2. to present a likeness of. 3. to describe. 4. to stand for; symbolize. 5. to be the equivalent of. 6. to act (a role). 7. to act in place of, esp. by conferred authority. 8. to serve as a specimen, example, etc. of.

**rep′re·sen·ta′tion,** *n.* 1. a representing or being represented. 2. a likeness, picture, etc. 3. *often in pl.* a statement of claims, protest, etc. 4. representatives collectively.

**rep′re·sent′a·tive,** *adj.* 1. representing. 2. of or based on representation of the people by elected delegates. 3. typical. *n.* 1. a type; example. 2. one authorized to act for others. 3. [R-], a member of the lower house of Congress or of a State legislature.

**re·press** (ri-pres′), *v.t.* [see RE- & PRESS (squeeze)], 1. to hold back; restrain. 2. to put down; subdue. 3. in *psychiatry*, to force (painful ideas, etc.) into the unconscious. —**re·pres′sion,** *n.* —**re·pres′sive,** *adj.*

**re·prieve** (ri-prēv′), *v.t.* [-PRIEVED, -PRIEVING], [< Fr. *reprendre*, take back], 1. to postpone the execution of (a condemned person). 2. to give temporary relief to. *n.* a reprieving or being reprieved.

**rep·ri·mand** (rep′rə-mand′), *n.* [< L. *reprimere*, repress], a severe or formal rebuke. *v.t.* to rebuke severely or formally.

**re·pris·al** (ri-prī′z'l), *n.* [see REPREHEND], injury done for injury received; retaliation, esp. in war.

**re·proach** (ri-prōch′), *v.t.* [< L. *re-*, back + *prope*, near], to accuse of a fault; rebuke. *n.* 1. shame, disgrace, etc. incurred. 2. a cause of shame, etc. 3. censure; rebuke.

**rep·ro·bate** (rep′rə-bāt′), *adj.* [< LL. *reprobare*, reprove], depraved; unprincipled. *n.* a depraved person. —**rep′ro·ba′tion,** *n.*

**re·pro·duce** (rē′prə-dōōs′, -dūs′), *v.t.* [-DUCED, -DUCING], to produce again; specif., *a*) to produce by propagation. *b*) to make a copy of. *v.i.* to produce offspring.

**re′pro·duc′tion** (-duk′shən), *n.* 1. a copy; imitation. 2. the process by which animals and plants produce new individuals. —**re′pro·duc′tive,** *adj.*

**re·proof** (ri-prōōf′), *n.* a reproving; rebuke.

**re·prove** (ri-prōōv′), *v.t.* [-PROVED, -PROVING], [see RE- & PROVE], to rebuke; find fault with; censure. —**re·prov′ing·ly,** *adv.*

**rep·tile** (rep′til, -tīl), *n.* [< L. *repere*, creep], a cold-blooded, creeping vertebrate, as a snake, lizard, turtle, etc. —**rep·til·i·an** (rep-til′i-ən), *adj. & n.*

**re·pub·lic** (ri-pub′lik), *n.* [< L. *res publica*, public thing], a state or government in which the power is exercised by representatives elected by citizens eligible to vote.

**re·pub′li·can** (-li-kən), *adj.* 1. of or like a republic. 2. [R-], of or belonging to the Republican Party. *n.* 1. one who favors a republic. 2. [R-], a member of the Republican Party. —**re·pub′li·can·ism,** *n.*

**Republican Party,** one of the two major U.S. political parties.

**re·pu·di·ate** (ri-pū′di-āt′), *v.t.* [-ATED, -ATING], [< L. *repudium*, separation], 1. to disown. 2. to refuse to acknowledge; deny. —**re·pu′di·a′tion,** *n.* —**re·pu′di·a′tor,** *n.*

**re·pug·nant** (ri-pug′nənt), *adj.* [< L. *re-*, back + *pugnare*, fight], 1. contradictory or opposed. 2. causing extreme dislike or aversion; distasteful. —**re·pug′nance,** *n.*

**re·pulse** (ri-puls′), *v.t.* [-PULSED, -PULSING], [see REPEL], 1. to drive back, as an attack. 2. to refuse or reject with discourtesy; rebuff. *n.* 1. a repelling or being repelled. 2. a refusal or rebuff.

**re·pul′sion,** *n.* 1. a repelling or being repelled. 2. strong dislike, distaste, etc.

**re·pul′sive,** *adj.* causing strong dislike or aversion; disgusting. —**re·pul′sive·ness,** *n.*

**rep·u·ta·ble** (rep′yoo-tə-b'l), *adj.* having a good reputation; respectable. —**rep′u·ta·bil′i·ty,** *n.* —**rep′u·ta·bly,** *adv.*

**rep·u·ta·tion** (rep′yoo-tā′shən), *n.* [see REPUTE], 1. estimation in which a person or thing is commonly held. 2. favorable estimation. 3. fame.

**re·pute** (ri-pūt′), *v.t.* [-PUTED, -PUTING], [< L. *re-*, again + *putare*, think], to consider to be as specified: as, he is *reputed* to be rich. *n.* 1. reputation. 2. good reputation.

**re·quest** (ri-kwest′), *n.* [see REQUIRE], 1. an asking for something. 2. what is asked for. 3. the state of being asked for; demand. *v.t.* 1. to ask for. 2. to ask (a person) to do something.

**Re·qui·em, re·qui·em** (rē′kwi-əm, rek′wi-), *n.* [L., rest], in the *R.C. Church*, 1. a Mass for the repose of the dead. 2. its musical setting.

**re·quire** (ri-kwīr′), *v.t.* [-QUIRED, -QUIRING], [< L. *re-*, again + *quaerere*, ask], 1. to insist upon; demand; order. 2. to need: as, man *requires* food. —**re·quire′ment,** *n.*

**req·ui·site** (rek′wə-zit), *adj.* [see REQUIRE], required; necessary; indispensable. *n.* something requisite. —**req′ui·site·ly,** *adv.*

**req·ui·si·tion** (rek′wə-zish′ən), *n.* 1. a requiring; demanding. 2. a formal written order, as for equipment. *v.t.* to demand or take, as by authority.

**re·quite** (ri-kwīt′), *v.t.* [-QUITED, -QUITING], [*re-* + *quite*, obs. var. of *quit*], to repay for (a benefit, service, etc., or an injury, wrong, etc.). —**re·quit′al,** *n.* —**re·quit′er,** *n.*

**re·route** (rē-rōōt′, -rout′), *v.t.* [-ROUTED, -ROUTING], to send by a new or different route.

**re·scind** (ri-sind′), *v.t.* [< L. *re-*, back + *scindere*, to cut], to annul; cancel, as a law.

**res·cue** (res′kū), *v.t.* [-CUED, -CUING], [ult. < L. *re-*, again + *ex-*, off + *quatere*, to shake], to free or save from danger, evil, etc. *n.* a rescuing. —**res′cu·er,** *n.*

**re·search** (ri-sũrch′, rē′sũrch), ***n.*** [see RE- & SEARCH], *often in pl.* careful, systematic study and investigation in some field of knowledge. —**re·search′er,** ***n.***

**re·sec·tion** (ri-sek′shən), ***n.*** [< L. *re-*, back + *secare*, to cut], the surgical removal of part of an organ, bone, etc.

**re·sem·blance** (ri-zem′bləns), ***n.*** similarity of appearance, character, etc.; likeness.

**re·sem·ble** (ri-zem′b'l), ***v.t.*** [-BLED, -BLING], [ult. < L. *re-*, again + *simulare*, to feign], to be like or similar to.

**re·sent** (ri-zent′), ***v.t.*** [< L. *re-*, again + *sentire*, feel], to feel or show displeasure and indignation at (a person, act, etc.). —**re·sent′ful.** ***adj.*** —**re·sent′ment,** ***n.***

**res·er·va·tion** (rez′ẽr-vā′shən), ***n.*** 1. a reserving; withholding. 2. something reserved or withheld. 3. a limiting condition. 4. public land set aside for some special use, as for Indians. 5. a reserving, as of a hotel room, train ticket, etc., until called for.

**re·serve** (ri-zũrv′), ***v.t.*** [-SERVED, -SERVING], [see RE- & SERVE], 1. to keep back; set apart for later or special use. 2. to keep back for oneself. ***n.*** 1. something kept back or stored up, as for later use. 2. a limitation: as, without *reserve.* 3. the practice of keeping one's thoughts, feelings, etc. to oneself. 4. reticence; silence. 5. *pl.* troops not on active duty but subject to call. —**in reserve,** reserved for later use.

**re·served′,** ***adj.*** 1. kept in reserve; set apart. 2. reticent; self-restrained.

**res·er·voir** (rez′ẽr-vwär′, -vôr′), ***n.*** [< Fr.; see RESERVE], 1. a place where water is collected and stored for use. 2. a large supply or store of something.

**re·set** (rē-set′), ***v.t.*** [-SET, -SETTING], to set again, as a broken arm, type, etc.

**re·side** (ri-zīd′), ***v.i.*** [-SIDED, -SIDING], [< L. *re-*, back + *sedere*, sit], 1. to dwell for some time; live (*in* or *at*). 2. to be present or inherent (*in*): said of qualities, etc.

**res·i·dence** (rez′i-dəns), ***n.*** 1. a residing. 2. the place where one resides; home. —**res′i·den′tial** (-den′shəl), ***adj.***

**res′i·dent,** ***adj.*** residing; esp., living in a place while working there: as, a *resident* surgeon. ***n.*** one who lives in a place, not a visitor or transient.

**re·sid·u·al** (ri-zij′o͞o-əl), ***adj.*** of or being a residue; remaining. ***n.*** a remainder.

**res·i·due** (rez′ə-do͞o′, -dū′), ***n.*** [< L. *residuus*, remaining], that which is left after part is removed; remainder.

**re·sign** (ri-zīn′), ***v.t. & v.i.*** [< L. *re-* back + *signare*, to sing], to give up (a claim, an office, etc.). —**resign oneself,** to submit.

**res·ig·na·tion** (rez′ig-nā′shən), ***n.*** 1. the act of resigning. 2. formal notice of this. 3. patient submission.

**re·signed** (ri-zīnd′), ***adj.*** feeling or showing resignation; submissive.

**re·sil·i·ent** (ri-zil′i-ənt), ***adj.*** [< L. *re-*, back + *salire*, to jump], 1. springing back into shape or position; elastic. 2. recovering strength, spirits, etc. quickly. —**re·sil′i·ence, re·sil′i·en·cy,** ***n.***

**res·in** (rez′'n), ***n.*** [L. *resina*], 1. a substance exuded from various plants and trees, as the pines, and used in medicines, varnish, etc. 2. rosin. —**res′in·ous, res′in·y,** ***adj.***

**re·sist** (ri-zist′), ***v.t.*** [< L. *re-*, back + *sistere*, to set], 1. to withstand; fend off. 2. to oppose actively; fight against. ***v.i.*** to oppose or withstand something. —**re·sist′i·ble,** ***adj.***

**re·sist′ance,** ***n.*** 1. a resisting. 2. power to resist; specif., the ability of an organism to ward off disease. 3. opposition of some force, thing, etc. to another, as to the passage of an electric current. —**re·sist′ant,** ***adj.***

**re·sis′tor,** ***n.*** a device used in an electric circuit to provide resistance.

**res·o·lute** (rez′ə-lo͞ot′), ***adj.*** [see RE- & SOLVE], fixed and firm in purpose; determined. —**res′o·lute′ly,** ***adv.***

**res′o·lu′tion,** ***n.*** 1. the act or result of resolving something. 2. the thing determined upon; decision as to future action. 3. a resolute quality of mind. 4. a formal statement of opinion or determination by an assembly. 5. a solving; solution.

**re·solve** (ri-zolv′), ***v.t.*** [-SOLVED, -SOLVING], [see RE- & SOLVE], 1. to break up into separate parts; analyze. 2. to determine; reach as a decision. 3. to solve, as a problem. 4. to decide by vote. ***v.i.*** 1. to be resolved (*into* or *to*), as by analysis. 2. to determine; come to a decision. ***n.*** 1. firm determination. 2. a formal resolution.

**re·solved′,** ***adj.*** resolute; determined.

**res·o·nant** (rez′ə-nənt), ***adj.*** [< L. *resonare*, resound], 1. resounding; re-echoing. 2. intensifying sound: as, *resonant* walls. 3. vibrant; sonorous, as a voice. —**res′o·nance,** ***n.*** —**res′o·nant·ly,** ***adv.***

**re·sort** (ri-zôrt′), ***v.i.*** [< OFr. *re-*, again + *sortir*, go out], 1. to go; esp., to go often. 2. to have recourse, as for help: as, to *resort* to threats. ***n.*** 1. a place to which people go often, as on vacation. 2. a source of help, support, etc.; recourse.

**re·sound** (ri-zound′), ***v.i.*** [< L. *resonare*], to make a loud, echoing sound; reverberate. —**re·sound′ing,** ***adj.*** —**re·sound′ing·ly,** ***adv.***

**re·source** (ri-sôrs′, rē′sôrs), ***n.*** [< OFr. *re-*, again + *sourdre*, spring up], 1. something that lies ready for use or can be drawn upon in an emergency. 2. *pl.* wealth; assets. 3. resourcefulness.

**re·source′ful,** ***adj.*** able to deal effectively with problems, etc. —**re·source′ful·ness,** ***n.***

**re·spect** (ri-spekt′), ***v.t.*** [< L. *re-*, back + *specere*, look at], 1. to feel or show honor or esteem for. 2. to show consideration for. 3. to concern; relate to. ***n.*** 1. honor or esteem. 2. consideration: as, *respect* for her grief. 3. *pl.* expressions of respect. 4. a particular detail: as, in this *respect* it's bad. 5. reference; relation: as, with *respect* to his job.—**re·spect′ful,** ***adj.***—**re·spect′ful·ly,** ***adv.***

**re·spect′a·ble,** ***adj.*** 1. worthy of respect or esteem. 2. having a good reputation. 3. of moderate quality or size. —**re·spect′a·bil′i·ty,** ***n.*** — **re·spect′a·bly,** ***adv.***

**re·spect′ing,** ***prep.*** concerning; about.

**re·spec·tive** (ri-spek′tiv), ***adj.*** relating individually to each one.

**re·spec′tive·ly,** ***adv.*** with respect to each in the order named: as, the first and second prizes went to John and Mary, *respectively.*

**res·pi·ra·tion** (res′pə-rā′shən), ***n.*** act or process of breathing. —**re·spir·a·to·ry** (ri-spīr′ə-tôr′i, res′pẽr-), ***adj.***

**res′pi·ra′tor,** ***n.*** 1. a mask, as of gauze, to prevent the inhaling of harmful substances. 2. an apparatus to maintain breathing by artificial means.

**re·spire** (ri-spīr′), ***v.t. & v.i.*** [-SPIRED, -SPIRING], [< L. *re-*, back + *spirare*, breathe], to breathe.

**res·pite** (res′pit), ***n.*** [see RESPECT], 1. a delay or postponement. 2. temporary relief, as from pain, work, etc.; rest.

**re·splend·ent** (ri-splen′dənt), ***adj.*** [< L. *re-*, again + *splendere*, to shine], shining brightly; dazzling. —**re·splend′ence,** ***n.***

**re·spond** (ri-spond′), ***v.i.*** [< L. *re-*, back + *spondere*, to pledge], 1. to answer; reply. 2. to react, as to a stimulus. ***v.t.*** to reply.

**re·spond′ent,** ***adj.*** responding. ***n.*** 1. one who responds. 2. in *law*, a defendant.

**re·sponse** (ri-spons′), ***n.*** 1. something said or done in responding; reply. 2. words sung or spoken by the congregation or choir in answer to the clergyman. 3. any reaction to a stimulus.

**re·spon·si·bil·i·ty** (ri-spon'sə-bil'ə-ti), *n.* [*pl.* -TIES], 1. a being responsible; obligation. 2. a thing or person for whom one is responsible.

**re·spon'si·ble** (-sə-b'l), *adj.* 1. obliged to account (*for*); answerable (*to*). 2. involving obligation or duties. 3. accountable for one's behavior or for an act. 4. trustworthy; dependable. —**re·spon'si·bly**, *adv.*

**re·spon·sive** (ri-spon'siv), *adj.* reacting readily, as to appeal. —**re·spon'sive·ness**, *n.*

**rest** (rest), *n.* [AS.], 1. sleep or repose. 2. ease or inactivity after exertion. 3. relief from anything distressing, tiring, etc. 4. absence of motion. 5. a resting place. 6. a support, as for a gun. 7. in *music*, an interval of silence between tones, or a symbol for this. *v.i.* 1. to get ease and refreshment by sleeping or by ceasing from work. 2. to be at ease. 3. to be or become still. 4. to be supported; lie or lean (*in*, *on*, etc.). 5. to be found: as, the fault *rests* with him. 6. to rely (*on* or *upon*); depend. *v.t.* 1. to cause to rest. 2. to put for ease, etc.: as, *rest* your head here.

**rest** (rest), *n.* [< L. *restare*, remain], 1. what is left; remainder. 2. [construed as pl.], those that are left. *v.i.* to go on being: as, *rest* assured.

**res·tau·rant** (res'tə-rənt, -ränt'), *n.* [Fr.; see RESTORE], a place where meals can be bought and eaten.

**res·tau·ra·teur** (res'tə-rə-tũr'), *n.* [Fr.], one who owns or operates a restaurant.

**rest·ful** (rest'fəl), *adj.* 1. full of or giving rest. 2. quiet; tranquil. —**rest'ful·ly**, *adv.*

**res·ti·tu·tion** (res'tə-tōō'shən, -tū'-), *n.* [< L. *re-*, again + *statuere*, set up], 1. a giving back of something that has been lost or taken away; restoration. 2. payment for loss or damage; reimbursement.

**res·tive** (res'tiv), *adj.* [< OFr. *rester*, remain], 1. nervous or impatient under restraint; restless. 2. unruly.

**rest'less,** *adj.* 1. unable to relax; uneasy. 2. giving no rest; disturbed: as, a *restless* sleep. 3. rarely quiet or still; active.

**res·to·ra·tion** (res'tə-rā'shən), *n.* 1. a restoring or being restored. 2. something restored.

**re·stor·a·tive** (ri-stôr'ə-tiv), *adj.* restoring health, consciousness, etc.

**re·store** (ri-stôr'), *v.t.* [-STORED, -STORING], [< L. *re-*, again + *staurare*, make strong], 1. to give back (something taken, lost, etc.). 2. to return to a former or normal state, or to a position, rank, etc. 3. to bring back to health, consciousness, etc.

**re·strain** (ri-strān'), *v.t.* [< L. *re-*, back + *stringere*, draw tight], to hold back from action; check; curb. —**re·strain'a·ble**, *adj.*

**re·straint** (ri-strānt'), *n.* 1. a restraining or being restrained. 2. a means of restraining. 3. confinement. 4. control of emotions, etc.

**re·strict** (ri-strikt'), *v.t.* [see RESTRAIN], to keep within limits; confine; limit. —**re·strict'ed**, *adj.* —**re·stric'tion**, *n.*

**re·stric'tive,** *adj.* 1. restricting. 2. in *grammar*, designating a subordinate clause or phrase felt as limiting the application of the word it modifies, and not set off by commas (e.g., a man *with money* is needed).

**rest'-room',** *n.* a room (in a public building) equipped with toilets, washbowls, etc.: also **rest room.**

**re·sult** (ri-zult'), *v.i.* [< L. *resultare*, to rebound], 1. to happen as an effect of some cause. 2. to end as a consequence (*in* something). *n.* 1. anything that issues as an effect. 2. the number, etc. obtained by a mathematical calculation. —**re·sult'ant**, *adj.*

**re·sume** (ri-zōōm', -zūm'), *v.t.* [-SUMED, -SUMING], [< L. *re-*, again + *sumere*, take], 1. to take or occupy again. 2. to continue after interruption. *v.i.* to proceed after interruption. —**re·sump·tion** (ri-zump'shən) *n.*

**ré·su·mé** (rā'zoo-mā', rez'yoo-), *n.* [Fr.; see RESUME], a summary.

**re·sur·gent** (ri-sũr'jənt), *adj.* rising or tending to rise again. —**re·sur'gence**, *n.*

**res·ur·rect** (rez'ə-rekt'), *v.t.* [< *resurrection*], 1. to bring back to life. 2. to bring back into use, etc. —**res'ur·rect'or**, *n.*

**res'ur·rec'tion,** *n.* [< L. *resurgere*, rise again], 1. a rising from the dead. 2. a coming back into use, etc.; revival. 3. the state of having risen from the dead. —**the Resurrection**, in *Christian theology*, the rising of Jesus from the dead.

**re·sus·ci·tate** (ri-sus'ə-tāt'), *v.t. & v.i.* [-TATED, -TATING], [< L. *re-*, again + *suscitare*, revive], to revive, as a person apparently dead, in a faint, etc. —**re·sus'ci·ta'tion**, *n.*

**re·tail** (rē'tāl), *n.* [< OFr. *re-*, again + *tailler*, to cut], the sale of goods in small quantities directly to the consumer. *adj.* of or engaged in such sale. *v.t. & v.i.* to sell or be sold at retail. —**re'tail·er**, *n.*

**re·tain** (ri-tān'), *v.t.* [< L. *re-*, back + *tenere*, to hold], 1. to keep in possession, use, etc. 2. to keep in mind. 3. to engage (a lawyer) by paying a fee. —**re·tain'a·ble**, *adj.*

**re·tain'er,** *n.* 1. a person or thing that retains. 2. a person serving someone of rank or wealth. 3. a fee paid to engage a lawyer's services.

**re·take** (rē-tāk'), *v.t.* [-TOOK, -TAKEN, -TAKING], 1. to take again; recapture. 2. to photograph again. *n.* (rē'tāk'), a scene, etc. photographed again.

**re·tal·i·ate** (ri-tal'i-āt'), *v.i.* [-ATED, -ATING], [< L. *re-*, back + *talio*, punishment in kind], to return like for like, esp. injury for injury. —**re·tal'i·a'tion**, *n.* —**re·tal'i·a·to'ry** (-ə-tôr'i), **re·tal'i·a'tive**, *adj.*

**re·tard** (ri-tärd'), *v.t.* [< L. *re-*, back + *tardare*, hinder], to hinder, delay, or slow the progress of. *v.i.* to be delayed. —**re·tar·da·tion** (rē'tär-dā'shən), *n.*

**retch** (rech), *v.i.* [AS. *hræcan*, to spit], to make a straining, involuntary effort to vomit.

**re·ten·tion** (ri-ten'shən), *n.* 1. a retaining or being retained. 2. capacity for retaining. 3. memory. —**re·ten'tive**, *adj.*

**ret·i·cent** (ret'ə-s'nt), *adj.* [< L. *re-*, again + *tacere*, be silent], disinclined to speak; taciturn. —**ret'i·cence**, *n.*

**ret·i·na** (ret''n-ə), *n.* [*pl.* -NAS, -NAE (-ē')], [prob. < L. *rete*, a net], the innermost coat of the back part of the eyeball, on which the image is formed. —**ret'i·nal**, *adj.*

**ret·i·nue** (ret''n-ōō', -i-nū'), *n.* [see RETAIN], a group of persons in attendance on a person of rank.

**re·tire** (ri-tīr'), *v.i.* [-TIRED, -TIRING], [< Fr. *re-*, back + *tirer*, draw], 1. to withdraw to a secluded place. 2. to go to bed. 3. to retreat, as in battle. 4. to withdraw from business, active service, etc., esp. because of age. *v.t.* 1. to withdraw, as troops. 2. to take out of circulation, as bonds. 3. to remove from a position or office: as, to *retire* a general. 4. in *baseball*, to put out (a batter, side, etc.). —**re·tire'ment**, *n.*

**re·tir'ing,** *adj.* reserved; modest; shy.

**re·tort** (ri-tôrt'), *v.t.* [< L. *re-*, back + *torquere*, to twist], 1. to turn (an insult, etc.) back upon its originator. 2. to say in reply. *v.i.* to make a sharp or witty reply. *n.* a sharp or witty reply; sharp retaliation.

**re·tort** (ri-tôrt'), *n.* [< ML. *retorta*; see prec.], a glass container in which substances are distilled or decomposed by heat.

**re·touch** (rē-tuch'), *v.t.* to touch up details in (a painting, photograph, etc.) so as to improve or change it.

**re·trace** (ri-trās'), *v.t.* [-TRACED, -TRACING],

[see RE- & TRACE], to go back over again: as, he *retraced* his steps.

**re·tract** (ri-trakt′), *v.t. & v.i.* [< L. *re-*, back + *trahere*, draw], 1. to draw back or in. 2. to withdraw (a statement, charge, etc.). —**re·tract′a·ble,** *adj.* —**re·trac′tion,** *n.*

**re·trac′tile** (-t'l), *adj.* [Fr.], that can be drawn back or in, as claws.

**re·tread** (rē′tred′), *v.t.* [-TREADED, -TREADING], to recap. *n.* (rē′tred′), a recap.

**re·treat** (ri-trēt′), *n.* [< L. *re-*, back + *trahere*, draw], 1 a withdrawal, or giving ground. 2. a safe, quiet place. 3. a period of seclusion, esp. for contemplation. 4. *a*) the forced withdrawal of troops under attack. *b*) a signal for this. *c*) a signal by drum or bugle at sunset for lowering the national flag. *v.i.* to withdraw; go back.

**re·trench** (ri-trench′), *v.t. & v.i.* [see RE- & TRENCH], to cut down; reduce (expenses); economize. —**re·trench′ment,** *n.*

**ret·ri·bu·tion** (ret′rə-bū′shən), *n.* [< L. *re-*, back + *tribuere*, to pay], deserved reward or, esp., punishment. —**re·trib·u·tive** (ri-trib′-yoo-tiv), **re·trib′u·to′ry** (-tôr′i), *adj.*

**re·trieve** (ri-trēv′), *v.t.* [-TRIEVED, -TRIEVING], [< OFr. *re-*, again + *trouver*, find], 1. to get back; recover. 2. to restore: as, he *retrieved* his spirits. 3. to make amends for (a loss, etc.). 4. to find and bring back (killed or wounded game): said of hunting dogs. *v.i.* to retrieve game.

**re·triev·er,** *n.* 1. one who retrieves. 2. a dog trained to retrieve game.

**retro-,** [< L.], a combining form meaning *backward, back, behind.*

**ret·ro·ac·tive** (ret′rō-ak′tiv), *adj.* having effect on things done prior to its enactment, etc., as a law. —**ret′ro·ac′tive·ly,** *adv.*

**ret·ro·fire** (ret′rə-fīr′). *v.t.* [-FIRED, -FIRING], to fire (a retrorocket).

**ret·ro·grade** (ret′rə-grād′), *adj.* [see RETRO- & GRADE], 1. moving backward. 2. going back to a worse condition. *v.i.* [-GRADED, -GRADING], 1. to go backward. 2. to become worse.

**ret·ro·gress** (ret′rə-gres′), *v.i.* [see RETROGRADE], to move backward, esp. into a worse condition. —**ret′ro·gres′sion,** *n.*

**ret·ro·rock·et, ret·ro-rock·et** (ret′rō-rok′-it), *n.* a small rocket, as on a spacecraft, that produces thrust in a backward direction, as for reducing speed for landing.

**ret·ro·spect** (ret′rə-spekt′), *n.* [< L. *retro-*, + *specere*, to look], contemplation of the past. —**ret′ro·spec′tion,** *n.* —**ret′ro·spec′tive,** *adj.* —**ret′ro·spec′tive·ly,** *adv.*

**re·turn** (ri-tũrn′), *v.i.* [see RE- & TURN], 1. to go or come back. 2. to reply. *v.t.* 1. to bring, send, or put back. 2. to do in reciprocation: as, to *return* a visit. 3. to yield, as a profit. 4. to report officially. 5. to elect or re-elect. *n.* 1. a coming or going back. 2. a bringing, sending, or putting back. 3. something returned. 4. a recurrence. 5. repayment; requital. 6. *often in pl.* yield or profit, as from investments. 7. a reply. 8. an official report: as, election *returns.* *adj.* 1. of or for a return. 2. given, sent, done, etc. in return. —**in return,** as a return. —**re·turn′a·ble,** *adj.*

**re·un·ion** (re-ūn′yən), *n.* a coming together again, as after separation.

**re·u·nite** (rē′yoo-nīt′), *v.t. & v.i.* [-NITED, -NITING], to unite again.

**rev** (rev), *v.t. & v.i.* [REVVED, REVVING], [Colloq.], to change the rate of revolutions of (a motor): usually in *rev up*, to accelerate.

**Rev.,** [*pl.* REVS.], Reverend.

**re·vamp** (rē-vamp′), *v.t.* to vamp again; specif., to renovate; redo.

**re·veal** (ri-vēl′), *v.t.* [< L. *re-*, back + *velum*, veil], 1. to make known (something hidden or secret). 2. to expose to view.

**re·veil·le** (rev′ə-li), *n.* [< Fr. < L. *re-*, again + *vigilare*, to watch], a signal on a bugle, drum, etc. in the morning to waken soldiers or sailors.

**rev·el** (rev′'l), *v.i.* [-ELED or -ELLED, -ELING or -ELLING], [see REBEL], 1. to be noisily festive. 2. to take much pleasure (*in*). *n.* merrymaking. —**rev′el·ry** [*pl.*-RIES], *n.*

**rev·e·la·tion** (rev′ə-lā′shən), *n.* 1. a revealing. 2. something disclosed; esp., a striking disclosure. 3. in *theology*, God's disclosure of himself to man. 4. [R-], *also pl.* the last book of the New Testament.

**re·venge** (ri-venj′), *v.t.* [-VENGED, -VENGING], [< OFr. *re-*, again + *vengier*, take vengeance], to inflict harm in return for (an injury, etc.). *n.* 1. a revenging. 2. what is done in revenging. 3. desire to take vengeance. —**re·venge′ful,** *adj.*

**rev·e·nue** (rev′ə-nōō′, -nū′), *n.* [< OFr. *revenu*, returned], income, esp. of a government from taxes, duties, etc.

**re·ver·ber·ate** (ri-vũr′bə-rāt′), *v.t. & v.i.* [-ATED, -ATING], [< L. *re-*, again + *verberare*, to beat], to throw back (sound); re-echo. —**re·ver′ber·a′tion,** *n.*

**re·vere** (ri-vêr′), *v.t.* [-VERED, -VERING], [< L. *re-*, again + *vereri*, to fear], to regard with deep respect, love, etc.

**rev·er·ence** (rev′ẽr-əns), *n.* a feeling of deep respect, love, and awe. *v.t.* [-ENCED, -ENCING], to revere.

**rev·er·end** (rev′ẽr-ənd), *adj.* worthy of reverence: used [usually R-], as a title of respect for a clergyman.

**rev′er·ent,** *adj.* feeling or showing reverence: also **rev′er·en′tial** (-ə-ren′shəl).

**rev·er·ie** (rev′ẽr-i), *n.* [< Fr. *rêver*, to dream], 1. daydreaming. 2. a fanciful notion. Also sp. **revery** [*pl.* -IES].

**re·vers** (rə-vêr′, vâr′), *n.* [*pl.* -VERS (-vêrz′, -vârz′)], [Fr.; see REVERSE], a part (of a garment) turned back to show the reverse side, as a lapel: also **re·vere** (ri-vêr′).

**re·verse** (ri-vũrs′), *adj.* [see REVERT], 1. turned backward; opposite or contrary. 2. causing movement in the opposite direction. *n.* 1. the opposite or contrary. 2. the back of a coin, medal, etc. 3. a change from good fortune to bad. 4. a mechanism for reversing, as a gear on a machine. *v.t.* [-VERSED, -VERSING], 1. to turn about, upside down, or inside out. 2. to change to the opposite. 3. to revoke or annul (a decision, etc.). *v.i.* to go or turn in the opposite direction. —**re·ver′sal** (-vũr′s'l), *n.* —**re·vers′i·ble,** *adj.*

**re·ver·sion** (ri-vũr′zhən), *n.* act or instance of reverting.

**re·vert** (ri-vũrt′), *v.i.* [< L. *re-*, back + *vertere*, to turn], 1. to go back, as to a former state, practice, etc. 2. in *biology*, to return to an earlier type. 3. in *law*, to go back to a former owner or his heirs.

**re·view** (ri-vū′), *n.* [< L. *re-*, again + *videre*, see], 1. a viewing or studying again. 2. a general survey or report. 3. a looking back, as on past events. 4. a re-examination, as of the decision of a lower court. 5. a critical discussion of a book, play, etc. 6. a formal inspection, as of troops on parade. *v.t.* 1. to study again. 2. to look back on. 3. to survey. 4. to inspect formally, as troops. 5. to write a critical discussion of (a book, etc.). —**re·view′er,** *n.*

**re·vile** (ri-vil′), *v.t. & v.i.* [-VILED, -VILING], [see RE- & VILE], to use abusive language (to or about). —**re·vile′ment,** *n.*

**re·vise** (ri-vīs′), *v.t.* [-VISED, -VISING], [< L. *re-*, back + *visere*, to survey], 1. to read over carefully, as a manuscript, etc., to correct and improve. 2. to change or amend. —**re·vi·sion** (ri-vizh′ən), *n.*

**re·viv·al** (ri-vī′v'l), *n.* 1. a reviving or being

revived. 2. a bringing or coming back into use, being, etc. 3. a new presentation of an earlier play, etc. 4. restoration to vigor or activity. 5. a stirring up of religious faith. 6. a meeting aimed at this, with fervid preaching, etc.; in full, **revival meeting.**

**re·viv′al·ist,** *n.* one who promotes or conducts religious revivals.

**re·vive** (ri-vīv′), *v.i. & v.t.* [-VIVED, -VIVING], [< L. *re-*, again + *vivere*, to live], 1. to return to life or consciousness. 2. to return to health and vigor. 3. to bring back or come back into use or attention.

**re·voke** (ri-vōk′), *v.t.* [-VOKED, -VOKING], [< L. *re-*, back + *vocare*, to call], to withdraw, repeal, or cancel, as a law. **—rev·o·ca·ble** (rev′ə-kə-b'l), **re·vok′a·ble,** *adj.* **—rev′o·ca′tion** (-kā′shən), *n.*

**re·volt** (ri-vōlt′), *n.* [see REVOLVE], a rebelling against the government or any authority. *v.i.* 1. to rebel against authority. 2. to be disgusted (with *at, against,* or *from*). *v.t.* to disgust. **—re·volt′ing,** *adj.*

**rev·o·lu·tion** (rev′ə-lōō′shən), *n.* [see REVOLVE], 1. movement of a body in an orbit. 2. a turning around a center or axis; rotation. 3. a complete cycle. 4. a complete change. 5. complete overthrow of a government, social system, etc. **—rev′o·lu′tion·ar′y,** *adj. & n.* [*pl.* -IES] **—rev′o·lu′tion·ist,** *n.*

**Revolutionary War,** the war (1775–1783), by which the American colonies won their independence from England.

**rev′o·lu′tion·ize′** (-īz′), *v.t.* [-IZED, -IZING], to make a drastic change in.

**re·volve** (ri-volv′), *v.t.* [-VOLVED, -VOLVING], [< L. *re-*, back + *volvere*, to roll], 1. to turn over in the mind. 2. to cause to travel in orbit. 3. to cause to rotate. *v.i.* 1. to move in an orbit. 2. to rotate. 3. to recur at intervals. **—re·volv′a·ble,** *adj.*

**re·volv′er,** *n.* a pistol with a revolving cylinder holding several cartridges.

**re·vue** (ri-vū′), *n.* [Fr.; see REVIEW], a musical show with skits, dances, etc., often parodying recent events, etc.

**re·vul·sion** (ri-vul′shən), *n.* [< L. *re-*, back + *velere*, to pull], an abrupt, strong reaction; esp., disgust.

**re·ward** (ri-wôrd′), *n.* [see REGARD], 1. something given in return for something done. 2. money offered, as for capturing a criminal. *v.t.* to give a reward to (someone) for (service, etc.). **—re·ward′a·ble,** *adj.*

**re·word** (rē-wûrd′), *v.t.* 1. to change the wording of. 2. to state again.

**re·write** (rē-rīt′), *v.t. & v.i.* [-WROTE, -WRITTEN, -WRITING], 1. to write again. 2. to revise. 3. in *journalism,* to write (news turned in) for publication.

**RFD, R.F.D.,** Rural Free Delivery.

**rhap·so·dize** (rap′sə-dīz′), *v.i. & v.t.* [-DIZED, -DIZING], to speak, write, etc. in a rhapsodical manner. **—rhap′so·dist,** *n.*

**rhap′so·dy** (-di), *n.* [*pl.* -DIES], [< Gr. *rhaptein*, stitch together + *ōidē*, song], 1. any ecstatic or enthusiastic speech or writing. 2. in *music,* an instrumental composition of free, irregular form, suggesting improvisation. **—rhap·sod′i·cal** (-sod′i-k'l), **rhapsod′ic,** *adj.* **—rhap·sod′i·cal·ly,** *adv.*

**rhe·a** (rē′ə), *n.* [< *Rhea*, Gr. goddess], a large S. American nonflying bird.

**rhe·o·stat** (rē′ə-stat′), *n.* [< Gr. *rheos*, current + *statos*, standing still], a device for regulating strength of an electric current by varying the resistance without opening the circuit.

**rhe·sus (monkey)** (rē′səs), [< Gr. proper name], a small, brownish monkey of India: used in medical experiments.

**rhet·o·ric** (ret′ə-rik), *n.* [< Gr. *rhētōr*, orator], 1. the art of using words effectively; esp., the art of prose composition. 2. artificial eloquence. **—rhe·tor·i·cal** (ri-tôr′i-k'l), *adj.* **—rhet′o·ri′cian** (-rish′ən), *n.*

**rhetorical question,** a question asked only for rhetorical effect, no answer being expected.

**rheum** (rōōm), *n.* [< Gr. *rheuma*, a flow], watery discharge from the eyes, nose, etc., as in a cold. **—rheum′y** [-IER, -IEST], *adj.*

**rheumatic fever,** an infectious disease, usually of children, with fever, inflammation of the heart valves, etc.

**rheu·ma·tism** (rōō′mə-tiz'm), *n.* [see RHEUM], a painful condition of the joints and muscles. **—rheu·mat′ic** (-mat′ik), *adj. & n.* **—rheu′ma·toid′** (-toid′), *adj.*

**Rh factor,** [first discovered in *rh*esus monkeys], an agglutinating factor, usually present in human blood: people who have this factor are *Rh positive*; those who do not are *Rh negative.*

**rhine·stone** (rīn′stōn′), *n.* an artificial gem of colorless, bright glass or paste.

**rhi·ni·tis** (rī-nī′tis), *n.* [< Gr. *rhis*, nose; + *-itis*], inflammation of the nasal mucous membrane.

**rhi·no** (rī′nō), *n.* [*pl.* -NOS], [Colloq.], a rhinoceros.

**rhi·noc·er·os** (rī-nos′ẽr-əs), *n.* [< Gr. *rhis*, nose + *keras*, horn], a large, thick-skinned, plant-eating mammal of Africa and Asia, with one or two upright horns on the snout.

**rhi·zome** (rī′zōm), *n.* [Gr. *rhiza*, a root], a horizontal, rootlike stem, which usually sends out roots below and leafy shoots above the ground.

**rho** (rō), *n.* the seventeenth letter of the Greek alphabet (Ρ, ρ).

**rho·do·den·dron** (rō′də-den′drən), *n.* [< Gr. *rhodon*, rose + *dendron*, tree], a tree or shrub, usually evergreen, with pink, white, or purple flowers.

**rhom·boid** (rom′boid), *n.* [see RHOMBUS & -OID], a parallelogram with oblique angles and only the opposite sides equal.

**rhom·bus** (rom′bəs), *n.* [*pl.* -BUSES, -BI (-bī)], [< Gr. *rhombos*], an equilateral parallelogram with oblique angles: also **rhomb.**

**rhu·barb** (rōō′bärb), *n.* [< Gr. *rhēon*, plant from the *Rha* (the Volga River) + *barbaron*, foreign], 1. a plant with large leaves and fleshy, acid leafstalks. 2. the leafstalks made into a sauce or used in pies. 3. [Slang], a heated argument.

**rhyme** (rīm), *n.* [prob. < L. *rhythmus*, rhythm], 1. correspondence of end sounds in lines of verse or in words. 2. poetry or (a) verse employing this. 3. a word that rhymes with another. *v.i.* [RHYMED, RHYMING], 1. to make rhymes. 2. to form a rhyme: as "more" *rhymes* with "door." *v.t.* 1. to put into rhyme. 2. to use as a rhyme. Also sp. **rime. —rhym′er,** *n.*

**rhyme·ster** (rīm′stẽr), *n.* a maker of mediocre rhymes or poems; poetaster.

**rhythm** (rith″m, -əm), *n.* [< Gr. *rhythmos*, measure], 1. movement characterized by a regular recurrence, as of beat, accent, etc. 2. the pattern of this in music, verse, etc. **—rhyth′mi·cal** (-mi-k'l), **rhyth′mic,** *adj.*

**rhythm method,** a method of birth control involving abstinence from sexual intercourse during the woman's ovulation periods.

**rib** (rib), *n.* [AS.], 1. any of the arched bones attached to the spine and enclosing the chest cavity. 2. something like a rib in appearance or arrangement. *v.t.* [RIBBED, RIBBING], 1. to form with ribs. 2. [Slang], to tease. **—ribbed,** *adj.*

**rib·ald** (rib′əld), *adj.* [OFr. *ribauld*], coarsely joking; offensive or vulgar in language. *n.* a ribald person. **—rib′ald·ry,** *n.*

**rib·bon** (rib′ən), *n.* [< OFr. *riban*], 1. a narrow strip as of silk or rayon, used for decorating, tying, etc. 2. *pl.* torn shreds. 3. a strip of cloth inked for use on a typewriter, etc. —**rib′bon·like′**, *adj.*

**ri·bo·fla·vin** (rī′bə-flā′vin), *n.* [< *ribose*, a sugar + L. *flavus*, yellow], a factor of the vitamin B complex, found in milk, eggs, fruits, etc.: also called *vitamin* $B_2$.

**rice** (rīs), *n.* [< Gr. *oryza*], 1. a cereal grass grown widely in warm climates, esp. in the Orient. 2. the starchy grain of this grass, used as food. *v.t.* [RICED, RICING], to reduce (potatoes, etc.) to a ricelike consistency.

**rich** (rich), *adj.* [< AS. *rice*, noble], 1. having much money or property; wealthy. 2. well supplied; abounding (*in* or *with*). 3. valuable or costly: as, *rich* gifts. 4. full of choice ingredients, as butter, sugar, etc. 5. *a*) full and mellow: said of sound. *b*) deep; vivid: said of colors. *c*) very fragrant. 6. abundant. 7. yielding in abundance, as soil, etc. 8. [Colloq.], very amusing. —**the rich**, wealthy people collectively.

**rich·es** (rich′iz), *n.pl.* [orig. sing.], [< OFr. *richesse*], wealth; money, real estate, etc.

**rick** (rik), *n.* [AS. *hreac*], a stack of hay, straw, etc. *v.t.* to form into a rick or ricks.

**rick·ets** (rik′its), *n.* [? < Gr. *rhachis*, spine], a disease, chiefly of children, characterized by a softening and, often, bending of the bones.

**rick·et·y** (rik′i-ti), *adj.* 1. having rickets. 2. feeble; weak; shaky. —**rick′et·i·ness**, *n.*

**rick·ey** (rik′i), *n.* [? < a Col. *Rickey*], a drink of carbonated water, lime juice, and an alcoholic liquor, esp. gin (*gin rickey*).

**ric·o·chet** (rik′ə-shā′), *n.* [Fr.], the glancing rebound(s) of an object from a flat surface. *v.i.* [-CHETED (-shād′), -CHETING (-shā′iŋ)], to move with such rebound(s).

**rid** (rid), *v.t.* [RID or RIDDED, RIDDING], [< ON. *rythja*, to empty], to free or relieve, as of something undesirable. —**get rid of**, to dispose of.

**rid·dance** (rid′′ns), *n.* a ridding or being rid; clearance or removal.

**rid·den** (rid′′n), pp. of **ride**.

**rid·dle** (rid′′l), *n.* [< AS. *rædan*, to guess], 1. a puzzling question, etc. requiring some ingenuity to answer. 2. a puzzling person or thing. *v.i.* to propound riddles.

**rid·dle** (rid′′l), *v.t.* [-DLED, -DLING], [< AS. *hriddel*], to make holes in; perforate.

**ride** (rīd), *v.i.* [RODE, RIDDEN, RIDING], [AS. *ridan*], 1. to be carried by a horse, in a vehicle, etc. 2. to be supported in motion (*on* or *upon*): as, tanks *ride* on treads. 3. to move or float on water. 4. to admit of being ridden: as the car *rides* smoothly. *v.t.* 1. to sit on or in so as to move along. 2. to move over, along, or through (a road, area, etc.) by horse, etc. 3. to engage in by riding: as, to *ride* a race. 4. to control, dominate, etc.: as, *ridden* by fear. 5. [Colloq.], to torment, as with ridicule. *n.* a riding; journey.

**rid′er**, *n.* 1. one who rides. 2. an addition or amendment to a document.

**ridge** (rij), *n.* [AS. *hrycg*], 1. the long, narrow crest of something. 2. a long, narrow elevation of land. 3. any narrow raised strip. 4. the horizontal line formed by the meeting of two sloping surfaces. *v.t. & v.i.* [RIDGED, RIDGING], to mark with, or form into, ridges.

**rid·i·cule** (rid′i-kūl′), *n.* [< L. *ridere*, to laugh], 1. the act or practice of making one the object of contemptuous laughter. 2. remarks, etc. intended to produce such laughter. *v.t.* [-CULED, -CULING], to make fun of with ridicule. —**rid′i·cul′er**, *n.*

**ri·dic·u·lous** (ri-dik′yoo-ləs), *adj.* deserving ridicule; absurd. —**ri·dic′u·lous·ly**, *adv.*

**rife** (rīf), *adj.* [AS.], 1. frequently occurring; widespread. 2. abounding (*with*).

**rif·fle** (rif′′l), *n.* [prob. < *ripple*], 1. a ripple in a stream, produced by a reef, etc. 2. a method of shuffling cards.

**riff·raff** (rif′raf′), *n.* [see RIFLE (rob) & RAFFLE], those people regarded as of no consequence or merit.

**ri·fle** (rī′f′l), *v.t.* [-FLED, -FLING], [Fr. *rifler*, to scrape], to cut spiral grooves within (a gun barrel, etc.). *n.* a firearm with spiral grooves in the barrel to spin the bullet and so give it greater accuracy.

**ri·fle** (rī′f′l), *v.t.* [-FLED, -FLING], [< OFr. *rifler*], 1. to ransack and rob. 2. to take as plunder; steal. —**ri′fler**, *n.*

**ri′fle·man** (-mən), *n.* [*pl.* -MEN], a soldier armed with a rifle.

**rift** (rift), *n.* [< ON. *ripta*, break (a bargain)], an opening caused by splitting; cleft. *v.t. & v.i.* to split.

**rig** (rig), *v.t.* [RIGGED, RIGGING], [? < ON. *rigga*, wrap around], 1. to fit (a ship, mast, etc.) with (sails, shrouds, etc.). 2. to equip. 3. to arrange dishonestly. 4. [Colloq.], to dress. *n.* 1. the arrangement of sails, masts, etc. on a vessel. 2. equipment; gear.

**rig′ging**, *n.* 1. the chains, ropes, etc. that support and work the masts, sails, etc. of a vessel. 2. equipment; tackle.

**right** (rīt), *adj.* [AS. *riht*], 1. straight. 2. in accordance with justice, law, etc.; virtuous. 3. correct. 4. fitting; suitable. 5. mentally or physically sound. 6. designating the side meant to be seen. 7. *a*) designating or of that side toward the east when one faces north. *b*) designating or of the corresponding side of anything. *c*) closer to the right side of one facing the thing mentioned. *n.* 1. what is right, just, etc. 2. a power, privilege, etc. belonging to one by law, nature, etc. 3. the right side. 4. [often R-], in *politics*, a conservative or reactionary position, party, etc. (often with *the*). *adv.* 1. in a straight line; directly: as, go *right* home. 2. properly; fittingly. 3. completely. 4. exactly: as, *right* here. 5. according to law, justice, etc. 6. correctly. 7. on or toward the right hand. 8. very: in certain titles, as, the *right* honorable. *v.t.* 1. to put upright. 2. to correct. 3. to put in order. —**right away** (or **off**), at once.

**right′a·bout′-face′**, *n.* 1. a turning directly about to the opposite direction. 2. a complete reversal, as of belief.

**right angle**, an angle of 90 degrees.

**right·eous** (rī′chəs), *adj.* 1. acting in a just, upright manner; virtuous. 2. morally right or justifiable. —**right′eous·ly**, *adv.*

**right′ful**, *adj.* 1. right; just; fair. 2. having a lawful claim. —**right′ful·ly**, *adv.*

**right′-hand′**, *adj.* 1. on or directed toward the right. 2. of, for, or with the right hand. 3. most helpful or reliable: as, my *right-hand* man.

**right′-hand′ed**, *adj.* 1. using the right hand more skillfully than the left. 2. done with or made for use with the right hand.

**right′ist**, *n. & adj.* in *politics*, conservative or reactionary.

**right of way**, 1. the right to move first at intersections. 2. land over which a road, power line, etc. passes. Also **right′-of-way′**.

**right wing**, in *politics*, the more conservative or reactionary section of a party, group, etc. —**right′-wing′**, *adj.*

**rig·id** (rij′id), *adj.* [< L. *rigere*, be stiff], 1. not bending or flexible; stiff. 2. not moving; set. 3. severe; strict. 4. having a rigid framework: said of airships. —**ri·gid′i·ty** [*pl.* -TIES], *n.* —**rig′id·ly**, *adv.*

**rig·ma·role** (rig′mə-rōl′), *n.* [< ME. *rageman*, document], nonsense.

**rig·or** (rig′ẽr), *n.* [see RIGID], 1. severity; strictness; hardship. 2. stiffness; rigidity. Also, Brit. sp., **rigour**. —**rig′or·ous**, *adj.*

**‡ri·gor mor·tis** (rī′gôr môr′tis, rig′ẽr), [L.,

stiffness of death], the stiffening of the muscles after death.

**rile** (rīl), *v.t.* [RILED, RILING], [< *roil*], [Colloq.], to anger; irritate.

**rill** (ril), *n.* [cf. D. *ril*], a little brook.

**rim** (rim), *n.* [AS. *rima*, edge], 1. the edge, border, or margin, esp. of something circular. 2. the outer part of a wheel. *v.t.* [RIMMED, RIMMING], to put or form a rim on or around. **—rimmed**, *adj.*

**rime** (rīm), *n.*, *v.t.* & *v.i.* [RIMED, RIMING], rhyme.

**rime** (rīm), *n.* [AS. *hrim*], hoarfrost. *v.t.* [RIMED, RIMING], to coat with rime.

**rind** (rīnd), *n.* [AS.], a firm outer layer or coating: as, the *rind* of cheese or fruit.

**ring** (riŋ), *v.i.* [RANG, or *rarely* RUNG, RUNG, RINGING], [AS. *hringan*], 1. to give forth the resonant sound of a bell. 2. to seem: as, to *ring* true. 3. to sound a bell, as a summons, etc. 4. to resound: as, to *ring* with laughter. 5. to have a ringing sensation, as the ears. *v.t.* 1. to cause (a bell, etc.) to sound. 2. to signal, announce, etc. as by ringing. 3. to call by telephone. *n.* 1. the sound of a bell. 2. any similar sound. 3. a characteristic sound or quality: as, the *ring* of truth. 4. act of ringing a bell, etc. 5. a telephone call.

**ring** (riŋ), *n.* [AS. *hring*], 1. an ornamental circular band worn on a finger. 2. any of various circular bands: as, a key *ring*. 3. a circular line, mark, or figure. 4. the outer edge of something circular. 5. a group of people or things in a circle. 6. a group working to advance its own selfish interests. 7. an enclosed area for contests, exhibitions, etc.: as, a boxing *ring*. 8. prize fighting (with *the*). *v.t.* [RINGED, RINGING], 1. to encircle. 2. to form into, or furnish with, a ring or rings. **—toss one's hat in the ring**, to announce one's candidacy for office. **—ringed**, *adj.*

**ring'er**, *n.* a person or thing that encircles; specif., a horseshoe, etc. thrown so that it encircles the peg.

**ring'er**, *n.* 1. one that rings a bell, etc. 2. [Slang], *a*) a player, horse, etc. dishonestly entered in a competition. *b*) a person or thing that very much resembles another.

**ring'lead'er**, *n.* one who leads others, esp. in unlawful acts, etc.

**ring'let** (-lit), *n.* a curl, esp. a long one.

**ring'worm'**, *n.* a contagious skin disease caused by a fungus.

**rink** (riŋk), *n.* [< OFr. *renc*, course], 1. a smooth expanse of ice for skating. 2. a smooth floor for roller skating.

**rinse** (rins), *v.t.* [RINSED, RINSING], [ult. < L. *recens*, fresh], 1. to wash lightly. 2. to remove soap, dirt, etc. from with clean water. *n.* a rinsing. **—rins'er**, *n.*

**ri·ot** (rī'ət), *n.* [< L. *rugire*, to roar], wild or violent disorder, confusion, etc.; esp., a violent disturbance of the peace. *v.i.* 1. to take part in a riot. 2. to revel. **—run riot**, to act in a wild, unrestrained manner. **—ri'ot·er**, *n.* **—ri'ot·ous**, *adj.* **—ri'ot·ous·ly**, *adv.*

**rip** (rip), *v.t.* [RIPPED, RIPPING], [prob. < LG.], 1. *a*) to cut or tear apart roughly. *b*) to sever the threads of (a seam). 2. to remove as by tearing roughly (with *off*, *out*, etc.). 3. to saw (wood) along the grain. *v.i.* to become torn. *n.* a torn place, as in cloth. **—rip'per**, *n.*

**ri·par·i·an** (ri-pâr'i-ən, rī-), *adj.* [< L. *ripa*, a bank], of or on the bank of a river, etc.

**rip cord**, a cord, etc. for opening a parachute during descent.

**ripe** (rīp), *adj.* [AS.], 1. ready to be harvested, as grain or fruit. 2. sufficiently developed for use; mature. 3. fully prepared: as, *ripe* for trouble. 4. sufficiently advanced (*for*): said of time. **—ripe'ness**, *n.*

**rip·en** (rīp'ən), *v.i.* & *v.t.* to become or make ripe; mature. **—rip'en·er**, *n.*

**rip·ple** (rip''l), *v.i.* & *v.t.* [-PLED, -PLING], [prob. < *rip*], to form little waves on the surface (of), as water stirred by a breeze. *n.* such a wave, or a movement, appearance, etc. like this. **—rip'ply**, *adj.*

**rip-roar·ing** (rip'rôr'iŋ), *adj.* [Slang], very lively and noisy; boisterous.

**rip'saw'**, *n.* a saw with coarse teeth, for cutting wood along the grain.

**rise** (rīz), *v.i.* [ROSE, RISEN (riz''n), RISING], [AS. *risan*], 1. to stand or sit up from a sitting or lying position. 2. to rebel; revolt. 3. to go up; ascend. 4. to appear above the horizon: as, the moon *rose*. 5. to attain a higher level, status, rank, etc. 6. to extend upward: as, the hills *rise* steeply. 7. to increase in amount, degree, etc. 8. to expand or swell, as dough with yeast. 9. to originate; begin. *n.* 1. upward motion; ascent. 2. an advance in status, rank, etc. 3. a slope upward. 4. an increase in degree, amount, etc. 5. a beginning; origin. **—give rise to**, to bring about; begin.

**ris'er**, *n.* 1. a person or thing that rises. 2. a vertical piece between the steps in a stairway.

**ris·i·ble** (riz'ə-b'l), *adj.* [< L. *ridere*, to laugh], 1. able or inclined to laugh. 2. causing laughter; funny. **—ris'i·bil'i·ty** [*pl.* -TIES], *n.*

**ris·ing** (rīz'iŋ), *adj.* 1. that rises; ascending, advancing, etc. 2. growing; maturing: as, the *rising* generation. *n.* 1. a revolt. 2. something that rises; projection.

**risk** (risk), *n.* [< Fr. < It. *risco*], the chance of injury, damage, or loss; hazard. *v.t.* 1. to expose to risk: as, to *risk* one's life. 2. to incur the risk of: as, to *risk* a war. **—risk'y** [-IER, -IEST], *adj.*

**ris·qué** (ris-kā'), *adj.* [< Fr. *risquer*, to risk], very close to being improper or indecent; suggestive.

**rite** (rīt), *n.* [L. *ritus*], a solemn, ceremonial act, as in a religion.

**rit·u·al** (rich'ōō-əl), *adj.* of, like, or done as a rite. *n.* a system or form of rites, religious or otherwise. **—rit'u·al·ly**, *adv.*

**rit'u·al·ism**, *n.* the observance of, or insistence on, ritual. **—rit'u·al·is'tic**, *adj.*

**ri·val** (rī'v'l), *n.* [< L. *rivalis*], one who is trying to get the same thing as another or to equal or surpass another; competitor. *adj.* acting as a rival; competing. *v.t.* [-VALED or -VALLED, -VALING or -VALLING], 1. to try to equal or surpass. 2. to equal in some way. **—ri'val·ry** [*pl.* -RIES], *n.*

**rive** (rīv), *v.t.* & *v.i.* [RIVED, RIVED or RIVEN (riv''n), RIVING], [ON. *rifa*], 1. to rend. 2. to split; cleave. **—riv'er**, *n.*

**riv·er** (riv'ẽr), *n.* [< L. *ripa*, a bank], a natural stream of water larger than a creek, emptying into an ocean, lake, etc.

**river basin**, the area drained by a river and its tributaries.

**riv'er·side'**, *n.* the bank of a river. *adj.* on or near the bank of a river.

**riv·et** (riv'it), *n.* [< OFr. *river*, to clinch], a metal bolt used to fasten parts together by hammering the ends into heads. *v.t.* to fasten firmly, as with rivets. **—riv'et·er**, *n.*

**riv·u·let** (riv'yoo-lit), *n.* [< L. *rivus*, a brook], a little stream.

**rm.**, [*pl.* RMS.], 1. ream. 2. room.

**R.N.**, registered nurse.

**roach** (rōch), *n.* [*pl.* ROACH, ROACHES], [< OFr. *roche*], a fresh-water fish of the carp family.

**road** (rōd), *n.* [< AS. *rad*, a ride], 1. a way made for traveling; highway. 2. a way; course: as, the *road* to fortune. 3. *often in pl.* a place near shore where ships can ride at anchor.

**road′bed′,** *n.* the foundation laid for railroad tracks or for a highway, etc.
**road′block′,** *n.* a blockade set up in a road to prevent movement of vehicles.
**road′side′,** *n.* the side of a road. *adj.* on or at the side of a road.
**road·ster** (rōd′stēr), *n.* an open automobile with a single cross seat.
**road′way′,** *n.* 1. a road. 2. that part of a road used by cars, trucks, etc.
**roam** (rōm), *v.i.* [ME. *romen*], to travel without purpose or plan; wander. *v.t.* to wander through or over.
**roan** (rōn), *adj.* [< Sp. *ruano*], grayish-yellow or reddish-brown with a thick sprinkling of gray or white: said chiefly of horses. *n.* 1. a roan color. 2. a roan horse.
**roar** (rôr), *v.i.* [AS. *rarian*], 1. to utter or make a loud, deep, rumbling sound. 2. to laugh boisterously. *v.t.* to utter with a roar. *n.* a loud, deep, rumbling sound.
**roast** (rōst), *v.t.* [< OHG. *rost*, gridiron], 1. to cook (meat, etc.) over an open fire or in an oven; bake. 2. to process, as coffee, by exposure to heat. 3. to expose to great heat. 4. [Colloq.], to criticize severely. *v.i.* 1. to undergo roasting. 2. to become very hot. *n.* 1. roasted meat. 2. a cut of meat for roasting. *adj.* roasted: as, *roast* pork.
**rob** (rob), *v.t.* [ROBBED, ROBBING], [< OHG. *roubon*], 1. to take property from unlawfully by force. 2. to deprive of something by stealth or fraud. *v.i.* to commit robbery.
**rob′ber·y** (-ēr-i), *n.* [*pl.* -IES], a robbing; the taking of another's property by violence or intimidation.
**robe** (rōb), *n.* [OHG. *roub*, plunder], 1. a long, loose, usually outer, garment. 2. such a garment worn, as by a judge, to show rank or office. 3. *pl.* clothes; costume. 4. a covering or wrap: as, a lap *robe*. *v.t.* & *v.i.* [ROBED, ROBING], to dress in a robe.
**rob·in** (rob′in), *n.* [OFr. dim. of *Robert*], a large North American thrush with a dull-red breast: also **robin redbreast**.
**Robin Hood,** in *English legend*, the leader of a band of outlaws that robbed the rich to help the poor.
**Rob·in·son Cru·soe** (rob′in-s'n kroo͞′sō), the title hero of Daniel Defoe's novel (1719) about a shipwrecked sailor.
**ro·bot** (rō′bət, rob′ət), *n.* [< such beings in K. Čapek's play *R.U.R.*; < Czech *robotnik*, serf], 1. a manlike device with a mechanism that enables it to move or work of itself. 2. one who acts or works mechanically.
**ro·bust** (rō-bust′), *adj.* [< L. *robur*, a hard oak], strong and healthy; hardy.
**rock** (rok), *n.* [< OFr. *roche*], 1. a large mass of stone. 2. broken pieces of stone. 3. mineral matter formed in masses in the earth's crust. 4. anything like a rock; esp., a firm support, etc. 5. [Colloq.], a stone. —**on the rocks,** [Colloq.], 1. ruined; bankrupt. 2. served over ice cubes, as whisky.
**rock** (rok), *v.t.* & *v.i.* [< AS. *roccian*], 1. to move back and forth or from side to side. 2. to sway strongly; shake. *n.* 1. a rocking motion. 2. rock-and-roll.
**rock′-and-roll′,** *n.* a form of popular music with a strong, regular beat, which evolved from jazz and the blues.
**rock bottom,** the lowest level; very bottom.
**rock′-bound′,** *adj.* surrounded or hemmed in by rocks.
**rock′er,** *n.* 1. either of the curved pieces on which a cradle, etc. rocks. 2. a chair mounted on such pieces: also **rocking chair**.
**rock·et** (rok′it), *n.* [It. *rocchetta*, spool], a projectile driven forward by the escape of gases in the rear: rockets are used in fireworks, weapons, aircraft, etc.
**rock′et·ry** (-ri), *n.* the science of designing, building, and launching rockets.
**rocking horse,** a child's toy horse of wood, etc., set on rockers or springs.
**rock′-ribbed′,** *adj.* 1. having rocky ridges. 2. firm; unyielding.
**rock salt,** common salt in solid masses.
**rock wool,** a fibrous material made from molten rock, used for insulation.
**rock·y** (rok′i), *adj.* [-IER, -IEST], 1. full of rocks. 2 consisting of rock. 3. like a rock; firm, hard, etc. —**rock′i·ness,** *n.*
**rock′y,** *adj.* [-IER, -IEST], inclined to rock; unsteady. —**rock′i·ness,** *n.*
**ro·co·co** (rə-kō′kō), *n.* [Fr. < *rocaille*, shellwork], an elaborate style of architecture and decoration, imitating foliage, scrolls, etc. *adj.* 1. of or in rococo. 2. too elaborate.
**rod** (rod), *n.* [AS. *rodd*], 1. a straight stick or bar. 2. a stick for beating as punishment. 3. a scepter carried as a symbol of office. 4. a measure of length equal to 5½ yards. 5. a pole for fishing. 6. [Slang], a pistol.
**rode** (rōd), pt. of **ride**.
**ro·dent** (rō′d'nt), *n.* [< L. *rodere*, gnaw], any of several gnawing mammals, as rats, mice, rabbits, etc. *adj.* gnawing.
**ro·de·o** (rō′di-ō′, rō-dā′ō), *n.* [*pl.* -DEOS], [Sp. < L. *rotare*, to turn], 1. a roundup of cattle. 2. a public exhibition of the skills of cowboys, as horsemanship, lassoing, etc.
**roe** (rō), *n.* [prob. < ON. *hrogn*], 1. fish eggs, esp. when still massed in the ovarian membrane. 2. fish sperm; milt.
**roe** (rō), *n.* [*pl.* ROE, ROES], [< AS. *ra*, *raha*], a small, agile European and Asiatic deer.
**roe·buck** (rō′buk′), *n.* the male of the roe.
**roent·gen** (rent′gən), *n.* [< W. K. *Roentgen*, 1845–1923, G. physicist], the unit for measuring the radiation of X rays (**Roentgen rays**) or gamma rays.
**Rog·er** (roj′ēr), *interj.* [< name of signal flag for R], [also r-], 1. received: code word used to indicate reception of a radio message. 2. [Slang], O.K.!
**rogue** (rōg), *n.* [< ?], 1. a scoundrel. 2. a funloving, mischievous person. —**ro·guer·y** (rō′gə-ri), *n.* —**ro·guish** (rō′gish), *adj.*
**roil** (roil), *v.t.* [< L. *robigo*, rust], 1. to make (a liquid) cloudy, muddy, etc. by stirring up the sediment. 2. to displease; vex.
**roist·er** (rois′tēr), *v.i.* [see RUSTIC], 1. to swagger. 2. to be lively and noisy; revel.
**role, rôle** (rōl), *n.* [Fr. *rôle*, orig., the roll containing the actor's part], 1. a part, or character, played by an actor. 2. a function assumed by someone: as, an advisory *role*.
**roll** (rōl), *v.i.* [< L. *rota*, wheel], 1. to move by turning over and over. 2. to move on wheels. 3. to pass: as, the years *roll* by. 4. to extend in gentle swells. 5. to make a loud, rising and falling sound: as, thunder *rolls*. 6. to turn in a circular motion. 7. to move in a rocking motion, as a ship. *v.t.* 1. to move by turning over and over. 2. to move on wheels or rollers. 3. to utter with full, flowing sound. 4. to say with a trill: as, he *rolls* his r's. 5. to give a swaying motion to. 6. to move around or from side to side: as, she *rolled* her eyes. 7. to wind into a ball or cylinder: as, *roll* up the rug. 8. to flatten or spread with a roller, etc. *n.* 1. a rolling. 2. a scroll. 3. a list of names. 4. something rolled into a cylinder. 5. a small cake of bread, etc. 6. a swaying motion. 7. a loud, reverberating sound, as of thunder. 8. a slight swell on a surface.
**roll call,** the reading aloud of a roll to find out who is absent.
**roll′er,** *n.* 1. one that rolls. 2. a cylinder of metal, wood, etc. on which something is rolled, or one used to crush, smooth, or spread something. 3. a heavy, swelling wave.
**roller coaster,** an amusement ride in which small cars move on tracks that curve and dip sharply.

**roller skate,** a skate having four small wheels, instead of a runner. **—roll'er-skate'** [-SKATED, -SKATING], ***v.i.***

**rol·lick** (rol'ik), ***v.i.*** [prob. blend of *romp & frolic*], to be gay, carefree, etc. in play. **—rol'lick·ing,** ***adj.***

**rolling pin,** a heavy, smooth cylinder of wood, etc. used to roll out dough.

**rolling stock,** railroad vehicles.

**ro·ly-po·ly** (rō'li-pō'li), ***adj.*** [< *roll*], short and plump; pudgy.

**Rom.,** Roman.

**Ro·man** (rō'mən), ***adj.*** 1. of or characteristic of ancient or modern Rome, its people, etc. 2. of the Roman Catholic Church. 3. [usually r-], designating or of the usual, upright style of printing types. ***n.*** 1. a native or inhabitant of ancient or modern Rome. 2. [usually r-], roman type or characters.

**Roman Catholic,** 1. of the Christian church (**Roman Catholic Church**) headed by the Pope. 2. a member of this church.

**ro·mance** (rō-mans', rō'mans), ***adj.*** [ult. < L. *Romanicus*, Roman], [R-], designating or of any of the languages derived mainly from Latin, as French, Italian, Spanish, etc. ***n.*** 1. a long poem or tale, originally written in a Romance dialect, about knights, adventure, and love. 2. a novel of love, adventure, etc. 3. the quality of excitement, love, etc. found in such literature. 4. a love affair. ***v.t. & v.i.*** [-MANCED, -MANCING], 1. to write or tell romances. 2. [Colloq.], to make love (to). **—ro·manc'er,** ***n.***

**Roman Empire,** the empire of ancient Rome, existing from 27 B.C. until 395 A.D.

**Ro'man·ize',** ***v.t. & v.i.*** [-IZED, -IZING], to make or become Roman in character, spirit, etc.

**Roman numerals,** Roman letters used as numerals: I = 1, V = 5, X = 10, L = 50, C = 100, D = 500, and M = 1,000.

**ro·man·tic** (rō-man'tik), ***adj.*** 1. of, like, or characterized by romance. 2. fanciful; fictitious. 3. not practical; visionary. 4. full of thoughts, feelings, etc. of romance. 5. of or in the spirit of, a 19th-c. cultural movement characterized by liberalism, feeling, imagination, etc. 6. suitable for romance. ***n.*** a romantic person. **—ro·man'ti·cal·ly,** ***adv.***

**ro·man'ti·cism** (-tə-siz'm), ***n.*** romantic spirit, outlook, etc.

**Rom·a·ny** (rom'ə-ni), ***n.*** [< Gypsy *rom*, man], [*pl.* -NY, -NIES], a gypsy. ***adj.*** of the gypsies, their language, etc.

**Ro·me·o** (rō'mi-ō'), ***n.*** 1. the hero of Shakespeare's tragedy *Romeo and Juliet* (c. 1595), lover of Juliet. 2. [*pl.* -OS], a lover.

**romp** (romp), ***n.*** [prob. < OFr. *ramper*, climb], boisterous, lively play. ***v.i.*** to play in a boisterous, lively way.

**romp'er,** ***n.*** 1. one who romps. 2. ***pl.*** a young child's loose-fitting outer garment, combining a waist with pants.

**Rom·u·lus** (rom'yoo-ləs), ***n.*** in *Rom. myth.*, the founder and first king of Rome: a she-wolf reared him and his twin brother Remus, whom he later killed.

**rood** (ro͞od), ***n.*** [AS. *rod*], 1. a crucifix. 2. a measure of area usually equal to ¼ acre.

**roof** (ro͞of, roof), ***n.*** [*pl.* ROOFS], [AS. *hrof*], 1. the outside top covering of a building. 2. anything like this: as, the *roof* of the mouth. ***v.t.*** to cover as with a roof. **—roof'less,** ***adj.***

**roof'ing,** ***n.*** material for roofs.

**rook** (rook), ***n.*** [AS. *hroc*], a European crow. ***v.t. & v.i.*** to swindle; cheat.

**rook** (rook), ***n.*** [< Per. *rukh*], in *chess*, a castle.

**rook'er·y,** ***n.*** [*pl.* -IES], a breeding place or colony of rooks.

**rook·ie** (rook'i), ***n.*** [Slang], an inexperienced recruit, as in the army.

**room** (ro͞om, room), ***n.*** [AS. *rum*], 1. space to hold something. 2. opportunity: as, *room* for doubt. 3. an interior space enclosed or set apart by walls. 4. ***pl.*** living quarters. 5. the people in a room. ***v.i. & v.t.*** to have or provide with lodgings. **—room'ful,** ***n.*** **—room'y** [-IER, -IEST], ***adj.***

**room and board,** lodging and meals.

**room'er,** ***n.*** one who rents a room or rooms to live in; lodger.

**room·ette'** (-et'), ***n.*** a small bedroom in some railroad sleeping cars.

**rooming house,** a house with furnished rooms for renting.

**room'mate',** ***n.*** a person with whom one shares a room or rooms.

**roost** (ro͞ost), ***n.*** [AS. *hrost*], 1. a perch on which birds, esp. domestic fowls, can rest or sleep. 2. a place with perches for birds. 3. a place for resting, sleeping, etc. ***v.i.*** 1. to perch on a roost. 2. to settle down, as for the night.

**roost·er** (ro͞os'tẽr), ***n.*** the male of the chicken.

**root** (ro͞ot, root), ***n.*** [< ON. *rot*], 1. the part of a plant, usually underground, that anchors the plant, draws water from the soil, etc. 2. the embedded part of a tooth, a hair, etc. 3. a source or cause. 4. a supporting or essential part. 5. a quantity that, multiplied by itself a specified number of times, produces a given quantity. 6. the part of a word to which affixes are added. ***v.i.*** to take root. ***v.t.*** 1. to fix the roots of in the ground. 2. to establish; settle. **—take root,** 1. to begin growing by putting out roots. 2. to become fixed, settled, etc.

**root** (ro͞ot, root), ***v.t.*** [< AS. *wrot*, snout], to dig up with the snout, as a pig. ***v.i.*** 1. to search by rummaging. 2. [Slang], to encourage a team, etc. **—root'er,** ***n.***

**root beer,** a carbonated drink made of root extracts from certain plants.

**root'let** (-lit), ***n.*** a little root.

**rope** (rōp), ***n.*** [AS. *rap*], 1. a thick, strong cord made of intertwisted strands of fiber, etc. 2. a ropelike string, as of beads. ***v.t.*** [ROPED, ROPING], 1. to fasten or tie with a rope. 2. to mark off or enclose with a rope. 3. to catch with a lasso. **—know the ropes,** [Colloq.], to be acquainted with a procedure. **—rope in,** [Slang], to entice; persuade.

**Roque·fort (cheese)** (rōk'fẽrt), [< *Roquefort*, France, where orig. made], a strong cheese with a bluish mold.

**ro·sa·ry** (rō'zə-ri), ***n.*** [*pl.* -RIES], [ML. *rosarium*], in the *R.C. Church*, a string of beads used to keep count in saying prayers.

**rose** (rōz), ***n.*** [< L. *rosa*], 1. a plant with prickly stems and flowers of red, pink, white, yellow, etc. 2. its flower. 3. pinkish red or purplish red: also **rose color.** ***adj.*** rose-colored. **—bed of roses,** luxury or idleness.

**rose** (rōz), pt. of **rise.**

**ro·se·ate** (rō'zi-it), ***adj.*** rose-colored; rosy.

**rose'bud',** ***n.*** the bud of a rose.

**rose'bush',** ***n.*** a shrub bearing roses.

**rose'-col'ored,** ***adj.*** 1. pinkish-red or purplish-red. 2. cheerful or optimistic.

**rose·mar·y** (rōz'mâr'i), ***n.*** [ult. < L. *ros marinus*, dew of the sea], an evergreen shrub of the mint family, with fragrant leaves used in perfumery, cooking, etc.

**ro·sette** (rō-zet'), ***n.*** an ornament, arrangement, etc. suggesting a rose.

**rose water,** a preparation of water and oil of roses, used as a perfume.

**rose'wood',** ***n.*** [< its odor], 1. a hard, reddish wood, used in furniture, etc. 2. a tropical tree yielding this wood.

**Rosh Ha·sha·na** (rōsh' hä-shä'nə), the Jewish New Year: also sp. **Rosh Hashona.**

**ros·in** (roz''n, -in), ***n.*** [see RESIN], resin; specif., the hard, brittle resin left after the distillation of crude turpentine; it is rubbed on violin bows, used in making varnish, etc. ***v.t.*** to put rosin on.

**ros·ter** (ros′tẽr), *n.* [< D. *rooster*], a list or roll, as of military personnel.

**ros·trum** (ros′trəm), *n.* [*pl.* -TRUMS, -TRA (-trə)], [L., beak, hence the speakers' platform in the Forum, decorated with ramming beaks from captured ships], a platform for public speaking. —**ros′tral,** *adj.*

**ros·y** (rō′zi), *adj.* [-IER, -IEST], 1. rose red or pink: as, *rosy* cheeks. 2. bright, promising, etc.: as, a *rosy* future. —**ros′i·ness,** *n.*

**rot** (rot), *v.i. & v.t.* [ROTTED, ROTTING], [AS. *rotian*], to decompose; decay; spoil. *n.* 1. a rotting or something rotten. 2. any of various plant and animal diseases characterized by decay. 3. [Slang], nonsense.

**ro·ta·ry** (rō′tə-ri), *adj.* [< L. *rota,* wheel], 1. turning around a central point or axis, as a wheel. 2. having rotating parts: as, a *rotary* press.

**ro·tate** (rō′tāt, rō-tāt′), *v.i. & v.t.* [-TATED, -TATING], [< L. *rota,* wheel], 1. to move or turn around, as a wheel. 2. to go or cause to go in a regular and recurring succession of changes. —**ro·ta′tion,** *n.* —**ro′ta·tor,** *n.*

**ro·ta·to·ry** (rō′tə-tôr′i), *adj.* 1. of, or having the nature of, rotation. 2. rotary. 3. following in rotation.

**R.O.T.C.,** Reserve Officers' Training Corps.

**rote** (rōt), *n.* [ME., var. of *route* (road)], a fixed, mechanical way of doing something. —**by rote,** by memory alone, without thought.

**ro·tis·ser·ie** (rō-tis′ẽr-i), *n.* [Fr. < *rôtir,* to roast], a portable electric grill with a turning spit.

**ro·to·gra·vure** (rō′tə-grə-vyoor′), *n.* [< L. *rota,* a wheel + Fr. *gravure,* engraving], 1. a process of printing pictures, etc. on a rotary press using cylinders etched from photographic plates. 2. a newspaper pictorial section printed by this process.

**rot·ten** (rot′'n), *adj.* [ON. *rotinn*], 1. decayed; spoiled. 2. foul-smelling. 3. morally corrupt. 4. unsound, as if decayed within. 5. [Slang], very bad, unpleasant, etc.

**rot′ter,** *n.* [< *rot*], [Chiefly Brit. Slang], a scoundrel.

**ro·tund** (rō-tund′), *adj.* [L. *rotundus*], round or rounded out; plump. —**ro·tun′di·ty,** *n.*

**ro·tun·da** (rō-tun′də), *n.* [< L. *rotundus,* rotund], a round building, hall, or room, esp. one with a dome.

**rou·é** (rōō-ā′), *n.* [Fr. < *rouer,* to break on the wheel (instrument of torture)], a dissipated man; rake.

**rouge** (rōōzh), *n.* [Fr., red], 1. a reddish cosmetic powder, paste, etc. for coloring the cheeks and lips. 2. a reddish powder used for polishing jewelry, etc. *v.t. & v.i.* [ROUGED, ROUGING], to use cosmetic rouge (on).

**rough** (ruf), *adj.* [AS. *ruh*], 1. not smooth or level; uneven. 2. shaggy: as, a *rough* coat. 3. stormy: as, *rough* weather. 4. disorderly or riotous: as, *rough* play. 5. harsh; not gentle: as, *rough* manners. 6. lacking comforts and conveniences. 7. not refined or polished; natural, crude, etc. 8. not finished, perfected, etc.: as, a *rough* sketch. 9. [Colloq.], difficult: as, a *rough* time. *n.* 1. [Chiefly Brit.], a rowdy. 2. in *golf,* any part of the course where grass, etc. grows uncut. *adv.* in a rough manner. *v.t.* 1. to make rough. 2. to treat roughly (often with *up*). 3. to make or shape roughly (usually with *in* or *out*). *v.i.* to become rough. —**rough it,** to live without conveniences and comforts.

**rough′age** (-ij), *n.* rough or coarse food or fodder, as bran, straw, etc.

**rough′en,** *v.t. & v.i.* to make or become rough.

**rough′-hew′,** *v.t.* [-HEWED, -HEWED or -HEWN, -HEWING], 1. to hew (timber, stone, etc.) roughly, without smoothing. 2. to form roughly. Also **roughhew.**

**rough′house′** (-hous′), *n.* [Slang], rough, boisterous play, fighting, etc. *v.t. & v.i.* [-HOUSED, -HOUSING], [Slang], to treat or act roughly.

**rough′ly,** *adv.* 1. in a rough manner. 2. approximately.

**rough′neck′,** *n.* [Slang], a rowdy.

**rough′shod′,** *adj.* shod with horseshoes having calks to prevent slipping. —**ride roughshod over,** to treat harshly.

**rou·lette** (rōō-let′), *n.* [Fr. < L. *rota,* wheel], a gambling game played with a small ball in a whirling shallow bowl (**roulette wheel**) with red and black numbered compartments.

**round** (round), *adj.* [< L. *rotundus,* rotund], 1. shaped like a ball, circle, or cylinder. 2. plump. 3. full; complete: as, a *round* dozen. 4. expressed by a whole number, or in tens, hundreds, etc. 5. large; considerable: as, a *round* sum. 6. mellow and full in tone, as a sound. 7. brisk; vigorous: as, a *round* pace. *n.* 1. something round. 2. the part of a beef animal between the rump and the leg. 3. movement in a circular course. 4. a course or series: as, a *round* of parties. 5. *often in pl.* a regular, customary circuit: as, a watchman's *rounds.* 6. a single shot from a rifle, etc. or from a number of rifles fired together. 7. ammunition for such a shot. 8. a single outburst, as of applause. 9. a single division as of a boxing match. 10. a short song which one group begins singing when another has reached the second phrase, etc. *v.t.* 1. to make round. 2. to make plump. 3. to complete; finish. 4. to pass around. 5. to encircle; surround. *v.i.* 1. to make a circuit. 2. to turn; reverse direction. 3. to become plump. *adv.* 1. in a circle. 2. through a recurring period of time: as, spring came *round.* 3. from one to another: as, the peddler went *round.* 4. in circumference: as, ten feet *round.* 5. on all sides. 6. about; near. 7. in a roundabout way. 8. here and there. 9. with a rotating movement. 10. in the opposite direction. *prep.* 1. so as to encircle: as, tie the rope *round* the tree. 2. on all sides of. 3. in the vicinity of. 4. in a circuit through: as, go *round* the city. —**round about,** in or to the opposite direction. —**round up,** to collect in a herd, group, etc. —**round′ish,** *adj.*

**round′a·bout′,** *adj.* 1. indirect; circuitous. 2. encircling; enclosing.

**roun·de·lay** (roun′də-lā′), *n.* [< OFr. *rondel,* a short lyrical poem], a simple song in which some phrase, line, etc. is continually repeated.

**round′house′,** *n.* a circular building with a turntable, for storing and repairing locomotives.

**round′ly,** *adv.* 1. in a round form. 2. vigorously. 3. fully; completely.

**round′-shoul′dered,** *adj.* having the shoulders bent forward.

**Round Table,** 1. the table around which King Arthur and his knights sat. 2. [r- t-], a group gathered for an informal discussion.

**round trip,** a trip to a place and back to the starting point.

**round′up′,** *n.* 1. a driving together of cattle, etc. on the range, as for branding. 2. any similar collecting.

**round′worm′,** *n.* any of various round, unsegmented worms, as the hookworm.

**rouse** (rouz), *v.t. & v.i.* [ROUSED, ROUSING], [? < OFr.], 1. to stir up; excite or become excited. 2. to wake. *n.* a rousing.

**roust·a·bout** (roust′ə-bout′), *n.* [< *rouse* + *about*], an unskilled, transient laborer on wharves, in circuses, etc.

**rout** (rout), *n.* [< L. *rupta,* broken], 1. the rabble. 2. a disorderly flight. 3. an overwhelming defeat. *v.t.* 1. to put to disorderly flight. 2. to defeat overwhelmingly.

**rout** (rout), *v.t.* [< *root* (dig)], 1. to gouge out. 2. to force out. —**rout′er**, *n.*

**route** (ro͞ot, rout), *n.* [< L. *rupta* (*via*), broken (path)], a road or course to be traveled; often, a regular course, as in delivering milk, mail, etc. *v.t.* [ROUTED, ROUTING], 1. to send by a certain route. 2. to arrange the route for.

**rou·tine** (ro͞o-tēn′), *n.* [see ROUTE], a regular procedure, customary or prescribed. *adj.* like or using routine. —**rou·tine′ly**, *adv.*

**rove** (rōv), *v.i.* & *v.t.* [ROVED, ROVING], [prob. < AS. *arafian*, set free], to wander about; roam. —**rov′er**, *n.*

**row** (rō), *n.* [AS. *raw*], 1. a number of people or things in a line. 2. any of the lines of seats in a theater, etc.

**row** (rō), *v.t.* & *v.i.* [AS. *rowan*], 1. to propel (a boat) by using oars. 2. to carry in a rowboat. *n.* a trip by rowboat. —**row′er**, *n.*

**row** (rou), *n.* & *v.i.* [prob. < *rouse*], ]Colloq.], quarrel, squabble, or brawl.

**row′boat′**, *n.* a boat designed to be rowed.

**row·dy** (rou′di), *n.* [*pl.* -DIES], [ ? < *row* (quarrel)], a rough, quarrelsome, and disorderly person. *adj.* [-DIER, -DIEST], rough, quarrelsome, etc. —**row′di·ness**, *n.*

**row·el** (rou′əl), *n.* [ult. < L. *rota*, wheel], a small wheel with sharp points, as at the end of a spur.

**roy·al** (roi′əl), *adj.* [< L. *regalis*], 1. of a king or queen. 2. being a king or queen. 3. of a kingdom, its government, etc. 4. like or suitable for a king or queen; magnificent, splendid, etc. —**roy′al·ly**, *adv.*

**roy′al·ist**, *n.* one who supports a monarch or monarchy. —**roy′al·ism**, *n.*

**roy′al·ty**, *n.* [*pl.* -TIES], 1. the rank or power of a king or queen. 2. a royal person or persons. 3. royal quality. 4. a share of the proceeds paid to the owner for the use of a patent, the work of an author, etc.

**r.p.m.**, revolutions per minute.

**R.R.**, railroad.

**R.S.V.P., r.s.v.p.**, *répondez s'il vous plaît*, [Fr.], please reply.

**rub** (rub), *v.t.* [RUBBED, RUBBING], [prob. < MLG. or MD.], 1. to move (one's hand, a cloth, etc.) over (something) with pressure and friction. 2. to spread (polish, etc.) on something. 3. to move (things) over each other with pressure and friction. 4. to make sore by rubbing. 5. to remove by rubbing. *v.i.* 1. to move with pressure and friction (*against*). 2. to rub something. *n.* 1. a rubbing. 2. an obstacle or difficulty. 3. something that irritates, etc., as a jeer. —**rub down**, 1. to massage. 2. to smooth, polish, etc. by rubbing. —**rub it in**, [Slang], to keep reminding someone of his failure or mistake. —**rub the wrong way**, to irritate or annoy.

**rub′ber**, *n.* 1. one that rubs. 2. [< use as eraser], an elastic substance made from the milky sap of various tropical plants, or synthetically. 3. something made of this substance; specif., *usually in pl.* an overshoe. *adj.* made of rubber. —**rub′ber·y**, *adj.*

**rub·ber** (rub′ẽr), *n.* [? < OFr. *a rebours*, backward], the deciding game in a series.

**rub′ber·ize′** (-īz′), *v.t.* [-IZED, -IZING], to coat or impregnate with rubber.

**rubber stamp**, 1. a stamp of rubber, inked and used to print signatures, etc. 2. [Colloq.], a person, bureau, etc. that approves something mechanically. —**rub′ber-stamp′**, *v.t.*

**rub·bish** (rub′ish), *n.* [< ML. *rubbosa*, rubble], 1. any material thrown away as worthless; trash. 2. nonsense.

**rub·ble** (rub′'l), *n.* [prob. akin to *rubbish*], rough, broken pieces of stone, brick, etc.

**rub′down′**, *n.* a massage.

**rube** (ro͞ob), *n.* [< given name *Reuben*], [Slang], a rustic.

**ru·bel·la** (ro͞o-bel′ə), *n.* [< L. *ruber*, red], a mild, infectious, communicable disease causing small red spots on the skin.

**ru·bi·cund** (ro͞o′bi-kund′), *adj.* [< L. *ruber*, red], reddish; ruddy.

**ru·ble** (ro͞o′b'l), *n.* [Russ. *rubl′*], the monetary unit and a silver coin of the U.S.S.R.

**ru·bric** (ro͞o′brik), *n.* [< L. *ruber*, red], a heading, title, initial letter, etc., usually written or printed in red.

**ru·by** (ro͞o′bi), *n.* [*pl.* -BIES], [ult. < L. *rubeus*, red], 1. a clear, deep-red precious stone: a variety of corundum. 2. deep red. *adj.* deep-red.

**ruch·ing** (ro͞osh′iŋ), *n.* [Fr.; ult. < L. *rusca*, bark], 1. a trimming for women's dresses, made of frills or pleats of lace, ribbon, etc. 2. material used for this.

**ruck·us** (ruk′əs), *n.* [prob. merging of *rumpus* & *ruction*, uproar], [Colloq.], noisy confusion; disturbance.

**rud·der** (rud′ẽr), *n.* [AS. *rother*, a paddle], 1. a broad, flat, movable piece hinged vertically to the stern of a ship, used for steering. 2. a piece like this in an aircraft, etc.

**rud·dy** (rud′i), *adj.* [-DIER, -DIEST], [AS. *rudig*], 1. having a healthy red color. 2. reddish. —**rud′di·ly**, *adv.* —**rud′di·ness**, *n.*

**rude** (ro͞od), *adj.* [< L. *rudis*], 1. coarse; rough; crude. 2. barbarous or ignorant. 3. uncouth; impolite. —**rude′ly**, *adv.*

**ru·di·ment** (ro͞o′də-mənt), *n.* [< L. *rudis*, rude], 1. a first principle or element, as of a subject to be learned. 2. a first slight beginning of something. —**ru′di·men′ta·ry** (-men′tẽr-i), *adj.*

**rue** (ro͞o), *v.t.* & *v.i.* [RUED, RUING], [AS. *hreowan*], 1. to feel remorse for (a sin, fault, etc.). 2. to wish (an act, etc.) undone; regret. *n.* [Archaic], sorrow. —**rue′ful**, *adj.*

**rue** (ro͞o), *n.* [< Gr. *rhytē*], a strong-scented herb with bitter leaves.

**ruff** (ruf), *n.* [< *ruffle*], 1. a high, frilled, starched collar worn in the 16th and 17th centuries. 2. a stripe of colored feathers or fur around the neck of an animal.

**ruf·fi·an** (ruf′i-ən, ruf′yən), *n.* [< It. *ruffiano*, pander], a brutal, lawless person.

**ruf·fle** (ruf′'l), *v.t.* [-FLED, -FLING], [< ON. or MLG.], 1. to disturb the smoothness of. 2. to fold into ruffles. 3. to make (feathers, etc.) stand up. 4. to disturb or annoy. *v.i.* 1. to become uneven. 2. to become disturbed, irritated, etc. *n.* 1. a narrow, pleated trimming of cloth, lace, etc. 2. a disturbance. 3. a ripple.

**rug** (rug), *n.* [< Scand.], 1. a piece of thick fabric used as a floor covering. 2. [Chiefly Brit.], a lap robe.

**rug·ged** (rug′id), *adj.* [< Scand.], 1. uneven; rough. 2. heavy and irregular, as a face. 3. stormy. 4. harsh; severe; hard. 5. not polished or refined. 6. strong; robust.

**ru·in** (ro͞o′in), *n.* [< L. *ruere*, to fall], 1. *pl.* the remains of something destroyed, decayed, etc. 2. anything destroyed, etc. 3. downfall, destruction, etc. 4. anything causing this. *v.t.* & *v.i.* to bring or come to ruin. —**ru′in·a′tion**, *n.* —**ru′in·ous**, *adj.*

**rule** (ro͞ol), *n.* [< L. *regere*, lead straight], 1. an established guide for conduct, procedure, etc. 2. custom; usage. 3. a criterion or standard. 4. the customary course. 5. government; reign. 6. a ruler (sense 2). *v.t.* & *v.i.* [RULED, RULING], 1. to have an influence (over); guide. 2. to govern. 3. to determine officially. 4. to mark lines (on) as with a ruler. —**as a rule**, usually. —**rule out**, to exclude by decision.

**rule of thumb**, a practical, though crude or unscientific, method.

**rul′er**, *n.* 1. one who governs. 2. a thin

strip of wood, metal, etc. with a straight edge, used in drawing lines, measuring, etc.
**rul'ing,** *adj.* 1. governing. 2. predominating. *n.* a court decision.
**rum** (rum), *n.* [? < *Rambouillet,* France], 1. an alcoholic liquor distilled from fermented molasses, sugar cane, etc. 2. any alcoholic liquor.
**rum** (rum), *adj.* [< obs. *rum,* good], [Brit. Slang], odd; queer.
**rum** (rum), *n.* rummy.
**rum·ba** (rum'bə), *n.* [Sp.], 1. a dance of Cuban Negro origin. 2. music for this dance.
**rum·ble** (rum'b'l), *v.i. & v.t.* [-BLED, -BLING], [prob. < MD. *rommelen*], 1. to make or cause to make a deep, continuous, rolling sound. 2. to move with such a sound. *n.* 1. a rumbling sound. 2. a space for luggage or for a small seat (**rumble seat**) in the rear of an automobile, etc. —**rum'bling,** *adj.*
**ru·mi·nant** (ro͞o'mə-nənt), *adj.* [see RUMINATE], 1. chewing the cud. 2. meditative. *n.* any of a group of four-footed, cud-chewing mammals, as cattle, sheep, deer, etc.
**ru·mi·nate** (ro͞o'mə-nāt'), *v.t. & v.i.* [-NATED, -NATING], [< L. *ruminare*], 1. to chew (the cud). 2. to meditate or reflect (on). —**ru'mi·na'tion,** *n.* —**ru'mi·na'tive,** *adj.*
**rum·mage** (rum'ij), *v.t. & v.i.* [-MAGED, -MAGING], [< AS. *rum,* room], to search through (a place) thoroughly.
**rummage sale,** a sale of miscellaneous articles.
**rum·my** (rum'i), *n.* [< *rum* (odd)], any of certain card games whose object is to match sets and sequences.
**ru·mor** (ro͞o'mẽr), *n.* [L., noise], 1. general talk not based on definite knowledge. 2. an unconfirmed report, story, etc. in general circulation. *v.t.* to tell or spread by rumor. Also, Brit. sp., **rumour.**
**rump** (rump), *n.* [< ON. *rumpr*], 1. the hind part of an animal, where the legs and back join. 2. the buttocks.
**rum·ple** (rum'p'l), *n.* [< MD. *rompe*], an uneven crease; wrinkle. *v.t. & v.i.* [-PLED, -PLING], to wrinkle; muss. —**rum'ply,** *adj.*
**rum·pus** (rum'pəs), *n.* [prob. < Swiss G. student slang], [Colloq.], noisy disturbance.
**run** (run), *v.i.* [RAN, RUN, RUNNING], [< ON.], 1. to go by moving the legs faster than in walking. 2. to go, move, etc. easily and freely. 3. to make a quick trip (*up to, down to,* etc.). 4. to flee. 5. to compete in a race, election, etc. 6. to ply (between two points), as a train. 7. to climb or creep, as a vine. 8. to ravel, as a stocking. 9. to operate, as a machine. 10. to flow. 11. to spread over cloth, etc. when moistened, as colors. 12. to discharge pus, etc. 13. to extend in time or space; continue. 14. to pass into a specified condition, etc.: as, he *ran* into trouble. 15. to be written, etc. in a specified way. 16. to be at a specified size, price, etc.: as, eggs *run* high. *v.t.* 1. to follow (a specified course). 2. to perform as by running: as, to *run* a race. 3. to incur (a risk, etc.). 4. to get past: as, to *run* a blockade. 5. to sew with continuous stitches. 6. to cause to run, move, compete, etc. 7. to drive into a specified condition, place, etc. 8. to drive (an object) into or against (something). 9. to make flow in a specified way, place, etc. 10. to manage as a business. 11. to trace. 12. to undergo (a fever, etc.). 13. to publish (a story, etc.) in a newspaper. *n.* 1. an act or period of running. 2. the distance covered in running. 3. a trip; journey. 4. a route: as, a milkman's *run.* 5. *a*) movement onward; progression. *b*) the tendency, as of events. 6. a continuous course or period: as, a *run* of good luck. 7. a continuous course of performances, etc., as of a play. 8. a continued series of demands, as on a bank. 9. a brook. 10. a kind or class; esp., the average kind. 11. an enclosed area for domestic animals. 12. freedom to move about at will: as, the *run* of the house. 13. a large number of fish migrating together. 14. a ravel, as in a stocking. 15. in *baseball,* a scoring point, made by a successful circuit of the bases. —**in the long run,** ultimately. —**on the run,** running or running away. —**run across,** to encounter by chance: also **run into.** —**run down,** 1. to stop operating. 2. to run against so as to knock down. 3. to pursue and capture or kill. 4. to speak of disparagingly. —**run out,** to come to an end; expire. —**run out of,** to use up. —**run over,** 1. to ride over. 2. to overflow. 3. to examine, rehearse, etc. rapidly. —**run through,** 1. to use up quickly or recklessly. 2. to pierce. —**run up,** to raise or rise rapidly.
**run'-a·round',** *n.* [Slang], a series of evasions: also **run'round'.**
**run'a·way',** *n.* 1. a fugitive. 2. a horse, etc. that runs away. *adj.* 1. escaping or having escaped. 2. easily won, as a race. 3. rising rapidly, as prices.
**run'-down',** *adj.* 1. not wound and therefore not running, as a watch. 2. in poor physical condition, as from overwork. 3. fallen into disrepair; dilapidated. *n.* a quick summary.
**rune** (ro͞on), *n.* [AS. *run*], 1. any of the characters of an ancient Germanic alphabet. 2. any similar mark having mysterious meaning. —**ru'nic,** *adj.*
**rung** (ruŋ), *n.* [AS. *hrung,* a staff], a rod forming a step of a ladder, a crosspiece on a chair, a spoke of a wheel, etc.
**rung** (ruŋ), pp. of **ring** (to sound).
**run'ner,** *n.* 1. one that runs, as a racer, messenger, etc. 2. a long, narrow cloth or rug. 3. a ravel, as in hose. 4. a long, trailing stem, as of a strawberry. 5. something on or in which something else moves. 6. either of the long, narrow pieces on which a sled, etc. slides.
**run'ner-up',** *n.* a person or team that finishes second in a race, contest, etc.
**run'ning,** *n.* the act of one that runs; racing, management, etc. *adj.* 1. that runs (in various senses). 2. measured in a straight line: as, a *running* foot. 3. continuous: as, a *running* commentary. 4. successive: as, for five days *running.*
**running mate,** a candidate for a lesser office, running together with his party's candidate for the greater.
**run'-off',** *n.* a deciding, final contest.
**runt** (runt), *n.* [cf. AS. *hrindan,* to thrust], a stunted animal, plant, or (in a contemptuous sense) person. —**runt'y,** *adj.*
**run·way** (run'wā'), *n.* a channel, track, etc. in, on, or along which something moves; esp., a strip of leveled ground used by airplanes in taking off and landing.
**ru·pee** (ro͞o-pē'), *n.* [< Sans. *rūpya,* wrought silver], the monetary unit of India or of Pakistan.
**rup·ture** (rup'chẽr), *n.* [< L. *rumpere,* to break], 1. a breaking apart or being broken apart; breach. 2. hernia. *v.t. & v.i.* [-TURED, -TURING], 1. to break; burst. 2. to affect with or undergo a hernia.
**ru·ral** (roor'əl), *adj.* [< L. *rus,* the country], of, like, or living in the country; rustic.
**ruse** (ro͞oz), *n.* [< OFr. *ruser,* to dodge], a stratagem, trick, or artifice.
**rush** (rush), *v.i. & v.t.* [< OFr. *reüsser,* get out of the way], 1. to move, push, drive, etc. swiftly or impetuously. 2. to make a sudden attack (on). 3. to pass, go, send, act, do, etc. with unusual haste; hurry. 4. [Slang], to lavish attentions (on), as in

courting. **n.** 1. a rushing. 2. an eager movement of many people to get to a place. 3. busyness; haste: as, the *rush* of modern life. 4. a press, as of business, necessitating unusual haste.

**rush** (rush), **n.** [AS. *rysce*], a grasslike plant with a hollow or pithy stem, growing in wet places.

**rusk** (rusk), **n.** [< Sp. *rosca*, twisted bread roll], 1. a piece of bread or cake toasted in an oven. 2. a light, soft, sweetened biscuit.

**Russ.,** 1. Russia. 2. Russian.

**rus·set** (rus′it), **n.** [< L. *russus*, reddish], 1. yellowish (or reddish) brown. 2. a winter apple with a mottled skin. **adj.** yellowish-brown or reddish-brown.

**Rus′sian,** **adj.** of Russia, its people, language, etc. **n.** 1. a native of Russia. 2. the East Slavic language of the Russians.

**rust** (rust), **n.** [AS.], 1. the reddish-brown coating formed on iron and steel during exposure to air and moisture. 2. any stain resembling this. 3. a reddish brown. 4. a plant disease caused by parasitic fungi, spotting stems and leaves. **v.i. & v.t.** 1. to form rust (on). 2. to deteriorate, as through disuse.

**rus·tic** (rus′tik), **adj.** [< L. *rus*, the country], 1. of the country; rural. 2. simple; artless. 3. rough; uncouth. **n.** an unsophisticated country person. —**rus′ti·cal·ly,** **adv.** —**rus·tic′i·ty** (-tis′ə-ti), **n.**

**rus·ti·cate** (rus′ti-kāt′), **v.i. & v.t.** [-CATED, -CATING], 1. to go or send to live in the country. 2. to become or make rustic. —**rus′ti·ca′tion,** **n.** —**rus′ti·ca′tor,** **n.**

**rus·tle** (rus′'l), **v.i. & v.t.** [-TLED, -TLING], [ult. echoic], to make, or move so as to make, soft, rubbing sounds, as of moving leaves, etc. **n.** a series of such sounds.

**rus·tle** (rus′'l), **v.i. & v.t.** [-TLED, -TLING], [< ?], [Colloq.], to steal (cattle, etc.). —**rustle up,** [Colloq.], to collect or get together. —**rus′tler,** **n.**

**rust′proof′,** **adj.** resistant to rust.

**rust·y** (rus′ti), **adj.** [-IER, -IEST], 1. coated with rust, as a metal. 2. *a*) impaired by disuse, neglect, etc. *b*) having lost facility through lack of practice. 3. rust-colored.

**rut** (rut), **n.** [see ROUTE], 1. a groove, track, etc., as made by wheels. 2. a fixed, routine procedure, course of action, etc. **v.t.** [RUTTED, RUTTING], to make ruts in.

**rut** (rut), **n.** [< L. *rugire*, to roar], the periodic sexual excitement of many male mammals. **v.i.** [RUTTED, RUTTING], to be in rut.

**ru·ta·ba·ga** (ro͞o′tə-bā′gə), **n.** [Sw. dial. *rotabagge*], a turnip with a large, yellow root.

**Ruth** (ro͞oth), **n.** in the *Bible*, a woman who left her own people out of devotion to her mother-in-law, Naomi.

**ruth·less** (ro͞oth′lis), **adj.** [< AS. *hreowian*, to rue], without pity or compassion.

**Rwy., Ry.,** Railway.

**rye** (rī), **n.** [AS. *ryge*], 1. a hardy cereal grass. 2. its grain or seeds, used for making flour, etc. and as feed for livestock. 3. whisky distilled from this grain.

# S

**S, s** (es), **n.** [*pl.* S's, s's, Ss, ss], the nineteenth letter of the English alphabet.

**S,** in *chem.*, sulfur.

**-s,** [alt. of *-es*], 1. the plural ending of most nouns, as in *lips*. 2. the ending of the third person singular, present indicative, of verbs.

**-'s,** [AS. *-es*], the ending of the possessive singular of nouns (and some pronouns) and of the possessive plural of nouns not ending in *s*: as, boy'*s*, women'*s*.

**-'s,** the assimilated form of: 1. *is*, as in *he's here*. 2. *has*, as in *she's gone*. 3. *us*, as in *let's go*.

**S, s,** southern.

**S., s.,** 1. [*pl.* SS., ss.], saint. 2. school. 3. south.

**s.,** 1. second(s). 2. shilling(s).

**S.A.,** 1. South Africa. 2. South America.

**Sab·bath** (sab′əth), **n.** [< Heb. *shābath*, to rest], 1. the seventh day of the Jewish week, set aside for rest and worship; Saturday. 2. Sunday: so called by most Protestants.

**Sab·bat·i·cal** (sə-bat′i-k'l), **adj.** 1. of the Sabbath. 2. [s-], bringing a period of rest: as, a *sabbatical* leave. **n.** [s-], a sabbatical year. Also **Sab·bat′ic.**

**sa·ber, sa·bre** (sā′bẽr), **n.** [< MHG. *sabel*], a heavy cavalry sword with a slightly curved blade. **v.t.** [-BERED or -BRED, -BERING or -BRING], to strike, wound, or kill with a saber.

**sa·ble** (sā′b'l), **n.** [< ML. *sabelum*], 1. a flesh-eating, weasellike mammal valued for its glossy, dark fur. 2. this fur.

**sa·bot** (sab′ō; Fr. sä′bō′), **n.** [Fr.; ult. < Ar. *sabbāt*, sandal], a wooden shoe worn by peasants in Europe.

**sab·o·tage** (sab′ə-täzh′), **n.** [Fr. < *sabot*: from damage done to machinery by wooden shoes in early labor disputes], deliberate destruction of railroads, bridges, etc., as by enemy agents or an underground resistance, in time of war. **v.t. & v.i.** [-TAGED, -TAGING], to commit sabotage (on).

**sab′o·teur′** (-tũr′), **n.** [Fr.], one who engages in sabotage.

**sac** (sak), **n.** [see SACK (bag)], a pouchlike part in a plant or animal.

**sac·cha·rin** (sak′ə-rin), **n.** [< Gr. *sakcharon*], a white, crystalline coal-tar compound used for sweetening in place of sugar.

**sac′cha·rine** (-rin), **adj.** 1. of or like sugar. 2. very sweet: as, a *saccharine* voice: used derisively. **n.** saccharin.

**sac·er·do·tal** (sas′ẽr-dō′t'l), **adj.** [< L. *sacerdos*, priest], of priests or the office of priest.

**sa·chem** (sā′chəm), **n.** [Am. Ind.], among some American Indian tribes, the chief.

**sa·chet** (sa-shā′), **n.** [Fr. < *sac*, a bag], a small bag, pad, etc. filled with perfumed powder, used to scent clothing.

**sack** (sak), **n.** [ult. < Heb. *saq*], 1. a bag; esp., a large bag of coarse cloth, for holding grain, etc. 2. [Slang], discharge (with *the*). 3. [Slang], a bed. **v.t.** 1. to put into sacks. 2. [Slang], to discharge (a person).

**sack** (sak), **n.** [akin to SACK (a bag)], the plundering of a captured city or town. **v.t.** to plunder; pillage. —**sack′er,** **n.**

**sack** (sak), **n.** [< L. *siccus*, dry], a dry white wine from Spain, etc.

**sack′cloth′,** **n.** 1. coarse cloth used for sacks: also called **sack′ing.** 2. coarse, rough cloth worn as a symbol of mourning.

**sac·ra·ment** (sak′rə-mənt), **n.** [< L. *sacer*, sacred], 1. any of certain rites observed by Christians, as baptism, the Eucharist, etc. 2. something regarded as sacred. —**sac′ra·men′tal,** **adj.** —**sac′ra·men′tal·ly,** **adv.**

**sa·cred** (sā′krid), **adj.** [< L. *sacer*, holy], 1. consecrated to a god or God; holy. 2. having to do with religion. 3. venerated; hallowed. 4. inviolate. —**sa′cred·ly,** **adv.**

**sac·ri·fice** (sak′rə-fīs′), **n.** [< L. *sacer*, sacred + *facere*, make], 1. an offering, as of a life or object, to a deity. 2. a giving up of one thing for the sake of another. 3. a loss incurred in selling. ***v.t. & v.i.*** [-FICED, -FICING], 1. to offer (something) to a deity. 2. to give up (one thing) for the sake of another. 3. to incur a loss in selling. —**sac′ri·fi′cial** (-fish′əl), ***adj.***

**sac·ri·lege** (sak′rə-lij), ***n.*** [< L. *sacer*, sacred + *legere*, take away], desecration of what is sacred. —**sac′ri·le′gious** (-lē′jəs, -lij′əs), ***adj.*** —**sac′ri·le′gious·ly,** ***adv.***

**sac·ro·sanct** (sak′rō-saŋkt′), ***adj.*** [< L. *sacer*, sacred + *sanctus*, holy], very sacred, holy, or inviolable. —**sac′ro·sanc′ti·ty,** ***n.***

**sad** (sad), ***adj.*** [SADDER, SADDEST], [AS. *sæd*, sated], 1. having or expressing low spirits; unhappy; sorrowful. 2. causing dejection, sorrow, etc. 3. [Colloq.], very bad.

**sad′den,** ***v.t. & v.i.*** to make or become sad.

**sad·dle** (sad′'l), ***n.*** [AS. *sadol*], 1. a padded leather seat for a rider on a horse, bicycle, etc. 2. a cut of mutton, etc. including part of the backbone. ***v.t.*** [-DLED, -DLING], 1. to put a saddle upon. 2. to encumber, as with a burden.

**sad′dle·bag′,** ***n.*** a large bag, usually one of a pair, hung over a horse's back behind the saddle.

**saddle horse,** a horse trained to be ridden.

**saddle shoes,** flat-heeled sport shoes with a band of leather across the instep.

**Sad·du·cee** (saj′oo-sē′), ***n.*** a member of an ancient Jewish sect that adhered strictly to the written law. —**Sad′du·ce′an,** ***adj.***

**sad·ism** (sad′iz'm, sā′diz'm), ***n.*** [< Count de *Sade*, 18th-c. Fr. writer], the getting of pleasure from mistreating others. —**sad′ist,** ***n.*** —**sa·dis′tic,** ***adj.*** —**sa·dis′ti·cal·ly,** ***adv.***

**sa·fa·ri** (sə-fä′ri), ***n.*** [*pl.* -RIS], [< Ar. *safara*, travel], a journey or hunting expedition, esp. in Africa.

**safe** (sāf), ***adj.*** [SAFER, SAFEST], [< L. *salvus*], 1. free from damage, danger, etc. 2. having escaped injury; unharmed. 3. giving protection. 4. trustworthy. 5. prudent; cautious. ***n.*** a locking metal container for valuables. —**safe′ly,** ***adv.*** —**safe′ness,** ***n.***

**safe′-con′duct,** ***n.*** permission, usually written, to travel safely through enemy regions.

**safe′-de·pos′it box,** a box for storing valuables, as in a bank vault.

**safe′guard′,** ***n.*** a protection; precaution. ***v.t.*** to protect or guard.

**safe′keep′ing,** ***n.*** a keeping or being kept in safety; protection.

**safe′ty,** ***n.*** [*pl.* -TIES], 1. a being safe; security. 2. any device for preventing accident. ***adj.*** giving safety.

**safety belt,** a seat belt securing a passenger in an airplane or automobile.

**safety glass,** shatterproof glass.

**safety match,** a match that lights only when struck on a prepared surface.

**safety pin,** a pin bent back on itself and having the point held in a guard.

**safety razor,** a razor with a detachable blade fitted into a holder with guards.

**safety valve,** an automatic valve which releases steam if the pressure in a boiler, etc. becomes excessive.

**saf·flow·er** (saf′lou′ər), ***n.*** [ult. < Ar.], a thistlelike plant with large, orange flower heads and seeds that yield an edible oil.

**saf·fron** (saf′rən), ***n.*** [< Ar. *za'farān*], 1. a plant with orange stigmas yielding a dye and seasoning. 2. its dried stigmas. 3. orange yellow.

**S. Afr. D.,** South African Dutch.

**sag** (sag), ***v.i.*** [SAGGED, SAGGING], [prob. < ON.], 1. to sink, esp. in the middle, from weight or pressure. 2. to hang down unevenly. 3. to weaken through weariness, age, etc. ***n.*** 1. a sagging. 2. a sagging place.

**sa·ga** (sä′gə), ***n.*** [ON., a tale], 1. a medieval Scandinavian story of battles, legends, etc. 2. any long story of heroic deeds.

**sa·ga·cious** (sə-gā′shəs), ***adj.*** [< L. *sagax*, wise], keenly perceptive; shrewd. —**sa·ga′cious·ly,** ***adv.*** —**sa·gac′i·ty** (-gas′ə-ti), ***n.***

**sage** (sāj), ***adj.*** [SAGER, SAGEST], [ult. < L. *sapere*, know], 1. wise and perceptive. 2. showing wisdom: as, a *sage* comment. ***n.*** a very wise man. —**sage′ly,** ***adv.***

**sage** (sāj), ***n.*** [< L. *salvus*, safe: it reputedly had healing powers], 1. a plant of the mint family with grayish-green leaves used for flavoring meats, etc. 2. sagebrush.

**sage′brush′,** ***n.*** a shrub with a sagelike odor, found chiefly on western U.S. plains.

**Sag·it·ta·ri·us** (saj′i-târ′i-əs), ***n.*** [L., archer], the ninth sign of the zodiac.

**sa·hib** (sä′ib), ***n.*** [< Ar.], master: title formerly used by natives in India when speaking to or of a European.

**said** (sed), pt. and pp. of **say.** ***adj.*** aforesaid.

**sail** (sāl), ***n.*** [AS. *segl*], 1. a sheet, as of canvas, spread to catch the wind so as to drive a vessel forward. 2. sails collectively. 3. a trip in any vessel. 4. anything like a sail. ***v.i.*** 1. to be moved forward by means of sails. 2. to travel on water. 3. to begin a voyage by water. 4. to navigate a sailboat. 5. to glide or move smoothly, like a ship in full sail. ***v.t.*** 1. to move upon (a body of water) in a vessel. 2. to manage (a vessel). —**sail into,** [Colloq.], 1. to begin vigorously. 2. to criticize severely. —**set sail,** to begin a trip by water. —**under sail,** sailing.

**sail′boat′,** ***n.*** a boat propelled by a sail or sails.

**sail′fish′,** ***n.*** [*pl.* see FISH], a large tropical marine fish with a large saillike dorsal fin.

**sail′or,** ***n.*** 1. one who makes his living by sailing. 2. an enlisted man in the navy. 3. a hat with a flat crown and brim.

**saint** (sānt), ***n.*** [< L. *sanctus*, holy], 1. a holy person. 2. a person who is exceptionally patient, charitable, etc. 3. in certain churches, a person officially recognized as having attained heaven after an exceptionally holy life, and duly venerated. —**saint′ly** [-LIER, -LIEST], ***adj.*** —**saint′li·ness,** ***n.***

**Saint Ber·nard** (bẽr-närd′), a large dog of a breed formerly kept at St. Bernard hospice in the Swiss Alps to rescue lost travelers.

**Saint Patrick's Day,** March 17, observed by the Irish in honor of the patron saint of Ireland.

**Saint Valentine's Day,** February 14, observed in honor of a martyr of the 3d century, now a day for sending valentines, candy, etc. to sweethearts.

**saith** (seth), [Archaic], says.

**sake** (sāk), ***n.*** [AS. *sacu*, suit at law], 1. motive; cause: as, for the *sake* of money. 2. advantage; behalf: as, for my *sake*.

**sa·ke** (sä′ki), ***n.*** [Japan.], a Japanese alcoholic beverage made from fermented rice.

**sal** (sal), ***n.*** [L.], in *pharmacy*, etc., salt.

**sa·laam** (sə-läm′), ***n.*** [Ar. *salām*, peace], an Oriental greeting, etc. made by bowing low in respect or obeisance. ***v.i.*** to make a salaam.

**sal·a·ble** (sāl′ə-b'l), ***adj.*** that can be sold; marketable: also sp. **saleable.**

**sa·la·cious** (sə-lā′shəs), ***adj.*** [< L. *salire*, to leap], 1. lecherous; lustful. 2. obscene.

**sal·ad** (sal′əd), ***n.*** [< L. *salata*, salted], a dish, usually cold, of fruits, vegetables (esp. lettuce), meat, eggs, etc. in various combinations, prepared with a salad dressing.

**salad days,** time of youth and inexperience.

**salad dressing,** a preparation of oil, vinegar, spices, etc. put on a salad.

**sal·a·man·der** (sal′ə-man′dẽr), ***n.*** [< Gr. *salamandra*], 1. a mythological reptile able to live in fire. 2. a scaleless, lizardlike amphibian.

**sa·la·mi** (sə-lä′mi), ***n.*** [It. < L. *sal*, salt], a spiced, salted sausage.

**sal·a·ry** (sal'ə-ri), *n.* [*pl.* -RIES], [< L. *salarium*, orig., part of a soldier's pay for buying salt < *sal*, salt], a fixed payment at regular intervals for work or services. —**sal'a·ried** (-rid), *adj.*

**sale** (sāl), *n.* [< ON. *sala*], 1. a selling. 2. a market; opportunity to sell. 3. an auction. 4. a special offering of goods at reduced prices. —**for** (or **on**) **sale**, to be sold.

**sales·man** (sālz'mən), *n.* [*pl.* -MEN], a man employed to sell goods. —**sales'girl'**, **sales'-la'dy** [*pl.* -DIES], **sales'wom'an**, [*pl.* -WOMEN], *n.fem.* —**sales'man·ship'**, *n.*

**sales'per'son,** *n.* a person employed to sell goods, esp. in a store.

**sales tax,** a tax on receipts from sales.

**sal·i·cyl·ic acid** (sal'ə-sil'ik), [< *salicin* (substance obtained from certain willows)], a white, crystalline compound, used, as in aspirin, to relieve pain, etc.

**sa·li·ent** (sā'li-ənt), *adj.* [< L. *salire*, to leap], 1. pointing outward; jutting. 2. prominent; conspicuous. *n.* a salient angle, part, etc. —**sa'li·ence**, *n.*

**sa·line** (sā'līn), *adj.* [< L. *sal*, salt], of, like, or containing salt; salty.

**sa·li·va** (sə-lī'və), *n.* [L.], a thin, watery fluid secreted by glands in the mouth: it aids in digestion. —**sal·i·var·y** (sal'ə-ver'i), *adj.*

**sal·i·vate** (sal'ə-vāt'), *v.i.* [-VATED, -VATING], [< L. *salivare*], to secrete saliva. —**sal'i-va'tion**, *n.*

**sal·low** (sal'ō), *adj.* [AS. *salu*], of a sickly, pale-yellowish complexion.

**sal·ly** (sal'i), *n.* [*pl.* -LIES], [< L. *salire*, to leap], 1. a sudden rushing forth, as to attack. 2. any sudden start into activity. 3. a quick witticism; quip. 4. an excursion; jaunt. *v.i.* [-LIED, -LYING], to rush or start (*out* or *forth*) on a sally.

**sal·ma·gun·di** (sal'mə-gun'di), *n.* [< Fr. *salmigondis*], 1. a dish of chopped meat, eggs, onions, anchovies, etc. 2. any mixture.

**salm·on** (sam'ən), *n.* [*pl.* -ON, -ONS], [< L. *salmo*], 1. a large game and food fish with yellowish-pink flesh, that lives in salt water and spawns in fresh water. 2. yellowish pink: also **salmon pink**. *adj.* yellowish-pink: also **salmon-pink**.

**Sa·lo·me** (sə-lō'mi), *n.* in the *Bible*, a dancer at whose request John the Baptist was beheaded: Matt. 14:8.

**sa·lon** (sə-lon'), *n.* [Fr.; see SALOON], 1. a large reception hall or drawing room. 2. a regular gathering of distinguished guests.

**sa·loon** (sə-lōōn'), *n.* [< Fr. < It. *sala*, hall], 1. any large room or hall for receptions, exhibitions, etc. 2. a public place where alcoholic drinks are sold.

**salt** (sôlt), *n.* [AS. *sealt*], 1. a white, crystalline substance, sodium chloride, found in natural beds, in sea water, etc., and used for seasoning food, etc. 2. a chemical compound derived from an acid by replacing hydrogen with a metal. 3. tang or piquancy. 4. sharp, pungent humor. 5. *pl.* *a*) mineral salts used as a cathartic. *b*) smelling salts. 6. [Colloq.], a sailor. *adj.* containing, preserved with, or tasting of salt. *v.t.* to sprinkle, season, or preserve with salt. —**salt of the earth**, any person or persons regarded as the finest, etc. —**with a grain of salt**, with allowance for exaggeration, etc. —**salt'y** [-IER, -IEST], *adj.*

**salt'cel'lar** (-sel'ẽr), *n.* [< *salt* + Fr. *salière*, saltcellar], 1. a small dish for salt. 2. a salt shaker.

**salt lick,** an exposed natural deposit of rock salt which animals come to lick.

**salt·pe·ter, salt·pe·tre** (sôlt'pē'tẽr), *n.* [< L. *sal*, salt + *petra*, a rock], 1. potassium nitrate. 2. sodium nitrate: also **Chile saltpeter.**

**salt pork,** pork cured in salt.

**salt shaker,** a container for salt with a perforated top.

**salt water,** water containing much salt; esp., sea water. —**salt'-wa'ter**, *adj.*

**sa·lu·bri·ous** (sə-lōō'bri-əs), *adj.* [< L. *salus*, health], healthful; wholesome.

**sal·u·tar·y** (sal'yoo-ter'i), *adj.* [< L. *salus*, health], 1. healthful. 2. beneficial.

**sal·u·ta·tion** (sal'yoo-tā'shən), *n.* [see SALUTE], 1. the act of greeting, paying respect, etc. 2. a form of greeting, as the "Dear Sir" of a letter.

**sa·lute** (sə-lōōt'), *v.t. & v.i.* [-LUTED, -LUTING], [< L. *salus*, health], 1. to greet with a salute. 2. to honor ceremonially as a mark of official respect. *n.* an act, words, etc. expressing welcome, respect, etc.; specif., a prescribed formal gesture, as raising the hand to the head, in military and naval practice.

**sal·vage** (sal'vij), *n.* [see SAVE], 1. the rescue of a ship, crew, and cargo from shipwreck, etc. 2. compensation paid for such rescue. 3. in *insurance*, *a*) the rescue of property from fire. *b*) the property so rescued. *v.t.* [-VAGED, -VAGING], 1. to save from shipwreck, fire, etc. 2. to restore (sunken ships). 3. to utilize (waste, damaged goods, etc.).

**sal·va·tion** (sal-vā'shən), *n.* [< L. *salvare*, save], 1. a saving or being saved. 2. a person or thing that saves or rescues. 3. in *theology*, the saving of the soul from sin and death.

**Salvation Army,** a religious and charitable organization to aid the poor.

**salve** (sav, säv), *n.* [AS. *sealf*], 1. any soothing or healing ointment for wounds, burns, etc. 2. something that soothes or heals. *v.i.* [SALVED, SALVING], 1. to apply salve to. 2. to soothe; assuage.

**sal·ver** (sal'vẽr), *n.* [ult. < L. *salvare*, save], a tray.

**sal·vo** (sal'vō), *n.* [*pl.* -VOS, -VOES], [< It. < L. *salve*, hail!], a discharge of a number of guns, either in salute or at a target.

**S. Am., S. Amer.,** South America(n).

**same** (sām), *adj.* [< ON. *samr*], 1. being the very one; identical. 2. alike in kind, quality, amount, etc. 3. unchanged: as, he kept the *same* expression. 4. before-mentioned. *pron.* the same person or thing. *adv.* in like manner. —**all the same**, 1. nevertheless. 2. of no importance. —**just the same**, 1. in the same way. 2. nevertheless. —**same'ness**, *n.*

**sam·o·var** (sam'ə-vär'), *n.* [Russ.], a Russian metal urn with an internal tube for heating water in making tea.

**sam·pan** (sam'pan), *n.* [Chin. < Sp. *champán*, canoe], a small boat used in China and Japan, rowed with a scull from the stern.

**sam·ple** (sam'p'l, säm'-), *n.* [see EXAMPLE], 1. a part taken as representative of a whole thing, group, etc.; specimen. 2. an example. *adj.* being a sample. *v.t.* [-PLED, -PLING], to take or test a sample of.

**sam'pler,** *n.* 1. one who samples. 2. a piece of cloth embroidered with designs, letters, etc., as to display skill in needlework.

**Sam·son** (sam's'n), *n.* in the *Bible*, an Israelite with great strength: see Judges 13–16.

**Sam·u·el** (sam'ū-əl), *n.* in the *Bible*, a Hebrew judge and prophet.

**sam·u·rai** (sam'oo-rī'), *n.* [*pl.* -RAI], [Japan.], a member of a military caste in feudal Japan.

**san·a·to·ri·um** (san'ə-tôr'i-əm), *n.* [*pl.* -UMS, -A (-ə)], [< L. *sanare*, heal], a sanitarium.

**sanc·ti·fy** (saŋk'tə-fī'), *v.t.* [-FIED, -FYING], [< L. *sanctus*, holy + *facere*, make], 1. to make free from sin. 2. to set apart as holy; consecrate. —**sanc'ti·fi·ca'tion**, *n.*

**sanc·ti·mo·ni·ous** (saŋk'tə-mō'ni-əs), *adj.* pretending to be pious.

**sanc'ti·mo'ny,** *n.* [< L. *sanctus*, holy], pretended piety; religious hypocrisy.

**sanc·tion** (saŋk'shən), *n.* [< L. *sancire*,

make sacred], 1. authorization. 2. support; approval. 3. *usually in pl.* a punitive measure, as an official trade boycott, against a nation defying international law. *v.t.* 1. to authorize; confirm. 2. to approve.

**sanc·ti·ty** (saŋk′tə-ti), *n.* [*pl.* -TIES], [< L. *sanctus*, holy], 1. saintliness; holiness. 2. sacredness. 3. binding force.

**sanc·tu·ar·y** (saŋk′chōō-er′i), *n.* [*pl.* -IES], [< L. *sanctus*, sacred], 1. a holy place; specif., a church, temple, etc. 2. a place of refuge or protection.

**sanc·tum** (saŋk′təm), *n.* [*pl.* -TUMS, -TA (-tə)], [L. < *sancire*, consecrate], 1. a sacred place. 2. a private room where one is not to be disturbed.

**sand** (sand), *n.* [AS.], 1. loose, gritty grains of disintegrated rock, as on beaches, in deserts, etc. 2. *usually pl.* a tract of sand. *v.t.* 1. to sprinkle or fill with sand. 2. to smooth or polish as with sandpaper.

**san·dal** (san′d'l), *n.* [< Gr. *sandalon*], 1. a shoe made of a sole fastened to the foot by straps. 2. a slipper having the upper slashed with openwork. —**san′daled, san′dalled,** *adj.*

**san′dal·wood′,** *n.* [ult. < Sans.], 1. the hard, sweet-smelling heartwood of an Asiatic tree. 2. this tree.

**sand′bag′,** *n.* a bag filled with sand and used for fortifications, ballast in ships, etc.

**sand bar,** a ridge of sand formed in a river or along a shore.

**sand′blast′,** *n.* a current of air or steam carrying sand at a high velocity, used in cleaning stone, etc. *v.t.* to clean with a sandblast. —**sand′blast′er,** *n.*

**sand′box′,** *n.* a box filled with sand, as for children to play in.

**sand′hog′,** *n.* a laborer in underground or underwater construction.

**sand′-lot′,** *adj.* of, having to do with, or played in a sandy lot or field in or near a city: as, *sand-lot* baseball.

**sand′man′,** *n.* a mythical person supposed to make children sleepy by dusting sand on their eyes.

**sand′pa′per,** *n.* paper coated on one side with sand, used for smoothing and polishing. *v.t.* to smooth or polish with sandpaper.

**sand′pip′er** (-pīp′ẽr), *n.* a shore bird with a long, soft-tipped bill.

**sand′stone′,** *n.* a sedimentary rock consisting of sand grains cemented together by silica, lime, etc.

**sand′storm′,** *n.* a windstorm in which sand is blown about in large clouds.

**sand·wich** (sand′wich, san′-), *n.* [< 4th Earl of *Sandwich* (1718–1792)], two or more slices of bread with meat, cheese, etc. between them. *v.t.* to place between other persons, things, etc.

**sand·y** (san′di), *adj.* [-IER, -IEST], 1. of or like sand. 2. pale reddish-yellow: as, *sandy* hair.

**sane** (sān), *adj.* [L. *sanus*, healthy], 1. mentally healthy; rational. 2. showing good sense; sound: as, a *sane* policy.

**San·for·ize** (san′fə-rīz′), *v.t.* [-IZED, -IZING], [< *Sanford* L. Cluett (1874–1968), U.S. inventor], to preshrink (cotton or linen cloth) permanently by a patented process before making it into clothes.

**sang** (saŋ), pt. of **sing.**

**san·gui·nar·y** (saŋ′gwi-ner′i), *adj.* [< L. *sanguis*, blood], 1. accompanied by much bloodshed, or murder. 2. bloodthirsty.

**san·guine** (saŋ′gwin), *adj.* [< L. *sanguis*, blood], 1. of the color of blood; ruddy. 2. cheerful; confident. —**san′guine·ly,** *adv.*

**san·i·tar·i·um** (san′ə-târ′i-əm), *n.* [*pl.* -UMS, -A (-ə)], [Mod. L. < *sanitas*, health], 1. a resort where people go to regain health. 2. an institution for the care of invalids or convalescents.

**san·i·tar·y** (san′ə-ter′i), *adj.* [< L. *sanitas*, health], 1. of health or the rules and conditions of health. 2. in a clean, healthy condition.

**san·i·ta·tion** (san′ə-tā′shən), *n.* 1. the science and practice of effecting hygienic conditions. 2. drainage and disposal of sewage.

**san·i·tize** (san′ə-tīz′), *v.t.* [-TIZED, -TIZING], to make sanitary.

**san·i·ty** (san′ə-ti), *n.* 1. the state of being sane. 2. soundness of judgment.

**sank** (saŋk), pt. of **sink.**

**sans** (sanz; Fr. sän), *prep.* [< L. *absentia*, absence] without.

**San·skrit, San·scrit** (san′skrit), *n.* the classical literary language of ancient India.

**San·ta** (san′tə, sän′tä), *adj.* [Sp. & It., saint, fem.], holy or saint: used in combinations.

**San·ta Claus, San·ta Klaus** (san′tə klôz′), [< D. *Sant Nikolaas*, St. Nicholas], in *folklore*, a fat, white-bearded, jolly old man in a red suit, who distributes gifts at Christmas.

**sap** (sap), *n.* [AS. *sæp*], 1. the juice that circulates through a plant, bearing water, food, etc. 2. vigor; energy. 3. [Slang], a fool. —**sap′less,** *adj.*

**sap** (sap), *v.t.* [SAPPED, SAPPING], [< It. *zappe*, spade], 1. to undermine by digging away foundations. 2. to weaken; exhaust.

**sa·pi·ent** (sā′pi-ənt), *adj.* [< L. *sapere*, to taste, know], wise; full of knowledge. —**sa′pi·ence, sa′pi·en·cy,** *n.* —**sa′pi·ent·ly,** *adv.*

**sap·ling** (sap′liŋ), *n.* a young tree.

**sap·phire** (saf′īr), *n.* [< Gr. *sappheiros*], 1. a hard precious stone of a clear, deep-blue corundum. 2. its color. *adj.* deep-blue.

**sap·py** (sap′i), *adj.* 1. full of sap; juicy. 2. energetic; vigorous. 3. [Slang], foolish; silly. —**sap′pi·ly,** *adv.* —**sap′pi·ness,** *n.*

**sap′suck′er,** *n.* a small American woodpecker that drills holes in certain trees and drinks the sap.

**sar·a·band** (sar′ə-band′), *n.* [ult. < Per. *sarband*, a dance], 1. a stately, slow Spanish dance. 2. music for this.

**Sar·a·cen** (sar′ə-s'n), *n.* formerly, *a*) a Moslem, esp. as opposed to the Crusaders. *b*) an Arab. —**Sar′a·cen′ic** (-sen′ik), *adj.*

**Sar·ah** (sâr′ə), *n.* in the *Bible*, the wife of Abraham and mother of Isaac.

**sa·ran** (sə-ran′), *n.* [a coinage], a thermoplastic substance used in making various fabrics, a transparent wrapping material, etc.

**sar·casm** (sär′kaz'm), *n.* [< Gr. *sarkazein*, to tear flesh], 1. a taunting or caustic remark, generally ironical. 2. the making of such remarks. 3. sarcastic quality.

**sar·cas·tic** (sär-kas′tik), *adj.* 1. of or characterized by sarcasm; sneering; caustic. 2. using, or fond of using, sarcasm. —**sar·cas′ti·cal·ly,** *adv.*

**sar·co·ma** (sär-kō′mə), *n.* [*pl.* -MAS, -MATA (-mə-tə)], [< Gr. *sarx*, flesh], a malignant tumor in connective tissue.

**sar·coph·a·gus** (sär-kof′ə-gəs), *n.* [*pl.* -GI (-jī′), -GUSES], [< Gr. *sarx*, flesh + *phagein*, to eat: limestone coffins hastened disintegration], a stone coffin, esp. an ornamented one in a tomb.

**sar·dine** (sär-dēn′), *n.* [< Gr. *sarda*, a fish], any of various small fishes of the herring family edible when preserved in oil.

**sar·don·ic** (sär-don′ik), *adj.* [< Gr. *sardanios*, bitter], scornfully or bitterly sarcastic. —**sar·don′i·cal·ly,** *adv.*

**sa·ri** (sä′rē), *n.* [*pl.* -RIS], [< Sans.], an outer garment of Hindu women, a long cloth wrapped around the body.

**sa·rong** (sə-rôŋ′), *n.* [Malay *sāron*], a garment of men and women in the East Indies, etc. consisting of a cloth, often brightly colored, worn like a skirt.

**sar·sa·pa·ril·la** (sär′sə-pə-ril′ə, sas′pə-), *n.* [< Sp. *zarza*, bramble + *parra*, vine], 1. a tropical American plant with fragrant roots. 2. a carbonated drink flavored with an extract from the dried roots.

**sar·to·ri·al** (sär-tôr′i-əl), *adj.* [< LL. *sartor*, tailor], 1. of tailors or their work. 2. of men's dress. —**sar·to′ri·al·ly,** *adv.*

**sash** (sash), *n.* [Ar. *shāsh*, turban], an ornamental band, ribbon, etc. worn over the shoulder or around the waist.

**sash** (sash), *n.* [< Fr. *châssis*, a frame], a frame for holding the glass pane of a window or door, esp. a sliding frame.

**sa·shay** (sa-shā′), *v.i.* [< Fr. *chassé*, a dance], [Colloq.], to glide or go.

**sas·sa·fras** (sas′ə-fras′), *n.* [Sp. *sasafras*], 1. a slender tree with yellow flowers and bluish fruit. 2. its dried root bark, used in medicine and for flavoring.

**sass·y** (sas′i), *adj.* [-IER, -IEST], [var. of *saucy*], [Dial. or Colloq.], impudent; saucy.

**sat** (sat), pt. and pp. of **sit.**

**Sat.,** 1. Saturday. 2. Saturn.

**Sa·tan** (sā′t'n), *n.* [< Heb. *sātān*, enemy], the Devil. —**Sa·tan·ic** (sā-tan′ik, sə-), *adj.*

**sa·tan·ic** (sā-tan′ik, sə-), *adj.* like Satan; devilish; wicked. —**sa·tan′i·cal·ly,** *adv.*

**satch·el** (sach′əl), *n.* [< L. *saccus*, a sack], a small traveling bag.

**sate** (sāt), *v.t.* [SATED, SATING], [prob. < L. *satiare*, satisfy], 1. to satisfy (an appetite, desire, etc.) to the full. 2. to satiate.

**sa·teen** (sa-tēn′), *n.* [< *satin*], a cotton cloth made to imitate satin.

**sat·el·lite** (sat′ə-līt′), *n.* [< L. *satelles*, an attendant], 1. an attendant of some important person. 2. a small planet revolving around a larger one. 3. a man-made object put into orbit around the earth, the sun, or some other heavenly body. 4. a small state that is economically dependent on a larger state.

**sa·ti·a·ble** (sā′shi-ə-b'l, -shə-b'l), *adj.* that can be sated or satiated. —**sa′ti·a·bil′i·ty,** *n.*

**sa·ti·ate** (sā′shi-āt′), *v.t.* [-ATED, -ATING], [< L. *satis*, sufficient], to gratify with more than enough, so as to weary or disgust; glut.

**sa·ti·e·ty** (sə-tī′ə-ti), *n.* a being satiated.

**sat·in** (sat′'n), *n.* [< Ar. *zaitūni*, of *Zaitūn*, former name of a Chinese seaport], a silk, nylon, or rayon cloth with a smooth, glossy finish on one side. —**sat′in·y,** *adj.*

**sat′in·wood′,** *n.* 1. a smooth wood used in fine furniture. 2. an East Indian tree, yielding such a wood.

**sat·ire** (sat′īr), *n.* [< L. *satira*], 1. a literary work in which vices, follies, etc. are held up to ridicule and contempt. 2. the use of ridicule, sarcasm, etc. to attack vices, follies, etc. —**sa·tir·i·cal** (sə-tir′i-k'l), **sa·tir′ic,** *adj.* —**sat·i·rist** (sat′ə-rist), *n.*

**sat·i·rize** (sat′ə-rīz′), *v.t.* [-RIZED, -RIZING], to attack with satire. —**sat′i·riz′er,** *n.*

**sat·is·fac·tion** (sat′is-fak′shən), *n.* 1. a satisfying or being satisfied. 2. something that satisfies; specif., *a*) settlement of debt. *b*) anything that brings pleasure or contentment.

**sat′is·fac′to·ry** (-tēr-i), *adj.* satisfying; fulfilling all needs, desires, etc. —**sat′is·fac′to·ri·ly,** *adv.* —**sat′is·fac′to·ri·ness,** *n.*

**sat·is·fy** (sat′is-fī′), *v.t.* [-FIED, -FYING], [< L. *satis*, enough + *facere*, make], 1. to fulfill the needs and desires of; content. 2. to fulfill the requirements of. 3. to free from doubt; convince. 4. *a*) to give what is due to. *b*) to discharge (a debt, etc.). *v.i.* to give satisfaction.

**sa·trap** (sā′trap, sat′rəp), *n.* [< OPer.], a petty tyrant.

**sat·u·rate** (sach′oo-rāt′), *v.t.* [-RATED, -RATING], [< L. *satur*, full], 1. to cause to be thoroughly soaked. 2. to cause to be so completely filled or charged that no more can be taken up. —**sat′u·ra′tion,** *n.*

**Sat·ur·day** (sat′ēr-di), *n.* [< AS. *Sæterdæg*, Saturn's day], the seventh and last day of the week.

**Sat·urn** (sat′ērn), *n.* 1. the Roman god of agriculture. 2. the second largest planet in the solar system, notable for the three rings which revolve around it: cf. **planet.**

**sat·ur·nine** (sat′ēr-nīn′), *adj.* [< supposed influence of planet Saturn], reserved, sluggish, grave, etc. —**sat′ur·nine′ly,** *adv.*

**sat·yr** (sat′ēr, sā′tēr), *n.* [< Gr. *satyros*], in *Gr. myth.*, a lecherous woodland deity, represented as a man with a goat's legs, ears, and horns.

**sauce** (sôs), *n.* [< L. *sal*, salt], 1. a liquid or soft dressing served with food as a seasoning. 2. mashed, stewed fruit. 3. [Colloq.], impudence. *v.t.* [SAUCED, SAUCING], 1. to flavor with sauce. 2. [Colloq.], to be saucy to.

**sauce′pan′,** *n.* a small metal pot with a long handle, used for cooking.

**sau·cer** (sô′sēr), *n.* [see SAUCE], a shallow dish, esp. one designed to hold a cup.

**sau·cy** (sô′si), *adj.* [-CIER, -CIEST], [< *sauce* + *-y*], 1. rude; impudent. 2. pert; sprightly. —**sau′ci·ly,** *adv.* —**sau′ci·ness,** *n.*

**sauer·kraut** (sour′krout′), *n.* [G.; *sauer*, sour + *kraut*, cabbage], chopped cabbage fermented in brine.

**Saul** (sôl), *n.* in the *Bible*, the first king of Israel.

**sau·na** (sou′nə, sô′-), *n.* [Finn.], a Finnish bath consisting of exposure to hot, dry air.

**saun·ter** (sôn′tēr), *v.i.* [< ME. *santre(n)*, to muse], to walk about idly; stroll. *n.* a leisurely walk. —**saun′ter·ing·ly,** *adv.*

**sau·ri·an** (sô′ri-ən), *adj.* [< Gr. *saura*, lizard], of, or having the characteristics of, lizards, crocodiles, or dinosaurs.

**sau·sage** (sô′sij), *n.* [see SAUCE], meat, usually pork, chopped fine, seasoned, and often stuffed into a casing.

**sau·té** (sô-tā′), *adj.* [Fr. < *sauter*, to leap], fried quickly in a little fat. *v.t.* [-TÉED, -TÉING], to fry quickly in a little fat.

**sau·terne** (sō-tũrn′), *n.* [< *Sauternes*, town in France], a white table wine.

**sav·age** (sav′ij), *adj.* [< L. *silva*, a wood], 1. wild; uncultivated: as, a *savage* forest. 2. fierce; untamed: as, a *savage* tiger. 3. primitive; barbarous: as, a *savage* tribe. *n.* 1. a human being living in an uncivilized, primitive way. 2. a brutal person.

**sav′age·ry,** *n.* [*pl.* -RIES], 1. the condition of being savage. 2. savage act or behavior.

**sa·vant** (sə-vänt′, sav′ənt), *n.* [Fr. < *savoir*, to know], a learned person.

**save** (sāv), *v.t.* [SAVED, SAVING], [< L. *salvus*, safe], 1. to rescue or preserve from harm or danger. 2. to preserve for future use. 3. to prevent or lessen: as, *save* expense. 4. to prevent loss or waste of: as, it *saves* hours. 5. in *theology*, to deliver from sin. *v.i.* 1. to avoid expense, waste, etc. 2. to store up money or goods. —**sav′a·ble,** *adj.* —**sav′er,** *n.*

**save** (sāv), *prep. & conj.* [< L. *salvus*, safe], except; but: also **sav′ing.**

**sav·ing** (sāv′iŋ), *adj.* that saves; specif., *a*) rescuing. *b*) economical. *c*) redeeming. *n.* 1. any reduction in time, expense, etc. 2. what is saved; esp., *pl.* sums of money saved.

**sav·ior, sav·iour** (sāv′yēr), *n.* [< L. *salvare*, to save], one who saves. —**the Saviour,** Jesus Christ.

**sa·voir-faire** (sav′wär-fâr′), *n.* [Fr., to know (how) to do], ready knowledge of what to do or say; tact.

**sa·vor** (sā′vēr), *n.* [< L. *sapor*], 1. a particular taste or smell. 2. characteristic quality. *v.i.* to have the characteristic taste, smell, or quality (*of*). Also, Brit. sp., **savour.**

**sa′vor·y,** *adj.* [-IER, -IEST], 1. pleasing to the taste or smell. 2. agreeable; pleasing. Also, Brit. sp., **savoury.** —**sa′vor·i·ness,** *n.*

**sav·vy** (sav′i), *v.i.* [-VIED, -VYING], [alt. < Sp. *sabe* (*usted*), do (you) know], [Slang], to understand. *n.* [Slang], common sense.
**saw** (sô), *n.* [AS. *saga*], a cutting tool consisting of a thin, metal blade or disk with sharp teeth. *v.t.* [SAWED, SAWED or SAWN, SAWING], to cut or shape with a saw. *v.i.* 1. to cut with or as a saw. 2. to be cut with a saw.
**saw** (sô), *n.* [AS. *sagu*], a saying; maxim.
**saw** (sô), pt. of **see.**
**saw·buck** (sô′buk′), *n.* [D. *zaagbuk*], 1. a sawhorse. 2. [Slang], a ten-dollar bill.
**saw·dust** (sô′dust′), *n.* fine particles of wood formed in sawing wood.
**saw·horse** (sô′hôrs′), *n.* a rack on which wood is placed for sawing.
**saw·mill** (sô′mil′), *n.* a place where logs are sawed into boards.
**saw′toothed′**, *adj.* having teeth like those of a saw; serrate.
**saw·yer** (sô′yẽr), *n.* one whose work is sawing wood, as into planks and boards.
**Sax·on** (sak′s'n), *n.* 1. a member of an ancient Germanic people of N Germany, some of whom settled in England. 2. an Anglo-Saxon (senses 1 & 3). 3. Old Saxon. *adj.* of the ancient Saxons, their language, etc.
**sax·o·phone** (sak′sə-fōn′), *n.* [< A. J. *Sax*, 19th-c. Belgian inventor + Gr. *phōnē*, sound], a single-reed, keyed, metal wind instrument. —**sax′o·phon′ist**, *n.*
**say** (sā), *v.t.* [SAID, SAYING], [AS. *secgan*], 1. to utter; speak. 2. to state; express in words; tell. 3. to state positively or as an opinion: as, I cannot *say* who won. 4. to recite: as, *say* your prayers. 5. to assume: as, he is, *say*, forty. *n.* 1. what a person says. 2. a chance to speak: as, I had my *say*. 3. authority, as to make a final decision: often with *the*. —**that is to say**, in other words.
**say′ing**, *n.* something said; esp., an adage, proverb, or maxim.
**say′-so′**, *n.* [Colloq.], 1. an unsupported statement. 2. right of decision. 3. a dictum.
**Sb**, *stibium*, [L.], in *chem.*, antimony.
**scab** (skab), *n.* [AS. *sceabb*], 1. a crust forming over a sore during healing. 2. a worker who refuses to join a union, or one who takes the place of a striking worker. *v.i.* [SCABBED, SCABBING], 1. to become covered with a scab. 2. to act as a scab. —**scab′by** [-BIER, -BIEST], *adj.*
**scab·bard** (skab′ẽrd), *n.* [? < OHG. *scar*, sword + *bergan*, hide], a sheath for the blade of a sword, dagger, etc.
**sca·bi·es** (skā′bi-ēz′, -bēz), *n.* [< L. *scabere*, to scratch], a contagious skin disease caused by mites; the itch.
**scads** (skadz), *n.pl.* [? < *scat*, a tax], [Colloq.], a very large amount.
**scaf·fold** (skaf′'ld, -ōld), *n.* [< OFr. *escafalt*], 1. a temporary framework for supporting men working on a building, etc. 2. a raised platform on which criminals are executed. 3. any raised framework.
**scaf′fold·ing**, *n.* 1. the materials forming a scaffold. 2. a scaffold.
**scal·a·wag** (skal′ə-wag′), *n.* a rascal.
**scald** (skôld), *v.t.* [< L. *ex-*, intens. + *caldus*, hot], 1. to burn with hot liquid or steam. 2. to heat almost to the boiling point. 3. to use boiling liquid on. *n.* a burn caused by scalding.
**scale** (skāl), *n.* [< L. *scala*, ladder], 1. a series of marks along a line used in measuring: as, the *scale* of a thermometer. 2. any instrument so marked. 3. the proportion that a map, etc. bears to the thing it represents: as, a *scale* of one inch to a mile. 4. *a*) a series of degrees classified by size, amount, etc.: as, a wage *scale*. *b*) any degree in such a series. 5. in *music*, a sequence of tones, rising or falling in pitch, according to a system of intervals. *v.t.* [SCALED, SCALING], 1. to climb up or over. 2. to make according to a scale. 3. to reduce according to a fixed ratio: as, to *scale* down prices.
**scale** (skāl), *n.* [< OFr. *escaille*], 1. any of the thin, flat, horny plates covering many fishes, reptiles, etc. 2. any thin, platelike layer or piece. *v.t.* [SCALED, SCALING], to scrape scales from. *v.i.* to flake or peel off in scales. —**scal′y** [-IER, -IEST], *adj.*
**scale** (skāl), *n.* [< ON. *skāl*, bowl], 1. either pan of a balance. 2. *usually pl. a*) a balance. *b*) any weighing machine. *v.t.* [SCALED, SCALING], to weigh.
**scal·lion** (skal′yən), *n.* [< L. (*caepa*) *Ascalonia*, (onion of) Ascalon (Philistine city)], any of various onions, as the leek or a green onion, with a thick stem and an almost bulbless root.
**scal·lop** (skäl′əp, skal′-), *n.* [OFr. *escalope*], 1. any of various edible mollusks with two curved, deeply grooved, hinged shells. 2. one of the shells. 3. one of a series of curves, etc. forming an ornamental edge. *v.t.* 1. to cut the edge of in scallops. 2. to bake with a milk sauce and bread crumbs; escalop.
**scalp** (skalp), *n.* [prob. < ON. *skālpr*, sheath], the skin on the top and back of the head, usually covered with hair. *v.t.* 1. to cut or tear the scalp from. 2. [Colloq.], to buy (theater tickets, etc.) and resell them at higher prices. —**scalp′er**, *n.*
**scal·pel** (skal′pəl), *n.* [< L. *scalprum*, knife], a small, sharp, straight knife used in surgery and anatomical dissections.
**scamp** (skamp), *n.* [< *scamper*], a worthless fellow; rascal. —**scamp′ish**, *adj.*
**scam·per** (skam′pẽr), *v.i.* [< L. *ex*, out + *campus*, field], to run or go quickly. *n.* a scampering.
**scan** (skan), *v.t.* [SCANNED, SCANNING], [< L. *scandere*], 1. to analyze (verse) by marking off the metrical feet. 2. to look at closely; scrutinize. 3. to glance at quickly. 4. in *TV*, to traverse (a surface) rapidly with a beam of light or electrons in transmitting or reproducing a picture. *v.i.* to conform to metrical principles: said of verse.
**Scand., Scan.**, Scandinavian.
**scan·dal** (skan′d'l), *n.* [< Gr. *skandalon*, snare], 1. anything that offends morals and leads to disgrace. 2. shame, outrage, etc. caused by this; disgrace. 3. malicious gossip.
**scan′dal·ize′**, *v.t.* [-IZED, -IZING], to outrage the moral feelings of by improper conduct.
**scan′dal·mon′ger** (-muŋ′gẽr), *n.* one who spreads scandal, or gossip.
**scan′dal·ous**, *adj.* 1. causing scandal; shameful. 2. spreading slander; libelous.
**Scan′di·na′vi·an**, *adj.* of Scandinavia, its people, languages, etc. *n.* 1. one of the people of Scandinavia. 2. the subbranch of the Germanic languages spoken by them.
**scan·sion** (skan′shən), *n.* the act of scanning verse.
**scant** (skant), *adj.* [< ON. *skammr*, short], 1. inadequate; meager. 2. not quite up to full measure. *v.t.* to stint. —**scant′ness**, *n.*
**scant′y**, *adj.* [-IER, -IEST], 1. barely sufficient; meager. 2. insufficient; not enough. —**scant′i·ly**, *adv.* —**scant′i·ness**, *n.*
**scape·goat** (skāp′gōt′), *n.* [< *escape* + *goat*: see Lev. 16:8–22], one who bears the blame for the mistakes of others.
**scape′grace′**, *n.* [< *escape* + *grace*], a graceless, unprincipled fellow; rogue; scamp.
**scap·u·la** (skap′yoo-lə), *n.* [*pl.* -LAE (-lē′), -LAS], [L.], the shoulder blade.
**scap·u·lar** (skap′yoo-lẽr), *adj.* of the shoulder or scapula. *n.* 1. a sleeveless outer garment worn by monks. 2. two pieces of cloth joined by strings, worn front and back as a token of religious devotion.

**scar** (skär), *n.* [< Gr. *eschara*, fireplace], a mark left after a wound, burn, etc. has healed. *v.t.* [SCARRED, SCARRING], to mark as with a scar. *v.i.* to form a scar in healing.
**scar·ab** (skar′əb), *n.* [< L. *scarabeus*], a beetle.
**scarce** (skârs), *adj.* [ult. < L. *excerpers*, pick out], 1. not common; rarely seen. 2. not plentiful; hard to get. *adv.* scarcely: a literary usage. —**scarce′ness,** *n.*
**scarce′ly,** *adv.* 1. hardly; not quite. 2. probably not or certainly not.
**scar·ci·ty** (skâr′sə-ti), *n.* [*pl.* -TIES], 1. a being scarce; inadequate supply; lack. 2. rarity; uncommonness.
**scare** (skâr), *v.t.* [SCARED, SCARING], [< ON. *skiarr*, shy], 1. to fill with sudden fear. 2. to drive (*away* or *off*) by frightening. *v.i.* to be frightened. *n.* a sudden fear. —**scare up,** [Colloq.], to produce or gather quickly.
**scare′crow′,** *n.* the roughly dressed figure of a man put in a field to scare crows, etc. away from crops.
**scarf** (skärf), *n.* [*pl.* SCARFS, SCARVES (scärvz)], [< OFr. *escreppe*, purse hung from the neck], 1. a long, broad piece of cloth worn about the neck, head, etc. 2. a long, narrow covering for a table, etc.
**scarf** (skärf), *n.* [? < ON. *skarfr*], a joint made by cutting the ends of two pieces and fastening them into one continuous piece.
**scar·la·ti·na** (skär′lə-tē′nə), *n.* [< It.], scarlet fever, esp. in a mild form.
**scar·let** (skär′lit), *n.* [< ML. *scarlatum*], very bright red. *adj.* 1. of this color. 2. sinful.
**scarlet fever,** an acute contagious disease characterized by sore throat, fever, and a scarlet rash.
**scarp** (skärp), *n.* [< It. *scarpa*], a steep slope.
**scar·y** (skâr′i), *adj.* [-IER, -IEST], [< *scare*], [Colloq.], 1. frightening. 2. easily frightened. —**scar′i·ly,** *adv.*
**scat** (skat), *v.i.* [SCATTED, SCATTING], [? a hiss + *cat*], [Colloq.], to go away: usually imperative.
**scath·ing** (skāth′iŋ), *adj.* [< ON. *skathi*, harm], searing; blasting: usually figurative, as, *scathing* remarks. —**scath′ing·ly,** *adv.*
**scat·ter** (skat′ẽr), *v.t.* [ME. *sc(h)ateren*], 1. to throw about; sprinkle here and there. 2. to separate and drive in several directions; disperse. *v.i.* to move apart in several directions. *n.* a scattering.
**scat′ter·brain′,** *n.* one who is incapable of concentrated thinking.
**scatter rug,** a small rug for covering only part of a floor.
**scav·eng·er** (skav′in-jẽr), *n.* [ult. < Fl. *scauwen*, to see], 1. one who collects and disposes of filth, garbage, etc. 2. any animal that eats refuse and decaying matter. —**scav′enge** (-inj), [-ENGED, -ENGING], *v.i. & v.t.*
**sce·na·rio** (si-nâr′i-ō′, -nä′ri-), *n.* [*pl.* -OS], [see SCENE], an outline of a motion picture, indicating the action, scenes, characters, etc. —**sce·na·rist** (si-nâr′ist, -när′ist), *n.*
**scene** (sēn), *n.* [< Gr. *skēnē*, stage], 1. the place where an event occurs. 2. the setting of the action of a play, story, etc. 3. a division of a play, usually part of an act. 4. a particular incident, as of a story. 5. the scenery of a play, motion picture, etc. 6. a view of people or places. 7. a display of strong feeling: as, she made a *scene* in court.
**scen·er·y** (sēn′ẽr-i), *n.* [*pl.* -IES], 1. painted screens, backdrops, etc. used on the stage to represent places. 2. the general appearance of a place; features of a landscape.
**sce·nic** (sē′nik, sen′ik), *adj.* 1. of stage scenery. 2. of natural scenery; picturesque. Also **sce′ni·cal.** —**sce′ni·cal·ly,** *adv.*
**scent** (sent), *v.t.* [< L. *sentire*, to feel], 1. to smell. 2. to have a suspicion of. 3. to fill with an odor; perfume. *n.* 1. an odor. 2. the sense of smell. 3. a perfume. 4. an odor left by an animal, by which it is tracked.
**scep·ter, scep·tre** (sep′tẽr), *n.* [< Gr. *skēptron*, staff], a staff held by a ruler as a symbol of sovereignty.
**scep·tic** (skep′tik), *n.* skeptic. —**scep′ti·cal,** *adj.* —**scep′ti·cism,** *n.*
**sched·ule** (skej′ool), *n.* [< L. *sceda*, a leaf of paper], 1. a list of details. 2. a list of the times certain things are to happen; timetable. 3. a timed plan for a project. *v.t.* [-ULED, -ULING], 1. to place in a schedule. 2. to make a schedule of.
**sche·mat·ic** (skē-mat′ik), *adj.* of or like a scheme, outline, etc.; diagrammatic.
**scheme** (skēm), *n.* [< Gr. *schēma*, a form], 1. a systematic plan for attaining some object. 2. an orderly combination of things on a definite plan. 3. a plot; intrigue. 4. a diagram. *v.t. & v.i.* [SCHEMED, SCHEMING], to devise; plot; contrive. —**schem′er,** *n.*
**scher·zo** (sker′tsō), *n.* [*pl.* -ZOS, -ZI (-tsē)], [It. < G. *scherz*, a jest], a lively movement, as of a symphony, in ¾ time.
**schism** (siz′'m), *n.* [< Gr. *schizein*, cleave], a split, esp. in a church, because of difference of opinion, doctrine, etc. —**schis·mat′ic** (-mat′ik), *adj.* —**schis·mat′i·cal·ly,** *adv.*
**schist** (shist), *n.* [< Gr. *schizein*, cleave], a crystalline rock easily split into layers.
**schiz·o·phre·ni·a** (skiz′ə-frē′ni-ə), *n.* [< Gr. *schizein*, cleave + *phrēn*, mind], a mental disorder characterized by indifference, withdrawal, hallucinations, etc. —**schiz′oid** (-oid), *n.* —**schiz′o·phren′ic** (-fren′ik), *adj. & n.*
**schmaltz** (shmälts), *n.* [< G. *schmalz*, melted fat], [Slang], anything very sentimental.
**schnapps, schnaps** (shnäps), *n.* [G., a dram], alcoholic liquor.
**schnau·zer** (shnou′zẽr), *n.* [G. < *schnauzen*, to snarl], a small terrier with a wiry coat.
**schol·ar** (skol′ẽr), *n.* [< L. *schola*, school], 1. a learned person. 2. a student or pupil. —**schol′ar·ly,** *adj. & adv.* —**schol′ar·li·ness,** *n.*
**schol′ar·ship′,** *n.* 1. the systematized knowledge of a scholar. 2. a gift of money, etc. to help a student.
**scho·las·tic** (skə-las′tik), *adj.* [see SCHOOL], of schools, colleges, students, teachers, etc.; academic; educational.
**school** (sko͞ol), *n.* [< Gr. *scholē*], 1. a place or institution, with its buildings, etc., for teaching and learning. 2. all of its students and teachers. 3. a regular session of teaching. 4. the process of being educated: as, he likes *school.* 5. any situation through which one gains knowledge, etc.: as, the *school* of hard knocks. 6. a particular division of a university. 7. a group following the same beliefs, methods, etc. *v.t.* 1. to train; teach. 2. to discipline; control. *adj.* of a school or schools.
**school** (sko͞ol), *n.* [D., crowd], a group of fish, etc. swimming together.
**school board,** a group of people in charge of local public schools.
**school′book′,** *n.* a textbook.
**school′boy′,** *n.* a boy attending school. —**school′girl′,** *n.fem.*
**school′house′,** *n.* a building used as a school.
**school′ing,** *n.* instruction at school; education; training.
**school′marm′** (-mäm′, -märm′), *n.* [Colloq.], a woman schoolteacher, esp. one regarded as prudish or prim.
**school′mas′ter,** *n.* a man who teaches in, or is head of, a school. —**school′mis′tress,** *n.fem.*
**school′mate′,** *n.* one educated at the same school and at the same time as another.
**school′room′,** *n.* a room where pupils are taught, as in a school.
**school′teach′er,** *n.* one who teaches in a school.

**school year,** the part of a year when school is in session.
**schoon·er** (skōōn′ẽr), *n.* [< New England *scoon*, skim upon water], 1. a ship with two or more masts, rigged fore and aft. 2. a large beer glass.
**schwa** (shwä), *n.* [G. < Heb. *sh'wa*], 1. the neutral vowel sound of most unstressed syllables in English, as of *a* in *ago*. 2. the symbol (ə) for this.
**sci·at·i·ca** (sī-at′i-kə), *n.* [< Gr. *ischion*, hip], any painful condition in the hip or thighs; esp., neuritis of the long nerve (**sciatic nerve**) down the back of the thigh.
**sci·ence** (sī′əns), *n.* [< L. *scire*, know], 1. systematized knowledge derived from observation, study, etc. 2. a branch of knowledge, esp. one that systematizes facts, principles, and methods. 3. skill or technique.
**science fiction,** highly imaginative stories about some projected, often fantastic, scientific development.
**sci·en·tif·ic** (sī′ən-tif′ik), *adj.* 1. of or dealing with science. 2. based on, or using, the principles and methods of science; systematic and exact. —**sci′en·tif′i·cal·ly,** *adv.*
**sci′en·tist,** *n.* a specialist in science.
**scim·i·tar, scim·i·ter** (sim′ə-tẽr), *n.* [It. *scimitarra*], a short, curved sword used by Turks, Arabs, etc.
**scin·til·la** (sin-til′ə), *n.* [L.], 1. a spark. 2. a particle; the least trace.
**scin·til·late** (sin′tə-lāt′), *v.i.* [-LATED, -LATING], [< *scintilla*, a spark], 1. to sparkle or twinkle. 2. to be brilliant and witty. —**scin′til·lat′ing,** *adj.* —**scin′til·la′tion,** *n.*
**sci·on** (sī′ən), *n.* [OFr. *cion*], 1. a shoot or bud of a plant, used for grafting. 2. a descendant.
**scis·sors** (siz′ẽrz), *n.pl.* [< LL. *cisorium*, cutting tool], a cutting instrument with two opposing blades pivoted together so that they slide over each other: also **pair of scissors.**
**scle·ro·sis** (skli-rō′sis), *n.* [*pl.* -SES (-sēz)], [< Gr. *sklēros*, hard], a hardening of body tissues. —**scle·rot′ic** (-rot′ik), *adj.*
**scoff** (skôf, skof), *n.* [prob. < ON.], an expression of scorn or derision. *v.t.* & *v.i.* to mock or jeer (at). —**scoff′er,** *n.*
**scold** (skōld), *n.* [prob. < ON. *skald*, poet (in allusion to satirical verses)], a woman who habitually uses abusive language. *v.t.* to find fault with angrily; rebuke. *v.i.* 1. to find fault angrily. 2. to use abusive language. —**scold′er,** *n.* —**scold′ing,** *adj.* & *n.*
**sconce** (skons), *n.* [ult. < L. *absconsus*, hidden], a wall bracket for holding candles, etc.
**sconce** (skons), *n.* [D. *schans*], a small fort.
**scone** (skōn), *n.* [Scot. < MD. *schoonbrot*, fine bread], a kind of tea cake resembling a baking powder biscuit.
**scoop** (skōōp), *n.* [< MD. *schope*, bucket & *schoppe*, a shovel], 1. any of various small, shovellike utensils, as for taking up flour, ice cream, etc. 2. the deep bucket of a dredge or steam shovel. 3. a scooping, or the amount scooped up at one time. 4. a motion as of scooping. 5. [Slang], a publishing of news before rival newspapers. *v.t.* 1. to take up or out as with a scoop. 2. to hollow out. 3. [Slang], to publish news before (a rival). —**scoop′ful′** [*pl.* -FULS], *n.*
**scoot** (skōōt), *v.i.* [prob. < ON. *skiōta*, to shoot], [Colloq.], to go quickly; scurry off.
**scoot′er,** *n.* 1. a child's two-wheeled vehicle moved by pushing one foot against the ground. 2. a similar vehicle propelled by a motor: in full, **motor scooter.**
**scope** (skōp), *n.* [< Gr. *skopos*, watcher], 1. the area that the mind can cover. 2. range or extent of action, observation, inclusion, etc. 3. room for achievement; opportunity.
**-scope,** [< Gr. *skopein*, to see], a combining form meaning (an instrument, etc. for) *observing*, as in *telescope*.
**scor·bu·tic** (skôr-bū′tik), *adj.* [< MD. *scorft*], of, like, or having scurvy.
**scorch** (skôrch), *v.t.* & *v.i.* [< L. *ex-*, out + *cortex*, bark], 1. to burn slightly or on the surface. 2. to parch; shrivel with heat. *n.* a superficial burn.
**scorch′er,** *n.* one that scorches; specif., [Colloq.], *a*) a very hot day. *b*) a severe rebuke.
**score** (skôr), *n.* [< ON. *skor*], 1. a scratch, mark, notch, incision, etc. 2. a debt or account. 3. a reason; motive. 4. the number of points made, as in a game. 5. a grade, as on a test. 6. twenty people or objects. 7. *pl.* very many. 8. a copy of a musical composition, showing all parts for the instruments or voices. *v.t.* [SCORED, SCORING], 1. to mark or mark out with notches, lines, etc. 2. *a*) to make (runs, points, etc.) in a game. *b*) to record the score of. 3. to upbraid. 4. to evaluate, as in testing. 5. to achieve, as a success. 6. in *music*, to arrange in a score. *v.i.* 1. to make points, as in a game. 2. to keep score in a game. —**scor′er,** *n.*
**score card,** 1. a card for recording the score of a game, etc. 2. a card printed with players' names, positions, etc. at a sports event.
**scorn** (skôrn), *v.t.* [< OFr. *escarnir*], 1. to regard with contempt; treat disdainfully. 2. to refuse or reject as contemptible. *n.* a feeling of anger and contempt. —**scorn′ful,** *adj.* —**scorn′ful·ly,** *adv.*
**Scor·pi·o** (skôr′pi-ō′), *n.* [L., scorpion], the eighth sign of the zodiac.
**scor·pi·on** (skôr′pi-ən), *n.* [< Gr. *skorpios*], an arachnid found in warm regions, with a long tail ending in a poisonous sting.
**Scot** (skot), *n.* a native of Scotland.
**Scot.,** 1. Scotch. 2. Scotland. 3. Scottish.
**Scotch** (skoch), *adj.* Scottish. *n.* 1. the English spoken in Scotland. 2. Scotch whisky.
**scotch** (skoch), *v.t.* [akin to Fr. *coche*, a nick], 1. to cut or maim. 2. to put down; stifle: as, to *scotch* a rumor.
**Scotch′man** (-mən), *n.* [*pl.* -MEN], a Scot; Scotsman: cf. **Scotsman.**
**Scotch tape,** a thin, paperlike adhesive tape: a trademark.
**Scotch whisky,** whisky distilled in Scotland from malted barley.
**scot-free** (skot′frē′), *adj.* [< earlier *scot*, a tax + *free*], unharmed or unpunished; safe.
**Scotland Yard,** the London police headquarters, esp. its detective bureau.
**Scots** (skots), *adj.* & *n.* Scottish.
**Scots′man** (-mən), *n.* [*pl.* -MEN], a Scot: the current term in Scotland.
**Scot·tish** (skot′ish), *adj.* of Scotland, its people, their English dialect, etc. *n.* the English spoken in Scotland. —**the Scottish,** the Scottish people. *Scottish* is formal usage, but with some words, *Scotch* is used (e.g., tweed, whisky), with others, *Scots* (e.g., law).
**scoun·drel** (skoun′drəl), *n.* [< L. *ex-*, from + *condere*, to hide], an unscrupulous person; villain. —**scoun′drel·ly,** *adj.*
**scour** (skour), *v.t.* & *v.i.* [< L. *ex-*, intens. + *cura*, care], 1. to clean by vigorous rubbing, as with abrasives. 2. to remove dirt and grease from (wool, etc.).
**scour** (skour), *v.t.* [prob. < L. *ex-*, out + *currere*, to run], to pass over quickly, or range over, as in search: as, to *scour* a library for a book.
**scourge** (skũrj), *n.* [< L. *ex*, off + *corrigia*, a whip], 1. a whip. 2. any punishment, affliction, etc. *v.t.* [SCOURGED, SCOURGING], 1. to whip; flog. 2. to punish or afflict severely.
**scout** (skout), *n.* [< L. *auscultare*, listen], 1. a person, plane, etc. sent to spy out the ene-

my's strength, actions, etc. 2. a Boy Scout or Girl Scout. 3. a person sent out to survey a competitor, find new talent, etc. *v.t. & v.i.* 1. to reconnoiter. 2. to go in search of (something). —**scout′er,** *n.*

**scout** (skout), *v.t.* [< ON. *skūta*, a taunt], to reject as absurd; scoff at.

**scout′mas′ter,** *n.* the adult leader of a troop of Boy Scouts.

**scow** (skou), *n.* [< D. *schouw*], a large, flat-bottomed boat with square ends, used for carrying freight, usually towed by a tug.

**scowl** (skoul), *v.i.* [prob. < ON.], to look angry, sullen, etc., as by contracting the eyebrows. *n.* a scowling; angry frown.

**scrab·ble** (skrab′'l), *v.i.* [-BLED, -BLING], [< D. *schrabben*, to scrape], 1. to scratch, scrape, etc. as though looking for something. 2. to struggle. 3. to scribble.

**scrag·gly** (skrag′li), *adj.* [-GLIER, -GLIEST], [prob. < ON.], unkempt; rough; jagged.

**scram** (skram), *v.i.* [SCRAMMED, SCRAMMING], [< *scramble*], [Slang], to go away.

**scram·ble** (skram′b'l), *v.i.* [-BLED, -BLING], [< ?], 1. to climb, crawl, etc. with the hands and feet. 2. to scuffle or struggle for something. *v.t.* 1. to mix haphazardly. 2. to cook (eggs) after mixing the white and yolk together. *n.* 1. a hard climb or advance, as over rough ground. 2. a disorderly struggle, as for something prized.

**scrap** (skrap), *n.* [< ON. *skrap*], 1. a small piece; fragment. 2. discarded material. 3. *pl.* bits of food. *adj.* 1. in the form of pieces, leftovers, etc. 2. used and discarded. *v.t.* [SCRAPPED, SCRAPPING], 1. to make into scraps. 2. to discard; junk. —**scrap′per,** *n.*

**scrap** (skrap), *n. & v.i.* [SCRAPPED, SCRAPPING], [Slang], fight or quarrel.

**scrap′book′,** *n.* a book of blank pages in which to paste clippings, pictures, etc.

**scrape** (skrāp), *v.t.* [SCRAPED, SCRAPING], [< ON. *skrapa*], 1. to make smooth or clean by rubbing with a tool or abrasive. 2. to remove in this way (with *off*, *out*, etc.). 3. to scratch, abrade, etc. 4. to gather slowly and with difficulty: as, to *scrape* up some money. *v.i.* 1. to rub against something harshly; grate. 2. to save money, etc. slowly and with difficulty. 3. to get along, but with difficulty. *n.* 1. a scraping. 2. a scraped place. 3. a harsh, grating sound. 4. a predicament. —**scrap′er,** *n.*

**scrap·py** (skrap′i), *adj.* [-PIER, -PIEST], 1. made of scraps. 2. disconnected: as, *scrappy* thinking. —**scrap′pi·ness,** *n.*

**scrap′py,** *adj.* [-PIER, -PIEST], [< *scrap* (fight)], [Slang], fond of fighting.

**scratch** (skrach), *v.t.* [prob. a fusion of ME. *scratten & cracchen*], 1. to scrape or cut the surface of slightly. 2. to tear or dig with the nails or claws. 3. to scrape lightly to relieve itching. 4. to scrape with a grating noise. 5. to write or draw hurriedly or carelessly. 6. to strike out (writing, etc.). 7. in *sports*, to withdraw (a contestant, etc.). *v.i.* 1. to use nails or claws in digging or wounding. 2. to scrape. *n.* 1. the act of scratching. 2. a mark, tear, etc. made by scratching. 3. a grating sound; scraping. *adj.* used for hasty notes, figuring, etc.: as, *scratch* paper. —**from scratch,** from nothing; without advantage. —**up to scratch,** [Colloq.], up to a standard. —**scratch′y** [-IER, -IEST], *adj.*

**scrawl** (skrôl), *v.t. & v.i.* [prob. alt. form of *crawl*], to write or draw hastily, carelessly, etc. *n.* sprawling, often illegible handwriting. —**scrawl′y** [-IER, -IEST], *adj.*

**scraw·ny** (skrô′ni), *adj.* [-NIER, -NIEST], [prob. < ON.], lean; thin. —**scraw′ni·ness,** *n.*

**scream** (skrēm), *v.i.* [< ON. *skraema*, terrify], 1. to utter a shrill, piercing cry as in pain or fright. 2. to shout, laugh, etc. hysterically. *v.t.* to utter as with a scream. *n.* 1. a sharp, piercing cry or sound. 2. [Colloq.], a hilariously funny person or thing.

**screech** (skrēch), *v.i. & v.t.* [ult. echoic], to utter (with) a shrill, high-pitched cry. *n.* such a cry. —**screech′y** [-IER, -IEST], *adj.*

**screed** (skrēd), *n.* [ME. *screde*; var. of *shred*], a long, tiresome speech or writing.

**screen** (skrēn), *n.* [prob. < OHG. *scerm*, a guard], 1. a curtain or partition used to separate, conceal, protect, etc. 2. anything that shields, conceals, etc.: as, a smoke *screen*. 3. a coarse mesh of wire, etc., used as a sieve. 4. a frame covered with a mesh, used, as on a window, to keep insects out. 5. a surface upon which motion pictures, etc. are projected. 6. the motion-picture industry: with *the*. *v.t.* 1. to conceal, shelter, or protect as with a screen. 2. to sift through a screen. 3. to interview or test in order to separate according to skills, etc. 4. to show (a motion picture) upon a screen.

**screen′play′,** *n.* a story written in a form suitable for a motion picture.

**screw** (skrōō), *n.* [< OFr. *escroue*, hole in which a screw turns], 1. a naillike metal piece grooved in an advancing spiral, for fastening things by being turned. 2. any spiral thing like this. 3. a hollow, threaded cylinder into which the male screw fits: **female** (or **internal**) **screw.** 4. a propeller with blades arranged on the hub in a spiral, used on ships, aircraft, etc.: in full, **screw propeller.** *v.t.* 1. to turn; twist. 2. to fasten, tighten, etc. as with a screw. 3. to contort. *v.i.* 1. to come apart or go together by being turned like a screw: as, the lid *screws* on. 2. to be fitted for screws. —**put the screws on** (or **to**), to subject to force or pressure.

**screw′ball′,** *n.* [Slang], an erratic, irrational, or unconventional person.

**screw′driv′er,** *n.* a tool used for turning screws: also **screw driver.**

**screw′y,** *adj.* [-IER, -IEST], [Slang], irrational, peculiar, absurd, etc.

**scrib·ble** (skrib′'l), *v.t. & v.i.* [-BLED, -BLING], [< L. *scribere*, write], 1. to write carelessly, hastily, etc. 2. to make meaningless or illegible marks (on). *n.* scribbled writing.

**scribe** (skrīb), *n.* [< L. *scribere*, write], 1. a writer; author. 2. one who copied manuscripts before the invention of printing.

**scrim·mage** (skrim′ij), *n.* [< *skirmish*], 1. a confused struggle. 2. in *football*, *a*) the play that follows the pass from center. *b*) a practice game. *v.i.* [-MAGED, -MAGING], to take part in a scrimmage. —**line of scrimmage,** in *football*, an imaginary line along which the two teams line up for each play.

**scrimp** (skrimp), *v.t.* [prob. < AS. *scrimman*, shrink], 1. to make too small, short, etc. 2. to treat stingily. *v.i.* to be sparing and frugal.

**scrip** (skrip), *n.* [< *script*], a certificate of a right to receive something, as stocks, money, etc.

**script** (skript), *n.* [< L. *scribere*, write], 1. handwriting. 2. a working copy of a play, radio show, etc.

**Scrip·ture** (skrip′chẽr), *n.* [see SCRIPT], 1. *usually pl.* the Bible: also (**the**) **Holy Scripture** (or **Scriptures**). 2. [s-], any sacred writing. —**Scrip′tur·al, scrip′tur·al,** *adj.*

**scrive·ner** (skriv′nẽr), *n.* [< L. *scribere*, write], [Archaic], 1. a public clerk, copyist, etc. 2. a notary.

**scrof·u·la** (scrof′yoo-lə), *n.* [< L. *scrofa*, a sow], tuberculosis of the lymphatic glands, esp. of the neck. —**scrof′u·lous,** *adj.*

**scroll** (skrōl), *n.* [< ME. *scrowe*], 1. a roll of parchment or paper, usually with writing upon it. 2. an ornamental design in coiled or spiral form.

**scro·tum** (skrō′təm), *n.* [*pl.* -TA (-tə), -TUMS], [L.], the pouch of skin containing the testicles.

**scrounge** (skrounj), *v.t. & v.i.* [SCROUNGED, SCROUNGING], [< ?], [Slang], to pilfer.
**scrub** (skrub), *n.* [dial. var. of *shrub*], 1. a thick growth of stunted trees or bushes. 2. any person or thing smaller than the usual, or inferior. 3. in *sports*, a substitute player. *adj.* 1. poor; inferior. 2. undersized. —**scrub′by** [-BIER, -BIEST], *adj.*
**scrub** (skrub), *v.t. & v.i.* [SCRUBBED, SCRUBBING], [prob. < ON.], 1. to clean or wash by rubbing hard. 2. to rub hard. *n.* the act of scrubbing. —**scrub′ber**, *n.*
**scruff** (skruf), *n.* [ult. < *scurf*], the nape of the neck.
**scrump·tious** (skrump′shəs), *adj.* [< *sumptuous*], [Slang], first-rate.
**scru·ple** (skrōō′p'l), *n.* [< L. *scrupulus*, small stone], 1. a very small quantity. 2. a doubt arising from difficulty in deciding what is right, proper, etc. *v.t. & v.i.* [-PLED, -PLING], to hesitate (at) from doubt.
**scru′pu·lous** (-pyoo-ləs), *adj.* 1. having or showing scruples; conscientiously honest. 2. careful of details; precise.
**scru·ti·nize** (skrōō′t'n-īz′), *v.t.* [-NIZED, -NIZING], to look at carefully; examine closely.
**scru·ti·ny** (skrōō′t'n-i), *n.* [*pl.* -NIES], [< L. *scrutari*, examine], a close examination.
**scu·ba** (skōō′bə), *n.* [*s*elf-*c*ontained *u*nderwater *b*reathing *a*pparatus], a diver's apparatus with compressed-air tanks for breathing under water.
**scud** (skud), *v.i.* [SCUDDED, SCUDDING], [? < dial. *scut*, tail], 1. to move swiftly. 2. to be driven before the wind. *n.* 1. a scudding. 2. clouds or spray driven by the wind.
**scuff** (skuf), *v.t.* [prob. < ON. *skūfa*, to shove], 1. to scrape (the ground, etc.) with the feet. 2. to wear a rough place on the surface of. *v.i.* to walk without lifting the feet; shuffle. *n.* 1. a scuffing. 2. a worn or rough spot.
**scuf·fle** (skuf′'l), *v.i.* [-FLED, -FLING], [< *scuff*], 1. to struggle or fight in rough confusion. 2. to drag the feet. *n.* 1. a rough, confused fight. 2. a shuffling of feet.
**scull** (skul), *n.* [ME. *skulle*], 1. an oar twisted from side to side over the stern of a boat to move it forward. 2. a light rowboat for racing. *v.t. & v.i.* to propel (a boat) with a scull. —**scull′er**, *n.*
**scul·ler·y** (skul′ẽr-i), *n.* [*pl.* -IES], [< L. *scutella*, tray], a room where the kitchen utensils, etc. are cleaned.
**scul·lion** (skul′yən), *n.* [ult. < L. *scopa*, broom], [Archaic], a servant who does rough kitchen work.
**sculp·tor** (skulp′tẽr), *n.* an artist who creates works of sculpture. —**sculp′tress**, *n.fem.*
**sculp·ture** (skulp′chẽr), *n.* [< L. *sculpere*, carve], 1. the art of forming stone, clay, wood, etc. into statues, figures, or the like. 2. a work or works of sculpture. *v.t.* [-TURED, -TURING], 1. to cut, carve, chisel, etc., as statues, figures, etc. 2. to decorate with sculpture. —**sculp′tur·al**, *adj.*
**scum** (skum), *n.* [< MD. *schum*], 1. a thin layer of impurities on the top of a liquid. 2. refuse. 3. low, despicable people. —**scum′my** [-MIER, -MIEST], *adj.*
**scup·per** (skup′ẽr), *n.* [prob. < OFr. *escope*, bailing scoop], an opening in a ship's side to let water run off the deck.
**scurf** (skũrf), *n.* [AS.], 1. little, dry scales shed by the skin, as dandruff. 2. any scaly coating. —**scurf′y** [-IER, -IEST], *adj.*
**scur·ril·ous** (skũr′i-ləs), *adj.* [< L. *scurra*, buffoon], coarse; vulgar; abusive. —**scur·ril·i·ty** (skə-ril′ə-ti), [*pl.* -TIES], *n.*
**scur·ry** (skũr′i), *v.i.* [-RIED, -RYING], [< ?], to run hastily; scamper. *n.* a scampering.
**scur·vy** (skũr′vi), *adj.* [-VIER, -VIEST], [< *scurf*], low; mean. *n.* a disease resulting from a vitamin C deficiency, characterized by weakness, anemia, spongy gums, etc. —**scur′vi·ly**, *adv.* —**scur′vi·ness**, *n.*
**scutch·eon** (skuch′ən), *n.* escutcheon.
**scut·tle** (skut′'l), *n.* [< L. *scutella*, a dish], a bucket for carrying coal.
**scut·tle** (skut′'l), *v.i.* [-TLED, -TLING], [< *scud*], to scurry; scamper. *n.* a scamper.
**scut·tle** (skut′'l), *n.* [< Sp. *escotilla*], an opening fitted with a cover, as in the hull or deck of a ship. *v.t.* [-TLED, -TLING], to cut holes through the lower hull of (a ship) to sink it. —**scut′tler**, *n.*
**scut·tle·butt** (skut′'l-but′), *n.* [< *scuttled butt*, lidded cask], [Slang], 1. a drinking fountain on shipboard. 2. rumor or gossip.
**scythe** (sīth), *n.* [AS. *sithe*], a tool with a long, single-edged blade on a bent wooden shaft, for cutting grass, grain, etc. by hand.
**SE, S.E., s.e.,** southeast(ern).
**sea** (sē), *n.* [< AS. *sæ*], 1. the ocean. 2. any of various smaller bodies of salt water: as, the Red *Sea*. 3. a large body of fresh water: as, the *Sea* of Galilee. 4. the state of the surface of the ocean: as, a calm *sea*. 5. a heavy wave: as, swamped by the *seas*. 6. a very great amount. —**at sea**, 1. on the open sea. 2. uncertain; bewildered.
**sea anemone,** a sea polyp having a firm, gelatinous body topped with colored, petal-like tentacles.
**sea′board′**, *n.* land bordering on the sea. *adj.* bordering on the sea.
**sea′coast′**, *n.* land on or near the sea.
**sea dog,** a sailor, esp. an experienced one.
**sea′far′er** (-fâr′ẽr), *n.* one who travels on the sea.
**sea′far′ing,** *adj.* of or engaged in life at sea.
**sea food,** food prepared from or consisting of salt-water fish or shellfish.
**sea′girt′** (-gũrt′), *adj.* surrounded by the sea.
**sea′go′ing,** *adj.* 1. made for use on the open sea. 2. seafaring.
**sea gull,** a gull (bird).
**sea horse,** a small, semitropical fish with a slender tail, plated body, and a head somewhat like that of a horse.
**seal** (sēl), *n.* [< L. *sigillum*], 1. a design or initial impressed, often over wax, on a letter or document as proof of authenticity. 2. a stamp or ring for making such an impression. 3. a piece of paper, etc. bearing an impressed design recognized as official. 4. something that seals or closes tightly. 5. something that guarantees; pledge. 6. an ornamental paper stamp: as, Easter *seals*. *v.t.* 1. to mark with a seal, as to authenticate or certify. 2. to close or shut tight as with a seal: as, an envelope *sealed* with mucilage, a *sealed* door. 3. to confirm the genuineness of (a promise, etc.). 4. to settle finally.
**seal** (sēl), *n.* [< AS. *seolh*], 1. a sea mammal with a torpedo-shaped body and four flippers: *fur seals* are hunted for their valuable fur. 2. this fur. 3. leather made from sealskin. *v.i.* to hunt seals. —**seal′er**, *n.*
**sea legs,** the ability to walk without loss of balance on board ship, esp. in a rough sea.
**sea level,** the mean level of the surface of the sea.
**sea lion,** a large seal of the North Pacific.
**seal′skin′**, *n.* 1. the skin of the seal. 2. a garment made of this.
**seam** (sēm), *n.* [AS.], 1. a line formed by sewing together two pieces of material. 2. any line marking joining edges. 3. a mark like this, as a scar, wrinkle, etc. 4. a stratum of ore, coal, etc. *v.t.* 1. to join together so as to form a seam. 2. to mark with a seamlike line, etc. —**seam′less**, *adj.*
**sea′man** (-mən), *n.* [*pl.* -MEN], 1. a sailor. 2. an enlisted man ranking below a petty officer in the navy. —**sea′man·like′**, *adj.*
**sea′man·ship′**, *n.* skill in sailing or working a ship.

**seam·stress** (sēm′stris), *n.* a woman whose occupation is sewing.
**seam′y,** *adj.* [-IER, -IEST], having or showing seams. —**the seamy side,** the least attractive aspect. —**seam′i·ness,** *n.*
**sé·ance** (sā′äns), *n.* [Fr. < OFr. *seoir,* sit], a meeting at which spiritualists try to communicate with the dead.
**sea′plane′,** *n.* any airplane designed to land on or take off from water.
**sea′port′,** *n.* 1. a port or harbor used by ocean ships. 2. a city having such a port.
**sear** (sêr), *adj.* [AS.], withered. *v.t.* 1. to wither. 2. to scorch or burn the surface of. 3. to make callous or unfeeling.
**search** (sũrch), *v.t.* [< L. *circare,* go about], 1. to go over and look through in order to find something. 2. to examine (a person) for something concealed. 3. to examine carefully; probe. 4. to pierce; penetrate. *v.i.* to make a search. *n.* a searching. —**in search of,** making a search for.
**search′ing,** *adj.* 1. examining thoroughly. 2. keen; piercing. —**search′ing·ly,** *adv.*
**search′light′,** *n.* 1. an apparatus, as on a swivel, that projects a strong beam of light. 2. the beam of light.
**search warrant,** a legal document authorizing a police search, as for stolen goods.
**sea′scape′** (-skāp′), *n.* [*sea* + land*scape*], 1. a view of the sea. 2. a picture of this.
**sea shell,** a salt-water mollusk shell.
**sea′shore′,** *n.* land along the sea; seacoast.
**sea′sick′ness,** *n.* nausea, dizziness, etc. caused by the rolling of a ship at sea. —**sea′sick′,** *adj.*
**sea′side′,** *n.* seashore.
**sea·son** (sē′z'n), *n.* [< LL. *satio,* sowing time], 1. any of the four divisions of the year; spring, summer, fall, or winter. 2. the time when something takes place, is popular, permitted, etc. 3. the fitting time. *v.t.* 1. to add to, or change, the flavor of (food); flavor. 2. to add zest to. 3. to make more usable, as by aging. 4. to make used to; accustom. *v.i.* to become seasoned, or more usable.
**sea′son·a·ble,** *adj.* 1. suitable to the season. 2. opportune; timely.
**sea′son·al,** *adj.* of or depending on the season. —**sea′son·al·ly,** *adv.*
**sea′son·ing,** *n.* any flavoring added to food.
**seat** (sēt), *n.* [ON. *sæti*], 1. a place to sit. 2. a thing to sit on; chair, etc. 3. the buttocks. 4. the part of a chair, garment, etc. that one sits on. 5. the right to sit as a member: as, a *seat* on the council. 6. the chief location, or center: as, the *seat* of government. *v.t.* 1. to set in or on a seat. 2. to have seats for: as, the car *seats* six.
**SEATO** (sē′tō), Southeast Asia Treaty Organization.
**sea′ward** (-wẽrd), *adj.* & *adv.* toward the sea.
**sea′way′,** *n.* an inland waterway to the sea for ocean-going ships.
**sea′weed′,** *n.* any sea plant or plants.
**sea′wor′thy** (-wũr′*th*i), *adj.* fit for travel on the sea: said of a ship.
**se·ba·ceous** (si-bā′shəs), *adj.* [< L. *sebum,* tallow], of, like, or secreting fat, etc.
**SEC, S.E.C.,** Securities and Exchange Commission.
**sec.,** 1. second(s). 2. secretary.
**se·cant** (sē′kənt, -kant), *n.* [< L. *secare,* to cut], 1. any straight line intersecting a curve at two or more points. 2. in *trigonometry,* the ratio of the hypotenuse of a right triangle to either of the other sides with reference to the enclosed angle.
**se·cede** (si-sēd′), *v.i.* [-CEDED, -CEDING], [< L. *se-,* apart + *cedere,* to go], to withdraw formally from a group, organization, etc.
**se·ces·sion** (si-sesh′ən), *n.* 1. a seceding. 2. [often S-], the withdrawal of the Southern States from the Federal Union in 1860-1861. —**se·ces′sion·ist,** *n.*
**se·clude** (si-klōōd′), *v.t.* [-CLUDED, -CLUDING], [< L. *se-,* apart + *claudere,* shut], to shut off from others; isolate.
**se·clu·sion** (si-klōō′zhən), *n.* a secluding or being secluded; retirement; privacy. —**se·clu′sive,** *adj.* —**se·clu′sive·ly,** *adv.*
**sec·ond** (sek′ənd), *adj.* [< L. *sequi,* follow], 1. coming next after the first; 2d. 2. another of the same kind; other: as, a *second* chance, a *second* Caesar. 3. next below the first in rank, value, merit, etc. *n.* 1. one that is second. 2. an article of merchandise not of first quality. 3. an aid or assistant, as to a boxer. *v.t.* 1. to assist; support. 2. to indicate formal support of (a motion) as a preliminary to discussion or a vote. *adv.* in the second place, group, etc.
**sec·ond** (sek′ənd), *n.* [< ML. *secunda minuta,* lit., second minute], 1. 1/60 of a minute of time or of angular measure. 2. a very short time; instant.
**sec·ond·ar·y** (sek′ən-der′i), *adj.* 1. second in order, rank, importance, etc. 2. subordinate; minor. 3. derived, not primary.
**secondary accent,** in a word with two or more syllables accented, any accent (′) weaker than the primary accent.
**secondary school,** a school, esp. a high school, giving education (**secondary education**) between the primary and collegiate levels.
**sec′ond-class′,** *adj.* 1. of the class, rank, etc. next below the highest. 2. inferior.
**sec′ond-guess′,** *v.t.* & *v.i.* [Colloq.], to use hindsight in criticizing (someone), remaking (a decision), etc.
**sec′ond·hand′,** *adj.* 1. not direct from the original source. 2. used before; not new. 3. dealing in used merchandise.
**second lieutenant,** a commissioned army officer of the lowest rank.
**sec′ond·ly,** *adv.* in the second place; second.
**second nature,** an acquired habit, etc. deeply fixed in one's nature.
**second person,** that form of a pronoun or verb which refers to the person spoken to.
**sec′ond-rate′,** *adj.* 1. second in quality, etc. 2. inferior. —**sec′ond-rat′er,** *n.*
**se·cre·cy** (sē′krə-si), *n.* [*pl.* -CIES], 1. a being secret. 2. the ability or a tendency to keep secrets.
**se·cret** (sē′krit), *adj.* [< L. *se-,* apart + *cernere,* sift], 1. kept from or acting without the knowledge of others. 2. beyond general understanding; mysterious. 3. concealed from sight; hidden. *n.* a secret fact, cause, process, etc. —**se′cret·ly,** *adv.*
**sec·re·tar·i·at, sec·re·tar·i·ate** (sek′rə-târ′i-it), *n.* a staff headed by a secretary.
**sec·re·tar·y** (sek′rə-ter′i), *n.* [*pl.* -IES], [< ML. *secretarius,* one entrusted with secrets], 1. one who keeps records, handles correspondence, etc. for an organization or person. 2. the head of a department of government. 3. a writing desk. —**sec′re·tar′i·al** (-târ′i-əl), *adj.* —**sec′re·tar′y·ship′,** *n.*
**se·crete** (si-krēt′), *v.t.* [-CRETED, -CRETING], [see SECRET], 1. to hide; conceal. 2. in *biology,* to separate and develop (a substance) from the blood or sap for use or excretion. —**se·cre′tor** (-krē′tẽr), *n.*
**se·cre·tion** (si-krē′shən), *n.* a substance secreted by an animal or plant.
**se·cre·tive** (si-krē′tiv, sē′krə-), *adj.* reticent; not frank or open. —**se·cre′tive·ly,** *adv.*
**Secret Service,** a division of the U.S. Treasury Department for uncovering counterfeiters, guarding the President, etc.
**sect** (sekt), *n.* [< L. *sequi,* follow], 1. a group of people having a common philosophy, set of beliefs, etc. 2. a religious denomination.
**sec·tar·i·an** (sek-târ′i-ən), *adj.* 1. of or

characteristic of a sect. 2. devoted to some sect. 3. narrow-minded.
**sec·tion** (sek′shən), *n.* [< L. *secare*, to cut], 1. a cutting apart. 2. a part cut off; portion. 3. any distinct or separate part. 4. a drawing, etc. of something as it would appear if cut straight through.
**sec′tion·al,** *adj.* 1. of or characteristic of a given section or district. 2. made up of sections. —**sec′tion·al·ly,** *adv.*
**sec′tion·al·ism,** *n.* undue concern for the interests of a particular section of the country.
**sec·tor** (sek′tẽr), *n.* [< L. *secare*, to cut], 1. part of a circle bounded by any two radii and the included arc. 2. any of the districts into which an area is divided for military operations.
**sec·u·lar** (sek′yoo-lẽr), *adj.* [< L. *saeculum*, age], 1. not religious; not connected with a church. 2. not bound by a monastic vow: as, *secular* clergy. —**sec′u·lar·ism,** *n.*
**sec′u·lar·ize′** (-lə-rīz′), *v.t.* [-IZED, -IZING], 1. to convert from religious to civil ownership or use. 2. to remove any religious character, influence, etc. from. —**sec′u·lar·i·za′tion,** *n.*
**se·cure** (si-kyoor′), *adj.* [< L. *se-*, free from + *cura*, care], 1. free from fear, care, etc. 2. free from danger; safe. 3. firm; stable: as, make the knot *secure*. 4. sure; certain. *v.t.* [-CURED, -CURING], 1. to make secure; protect. 2. to make certain, as with a pledge: as, to *secure* a loan. 3. to make firm, fast, etc. 4. to obtain; acquire.
**se·cu·ri·ty** (si-kyoor′ə-ti), *n.* [*pl.* -TIES], 1. a feeling of being free from fear, danger, etc. 2. freedom from doubt; certainty. 3. protection; safeguard. 4. something given as a pledge of repayment, etc.; guarantee. 5. *pl.* bonds, stocks, etc.
**Security Council,** the organ of the UN responsible for maintaining international peace and security.
**secy., sec′y.,** secretary.
**se·dan** (si-dan′), *n.* [prob. < L. *sedere*, sit], a type of closed automobile with front and rear seats.
**se·date** (si-dāt′), *adj.* [< L. *sedare*, settle], 1. calm; composed. 2. serious; dignified.
**sed·a·tive** (sed′ə-tiv), *adj.* [see SEDATE], tending to soothe or quiet; reducing pain, excitement, etc. *n.* a sedative medicine. —**se·da·tion** (si-dā′shən), *n.*
**sed·en·tar·y** (sed′'n-ter′i), *adj.* [< L. *sedere*, sit], characterized by much sitting: as, a *sedentary* task. —**sed′en·tar′i·ness,** *n.*
**sedge** (sej), *n.* [AS. *secg*], a coarse, grasslike plant usually growing in wet ground.
**sed·i·ment** (sed′ə-mənt), *n.* [< L. *sedere*, sit], 1. matter that settles to the bottom of a liquid. 2. in *geology*, matter deposited by water or wind.
**sed′i·men′ta·ry** (-men′tẽr-i), *adj.* 1. of, like, or containing sediment. 2. formed by the deposit of sediment, as rocks.
**se·di·tion** (si-dish′ən), *n.* [< L. *sed-*, apart + *itio*, a going], a stirring up of rebellion against the government. —**se·di′tious,** *adj.*
**se·duce** (si-dōōs′, -dūs′), *v.t.* [-DUCED, -DUCING], [< L. *se-*, apart + *ducere*, to lead], 1. to tempt to wrongdoing; lead astray. 2. to induce to give up one's chastity. —**se·duc′er,** *n.* —**se·duc·tion** (si-duk′shən), *n.* —**se·duc′tive,** *adj.* —**se·duc′tive·ly,** *adv.*
**sed·u·lous** (sej′oo-ləs), *adj.* [L. *sedulus*], diligent and persistent. —**sed′u·lous·ness,** *n.*
**see** (sē), *v.t.* [SAW, SEEN, SEEING], [AS. *seon*], 1. to get knowledge of through the eyes; look at. 2. to understand: as, I *see* your point. 3. to learn; find out. 4. to experience: as, to *see* war service. 5. to make sure: as, *see* that he goes. 6. to escort: as, *see* her to the door. 7. to encounter. 8. to call on; consult. 9. to receive: as, too ill to *see* people. *v.i.* 1. to have the power of sight. 2. to understand. 3. to think: as, let me *see*, who's next? —**see through,** 1. to understand the true nature of. 2. to finish. 3. to help through difficulty. —**see to** (or **about**), to attend to.
**see** (sē), *n.* [< L. *sedes*, a seat], the official seat, or center of authority, of a bishop.
**seed** (sēd), *n.* [*pl.* SEEDS, SEED], [AS. *sæd*], 1. the part of a plant, containing the embryo, from which a new plant will grow. 2. seeds collectively. 3. the source of anything. 4. descendants; posterity. 5. sperm; semen. *v.t.* 1. to plant with seed. 2. to remove the seeds from. 3. to distribute (contestants in a tournament) so that the best players are not matched in early rounds. *v.i.* to produce seed. —**go to seed,** 1. to shed seeds after flowering. 2. to deteriorate; weaken, wane, etc. —**seed′er,** *n.* —**seed′less,** *adj.*
**seed leaf,** a cotyledon.
**seed′ling** (-liŋ), *n.* 1. a plant grown from a seed. 2. a young tree.
**seed′y,** *adj.* [-IER, -IEST], 1. full of seed. 2. gone to seed. 3. shabby, unkempt, etc.
**see·ing** (sē′iŋ), *n.* the sense of sight; vision. *conj.* in view of the fact; considering.
**seek** (sēk), *v.t.* [SOUGHT, SEEKING], [AS. *secan*], 1. to try to find; search for. 2. to try to get; aim at. 3. to try; attempt: as, he *sought* to lower taxes. —**seek′er,** *n.*
**seem** (sēm), *v.i.* [prob. < ON. *sæma*, conform to], 1. to appear to be; appear: as, he *seems* glad. 2. to appear to one's own mind: as, I *seem* to hear voices.
**seem′ing,** *adj.* apparent; not actual. —**seem′ing·ly,** *adv.*
**seem′ly,** *adj.* [-LIER, -LIEST], suitable; proper.
**seen** (sēn), pp. of **see.**
**seep** (sēp), *v.i.* [< AS. *sipian*, to soak], to leak through small openings; ooze. —**seep′age** (-ij), *n.* —**seep′y,** *adj.*
**seer** (sêr), *n.* one who foretells the future; prophet. —**seer′ess** (-is), *n.fem.*
**seer·suck·er** (sêr′suk′ẽr), *n.* [< Per. *shir u shakar*, lit., milk and sugar], a light, crinkled fabric of linen, cotton, etc.
**see·saw** (sē′sô′), *n.* [redupl. of *saw*], 1. a plank balanced at the middle on which children at play, riding the ends, rise and fall alternately. 2. any back-and-forth or up-and-down motion, tendency, etc. *v.t. & v.i.* to move in such a way.
**seethe** (sē*th*), *v.i.* [SEETHED, SEETHING], [AS. *sēothan*], 1. to boil. 2. to surge or bubble, as boiling liquid. 3. to be violently agitated.
**seg·ment** (seg′mənt), *n.* [< L. *secare*, to cut], any of the parts into which something is separated; section. *v.t. & v.i.* to divide into segments. —**seg′men·ta′tion,** *n.*
**seg·re·gate** (seg′ri-gāt′), *v.t.* [-GATED, -GATING], [< L. *se-*, apart + *grex*, a flock], to set apart from others; isolate; specif., to compel (racial groups) to live, go to school, etc. apart from each other. —**seg′re·ga′tion,** *n.*
**seine** (sān), *n.* [< Gr. *sagēnē*], a large fishing net with floats along the top edge and weights along the bottom. *v.t. & v.i.* [SEINED, SEINING], to catch with a seine.
**seis·mic** (sīz′mik), *adj.* [< Gr. *seiein*, to shake], of or caused by an earthquake.
**seis·mo·graph** (sīz′mə-graf′, -gräf′), *n.* [< Gr. *seismos*, earthquake; + *-graph*], an instrument that records the direction, intensity, and time of earthquakes. —**seis′mo·graph′ic,** *adj.*
**seis·mol′o·gy** (-mol′ə-ji), *n.* the study of earthquakes and related matters. —**seis·mol′o·gist,** *n.*
**seize** (sēz), *v.t.* [SEIZED, SEIZING], [< LL. *sacire*], 1. to take legal possession of. 2. to take possession of suddenly and by force. 3. to attack: as, *seized* with pain. 4. to capture; arrest. 5. to grasp suddenly.

**sei·zure** (sē'zhẽr), *n.* 1. a seizing or being seized. 2. a sudden attack, as of disease.
**sel·dom** (sel'dəm), *adv.* [AS. *seldum*], rarely; infrequently; not often.
**se·lect** (sə-lekt'), *adj.* [< L. *se-*, apart + *legere*, choose], 1. chosen in preference to others. 2. choice; excellent; exclusive. 3. careful in choosing. *v.t. & v.i.* to choose; pick out. —**se·lec'tor**, *n.*
**se·lec'tion**, *n.* 1. a selecting or being selected. 2. that or those selected. —**se·lec'tive**, *adj.* —**se·lec'tiv'i·ty**, *n.*
**selective service**, compulsory military service according to age, physical fitness, etc.
**se·lect'man** (-mən), *n.* [*pl.* -MEN], one of a board of governing officers in New England towns.
**self** (self), *n.* [*pl.* SELVES], [AS. *se(o)lf*], 1. the identity, character, etc. of any person or thing. 2. one's own identity, personality, etc. 3. one's own welfare or interest. *pron.* [Colloq.], myself, himself, etc.: as, for *self* and wife. *adj.* of the same kind, color, etc. as the rest: as, *self* lining.
**self-**, a prefix meaning *of*, *by*, *in*, *on*, *to*, or *with oneself* or *itself*. The following list includes some common compounds formed with *self-* that do not have special meanings.

**self-abnegation**
**self-appointed**
**self-assertion**
**self-command**
**self-complacent**
**self-deceit**
**self-deception**
**self-destruction**
**self-discipline**
**self-examination**
**self-fertilization**
**self-help**
**self-imposed**
**self-improvement**
**self-induced**
**self-indulgence**
**self-indulgent**
**self-inflicted**
**self-knowledge**
**self-love**
**self-pity**
**self-pollinated**
**self-protection**
**self-reproach**
**self-sealing**
**self-support**
**self-supporting**
**self-sustaining**

**self'-ad·dressed'**, *adj.* addressed to oneself: as, a *self-addressed* envelope.
**self'-as·sur'ance**, *n.* confidence in oneself. —**self'-as·sured'**, *adj.*
**self'-cen'tered**, *adj.* concerned only with one's own affairs; selfish.
**self'-con·ceit'**, *n.* too high an opinion of oneself; vanity. —**self'-con·ceit'ed**, *adj.*
**self'-con'fi·dent**, *adj.* confident of one's own ability; sure of oneself. —**self'-con'fi·dence**, *n.*
**self'-con'scious**, *adj.* unduly conscious of oneself as an object of notice; ill at ease. —**self'-con'scious·ly**, *adv.*
**self'-con·tained'**, *adj.* 1. keeping one's affairs to oneself. 2. showing self-control. 3. self-sufficient.
**self'-con'tra·dic'tion**, *n.* 1. contradiction of oneself or itself. 2. any statement having elements that contradict each other. —**self'-con'tra·dic'to·ry**, *adj.*
**self'-con·trol'**, *n.* control of one's emotions, desires, etc. —**self'-con·trolled'**, *adj.*
**self'-de·fense'**, *n.* defense of oneself or of one's property, rights, etc.
**self'-de·ni'al**, *n.* denial or sacrifice of one's own desires or pleasures.
**self'-de·ter'mi·na'tion**, *n.* 1. determination according to one's own mind; free will. 2. the right of a people to choose its own form of government.
**self'-de·vo'tion**, *n.* devotion of oneself to the interests of others; self-sacrifice.
**self'-ed'u·cat'ed**, *adj.* educated by oneself, with little formal schooling.
**self'-ef·face'ment**, *n.* modest, retiring behavior. —**self'-ef·fac'ing**, *adj.*
**self'-es·teem'**, *n.* 1. belief in oneself; self-respect. 2. undue pride in oneself; conceit.
**self'-ev'i·dent**, *adj.* evident without explanation or proof.
**self'-ex·plan'a·to'ry**, *adj.* explaining itself; obvious.
**self'-ex·pres'sion**, *n.* the expression of one's personality, as through art.
**self'-gov'ern·ment**, *n.* government of a group by the action of its own members. —**self'-gov'ern·ing**, *adj.*
**self'-im·por'tance**, *n.* an exaggerated opinion of one's own importance. —**self'-im·por'tant**, *adj.*
**self'-in'ter·est**, *n.* 1. one's own interest or advantage. 2. an exaggerated regard for this. —**self'-in'ter·est·ed**, *adj.*
**self'ish**, *adj.* overly concerned with one's own interests and advantage, so that the welfare of others is neglected. —**self'ish·ly**, *adv.* —**self'ish·ness**, *n.*
**self'less**, *adj.* without regard for oneself or one's own interests; unselfish.
**self'-made'**, *adj.* 1. made by oneself or itself. 2. successful through one's own efforts.
**self'-o·pin'ion·at'ed**, *adj.* 1. stubborn in holding to one's opinion. 2. conceited.
**self'-pos·ses'sion**, *n.* the full control of one's faculties or feelings; self-control; composure. —**self'-pos·sessed'**, *adj.*
**self'-pres·er·va'tion**, *n.* preservation of oneself from injury or death.
**self'-pro·pelled'**, *adj.* producing its own power of movement.
**self'-re·li'ance**, *n.* reliance upon one's own judgment, abilities, etc.—**self'-re·li'ant**, *adj.*
**self'-re·spect'**, *n.* a proper respect for oneself, one's character, etc. —**self'-re·spect'ing**, *adj.*
**self'-re·straint'**, *n.* restraint imposed on oneself by oneself; self-control. —**self'-re·strained'**, *adj.*
**self'-right'eous**, *adj.* righteous, moral, etc. in one's own opinion.
**self'-sac'ri·fice**, *n.* the sacrifice of oneself or one's interests, usually for the advantage of others. —**self'-sac'ri·fic'ing**, *adj.*
**self'same'**, *adj.* identical; (the) very same.
**self'-sat'is·fied'**, *adj.* feeling or showing satisfaction with oneself. —**self'-sat·is·fac'tion**, *n.*
**self'-seek'er**, *n.* one who seeks mainly to further his own interests. —**self'-seek'ing**, *n. & adj.*
**self'-serv'ice**, *n.* the practice of serving oneself in a cafeteria, store, etc.
**self'-start'er**, *n.* a device for automatically starting an internal-combustion engine.
**self'-styled'**, *adj.* named (as such) by oneself: as he is a *self-styled* patriot.
**self'-suf·fi'cient**, *adj.* able to get along without help; independent. —**self'-suf·fi'cien·cy**, *n.* —**self'-suf·fi'cient·ly**, *adv.*
**self'-taught'**, *adj.* taught through one's own efforts.
**self'-willed'**, *adj.* stubborn; obstinate.
**self'-wind'ing**, *adj.* wound automatically, as some watches, etc.
**sell** (sel), *v.t.* [SOLD, SELLING], [AS. *sellan*, give], 1. to exchange (goods or services) for money, etc. 2. to offer for sale. 3. to promote the sale of. *v.i.* 1. to engage in selling. 2. to be sold (*for*). —**sell out**, 1. to get rid of completely by selling. 2. [Colloq.], to betray. —**sell'er**, *n.*
**Selt·zer (water)** (selt'sẽr), [< *Nieder Selters*, Germany], 1. a mineral water. 2. [often s-], carbonated water.
**sel·vage, sel·vedge** (sel'vij), *n.* [< *self* + *edge*], a specially woven edge which prevents fabric from raveling.
**selves** (selvz), *n.* pl. of **self**.
**se·man·tics** (sə-man'tiks), *n.pl.* [construed sing.], [< Gr. *sēmainein*, to show], the study of the development and changes of the meanings of words. —**se·man'tic**, *adj.*
**sem·a·phore** (sem'ə-fôr'), *n.* [< Gr. *sēma*,

a sign + *pherein*, to bear], any apparatus or system for signaling, as by lights, flags, etc. —**sem'a·phor'ic**, *adj.*

**sem·blance** (sem'bləns), *n.* [< L. *similis*, like], 1. outward appearance. 2. resemblance. 3. a likeness, copy, etc.

**se·men** (sē'mən), *n.* [*pl.* SEMINA (sem'i-nə)], [L., seed], the fluid secreted by the male reproductive organs.

**se·mes·ter** (sə-mes'tẽr), *n.* [< L. *sex*, six + *mensis*, month], either of the two terms generally making up a school year.

**semi-**, [L.], a prefix meaning: 1. *half.* 2. *partly, not fully.* 3. *twice in a* (specified period).

**sem·i·an·nu·al** (sem'i-an'ū-əl), *adj.* 1. happening, coming, etc. every half year. 2. lasting half a year. —**sem'i·an'nu·al·ly**, *adv.*

**sem·i·cir·cle** (sem'ə-sũr'k'l), *n.* a half circle. —**sem'i·cir'cu·lar** (-kyoo-lẽr), *adj.*

**sem'i·co'lon** (-kō'lən), *n.* a mark of punctuation (;) indicating a degree of separation greater than that marked by the comma.

**sem'i·con·duc'tor** (-kən-duk'tər), *n.* a substance, as germanium or silicon, used as in transistors to control current flow.

**sem'i·con'scious,** *adj.* not fully conscious or awake. —**sem'i·con'scious·ly**, *adv.*

**sem'i·fi'nal,** *adj.* coming just before the final: said of the divisions of a contest. *n.* a semifinal match, etc.

**sem'i·month'ly,** *adj.* coming, done, etc. twice a month. *adv.* twice monthly.

**sem·i·nal** (sem'ə-n'l), *adj.* [see SEMEN], 1. of or containing seed or semen. 2. of reproduction. 3. like seed.

**sem·i·nar** (sem'ə-när'), *n.* 1. a group of supervised students doing research. 2. a course for such a group.

**sem·i·nar·y** (sem'ə-ner'i), *n.* [*pl.* -IES], [< L. *seminarium*, nursery], 1. a school, esp. a private school for young women. 2. a school where priests, ministers, etc. are trained.

**sem·i·pre·cious** (sem'ə-presh'əs), *adj.* designating stones, as the garnet, turquoise, etc., of lower value than precious stones.

**sem·i·pro** (sem'i-prō'), *n.* [< *semiprofessional*], [Colloq.], a person who engages in a sport for pay but not as a regular occupation.

**Sem·ite** (sem'īt), *n.* [< *Shem*, a son of Noah], a member of any of the peoples whose language is Semitic; now, specif., a Jew.

**Se·mit·ic** (sə-mit'ik), *adj.* 1. of or like the Semites. 2. designating or of a group of languages of SW Asia and N Africa, including Hebrew, Arabic, etc.

**sem·i·trop·i·cal** (sem'ə-trop'i-k'l), *adj.* partly tropical.

**sem'i·week'ly,** *adj.* coming, done, etc. twice a week. *adv.* twice weekly.

**Sen., sen.,** 1. Senate. 2. Senator. 3. senior.

**sen·ate** (sen'it), *n.* [< L. *senex*, old], 1. a lawmaking assembly. 2. [S-], the upper branch of the U.S. Congress or of a State legislature.

**sen·a·tor** (sen'ə-tẽr), *n.* a member of a senate. —**sen'a·to'ri·al** (-tôr'i-əl), *adj.*

**send** (send), *v.t.* [SENT, SENDING], [AS. *sendan*], 1. to cause to go or be transmitted; dispatch. 2. to cause (a person) to go. 3. to impel; drive. 4. to cause to happen, come, etc. —**send for**, 1. to summon. 2. to place an order for. —**send'er**, *n.*

**send'-off',** *n.* [Colloq.], 1. a farewell demonstration for someone starting out on a trip, career, etc. 2. a start given to someone or something.

**se·nile** (sē'nīl), *adj.* [< L. *senex*, old], 1. of or resulting from old age. 2. showing signs of old age; weak in mind and body. —**se·nil·i·ty** (sə-nil'ə-ti), *n.*

**sen·ior** (sēn'yẽr), *adj.* [L. < *senex*, old], 1. older: written *Sr.* after a father's name if it is the same as his son's. 2. of higher rank or longer service. 3. of seniors. *n.* 1. one who is older, of higher rank, etc. 2. a person in the graduating class of a high school or college.

**senior high school,** high school: usually the grades 10, 11, and 12.

**sen·ior·i·ty** (sēn-yôr'ə-ti), *n.* [*pl.* -TIES], 1. a being senior. 2. status, priority, etc. achieved by length of service in a given job.

**sen·na** (sen'ə), *n.* [< Ar. *sanā*, cassia plant], 1. the dried leaves of various cassia plants. 2. a laxative extracted from these leaves.

‡**se·nor** (se-nyôr'), *n.* [*pl.* -NORES (-nyô'res)], [Sp.], a man; gentleman: Spanish title equivalent to *Mr.* or *Sir.*

‡**se·no·ra** (se-nyô'rä), *n.* [Sp.], a married woman; lady: Spanish title equivalent to *Mrs.* or *Madam.*

‡**se·no·ri·ta** (se'nyô-rē'tä), *n.* [Sp.], an unmarried woman or girl; young lady: Spanish title equivalent to *Miss.*

**sen·sa·tion** (sen-sā'shən), *n.* [< L. *sensus*, sense], 1. the receiving of sense impressions through hearing, seeing, etc. 2. a conscious sense impression. 3. a generalized feeling: as, a *sensation* of joy. 4. a feeling of excitement or the cause of this: as, the play caused (or was) a *sensation.*

**sen·sa'tion·al,** *adj.* 1. arousing intense interest. 2. intended to excite, shock, etc. —**sen·sa'tion·al·ism**, *n.*

**sense** (sens), *n.* [< L. *sentire*, to feel], 1. any faculty of receiving impressions through body organs; sight, hearing, touch, smell, or taste. 2. feeling, perception, etc., through either the senses or the intellect. 3. an ability to understand some quality, as humor, honor, etc. 4. sound intelligence and judgment. 5. meaning, as of a word. *v.t.* [SENSED, SENSING], to perceive. —**in a sense**, to some extent. —**make sense**, to be intelligible or logical.

**sense'less,** *adj.* 1. unconscious. 2. stupid or foolish. 3. unreasonable.

**sen·si·bil·i·ty** (sen'sə-bil'ə-ti), *n.* [*pl.* -TIES], 1. the capacity for physical sensation. 2. *often pl.* the capacity for being affected emotionally, intellectually, or aesthetically.

**sen·si·ble** (sen'sə-b'l), *adj.* 1. that can cause physical sensation. 2. easily perceived. 3. aware; cognizant. 4. having or showing good sense; wise. —**sen'si·bly**, *adv.*

**sen·si·tive** (sen'sə-tiv), *adj.* 1. sensory. 2. very keenly susceptible to stimuli. 3. tender; raw: as, a *sensitive* bruise. 4. having or showing keen sensibilities. 5. easily offended; touchy. —**sen'si·tiv'i·ty**, *n.*

**sen'si·tize'** (-tīz'), *v.t.* [-TIZED, -TIZING], to make sensitive. —**sen'si·ti·za'tion**, *n.*

**sen·so·ry** (sen'sẽr-i), *adj.* of the senses or sensation: also **sen·so'ri·al** (-sôr'i-əl, -sō'ri-).

**sen·su·al** (sen'shoo-əl), *adj.* [< L. *sensus*, sense], 1. of the body and the senses as distinguished from the intellect. 2. connected or preoccupied with sexual pleasures. —**sen'su·al'i·ty** (-al'ə-ti), *n.*

**sen'su·al·ism** (-iz'm), *n.* 1. excessive indulgence in sexual pleasure. 2. the belief that sensual pleasures constitute the greatest good. —**sen'su·al·ist**, *n.*

**sen·su·ous** (sen'shoo-əs), *adj.* 1. of, derived from, or perceived by the senses. 2. enjoying sensation. —**sen'su·ous·ly**, *adv.*

**sent** (sent), pt. and pp. of **send.**

**sen·tence** (sen'təns), *n.* [< L. *sententia*, opinion], 1. a decision, as of a court. 2. *a*) the determination by a court of a punishment. *b*) the punishment. 3. a group of words stating something, usually containing a subject and predicate. *v.t.* [-TENCED, -TENCING], to pronounce punishment upon (a convicted person). —**sen'tenc·er**, *n.*

**sen·ten·tious** (sen-ten'shəs), *adj.* [see SEN-

TENCE], full of, or fond of using, maxims, proverbs, etc.; often, ponderously trite.

**sen·tient** (sen′shənt, -shi-ənt), *adj.* [< L. *sentire*, to feel], of or capable of feeling; conscious. —**sen′tience, sen′tien·cy,** *n.*

**sen·ti·ment** (sen′tə-mənt), *n.* [< L. *sentire*, to feel], 1. a complex combination of feelings and opinions. 2. an opinion, etc., often colored by emotion. 3. susceptibility to emotional appeal. 4. appeal to the emotions. 5. sentimentality; maudlin emotion.

**sen·ti·men·tal** (sen′tə-men′t'l), *adj.* 1. having or showing tenderness, emotion, etc. 2. affectedly emotional; maudlin. 3. of or caused by sentiment. —**sen′ti·men′tal·ist,** *n.* —**sen′ti·men·tal′i·ty** (-tal′ə-ti), *n.*

**sen·ti·nel** (sen′ti-n'l), *n.* [< It. *sentinella*], a guard or sentry.

**sen·try** (sen′tri), *n.* [*pl.* -TRIES], [prob. < ME. *centry* (sanctuary)], a person, esp. a soldier, stationed to guard a group against surprise.

**se·pal** (sē′p'l, sep′'l), *n.* [< L. *separatus*, separate + *petalum*, petal], any of the leaf divisions of a calyx.

**sep·a·ra·ble** (sep′ẽr-ə-b'l), *adj.* that can be separated.

**sep·a·rate** (sep′ə-rāt′; *for adj.*, -ẽr-it), *v.t.* [-RATED, -RATING], [< L. *se-*, apart + *parare*, arrange], 1. to set apart into parts, groups, etc.; divide. 2. to keep apart by being between. 3. to stop from living together. *v.i.* 1. to withdraw (*from*). 2. to part, become disconnected, etc. 3. to go in different directions. *adj.* 1. set apart from the rest or others. 2. not associated with others; distinct. 3. not shared: as, *separate* rooms. —**sep′a·rate·ly,** *adv.* —**sep′a·ra′tor,** *n.*

**sep·a·ra·tion** (sep′ə-rā′shən), *n.* 1. a separating or being separated. 2. the place where this occurs; break; division. 3. something that separates.

**sep′a·ra′tist** (-rā′tist), *n.* one who withdraws: esp., a member of a group that has seceded from a larger group.

**se·pi·a** (sē′pi-ə), *n.* & *adj.* [< Gr. *sēpia*, cuttlefish secreting brown fluid], (of) dark reddish brown.

**sep·sis** (sep′sis), *n.* [see SEPTIC], poisoning caused by the absorption into the blood of pathogenic microorganisms.

**Sep·tem·ber** (sep-tem′bẽr), *n.* [< L. *septem*, seven: seventh month in Rom. calendar], the ninth month of the year, having 30 days: abbrev. **Sept.**

**sep·tic** (sep′tik), *adj.* [< Gr. *sēpein*, to make putrid], 1. causing sepsis or putrefaction; infective. 2. of or resulting from sepsis.

**sep·ti·ce·mi·a, sep·ti·cae·mi·a** (sep′tə-sē′mi-ə), *n.* [< Gr. *sēptikos*, septic + *haima*, blood], blood poisoning from pathogenic microorganisms and their toxic products in the blood.

**septic tank,** a tank in which waste matter is decomposed through bacterial action.

**Sep·tu·a·gint** (sep′too-ə-jint′), *n.* [< L. *septuaginta*, seventy: in tradition, done in 70 days], a Greek translation of the Old Testament.

**sep·ul·cher** (sep′'l-kẽr), *n.* [< L. *sepelire*, bury], a vault for burial; tomb: also, Brit. sp., **sep′ul·chre.**

**se·pul·chral** (sə-pul′krəl), *adj.* 1. of sepulchers, burial, etc. 2. suggestive of the grave or burial; gloomy. 3. deep and melancholy: said of sound.

**seq.,** *sequentes* or *sequentia*, [L.], the following.

**se·quel** (sē′kwəl), *n.* [< L. *sequi*, follow], 1. something that follows; continuation. 2. something coming as a result of something else; consequence. 3. any literary work complete in itself but continuing a story begun in an earlier work.

**se·quence** (sē′kwəns), *n.* [< L. *sequi*, follow], 1. the coming of one thing after another; succession. 2. the order in which this occurs. 3. a series. 4. consequence. 5. a scene or episode, as in a film play.

**se·quen·tial** (si-kwen′shəl), *adj.* 1. subsequent or consequent. 2. characterized by a regular sequence of parts.

**se·ques·ter** (si-kwes′tẽr), *v.i.* [< L. *sequestrare*, remove], 1. to set off or apart. 2. to withdraw; seclude. —**se·ques·tra·tion** (sē′-kwes-trā′shən), *n.*

**se·quin** (sē′kwin), *n.* [ult. < Ar. *sikkah*, a stamp], a small, shiny spangle, esp. one of many sewn on fabric for decoration.

**se·quoi·a** (si-kwoi′ə), *n.* [< *Sikwâyi*, Indian inventor of Cherokee writing], a giant evergreen tree of California.

**se·rag·lio** (si-ral′yō, se-räl′-), *n.* [*pl.* -LIOS], [ult. < L. *sera*, a lock], the place where a Moslem keeps his wives or concubines; harem.

**se·ra·pe** (se-rä′pi), *n.* [Mex. Sp.], a bright-colored woolen blanket used as a garment in Mexico and Spanish America.

**ser·aph** (ser′əf), *n.* [*pl.* -APHS, -APHIM (-ə-fim′)], [< Heb. *sĕrāphim*, *pl.*], in *theology*, a member of the highest order of angels. —**se·raph·ic** (sə-raf′ik), *adj.*

**Serb** (sũrb), *n.* 1. one of a Slavic people of the Balkans. 2. their language. *adj.* Serbian.

**Ser·bi·an** (sũr′bi-ən), *adj.* of Serbia, the Serbs, or their language. *n.* 1. a native or inhabitant of Serbia. 2. the South Slavic language as spoken in Serbia.

**sere** (sêr), *adj.* [var. of *sear*], [Poetic], withered.

**ser·e·nade** (ser′ə-nād′), *n.* [ult. < L. *serenus*, clear], music played or sung at night, esp. by a lover under his sweetheart's window. *v.t.* & *v.i.* [-NADED, -NADING], to perform a serenade (to). —**ser′e·nad′er,** *n.*

**se·rene** (sə-rēn′), *adj.* [L. *serenus*], 1. clear; unclouded. 2. undisturbed; calm. —**se·rene′ly,** *adv.* —**se·ren′i·ty** (-ren′ə-ti), *n.*

**serf** (sũrf), *n.* [< L. *servus*, a slave], a person in feudal servitude, bound to his master's land and transferred with it to a new owner. —**serf′dom,** *n.*

**serge** (sũrj), *n.* [< L. *serica* (*lana*), (wool of the) *Seres*, prob. the Chinese], a twilled, worsted fabric.

**ser·geant** (sär′jənt), *n.* [< L. *servire*, serve], 1. a police officer ranking next below a captain or lieutenant. 2. a noncommissioned officer ranking just above a corporal. Abbrev. **Sgt., Sergt.** —**ser′gean·cy** [*pl.* -CIES], *n.*

**ser′geant-at-arms′,** *n.* [*pl.* SERGEANTS-AT-ARMS], an officer appointed to keep order, as in a court, social club, etc.

**se·ri·al** (sêr′i-əl), *adj.* [< L. *series*, an order], appearing in a series of continuous parts at regular intervals. *n.* any story, etc. presented in serial form. —**se′ri·al·i·za′tion,** *n.* —**se′ri·al·ize′** (-īz′), [-IZED, -IZING] *v.t.*

**serial number,** any one of a series of numbers used to identify.

**se·ries** (sêr′iz), *n.* [*pl.* SERIES], [L. < *serere*, join together], a number of similar things or persons arranged in a row or coming one after another.

**ser·if** (ser′if), *n.* [< D. *schreef*, a line], in *printing*, a fine line projecting from the main stroke of a letter.

**se·ri·ous** (sêr′i-əs), *adj.* [< L. *serius*], 1. earnest, grave, sober, etc. 2. not joking; sincere. 3. requiring careful consideration; important. 4. dangerous: as, a *serious* wound.

**ser·mon** (sũr′mən), *n.* [< L. *sermo*], 1. a speech on religion or morals, esp. by a clergyman. 2. any serious talk on behavior, duty, etc., esp. a tedious one. —**ser′mon·ize′** [-IZED, -IZING], *v.i.*

**Sermon on the Mount,** the sermon deliv-

ered by Jesus to his disciples: Matt. 5-7, Luke 6:20-49.
**se·rous** (sêr'əs), *adj.* 1. of or containing serum. 2. thin and watery.
**ser·pent** (sũr'pənt), *n.* [< L. *serpere*, to creep], a snake.
**ser'pen·tine'** (-pən-tēn', -tīn'), *adj.* of or like a serpent; esp., *a*) cunning; treacherous. *b*) twisted; winding.
**ser·rate** (ser'āt, -it), *adj.* [< L. *serra*, a saw], having sawlike notches along the edge, as some leaves. **—ser·ra'tion,** *n.*
**ser·ried** (ser'id), *adj.* [ult. < LL. *sera*, a bar], placed close together.
**se·rum** (sêr'əm), *n.* [*pl.* SERUMS, SERA (-ə)], [L., whey], 1. any watery animal fluid, esp. blood serum, the yellowish fluid which separates from the clot when blood coagulates. 2. blood serum used as an antitoxin, taken from an animal made immune to a specific disease by inoculation.
**ser·vant** (sũr'vənt), *n.* [OFr. < *servir*, serve], 1. a person employed by another, esp. to do household duties. 2. a slave. 3. a person devoted to another or to a cause, creed, etc.
**serve** (sũrv), *v.t.* [SERVED, SERVING], [< L. *servire*], 1. to be a servant to. 2. to do services for; aid; help. 3. to do military or naval service for. 4. to spend (a term of imprisonment, etc.): as, to *serve* ten years. 5. to provide (customers) with (goods or services). 6. to set (food, etc.) before (a person). 7. to be sufficient for. 8. to be used by: as, one hospital *serves* the city. 9. to function for: as, my memory *serves* me well. 10. to deliver (a summons, etc.) to (someone). 11. in *tennis*, etc., to hit (the ball) in order to start play. *v.i.* 1. to work as a servant. 2. to do service: as, he *served* in the navy. 3. to carry out the duties of an office. 4. to be of service. 5. to be sufficient. 6. to wait on table. 7. to be suitable: as, when the opportunity *serves*. **—serve one right**, to give one his just deserts.
**serv·ice** (sũr'vis), *n.* [< L. *servus*, a slave], 1. the occupation of a servant. 2. public employment. 3. a branch of this: as, the civil *service*. 4. the U.S. armed forces: with *the*. 5. work done for others: as, repair *service*. 6. a religious ceremony. 7. helpful or friendly action. 8. advantage; benefit. 9. the act or manner of serving food. 10. a set of articles used in serving: as, a tea *service*. 11. the act or method of providing people with some utility, as water or gas. 12. in *tennis*, etc., an act, manner, or turn of serving. *v.t.* [-ICED, -ICING], 1. to furnish with a service; supply. 2. to make fit for service, as by repairing. **—at one's service,** 1. ready to serve one. 2. ready for one's use. **—of service**, helpful.
**serv'ice·a·ble,** *adj.* 1. that can be of service; useful. 2. that will give good service; durable. 3. beneficial. **—serv'ice·a·bil'i·ty,** *n.*
**serv'ice·man',** *n.* [*pl.* -MEN], a member of the armed forces: also **service man.**
**service station,** a gas station.
**ser·vi·ette** (sũr'vi-et'), *n.* [Fr. < *servir*, serve], a table napkin.
**ser·vile** (sũr'v'l), *adj.* [< L. *servus*, a slave], 1. of slaves. 2. like that of slaves. 3. humbly submissive. **—ser'vile·ly,** *adv.* **—ser·vil'i·ty** (-vil'ə-ti) [*pl.* -TIES], *n.*
**ser·vi·tor** (sũr'və-tẽr), *n.* a servant.
**ser·vi·tude** (sũr'və-tōōd'), *n.* [< L. *servus*, a slave], 1. slavery. 2. work imposed as punishment for crime.
**ses·a·me** (ses'ə-mē'), *n.* [< Gr. *sēsamon*], 1. an East Indian plant whose edible seeds yield an oil. 2. its seeds.
**ses·qui·cen·ten·ni·al** (ses'kwi-sen-ten'i-əl), *adj.* [< L. *sesqui-*, more by a half; + *centennial*], of a period of 150 years. *n.* a 150th anniversary.
**ses·sion** (sesh'ən), *n.* [< L. *sedere*, sit], 1. the meeting of a court, legislature, etc. to do its work. 2. a series of such meetings. 3. the period of either of these. 4. a period of study, classes, etc. **—in session,** meeting.
**set** (set), *v.t.* [SET, SETTING], [AS. *settan*], 1. to cause to sit; seat. 2. to put in a specified place, condition, etc.: as, *set* the book on the table, he *set* the house on fire. 3. to put in proper condition; fix (a trap for animals), adjust (a clock or dial), arrange (a table for a meal), etc. 4. to put (a broken bone, etc.) into normal position. 5. to make settled, rigid, or fixed: as, pectin *sets* jelly. 6. to mount (gems). 7. to direct. 8. to appoint; establish; fix (boundaries, the time for an event, a rule, a quota, a price, etc.). 9. to furnish (an example) for others. 10. to fit (words) to music or (music) to words. 11. in *printing*, to compose (type) or put (copy) into type. *v.i.* 1. to sit on eggs: said of a fowl. 2. to become firm, hard, or fixed: as, the cement *set*. 3. to begin to move (*out*, *forth*, *off*, etc.). 4. to sink below the horizon: as, the sun *sets*. 5. to have a certain direction; tend. *adj.* 1. fixed; established: as, a *set* time. 2. intentional. 3. fixed; rigid; firm. 4. obstinate. 5. ready: as, get *set*. *n.* 1. a setting or being set. 2. the way in which a thing is set: as, the *set* of his jaw. 3. direction; tendency. 4. the scenery for a play, etc. 5. a group of persons or things classed or belonging together. 6. assembled equipment for radio or television reception, etc. 7. in *tennis*, a group of six or more games won by a margin of at least two. **—set about** (or **in, to**), to begin. **—set down,** to put in writing. **—set forth,** 1. to publish. 2. to state. **—set off,** 1. to make prominent by contrast. 2. to cause to explode. **—set on** (or **upon**), to attack. **—set up,** 1. to erect. 2. to establish.
**set'back',** *n.* a reversal in progress.
**set·tee** (se-tē'), *n.* 1. a seat or bench with a back. 2. a small sofa.
**set'ter,** *n.* 1. one that sets. 2. a long-haired dog trained to hunt game.
**set'ting,** *n.* 1. the act of one that sets. 2. a thing in or on which something is set. 3. time and place, environment, etc., as of a story, etc. 4. actual physical surroundings.
**set·tle** (set''l), *n.* [AS. *setl*], a long wooden bench with a back and arm rests.
**set·tle** (set''l), *v.t.* [-TLED, -TLING], [AS. *setlan*], 1. to put in order; arrange, as one's affairs. 2. to set in place so as to be firmly or comfortably situated. 3. to colonize. 4. to cause to sink and become more compact. 5. to free from disturbance, as the nerves. 6. to decide (a dispute, etc.). 7. to pay (a debt, etc.). *v.i.* 1. to stop moving and stay in one place. 2. to cast itself over a landscape, as fog, or over a person, as gloom. 3. to become localized, as a pain. 4. to take up permanent residence. 5. to sink: as, the house *settled*. 6. to become more dense by sinking, as sediment. 7. to become more stable. 8. to reach a decision (*with* or *on*). **—set'tler,** *n.*
**set'tle·ment,** *n.* 1. a settling or being settled. 2. a colonizing, as of new land. 3. a colony. 4. a village. 5. an agreement. 6. payment. 7. a community center for the underprivileged.
**set'up',** *n.* 1. the plan, make-up, etc. of equipment, an organization, etc. 2. [Slang], a contest, etc. arranged to result in an easy victory or success.
**sev·en** (sev''n), *adj.* & *n.* [AS. *seofon*], one more than six; 7; VII. **—sev'enth,** *adj.* & *n.*
**seven seas,** all the oceans of the world.
**sev'en·teen'** (-tēn'), *adj.* & *n.* seven more than ten; 17; XVII. **—sev'en·teenth'** (-tēnth'), *adj.* & *n.*

**sev·en·ty** (sev′'n-ti), *adj. & n.* [*pl.* -TIES], seven times ten; 70; LXX. —**the seventies,** the years from 70 through 79 (of a century or a person's age). —**sev′en·ti·eth** (-ith), *adj. & n.*

**sev·er** (sev′ẽr), *v.t. & v.i.* [< L. *separare*], to separate, divide, or break off. —**sev′er·a·ble,** *adj.* —**sev′er·ance,** *n.*

**sev·er·al** (sev′ẽr-əl), *adj.* [< L. *separ*], 1. separate; distinct. 2. different; respective. 3. more than two but not many; few. *n.* several persons or things. —**sev′er·al·ly,** *adv.*

**se·vere** (sə-vêr′), *adj.* [< L. *severus*], 1. harsh or strict, as in treatment; stern. 2. serious; grave, as in expression. 3. rigidly accurate or exact. 4. extremely plain: said of style. 5. violent; intense, as pain. 6. difficult; rigorous, as a rule or test. —**se·vere′ly,** *adv.* —**se·ver′i·ty** (-ver′ə-ti), **se·vere′ness,** *n.*

**sew** (sō), *v.t. & v.i.* [SEWED, SEWED or SEWN (sōn), SEWING], [AS. *si(o)wan*], 1. to fasten with stitches made with needle and thread. 2. to make, mend, etc. by sewing. —**sew up,** [Colloq.], to get full control of; monopolize.

**sew·age** (so͞o′ij, sū′-), *n.* the waste matter carried off by sewers or drains.

**sew·er** (so͞o′ẽr, sū′-), *n.* [ult. < L. *ex*, out + *aqua*, water], an underground pipe or drain for carrying off water and waste matter.

**sew′er·age** (-ij), *n.* 1. a system of sewers. 2. sewage.

**sew·ing** (sō′iŋ), *n.* 1. the act of one who sews. 2. material for sewing.

**sewing machine,** a machine with a mechanically driven needle for sewing.

**sex** (seks), *n.* [< L. *sexus*], 1. either of the two divisions of organisms distinguished as male or female. 2. the character of being male or female. 3. the attraction between the sexes.

**sex-,** [< L. *sex*, six], a combining form meaning *six*.

**sex appeal,** the physical charm that attracts those of the opposite sex.

**sex′ism,** *n.* the economic exploitation and social domination of members of one sex by the other, specif. of women by men.

**sex·tant** (seks′tənt), *n.* [< L. *sextans*, a sixth (part of a circle)], an instrument for measuring angular distance, esp. between a heavenly body and the horizon, as to determine position at sea.

**sex·tet, sex·tette** (seks-tet′), *n.* [ult. < L. *sex*, six], 1. a group of six. 2. a musical composition for six voices or instruments. 3. the six performers of this.

**sex·ton** (seks′tən), *n.* [ult. < L. *sacer*, sacred], a church official in charge of the maintenance of church property.

**sex·u·al** (sek′sho͞o-əl), *adj.* of or affecting sex, the sexes, the sex organs, etc. —**sex′u·al′i·ty** (-al′ə-ti), *n.* —**sex′u·al·ly,** *adv.*

**sex′y,** *adj.* [-IER, -IEST], [Slang], exciting or intended to excite sexual desire.

**Sgt.,** Sergeant.

**shab·by** (shab′i), *adj.* [-BIER, -BIEST], [< AS. *sceabb*, a scab], 1. worn out; dilapidated, ragged, etc. 2. wearing worn clothing. 3. mean; shameful: as, *shabby* treatment.

**shack** (shak), *n.* [? < Mex. Ind.], a small, crudely built cabin; shanty.

**shackle** (shak′'l), *n.* [AS. *sceacul*], 1. a metal fastening, usually in pairs, for the wrist or ankle of a prisoner; fetter. 2. anything that restrains freedom, as of expression. 3. a device for coupling, etc. *v.t.* [-LED, -LING], 1. to put shackles on. 2. to restrain in freedom, as of expression. —**shack′ler,** *n.*

**shad** (shad), *n.* [*pl.* SHAD, SHADS], [AS. *sceadd*], a salt-water fish related to the herring but spawning in rivers.

**shade** (shād), *n.* [AS. *sceadu*], 1. comparative darkness caused by cutting off rays of light. 2. an area with less light than its surroundings. 3. degree of darkness of a color. 4. *a*) a small difference: as, *shades* of opinion. *b*) a slight amount or degree. 5. [Poetic], a ghost. 6. a device used to screen from light: as, a window *shade*. *v.t.* [SHADED, SHADING], 1. to screen from light. 2. to darken; dim. 3. to represent shade in (a painting, etc.). *v.i.* to change slightly or by degrees.

**shad·ing** (shād′iŋ), *n.* 1. a shielding against light. 2. the representation of light or shade in a picture. 3. a small variation.

**shad·ow** (shad′ō), *n.* [< AS. *sceadu*, shade], 1. (a) shade cast by a body intercepting light rays. 2. gloom or that which casts gloom. 3. the shaded area of a picture. 4. a ghost. 5. a remnant, trace, etc. *v.t.* 1. to throw a shadow upon. 2. to follow closely, esp. in secret. —**shad′ow·y,** *adj.*

**shad·y** (shād′i), *adj.* [-IER, -IEST], 1. giving shade. 2. shaded, as from the sun; full of shade. 3. [Colloq.], of questionable character. —**on the shady side of,** beyond (a given age). —**shad′i·ness,** *n.*

**shaft** (shaft), *n.* [AS. *sceaft*], 1. an arrow or spear, or its stem. 2. anything hurled like a missile: as, *shafts* of wit. 3. a long, slender part or object. 4. either of the two poles between which an animal is harnessed to a vehicle. 5. a bar transmitting motion to a mechanical part, as of an engine. 6. a long, narrow opening sunk into the earth. 7. a vertical opening passing through a building, as for an elevator.

**shag** (shag), *n.* [< AS. *sceacga*], 1. [Rare], heavily matted wool or hair. 2. a heavy, rough nap. 3. cloth with such a nap.

**shag′gy,** *adj.* [-GIER, -GIEST], 1. covered with long, coarse hair or wool. 2. unkempt, as a person. 3. of coarse growth; straggly. 4. having a rough surface. —**shag′gi·ness,** *n.*

**shah** (shä), *n.* [Per. *shāh*], a title of the ruler of Iran.

**shake** (shāk), *v.t. & v.i.* [SHOOK, SHAKEN, SHAKING], [AS. *sceacan*], 1. to move quickly up and down, back and forth, etc. 2. to bring, force, come, etc. by brisk movement. 3. to tremble or cause to tremble. 4. *a*) to become or cause to become unsteady. *b*) to unnerve or become unnerved. 5. to clasp (another's hand), as in greeting. *n.* 1. an act of shaking. 2. [Colloq.], an earthquake. —**no great shakes,** [Colloq.], not unusual. —**shake down,** 1. to cause to fall by shaking. 2. [Slang], to extort money from. —**shake off,** to get rid of. —**shake up,** 1. to shake, esp. so as to mix. 2. to jar or shock. 3. to reorganize. —**the shakes,** [Colloq.], a convulsive trembling. —**shak′y,** *adj.*

**shake′down′,** *n.* [Slang], an extortion of money, as by blackmail.

**shak′er,** *n.* 1. a person or thing that shakes. 2. a device used in shaking.

**shake′-up′,** *n.* a shaking up; specif., an extensive reorganization.

**shale** (shāl), *n.* [< AS. *scealu*, a shell], a rock formed of hardened clay, that splits into thin layers.

**shall** (shal), *v.* [pt. SHOULD], [< AS. *sceal*], an auxiliary used in formal speech to express futurity in the first person, and determination, obligation, etc. in the second and third persons. *Shall* and *will* are used interchangeably in prevailing usage.

**shal·lot** (shə-lot′), *n.* [ult. < Fr. *eschaloigne*, scallion], 1. an onionlike plant whose bulbs are used for flavoring. 2. a small onion.

**shal·low** (shal′ō), *adj.* [prob. < AS. *sceald*], 1. not deep. 2. lacking depth of character or intellect. *n.* a shoal. —**shal′low·ness,** *n.*

**shalt** (shalt), archaic 2d pers. sing., pres. indic. of **shall.**

**sham** (sham), *n.* [? < *shame*], 1. an imitation; counterfeit. 2. one who falsely affects a certain character. *adj.* not real; false.

*v.t. & v.i.* [SHAMMED, SHAMMING], to pretend; feign. **—sham'mer,** *n.*

**sham·ble** (sham'b'l), *v.i.* [-BLED, -BLING], [orig. *adj.* referring to legs of a *shamble*, bench], to walk clumsily; shuffle. *n.* a shambling walk.

**sham·bles** (sham'b'lz), *n.pl.* [construed as sing.], [ult. < L. *scamnum*, bench: orig., butcher's bench], 1. a slaughterhouse. 2. a scene of great slaughter, destruction, or disorder.

**shame** (shām), *n.* [< AS. *scamu*], 1. a painful feeling of guilt, indecency, etc. 2. dishonor; disgrace. 3. something unfortunate or outrageous. *v.t.* [SHAMED, SHAMING], 1. to cause to feel shame. 2. to dishonor; disgrace. 3. to force by a sense of shame. **—put to shame,** 1. to cause to feel shame. 2. to surpass. **—shame'ful,** *adj.*

**shame'faced',** *adj.* 1. shy; bashful. 2. showing shame or guilt; ashamed.

**shame'less,** *adj.* having or showing no shame, modesty, or decency; brazen.

**sham·my** (sham'i), *n.* [*pl.* -MIES], chamois.

**sham·poo** (sham-pōō'), *v.t.* [-POOED, -POOING], [< Hind. *chāmpnā*, to press], 1. to wash (the hair of). 2. to wash (a carpet, etc.). *n.* 1. a shampooing. 2. a preparation used for this.

**sham·rock** (sham'rok), *n.* [< Ir. *seamar*, clover], a cloverlike plant with leaflets in groups of three; the emblem of Ireland.

**shang·hai** (shaŋ'hī, shaŋ-hī'), *v.t.* [-HAIED, -HAIING], [< *Shanghai*, China: after such kidnaping for crews on the China run], to kidnap, usually by drugging, for service aboard ship.

**shank** (shaŋk), *n.* [AS. *scanc*], 1. the part of the leg between the knee and the ankle in man, or a corresponding part in animals. 2. the whole leg. 3. a cut of beef from the upper leg. 4. the part between the handle and the working part (of a tool, etc.).

**shan't** (shant, shänt), shall not.

**shan·tung** (shan'tuŋ'), *n.* [< *Shantung*, a province in China], a fabric made from the silk of wild silkworms.

**shan·ty** (shan'ti), *n.* [*pl.* -TIES], [< Canad. Fr. *chantier*, workshop], a small, shabby dwelling; hut.

**shape** (shāp), *n.* [< AS. *scieppan*, create], 1. the quality of a thing that depends on the relative position of all points on its surface; physical form. 2. the contour of the body. 3. definite or regular form: as, his story is taking *shape*. 4. [Colloq.], condition: as, the victim is in bad *shape*. *v.t.* [SHAPED, SHAPING], 1. to give definite shape to; form. 2. to arrange, express, etc. in definite form. 3. to adapt: as, *shape* your plans to mine. **—shape up,** [Colloq.], to develop to a definite or satisfactory form, etc. **—take shape,** to show distinct development. **—shape'less,** *adj.*

**shape'ly,** *adj.* [-LIER, -LIEST], having good shape; well-proportioned. **—shape'li·ness,** *n.*

**shard** (shärd), *n.* [AS. *sceard*], a fragment or broken piece, esp. of pottery; potsherd.

**share** (shâr), *n.* [< AS. *sceran*, to cut], 1. a portion which belongs to an individual. 2. any of the equal parts of capital stock of a corporation. *v.t.* [SHARED, SHARING], 1. to distribute in shares. 2. to have a share of with others. *v.i.* to have a share; participate.

**share** (shâr), *n.* [AS. *scear*], a plowshare.

**share'crop',** *v.i. & v.t.* [-CROPPED, -CROPPING], to work (land) for a share of the crop. **—share'crop'per,** *n.*

**share'hold'er,** *n.* one who owns shares of stock.

**shark** (shärk), *n.* [prob. < G. *schurke*, scoundrel], 1. a large marine fish with a tough gray skin: most sharks are fish-eaters. 2. a swindler. 3. [Slang], an expert.

**shark·skin** (shärk'skin'), *n.* a smooth, silky cloth of wool, rayon, etc.

**sharp** (shärp), *adj.* [< AS. *scearp*], 1. having a fine edge or point for cutting or piercing. 2. having a point or edge; not rounded. 3. not gradual; abrupt: as, a *sharp* turn. 4. distinct; clear: as, a *sharp* difference. 5. quick in perception; clever. 6. attentive; vigilant. 7. crafty; underhanded. 8. harsh; severe, as temper. 9. violent, as an attack. 10. brisk; active: as, a *sharp* run. 11. cold, as a wind. 12. intense, as pain. 13. pungent. 14. [Slang], well-groomed; handsome. 15. in *music*, above the true pitch. *n.* 1. [Colloq.], *a*) an expert. *b*) a sharper. 2. in *music*, *a*) a tone one half step above another. *b*) the symbol (#) for such a note. *v.t. & v.i.* to make or become sharp, as in pitch. *adv.* 1. in a sharp manner; specif., *a*) abruptly or briskly. *b*) attentively or alertly. *c*) in *music*, above the true pitch. 2. precisely.

**sharp'en,** *v.t. & v.i.* to make or become sharp or sharper. **—sharp'en·er,** *n.*

**sharp'er,** *n.* a swindler.

**sharp'shoot'er,** *n.* a good marksman.

**shat·ter** (shat'ẽr), *v.t. & v.i.* [ME. *sc(h)ateren*, scatter], 1. to break or burst into pieces. 2. to damage or be damaged severely.

**shave** (shāv), *v.t.* [SHAVED, SHAVED or SHAVEN, SHAVING], [< AS. *sceafan*], 1. to cut away thin slices or sections from. 2. *a*) to cut off (hair) at the surface of the skin. *b*) to cut the hair to the surface of (the face, etc.). *c*) to cut the beard of (a person). 3. to skim the surface of; graze. *v.i.* to cut off hair with a razor, etc. *n.* the act or result of shaving the beard. **—close shave,** [Colloq.], a narrow escape.

**shav'er,** *n.* 1. one who shaves. 2. an instrument used in shaving. 3. [Colloq.], a boy.

**shav'ing,** *n.* 1. the act of one who shaves. 2. a thin piece of wood, etc. shaved off.

**shawl** (shôl), *n.* [< Per. *shāl*], an oblong or square cloth worn, esp. by women, as a covering for the head and shoulders.

**shay** (shā), *n.* [< *chaise*, assumed as pl.], [Colloq.], a light carriage; chaise.

**she** (shē), *pron.* [for *pl.* see THEY], [< AS. *seo*], the girl, woman, or female animal previously mentioned. *n.* a girl, woman, or female animal.

**sheaf** (shēf), *n.* [*pl.* SHEAVES], [< AS. *sceaf*], 1. a bundle of cut stalks of grain, etc. 2. a collection, as of papers, bound in a bundle.

**shear** (shêr), *v.t.* [SHEARED, SHEARED or SHORN, SHEARING], [< AS. *sceran*], 1. to cut as with shears. 2. to remove (the hair, wool, etc.) by cutting. 3. to clip the hair, etc. from. 4. to strip (*of* a right, etc.). *n.* 1. a machine for cutting metal. 2. the act or result of shearing. **—shear'er,** *n.*

**shears,** *n.pl.* 1. large scissors. 2. a large tool or machine with two opposed blades, used to cut metal, etc.

**sheath** (shēth), *n.* [*pl.* SHEATHS (shēthz, shēths)], [< AS. *sceath*], 1. a case for the blade of a knife, sword, etc. 2. a covering resembling this.

**sheathe** (shēth), *v.t.* [SHEATHED, SHEATHING], 1. to put into a sheath. 2. to enclose in a case or covering. **—sheathed,** *adj.*

**sheave** (shēv), *v.t.* [SHEAVED, SHEAVING], to gather in a sheaf or sheaves, as grain.

**she·bang** (shə-baŋ'), *n.* [Slang], a particular matter of concern; affair, etc.

**shed** (shed), *n.* [< AS. *scead*], a small structure for shelter or storage.

**shed** (shed), *v.t.* [SHED, SHEDDING], [< AS. *sceadan*, to separate], 1. to pour out. 2. to cause to flow: as, to *shed* tears. 3. to radiate: as, to *shed* confidence. 4. to throw off: as, oilskin *sheds* water. 5. to cast off (a natural growth, as hair, etc.). *v.i.* to shed hair, etc. **—shed blood,** to kill by violent means.

**she'd** (shēd), 1. she had. 2. she would.
**sheen** (shēn), *n.* [< AS. *scene*, beautiful], brightness; luster. —**sheen'y**, *adj.*
**sheep** (shēp), *n.* [*pl.* SHEEP], [AS. *sceap*], 1. a cud-chewing mammal related to the goats, with heavy wool and edible flesh. 2. one who is meek, stupid, timid, etc.
**sheep'cote'** (-kōt'), *n.* [cf. COTE], a sheepfold.
**sheep dog,** a dog trained to herd sheep.
**sheep'fold',** *n.* an enclosure for sheep.
**sheep'ish,** *adj.* bashful or embarrassed.
**sheep'skin',** *n.* 1. the skin of a sheep. 2. parchment or leather made from the skin of a sheep. 3. [Colloq.], a diploma.
**sheer** (shêr), *v.t. & v.i.* [a form of *shear*], to turn aside or cause to turn aside from a course; swerve. *n.* deviation from a course.
**sheer** (shêr), *adj.* [< ON. *skiær*, bright], 1. very thin; transparent: said of textiles. 2. absolute; downright: as, *sheer* folly. 3. extremely steep. *adv.* 1. completely; utterly. 2. very steeply. —**sheer'ness,** *n.*
**sheet** (shēt), *n.* [AS. *sceat*], 1. a large piece of cotton, linen, etc., used as bedding. 2. *a*) a single piece of paper. *b*) a newspaper. 3. a broad, continuous surface, as of flame, water, etc. 4. a broad, thin piece of any material, as glass, tin, etc.
**sheet** (shēt), *n.* [< AS. *sceatline*], a rope for controlling the set of a sail.
**sheet'ing,** *n.* cotton or linen material used for making sheets.
**sheet metal,** metal rolled thin to the form of a sheet.
**sheet music,** music printed on unbound sheets of paper.
**sheik, sheikh** (shēk), *n.* [< Ar. *shaikh*, old man], the chief of an Arab family, tribe, or village.
**shek·el** (shek''l), *n.* [< Heb. *shāqal*, weigh], 1. a gold or silver coin of the ancient Hebrews. 2. *pl.* [Slang], money.
**shelf** (shelf), *n.* [*pl.* SHELVES], [< MLG. *schelf*, set of shelves], 1. a thin, flat board set horizontally against a wall, etc., used for holding things. 2. something like a shelf, as a ledge. 3. a sandbar or reef. —**on the shelf,** out of use, circulation, etc.
**shell** (shel), *n.* [AS. *sciel*], 1. a hard outer covering, as of an animal, egg, nut, etc. 2. something like a shell in being hollow, empty, a covering, etc. 3. a light, narrow rowboat for racing. 4. a missile fired from a large gun, containing high explosives, etc. 5. a cartridge. *v.t.* 1. to remove the shell or covering from: as, to *shell* peas. 2. to bombard. —**shell out,** [Colloq.], to pay out (money).
**she'll** (shēl), 1. she shall. 2. she will.
**shel·lac, shel·lack** (shə-lak'), *n.* [< *shell* + *lac*], 1. a resin usually produced in thin, flaky layers. 2. a thin varnish containing this resin and alcohol. *v.t.* [SHELLACKED, SHELLACKING], 1. to apply shellac to. 2. [Slang], *a*) to beat; flog. *b*) to defeat decisively.
**-shelled,** a combining form meaning *having a* (specified kind of) *shell*.
**shell'fish',** *n.* [*pl.* see FISH], any aquatic animal with a shell, as the oyster or clam.
**shell shock,** combat fatigue.
**shel·ter** (shel'tẽr), *n.* [< AS. *sceld*, shield + *truma*, a troop], 1. something that protects against the elements, danger, etc. 2. a being covered, protected, etc. *v.t.* to provide shelter for; protect. *v.i.* to find shelter.
**shelve** (shelv), *v.t.* [SHELVED, SHELVING], 1. to furnish with shelves. 2. to put on a shelf or shelves. 3. *a*) to lay aside: as, to *shelve* a debate. *b*) to retire from active service.
**shelves** (shelvz), *n.* pl. of **shelf.**
**shelv'ing,** *n.* 1. material for shelves. 2. shelves collectively.
**she·nan·i·gan** (shi-nan'i-gən), *n.* [? < Ir. *sionnachuighim*, I play the fox], *usually pl.* [Colloq.], trickery; mischief.
**shep·herd** (shep'ẽrd), *n.* [see SHEEP & HERD], 1. one who herds sheep. 2. a religious leader. *v.t.* to herd, guard, lead, etc. as a shepherd. —**shep'herd·ess,** *n.fem.*
**sher·bet** (shũr'bət), *n.* [< Ar. *sharbah*, a drink], a frozen dessert of fruit juice, sugar, and water, milk, or egg white.
**sher·iff** (sher'if), *n.* [< AS. *scir*, shire + *gerefa*, chief officer], the chief law-enforcement officer of a county. —**sher'iff·dom,** *n.*
**sher·ry** (sher'i), *n.* [< *Xeres*, Spain], 1. a strong, yellow or brownish Spanish wine. 2. any similar wine.
**she's** (shēz), 1. she is. 2. she has.
**shew** (shō), *n., v.t. & v.i.* [SHEWED, SHEWN, SHEWING], [Brit. or Archaic], show.
**shib·bo·leth** (shib'ə-ləth), *n.* [< Heb. *shibbōleth*, a stream], 1. in the *Bible*, a test word used to distinguish the enemy: Judg. 12:6. 2. any password.
**shied** (shīd), pt. and pp. of **shy.**
**shield** (shēld), *n.* [AS. *scield*], 1. a piece of armor carried on the arm to ward off blows, etc. 2. one that guards, protects, etc. 3. an escutcheon. 4. anything shaped like a shield. *v.t. & v.i.* to defend; protect.
**shift** (shift), *v.t.* [AS. *sciftan*, divide], 1. to move from one person or place to another. 2. to put another or others in place of. 3. to change the arrangement of (gears). *v.i.* 1. to change position, direction, etc. 2. to get along: as, to *shift* for oneself. *n.* 1. a plan of conduct, esp. for an emergency; expedient. 2. a trick; dodge. 3. a shifting; transfer. 4. a group of employees working in relay with another. 5. their daily work period. —**make shift (with),** to do the best one can (*with*) under difficulties.
**shift'less,** *adj.* inefficient, lazy, etc.
**shift'y,** *adj.* [-IER, -IEST], of a tricky nature; evasive. —**shift'i·ly,** *adv.* —**shift'i·ness,** *n.*
**shill** (shil), *n.* [Slang], a confederate, as of a carnival operator, who pretends to buy, bet, etc. so as to lure others.
**shil·le·lagh, shil·la·lah** (shi-lā'lə, shə-lā'li), *n.* [< *Shillelagh*, Ir. village], a cudgel.
**shil·ling** (shil'iŋ), *n.* [AS. *scylling*], a British money of account and silver coin, equal to 12 pence.
**shil·ly-shal·ly** (shil'i-shal'i), *v.i.* [-LIED, -LYING], [< *shall I?*], to be irresolute; vacillate.
**shim·mer** (shim'ẽr), *v.i.* [AS. *scymrian*], to shine with an unsteady light; glimmer. *n.* a shimmering light. —**shim'mer·y,** *adj.*
**shim·my, shim·mey** (shim'i), *n.* [*pl.* -MIES or -MEYS], [< Fr. *chemise*, a chemise: orig., a shaking dance], a marked vibration or wobble, as in automobile wheels. *v.i.* [-MIED, -MYING; -MEYED, -MEYING], to shake, vibrate, or wobble.
**shin** (shin), *n.* [AS. *scinu*], the front part of the leg between the knee and the ankle. *v.t. & v.i.* [SHINNED, SHINNING], to climb (a rope, etc.), gripping with hands and legs.
**shin'bone',** *n.* the tibia: also **shin bone.**
**shin·dig** (shin'dig), *n.* [< colloq. *shindy*, commotion], [Colloq.], a dance, party, or other social affair.
**shine** (shīn), *v.i.* [SHONE or, esp. for *v.t.* 2, SHINED, SHINING], [AS. *scinan*], 1. to emit or reflect light; gleam; glow. 2. to excel; be eminent. 3. to exhibit itself brightly: as, love *shone* from her face. *v.t.* 1. to cause to shine. 2. to make shiny by polishing. *n.* 1. brightness; radiance. 2. luster; polish. 3. a shoeshine. 4. splendor; brilliance. —**take a shine to,** [Slang], to develop a liking for.
**shin·er** (shin'ẽr), *n.* 1. a silvery minnow. 2. [Slang], a black eye.
**shin·gle** (shiŋ'g'l), *n.* [Norw. *singel*], 1. coarse, waterworn gravel, as on a beach. 2. an area covered with this.

**shin·gle** (shiŋ′g'l), ***n.*** [< L. *scindere*, to split], 1. a thin, wedge-shaped tile of wood, slate, etc. laid with others in overlapping rows, as for roofs. 2. [Colloq.], a small signboard, as of a doctor. ***v.t.*** [-GLED, -GLING], to cover (a roof, etc.) with shingles.
**shin·gles** (shiŋ′g'lz), ***n.*** [< L. *cingere*, to gird], an acute virus disease with eruption of blisters on the skin along the course of a nerve.
**Shin·to** (shin′tō), ***n.*** [Japan. < Chin. *shin*, god + *tao*, way], a religion of Japan, emphasizing ancestor worship: also **Shin′to·ism.**
**shin·y** (shīn′i), ***adj.*** [-IER, -IEST], 1. bright; shining. 2. smoothly polished; glossy.
**ship** (ship), ***n.*** [AS. *scip*], 1. any large vessel navigating deep water. 2. a ship's officers and crew. 3. any aircraft. ***v.t.*** [SHIPPED, SHIPPING], 1. to put or take on board a ship. 2. to send or transport by any carrier: as, to *ship* coal by rail. 3. to put in place on a vessel: as, *ship* the oars. 4. to engage for work on a ship. ***v.i.*** 1. to go aboard ship; embark. 2. to engage to serve on a ship. **—ship′per, *n.***
**-ship,** [AS. *-scipe*], a suffix meaning: 1. *the quality* or *state of*, as in *friendship*. 2. *a*) *the rank* or *office of*, as in *governorship*. *b*) *one having the rank of*, as in *lordship*. 3. *ability in*, as in *leadership*.
**ship′board′, *n.*** a ship. **—on shipboard**, on or in a ship.
**ship′build′er, *n.*** one whose business is building ships. **—ship′build′ing, *n. & adj.***
**ship′mate′, *n.*** a fellow sailor.
**ship′ment, *n.*** 1. the shipping of goods; consignment. 2. goods shipped.
**ship′ping, *n.*** 1. the act or business of transporting goods. 2. ships collectively, as of a nation or port, with reference to tonnage.
**ship′shape′, *adj.*** having everything neatly in place; trim. ***adv.*** in a shipshape manner.
**ship′wreck′, *n.*** 1. the remains of a wrecked ship. 2. the loss of a ship through storm, etc. 3. ruin; destruction. ***v.t.*** to cause to undergo shipwreck.
**ship′yard′, *n.*** a place where ships are built and repaired.
**shire** (shīr), ***n.*** [AS. *scire*, office], in Great Britain, a county.
**shirk** (shũrk), ***v.t. & v.i.*** [prob. < G. *schurke*, rascal], to neglect (a duty). ***n.*** one who shirks: also **shirk′er, *n.***
**shirr** (shũr), ***n.*** [< ?], a series of parallel rows of short stitches with gatherings between rows. ***v.t.*** 1. to make shirrs in (cloth). 2. to bake (eggs) with crumbs in buttered dishes.
**shirt** (shũrt), ***n.*** [AS. *scyrte*], 1. a garment worn by men on the upper part of the body. 2. an undershirt. **—keep one's shirt on,** [Slang], to be patient or calm.
**shiv·a·ree** (shiv′ə-rē′), ***n.*** [< Fr. *charivari*], a mock serenade, as to newlyweds, with kettles, horns, etc.
**shiv·er** (shiv′ẽr), ***n.*** [ME. *schivere*], a fragment or splinter. ***v.t. & v.i.*** to break into fragments or splinters. **—shiv′er·y, *adj.***
**shiv·er** (shiv′ẽr), ***v.i.*** [? < AS. *ceafi*, jaw], to shake or tremble, as from fear or cold. ***n.*** a shaking, trembling, etc. **—shiv′er·y, *adj.***
**shoal** (shōl), ***n.*** [AS. *scolu*], 1. a large group; crowd. 2. a school of fish.
**shoal** (shōl), ***n.*** [< AS. *sceald*, shallow], 1. a shallow place in a river, sea, etc. 2. a sand bar forming a shallow place.
**shoat** (shōt), ***n.*** [< ?], a young pig.
**shock** (shok), ***n.*** [< MD. *schokken*, collide], 1. a sudden, powerful blow, shake, etc. 2. *a*) a sudden emotional disturbance. *b*) the cause of this. 3. an extreme stimulation of the nerves by the passage of electric current through the body. 4. a disorder of the circulatory system, caused by injury or sudden psychic disturbance. ***v.t.*** 1. to disturb emotionally; astonish, horrify, etc. 2. to produce electrical shock in.
**shock** (shok), ***n.*** [? <MD.], a bunch of grain sheaves stacked together to cure and dry.
**shock** (shok), ***n.*** [< obs. *shock dog*, poodlelike dog], a thick, bushy or tangled mass, as of hair.
**shock′ing, *adj.*** 1. causing great surprise and distress. 2. disgusting.
**shock troops,** troops especially trained and equipped to lead an attack.
**shod** (shod), pt. and pp. of **shoe.**
**shod·dy** (shod′i), ***n.*** [*pl.* -DIES], [prob. < dial. *shode*, loose pieces], 1. an inferior woolen cloth made from used fabrics. 2. anything worth less than it seems to be. ***adj.*** [-DIER, -DIEST], 1. made of inferior material. 2. lacking the claimed quality.
**shoe** (sho͞o), ***n.*** [*pl.* SHOES], [< AS. *scoh*], 1. an outer covering for the foot. 2. a horseshoe. 3. the part of a brake that presses against a wheel. 4. the outer casing of a pneumatic tire. ***v.t.*** [SHOD, SHOEING], to furnish with shoes. **—fill one's shoes**, to take one's place.
**shoe′horn′, *n.*** an implement inserted at the back of a shoe to help slip it on the foot.
**shoe′lace′, *n.*** a length of cord, etc. used for lacing and fastening a shoe.
**shoe′mak′er, *n.*** one whose business is making and repairing shoes.
**shoe′shine′, *n.*** the cleaning and polishing of a pair of shoes.
**shoe′string′, *n.*** a shoelace. **—on a shoestring**, with very little money.
**shoe tree,** a shoe-shaped form inserted in a shoe to stretch it or preserve its shape.
**shone** (shōn), pt. and pp. of **shine.**
**shoo** (sho͞o), ***interj.*** go away! get out! ***v.t.*** [SHOOED, SHOOING], to drive away, as by crying "shoo."
**shook** (shook), pt. of **shake.**
**shoot** (sho͞ot), ***v.t.*** [SHOT, SHOOTING], [AS. *sceotan*], 1. to pass swiftly over, by, etc.: as, to *shoot* the rapids. 2. to variegate as with another color. 3. to thrust forth, as a branch, bud, etc. 4. to discharge (a bullet, arrow, etc.) or fire (a gun, etc.). 5. to send forth swiftly, or with force. 6. to take the altitude of, as a star. 7. to hit, wound, etc. with a missile from a weapon. 8. to photograph. 9. in *sports*, *a*) to throw or drive (a ball, etc.) toward the objective. *b*) to score (a goal, points, etc.). ***v.i.*** 1. to move swiftly. 2. to be felt suddenly, as pain. 3. to grow rapidly. 4. to jut out. 5. to fire a missile, as from a gun. 6. to be discharged, as a gun. 7. to hunt game. ***n.*** 1. a shooting trip, contest, etc. 2. a new growth; sprout.
**shooting star,** a meteor.
**shop** (shop), ***n.*** [< AS. *sceoppa*, booth], 1. a place where things are offered for sale; store. 2. a place where a particular kind of work is done. ***v.i.*** [SHOPPED, SHOPPING], to visit shops to examine or buy goods. **—talk shop**, to discuss one's work.
**shop′keep′er, *n.*** one who operates a shop, or store.
**shop′lift′er, *n.*** one who steals articles exposed for sale in a shop. **—shop′lift′ing, *n.***
**shop′per, *n.*** 1. one who shops. 2. one hired by a store to compare competitors' merchandise.
**shop′worn′, *adj.*** soiled, worn, etc. from being displayed in a shop.
**shore** (shôr), ***n.*** [prob. < MLG. *schore*], land at the edge of a body of water.
**shore** (shôr), ***n.*** [< MD. *schōre*], a beam, etc. used as a prop. ***v.t.*** [SHORED, SHORING], to support with shores; prop (*up*).
**shore patrol,** a detail of the U.S. Navy, Coast Guard, or Marine Corps acting as military police on shore.
**shorn** (shôrn), alt. pp. of **shear.**

**short** (shôrt), *adj.* [< AS. *sc(e)ort*], 1. not measuring much from end to end in space or time. 2. not great in range or scope. 3. not tall. 4. brief; concise. 5. not retentive: as, a *short* memory. 6. curt; brusque. 7. less than a sufficient or correct amount. 8. tending to crumble, as pastry. 9. designating a sale of securities, etc. which the seller expects to buy at a lower price before the date of delivery. *n.* 1. something short. 2. *pl.* short trousers or drawers. 3. a short circuit. *adv.* 1. abruptly; suddenly. 2. briefly; concisely. 3. so as to be short: as, cut it *short.* *v.t. & v.i.* to short-circuit. **—fall** (or **come**) **short,** to fail to reach, suffice, etc. **—in short,** briefly. **—run short,** to have less than enough.**—short of,** less than or lacking. **—short′ness,** *n.*

**short′age,** *n.* 1. an insufficient amount; deficiency. 2. a deficit.

**short′bread′,** *n.* a rich, crumbly cake or cooky made with shortening.

**short′cake′,** *n.* a light biscuit or a sweet cake served with fruit, etc. as a dessert.

**short′change′,** *v.t. & v.i.* [-CHANGED, -CHANGING], [Colloq.], 1. to give less money than is due in change. 2. to cheat.

**short circuit,** 1. a side circuit of low relative resistance connecting two points in an electric circuit of higher resistance so as to deflect most of the current. 2. loosely, a disrupted electric circuit resulting from this. **—short′-cir′cuit,** *v.t. & v.i.*

**short′com′ing,** *n.* a fault, deficiency, defect, etc.

**short cut,** 1. a shorter route. 2. any way of saving time, effort, etc.

**short′en,** *v.t. & v.i.* to make short or shorter.

**short′en·ing,** *n.* fat used in baked goods to make them crisp or flaky.

**short′hand′,** *n.* any system of speed writing using symbols for letters, words, and phrases. *adj.* written in or using shorthand.

**short′-hand′ed,** *adj.* short of workers.

**short′horn′,** *n.* any of a breed of cattle with short, curved horns.

**short′-lived′** (-līvd′, -livd′), *adj.* living, lasting, or continuing only a short time.

**short′ly,** *adv.* 1. briefly. 2. soon. 3. abruptly.

**short order,** food quickly prepared after it has been ordered in a restaurant. **—in short order,** quickly. **—short′-or′der,** *adj.*

**short shrift,** very little care or attention. **—make short shrift of,** to make short work of: also **give short shrift.**

**short′sight′ed,** *adj.* 1. unable to see clearly at a distance. 2. lacking in foresight.

**short′stop′,** *n.* in *baseball,* the infielder stationed between second and third base.

**short′-tem′pered,** *adj.* easily angered.

**short wave,** a radio wave 60 meters or less in length. **—short′-wave′,** *adj.*

**short′-wind′ed** (-win′did), *adj.* easily put out of breath by exercise.

**shot** (shot), *n.* [AS. *sceot*], 1. the act of shooting. 2. range; scope. 3. an attempt; try. 4. a pointed, critical remark. 5. a stroke, throw, etc., as of a ball. 6. *a*) a projectile for a gun. *b*) projectiles collectively. 7. small pellets of lead for a shotgun. 8. a heavy metal ball cast overhand for distance by contestants: in phr. *to put the shot.* 9. a marksman. 10. a film sequence or photograph. 11. [Slang], a dose, as of morphine. 12. [Slang], a drink of liquor.

**shot** (shot), pt. and pp. of **shoot.** *adj.* 1. variegated, streaked, etc. with another color or substance. 2. [Colloq.], ruined; worn out.

**shot′gun′,** *n.* a smoothbore gun for firing a charge of small shot.

**shot′-put′,** *n.* 1. a contest in which athletes put the shot. 2. a throw of the shot.

**should** (shood), *v.* [AS. *sc(e)olde*], 1. pt. of **shall.** 2. an auxiliary used to express: *a*) obligation, duty, etc.: e.g., you *should* help. *b*) expectation or probability: e.g., he *should* be here by now. *c*) a future condition: e.g., if I *should* die.

**shoul·der** (shōl′dẽr), *n.* [AS. *sculdor*], 1. *a*) the joint connecting the arm or forelimb with the body. *b*) the part of the body including this joint. 2. *pl.* the two shoulders and the part of the back between them. 3. a shoulderlike projection. 4. the edge of a road. *v.t.* 1. to push through, as with the shoulder. 2. to carry upon the shoulder. 3. to assume the burden of. **—straight from the shoulder,** without reserve; frankly. **—turn** (or **give**) **a cold shoulder to,** to treat with disdain.

**shoulder blade,** either of the two flat bones in the upper back articulated with the humerus.

**should·n't** (shood′'nt), should not.

**shouldst** (shoodst), archaic 2d pers. sing. of **should:** also **should·est** (shood′ist).

**shout** (shout), *n.* [ME. *schoute*], a loud, sudden cry, call, etc. *v.t. & v.i.* to utter or cry out in a loud voice.

**shove** (shuv), *v.t. & v.i.* [SHOVED, SHOVING], [AS. *scufan*], 1. to push, as along a surface. 2. to push roughly. *n.* a push. **—shove off,** 1. to push (a boat) away from shore. 2. [Colloq.], to start off; leave.

**shov·el** (shuv′'l), *n.* [AS. *sceofol*], a tool with a broad scoop and long handle, for lifting and moving loose material. *v.t.* [-ELED or ELLED, -ELING or -ELLING], 1. to lift and move with a shovel. 2. to dig out with a shovel.

**show** (shō), *v.t.* [SHOWED, SHOWN or SHOWED, SHOWING], [< AS. *sceawian,* to look], 1. to bring or put in sight. 2. to guide; conduct. 3. to point out. 4. to reveal: as, *show* no anger. 5. to prove; demonstrate. 6. to bestow (favor, grace, etc.). *v.i.* 1. to be or become seen; appear. 2. to be noticeable. 3. to finish third in a horse race. *n.* 1. a showing or demonstration. 2. a public display or exhibition. 3. a pompous display. 4. pretense: as, his anger was mere *show.* 5. a presentation of entertainment. **—show off,** to make a display of, esp. a vain display. **—show up,** 1. to be seen. 2. to arrive. 3. [Colloq.], to be superior to.

**show′boat′,** *n.* a boat with a theater and actors who play river towns.

**show business,** the theater, motion pictures, etc. as a business or industry.

**show′case′,** *n.* a glass-enclosed case for displaying things as in a store.

**show′down′,** *n.* [Colloq.], a disclosure, as of the true nature of a situation.

**shower** (shou′ẽr), *n.* [AS. *scur*], 1. a brief fall of rain, hail, or sleet. 2. a sudden, abundant fall, as of sparks, praise, etc. 3. a party during which gifts are presented to the guest of honor. 4. a shower bath. *v.t.* 1. to spray with water, etc. 2. to give abundantly. *v.i.* 1. to fall or come in a shower. 2. to take a shower bath. **—show′er·y,** *adj.*

**shower bath,** a bath in which the body is sprayed with fine streams of water.

**show·man** (shō′mən), *n.* [*pl.* -MEN], 1. one whose business is producing shows. 2. a person skilled at presenting anything in a striking manner. **—show′man·ship′,** *n.*

**shown** (shōn), pp. of **show.**

**show′-off′,** *n.* [Colloq.], one who shows off.

**show′room′,** *n.* a room where goods are displayed for advertising or sale.

**show′y,** *adj.* [-IER, -IEST], 1. of striking appearance. 2. attracting attention in a cheap way; flashy.**—show′i·ly,** *adv.***—show′i·ness,** *n.*

**shrank** (shraŋk), pt. of **shrink.**

**shrap·nel** (shrap'nəl), *n.* [< Gen. *Shrapnel* (1761–1842), its Brit. inventor], 1. an artillery shell filled with an explosive charge and small metal balls. 2. these balls or shell fragments scattered on explosion.

**shred** (shred), *n.* [AS. *screada*], 1. an irregular strip cut or torn off. 2. a fragment: as, not a *shred* of truth. *v.t.* [SHREDDED or SHRED, SHREDDING], to tear or cut into shreds. —**shred'der**, *n.*

**shrew** (shro͞o), *n.* [AS. *screawa*], 1. a small, mouselike mammal with a long snout. 2. a nagging, evil-tempered woman. —**shrew'ish**, *adj.* —**shrew'ish·ness**, *n.*

**shrewd** (shro͞od), *adj.* [ME. *schrewe*, shrew], clever or sharp in practical affairs; astute.

**shriek** (shrēk), *v.i. & v.t.* [prob. < ON.], to make or utter with a loud, piercing cry; screech. *n.* such a cry. —**shriek'er**, *n.*

**shrift** (shrift), *n.* [ult. < L. *scribere*, write], [Archaic], confession to and absolution by a priest.

**shrike** (shrīk), *n.* [< AS. *scric*], a shrill-voiced bird of prey with a hooked beak: some types hang their prey on thorns after the kill.

**shrill** (shril), *adj.* [echoic], having or producing a high, thin, piercing sound. *adv.* in a shrill tone, voice, etc. *v.t. & v.i.* to utter (with) a shrill sound. —**shrill'ness**, *n.*

**shrimp** (shrimp), *n.* [< AS. *scrimman*, shrink], 1. a small, long-tailed crustacean, valued as food. 2. [Colloq.], a small or insignificant person.

**shrine** (shrīn), *n.* [< L. *scrinium*, box], 1. a container holding sacred relics. 2. the tomb of a saint. 3. a place of worship. 4. a place or thing hallowed because of its history or associations.

**shrink** (shriŋk), *v.i.* [SHRANK or SHRUNK, SHRUNK or SHRUNKEN, SHRINKING], [AS. *scrincan*], 1. to contract, as from heat, cold, wetting, etc. 2. to lessen, as in amount. 3. to draw back. *v.t.* to cause to shrink.

**shrink'age**, *n.* 1. a shrinking. 2. the amount of shrinking.

**shrive** (shrīv), *v.t.* [SHRIVED or SHROVE (shrōv), SHRIVEN (shriv''n) or SHRIVED, SHRIVING], [< L. *scribere*, write], [Archaic], to hear the confession of and give absolution to.

**shriv·el** (shriv''l), *v.t. & v.i.* [-ELED or -ELLED, -ELING or -ELLING], [cf. Sw. *skryvla*, to wrinkle], to curl up or wrinkle; wither.

**shroud** (shroud), *n.* [AS. *scrud*], 1. a cloth used to wrap a corpse for burial. 2. something that covers, protects, etc. 3. any of the ropes stretched from a ship's side to a masthead. *v.t.* to hide; cover.

**Shrove Tuesday**, [cf. alt. pt. of *shrive*], the last day before Lent.

**shrub** (shrub), *n.* [prob. < AS. *scrybb*, brushwood], a woody plant with a number of main stems; bush. —**shrub'by**, *adj.*

**shrub'ber·y**, *n.* [*pl.* -IES], shrubs collectively.

**shrug** (shrug), *v.t. & v.i.* [SHRUGGED, SHRUGGING], [ME. *schruggen*], to draw up (the shoulders), as in doubt, indifference, etc. *n.* the gesture so made.

**shrunk** (shruŋk), alt. pt. and pp. of **shrink**.

**shrunk'en**, alt. pp. of **shrink**. *adj.* contracted in size.

**shuck** (shuk), *n.* [? < *husk*], a shell, pod, or husk. *v.t.* to remove the shucks of.

**shucks** (shuks), *interj.* an exclamation of disappointment or disgust.

**shud·der** (shud'ẽr), *v.i.* [< AS. *scudan*, to hurry], to shake or tremble violently, as in horror. *n.* a shuddering.

**shuf·fle** (shuf''l), *v.t. & v.i.* [-FLED, -FLING], [prob. < LG. *schuffeln*], 1. to move (the feet) with a dragging gait. 2. to mix (playing cards). 3. to mix together in a jumble. *n.* a shuffling. —**shuf'fler**, *n.*

**shuf'fle·board'**, *n.* [< *shovel board*], a game in which disks are pushed with a cue toward numbered squares.

**shun** (shun), *v.t.* [SHUNNED, SHUNNING], [AS. *scunian*], to keep away from; avoid scrupulously. —**shun'ner**, *n.*

**shunt** (shunt), *v.t. & v.i.* [prob. < AS. *scyndan*, hasten], 1. to move or turn to one side. 2. to switch, as a train, from one track to another. *n.* 1. a shunting. 2. a railroad switch.

**shush** (shush), *interj.* [echoic], hush! be quiet! *v.t.* to say "shush" to.

**shut** (shut), *v.t.* [SHUT, SHUTTING], [AS. *scyttan*], 1. to move (a door, lid, etc.) so as to close an opening. 2. to close (an opening, container, etc.). 3. to prevent entrance to. 4. to fold up the parts of, as an umbrella, etc. *v.i.* to be or become shut. *adj.* closed, fastened, etc. —**shut down**, to cease operating. —**shut off**, to prevent passage of or through. —**shut out**, 1. to deny entrance to. 2. to prevent from scoring. —**shut up**, 1. to enclose or confine. 2. [Colloq.], to stop or cause to stop talking.

**shut'down'**, *n.* a stoppage of activity, esp. in a factory temporarily.

**shut'-in'**, *n.* an invalid who cannot go out. *adj.* unable to go out; confined.

**shut'out'**, *n.* in *sports*, a game in which the opposing team is prevented from scoring.

**shut'ter**, *n.* 1. a person or thing that shuts. 2. a movable cover for a window. 3. a device that snaps open and shut in front of a camera lens. *v.t.* to close with shutters.

**shut·tle** (shut''l), *n.* [AS. *scytel*, missile], 1. an instrument that carries the woof thread back and forth in weaving. 2. anything that moves back and forth. *v.t. & v.i.* [-TLED, -TLING], to move rapidly to and fro.

**shut'tle·cock'**, *n.* a rounded piece of cork having a flat end stuck with feathers: used in badminton.

**shy** (shī), *adj.* [SHIER or SHYER, SHIEST or SHYEST], [< AS. *sceoh*], 1. easily frightened; timid. 2. avoiding contact with others; bashful. 3. distrustful; wary. 4. [Slang], lacking. *v.i.* [SHIED, SHYING], 1. to move suddenly as if startled. 2. to be or become hesitant, etc. —**shy'ly**, *adv.* —**shy'ness**, *n.*

**shy** (shī), *v.t. & v.i.* [SHIED, SHYING], [< ?], to fling, esp. sidewise with a jerk.

**shy·ster** (shī'stẽr), *n.* [? ult. < G. *scheisser*, defecator], [Slang], an unethical lawyer.

**Si**, in *chem.*, silicon.

**Si·a·mese** (sī'ə-mēz'), *n.* 1. [*pl.* -MESE], a native of Siam, or Thailand. 2. the language of the Siamese; Thai. *adj.* of Siam, its people, language, etc.

**Siamese twins**, [after such a pair born in Siam], any pair of twins born joined to each other.

**sib·i·lant** (sib''l-ənt), *adj.* [< L. *sibilare*, to hiss], having or making a hissing sound. *n.* a hissing sound, as *s*, *sh*, *z*, *zh*, etc.

**sib·ling** (sib'liŋ), *n.* [< AS. *sib*(*b*), kin; + *-ling*], a brother or sister.

**sib·yl** (sib''l), *n.* [< Gr. *sibylla*], a prophetess of ancient Greece or Rome.

‡**sic** (sik), *adv.* [L.], thus; so: used within brackets, [*sic*], to show that a quoted passage, often containing some error, is precisely reproduced.

**Si·cil·i·an** (si-sil'i-ən, -sil'yən), *adj.* of Sicily, its people, dialect, etc. *n.* 1. a native of Sicily. 2. the Italian dialect of the Sicilians.

**sick** (sik), *adj.* [AS. *seoc*], 1. suffering from disease; ill. 2. having nausea. 3. of or for sick people. 4. deeply disturbed, as by grief, failure, longing, etc. 5. disgusted by an excess: as, he is *sick* of puns. *n.* sick people (with *the*).

**sick, sic** (sik), *v.t.* [SICKED, SICKING], [< *seek*], to urge (a dog) to attack.

**sick′bed′**, *n.* the bed of a sick person.
**sick′en**, *v.t. & v.i.* to make or become sick.
**sick′en·ing**, *adj.* 1. causing sickness or nausea. 2. disgusting.
**sick·le** (sik′'l), *n.* [ult. < L. *secare*, to cut], a tool having a crescent-shaped blade on a short handle for cutting tall grass, etc.
**sick·ly** (sik′li), *adj.* [-LIER, -LIEST], 1. in poor health. 2. produced by sickness: as, a *sickly* pallor. 3. faint; pale, as light or color. 4. weak: insipid. — **sick′li·ness**, *n.*
**sick′ness**, *n.* 1. a being sick or diseased. 2. a malady. 3. nausea.
**side** (sīd), *n.* [AS.], 1. the right or left half, as of the body. 2. *a)* any of the lines or surfaces that bound something. *b)* either of the two opposed vertical surfaces of an object that are not the front or back. 3. either of the two surfaces of paper, cloth, etc. 4. an aspect: as, his cruel *side*. 5. any location, etc. with reference to a central point. 6. the position or attitude of one person or faction opposing another. 7. one of the parties in a contest, conflict, etc. 8. a line of descent. *adj.* 1. of, at, or on a side. 2. to or from one side: as, a *side* glance. 3. secondary: as, a *side* interest. *v.t.* [SIDED, SIDING], to furnish with sides or siding. — **side by side**, beside each other. —**side with**, to support (one faction, etc.) against another. —**take sides**, to support one side in a dispute, etc.
**side′board′**, *n.* a piece of furniture for holding table linen, china, etc.
**side·burns** (sīd′būrnz′), *n.pl.* [< *burnsides*, side whiskers worn by A. E. *Burnside*, Civil War general], the hair growing on the cheeks, alongside the ears.
**side light**, incidental information.
**side line**, 1. either of two lines marking the side limits of a playing area, as in football. 2. a secondary line of merchandise, business, etc.
**side′long′**, *adv.* toward the side; obliquely. *adj.* directed to the side, as a glance.
**si·de·re·al** (sī-dêr′i-əl), *adj.* [< L. *sidus*, a star], 1. of the stars or constellations. 2. measured by the apparent motion of fixed stars.
**side show**, a small show apart from the main show, as of a circus.
**side′slip′**, *v.i. & v.t.* [-SLIPPED, -SLIPPING], to slip or cause to slip sideways, as on skis. *n.* a slip or skid to the side.
**side′-step′**, *v.t. & v.i.* [-STEPPED, -STEPPING], to avoid as by stepping aside; dodge.
**side′swipe′** (-swīp′), *v.t. & v.i.* [-SWIPED, -SWIPING], to hit along the side in passing. *n.* a glancing blow of this kind.
**side′track′**, *v.t. & v.i.* 1. to switch (a train) to a siding. 2. to turn away from the main issue. *n.* a railroad siding.
**side′walk′**, *n.* a path, usually paved, at the side of a street, for pedestrians.
**side′ways′** (-wāz′), *adj. & adv.* 1. toward or from one side. 2. with one side forward. Also **side′way′**, **side′wise′** (-wīz′).
**sid·ing** (sīd′iŋ), *n.* 1. boards, etc. for covering the outside of a frame building. 2. a short railway track, for unloading, etc., connected with a main track by a switch.
**si·dle** (sī′d'l), *v.i.* [-DLED, -DLING], [prob. < *sideling*, sideways], to move sideways cautiously or stealthily.
**siege** (sēj), *n.* [< L. *sedere*, sit], 1. the encirclement of a fortified place by an enemy intending to take it. 2. a persistent attempt to gain an objective. 3. [Colloq.], a long, distressing period, as of illness. —**lay siege to**, to subject to a siege.
**si·en·na** (si-en′ə), *n.* [It. *terra di Siena*, earth of Siena (city in Italy)], 1. a yellowish-brown earth pigment. 2. a reddish-brown pigment made by burning this.
**si·er·ra** (si-er′ə), *n.* [Sp. < L. *serra*, a saw], a range of mountains with a saw-toothed appearance.
**si·es·ta** (si-es′tə), *n.* [Sp. < L. *sexta* (*hora*), sixth (hour), noon], a brief nap or rest, esp. at midday or in the afternoon.
**sieve** (siv), *n.* [< AS. *sife*], a utensil with many small holes for straining liquids or fine particles of matter.
**sift** (sift), *v.t.* [AS. *siftan*], 1. to pass through a sieve so as to separate the coarse from the fine particles. 2. to examine with care, as evidence. 3. to separate: as, he *sifted* fact from fable. *v.i.* to pass through or as through a sieve. —**sift′er**, *n.*
**sigh** (sī), *v.i.* [< AS. *sican*], 1. to take in and let out a long, deep, audible breath, as in sorrow, relief, etc. 2. to feel longing or grief (*for*). *n.* the act or sound of sighing.
**sight** (sīt), *n.* [< AS. *seon*, to see], 1. something seen or worth seeing. 2. the act of seeing. 3. aim or an observation taken as with a gun or telescope. 4. the power of seeing; eyesight. 5. range of vision. 6. a device to aid the eyes in aiming a gun, etc. 7. [Colloq.], anything that looks unpleasant, odd, etc. *v.t.* 1. to discern; see. 2. to adjust the sights of (a gun, etc.). *v.i.* to look carefully: as, *sight* along the line. —**a sight for sore eyes**, [Colloq.], a person or thing pleasant to see. —**at** (or **on**) **sight**, as soon as seen. —**by sight**, by appearance. —**not by a long sight**, 1. not nearly. 2. not at all.
**sight′less**, *adj.* blind. —**sight′less·ness**, *n.*
**sight′ly**, *adj.* [-LIER, -LIEST], pleasant to the sight. —**sight′li·ness**, *n.*
**sight′-see′ing**, *n.* a visiting of places and things of interest. —**sight′-se′er**, *n.*
**sig·ma** (sig′mə), *n.* the eighteenth letter of the Greek alphabet (Σ, σ, ς).
**sign** (sīn), *n.* [< L. *signum*], 1. something that indicates a fact, quality, etc.: as, black is a *sign* of mourning. 2. a gesture that conveys information, etc. 3. a mark or symbol having a specific meaning: as, a dollar *sign* ($). 4. a publicly displayed board, etc. bearing information or advertisement. 5. any trace, indication, or vestige. *v.t.* 1. to write (one's name) on (a letter, check, contract, etc.). 2. to hire by written contract. *v.i.* to write one's signature. —**sign off**, in *radio & TV*, to stop broadcasting. —**sign′er**, *n.*
**sig·nal** (sig′n'l), *n.* [< L. *signum*, a sign], 1. a sign; token. 2. a sign given by gesture, a device, etc. to convey command, warning, etc. 3. in *radio*, *TV*, etc., the sound or picture elements, etc. transmitted or received. *adj.* 1. conspicuous; notable. 2. used as a signal. *v.t. & v.i.* [-NALED or -NALLED, -NALING or -NALLING], to make a signal or signals (to).
**sig′nal·ize** (-īz′), *v.t.* [-IZED, -IZING], 1. to make signal, or noteworthy. 2. to point out.
**sig·na·to·ry** (sig′nə-tôr′i), *adj.* taking part in the signing of a pact, etc. *n.* [*pl.* -RIES], a signatory nation, person, etc.
**sig·na·ture** (sig′nə-chēr), *n.* [< L. *signare*, to sign], 1. a person's name written by himself. 2. in *music*, signs placed at the beginning of a staff to show key or time.
**sign·board** (sīn′bôrd′), *n.* a board bearing a sign or advertisement.
**sig·net** (sig′nit), *n.* [< OFr. *signe*, a sign], a small seal used in marking documents as official, etc.
**sig·nif·i·cance** (sig-nif′ə-kəns), *n.* 1. that which is signified; meaning. 2. the quality of being significant; expressiveness. 3. importance; consequence.
**sig·nif·i·cant** (sig-nif′ə-kənt), *adj.* [< L. *significare*, signify], 1. having or expressing a meaning, esp. a special or hidden one. 2. full of meaning. 3. important; momentous. —**sig·nif′i·cant·ly**, *adv.*

**sig·ni·fy** (sig'nə-fī'), *v.t.* [-FIED, -FYING], [< L. *signum*, a sign + *facere*, make], 1. to be an indication of; mean. 2. to make known, as by a sign, words, etc. *v.i.* to be important. —**sig'ni·fi·ca'tion**, *n.*
‡**si·gnor** (sē-nyôr'), *n.* [It.], a gentleman; man: as a title [S-], equivalent to *Mr.*
‡**si·gno·ra** (sē-nyô'rä), *n.* [*pl.* -RE (-re)], [It.], woman; lady: as a title [S-], equivalent to *Mrs.*
‡**si·gno·ri·na** (sē'nyô-rē'nä), *n.* [*pl.* -NE (-ne)], [It.], an unmarried woman or girl: as a title [S-], equivalent to *Miss.*
**sign'post'**, *n.* 1. a post bearing a sign. 2. an obvious clue, symptom, etc.
**si·lage** (sī'lij), *n.* green fodder preserved in a silo.
**si·lence** (sī'ləns), *n.* 1. a keeping silent or still. 2. absence of sound or noise; stillness. 3. omission of mention. *v.t.* [-LENCED, -LENCING], 1. to cause to be silent. 2. to put down; repress. *interj.* be silent!
**si'lenc·er**, *n.* 1. one that silences. 2. a device for deadening the sound of a gun.
**si·lent** (sī'lənt), *adj.* [< L. *silere*, be silent], 1. not speaking; mute. 2. not talkative. 3. free from noise; quiet; still. 4. not spoken; tacit: as, *silent* longing. 5. inactive: as, a *silent* partner. —**si'lent·ly**, *adv.*
**sil·hou·ette** (sil'oo-et'), *n.* [< E. de *Silhouette*, 18th-c. Fr. statesman], 1. a solid, usually black, outline drawing, esp. a profile. 2. any dark shape seen against a light background. *v.t.* [-ETTED, -ETTING], to show or project in a silhouette.
**sil·i·ca** (sil'i-kə), *n.* [< L. *silex*, flint], a hard, glassy mineral found in various forms, as quartz, sand, etc.
**sil·i·cate** (sil'i-kit), *n.* a salt or ester derived from silica.
**sil·i·con** (sil'i-kən), *n.* [< L. *silex*, flint], a nonmetallic chemical element, found always in combination: symbol Si.
**sil·i·cone** (sil'ə-kōn'), *n.* a synthetic resin, oil, plastic, etc. in which the carbon has been replaced by silicon.
**sil'i·co'sis** (-ə-kō'sis), *n.* [< *silicon* + *-osis*], a disease of the lungs caused by continued inhaling of silica dust, as in quarrying stone.
**silk** (silk), *n.* [< L. *sericus*, fabric of the *Seres*, the Chinese], 1. the fine, soft fiber produced by silkworms. 2. thread or fabric made from this. 3. any silklike substance. *adj.* of or like silk. —**silk'en**, **silk'y** [-IER, -IEST], *adj.*
**silk'worm'** (-wũrm'), *n.* any of certain moth caterpillars that produce cocoons of silk fiber.
**sill** (sil), *n.* [AS. *syl(l)*], 1. a heavy, horizontal timber or line of masonry supporting a house wall, etc. 2. a horizontal piece forming the bottom frame of a door or window.
**sil·ly** (sil'i), *adj.* [-LIER, -LIEST], [< AS. *sælig*, happy], having or showing little sense or judgment; foolish, absurd, etc. *n.* [*pl.* -LIES], [Colloq.], a silly person. —**sil'li·ness**, *n.*
**si·lo** (sī'lō), *n.* [*pl.* -LOS], [< Gr. *siros*], 1. an airtight pit or tower in which green fodder is preserved. 2. an underground structure for storing and launching a large ballistic missile.
**silt** (silt), *n.* [prob. < ON.], fine particles of soil, sand, etc. suspended in or deposited by water. *v.t.* & *v.i.* to fill or choke up with silt. —**silt'y** [-IER, -IEST], *adj.*
**sil·ver** (sil'vẽr), *n.* [< AS. *seolfer*], 1. a white, precious, metallic chemical element that is very ductile and malleable: symbol, Ag. 2. silver coin. 3. money; wealth. 4. silverware. 5. a lustrous, grayish white. *adj.* 1. of, containing, or plated with silver. 2. of the color of silver. *v.t.* to cover with or as with silver.
**sil'ver·fish'**, *n.* a wingless insect with silvery scales, found in damp places.
**silver nitrate**, a colorless crystalline salt, used in photography, as an antiseptic, etc.
**sil'ver·smith'**, *n.* a skilled worker who makes articles of silver.
**sil'ver-tongued'**, *adj.* eloquent.
**sil'ver·ware'**, *n.* articles, esp. tableware, made of or plated with silver.
**sil'ver·y**, *adj.* 1. having the appearance of silver. 2. softly and clearly ringing: as, a *silvery* tone. 3. covered with or containing silver. —**sil'ver·i·ness**, *n.*
**sim·i·an** (sim'i-ən), *adj.* [< L. *simia*, an ape], of or like an ape or monkey. *n.* an ape or monkey.
**sim·i·lar** (sim'ə-lẽr), *adj.* [< L. *similis*], 1. nearly but not exactly the same or alike. —**sim'i·lar'i·ty** (-lar'ə-ti), [*pl.* -TIES], *n.*
**sim·i·le** (sim'ə-lē'), *n.* [*pl.* -LES], [L. < *similis*, like], a figure of speech in which one thing is likened to another, dissimilar thing (e.g., a heart as big as a whale).
**si·mil·i·tude** (sə-mil'ə-tood', -tūd'), *n.* [< L. *similitudo*], likeness.
**sim·mer** (sim'ẽr), *v.i.* [echoic], 1. to boil gently. 2. to be about to break out, as in anger. *v.t.* to keep close to the boiling point. *n.* the state of simmering.
**Si·mon Le·gree** (sī'mən lə-grē'), 1. the villainous slave overseer in H. B. Stowe's *Uncle Tom's Cabin*. 2. any relentless taskmaster.
**si·mon-pure** (sī'mən-pyoor'), *adj.* [< *Simon Pure*, a character in an 18th-c. play], genuine; authentic.
**sim·o·ny** (sī'mə-ni, sim'ə-), *n.* [< *Simon Magus*, a magician in the Bible: Acts 8:9-24], the buying or selling of church pardons, offices, etc. —**si'mon·ist**, *n.*
**sim·per** (sim'pẽr), *v.i.* [cf. MD. *simper*, affected], to smile in a silly, affected way; smirk. *n.* such a smile. —**sim'per·er**, *n.*
**sim·ple** (sim'p'l), *adj.* [-PLER, -PLEST], [< L. *simplex*], 1. having but one or a few parts; uncomplicated. 2. easy to do or understand, as a task. 3. without additions: as, the *simple* facts. 4. not ornate or luxurious; plain. 5. without guile or deceit. 6. without ostentation; natural. 7. of low rank or position; common. 8. foolish; stupid.
**sim'ple-mind'ed**, *adj.* 1. foolish. 2. feebleminded. —**sim'ple-mind'ed·ness**, *n.*
**sim·ple·ton** (sim'p'l-tən), *n.* a fool.
**sim·plic·i·ty** (sim-plis'ə-ti), *n.* [*pl.* -TIES], 1. a being simple; freedom from complexity, difficulty, etc. 2. absence of luxury, elegance. 3. plainness, as of way of life.
**sim·pli·fy** (sim'plə-fī'), *v.t.* [-FIED, -FYING], to make more simple; make easier. —**sim'pli·fi·ca'tion**, *n.* —**sim'pli·fi'er**, *n.*
**sim·plis·tic** (sim-plis'tik), *adj.* simplified to an unrealistic degree by the avoidance of complexities. —**sim·plis'ti·cal·ly**, *adv.*
**sim·ply** (sim'pli), *adv.* 1. in a simple manner. 2. merely; just: as, his reply was *simply* this. 3. completely: as, it is *simply* absurd.
**sim·u·late** (sim'yoo-lāt'), *v.t.* [-LATED, -LATING], [< L. *simulare*], 1. to give a false appearance of; feign. 2. to look or act like. —**sim'u·la'tion**, *n.* —**sim'u·la'tive**, *adj.*
**si·mul·cast** (sī'm'l-kast', -käst'), *v.t.* [-CAST, -CASTING], [*simul*taneous + broad*cast*], to transmit simultaneously by radio and television. *n.* a program so transmitted.
**si·mul·ta·ne·ous** (sī'm'l-tā'ni-əs, sim''l-), *adj.* [< L. *simul*, at the same time], occurring, done, etc. at the same time.
**sin** (sin), *n.* [< AS. *synne*], 1. the willful breaking of religious or moral law. 2. any offense or fault. *v.i.* [SINNED, SINNING], to commit a sin. —**sin'ful**, *adj.* —**sin'ner**, *n.*
**Si·nai, Mount** (sī'nī), in the *Bible*, the mountain where Moses received the law from God.

**since** (sins), *adv.* [ult. < AS. *sith*, after + *thæt*, that], 1. from then until now: as, he came in May and has been here ever *since*. 2. at some time between then and now: as, he was ill last week but has *since* recovered. 3. before now; ago: as, he disappeared long *since*. *prep.* 1. continuously from (then) until now: as, I've walked *since* noon. 2. during the period between (then) and now: as, he's moved twice *since* May. *conj.* 1. during the period following the time when: as, he's died *since* they met. 2. continuously from the time when: as, she's been unhappy *since* she left. 3. because: as, *since* I can, I will.

**sin·cere** (sin-sêr'), *adj.* [-CERER, -CEREST], [< L. *sincerus*, pure], 1. without deceit or pretense. 2. genuine: as, *sincere* grief. **—sin·cere'ly,** *adv.* **—sin·cer'i·ty** (-ser'ə-ti), *n.*

**si·ne·cure** (sī'ni-kyoor', sin'ə-), *n.* [< L. *sine*, without + *cura*, care], any position that brings profit without involving much work.

**sin·ew** (sin'ū), *n.* [AS. *seonwe*], 1. a tendon. 2. muscular power; strength.

**sing** (siŋ), *v.i.* [SANG or *rarely* SUNG, SUNG, SINGING], [< AS. *singan*], 1. to produce musical sounds with the voice; perform songs, etc. vocally. 2. to produce musical notes, as a songbird, etc. 3. to hum, buzz, etc., as an insect. *v.t.* 1. to utter or perform by singing. 2. to celebrate in song: as, we *sing* his praises. 3. to bring or put, as to sleep, by singing. *n.* informal singing by a group. **—sing'er,** *n.*

**sing.,** singular.

**singe** (sinj), *v.t.* [SINGED, SINGEING], [< AS. *sengan*], 1. to burn superficially or slightly. 2. to expose (a carcass) to flame in removing feathers, etc. *n.* 1. a singeing. 2. a slight burn.

**Sin·gha·lese** (siŋ'gə-lēz'), *adj.* of Ceylon, its people, language, etc. *n.* 1. [*pl.* -LESE], one of the Singhalese people. 2. their language.

**sin·gle** (siŋ'g'l), *adj.* [< LL. *singulus*], 1. one only. 2. alone. 3. of or for one person or family. 4. between two persons only: as, *single* combat. 5. unmarried. 6. having only one part; not multiple, etc. 7. honest; sincere. *v.t.* [-GLED, -GLING], to select from others, (usually with *out*). *v.i.* in *baseball*, to make a single. *n.* 1. a single person or thing. 2. in *baseball*, a hit by which the batter reaches first base only. 3. *pl.* in *tennis*, etc., a game with only one player on each side. **—sin'gle·ness,** *n.*

**sin'gle-breast'ed,** *adj.* overlapping the front of the body only enough to fasten, as a coat.

**single file,** a single column of persons or things, one behind another.

**sin'gle-hand'ed,** *adj.* 1. using only one hand. 2. done or working alone.

**sin'gle-mind'ed,** *adj.* 1. honest; sincere. 2. with only one aim or purpose.

**sin'gle·ton** (-tən), *n.* 1. a playing card that is the only one of a suit held by a player. 2. a single thing.

**sin·gle·tree** (siŋ'g'l-trē'), *n.* [< ME. *swingle*, rod + *tre*, tree], the crossbar on a wagon, etc. to which the traces of a horse's harness are hooked.

**sin·gly** (siŋ'gli), *adv.* 1. alone. 2. one by one. 3. unaided.

**sing'song,'** *n.* a rising and falling tone in a monotonous cadence. *adj.* characterized by such tone or cadence.

**sin·gu·lar** (siŋ'gyoo-lẽr), *adj.* [< L. *singulus*, single], 1. sole; unique. 2. individual; separate. 3. strange; unusual. 4. exceptional; remarkable. 5. in *grammar*, denoting only one. *n.* in *grammar*, the singular number or form of a word. **—sin'gu·lar'i·ty** (-lar'ə-ti), *n.* **—sin'gu·lar·ly,** *adv.*

**sin·is·ter** (sin'is-tẽr), *adj.* [< L. *sinister*, left (hand)], 1. orig., on or to the left-hand side. 2. threatening, as with misfortune. 3. wicked, evil, or dishonest. 4. disastrous.

**sink** (siŋk), *v.i.* [SANK, or SUNK, SUNK, SINKING], [AS. *sincan*], 1. to go beneath the surface of water, etc. 2. to go down slowly. 3. to appear to descend, as the sun. 4. to become lower, as in level, value, rank, etc. 5. to subside, as wind, a voice, etc. 6. to become hollow, as the cheeks. 7. to pass gradually (*into* sleep, etc.). 8. to approach death: as, he is *sinking* rapidly. *v.t.* 1. to cause to sink or go down. 2. to make (a well, design, etc.) by digging, cutting, etc. 3. to invest. 4. to defeat; undo: as, if they see us we're *sunk*. *n.* 1. a cesspool, drain, or sewer. 2. a basin, as in a kitchen, with a drainpipe. 3. an area of sunken land.

**sink'er,** *n.* 1. one that sinks. 2. a lead weight used on a fishing line.

**Sino-,** [< Gr. *Singai*], a combining form meaning *Chinese and*.

**sin·u·ous** (sin'ū-əs), *adj.* [< L. *sinus*, a bend], 1. bending or winding in or out; wavy. 2. devious; crooked; not honest. **—sin'u·os'i·ty** (-os'ə-ti), *n.*

**si·nus** (sī'nəs), *n.* [*pl.* -NUSES, -NUS], [L., bent surface], 1. a cavity, hollow, etc.; specif., any of the air cavities in the skull opening into the nasal cavities. 2. popularly, sinusitis.

**si'nus·i'tis** (-ī'tis), *n.* inflammation of the sinuses, esp. of the skull.

**-sion,** [< L. *-sio*], a suffix meaning *the act, state*, or *result of*, as in *fusion*.

**Sioux** (so͞o), *n.* [*pl.* SIOUX (so͞o, so͞oz)], a member of a confederation of Indian tribes that lived in the northern U.S. *adj.* of these tribes. **—Siou'an,** *adj.*

**sip** (sip), *v.t. & v.i.* [SIPPED, SIPPING], [prob. < AS. *sypian*, drink in], to drink a little at a time. *n.* 1. the act of sipping. 2. a small quantity sipped. **—sip'per,** *n.*

**si·phon** (sī'fən), *n.* [< Gr. *siphōn*, tube], 1. a bent tube for carrying liquid out over the edge of a container to a lower level, through the air pressure on the liquid. 2. a sealed bottle from which carbonated water may be released: in full, **siphon bottle.** *v.t.* to drain off through a siphon.

**sir** (sũr), *n.* [< *sire*], 1. [sometimes S-], a respectful term of address used to a man: not followed by the name. 2. [S-], the title used before the given name of a knight or baronet.

**sire** (sīr), *n.* [see SENIOR], 1. a title of respect used esp. in addressing a king. 2. [Poetic], a father or forefather. 3. the male parent of a quadruped. *v.t.* [SIRED, SIRING], to beget: said esp. of quadrupeds.

**si·ren** (sī'rən), *n.* [< Gr. *seirēn*], 1. in *Gr. & Rom. myth.*, any of several sea nymphs whose singing lured sailors to their death on rocky coasts. 2. a seductive woman. 3. a device that produces a wailing sound as a warning signal, etc. *adj.* seductive.

**sir·loin** (sũr'loin), *n.* [< OFr. *sur*, over + *longe*, loin], a choice cut of beef from the loin end in front of the rump.

**si·roc·co** (sə-rok'ō), *n.* [*pl.* -COS], [It. < Ar. *sharq*, the east], a hot, oppressive wind; esp., one blowing from the deserts of N Africa into S Europe.

**sir·up** (sir'əp, sũr'-), *n.* [< Ar. *shariba*, to drink], any sweet, thick liquid; specif., *a*) a solution made by boiling sugar with water, fruit juices, etc. *b*) maple sirup, etc. Also sp. **syrup.** **—sir'up·y,** *adj.*

**sis** (sis), *n.* [Colloq.], sister.

**si·sal** (sī's'l), *n.* [< *Sisal*, in SE Mexico], a strong fiber obtained from the leaves of an agave, used for making rope.

**sis·sy** (sis'i), *n.* [*pl.* -SIES], [dim. of *sis*],

[Colloq.], a boy or man whose behavior, tastes, etc. seem more feminine than masculine. —**sis'sy·fied'**, *adj.*

**sis·ter** (sis'tẽr), *n.* [< ON. *systir*], 1. a female related to one by having the same parents. 2. a female fellow member of the same race, creed, organization, etc. 3. a nun. 4. one of the same kind, model, etc. —**sis'ter·hood'**, *n.* —**sis'ter·ly**, *adj. & adv.*

**sis'ter-in-law'**, *n.* [*pl.* SISTERS-], 1. the sister of one's spouse. 2. the wife of one's brother. 3. the wife of the brother of one's spouse.

**sit** (sit), *v.i.* [SAT, SITTING], [< AS. *sittan*], 1. to rest oneself upon the buttocks, as on a chair. 2. to rest on the haunches with the forelegs braced, as a dog. 3. to perch, as a bird. 4. to cover eggs for hatching, as a hen. 5. to occupy a seat as a judge, legislator, etc. 6. to be in session, as a court. 7. to pose, as for a portrait. 8. to be located. 9. to fit: as, this hat *sits* well. 10. to rest or lie: as, his duties *sit* lightly on him. 11. to baby-sit. *v.t.* 1. to cause to sit. 2. to keep one's seat on (a horse, etc.). —**sit down**, to take a seat. —**sit in (on)**, to attend. —**sit up**, 1. to sit erect. 2. to stay up beyond one's bedtime. 3. [Colloq.], to be startled. —**sit'ter**, *n.*

**si·tar** (si-tär'), *n.* [Hindi *sitār*], a lutelike instrument of India with a long, fretted neck.

**site** (sīt), *n.* [< L. *situs*, position], the location or scene of anything.

**sit'-in'**, *n.* an act of civil disobedience inside a public place, in which demonstrators sit down and refuse to leave voluntarily.

**sit'ting**, *n.* 1. the act or position of one that sits. 2. a period of being seated. 3. a session, as of a court.

**sit·u·ate** (sich'o͞o-āt'), *v.t.* [-ATED, -ATING], [< L. *situs*, position], to put in a certain place; locate.

**sit'u·a'tion**, *n.* 1. location; position; place. 2. condition with regard to circumstances. 3. a state of affairs. 4. a position of employment.

**Si·va** (sē'və), *n.* Hindu god of destruction and reproduction: see **Brahma**.

**six** (siks), *adj. & n.* [AS. *sex*], one more than five; 6; VI. —**sixth** (siksth), *adj. & n.*

**six'pence** (-pəns), *n.* the sum of, or a British coin worth, six pence.

**six'teen'** (-tēn'), *adj. & n.* [AS. *syxtene*], six more than ten; 16; XVI. —**six'teenth'**, *adj. & n.*

**sixteenth note**, in *music*, a note having one sixteenth the duration of a whole note.

**sixth sense**, intuition.

**six·ty** (siks'ti), *adj. & n.* [AS. *sixtig*], six times ten; 60; LX. —**the sixties**, the years sixty through sixty-nine (of a century or a person's age). —**six'ti·eth** (-ith), *adj. & n.*

**siz·a·ble, size·a·ble** (sīz'ə-b'l), *adj.* of considerable size or bulk; large.

**size** (sīz), *n.* [ult. < L. *assidere*, to assess], 1. that quality of a thing which determines how much space it occupies; dimensions or magnitude. 2. any of a series of graded classifications according to this: as, *size* nine shoes. *v.t.* [SIZED, SIZING], to arrange according to size. —**size up**, [Colloq.], 1. to make an estimate or judgment of. 2. to meet requirements.

**size** (sīz), *n.* [< Fr. *assise*, layer], a pasty substance used as a glaze or filler on paper, cloth, etc. *v.t.* [SIZED, SIZING], to fill, stiffen, or glaze with size. —**siz'y**, *adj.*

**-sized**, a combining form meaning *of* (a specified) *size*, as in *small-sized*: also **-size**.

**siz'ing**, *n.* 1. size (glaze or filler). 2. the act or process of applying this.

**siz·zle** (siz''l), *v.i.* [-ZLED, -ZLING], [echoic], to make a hissing sound when in contact with heat. *n.* such a sound.

**skate** (skāt), *n.* [< OFr. *escache*, stilt], 1. *a*) a bladelike metal runner in a frame, fastened to a shoe for gliding on ice. *b*) a shoe with such a runner attached. Also **ice skate**. 2. a roller skate. *v.i.* [SKATED, SKATING], to glide or roll on skates. —**skate on thin ice**, to be in a precarious situation. —**skat'er**, *n.*

**skate** (skāt), *n.* [< ON. *skata*], a salt-water food fish of the ray family.

**ske·dad·dle** (ski-dad''l), *v.i.* [-DLED, -DLING], [< ?], [Colloq.], to scurry away.

**skein** (skān), *n.* [< OFr. *esca(i)gne*], a quantity of thread or yarn in a coil.

**skel·e·ton** (skel'ə-t'n), *n.* [< Gr. *skeleton* (*sōma*), dried (body)], 1. the hard framework of bones of an animal body. 2. a supporting framework. 3. an outline, as of a book. *adj.* of or like a skeleton. —**skel'e·tal**, *adj.*

**skeleton key**, a key with a slender bit that can open many simple locks.

**skep·tic** (skep'tik), *adj.* [< Gr. *skeptikos*, inquiring], skeptical. *n.* 1. an adherent of skepticism. 2. one who habitually questions matters generally accepted. 3. one who doubts religious doctrines.

**skep'ti·cal**, *adj.* doubting; questioning: also sp. **sceptical**. —**skep'ti·cal·ly**, *adv.*

**skep'ti·cism** (-tə-siz'm), *n.* 1. the doctrine that the truth of all knowledge must always be in question. 2. skeptical attitude. 3. disbelief of religious doctrines.

**sketch** (skech), *n.* [ult. < Gr. *schedios*, extempore], 1. a rough drawing or design, done rapidly. 2. a brief outline. 3. a short, light story, play, etc. *v.t. & v.i.* to make a sketch (of). —**sketch'y** [-IER, -IEST], *adj.*

**skew·er** (skū'ẽr), *n.* [< ON. *skifa*, a slice], a long pin used to hold meat together while cooking. *v.t.* to fasten with skewers.

**ski** (skē), *n.* [*pl.* SKIS, SKI], [Norw. < ON. *skith*, snowshoe], one of a pair of long, wood runners fastened to the feet for gliding over snow. *v.i.* [SKIED, SKIING], to glide over snow on skis. —**ski'er**, *n.*

**skid** (skid), *n.* [< ON. *skith*, wooden billet], 1. a plank, log, etc. used as a track upon which to slide a heavy object. 2. a low, wooden platform for holding loads. 3. a runner on an aircraft landing gear. 4. a sliding wedge used to brake a wheel. 5. the act of skidding. *v.t. & v.i.* [SKIDDED, SKIDDING], 1. to slide without turning, as a wheel on a slippery surface. 2. to slide or slip sideways, as a vehicle on ice. —**on the skids**, [Slang], falling from power, losing prestige, etc. —**skid'der**, *n.*

**skid row**, [Slang], a section of a city frequented by hobos, vagrants, etc.

**skiff** (skif), *n.* [< OHG. *scif*], a light rowboat, esp. one with a small sail.

**skill** (skil), *n.* [< ON. *skil*, distinction], 1. great ability or proficiency. 2. an art, craft, etc., esp. one involving the use of the hands or body. 3. ability in such an art, etc. —**skilled**, *adj.* —**skill'ful**, **skil'ful**, *adj.*

**skil·let** (skil'it), *n.* [? < L. *scutra*, a dish], a frying pan.

**skim** (skim), *v.t. & v.i.* [SKIMMED, SKIMMING], [< OHG. *scum*, scum], 1. to remove (floating matter) from (a liquid). 2. to read or look through (a book, etc.) in a cursory manner. 3. to glide lightly (over).

**skim milk**, milk from which the cream has been removed.

**skimp** (skimp), *v.t. & v.i.* [Colloq.], to scrimp.

**skimp'y**, *adj.* [-IER, -IEST], [Colloq.], 1. barely enough; scanty. 2. stingy.

**skin** (skin), *n.* [< ON. *skinn*], 1. the outer covering of the animal body. 2. a pelt. 3. something like skin, as fruit rind, etc. *v.t.* [SKINNED, SKINNING], 1. to remove the skin of. 2. [Colloq.], to swindle. —**get under one's skin**, [Slang], to irritate one.

**skin′-deep′,** *adj.* 1. penetrating no deeper than the skin. 2. superficial.
**skin diving,** underwater diving in which the swimmer uses portable compressed-air equipment. —**skin diver.**
**skin′flint′,** *n.* [lit., one who would skin a flint for economy], a miser.
**skinned** (skind), *adj.* having a (specified kind of) skin: as, dark-*skinned.*
**skin′ny,** *adj.* [-NIER, -NIEST], emaciated; thin. —**skin′ni·ness,** *n.*
**skip** (skip), *v.i. & v.t.* [SKIPPED, SKIPPING], [prob. < ON.], 1. to leap lightly and quickly (over). 2. to ricochet or bounce. 3. to pass from one point to another, omitting or ignoring (what lies between). 4. [Colloq.], to leave (a place) hurriedly. *n.* 1. *a*) an act of skipping. *b*) a gait of alternating hops and steps. 2. an omitting.
**skip·per** (skip′ẽr), *n.* [< MD. *schip,* a ship], the captain of a ship.
**skir·mish** (skũr′mish), *n.* [< OFr. *eskirmir* < Gmc.], 1. a brief fight between small groups, as in a war. 2. any slight, unimportant conflict. *v.i.* to take part in a skirmish.
**skirt** (skũrt), *n.* [< ON. *skyrt,* shirt], 1. that part of a dress, coat, etc. that hangs below the waist. 2. a woman's separate garment that hangs from the waist. 3. something like a skirt. 4. [Slang], a woman. *v.t. & v.i.* to be on, or move along, the edge (of).
**skit** (skit), *n.* [prob. ult. < ON. *skjota,* to shoot], a short humorous sketch, as in the theater.
**skit·tish** (skit′ish), *adj.* [< *skit* + *-ish*], 1. lively; playful; coy. 2. easily frightened; nervous. 3. fickle. —**skit′tish·ly,** *adv.*
**skoal** (skōl), *interj.* [< ON. *skāl,* a bowl], to your health: a toast.
**Skr., Skrt., Skt.,** Sanskrit.
**skul·dug·ger·y** (skul-dug′ẽr-i), *n.* [< OFr. *escoulourgier,* to slip], [Colloq.], mean trickery; craftiness.
**skulk** (skulk), *v.i.* [prob. < ON.], to move in a stealthy manner; slink. —**skulk′er,** *n.*
**skull** (skul), *n.* [< Scand.], 1. the bony framework of the head, enclosing the brain. 2. the head; mind.
**skull′cap′,** *n.* a light, closefitting, brimless cap, usually worn indoors.
**skunk** (skuŋk), *n.* [< Am. Ind. *segonku*], 1. a small, bushy-tailed mammal having black fur with white stripes down its back: it ejects a foul-smelling liquid when molested. 2. its fur. 3. [Colloq.], a despicable person.
**sky** (skī), *n.* [*pl.* SKIES], [< ON. *sky,* cloud], 1. *often pl.* the upper atmosphere: as, blue *skies.* 2. the firmament. 3. heaven.
**sky′div′ing, sky′-div′ing,** *n.* the sport of parachuting from an airplane, delaying the opening of the parachute to the last possible moment. —**sky′div′er, sky′-div′er,** *n.*
**sky′-high′,** *adj. & adv.* very high.
**sky′jack′,** *v.t.* [Colloq.] to force (an aircraft) to make a nonscheduled flight.
**sky′lark′,** *n.* the Old World lark, famous for the song it utters as it soars. *v.i.* to frolic.
**sky′light′,** *n.* a window in a roof or ceiling.
**sky′line′,** *n.* 1. the visible horizon. 2. the outline of a city, etc. seen against the sky.
**sky′rock′et,** *n.* a firework rocket that explodes in mid-air. *v.i.* [Colloq.], to rise rapidly, as prices, etc.
**sky′scrap′er,** *n.* a very tall building.
**sky′ward** (-wẽrd), *adj. & adv.* toward the sky: also **sky′wards,** *adv.*
**sky′writ′ing,** *n.* the tracing of words, etc. in the sky by trailing smoke from an airplane. —**sky′writ′er,** *n.*
**slab** (slab), *n.* [ME. *sclabbe*], a flat, broad, and fairly thick piece.
**slack** (slak), *adj.* [< AS. *slæc*], 1. slow; sluggish. 2. not busy: dull: as, a *slack* period. 3. loose; not tight. 4. careless: as, a *slack* workman. *v.t. & v.i.* to slacken. *n.* 1. a part that is slack or hangs loose. 2. a lack of tension, as in rope. 3. a dull period; lull. —**slack off,** to slacken. —**slack up,** to go more slowly. —**slack′ly,** *adv.* —**slack′ness,** *n.*
**slack** (slak), *n.* [< MLG.], a mixture of small pieces of coal, coal dust, and dirt left from the screening of coal.
**slack·en** (slak′ən), *v.t. & v.i.* 1. to make or become less active, brisk, etc. 2. to loosen or relax, as rope.
**slack′er,** *n.* one who shirks duties, etc.
**slacks** (slaks), *n.pl.* full-cut trousers for casual wear by men and women.
**slag** (slag), *n.* [< MLG. *slagge*], 1. the fused refuse separated from a metal in smelting. 2. lava resembling this. —**slag′gy,** *adj.*
**slain** (slān), pp. of **slay.**
**slake** (slāk), *v.t.* [SLAKED, SLAKING], [< AS. *slæc,* slack], 1. to make less intense by satisfying, as thirst, etc. 2. to produce a chemical change in (lime) by combination with water. *v.i.* to become slaked.
‡**sla·lom** (slä′lōm), *n.* [Norw.], a downhill skiing race. *v.i.* to ski in a slalom.
**slam** (slam), *v.t. & v.i.* [SLAMMED, SLAMMING], [prob. < ON.], 1. to shut or hit, put, etc. with force and noise. 2. [Colloq.], to criticize severely. *n.* 1. a heavy impact, etc. 2. the noise made by this. 3. [Colloq.], severe criticism. 4. in *card games,* the winning of all the tricks in one deal: in *bridge,* called **grand slam.**
**slan·der** (slan′dẽr), *n.* [see SCANDAL], 1. the oral utterance or spreading of a falsehood, harmful to another's reputation. 2. such a falsehood. *v.t.* to make a slanderous statement about. —**slan′der·ous,** *adj.*
**slang** (slaŋ), *n.* [? akin to *sling*], vigorous, colloquial language, usually short-lived, that is outside formal usage. —**slang′y** [-IER, -IEST], *adj.* —**slang′i·ness,** *n.*
**slant** (slant), *v.t. & v.i.* [prob. < ON.], 1. to incline; slope. 2. [Colloq.], to tell so as to express a particular bias. *n.* 1. an oblique surface, line, etc. 2. [Colloq.], a point of view; attitude. *adj.* sloping. —**slant′ing,** *adj.*
**slap** (slap), *n.* [echoic], 1. a blow with something flat, as the palm of the hand. 2. an insult; rebuff. *v.t.* [SLAPPED, SLAPPING], 1. to strike with something flat. 2. to put, hit, etc. with force. *adv.* [Colloq.], suddenly.
**slap′stick′,** *n.* crude comedy full of violent activity, horseplay, etc. *adj.* characterized by such comedy.
**slash** (slash), *v.t.* [? < OFr. *esclachier,* break], 1. to cut with sweeping strokes, as of a knife. 2. to gash. 3. to cut slits in. 4. to reduce drastically, as prices. *v.i.* to make a sweeping stroke as with a knife. *n.* 1. a slashing. 2. a cut made by slashing.
**slat** (slat), *n.* [< OFr. *esclat,* fragment], a narrow strip of wood, etc. *v.t.* [SLATTED, SLATTING], to provide with slats.
**slate** (slāt), *n.* [see SLAT], 1. a hard rock that cleaves into thin, smooth layers. 2. its bluish-gray color. 3. a roofing tile, etc. made of slate. 4. a list of proposed candidates. *v.t.* [SLATED, SLATING], 1. to cover with slate. 2. to designate, as for candidacy.
**slat·tern** (slat′ẽrn), *n.* [prob. < dial. *slatter,* to slop], a woman who is untidy in her habits, appearance, etc. —**slat′tern·ly,** *adj. & adv.*
**slaugh·ter** (slô′tẽr), *n.* [< ON. *slātr,* slain flesh], 1. the killing of animals for food. 2. the brutal killing of a person. 3. the killing of people in large numbers. *v.t.* 1. to kill (animals) for food. 2. to kill (people) brutally or in large numbers.
**slaugh′ter·house′,** *n.* a place where animals are butchered for food.

**Slav** (släv, slav), *n.* a member of a group of peoples of E and SE Europe, including the Russians, Poles, Czechs, etc. *adj.* Slavic.
**slave** (slāv), *n.* [< LGr. *Sklabos*: first applied to captive Slavs], 1. a human being who is owned by another human being. 2. one who is dominated by some influence, habit, etc. 3. one who slaves. *v.i.* [SLAVED, SLAVING], to work like a slave; drudge; toil.
**slave driver,** 1. one who oversees slaves. 2. any merciless taskmaster.
**slav·er** (slav'ẽr), *v.i.* [prob. < ON. *slafra*], to drool. *n.* saliva drooling from the mouth.
**slav·er·y** (slāv'ẽr-i), *n.* 1. the owning of slaves as a practice or institution. 2. the condition of a slave; bondage. 3. drudgery.
**Slav·ic** (släv'ik, slav'-), *adj.* of the Slavs, their languages, etc. *n.* a family of languages, including Russian, Polish, Czech, Bulgarian, etc.: abbrev. **Slav.**
**slav·ish** (slāv'ish), *adj.* 1. of or like slaves; servile. 2. of or like slavery; oppressive. 3. blindly dependent or imitative.
**slaw** (slô), *n.* [D. *sla* < Fr. *salade*, salad], shredded cabbage served as a salad.
**slay** (slā), *v.t.* [SLEW, SLAIN, SLAYING], [< AS. *slean*], to kill by violent means.
**slea·zy** (slē'zi, slā'-), *adj.* [-ZIER, -ZIEST], [< obs. *Sleasie*, cloth made in Silesia, Germany], flimsy or thin in substance.
**sled** (sled), *n.* [< MLG. *sledde*], a vehicle on runners for moving over snow, ice, etc. *v.t. & v.i.* [SLEDDED, SLEDDING], to carry or ride on a sled. —**sled'ding,** *n.*
**sledge** (slej), *n.* [< AS. *slecge*], a long, heavy hammer, usually used with both hands: also **sledge hammer.**
**sledge** (slej), *n.* [MD. *sleedse*], a sled or sleigh.
**sleek** (slēk), *adj.* [< *slick*], 1. smooth and shiny; glossy. 2. of well-fed or well-groomed appearance. 3. suave. *v.t.* to make sleek. —**sleek'ly,** *adv.* —**sleek'ness,** *n.*
**sleep** (slēp), *n.* [AS. *slæp*], 1. a natural, regularly recurring state of rest for the body and mind, during which there is little or no conscious thought. 2. any condition like this. *v.i.* [SLEPT, SLEEPING], to be in the state of, or a state like, sleep. —**sleep off,** to rid oneself of by sleeping. —**sleep'less,** *adj.* —**sleep'less·ness,** *n.*
**sleep'er,** *n.* 1. one who sleeps. 2. a railway car with berths, compartments, etc. for sleeping: also **sleeping car.** 3. something that achieves an unexpected success.
**sleeping sickness,** an infectious, usually fatal disease, esp. of Africa, characterized by lethargy, coma, etc.
**sleep'walk'ing,** *n.* the act or practice of walking while asleep. —**sleep'walk'er,** *n.*
**sleep'y,** *adj.* [-IER, -IEST], 1. ready or inclined to sleep; drowsy. 2. dull; idle: as, a *sleepy* town. —**sleep'i·ness,** *n.*
**sleet** (slēt), *n.* [< AS. hyp. *sliete*], 1. partly frozen rain. 2. a mixture of rain with snow. *v.i.* to shower in the form of sleet. —**sleet'y,** *adj.*
**sleeve** (slēv), *n.* [AS. *sl(i)efe*], 1. that part of a garment that covers the arm. 2. a tubelike part fitting around another part. —**laugh up** (or **in**) **one's sleeve,** to be secretly amused. —**up one's sleeve,** hidden but ready at hand. —**sleeve'less,** *adj.*
**sleigh** (slā), *n.* [D. *slee*], a light vehicle on runners, for travel on snow and ice.
**sleight of hand** (slīt), [< ON. *slægr*, crafty], 1. skill with the hands, esp. in deceiving onlookers, as in magic. 2. tricks thus performed.
**slen·der** (slen'dẽr), *adj.* [ME. *s(c)lendre*], 1. long and thin; slim. 2. small in amount, size, etc. 3. small in force; feeble.
**slen'der·ize',** *v.t. & v.i.* [-IZED, -IZING], to make or become slender.
**slept** (slept), pt. and pp. of **sleep.**
**sleuth** (slōōth), *n.* [< ON. *sloth*, a track], [Colloq.], a detective.
**slew** (slōō), *n.* [< ?], [Colloq.], a large number, group, or quantity: also sp. **slue.**
**slew** (slōō), pt. of **slay.**
**slice** (slīs), *n.* [ult. < OHG. *slizan*, to split], 1. a relatively thin, broad piece cut from something. 2. a part or share. *v.t.* [SLICED, SLICING], 1. to cut into slices. 2. to cut as a slice (with *off, from*, etc.). 3. to give a glancing stroke. —**slic'er,** *n.*
**slick** (slik), *v.t.* [prob. < AS. *-slician*, smooth by hammering], 1. to make smooth. 2. [Colloq.], to make smart, neat, etc. (with *up*). *adj.* 1. sleek; smooth. 2. slippery. 3. adept; clever. 4. [Colloq.], smooth but superficial, tricky, etc. *n.* a smooth area on the water, as from a film of oil.
**slick'er,** *n.* a loose, waterproof coat.
**slide** (slīd), *v.i.* [SLID (slid), SLID or SLIDDEN, SLIDING], [AS. *slidan*], 1. to move along in constant contact with a smooth surface, as on ice. 2. to glide. 3. to slip: as, it *slid* from his grasp. *v.t.* 1. to cause to slide. 2. to place quietly or dexterously (with *in* or *into*). *n.* 1. a sliding. 2. a smooth, often inclined surface for sliding. 3. something that operates by sliding. 4. a transparent plate bearing a picture for projection on a screen. 5. a small glass plate on which objects are mounted for microscopic study. 6. the fall of a mass of rock, snow, etc. down a slope. —**slid'er,** *n.*
**slide fastener,** a device used to fasten and unfasten two edges of material: it consists of interlocking tabs worked by a sliding part.
**slide rule,** an instrument for rapid calculations, consisting of a ruler with a central sliding piece, both marked with logarithmic scales.
**slight** (slīt), *adj.* [ME. *sliht*], 1. light in build; slender. 2. frail; fragile. 3. lacking strength, importance, etc. 4. small in amount or extent. *v.t.* 1. to neglect. 2. to treat with disrespect. 3. to treat as unimportant. *n.* a slighting or being slighted (sense 2 of *v.*). —**slight'ly,** *adv.*
**slim** (slim), *adj.* [SLIMMER, SLIMMEST], [< D. *slim*, bad], 1. small in girth; slender. 2. small in amount, degree, etc.; meager. *v.t. & v.i.* [SLIMMED, SLIMMING], to make or become slim. —**slim'ly,** *adv.* —**slim'ness,** *n.*
**slime** (slīm), *n.* [AS. *slim*], any soft, moist, slippery, often sticky matter. *v.t.* [SLIMED, SLIMING], to cover with slime. —**slim'y** [-IER, -IEST], *adj.*
**sling** (sliŋ), *n.* [< AS. *slingan*, twist oneself], 1. a primitive instrument whirled by hand for throwing stones, etc. 2. a cast; fling; throw. 3. a supporting band, etc. as for raising a heavy object. 4. a cloth looped from the neck under an injured arm for support. *v.t.* [SLUNG, SLINGING], 1. to throw, cast, etc. 2. to hang in a sling. —**sling'er,** *n.*
**sling** (sliŋ), *n.* [< ?], an iced drink made with alcoholic liquor, water, sugar, and, usually, lemon juice.
**sling'shot',** *n.* a Y-shaped piece of wood, etc. with an elastic band attached to the upper tips for shooting stones, etc.
**slink** (sliŋk), *v.i.* [SLUNK, SLINKING], [AS. *slincan*, to creep], to move in a furtive or sneaking way. —**slink'y** [-IER, -IEST], *adj.*
**slip** (slip), *v.i.* [SLIPPED, SLIPPING], [MLG. *slippen*], 1. to go quietly or secretly: as, he *slipped* away. 2. to pass smoothly or easily. 3. to escape from one's mind, etc. 4. to slide accidentally, lose footing, etc. 5. to make a mistake; err. 6. to become worse. *v.t.* 1. to cause to slip. 2. to put, pass, etc. quickly or deftly: as, she *slipped* a pill into her mouth. 3. to escape from (the mind). *n.* 1. a dock for ships between piers. 2. a woman's undergarment, about the length of

a dress. 3. a pillowcase. 4. a slipping or falling down. 5. an error or mistake. **—let slip,** to say without intending to.

**slip** (slip), *n.* [< MD. *slippen*, to cut], 1. a stem, root, etc. of a plant, used for planting or grafting. 2. a young, slender person. 3. a small piece of paper. *v.t.* [SLIPPED, SLIPPING], to take a slip from (a plant).

**slip′knot′,** *n.* a knot made so that it will slip along the rope around which it is tied.

**slip·per** (slip′ẽr), *n.* a light, low shoe easily slipped onto the foot. **—slip′pered,** *adj.*

**slip·per·y** (slip′ẽr-i), *adj.* [-IER, -IEST], 1. liable to cause slipping, as a wet surface. 2. tending to slip away, as from a hold. 3. evasive; unreliable. **—slip′per·i·ness,** *n.*

**slip·shod** (slip′shod′), *adj.* [after obs. *slipshoe*, a slipper], careless or slovenly.

**slip′-up′,** *n.* [Colloq.], an error; oversight.

**slit** (slit), *v.t.* [SLIT, SLITTING], [< AS. *slitan*, to cut], 1. to cut or split open, esp. by a lengthwise incision. 2. to cut into strips. *n.* a straight, narrow cut, opening, etc.

**slith·er** (sli*th*′ẽr), *v.i.* [< AS. *slidan*, to slide], to slip, slide, or glide along. *n.* a slithering

**sliv·er** (sliv′ẽr), *n.* [< AS. *slifan*, to cut], a thin, often pointed piece, cut or split off; splinter. *v.t. & v.i.* to cut or split into slivers.

**slob** (slob), *n.* [< Ir. *slab*, mud], [Colloq.], a coarse, sloppy, stupid person.

**slob·ber** (slob′ẽr), *v.i.* [prob. < D. *slobberen*], 1. to drool. 2. to speak with excessive sentimentality. *n.* drool. **—slob′ber·y,** *adj.*

**sloe** (slō), *n.* [AS. *sla*], 1. the blackthorn. 2. its small, blue-black fruit.

**sloe′-eyed′,** *adj.* having large, dark eyes.

**sloe gin,** alcoholic liquor distilled from grain and flavored with sloes.

**slog** (slog), *v.t. & v.i.* [SLOGGED, SLOGGING], [prob. < ON.], to make (one's way) heavily and with effort; plod. **—slog′ger,** *n.*

**slo·gan** (slō′gən), *n.* [< Gael. *sluagh*, a host + *gairm*, a call: orig., a battle cry], 1. a catchword or motto associated with a political party, etc. 2. a catch phrase advertising a product.

**sloop** (slōōp), *n.* [< D. < LG. *slupen*, to glide], a small boat with a single mast and a jib.

**slop** (slop), *n.* [AS. *sloppe*], 1. watery snow or mud; slush. 2. a splash or puddle of spilled liquid. 3. unappetizing liquid or semiliquid food. 4. *often pl.* liquid waste of any kind. *v.i. & v.t.* [SLOPPED, SLOPPING], to spill; splash.

**slope** (slōp), *n.* [< AS. *slupan*, to glide], 1. rising or falling ground. 2. any inclined line, surface, etc.; slant. 3. the amount or degree of this. *v.i.* [SLOPED, SLOPING], to have an upward or downward inclination; slant. *v.t.* to cause to slope.

**slop·py** (slop′i), *adj.* [-PIER, -PIEST], [see SLOP], 1. splashy; slushy. 2. [Colloq.], *a*) slovenly. *b*) slipshod. **—slop′pi·ness,** *n.*

**slosh** (slosh), *v.t.* [var of *slush*], to shake or agitate (a liquid). *v.i.* to splash clumsily through water, mud, etc. *n.* slush.

**slot** (slot), *n.* [< OFr. *esclot*, hollow between the breasts], a narrow opening, as for a coin in a vending machine. *v.t.* [SLOTTED, SLOTTING], to make a slot in.

**sloth** (slōth, slôth), *n.* [< AS. *slaw*, slow], 1. disinclination to work or exert oneself; laziness. 2. a slow-moving, tree-dwelling South American mammal. **—sloth′ful,** *adj.*

**slouch** (slouch) *n.* [akin to ON. *slōkr*, lazy fellow], 1. a lazy or incompetent person. 2. a drooping or slovenly posture. 3. a drooping, as of a hat brim. *v.i.* to have a drooping or slovenly posture. **—slouch′y** [-IER, -IEST], *adj.* **—slouch′i·ness,** *n.*

**slough** (sluf), *n.* [ME. *slouh*], a castoff layer or covering, as the skin of a snake. *v.t.* to throw off; discard. **—slough′y,** *adj.*

**slough** (slou), *n.* [AS. *sloh*], 1. a place full of soft, deep mud. 2. deep, hopeless discouragement. 3. (slōō), a swamp, bog, etc.

**Slo·vak** (slō′vak, -väk), *n.* 1. any of a Slavic people living chiefly in E Czechoslovakia. 2. their language. *adj.* of the Slovaks, their language, etc.

**slov·en** (sluv′ən), *n.* [prob. < MD. *slof*], an untidy person.

**Slo·vene** (slō-vēn′, slō′vēn), *n.* 1. any of a Slavic people living chiefly in Slovenia. 2. their language. *adj.* of the Slovenes, their language, etc.

**slov·en·ly** (sluv′ən-li), *adj.* [-LIER, -LIEST], [see SLOVEN], careless in appearance, habits, work, etc.; untidy. **—slov′en·li·ness,** *n.*

**slow** (slō), *adj.* [< AS. *slaw*], 1. not quick in understanding. 2. taking a longer time than is usual. 3. marked by low speed, etc.; not fast. 4. behind the correct time, as a clock. 5. passing tediously; dull. *v.t. & v.i.* to make or become slow or slower (often with *up* or *down*). *adv.* in a slow manner. **—slow′ly,** *adv.* **—slow′ness,** *n.*

**sludge** (sluj), *n.* [dial. var. of *slutch*], 1. mud, mire, or ooze. 2. any heavy, slimy deposit, sediment, etc. **—sludg′y,** *adj.*

**slug** (slug), *n.* [ME. *slugge*, clumsy one], a small mollusk resembling a land snail, but having no outer shell.

**slug** (slug), *n.* [prob. < LG.], 1. a small piece of metal; specif., a bullet. 2. in *printing*, a line of type made in one piece.

**slug** (slug), *v.t.* [SLUGGED, SLUGGING], [< dial.], [Colloq.], to hit hard, esp. with the fist. *n.* [Colloq.], a hard blow. **—slug′ger,** *n.*

**slug·gard** (slug′ẽrd), *n.* [< ME. *sluggen*, be lazy], a lazy person. *adj.* lazy.

**slug·gish** (slug′ish), *adj.* [< *slug* (mollusk)], 1. lacking in energy; lazy. 2. slow or slow-moving. 3. lacking normal vigor.

**sluice** (slōōs), *n.* [< L. *ex-*, out + *claudere*, shut], 1. an artificial channel for water, with a gate to regulate the flow. 2. such a gate: also **sluice gate.** 3. any channel for excess water. 4. a sloping trough, as for washing gold ore. *v.t.* [SLUICED, SLUICING], 1. to draw off through a sluice. 2. to wash with water from a sluice.

**slum** (slum), *n.* [< ?], a populous area in which housing and living conditions are extremely poor. *v.i.* [SLUMMED, SLUMMING], to visit slums.

**slum·ber** (slum′bẽr), *v.i.* [< AS. *sluma*, *n.*], 1. to sleep. 2. to be inactive. *n.* 1. sleep. 2. an inactive state.

**slump** (slump), *v.i.* [prob. < LG. *slumpen*, come about by accident], 1. to fall or sink suddenly. 2. to have a drooping posture. *n.* a sudden fall.

**slung** (sluŋ), pt. and pp. of **sling.**

**slunk** (sluŋk), pt. and pp. of **slink.**

**slur** (slũr), *v.t.* [SLURRED, SLURRING], [prob. < MD. *sleuren*, to drag], 1. to pass (*over*) quickly and carelessly. 2. to pronounce indistinctly. 3. to disparage. 4. in *music*, to produce (successive notes) by gliding without a break. *n.* 1. a slurring. 2. something slurred, as a pronunciation. 3. an aspersion. 4. in *music*, slurred notes or a mark (‿ or ⁀) connecting them. **—slur′ring·ly,** *adv.*

**slush** (slush), *n.* [prob. < ON.], 1. partly melted snow. 2. soft mud. 3. grease. 4. sentimentality. **—slush′y** [-IER, -IEST], *adj.*

**slut** (slut), *n.* [cf. MLG. *slōt*, puddle], 1. a slovenly woman. 2. a promiscuous woman.

**sly** (slī), *adj.* [SLIER or SLYER, SLIEST or SLYEST], [< ON. *slægr*], 1. skillful at trickery; crafty. 2. cunningly underhanded. 3. playfully mischievous. **—on the sly,** secretly.

**smack** (smak), *n.* [< AS. *smæc*], 1. a slight but distinctive taste or flavor. 2. a small amount; trace. *v.i.* to have a smack (*of*).

**smack** (smak), *n.* [echoic], 1. a sharp noise made by parting the lips suddenly. 2. a loud kiss. 3. a slapping blow. *v.t.* 1. to move (the lips) so as to make a smack. 2. to kiss or slap loudly. *adv.* 1. with a smack; violently. 2. directly.

**smack** (smak), *n.* [prob. < D. & LG. *smak*], a fishing vessel fitted with a well for keeping fish alive.

**small** (smôl), *adj.* [< AS. *smæl*], 1. comparatively little in size; not large. 2. little in quantity, extent, duration, etc. 3. of little importance; trivial. 4. mean; petty. *n.* a small part: as, the *small* of the back. **—feel small,** to feel shame. **—small′ish,** *adj.*

**small′pox′** (-poks′), *n.* an acute, infectious virus disease characterized by fever and pustular eruptions.

**smart** (smärt), *v.i.* [< AS. *smeortan*], 1. to cause sharp, stinging pain, as a slap. 2. to feel such pain. 3. to feel distress; suffer. *n.* a smarting sensation. *adj.* 1. causing keen pain: as, a *smart* blow. 2. sharp; intense, as pain. 3. brisk; lively: as, a *smart* pace. 4. alert; clever. 5. neat; clean. 6. stylish. **—smart′ly,** *adv.* **—smart′ness,** *n.*

**smart·en** (smär′t'n), *v.t.* 1. to make smart, neat, or stylish. 2. to make brisk or alert.

**smash** (smash), *n.* [prob. < *mash*], 1. a hard, heavy hit. 2. a violent, noisy breaking. 3. a violent collision. 4. total failure, esp. in business. *v.t. & v.i.* 1. to break into pieces with noise or violence. 2. to hit, move, or collide with force. 3. to destroy or be destroyed.

**smash′up′,** *n.* 1. a violent wreck or collision. 2. total failure; ruin.

**smat·ter·ing** (smat′ẽr-iŋ), *n.* [< ON.], slight or superficial knowledge (with *of*).

**smear** (smêr), *v.t.* [< AS. *smerian*, anoint], 1. to cover or soil with something greasy, sticky, etc. 2. to apply (something greasy, etc.). 3. to slander. *v.i.* to be or become smeared. *n.* 1. a mark made by smearing. 2. slander. **—smear′y** [-IER, -IEST], *adj.*

**smell** (smel), *v.t.* [SMELLED or SMELT, SMELLING], [< ME. *smellen*], 1. to be aware of through the nose; catch the odor of. 2. to sense the presence of: as, to *smell* trouble. *v.i.* 1. to use the sense of smell; sniff. 2. to have an odor: as, to *smell* fresh. *n.* 1. the sense by which odors are perceived. 2. something that is smelled; odor; scent. 3. an act of smelling.

**smell′y,** *adj.* [-IER, -IEST], giving off an unpleasant odor.

**smelt** (smelt), *n.* [AS.], a small, silvery food fish found in northern seas.

**smelt** (smelt), *v.t.* [< MD. *smelten*], 1. to melt or fuse (ore, etc.) so as to separate impurities from pure metal. 2. to refine (metal) in this way.

**smelt′er,** *n.* 1. one whose work is smelting. 2. a place where smelting is done.

**smi·lax** (smī′laks), *n.* [Gr.], 1. any of various prickly vines, as the sarsaparilla. 2. a greenhouse vine with bright-green leaves.

**smile** (smīl), *v.i.* [SMILED, SMILING], [ME. *smilen*], to show pleasure, amusement, affection, etc. by an upward curving of the mouth. *v.t.* 1. to express with a smile. 2. to affect by smiling. *n.* 1. the act or expression of smiling. 2. a bright, pleasant aspect. **—smil′ing,** *adj.* **—smil′ing·ly,** *adv.*

**smirch** (smũrch), *v.t.* [prob. < OFr. *esmorcher*, to hurt], 1. to soil or smear. 2. to dishonor. *n.* 1. a smudge; smear. 2. a stain on reputation.

**smirk** (smũrk), *v.i.* [< AS. *smercian*, to smile], to smile in a conceited or complacent way. *n.* such a smile.

**smite** (smīt), *v.t.* [SMOTE, SMITTEN or SMIT (smit) or SMOTE, SMITING], [AS. *smitan*], 1. to hit or strike hard. 2. to affect strongly.

**smith** (smith), *n.* [AS.], 1. one who makes or repairs metal objects. 2. a blacksmith.

**smith·er·eens** (smi*th*′ə-rēnz′), *n.pl.* [Ir. *smidirin*], [Colloq.], fragments; bits.

**smith·y** (smith′i), *n.* [*pl.* -IES], the workshop of a smith, esp. a blacksmith; forge.

**smock** (smok), *n.* [< AS. *smoc* or ON. *smokkr*], a loose, shirtlike, outer garment worn to protect the clothes.

**smock′ing,** *n.* decorative stitching that gathers cloth to make it hang in folds, as on smocks.

**smog** (smog), *n.* [*sm*oke + f*og*], a mixture of fog and smoke.

**smoke** (smōk), *n.* [< AS. *smoca*], 1. the vaporous matter arising from something burning. 2. any vapor, etc. like this. 3. an act of smoking tobacco, etc. 4. a cigarette, cigar, etc. *v.i.* [SMOKED, SMOKING], 1. to give off smoke. 2. to draw in and exhale the smoke of tobacco; use cigarettes, etc. *v.t.* 1. to cure (meats, etc.) with smoke. 2. to use (a pipe, cigarette, etc.) in smoking. **—smoke out,** to force out of hiding, etc. **—smoke′less,** *adj.*

**smoke′house′,** *n.* a place where meats, fish, etc. are cured with smoke.

**smok·er** (smōk′ẽr), *n.* 1. one who smokes tobacco. 2. a railroad car in which smoking is allowed: also **smoking car.** 3. an informal gathering for men.

**smoke screen,** a cloud of artificial smoke spread to screen the movements of troops, ships, etc.

**smoke′stack′** (-stak′), *n.* a pipe for discharging smoke from a factory, etc.

**smok·y** (smōk′i), *adj.* [-IER, -IEST], 1. giving off smoke, esp. to excess. 2. of, like, or of the color of, smoke. 3. filled with smoke.

**smol·der** (smōl′dẽr), *v.i.* [ME. *smoldren*], 1. to burn and smoke without flame. 2. to exist in a suppressed state. *n.* a smoldering. Also sp. **smoulder.**

**smooth** (smōō*th*), *adj.* [AS. *smoth*], 1. having an even surface, with no roughness. 2. without lumps. 3. even or gentle in movement: as, a *smooth* voyage. 4. free from interruptions, difficulties, etc. 5. pleasing to the taste; bland. 6. having an easy, flowing rhythm or sound. 7. polished or ingratiating, esp. in an insincere way. *v.t.* 1. to make level or even. 2. to free from difficulties, etc. 3. to make calm; soothe. 4. to polish; refine. *adv.* in a smooth manner. **—smooth over,** to make light of.

**smör·gås·bord, smor·gas·bord** (smôr′gəs-bôrd′, smũr′-), *n.* [Sw.], 1. hors d'oeuvres, esp. as served buffet style. 2. a restaurant serving these.

**smote** (smōt), pt. and alt. pp. of **smite.**

**smoth·er** (smu*th*′ẽr), *v.t.* [< ME. *smorther*, dense smoke], 1. to prevent from getting air; suffocate. 2. to cover over thickly. 3. to stifle, as a yawn. *v.i.* to be suffocated.

**smudge** (smuj), *n.* [< *smutch*], 1. a dirty spot. 2. a fire made to produce dense smoke. 3. such smoke, as used in protecting plants from frost, etc. *v.t. & v.i.* [SMUDGED, SMUDGING], to streak with dirt.

**smug** (smug), *adj.* [SMUGGER, SMUGGEST], [prob. < LG. *smuk*, trim], annoyingly self-satisfied. **—smug′ly,** *adv.* **—smug′ness,** *n.*

**smug·gle** (smug′'l), *v.t. & v.i.* [-GLED, -GLING], [< LG. *smuggeln*], 1. to bring into or take out of a country secretly or illegally. 2. to bring, take, etc. secretly.

**smut** (smut), *n.* [< LG. *smutt*], 1. sooty matter. 2. a soiled spot. 3. obscene talk or writing. 4. a plant disease. **—smut′ty,** *adj.*

**Sn,** *stannum*, [L.], in *chem.*, tin.

**snack** (snak), *n.* [prob. < MD. *snacken*, to snap], a light, quick meal.

**snag** (snag), *n.* [< ON.], 1. a sharp point or projection. 2. an underwater tree stump or branch. 3. a tear, as in cloth, made by a snag, etc. 4. an unexpected or hidden diffi-

culty. *v.t.* [SNAGGED, SNAGGING], 1. to damage on a snag. 2. to impede with a snag.
**snail** (snāl), *n.* [AS. *snegl*], a slow-moving mollusk having a wormlike body and a protective, spiral shell.
**snake** (snāk), *n.* [AS. *snaca*], 1. a long, scaly, limbless reptile with a tapering tail. 2. a treacherous or deceitful person. *v.i.* [SNAKED, SNAKING], to move, twist, etc. like a snake.
**snak'y,** *adj.* [-IER, -IEST], 1. of or like a snake or snakes. 2. winding; twisting. 3. cunningly treacherous.
**snap** (snap), *v.i. & v.t.* [SNAPPED, SNAPPING], [< MLG. *snappen*], 1. to bite or grasp suddenly (often with *at*). 2. to shout (*at*) or utter sharply. 3. to break suddenly. 4. to make or cause to make a sudden, cracking sound. 5. to close, fasten, etc. with this sound. 6. to move or cause to move suddenly and smartly: as, *snap* to attention. 7. to take a snapshot (of). *n.* 1. a sudden bite, grasp, etc. 2. a sharp cracking sound. 3. a short, angry utterance. 4. a brief period: said of cold weather. 5. a fastening that closes with a click. 6. a hard, thin cooky. 7. [Colloq.], alertness, vigor, etc. 8. [Slang], an easy job, problem, etc. *adj.* 1. made or done quickly: as, a *snap* decision. 2. that fastens with a snap. 3. [Slang], easy. **—snap out of it,** to improve or recover quickly.
**snap'drag'on,** *n.* [< *snap* + *dragon:* from the mouth-shaped flowers], a plant with saclike, two-lipped flowers.
**snap'per,** *n.* 1. a person or thing that snaps. 2. any of various tropical basslike food fishes; esp., the red snapper.
**snap'py,** *adj.* [-PIER, -PIEST], 1. cross; irritable. 2. that snaps. 3. [Colloq.], full of vigor; brisk. 4. [Colloq.], stylish; smart.
**snap'shot',** *n.* a photograph taken in an instant with a hand camera.
**snare** (snâr), *n.* [< ON. *snara* or MD. *snare*], 1. a trap for small animals. 2. anything dangerous, etc. that tempts or attracts. 3. a length of wire or gut across the bottom of a drum. *v.t.* [SNARED, SNARING], to catch as in a snare; trap.
**snarl** (snärl), *v.i.* [< earlier *snar*, to growl], 1. to growl fiercely, baring the teeth, as a dog. 2. to speak sharply, as in anger. *v.t.* to utter with a snarl. *n.* 1. a fierce growl. 2. an angry utterance.
**snarl** (snärl), *n., v.t. & v.i.* [< *snare*], tangle.
**snatch** (snach), *v.t.* [prob. < ME. *snakken*, seize], to seize or take suddenly, eagerly, without right, etc.; grab. *n.* 1. a snatching. 2. a brief period. 3. a fragment; bit. **—snatch at,** 1. to try to seize. 2. to take advantage of (a chance, etc.) quickly.
**sneak** (snēk), *v.i. & v.t.* [AS. *snican*], to move, act, give, put, take, etc. secretly or stealthily. *n.* 1. one who sneaks. 2. an act of sneaking. **—sneak'y** [-IER, -IEST], *adj.*
**sneak'ers,** *n.pl.* [Colloq.], canvas shoes with heelless, soft rubber soles.
**sneak'ing,** *adj.* 1. cowardly; stealthy; furtive. 2. not admitted; secret: as, a *sneaking* fondness for jazz. **—sneak'ing·ly,** *adv.*
**sneer** (snêr), *v.i.* [ME. *sneren*], 1. to show scorn by a derisive smile. 2. to express derision, etc. in speech or writing. *n.* 1. an act of sneering. 2. a sneering expression, etc.
**sneeze** (snēz), *v.i.* [SNEEZED, SNEEZING], [ME. *snesen*], to expel breath from the nose and mouth in an involuntary, explosive action. *n.* an act of sneezing.
**snick·er** (snik'ẽr), *v.i.* [echoic], to laugh in a sly, partly stifled manner; giggle; titter. *n.* a sly, partly stifled laugh.
**snide** (snīd), *adj.* [prob. < D. dial.], [Slang], sly and malicious. **—snide'ly,** *adv.*
**sniff** (snif), *v.i. & v.t.* [echoic], 1. to breathe in forcibly through the nose. 2. to express (contempt, etc.) by sniffing. 3. to smell by sniffing. *n.* 1. an act or sound of sniffing. 2. something sniffed.
**snif·fle** (snif''l), *v.i.* [-FLED, -FLING], to sniff repeatedly so as to check mucus running from the nose. *n.* an act or sound of sniffling. **—the sniffles,** [Colloq.], a head cold.
**snig·ger** (snig'ẽr), *n., & v.i.* snicker.
**snip** (snip), *v.t. & v.i.* [SNIPPED, SNIPPING], [D. *snippen*], to cut or cut off in a short, quick stroke, as with scissors. *n.* 1. a small piece cut off. 2. [Colloq.], a small or young person.
**snipe** (snīp), *n.* [ON. *snipa*], a long-billed wading bird. *v.i.* [SNIPED, SNIPING], 1. to hunt snipe. 2. to shoot at individuals from a hidden position. **—snip'er,** *n.*
**snip·pet** (snip'it), *n.* [dim. of *snip*], a small fragment, esp. one snipped off.
**snip·py** (snip'i), *adj.* [-PIER,-PIEST], [Colloq.], insolently curt, sharp, etc.
**snitch** (snich), *v.t.* [Slang], to steal. *v.i.* [Slang], 1. to steal. 2. to be an informer (*on*).
**sniv·el** (sniv''l), *v.i.* [-ELED or -ELLED, -ELING or -ELLING], [ME. *snivelen*], 1. to cry and sniffle, as in complaint. 2. to make a tearful, often false display of grief.
**snob** (snob), *n.* [< ?], one who attaches too much importance to wealth, social position, etc., having contempt for those he considers inferior. **—snob'bish,** *adj.* **—snob'bish·ness, snob'ber·y,** *n.*
**snood** (snōōd), *n.* [< AS. *snod*], a netlike bag worn at the back of a woman's head to hold the hair.
**snoop** (snōōp), *v.i.* [D. *snoepen*], [Colloq.], to pry about in a sneaking way. *n.* [Colloq.], one who snoops. **—snoop'y,** *adj.*
**snoot** (snōōt), *n.* [see SNOUT], [Colloq.], 1. the nose. 2. the face.
**snoot'y,** *adj.* [-IER, -IEST], [Colloq.], haughty; snobbish. **—snoot'i·ness,** *n.*
**snooze** (snōōz), *n.* [prob. < LG. *snūsen*, to snore], [Colloq.], a brief sleep. *v.i.* [SNOOZED, SNOOZING], [Colloq.], to nap; doze.
**snore** (snôr), *v.i.* [SNORED, SNORING], [echoic], to breathe with a harsh sound while asleep. *n.* a snoring. **—snor'er,** *n.*
**snor·kel** (snôr'k'l), *n.* [G. *schnörkel*, spiral], 1. a device for submarines, with air intake and exhaust tubes, permitting submergence for long periods. 2. a breathing tube extending above the surface of the water, used in swimming just below the surface.
**snort** (snôrt), *v.i.* [prob. < *snore*], 1. to force breath audibly through the nostrils. 2. to express contempt, etc. by a snort. *n.* 1. the act or sound of snorting. 2. a small drink of liquor. **—snort'er,** *n.*
**snot** (snot), *n.* [AS. (*ge*)*snot*, mucus], 1. nasal mucus: vulgar term. 2. [Slang], an offensive or impudent person. **—snot'ty** [-TIER, -TIEST], *adj.* **—snot'ti·ness,** *n.*
**snout** (snout), *n.* [prob. < MD. *snute*], the projecting nose and jaws of an animal.
**snow** (snō), *n.* [AS. *snaw*], 1. frozen particles of water vapor that fall to earth as white, crystalline flakes. 2. a falling of snow. 3. a mass of fallen snow. *v.i.* to fall as or like snow. **—snow in** (or **under**), to cover, enclose, etc. with or as with snow. **—snow'y** [-IER, -IEST], *adj.* **—snow'i·ness,** *n.*
**snow'ball',** *n.* a mass of snow packed together into a ball. *v.i.* to increase rapidly like a rolling ball of snow.
**snow'-blind',** *adj.* blinded temporarily by exposure to the rays of the sun reflected from snow. **—snow blindness.**
**snow'-bound',** *adj.* confined by snow.
**snow'-clad',** *adj.* covered with snow.
**snow'drift',** *n.* a pile of snow heaped up by the wind.
**snow'fall',** *n.* a fall of snow or the amount of snow falling in a given area or time.
**snow'flake',** *n.* a single crystal of snow.

**snow line** (or **limit**), the lower boundary of a high region in which snow never melts.
**snow′mo·bile′** (-mō-bēl′), *n.* a motor vehicle for traveling over snow, with steerable runners in front and tractor treads at the rear.
**snow′plow′**, *n.* a plowlike machine used to clear snow off a road, etc.
**snow′shoe′**, *n.* a racket-shaped wooden frame crisscrossed with leather, etc., worn on the feet to prevent sinking in deep snow.
**snow′storm′**, *n.* a snow accompanied by a strong wind.
**snub** (snub), *v.t.* [SNUBBED, SNUBBING], [< ON. *snubba*, chide], 1. to treat with scorn, disregard, etc. 2. to check the movement of suddenly. *n.* a deliberate slight. *adj.* short and turned up, as a nose.
**snub′-nosed′**, *adj.* having a snub nose.
**snuff** (snuf), *v.t.* [ME.], 1. to trim off the charred end of (a wick). 2. to put out (a candle). —**snuff out**, 1. to extinguish. 2. to destroy. —**snuff′er**, *n.*
**snuff** (snuf), *v.t. & v.i.* [MD. *snuffen*], to sniff or smell. *n.* 1. a sniff. 2. powdered tobacco taken up into the nose or applied to the gums. —**up to snuff**, [Colloq.], up to the usual standard.
**snuff′box′**, *n.* a small box for snuff.
**snuf·fle** (snuf′'l), *n. & v.i.* [-FLED, -FLING], [< *snuff* (to sniff)], sniffle.
**snug** (snug), *adj.* [SNUGGER, SNUGGEST], [*prob.* < LG.], 1. comfortable; cozy. 2. compact; neat: as, a *snug* cottage. 3. tight in fit: as, a *snug* coat. 4. hidden: as, he kept *snug* in the corner. —**snug′ly**, *adv.*
**snug·gle** (snug′'l), *v.i. & v.t.* [-GLED, -GLING], [< *snug*], to cuddle; nestle.
**so** (sō), *adv.* [AS. *swa*], 1. as shown or described: as, hold your bat *so*. 2. *a*) to such an extent: as, why are you *so* late? *b*) very: as, they are *so* happy. *c*) [Colloq.], very much. 3. therefore: as, they were late, and *so* didn't go. 4. more or less: as, he won ten dollars or *so*. 5. also; likewise: as, I'm going and *so* are you. 6. then: as, *so* you really don't care. *conj.* 1. in order (*that*). 2. [Colloq.], with the result (*that*). *pron.* that which has been specified or named. *interj.* an exclamation of surprise, triumph, etc. —**and so on** (or **forth**), and the rest; et cetera. —**so as**, with the result or purpose. —**so what?** [Colloq.], even if so, what then?
**soak** (sōk), *v.t.* [AS. *socian*], 1. to make thoroughly wet. 2. to drink in; absorb (with *up*). 3. [Slang], to charge excessively. *v.i.* 1. to remain in liquid so as to become thoroughly wet. 2. to penetrate. *n.* 1. a soaking or being soaked. 2. [Slang], a drunkard.
**soap** (sōp), *n.* [AS. *sape*], a substance mixed with water to produce suds for washing: prepared by the action of an alkali, as potash, on a fat. *v.t.* to rub with soap. —**no soap**, [Slang], (it is) not acceptable. —**soap′y** [-IER, -IEST], *adj.* —**soap′i·ness**, *n.*
**soap′box′**, *n.* a box used as a platform by one speaking to a street audience.
**soap opera**, [Colloq.], a daytime radio or television serial drama of a melodramatic, sentimental nature.
**soap′stone′**, *n.* a soft talc in rock form used for griddles, bed warmers, etc.
**soap′suds′**, *n.pl.* foamy, soapy water.
**soar** (sôr), *v.i.* [ult. < L. *ex-*, out + *aura*, air], 1. to fly high into the air. 2. to glide along high in the air. 3. to rise to great heights. —**soar′er**, *n.*
**sob** (sob), *v.i.* [SOBBED, SOBBING], [< AS. *supan*, to swallow], to weep aloud with short, gasping breaths. *v.t.* to utter with sobs. *n.* the act or sound of sobbing.
**so·ber** (sō′bẽr), *adj.* [< L. *sobrius*], 1. temperate, esp. in the use of liquor. 2. not drunk. 3. serious, sedate, reasonable, etc. 4. quiet; plain, as color, clothes, etc. *v.t. & v.i.* to make or become sober (often with *up* or *down*). —**so′ber·ly**, *adv.* —**so′ber·ness**, *n.*
**so·bri·e·ty** (sō-brī′ə-ti), *n.* a being sober; specif., *a*) temperance, esp. in the use of drink. *b*) seriousness, sedateness, etc.
**so·bri·quet** (sō′bri-kā′), *n.* [Fr.], 1. a nickname. 2. an assumed name.
**Soc., soc.,** society.
**so′-called′**, *adj.* known by this term, but usually inaccurately so.
**soc·cer** (sok′ẽr), *n.* [alt. < *association* football], a kind of football played by kicking a round ball.
**so·cia·ble** (sō′shə-b'l), *adj.* [see SOCIAL], 1. friendly; affable. 2. characterized by informal conversation and companionship. *n.* a social. —**so′cia·bil′i·ty** [*pl.* -TIES], *n.*
**so·cial** (sō′shəl), *adj.* [< L. *socius*, companion], 1. of or having to do with human beings in their living together. 2. living with others; gregarious: as, modern man is *social*. 3. of or having to do with society, esp. fashionable society. 4. sociable. 5. of or for companionship. 6. of or engaged in welfare work. *n.* an informal gathering; party. —**so′cial·ly**, *adv.*
**so′cial·ism** (-iz'm), *n.* 1. the theory of the ownership and operation of the means of production and distribution by society, with all members sharing in the work and the products. 2. [often S-], a political movement for establishing such a system. —**so′cial·ist**, *n. & adj.* —**so′cial·is′tic**, *adj.*
**so·cial·ite** (sō′shə-līt′), *n.* [Colloq.], a person prominent in fashionable society.
**so′cial·ize′** (-līz′), *v.t.* [-IZED, -IZING], 1. to make social. 2. to put under government ownership or control. *v.i.* [Colloq.], to take part in social activity. —**so′cial·i·za′tion**, *n.*
**social register**, a book containing a list of socially prominent people.
**social science**, sociology.
**social security**, a federal system of old-age, unemployment, or disability insurance.
**social work**, the promotion of the welfare of the community and the individual, as through counseling agencies, recreation centers, etc. —**social worker.**
**so·ci·e·ty** (sə-sī′ə-ti), *n.* [*pl.* -TIES], [< L. *socius*, companion], 1. a group of persons forming a single community. 2. all people, collectively. 3. a particular system of group living. 4. companionship. 5. an organized group with some interest in common. 6. the wealthy, fashionable class. —**so·ci′e·tal**, *adj.*
**Society of Friends**, a Christian religious sect that believes in plainness of manners and worship, in pacifism, etc.: see **Quaker.**
**so·ci·ol·o·gy** (sō′si-ol′ə-ji), *n.* [see -LOGY], the study of the development, organization, and problems of society. —**so′ci·o·log′i·cal** (-ə-loj′i-k'l), *adj.* —**so′ci·ol′o·gist**, *n.*
**sock** (sok), *n.* [< L. *soccus*, light shoe], a short stocking.
**sock** (sok), *v.t.* [Slang], to hit with force. *n.* [Slang], a blow. *adv.* [Slang], directly.
**sock·et** (sok′it), *n.* [< OFr. *soc*, plowshare], a hollow part into which something fits: as, an eye *socket*. *v.t.* to fit into a socket.
**sod** (sod), *n.* [prob. < MD. *sode*], 1. a surface layer of earth containing grass; turf. 2. a piece of this. *v.t.* [SODDED, SODDING], to cover with sod.
**so·da** (sō′də), *n.* [ML.], 1. sodium carbonate. 2. sodium bicarbonate. 3. sodium hydroxide. 4. soda water. 5. a beverage of soda water, sirup, etc., often with ice cream.
**soda cracker**, a light, crisp cracker.
**soda fountain**, a counter for making and serving soft drinks, sodas, etc.
**soda pop**, a soft drink of flavored carbonated water.

**soda water,** water charged under pressure with carbon dioxide gas.
**sod·den** (sod''n), *adj.* [obs. pp. of *seethe*], 1. soaked through. 2. moist from improper cooking. 3. dull or stupid, as from fatigue.
**so·di·um** (sō'di-əm), *n.* [Mod. L. < *soda*], a white, alkaline metallic chemical element: symbol, Na.
**sodium bicarbonate,** see **baking soda.**
**sodium carbonate,** a crystalline carbonate of sodium, used in washing.
**sodium chloride,** common salt.
**sodium fluoride,** a colorless, soluble salt, used in fluoridation of water.
**sodium hydroxide,** a white, strongly alkaline substance: also called *caustic soda, lye.*
**sodium nitrate,** a clear, crystalline salt, used in making explosives, fertilizers, etc.
**Sod·om and Go·mor·rah** (sod'əm and gə-môr'ə), in the *Bible,* two sinful cities destroyed by fire.
**sod·om·y** (sod'əm-i), *n.* [< *Sodom*], abnormal sexual intercourse, as between persons of the same sex. **—sod'om·ite'** (-īt'), *n.*
**so·fa** (sō'fə), *n.* [< Ar. *suffah*], an upholstered couch with fixed back and arms.
**soft** (sôft), *adj.* [AS. *softe*], 1. giving way easily under pressure. 2. easily cut, worked, etc.: as, a *soft* metal. 3. not as hard as is normal, desirable, etc.: as, *soft* butter. 4. smooth to the touch. 5. nonalcoholic: said of drinks. 6. having few of the mineral salts that keep soap from lathering: said of water. 7. mild: as, a *soft* breeze. 8. weak; not vigorous. 9. easy: as, a *soft* job. 10. kind; gentle; lenient. 11. not bright: said of color. 12. gentle; low: said of sound. *adv.* gently. **—soft'ly,** *adv.* **—soft'ness,** *n.*
**soft'ball',** *n.* 1. a kind of baseball played with a ball larger and softer than in ordinary baseball. 2. this ball.
**soft'-boiled',** *adj.* boiled only a short time so that the yolk is soft: said of eggs.
**sof·ten** (sôf''n), *v.t. & v.i.* to make or become soft or softer. **—sof'ten·er,** *n.*
**soft'heart'ed,** *adj.* 1. full of compassion. 2. not strict or severe, as in discipline.
**soft palate,** the soft, fleshy part at the rear of the roof of the mouth; velum.
**soft'-ped'al,** *v.t.* [-ALED or -ALLED, -ALING or -ALLING], [from pedal action in piano, etc.], [Colloq.], to tone down; make less emphatic.
**sog·gy** (sog'i), *adj.* [-GIER, -GIEST], [prob. < ON. *sog,* a sucking], soft and heavy with moisture. **—sog'gi·ly,** *adv.* **—sog'gi·ness,** *n.*
**soil** (soil), *n.* [< L. *solum*], 1. the surface layer of earth, supporting plant life. 2. country: as, foreign *soil.* 3. ground; earth.
**soil** (soil), *v.t.* [ult. < L. *sus,* pig], 1. to make dirty; stain. 2. to disgrace. *v.i.* to become soiled. *n.* 1. a soiled spot. 2. excrement.
**soi·ree, soi·rée** (swä-rā'), *n.* [< Fr. *soir,* evening], an evening party or gathering.
**so·journ** (sō'jūrn; *also, for v.,* sō-jūrn'), *v.i.* [< L. *sub-,* under + *diurnus,* of a day], to live somewhere temporarily. *n.* a brief stay.
**sol** (sōl), *n.* [It.], in *music,* the fifth tone of the diatonic scale.
**sol·ace** (sol'is), *n.* [< L. *solari,* to comfort], 1. an easing of grief, loneliness, etc. 2. something that relieves; comfort. *v.t.* [-ACED, -ACING], to comfort; console.
**so·lar** (sō'lẽr), *adj.* [< L. *sol,* sun], 1. of or having to do with the sun. 2. produced by or coming from the sun: as, *solar* energy.
**so·lar·i·um** (sō-lâr'i-əm), *n.* [*pl.* -LARIA (-ə)], [L. < *sol,* sun], a glassed-in room for sunning.
**solar plexus,** a network of nerves in the abdomen behind the stomach.
**solar system,** the sun and all the planets, etc. revolving around it.
**sold** (sōld), pt. and pp. of **sell.**
**sol·der** (sod'ẽr), *n.* [< L. *solidare,* make firm], a metal alloy used when melted to join or patch metal parts, etc. *v.t. & v.i.* to join with solder. **—sol'der·er,** *n.*
**sol·dier** (sōl'jẽr), *n.* [< OFr. *solde,* pay], 1. a member of an army. 2. an enlisted man, as distinguished from an officer. 3. one who works for a specified cause. *v.i.* 1. to serve as a soldier. 2. to shirk one's duty, as by feigning illness. **—sol'dier·ly,** *adj.*
**soldier of fortune,** a military adventurer, serving in foreign armies.
**sole** (sōl), *n.* [ult. < L. *solum,* a base], 1. the bottom surface of the foot. 2. the part of a shoe, sock, etc. corresponding to this. *v.t.* [SOLED, SOLING], to furnish (a shoe, etc.) with a sole.
**sole** (sōl), *adj.* [< L. *solus*], without another; single; one and only.
**sole** (sōl), *n.* [*pl.* SOLE, SOLES], [< L. *solea,* sole of a shoe: from its shape], a sea flatfish valued as food.
**sol·e·cism** (sol'ə-siz'm), *n.* [< Gr. *soloikos,* speaking incorrectly], a violation of the conventional usage, grammar, etc. of a language. **—sol'e·cis'tic,** *adj.*
**sole·ly** (sō'li), *adv.* 1. alone. 2. only, exclusively, or merely.
**sol·emn** (sol'əm), *adj.* [< L. *sollus,* all + *annus,* year], 1. sacred. 2. formal. 3. serious; grave; earnest. 4. awe-inspiring.
**so·lem·ni·ty** (sə-lem'nə-ti), *n.* [*pl.* -TIES], 1. solemn ritual. 2. seriousness; gravity.
**sol·em·nize** (sol'əm-nīz'), *v.t.* [-NIZED, -NIZING], 1. to celebrate formally or according to ritual. 2. to perform (a ceremony).
**sol-fa** (sōl'fä'), *n.* [It. *solfa*], the syllables *do, re, mi, fa, sol, la, ti, do,* used for the tones of a scale.
**sol·feg·gio** (sol-fej'ō, -i-ō'), *n.* [*pl.* -GIOS, -GI (-fej'i)], [It.], voice practice of scales to the sol-fa syllables.
**so·lic·it** (sə-lis'it), *v.t.* [see SOLICITOUS], 1. to ask or seek earnestly; entreat. 2. to entice or lure. *v.i.* to make a plea or request. **—so·lic'i·ta'tion,** *n.*
**so·lic·i·tor** (sə-lis'ə-tẽr), *n.* 1. one who solicits trade, contributions, etc. 2. in England, a lawyer other than a barrister. 3. the law officer for a city, department, etc.
**so·lic·i·tous** (sə-lis'ə-təs), *adj.* [< L. *sollus,* whole + *ciere,* set in motion], 1. showing care or concern: as, *solicitous* for their welfare. 2. desirous; eager. 3. full of anxiety; troubled. **—so·lic'i·tous·ly,** *adv.*
**so·lic'i·tude'** (-tōōd', -tūd'), *n.* a being solicitous; care, concern, etc.
**sol·id** (sol'id), *adj.* [< L. *solidus*], 1. relatively firm or compact; neither liquid nor gaseous. 2. not hollow. 3. in three dimensions; cubic. 4. substantial; firm; sound. 5. having no breaks or divisions. 6. of one color, material, etc. throughout. 7. showing unity; unanimous. 8. [Colloq.], firm or dependable. *n.* 1. a solid substance, neither a liquid nor gas. 2. an object having length, breadth, and thickness.
**sol·i·dar·i·ty** (sol'ə-dar'ə-ti), *n.* [*pl.* -TIES], complete unity, as of purpose, interest, etc.
**so·lid·i·fy** (sə-lid'ə-fī'), *v.t. & v.i.* [-FIED, -FYING], 1. to make or become solid, hard, etc. 2. to crystallize. **—so·lid'i·fi·ca'tion,** *n.*
**so·lid·i·ty** (sə-lid'ə-ti), *n.* [*pl.* -TIES], a being solid; firmness, soundness, etc.
**sol'id-state',** *adj.* 1. of the branch of physics dealing with the structure, properties, etc. of solids. 2. equipped with transistors, etc.
**so·lil·o·quy** (sə-lil'ə-kwi), *n.* [*pl.* -QUIES], [< L. *solus,* alone + *loqui,* speak], 1. a talking to oneself. 2. lines in a drama spoken by a character as if to himself. **—so·lil'o·quize'** (-kwīz') [-QUIZED, -QUIZING], *v.i. & v.t.*
**sol·i·taire** (sol'ə-târ', sol'ə-târ'), *n.* [Fr.; see SOLITARY], 1. a single gem, esp. a diamond.

set by itself. 2. a card game for one person.
**sol·i·tar·y** (sol′ə-ter′i), *adj.* [< L. *solus*, alone], 1. living or being alone. 2. single; only: as, a *solitary* example. 3. lonely; remote. 4. done in solitude. —**sol′i·tar′i·ness,** *n.*
**sol′i·tude′** (-tōōd′, -tūd′), *n.* [< L. *solus*, alone], 1. a being solitary, or alone; seclusion. 2. a secluded place.
**so·lo** (sō′lō), *n.* [*pl.* -LOS; *rarely* -LI (-lē)], [It. < L. *solus*, alone], 1. a musical piece or passage to be performed by one person. 2. any performance by one person alone. *adj.* for or by a single performer. —**so′lo·ist,** *n.*
**so long,** [< ?], [Colloq.], good-by.
**sol·stice** (sol′stis), *n.* [< L. *sol*, sun + *sistere*, to halt], 1. either of the two points on the sun's ecliptic at which it is farthest north or south of the equator. 2. the time during the summer (**summer solstice**) or winter (**winter solstice**) when the sun reaches either of these points: in the Northern Hemisphere, June 21 or 22 and December 21 or 22, respectively.
**sol·u·ble** (sol′yoo-b'l), *adj.* [see SOLVE], 1. that can be dissolved. 2. that can be solved. —**sol′u·bil′i·ty,** *n.* —**sol′u·bly,** *adv.*
**so·lu·tion** (sə-lōō′shən), *n.* [see SOLVE], 1. the act or process of solving a problem. 2. an explanation, answer, etc. 3. the dispersion of one or more substances in another, usually a liquid, so as to form a homogeneous mixture. 4. the mixture so produced.
**solve** (solv), *v.t.* [SOLVED, SOLVING], [< L. *se-*, apart + *luere*, let go], to find the answer to (a problem, etc.); explain. —**solv′a·bil′i·ty,** *n.* —**solv′a·ble,** *adj.* —**solv′er,** *n.*
**sol·vent** (sol′vənt), *adj.* [see SOLVE], 1. able to pay all one's debts. 2. that can dissolve another substance. *n.* a substance used for dissolving another one. —**sol′ven·cy,** *n.*
**so·mat·ic** (sō-mat′ik), *adj.* [< Gr. *sōma*, the body], of the body; physical.
**som·ber, som·bre** (som′bẽr), *adj.* [< L. *sub*, under + *umbra*, shade], 1. dark and gloomy or dull. 2. dismal; melancholy; sad.
**som·bre·ro** (som-brâr′ō), *n.* [*pl.* -ROS], [Sp. < *sombra*, shade], a broad-brimmed hat worn in Spain, Latin America, etc.
**some** (sum), *adj.* [AS. *sum*], 1. certain but not specified or known: as, *some* people smoke. 2. of a certain unspecified quantity, degree, etc.: as, have *some* butter. 3. about: as, *some* ten of us. 4. [Colloq.], remarkable, striking, etc.: as, that was *some* fight. *pron.* a certain unspecified quantity, degree, etc.: as, *some* of the time.
**-some,** [AS. *-sum*], a suffix meaning *like*, *apt*, or *tending to* (*be*), as in *lonesome*, *tiresome*.
**-some,** [< Gr. *sōma*, body], a combining form meaning *body*, as in *chromosome*.
**some·bod·y** (sum′bud′i, -bod′i), *n.* [*pl.* -IES], a person of importance. *pron.* a person unknown or not named; some person.
**some·day** (sum′dā′), *adv.* at some future time.
**some·how** (sum′hou′), *adv.* in a way or by a method not known or stated.
**some·one** (sum′wun′), *pron.* somebody.
**som·er·sault** (sum′ẽr-sôlt′), *n.* [< L. *supra*, over + *saltus*, a leap], an acrobatic stunt performed by turning the body one full revolution, heels over head. *v.i.* to perform a somersault. Also **som′er·set′** (-set′).
**some′thing,** *n.* 1. a thing not definitely known, understood, etc.: as, *something* went wrong. 2. a definite but unspecified thing: as, he has *something* for you.
**some′time′,** *adv.* at some unspecified or future time. *adj.* former.
**some′times′,** *adv.* occasionally.
**some·what** (sum′hwät′, -wət), *n.* some part, amount, etc. *adv.* to some extent, degree, etc.; a little.
**some·where** (sum′hwâr′), *adv.* 1. in, to, or at some place not known or specified. 2. at some unspecified point, as in time (with *about* or *in*). *n.* an unspecified place.
**som·nam·bu·late** (som-nam′byoo-lāt′), *v.i.* & *v.t.* [-LATED, -LATING], [< L. *somnus*, sleep + *ambulare*, to walk], to walk in a trancelike state while asleep. —**som·nam′bu·lant,** *adj.*
**som·nam′bu·lism** (-liz'm), *n.* sleepwalking. —**som·nam′bu·list,** *n.*
**som·no·lent** (som′nə-lent), *adj.* [< L. *somnus*, sleep], 1. sleepy. 2. inducing drowsiness. —**som′no·lence,** *n.*
**son** (sun), *n.* [AS. *sunu*], 1. a boy or man in his relationship to either or both parents. 2. a male descendant.
**so·nar** (sō′när), *n.* [*so*und *na*vigation *r*anging], an apparatus for transmitting sound waves in water, used in detecting submarines, finding depths of oceans, etc.
**so·na·ta** (sə-nä′tə), *n.* [It. < L. *sonare*, to sound], a musical composition for solo instrument or instruments, in several movements having unity of subject but differing in tempo, rhythm, etc.
**song** (sôŋ), *n.* [AS.], 1. the act or art of singing. 2. a piece of music for singing. 3. *a*) poetry. *b*) a ballad or lyric set to music. 4. a singing sound. —**for a song,** cheaply.
**song′bird′,** *n.* 1. a bird that makes vocal sounds like singing. 2. a woman singer.
**song′ster** (-stẽr), *n.* [AS. *sangestre*], a singer. —**song′stress** (-stris), *n.fem.*
**son·ic** (son′ik), *adj.* [< L. *sonus*, sound], of or having to do with sound or the speed of sound (about 738 miles per hour).
**son′-in-law′,** *n.* [*pl.* SONS-IN-LAW], the husband of one's daughter.
**son·net** (son′it), *n.* [< L. *sonus*, a sound], a poem normally of fourteen lines in any of several rhyme schemes.
**so·no·rous** (sə-nôr′əs), *adj.* [< L. *sonor*, a sound], 1. producing sound; resonant. 2. full, deep, or rich in sound. —**so·nor·i·ty** (sə-nôr′ə-ti, sə-nor′-), *n.* —**so·no′rous·ly,** *adv.*
**soon** (sōōn), *adv.* [AS. *sona*, at once], 1. in a short time: as, come see us *soon*. 2. promptly; quickly: as, as *soon* as possible. 3. ahead of time; early: as, he left too *soon*. 4. readily; willingly: as, I'd as *soon* go as stay. —**sooner or later,** eventually.
**soot** (soot, sōōt), *n.* [AS. *sot*], a black substance, chiefly carbon particles, in the smoke of burning matter. —**soot′y** [-IER, -IEST], *adj.* —**soot′i·ness,** *n.*
**sooth** (sōōth), *n.* [AS. *soth*], [Archaic], truth.
**soothe** (sōōth), *v.t.* [SOOTHED, SOOTHING], [< AS. *soth*, truth], 1. to make calm or composed, as by gentleness, flattery, etc. 2. to relieve, as pain. —**sooth′er,** *n.*
**sooth·say·er** (sōōth′sā′ẽr), *n.* [see SOOTH], one who claims to foretell the future. —**sooth′say′ing,** *n.*
**sop** (sop), *n.* [AS. *sopp*], 1. a piece of food, as bread, soaked in milk, etc. 2. something given to appease; bribe. *v.t.* & *v.i.* [SOPPED, SOPPING], 1. to soak, steep, etc. 2. to take (*up*), as water, by absorption.
**soph·ism** (sof′iz'm), *n.* [< Gr. *sophos*, clever], a clever and plausible but fallacious argument.
**soph·ist** (sof′ist), *n.* one who uses clever, specious reasoning.
**so·phis·ti·cate** (sə-fis′tə-kāt′; *also, for n.,* -kit), *v.t.* [-CATED, -CATING], [see SOPHISM], to change from a natural or simple state; make wordly-wise. *n.* a sophisticated person.
**so·phis′ti·ca′ted,** *adj.* 1. worldy-wise; not naive. 2. for sophisticates. 3. highly complex or developed in form, technique, etc., as equipment. —**so·phis′ti·ca′tion,** *n.*
**soph·is·try** (sof′is-tri), *n.* [*pl.* -TRIES], mis-

leading but clever and plausible reasoning.
**soph·o·more** (sof′ə-môr′), *n.* [< obs. *sophumer*, sophist], a student in the second year of college or high school. *adj.* of sophomores.
**soph′o·mor′ic,** *adj.* of or like sophomores; opinionated, immature, etc.
**-sophy,** [< Gr. *sophia*, skill, wisdom], a suffix meaning *knowledge*, as in *philosophy*.
**so·po·rif·ic** (sop′ə-rif′ik, sō′pə-), *adj.* [< L. *sopor*, sleep; + *-fic*], 1. causing sleep. 2. sleepy. *n.* a drug, etc. that causes sleep.
**sop·ping** (sop′iŋ), *adj.* [ppr. of *sop*], thoroughly wet; drenched; soaking.
**so·pra·no** (sə-pran′ō, -prä′nō), *n.* [*pl.* -PRANOS, -PRANI (-prä′nē)], [It. < *sopra*, above], 1. the highest singing voice of women and children. 2. a singer with such a range. 3. a part for a soprano. *adj.* of or for a soprano.
**sor·cer·y** (sôr′sẽr-i), *n.* [*pl.* -IES], [< L. *sors*, fate], the supposed use of an evil supernatural power over people; witchcraft. —**sor′cer·er,** *n.* —**sor′cer·ess** (-is), *n.fem.*
**sor·did** (sôr′did), *adj.* [< L. *sordes*, filth], 1. dirty; filthy. 2. squalid; wretched. 3. base; ignoble. —**sor′did·ly,** *adv.* —**sor′did·ness,** *n.*
**sore** (sôr), *adj.* [AS. *sar*], 1. giving or feeling pain; painful. 2. filled with grief, etc.: as, *sore* at heart. 3. causing sadness, misery, etc.: as, a *sore* hardship. 4. [Colloq.], angry; offended. *n.* 1. a place on the body where the tissue is injured. 2. any source of pain, irritation, etc. —**sore′ness,** *n.*
**sore′ly,** *adv.* 1. grievously; painfully. 2. urgently: as, *sorely* needed.
**sor·ghum** (sôr′gəm), *n.* [< It. *sorgo*], 1. a cereal grass grown for grain, fodder, sirup, etc. 2. a sirup made from the juice of its stalk.
**so·ror·i·ty** (sə-rôr′ə-ti), *n.* [*pl.* -TIES], [< L. *soror*, sister], a group of women or girls joined together for fellowship, etc., as in some colleges.
**sor·rel** (sôr′əl, sor′-), *n.* [< OHG. *sur*, sour], a plant with sour, fleshy leaves used in salads.
**sor·rel** (sôr′əl, sor′-), *n.* [< OFr. *sor*, a hawk with red plumage], 1. reddish brown. 2. a reddish-brown horse, etc. *adj.* reddish-brown.
**sor·row** (sor′ō, sôr′ō), *n.* [< AS. *sorg*], 1. mental suffering caused by loss, disappointment, etc.; grief. 2. that which produces grief. *v.i.* to feel sorrow; grieve. —**sor′row·ful,** *adj.* —**sor′row·ful·ly,** *adv.*
**sor·ry** (sôr′i, sor′i), *adj.* [-RIER, -RIEST], [< AS. *sar*, sore], 1. full of sorrow, pity, or regret. 2. inferior; poor. 3. wretched.
**sort** (sôrt), *n.* [< L. *sors*, a lot], 1. any group of related things; kind; class. 2. quality; type. 3. [Archaic], manner; way. *v.t.* to arrange according to class or kind. —**of sorts,** of an inferior kind: also **of a sort.** —**out of sorts,** [Colloq.], not in good humor or health. —**sort of,** [Colloq.], somewhat.
**sor·tie** (sôr′ti), *n.* [Fr. < *sortir*, to issue], 1. a sudden attack by forces of a besieged place. 2. one mission by a single military plane.
**SOS** (es′ō′es′), a signal of distress, as in wireless telegraphy.
**so-so** (sō′sō′), *adv.* indifferently: just passably. *adj.* not very good; rather poor.
**sot** (sot), *n.* [< LL. *sottus*, stupid], a habitual drunkard. —**sot′tish,** *adj.*
**sot·to vo·ce** (sot′ō vō′chi), [It., under the voice], in an undertone, so as not to be overheard.
**sou** (sōō), *n.* [*pl.* SOUS (sōōz: Fr. sōō)], [< L. *solidus*, coin], a former French coin of small value.
**souf·flé** (sōō′flā′, sōō′flā), *adj.* [Fr. < *souffler*, to blow], in *cooking*, light and puffy: also **souffléed.** *n.* a baked food made light and puffy by adding beaten egg whites before baking.
**sough** (suf, sou), *n.* [< AS. *swogan*, to sound], a soft murmuring, sighing, or rustling sound. *v.i.* to make a sough.
**sought** (sôt), pt. and pp. of **seek.**
**soul** (sōl), *n.* [AS. *sawol*], 1. an entity without material reality, regarded as the spiritual part of the person. 2. the moral or emotional nature of man. 3. spiritual or emotional warmth, force, etc. 4. vital or essential part, quality, etc. 5. a person: as, I didn't see a *soul.*
**soul′ful,** *adj.* full of or showing deep feeling.
**soul′less,** *adj.* lacking deep feeling.
**sound** (sound), *n.* [< L. *sonus*], 1. that which is heard, resulting from stimulation of auditory nerves by vibrations in the air. 2. the distance within which a sound may be heard. 3. mental impression: as, I like the *sound* of his report. *v.i.* 1. to make a sound. 2. to seem through sound: as, she *sounds* sad. *v.t.* 1. to cause to sound. 2. to express, signal, etc.: as, *sound* the alarm. 3. to pronounce: as, he doesn't *sound* his r's. —**sound′less,** *adj.*
**sound** (sound), *adj.* [AS. (*ge*)*sund*], 1. free from defect, damage, or decay. 2. healthy: as, a *sound* body. 3. firm; safe: as, a *sound* bank. 4. based on valid reasoning; sensible. 5. deep and undisturbed: said of sleep. 6. honest, loyal, etc. *adv.* in a sound manner.
**sound** (sound), *n.* [< AS. & ON. *sund*], 1. a wide channel linking two large bodies of water or separating an island from the mainland. 2. a long arm of the sea.
**sound** (sound), *v.t. & v.i.* [< L. *sub*, under + *unda*, a wave], 1. to measure the depth of (water), esp. with a weighted line. 2. to try to find out the opinions of (someone) on a matter (often with *out*). —**sound′ing,** *n.*
**sound′ing,** *adj.* 1. giving forth sound. 2. resonant; sonorous.
**sounding board,** 1. a board, etc. used to reflect sound. 2. a person on whom one tests one's ideas, etc.
**sound′proof′,** *adj.* impervious to sound. *v.t.* to make soundproof.
**sound track,** the sound record along one side of a motion-picture film.
**soup** (sōōp), *n.* [Fr. *soupe*], a liquid food made by cooking meat, vegetables, etc. in water, milk, etc. —**soup up,** [Slang], to increase the capacity for speed, as an engine.
**soup·çon** (sōōp′sōn′), *n.* [Fr.], 1. literally, a suspicion. 2. a suggestion or trace, as of a flavor.
**sour** (sour), *adj.* [AS. *sur*], 1. having a sharp, acid taste, as vinegar, etc. 2. spoiled by fermentation. 3. cross; disagreeable. 4. distasteful or unpleasant. *v.t. & v.i.* to make or become sour.—**sour′ly,** *adv.*—**sour′ness,** *n.*
**source** (sôrs), *n.* [< L. *surgere*, to rise], 1. a spring, etc. from which a stream arises. 2. a place of origin; prime cause. 3. a person, book, etc. from which information is gotten.
**sour′dough′,** *n.* 1. fermented dough kept for use as leaven. 2. a prospector, as in the western U.S., Canada, or Alaska.
**sour grapes,** something scorned only because it cannot be had.
**souse** (sous), *n.* [< OHG. *sulza*, brine], 1. a pickled food, as pig's feet. 2. liquid for pickling; brine. 3. a plunging into a liquid. 4. [Slang], a drunkard. *v.t. & v.i.* [SOUSED, SOUSING], 1. to pickle. 2. to plunge or steep in a liquid. 3. to make or become soaking wet.
**south** (south), *n.* [AS. *suth*], 1. the direction to the left of one facing the sunset (180° on the compass). 2. [often S-], a region in or toward this direction. *adj.* 1. in, of, or toward the south. 2. from the south. *adv.* in or toward the south.
**south′east′,** *n.* 1. the direction halfway between south and east. 2. a region in or

toward this direction. *adj.* 1. in, of, or toward the southeast. 2. from the southeast. *adv.* in, toward, or from the southeast. **—south'east'er·ly**, *adj. & adv.* **—south'east'ern**, *adj.* **—south'east'ward** (-wẽrd), *adv. & adj.* **—south'east'wards**, *adv.*

**south·er·ly** (suth'ẽr-li), *adj. & adv.* 1. toward the south. 2. from the south.

**south·ern** (suth'ẽrn), *adj.* 1. in, of, or toward the south. 2. from the south. 3. [S-], of the South. **—south'ern·most'**, *adj.*

**south'ern·er**, *n.* a native or inhabitant of the south, esp. [S-] of a Southern State.

**south·paw** (south'pô'), *n.* [Slang], in *sports*, a left-handed player.

**South Pole**, the southern end of the earth's axis.

**south'ward** (-wẽrd), *adj. & adv.* toward the south: also **south'wards**, *adv.*

**south'west'**, *n.* 1. the direction halfway between south and west. 2. a region in or toward this direction. *adj.* 1. in, of, or toward the southwest. 2. from the southwest. *adv.* in, toward, or from the southwest. **—south'west'er·ly**, *adj. & adv.* **—south'west'ern**, *adj.* **—south'west'ward** (-wẽrd), *adv. & adj.* **—south'west'wards**, *adv.*

**south·west·er** (south'wes'tẽr, sou-), *n.* 1. a storm or wind from the southwest. 2. a sailor's waterproof hat with a broad brim in the back. Also **sou'west'er, sou·west'er** (sou-).

**sou·ve·nir** (sōō'və-nêr'), *n.* [Fr. < L. *subvenire*, come to mind], something kept as a reminder; memento.

**sov·er·eign** (sov'rin), *adj.* [< L. *super*, above], 1. above all others; chief; supreme. 2. supreme in power, rank, etc. 3. independent of all others: as, a *sovereign* state. *n.* 1. a person having sovereign authority. 2. a British gold coin worth one pound.

**sov'er·eign·ty**, *n.* [*pl.* -TIES], 1. the status, rule, etc. of a sovereign. 2. supreme and independent political authority.

**so·vi·et** (sō'vi-it), *n.* [Russ., lit., council], 1. a council of delegates. 2. in the Soviet Union, any of the various elected governing councils, from the village and town soviets to the Supreme Soviet. *adj.* [S-], of or connected with the Soviet Union.

**sow** (sou), *n.* [AS. *sugu*], an adult female pig.

**sow** (sō), *v.t.* [SOWED, SOWN (sōn) or SOWED, SOWING], [AS. *sawan*], 1. to scatter or plant (seed) for growing. 2. to plant (a field, etc.) with seed. 3. to spread. *v.i.* to sow seed.

**soy** (soi), *n.* [Japan. < Chin. *chiang*, salted bean + *yu*, oil], an oriental sauce made from fermented soybeans.

**soy'bean'**, *n.* 1. a plant with white or purple flowers and brown pods. 2. its seed, which yields flour, oil, and other products.

**Sp.**, 1. Spain. 2. Spaniard. 3. Spanish.

**spa** (spä), *n.* [< *Spa*, resort in Belgium], 1. a mineral spring. 2. a resort having a mineral spring.

**space** (spās), *n.* [< L. *spatium*], 1. the boundless expanse within which all things are contained. 2. distance, area, etc. between or within things. 3. room for some purpose: as, a parking *space*. 4. interval of time: as, *space* between wars. 5. the universe outside the earth's atmosphere: in full, **outer space**. *v.t.* [SPACED, SPACING], to arrange with spaces between. **—spac'er**, *n.*

**space'craft'**, *n.* [*pl.* -CRAFT], a spaceship or satellite designed for travel, exploration, etc. in outer space.

**space'ship'**, *n.* a rocket-propelled vehicle for travel in outer space.

**spa·cious** (spā'shəs), *adj.* 1. having more than enough space; vast. 2. great; large.

**spade** (spād), *n.* [AS. *spadu*], a flat-bladed, long-handled digging tool, like a shovel. *v.t. & v.i.* [SPADED, SPADING], to dig with a spade. **—spade'ful'**, *n.*

**spade** (spād), *n.* [ult. < Gr. *spathē*, flat blade], 1. the black figure (♠) marking one of the four suits of playing cards. 2. a card of this suit.

**spade'work'**, *n.* any tiresome work necessary to make a beginning.

**spa·ghet·ti** (spə-get'i), *n.* [It. < *spago*, small cord], a food consisting of long strings of flour paste, cooked by boiling or steaming.

**spake** (spāk), archaic pt. of **speak**.

**span** (span), *n.* [AS.], 1. the distance (about 9 in.) between the tips of the thumb and little finger when extended. 2. *a*) the full extent between any two limits. *b*) a part between two supports. 3. a short space of time. 4. a team of two animals. *v.t.* [SPANNED, SPANNING], 1. to measure, esp. by the span of the hand. 2. to extend over.

**span·gle** (spaŋ'g'l), *n.* [< AS. *spang*, a clasp], a small piece of bright metal sewed on fabric for decoration. *v.t.* [-GLED, -GLING], to decorate with spangles.

**Span·iard** (span'yẽrd), *n.* a native of Spain.

**span·iel** (span'yəl), *n.* [< OFr. *espagneul*, Spanish dog], any of several breeds of dog with a silky coat, large drooping ears, and short legs.

**Span·ish** (span'ish), *adj.* of Spain, its people, their language, etc. *n.* the Romance language of Spain and Spanish America. **—the Spanish**, the Spanish people.

**spank** (spaŋk), *v.t.* [echoic], to strike with something flat, as the open hand, esp. on the buttocks, as in punishment. *n.* a smart slap given in spanking. **—spank'er**, *n.*

**spank'ing**, *adj.* 1. swiftly moving; rapid. 2. brisk; strong, as a wind.

**spar** (spär), *n.* [< ON. *sparri*], any pole, as a mast or yard, supporting a sail on a ship.

**spar** (spär), *v.i.* [SPARRED, SPARRING], [< It. *parare*, to parry], 1. to box with caution, landing few heavy blows. 2. to wrangle.

**spare** (spâr), *v.t.* [SPARED, SPARING], [AS. *sparian*], 1. to refrain from killing, hurting, etc. 2. to save or free a (person) from (something). 3. to avoid using or use frugally. 4. to do without; give up, as time or money. *adj.* 1. not in regular use; extra. 2. free: said of time. 3. meager; scanty. 4. lean; thin. *n.* 1. a spare, or extra, thing. 2. in *bowling*, a knocking down of all the pins with two bowls. **—spare'ness**, *n.*

**spare'rib'**, *n.* [prob. < MLG. *ribbespēr*], the thin end of pork rib.

**spar'ing**, *adj.* 1. careful; frugal. 2. scanty; meager. **—spar'ing·ly**, *adv.*

**spark** (spärk), *n.* [AS. *spearca*], 1. a small, glowing piece of matter, esp. one thrown off by a fire. 2. any flash or sparkle. 3. a particle: as, a *spark* of hope. 4. the small flash of light accompanying an electrical discharge across a gap. *v.i.* to produce sparks or come forth as sparks. *v.t.* to kindle into activity.

**spark** (spärk), *n.* [< ON. *sparkr*, lively], a beau or lover. *v.t. & v.i.* [Colloq.], to woo.

**spar·kle** (spär'k'l), *v.i.* [-KLED, -KLING], 1. to give off sparks. 2. to glitter. 3. to effervesce. *n.* 1. a spark; glowing particle. 2. a sparkling. 3. brilliance. **—spar'kler** (-klẽr), *n.*

**spark plug**, a piece fitted into a cylinder of an engine to ignite the fuel mixture by making sparks.

**spar·row** (spar'ō), *n.* [AS. *spearwa*], any of several small finches.

**sparse** (spärs), *adj.* [< L. *spargere*, scatter], thinly spread; not dense; meager.

**Spar·tan** (spär't'n), *adj.* 1. of ancient Sparta, its people, culture, etc. 2. like the Spartans; warlike, hardy, disciplined, etc. *n.* a Spartan person. **—Spar'tan·ism**, *n.*

**spasm** (spaz'm), *n.* [< Gr. *spān*, to pull], 1. a sudden, involuntary muscular contrac-

tion. 2. any sudden, violent, temporary activity, feeling, etc. —**spas′mic**, *adj.*
**spas·mod·ic** (spaz-mod′ik), *adj.* [< Gr. *spasmos*, spasm + *eidos*, likeness], of or like spasms; fitful; intermittent: also **spas-mod′i·cal.** —**spas·mod′i·cal·ly**, *adv.*
**spas·tic** (spas′tik), *adj.* of or characterized by muscular spasms. *n.* one having a spastic condition. —**spas′ti·cal·ly**, *adv.*
**spat** (spat), *n.* [prob. echoic], [Colloq.], a brief, petty quarrel or dispute. *v.i.* [SPATTED, SPATTING], to engage in a spat.
**spat** (spat), *n.* [< *spatterdash*, a legging], *usually in pl.* a short gaiter covering the instep and ankle.
**spat** (spat), alt. pt. and pp. of **spit.**
**spate** (spāt), *n.* [? < OFr. *espoit*], 1. [Brit.], a heavy rain. 2. an unusually large outpouring, as of words.
**spa·tial** (spā′shəl), *adj.* [< L. *spatium*, space], of, or existing in, space.
**spat·ter** (spat′ẽr), *v.t. & v.i.* [< LG.], 1. to scatter or spurt out in drops. 2. to splash. *n.* 1. a spattering. 2. a mark caused by spattering. —**spat′ter·ing·ly**, *adv.*
**spat·u·la** (spach′oo-lə), *n.* [L. < Gr. *spathē*, flat blade], an implement with a broad, flexible blade for spreading or blending foods, paints, etc. —**spat′u·lar**, *adj.*
**spav·in** (spav′in), *n.* [OFr. *esparvain*], a disease of horses affecting the hock joint and causing lameness. —**spav′ined**, *adj.*
**spawn** (spôn), *v.t. & v.i.* [< L. *ex-*, out + *pandere*, spread], 1. to produce or deposit (spawn). 2. to bring forth or produce prolifically. *n.* 1. the mass of eggs emitted by fishes, mollusks, etc. 2. something produced, esp. in great quantity, as offspring.
**spay** (spā), *v.i.* [< Gr. *spathē*, flat blade], to remove the ovaries of (a living animal).
**speak** (spēk), *v.i.* [SPOKE or *archaic* SPAKE, SPOKEN, SPEAKING], [AS. *sp(r)ecan*], 1. to utter words; talk. 2. to communicate as by talking. 3. to make a speech. *v.t.* 1. to make known as by speaking. 2. to use (a given language) in speaking. 3. to utter orally, as words. —**speak for**, to ask for. —**speak of**, to talk about. —**speak out** (or **up**), to speak clearly or freely.
**speak-eas·y** (spēk′ēz′i), *n.* [*pl.* -IES], [Slang], a place where alcoholic drinks are sold illegally.
**speak′er**, *n.* 1. one who speaks; esp., an orator. 2. [S-], the presiding officer of various lawmaking bodies.
**speak′ing**, *adj.* 1. that speaks or seems to speak; vivid. 2. allowing or admitting of speech: as, on *speaking* terms. *n.* the act or art of one who speaks.
**spear** (spêr), *n.* [AS. *spere*], 1. a weapon with a long shaft and a sharp head, for thrusting. 2. [var. of *spire* (stem)], a long blade or shoot, as of grass. *v.t.* 1. to pierce or stab as with a spear. 2. to catch, as fish, with a spear.
**spear′head′**, *n.* 1. the point of a spear. 2. the leading person or group, as in an attack. *v.t.* to serve as the spearhead of (an attack, etc.).
**spear′mint′**, *n.* [from its flower spikes], a fragrant plant of the mint family, used for flavoring.
**spe·cial** (spesh′əl), *adj.* [< L. *species*, kind], 1. distinctive or unique. 2. unusual; exceptional. 3. especial; chief. 4. of or for a particular purpose. 5. not general; specific. *n.* a special person or thing.
**special delivery**, mail delivery by a special messenger, for an extra fee.
**spe′cial·ist**, *n.* one who specializes in a particular study, work, etc.
**spe′cial·ize′** (-īz′), *v.i.* [-IZED, -IZING], to concentrate on a special branch of study, work, etc. —**spe′cial·i·za′tion**, *n.*
**spe′cial·ty** (-ti), *n.* [*pl.* -TIES], 1. a special quality, feature, etc. 2. an article with special features, superior quality, etc. 3. a special interest, study, etc.
**spe·cie** (spē′shi), *n.* [< L. *species*], coin, as distinguished from paper money.
**spe·cies** (spē′shiz), *n.* [*pl.* -CIES], [L., appearance], 1. a distinct kind; sort. 2. a single, distinct kind of plant or animal, having certain distinguishing characteristics.
**specif.**, specifically.
**spe·ci·fic** (spi-sif′ik), *adj.* [see SPECIFY], 1. definite; explicit. 2. peculiar to or characteristic of something. 3. of a particular sort or kind. 4. specially indicated as a cure for some disease. *n.* a specific cure. —**spe-cif′i·cal·ly**, *adv.*
**spec·i·fi·ca·tion** (spes′ə-fi-kā′shən), *n.* 1. *usually pl.* an enumeration of particulars, as to size, quality, etc. 2. something specified.
**specific gravity**, the ratio of the weight of a given volume of a substance to that of an equal volume of another substance (as water) used as a standard.
**spec·i·fy** (spes′ə-fī′), *v.t.* [-FIED, -FYING], [< L. *species*, kind + *facere*, to make], to mention or describe in detail; state explicitly.
**spec·i·men** (spes′ə-mən), *n.* [L. < *specere*, see], a part or individual used as a sample of a whole or group.
**spe·cious** (spē′shəs), *adj.* [< L. *species*, appearance], seeming to be good, sound, correct, etc. without really being so.
**speck** (spek), *n.* [AS. *specca*], 1. a small spot, mark, etc. 2. a very small bit. *v.t.* to mark with specks; spot.
**speck·le** (spek′'l), *n.* a small speck. *v.t.* [-LED, -LING], to mark with speckles.
**spec·ta·cle** (spek′tə-k'l), *n.* [< L. *specere*, see], 1. something remarkable to look at. 2. a large public show. 3. *pl.* a pair of eyeglasses. —**spec′ta·cled** (-k'ld), *adj.*
**spec·tac·u·lar** (spek-tak′yoo-lẽr), *adj.* 1. of or like a spectacle, or show. 2. unusual to a striking degree. *n.* an elaborate, extended television production.
**spec·ta·tor** (spek′tā-tẽr), *n.* [L. *spectare*, behold], one who watches without taking an active part.
**spec·ter** (spek′tẽr), *n.* [< L. *spectare*, behold], a ghost; apparition: also, Brit. sp., **spectre.** —**spec′tral**, *adj.* —**spec′tral·ly**, *adv.*
**spec·tro·scope** (spek′trə-skōp′), *n.* [< L. *spectare*, behold; + *-scope*], an optical instrument used for forming spectra for study. —**spec′tro·scop′ic** (-skop′ik), *adj.*
**spec·trum** (spek′trəm), *n.* [*pl.* -TRA (-trə), -TRUMS], [< L.; see SPECTER], a series of colored bands diffracted and arranged in order of their respective wave lengths by passage of white light through a prism, etc.
**spec·u·late** (spek′yoo-lāt′), *v.i.* [-LATED, -LATING], [< L. *specere*, see], 1. to think reflectively; ponder; conjecture. 2. to engage in a risky business venture on the chance of making huge profits. —**spec′u-la′tion**, *n.* —**spec′u·la′tive**, *adj.* —**spec′u-la′tor**, *n.*
**speech** (spēch), *n.* [< AS. *sp(r)ecan*, speak], 1. the act or manner of speaking. 2. the power to speak. 3. that which is spoken; utterance, remark, etc. 4. a talk given in public. 5. the language of a certain people.
**speech·i·fy** (spē′chə-fī′), *v.i.* [-FIED, -FYING], to make speeches: used humorously.
**speech′less**, *adj.* 1. incapable of speech. 2. silent, as from shock. —**speech′less·ly**, *adv.*
**speed** (spēd), *n.* [AS. *sped*, success], 1. rapid motion; swiftness. 2. rate of movement; velocity. *v.i.* [SPED or SPEEDED, SPEEDING], to move rapidly, esp. too rapidly. *v.t.* 1. to cause to speed. 2. to increase the speed of. 3. to help to succeed; aid. —**speed up**, to increase in speed. —**speed′er**, *n.*

**speed·om·e·ter** (spi-dom′ə-tẽr), *n.* a device attached to an automobile, etc. to indicate speed.

**speed′way′**, *n.* 1. a track for racing automobiles. 2. a road built for high-speed traffic.

**speed′y**, *adj.* [-IER, -IEST], 1. rapid; swift. 2. without delay; prompt: as, a *speedy* reply. —**speed′i·ly**, *adv.* —**speed′i·ness**, *n.*

**spell** (spel), *n.* [AS. *spel*, a saying], 1. a word or formula supposed to have some magic power. 2. irresistible influence; magical charm; fascination.

**spell** (spel), *v.t.* [SPELLED or SPELT, SPELLING], [< OFr. *espeler*], 1. to name in order the letters of (a word). 2. to make up (a word): said of specified letters. 3. to mean: as, red *spells* danger. *v.i.* to spell words.

**spell** (spel), *v.t.* [SPELLED, SPELLING], [AS. *spelian*], [Colloq.], to serve in place of (another) for an interval; relieve. *n.* 1. a period of work, duty, etc. 2. a period of anything: as, a *spell* of brooding. 3. [Colloq.], a fit of illness.

**spell′bind′** (-bīnd′), *v.t.* [-BOUND, -BINDING], to cause to be spellbound; fascinate.

**spell′bound′** (-bound′), *adj.* held by or as by a spell; fascinated.

**spell′er**, *n.* 1. one who spells words. 2. a textbook used to teach spelling.

**spell′ing**, *n.* 1. the act of forming words from letters. 2. the study of this. 3. the way a word is spelled.

**spe·lunk·er** (spi-luŋ′kẽr), *n.* [< L. *spelunca*, a cave], a cave explorer.

**spend** (spend), *v.t.* [SPENT, SPENDING], [< L. *expendere*, expend], 1. to use up, exhaust, etc.: as, his fury was *spent*. 2. to pay out (money). 3. to devote, as time, labor, etc., to something. 4. to pass (time). 5. to waste; squander. *v.i.* to pay out or use up money, etc. —**spend′er**, *n.*

**spend′thrift′** (-thrift′), *n.* one who wastes money. *adj.* wasteful.

**spent** (spent), pt. and pp. of **spend**. *adj.* 1. tired out; physically exhausted. 2. used up; worn out.

**sperm** (spũrm), *n.* [< Gr. *sperma*, seed], 1. the male generative fluid; semen. 2. any of the germ cells in it.

**sper·ma·to·zo·on** (spũr′mə-tə-zō′on), *n.* [*pl.* -ZOA (-zō′ə)], [< Gr. *sperma*, seed + *zōion*, animal], the male germ cell, found in semen, which penetrates the female egg to fertilize it.

**spew** (spū), *v.t. & v.i.* [AS. *spiwan*], to throw up from or as from the stomach; vomit; eject. *n.* spewed matter. —**spew′er**, *n.*

**sphere** (sfêr), *n.* [< Gr. *sphaira*], 1. any round body having the surface equally distant from the center at all points; globe; ball. 2. the place or range of action or existence; field of knowledge, experience, etc. *v.t.* [SPHERED, SPHERING], 1. to put in or as in a sphere. 2. to form into a sphere. —**spher·i·cal** (sfer′i-k'l), *adj.*

**sphe·roid** (sfêr′oid), *n.* a body that is almost but not quite spherical. —**sphe·roi·dal** (sfi-roi′d'l), *adj.*

**sphinc·ter** (sfiŋk′tẽr), *n.* [< Gr. *sphingein*, to draw close], a ring-shaped muscle at a body orifice. —**sphinc′ter·al**, *adj.*

**Sphinx** (sfiŋks), *n.* [< Gr. *sphinx*, strangler], 1. statue with a lion's body and a man's head, near Cairo, Egypt. 2. in *Gr. myth.*, a winged monster with a lion's body and a woman's head: it strangled passers-by unable to answer its riddle. 3. [s-], one whose character seems mysterious.

**spice** (spīs), *n.* [< L. *species*, sort], 1. any of various aromatic substances, as clove, pepper, etc., used to season food. 2. that which gives zest or piquancy. *v.t.* [SPICED, SPICING], 1. to season with spice. 2. to add zest to. —**spic′y** [-IER, -IEST], *adj.*

**spick-and-span** (spik′'n-span′), *adj.* [< *spike*, nail; + ON. *spānn*, a chip], 1. new; fresh. 2. neat and clean; tidy.

**spi·der** (spī′dẽr), *n.* [< AS. *spinnan*, spin], 1. any of various small arachnids that have eight legs and spin webs. 2. a frying pan.

**spiel** (spēl), *n.* [G., play], [Slang], a talk or harangue, as by a salesman. —**spiel′er**, *n.*

**spig·ot** (spig′ət), *n.* [ME. *spigote*], 1. a plug to stop the vent in a cask, etc. 2. a faucet.

**spike** (spīk), *n.* [prob. < ON. *spikr*], 1. a sharp-pointed projection, as (in *pl.*) on the sole of a shoe to prevent slipping. 2. a long, heavy nail. *v.t.* [SPIKED, SPIKING], 1. to fasten or fit as with spikes. 2. to pierce with, or impale on, a spike. 3. to thwart, as a scheme. 4. [Slang], to add alcoholic liquor to (a drink). —**spik′y**, *adj.*

**spike** (spīk), *n.* [L. *spica*], 1. an ear of grain. 2. a long flower cluster.

**spill** (spil), *v.t.* [SPILLED or SPILT (spilt), SPILLING], [AS. *spillan*, destroy], 1. to allow (a fluid), esp. unintentionally, to run, scatter, or flow over from a container. 2. to shed (blood). 3. [Colloq.], to throw off (a rider, etc.). *v.i.* to be spilled; overflow. *n.* 1. a spilling. 2. [Colloq.], a fall, as from a horse.

**spill′way′**, *n.* a channel to carry off excess water.

**spin** (spin), *v.t.* [SPUN, SPINNING], [AS. *spinnan*], 1. to draw out and twist fibers of (wool, cotton, etc.) into thread. 2. to make (thread, etc.) thus. 3. to make (a web, cocoon, etc.), as a spider. 4. to tell (a story) slowly and in detail. 5. to rotate swiftly. *v.i.* 1. to spin thread or yarn. 2. to form a web, cocoon, etc. 3. to whirl. 4. to seem to be spinning from dizziness. 5. to move along swiftly and smoothly. *n.* 1. a whirling or spiral movement. 2. a swift ride in a vehicle. —**spin′ner**, *n.*

**spin·ach** (spin′ich, -ij), *n.* [< Sp. < Ar. *isbānah*], a plant with dark-green, juicy, edible leaves, usually eaten cooked.

**spi·nal** (spī′n'l), *adj.* of the spine or spinal cord. —**spi′nal·ly**, *adv.*

**spinal column**, the series of joined vertebrae forming the axial support for the skeleton; backbone.

**spinal cord**, the thick cord of nerve tissue in the spinal column.

**spin·dle** (spin′d'l), *n.* [< AS. *spinnan*, spin], 1. a long, slender rod or pin used in spinning for twisting, winding, or holding thread. 2. something shaped like a spindle. 3. any rod, pin, etc. that revolves or serves as an axis for a revolving part.

**spin·dling** (spin′dliŋ), *adj.* slender in proportion to length or height.

**spin·dly** (spin′dli), *adj.* [-DLIER, -DLIEST], spindling. —**spin′dli·ness**, *n.*

**spine** (spīn), *n.* [< L. *spina*, thorn], 1. a sharp, stiff projection, as a thorn of the cactus, or a porcupine's quill. 2. anything like this. 3. the spinal column. 4. anything like this, as the back of a book. —**spin′y** [-IER, -IEST], *adj.*

**spine′less**, *adj.* 1. having no spine or spines. 2. without courage or will power.

**spin·et** (spin′it), *n.* [prob. < G. *Spinetti* (c. 1500), It. inventor], a small upright piano.

**spinning wheel**, a simple spinning machine with one spindle driven by a large wheel.

**spin·ster** (spin′stẽr), *n.* [ME. < *spinnen*, to spin], an unmarried woman, esp. an older one; old maid. —**spin′ster·hood′**, *n.*

**spi·rae·a, spi·re·a** (spī-rē′ə), *n.* [< Gr. *speira*, a coil], a shrub of the rose family with clusters of small pink or white flowers.

**spi·ral** (spī′rəl), *adj.* [< Gr. *speira*], circling continuously around a point in constantly increasing (or decreasing) curves, or in constantly changing planes. *n.* a spiral curve or coil. *v.i. & v.t.* [-RALED or -RALLED, -RALING or -RALLING], to move in or form (into) a spiral. —**spi′ral·ly**, *adv.*

**spire** (spīr), *n.* [AS. *spir*], 1. a sprout, spike, or stalk of a plant. 2. the top part of a pointed, tapering object. 3. anything that tapers to a point, as a steeple. *v.i.* [SPIRED, SPIRING], to taper upward to a point.

**spir·it** (spir′it), *n.* [< L. *spirare*, breathe], 1. the soul. 2. [also S-], life, will, thought, etc., regarded as separate from matter. 3. a supernatural being, as a ghost, angel, fairy, etc. 4. an individual: as, a brave *spirit*. 5. *often pl.* disposition; mood: as, high *spirits*. 6. vivacity, courage, etc. 7. enthusiastic loyalty: as, school *spirit*. 8. true intention: as, the *spirit* of the law. 9. a pervading animating principle; essential quality: as, the *spirit* of the times. 10. *often pl.* distilled alcoholic liquor. *v.t.* to carry (*away* or *off*) secretly and swiftly. —**spir′it·less**, *adj.*

**spir′it·ed,** *adj.* lively; vigorous.

**spir·it·u·al** (spir′i-chōō-əl), *adj.* 1. of the spirit or soul, in a religious or moral aspect. 2. of or consisting of spirit; not corporeal. 3. religious; sacred. *n.* a religious folk song of American Negro origin. —**spir′it·u·al′i·ty** (-al′ə-ti) [*pl.* -TIES], *n.* —**spir′it·u·al·ly**, *adv.*

**spir′it·u·al·ism,** *n.* the belief that the dead survive as spirits which can communicate with the living. —**spir′it·u·al·ist**, *n.* —**spir′-it·u·al·is′tic**, *adj.*

**spir′it·u·al·ize′** (-ə-līz′), *v.t.* [-IZED, -IZING], to make spiritual. —**spir′it·u·al·i·za′tion**, *n.*

**spi·ro·chete** (spī′rə-kēt′), *n.* [< Gr. *speira*, spiral + *chaitē*, hair], any of various spiral-shaped bacteria, some of which cause disease.

**spit** (spit), *n.* [AS. *spitu*], 1. a thin, pointed rod on which meat is roasted over a fire. 2. a narrow point of land extending from the shore. *v.t.* [SPITTED, SPITTING], to impale as on a spit.

**spit** (spit), *v.t.* [SPAT or SPIT, SPITTING], [AS. *spittan*], 1. to eject from the mouth. 2. to eject explosively. *v.i.* to eject saliva from the mouth. *n.* 1. a spitting. 2. saliva. —**spit and image**, [Colloq.], perfect likeness.

**spite** (spīt), *n.* [< *despite*], ill will; malice; grudge. *v.t.* [SPITED, SPITING], to vent one's spite upon by hurting, frustrating, etc. —**in spite of**, regardless of. —**spite′ful**, *adj.*

**spit·tle** (spit′'l), *n.* spit; saliva.

**spit·toon** (spi-tōōn′), *n.* a container to spit into.

**splash** (splash), *v.t.* [< *plash*], 1. to cause (a liquid) to scatter. 2. to dash a liquid, mud, etc. on, so as to wet or soil. *v.i.* to move, strike, etc. with a splash. *n.* 1. the act or sound of splashing. 2. a spot made as by splashing. —**make a splash**, [Colloq.], to attract great attention. —**splash′y**, *adj.*

**splat·ter** (splat′ẽr), *n., v.t. & v.i.* spatter; splash.

**splay** (splā), *adj.* [< *display*], spreading out. *v.t. & v.i.* to spread out.

**splay′foot′**, *n.* [*pl.* -FEET], a foot that is flat and turned outward.

**spleen** (splēn), *n.* [< Gr. *splēn*], 1. a large ductless organ in the upper left part of the abdomen: it modifies the blood structure. 2. malice; spite. —**spleen′ful**, *adj.*

**splen·did** (splen′did), *adj.* [< L. *splendere*, to shine], 1. shining; brilliant. 2. magnificent; gorgeous. 3. grand; glorious. 4. [Colloq.], very good; fine. —**splen′did·ly**, *adv.*

**splen·dor** (splen′dẽr), *n.* [< L. *splendere*, to shine], 1. great luster; brilliance. 2. magnificent richness or glory. Also, Brit. sp., **splendour.** —**splen′dor·ous**, **splen′drous**, *adj.*

**sple·net·ic** (spli-net′ik), *adj.* 1. of the spleen. 2. irritable; peevish.

**splice** (splīs), *v.t.* [SPLICED, SPLICING], [< MD. *splissen*], 1. to join, as ropes, by weaving together the end strands. 2. to join (pieces of wood) by overlapping the ends. *n.* a joint made by splicing.

**splint** (splint), *n.* [< MD. *splinte*], 1. a thin strip of wood, etc. woven with others to make baskets, chair seats, etc. 2. a strip of wood, etc. used to hold a broken bone in place.

**splin·ter** (splin′tẽr), *v.t. & v.i.* [see SPLINT], to break or split into thin, sharp pieces. *n.* a thin, sharp piece, as of wood, made by splitting, etc. —**splin′ter·y**, *adj.*

**split** (split), *v.t. & v.i.* [SPLIT, SPLITTING], [MD. *splitten*], 1. to separate lengthwise into two or more parts. 2. to break or tear apart. 3. to divide into shares. 4. to disunite. 5. *a*) to break into atoms: said of a molecule. *b*) to produce nuclear fission in or undergo nuclear fission: said of an atom. *n.* 1. a splitting. 2. a break; crack. 3. a division in a group, etc. *adj.* divided; separated.

**split infinitive,** in *grammar*, an infinitive with the verb and the *to* separated by an adverb. Example: *to slowly change*.

**split′-lev′el,** *adj.* designating or of a type of house in which each floor level is about a half story above or below the adjacent one.

**split′ting,** *adj.* 1. that splits. 2. severe or sharp, as a headache.

**splotch** (sploch), *n.* [prob. < *spot* + *blotch*], an irregular spot, splash, or stain. *v.t.* to mark with splotches. —**splotch′y**, *adj.*

**splurge** (splũrj), *n.* [echoic], [Colloq.], any very showy display, effort, etc. *v.i.* [SPLURGED, SPLURGING], [Colloq.], to make a splurge. —**splurg′er**, *n.*

**splut·ter** (splut′ẽr), *v.i.* [var. of *sputter*], 1. to make hissing or spitting sounds. 2. to speak hurriedly and confusedly. *n.* a spluttering. —**splut′ter·er**, *n.*

**spoil** (spoil), *v.i.* [SPOILED or SPOILT, SPOILING], [< L. *spolium*, plunder], 1. to damage so as to make useless, etc. 2. to impair the enjoyment, etc. of. 3. to cause to expect too much by overindulgence. 4. [Archaic], to rob; plunder. *v.i.* to become spoiled; decay, etc., as food. *n. usually pl.* goods taken by force; booty. —**spoil′age**, *n.*

**spoil′sport′**, *n.* one whose actions spoil the pleasure of others.

**spoils system,** the treating of public offices as the booty of a successful political party.

**spoke** (spōk), *n.* [AS. *spaca*], 1. any of the braces extending from the hub to the rim of a wheel. 2. a ladder rung.

**spoke** (spōk), pt. of **speak.**

**spo·ken** (spō′kən), pp. of **speak.** *adj.* 1. uttered; oral. 2. having a (specified kind of) voice: as, *soft-spoken*.

**spokes·man** (spōks′mən), *n.* [*pl.* -MEN], one who speaks for another or others.

**spo·li·a·tion** (spō′li-ā′shən), *n.* [< L. *spoliare*, spoil], robbery; plundering.

**sponge** (spunj), *n.* [< Gr. *spongia*], 1. a plantlike sea animal with a porous structure. 2. the highly absorbent skeleton of such animals, used for washing surfaces, etc. 3. any substance like this, as a synthetic sponge of plastic. 4. a sponge bath. *v.t.* [SPONGED, SPONGING], 1. to wipe, dampen, absorb, etc. as with a sponge. 2. [Colloq.], to get as by begging, imposition, etc. *v.i.* [Colloq.], to live as a parasite upon others. —**spong′er**, *n.* —**spon′gy** [-GIER, -GIEST], *adj.*

**sponge bath,** a bath taken by using a wet sponge or cloth without getting into water.

**sponge′cake′**, *n.* a light, porous kind of cake: also **sponge cake.**

**spon·sor** (spon′sẽr), *n.* [L. < *spondere*, promise solemnly], 1. one who assumes responsibility as surety for, or endorser of, some person or thing. 2. a godparent. 3. a business firm, etc. that pays for a radio or television program advertising its product. *v.t.* to be a sponsor of. —**spon′sor·ship′**, *n.*

**spon·ta·ne·i·ty** (spon′tə-nē′ə-ti), *n.* 1. a being spontaneous. 2. [*pl.* -TIES], a spontaneous movement, action, etc.

**spon·ta·ne·ous** (spon-tā′ni-əs), *adj.* [< L. *sponte*, of free will], 1. moved by a natural feeling or impulse, without constraint, effort, etc. 2. acting by internal energy, force, etc. —**spon·ta′ne·ous·ly**, *adv.*

**spontaneous combustion,** the process of catching fire as a result of heat generated by internal chemical action.

**spoof** (spōōf), *n.* [Slang], a hoax or joke. *v.t. & v.i.* [Slang], to fool; deceive; trick.

**spook** (spōōk), *n.* [D.], [Colloq.], a ghost. —**spook′y** [-IER, -IEST], *adj.*

**spool** (spōōl), *n.* [< MD. *spoele*], a cylinder upon which thread, wire, etc. is wound.

**spoon** (spōōn), *n.* [< AS. *spon*, a chip], 1. a utensil consisting of a small, shallow bowl with a handle, used for eating, stirring, etc. 2. something shaped like a spoon. 3. a wooden-headed golf club with more loft than a driver. *v.t.* to take up with a spoon. *v.i.* [Colloq.], to make love, as by kissing and hugging. —**spoon′ful′** [*pl.* -FULS], *n.*

**spoon·er·ism** (spōōn′ẽr-iz′m), *n.* [< Prof. W. A. *Spooner* of Oxford], an unintentional interchange of initial sounds in words. Example: It is kistumary to cuss the bride.

**spoon′feed′**, *v.t.* [-FED, -FEEDING], 1. to feed with a spoon. 2. to pamper; coddle.

**spoor** (spoor, spôr), *n.* [D.], the track or trail of a wild animal.

**spo·rad·ic** (spô-rad′ik), *adj.* [< Gr. *sporas*, scattered], happening or appearing in isolated instances: as, *sporadic* storms. —**spo·rad′i·cal·ly**, *adv.*

**spore** (spôr), *n.* [< Gr. *spora*, a seed], 1. a small reproductive body produced by mosses, ferns, etc. and capable of giving rise to a new individual. 2. any seed, germ, etc. *v.i.* [SPORED, SPORING], to develop spores.

**sport** (spôrt), *n.* [< *disport*], 1. any recreational activity; specif., a game, competition, etc. requiring bodily exertion. 2. fun; play. 3. a thing joked about. 4. [Colloq.], a sportsmanlike person. 5. [Colloq.], a gay, fast, showy person. 6. in *biology*, a plant or animal markedly different from the normal type. *v.t.* [Colloq.], to display: as, to *sport* a new tie. *v.i.* 1. to play. 2. to joke. *adj.* 1. of or for sports. 2. suitable for casual wear: said of clothes. —**in** (or **for**) **sport**, in jest. —**make sport of**, to mock or ridicule.

**sport′ing,** *adj.* 1. of or interested in sports. 2. sportsmanlike; fair. 3. of games, etc. involving gambling.

**sports,** *adj.* sport: as, *sports* clothes.

**sports′man,** *n.* [*pl.* -MEN], 1. a man who takes part in sports, esp. fishing, hunting, etc. 2. one who plays fair and can lose without complaint or win without boasting. —**sports′man·like′**, *adj.* —**sports′man·ship′**, *n.*

**spot** (spot), *n.* [prob. < MD. *spotte*], 1. a small area differing in color, etc. from the surrounding area. 2. a stain, speck, etc. 3. a flaw or defect. 4. a locality; place. *v.t.* [SPOTTED, SPOTTING], 1. to mark with spots. 2. to stain; blemish. 3. to place; locate. 4. [Colloq.], to see; recognize. 5. [Colloq.], to allow as a handicap. *v.i.* 1. to become marked with spots. 2. to make a stain, as ink. *adj.* 1. ready: as, *spot* cash. 2. made at random: as, a *spot* check. —**hit the spot**, [Colloq.], to satisfy a craving. —**in a spot**, [Colloq.], in trouble. —**on the spot**, [Slang], in a bad or demanding situation. —**spot′less**, *adj.* —**spot′ted**, *adj.*

**spot′light′**, *n.* 1. a strong beam of light focused on a particular person, thing, etc. 2. a lamp used to project such a light. 3. public notice.

**spot′ter,** *n.* one whose duty is to keep a lookout, as for enemy aircraft.

**spot′ty,** *adj.* [-TIER, -TIEST], 1. having, occurring in, or marked with spots. 2. not uniform or consistent. —**spot′ti·ness**, *n.*

**spous·al** (spou′z′l), *adj.* [< *espousal*], nuptial.

**spouse** (spous, spouz), *n.* [< L. *sponsus*, betrothed], a husband or wife.

**spout** (spout), *n.* [< MD. *spuiten*, to spout], 1. a projecting pipe or orifice by which a liquid is poured. 2. a stream, etc. as of a liquid from a spout. *v.t. & v.i.* 1. to shoot out (liquid, etc.) as from a spout. 2. to utter or speak in a loud, pompous manner.

**sprain** (sprān), *v.t.* [< L. *ex*, out + *premere*, to press], to wrench a ligament or muscle of (a joint) without dislocating the bones. *n.* an injury resulting from this.

**sprang** (spraŋ), pt. of **spring.**

**sprat** (sprat), *n.* [AS. *sprot*], a small European fish of the herring family.

**sprawl** (sprôl), *v.i.* [AS. *spreawlian*], 1. to sit or lie with the limbs in a relaxed or awkward position. 2. to spread awkwardly, as handwriting, etc. *v.t.* to cause to sprawl. *n.* a sprawling movement or position.

**spray** (sprā), *n.* [prob. < LG.], 1. a mist of fine liquid particles. 2. a jet of such particles, as from a spray gun. 3. a device for spraying. 4. something likened to a spray. *v.t. & v.i.* 1. to direct a spray (upon). 2. to scatter or shoot out in a spray.

**spray** (sprā), *n.* [ME. *sprai*], a small branch of a tree, etc., with leaves, flowers, etc.

**spray gun,** a device that shoots out a spray of liquid, as paint or insecticide.

**spread** (spred), *v.t. & v.i.* [SPREAD, SPREADING], [AS. *sprædan*], 1. to open out; expand; unfold. 2. to stretch out; extend. 3. to distribute or be distributed over an area. 4. to extend over a certain period of time. 5. to make or be made widely known, felt, etc. 6. to cover or be covered with something, as in a thin layer. 7. to set (a table) for a meal. 8. to push or be pushed apart. *n.* 1. the act or extent of spreading. 2. an expanse. 3. a cloth cover for a table, bed, etc. 4. butter, jam, etc. used on bread. 5. [Colloq.], a meal. —**spread′er**, *n.*

**spree** (sprē), *n.* [< earlier *spray*], 1. a noisy frolic. 2. a drinking bout.

**sprig** (sprig), *n.* [ME. *sprigge*], a little twig or spray.

**spright·ly** (sprīt′li), *adj.* [-LIER, -LIEST], [see SPRITE], gay; lively. *adv.* gaily; briskly.

**spring** (spriŋ), *v.i.* [SPRANG or SPRUNG, SPRUNG, SPRINGING], [AS. *springan*], 1. to leap; bound. 2. to appear, come, etc. suddenly. 3. to be resilient or elastic. 4. to arise from some source; grow or develop. 5. to become warped, split, etc. 6. to rise up above surrounding objects. Often followed by *up*. *v.t.* 1. to cause to leap forth suddenly. 2. to leap over. 3. to cause to snap shut, as a trap. 4. to cause to warp, split, etc. 5. to make known suddenly. 6. [Slang], to get (someone) released from jail. *n.* 1. a leap, or the distance so covered. 2. a sudden flying back. 3. resilience; elasticity. 4. a device, as a coil of wire, that returns to its original form after being forced out of shape. 5. a flow of water from the ground. 6. a source or origin. 7. that season of the year following winter, in which plants begin to grow again. 8. any period of beginning. 9. a bending, warping, etc. *adj.* 1. of, for, appearing in, or planted in the spring. 2. having, or supported on, springs. 3. coming from a spring, as water. —**spring a leak**, to begin to leak suddenly.

**spring′board′**, *n.* a flexible, springy board used as a take-off in leaping or diving.

**spring fever,** the listlessness that many people feel during the first warm days of spring.
**spring′time′,** *n.* the season of spring: also **spring′tide′.**
**spring′y,** *adj.* [-IER, -IEST], flexible; elastic; resilient. —**spring′i·ly,** *adv.* —**spring′i·ness,** *n.*
**sprin·kle** (spriŋ′k'l), *v.t.* & *v.i.* [-KLED, -KLING], [< ME. *sprengen*, scatter], 1. to scatter or fall in drops or particles. 2. to scatter drops or particles (upon). 3. to rain lightly. *n.* 1. a sprinkling. 2. a light rain. —**sprin′kler,** *n.*
**sprint** (sprint), *v.i.* & *n.* [ME. *sprenten*], run or race at full speed for a short distance.
**sprit** (sprit), *n.* [AS. *sprēot*], a pole extended upward from a mast to the corner of a fore-and-aft sail.
**sprite** (sprīt), *n.* [< L. *spiritus*, spirit], an elf, pixie, fairy, or goblin.
**sprock·et** (sprok′it), *n.* [prob. < LG.], 1. any of the teeth, as on a wheel, arranged to fit the links of a chain. 2. a wheel fitted with sprockets: in full, **sprocket wheel.**
**sprout** (sprout), *v.i.* [AS. *sprutan*], to begin to grow; give off shoots or buds. *v.t.* to cause to sprout. *n.* 1. a young growth on a plant; shoot. 2. a new growth from a bud, etc.
**spruce** (sprōōs), *n.* [< ME. *Spruce*, Prussia], 1. an evergreen tree with needle-shaped leaves. 2. its wood.
**spruce** (sprōōs), *adj.* [SPRUCER, SPRUCEST], [< *Spruce* (Prussian) leather; see prec.], neat; trim; smart. *v.t.* & *v.i.* [SPRUCED, SPRUCING], to make or become spruce (with *up*). —**spruce′ly,** *adv.* —**spruce′ness,** *n.*
**sprung** (spruŋ), pp. and alt. pt. of **spring.**
**spry** (sprī), *adj.* [SPRIER or SPRYER, SPRIEST or SPRYEST], [< ON.], full of life; active; agile. —**spry′ly,** *adv.* —**spry′ness,** *n.*
**spud** (spud), *n.* [Colloq.], a potato.
**spume** (spūm), *n.* [< L. *spuere*, spit out], foam, froth, or scum.
**spun** (spun), pt. and pp. of **spin.** *adj.* formed by or as if by spinning.
**spunk** (spuŋk), *n.* [< Gael. *sponc*, tinder], [Colloq.], courage; spirit; pluck. —**spunk′y,** [-IER, -IEST], *adj.* —**spunk′i·ness,** *n.*
**spur** (spũr), *n.* [AS. *spura*], 1. a pointed device worn on the heel by horsemen, used to urge the horse forward. 2. anything that urges; stimulus. 3. any spurlike projection. 4. a short railroad track connected with the main track. *v.t.* [SPURRED, SPURRING], 1. to prick with spurs. 2. to urge; incite. *v.i.* to hurry; hasten. —**on the spur of the moment,** abruptly and impulsively.
**spu·ri·ous** (spyoor′i-əs), *adj.* [L. *spurius*], 1. illegitimate. 2. false; not genuine.
**spurn** (spũrn), *v.t.* [AS. *spurnan*], to reject with contempt; scorn.
**spurt** (spũrt), *v.t.* & *v.i.* [< AS. *sprutan*, to sprout], 1. to shoot forth in a gush or jet. 2. to show a sudden, brief burst of energy. *n.* 1. a sudden shooting forth; jet. 2. a sudden, brief burst of energy or activity.
**sput·nik** (spoot′nik, sput′-), *n.* [Russ.; lit., co-traveler], any of the artificial earth satellites put into orbit by the U.S.S.R., beginning in October, 1957.
**sput·ter** (sput′ẽr), *v.i.* & *v.t.* [< *spout* + *-er*], 1. to spit or throw out (bits or drops) in an explosive manner. 2. to speak in a confused, explosive manner. *n.* a sputtering, as of frying fat. —**sput′ter·er,** *n.*
**spu·tum** (spū′təm), *n.* [*pl.* -TA (-tə)], [< L. *spuere*, to spit], 1. saliva. 2. saliva, mucus, etc. spat out.
**spy** (spī), *v.t.* [SPIED, SPYING], [< OHG. *spehōn*, examine], 1. to watch closely and secretly (usually with *out*). 2. to catch sight of; see. 3. to discover by close examination. *v.i.* to watch closely and secretly; act as a spy. *n.* [*pl.* SPIES], 1. one who keeps close and secret watch on others. 2. a person employed by a government to get secret information on the military affairs, etc. of another government.
**spy′glass′,** *n.* a small telescope.
**Sq., sq.,** square.
**squab** (skwäb), *n.* [prob. < ON.], a nestling pigeon.
**squab·ble** (skwäb′'l), *v.i.* [-BLED, -BLING], [< Scand.], to quarrel noisily over a small matter; wrangle. *n.* a noisy, petty quarrel.
**squad** (skwäd), *n.* [see SQUARE], 1. a small group of soldiers, subdivision of a platoon. 2. any small group of people acting together.
**squad·ron** (skwäd′rən), *n.* [< It. *squadra*, a square], a unit of warships, cavalry, military aviation, etc.
**squal·id** (skwäl′id), *adj.* [< L. *squalere*, be foul], 1. foul; unclean. 2. wretched.
**squall** (skwôl), *n.* [prob. < Scand.], a brief, violent windstorm, usually with rain or snow. *v.i.* to storm briefly. —**squall′y,** *adj.*
**squall** (skwôl), *v.t.* & *v.i.* [prob. echoic], to cry or scream loudly and harshly. *n.* a harsh, loud cry. —**squall′er,** *n.*
**squal·or** (skwäl′ẽr), *n.* [L., foulness], a being squalid; filth and wretchedness.
**squand·er** (skwän′dẽr), *v.t.* [prob. < dial. *squander*, to scatter], to spend or use wastefully. *n.* a squandering.
**square** (skwâr), *n.* [< L. *ex-*, out + *quadrere*, to square], 1. a plane figure having four equal sides and four right angles. 2. anything of or approximating this shape. 3. an area bounded by streets on four sides. 4. one side of such an area. 5. an open area bounded by several streets, used as a park, etc. 6. an instrument used for making or testing right angles. 7. the product of a number multiplied by itself. 8. [Slang], an old-fashioned or unsophisticated person. *v.t.* [SQUARED, SQUARING], 1. to make into a square (sense 1). 2. to make straight, even, right-angled, etc. 3. to settle; adjust: as, to *square* accounts. 4. to adapt; regulate: as, *square* these figures with that chart. 5. to multiply (a quantity) by itself. *v.i.* to fit; agree; accord. *adj.* 1. having four equal sides and four right angles. 2. forming a right angle. 3. straight, level, even, etc. 4. leaving no balance; balanced. 5. just; fair. 6. direct; straightforward. 7. designating or of a unit of surface measure in the form of a square: as, a *square* foot. 8. solid; thickset: as, a *square* build. 9. [Colloq.], satisfying; substantial: as, a *square* meal. *adv.* in a square manner. —**square off** (or **away**), to assume a posture of attack or self-defense. —**square oneself,** [Colloq.], to make amends.
**square dance,** a dance in which the couples are grouped in a given form, as a square.
**square′-rigged′,** *adj.* rigged with four-sided sails on a yard suspended horizontally across the mast. —**square′-rig′ger,** *n.*
**square root,** the quantity which when squared will produce a given quantity: as, the *square root* of 9 is 3.
**squash** (skwäsh), *v.t.* [< L. *ex-*, intens. + *quatere*, to shake], 1. to beat or press into a soft, flat mass; crush. 2. to quash; suppress. *v.i.* 1. to be squashed or crushed. 2. to make a sound of squashing. *n.* 1. something squashed. 2. the act or sound of squashing. 3. a game played in a walled court with rackets and a rubber ball.
**squash** (skwäsh), *n.* [< Algonquian], the fleshy fruit of various plants of the gourd family, eaten as a vegetable.
**squash·y** (skwäsh′i), *adj.* [-IER, -IEST], 1. soft and wet; mushy. 2. easily squashed or crushed. —**squash′i·ness,** *n.*
**squat** (skwät), *v.i.* [SQUATTED or SQUAT, SQUATTING], [< L. *ex-*, intens. + *cogere*, to force], 1. to sit on the heels with the knees

bent. 2. to crouch with the feet drawn in close to the body. 3. to settle on land without right or title. 4. to settle on public land in order to get title to it. *adj.* short and heavy or thick: also **squat'ty.** *n.* the position of squatting. —**squat'ter,** *n.*

**squaw** (skwô), *n.* [< Algonquian], an American Indian woman or wife.

**squawk** (skwôk), *v.i.* [echoic], 1. to utter a loud, harsh cry. 2. [Slang], to complain loudly. *n.* 1. a loud, harsh cry. 2. [Slang], a raucous complaint. —**squawk'er,** *n.*

**squeak** (skwēk), *v.i.* [echoic], to utter or make a thin, sharp, high-pitched cry or sound. *v.t.* to say in a squeak. *n.* a high, sharp cry or sound. —**narrow** (or **close** or **near**) **squeak,** [Colloq.], a narrow escape. —**squeak'y** [-IER, -IEST], *adj.*

**squeal** (skwēl), *v.i.* [prob. echoic], 1. to utter a sharp, high-pitched, prolonged cry. 2. [Slang], to act as an informer. *v.t.* to utter in a squeal. *n.* a squealing. —**squeal'er,** *n.*

**squeam·ish** (skwēm'ish), *adj.* [ME. *squaimous*], 1. easily nauseated. 2. easily shocked; prudish; fastidious.

**squee·gee** (skwē'jē), *n.* [prob. < *squeeze*], a rubber-edged tool for scraping water from a flat surface.

**squeeze** (skwēz), *v.t.* [SQUEEZED, SQUEEZING], [< AS. *-cwysan*, crush], 1. to press hard, esp. from two or more sides. 2. to extract by pressure: as, to *squeeze* juice from a lime. 3. to force by pressing: as, we can *squeeze* it in. 4. to embrace closely; hug. *v.i.* 1. to yield to pressure. 2. to exert pressure. 3. to force one's way by pushing. *n.* 1. a squeezing or being squeezed. 2. a close embrace; hug. 3. the state of being closely pressed or packed; crush. —**squeez'er,** *n.*

**squelch** (skwelch), *n.* [< fusion of *quell* + *crush*], [Colloq.], a crushing retort, etc. *v.t.* to crush or suppress or silence completely.

**squib** (skwib), *n.* [prob. echoic], 1. any firework that burns with a hissing noise, ending in an explosion. 2. a short, witty verbal attack; lampoon.

**squid** (skwid), *n.* [prob. < dial. for *squirt*], a long, slender sea mollusk with ten arms, two much longer than the others.

**squint** (skwint), *v.i.* [cf. D. *schuinte*, slant], 1. to peer with the eyes partly closed. 2. to look sideways or askance. 3. to be cross-eyed. *n.* 1. a squinting. 2. a being cross-eyed. 3. [Colloq.], a quick or sidelong glance.

**squire** (skwīr), *n.* [contr. of *esquire*], 1. in England, a title of respect for a large rural landowner. 2. a title of respect for a justice of the peace, etc. 3. an attendant; esp., a man escorting a woman. *v.t.* & *v.i.* [SQUIRED, SQUIRING], to act as a squire (to).

**squirm** (skwũrm), *v.i.* [prob. echoic], 1. to twist and turn the body; wriggle. 2. to show or feel distress. —**squirm'y,** *adj.*

**squir·rel** (skwũr'əl), *n.* [< Gr. *skia*, a shadow + *oura*, tail], 1. a small, tree-dwelling rodent with heavy fur and a long, bushy tail. 2. its fur.

**squirt** (skwũrt), *v.t.* & *v.i.* [< LG. *swirtjen*], 1. to spurt; shoot out in a jet. 2. to wet with liquid so shot out. *n.* 1. a squirting or jet. 2. [Colloq.], a small or insignificant person.

**Sr.,** in *chem.*, strontium.

**Sr.,** Senior.

**S.R.O.,** standing room only.

**S.S., SS, S/S,** steamship.

**St.,** 1. Saint. 2. Strait. 3. Street.

**stab** (stab), *v.t.* & *v.i.* [STABBED, STABBING], [< ME. *stob*, a stake], 1. to pierce or wound as with a knife. 2. to thrust (a knife, etc.) into a thing. 3. to pain sharply. *n.* 1. a wound made by stabbing. 2. a thrust, as with a knife. 3. a sharp pain. 4. [Colloq.], an attempt. —**stab'ber,** *n.*

**sta·bil·i·ty** (stə-bil'ə-ti), *n.* [*pl.* -TIES], 1. a being stable, or fixed; steadiness. 2. firmness of character, purpose, etc. 3. permanence.

**sta·bi·lize** (stā'bə-līz'), *v.t.* [-LIZED, -LIZING], 1. to make stable, or firm. 2. to keep from changing, as in price. —**sta'bi·li·za'tion,** *n.*

**sta·ble** (stā'b'l), *adj.* [< L. *stare*, to stand], 1. not likely to break down, fall over, or give way; firm. 2. firm in character, purpose, etc. 3. resisting change; permanent.

**sta·ble** (stā'b'l), *n.* [< L. *stare*, to stand], 1. a building in which horses or cattle are sheltered and fed. 2. all the race horses belonging to one owner. *v.t.* & *v.i.* [-BLED, -BLING], to lodge, keep, or be kept in a stable.

**stac·ca·to** (stə-kä'tō), *adj.* [It., detached], in *music*, with distinct breaks between successive tones; abrupt.

**stack** (stak), *n.* [< ON. *stakkr*], 1. a large, symmetrical pile of straw, hay, etc. 2. any orderly pile. 3. a chimney or smokestack. 4. a set of bookshelves. *v.t.* to arrange in a stack. —**stack the cards** (or **deck**), 1. to arrange a deck of playing cards secretly so as to control the dealing. 2. to prearrange circumstances unfairly.

**sta·di·um** (stā'di-əm), *n.* [*pl.* -UMS], [< Gr. *stadion*, a unit of length], a place for outdoor games, meetings, etc. surrounded by tiers of seats.

**staff** (staf, stäf), *n.* [*pl.* STAVES; *also, and for 3, 4, 5 always,* STAFFS], [AS. *stæf*], 1. a stick or rod used as for support, a symbol of authority, etc. 2. figuratively, a support. 3. a group of people assisting a leader. 4. a group of advisory officers serving a military or naval commanding officer. 5. a specific group of workers: as, a teaching *staff*. 6. the five horizontal lines and four intermediate spaces on which music is written. *v.t.* to provide with a staff, as of workers.

**stag** (stag), *n.* [AS. *stagga*], a full-grown male deer. *adj.* for men only: as, a *stag* party.

**stage** (stāj), *n.* [< L. *stare*, to stand], 1. a platform. 2. an area or platform upon which plays, etc. are presented. 3. the theater, or acting as a profession. 4. the scene of an event. 5. a stopping place, or the distance between stops, on a journey. 6. a stagecoach. 7. a period in a process of development, etc.: as, the larval *stage*. 8. one of two or more propulsion systems used in sequence to power a rocket into outer space: when each is exhausted, it separates from the rest. *v.t.* [STAGED, STAGING], 1. to present as on a stage. 2. to plan and carry out: as, to *stage* an attack.

**stage'coach',** *n.* a horse-drawn public coach traveling a regular route.

**stage'hand',** *n.* one who sets up scenery, lights, etc. on a stage.

**stage'-struck',** *adj.* intensely eager to become an actor or actress.

**stag·ger** (stag'ẽr), *v.i.* [< ON. *stakra*, cause to stumble], 1. to totter or reel, as from a blow, fatigue, etc. 2. to falter; waver. *v.t.* 1. to cause to stagger, as with a blow. 2. to affect strongly, as with grief. 3. to make zigzag in arrangement. 4. to arrange (periods, duties, etc.) so as to eliminate crowding. *n.* 1. a staggering; reeling. 2. *pl.* [construed as sing.], a nervous disease of horses, etc. —**stag'ger·ing·ly,** *adv.*

**stag·ing** (stāj'iŋ), *n.* 1. scaffolding. 2. the act of presenting a play on the stage.

**stag·nant** (stag'nənt), *adj.* [< L. *stagnare*, stagnate], 1. not flowing or moving. 2. foul from lack of movement: said of water, etc. 3. dull; sluggish: as, a *stagnant* mind.

**stag·nate** (stag'nāt), *v.i.* [-NATED, -NATING], to be or become stagnant. —**stag·na'tion,** *n.*

**staid** (stād), *adj.* [archaic pt. & pp. of *stay* (to remain)], sober; sedate. —**staid'ly,** *adv.*

**stain** (stān), *v.t.* [< *distain* < L. *dis-*, from + *tingere*, to color], 1. to spoil by discoloring or soiling. 2. to corrupt; dishonor. 3. to color (wood, etc.) with a dye. *n.* 1. a color or spot resulting from staining. 2. a moral blemish; dishonor. 3. a dye for staining wood, etc.

**stainless steel,** steel alloyed with chromium, etc., virtually immune to rust and corrosion.

**stair** (stâr), *n.* [< AS. *stæger*], 1. *usually pl.* a staircase. 2. one of a series of steps between levels.

**stair'case',** *n.* a flight of stairs with a handrail: also **stair'way'**.

**stake** (stāk), *n.* [AS. *staca*], 1. a pointed length of wood or metal for driving into the ground. 2. the post to which one is tied for execution by burning. 3. *often pl.* money, etc. risked as in a wager. 4. *often pl.* the winner's prize in a race, etc. *v.t.* [STAKED, STAKING], 1. to mark the boundaries of: as, to *stake* out a claim. 2. to fasten to stakes. 3. to gamble. 4. [Colloq.], to furnish with money, etc., as for a business venture. **—at stake,** being risked. **—pull up stakes,** [Colloq.], to change one's residence, etc.

**sta·lac·tite** (stə-lak'tīt), *n.* [< Gr. *stalaktos*, dripping], an icicle-shaped lime deposit hanging from the roof or sides of a cave.

**sta·lag·mite** (stə-lag'mīt), *n.* [< Gr. *stalagmos*, a dropping], a cone-shaped deposit on the floor of a cave, often beneath a stalactite.

**stale** (stāl), *adj.* [prob. < LG.], 1. no longer fresh; flat, tasteless, dry, stagnant, etc. 2. trite, as a joke. 3. out of condition physically or mentally. *v.t. & v.i.* [STALED, STALING], to make or become stale.

**stale·mate** (stāl'māt'), *n.* [prob. < OHG. *stal*, a place; + *mate* (checkmate)], 1. in *chess*, a situation in which a player cannot move without placing his king in check: it results in a draw. 2. a deadlock. *v.t.* [-MATED, -MATING], to bring into a stalemate.

**stalk** (stôk), *v.i. & v.t.* [AS. *stealcian*], 1. to walk (through) in a stiff, haughty manner. 2. to pursue (game, etc.) stealthily. *n.* 1. a stiff, haughty walk. 2. a stalking.

**stalk** (stôk), *n.* [AS. *stæla*], 1. the stem of a plant. 2. any part like this.

**stall** (stôl), *n.* [AS. *st(e)all*], 1. a stable. 2. a section for one animal in a stable. 3. *a*) a booth, etc. as at a market. *b*) a pew, as in a church. 4. a stop or standstill, esp. when unintentional. *v.t. & v.i.* 1. to keep or be kept in a stall. 2. to bring or come to a standstill, esp. unintentionally.

**stall** (stôl), *v.i. & v.t.* [< obs. *stale*, a decoy], [Colloq.], to act evasively or hesitantly so as to deceive or delay. *n.* [Colloq.], any action used in stalling.

**stal·lion** (stal'yən), *n.* [< OHG. *stal*, a stall], an uncastrated male horse.

**stal·wart** (stôl'wẽrt), *adj.* [< AS. *stathol*, foundation + *wyrthe*, worth], 1. strong; sturdy. 2. valiant. 3. firm; resolute. *n.* a stalwart person. **—stal'wart·ly,** *adv.*

**sta·men** (stā'mən), *n.* [L., thread], the pollen-bearing organ in a flower.

**stam·i·na** (stam'ə-nə), *n.* [L., pl. of *stamen*], resistance to fatigue, illness, hardship, etc.; endurance.

**stam·mer** (stam'ẽr), *v.t. & v.i.* [AS. *stamerian*], to speak or say with involuntary pauses and rapid repetitions. *n.* a stammering. **—stam'mer·er,** *n.*

**stamp** (stamp), *v.t.* [ME. *stampen*], 1. to bring (the foot) down forcibly. 2. to crush or pound with the foot. 3. to cut out by pressing with a die. 4. to impress or imprint with a design, etc. 5. to put a stamp on. 6. to characterize. *v.i.* 1. to bring the foot down forcibly. 2. to walk with loud, heavy steps. *n.* 1. a stamping. 2. a machine, tool, or die for stamping. 3. a mark or form made by stamping. 4. any of various seals, gummed pieces of paper, etc. used to show that a fee, as for postage, has been paid. 5. kind; class. **—stamp'er,** *n.*

**stam·pede** (stam-pēd'), *n.* [< Sp. *estampar*, to stamp], a sudden, headlong rush or flight, as of a herd of cattle. *v.i. & v.t.* [-PEDED, -PEDING], to move in a stampede.

**stance** (stans), *n.* [< L. *stare*, to stand], the way one stands; esp., the position of the feet.

**stanch** (stänch, stanch), *v.t.* [< L. *stare*, to stand], to check the flow of (blood, etc.) from (a cut, etc.). *adj.* 1. watertight. 2. trustworthy; loyal. 3. strong; firm.

**stan·chion** (stan'shən), *n.* [see STANCE], an upright post or support.

**stand** (stand), *v.i.* [STOOD, STANDING], [AS. *standan*], 1. to be in, or assume, an upright position, as on the feet. 2. to take or maintain a (specified) position, condition, etc. 3. to have a (specified) height when standing. 4. to be placed or situated. 5. to gather and remain, as water. 6. to remain unchanged. 7. to make resistance. 8. *a*) to halt. *b*) to be stationary. *v.t.* 1. to place upright. 2. to endure. 3. to withstand; resist. 4. to undergo: as, *stand* trial. *n.* 1. a standing; esp., a halt or stop. 2. a position; station. 3. a view, opinion, etc. 4. a structure to stand or sit on. 5. a place of business. 6. a rack, etc. for holding things. 7. a growth (of trees). **—stand by,** 1. to be near and ready if needed. 2. to aid. **—stand for,** 1. to represent. 2. [Colloq.], to tolerate. **—stand off,** 1. to keep at a distance. 2. to put off, as an assailant. **—stand on,** 1. to be based upon. 2. to demand. **—stand out,** 1. to project. 2. to be distinct, prominent, etc. **—stand up,** 1. to take a standing position. 2. to prove valid, durable, etc. 3. [Colloq.], to fail to keep a date with.

**stand·ard** (stan'dẽrd), *n.* [< OFr. *estendard*], 1. a flag, banner, etc. as an emblem of a people, military unit, etc. 2. something established or used as a rule or basis of comparison in measuring quantity, quality, value, etc. 3. an upright support. *adj.* 1. used as, or conforming to, a standard, rule, model, etc. 2. generally recognized as excellent and authoritative. 3. ordinary; typical.

**stand'ard-bear'er,** *n.* 1. one who carries the standard, or flag. 2. the leader, as of a political party.

**stand'ard·ize',** *v.t.* [-IZED, -IZING], to make standard or uniform. **—stand'ard·i·za'tion,** *n.*

**standard time,** the official civil time for any given region: the earth is divided into 24 time zones, four of them (*Eastern, Central, Mountain,* and *Pacific*) falling in the U.S.; adjacent zones are one hour apart.

**stand'-by',** *n.* [*pl.* -BYS], a person or thing that can always be depended upon or used.

**stand'-in',** *n.* a temporary substitute, as for a film star at rehearsals.

**stand'ing,** *n.* 1. status, rank, or reputation: as, in good *standing*. 2. duration of service, existence, etc.: as, a rule of long *standing*. *adj.* 1. that stands; upright. 2. done from a standing position: as, a *standing* jump. 3. stagnant: said of water. 4. permanent or continuing: as, a *standing* order.

**stand'off',** *n.* a tie in a contest.

**stand'off'ish,** *adj.* aloof; reserved.

**stand'point',** *n.* point of view.

**stand'still',** *n.* a stop or halt.

**stank** (staŋk), pt. of **stink**.

**stan·za** (stan'zə), *n.* [It.; ult. < L. *stare*, to stand], a group of lines of verse forming a division of a poem. **—stan·za'ic** (-zā'ik), *adj.*

**sta·ple** (stā'p'l), *n.* [< MD. *stapel*, mart], 1.

a chief commodity made or grown in a particular place. 2. raw material. 3. a regularly stocked item of trade, as flour, salt, etc. 4. the fiber of cotton, wool, etc. *adj.* 1. regularly stocked, produced, or used. 2. most important; principal.

**sta·ple** (stā′p'l), *n.* [AS. *stapol*, a post], a U-shaped piece of metal with sharp ends, driven into wood, etc. as to hold a hook or wire, or through papers, etc. as a binding. *v.t.* [-PLED, -PLING], to fasten with a staple. —**sta′pler,** *n.*

**star** (stär), *n.* [AS. *steorra*], 1. any heavenly body seen as a small fixed point of light, esp. one that is a distant sun. 2. a conventionalized figure with five or six points, representing a star. 3. anything like such a figure, as an asterisk. 4. one who excels, as in a sport. 5. a leading actor or actress. *v.t.* [STARRED, STARRING], 1. to mark with stars as a decoration, etc. 2. to present (an actor or actress) in a leading role. *v.i.* 1. to perform brilliantly. 2. to play a leading role. *adj.* 1. outstanding for skill and talent. 2. of a star. —**star′less,** *adj.*

**star·board** (stär′bẽrd, -bôrd′), *n.* [< AS. *steoran*, to steer (the old rudder was on the right side)], the right side of a ship, etc. as one faces forward. *adj.* of or on the starboard. *adv.* to or toward the starboard.

**starch** (stärch), *n.* [< AS. *stearc*, stiff], 1. a white, tasteless, odorless food substance found in potatoes, cereals, etc. 2. a powdered form of this used in water for stiffening cloth, etc. *v.t.* to stiffen as with starch. —**starch′y** [-IER, -IEST], *adj.*

**Star Chamber,** [also s- c-], an unjust and arbitrary tribunal, etc.

**star′dom** (-dəm), *n.* the status of a star in the theater, etc.

**stare** (stâr), *v.i.* [STARED, STARING], [AS. *starian*], 1. to gaze steadily and intently. 2. to be conspicuous: said esp. of color. *v.t.* to stare at. *n.* a steady, intent look.

**star′fish′,** *n.* [*pl.* see FISH], a small, star-shaped sea animal.

**star′gaze′,** *v.i.* [-GAZED, -GAZING], 1. to gaze at the stars. 2. to indulge in dreamy thought. —**star′gaz′er,** *n.*

**stark** (stärk), *adj.* [AS. *stearc*], 1. rigid, as a corpse. 2. standing in sharp outline. 3. bleak; desolate. 4. sheer; downright. *adv.* utterly; entirely. —**stark′ly,** *adv.*

**stark′-nak′ed,** *adj.* [< AS. *steort*, tail], entirely naked.

**star′light′,** *n.* light given by the stars. *adj.* lighted by the stars: also **star′lit′** (-lit′).

**star·ling** (stär′liŋ), *n.* [AS. *stær*], any of various birds with iridescent plumage, native to Europe.

**star′ry,** *adj.* [-RIER, -RIEST], 1. shining like stars; bright. 2. lighted by or full of stars.

**Stars and Stripes,** the flag of the U.S.

**star′-span′gled,** *adj.* studded or spangled with stars.

**Star-Spangled Banner,** 1. the flag of the U.S. 2. the U.S. national anthem.

**start** (stärt), *v.i.* [AS. *styrtan*], 1. to move suddenly or involuntarily; jump, etc. 2. to go into action or motion; begin; commence. 3. to spring into being, activity, etc. *v.t.* 1. to rouse; flush, as game. 2. to displace, loosen, etc.: as, to *start* a seam. 3. to set into motion or action. 4. to begin using, doing, etc. 5. to cause to be an entrant in a race, etc. *n.* 1. a sudden, brief shock. 2. a sudden, startled movement. 3. *pl.* sudden bursts of activity; usually in *by fits and starts*. 4. a starting, or beginning. 5. a place or time of beginning. 6. a lead, etc. giving an advantage. 7. an opportunity of beginning a career. —**start in,** to begin a task, etc. —**start out,** to start a journey, project, etc. —**start′er,** *n.*

**star·tle** (stär′t'l), *v.t.* [-TLED, -TLING], [< ME. *sterten*, to start], 1. to frighten or alarm suddenly. 2. to surprise. *v.i.* to be startled. *n.* a start or shock. —**star′tling,** *adj.*

**starve** (stärv), *v.i.* [STARVED, STARVING], [< AS. *steorfan*, to die], 1. to die from lack of food. 2. to suffer from hunger or poverty. *v.t.* 1. to cause to starve. 2. to compel by starvation. —**star·va·tion** (stär-vā′shən), *n.*

**starve′ling** (-liŋ), *n.* a person or animal that is starving. *adj.* starving.

**stash** (stash), *v.t. & v.i.* [? a blend of *store* and *cache*], [Slang], to put or hide away (money, valuables, etc.).

**-stat,** [Gr. *-statēs*], a combining form meaning *stationary*, as in *thermostat*.

**state** (stāt), *n.* [< L. *stare*, to stand], 1. a set of circumstances, etc. characterizing a person or thing; condition. 2. condition as regards structure, form, etc. 3. ceremonious or luxurious display or style of living. 4. [sometimes S-], a body of people politically organized under one government; nation. 5. [usually S-], any of the political units forming a federal government, as in the U.S. 6. civil government: as, matters of *state*. *adj.* 1. formal; ceremonial. 2. [sometimes S-], of the body politic, government, or state. *v.t.* [STATED, STATING], 1. to establish by specifying. 2. to set forth in words; express; declare. —**lie in state,** to be displayed formally before burial. —**the States,** [Colloq.], the United States.

**stat·ed** (stāt′id), *adj.* 1. fixed; regular. 2. declared; alleged. 3. formulated.

**state′ly,** *adj.* [-LIER, -LIEST], 1. imposing; majestic. 2. slow, dignified, etc. *adv.* in a stately manner. —**state′li·ness,** *n.*

**state′ment,** *n.* 1. a setting forth in words. 2. something stated; declaration. 3. an abstract of a financial account, esp. of money due.

**state′room′,** *n.* 1. a cabin on a ship. 2. a private room in a railroad car.

**states′man,** *n.* [*pl.* -MEN], one who is wise or experienced in the business of government. —**states′man·ship′,** *n.*

**stat·ic** (stat′ik), *adj.* [< Gr. *statikos*, causing to stand], 1. of masses, forces, etc. at rest or in equilibrium. 2. at rest; inactive; stationary. 3. designating, of, or producing stationary electrical charges, as from friction. 4. of or having to do with static. *n.* 1. electrical discharges in the atmosphere that interfere with radio reception, etc. 2. interference so produced.

**sta·tion** (stā′shən), *n.* [< L. *stare*, to stand], 1. the place or building where one stands or is located; esp., an assigned post. 2. a regular stopping place, as for trains, or a building at such a place. 3. social standing. 4. a place equipped for radio or television transmission. *v.t.* to assign to a station; place; post.

**sta·tion·ar·y** (stā′shən-er′i), *adj.* [see STATION], 1. not moving; fixed. 2. unchanging. 3. not itinerant.

**sta·tion·er** (stā′shən-ẽr), *n.* [< ML. *stationarius*, shopkeeper], a person who sells paper, ink, pens, etc.

**sta·tion·er·y** (stā′shən-er′i), *n.* writing materials, as paper and envelopes.

**station wagon,** an automobile with folding or removable rear seats and a back end that opens.

**sta·tis·tics** (stə-tis′tiks), *n.pl.* [< L. *status*, standing], 1. numerical facts assembled and classified so as to present significant information. 2. [construed as sing.], the science of compiling such facts. —**sta·tis′ti·cal,** *adj.* —**stat·is·ti·cian** (stat′is-tish′ən), *n.*

**stat·u·ar·y** (stach′ōō-er′i), *n.* [*pl.* -IES], statues collectively.

**stat·ue** (stach′ōō), *n.* [< L. *statuere*, to set],

the form of a person or animal carved in stone, etc., modeled in clay, etc., or cast in bronze, etc.

**stat·u·esque** (stach'ōō-esk'), *adj.* of or like a statue; stately; imposing.

**stat'u·ette'** (-et'), *n.* a small statue.

**stat·ure** (stach'ẽr), *n.* [< L. *statura*], 1. the natural height of the body. 2. growth or height reached: as, moral *stature.*

**sta·tus** (stā'təs, stat'əs), *n.* [*pl.* -TUSES], [L., standing], 1. legal condition: as, the *status* of a minor. 2. position; rank. 3. high position, or prestige. 4. state, as of affairs.

**‡status quo** (kwō), [L., the state in which], the existing state of affairs.

**stat·ute** (stach'oot), *n.* [see STATUE], 1. an established rule or law. 2. a law passed by a legislative body.

**stat·u·to·ry** (stach'oo-tôr'i), *adj.* 1. fixed or authorized, by statute. 2. punishable by statute, as an offense.

**staunch** (stônch, stänch), *adj., v.t. & v.i.* stanch. —**staunch'ly,** *adv.*

**stave** (stāv), *n.* [< *staves*, pl. of *staff*], 1. one of the shaped strips of wood that form the wall of a barrel, bucket, etc. 2. a stick or staff. 3. a stanza. *v.t.* [STAVED or STOVE, STAVING], to puncture, as by breaking in staves. —**stave off,** to hold or put off.

**staves** (stāvz), *n.* 1. alt pl. of **staff.** 2. pl. of **stave.**

**stay** (stā), *n.* [AS. *stæg*], a heavy rope or cable used as a brace, as for the masts of a ship; guy. *v.t.* to brace with stays.

**stay** (stā), *n.* [OFr. *estai*], 1. a support; prop. 2. a strip of stiffening material used in a corset, shirt collar, etc. *v.t.* to support; prop up. —**stay'er,** *n.*

**stay** (stā), *v.i.* [< OFr. *ester*, to stand], 1. to continue in the place or condition specified; remain. 2. to live; dwell. 3. to stop; halt. 4. to pause; delay. 5. [Colloq.], to hold out; last. *v.t.* 1. to stop or check. 2. to hinder; detain. 3. to postpone (legal action). 4. to satisfy for a time (hunger, etc.). 5. to remain to the end of. *n.* 1. *a*) a stopping or being stopped. *b*) a halt or pause. 2. a postponement in legal action. 3. the action of remaining, or the time spent, in a place.

**Ste.,** *Sainte*, [Fr.], Saint (female).

**stead** (sted), *n.* [AS. *stede*], the place or position of a person or thing as filled by a substitute. —**stand (one) in good stead,** to give (one) good service.

**stead·fast** (sted'fast', -fäst'), *adj.* [< AS. *stedefæst*], 1. firm; fixed. 2. constant.

**stead·y** (sted'i), *adj.* [-IER, -IEST], [< AS. *stede*, stead], 1. firm; stable; not shaky. 2. regular, uniform, continuous, etc.: as, a *steady* gaze. 3. constant in behavior, loyalty, etc. 4. calm and controlled: as, *steady* nerves. 5. sober; reliable. *v.t. & v.i.* [-IED, -YING], to make or become steady. —**go steady,** [Colloq.], to be sweethearts.

**steak** (stāk), *n.* [< ON. *steikja*, to roast on a spit], a thick slice of meat or fish, esp. beef, for broiling or frying.

**steal** (stēl), *v.t.* [STOLE, STOLEN, STEALING], [AS. *stælan*], 1. to take (another's property, etc.) dishonestly, esp. in a secret manner. 2. to take slyly, as a look. 3. to gain insidiously or artfully: as, he *stole* her heart. 4. to move or put stealthily. 5. in *baseball*, to gain (a base) safely without the help of a hit or error. *v.i.* 1. to practice theft. 2. to move stealthily. *n.* [Colloq.], a thing obtained at a ludicrously low cost.

**stealth** (stelth), *n.* secret or furtive action. —**stealth'y** [-IER, -IEST], *adj.*

**steam** (stēm), *n.* [AS.], 1. water as converted into a vapor by being heated to the boiling point. 2. the power of compressed steam. 3. [Colloq.], power; energy. *adj.* using or operated by steam. *v.i.* 1. to give off steam. 2. to move by steam power. *v.t.* to expose to steam, as in cooking. —**steam'y,** *adj.*

**steam'boat',** *n.* a steamship.

**steam engine,** an engine using steam under pressure to supply mechanical energy.

**steam'er,** *n.* something operated by steam; steamship, steam engine, etc.

**steam fitter,** a mechanic who installs and maintains the boilers, pipes, etc. in steam pressure systems. —**steam fitting.**

**steam'-roll'er,** *v.t. & v.i.* to move, override, etc. as with a steam roller.

**steam roller,** a heavy, steam-driven roller used in road building, etc.

**steam'ship',** *n.* a ship driven by steam.

**steam shovel,** a large, mechanically operated digger, powered by steam.

**steed** (stēd), *n.* [AS. *steda*], a horse.

**steel** (stēl), *n.* [AS. *stiele*], 1. a hard, tough alloy of iron with a little carbon, etc. 2. something made of steel. 3. great strength or hardness. *adj.* of or like steel. *v.t.* to make hard, tough, etc. —**steel'y** [-IER, -IEST], *adj.*

**steel wool,** long, hairlike shavings of steel, used for cleaning, etc.

**steel'yard'** (-yärd', stil'yẽrd), *n.* [*steel* + obs. *yard*, rod], a balance scale consisting of a metal arm suspended from above.

**steep** (stēp), *adj.* [AS. *steap*, lofty], 1. having a sharp rise or slope; precipitous. 2. [Colloq.], excessive; extreme. *n.* a steep slope.

**steep** (stēp), *v.t. & v.i.* [< ON. *steypa*], to soak, saturate, imbue, etc. —**steep'er,** *n.*

**stee·ple** (stē'p'l), *n.* [AS. *stypel*], 1. a tower rising above the main structure, as of a church. 2. a spire.

**stee'ple·chase',** *n.* a horse race over a course obstructed with ditches, hedges, etc.

**stee'ple·jack',** *n.* one who paints or repairs steeples, smokestacks, etc.

**steer** (stêr), *v.t. & v.i.* [AS. *stieran*], 1. to guide (a ship, etc.) with a rudder. 2. to direct the course of (an automobile, etc.). 3. to follow (a course).

**steer** (stêr), *n.* [AS. *steor*], 1. a young castrated ox. 2. any male of beef cattle.

**steer'age,** *n.* 1. a steering. 2. the section of a ship occupied by passengers paying the lowest fare.

**steers'man** (-mən), *n.* [*pl.* -MEN], one who steers a ship or boat.

**stein** (stīn), *n.* [G.], a beer mug.

**stel·lar** (stel'ẽr), *adj.* [< L. *stella*, star], 1. of or like a star. 2. excellent, leading, chief, etc.

**stem** (stem), *n.* [AS. *stemn*], 1. the main stalk of a plant. 2. any stalk supporting leaves, flowers, or fruit. 3. a stemlike part, as of a goblet, pipe, etc. 4. the prow of a ship; bow. 5. the part of a word to which inflectional endings are added. *v.t.* [STEMMED, STEMMING], to make headway against: as, to *stem* the tide. *v.i.* to originate or derive.

**stem** (stem), *v.t.* [STEMMED, STEMMING], [< Scand.], to stop or check by or as if by damming up.

**stench** (stench), *n.* [< AS. *stincan*, to stink], an offensive smell; stink.

**sten·cil** (sten's'l), *v.t.* [-CILED or -CILLED, -CILING or -CILLING], [ult. < L. *scintilla*, a spark], to mark or paint with a stencil. *n.* a thin sheet, as of paper, perforated in such a way that when ink or paint is applied, designs, letters, etc. form on the surface beneath the sheet.

**ste·nog·ra·phy** (stə-nog'rə-fi), *n.* [< Gr. *stenos*, narrow; + *-graphy*], shorthand writing for later transcription in typewriting. —**ste·nog'ra·pher,** *n.* —**sten·o·graph·ic** (sten'ə-graf'ik), *adj.*

**sten·to·ri·an** (sten-tôr'i-ən), *adj.* [< *Stentor*, a Greek herald in the *Iliad*], very loud.

**step** (step), *n.* [AS. *stepe*], 1. a single movement of the foot, as in walking. 2. the distance covered by such a movement. 3. a short distance. 4. a manner of stepping. 5. the sound of stepping. 6. a rest for the foot in climbing, as a stair. 7. a degree; rank; level. 8. any of a series of acts, processes, etc. 9. a basic sequence of movements in dancing. *v.i.* [STEPPED, STEPPING], 1. to move by executing a step. 2. to walk a short distance. 3. to enter (*into* a situation, etc.). 4. to press the foot down (*on*). *v.t.* 1. to measure by taking steps (with *off*). 2. to arrange in a series of degrees, etc. —**in** (or **out of**) **step**, (not) conforming to a rhythm in marching, regular procedure, etc. —**step up**, 1. to advance. 2. to increase, as in rate.

**step·broth·er** (step'bruth'ẽr), *n.* one's stepparent's son by a former marriage.

**step'child'**, *n.* [*pl.* -CHILDREN], [AS. *steop-* < base of *astypan*, to orphan], a child (**stepdaughter** or **stepson**) by a former marriage of one's spouse.

**step'lad'der**, *n.* a four-legged ladder having broad, flat steps.

**step·par·ent** (step'pâr'ənt), *n.* the person (**stepfather** or **stepmother**) who has married one's parent after the death or divorce of the other parent.

**steppe** (step), *n.* [< Russ. *step'*], one of the great plains of SE Europe and Asia, having few trees.

**step'ping·stone'**, *n.* 1. a stone used to step on, as in crossing a stream, etc. 2. a means for advancement. Also **stepping stone**.

**step·sis·ter** (step'sis'tẽr), *n.* one's stepparent's daughter by a former marriage.

**-ster**, [AS. *-estre*], a suffix meaning *one who is, does*, or *creates* (something specified), as in *oldster, punster*.

**stereo-**, [< Gr. *stereos*, hard], a combining form meaning *solid, firm, three-dimensional*, as in *stereoscope*.

**ster·e·o·phon·ic** (ster'i-ə-fon'ik, stêr'-), *adj.* [< *stereo-*; + Gr. *phōnē*, a sound], designating sound reproduction, as in motion pictures, employing a number of loud-speakers so as to reproduce sounds from the directions in which they were recorded.

**ster'e·o·scope'** (-skōp'), *n.* [*stereo-* + *-scope*], an instrument with two eyepieces that gives a three-dimensional effect to photographs viewed in it.

**ster'e·o·type'** (-tīp'), *n.* [see STEREO- & -TYPE], 1. a printing plate cast from a mold, as of a page of set type. 2. a fixed or conventional expression, notion, etc. —**ster'e·o·typed'**, *adj.*

**ster·ile** (ster''l, -il), *adj.* [L. *sterilis*], 1. incapable of producing offspring, fruit, etc.; barren. 2. free from living microorganisms. —**ste·ril·i·ty** (stə-ril'ə-ti), [*pl.* -TIES], *n.*

**ster'i·lize'** (-ə-līz'), *v.t.* [-LIZED, -LIZING], to make sterile; specif., *a*) to make incapable of reproduction. *b*) to free from living microorganisms. —**ster'i·li·za'tion**, *n.*

**ster·ling** (stũr'liŋ), *n.* [< ME. *sterlinge*, Norman coin], 1. sterling silver or articles made of it. 2. British money. *adj.* 1. of standard quality (92.5% pure): said of silver. 2. of British money. 3. made of sterling silver. 4. excellent: as, *sterling* principles.

**stern** (stũrn), *adj.* [AS. *styrne*], 1. hard; severe: as, *stern* treatment. 2. grim: as, a *stern* face. 3. relentless. —**stern'ly**, *adv.*

**stern** (stũrn), *n.* [prob. < ON. *styra*, to steer], the rear end of a ship, etc.

**ster·num** (stũr'nəm), *n.* [*pl.* -NA (-nə), -NUMS], [< Gr. *sternon*], a flat, bony structure to which most of the ribs are attached in the front of the chest; breastbone. —**ster'nal** (-n'l), *adj.*

**stet** (stet), [L.], let it stand: a printer's term used to indicate that matter previously struck out is to remain. *v.t.* [STETTED, STETTING], to cancel a correction or deletion by marking with the word *stet*.

**steth·o·scope** (steth'ə-skōp'), *n.* [< Gr. *stethos*, chest; + *-scope*], in *medicine*, a hearing instrument used to examine the heart, lungs, etc. by listening to the sounds they make.

**ste·ve·dore** (stē'və-dôr'), *n.* [< L. *stipare*, to cram], a person employed at loading and unloading ships.

**stew** (stōō, stū), *v.t.* & *v.i.* [< L. *ex*, out + Gr. *typhos*, steam], 1. to cook by boiling slowly; simmer. 2. [Colloq.], to worry. *n.* 1. a dish, esp. of meat and vegetables, cooked by slow boiling. 2. [Colloq.], a state of worry.

**stew·ard** (stōō'ẽrd, stū'-), *n.* [< AS. *sti(g)*, hall + *weard*, keeper], 1. a person hired to supervise a large estate. 2. an administrator, as of another's finances and property. 3. one in charge of the provisions, kitchen, etc. as in a club or dining car. 4. one of the staff of servants on a passenger ship. —**stew'ard·ship'**, *n.*

**stew'ard·ess** (-ẽr-dis), *n.* a woman steward, esp. as on an airplane.

**stick** (stik), *n.* [AS. *sticca*], 1. a twig or branch broken or cut off. 2. a long, slender piece of wood, as a staff, club, cane, etc. 3. any sticklike piece: as, a *stick* of gum. 4. [Colloq.], a dull or stupid person. *v.t.* [STUCK, STICKING], 1. to pierce, as with a pointed instrument. 2. to press (a knife, pin, etc.) so as to pierce. 3. to thrust: as, *stick* out your hand. 4. to attach as by pinning, gluing, etc. 5. to obstruct, detain, etc.: as, the wheels were *stuck*. 6. [Colloq.], to put, set, etc. 7. [Colloq.], to puzzle; baffle. 8. [Slang], to impose a burden, etc. upon. 9. [Slang], to endure: often with *out*. *v.i.* 1. to be fixed by a pointed end, as a nail, etc. 2. to adhere; cleave; cling. 3. to persevere: as, *stick* at the job. 4. to remain firm and resolute: as, he *stuck* with us. 5. to become embedded, jammed, etc. 6. to hesitate; scruple: as, he'll *stick* at nothing. 7. to protrude or extend (with *out, up*, etc.). —**stick up**, [Slang], to commit armed robbery upon. —**stick up for**, [Colloq.], to uphold; defend. —**the sticks**, [Colloq.], the rural districts.

**stick'er**, *n.* a person or thing that sticks; specif., a gummed label.

**stick·le** (stik''l), *v.i.* [-LED, -LING], [< AS. *stihtan*, arrange], to be stubbornly precise, etc., usually about trifles. —**stick'ler**, *n.*

**stick'y**, *adj.* [-IER, -IEST], 1. that sticks; adhesive. 2. [Colloq.], humid: as, *sticky* heat.

**stiff** (stif), *adj.* [AS. *stif*], 1. hard to bend; rigid; firm. 2. sore or limited in movement: said of joints and muscles. 3. not fluid; thick: as, a *stiff* sauce. 4. moving swiftly, as a breeze. 5. harsh: as, *stiff* punishment. 6. difficult: as, a *stiff* climb. 7. not relaxed; constrained or awkward. 8. [Colloq.], high: said of prices. *n.* [Slang], a corpse.

**stiff'en**, *v.t.* & *v.i.* to make or become stiff or stiffer. —**stiff'en·er**, *n.*

**stiff'-necked'** (-nekt'), *adj.* stubborn.

**sti·fle** (stī'f'l), *v.t.* [-FLED, -FLING], [< ON. *stīfla*, stop up], 1. to suffocate; smother. 2. to suppress or check; stop: as, she *stifled* her sobs. *v.i.* to die or suffer from lack of air.

**stig·ma** (stig'mə), *n.* [*pl.* -MAS, -MATA (-mə-tə)], [L.; Gr., a mark], 1. a brand or mark of disgrace or disrepute. 2. the upper tip of the pistil of a flower, receiving the pollen. 3. in *medicine*, a spot on the skin, esp. one that bleeds in certain nervous tensions. —**stig·mat'ic** (-mat'ik), **stig·mat'i·cal**, *adj.*

**stig'ma·tize'**, *v.t.* [-TIZED, -TIZING], 1. to brand with a stigma. 2. to mark as disgraceful. —**stig'ma·ti·za'tion**, *n.*

**stile** (stīl), *n.* [< AS. *stigan*, to climb], 1. a step or set of steps used in climbing over a fence or wall. 2. a turnstile.

**sti·let·to** (sti-let'ō), *n.* [*pl.* -TOS, -TOES], [It.

< L. *stilus*, stylus], a small dagger with a slender, tapering blade.

**still** (stil), *adj.* [AS. *stille*], 1. without sound; quiet. 2. soft or low in sound. 3. stationary; motionless. 4. tranquil; calm. 5. designating or of a single photograph taken from a motion-picture film. *n.* 1. [Poetic], silence; quiet. 2. a still photograph. *adv.* 1. at or up to the time indicated. 2. even; yet: as, *still* colder. 3. nevertheless; yet: as, though old, he *still* works. *conj.* nevertheless; yet. *v.t. & v.i.* to make or become still.

**still** (stil), *n.* [< obs. *still*, to distill], an apparatus for distilling liquids, esp. alcoholic liquors.

**still′born′,** *adj.* dead when born.

**still life,** a painting or picture of inanimate objects, as fruit, flowers, etc.

**stilt** (stilt), *n.* [prob. < LG.], 1. either of a pair of poles fitted with a footrest along its length and used for walking, as in play. 2. a long post or pole used to hold something above the ground or out of the water.

**stilt·ed** (stil′tid), *adj.* artificially formal or dignified; pompous. **—stilt′ed·ness,** *n.*

**stim·u·lant** (stim′yoo-lənt), *adj.* stimulating. *n.* anything, as a drug, that stimulates.

**stim′u·late′** (-lāt′), *v.t.* [-LATED, -LATING], [ult. < L. *stimulus*, a goad], to rouse to action; excite to activity or increased activity. **—stim′u·la′tion,** *n.*

**stim·u·lus** (stim′yoo-ləs), *n.* [*pl.* -LI (-lī′)], [L., a goad], 1. any action or agent that causes an activity in an organism, organ, etc. 2. an incentive.

**sting** (stiŋ), *v.t.* [STUNG, STINGING], [AS. *stingan*], 1. to prick or wound with a sting. 2. to cause sudden, pricking pain to. 3. to cause to suffer mentally. 4. to spur into action. *v.i.* to cause to feel sharp, smarting pain. *n.* 1. a stinging. 2. a pain or wound resulting from stinging. 3. a sharp-pointed organ, as in insects and plants, that pricks, wounds, etc. **—sting′er,** *n.*

**stin·gy** (stin′ji), *adj.* [-GIER, -GIEST], [< dial. *stinge*, a sting], 1. giving or spending grudgingly; miserly. 2. scanty; less than needed. **—stin′gi·ly,** *adv.* **—stin′gi·ness,** *n.*

**stink** (stiŋk), *v.i.* [STANK or STUNK, STUNK, STINKING], [AS. *stincan*], to have a strong, unpleasant smell. *n.* a strong, unpleasant smell; stench. **—stink′er,** *n.*

**stint** (stint), *v.t.* [< AS. *styntan*, to blunt], to restrict to a certain quantity, often small. *v.i.* to be sparing in giving or using. *n.* 1. restriction; limit. 2. an assigned task.

**sti·pend** (stī′pend), *n.* [< L. *stips*, small coin + *pendere*, to pay], a regular or fixed payment, as a salary.

**stip·ple** (stip′'l), *v.t.* [-PLED, -PLING], [< D. *stippel*, a speckle], to paint, draw, or engrave in small dots. **—stip′pling,** *n.*

**stip·u·late** (stip′yoo-lāt′), *v.t.* [-LATED, -LATING], [< L. *stipulari*, to bargain], 1. to arrange definitely, as in a contract. 2. to specify as an essential condition of an agreement. **—stip′u·la′tion,** *n.*

**stir** (stũr), *v.t. & v.i.* [STIRRED, STIRRING], [AS. *styrian*], 1. to move, esp. slightly. 2. to rouse from dormancy, lethargy, etc.; set or be in motion. 3. to mix (a liquid, etc.) as by agitating with a spoon. 4. to excite the feelings (of). 5. to incite (often with *up*). *n.* 1. a stirring, as with a spoon. 2. movement; activity. 3. commotion.

**stir′ring,** *adj.* 1. active; busy. 2. moving; rousing: as, *stirring* music.

**stir·rup** (stũr′əp, stir′-), *n.* [< AS. *stigan*, to climb + *rap*, a rope], a flat-based ring hung from a saddle and used as a footrest.

**stitch** (stich), *n.* [AS. *stice*, a puncture], 1. a single complete in-and-out movement of a needle in sewing, knitting, etc. 2. a loop, etc. made by stitching. 3. a particular kind of stitch or stitching. 4. a sudden, sharp pain. 5. [Colloq.], a bit. *v.i. & v.t.* to make stitches (in); sew. **—stitch′er,** *n.*

**stoat** (stōt), *n.* [ME. *stote*], an ermine, esp. when in its brown summer coat.

**stock** (stok), *n.* [AS. *stocc*], 1. the trunk of a tree. 2. *a*) descent; ancestry. *b*) a strain, race, etc. of animals or plants. 3. the body or handle of an implement, etc., as the part of a rifle holding the barrel. 4. *pl.* a wooden frame with holes for confining the ankles or wrists, formerly used for punishment. 5. raw material: as, paper *stock*. 6. water in which meat, fish, etc. was boiled, used in soups. 7. livestock. 8. a supply of goods on hand in a store, etc. 9. shares of corporate capital, or the certificates showing such ownership. 10. a stock company (sense 2). 11. a former kind of wide cravat. *v.t.* 1. to furnish with stock, as a farm or shop. 2. to keep a supply of for sale or for future use. *v.i.* to put in a stock, or supply (with *up*). *adj.* 1. kept in stock: as, *stock* sizes. 2. common or trite: as, a *stock* joke. 3. that deals with stock. 4. of or relating to a stock company. **—in** (or **out of**) **stock,** (not) available for sale or use. **—take stock,** to inventory the stock on hand. **—take stock in,** [Colloq.], to have faith in.

**stock·ade** (sto-kād′), *n.* [< Pr. *estaca*, a stake], a barrier made of stakes driven into the ground side by side, for defense against attack. *v.t.* [-ADED, -ADING], to surround, protect, etc. with a stockade.

**stock′bro′ker,** *n.* a broker who buys and sells stocks and bonds.

**stock car,** a standard automobile, but modified in certain ways, used in races.

**stock company,** 1. a company whose capital is divided into shares. 2. a theatrical company presenting a repertoire of plays.

**stock exchange,** 1. a place for the sale of stocks and bonds. 2. an association of stockbrokers.

**stock′hold′er** (-hōl′dẽr), *n.* an owner of shares of stock in a company.

**stock·ing** (stok′iŋ), *n.* [< obs. sense of *stock*], a closefitting covering, usually knitted, for the leg and foot.

**stock market,** a stock exchange.

**stock′pile′** (-pīl′), *n.* a reserve supply of goods, raw materials, etc.: also **stock pile.** *v.t. & v.i.* [-PILED, -PILING], to accumulate a stockpile (of).

**stock′-still′,** *adj.* motionless.

**stock′y,** *adj.* [-IER, -IEST], heavily built; thickset and short. **—stock′i·ness,** *n.*

**stock′yard′,** *n.* an enclosure for keeping cattle, hogs, etc. to be slaughtered.

**stodg·y** (stoj′i), *adj.* [-IER, -IEST], [< dial. *stodge*, heavy food], dull; uninteresting.

**Sto·ic** (stō′ik), *n.* [< Gr. *stoa*, colonnade: the Stoics met in a colonnade], 1. a member of an ancient Greek school of philosophy. 2. [s-], a stoical person. *adj.* [s-], stoical. **—Sto′i·cism, sto′i·cism,** *n.*

**sto·i·cal** (stō′i-k'l), *adj.* showing indifference to joy, grief, pain, etc.; impassive.

**stoke** (stōk), *v.t. & v.i.* [STOKED, STOKING], [< D. *stoken*, to poke], 1. to stir up and feed fuel to (a fire). 2. to tend (a furnace, etc.).

**stole** (stōl), *n.* [< Gr. *stolē*, garment], 1. a long strip of cloth worn like a scarf by some clergymen. 2. a woman's long scarf of cloth or fur worn with the ends hanging in front.

**stole** (stōl), pt. of **steal.**

**stol·en** (stōl′ən), pp. of **steal.**

**stol·id** (stol′id), *adj.* [< L. *stolidus*, slow], having or showing little or no emotion; unexcitable. **—sto·lid·i·ty,** (stə-lid′ə-ti), *n.*

**stom·ach** (stum′ək), *n.* [ult. < Gr. *stoma*, mouth], 1. the saclike, digestive organ into which food passes from the esophagus. 2. the abdomen; belly. 3. appetite. 4. desire or inclination. *v.t.* 1. to be able to eat or digest. 2. to tolerate; bear.

**stom′ach·er,** *n.* an ornamented piece of cloth formerly worn over the chest and abdomen, esp. by women.

**stone** (stōn), *n.* [AS. *stan*], 1. the hard, solid, nonmetallic mineral matter of rock. 2. a piece of rock. 3. the seed of certain fruits. 4. a precious gem. 5. [*pl.* STONE], in Great Britain, 14 pounds avoirdupois. 6. an abnormal stony mass formed in the kidney, bladder, etc. *v.t.* [STONED, STONING], 1. to throw stones at. 2. to remove the stone from, as a peach. *adj.* of stone.

**stone-,** [< *stone, n.*], a combining form meaning *completely*, as in *stone-blind*.

**Stone Age,** the early period in human culture when stone implements were used.

**stone's throw,** a relatively short distance.

**ston′y,** *adj.* [-IER, -IEST], 1. full of stones. 2. of or like stone; specif., unfeeling; pitiless. **—ston′i·ly,** *adv.* **—ston′i·ness,** *n.*

**stood** (stood), pt. and pp. of **stand.**

**stooge** (stōōj), *n.* [< ?], [Colloq.], 1. an actor who serves as the victim of a comedian's jokes, pranks, etc. 2. anyone who acts as a foil or underling to another. *v.i.* [STOOGED, STOOGING], [Colloq.], to be a stooge (*for* someone).

**stool** (stōōl), *n.* [AS. *stol*], 1. a single seat having no back or arms. 2. feces.

**stool pigeon,** [Colloq.], a police spy or informer.

**stoop** (stōōp), *v.i.* [AS. *stupian*], 1. to bend the body forward or in a crouch. 2. to carry the head and shoulders habitually bent forward. 3. to degrade oneself. *n.* the position of stooping the body.

**stoop** (stōōp), *n.* [D. *stoep*], a small porch or platform at the entrance of a house.

**stop** (stop), *v.t.* [STOPPED, STOPPING], [< LL. *stuppare*, stop up], 1. to close by filling, shutting off, etc. 2. to cause to cease motion, activity, etc. 3. to block; obstruct; prevent. 4. to cease; desist from: as, *stop* talking. *v.i.* 1. to cease moving, etc.; halt. 2. to leave off doing something. 3. to cease operating. 4. to become clogged. 5. to tarry; stay. *n.* 1. a stopping or being stopped. 2. a finish; end. 3. a stay or sojourn. 4. a place stopped at, as on a bus route. 5. something that stops; obstruction, plug, etc. 6. a finger hole in a wind instrument, closed to produce a desired pitch. 7. a pull, lever, etc. for putting a set of organ pipes into or out of operation. **—stop off,** to stop for a while.

**stop′gap′,** *n.* a person or thing serving as a temporary substitute.

**stop′o′ver,** *n.* a brief stop or stay at a place in the course of a journey.

**stop′page** (-ij), *n.* 1. a stopping or being stopped. 2. an obstructed condition; block.

**stop′per,** *n.* something inserted to close an opening; plug. *v.t.* to close with a stopper.

**stop watch,** a watch with a hand that can be started and stopped instantly to time races, etc.

**stor·age** (stôr′ij), *n.* 1. a storing or being stored. 2. a place or space for storing goods. 3. the cost of storing goods.

**store** (stôr), *n.* [< L. *instaurare*, restore], 1. a supply (*of* something) for use when needed; stock. 2. *pl.* supplies, esp. of food, clothing, etc. 3. an establishment where goods are offered for sale. 4. a storehouse. *v.t.* [STORED, STORING], 1. to put aside for use when needed. 2. to furnish with a supply. 3. to put in a warehouse for safekeeping. **—in store,** set aside for the future; in reserve. **—set store by,** to value.

**store′house′,** *n.* a place where things are stored; esp., a warehouse.

**store′keep′er,** *n.* a person in charge of a store or stores.

**store′room′,** *n.* a room where things are stored.

**sto·ried** (stôr′id), *adj.* famous in story or history.

**stork** (stôrk), *n.* [AS. *storc*], a large, long-legged wading bird with a long neck and bill.

**storm** (stôrm), *n.* [AS.], 1. a strong wind, with rain, snow, thunder, etc. 2. any heavy fall of rain, snow, etc. 3. a strong, emotional outburst. 4. any strong disturbance. 5. a sudden, strong attack on a fortified place. *v.i.* 1. to blow violently, rain, snow, etc. 2. to rage; rant. 3. to rush violently: as, he *stormed* into the office. *v.t.* to attack violently.

**storm door** (or **window),** an extra door (or window) placed outside of the regular one as added protection.

**storm′y,** *adj.* [-IER, -IEST], 1. of or characterized by storms. 2. violent; raging.

**sto·ry** (stôr′i), *n.* [*pl.* -RIES], [< Gr. *historia*, history], 1. the telling of an event or series of events; account; narration. 2. a fictitious narrative shorter than a novel. 3. the plot of a novel, play, etc. 4. [Colloq.], a falsehood. 5. in *journalism*, a news article.

**sto·ry** (stôr′i), *n.* [*pl.* -RIES], [< prec. entry], a horizontal division of a building between successive floors.

**sto·ry·tell·er** (stôr′i-tel′ẽr), *n.* 1. one who tells stories. 2. [Colloq.], a liar. **—sto′ry-tell′ing,** *n. & adj.*

**stoup** (stōōp), *n.* [< ON. *staup*], a basin for holy water in a church.

**stout** (stout), *adj.* [< OFr. *estout*, bold], 1. courageous; brave. 2. strong; sturdy; firm. 3. powerful; forceful. 4. fat; thickset. *n.* strong, dark-brown beer. **—stout′ly,** *adv.*

**stout′heart′ed,** *adj.* brave.

**stove** (stōv), *n.* [MD., heated room], an apparatus for heating, cooking, etc.

**stove** (stōv), alt. pt. and pp. of **stave.**

**stove′pipe′,** *n.* a metal pipe used to carry off smoke from a stove.

**stow** (stō), *v.t.* [< AS. *stow*, a place], 1. to pack in an orderly manner. 2. to fill by packing thus. **—stow away,** 1. to put or hide away. 2. to be a stowaway.

**stow′a·way′,** *n.* one who hides aboard a ship, train, etc. to obtain free passage or evade port officials, etc.

**strad·dle** (strad′'l), *v.i. & v.t.* [-DLED, -DLING], [< *stride*], 1. to sit astride, or stand or walk with the legs wide apart. 2. [Colloq.], to appear to take both sides of (an issue). *n.* 1. a straddling. 2. the space between the legs in straddling. **—strad′dler,** *n.*

**Strad·i·var·i·us** (strad′ə-vâr′i-əs), *n.* a violin, cello, etc. made by Antonio Stradivari (1644–1737) of Italy.

**strafe** (strāf), *v.t.* [STRAFED, STRAFING], [< G. *Gott strafe England* (God punish England)], to attack with machine-gun fire from low-flying aircraft. **—straf′er,** *n.*

**strag·gle** (strag′'l), *v.i.* [-GLED, -GLING], [prob. < ME. *straken*, roam], 1. to wander from the main group. 2. to be scattered over a wide area; ramble. **—strag′gler,** *n.* **—strag′gly** [-GLIER, -GLIEST], *adj.*

**straight** (strāt), *adj.* [< AS. *streccan*, stretch], 1. having the same direction throughout its length; not crooked, bent, etc. 2. direct; undeviating. 3. in order; properly arranged, etc. 4. honest; sincere. 5. unmixed; undiluted: as, *straight* whisky. *adv.* 1. in a straight line. 2. upright; erectly. 3. without deviation, etc.; directly. *n.* in *poker*, a series of five cards in sequence. **—straight away** (or **off),** without delay.

**straight′en,** *v.i. & v.t.* to make or become straight. **—straight′en·er,** *n.*

**straight′for′ward,** *adj.* 1. moving or leading straight; direct. 2. honest; frank. *adv.* in a straightforward manner.

**straight′way′,** ***adv.*** at once; without delay.

**strain** (strān), ***v.t.*** [< L. *stringere*], 1. to draw or stretch tight. 2. to exert, use, etc. to the utmost. 3. to injure by exertion; sprain, as a muscle. 4. to stretch beyond normal limits. 5. to pass through a screen, sieve, etc.; filter. ***v.i.*** 1. to make violent efforts; strive hard. 2. to filter, ooze, etc. ***n.*** 1. a straining or being strained. 2. great effort, exertion, etc. 3. a sprain or wrench. 4. stress; force. 5. an excessive demand on one's emotions, resources, etc.

**strain** (strān), ***n.*** [< AS. *strynan*, to produce], 1. ancestry; lineage. 2. race; stock; line. 3. a line of individuals differentiated from its main species. 4. an inherited tendency. 5. a trace; streak. 6. *often pl.* a passage of music; tune.

**strain′er,** ***n.*** a device for straining, sifting, or filtering; sieve, filter, etc.

**strait** (strāt), ***adj.*** [< L. *stringere*, draw tight], [Archaic], 1. narrow; tight. 2. strict; rigid. ***n.*** 1. *often in pl.* a narrow waterway connecting two large bodies of water. 2. *often in pl.* difficulty; distress.

**strait′en,** ***v.t.*** 1. to make strait or narrow; limit. 2. to bring into difficulties: esp. in *in straitened circumstances*, lacking sufficient money.

**strait jacket,** a coatlike device for restraining the mentally deranged, etc.

**strait′-laced′** (-lāst′), ***adj.*** narrowly strict in behavior or opinions; prudish.

**strand** (strand), ***n.*** [AS.], shore, esp. ocean shore. ***v.t. & v.i.*** 1. to run or drive aground, as a ship. 2. to put or come into a helpless position: as, *stranded* in the desert.

**strand** (strand), ***n.*** [< OFr. *estran*], 1. any of the threads, fibers, wires, etc. that are twisted together to form a string, rope, cable, etc. 2. any string, thread, etc.: as, a *strand* of beads.

**strange** (strānj), ***adj.*** [STRANGER, STRANGEST], [< L. *extraneus*, foreign], 1. not previously known, seen, etc.; unfamiliar. 2. unusual; extraordinary. 3. peculiar; odd. 4. reserved; distant. 5. unaccustomed (*to*); unversed (*in*). ***adv.*** in a strange manner.

**stran·ger** (strān′jẽr), ***n.*** 1. a newcomer. 2. a person not known to one.

**stran·gle** (straŋ′g'l), ***v.t. & v.i.*** [-GLED, -GLING], [< Gr. *strangalē*, halter], 1. to choke to death. 2. to suppress; stifle.

**stran·gu·late** (straŋ′gyoo-lāt′), ***v.t.*** [-LATED, -LATING], 1. to strangle. 2. to block (a tube) by constricting. **—stran′gu·la′tion,** ***n.***

**strap** (strap), ***n.*** [ult. < Gr. *strophos*, a band], a narrow strip of leather, etc., for binding or securing things. ***v.t.*** [STRAPPED, STRAPPING], to fasten with a strap.

**strap·ping** (strap′iŋ), ***adj.*** [Colloq.], tall and well-built; strong; robust.

**stra·ta** (strā′tə, strat′ə), ***n.*** pl. of **stratum.**

**strat·a·gem** (strat′ə-jəm), ***n.*** [< Gr. *stratos*, army + *agein*, to lead], 1. a trick, device, etc. for deceiving an enemy in war. 2. any tricky ruse.

**stra·te·gic** (strə-tē′jik), ***adj.*** 1. of strategy. 2. sound in strategy. 3. essential to effective military strategy. Also **stra·te′gi·cal. —stra·te′gi·cal·ly,** ***adv.***

**strat·e·gy** (strat′ə-ji), ***n.*** [*pl.* -GIES], 1. the science of planning and directing military operations. 2. skill in managing or planning, esp. by using stratagem. **—strat′e·gist,** ***n.***

**strat·i·fy** (strat′ə-fī′), ***v.t. & v.i.*** [-FIED, -FYING], to form or arrange in layers or strata. **—strat′i·fi·ca′tion,** ***n.***

**strat·o·sphere** (strat′ə-sfêr′), ***n.*** [see STRATUM], the part of the earth's atmosphere from an altitude of about seven miles to the ionosphere.

**stra·tum** (strā′təm, strat′əm), ***n.*** [*pl.* -TA, -TUMS], [L. < *stratus*, a spreading], 1. a horizontal layer of matter; specif., a single layer of sedimentary rock. 2. a level of society.

**stra·tus** (strā′təs), ***n.*** [*pl.* -TI (-tī)], [see STRATUM], a cloud formation extending in a long, low layer.

**straw** (strô), ***n.*** [AS. *streaw*], 1. hollow stalks of grain after threshing. 2. a single one of these. 3. a tube used for sucking beverages. 4. a trifle. ***adj.*** 1. straw-colored; yellowish. 2. made of straw. 3. worthless.

**straw·ber·ry** (strô′ber′i, -bẽr-i), ***n.*** [*pl.* -RIES], [prob. from the strawlike particles on the fruit], 1. the small, red, fleshy fruit of a vinelike plant of the rose family. 2. this plant.

**straw boss,** [Colloq.], a person having subordinate authority.

**straw vote,** an unofficial vote taken to determine general group opinion.

**stray** (strā), ***v.i.*** [prob. < L. *extra vagare*, wander outside], 1. to wander from a given place, course, etc. 2. to deviate (*from* what is right). ***n.*** one that strays; esp., a lost domestic animal. ***adj.*** 1. having strayed; lost. 2. isolated: as, a few *stray* words.

**streak** (strēk), ***n.*** [< AS. *strica*], 1. a long, thin mark or stripe. 2. a layer, as of fat in meat. 3. a tendency in behavior, etc.: as, a nervous *streak*. 4. [Colloq.], a period, as of luck. ***v.t.*** to mark with streaks. ***v.i.*** 1. to become streaked. 2. to go fast. **—like a streak,** [Colloq.], swiftly. **—streak′y,** ***adj.***

**stream** (strēm), ***n.*** [AS.], 1. a current of water; specif., a small river. 2. any steady flow, as of air, light, etc. 3. a continuous series: as, a *stream* of cars. ***v.i.*** 1. to flow as in a stream. 2. to flow (*with*): as, eyes *streaming* with tears. 3. to move swiftly.

**stream′er,** ***n.*** 1. a long, narrow flag. 2. any long, narrow, flowing strip. 3. a newspaper headline across the page.

**stream′line′,** ***adj.*** designating, of, or having a contour designed to offer the least resistance in moving through air, water, etc.: also **stream′lined′.** ***v.t.*** [-LINED, -LINING], to give a streamline form to.

**street** (strēt), ***n.*** [< L. *strata via*, paved road], 1. a public road in a city or town; esp., a paved thoroughfare with its sidewalks and buildings. 2. such a road apart from its sidewalks.

**street′car′,** ***n.*** a car on rails for public transportation along the streets.

**street′walk′er,** ***n.*** a prostitute.

**strength** (streŋth, streŋkth), ***n.*** [AS. *strengthu*], 1. the state or quality of being strong; force. 2. toughness; durability. 3. the power to resist attack. 4. potency, as of drugs. 5. intensity, as of sound, etc. 6. force of an army, etc. as measured in numbers.

**strength′en,** ***v.t. & v.i.*** to make or become stronger. **—strength′en·er,** ***n.***

**stren·u·ous** (stren′ū-əs), ***adj.*** [L. *strenuus*], requiring or characterized by great effort or energy. **—stren′u·ous·ly,** ***adv.***

**strep·to·coc·cus** (strep′tə-kok′əs), ***n.*** [*pl.* -COCCI (-kok′sī)], [< Gr. *streptos*, bent + *kokkos*, a grain], any of various spherical bacteria occurring in chains: some cause serious diseases.

**strep·to·my·cin** (strep′tə-mī′sin), ***n.*** [< Gr. *streptos*, bent + *mykēs*, fungus], an antibiotic drug obtained from molds and used in treating various diseases.

**stress** (stres), ***n.*** [< L. *strictus*, strict], 1. strain; pressure; esp., force that strains or deforms. 2. urgency; importance. 3. tension; strained exertion. 4. the relative force of utterance given a syllable or word; accent. ***v.t.*** 1. to put stress or pressure on. 2. to accent. 3. to emphasize.

**stretch** (strech), ***v.t.*** [AS. *streccan*], 1. to reach out (a hand, etc.). 2. to draw out to full extent or to greater size. 3. to extend beyond normal limits; strain. 4. to exaggerate. *v.i.* 1. *a*) to spread out to full extent or beyond normal limits. *b*) to extend over a given distance. 2. to extend the body or limbs to full length. 3. to become stretched. 4. to lie down (usually with *out*). *n.* 1. a stretching or being stretched. 2. an unbroken period: as, a *stretch* of ten years. 3. an unbroken length, tract, etc. 4. one of the straight sections of a race track.

**stretch′er,** *n.* 1. one that stretches. 2. a light, canvas-covered frame for carrying the sick or injured.

**strew** (strōō), *v.t.* [STREWED, STREWED or STREWN, STREWING], [AS. *streowian*], 1. to scatter; spread here and there as by sprinkling. 2. to cover as by scattering.

**stri·at·ed** (strī′āt-id), *adj.* [< L. *striare*, to groove], marked with thin, parallel lines.

**strick·en** (strik′ən), alt. pp. of **strike.** *adj.* 1. struck or wounded. 2. afflicted, as by something painful.

**strict** (strikt), *adj.* [< L. *stringere*, draw tight], 1. exact; precise. 2. perfect; absolute. 3. *a*) enforcing rules carefully. *b*) closely enforced. **—strict′ly,** *adv.* **—strict′ness,** *n.*

**stric·ture** (strik′chẽr), *n.* [see STRICT], 1. adverse criticism. 2. an abnormal narrowing of a passage in the body.

**stride** (strīd), *v.i.* & *v.t.* [STRODE, STRIDDEN (strid′′n), STRIDING], [AS. *stridan*], 1. to walk with long steps. 2. to cross with a single, long step. 3. to straddle. *n.* 1. a long step. 2. the distance covered by a stride.

**stri·dent** (strī′d′nt), *adj.* [< L. *stridere*, to rasp], harsh-sounding; shrill; grating.

**strife** (strīf), *n.* [< OFr. *estrif*], 1. contention. 2. a quarrel; struggle.

**strike** (strīk), *v.t.* [STRUCK, STRUCK or STRICKEN, STRIKING], [< AS. *strican*, to go], 1. *a*) to give a blow to; hit. *b*) to give (a blow, etc.). 2. to make by stamping, etc.: as, to *strike* coins. 3. to announce (time), as with a bell: said of clocks, etc. 4. to ignite (a match) or produce (a light, etc.) by friction. 5. to collide with or cause to collide: as, he *struck* his arm on the door. 6. to attack. 7. to come upon; notice, find, discover, etc. 8. to affect as if by contact, a blow, etc.; to occur to: as, an idea *strikes* me. 9. to make (a bargain, truce, etc.). 10. to lower (a sail, flag, etc.). 11. to assume (a pose, etc.). *v.i.* 1. to hit (*at*). 2. to attack. 3. to make sounds as by being struck, as a bell, clock, etc. 4. to collide; hit (*against*, *on*, or *upon*). 5. to come suddenly (*on* or *upon*). 6. to refuse to continue to work until certain demands are met. 7. to proceed: as, *strike* south. *n.* 1. a striking; blow. 2. a refusal by employees to go on working in an attempt to gain better working conditions. 3. a finding of a rich deposit of oil, etc. 4. in *baseball*, a pitched ball which is struck at but missed, fairly delivered but not struck at, etc. 5. in *bowling*, a knocking down of all the pins on the first bowl. **—strike out,** 1. to erase. 2. in *baseball*, to put out, or be put out, on three strikes. **—strike up,** to begin. **—strik′er,** *n.*

**strike′break′er,** *n.* one who tries to break up a workers' strike as by working as a scab, supplying scabs, etc.

**strik′ing,** *adj.* very attractive, impressive, conspicuous, etc. **—strik′ing·ly,** *adv.*

**string** (striŋ), *n.* [AS. *streng*], 1. a thin line of fiber, leather, wire, etc., used as for tying or pulling. 2. a number of objects on a string: as, a *string* of pearls. 3. a row, series, etc.: as, a *string* of houses. 4. *a*) a slender cord bowed, plucked, etc. to make a musical sound, as on a violin. *b*) *pl.* all the stringed instruments of an orchestra. 5. a fiber of a plant. 6. [Colloq.], a condition attached to a plan, offer, etc. *v.t.* [STRUNG, STRINGING], 1. to provide with strings. 2. to thread on a string. 3. to tie, hang, etc. with a string. 4. to make excited or tense. 5. to remove strings from (beans, etc.). 6. to arrange in a row. 7. to extend: as, *string* a cable. 8. [Colloq.], to hoax (often with *along*). *v.i.* to stretch out in a line. **—pull strings,** to use influence, esp. secretly, to gain advantage. **—string′y,** *adj.*

**string bean,** a bean whose thick, unripe pods are eaten as a vegetable.

**strin·gent** (strin′jənt), *adj.* [< L. *stringere*, draw tight], strict; severe. **—strin′gen·cy** [*pl.* -CIES], *n.* **—strin′gent·ly,** *adv.*

**strip** (strip), *v.t.* [STRIPPED, STRIPPING], [< AS. *strypan*], 1. to remove (the clothing, etc.) from (a person). 2. to dispossess of honors, titles, etc. 3. to plunder; rob. 4. to take off (the covering, skin, etc. of something). 5. to make bare by taking away removable parts, etc. 6. to break the thread of (a bolt), the teeth of (a gear), etc. *v.i.* to take off one's clothing. **—strip′per,** *n.*

**strip** (strip), *n.* [< STRIPE], 1. a long, narrow piece, as of land, tape, etc. 2. a runway for airplanes: also **landing strip.**

**stripe** (strīp), *n.* [< MD.], 1. a long, narrow band or mark differing from the surrounding area. 2. a strip of cloth on a uniform to show rank, years served, etc. 3. kind; sort. *v.t.* [STRIPED, STRIPING], to mark with stripes.

**strip·ling** (strip′liŋ), *n.* a youth.

**strive** (strīv), *v.i.* [STROVE, STRIVEN (striv′′n) or STRIVED, STRIVING], [< OFr. *estrif*, effort], 1. to make great efforts; try very hard. 2. to struggle: as, *strive* against tyranny.

**strode** (strōd), pt. of **stride.**

**stroke** (strōk), *n.* [< AS. *strican*, to hit], 1. a sweeping blow, as of an ax. 2. a sudden action or event: as, a *stroke* of luck. 3. a sudden attack, esp. of apoplexy. 4. a single strong effort. 5. the sound of striking, as of a clock. 6. *a*) a single movement of the arms, hands, etc. or of something held. *b*) any of a series of motions made in swimming, rowing, etc. 7. the rower who sets the rate of rowing. 8. a mark made by a pen, etc. *v.t.* [STROKED, STROKING], to draw one's hand, etc. gently over the surface of.

**stroll** (strōl), *v.i.* [? < G. *strolchen*], 1. to walk about leisurely; saunter. 2. to wander. *v.t.* to stroll along or through. *n.* a leisurely walk.

**stroll′er,** *n.* 1. one who strolls. 2. a small cart for infants learning to walk.

**strong** (strôŋ), *adj.* [AS. *strang*], 1. *a*) physically powerful. *b*) healthy; sound. 2. morally or intellectually powerful: as, a *strong* will. 3. firm; durable: as, a *strong* fort. 4. powerful in wealth, numbers, etc. 5. vigorously effective. 6. intense in degree or quality: as, *strong* coffee, a *strong* light, *strong* colors, etc. 7. forceful, vigorous, etc.

**strong′-arm′,** *adj.* [Colloq.], using physical force. *v.t.* [Colloq.], to use force upon.

**strong′box′,** *n.* a heavily made box or safe for storing valuables.

**strong′hold′,** *n.* a fortress.

**strong′-mind′ed,** *adj.* determined; unyielding: also **strong′-willed′.**

**stron·ti·um** (stron′shi-əm), *n.* [< *Strontian*, Scotland, where first found], a metallic chemical element resembling calcium in properties: symbol, Sr.

**strop** (strop), *n.* [cf. STRAP], a leather strap, esp. one used for putting a fine edge on razors. *v.t.* [STROPPED, STROPPING], to sharpen on a strop. **—strop′per,** *n.*

**strove** (strōv), pt. of **strive.**

**struck** (struk), pt. and pp. of **strike.**

**struc·ture** (struk′chẽr), *n.* [< L. *struere*, arrange], 1. something built or constructed; building, etc. 2. the arrangement of all the parts of a whole. 3. something composed of parts. —**struc′tur·al**, *adj.*

**stru·del** (stroo͞′d′l), *n.* [G.], a pastry made of a thin sheet of dough filled with apples, etc. and rolled.

**strug·gle** (strug′′l), *v.i.* [-GLED, -GLING], [ME. *strogelen*], 1. to fight violently with an opponent. 2. to make great efforts; strive; labor. *n.* 1. great effort. 2. conflict; strife. —**strug′gler**, *n.*

**strum** (strum), *v.t. & v.i.* [STRUMMED, STRUMMING], [echoic], to pluck (a guitar, etc.) carelessly, idly, etc. —**strum′mer**, *n.*

**strum·pet** (strum′pit), *n.* [ME.], a prostitute.

**strung** (struŋ), pt. and pp. of **string**.

**strut** (strut), *v.i.* [STRUTTED, STRUTTING], [< AS. *strutian*, stand rigid], to walk in a vain, swaggering manner. *n.* 1. a strutting walk. 2. a brace fitted into a framework to resist pressure. —**strut′ting·ly**, *adv.*

**strych·nine** (strik′nin, -nēn, -nin), *n.* [< Gr. *strychnos*, nightshade], a highly poisonous crystalline alkaloid: used in small doses as a stimulant: also **strych′nin** (-nin).

**stub** (stub), *n.* [AS. *stubb*], 1. a tree stump. 2. a short piece left over. 3. any short or blunt projection or thing. 4. a short piece of a leaf in a checkbook, etc. kept as a record. *v.t.* [STUBBED, STUBBING], to strike (one's toe, etc.) against something.

**stub·ble** (stub′′l), *n.* [< L. *stipula*, a stalk], 1. the short stumps of grain left standing after the harvest. 2. any growth like this, as of beard. —**stub′bly**, *adj.*

**stub·born** (stub′ẽrn), *adj.* [prob. < AS. *stubb*, a stub], 1. refusing to yield or comply; obstinate. 2. done in an obstinate or persistent manner. 3. hard to handle, etc. —**stub′born·ly**, *adv.* —**stub′born·ness**, *n.*

**stub′by**, *adj.* [-BIER, -BIEST], 1. covered with stubs or stubble. 2. short and dense. 3. short and thickset. —**stub′bi·ness**, *n.*

**stuc·co** (stuk′ō), *n.* [*pl.* -COES, -COS], [It.], a kind of fine plaster used for surfacing walls, etc. *v.t.* [-COED, -COING], to cover with stucco.

**stuck** (stuk), pt. and pp. of **stick**.

**stuck′-up′**, *adj.* [Colloq.], snobbish.

**stud** (stud), *n.* [AS. *studu*, post], 1. any of a series of small knobs, etc. used to ornament a surface. 2. a small, buttonlike device for fastening collars, etc. 3. an upright piece in a building frame, to which laths, etc. are nailed. *v.t.* [STUDDED, STUDDING], 1. to set or decorate with studs, etc. 2. to be set thickly on: as, rocks *stud* the hill.

**stud** (stud), *n.* [AS. *stod*], a place where horses are kept for breeding.

**stu·dent** (stoo͞′d′nt, stū′-), *n.* [< L. *studere*, to study], 1. one who studies something. 2. one who is enrolled for study at a school, college, etc.

**stud·ied** (stud′id), *adj.* 1. prepared by careful study. 2. deliberate.

**stu·di·o** (stoo͞′di-ō, stū′-), *n.* [*pl.* -OS], [It., a study], 1. a room, etc. in which an artist works. 2. a place where motion pictures, or radio or television programs, are produced.

**stu·di·ous** (stoo͞′di-əs, stū′-), *adj.* 1. fond of study. 2. attentive; zealous.

**stud·y** (stud′i), *n.* [*pl.* -IES], [< L. *studere*, to study], 1. the acquiring of knowledge, as by reading, etc. 2. careful examination of a subject, event, etc. 3. a branch of learning. 4. *pl.* education; schooling. 5. earnest effort or deep thought. 6. a room for study, etc. *v.t.* [-IED, -YING], 1. to try to learn by reading, etc. 2. to investigate carefully. 3. to scrutinize; peruse. *v.i.* 1. to seek knowledge. 2. to be a student. 3. to meditate.

**stuff** (stuf), *n.* [< OFr. *estoffe*], 1. the material out of which anything is made. 2. essence; character. 3. any kind of matter, indefinitely. 4. cloth, esp. woolen cloth. 5. objects; things. 6. worthless objects; junk. *v.t.* 1. to fill or pack; specif., *a*) to fill the skin of (a dead animal) in order to preserve it. *b*) to fill (a fowl, etc.) with seasoning, bread crumbs, etc. before roasting. 2. to fill too full; cram. 3. to plug; block. *v.i.* to eat too much.

**stuffed shirt**, [Slang], a pompous, but actually unimportant person.

**stuff′ing**, *n.* something used to stuff, as padding in upholstery, a bread-crumb filling for roast fowl, etc.

**stuff′y**, *adj.* [-IER, -IEST], 1. poorly ventilated; close. 2. having the nasal passages stopped up, as from a cold. 3. [Colloq.], dull; stodgy. —**stuff′i·ness**, *n.*

**stul·ti·fy** (stul′tə-fī′), *v.t.* [-FIED, -FYING], [< L. *stultus*, foolish + *facere*, make], 1. to cause to appear foolish, stupid, etc. 2. to make worthless, etc. —**stul′ti·fi·ca′tion**, *n.*

**stum·ble** (stum′b′l), *v.i.* [-BLED, -BLING], [< ME. *stomblen*], 1. to trip in walking, running, etc. 2. to walk unsteadily. 3. to speak, act, etc. in a blundering manner. 4. to do wrong. 5. to come by chance. *n.* 1. a stumbling. 2. a blunder, error, or sin.

**stump** (stump), *n.* [prob. < ON.], 1. the end of a tree or plant left in the ground after cutting off the upper part. 2. the part of a leg, tooth, etc. left after the rest has been removed. 3. the place where a political speech is made. *v.t.* 1. to remove stumps from (land). 2. to travel over (a district) making political speeches. 3. [Colloq.], to puzzle, perplex. *v.i.* 1. to walk heavily. 2. to travel about making political speeches.

**stun** (stun), *v.t.* [STUNNED, STUNNING], [< L. *ex-*, intens. + *tonare*, to crash], 1. to make unconscious, as by a blow. 2. to daze; astound. *n.* a being stunned.

**stung** (stuŋ), pt. and pp. of **sting**.

**stunk** (stuŋk), pp. and alt. pt. of **stink**.

**stun·ning** (stun′iŋ), *adj.* [Colloq.], remarkable for beauty, smartness, etc.

**stunt** (stunt), *v.t.* [< AS. *stunt*, stupid], 1. to check the growth or development of. 2. to hinder (growth, etc.). *n.* a stunting.

**stunt** (stunt), *n.* [? akin to *stint*], [Colloq.], something done to attract attention; exhibition of skill or daring. *v.i.* [Colloq.], to perform a stunt. —**stunt′er**, *n.*

**stu·pe·fy** (stoo͞′pə-fī′, stū′-), *v.t.* [-FIED, -FYING], [< L. *stupere*, be stunned + *facere*, to make], 1. to stun; make dull, etc. 2. to amaze; astonish. —**stu′pe·fac′tion** (-fak′shən), *n.*

**stu·pen·dous** (stoo͞-pen′dəs, stū-), *adj.* [< L. *stupere*, be stunned], astonishingly great.

**stu·pid** (stoo͞′pid, stū′-), *adj.* [< L. *stupere*, be stunned], 1. slow-witted; dull. 2. resulting from a lack of intelligence; foolish. 3. dull, tiresome, etc. —**stu·pid′i·ty** [*pl.* -TIES], *n.* —**stu′pid·ly**, *adv.*

**stu·por** (stoo͞′pẽr, stū′-), *n.* [L.], a state in which the mind and senses are dulled; loss of sensibility. —**stu′por·ous**, *adj.*

**stur·dy** (stũr′di), *adj.* [-DIER, -DIEST], [< OFr. *estourdi*, stunned], 1. firm; resolute. 2. strong; vigorous. —**stur′di·ly**, *adv.*

**stur·geon** (stũr′jən), *n.* [< Gmc.], a large food fish valuable as a source of caviar.

**stut·ter** (stut′ẽr), *n., v.t. & v.i.* [< ME. *stutten*], stammer. —**stut′ter·er**, *n.*

**sty** (stī), *n.* [*pl.* STIES], [AS. *sti*], 1. a pen for pigs. 2. any filthy place.

**sty, stye** (stī), *n.* [*pl.* STIES], [ult. < AS. *stigan*, to rise], a small, inflamed swelling on the rim of the eyelid.

**style** (stīl), *n.* [< L. *stilus*, pointed writing tool], 1. a stylus. 2. *a*) manner of expression in writing or speaking. *b*) characteristic manner of expression, execution, etc. in any art, period, etc. *c*) distinction, originality, etc. in expression. 3. fashion or fashionable mode: as, to dress in *style*. *v.t.* [STYLED, STYLING], 1. to name; call. 2. to design the style of.

**styl'ish,** *adj.* conforming to current style in dress, etc.; fashionable. —**styl'ish·ly,** *adv.*

**styl'ist,** *n.* a writer, etc. whose work has style (sense 2*c*).

**styl'ize** (-īz), *v.t.* [-IZED, -IZING], to make conform to a given style; make conventional.

**sty·lus** (stī'ləs), *n.* [*pl.* -LUSES, -LI (-lī)], [L. < *stilus*, pointed tool], 1. a sharp, pointed marking device. 2. *a*) a pointed device for cutting the grooves of a phonographic record. *b*) a phonograph needle.

**sty·mie** (stī'mi), *n.* [prob. < Scot. *stymie*, person partially blind], in *golf*, the state of having an opponent's ball lying between one's ball and the hole on a putting green. *v.t.* [-MIED, -MIEING], to obstruct as with a stymie. Also sp. **stymy** [-MIED, -MYING].

**styp·tic** (stip'tik), *adj.* [< Gr. *styphein*, to contract], that halts bleeding; astringent.

**Styx** (stiks), *n.* in *Gr. myth.*, a river over which dead souls were ferried into Hades.

**suave** (swäv), *adj.* [Fr. < L. *suavis*, sweet], smoothly gracious or polite; polished. — —**suav·i·ty** (swav'ə-ti, swä'və-) [*pl.* -TIES], *n.*

**sub** (sub), *n.* [Colloq.], *a contracted form of* submarine, substitute, etc. *v.i.* [SUBBED, SUBBING], [Colloq.], to be a substitute (*for*).

**sub-,** [< L. *sub*, under], a prefix meaning: 1. *beneath*, as in *subsoil*. 2. *lower than*, as in *subaltern*. 3. *to a lesser degree than*, as in *subtropical*.

**sub.,** 1. substitute(s). 2. suburb(an).

**sub·al·tern** (səb-ôl'tērn), *n.* [< L. *sub-*, under + *alternus*, alternate], [Chiefly Brit.], an army officer holding a rank below captain.

**sub'com·mit'tee,** *n.* a subordinate committee chosen from a main committee.

**sub·con'scious,** *adj.* occurring with little or no conscious perception on the part of the individual: said of mental processes. *n.* subconscious mental activity.

**sub·con'tract,** *n.* a secondary contract undertaking some of the obligations of the main contract. —**sub'con'trac·tor,** *n.*

**sub·cu·ta·ne·ous** (sub'kū-tā'ni-əs), *adj.* beneath the skin.

**sub'di·vide',** *v.t. & v.i.* [-VIDED, -VIDING], 1. to divide further. 2. to divide (land) into small parcels. —**sub'di·vi'sion,** *n.*

**sub·due** (səb-dōō', -dū'), *v.t.* [-DUED, -DUING], [< L. *subducere*, to remove], 1. to conquer; vanquish. 2. to overcome, as by persuasion; control. 3. to make less intense; diminish; soften. —**sub·du'a·ble,** *adj.*

**subj.,** 1. subject. 2. subjunctive.

**sub·ject** (sub'jikt), *adj.* [< L. *sub-*, under + *jacere*, to throw], 1. under the authority or control of another. 2. having a tendency: as, *subject* to temptation. 3. exposed: as, *subject* to censure. 4. contingent upon: as, *subject* to approval. *n.* 1. a person under the authority or control of another. 2. someone or something undergoing a treatment, experiment, etc. 3. something dealt with in discussion, study, etc.; topic. 4. in *grammar*, the word or words in a sentence about which something is said. *v.t.* (səb-jekt'), 1. to bring under the authority or control of. 2. to cause to undergo something: as, they *subjected* him to indignities. —**sub·jec'tion,** *n.*

**sub·jec·tive** (səb-jek'tiv), *adj.* of or resulting from the feelings of the person thinking rather than the attributes of the object thought of. —**sub·jec'tive·ly,** *adv.* —**sub·jec·tiv·i·ty** (sub'jek-tiv'ə-ti), *n.*

**sub·join** (səb-join'), *v.t.* [see SUB- & JOIN], to add (something) at the end; append.

**sub·ju·gate** (sub'joo-gāt'), *v.t.* [-GATED, -GATING], [< L. *sub-*, under + *jugum*, a yoke], to conquer or make subservient. —**sub'ju·ga'tion,** *n.* —**sub'ju·ga'tor,** *n.*

**sub·junc·tive** (səb-juŋk'tiv), *adj.* [< L. *subjungere*, subjoin], designating or of that mood of a verb used to express supposition, possibility, desire, etc., rather than to state an actual fact.

**sub·lease** (sub'lēs'), *n.* a lease granted by a lessee. *v.t.* (sub-lēs'), [-LEASED, -LEASING], to grant or hold a sublease of.

**sub·let** (sub-let'), *v.t.* [-LET, -LETTING], 1. to lease to another (property leased to oneself). 2. to let out (work) to a subcontractor.

**sub·li·mate** (sub'lə-māt'), *v.t. & v.i.* [-MATED, -MATING], 1. to sublime (a solid). 2. to express (certain impulses or drives) in constructive, socially acceptable forms. —**sub'li·ma'tion,** *n.*

**sub·lime** (sə-blīm'), *adj.* [< L. *sub-*, up to + *limen*, lintel], 1. noble; exalted. 2. inspiring awe or admiration. *n.* something sublime (with *the*). *v.t.* [-LIMED, -LIMING], to purify (a solid) by heating to a gaseous state and condensing the vapor back into solid form. —**sub·lim'i·ty** (-blim'ə-ti), *n.*

**sub·lim·i·nal** (sub-lim'ə-n'l), *adj.* [< *sub-* + L. *limen*, threshold], too slight to be perceived; subconscious.

**sub·ma·chine gun** (sub'mə-shēn'), a portable, automatic firearm.

**sub·ma·rine** (sub'mə-rēn'), *adj.* being, living, etc. beneath the surface of the sea. *n.* (sub'mə-rēn'), a kind of warship that can operate under water.

**sub·merge** (səb-mūrj'), *v.t. & v.i.* [-MERGED, -MERGING], [< L. *sub-*, under + *mergere*, to plunge], to place or sink under the surface, as of water. —**sub·mer'gence,** *n.*

**sub·merse** (səb-mūrs'), *v.t.* [-MERSED, -MERSING], to submerge. —**sub·mer'sion,** *n.*

**sub·mis·sion** (səb-mish'ən), *n.* 1. a submitting or surrendering. 2. resignation; obedience. —**sub·mis'sive,** *adj.*

**sub·mit** (səb-mit'), *v.t.* [-MITTED, -MITTING], [< L. *sub-*, under + *mittere*, send], 1. to present to others for consideration, etc. 2. to yield to the control of another; surrender. 3. to offer as an opinion. *v.i.* to yield.

**sub·nor·mal** (sub-nôr'm'l), *adj.* below normal, esp. in intelligence.

**sub·or·di·nate** (sə-bôr'də-nit), *adj.* [< L. *sub-*, under + *ordinare*, to order], 1. below another in rank, importance, etc. 2. under the authority of another. 3. introducing a subordinate clause: as, *if* is a *subordinate* conjunction. *n.* a subordinate person or thing. *v.t.* (-nāt'), [-NATED, -NATING], to place in a subordinate position.

**subordinate clause,** a clause that is dependent upon another clause and is not itself a sentence.

**sub·orn** (sə-bôrn'), *v.t.* [< L. *sub-*, under + *ornare*, furnish], to induce (another) to commit perjury. —**sub·or·na·tion** (sub'ôr-nā'shən), *n.*

**sub·poe·na** (sə-pē'nə, səb-), *n.* [< L. *sub*, under + *poena*, penalty], a written legal order directing a person to appear in court to testify, etc. *v.t.* [-NAED, -NAING], to summon with such an order. Also sp. **subpena.**

**‡sub ro·sa** (sub rō'zə), [L., under the rose], secretly; privately.

**sub·scribe** (səb-skrīb'), *v.t. & v.i.* [-SCRIBED, -SCRIBING], [< L. *sub-*, under + *scribere*, write], 1. to sign (one's name) to a document, etc. 2. to give support or consent (to). 3. to promise to contribute (money). —**subscribe to,** to agree to receive and pay for (a periodical, etc.). —**sub·scrib'er,** *n.*

**sub·script** (sub'skript), *adj.* [see SUBSCRIBE], written underneath. *n.* a figure, symbol, etc. that is written underneath, as $x$ in $3_x$.

**sub·scrip·tion** (səb-skrip′shən), *n.* 1. a subscribing. 2. money subscribed. 3. a formal agreement to receive and pay for a periodical, etc.
**sub·se·quent** (sub′si-kwənt), *adj.* [< L. *sub-*, after + *sequi*, follow], coming after; following. **—sub′se·quent·ly,** *adv.*
**sub·ser·vi·ent** (səb-sũr′vi-ənt), *adj.* 1. that is of service, esp. in a subordinate capacity. 2. submissive; servile. **—sub·ser′vi·ence,** *n.*
**sub·side** (səb-sīd′), *v.i.* [-SIDED, -SIDING], [< L. *sub-*, under + *sidere*, settle], 1. to sink to a lower level or the bottom. 2. to become less active, intense, etc.
**sub·sid·i·ar·y** (səb-sid′i-er′i), *adj.* [see SUBSIDY], giving aid, service, etc., esp. in a subordinate capacity; supplementary. *n.* [*pl.* -IES], 1. one that is subsidiary. 2. a company controlled by another company.
**sub·si·dize** (sub′sə-dīz′), *v.t.* [-DIZED, -DIZING], to support with a subsidy. **—sub′si·di·za′tion,** *n.* **—sub′si·diz′er,** *n.*
**sub·si·dy** (sub′sə-di), *n.* [*pl.* -DIES], [< L. *subsidium*, reserve troops], a grant of money, as from a government to a private enterprise considered of benefit to the public.
**sub·sist** (səb-sist′), *v.i.* [< L. *sub-*, under + *sistere*, stand], 1. to continue to be; exist. 2. to continue to live (*on* or *by*).
**sub·sist′ence,** *n.* 1. a subsisting. 2. the act of providing sustenance. 3. means of support or livelihood. **—sub·sist′ent,** *adj.*
**sub·soil** (sub′soil′), *n.* the layer of soil beneath the surface soil.
**sub·stance** (sub′stəns), *n.* [< L. *substare*, exist], 1. the real or essential part of anything; essence. 2. the physical matter of which a thing consists; material. 3. *a*) solid or substantial quality. *b*) body; consistency. 4. the essential meaning. 5. wealth.
**sub·stand·ard** (sub-stan′dẽrd), *adj.* below standard.
**sub·stan·tial** (səb-stan′shəl), *adj.* 1. of or having substance. 2. real; true. 3. strong; solid. 4. ample; large. 5. important. 6. well-to-do. 7. with regard to essential parts.
**sub·stan·ti·ate** (səb-stan′shi-āt′), *v.t.* [-ATED, -ATING], [see SUBSTANCE], to show to be true or real by giving evidence. **—sub·stan′ti·a′tion,** *n.*
**sub·stan·tive** (sub′stən-tiv), *n.* [see SUBSTANCE], in *grammar*, 1. a noun. 2. any word or words used as a noun.
**sub·sti·tute** (sub′stə-to͞ot′, -tūt′), *n.* [ult. < L. *sub-*, under + *statuere*, put], a person or thing acting or used in place of another. *v.t. & v.i.* [-TUTED, -TUTING], 1. to use or be used in place of another. 2. to serve in place of (another). *adj.* that is a substitute. **—sub′sti·tu′tion,** *n.*
**sub·stra·tum** (sub-strā′təm), *n.* [*pl.* -TA (-tə), -TUMS], [see SUB- & STRATUM], a part, substance, etc. which lies beneath and supports another.
**sub·ter·fuge** (sub′tẽr-fūj′), *n.* [< L. *subter-*, below + *fugere*, flee], any plan or action used to evade something difficult or unpleasant.
**sub·ter·ra·ne·an** (sub′tə-rā′ni-ən), *adj.* [< L. *sub-*, under + *terra*, earth], 1. underground. 2. secret; hidden.
**sub′ti′tle,** *n.* 1. a secondary or explanatory title. 2. in *motion pictures*, descriptive titles, translations, etc. thrown on the screen between scenes or superimposed on the film.
**sub·tle** (sut′'l), *adj.* [< L. *subtilis*, orig. closely woven], 1. thin; not dense. 2. keen; discriminating. 3. deft; ingenious. 4. crafty; wily. 5. sly: as, a *subtle* wink. 6. hard to solve; intricate. **—sub′tle·ty** [*pl.* -TIES], *n.*
**sub·tract** (səb-trakt′), *v.t. & v.i.* [< L. *sub-*, under + *trahere*, to draw], to take away or deduct, as a part from a whole or one quantity from another. **—sub·trac′tion,** *n.*
**sub·tra·hend** (sub′trə-hend′), *n.* a quantity to be subtracted from another.
**sub·trop·i·cal** (sub-trop′i-k'l), *adj.* designating, of, or characteristic of regions bordering on the tropics.
**sub·urb** (sub′ẽrb), *n.* [< L. *sub-*, under + *urbs*, town], a district, town, etc. on the outskirts of a city. **—sub·ur·ban** (sə-bũr′bən), *adj.*
**sub·ur′bi·a** (-bi-ə), *n.* the suburbs collectively: usually connoting the attitudes, etc. regarded as typical of suburban life.
**sub·ver·sive** (səb-vũr′siv), *adj.* tending to subvert (something established). *n.* a person regarded as subversive.
**sub·vert** (səb-vũrt′), *v.t.* [< L. *sub-*, under + *vertere*, to turn], 1. to overthrow or destroy (something established). 2. to corrupt, as in morals. **—sub·ver′sion** (-vũr′zhən), *n.*
**sub·way** (sub′wā′), *n.* an underground, metropolitan electric railway.
**suc-,** sub-: used before *c*.
**suc·ceed** (sək-sēd′), *v.i.* [< L. *sub-*, under + *cedere*, to go], 1. to come next after; follow, as in office. 2. to accomplish something planned or attempted. *v.t.* to follow; to come after. **—suc·ceed′er,** *n.*
**suc·cess** (sək-ses′), *n.* 1. a favorable result. 2. the gaining of wealth, fame, etc. 3. a successful person or thing.
**suc·cess′ful,** *adj.* 1. having a favorable result. 2. wealthy, famous, etc.
**suc·ces·sion** (sək-sesh′ən), *n.* 1. the act of succeeding or following another. 2. the right to succeed to an office, etc. 3. a number of persons or things coming one after another.
**suc·ces′sive** (-ses′iv), *adj.* coming in succession; consecutive. **—suc·ces′sive·ly,** *adv.*
**suc·ces′sor,** *n.* one who follows or succeeds another, as to an office.
**suc·cinct** (sək-siŋkt′), *adj.* [< L. *sub-*, under + *cingere*, to gird], clearly and briefly stated; terse. **—suc·cinct′ly,** *adv.*
**suc·cor** (suk′ẽr), *v.t.* [< L. *sub-*, under + *currere*, to run], to help in time of need. *n.* aid; relief. Also, Brit. sp., **succour.**
**suc·co·tash** (suk′ə-tash′), *n.* [< Am. Ind.], beans and corn kernels cooked together as a dish.
**suc·cu·lent** (suk′yoo-lənt), *adj.* [< L. *sucus*, juice], 1. full of juice; juicy. 2. interesting; not dry or dull. **—suc′cu·lence, suc′cu·len·cy,** *n.* **—suc′cu·lent·ly,** *adv.*
**suc·cumb** (sə-kum′), *v.i.* [< L. *sub-*, under + *cumbere*, to lie], 1. to give way; yield (often with *to*). 2. to die.
**such** (such), *adj.* [AS. *swylc*], 1. of this or that kind; similar to something suggested. 2. not named; some: as, on *such* a day as you may go. 3. as extreme, as much, etc.: as, *such* an honor. *adv.* [Colloq.], to such a degree: as, *such* a good man. *pron.* 1. such a person or thing. 2. that suggested: as, *such* was his nature. **—as such,** 1. as being what is indicated. 2. in itself. **—such as,** for example.
**suck** (suk), *v.t.* [< AS. *sucan*], 1. to draw (liquid) into the mouth. 2. to take in as if by sucking. 3. to suck liquid from (fruit, etc.). 4. to dissolve by holding in the mouth or licking. *v.i.* to suck something. *n.* the act of sucking.
**suck′er,** *n.* 1. one that sucks. 2. a fish of the carp family. 3. a part used, as by the leech, for sucking or holding fast to something. 4. a shoot from the roots or stem of a plant. 5. [Slang], one easily cheated. 6. [Colloq.], a lollipop.
**suck·le** (suk′'l), *v.i. & v.t.* [-LED, -LING], [freq. of *suck*], 1. to feed at the breast or udder. 2. to rear; foster. **—suck′ler,** *n.*
**suck′ling,** *n.* an unweaned child or young animal.

**su·crose** (sōō′krōs, sū′-), *n.* [< Fr. *sucre*, sugar], a sugar found in sugar cane, sugar beets, etc.
**suc·tion** (suk′shən), *n.* [< L. *sugere*, to suck], 1. a sucking. 2. the production of a partial vacuum in a space so that the surrounding fluid, etc. is sucked in. *adj.* operating by suction.
**sud·den** (sud′'n), *adj.* [ult. < L. *sub-*, under + *ire*, go], 1. happening or appearing unexpectedly. 2. taking place quickly or abruptly. —**all of a sudden**, in a sudden manner.
**suds** (sudz), *n.pl.* [prob. < MD. *sudse*, marsh water], 1. soapy water. 2. froth or foam. —**suds′y** [-IER, -IEST], *adj.* —**suds′i·ness**, *n.*
**sue** (sōō, sū), *v.t. & v.i.* [SUED, SUING], [< L. *sequi*, follow], 1. to appeal (to); petition. 2. to prosecute in a court in seeking redress of wrongs, etc. —**su′er**, *n.*
**suede, suède** (swād), *n.* [< Fr. *gants de Suède*, gloves of Sweden], 1. tanned leather having the flesh side buffed into a nap. 2. a cloth like this.
**su·et** (sōō′it, sū′-), *n.* [< L. *sebum*, fat], the hard fat of cattle and sheep: used in cooking and as tallow. —**su′et·y**, *adj.*
**suf-**, sub-: used before *f.*
**suf·fer** (suf′ẽr), *v.t. & v.i.* [< L. *sub-*, under + *ferre*, to bear], 1. to undergo or endure (pain, injury, loss, etc.). 2. to experience (any process). 3. to permit; tolerate. —**suf′fer·a·ble**, *adj.* —**suf′fer·er**, *n.*
**suf′fer·ance**, *n.* 1. the capacity to endure pain, etc. 2. consent, permission, etc. implied by failure to prohibit.
**suf′fer·ing**, *n.* 1. the bearing of pain, distress, etc. 2. something suffered.
**suf·fice** (sə-fīs′), *v.i. & v.t.* [-FICED, -FICING], [< L. *sub-*, under + *facere*, make], to satisfy; be enough (for). —**suf·fic′er**, *n.*
**suf·fi·cient** (sə-fish′ənt), *adj.* as much as is needed; enough; adequate. —**suf·fi′cien·cy**, *n.* —**suf·fi′cient·ly**, *adv.*
**suf·fix** (suf′iks), *n.* [< *sub-*, under + *figere*, fix], a syllable or syllables added at the end of a word to alter its meaning, etc., as *-ness* in *darkness*.
**suf·fo·cate** (suf′ə-kāt′), *v.t.* [-CATED, -CATING], [< L. *sub-*, under + *fauces*, throat], 1. to kill by cutting off the supply of air for breathing. 2. to smother, stifle, etc. *v.i.* 1. to die by being suffocated. 2. to choke; stifle; smother. —**suf′fo·ca′tion**, *n.*
**suf·frage** (suf′rij), *n.* [< L. *suffragium*], 1. a vote or voting. 2. the right to vote.
**suf·fra·gette** (suf′rə-jet′), *n.* a woman who advocated female suffrage.
**suf·fuse** (sə-fūz′), *v.t.* [-FUSED, -FUSING], [< L. *sub-*, under + *fundere*, pour], to overspread, as with a liquid, light, etc. —**suf·fu′sion**, *n.* —**suf·fu′sive**, *adj.*
**sug·ar** (shoog′ẽr), *n.* [< Sans. *śarkarā*], any of a class of sweet, soluble carbohydrates, as sucrose, glucose, etc.; specif., the sucrose extracted from sugar cane and sugar beets. *v.t.* 1. to sweeten, cover, etc. with sugar. 2. to make less disagreeable. *v.i.* to form sugar crystals. —**sug′ar·y**, *adj.*
**sugar beet**, a beet having a white root with a high sugar content.
**sugar cane**, a very tall tropical grass cultivated as the main source of sugar.
**sug′ar-coat′**, *v.t.* 1. to coat with sugar. 2. to make seem more pleasant.
**sug′ar·plum′** (-plum′), *n.* a round piece of sugary candy; bonbon.
**sug·gest** (səg-jest′), *v.t.* [< L. *sub-*, under + *gerere*, carry], 1. to bring (a thought, etc.) to the mind. 2. to call to mind by association of ideas. 3. to propose as a possibility. 4. to show indirectly; imply.
**sug·ges·tion** (səg-jes′chən), *n.* 1. a suggesting or being suggested. 2. something suggested. 3. a faint hint; trace.
**sug·ges′tive**, *adj.* 1. that tends to suggest ideas. 2. tending to suggest something considered improper or indecent.
**su·i·cide** (sōō′i-sīd′, sū′-), *n.* [L. *sui*, of oneself; + *-cide*], 1. the act of killing oneself intentionally. 2. one who commits suicide. —**su′i·cid′al**, *adj.* —**su′i·cid′al·ly**, *adv.*
**suit** (sōōt, sūt), *n.* [< L. *sequi*, follow], 1. a set of clothes; esp., a coat and trousers (or skirt). 2. any of the four sets of playing cards. 3. action to secure justice in a court of law. 4. an act of suing, pleading, etc. *v.t.* 1. to be suitable for. 2. to make suitable or appropriate; fit. 3. to please; satisfy: as, nothing *suits* him. —**follow suit**, to follow the example set. —**suit oneself**, to act according to one's own wishes.
**suit′a·ble**, *adj.* that suits a given purpose, etc.; appropriate. —**suit′a·bil′i·ty**, *n.* —**suit′a·bly**, *adv.*
**suit′case′**, *n.* a flat, rectangular traveling bag, or valise.
**suite** (swēt), *n.* [Fr.; see SUIT], 1. a group of attendants; staff. 2. a group of connected rooms used as a unit. 3. (*occas.* sōōt, sūt), a set of matched furniture for a given room.
**suit′ing**, *n.* cloth for making suits.
**suit·or** (sōō′tẽr, sū′-), *n.* a man who courts a woman.
**sul·fa** (sul′fə), *adj.* designating or of a family of drugs of the sulfanilamide type, used in combating certain bacterial infections.
**sul·fa·nil·a·mide** (sul′fə-nil′ə-mīd′), *n.* a white crystalline sulfa drug used in treating gonorrhea, streptococcus infections, etc.
**sul·fate** (sul′fāt), *n.* a salt of sulfuric acid.
**sul·fide** (sul′fīd), *n.* a compound of sulfur with another element or a radical.
**sul·fur** (sul′fẽr), *n.* [L. *sulphur*, sulfur], a pale-yellow, nonmetallic chemical element: it burns with a blue flame and a stifling odor: symbol, S: also sp. **sulphur**.
**sul·fu·ric** (sul-fyoor′ik), *adj.* of or containing sulfur.
**sulfuric acid**, an oily, colorless, corrosive liquid used in explosives, fertilizers, etc.
**sul·fu·rous** (sul-fyoor′əs, sul′fẽr-), *adj.* 1. of or containing sulfur. 2. like burning sulfur in odor, color, etc.
**sulk** (sulk), *v.i.* [< *sulky*], to be sulky. *n.* *often pl.* a sulky mood or state. —**sulk′er**, *n.*
**sulk·y** (sul′ki), *adj.* [-IER, -IEST], [prob. < AS. *solcen*, remiss], sullen; glum. *n.* [*pl.* -IES], a light, two-wheeled carriage for one person. —**sulk′i·ly**, *adv.* —**sulk′i·ness**, *n.*
**sul·len** (sul′ən), *adj.* [< L. *solus*, alone], 1. showing resentment and ill-humor by morose, unsociable withdrawal; glum. 2. gloomy; dismal. —**sul′len·ly**, *adv.*
**sul·ly** (sul′i), *v.t. & v.i.* [-LIED, -LYING], [prob. < Fr. *souiller*], to soil, stain, defile, etc. *n.* [*pl.* -LIES], a stain or tarnish.
**sul·pha** (sul′fə), *adj.* sulfa.
**sul·phur** (sul′fẽr), *n.* sulfur.
**sul·tan** (sul′t'n), *n.* [< Ar. *sulṭān*], a Moslem ruler.
**sul·tan·ate** (sul′t'n-it, -āt′), *n.* 1. the authority or position of a sultan. 2. the territory of a sultan. Also **sul′tan·ship′**.
**sul·try** (sul′tri), *adj.* [-TRIER, -TRIEST], [< *swelter*], 1. oppressively hot and moist; close. 2. inflamed, as with passion. —**sul′tri·ness**, *n.*
**sum** (sum), *n.* [< L. *summus*, highest], 1. an amount of money. 2. the whole amount. 3. gist; summary. 4. the result obtained by adding together two or more quantities; total. 5. [Colloq.], a problem in arithmetic. *v.t.* [SUMMED, SUMMING], 1. to collect into a whole. 2. to summarize. Usually with *up*.
**su·mac, su·mach** (shōō′mak, sōō′-), *n.* [< Ar. *summaq*], any of various plants with lance-shaped leaves and cone-shaped clusters of red fruit.

**sum·ma·rize** (sum'ə-rīz'), *v.t.* [-RIZED, -RIZING], to make or be a summary of.
**sum·ma·ry** (sum'ə-ri), *adj.* [< L. *summa*, a sum], 1. summarizing; concise. 2. done without delay or ceremony. *n.* [*pl.* -RIES], a brief statement covering the main points; digest. —**sum·ma·ri·ly** (sum'ə-rə-li, su-mer'ə-li), *adv.* —**sum'ma·ri·ness,** *n.*
**sum·ma·tion** (sum-ā'shən), *n.* 1. the act of finding a total. 2. a final summing up of arguments, as in a trial.
**sum·mer** (sum'ẽr), *n.* [AS. *sumor*], the warmest season of the year, following spring. *adj.* of or for summer. *v.i.* to pass the summer. —**sum'mer·y,** *adj.*
**sum'mer·house',** *n.* an open structure, as in a park, providing a shady rest.
**sum'mer·time',** *n.* the summer season.
**sum·mit** (sum'it), *n.* [< L. *summus*, highest], 1. the highest point; top. 2. the highest degree or state; acme. 3. the highest level of officialdom, involving heads of government: as, a meeting at the *summit.*
**sum·mon** (sum'ən), *v.t.* [< L. *sub-*, secretly + *monere*, warn], 1. to call together; order to convene. 2. to call or send for with authority. 3. to call forth; rouse: as, *summon* (*up*) your strength. —**sum'mon·er,** *n.*
**sum·mons** (sum'ənz), *n.* [*pl.* -MONSES], [see SUMMON], 1. a call or order to come, attend, etc. 2. in *law*, an official order to appear in court.
**sump·tu·ous** (sump'chōō-əs), *adj.* [< L. *sumptus*, expense], 1. costly; lavish. 2. magnificent; splendid.
**sun** (sun), *n.* [AS. *sunne*], 1. the incandescent body of gases about which the earth and other planets revolve. 2. the heat or light of the sun. 3. any similar body that is the center of a system of satellites. *v.t.* [SUNNED, SUNNING], to warm, dry, tan, etc. in the sunlight. —**sun'less,** *adj.*
**Sun.,** Sunday.
**sun'-bathe'** (-bāth'), *v.i.* [-BATHED, -BATHING], to expose the body to sunlight. —**sun bath.**
**sun'beam',** *n.* a beam of sunlight.
**sun'bon'net,** *n.* a bonnet for shading the face and neck from the sun.
**sun'burn'** (-būrn'), *n.* inflammation of the skin from exposure to the sun. *v.t.* & *v.i.* [-BURNED or -BURNT, -BURNING], to give or get sunburn.
**sun·dae** (sun'di), *n.* [? < *Sunday*], a serving of ice cream covered with sirup, fruit, nuts, etc.
**Sun·day** (sun'di), *n.* [< AS. *sunnan dæg*, day of the sun], the first day of the week: set aside as a day of rest and worship by most Christians.
**sun·der** (sun'dẽr), *v.t.* & *v.i.* [< AS. *sundor*, asunder], to break apart; split.
**sun·di·al** (sun'dī'əl, -dīl'), *n.* an instrument that shows time by the shadow of a pointer cast by the sun on a dial.
**sun'down'** (-doun'), *n.* sunset.
**sun'dries** (-driz), *n.pl.* sundry items.
**sun·dry** (sun'dri), *adj.* [< AS. *sunder*, apart], various; miscellaneous.
**sun'fish',** *n.* [*pl.* see FISH], 1. a small, freshwater fish of N. America. 2. a large ocean fish with a short, thick body.
**sun'flow'er,** *n.* a tall plant having yellow, daisylike flowers containing edible seeds.
**sung** (suŋ), pp. and rare pt. of **sing.**
**sunk** (suŋk), pp. and alt. pt. of **sink.**
**sunk·en** (suŋk'ən), *adj.* 1. sunk in liquid; esp., at the bottom of a body of water. 2. below the general level: as, a *sunken* room. 3. depressed; hollow: as, *sunken* cheeks.
**sun lamp,** an ultraviolet-ray lamp, used therapeutically, etc.
**sun'light',** *n.* the light of the sun.
**sun'lit',** *adj.* lighted by the sun.
**sun'ny** (-i), *adj.* [-NIER, -NIEST], 1. full of sunshine. 2. of or like the sun. 3. cheerful; bright. —**sun'ni·ness,** *n.*
**sun'rise'** (-rīz'), *n.* 1. the daily appearance of the sun above the eastern horizon. 2. the time of this.
**sun'set'** (-set'), *n.* 1. the daily disappearance of the sun below the western horizon. 2. the time of this.
**sun'shine',** *n.* 1. the shining of the sun. 2. light and heat from the sun. 3. cheerfulness, happiness, etc. —**sun'shin'y,** *adj.*
**sun'spot',** *n.* any of the dark spots sometimes seen on the surface of the sun.
**sun'stroke',** *n.* a condition caused by excessive exposure to the sun, characterized by fever, convulsions, etc.
**sun tan,** darkened skin resulting from exposure to the sun. —**sun'-tanned',** *adj.*
**sun'up',** *n.* sunrise.
**sup** (sup), *v.i.* [SUPPED, SUPPING], [< OFr. *soper*], to have supper.
**super-,** [L. < *super*, above], a prefix meaning: 1. *over, above*, as in *superscribe.* 2. *superior to*, as in *supervisor.* 3. *a*) *surpassing*, as in *superabundant.* *b*) *greater than others of its kind*, as in *supermarket.*
**su·per·a·bun·dant** (sōō'pẽr-ə-bun'dənt, sū'-), *adj.* being more than enough. —**su'per·a·bun'dance,** *n.*
**su'per·an'nu·at'ed** (-an'ū-āt'id), *adj.* [< L. *super annum*, beyond a year], 1. retired on a pension because of old age or infirmity. 2. too old for work.
**su·perb** (soo-pūrb', syoo-), *adj.* [< L. *super*, above], 1. noble; majestic. 2. rich; luxurious. 3. extremely fine; excellent.
**su·per·car·go** (sōō'pẽr-kär'gō, sū'-), *n.* [*pl.* -GOES, -GOS], an officer on a merchant ship in charge of the cargo.
**su'per·charge'** (-chärj'), *v.t.* [-CHARGED, -CHARGING], to increase the power of (an engine) as with a device (**supercharger**) that forces air into the cylinders.
**su·per·cil·i·ous** (sōō'pẽr-sil'i-əs, sū'-), *adj.* [< L. *super-*, above + *cilium*, eyelid, hence (in allusion to raised eyebrows) haughtiness], disdainful or contemptuous; haughty.
**su·per·e·go** (sōō'pẽr-ē'gō, sū'-), *n.* in *psychoanalysis*, that part of the psyche which controls the impulses of the id.
**su·per·fi·cial** (sōō'pẽr-fish'əl, sū'-), *adj.* [< L. *super-*, above + *facies*, face], 1. of or being on the surface. 2. concerned with and understanding only the obvious; shallow. 3. quick and cursory. 4. apparent, but not real. —**su'per·fi'ci·al'i·ty** (-i-al'ə-ti) [*pl.* -TIES], *n.* —**su'per·fi'cial·ly,** *adv.*
**su·per·fine** (sōō'pẽr-fīn', sū'-), *adj.* 1. too refined; overnice. 2. very fine; excellent: said of goods.
**su·per·flu·ous** (soo-pūr'flōō-əs, syoo-), *adj.* [< L. *super-*, above + *fluere*, to flow], being more than is needed, useful, etc.; excessive. —**su·per·flu·i·ty** (sōō'pẽr-flōō'ə-ti, sū'-), *n.*
**su'per·hu'man,** *adj.* 1. regarded as having a nature above that of man; divine. 2. greater than that of a normal human being.
**su'per·im·pose',** *v.t.* [-POSED, -POSING], to impose or lay (something) on top of something else.
**su'per·in·tend'** (-in-tend'), *v.t.* to act as superintendent of; manage; supervise.
**su'per·in·tend'ent,** *n.* [see SUPER- & INTEND], a person in charge of a department, institution, etc.; director. *adj.* superintending. —**su'per·in·tend'ence,** *n.*
**su·pe·ri·or** (sə-pêr'i-ẽr, soo-), *adj.* [< L. *superus*, that is above], 1. higher in position, rank, authority, etc. 2. greater in quality, amount, etc. 3. of very high quality, ability, etc.; excellent. 4. showing a feeling that one is better than others; haughty. *n.* 1. one who is superior, as in rank, merit, etc.

2. the head of a monastery, convent, etc. **—superior to,** unaffected by; not yielding to (something painful, etc.). **—su·pe'ri·or'i·ty** (-ôr'ə-ti, -or'-), *n.*
**superl.,** superlative.
**su·per·la·tive** (soo-pũr'lə-tiv, syoo-), *adj.* [< L. *super-*, above + *latus*, pp. of *ferre*, carry], 1. superior to all others; supreme. 2. in *grammar*, expressing the extreme degree of comparison of adjectives and adverbs. *n.* 1. the highest degree; acme. 2. in *grammar*, the superlative degree: as, *loveliest* is the *superlative* of *lovely*.
**su·per·man** (soo'pẽr-man', sū'-), *n.* [*pl.* -MEN], an apparently superhuman man.
**su'per·mar'ket,** *n.* a large, self-service food store: also **super market.**
**su·per·nal** (soo-pũr'n'l, sū-), *adj.* [< L. *supernus*, upper], 1. high in rank, power, etc.; exalted. 2. celestial; heavenly.
**su·per·nat·u·ral** (soo'pẽr-nach'ẽr-əl, sū'-), *adj.* attributed to hypothetical forces beyond nature; miraculous; divine.
**su'per·nu'mer·ar'y** (-noo'mẽr-er'i), *adj.* [< L. *super*, above + *numerus*, number], extra. *n.* [*pl.* -IES], 1. an extra person or thing. 2. an actor having a small nonspeaking part.
**su'per·scribe'** (-skrīb'), *v.t.* [-SCRIBED, -SCRIBING], [< L. *super-*, above + *scribere*, write], to write (something) on the top or outer surface. **—su'per·scrip'tion** (-skrip'shən), *n.*
**su·per·sede** (soo'pẽr-sēd', sū'-), *v.t.* [-SEDED, -SEDING], [< L. *super-*, above + *sedere*, sit], 1. to set aside as inferior or obsolete. 2. to replace, succeed, or supplant.
**su'per·son'ic** (-son'ik), *adj.* [< *super* (above) + L. *sonus*, sound], 1. having higher frequencies than those normally audible. 2. surpassing the speed of sound. 3. traveling at such a speed.
**su·per·sti·tion** (soo'pẽr-stish'ən, sū'-), *n.* [< L. *superstitio*, lit., a standing (in awe) over], 1. any belief that is inconsistent with known facts or rational thought, esp. such a belief in omens, the supernatural, etc. 2. any action or practice based on such a belief. **—su'per·sti'tious,** *adj.*
**su'per·struc'ture,** *n.* 1. a structure built on top of another, as above the main deck of a ship. 2. that part of a building above the foundation.
**su·per·vene** (soo'pẽr-vēn', sū'-), *v.i.* [-VENED, -VENING], [< L. *super-*, over + *venire*, come], to come or happen as something additional or unexpected.
**su·per·vise** (soo'pẽr-vīz', sū'-), *v.t. & v.i.* [-VISED, -VISING], [< L. *super-*, over + *videre*, see], to oversee or direct (work, workers, a project, etc.); superintend. **—su'per·vi'sion** (-vizh'ən), *n.* **—su'per·vi'sor,** *n.* **—su'per·vi'so·ry,** *adj.*
**su·pine** (soo-pīn', sū-), *adj.* [L. *supinus*], 1. lying on the back, face upward. 2. sluggish; listless; inactive. **—su·pine'ly,** *adv.*
**supp., suppl.,** supplement.
**sup·per** (sup'ẽr), *n.* [< OFr. *soper*, to sup], the last meal of the day.
**sup·plant** (sə-plant'), *v.t.* [< L. *sub-*, under + *planta*, sole of the foot], 1. to take the place of, esp. by force. 2. to remove in order to replace with something else.
**sup·ple** (sup''l), *adj.* [see SUPPLICATE], 1. easily bent; flexible. 2. lithe; limber. 3. easily influenced; adaptable.
**sup·ple·ment** (sup'lə-mənt), *n.* [see SUPPLY], 1. something added, esp. to make up for a lack. 2. a section of additional material in a book, newspaper, etc. *v.t.* (-ment'), to provide a supplement to. **—sup'ple·men'ta·ry** (-men'tẽr-i), **sup'ple·men'tal,** *adj.*
**sup·pli·ant** (sup'li-ənt), *n.* one who supplicates. *adj.* supplicating. Also **sup'pli·cant** (-lə-kənt).
**sup·pli·cate** (sup'lə-kāt'), *v.t. & v.i.* [-CATED, -CATING], [< L. *sub-*, under + *plicare*, to fold], 1. to ask for (something) humbly. 2. to make a humble request (of). **—sup'pli·ca'tion,** *n.* **—sup'pli·ca'tor,** *n.*
**sup·ply** (sə-plī'), *v.t.* [-PLIED, -PLYING], [< L. *sub-*, under + *plere*, fill], 1. to furnish; provide. 2. to compensate for (a deficiency, etc.). 3. to meet the needs of. *n.* [*pl.* -PLIES], 1. a supplying. 2. the amount available for use or sale; stock. 3. *pl.* needed materials, etc. **—sup·pli'er,** *n.*
**sup·port** (sə-pôrt'), *v.t.* [< L. *sub-*, under + *portare*, carry], 1. to carry the weight of; hold up. 2. to encourage; help. 3. to give approval to; advocate; uphold. 4. to maintain (a person, institution, etc.), with money or subsistence. 5. to help prove, vindicate, etc. 6. to bear; endure. 7. to keep up; maintain. 8. to have a role subordinate to (a star) in a play. *n.* 1. a supporting or being supported. 2. a person or thing that supports. 3. a means of support. **—sup·port'a·ble,** *adj.* **—sup·port'er,** *n.*
**sup·pose** (sə-pōz'), *v.t.* [-POSED, -POSING], [< L. *sub*, under + OFr. *poser*, put], 1. to assume to be true, as for argument's sake. 2. to imagine; think. 3. to consider as a possibility: as, *suppose* I go. 4. to expect: as, I'm *supposed* to sing. *v.i.* to conjecture. **—sup·posed',** *adj.* **—sup·pos'ed·ly,** *adv.*
**sup·po·si·tion** (sup'ə-zish'ən), *n.* 1. a supposing. 2. something supposed; theory.
**sup·pos·i·to·ry** (sə-poz'ə-tôr'i), *n.* [*pl.* -RIES], [< L. *sub-*, under + *ponere*, to place], a small piece of medicated substance, introduced into the rectum, vagina, etc., where it melts.
**sup·press** (sə-pres'), *v.t.* [< L. *sub-*, under + *premere*, to press], 1. to put down by force; quell. 2. to keep back; restrain. 3. to prevent the publication of (a book, etc.). 4. in *psychiatry*, to withhold from consciousness. **—sup·pres'sion** (-presh'ən), *n.*
**sup·pu·rate** (sup'yoo-rāt'), *v.i.* [-RATED, -RATING], [< L. *sub-*, under + *pus*, pus], to form or discharge pus. **—sup'pu·ra'tion,** *n.*
**su·prem·a·cy** (sə-prem'ə-si, syoo-), *n.* [*pl.* -CIES], supreme power or authority.
**su·preme** (sə-prēm', syoo-), *adj.* [< L. *superus*, that is above], 1. highest in rank, power, etc. 2. highest in quality, achievement, etc. 3. highest in degree. 4. final; ultimate.
**Supreme Being,** God.
**Supreme Court,** 1. the highest Federal court. 2. the highest court in any State.
**Supt., supt.,** Superintendent.
**sur-,** [< L. *super*, over], a prefix meaning *over, upon, above, beyond.*
**sur-,** sub-: used before *r.*
**sur·cease** (sũr-sēs'), *n.* [< L. *supersedere*, refrain from], [Archaic], end; cessation.
**sur·charge** (sũr-chärj'), *v.t.* [-CHARGED, -CHARGING], 1. to overcharge. 2. to overload. 3. to mark (a postage stamp) with a surcharge. *n.* (*usually* sũr'chärj'), 1. an additional charge. 2. a new valuation overprinted on a postage stamp.
**sur·cin·gle** (sũr'siŋ'g'l), *n.* [< OFr. *sur-*, over + L. *cingulum*, a belt], a strap passed around a horse's body to bind on a saddle, pack, etc.
**sur·coat** (sũr'kōt'), *n.* [OFr. *surcote*], an outer coat, esp. a short one.
**sure** (shoor), *adj.* [< L. *securus*], 1. that will not fail; reliable: as, a *sure* method. 2. that cannot be doubted, questioned, etc. 3. having no doubt; confident: as, I'm *sure* of my facts. 4. bound to be or happen: as, a *sure* defeat. 5. bound (to do, etc.): as, he is *sure* to lose. *adv.* [Colloq.], surely. **—for sure,** certainly. **—sure enough,** [Colloq.], without doubt. **—sure'ness,** *n.*

**sure′ly,** ***adv.*** 1. with confidence. 2. without a doubt; certainly.

**sure·ty** (shoor′ti, -ə-ti), ***n.*** [*pl.* -TIES], 1. a being sure. 2. something that makes sure, protects, etc. 3. one who makes himself responsible for another. **—sure′ty·ship′,** ***n.***

**surf** (sũrf), ***n.*** [prob. < *sough*, rustle], the waves of the sea breaking on the shore or a reef. ***v.i.*** to ride a surfboard. **—surf′er,** ***n.***

**sur·face** (sũr′fis), ***n.*** [< Fr. *sur-*, over + *face*, a face], 1. *a*) the exterior of an object. *b*) any of the faces of a solid. 2. superficial features. ***adj.*** 1. of, on, or at the surface. 2. exterior; superficial. ***v.t.*** [-FACED, -FACING], to give a specified kind of surface to. ***v.i.*** to rise to the surface of the water.

**surf′board′,** ***n.*** a long, narrow board used in the sport of surfing.

**sur·feit** (sũr′fit), ***n.*** [< OFr. *sur-*, over + *faire*, make], 1. too great an amount or supply. 2. overindulgence, esp. in food or drink. 3. disgust, nausea, etc. resulting from excess. ***v.i.*** to overindulge.

**surf·ing** (sũr′fiŋ), ***n.*** the sport of riding in toward shore on the crest of a wave, esp. on a surfboard.

**surge** (sũrj), ***n.*** [< L. *surgere*, to rise], 1. a large wave of water. 2. a strong swelling or rolling like a wave: as, a *surge* of power. ***v.i.*** [SURGED, SURGING], to move in a surge.

**sur·geon** (sũr′jən), ***n.*** a doctor who practices surgery.

**sur·ger·y** (sũr′jẽr-i), ***n.*** [*pl.* -IES], [ult. < Gr. *cheir*, the hand + *ergein*, to work], 1. the treatment of disease, injury, etc. by manual or instrumental operations. 2. the operating room of a surgeon or hospital.

**sur′gi·cal** (-ji-k'l), ***adj.*** of surgeons or surgery.

**sur·ly** (sũr′li), ***adj.*** [-LIER, -LIEST], [earlier *sirly*, imperious < *sir*], bad-tempered; uncivil; sullenly rude. **—sur′li·ness,** ***n.***

**sur·mise** (sẽr-mīz′), ***n.*** [< OFr. *sur-*, upon + *mettre*, put], a conjecture; guess. ***v.t. & v.i.*** [-MISED, -MISING], to guess.

**sur·mount** (sẽr-mount′), ***v.t.*** [see SUR- (over) & MOUNT], 1. to overcome (a difficulty). 2. to be or rise above. 3. to climb up and across (a height, etc.).

**sur·name** (sũr′nām′), ***n.*** [< OFr. *sur-*, over; + *name*], a family name; last name.

**sur·pass** (sẽr-pas′, -päs′), ***v.t.*** [< OFr. *sur-*, beyond + *passer*, to pass], 1. to excel or be superior to. 2. to go beyond the limit, capacity, etc. of. **—sur·pass′ing,** ***adj.***

**sur·plice** (sũr′plis), ***n.*** [< LL. *super-*, above + *pelliceum*, fur robe], a loose, white gown worn over the cassock by the clergy and choir in some churches. **—sur′pliced,** ***adj.***

**sur·plus** (sũr′plus), ***n.*** [< OFr. < *sur-*, above + L. *plus*, more], a quantity over what is needed or used. ***adj.*** forming a surplus.

**sur·prise** (sẽr-prīz′), ***v.t.*** [-PRISED, -PRISING], [< OFr. *sur-*, above + *prendere*, take], 1. to come upon suddenly or unexpectedly; take unawares. 2. to attack without warning. 3. to amaze; astonish. ***n.*** 1. a surprising or being surprised. 2. something that surprises. **—sur·pris′ing,** ***adj.***

**sur·re·al·ism** (sə-rē′əl-iz'm), ***n.*** [< Fr. *sur-*, above + *réalisme*, realism], a modern movement in the arts, trying to depict the workings of the subconscious mind. **—sur·re′al·ist,** ***adj. & n.*** **—sur·re′al·is′tic,** ***adj.***

**sur·ren·der** (sə-ren′dẽr), ***v.t.*** [< OFr. *sur-*, up + *rendre*, render], 1. to give up possession of; yield to another on compulsion. 2. to give up or abandon. ***v.i.*** to give oneself up, esp. as a prisoner. ***n.*** the act of surrendering.

**sur·rep·ti·tious** (sũr′əp-tish′əs), ***adj.*** [< L. *sub-*, under + *rapere*, seize], done, obtained, acting, etc. in a secret, stealthy way.

**sur·rey** (sũr′i), ***n.*** [*pl.* -REYS], [< *Surrey*, county in England], a light, four-wheeled carriage with two seats.

**sur·ro·gate** (sũr′ə-gāt′), ***n.*** [< L. *sub-*, in place of + *rogare*, to elect], 1. a deputy or substitute. 2. in some States, a probate court judge.

**sur·round** (sə-round′), ***v.t.*** [< L. *super*, over + *undare*, to rise], to encircle on all or nearly all sides. **—sur·round′er,** ***n.***

**sur·round′ings,** ***n.pl.*** the things, conditions, etc. that surround one; environment.

**sur·tax** (sũr′taks′), ***n.*** an extra tax on something already taxed.

**sur·veil·lance** (sẽr-vā′ləns), ***n.*** [Fr. < *sur-*, over + *veiller*, to watch], 1. watch kept over a person, esp. a suspect. 2. supervision.

**sur·vey** (sẽr-vā′), ***v.t.*** [< OFr. *sur-*, over + *veoir*, see], 1. to examine or consider in detail or comprehensively. 2. to determine the location, form, or boundaries of (a tract of land). ***n.*** (*usually* sũr′vā), [*pl.* -VEYS], 1. a general study, as by sampling opinion. 2. a comprehensive study or examination. 3. the process of surveying an area. 4. a written description of the area surveyed. **—sur·vey′or,** ***n.***

**sur·vive** (sẽr-vīv′), ***v.t.*** [-VIVED, -VIVING], [< L. *super-*, above + *vivere*, live], to remain alive or in existence after. ***v.i.*** to continue living. **—sur·viv′al,** ***n.*** **—sur·vi′vor,** ***n.***

**sus·cep·ti·ble** (sə-sep′tə-b'l), ***adj.*** [< L. *sus-*, under + *capere*, take], easily affected emotionally. **—susceptible of,** admitting; allowing: as, testimony *susceptible of* error. **—susceptible to,** easily influenced or affected by. **—sus·cep′ti·bil′i·ty,** ***n.***

**sus·pect** (sə-spekt′; *for adj. & n., usually* sus′pekt), ***v.t.*** [< L. *sub-*, under + *spicere*, to look], 1. to believe to be guilty on little or no evidence. 2. to believe to be bad, wrong, etc.; distrust. 3. to surmise. ***adj.*** suspected. ***n.*** one suspected, as of a crime.

**sus·pend** (sə-spend′), ***v.t.*** [< L. *sub-*, under + *pendere*, hang], 1. to exclude for a time from an office, privilege, etc. as a penalty. 2. to make inoperative for a time. 3. to hold back (judgment, sentence, etc.). 4. to hang by a support from above. 5. to hold without attachment, as dust in the air. ***v.i.*** to stop temporarily.

**sus·penders,** ***n.pl.*** 1. a pair of straps passed over the shoulders to support the trousers. 2. [Brit.], garters.

**sus·pense** (sə-spens′), ***n.*** [< L. *suspendere*, suspend], 1. the state of being uncertain. 2. anxiety; uncertainty.

**sus·pen·sion** (sə-spen′shən), ***n.*** 1. a suspending or being suspended (in various senses). 2. a supporting device upon or from which something is suspended.

**suspension bridge,** a bridge suspended from cables anchored at either end and supported by towers at intervals.

**sus·pi·cion** (sə-spish′ən), ***n.*** [< L. *suspicere*, to suspect], 1. a suspecting or being suspected. 2. the feeling or state of mind of one who suspects. 3. a very small amount; trace. ***v.t.*** [Dial.], to suspect.

**sus·pi′cious,** ***adj.*** 1. arousing suspicion. 2. showing or feeling suspicion.

**sus·tain** (sə-stān′), ***v.t.*** [< L. *sub-*, under + *tenere*, hold], 1. to maintain; keep in existence; prolong. 2. to keep supplied with necessities. 3. to support; carry the weight of. 4. to endure; withstand. 5. to suffer, as an injury or loss. 6. to uphold the validity of: as, the court *sustained* his claim. 7. to confirm; corroborate. **—sus·tain′a·ble,** ***adj.***

**sus·te·nance** (sus′ti-nəns), ***n.*** 1. a sustaining. 2. means of livelihood. 3. that which sustains life; food.

**su·ture** (sōō′chẽr, sū′-), ***n.*** [< L. *suere*, sew], 1. the line of junction of two things, esp. of bones of the skull. 2. *a*) the stitching together of the two edges of a wound or incision. *b*) any of the stitches so used.

**svelte** (svelt), *adj.* [Fr.], slender and graceful.
**SW, S.W., s.w.,** southwest(ern).
**Sw.** 1. Sweden 2. Swedish.
**swab** (swäb), *n.* [< D. *zwabben*, do dirty work], 1. a mop for scrubbing. 2. a small piece of cotton, etc. used to medicate or clean the throat, mouth, etc. *v.t.* [SWABBED, SWABBING], to use a swab on. **—swab′ber,** *n.*
**swad·dle** (swäd′'l), *v.t.* [-DLED, -DLING], [< AS. *swathian*, swathe], to wrap (a newborn baby) in long narrow bands of cloth.
**swag** (swag), *n.* [prob. < ON.], [Slang], stolen money or property; loot.
**swag·ger** (swag′ẽr), *v.t.* [prob. < *swag*, sway], 1. to walk with a bold or arrogant stride; strut. 2. to boast or brag loudly. *n.* swaggering walk or manner.
**swain** (swān), *n.* [< ON. *sveinn*, boy], [Poetic], 1. a country youth. 2. a young rustic lover. 3. a lover.
**swal·low** (swäl′ō), *n.* [AS. *swalewe*], a small, swift-flying bird with long, pointed wings and a forked tail.
**swal·low** (swäl′ō), *v.t.* [AS. *swelgan*], 1. to pass (food, etc.) from the mouth into the stomach. 2. to take in; absorb: often with *up*. 3. to retract (words said). 4. to put up with: as, to *swallow* insults. 5. to suppress: as, to *swallow* one's pride. 6. [Colloq.], to accept as true without question. *v.i.* to perform the actions of swallowing something, esp. as in emotion. *n.* 1. the act of swallowing. 2. the amount swallowed at one time.
**swal′low-tailed′ coat,** a man's full-dress, cutaway coat.
**swam** (swam), pt. of **swim.**
**swamp** (swämp, swômp), *n.* [prob. < D. *zwamp*], a piece of wet, spongy land; bog: also **swamp′land′**. *v.t.* 1. to plunge in a swamp, water, etc. 2. to flood as with water. 3. to overwhelm: as, debts *swamped* them. 4. to sink (a boat) by filling with water. **—swamp′y** [-IER, -IEST], *adj.*
**swan** (swän, swôn), *n.* [AS.], a large, web-footed, usually white, water bird with a long, graceful neck.
**swank** (swaŋk), *n.* [prob. akin to AS. *swancor*, pliant], [Slang], stylish display or ostentation in dress, etc. *adj.* [Slang], ostentatiously stylish: also **swank′y** [-IER, -IEST].
**swan's′-down′,** *n.* 1. the soft, fine under-feathers, or down, of the swan, used for trimming clothes, etc. 2. a soft, thick fabric, as of wool and cotton, used for making baby clothes, etc. Also **swans′down′**.
**swan song,** [after the song sung, in ancient fable, by a dying swan], the last act, final work, etc. of a person.
**swap** (swäp, swôp), *n., v.t. & v.i.* [SWAPPED, SWAPPING], [ME. *swappen*, to strike], [Colloq.], trade; barter. **—swap′per,** *n.*
**sward** (swôrd), *n.* [< AS. *sweard*, skin], grass-covered soil; turf. **—sward′y,** *adj.*
**swarm** (swôrm), *n.* [AS. *swearm*], 1. a number of bees leaving a hive to start a new colony. 2. a colony of bees in a hive. 3. a large, moving mass of insects. 4. a moving throng. *v.i.* 1. to fly off in a swarm: said of bees. 2. to move, collect, etc. in large numbers. 3. to be filled (*with*); teem.
**swarth·y** (swôr′*th*i, -thi), *adj.* [-IER, -IEST], [< AS. *sweart*], having a dark skin: also **swart** (swôrt). **—swarth′i·ness,** *n.*
**swash** (swäsh, swôsh), *v.i.* [echoic], to dash, strike, etc. with a splash.
**swash′buck′ler** (-buk′lẽr), *n.* [*swash*, to swagger + *buckler*, a shield], a blustering, swaggering, fighting man. **—swash′buck′ling,** *n. & adj.*
**swas·ti·ka** (swäs′ti-kə), *n.* [< Sans. *svasti*, well-being], 1. an ancient design in the form of a Greek cross with each arm bent in a right angle. 2. this design with the arms going clockwise: used as the Nazi emblem.
**swat** (swät), *v.t.* [SWATTED, SWATTING], [echoic], [Colloq.], to hit with a quick, sharp blow. *n.* [Colloq.], a quick, sharp blow. **—swat′ter,** *n.*
**swatch** (swäch), *n.* [< N. dial.], a sample piece of cloth, etc.
**swath** (swäth, swôth), *n.* [AS. *swathu*, a track], 1. the space covered with one cut of a scythe or other mowing device. 2. a strip, row, etc. mowed.
**swathe** (swā*th*), *v.t.* [SWATHED, SWATHING], [AS. *swathian*], 1. to wrap up in a bandage. 2. to envelop.
**sway** (swā), *v.i.* [< ON. *sveigja*], 1. to swing from side to side or to and fro. 2. to lean to one side; veer. 3. to incline in judgment or opinion. 4. to have control or influence; rule. *v.t.* 1. to cause to sway. 2. to divert from a course: as, his threats *swayed* us. *n.* 1. a swaying or being swayed. 2. influence; rule: as, the *sway* of passion.
**sway′-backed′** (-bakt′), *adj.* having an abnormal inward curve in the spine: said of a horse, etc. **—sway′-back′,** *n. & adj.*
**swear** (swâr), *v.i.* [SWORE, SWORN, SWEARING], [AS. *swerian*], 1. to make a solemn declaration with an appeal to God to confirm it. 2. to make a solemn promise; vow. 3. to use profane language; curse. *v.t.* 1. to declare, pledge, or vow on oath. 2. to administer a legal oath to. **—swear by,** to have great faith in. **—swear off,** to renounce. **—swear out,** to obtain (a warrant for arrest) by making a charge under oath.
**sweat** (swet), *v.i. & v.t.* [SWEAT or SWEATED, SWEATING], [< AS. *swat*, sweat], 1. to give forth or cause to give forth a salty moisture through the pores of the skin; perspire. 2. to give forth or condense (moisture) on its surface. 3. to work so hard as to cause sweating. 4. [Colloq.], to subject (someone) to the third degree. *n.* 1. the salty liquid given forth in perspiration. 2. moisture collected in droplets on a surface. 3. a sweating or being sweated. 4. a condition of eagerness, anxiety, etc. **—sweat out,** to wait anxiously for or through. **—sweat′y,** *adj.*
**sweat′er,** *n.* a knitted or crocheted outer garment for the upper body.
**sweat shirt,** a heavy cotton jersey, worn to absorb sweat, as after exercise.
**sweat′shop′,** *n.* a shop or plant where employees work long hours at low wages under poor working conditions.
**Swed.,** 1. Sweden. 2. Swedish.
**Swede** (swēd), *n.* a native of Sweden.
**Swed·ish** (swē′dish), *adj.* of Sweden, its people, language, etc. *n.* the language of Sweden. **—the Swedish,** the Swedish people.
**sweep** (swēp), *v.t.* [SWEPT, SWEEPING], [AS. *swapan*], 1. to clean (a room, etc.) as by brushing with a broom. 2. to remove (dirt, etc.) as with a broom. 3. to strip, carry away, or destroy with force of movement. 4. to touch in moving across: as, her dress *swept* the floor. 5. to pass swiftly over or across. 6. [Colloq.], to win overwhelmingly. *v.i.* 1. to clean a surface, etc. as with a broom. 2. to move steadily with speed, force, or gracefulness. 3. to extend in a long curve or line: as, the road *sweeps* up the hill. *n.* 1. the act of sweeping, as with a broom. 2. a steady sweeping movement. 3. range or scope. 4. a stretch; extent, as of land. 5. a line, curve, etc. that seems to flow or move. 6. one whose work is sweeping.
**sweep′stakes′,** *n.* [*pl.* -STAKES], a lottery in which the winner or winners of the common fund of stakes put up are determined by a horse race or other contest: also **sweep′stake′**.
**sweet** (swēt), *adj.* [AS. *swete*], 1. having a taste of, or like that of, sugar. 2. *a*) agreeable in taste, smell, sound, etc. *b*) gratifying.

*c*) friendly, pleasant, etc. 3. not salty or salted. 4. not spoiled; fresh. *n.* something sweet, as a candy. —**sweet'ish,** *adj.*

**sweet'bread'** (-bred'), *n.* the pancreas or the thymus of a calf, etc., when used as food.

**sweet'bri'er, sweet'bri'ar** (-brī'ẽr), *n.* a rose with pink flowers and prickly stems.

**sweet corn,** a variety of Indian corn eaten unripe as a table vegetable.

**sweet'en,** *v.t.* 1. to make sweet. 2. to make pleasant or agreeable. —**sweet'en·er,** *n.*

**sweet'heart',** *n.* a lover; loved one.

**sweet'meat',** *n.* a candy.

**sweet pea,** a climbing plant with large, variously colored, fragrant flowers.

**sweet potato,** 1. a tropical trailing plant with a large, fleshy, orange or yellow root used as a vegetable. 2. its root.

**swell** (swel), *v.i. & v.t.* [SWELLED, SWELLED or SWOLLEN, SWELLING], [AS. *swellan*], 1. to expand as a result of pressure from within. 2. to curve out; bulge. 3. to fill (*with* pride, etc.). 4. to increase in size, force, intensity, etc. *n.* 1. a part that swells; specif., a large, rolling wave. 2. an increase in size, amount, etc. 3. a crescendo. 4. [Colloq.], one who is strikingly stylish. *adj.* [Colloq.], stylish.

**swell'ing,** *n.* 1. an increase in size, volume, etc. 2. a swollen part.

**swel·ter** (swel'tẽr), *v.i.* [< AS. *sweltan*, to die], to feel oppressed with great heat.

**swel'ter·ing,** *adj.* very hot; sultry.

**swept** (swept), pt. and pp. of **sweep.**

**swerve** (swũrv), *v.i. & v.t.* [SWERVED, SWERVING], [< AS. *sweorfan*, to scour], to turn aside from a straight line, course, etc. *n.* a swerving. —**swerv'er,** *n.*

**swift** (swift), *adj.* [AS.], 1. moving with great speed; fast. 2. coming, acting, etc. quickly. *n.* a brown, swift bird resembling the swallow. —**swift'ly,** *adv.* —**swift'ness,** *n.*

**swig** (swig), *v.t. & v.i.* [SWIGGED, SWIGGING], [<?], [Colloq.], to drink in gulps. *n.* [Colloq.], a deep draft, as of liquor.

**swill** (swil), *v.t. & v.i.* [AS. *swilian*, wash], to drink greedily in large quantities. *n.* 1. liquid garbage fed to pigs. 2. garbage.

**swim** (swim), *v.i.* [SWAM, SWUM, SWIMMING], [AS. *swimman*], 1. to move through water by moving arms, legs, fins, etc. 2. to move along smoothly. 3. to float on or in a liquid. 4. to overflow: as, eyes *swimming* with tears. *v.t.* to swim in or across. *n.* the act of swimming. —**in the swim,** active in, or conforming to, current society, etc. —**swim'mer,** *n.*

**swim** (swim), *n.* [AS. *swima*], a being dizzy. *v.i.* [SWAM, SWUM, SWIMMING], to be dizzy.

**swin·dle** (swin'd'l), *v.t. & v.i.* [SWINDLED, SWINDLING], [< G. *schwindeln*, to cheat], to defraud (others) of money or property; cheat. *n.* an act of swindling. —**swin'dler,** *n.*

**swine** (swin), *n.* [*pl.* SWINE], [AS. *swin*], 1. a pig or hog: usually used collectively. 2. a vicious, contemptible person. —**swin'ish,** *adj.* —**swin'ish·ly,** *adv.*

**swing** (swiŋ), *v.i. & v.t.* [SWUNG, SWINGING], [AS. *swingan*], 1. to sway or move backward and forward. 2. to walk, trot, etc. with freely swaying movements. 3. to turn, as on a hinge. 4. to move on a swing (*n.*, 8). 5. to move (a bat, etc.) with a sweeping motion. 6. to cause to come about successfully: as, to *swing* an election. *n.* 1. a swinging. 2. the arc through which something swings. 3. the manner of swinging a golf club, etc. 4. a relaxed motion, as in walking. 5. a sweeping blow or stroke. 6. the course of some activity, etc. 7. rhythm, as of music. 8. a seat hanging from ropes, etc., on which one can swing. 9. a style of jazz characterized by large bands, contrapuntal improvisation, etc.

**swing shift,** [Colloq.], in factories, the work shift from mid-afternoon to about midnight.

**swipe** (swīp), *n.* [< ON. *svipr*, a stroke], [Colloq.], a hard, sweeping blow. *v.t.* [SWIPED, SWIPING], 1. [Colloq.], to hit with a hard, sweeping blow. 2. [Slang], to steal.

**swirl** (swũrl), *v.i. & v.t.* [prob. < ON. *svirla*, to whirl], to move or cause to move with a whirling motion. *n.* 1. a whirl; eddy. 2. a twist; curl. —**swirl'y,** *adj.*

**swish** (swish), *v.i. & v.t.* [echoic], 1. to move with a sharp, hissing sound, as a cane swung through the air. 2. to rustle, as skirts. *n.* a swishing sound or movement.

**Swiss** (swis), *adj.* of Switzerland, its people, etc. *n.* [*pl.* SWISS], a native of Switzerland.

**Swiss cheese,** a pale-yellow hard cheese with many large holes.

**Swiss steak,** a thick cut of round steak pounded with flour and braised.

**switch** (swich), *n.* [prob. < LG.], 1. a thin, flexible stick used for whipping. 2. a sharp lash, as with a whip. 3. a device used to open, close, or divert an electric circuit. 4. a device used in transferring a train from one track to another. 5. a shift; change. *v.t.* 1. to whip as with a switch. 2. to jerk sharply. 3. to shift; change. 4. to turn (an electric light, etc.) *on* or *off.* 5. to transfer (a train, etc.) to another track. 6. [Colloq.], to change or exchange. *v.i.* to shift.

**switch'board'** (-bôrd'), *n.* a panel equipped with apparatus for controlling a system of electric circuits, as in a telephone exchange.

**switch'man** (-mən), *n.* [*pl.* -MEN], a railroad worker who is in charge of switches.

**swiv·el** (swiv''l), *n.* [< AS. *swifan*, to revolve], a fastening that allows free turning of the parts attached to it. *v.i. & v.t.* [-ELED or -ELLED, -ELING or -ELLING], to turn or cause to turn as on a swivel or pivot.

**swol·len** (swō'lən), alt. pp. of **swell.** *adj.* blown up; distended; bulging.

**swoon** (swōōn), *v.i. & n.* [< AS. *geswogen*, unconscious], faint. —**swoon'ing·ly,** *adv.*

**swoop** (swōōp), *v.i.* [< AS. *swapan*, sweep along], to pounce or sweep (*down* or *upon*), as a bird in hunting. *n.* the act of swooping.

**swop** (swop), *n., v.t. & v.i.* [SWOPPED, SWOPPING], swap.

**sword** (sôrd), *n.* [AS. *sweord*], a hand weapon having a hilt and a long, sharp, pointed blade. —**at swords' points,** ready to quarrel or fight. —**sword'like,** *adj.*

**sword'fish',** *n.* [*pl.* see FISH], a large marine food fish with the upper jawbone extending in a swordlike point.

**sword'play'** (-plā'), *n.* the act or art of using a sword; fencing.

**swords'man,** *n.* [*pl.* -MEN], 1. one who uses a sword in fencing or fighting. 2. one skilled in using a sword.

**swore** (swôr), pt. of **swear.**

**sworn** (swôrn), pp. of **swear.** *adj.* bound, pledged, etc. by an oath.

**swum** (swum), pp. of **swim.**

**swung** (swuŋ), pt. and pp. of **swing.**

**syb·a·rite** (sib'ə-rīt'), *n.* [< *Sybaris*, ancient Gr. city in Italy, famed for its luxury], anyone very fond of luxury and pleasure. —**syb'a·rit'ic** (-rit'ik), *adj.*

**syc·a·more** (sik'ə-môr'), *n.* [< Gr. *sykomoros*], 1. a maple tree of Europe and Asia. 2. an American tree with large leaves and streaky, shedding bark.

**syc·o·phant** (sik'ə-fənt), *n.* [< Gr. *sykophantēs*, informer], one who seeks favor by flattering people of wealth or influence.

**syl·lab·i·cate** (si-lab'i-kāt'), *v.t.* [-CATED, -CATING], to syllabify. —**syl·lab'i·ca'tion,** *n.*

**syl·lab·i·fy** (si-lab'ə-fī'), *v.t.* [-FIED, -FYING], [< L. *syllaba*, syllable + *facere*, make], to form or divide into syllables. —**syl·lab'i·fi·ca'tion,** *n.*

**syl·la·ble** (sil'ə-b'l), *n.* [< Gr. *syn-*, together + *lambanein*, to hold], 1. a word (e.g., *sun*) or part of a word (e.g., *per·me·ate*) pronounced with a single, uninterrupted sounding of the voice. 2. one or more letters written to represent a spoken syllable. —**syl·lab·ic** (si-lab′ik), *adj.*

**syl·la·bus** (sil′ə-bəs), *n.* [*pl.* -BUSES, -BI (-bī′)], [< Gr. *syttyba*, parchment label], a summary or outline, esp. of a course of study.

**syl·lo·gism** (sil′ə-jiz'm), *n.* [< Gr. *syn-*, together + *logizesthai*, to reason], a form of reasoning in which two premises are made and a logical conclusion drawn from them.

**sylph** (silf), *n.* [? < L. *sylvestris*, of a forest + *nympha*, nymph], 1. any of a class of imaginary beings supposed to inhabit the air. 2. a slender, graceful woman or girl.

**syl·van** (sil′vən), *adj.* [< L. *silva*, a wood], 1. of, characteristic of, or living in the woods or forest. 2. wooded.

**sym·bol** (sim′b'l), *n.* [< Gr. *syn-*, together + *ballein*, to throw], 1. an object used to represent something else: as, the dove is a *symbol* of peace. 2. a mark, letter, etc. standing for a quality, process, etc., as in music or chemistry. —**sym·bol′ic** (-bol′ik), **sym·bol′i·cal**, *adj.* —**sym·bol′i·cal·ly**, *adv.*

**sym·bol·ism** (sim′b'l-iz'm), *n.* 1. representation by symbols. 2. a system of symbols. 3. symbolic meaning. —**sym′bol·ist** (-ist), *n.*

**sym′bol·ize′**, *v.t.* [-IZED, -IZING], 1. to be a symbol of; stand for. 2. to represent by a symbol or symbols. —**sym′bol·i·za′tion**, *n.*

**sym·me·try** (sim′ə-tri), *n.* [*pl.* -TRIES], [< Gr. *syn-*, together + *metron*, a measure], 1. correspondence of opposite parts in size, shape, and position. 2. excellence of form or balance resulting from this. —**sym·met·ri·cal** (si-met′ri-k'l), *adj.*

**sym·pa·thet·ic** (sim′pə-thet′ik), *adj.* 1. of, feeling, or showing sympathy. 2. in agreement with one's tastes, mood, etc. —**sym′pa·thet′i·cal·ly**, *adv.*

**sym′pa·thize′** (-thīz′), *v.i.* [-THIZED, -THIZING], 1. to share the feelings or ideas of another. 2. to feel or express sympathy.

**sym·pa·thy** (sim′pə-thi), *n.* [*pl.* -THIES], [< Gr. *syn-*, together + *pathos*, feeling], 1. sameness of feeling. 2. agreement in qualities; accord. 3. mutual liking or understanding. 4. ability to share another's ideas, emotions, etc.; esp., pity or compassion for another's trouble, etc.

**sym·pho·ny** (sim′fə-ni), *n.* [*pl.* -NIES], [< Gr. *syn-*, together + *phōnē*, sound], 1. harmony, as of sounds, color, etc. 2. an extended musical composition in several movements, for full orchestra. 3. a large orchestra for playing symphonic works: also **symphony orchestra**. —**sym·phon′ic** (-fon′ik), *adj.*

**sym·po·si·um** (sim-pō′zi-əm), *n.* [*pl.* -UMS, -A (-ə)], [< Gr. *syn-*, together + *posis*, a drinking], 1. a conference for discussing some subject. 2. a collection of opinions on a given subject. —**sym·po′si·ac′** (-ak′), *adj.*

**symp·tom** (simp′təm), *n.* [< Gr. *syn-*, together + *piptein*, to fall], any circumstance or condition that indicates the existence of something, esp. of a particular disease. —**symp′to·mat′ic** (-tə-mat′ik), *adj.*

**syn-**, [Gr.], a prefix meaning *with, together with, at the same time.*

**syn·a·gogue** (sin′ə-gôg′, -gog′), *n.* [< Gr. *syn-*, together + *agein*, bring], 1. an assembly of Jews for worship and religious study. 2. a building or place for such assembly.

**syn·chro·nism** (siŋ′krə-niz'm), *n.* the fact or state of being synchronous.

**syn·chro·nize** (siŋ′krə-nīz′), *v.i.* [-NIZED, -NIZING], [< Gr. *syn-*, together + *chronos*, time], to move or occur at the same time or rate. *v.t.* to cause to agree in time or rate of speed. —**syn′chro·ni·za′tion**, *n.*

**syn′chro·nous**, *adj.* happening at the same time; simultaneous.

**syn·co·pate** (siŋ′kə-pāt′), *v.t.* [-PATED, -PATING], [< Gr. *syn-*, together + *koptein*, cut], in *music*, to begin (a tone) on an unaccented beat and continue it through the next accented beat. —**syn′co·pa′tion**, *n.*

**syn·dic** (sin′dik), *n.* [< Gr. *syn-*, together + *dikē*, justice], 1. the business manager of a corporation as a university. 2. a civil magistrate.

**syn·di·cate** (sin′di-kit), *n.* [see SYNDIC], 1. an association of bankers, corporations, etc. formed for a project requiring much capital. 2. an organization selling articles or features to newspapers for simultaneous publication. *v.t.* (-kāt′), [-CATED, -CATING], 1. to manage as or form into a syndicate. 2. to sell (an article, etc.) through a syndicate. *v.i.* (-kāt′), to form a syndicate. —**syn′di·ca′tion**, *n.*

**syn·od** (sin′əd), *n.* [< Gr. *syn-*, together + *hodos*, way], 1. a council of churches or church officials. 2. any council.

**syn·o·nym** (sin′ə-nim), *n.* [< Gr. *syn-*, together + *onyma*, name], a word having the same or nearly the same meaning as another in the same language.—**syn·on·y·mous** (si-non′ə-məs), *adj.* —**syn·on′y·my** (-mi) [*pl.* -MIES], *n.*

**syn·op·sis** (si-nop′sis), *n.* [*pl.* -SES (-sēz)], [< Gr. *syn-*, together + *opsis*, a sight], a statement giving a brief, general review or condensation; summary.

**syn·tax** (sin′taks), *n.* [< Gr. *syn-*, together + *tassein*, arrange], the arrangement of words as elements in a sentence to show their relationship. —**syn·tac′ti·cal** (-tak′ti-k'l), *adj.*

**syn·the·sis** (sin′thə-sis), *n.* [*pl.* -SES, (-sēz′)], [< Gr. *syn-*, together + *tithenai*, to place], the combining of parts or elements so as to form a whole, a compound, etc. —**syn′the·size′** (-sīz′) [-SIZED, -SIZING], *v.t.*

**syn·thet′ic** (-thet′ik), *adj.* 1. of or involving synthesis. 2. produced by chemical synthesis, rather than of natural origin. 3. artificial; not real. *n.* something synthetic. —**syn·thet′i·cal·ly**, *adv.*

**syph·i·lis** (sif′ə-lis), *n.* [< *Syphilus*, hero of a L. poem (1530)], an infectious venereal disease. —**syph′i·lit′ic** (-lit′ik), *adj.* & *n.*

**Syr.**, 1. Syria. 2. Syrian.

**Syr·i·an** (sêr′i-ən), *adj.* of Syria, its people, language, etc. *n.* 1. a member of the Semite people of Syria. 2. their Arabic dialect.

**syr·inge** (sə-rinj′, sir′inj), *n.* [< Gr. *syrinx*, a tube], a device consisting of a tube with a rubber bulb or piston at one end for drawing in a liquid and then ejecting it in a stream: used to inject fluids into the body, cleanse wounds, etc.

**syr·up** (sir′əp, sũr′-), *n.* sirup.

**sys·tem** (sis′təm), *n.* [< Gr. *syn-*, together + *histanai*, to set], 1. a set or arrangement of things so related as to form a whole: as, a solar *system*, supply *system*. 2. the body, or a number of bodily organs, functioning as a unit. 3. a set of facts, rules, etc. arranged to show a plan. 4. a method; plan. 5. a regular, orderly way of doing something.

**sys′tem·at′ic** (-tə-mat′ik), *ad* . 1. constituting or based on a system. 2. according to a system; orderly; methodical. Also **sys′tem·at′i·cal**. —**sys′tem·at′i·cal·ly**, *adv.*

**sys′tem·a·tize′** (-ə-tīz′), *v.t.* [-TIZED, -TIZING], to arrange according to a system; make systematic. —**sys′tem·a·ti·za′tion**, *n.*

**sys·tem·ic** (sis-tem′ik), *adj.* of or affecting the body as a whole. —**sys·tem′i·cal·ly**, *adv.*

**sys·tem·ize** (sis′təm-īz′), *v.t.* [-IZED, -IZING], to systematize. —**sys′tem·i·za′tion**, *n.*

**sys·to·le** (sis′tə-lē′), *n.* [ult. < Gr. *syn-*, together + *stellein*, to draw], the usual rhythmic contraction of the heart. —**sys·tol′ic** (-tol′ik), *adj.*

# T

**T, t** (tē), *n.* [*pl.* T's, t's, Ts, ts], the twentieth letter of the English alphabet. **—to a T,** to perfection.

**'t,** it: a contraction, as in *'twas.*

**t.,** 1. teaspoon(s). 2. temperature. 3. tense. 4. time. 5. ton. 6. transitive.

**Ta,** in *chem.*, tantalum.

**tab** (tab), *n.* [< Eng. dial.], 1. a small, flat loop or strap fastened to something. 2. a projecting piece of a card or paper, useful in filing. 3. [Colloq.], a reckoning. **—keep tab** (or **tabs**) **on,** [Colloq.], to keep a check on.

**Ta·bas·co** (tə-bas'kō), *n.* a very hot pepper sauce: a trademark.

**tab·by** (tab'i), *n.* [*pl.* -BIES], [ult. < Ar.], a domestic cat, esp. a female.

**tab·er·nac·le** (tab'ẽr-nak''l), *n.* [< L. *taberna*, hut], 1. [T-], the portable sanctuary carried by the Jews during the Exodus. 2. a large place of worship.

**ta·ble** (tā'b'l), *n.* [< L. *tabula*, board], 1. a thin slab of metal, stone, etc.; tablet. 2. a piece of furniture having a flat top set on legs. 3. such a table set with food. 4. food served. 5. the people seated at a table. 6. a systematic list of details, contents, etc. 7. an orderly arrangement of facts, figures, etc. 8. any flat, horizontal surface, piece, etc. *v.t.* [-BLED, -BLING], 1. to put on a table. 2. to postpone consideration of, as a legislative bill. **—turn the tables,** to reverse a situation.

**tab·leau** (tab'lō), *n.* [*pl.* -LEAUX (-lōz), -LEAUS], [Fr., dim. of *table*], a representation of a scene, picture, etc. by a person or group posed in costume.

**ta'ble·cloth',** *n.* a cloth for covering a table.

**ta·ble d'hôte** (tä'b'l dōt'), [Fr., table of the host], a complete meal served at a restaurant for a set price: cf. **à la carte.**

**ta·ble·land** (tā'b'l-land'), *n.* a plateau.

**ta'ble·spoon',** *n.* a large spoon for serving, measuring, etc., holding ½ fluid ounce. **—ta'ble·spoon'ful** [*pl.* -FULS], *n.*

**tab·let** (tab'lit), *n.* [< OFr. dim. of *table*], 1. a flat, thin piece of stone, metal, etc. with an inscription. 2. a writing pad of paper sheets fastened at one edge. 3. a small, flat piece of compressed material, as medicine.

**table tennis,** ping-pong.

**ta'ble·ware'** (-wâr'), *n.* dishes, knives, forks, spoons, etc. used at table.

**tab·loid** (tab'loid), *n.* [< *tablet* + *-oid*], a newspaper, usually half size, with many pictures and short news stories.

**ta·boo** (tə-bōō', ta-), *n.* [*pl.* -BOOS], [S Pacific native term *tabu*], 1. among primitive tribes, a sacred prohibition making certain people or things untouchable, etc. 2. any conventional social restriction. *adj.* prohibited or restricted by taboo. *v.t.* [-BOOED, -BOOING], to put under taboo; prohibit. Also sp. **tabu.**

**ta·bor, ta·bour** (tā'bẽr), *n.* [< Persian *tabīrah*], a small drum.

**tab·u·lar** (tab'yoo-lẽr), *adj.* [< L. *tabula*, table], of, arranged in, or computed from a table or list.

**tab·u·late** (tab'yoo-lāt'), *v.t.* [-LATED, -LATING], to put (facts, statistics, etc.) in a table. **—tab'u·la'tion,** *n.* **—tab'u·la'tor,** *n.*

**tac·it** (tas'it), *adj.* [< L. *tacere*, be silent], 1. unspoken; silent. 2. not expressed openly, but implied. **—tac'it·ly,** *adv.* **—tac'it·ness,** *n.*

**tac·i·turn** (tas'ə-tũrn'), *adj.* [see TACIT], almost always silent; not liking to talk.

**tack** (tak), *n.* [< OFr. *tache*, a nail], 1. a short nail with a sharp point and a large, flat head. 2. a basting stitch. 3. a zigzag course. 4. a course of action. 5. *a*) the direction a ship goes in relation to the position of the sails. *b*) a change of a ship's direction. *v.t.* 1. to fasten with tacks. 2. to attach or add. 3. to change the course of (a ship). *v.i.* to change course suddenly.

**tack·le** (tak''l), *n.* [prob. < LG.], 1. apparatus; equipment; gear. 2. a system of ropes and pulleys, for moving weights. 3. the act of tackling. 4. in *football*, a player next to the end in the line. *v.t.* [-LED, -LING], 1. to take hold of; seize. 2. to undertake; attempt. 3. in *football*, to throw (the ball carrier).

**tack·y** (tak'i), *adj.* [-IER, -IEST], 1. sticky, as glue. 2. [Colloq.], shabby.

**ta·co** (tä'kō), *n.* [Sp., light lunch], a fried, folded tortilla filled with chopped meat, shredded lettuce, etc.

**tact** (takt), *n.* [< L. *tangere*, touch], delicate perception of the right thing to say or do without offending. **—tact'ful,** *adj.* **—tact'ful·ly,** *adv.* **—tact'less,** *adj.* **—tact'less·ly,** *adv.*

**tac·tics** (tak'tiks), *n.pl.* [< Gr. *tassein*, arrange], 1. [construed as sing.], the science of maneuvering military and naval forces. 2. any skillful methods to gain an end. **—tac'ti·cal,** *adj.* **—tac·ti'cian** (-tish'ən), *n.*

**tac·tile** (tak't'l, -til), *adj.* [< L. *tangere*, touch], of or perceived by the sense of touch.

**tad·pole** (tad'pōl'), *n.* [ME. *tade*, toad + *poll*, head], the larva of a frog or toad, having gills and a tail and living in water.

**taf·fe·ta** (taf'i-tə), *n.* [< Persian *tāftan*, weave], a fine, stiff cloth of silk, rayon, etc.

**taf·fy** (taf'i), *n.* [< *toffee*], a chewy candy made of sugar or molasses.

**tag** (tag), *n.* [prob. < ON.], 1. a hanging end or part. 2. a hard-tipped end on a string or lace. 3. a card, etc. attached as a label. 4. the last line or lines of a speech, story, etc. 5. a children's game in which one player chases the others until he touches one. *v.t.* [TAGGED, TAGGING], 1. to provide with a tag. 2. to touch as in the game of tag. 3. [Colloq.], to follow close behind. *v.i.* [Colloq.], to follow closely (with *along*, *after*, etc.).

**Ta·hi·ti·an** (tä-hē'ti-ən, -hē'shən), *adj.* of Tahiti, its people, language, etc. *n.* 1. a native of Tahiti. 2. the Tahitian language.

**tail** (tāl), *n.* [AS. *tægel*], 1. the rear end of an animal's body, esp. when a distinct appendage. 2. anything like an animal's tail in form or position. 3. the hind, bottom, last, or inferior part of anything. 4. *usually pl.* the side of a coin opposite the head. 5. *pl.* [Colloq.], the swallow-tailed coat of men's full-dress attire. *v.t. & v.i.* [Colloq.], to follow close behind. *adj.* 1. at the rear or end. 2. from the rear: as, a *tail* wind.

**tail'board',** *n.* the hinged or removable board forming the back of a wagon, truck, etc.: also **tail'gate'.**

**tail'light',** *n.* a light at the back of a vehicle to warn approaching vehicles of its presence at night.

**tai·lor** (tā'lẽr), *n.* [< LL. *taliare*, to cut], one who makes, repairs, or alters clothes. *v.i.* to work as a tailor. *v.t.* 1. to make by tailor's work. 2. to form, alter, etc. so as to meet certain conditions: as, a novel *tailored* to popular taste. **—tai'lor·ing,** *n.*

**tai'lor-made',** *adj.* made by or as by a tailor; specif., made to order.

**tail'spin',** *n.* the descent of an airplane with nose down and tail spinning in circles: often used figuratively: also **(tail) spin.**

**taint** (tānt), ***v.t.*** [ult. < L. *tangere*, to touch], 1. to affect with something injurious, unpleasant, etc.; infect. 2. to make morally corrupt. ***v.i.*** to become tainted. ***n.*** a trace of contamination, corruption, etc.

**take** (tāk), ***v.t.*** [TOOK, TAKEN, TAKING], [< ON. *taka*], 1. to get possession of; capture, seize, etc. 2. to get hold of. 3. to capture the fancy of. 4. to obtain, assume, receive, etc. 5. to use, consume, etc. 6. to assume as a responsibility, task, etc.: as, he *took* the job. 7. to support (one side) in a quarrel, etc. 8. to select; choose. 9. to travel by: as, *take* a bus. 10. to deal with; consider. 11. to occupy: as, *take* a chair. 12. to derive, as a name, quality, etc., from. 13. to extract, as for quotation. 14. to write down: as, *take* notes. 15. to make by photographing. 16. to win, as a prize. 17. to undergo: as, *take* punishment. 18. to engage in: as, *take* a nap. 19. to accept (an offer, bet, etc.). 20. to react to: as, he *took* the joke in earnest. 21. to contract (a disease, etc.). 22. to understand. 23. to suppose; presume. 24. to feel: as, *take* pity. 25. to lead, escort, etc. 26. to carry. 27. to remove as by stealing. 28. to subtract. 29. to require: as, it *takes* money. 30. [Slang], to cheat; trick. ***v.i.*** 1. to take root: said of a plant. 2. to gain favor, success, etc. 3. to catch: as, the fire *took*. 4. to be effective: as, the vaccination *took*. 5. to go: as, *take* to the hills. 6. [Colloq.], to become (sick). ***n.*** 1. a taking. 2. the amount taken. —**take after,** to be, act, or look like. —**take back,** to retract (something said, etc.). —**take down,** to put in writing; record. —**take in,** 1. to admit; receive. 2. to make smaller. 3. to understand. 4. to cheat; trick. —**take off,** 1. to leave the ground, etc. in flight, as an airplane. 2. [Colloq.], to start. 3. [Colloq.], to imitate in a burlesque manner. —**take on,** 1. to acquire; assume. 2. to employ. 3. to undertake, as a task. —**take over,** to begin controlling, managing, etc. —**take to,** to become fond of. —**take up,** 1. to make tighter or shorter. 2. to absorb (a liquid). 3. to become interested in, as a study, etc.

**tak·en** (tā′k'n), pp. of **take.** —**taken aback,** suddenly confused or startled.

**take′-off′,** ***n.*** 1. the act of leaving the ground, as in jumping or flight. 2. [Colloq.], an amusing or mocking imitation; caricature; burlesque.

**tak·ing** (tāk′iŋ), ***adj.*** attractive; winning. ***n.*** 1. the act of one that takes. 2. *pl.* earnings; profits.

**talc** (talk), ***n.*** [< Per. *talk*], a soft mineral used to make talcum powder, etc.

**tal·cum (powder)** (tal′kəm), [ML.; see TALC], a powder for the body and face made of purified talc.

**tale** (tāl), ***n.*** [AS. *talu*], 1. a true or fictitious story; narrative. 2. idle or malicious gossip. 3. a fiction; lie. 4 a tally; total.

**tale′bear′er** (-bâr′ẽr), ***n.*** one who gossips or tells secrets, etc. —**tale′bear′ing,** ***n. & adj.***

**tal·ent** (tal′ənt), ***n.*** [< Gr. *talanton*, thing weighed], 1. an ancient unit of weight or money. 2. any natural ability or power. 3. a special, superior ability in art, etc. 4. people who have talent. —**tal′ent·ed,** ***adj.***

**tales·man** (tālz′mən), ***n.*** [*pl.* -MEN], [< L. *talis*, such; + *man*], a person summoned to fill a vacancy in a jury.

**tal·is·man** (tal′is-mən), ***n.*** [*pl.* -MANS], [< Gr. *telesma*, religious rite], a ring, stone, etc. bearing engraved figures supposed to bring good luck, avert evil, etc.; charm.

**talk** (tôk), ***v.i.*** [prob. < AS. *talian*, reckon], 1. to put ideas into words; speak. 2. to express ideas by speech substitutes: as, *talk* by signs. 3. to chatter; gossip. 4. to confer; consult. ***v.t.*** 1. to use in speaking: as, to *talk* French. 2. to discuss. 3. to put or influence by talking. ***n.*** 1. the act of talking. 2. conversation. 3. a speech. 4. a conference. 5. gossip. 6. the subject of conversation, gossip, etc. 7. frivolous discussion. —**talk back,** to answer impertinently. —**talk down to,** to patronize by pointedly simple speech. —**talk′er,** ***n.***

**talk′a·tive** (-ə-tiv), ***adj.*** talking a great deal; loquacious: also **talk′y.** —**talk′a·tive·ness,** ***n.***

**tall** (tôl), ***adj.*** [AS. (*ge*)*tæl*, swift], 1. higher than the average in stature. 2. having a stated height. 3. [Colloq.], exaggerated: as, a *tall* tale. 4. [Colloq.], large: as, a *tall* drink. —**tall′ish,** ***adj.*** —**tall′ness,** ***n.***

**tal·low** (tal′ō), ***n.*** [prob. < MLG. *talg*], the hard, coarse fat in cows, sheep, etc., used to make candles, soap, etc. —**tal′low·y,** ***adj.***

**tal·ly** (tal′i), ***n.*** [*pl.* -LIES], [< L. *talea*, a stick (notched to keep accounts)], 1. anything used as a record for an account. 2. an account; reckoning. 3. a tag or label. ***v.t.*** -LIED, -LYING], 1. to put on or as on a tally. 2. to count (*up*). ***v.i.*** 1. to record a score, etc. 2. to agree; correspond.

**tal·ly·ho** (tal′i-hō′), ***interj.*** [< Fr. *taiaut*], the cry of a hunter on sighting the fox. ***n.*** (tal′i-hō′), 1. a cry of "tallyho." 2. a coach drawn by four horses.

**Tal·mud** (tal′mud, täl′mood), ***n.*** [< Heb. *lāmadh*, learn], the body of early Jewish civil and religious law. —**Tal′mud·ist,** ***n.***

**tal·on** (tal′ən), ***n.*** [< L. *talus*, an ankle], *usually in pl.* the claw of an animal or bird of prey. —**tal′oned,** ***adj.***

**tam** (tam), ***n.*** a tam-o'-shanter.

**ta·ma·le** (tə-mä′li), ***n.*** [< Mex. Sp.], a Mexican food of minced meat and red peppers cooked in corn husks.

**tam·a·rack** (tam′ə-rak′), ***n.*** [< Am. Ind.], any of various larch trees usually found in swamps.

**tam·a·rind** (tam′ə-rind′), ***n.*** [< Ar. *tamr hindī*, date of India], 1. a tropical tree with yellow flowers and brown, acid pods. 2. its fruit, used in foods, medicine, etc.

**tam·bou·rine** (tam′bə-rēn′), ***n.*** [see TAMBOUR], a shallow, one-headed drum with jingling metal disks around it: played by shaking, hitting, etc.

**tame** (tām), ***adj.*** [TAMER, TAMEST], [AS. *tam*], 1. taken from a wild state and trained for man's use. 2. gentle; docile. 3. without spirit or force; dull. ***v.t.*** [TAMED, TAMING], 1. to make tame, or domestic. 2. to make gentle, etc.; subdue. —**tam′a·ble, tame′a·ble,** ***adj.*** —**tame′ly,** ***adv.*** —**tame′ness,** ***n.***

**Tam·il** (tam′il, tum′-), ***n.*** the non-Indo-European language of the Tamils, a people of S India and N Ceylon.

**tam-o'-shan·ter** (tam′ə-shan′tẽr), ***n.*** [< title character of Burns's poem], a Scottish cap with a round, flat top.

**tamp** (tamp), ***v.t.*** [? < Fr. *tampon*, a plug], to pack or pound down by a series of taps.

**tam·per** (tam′pẽr), ***v.i.*** [< *temper*], to plot; scheme. —**tamper with,** 1. to interfere with; meddle. 2. to make corrupt, illegal, etc. by meddling. —**tam′per·er,** ***n.***

**tan** (tan), ***n.*** [< ML. *tannum*], 1. tanbark. 2. a yellowish-brown color. 3. the color of sun tan. ***adj.*** [TANNER, TANNEST], yellowish-brown. ***v.t.*** [TANNED, TANNING], 1. to change (hide) into leather by soaking in tannic acid. 2. to produce a sun tan in. 3. [Colloq.], to whip. ***v.i.*** to become tanned.

**tan′bark′,** ***n.*** any bark containing tannic acid used to tan hides.

**tan·dem** (tan′dəm), ***adv.*** [< punning use of L. *tandem*, at length (of time)], one behind another; in single file. ***n.*** 1. a bicycle with two seats and two sets of pedals placed tandem. 2. a two-wheeled carriage drawn by horses harnessed tandem.

**tang** (taŋ), *n.* [< ON. *tangi*, a sting], 1. a prong on a chisel, file, etc. to fit into the handle. 2. a strong, penetrating taste or odor. —**tang'y** [-IER, -IEST], *adj.*

**tan·gent** (tan'jənt), *adj.* [< L. *tangere*, to touch], 1. touching. 2. in *geometry*, meeting a curve or surface at one point but not intersecting it. *n.* a tangent curve, line, or surface. —**go** (or **fly**) **off at** (or **on**) **a tangent**, to change suddenly to another line of action. —**tan·gen'tial** (-jen'shəl), *adj.*

**tan·ge·rine** (tan'jə-rēn'), *n.* [< *Tangier*, a city in N. Africa], 1. a small, loose-skinned orange with easily separated segments. 2. reddish yellow.

**tan·gi·ble** (tan'jə-b'l), *adj.* [< L. *tangere*, to touch], 1. that can be touched or felt by touch. 2. definite; objective. *n. pl.* property that can be appraised for value. —**tan'gi·bil'i·ty**, *n.* —**tan'gi·bly**, *adv.*

**tan·gle** (taŋ'g'l), *v.t.* [-GLED, -GLING], [< ON.], 1. to catch as in a snare; trap. 2. to make a snarl of: intertwine. *v.i.* to become tangled. *n.* 1. an intertwined, confused mass. 2. a jumbled, confused condition.

**tan·go** (taŋ'gō), *n.* [*pl.* -GOS], [< Sp.], 1. a South American dance with long, gliding steps. 2. music for this. *v.i.* [-GOED, -GOING], to dance the tango.

**tank** (taŋk), *n.* [< L. *stagnum*, pond], 1. any large container for liquid or gas. 2. an armored vehicle carrying guns and moving on endless treads. —**tank'ful** [*pl.* -FULS], *n.*

**tank·ard** (taŋk'ẽrd), *n.* [< OFr. *tanquart*], a large drinking cup with a handle and a hinged lid.

**tank·er** (taŋk'ẽr), *n.* a ship equipped to transport oil or other liquids.

**tan·ner** (tan'ẽr), *n.* one whose work is making leather by tanning hides.

**tan'ner·y**, *n.* [*pl.* -IES], a place where hides are tanned.

**tan·nic acid** (tan'ik), a yellowish, astringent substance used in tanning, dyeing, etc.: also **tan'nin** (-in), *n.*

**tan·ta·lize** (tan'tə-līz'), *v.t.* [-LIZED, -LIZING], [< *Tantalus*], to promise or show something desirable to (a person) and then remove or withhold it; tease.

**tan·ta·lum** (tan'tə-ləm), *n.* [< *Tantalus*: from difficulty in extracting it], a rare, steel-blue,. corrosion-resisting, metallic chemical element used for electric light filaments, etc.: symbol, Ta.

**Tan·ta·lus** (tan'tə-ləs), *n.* in *Gr. myth.*, a king punished in Hades by being unable to drink water in which he stood or eat fruit which hung above him.

**tan·ta·mount** (tan'tə-mount'), *adj.* [< L. *tantus*, so much + OFr. *amont*, upward], equal in value, effect, etc.; equivalent.

**tan·trum** (tan'trəm), *n.* [<?], a violent, willful outburst of rage, etc.

**Tao·ism** (tou'iz'm), *n.* [Chin. *tao*, the way], a Chinese religion and philosophy advocating simplicity, selflessness, etc. —**Tao'ist**, *n.*

**tap** (tap), *v.t.* & *v.i.* [TAPPED, TAPPING], [echoic], 1. to strike lightly. 2. to make or do by tapping: as, to *tap* a message. *n.* 1. a light, rapid blow. 2. *pl.* a military bugle call or drum signal to put out lights in retiring for the night.

**tap** (tap), *n.* [AS. *tæppe*], 1. a faucet or spigot. 2. a plug, cork, etc. for stopping a hole in a cask, etc. 3. a place in an electric circuit where a connection can be made. *v.t.* [TAPPED, TAPPING], 1. to put a hole in, or pull the plug from, for drawing off liquid. 2. to draw off (liquid). 3. to make a connection with (a water main, etc.). —**on tap**, 1. ready to be drawn from a tapped cask. 2. [Colloq.], ready for consideration or action.

**tape** (tāp), *n.* [AS. *tæppe*, a fillet], 1. a strong, narrow strip of cloth, paper, etc. used for binding, tying, etc. 2. a tapeline. *v.t.* [TAPED, TAPING], to bind, tie, etc. with tape.

**tape'line'** (-līn'), *n.* a tape marked in inches, feet, etc. for measuring: also **tape measure.**

**ta·per** (tā'pẽr), *n.* [AS. *tapur*], 1. a slender candle. 2. a gradual decrease in width or thickness. *v.t.* & *v.i.* 1. to decrease gradually in width or thickness. 2. to lessen; diminish. Often with *off*.

**tape recorder**, a machine for recording sound on a thin magnetic tape and for playing it back.

**tap·es·try** (tap'is-tri), *n.* [*pl.* -TRIES], [< Gr. *tapēs*, a carpet], a heavy woven cloth with decorative designs and pictures, used as a wall hanging, furniture covering, etc.

**tape'worm'**, *n.* a tapelike worm that lives as a parasite in the intestines of man and other animals.

**tap·i·o·ca** (tap'i-ō'kə), *n.* [< S. Am. Ind.], a starchy, granular substance prepared from cassava roots, used for puddings, etc.

**ta·pir** (tā'pẽr), *n.* [< S. Am. Ind.], a large, hoglike mammal found mostly in tropical America: tapirs have flexible snouts.

**tap'room'**, *n.* a barroom.

**tap'root'**, *n.* [*tap* (faucet) + *root*], a main root from which branch roots spread out.

**tar** (tär), *n.* [AS. *teru*], a thick, sticky, black liquid obtained by the destructive distillation of wood, coal, etc. *v.t.* [TARRED, TARRING], to cover or smear with tar. —**tar'ry** [-RIER, -RIEST], *adj.*

**tar** (tär), *n.* [< *tarpaulin*], [Colloq.], a sailor.

**tar·an·tel·la** (tar'ən-tel'ə), *n.* [< *Taranto*, city in Italy], 1. a fast, whirling Italian dance for couples. 2. music for this.

**ta·ran·tu·la** (tə-ran'choo-lə), *n.* [see prec.], a large, hairy, somewhat poisonous spider of S Europe and tropical America.

**tar·dy** (tär'di), *adj.* [-DIER, -DIEST], [< L. *tardus*, slow], 1. slow; slow-moving. 2. late; delayed; dilatory. —**tar'di·ness**, *n.*

**tare** (târ), *n.* [prob. < MD. *tarwe*, wheat], 1. vetch, a plant grown for fodder. 2. in the *Bible*, a noxious weed.

**tare** (târ), *n.* [< Ar. *taraha*, to reject], the deduction of the weight of a container from the total weight to determine the weight of the contents.

**tar·get** (tär'git), *n.* [< OFr. *targe*, a shield], 1. a board, etc. marked as with concentric circles, aimed at in archery, rifle practice, etc. 2. any object that is shot at. 3. an object of attack, etc.

**tar·iff** (tar'if), *n.* [< Ar. *ta'rif*, information], 1. a list or system of taxes upon exports or imports. 2. a tax of this kind, or its rate. 3. any list of prices, charges, etc.

**tar·nish** (tär'nish), *v.t.* [< Fr. *terne*, dull], 1. to dull the luster of. 2. to sully (a reputation, etc.). *v.i.* 1. to lose luster; discolor. 2. to become sullied. *n.* dullness; discoloration; stain. —**tar'nish·a·ble**, *adj.*

**ta·ro** (tä'rō), *n.* [*pl.* -ROS], [Tahitian], a tropical plant with a starchy, edible root.

**tar·pau·lin** (tär-pô'lin, tär'pə-), *n.* [< *tar* + *pall*, a covering], 1. canvas waterproofed with tar, paint, etc., or a sheet of this used as a protective cover. 2. a hat or coat of tarpaulin.

**tar·pon** (tär'pon), *n.* [prob. < W. Ind. native name], a large, silvery game fish found in the warmer parts of the W Atlantic.

**tar·ry** (tar'i), *v.i.* [-RIED, -RYING], [merging of AS. *tergan*, to vex & OFr. *targer*, to delay], 1. to delay; linger; loiter. 2. to stay for a time. 3. to wait.

**tart** (tärt), *adj.* [AS. *teart*], 1. sharp in taste; sour; acid. 2. sharp in meaning; cutting: as, a *tart* answer. —**tart'ly**, *adv.* —**tart'ness**, *n.*

**tart** (tärt), *n.* [< OFr. *tarte*], a small pastry shell filled with jam, jelly, etc.

**tart** (tärt), *n.* [orig., slang for *sweetheart*], a prostitute or any woman of loose morals.

**tar·tan** (tär′t'n), *n.* [cf. ME. *tirtaine*, mixed fabric], a woolen cloth in any of various woven plaid patterns, worn esp. in the Scottish Highlands.

**Tar·tar** (tär′tẽr), *n.* a Tatar.

**tar·tar** (tär′tẽr), *n.* [< MGr. *tartaron*], 1. a potassium salt forming a reddish, crustlike deposit in wine casks: in purified form called *cream of tartar*. 2. a hard deposit forming on the teeth.

**task** (task, täsk), *n.* [ult. < L. *taxare*, to rate], 1. a piece of work to be done. 2. any difficult undertaking. *v.t.* to burden; strain. **—take to task**, to reprimand.

**task force,** a specially trained military unit assigned a specific task.

**task′mas′ter,** *n.* one who assigns tasks to others, esp. when severe.

**tas·sel** (tas′'l), *n.* [OFr., a knob], 1. an ornamental tuft of threads, etc. hanging loosely from a knob. 2. something like this, as a tuft of corn silk.

**taste** (tāst), *v.t.* [TASTED, TASTING], [< OFr. *taster*], 1. to test the flavor of by putting a little in one's mouth. 2. to detect the flavor of by the sense of taste. 3. to eat or drink a small amount of. 4. to experience: as, to *taste* defeat. *v.i.* to have a specific flavor. *n.* 1. the sense by which flavor is perceived through stimulation of the taste buds on the tongue. 2. the quality so perceived; flavor. 3. a small amount tasted as a sample. 4. a bit; trace. 5. the ability to appreciate what is beautiful, appropriate, etc. 6. a liking; inclination. 7. a specific preference. **—in bad** (or **good**) **taste**, in a style or manner showing a bad (or good) sense of beauty, fitness, etc. **—taste′less**, *adj.* **—tast′er**, *n.*

**taste bud,** any of the clusters of cells on the tongue, functioning as the sense organs of taste.

**taste′ful,** *adj.* having or showing good taste (*n.* 5). **—taste′ful·ly**, *adv.* **—taste′ful·ness**, *n.*

**tast′y,** *adj.* [-IER, -IEST], that tastes good.

**tat** (tat), *v.t.* [TATTED, TATTING], to make by tatting. *v.i.* to do tatting.

**Ta·tar** (tä′tẽr), *n.* a member of any of the E Asiatic tribes who invaded W Asia and E Europe in the Middle Ages.

**tat·ter** (tat′ẽr), *n.* [< ON. *töturr*, rags], 1. a torn and hanging piece, as of a garment. 2. *pl.* torn, ragged clothes. *v.t. & v.i.* to make or become ragged. **—tat′tered**, *adj.*

**tat·ting** (tat′iŋ), *n.* [prob. < Brit. dial. *tat*, to tangle], 1. a kind of lace made by looping and knotting. 2. the process of making this.

**tat·tle** (tat′'l), *v.i.* [-TLED, -TLING], [< MD. *tatelen*], 1. to talk idly. 2. to reveal others' secrets. *v.t.* to reveal (a secret) by gossiping. *n.* idle talk; chatter. **—tat′tler**, *n.*

**tat′tle·tale′,** *n.* a talebearer.

**tat·too** (ta-tōō′), *v.t.* [-TOOED, -TOOING], [< Tahitian *tatu*], to make (permanent designs) on (the skin) by puncturing it and inserting indelible colors. *n.* [*pl.* -TOOS], a tattooed mark or design. **—tat·too′er**, *n.*

**tat·too** (ta-tōō′), *n.* [*pl.* -TOOS], [< D. *tap toe*, shut the tap: a signal for closing barrooms], 1. a signal on a drum, bugle, etc. summoning soldiers, etc. to their quarters at night. 2. a drumming, rapping, etc.

**tau** (tô, tou), *n.* the nineteenth letter of the Greek alphabet (Τ, τ).

**taught** (tôt), pt. and pp. of **teach.**

**taunt** (tônt, tänt), *v.t.* [? < Fr. *tant pour tant*, tit for tat], to reproach scornfully or sarcastically. *n.* a scornful remark.

**taupe** (tōp), *n.* [< L. *talpa*, a mole], a dark, brownish gray, the color of moleskin.

**Tau·rus** (tôr′əs), *n.* [L., a bull], the second sign of the zodiac.

**taut** (tôt), *adj.* [ME. *toght*, tight], 1. tightly stretched, as a rope. 2. tense: as, a *taut* smile. 3. neat; trim. **—taut′ly**, *adv.*

**tau·tol·o·gy** (tô-tol′ə-ji), *n.* [*pl.* -GIES], [< Gr. *to auto*, the same; + *-logy*], needless repetition of an idea in a different word, phrase, etc.; redundancy. Example: necessary essentials.

**tav·ern** (tav′ẽrn), *n.* [< L. *taberna*], 1. a saloon; bar. 2. an inn.

**taw** (tô), *n.* 1. a marble used to shoot with. 2. a game of marbles.

**taw·dry** (tô′dri), *adj.* [-DRIER, -DRIEST], [< *tawdry* (< *St. Audrey*) *laces*, sold at St. Audrey's fair, Norwich, England], gaudy and cheap. **—taw′dri·ness**, *n.*

**taw·ny** (tô′ni), *adj.* [-NIER, -NIEST], [< OFr. *tanner*, to tan], brownish-yellow; tan. *n.* a tawny color. **—taw′ni·ness**, *n.*

**tax** (taks), *v.t.* [< *taxare*, appraise], 1. to require to pay a tax. 2. to assess a tax on (income, purchases, etc.). 3. to impose a burden or strain on. 4. to accuse; charge. *n.* 1. a compulsory payment of a percentage of income, property value, etc. for the support of government. 2. a heavy demand; burden. **—tax′a·ble**, *adj.* **—tax′er**, *n.*

**tax·a·tion** (tak-sā′shən), *n.* 1. a taxing or being taxed. 2. taxes paid.

**tax·i** (tak′si), *n.* [*pl.* -IS], a taxicab. *v.i.* [-IED, -IING or -YING], 1. to travel by taxi. 2. to move along the ground or water under its own power: said of an airplane.

**tax′i·cab′,** *n.* [short for *taximeter cab*], an automobile in which passengers are carried for a fare.

**tax·i·der·my** (tak′si-dũr′mi), *n.* [< Gr. *taxis*, arrangement + *derma*, skin], the art of preparing, stuffing, and mounting the skins of animals to make them appear lifelike. **—tax′i·der′mal**, *adj.* **—tax′i·der′mist**, *n.*

**tax·i·me·ter** (tak′si-mē′tẽr), *n.* [< Fr. *taxe*, a tax + *metre*, meter], an automatic device in taxicabs to register fare due.

**tax·on·o·my** (tak-son′ə-mi), *n.* [< Gr. *taxis*, arrangement + *nomos*, law], classification, esp. of animals and plants. **—tax·on′o·mist**, *n.*

**tax′pay′er,** *n.* one who pays a tax.

**TB, T.B., tb., t.b.,** tuberculosis.

**T-bone steak** (tē′bōn′), a steak, as a porterhouse, with a T-shaped bone.

**tbs., tbsp.,** tablespoon; tablespoons.

**tea** (tē), *n.* [< Chin. dial. *t'e*], 1. an evergreen plant grown in China, India, etc. 2. its dried leaves, steeped in boiling water to make a beverage. 3. this beverage. 4. a tealike extract made as from other plants. 5. [Chiefly Brit.], a light meal in the late afternoon. 6. a social gathering in the afternoon at which tea, coffee, etc. are served.

**tea bag,** a small, porous bag of cloth or paper, containing tea leaves and used in making an individual cup of tea.

**teach** (tēch), *v.t.* [TAUGHT, TEACHING], [AS. *tæcan*], 1. to show how to do something; train; give lessons to; instruct. 2. to give lessons in (a subject). 3. to provide with knowledge, insight, etc. *v.i.* to be a teacher. **—teach′a·ble**, *adj.* **—teach′ing**, *n.*

**teach′er,** *n.* one who teaches, esp. as a profession.

**tea′cup′,** *n.* a cup for drinking tea, etc.

**teak** (tēk), *n.* [< Malayalam *tēkka*], 1. a large East Indian tree with hard, yellowish-brown wood. 2. its wood. Also **teak′wood′.**

**tea′ket′tle,** *n.* a covered kettle with a spout, used to heat water as for tea.

**teal** (tēl), *n.* [prob. < AS.], 1. a small, short-necked, fresh-water duck. 2. a dark grayish blue: also **teal blue.**

**team** (tēm), *n.* [AS., offspring], 1. two or more horses, oxen, etc. harnessed to the same plow, etc. 2. a group of people working or playing together: as, a baseball *team*. *v.t.* to harness together in a team. *v.i.* to join in co-operative activity (with *up*).

**team′mate′**, *n.* one on the same team.

**team′ster** (-stẽr), *n.* one who drives a team, or truck, for hauling loads.

**team′work′**, *n.* 1. joint action by a group of people. 2. work done by or with a team.

**tea′pot′**, *n.* a pot with a spout, handle, and lid, for brewing and pouring tea.

**tear** (târ), *v.t.* [TORE, TORN, TEARING], [AS. *teran*, rend], 1. to pull apart into pieces by force; rip. 2. to make by tearing: as, to *tear* a hole. 3. to lacerate. 4. to disrupt; split: as, *torn* by dissension. 5. to divide with doubt, etc.: as, *torn* between two loves. 6. to remove as by tearing, pulling, etc. (with *out*, *off*, etc.). *v.i.* 1. to be torn. 2. to move violently or with speed. *n.* 1. a tearing. 2. the result of a tearing; rent. 3. a violent outburst. 4. [Slang], a spree. **—tear down**, to dismantle; wreck.

**tear** (têr), *n.* [AS.], 1. a drop of the salty fluid which flows from the eye, as in weeping. 2. *pl.* sorrow; grief. **—in tears**, weeping. **—tear′ful**, *adj.* **—tear′ful·ly**, *adv.*

**tear′drop′** (têr′-), *n.* a tear.

**tear gas** (têr), a gas causing irritation of the eyes, a flow of tears.

**tea′room′**, *n.* a restaurant that serves tea, coffee, light lunches, etc.

**tease** (tēz), *v.t.* [TEASED, TEASING], [AS. *tæsan*], 1. to card or comb (flax, wool, etc.). 2. to raise a nap on (cloth) by brushing with teasels. 3. to annoy by irritating acts or remarks, or by poking fun at. 4. to beg; importune. *v.i.* to indulge in irritating acts, etc. *n.* 1. a teasing or being teased. 2. one who teases. **—teas′er**, *n.* **—teas′ing·ly**, *adv.*

**tea′spoon′**, *n.* a spoon for use at the table and as a measuring unit holding ⅓ tablespoonful. **—tea′spoon·ful′** [*pl.* -FULS], *n.*

**teat** (tēt), *n.* [< OFr. *tete*], the nipple on a breast or udder.

**tech.**, 1. technical(ly). 2. technology.

**tech·ni·cal** (tek′ni-k′l), *adj.* [< Gr. *technē*, an art], 1. dealing with the industrial or mechanical arts of the applied sciences. 2. of a specific science, art, craft, etc. 3. of, in, or showing technique.

**tech′ni·cal′i·ty** (-kal′ə-ti), *n.* [*pl.* -TIES], 1. the state or quality of being technical. 2. a technical point, detail, etc. 3. a minute point, detail, etc. brought to bear on a main issue.

**tech·ni·cian** (tek-nish′ən), *n.* one skilled in the technique of some art, craft, or science.

**tech·ni·col·or** (tek′ni-kul′ẽr), *n.* a process of reproducing colors on a motion-picture film: a trademark (**Technicolor**).

**tech·nique** (tek-nēk′), *n.* [Fr., see TECHNICAL], 1. the method of procedure in artistic work, scientific operation, etc. 2. the degree of expertness in this.

**tech·noc·ra·cy** (tek-nok′rə-si), *n.* [< Gr. *technē*, an art; + *-cracy*], government by scientists and engineers. **—tech′no·crat′** (-nə-krat′), *n.* **—tech′no·crat′ic**, *adj.*

**tech·nol·o·gy** (tek-nol′ə-ji), *n.* [< Gr. *technologia*, systematic treatment], 1. the science of the practical or industrial arts. 2. applied science. **—tech′no·log′i·cal** (-nə-loj′i-k′l), *adj.* **—tech·nol′o·gist**, *n.*

**ted·dy bear** (ted′i), [< *Teddy* (*Theodore*) Roosevelt, 26th President], a child's toy somewhat like a small, stuffed bear.

**te·di·ous** (tē′di-əs), *adj.* full of tedium; long and wearisome; tiresome; boring.

**te·di·um** (tē′di-əm), *n.* [< L. *taedet*, it offends], the condition or quality of being tiresome, wearisome, or monotonous.

**tee** (tē), *n.* [*pl.* TEES], 1. the letter T, t. 2. anything shaped like a T. *adj.* shaped like a T. **—to a tee**, exactly; precisely.

**tee** (tē), *n.* [prob. < Scot. dial. *teaz*], in *golf*, 1. a small mound of earth, or a small peg, from which the player drives the ball. 2. the place from which a player makes the first stroke on each hole. *v.i.* [TEED, TEEING], to play a golf ball from a tee (with *off*).

**teem** (tēm), *v.i.* [< AS. *team*, progeny], to be prolific; abound: swarm. **—teem′ing**, *adj.*

**teen-age** (tēn′āj), *adj.* 1. in one's teens. 2. of or for persons in their teens. **—teen′-ag′er**, *n.*

**teens** (tēnz), *n.pl.* the years of one's age between 13 and 19 inclusive.

**tee·pee** (tē′pē), *n.* a tepee.

**tee·ter** (tē′tẽr), *n.*, *v.i.* & *v.t.* [< ON. *titra*, to tremble], seesaw; waver.

**tee′ter-tot′ter** (-tot′ẽr, -tô′tẽr), *n.* & *v.i.* seesaw.

**teeth** (tēth), *n.* pl. of **tooth.**

**teethe** (tē*th*), *v.i.* [TEETHED, TEETHING], to grow teeth; cut one's teeth.

**tee·to·tal** (tē-tō′t'l), *adj.* [< doubling of initial *t* in *total*], 1. [Colloq.], entire; complete. 2. practicing total abstinence from alcoholic liquor. **—tee·to′tal·er**, *n.*

**tel.**, 1. telegram. 2. telephone.

**tele-**, [< Gr. *tēle*, far off], a combining form meaning: 1. *operating at a distance*, as in *telegraph*. 2. *of*, *in*, or *by television*.

**tel·e·cast** (tel′ə-kast′, -käst′), *v.t.* & *v.i.* [-CAST or -CASTED, -CASTING], to broadcast by television. *n.* a television broadcast.

**tel·e·gram** (tel′ə-gram′), *n.* a message transmitted by telegraph.

**tel·e·graph** (tel′ə-graf′, -gräf′), *n.* [see TELE- & -GRAPH], an apparatus or system for transmitting messages by electric impulses sent through a wire or converted into radio waves. *v.t.* & *v.i.* to send (a message) to (a person) by telegraph. **—tel′e·graph′ic**, *adj.*

**te·leg·ra·phy** (tə-leg′rə-fi), *n.* the operation of telegraph apparatus. **—te·leg′ra·pher**, *n.*

**tel·e·me·ter** (tel′ə-mē′tẽr, tə-lem′ə-tẽr), *n.* a device for measuring and transmitting data about radiation, temperature, etc. from a remote point: used in space studies, etc.

**te·lep·a·thy** (tə-lep′ə-thi), *n.* [*tele-* + *-pathy*], supposed communication between minds by means other than the normal sensory channels. **—tel·e·path·ic** (tel′ə-path′ik), *adj.*

**tel·e·phone** (tel′ə-fōn′), *n.* [*tele-* + *-phone*], an instrument or system for conveying speech over distances by converting sound into electric impulses sent through a wire. *v.t.* & *v.i.* [-PHONED, -PHONING], to convey (a message) to (a person) by telephone. **—tel′e·phon′ic** (-fon′ik), *adj.*

**te·leph·o·ny** (tə-lef′ə-ni), *n.* the making or operating of telephones.

**tel·e·pho·to** (tel′ə-fō′tō), *adj.* designating or of a camera lens that produces a large image of a distant object.

**tel′e·pho′to·graph′**, *n.* 1. a photograph taken with a telephoto lens. 2. a photograph transmitted by telegraph or radio. *v.t.* & *v.i.* 1. to take (photographs) with a telephoto lens. 2. to transmit (telephotographs). **—tel′e·pho·tog′ra·phy**, *n.*

**Tel·e·promp·ter** (tel′ə-promp′tẽr), *n.* an electronic device that unrolls a script line by line as a prompting aid: a trademark.

**tel·e·scope** (tel′ə-skōp′), *n.* [< Gr. *tēle*, far off + *skopein*, to view], an instrument with lenses for making distant objects appear nearer and larger. *v.i.* & *v.t.* [-SCOPED, -SCOPING], to slide one into another, as the tubes of a collapsible telescope. **—tel′e·scop′ic** (-skop′ik), *adj.*

**Tel·e·type** (tel′ə-tīp′), *n.* [often t-], a form of telegraph in which the receiver prints messages typed on the transmitter: a trademark.

**tel·e·vise** (tel′ə-vīz′), *v.t.* [-VISED, -VISING], to transmit by television.

**tel·e·vi·sion** (tel'ə-vizh'ən), *n.* 1. the process of transmitting images by electronically converting light rays into radio waves: the receiver reconverts the waves so that the images are reproduced on a screen. 2. television broadcasting.

**tell** (tel), *v.t.* [TOLD, TELLING], [< AS. *tellan*, calculate], 1. to enumerate; count. 2. to narrate; relate, as stories. 3. to express in words; say: as, *tell* the facts. 4. to report; announce. 5. to reveal; disclose. 6. to recognize; distinguish; know: as, to *tell* twins apart. 7. to let know; inform: as, *tell* me later. 8. to request; order: as, *tell* her to go. *v.i.* 1. to give an account or evidence (*of* something). 2. to be effective: as, each blow *told*. —**tell off,** [Colloq.], to criticize severely. —**tell on,** 1. to tire. 2. [Colloq.], to inform against.

**tell'er,** *n.* 1. one who tells (a story, etc.). 2. one who counts, as a bank clerk who pays out or receives money. —**tell'er·ship,** *n.*

**tell'ing,** *adj.* having an effect; forceful: as, a *telling* blow. —**tell'ing·ly,** *adv.*

**tell'tale',** *n.* an outward indication of something secret.

**te·mer·i·ty** (tə-mer'ə-ti), *n.* [< L. *temere*, rashly], foolish boldness; rashness.

**temp.,** 1. temperature. 2. temporary.

**tem·per** (tem'pẽr), *v.t.* [< L. *temperare*, regulate], 1. to moderate, as by mingling with something else: as, *temper* blame with praise. 2. to bring to the proper condition by some treatment: as, to *temper* steel. *n.* 1. the degree of hardness and resiliency of a metal. 2. frame of mind; disposition. 3. calmness of mind: in *lose* (or *keep*) *one's temper*. 4. anger; rage.

**tem·per·a** (tem'pẽr-ə), *n.* [It.; see TEMPER], a process of painting with pigments mixed with size, casein, or egg.

**tem·per·a·ment** (tem'prə-mənt, tem'pẽr-ə-), *n.* [see TEMPER], 1. frame of mind. 2. a moody, rebellious disposition.

**tem'per·a·men'tal** (-men't'l), *adj.* 1. of or caused by temperament. 2. excitable; easily upset; moody.

**tem·per·ance** (tem'pẽr-əns), *n.* 1. self-restraint; moderation, as in indulging the appetites. 2. moderation in drinking alcoholic liquors. 3. total abstinence from alcoholic liquors.

**tem·per·ate** (tem'pẽr-it), *adj.* [see TEMPER], 1. moderate, as in eating or drinking. 2. self-restrained in actions, speech, etc. 3. neither very hot nor very cold: said of climate, etc. —**tem'per·ate·ly,** *adv.*

**Temperate Zone,** either of two zones (*North* or *South Temperate Zone*) between the tropics and the polar circles.

**tem·per·a·ture** (tem'pẽr-ə-chẽr), *n.* [< L. *temperatus*, temperate], 1. the degree of hotness or coldness of anything. 2. excess of body heat over the normal; fever.

**tem·pered** (tem'pẽrd), *adj.* 1. having been given the desired temper, hardness, etc.: as, *tempered* steel. 2. having a (specified) temper: as, *bad-tempered*.

**tem·pest** (tem'pist), *n.* [< L. *tempus*, time], a violent wind, esp. one accompanied by rain, snow, etc.

**tem·pes·tu·ous** (tem-pes'cho͞o-əs), *adj.* of or like a tempest; stormy; violent.

**tem·ple** (tem'p'l), *n.* [< L. *templum*], 1. a building for the worship of God or gods. 2. a large building for some special purpose: as, a *temple* of art. —**tem'pled,** *adj.*

**tem·ple** (tem'p'l), *n.* [< L. *tempus*, fatal spot], the flat surface behind the forehead and in front of the ear.

**tem·po** (tem'pō), *n.* [*pl.* -POS, -PI (-pi)], [It. < L. *tempus*, time], 1. the rate of speed at which a musical work is, or is supposed to be, played. 2. rate of activity.

**tem·po·ral** (tem'pẽr-əl), *adj.* [< L. *tempus*, time], 1. temporary; transitory. 2. of this world; worldly. 3. secular. 4. of or limited by time. —**tem'po·ral·ly,** *adv.*

**tem·po·ral** (tem'pẽr-əl), *adj.* of or near the temples (of the head).

**tem·po·rar·y** (tem'pə-rer'i), *adj.* [< L. *tempus*, time], lasting only a while; not permanent. —**tem'po·rar'i·ly,** *adv.*

**tem·po·rize** (tem'pə-rīz'), *v.i.* [-RIZED, -RIZING], to give temporary compliance, evade decision, etc. so as to gain time or avoid argument. —**tem'po·ri·za'tion,** *n.*

**tempt** (tempt), *v.t.* [< L. *tentare*, to test], 1. to induce; entice, as to something immoral. 2. to be inviting to; attract. 3. to provoke or risk provoking (fate, etc.). 4. to incline strongly: as, I am *tempted* to go. —**temp·ta·tion** (temp-tā'shən), *n.*

**ten** (ten), *adj.* & *n.* [AS.], one more than nine; 10; X.

**ten·a·ble** (ten'ə-b'l), *adj.* [< L. *tenere*, to hold], that can be held, defended, or maintained. —**ten'a·bil'i·ty,** *n.* —**ten'a·bly,** *adv.*

**te·na·cious** (ti-nā'shəs), *adj.* [< L. *tenere*, to hold], 1. holding firmly: as, a *tenacious* grip. 2. retentive: as, a *tenacious* memory. 3. strongly cohesive or adhesive. 4. persistent; stubborn. —**te·nac'i·ty** (-nas'ə-ti), *n.*

**ten·ant** (ten'ənt), *n.* [< L. *tenere*, to hold], 1. one who pays rent to occupy or use land, a building, etc. 2. an occupant. *v.t.* to hold as a tenant; occupy. —**ten'an·cy** [*pl.* -CIES], *n.* —**ten'ant·less,** *adj.*

**Ten Commandments,** in the *Bible*, the ten rules of moral and religious behavior given to Moses by God: Ex. 20:2-17.

**tend** (tend), *v.t.* [see ATTEND], to take care of; cultivate; manage.

**tend** (tend), *v.i.* [< L. *tendere*, to stretch], 1. to be inclined or disposed (*to*). 2. to be directed (*to* or *toward*).

**tend·en·cy** (ten'dən-si), *n.* [*pl.* -CIES], [see TEND, *v.i.*], 1. an inclination to move or act in a particular direction or way. 2. a course toward some object, purpose, or result.

**ten·der** (ten'dẽr), *adj.* [< L. *tener*, soft], 1. easily chewed, broken, cut, etc.; soft. 2. physically weak. 3. immature. 4. that requires careful handling. 5. light; gentle: as, a *tender* smile. 6. acutely sensitive, as to pain. 7. sensitive to emotions, other's feelings, etc. —**ten'der·ly,** *adv.* —**ten'der·ness,** *n.*

**ten·der** (ten'dẽr), *v.t.* [< L. *tendere*, to stretch], to present for acceptance. *n.* 1. a formal offer. 2. something offered in payment, esp. money. —**ten'der·er,** *n.*

**tend'er,** *n.* 1. one who tends something. 2. a small ship for supplying a large one. 3. a railroad car attached behind, and carrying coal and water for, a steam locomotive.

**ten'der·foot',** *n.* [*pl.* -FOOTS, -FEET], 1. a newcomer to the ranching country of the West, unused to hardships. 2. any newcomer, novice, etc.

**ten'der·ize'** (-īz'), *v.t.* [-IZED, -IZING], to make tender, as meat. —**ten'der·iz'er,** *n.*

**ten'der·loin',** *n.* the tenderest part of a loin of beef, pork, etc.

**ten·don** (ten'dən), *n.* [< Gr. *tenein*, to stretch], any of the inelastic cords of tough connective tissue by which muscles are attached to bones, etc.; a sinew.

**ten·dril** (ten'dril), *n.* [prob. < Fr. *tendre*, stretch out], a threadlike, clinging part of a climbing plant, serving to support it.

**ten·e·ment** (ten'ə-mənt), *n.* [< L. *tenere*, to hold], 1. a room or suite tenanted as a separate dwelling. 2. a building divided into tenements, esp. one that is overcrowded, dirty, etc.: also **tenement house.**

**ten·et** (ten'it), *n.* [L., he holds], a principle, doctrine, or opinion maintained, as by a school of thought.

**ten'fold'**, *adj. & adv.* (having) ten times as much or as many.

**ten·nis** (ten'is), *n.* [prob. < OFr. *tenez*, hold (imperative)], a game in which players in a marked court bat a ball back and forth with rackets over a net.

**tennis shoe**, a rubber-soled, heelless shoe of canvas, worn for tennis, etc.

**ten·on** (ten'ən), *n.* [ult. < L. *tenere*, to hold], a projecting part cut on the end of a piece of wood for insertion into a mortise to make a joint.

**ten·or** (ten'ẽr), *n.* [< L. *tenere*, to hold], 1. general course or tendency. 2. general meaning; drift. 3. *a*) the highest adult male singing voice. *b*) a part for this voice. *c*) a person or instrument having a tenor range.

**ten'pins'**, *n.pl.* 1. [construed as sing.], a game in which ten wooden pins are set up in a triangle and bowled at. 2. these pins.

**tense** (tens), *adj.* [TENSER, TENSEST], [< L. *tendere*, stretch], 1. stretched tight; taut. 2. undergoing or characterized by mental or nervous strain. *v.t. & v.i.* [TENSED, TENSING], to make or become tense. **—tense'ly**, *adv.* **—tense'ness, ten'si·ty**, *n.*

**tense** (tens), *n.* [< L. *tempus*, time], any of the forms of a verb that show the time of its action or existence.

**ten·sile** (ten's'l, -sil), *adj.* 1. of, undergoing, or exerting tension. 2. capable of being stretched. **—ten·sil'i·ty**, *n.*

**ten·sion** (ten'shən), *n.* 1. a tensing or being tensed. 2. mental or nervous strain. 3. a state of strained relations due to mutual hostility. 4. voltage. 5. stress on a material produced by the pull of forces tending to cause extension. **—ten'sion·al**, *adj.*

**ten·sor** (ten'sẽr, -sôr), *n.* [< L. *tendere*, stretch], any muscle that stretches, or tenses, some part of the body.

**tent** (tent), *n.* [< L. *tendere*, stretch], a portable shelter made of canvas, etc. stretched over poles. *v.i. & v.t.* to lodge in a tent or tents. **—tent'like'**, *adj.*

**ten·ta·cle** (ten'tə-k'l), *n.* [< L. *tentare*, to touch], a long, slender, flexible growth about the head of some invertebrates, used to feel, grasp, etc.

**ten·ta·tive** (ten'tə-tiv), *adj.* [< L. *tentare*, try], made or done as a trial or provisionally.

**ten·ter·hook** (ten'tẽr-hook'), *n.* [ult. < L. *tendere*, stretch], any of the hooks that hold cloth stretched on a frame to dry. **—on tenterhooks**, in suspense; anxious.

**tenth** (tenth), *adj.* preceded by nine others in a series; 10th. *n.* 1. the one following the ninth. 2. any of the ten equal parts of something; 1/10.

**ten·u·ous** (ten'ū-əs), *adj.* [< L. *tenuis*, thin], 1. physically thin or fine. 2. rare; not dense, as air at high altitudes. 3. unsubstantial.

**ten·ure** (ten'yẽr), *n.* [< OFr. *tenir*, hold], 1. a holding, as of property, office, etc. 2. the right to hold or possess something. 3. the length of time, or the conditions, of possession. **—ten·u'ri·al** (-yoor'i-əl), *adj.*

**te·pee** (tē'pē), *n.* [< Siouan *ti*, dwell + *pi*, used for], a cone-shaped tent used by American Indians.

**tep·id** (tep'id), *adj.* [< L. *tepidus*], moderately warm; lukewarm. **—tep'id·ness**, *n.*

**te·qui·la** (ti-kē'lä), *n.* [< *Tequila*, Mex. district], an alcoholic liquor distilled from a Mexican agave.

**ter·cen·te·nar·y** (tẽr-sen'tə-ner'i, tũr'senten'ə-ri), *n.* [*pl.* -IES], [L. *ter*, three times; + *centenary*], a 300th anniversary. *adj.* of a period of 300 years.

**term** (tũrm), *n.* [< L. *terminus*, a limit], 1. a date set for payment, etc. 2. a fixed period of time: as, school *term*, *term* of office. 3. *pl.* conditions of a contract, etc. 4. *pl.* mutual relationship between persons: as, on speaking *terms*. 5. a word or phrase, esp. as used in some science, art, etc. 6. *pl.* manner of speech: as, he spoke in unkind *terms*. 7. in *math.*, *a*) either quantity of a fraction or a ratio. *b*) each quantity in a series or algebraic expression. *v.t.* to call by a term; name. **—bring** (or **come**) **to terms**, to force into (or arrive at) an agreement.

**ter·ma·gant** (tũr'mə-gənt), *n.* [< OFr. *Tervagant*, imaginary Moslem deity], a boisterous, quarrelsome, scolding woman.

**ter·mi·na·ble** (tũr'mi-nə-b'l), *adj.* that can be, or is, terminated. **—ter'mi·na·bly**, *adv.*

**ter·mi·nal** (tũr'mə-n'l), *adj.* [< L. *terminalis*], 1. of, at, or forming the end or extremity. 2. concluding; final. 3. connected with a railroad terminus. *n.* 1. an end; extremity. 2. either end of an electric circuit. 3. either end of a transportation line; esp., a main railroad station. **—ter'mi·nal·ly**, *adv.*

**ter·mi·nate** (tũr'mə-nāt'), *v.t.* [-NATED, -NATING], [< L. *terminus*, a limit], 1. to form the end or conclusion of. 2. to put an end to; stop. *v.i.* 1. to come to an end. 2. to have its end (*in* something): as, the road *terminates* in woods. **—ter'mi·na'tion**, *n.*

**ter·mi·nol·o·gy** (tũr'mə-nol'ə-ji), *n.* [*pl.* -GIES], the terms used in a specific art, science, etc.

**ter·mi·nus** (tũr'mə-nəs), *n.* [*pl.* -NI (-nī'), -NUSES], [L., a limit], 1. an end; extremity or goal. 2. either end of a railroad, bus, or air line.

**ter·mite** (tũr'mīt), *n.* [L. *termes*, wood-boring worm], a social insect that is very destructive to wooden structures: also called *white ant*.

**tern** (tũrn), *n.* [< ON. *therna*], a sea bird related to the gull, but smaller.

**terp·si·cho·re·an** (tũrp'si-kə-rē'ən), *adj.* [< *Terpsichore*, Gr. Muse of dancing], of dancing.

**ter·race** (ter'is), *n.* [< L. *terra*, earth], 1. a raised, flat mound of earth with sloping sides, often one in a series on a hillside. 2. an unroofed, paved area next to a house and overlooking a garden. 3. a row of houses on ground raised from the street. 4. the street itself. *v.t.* [-RACED, -RACING], to form into a terrace or terraces.

**ter·ra cot·ta** (ter'ə kot'ə), [It., baked earth], 1. a hard, brown-red earthenware. 2. its brown-red color. **—ter'ra-cot'ta**, *adj.*

**terra fir·ma** (fũr'mə), [L.], firm or solid ground.

**ter·rain** (tə-rān', ter'ān), *n.* [< L. *terra*, earth], a tract of ground, esp. with regard to its features or fitness for some use.

**ter·ra·my·cin** (ter'ə-mī'sin), *n.* [< L. *terra*, earth + Gr. *mykēs*, fungus], an antibiotic drug, effective against certain viruses, etc.

**ter·ra·pin** (ter'ə-pin), *n.* [< Algonquian], 1. any of various American fresh-water or tidewater turtles. 2. its edible flesh.

**ter·res·tri·al** (tə-res'tri-əl), *adj.* [< L. *terra*, earth], 1. worldly; mundane. 2. of or constituting the earth. 3. consisting of land, not water. 4. living on land.

**ter·ri·ble** (ter'ə-b'l), *adj.* [< L. *terrere*, frighten], 1. causing terror; dreadful. 2. extreme; intense. 3. [Colloq.], very unpleasant, bad, etc. **—ter'ri·bly**, *adv.*

**ter·ri·er** (ter'i-ẽr), *n.* [< Fr. (*chien*) *terrier*, hunting (dog)], any of several breeds of active, typically small dog.

**ter·rif·ic** (tə-rif'ik), *adj.* [< L. *terrere*, frighten], 1. causing great fear; terrifying. 2. [Colloq.], very great, intense, etc.

**ter·ri·fy** (ter'ə-fī'), *v.t.* [-FIED, -FYING], to fill with terror; frighten greatly.

**ter·ri·to·ry** (ter'ə-tôr'i), *n.* [*pl.* -RIES], [< L. *terra*, earth], 1. an area under the jurisdiction of a nation, ruler, etc. 2. a part of a country, etc. lacking full status; specif., [T-], formerly a part of the U.S. not a State: Hawaii was the last U.S. Territory. 3. any large tract of land. 4. area or sphere of action. —**ter′ri·to′ri·al,** *adj.*

**ter·ror** (ter′ẽr), *n.* [< L. *terrere,* frighten], 1. intense fear. 2. *a*) one that causes intense fear. *b*) the quality of causing dread.

**ter′ror·ism,** *n.* the use of terror and violence to intimidate, etc., esp. as a political policy. —**ter′ror·ist,** *n. & adj.*

**ter′ror·ize′** (-ə-rīz′), *v.t.* [-IZED, -IZING], 1. to terrify. 2. to coerce, hold power, etc. by inducing terror. —**ter′ror·i·za′tion,** *n.*

**ter·ry** (ter′i), *n.* [prob. < Fr. *tirer,* to draw], a cloth having a pile in which the loops are left uncut: also **terry cloth.**

**terse** (tũrs), *adj.* [TERSER, TERSEST], [< L. *tergere,* to wipe], free of superfluous words; concise; succinct. —**terse′ness,** *n.*

**ter·ti·ar·y** (tũr′shi-er′i), *adj.* [< L. *teritus,* third], of the third rank, order, etc.

**tes·sel·late** (tes′ə-lāt′), *v.t.* [-LATED, -LATING], [< L. *tessella,* little square stone], to lay out in a mosaic pattern of small, square stones. —**tes′sel·la′tion,** *n.*

**test** (test), *n.* [OFr., assaying cup], 1. *a*) an examination or trial, as of something's value. *b*) the method or a criterion used in this. 2. an event, etc. that tries one's qualities. 3. a set of questions, problems, etc. for determining one's knowledge, abilities, etc. 4. in *chem.,* a trial or reaction for identifying a substance. *v.t.* to subject to, or examine by, a test. —**test′er,** *n.*

**tes·ta·ment** (tes′tə-mənt), *n.* [< L. *testis,* a witness], 1. a covenant. 2. [T-], either of the two parts of the Bible, the *Old Testament* and the *New Testament.* 3. in *law,* a will.

**tes′ta·men′ta·ry** (-men′tə-ri), *adj.* 1. of a testament, or will, or its administration. 2. bequeathed by, or contained in, a will.

**tes·tate** (tes′tāt), *adj.* [< L. *testari,* testify], having left a legally valid will.

**tes′ta·tor,** *n.* one who has made a will.

**tes·ti·cle** (tes′ti-k'l), *n.* [< L. *testis*], the male sex gland.

**tes·ti·fy** (tes′tə-fī), *v.i.* [-FIED, -FYING], [< L. *testis,* a witness + *facere,* make], 1. to give evidence, esp. under oath in court. 2. to serve as evidence. *v.t.* 1. to bear witness to; give as evidence. 2. to indicate.

**tes·ti·mo·ni·al** (tes′tə-mō′ni-əl), *n.* 1. a written statement recommending a person or thing. 2. something given as an expression of gratitude or as a tribute. *adj.* given as a testimonial.

**tes·ti·mo·ny** (tes′tə-mō′ni), *n.* [*pl.* -NIES], [< L. *testis,* a witness], 1. a statement made to establish a fact, esp. one made under oath. 2. any affirmation or declaration. 3. any form of evidence; indication.

**tes·tos·ter·one** (tes-tos′tə-rōn′), *n.* [see TESTICLE], a male sex hormone.

**test tube,** a tube of thin, clear glass closed at one end, used in chemical experiments, etc.

**tes·ty** (tes′ti), *adj.* [-TIER, -TIEST], [< L. *testa,* skull], irritable; touchy. —**tes′ti·ly,** *adv.*

**tet·a·nus** (tet′ə-nəs), *n.* [< Gr. *tetanos,* spasm], an acute infectious disease, often fatal, caused by toxins and characterized by spasmodic contractions and rigidity of muscles.

**tête-à-tête** (tāt′ə-tāt′), *n.* [Fr., head to head], a private conversation between two people. *adj.* for or of two people in private.

**teth·er** (teth′ẽr), *n.* [< ON. *tiōthr*], 1. a rope, etc. fastened to an animal to keep it within bounds. 2. the range of one's abilities, resources, etc. *v.t.* to fasten with a tether.

**tetra-,** [Gr. < *tettares,* four], a combining form meaning *four.*

**tet·ra·eth·yl lead** (tet′rə-eth′əl), see **ethyl.**

**tet·ra·he·dron** (tet′rə-hē′drən), *n.* [*pl.* -DRONS, -DRA (-drə)], [see TETRA- & -HEDRON], a solid figure with four triangular surfaces.

**Teut.,** 1. Teuton. 2. Teutonic.

**Teu·ton·ic** (too͞-ton′ik), *adj.* designating or of a group of north European peoples, esp. the German. —**Teu′ton** (-t'n), *n.*

**text** (tekst), *n.* [< L. *texere,* to weave], 1. the actual words of an author, as distinguished from notes, etc. 2. any form in which a writing exists: as, a corrupt *text.* 3. the principal matter on a printed page, as distinguished from notes, illustrations, etc. 4. a Biblical passage used as the topic of a sermon, etc. 5. a topic; subject. —**tex·tu·al** (teks′choo͞-əl), *adj.* —**tex′tu·al·ly,** *adv.*

**text′book′,** *n.* a book giving instruction in a subject of study.

**tex·tile** (teks′t'l, -tīl), *adj.* [see TEXT], 1. having to do with weaving. 2. woven. 3. that can be woven. *n.* 1. a woven fabric; cloth. 2. raw material suitable for weaving.

**tex·ture** (teks′chẽr), *n.* [< L. *texere,* to weave], 1. the character of a fabric, determined by the arrangement of its threads. 2. the arrangement of the constituent parts of anything; structure. —**tex′tur·al,** *adj.*

**-th,** [< AS.], a suffix meaning: 1. *the action of -ing,* as in *stealth.* 2. *the state* or *quality of being* or *having,* as in *wealth.*

**-th,** [< AS.], a suffix used in forming ordinal numbers, as *fourth.*

**Th,** in *chem.,* thorium.

**Th.,** Thursday.

**Tha·i** (tä′ē, tī), *n.* 1. a branch of the Indo-chinese languages, including Siamese. 2. a member of a group of Thai-speaking peoples in Indochina.

**thal·a·mus** (thal′ə-məs), *n.* [*pl.* -MI (-mī′)], [< Gr. *thalamos,* inner room], a large mass of gray matter at the base of the brain, involved in the transmission of certain sensations.

**than** (*th*an, *th*en), *conj. & prep.* [< AS. *thenne*], a particle used to introduce the second element in a comparison: as, I am taller *than* Bill.

**thank** (thaŋk), *v.t.* [< AS. *thancian*], 1. to give one's thanks to. 2. to hold responsible: an ironic use. —**have oneself to thank,** to be oneself the cause of (something unpleasant).

**thank′ful,** *adj.* feeling or expressing thanks.

**thank′less,** *adj.* 1. not feeling or expressing thanks; ungrateful. 2. unappreciated.

**thanks,** *n.pl.* an expression of gratitude. *interj.* I thank you. —**thanks to,** 1. thanks be given to. 2. on account of.

**thanks′giv′ing,** *n.* 1. a formal public expression of thanks to God. 2. [T-], an annual U.S. holiday, usually the fourth Thursday of November.

**that** (*th*at), *pron.* [*pl.* THOSE], [AS. *thæt*], 1. the person or thing mentioned: as, *that* is John. 2. the farther one or other one: as, this is better than *that.* 3. who, whom, or which: as, the road *that* we took. 4. where: as, the place *that* I saw him. 5. when: as, the year *that* he died. *adj.* 1. designating the one mentioned: as, *that* man is John. 2. designating the farther one or other one: as, this car is newer than *that* one. *conj. that* is used: 1. to introduce a noun clause (*that* he's gone is obvious) or an elliptical sentence expressing surprise, desire, etc. (oh, *that* he were here!). 2. to introduce a clause expressing purpose (he died *that* I might live), result (he ran so fast *that* I lost him), or cause (I'm sorry *that* I won). *adv.* to that extent; so: as, I can't see *that* far. —**at that,** [Colloq.], 1. at that point. 2. all things considered. —**in that,** because.

**thatch** (thach), *n.* [< AS. *thæc*], 1. a roof of straw, rushes, palm leaves, etc. 2. material for such a roof: also **thatch′ing.** ***v.t.*** to cover as with thatch. —**thatch′y,** ***adj.***

**thaw** (thô), ***v.i.*** [< AS. *thawian*], 1. to melt, as ice, snow, etc. 2. to become warmer, so that ice, snow, etc. melts. 3. to lose one's coldness of manner. ***v.t.*** to cause to thaw. ***n.*** 1. a thawing. 2. a spell of weather warm enough to allow a thawing.

**the** (*thə*; *before vowels, thi*), ***adj., definite article*** [< AS. *se, the*], *the* (as opposed to *a, an*) refers to: 1. a particular person or thing: as, *the* story ended, *the* President. 2. a person or thing considered generically: as, *the* cow is a mammal, *the* rich and *the* poor. ***adv.*** 1. that much: as, *the* better to see you. 2. by how much . . . by that much: as, *the* sooner *the* better.

**the·a·ter, the·a·tre** (thē′ə-tẽr), ***n.*** [< Gr. *theasthai*, to view], 1. a place or building where plays, motion pictures, etc. are presented. 2. any similar place with rows of seats. 3. any scene of events. 4. *a*) the dramatic art. *b*) the theatrical world.

**the·at·ri·cal** (thi-at′ri-k'l), ***adj.*** 1. having to do with the theater. 2. dramatic; histrionic; esp., melodramatic or affected.

**thee** (*thē*), ***pron.*** [AS. *the*], the objective case of **thou:** used for **thou** by Friends (Quakers).

**theft** (theft), ***n.*** [AS. *thiefth*], the act or an instance of stealing; larceny.

**their** (*thâr*), ***pron.*** [< ON. *theirra*], possessive form of **they.** ***poss. pronominal adj.*** of, belonging to, or done by them.

**theirs** (*thârz*), ***pron.*** that or those belonging to them: as, *theirs* are better.

**the·ism** (thē′iz'm), ***n.*** [< Gr. *theos*, god], 1. belief in a god or gods. 2. monotheism. —**the′ist,** ***n. & adj.*** —**the·is′tic,** ***adj.***

**them** (*them*), ***pron.*** [< ON. *theim*], the objective case of **they.**

**theme** (thēm), ***n.*** [< Gr. *thema*, what is set down], 1. a topic, as of a lecture, etc. 2. a short essay. 3. a short melody constituting the subject of a musical composition. 4. the principal song of a musical play, etc.: also **theme song.** —**the·mat′ic** (-mat′ik), ***adj.***

**them·selves** (*thəm*-selvz′), ***pron.*** 1. the intensive form of **they:** as, they went *themselves.* 2. the reflexive form of **they:** as, they hurt *themselves.*

**then** (*then*), ***adv.*** [see THAN], 1. at that time: as, I did it *then.* 2. next in time or order: as, he ate and *then* slept. 3. in that case; accordingly: as, if he read it, *then* he knows. 4. besides; moreover: as, I like to walk, and *then* it's cheaper. 5. at another time: as, now she's sullen, *then* gay. ***adj.*** being such at that time: as, the *then* director. ***n.*** that time: as, by *then*, they were gone.

**thence** (*thens*, thens), ***adv.*** [< AS. *thanan*], 1. from that place. 2. thenceforth; thereafter. 3. therefore.

**thence′forth′** (-fôrth′), ***adv.*** from that time onward; thereafter: also **thence′for′ward.**

**the·oc·ra·cy** (thē-ok′rə-si), ***n.*** [*pl.* -CIES], [< Gr. *theos*, god + *kratein*, to rule], (a) government by priests claiming to rule with divine authority.

**the·o·lo·gi·an** (thē′ə-lō′jən, -ji-ən), ***n.*** a student of or authority on theology.

**the·ol·o·gy** (thē-ol′ə-ji), ***n.*** [*pl.* -GIES], [< Gr. *theos*, god + *logos*, discourse], the study of God and of religious doctrines and matters of divinity. —**the′o·log′i·cal** (-ə-loj′i-k'l), ***adj.*** —**the′o·log′i·cal·ly,** ***adv.***

**the·o·rem** (thē′ə-rəm), ***n.*** [< Gr. *theōrein*, to view], 1. a proposition that can be proved from accepted premises; a law or principle. 2. a proposition embodying something to be proved.

**the·o·ret·i·cal** (thē′ə-ret′i-k'l), ***adj.*** 1. limited to or based on theory; hypothetical. 2. tending to theorize; speculative. Also **the′o·ret′ic.** —**the′o·ret′i·cal·ly,** ***adv.***

**the·o·rize** (thē′ə-rīz′), ***v.i.*** [-RIZED, -RIZING], to form theories; speculate. —**the′o·rist** (-rist), **the′o·riz′er,** ***n.*** —**the′o·ri·za′tion,** ***n.***

**the·o·ry** (thē′ə-ri), ***n.*** [*pl.* -RIES], [< Gr. *theōrein*, to view], 1. an idea or plan. 2. a formulation of underlying principles of certain observed phenomena which has been verified to some degree. 3. the principles of an art or science rather than its practice. 4. a mere conjecture; guess.

**ther·a·peu·tic** (ther′ə-pū′tik), ***adj.*** [< Gr. *therapeuein*, to nurse], serving to cure or heal; curative: also **ther′a·peu′ti·cal.**

**ther′a·peu′tics,** ***n.pl.*** [construed as sing.], the branch of medicine dealing with the treatment and cure of disease; therapy.

**ther·a·py** (ther′ə-pi), ***n.*** [*pl.* -PIES], therapeutics. —**ther′a·pist,** ***n.***

**there** (*thâr*), ***adv.*** [AS. *ther*], 1. at or in that place: often used as an intensive, as, John *there* is a good boy. 2. to or into that place: as, go *there.* 3. at that point; then. 4. in that respect: as, *there* you are wrong. *There* is also used in clauses in which the real subject follows the verb (e.g., *there* is joy here). ***n.*** that place: as, we left *there* at six. ***interj.*** an exclamation of defiance, dismay, sympathy, etc.

**there′a·bouts′,** ***adv.*** 1. near that place. 2. near that time, number, amount, etc. Also **there′a·bout′.**

**there·aft′er,** ***adv.*** 1. after that; subsequently. 2. [Rare], accordingly.

**there·at′,** ***adv.*** 1. at that place; there. 2. at that time. 3. for that reason.

**there·by′,** ***adv.*** 1. by that means. 2. connected with that. 3. thereabouts.

**there′fore′** (-fôr′), ***adv. & conj.*** for this or that reason; hence.

**there·in′,** ***adv.*** 1. in or into that place. 2. in that matter, detail, etc.

**there·of′,** ***adv.*** 1. of that; of it. 2. from that as a cause, reason, etc.

**there·on′,** ***adv.*** 1. on that. 2. immediately following that; thereupon.

**there·to′,** ***adv.*** to that place, thing, etc.

**there′to·fore′,** ***adv.*** up to that time.

**there′up·on′,** ***adv.*** 1. immediately following that. 2. as a consequence of that. 3. concerning that subject, etc.

**there·with′,** ***adv.*** 1. with that or this. 2. immediately thereafter.

**there′with·al′** (-with-ôl′), ***adv.*** 1. in addition; besides. 2. [Obs.], with that or this.

**ther·mal** (thũr′m'l), ***adj.*** [< Gr. *thermē*, heat], having to do with heat.

**thermo-,** [< Gr. *thermē*, heat], a combining form meaning *heat.*

**ther·mo·dy·nam·ics** (thũr′mō-dī-nam′iks), ***n.pl.*** [construed as sing.], the science that deals with the relationship of heat and mechanical energy. —**ther′mo·dy·nam′ic,** ***adj.***

**ther·mom·e·ter** (thẽr-mom′ə-tẽr), ***n.*** [*thermo-* + *-meter*], an instrument for measuring temperatures, as a graduated glass tube in which mercury, etc. rises or falls as it expands or contracts from changes in temperature: see **centigrade, Fahrenheit.**

**ther·mo·nu·cle·ar** (thũr′mō-nōō′kli-ẽr, -nū′-), ***adj.*** designating, of, or employing the heat energy released in nuclear fission.

**ther·mo·plas·tic** (thũr′mə-plas′tik), ***adj.*** soft and moldable when subjected to heat: said of certain plastics. ***n.*** a thermoplastic substance.

**ther·mos bottle** (or **flask, jug**) (thũr′məs), [Gr. *thermos*, hot], a bottle, flask, or jug for keeping liquids at almost their original temperature: a trademark **(Thermos).**

**ther·mo·stat** (thũr′mə-stat′), ***n.*** [*thermo-* + *-stat*], an apparatus for regulating temperature, esp. one that automatically controls a heating unit. —**ther′mo·stat′ic,** ***adj.***

**the·sau·rus** (thi-sô′rəs), *n.* [*pl.* -RI (-rī), -RUSES], [< Gr. *thēsauros*, a treasure], 1. a storehouse. 2. a book containing a store of words, as a dictionary, book of synonyms, etc.
**these** (*th*ēz), *pron. & adj.* pl. of **this**.
**The·seus** (thē′sūs, -si-əs), *n.* a legendary Greek hero who killed the Minotaur.
**the·sis** (thē′sis), *n.* [*pl.* -SES (-sēz)], [< Gr. *tithenai*, to put], 1. a proposition to be defended in argument. 2. an essay presented by a candidate for an academic degree.
**Thes·pi·an** (thes′pi-ən), *adj.* [< *Thespis*, ancient Gr. poet], having to do with the drama, esp. with tragedy. *n.* an actor.
**the·ta** (thā′tə, thē′-), *n.* the eighth letter of the Greek alphabet (Θ, θ).
**thews** (thūz), *n.pl.* [sing. THEW], [< AS. *theaw*, habit], muscles or sinews.
**they** (*th*ā), *pron.* [for *sing.* see HE, SHE, IT], [< ON. *their*], 1. the persons, animals, or things previously mentioned. 2. people generally or indefinitely: as, *they* say it will rain.
**they'd** (*th*ād), 1. they had. 2. they would.
**they'll** (*th*āl), 1. they will. 2. they shall.
**they're** (*th*âr), they are.
**they've** (*th*āv), they have.
**thi·a·mine** (thī′ə-mēn′, -min), *n.* [ult. < Gr. *theion*, brimstone], a factor of the vitamin B complex, found in cereal, egg yolk, liver, etc.: also called *vitamin* $B_1$.
**thick** (thik), *adj.* [AS. *thicce*], 1. of relatively great extent from side to side. 2. measured between opposite surfaces: as, one inch *thick*. 3. dense; compact: as, *thick* woods. 4. close and abundant. 5. heavy; not clear: as, *thick* soup. 6. husky; hoarse: as, a *thick* voice. 7. stupid; dull. 8. [Colloq.], very friendly. *adv.* thickly. *n.* the thickest part.
**thick′en,** *v.t. & v.i.* 1. to make or become thick or thicker. 2. to make or become more complex or involved. **—thick′en·er,** *n.*
**thick·et** (thik′it), *n.* [see THICK], a thick growth of shrubs or small trees.
**thick′set′,** *adj.* 1. planted thickly or closely. 2. thick in body; stout.
**thick′-skinned′,** *adj.* 1. having a thick skin. 2. insensitive, as to insult.
**thief** (thēf), *n.* [*pl.* THIEVES (thēvz)], [AS. *theof*], one who steals, esp. secretly.
**thieve** (thēv), *v.t. & v.i.* [THIEVED, THIEVING], to steal. **—thiev′ish,** *adj.*
**thiev′er·y,** *n.* [*pl.* -IES], the act or an instance of stealing; theft.
**thigh** (thī), *n.* [AS. *theoh*], the part of the leg between the knee and the hip.
**thigh′bone′,** *n.* the bone of the leg between the knee and the hip: also **thigh bone.**
**thim·ble** (thim′b'l), *n.* [< AS. *thuma*, thumb], a small cap worn on the finger in sewing to protect it in pushing the needle.
**thin** (thin), *adj.* [THINNER, THINNEST], [AS. *thynne*], 1. of relatively little extent from side to side. 2. lean; slender. 3. not dense or compact; sparse. 4. very fluid or tenuous: as, *thin* milk, *thin* air. 5. high-pitched and weak: as, a *thin* voice. 6. transparent; flimsy; slight: as, *thin* fabric, a *thin* excuse. 7. lacking depth, intensity, etc. *v.t. & v.i.* [THINNED, THINNING], to make or become thin or thinner. **—thin′ly,** *adv.* **—thin′ness,** *n.*
**thine** (*th*īn), *pron.* [AS. *thin*], possessive form of **thou.** *adj.* thy.
**thing** (thiŋ), *n.* [AS., council], 1. any matter, affair, or concern. 2. a happening, act, incident, etc. 3. a tangible object. 4. an inanimate object. 5. an item, detail, etc. 6. *pl. a*) personal belongings. *b*) clothes. 7. [Colloq.], a person or creature.
**think** (thiŋk), *v.t.* [THOUGHT, THINKING], [AS. *thencan*], 1. to form or have in the mind: as, to *think* bad thoughts. 2. to judge; consider: as, he is *thought* wise. 3. to believe; expect: as, I *think* I can. *v.i.* 1. to use the mind; reflect; reason. 2. to have an opinion, belief, etc. **—think of,** 1. to remember. 2. to have an opinion of. 3. to conceive of: also **think up.** 4. to consider. **—think′er,** *n.*
**thin′-skinned′,** *adj.* 1. having a thin skin. 2. sensitive, as to insult.
**third** (thũrd), *adj.* [AS. *thridda*], preceded by two others in a series; 3(r)d. *n.* 1. the one following the second. 2. any of the three equal parts of something; 1/3.
**third degree,** severe treatment or torture by police, etc. to force a confession or information.
**third person,** that form of a pronoun or verb which refers to the person or thing spoken of.
**third′-rate′,** *adj.* 1. third in quality or other rating. 2. very poor.
**thirst** (thũrst), *n.* [AS. *thurst*], 1. the discomfort caused by a need for drink. 2. a strong desire; craving. *v.i.* 1. to feel thirst. 2. to have a strong desire or craving. **—thirst′i·ly,** *adv.* **—thirst′y** [-IER, -IEST], *adj.*
**thir·teen** (thũr′tēn′), *adj. & n.* [AS. *threotyne*], three more than ten; 13; XIII. **—thir′teenth′,** *adj. & n.*
**thir·ty** (thũr′ti), *adj. & n.* [*pl.* -TIES], [AS. *thritig*], three times ten; 30; XXX. **—the thirties,** the years from 30 through 39 (of a century or a person's age). **—thir′ti·eth,** *adj. & n.*
**this** (*th*is), *pron.* [*pl.* THESE] *& adj.* [AS. *thes*], 1. (designating) the person or thing mentioned: as, *this* (man) is John. 2. (designating) the nearer one or other one: as, *this* (car) is better than that. 3. (designating) something about to be stated: as, now hear *this* (news). *adv.* to this extent: as, it was *this* big.
**this·tle** (this′'l), *n.* [AS. *thistel*], a plant with prickly leaves and white, purple, etc. flowers. **—this′tly** [-TLIER, -TLIEST], *adj.*
**thith·er** (thi*th*′ẽr, *th*i*th*′-), *adv.* [AS. *thider*], to or toward that place; there.
**tho, tho'** (*th*ō), *conj. & adv.* though.
**thong** (thôŋ), *n.* [AS. *thwang*], a narrow strip of leather, etc. used as a lace, strap, etc.
**Thor** (thôr), *n.* in *Norse myth.*, the god of thunder, war, and strength.
**tho·rax** (thôr′aks), *n.* [*pl.* -RAXES, -RACES (-ə-sēz′)], [< Gr.], 1. the part of the body between the neck and the abdomen; chest. 2. the middle one of the three segments of an insect. **—tho·rac·ic** (thô-ras′ik), *adj.*
**tho·ri·um** (thôr′i-əm), *n.* [< *Thor*], a rare, grayish, radioactive chemical element: symbol, Th.
**thorn** (thôrn), *n.* [AS.], 1. a very short, hard, leafless stem with a sharp point. 2. any small tree or shrub bearing thorns. 3. any tenacious cause of hurt, irritation, etc. — **thorn′y** [-IER, -IEST], *adj.*
**thor·ough** (thũr′ō), *adj.* [var. of *through*], 1. done or proceeding through to the end; complete. 2. absolute: as, a *thorough* rascal. 3. very exact, accurate, or painstaking.
**thor·ough·bred** (thũr′ə-bred′), *adj.* of pure stock or official pedigree. *n.* a thoroughbred animal; specif., [T-], any of a breed of race horses.
**thor·ough·fare** (thũr′ə-fâr′), *n.* a public, unobstructed street open at both ends, esp. a main road or highway.
**thor′ough·go′ing,** *adj.* very thorough.
**those** (*th*ōz), *adj. & pron.* pl. of **that.**
**thou** (*th*ou), *pron.* [AS. *thu*], you (nom. sing.): in poetic or religious use.
**though** (*th*ō), *conj.* [< AS. *theah*], 1. in spite of the fact that: as, *though* it rained, he went. 2. all the same; yet: as, they did it, *though* not very well. 3. even if: as, *though* he may fail, he will have tried. *adv.* however; nevertheless.

**thought** (thôt), *n.* [AS. *thoht*], 1. the act or process of thinking. 2. the power of reasoning. 3. an idea, concept, opinion, etc. 4. attention; consideration. 5. a little: as, be a *thought* more careful.
**thought** (thôt), pt. and pp. of **think.**
**thought'ful,** *adj.* 1. full of thought; meditative. 2. considerate. —**thought'ful·ly,** *adv.*
**thought'less,** *adj.* 1. not stopping to think; careless. 2. ill-considered; rash. 3. inconsiderate; remiss. 4. stupid; dull-witted.
**thou·sand** (thou'z'nd), *adj. & n.* [AS. *thusend*], ten hundred; 1,000; M. —**thou'sandth** (-z'ndth), *adj. & n.*
**thrall** (thrôl), *n.* [< ON. *thræll*], 1. a slave. 2. slavery. —**thrall'dom, thral'dom** (-dəm), *n.*
**thrash** (thrash), *v.t.* [AS. *threscan*], 1. to thresh. 2. to beat; flog. *v.i.* 1. to thresh. 2. to toss about violently. *n.* a thrashing. —**thrash out,** to discuss thoroughly and conclusively. —**thrash'er,** *n.*
**thrash·er** (thrash'ẽr), *n.* [Eng. dial. *thresher*], a thrushlike songbird.
**thread** (thred), *n.* [AS. *thræd*], 1. a very fine cord composed of strands of spun silk, cotton, etc., used in sewing. 2. a threadlike filament, line, vein, etc. 3. something like a thread in its length, sequence, etc.: as, the *thread* of a story. 4. the spiral ridge of a screw, nut, etc. *v.t.* 1. to put a thread through (a needle, etc.). 2. to make (one's way) in a threadlike, winding path. 3. to fashion a thread (sense 4) on or in.
**thread'bare',** *adj.* 1. worn down so that the threads show. 2. wearing worn clothes; shabby. 3. stale; trite.
**threat** (thret), *n.* [AS. *threat*, pressure], 1. an expression of intention to hurt, destroy, punish, etc. 2. an indication of imminent danger: as, the *threat* of war.
**threat'en,** *v.t. & v.i.* 1. to make threats, as of injury (against). 2. to indicate (something dangerous, etc.). 3. to be a source of danger (to). —**threat'en·ing·ly,** *adv.*
**three** (thrē), *adj. & n.* [AS. *threo*], one more than two; 3; III.
**three'-deck'er** (-dek'ẽr), *n.* anything having three levels, layers, etc.
**three'fold',** *adj.* 1. having three parts. 2. having three times as much or as many. *adv.* three times as much or as many.
**three·score** (thrē'skôr'), *adj.* sixty.
**three'some** (-səm), *n.* a group of three persons.
**thren·o·dy** (thren'ə-di), *n.* [*pl.* -DIES], [< Gr. *thrēnos*, lamentation + *ōdē*, song], a song of lamentation; dirge.
**thresh** (thresh), *v.t. & v.i.* [AS. *threscan*], 1. to beat out (grain) from its husk, as with a flail. 2. to thrash. —**thresh'er,** *n.*
**thresh·old** (thresh'ōld, -hōld), *n.* [< AS. *therscan*, tread down], 1. a piece of wood, stone, etc. set under a door; doorsill. 2. the beginning point.
**threw** (thro͞o), pt. of **throw.**
**thrice** (thrīs), *adv.* [ME. *thries*], 1. three times. 2. threefold. 3. very; greatly.
**thrift** (thrift), *n.* [< ON. *thrifa*, to grasp], economical management; saving. —**thrift'less,** *adj.* —**thrift'y** [-IER, -IEST], *adj.*
**thrill** (thril), *v.i. & v.t.* [< AS. *thurh*, through], 1. to feel or cause to feel emotional excitement. 2. to quiver or cause to quiver; tremble. *n.* 1. a thrilling or being thrilled. 2. a tremor; quiver. —**thrill'er,** *n.*
**thrive** (thrīv), *v.i.* [THROVE or THRIVED, THRIVED or THRIVEN, THRIVING], [< ON. *thrifa*, to grasp], 1. to prosper; be successful. 2. to grow luxuriantly. —**thriv'er,** *n.*
**throat** (thrōt), *n.* [AS. *throte*], 1. the front part of the neck. 2. the upper passage from the mouth to the stomach and lungs. 3. any narrow passage.
**throat'y,** *adj.* [-IER, -IEST], produced in the throat, as some sounds; husky.
**throb** (throb), *v.i.* [THROBBED, THROBBING], [ME. *throbben*], 1. to beat, pulsate, vibrate, etc., esp. strongly or fast. 2. to feel excitement. *n.* a throbbing; strong beat or pulsation. —**throb'ber,** *n.*
**throe** (thrō), *n.* [prob. < AS. *thrawu*, pain], 1. a spasm or pang of pain. 2. *pl.* desperate struggle; agony.
**throm·bo·sis** (throm-bō'sis), *n.* [< Gr. *thrombos*, a clot], coagulation of blood in the circulatory system, forming a clot that obstructs circulation.
**throne** (thrōn), *n.* [< Gr. *thronos*, a seat], 1. the chair on which a king, cardinal, etc. sits on formal occasions. 2. the power or rank of a king, etc. 3. a sovereign, etc.
**throng** (thrôŋ), *n.* [< AS. *thringan*, to crowd], 1. a crowd. 2. any great number of things considered together. *v.i.* to gather together in a throng. *v.t.* to crowd into.
**throt·tle** (throt''l), *n.* [< *throat*], the valve in an engine that regulates the amount of fuel vapor entering the cylinders. *v.t.* [-TLED, -TLING], 1. to choke; strangle. 2. to suppress; silence. 3. to reduce the flow of (fuel vapor) by means of a throttle. 4. to slow (*down*) by this means.
**through** (thro͞o), *prep.* [AS. *thurh*], 1. in one side and out the other side of. 2. in the midst of; among. 3. by way of. 4. around: as, to tour *through* France. 5. from beginning to end of; throughout. 6. by means of. 7. as a result of. *adv.* 1. in one side and out the other. 2. from the beginning to the end. 3. completely to the end: as, see it *through.* 4. completely: as, soaked *through.* *adj.* 1. extending from one place to another: as, a *through* street. 2. traveling to the destination without stops: as, a *through* train. 3. finished.
**through·out',** *prep.* all the way through. *adv.* in every part; everywhere.
**throve** (thrōv), pt. of **thrive.**
**throw** (thrō), *v.t.* [THREW, THROWN, THROWING], [AS. *thrawan*, to twist], 1. to send through the air by a rapid motion of the arm, etc. 2. to cause to fall; upset. 3. to send rapidly: as, to *throw* troops into battle. 4. to put suddenly into a specified state, etc.: as, *thrown* into confusion. 5. to move (a switch, etc.) so as to connect, disconnect, etc. 6. to direct, cast, etc.: as, *throw* a glance. 7. [Colloq.], to lose (a contest) deliberately. 8. [Slang], to give (a party, etc.). *v.i.* to cast or hurl something. *n.* 1. the act of one who throws. 2. the distance something is or can be thrown: as, a stone's *throw.* 3. a spread for a bed, etc. —**throw away,** 1. to discard. 2. to waste. —**throw in,** to add extra or free. —**throw off,** 1. to rid oneself of. 2. to expel, emit, etc. —**throw oneself at,** to try very hard to win the love, etc. of. —**throw out,** 1. to discard. 2. to reject. —**throw over,** 1. to give up; abandon. 2. to jilt. —**throw together,** to make or assemble hurriedly. —**throw up,** 1. to give up; abandon. 2. to vomit.
**throw'back',** *n.* (a) reversion to an ancestral type.
**thru** (thro͞o), *prep., adv., adj.* through.
**thrum** (thrum), *v.t. & v.i.* [THRUMMED, THRUMMING], [echoic], 1. to strum (a stringed instrument). 2. to drum (on) with the fingers. *n.* act or sound of thrumming.
**thrush** (thrush), *n.* [AS. *thrysce*], any of a large group of songbirds, including the robin, bluebird, etc.
**thrust** (thrust), *v.t. & v.i.* [THRUST, THRUSTING], [< ON. *thrysta*], 1. to push with sudden force. 2. to stab. 3. to force or compel. *n.* 1. a sudden, forceful push. 2. a stab. 3. continuous pressure, as of a rafter

against a wall. 4. *a*) the driving force of a propeller. *b*) the forward force produced in jet propulsion. —**thrust'ing·ly**, *adv.*

**thud** (thud), *n.* [? < AS. *thyddan*, to strike], a dull sound, as of something heavy dropping on a soft, solid surface. *v.i.* [THUDDED, THUDDING], to hit with a thud.

**thug** (thug), *n.* [< Hind. *ṭhag*], an assassin or ruffian.

**Thu·le** (thōō'li, thū'lē), *n.* [L.], among the ancients, the northernmost region of the world.

**thumb** (thum), *n.* [AS. *thuma*], the short, thick, inner digit of the hand. *v.t.* 1. to handle, soil, etc. as with the thumb. 2. [Colloq.], to solicit (a ride) in a passing automobile by signaling with the thumb. —**all thumbs**, clumsy. —**thumbs down**, a signal of disapproval. —**under one's thumb**, under one's influence.

**thumb'nail'**, *n.* the nail of the thumb. *adj.* very small or brief.

**thumb'screw'**, *n.* a screw that may be turned with the thumb and fingers.

**thumb'tack'**, *n.* a tack with a wide, flat head, that can be pressed into a board, etc. with the thumb.

**thump** (thump), *n.* [echoic], 1. a blow with something heavy and blunt. 2. the dull sound made by such a blow. *v.t.* to strike with a thump. *v.i.* 1. to hit or fall with a thump. 2. to make a dull, heavy sound; pound; throb. —**thump'er**, *n.*

**thun·der** (thun'dẽr), *n.* [AS. *thunor*], 1. the sound that follows a flash of lightning. 2. any sound like this. *v.i.* to produce thunder or a sound like thunder. *v.t.* to utter, etc. with a thundering sound. —**steal one's thunder**, to make something done by one less effective by doing it first. —**thun'derous**, *adj.*

**thun'der·bolt'** (-bōlt'), *n.* 1. a flash of lightning and the accompanying thunder. 2. something that stuns or acts with sudden violence.

**thun'der·show'er**, *n.* a shower accompanied by thunder and lightning.

**thun'der·storm'**, *n.* a storm accompanied by thunder and lightning.

**thun'der·struck'**, *adj.* struck with amazement, terror, etc.; astonished.

**Thurs·day** (thũrz'di), *n.* [after *Thor*], the fifth day of the week: abbrev. **Thur.**, **Thurs.**

**thus** (*th*us), *adv.* [AS.], 1. in this or that manner. 2. to this or that degree or extent; so. 3. therefore.

**thwack** (thwak), *v.t.* [ult. echoic], to strike with something flat; whack. *n.* a whack.

**thwart** (thwôrt), *v.t.* [< ON. *thvert*, athwart], to obstruct, frustrate, or defeat (a person, plans, etc.).

**thy** (*th*ī), *poss. pronominal adj.* [< ME. *thin*], of, belonging to, or done by thee: archaic or dial. var. of *your*.

**thyme** (tīm), *n.* [Gr. *thymon*], a plant of the mint family, with leaves used for seasoning.

**thy·mus** (thī'məs), *n.* [< Gr. *thymos*], a ductless, glandlike body situated near the throat: also **thymus gland**.

**thy·roid** (thī'roid), *adj.* [Gr. *thyreoeidēs*, shield-shaped], designating or of a large ductless gland near the trachea, secreting a hormone which regulates growth. *n.* 1. the thyroid gland. 2. an animal extract of this gland, used in treating goiter, etc.

**thy·self** (*th*ī-self'), *pron.* the reflexive or intensive form of **thou**.

**ti** (tē), *n.* in *music*, the seventh tone in the diatonic scale.

**Ti**, in *chem.*, titanium.

**ti·ar·a** (tī-âr'ə, ti-ä'rə), *n.* [< Gr. *tiara*, headdress], a woman's crownlike headdress of jewels, flowers, etc.

**tib·i·a** (tib'i-ə), *n.* [*pl.* -AE (-ē'), -AS], [L.], the inner and thicker of the two bones of the lower leg; shinbone. —**tib'i·al**, *adj.*

**tic** (tik), *n.* [Fr. < Gmc.], any involuntary, regularly repeated, spasmodic contraction of a muscle.

**tick** (tik), *n.* [prob. echoic], 1. a light clicking sound, as of a clock. 2. a mark made to check off items. *v.i.* to make a tick or ticks. *v.t.* to record, mark, or check by ticks.

**tick** (tik), *n.* [AS. *ticia*], any of various wingless, blood-sucking insects that infest man, cattle, etc.

**tick** (tik), *n.* [< Gr. *thēkē*, case], the cloth case of a mattress or pillow.

**tick'er**, *n.* 1. one that ticks. 2. a telegraphic device that records stock market quotations, etc. on paper tape (**ticker tape**).

**tick·et** (tik'it), *n.* [< OFr. *estiquer*, to stick], 1. a printed card, etc. that gives one a right, as to attend a theater. 2. a license or certificate. 3. a label fastened to goods to tell the size, price, etc. 4. the list of candidates nominated by a political party in an election. 5. [Colloq.], a court summons for a traffic violation. *v.t.* 1. to put a ticket on; tag. 2. to give a ticket to.

**tick'ing**, *n.* strong, heavy cotton or linen cloth for making pillow ticks, etc.

**tick·le** (tik''l), *v.t.* [-LED, -LING], [ME. *tikelen*], 1. to gratify, amuse, delight, etc. 2. to stroke lightly so as to cause involuntary twitching, laughter, etc. *v.i.* to react to being tickled. *n.* a sensation of being tickled.

**tick·ler** (tik'lẽr), *n.* a memorandum pad, file, etc. for aiding the memory.

**tick·lish** (tik'lish), *adj.* 1. sensitive to tickling. 2. needing careful handling; delicate; touchy. —**tick'lish·ness**, *n.*

**tick·tock** (tik'tok'), *n.* the sound made by a clock or watch. *v.i.* to make this sound.

**tid·al** (tī'd'l), *adj.* of, having, or caused by a tide or tides.

**tidal wave**, an unusually great, destructive wave sent inshore by an earthquake or very strong wind.

**tid·bit** (tid'bit'), *n.* [dial. *tid*, tiny object], a choice bit of food, gossip, etc.: also **titbit**.

**tide** (tīd), *n.* [AS. *tid*, time], 1. a period of time, as in *Eastertide*. 2. the alternate rise and fall, about twice a day, of the surface of oceans, seas, etc., caused by the attraction of the moon and sun. 3. something that rises and falls like the tide. 4. a stream, current, etc.: as, the *tide* of public opinion. *v.t.* [TIDED, TIDING], to carry as with the tide. —**tide over**, to help temporarily.

**tide'wa'ter**, *n.* 1. water that is affected by the tide. 2. a seaboard. *adj.* of or along a tidewater.

**ti·dings** (tī'diŋz), *n.pl.* [AS. *tidung*], news.

**ti·dy** (tī'di), *adj.* [-DIER, -DIEST], [< AS. *tid*, time], 1. neat in appearance, arrangement, etc.; orderly. 2. [Colloq.], rather large. *v.t. & v.i.* [-DIED, -DYING], to make (things) tidy: often with *up*.

**tie** (tī), *v.t.* [TIED, TYING], [< AS. *teag*, rope], 1. to bind with string, rope, etc. 2. to knot the laces, etc. of. 3. to make (a knot) in. 4. to fasten or join in any way. 5. to equal (the score of) in a contest. *v.i.* to make the same score in a contest. *n.* 1. a string, cord, etc. used to tie things. 2. something that connects, binds, etc. 3. a necktie. 4. a beam, rod, etc. that holds parts together. 5. any of the crossbeams to which the rails of a railroad are fastened. 6. an equality of scores in a contest. 7. a contest in which this occurs. —**tie down**, to confine; restrict. —**tie up**, 1. to wrap up and tie. 2. to moor to a dock. 3. to obstruct. 4. to cause to be already in use, committed, etc.

**tier** (têr), *n.* [< OFr. *tire*, order], any of a series of rows, as of seats, arranged one above or behind another. —**tiered**, *adj.*
**tie-up** (tī'up'), *n.* 1. a temporary stoppage of production, traffic, etc. 2. [Colloq.], connection; relation.
**tiff** (tif), *n.* [? echoic], 1. a slight fit of anger. 2. a slight quarrel. *v.i.* to be in or have a tiff.
**ti·ger** (tī'gẽr), *n.* [< Gr. *tigris*], a large, flesh-eating animal of the cat family, native to Asia, having a tawny coat striped with black. —**ti'ger·ish, ti'grish,** *adj.*
**tight** (tīt), *adj.* [< AS. *thiht*, strong], 1. so compact in structure that water, air, etc. cannot pass through. 2. drawn, packed, etc. closely together. 3. fixed securely; firm. 4. fully stretched; taut. 5. fitting so closely as to be uncomfortable. 6. difficult: esp. in *a tight corner, squeeze*, etc., a difficult situation. 7. difficult to get; scarce. 8. [Colloq.], stingy. *adv.* closely. —**sit tight**, to maintain one's position, etc.
**tight'en,** *v.t. & v.i.* to make or become tight or tighter. —**tight'en·er,** *n.*
**tight'fist'ed,** *adj.* stingy.
**tight'-lipped'** (-lipt'), *adj.* not saying much; secretive.
**tight'rope',** *n.* a tightly stretched rope on which acrobats perform.
**tights,** *n.pl.* a tightly fitting garment for the lower half of the body, worn by acrobats, dancers, etc.
**tight'wad'** (-wäd', -wôd'), *n.* [*tight* + *wad* (roll of money)], [Slang], a stingy person.
**ti·gress** (tī'gris), *n.* a female tiger.
**til·de** (til'də), *n.* [Sp. < L. *titulus*, title], a diacritical mark (~) variously used.
**tile** (tīl), *n.* [< L. *tegula*], 1. a thin piece of fired clay, stone, etc., used for roofing, flooring, walls, etc. 2. a similar piece of plastic, etc. 3. a drain of earthenware pipe. *v.t.* [TILED, TILING], to cover with tiles.
**till** (til), *prep. & conj.* [AS. *til*], until.
**till** (til), *v.t. & v.i.* [AS. *tilian*, strive for], to prepare (land) for raising crops, as by plowing, etc. —**till'a·ble,** *adj.* —**till'er,** *n.*
**till** (til), *n.* [prob. < ME. *tyllen*, to draw], a drawer for keeping money.
**till'age** (-ij), *n.* 1. the tilling of land. 2. the state of being tilled.
**till·er** (til'ẽr), *n.* [< ML. *telarium*, weaver's beam], a bar or handle for turning a boat's rudder.
**tilt** (tilt), *v.t.* [AS. *tealt*, shaky], to cause to slope; tip. *v.i.* 1. to slope; incline. 2. to thrust one's lance in a tilt. 3. to engage in a tilt. *n.* 1. a medieval contest in which two horsemen fight with lances. 2. any spirited contest. 3. a slope. —**(at) full tilt**, at full speed.
**tim·ber** (tim'bẽr), *n.* [AS.], 1. wood for building houses, ships, etc. 2. a wooden beam used in building. 3. trees collectively. —**tim'bered,** *adj.* —**tim'ber·ing,** *n.*
**timber line,** the imaginary line on mountains and in polar regions beyond which trees do not grow. —**tim'ber-line',** *adj.*
**tim·bre** (tim'bẽr, tam'-), *n.* [see TIMBREL], the quality of sound that distinguishes one voice from another.
**time** (tīm), *n.* [AS. *tima*], 1. the period during which something exists, happens, etc. 2. *often pl.* a period of history; age, era, etc. 3. *usually pl.* prevailing conditions: as, *times* are bad. 4. a set period or term, as of work, confinement, etc. 5. standard rate of pay. 6. rate of speed in marching, driving, etc. 7. in *music*, *a*) rhythm as determined by the grouping of beats into measures. *b*) tempo. 8. a precise instant, minute, day, etc. 9. the usual or designated moment or period: as, *time* to get up. 10. an occasion: as, this is the fifth *time* I've gone. 11. every moment there has ever been or ever will be. 12. a system of measuring duration: as, standard *time*. *v.t.* [TIMED, TIMING], 1. to arrange the time of so as to be suitable, opportune, etc. 2. to adjust, set, etc. so as to coincide in time: as, *time* your watches. 3. to record the pace, speed, etc. of. *adj.* 1. having to do with time. 2. set to explode, open, etc. at a given time. 3. having to do with paying in installments. —**ahead of time**, early. —**at the same time**, however. —**at times**, occasionally. —**for the time being**, temporarily.—**from time to time**, now and then. —**in time**, 1. eventually. 2. before it is too late. 3. keeping the set tempo, pace, etc. —**make time**, to travel, work, etc. rapidly. —**on time**, 1. at the appointed time. 2. for or by payment by installments. —**time after time**, again and again: also **time and again.** —**times**, multiplied by.
**time clock,** a clock with a mechanism for recording the time an employee begins and ends a work period.
**time'-hon'ored,** *adj.* honored because in existence or usage for a long time.
**time'keep'er,** *n.* 1. a timepiece. 2. one who keeps account of hours worked by employees, or of elapsed time in races, games, etc.
**time'less** (-lis), *adj.* eternal.
**time'ly,** *adj.* [-LIER, -LIEST], well-timed; opportune. —**time'li·ness,** *n.*
**time out,** in *sports*, etc., any temporary suspension of play, as to discuss strategy, etc.
**time'piece',** *n.* a clock or watch.
**tim'er,** *n.* 1. a timekeeper. 2. a device for controlling the timing of some mechanism.
**time'ta'ble** (-tā'b'l), *n.* a schedule of the times of arrival and departure of trains, buses, etc.
**tim·id** (tim'id), *adj.* [< L. *timere*, to fear], 1. easily frightened; shy. 2. showing lack of self-confidence.—**ti·mid·i·ty** (ti-mid'ə-ti), *n.*
**tim·ing** (tīm'iŋ), *n.* the regulation of time or speed so as to achieve the most effective performance.
**tim·or·ous** (tim'ẽr-əs), *adj.* [< L. *timor*, fear], full of fear; timid.
**tim·o·thy** (tim'ə-thi), *n.* [after *Timothy* Hanson, c. 1720], a grass with bearded spikes, used for fodder: also **timothy grass.**
**tim·pa·ni** (tim'pə-ni), *n.pl.* [It.; see TYMPANUM], kettledrums, esp. a set of them played by one performer. —**tim'pa·nist,** *n.*
**tin** (tin), *n.* [AS.], 1. a soft, silver-white, metallic chemical element: symbol, Sn. 2. tin plate. 3. a pan, box, etc. made of tin plate. *adj.* of tin or tin plate. *v.t.* [TINNED, TINNING], to plate with tin.
**tinc·ture** (tiŋk'chẽr), *n.* [< L. *tingere*, to dye], 1. a light color; tinge. 2. a slight trace. 3. a medicinal substance in solution, esp. in alcohol. *v.t.* [-TURED, -TURING], to tinge.
**tin·der** (tin'dẽr), *n.* [AS. *tynder*], any dry, easily inflammable material.
**tine** (tīn), *n.* [AS. *tind*], a sharp, projecting point; prong: as, fork *tines*. —**tined,** *adj.*
**tin foil,** a very thin sheet of tin or of an alloy of tin and lead, used to wrap candy, cigarettes, etc. —**tin'-foil',** *adj.*
**ting** (tiŋ), *n.* [echoic], a single, light, ringing sound, as of a small bell.
**tinge** (tinj), *v.t.* [TINGED, TINGEING or TINGING], [< L. *tingere*, to dye], 1. to color slightly; tint. 2. to give a trace, slight flavor, etc. to. *n.* 1. a slight coloring; tint. 2. a slight trace, flavor, etc.
**tin·gle** (tiŋ'g'l), *v.i.* [-GLED, -GLING], [var. of *tinkle*], to have a prickling, slightly stinging feeling, as from cold, excitement, etc. *n.* this feeling. —**tin'gly,** *adj.*
**tink·er** (tiŋ'kẽr), *n.* [ult. echoic], 1. one who mends pots, pans, etc. 2. a bungler. *v.i.* 1. to work as a tinker. 2. to make

clumsy attempts to mend something. 3. to putter aimlessly. —**tink′er·er**, *n.*
**tin·kle** (tiŋ′k'l), *v.i.* [-KLED, -KLING], [echoic], to make a series of light, clinking sounds as of a small bell. *v.t.* to cause to tinkle. *n.* a tinkling sound. —**tin′kly**, *adj.*
**tin·ny** (tin′i), *adj.* [-NIER, -NIEST], 1. of tin. 2. like tin; bright but cheap; not durable.
**tin plate,** thin sheets of iron or steel plated with tin. —**tin′-plate′** [-PLATED, -PLATING], *v.t.*
**tin·sel** (tin′s'l), *n.* [< L. *scintilla*, a flash], 1. thin strips or threads of tin, metal foil, etc., used for decoration. 2. something that glitters but has little worth.
**tin′smith′**, *n.* one who works in tin or tin plate: also **tin′ner.**
**tint** (tint), *n.* [< L. *tingere*, to dye], 1. a delicate color. 2. a gradation of a color; shade. *v.t.* to give a tint to. —**tint′er**, *n.*
**tin·tin·nab·u·la·tion** (tin′ti-nab-yoo-lā′shən), *n.* [< L. *tintinnabulum*, little bell], the ringing sound of bells.
**tin·type** (tin′tīp′), *n.* a photograph taken directly on a sensitized plate of enameled tin or iron.
**ti·ny** (tī′ni), *adj.* [-NIER, -NIEST], [< ME. *tine*, a little], very small. —**ti′ni·ness**, *n.*
**-tious,** a suffix used in forming adjectives corresponding to nouns in *-tion*, as *cautious.*
**tip** (tip), *n.* [ME. *tippe*], 1. the point or end of something. 2. something attached to the end, as a cap, etc. *v.t.* [TIPPED, TIPPING], 1. to form a tip on. 2. to cover the tip of.
**tip** (tip), *v.t.* [TIPPED, TIPPING], [< ?], 1. to strike lightly and sharply. 2. to give a gratuity to (a waiter, etc.). 3. [Colloq.], to give secret information to: often with *off.* *v.i.* to give a tip or tips. *n.* 1. a light, sharp blow. 2. a piece of information given confidentially. 3. a suggestion, hint, warning, etc. 4. a gratuity. —**tip′per**, *n.*
**tip** (tip), *v.t.* & *v.i.* [TIPPED, TIPPING], [prob. < ON.], 1. to overturn or upset: often with *over.* 2. to tilt or slant. *n.* a tilt; slant. —**to tip one's hat**, to greet by raising one's hat slightly. —**tip′per**, *n.*
**tip′-off′**, *n.* a tip; confidential hint, warning, etc.
**tip·pet** (tip′it), *n.* [prob. < *tip*, a point], a long scarf, as of fur.
**tip·ple** (tip′'l), *v.i.* & *v.t.* [-PLED, -PLING], [prob. < *tip* (to upset)], to drink (alcoholic liquor) habitually. *n.* alcoholic liquor.
**tip·ster** (tip′stẽr), *n.* [Colloq.], one who sells tips, as on horse races.
**tip·sy** (tip′si), *adj.* [-SIER, -SIEST], 1. that tips easily; not steady. 2. somewhat drunk.
**tip′toe′**, *n.* the tips of the toes. *v.i.* [-TOED, -TOEING], to walk stealthily or cautiously on one's tiptoes. —**on tiptoe**, 1. eager or eagerly. 2. silently.
**tip′top′**, *n.* [*tip* (end) + *top*], 1. the highest point. 2. [Colloq.], the best. *adj.* & *adv.* 1. at the highest point. 2. [Colloq.], at the highest point of excellence, health, etc.
**ti·rade** (tī′rād, ti-rād′), *n.* [< It. *tirare*, to fire], a long, vehement speech or denunciation; harangue.
**tire** (tīr), *v.t.* & *v.i.* [TIRED, TIRING], [AS. *tiorian*], to make or become weary, exhausted, bored, etc. —**tire of**, to become bored by.
**tire** (tīr), *n.* [< ME. contr. of *attire*, equipment], a hoop of iron or rubber, or a rubber tube filled with air, fixed around the wheel of a vehicle.
**tired** (tīrd), *adj.* fatigued; weary.
**tire′less,** *adj.* that does not become tired.
**tire′some,** *adj.* tiring; boring.
**tis·sue** (tish′o͞o), *n.* [< L. *texere*, to weave], 1. light, thin cloth. 2. an interwoven mass; mesh; network. 3. tissue paper. 4. the substance of an organic body, consisting of cells and intercellular material.
**tissue paper,** very thin, unsized, nearly transparent paper for wrapping, for toilet use, etc.
**tit** (tit), *n.* [AS. *titt*], a teat; nipple.
**ti·tan** (tī′t'n), *n.* [< Gr. *Titan*, a giant deity], any person or thing of great size or power. *adj.* titanic.
**ti·tan·ic** (tī-tan′ik), *adj.* of great size, strength, or power.
**ti·ta·ni·um** (tī-tā′ni-əm, ti-), *n.* [see TITAN], a metallic chemical element used as a deoxidizing agent in molten steel, etc.: symbol, Ti.
**tit for tat,** [earlier *tip for tap*], blow for blow; retaliation in kind.
**tithe** (tīth), *n.* [AS. *teothe*, a tenth], 1. a tenth of one's income paid as a tax to a church. 2. a tenth part. *v.t.* & *v.i.* [TITHED, TITHING], to pay a tithe of (one's income, etc.).
**ti·tian** (tish′ən), *n.* & *adj.* [< *Titian* (1477–1576), Venetian painter], reddish yellow; auburn.
**tit·il·late** (tit′'l-āt′), *v.t.* [-LATED, -LATING], [< L. *titillare*], 1. to tickle. 2. to excite pleasurably. —**tit′il·la′tion**, *n.*
**ti·tle** (tī′t'l), *n.* [< L. *titulus*], 1. the name of a poem, book, picture, etc. 2. an epithet. 3. an appellation indicating one's rank, position, or profession. 4. a claim or right. 5. in *law*, *a*) a right to ownership, esp. of real estate. *b*) a deed. 6. in *sports*, etc., a championship. *v.t.* [TITLED, TITLING], to give a title to; name. —**ti′tled**, *adj.*
**title page,** the page in the front of a book that gives the title, author, publisher, etc.
**tit·mouse** (tit′mous′), *n.* [*pl.* -MICE], [ME. *titemose*], a small bird with dull-colored feathers.
**tit·ter** (tit′ẽr), *v.i.* [echoic], to laugh in a half-suppressed way; giggle. *n.* a tittering; giggle. —**tit′ter·er**, *n.* —**tit′ter·ing·ly**, *adv.*
**tit·tle** (tit′'l), *n.* [ME. *titel*], a very small particle; iota; jot.
**tit·u·lar** (tich′oo-lẽr, tit′yoo-), *adj.* [< L. *titulus*, title], 1. of a title. 2. being or having a title. 3. in name only: as, a *titular* chief. —**tit′u·lar·ly**, *adv.*
**tiz·zy** (tiz′i), *n.* [*pl.* -ZIES], [Slang], a state of frenzied excitement, esp. over a triviality.
**tn.,** ton; tons.
**TNT, T.N.T.,** [< *tri*nitro*t*oluene], a high explosive used for blasting, in artillery shells, etc.
**to** (to͞o, too, tə), *prep.* [AS.], 1. toward: as, turn *to* the left. 2. so as to reach: as, he went *to* Boston. 3. as far as: as, wet *to* the skin. 4. into a condition of: as, a rise *to* fame. 5. on, onto, against, at, etc.: as, tie it *to* the post. 6. until: as, from noon *to* night. 7. for the purpose of: as, come *to* my aid. 8. in respect of: as, open *to* attack. 9. so as to produce: as, torn *to* pieces. 10. along with: as, add this *to* the rest. 11. belonging with: as, the coat *to* this suit. 12. compared with: as, a score of 7 *to* 0. 13. in agreement with: as, not *to* my taste. 14. constituting: as, ten *to* the peck. 15. with (a specified person or thing) as the recipient, or indirect object, of the action: as, give it *to* me. 16. in honor of: as, a toast *to* you. *To* is also a sign of the infinitive (e.g., I want *to* stay). *adv.* 1. forward: as, his hat is on wrong side *to.* 2. shut; closed: as, the door was blown *to.* 3. to the matter at hand: as, fall *to!*
**toad** (tōd), *n.* [AS. *tade*], a small, froglike animal that lives on land.
**toad′stool′** (-sto͞ol′), *n.* a mushroom; esp., any poisonous mushroom.
**toad·y** (tōd′i), *n.* [*pl.* -IES], [short for *toadeater*, quack doctor's assistant], a servile flatterer. *v.t.* & *v.i.* [-IED, -YING], to be a toady (to).

**to-and-fro** (to͞o′ən-frō′, -ənd-), *adj.* moving forward and backward.
**toast** (tōst), *v.t.* [< L. *torrere*, parch], 1. to brown the surface of (bread, etc.) by heating. 2. to warm thoroughly. *v.i.* to become toasted. *n.* sliced bread browned by heat.
**toast** (tōst), *n.* [< the toasted bread formerly put in wine], 1. a person or thing in honor of which persons raise their glasses and drink. 2. a proposal to drink, or a drink, in honor of some person, etc. *v.t. & v.i.* to propose or drink a toast (to). —**toast′er,** *n.*
**toast′mas′ter,** *n.* the person at a banquet who proposes toasts, introduces after-dinner speakers, etc.
**to·bac·co** (tə-bak′ō), *n.* [*pl.* -COS], [< W. Ind. *tabaco*, smoking pipe], 1. a plant with large leaves that are prepared for smoking, chewing, or snuffing. 2. the leaves so prepared. 3. cigars, cigarettes, snuff, etc.
**to·bac′co·nist** (-ə-nist), *n.* [Chiefly Brit.], a dealer in tobacco.
**to·bog·gan** (tə-bog′ən), *n.* [< Algonquian], a long, flat sled without runners or with very low runners, used for coasting downhill. *v.i.* [-GANED, -GANING], 1. to coast downhill on a toboggan. 2. to decline rapidly.
**toc·sin** (tok′sin), *n.* [Fr. < Pr. *toc*, a stroke + *senh*, a bell], an alarm bell.
**to·day, to-day** (tə-dā′, too-), *adv.* [AS. *to dæg*], 1. on or during the present day. 2. in the present time or age. *n.* 1. the present day. 2. the present time or age.
**tod·dle** (tod′'l), *v.i.* [-DLED, -DLING], [? < *totter*], to walk with short, uncertain steps, as a child. *n.* a toddling. —**tod′dler,** *n.*
**tod·dy** (tod′i), *n.* [*pl.* -DIES], [< Hind.], a drink of whisky, etc. mixed with hot water, sugar, etc.
**to-do** (tə-do͞o′), *n.* [Colloq.], a commotion.
**toe** (tō), *n.* [AS. *ta*], 1. any of the digits of the foot. 2. the fore part of the foot. 3. anything like a toe in location, shape, or use. *v.t.* [TOED, TOEING], to touch, kick, etc. with the toes. *v.i.* to stand, walk, etc. with the toes in a specified position: as, he *toes* in. —**on one's toes,** [Colloq.], mentally or physically alert.
**toed** (tōd), *adj.* having (a specified kind or number of) toes: as, *two-toed*.
**tof·fee, tof·fy** (tôf′i, tof′i), *n.* [? < *tafia*, a rum made from molasses], a kind of taffy.
**to·ga** (tō′gə), *n.* [*pl.* -GAS, -GAE (-jē)], [L. < *tegere*, to cover], 1. in ancient Rome, a loose outer garment worn in public by citizens. 2. a robe of office.
**to·geth·er** (tə-geth′ẽr, too-), *adv.* [AS. < *to*, to + *gædre*, together], 1. in or into one group, place, etc.: as, we ate *together*. 2. in or into contact, union, etc.: as, they bumped *together*. 3. considered collectively: as, he lost more than all of us *together*. 4. at the same time: as, the shots were fired *together*. 5. continuously: as, he worked two days *together*. 6. in or into agreement, etc.: as, let's get *together*.
**togs** (togz, tôgz), *n.pl.* [prob. < *toga*], [Colloq.], clothes.
**toil** (toil), *v.i.* [< L. *tudiculare*, stir about], 1. to work hard and continuously. 2. to proceed laboriously. *n.* hard, exhausting work or task. —**toil′er,** *n.*
**toi·let** (toi′lit), *n.* [< Fr. *toile*, cloth < L. *tela*, a web], 1. the act of dressing or grooming oneself. 2. dress; attire. 3. *a*) a room equipped with a washbowl, water closet, etc. *b*) a water closet.
**toi′let·ry** (-ri), *n.* [*pl.* -RIES], soap, powder, etc. used in grooming oneself.
**toi·lette** (toi-let′, twä-), *n.* [Fr.], 1. the process of grooming oneself: said of a woman. 2. dress; attire.
**toilet water,** a perfumed liquid, as cologne.
**toils** (toilz), *n.pl.* [< L. *tela*, a web], any snares, etc. suggestive of a net.
**to·ken** (tō′kən), *n.* [AS. *tacn*], 1. a sign, indication, symbol, etc.: as, a *token* of affection or of authority. 2. a keepsake. 3. a metal disk with a face value higher than its real value, issued as a substitute for currency or used for transportation fares, etc. *adj.* merely simulated: as, *token* resistance. —**by this** (or **the same**) **token,** furthermore.
**told** (tōld), pt. and pp. of **tell.** —**all told,** all (being) counted.
**tol·er·a·ble** (tol′ẽr-ə-b'l), *adj.* 1. endurable. 2. fairly good; passable. —**tol′er·a·bly,** *adv.*
**tol·er·ance** (tol′ẽr-əns), *n.* 1. a being tolerant of others' beliefs, practices, etc. 2. the amount of variation allowed from a standard, accuracy, etc. 3. in *medicine*, the ability to endure, or resist the effects of, a drug, poison, etc.
**tol′er·ant,** *adj.* inclined to tolerate others' beliefs, practices, etc.
**tol·er·ate** (tol′ə-rāt′), *v.t.* [-ATED, -ATING], [< L. *tolerare*, to bear], 1. to allow; permit. 2. to recognize and respect (others' beliefs, practices, etc.) without necessarily agreeing. —**tol′er·a′tion,** *n.*
**toll** (tōl), *n.* [prob. ult. < Gr. *telos*, tax], 1. a tax or charge for a privilege, as for the use of a bridge. 2. a charge for some service, as for a long-distance telephone call. 3. the number lost, etc.: as, war took a heavy *toll* of lives.
**toll** (tōl), *v.t.* [ME. *tollen*, pull], 1. to ring (a bell, etc.) with slow, regular strokes. 2. to announce, summon, etc. by this. *v.i.* to sound or ring slowly: said of a bell. *n.* the sound of tolling a bell.
**toll′gate′,** *n.* a gate for stopping travel at a point where toll is taken.
**tom** (tom), *adj.* [< the name *Tom*], male: as, *tomcat*, *tom* turkey.
**tom·a·hawk** (tom′ə-hôk′), *n.* [< Algonquian], a light ax used by N. American Indians as a tool and a weapon.
**to·ma·to** (tə-mā′tō, -mä′-), *n.* [*pl.* -TOES], [< Mex. Ind.], 1. a red or yellowish, round fruit, with a juicy pulp, used as a vegetable. 2. the plant it grows on.
**tomb** (to͞om), *n.* [< Gr. *tymbos*], 1. a vault or grave for the dead. 2. a tombstone. *v.t.* [Rare], to entomb. —**the tomb,** death.
**tom·boy** (tom′boi′), *n.* a girl who behaves like a boisterous boy. —**tom′boy′ish,** *adj.*
**tomb·stone** (to͞om′stōn′), *n.* a stone marking a tomb or grave.
**tom·cat** (tom′kat′), *n.* [see TOM], a male cat.
**tome** (tōm), *n.* [< Gr. *tomos*, piece cut off], a book, esp. a large one.
**tom·fool·er·y** (tom′fo͞ol′ẽr-i), *n.* [*pl.* -IES], foolish behavior; silliness.
**tom·my·rot** (tom′i-rot′), *n.* [Slang], nonsense; foolishness.
**to·mor·row, to-mor·row** (tə-mor′o, -môr′-), *adv.* [AS. *to morgen*], on the day after today. *n.* the day after today.
**tom·tit** (tom′tit′), *n.* 1. [Brit.], a titmouse. 2. any small bird, as a wren.
**tom-tom** (tom′tom′), *n.* [Hind. *tam-tam*], a primitive drum, usually beaten with the hands.
**ton** (tun), *n.* [AS. *tunne*], 1. a unit of weight (in full, **short ton**) equal to 2,000 pounds avoirdupois. 2. in Great Britain, a unit of weight equal to 2,240 pounds avoirdupois: also **long ton.**
**ton·al** (tō′n'l), *adj.* of a tone. —**ton′al·ly,** *adv.*
**to·nal·i·ty** (tō-nal′ə-ti), *n.* [*pl.* -TIES], in *music*, 1. a key. 2. tonal character as determined by the relationship of the tones to the keynote.
**tone** (tōn), *n.* [< Gr. *teinein*, to stretch], 1. a vocal or musical sound, or its quality as to

pitch, intensity, etc. 2. a manner of expression showing a certain attitude: as, a friendly *tone*. 3. style, character, spirit, etc. 4. elegant style. 5. a quality of color; shade. 6. normal, healthy condition of a muscle, organ, etc. 7. in *music*, *a*) a sound of distinct pitch. *b*) any of the full intervals of a diatonic scale. ***v.t.*** [TONED, TONING], to give a tone to. **—tone down** (or **up**), to give a less (or more) intense tone to.

**tone′-deaf′**, ***adj.*** unable to distinguish accurately differences in musical pitch.

**tong** (tôŋ, toŋ), [Chin. *t'ang*, meeting place], in the U.S., a Chinese society or association.

**tongs** (tôŋz, toŋz), ***n.pl.*** [also construed as sing.], [AS. *tange*], a device for seizing, lifting, etc., consisting of two hinged arms.

**tongue** (tuŋ), ***n.*** [AS. *tunge*], 1. the movable muscular structure in the mouth, used in eating, tasting, and (in man) speaking. 2. talk; speech. 3. the act, power, or manner of speaking. 4. a language or dialect. 5. something like a tongue in shape, position, use, etc., as the flap under the laces of a shoe.

**tongue-and-groove joint,** a kind of joint in which a projection on one board fits into a groove in another.

**tongue′-tied′**, ***adj.*** speechless from amazement, embarrassment, etc.

**ton·ic** (ton′ik), ***adj.*** [see TONE], 1. of or producing good muscular tone. 2. in *music*, designating or based on a keynote. ***n.*** 1. anything that invigorates; specif., a tonic medicine. 2. in *music*, a keynote.

**to·night, to-night** (tə-nīt′, too-), ***adv.*** [AS. *to niht*], on or during the present or coming night. ***n.*** the present or the coming night.

**ton·nage** (tun′ij), ***n.*** 1. the total amount of shipping of a country or port, calculated in tons. 2. the carrying capacity of a ship.

**ton·sil** (ton′s'l), ***n.*** [L. *tonsillae*, *pl.*], either of a pair of oval masses of lymphoid tissue at the back of the mouth.

**ton′sil·lec′to·my** (-ek′tə-mi), ***n.*** [*pl.* -MIES], [see -ECTOMY], the surgical removal of the tonsils.

**ton′sil·li′tis** (-ī′tis), ***n.*** inflammation of the tonsils. **—ton′sil·lit′ic** (-it′ik), ***adj.***

**ton·sure** (ton′shẽr), ***n.*** [< L. *tondere*, to clip], 1. the act of shaving the head or crown of one entering the priesthood or a monastic order. 2. the part so shaven.

**too** (to͞o), ***adv.*** [< *to*], 1. in addition; also. 2. more than enough: as, the hat's *too* big. 3. very; extremely: as, that's *too* bad.

**took** (took), pt. of **take**.

**tool** (to͞ol), ***n.*** [AS. *tol*], 1. any hand implement, instrument, etc. used for some work. 2. any similar instrument that is part of a machine, as a drill. 3. anything that serves as a means. 4. a stooge. ***v.t.*** 1. to shape or work with a tool. 2. to impress designs, etc., as on leather, with a tool.

**toot** (to͞ot), ***v.i. & v.t.*** [echoic], to sound (a horn, whistle, etc.) in short blasts. ***n.*** a short blast of a horn, etc. **—toot′er**, ***n.***

**tooth** (to͞oth), ***n.*** [*pl.* TEETH], [AS. *toth*], 1. any of the hard, bonelike structures in the jaws, used for biting, chewing, etc. 2. a toothlike part, as on a saw, comb, gear, etc. 3. something that bites like a tooth: as, the *teeth* of a storm. **—in the teeth of,** 1. directly against. 2. defying. **—tooth and nail,** with all one's strength.

**tooth′ache′**, ***n.*** an ache in a tooth.

**tooth′brush′**, ***n.*** a small brush for cleaning the teeth.

**tooth paste** (or **powder**), a paste (or powder) for brushing the teeth.

**tooth′pick′**, ***n.*** a slender, pointed instrument, as a sliver of wood, etc., for dislodging food particles from between the teeth.

**tooth′some** (-səm), ***adj.*** tasty.

**top** (top), ***n.*** [AS.], 1. the head or crown. 2. the highest point or surface of anything. 3. the part of a plant above ground. 4. the uppermost part or covering, as a lid, cap, etc. 5. the highest degree: as, at the *top* of his voice. 6. the highest rank, position, etc.: as, the *top* of the class. ***adj.*** of, at, or being the top; highest. ***v.t.*** [TOPPED, TOPPING], 1. to remove the top of (a plant, etc.). 2. to provide with a top. 3. to be a top for. 4. to reach the top of. 5. to exceed in amount, etc. 6. to surpass; outdo. **—blow one's top,** [Slang], to lose one's temper. **—on top,** successful. **—on top of,** 1. resting upon. 2. besides. **—top off,** to complete with a finishing touch.

**top** (top), ***n.*** [AS.], a child's cone-shaped toy with a point upon which it is spun.

**to·paz** (tō′paz), ***n.*** [< Gr. *topazos*], any of various yellow gems, esp. a variety of aluminum silicate.

**top′coat′**, ***n.*** a lightweight overcoat.

**top′-drawer′**, ***adj.*** of first importance.

**tope** (tōp), ***v.t. & v.i.*** [TOPED, TOPING], to drink (alcoholic liquor) in large amounts.

**top-flight** (top′flīt′), ***adj.*** [Colloq.], best; first-rate.

**top hat,** a man's tall, black, cylindrical silk hat, worn in formal dress.

**top′-heav′y**, ***adj.*** too heavy at the top, so as to be unstable. **—top′-heav′i·ness**, ***n.***

**top·ic** (top′ik), ***n.*** [ult. < Gr. *topos*, place], 1. the subject of a speech, essay, discussion, etc. 2. a heading in an outline.

**top′i·cal**, ***adj.*** dealing with topics of the day; of current or local interest.

**top′knot′** (-not′), ***n.*** a tuft of hair or feathers on the top of the head.

**top′mast′**, ***n.*** the second mast above the deck of a sailing ship.

**top·most** (top′mōst′, -məst), ***adj.*** of the very top; uppermost; highest.

**top-notch** (top′noch′), ***adj.*** [Colloq.], first-rate.

**to·pog·ra·phy** (tə-pog′rə-fi), ***n.*** [*pl.* -PHIES], [< Gr. *topos*, a place + *graphein*, write], 1. the science of representing, as on maps and charts, the surface features of a region. 2. these surface features. **—top·o·graph·i·cal** (top′ə-graf′i-k'l), **top′o·graph′ic**, ***adj.***

**top·ping** (top′iŋ), ***n.*** something put on top of something else.

**top·ple** (top′'l), ***v.i.*** [-PLED, -PLING], [< *top*, *v.*], to fall top forward; fall (*over*) from top-heaviness, etc. ***v.t.*** to cause to topple.

**top·sail** (top′s'l, -sāl′), ***n.*** in a square-rigged vessel, the sail next above the lowest sail on a mast.

**top′-se′cret**, ***adj.*** designating or of information of the greatest secrecy.

**top′soil′**, ***n.*** the upper layer of soil, usually richer than the subsoil.

**top·sy-tur·vy** (top′si-tũr′vi), ***adv. & adj.*** [prob. < *top*, highest part + ME. *terven*, to roll], 1. upside down; in a reversed condition. 2. in confusion or disorder.

**toque** (tōk), ***n.*** [Fr.], a woman's small, round hat, with little or no brim.

**to·rah, to·ra** (tō′rə), ***n.*** [*pl.* -ROTH (-rōth, -rōs)], [Heb., law], 1. the body of Jewish scriptures. 2. [usually T-], the Pentateuch, or a scroll containing it.

**torch** (tôrch), ***n.*** [< L. *torquere*, to twist], 1. a portable, flaming light. 2. a source of enlightenment, inspiration, etc. 3. a device for producing a very hot flame, as in welding. 4. [Brit.], a flashlight.

**torch′light′**, ***n.*** the light of a torch or torches. ***adj.*** done by torchlight.

**tore** (tôr), pt. of **tear** (pull apart).

**tor·e·a·dor** (tôr′i-ə-dôr′), ***n.*** [Sp. < L. *taurus*, a bull], a bullfighter.

**tor·ment** (tôr′ment), ***n.*** [< L. *torquere*, to twist], 1. great pain or anguish; agony. 2.

a source of pain, anxiety, or annoyance. *v.t.* (tôr-ment′), 1. to cause great physical or mental pain in. 2. to annoy; harass. —**tor·men′tor, tor·ment′er,** *n.*

**torn** (tôrn), pp. of **tear** (pull apart).

**tor·na·do** (tôr-nā′dō), *n.* [*pl.* -DOES, -DOS], [< Sp. < L. *tonare*, to thunder], a violent, destructive wind accompanied by a whirling, funnel-shaped cloud that moves in a narrow path. —**tor·nad′ic** (-nad′ik), *adj.*

**tor·pe·do** (tôr-pē′dō), *n.* [*pl.* -DOES], [L., an electric ray (fish)], 1. a large, cigar-shaped, self-propelled, underwater projectile containing explosives. 2. any of various explosive devices. *v.t.* [-DOED, -DOING], to attack, destroy, etc. as with a torpedo.

**tor·pid** (tôr′pid), *adj.* [< L. *torpere*, to be numb], 1. dormant; inactive and unfeeling, as a hibernating animal. 2. dull; sluggish.

**tor·por** (tôr′pẽr), *n.* 1. a torpid state. 2. sluggishness; apathy.

**torque** (tôrk), *n.* [< L. *torques*, twisted metal necklace], in *physics*, a force that produces or tends to produce a twisting or rotating motion.

**tor·rent** (tôr′ənt, tor′-), *n.* [< L. *torrens*, boiling], 1. a swift, violent stream, as of water. 2. a rapid or violent flow, as of words. —**tor·ren·tial** (tô-ren′shəl), *adj.*

**tor·rid** (tôr′id, tor′-), *adj.* [< L. *torrere*, to parch], 1. subjected to intense heat, esp. of the sun; parched; arid. 2. very hot.

**tor·sion** (tôr′shən), *n.* [< L. *torquere*, to twist], a twisting or being twisted, esp. along the length of an axis. —**tor′sion·al,** *adj.*

**tor·so** (tôr′sō), *n.* [*pl.* -SOS, -SI (-sē)], [< Gr. *thyrsos*, a stem], 1. the trunk of the human body. 2. a statue of the human trunk.

**tort** (tôrt), *n.* [< L. *torquere*, to twist], in *law*, a wrongful act or damage (not involving a breach of contract), for which a civil action can be brought.

**tor·til·la** (tôr-tē′yä), *n.* [Sp., dim. of *torta*, a cake], a flat, unleavened corn cake, a food staple of Mexico.

**tor·toise** (tôr′təs), *n.* [prob. < Gr. *tartaruchos*, demon], a turtle, esp. one that lives on land.

**tortoise shell,** the hard, mottled, yellow-and-brown shells of some turtles.

**tor·tu·ous** (tôr′chōō-əs), *adj.* [< L. *torquere*, to twist], full of twists, turns, etc.; winding; crooked. —**tor′tu·ous·ly,** *adv.*

**tor·ture** (tôr′chẽr), *n.* [< L. *torquere*, to twist], 1. the inflicting of severe pain, as to force information or confession. 2. any severe physical or mental pain; agony. *v.t.* [-TURED, -TURING], 1. to subject to torture. 2. to twist or distort (meaning, etc.).

**To·ry** (tôr′i), *n.* [*pl.* -RIES], [< Ir. *tōruidhe*, robber], 1. formerly, a member of the major conservative party of England. 2. in the American Revolution, one who favored allegiance to Great Britain.

**toss** (tôs, tos), *v.t.* [TOSSED, TOSSING], [prob. < ON.], 1. to throw about: as, waves *tossed* the boat. 2. to throw lightly from the hand. 3. to jerk upward: as, to *toss* one's head. *v.i.* 1. to be thrown about. 2. to fling oneself about in sleep, etc. *n.* a tossing or being tossed. —**toss up,** to toss a coin for deciding something according to which side lands uppermost.

**toss′up′,** *n.* 1. the act of tossing up. 2. an even chance.

**tot** (tot), *n.* [prob. < ON. *tuttr*, dwarf], 1. a small amount. 2. a young child.

**tot** (tot), *v.t.* [TOTTED, TOTTING], [Brit. Colloq.], to add up; total (with *up*).

**to·tal** (tō′t'l), *adj.* [< L. *totus*, all], 1. constituting a whole. 2. complete; utter: as, a *total* loss. *n.* the whole amount; sum. *v.t.* [-TALED or -TALLED, -TALING or -TALLING], 1. to find the total of. 2. to add up to. *v.i.* to amount (*to*) as a whole. —**to′tal·ly,** *adv.*

**to·tal·i·tar·i·an** (tō-tal′ə-târ′i-ən), *adj.* [< *totality*], designating or of a government in which one political group maintains absolute control. *n.* one who favors such a government. —**to·tal′i·tar′i·an·ism,** *n.*

**to·tal·i·ty** (tō-tal′ə-ti), *n.* the total amount.

**to·tal·i·za·tor** (tō′t'l-ə-zā′tẽr), *n.* a machine for registering the total number of bets, as at a horse race.

**tote** (tōt), *v.t.* [TOTED, TOTING], [< ?], [Colloq.], to carry or haul. —**tot′er,** *n.*

**to·tem** (tō′təm), *n.* [< Algonquian], 1. among primitive peoples, an animal or natural object taken as the symbol of a family or clan. 2. an image of this.

**totem pole,** a pole carved and painted with totems by Indian tribes of NW North America.

**tot·ter** (tot′ẽr), *v.i.* [prob. < ON.], 1. to rock as if about to fall. 2. to be unsteady on one's feet; stagger. *n.* a tottering.

**tou·can** (tōō′kan, too-kän′), *n.* [< S. Am. Ind.], a brightly colored bird of tropical America, with a huge beak.

**touch** (tuch), *v.t.* [< OFr. *tochier*], 1. to put the hand, etc. on, so as to feel. 2. to bring (something), or come, into contact with (something else). 3. to border on. 4. to strike lightly. 5. to give a light tint, aspect, etc. to: as, *touched* with pink. 6. to stop at, as a ship. 7. to handle; use. 8. to come up to; reach. 9. to compare with; equal. 10. to affect; concern. 11. to arouse sympathy, gratitude, etc. in. 12. [Slang], to seek a loan or gift of money from. *v.i.* 1. to touch a person or thing. 2. to be or come in contact. *n.* 1. a touching or being touched; specif., a light tap. 2. the sense by which physical objects are perceived by feeling. 3. a subtle change or addition in a painting, story, etc. 4. a trace, tinge, etc. 5. a slight attack: as, a *touch* of the flu. 6. [Slang], the act of seeking a gift or loan of money. 7. in *music*, the manner of striking the keys of a piano, etc. —**in** (or **out of) touch with,** in (or no longer in) communication with. —**touch on** (or **upon),** 1. to verge on. 2. to merely mention. —**touch up,** to improve or finish (a painting, story, etc.) by minor changes or additions. —**touch′a·ble,** *adj.*

**touch and go,** an uncertain or dangerous situation. —**touch′-and-go′,** *adj.*

**touch′down′,** *n.* in *football*, a scoring play in which a player grounds the ball past the opponents' goal line.

**touched** (tucht), *adj.* 1. emotionally affected. 2. mentally unbalanced.

**touch′ing,** *adj.* arousing tender emotion; moving. —**touch′ing·ly,** *adv.*

**touch′stone′,** *n.* 1. a stone formerly used to test the purity of gold or silver. 2. any test of genuineness.

**touch′y,** *adj.* [-IER, -IEST], [< OFr. *tache*, a mark], 1. easily offended; irritable. 2. very risky or precarious. —**touch′i·ness,** *n.*

**tough** (tuf), *adj.* [AS. *toh*], 1. that will bend without tearing or breaking. 2. not easily cut or chewed: as, *tough* steak. 3. strong; hardy. 4. stubborn. 5. brutal; rough. 6. very difficult; toilsome. *n.* a tough person; thug. —**tough′ly,** *adv.* —**tough′ness,** *n.*

**tough′en,** *v.t.* & *v.i.* to make or become tough or tougher. —**tough′en·er,** *n.*

**tou·pee** (tōō-pā′, -pē′), *n.* [< Fr. < OFr. *toup*, tuft of hair], a small wig.

**tour** (toor), *n.* [OFr. < *to(u)rner*, to turn], 1. a turn, period, etc., as of work. 2. a long trip, as for sightseeing. 3. any trip, as for inspection, giving performances, etc.. *v.i.* & *v.t.* to go on a tour (through).

**tour′ism,** *n.* tourist travel, esp. when regarded as a source of income for a country, etc.

**tour′ist,** *n.* one who tours, esp. for pleasure. *adj.* of or for tourists.

**tour·ma·line** (toor′mə-lin, -lēn′), *n.* [Fr. < Singhalese], a semiprecious mineral.

**tour·na·ment** (toor′nə-mənt, tũr′-), *n.* [< OFr. *tourner*, to turn], 1. a contest between knights on horseback who tried to unseat one another with lances. 2. a series of contests in competition for a championship.

**tour·ney** (toor′ni, tũr′-), *n.* [*pl.* -NEYS], a tournament.

**tour·ni·quet** (toor′ni-ket′, tũr′-), *n.* [Fr. < *tourner*, to turn], a device for compressing a blood vessel to stop bleeding, as a bandage twisted tight.

**tou·sle** (tou′z'l), *v.t.* [-SLED, -SLING], [< ME. *tusen*, to pull], to disorder, dishevel, etc.

**tout** (tout), *v.i.* & *v.t.* [< AS. *totian*, to peep], 1. [Colloq.], to praise highly. 2. [Slang], to sell betting tips on (race horses). *n.* one who touts. —**tout′er**, *n.*

**tow** (tō), *v.t.* [AS. *togian*], to pull as by a rope or chain. *n.* 1. a towing or being towed. 2. something towed. 3. a towline. —**in tow**, 1. being towed. 2. in one's company or charge.

**tow** (tō), *n.* [AS. *tow-*, for spinning], the broken fibers of hemp, flax, etc. before spinning.

**to·ward** (tôrd, tə-wôrd′), *prep.* [see TO & -WARD], 1. in the direction of. 2. facing. 3. along a likely course to: as, efforts *toward* peace. 4. concerning. 5. just before: as, *toward* noon. 6. for: as, save *toward* a car. Also **to′wards.**

**tow·el** (tou′'l), *n.* [< OFr. *toaille*], a piece of cloth or paper for wiping or drying things.

**tow′el·ing, tow′el·ling,** *n.* material for making towels.

**tow·er** (tou′ẽr), *n.* [< L. *turris*], 1. a high structure, often part of another building. 2. such a structure used as a fortress. *v.i.* to rise high like a tower. —**tow′er·ing,** *adj.*

**tow·head** (tō′hed′), *n.* 1. a head of pale-yellow hair. 2. a person with such hair.

**tow′line′,** *n.* a rope, chain, etc. for towing.

**town** (toun), *n.* [AS. *tun*], 1. a concentration of houses, etc., somewhat larger than a village. 2. a township. 3. the business center of a city. 4. a city. 5. the people of a town. —**go to town,** [Slang], 1. to act fast and efficiently. 2. to be successful. —**on the town,** [Slang], out for a good time. —**paint the town red,** [Slang], to carouse.

**town hall,** a building in a town, housing the offices of officials, the council chamber, etc.

**town meeting,** a meeting of the voters of a town, as in New England.

**town′ship,** *n.* 1. a division of a county, constituting a unit of local government. 2. a unit of land in the U.S. land survey, generally 6 miles square.

**towns·man** (tounz′mən), *n.* [*pl.* -MEN], 1. a person who lives in a town. 2. a fellow resident of a town.

**towns′peo′ple,** *n.pl.* the people of a town: also **towns′folk′** (-fōk′).

**tox·e·mi·a, tox·ae·mi·a** (tok-sē′mi-ə), *n.* [see TOXIC], blood poisoning, esp. as caused by bacterial toxins.

**tox·ic** (tok′sik), *adj.* [< L. *toxicum*, a poison], 1. of, affected by, or caused by a toxin. 2. poisonous. —**tox′i·cal·ly,** *adv.*

**tox·i·col·o·gy** (tok′si-kol′ə-ji), *n.* [see TOXIC & -LOGY], the science of poisons, their effects, antidotes, etc. —**tox′i·col′o·gist,** *n.*

**tox·in** (tok′sin), *n.* [< *toxic* + *-ine*], 1. a poison produced by microorganisms and causing certain diseases. 2. any poison secreted by plants or animals.

**toy** (toi), *n.* [< D. *tuig*, tools], 1. a trifle. 2. a bauble; trinket. 3. a plaything for children. *adj.* 1. like a toy in size, use, etc. 2. made as a toy. *v.i.* to trifle (*with* food, an idea, etc.).

**tr.,** 1. transpose. 2. treasurer.

**trace** (trās), *n.* [< L. *trahere*, to draw], 1. a mark, track, sign, etc. left by a person, animal, or thing. 2. a barely observable amount. *v.t.* [TRACED, TRACING], 1. to follow (a route, etc.). 2. to follow the trail of; track. 3. *a*) to follow the development or history of. *b*) to determine (a source, etc.) thus. 4. to draw, outline, etc. 5. to copy (a drawing, etc.) by following its lines on a superimposed transparent sheet. —**trace′a·ble,** *adj.* —**trac′er,** *n.*

**trace** (trās), *n.* [see TRAIT], either of two straps, chains, etc. connecting a draft animal's harness to the vehicle.

**trac·er·y** (trās′ẽr-i), *n.* [*pl.* -IES], [< *trace*, *v.* + *-ery*], ornamental work of interlacing or branching lines.

**tra·che·a** (trā′ki-ə), *n.* [*pl.* -AE (-ē′)], [< Gr. *tracheia* (*arteria*), rough (windpipe)], the passage that conveys air from the larynx to the bronchi; windpipe. —**tra′che·al,** *adj.*

**trac·ing** (trās′iŋ), *n.* something traced; specif., a copy of a drawing, etc.

**tracing paper,** thin, strong, transparent paper on which tracings may be made.

**track** (trak), *n.* [< OFr. *trac*], 1. a mark left in passing, as a footprint, wheel rut, etc. 2. a path or trail. 3. a circuit laid out for racing, etc. 4. a pair of parallel metal rails on which trains, etc. run. 5. a sequence of ideas, events, etc. 6. *a*) sports performed on a track, as running, hurdling, etc. *b*) these sports along with other contests in jumping, throwing, etc. *v.t.* 1. to follow the track of. 2. to trace by means of evidence, etc. 3. to leave tracks of (mud, etc.) on (often with *up*). —**in one's tracks,** where one is at the moment. —**keep** (or **lose**) **track of,** to stay (or fail to stay) informed about.

**track′less trolley,** a trolley bus.

**tract** (trakt), *n.* [< L. *trahere*, to draw], 1. a continuous expanse of land. 2. a system of organs having some special function: as, the digestive *tract*.

**tract** (trakt), *n.* [< L. *tractatus*, a treatise], a pamphlet or leaflet, esp. one on a religious subject.

**trac·ta·ble** (trak′tə-b'l), *adj.* [< L. *trahere*, to draw], 1. easily managed; docile. 2. easily worked; malleable. —**trac′ta·bil′i·ty,** *n.*

**trac·tion** (trak′shən), *n.* [< L. *trahere*, to draw], 1. *a*) a pulling or drawing. *b*) a being pulled or drawn. 2. the pulling power of a locomotive, etc. 3. adhesive friction.

**trac·tor** (trak′tẽr), *n.* [see TRACTION], 1. a small, powerful, motor-driven vehicle for pulling farm machinery, etc. 2. a driver's cab for hauling large vans, etc.

**trade** (trād), *n.* [MLG., a track], 1. an occupation; esp., skilled labor. 2. buying and selling; commerce. 3. all the persons in a particular business. 4. customers. 5. a purchase or sale. 6. an exchange; swap. *v.i.* [TRADED, TRADING], 1. to carry on a business. 2. to have business dealings (*with*). 3. to make an exchange (*with*). 4. [Colloq.], to be a customer (*at* a certain store). *v.t.* to exchange; swap. —**trade on** (or **upon**), to take advantage of.

**trade′-in′,** *n.* a thing given or taken as part payment for something else.

**trade′mark′, trade′-mark′,** *n.* a symbol, word, etc. used by a manufacturer or dealer to distinguish his products: usually registered and protected by law.

**trade name,** a name used as a trademark.

**trad′er,** *n.* 1. one who trades; merchant. 2. a ship used in trade.

**trades·man** (trādz′mən), *n.* [*pl.* -MEN], a storekeeper.

**trade union,** a labor union: also **trade′-un′ion.** —**trade′-un′ion,** *adj.*

**trade wind,** a wind that blows toward the equator from either side of it.

**trad′ing post,** a store in an outpost, settlement, etc. where trading is done.
**tra·di·tion** (trə-dish′ən), *n.* [< L. *tradere*, deliver], 1. the handing down orally of customs, beliefs, stories, etc. from generation to generation. 2. a custom, belief, etc. handed down this way.
**tra·di′tion·al,** *adj.* of, handed down by, or conforming to tradition.
**tra·duce** (trə-dōōs′, -dūs′), *v.t.* [-DUCED, -DUCING], [< L. *trans*, across + *ducere*, to lead], to defame; slander. —**tra·duc′er,** *n.*
**traf·fic** (traf′ik), *n.* [< It. < L. *trans*, across + It. *ficcare*, bring], 1. buying and selling; trade. 2. dealings (*with* someone). 3. the movement or number of automobiles, pedestrians, etc. along a street, etc. 4. the business done by a transportation company. *v.i.* [-FICKED, -FICKING], 1. to carry on traffic (*in* a commodity). 2. to have dealings (*with* someone). —**traf′fick·er,** *n.*
**tra·ge·di·an** (trə-jē′di-ən), *n.* an actor of tragedy. —**tra·ge′di·enne′** (-en′), *n.fem.*
**trag·e·dy** (traj′ə-di), *n.* [*pl.* -DIES], [< Gr. *tragos*, goat + *ōidē*, song], 1. a serious play with an unhappy ending. 2. a very sad or tragic event.
**trag·ic** (traj′ik), *adj.* 1. of, or having the nature of, tragedy. 2. very sad, disastrous, etc. Also **trag′i·cal.** —**trag′i·cal·ly,** *adv.*
**trail** (trāl), *v.t.* [< L. *trahere*, to drag], 1. to drag or let drag behind one. 2. to follow the tracks of. 3. to hunt by tracking. 4. to follow behind. *v.i.* 1. to drag along on the ground, etc. 2. to grow along the ground, etc., as some plants. 3. to stream behind, as smoke. 4. to follow or lag behind; straggle. 5. to dwindle, as a sound. *n.* 1. something that trails behind. 2. a mark, scent, etc. left by a person, animal, or thing that has passed. 3. a beaten path.
**trail′er,** *n.* 1. one that trails. 2. *a*) a wagon, van, etc. designed to be pulled by an automobile, truck, or tractor. *b*) such a vehicle designed to be lived in.
**train** (trān), *n.* [< L. *trahere*, to pull], 1. something that drags along behind, as a trailing skirt. 2. a group of followers; retinue. 3. a procession; caravan. 4. any connected sequence: as, a *train* of thought. 5. a line of connected railroad cars pulled by a locomotive. *v.t.* 1. to guide the growth of (a plant). 2. to guide the mental, moral, etc. development of; rear. 3. to instruct so as to make proficient. 4. to make fit for an athletic contest, etc. 5. to aim (a gun, etc.). *v.i.* to undergo training. —**train·ee′** (-ē′), *n.* —**train′er,** *n.* —**train′ing,** *n.*
**train′man** (-mən), *n.* [*pl.* -MEN], one who works on a railroad train.
**traipse** (trāps), *v.i.* [TRAIPSED, TRAIPSING], [see TRESPASS], [Dial.], to walk or wander idly; trudge; saunter.
**trait** (trāt), *n.* [< L. *trahere*, to draw], a distinguishing quality or characteristic.
**trai·tor** (trā′tẽr), *n.* [< L. *tradere*, betray], one who betrays his country, friends, etc. —**trai′tor·ous,** *adj.* —**trai′tor·ous·ly,** *adv.*
**tra·jec·to·ry** (trə-jek′tẽr-i), *n.* [*pl.* -RIES], [< L. *trans*, across + *jacere*, to throw], the curved path of something hurtling through space, especially that of a projectile.
**tram** (tram), *n.* [prob. < LG. *traam*, a beam], 1. an open railway car used in mines. 2. [Brit.], a streetcar: also called **tram′car′.**
**tram·mel** (tram′'l), *n.* [< L. *tres*, three + *macula*, a mesh], 1. a shackle for a horse. 2. *often pl.* something that confines or restrains. *v.t.* [-MELED or -MELLED, -MELING or -MELLING], to confine, restrain, or shackle.
**tramp** (tramp), *v.i.* [ME. *trampen*], 1. to walk firmly and heavily. 2. to travel about on foot, esp. as a vagrant. *v.t.* 1. to step on heavily. 2. to walk through. *n.* 1. a vagrant; hobo. 2. the sound of heavy steps. 3. a journey on foot; hike. 4. a freight ship that picks up cargo wherever it may be.
**tram·ple** (tram′p'l), *v.i.* [-PLED, -PLING], [see TRAMP], to tread heavily. *v.t.* to crush as by treading heavily on. *n.* the sound of trampling. —**tramp′ler,** *n.*
**trance** (trans, träns), *n.* [< L. *trans*, across + *ire*, go], 1. a sleeplike state in which consciousness may remain, as in hypnosis. 2. a daze; stupor. 3. a state of great mental abstraction, as that of a religious mystic.
**tran·quil** (traŋ′kwil), *adj.* [-QUILER or -QUILLER, -QUILEST or -QUILLEST], [< L. *trans-*, beyond + *quies*, rest], calm; serene; quiet. —**tran·quil′li·ty, tran·quil′i·ty,** *n.*
**tran′quil·ize′, tran′quil·lize′** (-īz′), *v.t. & v.i.* [-IZED, -IZING; -LIZED, -LIZING], to make or become tranquil; quiet; calm.
**tran′quil·iz′er, tran′quil·liz′er,** *n.* a drug used to tranquilize the mentally ill or emotionally disturbed.
**trans-,** [L. < *trans*, across], a prefix meaning *over, across, beyond*: as in *transatlantic.*
**trans.,** 1. translated. 2. translation.
**trans·act** (tran-sakt′, -zakt′), *v.t.* [< L. *trans-*, over + *agere*, to drive], to carry on or complete (business, etc.). —**trans·ac′tor,** *n.*
**trans·ac′tion,** *n.* 1. a transacting. 2. something transacted; specif., *a*) a piece of business; deal. *b*) *pl.* a record of proceedings, as of a society.
**trans·at·lan·tic** (trans′ət-lan′tik), *adj.* 1. crossing the Atlantic. 2. on the other side of the Atlantic.
**tran·scend** (tran-send′), *v.t.* [< L. *trans*, over + *scandere*, climb], 1. to go beyond the limits of; exceed. 2. to surpass; excel. —**tran·scend′ent,** *adj.*
**tran·scen·den·tal** (tran′sen-den′t'l), *adj.* 1. supernatural. 2. abstract.
**trans·con·ti·nen·tal** (trans′kon-tə-nen′t'l), *adj.* 1. that crosses a continent. 2. on the other side of a continent.
**tran·scribe** (tran-skrīb′), *v.t.* [-SCRIBED, -SCRIBING], [< L. *trans-*, over + *scribere*, write], 1. to make a written or typewritten copy of (shorthand notes, etc.). 2. in *music & radio*, to make a transcription of.
**tran·script** (tran′skript′), *n.* 1. a written or typewritten copy. 2. any copy.
**tran·scrip′tion** (-skrip′shən), *n.* 1. a transcribing. 2. a transcript. 3. an arrangement of a piece of music for some other instrument or voice. 4. a recording of a program, etc. for radio broadcasting.
**tran·sept** (tran′sept), *n.* [< L. *transversus*, transverse + *septum*, enclosure], the part of a cross-shaped church at right angles to the nave.
**trans·fer** (trans-fũr′, trans′fẽr), *v.t.* [-FERRED, -FERRING], [< L. *trans-*, across + *ferre*, to bear], 1. to carry, send, etc. to another person or place. 2. to make over the ownership of to another. 3. to convey (a picture, etc.) from one surface to another. *v.i.* 1. to transfer oneself or be transferred. 2. to change to another bus, etc. *n.* (trans′fẽr), 1. a transferring or being transferred. 2. one that is transferred. 3. a ticket entitling the bearer to change to another bus, etc. —**trans·fer′a·ble,** *adj.* —**trans·fer′ence,** *n.*
**trans·fig·u·ra·tion** (trans-fig′yoo-rā′shən), *n.* 1. a transfiguring. 2. [T-], the change in the appearance of Jesus on the mountain: Matt. 17.
**trans·fig·ure** (trans-fig′yoor), *v.t.* [-URED, -URING], [< L. *trans-*, across + *figura*, figure], 1. to change the form or appearance of. 2. to transform so as to exalt or glorify.
**trans·fix** (trans-fiks′), *v.t.* [< L. *trans-*, through + *figere*, to fix], 1. to pierce through; impale. 2. to make motionless, as with horror.

**trans·form** (trans-fôrm′), *v.t.* [ult. < L. *trans-*, over + *forma*, a shape], 1. to change the form or appearance of. 2. to change the condition, character, or function of. —**trans′for·ma′tion**, *n.*

**trans·form′er,** *n.* 1. one that transforms. 2. an apparatus for changing an electric current in potential or type.

**trans·fuse** (trans-fūz′), *v.t.* [-FUSED, -FUSING], [< L. *trans-*, across + *fundere*, pour], 1. to instill; imbue. 2. to transfer (blood) from one individual into another. —**trans-fu′sion,** *n.* —**trans·fu′si·ble,** *adj.*

**trans·gress** (trans-gres′), *v.t. & v.i.* [< L. *trans-*, over + *gradi*, to step], 1. to break (a law, commandment, etc.); sin (against). 2. to go beyond (a limit, etc.). —**trans·gres′sion** (-gresh′ən), *n.* —**trans·gres′sor,** *n.*

**tran·sient** (tran′shənt), *adj.* [< L. *trans-*, over + *ire*, go], 1. passing away with time; temporary. 2. passing quickly; fleeting. *n.* a transient person; esp., a temporary lodger, etc. —**tran′sience, tran′sien·cy,** *n.*

**tran·sis·tor** (tran-zis′tẽr, -sis′-), *n.* [< *transfer* + *resistor*], a minute electronic device, used like an electronic tube, which controls current flow by means of germanium.

**tran·sis′tor·ized′** (-īzd′), *adj.* equipped with a transistor or transistors.

**trans·it** (tran′sit), *n.* [< L. *trans-*, over + *ire*, go], 1. passage through or across. 2. a carrying through or across; conveyance. 3. a surveying instrument for measuring horizontal angles.

**tran·si·tion** (tran-zish′ən), *n.* a passing from one condition, place, etc. to another.

**tran·si·tive** (tran′sə-tiv), *adj.* taking a direct object to complete the meaning: said of certain verbs. *n.* a transitive verb.

**tran·si·to·ry** (tran′sə-tôr′i), *adj.* not enduring; temporary; fleeting.

**trans·late** (trans-lāt′), *v.t.* [-LATED, -LATING], [< L. *translatus*, transferred], 1. to change from one place, condition, etc. to another. 2. to change from one language into another. 3. to put into different words. —**trans-la′tor,** *n.*

**trans·la′tion,** *n.* 1. a translating. 2. a translated version of a literary work.

**trans·lit·er·ate** (trans-lit′ə-rāt′), *v.t.* [-ATED, -ATING], [< *trans-* + L. *litera*, letter], to write (words, etc.) in the characters of another alphabet.

**trans·lu·cent** (trans-lōō′s'nt), *adj.* [< L. *trans-*, through + *lucere*, to shine], letting light pass through but not transparent.

**trans·mi·grate** (trans-mī′grāt), *v.i.* [-GRATED, -GRATING], [see TRANS- & MIGRATE], 1. to move from one country, etc. to another. 2. in some religions, to pass into another body at death: said of the soul. —**trans′mi·gra′-tion,** *n.*

**trans·mis·sion** (trans-mish′ən), *n.* 1. a transmitting. 2. something transmitted. 3. the part of an automobile that transmits motive force from the engine to the wheels, as by gears.

**trans·mit** (trans-mit′), *v.t.* [-MITTED, -MITTING], [< L. *trans-*, over + *mittere*, send], 1. to cause to go to another person or place; transfer. 2. to hand down by heredity, inheritance, etc. 3. to pass (light, heat, etc.) through some medium. 4. to convey; conduct (sound, force, movement, etc.). 5. to send out (radio or television signals).

**trans·mit′ter,** *n.* one that transmits; specif., the apparatus that transmits signals, sounds, etc. in telegraphy, radio, etc.

**trans·mute** (trans-mūt′), *v.t.* [-MUTED, -MUTING], [< L. *trans-*, over + *mutare*, change], to change from one form, nature, substance, etc. into another; transform.

**trans·o·ce·an·ic** (trans′ō-shi-an′ik), *adj.* crossing or across the ocean.

**tran·som** (tran′səm), *n.* [prob. < L. *transtrum*, crossbeam], 1. a horizontal crossbar, as across the top of a door or window. 2. a small window just above a door or window.

**trans·par·ent** (trans-pâr′ənt), *adj.* [< L. *trans-*, through + *parere*, appear], 1. transmitting light rays so that objects on the other side may be seen. 2. so fine in texture as to be seen through. 3. easily understood or detected; obvious. —**trans·par′en·cy** [*pl.* -CIES], *n.* —**trans·par′ent·ly,** *adv.*

**tran·spire** (tran-spīr′), *v.i.* [-SPIRED, -SPIRING], [< L. *trans*, through + *spirare*, breathe], 1. to give off vapor, moisture, etc., as through pores. 2. to become known. 3. to happen: regarded by some as a loose usage. —**tran′spi·ra′tion** (-spə-rā′shən), *n.*

**trans·plant** (trans-plant′, -plänt′), *v.t.* 1. to remove from one place and plant, resettle, etc. in another. 2. in *surgery*, to graft (tissue, etc.).

**trans·port** (trans-pôrt′), *v.t.* [< L. *trans-*, over + *portare*, carry], 1. to carry from one place to another. 2. to carry away with emotion. 3. to banish to a penal colony, etc. *n.* (trans′pôrt), 1. a transporting; transportation. 2. rapture. 3. a ship, airplane, etc. used for transporting.

**trans·por·ta·tion** (trans′pẽr-tā′shən), *n.* 1. a transporting or being transported. 2. a means of conveyance. 3. fare.

**trans·pose** (trans-pōz′), *v.t. & v.i.* [-POSED, -POSING], [see TRANS- & POSE], 1. to change the usual or relative order or position of; interchange. 2. to write or play (a musical composition) in a different key. —**trans′-po·si′tion** (-pə-zish′ən), **trans·pos′al,** *n.*

**tran·sub·stan·ti·a·tion** (tran′səb-stan′shi-ā′shən), *n.* [< L. *trans-*, over + *substantia*, substance], 1. the changing of one substance into another. 2. in *R.C. & Orthodox Eastern doctrine*, the changing, in the Eucharist, of the whole substance of the bread and wine into the body and blood of Christ.

**trans·u·ran·ic** (trans′yoo-ran′ik), *adj.* designating or of the elements, as plutonium, having atomic numbers higher than that of uranium.

**trans·verse** (trans-vũrs′), *adj.* [< L. *trans-*, across + *vertere*, to turn], situated, placed, etc. across; crosswise. *n.* a transverse part, beam, etc. —**trans·verse′ly,** *adv.*

**trap** (trap), *n.* [< AS. *træppe*], 1. a device for catching animals. 2. any stratagem, etc. designed to catch or trick. 3. a device, as in a drainpipe, for preventing the escape of gas, etc. 4. a light, two-wheeled carriage. 5. *pl.* drums, cymbals, etc., as in a band. *v.t.* [TRAPPED, TRAPPING], to catch as in a trap. *v.i.* to set traps to catch animals, esp. for their furs. —**trap′per,** *n.*

**trap door,** a hinged or sliding door in a roof or floor.

**tra·peze** (trə-pēz′, tra-), *n.* [< L. *trapezium*, a four-sided figure], a short horizontal bar, hung high by two ropes, on which acrobats, etc. swing.

**trap·e·zoid** (trap′ə-zoid′), *n.* [< Gr. *trapeza*, table], a plane figure with four sides, two of which are parallel.

**trap·pings** (trap′iŋz), *n.pl.* [prob. < OFr. *drap*, cloth], 1. an ornamental covering for a horse. 2. adornments.

**trash** (trash), *n.* [cf. Norw. dial. *trask*], 1. worthless or waste things; rubbish. 2. a disreputable person or people. —**trash′y** [-IER, -IEST], *adj.*

**trau·ma** (trô′mə, trou′-), *n.* [*pl.* -MATA (-mə-tə), -MAS], [Gr.], 1. an injury violently produced. 2. an emotional shock having a lasting psychic effect. —**trau·mat·ic** (trô-mat′ik), *adj.*

**trav·ail** (trav′āl, -′l), *n.* [< LL. *tria*, three + *palus*, stake: referring to a torture device],

1. very hard work. 2. intense pain; agony.

**trav·el** (trav''l), *v.i.* [-VELED or -VELLED, -VELING or -VELLING], [< *travail*], 1. to go from one place to another. 2. to move, pass, or be transmitted. *v.t.* to make a journey over or through. *n.* a traveling; trip. —**trav'el·er, trav'el·ler,** *n.*

**trav·e·logue, trav·e·log** (trav'ə-lôg'), *n.* an illustrated lecture or motion picture of travels.

**tra·verse** (trav'ẽrs, trə-vũrs'), *v.t.* [-VERSED, -VERSING], [< L. *trans-*, over + *vertere*, to turn], to pass over, across, or through. *n.* something that traverses or crosses, as a crossbar. *adj.* 1. extending across. 2. designating or of drapes drawn by pulling cords at the side. —**trav'ers·a·ble,** *adj.*

**trav·es·ty** (trav'is-ti), *n.* [*pl.* -TIES], [< L. *trans*, over + *vestire*, to dress], 1. a farcical imitation in ridicule. 2. a crude and ridiculous representation. *v.t.* [-TIED, -TYING], to make a travesty of.

**trawl** (trôl), *n.* [prob. < *trail*], 1. a large net dragged along the bottom of a fishing bank. 2. a long line supported by buoys, from which fishing lines are hung: also **trawl line.** *v.t. & v.i.* to fish or catch with a trawl.

**trawl'er,** *n.* a boat used in trawling.

**tray** (trā), *n.* [< AS. *treg*, wooden board], a flat receptacle with low sides, for holding or carrying articles.

**treach·er·ous** (trech'ẽr-əs), *adj.* 1. characterized by treachery; traitorous. 2. untrustworthy. —**treach'er·ous·ly,** *adv.*

**treach·er·y** (trech'ẽr-i), *n.* [*pl.* -IES], [OFr. *trichier*, to trick], 1. betrayal of trust; deceit. 2. treason.

**trea·cle** (trē'k'l), *n.* [< Gr. *thēriakē*, antidote for venom], [Brit.], molasses.

**tread** (tred), *v.t.* [TROD, TRODDEN or TROD, TREADING], [AS. *tredan*], 1. to walk on, in, along, etc. 2. to do or follow by walking, dancing, etc. 3. to press or beat with the feet. *v.i.* 1. to walk. 2. to set one's foot (*on* or *upon*). 3. to trample (*on* or *upon*). *n.* 1. manner or sound of treading. 2. something on which a person or thing treads or moves, as a shoe sole, wheel rim, upper surface of a stair, etc. —**tread water,** [*pt.* usually TREADED], in *swimming*, to stay upright by moving the legs up and down.

**trea·dle** (tred''l), *n.* [< AS. *tredan*, to tread], a lever moved by the foot to operate a sewing machine, etc. *v.i.* [-DLED, -DLING], to work a treadle.

**tread'mill',** *n.* a mill wheel turned by an animal treading an endless belt.

**treas.,** 1. treasurer. 2. treasury.

**trea·son** (trē'z'n), *n.* [< L. *trans*, over + *dare*, give], betrayal of one's country to an enemy. —**trea'son·a·ble, trea'son·ous,** *adj.*

**treas·ure** (trezh'ẽr), *n.* [< Gr. *thēsauros*], 1. accumulated wealth, as money, jewels, etc. 2. any person or thing considered valuable. *v.t.* [-URED, -URING], 1. to save up for future use. 2. to value greatly.

**treas'ur·er,** *n.* one in charge of a treasury, as of a government, corporation, etc.

**treas'ure-trove'** (-trōv'), *n.* [*trove* < OFr. *trover*, find], treasure found hidden, the owner of which is unknown.

**treas·ur·y** (trezh'ẽr-i), *n.* [*pl.* -IES], 1. a place where treasure or funds are kept. 2. the funds or revenues of a state, corporation, etc. 3. [T-], the governmental department in charge of revenue, taxation, etc.

**treat** (trēt), *v.i.* [ult. < L. *trahere*, to draw], 1. to carry on business (*with*). 2. to pay for another's entertainment. *v.t.* 1. to deal with (a subject) in writing, music, etc. in a certain manner. 2. to act toward (someone or something) in a specified manner. 3. to pay for the food, etc. of (another). 4. to subject to some process; specif., to give medical care to. *n.* 1. a meal, drink, etc. paid for by another. 2. anything that gives great pleasure. —**treat of,** to deal with in speaking or writing.

**trea·tise** (trē'tis), *n.* [see TREAT], a formal, systematic essay or book on some subject.

**treat·ment** (trēt'mənt), *n.* 1. act, manner, method, etc. of treating. 2. medical or surgical care.

**trea·ty** (trē'ti), *n.* [*pl.* -TIES], [< L. *tractare*, manage], a formal agreement between two or more nations.

**tre·ble** (treb''l), *adj.* [< L. *triplus*, triple], 1. threefold; triple. 2. of, for, or performing the treble. *n.* 1. the highest part in musical harmony; soprano. 2. a high-pitched voice or sound. *v.t. & v.i.* [-BLED, -BLING], to make or become threefold.

**tree** (trē), *n.* [AS. *treow*], 1. a large, woody perennial plant with one main trunk and many branches. 2. anything suggesting a tree; specif., a diagram of family descent (**family tree**). *v.t.* [TREED, TREEING], to chase up a tree. —**tree'less,** *adj.*

**tre·foil** (trē'foil), *n.* [< L. *tri-*, three + *folium*, leaf], 1. a plant with leaves divided into three leaflets, as the clover. 2. any ornament, etc. resembling a threefold leaf.

**trek** (trek), *v.i.* [TREKKED, TREKKING], [S. Afr.D. < D. *trekken*, to draw], to travel slowly or laboriously. *n.* 1. a journey. 2. a migration.

**trel·lis** (trel'is), *n.* [< L. *tri-*, three + *licium*, a thread], a lattice, esp. one on which vines are trained.

**trem·ble** (trem'b'l), *v.i.* [-BLED, -BLING], [< L. *tremere*], 1. to shake or shiver, as from cold, fear, etc. 2. to feel great fear or anxiety. 3. to quiver, vibrate, etc. *n.* 1. a trembling. 2. *sometimes pl.* a fit or state of trembling. —**trem'bling·ly,** *adv.*

**tre·men·dous** (tri-men'dəs), *adj.* [< L. *tremere*, tremble], 1. such as to make one tremble; terrifying. 2. [Colloq.], *a*) very large; great. *b*) wonderful, amazing, etc.

**trem·o·lo** (trem'ə-lō'), *n.* [*pl.* -LOS], [It.], a tremulous effect produced by rapid reiteration of the same tone.

**trem·or** (trem'ẽr, trē'mẽr), *n.* [< L. *tremere*, tremble], 1. a trembling, shaking, etc. 2. a vibratory motion. 3. a nervous thrill.

**trem·u·lous** (trem'yoo-ləs), *adj.* [< L. *tremere*, tremble], 1. trembling; quivering; vibrating. 2. fearful; timid.

**trench** (trench), *v.t.* [< L. *truncare*, cut off], to dig a ditch or ditches in. *n.* 1. a deep furrow. 2. a long, narrow ditch with earth banked in front, used in battle for cover, etc.

**trench·ant** (tren'chənt), *adj.* [see TRENCH], 1. sharp; keen; incisive: as, *trenchant* words. 2. forceful; vigorous: as, a *trenchant* argument. —**trench'ant·ly,** *adv.*

**trench coat,** a belted raincoat in a military style.

**trench'er·man** (-mən), *n.* [*pl.* -MEN], an eater: esp., a heavy eater.

**trench mouth,** an infectious disease of the mucous membranes of the mouth and throat.

**trend** (trend), *v.i.* [AS. *trendan*], to have a general direction or tendency. *n.* a general direction or tendency; course, drift, etc.

**tre·pan** (tri-pan'), *n.* [< Gr. *trypan*, to bore], 1. an obsolete form of the trephine. 2. a heavy boring tool. *v.t.* [-PANNED, -PANNING], to trephine.

**tre·phine** (tri-fīn', -fēn'), *n.* [< L. *tres*, three + *fines*, ends], a surgical saw for removing disks of bone from the skull. *v.t.* [-PHINED, -PHINING], to operate on with a trephine.

**trep·i·da·tion** (trep'ə-dā'shən), *n.* [< L. *trepidus*, disturbed], 1. trembling movement. 2. fear; dread.

**tres·pass** (tres'pəs), *v.i.* [< L. *trans-*, across + *passare*, to pass], 1. to go beyond the limits of what is considered right; transgress; sin. 2. to enter another's property unlawfully. *n.* 1. a trespassing. 2. an offense; sin. —**tres'pass·er**, *n.*

**tress** (tres), *n.* [< LL. *tricia*], 1. orig., a braid of hair. 2. a lock, or curl of hair. 3. *pl.* a woman's or girl's hair. —**tressed**, *adj.*

**tres·tle** (tres''l), *n.* [< L. *transtrum*, a beam], 1. a horizontal beam fastened to two pairs of spreading legs, used as a support. 2. a framework of uprights and crosspieces, supporting a bridge, etc.

**trey** (trā), *n.* [< L. *tres*, three], a playing card or side of a die with three spots.

**tri-**, [< Fr., L., or Gr.], a combining form meaning: 1. *of three, having three parts*, etc. 2. *three times, into three*. 3. *every third*.

**tri·ad** (trī'ad), *n.* [< Gr. *treis*, three], a group of three.

**tri·al** (trī'əl), *n.* [see TRY], 1. the act or process of trying, testing, etc.; test; probation. 2. a hardship, pain, etc. 3. a source of annoyance. 4. a formal examination and decision of a case by a court of law. 5. an attempt; effort. *adj.* 1. of a trial. 2. for the purpose of trying, testing, etc.

**trial and error**, the process of making repeated trials, tests, etc. to find a desired result.

**trial balloon**, an action, statement, etc. intended to test public opinion on an issue.

**tri·an·gle** (trī'aŋ'g'l), *n.* [see TRI- & ANGLE], 1. a plane figure having three angles and three sides. 2. any three-sided or three-cornered object. 3. a group of three involved in some situation: as, a love *triangle*. —**tri·an'gu·lar** (-gyoo-lẽr), *adj.*

**tri·an'gu·late'** (-gyoo-lāt'), *v.t.* [-LATED, -LATING], to divide into triangles, as in surveying. —**tri·an'gu·la'tion**, *n.*

**tribe** (trīb), *n.* [< L. *tribus*], 1. a group of persons or clans descended from a common ancestor and, often, under common leadership. 2. any group or class of animals, plants, etc. —**trib'al**, *adj.* —**tribes'man**, *n.*

**trib·u·la·tion** (trib'yoo-lā'shən), *n.* [< L. *tribulare*, thrash], great misery or distress, or the cause of it.

**tri·bu·nal** (tri-bū'n'l, trī-), *n.* [see TRIBUNE], 1. a seat for a judge in a court. 2. a court of justice.

**trib·une** (trib'ūn, tri-būn'), *n.* [< L. *tribus*, tribe], 1. in ancient Rome, a magistrate appointed to protect the rights of plebians. 2. a champion of the people.

**trib·u·tar·y** (trib'yoo-ter'i), *adj.* 1. paying tribute. 2. subject: as, a *tributary* nation. 3. making additions: as, *tributary* streams. *n.* [*pl.* -IES], 1. a tributary nation. 2. a river that flows into a larger one.

**trib·ute** (trib'ūt), *n.* [< L. *tribuere*, allot], 1. money paid regularly by one nation to another as acknowledgment of subjugation, for protection, etc. 2. any forced payment or levy. 3. a gift, etc. that shows gratitude, respect, or honor. 4. praise.

**tri·chi·na** (tri-kī'nə), *n.* [*pl.* -NAE (-nē)], [< Gr. *trichinos*, hairy], a very small worm whose larvae cause trichinosis.

**trich·i·no·sis** (trik'ə-nō'sis), *n.* a disease caused by trichinae in the intestines and muscle tissues, usually acquired from eating insufficiently cooked pork.

**trick** (trik), *n.* [< OFr. *trichier*, *v.*], 1. something designed to deceive, swindle, etc. 2. a practical joke; prank. 3. *a*) a clever act intended to amuse. *b*) any feat requiring skill. 4. a personal mannerism. 5. a round of duty; shift. 6. in *card games*, the cards played in a single round. *v.t.* to deceive or cheat. —**do** (or **turn**) **the trick**, to produce the desired result. —**trick'er·y** [*pl.* -IES], *n.*

**trick·le** (trik''l), *v.i.* [-LED, -LING], [prob. < ME. *striken*, to strike], 1. to flow slowly in a thin stream or fall in drops. 2. to move slowly: as, the crowd *trickled* away. *n.* a slow flow or drip. —**trick'ling·ly**, *adv.*

**trick'y**, *adj.* [-IER, -IEST], 1. given to or characterized by trickery. 2. like a trick; intricate; catchy. —**trick'i·ness**, *n.*

**tri·col·or** (trī'kul'ẽr), *n.* a flag having three colors in large areas; esp., the flag of France.

**tri·cy·cle** (trī'si-k'l), *n.* [Fr.], a three-wheeled vehicle operated by pedals.

**tri·dent** (trī'd'nt), *n.* [< L. *tri-*, three + *dens*, tooth], a three-pronged spear. *adj.* three-pronged.

**tried** (trīd), pt. and pp. of **try**. *adj.* 1. tested; proved. 2. trustworthy.

**tri·fle** (trī'f'l), *n.* [< OFr. *truffe*, mockery], 1. something of little value or importance. 2. a small amount or sum. *v.i.* [-FLED, -FLING], 1. to talk or act jokingly. 2. to play or toy (*with*). *v.t.* to spend idly; waste (time, etc.). —**tri'fler**, *n.*

**tri'fling**, *adj.* 1. frivolous; shallow. 2. of little importance; trivial.

**trig** (trig), *adj.* [< ON. *trygar*, true], 1. trim; neat. 2. strong; sound.

**trig·ger** (trig'ẽr), *n.* [< D. *trekken*, pull], a lever pulled to release a catch, etc., esp. one releasing the firing hammer on a firearm. *v.t.* [Colloq.], to initiate (an action).

**trig·o·nom·e·try** (trig'ə-nom'ə-tri), *n.* [< Gr. *trigōnon*, triangle + *-metria*, measurement], the branch of mathematics analyzing, and making calculations from, the relations between the sides and angles of triangles. —**trig'o·no·met'ric** (-nə-met'rik), *adj.*

**tri·lat·er·al** (trī-lat'ẽr-əl), *adj.* [< L. *tri-*, three + *latus*, side], having three sides.

**trill** (tril), *n.* [ult. echoic], 1. a rapid alternation of two musical tones a degree apart. 2. a warble. 3. a rapid vibration of the tongue or uvula. *v.t.* & *v.i.* to sound, speak, sing, or play with a trill.

**tril·lion** (tril'yən), *n.* 1. in the U.S. and France, a thousand billions. 2. in Great Britain and Germany, a million billions. —**tril'lionth**, *adj.* & *n.*

**tril·o·gy** (tril'ə-ji), *n.* [*pl.* -GIES], [see TRI- & -LOGY], a set of three related plays, novels, etc.

**trim** (trim), *v.t.* [TRIMMED, TRIMMING], [< AS. *trymian*, make firm], 1. to put in proper order; make neat or tidy: as, to *trim* hair. 2. to clip, lop, cut, etc. 3. to decorate, as a Christmas tree. 4. *a*) to balance (a ship) by shifting cargo, etc. *b*) to put (sails) in order for sailing. 5. [Colloq.], to beat, punish, defeat, cheat, etc. *v.i.* to adjust according to expediency. *n.* 1. order; arrangement. 2. good condition. 3. a trimming. 4. decorative parts or borders. *adj.* [TRIMMER, TRIMMEST], 1. orderly; neat. 2. well-proportioned. 3. in good condition.

**trim'ming**, *n.* 1. decoration; ornament. 2. *pl.* parts trimmed off.

**trin·i·ty** (trin'ə-ti), *n.* [*pl.* -TIES], [< L. *trinus*, triple], 1. a set of three. 2. [T-], in *Christian theology*, the union of Father, Son, and Holy Ghost in one Godhead.

**trink·et** (triŋ'kit), *n.* [< ME. *trenket*], 1. a small ornament, piece of jewelry, etc. 2. a trifle or toy.

**tri·o** (trē'ō), *n.* [*pl.* -os], [< L. *tres*, three], 1. a musical composition for three voices or three instruments. 2. the three performers of such a composition. 3. a set of three.

**trip** (trip), *v.i.* & *v.t.* [TRIPPED, TRIPPING], [prob. < MD. *trippen*], 1. to move or perform with light, rapid steps. 2. to stumble or cause to stumble, as by catching the foot. 3. to make or cause to make a mistake. 4. to release or run past (a spring, wheel, etc.). *n.* 1. a light, quick tread. 2. a journey, voyage, etc. 3. a stumble or a causing to stumble; slip. 4. a mistake. —**trip up**, to catch in a lie, error, etc. —**trip'per**, *n.*

**tri·par·tite** (trī-pär'tīt), *adj.* [< L. *tri-*, three + *partiri*, divide], 1. having three parts. 2. made between three parties, as an agreement.

**tripe** (trīp), *n.* [< Ar. *tharb*, entrails], 1. part of the stomach of an ox, etc. used as food. 2. [Slang], anything worthless, etc.

**trip'ham'mer**, *n.* a heavy, power-driven hammer, alternately raised and allowed to fall by a tripping device: also **trip hammer**.

**tri·ple** (trip''l), *adj.* [< L. *tri-*, three + *-plus*, -fold], 1. consisting of three; threefold. 2. three times as much or as many. *n.* 1. an amount three times as much or as many. 2. a group of three. 3. in *baseball*, a hit by which the batter reaches third base. *v.t.* [-PLED, -PLING], to make three times as much or as many. *v.i.* to be tripled.

**tri·plet** (trip'lit), *n.* 1. *pl.* three offspring born at a single birth. 2. any one of these. 3. a group of three musical notes to be played in the time of two of the same value.

**trip·li·cate** (trip'lə-kit; *for v.*, -kāt'), *adj.* [< L. *triplex*, threefold], 1. made in three identical copies. 2. threefold. *n.* one of three identical copies. *v.t.* [-CATED, -CATING], 1. to make three copies of. 2. to triple.

**tri·pod** (trī'pod), *n.* [< L. *tri-*, three + *pous*, a foot], 1. a three-legged caldron, stool, etc. 2. a three-legged support for a camera, etc.

**trip·tych** (trip'tik), *n.* [< Gr. *tri-*, three + *ptyx*, a fold], a set of three panels with pictures, carvings, etc., often hinged: used as an altarpiece.

**tri·sect** (trī-sekt'), *v.t.* [< *tri-* + L. *secare*, to cut], to cut or divide into three parts.

**trite** (trīt), *adj.* [TRITER, TRITEST], [< L. *terere*, wear out], worn out by constant use; stale. —**trite'ly**, *adv.* —**trite'ness**, *n.*

**Tri·ton** (trī't'n), *n.* in *Gr. myth.*, a sea god.

**trit·u·rate** (trich'ə-rāt'), *v.t.* [-RATED, -RATING], [< L. *terere*, rub], to grind to a powder. *n.* a triturated substance. —**trit'u·ra'tion**, *n.*

**tri·umph** (trī'əmf), *n.* [< Gr. *thriambos*, hymn to Bacchus], 1. a victory; success. 2. exultation or joy for a victory, etc. *v.i.* 1. to gain victory or success. 2. to rejoice over victory, etc. —**tri·um'phal** (-um'f'l), *adj.*

**tri·um'phant** (-um'fənt), *adj.* 1. successful; victorious. 2. rejoicing for victory; elated.

**tri·um·vir** (trī-um'vẽr), *n.* [*pl.* -VIRS, -VIRI (-vi-rī')], [< L. *trium virorum*, of three men], in ancient Rome, any of three administrators sharing authority. —**tri·um'vi·ral**, *adj.*

**tri·um·vi·rate** (trī-um'vẽr-it), *n.* government by a group of three men.

**triv·et** (triv'it), *n.* [< L. *tripes*, tripod], a three-legged stand for holding pots, kettles, etc. near a fire.

**triv·i·a** (triv'i-ə), *n.pl.* unimportant matters; trivialities; trifles.

**triv·i·al** (triv'i-əl), *adj.* [< L. *trivialis*, commonplace], unimportant; insignificant. —**triv'i·al'i·ty** (-al'ə-ti) [*pl.* -TIES], *n.*

**-trix**, [*pl.* -TRIXES, -TRICES], [L.], an ending of some feminine nouns of agent, as in *aviatrix*.

**tro·che** (trō'ki), *n.* [< Gr. *trochos*, a wheel], a small medicinal lozenge.

**tro·chee** (trō'kē), *n.* [< Gr. *trechein*, run], a metrical foot of an accented syllable followed by an unaccented one. —**tro·cha'ic** (-kā'ik), *adj.*

**trod** (trod), pt. and alt. pp. of **tread**.

**trod·den** (trod''n), pp. of **tread**.

**trog·lo·dyte** (trog'lə-dīt'), *n.* [< Gr. *trōglē*, cave + *dyein*, enter], 1. a cave dweller. 2. a hermit.

**Tro·jan** (trō'jən), *adj.* of Troy, its people, etc. *n.* 1. a native or inhabitant of Troy. 2. a person of energy and determination.

**Trojan horse**, in *Gr. legend*, a huge, hollow wooden horse filled with Greek soldiers: it was taken into Troy as an ostensible gift, thus leading to the destruction of the city.

**Trojan War**, in *Gr. legend*, the war waged against Troy by the Greeks in order to get back Helen.

**troll** (trōl), *v.t. & v.i.* [< MHG. *trollen*, take short steps], 1. to sing the parts of (a round, etc.) in succession. 2. to sing in a full voice. 3. to fish with a moving line. *n.* 1. a round (song). 2. a lure and line used in trolling.

**troll** (trōl), *n.* [ON., wanderer], in *Scand. folklore*, a supernatural being, as a giant or dwarf, living underground or in caves.

**trol·ley** (trol'i), *n.* [*pl.* -LEYS], [< *troll*, *v.*], 1. a wheeled basket, etc. that runs suspended from an overhead track. 2. a small wheel at the end of a pole, that transmits electric current from an overhead wire to a streetcar, etc. 3. a trolley car.

**trolley bus** (or **car**), an electric bus (or streetcar) powered from an overhead wire by means of a trolley.

**trol·lop** (trol'əp), *n.* [Scot. < ME. *trollen*, to troll], 1. an untidy woman. 2. a prostitute.

**trom·bone** (trom'bōn), *n.* [< It. *tromba*, a trumpet], a large brass-wind instrument, usually with a slide, or movable section. (also **slide trombone**). —**trom'bon·ist**, *n.*

**troop** (trōōp), *n.* [< LL. *troppus*, a flock], 1. a group of persons or animals. 2. *usually pl.* a body of soldiers. 3. a subdivision of a cavalry regiment. 4. a unit of boy scouts or girl scouts. *v.i.* 1. to gather or go as in troops. 2. to walk, go, etc.

**troop'er**, *n.* [*troop* + *-er*], 1. a cavalryman. 2. a mounted policeman.

**troop'ship'**, *n.* a ship used for carrying troops; transport.

**tro·phy** (trō'fi), *n.* [*pl.* -PHIES], [< Gr. *tropaion*], a memorial of victory in war, sports competition, etc.; prize.

**trop·ic** (trop'ik), *n.* [< Gr. *tropikos*, marking a turn (of the sun at the solstices)], 1. either of two parallels of latitude, one, the **Tropic of Cancer**, 23°27′ north of the equator, and the other, the **Tropic of Capricorn**, 23°27′ south. 2. [also T-], *pl.* the region between these parallels. *adj.* of the tropics; tropical.

**trop'i·cal** (-i-k'l), *adj.* 1. of, in, or characteristic of the tropics. 2. very hot; sultry.

**tro·pism** (trō'piz'm), *n.* [< Gr. *tropē*, a turn], the tendency of a plant or animal to move or turn in response to an external stimulus, as light.

**trot** (trot), *v.i. & v.t.* [TROTTED, TROTTING], [< OHG. *trottōn*, to tread], 1. to go, ride, etc. at a trot. 2. to hurry; run. *n.* 1. a gait of a horse, etc. in which the legs are lifted in alternating diagonal pairs. 2. a jogging gait of a person. —**trot'ter**, *n.*

**troth** (trôth, trōth), *n.* [AS. *treowth*], [Archaic], 1. faithfulness; loyalty. 2. truth. 3. betrothal. *v.t.* [Archaic], to pledge.

**trou·ba·dour** (trōō'bə-dôr'), *n.* [Fr. < Pr. *trobar*, to compose in verse], any of a class of late-medieval lyric poets of S France and N Italy.

**trou·ble** (trub''l), *v.t.* [-BLED, -BLING], [< L. *turba*, tumult], 1. to disturb or agitate. 2. to worry; harass. 3. to cause inconvenience to: as, may I *trouble* you to move? *v.i.* to take pains; bother: as, don't *trouble* about a reply. *n.* 1. a state of mental distress; worry. 2. a misfortune; calamity. 3. a person, event, etc. causing annoyance, distress, etc. 4. public disturbance. 5. effort; pains: as, take the *trouble* to listen.

**trou'ble-shoot'er,** *n.* one employed to locate and correct sources of trouble in any flow of work: also **trouble shooter.**
**trou'ble·some** (-səm), *adj.* characterized by or causing trouble.
**trough** (trôf), *n.* [AS. *trog*], 1. a long, narrow, open container for holding water or food for animals. 2. any similarly shaped vessel, as a gutter for carrying off rain water. 3. a long, narrow hollow, as between waves.
**trounce** (trouns), *v.t.* [TROUNCED, TROUNCING], [<?], 1. to beat; flog. 2. [Colloq.], to defeat.
**troupe** (trōōp), *n.* [Fr.], a troop, esp. of actors, singers, etc. —**troup'er,** *n.*
**trou·sers** (trou'zẽrz), *n.pl.* [< Ir. *triubhas*], a two-legged outer garment, esp. for men and boys, reaching from the waist to the ankles.
**trous·seau** (trōō-sō'), *n.* [*pl.* -SEAUX, -SEAUS (-sōz')], [< Fr., small bundle], a bride's outfit of clothes, linen, etc.
**trout** (trout), *n.* [*pl.* TROUT, TROUTS], [< Gr. *trōgein*, gnaw], any of various food and game fishes of the salmon family, found chiefly in fresh water.
**trow** (trō, trou), *v.i. & v.t.* [< AS. *treowa*, faith], [Archaic], to think.
**trow·el** (trou'əl), *n.* [< L. *trua*, ladle], 1. a flat tool for smoothing plaster or applying mortar. 2. a pointed, scooplike tool for loosening soil, digging holes, etc.
**troy** (troi), *adj.* by troy weight.
**troy weight,** [< *Troyes*, a city in France], a system of weights for gold, silver, gems, etc.
**tru·ant** (trōō'ənt), *n.* [OFr., a beggar], 1. a pupil who stays away from school without permission. 2. one who shirks his duties. *adj.* 1. that is a truant. 2. errant; straying. —**tru'an·cy** [*pl.* -CIES], *n.*
**truce** (trōōs), *n.* [< AS. *treowa*, faith], 1. a temporary cessation of warfare by agreement between the belligerents. 2. respite from trouble, pain, etc. —**truce'less,** *adj.*
**truck** (truk), *n.* [prob. < Gr. *trochos*, wheel], 1. a vehicle for carrying heavy articles; esp., an automotive vehicle for hauling loads along highways, etc. 2. a swiveling frame, with two or more pairs of wheels, under each end of a railroad car, etc. *v.t.* to carry on a truck. *v.i.* to drive a truck.
**truck** (truk), *v.t. & v.i.* [Fr. *troquer*], to exchange; barter. *n.* 1. small articles of little value. 2. vegetables raised for market. 3. [Colloq.], dealings. 4. [Colloq.], rubbish.
**truck'er,** *n.* a person or company engaged in trucking: also **truck'man.**
**truck farm,** a farm where vegetables are grown to be marketed. —**truck farmer.**
**truck'ing,** *n.* the business of transporting goods by truck.
**truck·le** (truk''l), *n.* [< Gr. *trochos*, wheel], a low bed on wheels (in full, **truckle bed**), that can be rolled under another bed when not in use. *v.i.* [-LED, -LING], to be servile; toady (with *to*). —**truck'ler,** *n.*
**truc·u·lent** (truk'yoo-lənt, trōō'kyoo-), *adj.* [< L. *trux*], fierce; savage; cruel. —**truc'u·lence, truc'u·len·cy,** *n.*
**trudge** (truj), *v.i.* [TRUDGED, TRUDGING], [prob. < AS.], to walk, esp. wearily or laboriously. —**trudg'er,** *n.*
**true** (trōō), *adj.* [TRUER, TRUEST], [AS. *treowe*], 1. faithful; loyal. 2. in accordance with fact; not false. 3. truthful. 4. conforming to a standard, etc.; exact; accurate. 5. rightful; lawful. 6. accurately fitted, shaped, etc. 7. real; genuine. *adv.* truly. *v.t.* [TRUED, TRUING or TRUEING], to make true; esp., to fit, shape, etc. accurately. *n.* that which is true (with *the*).
**true'-blue',** *adj.* very loyal; stanch.
**truf·fle** (truf''l), *n.* [< L. *tuber*, knob], a fleshy, edible, underground fungus.

**tru·ism** (trōō'iz'm), *n.* a statement the truth of which is obvious and well known.
**tru'ly,** *adv.* 1. in a true manner; accurately, genuinely, etc. 2. in fact; really.
**trump** (trump), *n.* [< *triumph*], 1. any playing card of a suit ranked higher than any other suit for a given hand. 2. such a suit. *v.t. & v.i.* to take (a trick, etc.) by playing a trump. —**trump up,** to devise deceitfully.
**trump·er·y** (trum'pẽr-i), *n.* [*pl.* -IES], [< Fr. *tromper*, deceive], something showy but worthless. *adj.* showy but worthless.
**trum·pet** (trum'pit), *n.* [< OFr. *trompe*], 1. a brass-wind instrument consisting of a looped tube ending in a flared bell. 2. a trumpetlike device for channeling sound, as a hearing aid. 3. a sound like that of a trumpet. *v.i.* to make a sound like a trumpet. *v.t.* to proclaim loudly. —**trum'pet·er,** *n.*
**trun·cate** (truŋ'kāt), *v.t.* [-CATED, -CATING], [< L. *truncus*, stem], to cut off a part of; lop.
**trun·cheon** (trun'chən), *n.* [< L. *truncus*, stem], a policeman's club.
**trun·dle** (trun'd'l), *v.t. & v.i.* [-DLED, -DLING], [< AS. *trendan*, to roll], 1. to roll along. 2. to rotate. —**trun'dler,** *n.*
**trunk** (truŋk), *n.* [< L. *truncus*], 1. the main stem of a tree. 2. a human or animal body, not including the head and limbs. 3. a long snout, as of an elephant. 4. a large, reinforced box to hold clothes, etc. in travel. 5. *pl.* very short breeches worn as for athletics. *adj.* designating or of a main line of a railroad, telephone system, etc.
**truss** (trus), *v.t.* [< OFr. *trousser*], 1. originally, to bundle. 2. to tie, fasten, or tighten. 3. to support or strengthen with a truss (*n.* 2). *n.* 1. a bundle or pack. 2. a framework for supporting a roof, bridge, etc. 3. a padded device for giving support in cases of hernia.
**trust** (trust), *n.* [< ON. *traust*], 1. firm belief in the honesty, reliability, etc. of another; faith. 2. the one trusted. 3. confident expectation, hope, etc. 4. the responsibility resulting from confidence placed in one. 5. care; custody. 6. something entrusted to one. 7. credit (*n.* 9). 8. a combination of corporations organized to establish a monopoly. 9. in *law*, *a*) the fact of having nominal ownership of property to keep, use, or administer for another. *b*) such property. *v.i.* to be confident. *v.t.* 1. to have confidence in. 2. to commit (something) (*to* another's care). 3. to allow to do something without misgivings. 4. to believe. 5. to hope; expect. 6. to give business credit to. *adj.* 1. relating to a trust. 2. acting as trustee. —**in trust,** entrusted to another's care.
**trus·tee** (trus-tē'), *n.* 1. one to whom another's property or its management is entrusted. 2. a member of a board controlling a college, hospital, etc. —**trus·tee'ship,** *n.*
**trust'ful,** *adj.* full of trust; ready to confide.
**trust'ing,** *adj.* trustful. —**trust'ing·ly,** *adv.*
**trust territory,** a region placed by the UN under the administrative authority of a country.
**trust'wor'thy,** *adj.* worthy of trust; reliable.
**trust·y** (trus'ti), *adj.* [-IER, -IEST], dependable; trustworthy. *n.* [*pl.* -IES], a convict granted special privileges because of good behavior. —**trust'i·ness,** *n.*
**truth** (trōōth), *n.* [*pl.* TRUTHS (trōōthz, trōōths)], [AS. *treowth*], 1. a being true; specif., *a*) sincerity; honesty. *b*) conformity with fact. *c*) reality; actual existence. *d*) agreement with a standard, etc.; correctness. 2. that which is true. 3. an established fact, etc. —**in truth,** truly; in fact.
**truth'ful,** *adj.* 1. telling the truth; honest. 2. corresponding with fact or reality.

**try** (trī), *v.t.* [TRIED, TRYING], [OFr. *trier*], 1. to melt out or render, as fat. 2. to conduct the trial of in a law court. 3. to put to the proof; test. 4. to subject to trials, etc.; afflict. 5. to experiment with: as, *try* this recipe. 6. to attempt; endeavor. *v.i.* to make an effort, attempt, etc. *n.* [*pl.* TRIES], an attempt; effort; trial.
**try'ing,** *adj.* that tries; vexing; annoying.
**try'out',** *n.* [Colloq.], a test to determine fitness or qualifications.
**tryst** (trist), *n.* [< OFr. *tristre*, hunting station], 1. an appointment to meet, esp. one made by lovers. 2. an appointed meeting or meeting place: also **trysting place.**
**tsar** (tsär), *n.* a czar. —**tsa·ri·na** (tsä-rē'nə), *n.fem.*
**tset·se** (tset'si), *n.* [< native name], a small fly of central and S Africa: one kind is a carrier of sleeping sickness: also **tsetse fly.**
**T'-shirt',** *n.* a collarless pull-over shirt with very short sleeves.
**tsp.,** teaspoon; teaspoons.
**T square,** a T-shaped ruler for drawing parallel lines.
**Tu.,** Tuesday.
**tub** (tub), *n.* [< MD. *tubbe*], 1. a round, open wooden container, usually with staves and hoops. 2. any large, open container of metal, etc. 3. a bathtub. 4. [Brit. Colloq.], a bath in a tub.
**tu·ba** (to͞o'bə, tū'-), *n.* [*pl.* -BAS, -BAE (-bē)], [L., a trumpet], a large, deep-toned, brass-wind instrument.
**tub'by,** *adj.* [-BIER, -BIEST], 1. shaped like a tub. 2. short and fat. —**tub'bi·ness,** *n.*
**tube** (to͞ob, tūb), *n.* [< L. *tubus*, pipe], 1. a slender, hollow pipe of metal, glass, etc., for conveying fluids. 2. a tubelike container, as for holding toothpaste. 3. a tubelike part, organ, etc. 4. a vacuum tube. 5. a subway.
**tu·ber** (to͞o'bẽr, tū'-), *n.* [L., lit,. a swelling], a short, thickened, fleshy part of an underground stem, as a potato. —**tu'ber·ous,** *adj.*
**tu'ber·cle** (-k'l), *n.* [see TUBER], 1. a small, rounded projection, as on a bone or a plant root. 2. any abnormal hard nodule or swelling: esp., the lesion of tuberculosis.
**tu·ber·cu·lar** (to͞o-bũr'kyoo-lẽr, tū-), *adj.* 1. of, like, or having tubercles. 2. having tuberculosis. *n.* one having tuberculosis.
**tu·ber'cu·lin** (-lin), *n.* a solution injected into the skin as a test for tuberculosis.
**tu·ber'cu·lo'sis** (-lō'sis), *n.* [see TUBERCLE + -OSIS], an infectious disease characterized by the formation of tubercles in body tissues; esp., tuberculosis of the lungs; consumption. —**tu·ber'cu·lous,** *adj.*
**tube·rose** (to͞ob'rōz', tūb'-), *n.* [see TUBER], a plant with a bulblike root and sweet, white, funnel-shaped flowers.
**tub·ing** (to͞ob'iŋ, tūb'-), *n.* 1. a series or system of tubes. 2. tubes collectively. 3. material in the form of a tube.
**tu·bu·lar** (to͞o'byoo-lẽr, tū'-), *adj.* [< L. *tubus*, pipe], 1. of or like a tube or tubes. 2. made with tubes. —**tu'bu·lar·ly,** *adv.*
**tuck** (tuk), *v.t.* [< MD. *tucken*], 1. to pull (*up*) or gather (*up*) in a fold or folds. 2. to thrust the edges of (a sheet, etc.) under or in, in order to make secure. 3. to press snugly into a small space. 4. to make tucks in (a garment). *n.* a sewed fold.
**tuck'er,** *v.t.* [prob. < *tuck*], [Colloq.], to tire; weary (usually with *out*).
**-tude,** [< L. *-tudo*], a suffix corresponding to *-ness*, as in *certitude*.
**Tues·day** (to͞oz'di, tūz'-), *n.* [AS. *Tiwes daeg*, day of the god of war *Tiw*], the third day of the week.
**tuft** (tuft), *n.* [< OFr. *tuffe*], 1. a bunch of hairs, grass, etc. growing or tied closely together. 2. any cluster, as of trees. *v.t.* 1. to provide with tufts. 2. to secure the padding of (a mattress, etc.) by tufts of thread.
**tug** (tug), *v.i.* & *v.t.* [TUGGED, TUGGING], [prob. < ON. *toga*, to draw], 1. to pull with great force; drag. 2. to tow with a tugboat. *n.* 1. a hard pull. 2. a great effort. 3. a tugboat.
**tug'boat',** *n.* a small, sturdy boat for towing or pushing ships, etc.
**tug of war,** a contest in which two teams pull at opposite ends of a rope.
**tu·i·tion** (to͞o-ish'ən, tū-), *n.* [< L. *tueri*, protect], 1. instruction. 2. the charge for instruction. —**tu·i'tion·al, tu·i'tion·ar'y,** *adj.*
**tu·la·re·mi·a, tu·la·rae·mi·a** (to͞o-lə-rē'mi-ə), *n.* [< *Tulare* County, Calif.], an infectious disease of rabbits, etc., sometimes transmitted to man.
**tu·lip** (to͞o'lip, tū'-), *n* [< Turk. *dülbend*, turban: from its shape], 1. a bulb plant with a cup-shaped flower. 2. the flower.
**tulle** (to͞ol; Fr. töl), *n.* [< *Tulle*, city in France], a fine silk, rayon, or nylon netting used for veils, etc.
**tum·ble** (tum'b'l), *v.i.* [-BLED, -BLING], [< AS. *tumbian*, to jump], 1. to do somersaults or other acrobatic feats. 2. to fall suddenly or helplessly. 3. to toss or roll about. 4. to move in a hasty, disorderly manner. *v.t.* 1. to cause to tumble. 2. to disorder; disarrange. *n.* 1. a fall. 2. disorder.
**tum'ble-down',** *adj.* dilapidated.
**tum'bler** (-blẽr), *n.* 1. one who tumbles (*v.i.* 1); acrobat. 2. a drinking glass. 3. a part of a lock whose position must be changed by a key in order to release the bolt.
**tum'ble·weed',** *n.* a plant which breaks off near the ground in autumn and is blown about by the wind.
**tum·brel, tum·bril** (tum'brəl), *n.* [< OFr. *tomber*, to fall], a cart, esp. one that may be tilted for emptying.
**tu·mid** (to͞o'mid, tū'-), *adj* [< L. *tumere*, to swell], 1. swollen; bulging. 2. inflated; pompous. —**tu·mid'i·ty,** *n.*
**tum·my** (tum'i), *n.* [*pl.* -MIES], stomach: a child's word.
**tu·mor** (to͞o'mẽr, tū'-), *n.* [< L. *tumere*, to swell], a swelling on the body; esp., an abnormal growth of new tissue, independent of its surrounding structures: Brit. spelling **tumour.** —**tu'mor·ous,** *adj.*
**tu·mult** (to͞o'mult, tū'-), *n.* [< L. *tumere*, to swell], 1. noisy commotion; uproar. 2. confusion; agitation.
**tu·mul'tu·ous** (-mul'cho͞o-əs), *adj.* full of tumult, uproar, agitation, etc.
**tun** (tun), *n.* [AS. *tunne*], a large cask.
**tu·na** (to͞o'nə), *n.* [*pl.* -NA, -NAS], [Am. Sp.], a tunny: also **tuna fish.**
**tun·dra** (tun'drə), *n.* [Russ.], any of the vast, nearly level, treeless arctic plains.
**tune** (to͞on, tūn), *n.* [see TONE], 1. a rhythmical succession of musical tones; melody. 2. proper musical pitch: as, he's out of *tune*. 3. agreement; concord. *v.t.* [TUNED, TUNING], 1. to adjust (a musical instrument) to some standard of pitch. 2. to adapt to some condition, mood, etc. —**tune in (on),** to adjust a radio receiver so as to receive (a station, etc.). —**tun'er,** *n.*
**tune'ful,** *adj.* 1. full of music or melody; melodious. 2. producing musical sounds.
**tune'-up',** *n.* an adjusting, as of a motor, to the proper condition.
**tung·sten** (tuŋ'stən), *n.* [Sw. < *tung*, heavy + *sten*, stone], a hard, heavy, metallic chemical element, used in steel, etc.: symbol, W: also called *wolfram*.
**tu·nic** (to͞o'nik, tū'-), *n.* [< L. *tunica*], 1. a loose, gownlike garment worn by men and women in ancient Greece and Rome. 2. a blouselike garment extending to the hips, usually belted.

**tun·nel** (tun′'l), ***n.*** [< Fr. *tonnelle*, vault], 1. an underground passageway, as for autos, etc. 2. any tunnellike passage, as in a mine. ***v.t.* & *v.i.*** [-NELED or NELLED, -NELING or -NELLING], to make a tunnel (through or under). **—tun′nel·er, tun′nel·ler, *n.***

**tun·ny** (tun′i), ***n.*** [< Gr. *thynnos*], a large, edible sea fish of the mackerel group, with coarse, oily flesh; tuna.

**tur·ban** (tũr′bən), ***n.*** [< Ar. & Per. *dul*, a turn + *band*, a band], 1. a Moslem headdress, consisting of a cap with a scarf wound round it. 2. a similar headdress consisting of a scarf wound round the head.

**tur·bid** (tũr′bid), ***adj.*** [< L. *turba*, a crowd], 1. having the sediment stirred up; muddy. 2. thick, dense, or dark, as clouds. 3. confused. **—tur′bid·ly, *adv.***

**tur·bine** (tũr′bin, -bīn), ***n.*** [< L. *turbo*, whirl], an engine driven by the pressure of steam, water, or air against the curved vanes of a wheel.

**tur·bo·jet (engine)** (tũr′bō-jet′), in *aeronautics*, a jet engine in which the energy of the jet operates a turbine which drives the air compressor.

**tur′bo·prop′ (engine)** (-prop′), in *aeronautics*, a jet engine in which the energy of the jet operates a turbine which drives the propeller.

**tur·bot** (tũr′bət), ***n.*** [*pl.* -BOT, -BOTS], [< OFr. *tourbout*], a large, edible European flatfish.

**tur·bu·lent** (tũr′byoo-lənt), ***adj.*** [see TURBID], 1. causing disturbance; disorderly. 2. disturbed; agitated. **—tur′bu·lence, *n.***

**tu·reen** (too-rēn′), ***n.*** [< Fr. *terrine*, earthen vessel], a large, deep dish with a lid, for serving soup, etc.

**turf** (tũrf), ***n.*** [AS.], 1. a surface layer of earth containing grass plants with their matted roots; sod. 2. a piece of this. 3. peat. ***v.t.*** to cover with turf. **—the turf,** 1. a track for horse racing. 2. horse racing.

**tur·gid** (tũr′jid), ***adj.*** [< L. *turgere*, to swell], 1. swollen; bloated. 2. bombastic; pompous. **—tur·gid′i·ty, tur′gid·ness, *n.***

**Turk** (tũrk), ***n.*** a native of Turkey.

**Turk.,** 1. Turkey. 2. Turkish.

**tur·key** (tũr′ki), ***n.*** [< similarity to a fowl formerly imported through Turkey], 1. a large North American bird with a small head and spreading tail. 2. its flesh, used as food.

**turkey buzzard,** a dark-colored vulture of the Southwest and S. America.

**Tur·ki** (toor′kē), ***adj.*** designating or of a group of Asiatic languages, including Turkish. ***n.*** the Turki languages.

**Turk·ish** (tũr′kish), ***adj.*** of Turkey, the Turks, etc. ***n.*** the language of Turkey.

**Turkish bath,** a bath with steam rooms, showers, massage, etc.

**tur·mer·ic** (tũr′mẽr-ik), ***n.*** [< ML. *terra merita*, deserving earth], an East Indian plant whose powdered root is used as a yellow dye, seasoning, etc.

**tur·moil** (tũr′moil), ***n.*** [< OFr. *trumel*], tumult; commotion; confusion.

**turn** (tũrn), ***v.t.*** [ult. < Gr. *tornos*, lathe], 1. to rotate (a wheel, etc.). 2. to move around or partly around: as, *turn* the key. 3. to give form to, as in a lathe. 4. to change the position or direction of. 5. to ponder (*over*). 6. to reverse: as, to *turn* pages. 7. to upset (the stomach). 8. to divert; avert: as, to *turn* a blow. 9. to cause to change one's actions, beliefs, aims, etc. 10. to pass (a certain age, amount, etc.). 11. to repel, as an attack. 12. to drive, set, let go, etc.: as, to *turn* loose. 13. to direct, point, aim, etc. 14. to change: as, to *turn* cream into butter. 15. to make sour. 16. to affect in some way: as, it *turns* her sick. ***v.i.*** 1. to rotate; revolve; pivot. 2. to move around or partly around. 3. to reel; whirl: has, my ead is *turning*. 4. to become curved or bent. 5. to become upset, as the stomach. 6. to change or reverse course, direction, etc., or one's feelings, allegiance, etc. 7. to direct or shift one's attention, skills, etc.: as, he *turned* to music. 8. to become: as, the milk *turned* sour. 9. to change to another form: as, the rain *turned* to snow. 10. to become rancid, sour, etc. ***n.*** 1. a turning around; rotation; revolution. 2. a single twist, winding, etc. 3. a change or reversal of course or direction. 4. a short walk, ride, etc., as for exercise. 5. a bend; curve: as, a *turn* in a road. 6. a change in trend, events, etc. 7. a turning point. 8. an action or deed: as, a good *turn*. 9. a bout; spell; try; chance: as, it's my *turn* to go. 10. a distinctive form, detail, etc.: as, a quaint *turn* to her speech. 11. natural inclination. 12. [Colloq.], a momentary shock, as from fright. **—in** (or **out of**) **turn,** (not) in proper sequence. **—turn down,** to reject (a request, etc.). **—turn in,** 1. to deliver; hand in. 2. [Colloq.], to go to bed. **—turn off,** 1. to shut off. 2. to put out (a light). **—turn on,** 1. to start the flow of; open. 2. to cause (a light) to go on. 3. to attack suddenly. 4. to depend on. **—turn out,** 1. to shut off. 2. to put out (a light). 3. to put outside. 4. to dismiss. 5. to come or go out: as, to *turn out* for a picnic. 6. to produce. 7. to result. 8. to prove to be. 9. to become. **—turn to,** 1. to refer to. 2. to rely on.

**turn′a·bout′,** ***n.*** a shift or reversal of position, allegiance, opinion, etc.

**turn′buck′le** (-buk′'l), ***n.*** a coupling for lengths of rod or wire, consisting of a metal loop with opposite internal threads at each end or with a swivel at one end.

**turn′coat′,** ***n.*** a renegade.

**turn′ing,** ***n.*** 1. a revolving, winding, inverting, etc. 2. a place where a road, etc. turns.

**turning point,** a point in time at which a decisive change occurs; crisis.

**tur·nip** (tũr′nip), ***n.*** [prob. < Fr. *tour*, round + ME. *nepe*, turnip], 1. a plant of the mustard family with a roundish, light-colored, edible root. 2. the root.

**turn′key′,** ***n.*** [*pl.* -KEYS], a jailer.

**turn′out′, turn′-out′,** ***n.*** 1. a turning out. 2. a gathering of people, as at a meeting. 3. output. 4. equipment; outfit.

**turn′o′ver,** ***n.*** 1. a turning over; upset. 2. a small pie with one half of the crust folded back over the other. 3. *a*) the selling out and replenishing of a stock of goods. *b*) the amount of business done during a given period. 4. rate of replacment of workers.

**turn′pike′** (-pīk′), ***n.*** [ME. *turnpyke*, a spiked road barrier], 1. a tollgate. 2. a road with tollgates. 3. loosely, any highway.

**turn′stile′** (-stīl′), ***n.*** a device, as a post with revolving bars, placed in an entrance to allow the passage of persons one at a time.

**turn′ta′ble,** ***n.*** a circular revolving platform, as in a roundhouse, or of a phonograph.

**tur·pen·tine** (tũr′pən-tīn′), ***n.*** [< Gr. *terebinthos*, tree yielding this substance], a light-colored, volatile oil distilled from various coniferous trees: used in paints, etc.

**tur·pi·tude** (tũr′pə-tōōd′, -tūd′), ***n.*** [< L. *turpis*, vile], baseness; vileness.

**tur·quoise** (tũr′koiz, -kwoiz), [illegible] [< OFr. *turqueis*, Turkish], a greenish-blue semi-precious stone, or its color. ***adj.*** greenish-blue.

**tur·ret** (tũr′it), ***n.*** [see TOWER], 1. a small tower projecting from a building, usually at a corner. 2. an armored, usually revolving, structure for guns, as on a warship, tank, etc. 3. a rotating attachment for a lathe, etc., holding several cutting tools for successive use.

**tur·tle** (tũr′t'l), *n.* [< Fr. *tortue* or Sp. *tortuga*, tortoise], any of various land and water reptiles having a soft body encased in a hard shell. —**turn turtle,** to turn upside down.
**tur′tle·dove′,** *n.* [< L. *turtur*; echoic], a wild dove noted for its mournful call.
**turtle neck,** a high, turned-down collar that fits snugly about the neck.
**tusk** (tusk), *n.* [AS. *tucs*], a long, pointed, projecting tooth, as of the elephant.
**tus·sle** (tus′'l), *n.* & *v.i.* [-SLED, -SLING], [< ME. *tusen* (in comp.), to pull], struggle; wrestle.
**tut** (tut), *interj.* an exclamation of impatience, annoyance, contempt, etc.
**tu·te·lage** (tōō′t'l-ij, tū′-), *n.* [< L. *tutela*, protection], 1. guardianship; care, protection, etc. 2. instruction. —**tu′te·lar′y** (-er′i), **tu′te·lar,** *adj.*
**tu·tor** (tōō′tẽr, tū′-), *n.* [< L. *tueri*, to guard], a private teacher. *v.t.* & *v.i.* to act as a tutor (to); teach. —**tu·to′ri·al** (-tôr′i-əl), *adj.*
**tut·ti-frut·ti** (tōō′ti-frōō′ti), *n.* [It., all fruits], an ice cream, candy, etc. made or flavored with mixed fruits.
**tux** (tuks), *n.* [Colloq.], a tuxedo.
**tux·e·do** (tuk-sē′dō), *n.* [*pl.* -DOS], [< a country club near *Tuxedo* Lake, N.Y.], a man's semiformal suit with a tailless jacket.
**TV,** television.
**TVA,** Tennessee Valley Authority.
**twad·dle** (twäd′'l), *n.* [akin to *tattle*], foolish, empty talk or writing; nonsense. *v.t.* & *v.i.* [-DLED, -DLING], to talk or write foolishly.
**twain** (twān), *n.* & *adj.* [AS. *twegen*, two], [Archaic or Poetic], two.
**twang** (twaŋ), *n.* [echoic], 1. a sharp, vibrating sound, as of a plucked string. 2. a sharp, nasal speech sound. *v.i.* & *v.t.* 1. to make or cause to make a twang. 2. to utter with a twang. —**twang′y,** *adj.*
**'twas** (twuz, twäz; *unstressed* twəz), it was.
**twat·tle** (twät′'l), *n., v.i.* & *v.t.* [-TLED, -TLING], [< *tattle*], twaddle.
**tweak** (twēk), *v.t.* [AS. *twiccan*, to twitch], to seize and pull (the nose, ear, etc.) with a sudden jerk. *n.* a sudden, twisting pinch.
**tweed** (twēd), *n.* [< misreading of *tweel*, Scot. form of *twill*], 1. a rough wool fabric in a weave of two or more colors. 2. *pl.* clothes of tweed.
**twee·dle·dum and twee·dle·dee** (twē′d'l-dum′ 'n twē′d'l-dē′), two persons or things very much alike.
**'tween** (twēn), *prep.* [Poetic], between.
**tweet** (twēt), *n.* & *interj.* [echoic], the chirping sound of a small bird. *v.i.* to utter this sound.
**tweez·ers** (twēz′ẽrz), *n.pl.* [< obs. *tweeze*, set of instruments], small pincers for plucking out hairs, etc.: often **pair of tweezers.**
**twelfth** (twelfth), *adj.* [AS. *twelfta*], preceded by eleven others; 12th. *n.* 1. the one following the eleventh. 2. any of the twelve equal parts of something; 1/12.
**Twelfth′-night′,** *n.* the eve of Epiphany (**Twelfth-day**, as reckoned from Christmas).
**twelve** (twelv), *adj.* & *n.* [< AS. *twelf*], two more than ten; 12; XII.
**twen·ty** (twen′ti), *adj.* & *n.* [*pl.* -TIES], [AS. *twentig*], two times ten; 20; XX. —**the twenties,** the years from 20 through 29 (of a century or a person's age). —**twen′ti·eth** (-ith), *adj.* & *n.*
**'twere** (twũr), it were.
**twice** (twīs), *adv.* [AS. *twiga*], 1. two times. 2. in twofold amount.
**twid·dle** (twid′'l), *v.t.* & *v.i.* [-DLED, -DLING], [prob. < ON. *tvidla*, to stir], to twirl or play with (something) lightly. —**twiddle one's thumbs,** to be idle. —**twid′dler,** *n.*
**twig** (twig), *n.* [AS. *twigge*], a small branch of a tree or shrub.
**twi·light** (twī′līt′), *n.* [ME. < *twi-*, two + *light*], 1. the subdued light just after sunset or, sometimes, just before sunrise. 2. the period from sunset to dark. *adj.* of or like twilight.
**twill** (twil), *n.* [< AS. *twi-*, two; cf. DRILL (cloth)], a cloth woven with parallel diagonal lines. —**twilled,** *adj.*
**'twill** (twil), it will.
**twin** (twin), *adj.* [AS. *twinn*, double], 1. consisting of, or being one of a pair of, two identical things. 2. being a twin or twins. *n.* 1. either of two born at the same birth. 2. either of two persons or things very much alike.
**twine** (twīn), *n.* [AS. *twin*], strong thread, string, etc. of strands twisted together. *v.t.* & *v.i.* [TWINED, TWINING], 1. to twist together; interweave. 2. to wind around.
**twinge** (twinj), *v.t.* & *v.i.* [TWINGED, TWINGING], [AS. *twengan*, squeeze], to have or give a sudden, sharp pain, qualm, etc. *n.* such a pain, etc.
**twin·kle** (twiŋ′k'l), *v.i.* [-KLED, -KLING], [AS. *twinclian*], 1. to shine in rapid, intermittent gleams; sparkle. 2. to light up, as with amusement: said of the eyes. 3. to move rapidly to and fro, as dancers' feet. *v.t.* to cause to twinkle. *n.* 1. a glint in the eye. 2. a gleam. 3. an instant. —**twin′kler,** *n.*
**twirl** (twũrl), *v.t.* & *v.i.* [< ME. *trillen*, to turn], 1. to rotate rapidly; spin. 2. to whirl in a circle. 3. in *baseball*, to pitch. *n.* 1. a twirling. 2. a twist, coil, etc. —**twirl′er,** *n.*
**twist** (twist), *v.t.* [AS., rope], 1. to wind (strands, etc.) around one another. 2. to wind (rope, etc.) around something. 3. to give spiral shape to. 4. to subject to torsion. 5. to wrench; sprain. 6. to contort or distort. 7. to confuse. 8. to break (*off*) by turning the end. 9. to pervert the meaning of. 10. to revolve or rotate. *v.i.* 1. to undergo twisting. 2. to spiral, twine, etc. (*around* or *about*). 3. to revolve or rotate. 4. to turn to one side. 5. to wind, as a path. 6. to squirm; writhe. *n.* 1. a thread or cord of twisted strands. 2. something twisted, as a roll of tobacco. 3. a twisting or being twisted. 4. torsional stress. 5. a contortion. 6. a wrench or sprain. 7. a turn; bend. 8. a distorting of meaning.
**twist′er,** *n.* 1. a person or thing that twists. 2. a tornado or cyclone.
**twit** (twit), *v.t.* [TWITTED, TWITTING], [< AS. *æt*, at + *witan*, accuse], to reproach, taunt, etc. *n.* a taunt.
**twitch** (twich), *v.t.* & *v.i.* [< AS. *twiccian*, to pluck], to pull (at) or move with a quick, sudden jerk. *n.* 1. a twitching. 2. a sudden, quick motion, esp. a spasmodic one.
**twit·ter** (twit′ẽr), *v.i.* [ME. *twiteren*], 1. to chirp rapidly. 2. to tremble with excitement. 3. to titter. *n.* 1. a twittering. 2. a condition of tremulous excitement.
**two** (tōō), *adj.* & *n.* [AS. *twa*], one more than one; 2; II. —**in two,** in two parts.
**two bits,** [Slang], twenty-five cents. —**two′-bit′,** *adj.*
**two′-by-four′,** *n.* a piece of lumber two inches thick and four inches wide.
**two′-edged′,** *adj.* 1. that has two edges. 2. that can have a double meaning.
**two′-faced′,** *adj.* 1. having two faces. 2. deceitful; hypocritical.
**two′-fist′ed,** *adj.* [Colloq.], 1. able to use both fists. 2. vigorous; virile.
**two′fold′,** *adj.* 1. having two parts. 2. having twice as much or as many. *adv.* twice as much or as many.
**two′-hand′ed,** *adj.* 1. that needs to be used with both hands. 2. needing two people to operate, play, etc.
**two·pence** (tup′'ns), *n.* 1. two pence. 2. a British coin of this value.

**two'-piece'**, *adj.* consisting of two separate parts.
**two'-ply'**, *adj.* having two layers, strands, etc.
**two'some** (-səm), *n.* two people; couple.
**two'-step'**, *n.* a ballroom dance in 2/4 time.
**two'-time'**, *v.t.* [-TIMED, -TIMING], [Slang], to be unfaithful to. —**two'-tim'er**, *n.*
**two'-way'**, *adj.* allowing passage in either direction.
**-ty**, [< L. *-tas*], a suffix meaning *quality of, condition of.*
**ty·coon** (tī-ko͞on'), *n.* [< Japan. < Chin. *ta*, great + *kiun*, prince], [Colloq.], a wealthy and powerful industrialist, financier, etc.
**ty·ing** (tī'iŋ), ppr. of **tie.**
**tyke** (tīk), *n.* [< ON. *tik*, bitch], 1. a dog. 2. [Colloq.], a small child.
**tym·pa·ni** (tim'pə-ni), *n.pl.* timpani.
**tym·pa·num** (tim'pə-nəm), *n.* [*pl.* -NUMS, -NA (-nə)], [L., a drum], 1. the middle ear, a cavity connected to the external ear by the eardrum. 2. the eardrum. —**tym·pan'ic** (-pan'ik), *adj.*
**type** (tīp), *n.* [< Gr. *typos*, a mark], 1. the characteristic form, plan, style, etc. of a class or group. 2. a class, group, etc. with characteristics in common. 3. a person, animal, or thing representative of a class. 4. a perfect example; model. 5. *a*) a rectangular piece as of metal, with a raised letter, etc. in reverse on its upper end, used in printing. *b*) such pieces collectively. 6. a printed character or characters. *v.t.* [TYPED, TYPING], 1. to typify; represent. 2. to classify. 3. to typewrite. *v.i.* to typewrite.
**-type**, a combining form meaning: 1. *type, example*, as in *prototype*. 2. *stamp, print*, as in *daguerreotype*.
**type'set'ter**, *n.* 1. a person who sets type. 2. a machine for setting type.
**type'write'**, *v.t. & v.i.* [-WROTE, -WRITTEN, -WRITING], to write with a typewriter: now usually **type.** —**type'writ'ing**, *n.*
**type'writ'er**, *n.* 1. a writing machine with a keyboard for reproducing letters, figures, etc. resembling printed ones. 2. a typist.
**ty·phoid** (tī'foid), *adj.* [< Gr. *typhos*, fever; + *-oid*], designating or of an infectious disease **(typhoid fever)** acquired from infected food, water, etc. and characterized by fever, intestinal disorders, etc. *n.* typhoid fever.
**ty·phoon** (tī-fo͞on'), *n.* [< Chin. *tai-fung*, great wind], a violent cyclonic storm, esp. in the W Pacific. —**ty·phon'ic** (-fon'ik), *adj.*
**ty·phus** (tī'fəs), *n.* [< Gr. *tyhpos*, fever], an acute infectious disease transmitted to man by fleas, lice, etc. and characterized by fever, skin rash, etc.: also **typhus fever.**
**typ·i·cal** (tip'i-k'l), *adj.* 1. serving as a type; symbolic. 2. having the distinguishing characteristics of a class, group, etc.; representative. 3. belonging to a type; characteristic. —**typ'i·cal·ly**, *adv.*
**typ·i·fy** (tip'ə-fī), *v.t.* [-FIED, -FYING], 1. to be a type of; symbolize. 2. to have the characteristics of; exemplify.
**typ·ist** (tīp'ist), *n.* a person who operates a typewriter.
**ty·pog·ra·phy** (tī-pog'rə-fi), *n.* [see TYPE & -GRAPHY], 1. the setting of, and printing with, type. 2. the arrangement, style, etc. of matter printed from type. —**ty·pog'ra·pher**, *n.* —**ty'po·graph'i·cal** (-pə-graf'i-k'l), *adj.* —**ty'po·graph'i·cal·ly**, *adv.*
**ty·ran·ni·cal** (ti-ran'i-k'l), *adj.* 1. of or suited to a tyrant. 2. harsh, cruel, unjust, etc. Also **ty·ran'nic.** —**ty·ran'ni·cal·ly**, *adv.*
**tyr·an·nize** (tir'ə-nīz'), *v.i.* [-NIZED, -NIZING], 1. to govern as a tyrant. 2. to rule with cruelty, injustice, etc. *v.t.* to treat tyrannically.
**tyr'an·ny** (-ni), *n.* [*pl.* -NIES], 1. the authority, government, etc. of a tyrant. 2. cruel and unjust use of power. 3. a tyrannical act.
**ty·rant** (tī'rənt), *n.* [< Gr. *tyrannos*, lord], 1. an absolute ruler. 2. a cruel, oppressive ruler, etc.
**ty·ro** (tī'rō), *n.* [*pl.* -ROS], [< L. *tiro*, recruit], a beginner in learning something; novice.
**tzar** (tsär), *n.* a czar. —**tza·ri·na** (tsä-rē'nə), *n.fem.*

# U

**U, u,** (ū), *n.* [*pl.* U's, u's, Us, us], the 21st letter of the English alphabet.
**U,** in *chem.*, uranium.
**U.,** 1. Union. 2. University.
**u·biq·ui·tous** (ū-bik'wə-təs), *adj.* [< L. *ubique*, everywhere], (seemingly) present everywhere at the same time. —**u·biq'ui·ty**, *n.*
**U-boat** (ū'bōt'), *n.* [< G. *Unterseeboot*, undersea boat], a German submarine.
**u.c.,** in *typography*, upper case.
**ud·der** (ud'ẽr), *n.* [AS. *udr*], a large, pendulous, milk-secreting gland with two or more teats, as in cows.
**UFO,** unidentified flying object.
**ugh** (ookh, ug, *etc.*) *interj.* [echoic], an exclamation of disgust, horror, etc.
**ug·ly** (ug'li), *adj.* [-LIER, -LIEST], [< ON. *uggr*, fear], 1. very unpleasant to the sight. 2. bad; vile; repulsive. 3. ominous. 4. [Colloq.], cross; quarrelsome. —**ug'li·ness**, *n.*
**UHF,** ultrahigh frequency.
**u·kase** (ū'kās, ū-kāz'), *n.* [Russ. *ukaz*, edict], 1. in Czarist Russia, an imperial decree. 2. any official decree.
**u·ku·le·le** (ū'kə-lā'li), *n.* [Haw., flea], a small, four-stringed musical instrument of the guitar family: also [Colloq.], **uke** (ūk).
**ul·cer** (ul'sẽr), *n.* [< L. *ulcus*], 1. an open sore on the skin or some mucous membrane, discharging pus. 2. any corrupt condition. —**ul'cer·ous**, *adj.*
**ul·cer·ate** (ul'sə-rāt'), *v.t. & v.i.* [-ATED, -ATING], to make or become ulcerous. —**ul'cer·a'tion**, *n.* —**ul'cer·a'tive**, *adj.*
**-ulent,** [< L. *-ulentus*], a suffix meaning *full of*, as in *fraudulent*.
**ul·na** (ul'nə), *n.* [*pl.* -NAE (-nē), -NAS], [L., elbow], the larger of the two bones of the forearm. —**ul'nar** (-nẽr), *adj.*
**ul·ster** (ul'stẽr), *n.* [< *Ulster*, in Northern Ireland], a long, loose, heavy overcoat.
**ult.,** ultimate(ly).
**ul·te·ri·or** (ul-têr'i-ẽr), *adj.* [L. < *ulter*, beyond], 1. lying beyond or on the farther side. 2. beyond what is expressed or implied; undisclosed. —**ul·te'ri·or·ly**, *adv.*
**ul·ti·mate** (ul'tə-mit), *adj.* [< L. *ultimus*, last], 1. beyond which it is impossible to go. 2. final; concluding. 3. beyond further analysis. 4. greatest possible; maximum. *n.* a final point or result.
**ul·ti·ma·tum** (ul'tə-mā'təm), *n.* [*pl.* -TUMS, -TA (-tə)], [see ULTIMATE], a final offer or demand, as in diplomatic negotiations.
**ul·tra** (ul'trə), *adj.* [L., beyond], going beyond the usual limit; extreme.
**ultra-,** [L.], a prefix meaning: 1. *beyond*, as in *ultraviolet*. 2. *excessively*, as in *ultramodern*.
**ul·tra·high frequency** (ul'trə-hī'), in *radio & TV*, any frequency of 300 megacycles or higher.

**ul'tra·ma·rine'** (-mə-rēn'), *adj.* 1. beyond the sea. 2. deep-blue. *n.* deep blue.
**ul'tra·vi'o·let,** *adj.* lying just beyond the violet end of the visible spectrum: said of certain light rays.
**ul·u·late** (ūl'yoo-lāt', ul'-), *v.i.* [-LATED, -LATING], [< L. *ululare*; echoic], to howl, hoot, or wail. **—ul'u·la'tion,** *n.*
**U·lys·ses** (yoo-lis'ēz), *n.* [L.], Odysseus.
**um·bel** (um'b'l), *n.* [see UMBRELLA], a cluster of flowers with stalks of nearly equal length which spring from about the same point. **—um'bel·late** (-it, -āt'), *adj.*
**um·ber** (um'bēr), *n.* [< It. (*terra d'*) *ombra*, (earth of) shade], 1. a kind of earth used as a reddish-brown pigment. 2. a reddish-brown color.
**um·bil·i·cal** (um-bil'i-k'l), *adj.* [< L. *umbilicus*, navel], designating or of a cordlike structure (**umbilical cord**) connecting a fetus with the placenta and serving to convey food to the fetus.
**um·bil·i·cus** (um-bil'i-kəs, um'bi-lī'-), *n.* [*pl.* -CI (-sī', -sī)], [L.], the navel.
**um·bra** (um'brə), *n.* [*pl.* -BRAE (-brē)], [L., a shade], shade; shadow.
**um·brage** (um'brij), *n.* [< L. *umbra*, a shade], resentment and displeasure.
**um·brel·la** (um-brel'ə), *n.* [< L. *umbra*, shade], 1. a screen, usually of cloth on a folding radial frame, carried for protection against the rain or sun. 2. something suggestive of this.
**u·mi·ak, u·mi·ack** (ōō'mi-ak'), *n.* [Esk.], a large open boat made of skins stretched on a wooden frame, used by Eskimos.
**um·laut** (oom'laut), *n.* [G. < *um*, about + *laut*, a sound], in *linguistics*, 1. a vowel changed in sound by its assimilation to another vowel. 2. the mark (¨) placed over such a vowel, especially in German.
**um·pire** (um'pīr), *n.* [< OFr. *nomper*, uneven, hence a third person], a person chosen to judge a dispute; arbiter; esp., an official who administers the rules in certain sports, as baseball. *v.t. & v.i.* [-PIRED, -PIRING], to act as umpire (in or of).
**UN, U.N.,** United Nations.
**un-,** either of two prefixes, meaning: 1. [AS. *un-*], *not, lack of, the opposite of*, as in *unhappy, untruth.* 2. [AS. *un-, on-*], *back*: indicating a reversal of action, as in *unfasten.* The following list includes some of the more common compounds formed with *un-* (either prefix) that do not have special meanings.

**unabashed**
**unabated**
**unable**
**unabridged**
**unaccented**
**unacceptable**
**unaccommodating**
**unaccompanied**
**unacquainted**
**unadorned**
**unadulterated**
**unafraid**
**unaided**
**unalterable**
**unambitious**
**unannounced**
**unanswerable**
**unappreciated**
**unashamed**
**unasked**
**unassailable**
**unassisted**
**unattainable**
**unattended**
**unattractive**
**unauthorized**
**unavailable**
**unavoidable**
**unbearable**
**unbefitting**
**unbelievable**
**unbiased**
**unbind**
**unbleached**
**unblemished**
**unbounded**
**unbreakable**
**unbroken**
**unbuckle**
**unburied**
**unburned**
**unbusinesslike**
**unbutton**
**uncap**
**unceasing**
**uncensored**
**unchain**
**unchallenged**
**unchanged**
**unchanging**
**uncharitable**
**uncharted**
**unchecked**
**uncivil**
**uncivilized**
**unclaimed**
**unclean**
**unclothed**
**uncommitted**
**uncomplaining**
**uncompleted**
**uncomplimentary**
**unconcealed**
**unconfirmed**
**unconnected**
**unconquerable**
**unconstrained**
**uncontrollable**
**uncontrolled**
**unconventional**
**unconvinced**
**unconvincing**
**uncooked**
**uncorrupted**
**uncultivated**
**undamaged**
**undated**
**undeceive**
**undecipherable**
**undeclared**
**undefeated**
**undefended**
**undefiled**
**undefinable**
**undefined**
**undemocratic**
**undemonstrative**
**undependable**
**undeserved**
**undeserving**
**undesirable**
**undetermined**
**undeterred**
**undeveloped**
**undeviating**
**undifferentiated**
**undigested**
**undiluted**
**undiminished**
**undisciplined**
**undiscovered**
**undiscriminating**
**undisguised**
**undismayed**
**undisputed**
**undistinguished**
**undisturbed**
**undivided**
**unearned**
**uneconomical**
**uneducated**
**unemotional**
**unending**
**unendurable**
**unenlightened**
**uneventful**
**unexceptional**
**unexpired**
**unexplained**
**unexplored**
**unexpressed**
**unexpurgated**
**unfaded**
**unfading**
**unfair**
**unfaltering**
**unfashionable**
**unfasten**
**unfathomed**
**unfavorable**
**unfettered**
**unfit**
**unflattering**
**unforeseeable**
**unforeseen**
**unforgettable**
**unforgivable**
**unforgiven**
**unforgiving**
**unforgotten**
**unformed**
**unfrequented**
**unfruitful**
**unfulfilled**
**unfurnished**
**ungenerous**
**ungentlemanly**
**ungoverned**
**ungrammatical**
**ungrateful**
**ungrudging**
**unhampered**
**unhandy**
**unharmed**
**unharness**
**unhealthful**
**unheeded**
**unhesitating**
**unhitch**
**unhook**
**unhurried**
**unhurt**
**unhygienic**
**unidentified**
**unimaginable**
**unimaginative**
**unimpaired**
**unimportant**
**unimproved**
**unincorporated**
**uninformed**
**uninhabitable**
**uninhabited**
**uninhibited**
**uninjured**
**uninspired**
**uninsured**
**unintelligent**
**unintelligible**
**unintended**
**unintentional**
**uninterested**
**uninteresting**
**uninterrupted**
**unintimidated**
**uninvited**
**uninviting**
**unjustifiable**
**unkind**
**unknowable**
**unknowing**
**unlace**
**unlamented**
**unlatch**
**unleavened**
**unlicensed**
**unlit**
**unloved**
**unlovely**
**unmanageable**
**unmannerly**
**unmarked**
**unmarried**
**unmatched**
**unmeasured**
**unmentioned**
**unmindful**
**unmixed**
**unmolested**
**unmoved**
**unmoving**
**unmusical**
**unnamed**
**unnaturalized**
**unnavigable**
**unnoticed**
**unobserved**
**unobstructed**
**unobtrusive**
**unoccupied**
**unofficial**
**unopened**
**unopposed**
**unorthodox**

**unostentatious**
**unpaid**
**unpalatable**
**unpardonable**
**unpaved**
**unperturbed**
**unpin**
**unplanned**
**unpleasing**
**unplowed**
**unpolished**
**unpredictable**
**unprejudiced**
**unpremeditated**
**unprepared**
**unpretentious**
**unproductive**
**unprofitable**
**unpromising**
**unpronounceable**
**unprotected**
**unprovided**
**unprovoked**
**unpruned**
**unpublished**
**unpunished**
**unquenchable**
**unquestioned**
**unquestioning**
**unreadable**
**unready**
**unrealized**
**unreasoned**
**unrecognizable**
**unrecognized**
**unrecorded**
**unrefined**
**unrelated**
**unreliable**
**unrelieved**
**unrequited**
**unrestricted**
**unrighteous**
**unrightful**
**unsafe**
**unsaid**
**unsalable**
**unsaleable**
**unsanitary**
**unsatisfactory**
**unsatisfied**
**unscientific**
**unseasoned**
**unseeing**
**unseen**
**unselfish**
**unshaded**
**unshakable**
**unshaven**
**unshed**
**unsighted**
**unsightliness**
**unsightly**
**unsmiling**
**unsociable**
**unsold**
**unsolicited**
**unsought**
**unspoiled**
**unsportsmanlike**
**unsprung**
**unstained**
**unstrained**
**unstuck**
**unsubdued**
**unsuccessful**
**unsuitable**
**unsuited**
**unsullied**
**unsupported**
**unsure**
**unsurpassed**
**unsuspected**
**unsuspicious**
**unsweetened**
**unswept**
**unswerving**
**unsympathetic**
**unsympathizing**
**untainted**
**untamed**
**untarnished**
**untasted**
**unteachable**
**untenable**
**untiring**
**untouched**
**untrained**
**untraveled**
**untried**
**untrimmed**
**untroubled**
**untrue**
**untwist**
**unuttered**
**unvarying**
**unverified**
**unvisited**
**unwanted**
**unwarranted**
**unwashed**
**unwavering**
**unwed**
**unworkable**
**unworldly**
**unyielding**

**un·ac·count·a·ble** (un'ə-koun'tə-b'l), ***adj.*** 1. that cannot be explained; strange. 2. not responsible. **—un'ac·count'a·bly, *adv.***
**un'ac·cus'tomed, *adj.*** 1. not accustomed (*to*). 2. uncommon; strange.
**un'ad·vised', *adj.*** 1. without counsel or advice. 2. indiscreet; hasty.
**un'af·fect'ed, *adj.*** 1. not affected, or influenced. 2. without affectation; sincere.
**un'-A·mer'i·can, *adj.*** regarded as not properly American, i.e., as opposed to the U.S., its institutions, etc.
**u·nan·i·mous** (yoo-nan'ə-məs), ***adj.*** [< L. *unus*, one + *animus*, the mind], in total agreement; without dissent. **—u·na·nim·i·ty** (ū'nə-nim'ə-ti), ***n.***
**un'ap·proach'a·ble, *adj.*** 1. not to be approached; inaccessible; aloof. 2. having no equal; unmatched.
**un·arm', *v.t. & v.i.*** to disarm.
**un'as·sum'ing, *adj.*** not assuming, pretending, or forward; modest.
**un'at·tached', *adj.*** 1. not attached. 2. not engaged or married.
**un'a·vail'ing, *adj.*** not availing; futile.
**un'a·ware', *adj.*** 1. not aware or conscious. 2. unwary; heedless. ***adv.*** unawares.
**un'a·wares'** (-wârz'), ***adv.*** 1. unintentionally. 2. unexpectedly; by surprise.
**un·bal'anced, *adj.*** 1. not in balance. 2. *a*) deranged; mentally ill. *b*) not stable, steady, etc., as in judgment.
**un·bar', *v.t. & v.i.*** [-BARRED, -BARRING], to unlock; unbolt; open.
**un'be·com'ing, *adj.*** 1. not becoming; not suited. 2. not proper or decent.
**un'be·lief', *n.*** lack of belief, esp. in religion. **—un'be·liev'er, *n.***
**un·bend', *v.t. & v.i.*** [-BENT or -BENDED, -BENDING], 1. to release or be released from tension. 2. to relax, as from formality. 3. to straighten.
**un·bend'ing, *adj.*** 1. rigid; stiff; inflexible. 2. firm; unyielding. **—un·bend'ing·ly, *adv.***
**un·bid'den, *adj.*** 1. not commanded. 2. uninvited.
**un·bolt', *v.t. & v.i.*** to withdraw the bolt or bolts of (a door, etc.); open.
**un·born', *adj.*** 1. not born. 2. not yet born; yet to come or be; future.
**un·bos'om** (un-booz'əm, -bōō'zəm), ***v.t. & v.i.*** to tell or reveal (feelings, secrets, etc.). **—unbosom oneself,** to reveal one's feelings, etc.
**un·bri'dled, *adj.*** 1. having no bridle on, as a horse. 2. unrestrained; uncontrolled.
**un·bur'den, *v.t.*** 1. to free from a burden. 2. to relieve, as one's soul, mind, etc., by disclosing guilt, etc.
**un·called'-for', *adj.*** 1. not called for. 2. unnecessary and out of place; impertinent.
**un·can·ny** (un-kan'i), ***adj.*** 1. mysterious and eerie; weird. 2. so good, acute, etc. as to seem preternatural: as, *uncanny* vision.
**un'cer·e·mo'ni·ous, *adj.*** 1. not ceremonious; informal. 2. curt; abrupt.
**un·cer'tain, *adj.*** 1. not surely or certainly known. 2. not sure or certain in knowledge; doubtful. 3. vague. 4. not dependable or reliable. 5. varying. **—un·cer'tain·ly, *adv.*** **—un·cer'tain·ty** [*pl.* -TIES], ***n.***
**un·chris'tian, *adj.*** 1. not Christian. 2. unworthy of any decent, civilized person.
**un·cir'cum·cised', *adj.*** 1. not circumcised. 2. Gentile. 3. heathen.
**un·clasp', *v.t.*** 1. to loosen the clasp of. 2. to release from a clasp.
**un·cle** (uŋ'k'l), ***n.*** [< L. *avunculus*], 1. the brother of one's father or mother. 2. the husband of one's aunt.
**Uncle Sam,** [< abbrev. U.S.], [Colloq.], the U.S. (government or people), personified as a tall, spare man with chin whiskers.
**un·cloak', *v.t. & v.i.*** 1. to remove a cloak (from). 2. to reveal; expose.
**un·clothe', *v.t.*** [-CLOTHED or -CLAD, -CLOTHING], to undress, uncover, etc.
**un·coil', *v.t. & v.i.*** to unwind.
**un·com'fort·a·ble, *adj.*** 1. feeling discomfort. 2. causing discomfort. 3. ill at ease.
**un·com'mon, *adj.*** 1. rare; not common or usual. 2. strange; remarkable.
**un'com·mu'ni·ca'tive, *adj.*** not communicative; reserved; silent.
**un·com'pro·mis'ing, *adj.*** not yielding; firm; inflexible.
**un'con·cern', *n.*** 1. indifference. 2. lack of concern; freedom from anxiety.
**un'con·cerned', *adj.*** not solicitous or anxious; indifferent.
**un'con·di'tion·al, *adj.*** without conditions or reservations; absolute.
**un·con·scion·a·ble** (un-kon'shən-ə-b'l), ***adj.*** 1. not guided or restrained by conscience; unscrupulous. 2. unreasonable.
**un·con'scious, *adj.*** 1. deprived of consciousness. 2. not aware (*of*). 3. not intended by the person himself: as, an *unconscious* act. **—the unconscious,** in *psychoanalysis,*

the sum of all thoughts, impulses, etc. of which the individual is not conscious but which influence his behavior.

**un'con·sti·tu'tion·al,** *adj.* not in accordance with the principles of the constitution.

**un·cork',** *v.t.* to pull the cork out of.

**un·count'ed,** *adj.* 1. not counted. 2. inconceivably numerous; innumerable.

**un·cou'ple,** *v.t.* [-PLED, -PLING], to unfasten (something coupled); disconnect.

**un·couth** (un-kōōth'), *adj.* [AS. < *un-*, not + *cunnan*, know], 1. awkward; ungainly. 2. uncultured; crude.

**un·cov'er,** *v.t.* 1. to disclose. 2. to remove the cover from. 3. to remove the hat, etc. from (the head). *v.i.* to bare the head, as in respect.

**unc·tion** (uŋk'shən), *n.* [< L. *ungere*, anoint], 1. the act of anointing, as for medical or religious purposes. 2. the oil, ointment, etc. used for this. 3. anything that soothes or comforts.

**unc·tu·ous** (uŋk'chōō-əs), *adj.* [< L. *ungere*, anoint], 1. oily or greasy. 2. characterized by a smooth pretense of fervor or earnestness; too suave, bland, etc.

**un·cut',** *adj.* not cut; specif., not ground to shape: said of a gem.

**un·daunt'ed,** *adj.* not daunted; fearless, etc.

**un'de·cid'ed,** *adj.* 1. not decided. 2. not having come to a decision.

**un'de·ni'a·ble,** *adj.* 1. that cannot be denied. 2. unquestionably good. **—un'de·ni'a·bly,** *adv.* **—un'de·ni'a·ble·ness,** *n.*

**un·der** (un'dẽr), *prep.* [AS.], 1. in, at, or to a position down from; below. 2. covered by: as, a gun *under* his coat. 3. beneath the surface of. 4. lower in rank, position, amount, etc. than. 5. lower than the required degree of: as, *under* age. 6. below and to the other side of: as, drive *under* the bridge. 7. subject to the control, etc. of. 8. bound by: as, *under* oath. 9. undergoing: as, *under* repair. 10. with the disguise of: as, to go *under* an alias. 11. in (the designated class, division, etc.). 12. in the time of: as, France *under* Louis XV. 13. being the subject of: as, the topic *under* debate. 14. because of: as, *under* the circumstances. 15. by authorization of; in accordance with. *adv.* 1. in or to a lower position or state. 2. so as to be covered, concealed, etc. *adj.* lower in position, authority, amount, etc. **—go under,** to fail, as in business.

**under-,** a prefix meaning: 1. *in, on, to,* or *from a lower place*; *beneath*, as in *undershirt, undergarment.* 2. *in a subordinate position,* as in *undergraduate.* 3. *to a degree below standard, insufficiently,* as in *underdevelop, underdone, underexpose, underpay.*

**un'der·age',** *adj.* 1. not of mature age. 2. below the required age.

**un'der·arm',** *adj.* under the arm; in the armpit. *adv.* with an underhand delivery or motion.

**un'der·brush',** *n.* small trees, shrubs, etc. that grow beneath large trees in woods.

**un'der·car'riage,** *n.* 1. a supporting frame, as of an automobile. 2. the landing gear of an airplane.

**un'der·charge',** *v.t.* [-CHARGED, -CHARGING], to charge less than is usual or correct (for). *n.* (un'dẽr-chärj'), an insufficient charge.

**un'der·clothes',** *n.pl.* clothes worn next to the skin, or under a suit, dress, etc.: also **un'der·cloth'ing** (-klōth'iŋ).

**un'der·coat',** *v.t.* to apply a tarlike coating to the underside of an automobile to prevent rust, etc. *n.* such a coating.

**un'der·cov'er,** *adj.* acting or carried out in secret.

**un'der·cur'rent,** *n.* 1. a current flowing beneath the surface. 2. a hidden or underlying tendency, opinion, etc.

**un'der·cut',** *v.t.* [-CUT, -CUTTING], 1. to make a cut below or under. 2. to undersell or work for lower wages than. 3. in *sports*, to strike so as to give backward rotation to (a ball).

**un'der·dog',** *n.* a person, group, etc. that is underprivileged, unfavored, losing, etc.

**un'der·es'ti·mate',** *v.t.* & *v.i.* [-MATED, -MATING], to estimate below the actual value, amount, etc.

**un'der·foot',** *adv.* & *adj.* 1. under the foot or feet; hence, 2. in the way.

**un'der·go',** *v.t.* [-WENT, -GONE, -GOING], to experience; endure; be subjected to.

**un'der·grad'u·ate,** *n.* a college student who does not yet have a degree.

**un'der·ground',** *adj.* 1. occurring, working, etc. beneath the surface of the earth. 2. secret; undercover. *adv.* 1. beneath the surface of the earth. 2. (in)to secrecy or hiding. *n.* (un'dẽr-ground'), 1. the region beneath the surface of the earth. 2. a secret movement opposing the government or enemy occupation forces. 3. [Brit.], a subway.

**un'der·growth',** *n.* underbrush.

**un'der·hand',** *adj.* 1. done with the hand below the level of the elbow or shoulder. 2. secret; sly; deceitful. *adv.* 1. with an underhand motion. 2. slyly; secretly.

**un'der·hand'ed,** *adj.* underhand; secret.

**un'der·lie',** *v.t.* [-LAY, -LAIN, -LYING], 1. to be beneath. 2. to form the basis or foundation of.

**un'der·line',** *v.t.* [-LINED, -LINING], 1. to draw a line beneath. 2. to stress.

**un·der·ling** (un'dẽr-liŋ), *n.* [AS.; see UNDER & -LING], one who has little rank or authority; a subordinate.

**un'der·ly'ing,** *adj.* 1. lying under; placed beneath. 2. fundamental; basic.

**un'der·mine',** *v.t.* [-MINED, -MINING], 1. to dig beneath, so as to form a tunnel or mine. 2. to wear away at the foundation. 3. to injure, weaken, etc., esp. by subtle or stealthy means. **—un'der·min'er,** *n.*

**un'der·most',** *adj.* & *adv.* lowest in place, position, rank, etc.

**un'der·neath',** *adv.* & *prep.* under; below; beneath. *n.* the under part.

**un'der·nour'ish,** *v.t.* to give insufficient nourishment to. **—un'der·nour'ished,** *adj.*

**un'der·pass',** *n.* a passage under something, as a road under a railway or highway.

**un'der·pay',** *v.t.* [-PAID, -PAYING], to pay less than is right; pay insufficiently.

**un·der·pin·ning** (un'dẽr-pin'iŋ), *n.* 1. a supporting structure, esp. one placed beneath a wall. 2. *pl.* [Colloq.], the legs.

**un'der·priv'i·leged,** *adj.* deprived of basic social rights, or privileges, through poverty, discrimination, etc.

**un'der·rate',** *v.t.* [-RATED, -RATING], to rate too low; underestimate.

**un'der·score',** *v.t.* [-SCORED, -SCORING], to underline. *n.* a line underneath a printed or written word, etc.

**un'der·sea',** *adj.* & *adv.* beneath the surface of the sea.: also **un'der·seas',** *adv.*

**un'der·sec're·tar'y,** *n.* [*pl.* -IES], an assistant secretary.

**un'der·sell',** *v.t.* [-SOLD, -SELLING], to sell at a lower price than.

**un'der·shot',** *adj.* 1. protruding: said of the lower jaw. 2. turned by water passing beneath: said of a water wheel.

**un'der·side',** *n.* the side or surface that is underneath.

**un'der·sign',** *v.t.* to sign one's name at the end of (a letter, document, etc.). **—the undersigned,** the person or persons undersigning.

**un'der·stand',** *v.t.* [-STOOD (-stood'), -STANDING], [AS. *understandan*, stand under], 1.

to perceive the meaning of. 2. to take as the meaning; infer. 3. to take as meant; interpret. 4. to take as a fact. 5. to learn. 6. to know the nature, character, etc. of. *v.i.* 1. to have understanding, comprehension, etc. 2. to be informed; believe. **—un′der·stand′a·ble,** *adj.*

**un′der·stand′ing,** *n.* 1. comprehension. 2. the power to think and learn; intelligence. 3. a specific interpretation. 4. mutual agreement, esp. one that settles differences. *adj.* that understands; sympathetic.

**un′der·state′,** *v.t. & v.i.* [-STATED, -STATING], to make a weaker statement (of) than is warranted by truth, importance, etc. **—un′der·state′ment,** *n.*

**un′der·stud′y,** *n.* [*pl.* -IES], an actor prepared to substitute for another. *v.t. & v.i* [-IED, -YING], to learn (a part) as an understudy (to).

**un′der·take′,** *v.t.* [-TOOK, -TAKEN, -TAKING], 1. to take upon oneself (a task, etc.). 2. to promise; guarantee.

**un′der·tak′er,** *n.* a person whose business is to prepare the dead for burial and manage funerals.

**un′der·tak′ing** (*for* 3, un′dẽr-tāk′iŋ), *n.* 1. something undertaken; task; enterprise. 2. a promise; guarantee. 3. the business of an undertaker.

**un′der·tone′,** *n.* 1. a low tone of voice. 2. a subdued color. 3. an underlying quality, factor, etc.

**un′der·tow′** (-tō′), *n.* a current of water moving beneath the surface water and in a different direction.

**un′der·wa′ter,** *adj.* being done, etc. beneath the surface of the water.

**un′der·wear′,** *n.* underclothes.

**un′der·weight′,** *adj.* weighing too little. *n.* weight below what is normal, required, etc.

**un′der·went′,** pt. of **undergo.**

**un′der·world′,** *n.* 1. Hades; hell. 2. the criminal members of society.

**un′der·write′,** *v.t.* [-WROTE, -WRITTEN, -WRITING], 1. to write under something; subscribe. 2. to agree to buy (an issue of stocks, bonds, etc., often that part of an issue remaining unsubscribed). 3. to agree to finance (an undertaking, etc.). 4. to sign one's name to (an insurance policy), thus assuming liability. **—un′der·writ′er,** *n.*

**un·do′,** *v.t.* [-DID, -DONE, -DOING], 1. to open, untie, etc. 2. to reverse the doing of; annul. 3. to bring to ruin. **—un·do′er,** *n.*

**un·do′ing,** *n.* 1. an annulling; reversal. 2. a bringing to ruin. 3. the cause of ruin.

**un·done′,** *adj.* 1. not done; not performed, accomplished, etc. 2. ruined.

**un·doubt′ed,** *adj.* not doubted or called in question; accepted. **—un·doubt′ed·ly,** *adv.*

**un·dress′,** *v.t.* to take off the clothing of. *v.i.* to take off one's clothing.

**un·due′,** *adj.* 1. improper; not appropriate. 2. not just, legal, etc. 3. excessive.

**un·du·lant** (un′joo-lənt, -doo-), *adj.* undulating.

**un·du·late** (un′joo-lāt′, -doo-), *v.i. & v.t.* [-LATED, -LATING], [< L. *unda*, a wave], 1. to move or cause to move in waves. 2. to have or cause to have a wavy form or surface. **—un′du·la′tion,** *n.*

**un·du·ly** (un-dōō′li, -dū′-), *adv.* 1. improperly; unjustly. 2. excessively.

**un·dy′ing,** *adj.* immortal; eternal.

**un·earth′,** *v.t.* 1. to dig up from the earth. 2. to bring to light; disclose.

**un·earth′ly,** *adj.* 1. supernatural. 2. weird; mysterious. 3. [Colloq.], fantastic; outlandish. **—un·earth′li·ness,** *n.*

**un·eas′y,** *adj.* [-IER, -IEST], 1. having, showing, or allowing no ease of body or mind; uncomfortable, disturbed, perturbed, restless, etc. 2. awkward; constrained.

**un′em·ployed′,** *adj.* 1. not employed; without a job. 2. not being used. **—un′employ′ment,** *n.*

**un·e′qual,** *adj.* 1. not of the same size, strength, ability, value, etc. 2. not balanced, even, regular, etc. 3. not adequate (*to*). 4. unjust; unfair. **—un·e′qual·ly,** *adv.*

**un·e′qualed, un·e′qualled,** *adj.* not equaled; unmatched; unrivaled; supreme.

**un′e·quiv′o·cal,** *adj.* not equivocal; straightforward; clear.

**un·err′ing,** *adj.* 1. free from error. 2. not missing or failing; sure; exact.

**UNESCO** (yoo-nes′kō), *n.* the United Nations Educational, Scientific, and Cultural Organization.

**un·e′ven,** *adj.* 1. not even; not level, smooth, regular, etc. 2. unequal. 3. in *math.*, odd. **—un·e′ven·ly,** *adv.*

**un′ex·am′pled,** *adj.* having no parallel or precedent; unprecedented.

**un′ex·pect′ed,** *adj.* not expected; sudden.

**un·fail′ing,** *adj.* 1. not failing. 2. never ceasing or falling short; inexhaustible. 3. always reliable. **—un·fail′ing·ly,** *adv.*

**un·faith′ful,** *adj.* 1. lacking or breaking faith or loyalty. 2. not true, accurate, etc. 3. adulterous. **—un·faith′ful·ness,** *n.*

**un′fa·mil′iar,** *adj.* 1. not well known; strange. 2. not acquainted (*with*).

**un·feel′ing,** *adj.* 1. incapable of feeling; insensible. 2. hardhearted; cruel.

**un·feigned′** (-fānd′), *adj.* real; true.

**un·fin′ished,** *adj.* 1. not finished; incomplete. 2. having no finish, or final coat, as of paint.

**un·flinch′ing,** *adj.* steadfast; firm.

**un·fold′,** *v.t.* 1. to open the folds of; spread out. 2. to lay open to view; reveal, explain, etc. 3. to develop. *v.i.* to become unfolded.

**un·for′tu·nate,** *adj.* characterized by bad fortune; unsuccessful, unlucky, etc. *n.* an unfortunate person.

**un·found′ed,** *adj.* 1. not founded on fact or truth. 2. not established.

**un·friend′ly,** *adj.* 1. not friendly or kind. 2. not favorable. *adv.* in an unfriendly manner. **—un·friend′li·ness,** *n.*

**un·frock′** (-frok′), *v.t.* to deprive of the rank of priest or minister.

**un·furl′,** *v.t. & v.i.* to open or spread out from a furled state; unfold.

**un·gain·ly** (un-gān′li), *adj.* [< ME. < *un-*, not + ON. *gegn*, steady], awkward; clumsy.

**un·god′ly,** *adj.* 1. not godly or religious. 2. [Colloq.], outrageous. **—un·god′li·ness,** *n.*

**un·gov′ern·a·ble,** *adj.* that cannot be governed or restrained; unruly.

**un·gra′cious,** *adj.* 1. unacceptable; unpleasant. 2. rude; discourteous.

**un·guard′ed,** *adj.* 1. unprotected. 2. careless; imprudent. **—un·guard′ed·ly,** *adv.*

**un·guent** (uŋ′gwənt), *n.* [< L. *unguere*, anoint], a salve or ointment.

**un·gu·late** (uŋ′gyoo-lit, -lāt′), *adj.* [< L. *unguis*, a hoof], having hoofs. *n.* a mammal having hoofs.

**un·hand′,** *v.t.* to loose or release from the hand or hands; let go of.

**un·hap′py,** *adj.* [-PIER, -PIEST], 1. unfortunate. 2. sad; wretched. 3. not suitable.

**un·health′y,** *adj.* [-IER, -IEST], 1. sickly; not well. 2. harmful to health. 3. harmful to morals. **—un·health′i·ness,** *n.*

**un·heard′,** *adj.* 1. not perceived by the ear. 2. not given a hearing.

**un·heard′-of′,** *adj.* not heard of before; unprecedented or unknown.

**un·hinge′,** *v.t.* [-HINGED, -HINGING], 1. to remove from the hinges. 2. to dislodge or detach. 3. to unbalance (the mind).

**un·ho′ly,** *adj.* [-LIER, -LIEST], 1. not sacred, hallowed, etc. 2. wicked; profane. 3. [Colloq.], frightful; dreadful.

**un·horse′,** *v.t.* [-HORSED, -HORSING], to throw (a rider) from a horse.
**uni-,** [< L. *unus*, one], a combining form meaning *having* or *consisting of one only*.
**u·ni·cam·er·al** (ū′ni-kam′ēr-əl), *adj.* [< *uni-* + LL. *camera*, chamber], of or having a single legislative chamber.
**UNICEF** (yōō′nə-sef′), *n.* United Nations Children's (Emergency) Fund.
**u·ni·corn** (ū′nə-kôrn′), *n.* [< L. *unus*, one + *cornu*, horn], a mythical horselike animal with a single horn in its forehead.
**u·ni·fi·ca·tion** (ū′nə-fi-kā′shən), *n.* 1. a unifying or being unified. 2. an instance of this.
**u·ni·form** (ū′nə-fôrm′), *adj.* [< L. *unus*, one + *forma*, a form], 1. not varying in form, rate, degree, etc. 2. not varying among themselves; all alike. *n.* the distinctive clothes of a particular group: as, a military *uniform*. *v.t.* to supply with a uniform. —**u′ni·form′it·y** (-fôr′mə-ti), *n.*
**u·ni·fy** (ū′nə-fī′), *v.t.* [-FIED, -FYING], [ult. < L. *unus*, one + *facere*, make], to cause to become one; unite. —**u′ni·fi′a·ble**, *adj.*
**u·ni·lat·er·al** (ū′ni-lat′ēr-əl), *adj.* 1. of, occurring on, or affecting one side only. 2. involving one only of several parties; not reciprocal. —**u′ni·lat′er·al·ly**, *adv.*
**un·im·peach·a·ble** (un′im-pēch′ə-b'l), *adj.* that cannot be doubted or discredited; irreproachable. —**un′im·peach′a·bly**, *adv.*
**un·ion** (ūn′yən), *n.* [< L. *unus*, one], 1. a uniting or being united; combination. 2. a grouping together of nations, etc. for some specific purpose. 3. marriage. 4. something united. 5. a device symbolizing political union, used as in a flag. 6. a labor union. 7. a device for joining together parts.
**un′ion·ize′,** *v.t. & v.i.* [-IZED, -IZING], to organize into a labor union.
**union jack,** 1. a flag, esp. a national flag, consisting only of a union. 2. [U- J-], the national flag of the United Kingdom.
**u·nique** (ū-nēk′), *adj.* [Fr. < L. *unicus*, single], 1. one and only; sole. 2. without like or equal. 3. unusual; rare.
**u·ni·son** (ū′nə-s'n, -z'n), *n.* [< L. *unus*, one + *sonus*, a sound], 1. identity of musical pitch, as of two or more tones or voices. 2. agreement; harmony. —**in unison**, with all the voices or instruments performing the same part.
**u·nit** (ū′nit), *n.* [< *unity*], 1. the smallest whole number; one. 2. a standard basic quantity, measure, etc. 3. a single person or group, esp. as a part of a whole. 4. a distinct object with a specific purpose.
**U·ni·tar·i·an** (ū′nə-târ′i-ən), *n.* a member of a Protestant sect holding that God is a single being. —**U′ni·tar′i·an·ism**, *n.*
**u·nite** (yoo-nīt′), *v.t. & v.i.* [UNITED, UNITING], [< L. *unus*, one], 1. to put or join together so as to make one; combine. 2. to bring or come together in common cause, action, etc. —**u·nit′er**, *n.*
**u·nit′ed,** *adj.* 1. combined; joined. 2. of or resulting from joint action or association. 3. in agreement. —**u·nit′ed·ly**, *adv.*
**United Nations,** an international organization for world peace and security, formed in 1945 around the nucleus of allies opposing the Axis.
**u·ni·ty** (ū′nə-ti), *n.* [*pl.* -TIES], [< L. *unus*, one], 1. a being united; oneness. 2. a single, separate thing. 3. harmony; agreement. 4. a complex that is a union of related parts. 5. a harmonious, unified arrangement of parts in an artistic work. 6. constancy or continuity of purpose, action, etc. 7. in *math.*, any quantity, etc. identified as a unit or 1.
**u·ni·valve** (ū′nə-valv′), *n.* 1. a mollusk having a one-piece shell, as a snail. 2. such a one-piece shell.
**u·ni·ver·sal** (ū′nə-vũr′s'l), *adj.* 1. of, for, or including all or the whole; unlimited. 2. of the universe; present everywhere. 3. used, or intended to be used, for all kinds, sizes, etc. or by all people. —**u′ni·ver·sal′i·ty** (-vẽr-sal′ə-ti), *n.*
**universal joint** (or **coupling**), a joint or coupling that permits a swing of limited angle in any direction.
**u′ni·ver′sal·ly,** *adv.* 1. in every instance. 2. in every part or place.
**u·ni·verse** (ū′nə-vũrs′), *n.* [< L. *unus*, one + *vertere*, to turn], 1. the totality of all things that exist. 2. the world.
**u·ni·ver·si·ty** (ū′nə-vũr′sə-ti), *n.* [*pl.* -TIES], [see UNIVERSE], an educational institution of the highest level, variously composed of undergraduate and graduate colleges.
**un·just** (un-just′), *adj.* not just or right; unfair. —**un·just′ly**, *adv.* —**un·just′ness**, *n.*
**un·kempt** (un-kempt′), *adj.* [*un-* + *kempt* < dial. *kemben*, to comb], 1. not combed. 2. untidy; messy. —**un·kempt′ness**, *n.*
**un·known′,** *adj.* 1. not known; unfamiliar; strange. 2. not discovered, identified, etc. *n.* an unknown person or thing.
**un·law′ful,** *adj.* 1. against the law; illegal. 2. illegitimate. —**un·law′ful·ly**, *adv.*
**un·learn′,** *v.t.* [-LEARNED or -LEARNT, -LEARNING], to forget (something learned).
**un·learn′ed** (-lũr′nid), *adj.* 1. not educated; ignorant. 2. (-lũrnd′), not learned.
**un·leash′,** *v.t.* to release from a leash.
**un·less** (ən-les′), *conj.* [earlier *on lesse that*, at less than], if not; in any case other than; except that.
**un·let′tered,** *adj.* 1. not lettered; ignorant; uneducated. 2. illiterate.
**un·like′,** *adj.* not alike; different. *prep.* different from; not like. —**un·like′ness**, *n.*
**un·like′ly,** *adj.* 1. not likely; improbable. 2. not likely to succeed.
**un·lim′it·ed,** *adj.* 1. without limits or restrictions. 2. vast; illimitable.
**un·load′,** *v.t. & v.i.* 1. to remove (a load). 2. to relieve of something that troubles, etc. 3. to take a load from. 4. to remove the charge from (a gun). 5. to get rid of.
**un·lock′,** *v.t.* 1. to open or unfasten as by undoing a lock. 2. to reveal.
**un·looked′-for′,** *adj.* not looked for; not expected or foreseen.
**un·loose′,** *v.t.* [-LOOSED, -LOOSING], to loose; set free, release, etc.
**un·luck′y,** *adj.* [-IER, -IEST], having or bringing bad luck; unfortunate.
**un·man′,** *v.t.* [-MANNED, -MANNING], to deprive of the qualities considered manly; make weak, timid, etc. —**un·man′ly**, *adv.*
**un·mask′,** *v.t. & v.i.* 1. to remove a mask or disguise (from). 2. to disclose the true nature or character (of).
**un·mean′ing,** *adj.* lacking in meaning.
**un·men′tion·a·ble,** *adj.* considered improper for polite conversation. *n. pl.* things regarded as unfit for mention; specif., undergarments. —**un·men′tion·a·bly**, *adv.*
**un·mer′ci·ful,** *adj.* having or showing no mercy; cruel; pitiless.
**un′mis·tak′a·ble,** *adj.* that cannot be mistaken or misinterpreted; clear.
**un·mit′i·gat′ed,** *adj.* 1. not lessened or eased. 2. clear-cut; absolute.
**un·mor′al,** *adj.* neither moral nor immoral; amoral.
**un·nat′u·ral,** *adj.* 1. contrary to nature; abnormal. 2. artificial. 3. abnormally cruel. —**un·nat′u·ral·ly**, *adv.*
**un·nec′es·sar′y,** *adj.* not necessary; needless. —**un·nec′es·sar′i·ly**, *adv.*
**un·nerve′,** *v.t.* [-NERVED, -NERVING], to deprive of nerve, courage, etc.
**un·num′bered,** *adj.* 1. countless. 2. not numbered. 3. not counted.

**un·or′gan·ized′**, *adj.* not organized; specif., not belonging to a labor union.
**un·pack′**, *v.t. & v.i.* 1. to remove (the contents of a trunk, package, etc.). 2. to take things out of (a trunk, etc.).
**un·par′al·leled′**, *adj.* that has no parallel, equal, or counterpart.
**un·pleas′ant**, *adj.* not pleasant; offensive.
**un·pop′u·lar**, *adj.* not liked by the public or by the majority. **—un′pop·u·lar′i·ty** (-lar′ə-ti), *n.* **—un·pop′u·lar·ly**, *adv.*
**un·prac′ticed** (-prak′tist), *adj.* 1. not habitually or repeatedly done. 2. not skilled or experienced; inexpert.
**un·prec′e·dent′ed**, *adj.* having no precedent or parallel; unique; novel.
**un·prin′ci·pled** (-p'ld), *adj.* lacking moral principles; unscrupulous.
**un·print′a·ble**, *adj.* not fit to be printed, as because of obscenity.
**un′pro·fes′sion·al**, *adj.* not professional; esp., violating the ethical code of a given profession. **—un′pro·fes′sion·al·ly**, *adv.*
**un·qual′i·fied′**, *adj.* 1. lacking the necessary qualifications. 2. not modified or limited; absolute. **—un·qual′i·fied′ly**, *adv.*
**un·ques′tion·a·ble**, *adj.* not to be questioned, doubted, or disputed; certain.
**un·quote′**, *v.t. & v.i.* [-QUOTED, -QUOTING], to end (a quotation).
**un·rav′el**, *v.t.* [-ELED or -ELLED, -ELING or -ELLING], 1. to separate the threads of (something woven, tangled, etc.). 2. to make clear; solve. *v.i.* to become unraveled.
**un·read′** (-red′), *adj.* 1. not having been read, as a book, etc. 2. having read little.
**un·re′al**, *adj.* not real or actual; fantastic; imaginary; fanciful.
**un·rea′son·a·ble**, *adj.* 1. not reasonable or rational. 2. excessive; immoderate.
**un·rea′son·ing**, *adj.* not reasoning; thoughtless; irrational.
**un′re·gen′er·ate**, *adj.* 1. not spiritually reborn. 2. wicked; sinful.
**un′re·lent′ing**, *adj.* 1. inflexible; relentless. 2. without mercy; cruel. 3. not relaxing in effort, speed, etc.
**un′re·mit′ting**, *adj.* not stopping, relaxing, etc.: incessant; persistent.
**un′re·served′**, *adj.* 1. not reserved in speech or behavior. 2. not restricted or qualified. **—un′re·serv′ed·ly** (-zũr′vid-li), *adv.*
**un·rest′**, *n.* 1. restlessness; disquiet. 2. angry discontent verging on revolt.
**un·ripe′**, *adj.* not ripe or mature; green.
**un·ri′valed, un·ri′valled**, *adj.* having no rival, equal, or competitor.
**un·roll′**, *v.t.* 1. to open or extend (something rolled up). 2. to present to view; display. *v.i.* to become unrolled.
**un·ruf′fled**, *adj.* not ruffled or disturbed; calm; smooth; serene.
**un·rul·y** (un-rōō′li), *adj.* [-IER, -IEST], hard to control, restrain, or keep in order; disobedient. **—un·rul′i·ness**, *n.*
**un·sad′dle**, *v.t.* [-DLED, -DLING], 1. to take the saddle off (a horse, etc.). 2. to throw from the saddle; unhorse.
**un·sa′vor·y**, *adj.* 1. tasteless. 2. unpleasant to taste or smell. 3. morally offensive.
**un·say′**, *v.t.* [-SAID, -SAYING], to take back or retract (what has been said).
**un·scathed** (un-skāthd′), *adj.* [*un-* + archaic *scathe*, injure], uninjured.
**un·scram′ble**, *v.t.* [-BLED, -BLING], [Colloq.], to cause to be no longer scrambled, disordered, or mixed up.
**un·screw′**, *v.t.* to detach or loosen by removing a screw or screws.
**un·scru′pu·lous**, *adj.* having no moral principles or scruples; unprincipled.
**un·seal′**, *v.t.* to break the seal of; open.
**un·sea′son·a·ble**, *adj.* 1. not usual for the season. 2. at the wrong time.
**un·seat′**, *v.t.* 1. to dislodge from a seat. 2. to remove from office. 3. to unhorse.
**un·seem′ly**, *adj.* not seemly, decent, or becoming; improper. **—un·seem′li·ness**, *n.*
**un·set′tle**, *v.t. & v.i.* [-TLED, -TLING], to make or become unstable; disturb or displace.
**un·shack′le**, *v.t.* [-LED, -LING], 1. to remove the shackles from. 2. to free.
**un·sheathe′** (-shēth′), *v.t.* [-SHEATHED, -SHEATHING], to remove (a sword, etc.) from a sheath.
**un·skilled′**, *adj.* having or requiring no special skill or training.
**un·skill′ful, un·skil′ful**, *adj.* having little or no skill; awkward.
**un·snap′**, *v.t.* [-SNAPPED, -SNAPPING], to detach by undoing the snaps of.
**un·snarl′** (-snärl′), *v.t.* to untangle.
**un′so·phis′ti·cat′ed**, *adj.* not sophisticated; artless; simple.
**un·sound′**, *adj.* 1. not sound, whole, or perfect. 2. at variance with fact; false. 3. not safe, firm, etc.; insecure. 4. not deep: said of sleep. **—un·sound′ly**, *adv.*
**un·spar′ing**, *adj.* 1. not sparing; lavish. 2. not merciful; severe. **—un·spar′ing·ly**, *adv.*
**un·speak′a·ble**, *adj.* 1. that cannot be spoken. 2. inexpressibly bad, evil, etc.
**un·sta′ble**, *adj.* 1. not stable; easily upset, shifted, etc. 2. changeable; variable. 3. unreliable; fickle. **—un·sta′bly**, *adv.*
**un·stead′y**, *adj.* 1. not steady or firm; shaky. 2. changeable; inconstant. 3. erratic in habits, purpose, etc. **—un·stead′i·ly**, *adv.*
**un·stop′**, *v.t.* [-STOPPED, -STOPPING], 1. to remove the stopper from. 2. to clear (a pipe, etc.) of an obstruction.
**un·strung′**, *adj.* 1. nervous; upset. 2. with the strings loosened or detached.
**un·stud′ied**, *adj.* not got by study or conscious effort; spontaneous; natural.
**un′sub·stan′tial**, *adj.* 1. having no material substance. 2. not solid; flimsy. 3. unreal; visionary. **—un′sub·stan′tial·ly**, *adv.*
**un·sung′**, *adj.* 1. not sung. 2. not honored or celebrated, as in song or poetry.
**un·tan′gle**, *v.t.* [-GLED, -GLING], 1. to free from a snarl or tangle. 2. to put in order.
**un·taught′**, *adj.* 1. not taught; uneducated. 2. got without teaching.
**un·think′a·ble**, *adj.* that cannot be thought, conceived, or considered.
**un·think′ing**, *adj.* thoughtless; heedless.
**un·ti′dy**, *adj.* not tidy; slovenly; careless.
**un·tie′**, *v.t.* [-TIED, -TYING or -TIEING], 1. to unfasten (something tied or knotted). 2. to free, as from restraint.
**un·til** (ən-til′), *prep.* [ME. *untill*], 1. up to the time of: as, work *until* dusk. 2. before: as, don't eat *until* noon. *conj.* 1. up to the time when or that. 2. to the point, degree, etc. that: as, he ate *until* he was full. 3. before: as, don't go *until* he does.
**un·time′ly**, *adj.* 1. before the proper time; premature. 2. at the wrong time; inopportune. *adv.* 1. inopportunely. 2. prematurely.
**un·to** (un′tōō, -too), *prep.* [ME.], [Archaic or Poetic], 1. to. 2. until.
**un·told′**, *adj.* 1. not told or revealed. 2. too many to be counted; vast.
**un·touch′a·ble**, *adj.* 1. out of reach. 2. not to be touched. *n.* in India, formerly, a member of the lowest caste.
**un·toward** (un-tôrd′), *adj.* 1. hard to manage; perverse. 2. inconvenient; unfavorable. 3. unseemly. **—un·toward′ly**, *adv.*
**un·truth′**, *n.* 1. falsity. 2. a falsehood; lie. **—un·truth′ful**, *adj.* **—un·truth′ful·ly**, *adv.*
**un·tu′tored**, *adj.* uneducated.
**un·used′**, *adj.* 1. not in use. 2. unaccustomed. 3. that has never been used.
**un·u′su·al**, *adj.* not usual or common; rare.
**un·ut′ter·a·ble**, *adj.* that cannot be pronounced, expressed, or described.

**un·var'nished,** *adj.* 1. not varnished. 2. plain; simple; unadorned.
**un·veil',** *v.t.* to remove a veil from; disclose. *v.i.* to take off one's veil.
**un·war'y,** *adj.* not wary or cautious.
**un·well',** *adj.* not well; ill; sick.
**un·whole'some,** *adj.* 1. harmful to body or mind. 2. of unsound health, or unhealthy appearance. 3. morally harmful.
**un·wield'y,** *adj.* [-IER, -IEST], 1. hard to wield, manage, etc., as because of large size. 2. awkward; clumsy. **—un·wield'i·ness,** *n.*
**un·will'ing,** *adj.* 1. not willing; reluctant. 2. done, said, etc. reluctantly.
**un·wind',** *v.t.* [-WOUND, -WINDING], 1. to wind off or undo (something wound). 2. to untangle (something involved). *v.i.* to become unwound.
**un·wise',** *adj.* having or showing a lack of wisdom or sound judgment.
**un·wit·ting** (un-wit'iŋ), *adj.* 1. not knowing or aware. 2. unintentional.
**un·wont·ed** (un-wun'tid), *adj.* 1. not accustomed (*to*). 2. uncommon; rare.
**un·wor'thy,** *adj.* [-THIER, -THIEST], 1. without merit or value; worthless. 2. not deserving (*of*). 3. not fit, becoming, etc. (with *of*). 4. shameful; despicable.
**un·wrap',** *v.t.* [-WRAPPED, -WRAPPING], to take off the wrapping of.
**un·writ'ten,** *adj.* 1. not in writing. 2. operating only through custom or tradition: said of laws, etc. 3. not written on; blank.
**un·yoke',** *v.t.* [-YOKED, -YOKING], 1. to release from a yoke. 2. to disconnect.
**up** (up), *adv.* [AS.], 1. to, in, or on a higher place or level. 2. in or to a higher condition, amount, etc. 3. to a later period. 4. in or into a standing position. 5. in or into action, view, consideration, etc. 6. aside; away: as, to lay *up* grain. 7. so as to be even with in time, degree, etc. 8. in or into a close space: as, fold *up* the table. 9. completely; thoroughly. 10. in *baseball*, to one's turn at batting. The adverb *up* is also used: *a*) to alter the meaning of a verb (e.g., look *up* this word). *b*) as an intensive with verbs (e.g., dress *up*). *prep.* up toward, along, through, into, or upon. *adj.* 1. directed toward a higher position. 2. in a higher place, position, etc. 3. advanced in amount, degree, etc.: as, rents are *up*. 4. in a standing position. 5. in an active or excited state. 6. at an end; over: as, time's *up*. 7. [Colloq.], going on: as, what's *up?* 8. in *baseball*, at bat. *n.* 1. an upward slope. 2. an upward movement, etc. *v.i.* [UPPED, UPPING], [Colloq.], to get up; rise. *v.t.* [Colloq.], 1. to put up, lift up, etc. 2. to increase, as prices. **—on the up and up,** [Slang], honest. **—up against,** [Colloq.], confronted with. **—up on** (or **in**), [Colloq.], well informed concerning. **—ups and downs,** changes in fortune. **—up to,** [Colloq.], 1. doing or scheming. 2. capable of (doing, etc.). 3. to be decided by. 4. incumbent upon.
**up** (up), *adv.* [phonetic respelling of *ap*iece], apiece: as, a score of two *up*.
**up-,** a combining form meaning *up*.
**up-and-com·ing** (up''n-kum'iŋ), *adj.* [Colloq.], enterprising, promising, etc.
**up·braid** (up-brād'), *v.t.* & *v.i.* [< AS. *up-*, up + *bregdan*, to pull], to scold, reproach, or reprove for some wrongdoing, offense, etc.
**up'bring'ing,** *n.* the training and education received during childhood; rearing.
**up'coun'try,** *adj.* & *adv.* in or toward the interior of a country. *n.* the interior of a country.
**up·end',** *v.t.* & *v.i.* to set, turn, or stand on end. **—up·end'ed,** *adj.*
**up'grade',** *n.* an upward slope. *adj.* & *adv.* uphill. *v.t.* [-GRADED, -GRADING], to raise to a higher grade, rank, etc.
**up·heav·al** (up-hē'v'l), *n.* 1. a heaving up. 2. a sudden, violent change.
**up'hill',** *adj.* 1. going or sloping up. 2. tiring; difficult. *n.* a sloping rise. *adv.* upward as on a hillside.
**up·hold',** *v.t.* [-HELD, -HOLDING], 1. to hold up. 2. to keep from falling; support. 3. to confirm; sustain. **—up·hold'er,** *n.*
**up·hol·ster** (up-hōl'stẽr), *v.t.* [ult. < ME. *upholder*, tradesman], to fit out (furniture) with coverings, springs, padding, etc.
**up·hol'ster·y,** *n.* [*pl.* -IES], 1. the material used in upholstering. 2. the work of an upholsterer.
**up'keep',** *n.* 1. maintenance. 2. state of repair. 3. the cost of maintenance.
**up'land** (-lənd, -land'), *n.* land elevated above other land. *adj.* of or situated in up land.
**up·lift',** *v.t.* 1. to lift up. 2. to raise to a higher moral, social, or spiritual level. *n.* (up'lift'), 1. a lifting up. 2. a movement for moral, social, or spiritual betterment.
**up'most',** *adj.* uppermost.
**up·on** (ə-pon'), *prep.* on or up and on. *adv.* on. Used interchangeably with *on*.
**up·per** (up'ẽr), *adj.* 1. higher in place. 2. higher in rank; superior. *n.* the part of a shoe above the sole. **—on one's uppers,** [Colloq.], 1. wearing worn-out shoes. 2. poor.
**upper case,** capital-letter type used in printing, as distinguished from small letters (*lower case*). **—up'per-case',** *adj.*
**up'per-class',** *adj.* 1. of or characteristic of the aristocracy or very wealthy class. 2. of or characteristic of the junior and senior classes in a school, college, etc.
**up'per·cut',** *n.* in *boxing*, a short, swinging blow directed upward.
**upper hand,** the position of advantage.
**up'per·most',** *adj.* highest in place, power, authority, etc. *adv.* in the highest place, rank, etc.; first.
**up·pish** (up'ish), *adj.* [Colloq.], haughty, arrogant, snobbish, etc.: also **up'pi·ty** (-ə-ti).
**up·raise',** *v.t.* [-RAISED, -RAISING], to raise up; lift; elevate.
**up·rear',** *v.t.* 1. to rear up; raise. 2. to exalt. 3. to bring up.
**up'right',** *adj.* 1. standing, pointing, etc. straight up; erect. 2. honest; just. *adv.* (*also* up-rīt'), in an upright position or direction. *n.* something having an upright position.
**upright piano,** a piano with a rectangular body mounted vertically.
**up'ris'ing,** *n.* 1. a rising up. 2. a revolt.
**up·roar** (up'rôr'), *n.* [D. *oproer*, a stirring up], 1. a violent disturbance; tumult. 2. loud, confused noise; din.
**up·roar'i·ous,** *adj.* 1. making, or full of, an uproar. 2. loud and boisterous, as laughter.
**up·root',** *v.t.* 1. to tear up by the roots. 2. to destroy or remove utterly.
**up·set',** *v.t.* [-SET, -SETTING], 1. to tip over; overturn. 2. to disturb the functioning of: as, the food *upset* his stomach. 3. to defeat unexpectedly. 4. to perturb. *v.i.* to become overturned or upset. *n.* (up'set'), 1. an upsetting. 2. a disturbance. 3. an unexpected defeat. *adj.* 1. tipped over. 2. disturbed; disordered. 3. perturbed; distressed.
**up'shot',** *n.* [orig., final shot in an archery match], the conclusion; result.
**upside down,** 1. with the upper part underneath. 2. in disorder. **—up'side'-down',** *adj.*
**up·si·lon** (ūp'sə-lon'), *n.* the twentieth letter of the Greek alphabet (Υ, υ).
**up'stage',** *adv.* toward or at the rear of the stage. *adj.* 1. of or having to do with the rear of the stage. 2. [Colloq.], aloof, haughty, etc.
**up'stairs',** *adv.* 1. up the stairs. 2. in, on, or toward an upper floor. *adj.* of or on an upper floor. *n.* an upper story or stories.

**up·stand′ing,** *adj.* 1. erect. 2. honorable; straightforward.
**up′start′,** *n.* one who has recently come into wealth, power, etc.; esp., such a person who is pushing, presumptuous, etc.
**up′state′,** *adj.* of or from the more northerly or inland part of a State. *adv.* in or toward such a part of a State.
**up′stream′,** *adv. & adj.* in, toward, or of the upper part of a stream.
**up′-tight′, up′tight′,** *adj.* [Slang], very tense, nervous, anxious, etc.
**up′-to-date′,** *adj.* 1. extending to the present time. 2. keeping up with what is most recent, modern, etc. **—up′-to-date′ness,** *n.*
**up′town′,** *adj. & adv.* of, in, or toward the upper part of a city or town. *n.* the upper part of a city or town.
**up·turn′,** *v.t. & v.i.* to turn up or over. *n.* (up′tũrn′), an upward turn, curve, or trend.
**up′ward** (-wẽrd), *adv. & adj.* toward a higher place, position, etc.: also **up′wards,** *adv.* **—upward of,** more than.
**u·ra·ni·um** (yoo-rā′ni-əm), *n.* [< *Uranus*], a very hard, heavy, radioactive metallic chemical element: used in work on atomic energy: symbol, U.
**U·ra·nus** (yoor′ə-nəs), *n.* [< Gr. *ouranos,* heaven], a planet of the solar system: cf. **planet.**
**ur·ban** (ũr′bən), *adj.* [< L. *urbs,* city], 1. of, in, or constituting a city. 2. characteristic of a city.
**ur·bane** (ũr-bān′), *adj.* [see prec.], suave; smooth and polished in manner. **—ur·bane′ly,** *adv.* **—ur·ban′i·ty** (-ban′ə-ti), *n.*
**ur′ban·ize′** (-iz′), *v.t.* [-IZED, -IZING], to change from rural to urban. **—ur′ban·i·za′tion,** *n.*
**ur·chin** (ũr′chin), *n.* [< L. *ericius,* hedgehog], a small child; esp., a mischievous boy.
**-ure,** [< L. *-ura*], a suffix meaning *act, result* or *agent of an action, state of being,* etc., as in *exposure.*
**u·re·a** (yoo-rē′ə), *n.* [< Gr. *ouron,* urine], a soluble, crystalline solid found in urine.
**u·re·mi·a** (yoo-rē′mi-ə), *n.* [< Gr. *ouron,* urine + *haima,* blood], a toxic condition caused by the retention in the blood of waste products normally eliminated in the urine: also sp. **uraemia. —u·re′mic,** *adj.*
**u·re·ter** (yoo-rē′tẽr), *n.* [< Gr. *ourein,* urinate], a tube carrying urine from a kidney to the bladder.
**u·re·thra** (yoo-rē′thrə), *n.* [*pl.* -THRAE (-thrē), -THRAS], [< Gr. *ouron,* urine], the canal through which urine is discharged from the bladder: in males, also the duct for semen. **—u·re′thral,** *adj.*
**urge** (ũrj), *v.t.* [URGED, URGING], [< L. *urgere,* press hard], 1. to press upon the attention; advocate. 2. to drive or force onward. 3. to plead with; ask. 4. to force; incite. *v.i.* 1. to make an earnest presentation of arguments, claims, etc. 2. to exert a driving force. *n.* 1. an urging. 2. an impulse.
**ur·gent** (ũr′jənt), *adj.* [see URGE], 1. calling for haste, immediate action, etc. 2. insistent. **—ur′gen·cy** [*pl.* -CIES], *n.*
**-urgy,** [< Gr. *-ourgos,* worker], a combining form meaning a *fabricating* or *working of.*
**u·ric** (yoor′ik), *adj.* of, contained in, or derived from urine.
**u·ri·nal** (yoor′ə-n′l), *n.* 1. a receptacle for urine. 2. a place for urinating.
**u·ri·nal·y·sis** (yoor′ə-nal′ə-sis), *n.* chemical analysis of the urine.
**u·ri·nar·y** (yoor′ə-ner′i), *adj.* 1. of urine. 2. of the organs that secrete or discharge urine.
**u·ri·nate** (yoor′ə-nāt′), *v.i.* [-NATED, -NATING], to discharge urine from the body. **—u′ri·na′tion,** *n.*
**u·rine** (yoor′in), *n.* [< L. *urina*], the yellowish fluid containing waste products secreted by the kidneys and discharged through the urethra.
**urn** (ũrn), *n.* [L. *urna*], 1. a vase with a pedestal, esp. one used to hold the ashes of a cremated body. 2. a metal container with a faucet, for making or serving coffee, etc.
**ur·sine** (ũr′sin, -sin), *adj.* [< L. *ursus,* a bear], of or like a bear.
**us** (us), *pron.* [AS.], the objective case of **we.**
**U.S., US,** United States.
**U.S.A., USA,** 1. United States of America. 2. United States Army.
**us·a·ble, use·a·ble** (ūz′ə-b′l), *adj.* that can be used; fit for use.
**U.S.A.F., USAF,** United States Air Force.
**us·age** (ūs′ij, ūz′-), *n.* 1. the act or way of using; treatment. 2. established practice; custom. 3. the way in which a word, phrase, etc. is used to express a particular idea.
**use** (ūz; *for n.,* ūs), *v.t.* [USED, USING], [< L. *uti*], 1. to put or bring into action or service. 2. to exercise: as, *use* your judgment. 3. to deal with; treat. 4. to consume, expend, etc.: as, *use* up the time. 5. to accustom: as, *used* to the cold. *v.i.* to be accustomed: as, he *used* to play golf. *n.* 1. a using or being used. 2. the ability to use. 3. the right to use. 4. the need or opportunity to use. 5. way of using. 6. usefulness; utility. 7. the purpose for which something is used. 8. function; service. **—us′er,** *n.*
**use·ful** (ūs′fəl), *adj.* that can be used; serviceable; helpful. **—use′ful·ly,** *adv.*
**use′less,** *adj.* having or of no use; worthless.
**ush·er** (ush′ẽr), *n.* [< L. *ostium,* door], 1. an official doorkeeper. 2. one who shows people to their seats in a church, theater, etc. 3. a bridegroom's attendant. *v.t.* 1. to escort (others) to seats, etc. 2. to be a forerunner of.
**USMC, U.S.M.C.,** United States Marine Corps.
**U.S.N., USN,** United States Navy.
**U.S.S.R., USSR,** Union of Soviet Socialist Republics.
**u·su·al** (ū′zhōō-əl), *adj.* [see USE], such as is in common or ordinary use; customary; habitual. **—u′su·al·ly,** *adv.*
**u·surp** (ū-zũrp′, -sũrp′), *v.t. & v.i.* [< L. *usus,* a use + *rapere,* seize], to take and hold (power, position, etc.) by force or without right. **—u·sur·pa·tion** (ū′zẽr-pā′shən, -sẽr-), *n.* **—u·surp′er,** *n.*
**u·su·ry** (ū′shoo-ri), *n.* [*pl.* -RIES], [see USE], 1. the lending of money at an excessive rate of interest. 2. such a rate of interest. **—u′su·rer,** *n.* **—u·su′ri·ous** (-zhoor′i-əs), *adj.*
**u·ten·sil** (ū-ten′s'l), *n.* [< L. *uti,* to use], an implement or container, esp. one used in a kitchen, dairy, etc.
**u·ter·us** (ū′tẽr-əs), *n.* [*pl.* -TERI (-ī′)], [L.], a hollow organ of female mammals in which the embryo and fetus are developed and protected. **—u′ter·ine** (-in, -īn′), *adj.*
**u·til·i·tar·i·an** (ū-til′ə-târ′i-ən), *adj.* 1. of or having to do with utility. 2. stressing utility over beauty, decorativeness, etc.
**u·til′i·tar′i·an·ism,** *n.* the doctrine that the purpose of all action should be to bring about the greatest happiness of the greatest number.
**u·til·i·ty** (ū-til′ə-ti), *n.* [*pl.* -TIES], [< L. *uti,* to use], 1. usefulness. 2. something useful, as the service to the public of gas, water, etc. 3. a company providing such a service.
**u·ti·lize** (ū′t'l-iz′), *v.t.* [-LIZED, -LIZING], to put to profitable use; make use of. **—u′ti·liz′a·ble,** *adj.* **—u′ti·li·za′tion,** *n.*
**ut·most** (ut′mōst′), *adj.* [< AS. superl. of *ut,* out], 1. most extreme or distant; farthest. 2. of the greatest degree, amount, etc.; greatest. *n.* the most that is possible.
**U·to·pi·a** (ū-tō′pi-ə), *n.* [< Gr. *ou,* not + *topos,* a place], 1. the imaginary island of

Sir Thomas More's *Utopia* (1516), with a perfect political and social system. 2. [often u-), *a*) any place of ideal perfection. *b*) any visionary scheme for a perfect social order. —**U·to′pi·an, u·to′pi·an,** *adj. & n.*

**ut·ter** (ut′ẽr), *adj.* [< AS. compar. of *ut*, out], 1. complete; total. 2. unqualified; absolute.

**ut·ter** (ut′ẽr), *v.t.* [< ME. *ut*, out], 1. to speak or say, as words. 2. to express in any way. 3. to make known; divulge; reveal.

**ut′ter·ance,** *n.* 1. an uttering. 2. the power or style of speaking. 3. that which is uttered.

**ut′ter·most′** (-mōst′), *adj. & n.* utmost.

**u·vu·la** (ū′vyoo-lə), *n.* [*pl.* -LAS, -LAE (-lē′)], [< L. *uva*, grape], the small, fleshy process hanging down from the soft palate above the back of the tongue. —**u′vu·lar,** *adj.*

# V

**V, v,** (vē), *n.* [*pl.* V's, v's, Vs, vs], the 22d letter of the English alphabet.

**V,** *n.* 1. an object shaped like V. 2. a Roman numeral for 5. 3. in *chem.*, vanadium.

**V, v,** 1. velocity. 2. volt(s).

**v.,** 1. verb. 2. versus. 3. volume.

**VA, V.A.,** Veterans' Administration.

**va·can·cy** (vā′kən-si), *n.* [*pl.* -CIES], 1. a being vacant. 2. empty or vacant space. 3. an unoccupied office, quarters, etc.

**va·cant** (vā′kənt), *adj.* [< L. *vacare*, be empty], 1. having nothing in it; empty. 2. not held, filled, etc., as a seat, house, etc. 3. free from work; leisure. 4. foolish or stupid. —**va′cant·ly,** *adv.*

**va·cate** (vā′kāt), *v.t. & v.i.* [-CATED, -CATING], [see prec. entry], 1. to make vacant, as an office, house, etc. 2. to make void; annul.

**va·ca·tion** (və-kā′shən, vā-), *n.* [< L. *vacatio*], a specific interval of rest from work, study, etc. *v.i.* to take one's vacation.

**vac·ci·nate** (vak′sə-nāt′), *v.t. & v.i.* [-NATED, -NATING], to inoculate with a vaccine to prevent a disease, specif. smallpox. —**vac′ci·na′tion,** *n.*

**vac·cine** (vak′sēn), *n.* [< L. *vacca*, cow], 1. a substance containing the causative virus of cowpox, used in vaccination against smallpox. 2. any preparation used to produce immunity against a specific disease.

**vac·il·late** (vas′ə-lāt′), *v.i.* [-LATED, -LATING], [< L. *vacillare*], 1. to sway to and fro; waver. 2. to fluctuate. 3. to show indecision. —**vac′il·la′tion,** *n.*

**va·cu·i·ty** (va-kū′ə-ti), *n.* [*pl.* -TIES], [< L. *vacuus*, empty], 1. emptiness. 2. an empty space; void. 3. lack of intelligence, thought, etc. 4. inanity.

**vac·u·ous** (vak′ū-əs), *adj.* [see prec. entry], 1. empty. 2. stupid; senseless.

**vac·u·um** (vak′ū-əm, vak′yoom), *n.* [*pl.* -UMS, -A (-ə)], [L.], 1. space with nothing at all in it. 2. a space from which most of the air or gas has been taken. 3. a void. *adj.* 1. of, or used to make, a vacuum. 2. having or working by a vacuum. *v.t.* [Colloq.], to clean with a vacuum cleaner.

**vacuum cleaner,** a machine for cleaning carpets, floors, upholstery, etc. by suction.

**vacuum tube,** a sealed tube containing a rarefied air or gas and electrodes for controlling the flow of electrons: used in radio, etc.

**vag·a·bond** (vag′ə-bond′), *adj.* [< L. *vagari*, wander], 1. wandering. 2. vagrant; shiftless; worthless. *n.* one who wanders from place to place; esp., a vagrant; tramp.

**va·gar·y** (və-gâr′i), *n.* [*pl.* -IES], [see prec.], 1. an odd or eccentric action. 2. a whimsical or freakish idea or notion; caprice.

**va·gi·na** (və-jī′nə), *n.* [*pl.* -NAS, -NAE (-nē)], [L., sheath], in female mammals, the canal from the vulva to the uterus. —**vag·i·nal** (vaj′ə-n'l), *adj.*

**va·grant** (vā′grənt), *n.* [prob. < OFr. *wa(u)crer*, wander about], one who wanders from place to place; esp., one without a regular job, supporting himself by begging, etc.; tramp. *adj.* 1. wandering; nomadic. 2. of or like a vagrant. 3. wayward; irregular. —**va′gran·cy** [*pl.* -CIES], *n.*

**vague** (vāg), *adj.* [< L. *vagus*, wandering], 1. indefinite in shape or form. 2. not sharp, clear, certain, etc. in thought or expression.

**vain** (vān), *adj.* [< L. *vanus*, empty], 1. having no real value; worthless: as, *vain* pomp. 2. without effect; futile: as, a *vain* endeavor. 3. having an excessively high regard for one's self, looks, etc.; conceited. —**in vain,** 1. without success. 2. profanely.

**vain·glo·ry** (vān′glôr′i), *n.* [see VAIN & GLORY], boastful pride or vanity. —**vain′glo′ri·ous,** *adj.* —**vain′glo′ri·ous·ly,** *adv.*

**val·ance** (val′əns), *n.* [prob. < OFr. *avaler*, to hang], a short drapery or curtain forming a border, esp. across the top of a window.

**vale** (vāl), *n.* [Poetic], a valley.

**val·e·dic·to·ri·an** (val′ə-dik-tôr′i-ən), *n.* the student who delivers the valedictory at graduation.

**val′e·dic′to·ry** (-tə-ri), *n.* [*pl.* -RIES], [< L. *vale*, farewell + *dicere*, to say], a farewell speech, esp. at a graduation.

**va·lence** (vā′ləns), *n.* [< L. *valere*, be strong], in *chem.*, the combining capacity of an element as measured by the number of hydrogen atoms which one atom of the element will combine with or replace. Also **va′len·cy.**

**val·en·tine** (val′ən-tīn′), *n.* 1. a sweetheart chosen or complimented on Saint Valentine's Day. 2. a greeting card or gift sent on this day.

**val·et** (val′it, -ā), *n.* [Fr.], 1. a personal manservant who takes care of one's clothes, helps one in dressing, etc. 2. a hotel employee who cleans or presses clothes, etc.

**Val·hal·la** (val-hal′ə), *n.* in *Norse myth.*, the great hall where Odin receives and feasts the souls of heroes slain in battle.

**val·iant** (val′yənt), *adj.* [< L. *valere*, be strong], brave; courageous. —**val′ian·cy** (-si), *n.* —**val′iant·ly,** *adv.*

**val·id** (val′id), *adj.* [< L. *valere*, have power], 1. having legal force. 2. well grounded on principles or evidence, as an argument.

**val·i·date** (val′ə-dāt′), *v.t.* [-DATED, -DATING], 1. to make legally valid. 2. to prove to be valid. —**val′i·da′tion,** *n.*

**va·lid·i·ty** (və-lid′ə-ti), *n.* [*pl.* -TIES], the state, quality, or fact of being valid; (legal) soundness.

**va·lise** (və-lēs′), *n.* [Fr. < It. *valigia*], a traveling bag; suitcase.

**Val·kyr·ie** (val-kêr′i, val′ki-ri), *n.* in *Norse myth.*, any of the maidens of Odin who conduct the souls of heroes slain in battle to Valhalla.

**val·ley** (val′i), *n.* [*pl.* -LEYS], [< L. *vallis*], 1. low land lying between hills or mountains. 2. the land drained by a river system. 3. any valleylike dip or hollow.

**val·or** (val′ẽr), *n.* [< L. *valere*, be strong], courage; fearlessness: also, Brit. sp., **valour.** —**val′or·ous,** *adj.* —**val′or·ous·ly,** *adv.*

**val·u·a·ble** (val′yoo-b'l, -ū-ə-b'l), *adj.* 1.

having material value. 2. of great monetary value. 3. highly thought of; prized. *n. usually in pl.* an article of value.

**val·u·a·tion** (val'ū-ā'shən), *n.* 1. the determining of the value of anything. 2. determined or estimated value.

**val·ue** (val'ū), *n.* [< L. *valere*, be worth], 1. the worth of a thing in money or goods. 2. estimated worth. 3. purchasing power. 4. that quality of a thing which makes it more or less desirable, useful, etc. 5. distinct quality or quantity. 6. relative duration, intensity, etc. *v.t.* [-UED, -UING], 1. to estimate the value of; appraise. 2. to place an estimate of worth on: as, I *value* health above wealth. 3. to think highly of; prize. **—val'ue·less,** *adj.*

**val'ued,** *adj.* highly thought of; esteemed.

**valve** (valv), *n.* [< L. *valva*, leaf of a folding door], 1. in *anatomy*, a membranous structure which permits body fluids to flow in one direction only, or opens and closes a tube, etc. 2. any device in a pipe, etc. that regulates the flow by means of a flap, lid, etc. 3. in *music*, a device, as in the trumpet, that changes the tube length so as to change the pitch. 4. in *zoology*, one of the parts making up the shell of a mollusk, clam, etc.

**val·vu·lar** (val'vyoo-lẽr), *adj.* 1. having a valve or valves. 2. of a valve or valves; esp., of the valves of the heart.

**va·moose** (va-mōōs'), *v.i.* [-MOOSED, -MOOSING], [Sp. *vamos*, let us go], [Slang], to leave quickly.

**vamp** (vamp), *n.* [< OFr. *avant*, before + *pié*, a foot], 1. the part of a boot or shoe covering the instep and toe. 2. something patched up to seem new. *v.t.* to patch (*up*).

**vamp** (vamp), *n.* [Slang], a vampire (sense 3). *v.t. & v.i.* [Slang], to flirt with or beguile (a man).

**vam·pire** (vam'pīr), *n.* [< Slav.], 1. in *folklore*, a reanimated corpse that sucks the blood of sleeping persons. 2. one who preys ruthlessly on others. 3. a beautiful but unscrupulous woman who seduces then ruins men. 4. a vampire bat.

**vampire bat,** a tropical American bat that lives on the blood of animals.

**van** (van), *n.* the vanguard.

**van** (van), *n.* [< *caravan*], a large closed truck or wagon for carrying furniture, etc.

**va·na·di·um** (və-nā'di-əm), *n.* [< ON. *Vanadis*, goddess of love], a ductile metallic chemical element used in steel alloys: symbol, V.

**Van·dal** (van'd'l), *n.* 1. a member of a Germanic tribe that sacked Rome (455 A.D.). 2. [v-], one who maliciously destroys works of art, public property, etc. **—van'dal·ism,** *n.*

**van'dal·ize,** *v.t.* [-IZED, -IZING], to destroy or damage public property, etc. maliciously.

**Van·dyke (beard)** (van-dīk'), a closely trimmed, pointed beard.

**vane** (vān), *n.* [< AS. *fana*, flag], 1. a free-swinging piece of metal, etc. that shows which way the wind is blowing; weather vane. 2. any of the flat blades set around an axle, forming a wheel to be rotated by, or to rotate, air, water, etc.: as, the *vanes* of a windmill.

**van·guard** (van'gärd'), *n.* [< OFr. *avant*, before + *garde*, guard], 1. the front part of an army in an advance; the van. 2. the leading position in a movement. 3. those leading a movement.

**va·nil·la** (və-nil'ə), *n.* [< Sp. *vaina*, pod], 1. a climbing orchid with podlike capsules **(vanilla beans).** 2. a flavoring made from these capsules.

**van·ish** (van'ish), *v.i.* [see EVANESCE], 1. to disappear; pass suddenly from sight. 2. to cease to exist. **—van'ish·er,** *n.*

**van·i·ty** (van'ə-ti), *n.* [*pl.* -TIES], [< L. *vanus*, vain], 1. anything vain, or futile. 2. worthlessness; futility. 3. a being vain, or too proud of oneself. 4. a small case for carrying cosmetics: in full, **vanity case.**

**van·quish** (vaŋ'kwish), *v.t.* [< L. *vincere*], to conquer or defeat. **—van'quish·er,** *n.*

**van·tage** (van'tij), *n.* advantage.

**vap·id** (vap'id), *adj.* [L. *vapidus*], tasteless; flavorless; dull. **—va·pid·i·ty** (və-pid'ə-ti), **vap'id·ness,** *n.* **—vap'id·ly,** *adv.*

**va·por** (vā'pẽr), *n.* [L.], 1. *a*) visible particles of moisture floating in the air; fog; steam. *b*) smoke, fumes, etc. 2. the gaseous form of any substance normally a liquid or a solid. *v.i.* to pass off as vapor; evaporate. Also, Brit. sp., **vapour.**

**va'por·ize'** (-īz'), *v.t. & v.i.* [-IZED, -IZING], to change into vapor. **—va'por·i·za'tion,** *n.*

**va'por·ous,** *adj.* 1. forming vapor. 2. full of vapor; foggy. 3. like vapor. 4. fleeting, fanciful, etc.

**var.,** 1. variant. 2. various.

**var·i·a·ble** (vâr'i-ə-b'l), *adj.* 1. apt to change or vary; changeable, inconstant, etc. 2. that can be changed or varied. *n.* anything changeable; thing that varies. **—var'i·a·bil'i·ty,** *n.* **—var'i·a·bly,** *adv.*

**var·i·ance** (vâr'i-əns), *n.* 1. a varying or being variant. 2. degree of change or difference; discrepancy. 3. a quarrel; dispute. **—at variance,** disagreeing; differing.

**var·i·ant** (vâr'i-ənt), *adj.* 1. varying; different in some way from others of the same kind. 2. variable; changeable. *n.* anything variant, as a different spelling of the same word.

**var·i·a·tion** (vâr'i-ā'shən), *n.* 1. a varying change in form, extent, etc. 2. the degree of such change. 3. a thing somewhat different from another of the same kind.

**var·i·col·ored** (vâr'i-kul'ẽrd), *adj.* 1. of several or many colors. 2. varied.

**var·i·cose** (var'ə-kōs'), *adj.* [< L. *varix*, enlarged vein], abnormally and irregularly swollen: as, *varicose* veins.

**var·ied** (vâr'id), *adj.* 1. of different kinds; various. 2. changed; altered.

**var·i·e·gat·ed** (vâr'i-ə-gāt'id), *adj.* [< L. *varius*, various], 1. of different colors in spots, streaks, etc. 2. varied.

**va·ri·e·ty** (və-rī'ə-ti), *n.* [*pl.* -TIES], 1. a being various or varied. 2. a different form of some thing, condition, etc.; kind: as, *varieties* of cloth. 3. a collection of different things. 4. vaudeville: in full, **variety show.**

**var·i·ous** (vâr'i-əs), *adj.* [L. *varius*, diverse], 1. differing one from another; of several kinds. 2. several; many. **—var'i·ous·ly,** *adv.*

**var·let** (vär'lit), *n.* [OFr., a valet], [Archaic], a rascal; scoundrel.

**var·mint, var·ment** (vär'mənt), *n.* [Dial.], vermin; esp., a person or animal regarded as objectionable.

**var·nish** (vär'nish), *n.* [< ML. *veronix*, resin], 1. a preparation of resinous substances dissolved in oil, alcohol, etc., used to give a glossy surface to wood, metal, etc. 2. this smooth, glossy surface. 3. an outward, deceptive attractiveness. *v.t.* 1. to cover with varnish. 2. to give a superficial attractiveness to.

**var·si·ty** (vär'sə-ti), *n.* [*pl.* -TIES], [< *university*], a team representing a university, school, etc., as in a sport.

**var·y** (vâr'i), *v.t.* [-IED, -YING], [< L. *varius*, various], 1. to change; alter. 2. to make different from one another. 3. to give variety to: as, *vary* your reading. *v.i.* 1. to undergo change. 2. to be different. 3. to deviate (*from*). **—var'y·ing·ly,** *adv.*

**vas·cu·lar** (vas'kyoo-lẽr), *adj.* [< L. *vas*, vessel], of or having vessels or ducts for conveying blood, sap, etc.

**vase** (vās, vāz; Brit. väz), *n.* [< L. *vas*, vessel], an open container used for decoration, displaying flowers, etc.

**vas·e·line** (vas′ə-lēn′), *n.* [< G. *wasser*, water + Gr. *elaion*, oil], a greasy, jellylike substance obtained from petroleum, used as a lubricant or ointment: a trademark **(Vaseline).**

**vas·o·mo·tor** (vas′ō-mō′tēr), *adj.* [< L. *vas*, vessel; + *motor*], regulating the size, or diameter, of blood vessels: said of a nerve, drug, etc.

**vas·sal** (vas′'l), *n.* [< ML. *vassus*, servant], 1. in the Middle Ages, one who held land under the feudal system, pledging fealty to an overlord. 2. a subordinate. 3. a servant. 4. a slave. **—vas′sal·age** (-ij), *n.*

**vast** (vast, väst), *adj.* [L. *vastus*], 1. of very great size or extent; immense. 2. very great in quantity or degree. **—vast′ly,** *adv.*

**vat** (vat), *n.* [< AS. *fæt*, cask], a large tank, tub, or cask for liquids.

**Vat·i·can** (vat′i-kən), *n.* 1. the papal palace in Vatican City. 2. the papal government.

**vaude·ville** (vōd′vil, vô′də-vil), *n.* [Fr. < *Vau-de-Vire*, a valley in Normandy, famous for convivial songs], a stage show consisting of various acts of songs, dances, skits, etc.

**vault** (vôlt), *n.* [< L. *volvere*, to roll], 1. an arched roof or ceiling. 2. an arched chamber or space. 3. a cellar room used for storage. 4. a burial chamber. 5. a room for the safekeeping of valuables, as in a bank. *v.t.* to cover with, or build as, a vault.

**vault** (vôlt), *v.i.* & *v.t.* [< OFr. *volter*], to jump, leap, etc.; esp., to leap over (a barrier) with the hands supported on the barrier, or holding a long pole. *n.* a vaulting.

**vaunt** (vônt, vänt), *n., v.i.* & *v.t.* [< L. *vanus*, vain], boast; brag. **—vaunt′ing·ly,** *adv.*

**V.D., VD,** venereal disease.

**veal** (vēl), *n.* [< L. *vitulus*, a calf], the flesh of a calf used as food.

**veer** (vêr), *v.i.* & *v.t.* [< Fr. *virer*, turn around], to change in direction; shift; turn. *n.* a change of direction. **—veer′ing·ly,** *adv.*

**veg·e·ta·ble** (vej′tə-b'l, vej′i-tə-), *n.* [see VEGETATE], 1. any plant, as distinguished from animal or inorganic matter. 2. a plant eaten whole or in part, raw or cooked, as in a salad or with an entree, as the tomato, potato, lettuce, etc. *adj.* 1. of, like, or made from edible vegetables. 2. of plants in general.

**veg′e·tar′i·an** (-ə-târ′i-ən), *n.* one who eats no meat. *adj.* 1. of vegetarians. 2. consisting only of vegetables.

**veg·e·tate** (vej′ə-tāt′), *v.i.* [-TATED, -TATING], [< L. *vegere*, quicken], 1. to grow as plants. 2. to lead a very inactive life. **—veg′e·ta′tive,** *adj.* **—veg′i·ta′tive·ly,** *adv.*

**veg′e·ta′tion,** *n.* 1. a vegetating. 2. plant life in general.

**ve·he·ment** (vē′ə-mənt), *adj.* [< L. *vehere*, carry], 1. violent; impetuous. 2. having or showing intense feeling; passionate. **—ve′he·mence, ve′he·men·cy,** *n.*

**ve·hi·cle** (vē′ə-k'l), *n.* [< L. *vehere*, carry], 1. any device on wheels or runners for conveying persons or objects. 2. any means of carrying, conveying, or communicating. **—ve·hic′u·lar** (-hik′yoo-lēr), *adj.*

**veil** (vāl), *n.* [< L. *velum*, cloth], 1. a piece of light fabric, as of net, worn, esp. by women, over the face or head. 2. anything used to conceal, separate, etc.: as, a *veil* of silence. 3. a part of a nun's headdress. *v.t.* 1. to cover with a veil. 2. to conceal; hide or disguise. **—take the veil,** to become a nun.

**veiled** (vāld), *adj.* 1. wearing, or covered with, a veil. 2. concealed; hidden. 3. not openly expressed.

**vein** (vān), *n.* [< L. *vena*], 1. any blood vessel carrying blood to the heart. 2. any of the ribs of an insect's wing or of a leaf blade. 3. a fissure in rock, filled with a mineral. 4. a stratum of coal, etc. 5. a streak of a different color, etc., as in marble. 6. a distinctive quality in one's character, speech, etc. *v.t.* to mark as with veins.

**veld, veldt** (velt, felt), *n.* [D. *veld*, field], in S Africa, open grassy country with few bushes and almost no trees; grassland.

**vel·lum** (vel′əm), *n.* [< L. *vitulus*, calf], 1. a fine parchment prepared from calfskin, lambskin, etc., used for writing on or for binding books. 2. paper resembling this.

**ve·loc·i·pede** (və-los′ə-pēd′), *n.* [< L. *velox*, swift + *pes*, foot], a tricycle.

**ve·loc·i·ty** (və-los′ə-ti), *n.* [*pl.* -TIES], [< L. *velox*, swift], 1. quickness of motion; speed. 2. rate of motion in relation to time.

**ve·lours, ve·lour** (və-loor′), *n.* [*pl.* -LOURS], [Fr.; see VELURE], a fabric with a nap like velvet used for upholstery, draperies, etc.

**ve·lum** (vē′ləm), *n.* [*pl.* -LA (-lə)], [L., veil], the soft palate. **—ve′lar** (-lēr), *adj.*

**ve·lure** (və-loor′), *n.* [< Fr. < L. *villus*, shaggy hair], velvet or a fabric like velvet.

**vel·vet** (vel′vit), *n.* [see prec.], 1. a rich fabric of silk, rayon, etc. with a soft, thick pile. 2. anything like velvet in texture. 3. [Slang], clear profit. *adj.* 1. made of velvet. 2. like velvet. **—vel′vet·y,** *adj.*

**vel′vet·een′** (-və-tēn′), *n.* a cotton cloth with a short, thick pile, like velvet.

**ve·nal** (vē′n'l), *adj.* [< L. *venum*, sale], open to, or characterized by, corruption or bribery. **—ve·nal′i·ty** (-nal′ə-ti) [*pl.* -TIES], *n.*

**vend** (vend), *v.t.* & *v.i.* [< L. *vendere* < *venum dare*, offer for sale], to sell. **—ven′dor, vend′er,** *n.*

**ven·det·ta** (ven-det′ə), *n.* [*pl.* -TAS], [It. < L. *vindicta*, vengeance], a family feud arising from a murder.

**ve·neer** (və-nêr′), *v.t.* [< Fr. *fournir*, furnish], to cover with a thin layer of something fine, esp., to cover (wood) with wood of a finer quality. *n.* 1. a thin surface layer, as of wood, laid over a base of common material. 2. any attractive but superficial appearance: as, a *veneer* of culture.

**ven·er·a·ble** (ven′ēr-ə-b'l), *adj.* worthy of respect or reverence because of age, dignity, etc. **—ven′er·a·bil′i·ty,** *n.*

**ven·er·ate** (ven′ə-rāt′), *v.t.* [-ATED, -ATING], [< L. *venerari*, worship], to look upon with feelings of deep respect; revere. **—ven′er·a′tion,** *n.*

**ve·ne·re·al** (və-nêr′i-əl), *adj.* [< *Venus*], 1. of sexual intercourse. 2. transmitted by sexual intercourse, as a disease. 3. infected with venereal disease.

**ven·er·y** (ven′ēr-i), *n.* [< L. *venari*, to hunt], hunting, as a sport.

**Ve·ne·tian** (və-nē′shən), *adj.* of Venice, its people, etc. *n.* a native of Venice.

**Venetian blind,** a window blind made of a number of thin wooden or metal slats that can be set at an angle.

**venge·ance** (ven′jəns), *n.* [< L. *vindicare*, avenge], the return of an injury for an injury as in retribution; revenge. **—with a vengeance,** 1. with great force or fury. 2. extremely.

**venge·ful** (venj′fəl), *adj.* seeking revenge; vindictive. **—venge′ful·ness,** *n.*

**ve·ni·al** (vē′ni-əl, vēn′yəl), *adj.* [< L. *venia*, grace], that may be forgiven; pardonable, as a sin. **—ve′ni·al′i·ty** (-al′ə-ti), *n.*

**ve·ni·re·man** (vi-nī′ri-mən), *n.* [*pl.* -MEN], [< L. *venire facias*, cause to come], a person called to jury service.

**ven·i·son** (ven′i-z'n), *n.* [< L. *venari*, to hunt], the flesh of deer, used as food.

**ven·om** (ven′əm), *n.* [< L. *venenum*, a poison], 1. the poison secreted by some snakes, spiders, etc. 2. spite; malice.
**ven′om·ous,** *adj.* 1. full of venom; poisonous. 2. spiteful; malicious.
**ve·nous** (vē′nəs), *adj.* 1. of or having veins. 2. designating blood carried in veins.
**vent** (vent), *n.* [< OFr. *fente*, a rift], 1. a means of escaping; outlet. 2. expression; release: as, giving *vent* to emotion. 3. a small opening to permit passage, as of a gas. 4. a slit in a garment. *v.t.* give release to; let out. **—vent′less,** *adj.*
**ven·ti·late** (ven′t'l-āt′), *v.t.* [-LATED, -LATING], [< L. *ventus*, a wind], 1. to circulate fresh air in (a room, etc.). 2. to provide with an opening for the escape of foul air, gas, etc. **—ven′ti·la′tion,** *n.*
**ven′ti·la′tor,** *n.* an opening or device for replacing foul air with fresh air.
**ven·tral** (ven′trəl), *adj.* [< L. *venter*, belly], of, near, or on the belly. **—ven′tral·ly,** *adv.*
**ven·tri·cle** (ven′tri-k'l), *n.* [< L. *venter*, belly], either of the two lower chambers of the heart.
**ven·tril·o·quism** (ven-tril′ə-kwiz'm), *n.* [< L. *venter*, belly + *loqui*, speak], the art of speaking so that the voice seems to come from some source other than the speaker. **—ven·tril′o·quist,** *n.*
**ven·ture** (ven′chẽr), *n.* [see ADVENTURE], 1. a risky undertaking, as in business. 2. something on which a risk is taken. *v.t.* [-TURED, -TURING], 1. to expose to danger or chance of loss. 2. to take the risk of; brave. 3. to express at the risk of criticism: as, to *venture* an opinion. *v.i.* to dare.
**ven′ture·some** (-səm), *adj.* 1. inclined to venture; daring. 2. risky; hazardous.
**ven′tur·ous,** *adj.* venturesome.
**ven·ue** (ven′ū, -ōō), *n.* [< OFr. *venir*, to come], in *law*, 1. the locality in which a cause of action or a crime occurs. 2. the locality in which a case is tried.
**Ve·nus** (vē′nəs), *n.* 1. the Roman goddess of love and beauty. 2. the most brilliant planet in the solar system: cf. **planet**.
**ve·ra·cious** (və-rā′shəs), *adj.* [< L. *verus*, true], 1. habitually truthful; honest. 2. true; accurate. **—ve·ra′cious·ly,** *adv.*
**ve·rac′i·ty** (-ras′ə-ti), *n.* [*pl.* -TIES], 1. honesty. 2. accuracy or precision. 3. truth.
**ve·ran·da, ve·ran·dah** (və-ran′də), *n.* [< Hind.], an open porch, usually roofed, along the side of a building.
**verb** (vũrb), *n.* [< L. *verbum*, a word], in *grammar*, a word expressing action, existence, or occurrence.
**ver·bal** (vũr′b'l), *adj.* 1. of, in, or by means of words. 2. in speech; oral. 3. word for word; literal. 4. of, having the nature of, or derived from a verb. **—ver′bal·ly,** *adv.*
**verbal noun,** in *grammar*, a noun derived from a verb, esp. a gerund or an infinitive (e.g., *swimming* is fun, *to err* is human).
**ver·ba·tim** (vẽr-bā′tim), *adv.* & *adj.* [< L. *verbum*, a word], word for word.
**ver·bi·age** (vũr′bi-ij), *n.* [< L. *verbum*, a word], an excess of words; wordiness.
**ver·bose** (vẽr-bōs′), *adj.* [< L. *verbum*, a word], using too many words; wordy.
**ver·dant** (vũr′d'nt), *adj.* [prob. < *verdure* + *-ant*], 1. covered with green vegetation. 2. inexperienced; innocent. **—ver′dan·cy,** *n.*
**ver·dict** (vũr′dikt), *n.* [< L. *vere*, truly + *dicere*, say], 1. the formal finding of a jury. 2. a decision; judgment.
**ver·di·gris** (vũr′di-grēs′, -gris), *n.* [< OFr. *verd*, green + *de*, of + *Grece*, Greece], a greenish coating that forms like rust on brass, bronze, or copper.
**ver·dure** (vũr′jẽr), *n.* [OFr. < *verd*, green], 1. the fresh green color of growing things. 2. green vegetation.
**verge** (vũrj), *n.* [< L. *virga*, rod], the edge, brink, or margin (*of* something). *v.i.* [VERGED, VERGING], to be on the verge; border (with *on* or *upon*).
**ver·i·fy** (ver′ə-fī′), *v.t.* [-FIED, -FYING], [< L. *verus*, true + *facere*, make], 1. to prove to be true by evidence, etc.; confirm. 2. to test the accuracy of. **—ver′i·fi′a·ble,** *adj.* **—ver′i·fi·ca′tion,** *n.* **—ver′i·fi′er,** *n.*
**ver·i·ly** (ver′ə-li), *adv.* [Archaic], in fact; really.
**ver·i·si·mil·i·tude** (ver′ə-si-mil′ə-tōōd′, -tūd′), *n.* [< L. *verus*, true + *similis*, like], the appearance of being true or real.
**ver·i·ta·ble** (ver′i-tə-b'l), *adj.* [< L. *veritas*, truth], true; real; genuine.
**ver·i·ty** (ver′i-ti), *n.* [*pl.* -TIES], [< L. *verus*, true], 1. truth; reality. 2. a principle, belief, etc. taken to be fundamentally true.
**ver·mi·cel·li** (vũr′mə-sel′i, -chel′i), *n.* [It. < L. *vermis*, worm], a kind of spaghetti in very thin threads.
**ver·mi·form** (vũr′mə-fôrm′), *adj.* [< L. *vermis*, worm; + *-form*], shaped like a worm.
**vermiform appendix,** a small, saclike appendage of the large intestine.
**ver·mil·ion** (vẽr-mil′yən), *n.* [< L. *vermis*, worm], 1. a bright red pigment. 2. bright yellowish red. *adj.* of this color.
**ver·min** (vũr′min), *n.* [*pl.* -MIN], [< L. *vermis*, worm], 1. any of various small, destructive animals, as flies, lice, rats, etc. 2. an offensive person. **—ver′min·ous,** *adj.*
**ver·mouth** (vẽr-mōōth′, vũr′mōōth), *n.* [< G. *wermuth*, wormwood], a fortified white wine flavored with aromatic herbs.
**ver·nac·u·lar** (vẽr-nak′yoo-lẽr), *adj.* [< L. *vernaculus*, native], 1. of, in, or using the native language of a place. 2. native to a country. *n.* 1. the native language or dialect of a country or place. 2. the common everyday language of a people. 3. the shoptalk of a profession, trade, etc.
**ver·nal** (vũr′n'l), *adj.* [< L. *ver*, spring], 1. of or in the spring. 2. springlike. 3. youthful.
**ver·ni·er** (vũr′ni-ẽr, -nêr), *n.* [< P. *Vernier*, 17th-c. Fr. mathematician], a short scale used to indicate fractional parts of divisions of a longer scale: also **vernier scale.**
**ver·sa·tile** (vũr′sə-til), *adj.* [< L. *vertere*, to turn], competent in many things. **—ver′sa·tile·ly,** *adv.* **—ver′sa·til′i·ty,** *n.*
**verse** (vũrs), *n.* [< L. *vertere*, to turn], 1. a single line of poetry. 2. poetry. 3. a particular form of poetry. 4. a poem. 5. a stanza. 6. in the *Bible*, any of the short divisions of a chapter.
**versed** (vũrst), *adj.* [< L. *versari*, be busy], acquainted by experience and study; skilled.
**ver·si·fi·ca·tion** (vũr′sə-fi-kā′shən), *n.* 1. a versifying. 2. the art, practice, or theory of poetic composition. 3. metrical structure.
**ver·si·fy** (vũr′sə-fī′), *v.i.* [-FIED, -FYING], [< L. *versus*, verse + *facere*, make], to compose verses. *v.t.* 1. to tell in verse. 2. to rewrite (prose) in verse form. **—ver′si·fi′er,** *n.*
**ver·sion** (vũr′zhən), *n.* [see VERSE], 1. a translation, esp. of the Bible. 2. an account showing one point of view. 3. a particular form of something. **—ver′sion·al,** *adj.*
**ver·sus** (vũr′səs), *prep.* [L.], against.
**ver·te·bra** (vũr′tə-brə), *n.* [*pl.* -BRAE (-brē′), -BRAS], [L. < *vertere*, to turn], any of the single bones of the spinal column. **—ver′te·bral,** *adj.*
**ver′te·brate′** (-brāt′, -brit), *adj.* 1. having a backbone, or spinal column. 2. of the vertebrates. *n.* any of a large division of animals having a spinal column.
**ver·tex** (vũr′teks), *n.* [*pl.* -TEXES, -TICES (-tə-sēz′)], [L. < *vertere*, to turn], 1. the highest point; top. 2. in *geometry*, the point opposite to the base and farthest from it.
**ver·ti·cal** (vũr′ti-k'l), *adj.* 1. of or at the

vertex. 2. upright; straight up and down. *n.* a vertical line, plane, etc.

**ver·tig·i·nous** (vẽr-tij′ə-nəs), *adj.* 1. rotating; whirling. 2. of, having, or causing vertigo; dizzy. 3. unstable.

**ver·ti·go** (vũr′ti-gō′), *n.* [L. < *vertere*, to turn], a sensation of dizziness.

**verve** (vũrv), *n.* [prob. < L. *verbum*, word], vigor; energy; enthusiasm.

**ver·y** (ver′i), *adj.* [-IER, -IEST], [< L. *verus*, true], 1. complete; absolute: as, the *very* opposite. 2. the same: as, the *very* hat I lost. 3. even: used as an intensive, as, the *very* rafters shook. 4. actual: as, caught in the *very* act. *adv.* 1. extremely. 2. truly; really: used as an intensive, as, the *very* same man.

**very high frequency,** in *radio & TV*, any frequency of between 30 and 300 megacycles.

**ves·i·cle** (ves′i-k'l), *n.* [< L. *vesica*, bladder], a small membranous cavity, sac, or cyst; specif., a blister. —**ve·sic·u·lar** (və-sik′yoo-lẽr), **ve·sic′u·late** (-lit), *adj.*

**ves·per** (ves′pẽr), *n.* [L.], 1. evening. 2. *often in pl.* an evening prayer, church service, etc.: also **vespers.**

**ves·sel** (ves′'l), *n.* [< L. *vas*], 1. a utensil for holding something, as a bowl, kettle, etc. 2. a ship or boat. 3. an airship. 4. a tube of the body, as a vein, circulating a fluid.

**vest** (vest), *n.* [< L. *vestis*, garment], 1. a short, sleeveless garment worn under a suit coat by men. 2. an undershirt. *v.t.* 1. to dress. 2. to place (authority, etc.) *in* someone. 3. to put (a person) in control of, as power, etc. *v.i.* to become vested (*in* a person), as property.

**ves·tal** (ves′t'l), *adj.* [< L. *Vesta*, goddess of the hearth], chaste; pure. *n.* 1. a virgin. 2. a nun.

**vest·ed** (ves′tid), *adj.* 1. clothed, esp. in church vestments. 2. in *law*, fixed; settled; absolute: as, a *vested* interest.

**ves·ti·bule** (ves′tə-būl′), *n.* [L. *vestibulum*], 1. a small entrance hall, as to a building. 2. the enclosed passage between passenger cars of a train.

**ves·tige** (ves′tij), *n.* [< L. *vestigium*, footprint], 1. a trace, mark, or sign, esp. of something which has passed away. 2. in *biology*, a degenerate part, more fully developed in an earlier stage. —**ves·tig′i·al,** *adj.*

**vest·ment** (vest′mənt), *n.* [< L. *vestire*, clothe], a garment or robe, esp. one worn by a clergyman. —**vest′men·tal,** *adj.*

**ves·try** (ves′tri), *n.* [*pl.* -TRIES], [< L. *vestis*, garment], 1. a room in a church, where vestments, etc. are kept. 2. a room in a church used as a chapel. 3. a group of church members who manage temporal affairs. —**ves′try·man** (-mən) [*pl.* -MEN], *n.*

**vet** (vet), *n.* [Colloq.], a veterinarian.

**vet** (vet), *n.* [Colloq.], a veteran.

**vetch** (vech), *n.* [< L. *vicia*], a plant of the pea family grown for fodder.

**vet·er·an** (vet′ẽr-ən), *adj.* [< L. *vetus*, old], 1. old and experienced. 2. of veterans. *n.* 1. a person of long service in some position. 2. one who has served in the armed forces.

**Veterans' Day,** November 11; formerly called *Armistice Day.*

**vet·er·i·nar·i·an** (vet′ẽr-ə-nâr′i-ən), *n.* one who practices veterinary medicine.

**vet′er·i·nar′y** (-ner′i), *adj.* [< L. *veterina*, beasts of burden], designating or of the medical or surgical treatment of animals. *n.* [*pl.* -IES], a veterinarian.

**ve·to** (vē′tō), *n.* [*pl.* -TOES], [L., I forbid], 1. an order prohibiting some act. 2. the power to prohibit action. 3. *a*) the right of one branch of a government to reject bills passed by another. *b*) the exercise of this right. *v.t.* [-TOED, -TOING], 1. to prevent (a bill) from becoming law by a veto. 2. to forbid.

**vex** (veks), *v.t.* [< L. *vexare*, agitate], 1. to disturb; annoy, esp. in little things. 2. to trouble seriously. —**vexed,** *adj.*

**vex·a·tion** (vek-sā′shən), *n.* 1. a vexing or being vexed. 2. something that vexes. —**vex·a′tious** (-shəs), *adj.*

**VHF,** very high frequency.

**v.i.,** intransitive verb.

**vi·a** (vī′ə), *prep.* [L., way], by way of.

**vi·a·ble** (vī′ə-b'l), *adj.* [< L. *vita*, life], sufficiently developed to be able to live outside the uterus: said of a fetus. —**vi′a·bil′i·ty,** *n.*

**vi·a·duct** (vī′ə-dukt′), *n.* [(after *aqueduct*) < L. *via*, way], a bridge consisting of a series of short spans supported on piers or towers.

**vi·al** (vī′əl), *n.* [< Gr. *phialē*, shallow cup], a small vessel, usually of glass, for containing medicines or other liquids.

**vi·and** (vī′ənd), *n.* [< L. *vivere*, live], 1. an article of food. 2. *pl.* food.

**vi·brant** (vī′brənt), *adj.* 1. quivering; vibrating. 2. produced by vibration; resonant: said of sound. 3. vigorous; energetic. —**vi′bran·cy,** *n.* —**vi′brant·ly,** *adv.*

**vi·brate** (vī′brāt), *v.t.* [-BRATED, -BRATING], [< L. *vibrare*], to set in to-and-fro motion. *v.i.* 1. to swing back and forth. 2. to move rapidly back and forth; quiver. 3. to be emotionally stirred; thrill. —**vi·bra′tion,** *n.* —**vi′bra·tor,** *n.* —**vi′bra·to′ry** (-brə-tôr′i), *adj.*

**vic·ar** (vik′ẽr), *n.* [< L. *vicis*, a change], 1. in the *Anglican Church*, a parish priest who receives a salary instead of the tithes. 2. in the *R.C. Church*, a priest or other deputy of a bishop. —**vic′ar·ship′,** *n.*

**vic′ar·age** (-ij), *n.* 1. the residence of a vicar. 2. the benefice of a vicar.

**vi·car·i·ous** (vī-kâr′i-əs), *adj.* [< L. *vicis*, a change], 1. taking the place of another. 2. endured or performed by one person in place of another. 3. delegated. 4. felt by imagined participation in another's experience: as, a *vicarious* thrill. —**vi·car′i·ous·ly,** *adv.*

**vice** (vīs), *n.* [< L. *vitium*], 1. a serious fault of character. 2. evil conduct; depravity. 3. a degrading habit. 4. a fault, defect, etc.

**vi·ce** (vī′si), *prep.* [< L. *vicis*, a change], in the place of; instead of.

**vice-,** [see prec.], a prefix meaning *subordinate, deputy*, as in *vice-president.*

**vice·ge·rent** (vīs′jêr′ənt), *n.* [< *vice*, prep. + L. *gerere*, to direct], a deputy.

**vice-pres·i·dent** (vīs′prez′ə-dənt), *n.* an executive assistant to a president, acting in his place during his absence: also **vice president.** —**vice′-pres′i·den·cy,** *n.*

**vice·roy** (vīs′roi), *n.* [< Fr. *vice-* (see VICE-) + *roi*, a king], a person ruling a country, province, etc. as the deputy of a sovereign.

**vi·ce ver·sa** (vī′si, *or* vīs′, vũr′sə), [L.], the order or relation being reversed.

**Vi·chy water** (vish′i, vē′shi), 1. a mineral water found at Vichy, a city in France. 2. a natural or manufactured water like this.

**vi·cin·i·ty** (və-sin′ə-ti), *n.* [*pl.* -TIES], [< L. *vicinus*, near], 1. nearness; proximity. 2. a near-by region; neighborhood.

**vi·cious** (vish′əs), *adj.* [< L. *vitium*, vice], 1. characterized by vice or evil; depraved. 2. faulty: as, a *vicious* argument. 3. unruly: as, a *vicious* horse. 4. malicious; spiteful: as, a *vicious* rumor. 5. debasing; corrupting. 6. [Colloq.], very intense, sharp, etc.

**vicious circle,** a situation in which the solution to each problem gives rise to another, eventually bringing back the first problem.

**vi·cis·si·tude** (vi-sis′ə-tōōd′, -tūd′), *n.* [< L. *vicis*, a turn], *usually pl.* irregular changes in the course of something; esp., change of circumstances in life; hazards of fortune.

**vic·tim** (vik′tim), *n.* [L. *victima*], 1. someone or something killed, destroyed, sacrificed, etc. 2. one who suffers some loss, esp. by being swindled.

**vic′tim·ize′** (-īz′), *v.t.* [-IZED, -IZING], to make a victim of. —**vic′tim·iz′er,** *n.*
**vic·tor** (vik′tẽr), *n.* [L. < *vincere,* conquer], a winner or conqueror.
**vic·to·ri·a** (vik-tôr′i-ə), *n.* [< *Victoria* (1819–1901), queen of England], a low four-wheeled carriage for two, with a folding top.
**Vic·to′ri·an,** *adj.* [see prec.], 1. of or characteristic of the time of Queen Victoria. 2. showing the respectability, prudery, etc. attributed to the Victorians. *n.* a person, esp. a writer, of the time of Queen Victoria.
**vic·to·ri·ous** (vik-tôr′i-əs), *adj.* 1. having won a victory; conquering. 2. of or bringing about victory. —**vic·to′ri·ous·ly,** *adv.*
**vic·to·ry** (vik′tə-ri), *n.* [*pl.* -RIES], [< L. *vincere,* conquer], 1. final supremacy in battle or war. 2. success in any struggle.
**vict·ual** (vit′'l), *n.* [< L. *victus,* food], *pl.* [Dial. or Colloq.], articles of food. *v.t. & v.i.* [-UALED or -UALLED, -UALING or -UALLING], to supply with, or take on, victuals.
‡**vi·de** (vī′di), [L.], see (the indicated page, etc.): abbrev. **v., vid.**
**vid·e·o** (vid′i-ō′), *adj.* [L., I see], of television, esp. of the picture phase of a broadcast. *n.* television.
**vie** (vī), *v.i.* [VIED, VYING], [< L. *invitare,* invite], to struggle for superiority (*with* someone); compete. —**vi′er,** *n.*
**view** (vū), *n.* [< L. *videre,* to see], 1. a seeing or looking, as in inspection. 2. range of vision. 3. mental survey: as, a correct *view* of the affair. 4. *a*) a scene or prospect, as of a landscape. *b*) a picture of such a scene. 5. manner of regarding something; opinion. 6. an object; aim; goal. *v.t.* 1. to inspect; look at closely. 2. to see; behold. 3. to survey mentally; consider. —**in view,** 1. in sight. 2. under consideration. 3. as a goal or hope. —**in view of,** because of. —**on view,** displayed publicly. —**view′er,** *n.*
**view finder,** a finder (sense 2).
**view′point′,** *n.* 1. place of observation. 2. mental attitude. Also **point of view.**
**vig·il** (vij′əl), *n.* [< L. *vigere,* be lively], 1. a watchful staying awake. 2. a watch kept. 3. the eve of a church festival. 4. a devotional watch kept on such an eve.
**vig·i·lant** (vij′ə-lənt), *adj.* [< L. *vigil,* awake], characterized by wakefulness; alert to danger; watchful. —**vig′i·lance,** *n.*
**vig·i·lan·te** (vij′ə-lan′ti), *n.* [Sp., vigilant], one of an unauthorized group organized professedly to keep order and punish crime.
**vi·gnette** (vin-yet′), *n.* [< Fr. *vigne,* vine], 1. an ornamental design used as a border, inset, etc. on a page. 2. a photograph, etc. shading off gradually at the edges. 3. a short, subtle, compact literary composition.
**vig·or** (vig′ẽr), *n.* [< L. *vigere,* be strong], active force; vitality, intensity, or energy: also, Brit. sp., **vigour.**
**vig′or·ous,** *adj.* of or characterized by vigor; forceful; strong; energetic.
**vik·ing** (vī′kiŋ), *n.* [< ON. *vikingr*], any of the Scandinavian pirates of the 8th to 10th centuries.
**vile** (vīl), *adj.* [< L. *vilis,* cheap, base], 1. morally evil; wicked. 2. repulsive; disgusting. 3. degrading; mean: as, *vile* conditions. 4. of poor quality; bad: as, *vile* weather.
**vil·i·fy** (vil′ə-fī′), *v.t.* [-FIED, -FYING], [< L. *vilis,* base + *facere,* make], to use abusive language about or of; defame. —**vil′i·fi·ca′tion,** *n.* —**vil′i·fi′er,** *n.*
**vil·la** (vil′ə), *n.* [It. < L.], 1. orig., a country house. 2. a pretentious rural residence.
**vil·lage** (vil′ij), *n.* [see VILLA], 1. a community smaller than a town. 2. the people of a village, collectively. —**vil′lag·er,** *n.*
**vil·lain** (vil′ən), *n.* [< LL. *villanus,* a farm servant], a person guilty of evil deeds; scoundrel. —**vil′lain·ess,** *n.fem.*
**vil′lain·ous,** *adj.* 1. of or like a villain; evil. 2. very bad. —**vil′lain·ous·ly,** *adv.*
**vil′lain·y,** *n.* [*pl.* -IES], 1. a being villainous. 2. wickedness; evil. 3. a villainous act.
**vim** (vim), *n.* [< L. *vis,* strength], energy; vigor.
**vin·di·cate** (vin′də-kāt′), *v.t.* [-CATED, -CATING], [< L. *vis,* force + *dicere,* say], 1. to clear from criticism, blame, etc. 2. to defend against opposition. 3. to justify. —**vin′di·ca′tion,** *n.* —**vin′di·ca′tor,** *n.*
**vin·dic·tive** (vin-dik′tiv), *adj.* [see VINDICATE], 1. revengeful in spirit. 2. said or done in revenge. —**vin·dic′tive·ly,** *adv.*
**vine** (vīn), *n.* [< L. *vinum,* wine], 1. a plant with a long stem that grows along the ground or climbs a support. 2. a grapevine.
**vin·e·gar** (vin′i-gẽr), *n.* [< OFr. *vin,* wine + *aigre,* sour], a sour liquid containing acetic acid, made by fermenting cider, wine, etc. and used as a condiment and preservative. —**vin′e·gar·y,** *adj.*
**vine·yard** (vin′yẽrd), *n.* land devoted to cultivating grapevines.
**vin·tage** (vin′tij), *n.* [< L. *vinum,* wine + *demere,* remove], 1. the crop of grapes of a single season. 2. the wine of a particular region and year. 3. an earlier model or type: as, a car of ancient *vintage.* *adj.* of choice vintage: as, *vintage* wine.
**vint·ner** (vint′nẽr), *n.* [< OFr. *vin,* wine], [Chiefly Brit.], a wine merchant.
**vin·yl** (vī′nil, vin′il), *adj.* [< L. *vinum,* wine; + *-yl*], designating or of a group of compounds used in making many plastics (**vinyl plastics**).
**vi·ol** (vī′əl), *n.* [< L. *vitula*], 1. an early stringed instrument like the violin. 2. any instrument of the violin family.
**vi·o·la** (vi-ō′lə, vī-), *n.* [It.], a stringed instrument of the violin family, slightly larger than a violin.
**vi·o·la·ble** (vī′ə-lə-b'l), *adj.* that can be violated; easily violated. —**vi′o·la·bly,** *adv.*
**vi·o·late** (vī′ə-lāt′), *v.t.* [-LATED, -LATING], [< L. *violare*], 1. to break (a law, promise, etc.). 2. to infringe on. 3. to rape. 4. to desecrate, as a sacred place. 5. to break in on; disturb. —**vi′o·la′tor,** *n.*
**vi′o·la′tion,** *n.* a violating or being violated; specif., *a*) infringement, as of a law. *b*) rape. *c*) desecration of something sacred. *d*) disturbance.
**vi·o·lence** (vī′ə-ləns), *n.* [< L. *violentus,* violent], 1. physical force used so as to injure or damage. 2. intensity; severity: as, the *violence* of the storm. 3. desecration. 4. great force of feeling, etc.; passion.
**vi·o·lent** (vī′ə-lənt), *adj.* 1. acting with or having great physical force. 2. caused by violence. 3. passionate: as, *violent* language. 4. intense: as, a *violent* storm.
**vi·o·let** (vī′ə-lit), *n.* [< L. *viola*], 1. a low plant with fragrant white, blue, purple, or yellow flowers. 2. a bluish purple. *adj.* bluish-purple.
**vi·o·lin** (vī′ə-lin′), *n.* [< It. *viola,* viol], any instrument of the family of four-stringed instruments played with a bow; specif., the smallest and highest-pitched instrument of this family. —**vi′o·lin′ist,** *n.*
**vi·ol·ist** (vi-ō′list), *n.* a player on the viola.
**vi·o·lon·cel·lo** (vē′ə-lon-chel′ō, vī′ə-lən-), *n.* [*pl.* -LOS], a cello.
**V.I.P., VIP,** [Slang], very important person.
**vi·per** (vī′pẽr), *n.* [prob. < L. *vivus,* living + *parere,* to bear], 1. a venomous snake. 2. a malicious or treacherous person. —**vi′perous, vi′per·ish,** *adj.*
**vi·ra·go** (vi-rā′gō, vī-), *n.* [*pl.* -GOES, -GOS], [< L. *vir,* a man], a bold, shrewish woman.
**vir·gin** (vũr′jin), *n.* [< L. *virgo,* maiden], 1. a person, esp. a woman, who has not had sexual intercourse. 2. [V-], Mary, the

mother of Jesus: with *the.* ***adj.*** 1. being a virgin. 2. chaste; modest. 3. untouched, unused, clean, etc.: as, *virgin* snow.
**vir′gin·al,** ***adj.*** 1. of or like a virgin; maidenly. 2. pure; fresh; unsullied.
**Vir·gin·ia creeper** (vēr-jin′yə), a climbing vine with bluish-black berries.
**Virginia reel,** an American reel, danced by couples facing in two lines.
**vir·gin·i·ty** (vēr-jin′ə-ti), ***n.*** a virgin state; maidenhood; chastity.
**Vir·go** (vũr′gō), ***n.*** [L., virgin], the sixth sign of the zodiac.
**vir·ile** (vir′əl), ***adj.*** [< L. *vir*, a man], 1. of or characteristic of a man; masculine. 2. having manly strength or vigor. 3. capable of procreation. **—vi·ril·i·ty** (vi-ril′ə-ti), ***n.***
**vir·tu** (vēr-too′, vũr′too), ***n.*** [It.; see VIRTUE], 1. a knowledge of, or taste for, artistic objects. 2. beautiful or rare objects of art, collectively.
**vir·tu·al** (vũr′choo-əl), ***adj.*** being so in effect or essence, although not in actual fact or name. **—vir′tu·al·ly,** ***adv.***
**vir·tue** (vũr′choo), ***n.*** [< L. *virtus*, manliness, worth], 1. general moral excellence. 2. a specific moral quality regarded as good. 3. chastity. 4. *a*) excellence in general. *b*) a good quality. 5. efficacy, as of a medicine. **—by** (or **in**) **virtue of,** because of.
**vir·tu·os·i·ty** (vũr′choo-os′ə-ti), ***n.*** [*pl.* -TIES], [< *virtuoso*], great technical skill in some fine art, esp. in music.
**vir·tu·o·so** (vũr′choo-ō′sō), ***n.*** [*pl.* -SOS, -SI (-si)], [It., skilled], 1. a collector or connoisseur of art. 2. a person displaying virtuosity.
**vir·tu·ous** (vũr′choo-əs), ***adj.*** 1. having, or characterized by, moral virtue. 2. chaste: said of a woman. **—vir′tu·ous·ly,** ***adv.***
**vir·u·lent** (vir′yoo-lənt, -oo-), ***adj.*** [< L. *virus*, a poison], 1. poisonous; deadly. 2. bitterly hostile; full of hate. 3. in *medicine*, violent and rapid in its course, as a disease; highly infectious. **—vir′u·lence,** ***n.***
**vi·rus** (vī′rəs), ***n.*** [L., a poison], 1. any of a group of very small infective agents that cause various diseases, as smallpox. 2. a harmful influence.
**vi·sa** (vē′zə), ***n.*** [< L. *videre*, see], an endorsement on a passport, granting entry into a country.
**vis·age** (viz′ij), ***n.*** [< L. *videre*, see], 1. the face; countenance. 2. aspect; look.
**vis-à-vis** (vē′zə-vē′), ***adj. & adv.*** [Fr.], face to face; opposite. ***prep.*** face to face with.
**vis·cer·a** (vis′ēr-ə), ***n.pl.*** [sing. (rare) VISCUS (-kəs)], [L.], the internal organs of the body, as the heart, lungs, intestines, etc. **—vis′cer·al,** ***adj.***
**vis·cid** (vis′id), ***adj.*** [< L. *viscum*, birdlime], thick, sirupy, and sticky. **—vis′cid·ness,** ***n.***
**vis·cose** (vis′kōs), ***n.*** a sirupy solution of cellulose, used in making rayon, cellophane, etc. ***adj.*** 1. viscous. 2. of viscose.
**vis·cos·i·ty** (vis-kos′ə-ti), ***n.*** [*pl.* -TIES], 1. a viscous quality or state. 2. in *physics*, the internal resistance of a substance to being fluid, caused by molecular attraction.
**vis·count** (vī′kount), ***n.*** [< L. *vice*, in place of + *comes*, a count], a nobleman next below an earl or count and above a baron.
**vis·cous** (vis′kəs), ***adj.*** [see VISCID], 1. thick, sirupy, and sticky. 2. in *physics*, having viscosity. **—vis′cous·ness,** ***n.***
**vise** (vīs), ***n.*** [< L. *vitis*, vine, lit., that which winds], a device having two jaws opened and closed as by a screw, used for holding firmly an object being worked on. Also sp. **vice. —vise′like′,** ***adj.***
**vi·sé** (vē′zā, vē-zā′), ***n.*** [Fr.], visa.
**Vish·nu** (vish′noo), ***n.*** the second member of the Hindu trinity (Brahma, Vishnu, and Siva), called "the Preserver."
**vis·i·bil·i·ty** (viz′ə-bil′ə-ti), ***n.*** [*pl.* -TIES], 1. a being visible. 2. *a*) the relative possibility of being seen under prevailing conditions of distance, light, etc. *b*) range of vision.
**vis·i·ble** (viz′ə-b'l), ***adj.*** [< L. *videre*, to see], 1. that can be seen. 2. evident. **—vis′i·ble·ness,** ***n.*** **—vis′i·bly,** ***adv.***
**vi·sion** (vizh′ən), ***n.*** [< L. *videre*, to see], 1. the power of seeing. 2. something supposedly seen in a dream, trance, etc. 3. a mental image: as, *visions* of power. 4. the ability to foresee or perceive something, as through mental acuteness. 5. something or someone of great beauty. ***v.t.*** to see as in a vision. **—vi′sion·al,** ***adj.***
**vi′sion·ar′y** (-er′i), ***adj.*** 1. seen in a vision. 2. merely speculative and impractical, as an idea. ***n.*** [*pl.* -IES], 1. one who sees visions. 2. one who has impractical ideas.
**vis·it** (viz′it), ***v.t.*** [< L. *videre*, to see], 1. to go or come to see. 2. to stay with as a guest. 3. to afflict: as, a drought *visited* the valley. ***v.i.*** to make a visit, esp. a social call. ***n.*** a visiting; specif., *a*) a social call. *b*) a stay as a guest. *c*) an official call, as of a doctor.
**vis·it·ant** (viz′ə-tənt), ***n.*** a visitor.
**vis′it·a′tion** (-tā′shən), ***n.*** 1. a visiting; esp., an official visit as to inspect. 2. a reward or punishment, as sent by God.
**vis′i·tor,** ***n.*** a person making a visit.
**vi·sor** (vī′zēr), ***n.*** [< OFr. *vis*, a face], 1. the movable part of a helmet, covering the face. 2. a projecting brim, as on a cap, for shading the eyes. Also sp. **vizor.**
**vis·ta** (vis′tə), ***n.*** [< L. *videre*, to see], 1. a view, esp. as seen through a long passage. 2. a mental view of events.
**vis·u·al** (vizh′oo-əl), ***adj.*** [< L. *videre*, to see], 1. of or used in seeing. 2. that can be seen; visible. **—vis′u·al·ly,** ***adv.***
**vis′u·al·ize′,** ***v.t. & v.i.*** [-IZED, -IZING], to form a mental image of (something not visible). **—vis′u·al·i·za′tion,** ***n.***
**vi·tal** (vī′t'l), ***adj.*** [< L. *vita*, life], 1. of or concerned with life. 2. essential to life. 3. fatal: as, *vital* wounds. 4. *a*) essential; indispensable. *b*) of greatest importance. 5. full of life; energetic. ***n. pl.*** 1. the vital organs, as the heart, brain, etc. 2. any essential parts. **—vi′tal·ly,** ***adv.***
**vi·tal·i·ty** (vī-tal′ə-ti), ***n.*** [*pl.* -TIES], 1. power to live. 2. power to endure or survive. 3. mental or physical vigor; energy.
**vi·tal·ize** (vī′t'l-īz′), ***v.t.*** [-IZED, -IZING], to make vital; give life or vigor to.
**vital statistics,** data about births, deaths, marriages, etc.
**vi·ta·min** (vī′tə-min), ***n.*** [< L. *vita*, life], any of certain complex substances found variously in foods and essential to good health: some of the important vitamins are: **—vitamin A,** a fat-soluble alcohol found in fish-liver oil, egg yolk, carrots, etc.: a deficiency of this results in imperfect vision in the dark. **—vitamin B (complex),** a group of unrelated water-soluble substances including: *a*) **vitamin** $B_1$, thiamin. *b*) **vitamin** $B_2$, riboflavin. *c*) nicotinic acid. **—vitamin C,** a compound occurring in citrus fruits, tomatoes, etc.: a deficiency of this produces scurvy. **—vitamin D,** any of several related vitamins occurring in fish-liver oil, milk, egg yolk, etc.: a deficiency of this produces rickets. **—vitamin K,** a substance occurring in alfalfa leaves, fish meal, etc., that clots blood.
**vi·ti·ate** (vish′i-āt′), ***v.t.*** [-ATED, -ATING], [< L. *vitium*, a vice], 1. to make imperfect; spoil. 2. to make legally ineffective. **—vi′ti·at′ed,** ***adj.*** **—vi′ti·a′tion,** ***n.***
**vit·re·ous** (vit′ri-əs), ***adj.*** [< L. *vitrum*, glass], 1. of or like glass. 2. derived from or made of glass. **—vit′re·ous·ness,** ***n.***

**vit·ri·fy** (vit'rə-fī'), *v.t. & v.i.* [-FIED, -FYING], [< L. *vitrum*, glass + *facere*, make], to change into glass or a glasslike substance by heat. —**vit'ri·fi'a·ble,** *adj.*

**vit·ri·ol** (vit'ri-əl), *n.* [< L. *vitreus*, glassy], 1. any of several sulfates of metals, as of copper (*blue vitriol*), or iron (*green vitriol*). 2. sulfuric acid. 3. sharp or caustic speech, etc. —**vit'ri·ol'ic** (-ol'ik), *adj.*

**vi·tu·per·ate** (vī-tōō'pə-rāt', vi-tū'-), *v.t.* [-ATED, -ATING], [< L. *vitium*, fault + *parare*, make ready], to speak abusively to or about; berate. —**vi·tu'per·a'tion,** *n.*

‡**vi·va** (vē'vä), *interj.* [It.], (long) live (someone specified)! *n.* a shout of "viva!"

**vi·va·cious** (vi-vā'shəs, vī-), *adj.* [< L. *vivere*, to live], full of animation; spirited; lively.

**vi·vac'i·ty** (-vas'ə-ti), *n.* the quality or state of being vivacious.

‡**vive** (vēv), *interj.* [Fr.]. (long) live (someone specified)!

**viv·id** (viv'id), *adj.* [< L. *vivere*, to live], 1. full of life; vigorous. 2. bright; intense, as colors. 3. strong and clear; active: as, a *vivid* imagination. —**viv'id·ly,** *adv.*

**viv·i·fy** (viv'ə-fī'), *v.t.* [-FIED, -FYING], [< L. *vivus*, alive + *facere*, make], to give life to; animate. —**viv'i·fi·ca'tion,** *n.*

**vi·vip·a·rous** (vi-vip'ə-rəs), *adj.* [< L. *vivus*, alive + *parere*, produce], bearing living young instead of laying eggs.

**viv·i·sec·tion** (viv ə-sek'shən), *n.* [< L. *vivus*, alive; + *section*], surgery performed on a living animal in medical research. —**viv'i·sect',** *v.t. & v.i.* —**viv'i·sec'tion·ist,** *n.*

**vix·en** (vik's'n), *n.* [< AS. < base of *fox*], 1. a female fox. 2. an ill-tempered, shrewish woman. —**vix'en·ish,** *adj.*

**viz.** (viz), [< contr. for L. *videlicet*, one can see], that is; namely.

**vi·zier, vi·zir** (vi-zêr'), *n.* [< Ar. *wazara*, bear a burden], in Moslem countries, a high government official.

**vo·cab·u·lar·y** (vō-kab'yoo-ler'i), *n.* [*pl.* -IES], [ult. < L. *vocare*, to call], 1. a list of words, as a dictionary, glossary, etc. 2. all the words used in a language or by a particular person, class, etc.

**vo·cal** (vō'k'l), *adj.* [< L. *vox*, voice], 1. of or produced by the voice. 2. capable of making sounds. 3. speaking freely.

**vocal cords,** membranous folds in the larynx that vibrate to produce the voice.

**vo'cal·ist,** *n.* a singer.

**vo'cal·ize'** (-īz'), *v.t. & v.i.* [-IZED, -IZING], to utter, speak, or sing. —**vo'cal·i·za'tion,** *n.*

**vo·ca·tion** (vō-kā'shən), *n.* [< L. *vocare*, to call], 1. the career toward which one feels he is called. 2. any trade or occupation. —**vo·ca'tion·al,** *adj.* —**vo·ca'tion·al·ly,** *adv.*

**voc·a·tive** (vok'ə-tiv), *adj.* [< L. *vocare*, to call], in *grammar*, designating the case indicating the one addressed.

**vo·cif·er·ate** (vō-sif'ə-rāt'), *v.t. & v.i.* [-ATED, -ATING], [< L. *vox*, voice + *ferre*, to bear], to shout; clamor. —**vo·cif'er·a'tion,** *n.*

**vo·cif·er·ous** (vō-sif'ẽr-əs), *adj.* noisy; clamorous. —**vo·cif'er·ous·ly,** *adv.*

**vod·ka** (vod'kə), *n.* [Russ. < *voda*, water], a Russian alcoholic liquor distilled from wheat, rye, potatoes, etc.

**vogue** (vōg), *n.* [Fr.], 1. the current fashion; mode. 2. popularity; general acceptance.

**voice** (vois), *n.* [< L. *vox*], 1. sound made through the mouth, esp. by human beings. 2. the ability to make such sound. 3. any sound, influence, etc. regarded as like vocal utterance. 4. expressed wish, opinion, etc. 5. the right to express one's wish, etc.; vote. 6. expression. 7. in *grammar*, a form of a verb showing it as active or passive. 8. in *music*, *a*) singing ability. *b*) any of the parts of a work in harmony. *v.t.* [VOICED, VOICING], to give utterance to (a wish, etc.).

**void** (void), *adj.* [< L. *vacuus*, empty], 1. containing nothing; empty; vacant. 2. lacking: as, *void* of sense. 3. ineffective; useless. 4. of no legal force. *n.* an empty space. *v.t.* 1. to make empty. 2. to empty (the contents); evacuate. 3. to make void; annul. —**void'a·ble,** *adj.*

**voile** (voil), *n.* [Fr., a veil], a thin, sheer fabric of cotton, silk, rayon, etc.

**vol.,** [*pl.* VOLS.], volume.

**vol·a·tile** (vol'ə-t'l), *adj.* [< L. *volare*, to fly], 1. quickly evaporating. 2. changeable; fickle. —**vol'a·til'i·ty** (-til'ə-ti), *n.*

**vol'a·til·ize'** (-īz'), *v.t. & v.i.* [-IZED, -IZING], to evaporate. —**vol'a·til·i·za'tion,** *n.*

**vol·can·ic** (vol-kan'ik), *adj.* 1. of or caused by a volcano. 2. like a volcano; violently explosive. —**vol·can'i·cal·ly,** *adv.*

**vol·ca·no** (vol-kā'nō), *n.* [*pl.* -NOES, -NOS], [< L. *Volcanus*, Vulcan], 1. a vent in the earth's crust through which ash, molten rock, etc. are ejected. 2. a cone-shaped mountain of this material built up around the vent.

**vole** (vōl), *n.* [< ON. *völlr*, field], any of various burrowing rodents.

**vo·li·tion** (vō-lish'ən), *n.* [ult. < L. *velle*, to will], act or power of willing. —**vo·li'tion·al,** *adj.* —**vo·li'tion·al·ly,** *adv.*

**vol·ley** (vol'i), *n.* [*pl.* -LEYS], [< L. *volare*, to fly], 1. the simultaneous discharge of a number of weapons. 2. the missiles so discharged. 3. a rapid outpouring. 4. in *tennis*, etc., a return of a ball before it touches the ground. *v.t. & v.i.* [-LEYED, -LEYING], 1. to discharge or be discharged as in a volley. 2. in *tennis*, etc., to return (a ball) before it touches the ground.

**vol'ley·ball',** *n.* 1. a team game played by hitting a large ball back and forth over a net with the hands. 2. the ball.

**volt** (vōlt), *n.* [< A. *Volta* (1745–1827), It. physicist], the unit of electromotive force.

**volt·age** (vōl'tij), *n.* electromotive force, expressed in volts.

**vol·ta·ic** (vol-tā'ik), *adj.* 1. of electricity produced by chemical action: as, a *voltaic* battery. 2. designating or of electricity that moves in a current.

**vol·u·ble** (vol'yoo-b'l), *adj.* [< L. *volvere*, to roll], characterized by a great flow of words; talkative. —**vol'u·bil'i·ty,** *n.*

**vol·ume** (vol'yoom), *n.* [< L. *volumen*, scroll], 1. *a*) a book. *b*) one of a set of books. 2. the amount of space occupied in three dimensions. 3. a quantity, bulk, or amount. 4. a large quantity. 5. loudness of sound.

**vo·lu·mi·nous** (və-lōō'mə-nəs), *adj.* 1. producing or consisting of enough to fill volumes. 2. large; bulky; full.

**vol·un·tar·y** (vol'ən-ter'i), *adj.* [< L. *voluntas*, free will], 1. brought about by one's own free choice. 2. acting of one's own accord. 3. intentional; not accidental. 4. controlled by the will. —**vol'un·tar'i·ly,** *adv.*

**vol·un·teer** (vol'ən-têr'), *n.* one who offers to enter into any service, esp. military service, of his own free will. *adj.* 1. of volunteers. 2. voluntary. *v.t.* to offer or give of one's free will. *v.i.* to enter or offer to enter into service of one's own free will.

**vo·lup·tu·ar·y** (və-lup'chōō-er'i), *n.* [*pl.* -IES], [< L. *voluptas*, pleasure], one devoted to sensual pleasures.

**vo·lup·tu·ous** (və-lup'chōō-əs), *adj.* full of, producing, or fond of sensual pleasures.

**vo·lute** (və-lōōt'), *n.* [ult. < L. *volvere*, to roll], a spiral or whorl.

**vom·it** (vom'it), *n.* [< L. *vomere*, to vomit], matter ejected from the stomach through the mouth. *v.t. & v.i.* 1. to eject (the contents of the stomach) through the mouth; throw up. 2. to discharge or be discharged with force.

‡**von** (fôn; Eng. von), *prep.* [G.], of; from: a prefix in many German names.
**voo·doo** (vōō′dōō), *n.* [*pl.* -DOOS], [< a W. Afr. word], 1. a body of primitive rites and practices in the West Indies, based on a belief in sorcery, etc. 2. a charm, fetish, etc. used in voodoo. *v.t.* to affect by voodoo magic. **—voo′doo·ism,** *n.*
**vo·ra·cious** (vô-rā′shəs), *adj.* [< L. *vorare,* devour], 1. greedy in eating; ravenous. 2. very eager: as, a *voracious* reader. **—vo·rac′i·ty** (-ras′ə-ti), *n.*
**vor·tex** (vôr′teks), *n.* [*pl.* -TEXES, -TICES (-tə-sēz′)], [L. < *vertere,* to whirl], 1. a whirlpool. 2. a whirlwind. 3. anything like a whirl in its rush, irresistible power, etc.
**vo·ta·ry** (vō′tə-ri), *n.* [*pl.* -RIES], [< L. *vovere,* to vow], 1. one bound by a vow, esp. by religious vows. 2. one devoted to a cause, study, etc.
**vote** (vōt), *n.* [L. *votum,* a vow], 1. a decision on a proposal, etc., or a choice between candidates for office. 2. *a*) the expression of such a decision, etc. *b*) a ballot, etc. by which it is expressed. 3. the right to vote. 4. votes collectively. *v.i.* [VOTED, VOTING], to give or cast a vote. *v.t.* to decide or enact by vote. **—vot′er,** *n.*
**vo·tive** (vō′tiv), *adj.* [see VOTE], given, done, etc. in fulfillment of a vow.
**vouch** (vouch), *v.t.* [< L. *vocare,* to call], to affirm: as, *vouch* a statement. *v.i.* to give, or serve as, assurance, a guarantee, etc. (with *for*): as, *vouch* for one's honesty.
**vouch′er,** *n.* 1. one who vouches. 2. a paper attesting or serving as evidence, as of payment of a debt.
**vouch·safe′,** *v.t.* [-SAFED, -SAFING], [*vouch* + *safe*], to condescend to grant, do, etc.: as, *vouchsafe* a reply.
**vow** (vou), *n.* [< L. *votum*], 1. a solemn promise, esp. one made to God. 2. a promise of fidelity and love: as, marriage *vows.* *v.t.* & *v.i.* to promise or declare solemnly. **—take vows,** to enter a religious order.
**vow·el** (vou′əl), *n.* [< L. *vocalis,* vocal], 1. a speech sound in which the air passes in a continuous stream through the open mouth. 2. a letter representing such a sound, as *a, e, i, o, u.* **—vow′el·less,** *adj.*
**voy·age** (voi′ij), *n.* [< L. *via,* way], 1. a relatively long journey, esp. by water. 2. a journey by aircraft. *v.i.* & *v.t.* [-AGED, -AGING], to make a voyage (over or on).
**V.P., VP,** Vice-President.
**vs.,** versus.
**v.t.,** transitive verb.
**Vul·can** (vul′kən), *n.* the Roman god of fire and of metalworking.
**vul·can·ite** (vul′kən-īt′), *n.* [*Vulcan* + *-ite*], a hard rubber: used in combs, etc.
**vul′can·ize′,** *v.t.* & *v.i.* [-IZED, -IZING], to treat (crude rubber) with sulfur under great heat to increase its strength and elasticity. **—vul′can·i·za′tion,** *n.*
**vul·gar** (vul′gẽr), *adj.* [< L. *vulgus,* common people], 1. of people in general; popular. 2. lacking culture, taste, etc.; crude; boorish. **—vul′gar·ly,** *adv.* **—vul′gar·ness,** *n.*
**vul·gar′i·an** (-gâr′i-ən), *n.* a rich person with coarse, vulgar tastes.
**vul′gar·ism,** *n.* a word, phrase, etc. occurring only in informal usage, or, esp., in coarse speech.
**vul·gar′i·ty** (-gar′ə-ti), *n.* 1. the state or quality of being vulgar. 2. [*pl.* -TIES], a vulgar act, habit, usage in language, etc.
**vul′gar·ize′,** *v.t.* [-IZED, -IZING], to make vulgar. **—vul′gar·i·za′tion,** *n.*
**Vul·gate** (vul′gāt), *n.* [< ML. *vulgata* (*editio*), popular (edition)], a Latin version of the Bible, the authorized version of the Roman Catholic Church.
**vul·ner·a·ble** (vul′nẽr-ə-b'l), *adj.* [< L. *vulnus,* a wound], 1. that can be wounded or injured. 2. open to, or liable to be hurt by, criticism or attack. **—vul′ner·a·bil′i·ty,** *n.* **—vul′ner·a·bly,** *adv.*
**vul·pine** (vul′pīn), *adj.* [< L. *vulpes,* a fox], of or like a fox; clever; cunning.
**vul·ture** (vul′chẽr), *n.* [< L. *vultur*], 1. a large bird of prey that lives on carrion. 2. a greedy, ruthless person. **—vul′tur·ous,** *adj.*
**vul·va** (vul′və), *n.* [L., womb], the external genital organs of the female.
**vy·ing** (vī′iŋ), *adj.* that vies; that competes.

# W

**W, w** (dub′'l-yoo), *n.* [*pl.* W's, w's, Ws, ws], the 23rd letter of the English alphabet.
**W,** 1. watt(s). 2. west. 3. western. 4. in *chem.,* tungsten (wolfram).
**W.,** 1. Wednesday. 2. Western. 3. West.
**wab·ble** (wäb′'l), *n., v.i.* & *v.t.* [-BLED, -BLING], wobble. **—wab′bling, wab′bly,** *adj.*
**Wac** (wak), *n.* a member of the WAC.
**WAC, W.A.C.,** the Women's Army Corps.
**wack·y** (wak′i), *adj.* [-IER, -IEST], [? < *whack* + *-y*], [Slang], erratic, eccentric, or irrational: also sp. **whacky.**
**wad** (wäd, wôd), *n.* [akin to Sw. *vadd*], 1. a small, soft mass, as of cotton or paper. 2. a lump or small, compact roll. *v.t.* [WADDED, WADDING], 1. to compress, or roll up, into a wad. 2. to stuff with a wad or wadding.
**wad′ding,** *n.* any soft material for use in padding, packing, etc.
**wad·dle** (wäd′'l, wôd′-), *v.i.* [-DLED, -DLING], [< *wade*], to walk with short steps and a swaying motion from side to side, as a duck. *n.* a waddling gait.
**wade** (wād), *v.i.* [WADED, WADING], [< AS. *waden,* go], 1. to walk through any resisting substance, as water, mud, etc. 2. to proceed with difficulty: as, *wade* through a dull book. *v.t.* to cross by wading. **—wade in** (or **into**), [Colloq.], to begin with vigor.
**wad·er** (wād′ẽr), *n.* 1. one who wades. 2. a long-legged shore bird that wades the shallows. 3. *pl.* high waterproof boots.
**wa·di** (wä′di), *n.* [*pl.* -DIS, -DIES], [Ar. *wādī*], in N Africa, a river valley that is usually dry: also sp. **wady** [*pl.* -DIES].
**wa·fer** (wā′fẽr), *n.* [< D. *wafel*], 1. a thin, flat, crisp cracker or cake. 2. any disklike thing resembling this. **—wa′fer·like′,** *adj.*
**waf·fle** (wäf′'l, wôf′-), *n.* a crisp batter cake cooked in a waffle iron.
**waffle iron,** a utensil with two flat, studded plates pressed together so that a waffle bakes between them.
**waft** (waft, wäft), *v.t.* & *v.i.* [< D. *wachter,* watcher], to carry or move lightly over water or through the air, as sounds or odors. *n.* 1. an odor, sound, etc. carried through the air. 2. a gust of wind. 3. a wafting movement.
**wag** (wag), *v.i.* & *v.t.* [WAGGED, WAGGING], [prob. < ON.], to move rapidly back and forth, up and down, etc. *n.* 1. a wagging. 2. a comical person; wit.
**wage** (wāj), *v.t.* [WAGED, WAGING], [< OFr. *gage,* a pledge], to engage in; carry on: as, to *wage* war. *n. usually pl.* 1. money paid for work done. 2. what is given in return.
**wag·er** (wā′jẽr), *n.* [see WAGE], a bet. *v.t.* & *v.i.* to bet.

**wag·gish** (wag′ish), *adj.* 1. of or like a wag; roguishly merry. 2. playful; jesting.

**wag·gle** (wag′'l), *v.t. & v.i.* [-GLED, -GLING], to wag, esp. with short, abrupt movements. *n.* a waggling.

**wag·on** (wag′ən), *n.* [< D. *wagen*], a four-wheeled vehicle, esp. one for hauling heavy loads: also, Brit. sp., **waggon.** —**on the (water) wagon,** [Slang], no longer drinking alcoholic liquor.

**waif** (wāf), *n.* [< OFr. *gaif*], 1. anything found that is without an owner. 2. a homeless person, esp. a child.

**wail** (wāl), *v.i.* [< ON. *væ*, woe], to make long, loud, sad cries, as in grief or pain. *v.t.* to lament; mourn. *n.* 1. a long, sad cry, as of grief or pain. 2. a wailing. —**wail′er,** *n.*

**wain** (wān), *n.* [AS. *wægn*], [Archaic], a wagon.

**wain·scot** (wān′skət, -skot′), *n.* [< MLG. or MD.], a paneling of wood, etc. on the walls of a room. *v.t.* [-SCOTED or -SCOTTED, -SCOTING or -SCOTTING], to panel with wood, etc.

**wain′scot·ing, wain′scot·ting,** *n.* 1. wainscot. 2. material used for wainscots.

**wain·wright** (wān′rīt′), *n.* [*wain* + *wright*], one who builds or repairs wagons.

**waist** (wāst), *n.* [< AS. *weaxan*, grow], 1. the part of the body between the ribs and the hips. 2. the part of a garment that covers the body from the shoulders to the waistline. 3. a blouse. 4. the narrow part of an object that widens at the ends.

**waist′band′,** *n.* a band encircling the waist, as at the top of a skirt, trousers, etc.

**waist·coat** (wāst′kōt′, wes′kət), *n.* [Brit.], a man's vest.

**waist·line** (wāst′līn′), *n.* the line around the narrowest part of the waist.

**wait** (wāt), *v.i.* [< OHG. *wahta*, a guard], 1. to remain until something expected takes place. 2. to be ready. 3. to remain undone: as, it can *wait.* 4. to serve food. *v.t.* 1. to await. 2. to serve food at: as, he *waits* table. 3. [Colloq.], to put off serving: as, *wait* dinner. *n.* 1. act or duration of waiting. 2. an ambush; trap: usually in *lie in wait.* —**wait on** (or **upon**), 1. to act as a servant to. 2. to serve (a customer). —**wait up (for),** [Colloq.], to delay going to bed until the arrival of.

**wait′er,** *n.* one who waits; esp., a man who waits on table in a restaurant.

**wait′ing,** *adj.* 1. that waits. 2. of or for a wait. *n.* 1. the act of one that waits. 2. a period of waiting. —**in waiting,** in attendance, as on a king.

**waiting room,** a room in which people wait, as in a railroad station, dentist's office, etc.

**wait′ress** (-ris), *n.* a woman waiter.

**waive** (wāv), *v.t.* [WAIVED, WAIVING], [prob. < ON. *veifa*, fluctuate], 1. to give up or forego, as a right, claim, etc. 2. to postpone; defer.

**waiv′er,** *n.* in *law*, a waiving of a right, claim, etc.

**wake** (wāk), *v.i.* [WAKED or WOKE, WAKED, WAKING], [< AS. *wacian*, be awake & *wacan*, arise], 1. to come out of sleep; awake (often with *up*). 2. to stay awake. 3. to become active. 4. to become alert (*to* a realization, etc.). *v.t.* 1. to cause to wake: often with *up*. 2. to arouse, as passions. *n.* an all-night vigil over a corpse before burial.

**wake** (wāk), *n.* [D. *wak*], the track left in the water by a moving ship. —**in the wake of,** following closely.

**wake′ful,** *adj.* 1. alert; watchful. 2. unable to sleep. —**wake′ful·ness,** *n.*

**wak·en** (wāk′'n), *v.i. & v.t.* to wake.

**wale** (wāl), *n.* [AS. *walu*, a rod], 1. a welt raised by a whip, etc. 2. a ridge on the surface of cloth, as corduroy. *v.t.* [WALED, WALING], to mark (the skin) with wales.

**walk** (wôk), *v.i.* [AS. *wealcan*, to roll], 1. to go on foot at a moderate pace. 2. to follow a certain course: as, to *walk* in peace. 3. in *baseball*, to go to first base on four balls. *v.t.* 1. to walk along, over, etc. 2. to cause (a horse, etc.) to walk. 3. to accompany on a walk: as, I'll *walk* you home. 4. in *baseball*, to advance (a batter) to first base by pitching four balls. *n.* 1. the act or manner of walking. 2. a stroll or hike. 3. a distance walked: as, an hour's *walk.* 4. a sphere of activity, mode of living, etc.: as, people from all *walks* of life. 5. a path for walking. 6. in *baseball*, a walking. —**walk off with,** 1. to steal. 2. to win or gain. —**walk out on,** [Colloq.], to leave; desert. —**walk′er,** *n.*

**walk′ie-talk′ie** (-i-tôk′i), *n.* a portable radio transmitter and receiver.

**walking stick,** a cane.

**walk′out′,** *n.* [Colloq.], a labor strike.

**walk′-up′,** *n.* [Colloq.], an apartment house without an elevator.

**wall** (wôl), *n.* [< L. *vallum*], 1. an upright structure of wood, stone, etc. serving to enclose, divide, or protect. 2. something like a wall as in function. *v.t.* 1. to divide, enclose, etc. with a wall (often with *off*). 2. to close (an opening) with a wall (often with *up*). —**drive** (or **push**) **to the wall,** to place in a desperate position. —**walled,** *adj.*

**wal·la·by** (wäl′ə-bi), *n.* [*pl.* -BIES, -BY], [< Australian name], a small kangaroo.

**wall′board′,** *n.* fibrous material in thin slabs for making or covering walls.

**wal·let** (wäl′it, wôl′-), *n.* [ME. *walet*, knapsack], a flat pocketbook for carrying paper money, cards, etc.; billfold.

**wall·eye** (wôl′ī′), *n.* [< ON. *vagl*, film on the eye; + *eye*], 1. an eye that turns outward, showing much white. 2. a fish with large, staring eyes; specif., a N. American freshwater food fish of the perch family: in full, **wall′eyed′ pike.**

**wall′flow′er,** *n.* [Colloq.], a shy person who only looks on at a dance.

**Wal·loon** (wä-lo͞on′), *n.* 1. a member of a people living in S and SE Belgium and near-by parts of France. 2. the French dialect of the Walloons.

**wal·lop** (wäl′əp, wôl′-), *v.t.* [< OFr. *galoper*, to gallop], [Colloq.], 1. to beat or defeat soundly. 2. to strike hard. *n.* [Colloq.], a hard blow.

**wal·low** (wäl′ō, wôl′ō), *v.i.* [< AS. *wealwian*, roll around], 1. to roll about in mud, etc., as pigs. 2. to indulge oneself fully: as, to *wallow* in vice. *n.* an act of wallowing.

**wall′pa′per,** *n.* paper for covering the walls. *v.t.* to put wallpaper on or in.

**wal·nut** (wôl′nut), *n.* [< AS. *wealh*, foreign + *hnutu*, nut], 1. a roundish, edible nut with a two-lobed seed. 2. a tree bearing such a nut, as the *English walnut.* 3. the wood of such a tree, used in furniture, etc.

**wal·rus** (wôl′rəs, wäl′-), *n.* [prob. < ON. *hrosshvalr*, horse whale], a massive sea animal of the seal family, having two protruding tusks and a heavy layer of blubber.

**waltz** (wôlts, wôls), *n.* [< G. *walzen*, dance about], 1. a ballroom dance for couples, in ¾ time. 2. music for this. *v.i.* 1. to dance a waltz. 2. to move lightly and nimbly. *v.t.* to cause to waltz. —**waltz′er,** *n.*

**wam·pum** (wäm′pəm, wôm′-), *n.* [< Algonquian], small beads made of shells and used by N. American Indians as money.

**wan** (wän, wôn), *adj.* [WANNER, WANNEST], [AS. *wann*, dark], 1. sickly pale. 2. suggesting a sickly condition; feeble: as, a *wan* smile. —**wan′ly,** *adv.* —**wan′ness,** *n.*

**wand** (wänd, wônd), *n.* [ON. *vöndr*], 1. a slender stick or rod, as a musician's baton. 2. a staff of authority. 3. a rod of supposed magic power. —**wand′like′,** *adj.*

**wan·der** (wän′dẽr, wôn′-), ***v.i.*** [AS. *wandrian*], 1. to roam idly about; ramble. 2. to stray (*from* a path, etc.). 3. to go astray; specif., to be disjointed, incoherent, etc. 4. to meander, as a river. ***v.t.*** [Poetic], to roam in or over. **—wan′der·er, *n.***

**wan′der·lust′** (-lust′), ***n.*** [G.], an urge to wander or travel.

**wane** (wān), ***v.i.*** [WANED, WANING], [< AS. *wana*, lacking], 1. to grow gradually less in extent, as the moon after it is full. 2. to grow dim, as a light. 3. to decline in power, etc. 4. to approach the end. ***n.*** a waning.

**wan·gle** (waŋ′g'l), ***v.t.*** [-GLED, -GLING], [prob. < *angle*], [Colloq.], to get or cause by persuasion, influence, tricks, etc.

**want** (wänt, wônt), ***v.t.*** [< ON. *vanta*], 1. to lack. 2. to crave: as, he *wants* love. 3. to desire: as, he *wants* to go home. 4. to wish to see or apprehend: as, *wanted* by the police. 5. [Chiefly Brit.], to require. ***v.i.*** 1. to have a need or lack (with *for*). 2. to be destitute. ***n.*** 1. a lack; shortage. 2. poverty. 3. a craving. 4. something needed.

**want ad,** [Colloq.], an advertisement for something wanted, as a job.

**want′ing,** ***adj.*** 1. lacking. 2. not up to standard. ***prep.*** less; minus. **—wanting in,** deficient in (a quality).

**wan·ton** (wän′tən, wôn′-), ***adj.*** [< AS. *wan*, lacking + *teon*, bring up], 1. unchaste; lewd. 2. [Poetic], playful. 3. unprovoked or malicious. 4. recklessly disregardful of decency, etc. ***n.*** a wanton person; esp., an immoral woman. ***v.i.*** to be wanton. **—wan′ton·ly, *adv.* —wan′ton·ness, *n.***

**wap·i·ti** (wäp′ə-ti), ***n.*** [< Algonquian], a N. American deer with large, branching antlers; American elk.

**war** (wôr), ***n.*** [< OHG. *werra*, strife], 1. open armed conflict, as between nations. 2. any active hostility; strife. 3. military operations as a science. ***adj.*** of, in, or from war. ***v.i.*** [WARRED, WARRING], 1. to carry on war. 2. to contend; strive.

**war·ble** (wôr′b'l), ***v.t. & v.i.*** [-BLED, -BLING], [< Gmc.], to sing with trills, quavers, runs, etc., as a bird. ***n.*** a warbling; trill.

**war′bler,** ***n.*** one that warbles; esp., any of various songbirds.

**war cry,** 1. a slogan, etc. shouted in battle. 2. a phrase or a slogan in any conflict.

**ward** (wôrd), ***v.t.*** [AS. *weardian*, to watch], to turn aside; fend (*off*). ***n.*** 1. a being under guard. 2. *a*) guardianship. *b*) one under the care of a guardian or court. 3. a division of a jail, hospital, etc. 4. a division of a city or town, for purposes of voting, etc.

**-ward,** [AS. *-weard*], a suffix meaning *in a* (specified) *direction*, as in *backward:* also **-wards.**

**ward·en** (wôr′d'n), ***n.*** [< OFr. *gardein*], 1. one who guards, or has charge of, something: as, a game *warden.* 2. the head official of a prison.

**ward·er** (wôr′dẽr), ***n.*** a watchman; guard.

**ward heeler,** a hanger-on of a politician, etc.; ward worker: contemptuous term.

**ward·robe** (wôrd′rōb′), ***n.*** 1. a closet, cabinet, etc. for holding clothes. 2. one's supply of clothes.

**ward′room′,** ***n.*** in a warship, living or eating quarters for officers.

**ward′ship′,** ***n.*** 1. guardianship. 2. the condition of being a ward.

**ware** (wâr), ***n.*** [AS. *waru*], 1. *usually in pl.* anything for sale. 2. pottery.

**ware′house′,** ***n.*** a building where wares, or goods, are stored. ***v.t.*** [-HOUSED, -HOUSING], to place or store in a warehouse.

**war′fare′** (-fâr′), ***n.*** 1. the action of waging war. 2. conflict of any kind.

**war′head,** ***n.*** the front part of a torpedo, bomb, etc., containing the explosive charge.

**war horse,** [Colloq.], one who has engaged in many struggles.

**war·i·ly** (wâr′ə-li), ***adv.*** in a wary manner.

**war′like′,** ***adj.*** 1. fond of or ready for war. 2. of war. 3. threatening war.

**warm** (wôrm), ***adj.*** [AS. *wearm*], 1. having, feeling, or giving off a moderate degree of heat. 2. that keeps one heated: as, *warm* clothing. 3. ardent; enthusiastic. 4. lively, vigorous, etc. 5. fiery; quick to anger. 6. *a*) genial; cordial: as, a *warm* welcome. *b*) sympathetic or loving. 7. newly made; fresh, as a trail. 8. [Colloq.], close to discovering something. ***v.t. & v.i.*** to make or become warm. **—warm′ly, *adv.* —warm′ness, *n.***

**warm′-blood′ed,** ***adj.*** 1. having warm blood and a constant natural body heat: said of mammals and birds. 2. ardent; fervent.

**warm′heart′ed,** ***adj.*** 1. kind; sympathetic; friendly. 2. loving; ardent.

**war′mon′ger** (-muŋ′gẽr), ***n.*** one who advocates, or tries to bring about, war.

**warmth** (wôrmth), ***n.*** 1. a being warm. 2. mild heat. 3. excitement or vigor of feeling; ardor. 4. slight anger.

**warn** (wôrn), ***v.t. & v.i.*** [AS. *wearnian*], 1. to tell (a person) of a danger, coming evil, etc. 2. to advise to be wary or cautious. 3. to notify in advance; inform. **—warn′er, *n.***

**warn′ing,** ***n.*** 1. the act of one that warns. 2. that which warns. ***adj.*** that warns.

**warp** (wôrp), ***n.*** [< AS. *weorpan*, throw], 1. *a*) a distortion, as a twist or bend, in wood. *b*) any like distortion. 2. a mental quirk, bias, etc. 3. in *weaving*, the threads running lengthwise in the loom. ***v.t.*** 1. to bend or twist out of shape. 2. to distort, pervert, etc.: as, a *warped* mind. ***v.i.*** to become bent or twisted.

**war paint,** 1. paint applied to the face and body by primitive tribes before going to war. 2. [Slang], ceremonial dress.

**war′path′,** ***n.*** the path taken by N. American Indians on a warlike expedition. **—on the warpath,** 1. ready for war. 2. actively angry; ready to fight.

**war·rant** (wôr′ənt, wär′-), ***n.*** [< OHG. *weren*, warranty], 1. *a*) authorization, as by law. *b*) justification for some act, belief, etc. 2. something serving as a guarantee of some event or result. 3. in *law*, a writ authorizing an arrest, search, etc. 4. the certificate appointing a warrant officer. ***v.t.*** 1. to authorize. 2. to serve as justification for (an act, belief, etc.). 3. to guarantee.

**warrant officer,** a military officer ranking above an enlisted man but below a commissioned officer.

**war′ran·tor′** (-tôr′), **war′rant·er,** ***n.*** one who warrants or gives a warranty.

**war′ran·ty** (-ti), ***n.*** [*pl.* -TIES], 1. official authorization. 2. justification, as for some act. 3. a guarantee (sense 2*a*).

**war·ren** (wôr′ən, wär′-), ***n.*** [< OFr. *warir*, to preserve], 1. an area in which rabbits breed or are raised. 2. any crowded building or buildings.

**war·ri·or** (wôr′i-ẽr, wär′yẽr), ***n.*** [see WAR], a fighting man; veteran soldier.

**war·ship** (wôr′ship′), ***n.*** any ship for combat use, as a battleship, destroyer, etc.

**wart** (wôrt), ***n.*** [AS. *wearte*], 1. a small, usually hard, tumorous growth on the skin. 2. a small protuberance, as on a plant. **—wart′like′, *adj.* —wart′y, *adj.***

**wart hog,** a wild African hog with large tusks, and warts below the eyes.

**war·y** (wâr′i), ***adj.*** [-IER, -IEST], [< AS. *wær*, aware], full of or characterized by caution. **—wary of,** careful of.

**was** (wuz, wäz), [AS. *wæs*], 1st and 3d pers. sing., pt., of **be.**

**wash** (wôsh, wäsh), ***v.t.*** [AS. *wæscan*], 1. to clean with water or other liquid. 2. to purify. 3. to wet; moisten. 4. to flow over, past, or against: as, the sea *washed* the shore. 5. to soak out or pick up and carry (*off, out,* or *away*), as dirt, etc., with water. 6. to erode (with *out* or *away*): as, the flood *washed* out the road. 7. to cover with a thin coating of paint or metal. *v.i.* 1. to wash oneself. 2. to wash clothes. 3. to undergo washing. 4. to be removed by washing: as, the stain *washed* out. 5. to be worn or carried away by the action of water: as, the bridge had *washed* out. *n.* 1. a washing. 2. a quantity of clothes washed, or to be washed. 3. *a*) the rush or surge of water. *b*) the eddy of water caused by a propeller, etc. 4. silt, mud, etc. carried and dropped by running water. 5. a thin coating of paint or metal. 6. a liquid for cosmetic or toilet use: as, mouth *wash*. *adj.* that can be washed without damage: as, a *wash* dress. **—wash down,** to follow (a bite of food) with a drink. **—wash′a·ble,** *adj.*

**Wash.,** Washington (State).

**wash′board′,** *n.* a ridged board for scrubbing dirt out of clothes.

**wash′bowl′,** *n.* a bowl for use in washing one's hands, etc.: also **wash′ba′sin.**

**wash′cloth′,** *n.* a small cloth used in washing the body.

**washed′-out′,** *adj.* 1. faded. 2. [Colloq.], tired; spiritless; pale and wan.

**wash′er,** *n.* 1. one who washes. 2. a flat ring of metal, rubber, etc. used to make a seat for a bolt head or nut, to provide packing, etc. 3. a machine for washing.

**wash′er·wom′an,** *n.* [*pl.* -WOMEN], a woman whose work is washing clothes.

**wash′ing,** *n.* 1. the act of one that washes. 2. clothes, etc. to be washed.

**washing machine,** a machine for washing clothes, etc.

**washing soda,** sodium carbonate.

**wash′out′,** *n.* 1. a washing away of soil, etc. by water. 2. [Slang], a failure.

**wash′rag′,** *n.* a washcloth.

**wash′room′,** *n.* 1. a room for washing. 2. a rest-room.

**wash′stand′,** *n.* a table or plumbing fixture with a washbowl, etc.

**wash′tub′,** *n.* a tub for washing clothes, etc.

**wash′y,** *adj.* [-IER, -IEST], 1. watery; diluted. 2. insipid; feeble.

**was·n't** (wuz′′nt, wäz′-), was not.

**wasp** (wäsp, wôsp), *n.* [AS. *wæsp*], a winged insect with a slender body and, in the females and workers, a painful sting.

**wasp′ish,** *adj.* 1. of or like a wasp. 2. bad-tempered; snappish. **—wasp′ish·ness,** *n.*

**wasp waist,** a very slender waist.

**was·sail** (wäs′′l, -āl), *n.* [< ON. *ves heill,* be hearty], 1. a former toast in drinking healths. 2. the spiced ale, etc. with which such healths were drunk. 3. a drinking bout. *v.i.* & *v.t.* to drink a wassail (to).

**wast·age** (wās′tij), *n.* 1. loss by use, decay, etc. 2. what is wasted.

**waste** (wāst), *v.t.* [WASTED, WASTING], [< L. *vastare,* lay waste], 1. to devastate, as land. 2. to wear away. 3. to make weak or emaciated: as, *wasted* by age. 4. to use up needlessly; squander. 5. to fail to take advantage of. *v.i.* 1. to lose strength, etc., as by disease. 2. to be used up or worn down gradually. *adj.* 1. uncultivated or uninhabited; desolate. 2. left over; superfluous. 3. excreted from the body. 4. used for waste. *n.* 1. uncultivated or uninhabited land. 2. a devastated area. 3. a wasting or being wasted. 4. discarded material, as ashes, etc. 5. excretions from the body, as urine. **—go to waste,** to be wasted. **—lay waste,** to devastate. **—wast′er,** *n.*

**waste′bas′ket,** *n.* a container for wastepaper, etc.: also **wastepaper basket.**

**waste′ful,** *adj.* 1. characterized by waste. 2. using more than is needed; extravagant. **—waste′ful·ly,** *adv.* **—waste′ful·ness,** *n.*

**waste′land′,** *n.* barren land.

**waste′pa′per,** *n.* paper thrown away after use or as useless: also **waste paper.**

**wast·rel** (wās′trəl), *n.* 1. one who wastes; esp., a spendthrift. 2. a good-for-nothing.

**watch** (wäch, wôch), *n.* [AS. *wæcce*], 1. a keeping awake, esp. in order to guard. 2. close observation for a time. 3. a guard, or the period of duty of a guard. 4. a small timepiece worn on the wrist or carried in the pocket. 5. *a*) any of the periods of duty (usually four hours) on shipboard. *b*) the crew on duty during such a period. *v.i.* 1. to stay awake; keep vigil. 2. to keep guard. 3. to look; observe: as, just *watch*. 4. to be looking or waiting attentively. *v.t.* 1. to guard or tend. 2. to observe carefully. 3. to wait and look for. **—watch out,** to be alert or careful. **—watch′er,** *n.*

**watch′dog′,** *n.* 1. a dog kept to guard property. 2. any watchful guardian.

**watch′ful,** *adj.* alert; attentive; vigilant. **—watch′ful·ly,** *adv.* **—watch′ful·ness,** *n.*

**watch′mak′er,** *n.* one who makes or repairs watches. **—watch′mak′ing,** *n.*

**watch′man** (-mən), *n.* [*pl.* -MEN], a person hired to watch or guard, esp. at night.

**watch′tow′er,** *n.* a high tower from which watch is kept, as for forest fires.

**watch′word′,** *n.* 1. a password. 2. a slogan.

**wa·ter** (wô′tẽr, wä′tẽr), *n.* [AS. *wæter*], 1. the colorless liquid of rivers, lakes, etc., which falls as rain. 2. water with reference to its depth, surface, or level: as, above *water*. 3. a body secretion, as urine. 4. a wavy, lustrous finish given to linen, silk, metal, etc. *v.t.* 1. to give (an animal) water to drink. 2. to supply (crops, etc.) with water. 3. to moisten, soak, or dilute with water. 4. to give a wavy luster to (silk, etc.). *v.i.* 1. to fill with tears, as the eyes. 2. to secrete saliva: as, his mouth *watered*. 3. to take on a supply of water. 4. to drink water. *adj.* of, for, in, on, near, from, or by water. **—hold water,** to prove sound, logical, etc.

**water buffalo,** a slow, powerful, oxlike draft animal of Asia and Africa.

**water chestnut,** 1. a water plant with nutlike fruit. 2. its fruit.

**water closet,** 1. a small room with a bowl-shaped plumbing fixture in which to defecate or urinate. 2. this fixture.

**water color,** 1. a paint mixed with water instead of oil. 2. (a) painting done with water colors. **—wa′ter-col′or,** *adj.*

**wa′ter-cool′,** *v.t.* to cool by passing water over, into, or through.

**wa′ter·course′,** *n.* 1. a stream, river, etc. 2. a channel for water, as a canal.

**water cress,** a plant of the mustard family whose leaves are used in salads, etc.: it grows in water or wet soil.

**wa′ter·fall′,** *n.* a steep fall of water, as of a stream from a height.

**wa′ter·fowl′,** *n.* a water bird, esp. one that swims.

**water front,** land or docks at the edge of a stream, harbor, etc.: also **wa′ter·front′,** *n.*

**water glass,** 1. a drinking glass. 2. a silicate of sodium or potassium, dissolved in water to form a sirupy liquid used as a preservative for eggs, etc.

**water hole,** a pond or pool.

**water level,** 1. *a*) the surface of still water. *b*) the height of this. 2. water line.

**water lily,** 1. a water plant with large, flat, floating leaves and showy flowers. 2. the flower.

**water line,** the line to which the surface of the water comes on the side of a ship or boat: also **wa′ter·line′,** *n.*

**wa′ter-logged′**, *adj.* soaked or filled with water so as to be heavy and sluggish, as a boat.
**water main,** a main pipe in a system of pipes which carry water.
**wa′ter·mark′**, *n.* 1. a mark showing the limit to which water has risen. 2. a mark in paper, produced by the impression of a design, as in the mold. *v.t.* to mark (paper) with a watermark.
**wa′ter·mel′on,** *n.* a large, seedy melon with a green rind and juicy, red pulp.
**water moccasin,** a large, poisonous snake found along rivers and swamps of the southern U.S.
**water polo,** a water game played with a ball by two teams of swimmers.
**water power,** the power of running or falling water, used to drive machinery.
**wa′ter·proof′**, *adj.* that keeps out water, as a fabric treated with rubber, plastic, etc. *n.* waterproof material or garment. *v.t.* to make waterproof.
**water rat,** 1. a European vole that lives on the banks of streams, etc. 2. a muskrat.
**wa′ter·shed′** (-shed′), *n.* 1. a ridge dividing the areas drained by different river systems. 2. the area drained by a river system.
**wa′ter·side′**, *n.* land at the edge of a body of water.
**wa′ter-ski′**, *v.i.* [-SKIED, -SKIING], to be towed on ski-like boards by a line attached to a motorboat.
**water snake,** any of various nonpoisonous, fresh-water snakes.
**wa′ter·spout′**, *n.* a rotating, tubelike column of air full of moisture, extending downward from a storm cloud to a body of water.
**water table,** the level below which the ground is saturated with water.
**wa′ter·tight′**, *adj.* 1. so tight that no water can get in or through. 2. that cannot be misconstrued, nullified, etc., as a plan.
**water tower,** an elevated tank for water storage and for equalizing water pressure.
**wa′ter·way′**, *n.* 1. a channel through which water runs. 2. any body of water on which boats, ships, etc. can travel.
**water wheel,** a wheel turned by running water, as for power.
**water wings,** an inflated device used to keep one afloat while learning to swim.
**wa′ter·works′**, *n.pl.* [often construed as sing.], a system of reservoirs, pumps, etc. supplying water to a city.
**wa′ter·y**, *adj.* 1. of or like water. 2. full of water. 3. diluted; thin, weak, etc. 4. tearful.
**watt** (wät, wôt), *n.* [< J. *Watt*, 18th-c. Scottish inventor], a unit of electric power, equal to one ampere under one volt of pressure.
**watt′age** (-ij), *n.* amount of electric power expressed in watts.
**wat′tle** (wät′'l, wôt′'l), *n.* [AS. *watel*], 1. a woven work of sticks intertwined with twigs or branches. 2. a fleshy flap of skin hanging from the throat of a cock, etc. *v.t.* [-TLED, -TLING], 1. to intertwine (sticks, twigs, etc.). 2. to construct of wattle.
**Wave, WAVE** (wāv), *n.* [< *W*omen *A*ppointed for *V*oluntary *E*mergency Service], one of the Women's Reserve of the U.S. Naval Reserve (**WAVES**).
**wave** (wāv), *v.i.* [WAVED, WAVING], [AS. *wafian*], 1. to move or sway to and fro. 2. to signal by moving a hand, arm, etc. to and fro. 3. to have the form of a series of curves. *v.t.* 1. to cause to wave. 2. to brandish, as a weapon. 3. *a*) to move or swing (something) as a signal. *b*) to signal (something) to (someone) by doing this. 4. to give an undulating form to (hair, etc.). *n.* 1. a curving swell moving along the surface of the ocean, etc. 2. an undulation or curve, as in the hair. 3. a motion to and fro, as with the hand in signaling. 4. a thing like a wave in effect; specif., an upsurge: as, a crime *wave*. 5. in *physics*, any of the series of advancing impulses set up by a vibration, etc.
**wave length,** in *physics*, the distance, measured in the direction of progression of a wave, from any given point to the next point characterized by the same phase.
**wa·ver** (wā′vẽr), *v.i.* [< ME. *waven*, to wave], 1. to sway to and fro; flutter. 2. to show indecision; vacillate. 3. to falter, flicker, or tremble. *n.* a wavering. **—wa′ver·y,** *adj.*
**wav·y** (wāv′i), *adj.* [-IER, -IEST], 1. having or like waves. 2. moving in a wavelike motion. **—wav′i·ness,** *n.*
**wax** (waks), *n.* [AS. *weax*], 1. a plastic, dull-yellow substance secreted by bees; beeswax. 2. any plastic substance like this, as paraffin. *v.t.* to rub, polish, cover, or treat with wax. **—wax′er,** *n.*
**wax** (waks), *v.i.* [< AS. *weaxan*, grow], 1. to increase in strength, size, etc. 2. to become gradually full: said of the moon. 3. to become: as, *wax* old.
**wax bean,** a variety of string bean with long, edible yellow pods.
**wax·en** (wak′s'n), *adj.* 1. made of wax. 2. like wax; smooth, pale, plastic, etc.
**wax myrtle,** a shrub or tree bearing grayish berries coated with a waxy substance.
**wax paper,** a paper made moistureproof by a wax, or paraffin, coating.
**wax′wing′**, *n.* a bird with silky-brown plumage, a showy crest, and scarlet spines at the ends of the wings.
**wax′works′**, *n.pl.* [construed as sing.], an exhibition of wax figures.
**wax′y**, *adj.* [-IER, -IEST], of, full of, or like wax. **—wax′i·ness,** *n.*
**way** (wā), *n.* [AS. *weg*], 1. a road, street, path, etc. 2. room for passing. 3. a route or course. 4. movement along a route: as, lead the *way*. 5. habits of life: as, give up evil *ways*. 6. a method of doing something. 7. a manner of living, acting, etc.: as, his *ways* are odd. 8. distance: as, a long *way* off. 9. direction of movement. 10. respect; particular: as, right in some *ways*. 11. wish; will: as, I had my *way*. 12. *pl.* a timber framework on which a ship is built. 13. [Colloq.], *a*) a condition: as, he's in a bad *way*. *b*) a locality: as, out our *way*. *adv.* [Colloq.], away; far: as, *way* behind. **—by the way,** incidentally. **—by way of,** 1. passing through. 2. as a method, etc. of. **—give way,** 1. to yield. 2. to break down. **—make way,** to clear a passage. **—under way,** 1. moving. 2. making headway, as a boat: also **under weigh.**
**way′bill′**, *n.* a list of goods and shipping instructions, sent with goods in transit.
**way·far·er** (wā′fâr′ẽr), *n.* a traveler, esp. on foot. **—way′far′ing,** *adj. & n.*
**way′lay′**, *v.t.* [-LAID, -LAYING], 1. to lie in wait for and attack; ambush. 2. to wait for and accost by surprise.
**way′-out′**, *adj.* [Colloq.], 1. very advanced. 2. eccentric, bizarre, etc.
**-ways,** [< *way*], a suffix meaning *in a* (specified) *direction, position,* or *manner,* as in *endways*.
**ways and means,** methods and resources at the disposal of a person, company, etc.
**way′side′**, *n.* the edge of a road.
**way·ward** (wā′wẽrd), *adj.* [see AWAY & -WARD], 1. willful, disobedient, perverse, etc. 2. unpredictable; erratic.
**we** (wē), *pron.* [for *sing.* see I], [AS.], the persons speaking or writing: sometimes used by a person in referring to a group of which he is one, or, in place of *I*, by a king, editor, etc.

**weak** (wēk), *adj.* [< ON. *veikr*], 1. lacking physical strength; frail; feeble. 2. lacking moral strength or firmness of character. 3. lacking mental power. 4. lacking force, power, etc.: as, *weak* discipline. 5. easily broken, torn, etc.: as, a *weak* rail. 6. lacking in intensity: as, a *weak* voice. 7. diluted: as, *weak* tea. 8. unconvincing: as, a *weak* argument.

**weak′en,** *v.t. & v.i.* to make or become weak or weaker. **—weak′en·er,** *n.*

**weak′-kneed′,** *adj.* lacking in courage, firmness, etc.; timid.

**weak′ling,** *n.* one lacking physical or moral strength.

**weak′ly,** *adj.* [-LIER, -LIEST], sickly; feeble. *adv.* in a weak manner. **—weak′li·ness,** *n.*

**weak′-mind′ed,** *adj.* 1. not firm of mind; indecisive. 2. feeble-minded.

**weak′ness,** *n.* 1. a being weak. 2. a weak point; fault. 3. an unreasonable fondness (*for* something).

**weal** (wēl), *n.* [< *wale*], a mark raised on the skin, as by a blow; welt.

**weal** (wēl), *n.* [AS. *wela*], [Archaic], well-being; welfare.

**wealth** (welth), *n.* [< prec.], 1. much money or property; riches. 2. a large amount: as, a *wealth* of ideas. 3. valuable products, contents, etc. 4. everything having value in money.

**wealth′y,** *adj.* [-IER, -IEST], having wealth; rich. **—wealth′i·ness,** *n.*

**wean** (wēn), *v.t.* [AS. *wenian*], 1. to accustom (a child or young animal) to take food other than by suckling. 2. to withdraw (a person) as from a habit.

**wean′ling,** *n.* a child or young animal that has just been weaned. *adj.* recently weaned.

**weap·on** (wep′ən), *n.* [AS. *wæpen*], 1. any instrument used for fighting. 2. any means of attack or defense.

**wear** (wâr), *v.t.* [WORE, WORN, WEARING], [AS. *werian*], 1. to bear on the body, as clothing. 2. to show in one's appearance: as, she *wore* a smile. 3. to impair or diminish by use, friction, etc. 4. to make by rubbing, flowing, etc.: as, to *wear* a hole in the rug. 5. to tire or exhaust. *v.i.* 1. to become impaired or diminished, as by use. 2. to hold up in use: as, that suit *wears* well. 3. to become in time: as, my courage *wore* thin. *n.* 1. a wearing or being worn. 2. things worn; clothing: as, men's *wear.* 3. impairment or loss, as from use, friction, etc. **—wear off,** to diminish by degrees. **—wear out,** 1. to make or become useless from continued use. 2. to tire out. **—wear′a·ble,** *adj.* **—wear′er,** *n.*

**wear and tear,** loss and damage caused by use.

**wear′ing** (wâr′-), *adj.* 1. causing wear (sense 3). 2. wearying.

**wearing apparel,** garments; clothing.

**wea·ri·some** (wêr′i-səm), *adj.* causing weariness; tiresome; tedious.

**wea·ry** (wêr′i), *adj.* [-RIER, -RIEST], [AS. *werig*], 1. tired; worn out. 2. without further patience, zeal, etc. 3. tiring: as, *weary* work. 4. tedious. *v.t. & v.i.* [-RIED, -RYING], to make or become weary. **—wea′ri·less,** *adj.* **—wea′ri·ly,** *adv.* **—wea′ri·ness,** *n.*

**wea·sel** (wē′z'l), *n.* [AS. *wesle*], an agile, flesh-eating mammal, with a long, slender body, short legs, and a long tail.

**weath·er** (weth′ẽr), *n.* [AS. *weder*], 1. the condition of the atmosphere with regard to temperature, moisture, etc. 2. storm, rain, etc. *v.t.* 1. to expose to the action of weather. 2. to pass through safely: as, to *weather* a storm. 3. in *naut. usage,* to pass to the windward of. *v.i.* to become discolored, worn, etc. by exposure to the weather. **—under the weather,** [Colloq.], ill.

**weath′er-beat′en,** *adj.* showing the effect of exposure to sun, rain, etc.

**weath′er·board′,** *n.* a clapboard.

**Weather Bureau,** the National Weather Service: the former name.

**weath′er·cock′,** *n.* a weather vane in the form of a cock.

**weath′er·glass′,** *n.* an instrument used to forecast the weather by showing changes in atmospheric pressure, as a barometer.

**weath′er·man′** (-man′), *n.* [*pl.* -MEN], [Colloq.], a forecaster of the weather.

**weath′er·proof′,** *adj.* that can withstand exposure to the weather without damage. *v.t.* to make weatherproof.

**weath′er·strip′,** *n.* a thin strip of wood, metal, felt, etc. covering the joint between a door or window and the casing, to keep out drafts, etc.: also **weather strip.** *v.t.* [-STRIPPED, -STRIPPING], to fit or provide with weatherstrips: also **weath′er-strip′.**

**weath′er·strip′ping,** *n.* weatherstrips.

**weather vane,** a vane for showing which way the wind is blowing.

**weave** (wēv), *v.t.* [WOVE or *rarely* WEAVED, WOVEN or WOVE, WEAVING], [AS. *wefan*], 1. to make (a fabric, basket, etc.) by interlacing (threads, reeds, etc.), as on a loom. 2. to construct in the mind: as, to *weave* a tale. 3. to twist (something) into or through. 4. to spin (a web), as spiders do. *v.i.* 1. to do weaving. 2. to become interlaced. 3. to move from side to side or in and out. *n.* a method or pattern of weaving. **—weav′er,** *n.*

**web** (web), *n.* [AS. *webb*], 1. any woven fabric. 2. the network spun by a spider, etc. 3. a carefully woven trap. 4. a network. 5. a membrane joining the toes of various water birds, animals, etc. *v.t.* [WEBBED, WEBBING], to join by, or cover as with, a web. **—webbed,** *adj.*

**web′bing,** *n.* a strong fabric woven in strips and used for belts, in upholstery, etc.

**web′foot′,** *n.* [*pl.* -FEET], a foot with the toes webbed. **—web′-foot′ed,** *adj.*

**wed** (wed), *v.t. & v.i.* [WEDDED, WEDDED or WED, WEDDING], [AS. *weddian*], 1. to marry. 2. to unite.

**we'd** (wēd), 1. we had. 2. we should. 3. we would.

**Wed.,** Wednesday.

**wed·ded** (wed′id), *adj.* 1. married. 2. of marriage. 3. devoted: as, *wedded* to one's work. 4. united.

**wed′ding,** *n.* 1. the marriage ceremony. 2. a marriage anniversary.

**wedge** (wej), *n.* [AS. *wecg*], 1. a piece of wood, metal, etc. tapering to a thin edge: used to split wood, lift weights, etc. 2. anything shaped like a wedge. 3. any act serving to open the way for change, intrusion, etc. *v.t.* [WEDGED, WEDGING], 1. to force apart, or fix in place, with a wedge. 2. to crowd together or pack (*in*). *v.i.* to be forced as a wedge. **—wedge′like′,** *adj.* **—wedg′y,** *adj.*

**Wedg·wood (ware)** (wej′wood′), [< J. *Wedgwood,* 18th-c. Eng. potter], a fine English pottery with figures in relief.

**wed·lock** (wed′lok), *n.* [AS. *wedloc*], the state of being married; matrimony.

**Wednes·day** (wenz′di), *n.* [after *Woden,* Germanic god], the fourth day of the week.

**wee** (wē), *adj.* [WEER (wē′ẽr), WEEST (wē′ist)], [AS. *wege*], very small; tiny.

**weed** (wēd), *n.* [AS. *weod*], any undesired, uncultivated plant that crowds out desired ones. *v.t. & v.i.* 1. to remove weeds from (a garden, etc.). 2. to remove as useless, harmful, etc.: often with *out.* **—weed′er,** *n.*

**weeds** (wēdz), *n.pl.* [< AS. *wæde,* garment], black mourning clothes.

**weed′y,** *adj.* [-IER, -IEST], 1. full of weeds. 2. of or like a weed. 3. lean; lanky.

**week** (wēk), *n.* [AS. *wicu*], 1. a period of seven days, esp. the period from Sunday through Saturday. 2. the hours or days of work in this period.

**week′day′,** *n.* any day of the week except Sunday and, often, Saturday.

**week′end′, week′-end′,** *n.* the period from Friday night or Saturday to Monday morning: also **week end.** *v.i.* to spend the weekend (*at* or *in*).

**week′ly,** *adj.* 1. of, for, or lasting a week. 2. done, happening, etc. once every week. *adv.* once a week; every week. *n.* [*pl.* -LIES], a periodical published once a week.

**ween** (wēn), *v.i. & v.t.* [AS. *wenan*], [Archaic], to think; suppose; imagine.

**weep** (wēp), *v.i. & v.t.* [WEPT, WEEPING], [< AS. *wop*, outcry], 1. to shed (tears). 2. to mourn (*for*). 3. to drip or exude (water, etc.). —**weep′er,** *n.* —**weep′y,** *adj.*

**weep′ing,** *n.* the act of one who weeps. *adj.* 1. that weeps. 2. having graceful, drooping branches. —**weep′ing·ly,** *adv.*

**wee·vil** (wē′v'l), *n.* [AS. *wifel*], a beetle whose larvae attack cotton, grain, etc. by boring. —**wee′vil·y, wee′vil·ly,** *adj.*

**weft** (weft), *n.* [< AS. *wefan*, to weave], 1. in weaving, the woof. 2. something woven.

**weigh** (wā), *v.t.* [AS. *wegan*, carry], 1. to determine the heaviness of. 2. to consider and choose carefully: as, *weigh* one's words. 3. to burden (with *down*). 4. to hoist (an anchor). *v.i.* 1. to have (a specified) weight. 2. to have significance, importance, etc. 3. to be a burden. —**weigh′a·ble,** *adj.*

**weight** (wāt), *n.* [AS. (*ge*)*wiht*], 1. a quantity weighing a definite amount. 2. heaviness; attraction of a body, by gravitation, toward the earth. 3. amount of heaviness. 4. *a*) any unit of heaviness. *b*) any system of such units. *c*) a piece of standard heaviness used in weighing. 5. any mass used for its heaviness: as, a paper *weight*. 6. a burden, as of sorrow. 7. importance; consequence. 8. influence; power. *v.t.* 1. to add weight to. 2. to burden.

**weight′y,** *adj.* [-IER, -IEST], 1. very heavy. 2. burdensome. 3. significant; important.

**weir** (wêr), *n.* [AS. *wer*], 1. a low dam built to back up water, as for a mill. 2. a fence, as of brushwood, in a stream, etc., for catching fish.

**weird** (wêrd), *adj.* [< AS. *wyrd*, fate], 1. suggestive of ghosts, etc.; mysterious. 2. [Colloq.], queer; unusual. —**weird′ness,** *n.*

**welch** (welch), *v.i.* [Slang], to welsh.

**wel·come** (wel′kəm), *adj.* [< AS. *wilcuma*, welcome guest], 1. gladly received: as, a *welcome* guest, *welcome* news. 2. freely permitted: as, you are *welcome* to use my car. 3. under no obligation: in *you're welcome*. *n.* a welcoming. *v.t.* [-COMED, -COMING], to greet or receive with pleasure, etc.

**weld** (weld), *v.t.* [< *well* (to boil)], 1. to unite (pieces of metal) by heating until fused or soft enough to hammer or press together. 2. to unite closely. *v.i.* to be welded. *n.* 1. a welding. 2. the joint formed by welding. —**weld′er,** *n.*

**wel·fare** (wel′fâr′), *n.* [< ME. *wel*, well + AS. *faran*, to fare], state of health, happiness, and prosperity; well-being.

**wel·kin** (wel′kin), *n.* [< AS. *wolcen*], [Archaic or Poetic], the curved vault of the sky.

**well** (wel), *n.* [< AS. *weallan*, boil up], 1. a natural spring and pool. 2. a deep hole sunk into the earth to get water, oil, etc. 3. a source of abundant supply. 4. a shaft, etc. resembling a well. 5. a container for a liquid, as an inkwell. *v.i. & v.t.* to gush or flow as from a well (often with *up*, *forth*, etc.).

**well** (wel), *adv.* [BETTER, BEST], [AS. *wel*], 1. in a satisfactory, proper, or excellent manner: as, the affair ended *well*, she sings *well*. 2. prosperously: as, to live *well*. 3. with good reason: as, you may *well* ask. 4. to a considerable degree: as, *well* advanced. 5. thoroughly: as, stir it *well*. 6. with certainty; definitely. 7. familiarly: as, I know him *well*. *adj.* 1. suitable; proper. 2. in good health. 3. favorable; comfortable. *interj.* an exclamation of surprise, agreement, etc. —**as well (as),** 1. in addition (to). 2. equally (with).

**we'll** (wēl, wil), 1. we shall. 2. we will.

**well-ap·point·ed** (wel′ə-poin′tid), *adj.* excellently furnished.

**well′-bal′anced,** *adj.* 1. evenly proportioned. 2. sane, sensible, etc.

**well′-be·haved′,** *adj.* behaving well; displaying good manners.

**well′-be′ing,** *n.* the state of being well, happy, or prosperous; welfare.

**well′born′,** *adj.* born of good family.

**well′-bred′,** *adj.* showing good breeding; courteous and considerate.

**well′-dis·posed′,** *adj.* friendly (*toward* a person) or receptive (*to* an idea, etc.).

**well′-done′,** *adj.* 1. performed with skill. 2. thoroughly cooked, as meat.

**well′-fed′,** *adj.* plump; fat.

**well′found′ed,** *adj.* based on facts, good evidence, or sound judgment.

**well′-groomed′,** *adj.* clean and neat.

**well′-ground′ed,** *adj.* having a thorough basic knowledge of a subject.

**well′-heeled′,** *adj.* [Slang], rich.

**well′-in·formed′,** *adj.* having considerable knowledge of a subject or of many subjects.

**well′-in·ten′tioned,** *adj.* having or showing good or kindly intentions.

**well′-known′,** *adj.* 1. widely known; famous. 2. thoroughly known.

**well′-made′,** *adj.* skillfully and soundly put together.

**well′-man′nered,** *adj.* having or showing good manners; polite; courteous.

**well′-mean′ing,** *adj.* having or showing good or kindly intentions.

**well′-meant′,** *adj.* said or done with good intentions.

**well′-nigh′** (-nī′), *adv.* very nearly; almost.

**well′-off′,** *adj.* 1. in a fortunate condition or circumstance. 2. prosperous. Also **well off.**

**well′-read′,** *adj.* having read much.

**well′-spo′ken,** *adj.* 1. speaking easily or graciously. 2. aptly spoken.

**well′spring′,** *n.* 1. the source of a stream or spring. 2. a source of abundant supply.

**well′-thought′-of′,** *adj.* having a good reputation; of good repute.

**well′-to-do′,** *adj.* prosperous; wealthy: also **well to do.**

**well′-worn′,** *adj.* much worn or used.

**Welsh** (welsh), *adj.* of Wales, its people, etc. *n.* the Celtic language of Wales. —**the Welsh,** the people of Wales. —**Welsh′man** (-mən) [*pl.* -MEN], *n.*

**welsh** (welsh), *v.i.* [Slang], to fail to pay a debt, fulfill an obligation, etc.: often with *on*. —**welsh′er,** *n.*

**Welsh rabbit,** a dish of melted cheese served on crackers or toast: also **Welsh rarebit.**

**welt** (welt), *n.* [MG. *welte*], 1. a strip of leather in the seam between the sole and upper of a shoe. 2. a ridge raised on the skin by a slash or blow.

**welt·er** (wel′tẽr), *v.i.* [< MD. *welteren*], to roll about or wallow. *n.* a confusion; turmoil.

**welt·er·weight** (wel′tẽr-wāt′), *n.* [? < *welt*, to beat], a boxer or wrestler weighing between 136 and 147 lbs.

**wen** (wen), *n.* [AS. *wenn*], a benign skin tumor, esp. of the scalp.

**wench** (wench), *n.* [AS. *wencel*, child], 1. a young woman: derogatory or facetious term. 2. [Archaic], a female servant.

**wend** (wend), *v.i.* [AS. *wendan*, to turn], [Archaic], to go; journey. *v.t.* to direct (one's way).
**went** (went), pt. of **go.**
**wept** (wept), pt. and pp. of **weep.**
**were** (wũr), [AS. *wæron*], the pl. and 2d pers. sing., past indic., and the past subj., of **be.**
**we're** (wêr), we are.
**were·n't** (wũrnt), were not.
**were·wolf** (wêr'woolf', wũr'-), *n.* [*pl.* -WOLVES], [AS. *wer*, man + *wulf*, wolf], in *folklore*, a person changed into a wolf.
**Wes·ley·an** (wes'li-ən, wez'-), *adj.* of the Methodist Church or its founder, John Wesley, 18th-c. English clergyman. *n.* a follower of John Wesley; Methodist.
**west** (west), *n.* [AS.], 1. the direction in which sunset occurs (270° on the compass, opposite east). 2. a region in or toward this direction. *adj.* 1. in, of, or toward the west. 2. from the west. *adv.* in or toward the west.
**west'er·ly,** *adj. & adv.* 1. toward the west. 2. from the west.
**west'ern,** *adj.* 1. in, of, or toward the west. 2. from the west. *n.* a story or motion picture about cowboys, etc. in the western U.S. **—west'ern·most',** *adj.*
**west'ern·er,** *n.* a native of the west.
**west'ward** (-wẽrd), *adj. & adv.* toward the west: also **west'wards,** *adv.*
**wet** (wet), *adj.* [WETTER, WETTEST], [AS. *wæt*], 1. covered or saturated with water or other liquid. 2. rainy; misty. 3. not yet dry: as, *wet* paint. 4. permitting the sale of alcoholic liquor. *n.* 1. water or other liquid. 2. rain or rainy weather. 3. one who favors the sale of alcoholic liquor. *v.t. & v.i.* [WET or WETTED, WETTING], to make or become wet. **—all wet,** [Slang], wrong. **—wet'ness,** *n.*
**wet'back',** *n.* [Colloq.], a Mexican who illegally enters the U.S. to work.
**wet blanket,** one who dampens or discourages enthusiasm or pleasure.
**weth·er** (we*th*'ẽr), *n.* [AS.], a castrated male sheep.
**wet nurse,** a woman hired to suckle another's child. **—wet'-nurse'** [-NURSED, -NURSING], *v.t.*
**we've** (wēv), we have.
**whack** (hwak), *v.t. & v.i.* [echoic], [Colloq.], to strike or slap with a sharp, resounding blow. *n.* 1. [Colloq.], *a*) a sharp, resounding blow. *b*) the sound of this. 2. [Slang], an attempt. **—whack'er,** *n.*
**whack'ing,** *adj.* [Colloq.], very large.
**whale** (hwāl), *n.* [AS. *hwæl*], a large, warm-blooded sea mammal that breathes air. *v.i.* [WHALED, WHALING], to hunt for whales. **—a whale of a,** [Colloq.], an exceptionally large, fine, etc. specimen of.
**whale** (hwāl), *v.t.* [WHALED, WHALING], [< *wale*], [Colloq.], to thrash.
**whale'boat',** *n.* a long rowboat, pointed at both ends to increase maneuverability.
**whale'bone',** *n.* the horny elastic material hanging from the upper jaw of some whales: used in corset stays, etc.
**whal'er,** *n.* 1. a whaling ship. 2. a man whose work is whaling: also **whale'man.**
**whal'ing,** *n.* the hunting and killing of whales for their blubber, whalebone, etc.
**wham·my** (hwam'i), *n.* [*pl.* -MIES], [Slang], a jinx; evil eye.
**wharf** (hwôrf), *n.* [*pl.* WHARVES (hwôrvz), WHARFS], [< AS. *hwerf*, a dam], a structure on a shore, at which ships are loaded or unloaded; dock.
**wharf·age** (hwôr'fij), *n.* the use of a wharf, or the charge for this.
**what** (hwut, hwät), *pron.* [< AS. *hwa*, who], 1. which thing, event, etc.?: as, *what* is that object? 2. that which or those which: as, do *what* you will. *adj.* 1. which or which kind of: used interrogatively or relatively. 2. as much, or as many, as: as, take *what* men you need. 3. how great, surprising, etc.: as, *what* nonsense! *adv.* 1. partly: as, *what* with singing and joking, the time passed. 2. how greatly, etc.: as, *what* tragic news! *interj.* an exclamation of surprise, anger, etc. **—what for,** why? **—what have you,** [Colloq.], any similar thing: as, games or *what have you.* **—what if,** what would happen if.
**what·ev'er,** *pron.* 1. what: an emphatic variant. 2. anything that: as, say *whatever* you like. 3. no matter what: as, *whatever* you do, don't hurry. *adj.* 1. of no matter what type, number, etc.: as, give *whatever* aid you can. 2. being who it may be: as, *whatever* man said that, it's false.
**what'not',** *n.* a set of open shelves used for bric-a-brac, books, etc.
**what'so·ev'er,** *pron. & adj.* whatever: an emphatic form.
**wheal** (hwēl), *n.* [akin to AS. *hwelian*, suppurate], a pustule; pimple.
**wheat** (hwēt), *n.* [AS. *hwæte*], 1. a cereal grass having spikes filled with seeds. 2. the seed, used for making flour, cereals, etc.
**whee·dle** (hwē'd'l), *v.t. & v.i.* [-DLED, -DLING], [prob. < G. *wedeln*, flatter], to influence, persuade, or get by flattery, begging, etc.
**wheel** (hwēl), *n.* [AS. *hweol*], 1. a circular disk or frame turning on a central axis. 2. anything like a wheel in shape, movement, etc. 3. the steering wheel of a motor vehicle. 4. [Colloq.], a bicycle. 5. *usually pl.* machinery: as, the *wheels* of progress. 6. a turning movement. *v.t. & v.i.* 1. to move on or in a vehicle with wheels. 2. to turn, revolve, etc. 3. to turn so as to change direction. **—wheeled,** *adj.*
**wheel'bar'row** (-bar'ō), *n.* a shallow, open box for moving small loads, having a wheel in front, two legs in back, and two shafts for pushing the vehicle.
**wheel'base',** *n.* in a motor vehicle, the distance in inches from the front axle to the rear axle: also **wheel base.**
**wheel chair,** a mobile chair for invalids, mounted on large wheels.
**wheel'wright'** (-rīt'), *n.* one who makes and repairs wheels and wheeled vehicles.
**wheeze** (hwēz), *v.i.* [WHEEZED, WHEEZING], [< ON. *hvaesa*, to hiss], to make a whistling, breathy sound, as in asthma. *n.* 1. a wheezing. 2. [Slang], a trite joke.
**whelk** (hwelk), *n.* [AS. *wiloc*], a large marine snail with a spiral shell, esp. a variety used in Europe for food.
**whelm** (hwelm), *v.t.* [prob. < AS. *-hwelfan*, overwhelm & *helmian*, to cover], 1. to submerge, cover, etc. 2. to overwhelm; crush.
**whelp** (hwelp), *n.* [AS. *hwelp*], the young of a dog, etc.; puppy. *v.t. & v.i.* to bring forth (young), as an animal.
**when** (hwen), *adv.* [AS. *hwænne*], at what time?: as, *when* did he leave? *conj.* 1. at what time: as, tell me *when* to go. 2. at which time: as, he came at six, *when* the sun rose. 3. at the time that: as, *when* we were young. 4. as soon as: as, we will eat *when* he comes. 5. although: as, he read *when* he might play. *pron.* what or which time: as, until *when* will you stay? *n.* the time (*of* an event).
**whence** (hwens), *adv.* [AS. *hwanan*], from what place, source, cause, etc.; from where: as, *whence* do you come?
**whence'so·ev'er,** *adv. & conj.* from whatever place, source, or cause.
**when·ev'er,** *adv.* [Colloq.], when: an emphatic variant. *conj.* at whatever time: as, leave *whenever* you like.
**when'so·ev'er,** *adv. & conj.* whenever: an emphatic variant.
**where** (hwâr), *adv.* [AS. *hwær*], 1. in or at what place?: as, *where* is it? 2. to or toward

what place?: as, *where* did he go? 3. in what respect?: as, *where* is he at fault? 4. from what place or source?: as, *where* did he learn it? *conj.* 1. at what place: as, I see *where* it is. 2. at which place: as, I came home, *where* I ate. 3. wherever. 4. to the place to which: as, we go *where* you go. *pron.* 1. the place at which: as, a mile to *where* I live. 2. what place: as, *where* are you from? *n.* the place (*of* an event).

**where′a·bouts′** (-ə-bouts′), *adv.* near what place? where? *n.* the place where a person or thing is: as, do you know his *whereabouts*?

**where·as′** (-az′), *conj.* 1. in view of the fact that. 2. while on the contrary: as, she is slim, *whereas* he is fat.

**where·at′**, *conj.* at or upon which.

**where·by′**, *adv.* 1. by which: as, a plan *whereby* to grow rich. 2. by what? how?

**where′fore′** (-fôr′), *adv.* 1. for what reason? why? 2. for which. *conj.* because of which; therefore. *n.* the reason; cause.

**where·in′**, *adv.* 1. in what? 2. in which.

**where·of′**, *adv.* of what, which, or whom.

**where·on′**, *adv.* 1. on what? 2. on which.

**where′so·ev′er**, *adv.* & *conj.* wherever: an emphatic variant.

**where·to′**, *adv.* 1. to what place, end, etc.? 2. to which.

**where′up·on′**, *adv.* upon what or which? *conj.* at which; upon which.

**wher·ev·er** (hwâr-ev′ẽr), *adv.* [Colloq.], where: an emphatic variant. *conj.* in, at, or to whatever place: as, go *wherever* you like.

**where·with′**, *adv.* with which.

**where′with·al′** (-with-ôl′), *n.* the necessary means, esp. money.

**wher·ry** (hwer′i), *n.* [*pl.* -RIES], [? < *whir*], a light rowboat.

**whet** (hwet), *v.t.* [WHETTED, WHETTING], [< AS. *hwæt*, keen], 1. to sharpen by rubbing or grinding, as a knife. 2. to stimulate, as the appetite.

**wheth·er** (hweth′ẽr), *conj.* [AS. *hwæther*], 1. if it be the case that: as, ask *whether* she sings. 2. in case; in either case that: introducing alternatives, as, *whether* it rains or snows.

**whet·stone** (hwet′stōn′), *n.* an abrasive stone for sharpening knives, etc.

**whew** (hwū), *interj.* [echoic], an exclamation of relief, surprise, etc.

**whey** (hwā), *n.* [AS. *hwæg*], the thin, watery part of milk which separates from the curds.

**which** (hwich), *pron.* [AS. *hwylc*], 1. what one (or ones) of several?: as, *which* do you want? 2. the one (or ones) that: as, I know *which* I want. 3. that: as, the boat *which* sank. 4. any that: as, take *which* you like. *adj.* 1. what one (or ones): as, *which* man (or men) came? 2. whatever: as, use *which* plan is best.

**which·ev′er**, *pron.* & *adj.* 1. any one that: as, take *whichever* (seat) you like. 2. no matter which: as, *whichever* (horse) wins, he loses.

**whiff** (hwif), *n.* [echoic], 1. a light puff or gust of air or wind; breath. 2. a slight odor. *v.t.* & *v.i.* to blow or puff. —**whiff′er**, *n.*

**Whig** (hwig), *n.* [< *whiggamore* (contemptuous term for Scot. Presbyterians)], 1. a member of a former English political party, which championed popular rights. 2. a supporter of the American Revolution against England. 3. a member of a political party in the U.S. (c. 1836–1856).

**while** (hwil), *n.* [AS. *hwil*], a period of time: as, a long *while*. *conj.* 1. during the time that: as, let's talk *while* we eat. 2. although; whereas: as, *while* not poor, he's not rich. *v.t.* [WHILED, WHILING], to spend (time) in a pleasant way (often with *away*). —**the while**, during the same time.

**whi·lom** (hwī′ləm), *adv.* [< AS. *hwil*, while], [Archaic], at one time; formerly. *adj.* [Archaic], former: as, their *whilom* friends.

**whilst** (hwilst), *conj.* [Chiefly Brit.], while.

**whim** (hwim), *n.* [? < ON. *hvima*, wander with the eyes], a sudden fancy; caprice.

**whim·per** (hwim′pẽr), *v.i.* & *v.t.* [? < base of *whine*], to cry or utter with low, whining, broken sounds. *n.* a whimpering sound.

**whim·si·cal** (hwim′zi-k'l), *adj.* 1. full of whims or whimsy. 2. oddly out of the ordinary. —**whim′si·cal′i·ty** (-kal′ə-ti) [*pl.* -TIES], *n.* —**whim′si·cal·ly**, *adv.*

**whim·sy** (hwim′zi), *n.* [*pl.* -SIES], [prob. < *whim*], 1. an odd fancy; idle notion; whim. 2. quaint or fanciful humor. Also sp. **whim′sey** [*pl.* -SEYS].

**whine** (hwin), *v.i.* [WHINED, WHINING], [AS. *hwinan*], 1. to utter a low, plaintive cry. 2. to complain in a childish way. *n.* 1. a whining. 2. a complaint in a whining tone.

**whin·ny** (hwin′i), *v.i.* [-NIED, -NYING], [< *whine*], to neigh in a low and gentle way: said of a horse. *n.* [*pl.* -NIES], a whinnying.

**whip** (hwip), *v.t.* [WHIPPED or WHIPT, WHIPPING], [< MD. *wippen*, to swing], 1. to move, pull, throw, etc. suddenly: as, he *whipped* out a knife. 2. to strike, as with a strap; lash. 3. to wind (cord or thread) around a rope to prevent fraying. 4. to beat (eggs, cream, etc.) into a froth. 5. [Colloq.], to defeat. *v.i.* 1. to move quickly and suddenly. 2. to flap about in a whiplike manner. *n.* 1. a flexible instrument for striking or flogging. 2. a blow, etc. as with a whip. 3. a whipping motion. 4. a member of a legislature who enforces party discipline. 5. a dessert of fruit, sugar, whipped cream, etc.

**whip′cord′**, *n.* 1. a hard, twisted or braided cord. 2. a strong worsted cloth with a diagonally ribbed surface.

**whip′lash′**, *n.* 1. the lash of a whip. 2. a sudden, severe bending and jolting of the neck back and forth, as caused by the impact of an automobile collision.

**whip′per·snap′per**, *n.* an insignificant but presumptuous or impertinent person.

**whip·pet** (hwip′it), *n.* [< *whip*], a swift dog like a small greyhound, used in racing.

**whip′ping**, *n.* a flogging or beating.

**whip·ple·tree** (hwip′'l-trē′), *n.* [< *whip*], the pivoted crossbar at the front of a wagon or carriage, to which the traces of the harness are attached.

**whip·poor·will** (hwip′ẽr-wil′), *n.* [echoic], a N. American bird active at night.

**whir** (hwũr), *v.i.* & *v.t.* [WHIRRED, WHIRRING], [? < *whirl*], to fly, revolve, etc. with a buzzing sound. *n.* such a sound. Also sp. **whirr.**

**whirl** (hwũrl), *v.i.* [< ON. *hvirfla*], 1. to move rapidly in a circle or orbit. 2. to rotate or spin fast. 3. to seem to spin: as, my head is *whirling*. *v.t.* to cause to move, rotate, revolve, etc. rapidly. *n.* 1. a whirling or whirling motion. 2. a tumult; uproar. 3. a confused or giddy condition. —**whirl′er**, *n.*

**whirl·i·gig** (hwũr′li-gig′), *n.* a child's toy that whirls or spins.

**whirl′pool′**, *n.* water in violent, whirling motion tending to draw floating objects into its center.

**whirl′wind′**, *n.* 1. a current of air whirling violently in spiral form and having a forward motion. 2. anything like a whirlwind, as in destructiveness.

**whish** (hwish), *v.i.* [echoic], to move with a soft rushing sound. *n.* a sound so made.

**whisk** (hwisk), *v.t.* & *v.i.* [prob. < ON.], to move, pull, brush, etc. with a quick, sweeping motion. *n.* 1. a whisking or a motion like this. 2. a small broom for brushing clothes, etc.: in full, **whisk broom.**

**whisk′er**, *n.* 1. *pl.* the hair growing on a man's face, esp. on the cheeks. 2. any of

the long, bristly hairs on the upper lip of a cat, rat, etc. —**whisk′ered,** *adj.*
**whis·ky** (hwis′ki), *n.* [*pl.* -KIES], [< Ir. *uisge,* water + *beatha,* life], a strong alcoholic liquor distilled from the fermented mash of grain: also sp. **whis′key** [*pl.* -KEYS].
**whis·per** (hwis′pẽr), *v.i. & v.t.* [AS. *hwisprian*], 1. to speak or say very softly, esp. without vibrating the vocal cords. 2. to talk or tell furtively, as in gossip. 3. to make a soft, rustling sound. *n.* 1. a whispering. 2. something whispered. 3. a soft, rustling sound.
**whist** (hwist), *n.* [< *whisk*], a card game: forerunner of bridge.
**whis·tle** (hwis′'l), *v.i.* [-TLED, -TLING], [AS. *hwistlian*], 1. to make a clear, shrill sound as by forcing breath through the contracted lips. 2. to move with a shrill sound, as the wind. 3. *a*) to blow a whistle. *b*) to have its whistle blown, as a train. *v.t.* 1. to produce (a tune, etc.) by whistling. 2. to signal, etc. by whistling. *n.* 1. an instrument for making whistling sounds. 2. a whistling. —**whis′tler,** *n.*
**whit** (hwit), *n.* [< AS. *wiht,* a wight], the least bit; jot; iota: as, not a *whit* concerned.
**white** (hwit), *adj.* [AS. *hwit*], 1. having the color of pure snow or milk. 2. of a light or pale color. 3. pale; wan. 4. pure; innocent. 5. having a light-colored skin. *n.* 1. the color of pure snow or milk. 2. a white or light-colored thing, as the albumen of an egg, the white part of the eyeball, etc. 3. a person with a light-colored skin; Caucasian. —**white′ly,** *adv.* —**white′ness,** *n.*
**white ant,** a termite.
**white′cap′,** *n.* a wave with its crest broken into white foam.
**white′-col′lar,** *adj.* designating or of clerical or professional workers.
**white elephant,** 1. a rare, pale-gray elephant, held as sacred in SE Asia. 2. a thing expensive to maintain from which little profit or use is derived.
**white feather,** a symbol of cowardice.
**white′fish′,** *n.* [*pl.* see FISH], a white or silvery lake fish of the salmon family, found in northeastern U.S.
**white flag,** a white banner hoisted as a signal of truce or surrender.
**white gold,** gold alloyed with platinum, nickel, etc. to give it a white appearance.
**white heat,** 1. the degree of intense heat at which metal, etc. becomes glowing white. 2. a state of intense anger, etc. —**white′-hot′,** *adj.*
**White House, the,** 1. the official residence of the President of the U.S. in Washington, D.C. 2. the executive branch of the U.S. government.
**white lead,** a poisonous, white powder, lead carbonate, used in paint.
**white lie,** a lie about a trivial matter, without harmful intent.
**white′-liv′ered,** *adj.* cowardly.
**white meat,** any light-colored meat, as the breast of chicken, etc.
**whit·en** (hwit′'n), *v.t. & v.i.* to make or become white or whiter. —**whit′en·er,** *n.*
**white plague,** tuberculosis.
**white race,** loosely, the Caucasian division of mankind.
**white slave,** a woman forced into prostitution for others' profit. —**white′-slave′,** *adj.* —**white slaver.** —**white slavery.**
**white′wash′,** *n.* 1. a mixture of lime, chalk, water, etc. as for whitening walls. 2. a concealing of faults in order to exonerate. 3. [Colloq.], in *sports,* a defeat in which the loser scores no points. *v.t.* 1. to cover with whitewash. 2. to conceal the faults of. 3. [Colloq.], to defeat (an opponent), allowing him no points. —**white′wash′ing,** *n.*
**whith·er** (hwith′ẽr), *adv.* [AS. *hwider*], to what place, condition, etc.? where? *conj.* 1. to which place, condition, etc. 2. wherever. Chiefly in poetical usage.
**whit·ing** (hwīt′iŋ), *n.* [< MD. *wit,* white], 1. a European sea fish of the cod family. 2. any of various spiny-finned North American fishes.
**whit′ish,** *adj.* somewhat white.
**Whit·sun·day** (hwit′sun′di, -s'n-dā′), *n.* [AS. *Hwita Sunnandæg,* white Sunday], the seventh Sunday after Easter; Pentecost.
**Whit′sun·tide** (-s'n-tīd′), *n.* the week beginning with Whitsunday.
**whit·tle** (hwit′'l), *v.t.* [-TLED, -TLING], [< AS. *thwitan,* to cut], 1. *a*) to cut thin shavings from (wood) with a knife. *b*) to carve (an object) thus. 2. to reduce gradually. *v.i.* to whittle wood.
**whiz, whizz** (hwiz), *v.i.* [WHIZZED, WHIZZING], [echoic], 1. to make the hissing sound of something rushing through the air. 2. to speed by with this sound. *n.* 1. this sound. 2. [Slang], an expert: as, a *whiz* at golf. —**whiz′zer,** *n.*
**who** (hōō), *pron.* [*obj.* WHOM, *poss.* WHOSE], [AS. *hwa*], 1. what person or persons?: as, *who* came? 2. which person or persons: as, I know *who* came. 3. (the, or a, person or persons) that: as, a man *who* knows.
**whoa** (hwō), *interj.* stop!: a direction to a horse to stand still.
**who·dun·it** (hōō-dun′it), *n.* [Slang], a novel, play, etc. in which a crime is solved at the end.
**who·ev·er** (hōō-ev′ẽr), *pron.* 1. any person at all that. 2. no matter who: as, *whoever* did it, I didn't. 3. who?: an emphatic variant.
**whole** (hōl), *adj.* [AS. *hal*], 1. healthy; not diseased or injured. 2. not broken, damaged, etc.; intact. 3. containing all of its parts; complete. 4. not divided up; in a single unit. 5. having both parents in common: as, a *whole* brother. *n.* 1. the entire amount, etc.; totality. 2. a complete organization of parts; unity. —**on the whole,** all things considered. —**whole′ness,** *n.*
**whole′heart′ed,** *adj.* with all one's energy, enthusiasm, etc.; sincere.
**whole note,** in *music,* a note (○) having four times the duration of a quarter note.
**whole′sale′,** *n.* the sale of goods in large quantities, esp. to retailers. *adj.* 1. of or engaged in selling at wholesale. 2. sold in large quantities, usually at a lower cost. 3. extensive and general: as, *wholesale* destruction. *v.t. & v.i.* [-SALED, -SALING], to sell or be sold at wholesale. —**whole′sal′er,** *n.*
**whole·some** (hōl′səm), *adj.* [< ON. *heilsamr*], 1. promoting good health or well-being; healthful. 2. improving the mind or morals. 3. looking healthy and vigorous. —**whole′some·ly,** *adv.* —**whole′some·ness,** *n.*
**who'll** (hōōl), who shall (or will).
**whol·ly** (hō′li), *adv.* to the whole amount or extent; completely, exclusively, etc.
**whom** (hōōm), *pron.* obj. case of **who.**
**whom·ev′er** (-ev′ẽr), *pron.* obj. case of **whoever.**
**whoop** (hōōp, hwōōp), *n.* [< OFr. *houper,* cry out], 1. a loud shout, cry, etc., as of joy. 2. the convulsive intake of air following a coughing fit in whooping cough. *v.t. & v.i.* to utter (with) a whoop or whoops.
**whoop·ee** (hwōō′pē, hwoop′ē), *interj.* [< *whoop*], an exclamation expressing great enjoyment, gay abandon, etc.
**whooping cough,** an acute infectious disease, esp. of children, with coughing fits that end in a whoop.
**whop·per** (hwop′ẽr), *n.* [< dial. *whop,* to beat], [Colloq.], anything extraordinarily large; esp., a great lie. —**whop′ping,** *adj.*

**whore** (hôr), *n.* [< ON. *hora*], a prostitute.

**whorl** (hwũrl, hwôrl), *n.* [< dial. var. of *whirl*], anything that whirls or coils; any of the circular ridges forming the design of a fingerprint. —**whorled,** *adj.*

**who's** (hōōz), who is.

**whose** (hōōz), *pron.* [AS. *hwæs*], the poss. case of **who,** and now, usually, of **which.**

**who·so·ev·er** (hōō'sō-ev'ẽr), *pron.* whoever: an emphatic variant.

**why** (hwī), *adv.* [< AS. *hwa*, who], 1. for what reason, cause, or purpose: as, *why* go? 2. because of which: as, no reason *why* I must. 3. the reason for which: as, this is *why* he went. *n.* [*pl.* WHYS], the reason, cause, etc.: as, this is the *why* of it. *interj.* an exclamation of surprise, hesitation, etc.

**wick** (wik), *n.* [AS. *weoca*], a piece of cord, tape, etc., as in a candle or oil lamp, that absorbs the fuel and, when lighted, burns.

**wick·ed** (wik'id), *adj.* [< ME. *wikke*, evil], 1. morally bad; evil. 2. generally bad, unpleasant, etc.: as, a *wicked* storm. 3. naughty; mischievous. —**wick'ed·ly,** *adv.* —**wick'ed·ness,** *n.*

**wick·er** (wik'ẽr), *n.* [prob. < ON.], 1. a thin, flexible twig. 2. wickerwork. *adj.* made of or covered with wicker.

**wick'er·work'** (-wũrk'), *n.* 1. thin, flexible twigs woven together. 2. baskets, furniture, etc. made of such interwoven twigs.

**wick·et** (wik'it), *n.* [< ME. *wiket*], 1. a small door or gate, esp. one in or near a larger one. 2. a small window, as in a box office. 3. in *croquet*, any of the small wire arches through which the balls must be hit.

**wide** (wīd), *adj.* [AS. *wid*], 1. extending over a large area, esp. from side to side. 2. of a specified extent from side to side. 3. of great extent: as, a *wide* variety. 4. roomy; full: as, a *wide* blouse. 5. open fully: as, eyes *wide* with fear. 6. far from the point, etc. aimed at: as, *wide* of the mark. *adv.* 1. over a relatively large area. 2. to a large or full extent: as, *wide* open. 3. so as to miss the point, etc. aimed at; astray. —**wide'ly,** *adv.* —**wide'ness,** *n.*

**wide'-an'gle** (-aŋ'g'l), *adj.* designating or of any motion-picture system (trademarked as **CinemaScope, Cinerama,** etc.) using an especially wide, curved screen to simulate normal panoramic vision.

**wide'-a·wake',** *adj.* 1. completely awake. 2. alert. —**wide'-a·wake'ness,** *n.*

**wide'-eyed',** *adj.* with the eyes wide open.

**wid·en** (wīd''n), *v.t. & v.i.* to make or become wide or wider. —**wid'en·er,** *n.*

**wide'spread',** *adj.* occurring over a wide area or extent.

**widg·eon, wi·geon** (wij'ən), *n.* [< OFr. *vigeon*], a wild, fresh-water duck.

**wid·ow** (wid'ō), *n.* [< AS. *widewe*], a woman whose husband has died and who has not remarried. *v.t.* to cause to become a widow.

**wid'ow·er,** *n.* a man whose wife has died and who has not remarried.

**width** (width), *n.* 1. distance from side to side. 2. a piece of a specified width.

**wield** (wēld), *v.t.* [AS. *wealdan*], 1. to handle (a tool, etc.), esp. with skill. 2. to exercise (power, control, etc.).

**wield'y,** *adj.* [-IER, -IEST], that can be wielded easily; manageable: also **wield'a·ble.**

**wie·ner** (wē'nẽr), *n.* [< G. *Wiener wurst*, Vienna sausage], a smoked link sausage; frankfurter: also **wie'ner·wurst'** (-wũrst').

**wife** (wīf), *n.* [*pl.* WIVES], [AS. *wif*, woman], a married woman. —**wife'ly,** *adj.*

**wig** (wig), *n.* [< *periwig*], an artificial covering of hair for the head. —**wigged,** *adj.*

**wig·gle** (wig''l), *v.t. & v.i.* [-GLED, -GLING], [prob. < MD. *wiggen*], to move with short, jerky motions from side to side. *n.* a wiggling. —**wig'gly** [-GLIER, -GLIEST], *adj.*

**wight** (wīt), *n.* [AS. *wiht*], [Archaic], a human being; person.

**wig·wag** (wig'wag'), *v.t. & v.i.* [-WAGGED, -WAGGING], [< *wiggle*], 1. to move back and forth; wag. 2. to send (a message) by waving flags, lights, etc. according to a code. *n.* the sending of messages in this way.

**wig·wam** (wig'wäm), *n.* [< Algonquian], a N. American Indian shelter consisting of a conical framework of poles covered with hides, etc.

**wild** (wīld), *adj.* [AS. *wilde*], 1. living or growing in its original, natural state. 2. not lived in or cultivated; desolate. 3. not civilized; savage. 4. not easily restrained: as, a *wild* boy. 5. unbridled, unrepressed, etc.: as, a *wild* time. 6. turbulent; stormy. 7. enthusiastic: as, *wild* about golf. 8. fantastically impractical; reckless. 9. missing the target: as, a *wild* pitch. 10. in some card games, having any desired value: said of a card. *adv.* in a wild manner. *n. usually pl.* wilderness, waste, etc. —**wild'ly,** *adv.*

**wild'cat',** *n.* 1. any fierce, medium-sized, undomesticated animal of the cat family. 2. a fierce, aggressive person. 3. a productive oil well in an area not previously known to have oil. Also **wild cat.** *adj.* unsound or risky. *v.t. & v.i.* [-CATTED, -CATTING], to drill for oil in (an area previously considered unproductive). —**wild'cat'ter,** *n.*

**wil·de·beest** (wil'də-bēst'), *n.* [< D. *wild*, wild + *beeste*, beast], a gnu.

**wil·der·ness** (wil'dẽr-nis), *n.* [< AS. *wilde*, wild + *deor*, animal], an uncultivated, uninhabited region; waste.

**wild'-eyed',** *adj.* staring in a wild or distracted manner, as from fear.

**wild'fire',** *n.* an inflammable substance, difficult to extinguish: now mainly in phrase *spread like wildfire*, to spread widely and rapidly.

**wild'-goose' chase,** a futile attempt or enterprise; esp., a useless search or pursuit.

**wild oat** (or **oats**), a tall grass used for fodder. —**sow one's wild oats,** to be promiscuous or dissolute in youth.

**wile** (wīl), *n.* [AS. *wil*], 1. a sly trick; stratagem. 2. trickery; deceit. *v.t.* [WILED, WILING], to beguile; lure. —**wile away,** to while away (time, etc.).

**will** (wil), *n.* [AS. *willa*], 1. wish or desire; inclination. 2. something wished or ordered, esp. by one with authority. 3. strong determination. 4. the power of conscious and deliberate action or choice. 5. attitude toward others: as, ill *will*. 6. a legal document stating one's wishes concerning the disposal of his property after death. *v.t.* 1. to resolve firmly: as, he *willed* to survive. 2. to control as by hypnotic power. 3. to bequeath by a will. —**at will,** when one wishes.

**will** (wil), *v.* [pt. WOULD], [AS. *willan*], an auxiliary used: 1. to express futurity. 2. in formal speech, to express determination, obligation, etc. in the first person, and futurity in the second and third persons. See note following **shall.** 3. to express willingness: as, *will* you go? 4. to express ability or capacity: as, it *will* hold a pint. *v.t. & v.i.* to wish; desire: as, do as you *will*.

**will·ful** (wil'fəl), *adj.* 1. done or said deliberately. 2. obstinate; stubborn. Also sp. **wil'ful.** —**will'ful·ly,** *adv.* —**will'ful·ness,** *n.*

**will·ies** (wil'iz), *n.pl.* [< ?], [Slang], nervousness; jitters (with *the*).

**will·ing** (wil'iŋ), *adj.* 1. favorably disposed; consenting: as, *willing* to play. 2. acting, giving, etc., or done, given, etc., readily and cheerfully. —**will'ing·ness,** *n.*

**will-o'-the-wisp** (wil'ə-*thə*-wisp'), *n.* 1. a light seen at night over swamps, etc., believed to be marsh gas burning. 2. anything elusive, misleading, etc.

**wil·low** (wil′ō), *n.* [AS. *wilig*], 1. a tree with narrow leaves, and flexible twigs used in weaving baskets, etc. 2. its wood.

**wil′low·y** (-ō-i), *adj.* like a willow; slender, graceful, lithe, etc.

**will power,** strength of will, mind, or determination; self-control.

**wil·ly-nil·ly** (wil′i-nil′i), *adj. & adv.* [contr. < *will I, nill I; nill* < AS. *ne*, not + *wille*, to will], (happening) whether one wishes it or not.

**wilt** (wilt), *v.i.* [< obs. *welk*, wither], 1. to become limp, as from heat or lack of water; droop, as a plant. 2. to become weak or faint; lose strength or courage. *v.t.* to cause to wilt. —**wilt′ing·ly,** *adv.*

**Wil·ton (carpet** or **rug)** (wil′t'n), [< *Wilton*, England], a kind of carpet with a velvety pile of cut loops.

**wi·ly** (wī′li), *adj.* [-LIER, -LIEST], full of wiles; crafty; sly. —**wi′li·ness,** *n.*

**wim·ble** (wim′b'l), *n.* [< MD. *wimmel*, an auger], any of various boring tools, as a gimlet, auger, etc.

**wim·ple** (wim′p'l), *n.* [AS. *wimpel*], a nun's head covering so arranged as to leave only the face exposed.

**win** (win), *v.i.* [WON, WINNING], [< AS. *winnan*, to fight]. 1. to gain a victory; succeed. 2. to become by effort; get: as, he *won* free from the crowd. *v.t.* 1. to get by labor, struggle, etc. 2. to be victorious in (a contest, etc.). 3. to get to with effort: as, they *won* the camp by noon. 4. to influence; persuade (also with *over*). 5. to gain the sympathy, favor, etc. of. 6. to persuade to marry one. *n.* [Colloq.], a victory, as in a contest.

**wince** (wins), *v.i.* [WINCED, WINCING], [< MHG. *wenken*], to shrink or draw back suddenly; flinch. *n.* a wincing.

**winch** (winch), *n.* [AS. *wince*], 1. a crank with a handle for transmitting motion. 2. a type of windlass for hoisting or hauling.

**Win·ches·ter (rifle)** (win′ches′tẽr), [after O.F. *Winchester*, the manufacturer], a type of repeating rifle: a trademark.

**wind** (wīnd), *v.t.* [WOUND, WINDING], [AS. *windan*], 1. to turn: as, *wind* the crank. 2. to coil into a ball or around something else; twine. 3. to cover by entwining. 4. to make (one's way) in an indirect course. 5. to cause to move in a twisting course. 6. to tighten the spring of (a clock, etc.) as by turning a stem. *v.i.* 1. to move or go in a curving or sinuous manner. 2. to take a devious course. 3. to coil (*about* or *around* something). *n.* a turn; twist. —**wind up,** 1. to wind into a ball, etc. 2. to conclude; settle. 3. to excite greatly. 4. in *baseball*, to swing the arm preparatory to pitching.

**wind** (wind), *n.* [AS.]. 1. air in motion. 2. a strong current of air; gale. 3. air bearing a scent, as in hunting. 4. an intimation; hint: as, to get *wind* of something. 5. breath or the power of breathing. 6. empty talk. 7. gas in the intestines. 8. *pl.* the wind instruments of an orchestra. *v.t.* 1. to get the scent of. 2. to put out of breath. —**in the wind,** happening or about to happen.

**wind·bag** (wind′bag′), *n.* [Colloq], one who talks much but says little of importance.

**wind′break′,** *n.* a hedge, fence, or trees serving as a protection from wind.

**wind′break′er,** *n.* a jacket with close-fitting elastic waistband and cuffs: a trademark (**Windbreaker**).

**wind·ed** (win′did) *adj.* out of breath.

**wind′fall′,** *n.* 1. something blown down by the wind, as fruit from a tree. 2. an unexpected stroke of luck.

**wind·ing** (wīn′diŋ), *n.* 1. a coiling, turn, bend, etc. 2. something that winds or is wound around an object. *adj.* that winds.

**wind·ing sheet** (wīn′diŋ), a shroud.

**wind instrument** (wind), any musical instrument played by blowing air, esp. breath, through it.

**wind·jam·mer** (wind′jam′ẽr), *n.* a sailing ship or one of its crew.

**wind·lass** (wind′ləs), *n.* [< ON. *vinda*, to wind + *ass*, a beam], an apparatus for hauling or hoisting, having a cylinder upon which is wound the rope, etc. attached to the object to be lifted.

**wind′mill′,** *n.* a mill operated by the wind's rotation of large vanes radiating from a shaft: it is used for pumping water, etc.

**win·dow** (win′dō), *n.* [< ON. *vindr*, wind + *auga*, eye], 1. an opening in a building, vehicle, etc. for admitting light and air, usually having a pane or panes of glass in a movable frame. 2. such a pane of glass. 3. any opening resembling a window.

**window box,** a long, narrow box on or outside a window ledge, for growing plants.

**window dressing,** 1. the display of goods, etc. in a store window to attract customers. 2. statements or actions meant to give a misleading favorable impression.

**win′dow-shop′** (-shop′), *v.i.* [-SHOPPED, -SHOPPING], to look at goods in store windows without entering to buy.

**wind·pipe** (wind′pīp′), *n.* the trachea.

**wind·row** (wind′rō′, win′rō′), *n.* a row of hay, etc. raked together to dry.

**wind·shield** (wind′shēld′), *n.* in automobiles, etc., a glass screen in front, to protect the occupants from wind, etc.

**wind sock** (or **sleeve, cone**), a long, cone-shaped cloth bag attached to the top of a mast, as at an airfield, to show the direction of the wind.

**wind′storm′,** *n.* a storm with a strong wind but little or no rain.

**wind tunnel,** a tunnellike chamber through which air is forced for testing scale models of airplanes, etc. against the effects of wind pressure.

**wind·up** (wīnd′up′), *n.* 1. a conclusion; end. 2. in *baseball*, the swinging of the arm preparatory to pitching the ball.

**wind·ward** (wind′wẽrd), *n.* the direction from which the wind blows. *adv.* toward the wind. *adj.* 1. moving windward. 2. on the side from which the wind blows.

**wind·y** (win′di), *adj.* [-IER, -IEST], 1. with much wind: as, a *windy* day. 2. like wind; stormy, etc. 3. airy; intangible. 4. garrulous, boastful, etc. —**wind′i·ness,** *n.*

**wine** (wīn), *n.* [< L. *vinum*], 1. the fermented juice of grapes, used as an alcoholic beverage. 2. the fermented juice of other fruits or plants. *v.t.* [WINED, WINING], to entertain with wine. *v.i.* to drink wine.

**wine cellar,** 1. a cellar where wine is stored. 2. a stock of wine.

**wine′-col′ored,** *adj.* having the color of red wine; dark purplish-red.

**win′er·y** (-ẽr-i), *n.* [*pl.* -IES], an establishment where wine is made.

**Wine·sap** (wīn′sap′), *n.* a dark-red, medium-sized variety of winter apple.

**wing** (wiŋ), *n.* [< ON. *vaengr*], 1. either of the paired organs of flight of a bird, bat, or insect. 2. something like a wing in use, position, etc.; specif., *a*) one of the main supporting structures of an airplane. *b*) a subordinate, projecting part of a building. *c*) either side of a stage out of sight of the audience. 3. the right or left section of an army, fleet, team, etc. 4. a political group representing a certain shade of opinion. 5. a flying or manner of flying. 6. a unit of military aircraft. *v.t.* 1. to fly across, through, etc. 2. to provide with wings. 3. to hasten; speed: as, he *winged* his words. 4. to wound (a bird) in the wing or (a person) in the arm, etc. *v.i.* to fly. —**on the wing,** in flight. —**take wing,** to fly away. —**under the wing of,** under the protection, etc. of. —**winged** (wiŋd; *poetic* wiŋ′id), *adj.* —**wing′less,** *adj.*

**wing′spread′,** *n.* the distance between the tips of a pair of spread wings.

**wink** (wiŋk), *v.i.* [AS. *wincian*], 1. to close the eyelids and open them again quickly. 2. to close and open one eyelid quickly, as a signal, etc. 3. to twinkle. *v.t.* to make (an eye) wink. *n.* 1. a winking. 2. an instant. 3. a signal given by winking. 4. a twinkle. —**forty winks,** [Colloq.], a short nap.

**win·ner** (win′ẽr), *n.* one that wins.

**win·ning** (win′iŋ), *adj.* 1. victorious. 2. attractive; charming. *n.* 1. a victory. 2. *pl.* something won, esp. money.

**win·now** (win′ō), *v.t.* [AS. *wind*, wind], 1. to blow (the chaff) from (grain). 2. to scatter. 3. to sort out by sifting. *v.i.* to winnow grain.

**win·some** (win′səm), *adj.* [AS. *wynsum*, pleasant], attractive; charming; engaging. —**win′some·ly,** *adv.* —**win′some·ness,** *n.*

**win·ter** (win′tẽr), *n.* [AS.], 1. the coldest season of the year, following autumn. 2. a period of decline, distress, etc. *adj.* of or for winter. *v.i.* to pass the winter. *v.t.* to keep, maintain, etc. during the winter.

**win′ter·green′,** *n.* 1. an evergreen plant with white flowers and red berries. 2. an oil (**oil of wintergreen**) made from its leaves and used as a flavor. 3. this flavor.

**win′ter·ize′** (-īz′), *v.t.* [-IZED, -IZING], to put into condition for winter.

**win′ter·time′,** *n.* the winter season.

**win′try** (-tri), *adj.* [-TRIER, -TRIEST], of or like winter; cold, bleak, etc.

**wipe** (wīp), *v.t.* [WIPED, WIPING], [AS. *wipian*], 1. to clean or dry by rubbing with (a cloth, etc.). 2. to rub (a cloth, etc.) over something. 3. to apply or remove by rubbing with a cloth, etc. *n.* a wiping. —**wipe out,** 1. to remove. 2. to kill off. —**wip′er,** *n.*

**wire** (wīr), *n.* [AS. *wir*], 1. metal drawn into a long thread. 2. a length of this. 3. telegraph. 4. [Colloq.], a telegram. *adj.* made of wire. *v.t.* [WIRED, WIRING], 1. to furnish, connect, etc. with wire. 2. [Colloq.], to telegraph. *v.i.* [Colloq.], to telegraph. —**pull wires,** to use private influence.

**wire′hair′,** *n.* a fox terrier with a wiry coat: also **wire′-haired′ terrier.**

**wire′less,** *adj.* without wire; specif., operating with electric waves, not with conducting wire. *n.* 1. wireless telegraphy or telephony. 2. [Chiefly Brit.], radio.

**wire′pho′to,** *n.* a system of reproducing photographs, or a photograph reproduced, by electric impulses transmitted by wire: a trademark (**Wirephoto**).

**wire recorder,** a machine for recording sound by means of electric waves on a thin wire and for playing it back.

**wire tapper,** one who taps telephone wires, etc. to get information secretly.

**wir′ing,** *n.* a system of wires, as for carrying electricity.

**wir′y,** *adj.* [-IER, -IEST], 1. of wire. 2. like wire; stiff. 3. lean and strong. —**wir′i·ness,**

**wis·dom** (wiz′dəm), *n.* [AS.; see WISE- & -DOM], 1. the quality of being wise; good judgment; sagacity. 2. learning; knowledge.

**wisdom tooth,** the back tooth on each side of each jaw.

**wise** (wīz), *adj.* [AS. *wis*], 1. having or showing good judgment. 2. informed. 3. learned. 4. shrewd; cunning. 5. [Slang], conceited, impudent, etc. —**wise′ly,** *adv.*

**wise** (wīz), *n.* [AS.], way; manner; fashion.

**-wise,** [see prec.], a suffix meaning *in a* (specified) *direction, position,* or *manner,* as in *sidewise.*

**wise·a·cre** (wīz′ā′kẽr), *n.* [< OHG. *wizzago*, prophet], one who thinks he knows everything.

**wise′crack′,** *n.* [Slang], a flippant or facetious remark. *v.i.* [Slang], to make wisecracks. —**wise′crack′er,** *n.*

**wish** (wish), *v.t.* [AS. *wyscan*], 1. to have a longing for; want. 2. to express a desire concerning: as, I *wish* you well. 3. to request: as, I *wish* you to go. *v.i.* 1. to long; yearn. 2. to make a wish. *n.* 1. a wishing. 2. something wished for. 3. a request. 4. *pl.* expressed desire for one's health, etc.: as, best *wishes.*

**wish′bone′,** *n.* the forked bone in front of a bird's breastbone.

**wish′ful,** *adj.* having or showing a wish; desirous; longing. —**wish′ful·ly,** *adv.*

**wish·y-wash·y** (wish′i-wôsh′i), *adj.* 1. watery; thin. 2. weak; feeble.

**wisp** (wisp), *n.* [prob. < ON.], 1. a small bundle, as of straw. 2. a thin, slight, or filmy bit, as of smoke. 3. anything slight, frail, etc. —**wisp′y** [-IER, -IEST], *adj.*

**wist** (wist), pt. and pp. of **wit** (know).

**wis·te·ri·a** (wis-têr′i-ə), *n.* [< C. *Wistar*, Am. anatomist], a twining shrub with showy clusters of flowers: also **wis·ta′ri·a** (-târ′-).

**wist·ful** (wist′fəl), *adj.* [< earlier *wistly*, intently], having vague or pensive yearnings. —**wist′ful·ly,** *adv.* —**wist′ful·ness,** *n.*

**wit** (wit), *n.* [AS.], 1. *pl.* powers of thinking; mental faculties. 2. the ability to make clever remarks in a striking or ironic way. 3. one having this ability. —**at one's wits' end,** at a loss as to what to do.

**wit** (wit), *v.t.* & *v.i.* [WIST, WITTING], [AS. *witan*], [Archaic], to know or learn. —**to wit,** that is to say; namely.

**witch** (wich), *n.* [< AS. *wicca*, sorcerer], 1. a woman supposedly having supernatural power by a compact with evil spirits. 2. an ugly, old shrew. 3. [Colloq.], a fascinating woman.

**witch′craft′,** *n.* 1. the power or practices of witches. 2. bewitching attraction or charm.

**witch doctor,** among primitive tribes, a person who professes to counteract witchcraft.

**witch hazel,** [AS. *wice*], 1. a shrub with yellow flowers. 2. an alcoholic lotion of an extract from its bark.

**witch hunt,** an investigation of political dissenters, conducted with much publicity, supposedly to uncover subversion, etc.

**with** (w*th*, with), *prep.* [AS., against], 1. in opposition to: as, he argued *with* me. 2. *a*) alongside of; near to. *b*) in the company of. *c*) into; among: as, mix blue *with* red. 3. as a member of: as, he plays *with* a trio. 4. concerning: as, happy *with* his lot. 5. compared to. 6. as well as: as, he rides *with* the best. 7. in the opinion of: as, it's O.K. *with* me. 8. as a result of: as, faint *with* hunger. 9. having received: as, *with* your consent, I'll go. 10. having as a possession, attribute, etc. 11. in the keeping, care, etc. of: as, leave it *with* me. 12. in spite of. 13. in proportion to: as, grow wise *with* age. 14. to; onto: as, join this end *with* that one. 15. from: as, to part *with* one's gains.

**with-,** a prefix meaning: 1. *away, back,* as in *withdraw.* 2. *against, from,* as in *withhold.*

**with·al** (w*th*-ôl′), *adv.* [Archaic], 1. besides. 2. still. *prep.* [Archaic], with.

**with·draw** (w*th*-drô′, with-), *v.t.* [-DREW, -DRAWN, -DRAWING], 1. to take back; remove. 2. to retract or recall (a statement, etc.). *v.i.* to move back; go away; retreat. —**with·draw′al,** *n.*

**with·drawn′,** *adj.* shy, reserved, etc.

**withe** (with, wi*th*, wi*th*), *n.* [AS. *withthe*], a tough, flexible twig of willow, etc. used for binding.

**with·er** (wi*th*′ẽr), *v.i.* [< ME. *wederen*, to weather], 1. to dry up; shrivel; wilt, as plants. 2. to become decayed, etc. 3. to languish; weaken. *v.t.* 1. to cause to wither. 2. to cause to feel abashed.

**with·ers** (wi*th*′ẽrz), *n.pl.* [< AS. *wither*, against], the part of a horse's back between the shoulder blades.

**with·hold** (with-hōld′, wi*th*-), *v.t.* [-HELD, -HOLDING], 1. to hold back; restrain. 2. to refrain from granting. *v.i.* to refrain; forbear.

**withholding tax,** the amount of income tax withheld from wages or salaries.

**with·in** (wi*th*-in′, with-), *adv.* [AS. *withinnan*], 1. on or to the inside. 2. indoors. 3. inside the body, mind, etc. *prep.* 1. in the inner part of. 2. not beyond. 3. inside the limits of.

**with·out** (wi*th*-out′, with-), *adv.* [AS. *withutan*], 1. on or to the outside; externally. 2. out of doors. *prep.* 1. at, on, or to the outside of. 2. beyond. 3. lacking; free from: as, *without* fear. 4. with avoidance of: as, to pass *without* speaking.

**with·stand** (with-stand′, wi*th*-), *v.t. & v.i.* [-STOOD, -STANDING], to oppose, resist, or endure.

**wit·less** (wit′lis), *adj.* lacking wit; stupid. **—wit′less·ly,** *adv.* **—wit′less·ness,** *n.*

**wit·ness** (wit′nis), *n.* [< AS. *gewitnes*, knowledge], 1. evidence; testimony. 2. one who saw, or can give a firsthand account of, something. 3. one who testifies in court. 4. one who observes, and attests to, a signing, etc. *v.t.* 1. to testify to. 2. to serve as evidence of. 3. to act as witness of. 4. to be present at.

**witness stand,** the place from which a witness gives his testimony in a law court.

**wit·ti·cism** (wit′ə-siz′m), *n.* [< *witty*], a witty remark.

**wit·ting** (wit′iŋ), *adj.* [ME. *wything*], deliberate; intentional. **—wit′ting·ly,** *adv.*

**wit·ty** (wit′i), *adj.* [-TIER, -TIEST], [AS. *wittig*], having or showing wit; cleverly amusing. **—wit′ti·ly,** *adv.* **—wit′ti·ness,** *n.*

**wive** (wīv), *v.i. & v.t.* [WIVED, WIVING], [AS. *wifian*], to marry (a woman).

**wives** (wīvz), *n.* pl. of **wife.**

**wiz·ard** (wiz′ẽrd), *n.* [< ON. *viskr*, clever], 1. a magician; sorcerer. 2. [Colloq.], a very skillful person. **—wiz′ard·ly,** *adv.*

**wiz′ard·ry,** *n.* magic; sorcery.

**wiz·ened** (wiz′′nd), *adj.* [< AS. *wisnian*, wither], shriveled; dried up; withered

**wk.,** [*pl.* WKS.], 1. week. 2. work.

**woad** (wōd), *n.* [AS. *wad*], 1. a plant of the mustard family. 2. a blue dye made from its leaves.

**wob·ble** (wob′′l), *v.i.* [-BLED, -BLING], [<?], 1. to move unsteadily from side to side; shake. 2. to vacillate. *v.t.* [Colloq.], to cause to wobble. *n.* wobbling motion. **—wob′bly** [-BLIER, -BLIEST], *adj.*

**woe, wo** (wō), *n.* [AS. *wa*], 1. great sorrow; grief. 2. trouble. *interj.* alas!

**woe·be·gone, wo·be·gone** (wō′bi-gôn′), *adj.* of woeful appearance; looking mournful.

**woe·ful, wo·ful** (wō′fəl), *adj.* 1. full of woe; mournful. 2. of, causing, or involving woe. 3. pitiful; wretched. **—woe′ful·ly, wo′ful·ly,** *adv.*

**woke** (wōk), alt. pt. of **wake.**

**wolf** (woolf), *n.* [*pl.* WOLVES], [AS. *wulf*], 1. a wild, flesh-eating, doglike mammal of the Northern Hemisphere. 2. *a*) a cruel or greedy person. *b*) [Slang], a man who flirts with many women. *v.t.* to eat greedily. **—wolf′ish,** *adj.*

**wolf′hound′** (-hound′), *n.* a breed of large dog, once used for hunting wolves.

**wolf·ram** (wool′frəm), *n.* [G.], tungsten.

**wol·ver·ine, wol·ver·ene** (wool′və-rēn′), *n.* [< *wolf*], a stocky, flesh-eating mammal of North America.

**wolves** (woolvz), *n.* pl. of **wolf.**

**wom·an** (woom′ən), *n.* [*pl.* WOMEN], [< AS. *wif*, a female + *mann*, human being], 1. an adult female human being, or women collectively. 2. a female servant. 3. a wife. 4. womanly qualities: as, the *woman* in her.

**wom′an·hood′,** *n.* 1. the state of being a woman. 2. womanly qualities. 3. womankind.

**wom′an·ish,** *adj.* like a woman; feminine.

**wom′an·kind′,** *n.* women in general.

**wom′an·like′,** *adj.* womanly.

**wom′an·ly,** *adj.* 1. womanish. 2. characteristic of or suitable to a woman.

**womb** (wo͞om), *n.* [AS.], the uterus.

**wom·bat** (wom′bat), *n.* [< native name], a burrowing Australian marsupial resembling a small bear.

**wom·en** (wim′in), *n.* pl. of **woman.**

**wom′en·folk′,** *n.pl.* womankind.

**won** (wun), pt. and pp. of **win.**

**won·der** (wun′dẽr), *n.* [AS. *wundor*], 1. a person, thing, or event causing astonishment and admiration; marvel. 2. the feeling aroused by something strange, unexpected, etc. *v.i.* 1. to be filled with wonder; marvel. 2. to have doubt mingled with curiosity. *v.t.* to have doubt and curiosity about: as, I *wonder* why he came.

**won′der·ful,** *adj.* 1. that causes wonder; marvelous, 2. [Colloq.], fine; excellent. **—won′der·ful·ly,** *adv.* **—won′der·ful·ness,** *n.*

**won′der·land′,** *n.* 1. an imaginary land full of wonders. 2. any place of beauty, etc.

**won′der·ment,** *n.* amazement.

**won·drous** (wun′drəs), *adj.* wonderful. *adv.* surprisingly. **—won′drous·ly,** *adv.*

**wont** (wunt, wōnt, wônt), *adj.* [< AS. *wunian*, be used to], accustomed: as, he was *wont* to eat late. *n.* usual practice; habit.

**won't** (wōnt), will not.

**wont·ed** (wun′tid, wōn′-, wôn′-), *adj.* customary; accustomed.

**woo** (wo͞o), *v.t.* [AS. *wogian*], 1. to make love to or seek to marry. 2. to try to get; seek: as, she *wooed* fame. 3. to coax; urge. *v.i.* to woo a person. **—woo′er,** *n.*

**wood** (wood), *n.* [AS. *wudu*], 1. *often pl.* a thick growth of trees; forest. 2. the hard, fibrous substance beneath the bark of trees and shrubs. 3. lumber or timber. *adj.* 1. made of wood; wooden. 2. growing or living in woods. **—out of the woods,** [Colloq.], out of difficulty, danger, etc. **—wood′ed,** *adj.*

**wood alcohol,** methyl alcohol.

**wood′bine′** (-bīn′), *n.* [*wood* + *bine*, twining stem], 1. a climbing honeysuckle. 2. the Virginia creeper.

**wood′chuck′** (-chuk′), *n.* [< Algonquian *wejack*], a N. American burrowing and hibernating marmot: also called *ground hog.*

**wood′cock′** (-kok′), *n.* a small game bird with short legs and a long bill.

**wood′craft′,** *n.* 1. matters relating to the woods, as camping, hunting, etc. 2. woodwork (sense 1).

**wood′cut′** (-kut′), *n.* 1. a wooden block engraved with a picture, etc. 2. a print made from it.

**wood′en** (-'n), *adj.* 1. made of wood. 2. stiff, lifeless, etc. 3. dull or insensitive. **—wood′en·ly,** *adv.* **—wood′en·ness,** *n.*

**wood′land′** (-land′, -lənd), *n.* land covered with woods. *adj.* of or in the woods.

**wood′peck′er** (-pek′ẽr), *n.* a climbing bird with a strong, pointed bill used to peck holes in bark to get insects.

**wood′shed′**, *n.* a shed for storing firewood.
**woods·man** (woodz′mən). *n.* [*pl.* -MEN], 1. one who lives or works in the woods. 2. one skilled in woodcraft.
**wood′sy** (-zi), *adj.* of or like the woods.
**wood wind**, any of the wind instruments of an orchestra made, esp. orig., of wood; flute, clarinet, oboe, English horn, and bassoon.
**wood′work′**, *n.* 1. work done in wood. 2. things made of wood, esp. the interior moldings, doors, etc. of a house.
**wood′y**, *adj.* [-IER, -IEST], 1. covered with woods. 2. consisting of or forming wood. 3. like wood. —**wood′i·ness**, *n.*
**woof** (wōōf), *n.* [ult. < AS. *wefan*, to weave], the threads woven across the fixed threads of the warp in a loom; weft.
**wool** (wool), *n.* [AS. *wull*], 1. the soft, curly hair of sheep, or of some other animals, as the goat. 2. woolen yarn, cloth, clothing, etc. 3. anything with the texture of wool. *adj.* of wool or woolen goods.
**wool′en, wool′len** (-ən), *adj.* 1. made of wool. 2. of or relating to wool or woolen cloth. *n.pl.* woolen goods or clothing.
**wool·gath·er·ing** (wool′gath′ẽr-iŋ), *n.* absent-mindedness or daydreaming.
**wool·ly** (wool′i), *adj.* [-LIER, -LIEST], 1. of or like wool. 2. bearing or covered with wool. 3. rough and uncivilized: chiefly in *wild and wooly*. *n.* [*pl.* -LIES], a woolen garment. Also sp. **wooly**. —**wool′li·ness**, *n.*
**wooz·y** (wōō′zi, wooz′i), *adj.* [-IER, -IEST], [Slang], befuddled, as with liquor; muddled. —**wooz′i·ly**, *adv.* —**wooz′i·ness**, *n.*
**word** (wũrd), *n.* [AS.], 1. a brief remark: as, a *word* of advice. 2. a promise: as, he gave his *word*. 3. news; information. 4. *a*) a password; signal. *b*) a command; order. 5. *pl. a*) talk; speech. *b*) lyrics; text. *c*) a quarrel; dispute. 6. *a*) a speech sound or series of sounds having meaning as a unit of language. *b*) the written or printed representation of this. *v.t.* to express in words; phrase. —**eat one's words**, to retract a statement. —**in a word**, briefly. —**the Word**, the Bible. —**word for word**, in precisely the same words. —**word′less**, *adj.*
**word·ing** (wũr′diŋ), *n.* choice and arrangement of words; phrasing.
**word·y** (wũr′di), *adj.* [-IER, -IEST], containing or using many or too many words; verbose. —**word′i·ly**, *adv.* —**word′i·ness**, *n.*
**wore** (wôr), pt. of **wear**.
**work** (wũrk), *n.* [AS. *weorc*], 1. effort exerted to do or make something; labor; toil. 2. employment; occupation: as, out of *work*. 3. something one is making or doing; task. 4. something made or done; specif., *a*) *usually pl.* an act; deed: as, good *works*. *b*) *pl.* collected writings. *c*) *pl.* engineering structures. 5. *pl.* [construed as sing.], a place where work is done, as a factory. 6. *pl.* the working parts of a watch, etc. 7. workmanship. *adj.* of, for, or used in work. *v.i.* [WORKED or WROUGHT, WORKING], 1. to do work; labor; toil. 2. to be employed. 3. to function or operate, esp. effectively. 4. to ferment. 5. to move, proceed, etc. slowly and with difficulty. 6. to come or become, as by repeated movement: as, the door *worked* loose. *v.t.* 1. to cause; bring about: as, his idea *worked* wonders. 2. to mold; shape. 3. to weave, knit, etc. 4. to solve (a mathematical problem). 5. to manipulate; knead. 6. to bring into a specified condition: as, they *worked* it loose. 7. to cultivate (soil). 8. to operate; use. 9. to cause to work: as, he *works* his men hard. 10. to make (one's way etc.) by effort. 11. to provoke; rouse: as, he *worked* her into a rage. —**at work**, working. —**the works**, [Slang], everything. —**work off**, to get rid of. —**work on** (or **upon**), 1. to influence. 2. to try to persuade. —**work out**, 1. to accomplish. 2. to solve. 3. to result. 4. to develop. —**work up**, 1. to advance. 2. to develop. 3. to excite.
**work′a·ble** (-ə-b'l), *adj.* 1. that can be worked. 2. practicable; feasible.
**work·a·day** (wũr′kə-dā′), *adj.* 1. of workdays; everyday. 2. ordinary.
**work′bench′** (-bench′), *n.* a table at which work is done, as by a mechanic.
**work′day′**, *n.* 1. a day on which work is done. 2. the hours of a day during which work is done. *adj.* workaday.
**work·er** (wũr′kẽr), *n.* 1. one who works for a living. 2. any of various sterile ants, bees, etc. that do work for the colony.
**work′house′**, *n.* 1. [Brit.], a poorhouse. 2. a prison where petty offenders are confined and put to work.
**work′ing**, *adj.* 1. that works. 2. of or used in work. 3. sufficient to get work done: as, a *working* majority. *n.* the act of one that works.
**work′ing·man′**, *n.* [*pl.* -MEN], a worker; esp., an industrial or manual worker.
**work′man** (-mən), *n.* [*pl.* -MEN], a worker; laborer.
**work′man·like′**, *adj.* characteristic of a good workman; skillful.
**work′man·ship′**, *n.* skill as or of a workman, or the quality of this.
**work′out′**, *n.* [Colloq.], 1. a test, practice, etc. 2. any strenuous exercise, work, etc.
**work′shop′**, *n.* 1. a room or building where work is done. 2. a group of people who meet for a period of intensive study, work, etc.
**world** (wũrld), *n.* [AS. *weoruld*], 1. the earth. 2. the universe. 3. *a*) mankind. *b*) people generally; the public. 4. [also W-], some part of the earth: as, the Old *World*. 5. any sphere or domain: as, the dog *world*. 6. individual experience, outlook, etc.: as, his *world* is narrow. 7. secular life and interests, or people concerned with these. 8. *often pl.* a large amount: as, a *world* of good. —**for all the world**, in every respect.
**world′ly**, *adj.* [-LIER, -LIEST], 1. of this world; temporal or secular. 2. devoted to the affairs, pleasures, etc. of this world. 3. worldly-wise. —**world′li·ness**, *n.*
**world′ly-wise′**, *adj.* wise in the ways of the world; sophisticated.
**world′-wea′ry**, *adj.* weary of the world or of living.
**world′-wide′**, *adj.* extending throughout the world.
**worm** (wũrm), *n.* [< AS. *wyrm*, serpent], 1. a long, slender, soft-bodied, creeping animal. 2. an abject or contemptible person. 3. something wormlike or spiral in shape, etc., as the thread of a screw. 4. *pl.* any disease caused by parasitic worms in the intestines, etc. *v.i.* to proceed like a worm, in a winding or devious manner. *v.t.* 1. to bring about, make, etc. in a winding or devious manner. 2. to purge of intestinal worms. —**worm′y**, *adj.*
**worm gear**, a gear consisting of a rotating screw meshed with a toothed wheel.
**worm′wood′** (-wood′), *n.* [< AS. *wermod*], 1. a strong-smelling plant that yields a bitter-tasting oil used in making absinthe. 2. bitterness.
**worn** (wôrn), pp. of **wear**. *adj.* 1. damaged by use or wear. 2. exhausted.
**worn′-out′**, *adj.* 1. used until no longer effective, usable, etc. 2. tired out.
**wor·ri·some** (wũr′i-səm), *adj.* 1. causing worry. 2. tending to worry.
**wor·ry** (wũr′i), *v.t.* [-RIED, -RYING], [< AS. *wyrgan*, strangle], 1. to bite and shake with the teeth: as, the dog *worried* a shoe. 2. to annoy; bother. 3. to make troubled or

uneasy. *v.i.* 1. to bite or tear (*at* an object) with the teeth. 2. to be anxious, troubled, etc. 3. to manage to get (*along* or *through*). *n.* [*pl.* -RIES], 1. a troubled state of mind; anxiety. 2. a cause of this. —**wor′ri·er,** *n.*

**worse** (wũrs), *adj.* [compar. of *bad* & *ill*], [AS. *wiersa*], 1. bad, evil, harmful, etc. in a greater degree. 2. in poorer health; more ill. 3. in a more unsatisfactory situation. *adv.* [compar. of *badly* & *ill*], in a worse manner; to a worse extent. *n.* that which is worse.

**wors·en** (wũr′s'n), *v.t.* & *v.i.* to make or become worse.

**wor·ship** (wũr′ship), *n.* [< AS. *weorth*, worthy + *-scipe*, -ship], 1. a prayer, church service, etc. showing reverence for a deity. 2. intense love, admiration, etc. 3. [Chiefly Brit.], a title of honor, in addressing magistrates, etc. *v.t.* [-SHIPED or SHIPPED, -SHIPING or -SHIPPING], 1. to show religious reverence for. 2. to have intense love or admiration for. *v.i.* to engage in worship. —**wor′ship′er, wor′ship′per,** *n.*

**wor′ship·ful,** *adj.* honorable; respected.

**worst** (wũrst), *adj.* [superl. of *bad* & *ill*], [AS. *wyrsta*], bad, evil, harmful, etc. in the highest degree. *adv.* [superl. of *badly* & *ill*], in the worst manner; to the worst extent. *n.* that which is worst. *v.t.* to defeat.

**wor·sted** (woos′tid, woor′stid), *n.* [<*Worstead*, England], 1. a smooth, hard-twisted wool thread or yarn. 2. fabric made from this. *adj.* made of worsted.

**wort** (wũrt), *n.* [AS. *wyrt-*], a liquid prepared with malt which, after fermenting, becomes beer, ale, etc.

**wort** (wũrt), *n.* [AS. *wyrt*, a root], a plant or herb; now usually in compounds, as *liverwort*.

**worth** (wũrth), *n.* [AS. *woerth*], 1. material value, esp. as expressed in money. 2. importance, value, merit, etc. 3. the quantity to be had for a given sum: as, a dime's *worth*. *adj.* 1. deserving or worthy of. 2. equal in value to. 3. having wealth totaling.

**worth′less,** *adj.* without worth or merit; useless. —**worth′less·ness,** *n.*

**worth′-while′,** *adj.* worth the time or effort spent. —**worth′-while′ness,** *n.*

**wor·thy** (wũr′*th*i), *adj.* [-THIER, -THIEST], 1. having worth, value, or merit. 2. deserving. *n.* [*pl.* -THIES], a person of outstanding worth, etc. —**wor′thi·ly,** *adv.* —**wor′thi·ness,** *n.*

**would** (wood), [AS. *wolde*], pt. of **will.** *Would* is also used to express: 1. condition: as, if you *would*. 2. futurity: as, he said he *would* come. 3. a wish: as, *would* that she were here. 4. a request: as, *would* you help me?

**would′-be′,** *adj.* 1. wishing or pretending to be. 2. intended to be.

**would′n't,** would not.

**wound** (wōōnd), *n.* [AS. *wund*], 1. an injury in which skin or other tissue is cut, torn, etc. 2. a scar. 3. any hurt to the feelings, honor, etc. *v.t.* & *v.i.* to inflict a wound (on or upon); injure. —**wound′er,** *n.*

**wound** (wound), pt. and pp. of **wind** (to twist).

**wove** (wōv), pt. and alt. pp. of **weave.**

**wo·ven** (wō′v'n), pp. of **weave.**

**wow** (wou), *interj.* an expression of surprise, pleasure, etc. *n.* [Slang], a great success.

**wrack** (rak), *n.* [MD. *wrak*, wreck], ruin; destruction: as, *wrack* and ruin.

**wraith** (rāth), *n.* [Scot.], a ghost.

**wran·gle** (raŋ′g'l), *v.i.* [-GLED, -GLING], [akin to *wring*], to argue; quarrel, esp. angrily and noisily. *v.t.* to round up (livestock). *n.* an angry, noisy dispute. —**wran′gler,** *n.*

**wrap** (rap), *v.t.* [WRAPPED or WRAPT, WRAPPING], [ME. *wrappen*], 1 to wind or fold (a covering) around (something). 2. to enclose and fasten in paper, etc. *v.i.* to twine, coil, etc. (*over*, *around*, etc.). *n.* an outer covering or garment. —**wrapped up in,** absorbed in.

**wrap′per,** *n.* 1. one that wraps. 2. that in which something is wrapped. 3. a woman's dressing gown.

**wrap′ping,** *n.* *usually pl.* the material in which something is wrapped.

**wrath** (rath, räth), *n.* [AS., angry], 1. intense anger; rage; fury. 2. any action of vengeance. —**wrath′ful,** *adj.*

**wreak** (rēk), *v.t.* [AS. *wrecan*, to revenge], 1. to give vent to (anger, etc.). 2. to inflict (vengeance, etc.). —**wreak′er,** *n.*

**wreath** (rēth), *n.* [*pl.* WREATHS (rē*th*z)], [AS. *wræth*], 1. a twisted ring of leaves, flowers, etc. 2. something like this in shape: as, *wreaths* of smoke.

**wreathe** (rē*th*), *v.t.* [WREATHED, WREATHING], 1. to form into a wreath. 2. to coil or twist around; encircle. 3. to decorate with wreaths. *v.i.* to form a wreath.

**wreck** (rek), *n.* [akin to *wreak*], 1. a shipwreck. 2. the remains of something destroyed; ruin. 3. a run-down person. 4. a wrecking or being wrecked. *v.t.* 1. to destroy; ruin. 2. to tear down (a building, etc.). 3. to overthrow; thwart.

**wreck′age** (-ij), *n.* 1. a wrecking or being wrecked. 2. the remains of something wrecked.

**wreck′er,** *n.* 1. one who wrecks. 2. one that salvages or removes wrecks.

**wren** (ren), *n.* [AS. *wrenna*], a small songbird with a long bill and stubby, erect tail.

**wrench** (rench), *n.* [< AS. *wrencan*, to twist], 1. a sudden, violent twist or pull. 2. any injury caused by a twist, as to the back. 3. a sudden feeling of grief, etc. 4. a tool for turning nuts, bolts, pipes, etc. *v.t.* 1. to twist or jerk violently. 2. to injure with a twist. 3. to distort (a meaning, etc.).

**wrest** (rest), *v.t.* [AS. *wræstan*], 1. to pull or force away violently with a twisting motion. 2. to take by force; usurp. *n.* a wresting.

**wres·tle** (res′'l), *v.i.* & *v.t.* [-TLED, -TLING], [< AS. *wræstan*, to twist], 1. to struggle hand to hand with (an opponent) in an attempt to throw him. 2. to contend (with). *n.* a wrestling. —**wres′tler,** *n.* —**wres′tling,** *n.*

**wretch** (rech), *n.* [AS. *wercca*, outcast], 1. a miserable or unhappy person. 2. a person despised or scorned.

**wretch′ed** (-id), *adj.* 1. very unhappy; miserable. 2. distressing; depressing. 3. very inferior. 4. despicable. —**wretch′ed·ly,** *adv.* —**wretch′ed·ness,** *n.*

**wrig·gle** (rig′'l), *v.i.* [-GLED, -GLING], [MLG. *wriggeln*], 1. to twist and turn; squirm. 2. to move along with a twisting motion. 3. to make one's way by shifty means. *n.* a wriggling. —**wrig′gler,** *n.* —**wrig′gly,** *adj.*

**wright** (rīt), *n.* [< AS. *wyrcan*, to work], one who makes or constructs: used chiefly in compounds, as, *shipwright*.

**wring** (riŋ), *v.t.* [WRUNG, WRINGING], [AS. *wringan*], 1. to squeeze, press, or twist. 2. to force (*out* water, etc.) by this means. 3. to extract by force, threats, etc. *n.* a wringing.

**wring′er,** *n.* a machine with opposed rollers that squeeze water from wet clothes.

**wrin·kle** (riŋ′k'l), *n.* [AS. *wrincle*], 1. a small furrow in a normally smooth surface. 2. a crease in the skin. *v.t.* & *v.i.* [-KLED, -KLING], to make or form wrinkles (in). —**wrin′kly** [-KLIER, -KLIEST], *adj.*

**wrin·kle** (riŋ′k'l), *n.* [< AS. *wrenc*, a trick], [Colloq.], a clever trick, idea, etc.

**wrist** (rist), *n.* [AS.], the joint between the hand and forearm.

**wrist watch,** a watch worn on a strap or band around the wrist.
**writ** (rit), *n.* [AS. < *writan*, write], a formal legal document ordering or prohibiting some action.
**write** (rīt), *v.t.* [WROTE, WRITTEN, WRITING], [AS. *writan*], 1. to form (words, letters, etc.) on a surface, as with a pen. 2. to produce (a literary or musical composition); compose. 3. to communicate (with) in writing: as, he *wrote* (me) that he was ill. *v.i.* 1. to write words, etc. 2. to write books, etc. 3. to write a letter. **—write off,** to remove from accounts, as bad debts, etc. **—write out,** 1. to put into writing. 2. to write in full. **—write up,** to write an account of.
**writ′er,** *n.* one who writes, esp. as a business or occupation; author, journalist, etc.
**write′-up′,** *n.* [Colloq.], a written report.
**writhe** (rīth), *v.t.* [WRITHED, WRITHING], [AS. *writhan*, to twist], to cause to twist or turn. *v.i.* 1. to twist, or turn; squirm. 2. to suffer great emotional distress. *n.* a writhing.
**writ·ing** (rīt′iŋ), *n.* 1. the act of one who writes. 2. something written. 3. written form. 4. handwriting. 5. a literary work.
**writ·ten** (rit′′n), pp. of **write.**
**wrong** (rôŋ), *adj.* [< ON. *rangr*, twisted], 1. not morally right or just. 2. not in accordance with an established standard, etc. 3. not suitable or appropriate. 4. *a*) contrary to truth, fact, etc.; incorrect. *b*) mistaken. 5. not functioning properly. 6. not designed to be displayed: as, the *wrong* side of a fabric. *adv.* in a wrong manner, direction, etc. *n.* something wrong; esp., a wicked, unjust, or illegal act. *v.t.* to treat badly or unjustly. **—in the wrong,** wrong.
**wrong′do′ing,** *n.* any act or behavior that is wrong. **—wrong′do′er,** *n.*
**wrong′ful,** *adj.* 1. unjust; unfair; injurious. 2. unlawful. **—wrong′ful·ly,** *adv.*
**wrong′head′ed** (-hed′id), *adj.* stubbornly refusing to yield, agree, etc. even when wrong. **—wrong′head′ed·ness,** *n.*
**wrote** (rōt), pt. of **write.**
**wroth** (rôth; Brit. rōth), *adj.* [AS. *wrath*], angry; wrathful; incensed.
**wrought** (rôt), alt. pt. and pp. of **work.** *adj.* 1. formed; made. 2. shaped by hammering, etc.: said of metals.
**wrought iron,** tough, malleable iron containing little carbon. **—wrought′-i′ron,** *adj.*
**wrought′-up′,** *adj.* disturbed; excited.
**wrung** (ruŋ), pt. and pp. of **wring.**
**wry** (rī), *adj.* [WRIER, WRIEST], [< AS. *wrigian*, to turn], 1. twisted; distorted. 2. distorted in a grimace: as, a *wry* face. **—wry′ly,** *adv.* **—wry′ness,** *n.*
**wry′neck′,** *n.* a condition in which the neck is twisted by a muscle spasm.
**wt.,** weight.
**W.Va.,** West Virginia.

# XYZ

**X, x** (eks), *n.* [*pl.* X's, x's, Xs, xs], the 24th letter of the English alphabet.
**X** (eks), *n.* the Roman numeral for 10.
**x,** in *math.*, an unknown quantity.
**X chromosome,** a sex chromosome: fertilized eggs containing two X chromosomes (one from each parent germ cell) develop into females, those containing one X and one Y chromosome (male germ cells carry either) develop into males.
**Xe,** in *chem.*, xenon.
**xe·bec** (zē′bek), *n.* [< Ar. *shabbak*], a small, three-masted ship, once common in the Mediterranean.
**xe·non** (zē′non, zen′on), *n.* [Gr., strange], a heavy, colorless, inert, gaseous chemical element: symbol, Xe.
**xen·o·pho·bi·a** (zen′ə-fō′bi-ə), *n.* [< Gr. *xenos*, strange; + *-phobia*], fear or hatred of strangers or foreigners.
**xe·rog·ra·phy** (zi-rog′rə-fi), *n.* [< Gr. *xēros*, dry; + *-graphy*], a process for copying printed material, pictures, etc. by the action of light on an electrically charged surface.
**xi** (zī, sī), *n.* the fourteenth letter of the Greek alphabet (Ξ, ξ).
**Xmas** (kris′məs), *n.* Christmas.
**X-ray** (eks′rā′), *adj.* of or by X rays. *v.t.* to examine, treat, or photograph with X rays.
**X ray,** 1. a ray or radiation of very short wave length that can penetrate solid substances: used to study internal body structures and treat various disorders. 2. a photograph made with X rays.
**xy·lem** (zī′lem), *n.* [< Gr. *xylon*, wood], the woody tissue of a plant.
**xy·lo·phone** (zī′lə-fōn′), *n.* [< Gr. *xylon*, wood; + *phone*], a musical percussion instrument having a series of graduated wooden bars struck with small wooden hammers. **—xy′lo·phon′ist,** *n.*

**Y, y** (wī), *n.* [*pl.* Y's, y's, Ys, ys], the 25th letter of the English alphabet.
**-y,** [ME.], a suffix used to form diminutives, nicknames, etc., as in *kitty, Billy, daddy.*
**-y,** [AS. *-ig*], a suffix meaning: 1. *full of, having,* etc., as in *dirty.* 2. *somewhat,* as in *dusky.* 3. *tending to,* as in *sticky.*
**-y,** [< L. *-ia*], a suffix meaning *quality* or *state of (being)*, as in *jealousy.*
**-y,** [< L. *-ium*], a suffix meaning *action of,* as in *inquiry.*
**yacht** (yät), *n.* [D. *jacht*], a small ship for pleasure cruises, racing, etc. *v.i.* to sail in a yacht. **—yacht′ing,** *n.* **—yachts′man,** *n.*
**yah** (yä, ya, *etc.*), *interj.* an exclamation of derision, defiance, or disgust.
**Ya·hoo** (yä′hōō, yā′-), *n.* in Swift's *Gulliver's Travels*, any of a race of brutish, degraded creatures having the form and vices of man.
**Yah·weh, Yah·we** (yä′we), *n.* Jehovah: a modern transliteration.
**yak** (yak), *n.* [< native name *gyak*], the long-haired wild ox of C Asia.
**yam** (yam), *n.* [< W. Afr.], 1. the edible, starchy, tuberous root of a tropical climbing plant. 2. [Dial.], the sweet potato.
**Yank** (yaŋk), *n.* [Slang], a Yankee.
**yank** (yaŋk), *n., v.t. & v.i.* [< New England Dial.], [Colloq.], jerk.
**Yankee** (yaŋ′ki), *n.* [prob. < D. *Jan Kees*, a disparaging nickname], 1. a New Englander. 2. a native of the N part of the U.S. 3. a citizen of the U.S. *adj.* of or like Yankees. **—Yan′kee·ism,** *n.*
**yap** (yap) *v.i.* [YAPPED, YAPPING], [echoic], 1. to make a sharp, shrill bark. 2. [Slang], to talk noisily and stupidly. *n.* a sharp, shrill bark.
**yard** (yärd), *n.* [AS. *gyrd*, rod], 1. a measure of length, equal to 3 feet, or 36 inches. 2. in *naut. usage*, a slender rod or spar fastened across a mast to support a sail.
**yard** (yärd), *n.* [AS. *geard*, enclosure], 1. the ground surrounding or surrounded by a building, etc. 2. an enclosed place used for a particular purpose or business: as, a ship*yard.* 3. a rail center where trains are made up, switched, etc.

**yard·age** (yär′dij), *n.* 1. measurement in yards. 2. the extent so measured.
**yard′arm′**, *n.* in *naut. usage*, either end of a yard supporting a square sail.
**yard′stick′**, *n.* 1. a graduated measuring stick one yard in length. 2. any standard used in measuring, judging, etc.
**yarn** (yärn), *n.* [AS. *gearn*], 1. fibers of wool, cotton, etc., spun into strands for weaving, knitting, etc. 2. [Colloq.], a tale or story.
**yaw** (yô), *v.i.* [< ON. *jaga*, sway], to turn unintentionally from the intended heading: said of a ship. *n.* a yawing.
**yawl** (yôl), *n.* [< D. *jol*], a small, two-masted sailboat rigged fore and aft.
**yawn** (yôn), *v.i.* [AS. *ganian*], 1. to open the mouth wide involuntarily, as a result of fatigue, drowsiness, etc. 2. to open wide; gape. *n.* a yawning.
**yaws** (yôz), *n.pl.* [prob. < W. Ind.], a tropical skin disease.
**Y chromosome,** a sex chromosome: see **X chromosome.**
**y·clept, y-clept** (i-klept′), *pp.* [< AS. *clipian*, to call], [Archaic], called; named: also sp. **ycleped, y-cleped.**
**yd.,** 1. yard. 2. yards: also **yds.**
**ye** (*thə, thi*; yē *is incorrect*), *adj.* [Archaic], the.
**ye** (yē), *pron.* [AS. *ge*], [Archaic], you.
**yea** (yā), *adv.* [AS. *gea*], 1. yes. 2. indeed; truly. *n.* 1. an affirmative statement or vote. 2. a voter in the affirmative.
**yeah** (ye, ya), *adv.* [Colloq.], yes.
**year** (yêr), *n.* [AS. *gear*], 1. a period of 365 days (366 in leap year) beginning Jan 1. 2. the period of time, 365 days, 5 hours, 48 minutes, and 45.51 seconds, of one revolution of the earth around the sun: also **solar year.** 3. a period of 12 calendar months reckoned from any date. 4. an annual period of less than 365 days: as, a school *year.* 5. *pl. a*) age: as, old for his *years. b*) a long time.
**year′book′**, *n.* an annual book, esp. one giving data of the preceding year.
**year′ling** (yêr′liŋ, yũr′-), *n.* an animal one year old or in its second year.
**year′long,** *adj.* lasting for a full year.
**year′ly,** *adj.* 1. lasting a year. 2. once a year, or every year. 3. of a year, or each year. *adv.* every year.
**yearn** (yũrn), *v.i.* [< AS. *georn*, eager], 1. to be filled with longing or desire. 2. to be deeply moved, esp. with pity. **—yearn′ing,** *n. & adj.* **—yearn′ing·ly,** *adv.*
**yeast** (yēst), *n.* [AS. *gist*], 1. a yellow, frothy substance consisting of minute fungi that cause fermentation: used in making beer and as a leavening agent. 2. yeast mixed with flour or meal, made up in small cakes: also **yeast cake.** 3. foam; froth. 4. ferment; agitation.
**yeast′y,** *adj.* [-IER, -IEST], 1. of, like, or containing yeast. 2. frothy; light.
**yegg** (yeg), *n.* [Slang], a criminal.
**yell** (yel), *v.i. & v.t.* [AS. *gellan*], to cry out loudly; scream. *n.* 1. a loud outcry or shout; scream. 2. a rhythmic cheer given in unison.
**yel·low** (yel′ō), *adj.* [AS. *geolo*], 1. of the color of ripe lemons. 2. having a yellowish skin. 3. [Colloq.], cowardly. 4. sensational, as a newspaper. *n.* 1. a yellow color or pigment. 2. the yolk of an egg. *v.t. & v.i.* to make or become yellow. **—yel′low·ish,** *adj.*
**yellow fever,** an infectious tropical disease caused by a virus transmitted by the bite of a certain mosquito.
**yellow jacket,** a wasp or hornet having bright-yellow markings.
**yelp** (yelp), *v.i. & v.t.* [AS. *gilpan*, to boast], to utter or express by a short, sharp cry or bark, as a dog. *n.* a short, sharp cry or bark.
**yen** (yen), *n.* [*pl.* YEN], [Japan.], the monetary unit of Japan.
**yen** (yen), *n.* [Chin., opium], [Colloq.], a deep longing or desire.
**yeo·man** (yō′mən), *n.* [*pl.* -MEN], [ME. *yeman*], 1. orig., a freeholder of a class below the gentry. 2. in the *U.S. Navy*, a petty officer assigned to clerical duty.
**yeo′man·ry** (-ri), *n.* yeomen collectively.
**yes** (yes), *adv.* [AS. *gese*], 1. aye; it is so: expressing agreement, consent, etc. 2. not only that, but more: as, ready, *yes*, eager to go. *n.* [*pl.* YESES], an affirmative reply, vote, etc. *v.t. & v.i.* [YESSED, YESSING], to say *yes* (to.).
**yes man,** [Slang], one who indicates indiscriminate approval of every idea offered by his superior.
**yes·ter** (yes′tẽr), *adj.* [Archaic or Poetic], of yesterday, as in *yesterevening.*
**yes·ter·day** (yes′tẽr-di, -dā′), *n.* [< AS. *geostran*, yesterday + *dæg*, day], 1. the day before today. 2. a recent day or time. *adv.* 1. on the day before today. 2. recently.
**yet** (yet), *adv.* [AS. *giet*], 1. up to now; thus far: as, he has not *yet* come. 2. at the present time; now: as, we can't go just *yet.* 3. still; even now: as, there is *yet* a chance. 4. in addition; even: as, he was *yet* more kind. 5. nevertheless: as, she's kind, *yet* dull. *conj.* nevertheless; however: as, she seems well, *yet* she is ill. **—as yet,** up to now.
**yew** (ū), *n.* [AS. *iw*], 1. an evergreen tree of Europe and Asia. 2. its fine-grained wood.
**Yid·dish** (yid′ish), *n.* [< G. *jüdisch* < L. *Judaeus*, Jew], a language spoken by many European Jews, a High-German dialect written in the Hebrew alphabet.
**yield** (yēld), *v.t.* [AS. *gieldan*, to pay], 1. to produce as a crop, result, profit, etc. 2. to give up; surrender. 3. to concede; grant. *v.i.* 1. to produce or bear. 2. to give up; surrender. 3. to give way to physical force. 4. to lose precedence, etc. (often with *to*). *n.* the amount yielded.
**yield′ing,** *adj.* that yields; submissive.
**Y.M.C.A.,** Young Men's Christian Association.
**yo·del** (yō′d'l), *v.t. & v.i.* [-DELED or -DELLED, -DELING or -DELLING], [G. *jodeln*], to sing with abrupt alternating changes to the falsetto. *n.* a yodeling.
**yo·ga** (yō′gə), *n.* [Sans., union], in *Hindu philos.*, a practice involving complete concentration upon something, esp. the deity, in order to establish identity of consciousness with it.
**yo·gi** (yō′gi), *n.* [*pl.* -GIS], one who practices yoga: also **yo′gin** (-gin).
**yo·gurt, yo·ghurt** (yō′goort), *n.* [Turk. *yōghurt*], a thick, semisolid food made from fermented milk.
**yoicks** (yoiks), *interj.* [Brit.], a cry to urge on hounds in fox hunting.
**yoke** (yōk), *n.* [AS. *geoc*], 1. a wooden frame for harnessing together a pair of oxen, etc. 2. a pair of animals so harnessed. 3. bondage; servitude. 4. anything like a yoke, as: *a*) something that binds, unites, etc. *b*) a part of a garment fitted to the shoulders or hips as a support for the gathered parts below. *v.t.* [YOKED, YOKING], 1. to put a yoke on. 2. to harness (an animal) to (a plow, etc.). 3. to join together.
**yo·kel** (yō′k'l), *n.* a person from the country; bumpkin: used contemptuously.
**yolk** (yōk), *n.* [AS. *geolca*], the yellow, principal substance of an egg. **—yolk′y,** *adj.*
**Yom Kip·pur** (yom′ kip′ẽr; Heb. yōm′ ki-pōōr′), the Day of Atonement, a Jewish holiday and day of fasting.
**yon** (yon), *adj. & adv.* [AS. *geon*], [Archaic or Dial.], yonder.
**yon·der** (yon′dẽr), *adj. & adv.* [ME.], (being)

at or in that (specified or relatively distant) place; over there.
**yore** (yôr), ***adv.*** [AS. *geara*], [Obs.], long ago. **—of yore,** formerly.
**you** (ū), ***pron. sing. & pl.*** [< AS. *eow*, dat. of *ge*, ye], 1. the person or persons spoken to. 2. a person or people generally: as, *you* can never tell!
**you'd** (ūd), 1. you had. 2. you would.
**you'll** (ūl), 1. you will. 2. you shall.
**young** (yuŋ), ***adj.*** [AS. *geong*], 1. being in an early period of life or growth. 2. youthful; fresh; vigorous. 3. in an early stage. 4. inexperienced; immature. ***n.*** offspring; esp., young offspring, collectively. **—the young,** young people. **—with young,** pregnant. **—young'ish,** ***adj.*** **—young'ness,** ***n.***
**young'ster** (-stẽr), ***n.*** a child or youth.
**your** (yoor), ***pron.*** [AS. *eower*], possessive form of **you** (sing. & pl.). ***poss. pronominal adj.*** of, belonging to, or done by you: also used before some titles, as, *your* Honor.
**you're** (yoor, ūr), you are.
**yours** (yoorz), ***pron.*** that or those belonging to you: as, *yours* are better.
**your·self'** (-self'), ***pron.*** [*pl.* -SELVES], 1. the intensive form of **you:** as, you went *yourself.* 2. the reflexive form of **you:** as, you hurt *yourself.* 3. your true self: as, you're not *yourself* now.
**yours truly,** 1. a phrase used in ending a letter. 2. [Colloq.], I or me.
**youth** (ūth), ***n.*** [*pl.* YOUTHS (ūths, ū*th*z)], [AS. *geoguthe*], 1. the state or quality of being young. 2. the period of adolescence. 3. an early stage of development. 4. young people collectively. 5. a young person; esp., a young man.
**youth'ful,** ***adj.*** 1. young. 2. of, characteristic of, or suitable for youth. 3. fresh; vigorous. 4. new; early. **—youth'ful·ly,** ***adv.*** **—youth'ful·ness,** ***n.***
**you've** (ūv), you have.
**yowl** (youl), ***v.i. & n.*** [< ON. *gaula*], howl.
**yo-yo** (yō'-yō'), ***n.*** [arbitrary formation], a spoollike toy attached to one end of a string upon which it may be made to spin up and down: a trademark (**Yo-Yo**).
**yr.,** 1. [*pl.* YRS.], year. 2. your.
**yrs.,** 1. years. 2. yours.
**yuc·ca** (yuk'ə), ***n.*** [< Sp. *yuca*], 1. a plant of the lily family, with stiff leaves and white flowers. 2. its flower.
**Yu·go·slav** (ū'gō-släv'), ***adj.*** of Yugoslavia or its people. ***n.*** a native or inhabitant of Yugoslavia. Also sp. **Jugoslav.** **—Yu'go-slav'i·an,** ***adj. & n.***
**yule** (ūl), ***n.*** [AS. *geol*], Christmas or the Christmas season.
**yule log,** a large log formerly used for the ceremonial Christmas-Eve fire.
**yule'tide'** (-tīd'), ***n.*** Christmas time.
**Y.W.C.A.,** Young Women's Christian Association.

**Z, z** (zē; *Brit.* zed), ***n.*** [*pl.* Z's, z's, Zs, zs], the 26th and last letter of the English alphabet.
**za·ny** (zā'ni), ***n.*** [*pl.* -NIES], [< It. *zanni* < *Giovanni*, John], 1. a clown or buffoon. 2. a fool; dolt. ***adj.*** [-NIER, -NIEST], of or like a zany; foolish or comical. **—za'ni·ness,** ***n.***
**zeal** (zēl), ***n.*** [< Gr. *zēlos*], eagerness; enthusiasm; ardor; fervor.
**zeal·ot** (zel'ət), ***n.*** one who is zealous, esp. to a fanatic degree. **—zeal'ot·ry,** ***n.***
**zeal·ous** (zel'əs), ***adj.*** full of, characterized by, or showing zeal; fervent; enthusiastic. **—zeal'ous·ly,** ***adv.*** **—zeal'ous·ness,** ***n.***
**ze·bra** (zē'brə), ***n.*** [Port. < native name], an African animal related to the horse: it has dark stripes on a light body.
**ze·bu** (zē'bū), ***n.*** [Fr. *zébu*], an oxlike domestic animal of Asia and Africa: it has a large hump and short, curving horns.
**ze·nith** (zē'nith), ***n.*** [< Ar. *semt*, road], 1. the point in the sky directly overhead. 2. the highest point; peak.
**zeph·yr** (zef'ẽr), ***n.*** [< Gr. *zephyros*], 1. the west wind. 2. a gentle breeze.
**zep·pe·lin** (zep'ə-lin), ***n.*** [< F. von *Zeppelin* (1838-1917), G. inventor], [often Z-], a type of dirigible with a stiff framework.
**ze·ro** (zêr'ō), ***n.*** [*pl.* -ROS, -ROES], [< Ar. *sifr*, cipher], 1. the symbol 0; cipher; naught. 2. the point marked 0, from which quantities are reckoned on a graduated scale. 3. nothing. 4. the lowest point. ***adj.*** of or at zero. **—zero in,** to adjust the sight settings of (a rifle, etc.) by calibrated firing.
**zero hour,** the time set for beginning an attack, etc.; crucial point.
**zest** (zest), ***n.*** [Fr. *zeste*, orange peel], 1. something that gives flavor or relish. 2. stimulating or exciting quality; piquancy. 3. keen enjoyment: as, *zest* for life. **—zest'ful,** ***adj.*** **—zest'ful·ly,** ***adv.***
**ze·ta** (zā'tə, zē'-), ***n.*** the sixth letter of the Greek alphabet (Z, ζ).
**Zeus** (zōōs, zūs), ***n.*** the supreme deity of the ancient Greeks.
**zig·zag** (zig'zag'), ***n.*** [Fr.], 1. any of a series of short, sharp angles in alternate directions. 2. something characterized by such a series. ***adj.*** having the form of a zigzag. ***adv.*** so as to form a zigzag. ***v.t. & v.i.*** [-ZAGGED, -ZAGGING], to move or form in a zigzag.
**zil·lion** (zil'yən), ***n.*** [arbitrary coinage, after *million*, etc.], [Colloq.], an indefinitely large number.
**zinc** (ziŋk), ***n.*** [G. *zink*], a bluish-white, metallic chemical element, used in various alloys, as a protective coating for iron, etc.: symbol, Zn.
**zinc ointment,** a zinc-oxide salve.
**zinc oxide,** a white powder used in making glass, paints, ointments, etc.
**zing** (ziŋ), ***n.*** [echoic], [Slang], a shrill, high-pitched, whizzing sound.
**zin·ni·a** (zin'i-ə, zin'yə), ***n.*** [< J. *Zinn*, 18th-c. G. botanist], a plant of the aster family, having colorful, composite flowers.
**Zion** (zī'ən), ***n.*** 1. the Jewish people. 2. heaven.
**Zi'on·ism,** ***n.*** the movement that re-established, and now supports, the state of Israel. **—Zi'on·ist,** ***n. & adj.***
**zip** (zip), ***n.*** [echoic], 1. a short, sharp hissing sound, as of a passing bullet. 2. [Colloq.], energy; vim. ***v.i.*** [ZIPPED, ZIPPING], 1. to make, or move with, a zip. 2. [Colloq.], to move with speed. ***v.t.*** to fasten with a slide fastener.
**ZIP code,** [*z*one *i*mprovement *p*lan], a system to speed mail deliveries, using a code number assigned to individual regions and places.
**zip·per** (zip'ẽr), ***n.*** [after *Zipper*, trademark for an overshoe with a slide fastener], a slide fastener.
**zip'py,** ***adj.*** [-PIER, -PIEST], [Colloq.], full of zip, or vim; brisk; snappy.
**zir·con** (zũr'kon), ***n.*** [< Per. *zar*, gold], a crystalline silicate mineral often used as a gem.
**zith·er** (zith'ẽr, zi*th*'-), ***n.*** [< Gr. *kithara*, lute], a musical instrument with 30 to 40 strings played with a plectrum: also **zith'ern.**
**zlo·ty** (zlô'ti), ***n.*** [*pl.* -TYS], the monetary unit of Poland.
**Zn,** in *chem.*, zinc.
**zo·di·ac** (zō'di-ak'), ***n.*** [< Gr. *zōdiakos* (*kyklos*), (circle) of animals], 1. an imaginary belt in the heavens extending on either side of the apparent path of the sun and divided into twelve equal parts, or signs, named for constellations. 2. a diagram

representing this. **—zo·di′a·cal** (-dī′ə-k'l), *adj.*

**zom·bi** (zom′bi), *n.* [*pl.* -BIS], [of Afr. origin], 1. in West Indian superstition, a supernatural power by which a corpse may be animated. 2. a corpse so animated. Also sp. **zombie** [*pl.* -BIES].

**zone** (zōn), *n.* [< Gr. *zōne*], 1. [Poetic], a belt or girdle. 2. an encircling band, stripe, etc. 3. any of the five great latitudinal divisions of the earth's surface (the *torrid zone*, two *temperate zones*, and two *frigid zones*). 4. any region or district with reference to a particular use, etc.: as, a canal *zone*, postal *zone*. *v.t.* [ZONED, ZONING], 1. to mark off into zones. 2. to encircle. **—zon′al,** *adj.* **—zoned,** *adj.*

**zoo** (zōō), *n.* [< *zoo*logical garden], a place where a collection of wild animals is kept for public showing.

**zoo-,** [< Gr. *zōion*, animal], a combining form meaning *animal, animals*, etc., as in *zoology:* also **zoö-, zo-.**

**zo·oid** (zō′oid), *n.* [*zo(o)-* + *-oid*], 1. an independent animal organism produced by nonsexual methods, as by fission. 2. any of the distinct individuals of a compound organism. **—zo·oi′dal** (-oi′d'l), *adj.*

**zoological garden,** a zoo.

**zo·ol·o·gy** (zō-ol′ə-ji), *n.* [*zoo-* + *-logy*], the science that deals with animals and animal life. **—zo′o·log′i·cal** (-ə-loj′i-k'l), **zo′o·log′ic,** *adj.* **—zo·ol′o·gist,** *n.*

**zoom** (zōōm), *v.i.* [echoic], 1. to make a loud, buzzing sound. 2. to climb sharply: said of an airplane. *v.t.* to cause to zoom. *n.* a zooming.

**Zoo·mar** (zōō′mär), *n.* a system of lenses, as in a television camera, that can be rapidly adjusted as for close-up shots while keeping the image in focus: a trademark.

**zo·o·phyte** (zō′ə-fīt′), *n.* [< Gr. *zōion*, animal + *phyton*, plant], any animal, as a sponge, that looks, and grows somewhat like a plant. **—zo′o·phyt′ic** (-fit′ik), *adj.*

**zo·o·spore** (zō′ə-spôr′), *n.* an asexual spore, as of certain fungi, capable of independent motion usually by means of cilia.

**Zo·ro·as·tri·an·ism** (zō′rō-as′tri-ən-iz'm), *n.* [< *Zoroaster*, the founder], the religion of the ancient Persians.

**Zou·ave** (zōō-äv′), *n.* [< Ar. *Zouaoua*, Algerian tribe], a member of a French infantry unit with colorful oriental uniforms.

**zounds** (zoundz), *interj.* [alt. < oath *God's wounds*], [Archaic], a mild oath.

**zuc·chi·ni** (zōō-kē′ni), *n.* [It.], a cucumberlike summer squash.

**Zu·lu** (zōō′lōō), *n.* [*pl.* -LUS, -LU], 1. a member of a people of SE Africa. 2. their language. *adj.* of the Zulus, their language, etc.

**Zu·ñi** (zōō′nyi, sōō′-), *n.* [*pl.* -ÑI, -ÑIS], [Sp. <Am. Ind.], 1. a member of a pueblo-dwelling Indian tribe of New Mexico. 2. their language. *adj.* of this tribe, their language, etc. Also **Zu′ñi·an.**

**zwie·back** (tswē′bäk′, swī′bak), *n.* [G. < *zwie-*, twice + *backen*, bake], a kind of biscuit that is sliced and toasted after baking.

**zyme** (zīm), *n.* [Gr. *zymē*, leaven], 1. a ferment or enzyme. 2. the principle causing an infectious disease.

**zymo-,** [see ZYME], a combining form meaning *fermentation:* also **zym-.**

**zy·mur·gy** (zī′mẽr-ji), *n.* [*zym-* + *-urgy*], the chemistry of fermentation, as applied in brewing, etc.

# TABLES OF WEIGHTS AND MEASURES

**Linear Measure**

| | | | |
|---|---|---|---|
| 1 inch | | = | 2.54 centimeters |
| 12 inches | = 1 foot | = | 0.3048 meter |
| 3 feet | = 1 yard | = | 0.9144 meter |
| 5½ yards or 16½ feet | = 1 rod (or pole or perch) | = | 5.029 meters |
| 40 rods | = 1 furlong | = | 201.17 meters |
| 8 furlongs or 1,760 yards or 5,280 feet | = 1 (statute) mile | = | 1,609.3 meters |
| 3 miles | = 1 (land) league | = | 4.83 kilometers |

**Square Measure**

| | | | |
|---|---|---|---|
| 1 square inch | | = | 6.452 square centimeters |
| 144 square inches | = 1 square foot | = | 929 square centimeters |
| 9 square feet | = 1 square yard | = | 0.8361 square meter |
| 30¼ square yards | = 1 square rod (or square pole or square perch) | = | 25.29 square meters |
| 160 square rods or 4,840 square yards or 43,560 square feet | = 1 acre | = | 0.4047 hectare |
| 640 acres | = 1 square mile | = | 259 hectares or 2.59 square kilometers |

**Cubic Measure**

| | | |
|---|---|---|
| 1 cubic inch | | = 16.387 cubic centimeters |
| 1,728 cubic inches | = 1 cubic foot | = 0.0283 cubic meter |
| 27 cubic feet | = 1 cubic yard | = 0.7646 cubic meter |
| | (in units for cordwood, etc.) | |
| 16 cubic feet | = 1 cord foot | |
| 8 cord feet | = 1 cord | = 3.625 cubic meters |

**Nautical Measure**

| | | |
|---|---|---|
| 6 feet | = 1 fathom | = 1.829 meters |
| 100 fathoms | = 1 cable's length (ordinary) (In the U.S. Navy 120 fathoms or 720 feet = 1 cable's length; in the British Navy, 608 feet = 1 cable's length.) | |
| 10 cable's lengths | = 1 nautical mile (6,076.10333 feet, by international agreement in 1954) | = 1.852 kilometers |
| 1 nautical mile (Also called geographical, sea, or air mile, and, in Great Britain, Admiralty mile.) | = 1.1508 statute miles (the length of a minute of longitude at the equator) | |
| 3 nautical miles | = 1 marine league (3.45 statute miles) | = 5.56 kilometers |
| 60 nautical miles | = 1 degree of a great circle of the earth | |

**Dry Measure**

| | | | |
|---|---|---|---|
| 1 pint | | = 33.60 cubic inches | = 0.5505 liter |
| 2 pints | = 1 quart | = 67.20 cubic inches | = 1.1012 liters |
| 8 quarts | = 1 peck | = 537.61 cubic inches | = 8.8096 liters |
| 4 pecks | = 1 bushel | = 2,150.42 cuibc inches | = 35.2383 liters |

1 British dry quart = 1.032 U.S. dry quarts.

According to United States government standards, the following are the weights avoirdupois for single bushels of the specified grains: for wheat, 60 pounds; for barley, 48 pounds; for oats, 32 pounds; for rye, 56 pounds; for corn, 56 pounds. Some States have specifications varying from these.

**Liquid Measure**

| | | | |
|---|---|---|---|
| 1 gill | = 4 fluid ounces (see next table) | = 7.219 cubic inches | = 0.1183 liter |
| 4 gills | = 1 pint | = 28.875 cubic inches | = 0.4732 liter |
| 2 pints | = 1 quart | = 57.75 cubic inches | = 0.9463 liter |
| 4 quarts | = 1 gallon | = 231 cubic inches | = 3.7853 liters |

The British imperial gallon (4 imperial quarts) = 277.42 cubic inches = 4.546 liters. The barrel in Great Britain equals 36 imperial gallons, in the United States, usually 31½ gallons.

**Apothecaries' Fluid Measure**

| | | | |
|---|---|---|---|
| 1 minim | | = 0.0038 cubic inch | = 0.0616 milliliter |
| 60 minims | = 1 fluid dram | = 0.2256 cubic inch | = 3.6966 milliliters |
| 8 fluid drams | = 1 fluid ounce | = 1.8047 cubic inches | = 0.0296 liter |
| 16 fluid ounces | = 1 pint | = 28.875 cubic inches | = 0.4732 liter |

See table immediately preceding for quart and gallon equivalents.
The British pint = 20 fluid ounces.

**Circular (or Angular) Measure**

| | |
|---|---|
| 60 seconds (″) | = 1 minute (′) |
| 60 minutes | = 1 degree (°) |
| 90 degrees | = 1 quadrant or 1 right angle |
| 4 quadrants or 360 degrees | = 1 circle |

### Avoirdupois Weight

(The grain, equal to 0.0648 gram, is the same in all three tables of weight)

| | | | | |
|---|---|---|---|---|
| 1 dram or 27.34 grains | | | = | 1.772 grams |
| 16 drams or 437.5 grains | = | 1 ounce | = | 28.3495 grams |
| 16 ounces or 7,000 grains | = | 1 pound | = | 453.59 grams |
| 100 pounds | = | 1 hundredweight | = | 45.36 kilograms |
| 2,000 pounds | = | 1 ton | = | 907.18 kilograms |

In Great Britain, 14 pounds (6.35 kilograms) = 1 stone, 112 pounds (50.80 kilograms) = 1 hundredweight, and 2,240 pounds (1,016.05 kilograms) = 1 long ton.

### Troy Weight

(The grain, equal to 0.0648 gram, is the same in all three tables of weight)

| | | | | |
|---|---|---|---|---|
| 3.086 grains | = | 1 carat | = | 200 milligrams |
| 24 grains | = | 1 pennyweight | = | 1.5552 grams |
| 20 pennyweights or 480 grains | = | 1 ounce | = | 31.1035 grams |
| 12 ounces or 5,760 grains | = | 1 pound | = | 373.24 grams |

### Apothecaries' Weight

(The grain, equal to 0.0648 gram, is the same in all three tables of weight)

| | | | | |
|---|---|---|---|---|
| 20 grains | = | 1 scruple | = | 1.296 grams |
| 3 scruples | = | 1 dram | = | 3.888 grams |
| 8 drams or 480 grains | = | 1 ounce | = | 31.1035 grams |
| 12 ounces or 5,760 grains | = | 1 pound | = | 373.24 grams |

## THE METRIC SYSTEM

### Linear Measure

| | | | | |
|---|---|---|---|---|
| 10 millimeters | = | 1 centimeter | = | 0.3937 inch |
| 10 centimeters | = | 1 decimeter | = | 3.937 inches |
| 10 decimeters | = | 1 meter | = | 39.37 inches or 3.28 feet |
| 10 meters | = | 1 decameter | = | 393.7 inches |
| 10 decameters | = | 1 hectometer | = | 328 feet 1 inch |
| 10 hectometers | = | 1 kilometer | = | 0.621 mile |
| 10 kilometers | = | 1 myriameter | = | 6.21 miles |

### Square Measure

| | | | | |
|---|---|---|---|---|
| 100 square millimeters | = | 1 square centimeter | = | 0.15499 square inch |
| 100 square centimeters | = | 1 square decimeter | = | 15.499 square inches |
| 100 square decimeters | = | 1 square meter | = | 1,549.9 square inches or 1.196 square yards |
| 100 square meters | = | 1 square decameter | = | 119.6 square yards |
| 100 square decameters | = | 1 square hectometer | = | 2.471 acres |
| 100 square hectometers | = | 1 square kilometer | = | 0.386 square mile |

### Land Measure

| | | | | |
|---|---|---|---|---|
| 1 square meter | = | 1 centiare | = | 1,549.9 square inches |
| 100 centiares | = | 1 are | = | 119.6 square yards |
| 100 ares | = | 1 hectare | = | 2.471 acres |
| 100 hectares | = | 1 square kilometer | = | 0.386 square mile |

### Volume Measure

| | | | | |
|---|---|---|---|---|
| 1,000 cubic millimeters | = | 1 cubic centimeter | = | .06102 cubic inch |
| 1,000 cubic centimeters | = | 1 cubic decimeter | = | 61.02 cubic inches |
| 1,000 cubic decimeters | = | 1 cubic meter (the unit is called a *stere* in measuring firewood) | = | 35.314 cubic feet |

### Capacity Measure

| | | | | |
|---|---|---|---|---|
| 10 milliliters | = | 1 centiliter | = | .338 fluid ounce |
| 10 centiliters | = | 1 deciliter | = | 3.38 fluid ounces |
| 10 deciliters | = | 1 liter | = | 1.0567 liquid quarts or 0.9081 dry quart |
| 10 liters | = | 1 decaliter | = | 2.64 gallons or 0.284 bushel |
| 10 decaliters | = | 1 hectoliter | = | 26.418 gallons or 2.838 bushels |
| 10 hectoliters | = | 1 kiloliter | = | 264.18 gallons or 35.315 cubic feet |

### Weights

| | | | | |
|---|---|---|---|---|
| 10 milligrams | = | 1 centigram | = | 0.1543 grain |
| 10 centigrams | = | 1 decigram | = | 1.5432 grains |
| 10 decigrams | = | 1 gram | = | 15.432 grains |
| 10 grams | = | 1 decagram | = | 0.3527 ounce |
| 10 decagrams | = | 1 hectogram | = | 3.5274 ounces |
| 10 hectograms | = | 1 kilogram | = | 2.2046 pounds |
| 10 kilograms | = | 1 myriagram | = | 22.046 pounds |
| 10 myriagrams | = | 1 quintal | = | 220.46 pounds |
| 10 quintals | = | 1 metric ton | = | 2,204.6 pounds |

# STATES OF THE UNITED STATES

**Al·a·bam·a** (al′ə-bam′ə), southeast, on Gulf of Mexico: admitted, 1819; 51,609 sq. mi.; pop. 3,444,000; cap. Montgomery.

**A·las·ka** (ə-las′kə), northwest, on the Pacific: admitted, 1959; 586,400 sq. mi.; pop. 302,000; cap. Juneau.

**Ar·i·zo·na** (ar′ə-zō′nə), southwest, on Mexican border: admitted, 1912; 113,909 sq. mi.; pop. 1,772,000; cap. Phoenix.

**Ar·kan·sas** (är′kən-sô′), west south central: admitted, 1836; 53,104 sq. mi.; pop. 1,923,000; cap. Little Rock.

**Cal·i·for·ni·a** (kal′ə-fôr′nyə), southwest, on the Pacific: admitted, 1850; 158,693 sq. mi.; pop. 19,953,000; cap. Sacramento.

**Col·o·rad·o** (kol′ə-rad′o), west, in the Rockies: admitted, 1876; 104,247 sq. mi.; pop. 2,207,000; cap. Denver.

***Con·nect·i·cut** (kə-net′i-kət), northeast, on the Atlantic: 5,009 sq. mi.; pop. 3,032,000; cap. Hartford.

***Del·a·ware** (del′ə-war′), east, on the Atlantic: 2,057 sq. mi.; pop. 548,000; cap. Dover.

**District of Co·lum·bi·a** (kə-lum′bi-ə), east, surrounded by Maryland and Virginia: 69 sq. mi.; pop. 757,000.

**Flor·i·da** (flôr′i-də), southeast, on the Atlantic: admitted, 1845; 58,560 sq. mi.; pop. 6,789,000; cap. Tallahassee.

***Geor·gia** (jôr′jə), southeast, on the Atlantic: 58,876 sq. mi.; pop. 4,590,000; cap. Atlanta.

**Ha·wai·i** (hə-wä′ē), west, in the Pacific: admitted, 1959; 6,424 sq. mi.; pop. 769,000; cap. Honolulu.

**I·da·ho** (ī′də-hō′), northwest, on Canadian border: admitted, 1890; 83,557 sq. mi.; pop. 713,000; cap. Boise.

**Il·li·nois** (il′ə-noi′), east north central: admitted, 1818; 56,400 sq. mi.; pop. 11,114,000; cap. Springfield.

**In·di·an·a** (in′di-an′ə), east north central: admitted, 1816; 36,291 sq. mi.; pop. 5,194,000; cap. Indianapolis.

**I·o·wa** (ī′ə-wə), west north central: admitted, 1846; 56,290 sq. mi.; pop. 2,825,000; cap. Des Moines.

**Kan·sas** (kan′zəs), west north central: admitted, 1861; 82,264 sq. mi.; pop. 2,249,000; cap. Topeka.

**Ken·tuck·y** (kən-tuk′i), east south central: admitted, 1792; 40,395 sq. mi.; pop. 3,219,000; cap. Frankfort.

**Lou·i·si·an·a** (loo͞′i-zi-an′ə), south, on the Gulf of Mexico: admitted, 1812; 48,523 sq. mi.; pop. 3,643,000; cap. Baton Rouge.

**Maine** (mān), northeast, on the Atlantic: admitted, 1820; 33,215 sq. mi.; pop. 992,000; cap. Augusta.

***Mar·y·land** (mâr′i-lənd), east, on the Atlantic: 10,577 sq. mi.; pop. 3,922,000; cap. Annapolis.

***Mas·sa·chu·setts** (mas′ə-cho͞o′sits), northeast, on the Atlantic: 8,257 sq. mi.; pop. 5,689,000; cap. Boston.

**Mich·i·gan** (mish′ə-gən), east north central: admitted, 1837; 58,216 sq. mi.; pop. 8,875,000; cap. Lansing.

**Min·ne·so·ta** (min′i-sō′tə), west north central, on Canadian border: admitted, 1858; 84,068 sq. mi.; pop. 3,805,000; cap. St. Paul.

**Mis·sis·sip·pi** (mis′ə-sip′i), south: admitted, 1817; 47,716 sq. mi.; pop. 2,217,000; cap. Jackson.

**Mis·sour·i** (mi-zoor′i), west north central: admitted, 1821; 69,686 sq. mi.; pop. 4,677,000; cap. Jefferson City.

**Mon·tan·a** (mon-tan′ə), northwest, on Canadian border: admitted, 1889; 147,138 sq. mi.; pop. 694,000; cap. Helena.

**Ne·bras·ka** (nə-bras′kə), west north central: admitted, 1867; 77,227 sq. mi.; pop. 1,484,000; cap. Lincoln.

**Ne·vad·a** (nə-vad′ə), southwest: admitted, 1864; 110,540 sq. mi.; pop. 489,000; cap. Carson City.

***New Hamp·shire** (hamp′shir), northeast, on the Atlantic: 9,304 sq. mi.; pop. 738,000; cap. Concord.

***New Jer·sey** (jũr′zi), east, on the Atlantic: 7,836 sq. mi.; pop. 7,168,000; cap. Trenton.

**New Mex·i·co** (mek′si-kō′), southwest, on Mexican border: admitted, 1912; 121,666 sq. mi.; pop. 1,016,000; cap. Santa Fe.

***New York** (yôrk), east, on the Atlantic: 49,576 sq. mi.; pop. 18,191,000; cap. Albany.

***North Car·o·li·na** (kar′ə-lī′nə), southeast, on the Atlantic: 52,712 sq. mi.; pop. 5,082,000; cap. Raleigh.

**North Da·ko·ta** (də-kō′tə), west north central, on Canadian border: admitted, 1889; 70,665 sq. mi.; pop. 618,000; cap. Bismarck.

**O·hi·o** (ō-hī′ō), east north central: admitted, 1803; 41,222 sq. mi.; pop. 10,652,000; cap. Columbus.

**O·kla·ho·ma** (ō′klə-hō′mə), west south central: admitted, 1907; 69,919 sq. mi.; pop. 2,559,000; cap. Oklahoma City.

**Or·e·gon** (ôr′i-gon′), west, on the Pacific: admitted, 1859; 96,981 sq. mi.; pop. 2,091,000; cap. Salem.

***Penn·syl·va·ni·a** (pen′s′l-vān′yə), east: 45,333 sq. mi.; pop. 11,794,000; cap. Harrisburg.

***Rhode Is·land** (rōd ī′lənd), northeast, on the Atlantic: 1,214 sq. mi.; pop. 950,000; cap. Providence.

***South Carolina**, southeast, on the Atlantic: 31,055 sq. mi.; pop. 2,591,000; cap. Columbia.

**South Dakota**, west north central: admitted, 1889; 77,047 sq. mi.; pop. 666,000; cap. Pierre.

**Ten·nes·see** (ten′ə-sē′), east south central: admitted, 1796; 42,244 sq. mi.; pop. 3,924,000; cap. Nashville.

**Tex·as** (tek′səs), west south central, on Mexican border: admitted, 1845; 267,339 sq. mi.; pop. 11,197,000; cap. Austin.

**U·tah** (ū′tô), west: admitted, 1896; 84,916 sq. mi.: pop. 1,059,000; cap. Salt Lake City.

**Ver·mont** (vẽr-mont′), northeast, on Canadian border: admitted, 1791; 9,609 sq. mi.; pop. 444,000; cap. Montpelier.

***Vir·gin·ia** (vẽr-jin′yə), east, on the Atlantic: 40,815 sq. mi.; pop. 4,648,000; cap. Richmond.

**Wash·ing·ton** (wôsh′iŋ-tən), northwest, on the Pacific: admitted, 1889; 68,192 sq. mi.; pop. 3,409,000; cap. Olympia.

**West Virginia**, east: admitted, 1863; 24,181 sq. mi.; pop. 1,744,000; cap. Charleston.

**Wis·con·sin** (wis-kon′s′n), east north central: admitted, 1848; 56,154 sq. mi.; pop. 4,418,000; cap. Madison.

**Wy·o·ming** (wī-ō′miŋ), west: admitted, 1890; 97,914 sq. mi.; pop. 332,000; cap. Cheyenne.

---

*One of the 13 original States when the Constitution was ratified, 1787-88.

# POSSESSIONS OF THE UNITED STATES

**(Populations are the 1970 Census preliminary figures)**

**American Sa·mo·a** (sə-mō′ə), territory consisting of seven islands in the South Pacific, north of Tonga: 76 sq. mi.; pop. 27,769; cap. Pago Pago.

**Canal Zone**, leasehold in Panama, consisting of a strip of land on either side of the Panama Canal: 362 sq. mi.; pop. 44,650.

**Guam** (gwäm), island territory occupying the largest of the Mariana Islands in the western Pacific: 209 sq. mi.; pop. 86,926; cap. Agaña.

**Pacific Islands**, trust territory in the western Pacific, consisting of the Caroline, Marshall, and Mariana islands: 700 sq. mi.; pop. 98,009 (1969 est.)

**Puer·to Ri·co** (pwer′tə rē′kō), island commonwealth in the West Indies, east of Hispaniola: 3,421 sq. mi.; pop. 2,689,932; cap. San Juan.

**Virgin Islands**, territory consisting of a group of islands in the West Indies, east of Puerto Rico: 132 sq. mi.; pop. 63,200; cap. Charlotte Amalie.

# THE LARGEST CITIES IN THE UNITED STATES

| City | Population |
|---|---|
| New York, N.Y. | 7,867,760 |
| Chicago, Ill. | 3,366,957 |
| Los Angeles, Cal. | 2,816,061 |
| Philadelphia, Pa. | 1,948,609 |
| Detroit, Mich. | 1,511,482 |
| Houston, Tex. | 1,232,802 |
| Baltimore, Md. | 905,759 |
| Dallas, Tex. | 844,401 |
| Cleveland, O. | 750,903 |
| Indianapolis, Ind. | 744,624 |
| Milwaukee, Wis. | 717,099 |
| San Francisco, Cal. | 715,674 |
| San Diego, Cal. | 696,769 |
| San Antonio, Tex. | 654,153 |
| Boston, Mass. | 641,071 |
| Memphis, Tenn. | 623,530 |
| St. Louis, Mo. | 622,236 |
| New Orleans, La. | 593,471 |
| Phoenix, Ariz. | 581,562 |
| Columbus, O. | 539,677 |
| Seattle, Wash. | 530,831 |
| Jacksonville, Fla. | 528,865 |
| Pittsburgh, Pa. | 520,117 |
| Denver, Colo. | 514,678 |
| Kansas City, Mo. | 507,087 |
| Atlanta, Ga. | 496,973 |
| Buffalo, N.Y. | 462,768 |
| Cincinnati, O. | 452,524 |
| Nashville, Tenn. | 447,877 |
| San Jose, Cal. | 445,779 |
| Minneapolis, Minn. | 434,400 |
| Fort Worth, Tex. | 393,476 |
| Toledo, O. | 383,818 |
| Portland, Oreg. | 382,619 |
| Newark, N.J. | 382,417 |
| Oklahoma City, Okla. | 366,481 |
| Oakland, Cal. | 361,561 |
| Louisville, Ky. | 361,472 |
| Long Beach, Cal. | 358,633 |
| Omaha, Nebr. | 347,328 |
| Miami, Fla. | 334,859 |
| Tulsa, Okla. | 331,638 |
| Honolulu, Hawaii | 324,871 |
| El Paso, Tex. | 322,261 |
| St. Paul, Minn. | 309,980 |
| Norfolk, Va. | 307,951 |
| Birmingham, Ala. | 300,910 |
| Rochester, N.Y. | 296,233 |
| Tampa, Fla. | 277,767 |
| Wichita, Kans. | 276,554 |
| Akron, O. | 275,425 |
| Tucson, Ariz. | 262,933 |
| Jersey City, N.J. | 260,545 |
| Sacramento, Cal. | 254,413 |
| Austin, Tex. | 251,808 |
| Richmond, Va. | 249,621 |
| Albuquerque, N. Mex. | 243,751 |
| Dayton, O. | 243,601 |
| Charlotte, N.C. | 241,178 |
| St. Petersburg, Fla. | 216,232 |
| Corpus Christi, Tex. | 204,525 |
| Yonkers, N.Y. | 204,370 |
| Des Moines, Ia. | 200,587 |
| Grand Rapids, Mich. | 197,649 |
| Syracuse, N.Y. | 197,208 |
| Flint, Mich. | 193,317 |
| Mobile, Ala. | 190,026 |
| Shreveport, La. | 182,064 |
| Warren, Mich. | 179,260 |
| Providence, R.I. | 179,213 |
| Fort Wayne, Ind. | 177,671 |
| Worcester, Mass. | 176,572 |
| Salt Lake City, Ut. | 175,885 |
| Gary, Ind. | 175,415 |
| Knoxville, Tenn. | 174,587 |
| Arlington, Va. | 174,284 |
| Madison, Wis. | 173,258 |
| Virginia Beach, Va. | 172,106 |
| Spokane, Wash. | 170,516 |
| Kansas City, Kans. | 168,213 |
| Anaheim, Cal. | 166,701 |
| Fresno, Cal. | 165,972 |
| Baton Rouge, La. | 165,963 |
| Springfield, Mass. | 163,905 |
| Hartford, Conn. | 158,017 |
| Santa Ana, Cal. | 156,601 |
| Bridgeport, Conn. | 156,542 |
| Tacoma, Wash. | 154,581 |
| Columbus, Ga. | 154,168 |
| Jackson, Miss. | 153,968 |
| Lincoln, Nebr. | 149,518 |
| Lubbock, Tex. | 149,101 |
| Rockford, Ill. | 147,370 |
| Paterson, N.J. | 144,824 |
| Greensboro, N.C. | 144,076 |
| Riverside, Cal. | 140,089 |
| Youngstown, O. | 139,788 |
| Fort Lauderdale, Fla. | 139,590 |
| Evansville, Ind. | 138,764 |
| Newport News, Va. | 138,177 |
| Huntsville, Ala. | 137,802 |
| New Haven, Conn. | 137,707 |
| Metairie, La. | 135,816 |
| Colorado Springs, Colo. | 135,060 |
| Torrance, Cal. | 134,584 |
| Montgomery, Ala. | 133,386 |
| Winston-Salem, N.C. | 132,913 |
| Glendale, Cal. | 132,752 |
| Little Rock, Ark. | 132,483 |
| Lansing, Mich. | 131,546 |
| Erie, Pa. | 129,231 |
| Amarillo, Tex. | 127,010 |
| Peoria, Ill. | 126,963 |
| Las Vegas, Nev. | 125,787 |
| South Bend, Ind. | 125,580 |
| Topeka, Kans. | 125,011 |
| Garden Grove, Cal. | 122,524 |
| Macon, Ga. | 122,423 |
| Raleigh, N.C. | 121,577 |
| Hampton, Va. | 120,779 |
| Springfield, Mo. | 120,096 |
| Chattanooga, Tenn. | 119,082 |
| Savannah, Ga. | 118,349 |
| Berkeley, Cal. | 116,716 |
| Huntington Beach, Cal. | 115,960 |
| Beaumont, Tex. | 115,919 |
| Albany, N.Y. | 114,873 |
| Columbia, S.C. | 113,542 |
| Pasadena, Cal. | 113,327 |
| Elizabeth, N.J. | 112,654 |
| Independence, Mo. | 111,662 |
| Portsmouth, Va. | 110,963 |
| Alexandria, Va. | 110,938 |
| Cedar Rapids, Ia. | 110,642 |
| Livonia, Mich. | 110,109 |
| Canton, O. | 110,053 |
| Allentown, Pa. | 109,527 |
| Stamford, Conn. | 108,798 |
| Lexington, Ky. | 108,137 |
| Waterbury, Conn. | 108,033 |

# PRINCIPAL FOREIGN CITIES

| City | Population |
|---|---|
| Adelaide, Australia | *736,900 |
| Ahmedabad, India | 1,149,918 |
| Alexandria, UAR | 1,513,000 |
| Algiers, Algeria | 943,000 |
| Alma-Ata, USSR | 673,000 |
| Amsterdam, Netherlands | 857,635 |
| Ankara, Turkey | 905,700 |
| Anshan, China | 2,500,000 |
| Athens, Greece | *1,852,709 |
| Baghdad, Iraq | 1,745,328 |
| Baku, USSR | 1,224,000 |
| Bandung, Indonesia | 972,566 |
| Bangalore, India | 905,134 |
| Bangkok, Thailand | 2,040,000 |
| Barcelona, Spain | 1,697,102 |
| Belo Horizonte, Brazil | 693,328 |
| Berlin, East, E. Germany | 1,082,019 |
| Berlin, West, W. Germany | 2,163,306 |
| Birmingham, England | 1,074,940 |
| Bogotá, Colombia | *2,148,387 |
| Bombay, India | 4,152,056 |
| Brisbane, Australia | *719,140 |
| Brussels, Belgium | *1,079,181 |
| Bucureşti, Romania | 1,414,643 |
| Budapest, Hungary | 1,928,000 |
| Buenos Aires, Argentina | 2,966,816 |
| Cairo, UAR | 3,346,000 |
| Calcutta, India | 2,927,289 |
| Caracas, Venezuela | *2,000,000 |
| Casablanca, Morocco | 1,180,000 |
| Changchun, China | 1,150,000 |
| Changsha, China | 709,000 |
| Chelyabinsk, USSR | 851,000 |
| Chengtu, China | 1,135,000 |
| Chichihaerh, China | 704,000 |
| Chungking, China | 4,070,000 |
| Cologne, W. Germany | 854,482 |
| Copenhagen, Denmark | *1,377,605 |
| Delhi, India | 2,061,758 |
| Dnepropetrovsk, USSR | 837,000 |
| Donetsk, USSR | 855,000 |
| Durban, South Africa | 662,894 |
| Düsseldorf, W. Germany | 688,503 |
| Essen, W. Germany | 705,203 |
| Frankfurt, W. Germany | 662,351 |
| Fukuoka, Japan | 750,000 |
| Fushun, China | 1,019,000 |
| Genoa, Italy | 844,499 |
| Glasgow, Scotland | 960,527 |
| Gorky, USSR | 1,139,000 |
| Guadalajara, Mexico | 1,352,100 |
| Guayaquil, Ecuador | 680,209 |
| Hamburg, W. Germany | 1,832,560 |
| Hangchow, China | 794,000 |
| Harbin, China | 1,800,000 |
| Havana, Cuba | 787,765 |
| Huhehot, China | 860,000 |
| Hyderabad, India | 1,118,553 |
| Istanbul, Turkey | 1,743,000 |
| Jakarta, Indonesia | 4,500,000 |
| Johannesburg, South Africa | 1,294,800 |
| Kanpur, India | 895,106 |
| Karachi, Pakistan | 1,912,598 |
| Kawasaki, Japan | 855,000 |
| Kazan, USSR | 837,000 |
| Kharkov, USSR | 1,148,000 |
| Kiev, USSR | 1,476,000 |
| Kinshasa, Congo (Kinshasa) | 1,225,720 |
| Kitakyushu, Japan | 1,042,000 |
| Kobe, Japan | 1,217,000 |
| Kowloon, Hong Kong | 726,976 |
| Kuibyshev, USSR | 1,014,000 |
| Kunming, China | 730,000 |
| Kwangchow, China | 2,200,000 |
| Kyoto, Japan | 1,365,000 |
| Lahore, Pakistan | 1,296,477 |
| Lanchow, China | 699,000 |
| Leningrad, USSR | 3,752,000 |
| Lima, Peru | 1,795,100 |
| Lisbon, Portugal | 802,230 |
| Liverpool, England | 688,010 |
| Łódz, Poland | 749,000 |
| London, England | 3,200,484 |
| Lüta, China | 3,000,000 |
| Madras, India | 1,729,141 |
| Madrid, Spain | 2,866,728 |
| Manila, Philippines | 1,300,000 |
| Marseille, France | 889,029 |
| Medellín, Colombia | 912,982 |
| Melbourne, Australia | *2,108,499 |
| Mexico City, Mexico | 3,484,000 |
| Milan, Italy | 1,683,680 |
| Minsk, USSR | 818,000 |
| Monterrey, Mexico | 1,011,900 |
| Montevideo, Uruguay | 1,280,000 |
| Montreal, Canada | 1,222,255 |
| Moscow, USSR | 6,590,000 |
| Munich, W. Germany | 1,244,237 |
| Nagoya, Japan | 1,935,000 |
| Nanking, China | 2,700,000 |
| Naples, Italy | 1,263,358 |
| Novosibirsk, USSR | 1,079,000 |
| Odessa, USSR | 797,000 |
| Omsk, USSR | 800,000 |
| Osaka, Japan | 3,156,222 |
| Paotou, China | 1,500,000 |
| Paris, France | 2,590,771 |
| Peking, China | 4,000,000 |
| Perm, USSR | 811,000 |
| Prague, Czechoslovakia | 1,030,000 |
| Pusan, S. Korea | 1,429,726 |
| Pyongyang, N. Korea | 940,000 |
| Rangoon, Burma | 1,616,948 |
| Recife, Brazil | 797,234 |
| Riga, USSR | 694,000 |
| Rio de Janeiro, Brazil | 3,307,163 |
| Rome, Italy | 2,630,535 |
| Rosario, Argentina | 672,000 |
| Rostov, USSR | 773,000 |
| Rotterdam, Netherlands | 710,871 |
| Saigon, S. Vietnam | *2,000,000 |
| Santiago, Chile | 1,169,481 |
| São Paulo, Brazil | 3,825,351 |
| Sapporo, Japan | 821,000 |
| Saratov, USSR | 737,000 |
| Seoul, S. Korea | 3,805,261 |
| Shanghai, China | 10,000,000 |
| Shenyang, China | 2,423,000 |
| Shihchiachuang, China | 1,118,000 |
| Sian, China | 1,500,000 |
| Singapore, Singapore | 1,150,000 |
| Sofia, Bulgaria | 859,000 |
| Stockholm, Sweden | 767,606 |
| Suchow, China | 710,000 |
| Surabaya, Indonesia | 1,007,945 |
| Sverdlovsk, USSR | 981,000 |
| Sydney, Australia | *2,444,735 |
| Taegu, S. Korea | 847,494 |
| Taipei, China (Taiwan) | 1,221,112 |
| Taiyüan, China | 1,500,000 |
| Tangshan, China | 812,000 |
| Tashkent, USSR | 1,324,000 |
| Tbilisi, USSR | 866,000 |
| Teherán, Iran | 2,803,130 |
| Tientsin, China | 3,278,000 |
| Tokyo, Japan | 8,893,000 |
| Toronto, Canada | 672,000 |
| Tsinan, China | 882,000 |
| Tsingtao, China | 1,144,000 |
| Tunis, Tunisia | *764,000 |
| Turin, Italy | 1,131,621 |
| Tzupo, China | 875,000 |
| Ufa, USSR | 723,000 |
| Victoria, Hong Kong | *2,800,000 |
| Vienna, Austria | *1,640,106 |
| Volgograd, USSR | 756,000 |
| Warsaw, Poland | 1,283,000 |
| Wuhan, China | 2,500,000 |
| Yerevan, USSR | 698,000 |
| Yokohama, Japan | 1,789,000 |

*population is of metropolitan area (only figure available)

# PUNCTUATION

The usages for the marks of punctuation, italics, and capital letters given here are those generally observed by Americans today. The following is a practical, concise treatment of the most important usages. Practice in punctuation often differs in particulars among writers, publishing houses, etc., but the modern trend generally is toward simplification.

## PERIOD

The period (.) is used:
1) to mark the end of a sentence;
   *Ex.*: The sun has set.
2) after most abbreviations;
   *Ex.*: Colloq. Mr. U.S.
3) as one of a series (usually three) to indicate missing material or a break in continuity;
   *Ex.*: "I pledge allegiance to the flag . . . and to the Republic . . ."

## COMMA

The comma (,) is used:
1) between independent clauses of equal value that are short and have no commas within them;
   *Ex.*: He worked hard, he saved his money, and he bought a house.
2) between two independent clauses joined by coordinating or correlative conjunctions;
   *Ex.*: We went to the party, but Ralph wasn't there. Either the fuel pump is broken, or we are out of gas.
3) after a dependent clause, usually a fairly long one, that precedes an independent clause;
   *Ex.*: When it became apparent that they would not co-operate, we stopped all negotiations.
4) before and after a dependent clause that comes in the middle of a sentence;
   *Ex.*: The apples, although they had been freshly picked, became spoiled in shipment.
5) to set off a nonrestrictive, as distinguished from a restrictive, clause, phrase, or word;
   *Ex.*: Dick, who is my brother, is not in town. (But *not* in: The boy who is my brother is sitting on the left.) The President lives in the White House, in Washington. (But *not* in: Many buildings in Washington house government offices.) The planet on which we live, Earth, is between Venus and Mars. (But *not* in: The planet Earth is between Venus and Mars.)
6) after a phrase that begins a sentence, especially for rhetorical effect;
   *Ex.*: From this balcony, he spoke to the crowd.
7) to set off conjunctive adverbs, such as *however*, *moreover*, etc., or short transitional phrases;
   *Ex.*: We are pleased with your suggestion; moreover, we intend to put it into effect.
8) to separate clauses, phrases, or words in a series;
   *Ex.*: Find out who he is, what he wants, and where he comes from. I proceeded up the stairs, down the hall, and into the office. Ann, Lois, or Jane will be chosen.
9) after terms (e.g., i.e., namely) that introduce a series or example;
   *Ex.*: Some of our presidents, e.g., Jefferson, J. Q. Adams, and Buchanan, had previously been secretaries of state.
10) to set off a parenthetical clause, phrase, or word;
   *Ex.*: By the end of the month, when the bill is due, I will have the money. The family, along with the servants, has left for the summer. Come, please, and bring your wife and children.
11) between two adjectives which modify the same substantive and can be interchanged in position;
   *Ex.*: a large, modern building.
12) to indicate omitted material;
   *Ex.*: The infant becomes a child; the child, an adolescent; and the adolescent, an adult.
13) to set off the one spoken to in direct address;
   *Ex.*: "Go, Dick, and shut the window."
   "Yes, sir, I'm going."
14) to set off direct quotation;
   *Ex.*: He said, "Keep to the right." "Thank you," we replied.
15) to set off titles, addresses, names of places, etc.;
   *Ex.*: R. T. Fisher, Ph.D., Secretary, 110 Elm Street, Akron 6, Ohio, handles all correspondence for the society. He traveled from the Black Forest, Germany, to Paris, France, by bicycle.
16) before, and sometimes after, the year in dates;
   *Ex.*: Lincoln was born on February 12, 1809, in a log cabin.
17) after the salutation of a personal letter;
   *Ex.*: Dear Max and Alice,
18) after the complimentary close of letters;
   *Ex.*: Very truly yours, Peter B. Stewart
19) to separate thousands in numbers of one thousand or over;
   *Ex.*: The area of the earth is approximately 196,950,000 sq. mi.
20) to separate inverted names, phrases, etc., as in a bibliography, index, or catalogue;
   *Ex.*: Jones, Harold T.
   Persia, architecture of
   radios, portable

## SEMICOLON

The semicolon (;) is used:
1) in compound sentences between independent clauses not joined by connectives, especially if they are extended or have commas within them;
   *Ex.*: The problems of adequately financing and endowing an institution of higher learning have become increasingly difficult; specialists in investing and handling money are needed to assure that the wisest use is made of the funds.
   Detroit, on one side of the river, is in the U.S.; Windsor, on the other side, is in Canada.
2) in compound sentences between independent clauses joined by conjunctive adverbs;
   *Ex.*: We are pleased with your suggestion; moreover, we intend to put it into effect.
3) in a series where further division than that given by commas is needed;
   *Ex.*: The contestants came from Albany, New York; Seattle, Washington; and London, England.

## COLON

The colon(:) is used:
1) to introduce a series;
   *Ex.*: The following materials will be needed: pencil, pen, eraser, ruler, and notebook.
2) to introduce a part of a sentence that exemplifies, restates, or explains the preceding part;
   *Ex.*: Some of the greatest creative artists never became wealthy during their lifetime: Mozart died a very poor man and was buried in a pauper's grave.
3) before an extended quotation;
   *Ex.*: Lincoln arose and spoke as follows: "Fourscore and seven years ago . . ."
4) between the chapter and verse numbers in Biblical refernces;
   *Ex.*: The story of Noah begins in Gen. 5:28.
5) between the volume and page numbers in references;
   *Ex.*: The article is found in *U.S. Encyclopedia* 34:1747.
6) after the salutation of a business letter;
   *Ex.*: Dear Sir:
7) to separate the hours from the minutes in expressions of time;
   *Ex.*: The train will depart at 10:47 P.M.
8) to separate the parts of a ratio;
   *Ex.*: The birth rate and the mortality rate for this region are in the ratio 17:14.

### INTERROGATION (or QUESTION) MARK

The interrogation mark (?) is used:
1) after a direct question;
   *Ex.*: Who is the chairman?
2) to express doubt or uncertainty;
   *Ex.*: Socrates lived 470(?)-399 B.C. Saint Peter lived ?-76 A.D.

### EXCLAMATION MARK

The exclamation mark (!) is used after an exclamatory word, phrase, or sentence, to indicate surprise, strong emotion, etc.;
   *Ex.*: Ouch! That hurt!

### HYPHEN

The hyphen (-) is used:
1) to separate the parts of a compound word;
   *Ex.*: co-operate, re-cover, Pre-Cambrian, anti-Fascist, reddish-brown, foot-pound.
2) to indicate syllabification, as at the end of a line.

### DASH

The dash (—) is used:
1) to show a break in continuity or thought in a sentence;
   *Ex.*: Give it to John—I mean, to George.
2) before and after parenthetical material that is a result of a break in thought or continuity;
   *Ex.*: I wrote a letter—and what a chore it was —to my lawyer concerning the problem.
3) between numbers, dates, times, places, etc. that mark limits;
   *Ex.*: You will find it on pages 89–104. Franklin lived 1706–1790. The hotel is open June–September. The office hours are 8:00–5:00 daily. He will arrive on the New York–Chicago express.
4) to indicate the omission of letters, numbers, etc.;
   *Ex.*: Don't tell Mr. B—.
   One dark winter night in 18— two men were having dinner together.
5) before the citation of the author or source of a quotation, etc.;
   *Ex.*: "Every dog has his day."—Cervantes.
   "Great men are not always wise."—Job 32:9.

### QUOTATION MARKS

Double quotation marks (" ") are used:
1) to enclose a direct quotation;
   *Ex.*: I replied, "I will try to help them."
2) in general, to enclose the titles of divisions, parts, chapters, etc. of books, periodicals, etc. Titles of plays, operas, and other works of art are either set off by quotation marks or italicized. Cf. **italics**, 2;
   *Ex.*: I have just read "The Gold Bug" by Poe. "The Knight's Tale" is one of *The Canterbury Tales.* The motion picture "The Informer" was directed by John Ford.
3) to enclose words out of the grammatical context of the sentence;
   *Ex.*: The word silly originally meant "happy"; now it means "foolish."
4) to enclose terms that are technical, esoteric, ironical, humorous, coined, slang, etc.;
   *Ex.*: The cloud mass was "fracto-cumulus." Isn't it "considerate" of him to make us wait like this? He's not a "square," he's "hep."

Single quotation marks (' ') are used to enclose a direct quotation within other quoted material;
   *Ex.*: The teacher said, "William Hazlitt's dying words were 'It was a happy life.' "

N.B. Commas and periods are usually placed inside quotation marks;
   *Ex.*: "I am seven," he said. The answer was "No."
   Colons and semicolons are placed outside quotation marks;
   *Ex.*: Answer these questions on the "Gettysburg Address": In what year was it given? What was the occasion? How was it received?
   I had not read Francis Bacon's essay "Of Truth"; in fact, I had never heard of it.
   An interrogation mark or exclamation mark is placed outside or inside quotation marks according to whether it applies to the entire sentence or just to part of it.
   *Ex.*: "What did you say?" he repeated. Did I hear you say, "It's snowing"? "Never!" she exclaimed. You had better not call me "yellow"!

### APOSTROPHE

The apostrophe (') is used:
1) to indicate an omitted letter or letters in a word or contraction;
   *Ex.*: He is the sec'y of the club. He'll attend if he's in town.
2) with an added *s* to form the possessive of all nouns that do not end in an *s* or *z* sound;
   *Ex.*: Sam's, Edgar's, men's, children's
3) with an added *s* to form the possessive of monosyllabic, singular nouns that end in an *s* or *z* sound and proper nouns ending in *-ce*;
   *Ex.*: lass's, Horace's
4) without an added *s* to form the possessive case of all nouns that end in an *s* or *z* sound except monosyllabic, singular forms and forms ending in *-ce*';
   *Ex.*: Moses', wolves', horses'
5) with an added *s* to indicate the possessive case of some pronouns;
   *Ex.*: It is everyone's duty to vote.
6) in forming the plural of letters, numbers, etc.;
   *Ex.*: He pronounced his *th*'s like *s*'s. She made her *l*'s look like 7's.

### PARENTHESES

Parentheses, ( ), are used:
1) to enclose nonessential material placed in a sentence as explanation or comment;
   *Ex.*: He ran 1500 meters (a little less than a mile).
2) to enclose letters or numbers of references as in an outline form;
   *Ex.*: The candidate spoke on three subjects: (1) better housing; (2) improved roads; (3) expanded recreation facilities.
   Sometimes only the closing parenthesis is used, as in this dictionary.
3) to enclose a mathematical expression that is to be considered as one quantity instead of having its individual components treated separately;
   *Ex.*: $(3 + 2)^2 = 25$.

N.B. Periods, commas, etc. are placed inside or outside parentheses depending on the part of the sentence to which they apply;
   *Ex.: Veni, vidi, vici.* (I came, I saw, I conquered.) I have many faults (as does everybody else).

### BRACKETS

Brackets, [ ], are used:
1) for the same purposes as parentheses; if parenthetical material falls within other parenthetical material, the brackets are used inside of the parentheses;
   *Ex.*: This is an excellent example of a dichotomy (a continued dividing [or subdividing] into opposed groups).
2) to enclose comments, corrections, insertions, etc. made by a person other than the author of the material;
   *Ex.*: "Acute anterior poliomyelitis [commonly called polio] is an acute inflammation of the gray matter of the spinal cord." "He was a friend of the nineteenth-century British statesman [Randolph] Churchill."

## ITALICS

Italicized type is used:

1) to indicate foreign words;
   *Ex.*: His motto was *omnia vincit amor*, which means "love conquers everything."
2) in general, to set off the titles of books, periodicals, newspapers, etc. Titles of plays, operas, and other works of art are either italicized or set off by quotation marks. Cf. **quotation marks**, 2;
   *Ex.*: *David Copperfield* is to some extent an autobiographical novel. Verdi's *Requiem* requires a large chorus.
3) to indicate words whose meaning is stressed;
   *Ex.*: Please do *not* use this door.
4) to indicate terms, letters, numbers, etc. used as words instead of for their meanings;
   *Ex.*: *Charry* means "like charcoal." The expression *to wit* is being used less frequently nowadays. He always forgets to dot his *j*'s. The key that types *3* is broken on this typewriter.

## CAPITALIZATION

A capital letter is used:

1) for the pronoun *I* and the interjection *O*.
2) as the initial letter of the first word in a sentence;
   *Ex.*: The books are on the shelves.
3) as the initial letter of the first word in quoted material falling within a sentence;
   *Ex.*: He called, "Wait a minute and I'll be with you."
4) as the initial letter of the first word in a direct question falling within a sentence;
   *Ex.*: This story answers the question, Where does true happiness really lie?
5) as the initial letter of the first word in a line of poetry or verse;
   *Ex.*: "All I could see from where I stood
   Was three long mountains and a wood;
   I turned and looked the other way,
   And saw three islands in a bay."
6) as the initial letter of every word in all proper nouns or names;
   *Ex.*: Ronald Jones, London, Germany, Maine, North America, Fifth Avenue, Pacific Ocean, Rocky Mountains, Titanic, *Atlantic Monthly*
7) as the initial letter of every word, except conjunctions, articles, and short prepositions that are not the first word, in the titles of works of literature, music, art, etc.;
   *Ex.*: *Twelfth Night*, *The Decline and Fall of the Roman Empire*, *The Magic Flute*, *Winged Victory*
8) as the initial letter of every word, except conjunctions, articles, and short prepositions, in the names (or derived adjectives, verbs, etc.) of organizations, institutions, businesses, agencies, movements, religions, holidays, etc. Sometimes the initial article is capitalized as part of the official name;
   *Ex.*: the Boy Scouts of America, The World Publishing Company, Internal Revenue Service, Humanism, Buddhism, Labor Day
9) as the initial letter of every word in the names of periods of time, as days, months, eras, etc.;
   *Ex.*: Thursday, June, Iron Age, Paleozoic Era
10) in most abbreviations;
    *Ex.*: B.C., A.D., M.P.
    Many abbreviations may be capitalized or not, according to personal preference;
    *Ex.*: A.M., a.m.; P.M., p.m.
11) as the initial letter of a symbol for a chemical element;
    *Ex.*: Au is the symbol for gold.
12) as the initial letter of every word in forms of address;
    *Ex.*: Your Excellency; Dear Bishop Hathaway; The Honorable Edwin Stanton.
13) as the initial letter of nouns and, often, pronouns referring to the Deity;
    *Ex.*: God is in His heaven.
14) as the initial letter of the names of gods and goddesses of polytheistic religions;
    *Ex.*: Isis, Zeus, Venus, Thor
15) as the initial letter in the names of all heavenly bodies;
    *Ex.*: Mars, Sirius, Big Dipper
    However, earth, sun, and moon are not capitalized except when cited along with other heavenly bodies;
    *Ex.*: The moon shines by means of light reflected from the sun. (But: Mercury is the planet closest to the Sun.)
16) as the initial letter in the names of phyla, classes, orders, families, and genera (but not in the names of species).
17) as the initial letter of a title, rank, etc. followed by a proper name, or of an epithet used with or in place of a proper name.
    *Ex.*: Mr. Kauffman, President Wilson, Bishop Eaton, Lord Byron, Richard the Lionhearted, the Great Emancipator
18) as the initial letter in the names of abstract or inanimate things that are personified;
    *Ex.*: It was the work of Fate. And now Spring wafted her gentle breezes. It has been said that Justice is lame as well as blind.
19) as the initial letter in all salutations and complimentary closes of letters;
    *Ex.*: Gentlemen, Dear Sir, Very truly yours
20) as the initial letter in names of trademarks;
    *Ex.*: Jello, Vaseline